The Wise Garden
Encyclopedia

The Wise Garden Encyclopedia

HarperCollins*Publishers*

This is an updated and revised edition of *The Wise Garden Encyclopedia*, edited by E. L. D. Seymour, B.S.A., published in 1970.

First Edition

Created and produced by Storey Communications, Inc., of Pownal, VT 05261
    President, M. John Storey
    Executive Vice President, Martha M. Storey
    Publisher, Thomas Woll
    Editorial Director, Pamela B. Art

Text design and production, Wanda Harper
Editorial assistant, Louise Lloyd
Production, Caroline Burch

Color section design and text consultant, Elizabeth Woll
Jacket design, Neil Stuart

Printed in the United States by R.R. Donnelley, Crawfordsville, IN
Color separations by State Color, Schenectady, NY

Library of Congress Catalog Card Number: 89-46559
ISBN 0-06-016114-0

Library of Congress Cataloging-in-Publication Data

The Wise garden encyclopedia. — 1st ed.
    p.   cm.
  Rev. ed. of: The Wise garden encyclopedia / E.L.D. Seymour. 1970.
  ISBN 0-06-016114-0
  1. Gardening — Dictionaries. I. Seymour, E.L.D. (Edward Loomis Davenport),
1888– Wise garden encyclopedia.
  SB450.95.W57 1990
  635'.9' 30—dc20   89-46559

---

  90   91   92   93   94   10   9   8   7   6   5   4   3   2   1

ACKNOWLEDGMENTS

The creation and production of a reference work of this scope is the result of the combined efforts of a great many people. Carol Cohen, Vice-President and Associate Publisher, Director of Reference Publishing at HarperCollins Publishers, created the plan for the new edition. Henry W. Art, Ph.D., Professor of Biology, Williams College, provided the critical review of the original book and made suggestions for its revision. Kenneth Wright, Senior Editor of Adult Trade at HarperCollins, supervised and reviewed the development of the manuscript and illustrations. Linda Dingler and Jill Korey also provided valuable assistance from HarperCollins.

The development of the database and word processing programs for *The Wise Garden Encyclopedia* involved input from a number of people. Eric Wirth, George Alexander, and Steve Muskie helped Michael Barrow and others at Storey Communications to configure the computer systems. Those who entered data include Andrew Art, Cyndi Garrison, Barbara Hurley, Marjorie Davenport, and Jessica Storey.

The contributing editors are acknowledged individually in a separate section of the front matter. Many others provided valuable assistance in the development of this manuscript, including Robyn Bem, Linda Conway, Judie Evrard, Elizabeth Johnson, George McCullum, John Mickel, Nick Noyes and Jennifer Storey.

Many that helped in the production process are noted on the copyright page. Others to be acknowledged are Northern Cartographic, Inc., of Burlington, VT, producers of the hardiness zone map; and Arcata Graphics of Kingsport, TN, for the linotronic output.

Particular credit should be given for the sustained effort and careful attention to detail by Louise Lloyd in editorial and Wanda Harper in design and production.

Pamela B. Art
Project Editor

PHOTOGRAPHY

Photo Research, Debbie Needleman

Photographers and Photo Agencies:

Henry W. Art
Philip E. Keenan

PHOTO/NATS, Boston, MA 02166

Paul Martin Brown	Dorothy Long
Gay Bumgarner	John Lynch
Al Bussewitz	Robert Lyons
Priscilla Connell	A. Peter Margosian
Greg Crisci	Mary Nemeth
Debby Crowell	Ann Reilly
Betsy Fuchs	John Smith
Valerie Hodgson	David Stone
Hal Horwitz	Virginia Twinam-Smith
Don Johnston	Marilyn Wood

Tony Stone Worldwide, Chicago, IL 60611

Raymond Barnes	Peter Fronk
Harold Barnett	Lois Moulton
Gay Bumgarner	Rod Planck
George Cassidy	Bob Rashid
Doris Dewitt	L.L.T. Rhodes
Wally Eberhart	Brian Seed

ILLUSTRATIONS

Judy Eliason. Illustrations appear on pages: 2 left, 54, 58, 59 bottom, 60, 66, 87, 106 left, 120, 149, 185, 207 right, 258, 261 right, 280, 299, 304, 305 top, 305 bottom, 317, 361, 406, 413 right, 414, 419 left, 470, 543, 556, 557, 572 left, 573, 622, 628 right, 630, 635, 636 right, 668, 698, 739, 741 right, 743, 745, 746 upper left, 746 lower left, 780, 813, 838 left, 859 right, 862, 871, 892 top, 907, 913, 920 left, 921 right, 929, 949, 957, 966, 971, 972, 985 upper right, 1016, 1024, 1031, 1035

Brigita Fuhrmann. Illustrations appear on pages: 12 right, 202 left, 241 top, 419 right, 480 right, 501, 701, 727, 880, 921 left, 942, 1003

Carol Jessop. Illustrated symbols appearing in the color section.

Charles Joslin. Illustrations appear on pages: 23 right, 31, 46, 57 left, 85, 86 top, 182, 201, 202 right, 224, 234, 241 bottom, 273 right, 290, 420, 434, 436 left, 436 right, 437, 488 top, 488 bottom, 529, 530, 562, 564, 580 left, 619, 620, 625 left, 626, 653 top, 675, 690, 717, 741 left, 778, 838 right, 843 left, 845, 856, 858, 859 left, 881, 941, 947, 959 left and upper right, 978 left, 999 lower left

Alison Kolesar. Illustrations appear on pages: 18, 24, 38, 91, 103 right, 144, 209, 214, 219 left, 267, 274 right, 275, 307, 308 right, 335, 344 bottom, 348, 357, 374, 387 right, 390, 407, 415, 478, 496, 515, 565, 566, 568, 572 right, 596 lower left, 599, 641, 694, 707, 710, 730, 732, 748 right, 758, 768 left, 775, 807, 818 left, 839, 869, 902, 916, 925, 926, 948, 973, 975, 990

Mallory Lake. Illustrations appear on pages: 5, 9, 12 left, 15, 17, 19, 28, 35, 41, 43, 56, 74 right, 75, 81 left, 83, 86 lower left, 94 right, 99, 101, 109, 123, 124, 125, 141, 158, 184 right, 187, 189, 192 right, 205, 207 left, 216, 217, 218, 219 right, 226, 242, 244 bottom, 251, 261 left, 273 upper left, 278, 279, 289, 308 left, 322, 327, 331 lower left, 332, 334, 347, 349, 362 left, 363, 372 right, 375, 377, 379 right, 386, 410, 433 right, 441, 443, 469, 481, 482, 483, 484, 492, 494, 500, 507, 512, 513, 539, 553, 559, 563, 576, 593 left, 594, 595 top, 596 lower right, 602, 604, 605, 606, 608, 609, 614, 623, 649, 651, 657, 664, 672, 682, 697, 699, 703, 719, 734, 737 left, 755 right, 765, 768 right, 771, 777, 781 right, 785, 796, 808, 830 lower left, 853, 857, 860, 861, 866, 870, 876, 888 left, 904, 920 right, 928 top, 955, 956, 977, 980 right, 991, 999 upper left, 1000, 1005, 1038

Elayne Sears. Illustrations appear on pages: 21, 23 left, 25, 26, 32, 36, 40, 57 right, 59 top, 77, 103 left, 111, 113, 119, 121, 134, 135, 147, 155, 159, 160, 161, 171, 177, 179, 180, 181, 184 left, 197, 213, 240, 244 top, 269, 284, 303, 306, 319, 343, 344 top, 362 lower right, 370, 384, 387 left, 388, 395, 399, 405, 409, 413 left, 421, 430, 435, 452, 453, 454, 495, 509, 514, 551, 560 top, 570 bottom, 585, 591, 625 right, 628 left, 629, 636 left, 653 bottom, 658, 666, 683, 721, 748 left, 776, 779, 781 left, 782, 787, 805, 806 bottom, 809, 815, 816, 823, 848, 856, 878, 888 right, 891 left, 895, 897, 903, 917, 930, 931, 940 left, 963, 979, 999 right, 1022, 1027, 1036

Hyla M. Skudder. Illustrations appear on pages: 2 right, 11, 13, 30, 39, 42, 44, 45, 61, 74 left top and bottom, 81 right, 82 left, 88, 89, 98, 106 right, 139 right, 163, 164, 192 left, 193, 249, 250, 252, 254, 262, 273 lower left, 274 left, 277, 281, 309, 314, 326, 331 right and upper left, 345, 353, 362 upper right, 372 left, 378, 379 left, 380, 381, 382, 383 left, 416, 417, 427, 433 left, 438, 440, 476, 480 left, 487, 493, 511, 531, 532, 561, 571, 580 right, 581, 584, 589, 593 right, 595 bottom, 598, 600, 603, 612, 627, 637, 663, 676, 692, 695, 715, 720, 726, 729, 733, 737 right, 759, 766, 767, 799, 810, 814, 830 right, 832, 841, 843 right, 852, 855, 889, 890, 891 right, 892 bottom, 910, 928 bottom, 934, 959 lower right, 967, 976, 980 left, 1001, 1012, 1034, 1040

CONTRIBUTORS

Henry W. Art, Ph.D. Professor of Biology, Williams College; Ecological and environmental consultant, National Park Service. Served as Visiting Professor at University of Vermont, University of California at Santa Barbara, and as a Visiting Scholar at the Botany School of Cambridge University, England. Published titles include *A Garden of Wildflowers* (Garden Way Publishing), winner of 1986 Garden Writer's of America Quill and Trowel Award; and the regional series entitled *The Wildflower Gardener's Guide*, winner of 1987 Garden Writer's of America Quill and Trowel Award.

Michael J. Balick, Ph.D. Philecology Curator of Economic Botany and Director of the Institute of Economic Botany, New York Botanical Garden. Field research and grant projects include numerous agronomic, ecological, and botanical studies in the United States, the Middle East, and the South and Central American tropics. Published books include *Botanical Gardens and Arboreta: Future Directions* (New York Botanical Garden), *Useful Palms of the World: A Synoptic Bibliography* (Columbia University Press), as well as several titles in the *Advances in Economic Botany* series and many other publications including over 70 popular and scientific papers.

David E. Benner. Assistant Professor Emeritus of Ornamental Horticulture, Delaware Valley College. Botanical Consultant for Bowman's Hill Wildflower Preserve Committee. Lecturer on shade gardening and consultant on landscaping in the shade and identification and uses of native plant material. Published works include contributions to *Horticulture, Garden,* and *The Green Scene* magazines and author of *Native Plants of Pennsylvania* (Livingston Publishing).

Marianne Binetti, B.S. Degree in horticulture from Washington State University. Syndicated garden columnist for over 20 newspapers. Author of *Tips for Carefree Landscapes* (Garden Way Publishing). Contributed articles to *Woman's Day* and other magazines. Winner of the B.P.I. Garden Columnist Award, 1985, and the Annual Journalism Award from the National Gardening Bureau, 1988.

Derek G. Burch, Ph.D. President, Horticultural Masterworks and Horticultural Educational Services. Chief Horticulturist, Missouri Botanical Gardens. Published works include the *Checklist of the Woody Cultivated Plants of Florida*, as well as numerous articles on landscaping, crop production, and pest control that have appeared in botanical and horticultural journals and gardening trade publications. Received the President's Gold Medal award from the Florida State Horticultural Society.

William H. Carlson, Ph.D. Professor and Extension Specialist in Horticulture, Michigan State University. Executive Vice-President, Professional Plant Growers Association. Active in several horticultural education and research projects, including extension programs, horticultural societies, and patented plant growth methods. Editorial contributions to *American Vegetable Grower Magazine, Michigan Florist Magazine, BPI News,* and *Greenhouse Grower Magazine.* Winner of agricultural honors and awards, including the John Walker Award from the Society of American Florists and a fellowship from the American Society for Horticultural Science. Dr. Carlson was assisted by **Mark P. Kaczperski**, a graduate research assistant at the University of Georgia working towards a Ph.D. in horticulture.

Maria Cinque, M.S. Turfgrass Specialist, Cornell Cooperative Extension Service. Conducted field research on insect, disease, and cultural problems of grasses, trees, and shrubs. Freelance garden writer. Published weekly garden columns in *Newsday* and *New York Newsday*, as well as articles in trade magazines and journals. Appeared as a Turf and Horticultural Expert on *The CBS Morning News*, *ABC Eyewitness News*, and many local television and radio programs.

Jeff Cox. West Coast Editorial Director, Rodale Press. Consultant in publishing (editorial, creative, and desktop) and in landscape design. Freelance author, editor, and journalist. Regular columns appearing in *The San Francisco Chronicle* and *Organic Gardening*, as well as frequent freelance articles in various magazines. Other published titles include *From Vines to Wines* (Harper Collins/Garden Way Publishing), *The Perennial Garden* (Rodale Press), *Landscaping with Nature* (Rodale Press), and *Flowers for All Seasons* (Rodale Press). Winner of the 1986 Quill and Trowel Communications Award, Garden Writers' Association of America. Mr. Cox was assisted by freelance writer and editor **Jeff Silva.**

Beverley R. Dobson. Author, editor, lecturer. Recipient of the Silver Honor Medal from the New York State District of the American Rose Society, and former Secretary-Treasurer of the Rose Hybridizer's Association. Published works include an the annual publication "Combined Rose List," *Bev Dobson's Rose Letter*, chapters in *10,000 Gardening Questions Answered* (Harper Collins), and *Taylor's Guide to Roses* (Houghton Mifflin), as well as articles in other books and periodicals.

Dara Emery. Plant Breeder, Santa Barbara Botanic Garden. Gardening Educator in California school system and participant in numerous horticultural societies, specializing in California flora of ornamental value, low chill stone fruits, and seed propagation of California flora. Published *Seed Propagation of Native California Plants*.

Derek Fell. Garden writer, photographer. Former director of All-America Selections and the National Garden Bureau. Published 35 full-length books and calendars on gardening, including *Vegetables, How to Select, Grow & Enjoy* (H.P. Books), *Home Landscaping* (Simon & Schuster), and *How to Photograph Flowers, Plants & Landscapes* (H.P. Books) Photographic contributor to many national magazines. Winner of numerous awards from the Garden Writers' Association of America, including Best Book, Best Photography, and Best Magazine Article.

Catharine Osgood Foster, M.A. Professor Emeritus of Literature, Bennington College. Writer, active in gardening and conservation programs. Member of Royal Horticultural Society of London, the Garden Club of America, and Massachusetts Horticultural Society. Frequent lecturer on organic gardening. Winner Zone 1 Conservation Award, Garden Club of America, 1968. Published works include *The Organic Gardener* (Knopf), *Building Healthy Gardens* (Garden Way Publishing), *Organic Flower Gardening* (Rodale Press), and *Plants-a-Plenty* (Rodale Press), as well as garden related articles in *The Country Journal*, *Rodale's Organic Gardening*, *The New York Times*, *The Bennington Banner*, and *Horticulture*.

Charles Glass. Editor, *Cactus and Succulent Journal* (Cactus & Succulent Society of America, Inc.). Editor since 1965, partner-owner of Abbey Garden Press and co-founder of Abbey Garden Nursery, specializing in cacti and other succulents. Former director of Lotusland, a private botanical garden in Montecito, California, specializing in exotic plants. Field explorer and discoverer of many species of cacti, other succulents, and conch shells. Co-author of several new taxa from Mexico. Fellow of the Cacti and Succulent Society of America, Honorary life member of the Mexican Cactus & Succulent Society. Co-author of *Cacti & Succulents for the Amateur* as well as other books and numerous articles on cacti and other succulents.

Lewis and Nancy Hill. Accomplished garden writers and owners of Vermont Daylilies Nursery. Specialists in growing perennials, fruits (collecting antique apple varieties), and trees. Published works include *Christmas Trees, Cold-Climate Gardening, Fruits & Berries for the Home Garden, Pruning Simplified, Secrets of Plant Propagation*, and the Benjamin Franklin Award-winning *Successful Perennial Gardening* (all from Garden Way Publishing). Authors of articles in *The Country Journal, The American Nurseryman, Diversion, Horticulture, Harrowsmith, Organic Gardening*, and others.

Betty E. M. Jacobs. Veteran gardener and garden writer. Published books include *Growing and Using Herbs Successfully* (Garden Way Publishing), *Flowers That Last Forever* (Garden Way Publishing), *Profitable Herb Growing at Home* (Gray's Publishing, Ltd.), and *Growing Herbs and Plants for Dyeing* (Unicorn Publishing).

Sandra Ladendorf. Garden writer and photographer. President, American Rock Gardening Society. Columnist for *First* magazine and *The News and Observer*, Raleigh, North Carolina. Author of *Successful Southern Gardening, A Practical Guide to Year-round Beauty* (University of North Carolina Press). Winner of many garden writing awards, including three awards for excellence from the Garden Writers' Association of America.

Frederick Magdoff, Ph.D. Professor/Chairman, Department of Plant and Soil Science, University of Vermont; President, Northeast Branch of the American Society of Agronomy. Numerous research projects include studies in soils related to ecology and agriculture. Articles have appeared in scientific journals such as the *Journal of Environmental Quality, Agronomy Journal, Monthly Review, Plant & Soil*, as well as periodicals published by the United States Environmental Protection Agency and government agencies of Canada and Israel.

Annalee Cox Mann. Owner, Ann Mann's Orchids. Freelance writer, lecturer, teacher on epiphytes. On staff of *Florida Orchidist* (quarterly publication) and contributor to Leu Botanical Gardens newsletter. Accredited judge for the American Orchid Society. Vice-chair, Membership Committee, American Orchid Society. Publicity director, Central Florida Orchid Society. Published articles in *American Orchid Society Bulletin, Mother Earth News, Orlando Sentinal Star, Hoyan International*, and other periodicals. Books include *Ann Mann's Orchid Handbook, Ann Mann's Bromeliand Handbook*, and *Value-Engineered Greenhouse and Plant Culture Handbook*.

Elvin McDonald. Director of Special Projects, Brooklyn Botanic Garden. Board of Directors, American Horticultural Society. Chairman, Horticulture Advisory Council, New York City Board of Education. Founder, American Gloxinia Society. Syndicated columnist in newspapers throughout the United States and Canada. Published several best-selling books on indoor gardening, including *House Beautiful Living Outdoors* (Morrow), *Northeast Gardening* (Macmillan). Consultant for television and film productions including *Gardens of the World with Audrey Hepburn* (Perennial Productions for PBS), *Green Card* (Peter Weir Production), and *House Party with Steve Doocy* (NBC). Contributions to *Flower and Garden Magazine, Garden Design Magazine, Park's Floral Magazine, Popular Gardening Indoors, Family Circle, Good Housekeeping*, and many others.

Dee Peck. Former head bacteriologist at Cleveland City Hospital and researcher at Case Western Reserve and the University of Chicago. Freelance writer, lecturer, photographer, specializing in ferns and rock gardening. Affiliated with the Garden Writers of America. Published articles in *The Green Scene, Primroses* (Journal of the American Primrose Society), *Plants and Gardens* (Brooklyn Botanic Garden), *House Plants and Porch Gardens*, and *Fine Gardening*.

Roger Raiche. Horticulturist, Californian and Eastern North American Collections, University of California Botanical Garden at Berkeley. Board Member, Jepson Manual Horticultural Review Council. Found and named new species, as well as identifying numerous range extensions, especially in Northern California. Member, California Horticultural Society's Native Plant Study Group. Published articles in *Pacific Horticulture* and *Four Seasons,* a journal of native plants.

Philip Swindells, M.I. Horticulture, M.I.S.T.C., A.M.I.T.D., F.L.S. Horticultural Consultant. Former Director of Gardens, Wycliffe Hall Botanical Gardens (England). Former garden manager at Castle Kennedy in Stranraer and Curator at Harlow Car Gardens, North Yorkshire. Churchill Fellow. Nuffield Scholar. Member Royal Horticultural Society, Examination Board. Registrar for cultivated *Nymphaea* and *Nelumbo* through the International Society for Horticultural Science. Gardening correspondent for *The Northern Echo, Yorkshire Evening Post, Yorkshire Life, Lancashire Life, Garden Answers,* and BBC Radio Leeds. Author of sixteen full length books on horticulture.

David Tarrant. Education Coordinator, University of British Columbia Botanical Gardens. Co-host "The Canadian Gardener" (CBC-TV). Garden columnist, *The Vancouver Sun.* Published books include *David Tarrant's Pacific Gardening Guide, A Year in Your Garden, Gardening as Therapy, Highrise Horticulture* (Whitecap Books).

Ron Whitehurst. Technical writer specializing in biotechnology. Member, Committee for Sustainable Agriculture, Biodynamics Association, Greens, and Urban Ecology. Research includes studying indicator plants and soil quality, as well as developing a plant stress response monitor, a kit for testing compost, and a botanical insect repellent. Published *Reading Weeds* and many articles on organic gardening.

Katharine D. Widin, Ph.D. Plant Pathologist/Consultant. Founder and Operator, Plant Health Associates, Inc. City Forester, Inver Grove Heights, Minnesota. Plant Pathology Consultant, Northern States Power Company. Author, former biology professor, and lecturer specializing in the effects of insects and diseases on plants. Contributing editor to the *Taylor's Guides* (Houghton Mifflin). Columns and articles have appeared in *The Minnesota Horticulturalist* (Minnesota Horticultural Society magazine), *Minneapolis Star-Tribune, Minnesota Home and Design Magazine,* and *American Nurseryman.*

INTRODUCTION

The Wise Garden Encyclopedia was first published in 1936. Now, more than 50 years later, it has been carefully revised with the aim of presenting in simple, practical, interesting, and helpful form the information that will enable any person to get the most out of gardening.

HOW TO USE THIS BOOK

Cross References

References to related articles are given throughout the text. When a word appears in SMALL CAPITAL LETTERS, it signifies that there is further information at the indicated entry.

Botanical Names

With the exception of fruits and vegetables, the primary discussion of each plant is found under its Latin botanical name. The common name is listed separately, with a cross reference to the genus for further information. For the convenience of the reader, the main gardening information for fruits and vegetables is found under their common names; related ornamentals are discussed under their genus name.

Study the style in which the plant names are printed. A complete botanical name always appears in italics, such as *Rosa rugosa*; but the common name does not, such as rose. The first word of the botanical name is the genus (*Rosa*), which is always capitalized. The second word (*rugosa*) is the particular species name, which is not capitalized in *The Wise Garden Encyclopedia*, although some other sources of information do capitalize species names when they are derived from a proper noun.

If a botanical name is commonly known, such as iris or chrysanthemum, it is not italicized in general discussion unless the reference applies to the classification of the plant.

The botanical family name is not italicized. Using the above example, Rosaceae is the Latin name for the Rose Family. A family often contains more than one genus and can contain several dozen genera (the plural form of the word "genus"). Sometimes the members of different genera of the same family resemble each other, and sometimes they look nothing alike. Taxonomists who study botanical families are continually revising and regrouping specific plants based on the most current research findings.

As a general rule, botanical names in this volume follow the *International Code of Botanical Nomenclature* 1988, using *Hortus Third* (Macmillan, 1976) as a guide for spelling. Within each genus entry, the selected species are listed alphabetically by species, preceded by the genus name abbreviated to its initial letter. Botanical varieties are listed under the species from which they are derived; variety is abbreviated "var." Cultivated varieties, or cultivars, are indicated by a single quotation mark around their names and are preceded by the abbreviate "cv." that stands for the word cultivar. Hybrids, indicated by a multiplication sign (x) between the genus and species names, may have their own listing within the genus entry, or may be discussed under a parent species. For further information, see PLANT NAMES AND CLASSIFICATION.

Common Names

Common names vary from region to region and change over time. Sometimes the same common name refers to several unrelated plants. For these reasons, it is not reliable to use common names for the identification and discussion of specific plants. There is also a great deal of variety in the spelling of common names. This encyclopedia attempts to follow a few basic rules in the spelling of common names:

1. If the common name includes a botanical name that is misapplied, the name is hyphenated. For example, spider-lily is hyphenated because it is not a member of the Liliaceae (Lily Family), thus not a true lily. The hyphen is dropped, however, if the first word of the common name indicates that the plant name is misapplied. For example, mock orange, false spirea, and bastard indigo are not hyphenated.

2. Common names that contain plant terms that are correctly applied are not hyphenated. They are either run together or kept as separate words. For example, moonflower, pigweed, and nannyberry are not hyphenated.

3. A hyphen is used if the second word of the common name does not pertain to plants. For example, baby's-breath and lady's-slipper are hyphenated.

4. A common name of three or more words is generally hyphenated, such as lily-of-the-valley or jack-in-the-pulpit.

Chemicals in the Garden

The *Wise Garden Encyclopedia* contains relatively few recommendations for the use of harsh chemical treatments for insects, pests, and diseases. Gardeners are becoming increasingly aware of the dangers to the environment that can result from the indiscriminate use of chemical controls. It is preferable to approach gardening from a non-toxic perspective. Healthy, vigorous plants tend to resist pest and disease problems. When faced with a choice of control measures, begin with the most benign procedure. Something as simple as picking beetles off leaves can be quicker and more effective than the application of an insecticide. Even the use of botanical products is not without hazards; the concerned gardener will supplement this reference book with current articles in magazines and newspapers, as well as check out any chemical usage with the local Cooperative Extension Service (see Appendix for listings). Guidelines for the use of many products are seasonal and will depend upon local climatic conditions. Federal, state, and local laws may also govern the use of certain chemicals. Always follow the directions on the label carefully when using even the mildest products. For related articles, see INSECT CONTROL; INSECTS, BENEFICIAL; INTEGRATED PEST MANAGEMENT (IPM); BIOLOGICAL CONTROL.

Climate

As much as any one volume can cover such a vast and diversified geographical area, *The Wise Garden Encyclopedia* applies to the North Temperate Zone. Hardiness zones are listed for many plants, and the USDA 11-Zone Hardiness Map is included (see HARDINESS ZONES) for the United States, Canada, and Northern Mexico.

Color Section

The 64-page color section of *The Wise Garden Encyclopedia* is divided into eight sections: annuals; perennials and bulbs; herbs, vegetables, and fruit; roses; foliage plants; shrubs and trees; houseplants; and native plants and wildflowers. Each section is identified by its own plant symbol at the top of the page and a different background color throughout each section. The photographs represent a sampling of the type of plants that comprise each category. To find out more about a particular plant, refer to the genus entry in the alphabetical text section.

PRONUNCIATION KEY

The purpose of this key is to indicate the pronunciation of botanical names accurately without requiring the reader to know any specialized phonetic symbols. The major accented syllable is indicated by capital letters, as in *Acorus* (ah KOR us).

It should be kept in mind that the pronunciation of botanical names varies with different regions and accents. An attempt has been made to include the most common pronunciation.

a	*as in*	apple, cat	oh	*as in*	coat, go
ah	*as in*	calm, father, hot, on	oo	*as in*	boot, too
			<u>oo</u>	*as in*	book, foot
ahr	*as in*	arm, dark	oor	*as in*	cure, poor, tour
air	*as in*	bare, pair	or	*as in*	or, warn
aw	*as in*	all, jaw	ow	*as in*	how, ouch
ay	*as in*	pain, say	oy	*as in*	boy, oil
b	*as in*	box	p	*as in*	pot
ch	*as in*	church	r	*as in*	ring
d	*as in*	do	s	*as in*	so
e	*as in*	egg, pet	sh	*as in*	should, sure
ee	*as in*	easy, me, seem	t	*as in*	sat, tip
eer	*as in*	beer, ear, tier	th	*as in*	bath, thin
f	*as in*	far, leaf	<u>th</u>	*as in*	bathe, then
g	*as in*	give, egg	u	*as in*	cut, supper
h	*as in*	hot	uh	*as in*	the "a" in ago, the "e" in taken, the "i" in pencil, the "o" in salmon, and the "u" in circus
i	*as in*	it, wick			
ī	*as in*	hide, sky			
j	*as in*	jam, magic			
k	*as in*	call, king			
ks	*as in*	extra	ur	*as in*	purr, teller
kw	*as in*	quiet	v	*as in*	valve
l	*as in*	live, mull	w	*as in*	wine
m	*as in*	mat	y	*as in*	you
n	*as in*	not	z	*as in*	zone
ng	*as in*	hang, singer	zh	*as in*	leisure, pleasure

ABELIA (ah BEE lee ah). A genus of several small shrubs belonging to the Caprifoliaceae (Honeysuckle Family), native to Asia and Mexico, and, with a few exceptions, hardy only to Zone 7. They thrive best in a sunny, sheltered location. A well-drained, sandy loam with plenty of leaf mold encourages growth. Flowers are rather small, tubular or bell shaped, abundantly produced in summer on young growth, and varying in color from white to pink or rose.

Cuttings taken in late summer or fall are easily rooted. Young plants wintered in a cool greenhouse and planted out in spring grow and flower well that year.

A. floribunda is a handsome evergreen from Mexico. It is hardy only to Zone 8 but is sometimes grown in a cool greenhouse. Flowers are larger than most, nodding, purple-rose, blooming in early summer.

A. x *grandiflora*, growing to 6 ft., is a semi-evergreen hybrid with glossy dark green leaves that take on a lovely bronze tone in the fall. Flowers are pink and white, appearing from June through November. Hardy in Zones 6–9, the wood is injured by severe cold.

ABELMOSCHUS (a bel MAHS kus). A genus of flowering annual, biennial, or perennial herbs with large flowers, belonging to the Malvaceae (Mallow Family), and formerly included in the genus *Hibiscus*. New plants are easily grown from seed but are often propagated from cuttings or by grafting.

PRINCIPAL SPECIES

A. esculentus (okra, gumbo) is grown in the garden for its long, ribbed pods used in cooking; see OKRA.

A. manihot, a vigorous annual or perennial, grows to 10 ft. and has palmate leaves and yellow flowers to 9 in. across with a dark, velvety center. A perennial in the tropics, it can be grown in cool climates as an annual if seeds are sown early under glass.

A. moschatus (musk mallow), formerly listed as *Hibiscus abelmoschus*, grows to 6 ft. and has leaves variously lobed and large yellow flowers with a crimson center. It is an annual or biennial, largely grown in the tropics for the musk-scented seeds.

ABIES (AY beez). A large genus of coniferous evergreen trees belonging to the Pinaceae (Pine Family) and commonly known as fir. Some species are native in the United States, and a number are valuable as ornamentals. They are generally conical and of particular beauty in youth. Their upright cones and flat leaves distinguish them from the spruces, which have pendent cones and very angular leaves. New cones are showy, varying with different species through bright shades of purple, violet, blue, red-brown, and green. Their branches are stiff and the foliage is aromatic.

Firs are attractive in the garden while young, but they should be carefully placed if you do not intend to move them later. In the lawn they are suitable for grouping in the background or as majestic specimens.

Their fibrous root system permits transplanting them even in large sizes. Most firs prefer moist soil that is kept cool by shading from the sun. Like most other evergreens, they are not often pruned but may be made denser by removing the terminal buds of the branches, which causes the laterals to develop side branches of their own. Species are propagated from seed, and the various cultivars by grafting.

ENEMIES

Firs are subject to all the common wood and root diseases of conifers; see EVERGREENS. Though important in forests and wood lots, they are rarely seen in ornamental plantings.

Eight species of blister rust fungus occurring on needles of fir require certain ferns (*Aspidium, Asplenium, Onoclea, Osmunda, Polypodium,* and *Thelypteris*) as alternate hosts. Another rust fungus of fir causes a witches'-broom disease of species of *Vaccinium*.

The most important of the rust diseases is a witches'-broom that dwarfs young twigs and causes upright laterals to develop into a broom-like growth. Species of *Stellaria* and *Cerastium* (chickweed) are alternate hosts and so should be destroyed. Prune off all infected fir branches. See WITCHES'-BROOM.

Of the few insects that attack ornamental firs, the spruce budworm may injure balsam fir, and the spruce mite attacks various kinds. See also BUDWORM; EVERGREENS; MITES.

PRINCIPAL SPECIES

A. alba (silver fir), whose lustrous green needles are whitish beneath, becomes a large tree but is not satisfactory in the eastern states, usually losing its lower branches and becoming thin at the top. Hardy to Zone 6.

A. balsamea (balsam fir) is a very hardy species, common in wet soils in the North. Attractive in youth, it loses its lower branches, particularly in warmer regions and drier soils. Cv. 'Nana' is a popular dwarf form growing to 2 ft. Hardy in Zones 3–5.

Abies balsamea

A. cephalonica (Greek fir) does best from New York southward but is susceptible to sunburn in winter and so prefers a sheltered location on a wooded north slope.

A. concolor (white fir) is one of the most desirable species, holding its dense lower branches to maturity in a rich, well-mulched soil and enduring heat and dry weather in a good moist location. Its needles are bluish, and the new growth is light colored, giving it a more cheerful appearance than that of most evergreens. This is enhanced by the smooth, light-gray trunk and branches.

A. fraseri (Fraser fir), native to the southeastern states, grows to 75 ft. and has reddish branchlets and leaves to 1 in. long, notched at the tip.

A. homolepis (nikko fir), from Japan, is hardy and is often planted. Symmetrical and attractive while young, it grows to 75 ft. and becomes more open, developing a rounded head with dark green foliage. Hardy in Zones 5–6.

A. nordmanniana (Nordmann fir), a hardy, decorative tree from the Caucasus, is rather slow growing and needs protection from strong winter sun; it may lose some foliage during severe winters in New England. Hardy to Zone 5.

A. veitchii, a hardy species from Japan, is particularly ornamental in its youth, especially if made denser by trimming. The unusually long needles are crowded together, giving it an appearance of great density. The large, purple cones are borne on quite young trees. Hardy in Zones 4–5.

ABRONIA (ah BROH nee ah). A genus of low or trailing herbs, native to western North America, it has fragrant white, pink, or yellow showy flowers and is commonly known as sand-verbena. Grown as annuals and good for open places in light soil, or for containers, rockwork, and baskets. Peel off the husks and sow seed outdoors after danger of frost; or in pots or frames in early fall for planting outside the next spring. They prefer sunny locations and excellent drainage. Although quite tolerant of heat and drought, the plants will grow and flower longer if additional water is provided. In mild climates, plants will survive the winter or may self-sow. Most species are hardy as perennials in Zones 9–10.

winged fruit

Abronia villosa

PRINCIPAL SPECIES

A. latifolia is a prostrate grower with yellow flowers.

A. mellifera is a relatively stout, white-flowered, Pacific Coast form. Blossoming all summer, the plants are pleasingly fragrant in the evening.

A. umbellata, native to California and the best-known species, forms a mat to 9 in. tall and has pink flowers.

A. villosa (desert sand-verbena) grows in hot, dry regions of the southwestern United States. The plants appear after winter rains, producing mounds to 20 in. across. The oval, fleshy leaves and branching stems are covered with short sticky hairs. In early spring they bear rounded clusters of five to fifteen fragrant lavender-pink flowers.

ABRUS (AY brus). A genus of tropical creeping or climbing woody shrubs grown in Zones 9–11 for screens and sometimes in greenhouses for ornamental effect. The seeds are interesting and, because of the hard seed coat, are sometimes used for beads, but they are extremely poisonous if eaten. Propagation is from seed (preferably soaked before sowing) or from cuttings rooted under glass.

A. precatorius, growing to 10 ft. but usually trailing, has white, rose, or purple flowers and scarlet, black-spotted seeds. The brilliant red seeds are used in making Buddhist rosaries, hence the plant's common name, rosary-pea. It is also called crab's-eye vine and, sometimes, weather plant because it droops or "goes to sleep" during storms.

ABUTILON (ah BYOO til ahn). A genus of tropical or semitropical shrubby or sometimes herbaceous plants commonly known as flowering-maple. Many species produce numerous beautiful, long-lasting blossoms that are red, yellow, white, or striped. Others resemble miniature maple trees in form and leaf, which explains the common name. These are grown as houseplants, usually as annuals, being treated like geraniums or fuchsias—placed outdoors in the summer and brought indoors when the weather turns cold. The long-stalked, vinelike leaves are usually edged or mottled with white.

The pendent flowers, 1–3 in. long, usually vary in color from red to yellow and white, with many intermediate hues and tints.

Valuable plants for the greenhouse, window box, or conservatory, they are equally suited for use in hanging baskets, vases, or the summer bedding garden. Indoors they require a temperature of 60–70°F, full exposure to light, and frequent watering. They are easily grown from seed. If cut back and potted in fall, they will bear flowers during the winter, growing 3–4 ft. high and making charming ornaments. They can also be propagated from greenwood cuttings taken in autumn. From these new plants other cuttings can be taken and rooted any time during the winter. Thus one plant will produce a large supply for planting outdoors the following summer. Young plants are likely to become spindly unless the tip shoots are pinched back to induce formation of side branches.

Abutilon sp.

A virus disease, infectious chlorosis, causes a variegation or mosaic of the foliage, but since the variegated forms are considered desirable from an ornamental standpoint, the disease is intentionally fostered and transmitted by budding or grafting chlorotic stock on normal green plants. One type of chlorosis may be transmitted by seeds. If the leaves show irregular brown spots, which are caused by the fungus, they should be removed and destroyed, as should entire plants if they show signs of fusarium wilt or corticium stem rot.

For infestations of tortoise scale, mealybugs, and whiteflies, spray with a strong stream of water or use pyrethrum-soap solution as recommended for other GREENHOUSE PESTS. Fumigation also will clear up scale, whitefly, and young (not adult) mealybugs.

PRINCIPAL SPECIES

A. grandiflorum is usually an annual, but sometimes a perennial, that grows to 5 ft. high and has soft, velvety leaves up to 6 in. long.

A. hybridum has leaves slightly three-lobed or unlobed and spotted, and flowers of various colors. This is actually a group, which includes many of the common garden forms.

A. indicum , a shrubby perennial, grows to 5 ft. and has entire or toothed leaves 4 in. across and 1-in. yellow flowers.

A. insigne has 4-in., wavy-toothed, unlobed leaves. Flowers are white or rose with dark veins and are 2½ in. across.

A. megapotamicum, of drooping form, has 3-in. unlobed leaves, often arrow shaped. Flowers are 2 in. across with yellow petals and red calyx; stamens are exserted as in fuchsias.

A. mollissimum grows to 10 ft. and has ovate, pubescent leaves 6 in. long. Flowers are yellow and ½ in. across.

A. pictum has three-lobed, toothed, green or variegated leaves and orange or yellow flowers 1¼ in. across with crimson veins. Cv. 'Pleniflorum' has solid green leaves and double flowers.

A. theophrasti (velvet leaf, Indian malllow) is an annual herb growing to 5 ft. with pubescent, nearly entire or toothed leaves to 1 ft. across. Yellow flowers are ¾ in. across.

ACACIA (ah KAY shah). A genus of trees and shrubs distributed over the warmer parts of the world, belonging to the Fabaceae (Bean Family), including about 500 species, many commonly known in Australia as wattle. It is a variable group and serves many purposes, both useful and ornamental. Certain kinds provide forage, fibers, gums, medicine, tannin, and valuable wood, some of which is scented. In tropical America there is a

Acacia decurrens

group known as bullhorn acacias, remarkable for their large, inflated spines which are inhabited by fierce ants.

From a horticultural viewpoint, the most important species are those from Australia, where wattle is held in high esteem. A few species are grown in greenhouses, and a number are used outdoors in Zones 9–11. Some will stand a light freeze. The typical leaf in the genus is bipinnate, light, and feathery; but other species lose the leaflets as the plants mature and then carry on their photosynthesis with expanded midribs known as phyllodes, or even with leaves reduced to spines.

Many acacias are fast growing and short-lived. Others are slower growing and very tolerant of poor, dry conditions.

PRINCIPAL SPECIES

A. armata (kangaroo thorn) is large spreading when it has room to fully develop, but it can be grown successfully as a compact pot plant. It has dark green, half-rounded phyllodes and globular heads of yellow flowers.

A. auriculiformis (earleaf acacia) has leaves reduced to phyllodes, bright yellow flowers, and fast-growing, though brittle, wood.

A. baileyana is a shrub or small tree with attractive, feathery, gray foliage and a shower of golden flower heads.

A. calamifolia (broom wattle) is a tall shrub or small tree with slender, upright branches and narrow phyllodes—one of the most decorative species.

A. cultriformis is a tall shrub with bluish, knife-shaped phyllodes and crowded heads of flowers in a terminal raceme.

A. dealbata (silver wattle) is a beautiful tree with silvery leaves and yellow flower heads, which are the florist's "Mimosa."

A. decurrens (green wattle) is a handsome tree with feathery foliage and racemes of fluffy flower heads.

A. drummondii is a handsome species with feathery leaves and drooping spikes of pale lemon flowers; one of the best for pot culture.

A. farnesiana (sweet thorn), native to Florida and the Gulf Coast, has fragrant flowers that are used in perfumery.

A. longifolia (Sydney golden wattle) is a handsome shrub or small tree with long phyllodes and a long season of bloom with flowers in long, loose spikes.

A. melanoxylon (blackwood) is grown as a street tree in California and has wide phyllodes.

A. nilotica (gum Arabic tree), formerly listed as *A. arabica*, is grown for its sap.

A. podalyriifolia is attractive, with gray branches overlaid with soft, white, downy hairs and silvery phyllodes. Fluffy yellow flowers are freely borne in clusters.

A. pravissima (screwpod acacia) forms a small tree with long, drooping branches terminating in fingerlike divisions; seed pods are twisted.

A. pubescens (hairy wattle), a graceful plant with feathery leaves and fluffy heads, is one of the most decorative.

A. riceana is a tall shrub with slender, drooping branches giving a weeping-willow effect. It has narrow phyllodes and flowers in spikes.

A. verticillata (star-leaved acacia) is a spreading, prickly shrub of graceful habit with flowers in spikes.

False, black-, and yellow-acacia are common names for *Robinia pseudoacacia*; rose-acacia is *R. hispida*; see ROBINIA.

ACALYPHA (ak ah LĪ fah). A tropical and warm-temperate genus of shrubs or weedy herbs, hardy only to Zone 10. A few species have been taken up in cultivation, and from these, many colored-leaved or showy-flowered types have developed.

For bedding purposes, plants from 4-in. pots should be set out in late spring. They are easily propagated by cuttings taken from outdoor plants in the fall, from outdoor plants taken indoors and cut back, or, in summer, from plants kept over a second year indoors. The latter method, which provides well-ripened wood, is preferred. In the greenhouse, the plants should be guarded against red spiders, mealy bugs, and scale. Control Cercospora leaf spot and Rhizoctonia stem rot by sanitary measures, such as removing spotted leaves and destroying wilted plants.

A. hispida (chenille plant, red-hot-cat's-tail) is a medium-sized shrub for hot areas. Only female flowers are known in the United States; these form drooping spikes to about 18 in. long in red or white.

A. wilkesiana (copperleaf) is a medium-sized shrub with copper-colored leaves, mottled or margined with green. It is sometimes cultivated in northern greenhouses and is often grown in warmer regions as a hedge or lawn plant. Several color forms or types with interesting leaf shapes have been selected and named. A new herbaceous plant with shorter red catkins is becoming popular as a basket plant in Florida.

ACANTHOPANAX (ak an thoh PAN aks). A genus of deciduous shrubs and trees with handsome foliage and prickly stems, belonging to the Araliaceae (Aralia Family), native to Asia. One shrubby species in cultivation, *A. sieboldianus* (fiveleaf aralia), is an erect shrub growing to 8 ft., with arching stems and bright green leaves. An excellent plant as a screen or barrier in sun or shade, it thrives in any soil, takes pruning well, and has no disease or insect problems. Cv. 'Variegatus' has leaves edged with white. Hardy in Zones 5–8.

ACANTHUS (ah KAN thus). A genus of European perennial herbs or small, thistlelike shrubs belonging to the Acanthaceae (Acanthus Family) and commonly known as bear's-breech. They have leaves from 12–24 in. long and 6–12 in. wide. Whitish, rose, or lilac flowers are borne on spikes 18 in. long. They do best in rich, well-drained soil and full sunlight and are especially useful for background plantings. Although semihardy, Zones 5–9, they need winter protection. Seed can be sown in spring; plants will flower in late summer. Propagation by division of the roots can be done in spring or in early autumn.

Acanthus mollis
var. *latifolius*

PRINCIPAL SPECIES

A. balcanicus is a hardy species from southern Europe. It grows up to 4 ft. high and has pinkish purple flowers with oval-lobed calyxes. The leaves have deep pinnate lobes with toothed edges and become narrow toward the base.

A. mollis (artist's acanthus) is the most commonly cultivated species. It grows to 2 ft. tall and has spineless leaves 2 ft. long and rose, lilac, or whitish flowers. It is a pretty plant but somewhat tender. Var. *latifolius* is hardier, has even larger leaves, grows to 3 ft., and is much better for most gardens. Hardy to Zone 8.

A. montanus, native to the African tropics, has spiny leaves 1 ft. long. The rose-tinted flowers are borne on terminal spikes about 10 in. long.

A. spinosissimus, also listed as *A. spinosus*, has purplish flowers on dense spikes. The lobed leaves of this southern European species are reputed to be the inspiration for important forms in early art, including the Greek Corinthian column. Hardy in Zones 5–6.

ACAULESCENT. A term describing plants and flowers that are stemless or have very short stems. Compare CAULESCENT.

ACER (AY sur). A genus of hardy native and foreign trees commonly known as maple. These handsome, deciduous, usually long-lived trees all have opposite, often lobed leaves and bear clusters of small flowers followed by two-winged fruits called samaras or keys. Nearly all the maples are hardy in the North, and many are among the most attractive street, lawn, and specimen trees. They are quite indifferent as to soil, although the silver and red maples require considerable moisture and many tend to do best in swampy situations.

The sugar maple, valuable for its sap and timber, as well as for shade and ornament, is one of the most beautiful and symmetrical of hardy trees for average planting. The red maple is a most satisfactory tree for yard or street, beautiful at all times but especially in the early spring when covered with vivid red flowers, in May when hung with red keys, and in the fall because of the brilliant crimson coloration of the foliage. The ash-leaved maple, because of its rapidity of growth and abundant foliage, has been widely planted through the midwestern states but unfortunately is a short-lived tree with brittle limbs; stronger maple species, ash, or elm should be grown in its place. The silver maple, also a rapid-growing tree with easily broken limbs, has been extensively planted in the Mississippi Valley, where the red maple should be given preference. The Japanese maple species are most decorative dwarf trees for lawns, having many fine cultivars with finely cut or brightly colored leaves.

Most maples are grown from seed, sown as soon as ripe, or stratified and planted in spring; the Japanese species and other cultivars are grown from cuttings or are grafted.

ENEMIES

DISEASES

Maples are subject to various fungus diseases and insect pests, but one of the most common troubles—leaf scorch—is caused not by an organism, but by insufficient soil moisture. Sugar, soft, and Japanese maples are especially susceptible to this problem. Since maples leaf out early and bear large, thin leaves, moisture may be lost from the foliage faster than it can be supplied by the roots, especially in early spring and dry summers. Leaf scorch appears as irregular blotches or a streaking of the veins and a yellowing of the entire leaf. The best treatment for trees subject to scorch is to prune during the winter and to provide additional water during spring droughts. Also, cultivate the soil in spring and fertilize well; during hot weather, water thoroughly and frequently.

Maple wilt, caused by a fungus that enters mostly through wounds, is most destructive to Norway and sugar maples. At first the leaves and branches suddenly wilt while green; this is followed by the death of other branches and, usually, of the entire tree, which shows long, conspicuous green streaks in the sapwood. Control by preventing wounds, painting fresh pruning cuts, and eliminating sources of infection by destroying diseased trees immediately, being sure to remove roots as well. See TREE SURGERY.

Maple decline in the northeastern states is caused by a group of disease-causing fungi, including a phythoptora disease especially prevalent in New Jersey and characterized by a thin crown, decrease in number and size of leaves, and reddish discoloration of bark. In New England, another species of this canker causes bleeding canker, which begins with a reddish ooze coming from fissures in trunk and branches and eventually causes large trunk cankers.

All kinds of maples are subject to a number of leaf spot diseases, which may cause large brown spots bordered by a reddish purple zone, small light brown or whitish spots, a scorched appearance (usually called ANTHRACNOSE), or large, tarlike blotches. Practically all of them can be controlled with BORDEAUX MIXTURE.

INSECT PESTS

Several species of APHIDS infest maples and are particularly obnoxious because they are often followed by the black sooty mold fungus. Spray with a sulfur or insecticidal soap solution. The cottony maple scale and the woolly maple-leaf scale are best controlled with a dormant oil spray. Maple foliage may be fed upon by saddle-prominent caterpillars, cankerworms, the green-striped maple moth, brown-tailed moth, bagworm, white-marked tussock moth, and Japanese beetle, all of which can be controlled by spraying thoroughly with insecticide.

Several BORERS operate on maples. The maple borer, especially destructive to sugar maples, can be controlled by injecting nicotine-sulfate or other insecticide directly into the burrows. There is no control for the leafstem borer, which tunnels the leaf stalks and causes serious dropping of the leaves. Galls on the leaves, caused by a mite, are more unsightly than injurious; spray in spring with dormant-strength lime-sulfur during the blossom period.

PRINCIPAL SPECIES

A. circinatum (vine maple) is a small tree that grows to 40 ft.; when growing in dense forests of larger trees, it produces long, slender, trailing branches. In the open, the circular, finely lobed leaves begin to color in August, turning brilliant orange and red.

A. ginnala (Amur maple) is a graceful, shrubby tree from northern China and Japan with foliage that turns yellow or orange-red in the fall. An unusual small maple with a multiple trunk and yellowish white fragrant flowers, it is extremely hardy, thriving in Zones 3–6, and can be planted where the Japanese maple is winter-killed.

A. griseum (paperbark maple) is a small, oval-shaped tree, growing to 30 ft., with attractive cinnamon-brown peeling bark that makes an effective display in winter. Hardy in Zones 5–8.

A. macrophyllum (big-leaf maple) is a western species not hardy in the North. A forest tree of the West Coast, it is now extensively planted in that region and abroad for outlying avenues and for shade in gardens. A stately, wide-spreading tree, it grows to 75 ft. high and bears remarkable large, lobed leaves.

A. negundo (box-elder) possesses few of the virtues of its relatives except that it propagates easily from seed and grows rapidly under unfavorable circumstances. It is therefore used for windbreaks in the prairie region, but leaves drop early after turning yellow, and trunk decay follows rapidly after injuries. Hardy in Zones 2–9.

A. palmatum (Japanese maple) is a small tree growing to 25 ft. or less, usually with rounded shape, layered branching, and dainty, five- to nine-lobed leaves. It is rather slow growing and expensive but extremely popular, with many uses in the landscape. There are hundreds of cultivars, most of them originating in Japan. Of the better known ones, 'Bloodgood' has red leaf color all summer. 'Burgundy Lace' has finely cut leaves that are purplish red in summer. 'Senkaki' has coral-red twigs and branches. 'Waterfall' is a new cultivar with very finely dissected green leaves overlapping each other. 'Dissectum' has deeply cut lobed leaves with weeping branches and is a choice specimen plant with its golden orange fall color and a fantastic shape with twisted branches. Hardy in Zones 6–8.

A. pensylvanicum (moosewood, striped maple) is a charming species of slender growth, sometimes reaching a height of 25 ft. The graceful trunks are striped green and white, and the large, rather long leaves turn clear yellow when mature. Found only in cool, rich woods, this maple can be grown in the shady shrubbery border or naturalized in the wild garden as a shrub.

A. platanoides (Norway maple) is a large, handsome, European tree with a broad, rounded head. The leaves turn yellow in the late fall and remain long on the tree. It is used extensively as a street and shade tree. This is the best species to grow for quick, dense shade. A few of the many fine cultivars that should be considered are: 'Crimson King', with striking maroon-colored leaves from spring to fall; 'Erectum', a very narrow, upright tree; and 'Summershade', rapid-growing and heat-resistant with upright, oval shape. Hardy in Zones 4–7.

A. pseudoplatanus (sycamore maple) grows to 70 ft. and has coarse-toothed leaves like those of the buttonwood or sycamore; it is an important hardwood tree in Europe. It grows well, even in exposed situations, but unfortunately is short-lived in the United States.

A. rubrum (red, soft, or swamp maple) grows to 60 ft. with strong, upright branches that make it resistant to storm and winds. The leaves, 3–4 in. long, are three- to five-lobed and turn scarlet or orange in the fall. There are some excellent cultivars: 'Columnare' has narrow, upright growth; 'Autumn Flame' has early red fall color; 'October Glory' and 'Red Sunset' have orange to red fall foliage; and 'Scanlon' is a compact tree with dense branches and good red color in autumn. Red maples grown from seed will have fall color ranging from a poor yellow to orange and red. The cultivars will be the same color for each tree with that name. This is true for other maples and in general for other trees with fall color. For example, twelve 'Red Sunset' trees will produce a spectacular orange-to-red fall display, all turning the same color at the same time. It is also usually quite disease resistant. Hardy in Zones 4–9.

A. saccharinum (silver or white maple) is a quick-growing tree that stands considerable heat, drought, and poor soils. In spite of being short-lived, brittle, and of no special timber value, it is sometimes used as a shade tree where quick results are sought in some of the more difficult sections of the Southwest.

Acer saccharinum

A. saccharum (sugar, hard, or rock maple) is a large tree reaching over 75 ft. in height with 6-in. lobed leaves turning bright orange and red. It does well in any soil and is one of the most beautiful shade trees of the eastern forests. A few choice cultivars are 'Bonfire', fast growing with red fall foliage; 'Green Mountain', with dark green, leathery foliage, is more tolerant of heat and drought; and 'Columnar', of narrow, upright growth with yellow-orange fall color. Hardy in Zones 4–8.

Acer saccharum

ACHILLEA (ah kil EE ah). A genus of hardy, herbaceous perennials belonging to the Asteraceae (Aster Family) and commonly known as yarrow or milfoil. They are easily recognizable by their bitter, aromatic odor and taste. The leaves and flowers have been used in medicines for centuries.

Easily grown in any good garden soil in a sunny location, they are good for border and rock garden plantings. All summer the plants bear clusters of small white, yellow, or pink flowers that are excellent for cutting. If seeds are planted indoors during the spring in leaf mold and sandy garden soil, well mixed and finely sifted, and are set outdoors in early summer, the plants will probably flower the first season. Seed can also be started outdoors and the plants set in their permanent places in the fall to bloom the next year. They grow to a height of 1½–3 ft. and should be set about 1 ft. apart. They can also be propagated by root division.

Achillea filipendulina

A handful of bonemeal around every plant in late spring will promote growth. Various species are hardy in Zones 3–10.

PRINCIPAL SPECIES

A. ageratum (sweet yarrow) bears yellow, pleasantly scented blossoms on compact plants.

A. clavennae, growing to 6–8 in., has ¾–1 in. white flowers in small, flat heads all summer long. The silver-gray foliage is deeply cut.

A. filipendulina (fernleaf yarrow) has yellow flowers on tall, 4–5 ft. plants with dark green, fernlike leaves. Commonly available cultivars include 'Coronation Gold' and 'Cloth of Gold', both with yellow flower heads. Hardy to Zone 4.

A. millefolium (common yarrow, milfoil) has finely cut foliage and yellow flowers. Var. *rose-um* bears dense heads of rosy pink flowers from midsummer until late fall. Hardy to Zone 3.

A. ptarmica (sneezewort) has small white flowers and includes the popular double-flowered cultivar 'Pearl', which produces plants 2 ft. high. Hardy to Zone 4.

A. taygetea grows 18–24 in., bearing yellow, 3-in. flower heads throughout the summer and into early fall.

A. tomentosa, with woolly foliage, grows 10–12 in. and bears yellow flowers in summer.

ACHIMENES (ah KIM en eez). A genus of tropical American plants belonging to the Gesneriaceae (Gesneria Family); included are many hybrids and some of the most valuable of all summer-flowering plants, both in window gardens and outdoors in partially shaded places. The tubular five-lobed blossoms resemble small petunias or cattleyas (hence nut-orchid is one of many common names), and the effect of the plant as a whole is similar to impatiens. They are grown in greenhouses for their showy flowers and are occasionally planted out in the garden in the summer. The latest hybrids have extra rows of petals, thus giving a double, hose-in-hose kind of flower. Colors include white, pink, rose, red, violet, purple, and blue. Some are solid, and others may be veined or dotted with contrasting colors. There is also variation in leaf shape, color, and in the manner of growth. Generally the plants are low and hairy with toothed, elmlike leaves. Flowers arise from the leaf axils and are borne singly, paired, or even several on one peduncle.

Plants of achimenes grow from scaly underground rhizomes or small tubercles. Small catkinlike bodies of similar appearance sometimes appear in the leaf axils or among the flowers and can be used for propagation. While a scaly rhizome may not look like much to the eye accustomed to planting dahlia tubers or potatoes, if six are planted in a 6-in. pot and the growing tips pinched out when plants are 2–3 in. tall, you will be amazed at the floral display from midsummer until fall. Their only drawback is sensitivity to ozone in the air. They do not grow well in New York City, for example, but thrive in gardens on Long Island.

Culture. Plants require light, semisunny to semishady conditions at average house temperatures with 30% or more humidity. Soil should be equal parts loam, sand, peat moss, and leaf mold and kept evenly moist when plants are in active growth and nearly dry during fall and winter dormancy. When active, they can be stored at 50–55°F. Hardy in Zones 10–11.

Order achimenes rhizomes from mid-winter to early spring, cover with ½–1 in. soil, and start with gentle bottom heat (70–80°F). Fertilize biweekly while plants are making active growth. When the plants begin to go dormant, either because of short days or lack of sufficient moisture, the scaly rhizomes can be left in the pot until replanting time in spring, or they can be shifted in autumn and stored through the winter in a cool place in a bag of dry vermiculite. Propagation is by breaking large rhizomes in two, by leaf or stem cuttings in summer, or by seed sown in midwinter.

Selections. Nearly 30 distinct species are in cultivation, mostly from Jamaica and from Mexico to Panama. Hybrids proliferated in the twentieth century. There are also bigeneric hybrids known in the trade as x *Achimenantha*, representing crosses between the genera *Achimenes* and *Smithiantha*. Some grow upright 12–18 in. high; others develop into cascades of similar size.

A. grandiflora has hairy, 6-in. ovate leaves and reddish purple flowers borne on 2-ft. stems.

A. longiflora (trumpet achimenes) has attractive, long-tubed, violet flowers that grow from the leaf axils.

ACHLYS (AK lis) **tryphylla.** A low-growing deciduous perennial belonging to the Berberidaceae (Barberry Family), commonly known as deerfoot or vanilla-leaf. Its leaves are divided into three fan-shaped leaflets, and it has a short spike of small flowers without petals. Native to the Pacific coast and hardy in Zones 7–11, this plant is found in shady woods and is useful for woodland or rock gardens.

ACID SOIL. In addition to exhibiting differences in texture or physical conditions, and in fertility, soils are either acid, neutral, or alkaline. The degree of acidity or alkalinity has an important bearing on the health of many plants.

Where underlying rocks are quartz, granite, gneiss, mica schist, sandstone, shale, or slate, the soil above or derived from them is usually acid, though some shales and sandstones are neutral or moderately alkaline instead. On the other hand, the soil above limestone, marble, or serpentine is nearly always alkaline. Where drinking water from shallow wells is "hard," expect the soil nearby to be alkaline (or "sweet"). If this hard water is used in sprinkling, it may injure plants that normally require acid conditions.

The soil condition can be roughly estimated from the kind of plants that grow naturally upon it. Where acid-soil plants predominate, look for acid soil, while alkaline-loving plants indicate soil alkalinity. Poor, sandy soils are often acid, as are peat or muck soils.

To decide definitely whether a soil is acid, neutral, or alkaline, samples can be tested by comparing the color developed when a little soil is mixed with buffer solutions (obtainable at garden supply stores) with a color chart. Inexpensive meters are also available for measuring soil acidity. More accurate test results may be obtained by sending soil samples away for laboratory tests; contact your local extension service to locate the nearest testing facility.

ACID-SOIL PLANTS

Lists of plants requiring acid soil have been published from time to time, but they are often contradictory. Most plants grow equally well in neutral, mildly alkaline, or mildly acid soils, with pH readings varying from 6 to 8 or even 5 to 9. True acid-soil plants prefer a soil that tests at 6.5 or under; they thrive best at a pH of 4 to 6. Acidity below pH 4 is too extreme even for most acid-loving plants.

Plants that seem to need a decidedly acid soil include: andromeda, azalea, baptisia, bayberry, blackberry, blueberry, butterfly weed, cardinal flower, chrysanthemum, cranberry, Dutchman's-breeches, fir, flax, galax, ground-pine, heath, heather, hemlock spruce, hickory, huckleberry, lady's-slipper, leatherleaf, ledum, leucothoâ, lupine, lily, magnolia, marigold, mountain-laurel, New-Jersey-tea, oak, orchid, pieris, pine, platycodon, radish, raspberry, rhododendron, sourwood, sweet-fern, sweet pepperbush, spicebush, spruce, swamp ferns, trailing-arbutus, wintergreen, and yew.

Plants of the Ericaceae (Heath Family), especially rhododendrons, are most extreme in their demand for acid soil and are frequently injured by alkalinity. Injury often follows their use as foundation plants. At the base of a wall, house builders are likely to discard and bury pieces of lime, concrete, mortar, stucco, and plaster, all of which are poisonous to acid-soil plants. Even evergreens of the Pinaceae (Pine Family), most of which prefer mildly acid soil, are often harmed or even killed by such alkaline materials. Consequently, before planting any acid-soil plant near the foundation, dig out all filled earth and replace it or screen it to remove debris. If the wall is concrete, stucco, brick, or stone with mortared joints, the drip from it will cause the surrounding soil to become gradually alkaline. To prevent this, keep the planting well away from the wall, add peat or leaf mold frequently, and water often; or add aluminum sulfate close to the wall.

Signs of alkaline poisoning in acid-soil plants are drooping, yellowing, and falling leaves; lack of root development; and poor health not otherwise explainable. If emergency measures are called for, water with a solution of 1 part commercial tannic acid to 50 parts water. Also, never use lime, bonemeal, or chemical fertilizers on acid-soil plants, except fertilizers known to contribute to acidity, such as sulfate of potash, ferrous sulfate, or superphosphate. Even these should be used with caution. See also ALKALINE SOIL; NEUTRAL SOIL; pH.

ACONITE.

Common name for ACONITUM, a genus of perennials with a characteristic hooded shape to the flowers. Winter-aconite refers to the genus ERANTHIS.

ACONITUM

(ak ah NĪ tum). A genus of herbaceous perennials belonging to the Ranunculaceae (Buttercup Family), and commonly known as monkshood or aconite. The latter common name reflects the characteristic hooded or helmet-

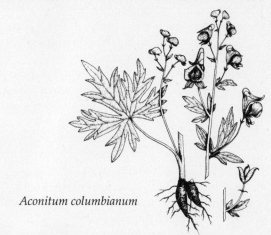

Aconitum columbianum

shaped sepals of the large, showy, usually blue flowers, which grow in spikes. Roots and sometimes flowers contain violent poisons and therefore should not be placed in the mouth; nor should plants be grown near the vegetable garden. Various species are hardy in Zones 2–7.

Seed, which germinates slowly, can be sown outdoors in rich soil and partial shade in early summer, or it can be started indoors in the spring, though the plants do better if not moved. When well up they should be thinned to stand 18 in. apart. Plants can also be propagated by divisions of the thickened, tuberous roots. Purchased plants should go into the garden in early summer or early fall. Any transplanting should be done in the fall and the soil enriched with bonemeal.

Blue or white flowers are borne in the summer of the second year on plants that attain heights of 3–6 ft. and are excellent for cutting. The plants do best under trees or in other semishaded locations, though they sometimes do well in rear borders, forming bushy clumps. Feed with bonemeal dug in carefully around the plants once every six weeks as well as when setting out.

Sudden wilting of plants may be due to CROWN ROT or to the VERTICILLIUM WILT, recognized by brown or black streaks seen in the tissues when a stem is cut slantwise. Powdery MILDEW can be controlled by dusting with sulfur beginning when the disease first appears. A drying of the lower leaves seen in many plants is apparently a physiological symptom due to hot, dry summers and locations that are too exposed. The cyclamen mite blackens and distorts the bulbs; see MITES.

PRINCIPAL SPECIES

A. anthora (Pyrenees monkshood) has pale yellow flowers with rounded helmets ending in short beaks. Var. *aureum* has deeper yellow flowers.

A. carmichaelii, formerly listed as *A. fischeri*, grows to 6 ft. and sometimes requires staking. The blue or white flowers have helmets as wide as they are long, with spurlike visors. This group is extremely variable and includes many named garden sorts. Hardy in Zones 3–4.

A. columbianum, native to western North America, is a stout, erect grower to 5 ft.; it has thin leaves 2–4 in. wide and deeply cut into three or five toothed segments. Helmet-shaped blue or purple flowers up to 1 in. long are borne in long, loose clusters.

A. lycoctonum (wolfsbane) is a tall European species grown as a specimen plant in borders.

A. napellus, a European native, is the best known and most poisonous species, yielding the drug aconite. It grows to 4 ft. and bears blue flowers with wide helmets and beaklike visors. Var. *album* has white flowers. Var. *bicolor* has blue and white blossoms. Hardy to Zone 5.

A. uncinatum, native from Pennsylvania to Wisconsin and Louisiana, grows to 5 ft., partially climbing. Its flowers are blue with decurved beaks.

Aconitum napellus

A. volubile is a climbing species, producing lilac-colored blooms in late summer.

A. vulparia, similar to *A. lycoctonum* but has more branching inflorescences. It grows 2–6 ft. and bears many small spikes of ¾-in. flowers.

ACORUS (ah KOR us). A small genus of hardy, swamp-loving herbs belonging to the Araceae (Arum Family). They have slender, grassy leaves and inconspicuous, greenish flowers on a thick spike, or spadix, partially surrounded by a bract, or spathe. They are often planted in the bog garden and are increased by division.

PRINCIPAL SPECIES

A. calamus (sweet-flag) grows as high as 6 ft. with attractive long, narrow foliage and a spadix 4 in. long. The roots have been dug and then boiled in syrup to make a spicy candy. Hardy to Zone 3.

A. gramineus and its var. *variegatus* are relatively small plants that are often used in hanging baskets, in the rock garden, for cutting, and also sometimes as houseplants. Hardy to Zone 5.

A. pusillus, sometimes used in miniature gardens, has leaves less than 1 in. long.

Acorus calamus

ACROCOMIA (ak roh KOH mee ah). A genus of palm trees native to the American tropics characterized by handsome crowns of feathery leaves and tall, sometimes swollen trunks often covered with sharp-pointed spines. Hardy from Zone 11 to parts of Zone 9, some species are cultivated in California and Florida. For other culture information, see PALMS.

PRINCIPAL SPECIES

A. aculeata (grugru palm), a West Indian native often distributed as *A. sclerocarpa*, grows to 50 ft. and has leaves 10 ft. or longer with 2–3 ft.

leaflets that are dark green above and whitish underneath. The small nuts hang in long clusters and yield an oil used locally in soap and other cosmetics.

   A. mexicana (Coyoli palm) has a regal, symmetrical crown on top of a brown, woolly trunk covered with long spines. It is frequently grown in California but is tender and should not be exposed to frost or cold winds.

   A. totai, from South America, has a trunk growing to 30 ft. and is covered with sharp spines that become smooth as the leaf stalks drop off. It is surmounted by a decorative crown of bluish green leaves. Widely grown in Florida, this species is hardy to the lower portions of Zone 9. Plant in a protected position and, to produce fine specimens quickly, feed frequently, always giving a mulch of well-rotted manure during the rainy seasons.

ACROSTICHUM (ak RAWS ti kum). A genus of large (up to 12 ft.), coarse ferns with sturdy, erect rhizomes found in the tropics, mainly in mangrove swamps. They can make large, handsome plants under tropical greenhouse conditions, but the pots must always have plenty of water. They are distinguished by sori that cover the entire lower surface of the pinnae. Of the principal species, *A. aureum* is the handsomest, with pinnate fronds up to 8 ft. long. Only the small upper pinnae are fertile.

ACTAEA (ak TEE ah). A genus that includes a few species of perennial herbs, belonging to the Ranunculaceae (Buttercup Family) and commonly known as baneberry or cohosh. The small white flowers, borne in showy terminal clusters in spring, develop into brightly colored or white berries in summer and fall. Growing to 2 ft., the plants are

Actaea pachypoda

admirably adapted to rockeries, wild gardens, or borders; they are vigorous growers in shady locations. Propagation is by root divisions in spring or by seed sown in late fall or early spring. Most species are hardy to Zone 3.

PRINCIPAL SPECIES

   A. pachypoda (white baneberry, doll's-eyes), formerly listed as *A. alba*, has white berries.

   A. rubra (red baneberry) has red berries.

   A. spicata (herb Christopher) has white or bluish flowers and purplish black berries.

ACTINIDIA (ak ti NID ee ah). A genus of deciduous climbing vines of twining habit and vigorous growth, belonging to the Actinidiaceae (Actinidia Family). Several of the species thrive in cool climates, and some are grown for their fruit. They grow well in good garden soil and are equally at home in sun or partial shade. They are well adapted to cover arbors and can be trained on a wall or to trail up a tree. Propagation is by seed, cuttings, or layers.

PRINCIPAL SPECIES

   A. arguta (tara vine), growing to more than 50 ft., bears attractive large green leaves and clusters of whitish flowers. Edible fruits resemble gooseberries, but not all of the plants bear fruit because some have flowers of one sex only. Native to Asia, it is a fast-growing vine for quickly shading a patio. Hardy in Zones 5–8.

   A. chinensis (kiwi, yangtao) is the most handsome species, but reliably hardy only to Zone 7. Red hairs clothe the branches when young, and it bears large flowers and tasty fruit. It is grown commercially in New Zealand and elsewhere. See also KIWI.

   A. kolomikta, growing to 18 ft., is handsome with pink or white variegated leaves on the male plants. Hardy in Zones 5–7.

   A. polygama (silvervine), growing to 15 ft., takes its common name from the silvery young leaves on male plants. Mature specimens have white or yellowish variegated leaves and small, white, fragrant flowers followed by yellow fruit. Since it attracts cats, this species may need protection from their attention. Hardy in Zones 4–6.

ACUMINATE. A term applied to leaves that taper to a long, slender tip.

ACUTE. Sharp; used to describe a leaf, such as the chestnut, that ends decisively in a point at the apex, forming an angle of less than 90°. Compare ACUMINATE.

ADAM'S-NEEDLE. Common name for *Yucca filamentosa*, a hardy succulent whose leaves are edged with fine white threads; see YUCCA.

ADDER'S-TONGUE. A common name for ERYTHRONIUM, a genus of lilies also known as dog-tooth-violet. The Adder's-tongue Family is Ophioglossaceae. Adder's-tongue fern is OPHIOGLOSSUM, an important and diverse genus of ferns.

ADENANDRA (ad en AN drah). A genus of small, tender evergreen shrubs belonging to the Rutaceae (Rue Family) and native to the Cape of Good Hope region of Africa. Of the 20 or more species known, some are found in large greenhouse collections. They are occasionally found in botanical gardens where they are wintered under glass and grown outdoors in summer. Propagation is by cuttings of half-ripened wood rooted in a fibrous loam. *A. fragrans* (breath-of-heaven), the principal species, is a summer-blooming shrub sometimes grown in California. Others are available in various color forms.

ADENIUM (a DEE nee um). A genus of bushy to treelike stem succulents in the Apocynaceae (Dogbane Family), found from southern Africa to Arabia. They have tufts of rounded leaves at the branch tips and lovely pink-to-red and white flowers, and are sometimes called desert-rose. They are grown extensively from cuttings, especially in southeast Asia, and are sometimes used for ornamental hedges. *A. obesum* is most commonly encountered and is quite free-flowering.

ADENOPHORA (ad en AWF oh rah). A genus of perennial herbs belonging to the Campanulaceae (Bellflower Family), and commonly known as ladybell. Very similar to the campanulas, they are grown in the same way, preferring rich soil and full sun or partial shade. The flowers are bell shaped, blue, and nodding, in racemes or erect panicles. They are hardy in Zones 3–9 and are propagated by cuttings or seed, since they resent disturbance of their roots when well established.

A. liliifolia grows to 3 ft. and has pale blue, fragrant flowers, 1¼ in. long, borne freely in late summer.

ADIANTUM (ad ee AN tum). A fairly large genus of ferns, popular both as house- and greenhouse plants; the hardier species are useful for naturalizing in woodland situations. Commonly known as maidenhair ferns, they are distinguished by their wedge-shaped, stalked pinnules, which bear the sori under brief, reflexed marginal segments. The rhizomes creep just below the surface. Fronds are usually forked, and the stipes and main branches are shiny brown-black or purplish and wiry. The new growth is frequently of a showy, rosy hue.

Faithful watering and excellent drainage, combined with proper humidity, are essential for its survival in the home; centrally heated houses often preclude its use unless special efforts are made. These may range from placing pots on trays of wet pebbles to installing a room humidifier. Cool room temperatures are very important, even more so than with most other ferns. Removing old fronds at the end of the dormant period brings on a flush of new growth.

The outdoor types respond readily to careful cultivation. They grow in moist woods and prefer a somewhat limey soil. High shade and good drainage are also essential. Protect with leaf cover in winter.

PRINCIPAL SPECIES

A. capillus-veneris (southern maidenhair, Venus-hair fern) is widely distributed throughout the world, familiar in the far South and common as far north as Virginia. It is more a rock plant than the northern species and is usually seen hanging on dripping, shaded cliffs. Greenhouse varieties will grow larger than those in the wild, but smaller specimens are good for terraria and pots. Cv. 'Mariesii', a frequently seen cultivar, is more hardy than the parent.

A. caudatum (trailing maidenhair, walking fern) makes a beautiful hanging basket and can be propagated readily from tiny plantlets that form on the tips of the fronds. The pendent gray-green fronds, growing to 1½ ft. long, are once pinnate, not forking.

A. concinnum (brittle maidenhair fern), from South America, Mexico, and the West Indies, is highly decorative, with bipinnate fronds except at the tapering tip.

A. diaphanum (filmy maidenhair fern) grows erect, 6–10 in. high, is branched at the base of the blades, and has a delicate texture. Excellent for edging greenhouse benches or beds, it thrives as a container plant. Small tubers that form on the roots are an interesting characteristic.

A. formosum (Australian maidenhair) grows erect and branching 1½–3 ft. high and is quadripinnate, with pinnules oblique. Easily grown indoors, it reproduces freely and can be grown outside in Zones 10–11.

A. hispidulum (rosy maidenhair) grows 10–20 in. high. An easy and adaptable houseplant if drainage is good and humidity is not too low, it is a good first maidenhair to try. The new growth is an attractive pink color.

A. jordanii (California maidenhair) is native to the southwestern states and is similar to *A. capillus-veneris*, requiring the same care.

A. pedatum (northern maidenhair) is a universally recognized fern that does best in cooler regions and is deciduous in winter. It needs plenty of moisture and woodland shade and prefers a humusy loam; it does not make a good pot plant. The fronds branch like a bird's foot, and there are eight to twelve pinnae on each frond. The stipes are almost black. It is distributed widely in North America, from British Columbia to Nova Scotia and as far south as Georgia and Arkansas; it crosses the Aleutians into Japan. There are two recognized varieties. Var. *aleuticum* is very hardy, growing throughout Canada, Alaska, and the northwestern states; it is distinguished by fewer pinnules. Var. *subpumilum*, originally from Vancouver Island, is a charming dwarf fern, growing 3–9 in. high; it has glaucous, overlapping pinnules resulting in a dense, compact appearance. It retains its smallest size best under lean rock garden conditions rather than in woodland humus. It comes true from spores and is easily grown in areas where the climate

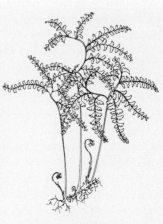

Adiantum pedatum

suits, but it may be a frustrating subject if conditions are not ideal.

A. peruvianum (silver-dollar maidenhair) is a tender fern with large pinnules. It requires plenty of humidity, moving air, and bright indirect light; sparse watering is essential during winter dormancy.

A. raddianum (delta maidenhair), an exotic from Brazil, is a standard for the greenhouse and a favorite houseplant. Fronds are 1–2 ft. and tripinnate to quadripinnate. There are many cultivars, including 'Fritz Luthii', 'Gracillimum', 'Ocean Spray', 'Pacific Maid', 'Tuffy Tips', and 'Variegatum'. All need basically the same treatment as the species.

A. reniforme is a small, delicate, difficult fern from Africa, Madeira, and the Canary Isles. The fronds are simple and kidney shaped.

A. tenerum (brittle maidenhair fern) is a brilliant green fern, three- to four-pinnate, with black-stalked pinnules. An excellent greenhouse subject, this 1½–2 ft. tall plant is found in peninsular Florida, the West Indies, and Central and South America.

A. venustum (Himalayan maidenhair) is a small (12 in.), spreading fern. If protected, it is hardy to Zone 7.

ADLUMIA (ad LOO mee ah) **fungosa.** An attractive, hardy biennial vine native in eastern North America, commonly known as Allegheny vine, mountain-fringe, or climbing-fumitory. Fragile and delicate, it clambers to a height of 15 ft. Hardy to Zone 4, it tolerates shade and prefers a moist soil with protection from wind. With delicately cut leaves and a profusion of pale pink flowers, it makes a charming picture, especially when draping an old bush with its light festoons. Propagation is by seed, often self-sown.

ADNATE. A term applied to unlike structures fused together to form what appears to be a single part or organ; the ovary of the apple is said to be adnate to the calyx-tube within which it is buried.

ADONIS (ah DOH nis). A genus of annual and perennial herbs, named for the youthful hunter of Greek mythology beloved by Aphrodite. They thrive in light, sandy soil and are commonly known as pheasant's-eye.

The annual species are hardy and grow well under trees or in other shaded locations. The foliage is dark green and finely cut, and the terminal flowers, solitary crimson or scarlet with a dark-colored base, appear in late spring. Plants grow about 1 ft. tall and are good for border use. Seeds can be sown outdoors in spring or started indoors a few weeks earlier.

The perennial species are also desirable in border plantings, growing 1 ft. tall and producing large yellow flowers in late spring. Hardy in Zones 2–3, they can be grown from seed sown in spring or fall, or the roots can be divided in spring.

PRINCIPAL SPECIES

A. aestivalis (summer Adonis) is an annual with scarlet flowers from June to August.

A. annua (autumn or flos Adonis) is an annual bearing small crimson flowers with dark centers in early summer.

A. vernalis (spring Adonis) is a perennial with delicate foliage; it bears yellow flowers in early summer.

ADROMISCHUS (a droh MIS kus). A genus of succulent herbs or small bushes belonging to the Crassulaceae (Orpine Family), from southern Africa. They have fat, succulent, often highly colored and attractively marked leaves that root rather readily and thus form new plants of the same clone, that is, genetically exactly the same as the parent plant. Popular species are *A. cooperi* (also listed as *A. festivus*), with leaves like elongate speckled eggs, and *A. maculatus*, with rounded, flattened, spotted leaves.

ADVENTITIOUS. A term applied to a plant part or organ that appears other than in its regular position, such as a bud arising from a root, a leaf, or the trunk of a tree.

AECHMEA (ek MEE ah). A genus of highly ornamental South American epiphytic herbs belonging to the Bromeliaceae (Pineapple Family). The leaf rosettes of aechmeas are vaselike in their ability to hold water, hence the common name, living-vase plant.

In the tropics it is not uncommon to see orchid or hibiscus flowers placed within these "vases" to give additional color to plants not in bloom. Since these flowers do not require water in order to stay fresh for short periods of time and neither has a long stem that can penetrate to the base of a rosette, this does no harm. Many amateur growers have taken up this practice, however, often using cut flowers that use up water and, even worse, have long stiff stems that can easily damage the heart of the plant where its own flower spike develops. If you have an aechmea, do not risk injury to the plant by trying to "gild the lily." Have patience, and plants will send up their own magnificent spikes of long-lasting, highly colored bracts and blossoms.

Culture. Aechmeas thrive in light, sunny to semisunny conditions at common room temperature and humidity; however, to grow well they need 30% more humidity. They should be planted in a medium of osmunda fiber, shredded bark, or coarse leaf mold, and roots should be watered generously by drenching the growing medium several times weekly in warm sunny weather, perhaps once every five to seven days in winter; always keep the vases filled with fresh water. Propagation is by offsets removed from the parent plant when they are large enough to handle.

Selections. About 168 species are known. Principal cultivated forms include *A. fasciata*, which grows to 1½ ft, and its cultivar 'Purpurea', with purple-to-maroon bands with silver markings on the leaves. In late summer, a flower spike bearing pink bracts and blue flowers appears. They age purple to rose and may last five months. Cv. 'Foster's Favorite', sometimes listed as *A. fosterana*, is one of the most colorful aechmeas. It has glossy wine-red leaves and pendent spikes of deep blue flowers in winter followed by blue berries. Other aechmeas bloom at various seasons with long-lasting flowers, making it possible to have a continuous display from these bromeliads.

AEGOPODIUM (ee goh POH dee um). A genus of coarse, fast-growing, weedy, perennial herbs belonging to the Apiaceae (Celery Family) and native to Europe and Asia. They have creeping rootstocks, divided leaves, and very small white or yellow flowers clustered in umbels. Weedy in growth, they are easily propagated by division of the roots. Hardy in Zones 3–9.

A. podagraria (goutweed, bishop's weed) has white or yellow flowers in umbels and grows to 14 in. high. Var.

Aegopodium podagraria

variegatum (snow-on-the-mountain) bears leaves margined with white, which form mats of attractive foliage. Sometimes used as an edging, it will grow in shady places next to buildings or in soil too poor for other plants. It is often found naturalized in the eastern states.

AEONIUM (ee OH nee um). A genus of succulents belonging to the Crassulaceae (Orpine Family), from the Canary Islands. Each head has a terminal, saucer-shaped rosette of leaves, which eventually produces a terminal, pyramidal raceme of yellow, white, pink, or red flowers. One of the most attractive is *A. arboreum* cv. 'Swartkopf', a shrubby cultivar with dark, shiny, purple-black leaves that is quite striking; one of the most interesting species is *A. tabuliforme*, consisting of a flat, stemless, saucer-shaped rosette.

AERANGIS (air ANG is). A genus of about 120 species of epiphytic angraecoid orchids, distributed throughout tropical Africa and Madagascar, with one species from Sri Lanka. Endemic to rain and montane forests, sometimes savannas, the plants are mostly epiphytic and are small to medium size, with short stems. The leaves are coriaeceous and lie in one plane. Inflorescences are arching to pendent, with three to many flowers. Stellate flowers are white to green, sometimes flushed with pink, and have a long slender spur (nectary). The plants are frequently hybridized with other angraecoids. Hardy in Zones 9–11 with frost protection, they should be mounted on cork, coconut husk, or bark plaques (as the aerial roots must dry out quickly) and grown in a shady, humid area. Appropriate midwinter temperature is 55–60°F. *A. brachycarpa* is the type species.

AERANTHES (air ANTH eez). A genus of 30 species of unusual epiphytic angraecoid orchids from Madagascar and the Comoro and Mascarene Islands. One species is found on the African continent. These orchids have fleshy leaves arranged in ranks on short stems. Spurred, medium-sized flowers are translucent green, dangling from long, wiry inflorescences, five or six flowers to a scape. They do well in baskets with a porous, well-draining compost and require a warm, humid atmosphere with moderate shade. They are often hybridized with other angraecoids. Hardy in Zones 9–10 with frost protection, they require minimum winter temperatures of 55–60°F. The type species is *A. grandiflora*.

AERATION. The healthy growth of plants is dependent to a considerable degree on the aeration or air content and circulation of air in the soil. While soil may appear solid and compact, actually, unless it is waterlogged, there is air in the myriad of tiny spaces between the soil particles. This air is the source of oxygen that plant roots must have. Also, by supporting certain kinds of bacteria, it facilitates the formation of nitrates and other nutrients, and thereby renders the fertilizing constituents of the soil more easily soluble.

To ensure good aeration, there must be proper drainage so that excess water can pass through freely and allow fresh air to enter. Cultivation and the maintenance of a loose, friable condition also helps. In general, a light, sandy soil is likely to be better aerated than a heavy, stiff, clay soil.

See also SOIL.

AERATOR. Soil-puncturing device for lawn care that allows air, water, and/or fertilizer to reach deep grass roots. Aerators may be as simple as a pair of flat plastic pieces that strap onto one's

Aerator

shoes with spikes protruding from the bottoms, to make a number of aerating holes 1–2 in. deep with each step. Core aerators make a series of 2–3 in. deep holes (the deeper the better), removing small, well-defined cores as they work. The cores remain above ground where they eventually break down and revert to the soil. Hand core aer-

ators and spiking forks are available for aerating small lawns. For large lawns, mechanical aerators are more practical. Both spike and core aerators are available as garden tractor accessories.

AERIDES (AIR ud eez). A "foxtail" orchid native to southeastern Asia. The genus contains about 60 species of evergreen epiphytic orchids. One type has leathery, curving leaves, while in a second section the leaves are terete. The many fragrant flowers are long-lasting and showy, and hang in dense racemes. They are fleshy and spurred at the base of the lip, usually white suffused with amethyst. They are used in hybridizing with other vandaceous orchids. Hardy in Zones 9–11 if protected from frost, they do best in baskets in a porous compost with their long aerial roots hanging free. Ideal cultural conditions include a minimum winter temperature of 60°F, high humidity, fresh air, and bright filtered light. The type species is *A. odoratum*.

AESCHYNANTHUS (ees ki NANTH us). A genus of shrubby, climbing plants from the tropics, belonging to the Gesneriaceae (Gesneria Family) and formerly listed as the genus *Trichosporum*. In cultivation they are usually grown in pans or baskets and are hung from the roof of a warm greenhouse. They can also be grown as pyramids by training them to moss-covered blocks of wood. A mixture of osmundine, sphaghum moss, and broken charcoal suits them well. When growing freely, they appreciate liquid manure now and again. They have attractive foliage and showy flowers. Propagation is by cuttings.

PRINCIPAL SPECIES

A. fulgens has slender, oval, pointed leaves and long, pointed, bright crimson flowers.

A. radicans, formerly listed as *A. lobbianus*, (lipstick plant), perhaps the most commonly grown, has ovate leaves and scarlet flowers with yellow throats emerging from large, bell-shaped, purple calyxes.

A. tricolor has small, oval leaves and flowers of deep red with orange and black markings.

AESCULUS (ESK yoo lus). A genus of deciduous trees or large shrubs belonging to the Hippocastanaceae (Horse-chestnut Family) and commonly known as horse-chestnut or buckeye. They are ornamental in leaf and have conspicuous panicles of flowers followed by large, spiny fruit burrs. Of fairly rapid growth, most of the 20-odd species are hardy. Its fruits are not edible and should not be confused with *Castanea*, the true chestnuts.

Native species are generally called buckeyes, especially in the Midwest, the West, and the South. They are well worth a place in the general landscape, their pyramidal form being intensified by repetition in the large panicles of blossoms. There are numerous species native to various parts of the country, ranging in height from 7–90 ft. and in color of their blossoms from white through yellow, pink, and greenish to shades of purple or red. The large, highly varnished, sticky buds provide a striking winter and spring feature, as do the characteristic stout stem and branch structure.

Propagation is by seed sown in autumn, or by grafting, budding, or root cuttings.

ENEMIES

Leaf scorch is a physiological disease occurring in the same trees year after year, but being more pronounced in dry seasons. It is apparently due to inadequate or damaged root systems or to poor soil conditions; it cannot be controlled by spraying but only by improving the soil, feeding, and giving plenty of water.

Leaf blotch (caused by *Guignardia aesculi*), which is often confused with scorch, gives rise to irregular brown spots on the leaves, with small black fungus fruiting bodies in the center. Defoliation follows and the overwintering spores are formed in dead leaves on the ground. Control by raking and burning such leaves and by spraying developing foliage with BORDEAUX MIXTURE. The white-marked tussock moth thrives on horse-chestnut. Collect its frothy white egg cases over winter and spray the foliage with insecticide. This will also protect against Japanese beetles, which are especially fond of this tree. See TUSSOCK MOTH for further control measures.

PRINCIPAL SPECIES

A. glabra (Ohio buckeye) is a native species with yellow flowers, hardy in Zones 4–7.

A. hippocastanum, the most commonly planted species, is too often used as a street tree, for which purpose the litter it causes makes it unsuitable. It suffers from dryness, so for best results it should be planted in heavy, moist soil. More or less narrowly pyramidal varieties are well adapted to more confined spaces, and the double-flowered forms are desirable, since the blossoms last longer and are not followed by burrs and nuts.

A. octandra is a large tree with yellow blossoms, well suited to the South. Hardy in Zones 4–8.

A. pavia is a small southern tree with dark red panicles.

AETHIONEMA (ee thee oh NEE mah). A genus of dwarf, sometimes woody, annual, biennial, or perennial herbs belonging to the Brassicaceae (Mustard Family), and commonly known as stonecress. They are closely related to the perennial candytuft and have similar small, four-petaled flowers in terminal racemes, usually in

Aethionema sp.

charming shades of pink, lilac, or purple, occasionally white, and very seldom yellow. Less well known than the candytufts, they are really superior to them for cut flowers, lasting much longer in water. They have small, narrow leaves, often with a bloom.

Since they are natives of hot, dry regions, particularly the Mediterranean, they enjoy a sandy, gritty soil in a sunny location in the rock garden, along a dry wall facing south or along the edge of the border. The perennial species are propagated by cuttings and division in the summer or by seed in the spring. The annuals and biennials are propagated by seed. Old plants are difficult to transplant, but if given good drainage, they will grow steadily for many years. Most are hardy in Zones 3–9.

PRINCIPAL SPECIES

A. armenum is excellent to place in rock crevices. It grows only 3–4 in. high and has blue-gray foliage and veined pink flowers in rounded heads.

A. coridifolium (Lebanon stonecress) has relatively small, rosy lilac flowers in fairly short racemes and is an excellent plant for edging the border.

A. grandiflorum (Persian stonecress), sometimes listed as *A. pulchellum*, grows 1 ft. high and has 1-ft.-long, slender branches that lie among the rocks. The handsome, rose-colored flowers grow in racemes at the ends of branches. It is one of the best species for both the rock garden and dry wall with a southern exposure.

A. schistosum, growing 5–10 in., has fragrant rose-colored flowers and erect, solitary stems bearing many ½-in., bluish leaves.

A. x *warleyense* (Warley-rose), the most commonly cultivated species, is a hybrid growing to 8 in. high with dense clusters of fragrant pink flowers and fine, needlelike, blue-gray foliage.

AFRICAN DAISY.

Common name for *Arctotis stoechadifolia*, a bushy plant with toothed leaves and colorful, solitary flowers, known in California as freeway daisy; see ARCTOTIS. The name also refers to *Lonas*, from the Mediterranean, with yellow flowers; and sometimes GERBERA, better known as Transvaal daisy. African golden daisy refers to species of DIMORPHOTHECA, better known as cape-marigold. South African daisy is GAZANIA, a genus of tender perennials with orange, yellow, or scarlet flowers.

AFRICAN-LILY.

A common name for species of AGAPANTHUS, a genus of herbs popularly grown in greenhouses for their bright flowers.

AFRICAN-VIOLET.

Common name for *Saintpaulia ionantha*, a tropical African perennial that is very commonly cultivated as a houseplant and also known as Usambara-violet; see SAINTPAULIA.

AGAPANTHUS

(ag uh PAN thus). A genus of semihardy African herbs that form rhizomes with thick, fleshy roots. They belong to the Amaryllidaceae (Amaryllis Family) and are commonly known as African-lily. In colder climates they are popular plants for house decoration, grown in large pots or tubs and brought indoors during the winter. Outdoors in warm regions, especially in the West, they are favored for locations that are not closely tended, such as along highways. They are drought resistant, tolerant of poor soils, and hardy in Zones 9–11.

The large umbels of funnel-shaped, bright blue flowers appear above strap-shaped leaves. There are varieties with dark blue and also white flowers and with striped foliage. Easily propagated by division of roots, plants can be allowed to bloom for several years without shifting if fed with liquid manure.

PRINCIPAL SPECIES

A. africanus is an evergreen species with flower stalks that grow to 2 ft. and bear blue flowers from July through September. Among its several varieties, *albus* has white flowers. Cv. 'Peter Pan' is a dwarf form, and 'Queen Anne', of intermediate size, has bright blue flowers.

A. campanulatus, growing 2–4 ft. high and 18 in. in diameter, is deciduous and has rather flat, blue flower heads. It is one of the hardier species.

A. inapertus is a deciduous species with weeping stalks of blue flowers.

A. orientalis is a popularly cultivated species that grows to 3 ft.

A. umbellatus (lily-of-the-Nile) is a tender pot plant with bright blue flowers.

AGATHIS (AG ah this). A genus of tall evergreen trees belonging to the Araucariaceae (Araucaria Family), native to the Southern Hemisphere and commonly known as dammar-pine. They have broad, leathery leaves, bear round or oval cones to 4 in. long, and yield a pitchy sap from which is obtained dammar resin. They are not hardy in the North but are occasionally cultivated in greenhouses and grown outdoors in Zones 10–11.

A. australis (Kauri-pine), growing to 150 ft., is a native forest tree of New Zealand. Leaves on young trees are sometimes 4 in. long, while those on older trees are less than half as long.

A. robusta, to 130 ft., is an Australian species with rather wide-spreading, horizontal branches, frequently seen in California.

AGAVACEAE (ah gah VAY see ee). The Agave Family. A group of plants, including the century plants (*Agave americana* and *A. attenuata*), of monocotyledonous plants with six petal-like parts, six stamens, and an inferior ovary. They are considered by many botanists to be a subfamily of the Amaryllidaceae (Amaryllis Family); however, others consider the presence of stiff, fleshy leaves, often with spines, to sufficiently distinguish them as a separate family.

AGAVE (ah GAH vay). A genus containing many species of handsome plants with long, mostly stiff, evergreen, succulent leaves, usually armed with terminal, and sometimes with marginal, spines; they form clumps of rosettes from which rise the tall, bare flower stems. The name *agave* is usually translated from the Greek as "majestic," but it undoubtedly refers to a follower of Bacchus, the god of wine in Greek mythology; the queen Agave, in a drunken stupor, helped murder her own son—an appropriate epithet for the plants that give us pulque and mescals such as Tequila. They belong to the AGAVACEAE (Agave Family) and are natives of warm arid and semi-arid regions of the Americas.

These plants are of great economic importance, with rope manufactured from the fiber, and food, beverages, soap, and other products from the pulp. Some bloom annually, but most bloom at much longer intervals, and some species die after flowering. In the South, some kinds are planted as lawn specimens or around the foundations of houses, but only the species *A. americana* is com-

Agave sp.

mon as a house or porch plant in the North. Agaves are variously propagated—by seed, from the bulbils, or by underground stems. The soil should be a mixture of sand and loam and be thoroughly drained. If anthracnose spots occur on the leaves, these should be removed and burned.

A. americana (century plant) has leaves sometimes 6 ft. long and a flower stalk up to 40 ft. high. It is often erroneously believed to bloom only when 100 years old. As a matter of fact, it typically blooms after it is ten years old; the plant then dies, but new plants develop from suckers at the base. The greenish flowers, about 2½ in. across, are borne on many horizontal branches at the top of the stalk. This species is often used as a potted specimen in the North, especially var. *marginata*, which has white-margined leaves.

Other interesting species of horticultural or economic importance are *A. attenuata*, a graceful, soft-leaved, spineless agave very popular for landscaping in the milder parts of the American southwest; *A. atrovirens*, one of the species from which pulque, a fermented drink, is made; *A. sisalana* (sisal-hemp), which produces rope fiber; *A. tequilana*, from which mescal tequila is distilled (but only in the town of Tequila); *A.*

yaquiana (also listed as *A. pacifica*), from which the bootleg Sonoran mescal Bacanora is made; and *A. sisalana*, extensively cultivated for fiber.

AGAVE CACTUS. Common name for the cactus *Leuchtenbergia principis*, which shows features resembling the agaves; see LEUCHTENBERGIA.

AGERATUM (ah jur AY tum). A genus of attractive annual herbs belonging to the Asteraceae (Aster Family), native to Mexico and commonly known as flossflower. Among the most popular summer-flowering plants, they are easily propagated from seed or stem cuttings. They are covered with blooms from early summer until frost and are excellent for borders, edgings, or pots. The popularity of ageratum is due not only to the profusion with which it bears flowers, but also to the fact that rain does not fade or otherwise spoil the blossoms.

The so-called hardy- or perennial-ageratums are actually species of EUPATORIUM.

The taller varieties of *Ageratum* are good for cutting, though most species growing 3–10 in. high have stems too short for that purpose. Most varieties bear blue flowers, but white and pink are produced by some. The individual flowers, small in size and ball shaped, last for a long time after being cut. While most of the common annuals are too spreading to permit them to be used in a small rockery, the dwarf forms are ideally adapted for such use and will give a quick effect at trifling cost.

For early flowering, seed should be started indoors in early spring and plants set out 9–12 in. apart in late spring. Since ageratums are one of the most frost-tender bedding plants, do not plant outdoors until night temperatures remain above 50°F. Seed can be sown outdoors after danger of frost is past, but the plants will not flower until late summer.

After their season of bloom has ended, take up the smallest plants, cut them back severely, and pot them up for the winter, placing them in the smallest pots available. Set these in a shady spot in the garden. The plants will recover quickly and then can be brought indoors, where they will flower for a while.

In the greenhouse or home, ageratums are often infested with whiteflies, mealybugs, and red spiders. Spray frequently with clear water or, if the pests become serious, use control measures for other greenhouse pests. Pale green caterpillars called leaf tiers may attack plants both under glass and outdoors, and subsequently plants may show damage from rust diseases. Plants affected by corticium stem rot should be removed and burned. See INSECT CONTROL.

A. conyzoides, growing 1½–2 ft., bears heads of blue or white flowers ¼ in. across all summer long.

A. houstonianum is the species most commonly grown in the garden. Flower colors range from deep violet-blue to pink or white. Their clean, neat habit makes them popular for bedding, borders, pots, and rock gardens.

AGLAOMORPHA (ag low MORF ah). A genus of about ten tropical or subtropical epiphytic ferns. All are large with coarse, leathery, dark green fronds broad at the base, without stipes, designed to trap organic litter and moisture. The sizable fleshy rhizomes are covered with scales that are so long they resemble brown, woolly hair. Their sori have no indusium. They are excellent basket plants, most needing coarse, well-draining potting mix and generous moisture, humidity, and light. They are similar to species of *Drynaria, Merinthosorus*, and *Pseudodrynaria* (including *P. coronans* which is often distributed as *Aglaomorpha coronans*).

A. heraclea and *A. myeniana* (bear's-paw fern) are typical of the genus. The latter has unique fertile fronds that end in constricted beadlike lobes. It is more hardy than most species, ranging into the lower temperate zone.

A. 'Roberts' is a sterile form of unknown origin, possibly a hybrid of *A. meyeniana*.

AGLAONEMA (ag loh NEE mah). A genus of perennial herbs from tropical Asia, belonging to the Araceae (Arum Family). They are grown outdoors in the warm, shaded areas of Zones 10–11. The plants are an important part of the interior landscaping industry, because they are vigorous house-plants that produce attractive plain green or variegated leaves borne on short, upright stems. Many combinations with light and darker green, silver, and white are found, and breeding work has introduced white or pink stems and leaf stalks, and varying degrees of uprightness or spread to leaves that range in shape from long and slender to almost round.

Aglaonema sp.

Culture is simple in a moist but free-draining, rich soil. Plants can be propagated by cuttings or by division when basal shoots have formed a large clump.

The hybrids most commonly found in nurseries include 'Silver Queen' and 'Emerald Beauty', but many other hybrids and true species are available from specialists.

A. modestum (Chinese evergreen) is an evergreen shrub from Africa, China, and the East Indies; it has attractive, sometimes variegated foliage valued for its large, glossy, dark green leaves growing two, three, and occasionally more on the top of a stalk, which rarely has side shoots. The stalk is thick and solid, averaging 15 in. tall. A bloom resembling a small green calla sometimes appears, seemingly stimulated by an overcrowded root system that has been in the same pot for a number of years. This plant is often grown in water only; small branches or rooted cuttings kept in water or wet soil make decorative houseplants. It can also be potted in soil or peat moss, thriving best in a vase with a soil mixture of equal parts sand, garden soil, and compost kept flooded with water. Charcoal can be added to make the soil mixture sweet. This plant has no use for direct sunlight and prospers in hallways or room corners where many other houseplants would fail. Stalks can be encouraged to grow in different shapes and curves by placing them sideways in a bowl.

AGRIMONIA (ag ri MOH nee ah) **eupatoria.** A hardy perennial herb belonging to the Rosaceae (Rose Family), commonly known as agrimony. Native from southern Europe to western Asia and northern Africa, it has been variously used for medicine, dye, or tea. It grows 2–3 ft. tall and bears alternate oblong leaves with coarse gray hairs on the undersides. The five-petaled, golden-yellow flowers resembling tiny roses are borne in loose clusters. As the petals fall, the calyx forms small, bristly green fruits. The flowers are not showy, but

Agrimonia eupatoria

plants are occasionally grown in the herb garden for their aromatic leaves.

Agrimony thrives in ordinary, well-drained soil and some shade. Propagation is generally by root cuttings taken in spring or fall. It can also be done by seed, but germination is difficult. The plants should stand about 10 in. apart.

AGRIMONY. Common name for AGRIMONIA, a genus of aromatic herbs with roselike flowers.

AGROPYRON. A genus of grasses including a number of valuable forage crops, though considered weeds in the garden, growing in Zones 3–7.

A. repens (quack or couch grass) has some value as a pasture or hay crop; its root stocks are efficient soil builders on slopes, embankments, and sandy soils where sod is necessary. It can be a serious weed, however, in pastures, fields, gardens, and lawns.

A. smithii (western wheat grass) is a native grass with blue-green stems and leaves that roll up lengthwise.

AGROSTEMMA (ag roh STEM ah). A small, European genus of herbs belonging to the Caryophyllaceae (Pink Family); it includes both weeds and garden subjects. The genus is closely related to and often confused with *Lychnis*.

A. coronaria (mullein pink, rose campion) is now listed as *Lychnis coronaria*; see LYCHNIS.

A. githago (corn cockle), a common weed, found in abundance in grain fields. The seeds are poisonous to animals, and when mixed with grain, render the flour or meal unwholesome. The showy plants are tall, erect, branching, grayish, and silky. They are sometimes cultivated in the garden for their flat-topped, purplish red flowers, 1 in. across. The plant grows in a wide range of soils, being indeterminate for nitrogen, water, and pH.

AGROSTIS (ah GRAWS tis). A large genus of mostly low-growing and spreading bent grasses including some valuable, high-class lawn grasses as well as the important pasture grass, redtop.

The species are annual or perennial, have somewhat rough, flat, or slightly rolled leaves, and bear loose panicles of small reddish flowers. While some of the forms are grown from seed, those used for fine lawns and putting greens are of the creeping type and are increasingly being grown vegetatively. A good bent grass turf is a joy to the eye as well as to walk on, but it calls for very well prepared soil and also for constant, intelligent attention.

Bent grasses do well in sun or partial shade but are not in any sense shade plants. The soil should be well supplied with thoroughly rotted manure or peat moss and receive a good application of a balanced complete fertilizer before planting time. See also LAWN; ORNAMENTAL GRASSES.

PRINCIPAL SPECIES

A. canina (velvet bent) is a dense turf used also in temperate shore climates.

A. gigantea (redtop), also listed as *A. alba*, is an unattractive European grass now naturalized in North America; it is no longer used as a nurse grass but is often used in pasture and somewhat in low-grade lawn seed mixtures. It has coarse leaves and will grow in good soil almost anywhere except in the extreme South and arid regions. It is tolerant of, if not actually benefited by, an acid soil.

A. hiemalis (hair or silk grass) is a perennial ornamental that grows to 2 ft. and has short, narrow, basal leaves and delicate purplish panicles up to 1 ft. long.

A. nebulosa (cloud grass) is a dwarf annual species with panicles 6 in. long; it is composed of many fine branches that grow to 2 ft. and has leaves 8 in. long.

A. palustris (creeping bent) is the species to which the best of the fine, lawn bent grasses belong. It is smaller and more stoloniferous in habit than redtop and withstands close cutting.

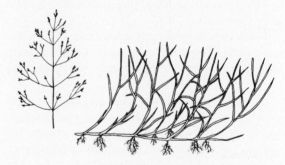

Agrostis palustris

A. tenuis (colonial bent) is a fine-textured grass particularly adaptable to temperate shore conditions.

AILANTHUS (ay LAN thus). A genus of Asiatic trees, sometimes known as varnish tree. One species, *A. altissima* (tree-of-heaven), is widely planted and is especially useful for city yards. It grows rapidly and can attain 60 ft.; it is hardy, deciduous, and of tropical appearance. The pinnate compound leaves, resembling those of sumac, have an unpleasant odor when crushed but are not often troubled by insects or disease and are highly resistant to air pollution. The staminate flowers have a strong odor, offensive to some, so it is best to plant the female tree, which bears large panicles of persistent red fruit. A high hedge can be made quickly by setting trees close together and topping them at the desired height each spring. Easily grown from seed, the ailanthus frequently self-sows so freely that it becomes a nuisance. It can also be propagated from root cuttings.

Although considered particularly healthy because of its ability to withstand city smoke and insect attacks, the ailanthus is sometimes killed by VERTICILLIUM WILT. Nectria canker and cercospora leaf spot may also occur. It is generally hardy in Zones 5–8.

AIPHANES (AY fan eez). A genus of very spiny feather palms from the American tropics, formerly included in the genus *Martinezia*, and commonly known as ruffle palm. They are sometimes called thorny-fishtail palms because the ornamental, pinnately divided leaves are broader toward the tip, resembling those of the true fishtail palms.

Some species are grown in Zones 10–11, requiring well-fertilized soil. A few are occasionally grown indoors as potted plants but are not attractive because of the spiny growths on all parts of the plant.

A. caryotifolia (ruffle or spine palm), thriving in south Florida, grows 25–30 ft. and has a very slender trunk ringed with long black spines and leaves 3–6 ft. long.

AIR LAYERING. Some woody plants, such as tall shrubs and flowering trees, are difficult to propagate by layering because they have no branches that can be bent over to root in the ground. However, often it is possible to root these high branches by bringing the earth to them in a method called air layering. Although only one layer can conveniently be placed on each branch, on a large plant a great many branches can be air layered at once, so a lot of new plants can be started.

PROCEDURE

The main stem is notched, girdled, or preferably slit, with a small wad of damp sphagnum moss inserted to keep the slit open (A). A large handful of wet sphagnum moss is placed about the stem (B), wrapped with clear polyethylene film, and sealed tightly, enclosing all strands of moss (C). Roots will develop at varying rates depending upon the species. When they are abundant, filling the sphagnum ball, the stem is cut at the bottom (D), all the plastic is removed, and the new rooted plant is potted (E, next page).

When potted, the small root system is insufficient for the large top. Therefore, the top is enclosed in a large, clear polyethylene bag (dry-cleaner bag) until the top growth starts. At this time, the bag is gradually removed over a two- or three-week period by mak-

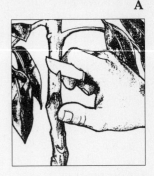

A

B

C

D

ing a few holes at a time every few days. During this aclimatizing period, the plant should be kept out of direct sun. The old stem, if kept, will send out new shoots. See also LAYERING; PROPAGATION.

E

AIR PLANT. Common term for EPIPHYTE, a plant that grows without soil on other plants.

AIR POLLUTION. Conspicuous plant injury in and around industrial centers is caused by discharged smoke, poisonous gases, and chemical pollutants. Certain species of plants may be killed and others chronically injured for miles around; acute injury has been traced for distances of ten to fifteen miles from the source and chronic injury for over 100 miles. Some pollutants contribute to acid rain, which may damage plants.

Smoke injury can result from the coating of soot deposited on the leaves as well as from the pollutants accompanying the smoke. The combination of soot and gases causes the leaves to turn brown in spots and then die; then the plant makes little growth. Coniferous trees are particularly susceptible. The common garden bean succumbs quickly to smoke injury and can be used as an indicator or detector of possible damage to valuable trees.

AIZOACEAE (ay ī zoh AY see ee). The Carpetweed Family, a group of low herbs and subshrubs, is widely distributed but grows principally in warm regions, mostly in southern Africa, where they inhabit deserts and seashores. The plants are characterized by showy, many-petaled flowers and paired, fat, succulent leaves. The family is of garden interest due to a few useful plants. *Mesembryanthemum* (fig-marigold) includes the common iceplant. *Aridaria*, *Conophytum*, *Doreanthus*, *Lithops*, *Oscularia*, and *Pleiospilos* (living-rock) are other cultivated genera.

AJUGA (ah JOO gah). A genus of European annual and perennial herbs belonging to the Lamiaceae (Mint Family), and commonly known as bugle or bugleweed. They are especially suitable for growing in the rock garden, though often used in the border. Growing from 6–14 in. tall, ajugas bloom early, generally in late spring, and occasionally again in the fall, bearing blue, purple, rose, or white flowers in dense whorls on terminal spikes. Of simple cultivation and thriving in any ordinary garden soil, they will do well in shade or sun. Propagation is by seed or division. Most are hardy to Zone 2.

A. reptans is particularly subject to the fungus disease known as CROWN ROT. In humid weather the white mycelian growth quickly creeps over the crowns of the plants, often destroying large areas in a few days. Remove diseased plants and sterilize the soil.

PRINCIPAL SPECIES

A. genevensis (Geneva bugle) is a tall species with blue flowers and is often used as a ground cover for shady places.

A. metallica cv. 'Crispa' is a dwarf horticultural form with metallic blue flowers.

A. reptans (carpet bugle) has stems to 12 in. long, though somewhat prostrate, and white, blue, or purplish flowers. Cv. 'Argentea' (kingwood) has blue flowers and silver foliage. Var. *atropurpurea* has blue-purple flowers and bronze-purple leaves. Cv. 'Burgundy Glow' is a spreading form with pink, white, and green markings on the foliage and blue flowers. Var. *multicolor* has red, brown, and yellow foliage. Cv. 'Pink Beauty' has green foliage and long-lasting pink flowers. Var. *rubra* has dark purple foliage. Cv. 'Silver Beauty' has green and white variegated foliage and blue flowers.

AKEBIA (ah KEE bee ah). A genus of hardy (Zones 5–8) deciduous or semi-evergreen twining vines from China and Japan, belonging to the Lardizabalaceae (Lardizabala Family). Their habit of growth is light and graceful, extending to about 30 ft. They appear to advantage on arbors and fences and will grow in any fairly good soil, producing their dark-colored flowers in early spring. Male and female fragrant flowers are separate in the same cluster, the latter being larger, darker in color, and opening first. The grayish purple sausage-shaped fruits are attractive but seldom seen. Apparently hand-pollination of the flowers is necessary to produce them. Sweet and pulpy, they are eaten in Japan, and the pliable stems are often used in wicker work.

The best-known species is *A. quinata*, with five-foliate leaves and chocolate-purple fragrant flowers. *A. trifoliata* has three leaflets and smaller flowers.

ALBA ROSE. This variety is thought to have developed not from one species, but from a cross of ancient species roses; *R. canina* and *R. gallica* have been suggested by some rose experts. Well-known rose authorities have identified alba roses in Renaissance paintings, and they are thought to have been grown from very early times. They are tall, upright, sturdy bushes with bluish green foliage and white or pink blooms. They have exquisite fragrance, and *R. alba semi-plena* or *R. alba suaveolens* is used as hedges around plantings of *R. damascena trigintipetala*, where it is grown for the perfume industry in the Kazanlik Valley of Bulgaria. Some well-known cultivars include 'Belle Amour', 'Celeste' or 'Celestial', 'Great Maiden's Blush', 'Königin von Dänemark', and 'Maxima'.

ALBIZIA (al BIZ ee ah). A genus of small deciduous trees or shrubs belonging to the Fabaceae (Bean Family) and closely allied to *Acacia*. Being natives of tropical and subtropical regions, they can be grown outdoors only in the warmer parts of the United States. One or two species are sometimes grown in greenhouses. They have graceful, feathery foliage and clusters of tassel-like flowers, followed by strap-shaped dry pods. They are easily raised from seed under glass.

A. julibrissin (silk tree, mimosa), the principal species, is a handsome, wide-spreading tree that grows to 40 ft. It can be grown as far north as Zone 6 and hardier varieties survive even farther

north. It has the longest blooming period of any northern ornamental tree, early summer through early autumn. Flowers are light to deep pink with many long stamens in ball-like clusters. Cv. 'Rosea' is a shorter plant, hardier, with brighter pink flowers. This tree is very susceptible, especially in the South, to a vascular wilt disease for which there is no cure. Webworm is another problem on the foliage, and though unsightly, does not harm the tree. Hardy in Zones 6–9.

ALBUCA (al BYOO kah). A genus of bulbs native to the Cape of Good Hope and cultivated in the greenhouse, belonging to the Liliaceae (Lily Family), and closely allied to ORNITHOGALUM. About 20 species are known, and many hybrids have been produced. Blooming in the late spring or early summer, with large white or yellow flowers, they are grown in a compost of loam, peat, and sand. The bulbs should be set deep in pots and kept in the dark until growth begins. Propagation is also by seed or by offsets taken in the spring.

ALCEA (al SEE ah). A genus of annual, biennial, or perennial herbs belonging to the Malvaceae (Mallow Family), and commonly known as hollyhock. There are about 60 species. Attaining a height of 5–9 ft., they blossom from midsummer until early fall, bearing large, wide-open, single or double flowers along the leafy main stem, which is generally hairy. The flowers may be white, red, rose, yellowish, or salmon, often in beautiful, delicate pastel shades. A tall group among shrubs or against a clump of evergreens is most effective, and a row along a garden wall or fence is charming.

CULTURE

Hollyhocks require a rich, well-drained soil, deeply dug and enriched with rotted manure. Heavy soil should be made looser by the addition of sand. Full sunlight and group planting are best. Most are hardy in Zones 2–9. New plants should be set out every two years because, although semiperennial, they are best treated as biennials.

Plants will bloom longer if dead blossoms are picked off the flower stalks, which should be cut down to the ground when all the flowers have faded, unless you wish to collect the seeds. Since seedlings cannot be depended on to come true to color, an unusual shade can be increased by root division in the early fall. This rather difficult operation consists of separating the auxiliary taproots from the main taproot of an old plant.

Seed is usually sown in midsummer in a coldframe or seedbed about ½ in. deep, and the plants set out 2 ft. apart the following spring to bloom that summer. They can also be started in their permanent locations. The newer annual strains produce flowers the first summer if seeds are sown indoors in midwinter.

ENEMIES

The most common disease of hollyhocks is rust, characterized by reddish brown spore pustules on the under-leaf surfaces. Severe infections cause yellowed foliage and very sickly looking plants. Control by carefully dusting underneath the leaves with fine sulfur dust beginning very early in the spring, and keep the new growth protected in the fall. Cut the old flower stalks down to the ground as soon as they finish blooming, and destroy the common succulent weed *Malva rotundifolia* (cheeses), which is also a host for the fungus. See RUSTS.

Several other fungi cause leaf spots, but removal and burning of all old plant parts in the fall will keep them in check. Removal of old stalks will also keep the common stalk BORERS from becoming too numerous. Hollyhocks are sometimes subject to injury by SLUGS and various chewing insects.

PRINCIPAL SPECIES

A. ficifolia (Antwerp hollyhock) is very similar to *A. rosea*, though not as commonly grown. It differs only in having figlike, deeply lobed leaves.

A. rosea (garden hollyhock), native to China, is by far the most commonly grown in American gardens. It produces stately, hardy biennial or semiperennial (though often cultivated as annual) plants. Their graceful, tall growth makes them

especially suitable for background borders, against walls or trellises, and as a screen for unsightly views or fences. Natural and cultivated varieties are available in many forms and colors. Cv. 'Allegheny' is a semidouble form that grows to 7 ft. tall and has large, fringe-edged flowers. Cv. 'Nigra' produces deep maroon blooms with nearly black centers. Cv. 'Prince of Orange' is an orange, double variety. Cv. 'Summer Carnival', an A.A.S. bronze medal winner, flowers the first summer after spring sowing, producing a display of double

Alcea rosea

blooms beginning very low on the stem and in a wide range of colors.

ALCHEMILLA (al ke MIL ah). A genus of low-growing, perennial, sometimes annual herbs belonging to the Rosaceae (Rose Family), and commonly known as lady's-mantle. Generally hardy, with matlike foliage and greenish or yellowish flowers blooming in midsummer, they are desirable for rock gardens or low borders. They are easily cultivated. Sow seed where it is to grow, in autumn or spring, in well-drained soil with partial shade.

Alchemilla vulgaris

Roots can be divided in late fall or early spring.

PRINCIPAL SPECIES

A. alpina grows to 9 in. and has silvery foliage and compound clusters of green flowers.

A. arvensis is an annual that grows to 6 in. and is widely naturalized in North America.

A. mollis (lady's-mantle) grows to 18 in. and bears many yellow flowers in attractive 3-in. clusters. Hardy to Zone 4.

A. vulgaris is the most commonly cultivated species. It grows to 1½ ft. and has gray woody foliage.

ALDER. Common name for ALNUS, a genus that includes about 30 species and numerous cultivars of hardy deciduous trees and shrubs of the Betulaceae (Birch Family).

ALFALFA. Common name for *Medicago sativa*, a leguminous perennial forage plant extensively grown for hay and pastures; see MEDICAGO.

ALISMA (ah LIZ mah). A genus of hardy perennial aquatic herbs that includes a few cultivated species, commonly known as water-plantain. Varying only slightly, they are used for planting along stream or pond margins or in bogs because of their decorative foliage and attractive bloom. The flowers are small, usually white but sometimes tinged with rose. The large heart-shaped leaves are effective, either floating or rising well above the water on long stalks. They are hardy in Zones 3–11 and are propagated by root division or by seed.

ALKALINE SOIL. Alkaline (or "sweet") soil, the opposite of acid soil, is usually found in limestone country and is associated with "hard" water. Also, many soils in acid and semiacid regions tend to be alkaline. Extreme alkalinity, as found in the western "badlands," is injurious to most plants. It follows lack of sufficient rain to wash away the alkali salts and continued irrigation with hard water, which leaves a constantly increasing accumulation of salts as it evaporates.

Simple tests will determine whether a soil is alkaline (see ACID SOIL). Readings higher than pH 7 show alkalinity, but a slight tendency in this direction is not a disadvantage in gardening, except where certain acid-loving plants are to be grown. In fact, it has long been customary to add lime to cultivated soils. See SOIL.

Much of the benefit from lime comes from the release of mineral foods, but there is also an increase in pH reading as the soil is made neutral or alkaline. Old, exhausted soil is usually acid (sour), and here lime is particularly valuable to increase fertility. Sometimes a soil is acid because it is not well drained, in which case ditching or underdraining will help neutralize the acidity. When peat, tree leaves, leaf mold, or other acid materials are used in growing alkaline-soil plants, lime, limestone, or bonemeal should be added immediately in sufficient quantity to counteract the acidity.

ALKALINE SOIL PLANTS

Moderately alkaline soil favors the growth and productiveness of many garden plants; others prefer acidity or are apparently indifferent. The use of lime creates or increases alkalinity, but it must be renewed, since rains wash it away and allow a naturally acid soil to become acid again. Clovers and other members of the Fabaceae (Bean Family) usually require an alkaline soil to aid the nitrogen-collecting bacteria in their roots. These and other alkaline-soil plants may become stunted, sickly, and yellow or reddish in acid soil.

Plants thriving in alkaline soil include alyssum, asparagus, bean, beet, cabbage, carnation, cantaloupe, cauliflower, celery, cucumber, geum, iris, lettuce, mignonette, nasturtium, onion, parsnip, pea, phlox, rhubarb, salsify, squash, and sweet pea.

ALKANET. Common name for ANCHUSA, a genus of summer-flowering perennial herbs, sometimes used to produce dyes.

ALLAMANDA (al ah MAN dah). A genus of shrubs or climbers from Brazil, belonging to the Apocynaceae (Dogbane Family). They are grown in greenhouses in the North and are planted outside by walls and fences in the far South. When grown outdoors to allow pollination, large yellow or showy purplish flowers are followed by large prickly fruits. Plants should be generously fed during the growing season (from late winter to autumn). They should be kept nearly dry until

February or March, when they are cut back, watered, started into growth, and repotted before the new shoots have made much headway. Propagation is by cuttings of new or old wood. Numerous cultivars have been developed within this genus; these include a wide range of colors, including creamy red, pink, rose, and dark reddish purple.

A. cathartica (common allamanda) has golden-yellow flowers 3 in. across. In several varieties, the flowers show various markings in their throats.

A. neriifolia (oleander allamanda) is a bushy grower, 4–5 ft. high and semierect, with dark green oblong leaves and yellow 1-in. flowers striped reddish inside and green at the base.

ALLEGHENY VINE. A common name for *Adlumia fungosa*, an attractive vine with delicate leaves and profuse flowers; see ADLUMIA.

ALLIUM (AL ee um). A genus of strong-smelling bulbous herbs of the Liliaceae (Lily Family) including onions, garlic, leeks, chives, and their relatives. Some 300 species are known in North Temperate regions, and about 70 of these are cultivated, all in the open ground, mostly as vegetables, but a few as ornamentals. A few species of Asian origin are treated as greenhouse plants. The hardy varieties have flat or tubular leaves with tapering tips and flowers at the end of erect bare stems in spherical clusters or slender spikes—the colors ranging from white to yellow, and through pinks to purple. Alliums require rich, loamy soil. Various species can be grown from seed, offsets, or small, aerial bulblets in the flower heads.

PRINCIPAL SPECIES

A. ampeloprasum var. *porrum* (leek) is a hardy biennial whose flat solid leaves and enclosed stems are used in cooking; see LEEK.

A. ascalonicum (shallot, scallion) is a hardy perennial bulb cultivated for its distinctive flavor; see SHALLOT.

A. cepa (onion) is the common bulb that is known and eaten in many forms. Var. *proliferum*

(top, tree, or Egyptian onion) is an unusual member of the family, with swollen stem bases from which typical onion leaves grow, but each of the white flowers at the end of a 24-in. stem develops a cluster of tiny bulblets instead of seed. For culture, see ONION.

A. cernuum (nodding wild onion) is an attractive midsummer wildflower found in moist prairies and woodlands of the central United States. It has soft, grasslike leaves and 12–24 in. leafless flower stalks (scapes) topped by nodding clusters of white to pink or lavender flowers with

Allium cernuum

three petals and three sepals all joined at the base.

A. fistulosum (Welsh or Japanese bunching onion) is a hardy perennial with tightly bunched leaves, which are generally used like scallions; see WELSH ONION.

A. giganteum (giant onion) is an attractive species often grown for ornament. From oval bulbs, it produces narrow leaves to 18 in. long and leafless flower stalks (scapes) to 4 ft. bearing bright lilac flowers in dense umbels 4 in. across.

A. sativum (garlic) is a hardy perennial bulb grown for its bulbs that divide into sections and are used as a flavoring; see GARLIC.

A. schoenoprasum (chives) is a hardy perennial grown for its thin, hollow foliage that is commonly used as a seasoning; see CHIVES.

A. scorodoprasum (giant or elephant garlic, sand leek) is very similar to *A. sativum*,

Allium tricoccum

but the plant is smaller and flowers are purple. It is grown and used like common onions; see ELE-PHANT GARLIC.

A. tricoccum (wild leek) is a favorite among edible wild plant fanciers. Groups of two to three fleshy leaves up to 12 in. long emerge in the early spring. The leaves stay green about a month, then wither as the flowering begins. As the leaves disappear, a hooded flower stalk emerges from the ground and reaches 6–12 in. in height. A cluster of small, six-petaled flowers burst from the top of the stalk.

A. tuberosum (gar-lic chives) is a hardy perennial similar to *A. schoenoprasum* but with leaves that are not hollow; they are triangular in cross section. See GARLIC CHIVES.

Allium tuberosum

ALLOPLECTUS (al oh PLEK tus). A genus of shrubby, tropical evergreen plants belonging to the Gesneriaceae (Gesneria Family). The leaves are opposite, one in each pair being smaller than the other. Tubular flowers are mostly red and yellow. They do well in the warm greenhouse under the same cultural treatment as COLUMNEA.

ALLSPICE. Common name for species of PIMEN-TA, especially *P. dioica* or *P. officinalis*, a tropical evergreen tree and its berrylike fruits, used for flavoring.

Carolina-allspice is *Calycanthus floridus*, a sweet-scented shrub; see CALYCANTHUS.

ALMOND. The common name of two groups of plants of the genus *Prunus*, one of value in gar-dens, the other primarily as an orchard or com-mercial subject.

The garden or ornamental types are small or medium-sized shrubs that are covered in early spring with pink or white, single or double flow-ers about the size of pompon or "button" chrysanthemums. Common species are *P. glan-dulosa* and *P. triloba*; *P. japonica* and *P. tenella* (the true dwarf almond) are not often seen.

P. glandulosa is hardy to Zone 4 and thrives in any well-drained soil, but it does best in sandy loam. Grown on its own roots (that is, not graft-ed), it becomes bushy and, even under neglect, blooms profusely. If grafted (usually on plum stock) two things must be watched—shoots from the plum root, which must be promptly removed, and attacks by peach borers. These pests, entering the tree at or just below the ground, can soon weaken it and may kill it. Grafted plants therefore should be carefully examined for signs of borer infestation before planting. The point of graft union should be planted at least 6 in. deep to encourage the devel-opment of many stems from dormant buds of the almond. "Worming" of any grafted plants (that is, the killing of any borers that may enter later, by thrusting a pointed, flexible wire into their burrows) should thereafter be done annually in late fall. See also PEACH.

The edible almond species include *P. amyg-dalus*, *P. communis*, and *P. dulcis* var. *dulcis*, a small peachlike tree that produces the familiar thin-shelled nuts. These are really the pits of the small, peachlike but thin-fleshed, inedible fruits. Grown commercially in California, it is frequent-ly planted elsewhere for its abundant, large pink flowers. Double varieties are even more popular, but they are sterile. It is hardy to Zone 5 but blooms so early it is frequently frost damaged.

The Indian- or tropical-almond belongs to a different family. See TERMINALIA.

ALNUS (AL nus). A genus of hardy deciduous shrubs and trees belonging to the Betulaceae (Birch Family), and commonly known as alder. There are about 30 species and numerous culti-vars. Most grow in cool or cold climates and moist or wet soils. Most alders do not have showy flowers or fruits, or fall color, and they are usually short-lived trees. Their primary use in gardening is for growing in moist or wet soils around ponds and along stream banks.

Propagation is by seed sown in the fall. If seeds are kept until spring, a three-month moist-cold treatment at 41°F is necessary. Shrub species will grow easily from suckers or hardwood cuttings. Cultivars are grafted onto seedling plants. Alders have numerous insect problems where they grow in the wild, but when cultivated they are usually free of serious injury.

PRINCIPAL SPECIES

A. glutinosa (common or black alder) is a tree that grows to 75 ft. and has cut leaves. There are several cultivars. Hardy in Zones 4–7.

A. incana (white alder) is a tree that grows to 50 ft. and is suited for cold and wet areas. Cv. 'Aurea' has yellow leaves and stems; 'Incana' has finely cut leaves. Hardy to Zone 3.

A. cordata (Italian alder), a round-headed tree growing to 50 ft., is the most beautiful of all alders but is not well known or grown. Hardy in Zones 6–7.

ALOCASIA (al oh KAY zhee ah). A genus of tropical herbs from southern Asia and the East Indies, belonging to the Araceae (Arum Family) and allied to *Colocasia* and *Caladium* (both known as elephant's-ear). Alocasias are grown under glass for their ornamental foliage—the large, hanging green leaves are veined, spotted, and marbled with striking colors and sometimes show a metallic gloss.

About 70 species are known, and with all the hybrids, a collection of 100 or more kinds is possible. The species fall into two divisions: evergreen and herbaceous. The herbaceous kinds have a resting period each year, during which they shed their leaves. Plants require a night temperature of not less than 60°F. When active growth begins in March, abundant water should be given and the temperature maintained at 70°F at night and 85°F during the day.

The soil for evergreen kinds is composed of fibrous peat and sphagnum moss intermixed with chunks of fibrous loam and small broken charcoal. The herbaceous kinds require 2 parts of a good fibrous loam with 1 part old, well-rotted cow manure. Perfect drainage is required, and on the surface of the pots, evergreens should have sphagnum moss packed up conically around the stem. Propagation is by suckers or root cuttings planted in pots, which are plunged in sand with bottom heat. Seed of new hybrids should be sown in a bed kept at 75°F.

ALOE (AL oh). A genus of perennial succulent herbs, native to southern and tropical Africa and neighboring Madagascar, belonging to the Liliaceae (Lily Family). They should not be confused with the agaves, which they somewhat resemble.

Their leaves are fleshy, stiff, and spiny along the edges, often large, and crowded together into a crude but picturesque rosette, making them attractive ornamental plants. The flowers, produced in irregular, showy spikes, sometimes

Aloe sp.

extending 20 ft. above the ground, are mostly of reddish shades but are sometimes yellow, orange, or whitish green.

Upwards of 325 species and numerous additional hybrids are recognized. Of the smaller species, *A. striata* (coral aloe), with coral pink flowers, is fairly common in collections, as is *A. variegata* (partridge-breast aloe), and *A. vera* (also listed as *A. barbadensis*), which is used extensively in cosmetics and as treatment for burns. Water-aloe is a name sometimes given to *Stratiotes aloides*, the water-soldier.

The plants are grown in pots in a sandy loam soil with a little peat, old manure, and some chunks of old lime-mortar. As this is filled in around the roots, bits of broken bricks are added, the coarser pieces being placed at the bottom.

The soil must be tightly packed around the roots. Unless active growth is evident, very little water is needed. Plants should remain in the same pots and soil for several years. Propagation is by suckers, cuttings, sprouts at the base of leaves, or seeds.

ALONSOA (al ahn SOH ah). A genus of tender or half-hardy herbs and small shrubs belonging to the Scrophulariaceae (Figwort Family) and commonly known as maskflower. They have dark green foliage and bear an abundance of two-lipped scarlet or orange flowers, turned upside down by the twisting of the pedicels.

Native to the tropical Americas and hardy only to Zones 9–11, they are grown as garden annuals or indoors. Thriving in warm, open places, they are best propagated by seed sown indoors in spring. For winter bloom, seeds can be sown outdoors in summer or stem cuttings can be rooted. Young plants taken up in the fall will become shrubby in form and bloom for a long period.

PRINCIPAL SPECIES

A. caulialata is a dwarf species that grows 12 in. tall and produces scarlet blooms.

A. incisifolia, from Chile, grows to 3 ft. and has deeply serrated leaves. The ⅝-in. flowers have deep scarlet corollas and purple-black throats.

A. warscewiczii, one of the best species for cultivation, is bushy, grows to 3 ft., and bears vermilion-scarlet blossoms.

ALOYSIA (ah loh IS ee ah). A genus of tender herbs and shrubs of the Verbenaceae (Verbena Family) with rose, purple, or white flowers in clusters of spikes. Only one species is commonly grown. *A. triphylla* (lemon verbena), formerly listed as *Lippia citriodora*, is a small shrub from South America with delightful lemon-scented foliage and long leaves growing in whorls. Hardy in Zones 10–11, it can be grown in warm climates as a standard to a height of 10 ft. In the North, it is treated as a houseplant or greenhouse subject. Pots can be put outside in summer but must be taken in before frost. This is an excellent indoor foliage plant during the winter. Leaves make a wonderful hot tea. Propagation is by cuttings started in moist sand.

ALPINE PLANTS. In North American gardening, this refers to plants not strictly native to the Alps, but rather those kinds that grow naturally on the rocky slopes above the mountain meadows, at timberline or higher. Here the growing season is very short (100 to 120 days), and the winters are long and cold with profuse snowfall that affords ample winter protection. During the short summer the plants are exposed to brilliant sunlight, and the roots are kept constantly supplied with ice-cold water from the melting snows above. They are generally of miniature growth and often shrubby; many are perennial, though there are a few attractive annuals. They often make brilliant displays of color, as one species sometimes covers a wide area of ground, blooming profusely through the short season.

From among the alpines come our choicest rock garden subjects, although the true alpine garden is only a special form of rock garden, perhaps forming a part of the rock garden and differing from the rest because it is usually provided with a system of underground irrigation. See ROCK GARDEN entry and chart.

ALPINE-AZALEA. Common name for LOISE-LEURIA, a genus of trailing, shrubby, evergreen mountain plants.

ALPINIA (al PIN ee ah). A genus of Asiatic, leafy, perennial herbs of the Zingiberaceae (Ginger Family), grown for their showy flowers borne in racemes and also for their handsome foliage. They grow outdoors in Zones 10–11 and in greenhouses in cooler regions, where they require moist air, a temperature of 60°F, a rich soil, and abundant water. Propagation is by division in the spring.

A. purpurata (red ginger) has bright red (rarely pink) bracts in a terminal spike up to 18 in. long, which are favored as cut flowers.

A. zerumbet (shellflower, shell ginger), formerly listed as *A. speciosa*, grows 10–12 ft. high. The leaves are long and veined, and the flowers are white, tinged purple with a lip crinkled and variegated red and brown. It grows well outdoors in tropical areas. A form with yellow variegated leaves is available.

ALSOPHILA (al SAW fil ah). One of several genera of large, tropical ferns, often elaborately pinnate, and suitable for greenhouse use; see TREE FERNS.

ALSTROEMERIA (al stre MEE ree ah). A genus of South American plants, commonly known as Peruvian- or herb-lilies. They are closely allied to the Amaryllidaceae (Amaryllis Family), but in the strictest sense they comprise their own family. Usually grown in the greenhouse, they grow from tuberous roots that are treated like bulbs and require deep planting in rich soil. They are sometimes grown outdoors (Zones 7–11) in a moist, fairly sunny spot, but the tender ones must be brought to a fairly warm storehouse when cool weather comes. Whether grown in pots or in the soil, the tuberous roots need dividing once a year. Plants raised from fresh seed sown in August, or later in pots in a good rich soil, will bloom in the garden the following summer.

Selections. The recently developed Ligtu hybrids have become stock items in cut-flower markets around the world. They are showy and long-lasting and can be produced efficiently in greenhouses with rooms kept at 50–55°F in the twelve weeks preceding bloom, thus saving energy and lowering production costs. In warm climates, they make splendid garden plants.

A. haemantha is fairly hardy with copper-colored flowers. Cv. 'Rosea' blooms in rose or pink.

A. pelegrina has lilac-colored flowers spotted with dark purple and has been grown successfully outdoors without special winter protection as far north as Zone 6. Cv. 'Alba', with white flowers, is recommended for greenhouse use.

ALTERNANTHERA (awl tur nan THEE rah). A genus of tender shrubs or herbs belonging to the Amaranthaceae (Amaranth Family). Some species are cultivated for their foliage and as car-

pet bedding; they are placed in the genera *Achyranthes* and *Telanthera* by botanists but are still called *Alternanthera* by many gardeners.

The flowers are minute; the plants are grown for their variously colored leaves and are kept dwarf and compact by shearing. They grow best where they have full sun and are easily propagated by division (the preferable method) or by cuttings made in the garden in late summer and kept over the winter in the greenhouse or hotbed. Cuttings may be subject to DAMPING-OFF. Most species are hardy in Zones 8–11.

PRINCIPAL SPECIES

A. besteri var. *mosaica* is a light yellow marbled with crimson.

A. ficoidea is trailing or erect with white or yellowish flowers and ovate leaves tipped with short spines. Cv. 'Amoena' is a very dwarf plant with leaves that have conspicuous green veins and are variously marbled with red and orange. Cv. 'Bettzickiana' has narrow leaves variegated with creamy yellow and red.

A. versicolor (copper alternanthera) has roundish leaves of copper or blood red.

ALTERNARIA. A disease caused by various species of the fungus genus *Alternaria*. On potatoes and tomatoes it is called early blight and appears as brown spots on the leaves; on some other vegetables and fruits it produces a soft rot. It also causes leaf spotting of many ornamentals, especially carnation, violet, and zinnia. The spots are usually light colored, often with concentric rings or circles. The dark centers are caused by the growth of the brown fungus mycelium and spores.

Control by cleaning up all old plant debris. Fungicidal sprays may be effective. Consult your local extension service for safe guidelines for your location. It also helps to keep the foliage dry, so water should be applied directly to the soil.

ALTERNATE. An arrangement of leaves or buds in which they are placed singly along the stem. "Leaves opposite" refers to two leaves arising from two sides of the same node or stem joint; more than two leaves arranged at the same point are called "whorled."

ALTHAEA. Alternative name for ALCEA, a genus of flowering herbs commonly known as hollyhock. The common name, shrub-althaea refers to the the summer-flowering shrub *Hibiscus syriacus*, which is better known as rose-of-sharon; see HIBISCUS.

ALUMINUM SULFATE. A chemical used to acidify a neutral or alkaline soil in order to make it suitable for acid-loving plants, such as rhododendrons, azaleas, and other members of the Ericaceae (Heath Family). It should be applied at the rate of up to 1 lb. per square yard on loams of ordinary fertility and thoroughly mixed with the soil, which should then be watered well. When used this way, it also causes hydrangea plants to produce blue flowers instead of pink ones. It can also be used to overcome excessive alkalinity or "hardness" of water, which is sometimes injurious to plants.

ALUMROOT. Common name for HEUCHERA, a genus of dwarf perennial herbs belonging to the Saxifragaceae (Saxifrage Family). False alumroot is the woodland perennial, *Tellima grandiflora*; see TELLIMA.

ALYSSUM (ah LIS um). A genus of annual and perennial herbs belonging to the Brassicaceae (Mustard Family); they are sometimes known as madwort. The plants grow 6–12 in., forming a mound of grayish foliage and small yellow or gold flowers. They are easily grown from seed in any good garden soil and are especially

Alyssum saxatile

suited for use in rock gardens and for edging in open sunny areas, or for use in beds, baskets, and window boxes. Seeds can be sown outdoors early in the spring or started indoors for earlier bloom. Most of the perennial species are hardy to Zone 3.

As a common name, sweet-alyssum refers to *Lobularia maritima*, a flowering perennial grown as an annual; see LOBULARIA.

PRINCIPAL SPECIES

A. murale (yellowtuft), sometimes listed as *A. argenteum*, is a perennial growing to 15 in. and is useful for light yellow flower color in the rock garden.

A. saxatile (basket-of-gold, goldentuft), a popular rock garden subject, is now listed as *Aurinia saxatilis*; see AURINIA.

A. spinosum is a low, branching, spiny plant with white or pinkish flowers.

AMARANTH. Common name for AMARANTHUS, a highly versatile genus of garden herbs. The Amaranth Family is AMARANTHACEAE. Globe amaranth, grown for dried bouquets, belongs to the same family but is a different genus; see GOMPHRENA.

AMARANTHACEAE (am ah ran THAY see ee). The Amaranth Family, an extensive family of weedlike herbs resembling those of the Chenopodiaceae (Goosefoot Family), mostly native to warm regions. The flowers are small, petal-less, usually green or white, of a shriveled texture, and usually in terminal spikes or heads, made showy by dry, chaffy bracts or scales. While many members of the family are weeds, others are popular garden subjects, and a few are potherbs. All are easily grown either from seed or cuttings in an open, sunny position. Among the principal cultivated genera are *Amaranthus*, *Celosia* (cockscomb), *Gomphrena*, and *Iresine*.

AMARANTHUS (am ah RAN thus). A genus of coarse, annual, warm-climate herbs, commonly known as amaranth. Some have edible and medicinal uses, but they are generally grown in the garden for their colorful foliage and some species for their showy, tassel-like heads made up of many red or brownish red flowers, which individually are tiny and inconspicuous. Of the 50 or more species, two are well known and satisfactory for garden use. There are also some bad weeds, such as pigweed and tumbleweed, which may be one reason why the ornamental kinds are not more popular. The genus lends its name to the AMARANTHACEAE (Amaranth Family), to which it belongs.

Amaranthus hybridus

The poorer the soil, the more brilliant the foliage of the *Amaranthus*; if the soil is very fertile, the gardener is likely to be disappointed. Plants grow readily from seed and prefer a sunny location. They can be started in the open in late spring, but since they require considerable space, they should be thinned or transplanted to stand at least 18–24 in. apart.

In warm climates, *Amaranthus* may be a host of the red- and black-spotted harlequin bugs, which are pests of cabbage and other crucifers. The roots are sometimes attacked by the carrot beetle, and there is no satisfactory control measure. Stem rots caused by fungi are best controlled by sanitary measures.

PRINCIPAL SPECIES

A. caudatus (love-lies-bleeding, tassel flower), reaches heights 3–6 ft. tall, growing coarsely and branching freely. Its odd crimson flower spikes have a texture like that of chenille and are either long and drooping or thick and short.

A. hybridus (pigweed) is a common weed, but its var. *erythrostachys* (prince's-feather) is graceful with much-branched, showy panicles.

A. tricolor (Joseph's-coat) is coarse and erect, 1–4 ft. high, and has grayish leaves 2–4 in. wide, sometimes blotched or splashed with green, yellow, and scarlet, hence the common name. Var.

nanus (fire amaranth) is a dwarf, especially good for potting, with brilliant coloring, the leaves being carmine with spots of yellow, red, and dark green. Var. *salicifolius* (fountain plant) has orange-bronze leaves of drooping habit and grows to 3 ft. Cv. 'Oriflamme' is of pyramidal growth to 5 ft. tall and has large leaves of glossy maroon; its central and side branches are topped with bright scarlet leaves.

AMARCRINUM (am ahr KRĪ num). A group or artificial genus of hybrids, similar to the belladonna-lily, produced by crossing plants of the genera AMARYLLIS and CRINUM. They are not widely available but are suitable for pot culture and have evergreen foliage in warmer climates. One species, *A. howardii*, has soft pink, fragrant flowers in large clusters on a 4-ft. stalk.

AMARYLLIDACEAE (am ah ri li DAY see ee). The Amaryllis Family, a large group of widely distributed perennial herbs growing from bulbs, rhizomes, or fibrous roots, and differing from the Liliaceae (Lily Family) by having the ovary below the floral parts (inferior) rather than above them (superior). This family is associated with warm, dry climates, some of its members often bearing leaves only during the rainy season. Here belong some of the most attractive and useful of garden and greenhouse genera, such as *Amaryllis*, *Amarcrinum*, *Clivia*, *Eucharis*, *Galanthus*, *Haemanthus*, *Hippeastrum*, *Hymenocallis*, *Narcissus*, *Nerine*, *Pancratium*, and *Zephyranthes*.

AMARYLLIS (am ah RIL is). A genus of South African bulbous plants that bear several large, fragrant, lilylike, pink, white, rose-red, or purple flowers on a single solid stem from midsummer to early autumn. Many closely related subjects are also commonly known or botanically listed as *Amaryllis*, especially several species and many hybrids of the South American genus HIPPEASTRUM. The genus LYCORIS, also known as amaryllis, is native to China and Japan. The Amaryllis Family is AMARYLLIDACEAE.

The only true species is *A. belladonna* (bel-ladonna-lily, naked-lady-lily), which grows well and blooms freely outdoors in California (Zones 9–11). In the East, it seems to defy every attempt to establish it outdoors. For indoor flowering, it requires a soil of fibrous loam, leaf mold, and sand with liquid manure during the blooming season. The bulbs are poisonous if eaten.

Amaryllis sp.

The leaf scorch common on narcissus also occurs on amaryllis, the fungus apparently over-wintering on the bulbs, which should be treated with a disinfectant. Bulbs showing the black resting bodies (sclerotia) of the botrytis fungus should be discarded. See BULBS; DISINFECTION.

AMAZON-LILY. A common name for *Eucharis grandiflora*, an attractive bulbous herb with broad basal leaves and clusters of fragrant green-and-white flowers; see EUCHARIS.

AMBERBOA (am bur BOH ah). A genus of rather weedy annual plants belonging to the Asteraceae (Aster Family), with jaggedly cut or divided leaves and heads of purple, blue, or pink flowers. They resemble bachelor's-button and are occasionally grown in the flower garden. Their culture is simple; the seed should be sown where the plants are to flower.

A. muricata, native to Spain and Morocco, is the most attractive species, growing 2 ft. high, with narrow leaves and heads of pink or purple flowers.

AMELANCHIER (am el ANK ee ur). A genus of hardy deciduous shrubs or small trees of the Rosaceae (Rose Family), commonly known as shadbush or serviceberry, including about 25 species, most of them native in North America. Their racemes of white flowers, freely produced in early spring, rank them among the most conspicuous of woody plants at that season. The flowers open in advance of, or with the unfolding of, the leaves. In most species, the young leaves attract attention by reason of a covering of soft woolly white hairs. In the fall, the tinted foliage adds to the display of that season. Some species are grown for their edible fruits, which are purple-black juicy berries. These are usually the stoloniferous kinds, which soon make a large patch.

Amelanchiers are not especially particular as to soil but prefer acid types. Some prefer wet environments, but in general the group is very tolerant. Propagation is by seed, layers, and, in some obvious cases, by suckers.

Yellow spots on shadbush leaves indicate infection by one of the juniper rusts (*Gymnosporangium* sp.). If it is present in abundance and if the two kinds of plants are growing close together, the best procedure is to remove all the plants of the least valuable kind.

Blighted twigs should also be removed. Clearing away fallen leaves and fruits will tend to prevent fruit and twig blight. See also FIRE BLIGHT; BROWN ROT.

PRINCIPAL SPECIES

A. alnifolia is a shrub or slender tree that grows to 25 ft. and is widespread in the region of Lake Superior. Bearing the largest fruit of any kind, up to ¾ in. across, it was an important food for the Indians of that region. Hardy to Zone 5.

A. arborea, growing to 30 ft., has outstanding apricot fall color and smooth gray bark; it grows in Zones 5–9.

A. canadensis is a bushy tree that grows to 15 ft. or more. It is widespread in the eastern United States and is the earliest species to bloom. Both sides of the young leaves are covered with short, dense, woolly hairs, giving the tree a very silvery appearance for a short time. It is similar to *A. arborea* but is smaller and grows in wet areas.

A. florida, native to the northwestern United States, makes a clump of upright stems to 8 ft. or more and displays rich yellow foliage in the fall. Hardy in Zones 3–6.

A. x *grandiflora*, a natural hybrid between *A. arborea* and *A. canadensis*, is a small tree with the largest flowers of any American shadbush. Hardy in Zones 5–8, it grows wild in upstate New York. Var. *rubescens* has pinkish flowers.

A. laevis is one of the most graceful and attractive of North American small trees, hardy in Zones 5–8. Especially beautiful in spring, it bears nodding racemes of white flowers among the bronze-tinted young leaves, which are a distinguishing feature. The fruit is sweet and black.

A. oblongifolia is the largest of the shrubby species and common in eastern North America. It is conspicuous in spring with its flowers and whitish leaves, in June with its abundant fruit, and in fall with its richly tinted leaves.

A. sanguinea is a slender shrub that grows to 6–8 ft. and is found across the northern United States. Hardy in Zones 5–7, it does well in dry soil and is one of the best for fruit.

AMENT. The botanical term for catkin, one of the blossoms or flowering parts of certain shrubs and trees, notably willow, poplar, and birch. It consists of a number of small flowers closely clustered on a drooping, tassel-like spike. Only the reproductive parts of these flowers, that is, the stamens and pistils, are present; they are protected, not by petals and sepals, but by scaly bracts. Catkins are either staminate (male) or pistillate (female), the two types being sometimes borne on separate (monoecious) plants and sometimes on different parts of the same (dioecious) plant.

AMIANTHIUM (am ee ANTH ee um) **muscitoxicum.** A perennial bulbous plant belonging to the Liliaceae (Lily Family). Sometimes known as fly-poison or cow-poison, the bulb is extremely poisonous. The flowers are white and borne in racemes not unlike *Zigadenus*, where it was once included. The leaves are grasslike and basal. The only member of the genus, it is widespread from New York to Florida and westward to Missouri and Oklahoma.

AMMOBIUM (ah MOH bee um). A genus of annual herbs, native to Australia, and grown as everlastings. The name, a combination of Latin words meaning "sand" and "life," indicates that the plant prefers a sandy soil. Plants are 18 in. tall and bear a profusion of small white flowers with yellow centers, which brighten the garden. They are easily cultivated; seed can be sown either in the spring or in the fall for next season's bloom. Flowers will remain white if cut before they have reached full bloom and hung in a shady, airy place to dry; later they become yellowish.

A. alatum (winged everlasting, everlasting sandflower) derives one common name from the peculiar winged formation of the branches. It grows to 3 ft. high, and flower heads are almost 2 in. across.

AMMONIUM SULFATE. A chemical used as a fertilizer. Containing about 20% nitrogen in comparatively available form, as a plant food it is classed among the quick-acting nitrogenous materials, such as nitrate of soda. Its continued use tends to make the soil acid, which renders it very satisfactory for ericaceous plants (such as rhododendrons), bent grasses, and other acid-loving plants. Use with caution, however, since overuse can kill plants quickly.

AMMOPHILA (a MOHF i lah). A genus of tall, perennial grasses with long, creeping root stocks useful for sand-binding in gardens near the water. They have been used extensively for that purpose in Europe, on Cape Cod in Massachusetts, and in Golden Gate Park in San Francisco, California. They are hardy to Zone 5.

Either start seed in flats of mixed sand and leaf mold and set out

Ammophila breviligulata

the small plants directly in the sand, or sow seed where the grass is to grow. In both cases, throw evergreen boughs or straw over the area planted in order to hold the sand in place and provide a little protecting shade. When the seedlings have taken hold, remove the protection and reinforce them with plantings of low-growing grasses.

A. arenaria (marram grass, sea sand-reed), common along the north Atlantic coast and shores of the Great Lakes, grows to 3 ft., has panicled flowers to 1 ft., and has very long, hard, branching root stocks that make it an excellent sand-binder.

A. breviligulata (American beach grass), which grows abundantly and to nearly 2 ft. on the shores of the Atlantic and the Great Lakes, is another fine sand-binder.

AMORPHA (ah MOR fah). A genus of deciduous shrubs native to North America, belonging to the Fabaceae (Bean Family), and commonly known as false indigo. They are summer blooming with small, dark blue or purple flowers in dense terminal spikes. The foliage is fine and fernlike, turning yellow in the fall. They prefer a sunny location and can stand dry soil better than many shrubs. Old plants get straggly, but they can be returned to good growth with hard pruning in spring. Hardy to Zone 5.

A. canescens (leadplant) grows to 4 ft. and has small, white-hairy leaflets.

A. fruticosa (bastard indigo) grows to 20 ft. and

Amorpha canescens

has smooth oval leaves to 1½ in. long and dark purple to light blue flowers with white calyxes clustered in spikes to 6 in. long.

AMORPHOPHALLUS (ah mor foh FAL us). A genus of large, tropical Asiatic herbs belonging to the Araceae (Arum Family), and commonly known as krubi. They have immense, bulblike tuberous roots. Very large, funnel-shaped flowers (resembling huge callas in shape) are thrust up from the bulb on a long naked stem in advance of the three-parted leaves, which may be 3 ft. or more across. The flower is of a chocolate or reddish maroon color and emits a nauseous odor in some species.

In temperate regions, these plants are grown in tubs as greenhouse curiosities and are sometimes transplanted to the open in summer and allowed to dry off under the greenhouse bench in the fall. The soil required is a mixture of light, sandy loam, leaf mold, and rotted manure. Propagation is by the small tubers that offset from the parent root. These should be placed in pots just large enough to hold them and shifted as they grow.

A. rivieri (devil's-tongue), formerly listed as **Hydrosme rivieri**, is a large tropical herb with leaves to 4 ft. long cut into segments. The large, calla-like flowers are 12 in. long, green spotted with purple; they appear before the leaves and have an offensive odor. The plant is sometimes grown as an exotic in the greenhouse; it needs a soil rich in humus and a high temperature.

A. titanum (krubi) is a tropical Asiatic plant reputed to bear the largest flowers known. Actually its flower is an inflorescence consisting, like that of the calla, of a petal-like sheath or spathe surrounding a spikelike spadix on which many true flowers are clustered. The inflorescences have been known to grow nearly 9 ft. across.

AMPELOPSIS (am pel AHP sis). A genus of tendril-climbing deciduous vines belonging to the Vitaceae (Grape Family), and native to North America and Asia. About 20 species are known, not all of them hardy in the North. Not particular as to soil and location, they are useful in gardens to cover walls, arbors, or to ramble over rocks. Propagation is by seed, cuttings, and by layering.

PRINCIPAL SPECIES

A. aconitifolia is a slender grower with dissected leaves, native to China and hardy in Zones 5–7. Its fruit starts bluish and turns yellow or orange.

A. arborea (peppervine) is native from Virginia to Florida and is hardy only in Zones 7–9. A shrub of slender, graceful, tendril-climbing habit, with finely cut leaves and dark purple fruit, it is very aggressive and is often a pest.

A. brevipendunculata (porcelain-berry) is one of the best Asiatic species. A strong grower and well adapted to clothe low walls and sprawl in rocky places, it is beautiful in fall with berries varying in color from pale lilac through copper-green to turquoise-blue. Var. *elegans* makes a lovely porch vine, being a smaller and slower grower. The young leaves show white, green, and pink variegation. Hardy in Zones 5–8.

A. japonica is a somewhat tender vine with a tuberous root. The leaves are handsome, lustrous, and finely cut, and the fruit is small and blue. Hardy in Zones 6–9.

AMPHIBIANS. The many species of amphibians, including toads, frogs, and lizards, are powerful enemies of insect pests and definitely an asset in the garden. Besides their usefulness, their amusing behavior and bright colorings make them an attractive feature at the edge of the water garden, in the pool, or in the bog garden.

That familiar and friendly dweller in garden and field, the toad, although still regarded with suspicion by the uninformed, has been proven to be a most valuable gardener's helper. Though they are probably happier if not handled, there is no truth in the old belief that contact with toads causes warts. In short, toads are distinct assets and should be protected and encouraged to reside in the garden.

Toad

Toads consume many undesirable insects, worms, and slugs, both plant pests and biting insects such as mosquitos. A series of studies has revealed that they devour nightly an astonishing variety and quantity of material. Up to 3000 insects or their larvae may be destroyed by a single toad in a summer month. Prominent in this insect harvest are ants, ground beetles, click beetles, weevils, sowbugs, and cutworms.

Primarily land animals, toads usually burrowing in the earth in the daytime and coming out to feed at night. During the breeding season they seek water in which to lay their eggs, and the tailed, swimming young, called tadpoles, live for a few weeks before reaching the adult stage.

To make toads more comfortable, clay pots can be buried on their sides to provide short tunnels or shelters under plants. Rotenone and several other insecticides also kill toads, salamanders, and fish, so avoid using them if you value your amphibians.

Frogs are similar to toads in appearance and diet; however, they consistently stay close to water. The larger bullfrogs, whose characteristic croaking reverberates around many ponds, sometimes prey on meadow mice, which may do damage to garden subjects.

Frog

In the southern and the western states, lizards of several species sometimes frequent gardens in search of food, which includes insects and insect larvae. They are absolutely harmless, and the gardener should try, for the garden's sake, to welcome them.

AMPHICARPAEA (am fi KAHR pay ah). A genus of perennial herbs belonging to the Fabaceae (Bean Family), and commonly known as hog-peanut. Native to the eastern states and India, they have little horticultural interest. The flowers, white or purple, are of two kinds—the upper ones showy, and the lower ones without petals but followed by rather conspicuous pods.

A. bracteata has rose, purplish, or white blossoms. It can be used to trail over bulb beds in shady spots, but it often becomes a pestiferous weed.

AMSONIA (am SOH nee ah). A genus of perennial herbs belonging to the Apocynaceae (Dogbane Family); it is commonly known as bluestar. They grow 1–3 ft. high and have peculiar tough bark and quite narrow leaves. The panicles of inconspicuous blue or bluish flowers are followed by rather attractive, milkweed-like pods. Occasionally they are planted in the border or with shrubbery; some of them hold their leaves well into the fall. Hardy to Zone 5, they will grow in ordinary garden soil and are propagated by division, cuttings in summer, or seed.

Amsonia ciliata

A. ciliata grows to 3 ft. and has erect stems and blue star-shaped flowers. Native to pinelands from the Carolinas to Missouri, this perennial flowers in early summer.

A. tabernaemontana grows 2–3 ft. high and produces soft-blue flowers, hairy outside, from May to July. It is found in low ground from New Jersey to Florida and Texas.

ANACAMPSEROS (an ah KAMP sur ohs). A genus of most unusual succulents of the Portulacaceae (Portulaca Family), mostly from southern Africa. The most remarkable species are *A. papyracea*, with thin, elongate stems completely covered with silvery white, papery scales, and *A. alstonii*, similar but with even tinier branches arising from a large caudex and very large, showy white flowers over an inch in diameter.

ANACARDIACEAE (an ah kahr dee AY see ee). The Cashew Family, a group of trees or woody shrubs found mostly in the tropics, with acrid, resinous,

or caustic juice. Some kinds are grown for their plum- or cherry-like fruit, which encloses a nut, and others for ornamental, tanning, or medicinal products. The principal genera are *Rhus* (which includes sumac, poison-ivy, and lacquer tree), *Pistacia*, *Anacardium*, *Schinus*, and *Spondias*.

ANACARDIUM (an ah KAHRD ee um) **occidentale.** An evergreen tree, which in the United States is cultivated only in Zone 11 and the extreme southern part of Zone 10. They yield a milky juice, used in making insecticidal varnish, and they produce the nuts that are commonly known as CASHEW.

ANACYCLUS (an ah SĪK lus). A genus of prostrate perennials belonging to the Asteraceae (Aster Family) and native to Morocco. They do best in the rock garden, preferring very well drained soil and much sun. Hardy to Zone 6.

A. atlanticus blooms in late spring to early summer, producing single, 1–2 in., daisylike flowers, white with red on the reverse side. The leaves are gray, hairy, and finely cut.

A. depressus is similar to *A. atlanticus* but has brighter red reverses.

ANAGALLIS (an ah GAL is). A genus of low-growing annual, biennial, or perennial herbs belonging to the Primulaceae (Primrose Family), and commonly known as pimpernel. They have delightful little starlike flowers of red, blue, or white growing out of the leaf axils on hairlike stems. Plants are free flowering, some species being most attractive in the rock garden. They require the simplest culture; seed for the annuals can be sown where the flowers are to grow, and the perennial kinds are easily propagated by root division and cuttings. They all thrive in a loose, warm soil.

A. arvensis (poor-man's-weatherglass) has its common name because of its flowers, which close at the approach of bad weather. An annual native to Europe and Asia, also naturalized in North America, it has trailing stems and scarlet or white flowers ¼ in. across.

A. monelli var. *linifolia*, a perennial or biennial, sometimes grows 1½ ft. high and bears blue flowers, reddish beneath, on woody stems.

ANANAS (ah NAH nas). A genus of stiff perennial herbaceous plants native to tropical America; it includes the popular PINEAPPLE.

ANAPHALIS (ah NAF al is). A genus of hardy, herbaceous perennials with woolly foliage, belonging to the Asteraceae (Aster Family), and commonly known as pearl or pearly everlasting because of the prominent whitish bracts in the small flower heads. The persistent flower formation makes the plant valuable for dried bouquets. For such use, the flower stalk is cut just before the flowers mature. Hardy in Zones 3–8.

Anaphalis margaritacea

A. margaritacea attains a height of 3 ft. Leafy stems and woolly appearance make them good subjects for hardy borders and rock gardens.

A. triplinervis bears pearly white flowers above silver-gray foliage.

ANASTATICA (an as TAT ik ah) **hierochuntica.** An annual plant belonging to the Brassicaceae (Mustard Family), commonly known as rose-of-Jericho or resurrection plant (both common names also refer to *Selaginella lepidophylla*). Native to sandy deserts of the Middle East, it curls up when dry and opens out again when supplied with moisture. It grows 6 in. tall and has small, broadly oval leaves. Small white flowers borne in spikes are followed by a short, broad fruit bearing two seeds.

This resurrection plant can be raised indoors from seed started in light soil in February. Transplant seedlings to 4-in. pots when they have formed their true leaves, then let the plants stay in pots until they have bloomed and fruited.

For ages, fantastic stories have been told about this fascinating plant, which was first brought to Europe by the crusaders; it is believed to be "the rolling thing before the whirlwind" mentioned in the Bible. After forming its fruit, the little plant sheds its leaves and rolls up into a dry ball consisting of the interlaced branches. This is soon unrooted by the wind and rolls rapidly over the desert sand until it reaches some damp soil or until rain falls, when the dry branches soften and unroll, and the seeds fall out and immediately start to germinate.

ANCHUSA (an KOO sah). A genus of herbaceous plants belonging to the Boraginaceae (Borage Family), and commonly known as alkanet, bugloss, and summer-forget-me-not. The botanical name comes from a Greek word meaning "paint for the skin," the ancients having made a kind of rouge from the root of the plant. The genus includes hardy, easily grown, perennial and biennial herbaceous plants excellent for the summer border in a sunny location. They make good-sized clumps of rather coarse, usually hairy foliage. From midsummer to early fall, 1½–5 ft. tall, leafy stalks bear loose masses of small flowers, sometimes white but usually blue and often in intense, striking shades.

Anchusas do well even in ordinary soil, but given plenty of well-rotted manure, they prove heavy feeders and respond vigorously. Propagation is from seed sown in a hotbed or coldframe in spring or outside in early summer. The biennial kinds are usually treated as annuals and can be sown where they are to bloom; the plants are later thinned to 1 ft. apart. Otherwise, transplant in the early fall or spring, handling them carefully so as not to break the taproot and setting them 12–18 in. apart. Some species self-sow freely in mild locations. After flowering, cut off the flower stems and give a little fertilizer or liquid manure to stimulate a second blossoming until frost; then cut back again. In severe locations, after the ground freezes, mulch with straw or leaves—but lightly to avoid rotting the crown. Various species are hardy in Zones 3–8.

PRINCIPAL SPECIES

A. azurea (Italian bugloss), formerly listed as *A. italica*, is a perennial that grows to 5½ ft. Popular cultivars are 'Dropmore' with deep blue flowers and 'Opal' with lighter blue flowers.

A. barrelieri is a perennial growing to 2 ft. that has blue spring flowers with white and yellow centers.

A. capensis (cape-forget-me-not) is a biennial that grows to 1½ ft.; it is offered by seed growers as an annual. Its blue flowers have red edges and white throats.

A. myosotidiflora is correctly listed as *Brunnera myosotidiflora*; see BRUNNERA.

Anchusa azurea

A. officinalis (bugloss) is a perennial or biennial that grows to 2 ft. Its bright blue or purple flowers bloom in summer and fall.

ANDROMEDA (an DRAH muh dah). Common

name for a group of attractive shrubs of several genera in the Ericaceae (Heath Family). Also, the botanical name for two dwarf, hardy evergreen shrubs of the same group, commonly called bog-rosemary. They grow naturally in peaty bogs of the temperate and colder regions of the Northern Hemisphere; hardy in Zones 2–4. In habit rather thin, they are interesting when clumped in front of evergreens or azaleas. They need a moist, peaty soil in a partly shaded position, since they will not stand becoming dry at the roots.

A. polifolia, growing to 1–2 ft., is found in Europe, Asia, and North America. It has small narrow leaves that are glaucous beneath. The pinkish urn-shaped flowers are in clusters at the end of branches. *A. glaucophylla*, native only in North America, is very similar, but the leaves are white beneath.

Other species formerly in this genus are now included under *Cassiope, Chamaedaphne, Leu-*

cothoâ, Pieris, and *Zenobia*. Among these is Japanese-andromeda (*Pieris japonica*).

ANDROSACE (an DROHS ah see). A genus of true

alpine plants belonging to the Primulaceae (Primrose Family) and commonly known as rock jessamine or rock jasmine. They grow in rock crevices and mountain screes above timberline. Their leaves are often woolly and usually tufted or in rosettes. The small white, pink, red, or lavender flowers are usually borne in flattened,

Androsace sp.

round clusters. They can be grown from seed, divisions, or cuttings. In the garden, they need a gritty soil and sharp drainage and should never be allowed to dry out. Most species are not successful in hot, humid climates.

PERENNIAL SPECIES

A. carnea is perhaps the easiest *Androsace* for the rock garden, particularly in humid regions where woolly-leaved plants often rot during the summer. Its leaves are smooth and bright green. Three to eight rose-pink, yellow-throated flowers grow in a loose umbel on a stalk 3 in. high.

A. chamaejasme has rosettes of hairy leaves that form a mat. The ⅜-in. white flowers have yellow eyes that turn deep pink with age. The flower umbels are supported by 1–5 in. stems. It does best in full sun.

A. lanuginosa is a trailer with narrow foliage covered with silvery woolly hairs. The lilac-pink flowers, in dense umbels on stems 2 in. high, recommend it for its late-summer flowering period.

A. sarmentosa has woolly leaves clustered at the base and increases by rooting stems that end in new rosettes. The many rose-pink flowers appear on stems up to 5 in. high. It is easily grown in gritty soil.

A. sempervivoides forms rosettes of leathery leaves. The pink flowers, ¼ in. across, grow in umbels on 2–3 in. stems. It can be easily propagated by pegging down the runners.

ANNUAL SPECIES

A. lactiflora produces airy umbels of small white flowers. It will self-sow when established but is easy to weed out and is never a pest.

ANEMIA (ah NEE mee ah). A genus of small to medium (6–18 in.), slow-growing ferns of the "flowering" type, with spore clusters borne in a separate panicle. They are native to the tropical Americas and can be grown outdoors in Zones 10–11 but are somewhat difficult as houseplants.

PRINCIPAL SPECIES

A. adiantifolia (pine fern) grows in rocky pine forests and sometimes in limey soils. It has sterile, bipinnate fronds that resemble those of the maidenhair fern.

A. mexicana (flowering fern) has pinnate fronds and adapts very well to cultivation.

A. phyllitidis has pinnate fronds and is the most commonly available species.

A. rotundifolia is unique in that it often roots at the tips.

ANEMONE (ah NEM oh nee). A large genus of perennial herbs with cup-shaped white, purple, or red flowers, belonging to the Ranunculaceae (Buttercup Family), and commonly known as windflower or pasqueflower. Different species are suitable for the border, the wild garden, or the rock garden. The most popular types are the autumn-flowering, fibrous-rooted kinds (Japanese anemones) and the spring-flowering, tuberous-rooted kinds (poppy anemones). The best rock garden species are among the lesser-known kinds. Most species are hardy in Zones 5–8, but the rock garden kinds may be hardier. The common name rue-anemone refers to the

monotypic genus ANEMONELLA.

Enemies. A smut sometimes causes abnormally large and deformed flowers of *A. nemorosa*, and diseased plants should be destroyed. In California, *A. coronaria* is severely attacked by a rust that causes the leaves to become abnormally thickened, puffy, and rigid and to die prematurely. This rust passes another stage on stone fruits (such as almond, apricot, cherry, or peach). To control it, promptly remove infected plants and avoid growing alternate hosts in

Anemone canadensis

the same locality. Blister beetles that may harm *A. japonica* are difficult to control. See BLISTER BEETLE; RUSTS.

AUTUMN-FLOWERING SPECIES

The Japanese anemone and its attractive varieties with pink and white flowers are beautiful in the border or naturalized, the graceful flowers on slender stems rising above the sturdy clumps of good-sized leaves. They should be planted in a moist soil, rich in humus (including well-rotted manure) in a somewhat shaded spot. Never allow the plants to dry out in summer; frequent watering and a mulch of decayed leaves will materially increase the beauty of the flowers. The clumps with their fibrous roots can be propagated by division in spring, although the plants resent disturbance.

A. japonica (Japanese anemone) grows to 3 ft. with flowers of white or tinged rose or purplish, to 3 in. across, blooming from early fall to heavy frost. Among the numerous varieties are *alba*, pure white; *rosea superba*, rose; and *rubra*, waxy red. Cultivars include 'Queen Charlotte', with semidouble white flowers; 'Alice', flowering rose pink with lilac centers; and 'September Charm', with silvery pink blooms. The plant formerly listed as *A. hupehensis*, with pink or mauve flowers shaded lavender-rose on the reverse, is considered a dwarf, early-flowering form of this species.

SPRING-FLOWERING SPECIES

The poppy-flowered anemones are very beautiful, with both single and double flowers shaped like large buttercups, and of many colors. They are more difficult to grow, except in temperate climates, since they succumb to both the heat of summer and a severe winter.

They are occasionally planted outdoors in cool climates, either in the open in a shady, sheltered spot and covered over with a thick but loose layer of leaves held in place with evergreen boughs, or in a coldframe. Set the tubers in leaf mold and sand, and then in the spring sift rich soil around those growing in the coldframe, giving them frequent ventilation and removing the frames after the danger from frost is over. At the same time, remove the leaves from those growing in the open. Poppy anemones can be propagated by division of the tubers or from seed.

A. baldensis (moraine anemone), growing about 5 in. tall, is an alpine species that has creamy white blossoms up to 2 in. across.

A. canadensis (Canada anemone) is one of the easiest northeastern wildflowers to grow. A hardy perennial, it grows to 2 ft. tall and has white flowers. The roots were used medicinally by Native Americans.

A. coronaria (poppy-flowered or poppy anemone) grows to 1½ ft. and has finely cut leaves and solitary flowers to 2½ in. across in white and brilliant shades and combinations of purple, red, and blue. Cv. 'St. Brigid' is a popular strain used frequently for forcing by florists.

A. x *fulgens* (flame or scarlet anemone) grows to 1 ft. It is frequently forced, producing vivid scarlet flowers to 2 in. across with numerous black stamens.

A. hortensis (broad-leaved garden anemone), growing to 10 in., differs from *A. coronaria* in having broad, irregularly cut leaves and slightly smaller flowers in shades of red, rose-purple, or white. It is also used for forcing, and many garden forms have been developed.

A. x *lesseri*, growing to 18 in., is the progeny of *A. multifida* and *A. sylvestris*. It has red flowers with yellow centers borne on erect stems over ferny foliage.

A. sylvestris (snowdrop anemone), growing 6–18 in., has semipendent, 1½–3 in. white blooms that give way to woolly white seed heads. It prefers a partially shaded site.

ROCK GARDEN SPECIES

Many anemones are native to mountainous areas and are fine candidates for rock gardens. Many taxonomists have moved some of this group into its own genus, *Pulsatilla*; others classify them all under *Anemone*.

A. blanda (windflower) is a lovely ground-hugging species, available in several color forms, including white and a clear sky blue.

A. nemorosa (European wood anemone, windflower), growing to 8 in., has delicate, airy white flowers 1 in. across. It adds an airy charm to shady rock gardens or a shady part of the border. Var. *robinsoniana* has larger flowers, occasionally blue. Var. *alba*, with white flowers, has a beautiful semidouble cultivar.

A. patens was originally listed in the genus *Pulsatilla*. Var. *nuttalliana* (American pasque-flower), growing 4–9 in., has silky, hairy foliage and bluish purple, erect flowers followed by plumed, seedlike fruits. It should be placed in a low spot in the rock garden in full sun.

A. pavoniana has flowers of brilliant scarlet.

A. pulsatilla (pasqueflower), also listed as *Pulsatilla vulgaris*, grows to 12 in. and has hairy foliage and large, erect, single, blue or purple,

Anemone patens

bell-shaped flowers. It does well in dry, rocky soil. Even more choice is Cv. 'Rubra' with wine-red flowers. There is also a slightly muddy white form.

A. quinquefolia (American wood anemone, windflower), of the eastern states, is much like its European counterpart, *A. nemorosa*.

A. vernalis grows to 6 in. high and has white flowers.

ANEMONELLA (ah nem oh NEL ah) **thalictroides.** A delicate perennial herb, the only member of its genus, belonging to the Ranunculaceae (Butter-cup Family), and commonly known as rue-anemone. The plant grows about 9 in. tall from tuberous roots and bears pink or white flowers 1 in. across in spring. Var. *flore-pleno* produces double flowers. Native to eastern North America, they can be grown in colonies and are often a nice addition to a wildflower garden, thriving in light, moist soil and partial shade. Propagation is by division of the roots in spring or fall.

ANETHUM (AN e thum) **graveolens.** An annual herb belonging to the Apiaceae (Celery Family), commonly known as dill. It is grown for both the seed heads, used in pickling, and for its feathery, sweet-tasting foliage, which can be used in salads. Early in spring, sow the seeds in rows 15 in. apart in a sunny spot. Thin the seedlings while still small to stand 1–10 in. apart. Do not transplant. Cultivate frequently. In midsummer, cut the ripening heads and spread thinly on sheets.

Anethum graveolens

When dry, shake, beat, or rub the seeds off. Clean and store them in a dry place. See also HERBS; EVERLASTINGS.

ANGELICA (an JEL ik ah). A genus of herbs belonging to the Apiaceae (Celery Family), and resembling species of *Delphinium*. Several of them are native to North America and other temperate parts of the world. They have large, much-divided leaves and large, round, flattened clusters (umbels) of white or greenish flowers on tall, stout stalks. They are easily propagated by seed or division and are sometimes planted in the border where height is needed or along roadsides for the striking, almost tropical effect of their profuse foliage. Hardiness varies depending on the species. The genus name was derived from their supposed angelic healing properties.

Angelica archangelica

A. archangelica is a stout herb that grows to 6 ft.; in low ground it makes a striking picture beside a stream.

A. triquinata, formerly listed as *A. curtisii*, is found from Pennsylvania to North Carolina; it grows 2–5 ft. high and has finely cut, ample foliage. The white flowers are borne in umbels 6 in. across.

ANGELICA TREE. Common name for various species of ARALIA, a genus of flowering herbs, shrubs, and trees.

ANGEL'S-EYES. A common name for *Veronica chamaedrys*, a spreading, flowering perennial, native to Europe but naturalized in North America; see VERONICA.

ANGEL'S-TRUMPET. Common name for BRUGMANSIA, a genus of poisonous, small, flowering trees.

ANGIOPTERIS (an jee AHP tur is). A genus of greenhouse ferns of large size (10–20 ft.) and rampant habit, commonly known as elephant or turnip ferns. They are native to swamps and woodlands in tropical to subtropical Asia and require acid soil. The trunklike rhizome is heavy, almost globose, inspiring the common names.

A. crinata shows a glaucous, waxy deposit on the undersurface of the fronds.

A. evecta, the best species for culture, attains a height of 16 ft.

ANGRAECUM (an GRAY kum). A genus containing about 200 species of epiphytic and lithophytic vandaceous orchids native to tropical and southern Africa, Madagascar, and the Comoro and Seychelles Islands, including *A. sesquipedale*, the Christmas-star or comet orchid. Plants range from very small to stately, with leaves from ½–12 in. and stems up to 3 ft. long. Their habitats are varied, from humid lowlands to hillsides, even open savannas. Species from montane areas need cool temperatures, high light levels, and abundant water. Those from warmer forest habitats require abundant water, filtered shade, and warm temperatures (minimum winter temperature 60°F). Flowers are fragrant at night, have open stellate shape, and are always spurred. They are usually white to green and attract night-flying moths.

Hardy in Zones 10–11 (some to Zone 9 with frost protection), most species do best in baskets with a loose, fast-draining compost. Small varieties do well mounted on cork, coconut husk, or plaques of tree-fern bark. They are used in hybridizing with other angraecoid and vandaceous orchids. The type species is *A. eburneum*.

ANISE. Common name for the flavoring herb *Pimpinella anisum*; see PIMPINELLA. The name is sometimes incorrectly applied to fennel; see FOENICULUM. Star-anise is *Illicium verum*.

ANNONA (a NOH nah). A genus of South American, mostly tropical, small trees and woody shrubs, grown in Zones 10–11 for their edible fruits. A few of the 50 or more species are grown in southern California and Florida, where they require a light, well-drained soil.

PRINCIPAL SPECIES

A. cherimola, the most popular of the fruit-bearing species, is grown in the Florida Keys and southern California. Its heart-shaped, fragrant, acidulous, white-fleshed fruits range from the size of an orange to 2 lb. or more and are considered almost as delicious as the mangosteen. The tree, which often reaches 30 ft., has drooping branches and oblong leaves. Its flowers, when abundant, are almost overpowering in their delightful fragrance.

A. glabra (pond-apple) is grown mainly as a stock for grafting.

A. muricata (soursop), *A. reticulata* (custard-apple, bullock's-heart), and *A. squamosa* (sweetsop, sugar-apple) are tropical, half-evergreen trees.

ANNUALS. Plants that grow from seed, attain their growth, flower, and produce seed in one year (or less), and then die. The word "annual" is derived from the Latin word meaning "year" and is, of course, used as an adjective as well as a noun. Many annuals are apparently perennial, seeming to live on from year to year; in reality they self-sow (that is, scatter seed, which lives over the winter and gives rise to new plants) and thus perpetuate themselves.

SELECTION

Plant choice is a matter of personal preference. There are, however, considerations of climate, maintenance requirements, and garden design that will influence selection. Quick-growing annuals can be grown for a season to fill gaps while slower perennials become established. Annuals also allow the gardener to make changes in the garden design every spring. Seed or nursery stock of different colored and shaped annuals can be planted in varying locations each spring.

The accompanying annuals selection chart can be useful in choosing species appropriate for the intended location and use.

ANNUALS SELECTION GUIDE

LATIN NAME (common name)	MAINTENANCE	PLANT HEIGHT	LIGHT
Ageratum houstonianum (ageratum)	low	4–8 in.	S, PSh
Amaranthus caudatus (love-lies-bleeding)	medium	1½–3 ft.	S
Anchusa capensis (cape-forget-me-not)	medium	9–18 in.	S
Antirrhinum majus (snapdragon)	medium	6–15 in.	S
Arctotis stoechadifolia (African daisy)	medium	10–12 in.	S
Begonia semperflorens (wax begonia)	low	6–8 in.	S, PSh, Sh
Begonia x *tuberhybrida* (tuberous begonia)	low	8–10 in.	PSh, Sh
Brassica oleracea (ornamental cabbage, kale)	low	15–18 in.	S
Browallia speciosa (browallia)	low	10–15 in.	PSh, Sh
Calendula officinalis (pot-marigold)	high	1–2 ft.	S, LSh
Callistephus chinensis (China aster)	high	6–30 in.	S, PSh
Capsicum annuum (ornamental pepper)	low	4–8 in.	S, PSh
Catharanthus roseus (Madagascar-periwinkle)	low	4–12 in.	S, PSh
Celosia cristata (cockscomb)	low	6–15 in.	S
Centaurea cyanus (bachelor's-buttons)	medium	1–3 ft.	S
Chrysanthemum spp. (annual chrysanthemum)	medium	4–36 in.	S
Clarkia spp. (farewell-to-spring)	high	1½–2 ft.	S, LSh
Cleome spp. (cleome)	low	2½–4 ft.	S
Coleus x *hybridus* (coleus)	low	10–24 in.	PSh, Sh
Coreopsis tinctoria (calliopsis)	medium	8–36 in.	S
Cosmos spp. (cosmos)	medium	18–30 in.	S
Dahlia spp. (dahlia)	high	8–15 in.	S, LSh
Dianthus chinensis (annual pink)	low	6–10 in.	S, PSh
Dimorphotheca plurialis (cape-marigold)	low	4–16 in.	S
Eschscholzia californica (California poppy)	low	12–24 in.	S

SYMBOLS:

LIGHT	MOISTURE	TEMPERATURE
S—full sun	d—dry	c—cool (below 70°F)
LSh—light shade	a—average	m—moderate
PSh—part shade	m—moist	h—hot (above 85°F)
Sh—full shade		

ANNUALS SELECTION GUIDE

MOISTURE	TEMPERATURE	HARDINESS	SPACING (inches)	GERMINATION TIME (days)	BEST USES
a–m	m	HH	9–12	5–10	b, c
d	m–h	HH	12–24	10–15	b, e
d	m–h	HH	8–10	14–21	b
a	c–m	VH	6–8	10–14	b, c, f
d	c	H	10–12	21–35	b, e
a	m	HH	6–8	15–20	b, h
m	h	T	8–10	15–40	h
m	c	VH	12–15	10–18	
m	c	HH	8–10	14–21	h
m	c–m	H	10–12	10–14	c
m	m	HH	6–15	10–14	b, c
m	m–h	HH	6–8	21–25	b
any	m–h	HH	8–10	15–20	b, h
d	m–h	HH	6–12	10–15	
d–a	m	VH	6–12	7–14	b, c, e
a–m	c–m	T	4–18	10–18	
d–a	c	H	8–10	5–10	
d	m–h	HH	24–30	10–14	c, f
a–m	m–h	T	10–12	10–15	b, h
d	m	HH	4–12	5–10	
d–a	m	HH	9–18	5–10	b, c
a–m	m	HH	9–18	5–10	d
a	c–m	HH	6–12	5–10	b, f
d	c–m	HH	4–8	10–15	
d–a	any	VH	6–8	10–12	

HARDINESS

VH—very hardy, withstands heavy frost
H—hardy, withstands light frost
HH—half-hardy, withstands cool weather but not frost
T—tender, does poorly in cool weather, does not withstand frost

USES

b—border
c—cut flowers
e—everlasting
f—fragrant
h—hanging basket

LATIN NAME (common name)	MAINTENANCE	PLANT HEIGHT	LIGHT
Euphorbia spp. (spurge)	low	2–3 ft.	S
Gaillardia pulchella (blanket flower)	medium	10–18 in.	S, LSh
Gazania ringens (South African daisy)	high	6–10 in.	S
Gerbera jamesonii (Transvaal daisy)	medium	12–18 in.	S
Gomphrena globosa (globe amaranth)	medium	9–30 in.	S
Heilanthus spp. (sunflower)	high	1–15 ft.	S
Helichrysum bracteatum (strawflower)	medium	1–3 ft.	S
Hibiscus spp. (rose mallow)	medium	4–5 ft.	S, LSh
Iberis spp. (candytuft)	low	8–10 in.	S
Impatiens balsamina (balsam)	low	1–3 ft.	S, PSh
Impatiens hybrids (New Guinea impatiens)	low	10–12 in.	S, LSh
Impatiens wallerana (impatiens)	low	6–18 in.	PSh, Sh
Ipomoea spp. (morning-glory)	medium	3–30 ft.	S
Kochia scoparia (Belvedere)	low	2–3 ft.	S
Lathyrus odoratus (sweet pea)	medium	2–5 ft.	S
Lavatera trimestris (tree mallow)	medium	2–6 ft.	S
Limonium sinuatum (statice)	medium	1–3 ft.	S
Lobelia erinus (lobelia)	low	3–5 in.	S, PSh
Lobularia maritima (sweet-alyssum)	low	3–5 in.	S, PSh
Matthiola incana (stock)	high	12–24 in.	S
Mimulus spp. (monkey flower)	low	6–8 in.	PSh, Sh
Mirabilis jalapa (four-o'clock)	low	1½–3 ft.	S
Moluccella laevis (bells-of-Ireland)	medium	2–3 ft.	S, LSh
Myosotis sylvatica (forget-me-mot)	low	8–24 in.	PSh
Nemesia strumosa (nemesia)	high	24 in.	S, LSh
Nemophila menziesii (baby-blue-eyes)	low	6–8 in.	S, LSh

SYMBOLS:

LIGHT	MOISTURE	TEMPERATURE
S—full sun	d—dry	c—cool (below 70°F)
LSh—light shade	a—average	m—moderate
PSh—part shade	m—moist	h—hot (above 85°F)
Sh—full shade		

MOISTURE	TEMPERATURE	HARDINESS	SPACING (INCHES)	GERMINATION TIME (DAYS)	BEST USES
d	m–h	T	8–12	10–15	
d–a	m–h	T	8–12	15–20	b, f
d–a	m–h	HH	8–12	8–12	b
m	m	HH	10–12	15–25	b, c
d	m–h	HH	10–15	14–20	c, e
d	h	T	24–36	10–14	b
d	m–h	H	8–12	7–10	h, e
m	m	H	24–30	10–20	
d–a	m	HH	6–8	10–15	b
m	h	T	10–12	8–14	b
m	m	T	10–12	14–21	b, h
m	m	T	8–12	15–20	b, h
d	m	T	12–18	5–7	
d	m–h	HH	15–18	10–15	
m	c–m	H	12–15	20–30	b
d–a	m	H	18–24	15–20	b
d	m–h	HH	12–24	15–20	c, e
m	c–m	HH	6–10	15–20	b, h
a–m	m	H	5–8	8–15	b, f, h
d	m–h	HH	12–15	7–10	f, c
m	c	HH	6–8	8–12	b
d–a	m	T	12–18	7–10	f
a	m	HH	12–15	25–35	
m	c	H	8–12	7–15	
m	c	HH	6–8	7–14	
a	c	HH	6–12	7–12	

HARDINESS

VH—very hardy, withstands heavy frost
H—hardy, withstands light frost
HH—half-hardy, withstands cool weather but not frost
T—tender, does poorly in cool weather, does not withstand frost

USES

b—border
c—cut flowers
e—everlasting
f—fragrant
h—hanging basket

LATIN NAME (common name)	MAINTENANCE	PLANT HEIGHT	LIGHT
Nicotiana alata (flowering tobacco)	low	to 5 ft.	S, PSh
Nierembergia spp. (cupflower)	low	4–6 in.	S, LSh
Pelargonium hybrids (geranium)	high	10–15 in.	S
Pelargonium peltatum (ivy geranium)	medium	2–3 ft.	S
Petunia x *hybrida* (petunia)	medium	6–12 in.	S
Phlox drummondii (annual phlox)	low	6–10 in.	S
Portulaca grandiflora (rose-moss)	low	4–6 in.	S
Reseda odorata (mignonette)	medium	12–18 in.	S, LSh
Rudbeckia hirta (black-eyed-Susan)	low	1½–3 ft.	S, LSh
Salpiglossis sinuata (painted-tongue)	medium	18–24 in.	S
Salvia splendens (scarlet sage)	low	12–24 in.	S, PSh
Sanvitalia procumbens (sanvitalia)	medium	5–16 in.	S
Scabiosa caucasia (pincushion flower)	high	12–24 in.	S
Schizanthus x *wisetonensis* (poor-man's-orchid)	medium	12–24 in.	S, LSh
Tagetes erecta (Aztec marigold)	high	1½–3 ft.	S
Tagetes patula (French marigold)	high	5–10 in.	S
Thunbergia alata (black-eyed-susan vine)	medium	3–6 in.	S, PSh
Tithonia rotundifolia (Mexican-sunflower)	medium	4–5 ft.	S
Torenia spp. (wishbone flower)	low	8–12 in.	PSh, Sh
Trapaeolum majus (garden nasturtium)	low	12–24 in.	S, LSh
Verbena x *hybrida* (garden verbena)	medium	6–8 in.	S
Viola spp. (pansy)	medium	4–8 in.	S, PSh
Zinnia elegans (youth-on-old-age)	high	4–36 in.	S

SYMBOLS:

LIGHT	MOISTURE	TEMPERATURE
S—full sun	d—dry	c—cool (below 70°F)
LSh—light shade	a—average	m—moderate
PSh—part shade	m—moist	h—hot (above 85°F)
Sh—full shade		

MOISTURE	TEMPERATURE	HARDINESS	SPACING (INCHES)	GERMINATION TIME (DAYS)	BEST USES
m	m–h	HH	10–12	10–20	b
m	m	T	6–12	15–20	
a–m	m	T	10–12	5–15	b
a	m	T	10–12	5–15	h
d	m–h	HH	10–12	10–12	b, h
m	c–m	H	6–8	10–15	b
d	h	T	12–15	10–15	h
m	c	VH	10–12	5–10	
a	m–h	HH	12–24	5–10	c
m	c	HH	8–12	15–20	
a–m	m–h	HH	6–8	7–14	
d–a	m–h	HH	5–7	10–15	b, h
m	m	H	8–12	7–21	b, f, e
m	c	HH	10–15	20–25	
a	m	HH	12–18	5–7	b, c
a	m	HH	6–8	5–7	b, c
m	m	HH	10–12	10–15	h
d	m–h	T	24–30	5–10	c
m	c	HH	6–8	15–20	b
d	c–m	T	8–12	7–12	
d–a	h	T	6–8	20–25	c, h
m	c	VH	4–6	10–20	
d–a	m–h	T	6–18	5–7	c

HARDINESS	USES
VH—very hardy, withstands heavy frost	b—border
H—hardy, withstands light frost	c—cut flowers
HH—half-hardy, withstands cool weather but not frost	e—everlasting
T—tender, does poorly in cool weather, does not withstand frost	f—fragrant
	h—hanging basket

In gardening, many plants of the biennial or perennial classes, but which bloom the first year from seed, are considered and used as annuals; directions for their culture, similar to that given the true annuals, are included in this article.

Annuals come to us from almost all parts of the world. Properly chosen, they can provide bloom and fragrance in the garden from early spring to late fall. As they come in many forms, heights, and colors, they lend themselves to many uses, and a very brilliant effect can be secured from a few packets of seeds. Some are excellent in beds or borders, either massed by themselves, in varied combinations, as fillers among perennials, or to follow spring-blooming bulbs. Others are attractive vines; many are suitable to grow as screens or in window boxes and hanging baskets, and still others can be used for edging and for prolonging bloom in the rock garden after the normal season of many of the best rock garden subjects. They are invaluable as cut flowers, and some can be dried for winter bouquets.

CULTURE

Two things must be remembered in growing annuals. The first is the necessity of obtaining the best seed from a well-known, established distributor that guarantees the purity of the strains it offers. Gardeners should be able to count on the right color and the desired quality in plants that they grow from carefully selected and nurtured

Deadheading

seeds. The second thing to remember is that the blooming period of an annual can be prolonged if the flowers are picked before they fade (or immediately thereafter) and before any seed forms. A true annual has a slight root system, since it stores no food for future seasons, and it lives to bloom quickly, set seed, and finish its existence. Constant picking conserves the plant's energy and stimulates it to produce new blossoms as fast as the old ones are removed.

In starting all seeds in flats, it is necessary to place the ones that germinate rapidly in one flat and those slow to appear in another to allow appropriate care for plants of various needs.

Seedlings started indoors benefit and are made more stocky by being shifted at least once before being set outdoors. As soon as several true leaves have appeared, seedlings should be pricked off into small individual pots or into another box or flat. An old kitchen fork is an excellent tool to use in this work, or a small garden label with the end notched. These transplanted seedlings form a better root system and grow compact and sturdy instead of tall and spindly as they would if left in a crowded row.

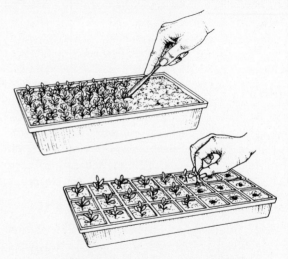

Transplanting seedlings into individual pots

By late spring these plants, which should have been gradually hardened-off by increasing ventilation and exposure to the outdoor temperature, should be ready to set in the open. Several hours before they are moved, water both the plants and the spot where they will be set. Separate the little plants carefully and set them far enough apart in the ground to allow them to develop without crowding.

TYPES OF ANNUALS

Annuals can be divided into three classes. Hardy forms can withstand a light spring frost and can therefore be started from seed sown in the open as soon as the soil can be worked. Half-hardy plants have cold-resistant seeds, but the plants will not survive a frost. They require a long season to attain maturity and can be given an early start inside. Tender kinds are easily injured by frost and must be planted outdoors only after all danger of frost is over.

Hardy Annuals. The seed of hardy annuals sown in the open should be planted in well-prepared loamy soil into which well-rotted manure has been dug the previous autumn. The surface soil should be so light and fine that the tender seedlings can penetrate it easily. If the soil is stiff or heavy, add sand or any sort of humus to help lighten the texture. No commercial fertilizer should be used in this seedbed, with the possible exception of bonemeal.

Some of the hardy annuals can be started in the fall; so handled, they will flower much earlier than those grown from spring-sown seed. Ordinarily they can be sown slightly deeper than in spring planting. The idea is not to have them grow above ground in the fall, but to get the seed in place and ready to grow with the first favorable weather of spring, even before the soil could normally be worked. For this reason some protection should be applied after the soil freezes, in order to prevent excessively deep freezing.

Half-hardy Annuals. These can be started in pots or boxes of well-pulverized soil in a sunny window in the house, or in flats in the greenhouse or hotbed. If only a few plants are desired, use the pots. First scrub them clean, then place pieces of broken crockery or pebbles over the hole in the bottom and fill to within 4 in. of the top of the pot with coarse soil. The next 2 in. should be finely sifted soil composed of equal parts of garden loam, humus, and sand. Plant the seeds in this mixture, scattering them thinly over the surface if very fine and planting larger seeds in a spiral row in order to have room for weeding. Very fine seeds should be pressed into the soil and not covered; larger ones should be covered according to their size—about as deep as their diameter is a common rule. Water, if necessary, with a fine spray. A piece of glass can now be placed over the top of the pot, which should be shaded with newspaper until germination takes place; then the paper and glass should be removed and the pot brought in to full sunlight.

If a greater quantity of plants is desired, use boxes or flats about 4 in. deep, making sure there is adequate drainage. Partly fill the boxes with coarse soil, finishing as in the pots, with an inch of the soil mixture given above. Sow the seeds in rows 1 in. apart. Very fine seeds can be covered with burlap, which is watered often enough to stay moist and left in place until germination occurs.

Tender Annuals. These can be started in the same way as the half-hardy annuals, but in late winter in the greenhouse or early spring in the hotbed. They should not be planted outside until the ground has warmed and all danger of frost is past.

ANOGRAMMA (an oh GRAM ah). A genus of small ferns with only a few much-divided, pale green fronds. Of subtropical origin, they will do well in small pots if given moist, shady conditions. They grow readily from spores and die down rather quickly but form small tuberous prothallia which are perennial. They can become pests in the greenhouse.

ANREDERA (an RED ur ah). A genus of tropical American perennial vines, formerly classified as *Boussingaultia*. *A. cordifolia* (mignonette or Madeira-vine) is a vigorous species popular for greenhouse and outdoor use, frequently grown as a porch or arbor vine. It has tuberous roots that may sometimes live over winter in the North but can be lifted and stored. It is a tall, rapid grower. The foliage is clean, fleshy, and attractive. Late in the summer, the plant bears long spikes of small, white, fragrant flowers. It is easily propagated by root division, from seeds, or from small tubercles that develop along the stems in the leaf axils.

ANTENNARIA (an te NAY ree ah). A genus of perennial herbs belonging to the Asteraceae (Aster Family), commonly known as everlastings or pussy-toes or cat's-ear. The white-woolly leaves are clustered at the base of the stems, and the flowers are borne in heads. Plants are common in fields and only occasionally are offered by dealers for planting in the wild or rock garden. They are sometimes cultivated for dried winter bouquets. They will grow in poor soil and are easily propagated by seed or division.

A. plantaginifolia (ladies'-tobacco), found in eastern North America, makes broad patches in old fields and pastures, with woolly leaves and small flowers appearing in early spring. It provides attractive foliage for a dry stone wall or rock garden.

A. rosea, found in western North America, grows to 18 in., spreading by means of underground stems. The foliage is distinctly white-woolly, and the bracts of the flower heads are rose-colored.

ANTHEMIS (AN them is). A genus of perennial herbs of the Asteraceae (Aster Family), sometimes referred to as chamomile. They have scented, finely cut foliage and solitary flowers with yellow disks. Hardy to Zone 3, seed should be sown outdoors in late spring but can be started indoors earlier. Mature plants can be propagated by division of the roots. All species flower from early summer until the first frost.

Anthemis tinctoria

PRINCIPAL SPECIES

A. cinerea, cushion forming, grows to 1 ft. and has grayish, woolly foliage. The large flower heads are made up of white ray flowers that are longer than the disk diameter.

A. montana, cushion forming, grows to 10 in. and has silky flowers and white ray flowers.

A. nobilis is now listed as *Chamaemelum nobilis;* see CHAMAEMELUM.

A. tinctoria (golden-marguerite), a popular but short-lived perennial, grows to 3 ft. and has golden ray flowers 2 in. across. Cv. 'Kelwayi' (hardy-arguerite) has finely cut foliage and flowers of deeper yellow.

ANTHER. A pollen-bearing sac attached to the usually threadlike stalk (filament) of a stamen located just within the floral envelope. At maturity each anther splits to release pollen grains containing the male germ elements of the plant. See FLOWER.

ANTHERICUM (an THUR ik um). A genus of tuberous-rooted herbs belonging to the Liliaceae (Lily Family), and commonly known as St. Bruno's or St. Bernard's lily. They produce racemes of small, white, lilylike flowers and long, narrow, grassy leaves. In mild climates, anthericums can be grown in the open, and in cooler areas, they will live through the winter in the border if given protection. They also make decorative subjects for the cool greenhouse and for use in container gardens in the summer. Easily cultured, they should be grown in rich, fibrous loam. When in bloom, they require plenty of water. They are hardy in Zones 3–9 and are propagated by cuttings of the stolons or by division.

A. bichetii, native to Africa, has variegated leaves and is occasionally cultivated.

A. liliago, the most frequently cultivated, grows to 3 ft. and has clustered flowers 1 in. across. Hardy to Zone 5.

ANTHRACNOSE. A term, originally used in France, to designate the slightly raised, scablike leaf spot of grapes caused by the "bird's-eye" fungus. Later it was used in the United States to describe the sunken black spots on bean pods. At present the word "anthracnose" usually represents a variety of different diseases typically manifested by circular leaf spots with a gray or white center and a reddish border, especially on roses and grapes. On beans the black pod spots are more prominent than the angular leaf lesions. Anthracnose diseases of shade trees are widespread. Sycamore and oak are particularly subject to them, but the same type of disease occurs on maple, horse-chestnut, and linden. Large areas on the leaves appear brown and scorched; defoliation, twig and limb blights, and, rarely, the death of the tree may follow. In general, anthracnose diseases have been treated by spraying with a fungicide; however, the effectiveness of this is questionable. The best prevention is by maintaining vigorous plants and choosing disease-resistant varieties.

ANTHRISCUS (an THRIS kus). A genus of the Apiaceae (Celery Family) native to Europe and Asia. *A. cerefolium* (salad chervil) is a hardy, annual, leafy herb that is used raw to flavor salads or as a flavoring in cooked foods. The foliage lies close to the ground, though its flower stems may reach a height of 18 in. or more. Seed sown in early spring or early autumn in any good garden soil, preferably in partial shade, will yield leaves ready for gathering in six to ten weeks.

Anthriscus cerefolium

ANTHURIUM (an THOOR ee um). A genus of tropical plants in the Araceae (Arum Family), commonly known as tailflower. They are grown for the heart- or strap-shaped leaves, which are sometimes white-veined and frosted. The flowers are borne in a spike with a bract folded back at the base. In a few species, these are brightly colored and are important items in the cut-flower trade.

These plants are hardy in Zones 10–11 and can be grown in greenhouses in cooler climates. Many species and hybrids have been introduced and are popular as house or landscape items. They require a moist but free-draining rich medium, moist air, and partial shade.

PRINCIPAL SPECIES

A. andraeanum (flamingo flower), is the florist's anthurium, a perennial with large heart-shaped leaves and brilliant orange-red to white, calla-like bracts surrounding the flowers, and occasionally bicolored spathes. It is native to the tropical Americas and popular for greenhouse culture.

A. crystallinum has beautiful, white-veined, frosted, heart-shaped leaves about 15 in. long.

A. hookeri is one of many "bird's nest" types whose strap-shaped leaves form an upright rosette.

A. scherzeranum (pigtail anthurium) has a smaller solid orange or orange- and white-flecked spathe and a flower spike coiled like the tail of a pig.

Anthurium scherzeranum

ANTIGONON (an TIG oh nahn) **leptopus.** A tendril climber belonging to the Polygonaceae (Buckwheat Family), native to Mexico, and commonly known as rosa-de-montana (mountain-rose), or coralvine. Grown in cold regions as a greenhouse vine, it is a popular, hardy climber in the South, where it has a long season of bloom, with handsome, bright rose-pink flowers borne in racemes. Cv. 'Albus' has white flowers.

Antigonon will grow more than 30 ft. in good soil, but if overfed it makes a rank growth. In the greenhouse it needs plenty of light and not too much root run. It blooms in the summer and needs plenty of water when growth is active, supplemented with liquid manure if in a tub or pot. It makes a large tuberous root and must be kept dry during the winter resting period.

ANTIRRHINUM (an ti RĪ num). A genus of erect, trailing, or half-shrubby plants belonging to the Scrophulariaceae (Figwort Family) and commonly known as snapdragon. The saclike, two-lipped flowers have been developed into many strains outstanding in beauty of form, color, and fragrance. Both the annual and perennial species are usually treated as annuals, since they flower from seed the first year.

Seed should be sown indoors in early spring. It may be slow in germinating, but after the true leaves have formed, the growth is usually rapid. The small plants can be transplanted to the open as soon as danger of frost is over. They will flower from midsummer until frost if the blossoms are picked as soon as they fade. Seed can also be planted in the open in late summer and the seedlings transplanted to pots for winter bloom, or the plants can be covered with a mulch over winter to give earlier summer flowers.

The growth of flower-bearing side branches can be encouraged by pinching out the central bud when transplanting, followed by occasional pinching of other too-vigorous shoots. This will result in a compact oval plant covered with short racemes of flowers.

To prevent taller varieties from falling over, put in stakes when setting out the young plants, tying them as

Snapdragon with support

soon as they show signs of flopping. Branched twigs set among the plants make excellent supports.

Enemies. Snapdragons may be infested by several insect pests. Among these are the LEAF MINER, RED SPIDER MITE, WHITEFLY, and APHIDS. Several good chemical and natural insecticides are available to control these pests; see individual pest entries. Snapdragons may also experience disease problems such as DAMPING-OFF, VERTICILLIUM WILT, RUSTS, and powdery MILDEW. The gardener should select rust- and wilt-resistant cultivars

whenever possible. Plants should be watered early in the day so that the leaves can dry before night. Many good fungicides are available and can be applied if disease problems develop.

PRINCIPAL SPECIES

A. coulteranum (chaparral snapdragon), native to California, is an annual growing to 3 ft. with small flowers varying from white to purplish.

A. majus (snapdragon), the most important species, is annual or perennial and grows to 3 ft. Naturally it has white to purplish red flowers to 1½ in. long; many beautiful hybrids of intermediate shades have been developed and are grouped according to height. The dwarf or Tom Thumb varieties, 6–9 in., are excellent for edging. Intermediate or half-dwarf sorts, 15–18 in. high, are good for massing in beds. The tall types, 2–3 ft., are good for use in border groupings.

A. orontium, a Eurasian species, is often found naturalized in North America.

ANTS. The 560 species of ants in North America are all social. There are three castes: males, queens, and wingless, sterile workers, which make up the majority. After mating, the male dies and the female tears off her wings, makes a nest, and lays up to 1500 eggs. These and the young larvae are tended by the young females until they mature to workers. Workers tend the queen and her young. New young queens leave to start new colonies, though many are caught by predators and birds.

Ants are omnivorous: some like fats, some sweets, and some even consume other insects. Their taste for sweets leads many ants to collect and tend aphids for the honeydew they exude after sucking up sweet sap. The cornfield ant carries the strawberry-root aphid to a burrow near strawberry roots, where the aphids can get at the roots to attack them. Carpenter ants infest decaying wood and hollow logs, eating the dead insects there. Thief ants and pharaoh ants enter houses to obtain fats, proteins, and sweets. The omnivorous Argentine ant aggressively drives out other ants. A particular menace is the Texas leaf-cutting ant, which strips plants of leaves and snips them to small pieces to support the fungi that the ants eat. Many ants nurse aphid eggs over the winter and release them near the roots of high-sugar plants, such as corn, for maturing.

The dangerous fire ant, imported from South America, has been spreading westward from Alabama. One, *Solenopsis saeuissima-richteri*, is a ferocious pest that builds many high mounds in fields and attacks humans and livestock. The repeated stings of fire ants are very painful and, to those allergic to them, even lethal.

CONTROLS

Repellents for ants include plants like tansy, mint, pennyroyal, and anise, and various kinds of sticky bands put around the stems or trunks of plants. Bonemeal, powdered charcoal, and lemon juice with rind placed at entrance holes are also repellent. One predatory ant, *Formica polyctena*, has been known to save oak trees from bud-moth defoliation.

Control is extremely difficult and many methods have been explored, including electrical devices, a South American nematode, and a soil microorganism available as Avermectin. Boiling water, kerosene, steamed bonemeal, and pepper have been used down the holes of anthills in efforts to eliminate the nests, with more or less success. Alkaline soils are not conducive to ant infestations. Biological controls include ant lions (Myrmeleontidae), the larvae of an adult insect similar to a dragonfly. The sickle-jawed larvae, called doodlebugs in the South, dig pits in sandy soil where they wait for ants to fall in (not a very effective control). *Neoaplectana carpocapsae* (Nc) nematodes in a carrier can be washed into the ant holes at dusk, aimed at the center of a colony. Pyrethrum applied directly on ants may be as effective as a soap and lime spray. Use peanut butter or sugar as bait to locate hidden ant colonies.

APETALOUS. A term meaning without petals. When a flower is lacking one set of floral leaves, it is customary to regard the missing set as the corolla, even though the remaining set may be petal-like. See FLOWER.

APHELANDRA (af ee LAN drah). A genus of evergreen shrubs from the tropical Americas, including a few choice species grown as greenhouse plants. They are prized for their handsome leaves, which are variegated in some species. All have showy terminal flower spikes in shades of orange or scarlet, often supplemented by large colored bracts that outlast the flowers. The usual flowering time is fall and winter. Old plants can be cut back when rested and grown again, or young plants can be grown annually from cuttings.

A. squarrosa (zebra plant), a Brazilian native, has glossy green,

Aphelandra squarrosa

more or less succulent ovate leaves marked with veins.

APHID LION. Larvae of the LACEWING, a beneficial insect that preys on aphids and other small soft-bodied insects.

APHID MIDGE. A tiny beneficial gall midge, *Aphidoletes aphidimyza* is a fierce predator of aphids. The females lay shiny orange eggs near colonies of aphids. When the larvae hatch, they feed on all the aphids they can find. The midge larvae are pale orange to red, about the same size

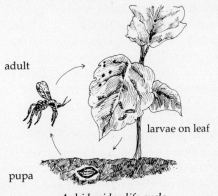

Aphid midge life cycle

as the aphids they feed on. They are especially useful in greenhouses where they pupate and stay from year to year, in contrast to lady beetles, which tend to go away when the aphids of the infestation have been consumed, or to lacewings, which need to be reintroduced each year. They can be purchased or are sometimes found on roses and moved into the greenhouse. They work best if there are about 30 to 50 aphids on the infested plant to be treated, and if the temperature is 68–70°F. Order the midges as pupae and keep them moist before releasing in a shady place. Make three to four releases within a week or two. Use a magnifying glass to check on the aphids to see whether they are dead. These midges will work at night if given light from 60-watt bulbs every 40 ft.

APHIDS. These tiny, soft-bodied insects are pests in gardens and greenhouses worldwide. Only 1/10–1/2 in. long, they are green or sometimes brown, yellow, pink, or black. They feed by thrusting a sharp stylet into plant cells and sucking out the sap. Loss of vitality in the plant shows as curling of leaves, brown spots, or blighted fruits and flowers. Aphids also transmit diseases such as bacterial blight and mosaic.

They overwinter as fertile eggs in plant crevices, emerge in the spring as nymphs, then grow to adults called stem mothers. At this stage they produce young females parthenogenically, and those, in turn, produce again; so large colonies are quickly formed. Some develop wings and migrate to other kinds of plants. After more generations, winged males and females are produced. The female wingless nymphs, borne of the original perennial species of the spring hatching, mate with the winged males of the preceding generation, lay one to four eggs, and die. In a greenhouse they produce generations without mating.

Because aphids suck so much sweet sap, they excrete a sweet honeydew that supports the sooty mold fungus and attracts ants. Ants nurse aphids, carry them to their underground colonies, and feed on the honeydew. Aphids

cause spruce galls, phylloxera of grapes, and leaf curl of apples, cherries, and snowballs. Green aphids suck rose shoots.

Dryness of the garden attracts aphids; they are less likely to attack where there is a good, rich, moist loam soil. Fall plowing or spading helps to kill overwintering aphid eggs. Mint interplanted with crops is sometimes helpful.

aphid colony

A strong spray of water from a hose will wash off many aphids. A pan lined with a light yellow coating and filled with water and a little detergent will attract and drown them because the surface tension is more than they can combat. A spray of insecticidal soap is also effective, as are homemade soap, lime, and potent garlic sprays; see SPRAYING. The most spectacular controls have been biological ones—by lady beetles, lacewings, aphid lions, aphid midges, and parasitic wasps. Pyrethrum and dormant oil sprays have also been effective, but it is amazing to see a badly infested plant completely cleaned by a few blasts of water from a strong hose. Other possible controls include teas made from rhubarb leaves or larkspur. Companion plants to try are nasturtium (though there is one aphid that infests them), garlic, chives, petunias, and coriander.

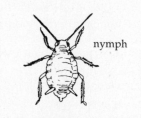

nymph

adult

Aphids

APIACEAE (ay pee AY see ee). The Celery, Carrot, or Parsnip family, formerly called Umbelliferae, a distinctive group of hollow-stemmed herbaceous plants, sometimes reaching great size, widely distributed throughout temperate and subtropical regions. The old family name was derived from its typical inflorescence, an umbel, or flattened cluster in which several flower stalks spring like rays from one point; many forms have compound umbels in which this arrangement is repeated in the branches of the clusters.

Many species are ornamental; others are grown for food and medicine, as carrot, celery, asafetida, anise, and caraway. The family also includes some bad weeds. Important genera are *Aegopodium, Anethum, Anthriscus, Apium* (celery), *Astrantia, Carum* (caraway), *Chaerophyllum, Conium, Coriandrum, Cuminum, Daucus* (carrot), *Eryngium, Ferula, Foeniculum, Levisticum, Myrrhis, Pastinaca* (parsnip), *Petroselinum, Pimpinella, Sium*, and *Trachymene* (blue laceflower).

APIOS (AY pee ohs) **americana.** A hardy perennial vine belonging to the Fabaceae (Bean Family), commonly known as groundnut or wild bean. Although long cultivated in Europe for its edible tubers and as bee plants, it is not often cultivated in North America. The stems grow only 1–2 ft. high but will climb along the ground or over shrubs and other obstacles. In summer, fragrant, nectar-rich, brownish purple flowers are borne in clusters.

Groundnut grows best in open or partially shaded locations and moist soil. In late summer, the 2–3 in. pods produce small, black, rectangular seeds, which are not always viable; propagation is generally

Apios americana

by seed in warm climates and by vegetative means in northern regions. The numerous walnut-sized tubers are edible, tasting like green peas and giving the plant its common name. In the fall, the plant dies back as the tubers grow larger. Hardy in Zones 3–9.

APIUM (AY pee um). A genus of annual or biennial herbs of the Apiaceae (Celery Family), native in the Mediterranean region of Europe. One species, *A. graveolens*, includes two familiar vegetables: celery, which is the var. *dulce*; and celeriac, which is the var. *rapaceum*.

See CELERY; CELERIAC.

APLECTRUM (ap LEK trum) **hyemale.** A hardy orchid native to North America and commonly known as puttyroot or (regionally) Adam-and-Eve. It has yellowish brown flowers with three-lobed lips, borne in racemes on 12-in. stems, with one leaf at the base. It is occasionally grown in bog gardens in very moist, acid soil. The common name "puttyroot" comes from the consistency of the sticky substance of the old bulbs, which has been used to mend broken china.

APOCYNACEAE (ah paw sin AY see ee). The Dogbane Family, a group of herbs, shrubs, or trees of a wide range but most abundant in the tropics; they are grown for ornament and in a few cases for their edible fruit and medicinal products. The juice of some species is an acrid, poisonous secretion. The principal cultivated genera are *Apocynum* (common dogbane), *Vinca* (periwinkle), *Nerium*, and *Tabernaemontana*.

APONOGETON (ah poh noh JEE tahn). A genus of perennial aquatic plants grown in indoor pools or aquariums and also outdoors in the summer in cool climates. Propagated by seed, division, or offsets, the plants should be grown in pots 18–24 in. deep in water. To favor seed production, hand-pollinate the flowers and keep them out of the water.

A. distachyus (cape-pondweed, waterhawthorn) has white or purplish flowers lifted slightly above the surface, with prominent white bracts and a delicious hawthornlike fragrance. The blunt, lance-shaped leaves, 3–6 in. long, float beside the flowers. Easily naturalized in warm water and suited to deeper ponds, it is hardy in Zones 7–11. It has tuberous rootstocks and in cold climates can be grown in a protected pool without moving indoors for the winter.

A. fenestralis (laceleaf, latticeleaf), the most popular species, has broad, elliptic lacy leaves that float just under the water surface and show only a network of veins. It is a tropical species and should be grown in a tub in a warm greenhouse (65–70°F) or in a heated aquarium.

APOROCACTUS (ap or oh KAK tus). A small genus of epiphytic cacti from the tropical Americas; the most common species is *A. flagelliformis* (rat-tail cactus), which has small crimson flowers and slender, bristly-spiny, pendent stems that can reach several feet in length and send out aerial roots. Most species do well enough in cultivation on their own roots, though they are often grafted onto some robust species of Cereanae or Hylocereanae.

APOTHECIUM. A cup-shaped, open, fungus fruiting body lined with sacs (asci) containing the sexual spores. See FUNGUS; compare PERITHECIUM.

APPLE. This is the most important temperate-climate fruit when measured by the extent of its culture, the number of uses to which it is adapted, and the length of the season covered by its varieties. The tree (of the genus MALUS) is presumably a native of Europe and adjacent Asia, home also of the true crabs (*M. baccata*) with which it has probably been hybridized to produce some of the larger crab apple varieties. The apple blossom is the state flower of Arkansas and Michigan.

SELECTION

Of all the fruits, the apple has been developed into the largest number of varieties; in the United States alone there are more than 4000, and new ones are introduced annually. Of those produced commercially, only a few are prominent, but for home gardens, where excellent flavor of the fruit is the important factor rather than its appearance and shipping quality, many kinds are well worth consideration. New varieties especially suited for the home garden have been developed recently, and many of those popular a century ago are once again being propagated.

When planting a home orchard, if space permits, choose varieties that, ripening successively, will cover the season between midsummer and the following spring. Some apples are best for cooking and others for eating fresh; some store well and others are good for cider. Among varieties that are popular with home growers are Cortland, Criterion, Duchess, Empire, Fameuse, Freedom, Gravenstein, Hazen, Liberty, Mutsu, and Viking. Those grown commercially include Red and Yellow Delicious, Cortland, Jonathan, McIntosh, Rome Beauty, Winesap, and, in areas with long growing seasons, Granny Smith.

Apples do not come true from seed and must be grafted or budded to obtain the desired variety. The kind of root stock used for grafting controls whether the size of the tree resulting from the graft is a standard, semidwarf, or dwarf. See GRAFTING.

In recent years, dwarf fruits have become very popular, and the Malling and East Malling rootstocks developed in England have made a wide variety of dwarf and semidwarf apple trees possible. The dwarfs and semidwarfs range in height and spread from 6–18 ft., so they are much more suitable for backyard and lawn plantings than standard trees, which may grow over 40 ft. tall and almost as wide. Dwarfs bear at a much earlier age than standards and are easier to spray, prune, thin, and harvest. They also make it possible to raise a wide variety of apples in a small space. See also DWARF FRUIT TREES.

In all the states and most of the Canadian provinces, apples of some kind can be grown. It is important to know the range of zones in which a tree can be grown, since varieties suited to the South require too long a season to ripen in the North and are likely to be injured or killed by northern winters. On the other hand, northern varieties tend to ripen earlier the farther they are taken southward. To illustrate, the Northern Spy, which ripens late and keeps well as a winter apple in northern New York, matures so much earlier in the lower Hudson Valley that it can rarely be kept in home storage after Christmas; and in Delaware it is a fall variety.

The length of time it takes newly planted trees to bear varies with the species. In general, trees that ripen early in the season tend to bear at a young age, sometimes after only a year or two. A winter-ripening apple may take up to ten years before bearing its first apple, but its first crop is usually large.

Cross-pollination of apples is necessary to obtain fruit, so two different varieties must be planted unless there are neighboring trees or wild apples within a quarter of a mile.

Apple trees are often planted as lawn ornamentals. The flowering crab apples are the best choice for this because they need little spraying and are attractive both in fruit and flower. Most of the trees hold their small fruits until they are eaten by birds, but if no fruit is wanted, there are varieties that are sterile. Crabs produce red, pink, or white blossoms and red, yellow, or purple fruits. Some also have red foliage, which is interesting in the summer but tends to hide the red flowers in spring and makes them barely noticeable. See CRAB APPLE.

CULTURE

Though some varieties of apples grow best and yield the best quality fruit only when grown on a certain kind of soil, most kinds do well on any type of soil. Best results are secured if the soil is deep, fairly rich, and well drained.

Apple trees bought by mail are usually bare root, and some are sold that way in garden centers or retail nurseries. Bare-rooted trees should be set in the spring in the North to give them the best chance of getting well established before winter. In the South, they can be planted safely in the fall. Many garden centers sell trees with their roots either growing in a large pot, or with roots in a ball of soil wrapped in plastic or burlap. The latter can be moved anytime with no setback or shock.

PLANTING

When planting trees, space them according to their ultimate size. Notice the spot on the trunk where the tree was grafted or budded. Usually nursery-grown trees are budded a few inches above ground level and grafted at about ground level. When planting dwarf apple trees that are grafted, it is important to set the graft union not more than an inch or so below the soil surface, or roots may sprout from the buried part above the graft and cause the tree to grow into a full-size specimen.

Bare-rooted trees should be cut back about a third after planting, to keep the tops from growing faster than the roots can supply food or moisture for them. An exception to this can be made, however, if one waters the tree daily and feeds it a liquid fertilizer at least once a week. Potted or balled trees need no cutting back at planting time. All newly planted trees benefit from daily watering if it does not rain.

If full-sized trees are planted, smaller fruit trees such as plums can be set between them to grow and produce for a few years before being removed. Neither vegetables nor berries that ripen early are good choices to plant between tree rows if toxic sprays will be used on the trees.

PRUNING

Frequent light pruning during the tree's early years will prevent the necessity for heavy corrective pruning later on—pruning that usually delays bearing. In order to develop a well-shaped tree with strong branching, it should be trained with a central trunk (leader), with branches coming from the trunk no closer than 30 degrees. Cut or pinch off any sprouts that are forming extra tops. Some varieties, such as Yellow Delicious, tend to grow upright and need careful pruning to get them into a spreading habit. McIntosh naturally grow in a more spreading form. Remove branches growing too close to the ground as soon as they are noticed.

Standard trees can be kept low by heavy pruning. Opening up the top after the tree has reached about 12 ft. is recommended so that more sunshine can enter the interior and ripen the fruit. Dwarf trees need far less pruning than standards, but on both types, the branches that are too close together should be thinned annually and older, unproductive wood removed. The fruit of some varieties is borne mostly on short, stubby spurs rather than along the branches. These spurs should be thinned so that the number of fruits will be decreased, and the size of

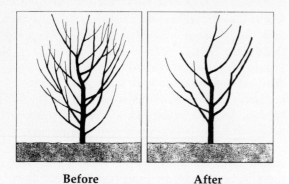

Before   After

Pruning a three-year-old apple tree

each fruit will be larger. Light pruning can be done anytime, but heavy pruning should be done when the tree is dormant and the wood is not frozen.

The quality of the fruit will be far better and the tree more likely to produce annually if the small fruits on the tree are thinned in early summer about the time they reach marble size, and after their natural "June drop." Usually, after the drop, there are still far too many fruits for each to develop into a large size. By thinning them to one apple per cluster, so that each is about 5 in. from the other, the "catalog quality" fruit will be produced. Also, by cutting down on seed production drastically, much of the tree's energy is saved, and a medium-sized crop of large fruit is produced annually, rather than a large crop of small apples every other year.

CULTIVATION

Though commercial orchards are often cultivated from spring to midsummer and then planted with a cover crop, they are also successfully managed under a sod mulch. This means that grass, clover, or alfalfa is grown between the trees and is cut two or three times a year while green; it is either allowed to decay where it falls or is raked beneath the trees and left there. In the home garden, as well, either of those methods can be followed. Alternative methods are to mulch the trees or grow them in a mowed lawn, preferably with a 1-ft. circle of bare earth around the base of each trunk to discourage attacks of the flat-headed tree borer, and to prevent damage from a lawn mower.

If grass or other cover crop is grown, it should be fertilized enough to increase the amount of humus it will provide and the amount of plant food in the soil. Trees need nitrogen especially, so superphosphate, bonemeal, potash, and phosphate rock, when used alone, do not provide enough nourishment. Cottonseed meal, manure, 10–5–5, or other nitrogenous fertilizers are best. A mature standard apple tree should receive 6–10 lb. of 10–5–5 or its equivalent annually; dwarf trees need from 1–2 lb. each.

HARVESTING

Color and taste are generally the best guides to the right time for picking different varieties. Most summer and early-autumn apple varieties ripen throughout several weeks, so they can be picked and used as they mature. Under home conditions, this early fruit can rarely be kept longer than a week or two without serious deterioration. Late autumn and winter varieties can be gathered as soon as the seeds in sample specimens have turned brown and while the fruit is still firm.

It is important that the stubby twigs or spurs that bear the fruit are not damaged. Give the fruit a gentle twist instead of pulling when removing them from the tree. Care must be taken to prevent bruising by rough handling because, though apples are apparently hard, such bruises turn brown, injure the appearance of the fruit, and lessen its keeping quality. As soon as it is gathered, the fruit should be placed out of the sun and, as soon as possible, removed to a cold cellar. Apples keep best at 33–34°F.

ENEMIES

DISEASES

Of the diseases that affect apple trees, scab is the most troublesome. Early, uncontrolled infection on the fruit stems may almost entirely prevent the setting of fruit; later infection by the fungus affects chiefly fruit and leaves; and severe leaf infection seriously weakens a tree and results in reducing crops in successive years.

On the leaves, scab shows first as dull, smoky areas that later become olive colored and velvety as masses of dark-colored spores develop. Typical fruit scab spots are olive-black surrounded by papery, broken skin. As the fruit grows, the center of the spot cracks, disclosing brown, corky tissue. The fruit may also be stunted.

The fungus overwinters in old leaves on the ground; in the spring, spores are carried by air currents to newly opened leaves. To prevent this infection, trees should be sprayed with a fungicide during the six to eight weeks when these spores are maturing. Later (secondary) infection is by summer spores developed on leaves or young fruit. Control of apple scab requires correct timing of sprays in relation to the growth of the trees. Get advice from your local extension service to supplement the general spray schedule given below.

Fire blight, which attacks apples, pears, quinces, and many ornamental trees and shrubs can be another devastating disease. Blossoms, leaves, and twigs appear to have been burned by fire, and cankers may be formed on larger limbs and trunks. This bacterial disease is spread by pruning tools, splashing rain, and insects—especially bees.

The best preventives are to plant blight-resistant varieties, sterilize pruning tools between trees with a chlorine solution, and cut away the infected areas as soon as they are discovered. Often disease will disappear quickly for no obvious reason, but if it persists, contact your extension service for advice on what remedy is currently being recommended. Blighted twigs and limbs should be removed with sanitary precautions as directed. See also FIRE BLIGHT.

Three apple rust diseases are caused by fungi that live part of their lives on red cedar and the remainder mostly on apple, hawthorn, and quince. Rust spots on fruit are orange with small fungus cups. The most effective control is the eradication of red cedar for at least a half-mile around the apple orchards. Spraying trees with lime sulfur or with a fungicide when the petals fall seems to help reduce fruit infection. See CEDAR-APPLE RUST.

Black rot causes the so-called New York apple tree canker on the limbs, a blossom end rot on the fruit, and leaf spot. The fungus enters through wounds, so all injured or dead branches should be removed, the wounds carefully painted, and the spray schedule given below followed.

Bitter rot of apple causes brown rotted spots filled with pink spore masses on the fruit and cankers on the limbs. Remove the cankers, paint the wounds, and follow the spray schedule.

INSECT PESTS

Many of the sucking insects, including San José scale (see SCALE INSECTS) and the common apple aphids are controlled by a delayed dormant spray, as described below. The principal aphids are the rosy apple aphid, which has a pinkish coating; the woolly apple aphid, which migrates from elm to apple and forms a bluish white cottony growth around scars and wounds, often causing galls; and the green apple aphid, which causes the familiar curling of leaves and tender shoots.

The European red mite is responsible for rusty brown foliage in midsummer and may call for a summer application of insecticide. See MITES.

The flat-headed apple-tree borer works in the sapwood of oak, apple, maple, and many other trees. The larvae construct broad feeding tunnels under the bark until late summer, when they bore into the sapwood and form pupal cells in which they spend the winter; the adults appear from May to July as dark copper-colored beetles about ½ in. long. The appearance of sawdust in or below holes in the bark indicates the presence of the borer, which may be killed by running a wire into the burrow or spraying it with an insecticide. Since borers do not usually work in healthy sapwood, the best control is prevention, that is, the promotion of vigor in your trees by feeding, watering, and pruning them. An insecticide can also be applied to the trunk.

The round-headed borer, which makes nearly round holes in the main trunk, sometimes seriously injuring young trees, is the larva of a long-horned, gray, white-striped beetle about an inch long. The shot-hole borer makes many small holes and burrows (filled with fine sawdust) up to 4 in. long; the adult, a small black beetle, is called the fruit-tree bark beetle. See BARK BEETLE; BORERS.

Chewing insects may attack twigs, leaves, or fruit. Weevils or snout beetles cut off small branches, buds, and newly set fruit. Leaves may be skeletonized by the spring or fall canker worm, or the apple-leaf skeletonizer, which also webs two or three leaves together. The budworm webs over the buds, and the eastern tent caterpillar, if neglected, forms large webs and defoliates the tree in spring, as does the fall webworm in late summer. For control measures see BUDWORM; CASEBEARER; TENT CATERPILLAR.

Other leaf-eating insects are the tussock, brown tail, and gypsy moths; and the Japanese beetle, which attacks both leaves and fruit.

Among the insects injurious to fruit, the codling moth is undoubtedly the best known. This pinkish, brown-headed worm burrows into the core, leaving brown castings protruding from the holes. The plum CURCULIO injures early-set apples with its crescent-shaped punctures; such fruit usually falls. The apple curculio causes knotty apples, as does red bug. The yellowish white apple maggot or railroad worm makes slender, brown, twisting mines through the fruit.

Apple maggot adult fly

The adult is a three-winged fly, somewhat smaller than a housefly, with conspicuous dark bands across the wings. The European sawfly causes raised markings around the mature apple in late summer.

PROTECTION PROGRAM

To help ensure high-quality fruit that is not chemically polluted, plant scab-resistant varieties, use insect traps, soap sprays, and other safer pesticides. If spraying is to be done, it is important that the timing be right to control the pest when it is most vulnerable. Unless you wish to mix your own ingredients, it is best to buy an already prepared orchard fruit spray and use the following spray schedule. (If you do not want to follow the complete schedule, items 1, 3, and 4 are the most important.)

1. Delayed Dormant Spray. Start when the fruit buds start to show silvery. Must be done before leaves appear. Use either a dormant oil spray or an all-purpose orchard spray to control scab, scale, mites, and aphids.

2. Pink Bud Spray. When the fruit buds begin to show color, use all-purpose orchard spray to control curculio, scab, canker worms, and chewing insects.

3. Petal Fall or Calyx Spray. Immediately after petals fall and before the calyx closes. Do not spray while the tree is in bloom, or bees will be killed. Controls codling moth, curculio, scab.

4. Ten days later, repeat step 3.

5. Three or four weeks after step 4, repeat step 3 again.

Commercial orchardists often spray several more times, and home orchardists should check their plantings frequently and take any necessary steps. Usually diseases, especially scab, are worst in wet, warm seasons; insects multiply faster in dry ones.

APRICOT. A tree (*Prunus armeniaca*) grown for its fruit—one of the stone fruits—which resembles a small, yellow, sweetish peach and is used for dessert, drying, canning, and preserves. The Japanese apricot (*P. mume*) is more often planted for ornament than for its fruit.

Different apricot varieties are available for each hardiness zone. Though they are grown commercially on the Pacific Coast and in parts of the Rocky Mountain region, they are less popular than they deserve to be in home gardens elsewhere in North America. This is partly because the flowers open so early that spring frosts often destroy them, and partly because the fruit that reaches eastern markets from the West is gathered while so immature that when eaten it gives a poor impression and does not inspire people to plant apricots even where they could be grown. By planting the trees where their buds may be retarded—that is, on a northern slope, the north or west side of a building, or shaded by tall trees to the eastward—a crop can sometimes be obtained where otherwise it would be impossible.

Apricot varieties suitable for home gardens are: Tillon, Wilson, Goldcot, Hungarian Rose, and Moongold. Most varieties are self-fruitful, but it is nevertheless advisable to plant at least two kinds to ensure the best crops.

Apricot varieties are budded or grafted on either seedling apricot, peach, or plum stocks. The first two are preferable for planting on light soils while plum stocks will do better on heavy soils.

CULTURE

One-year trees are better for planting than older ones because they can be trained as desired. Each should be allowed a spread of 25 ft. During the first five years, clean cultivation is necessary until midsummer, and cover cropping after that, at least as far as the branches spread, is highly desirable. This tends to develop deep rooting and helps the trees withstand dry weather. After the fifth year heavy mulching is satisfactory and saves labor. Should growth not be as good as desired, manure (about a bushel to the square yard) can be applied in spring, or a general fertilizer can be applied at the rate of 5 lb. per tree.

Training young trees consists in developing three to five well-spaced frame limbs and removing branches that crowd more desirable ones. See PRUNING; TRAINING PLANTS.

In general, apricots are attacked by the same enemies as plums, but brown rot fungus is especially characteristic of this host. Partial or complete blighting of the young fruit while still enclosed in the calyx sometimes results in entire crop losses. Plum curculio and San José scale are often destructive.

See also SCALE INSECTS; CURCULIO.

AQUARIUM. In keeping an aquarium for breeding fish or for cultivating aquatic plants, the gardener must recognize that each is necessary to the other. In the small aquarium especially, fish and plants are interdependent, and the exchange of oxygen and carbon dioxide is vital to the health of both. The gills of fish extract oxygen from the water and breathe out carbon dioxide. In a limited space, carbon dioxide saturates the water, and if there is no purifying agent, the fish die of suffocation. With plants, the reverse is true; they absorb and use the carbon dioxide and give off oxygen.

A balanced aquarium is one in which plant and animal material are so adjusted that no outside agent (such as a commercial filter) is needed to keep the environment healthy for both. AQUATIC PLANTS vary considerably in the amount of oxygen they liberate. To maintain a balance of oxygen and carbon dioxide, some kinds particularly rich in output, called "oxygenators," are used either alone or in combination with others that are less efficient but decorative. Any fish dealer can supply one or more of the staple oxygenating plants, which include CABOMBA, ELODEA, MYRIOPHYLLUM, SAGITTARIA, and VALLISNERIA.

Vallisneria and *Sagittaria*, both powerful oxygenators with beautiful foliage and bloom, can be used in the tank alone or as a background planting for smaller and more unusual plants, especially those with less oxygenating power. Both should be rooted in the sand of the tank bottom or grown in tiny buried pods.

Elodea, *Cabomba*, and *Myriophyllum*, all well-known oxygenating plants, can be grown successfully either floating free or rooted. They are especially good as a "cover planting" to keep the tank healthy and rich in green while rarer and more interesting plants are grown. *Cabomba* is attractive but tends to break up and discolor in less than ideal conditions; however, it is inexpensive and readily available, and it can be easily replaced as it decays. *Elodea* grows quickly, is a good oxygenator, and is satisfactory for general use. *Myriophyllum* is the most feathery of the aquatics, and two common varieties offer an opportunity for red and green color arrangement.

Fish keepers often limit their plantings to the most common species, but there are many unusual and beautiful plants available for anyone interested in aquatic plant culture.

Cryptocoryne is a good oxygenator with broad leaves and the ability to grow beautifully in less light than most other aquatic plants require.

In addition to submerged plants, a well-planted aquarium needs an assortment of floating plants. These may range in size from the tiny duckweeds and *Salvinia* to such flowering plants as the *Nymphoides* (floating-hearts) and, if the tank is large enough, perhaps even waterlilies.

AQUATIC PLANTS. The term "aquatic" applies not only to those plants that live entirely under water, but also to those, like the waterlily, that root in the bottom and project stems, leaves, and flowers up to float on or stand above the surface. It also includes plants that can adapt themselves to either terrestrial or aquatic conditions.

The true aquatics (those that grow entirely submerged) are mostly plants of simple structure whose greatest use is in supplying oxygen for fish in tanks or pools without artificial aeration mechanisms (see AQUARIUM). These water plants are almost always very decorative when seen through the sides of a glass tank that harbors a few colorful fish and thus can be a charming and satisfying solace for the winter-frustrated gardener.

Outdoors, in a natural pond, water course, or artificial pool, the greenery of submerged plants helps to create a setting for the bloom of surface plants and effectively hides unsightly containers in which larger waterlilies or other plants are usually grown.

Obviously the factors of location, temperature range, and size determine the selection of proper material. Wild ponds in cold climates are hardly suitable homes for the sweet-scented exotic lilies, but they are quite right for the hardy yellow-lotus, the spatterdock or cowlily, the lavender-flowered pickerelweed, and other North American natives. Among them and in such a setting,

the exotics would be inappropriate and difficult to grow.

WATERLILIES AND LOTUS

In the sheltered garden pool, formal or informal, shallow or deep, the tender tropical lilies show to best advantage. In any pool where *Nymphaea* (waterlily) or *Nelumbo* (lotus) is used, they are the feature, and other material is selected to supplement them. The surrounding shrubbery and trees, the border planting, and the other water material must all be considered, not only for its own sake but also for its contribution to the setting and to the well-being of the lilies. Cold northeast winds in the spring just after the lilies have been set in the pool may seriously check their growth and bloom.

If the pool is not naturally sheltered, a windbreak planting of evergreens, or large deciduous trees (such as oak, linden, or poplar) if space permits, is desirable. This can be supplemented and graded down to the pool by a marginal planting of laurel, rhododendron, or other shrubs. The southern exposures should be clear and unshaded to allow the maximum sunlight to reach the pool; hence large marginal planting should be confined to the north and northeast sides and also the northwest if cold winds can be expected from that direction.

Even if the situation of the pond, by reason of latitude or exposure, is unsuited to the tender tropical species, there is a wide variety in the form and color of the hardy *Nymphaea*. *N. odorata*, the large white pondlily of the eastern states, is most desirable. From its hybrids and those of exotic species, a selection of hardy varieties can provide beauty of leaf and bloom comparable to more tropical plants. It may be advisable for water gardeners to plant both hardy and tropical lilies to obtain a wider range of color and variation in height of bloom above the water.

To grow waterlilies, lotus, and their appropriate companions, good rich soil in abundance is imperative. If the soil is not rich enough, plants will produce small flowers and sparse, unhealthy foliage. In large ponds, it is sometimes necessary to plant directly in the pond bottom, but if possible, this should be avoided. It is much easier to enrich soil in a box or tub than a whole pond bottom. Also, the unrestricted roots of some lilies spread, crowding and stunting less robust varieties. For all except a few of the larger aquatics, container planting in rich soil is best. In boxes, tubs, or pots, lilies and other aquatics can be moved without check, but shifts are not easily done with bottom-rooted plants. See NYMPHAEA; NELUMBO.

PLANTS FOR SHALLOW WATERS

Aquatic plants other than lilies and lotus suitable for tub or pool comprise two general groups: those forming masses of foliage and bloom above the water surface and those floating on it. The first group includes plants for marginal and island planting. The second includes those for breaking the water surface into attractive arrangements of leaf and bloom.

The marginal aquatics are shallow-water plants and are best handled in pots submerged a few inches. Many of them, besides being useful outdoors, are excellent houseplants; the plants need only be removed from the pool (in the pots), repotted if necessary, and taken indoors in the fall. Attractive indoor gardens can be made with plants such as *Cyperus alternifolius* (umbrella plant), *Pontederia cordata* (pickerelweed), *Thalia dealbata* (water-canna), and *Ludwigia longifolia* (primrose-willow). As houseplants, these should be grown in pots set in trays or other containers kept filled with water. Good soil and a warm sunny location are also essential.

Among the most graceful of the high-growing, shallow-water plants are *Cyperus alternifolius* and *C. papyrus*. The latter has a mass of tall stems, each topped with a star of grasslike leaves, grows as much as 15 ft. in a summer, and is particularly useful placed at one end of a large pool.

Zizania aquatica (wild-rice), a North American native, is a tall, grassy plant suitable for the water's edge or island planting in the wild pond. It grows up to 10 ft. during the summer and readily reseeds itself. Besides having ornamental value, its grain attracts birds, particularly waterfowl.

Typha latifolia and *T. angustifolia* (cattails) are both native swamp plants especially good for planting in the shallows at the edge of a pool or water-course. Their narrow, dark green leaves and familiar soft brown cylindrical seed heads form a pleasant contrast to the broad, drooping leaves and gay blue-violet spikes of the pickerelweed and the distinctive leaves of *Sagittaria* (arrowheads) with their white bloom. *Sagittaria* varies in size from a few inches high to one species that grows up to 6 ft. high.

Any list of shallow-water plants would hardly be complete without mention of the water-loving *Iris*. Both *I. pseudacorus* (yellow flag) and *I. versicolor* (blue flag) planted in a few inches of water make fine heavy clumps of swordlike leaves, and they flower profusely.

A few members of the Araceae (Arum Family) are useful in shallow-water plantings. *Acorus calamus* (sweet-flag) has lance-shaped, erect leaves several feet high and aromatic roots. *Peltandra virginica* (water or arrow arum) has particularly handsome foliage, its large, arrow-shaped, dark green leaves held above the water on long stems. *Alisma* (water-plantain) includes plants of similar use and value.

The several species of *Colocasia* (Japanese-taro, elephant's-ear) have become popular for their rich foliage, not only for shallow-water planting but also as houseplants. Their large leaves give pools a tropical effect, as does *Thalia dealbata*, with its long stems and large leaves.

Among the shallow-water plants remarkable for their bloom as well as foliage, are *Caltha palustris* (marsh-marigold), with bright yellow flowers and luxuriant green leaves; *Ludwigia longifolia* (primrose water-willow), whose tall stems bear charming yellow flowers in the axils of reddish willowlike leaves; the hardy *Orontium aquaticum* (golden-club), with its spike of tiny golden flowers and handsome leaves; *Butomus umbellatus*, (flowering-rush), with clusters of rose flowers held high above clumps of three-cornered leaves; and *Saururus cernuus* (lizard-tail), with heart-shaped leaves and curved, lizard-tail spikes of tiny, fragrant white flowers.

AQUATIC PLANTS GUIDE

GENUS (common name)	HABIT	DEPTH OF WATER	HARDINESS
Acorus (sweet-flag)	upright	emergent, shallow	Zones 4–11
Azolla (azolla)	–	submergent, deep	Zones 5–11
Butomus (flowering-rush)	erect	emergent, shallow	Zones 4–11
Cabomba (water-shield)	bushy	submergent	Zones 4–11
Ceratophyllum (hornwort)	–	submergent	Zones 3–11
Cyperus (papyrus, umbrella plant)	upright	emergent, shallow	Zones 9–11
Eichhornia (water-hyacinth)	–	floating, deep or shallow	Zones 2–11
Elodea (waterweed)	–	submergent	Zones 3–11
Iris	upright	emergent, shallow	Zones 4–9
Ludwigia (primrose-willow)	recumbent	submergent, shallow	Zones 4–11
Myriophyllum (parrot's-feather)	bushy	floating or submergent	Zones 5 11
Nelumbo (lotus)	–	emergent, deep	Zones 4–11
Nymphaea (waterlily)	–	floating, deep	Zones 1–11 (tropical species Zones 10–11 only)
Nymphoides (floating-heart)	–	floating, shallow to a few feet deep	Zones 4–11
Orontium (golden-club)	upright	emergent, deep or shallow	Zones 3–11
Pontederia (pickerelweed)	upright	emergent, shallow	Zones 3–11
Sagittaria (arrowhead)	upright	emergent, shallow	Zones 5–11
Thalia (water-canna)	upright	emergent, shallow	Zones 6–11
Typha (cattails)	upright	emergent, shallow	Zones 2–11
Vallisneria (eelgrass)	upright	submergent	Zones 4–11
Zizania (wild-rice)	upright	shallow, swampy	Zones 3–11

AQUATIC PLANTS GUIDE

BLOOM TIME	FLOWERS	FOLIAGE	GOOD OXYGENATOR
May to August	yellow-green, fragrant when crushed	swordlike, aromatic	–
–	inconspicuous	tiny, mosslike changes color with light	yes
spring and fall	yellow, pink, or white	small, oblong	–
summer	white or yellowish feathery below	round above,	yes
–	inconspicuous	bristly, whorled	yes
late summer	reddish	palmlike	–
–	orchidlike; white, lilac, or blue	large, shiny green	–
summer	yellowish white, inconspicuous	tiny, lance-shaped	yes
early to late spring	blue, yellow, white, pink, or purple	green or variegated, bladelike	–
–	yellow	green or reddish, willow-like	–
–	inconspicuous	dark green, sometimes red; feathery	yes
–	pale yellow or red, some double	broad, olive or blue-green	–
early spring to frost	some fragrant; some night-blooming; red, yellow, blue, white, or pink; some change color	broad, olive green mottled with some red	–
late spring to early fall	buttercup-like, yellow	heart-shaped, olive green and brown mottled	–
spring	yellow spikes aging tored	narrow, lanceshaped	–
spring–summer	profuse blue-violet spikes	arrow-shaped on long stalks	–
July to October	white, some double	awl-shaped	yes
summer	small, purple	large leaves on long stalks	–
August to October	brown	bladelike	–
–	white, inconspicuous	ribbonlike	yes
–	inconspicuous	very tall, grassy	–

Nymphoides (floating-hearts) are splendid for planting, not only in the shallows, but in water up to a few feet deep. Their profusion of bloom and foliage makes them particularly good in the small tub garden. Under favorable conditions, they are more likely to need restraint than encouragement.

Other small, attractively flowered plants suitable for shallow water in the pool or tub garden or, in winter, the sunny aquarium are *Hydrocleys* spp. (water-poppies). Growing quickly, they reward the gardener with a summer-long profusion of poppylike yellow bloom held well above the masses of floating green foliage.

PLANTS FOR DEEPER WATERS
Deeper waters can be planted not only with lotus and water lilies, but also a sizable group of charming floating plants. *Nelumbo* (lotus), in any of its several species, presents large and beautiful blossoms that tower above masses of enormous blue-green leaves. They are best planted by themselves in a pool where the long roots can run at will. If this is not practical, however, they are quite successful planted in large containers and submerged in the deeper waters of the pond. They are also good subjects for the tub garden; one tuber can be planted in a tub or half-barrel filled to within 5–6 in. of the top with rich soil and then filled with water. Most forms flower in shades of pure white to rose, but there is also yellow form.

Nelumbo lutea (American lotus) and *Nuphar* spp. (cowlily, spatterdock), with its yellow, cup-shaped flowers and 12-in. heart-shaped leaves, are both hardy and especially suited to planting directly in the bottom of the wild pond.

The most common and showy of the large floating plants is *Eichhornia crassipes* (water-hyacinth). It is often used in aquariums and pools for its profuse spikes of yellow-blotched blue flowers kept afloat by curious bladderlike inflations of the leaf stems.

Aponogeton distachyus (water-hawthorn, cape-pondweed) is a fine aquatic for deeper waters. The blunt, lance-shaped leaves float beside twin spikes of fragrant white flowers.

Another floating plant useful indoors or out is *Ceratopteris thalictroides* (water-fern). In warm water and bright sun, it quickly builds up a mass of lettuce-green foliage, tiny new plants rapidly developing along the margins of older leaves.

The floating *Pistia stratiotes* (shellflower, water-lettuce) likes a shady place to display its rosette of elegantly fluted gray-green leaves. Its cluster of hanging roots makes a splendid nursery for very young fish.

Of the small floating plants useful in the pool or aquarium, *Azolla caroliniana* is one of the most curious and interesting. Because it turns reddish in bright sun, it can be used to indicate the amount of light in a tank or pool. Its larger relative, *Salvinia*, quickly forms large patterns of soft, velvety green on the surface of warm, sunny waters. *Lemna minor* (duckweed) forms spots like bright green confetti floating on the surface.

BOG GARDEN
Bog gardens are cultivated on the wet, usually low ground along a spring, stream, or pond.

SITE AND CONSTRUCTION
For success in such a special undertaking, it is important to have a genuine bog or swamp condition, or a little brook that can be slightly dammed and induced to saturate an area outside its natural banks. Low-lying land where water settles at rainy seasons only to disappear altogether as the summer advances will not suffice. Hence, it is desirable to have a spring or springs to maintain a constant water supply. Lacking these natural conditions, it is not advisable to attempt a bog garden, as artificial conditions are seldom successful or attractive. Given the proper conditions, however, it is sometimes advisable to excavate enough at the lowest portion of the land to provide moderate drainage for the entire space. Of course, such excavation, filling with water, will form a naturalistic little pool, which then will become a feature of the composition. Since it is necessary to walk immediately among plants in order to tend or enjoy them pathways are important. In such conditions, stepping stones justify themselves as nowhere else, because they provide the dry and firm footing

that no other kind of path can give. They should be evenly and securely set with their surfaces 2 in. above the earth—more if the water sometimes rises above its normal level. The local conditions must govern this.

PLANT MATERIALS

Trees especially adapted to sodden earth conditions are sour gum, black willow, swamp white oak, willow oak, hornbeam, black ash, bald-cypress, white and red birch, larch, and black spruce. Shrubs that thrive in such places are alder, spicebush, buttonbush, sweet pepperbush, clammy azalea, elder, steeplebush, and arrowwood. These shrubs and trees are not only able to do well in wet soil, but they bring the associated idea of natural bogs and swales into the composition. Thus they belong in such a garden, even though they also grow well under less saturated ground conditions. Naturally, they will be used as boundary planting rather than in the bog garden itself where smaller things will be used.

Bog plants themselves require special study. Of them all, perhaps the marsh-marigold and the pitcher plant are the most generally known. The cardinal flower is also popular, as is native sweet-flag, though it lacks conspicuous blossoms. Others include the native irises, ironweed, possibly bladderwort or rose-mallow (if not too far north), and countless other interesting plants.

AQUIFOLIACEAE (ak wi foh lee AY see ee). The Holly Family, a group of generally distributed trees and shrubs, often preferring moist woodlands. The two principal genera, *Ilex* (holly) and *Nemopanthus* (mountain holly), are widely used in horticulture as ornamental shrubs because of their glossy, handsome foliage and small, bright, berrylike fruits. Useful for wood and wood products, some species of *Ilex* are also sources of beverages. Appalachian-tea is derived from *I. cassine* (dahoon holly), and the well-known yerba de maté from *I. paraguaiensis*.

AQUILEGIA (ak wi LEE jee ah). A genus of perennials belonging to the Ranunculaceae (Buttercup Family), commonly known as columbine, and incorrectly identified as honeysuckle in some regions. This is one of the most valuable hardy perennials for its exquisite, durable, lobed foliage, which often turns to rich colors in autumn, and for its spurred, gracefully hung blossoms produced in early summer. The sepals as well as the petals are colored. Each of the petals has a downward extension that forms a hollow spear.

CULTURE

There are few spots in the garden that are not appropriate for some form of columbine. Many are suited to the perennial border, cutting garden, or wild garden; smaller kinds are ideal candidates for the rock garden. Various species are hardy in Zones 3–9.

Seed sown in spring or early summer will give plants that can be set into their permanent quarters in early fall. The following spring they will bloom abundantly, generally growing 1–3 ft. high. The seed may be slow to germinate, but it is reliable, provided the soil is kept fairly moist and shaded.

Young plants, too, should be shaded. When they are transplanted (preferably to rich humus to which bonemeal or well-decayed manure has been added), they should be given only partial sun and protection from the wind.

Most columbines (especially the garden hybrids) can also be propagated from root divisions. Made in autumn, these will produce well-established plants ready for flowering in the spring. To keep a constant supply, it is advisable to raise several new plants each season, since the hybrids are often short-lived.

Insect Pests. When borers (salmon-brown caterpillars of a moth) are found in the crowns, pull up and destroy infested plants and in the fall burn all waste grass, weeds, and other debris on which the eggs of this pest spend the winter. See BORERS.

A leaf miner often eats tunnels in the leaves, making winding white markings. Pick and burn such leaves and hoe the soil around the plants in the fall so the pests will be exposed to the elements and the birds. See LEAF MINER.

Diseases. Plant tops can be killed by either crown or stem rot. Remove and destroy infected clumps. Powdery mildew on the foliage may be controlled by dusting with fine sulfur. See CROWN ROT; STEM ROT; MILDEW.

PRINCIPAL SPECIES

A. alpina (alpine columbine) is an excellent rock garden plant from central Europe, low growing with large, deep blue flowers in midsummer.

A. bertolini (alpine-rock columbine) grows to six inches and has blue flowers on 2-in. stems and creates a compact cushion of blue-green foliage.

A. buergerana is a Japanese plant growing to 2 ft. with large purple-and-yellow flowers.

A. caerulea (Colorado columbine), the state flower of Colorado, is generally taller than *A. canadensis*, bearing large, showy blue flowers from spring to midsummer. Hybrids in white or in combinations, sometimes with pink or yellow, are available.

Aquilegia caerulea

A. canadensis (eastern columbine) is a dainty scarlet and yellow columbine of the midwestern and eastern states. It is smaller but more brilliant in color than the long-spurred hybrids and is especially attractive on a semishaded hillside. It self-sows readily and blooms in summer.

Aquilegia canadensis

A. chaplini, growing to 1 ft., is native to the southwestern states. It has finely cut leaves and small yellow flowers with long spurs and yellow stamens.

A. chrysantha (golden columbine), native to the Rocky Mountains, is a tall, branching plant bearing yellow flowers with long spurs all summer. Var. *jaeschkanii* is smaller and has red spurs.

A. discolor, introduced from Spain, is a choice small alpine species with relatively large blue-and-white flowers. It reseeds nicely but is never a difficult pest.

A. flabellata (fan columbine), also listed as *A. akitensis*, is a compact plant, 9–12 in., with glaucous leaves and lilac and white, nodding flowers. Cv. 'Nana Alba' is smaller, with pure white flowers, and is easy to grow. Var. *pumila* is only 6 in. tall, bearing flowers of blue or purple with yellow centers.

Aquilegia chrysantha

A. formosa (Sitka columbine), also listed as *A. eximea*, is native from California to Alaska and bears red and yellow, short-spurred flowers appearing from late spring through summer.

A. glandulosa (Altai columbine) is native to Siberia and is sometimes a difficult subject to keep, but it is worth an effort because of its bluish foliage and blue flowers tipped with white. It prefers a deep, sandy soil.

A. jonesii, native to the Rocky Mountains, especially north from Wyoming, is the most difficult columbine to grow but is very desirable in the rock garden. It has beautiful low, tight foliage and purplish blue flowers of appropriate scale. A number of rock gardeners have found the hybrid between this species and *A. saximontana* easy to grow.

A. leptoceras, a small species imported from Siberia, has greenish yellow and violet flowers.

A. x *nora barlow*, growing to 2 ft., has fully double flowers of pink and green. It is a favorite of florists and usually comes true from seed.

A. saximontana (Rocky Mountain columbine), growing 8–12 in., is an easily cultivated alpine species with small, light blue and white, semi-nodding flowers and very small, airy, twice-divided green leaves.

A. siberica (Siberian columbine) is an Asian species with large, lilac-blue flowers. Var. *spectabilis* has yellow-tipped petals.

A. skinneri (Mexican columbine) is a southern mountain species, growing in warm regions to 3 ft. It opens pale red and greenish yellow flowers from midsummer until fall.

A. vulgaris (granny's-bonnet) is the common columbine of Europe. Its blue flowers with short, knobbed, incurved spurs appear in midsummer. This plant is poisonous. Var. *plena* is a spurless, double form with violet, rose, and white flowers that bloom in spring.

ARABIS (AR ah bis). A widely cultivated genus of annuals, biennials, and perennials, belonging to the Brassicaceae (Mustard Family), and commonly known as rockcress. Species include delightful low-growing plants easily cultivated in the border or rock garden. Reaching heights of 6–12 in., they bear a profusion of white, pink, or purple flowers from midspring into early summer. Various species are hardy in Zones 3–7.

Arabis sp.

CULTURE

They prefer a sunny location but will get along in partial shade. Given a light, sandy soil enriched with bonemeal worked in around each plant when it is set out, these charming plants produce an abundance of blossoms and attractive mats of foliage later in the season after the blossoms.

They grow readily from seed, which can be sown outdoors in late spring. It should be covered to a depth twice its diameter. Mixing a little sand with the seeds will facilitate even sowing. Purchased plants should be set out in early fall, at which time plants grown from seed should be shifted to their permanent locations to flower the second season. They should stand 6 in. apart. After flowering, cut established plants back. When the ground freezes, cover them with 2–3 in. of leaves.

Propagation can also be done by division of roots soon after flowering. Lift the plant and separate the mass of roots by pulling it apart gently, using no knife unless necessary. Cuttings can be made of green growth as with CHRYSANTHEMUM.

PRINCIPAL SPECIES

A. alpina (mountain rockcress), growing to 6 in. and more slender than other species, produces sprays of four-petaled, white flowers and coarse-toothed, silvery gray foliage. It blooms for six to eight weeks in spring and is suitable for a large rock garden. Var. *rosea* has pink flowers. Cv. 'Snow Peak' is a compact version with profusions of pure white flowers.

A. androsacea, growing to 3 in., is native to the mountains of Turkey. It holds small white flowers just above its foliage.

A. aubretioides, growing to 6 in., has tufts of small leaves and pale pink flowers. It is native to Asia Minor.

A. blepharophylla (California rockcress, rose-cress), growing to 12 in., is native to California. It produces attractive rosettes of broad, glossy green leaves. Dense spikes of fragrant, rose-purple flowers bloom in late spring and continue to appear sporadically throughout the growing season. It can be a nuisance by self-sowing, but excess is easily weeded out.

A. caerula, growing to 3 in., is a small, tufted species bearing slate blue flowers in spring.

A. caucasica (wall rockcress, wallcress), also listed as *A. albida*, grows 6–9 in. high and has soft, silver-gray foliage and fragrant, ½–1 in. white flowers with yellow stamens. It blooms for six to eight weeks in spring. There are a number of varieties commercially available. Cv. 'Flore Pleno' is popular, growing to 12 in., and has fully double white flowers on long stems. Cv. 'Snow

Cap' grows to a compact 8 in. and has profusions of white flowers. Cv. 'Variegata' grows to 8 in. and has single white flowers and irregular white margins on the leaves. Hardy to Zone 4.

A. hirsuta is a biennial, growing to 10 in., tufted at the base, with hairy foliage and white or rose flowers.

A. procurrens is a choice species with small rosettes of green foliage and short sprays of white flowers. It spreads by runners into a tight ground cover.

A. sturii, perhaps the choicest species, grows to 8 in., forming a compact mat with small, glossy, bright green leaves and clusters of white blooms in spring.

ARACEAE (ahr AY see ee). The Arum Family, a group of herbs characterized by their extremely small, simple, unisexual flowers crowded around a column called a spadix, which is surrounded by a broad, petal-like or leaflike, often colored organ called a spathe. Plants belonging to this family are described as aroid. Principal cultivated members include *Anthurium* (tailflower), *Arisaema* (jack-in-the-pulpit), *Calla*, *Philodendron*, *Zantedeschia* (calla-lily).

ARACHNIODES (ah rak NOY deez). A genus of tropical ferns, including two from subtropic regions of Japan and China. As with most ferns, they require shade and moist, humusy soil. Hardy to Zone 7.

A. simplicior (variegated shield fern), often distributed as *A. aristata* 'Variegata', is a very slow-growing fern cherished only by collectors. It has attractive shining green fronds embellished with a pale gold band on each side of the midrib.

A. standishii (upside-down fern) is a medium-sized fern with narrow, 2–3 ft. long fronds. It is tripinnate, and the pinnae are thin in texture; the black sori show through the upper side, giving the plant its common name.

ARALIA (ah RAY lee ah). A genus of mostly hardy ornamental herbs, shrubs, or small trees, some with spiny stems, belonging to the Araliaceae (Ginseng Family). The larger species give a very imposing effect when grouped on the lawn or used as accent plants in the shrub border. The doubly pinnate leaves may exceed 3 ft. in length and 2 ft. in width. This fine foliage, together with the large clusters of small, creamy white flowers in late summer, creates a marked subtropical effect. The fruit is a soft, juicy black berry. Aralias send up suckers for a considerable distance around the plant and thrive in any good soil. Propagation is by seed, root cuttings, and suckers.

Several tender shrubby plants known as Aralias and grown in greenhouses for their ornamental foliage are now placed in other genera, including *Dizygotheca*, *Panax*, and *Polyscias*.

PRINCIPAL SPECIES

A. chinensis (Chinese angelica tree) is a large shrub that grows to 20 ft. or more and has spiny stems. The leaves are 2–4 ft., usually without prickles. Flower panicles nearly 2 ft. long bloom in August and September.

A. cordata (Udo) is a perennial herb from Japan, growing 4–8 ft. The young blanched shoots in spring are edible.

A. elata (Japanese angelica tree) is a large shrub or tree growing to 50 ft., usually with spiny stems. Leaflets are somewhat smaller than *A. chinensis*, but flower clusters are similar.

A. hispida (bristly sarsaparilla), native in North America, is an herb or subshrub that grows 1–3 ft. and has bark of medicinal value.

A. nudicalis (wild sarsaparilla) is a perennial that grows to 12 in. from rhizomes. It has pinnate leaves to 6 in. long and bare stems supporting terminal umbels, then black fruit.

A. racemosa (spikenard) is a perennial herb native in North American woodlands that grows 3–6 ft. and has small whitish flowers and purplish berries. The aromatic rootstock is used in medicine.

A. spinosa (angelica tree, Hercules'-club, devil's-walking-stick), native to the southeastern states, is a tree that grows to 40 ft. It makes a gaunt but interesting figure because of the spines on slender woody stems and upper leaf surfaces.

The leaves are fairly small, but the flower clusters, which bloom in August, are relatively larger than other species. It suckers freely and may become troublesome.

ARALIACEAE (ah ray lee AY see ee). The Aralia or Ginseng Family, a group of widely distributed, mostly woody herbs, shrubs, and trees, including a number of good garden subjects with ornamental foliage; some species yield medicinal products. The plants are characterized by small, regular whitish or greenish flowers borne in close heads as in the Apiaceae (Celery Family), which this family resembles. The foliage of many species is aromatic. The variable *Aralia* (including the devil's-walking-stick and wild sarsaparillas) is one well-known genus, others are *Acanthopanax*, *Dizygotheca*, *Hedera* (English ivy), and *Panax* (the source of ginseng root).

ARAUCARIA (ar aw KAY ree ah). A genus of evergreen trees related to the pines but separated in their own family, the Araucariaceae. They are native to temperate areas of the Southern Hemisphere and hardy in Zones 10–11, with one species, *A. araucana*, surviving into Zone 7. They are popular indoor plants where their main enemies are mealy bugs and mites.

Araucaria heterophylla

Propagation is best by seed. Cuttings will root, but those from side branches will usually continue to grow horizontally, rather than upright.

PRINCIPAL SPECIES

A. araucana (monkey-puzzle) is a stiff, ungainly tree with heavy, brittle branches, and sharp-pointed, overlapping, leathery needles, which supposedly make it a puzzle even for a monkey to climb. The hardiest of the species and native to Chile, it is grown in the open in the south of England and Ireland and also in the western United States.

A. bidwillii (bunya-bunya) is a thick-leaved evergreen tree from Australia.

A. heterophylla (Norfolk-Island-pine) was formerly listed as *A. excelsa*. It is a stiff and formal tree with whorls of branches regularly spaced up the trunk. It grows to a large tree in tropical areas but responds well to confinement in a pot to limit its size.

ARBOR. A shelter of branches or interwoven vines, or a trellis over which vines are trained. The primitive form of arbor consists of tree trunks grown in conveniently spaced rows. The tree tops are removed and branch stubs are left, over which vines, such as grapevines, are trained and woven into a green canopy from which fruit clusters hang. Modern arbors are open, light, and airy structures built to support vines. In addition to providing support and increased sunlight for vines, the arbor can serve overall garden design, act as a wind or sunscreen, and provide a shady, private retreat.

ARBORETUM. A collection of trees and other woody plants used for scientific or educational purposes. On private land the collection can reflect the personal interest of the owner, but most arboretums are established as part of a university or public park, and the plant material is chosen to show a wide range of specimens. To be of maximum value, the trees are often grouped according to families or genus. This arrangement gives students a clearer picture of the plant relationships.

An arboretum can be an outdoor museum only, or it can be maintained in connection with a greenhouse, library, herbarium, or collection of dried plant specimens. A large arboretum can also support a laboratory for research work and collections of drawings, paintings, photographs, and other plant identification material.

Bulletins, reports, and books are often issued from arboretums that support research centers. The information and plant displays in a public arboretum are very useful to the home gardener as well as the botany student. A walk through an arboretum will acquaint the visitor with a vast amount of plant material, both native and exotic, that can be grown in the climate and soil conditions of a given area.

ARBORVITAE. Common name for THUJA, a genus of hardy evergreen trees of compact pyramidal or columnar form.

ARBUTUS (ahr BYOO tus). A genus of evergreen trees and shrubs belonging to the Ericaceae (Heath Family). They are attractive outdoors in warm-temperate regions, Zones 7–9, but in the North can only be grown indoors. They have red-barked branches and dark green foliage.

A. menziesii (madrone, madroña), a native tree of California, is the largest of the family, growing to 50 ft. It bears white flowers in panicles followed by small red fruits. A destructive LEAF SPOT disease may cause defoliation in the Pacific Northwest.

A. unedo (strawberry tree), the best-known species, is native to Ireland and southern Europe. It grows to 25 ft. and has several attractive varieties. The drooping clusters of white or pinkish flowers appear in the fall, along with the ripe, strawberrylike berries from flowers of the previous year. These are edible but lack flavor.

ARCHONTOPHOENIX (ark ahn toh FEE niks). A genus of elegant feather palms, commonly known as king palm. They have stout, ringed stems and feathered leaves drooping from smooth green sheaths. Native to Australia, the trees are grown outdoors in tropical regions (Zones 10–11). They are attractive not only for their feathery foliage, but also for their white or purple flower trusses, which are followed by clusters of bright red pealike fruits. In cooler climates they can be planted in a temperate greenhouse in a rich, fibrous soil. Propagation is by seed, which must have heat and moisture.

A. alexandrae (Alexandra palm), the tallest type—growing to 80 ft.—has white or creamy flowers.

A. cunninghamiana (piccabeen palm), with lilac flowers, is sometimes called *Seaforthia elegans* in trade.

ARCTIUM (ARK tee um). A small genus of coarse, strong-smelling biennials or perennials. They have large leaves and small, purplish flowers followed by burr-like heads, armed with hooked bristles that aid in spreading. They are European plants that are now widely distributed. Some species are much despised as weeds. A tea of the leaves of some species has been used for medicinal purposes.

To control weedy stands, dig out roots as early as possible and destroy seed heads to avoid spreading. See WEEDS.

A. lappa (great burdock) grows to 8 ft. and has large, heart-shaped leaves and white wool beneath. It is less common in the United States, but in Japan it is cultivated for the large, edible root called "gobo." It grows on soils rich in nitrogen and iron, but low in calcium. The seeds and leaves are sometimes used in herbal medicines.

A. minus (common burdock) is widely naturalized in the United States (Zones 3–7) on nitrogen-rich soils with low levels of available calcium and high levels of phosphorus and iron.

ARCTOSTAPHYLOS (ark tuh STAF uh lis). A genus of evergreens of the Ericaceae (Heath Family), mostly native to western North America, and commonly known as manzanita, which means "little apple" in Spanish. Ranging from creeping mats to small trees, they are generally characterized by small, leathery leaves; clusters of small, urnlike flowers in white or pink; small brown or red dryish fruits like little apples; and hard, mahoganylike branches that twist and gnarl attractively. Most species are not very hardy but are invaluable in milder climates for their picturesque growth and tolerance for drought and poor soils as long as drainage is excellent. Propagation is usually from cuttings in the late summer or fall in the greenhouse with bottom heat. Seed germination is usually quite slow and erratic.

PRINCIPAL SPECIES

A. bakeri (Baker manzanita) is a mid-sized, sprawling shrub that grows to 6 ft. and has lanceolate, grayish olive leaves and smooth, purplish bronze trunks. 'Louis Edmonds' flowers are rich pink. This plant adapts to many soils.

A. columbiana (hairy manzanita) grows to 25 ft. in an open form that branches with age. Its leaves are 3 in. long, grayish green; new stems are hairy; branches and trunks are smooth and reddish brown. The flowers are white. Hardy in Zones 7–9.

A. densiflora (Vine Hill manzanita) is a low, intricately branched, sprawling shrub growing to 5 ft. Its narrow, bright green leaves are clustered in terminal branchlets on smooth, reddish black branches; flowers are white or pinkish. Best named varieties are 'Howard McMinn', which is an adaptable, finely textured, mounding shrub that grows to 4 ft.; and 'Sentinel', which is upright to 6 ft. and has greyish green foliage.

A. edmundsii (Little Sur manzanita) is a low, billowy, tender ground cover that grows to 12 in. and has roundish leaves, bronze new growth, and pink flowers. Var. *parvifolia* is smaller in all respects. Cv. 'Carmel Sur' has ½-in. oval glossy leaves and whitish pink flowers; this is a good choice for rock garden or bonsai. Var. *parvifolia* is smaller in all respects. Cv. 'Little Sur' forms a dense mat to 8 in. tall.

A. hookeri (Monterey manzanita) forms a dense, mounding shrub 2–4 ft. high. It has glossy green, oval to lanceolate leaves; intricate branching; and smooth, dark red-brown bark. Cv. 'Monterey Carpet' has compact growth to 12 in. high. 'Wayside' is more open, often growing to 3 ft. or more.

A. manzanita (common manzanita), the native manzanita of California, is a large and crooked branched shrub or small tree that grows to 12 ft. It has a distinct appearance, with drooping panicles of white and rose flowers; bright green leaves; and smooth, dark purplish red bark. Hardy to Zone 7.

A. pajaroensis (Pajaro manzanita) grows in a mounding or small tree form to 12 ft. and has nearly clasping, grayish leaves and pinkish flowers. Cv. 'Paradise' has rich pink flowers and bronze new growth. 'Warren Roberts' has gray foliage and red new growth. 'Myrtle Wolf' has deep rose-red buds and soft pink flowers.

A. patula (greenleaf manzanita), growing as a low, attractively branched shrub to 6 ft., is one of the hardiest species. It has dark red-purple trunks, glossy, green roundish leaves, and pink flowers.

A. stanfordiana (Stanford manzanita), an intricately branched shrub that grows 6–8 ft. It has narrow, glossy, deep green foliage; pink flowers; and smooth, muscular, reddish brown bark. Var. *bakeri* has grayish olive, lanceolate leaves. Cv. 'Trinity Ruby' has especially deep rose-pink flowers. Hardy to Zone 7.

A. uva-ursi (bearberry, kinnikinick), a prostrate shrub with rooting branches, is the best-known species, widely spread throughout the Northern Hemisphere and hardy in Zones 2–6. The bright green teardrop-shaped leaves are small and leathery, taking on a bronzy tone in fall. Small white to rose flowers open in spring and are followed by mealy red berries produced from late summer to winter and said to be enjoyed by bears. Being a trailing evergreen only a few inches in height, it is a valuable ground cover plant for northern gardens, forming a prostrate mat on poor, sandy soils, but tolerant of many soil types. It thrives in acid soil, full sun (or part shade), and grows best in sandy, infertile soil; it is rather difficult to transplant but worth the effort. It is salt tolerant and useful for seashore plantings. Propagation is best done by cuttings of mature growth, which root readily under glass in late summer in a mixture of sand and peat. It is best to establish them in pots prior to planting them outside. Varieties have different shapes, sizes, and quality of growth habit, leaves, and fruit. Cv. 'Massachusetts' has dense growth of dark green leaves. 'Pt. Reyes' has roundish, dark green leaves and mounds to 3 ft. 'Radiant' has lighter green leaves and heavy fruit. 'Samoa' has glossy foliage and large, showy, scarlet fruit.

ARCTOTHECA (ahrk toh THEE kah) **calendula.** An evergreen perennial ground cover, native to Africa, belonging to the Asteraceae (Aster Family), and commonly known as capeweed. Hardy only to Zone 8, it is grown in California, but almost nowhere else in the United States. Two-inch yellow daisylike flowers are borne almost year-round, though primarily in the spring. Leaves are grayish green and deeply divided. A good choice for a wildflower garden, the plant can withstand light frost, and its culture is not demanding.

ARCTOTIS (ahrk TOH tis). A genus of attractive, daisylike, half-hardy annual herbs from South Africa. The somewhat white-woolly plants grow 6 in. to 3 ft. high, bearing solitary flowers in shades of white, orange, brown, or purple. The flowers are especially good for cutting, lasting up to ten days, but use is limited to the daytime because they close at night. An interesting feature of this plant is that undeveloped buds brought indoors and placed in water in a sunny window will open.

Plants can be set in any part of the garden, growing luxuriously in any good garden soil and a sunny location. Propagation is easily done from seed started indoors or out. Seeds germinate quickly, and plants grow rapidly to produce flowers all summer and fall.

A. breviscapa is a dwarf species with 6-in. leaves and 2-in. flowers with orange rays and dark centers.

A. stoechadifolia (African daisy) is a bushy plant 2–2½ ft. tall, with 4-in. toothed leaves. The ray flowers are white on the upper surface and lilac-blue beneath, and the center or disk is steel blue, giving rise to its common name, blue-eyed African daisy. Flowers, sometimes 3 in. across, are borne on strong stalks well above the leaves.

ARDISIA (ahr DIZ ee ah). An extensive genus of ornamental evergreen trees and shrubs of subtropical and tropical regions. They have simple, often leathery leaves and small rose or white flowers in terminal clusters. They are subject to attacks of the common, large, brown scale insect. See GREENHOUSE PESTS.

A. crenata, often listed as or confused with *A. crispa*, is the primary species grown in the United States, and it is one of the best red-berried greenhouse plants for Christmas decoration. The berries are very durable, sometimes hanging on until the next crop is ripe. After about three years, the plant becomes leggy, but when this happens the tops can be girdled and bound with damp moss. In a warm house, they soon root and can be cut off and potted; they should be kept in a close atmosphere until the roots are active. The old plant can then be cut back so it forms a new head, first allowing it to dry to prevent bleeding. Young shoots can be rooted as cuttings. The old plant can be shaken free of old soil, repotted, and grown on as a good specimen. Equal parts loam and peat with some sharp sand suits them well. At the final potting, some old, crumbly manure can be added to advantage. Seed germinates in a few weeks. The seedlings need to be grown in a warm house to make much progress the first year.

A. escallonioides (marlberry) is a small tree with white flowers and glistening black berries; hardy only in Zones 10–11.

ARECA (ah REE kah). A genus of slender-stemmed graceful feather palms from the Malayan peninsula and now common in south Florida. Outdoors the smooth, ringed trunks, growing to 100 ft. tall, are topped by a feathery cluster of leaves 6–8 ft. long. The heavily fragrant white flowers are followed by orange-colored fruits. In cooler climates, arecas are grown as potted plants and decorative material, thriving in a rich, fibrous soil. The seeds of *A. catechu* (betel palm) produces the edible betelnut. *A. triandra*, an excellent container plant, is a much smaller species, growing only 12 ft. tall.

ARENARIA (ar en AY ree ah). A genus of low-growing herbs belonging to the Caryophyllaceae (Pink Family) and commonly known as sandwort because they prefer a sandy soil. They constitute a large group of annuals and perennials, native throughout the world except in tropical regions, and include many true alpine plants found only at high altitudes. More than 120 species have been recognized, but comparatively few, chiefly perennials, are grown in gardens.

Their habit of growth in dense mats, picturesque tufts, or graceful trailing creepers has commended their use in carpet bedding and in rock gardens. Most of the perennials bear small white flowers, but red and purple flowers may be had if

Arenaria sp.

truly alpine conditions can be provided. They are quite indifferent as to soil, as long as it is light, sandy, and free from standing water. Most species are hardy in Zones 3–8. Propagation is by seed or division. In the case of rare forms, cuttings are rooted in sand under glass.

PRINCIPAL SPECIES

A. balearica (Corsican sandwort) forms a dense mat of foliage, 3 in. high. The flowers, blooming in late spring and early summer, are small and white. This species should be given copious amounts of water and is less hardy than other arenarias (to Zone 6).

A. montana, growing 2–4 in., has 1-in., star-shaped, single white flowers with yellow eyes and is the most commonly cultivated sandwort. Handsome and easy to grow, it thrives in full sun or partial shade.

A. verna (moss sandwort) is a very hardy, fast-growing plant with evergreen, mosslike foliage and tiny white flowers in late spring. It tolerates sun or partial shade and is often planted between stepping stones. Var. *aurea* has yellow leaves. Var. *caespitosa* (Irish-moss) is 2 in. high and has star-shaped white flowers.

ARETHUSA (air ee THOO zah). A genus of two species of North American and Asian terrestrial orchids, found in sphagnum bogs and dense swamps. The flowers are handsome, rose-purple, and fragrant, with large fringed lips. Hardy to Zone 5 with proper winter protection, these orchids require a constantly moist, acid compost in a shaded location and a minimum winter temperature of 50–55°F.

ARGEMONE (ahr je MOH nee). A genus of free-flowering, hardy annuals native to the southwestern states, belonging to the Papaveraceae (Poppy Family), and commonly known as prickly poppy. The large flowers, which bloom all summer, resemble white, yellow, or purplish poppies. Leaves, with slender prickles, resemble those of the thistle. The botanic name comes from the Greek word *argemon*, meaning "cataract," which the plant once was thought to heal.

Plants grow up to 4 ft. tall, and if set 10 in. apart in rows, make a good low screen or hedge, especially attractive when topped by their beautiful flowers. Thriving in any soil and a sunny exposure, they are

Argemone munita

grown from seed that should be sown where the plants are to grow, as they resent transplanting.

PRINCIPAL SPECIES

A. grandiflora grows to 3 ft. and bears white-veined leaves and white flowers 2 in. across, the sepals with long stout tips.

A. hispida (hedgehog poppy) is densely bristled besides having yellow prickles.

A. mexicana grows to 3 ft. with white-veined leaves and yellow or orange flowers 2 in. across.

A. munita (prickly poppy) is considered a noxious weed in range lands of the American West, but it is also a beautiful and adaptable wildflower that grows 1–3 ft. tall and has many showy blossoms mounted on the branch tips amid spiny sepals. The flowers are 2–5 in. across and are made up of six white petals, textured like crepe paper, surrounding the many yellow stamens and brown-purple, scallop-edged stigma. Although toxic if eaten by humans or range animals, the spines on the foliage and stems discourage consumption.

A. platyceras (crested prickly poppy), the most commonly cultivated species, grows to 4 ft. and has white, sometimes purple flowers.

A. polyanthemos, formerly listed as *A. alba*, has white flowers and foliage that is pale or covered with a whitish bloom.

A. sanguinea has brownish purple flowers.

ARIOCARPUS (air ee oh KAHR pus). A most outlandish genus of cacti from southern Texas and northeastern Mexico, belonging to the Aizoaceae (Carpetweed Family). Because they resemble rocks in form, color, and texture, they are appropriately called living-rock cactus. They are very slow-growing and a bit difficult to grow, requiring especially well-drained soil and little water but are well worth the trouble for their incredible mimicry appearance and beautiful, large white, pink, yellow, or magenta flowers. The most popular species, *A. fissuratus*, has a convex, fissured surface with areoles in the center groove and light magenta flowers. They are among the great oddities of the plant world.

ARISAEMA (a ri SEE mah). A genus of tuberous-rooted perennial herbs of worldwide distribution, belonging to the Araceae (Arum Family). About 60 species are known, some of which are successfully grown in gardens in moist, shaded places. Some varieties are grown in pots, in a

Arisaema triphyllum

soil mixture of loam and peat. Propagation is by division of the tubers and by seed.

A. dracontium (dragonroot) is a tall species with greenish flowerlike bracts that contain orange-red berries.

A. triphyllum (jack-in-the-pulpit, Indian-turnip), the most familiar species, is an interesting plant native to eastern North America. It grows 1–3 ft. tall and has large, three-part leaves and flowers consisting of a brown and green mottled spadix followed by a bunch of brilliant red berries. It grows naturally in moist soils but is tolerant of almost any average conditions.

ARISTOLOCHIA (ah ris toh LOH kee ah). A genus of nearly 200 species of evergreen and deciduous shrubs, commonly known as birthwort for their supposed medicinal virtues, and widely distributed throughout the temperate and warmer regions. Most are climbers of twining habit and are usually grown in greenhouses. They do best when planted

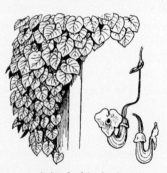

Aristolochia durior

out in rich garden soil, although some are grown successfully in pots when well fed. The flowers are remarkable for their extraordinary formation and peculiar coloring. In some species they are very large, with a long tail-like appendage, and most kinds have an offensive odor. Propagation is by seed or cuttings. Most are root-hardy to Zone 7.

PRINCIPAL SPECIES

A. durior (Dutchman's-pipe, pipevine) is a woody vine, tolerant of shade and dry soil, with large leaves. It is excellent for screening arbors or fences. The small pipe-shaped flowers lack the pronounced unpleasant family odor; their form gives the species its common name. Under ideal conditions it will grow to 30 ft. It is very hardy (to Zone 4) and free of insects and diseases.

A. elegans (calico flower) is a well-known, slender greenhouse climber that is hardy to Zone 8. The flowers are freely produced, about 3 in. across, and purple-brown with white markings and no bad odor.

A. grandiflora (pelican flower) is a large-leaved ornamental vine with flower buds resembling the body and neck of a large bird at rest. The expanded flowers are several inches across, heavily blotched and veined with purple on a white ground, and terminate in slender tails. Var. *sturtevantii* has flowers over 12 in. across, splashed with velvety crimson and with a tail 3 ft. or longer.

ARISTOTELIA (a ris toh TEE lee ah). A genus of evergreen trees and shrubs native to the Southern Hemisphere and grown in Zones 10–11. The foliage is handsome, but the flowers are small and not showy, with male and female often separate. The genus is named in honor of Aristotle, the Greek philosopher.

A. chilensis is a large shrub with purple-black berries, native to Chile but able to stand a few degrees of frost. There is a golden variegated variety.

A. racemosa (New Zealand wineberry), the principal species, is a small tree with thin, glossy leaves and pea-size, dark purple berries.

ARMERIA (ahr MER ee ah). A genus of hardy dwarf spring-blooming perennials, formerly classified as *Statice*, and commonly known as thrift or sea-pink. They grow in neat clumps of grassy, evergreen foli-age that is covered with small round heads of white, pink, red, or purplish flowers. They are easy, reliable plants for the rock garden and edge plantings. Most of the armerias available are forms of *A. maritima*.

Armeria maritima

ARMILLARIA ROOT ROT. Also called mushroom or shoestring root rot. A root and trunk decay of conifers, broad-leaved forest trees, fruit trees, and shrubs caused by the mushroom *Armillaria mellea*, often called the shoestring fungus or honey agaric. The symptoms are decline in vigor and tardy growth, followed by rotting of the bark, and finally, death of the tree. The fungus is seen as a white mycelium between the bark and cambium; it is also seen as black shoestring strands (rhizomorphs) growing out from the trunk and roots and through the soil; and finally, as honey-colored mushrooms growing in clusters around the trunk of the tree. The latter do not usually appear until the tree is almost or quite dead, which may be three or four years after the first signs of decline.

To prevent this rot, avoid planting trees in recently cleared lands. Instead, first grow farm crops for a season or two. Avoid injuring the roots of trees. Keeping trees in a vigorous condition by proper feeding and watering will render them less liable to attack by the fungus, which is a very weak parasite.

ARMORACIA (ahr mor AY see ah) **rusticana.** Botanical name for a hardy perennial from Europe, naturalized in moist ground in much of North America. Commercially cultivated as an annual, its roots are ground to produce the condiment HORSERADISH.

ARMY WORM. This striped caterpillar, *Pseudalita unipuncta*, moves in ranks like armies, devastating small grains, ornamental plants, and crops such as timothy, millet, and bluegrass. It feeds during the night but stays on the host plant during the day. The head is brown or black, the stripes yellow, and the young larvae white. The adult moth with 1½-in. wingspan is gray and mottled, and the hairy eggs in groups up to 150 are laid on the host plant. Adult moths migrate to the South for the winter and return in spring. The worm frequently feeds low on the plant, near the ground.

The effective control for larvae and caterpillars

is *Bacillus thuringiensis* (Bt, commonly available as Biotrol, Dipel, or Thuricide). Other controls include careful weeding, close mowing, fall plowing, and the introduction of predatory wasps, such as trichogramma, as well as predatory nematodes, lacewings, and the virus called NPV (nuclear polyhedrosis virus). Other toxins derive from bulbs of the *Chlorogalum pomeridianum* (California soap plant), from seeds of *Annona maricata* (soursop), and the powdered rhizome of *Dryoptera felix-mas* (shield fern). Similar species are the fall army worm and army cutworm.

ARNEBIA (ahr NEE bee ah) **decumbens.** An easily cultivated border or rock garden annual belonging to the Boraginaceae (Borage Family), formerly listed as *Arnebia cornuta*, and commonly known as Arabian-primrose. The plants grow 1–2 ft. tall and equally wide. All summer they bear a long profusion of beautiful flowers, which undergo a characteristic change in color. On opening the blossoms are primrose-yellow with black or purple spots. After the second day, the black spots become maroon and then disappear, leaving clear yellow blooms. They thrive in ordinary garden soil and a sunny location.

A. echioides is now classified as *Echioides longiflorum*; see ECHIOIDES.

ARNICA (AHR nik ah). A genus of perennial herbs, belonging to the Asteraceae (Aster Family). They have clustered, basal leaves and bright yellow flowers on long stalks. Only a few species are grown in the border or rock garden, though some of those native to the western states are effective when colonized in the wild garden. Arnicas grow readily in any good garden soil and spread so rapidly that they are most frequently propagated by division rather than seed. Hardy in Zones 3–8.

PRINCIPAL SPECIES

A. alpina, growing to 15 in., has soft, hairy foliage and heads of yellow flowers to 2 in. across. It is excellent in the sunny rock garden.

A. cordifolia, growing to 6–18 in., has flowers up to 3 in. in diameter and is good for cutting. It is a free-flowering plant that can be useful in a border, though not where children will come in contact with it, since it is poisonous.

A. montana (mountain-tobacco, mountain-snuff) is a central European plant that grows to 2 ft. tall; it is the source of the medicinal tincture of arnica. It has large heads of yellow ray and disk flowers in clusters of three or four and is attractive in an open sunny border.

AROID. Descriptive name for any plant belonging to the Araceae (Arum Family).

ARONIA (ah ROH nee ah). A genus of hardy, native, deciduous shrubs belonging to the Rosaceae (Rose Family) and commonly known as chokeberry. Valuable in the shrub border for all-around effect and for naturalizing in the garden, they are not especially particular as to soil and location but thrive best in rich, moist soil and full sun. The white flowers are attractive in spring and are followed by attractive fruit; the leaves are colorful in autumn. Propagation is by seed, cuttings, suckers, and layers. Some species are often listed in the genus *Pyrus* (pear).

PRINCIPAL SPECIES

A. arbutifolia (red chokeberry) grows to 10 ft. and bears a profusion of red berries, which remain colorful most of the winter. Cv. 'Brilliantissima' is a superior selection producing more flowers, glossier red fruit, and bright scarlet fall foliage. Hardy in Zones 5–9.

A. atropurpurea (purple chokeberry) grows to 12 ft. and has dark purple fruits that ripen in September but soon shrivel.

A. melanocarpa (black chokeberry) grows to about 4 ft. and has shining black fruits that ripen in August and drop early. Hardy in Zones 4–9.

ARRHENATHERUM (a re NA the rum). A genus of early perennial grasses commonly known as oat grass. Native to the Mediterranean region, they are cultivated in humid regions and frequently become naturalized, especially in the northern and eastern states. They are low growers with flat green-and-white leaf blades and narrow panicles of flowers; they are attractive as a border or single clump.

A. *elatius* (tall oat grass) has erect stems to 5 ft. tall and narrow leaves. It bears 12-in. panicles of glossy, pale green or purplish flowers.

See also ORNAMENTAL GRASSES.

ARROW ARUM. Common name for *Peltandra virginica*, a perennial bog herb with arrow-shaped leaves; see PELTANDRA.

ARROWHEAD. Common name for SAGITTARIA, a popular genus of flowering aquatic perennials.

ARROWROOT. Common name for *Maranta arundinacea*, a tropical herb whose starchy roots yield commercial arrowroot and tapioca; see MARANTA.

ARROWWOOD. Common name for *Viburnum dentatum*, a small tree with circular, toothed leaves and white flowers followed by black, berrylike fruits; see VIBURNUM.

ARTEMISIA (ahr te MEEZ ee ah). A genus of hardy, aromatic, usually perennial herbs or small shrubs belonging to the Asteraceae (Aster Family) and commonly known as wormwood or mugwort. Their small white or yellow heads are composed entirely of disk (tubular) flowers. The 50 or more species include the native sagebrushes of the western states, and many others are satisfactory for home garden culture.

Grown chiefly for their aromatic and medicinal qualities, the plants are also garden subjects and are good for cutting. They thrive in any average soil and bloom from late summer through the early fall.

Artemisia abrotanum

Species vary widely in shape and size, ranging from 6 in. to 12 ft. high. The foliage of many species is so densely hairy as to appear white. Propagation is generally by division, sometimes by seed. Most species are hardy in Zones 4–8.

PRINCIPAL SPECIES

A. *abrotanum* (southernwood, old-man) is a shrub that grows to 5 ft. and has leaves divided into threadlike segments and yellowish white flowers in heads growing in a loose cluster.

A. *absinthium* (absinthe, common wormwood), native to Europe, is a shrubby, aromatic perennial with silky white, segmented leaves. This is one of the sources of absinthe, a strong, green liquor.

A. *camphorata* is similar to A. *abrotanum*, but it has strongly scented foliage reminiscent of moth balls.

A. *dracunculus* (tarragon) is a perennial, hardy to Zone 5, and has long, narrow, smooth green leaves used for seasoning. See also HERBS.

Artemisia absinthium

A. *frigida* (mountain-fringe, fringed wormwood) is decorative in borders, grows 15 in. tall, and has delicate velvety leaves.

A. *gmelinii* (Russian wormwood), formerly listed as A. *sacrorum*, has whitish leaves. Cv. 'Viridis' (summer-fir) is tall and drought resistant, with finely cut, dark green leaves; it is useful in borders or for landscaping.

A. *lactiflora* (white mugwort) is fairly tall with deeply toothed, smooth, green foliage. The masses of fragrant white flower heads appear in autumn.

A. *lanata*, formerly listed as A. *pedemontana*, is a silvery-leaved plant, very effective in the rock garden.

A. *ludoviciana* (silverking), formerly listed as A. *albula* or A. *gnaphalodes*, is one of the showiest species, growing 3 ft. or taller. It is

native to the southwestern states but hardy to
Zone 5. The leaves, with fine white hair, are less
dissected than in other species and are often used
in winter as well as in
fresh bouquets. It works
well in borders but
requires considerable
moisture. Cv. 'Silver
Bouquet' has wider, larg-
er leaves than the species.

A. pontica (Roman
wormwood) has finely
cut leaves, whitish
beneath. Though it sel-
dom flowers, the foliage
is effective in the rock
garden.

Artemisia dracunculus

A. schmidtiana (silvermound, angel's-hair),
growing to 3 ft., has fine white hairs on deeply
cut leaves. Cv. 'Silvermound' is 8 in. high. Neither form has sig-
nificant flowers.

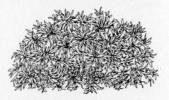

A. stellerana
(beach wormwood,
dusty miller) is
native to North
Temperate coastal
regions and is

Artemisia schmidtiana

especially suitable to seaside rock gardens. The
foliage is densely woolly.

A. tridentata (sagebrush), the state flower of
Nevada and native to the arid southwestern
states, is a rounded, evergreen shrub that grows
to 10 ft. and has silvery, aromatic foliage and panicles of tiny flowers. In some areas it is considered an aggressive weed, but it can be useful
where other shrubs will not grow.

A. vulgaris (mugwort) is a tall plant with
stems that are often purple and fragrant and
divided leaves that are green above and white
beneath. The yellow flowers appear in spikes.

ARTICHOKE. Common name for plants (and
their edible products) of three genera—*Cynara*,
Helianthus, and *Stachys*. The first two are
important garden crops. *Cynara scolymus* yields

the well-known flower buds whose scales are
blanched and eaten like asparagus. *Helianthus
tuberosum* is grown for its edible tubers; see
JERUSALEM-ARTICHOKE. The Chinese- or Japanese-
artichoke, *Stachys affinis*,
is an erect, hairy, herbaceous perennial that
grows to 1½ ft. It is cultivated in the United States
for its edible, slender,
knotty, white tubers.

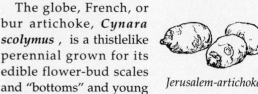

French artichoke

The globe, French, or
bur artichoke, *Cynara
scolymus*, is a thistlelike
perennial grown for its
edible flower-bud scales
and "bottoms" and young
suckers, which when
blanched are eaten like
asparagus. Though not
hardy in the North, it has
been wintered safely in
Massachusetts by placing
peck-size peach baskets

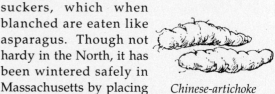

Jerusalem-artichoke

Chinese-artichoke

over the crowns to prevent smothering, and covering these with deep mulch.

When seed is sown indoors in early spring,
seedlings, pricked into small pots, hardened-off,
and later planted outdoors, often produce heads
by fall. Seedlings grown outdoors rarely bear
until the following summer. Set plants 3' x 3' or
2' x 4' in rich soil and give clean cultivation.
Gather flower heads before they bloom, and cut
back the stalks that bore them to the ground to
conserve the plants' strength and encourage
sucker production. Since plants rarely continue
to produce more than two or three years, and
since seedlings vary greatly, suckers of the best
ones should be used each spring to start new
plantings.

ARTIFICIAL LIGHT. It is possible to grow
healthy plants indoors by augmenting or replacing natural sunlight with artificial light. Plants
require primarily blue and red rays present in
light to carry on PHOTOSYNTHESIS. This balanced

lighting, supplied in appropriate intensities, is easily achieved and simulates sunlight. An arrangement of lights using fluorescent tubes and incandescent bulbs of low wattage can be used in a ratio of 100 total watts fluorescent to 40 total watts incandescent. Alternatively, a fixture containing one 40-watt cool-white fluorescent bulb and one 40-watt warm-white fluorescent bulb can be used. Special plant-growth lights, in the form of tubes, bulbs, or spotlights are also available, providing full-spectrum lighting and improving the visual effect of plants by making green leaves appear greener, red seem redder, etc. See also LIGHT.

Regardless of the type of lights used, it is important that the fixture be adjustable so the distance between the lights and the plants can be varied according to need. Because the light intensity decreases as the distance between the lamps and plants increases, it is necessary to group plants with the same light requirements together.

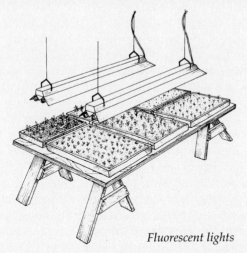

Fluorescent lights

Those plants that require high light intensities can be arranged directly under lights, while the more shade-tolerant ones should be placed further from the light source. Light intensity is described in terms of units called foot-candles and can be measured using a foot-candle meter or a photographic light meter. Most foliage houseplants will grow well at 250 foot-candles, and the flowering houseplants will blossom when provided with 250–650 foot-candles of light.

In addition to different light-intensity requirements, plants differ in their needs for day length. Constant light can be fatal; some plants require very specific ratios of light to darkness, but most respond well to fourteen to sixteen hours of light and eight to ten hours of dark in each 24-hour period. This day/night simulation is easily accomplished with the use of a timer that will automatically regulate the lighting schedule by turning the lights on and off for you.

ARTILLERY PLANT. Common name for *Pilea microphylla*, a tropical herb whose flowers "shoot out" their pollen when dry; see PILEA.

ARTOCARPUS (ahr toh KAHR pus). A genus of tropical trees of the Moraceae (Mulberry Family). These plants are not hardy in the United States mainland, though some are grown in the Florida Keys; specimens are rarely seen except in botanical gardens or in the southern United States as curiosities.

A. altilis (breadfruit) is grown for its edible fruit. After clusters of flowers, the large (to 8 in. across) oval fruits, prickly outside and pulpy inside, appear on a thickened stalk, which is cooked and eaten by native Malayans. In the usually cultivated form, the fruits are fleshy and seedless, but one seed-bearing form is called breadnut, although this name is also applied to the related plant *Brosimum alicastrum*. The large seeds of both are eaten roasted or boiled. Propagation of the breadfruit type is by suckers and root cuttings; the breadnut type, by seed.

A. heterophyllus (jackfruit) is another Malayan species of less importance.

ARUM (AIR um). A genus of tuberous herbs from Europe and Asia, from which the large family of aroides takes its name (Araceae). The plants resemble and are often known as callas (which are correctly *Zantedeschia*) and are sometimes called wild-ginger because of the acrid-tasting roots, which are poisonous in some species.

The name "arum" is frequently used in connection with unrelated plants. Arrow arum is *Peltandra virginica*. Ivy-arum is *Scindapsus*. Twist arum is *Helicodiceros muscivorus*. Water-arum is *Calla palustris*. The Arum Family is ARACEAE.

They have large leaves and variously colored spathes (the bracts surrounding a flower spike). Some species are tender and should be grown in the greenhouse, the tubers being planted deep in rich soil so that roots can form near the top, and the plants being shaded from intense sun and watered freely. The outdoor species should also have rich soil and a shaded position; leaf mulch in the fall is very beneficial. Propagation is by offsets of the tubers or by seed. Most are hardy in Zones 5–8.

PRINCIPAL SPECIES

A. italicum has yellow or white spadix, sometimes green or purplish. Though hardy, it is often grown in pots. The plant remains leafless until autumn. The roots are poisonous.

A. maculatum (lords-and-ladies, cuckoo-pint) is often mentioned in English poetry. A moisture-loving plant native to the Mediterranean region and hardy in Zones 7–8. It grows to 1 ft. high and has leaves and spathe both 10 in. long, the latter being green, spotted and margined with purple.

A. palaestinum (black-calla, Solomon's-lily) has a greenish spathe, black-purple within. Hardy only in Zones 9–11, it is grown in pots as an oddity.

ARUNCUS (ah RUN kus). A genus of herbaceous perennials belonging to the Rosaceae (Rose Family), and commonly known as goatsbeard. They have a brief bloom period in early summer when white flowers appear in clusters of spikes.

Aruncus diocus

Hardy in Zones 4–9, they are useful in the garden background, especially along shaded borders with moist, well-drained soil. Propagation is by seed or division. *A. diocus* (goat's-beard) grows from 4–6 ft., producing creamy white flowers.

ARUNDINARIA (ah roon di NAIR ee ah). One of the most important of several genera of tall-growing, woody members of the Poaceae (Grass Family), all of which are commonly known as BAMBOO. *Arundinarias* are treelike, with smooth, round, jointed stems; they often form great forests in the tropics from sea level to 15,000 ft.

Most of those grown in the United States are forms of *A. gigantea*, which in the southern states may reach 15 ft. or more. Hardiness varies according to species or subspecies, Zones 6–9.

A. macrosperma (cane reed, southern cane) is a tall grass native to wet ground from Virginia to the Gulf states.

ARUNDO (ah RUN doh). A genus of the Poaceae (Grass Family) containing, with the exception of the bamboos and uva grass, the tallest of the ornamental perennial grasses. Coming from regions of Europe, they are hardy to Zone 6 and are useful for bold effects in warm climates, growing from 8–20 ft. according to the location and soil. The stems are woody, the leaves broad, and the flowers have loose, feathery panicles 1–3 ft. long. It is from the stems of this plant that the reeds of musical instruments are made. See ORNAMENTAL GRASSES.

A. donax (great or giant reed) is capable of making from 10–20 ft. of growth in a season. Several varieties are available. Var. *versicolor*, growing to 12 ft., has white streaked leaves and is less hardy than the parent species, although both should be protected in northern regions during the winter months. Var. *macrophylla* has wide, glossy, green leaves and conspicuously close-jointed stems.

ASARINA (as ah RIN ah). A genus of slender, climbing perennial herbs belonging to the Scrophulariaceae (Figwort Family) and formerly listed as *Maurandia*. Native to Mexico and adjacent areas in the United States and hardy to Zone 7, they can be grown under glass for winter flowering. Thriving in a mixture of fibrous loam with leaf mold and well-rotted manure, they flower well in 7-in. pots. They can be treated as tender annuals for summer flowering outdoors and are attractive in baskets and vases or trained on trellises. Propagation is by seed or cuttings under glass.

PRINCIPAL SPECIES

A. antirrhinifolia,sometimes included in the genus *Antirrhinum*, is widespread in Texas and California. It climbs to 6 ft. and has hastate leaves and purple flowers.

A. barclaiana is the best-known species in cultivation. It has angular, heart-shaped leaves and purple flowers about 2 in. long. There are forms with rose and white flowers sometimes listed as *Maurandia varius*.

A. erubescens has triangular leaves and large rose-colored flowers.

ASARUM (AS ah rum). A genus of perennial herbs with many species native to Japan, found in moist woodlands and commonly known as wild-ginger. They are sometimes planted in gardens or used as ground cover. Hardiness varies (Zones 4–9) depending on the species.

Asarum canadense

A. canadense (wild-ginger) is a common native in the woods of the eastern states. A low herb with kidney-shaped leaves and chocolate-colored

flowers borne close to the ground, it is a good ground-cover plant for moist, shady locations.

A. caudatum is evergreen, with leaves 2–6 in. across; it is a common native in the Pacific states.

ASCLEPIADACEAE (as klee pee ah DAY see ee). The Milkweed Family, a group of widely distributed plants characterized by an abundant milky juice, the production of pollen grains in waxy masses, and a fruit that is a pod opening when ripe along one side to discharge light flat seeds tufted with long silky down. Generally herbs or shrubs, they vary widely, some genera being vines, like *Hoya*; or leafless and fleshy, like *Stapelia*. Many have medicinal properties, and some are grown for ornament, such as *Asclepias*, *Stephanotis*, and *Cynanchum*.

ASCLEPIAS (as KLEE pee us). A genus of perennial plants with milky juice, belonging to the Asclepiadaceae (Milkweed Family), commonly known as milkweed or silkweed. Many of them have gaily colored flowers and attractive seed pods. Plants are easily cultivated in the border or natural garden and are propagated by seed or division. Most species are hardy in Zones 3–9.

Asclepias tuberosa

PRINCIPAL SPECIES

A. curassavica (bloodflower) is a tropical species that can be grown in the greenhouse in cool regions and is easily naturalized in the wildflower garden in warm climates. It has brilliant flowers of orange and reddish purple.

A. incarnata (swamp milkweed) grows to 4 ft. and has rose-purple flowers. Var. *alba* is a white form, occasionally seen.

A. syriaca (common milkweed) is the species seen by the roadside in eastern North America. It grows to 5 ft. and has green or purplish flowers and interesting seed pods, which release masses of light, flat seeds with long, delicate, silky tassels.

A. tuberosa (butterfly weed, pleurisy root) is a rough-haired plant that grows 3 ft. high and has brilliant orange flowers in umbels (flattened clusters). Frequently found in dry places in the eastern states, it is most effective when planted in the border or wild garden but is also excellent as a cut flower. Var. *sulfurea* has primrose-yellow flowers.

ASCOCENTRUM (as koh SEN trum). A very important genus of only four or five species of epiphytic orchids. They are extensively hybridized with other vandaceous orchids, and the resulting crosses are among the most beautiful intergeneric orchid hybrids, including *Ascocenda* and *Ascofinetia*, among others. They are native to southeastern Asia, from the Himalayas through China, Java, and the Philippines.

The plants are no more than 6 in. high, with grooved, distichous leaves and long aerial roots. Erect inflorescences have many small, brilliantly colored flowers densely clustered on spikes. The colors are orange to crimson and violet, often with the lip contrasting with the petals and sepals. The flower has a small spur at the base of the lip. Plants produce offshoots readily. Hardy in Zones 9–11 with cold protection, they are best grown in baskets allowing the aerial roots to hang free. They need frequent watering, a humid atmosphere, strong light, and a minimum winter temperature of 60°F. The type species is *A. miniatum*.

ASCOCHYTA BLIGHT. Various species of the imperfect fungus *Ascochyta* cause such diseases as leaf spot and stem rot of clematis, a ray blight of chrysanthemum flowers, and a wilt of cucurbits. This blight is serious on peas, where it causes a purple leaf spot, stem and root lesions, and a pod spot somewhat similar to anthracnose of beans. Species of this fungus also cause diseases of alfalfa and other legumes, aster, columbine, cyclamen, hollyhock, horseradish, okra, rhubarb, strawberry, sweet pea, tomato, and walnut.

To control, choose disease resistant varieties. Seed grown in dry areas is less likely to be infected. If disease develops, remove the diseased plant material. Rotate crops to prevent soil contamination.

ASEXUAL REPRODUCTION. The propagation of plants by vegetative means, not by seed; that is, by such processes as grafting, cuttings, budding, layering, and division, which involve the use of an actual piece of the growing tissue of the plant that is propagated. Plants so produced are "true to type," whereas reproduction by seed may give rise to progeny quite different from the parents. See PROPAGATION.

ASH. Common name for FRAXINUS, a genus of hardy deciduous trees, including many native species and cultivars used as landscape subjects or sources of timber.

The name is also used for plants of other genera. Mountain-ash is SORBUS, a genus of deciduous flowering, fruit-bearing trees and shrubs. Prickly-ash is *Zanthoxylum americanum*, a spiny ornamental shrub; see ZANTHOXYLUM.

ASIATIC BEETLE. Three beetles of Japanese origin occur in the United States. One is the JAPANESE BEETLE; a second is the oriental beetle, *Anomala orientalis*; and the third, *Autoserica castanea*, is known as the Asiatic garden beetle.

The Asiatic beetle is particularly injurious to lawns. The adult beetles (about ⅜ in. long and varying greatly in color and markings) emerge in late June and July and lay their eggs about 6 in. deep in the soil. In three or four weeks, the recently hatched grubs ascend and begin to feed on grass roots near the surface. In late fall they descend a foot into the soil to hibernate. They again ascend to the surface in April, feed until early June, and then pupate at a 6-in. depth. There is only one generation per year.

Control is by milky spore disease (*Bacillus popilliae*) inserted into the lawn every 10 ft., at a rate of 2 lb. per acre, using 1 tsp. per insertion.

The spring tiphia wasp is a common parasite, laying eggs on the grubs underground. See also BEETLES; GRUBS.

ASIMINA (ah SIM in ah). A genus of deciduous or evergreen shrubs or small trees native to North America. Only one species, *A. triloba* (pawpaw), is hardy in the North. This is a small deciduous tree that grows to about 30 ft. and has large, drooping leaves that display attractive light-yellow color in the fall. Flowers are purple with a disagreeable odor and open before the leaves. The fruit is 3–5 in. long and is almost black when ripe, when it has a highly aromatic quality. It can be eaten raw when soft, baked, or made into pudding or pie filling. Some selection has been done recently for improved flavor, and a few cultivars are now available.

The plant thrives best in rich, moist soil, suckering freely, but it is not easy to transplant. Propagation is by seed sown in the fall and also by layers and root cuttings.

ASPARAGUS (ahs PAR ig us). Common and botanical name for a genus of about 150 species of European herbs, shrubs, and vines including several cultivated as ornaments and one as a vegetable. The most extensively grown species is *A. officinalis*. This choicest of all spring vegetables should be grown in every home garden, since better quality can be produced there than can usually be bought. Once established it requires less cultural attention than any other vegetable. If well fed and properly tended, it is a lifetime investment, annually producing successive crops of stalks for six to ten weeks.

PLANTING

In fall or spring, dig a trench about 10–12 in. deep and cover with 4–6 in. of rich garden loam or compost. On this bed, place plants 18–24 in. apart with their roots spread widely and their crowns (the buds) pointing upward; see (A). Then cover them with only 1–2 in. of soil packed firmly around them. At this point they should be about 6 in. below the ground level with only a thin layer of earth over them. In fall planting, the trench should then be filled with leaves or litter to be removed in the spring.

As the growing season advances, the soil in the trench must be slightly stirred with a narrow hoe or other implement about twice a week. This kills the weeds and works down a little earth from the sides each time, gradually increasing the cover over the roots and assuring better plant development than if the trench is completely filled at planting time. By the close of the season, the trench should be completely filled and the plants well established (B).

In many cases, beds are preferred to rows. Preparation of the soil is the same, except that all the earth is removed to the full width (5 ft.) and depth (15 in.) of the bed. The manure is spread and tramped down over the whole area, then covered with rich soil. One row of plants is placed down the center and one on each side 18 in. from the center and 12 in. from the edge. As in the garden row, set the plants closer together (18–24 in.) than in field planting, then compen-

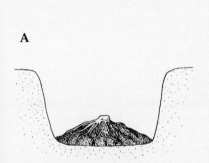
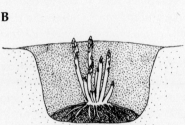
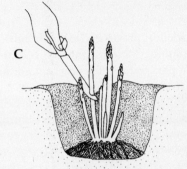

A   B   C

Trench planting asparagus

sate for this by intensive culture and lavish feeding. Though many beds are set with plants less than 12 in. apart, larger, finer quality spears are produced if the distance is 18–24 in.

In a heavy clay loam soil, especially if not naturally well drained, it is advisable to dig the trenches deeper than 15 in. Place the good topsoil in a pile by itself and replace part of the poorer subsoil with drainage material such as gravel, stones, or cinders. Then fill in with manure and rich compost to the planting level, and later use the topsoil originally removed to gradually level off as outlined above. If an outlet can be arranged, a line of tile can be placed below the trench. See also DRAINAGE.

CUTTING AND AFTER-CARE

Avoid cutting spears sooner than the third spring after planting; otherwise the plants will suffer and not yield as well in following years. Do not cut too liberally the first crop year; three cuttings is enough. Cutting too late in any season reduces the yield of sprouts the next season; it should stop as soon as early peas in local gardens are ready for the table, to give plants time to store up food for the next year's crop (C).

Careless cutting often injures or destroys sprouts still undeveloped below the surface. To cut properly, push the knife vertically down beside the sprout and, at the desired depth, give it a slight twist so the point will cut only the desired spear. Better still, snap off the sprouts by bending them across the finger with the thumb; this prevents injuring other sprouts and secures only the tender, edible parts of the stalks.

Blanching to yield white shoots, by mounding up soil around them as they grow, was once a common practice, especially with asparagus for canning. Modern preference is for natural green shoots produced by level cultivation.

FEEDING

At the close of each season, the tops should be cut close to the ground as soon as they have turned yellow or the berries become red. Avoid breaking off and scattering the berries, for any seeds that grow would become substandard plants. Then spread on the bed a heavy dressing of fresh manure, if available, to serve as a mulch and to enrich the soil. It is difficult to use too much, because asparagus is a gross feeder and responds with more and better spears. In the spring, remove the coarse, strawy part of the cover and fork the fine material into the upper 2–3 in. of soil. If fresh manure is not available in the fall, any coarse litter can be used as a mulch, and well-decayed manure can be spread and forked in when spring arrives. Poultry, pigeon, and pulverized animal manures can be liberally used in spring or early summer.

Chemical fertilizers can be used, especially those with a high phosphorus content, which stimulates strong root development. In addition, liming may be necessary in heavy or highly acid soils. Salt was once recommended, since it was found that asparagus could tolerate the salt while weed plants could not. A better method of weed control is mulching with straw or shredded leaves. Top dressings of compost applied twice a year—in spring before the shoots appear and again in fall after frost—are highly beneficial.

SELECTION

Beginners often make the mistake of buying two-year-old and older plants. Although these almost always cost more than yearlings of the same variety, they never give as satisfactory results because they have lost proportionally more roots and consequently take one or two years longer to produce usable stems. When buying yearling plants, select the highest grade stock and buy 25–50% more plants than are actually needed, then discard the poorest when planting to assure a uniform stand in the bed. The discarded plants can be planted in some odd corner, where usable shoots may appear a year or two later than those in a bed.

'Mary Washington' has been the most widely planted asparagus in North America, but the pure strain has been lost, and the stocks offered by seed suppliers and nurseries now have poor disease resistance, for which 'Mary Washington' was famous.

Growers are now favoring all-male hybrid asparagus, such as 'Ben Franklin', a cultivar developed in Holland from American technology, and 'Jersey Giant', developed by Rutgers University. All-male hybrids are up to four times heavier yielding than 'Mary Washington', since they produce no seed-bearing female plants with smaller fibrous stems. When a row of plants is all male, the edible stalks are not only consistently thicker and more succulent, but they do not set seeds to fall into the planting bed and compete with the parent plant like weeds.

All-male hybrid asparagus can be purchased as seed, as eight-week-old seedlings, and as year-old roots. Starting seed used to be discouraged among home gardeners because it would take an extra year to produce edible stalks, but seed of the new all-male hybrids is so vigorous that a fertile bed can produce a harvest at the same time as roots. Seedling asparagus are also popular because when a root is planted, nothing shows until it sprouts, by which time it can rot. When a seedling is transplanted, it is already green and viable, with wispy, chlorophyll-rich fronds remaining above the soil, shimmering in the breeze.

ENEMIES

Diseases. The rust fungus *Puccinia asparagi*, formerly a serious enemy, has been rendered far less prevalent by the development of resistant varieties. It can be recognized by dusty reddish pustules of summer spores and black pustules of winter spores. If susceptible varieties are grown, dust with fine sulfur three weeks after the last cutting and again a month later. Cut and burn all tops in the fall.

Fusarium wilt and stem rot seem to be increasing. If beds are badly diseased, start healthy stock in a different location. Destroy all wilting plants, including roots, as soon as noticed,

Insect Pests. Two species of beetles feed on asparagus tops. The common asparagus beetle is ¼ in. long, slender, and blue-black with three white spots and an orange margin on each wing. The adult hibernates under rubbish, emerges in spring, feeds on tender shoots, and lays eggs. These hatch into gray, black-legged grubs that attack the leaves and stalks. There are two to five generations each year. The twelve-spotted asparagus beetle is reddish brown or orange with six black spots on each wing cover. The adults may eat the shoots, but larvae feed on the berries of fruiting plants. There are two generations each year. See ASPARAGUS BEETLE for controls.

ORNAMENTAL SPECIES

A. asparagoides (florists' smilax), is a popular greenhouse vine, also planted outdoors in Florida to supply commercial needs. It is valued for its long trails of rich green foliage, useful for many decorative purposes. It is usually planted in solid beds, the growths being trained to strings and cut as needed. After cutting, plants need little water until new growth starts. In good soil and with liberal feeding, it is possible to keep the plants in good production for three or four years. Propagation is by seed, best sown early in the year.

A. densiflorus cv. 'Sprengeri' (Sprenger's asparagus), the most satisfactory species for house culture, is easily grown from seed sown during February. At room temperatures, the seed usually takes about a month to sprout. When seedlings are 2–3 in. high, prick them into moderately fertile potting soil in small flowerpots. Shift to larger pots when the roots form mats around the soil ball. Established plants bear open racemes of small, pinkish, fragrant flowers in May or June and coral-red berries about Christmas time.

A. setaceus (asparagus-fern), formerly listed as *A. plumosus*, is a tender twining vine with minutely divided leaves that suggest fern fronds. Several varieties are cultivated in commercial greenhouses for their cut sprays and the strings of lacy foliage, which remain attractive for a long time. This is a favorite florists' green for use with cut flowers and in table decorations.

ASPARAGUS BEETLE. This pest injures asparagus sprouts during the harvest season and attacks the fully grown tops later. The adult, about ¼ in. long, is dull blue-black with three orange-yellow spots along each wing. In the larval stage, its soft, wrinkled, wormlike body is about ½ in. long, colored olive green to dark gray with black legs and head. The beetle winters in weeds or other rubbish around the garden and then emerges in the spring to feed on the developing spears and to lay small, elongated, black eggs in rows. Later, both adults and larvae attack the fully developed plants. If they are left unchecked, these pests can cause crooked (which is more often due to cutworm feeding) and unsightly shoots and reduced yields the following season.

When checking for the common asparagus beetle in its larval stage, it is necessary to look carefully. It is big enough to be seen, but its coloring blends well with the plant. Removal of

Asparagus beetle

weeds, trash, and other hibernating sites from around the bed should help keep this pest away. It is also a good idea to turn over the soil around the plants in the fall to expose the beetles.

Planting tomatoes near the asparagus bed is often recommended since asparagus beetles find the strong tomato aroma objectionable. Asparagus will also help keep tomato nematodes in check, which makes this combination a good example of companion planting. Interplanting with garlic plants is also effective.

The beetles can be hand-picked early in the morning when it is too cool for them to fly. Bordering the patch with tomatoes, along with a program of early season hand-picking, is often sufficient pest control. For severe infestations, a rotenone dust can be applied, following the label instructions carefully.

ASPARAGUS-FERN. Common name for the foliage of *Asparagus*, chiefly *A. setaceus*, a tender species with minutely divided leaves suggesting fern fronds; see ASPARAGUS.

ASPEN. A common name for species of POPULUS, a widely distributed genus of hardy deciduous trees.

ASPERULA (as per ROOL ah). A genus of annual and perennial herbs of the Rubiaceae (Madder Family), and commonly known as woodruff. They have leaves in whorls and small lily-shaped flowers of white, blue, or pink. Used in rock gardens or for carpeting shady places, they thrive in moist soil and are of easy culture. Propagation is by seed or division of plants.

Asperula sp.

PRINCIPAL SPECIES

A. gussonei, a low-growing, tufted perennial suitable for the rock garden. The narrow leaves are grayish with soft hairs; flowers are rose colored but inconspicuous.

A. odorata (sweet woodruff) is now listed in the genus GALIUM.

A. orientalis, an annual, grows to 1 ft. and has sprays of dainty blue flowers. It is the best species for the open border.

ASPIDISTRA (as pi DIS trah). A genus of thick-rooted perennial herbs belonging to the Liliaceae (Lily Family), popular as foliage plants in homes and for window and porch boxes. They have stiff, glossy, evergreen leaves and will withstand much heat, dust, poor soil, and dim light. The flowers are dark colored and are not conspicuous, since they are borne close to the ground and hidden by the foliage. Propagation is done by dividing the roots in early spring.

A. elatior, sometimes listed as *A. lurida*, is the species commonly grown by florists. The leaves last well when cut and are sometimes used as foliage in arrangements with cut amaryllis blossoms. Var. *variegata*, with leaves striped green and white, is occasionally seen, but the variegation rapidly disappears if the plant is grown in rich soil.

ASPLENIUM (as PLEE nee um). A genus of ferns, mostly lime-loving, distributed throughout the world and represented in North America by several species commonly known as spleenworts. They are characterized by their tufted growth, wiry, usually black or polished brown stipes, and rather large and sparse linear or crescent-shaped sori. Both botanical and common names refer to the alleged antisplenetic curative properties.

Among our most charming and most distinctive rock plants, one or more spleenworts are found in nearly all mountainous parts of the United States; however, they should not be collected from the wild, as populations of many sorts are diminishing. They can be obtained from wildflower and rock garden nurseries or propagated from spores.

In the garden the spleenworts require well-drained, rocky soil, not too rich, with lime added. They do best in pockets between stones, and good drainage is essential. Do not remove old fronds, and protect plants with leaves in the fall. Because the many forms in cultivation are native to different ranges throughout the world, it must be understood that cultural needs will vary a great deal. Other than propagation from spores, many species can be increased by means of bulbils or plantlets found on the fronds; see FERNS. Some also have bulbils at the base of the fronds.

PRINCIPAL SPECIES

A. belangeri, a small fern from southeastern Asia, grows 8–20 in. and has greatly dissected fronds rising from a rosette. It makes a showy basket fern but is relished by slugs.

A. x *bradleyi*, native from New York to Georgia and Oklahoma, is a diminutive fern growing to 8 in. It is a fertile hybrid between *A. platyneuron* and *A. montanum*, and like its parents, does not require a calcareous soil as other American species do.

A. bulbiferum (mother or hen-and-chick fern), native to Australia and New Zealand, is an attractive fern that grows up to 4 ft. tall. It is readily available in nurseries and is not difficult to grow. The pinnules of the sterile fronds are broader than those of the fertile fronds, and the two dif-ferent textures make a very attractive plant. In addition, many bulbils and plantlets are scattered on the upper surfaces of the fronds; new plants are easily started from these.

A. caudatum is a tropical fern producing fronds to 2 ft. long, suddenly narrowed at the apex and terminating in a tail-like extension.

A. daucifolium is a medium-sized fern growing 1–2 ft. with finely dissected fronds that show off handsomely in a basket. Like *A. bulbiferum*, the fronds are generously supplied with plantlets.

A. incisum is a lovely dwarf fern (4–12 in.) that can be grown in pots. It is bipinnate, and the pinnae are sharply incised. The stipe and rachis are shining black. Native to China, Japan, and Korea, it needs acid soil in cultivation.

A. montanum (mountain spleenwort) is a small fern, growing only 5 in. tall. The smooth, shining fronds are bipinnate and triangular. It is found in the eastern states from New York to Georgia. It often hybridizes naturally with *Camptosorus rhizophyllus* to yield the fertile hybrid *Asplenosorus* x *pinnatifidus*.

A. nidus (bird's-nest fern) is a popular fern with highly polished, simple rich green fronds that grow 1–5 ft. It is epiphytic, living on trees and rocks in tropical jungles. There are several varieties. Cv. 'Crispum' (lasagna fern) is a fine houseplant if grown in warm, humid conditions.

A. platyneuron (ebony spleenwort) is a dwarf fern with fronds that grow to 15 in. long. It is pinnate, and the dark green, glossy pinnae have auricles. The fertile fronds are more erect than the sterile fronds. It is excellent for a well-drained rock garden and establishes well in walls. If potted, it should be kept on the dry side. It is native in eastern and central North America, thriving in Zones 5–7. Its sometimes fertile hybrid, produced with *Camptosorus rhizophyllus*, is known as *Asplenosorus* x *ebonoides*.

A. resiliens (black-stemmed spleenwort) is similar to *A. trichomanes* but is native to tropical and subtropical regions.

A. ruta-muraria (wall-rue) is a dainty, delicate-looking dwarf that grows only 3 in. tall. It is bipinnate to tripinnate, and the pinnules are round to oval. It grows on calcareous cliffs and loves to colonize walls, particularly those with mortar in the crevices, but it resents disturbance. Although it can be grown from spores, it is difficult to establish in the garden. It is native in northern regions of North America, Europe, and Asia.

A. scolopendrium is now listed as *Phyllitis scolopendrium*; see PHYLLITIS.

A. trichomanes (maidenhair spleenwort) is a miniature evergreen fern that grows in a clustered rosette 8 in. high. The fronds are pinnate, round to oval, and ½ in. wide. As many as 40 pinnules occur on opposite sides of the purple-black rachis. It grows readily in walls and shaded rock crevices if there is enough light. When grown in the rock garden, it needs limestone. It is widespread in North America and most of the temperate and subarctic regions of the world, even occasionally occurring in the high mountains of the tropics. Cv. 'Cristatum' is from Britain, with each frond branched into a crest.

A. viride (green spleenwort) is an 8-in. dwarf species similar to *A. trichomanes*, but it differs in its bright green fronds and rachis and deeply toothed pinnae.

Several other forms are now listed in the genus CETERACH.

ASPLENOSORUS (as plee noh SOR us). A group of bigeneric hybrids between *Asplenium* and *Camptosorus*.

A. x *ebonoides* (Scott's spleenwort) is a sometimes fertile hybrid between *C. rhizophyllus* and *Asplenium platyneuron*; it looks much like an irregularly lobed *Camptosorus*.

A. x *pinnatifidus* (lobed spleenwort), also listed as *Asplenium pinnatifidum*, is a fertile hybrid between *Asplenium montanum* and *C. rhizophyllus*. Its fronds sometimes take root at the tip. It is very rare, usually found growing on cliffs, and should not be collected.

ASSAI PALM. Common name for EUTERPE, a genus of palms whose terminal buds are harvested as hearts of palm.

ASTER (AS tur). This name, meaning "star," refers to two distinct genera of plants, both of which belong to the ASTERACEAE (Aster Family). First, it is the common and botanic name of the true, hardy asters, also called starworts or Michaelmas-daisies, many of which are native to the temperate zone of the United States. Second, it is the common name of *Callistephus chinensis*, the tender, so-called China aster including many annual garden hybrids; see CALLISTEPHUS.

In general, the true, hardy asters can be considered among the most desirable perennials from the perspective of simplicity of culture as well as the aesthetic point of view. They are usually characterized by leafy stems and opposite, often spear-shaped leaves, ranging from 1–4 in. in length. The small flowers are daisylike with yellow or orange centers and fine, often thickly growing petals. The stems are frequently branched near the top, producing large clusters of flowers that individually are less than 1–2 in. across. The colors range from deep purple through lavender, blue, pink, and rose to white. Most varieties bloom in the late summer and fall when other plants have finished blooming. For this reason, and because of their variation in height from 6 in. to 6 ft., they are adaptable to many purposes and are rightly considered plants of outstanding value.

Asters have been developed and used far more extensively in Europe than in North America, in spite of the fact that some of the principal species are natives of the United States. Many North American gardens have wild species under cultivation. The numerous superior varieties currently available or being developed offer gardeners an increasing selection.

In the flower border, the taller varieties can be used as background flowers, with smaller ones in front, arranged according to their respective heights. Since the taller varieties naturalize well, they can be satisfactorily used along the edge of fields to divide the lawn from uncultivated areas. They are also delightfully effective and grow well at the edge of a natural pond, bog, or brook, as long as their roots are above the water.

The dwarf types make ideal rock garden subjects, some blooming in the fall when there is a scarcity of flowering plants in this type of garden, and others flowering in early summer.

Wherever planted, the effect of asters is charming rather than striking. They blend with the landscape yet are very much in evidence. When planted in the border, the taller varieties will often need staking because the heavily branched spikes tend to weight themselves down.

CULTURE

Most of the asters like full sun and do well in an open location. Many enjoy a moist location, although they do not like to have their roots stand in water. A good average garden soil is more satisfactory than one that has been made very rich by fertilization. Most species are hardy in Zones 4–9.

Asters are easily raised from seed, almost invariably blooming the next year after a spring sowing. In some cases, even fall-sown seeds will give flowering plants the following year, although the plants may be smaller than older plants of the same variety. These seedlings bloom later than the older plants, extending the season of bloom. Cultivars cannot be depended upon to come true from seed, so they must be procured as plants. Because of their late flowering, these plants should be set out in the spring.

They can also be increased by cuttings made later in the spring when the growth has reached a height of about 3 in. These cuttings should be placed in damp sand in a coldframe that is kept closed to maintain a humid condition. They will root readily, and a large percentage will bloom in the fall of the same year. Division, however, is the more common and simpler method.

Mature specimens should be spaced at least 2 ft. apart, except in the case of the dwarf and alpine species, which need be only 8 in. apart. Most hardy asters thrive best when they are divided each spring. In this way the supply can be increased rapidly.

PRINCIPAL SPECIES

A. alpinus (mountain daisy), growing 6–10 in. tall, is suitable as a rock garden or edging plant.

Violet-blue flowers with one blossom per stem open in early summer. Var. *albus* has white flowers.

A. amellus (Italian starwort) is a semidwarf species, 2 ft. tall, with large purple flowers in late summer. Cv. 'King George' has violet-blue flowers in early fall.

A. cordifolius (blue wood aster), growing to 5 ft., has pale lavender flowers on graceful sprays in autumn.

A. dumosus (bushy aster, cushion aster), growing 1–3 ft., produces an abundance of blooms from late summer into the fall. It has many cultivars, including 'Alert' with crimson-red flowers, 'Peter Harrison' with pink flowers, and 'Professor Kippenburg' with blue flowers

A. ericoides (heath or North American aster), growing to 3 ft., has white or pinkish flowers in the fall.

A. x *frikartii* is a hybrid of *A. thompsonii* x *amellus*, growing 30–35 in. high, bears fragrant, purple-blue flowers 2½–3 in. in diameter. Hardy to Zone 6. Cv. 'Moench' produces flowers of clear blue with yellow centers over a long bloom period from summer until mid-autumn. Cv. 'Wonder of Staffa' is similar to 'Moench' but has purple-blue flowers.

A. grandiflorus (great aster) grows to 4 ft. and has purple ray flowers and yellow disk flowers. Relatively uncommon, it is found in dry areas along the coast from Virginia southward.

A. laevis (smooth aster) grows to 4 ft. in dry meadows over much of the eastern United States. It has late-summer ray flowers from white to lavender and heart-shaped leaves.

A. linosyris (Goldilocks) is a European perennial that grows to 2 ft. and has small heads of yellow flowers in clusters. It is a good late-summer-blooming plant that thrives in any soil.

A. novae-angliae (New England aster), growing to 5 ft., is a native species often cultivated in the United States. Although attractive in the wild, it improves considerably when planted in a good soil and given food and attention. Its deep purple flowers appear in late summer. Var. *roseus* has rose flowers which, if produced from fall-sown seeds, will bloom in the following year when the plants are only 18 in. high, in contrast with the 5-ft. height of mature plants. Cv. 'Barr's Pink' grows to 4½ ft. and has rose-pink flowers in autumn; 'Mrs F. W. Raynor' grows to 5 ft. with reddish rose flowers in autumn; 'Mrs. S. T. Wright' grows to 3 ft. with rose-mauve flowers in the fall; 'Roycroft Pink' grows to 4 ft., with bright pink flowers in the fall; 'Alma Potschke' has pink flowers on a relatively compact plant;

Aster novae-angliae

and 'Harrington's Pink' is a frost-resistant variety with salmon-pink flowers from late summer through autumn.

A. novi-belgii (New York aster) is a popular and attractive wild species cultivated in the United States. It grows to 3 ft. and has bright blue-violet flowers in the fall. Cv. 'Anita Ballard' grows to 4½ ft. with cornflower-blue blossoms in early fall. 'Beauty of Colwell' grows to 4 ft. with lavender flowers in early fall. 'Blue Gem' grows to 4 ft. with rich blue flowers in late fall. 'Climax' grows to 5 ft. with blue flowers on long sprays in late fall. 'Glory of Colwell' grows to 4½ ft. with silver-mauve flowers in late fall. 'King of the Belgians' grows to 5½ ft. with lavender-blue flowers in the fall. 'Nancy Bullard' grows to 3½ ft. with pink flowers in late fall. 'Peggy Ballard' grows to 3½ ft. with rosy mauve flowers in late fall. 'St. Egwin' grows to 3½ ft. with pink flowers in summer.

A. sericeus (silky aster) is a hardy perennial native to the dry prairie, with hairy, silvery leaves that turn red in the fall. The clusters

Aster sericeus

of flower heads top 2 ft. high stems and bloom a deep lavender.

A. tataricus, growing to 8 ft. high, is a very late blooming species with violet flowers, from Siberia.

A. tongolensis, also listed as *A. subcaeruleus*, has large, pale blue, solitary flowers in midsummer on branchless stems 2 ft. tall. The plants form thick mats.

A. yunnanensis grows to 15 in. and has soft blue flowers in late spring.

ASTERACEAE (as tur AY see ee). The Aster Family, formerly called Compositae (Composite, Daisy, or Sunflower Family), including nearly 1000 widely distributed genera of annual or perennial herbs and some shrubs. The plants are divided into several tribes based on the type of sap produced and details in the flower structure. Typical members are characterized by various combinations of ray and disk flowers, such as the common daisy, dandelion, or chamomile, including many popular subjects for drying or everlastings. While many members are considered pernicious weeds, others are cultivated in home and commercial gardens for ornament or food crops. Prominent members among the hundreds of cultivated genera include: *Ageratum*, *Artemisia* (sagebrush, wormwood), *Aster*, *Bellis* (English daisy), *Calendula* (pot-marigold), *Callistephus* (China aster), *Carthamus* (safflower), *Chamaemelum* (chamomile), *Chrysanthemum*, *Cosmos*, *Dimorphotheca* (cape marigold), *Felicia* (marguerite), *Gaillardia* (blanketflower), *Gazania* (South African daisy), *Helianthus* (sunflower, Jerusalem-artichoke), *Helichrysum* (strawflower), *Heliopsis* (oxeye), *Lactuca* (lettuce), *Onopordum* (thistle), *Rudbeckia* (coneflower, black-eyed-Susan), *Senecio* (groundsel, ragwort), *Solidago* (goldenrod), *Tagetes* (marigold), *Tanacetum* (tansy), *Taraxicum* (dandelion), and *Zinnia*.

ASTILBE (as TIL bee). A genus of strong, herbaceous perennials belonging to the Saxifragaceae (Saxifrage Family), often called spirea or

Japanese-spirea, although that name correctly refers to a genus of the Rosaceae (Rose Family). It grows from 1–6 ft. and bears feathery trusses of tiny whitish, pink, or red flowers and pleasing, finely cut foliage.

At one time a favorite garden and houseplant, especially popular at Easter, the astilbe was neglected for many years but has regained some popularity. There are a dozen or more species and many variable forms and hybrids that are often forced by florists for late winter and early spring sale. Easy to grow in either a sunny or partly shaded location, it does best in rich soil if supplied with great quantities of water. Hardy in Zones 5–8, it can be grown in the open border or forced in the greenhouse, where it requires ten weeks to four months to flower. Propagation can be done by seed or division.

Astilbe sp.

In growing astilbes for forcing, the gardener should plant the roots in 7-in. pots in the fall and plunge the pots into the ground until about midwinter. They should then be brought indoors, given plenty of light, and preferably, a temperature between 50 and 60°F. Constant moisture is necessary, and the pots should be kept in saucers filled with water. Grown indoors, the flowers are larger and purer in color than when grown outdoors. Plants should be washed at least once a month to control RED SPIDER MITE. After flowering in the house, a plant should be set out in the perennial border, where it will adapt itself and blossom year after year.

PRINCIPAL SPECIES

A. x *arendsii* (astilbe, false spirea) is a group of hybrids with flowers from purplish to almost white. Hardy to Zone 5.

A. astilboides (goatsherd astilbe), growing to 3 ft., is a Japanese native with sharp-toothed, hairy foliage and white flowers in dense spikes.

A. biternata, native to the mountains of the southern Atlantic states, grows to 6 ft. and has leaves 2 ft. across and numerous yellowish white flowers.

A. chinensis cv. 'Pumila' grows to 8 in. and has feathery leaves that create a dense mat, making it a common choice for ground cover. Rosy mauve flowers, blooming in late summer, are borne on stiff, 15-in. spikes. It requires moist soil conditions and is especially delightful in the rock garden. Hardy to Zone 5.

A. grandis, native to China, is somewhat hairy with creamy white flowers.

A. japonica is probably the most common species, well suited to use in the garden or for forcing indoors. Many cultivars are available.

A. x *rosea* is a hybrid of *A. japonica*, which it resembles, but it has pinkish flowers. The many cultivars include 'Peach Blossom', a light pink, and 'Queen Alexandra', a deeper pink.

A. simplicifolia (star astilbe), native to Japan, grows to 1 ft. and has starlike white flowers.

A. thunbergii, native to Japan, grows to 2 ft. and has toothed, hairy foliage and white flowers that often become pink.

ASTROLOGICAL GARDENING. Belief that the moon exerts a definite influence on the growth and development of plants has existed since early times. Gardeners who plant by the moon hold to the general theory that plants that bear their harvest above ground (as in beans, tomatoes, corn, and various flowers) should be planted during a waxing or increasing moon (before it is full), and plants that bear their harvest below the ground (such as carrots, potatoes, radishes, or beets) benefit if planted during a waning moon, that is, after the full moon.

Astrological gardeners believe that flower and vegetable gardens are influenced by phases (quarters) of the moon. Planetary rulership is also assigned for many plants, meaning that the signs of the zodiac have influence on certain crops. The best times to harvest, weed, mow the lawn, and water the garden are also researched by astrological gardeners.

ASTROPHYTUM (as troh FĪ tum). The star plants, a small genus of four to six species, often included in the larger group *Echinocactus*. Very popular cacti for the collector include *A. ornatum* (starcactus); *A. myriostigma* (bishop's-cap), a spineless species with the solitary, generally five-ribbed stem covered with tiny, white, woolly scales; *A. capricorne* (goat's-horn), with long, curving, papery spines; and *A. asterias* (sand-dollar cactus), another spineless species, this one with low, flattened ribs. They all have large, showy, silky, yellow to yellow-and-red flowers. They are of moderately easy culture, the touchiest being *A. asterias*.

ATHYRIUM (ah THIR ee um). A genus of ferns cultivated for their delicate, lacy fronds. Several species, called lady ferns, are commonly grown.

PRINCIPAL SPECIES

A. asplenioides (southern lady fern) is a moderately large fern that grows 2–4 ft. and has fronds spreading gracefully from a rosette. It is deciduous and turns brown with the frost; however, it is hardy and is found in the temperate to subtropical regions of North America.

A. deltoidifrons is a medium-sized fern growing 1–2 ft., with light green fronds that contrast nicely in plantings with darker ferns. Native to temperate and subtropical China, Korea, and Japan, it requires more light than most lady ferns.

A. distentifolium (alpine lady fern), also listed as *A. alpestre*, is a fairly large deciduous fern from damp woodlands and alpine meadows of temperate areas, native in North America, Europe, and Iceland.

A. filix-femina (lady fern), common in temperate regions, is a tough, cold-hardy fern. It is easily grown but is not suited to pot culture. Because the fronds are brittle, it must be handled carefully and often suffers breakage in extreme weather. It is winter deciduous but welcomes spring with handsome new growth. It has spread over most of the globe, being found in Europe, northern India, China, Japan, Java, northern Africa, the Azores, the Canary Islands, and most of the Americas. It is prone to genetic variation and has produced a huge number of graceful and interesting varieties. Among the many cultivars are 'Acrocladon', 'Clarissima', 'Corymbiferum', 'Cristatum', 'Fieldii', 'Frizelliae', 'Grandiceps', 'Plumosum', and 'Victoriae'. There are several attractive dwarf cultivars, including 'Caputmedusae', 'Congestum Cristatum', 'Congestum Minus', and 'Minutissimum'.

A. flexile is similar to but smaller than *A. distentifolium*, of which it is considered to be a variety by some botanists.

A. frangulum is a small Japanese fern that grows 6–18 in. and has triangular bipinnate or tripinnate fronds and a rachis of reddish purple. It is a good candidate for the rock garden.

A. niponicum 'Pictum' (Japanese painted fern) is deservedly the most desirable cultivar among those commercially available. It has 1–2 ft. fronds of grayish green marked with reddish blue. It is very hardy and is subdued only by heavy frost. It can also be grown in the subtropics. Under the usual fern-growing conditions, it will spread rapidly. If given more light and moisture, the colors will be intensified. The species *A. niponicum* is attractive in its own right but cannot compete in popularity with its colorful cultivar.

A. otophorum is a distinctive small fern that grows 1–2 ft. and has broad, triangular fronds of a pale lime-green color, which darkens some at maturity. The stipe and rachis are red-purple. It thrives in rich, humusy soil and shade. It is native to Japan, China, and Korea.

A. pycnocarpon (American glade fern, narrow-leaved spleenwort), native in eastern North America as far south as Georgia, is a moist woodland fern with 1–2 ft. fronds growing in a rosette. It is deciduous and very cold hardy, the fronds turning red-brown before they collapse. Slugs can be a problem on new spring growth.

A. thelypterioides (silvery glade fern, silvery spleenwort), also listed as *Lunathyrium thelypteroides*, is a fairly large, graceful fern that grows 2–4 ft. and is deciduous in winter. Its common name is derived from the silver color of its indusia. The spring growth is very attractive.

Common in eastern North America as far south as Georgia and also found in northern India and China, it likes damp woodland areas, especially near water.

ATRIPLEX (AT ri pleks). A genus of scaly herbs or shrubs of the Chenopodiaceae (Goosefoot Family), known in some regions as saltbush because they are usually found growing in salty situations in Zones 4–11. Of the many species, the great majority are weeds, though a few are valued as forage in arid regions; a very few are grown as ornamentals and potherbs.

PRINCIPAL SPECIES

A. breweri is sometimes grown as a hedge plant in southern California.

A. hortensis (garden orach, mountain-spinach) is an annual herb grown mainly as a potherb like spinach, and is sometimes used for medicinal purposes. Plants are generally salt tolerant and produce clusters of small greenish flowers. The red-leaved varieties, which often grow 6 ft. tall, are sometimes planted for ornament. Sow the seed in drills 12 in. apart in early spring and gather the seedlings when large enough to use and while still succulent. Though the plants resist heat better than spinach, it quickly runs to seed; so make successional sowings at biweekly intervals; see also GREENS.

A. lentiformis (quailbush) is a native shrub of southern California, hardy in Zones 8–11. Silvery gray foliage on this 6–10 ft. shrub makes it an attractive candidate for erosion control, wildlife enhancement, and large drought-tolerant landscapes.

A. patula is a widespread native, also called orach, grows as a weed on sandy saline or alkaline soils, and is edible. Control measures include clean cultivation early in the season and keeping compost piles clean of plants which pull moisture from the pile and would spread seeds.

ATROPA (AT roh pah) **belladonna.** A European perennial herb, commonly known as deadly nightshade or belladonna. It is generally not a garden subject but is important as the source of

atropine. All parts of the plant are poisonous, and the leaves and roots are used in medicine. Growing 3 ft. tall, it is a coarse plant producing dull purplish flowers 1 in. long, either solitary or paired and nodding in habit. The fruits are nearly globular, shiny, brownish black berries.

AUBRIETA (aw bree AY tah). A genus of low-growing perennials belonging to the Brassicaceae (Mustard Family), and commonly known as false or purple-rockcress. It includes excellent plants for borders, beds, or rock gardens, growing well in semishade. Attaining a maximum height of only 12 in., the attractive silvery green foliage covers the spaces between rocks and along borders. In spring and

Aubrieta deltoidea

early summer the flowers, when grown in masses, form a blanket of rosy purple, blue, or lilac. They look especially good combined with arabis or alyssum. Plants are grown from seed sown the previous season; or they can be propagated by layering the trailing shoots or by division of the mats or clumps. Hardy in Zones 4–9.

A. deltoidea and its many forms make easy, reliable, low drifts of springtime color in the rock garden. These are particularly effective flowing over a rock or spilling out of a wall planting. Various improved forms come in single or double flowers of white, pink, blue, purple, and lavender; others have variegated foliage. Some of the more popular are 'Bougainvillei', a dark blue; 'Graeca', a light blue, growing to 6 in.; 'Leichtlinii', bright reddish crimson, growing to 8 in.; 'Royal Blue'; and 'Royal Red'.

AUCUBA (ah KYOO bah). A genus of evergreen shrubs belonging to the Cornaceae (Dogwood Family), and commonly known as Japanese aucuba, Japanese-laurel, or gold-dust tree. They have large ornamental leaves; male and female flowers are borne on separate plants. To ensure a display of the attractive scarlet berries, the female flowers must be fertilized with pollen from the male plants. If kept dry, pollen retains its power for several weeks.

Often grown in pots or tubs in cool climates for porch or terrace decoration during the summer, they are tolerant of shade but are unable to withstand air pollutants and are hardy only in Zones 7–11. They can be wintered safely in a cool place if kept on the dry side.

A. japonica (gold-dust tree), the principal species, has glossy dark green leaves.

AURINIA (aw RIN ee ah) **saxatilis.** A hardy, mat-forming perennial formerly classified as *Alyssum saxatile* and commonly known as basket-of-gold, goldentuft, gold-dust, or rock madwort. Among the most popular early rock garden subjects, it is easy and reliable. It is not dainty, but the abundant, bright gold, double flowers are a wonderful addition to the springtime garden. It grows about 1 ft. tall with grayish persistent foliage. Since it tends to get woody in a few years, gardeners often replace old plants with new seedlings or plants raised from cuttings. A number of cultivars are commercially available, including 'Compactum', a dwarf form; 'Golden Queen', with clusters of light yellow flowers; and 'Plena', with double yellow flowers.

AUSTRALIAN-PINE. Common name for CASUARINA, a genus of tropical trees and shrubs.

AUTUMN-CROCUS. A common name for COLCHICUM, which bears large white to purple flowers directly from the corm in the autumn, after the leaves have died. Do not confuse with the autumn-flowering species of the true crocus.

AUTUMN FERN. Common name for *Dryopteris erythrosora*, a small, colorful fern with leathery fronds; see DRYOPTERIS.

AUXIN. A growth substance or "plant hormone" produced by the growing tips of plants.

As the substance travels down through the plant, it stimulates the growth of the cambium or living tissue just under the bark, causing the stem to become larger and thicker. Eventually it reaches the root, where it stimulates the formulation of new roots by increasing the rate of cell development. See ROOTING COMPOUNDS.

AVAILABILITY. A plant food is said to be "available" when it is in such form that plants can rapidly take it up and use it when it is added to the soil or other growing medium. A soil may contain great quantities of plant foods chemically speaking, but they may be in forms or combinations with other materials that render them useless to a crop.

Examples of plant foods immediately or readily available are: nitrate nitrogen, as found in nitrate of soda; the phosphorus and calcium in acid calcium phosphate (superphosphate); and the potassium in potassium chloride (muriate of potash), potassium sulfate, or potassium carbonate. All these compounds are soluble in water and thus quickly become part of the soil solution that is the source of a plant's sustenance.

Plant foods not immediately available are the organic nitrogenous fertilizers such as dried blood, fish scrap, cottonseed meal, and others, which are insoluble in water. Under the action of certain bacteria, their nitrogen is changed into the available nitrate form. Under usual conditions, much of the nitrogen in such substances, when applied to soils in spring, becomes available in time to be used that season.

Strictly speaking, a fertile soil is one that contains abundant plant food in available form at the time plants need the nutrients. Obviously, proper cultural practices that favor the growth and diversity of the microorganisms are essential to the maintenance of such a condition.

See also FERTILIZER; SOIL.

AVALANCHE LILY. Common name for *Erythronium grandiflorum*, a yellow-flowered bulbous plant native to Oregon and Washington; see ERYTHRONIUM.

AVENS (AV enz). Common name for GEUM, a genus of perennials useful for cut flowers and rock garden, border, or bed planting.

AVERRHOA (av er OH ah). A small genus of Malaysian trees, interesting botanically because most other members of the Oxalidaceae (Woodsorrel Family) are herbaceous plants. One species, *A. carambola*, is hardy in Zones 10–11 and is becoming an important tropical fruit crop in south Florida. Its common name, star fruit, comes from the star shape evident when the deeply ribbed, yellow, waxy-surfaced fruits are cut in cross sections.

AVOCADO. Common name for *Persea americana*, an evergreen tree of tropical and subtropical America, widely planted for its nutritious fruit, sometimes known as alligator-pear or avocado-pear. These vary in size from smaller than a tennis ball to larger than a softball and may be spherical or definitely pear shaped. The thick skins range from grass green to olive drab or darker, and there is some correlation with the place of origin and the oil content, although this has been obscured by the hybridization that has gone into the search for various characters. Those originating at higher altitudes in Guatemala and Mexico

Persea americana

are usually small, high in oil content, and dark skinned. These are the types most often grown in California. West Indian forms are softer skinned and lighter in color, less rich in oil, and more tender to cold. Most of the varieties grown in Florida have this type in their parentage.

An interesting houseplant can be grown by thrusting three toothpicks radially into the broad base of an avocado seed so it can be supported above a tumbler or wide-mouthed jar kept full of water; the bottom of the seed should just touch the surface. Within a few weeks the seed will sprout, first thrusting a long white root into the water and then a stem, bearing handsome glossy leaves, straight upward. It can be grown thus for some months; then by gradually adding soil to the water, the plant can be transferred from a water to a soil medium and carefully potted. If protected from frost, it can be grown to a good-sized plant or shrub, which can be plunged, pot and all, in the garden over summer and brought back indoors in the fall.

AWN. A bristlelike appendage, especially one of those at the tip of the bracts or glumes of grasses, which collectively make up the "beard" of barley, certain kinds of wheat, and similar plants.

AXIL. The angle formed by a branch, leaf stalk, or flower stalk, with the stem or another branch.

AXIS. The main line of development of a plant, as the principal root and its continuation, the stem; or the line of support of an organ or group of organs, such as stem, branch, or shoot. Also the main or base lines upon which a garden design or other landscape plan is built.

AXONOPUS (aks ah NOH pus). A genus of perennial herbs of the Poaceae (Grass Family). Hardiness varies according to species (Zones 5–7).

A. affinis (carpet grass) is regarded as only a pasture grass in the South and is not suitable for lawns. Established by seeding, it retains its color well in cool weather. *A. compressus* is similar but is not as winter hardy.

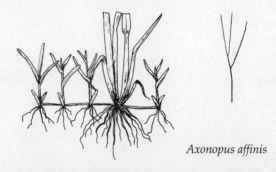

Axonopus affinis

AZALEA (ah ZAY lee ah). A subgenus of RHODO-DENDRON, including many popular hybrids of bright-flowered shrubs.

AZARA (ah ZAH rah). A genus of evergreen shrubs native to Chile and belonging to the Flacocourtiaceae (Flacortia Family). They are handsome shrubs of elegant habit up to 15 ft. high and have small, fragrant flowers without petals. They can be grown outdoors only in warm-temperate regions; hardy only to Zone 8. Propagation is by seed or cuttings of mature wood.

A. microphylla, the best known, is prized for its orange-colored berries as well as its graceful habit. It is hardy as far north as Washington, D.C., and is occasionally found in northern greenhouse collections.

A. petiolaris, with more conspicuous flowers and hollylike leaves, is considered the showiest member of the genus.

AZOLLA (ah ZOHL ah). A small genus of mosslike, aquatic ferns with divided, leaflike stems and tiny leaves. The plants multiply rapidly by self-division and, if not disturbed, will completely cover the water surface with solid mats in a short time. For this reason, they can be a nuisance in some areas.

Azollas do not have the usual fern structure but are made up of floating fronds whose usual greenish color turns reddish in the sun. They are also distinguished from other ferns by their production of both male and female spores, borne in a structure called a sporocarp. They are frost tender but are interesting to grow indoors in containers of water. There seems to be a symbiotic relationship between this genus and the blue-green algae *Anabaena*.

A. caroliniana, found floating on still water from Canada to Mexico and Florida, is one of the most curious and interesting of the small floating plants useful in the pool or aquarium. Since in bright sun it takes on a reddish tinge, it can be used as an indicator to show whether or not the tank or pool is getting enough direct light. It has been used in Panama to prevent the breeding of mosquitos.

Other useful species include *A. filiculoides*, *A. mexicana*, and *A. rubra*.

BABIANA (bab ee AY nah). A genus of low-growing, South African plants of the Iridaceae (Iris Family). Commonly known as baboonroot, the botanical name comes from a Dutch word for baboons, which eat the bulbs. Plants have sword-shaped, hairy leaves and a loose, spikelike cluster of showy red or purplish flowers in early spring. Grown from seed, or more often from corms, they succeed in very sandy soil. Hardy in Zones 10–11, they are grown in the North only indoors or in protected coldframes. In the South, plants can remain outdoors untouched, but they are better replanted every other year. The varieties obtainable (usually in mixtures) are probably all of the species *B. stricta*, which grow to 1 ft. and have red or purple to bluish and yellow flowers.

BABY-BLUE-EYES. Common name for *Nemophila menziesii*, an annual with bell-shaped blue flowers; see NEMOPHILA.

BABY'S-BREATH. Common name for *Gypsophila paniculata*, a popular perennial with fine white flowers often used in bouquets; see GYPSOPHILA. False baby's-breath is *Galium aristatum*; see GALIUM.

BABY'S-TEARS. Common name for *Soleirolia soleirolii*, a small, creeping perennial herb; see SOLEIROLIA.

BACCHARIS (BAK ah ris). A genus of ornamental shrubby plants of the Asteraceae (Aster Family), attaining heights of 5–12 ft. A few species are native to the United States, but more than 200 are native to South America. Most of the garden forms are easily grown in almost any well-drained soil in a sunny location and will do well even on dry, rocky slopes and in seashore plantings. Others are marsh plants. All have small white or yellowish flower heads borne in panicles or corymbs in late summer. Thereafter the glistening white bristles (pappus) of the fruits make an attractive, showy effect. Propagation can be done by seed or by cuttings rooted under glass.

B. halimifolia (groundsel bush) is a deciduous form that grows to 12 ft.; it is salt tolerant and is found in marshes and along the coast from New England to Texas. The hardiest (to Zone 6) and best-known species, it is attractive when in fruit.

B. pilularis, growing to 5 ft., is a handsome evergreen found on dry hills in California and Oregon. Hardy in Zones 7–9.

BACHELOR'S-BUTTON. Common name for *Centaurea cyanus*, frequently cultivated for its attractive flowers; see CENTAUREA. The name is also sometimes applied to *Gomphrena globosa* (globe amaranth) and to the double form of buttercup, *Ranunculus acris*.

BACILLUS POPILLIAE. A bacteria known as milky spore disease and commonly available as Doom, used for controlling insects, especially the larval or grub stage of Japanese beetles; see INSECT CONTROL.

BACILLUS THURINGIENSIS. A bacteria known as Bt and commonly available as Biotrol, Dipel, or Thuricide, used for controlling insects, especially caterpillars; see INSECT CONTROL.

BACTERIA. As the cause of diseases in humans, animals, and plants, bacteria are popularly called "microbes" and "germs," and are rightly regarded as dangerous; however, there are also many forms that are vitally useful in their relation to soil fertility and plant growth, and therefore to gardening. Some of them break down complex substances in the soil and in fertilizers and help convert them into simpler forms that the plant roots can take up as food. Others have the unique power of taking free nitrogen from the air and fixing it so that plants can use it, as in the nodules found on the roots of legumes. Still others are essential agents of fermentation, as in vinegar and wine making.

It is one of the gardener's tasks and opportunities to try to increase and make use of the helpful bacteria and to control or eliminate the harmful ones. This calls for a knowledge of the conditions that favor bacterial growth and activity—that is, moisture, the correct temperature range, and in most cases, the presence of air; also, knowledge of how to create and maintain such conditions or correct them as circumstances may require. It may mean the sterilization or disinfection of seeds, soil, or plants; the development of more resistant plant varieties; or the inoculation of soils or seeds with beneficial bacteria in the form of commercial preparations called "cultures" to bring about or hasten the desired growth stimulus or other effect.

By far the best practices for encouraging healthy biological activity in soils include 1) regular additions of organic materials or manures (grass clippings, leaf mold, etc.) and 2) maintaining good soil aeration by judicious cultivation.

BAGWORM. This brown worm, *Thyridopteryx ephemeraeformis*, lives inside a bag made of leaf parts that it sews together with its silk. It drags the bag along as it feeds on cedar, arborvitae, and other shrubs. Eggs laid in the bag overwinter and hatch in early spring. They pupate in late summer. Control is by hand picking and by *Bacillus thuringiensis* (Bt, commonly available as Biotrol, Dipel, or Thuricide).

Bagworm

Parasitic wasps also attack the bagworm, so refrain from using chemical sprays.

BAHIA GRASS. Common name for *Paspalum notatum*, a South American grass grown in the southeastern states for lawns, pastures, and ornament; see PASPALUM.

BAILEYA (BAY lee ah) **multiradiata.** A woolly wildflower native to the southwestern desert region of the United States, belonging to the Asteraceae (Aster Family), and commonly known as desert-marigold. In the garden it provides mounds of brilliant yellow ray and disk flowers in 1–2 in. heads throughout most of the growing season. The broadly lobed 1½–3 in. gray-green leaves are covered with dense, silky hairs. The stems, also hairy, grow 12–16 in. tall; they bear leaves toward the base but are entirely bare toward the top. The plants are poisonous to sheep and goats.

Baileya multiradiata

Being a desert species, the desert-marigold requires an open and sunny location with dry, well-drained soil. It is especially suited for rock gardens. In humid regions, it should be planted in gritty sands but will thrive in clay loam in arid regions. Although perennial or biennial in their native environment, plants can be cultivated as annuals elsewhere. Seed should be planted ¼ in. deep in the garden in spring or started earlier indoors and transplanted when all danger of frost is past. Hardy to Zone 7.

BAKING. A clay or silt soil is said to be "baked" when it becomes thoroughly dried out, as during a period of drought or under strong sun. Under such conditions (especially if puddled beforehand by being worked while wet), it becomes hard as raw bricks, and often as it shrinks, deep cracks develop through which evaporation of water from below is hastened. Only a generous amount of humus, well worked in over an extended period, can bring such a soil back to friable condition. Keeping a soil well mulched will lessen the extent of soil drying or baking.

In the case of small quantities, baking in the oven is a method often used for the sterilization of soil before seed-sowing or planting. This destroys weed seeds and disease-causing organisms such as bacteria and fungus spores but may also destroy certain beneficial soil organisms as well. See DISINFECTION.

BALD CYPRESS. Common name for *Taxodium distichum*, a tree belonging to the Pinaceae (Pine Family), which resembles an evergreen but sheds its leaves in the fall; see TAXODIUM.

BALLOONFLOWER. Common name for *Platycodon grandiflorum*, an herbaceous perennial whose buds resemble little balloons; see PLATYCODON.

BALLOONVINE. Common name for the genus CARDIOSPERMUM, especially *C. halicacabum*, a tropical climbing herb frequently grown for its interesting fruits.

BALM. Common name applied to many species of the Lamiaceae (Mint Family).

Bee-balm, *Monarda didyma*, is also known as Oswego-tea or fragrant-balm; see MONARDA.

Lemon-balm (also known as bee-, common-, or sweet-balm), *Melissa officinalis*; is grown for use in seasoning, liqueurs, and medicine; see MELISSA.

Molucca-balm, *Moluccella laevis*, is more commonly called bells-of-Ireland; see MOLUCCELLA.

BALSAM. Common name for *Impatiens balsamina*, an ornamental herb with colorful flowers; see IMPATIENS.

BALSAM-PEAR. Common name for *Momordica charantia*, an herbaceous vine with ornamental foliage, flowers, and fruit; see MOMORDICA.

BAMBOO. Common name for several genera making up a tribe (Bambusae) of the Poaceae (Grass Family). They comprise giant ornamental grasses, sometimes woody and treelike. The most important genera for the North American gardener are ARUNDINARIA, BAMBUSA, DENDROCALAMUS, PHYLLOSTACHYS, and SASA. These are distinguished from one another by botanical characteristics rather than horticultural uses, although it is valuable in deciding which plants

to use in the open ground to know if they form tight clumps like *Bambusa* and *Dendrocalamus*, or if they grow successive shoots from long horizontal runners to form a more open group.

In general, plants of the genus *Arundinaria* have cylindrical stems; those of *Bambusa* have stems growing in a zigzag manner; those of the *Dendrocalamus* are exceptionally large; the canes of *Phyllostachys* are flattened on one side; and *Sasa* includes dwarf shrubs, with cylindrical stems similar to those of *Arundinaria*.

Bamboos are of great importance in the tropics (especially in Asia) where they are used for many purposes including food products and building materials. Some species lend grace and beauty to gardens in mild climates and a few are hardy as far north as Philadelphia. In the southern and in the Pacific states they are common; their delicate stems and graceful, feathery foliage add much to the garden picture, especially when grown against a background composed of evergreens.

Bamboos thrive in partial shade and need a rich, deep loam and an abundance of moisture, preferably a supply of pure underground water. Some species grow in marshes. It takes at least three years to establish a sizable clump, and until the plants are growing strongly and have sent their roots firmly into the earth, they benefit from a constantly renewed mulch of well-rotted manure. They also need protection from harsh, cold winter winds, except the few species that will tolerate temperatures close to zero.

The larger types form excellent shelter belts, while some of the smaller ones make beautiful specimens in conservatories; or they can be used outdoors since potted plants in containers and wintered in a sun porch or cool greenhouse. It is difficult to secure seed, since the plants are unreliable and uneven seed bearers. Therefore, stock should be propagated by dividing the clumps before the year's growth starts, potting up the small pieces, and placing them in the greenhouse to form roots. They can also be propagated by layering young shoots. Spring is the best time for planting out, pruning, and propagating by layering or division.

BAMBOO FERN. Common name for *Coniogramme japonica*, an attractive tropical fern with a light herringbone pattern on the pinnae; see CONIOGRAMME.

BAMBUSA (bam BYOO sah). One of several genera commonly known as BAMBOO, this one including woody grasses, mostly of tropical and subtropical regions, numbering more than 200 species. Their stems are straight, tall, resilient, and of great strength. They grow rapidly, making very dense thickets. Different species thrive in wet to dry soils, and in localities from sea level to mountain slopes. Several species are grown in the United States.

PRINCIPAL SPECIES

B. arundinacea has yellow stems and dies after flowering. It can attain a height of 100 ft. in the tropics.

B. beecheyana is also a tropical or subtropical type and is a major source of bamboo sprouts in China.

B. glaucescens, reaching only 12–15 ft., is one of the most suitable for most south Florida gardens. There are a number of named cultivars, including 'Alphonse Kerr', 'Fernleaf', and 'Stripestem Fernleaf', each with their own characteristics.

B. oldhamii and *B. tuldoides* are tall-growing, slender species.

B. ventricosa (Buddha's-belly bamboo) has swollen areas between each node when grown as a potted plant with restricted root space.

BANANA. Common name for MUSA, a genus of large, perennial, tropical herbs whose rolled leaves form a sort of trunk, from which a stem emerges to bear fruits that hang in a bunch made of successive ranks or "hands," the whole cluster often weighing more than 50 lb. After bearing, the stem and leaves weaken or die; however, a sucker develops from the base and, in its turn, bears and ripens fruit about a year later. In commercial plantations, each plant may thus produce fruit for four or more years.

Since edible bananas produce no seed, suckers are used for propagating. Plants of *M. acuminata* cv. 'Cavendish' (Chinese or dwarf banana) are set 10 ft. apart; those of standard varieties, 15–20 ft. The plants thrive best in deep, rich, well-drained soils sheltered from hot sun and strong winds which break the leaves.

Dwarf bananas can be grown in the Gulf states and southern California, but the fruit and even the stems are sometimes destroyed by frost. Unless the underground parts are frozen, however, new shoots usually develop.

Some species are grown as ornamentals and greenhouse specimens; see MUSA. The Banana Family is MUSACEAE.

BANANA SHRUB. Common name for *Michelia figo*, a warm-climate shrub with banana-scented flowers; see MICHELIA.

BANDING TREES. Barriers can be used to trap and destroy insects that infest trees by crawling up the trunk. Bands are of no value against flying insects and should not be used indiscriminately since they may, if neglected, harbor certain pests. The simplest band, for catching caterpillars and wingless moths, is made by tying a strip of burlap or cotton batting 6–8 in. wide tightly around the trunk. Place a string around the center and fold the upper half down to form a flange. Wire screening, cut at the top to fit the tree but allowed to flare at the bottom, works well. Bands of tar building paper painted with sticky material, such as the commercial Tanglefoot, or with homemade mixtures of pine tar and molasses, glue, resin and oil, or roofing cement, can be tied around the tree over a layer of cotton that fills in the bark crevices. Sticky material applied directly to the tree may be injurious. A material called balsam wool combines a tough, brown, barklike outer layer over a soft, fibrous base and should prove excellent for banding trees where appearance is important. Such a paper band applied in early spring is effective against gypsy moth caterpillars, spring cankerworms, and later against fall cankerworms. All bands should be examined frequently and the trapped insects removed and destroyed to prevent later arrivals from ascending over the bridge formed by accumulated earlier victims. Bands are also effective as a pupation site for overwintering codling moths, and removal in late fall will eliminate large numbers of this pest.

BANEBERRY. Common name for ACTAEA, a genus of perennial herbs with white flowers and colored or white berries.

BANYAN. Common name for several species of fig growing in the tropics, noted for the age and size to which they grow, as well as the striking form presented by aerial roots growing downward from the branches and enlarging to become multiple trunks; see FICUS.

BAPTISIA (bap TIZ ee ah). A genus of sturdy, perennial leguminous herbs commonly known as wild- or false indigo. Native to the United States and growing wild from Pennsylvania to Mexico, they often reach a height of 6 ft. With deep green, cut foliage and indigo-blue, white, or yellow flowers resembling lupines in form and produced in long terminal racemes, these plants are imposing subjects for the border or wild garden. The flowers are good for cutting and bloom from spring to midsummer, followed by short, plump pods that turn black. Easily grown from seed in any good garden soil but preferring partial shade, plants should be started in the open ground.

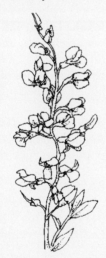

Baptisia australis

PRINCIPAL SPECIES

B. australis, the tallest species, bears profuse blossoms and has leaves 2½ in. long.

B. bracteata, growing to 2 ft., has 4-in. leaves and cream-colored flowers in May and June.

B. leucantha grows to 4 ft., bearing 2-in. leaves and white flowers in June and July.

B. tinctoria, growing to 4 ft., has leaves only 1 in. long and bright yellow flowers in June and July.

BARBAREA (bahr BAIR ee uh). A genus of European biennial and perennial herbs belonging to the Brassicaceae (Mustard Family), and commonly known as winter or upland cress. A few species are grown for ornament in the border, others are somewhat grown as potherbs or salads, and still others are roadside weeds. The cultivated species are easily grown in any rich garden soil and are propagated by seed. Most are hardy to Zone 3. For cultivating information, see CRESS.

PRINCIPAL SPECIES

B. rupicola grows to 1 ft., forming mats or sods covered with rather large yellow flowers.

B. verna is variously known as early winter, Belle Isle, American, land, or upland cress and is grown for use as a salad, seasoning, or garnish.

B. vulgaris, the common wintercress, rocket (not to be confused with roquette; see ERUCA), or yellow rocket, has become naturalized in North America, and in some areas it is a troublesome weed.

BARBERRY. Common name for BERBERIS, a genus of evergreen or deciduous spiny shrubs with yellow inner bark and wood. The Barberry Family is BERBERIDACEAE.

BARK BEETLE. Trees unhealthy because of disease, lack of water, inadequate fertilizing, or other causes may be attacked by a number of bark beetles belonging to the insect family Scolytidae. These small, black or brown beetles feed on the cambium of the trees, making many small burrows that cut off the flow of sap and eventually kill the trees. Females lay eggs along the sides of the burrows in the inner bark. Grubs tunnel into the trees for 2–3 in. Emergent beetles cut small holes to leave the tree and fly away to attack other trees.

Nearly all stone fruits are attacked by the peach-tree bark beetle. Hickory trees are often seriously damaged by the hickory bark beetle. The fruit-tree bark beetle (or shot-hole borer), which makes sawdust-filled burrows, is less likely to attack fruit trees if they are well fed with a nitrogenous fertilizer.

The most devastating of beetles has been the elm bark beetle (*Hylurgopinus rufipes* and *Scolytus multistriatus*), a small, black European import that carries the destructive fungus disease called DUTCH ELM DISEASE, common in Europe and the United States. Excellent sanitation and biological controls such as parasitic wasps, predatory beetles, and mites, or birds like woodpeckers, are the best controls. Sprays have not been noticeably effective. Pheromones (sex attractants) have been used with some success, but the future of the American elm is still in question.

BARLERIA (bahr LEE ree ah). A genus of tropical herbs and shrubs. They are easily grown in the greenhouse in any free-draining soil, and in Zones 10–11. They can become a minor pest when their seeds scatter.

B. cristata (Philippine-violet), the most common, has blue, white, or blue-and-white sectored flowers between green-toothed bracts.

B. lupulina is a spiny shrub that has narrow, dark green leaves with a yellow midrib. The flowers are yellow-orange and emerge from between bracts in a small, dense head.

BARREL CACTUS. Members of the genera FEROCACTUS and ECHINOCACTUS. Named for their barrel-like shape, they are rounded, generally elongate with pleated ribs, and usually have a fairly dense armament of spines, sometimes sharply hooked like fishhooks. One member, *F. wislizenii*, from the southwestern United States and northwestern Mexico, is called the compass-barrel, because it tends to lean toward the south, that is, toward the predominant sunlight. Perhaps the most popular barrel cactus in cultivation is the magnificent golden barrel, *E. grusonii*, from central Mexico, very rare in the wild, but grown commercially from seed by the millions in southern California alone. See also CACTUS.

BARREN-STRAWBERRY. Common name, along with false strawberry, for *Waldsteinia fragarioides*, a creeping, strawberrylike plant belonging to the Rosaceae (Rose Family); see WALDSTEINIA.

BASAL ROT. A serious fungus disease of the narcissus, crocus, hyacinth, and freesia (especially the narcissus), which rots the basal plate and sometimes the whole bulb, dwarfs the growth of the plant, and cripples the flower, if any.

Examine bulbs before planting, discarding those that are obviously softened by the rot. Provide good drainage. If disease develops, do not grow bulbs in that location the next year.

BASIL. Common name for *Ocimum basilicum*, a popular herb of the Lamiaceae (Mint Family) esteemed for flavoring; see OCIMUM.

BASKETFLOWER. Common name for *Centaurea americana*, an annual herb related to bachelor's-buttons; see CENTAUREA. The name also refers to species of HYMENOCALLIS, a genus of bulbous herbs better known as spider-lilies.

BASKET-OF-GOLD. Common name for *Aurinia saxatilis*, a yellow-flowered perennial popular for rock garden use; see AURINIA.

BASSWOOD. Common name for TILIA, a genus of handsome deciduous trees of the North Temperate Zone. The Basswood Family, better known as the Linden Family, is TILIACEAE.

BATS. It is not uncommon to see one of these small, unappreciated creatures flying around the garden at dusk. The bat is not a bird, but a highly specialized mammal whose front legs and feet have been modified into the wings with which it flits about in its nightly insect hunt. Bats are not necessarily attractive, it is true, but they are harmless and need cause no alarm even when they enter the house. Realize that the bat's nightly hunting saves the itch of many a mosquito bite.

Brown bat

BAUHINIA (baw HIN ee ah). A genus of tropical trees, shrubs, or vines in the Fabaceae (Bean Family), widely used in warm regions. In India, there are economic uses for the bark in tanning and dyeing, and the leaves and flower buds can be used as a vegetable. In the United States, the plants are purely decorative. Propagation is almost entirely by seed, except as noted.

PRINCIPAL SPECIES

B. galpinii is a vining shrub with orange flowers, well able to withstand drought.

B. monandra (Jerusalem-date, butterfly flower) is a tree native to South Africa.

B. purpurea is a tree with purple or white flowers appearing from late fall to spring.

B. variegata (orchid tree, mountain-ebony) is an Asiatic species popular in Zones 10–11 for its ornamental foliage and lavender flowers. It is similar to *B. purpurea*, and the two species are parents of the hybrid *B.* x *blakeana* (Hong-Kong-orchid). This has deep, rich purple flowers, but because of its hybrid nature, it does not seed and must be propagated by air layering or grafting.

BAY. Common name for LAURUS, a genus of evergreen shrubs or trees with long, oval, glossy leaves, also known as laurel.

Bull- or Red-bay is *Persea borbonia*, a large evergreen tree closely related to the avocado. Bull-bay also refers to *Magnolia grandiflora*, a large, flowering evergreen tree of the South.

Loblolly-bay is *Gordonia lasianthus*, a tender evergreen tree with showy flowers; see GORDONIA.

Sweet-bay is *Magnolia virginiana*, a shrubby tree native from Massachusetts to Florida and Texas; see MAGNOLIA.

BAYBERRY. Common name for *Myrica pensylvanica*, a hardy shrub with fragrant leaves and fruits; see MYRICA.

BEACH GRASS. Common name for *Ammophila breviligulata*, a vigorous grass used for binding sandy soil; see AMMOPHILA.

BEACH-HEATHER. Common name for *Hudsonia tomentosa*, a heathlike shrub that grows in southeastern coastal areas; see HUDSONIA.

BEACH PLUM. Common name for *Prunus maritima*, a shrub found chiefly in coastal areas. It has white flowers followed by fruits best used in jelly or jam; see PRUNUS.

BEACH WORMWOOD. Common name for *Artemisia stellerana*, a perennial foliage plant popular in rock gardens; see ARTEMISIA.

BEAD FERN. Common name for *Gleichenia* and ONOCLEA, two fern genera with growth features resembling beads.

BEAD PLANT. Common name for *Nertera granadensis*, a creeping perennial from the Southern Hemisphere sometimes grown in greenhouse or warm gardens as ground cover; see NERTERA.

BEAN. The name of many herbs of the FABACEAE (Bean Family) and their edible pods and seeds, but it is loosely applied to the pods or seeds of various trees and shrubs (as tamarind-coffee). In the United States, when used without qualification, the term refers to horticultural varieties of *Phaseolus vulgaris*.

COMMON OR KIDNEY BEANS

To this important species belong all the common garden, snap, string, and stringless beans whose immature pods are boiled and served as a vegetable and whole dried seeds (in the case of the field bean, of which the smallest are called navy, Boston pea, and California tree beans) are also baked. The fully formed but unripe seeds of the larger-seeded varieties are often "shelled" and cooked like garden peas. To this same group belong the French haricots, the Spanish frijoles, and the English kidney beans, so called because of their shape. In North America, the term "kidney bean" is limited to those varieties whose large, purplish brown seeds are used ripe like navy beans.

As these names suggest, the species has been greatly modified in cultivation, so much, in fact, that its original wild form is not known, although it is believed to be native to the American tropics. The plants range in habit of growth from low and bushy forms to tall and climbing "pole" beans, with many gradations in between. They also vary in foliage and seed characters, the latter especially as to size, color, and markings—large and small, mottled, eyed, and self-colors in white, black, brown, red, and yellow. About 200 types have been distinguished, and at least 500 varieties introduced. See PHASEOLUS.

Beans of this group are popularly classified as field and garden varieties. Each of these classes is subdivided into bush and pole or climbing groups. The kidney varieties include also green and butter (or wax) podded sorts. Of all these, the bush varieties are the most important.

Other terms are used to distinguish special uses. Snap or string beans are the varieties whose freshly gathered, immature pods, while thick and meaty, will break cleanly across when bent back without leaving a string along the back. Shell beans are large-seeded varieties whose immature but fully formed seeds are removed from the pods to be cooked like green peas. Beans allowed to mature fully are called "dry." There are also the double terms, green shell and dry shell, which are often used in descriptive literature. Many varieties, particularly of the white-seeded kinds of garden beans, are highly valued in all stages—snap, shell, and dry. Limas (discussed below) are never used as snap beans because they

are more highly valued for their shelled seeds and because the pods, when large enough to be worth gathering, are too fibrous and tough.

LIMA OR SUGAR BEANS

Ranking second in North America is the lima or sugar bean, *P. limensis* (often listed as a variety of *P. lunatus*), of which there are climbing, bush, and dwarf forms whose seeds are white, either small or large, flat or plump. The tall, climbing pole limas are slow growing, and the beans ripen late; hence they are often killed by early fall frosts before their pods mature. The earlier bush and dwarf varieties, especially var. *limenanus*, are more reliable.

The lima bean is an improved variety of the sieva or civet bean (*P. lunatus*), whose slender, bushy or low-climbing plants bear smaller pods containing two or three small beans that are either white, brown, or mottled when ripe. These varieties, popular in warm countries, mature even earlier than the dwarf limas and much earlier than the pole varieties.

GARDEN BEAN CULTURE

The two classes of garden beans cannot stand frost, but their varieties display wide differences in ability to resist cold and heat. In cold wet soil the seed of many types is almost sure to decay, while that of others will germinate and grow. Also, low temperatures over several days, even though well above freezing, will chill and stunt the plants of some varieties more than of others. The flowers of many kinds are often blasted by hot, dry weather, particularly in arid southwestern regions.

Excessive moisture in soil or air, and poor air circulation (particularly where the soil is rich), tend to cause lush growth and to favor disease of foliage and pods. It is important to select varieties and strains that are resistant to these drawbacks and to test various kinds and strains to determine which are most satisfactory for any particular locality or expected set of conditions. For the same reasons, it is rarely advisable to sow beans before the weather becomes settled and the ground thaws in spring; this means seed should not be sown outdoors more than a week earlier than the usual local date for the last spring frost.

In common with other legumes, beans are able to obtain much of their nitrogen from the air and from nitrogen-fixing bacteria that form nitrogen nodules on the roots. For this reason, they do not

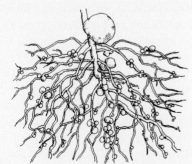

Nitrogen-fixing nodules

deplete the soil, but leave it in better condition for a succeeding crop than do nonleguminous crops. Hence, they are rated as soil-improving, not soil-impoverishing crops. When only the pods and their contents are gathered young, they consist mainly of water and cell tissue, and the harvest takes only trifling amounts of the mineral plant-food elements from the soil—especially if the vines are plowed under. Gathering beans while immature also stimulates the plants of many kinds to continue producing pods over a much longer season than if the earliest pods are allowed to mature.

Soil. When a choice of soil is possible, select fertile, humus-rich loams; second best are sandy or gravelly loams. Where no choice is possible, the garden soil, no matter what its character, can usually be improved sufficiently to meet the plants' needs. The soil must be well drained, fairly well supplied with humus, and moderately rich. If too rich in nitrogenous plant food, the plants are likely to make excessive leaf and stem development and produce few or no beans. So far as possible, rotate beans with other garden vegetables to help maintain soil fertility. See CROP ROTATION.

Composts and Fertilizers. Though beans gather much of their nitrogen from the soil bacteria and air, they are benefited, particularly from the time

buds form, by a top-dressing of compost. Apply this to bush varieties after the plants are growing well, and give pole varieties (especially limas) two or three such dressings at intervals of three or four weeks. Beans need potash and phosphorus more than nitrogen, so these elements should be supplied in applying fertilizer; a good formula is 5–10–10 or an equivalent ratio. Use proprietary (mixed) fertilizers carefully and never more than the manufacturer's directions advise.

Planting. Bush bean plants vary considerably in size, so the plant and row spacing should vary in proportion. In drills (shallow furrows) the seeds should be sown at least 2 in. apart, and preferably 4–6 in. Hills should be not less than 8 in. apart, and each should support only two or three plants. The hill method facilitates hand-hoeing and is believed to produce larger and finer beans than can be grown in drills, which for hoe and wheelhoe culture may be as close as 15 in. for the smaller-growing varieties and 18 in. for the large kinds. For garden tractor tillage, 30 in. is about the minimum.

The depth to plants seeds varies with the season and the character of the soil. Plant deeper in light loams, shallower in heavy ones. In general, early in the season, while the soil is moist, 2 in. or less is desirable. Later, in dry soil, plant deeper and firm the soil by tramping directly on the rows and afterward raking the surface loosely to prevent evaporation.

In home gardening, beans are often soaked in water overnight to accelerate germination. As they often swell to twice their dry size, provide plenty of water. Before planting, pour off any excess water and air-dry the beans for an hour to facilitate handling. As much as a week can be gained by doing this, but if cold, wet weather occurs soon after sowing, the seed is almost sure to decay. Therefore, do not try it until the weather has settled and the soil is somewhat dry.

Many varieties of bush beans mature like snap beans in six to eight weeks, so successional sowings can be made at two-week intervals until only enough time is left between the sowing date and the probable first local frost for the pods to reach edible size. Soaking the seed and thoroughly firming the soil when planting will hasten this last crop. In colder climates, the seasons are usually too short for successful successional sowings of dwarf limas; one main sowing should be made as early as it can be safely done.

Cultivation. Soils containing considerable clay tend to form crusts after hard rains. Bean seedlings find it difficult to break through such a crust, so it is important (especially with limas and other large-seeded varieties) to loosen the soil carefully above the seeds as soon as it is no longer sticky but before it bakes and becomes hard. After the plants are up, use the weeder along the rows, preferably in midafternoon when the plants are more limber and less likely to be broken than when full of water in the morning or late in the day.

Cultivation should be continuous, thorough, and clean to destroy weeds, maintain a loose and open surface, and conserve soil moisture. It must not be deep because beans are shallow-rooting plants. The scuffle hoe (or sweep) and the three-gang cultivator attachments of the wheelhoe are best for this, since they can be set to straddle the rows and work close to the plants without injuring them. For the last cultivation, use the shovel or hilling attachment to ridge up the soil and help support the plants. See HOE.

Never cultivate, pick weeds, or do any other work—even walk—among the bean rows or hills while the plants are wet with dew, because the spores of bean canker or anthracnose are thus spread from plant (or soil surface) to plant. Attacking the green parts of the plants, this disease renders them unsightly and sometimes unfit for food.

Harvesting. Gather snap beans while the seeds within are too small to give the pods an uneven outline; pick all of edible size to encourage continued pod production. For shell beans, leave the pods on the plants until the seeds are full size but not hard. If dry beans are wanted, leave the plants until they have dropped their leaves, then pull them by hand or cut with a bean-harvesting machine and lay them in shallow piles to cure for

a few days before placing them under cover. Should rain occur during this time, spread the piles out or turn them over daily for several days thereafter so they will dry evenly.

POLE BEAN CULTURE

Climbing beans, especially pole limas, require rich, warm soil and ample space. If they are to be grown on upright poles, these should be 8–9 ft. long, stout, and rough barked to aid the vines in clinging. Set them at least 4 ft. apart, at the center of hills and drive them 15 in. or more into the ground. Light bamboo poles thrust slantingly in the ground beside four adjacent hills and lashed together at the top will form a wigwam of vines much less likely to be blown over than single poles.

Temporary trellises can be made of woven wire, fencing, or stout cords stretched zigzag between two strands of number-10 wire fastened to firmly set posts several feet apart. Let the lower wire be about 6 in. above the ground and the upper one, 5–6 ft. Stakes, poles, and trellises should be placed before sowing or immediately afterward to avoid injuring the plants. Sow four or five seeds to each hill; or in rows, let the plants stand 12 in. apart. Sowing limas and other broad and large beans with the eye down, especially in heavy soil, is generally recommended but not essential. Thousands of acres of broad-seeded beans are planted by machines annually without any attention to this point. Cultivation is the same as for bush varieties.

ENEMIES

DISEASES

The chief symptoms of anthracnose (a fungus disease) are black, oval, sunken cankers (which may ooze salmon-colored spots in the center) on pods, stems, and cotyledons. Leaf symptoms are black marks on the veins. Control by selecting seed from healthy pods and resistant types. Avoid working in the bean rows during wet weather, since this spreads the spores from one plant to another.

Anthracnose is often referred to as a rust, but true rust is recognized by brown or black pustules on the leaves. Some varieties are resistant.

Bacterial blight produces large brown blotches on the leaves (which may drop off), stem-girdling so that the whole plant may topple over, and indefinite reddish-edged spots on the pods. Kidney beans are especially susceptible. Since the bacteria can enter the seed without infecting the pod, selection of clean pods does not ensure healthy seed. The safest plan is, therefore, to use disease-free seed grown by reputable nurseries in isolated valleys where the disease does not exist.

Mosaic is caused by a virus that lives in the seed and is carried from diseased to healthy plants by sucking insects. The cultivar 'Robust Pea' is fairly resistant.

Dry root rot (*Fusarium* spp.) results in stunting, wilting, and yellowing of plants. Proper disposal of infected bean refuse and a long (six-year) rotation are control measures.

In cold, moist weather lima beans are particularly subject to downy mildew, which covers the pods with white downy patches and distorts young shoots. Long rotation, use of healthy seed, and destruction of diseased vines in autumn are control measures.

INSECT PESTS

The Mexican bean beetle, *Epilachna corrupta*, is exceedingly destructive. The adults (tan with eight black spots on each wing cover) hibernate in plant rubbish and appear about the same time as the first bean leaves. After eating for a week or two, they lay yellow eggs in clusters on the undersides of leaves. Repulsive yellow larvae covered with spines hatch in six to fourteen days and eat entire leaves except the veins and upper epidermis. After three to five weeks, they pupate, the beetles emerging about a week later. There are two or more generations each year. To control, spray leaf surfaces and undersides with a combination pyrethrum-rotenone pesticide at weekly intervals and after rainfall.

In rainy seasons, the seed-corn maggot may destroy germinating seeds. To check it, plant shallow and avoid using barnyard manure.

MINOR BEAN SPECIES

There are many less important plants known as beans, grown for food or ornament.

Asparagus or Yard-long Bean. *Vigna unguiculata* var. *sesquipedalis*, though grown somewhat as a curiosity, is too unproductive to become popular. The species, *V. unguiculata* (cowpea), often called a bean, is widely grown for forage, fodder, and green manure.

Broad Bean. *Vicia faba*, the bean of history, variously known as field-tick, Windsor, English dwarf, and horse bean, is native to southwestern Asia and northern Africa, where it has been cultivated from prehistoric times and has spread throughout the world to be grown in cool climates and seasons for forage and human food. The plant differs from other beans in being hardy. It is stiffly erect with thick, very leafy, angular stems 2–4 ft. high; clusters of dull white flowers, each with a blue-black spot on the wing; thick pods 2–16 in. or longer; and flat, angular seeds larger than limas and six to eight weeks earlier in maturing. Though extensively grown in the Eastern Hemisphere, the broad bean is little grown in the United States, mainly because it fails when treated like other beans. Unless planted in earliest spring, it usually succumbs to aphids, blister beetles, or hot weather, and sets no pods. It succeeds, however, in the Canadian Maritime Provinces, British Columbia, Washington, and Oregon. In parts of California it is grown as a winter vegetable.

Chickasaw-lima or Jack Bean. *Canavalia ensiformis* is often grown in the southern states for its immature pods, which are used as snap beans. The plant is bushy and has purple flowers, pods often more than 12 in. long, and white seeds attached at right angles to the pods.

Hyacinth Bean. *Dolichos lablab* is grown in its native tropics for its edible pods and seeds. In temperate climates it is popular as an ornamental because of its rapid growth (often 20 ft. in a season), abundant large leaves, and purple or white flowers.

Scarlet Runner Bean. *Phaseolus coccineus*, formerly listed as *P. multiflora*, is a tall-climbing twiner and has tuberous roots in the tropics where it is a perennial. In cold climates it is grown as an annual, often as an ornamental for its long, naked racemes of large, brilliant red flowers. The 3–6 in. pods contain three or four large seeds which, if shelled and cooked while green, are delicious. If allowed to ripen, they are more or less unattractive because of their brown, red, and black coloring. The Dutch caseknife bean is a white-flowered variety.

Soybean or Soya Bean. *Glycine max*, a native of Japan and China, is a bushy annual growing 2–6 ft. high; it has clusters of small white flowers in the leaf axils and little pendent pods containing small yellow, brown, green, or black seeds. In the Orient, the ripe seeds are used for making oil and as a human food in fermented form, mainly as a sauce or as a protein substitute for meat. Special strains of soybeans, called edible soybeans, are grown as hot snacks; after the pods are boiled in water, the tender beans can be squirted out and eaten hot, like peanuts, and as a side dish. The plant is also an important animal forage and soil improver, being grown as a green manure or cover crop. See SOYBEAN.

Tepary Bean. *Phaseolus acutifolius* has long been cultivated in the arid southwestern states where it is native and highly prized as a vegetable. The plant grows erect on poor soils but is rather spreading on better ones. It bears short pods with two to seven white, yellow, or brown solid-colored or dotted seeds about the size of navy beans.

BEARBERRY. A common name for *Arctostaphylos uva-ursi*, a low shrub with small leaves and red berries; see ARCTOSTAPHYLOS.

BEARDTONGUE. Common name for the genus PENSTEMON, including many species of herbaceous perennials or shrubs.

BEAR-GRASS. Common name for XEROPHYLLUM, a genus of woody herbs bearing a center with narrow leaves and large flower stalks.

BEAR'S-PAW FERN. Common name for *Aglaomorpha myeniana*, a fern with fronds that end in constricted beadlike lobes; see AGLAOMORPHA.

Bear's-foot fern is *Humata tyermannii*, a popular epiphytic fern for basket culture; see HUMATA.

BEAUCARNEA (boh KAHR nee ah) **recurvata.** The most common and graceful species in cultivation of this genus of the Agavaceae (Agave Family) from south central Mexico, sometimes called ponytail-palm. The plants can attain heights of 18–24 ft. and form an enormous swollen caudex or caudiciform succulent trunk from which slender branches arise, tipped with rosettes of slender, gracefully recurving, pendent leaves 2–3 ft. long. A small seedling also makes a curious and attractive pot plant.

BEAUMONTIA (boh MON tee ah). A genus of vigorous woody vines of the tropics. One species, *B. grandiflora* (herald's-trumpet), is sometimes grown in warm greenhouses or outdoors in Zones 10–11. It has large, oval leaves and large, white, fragrant, trumpet-shaped flowers borne in terminal clusters in spring. The wood needs to be well ripened to induce flowering; afterward a hard pruning should be given to produce laterals for the next season's bloom. Propagation is by cuttings.

BEAUTYBERRY. A common name for CALLICARPA, a genus of deciduous or evergreen trees or shrubs grown for their showy flowers and fruit.

BEAUTYBUSH. Common name for KOLKWITZIA, a genus whose only member is an ornamental shrub belonging to the Caprifoliaceae (Honeysuckle Family).

BEDS. Flower beds are plantings of flowers and/or foliage plants, such as those in the center of a yard, that are accessible from all sides. Formal beds are usually square, rectangular, or circular. Informal beds are oval, kidney shaped, or free form. Size is best kept in scale with the rest of the property; a good rule of thumb is to keep beds less than one-third of the area in which it is located. The four main types of bedding are spring, summer, subtropical, and carpet bedding.

SPRING BEDDING

This style gives showy floral effects early in the season, and features such hardy bulbs in variety as crocus, hyacinth, narcissus, and tulips of both the early and late-flowering groups. Other plants used in connection with these are aubrietia, alyssum, arabis, bellis, myosotis, primulas of the polyanthus type, and pansies. One simple but effective combination is to carpet a bed of yellow tulips with forget-me-nots. As soon as the display is over, these spring plants are usually replaced with others that have been nursed indoors for summer display. Where bulbs alone are used, they can be planted over with annuals, either transplanted or sown in place.

SUMMER BEDDING

Plants for summer display are set out as soon as danger from frost is past. This group includes tender perennials propagated from cuttings, as well as perennials, biennials, or annuals raised from seed sown early in the year indoors or in hotbeds. Selection may depend on the length of the local growing season and time needed for plants to mature. Among the tender perennials that give a good floral display are the so-called geraniums (pelargoniums), heliotrope, lantana, cuphea, and fuchsia (in shady places).

Plants raised from seed include such kinds as ageratum (in both compact and spreading forms), varieties of *Begonia semperflorens*, California poppy (eschscholzia), various strains of dahlias, annual gaillardias, lobularia (sweet-alyssum), Japanese pinks, Drummond phlox, bedding petunias, sanvitalia, varieties of *Tagetes erecta* and *T. patula* (marigolds), torenia, garden verbenas, and *Verbena venosa*, which is sometimes hardy but succeeds best if handled as an annual.

For foliage effects, named varieties of coleus grown from cuttings are good in sunny situations. Good gray-leaved plants are *Centaurea cineraria*, *C. gymnocarpa* (both known as dusty-miller), and *Senecio leucostachys*; all usually raised from seed sown early in the year. Forms of *Chrysanthemum parehenium* (feverfew or golden-feather) are attractive with their golden leaves, often finely cut.

SUBTROPICAL BEDDING

Tropical plants are often arranged in beds or groups outdoors for the summer months. Bold and luxuriant effects can be obtained for a short season. For best results, sheltered positions should be selected. Permanent occupants of the conservatory or greenhouse can be moved outdoors for the summer, including tree ferns, palms, crotons, dracaenas, abutilons, acalyphas, cycads, and pittosporum. These are best plunged in the garden without being removed from their pots or tubs. Thus, they are easily returned indoors when cold weather approaches. Certain kinds are easily and quickly grown from seed. These include *Amaranthus, Albizzia lophantha, Eucalyptus globulus, Grevillea robusta, Melianthus, Nicotiana sylvestris, Ricinus*, and various species of *Solanum*, such as *S. marginatum, S. auculeatissimum, S. sisymbrifolium*, and *S. warscewicsi*. Cannas fit very well with this group, giving strong flower and foliage effects. Good grasses are the various forms of *Pennisetum* and *Miscanthus*.

CARPET BEDDING

This style has almost disappeared from the home garden as far as the elaborate geometrical layout of beds and intricate design of plant arrangements with coats-of-arms and similar picture work are concerned. Examples are still found in parks and other public places. While a most expensive and unnatural style, it calls for a high degree of technical skill in design, selection of plant material, and continuous grooming to keep the pattern well defined. The color effects in this style of planting are obtained from foliage rather than from flowers. Alternanthera, coleus, iresine, santolina, and dwarf forms of feverfew are good examples. *Antennaria dioica* and *Herniaria glabra* are useful edgers, as are such succulents as *Sedum acre, S. lydum, S. hispanicum, Aptenia cordifolia variegata, Senecio succulentus*, and various echeverias and sempervivums.

CARE OF BEDS

SOIL PREPARATION

To obtain the best results from bedding plants, one must give the preparation of the soil adequate attention. The effort spent on deep cultivation will be well repaid, as it is the best insurance against drought. This means providing good friable soil at least 12–18 in. deep, and for most plants it should be well enriched with old manure or leaf mold. Succulents and such flowering plants as geraniums and nasturtiums do best in a rather lean (sandy) mixture. Good drainage is essential, and if the subsoil is heavy and retentive, it can be improved by digging some sand, gravel, or coal ashes. If the soil is of a leachy character, a 6-in. layer of old sod or half-rotted leaves buried about 18 in. deep will offset this poor condition. Beds that are vacant over winter will be improved by double DIGGING in the fall; at this time, manure should be worked in and the surface left rough until planting time. The action of frost renders it more friable.

PLANTING

Perhaps the first planting will be done in early spring, using such things as pansies, daisies, and forget-me-nots that have been wintered in frames. Later on these would be replaced by more tender plants for summer display that have been kept indoors and held until danger from frost is safely past. It is advisable to harden-off such plants before planting by giving them gradually increased ventilation. If cloudy or rainy weather threatens around planting time, try to take advantage of such favorable conditions for moving plants.

As a rule, it is helpful to lay out the plants in position first, then make any necessary rearrangements, and finally begin to set them in the ground, working from the center of the area to the edges. In most cases, the planting shows to best advantage when the center of the bed is somewhat raised. After planting, unless rain falls promptly, give a good soaking to settle plants and soil in place. Future waterings depend on the conditions, but in general it is best to defer applying water until the plants definitely need it, then soak the soil thoroughly.

MAINTENANCE

Tidiness means a good deal in the success of a bedding scheme. Keep the soil lightly cultivated as long as it can be done without danger of injuring the plants, and pick off withered leaves and flowers as they appear. In some cases, some pinching back of wayward shoots may be necessary from time to time, especially if the design is formal. This pruning is less necessary if the right kinds of plants are chosen and if they are good, uniform stock. Neatly kept edges add much to an attractive appearance.

As frost approaches, cuttings of tender perennials in the beds can be taken as a source of future stock; or some old plants can be lifted and potted up to provide cuttings at a later date. When the summer display is finally over, the beds should be well dug and either planted with hardy bulbs for spring effects, or left in a rough state until planting time the following season.

BEE BALM. A common name for *Monarda didyma*, a perennial herb bearing clusters of scarlet flowers; see MONARDA.

BEECH. Common name for FAGUS, a genus of hardy deciduous trees related to oaks and chestnuts. The Beech Family is FAGACEAE.

Blue-beech is *Carpinus caroliniana*, a form of hornbeam; see CARPINUS.

BEECH FERN. Common name for some species of the fern genus THELYPTERIS.

BEES. Of the 2500 species of bees (of the order Hymenoptera) in North America, the Apidae (Honey Bee Family) is certainly most important, both for making and storing honey, and for pollination of fruits, flowers, and vegetables. Honey bees are social insects, living in colonies like the bumble bees (Bombidae). Both are excellent pollinators. Males and functional females of bumble bees appear late in the season. They mate; the males die, as do the year's workers; and the queens hibernate in holes in the ground, old mouse nests, and other snug places. A nest is made, lined with grass and moss, provided with pollen and nectar, and a waxen cell is made, into which eggs are laid. After the eggs hatch, in four or five days, the wax covering is enlarged for the larvae, who live about ten days. The resulting bees are all workers, who do the work of the colony while the queen goes on laying eggs. One advantage of the bumble bee as a collector of nectar and pollinator is a very long proboscis, making it possible for her to do jobs the honey bee and solitary bee (Adrenidae) cannot.

The common honey bee, *Apis mellifera*, cannot hibernate as the bumble bee does, but lives in a permanent colony. This makes it necessary to store plenty of honey for the winter. Though still cultivated for honey and beeswax, their main value is as pollinators, especially in commercial orchards, and for some 50 crops raised for food. Nurture of honey bees is essential since the habitats of native pollinators, the bumble bees and solitary bees, have been so widely destroyed by agriculture and development.

The worker honey bee, when visiting flower after flower, collects pollen from male stamens on her brushy hairs and stores it in pockets on her legs. As she visits other flowers, she leaves some pollen on the female pistils, causing fertilization.

Gardeners and greenhouse keepers as well as orchardists find keeping bees valuable and pleasurable. When working around the hive to inspect the bees for intruders or disease, or to collect honey, it is advisable to wear protective clothing and a screen helmet on the head. Bees are angered by disturbances and, on occasion, by people interrupting their path between flowers and the hive. Stings can be painful and for those allergic to bee poison, very dangerous. (People allergic to stings should seek medical treatment at once or carry a kit for quick treatment.) A few hives in a quiet corner, correctly handled and not molested, will seldom cause any trouble.

BEE SAGE. Common name for *Salvia apiana*, a shrubby, white-flowered herb of California; see SALVIA.

BEET. The name of about fifteen species of mostly biennial herbs of the genus *Beta*, native to Europe and the Middle East. *B. vulgaris* is of economic importance as the progenitor of the common garden beet, sugar beet, Swiss chard, and mangel, which have been cultivated for centuries.

Garden beet varieties are of two classes—long- and turnip-rooted. The former require five or more months to mature; along with the "half-long" types, they are famous for their fine flavor. The latter, developed mainly within the past 50 years, and reaching edible size in 3–4 months, include some varieties that compare favorably. Because turnip-rooted types, if spring sown, are likely to become tasteless and woody by fall, it is best to make successive sowings every fourteen days or so; or at least a second, midsummer sowing to provide a late fall and winter crop.

Beta vulgaris

Beets are semihardy and seed can be sown as early in spring as the ground can be worked; also, the roots can be left in the ground until heavy frosts threaten. At that point, they should be pulled, the tops cut (leaving an inch of stem), and the beets stored in pits or a cellar.

CULTURE

Though beets do best in deep, light, sandy loams, they will yield satisfactorily in any well-drained, properly managed garden. In soils underlain by hardpan or rock, grow only turnip-rooted varieties, for in shallow soil, the longer roots are likely to be deformed, rough, and of poor quality.

Soil preparation is the same as for other vegetables except that lime should not be added; it tends to cause the scab disease. Unrotted stable manure is undesirable as it tends to develop excessive tops at the expense of the roots; if well decayed, it is excellent. As a manure substitute, cover crops or green manures and a balanced commercial fertilizer can be used.

Strictly speaking, beet "seeds" are dried, shriveled fruits in which as many as eight seeds may be embedded. This explains the importance of thin sowing and also why seedlings appear in clusters even after thin sowing.

In home gardens seed is usually sown where the plants are to remain. If a hotbed or coldframe is available, crops can be started 4–6 weeks before the season opens and the seedlings transplanted outdoors when the first sowing is made there. An even earlier crop can be grown to maturity in a hotbed or frame, if space can be spared. In transplanting beets the taproots should be extended straight down into the holes, not cramped or doubled up.

Sowing should not be deeper than 1 in. while the soil is moist in early spring; in fact, the seed need only be firmed into the ground and lightly covered. In midsummer, the drier soil should be freshly turned and raked; the seed can then be covered 2 in. deep, and the rows tramped firm with loose soil raked over them to serve as a mulch and ensure a good stand of plants.

The distance between rows will depend upon the tillage methods and tools. In large scale operations, cultivation may require 24–30 in. spacing. In the small garden, 15–18 in., or even less, gives room for hand implements.

Thin when the plants are about 4 in. high. Those removed can be transplanted or cooked like greens. The distance left between plants varies with the variety; small-topped, globular sorts can stand as close as 3 in., while large, flat-rooted kinds need at least 5 in.

Plant breeders have developed some superior hybrids that are more tender and earlier than nonhybrids. 'Pacemaker' is one of the best. Among nonhybrids, 'Detroit Dark Red', 'Crosby's Egyptian', and 'Redball' are good choices. 'Lutz Green Leaf' grows extra luscious tops as delicious as top quality spinach. 'Burpee's Golden Beet' is a novelty, producing golden yellow

roots that do not bleed like red beets.

Enemies. A leaf spot is common but not serious; destroying diseased leaves will usually be enough control. Potato scab also occurs on beets (see POTATO). Curly-top, a virus disease of sugar beets causing great damage in the semiarid western regions, is spread by means of a leaf hopper. It causes dwarfed plants, curled leaves, and irregularly swollen veins. No certain control is known, but early planting helps.

See BETA; SWISS CHARD.

BEETLES. The order Coleoptera, including the families Carabidae, Silphidae, Elateridae, and many others, are all commonly known as beetles. This is the largest of all insect groups, comprising two out of five of all insects so far discovered and named. They have two pairs of wings, the front pair (called elytra) thickened and hornlike, meeting when at rest in a straight line down the back. They have chewing mouthparts and usually quite stout bodies. They go through a complete metamorphosis of egg, several larval instars (or stages) and molts, a pupal state, and adult. The wormlike larvae have six thoracic legs, except for the snout beetles, which are legless (they also have mouthparts modified into a snout). In the resting pupal stage, beetles are brown and often wriggly, living not in cocoons, but beneath bark or in burrows.

Cucumber beetle

Injurious beetles attack plants in both larval and adult phases, while the SNOUT BEETLE and several others are beneficial predators. Adult blister beetles attack plants but, as larvae, consume insect eggs of grasshoppers, for example, in the soil. Among highly beneficial beetles are lady beetles (ladybugs) and ground beetles. The Vedalia lady beetle was the first notable example of biological control when in 1888 it was imported to control the cottony-cushion scale in California. Soldier beetles are also beneficial.

Japanese beetles, rose chafers, and blister beetles, which attack flowers, are often controlled by
knocking them off into a container of water covered with a layer of kerosene, turpentine, or paint
thinner. As with other attacking insects, the
healthier the plant, the less severe the attack.
Increased amino acids from too much nitrogen in
the leaves are a magnet for chewing insects.
Pyrethrum spray on the leaves and poured
around the crown of vulnerable plants can be
effective. Asparagus beetles can be repelled by
interplanting with tomatoes and garlic. Flea beetles are repelled by sprinklings of DIATOMACEOUS
EARTH.

See also ASIATIC BEETLE; ASPARAGUS BEETLE; BARK
BEETLE; BLISTER BEETLE; CURCULIO; FLEA BEETLE;
GRUBS; LADY BEETLE; ROSE CHAFER; SNOUT BEETLE;
SOLDIER BEETLE; and WEEVIL.

BEGONIA (be GOH nee ah). A large and varied
genus of succulent herbs or partly shrubby
plants, widely distributed in warm regions of the
earth. A great many species have been introduced into cultivation, and countless hybrids and
forms have been developed in gardens. Some are
grown for their handsome foliage, and many others for their showy flowers, either for summer
bedding outdoors or for summer or winter flowering under glass. Many are fine plants for the
window garden.

They are divided roughly into three main categories: fibrous-rooted, rhizomatous-rooted, and
tuberous-rooted, but
due to interbreeding,
the lines are not clearly
defined in all cases.
Male and female flow-
ers are borne separately
in the same cluster.
The plants mostly dis-
like full exposure to
sun or very dry condi-
tions; they thrive best
in a mixture of fibrous

Begonia sp.

loam and leaf mold with well-rotted manure and
sand added.

Begonias are propagated by seed, which is
extremely small and should not be covered with
compost. They can also be propagated by stem
and leaf cuttings, and by division of the rhizomes
and tubers.

ENEMIES

The leaf nematode disease is a serious problem
on the semituberous type of begonia. The eelworms' feeding results in small brown spots on
the undersides of the leaves followed by dying of
foliage and stunting of plants, which may mean
the destruction of the entire stock of a greenhouse. To prevent this, take cuttings only from
healthy stock; discard infested soil; place pots so
that leaves of neighboring plants do not touch;
isolate infected plants; remove and burn infected
leaves; and, most important of all, do not wet
foliage when watering. Plants can be treated
with hot water at 117°F for three minutes.

To avoid bacterial leaf spot and resulting defoliation, botrytis blight, and pythium stem rot,
keep plants well spaced and the humidity not too
high. To prevent nematode root knot, use soil
free from infestation or sterilize it. See NEMA-
TODES; DISINFECTION.

The usual houseplant insects—mealybug,
brown scale, whitefly, aphids, and red spider
mites—seldom attack begonias. In the event they
do, use an insecticidal soap and water spray at
half the usual strength, and take great care not to
apply it while the plants are in direct sunlight or
in temperatures above 70°F.

PRINCIPAL SPECIES

B. x *argenteo-guttata* (trout begonia) has
leaves of shining green thickly spotted with
white, and blush pink flowers.

B. coccinea (scarlet or angel-wing begonia) has
tall smooth stems, oblique angular leaves with
red margins, and drooping clusters of coral-red
flowers.

B. corallina grows to 10 ft. or so and has glossy
green leaves and clusters of coral-red flowers. It
is one of the best to train against a pillar or over
rafters. Cv. 'Lucerna' is of strong, shrubby habit,
with leaves heavily spotted white and large,
showy, bright pink flowers.

B. dichroa is a good basket plant. It grows in a pendulous habit, bearing large green leaves and brick-red flowers.

B. x *digswelliana* has large green leaves tinged red and pendulous, rosy scarlet flowers.

B. dregei (grapeleaf begonia) grows to 3 ft. and has small thin leaves and a profusion of small white flowers. It is a semituberous species, native to South Africa. *B.* x *weltoniensis*, an old-time favorite in window gardens, is a *B. dregei* hybrid with pink flowers.

B. x *erythrophylla* has thick, roundish leaves, red beneath with hairy margins, and bright pink flowers borne on long stems.

B. foliosa (fern begonia) is a small plant good for basket culture, with slender stems, small, glossy, green, drooping leaves and small whitish flowers tinged pink. Var. *miniata* has tall slender stems, small leaves tinged red when young, and drooping scarlet flowers resembling fuchsias.

B. froebelii has green, heart-shaped leaves with fleshy purple hairs and large scarlet flowers in loose, drooping clusters.

B. glabra has glossy green leaves and small white flowers in round clusters. It is an excellent basket, window box, and climbing plant.

B. gracilis (hollyhock begonia) has lobed heart-shaped leaves and bears pink flowers in summer on erect succulent stems that may extend to 2 ft. tall or more. It is increased by leaf bulblets.

B. grandis (Evans or hardy begonia) is not showy but is unusual in being able to stand some frost, surviving winters to Zone 7 and even Zone 6 with winter protection. It has lobed leaves, red beneath, and flesh-colored flowers. It is propagated by bulblets from the leaf-axils.

B. heracleifolia (star begonia) has large bronzy green palmate leaves and rose-colored flowers on long hairy stems.

B. limmingheiana, a good basket plant, has somewhat pendulous stems with glaucous wavy-margined leaves and red flowers.

B. maculata has woody, branching stems with wavy green leaves blotched silvery white, and drooping clusters of pink flowers.

B. manicata has thick, fleshy, shining green leaves with stems covered in scalelike hairs, and loose panicles of small pink flowers. Cv. 'Aureo-maculata' is a form with leaves blotched yellowish white. Cv. 'Crispa' has leaves with heavily crinkled margins.

B. metallica is attractive with green leaves shaded a dark metallic color and clusters of blush-white to light rose colored flowers.

B. phyllomaniaca is a curious species with thick, fleshy, hairy stems and large fringed leaves bearing buds that produce young plants. It bears a profusion of small pink flowers.

B. rex (painted leaf begonia) is a dwarf species that has large wavy leaves of metallic green with purple margins and a silvery zone above and red beneath. It is the chief parent of the many named forms of the beautiful colored-leaved Rex begonias. While often grown in pots, these forms do much better when planted out in a greenhouse, where they show to advantage in rockwork with ferns or planted under staging.

B. sanguinea has a smooth and shining appearance with thick green leaves, red beneath, and small white flowers.

B. scharffii is a tall, handsome, red-hairy species with large hanging clusters of rose-pink flowers.

B. semperflorens (wax begonia, youth-and-old-age) is a dwarf compact grower, almost ever-blooming, and bears both green and white leaves at the same time. It is popular as a summer bedding plant and also for use in the house. Flowers are 1 in. wide, found in white, pink, red, single and double varieties. It needs water sparingly on the roots and not at all on the leaves. A good plan is to plant it in an unglazed clay pot that is set in peat moss in a large container and apply water only to the moss.

B. socotrana is a bulbous species that grows about 1 ft. high with large, round, dark green leaves and large rose-pink flowers in winter. After flowering, a cluster of bulbs is formed at the base of the stems from which new plants are started. Crossed with large-flowering tuberous varieties, it produced that fine white race known as winter-flowering begonias. The popular

Rieger hybrids are the newest additions to this class, although they can be found flowering in the marketplace almost any day of the year. Success depends on bright light, but not hot sun; fresh air circulation, but no icy drafts or hot blasts; moderate temperatures, 58–72°F, and a humus-rich growing medium kept evenly moist throughout to slightly dry at the surface. New plants should be started from tip cuttings taken in the spring or summer.

B. x *tuberhybrida* (tuberous begonia) is a class name for the showy and beautiful summer-flowering tuberous begonias in both single and double varieties. These have been developed from the following species native in the Peruvian Andes: *B. clarkei*, *B. boliviensis*, *B. davisi*, *B. pearcei*, *B. rosiflora*, and *B. veitchi*, which are interesting and beautiful in themselves but seldom seen outside botanical gardens. Tuberous begonias can be raised from seed, a good strain giving fine form and color variation. The tubers will be good for several years. Started early in spring they make good plants for summer flowering indoors or for bedding out in moist and partly shaded places.

B. venosa is an interesting upright species with thick fleshy leaves covered with silvery gray scales; it can be distinguished by very large, veined stipules or basal appendages.

B. x *verschaffeltii* has large, ovate, lobed green leaves and large clusters of rose flowers.

BELAMCANDA (bel am KAN dah) **chinensis.** A hardy East Asian plant belonging to the Iridaceae (Iris Family), commonly known as blackberry-lily or leopardflower. It has irislike leaves, orange flowers with red spots, and ornamental black fruit resembling a large-seeded blackberry. A strong-growing perennial, it delights in a rich, sandy

Belamcanda chinensis

soil in an open border in full sunlight. Propagation is easily done by division of the tubers in the fall or by seed. It blooms in midsummer, leaving ornamental seed pods that can be dried and used in floral arrangements. Hardy in Zones 4–11, winter mulching is advisable in cold regions. A favorite subject in old-fashioned gardens, it has become naturalized in some parts of North America.

BELLADONNA. Common name for *Atropa belladonna*, a European herb, not usually grown in gardens, but an important source of medicine; see ATROPA. The name is often mistakenly applied to *Delphinium cheilanthum*, better known as garland larkspur.

BELLADONNA-LILY. Common name for *Amaryllis belladonna*, a bulbous herb that bears fragrant, white or pink flowers from late summer to early autumn; see AMARYLLIS.

BELLFLOWER. Common name for CAMPANULA, a genus of excellent plants for gardens. The Bellflower Family is CAMPANULACEAE.

The name is sometimes applied to plants of other genera. Chilean-bellflower is *Lapageria rosea*. Giant bellflower is *Ostrowskia magnifica*. Gland bellflower is a catalog name for the genus *Adenophora*, also known as ladybell.

BELLIS (BEL is). A genus of annual or perennial herbs belonging to the Asteraceae (Aster Family), and often called English daisy (which correctly refers to *B. perennis*). Because of their dwarf nature—growing only 6–8 in. tall—they are best used for edgings and low beds. They are also satisfactory for potting. Blossoms are produced all summer.

They need fertile, moist soil and plenty of sun but are easily grown from seed sown in the fall. Wintered over in a coldframe, they flower early the next season. Plants bloom the first season, however, if seed is sown very early in the spring. Special varieties are best propagated by division in cool weather, since they do not always come true from seed. Most are hardy in Zones 3–9.

B. perennis (English daisy) produces red, rose, and white flowers borne in heads 2 in. across and blooming in spring and early summer. Var. *ranunculiflora* is a double form. This is the common "daisy" of literature.

B. rotundifolia has longer stalked, coarsely toothed leaves and usually white flower heads that are somewhat smaller than those of *B. perennis*. Var. *caerulescens* bears flowers with blue rays.

Bellis perennis

A number of cultivars are available, including 'Rose Carpet', 'White Carpet', and 'Nibelungen Mixed', a cutting variety with large double blooms of crimson, pink, rose, and white.

BELLWORT. Common name for UVULARIA, a genus of hardy perennials with drooping yellow flowers.

BELVEDERE. A permanent garden shelter, roofed over but open at the sides and located to command a broad, extensive view.

As common name this also refers to *Kochia scoparia*, a shrubby plant with cypresslike foliage; see KOCHIA.

BENEFICIAL INSECTS. See INSECTS, BENEFICIAL.

BENT GRASS. Common name for AGROSTIS, a widely distributed genus of tufted annual and perennial grasses.

BERBERIDACEAE (bur bay rid AY see ee). The Barberry Family, a group of herbs or shrubs, many of them ornamental, native in the Northern Hemisphere. Their spiny stems, black, red, or yellow berries, and attractive small leaves often held late into the winter, make them widely popular for hedges. The majority are deciduous and hardy;

the evergreen kinds are not hardy. One genus, *Berberis*, includes species that are host plants for the fungus that causes wheat rust; the elimination of these species is an important step in its control. Principal genera are *Berberis*, *Mahonia*, *Nandina*, *Epimedium*, and *Podophyllum*.

BERBERIS (BUR ber is). A genus of about 500 species of evergreen or deciduous spiny shrubs with yellow inner bark and wood, belonging to the Berberidaceae (Barberry Family), commonly known as barberry. Mostly native in Asia and South America, with some from North America, Europe, and North Africa, they are among the most useful and ornamental shrubs, with a good habit of growth. The flowers are not large but are numerous enough in many cases to be attractive in the spring or early summer. Some of the deciduous varieties rank among the best berried shrubs, and the leaves of several are brilliantly colored before falling. Of the evergreen species, mostly from China, some are hardy to Zone 5, and all have purple or blue-black berries.

Barberries are of easy cultivation and are adapted to various soils and situations. Purple and reddish foliage varieties need full sun for good color. Propagation is by seed, cuttings, suckers, and layers. The raising of barberries from seed has interesting possibilities. Some beautiful forms have been originated in this way and have been given distinctive names; they can be reproduced true only by vegetative means.

ENEMIES

Some relation has long been suspected between the common barberry and the black stem rust of wheat. Barberry eradication legislation was passed in France in 1660 and in Connecticut, Rhode Island, and Massachusetts in the middle of the 18th century, but it was not until 1865 that it was definitely proved that the rust on barberry and on wheat were stages in the life cycle of one fungus. Destruction of the common barberry in important wheat regions remains the chief means of control of the rust.

Since *B. thunbergii* (Japanese barberry) is not attacked by rust, it can safely be used for ornamental plantings. It is subject to a VERTICILLIUM WILT and a bacterial LEAF SPOT. These can be controlled by destroying wilted plants and diseased leaves.

PRINCIPAL SPECIES

EVERGREENS

B. buxifolia is a Chilean species with upright habit, growing to 10 ft., with solitary or paired flowers; among the hardiest, Zones 6–8. Var. *nana* is a useful dwarf and compact form.

B. darwinii, a Chilean native, is one of the most beautiful, with lustrous, dark green leaves and clusters of golden flowers. Hardy to Zone 7, it can withstand only a few degrees of frost.

B. gagnepainii is a bushy grower to 6 ft. and has yellowish stems armed with slender spines and narrow, spiny leaves with rolled edges. Hardy to Zone 6.

B. julianae is a tall, erect grower with light-colored branches and sharp spines. The dark green, spiny leaves are up to 3 in. long. Hardy in Zones 6–8, it is an excellent barrier or hedge plant with abundant showy yellow flowers and attractive bluish white fruit.

B. x *stenophylla* is a garden hybrid between *B. darwinii* and *B. empetrifolia*. A graceful shrub with slender, arching branches, it is hardy to Zone 6.

B. verruculosa has a low, arching form with glossy green leaves that are white beneath and assume a lovely bronze tone in autumn. The golden flowers are solitary or paired. Hardy in Zones 6–8.

DECIDUOUS SPECIES

These are mostly from western China.

B. koreana is a Korean species of vigorous, upright growth with large leaves that are brilliantly colored in autumn. The clusters of bright red berries persist long. Hardy in Zones 3–7.

B. x *mentorensis*, a hybrid produced from *B. julianae* and *B. thunbergii*, is excellent as an upright hedge plant, with uniform growth to about 6 ft. and sharp thorns; hardy in Zones 4–8.

B. thunbergii (Japanese barberry) is a popular hedge plant and is useful in general planting. Leaves open early in spring and color brilliantly in autumn. The red berries hang until spring. Cv. 'Atropurpurea', with lustrous bronzy red leaves, is one of the best shrubs with colored foliage. 'Minor' (box barberry) of low, dense form, makes a useful edging plant. 'Crimson Pygmy' is a dwarf shrub that grows to 2 ft. and has purplish red foliage. 'Erecta' maintains very upright growth to 4 ft. and has excellent fall color from yellow to red. 'Aurea' is slow growing to 3 ft. and has bright yellow leaves. There are many other fine varieties and cultivars of this species, most hardy in Zones 4–8.

B. vulgaris (common barberry), a European species naturalized in the United States, is one of the most ornamental with drooping clusters of coral red berries, but its cultivation in wheat-growing regions is prohibited by federal quarantine regulations because it is a host to wheat rust.

B. wilsoniae is a half-evergreen of low, bushy habit with clusters of salmon red berries, well-suited for the rock garden. Hardy to Zone 6.

BERGAMOT. Common name for *Citrus aurantium* var. *bergamia*, grown in Europe for its perfume-yielding oil and in the United States as a curiosity. Bergamot mint is a variety of *Mentha* x *piperita*; see MENTHA. Wild-bergamot refers to various species of MONARDA.

BERGENIA (bur JEE nee ah). A genus of hardy perennial herbs, closely related and quite similar to the saxifrages, but with much larger leaves. Native to Asia, they are often listed as *Saxifraga* or *Megasea*. Most species have large, fleshy, shining, almost evergreen leaves. The large, clear rose to pink or white flowers are borne on stems 1 ft. or taller and come quite early in the spring but are often partly hidden by the lush foliage. The leaves make good points of accent when planted at corners. Plants rapidly

Bergenia cordifolia

increase into large clumps or colonies when planted in the border. They will grow well in ordinary garden soil and are increased by seed or division.

B. cordifolia, the species most often found in catalogs, has heart-shaped leaves and is native to Siberia.

BERGEROCACTUS (bur jur oh KAK tus) **emoryi.** A species of cactus found in small groups in the extreme southern coastal areas of California. It is usually of low growth but sometimes forms thickets up to 8 ft. high. Its light, bright green color is modified by the completely enveloping yellow spines. Greenish yellow blossoms appear along the side of the stems. The dry fruit, resembling a chestnut burr, is persistent, so that buds, blossoms, and fruit are found together. It is hardy to Zone 9 and is easily cultivated but is not particularly desirable in the garden unless as part of a large collection. See CACTUS.

BERMUDA GRASS. Common name for the perennial grass *Cynodon dactylon*; see CYNODON.

BERRY. Botanically, the term is limited to fruits with thin skin, fleshy throughout, developed from one pistil, and containing one or more seeds, but no "stone." By such definition, currants, grapes, blueberries, tomatoes—even watermelons—are true berries.

The term is commonly and loosely applied to a number of different kinds of small, pulpy, often compound fruits. Examples are strawberry, which is a swollen "receptacle" with partially exposed seeds (achenes) that are embedded on the outside; blackberry, a union of many carpels forming drupelets; mulberry, resembling the blackberry but actually composed of flesh-covered achenes; and checkerberry (or wintergreen), a swollen calyx containing seeds.

ORNAMENTAL BERRY PLANTS

In gardening, ornamental berry plants are distinguished by their seed, which is produced within brightly colored seed vessels that are often decorative throughout the winter. This group does not include the edible bush fruits, although they too produce berries. The garden use of ornamental berry shrubs and small trees has grown with the developing appreciation of their value in winter landscapes and also with the increasing interest in attracting bird life.

Nursery catalogs usually list the type and color of berry yielded by each variety, as well as the period of bloom. Not all produce showy flowers, but most of them are sufficiently attractive to warrant their generous use in shrubbery plantings for their bloom as well as for their colorful berries; and they are a necessity in plantings for autumn effects.

According to whether the berries are especially favored by birds for food or are merely decorative, these plants fall into two groups. It is an advantage to the garden effect that the berries of some are almost never eaten by birds; these retain their decorative quality all winter, but because of the importance of bird-life conservation to the gardeners as well as to farmers, it is shortsighted to use only those that the birds do not like. A few of these can go into prominent places where all-winter color is greatly desired, but in the backgrounds and thickets those that provide for the birds are more desirable.

Most notable of these are the dogwood or cornel group, the flowering dogwood being the finest native ornamental berry tree. Native hawthorns, viburnums, chokeberries, Juneberries or shadbush, buckthorn, and bayberry all include varieties that will provide growth from low up to 20 ft. in height. All wild or species roses have bright fruits, many large and brilliant in color. The barberries are richly decorated with vivid berries.

BERTOLONIA (bur toh LOH nee ah). A genus of dwarf herbs from South America, sometimes grown in warm greenhouses or terrariums for their beautifully marked leaves, young plants being more colorful than old ones. To be seen at their best, they require dense shade and a close, moist atmosphere; often the only way to provide the proper conditions is to place them under a forcing cover or bell glass. They thrive in a soil of equal parts peat, leaf mold, and sand. Propagation is by cuttings.

B. maculata and *B. marmorata* are the principal species, and several hybrids with even more handsome foliage have been raised in Europe.

BESSERA (BES er ah) **elegans.** A name under which the native bulbous plant *Milla biflora* is often grown and sold. Common names are Mexican-star and coral-drops; see MILLA.

BETA (BEE tah). A genus of herbs native to Europe and the Middle East, mostly annual and biennial, grown for their edible roots or foliage, and commonly known as beets. The most important species, *B. vulgaris*, naturally a perennial, has four main botanical varieties: *crassa* (beetroot), grown for its thick roots and used as a vegetable or, commercially, as a source of sugar; *cruenta* (Victoria or foliage beet), small-rooted plants with large, brilliantly colored foliage; *cicla* (Swiss chard), small-rooted plants whose large, thick-stemmed leaves are used as greens; and *macrohiza* (mangel), enormous-rooted plants grown for cattle feeding.

See BEET; SWISS CHARD.

BETHLEHEM-SAGE. Common name for *Pulmonaria saccharata*, a flowering perennial with white-spotted leaves; see PULMONARIA.

BETULA (BET yoo lah). A genus including about 50 species of hardy deciduous trees, commonly known as birch. They belong to the Betulaceae (Birch Family), which also includes alder, hazelnut, and hornbeam.

Birches are usually of upright growth habit and of distinct decorative value, with their distinctive bark and catkins. The bark varies in color from gray to white in some species and in others, various shades of yellow, orange, red, brown, and almost black. They have thin, graceful branches and beautiful yellow leaves in fall. Unfortunately many species are short-lived and "bleed" profusely if pruned in early spring. All young birch

seedlings have dark-colored bark until they have trunks about an inch in diameter.

Those with gray or white bark are very effective in the landscape, especially in naturalistic plantings, on the edge of water, or in front of large evergreen trees. They are often planted in clumps to accent the bark.

Most of the birches thrive in moist, sandy loam with sandy or rocky subsoil, some others in dry locations. All bear catkins and soft cones. Propagation is by seed sown or stratified in sandy soil, by layers or greenwood cuttings under glass, and by grafting or budding.

Betula allegheniensis

Diseases. Several leaf diseases are common but not serious. Wood decays attack old trees. European CANKER, caused by a fungus, produces a large open canker with concentric rings of dead callus. It is serious only in weak trees, so feed them properly and dress any wounds.

Insect Pests. Presence of the bronze birch borer is indicated by dying tops and tortuous galleries formed underneath the bark. Dead or dying trees or limbs should be cut and burned in early spring before the beetles emerge. Later spraying with insecticide may help.

The introduced European birch sawfly or LEAF MINER has spread rapidly and can defoliate many kinds of birches. Since the larval and egg stages occur within the leaves, control is difficult. See INSECT CONTROL.

About every eleven years in the northern states, the birch-leaf skeletonizer defoliates many trees. It is usually not fatal to the tree, nor does it cause permanent damage.

PRINCIPAL SPECIES

B. allegheniensis (yellow birch), sometimes listed as *B. lutea*, grows to 90 ft. and has oval leaves to 5 in. long. Its bark is yellowish, silvery gray, or reddish brown on old trunks. The twigs are aromatic and somewhat bitter when young.

B. lenta (black, sweet, or cherry birch) grows to a height of about 65 ft. and about 40 ft. wide with a smooth, dark reddish black bark. Fall color of the leaves is a wonderful bright yellow. The young bark and twigs are very aromatic, smelling and tasting like wintergreen. An excellent hot tea can be made by pouring boiling water over crushed twigs and adding sugar or honey to taste. Hardy to Zone 4.

B. maximowicziana (monarch birch), native to Japan, is a tall tree that grows to 100 ft. and has orange-gray, flaking bark and large, cordate leaves. Hardy to Zone 5.

B. nana is a dwarf species from the Arctic, growing 2 ft. high or less in colder areas. Hardy to Zone 3.

B. nigra (river birch) is found mostly in moist lowlands and along stream banks, growing to about 75 ft. with a spread of about 50 ft. This is a good tree for wet areas with its attractive reddish brown and cream-colored, exfoliating bark. Hardy in Zones 5–9.

B. papyrifera (paper, white, or canoe birch) grows to 100 ft. with age and thrives best in colder climates. Making a bold display on hillsides and gracing the banks of many streams, it is a native species, very showy in the New England landscape, especially in light and rocky soils. It is very attractive, with chalky white, peely bark and larger foliage with good yellow color in autumn. Hardy in Zones 3–6.

B. pendula (European white birch) grows to about 60 ft. and has a pyramidal outline, graceful weeping branches, and white, exfoliating bark. Unfortunately this species is quite susceptible to two insect pests—the leaf miner and the bronze birch borer. Cv. 'Gracillis' is a small tree with finely cut leaves and drooping branches. 'Fastigiata' is of narrow, columnar growth habit. 'Youngii' has very weeping branches. Hardy in Zones 3–6.

B. populifolia (gray or white birch) is a short-lived tree growing to 30 ft. with black-marked, grayish white bark, which does not have the peely texture of *B. papyrifera*. It thrives in poor soils and dry or wet conditions and is usually a multiple-stemmed tree, but it can be trained to a single trunk and is best used for naturalizing. It is very susceptible to the birch leaf miner. There are many better birches with whiter bark, but this one has the advantage of surviving dusty, smoky city conditions better than other most species. Hardy in Zones 4–6.

BETULACEAE (bet yoo LAY see ee). The Birch Family, a group of hardy trees native to the cooler portions of the North Temperate Zone, and prominent as producers of timber, some edible fruits and medicinal oils, and in many cases ornamentals. One or two species of the genus *Betula* (birch) are planted extensively as ornamentals. *Carpinus* (hornbeam) is a small ornamental tree with smooth, fluted bark. Other popular genera include *Ostrya* (hop-hornbeam) and *Corylus* (hazelnut), which includes ornamental shrubs and nut producers.

BIDENS (BĪ denz). Plants of this genus of the Asteraceae (Aster Family), variously called bur marigold, sticktights, and tickseed, are closely related to *Cosmos*; they resemble it in having divided leaves and clustered heads with yellow or white ray flowers. As they are of weedy growth, they are seldom used in the flower garden. In the wild they grow principally in moist places throughout North America, springing up readily from seed. Some species are thought to have medicinal qualities.

B. bipinnata (Spanish-needles) is a native weed in cultivated and sandy soils, propagated by seeds that stick to clothing and animals.

B. ferulifolia (fern-leaved bidens) is an annual of Mexico with branching, divided leaves and bright yellow flowers less than 1 in. across.

BIENNIAL. A plant that, started from seed, requires two seasons to come to maturity. The first year it makes top growth and usually a fleshy root. The second year it produces flowers and seed, living on the food stored up on the root and then dying. Some biennials will bloom the first year if sown early enough indoors or in a hotbed; others require winter-chilling in order to bloom. Some perennials are so short-lived that they become biennial when cultivated. Examples of typical biennials are Canterbury-bells, foxglove, pansy, hollyhock, parsnip, and cabbage. In regions where winter-killing or rotting of the crowns is not a problem, biennials can be grown in the open garden from seed to maturity, seed being sown in June or July and seedlings transplanted later to permanent locations. As cold weather arrives, a loose mulch of leaves or straw should be given, though where the winter rosette of leaves is formed, these must be protected from the matting of the mulch by placing twigs or baskets under it. Where mulching is impracticable, plants can be wintered in a coldframe. Biennials require no different culture from that given other plants. Compare ANNUALS; PERENNIALS.

BIGNONIA (big NOH nee ah) **capreolata.** An evergreen climber growing to 50 ft. or more, belonging to the Bignoniaceae (Bignonia Family), and commonly known as crossvine or trumpet flower. It is found from Virginia south and westward but will grow considerably farther north as a trailing plant; hardy in Zones 6–9. The rather stiff leaves end in a branched tendril, which clings by means of small disks. In flower, it is a very showy vine with large clusters of yellowish red, tubular blossoms appearing in early summer. It is a very good wall plant. When trained on a wall, it should be pruned hard after flowering; later some of the weakest shoots should be thinned out. Propagation is by cuttings of half-ripened wood and by layering.

Although *B. capreolata* is the only member left in the genus, many former members are still commonly known as bignonias, including *Macfadyena unguis-cati*, see MACFADYENA, and *Pyrostegia venusta*, see PYROSTEGIA. These are vigorous warm-climate vines with showy flowers.

BIGNONIACEAE (big noh nee AY see ee). The Bignonia or Trumpet-creeper Family, a large group of trees, shrubs, and woody vines characterized in most cases by the beauty and profusion of the large, showy, often trumpet-shaped flowers. Preferring a moist, rich soil, members of the family are found chiefly in the tropics, but a few genera extend into temperate climates. *Bignonia* and *Tecoma* are evergreen vines extensively used as ornamentals, most species of *Bignonia* being hot-house climbers. Other cultivated genera include *Campsis, Catalpa, Crescentia* (calabash tree), *Eccremocarpus, Incarvillea, Jacaranda, Mactadyena, Pandorea, Pyrostegia*, and the handsome-foliaged *Spathodea*.

BIG TREE. Common name for SEQUOIADENDRON, a monotypic genus of giant coniferous trees.

BILLARDIERA (bil ahr dee AIR ah). A genus of evergreen climbing shrubs with twining stems, native to Australia, belonging to the Pittosporaceae (Pittosporum Family), and commonly known as apple-berry. These are ornamental plants for greenhouse culture or can be grown outside in warm climates; propagation is by seed or cutting. The fleshy, blue berries are edible.

B. cymosa bears clusters of violet-blue flowers; *B. longiflora* bears solitary flowers of greenish yellow changing to purple; *B. scandens* bears cream to purple flowers, sometimes in pairs.

BILLBERGIA (bil BUR jee ah). A genus of herbaceous epiphytes from the American tropics, belonging to the Bromiliaceae (Pineapple Family). Several species are grown in warm greenhouses and also make good houseplants. They thrive in a mixture of fern fiber and sphagnum moss with broken charcoal, and they require an abundance of water during the summer. They have long stiff leaves, usually spiny, in basal rosettes, and showy flowers, mostly with colorful bracts. Propagation is by suckers.

PRINCIPAL SPECIES

B. amoena has strap-shaped green leaves, striped on the back, 2 ft. long, and large, loose, drooping clusters of pale green, blue-tipped flowers and rosy bracts.

B. morelii has green leaves with few spiny teeth and drooping spikes of red-and-blue flowers with long red bracts.

B. nutans has narrow, long-pointed leaves and loose, drooping clusters of nodding green-and-blue flowers with red bracts.

B. pyramidalis has finely toothed leaves to 3 ft. long and a mealy erect flower cluster composed of red, violet-tipped flowers with red bracts.

B. sanderana has leathery leaves 1 ft. long and nodding racemes of green, blue-tipped flowers and rose bracts.

B. zebrina has leaves to 3 ft. long, spotted and banded with gray-white, and greenish yellow flowers with salmon-pink bracts.

BINDING PLANTS. A varied group of plants which, because of their underground running stems, or above-ground creeping and/or rooting stems, are valued in binding loose, shifting sands and light soils subject to erosion.

In Europe and along sections of our own coasts, *Ammophila* (beach grass) has done wonders in holding shifting sands in place. *Salix repens* (creeping willow) is equally effective under the same conditions. *S. alba* (white willow) has been used to advantage in checking sliding banks along streams; it can be established by sticking large pieces of stem into the banks to take root.

In dry, sandy regions, *Betula populifolia* (gray birch) and *Pinus rigida* (pitch pine) are good. *Robinia pseudoacacia* (black locust) is one of the most effective plants to use in almost any kind of soil subject to erosion. For dry banks, *Robinia hispida* (rose-acacia) and other shrubby plants of the Fabaceae (Bean Family), are both effective and decorative; and almost any shrub of spreading habit can be used where the soil is not too dry. Vines such as *Pueraria* spp. (kudzu), *Lonicera japonica* (Japanese honeysuckle), *Solanum dulcamara* (bittersweet), and *Parthenocissus quinquefolia* (Virginia creeper) are effective for covering large slopes. In sandy areas *Arctostaphylos uva-ursi* (bearberry) and *Calluna* spp. (heather) are useful and attractive.

BINDWEED. Common name for the genus CONVOLVULUS, which includes some troublesome weeds as well as a few species resembling morning-glories that are sometimes planted in gardens or hanging baskets.

BIO-DYNAMIC GARDENING. A branch of organic gardening and farming founded in the early 20th century by Dr. Rudolph Steiner and taught by Dr. Ehrenfried Pfeiffer. The key concept of interdependence of all living things includes the living soil and the planetary influences believed to affect the earth's living network, all seen as one organic unit.

The methods of bio-dynamic gardening include refraining from using synthetic commercial fertilizers and pest controls, and making and using well-composted manures to develop the humus in the soil. The compost made according to their procedures involves using an herbal activator, referred to as B-D starter, believed to improve the manures and plant residues in the compost heap. The compost is valuable for the feeding of essential microorganisms and macroorganisms necessary for plant health.

Bio-dynamic gardeners believe in planting and harvesting crops according to correct phases of the moon and other planets and the signs of the Zodiac through which the moon is moving at the time. See ASTROLOGICAL GARDENING.

Plants are seen as intimately interconnected with insects and other organisms in the soil and air necessary for pollination, beneficial predation, and for nutrient accessibility and antibiotics. Inorganic fertilizers and pest controls can be injurious to the entire organism—the planet earth.

BIOLOGICAL CONTROL. The forces of nature, left to themselves, tend to balance each other. If, however, natural controls are interrupted by heavy applications of wide-spectrum pesticides and soil amendments, the balance can be upset, sometimes resulting in new and greater buildups of pest populations and new pests developing out of previously innocuous species.

Gardeners and farmers who wish to restore or

promote the balance of nature use a number of biological or organic controls:

1. Beneficial predator and parasitic insects. Lady beetles prey on APHIDS and scales, and the Vedalia lady beetles on cottony-cushion scale found on citrus plants. Ground beetles will control gypsy moths and other caterpillars. Braconid and chalcid WASPS parasitize many BEETLES and MOTHS, as well as mealybugs and aphids. The tiny trichogramma wasp, useful against borers and tomato hornworms, is widely available commercially. So are lacewings, often used against army worms and Colorado potato bugs. Ambush and assassin bugs, praying mantises, and damsel bugs are voracious eaters of other insects. See also INSECTS, BENEFICIAL.

2. Beneficial bacilli are used to infect worms and grubs. Effective against many caterpillars is BACILLUS THURINGIENSIS (Bt), often used as dust or spray against cabbage worms on all brassicas or for corn earworms. Another control available is the BACILLUS POPILLIAE, milky spore disease, which attacks the larvae of the Japanese beetle when introduced among the roots where the grubs feed, especially in lawns. It spreads easily and so can be potent for up to fifteen years.

3. Beneficial plants, used both as materials for sprays and as companion plants for deterring insects from nearby crop plants or ornamentals. Garlic is the best example because its odor and aura of allyl sulfide is very repellent, both in sprays and as a companion for other plants. Onions and chives of the same family and hot peppers are protective and excellent for sprays. Helpful against aphids are those allium plants and also nasturtiums, coriander, anise, petunias, and basil. Sprays from basil help against potato bugs. Tansy will repel ants. Dormant oil sprays destroy pests on trees in the spring. See COMPANION PLANTING; SPRAYING.

Dusts made from wheat bran or flour and lime are effective against various bugs. Sprays or dusts made from the so-called botanicals ROTENONE, PYRETHRUM, ryania, and sabadilla are potent pest controls. Use rotenone only after the bees have gone to hive at dusk. See also DUSTING.

4. Various soaps can be helpful. Good plain kitchen soap mixed with water and lime will act on an insect's outer membrane and will control spider mites. Rinse sprayed plants an hour or so after using. Commercially obtainable insecticidal soaps are relatively mild but effective when sprayed directly on the insect. Any organic spray can be more clinging if soap or detergent is added, 1 tbsp. per gal. of spray.

5. Pheromones have been used to lure male insects to a sticky surface and to sterilize them, thus reducing future generations. It is not yet known what the long-range ecological effects of such a practice may be. See PHEROMONE.

6. Traps and other physical barriers, though not actually biological, are used in the form of snares or lures and scratchy or dehydrating deterrents. Traps baited with molasses will lure grasshoppers and codling moths. Sticky bands around trees prevent females from going up the trunk to lay eggs. Net covers protect trees and other plants subject to attack. Wood ashes, lime, and DIATOMACEOUS EARTH spread around the base of plants make barriers to repel soft-bodied pests.

7. A major way to reduce the danger of pests is to use the good garden practices that produce strong healthy plants. Excellent tilth and a well-balanced, nutritious soil promote healthy plants that are more disease- and pest-resistant. Weeding is necessary to remove plants that also attract pests; and careful cleanup of garden refuse will disturb larvae and, when burned, destroy them. Organic mulches, in place of herbicides, help to enrich the soil and can act as a deterrent when insects seek to reach the base of stems. Selection of resistant varieties of vegetables, flowers, and grains is always wise, both as insect prevention and protection against fungal and bacterial disease. When the above methods make up most of the practices of gardening and agricultural programs, the program is called INTEGRATED PEST MANAGEMENT (IPM). See also INSECT CONTROL.

BIRCH. Common name for BETULA, a genus of hardy, deciduous trees of distinct decorative value. The Birch Family is BETULACEAE.

BIRDFOOT VIOLET. Common name for *Viola pedata*, a species of violet with finely cut leaves that thrives in open gardens with sandy soil; see VIOLA.

BIRD-OF-PARADISE FLOWER. Common name for STRELITZIA, a genus of South African perennial herbs whose flower shape resembles a bird taking flight.

BIRDS. The aesthetic value of birds—with their sprightly movement, vigorous, usually pleasing songs, and dashing colors—cannot fail to attract attention and increase the pleasure of a garden. Birds add charm and character to even the smallest plot, their subtle instincts often astounding the intelligence of observers.

Efforts can be made to attract and protect these feathered creatures for economic reasons as well as for their charm and beauty. Usually gardeners appreciate the vast contribution birds make to the garden. For example, insects form a large part of avian sustenance, and birds are most numerous and active just at those times when harmful insect populations are at their peak. Birds also consume large quantities of weed seeds at a time when fall winds threaten to broadcast them over the land. In rural areas, birds of prey consume many small rodents troublesome in the garden. The abundance and voracious habits of some small birds, however, frequently present serious local problems; the English sparrow and European starling are common offenders.

PROTECTING THE BIRDS

Pesticides, cats, red squirrels, and snakes are the most troublesome enemies of birds in the garden. Most birds are exceedingly wary and must be assured of their safety before entering the garden. Individuals quickly communicate their caution to an entire flock, and months may pass before birds of some species will be comfortable in an area.

The extensive use of poisonous insecticides takes its toll on birds. Many dead ones are found in rainy weather after spraying programs have been conducted over wide areas, and some species are near extinction due to overuse of dangerous chemicals that leach into water systems. The use of the various effective nonpoisonous insecticides now available and other biological controls is recommended wherever practical.

ATTRACTING BIRDS TO THE GARDEN

Bird populations can be increased where the environment is congenial. There is no doubt that individual birds return to the same locality year after year. Studies show that many birds return to the same stations for several years. Water and food are the most potent attractions, and bird life is always abundant where these are provided.

Water can be supplied in shallow pans that deepen gradually toward the center. Cement or clay is better material for the birdbath since metal has too smooth a surface for secure footing. The bath should be placed in the open, away from shrubs or trees that might harbor enemies. Elevated positions are preferable, but the bath can be placed on the ground if in the open. The nesting population especially will increase where a constant supply of water is assured.

The birds' food supply in the garden can be classified as artificial or natural. The simplest types of artificial food accepted by all birds are commercial bird seed and small grains. Others include suet, nut meats, cereals, peppers, and a large variety of vegetable seeds. Although birds will usually eat bread crumbs and other baked goods, it is seldom advisable to give them anything with artificial ingredients that differ widely from their natural diet. Wild small fruits and weed seeds form a large part of the birds' diet whenever they are available. Birds especially enjoy uncultivated headlands along fences and property lines. Hedgerows of wild fruits and flowering shrubs will furnish food as well as nesting sites.

Providing food for the seed-eating birds presents some difficulty; they feed upon weeds which, obviously, are not cultivated. There are, however, a number of annuals that will prove attractive to this group if they can be sown in out-of-the-way corners and allowed to go to seed. These are *Amaranthus, Aster, Centaurea,*

(MILLET), *Helianthus* (sunflower), *Monarda* (bee balm), *Myosotis*, *Papaver* (poppy), *Portulaca*, and *Zinnia*. Other annuals adapted to local conditions can be added to this list by observing birds as they feed upon the plants. *Alnus* (alder), *Betula* (birch), *Cedrus* (cedar), *Fraxinus* (ash), *Larix* (larch), and *Pinus* (pine) are the trees most attractive to the seed-eating birds.

Catering to the needs and desires of fruit-eating birds is most important where fruit trees and small fruits are cultivated and must be protected. The raids of birds in gardens that have only one or two fruit trees are far more disastrous than those in orchards. The orchard provides many trees and generally the stealing is scattered over the whole area, whereas in the garden, one tree is usually stripped when the fruit is half ripe.

The following fruit trees and shrubs (listed in order of their value) are preferred by birds and help to protect cultivated trees: *Morus* (mulberry), *Myrica pensylvanica* (bayberry), *Rubus* (blackberry or raspberry), *Lonicera* (honeysuckle), *Vitis* (wild grape), *Vaccinium* (blueberry), *Rhus* (sumac), *Cornus* (dogwood), *Viburnum* (blackhaw), *Sambucus* (elder), *Malus* (dwarf apple), *Crataegus* (hawthorn), *Sassafras*, *Ilex* (holly), *Sorbus* (mountain-ash), and *Lindera benzoin* (spicebush). The widely planted *Berberis thunbergii* (Japanese barberry), frequently advocated by nurserymen for providing bird food, is actually of little value for this purpose. *Prunus* (wild cherries) are excellent bird food, but in many regions the trees are unpopular because they host tent caterpillars. In selecting varieties to protect cultivated fruits, try to use the wild forms of the same kinds that are cultivated and choose those that ripen earlier than the cultivated crops (such as wild cherry or chokecherry to protect sour cherry trees). Additional information on feeding birds can be obtained from your local extension service or Audubon Society.

NESTING AND NEST BOXES

Most migratory birds travel north in large flocks in the spring. The males of many species come several days in advance of the females and promptly begin to look for nesting sites and

mates. As they find mates they abandon the flock and locate a territory to which they lay claim. Many birds will fight to drive others of the same species from the land that they have staked out. This territory will be their nesting site, and if a garden offers the proper protection, water, and food, it will probably have several bird tenants.

It is during the nesting season that the greatest mortality occurs. Therefore, the most precaution for the birds' protection should be exercised at this time. The growing nestlings consume enormous quantities of insects, which are generally gathered from a comparatively small area around the nest. Hence the garden with several nests will reap the greatest benefits.

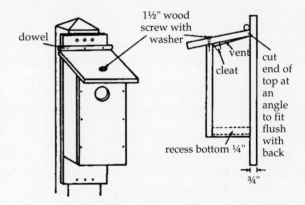

Simple, effective birdhouse

Birds that prefer holes in trees for nesting can be induced to accept nesting boxes. Bluebirds, house wrens, swallows, woodpeckers, and chickadees are some of the common birds that nest in birdhouses. Many types are offered for sale or can be made at home without difficulty. The roof should pitch sharply, the eaves should extend well beyond the box, and the entrance should be placed well up under the eaves. Box dimensions vary with the size and species of bird, but the average birdhouse should be about 6" x 6" x 8" with a round hole 1½ in. across for the entrance. There should be no perch next to the door, and the box should be set on a tree or pole at least 6 ft. off the ground. Houses for purple martins can contain many compartments and should be placed 15–20 ft. high. Boxes for other birds should have only one compartment.

Several species will nest around buildings, among them phoebes, chimney swifts, robins, barn swallows, and owls. Owls usually select cavities in trees, but nest boxes can be helpful. They require a larger house, usually 10" x 10" x 24". When they can be induced to nest in or near the garden, owls are especially valuable because moles, field mice, and other small rodents form the greater part of their diet.

Cedars and other coniferous trees are preferred by tree-nesting birds, which always select a dense growth in which to hide their nests. Closely planted trees and shrubs seldom fail to attract them. Ground-nesting birds like grassy fields. Unless the garden is a very large one, it is not likely to offer sites favorable to this class, but song sparrows will accept conditions offered in the garden more readily than other ground-nesting birds. As many as three families of song sparrows can be found in a garden where grass and low shrubs are allowed to grow wild along the borders.

PROTECTING FRUIT

Bird nets—light, thin plastic nets—are great for protecting a small fruit tree or bush just before the fruit is ripe. Birds dislike anything that interferes with their wings, especially if it is hard to see. Timing is everything. If put up too early, the birds will get accustomed to the net and find ways to get through it. If put up too late, after the birds have discovered the fruit, the birds claim ownership, and not much will dissuade them.

Birds have excellent eyesight, and good quality models of predatory birds will help to scare them. Inflatable plastic owls and hawks are available to hang in trees while fruit is ripening. Hawk silhouettes will also keep birds from flying into large glass windows. Plastic snakes and spirals printed with snake patterns hung in trees or near the object of a bird's attention, are also effective repellents.

Shiny aluminum pie pans or similar reflecting objects can be hung from lines so that they flap in a breeze. The resulting flashes of light irritate birds and will keep them away for a few days.

Sudden, sharp, and high-frequency sound set off at random or broadcast from speakers will repel birds; this is especially useful to keep them out of buildings. Although high-frequency sound is not audible to humans, it irritates them just the same and is not recommended for places where people work or animals are kept. Distress calls of pest birds broadcast from speakers will repel starlings and blackbirds in some areas.

BIRD'S-FOOT FERN. Common name for *Pellaea mucronata*, a tropical fern with fronds and pinnules often folded in half; see PELLAEA.

BIRD'S-FOOT TREFOIL. A common name for *Lotus corniculatus*, a leguminous perennial introduced from Europe; see LOTUS.

BIRD'S-NEST FERN. Common name for *Asplenium nidus*, a popular fern with highly polished fronds 1–5 ft. long; see ASPLENIUM.

BISHOP'S-CAP. Common name for MITELLA, a genus of woodland herbs with basal leaves and small flowers. Bishop's-cap cactus is *Astrophytum myriostigma*; see ASTROPHYTUM.

BISHOP'S WEED. Common name for *Aegopodium podagraria*, a coarse herb naturalized in North America and sometimes used as an edging; see AEGOPODIUM.

Protecting a tree with netting

BITTERROOT. Common name for *Lewisia rediviva,* the state flower of Montana, a deciduous herb with silky blossoms; see LEWISIA.

BITTERSWEET. Common name given to two unrelated, climbing vines. It most correctly applies to *Solanum dulcamara,* which bears poisonous red berries and is naturalized throughout North America; see SOLANUM.

Also known as bittersweet, *Celastrus scandens* is prized for its colored fruits; see CELASTRUS.

BIXA (BIK sah) **orellana.** A tree from the American tropics, commonly called annatto, grown in south Florida and elsewhere in Zones 10–11 for the orange-hued dye of that name obtained from the pulp surrounding the seeds in its small fruits. It is used to color butter, cheeses, and some silks. As a greenhouse plant, it is sometimes grown from cuttings of flowering branches, but outdoor trees are usually grown from seeds.

BLACKBERRY. Various tall, upright to trailing perennials with thorny biennial stems. All are brambles (members of the genus RUBUS) and therefore are closely related to raspberries. Dewberry is sometimes called trailing blackberry.

Blackberries thrive in well-drained, preferably clay-loam soils, liberally supplied with humus and moisture. They are propagated by suckers and root cuttings. Plants are set in early spring 3 ft. apart in rows 8 ft. apart. Common practice is clean cultivation until midsummer, when a COVER CROP is sown, but in home gardens deep mulching with cut weeds, lawn clippings, and any other vegetable debris available is preferable.

When the young shoots reach 30–36 in. in length, the tips should be pinched off to develop low branches and make the stems so stiff that they will need no supports. The following spring the branches can be shortened to 18 in. or less while the plants are dormant and again after the blossom buds have formed. Cutting back too severely while dormant, however, may destroy so many blossom buds as to seriously reduce the yield of fruit. After they have fruited, the old

stems should be cut out as already noted. They will die during the winter anyway, so their prompt removal and burning helps to clean up the patch, admits more air and light into the bushes, and controls plant diseases and insects.

Blackberries can be trained to a fence or trellis.

At picking time blackberries, like raspberries, should be so ripe that they fall off the vine when barely touched. If you must tug the fruit to harvest, the berry is not ripe.

PROBLEMS OF BLACKBERRIES

As a home garden fruit, the blackberry deserves high standing because the berries can be had in the perfection of full ripeness—which they do not have when purchased, since berries for market must be picked while still hard, rather acid, and lacking the delicious flavor that characterizes the best varieties when fully ripe. At this stage they drop into the hand at a slight touch.

On the other hand, blackberries offer three disadvantages under ordinary treatment. (1) The stems are often winter-killed, sometimes to the ground, so that no fruit forms the following summer. (2) Unless properly managed the plants are likely to spread in all directions by means of suckers and form impenetrable thickets. (3) The plants languish and fruits shrivel in hot, dry seasons (and in the arid Southwest), though this tendency can be partially overcome by mulching and irrigation.

Winter-killing can be partially, if not wholly, prevented by growing only varieties known to be generally hardy in the region, by cutting out all old canes and puny young shoots immediately after the fruiting season so as to direct the plant food and water they would consume into the sturdy canes chosen to bear fruit the following season, and by ripening the wood of these canes.

This ripening of the canes is dependent upon the amount of water and the quantity and character of plant food in the soil from midsummer to early fall. When water is ample during this period the plants develop strongly. When, however, it is insufficient then but is abundant later in the autumn, the plants are likely to make additional growth which, failing to ripen, is killed by the winter. Also, when nitrogenous plant food is too abundant from early fall onward, the canes continue to grow too late to become mature before winter, with the same result. It is, therefore, important to avoid supplying strongly nitrogenous fertilizers after midspring.

The problem of suckers springing up between the rows and in other places where they are not wanted can be largely solved by correct cultural practices. First, to get rid of such suckers, pull them up while less than a foot high. Do not cut them off, as new ones soon sprout from their cut stumps. Second, to prevent excessive suckering, avoid cutting or injuring the plant roots in the space between the rows. That means do not cultivate too deeply. In fact, a deep mulch left from year to year is preferable to clean cultivation, as it not only lessens the chance of suckers, but also maintains the cool, moist soil conditions that blackberries prefer.

The underside of the leaves is often covered with a bright orange rust. This fungus is perennial in the underground parts of the plants, so the only remedy is to pull up and burn diseased specimens. Crown gall is also common, and rose scale may be present. Remove and burn canes infested with cane and root borers at the annual pruning. Spray with an insecticide for leaf miners. See also INSECT CONTROL.

VARIETIES

Blackberries. The names of common varieties depend on the nursery distributing them. With two notable exceptions (the Oregon Evergreen and the Himalaya, imported from Europe), blackberry varieties grown in North America have been developed since about 1850 from native species, primarily from *R. allegheniensis*. Popular fruit producers are Alfred, Darrow, and Eldorado. Given proper winter protection, most can be hardy to Zone 4.

Dewberries. A group sometimes known as trailing blackberries, these include *R. flagellaris* (American dewberry) and *R. ursinus* (Pacific dewberry); there are several varieties of these species. They deserve a place in home gardens because the fruit can be allowed to ripen fully, thus excelling those purchased. Plants root at joints, and tips are propagated by the latter instead of by suckers as in blackberries. Also, they bear earlier by a week or two than the upright, nontrailing forms. Cultivated like blackberries, dewberries require support for their long, slender stems. Plants should be set 5–7 ft. apart during early spring, in light, well-drained loam, and the young shoots tied to poles the first year. The second spring these stems should be shortened to 4 or 5 ft. In summer, only four to six new shoots should be allowed to grow, and their tops should be pinched after they reach 5 ft. Attach to wires strung along posts.

Lucretia is the hardiest of the North American varieties (to Zone 4). Boysenberry, a hybrid of the Pacific varieties, is hardy to Zone 6 but does not usually do well in the eastern states. Its dark red berries ripen in midsummer and have an excellent flavor.

Loganberry, *R. ursinus* var. *loganobaccus*, originated in California and is extensively grown on the Pacific coast for its red fruits, which are used for eating and cooking, fresh, dried, canned, and for the production of juice. Hardy in Zones 7–9, the plants are tender to frost and cannot be grown successfully in cold regions, though the roots may live over winter.

Youngberry, *R. ursinus* cv. 'Young', developed from a cross between loganberry and the Mayes-Austin dewberry, is a vigorous, half-hardy (Zones 5–6), thorny vine bearing dark purple berries that turn black when thoroughly ripe. Produced over a long period of several months, they have a pleasant, sub-acid flavor and are excellent shippers.

See also RUBUS; RASPBERRY.

BLACKBERRY-LILY.
A common name for *Belamcanda chinensis*, a hardy perennial with orange flowers and blackberrylike fruit; see BELAMCANDA.

BLACK-EYED-SUSAN.
Common name for *Rudbeckia hirta*, a common wildflower with dark disks and yellow rays; see RUDBECKIA.

BLACKHAW.
Common name for *Viburnum prunifolium* and *V. rufidulum*, both North American shrubs or trees with handsome foliage, white flowers, and colored berries; see VIBURNUM.

BLACK LOCUST.
Common name for *Robinia pseudoacacia*, a tree with white flowers in dense racemes; see ROBINIA.

BLACK-OLIVE.
Common name now usually applied to *Bucida buceras*, a tropical shade tree; see BUCIDA. It was originally applied to a smaller tree, *Terminalia muelleri*; see TERMINALIA.

BLACK SPOT.
A fungus disease that quickly spreads its spores through the garden, causing black spots on the leaves followed by yellowing and defoliation. Probably the most widely distributed and generally destructive rose disease, black spot thrives in wet conditions. Keep foliage dry, avoid watering late in the day, and try a drip irrigation system. Clean up the rose garden each fall to prevent the disease from overwintering on dead plant material. Apply fresh mulch in the spring. When planning the garden, mix yellow roses, which are particularly susceptible, with more disease-resistant colors. See also ROSE.

BLADDERNUT.
Common name for STAPHYLEA, a genus of deciduous shrubs or trees found in temperate regions of the Northern Hemisphere.

BLADDERWORT.
Common name for UTRICULARIA, a genus of aquatic and terrestrial herbs.

BLANCH.
The process of whitening the shoots, leaves, or stems of a plant or preventing their becoming green by excluding light. Its main objectives are to modify the appearance, tenderness, pungency, acidity, bitterness, or other characteristics of vegetables and to improve their quality by enhancing palatability.

The desired results are attained by such methods as boarding up or EARTHING-UP such plants as celery, leek, cardoon, and Florence fennel; by breaking or tying the leaves of cauliflower and romaine lettuce over the newly forming heads; by covering endive plants with flowerpots a week or two before they are needed during the summer and fall; by covering sea-kale and rhubarb clumps with barrels, boxes, tile, or large flowerpots in early spring (the rhubarb does not actually turn white but becomes more pale and tender); and by forcing chicory roots in a dark cellar to produce barbe de capucin (or, if they are buried in manure or other soft material, to produce French endive, see CHICORY).

The principal precaution to observe in blanching is to see that free moisture is not enclosed in the blanched parts, where it can cause decay and spoilage.

BLANDFORDIA
(bland FOR dee ah). A genus of fibrous-rooted herbs from Australia, belonging to the Liliaceae (Lily Family). The large leaves are borne mostly at the base of the 2–3 ft. stems, which bear the large showy flowers, usually orange-red and yellow tipped, in drooping terminal spikes. Small bright fruits succeed the bloom. A plant for the greenhouse or for mild climates, it is difficult to grow. Air and moisture are essential, but drafts are fatal, and plants must be carefully shaded during the growing season. Soil should be chiefly peat with a little loam and charcoal. Plants should be potted in early spring after flowering and left undisturbed for two years. *B. grandiflora* is one of the best forms, with yellow to orange flowers, red at the base.

BLANKETFLOWER. Common name for the genus GAILLARDIA, specifically the perennial *G. aristata* and the annual *G. pulchella*, both popular garden flowers.

BLAST. Term often applied to the blighting or sudden death of young buds, flower clusters (inflorescences), or fruits. It can be a symptom or result of disease, or can be caused by some external influence, as weather, excess or insufficient moisture, or other reason.

BLAZING-STAR. Common name for at least three genera of flowering plants, including CHAMAELIRIUM, LIATRIS, and MENTZELIA.

BLECHNUM (BLEK num). A genus of ferns found mostly in the Southern Hemisphere, and commonly known only as houseplants. Some are hardy in the warmer temperate zones. The fronds vary in height and are pinnate or pinnatifid. They require plenty of moisture, and many species grow near water. The new growth of many species has a beautiful pink or red color.

PRINCIPAL SPECIES

B. discolor (crown fern) grows in a symmetrical rosette over a stout rhizome. The 2–4 ft., deeply pinnatifid, light green fronds have glossy black petioles. It is hardy in warmer temperate areas. Native to Australia and New Zealand, it prefers moist to wet soils where it will tolerate more sun.

B. gibbum (dwarf tree fern), from Fiji, New Caledonia, and New Hebrides, produces light green, pinnate fronds 1–2 ft. long. Older ferns develop a short trunk, up to 5 ft.

B. occidentale (hammock fern) is stoloniferous and makes a useful ground cover in subtropical to tropical regions, where it can be grown outside. The fronds are pinnate, about 18 in. long, and are a lovely salmon-pink when new. Found in Florida, Mexico, the West Indies, and South America, it can be grown as a houseplant.

B. penna-marina (dwarf hard fern) is a small, creeping fern that is moderately hardy. It grows among rocks in a loose, organic soil and can be an excellent ground cover where hardy. The fronds are pinnate and about 12 in. long. It is found in Australia, New Zealand, and South America.

B. serrulatum (saw fern) produces creeping rhizomes carrying 2–6 in. pinnate fronds along their length. Common in swamps and ditches from Florida through Central America, it is probably identical to *B. indicum* of Australia, Malaysia, and Polynesia.

B. spicant (deer fern), found in moist, coniferous forests and rock ledges, is a 6–24 in. pinnate fern that forms a terrestrial rosette. The fertile fronds stand erect at the center of the crown, surrounded by the shorter sterile fronds. Quite hardy, it is common in northwestern North America, northeast Asia, and Europe.

BLEEDING. The leaking of sap or pitch from any wound, especially one made in pruning. Deciduous trees will bleed more heavily after pruning than evergreen trees, but the loss of sap is not considered harmful to the tree. The moisture lost is only what would have been distributed to the removed branch.

BLEEDING-HEART. Common name for DICENTRA, a genus of hardy perennials with heart-shaped red or white flowers.

BLESSED-THISTLE. Common name for *Cnicus benedictus* whose tops, used as tonics, were said to be the origin of benedictine liqueur (see CNICUS) and for *Silybum marianum*, which is also known as holy-, St. Mary's-, or milk-thistle (see SILYBUM).

BLIGHT. A term commonly used to describe the browning of foliage, blossoms, or shoots suddenly caused by pathogenic (disease-causing) organisms. The word usually indicates death of plant tissues over an extended area rather than a local lesion, such as a leaf spot or canker, and is applied to various types of diseases, such as FIRE BLIGHT of pears and apples, CHESTNUT BLIGHT, ASCOCHYTA BLIGHT, ALTERNARIA and BOTRYTIS blights. See also DISEASE.

BLISTER BEETLE. This member of the insect family Meloidae is plant eating as an adult but beneficial in its larval stage. It spends one or two winters as a pseudopupa, then moves into the true pupal state. In June or July, swarms of these beetles appear and feed on flowers, vegetables, young trees, and vines. The females lay up to 100 eggs in holes in the ground. The eggs hatch in two or three weeks as larvae that eat many grasshopper eggs. There are four molts before they burrow down to form the cell for the pseudopupa. They are frequently found on asters.

Blister beetle

Of the 250 species in the United States, some are black, but others are gray, brown, or yellow. Blisters develop from their secreted oil (cantharidin), so when hand picking, be sure to wear gloves. To get them off plants, shake the plants so the beetles drop into a container with water and a layer of kerosene, turpentine, or paint thinner. A dust of lime and flour or sabadilla is effective. Floating row covers can also protect plants from the adults. This beetle used to be collected for use as "Spanish fly," an aphrodisiac plaster similar to a mustard plaster.

BLISTER RUST. A fungus disease prevalent on white pines, causing damage to all parts of the trees and eventually killing them; see WHITE PINE BLISTER RUST; RUSTS.

BLOOD, DRIED. This fairly quick acting organic or nitrogenous animal fertilizer is prepared by evaporating, drying, and grinding blood and nonfatty refuse at slaughterhouses. Varying in color from red to black, it also contains a varying but generally large amount of nitrogen, ranging from 13–15%. The red product is of better quality than the black, which is often mixed with more or less hair, dirt, and other useless or undesirable material with a nitrogen content rarely above 12%. Dried blood is usually applied to the soil as a constituent of a prepared complete fertilizer mixture. As a nitrogenous tonic it can be worked into the soil at the rate of 3–5 lb. per 100 sq. ft. three or four times during the growing season. It can also be mixed with potting soil at the rate of a 6-in. potful to each bushel of soil. See also FERTILIZER.

BLOODLEAF. Common name for IRESINE, a genus of herbs and shrubby plants grown for their colorful foliage.

BLOOD-LILY. Common name for HAEMANTHUS, a genus of showy bulbous plants with clustered red flowers.

BLOODROOT. Common name for *Sanguinaria canadensis*, a white-flowered perennial herb whose root contains red juice; see SANGUINARIA.

BLOOMERIA (bloo MEE ree ah). A genus of cormous plants from California and Mexico, hardy in Zones 9–11, and belonging to the Amaryllidaceae (Amaryllis Family).

B. crocea (golden-stars) is the species usually cultivated. It produces an 18-in. stem from amid basal, grasslike foliage, and it is topped with an airy 4-in. sphere of starry golden flowers, each petal having a dark stripe. Attractive and naturalized in mild regions in wild gardens or meadows, it is easily forced in pots in a cool greenhouse or coldframe.

Bloomeria crocea

BLOOMING-SALLY. A common name for *Epilobium augustifolium*, a perennial herb with long spikes of purple flowers; see EPILOBIUM.

BLUE AMARYLLIS. Common name for *Worsleya rayneri*, a summer-flowering bulb from South America; see WORSLEYA.

BLUEBEARD. Common name for CARYOPTERIS, a genus of shrubs with showy, late-blooming, lavender or white flowers.

BLUEBELL-CREEPER. Common name for *Sollya heterophylla*, a tender, climbing evergreen shrub with blue flowers; see SOLLYA.

BLUEBERRY. Common name for various North American species of VACCINIUM including *V. corymbosum* (highbush blueberry), *V. angustifolium* (lowbush blueberry), and *V. ashei* (rabbiteye blueberry).

Many cultivars of the highbush type have been developed and are ideal both for home gardens and commercial production. Among these are the popular Bluecrop, Blueray, Earliblue, Jersey, and Northland. The lowbush type is widely grown commercially where it is native in the northeastern states. Lowbush hybrids have also been developed and are better suited for colder regions than the *V. corymbosum* cultivars. The rabbit-eye blueberries are best grown in warm climates and include the Callaway, Garden Blue, Manditoo, Suwanee, and Tifblue.

Blueberries need a rich and acid soil—a pH of 4.5–5 is ideal. Since many garden soils are less acid than that, peat moss, composted oak leaves, and sulfur can be worked into the soil, and mulches of pine needles or oak leaves can be spread to increase acidity. Lime and wood ashes should not be used on the plants, nor should mulches of cedar chips or bark. Acid fertilizers, such as those used on broadleaf evergreens, provide the best nutrients.

Blueberry plants are grown mostly from cuttings, but the plants do not root easily. Some plants are currently being grown by tissue culture. Highbush blueberry plants grow from 5–10 ft. tall or more and should be set 6 ft. apart in rows spaced 8 ft. apart. Blueberry plants grow slowly, and although most begin to bear within two or three years, it may be ten years before they are mature, especially in the North.

Pruning methods depend on the climatic zone. In the South, they are pruned much like any bush fruit. Old wood is cut out every few years, and the bearing branches thinned. In Zones 3–4, very little pruning is necessary and consists mostly of the occasional thinning of twiggy tips of the branches. Such severe pruning as is necessary in warmer climates would make them unproductive for many years.

ENEMIES

Disease. Among the diseases that attack the blueberry are botrytis tip blight, which can kill the entire annual growth; and mummy berry, which makes the infected berries become brown and dry. Pruning the infected parts is the best control. Stunt is a virus disease that dwarfs both plants and berries; destroying the entire plant is the only control. Stem canker causes cracks on the stems, and only resistant varieties should be planted. Double spot leaf disease causes defoliation and can be controlled by spraying with a fungicide. The latter two diseases are most common in the South.

Insect Pests. Blueberry maggot, one of the most serious insect pests, is difficult to control without the use of poison sprays that would make the fruit unsafe. Rotenone and pyrethrum are favored insecticides because they wash off easily. Other pests can usually be controlled by spraying early in the season with an insecticide. Birds are among the worst pests, and covering the bushes with netting is usually the best way for home gardeners to protect their crop.

BLUEBLOSSOM. Common name for *Ceanothus thyrsiflorus*, an evergreen shrub or tree with pale blue to purplish flowers. See CEANOTHUS.

BLUECURLS. Common name for TRICHOSTEMA, a genus of shrubby herbs.

BLUE DAISY. Common name for species of FELICIA, a genus of tender herbs or subshrubs with yellow-centered, blue-petaled flowers.

BLUE-DICKS. Common name for *Dichelostemma pulchellum*, a cormous plant with small funnel-shaped lilac flowers; see DICHELOSTEMMA.

BLUE-EYED-GRASS. Common name for SISY-RINCHIUM, a genus of small perennial herbs that have grasslike foliage and small blue or yellow flowers.

BLUE-EYED-MARY. Common name for *Collinsia verna*, an annual herb with blue and purplish flowers.

BLUEGRASS. Common name for POA, a genus of perennial grasses, including many often used in lawns.

BLUE PALM. Common name for *Brahea armata*, a sturdy palm tree covered with a thick ruffle of old leaves; see BRAHEA.

BLUE-PALMETTO. Common name for *Rhapidophyllum hystrix*, a dwarf palm with needle-sharp foliage.

BLUESTAIN. Several species of fungi that, usually following attacks of bark beetles, stain the wood of living trees or fresh lumber a gray or blue color. Pines are especially subject to it. See BARK BEETLE.

BLUETS. Common name for *Hedyotis caerulea*, a small, tufted herb with attractive solitary flowers; see HEDYOTIS.

BLUEWEED. A common name for *Echium vulgare*, a Eurasian weed naturalized in dry places in the United States; see ECHIUM.

BOG GARDEN. Wet areas along the margins of ponds, springs, or streams can be dressed with specialized plants and techniques; see AQUATIC PLANTS.

BOLANDRA (boh LAN drah). A genus in the Saxifragaceae (Saxifrage Family) native to the northwestern United States and hardy to Zone 6. *B. oregana*, a small delicate herb with lobed, mottled leaves and small purple flowers is sometimes grown in woodland or shaded rock gardens.

BOLTONIA (bohl TOH nee ah). A genus of tall perennial herbs belonging to the Asteraceae (Aster Family), and commonly known as false chamomile. They are hardy in Zones 3–8 and are easily grown in the border or grouped in the wild garden.

Boltonia asteroides

B. asteroides, found in the eastern states, grows to 8 ft. and has small heads of asterlike flowers with white, purple, or lavender rays. Var. *latisquama*, found in the southwestern states, has larger, blue-violet ray flowers.

BOMAREA (boh MAY ree ah). A genus of South American twining plants sometimes grown in the cool greenhouse, or outdoors in warm climates, where they prefer partial shade. They make good pot plants with liberal feeding but do best under glass when planted in a bench or bed. Fibrous loam, leaf mold, and sand, with some old manure added, make a suitable compost. They need plenty of water when growing. Propagation is by seed or rooted divisions of the underground stems.

PRINCIPAL SPECIES
B. edulis (white-Jerusalem-artichoke) has tubers said to be edible and bears short clusters of rose-colored flowers tipped with green.

B. multiflora bears dense clusters of reddish flowers with brown spots.

B. oligantha has few-flowered clusters of dull red-and-yellow blossoms spotted brown.

BOMBAX (BAHM baks) **ceiba.** A large tree that grows to 90 ft. and has a massive trunk often made more impressive by tall, thin buttress roots running several feet up the tree. The common name, red silk-cotton tree, refers to the color of the flowers and the fiber in the pods. This native of tropical Asia is hardy in Zones 10–11, where it is used as a specimen tree.

BONEMEAL. This rather slow acting organic fertilizer is valuable principally for the phosphorus it contains, which may range from 23–25%. It also contains 1–3% nitrogen in readily available form. Depending on the fineness to which it is ground, bonemeal requires one to three years or even more for its plant-food elements to become available. While not, therefore, a source of a quick supply of phosphorus, it is a useful and popular fertilizer for garden use.

It is generally applied at the rate of about 10 lb. per 100 sq. ft. and is especially satisfactory for roses and other plants that prefer a neutral or slightly alkaline soil. It is absolutely safe and causes no burning such as may result from the heavy use of more rapidly available plant foods. It is a somewhat more expensive form of phosphorus than acid-phosphate (superphosphate), which is the most common phosphatic ingredient of mixed fertilizers, but it is a good material to keep on hand and use in potting-soil mixtures, in preparing garden soil, and in top-dressing perennials or other established plants.

BONESET. A common name for *Eupatorium perfoliatum*, a gray-flowered herb cultivated in old gardens for medicinal use; see EUPATORIUM.

BONSAI. This term refers to both the art of creating and the resulting trees that have been artificially dwarfed and trained into graceful or contorted shapes, to give them the appearance of old age or oddity. They grow from the normal seed of suitable tree species; there are no genetic bonsai. Practiced for centuries in China and Japan, the art of bonsai involves the selective pruning of a specimen's roots, branches, shoots, and foliage. By weighing, tying, or winding them with wire, the trunk and branches can be bent to a desired shape and direction to achieve upright, windswept, cascading, or weeping configurations. Bonsai can be grouped to create a miniature forest; rocks, figurines, pools, and paths can

be added to produce a tiny landscape in a dish.

Bonsai may be hundreds of years old. A mature bonsai is similar in age to that of its mature wild counterpart. Some are hardy and can be grown outdoors, while others require the constant warmth (59–70°F) of the indoors. All require high levels of filtered sunlight, high humidity, good ventilation, and must never dry out between watering. Good bonsai subjects include *Citrus* (lemon, orange, and grapefruit), *Crassula* (jade tree), *Ficus* (fig), *Pinus* (pine), *Punica* (pomegranate), and *Ulmus* (elm).

BORAGE. Common name for the genus BORAGO of hairy Mediterranean herbs. The Borage Family is BORAGINACEAE.

BORAGINACEAE (boh raj in AY see ee). The Borage Family, a group of plants grown in some cases as potherbs, in others for their ornamental foliage, and sometimes for their bright, usually small flowers. Mostly bristly herbs, a few are woody. The herbaceous kinds bear numerous small flowers on one side of a cyme resembling a spike, which is rolled at first, then straightening as the flowers develop. Among the genera of ornamental value are *Borago*, *Echium*, *Heliotropum*, *Mertensia* (Virginia-bluebells), *Myosotis* (forget-me-not), and *Onosma*.

BORAGO (boh RAY goh). A genus of hairy Mediterranean herbs, commonly known as borage. *B. laxiflora*, a low-growing perennial with blue flowers, is recommended for rock gardens. *B. officinalis*, is a rank-growing annual 2–3 ft. high whose young leaves, in Germany, are used for "greens." In the United States, it is sometimes planted as a honey plant and rarely for its ornamental loose racemes of blue flowers.

BORDEAUX MIXTURE. One of the oldest and most widely used fungicides, whose efficacy was discovered by accident. The vineyardists near Bordeaux, France, sprayed their vines with a bluish mixture of lime and copper sulfate to simulate a poison and thus prevent theft of the

grapes. In 1882, scientist Alexis Millardet reported that the mixture also protected the plants from
downy mildew. Bordeaux mixture was introduced to the United States in 1885 and is now
used for the control of many leaf spot and blight
diseases. Prepared Bordeaux mixture is obtainable at garden supply stores and is convenient
and economical for the small garden.

On certain crops the standard-strength mixture
can cause burning of the foliage or russeting of
apple and other leaves, which may be mistaken
for pest or disease injury; see SPRAYING. Continued use of Bordeaux mixture causes the leaves of
certain rose varieties to turn yellow and fall.

BORDERS. A border is a planting at the edge of
an area that is usually approached and viewed
from only one side. Borders can be located along
driveways, fences, foundations, walkways, or in
front of hedges and shrubs. Traditionally borders are proportional to their surroundings; for
instance, a very short walkway requires a narrow
border. Also, because borders can often be
accessed from only one side, they should be no
wider than five feet, or they will be very difficult
to maintain.

One border can be composed of evergreens:
coniferous, broad-leaved, flowering, or a mixture
of all three. Another can include deciduous
shrubs. Others can be comprised of hardy perennials, wild plants, or annuals and bedding plants.
However, such defined borders are usually less
effective—and some require more constant attention—than mixed plantings. Innumerable pleasing combinations can be made with plants
belonging to any or all of these groups. Changes
can be made occasionally, or even annually, so
that the border as a whole presents new effects
each year while the background remains constant. Thus, the well-planned, well-tended mixed
border offers the greatest opportunities for experiment and personal taste.

ANNUAL AND BULB BORDERS

If a border is to contain exclusively annuals, the
ground can be prepared in the spring if it is light;
if it is heavy, late autumn fitting is preferable.

For autumn conditioning, leave the ground
rough so the winter will soften and break up the
clods.

If the border will include hardy, large-flowering bulbs such as tulip, hyacinth, and crown-
imperial followed by annuals or bedding plants,
the soil should be prepared in autumn before
planting the bulbs. The bulbs can be either left in
the ground from year to year or dug after the
tops have died down, dried, cleaned, stored, and
replanted the following autumn. Though such
borders are attractive while in bloom, they are
less continuously interesting and involve more
work each year than do borders of perennials or
shrubs.

PERENNIAL AND SHRUB BORDERS

As perennial and shrubbery borders are permanent investments, they deserve thorough
preparation. This means deep digging and
preferably TRENCHING for deep-rooting, long-
lasting subjects such as peonies and dictamnus
(gasplant). The soil should be mixed with abundant humus (compost, leaf mold, commercial
humus, or peat moss) when forking it over.
Should the soil be heavy, these materials will
help lighten and loosen it. Late fall digging, leaving the clods scattered over winter, and scattering lime or wood ashes on the surface (about 1 lb.
to 10 sq. ft.) before raking in spring are also helpful. If the soil is wet, it must be drained. Naturally dry soil should be provided with some kind
of irrigation. Humus will also give body to a
loose, sandy soil and increase its ability to retain
moisture.

DESIGN AND CARE

In laying out a border, it is important to locate
the largest-growing subjects, especially the
shrubs first. They should go mostly in the background and always far enough apart to permit
development to full size without crowding.
Next, the plants that attain only medium size and
those that grow rapidly should be placed with
respect to each other and the larger plants. In
this way, all permanent plants are properly
placed regardless of how sparsely populated the
border may first appear. While the permanent

plants are developing to normal size and stature, any blank or bare spaces can be filled with annuals, bedding stock, and bulbous plants such as lilies, which include many tall and dwarf selections.

During the growing season, keep borders neat and clean by staking tall plants, destroying weeds, removing dead flower stems, feeding when necessary, stirring exposed soil to keep them loose and friable, and soaking the soil thoroughly whenever it becomes too dry. Just before winter, but after the ground freezes, apply a deep mulch, preferably of strawy stable manure, leaf mold, or both, if readily available; other good mulches are leaves, straw, compost, or any loose material. In spring, the coarse material including winter-killed tops and other debris should be raked off and added to the compost pile. The fine residual mulch material (or an application of pulverized manure and ground bone) should be worked into the soil by shallow forking. The only time a spade should be used in a border is when changes are to be made and plants removed, replaced, or reset.

Winter mulches that mat down, become sodden, and freeze solid should be avoided, especially where herbaceous perennials with leafy crowns are used. Evergreen branches and other loose materials are good. A deep covering of loose snow is an excellent natural blanket.

See also ANNUALS; BEDS; BULBS; PERENNIALS; SHRUBS.

BORERS. Borers are grubs or caterpillars, larvae of moths, or beetles that bore into both herbaceous and woody stems, attacking trees, shrubs, perennial and annual plants, and vegetables. Weak or newly set out plants attract them. Lack of sufficient water is a common cause, as well as insufficient nutrients. Several seasons of drought are usually followed by borer attacks, because of rootlet damage.

Flat-headed borers make shallow mines in the bark and sapwood of shade and fruit trees. Round-headed borers mine into the solid wood. The beetles of both are metallic and often beautifully colored. Their work on trees is usually obvious from little piles of sawdust near the hole. More often than not, the only way to deal with borers is to cut the stem and remove the pest, painting the wound afterward. They can be caught and killed by probing for them with a wire. Be vigilant in inspecting stalks and trunks on the south side, for borers seek the warmth of that side of plants. Cut off and burn infected branches, or stuff the hole with a paste of **Bacillus thuringiensis** (Bt). To prevent attacks, fertilize plants well. For iris borers, provide good drainage and parasitic nematodes. Wrap the trunks of young trees to prevent boring. Antidessicants on the trunks help. Clean up all debris: shred and plow down plant residues; trim perennials to the ground before winter; and pull up annuals in the fall.

Bent or broken tassels indicate the presence of the 1-in.-long European corn borer. This flesh-colored worm with small black spots hibernates in stalks and weeds and pupates in the spring. The adult brown moth lays eggs on the undersides of the leaves of corn, dahlias, and other plants. Larvae begin to emerge in a week or less and begin boring at once. European corn borers produce two generations each year, and it is the second brood

Peach tree borer, adult

that does the most damage. The first generation can be controlled in the home garden by water in holes each night, and newly hatched larvae will drown. Select resistant varieties and plant in late May, so the corn will mature when the danger of borer invasion is lowest. Soldier beetles are effective predatory insects against them. When removing borers by hand, make an insertion with your fingernail a little below the borer's entrance hole and slit the stalk to get at the pest.

The squash vine borer is a North American pest, occurring east of the Rocky Mountains. It can be very injurious when it infests pumpkins, gourds, cucumbers, muskmelons, and squashes. This borer winters as a larva or pupa in a silky cocoon, an inch or so below the surface of the soil. The adult moth is clear-winged and wasplike, with green, black, and orange markings. It appears about the time the vines begin to run and lays brown eggs on stems and petioles. Hatched borers emerge about a week later. When entered, the vines wilt and show greenish yellow excrement coming out of the bore holes. Later in the season, the borer enters the fruit as well. Slit the stems where the borers are with a knife or fingernail, kill the borer, and heap earth on the stem joints to promote new growth. After harvest, destroy the vines at once. Also, plant a second crop of summer squash for later maturing.

BORONIA (boh ROH nee ah). A genus of dwarf Australian shrubs of elegant habit, belonging to the Rutaceae (Rue Family). In cultivation they are usually grown as pot plants under cool greenhouse conditions. They have small fine leaves and are valued most for the delightful fragrance of their small flowers, which are mostly red or purple.

Propagation is by seed or cuttings, and plants bloom freely when young. After flowering, they should be cut back to encourage a good bushy growth. They can be plunged outdoors for the summer, but drainage and moisture should be monitored carefully since they will not stand drought or being waterlogged.

PRINCIPAL SPECIES

B. elatior has rosy red or purple flowers that do not open wide; they are borne in dense clusters along the ends of the branches.

B. heterophylla is the best kind for decorative purposes, with drooping pinkish flowers that stay partly closed.

B. megastigma has fragrant, open flowers of purplish maroon on the outside and yellow on the inside.

BORZICACTUS (bor zi KAK tus). A group of South American columnar cacti characterized by tubular, non-cleistogamous (wide opening, not closed as in CLEISTOCACTUS) flowers. Now considered to include, from a conservative point of view, many smaller groups such as *Arequipa*, *Arequipiopsis*, *Bolivicereus*, *Clistanthocereus*, *Loxanthocereus*, *Maritimocereus*, *Matucana*, *Morawetzia*, *Oreocereus*, *Seticereus*, *Submatucana*, and *Winterocereus*. Of particular interest is the *Oreocereus* group, with thick, tall stems; large, tubular, purplish red flowers; and long, silky, white hair in addition to heavy spines.

BOSTON FERN. Common name for *Nephrolepis exaltata* 'Bostoniensis', a fern popular for pot culture; see NEPHROLEPIS.

BOTANICALS. Insecticides made from plant material, including PYRETHRUM, ROTENONE, ryania, and sabadilla; see INSECT CONTROL.

BOTANIC GARDEN. Any collection of living plants maintained for scientific study, public display, and furthering of horticultural skill. Botanic (or botanical) gardens are often managed in conjunction with a library, greenhouse, museum, collection of dried plant material (herbarium), or laboratory for research work in botanical science and the application of horticultural skill.

These gardens, operated throughout the world and supported by public or private funds, are usually open to the public and are generally regarded and enjoyed as parks where beautiful trees, shrubs, flowering plants, and lawns can be enjoyed, and where special collections can be seen, including rose, perennial or annual, rock or alpine, aquatic, wildflower, and herb gardens. Students and other advanced horticulturists can make greater use of their scientific facilities.

The education of the public in knowledge and appreciation of the plant world and the encouragement of practical gardening is now considered just as important a function of a botanic garden as the advancement of botanical science. The greatest institutions of this kind, which have contributed most to botanical science and have been consistently supported, are those that have always recognized this twofold purpose.

Botanic gardens are training schools for advanced students in botany, horticulture, and forestry, but they may also offer elementary courses in these and related subjects or conduct lectures for the general public. Scientific literature and popular bulletins are offered for sale or issued to dues-paying members by many botanic gardens. See listing of botanic gardens in the APPENDIX.

BOTRYCHIUM (boh TRIK ee um). A genus of small (3–10 in.) succulent plants that are very primitive, commonly known as grape ferns. The name refers to the grapelike clusters of naked sporangia on the fertile fronds. They have fleshy, erect fronds that spring from a short subterranean rootstock. The fertile and sterile fronds are united below ground. The sterile fronds vary from pinnate to quadripinnate. Unlike other ferns, the fronds do not emerge in the form of croziers, or fiddleheads, but are simply folded back. Native to open woods and dry pastures, they are difficult to cultivate. They seem to require a symbiotic fungus. Because they are quite scarce and have no garden value, they should not be collected from the wild. There are many species in North America, but they are native to the temperate regions of both hemispheres.

PRINCIPAL SPECIES

B. australe (southern parsley fern) is a peculiar species from the Southern Hemisphere that is above ground for only part of the year. It is of interest to fern enthusiasts only.

B. dissectum (dissected grape fern) is an evergreen fern with leathery, triangular fronds 1½ ft. long. The barren frond is about half the length of the fertile frond. It is found in North America from Nova Scotia to Florida and in China and Japan.

B. lunaria (moonwort) is a rare, pinnate plant growing to 6 in. It grows in high meadows and open wastelands through the arctic and temperate zones of the world.

B. matricariifolium (daisy-leaved grape fern) is a little plant, growing 2–6 in., with pinnate-pin-natifid fronds. It is common in the moist woodlands of central and northeastern North America and usually disappears by midsummer.

B. multifidum (leathery grape fern) is the toughest and most leathery-textured of the grape ferns. It has semievergreen, sterile, pinnate to tripinnate fronds that are quite fernlike. It is found in North America throughout southern Canada into the northern states and also in Europe and Asia.

B. virginianum (rattlesnake fern) is a deciduous plant that grows to 2 ft. and has triangular bipinnate to tripinnate fronds. The only species of any garden merit, it requires light shade in deep, moist leaf mold and unstinting protection from slugs. It grows naturally in moist woodlands of North America, Asia, and Europe.

BOTRYTIS. A minute fungus responsible for many destructive blights. The genus *Botrytis* is one of the "imperfect fungi" (see FUNGUS), but many of its species are part stages in the life history of other fungi. The characteristic brownish gray mold of botrytis blights is produced by spores borne in clusters on little stalks all over the infected surfaces. The name comes from the Greek *botrys* and means "a grapelike cluster." A black resting body, sclerotium, is also typical of this genus; it is the form in which the fungus lives over the winter on infected plant parts or debris in the soil. Certain *Botrytis* species, such as those that blight peony, lily, and tulip, can attack only their respective host plant types, but *Botrytis cinerea* attacks many, causing gray mold rot of geranium, primrose, and other greenhouse plants; blossom blights of such garden flowers as rose, zinnia, and marigold; and a rot of lettuce and storage rots of fruits.

In general, to control botrytis troubles, burn all diseased plant parts and remove from the beds all old plant debris in autumn. If persistent, try spraying young shoots with a fungicide in early spring. Always follow label directions carefully. Avoid wetting leaves in watering greenhouse plants. Consult your local extension service for safe guidelines for your area. See also DISEASE.

BOTTLE GENTIAN. Common name for *Gentiana andrewsii*, a woodland herb bearing nearly closed purplish blue flowers in terminal clusters; see GENTIANA.

BOTTOM HEAT. The warmth artificially applied beneath seeds, cuttings, or plants to hasten germination or rooting and favor growth. It can be provided by fermenting material (as manure in a hotbed); warm flues (in sweet-potato plant production); hot water or steam pipes or radiators (as in dwellings or propagating benches); or by electricity carried by heating pads, wires, plates, cables, or grids below the soil surface. The expression "degrees of bottom heat" means the increase in temperature over that of the adjacent air. Generally, however, the heat applied to or needed in the soil is specified as actual soil temperature: 60°F, 70°F, etc.

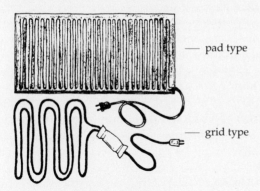

— pad type

— grid type

Heating elements

BOUGAINVILLEA (boo gin VIL ee ah). A genus of climbing vines from South America with thorny stems but a breathtaking display of color from three bracts that surround the flowers. In the tropics they are brilliant ornaments on arbors, fences, or rambling through trees; they are also grown in pots as bush or standard forms, especially in northern greenhouses. Propagation is by cuttings of almost any size or maturity of wood. Special care is needed at the transfer from the rooting bed or pot to the first growing container, since the roots are very brittle when first emerging from the stem.

Pruning should be directed at establishing a framework of branches and then cutting back the side shoots to two or three nodes after flowering to encourage more new growth upon which the flowering occurs. In Florida, the chief pest is a leaf rolling caterpillar that is hard to control unless caught before the protective leaf envelope is developed.

Some colors probably represent the true species, *B. glabra* or *B. spectabilis*, but most of the range from cream to pink, orange, and numerous shades of red are probably hybrids between the two. There are two varieties with two colors of flower mixed through the plant, and also cultivars with variegated leaves.

BOURBON ROSE. The result of a natural cross between *R. damascena semperflorens* (autumn damask rose) and the pink China rose, thought to be the same as 'Parson's Pink China'. These roses were planted as hedges on the Island of Reunion, then called Bourbon, and seeds were sent to France around 1817. The Bourbon roses can be thought of as forerunners of the hybrid perpetuals. For the most part, they are large, billowing bushes with very fragrant blooms in pink or red shades. Most are repeat flowering.

Well-known varieties are 'La Reine Victoria' and its sport 'Mme. Pierre Oger', Mme. Isaac Pereire' and its sport 'Mme. Ernst Calvat', and the nearly thornless climber 'Zéphirine Drouhin'.

BOUVARDIA (boo VAHR dee ah). A genus of small shrubs, mostly native to Mexico and Central America, belonging to the Rubiaceae (Madder Family). They are not grown as much as they once were but are still interesting shrubby plants for winter flowering in the greenhouse. Florists grow them for the rather waxy white flowers with four stout petals. Some bear yellow or red flowers. Those in cultivation are mostly sports or hybrids.

Bouvardias thrive in a mixture of fibrous loam, leaf mold, and sand. After they have flowered, keep them cooler and dryer for a few weeks, then cut back and start into new growth with heat and moisture. The shoots should be pinched from time to time to induce a good habit and free flowering. During the growth period, they need plenty of water; it is helpful to occasionally enrich the water with liquid manure. Plants can be flowered in pots or in the bench. Old plants can be set outdoors for the summer; if carefully handled and potted in the fall, kept in a close temperature and shaded for a few days, such specimens will produce a good supply of flowers for cutting. Propagation is by young stem cuttings taken with a heel and also by cutting up pieces of the thickest roots in 2-in. lengths.

B. longiflora, formerly listed as *B. humboldtii*, is perhaps the most handsome species. Unlike most species, it has opposite, glossy green leaves, and flowers before winter. Its fragrant white flowers are borne in large terminal clusters.

B. ternifolia, formerly listed as *B. triphylla*, has leaves in threes, and scarlet flowers. The earliest to be introduced, late in the 18th century, it has played an important part in the production of the improved forms now grown.

BOWER PLANT. Common name for *Pandorea jasminoides*, a tropical climbing shrub with white and pink flowers; see PANDOREA.

BOWIEA (BOH ee ah) **volubilis.** A twining South African plant belonging to the Liliaceae (Lily Family), formerly listed under the genus name *Schizobasopsis*, and commonly known as climbing-onion. It is grown as a greenhouse curiosity in North America. From its large green bulb above the ground springs a slender, leafless climbing stem that twines around a support. The small flowers are greenish white. The bulbs require a brief resting period in summer. Propagation is by seed or division of the bulbs.

BOX-ELDER. Common name for *Acer negundo*, a rapid growing and easily cultivated species of maple; see ACER.

BOX HUCKLEBERRY. Common name for *Gaylussacia brachycera*, a very rare, old, and unusual evergreen ground cover native to the United States; see GAYLUSSACIA.

BOX-THORN. Common name for LYCIUM, a genus of clambering shrubs with inconspicuous flowers and brightly colored berries.

BOXWOOD. Common name, along with box, for BUXUS, a genus of evergreen shrubs or small trees. The Box Family is BUXACEAE.

Brisbane-box is *Tristania conferta*; see TRISTANIA. Victorian-box is *Pittosporum undulatum*; see PITTOSPORUM.

BOYKINIA (boy KIN ee ah). A genus of herbaceous perennials in the Saxifragaceae (Saxifrage Family). Hardy to Zone 7 and native to moist, shaded woods of the western United States, they are useful in woodland, creek, or rock garden plantings.

B. elata has panicles of small white flowers on airy stems about 18 in. tall arising from a cluster of attractive lobed leaves.

B. major, growing to about 3 ft., is larger in all features.

BOYSENBERRY. Common name for a variety of *Rubus ursinis* (trailing blackberry); see BLACKBERRY.

BRACHONID WASP. A parasitic wasp beneficial for controlling pest insects; see WASPS.

BRACHYCHITON (bra ki KĪ ton). A genus of trees native to Australia, belonging to the Sterculiaceae (Sterculia Family), grown for ornamental effects in Zones 10–11. In some species, the trunks are swollen at ground level. Others, constricted both at the ground and near their tops, are swollen between, inspiring the common name bottletree. They have large, heavily lobed leaves; some species have showy flowers of red or scarlet. They succeed well in the soil of the high pinelands of Florida. Propagation is by seed or cuttings of ripe wood. *B. acerifolius* is commonly known as flame tree.

BRACHYCOME (brah KIK oh mee). A genus of annual and perennial herbs belonging to the Asteraceae (Aster Family). They have generally branching stems and solitary or loosely clustered heads of daisylike flowers.

B. *iberidifolia* (Swan River daisy) is a hardy annual that grows 10–18 in. tall and has branching stems and blue, rose, or white flowers about 1 in. across. An excellent plant for the rock garden, border, or edging, it is native to the Swan River region in Australia, along

Brachycome iberidifolia

whose banks its flowers first attracted attention. Its deeply cut, lacy foliage, compact growth, and free-flowering quality (which makes the plant resemble cineraria) have long combined to make it a garden favorite. It is easy to grow under any normal garden conditions, being started from seed, preferably rather early indoors, and handled like other hardy ANNUALS.

BRACHYSEMA (bra ki SEE mah). A genus of tender evergreen, semiclimbing shrubs with red, sweet-pealike flowers and generally silvery-hairy leaves. Attractive in flower and foliage, the plants are grown outdoors in Zones 10–11 and used as pillar climbers in northern greenhouses. B. *acuminatum* and B. *lanceolatum* are the species most frequently grown.

BRACKEN FERN. Common name for *Pteridium aquilinum*, an aggressive fern with attractive fronds found in woodlands, hillsides, and pastures; see PTERIDIUM.

BRACKET FUNGI. These are shelflike fruiting bodies of certain kinds of mushrooms (fungi) growing from the trunks of trees. They are commonly hard and woody but can be soft, fleshy, and sometimes edible. They often indicate diseased heartwood. See also FUNGUS; DISEASE.

BRACT. A small modified leaf with or without a stem, particularly one of the smaller scalelike leaves in a flower cluster. A bract's usual function is to protect the delicate tissue of the bud over which the bracts overlap; the "chaff" of wheat is an illustration. Some bracts are large and showy, resembling petals, as in the poinsettia and flowering dogwood.

BRAHEA (brah HEE ah). A genus of fan palms, formerly listed as *Erythea* and commonly known as rock or hesper palm. Native from Central America to southern California, they are often planted outdoors in Zones 9–11 and are sometimes seen as small specimens under glass.

PRINCIPAL SPECIES
B. *armata* (blue hesper or Mexican blue palm) is a robust grower to 40 ft. The trunk is covered with a thick, fibrous ruffle of old leaves. In the heavy crown of waxy, bluish green foliage, the leaf stems are armed with stout hooked spines.

B. *brandegeei* (San Jose hesper palm) grows to 40 ft. and has a slender trunk. Dark green leaves with pale undersides are borne on stems edged with recurved spines.

B. *edulis* (Guadalupe palm), native to the Guadalupe Islands of Mexico and frequently planted in southern California, has a stout trunk growing to 30 ft. or more and a crown of much-divided leaves with few prickles on the stems. The clusters of shining black fruits with sweet pulp are said to grow up to 50 lb.

B. *elegans* is a relatively slow growing dwarf tree with glaucous leaves and spiny stems.

BRAKE FERN. Common name for several different ferns, especially in the tropical genus PTERIS, a group of vigorous houseplants, including Australian or tender, Cretan, ladder, silver, and sword brake. Cliff-brake refers to two genera, PELLAEA, which grow in small tufts; and CRYPTOGRAMMA, a temperate genus of ferns with creeping rhizomes, also known as rock-brake.

BRAMBLE. Common name for the genus RUBUS, including raspberries, dewberries, blackberries, loganberries, and other small fruits. Thus it applies both to plants bearing thorns and to certain species or forms that are relatively or entirely thornless.

BRAN MASH. This is used as a bait to destroy cutworms, army worms, grasshoppers, and other chewing pests that attack young garden crops. To make it, combine 2 parts molasses with 1 part sawdust and 1 part wheat bran, plus enough water to saturate the bran and sawdust. If spread along a row, any slugs attracted to it will be covered so that as the mash dries, it hardens on the slug and prevents it from reentering its burrow; subsequent exposure to sun and wind will kill it.

BRASENIA (brah SEE nee ah) **schreberi.** A hardy aquatic herb native in North America, Asia, Africa, and Australia, belonging to the Nymphaeaceae (Waterlily Family), and commonly known as water-shield. Its leaves float on the water surface, and the underparts are coated with a transparent colloidal jelly. It has small purple flowers. Often grown in aquatic gardens, it thrives in deep water in Zones 7–11 and, except in warm climates, should receive some winter protection. Propagation is by division of the roots or by seed.

BRASSAVOLA (brah SAH voh lah). A genus of ten to fifteen epiphytic orchid species native to tropical America, including *B. nodosa* (lady-of-the-night). Plants in this genus hybridize readily with those of the Epidendreae (including *Laelia*, *Cattleya*, and *Broughtonia*). Their leaves are terete to semiterete, and inflorescences are several- to many-flowered. Pendent blossoms, often fragrant at night, are mostly white to green with a cordate lip and narrow petals and sepals. Mostly hardy in Zones 9–11, with a minimum winter temperature of 60°F, the plants do best either mounted on cork or bark or in baskets with a loose, well-drained compost. The type species is *B. cucullata.*

BRASSIA (BRAS ee ah). These are the exotic spider orchids, so called because of their elongated, narrow petals and sepals. The genus consists of 50 species native to tropical regions of the Americas. They are important in hybridizing programs using other orchids, and the intergeneric hybrids are bizarre and beautiful, with attenuated, twisted lateral sepals and fanciful markings on floral segments.

The plants are epiphytes, with ovoid or cylindrical pseudobulbs and long, thin leaves. The inflorescences are horizontal, with several to many flowers in ranks along horizontal stems. The flowers are large, light yellow-green to orange-yellow, with rich maroon or chestnut-brown blotches. Some have raised brown warts on the lip. The lateral sepals are the most prominent part of the flower, in some cases attaining a length of 10 in. or more. They do well in filtered light and need abundant water during growth, a little less after growth is made up. The roots should not be disturbed. Hardy only in Zones 10–11 they withstand minimum winter temperatures of 60–65°F. Some species flower several times a year. *B. maculata* is the type species.

BRASSICA (BRAS i kah). A genus of about 50 annual and biennial herbs and an important branch of the Brassicaceae (Mustard Family). Mostly they are natives of the old world, but many are naturalized as bad weeds in North America. Others are among the most important food plants of cool climates and seasons.

The roots of the annual species are fibrous, spreading, and shallow; those of the biennials, deep penetrating, and thickened; the foliage is mostly coarse or fleshy; the yellow flowers are borne usually in erect racemes. Under cultivation, species and varieties tend to thicken diverse parts. All parts of the plants have a characteristic pungent flavor.

DISEASES

Black-leg. This disease is widely distributed and attacks all varieties of cabbage as well as many other *Brassicas*, sometimes causing a 50–90% loss in commercial cabbage and cauliflower crops. The plants may be infected in the seedbed or later, the first symptoms being oval, depressed, light brown cankers near the base of the stem. As these enlarge, the stem is girdled and the dead tissue turns black, giving the disease its name. Small black dots (the fungus fruiting bodies) in the lesions and on leaves and stems also identify the disease. The fungus lives over on seed and in cabbage refuse. To avoid the trouble, use healthy seed, such as is produced in the Puget Sound region where the disease does not normally occur, and practice a four-year crop rotation. Disinfect seed that may be diseased by soaking in a fungicide solution, then rinse thoroughly in clear water and spread to dry. They can also be suspended in water held at 122°F for 30 minutes, then dipped in cold water before drying.

Black Rot. This bacterial disease causes dwarfing and rotting of plants, spotting or blighting of leaves, and sometimes death. Practically all brassicas are affected, cauliflower being particularly susceptible. The disease may affect seedlings or appear after the plants are set out into the field. The first symptom is a yellowing of the leaves accompanied by the blackening of veins, which begins at the leaf margin or around an insect injury. Disinfect seed as recommended for blackleg; use clean or disinfected soil in the seedbed; practice a four- or five-year crop rotation; control insect pests; and promptly remove and burn diseased plants.

Club Root. Called finger-and-toe disease in England and cabbage hernia in some other countries, this may occur wherever cabbage is grown. Nearly all kinds of brassicas can be affected, but while some varieties of turnips and radishes are very susceptible, others are practically immune. Above the ground the main symptom is a wilting of the tops on hot days, followed by a partial recovery at night. Leaves may appear yellowish and sickly. Young plants may die outright, and older ones may fail to produce marketable heads. The roots of diseased plants will be much enlarged and malformed, the enlargements varying from small swellings to huge clubbed masses,

often ten times normal size and cracked or furrowed on the surface. Later they decay and give off bad odors. This is one of the few diseases of economically important plants caused by a slime mold whose spores are liberated in vast numbers into the soil when the diseased roots decay. These spores can live in the soil for at least seven years and attack susceptible plants at any time during that period. To avoid the disease, start the seed in soil where cabbage has never been grown, and set the plants in soil that has been heavily limed three to six months before planting. Apply fungicide to the plants in the seedbed and, later, to those in the field once each week for several weeks. Cultivate the crop thoroughly, destroying all cruciferous weeds.

Cabbage Yellows. Caused by the fusarium fungus, which also affects cauliflower and kale, this is of particular importance in the southern central states, since the fungus, which lives in the soil, develops best at temperatures of 80–90°F. Diseased plants are sickly, yellow, and dwarfed, with pinkish spore masses on the stems. Planting resistant strains of cabbage is about the best control.

INSECT PESTS

Cabbage Worm. The imported cabbage worm *Artogenia rapae*, introduced in 1860, is now common throughout the United States and most of Canada. The velvety green worms, growing to 1¼ in. long with a slender orange stripe down the middle of the back, riddle the first formed leaves of cabbage and cauliflower, destroying so much leaf tissue that the heads are stunted or do not form at all. The adult is the small white cabbage butterfly, which emerges in spring and lays several hundred greenish

Cabbage worm and chrysalis

cylindrical eggs on both sides of the leaf in three to six generations each summer. The young green caterpillars hatch in about a week and become obvious because of the holes they make and the bright green excrement they leave. In some areas, natural enemies of the cabbage worm keep the pest in check.

If it becomes a problem, fight this pest by spraying or dusting plants with insecticide. Dusts tend to penetrate the foliage better but wash off more easily. Care should be taken to select an insecticide that will wash off readily or is not toxic to humans if the plants are grown for food, and any spraying or dusting treatment should be discontinued four weeks before the crop is gathered. Pyrethrum and rotenone can be used to control them, but the best defense is *Bacillus thuringiensis* (Bt, commonly available as Dipel, Thuricide, or Biotrol), as an infecting powder or spray that destroys the worm.

Cabbage Looper. This pest, *Trichoplusia ni*, attacks cabbage in the same manner as the cabbage worm. The light green caterpillar has four thin, lengthwise white lines and moves by humping or looping up the middle of the body like other inchworms because it has only two front legs. It winters in a white cocoon attached to a leaf. Adults are night-flying, inconspicuous grayish brown moths, which lay whitish eggs on the upper sides of leaves. There are three or more generations each year. Control by the same methods as the cabbage worm, but spraying or dusting must be thorough, since the worms are very active. Floating row covers provide protection; trichogramma wasps are good parasites; and the nuclear polyhedrosis virus (NPV) is lethal in a few days.

Aphid. Two species, the dusty gray cabbage aphid and the green turnip aphid, attack cabbage, cauliflower, and related crops, feeding on the undersides of the leaves, which crinkle and curl, forming cups completely lined with aphids. The plants are dwarfed and form light heads. Light infestations can be rinsed off with a stream of water. Insecticidal soaps or dusts will control both pests. They have been controlled by botanical sprays, such as rotenone and pyrethrum, but biological control by ladybugs or mechanical control by floating row covers are good alternatives.

Cabbage Maggot. This pest infests the stems of early-set cabbage and cauliflower plants as well as early turnips and late radish crops. It also creates problems by carrying bacterial soft rot and black-leg fungus diseases. The worms work in the stems just below the soil surface, causing the plants to wilt and die without forming heads. They hatch from eggs laid on the soil by slender gray flies, which emerge in late spring after passing the winter in the pupal stage in the soil. There are three broods each year. Control by placing a tar paper disk around the stem of each plant when setting it out, or by applying an insecticidal solution at the base of the plant. Surrounding the stems by gravel will help deter the pest. Floating row covers help against maggots as well as protecting plants from other pests. Where only a few plants are grown, they can be screened with cheesecloth to keep the flies from laying eggs near them.

Cabbage Flea Beetle. A newly hatched larva of this pest is recognizable by the black tubercules on its gray body. The adult is a small, yellowish green beetle with black bands and long dark hairs. The larvae grow to only ⅔ in. long, and they feed on the roots of cabbage, radish, and wild mustard. Cheesecloth screens afford protection, as does an application of fine tobacco dust or other insecticide, when the plants first appear.

Other Pests. The HARLEQUIN BUG, a gaudy, red-and-black spotted, sucking insect, is an injurious pest of brassicas in the southern states. Newly set plants or seedlings grown in the garden may be attacked by the CUTWORM, which girdles the stems. Bt will help control any of those, though the best repellent is a paper collar or stick beside the stem to prevent the cutworm from surrounding stems. Poison BRAN MASH is also effective.

See also INSECT CONTROL.

PRINCIPAL SPECIES

Immense diversity among varieties gives rise to a complicated system of classification, which groups varieties within some species.

B. hirta (white mustard), a somewhat hairy annual that grows to 4 ft. and has oval leaves, is one of the species that produces seeds used in commercial mustard and oil of mustard.

B. juncea (mustard greens) is an annual that

grows to 4 ft. and has large tufts of narrow, lobed leaves used for spring greens; it tends to become a weed in some areas. Var. *crispifolia* (curled mustard), with ruffled leaves, produces the most common mustard greens.

B. napus (rape) is an annual, but if seed is sown in late fall, the plants will grow and flower in spring. Annual crops are grown for the seed, which yields oil and birdseed. It has two primary variety groups.

The hardy Napobrassica group (rutabaga, Swedish turnip) forms bulblike roots with yellow or white flesh and a long neck or crown.

The Pabularia group (Siberian kale) includes low biennials whose narrow, lobed, bluish or purplish leaves have fringed edges; they are harvested for winter or spring use, but quickly go to seed in warm weather.

B. nigra (black mustard) is a branching annual that grows to 6 ft. under good conditions and has feathery leaves. It is one of the more common producers of the mustard seed used in oils and condiments.

B. oleracea (wild cabbage) is annual or perennial and has rounded or oval leaves that are thicker and lobed at the base. It includes the largest series of varieties.

The Acephala group (kale) has loose, large, spreading, sometimes very attractive leaves; they are planted for greens and for ornament.

The Botrytis group includes CAULIFLOWER, which forms a thickened, white, solid head of its flower-clusters, and BROCCOLI, which produces several smaller, looser heads, either white or green.

The Capitata group (CABBAGE) forms dense heads of leaves, which are firm or puckered, like in Savoy cabbage.

The Gemmifera group (BRUSSELS SPROUTS) has axillary buds that develop into little heads.

The Gongylodes group (kohlrabi) includes low, stout biennials with swollen globular stems that are cultivated and used like turnips.

The Italica group (Italian or asparagus broccoli) is similar to the Botrytis group, but leaves do not form compact heads.

The Tronchuda group (Tronchuda or Portuguese kale) includes low plants with loose, fleshy leaves that are used much like celery.

B. rapa (field mustard) is annual or biennial and has flat or globular roots and lobed leaves to 20 in. long.

The Chinensis group of varieties (pak-choi, celery mustard) has cabbagelike leaves and swollen, tuberous roots and is often grown for its succulent leaves, especially in Asia.

The Pekinensis group (pe-tsai, Chinese cabbage) is annual, forming loose, cylindrical heads with broad basal leaves with jagged edges.

The Perviridis group (spinach mustard) is usually annual, growing to 6 ft. in branching form with oblong, toothless leaves. It is grown in North America for its edible leaves, but the tuberous crown is commonly pickled in Asia.

The Rapifera group includes the common turnip, a stout biennial that is very leafy; it can be used in salad but is most commonly cultivated for its fleshy roots; see TURNIP.

The Ruvo group (rubo kale, turnip broccoli, Italian turnip) may be annual or biennial, depending on when seeds are sown; its dark green leaves are lobed and often glossy, and the taproots are edible.

BRASSICACEAE The Mustard or Crucifer family, a group of 1800 or more species, including many valuable vegetables, a number of useful garden flowers, and some troublesome weeds. A few of these are *Alyssum*, *Arabis* (rockcress), *Iberis* (candytuft), *Cheiranthus* (wallflower), *Matthiola* (stock), and *Brassica* (including mustard, turnip, and the rest of the cabbage tribe).

The former family name, Cruciferae, from the Latin words meaning "cross-bearing," refers to the flowers of all members of the family, which are composed of four petals arranged in the form of a cross, coming in shades of white, yellow, orange, rose, or purple. These are followed by characteristic, usually slender, pointed seed pods. A sharp, peppery flavor or fragrance is also characteristic of many plants in this useful and widely distributed group.

BREADFRUIT. Common name for both the tropical tree *Artocarpus altilis* and its large, pulpy fruit or thickened stalk; see ARTOCARPUS.

BREAKING. In tulips this applies to segregation of the color pigment into irregular stripes or flecks. Variegated tulips, thought by early growers to be special types or species, were encouraged and favored, but the condition is now known to be caused by a virus disease, or mosaic, transmitted by aphids. Apparently two distinct viruses can cause breaking. One results in loss of flower color, yellow-striped or mottled leaves, general stunting, and loss of vigor. The other causes darker streaks of color and seems not to have appreciable effect on the general health of the plant. Control by prompt removal of diseased plants and use contact insecticides against aphids.

BREYNIA (BRAY nee ah) **disticha.** A shrub belonging to the Euphorbiaceae (Spurge Family) and commonly known as snowbush. It is native to the Pacific but is now found in gardens throughout the tropics. The shoots and young leaves are white or pink and white, contrasting attractively with the older foliage that darkens to green or dark purple, and giving the plant its common name. Once established, it is tolerant of poor, dry conditions and can even become weedy as it spreads from root sprouts.

BRICKELLIA (bri KEL ee ah). A genus of herbs or shrubs belonging to the Asteraceae (Aster Family), found in high altitudes in western North America.

B. grandiflora (tassel flower), which appears to be the only cultivated species, is a perennial that grows to 3 ft. and is suitable for a moist, shady border. It bears drooping heads of yellowish white flowers in large panicles. Propagation is by cuttings under close conditions.

BRIDALWREATH. Common name for *Spiraea prunifolia*, a deciduous shrub with brilliant fall color and double flowers; see SPIRAEA.

BRIZA (BRĪ zah). A genus of small annual and perennial ornamental grasses, commonly called quaking grass because of the spikelets that tremble in the lightest breeze. They are native to Europe and Mexico, but several have been naturalized in the United States where they are hardy to Zone 5. When dried, these grasses add much to the beauty of bouquets of everlastings. They are easy to grow from seeds sown in the early spring in any garden soil. See ORNAMENTAL GRASSES.

BROAD BEAN. Common name for *Vicia faba*, an old-world vegetable and forage plant also called Windsor or horse bean. See BEAN; VICIA.

BROADCAST. In gardening, to scatter seed by hand or machine instead of sowing in rows or another pattern. It is most practiced when seeding a lawn, sowing cover crops, and starting seeds in flats. The soil is often prepared by raking before the seed is broadcast over the surface.

BROCCOLI. Easier to grow than cauliflower, which it resembles, broccoli (a variety of the Botrytis group of *Brassica oleracea*) is now one of the most popular vegetables for home gardens. While cauliflower forms a tight white head of tightly packed bud clusters, broccoli forms a looser green head. It grows faster than cauliflower, takes heat better, and yields more reliably under stress.

Broccoli is grown like cabbage, preferring heavy loam soils enriched with compost or well-rotted animal manure. High-nitrogen fertilizers are also beneficial. Sow seed in late winter indoors and set six-week-old plants outdoors. In the event of a week without natural rainfall, water thoroughly. Since broccoli will tolerate mild frosts, transplanting can be done several weeks before the last expected frost date. Direct seeding into the garden is generally unreliable, since broccoli seed prefers a 70°F soil temperature to germinate, even though it is a cool-season crop, performing best in spring and autumn when nights are cool. For autumn harvest, start seed in August for transplanting in September. Spaced 15 in. apart in rows set 3 ft. apart, many varieties will mature within 55 days of transplanting. To avoid disease problems, do not grow in the same place where any brassicas were grown earlier.

Popular broccoli varieties include 'Premium Crop', a hybrid that produces huge terminal heads up to 12 in. across, and 'Green Comet', one of the earliest hybrids. When the main head of broccoli is cut, smaller heads will usually appear on side shoots, so do not discard the plant. 'Sprouting Broccoli', also known as 'Broccoli Raab', produces lots of smaller heads and tender green leaves. 'Romanesco', a chartreuse-colored broccoli with heads that resemble sea coral, tastes

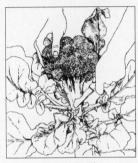 

main head   side shoots

Harvesting broccoli

more like cauliflower and needs 75 days of cool nights from transplanting to ready maturity. It is not as easy to grow as regular broccoli, but the attractive heads are reason enough to try it.

For pest and disease control, see BRASSICA.

BRODIAEA (broh di EE ah). This is the generic name for a large group of cormous or bulbous plants in the Amaryllidaceae (Amaryllis Family), generally divided by botanists into the genera *Brodiaea*, DICHELOSTEMMA, TRITELEIA, and IPHEION.

The true members of the genus *Brodiaea* are low to tall spring-flowering bulbs with waxy-petaled flowers, each petal with a central stripe. Hardy to Zone 7, they are useful for rock gardens or pot culture in warmer regions and in the North if protected in the winter.

PRINCIPAL SPECIES

B. appendiculata, *B. californica*, and *B. leptandra* are the largest species at 1½–2 ft. tall with 6–8 in. umbels of lilac-blue flowers in late spring.

B. coronaria, growing 1–10 in. tall with attractive lilac flowers above grassy foliage, is very similar to *B. jolonensis*, *B. minor*, and *B. stellaris*.

B. elegans (harvest brodiaea), with deep to mid-purple flowers in late spring, is perhaps the easiest to grow and is usually 1–2 ft. tall and has large umbels.

B. laxa (triplet-lily, Ithuriel's-spear) is now listed as *Triteleia laxa*; see TRITELEIA.

B. pulchella (bluedicks, wild hyacinth) is now listed as *Dichelostemma pulchellum*; see DICHELOSTEMMA.

B. terrestris (earth-stars) is a diminutive herb with nearly caespitose clusters of waxy, pale lilac-blue flowers.

BROMELIA (broh MEE lee ah). A genus of tropical American perennial herbs belonging to the Bromeliaceae (Pineapple Family). They have long, stiff leaves with spines along the margins set in an imposing basal rosette from which rises the 4-ft. flower stem crowned with racemes of bloom. They succeed outdoors in Zones 10–11 but are greenhouse plants in cooler climates. They require a well broken-up loam enriched with about a quarter decayed manure. Water should be given sparingly in winter. Propagation is by suckers.

Of the two dozen species, *B. pinguin* (pinguin, wild-pine) of Jamaica is the showiest. Its 6-ft. leaves with hooked prickles turn from bright green to red with age. Red flowers are followed by an edible, plumlike fruit sometimes used in native medicines.

BROMELIACEAE (broh mee lee AY see ee). The Pineapple or Bromelia Family, a group of herbs or subshrubs of the American tropics with persistent, stiff, channeled leaves in rosettes, crowded into a basal sheath. The bright flowers, provided with large, often colored and showy bracts, are borne in dense heads. Many bromeliads (as members of the family are called), grow on other plants (see EPIPHYTE), but some, like *Ananas* (pineapple) are terrestrial. They show great diversity, including such different forms as *Ananas*, *Tillandsia* (Spanish-moss), and *Pinguin*. In greenhouses some are grown in pots and baskets, making showy and effective subjects. Other genera grown for ornament include *Aechmea*, *Billbergia*, *Cryptanthus*, *Nidularium*, and *Vriesea*.

BROMUS. A genus of annual and perennial grasses with flat leaves and nodding spikes of bloom, natives of the North Temperate Zone of Europe and naturalized in North America. While most are of a weedy character, some have a special value as forage grasses on dry soils of the Midwest and South. There are several ornamental species valuable in the border.

PRINCIPAL SPECIES

B. briziformis (quake grass) forms effective clumps with long spikes of nodding bloom, which are often dried and used in winter bouquets.

B. inermis (awnless or Hungarian brome grass) is useful for its ability to hold earth banks in shape.

B. macrostachys, though less striking than the others, finds a place both in the garden and in dry bouquets.

B. madritensis has a beautiful feathery bloom.

BRONZE LEAF. Common name for *Rodgersia podophylla*, a perennial herb whose light green spring foliage turns bronzy in summer; see RODGERSIA.

BROOM. Common name for two closely related genera of attractive shrubs grown for indoor and outdoor ornament, especially *Genista hispanica* (Spanish broom), *Cytisus multiflorus* (white Spanish broom), and *C. scoparius* (Scotch broom); see CYTISUS; GENISTA.

The name is often applied to other plants. Broom-corn is a product of *Sorghum*. Broom wat-tle is the decorative shrub or tree listed as *Acacia calamifolia*. Butcher's-broom is *Ruscus aculeatus*. Spanish or weaver's-broom is *Spartium junceum*. WITCHES'-BROOM is a shrubby growth deformation caused by a rust fungus.

BROUGHTONIA (braw TOH nee uh). A genus of two small epiphytic orchids indigenous to Jamaica. They are important in hybridizing programs to produce windowsill orchids that stay small and produce large, showy flowers several times a year. Members of the Epidendreae tribe, they cross readily with *Cattleya*, *Laelia*, *Epidendrum*, and *Brassavola* to make a variety of small plants that produce large, bright flowers on each new growth.

Leathery leaves surmount small, flattened, wrinkled pseudobulbs. Many small fuchsia, pink, yellow, or white cattleya-type flowers cluster at the ends of long, wiry inflorescences. They do well mounted on plaques of cork, coconut husk, or tree fern, or in baskets of loose, well-drained compost. Plants do best in bright light with high humidity while growing, somewhat less when growth is completed. Hardy only to Zone 10, they withstand a minimum winter temperature of 65°F. The type species is *B. sanguinea*.

BROUSSONETIA (broo soh NEE shee ah). A genus of deciduous trees or shrubs belonging to the Moraceae (Mulberry Family). They are native in eastern Asia where the bark is used in paper making. *B. papyrifera* (paper mulberry), the best-known species, grows into a broad, rounded tree to 50 ft. and has smooth gray bark and large oval, usually lobed, leaves. Hardy to Zone 7, it has been used to some extent as a street tree and has become naturalized in some regions. 'Laciniata' is conspicuous because of its finely dissected leaves.

BROWALLIA (broh WAL ee ah). A genus of annual, free-flowering bedding plants belonging to the Solanaceae (Nightshade Family). They grow 1–1½ ft. tall and are used with best results in the blue section of the garden, where the winged flowers, of an intense blue color covering the plant, provide beauty throughout the summer and fall. Native to tropical America, this plant is easily cultivated in any good garden soil, needing practically no care as long as it has a sunny spot and plants are at least 6 in. apart. If lifted in the fall, potted, cut back, and brought indoors, browallia will bloom during the winter.

B. speciosa is the commonly cultivated species. Besides blue-flowered cultivars, shades of lilac to white are available. The 9–10 in. plants perform very well in pots or hanging baskets and can be successfully grown in full sun to partial shade.

BROWNING. A condition often seen on evergreens, especially arborvitae, in which the foliage becomes rusty and brownish. It varies in extent and degree from place to place, season to season, and year to year, and may indicate natural or abnormal conditions. In early fall it commonly accompanies the natural shedding or pruning of the older foliage (three- or four-year-old needles) comparable to what occurs in deciduous trees. A browning in very early spring may be caused by transpiration of moisture by the foliage faster than the roots can take it up from frozen soil. Shading from direct sunlight and protection against prevailing winds at this season to check excessive drying may be warranted in the case of valuable specimens. Summer browning is usually caused by insects, especially spruce mite, scale, and root and gall aphids; by unfavorable planting sites; hot, dry weather; or failure of newly transplanted trees to become established.

BROWN PATCH. A disease of grasses caused by a common soil fungus, *Rhizoctonia solani*. Definite, rather circular spots, bordered by a dark green ring, appear suddenly in the lawn during warm, humid weather. They may vary from an inch or so to several feet in diameter. A disease called small brown patch (caused by another species of the same fungus) is characterized by light brown patches never more than 2 in. across. For further notes, see LAWN.

BROWN ROT. A fungus disease of stone fruits—peaches, cherries, plums, prunes, nectarines, and apricots—and, to a slight extent, pome fruits. Symptoms appearing at different times in the season are blossom blight, twig blight, fruit rot, and canker.

The fungus *Monilinia fructicola* winters in the cankers and in the hard, wrinkled, fallen fruits called "mummies." When the flower buds begin to show color, small, mushroomlike cups (apothecia) grow out from the mummies. In moist weather millions of spores are literally shot from these cups and carried by air currents to the blossoms, which turn brown and wither. The disease then progresses down the twigs and eventually to the trunk, forming a canker there. Gummy substances on the twigs, cankers, and sometimes fruits are also evidence of brown rot. Gray spore tufts (masses of summer spores or conidia), which appear on the blighted blossoms and on mummies that cling to the trees over winter, are sources of infection of the young fruit, which, soon covered with its own spores, continues to spread infection throughout the season.

Sanitary measures are the best means of control. Knock clinging mummies from the trees, then plow under or rake up and burn all mummies and plant debris. Consult your local extension service about a spraying or dusting program for your locality. The first spray is generally applied when the blossoms are at the pink stage, the second when the petals are falling, the third two or three weeks later, and the fourth three or four weeks before the fruit ripens.

See also DISEASE.

BRUCKENTHALIA (bruk en THAY lee ah) **spiculifolia.** A small evergreen shrub of the Ericaceae (Heath Family), commonly known as spike heath. It has whorled needlelike leaves and spikes of small, nodding, bell-shaped rosy flowers. Resembling the dwarf ericas in growth, it is hardy to Zone 6 and is excellent for the rock garden, since its freely produced blossoms come in summer when bloom is needed. Thriving in acid soil, it grows readily from seed or cuttings.

BRUGMANSIA (brug MAN see ah). A genus of small trees commonly known as angel's trumpet. They bear pendent flowers of white, peach, or pink and are very fragrant but poisonous. Several were originally listed in the closely related genus *Datura*. Propagation is rapid by cuttings of mature wood. The plants respond well to fertilizer and water in any well-drained soil and are interesting greenhouse subjects.

PRINCIPAL SPECIES

B. arborea (angel's-trumpet) is treelike to 15 ft. and has soft-haired leaves to 8 in. long and white, green-veined flowers to 9 in. long.

B. cornigera grows to 4 ft. and is almost entirely covered with soft down. Leaves are chiefly at the ends of the branches. White or creamy flowers are very fragrant at night with floral lobes terminated by a long spreading or recurved point.

B. sanguinea (floripondio) is a native Peruvian shrub with shining leaves and drooping yellow-nerved, bright orange, scentless flowers followed by narcotic seeds.

B. suaveolens is treelike to 15 ft. and is often grown in tubs under glass. Frequently confused with *B. arborea*, it has larger, smoother leaves and distinguished sweet-scented flowers to 1 ft. long with an inflated calyx.

BRUNFELSIA (brun FEL zee ah). A genus of showy, winter-blooming shrubs and subshrubs of the tropical Americas, belonging to the Solanaceae (Nightshade Family). Grown in the open in the subtropics, they need a temperate greenhouse (50°F at night) in the North. The large, funnel-shaped or flattened, usually fragrant flowers grow singly or in loose terminal clusters. *Brunfelsias* need a rich, loose compost and plenty of food while growing; they bloom better when pot-bound than when newly started. Propagate from cuttings of ripened wood in spring or autumn, or from seed produced in the fleshy fruits a few months after flowering.

PRINCIPAL SPECIES

B. americana (lady-of-the-night) grows to 8 ft. and has solitary flowers of white fading to yellow, which are fragrant at night.

B. grandiflora and *B. pauciflora* (yesterday-today-and-tomorrow) have flowers that open blue and fade to white.

B. undulata is a magnificent, strong-growing evergreen that grows to 15 ft. and has creamy white, wavy margined flowers.

BRUNNERA (BROON er ah) **macrophylla.** A perennial herb growing to 18 in. with small, blue summer flowers resembling forget-me-nots; it is commonly known as Siberian bugloss. Hardy in Zones 3–8, it is good for rock garden use. This species is often referred to as *Anchusa myosotidiflora*.

Brunnera macrophylla

BRUSSELS SPROUTS. One of the seven distinct vegetables (the others being broccoli, cabbage, cauliflower, collards, kale, and kohlrabi) developed from the original wild cabbage *Brassica oleracea*. Included in Gemmifera variety group, it is distinguished as the plants mature by its sprouts, which are small, compact, more or less globular heads, very swollen buds, borne along the elongated, erect stem in the axils of the leaves. Its seeds and young plants are identical to those of other brassicas. The plant is entirely hardy.

Sprout formation starts near the ground and progresses steadily up the stem. As the buds approach edible size (1–2 in.), the lower leaves should be removed from the plant to make harvesting easier. More leaves—and more sprouts—develop above as the stalk grows until finally there remains a tall, lanky stem with a tuft of leaves at the top just above the remaining sprouts. Sprouts can be gathered from late September until well into winter, or plants can be dug with some soil before the ground freezes and transplanted to a cool, moist cellar or deep cold-frame. Here, if the soil is kept damp, many sprouts too small to use at transplanting time will develop to edible size, extending the crop season.

The varieties offered by seed distributors differ mainly in the height to which they grow and the spacing of sprouts on the stalk. For culture, see BRASSICA.

Brussels sprouts

BRYOPHYLLUM (brī oh FĪL um). Former name for plants now placed in the genus KALANCHOE.

BUCIDA (byoo SEE dah). A small genus belonging to the Combretaceae (Combretum Family), native to Central America and the West Indies. One species, *B. buceras*, is widely planted in all frost-free parts of south Florida. It used to be known as oxhorn bucida because of the long galls that form from its fruit when they are attacked by a tiny wasp. The name is seldom used, having been displaced by the name "black-olive" after some introductions of this species were confused with *Terminalia muelleri*, whose fruits really do resemble olives. The fruits of bucida are small and dry.

BUCKEYE. Common name, especially for the southern species of AESCULUS, a genus of native

North American trees more commonly known as horse-chestnut.

Mexican-, Texas-, or Spanish-buckeye is the shrubby tree *Ungnadia speciosa*.

BUCKLER FERN. Common name for species of DRYOPTERIS, especially *D. aemula* (hay-scented buckler fern), *D. carthusiana* (narrow buckler fern), and *D. dilatata* (broad buckler fern).

BUCKTHORN. Common name for RHAMNUS, a genus of shrubs or small trees. False buckthorn is *Bumelia*. Sea-buckthorn is HIPPOPHAE. The Buckthorn Family is RHAMNACEAE.

BUCKWHEAT. Common name for *Fagopyrum esculentum*, a quick-growing annual herb grown as a farm crop for its seed, which is ground into a dark-colored flour famous for making pancakes. It is also an important bee plant, though buckwheat honey is sometimes considered dark and rather strong-flavored.

Other plants known by this common name include several members of the POLYGONACEAE (Buckwheat Family). Wild-buckwheat is ERIOGONUM.

Because it is not particular as to soil, buckwheat is popular as a first crop on newly cleared land and in improving poor soil. So used, and also in orchards and gardens, it is grown as a GREEN MANURE or cover crop to be dug or plowed under while still green and succulent.

BUD. An incipient shoot together with the rudimentary leaves (or leaf parts in the form of scales) that invest and protect it. All growth of stems, foliage, branches, and flower-bearing shoots occurs from buds.

At the end of a season's growth, the stem has formed at its tip a leaf-bearing shoot that will continue the lengthwise growth of the stem the following season; this is the terminal bud. While each stem has only one terminal bud, there are numerous axillary buds that are formed in the upper angle between each leaf and the stem and may develop leaf shoots and flower shoots.

Accompanying an axillary bud may be one or more accessory buds, as in the red maple.

A bud is composed of embryonic leaves or flowers grouped around the growing point. Over winter this whole tiny shoot is covered by scale-like leaves of the past sea-son's growth that persist until the following season. The most conspicuous and highly specialized buds of temperate-climate shrubs and trees are the so-called resting buds that are remarkably well adapted to resisting unfavorable weather conditions. Many times they are covered with resinous secretions, hairy growths, waxy layers, or other coatings that protect them from unfavorable growing condi-tions, prevent their drying out, and guard them against premature development. It is these buds that, by refusing to grow until a certain period of cold weather has elapsed, make it difficult to force some kinds of plants or their branches to flower indoors in the winter; however, some treatments help overcome this natural tendency to seasonal dormancy.

Leaf and flower buds

See DORMANCY; FLOWER.

BUDDING. A special form of GRAFTING, also known as bud grafting, in which only a single bud of a desired variety with little or no wood is inserted in the stock. Many propagators prefer bud grafting because it is faster, easier, and less messy. No wax is necessary, and cambium layers need not be aligned. Although plants can be bud grafted in early spring with a dormant bud, it is usually done in the summer with a newly devel-oped latent bud that is taken from under the stem of a live leaf.

Although many professional and amateur propagators prefer budding to grafting, most agree that in the plant nursery there is a place for both. The side grafting of evergreens, splice grafting of cacti, and bench grafting of fruit trees cannot be satisfactorily duplicated by any kind of budding. Many plants, such as nut trees and cer-tain shade trees, have a better success rate when propagated by regular grafting, but most of the millions of roses and fruit trees that are sold each year are propagated by budding.

THE T-BUD

This is the most common budding method and is the easiest way for a beginner to graft a tree. Though perhaps a dozen methods of budding are used in special cases, the only one by which mil-lions of plants are annually propagated is "shield budding," so called because the scion bud is an elongated oval.

Budding is usually done outdoors from mid-summer until early autumn, while the bark of the plants to be "worked" will readily separate when gently pried from the young wood beneath. These "stocks" should be ½ in. or more in diame-ter and, to facilitate the work, be stripped of their lower leaves for about 6 in. As near the ground as possible, and where the bark is smooth, a ver-tical cut about 2 in. long is made with a budding knife, and at its upper end a horizontal cross cut (A). The two cuts, forming a T, must not be deeper than the bark or the wood may be wounded. The two upper corners of bark are then gently pried up just enough to permit inser-tion of the bud (B).

"Bud sticks" (young twigs of the current sea-son's growth) are cut from the variety it is desired to propagate and the leaves are cut off so that only about ½ in. of the stems are left (C). To prevent shriveling, they are wrapped in wet burlap or placed standing in water.

To cut a bud, start with the knife about ¾ in. below it, pass it up through the bark beneath the bud, and bring it about ¼ in. above, producing a shield-shaped sliver of bark and wood with a bud near its center (D). This, held by the stump of its leaf stem, is pushed down—bud pointing upward—beneath the raised bark of the T-cut (E). Its underside presses against the cambium layer (growing wood) of the stock. The operation is completed by wrapping raffia, adhesive graft-ing tape, or a rubber strip around the stock to hold the bud in place, without covering it (F).

If raffia (or any other tier that will not stretch as the stem grows) is used, it must later be cut through on the side opposite the inserted bud; an elastic tier will give and need not be cut. Buds that have "taken" or united with the stock will remain plump and later begin to grow; if the operation fails, the bud dies. In such a case, the stock can be rebudded.

The next spring, when the tree is still dormant, cut off the top of the tree about 4–6 in. above the bud. In cold climates the tree will still be dormant, but the bud will start to grow soon after the stock is cut back. Within three weeks the stubs should be cut back further, to about ½ in. above the new shoot, which may grow from 2–6 ft. during the season, depending on the kind of plant, the growing conditions, etc. All other sprouts that appear along the stock must be rubbed off while small and soft so all the plant food will go into the bud shoot. When the bud has grown a few inches, stake it to prevent injury and to promote straight growth. At the end of that season or during the following spring, the young budded plants can be transplanted.

BUDDLEIA (BUD lee ah). A genus of deciduous or semievergreen shrubs or trees belonging to the Loganiaceae (Logania Family), and commonly known as butterfly bush. The 100 or so species are found in tropical and temperate regions of the Americas, Asia, and South Africa. Most species are hardy only to Zone 7. Fast, rather coarse growers, with unusual, quadrangular stems, they grow 5–10 ft. high and thrive in rich, well-drained soil in a sunny location. The individual flowers are small but are produced in great profusion, mostly in long, dense racemes. Shades of lilac and purple predominate, but some have white and yellow flowers. Nearly all have a prominent orange eye and are sweetly fragrant. Butterflies attracted to the plant in gardens add to its interest. Propagation is easily accomplished by cuttings taken in early fall and wintered over in a cool spot.

PRINCIPAL SPECIES

B. alternifolia is a good-looking Chinese shrub growing to 12 ft. with wide-spreading, arching branches. It is one of the hardiest species, growing in Zones 6–9, as well as the only one with alternate leaves. The long, arching stems of the previous year are studded with compact clusters of lavender-purple flowers in spring. Shoots of the current season may flower in late summer.

B. davidii (summer-lilac), a native of China, is one of the best-known species. Hardy in Zones 6–9, given a protection of litter, the rootstock will survive most winters and send up vigorous shoots that flower from midsummer until frost.

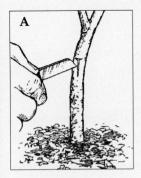
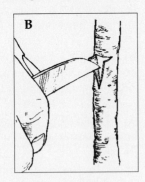

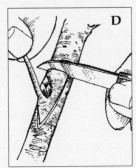
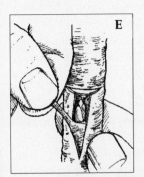

T-bud grafting

It is best to defer cutting them down until spring. The lilac-colored flowers are produced in terminal, tail-like spikes a foot or more long. Var. *magnifica* gives larger spikes and deeper colored flowers with crinkled and slightly reflexed petals. Cv. 'Black Knight' has dark purple flowers; 'Charming' has pink flowers; 'Empire Blue' has violet-blue flowers; 'White Bouquet' and 'White Profusion' have white flowers.

B. globosa (orange ball) is a handsome half-evergreen shrub from Chile, hardy to Zone 7, able to withstand a few degrees of frost. It is very striking in bloom with long-stalked round heads of orange-yellow flowers.

BUDWORM. The budworm, or bud moth as the adult form is called, feeds on the opening buds of various plants. Its most serious pest species is the spruce budworm, *Choristoneura fumiferana*, which infests all of the northern United States and much of Canada. Huge populations develop in spruce, balsam fir, and douglas fir forests, destroying the terminals and sometimes whole trees.

The mottled gray moths are just under an inch across and appear from late June into July. They lay oval, greenish eggs all along the needles, where the larvae feed before making cocoons. The 1-in. caterpillars feed at the base of needles and spin webs over the tops.

Birds, parasites, predators (including predatory wasps), and bad weather reduce the populations of these serious defoliators. *Bacillus thuringiensis* (Bt, commonly available as Biotrol, Dipel, or Thuricide) will curb the worm in home gardens. Other natural enemies include red squirrels, spiders, and spider mites.

Other budworms include tobacco budworm, *Heliothis virescens*, which infests cotton and tobacco in the South, and members of the Solanaceae (Nightshade Family), such as ground cherry and nightshade, as well as geraniums and ageratums. The very small caterpillars can be sprayed with Bt, and the single small eggs can be pinched or pushed off into kerosene from the undersides of the leaves.

Rose budworm, *Pyrrhia umbra*, infests the buds of roses, columbine, and other garden flowers. There are two kinds of caterpillars, one with black stripes on a green body, the other with pale orange markings on a green back. Control with Bt or a spray of rotenone after dusk when bees have gone to hive. Cut off and destroy infected buds.

The eyespotted bud moth infests blackberries, apples, hawthorns, larch, laurel, oak, and other forest and fruit trees. The small brown worms winter in silken cases on twigs or bud axils. The brown moths lay eggs on undersides of leaves for summer hatching.

BUGBANE. Common name for CIMICIFUGA, a genus of tall woodland plants with wands of small white flowers.

BUGLEWEED. Common name, along with bugle, for AJUGA, a genus of annual and perennial flowering herbs especially suited to rock garden or border planting. Bugleweed is also sometimes applied to species of LYCOPUS.

BUGLOSS. A common name for ANCHUSA, a genus of hairy herbs grown for their bright blue flowers. Viper's-bugloss refers to the genus ECHIUM. Siberian bugloss refers to BRUNNERA.

BULBIL. A small, bulblike bud or bulblet, produced generally in the axil of a leaf (as in the tiger lily) or in place of the flower (as the multiplier onion), and capable of developing into a new plant when planted.

BULBINELLA (bul bi NEL ah). A genus of perennial herbs belonging to the Liliaceae (Lily Family), native to South Africa and New Zealand. They have fleshy tuberous roots, grasslike leaves, and bright yellow or white flowers in dense clusters at the top of bare stalks. They should be planted in spring in a warm, sheltered place in the border or at the corner of the rock garden where a note of height is needed. They are propagated by division in the spring.

B. hookeri grows to 3 ft. and has bright yellow flowers in 10-in. racemes.

B. floribunda var. *latifolia* is white flowered and grows only 1 ft. high.

BULBLET BLADDER FERN.
Common name for *Cystopteris bulbifera*, a small, easily grown fern that has bulblike growths on the fronds; see CYSTOPTERIS.

BULBOCODIUM
(bul boh KOH dee um) **vernum.**
A small bulbous plant resembling a crocus, blooming very early in the spring in advance of the leaves; hardy to Zone 6. The rosy purple, funnelform flowers appear above the ground as early as the snowdrops. Plant the bulbs early in the fall, about 4 in. below the surface in good, well-drained soil in a sheltered spot in the rock garden, and mulch lightly with decayed leaves.

BULBOPHYLLUM
(bulb oh FIL um). A genus of orchids closely allied to and sometimes considered synonymous with *Cirrhopetalum*. There are probably 1000 species of creeping epiphytic orchids native to the tropical and subtropical areas of the world. Their sizes vary from very small to very large; the leaves are thin-textured or leathery. Wiry rhizomes connect the pseudobulbs from which the inflorescences rise. The flowers are of many sizes and shapes—some weird and foul-smelling.

Most species do best mounted on plaques of cork, cedar, fir bark, or coconut husk or in baskets with a loose, well-drained medium. All need high humidity during growth, less when fully grown, and moderate shade. They are hardy in Zones 7–11, depending on the species, and most withstand a minimum winter temperature of 60–65°F.

PRINCIPAL SPECIES
B. bufo, from Sierra Leone, has flattened, spiraled, erect flower stems on which small purplish flowers appear.

B. medusae has small pseudobulbs. The 6-in. flower stalk has a head of densely clustered fragrant flowers whose threadlike sepals may be 5 in. long. Its colors are yellow-orange to brown-purple.

B. nutans is the type species.

BULBS.
A bulb is an encased leaf bud, or flower bud, or sometimes a combination of the two, surrounded by fleshy layers or scales fastened upon a fibrous base from which the roots are produced. The onion is a typical example of a true bulb. Some bulbs, such as hyacinth or tulip, have the thickened fleshy layers wrapped all around them, while others, such as the lily, have overlapping scales. A great many other floral subjects, because of their resemblance, are commonly known as bulbs, but their true classifications are as follows:

CORMS
A corm, of which the gladiolus and crocus are typical, is a solid object, usually quite hard, instead of being formed of layers or scales like a true bulb. The method of growing is also entirely different. A true bulb can live indefinitely as a single unit or can multiply by splitting itself up, but a mature corm actually withers and dies after a year of growth, being replaced by a new corm

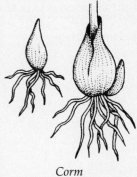

Corm

or corms that form usually on top of the old one, but sometimes beneath or alongside it.

TUBERS
These are shortened, congested, or swollen parts usually (though not always) protected underground. They may be modified stems, in which case they bear leaf buds or "eyes" in regular arrangement over their surface (the Irish potato is an example); or they may be swollen roots without eyes, as in the dahlia and sweet-potato, which sprout from buds on the stem end or "neck" of the tuber. The function of these fleshy tubers is to serve as reservoirs of plant food upon which the new shoots can subsist until their new

rooting system is able to provide nourishment by absorption through root hairs.

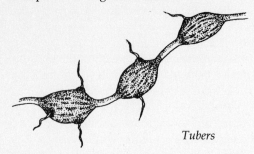

Tubers

RHIZOMES

A rhizome, or rootstock, is a thick, fleshy root that usually grows horizontally and often quite near the surface of the soil. The German iris is a typical example.

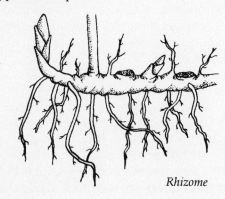

Rhizome

TRUE BULBS

A definite advantage of planting true bulbs for flower production is the fact that their flower buds, in well-matured, full-sized specimens, are actually encased within the bulb at the time of planting and surrounded with stored food material. That is why some kinds need little other than water to flower perfectly. Hyacinths, narcissus, and amaryllis can be flowered in water alone, and the autumn-crocus (**Colchicum**) will sometimes bloom without any soil or water if the temperature is favorable. The bud within a dormant bulb was created while the foliage was maturing the previous season. It is therefore important to remember that, in all true bulbs, next year's flowers are being produced while this

year's foliage is maturing. For this reason, just as much care should be given to bulbs after they flower as before.

This condition does not prevail with corms, tubers, or rhizomes, which have what can be called a progressive flower embryo. The treatment these subjects receive during their early growth determines to a great extent that same season's flowering results.

CLASSES OF BULBS

Seasonally this whole group of bulbs is divided into two main groups. The first and probably best known being the spring bulbs, which are usually planted in the fall. They include such well-known items as tulips, hyacinths, and narcissus. The other main group is the summer- and fall-blooming types, which are usually planted in the spring. These plants include gladiolus, schizostylis, and dahlias, the latter are not true bulbs, of course, but always get lumped in with this group.

Bulb

There is another important division of this whole group into hardy and tender bulbs. When a bulb—like any other plant—is spoken of as being hardy, it means that it will survive cold winter weather; tender subjects will not do this and therefore must not be allowed to freeze—either in the ground or out of it. Included in the so-called spring bulb class are many that are hardy and thus capable of remaining in the open ground during winter, among them the whole group of DUTCH BULBS. On the other hand, very few of the fall bulbs are hardy, which means that most of their group must come out of the ground in the fall and be placed in frost-free storage during the winter.

GROWING SPRING BULBS

September and October are the best months for planting. While the period can be extended into November or early December if the ground is still open, early planting is best since it provides sufficient time for rooting before the soil gets too cold. Spade the location thoroughly and if the soil is impoverished, work in liberal applications of bonemeal or well-rotted manure, but do not let any manure touch the bulbs.

Bulbs should be spaced in accordance with the floral effect that is desired. Generally speaking, a good plan to follow is to allow twice the diameter of a bulb between every two and to plant so that the top of the bulb is about 3 in. below the ground when covered, in the case of most of the larger bulbs, and 1½–2 in. below for smaller kinds such as crocus, galanthus, etc. Lily bulbs should go considerably deeper; see LILIUM. Since no bulb can flourish if crowded by other plants, it is important to select a location that provides ample light and space.

In the northern states, a winter covering is essential if the bulbs are to do their best, and for this purpose light mulch can be employed. It should be removed as the new growth starts peeking through in the spring and after danger of heavy frost is past. This covering is not intended to prevent frost from reaching the bulbs or even going below them, but it does prevent the alternate freezing and thawing that heaves the ground and injures many plants.

As the bulbs develop top growth in the spring, the soil should be continually loosened on the surface, but not deep enough to damage the roots. This treatment should be continued through the whole period of their growth and stopped only after all the foliage has completely died down. Remember that after the flower is spent, the bulb is making its flower bud for the next season, so it is important that the foliage be encouraged to stay green as long as possible. With bulbous subjects that make separate flower stems and leaves, such as narcissus, the picking of the flowers has only a slight effect on the building up of a flower bud for the next season. But for bulbs that bear flowers and leaves on the stems, such as tulips, any cutting of the flower that removes part of the foliage is detrimental to the next season's flower in proportion to the per-

centage of the foliage removed. Whatever the type, the flowers as they wither should be cut off near the top of the stem; this prevents the flower from going to seed, which draws heavily on the stored vitality of the bulb.

After the foliage has completely matured, usually during July, the bulb is dormant. If the planting is a recent one and the bulbs have not become crowded by increasing, they can remain in the same spot for years. When they have increased considerably, which will be shown by much additional foliage and fewer flowers, they should be taken up; separated by pulling apart those that hang loose; and then either immediately replanted, which is best, or stored over the summer months, then replanted in the early fall, as indicated above. A change of location when replanting is always beneficial.

GROWING FALL BULBS

It has been pointed out that a great many subjects commonly known as "fall bulbs" are not true bulbs at all but are either corms, tubers, or rhizomes. Since these depend for their bud development to a great extent upon the treatment they receive after planting, it is apparent that considerable care and attention must be given to their culture if the best flowering results are to be obtained. Select a spot that is fully exposed to the sun for at least three-quarters of the day, well away from tree or other roots that continually rob the soil of its moisture and vitality. Spade the location thoroughly and deeply, and mix in liberal applications of bonemeal or well-rotted manure. No simple rule can be given for spacing, as this will depend on the size of the growing plant. Gladiolus corms can be planted 6 in. apart, while dahlias should have at least 3 ft. between them.

Practically all these subjects can be planted as soon as the soil is warm in the spring and from then on the soil must be kept thoroughly loosened at the surface; this provides a mulch, which prevents the evaporation of moisture. Never disturb the soil deep enough to destroy any roots. Continue this treatment throughout the summer, and provide water whenever necessary. Applications of liquid manure aid greatly in producing extra fine blossoms. Successive plantings can be made during the early summer of such subjects as gladiolus; they will provide a continuity of blooms over a much longer period than if the bulbs are planted at the same time.

Some of the species will start to die off in the early fall, while others will remain in full growth until cut down by frost. In any case the bulbs should be lifted immediately and the top growth cut off with a sharp knife or shears. Then store the bulbs in a frost-free location for the winter. A hot, dry cellar is not a desirable storage place and if it is the only location available, the bulbs should be wrapped in several thicknesses of old newspaper to prevent evaporation of moisture. An ideal location is a part of the cellar partitioned off from any heating apparatus or pipes, where a constant temperature of about 45°F can be maintained with sufficient moisture in the atmosphere to preserve the roots in plump condition throughout the winter.

GROWING BULBS INDOORS

For indoor (home) culture, true bulbs are the easiest to flower successfully, because they contain their flower buds within them. However, the light and atmospheric conditions that prevail in the home tend to greatly limit the subjects that can be readily flowered there. A very dry atmosphere is a handicap to most plants and fatal to many. It can be overcome to some extent by humidifiers. A uniform temperature is also very desirable. Rooms that are maintained at a 70°F temperature in the daytime and allowed to fall much lower at night are not conducive to best results. Freedom from drafts is also important. The ideal room for indoor flower gardening is one that is light and airy, with a uniform temperature of about 65°F and with sufficient humidity and sunlight. The following is a list of the more popular bulbous subjects that can be readily flowered in the home.

Narcissus. The polyanthus, or many-flowered, forms of the species *N. tazetta* include the pure white cv. 'Paperwhite', the dark yellow 'Soleil d'Or', and the two-toned yellow var. *orientalis*, commonly known as Chinese sacred-lily or joss flower. The culture of all three kinds is simple. The dormant bulbs are available from August to January and can be planted at any time during that period. The earlier plantings will take several months to flower, while those made in December or January take only two or three weeks. This is because the flower bud progresses as the season advances. Water (and the right temperature) is all that is necessary to flower them perfectly, so any other material used in the container simply serves as a root anchorage to prevent the plants from toppling over after they have attained some height. The usual method of planting is to place a thin layer of gravel, stones, sand, peat moss, or similar material in the bottom of a bowl, then arrange the bulbs in an upright position in the manner desired, and then fill the space around the bulbs with the same material, allowing the tops (or so called "noses") of the bulbs to protrude. Water is then added, after which the bulbs will start to grow immediately. Small pieces of charcoal placed in the bowl will prevent the water from souring, but this can also be corrected by changing the water (which should be at room temperature) every few days.

Placing the bowl containing the planted bulbs in a dark place while the bulbs make their first root growth is sometimes recommended, but it is not desirable since it tends to create abnormally tall foliage and flower stems. So simply place the bowl in a light, sunny window, ideally maintaining a uniform temperature of 60°F, and except for the addition or change of water, no other attention is needed. The bulbs will come into flower in a few weeks. They must never be allowed to freeze.

Amaryllis are among the showiest and easiest of bulbous flowers to successfully grow in the home. For cultural instructions, see AMARYLLIS.

Fall-Flowering Crocus. Both this type of true crocus and COLCHICUM (autumn-crocus) are desirable house subjects. The bulbs are dormant for only a short time in late summer and will produce flowers even without being planted. The results are much better, however, if the bulbs are properly planted in shallow bowls and barely covered with peat moss, which should be lightly soaked. Add additional water as evaporation occurs. Because they have no foliage, the beauty of the flowers and the general effect will be much enhanced if a little lawn grass seed is planted in the bowls with them at the same time.

Zephyranthes (rain- or fairy-lily). All the zephyranthes (which are related to the amaryllis) are good house subjects and can be treated the same as crocus.

Hyacinth. The French Roman hyacinths adapt themselves well to house culture. The bulbs should be planted in early fall in well-dampened peat moss, then stored away in a dark closet. Water should be added as it evaporates. In early December they can be brought out into a light, sunny window where they will flower about Christmas time. Dutch hyacinths, while often recommended for growing in water in such receptacles as hyacinth glasses or milk bottles, are really quite difficult to handle in this manner. If the bulbs are not planted until late November or early December, the chances of success are much improved. In any event, after planting, they should be placed in a cool, dark closet and allowed to remain there until considerable root growth develops and the foliage and bud has attained a height of 1–2 in. The containers can then be removed to a light, sunny window in a warmer room.

Lily-of-the-valley. While this is grown from a "crown" or "pip," not a bulb, is easily flowered in the home and can well be mentioned here. The pips are held in a frozen condition in cold storage by importers and bulb dealers from one season to the next and are therefore available for forcing every day in the year. Their culture is most simple. The fibrous roots are usually too long for use in the popular shallow bowls but can be partially trimmed off to fit into such receptacles without suffering any damage. A bowl 6 in. across can well accommodate ten or twelve pips, which are placed in an upright position with their shoots extending above the top of the bowl. Pack sphagnum moss, sand, or peat moss firmly around the

roots. Fill with lukewarm water, and the pips will start to grow immediately. They will flower within three or four weeks in the usual room temperature.

Other Bulbs. With some preliminary outdoor handling, the list of bulbs that can be flowered in the home can be greatly enlarged. In view of the fact that any true bulb, if well rooted, can be brought into a heated room and flowered, a preliminary outdoor planting and storage followed by subsequent removal into warmer quarters duplicates what greenhouse growers call "forcing," which merely means the flowering of any plant before its normal period. Practically all the DUTCH BULBS and, in fact, nearly all true bulbs can be handled in this manner.

To cultivate bulbs for indoor use, in early fall plant the bulbs in the desired receptacle. An ordinary clay flowerpot with a drainage hole is best, but even fancy bowls without drainage can be employed. When clay pots are used, water well, then plunge or bury the whole pot outdoors from 1–2 ft. deep and cover it with ashes, soil, leaves, or straw. The latter is best as it can be more readily removed. A deep, unused cold-frame is a good place for this conditioning process. Leave the pots and bulbs undisturbed until February or early March, when the bulbs will have put out a good root system which is the secret of this whole operation. They are then ready for removal to a warmer temperature indoors.

When fancy bowls without drainage are used, the bulbs should be planted in dampened peat moss and the pots either plunged outdoors (which is best) or kept in a cool, dark place such as a root or fruit cellar. As before, when the bulbs are thoroughly rooted, they are transferred to the warmer location. The indoor temperature should at first be 45–50°F; it can be stepped up after the foliage and the buds develop. This method of indoor winter gardening is popular in Europe, where it provides flower lovers with a succession of blooming plants during the late winter and early spring months.

All the foregoing is intended only for those

who have the average home conditions or equipment. Where a greenhouse or a light, sunny porch is available, the list of bulbous plants that can be successfully flowered is much greater.

BULB ENEMIES

Bulbs are subject to a number of diseases and to attack by several serious insect pests, all of which can make rigid care necessary.

Virus and Bacterial Diseases. Most bulbous plants are subject to some form of virus disease. Mosaic produces mottling of the foliage, poor flowers, and stunted plants; it is often called the gray disease. Breaking refers to a change from a solid color to a streaking or splashing of the flowers; it is responsible for the variegated tulips that were formerly thought to be distinct varieties or types. A third kind of virus disease is typified by the "yellow flat" disease of lily. Roguing, which means a periodical inspection of plantings and the removal and destruction of every diseased or undesirable individual, is the only control method available against such diseases.

Hyacinth yellows, a bacterial disease, is confined to that genus, but bacterial soft rot is found in many types of bulbs, particularly callas.

Fungus Diseases. Fungi of the botrytis group cause a blight, or "fire disease," of lily, tulip, hyacinth, crocus, and narcissus. The most typical sign of this disease is the fuzzy grayish mold produced on the leaves and flowers, but small black resting bodies, sclerotia, can be found on the bulb scales and on plant debris in the soil. Sanitary measures such as removing all blossoms as soon as they fade and cutting off the leaves at the surface as soon as they ripen are the best means of control. Spraying with a weak BORDEAUX MIXTURE several times in the spring, starting when the young shoots first appear, is beneficial. See BOTRYTIS.

A basal bulb rot causes serious losses among narcissus, crocus, hyacinth, and freesia bulbs. The fungus rots the basal plate (or the entire bulb), dwarfing the plant and causing crippled flowers. Discard badly diseased bulbs and soak the rest in a mild fungicide solution for six hours. Where basal rot threatens, the hot water used to treat narcissus, iris, etc., for the control of nematodes and bulb flies as directed below should contain a diluted fungicide.

Bulb Flies. The greater narcissus fly (*Merodon equestris*) attacks narcissus, hyacinth, amaryllis, galtonia, and other bulbous plants over most of the United States. The adult is a shiny, yellow-and-black, hairy fly resembling a small bumblebee. It lays eggs in the base of the leaves or the neck of the bulb, which usually is penetrated by a whitish or yellowish maggot. As the latter grows, perhaps to ¾ in. long, it may consume most of the bulb, which becomes soft and shows brown scars on the outer scales. Examine bulbs that are either bought or dug up in the garden, and destroy any showing distinct evidence of fly infestation.

To sterilize the remainder, place them in a loosely woven bag, wood or wire rack, or other open container, and suspend in a tank of water kept at a constant temperature of 110°F for 2½ hours. (More time will be necessary for very large bulbs.) If any bulbs then develop poorly or fail completely in the spring, dig and destroy them immediately.

The lesser narcissus fly (*Eumeris strigatus*) causes somewhat similar injury, and the control measures are the same. The adult is a small, blackish green fly; the maggots, grayish or yellowish gray with wrinkled bodies, can sometimes be found in narcissus, hyacinth, amaryllis, onion, shallot, or iris bulbs.

Mites. The bulb mite attacks practically all types of bulbs but is a special pest of narcissus, tulip, hyacinth, crocus, lily, amaryllis, orchid, and dahlia. It is minute, whitish, eight legged, and usually visible only with the aid of a hand lens. The female lays from 50 to 100 eggs on the surface of a bulb. They hatch in four to seven days, and the young mites burrow into the bulb, growing rapidly as they feed on scales or root tissue. Preferring healthy bulbs, they migrate through the soil from decaying to sound ones. Infested bulbs stored under favorable conditions for the mites deteriorate rapidly. Control by burning all soft and rotted bulbs. Others can be

BULBS SELECTION GUIDE

SPRING FLOWERING

LATIN NAME (common name)	PLANT HEIGHT	BLOOMING TIME	PLANTING DEPTH
Allium giganteum (giant onion)	48″	late spring	10″
Anemone blanda (windflower)	5″	early spring	2″
Crocus spp. (crocus)	3–5″	early spring	3–4″
Fritillaria imperialis (crown-imperial)	30–48″	midspring	5″
Galanthus spp. (snowdrop)	4–6″	early spring	4″
Hyacinthus spp. (hyacinth)	12″	early spring	6″
Iris spp. (Dutch iris)	36″	late spring	4″
Muscari spp. (grape-hyacinth)	6–10″	early spring	3″
Narcissus spp. (daffodil)	12″	midspring	6″
Tulipa spp. (early tulips)	10–13″	early spring	6″
Tulipa spp. (Darwin hybrid tulips)	28″	midspring	6″
Tulipa spp. (late tulips)	36″	late spring	5″

SUMMER FLOWERING

LATIN NAME (common name)	PLANT HEIGHT	PLANTING TIME	PLANTING DEPTH	SPACING
Gladiolus canthus (Acidanthera)	20″	early spring	2″	5″
Anemone spp. (de Caen, St. Brigid)	18″	south—early fall to midwinter north—early spring	2″	3″
Dahlia spp. large varieties dwarf varieties	48″ 12″	after last frost	4″ 4″	24″ 6″
Galtonia (summer-hyacinth)	40″	spring	5″	10″
Gladiolus spp. large flowering small flowering	60″ 30″	spring spring	3–4″ 3–4″	6″ 6″
Lilium spp. (lily)	3–7′	fall or early spring	8″	8″
Ranunculus spp. (buttercup)	12″	south—fall to midwinter	2″	8″
Tigridia spp. (tiger flower)	16″	early spring	3″	6″
Tritonia, Crocosmia spp. (montbretia)	24″	midspring	4″	4″

immersed in a mild insecticide and water solution held at 122°F for 10 minutes. Or they can be treated with hot water at 110°F for 2½ hours, as directed under bulb flies above. These methods are safe for dormant bulbs, but they will kill young roots.

Eelworm or Nematode. The bulb or stem nematode *Anguillulina dipsaci* is a microscopic round eelworm that burrows through the cells and eventually destroys the bulb, which usually shows concentric brown rings when it is cut across. Use the hot water treatment described above, being careful to maintain the exact temperature, and plant treated bulbs in fresh or sterilized soil. See NEMATODES.

BULL-BAY. Common name for *Magnolia grandiflora*, an evergreen tree with large leaves and showy flowers; see MAGNOLIA. It also refers to *Persea borbonia*, a tender evergreen tree closely related to the avocado; see PERSEA.

BULNESIA (bul NEES ee ah) **arborea.** A South American tree, related to *Guaiacum* (lignum-vitae), belonging to the Zygophyllaceae (Caltrop Family), but much faster growing, and reaching about 50 ft. Chrome-yellow flowers about 2 in. across, formed several times a year, make this a good flowering tree for frost-free areas. Propagation is by seed or, with difficulty, by cuttings or air layering.

BULRUSH. Common name for SCIRPUS, a genus of coarse perennial sedges sometimes planted in pond borders or bog gardens.

BUNCHBERRY. Common name for *Cornus canadensis*, a low-growing herb with whorled leaves surrounding the flowers; see CORNUS.

BURDOCK. Common name for the genus ARCTIUM, including coarse, strong-smelling biennials or perennials of the Asteraceae (Aster Family).

BURNET (BUR net). Common name for plants of the genus SANGUISORBA of the Rosaceae (Rose Family), most species grown as ornamental border plants.

BURNING BUSH. Common name for *Euonymus atropurpurea*, a deciduous shrub or tree that displays yellow leaves and scarlet fruit in autumn, see EUONYMUS; also refers to DICTAMNUS, a genus of strong-scented bushy perennials.

BURSERA (BUR sur ah) **simaruba.** A tree of the American subtropics, belonging to the Burseraceae (Torchwood Family). Its smooth, ruddy bark has given it the common names of naked-Indian and tourist tree in Florida, as well as the more widely used gumbo limbo. Extremely salt- and drought-tolerant, this tree is being used in Zone 11 and the southern part of Zone 10 as a street tree, as well as for shade.

BURSTWORT. A common name for HERNIARIA, a genus of trailing herbs belonging to the Caryophyllaceae (Pink Family).

BUSH HONEYSUCKLE. Common name for DIERVILLA, a genus of low, spreading shrubs useful for ground cover to hold banks in shape.

BUSH POPPY. Common name, along with tree poppy, for *Dendromecon rigida*, a California evergreen shrub with yellow flowers; see DENDROMECON.

BUTOMUS (BYOO toh mus) **umbellatus.** An erect, perennial, aquatic herb commonly known as flowering-rush. It has 2–3 ft. leaves resembling those of the iris, and rose-colored flowers 1 in. across borne in clusters atop 4-ft. erect stems. Native to Europe and Asia, plants are hardy to Zone 4 and have often escaped from cultivation, especially in New England. It is easily grown in ponds or in a moist, rich, loamy soil. Propagation is by division.

BUTTER-AND-EGGS. Common name for *Linaria vulgaris*, a hardy field and roadside herb with orange-and-yellow flowers; see LINARIA.

BUTTERCUP. Common name for RANUNCULUS, a genus of familiar wildflowers, including many horticultural subjects. The Buttercup Family is RANUNCULACEAE.

BUTTERFLY BUSH. Common name for BUDDLEIA, a genus of tender evergreen shrubs or trees cultivated for their attractive flowers.

BUTTERFLY FLOWER. A common name for SCHIZANTHUS, a genus of annual or biennial herbs with showy, orchidlike flowers. The name is also applied to *Bauhinia monandra*, a leguminous tree; see BAUHINIA.

BUTTERFLY GARDENS. Sometimes plantings are designed specifically to attract butterflies to the garden. These colorful creatures feed on a variety of nectar, and they will commonly visit rich flowers in a sunny location that is sheltered from the wind. Since butterflies prefer to feed on the native wildflowers of their natural environment, consider sowing a wildflower seed mix in a nearby field or in a spot protected by a low wall, hedge, or other windbreak.

Butterflies have simple requirements that are easily met. To encourage butterflies to breed, provide plants with leaves that the larvae (caterpillars) can eat, and do not begrudge the damage they may do to ornamental effects. Because they are insects, butterflies may be adversely affected by any chemicals used in the garden. If you want to attract them, avoid using insecticides, herbicides, or fungicides.

Many wildflower and formal garden favorites will attract butterflies, including *Alyssum*, *Asclepias* (milkweed, butterfly weed), *Aster* (New England aster), *Daucus* (Queen-Anne's-lace, carrot), *Dianthus* (pinks, sweet-William), *Gaillardia* (blanketflower), *Monarda* (bergamot, bee balm), *Phlox* (annual or garden phlox), *Rudbeckia* (black-eyed-Susan), and *Syringa* (lilac).

Summer butterfly garden: (A) *Lythrum* sp. (lythrum), (B) *Asclepias tuberosa* (butterfly weed), (C) *Echinacea purpurea* (purple coneflower), (D) *Papaver orientale* (oriental poppy), (E) *Lupinus* sp. (lupine), (F) *Coreopsis* sp. (tickseed), (G) *Aquilegia canadensis* (eastern columbine)

BUTTERFLY PEA. Common name for CLITORIA, a genus of tropical, flowering vines and shrubs.

BUTTERNUT. Common name for *Juglans cinerea*, a large deciduous type of walnut tree, valuable for its nuts and hard wood. See JUGLANS.

BUTTONWOOD. Common name for *Platanus occidentalis*, a native tree grown for shade and for its unusual bark; see PLATANUS.

BUXACEAE (buks AY see ee). The Box Family, comprising about six genera of trees, shrubs, or herbs. *Buxus* (boxwood) and *Pachysandra* are the best-known representatives.

BUXUS (BUK sus). A genus including about 30 species of evergreen shrubs or small trees belonging to the Buxaceae (Box Family), and commonly known as box or boxwood. They have small leathery leaves and inconspicuous flowers. Boxwood foliage has an unpleasant odor that repels animals, who will not eat the foliage.

Boxwoods grow in any well-drained spot but seem to prefer partial shade and neutral to slightly alkaline soil. In cold climates, winter protection from sun and wind is usually necessary. They grow slowly but are valuable in gardens for many uses. One very dwarf form has been grown for centuries to edge walks and flower beds. Boxwoods are also amenable to hard trimming and can be cut into various shapes and figures if desired. See TOPIARY.

Propagation is by cuttings of mature shoots in early fall. Hardiness varies with species or cultivars, but most are hardy in Zones 5–9.

ENEMIES

Boxwood canker is prevalent and serious in the eastern states. In early summer, infected twigs show feeble growth and pale green foliage; late twigs and branches show a conspicuous dieback, the leaves fading and withering. Sometimes a branch suddenly turns straw-colored. On the undersides of leaves and on twigs and trunks appear salmon pink pustules containing thousands of spores, which may be washed or carried by air currents to other branches or plants. Infection may also be carried by the gardener working among the plants. Plants weakened by starvation and severe cold weather are especially susceptible; much loss attributed to winter injury is primarily due to nectria canker.

The LEAF MINER or midge, which is the worst pest of boxwoods, is a tiny orange fly that lays eggs in punctures in the lower leaf surface. The small maggots, which cause oval, blisterlike areas, winter in the leaves, and the young flies emerge in late spring or early summer. Damaged leaves should be removed and destroyed. A spray program can help to protect the plants during the three weeks the flies are active. Spray or dust thoroughly with insecticide, especially the lower surfaces and interior of the bushes. Apply as the first flies are emerging, and keep the plants covered by spraying again after each rain. See also INSECT CONTROL.

PRINCIPAL SPECIES

B. harlandii, an unusual species with long, narrow leaves and vase-shaped growth habit, resembles a miniature elm tree and is an excellent specimen plant.

B. microphylla is a compact shrub from Japan. It grows to 3 ft. but is often prostrate. Var. *koreana* is extremely hardy, but the foliage does turn brown in winter and is unsightly. Cv. 'Tide Hill' grows to only 15 in. but may spread to 5 ft. wide and has attractive, small, narrow green leaves that remain green in winter.

B. sempervirens (common box) is a shrub or small tree growing to 15 ft., found in southern Europe, northern Africa, and western Asia. Long in cultivation, there are several forms, variable in size, color, and shape of the leaves. Cultivars include 'Arborescens', the typical large form that grows to 25 ft.; 'Handsworthii', an upright, bushy form with very dark green leaves, which is considered the best for a hedge; and 'Myrtifolia', a dwarf form with narrow leaves.

CABBAGE. A biennial herb, *Brassica oleracea* var. *capitata*, whose thick, rounded, strongly veined leaves are compressed into huge buds or compact "heads" on a short, stout stock. Its numerous horticultural varieties include early and late types; smooth or crinkly and green or purple ("red") leaves; and oblong, conical, globular, or flattened heads. Chinese or celery cabbage refers to several oriental forms of BRASSICA.

Cabbage varieties display perhaps wider variation than those of any other vegetable, and not only in the color and form of the head. Early kinds (mostly of high quality) may form their small heads in less than 100 days from sowing seeds, and each requires only 1 sq. ft. to develop; late ones need twice as long and three times as much space. The early forms do best if they are planted in early

Cabbage head

spring, since they prefer cool, moist conditions. Midseason varieties should be started equally early to give them a good start before hot weather, which they tolerate better than the early kinds do. Late kinds are usually started in May or June and harvested in October or November. They are less susceptible to heat than the earlier kinds and form their heads during the cool fall weather.

For the home garden, early and midseason kinds are better than the late ones because late cabbage is a staple market vegetable. If any late variety is desired in the home garden, first choice should be one of the savory types, all of which are of the highest quality and are seldom available in the markets.

CULTURE

To grow best, cabbage requires full exposure to sun and a soil abundantly supplied with plant food and moisture. The soil can be of any type; the texture can be sandy, clay, mucky, or gravel-ly, but it can hardly be made too rich with stable manures and leguminous green manures. Without ample soil moisture the plants suffer and make few, poor, or no heads; however, they also fail in poorly drained soil. Hence, DRAINAGE is important.

Planting. For the earliest crop, sow seed under glass in seed pans or flats. When the seedlings have developed their second pair of true leaves, prick them off about 2 in. apart into other flats. The soil should be friable but not rich, so strong roots will develop rather than large tops. Keep where the night temperature is below 60°F, even down to 50°F, and give abundant air. When the plants are well established, place the flats in a coldframe and gradually harden the plants in readiness for transplanting them outdoors. Vigorous, stocky subjects are more easily transplanted and grow rapidly when properly handled. It is advisable to wrap a strip of paper 2 in. wide around each stem at ground level or use flat disks of tar paper to outwit CUTWORM pests.

Distances between plants depend on the variety, the soil, and the method of cultivation. Set early kinds 12 in. apart, or even closer, in rows 18 in. apart for wheelhoe or hoe culture. Leave 30 in. between rows if a tractor is used. Cultivate twice a week until there is danger of injuring the plants with the tools.

For the late crop, sow seed in early June in rows 12 in. or less apart in outdoor beds. Dig the soil freshly and rake it finely. It should be only moderately fertile. If the seed is sown thinly, the plants, without thinning, will grow sturdy and stocky enough for direct transplanting to the garden within a month after sowing.

Harvesting. To collect the heads, it is usually advisable to pull the plants up by the roots; however, if cut so as to leave a few inches of stalk, several small, loose heads may form along the stem for later gathering. The outer leaves and stems of large heads should be fed to livestock or poultry, or chopped up and buried in the compost pile to destroy insect pests that are very likely to be present in the leaf axils. Cut early cabbage only as needed because it does not keep well after cutting. To prevent excessive growth and splitting, bend or twist the stems of the largest heads to break or loosen some of the feeding roots. Harvest late cabbage as late in the season as possible before freezing. Trim off the outer leaves and store for winter use.

Enemies. The diseases and insect pests of cabbage are treated under BRASSICA.

CABBAGE PALMETTO. A common name for *Sabal palmetto*, a species of fan palm native from North Carolina to Florida; see SABAL.

CABOMBA (kah BOM bah). A small genus of aquatic plants native to the Western Hemisphere, belonging to the Nymphaeaceae (Waterlily Family), and commonly known as fanwort or watershield. Plants have tiny, white or yellowish flowers. The floating leaves are rounded and entire, but those below the surface are finely cut. Various species are hardy to Zone 4.

C. caroliniana, with white flowers, is the species commonly grown. Found in pools and slow streams from Illinois southward, it can easily be established in garden pools in Zones 7–11. It can also be used in aquariums, where it helps provide oxygen for fish but does not last long unless it can root in soil. Propagation is by cuttings, division, and seed.

CACAO. Common name for *Theobroma cacao*, a tropical tree whose fruit yields the cocoa and chocolate used for commercial purposes; see THEOBROMA.

CACTACEAE (kak TAY see ee). The Cactus Family. A group of plants native only to the Western Hemisphere and characterized by having succulent, often spiny stems with reduced leaves and usually showy flowers with many petal-like sepals and numerous petals and stamens. The inferior ovary produces a many-seeded berry, often covered with small spines and bristles. Common members include *Opuntia* (pricklypear), *Carnegiea gigantea* (saguaro), and *Echinocactus* (barrel cactus).

CACTUS. The CACTACEAE (Cactus Family) stands apart, with little to connect it to other plant families. It is dicotyledonous (that is, the seedlings have two seed-leaves), perennial, and all of its members are succulent. Succulent in this connection means capable of storing within itself sufficient moisture to enable it to withstand drought or arid conditions. In cacti this stored moisture is mucilaginous, which tends to retard evaporation.

Plants vary in shape from slender vines to huge, columnar, branched or unbranched forms; and from treelike growths to the small, flat, rounded forms of the MAMMILLARIA. Leaves, except in rare cases, which will be noted, are conspicuous by their absence. When present, they are small, inconspicuous, and soon fall. The roots also vary greatly; in most cases they are fibrous, but some are tuberous, some are aerial, and sometimes there is a taproot.

The blossoms are usually large and showy, with many petals and numerous stamens. The petals and sepals often integrate and are usually referred to as inner and outer perianth segments, the perianth being the floral envelope which includes both corolla and calyx. The fruits are berries with no partitions between the seeds. In many cases they are edible.

The cacti have one distinguishing characteristic found in no other plants: specialized organs that sprout branches, flowers, spines, glochids (barbed hairs), and, when present, leaves. These centers of growth are called areoles. Their position and number are determining factors in differentiating species, as are the number, form, and position of the spines.

Cacti (with a single doubtful exception, a species of *Rhipsalis*) are native to the Western Hemisphere. In North America their habitat extends into Canada, to Nova Scotia and British Columbia, and throughout the United States, especially in the Southwest. Mexico is undoubtedly entitled to be called "Cactus Land," leading all other localities in the number and variety of kinds found. They are also distributed over many parts of South America, where some of our most interesting species originate.

KINDS OF CACTI

Originally only a few species were known, grouped under a single genus, cactus. As our knowledge of these plants has grown and new species have been discovered, there are now between 1500 and 3000 species and subdivisions. Many changes in the nomenclature have occurred. As the most generally accepted authority in North America, names and classifications from the *The Cactaceae* by Britton and Rose, and the International Code of Botanical Nomenclature will be primarily followed in this article and other articles discussing cactus genera throughout this book.

The three tribes that form the first great subdivisions are:

PERESKIA

True leaves are persistent, and there is more or less resemblance to other plants; hence, by the uninitiated, they are often referred to other families; see PERESKIA.

OPUNTIA

This includes the genus *Nopalea* (prickly-pear) and *Cholla*, familiar to many. See also NOPALEA; OPUNTIA.

CEREUS

This is a very large and diverse category, divided into subtribes including the columnar giants; the slender, climbing plants, some of which are known as the night-blooming CEREUS and are frequently cultivated as houseplants; the ECHINOCEREUS types, delightful with their spines and lovely, colorful flowers; FEROCACTUS, which includes some of the most interesting specimens in the list of houseplants; the Coryphanthenae, including the largest single group—MAMMILLARIA, which lend themselves to even the smallest dish gardens; EPIPHYLLUM, wondrously beautiful, claiming the attention of professional and amateur alike; and the unique and curious RHIPSALIS.

Among these numerous representatives of the Cactus Family, many are little known, others are still difficult or impossible to obtain, and with others cultivation is impossible. Discussion will focus on those best suited to garden or home cultural purposes. Even there, the list is rich in specimens suited to large and small needs in almost any cultural condition.

CACTI IN THE GARDEN

Considering the culture of cacti, plants naturally fall into two classes: (1) those originating in the arid desert, and (2) those native to the tropics. This latter class, whose members are semiepiphytic in their habits, includes some of those longest known in cultivation and dearest to plant lovers, including night-blooming cereus, the *Epiphyllums*, and all greenhouse plants.

All cacti are succulent, built to store up any moisture obtainable, and to take it up sometimes too greedily. The one essential factor in the culture of all cacti is absolutely good drainage. They will not tolerate a soggy soil. A choice plant may be ruined in a single day by water standing at its roots.

In planning a cactus garden, a gentle slope is ideal. The ground must be dug up and a substratum of stones, broken brick, or similar substance placed. It should be filled with gravel and topped with a good sandy loam. Whether fertilizer should be used is debatable: some growers advise against it, while others use a richer soil with success. Most desert cacti like alkaline soil.

Climatic conditions vary so greatly that it is hard to make any rule that is applicable everywhere. In more northern and colder conditions, few cacti are hardy in the ground, but even into Canada, *Opuntia* is found. *O. opuntia* (also listed as *O. compressa*), for example, is found along the sandy Atlantic coast. Of somewhat straggly growth, it has a beautiful, roselike, clear yellow flower.

The hardy varieties can be potted and sunk into the ground—but here extra care must be taken with drainage in the pot and in the bed where it is sunk. In the colder season, these potted plants must be removed and taken indoors or otherwise protected.

In warmer climates, hardier specimens of normally smaller species can be planted in the garden and allowed to remain there. Under such conditions, a wider choice of plants is available. Not only can larger-growing species be included here, but larger specimens can be used than those that must be removed from the ground.

In planning a permanent outdoor garden, it is important to consider the growth patterns of specimens included, so that one that grows or spreads rapidly will not crowd its slower-growing neighbor. However, some of the smaller species like partial shade and may thrive in the shadow of larger plants.

A cactus garden is often designed to include other succulent plants requiring similar treatment. In this case it helps to have some low growing plant, succulent in character, as a ground cover.

Rock gardening is frequently a misunderstood subject. Too often a few boulders or cobblestones are strewn about, some cacti planted at random, and the result is dubbed a rock garden. Rocks are not necessary to a cactus garden (except as a substratum for drainage). If used, they should be carefully selected and placed as though they were there naturally.

WATERING

The care of a cactus garden after planting is simple. Weeds should be kept out, of course. The important question is watering—when to do it, how often, and how much?

Do not overwater. Requirements vary with climatic conditions. A drier atmosphere needs larger amounts of water. Closeness of planting also affects watering. Some growers recommend a light watering every few weeks while others prefer a thorough watering every four to six weeks. The soil should be moist but not wet. These directions apply to the blooming and growing season; otherwise little water is needed. If the soil does not drain well and dry out reasonably fast, the plant is probably being overwatered.

Of all things to be guarded against, rot is most important. A touch will sometimes disclose that a cactus is completely rotted inside; in that case, nothing can save it. This is caused by insufficient drainage or overwatering. A cactus in which rot has barely started, as the result of an abrasion, can be saved if the damage is not too advanced. Cut away all infected tissue; or if the injury is at the base, cut back to healthy tissue, leave to callus a few days, and treat as a cutting.

INSECT PESTS

Some insects must be guarded against. Cacti are susceptible to scale, mealybugs, aphids, and (in the case of *Opuntia*) the cochineal insect.

Protect against scale with an alcohol spray. Soapy water is usually effective and can be applied with a brush or as a spray. Use an oil emulsion spray only as a last resort, since it often spoils the appearance of the plants.

Mealybugs or aphids are sometimes found on the roots of cactus plants. An unhealthy appearance of the plant warrants investigation; if the insects are found, wash them off thoroughly with a brush, and treat, for mealybugs, with a reliable oil emulsion, and for aphids, with soap or sulfur solution. See APHIDS; MEALYBUG.

CACTI FOR THE GARDEN

The choice of cactus plants for garden culture depends on the space available, climatic conditions, etc. For summer gardens where plants will be grown in pots and protected in winter, some of the following smaller species can be used:

Ariocarpus fissuratus (living-rock);

Echinocactus johnsonii, with large, yellow flowers having maroon center;

Echinocereus fendleri, with large, violet-purple blossoms;

E. reichenbachii (merry-widow);

E. rigidissimus (rainbow cactus);

Ferocactus uncinatus, with colored spines and chocolate brown flowers;

Lophophora williamsii (dumpling cactus);

Mammillaria applanata, like a little Christmas wreath;

Opuntia erinacea, whose white spines give it the common name "grizzly-bear cactus";

O. leptocaulis, with persistent, colored fruits.

O. microdasys, with golden glochids;

O. monacantha, a free-blooming South American species with rapid growth;

O. pottsii, with pink, roselike flowers;

O. santa-rita, with colored pads;

O. subulata, with persistent awl-like leaves;

Pediocactus simpsonii (plains cactus).

In more permanent gardens, where plants can remain directly in the ground, the following species can be added:

Echinocactus grusonii (golden barrel cactus), which forms a perfect ball of gold;

Echinocereus engelmannii, with rose-purple blooms;

E. stramineus, with straw-colored spines and yellow flowers;

Lophocereus schottii, with curious, gray spines;

Echinocactus sp.

Opuntia basilaris, a mound of beauty when blooming;

Trichocereus spachianus, with a crown of white flowers.

CACTI IN THE HOME

Cacti are not restricted to the garden; some of the most beautiful can be contained in a single pot. The best cactus collection might even begin in this way, affording the opportunity to gain knowledge that can be applied to the care of other specimens later on.

If space is limited, an inside window garden can be constructed using brackets and plate-glass shelving. An interesting grouping might include a drooping *Aporocactus* at one corner and the center space filled with low-growing specimens. An outside window garden, if feasible, will allow the inclusion of larger specimens.

Suitable plants include the smaller *Coryphantha*, *Echinocereus*, *Echinopsis*, *Mammillarias*, and *Opuntia* already mentioned, or:

Astrophytum asterias, sometimes likened to a sea urchin;

A. myriostigma (bishop's-cap);

Coryphantha aggregata;

C. macromeris, with a pink blossom as large as the plant itself;

Dolichothele longimamma, with large, clear yellow blossoms; unique in that it can be propagated by rooting a single tubercle;

Mamillopsis senilis;

Mammillaria elegans;

M. hahniana, covered with white hair; it multiplies rapidly and can be propagated by separation;

M. parkinsonii.

CARE OF POTTED CACTI

In the culture of potted plants, the same drainage care must be exercised as described above for garden planting. Fill the pot at least one quarter full of broken pot, stone, or other material (it helps to include pieces of charcoal), fill in with gravel, and on top of this substratum place soil prepared according to the needs of the species being planted.

Desert cacti require little or no fertilizer but thrive in good, sandy loam with a little slaked lime (about a spoonful per medium-sized pot). *Epiphyllum* and cacti of similar habit use a rich loam containing peat moss over a substratum insuring drainage.

Watering a cactus in a pot is different from the practice in garden planting, since the roots are confined to a small space rather than permitted to reach out for moisture. Generally they should be treated much like other plants. Watch for signs of overwatering, and err on the side of too little rather than too much. Cacti will bear neglect to a surprising degree. They require more water during the blooming and growing periods than at other times and need rest after this time has passed.

CACTUS DISH GARDEN

If space is limited, consider a dish garden. Arrangements can be charming and provide the ideal solution for creating interest, requiring little care and attention.

For best results, use a double dish or one that somehow provides good drainage, or the specimen is doomed. The dish can be tiny, accommodating only one or two small subjects, or much larger, offering greater possibilities.

Special attention should be given to selecting plants. Since suitable varieties are limited, choice specimens should be chosen to provide all possible beauty.

The best arrangements consider balance of size, color, and texture. Old-man cactus, one of the more decorative *Opuntia* (*O. microdasys*), or the rare and interesting *O. vestita*, offer height to off-set smaller specimens.

In a smaller dish, the taller *Mammillaria elongata* works well surrounded by clusters of the tiny *Escobaria sneedii*. Also possible in these arrangements are:

Chamaecereus silvestri, called the peanut cactus, for the size and shape of its joints;

Epithelantha micromeris (button cactus), with tiny, scarlet fruits like little jewels;

Mammillaria denudata;

M. lasiacantha;

M. plumosa, a little ball of soft feathers.

Often dish gardens include other succulent plants, such as low-growing *Sedum*, for ground cover between the cacti.

PROPAGATING CACTI

Most species suited to house or small garden culture can be propagated from cuttings or from offshoots treated as cuttings. Handling these is simple and successful with the observance of a few precautions.

CUTTINGS

It is usually best to leave cuttings exposed to the air to callus for a few days before planting them. They can be rooted in a pot, or in a box prepared for the purpose and later transplanted. To prepare the box, first allow for drainage, as is necessary in any cultivation of cacti. Next, fill the box with sand and powdered charcoal, dampen it slightly, insert the cuttings, and water sparingly or not at all until roots begin to form. In the case of a tall or top-heavy cutting, add a support and tie the cutting to it, allowing the cutting to extend only a little way into the soil.

A cutting can be rooted directly into a pot by preparing the soil and drainage as for regular planting. Then make a small pocket filled with prepared sand and charcoal as above.

CACTI FROM SEED

The raising of cacti from seed by professional growers has become necessary. Government regulations allow importation for propagation purposes, under rigid inspection and supervision. Such propagation is the only way rare species can be obtained.

Collection of native plants is also becoming more restricted. Interstate regulations prevent their easy transportation. The ravaging of desert flora by collectors has aroused interest in conservation and more rigid enforcement of state laws.

Seeds, however, are available to growers from practically everywhere, and the propagation of cacti from seed has become one of the more popular and interesting details of their culture.

Seeds can be started in a small box with holes in the bottom, a flowerpot, a fern dish, or a regulation seed flat. As in all cactus planting, provide perfect drainage. Fill with a light mixture of sand, loam, and peat. Wet thoroughly and let stand overnight. Plant seed, cover with a light dusting of fine gravel, and place a glass over the seedbed, elevating the glass slightly as the seed begins to sprout. Keep soil moist, never allowing it to become too wet or too dry.

Cactus seed usually germinates quickly. The greatest danger is damping-off, the sudden killing of young seedlings by a rapidly spreading fungus; the seedlings will look flaccid or rotted. If there is any sign of this, use some disinfectant sold for the purpose.

When sowing rare seeds, it is a good idea to place them individually in small pots and sink these in propagating sand or peat.

The greatest requisite in raising cactus seedlings is patience, for though most seed germinates quickly, many species grow slowly.

GRAFTING CACTUS

The benefits of grafting include increasing the rate of growth, inducing a form of growth that better displays the plant, and preserving a delicate or rare specimen that may be suffering from some form of rot.

Whatever the purpose, the method is simple. Implements needed are a sharp knife and a few long, slender cactus spines to fasten scions in place. Do not use metal pins. Requisites to success are absolute cleanliness; sharp, clean cuts;

and immediate contact of cut surfaces. Also, cactus grafting should be done during the growing season.

The cuts can either form flat surfaces, as in grafting a small globose specimen to a columnar stock of similar diameter, in order to raise it above the danger point for rot; or the scion may be cut in wedge shape and inserted into a notch of similar size cut in the stock.

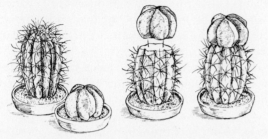

Grafting Astrophytum myriostigma (bishop's-cap) onto Echinocactus (barrel cactus).

Grafting stock is somewhat varied, depending on the scion to be used, the result to be obtained, the method used, and other details. Common stocks are *Opuntia, Acanthocereus, Nyctocereus serpentinus, Selenicereus macdonaldiae, Pereskia*, and others. The stock should be a well-rooted cutting of appropriate size and should be dry when the graft is made.

Plan the operation so that there will be no delay in bringing the cut surfaces in contact; fasten the stock and scion in place, and union will soon take place.

Some desirable possiblities are: an *Aporocactus* (rat-tail) grafted upon a columnar stock of suitable height for a drooping effect or upon a quick-growing stock so that its influence will cause more rapid growth. Similarly, *Schlumbergera truncata* can be grafted to form a pyramid, or at intervals along a climbing or erect stem of *Pereskia*, etc. *Epiphyllum* is often grafted upon a quick-growing stock to stimulate growth.

HINTS TO CACTUS BUYERS

In purchasing stock, choices are between collected specimens, propagations of collected specimens, and those that have been propagated from seed.

If any plants show broken or injured roots, trim these off and plant with a view to developing new roots. Do not plant injured specimens and run the risk of rot appearing at the root. If a bruise appears on the body of a plant, treat it with powdered charcoal and watch carefully to guard against rot.

Large shipments of desert plants are sometimes thrown on the market at low and tempting prices. Beware: not only are the specimens offered usually unattractive, mutilated, and worthless, but they may carry disease that will spread and ruin other plants.

CAESALPINIA (sez al PIN ee ah). A genus of tropical evergreen trees and shrubs of the Fabaceae (Bean Family), many species formerly classified under the genus *Poinciana*. A few species are climbers and some are armed with prickles. Caesalpinias are very popular in the tropics and, when in bloom, rank with the most decorative trees and shrubs. They bear loose clusters of showy yellow, orange, and red flowers followed by conspicuous, usually flattened seedpods. They are grown as ornamentals in Zones 10–11 or occasionally in greenhouses elsewhere. They require a rich, sandy soil and are propagated by seed which are best soaked before planting. Pot up as soon as seedlings can be handled.

C. gilliesii is a shrub of straggling habit and has mimosalike leaves and clusters of light yellow flowers with long stamens of brilliant red. It is known in California as bird-of-paradise.

C. pulcherrima (Barbados-pride, Barbados flowerfence, dwarf poinciana) is a somewhat prickly shrub to 10 ft. and has feathery foliage and red and yellow flowers with red stamens.

CAJANUS (kah JAH nus). A genus of tropical shrubs of the Fabaceae (Bean Family) and commonly known as pigeon-pea or cajan. One species, *C. cajan*, is widely cultivated in tropical countries for its nutritious seeds, good for humans and other animals. It grows to 10 ft. in height, and its stems, leaves, and seedpods are covered with soft, velvety hairs. The purple-spotted, yellow flowers are produced over a long season. It is often grown from seed as an annual.

CAJEPUT TREE. Common name for *Melaleuca quinquenervia*, an Australian tree with bark shredding in conspicuous strips. Planting this tree is prohibited in south Florida, where it has invaded large areas, crowding out the native vegetation; see MELALEUCA.

CALABASH-GOURD. Common name for the hard-shelled fruits of *Lagenaria siceraria*, occurring in various shapes and used for different purposes as dippers, bowls, etc.; see LAGENARIA.

CALABASH TREE. Common name for *Crescentia cujete*, a tropical American tree grown for its fruits, whose shells are grown and shaped to various purposes; see CRESCENTIA.

CALACINUM (kal ah SIN um). Former botanical name for MUEHLENBECKIA, a genus of tropical woody plants commonly known as wireplants.

CALADIUM (kah LAY dee um). A genus of striking, large-leaved herbs belonging to the Araceae (Arum Family), commonly known as elephant's-ear, native to the tropical Americas, and grown as bedding plants, or more commonly in a greenhouse or sunny room, for their ornamental veined and marbled foliage. Whether indoors or out, caladiums need plenty of food and plenty of moisture in loose, friable soil and, preferably, a humid atmosphere.

Indoors, caladiums can be started from seed, but they are usually grown from bulbs planted one to a 3–4 in. pot in

Caladium sp.

a mixture of 1 part light, sandy soil and 4 parts humus. This should be kept moist and the temperature should not go below 70°F, while it can go as high as 100°F without injury. When three or four leaves have developed, repot; then continue to shift as necessary, making the soil a little heavier each time by adding more loam and feeding with liquid manure every two or three weeks.

For outdoor planting, the dormant tubers should be set out about 2 in. deep in a semishaded location as soon as danger from frost is over. Plants started in the greenhouse and gradually hardened-off can be used instead of the tubers, setting them 12–24 in. apart. Cultivate and water frequently.

C. bicolor, the principal species, has produced many varieties and hybrids with brilliantly colored and variously marked leaves.

CALAMINT. Common name for *Calamintha nepeta*, a perennial aromatic herb belonging to the Lamiaceae (Mint Family); see CALAMINTHA.

CALAMINTHA (kal ah MIN thah) **nepeta.** A bushy perennial herb native to the Mediterranean region, belonging to the Lamiaceae (Mint Family), sometimes listed as *Satureja calamintha*, and commonly known as calamint. From creeping rhizomes, it grows to 2 ft. and bears whorls of white or lilac flowers among the tiny, grayish, hairy leaves. An attractive and aromatic evergreen, it is an old herb garden favorite, thriving under the same conditions as SATUREJA.

CALAMONDIN (kal ah MON din). Common name for a small, tropical or subtropical, evergreen tree, x *Citrofortunella mitis* (derived from *Citrus reticulata* x *Fortunella*), noted for its relative hardiness, ornamental form, and foliage. Its fruit—small, juicy, and with orange-red skin and deep orange flesh—is used in making beverages and preserves. It can be grown where the kumquat and the Satsuma orange thrive. See CITRUS FRUITS.

CALANDRINIA (kal an DRIN ee ah). A genus of low-growing, spreading, fleshy herbs of the Portulacaceae (Portulaca Family), native from British

Columbia to South America. They are occasionally grown as annuals in rock gardens, or as edging plants in sunny borders. The flowers, which are of short duration, range from orange-yellow and coppery rose to brick red, or from crimson-magenta to light purple. Propagation is by seed or cuttings.

C. ciliata (redmaids), formerly listed as *C. caulescens* var. *menziesii*, is an annual, fleshy herb with rose or crimson flowers.

CALANTHE (kuh LAN thee). A genus of nearly 150 medium-sized, terrestrial, evergreen or deciduous orchids native to tropical Asia. The evergreen types have cormlike pseudobulbs, while the deciduous ones have large, ovoid pseudobulbs with gray-green sheathing over the bulbs. The leaves are large and plicate. Usually seven to ten bright rose or white, long-lasting flowers rise from the apex of a wiry inflorescence emerging from the side of the pseudobulb. Evergreen types need less light than deciduous ones, which need about the same light as *Cattleya*.

They do well planted in a compost of sphagnum moss, peat, and sand. Abundant water should be given while the plants are growing, but after the leaves drop, the deciduous ones should be kept dry and cool. Evergreen types should never become completely dry. Hardy in Zones 10–11 (to Zone 9 in coastal areas), they withstand minimum winter temperatures of 55–60°F. The type species is *C. triplicata*.

CALATHEA (kal ah THEE ah). A genus of perennial plants of the Marantaceae (Maranta Family), with attractive colored foliage and flowers in cones among the leaves. They are tropical plants and should be grown in a close, moist greenhouse with a night temperature not lower than 65°F. The soil should retain moisture but be free draining, and a moist air will help prevent attacks by spider mites. In subtropical areas, some species can be grown outside with some protection during cold spells. Plants of this group are also proving useful in some interior landscaping situations.

Propagation is by division, less commonly by cuttings, and commercial production of some is from tissue-cultured plantlets. At least 30 species are now easily available in the trade with leaves in a wide range of colors and patterns.

Some of the leaves are as beautiful as any to be found in the plant kingdom. *C. zebrina* (zebra plant), from Brazil, is cultivated for its velvety, green-striped foliage. Flowers are not showy in most species, although *C. loeseneri* has long-lasting bracts that somewhat resemble a rosebud, and *C. rufibarba* produces a ring of fragrant, yellow flowers.

CALCEOLARIA (kal see oh LAIR ee ah). A genus of chiefly greenhouse-flowering plants belonging to the Scrophulariaceae (Figwort Family) and commonly known as slipper or pocketbook flower. They bear large numbers of mostly red and yellow, spotted flowers, each with a large, inflated pouch like a slipper toe or purse.

Native chiefly in South America, they have been so extensively hybridized that few original species are seen in cultivation. In England, the small shrubby types with mostly yellow or white, unspotted flowers are frequently used as edging plants, and these should be equally suitable on the West Coast of North America. Otherwise, *Calceolaria* is distinctly a florists' plant; its exacting demands,

Calceolaria sp.

especially when young, keeping it confined to commercial greenhouses or those on large estates.

Culture. A low temperature (not over 60°F) and a northern exposure are required for the germination of seeds. Early spring to midsummer is the best time for sowing, and the recommended soil mixture is 2 parts sand, 2 parts loose peat, and 1 part charcoal, all sifted. After the small seeds are pressed into the surface, they should be covered with fine sphagnum, and the seed pan should be moistened by setting it in a tub of water. The seedlings need fresh air constantly but will not tolerate sun until autumn, when they will require it in abundance. As the plants grow, dried cow manure and loam should be added to the mixture, until at the final shift, they are potted in 1 part manure, 2 parts sand and peat with a little charcoal, and 2 parts fibrous loam. When about to flower, they relish a dose of liquid cow manure twice a week. When propagating by cuttings, they are rooted in sand in the early fall and then are treated like the seedlings.

Insect Pests. Aphids, usually green, are notorious for their attraction to *Calceolaria*, especially young plants. Sometimes the insects can be washed away with a fairly stiff spray of tepid water. Although the practice is no longer recommended, gardeners once swore by fumigating with nicotine preparations or scattering tobacco stems to keep the plants insect free.

Disease. Gray mold or botrytis blight of leaves and flowers is kept down by removing infected parts and keeping foliage dry. Stem rot is reduced by clean culture, making sure that the hard, black sclerotia (resting bodies) do not fall from infected stems to the moist soil or cinders in the benches and there produce fruiting bodies that start general infection.

CALCIUM. This is one of the seventeen or so chemical elements essential to the growth and health of plants. In its pure state—as a light, silvery white, soft metal—it is rarely seen outside laboratories, and it never occurs in that form naturally. It is, however, present in many other forms in moist soils and in some mineral formations, such as limestone. In fact, calcium is best known in one form or another of lime, which may be the simple oxide (CaO), commonly known as quicklime, or hydrated or slaked lime ($Ca(OH)_2$) or the carbonate ($CaCO_2$), better known as raw limestone.

Calcium serves the plant in a number of ways and is especially important in the zones of active root and top growth. Since there is usually plenty of it in moist soils in forms that plants can use, it is rarely if ever necessary to apply lime to the soil as a fertilizer.

Its great usefulness is as a SOIL AMENDMENT, or conditioner or modifier. In that capacity, calcium is added to soils as ground limestone, or hydrated or agricultural lime. It is sometimes used in the form of ground shells, marl, bonemeal, or other material.

See also LIME.

CALENDULA (kah LEN dyoo lah). A genus of annual and perennial herbs belonging to the Asteraceae (Aster Family), but to gardeners the name indicates the old favorite, *C. officinalis*, called "Marygold" by Shakespeare and now commonly known as pot-marigold. The name "calendula" comes from the Latin *calendae*, meaning "first day of the month," for it was once supposed that some species bloomed every month of the year. Its yellow or orange heads of ray and disk flowers, with

Calendula officinalis

flowers closing at night, come in both single and double varieties and are borne on plants 1–2 ft. high. In early times, the pot-marigold was highly regarded not only for its medicinal qualities, but also as a flavoring for soups and stews.

CULTURE

This is one of the most easily grown annuals. Plants are best started from seed sown in the spring indoors or out. They should be thinned to about 9 in. Plants do well under any average soil conditions and in either full sun or semishade. Native to southern Europe, calendulas thrive in cool climates, and some excellent heat-tolerant varieties are also available. In the southern states, they bloom practically all year round, and in cooler regions, from late spring to frost.

Valuable for cutting, calendulas can also be used for pot culture, the smaller plants being cut back in the fall and potted up. They will bear flowers indoors for several weeks.

Calendulas are relatively pest and disease free but are occasionally subject to problems from APHIDS and SCLEROTINA ROT.

CALIBANUS (kal i BAN us). A most unusual genus of the Agavaceae (Agave Family), closely related to BEAUCARNEA, from which it differs in its hard, pealike seeds, which are not winged, and by a total lack of branches. There is only one species in this genus, which was named for Shakespeare's New World monster, Caliban, in *The Tempest*. *C. hookeri*, from central Mexico, bears numerous tufts of bluish green, very slender, almost linear, long, grasslike leaves about a foot long. The plants are unisexual and the tufts are monocarpic. The globose, highly succulent caudex is often mostly above ground and becomes barky, covered with deeply fissured, corky bark. It is propagated only from seed.

CALICO FLOWER. Common name for *Aristolochia elegans*, a slender climber with freely produced flowers of purple-brown with white markings; ARISTOLOCHIA.

CALIFORNIA-BLUEBELL. Common name for several species of arid annuals in the genus PHACELIA, especially *P. campanularia*, *P. viscida*, and *P. whitlavia*.

CALIFORNIA-FUSCHIA. Common name for several species of ZAUSCHNERIA, herbaceous or subshrubby, trailing plants with scarlet, tubular flowers in summer and fall.

CALIFORNIA LAUREL. Common name for *Umbellularia california*, a tall evergreen tree with lustrous foliage; see UMBELLULARIA.

CALIFORNIA-NUTMEG. Common name for *Torreya californica*, an evergreen of the Taxaceae (Yew Family); see TORREYA.

CALIFORNIA PITCHER-PLANT. Common name for *Darlingtonia californica*, named for its shape, which collects moisture in which to trap and digest insects. See DARLINGTONIA; INSECTIVOROUS PLANTS.

CALIFORNIA POPPY. Common name for *Eschscholzia californica*, a hardy, golden-flowered annual of the Papaveraceae (Poppy Family); it is the state flower of California, where it grows wild; see ESCHSCHOLZIA.

CALLA (KAL ah) **palustris.** A water-loving herb belonging to the Araceae (Arum Family) and commonly known as water arum or wild calla. It normally grows to 12 in. high in cold bogs of the Northern Temperate Zones. A white spathe (flowerlike bract), greenish outside, surrounds a yellow spadix (flower spike), which later bears a dense cluster of bright red berries. It is hardy in Zones 5–8.

As a common name, calla or calla-lily refers to the genus ZANTEDESCHIA. Black-calla is *Arum palaestinum*. Red-calla sometimes refers to varieties of *Sauromatum guttatum*.

CALLIANDRA (ka lee AN drah). A genus of shrubs and small trees from the tropical Americas, belonging to the Fabaceae (Bean Family). The flowers are formed in tight heads, and their long stamens make them look like a powderpuff, which is the common name for the group. The species most frequently grown outdoors in Zones 10–11 or in northern greenhouses is *C. haematocephala*, a bush that grows to about 10 ft. and has bright red, powderpuff flowers. Propagation is best by seed, but cuttings are possible. Growth is rapid in a rich, moist, but free-draining soil.

CALLICARPA (ka li KAHR pah). A genus of deciduous or evergreen shrubs or trees found in tropical and subtropical regions of Asia, Australia, North and Central America, belonging to the Verbenaceae (Verbena Family), and commonly known as beautyberry. The flowers are small, borne in short clusters in summer, and the plants are grown chiefly for their bright lilac- or violet-colored, berrylike fruits, very conspicuous in late autumn. Only a few of the species are at all hardy in cold climates and in severe winters, and these are generally killed back close to the ground. In such cases, however, vigorous new shoots start from below the following spring and usually flower and fruit the same season. They like rich soil in a sheltered location and are tolerant of shade. Propagation is by cuttings of growing and mature wood, layers, and seed.

PRINCIPAL SPECIES

C. americana (French-mulberry) is found from Virginia southward and grows to 6 ft. It has bluish flowers and in fruit is one of the showiest; the fruit is violet in the species and white in the tender var. *alba*.

C. bodinieri is a hardy Chinese species that grows to 10 ft. with pink flowers and violet fruit.

C. dichotoma, from Japan, is one of the hardiest species, growing to 4 ft. It has pink flowers and lilac-white fruit clustered in the leaf axils.

C. japonica is a fairly hardy shrub to 5 ft. and has pale pink flowers and violet fruit.

CALLIOPSIS (kal ee AHP sis). Another name for the genus COREOPSIS, commonly applied as a common name to the annual species *C. tinctoria*.

CALLIRHOE (kah LIR oh ee). A small genus of annual and perennial herbs native to North America, belonging to the Malvaceae (Mallow Family), and commonly known as poppy mallow. They have picturesque lobed foliage and showy flowers of pink, red, or reddish purple, which bloom through most of the summer. They thrive in poor soil, and their deeply penetrating, often tuberous roots make them suitable for dry situations. Trailing

Callirhoe involucrata

perennial forms are useful in the rock garden and are hardy to Zone 3. Propagation is usually by

seed, but the perennial sorts can also be increased by cuttings and division.

C. digitata, native to the southern central United States, is a perennial that grows 1–4 ft. and has unlobed or three-lobed leaflets. The 2-in. flowers are mostly white and bloom in spring.

C. involucrata (poppy mallow), the most common species, is a trailing perennial found in dry, sunny locations in the midwestern states. It grows to 12 in. high and bears deeply cut leaves. In summer, the pink to red or purplish solitary flowers are 2½ in. across with five heart-shaped petals.

CALLISTEMON (ka li STEM on). A genus of shrubs or small trees of Australia, belonging to the Myrtaceae (Myrtle Family). They are commonly planted in Zones 10–11 and are sometimes grown under glass. They have narrow, leathery leaves and remarkable, showy, cylindrical spikes of red or yellow flowers, mostly composed of stamens; these and the general shape of the spike suggest the popular name bottlebrush. They grow well in any good soil and are propagated by

Callistemon citrinus

seed or cuttings of ripened wood. To secure seed for spring sowing, gather the fruits in summer and keep in boxes or wrapped in paper until they open.

PRINCIPAL SPECIES

C. brachyandrus is a slender shrub with stiff, needlelike, gray leaves and spikes of dark red filaments bearing golden anthers.

C. citrinus, formerly listed as *C. lanceolatus*, is an upright species and *C. viminalis* has a weeping habit; both are red flowered and will tolerate a little frost.

C. salignus grows to 40 ft. and bears loose spikes of yellow or pink.

C. speciosus grows to 40 ft. and is the showiest species. These dense spikes bristle with bright red filaments tipped with yellow anthers.

CALLISTEPHUS (kal IS tef us) **chinensis.** A species of annual herbs belonging to the Asteraceae (Aster Family) and commonly known as aster or China aster. Originally native to China and Japan, many fine varieties have been developed and are popular in North American gardens. One of the premier cut flowers grown in the garden, its popularity waned early in the 1900s because of its susceptibility to aster yellows, but it has rebounded because of the development of resistant cultivars. Frequently confused with true members of the genus *Aster*, which are perennials, the annual China aster normally blooms in the garden in late summer.

In the late nineteenth century, the blossom of *Callistephus chinensis* was a small, simple, single, yellow-centered lavender flower. Today, with its varied, double, and greatly enlarged forms, it is a lush and frequently spectacular annual. The branching plants grow from 1–2½ ft. The flowers average 2½–3 in. across and often are so heavy that their weight is all the wiry stems can hold. They come in all shades of lavender, purple, rose, pink, crimson, and white. The foliage, plentiful near the base of the plant, is scanty or absent along the flower stems.

There are several features that make the modern China aster one of the most desirable of annual cut-flower subjects: their long stems, their excellent lasting quality, and the fact that they are not easily damaged. If leaves are allowed to stand in water for some time, however, they emit a foul odor. They should be removed from all parts of the stems that will stand under water. China asters are also used in beds, borders, planters and pots, as well as being forced in the greenhouse.

CULTURE

China asters are very easy to start from seeds, which can be started indoors in a flat in early spring or outdoors in the open after danger of heavy frosts has passed. In flats they will need a soil mixture of one-third each of garden soil, sand, and humus or leaf mold. It is a wise precaution to free this soil of possible insect and disease organisms by sterilizing it. See DISINFECTION.

The seeds germinate quickly and the seedlings should be transplanted at least once to stimulate growth. Whether the first crop of seeds is started early indoors or later outdoors, successional sowings should be made every two weeks for a period of at least six weeks in order to have a long season of bloom. Individual plants are short lived. Early and late varieties are available, and by using both, the season can be lengthened to some degree.

Pruning China asters

China asters produce a number of lateral branches, each of which bears a terminal flower and several buds on small side shoots. To promote the best blooms, cut off the side shoots and retain the main bud only.

Conditions. Best results are attained with China asters when they are grown in a little shade, although they often prosper in full sun. A moderately rich soil to which wood ashes have been added in early spring or at least two weeks before planting is most satisfactory. In the absence of wood ashes, well-rotted manure or a manure substitute can be used to advantage, but either of these is best applied in the fall previous to planting. A "light snow" of lime sprinkled on the soil surface a few weeks before planting is beneficial, since China asters like a sweet (alkaline) soil.

The most important point in growing China asters is to see that, once started from seed, they do not suffer from any check or setback until they have reached maturity. Setbacks usually occur as a result of overwatering, overcrowding of seedlings, or drought. Plants should be set to stand 1 ft. apart when mature. After they have been planted in their permanent location, it is important to cultivate and water them regularly. In cultivating, remember that the fine roots are shallow and must not be disturbed or broken; therefore, shallow cultivation near the plants is essential.

ENEMIES

China asters are relatively easy to grow if the soil is comparatively insect and disease free. Otherwise, their chief drawback is their susceptibility to insects and diseases; however, healthy plants given a good start usually escape trouble. Seed growers and breeders are making valuable progress on developing increasingly resistant forms or strains.

Insect Pests. The most serious of the insects that attack the China aster is the TARNISHED PLANT BUG, a flying creature about ½ in. long, difficult to control, and most likely to be present in long dry spells. The insects puncture new growth just below the flower buds, which droop or become deformed. Spraying or dusting with insecticide can be an effective treatment once an infestation has set in, but the destruction of weeds in which the insects can live and breed is a good preventive measure. These bugs do not seem to do as much damage in the shade.

The large, black or gray aster beetles (or blister beetles), which eat both foliage and flowers, will drop off a plant when disturbed. Holding a can of kerosene or kerosene-and-water under a plant as you tap it with a stick will catch many pests. See BLISTER BEETLE.

Root lice (aphids) are occasionally attracted to weak plants, sapping their strength and stunting them. Tobacco dust worked into the soil, or nicotine-sulfate solution poured in a depression around the crown is helpful. It is advisable not to plant China asters in the same place the year following a bad infestation of this pest. See APHIDS.

Diseases. A viral disease called yellows is responsible for severe aster losses. The dwarfed plants turn yellow, and if the flower heads open at all, they are malformed and greenish. The virus overwinters in various weed hosts and is carried back to new aster plants in the spring by leaf hoppers that attack them. Fall destruction of weed hosts plus spraying or dusting to destroy the insect carrier gives some control; also, use BORDEAUX MIXTURE to repel it. The greatest protection is obtained by growing asters under tents made of fine-mesh cheesecloth. Besides keeping off the insects and preventing inoculation with the disease, this protects the plants from hot sun, hail, wind, etc., and results in the production of finer flowers.

Wilt or STEM ROT, caused by a fungus (*Fusarium conglutinans*) that lives in the soil, is a serious disease among the China asters. The fungus attacks the roots first, then advances up the stem, which becomes black at the soil surface just as the buds form. The leaves wilt, and subsequently the whole plant wilts and dies, though sometimes only one of the branches becomes infected. The best prevention is to secure and grow only wilt-resistant varieties, of which seed is commercially available.

Orange-colored patches on the undersides of leaves are caused by rust fungi. See also RUSTS; DISEASE.

SELECTIONS

While modern China asters have all been developed from the one species, *C. chinensis*, the nomenclature, as far as types and varieties go, is rather confused. The following notes will help the gardener in selecting from the many kinds offered in seed catalogs. Varieties over 2 ft. are considered tall, and those under 2 ft. are dwarfs. Each of the types or varieties has its own list of segregated colors; many have more than a half-dozen different shades and tones.

Branching Types. These are compact, pyramidal plants with many lateral branches and are late-blooming unless otherwise specified. The flowers are loose and full. There are nonlateral strains with no side buds. The giant branching type has exceedingly long stems. Both types are extremely vigorous and easy to grow. Blooms cut just before they are mature will last almost two weeks if the water is changed daily and if the lower leaves are not allowed to foul it.

Comet Types. These may be either early or late, tall or dwarf. The flowers are large and the petals, fine and slightly curled, giving a feathery appearance. The crego is usually considered an improved comet, or in cases where the term "giant" is used, a branching comet. 'Giants of California', or 'California Giant Asters' (an improved form of crego), are exceedingly tall, with perhaps the largest flowers obtainable in the aster clan, and with long stems excellent for cutting. They bloom in midseason. Although "earliest blooming" claims are made for other varieties, 'Queen of the Market' is usually figured to open the China aster season. It is a dwarf and loosely branched kind, with neat, compact, and full flowers. The 'King' aster is the modern form of the 'Victoria' or 'Needle' type. The flowers are fairly flat and neatly formed, and the petals are semiquill-like, opening in a spiral swing. This fairly dwarf aster has a tendency to be upright and unbranched except when otherwise noted.

Mammoth Peony-flowered. This is the modern improvement of the 'Truffaut' or peony-flowered aster of past years. The flowers are globular, like a florist's chrysanthemum, exceptionally large, and borne on long stems. The plants themselves are extremely tall and late.

American Beauty. This has flowers of much the same appearance as the peony-flowered type; however, it blooms earlier, is very branched, and although one of the taller varieties, is not so tall as the mammoth peony-flowered type.

Sunshine Aster. In its improved form, 'Giant California Sunshine', this type has very large flowers, with a center of quills that radiate outward over a single row of ray petals of a contrasting shade.

Although single asters of today are large and fine and come in many colors, they do not enjoy the popularity of the various double forms. Usually of medium height and blooming in midseason, they are to be recommended.

CALLITRIS (kah LIT ris). A genus of several tender evergreen trees of the Cupressaceae (Cypress Family), known as cypress-pines. Natives of Australia, some of the species are grown in Zones 10–11 for ornament or timber.

CALLUNA (kah LOO nah). A genus of shrubs belonging to the Ericaceae (Heath Family), frequently confused with the genus ERICA, and commonly known as heather. They can be distinguished by their characteristic flowers and foliage. The leaves are short, overlapping, and scalelik. The flowers have a colored calyx that is longer than the corolla; also at the base of the calyx are four small, green bracts that at first glance might be mistaken for the calyx itself.

Heather is hardy to Zone 4 and well adapted to dry, sunny slopes, thriving in lime-free soil with plenty of leaf mold or peat. Kept sheared in spring, the plants make compact clumps. By planting several forms together, very pleasing foliage effects and summer flower-color variations can be achieved.

Over 600 forms of heather have all been derived from one species, *C. vulgaris*, which is native in Europe and Asia, and found in a few areas in the northeastern states. The type grows to 2 ft. or more and has rosy pink flowers in late summer. Among the best of the numerous named cultivars are 'Alba', with white flowers; 'County Wicklow', with double pink flowers; 'H. E. Beale', with silvery pink flowers; 'J. H. Hamilton', a double pink form; 'Mrs. Pat', with light purple and pink new foliage in spring; 'Mrs. Ronald Gray', with reddish color; 'Nana', a low spreader 4 in. tall, with purple flowers; and 'Searlei', with feathery growth and late, white flowers.

Calluna vulgaris

CALLUS. A growth, sometimes more or less protuberant, of hard or tough protective tissue developed over or around a wounded surface, such as that formed over the end of a cutting, and from which roots develop, or over a smooth wound caused by pruning. See PROPAGATION; PRUNING.

CALOCEDRUS (kal oh SEED rus). New botanical name for a genus of evergreen trees. Two Asian species are usually not cultivated. *C. decurrens* (California incense-cedar) is a tall, upright evergreen growing to 125 ft., native to the West Coast. It is a handsome specimen plant, growing to 50 ft. when cultivated. Heart rot is its one serious disease, caused by the fungus *Polyporus amarus*. Hardy in Zones 6–8.

CALOCHORTUS (kal oh KOHR tus). A genus of western North American plants in the Liliaceae (Lily Family), growing from corms and producing bell-shaped flowers in shades of white, cream, yellow, pink, lilac, and red, often with elaborate contrasting marks and hairs. Known variously as mariposa-, butterfly-, globe-, and star-tulips; mariposa, globe, or sego lilies; or fairy-lanterns, they are invariably plants of great beauty, exhibiting wide variability of flower shape, coloration, and form. Their three-petaled flowers are not unlike those of the TRILLIUM. Unfortunately, as a group they are considered very difficult to grow, even within the species' normal range, and are thus a challenge for the serious grower. Hardiness varies with the species, but most will thrive as far north as Zone 5. About 60 species are native to western North America from the Dakotas to British Columbia.

The plants are hardy in the northeastern states but must be protected against alternate freezing and thawing in winter. Fall or winter waterlogging will rot the bulbs. They need an open location, many requiring full sun, and a well-drained soil or raised bed. Most species require a dry summer dormancy so, in areas of summer rain, plants need to be lifted and stored; this is best done after flowering. Plants are generally easy to grow from seed but need three to five years to flower. Seedlings are best raised in pots or protected raised beds or frames. Plants will flower in pots but are not dependable for forcing.

PRINCIPAL SPECIES

This large genus is generally divided into three sections. The first comprises the globe lilies or fairy-lanterns, which have a single broad, grassy leaf from the base and rounded, nodding flowers on a graceful, leafy stem.

C. albus (white globe lily, fairy-lantern) grows about 1–2½ ft. high with lanceolate leaves and three to ten nodding, globose, white or white tinged pink, satiny blossoms, each petal fringed with hairs.

C. amabilis (yellow fairy-lantern) is similar but has smaller, deeper yellow flowers arranged in a pinwheel fashion.

C. amoenus (pink globe lily) has delicate, nodding, 1-in., rose-lilac flowers.

C. pulchellus (Mt. Diablo globe lily) is smaller and yellow.

The second group is made up of star-tulips or pussy-ears, native in western North America from Mexico to Oregon. They have generally small, upfacing flowers, variously streaked or spotted, typically with hairy inner petals.

C. coeruleus (cat's-ear, pussy-ears) has pale bluish lilac petals with dense, white hairs and is usually under 6 in. tall. Other species tend to be similar to these.

C. monophyllus has bright yellow cups, often marked with reddish bronze toward the base.

C. tolimei (pussy-ears) has delicate, hairy, white petals tinged purple toward the base and grows 6–12 in. tall.

C. uniflorus grows 6–10 in. tall and has pinkish lilac, 3-in. flowers with long hairs at the petal base; it is the easiest species to grow.

The third group includes the spectacular mariposa or butterfly lilies with generally large, tulip-like flowers of white, rose, yellow, or cream with contrasting eye spots on the petals of many species.

C. clavatus and *C. luteus* are both attractive species that grow 2 ft. tall and have golden yellow flowers and various markings and hairs.

C. leichtlinii has campanulate, white flowers tinged smoky blue or pink, with an outstanding dark blotch at the base of each petal.

C. splendens and *C. invenustus* have pale lilac-pink, satiny petals on 1–3 ft. stems.

C. venustus, *C. vestae*, and *C. superbus* are similar, growing 2–3 ft. tall on wiry stems with creamy white to yellowish petals and elaborate bronze or contrasting splotches on each petal.

CALONYCTION (kal oh NIK tee un). Former genus name for a group of vines from the tropical Americas, commonly known as moonflowers, and now placed in the genus IPOMOEA.

CALOPOGON (kal oh POH gahn). A genus of four handsome, terrestrial, North American orchids, commonly known as grass-pink orchids. They are found in swamps and bogs from the southeastern United States into eastern Canada.

Underground corms are topped by grasslike leaves. Flowers are produced in succession during warm weather and are about 1½ in. across, rose to white, with a large, yellow, bearded or fringed lip. Plants require an acid, moist compost of leaf mold, sand, peat, and sphagnum moss. Most species are hardy to Zone 5. *C. tuberosus* produces magenta flowers in midsummer.

CALTHA (KAL thah). A genus of small, perennial, succulent herbs, chiefly native to North America and belonging to the Ranunculaceae (Buttercup Family). They are hardy to Zone 4 and are best planted in marshland near running water but can be grown in moist spots in the border. They are especially useful in water-garden plantings, where they bloom abundantly in the spring and usually again in the fall. The flowers are without petals, but their yellow, white, or pink sepals are brilliantly showy and, because of their lasting quality, make good cut flowers.

Caltha palustris

C. palustris (marsh-marigold, cowslip) is a familiar species found in wet ground from the Carolinas to Canada and westward. A double-flowered variety is especially attractive for planting at the edge of a pond. Propagation is by division of the roots in autumn or by seed freshly gathered.

CALYCANTHUS (ka li KAN thus). A genus of ornamental deciduous shrubs of North America, favored for their aromatic fragrance, lending its name to the Calycanthaceae (Calycanthus Family), and commonly known as sweetshrub or sweet-scented shrub. They grow as well in shade as in open locations, and prefer a rather rich soil that does not get too dry. Propagation is by seed, layers, and divisions.

PRINCIPAL SPECIES

C. fertilis, more bushy than most, has leaves to 6 in. long, glaucous beneath. It bears unscented, chocolate-purple flowers a little later in the season and is hardy in Zones 6–9.

C. floridus (Carolina-allspice) is a shrub of rather open form that grows to 6 ft. or more. The best-known and hardiest species, it is beloved for its dark maroon or reddish brown, spicily fragrant flowers. Cv. 'Katherine' has yellow flowers and is very fragrant. Hardy in Zones 5–9.

C. occidentalis (California-allspice), the tallest grower, has leaves to 8 in. long. Its flowers are light brown and continue to late summer. Hardy to Zone 8.

CALYPSO (kah LIP soh) **bulbosa.** A terrestrial orchid, native and hardy in the North Temperate Zone of North America, Europe, and Asia. Tuberous roots are topped by a single folded leaf and one pendent flower. The flower is remarkable; it is heavily textured, fragrant, and showy, about 1½ in. long. Purple or white, narrow, twisting sepals and petals curve over a white or yellow, saccate lip, which has bright red spots inside and several rows of yellow cilia at the apex. It is difficult to cultivate and should be grown in cool shade in perfectly drained, humusy compost and given ample water. The roots should be disturbed as little as possible.

CALYPTRIDIUM (kal ip TRID ee um). A genus of small, half-hardy herbs belonging to the Portulacaceae (Portulaca Family), formerly listed as

Spraguea. Plants have fleshy leaves and small, white flowers borne in umbels on spikelike stems. The garden types are perennial but are grown as annuals.

C. umbellatum, native to the mountains of western North America, produces rose-tinged white flowers on 1-ft. plants. It is well suited for use in a rock garden when grown as an annual.

CALYX. The outer set of small, leaflike parts that, with the corolla, comprises the perianth or floral envelope of a flower. The individual leaves, called sepals, usually green, are sometimes fused to form a tube but more often are distinct. In some flowers, like the lily, the sepals may be petal-like and the calyx and corolla similar in appearance. See FLOWER.

CAMASSIA (kah MAS ee ah). A genus of North American bulbous plants with blue or white flowers in graceful racemes and grassy foliage, belonging to the Liliaceae (Lily Family), and commonly known as camass, camas, or quamash. They are perfectly hardy and should be planted in groups of nine or more, 3–4 in. apart in the border, or smaller species in the rock garden. The bulbs were once valued by the Indians for food. Plants can also be propagated by seed.

C. leichtlinii is a stout plant with regular flowers ranging from white to purple.

C. quamash (quamash, camas), the most common species, grows 2–3 ft., with flowers varying from white to deep blue. It is the most suitable form for the rock garden.

CAMBIUM. The layer of living tissue just below the bark, whose growth results in the increase in thickness of stems and perennial roots. In woody stems, its alternating growth and resting periods lead to the formation of the familiar annual rings seen in the cross section of a tree trunk.

CAMELLIA (kah MEL ee ah). A genus of evergreen trees and shrubs native to Asia and belonging to the Theaceae (Tea Family). They have long been prized for their handsome, glossy, green leaves, which in some species are brewed as tea, and showy, single, semidouble, and double flowers of white and shades of pink or red; yellow have more recently been introduced. In sheltered places they will tolerate some frost, but where winters are severe they need the protection of a greenhouse for a good part of the year. Attractive small specimens can be grown in large pots or tubs; they also do well planted out in a bed in the cool conservatory.

CULTURE

Camellias are propagated by seed (which germinates slowly), cuttings, layers, and grafting in the case of choice varieties.

POT CULTURE

Under the right conditions, camellias are not difficult to grow and flower, providing strict attention is paid to certain cultural details, especially watering. Bud dropping sometimes causes a considerable loss of flowers, and perhaps the chief reason for this is dryness at the roots, particularly after the buds have set. In pots or tubs the soil and roots are very likely to become compacted into a hard ball that gets dry in the center. When this occurs, the container should be completely immersed in water for a few hours so that the soil will be well soaked throughout.

While the plants need to be maintained in a moist state at the roots, perfect drainage is essential, since a sodden soil will also cause trouble. Equal parts of turfy loam and peat with a liberal dash of sharp sand make a good potting mixture. Camellias should never be overpotted. When repotting is called for, the best time to do it (or to renovate the soil) is immediately after flowering. This is also the time to thin out any overcrowded shoots and shorten back any straggly growth. The plants object to being forced into bloom but will tolerate heat and moisture after the flowers have passed and new growth is being made. When this is complete, harden them off by degrees. Those in pots or tubs will appreciate being outdoors for the summer in a partly shaded place. With a collection it is possible to have flowers over a period of several months from late fall to winter.

OUTDOOR CULTURE

Camellias do well outdoors in warm climates and grow in quite poor soil provided it is somewhat acid. They are very slow growers unless well cultivated and fed. A mulch of leaf mold or very old cow manure helps to maintain cool and moist conditions at the roots besides providing some food. A little commercial fertilizer now and then, with thorough waterings in a dry time, will also aid materially in promoting vigorous and healthy growth. The flowering season in the South is from October until hot weather comes, and the flowers are more satisfactory if the plants are in a somewhat shaded and moist place.

ENEMIES

Leaf spots may follow frost injury, and wounds may serve as starting points for cankers. Treat all large wounds with a disinfectant and paint with a wound dressing. A flower blight occurs in California. The only remedy is sanitation, consisting of the removal of all fallen blossoms for several consecutive seasons. In the South, spraying early in April and late in September with a white oil emulsion (3 tbsp. oil to 1 gal. water) controls various scales and mites.

PRINCIPAL SPECIES

C. japonica (common camellia) grows to 40 ft. under very favorable conditions. It has given rise to a great many forms of single, semidouble, and double named varieties in white, pink, red, and variegated colors.

C. sasanqua is a shrubby species of rather loose growth habit, with single white or pink flowers. There are several forms with semidouble and double flowers.

C. sinensis (tea), formerly listed as *Thea sinensis*, is a tender evergreen shrub or tree to 30 ft. that has leaves to 5 in. long and white, fragrant flowers more than an inch across. Of distinct ornamental as well as commercial value, it can be grown in warm regions. Cultivated especially in China and India for leaves, which yield the commercial tea crops, there are several forms, and certain districts are noted for specializing in particular varieties. It should be noted, however, the kinds of tea offered as "black" and "green" are the results of different ways of treating the leaves after picking, not the product of special varieties. Tea plantations are continually renewed by setting out vigorous plants, which are raised from seed.

C. reticulata makes a large shrub or small tree and is distinguished by dull green instead of glossy leaves. It has very large, semidouble, rose-colored flowers to 7 in. across. They look more like a semidouble peony than the stiff and formal flowers of the common camellia.

CAMOMILE. Spelling variation of CHAMOMILE.

CAMPANULA (kam PAN yoo lah). A genus of more than 300 biennial and perennial herbs and a few annuals, commonly known as bellflower, harebell, or bluebell. The attractive bell- or wheel-shaped flowers are white, blue, purple, or yellow and show lovely shades of deep rose and pink in the biennial types. With their great variations of size, campanulas form a most desirable group of garden flowers and are deservedly popular, providing many mainstays for the rock garden. Most are native to the Mediterranean region and easily grown from seed or cuttings.

The tall perennials, such as the chimney- and peach-leaved bellflowers and *C. lactiflora*, with its milky white or pale blue flowers, are excellent for the background of the border. The profusely blooming Canterbury-bells show interesting variation. The cup-and-saucer bellflowers, with their showy flowers in midsummer, are most desirable in masses. The low-growing perennials, including the Carpathian harebell and the Scotch bluebell are among the most charming plants for the rock garden.

The perennials and biennials are started from seed sown in the open in summer or under glass in early spring. The perennials are also propagated by division. The annuals start readily from spring-sown seed, sown either under glass or where they are to grow. Where winters are severe, the biennial Canterbury-bells should be mulched with leaves. Most species are hardy in Zones 3–8.

PRINCIPAL SPECIES

C. abietina is very low growing with flat, blue flowers on delicate stems.

C. alliarifolia grows in a small clump, 18–24 in. tall, and has gray to soft green leaves and spikes of 1-in., creamy white flowers.

C. allionii is quite small, 2–4 in., with lavender, lilac, or white blooms similar to those of *C. medium*, and a rosette of gray-green leaves.

C. alpina, growing to 6 in., produces pyramids of lavender, bell-shaped flowers on 6-in. stems. It should be grown in gritty soil.

C. americana (tall bellflower) grows 3–6 ft. and sends up tall spikes of 1-in., blue flowers all summer. A unique, attractive plant for the wildflower garden, it is an annual that can also be treated as a hardy biennial. Provide rich soil and partial shade. Divide for propagation in spring or fall.

C. barbata, 6–12 in., bears long, nodding, bell-shaped flowers in violet, royal, and azure shades of blue. Cv. 'Alba' has white flowers.

C. bononiensis (Russian bellflower) grows to 3 ft. Its small, lilac flowers are drooping bells about 1 in. long.

Campanula americana

C. carpatica (Carpathian harebell) is a low-growing perennial with broad tufts of heart-shaped leaves and charming, widely bell-shaped, blue flowers blooming all summer on the edge of the border and in the rock garden. Hardy to Zone 4. Var. *alba*, *coelestina*, and *turbinata* are desirable variations.

C. cochleariifolia, formerly listed as *C. pusilla*, is very dwarf and covered with exquisite, milky white bells. Wonderful in many rock gardens, it grows profusely in gritty soil but is difficult in very warm regions.

C. collina, growing 9–12 in., is a sturdy plant, useful in the border and bears large, funnel-shaped, dangling, violet blooms in early summer.

C. elatines var. *garganica* forms a mat of sharply toothed, green foliage, spraying starry, purple flowers over a rock bed, attractive throughout the season.

C. garganica, with dainty, wheel-shaped flowers, thrives in a rock crevice in full sun. Hardy to Zone 6.

C. glomerata, growing to 2 ft., has many-flowered spikes of lilac blooms in summer. It is easy to grow and spreads by runners. Cv. 'Crown of Snow' bears white flowers. Hardy to Zone 3.

C. isophylla var. *alba* is a tender perennial with starry, white flowers, exceedingly effective when used in window or porch boxes with a northern exposure.

C. lactiflora (milky bellflower), growing to 4 ft., bears large heads of lilac or slate blue flowers on sturdy stems. Hardy to Zone 4.

C. lanata has spikes of whitish flowers above silky, gray-green leaves. Hardy to Zone 6, it is usually a short-lived perennial.

C. lasiocarpa, growing 3–6 in., bears soft blue flowers on a sturdy stem. It requires gritty, very well drained soil.

C. latifolia (great bellflower) has large, single, tubular, purplish blue flowers and basil-like leaves 6 in. long. When the plant is not in bloom, the foliage creates a neat mound.

C. latiloba has spikes of large, bell-shaped, blue-purple flowers in summer. Leaves are long, lanceolate, and serrated at the edges. Hardy to Zone 5.

C. macrostyla is one of the few annual species. It blooms six months from seed, producing blue-purple flowers on 2-ft., branching plants. Named varieties are 'Angelus Bell', with deep rose flowers, and 'Liberty Bell', with violet-blue.

C. medium (Canterbury-bells) forms bushy biennial plants to 4 ft., loaded with large, bell-shaped

Campanula medium

flowers, white, blue, lavender, or pink in color. If started very early, they will bloom the first summer, but they produce much more profuse and handsome flowers the second year from summer-sown seed. Cv. 'Calycanthema' (cup-and-saucer bellflower) has a flaring, colored calyx and bell-shaped corolla.

C. orphanidea and several other minute beauties are monocarpic. It may take several years for them to flower, but then they die. The gardener must save seeds to maintain these plants.

C. patula, growing 12–36 in., is an autumn-flowering variety with upturned, purple, bell-shaped flowers.

C. persicifolia (peach-leaved bellflower) is the most beautiful of the perennial species, bearing in early summer a profusion of delicate blue blossoms on 3-ft., branching plants. They should be separated and reset in early fall or spring in order to keep them growing vigorously. Hardy to Zone 4.

C. portenschlagiana, with blue-purple flowers, delights in stony soil in a half-shady spot in the rock garden, where it forms attractive clumps of very dwarf foliage. Hardy to Zone 5.

C. poscharskyana is a vigorous, spreading plant up to 6 in. tall, but three times as wide. The plant blossoms in sprays of 1-in. stars of lavender-blue. Hardy to Zone 4.

C. pyramidalis (chimney bellflower), of spire-like growth to 4 ft. or more, has small, saucer-shaped, pale blue or white flowers. Most effective in the border, this perennial or biennial is still lovelier grown as a potted plant for the sun porch, where the flowers, not being pollinated by insects, remain unfaded for days.

C. raineri, growing 4–6 in., bears an abundance of 2-in. blooms above tufted, gray-green foliage and is well suited to the rock garden.

C. rapunculus (rampion) is a biennial whose roots and leaves are eaten raw as salad.

C. rotundifolia (bluebell, harebell, bluebells-of-Scotland) is a perennial species that grows 1–2 ft. Slender, wiry stems bear clear blue, dainty bells in long, loose clusters, reaching their greatest beauty in early summer but often blooming spar-ingly throughout the summer. There are varieties with white and more or less double flowers. Var. *soldanellaeflora* is an interesting type with partly double flowers slit into shreds. Hardy to Zone 3.

C. sarmatica sends up numerous tall, gray stems with 1-in., nodding, blue or lavender, bell-shaped flowers. The plant grows in mounds to 20 in. of erect, gray-green, hairy leaves.

C. sibirica, growing 12–18 in., produces panicles of many deep blue bells and is showy when in full bloom.

Campanula rotundifolia

C. thyrsoidea is a hardy biennial that grows 12–18 in. and has yellow flowers on a dense, pyramidal spike and foliage forming a flat rosette. It requires good surface drainage on alkaline soil with full sun.

C. tommasiniana grows as a miniature bush, 6–8 in. tall, and has slender stems that bear drooping, narrow, pale blue flowers.

C. versicolor grows to 3 ft. and has cup-shaped, starlike blooms of lavender with a dark purple eye.

C. vidalii, growing 1–2 ft., is native to the Azores Islands and is somewhat rare. It is a half-hardy perennial, best grown in a cool greenhouse in Zones 8–9. It bears 2-in., waxlike, white blooms with a yellow ring at the base.

CAMPANULACEAE (kam pan yoo LAY see ee). The Bellflower Family, so called for the shape of the blossoms, which defines the term "campanulate." Cultivated species are erect and frequently have milky juice. The characteristic flowers are usually blue but sometimes white or pink. The family includes herbs, shrubs, or rarely trees, widely distributed in both temperate and tropical regions, many of them fine ornamentals, such as **Adenophora**, **Campanula**, **Legousia**, **Phyteuma**, **Platycodon**, **Symphyandra**, and **Walhenbergia**.

CAMPERNELLE (KAM per nel). Common name for forms of *Narcissus* x *odorus*, one of the jonquil types of the genus; see NARCISSUS.

CAMPION. Common name for the genus SILENE and several species of LYCHNIS, both belonging to the Caryophyllaceae (Pink Family). Moss campion is *S. acaulis*. Rose campion is *L. coronaria*.

CAMPSIS (KAMP sis). A genus of ornamental deciduous shrubs belonging to the Bignoniaceae (Bignonia Family), commonly known as trumpet creeper or trumpet vine. Usually grown as climbers but adapted for covering banks and rambling over rocky places, they prefer rich soil in a sunny location and show to best advantage on posts and old tree trunks. If allowed on wooden buildings, they are likely to do damage by loosening shingles. To keep these plants in good form, the long lateral shoots should be cut back to about two nodes before growth begins. Propagation is by seed, cuttings of both green and mature wood, root cuttings, and layers.

PRINCIPAL SPECIES
C. grandiflora, formerly listed as *C. chinensis*, is not as high a climber as *C. radicans* but has larger, more brilliant orange-red flowers and produces fewer aerial roots. Hardy in Zones 7–9.

C. radicans (trumpet vine), the native species, is the hardiest and can be grown into Zone 5. It climbs to 30 ft. or more by means of stem rootlets and bears large, orange-red, tubular flowers in terminal clusters in late summer. It spreads rapidly and may become a troublesome weed if not controlled.

C. x *tagliabuana*, a hybrid from the two species, is intermediate in hardiness, Zones 6–9, with flowers almost as large and showy as those of the Chinese parent.

CAMPTOSORUS (kamp toh SOR us). A genus of two small terrestrial ferns that grow on mossy, shaded, limestone rocks. They are closely related to and sometimes classified with *Asplenium*; hybrids of the two genera are called *Asplenosorus*.

C. rhizophyllus (walking fern), also listed as *Asplenium rhizophyllum*, is a very unusual fern with elongated fronds that lie on the ground and produce roots at their tips, from which young plantlets grow. When the young plant is established, the plant usually withers but sometimes persists long enough for a grandchild to form. In this fashion, a colony is formed from each plant. The usual reproduction by spores also occurs. This curiously attractive plant would be a good candidate for shady rock gardens but is often prey to slugs and snails. It should be planted in a north-facing location on limestone rocks covered with shallow soil and plenty of moss. Hardy in Zones 3–8, it is found in the United States from the East Coast to the Midwest.

CANADA BLUEGRASS. Common name for *Poa compressa*, a coarse perennial grass sometimes used in lawns; see POA.

CANARY GRASS. Common name for *Phalaris canariensis*, an annual grass whose seed is fed to caged birds; see PHALARIS.

CANDLEWOOD. Common name for FOUQUIERIA, a small genus of flowering, cactuslike plants.

CANDYTUFT. Common name for IBERIS, a popular genus of annual or perennial flowering herbs.

CANE. In horticulture this may refer to a slender, jointed, woody, hollow or pithy, more or less flexible plant stem, like that of bamboo or rattan; the leafless yearling stems of grape and bramble fruits from which bearing- or fruiting-wood is chosen; or bamboo rods used for STAKING.

CANESCENT. Covered with gray or whitish hoar formed by a coating of fine hairs, as on twigs and leaves.

CANISTRUM (kah NIS trum). A genus of tropical herbs from Brazil, belonging to the Bromeliaceae

(Pineapple Family), including some occasionally grown in the greenhouse. Some are epiphytes, while others root in the ground. Plants form rosettes of long, pointed leaves with little spines along the edges; stems rise from the center of the rosettes, bearing flowers that are generally green but may be yellow, blue, or white in different species. They are usually grown in wire baskets of sphagnum moss or in pots with fibrous loam. Propagation is by suckers or sprouts that appear following a blooming period.

CANKER. Strictly speaking, this is a localized lesion or wound area resulting in the destruction of tissue, with the final production of an open wound area generally on woody tissues. The term has been used loosely to cover many types of lesions on woody or semiwoody parts of plants. Certain diseases are frequently named after this symptom, as in chestnut canker and brown canker of rose.

CANKERWORM. Several kinds of smooth, rather small caterpillars commonly known as loopers, inch worms, or measuring worms, referring to their method of progressing by alternately looping up and straightening their bodies as though measuring off distances. They feed on the foliage of apple, elm, maple, and many other fruit and shade trees. They appear early in the spring and cause greatest damage about the time trees obtain full foliage, often skeletonizing the leaves. When a caterpillar is disturbed, it drops from the leaf or twig and hangs suspended by a silken thread.

There are two common cankerworms, the so-called spring cankerworm (*Paleacrita vernata*) and the fall cankerworm (*Alosphila pometaria*). Both kinds are green or brown, sometimes slightly striped, and about an inch long when full grown. The adults are moths.

The spring cankerworm passes the winter as a pupa 1–4 in. deep in the soil around the base of trees. The wingless females crawl up the trees in early spring to lay clusters of yellowish green, oval eggs, which hatch about the same time the buds break. The moths of the fall cankerworm emerge from the soil in the autumn and lay eggs that do not hatch until the following spring.

Since the females are wingless, they can be prevented from ascending trees and laying eggs by keeping sticky bands around the trunks from September until April. Tanglefoot, obtainable commercially, or rosin and oil added to the banding improves the control (see BANDING TREES). Such bands, however, afford no protection against young caterpillars carried by the wind or dropping from other trees and rarely reduce infestation more than 10%. Additional control is by spraying with **Bacillus thuringiensis** (Bt, commonly available as Dipel, Biotrol, or Thuricide).

CANNA (KAN ah). A genus of tropical, summer-flowering plants of the Cannaceae (Canna Family) that grow from thick, fleshy, tuberlike roots. They are valued for both their large, tropical-looking foliage and their brilliantly colored blossoms. In the hands of modern hybridists, flowers have been developed to include shades that range from ivory and yellow through rose and salmon to scarlet and crimson-red. The foliage is either bronze or green. In the tropics and subtropics where they grow wild, they range from 2½–10 ft. high.

Canna sp.

In the North, where they are tender and handled as annuals, few of the true species are grown in gardens, the cultivated sorts being mainly hybrids and strains. Because of the hard, bullet-like seeds produced, any of these kinds are often called Indian-shot, though correctly this name applies only to *C. indica*. A wild species native to South Carolina and Florida, *C. flaccida*, with small, yellow flowers, is one of the principal parents of the modern kinds, but these have become so enlarged and glorified in the hands of hybridizers that there is now little resemblance.

Cannas show to best advantage when massed plantings are made in formal beds; thus their use is to a great extent confined to parks and larger gardens. In home gardens, however, their bold, colorful foliage provides good background material in formal effects. The roots should be planted as soon as the soil is warm in the early summer. Select an exposed spot and space them 18 in. apart. Since they require an abundance of plant food, the soil must be well and deeply prepared and generously enriched. After growth gets under way, they also require considerable water. In the fall, when the foliage starts to wither or is cut down by frost, the roots should be lifted and stored away from frost in a root cellar.

Propagation is easily done by division of the roots, which grow rapidly. Plants can also be grown from seed, which should be soaked in warm water or notched with a file to hasten germination. Seeds started in February or March in flats or open pots kept on a radiator or warm greenhouse bench may give blooming plants the first year. They may not, of course, be the same as their parents, but interesting new kinds may result.

DISEASES

Infection with a bacterial bud rot disease starts while the leaves are still rolled in the bud. When they unfold, they are either covered with minute white spots or partially or wholly blackened. The flowers may be ruined and the whole stalk killed. To avoid this trouble, select root stalks from healthy plants. Sterilize dormant corms by soaking for two hours in a fungicide solution. In greenhouses, keep young growth dry and the humidity low; outdoors, set out only disease-free plants and space them far apart. Be careful not to overwater.

Rust disease covers the leaves of most varieties with a powdery yellow coat by the end of the season. Control is difficult, and in areas where the disease is prevalent, it is best simply to accept that the season of beauty is shorter than it might otherwise be.

INSECT PESTS

In the Southeast, the worst pest is the larva of a skipper moth, which cuts into the leaves and rolls pieces over itself, making the plant very unsightly. Control is possible with many common insecticides, provided application penetrates the protective leaf covering. Japanese beetles are occasionally a problem and may feed on the blossoms.

PRINCIPAL VARIETIES

C. edulis of the West Indies and South America produces edible tubers, known in those regions as tous-les-mois.

C. flaccida, of the southeast United States, grows to 5 ft.

C. x *generalis*, which naturally shows great variation, includes most of the common garden varieties.

C. indica (Indian-shot), the other United States species, attains 4 ft. and has brilliant red flowers; the common name refers to its hard, black seeds.

C. latifolia is a stout plant from South America with scarlet flowers and green leaves that have purple margins when young.

C. x *orchiodes* (orchid-flowered Canna), from Australia, has large (6-in.) flowers that open wide with reflexed petals after the first day of bloom.

CANNABIS (KAN ah bis) **sativa.** An annual herb native to central Asia and the northwestern Himalayas but now naturalized in portions of North America, belonging to the Moraceae (Mulberry Family), and commonly known as hemp. There is only one species in the genus, though names have been given to different varieties of this plant. It has been grown commercially for the fiber contained in its inner bark. Because it is the source of marijuana, cultivation in the United States is only allowed under a federal permit.

CANTALOUPE. Common name for varieties of *Cucumis melo*, which are tender, annual, green or yellow fruits with hard, ribbed or warty rinds, also identified as muskmelons. The name derives from Cantalupo, Italy, where it was first grown in Europe. See also CUCUMIS; MELON.

CANTERBURY-BELLS. Common name for species of CAMPANULA, especially *C. medium*, a biennial herb with colorful flowers.

CANTUA (KAN tyoo ah). A genus of erect evergreen shrubs from South America, belonging to the Polemoniaceae (Phlox Family). Although usually grown as greenhouse plants, they will thrive outside where little frost occurs. *C. buxifolia*, the principal species, is a handsome shrub growing to 10 ft. The branch tips and young leaves are downy, and the showy, red, drooping flowers are borne in short, leafy terminal clusters. Propagation is by cuttings rooted under close, humid conditions.

CAPE-COWSLIP. Common name for LACHENALIA, a genus of small, bulbous herbs of the Liliaceae (Lily Family).

CAPE DAISY. Common name for *Venidium fastuosum*, an annual also known as monarch-of-the-veldt; see VENIDIUM.

CAPE-GOOSEBERRY. Common name for *Physalis peruviana*, a form of husk-tomato with edible, yellow berries; see PHYSALIS.

CAPE-HONEYSUCKLE. Common name for *Tecomaria capensis*, a climbing tropical shrub with showy flowers; see TECOMARIA.

CAPE-MARIGOLD. Common name for DIMORPHOTHECA, a genus of colorful herbs and shrubs native to South Africa.

CAPE-PONDWEED. Common name for *Aponogeton distachyus*, an aquatic herb with showy, fragrant flowers; see APONOGETON.

CAPE-PRIMROSE. Common name for STREPTOCARPUS, a genus of showy herbs with blue or purple blooms and broad basal leaves.

CAPITATE. Arranged in a very dense head, like that of the teasel.

CAPRIFOLIACEAE (kap ri foh lee AY see ee). The Honeysuckle Family, a group of widely distributed, largely woody shrubs, many of which are cultivated in North America for their showy, fragrant flowers and for medicinal purposes. Among the cultivated genera are *Abelia, Diervilla, Leycesteria, Linnaea, Lonicera* (honeysuckle), *Sambucus* (elder), *Symphoricarpos* (snowberry and coralberry), and *Viburnum*.

CAPSICUM (KAP si kum). A genus of plants belonging to the Solanaceae (Nightshade Family) and commonly known as pepper. The name "pimiento," from the Spanish word for pepper (*pimienta*) is sometimes applied to this genus or to certain cultivated varieties. Most of the plants are tropical shrubs grown as annuals in colder climates. They bear small flowers and attractive, edible fruit. For culture, see PEPPER.

Capsicum frutescens

PRINCIPAL SPECIES

C. annuum includes most of the cultivated sweet, hot, and ornamental forms. Var. *annuum* includes most of the cultivated forms grouped according to former variety names.

The Cerasiforme group (cherry pepper) produces erect or bending fruits, rounded to 1 in. across, yellow or purple, and very pungent.

The Conoides group (cone pepper) has erect, conical fruits to 2 in. long.

The Fasciculatum (red cluster pepper) has erect, slender, very hot, red fruits up to 3 in. long.

The Grossum group (bell or sweet pepper, pimiento) forms stout bushes with large, soft, irregularly compressed fruits of red or yellow and mild flavor, often used for salads or stuffed and cooked.

The Longum group (long pepper) includes the chili and cayenne sorts, with pendent, slender, very hot fruit, tapering to 1 ft. long.

C. frutescens (Tabasco pepper) produces hot (spicy) fruits.

CAPSULE. A dry, podlike fruit developed from a compound pistil and usually opening when mature. The pod or "fruit" of the poppy and the daylily are examples.

CARAGANA (kahr ah GAY nah). A genus of hardy ornamental shrubs belonging to the Fabaceae (Bean Family) and commonly known as pea tree or pea shrub. Hardy in Zones 3–7, and thriving in sunny places and light soils, they are grown chiefly for their bright yellow flowers and interesting growth habit. Propagation is by seed or cuttings of the cultivars.

C. arborescens (Siberian pea tree) is a tall shrub or small tree of stiff, upright habit, conspicuous in spring when crowded with small, yellow, pealike flowers. Var. *pendula*, a weeping form with stiffly hanging branches, is usually grafted high. Var. *nana* is a dwarf, stunted form with contorted branches.

CARAWAY. Common name for the herb *Carum carvi*, whose seeds are used to flavor bread, cake, confections, cheese, and other foods; see CARUM.

CARBON. This is one of the most important of all the chemical elements. It makes up about half of the dry matter in plants, which obtain it chiefly from carbon dioxide of the air. Also, combined with other elements, it forms the various carbonates and other compounds important in plant growth and soil handling.

CARDAMOM. Common name for *Elettaria cardamomum*, a perennial herb whose seeds are used as a spice; see ELETTARIA. The seeds of a related plant *Amomum compactum*, having similar properties, are sometimes offered and used in place of true cardamom seeds.

CARDINAL FLOWER. Common name for *Lobelia cardinalis*, a moisture-loving herb with spires of crimson flowers; see LOBELIA.

CARDIOCRINUM (kahr dee oh KRIN um). A genus of the Liliaceae (Lily Family) whose three species are all native to the Himalayas. While not commonly grown in North American gardens, they do well in the high rainfall and temperate regions of the Pacific Northwest.

C. giganteum is the most spectacular of this genus with flower spikes up to 12 ft. long and up to 20 blossoms per stem, sweetly scented. They are predominantly white with darker red-purple stripes inside the flowers. They do extremely well in moist woodland gardens.

CARDIOSPERMUM (kahr dee oh SPUR mum). A genus of hardy, annual or perennial, ornamental vines commonly known as heartseed or balloonvine. They are excellent for covering wire fences or trellises and with support will grow to a height of 10 ft. The seedpods are inflated like balloons, and each black seed is marked with a heart-shaped, white spot. The quick-growing vines are graceful, with their deeply cut leaves and small, white, four-petaled flowers.

Seed should be sown where the plants are to grow, or it can be started indoors in the spring, the plants later put outdoors, preferably in a light soil and sheltered location. Plants may self-sow in mild regions.

PRINCIPAL SPECIES

C. grandiflorum has relatively large, white flowers and pods growing to 2 in. long.

C. halicacabum (balloon vine, love-in-a-puff) is the most commonly grown species. It is an attractive vine native to the tropical Americas but is frequently grown as an annual climber because of its interesting, inflated fruits.

C. hirsutum has densely hairy stems.

CARDOON (kahr DOON). Common name for *Cynara cardunculus*, a sturdy, thistlelike plant belonging to the Asteraceae (Aster Family), closely related to the globe artichoke, *C. scolymus*, but grown for its blanched stalks and thick main roots. Sow seed in early spring where plants are to stand, either in hills 18–24 in. apart or in rows 3–4 ft. apart. In either case, thin the plants so they stand only one at a place. Water in dry spells, since lack of moisture makes the stalks pithy or hollow. In autumn, tie the mature leaves together, wrap them in blanching paper or straw, and bank them with earth. About a month later the stalks are ready to cut and use like celery or endive.

CARDUUS (KAHR doo us). A genus of vigorous herbs native to southeast Asia, commonly known as nodding-thistle or, more frequently, plumless-thistle because the flowers forming the composite head do not have the hairy plume of the true this-tles. They are robust, spiny-leaved annual and perennial plants with purple, tubular flowers. Striking in both flower and foliage, some species are distinctly ornamental. They grow well in ordinary garden soils and can be propagated by seed or division. They have escaped from gar-dens and become naturalized in parts of North America.

CAREX (KAY reks). A large genus including about 900 species of grasslike perennials commonly known as sedge. Hardy to Zone 1, depending on the species, they inhabit temperate and arctic regions, most of them growing on marshlands and often yielding crops of bog hay. Some kinds are planted by ponds and in bog gardens or used for naturalizing; the broad-leaved types are use-ful in rock gardens as a feature in corners or beside walls. A few species are grown as potted plants in the house or greenhouse. Their long, narrow leaves are sometimes used for making woven grass rugs and other fabrics. Propagation is by division of the clumps or by seed sown in the fall.

CARICA (KAR ik ah). A genus of tropical, treelike herbs, of which *C. papaya* is grown for its fruit; see PAPAYA.

CARICATURE PLANT. Common name for *Graptophyllum pictum*, a tropical shrub named for the designs in its mottled leaves; see GRAPTO-PHYLLUM.

CARISSA (kah RIS ah). A genus of branched, spiny, evergreen shrubs from South Africa, Asia, and Australia. They are grown as hedge plants and for the edible fruits in regions where only light frosts occur, mostly in Zones 9–11.

PRINCIPAL SPECIES

C. bispinosa (hedge-thorn) is a 10 ft. high, South African shrub with white flowers and red fruits.

C. carandas (caraunda) is a native of India, growing to 20 ft. in warmer regions of the United States. It has fragrant, white or pink flowers and cherrylike fruits that can be pickled when green or used in jelly.

C. macrocarpa (natal-plum), formerly listed as *C. grandiflora*, is a South African shrub with glossy, leathery leaves; fragrant, white, star-shaped flowers; and a scarlet, plumlike fruit. The original species was a large, spiny bush, but there are now a number of dwarf forms that make fine ground covers. All stand shearing well (or better still, close pruning by hand) and are tolerant of salt spray.

CARNATION. A common name for DIANTHUS, a large and variable genus of flowering annuals and perennials, especially for *D. caryophyllus*, the familiar greenhouse flower.

CARNEGIEA (kahr NEG ee ah) **gigantea.** One of the largest of cacti, commonly known as saguaro or desert cactus, and sometimes referred to by the older designation, *Cereus giganteus*. Its 4-in., white blossom is the state flower and an impor-tant symbol of Arizona, where it occurs in verita-ble forests ranging south throughout Sonora, Mexico. Saguaro National Monument is a pre-serve just east of Tucson, Arizona. The saguaro is very slow growing and may be 150 years old before it starts to branch. A large, many-armed specimen may be 250 to 300 years old. Its erect stem, often 2 ft. in diameter and attaining 60 ft., is heavily ribbed, covered with stout spines, and sometimes has a few branches jutting outward and upward. It bears white flowers and an edi-ble fruit. Although spectacular in appearance, it is best appreciated in its natural habitat. The plant does not do well in cultivation except in its natural habitat, and wild collection presents a serious threat to its survival.

CAROB. Common name for *Ceratonia siliqua*, an evergreen with edible pods; see CERATONIA.

CAROLINA-ALLSPICE. Common name for *Calycanthus floridus*, a hardy shrub with large, reddish, fragrant flowers; see CALYCANTHUS.

CARPEL. The ovule-bearing unit of a flower, comprising ovary, style, and stigma. A simple pistil consists of one carpel; a compound pistil is composed of several carpels, the ovaries of which are fused, while the styles and stigmas may be either fused or independent. See PISTIL.

CARPENTERIA (kahr pen TEE ree ah) **californica.** An evergreen shrub native in California, belonging to the Saxifragaceae (Saxifrage Family), and commonly known as California mock orange or tree-anemone. The only member of its genus, it is an attractive, 10-ft. shrub with long, narrow leaves, whitish beneath. The pure white, fragrant, 2–3 in. flowers clustered at the ends of the shoots have golden anthers and resemble single roses. It requires a well-drained soil in a sunny, sheltered location; hardy in Zones 7–8.

CARPENTER WORM. This borer is the larva of the moth *Prionoxystus robiniae* and is common on many shade trees, especially ash, oak, chestnut, maple, locust, and cottonwood. Trees are rarely killed, but the wide burrows in the trunk of the tree and often at the lower end (sometimes an inch or more in diameter), produce serious deformities. Signs of infestation are wilting of the twigs, accumulations of sawdust, and a discharge of dark-colored sap from the openings on the trunk. The full-grown worm is a reddish white caterpillar, 3 in. long, greenish underneath, with a shining black head. The life cycle covers three years. The large moths, mottled gray tinged with yellow, are around most of the summer. They lay eggs in crevices in the bark, preferably in old wounds, and the young borers work into the wood immediately on hatching, where they live, grow, and finally pupate.

Control is difficult. Since the moths prefer roughened places for laying eggs, smoothing off such areas and treating them with grafting wax or a wound dressing may help. Trunk wounds should be treated promptly; see TREE SURGERY. Spraying with *Bacillus thuringiensis* (Bt, commonly available as Biotrol, Dipel, or Thuricide) may also be effective.

CARPET GRASS. Common name for *Axonopus affinis*, a perennial grass used in pastures; see AXONOPUS. Carpet-grass is *Phyla nodiflora* var. *canescens*, a creeping herb used for ground cover or grass substitute in warm regions; see PHYLA.

CARPETWEED. Common name for AIZOACEAE, a family of mostly tropical, succulent plants.

CARPINUS (kahr PĪN us). A genus of hardy deciduous trees native to the Northern Hemisphere, belonging to the Betulaceae (Birch Family), and commonly known as hornbeam or ironwood. Most are small or medium-sized, of ornamental value, and usually of irregular form with delicate, wiry twigs; smooth, beechlike bark; muscular swellings along the trunk and lower limbs; and handsome, light green fruit clusters. They have rounded heads of foliage, which are rarely subject to insect attacks and assume attractive autumn tints. The exceedingly hard wood, once used to make ox yokes, takes on a glossy, hornlike polish when so used.

Some species stand severe pruning and have long been used for hedges in formal gardens. Although they grow very slowly, they are hardy and also of value as specimens on the lawn or for park planting, especially along brooks. They are raised from seed (which is slow to germinate), cuttings, or by grafting on common seedlings.

PRINCIPAL SPECIES

C. betulus (European hornbeam) grows to 70 ft. and has many landscape uses, including pruned hedges. A beautiful pyramidal-to-oval-shaped tree, it has no disease or insect problems. Cv. 'Fastigiata', with upright growth habit, is widely grown. 'Columnaris' has a slender, pyramidal shape. Hardy in Zones 5–7.

C. caroliniana (American hornbeam, blue-beech, ironwood) is a tree that grows to 40 ft., doing well in dense shade and tolerating wet soils. Best for naturalized areas, it has a very interesting smooth, gray, ridged trunk. Hardy in Zones 3–9.

C. japonica (Japanese hornbeam) grows to 30 ft. and has wide-spreading branches and dark green foliage. Hardy in Zones 5–6.

CARPOBROTUS (kahr poh BROH tus). A genus of plants of the Aizoaceae (Carpetweed Family), with fleshy leaves, showy, yellow to reddish and purple flowers, and edible fruit. They are used in mild climates as a ground cover but are hardy only to Zone 10. If grown in pots, they should have a light soil, full sunlight, and ample drainage.

C. edulis (hottentot-fig, iceplant) is a perennial originally from Natal, South Africa. It is frequently raised in greenhouses then planted outside and is now naturalized in California, where it is still commonly used in freeway landscaping. The paired, elongate, angled leaves are bronze-purple, and flowers are yellow varying to rose-purple, opening to 3 in. wide. The name *edulis* applies to the figlike fruits which are edible.

CARRION FLOWER. Common name for *Smilax herbacea*, a perennial herb with smelly flowers; see SMILAX.

CARROT. A biennial herb, *Daucus carota* var. *sativus*, whose cultivated forms are supposed to have been developed from the wild carrot, also known as Queen-Anne's-lace, which can be a pernicious weed in improperly managed land. Large-rooted, late kinds are used for livestock feed; small ones are used as a vegetable and in soups, stews, and salads. The Carrot (or Celery) Family is APIACEAE.

CULTURE

Carrots do best in deep, light, rich soils. Since the seedlings are hardy, sow seed thinly as soon as the soil can be worked. Make the rows 12–15 in. apart for hand tillage and 30 in. for power implements.

Because carrot seeds sprout slowly, sow some lettuce or forcing radish seed with it; these plants appear quickly, marking the carrot rows and permitting early cultivation to forestall weeds. The radishes or lettuce can be used within a month, or removed when the carrots are thinned to stand not less than 1 in. apart. Thin a second time a month later, leaving the plants 3–4 in. apart. Roots of the early or forcing varieties pulled at the second thinning should be large enough to eat.

For autumn and winter use, a more tender, better quality crop can be secured by sowing a forcing variety during August in freshly dug soil, tramping the seed firmly on the rows, then raking the surface ½ in. loose to promote germination and growth despite summer heat. Dig the winter crop before cold weather sets in, cut the tops ½ in. from the root crown, and store in a root cellar or pit.

Carrot stalk

ENEMIES

Diseases. Bacterial soft rot is significant both in the field and in storage. It occurs on many other vegetables and on some

Carrot root

ornamentals, particularly iris, and causes a soft, slimy disintegration of the tissues accompanied by a very disagreeable odor. Generally the outer skin is left intact. To prevent it, practice long crop rotations. When storing, dry the roots in the sun and save only perfectly healthy roots.

Two leaf blights turn leaves and petioles first yellow then brown, and one may kill the whole plant. The disease is worse in damp locations near large bodies of water. Destruction of diseased carrot refuse and planting on high, well-drained ground are advisable.

Insect Pests. The carrot rust fly, a small, shining, dark green fly with yellow head and red eyes, may cause serious problems on carrots, celery, and parsnips. Its slender, dark brown larvae ¼ in. long feed on the roots, and the injured plants show a rusty appearance. In the home garden, where this pest is bad, carrots can be grown under floating row covers. The growing plants can be protected by scattering a few moth balls along the rows, but their use should be restricted because they also kill beneficial elements in the soil.

Proper rotation of crops will prevent injury by the larvae of the dark brown carrot weevil. Destruction of weeds and decaying vegetation will keep down the reddish brown carrot beetle.

CARTHAMUS (KAHR tha mus). A genus of 20 species of spiny-leaved annuals of the Asteraceae (Aster Family), commonly known as safflower. They are native from the Canary Islands to Central Asia. The flower heads are purplish or yellow, and the plants form ornamental clumps in the garden.

C. tinctorius (false saffron) yields two dyes from its florets: one, a tint of orange soluble in water, is used for coloring soups and pickles; the other, a resinous red, affords shades of pink to

Carthamus tinctorius

cherry-red, which are used in dyeing silks and, when mixed with talc, for making rouge. Seeds are sown in April where the plants are to bloom.

CARUM (KAR um) **carvi.** A biennial or annual herb belonging to the Apiaceae (Celery Family) and commonly known as caraway. The seeds are used to flavor bread, cakes, confections, and cheese. It is hardy to Zone 3 and easily grown in any garden soil. Sow seed in early spring where the plants are to remain for two seasons, adding a few radish seeds to mark the rows. The young shoots and tender leaves can be used to flavor salads. The seeds are produced the second summer.

Carum carvi

CARYA (KAY ree ah). A genus of native, hardwood, deciduous trees including hickory and pecan, belonging to the Juglandaceae (Walnut Family). These are beautiful native American trees, and despite their slow growth, excellent for specimen planting. They have straight trunks and hold their foliage well above the ground. Hickory wood produces more heat when burned than any other native tree and is important in woodworking and for smoking meats.

The trees are rather tall, with large, pinnate (deeply divided) leaves with three to seventeen leaflets and greenish flowers followed by large, green fruits containing nuts that in some species are sweet and edible, and in others, exceedingly bitter. The nuts range from very hard and rough shelled to very smooth and thin shelled. Their golden autumn foliage and rugged form makes them desirable for ornamental purposes, while improved named varieties (especially of pecan) bearing edible nuts of high quality, are often cultivated in orchards.

CULTURE

Since caryas are rather difficult to transplant, it is better to plant seeds where the trees are to grow (if grown solely for ornament) or to buy young nursery-grown stock of grafted cultivars or strains if nuts are the first consideration, since they do not always come true from seed and are difficult to start from cuttings. They should be planted in rich, well-watered soil, though some of the species will grow in dry locations. Most species are hardy in Zones 5–6.

There are no serious or important diseases of caryas, but the hickory leaf aphid, the leaf stem gall, and certain borers do great damage. Plant lice, causing hollow green galls on the leaf stems, may kill as much as half of the new growth. Control them with dormant oil spray. Various twig borers and pruners can be kept in check by removing and burning infested wood. The hickory bark beetle, a close relative of the insect that spreads Dutch elm disease, is a particularly dangerous pest, its presence often not being noted until the whole top of the tree is dead. Trees found to have been entered by thousands of beetles should be cut and the bark burned before the insects can escape and attack other trees in spring. Encourage the vigorous growth of trees by giving plenty of food and water. See also INSECT CONTROL; SPRAYING.

PRINCIPAL SPECIES

C. aquatica (bitter pecan), growing to 90 ft., has shreddy, light brown bark and an angled, ridged nut with a very bitter kernel. It grows wild in swampy areas from Virginia to Florida and Texas.

C. cordiformis (bitternut), growing to 90 ft., is one of the fastest-growing species under cultivation and is excellent for park planting. The nuts are small, round, and bitter.

C. glabra (pignut) is a small tree that grows to 40 ft. and bears a ridged nuts with astringent, bitter kernels.

C. illinoinensis (pecan), also listed as *C. pecan*, grows to 150 ft. in nature but not when cultivated as an orchard crop. It is a most valuable nut tree but is only half-hardy. It is extensively planted in the South for its sweet-kerneled, light brown to reddish nut.

C. laciniosa (big shellbark hickory), growing to 120 ft., is a handsome tree with a yellowish white, sweet-kerneled nut, pointed at both ends.

C. ovata (shagbark hickory), growing to 75 ft., is a handsome ornamental tree with a broad, open head. It has gray bark that breaks up into shaggy shreds and pinnate leaves usually with five leaflets. It is hardy in the North and is often planted for its delicious, white, nearly round nuts. There are a number of improved cultivars.

C. tomentosa (mockernut), also listed as *C. alba*, grows to 90 ft. and has white, downy undersides on the leaves and very hard shelled nuts with sweet kernels.

CARYOPHYLLACEAE (kar ee oh fil AY see ee). The Pink Family, a group of widely distributed herbs and sometimes subshrubs, most abundant in temperate and cold regions. The stems are characteristically swollen at the joints, and the flowers are bright colored and mostly regular. The family contributes many fine annuals and perennials to the garden and greenhouse. Among the cultivated genera are *Cerastium*, *Dianthus* (carnation), *Gypsophila*, *Lychnis*, *Petrorhagia*, *Saponaria*, *Silene*, *Spergula*, and *Stellaria*.

CARYOPTERIS (kar ee AHP tur is). A genus of small deciduous shrubs or herbs from Asia, belonging to the Verbenaceae (Verbena Family), and commonly known as bluebeard. The leaves and flowers are aromatic and of an attractive gray tone. Plants show to advantage in the flower garden with dense flower clusters appearing in the fall, a season when any new flower in the garden is most welcome. The tops are usually killed back during northern winters, but young shoots that spring up from below as the weather becomes warm will flower the same season. These shrubs require a well-drained, light soil and sunny location. Hardy in Zones 5–8.

C. x *clandonensis* is a hybrid that grows to 2 ft. and should be cut back each winter. The following cultivars are grown: 'Blue Mist', with light blue flowers; 'Dark Knight', with deep purple flowers; and 'Heavenly Blue', which is a deeper blue. Hardy to Zone 5.

C. incana (blue-spirea), with lavender and blue flowers, is the best known. It grows to about 3 ft. high but may die back in winter. Cv. 'Candida' has white flowers, and a pink form has been introduced.

CARYOTA (kar ee OH tah). A genus of trees commonly known as fishtail palms because of the graceful, wide-spreading tips of the leaflets (pinnules). They have ringed brown trunks, which are smooth and unarmed (free from spines) after the leaf sheaths have fallen. Very large (12-ft.) flower clusters, which suggest horse tails, are borne in the leaf axils. The trees do not bloom until maturity and die after fruiting. Native to tropical Asia and Australia, they are easily grown in south Florida if given sufficient water and food, thriving in sun or shade. Potted specimens are most attractive on patios. In cooler climates, they are more appropriate for conservatories or other locations that will accommodate their large size.

C. urens (wine, sago, jaggery, or toddy palm), the best-known species, grows to 40 ft. The finely cut, stiff, dark green leaves are up to 20 ft. long and 10–15 ft. wide with prominently toothed edges. A graceful, decorative tree, it is frequently planted outdoors on the west coast of Florida, where it grows to perfection. In India this tree yields toddy or palm wine (some trees yielding 100 pints in 24 hours) and many other commercial products, such as sago, fiber, and timber.

C. mitis, with tufted stems, sometimes grown outdoors in Florida, and *C. rumphiana* are less common species.

See also PALMS.

CASEBEARER. Coleophoridae, a family of insects whose larvae live in portable cases, often in the shape of cigars or pistols, made from the woolly hairs of leaves. Some secrete the material used to make the cases between leaves that they web together. They mine leaves, flowers, and fruits and are especially vigorous on birches and alders. The birch casebearer is a very small, mottled, gray moth, which in caterpillar stage is light yellow to green with a black head. It is only ⅕ in. long and lives in a tube spun between the leaves. Rarely abundant, it can be controlled on apple trees, for instance, by *Bacillus thuringiensis* (Bt). Several parasites are useful for biological control. See also INSECT CONTROL.

CASHEW. Common name for *Anacardium occidentale*, a tropical tree that only survives in the United States in Zone 11 and the extreme southern parts of Zone 10. The tree is a spreading evergreen to 40 ft. and has milky juice that yields a gum used in making a varnish to protect woodwork and books against insects. It is propagated by seed, shield budding, or mature wood cuttings under glass. The nut, which is shaped like a kidney bean, is borne on the end of a red or yellow, fleshy, edible cashew "apple." The nut yields an oil and is prized for eating when roasted. Oil in the coat of the nut is very caustic and must be driven off by heat before the nut can be handled.

The Cashew Family is ANACARDIACEAE.

CASIMIROA (ka sim ir OH ah) **edulis.** A Mexican tree of the Rutaceae (Rue Family), commonly known as white-sapote. Trees grow to 50 ft. and have leathery, divided leaves; greenish flowers; and round, yellow-green fruit with creamy white, edible flesh. This tropical fruit is easily raised in warm climates in ordinary garden soil, propagated by seed and by shield budding.

CASSABANANA. Common name for *Sicana odorifera*, an annual vine producing edible, decorative fruits; see SICANA.

CASSIA (KASH ah). A genus of herbs, shrubs, and trees belonging to the Fabaceae (Bean Family) and common in tropical areas. The leaves and pods of several are useful in medicine, and a few species are grown for ornamental purposes and are very attractive, with finely cut foliage and showy flowers. Only one or two can stand more than a few degrees of frost. They are sun lovers, preferring a sandy loam. Propagation is by seed.

PRINCIPAL SPECIES

C. artemisioides is an Australian shrub with silvery, threadlike leaves and pale yellow flowers. It grows and flowers well in warm, dry places. Hardy to Zone 9.

C. corymbosa is a half-hardy shrub from South America, sometimes grown in pots or tubs for

decoration. The yellow flowers are freely produced all through the summer. Hardy to Zone 8.

C. fistula (golden-shower, pudding-pipe-tree)
is a small tree from India that grows to 30 ft. and
has long racemes of showy, yellow flowers and
pods 1–2 ft. long; these are the cassia pods of
commerce. Hardy in Zones 10–11.

C. grandis (pink-shower) is a tropical American
tree that grows to 50 ft.
and has long, drooping
racemes of rose-pink
flowers. Hardy in Zones
10–11.

C. marilandica (wild
senna) is a perennial herb
that grows to 4 ft. and is
native from New Eng-
land southward. It has
bright yellow flowers
that bloom in summer.
Hardy in Zones 6–9.

Cassia marilandica

C. tomentosa is a Mexican shrub with deep
golden flowers and leaves whitish beneath.
Hardy in Zones 10–11.

CASTANEA (kas TAY nee ah). A genus of hardy
deciduous trees and shrubs of the Fagaceae
(Beech Family) and commonly known as chestnut. They are valued for ornament and for their
edible nuts. The name is sometimes applied to
the Brazil- or Para-nut, produced by a tropical
tree, *Bertholletia excelsa*.

Chestnuts have slender, toothed leaves and
showy flowers. Unfortunately, the catkins have a
very disagreeable odor. They grow in any well-
drained soil and also tolerate acid soils. They are
easily propagated from seed or by budding and
grafting. They often sucker when cut to the
ground. The native species, *C. dentata*, has now
been exterminated throughout the United States
by the CHESTNUT BLIGHT.

PRINCIPAL SPECIES

C. crenata (Japanese chestnut) is a small,
rounded tree that grows to 30 ft. and bears nuts at
an early age. It is often planted for its 1-in. nuts
and resistance to the blight. Hardy in Zones 6–7.

C. dentata (American chestnut) was an important tree for its timber, edible nuts, and large size
(to 100 ft.). Since the spread of the chestnut
blight in the early 1900s, it has now been killed
off throughout the United States. Old stumps
keep suckering and occasionally grow large
enough to bear a few nuts before they are again
killed to the ground by the blight. This species
had the sweetest-tasting nut of any chestnut.
People used to own small woodlots for the sole
purpose of gathering chestnuts every year.
Hybrid crosses with a few remaining trees in
Ohio and elsewhere have been made with other
species. These are now being grown, and some
show resistance to the blight. It is hoped that we
can gather small, sweet chestnuts once again.
Hardy in Zones 5–7.

C. mollissima (Chinese chestnut) is a smaller
tree with a rounded shape, growing to 50 ft. This
is the most commonly planted chestnut, often
bearing 1-in. nuts two to three years after planting. This species is resistant to the blight. Hardy
in Zones 5–8.

C. pumila (chinquapin) is a small, southern
native tree that grows to 40 ft. and has small, edible nuts about ½ in. in size. The catkins have a
strong disagreeable odor. Hardy in Zones 6–7.

C. sativa (Spanish chestnut) grows to 100 ft.
and has larger nuts than *C. dentata* (1–3 in.
across). It is also susceptible to the blight but is
occasionally planted. Hardy in Zones 6–7.

CASTANOPSIS (kas tah NAWP sis). A small genus
of evergreen trees and shrubs belonging to the
Fagaceae (Beech Family) and commonly known
as chinquapin.

C. chrysophylla (giant chinquapin), a native
species, is grown in warmer regions. It has lustrous green leaves, often grows to 100 ft., and
thrives on poor, dry soils. Hardy in Zones 8–9.

CASTILLA (kas TIL ah) **elastica.** A tropical American tree of the Moraceae (Mulberry Family),
valuable commercially for its milky juice, from
which rubber is made. It grows to 60 ft. and has
large leaves, to 18 in., with dense, soft hair

beneath and flowers in close clusters. A native of Mexico, Central America, and northern South America, it was at one time extensively grown in the tropics. They can be raised from seed and the seedlings set in their permanent positions when 12 in. tall. The trees can be tapped when they are eight years old.

This plant belongs to the same family as the familiar rubber plant, *Ficus elastica*, though the latter is more closely related to the fig; see FICUS.

CASTILLEJA (kas til EE yah). A genus of herbs of the Scrophulariaceae (Figwort Family), commonly known as Indian-paintbrush or painted-cup. The plants are partially parasitic on the roots of surrounding vegetation, producing showy, red, orange, or yellow bracts that surround the small, true flowers. Although offering great potential for the garden, they have been notoriously difficult to transplant. Fresh seed sown around a host seedling (virtually any plant) gives good results, or seed can be directly sown outdoors near some other plant, grasses and woody composites working well as host.

PRINCIPAL SPECIES

C. affinis is a perennial that grows 1–2 ft. and has large, vivid bracts of scarlet or orange.

C. chromosa (great basin paintbrush), 1–2 ft. tall, has brilliant bracts of red through yellow and is excellent for drought-tolerant plantings.

C. foliolosa (woolly paintbrush), shrubby to 3 ft., is also good for arid situations and has attractive gray, woolly foliage with scarlet flower bracts.

C. franciscana (Franciscan-paintbrush) grows 1–3 ft. in height and has showy, orange or scarlet bracts arranged ladderlike on wiry stems.

C. latifolia is a perennial similar to *C. affinis*.

CASTOR-BEAN. Common name for *Ricinus communis*, a tropical plant grown for ornament and useful for repelling garden pests; see RICINUS.

CASUARINA (kas yoo ah RĪ nah). A genus of trees and shrubs from Australia and the Pacific Islands, comprising the only members of the Casuarinaceae (Casuarina Family). The common names include Australian-pine and she-oak, but the plants are not related to either pines or oaks. The leaves are reduced to tiny, pointed scales that occur in whorls around the slender branches to look like the horsetail plant. The flowers are not conspicuous, and the trees are mostly planted as windbreaks or to hold soil against erosion. One species spreads by root sprouts, and several drop quantities of branchlets that may also contain a chemical that inhibits other plants from growing under them. Hardiness varies with the species, but most will only survive in tropical climates (Zones 10–11).

CATALPA (kah TAL pah). Botanical and common name for a genus of deciduous, hardy, native North American and Asiatic trees belonging to the Bignoniaceae (Bignonia Family). They are ornamental because of their large, long-stalked leaves, showy terminal clusters of white or pinkish flowers in late spring, and long, slender pods. Catalpas are popular for lawn and avenue plantings, especially where a formal or exotic effect is desired.

Several species found in the North Temperate Zone are rapid growers and thrive in any good soil. Propagation is by seed sown in the spring with a little bottom heat and cuttings of green wood or roots. Most are hardy in Zones 5–9.

PRINCIPAL SPECIES

C. bignonioides (common catalpa, Indian-bean), a large tree of the southeastern states, is ornamental on lawns or in a garden background. It has large, white, yellow-striped flowers in loose panicles. Var. *nana*, a dwarf form, develops a dense, round head and is often grafted on straight, 6-ft. stems for use along paths or near doorways. It is often incorrectly called *C. bungei* after another Chinese species.

C. fargesi and *C. ovata* are Chinese species.

C. hybrida, the product of cross-breeding *C. bignonioides* and *C. ovata*, is a popular form whose leaves are purplish when young.

C. speciosa (western catalpa) is the most commonly planted in the North. A very rapid grower in favorable locations, it has leaves to 12 in. across, fuzzy beneath, and bears many panicles of brown-spotted white flowers 2 in. across.

CATANANCHE (kat ah NAN kee) **caerulea.** A hardy perennial herb from southern Europe, cultivated as a garden subject, commonly known as Cupid's-dart or blue suc-
cory. Distinguished by narrow, hairy leaves borne near the base of the stems and by long-stalked, sky blue, chafflike heads of ray and disk flowers, it grows 2 ft. tall and blossoms all summer the first year from seed. Hardy in Zones 3–9, the plants are excellent in beds and bor-
ders. Flowers are good for

Catananche caerulea

cutting, lasting well in water, or for drying to use as EVERLASTINGS in winter. Well-drained soil and sun are required. Propagation is by seed or division. The best method is to treat them as bienni-
als, sowing seed outdoors for the following season's bloom. Var. *alba* has blue rays edged with white.

CATASETUM (kat uh SEE tum). This group and its subgenus *Clowesia* consist of 50 to 100 species of unusual epiphytic or terrestrial orchids native to the tropical Americas. Large, fleshy pseudobulbs have plicate, deciduous leaves and few- or many-
flowered inflorescences that rise from the base.

The flowers of the genus are male and female, while those of the subgenus have perfect (hermaphroditic) flowers. Fragrant blossoms are yellow-green to brown-green with purple to black markings on sepals, petals, and helmet-
shaped lips. In the bisexual species, male and female flowers, which may be borne on the same plant, are dissimilar. Male flowers are often more fragrant than female flowers and "shoot" their pollinia when jostled by a pollinator. Petals and sepals in both types of flowers are broad and spreading.

Plants are hardy in Zones 10–11 (to Zone 9 if protected from cold) and are best grown in bas-
kets, in loose, well-drained compost, to permit the pendent flowers to hang freely. During growth, plants need bright light, abundant water, high humidity, and a minimum winter temperature of 65°F. After their leaves fall, they should rest in dry, cool (minimum 55°F) conditions. The type species is *C. macrocarpum*.

CATBRIER. Common name for *Smilax glauca*, a trailing vine with oval leaves and sometimes covered with bloom and black berries; see SMILAX.

CATCH CROP. A farming term applied to any crop used to occupy ground between the harvest-
ing of one more important crop and the planting of another. It can be plowed or dug under to improve the soil. See GREEN MANURE.

CATERPILLAR. The order Lepidoptera, cater-
pillars, including loopers, are the larvae of moths and butterflies. They are soft-bodied, with thirteen segments and a head. The first three seg-
ments have jointed legs, the next (usually five) segments have soft "prolegs" with hooks called "crochets." Of the thousands of caterpillars, some are smooth, some hairy, and some spiny. All have chewing mouthparts and, usually near the head, "spinnerets" for producing silk for cocoons, and a last proleg on the end segment. Caterpillars include budworms, cabbage loopers, cankerworms, cutworms, earworms, hornworms, leafminers, and webworms among the most common.

The woolly bear cater-
pillar is white, yellow, or brown, 2 in. long, and is covered with long, yellow to reddish brown hairs. It feeds on leaves in late summer and spins cocoons under rubbish.

Woolly bear caterpillar

Minor infestations can be controlled by picking off and destroying the caterpillars. On a larger scale, all are subject to control by *Bacillus thuringiensis* (Bt, commonly available as Dipel, Biotrol, or Thuricide) sprayed on the leaves they chew. Many are controlled by small wasps and other parasites, which lay their eggs in the bodies of the caterpillars with their piercing ovipositor.

Similar to caterpillars are the larvae of beetles, called GRUBS, which have only three pairs of thoracic legs and lack prolegs and crochets.

CATERPILLAR FERN. Common name for *Polypodium formosanum*, an attractive basket fern with wormlike rhizomes and hanging fronds; see POLYPODIUM.

CATHARANTHUS (kath ah RAN thus) **roseus.** A tender perennial belonging to the Apocynaceae (Dogbane Family), formerly listed as *Vinca rosea*, and commonly known as Madagascar-periwinkle. It is a good flower-garden plant with rosy purple flowers and is often used as a bedding plant. Hardy in Zones 10–11, it can be grown as an annual in cooler climates. Seeds should be sown early in the year in a warm greenhouse and transplanted several times before being set outdoors. There are varieties with white flowers and white ones with a reddish eye.

CATKIN. Common name for AMENT, a type of flower with scaly bracts and no petals or sepals.

CATNIP. Common name for *Nepeta cataria*, a hardy perennial herb attractive to cats, also known as catmint or catnep; see NEPETA. *Teucrium marum* (cat-thyme) is also popular with cats; see TEUCRIUM.

CAT'S-CLAW. Common name for *Macfadyena unguis-cati*, an evergreen vine; see MACFADYENA.

CAT'S-EAR. Common name for *Antennaria* and *Hypochoeris*, both genera belonging to the Asteraceae (Aster Family) and characterized by woolly leaves. The name is also applied to *Calochortus coeruleus*, whose blue flowers have hairy petals; see CALOCHORTUS.

CATTAIL. Common name for TYPHA, a genus of swamp-dwelling herbs with blunt flower spikes.

CATTLEYA (KAT lee uh). The best-known genus of orchids; the color known as "orchid" is synonymous with the distinctive flower color of *C. labiata*, the type species. About 65 species of epiphytic or lithophytic orchids comprise the genus, native to the tropical Americas, from Mexico to Argentina, and discovered by nineteenth-century English botanist John Lindley.

This significant genus is part of the tribe Epidendreae and is hybridized with innumerable members of the tribe, producing artificial intergeneric hybrids of incomparable beauty. The plants have more or less elongated, thickened pseudobulbs and stout rhizomes, with one or two thick, leathery leaves growing from the apex of the pseudobulbs from which the flowers emerge.

The genus *Cattleya* is divided into two sections: unifoliate (labiate types) and bifoliate types. Labiate types have one single, large, fleshy leaf growing from the apex of a fluted pseudobulb. The flowers are large, to 6½ in. across, very showy, and usually solitary, although occasionally more flowers are produced. In the bifoliate group, species have two, sometimes three, coriaceous leaves growing from the top of a long, cylindrical pseudobulb of smaller diameter than the unifoliate species. These plants produce up to 25 flowers per spike. The flowers are smaller than those of the labiate types, and they are usually of heavier substance than the unifoliate species. Flower shapes of both types are similar, with broad, spreading sepals and petals and a large showy lip or labellum. The lip is usually tubular, enclosing the column. The lip in some bifoliate species appears to have three lobes. Lips of the unifoliate types are broad, with ruffled or undulating edges. Colors are pale lavender to rich purple, white to yellow, even pale blue in some unifoliates. Some species have lips distinctly marked with gold eyes or striations, with the edges outlined in a contrasting color. Bifoliate *Cattleya* flowers are green, brown, yellow, orange, and mauve. Their lips are brightly colored, often contrasting with petals and sepals that may be spotted and blotched with chestnut-brown or maroon.

Hardy only in Zones 10–11, *Cattleya* withstands minimum winter temperatures of 60–65°F. The plants need bright light (4000 footcandles) and high humidity (70%). They are best grown in pots with a loose, well-drained compost and should be watered as needed, drying out between watering.

CAULESCENT. A term used in describing plants or flowers with an obvious stem. Compare ACAULESCENT.

CAULIFLOWER. A biennial herb from the Botrytis group of *Brassica oleracea* varieties, developed from the wild cabbage but distinguished from the cultivated cabbage by its swollen flower stems, which form white heads and suggest the name "stem flower."

Of all the members of the cauliflower group, cauliflower is the most finicky. When conditions are right, even the novice may succeed with it; otherwise, even the skilled grower may fail. Because the plant resents heat and dryness, it cannot be grown as a summer crop.

Cauliflower is a voracious but choosy feeder, requiring deep, rich, loamy soil abundantly supplied with quickly available plant food. Well-decayed horse manure is its best fertilizer, though green manures make fair substitutes.

After the ground is plowed or dug, but before planting, apply 1 lb. to 100 sq. ft. of a quickly available chemical fertilizer mixture made of 4% nitrogen, 8% phosphorus, and 10% potash, and preferably consisting of nitrate of soda, superphosphate, and sulfate of potash. Give a second application beside the plants when the heads begin to form.

For an early crop, start the plants indoors a week earlier than cabbage, prick them into flats when the second true leaves form, keep them growing steadily, and set them out a week or ten days later than cabbage. For a late crop, sow the seed thinly in partial shade in early June, in a moderately rich, friable, moist soil. Manage like late cabbage, setting the plants in the open in early summer, 2 ft. apart for hand tillage but leaving 36 in. between rows for rotary tiller or garden tractor.

Cultivate at least weekly until the leaves shade the ground. In dry weather, soak the soil weekly either by irrigation or by filling bowl-like hollows of hoed-up loose earth around the plants. When the young flower heads, or "buttons," are egg size, fold or tie some of the leaves up over them to keep them white.

Blanching cauliflower

The black leaf spot of cabbage causes brown spots on cauliflower heads, and a ring spot disease is sometimes destructive in the western states. Circular and irregular spots occur on the leaves, causing them to die prematurely. Use seed from healthy plants or treated with hot water as directed under BRASSICA.

CAULOPHYLLUM (kaw loh FIL um) **thalictroides.** A small-flowered, native perennial herb found in the eastern United States, belonging to the Berberidaceae (Barberry Family), and commonly known as blue-cohosh. The 3-ft. plants are of great beauty in the wild garden, with small, yellowish white flowers followed, after the foliage dies in September, by blue fruits. The plants transplant easily and are propagated by seed or division. They prefer partially shaded, rich woodland soil.

CEANOTHUS (see ah NOH thus). A genus of nearly 50 species of ornamental, deciduous or evergreen shrubby plants belonging to the Rhamnaceae (Buckthorn Family) and commonly known as wild-lilac, California-lilac, and blue-blossom. Ranging from dense ground cover mats to small trees, found in North America, they are native chiefly in the Pacific Coast area, where they grow on dry, rocky slopes. These handsome, free-flowering shrubs produce dense panicles of small, blue, white, or pink blossoms. Mostly hardy in Zones 5–9, only one or two can be grown outdoors in cooler regions. The evergreen species flower in spring and, in favorable climates, form bushes up to 20 ft. The deciduous species flower late in the season and so should be pruned fairly hard in spring to encourage good flowering shoots. They do best in a sunny, sheltered location in light, well-drained soil. They are subject to root rot in the garden and generally live only five to ten years.

PRINCIPAL SPECIES

EVERGREEN SPECIES

C. arboreus (felt-leaf ceanothus) is a tender shrub or small tree that grows to 25 ft. with 4-in., oval leaves and large plumes of pale blue flowers appearing early in summer. Cv. 'Ray Hartman' has dark green leaves and rich blue flowers.

C. coeruleus is a tender Mexican species that grows to 20 ft. and has deep blue to white flowers. It is often used in hybridization.

C. gloriosus (glory-mat) is a tender ground cover with small, hollylike, dark green leaves and blue-lilac flowers. Several named selections have varied foliage and flowers.

C. griseus is a tender shrub that grows to 12 ft. and has 3-in., dark green oval leaves and panicles of variably shaded blue flowers. Several varieties are available in forms suitable for ground cover. Var. *horizontalis*, a spreading ground cover about 2 ft. tall, has smaller, glossy leaves and light blue flowers. Several other varieties are available. Hardy to Zone 8.

C. impressus (Santa Barbara ceanothus), the most spectacular of all, is a tender shrub that forms a dense mass to 6 ft. and has small, cupped and impressed, oval leaves and dazzling cobalt blue flowers from bronze bud clusters. Many cultivars are available. Hardy to Zone 8.

C. maritimus (maritime ceanothus) is a good ground cover that forms a tender mat to 3 ft. and has small, leathery leaves and white to purple flowers, depending on the selection.

C. megacarpus is a tender shrub or small tree that grows to 15 ft. and has small, leathery, teardrop-shaped leaves and balls of white flowers appearing very early.

C. prostratus (Mahala-mat) may be hardy, growing less than 4 in., and is suitable as ground cover for sterile soils. It has small, hollylike foliage and usually blue-purple balls of flowers.

C. rigidus (Monterey ceanothus) is a tender, arching shrub that grows to 6 ft. and has small, toothed, teardrop-shaped leaves and violet-blue flowers. Varieties are available with white flowers and more spreading habit.

C. thyrsiflorus (blueblossom), the hardiest of the tall evergreen species (to Zone 8), it is a handsome, free-flowering shrub with pale blue to purplish or sometimes white flowers. Var. *repens* is prostrate to 4 ft.

C. velutinus (tobacco-brush) is a shrub to 15 ft. that has glossy, aromatic foliage and large panicles of whitish flowers.

DECIDUOUS SPECIES

C. americanus (New-Jersey-tea) is a low shrub of slender, upright growth to 3 ft., bearing clusters of white flowers in summer. Several hybrids have been raised, but they are only half-hardy (Zones 5–8). It is possible to carry them over, however, by digging them in the fall and wintering in a frost-free location.

C. x *delilianus* is a hybrid between *C. americanus* and *C. coeruleus*. There are various named forms, one of the most notable being the late-flowering cv. 'Gloire de Versailles'. Hardy to Zone 7.

C. integerrimus (deerbush), growing to 10 ft., is a semihardy shrub of open, branching habit with white to rich blue flowers.

C. ovatus is found from New England to Texas and is hardy to Zone 5. It is an upright shrub that grows to 3 ft. and has flowers similar to *C. americanus*, but smaller.

C. x *pallidus* is a hybrid of *C. delilianus* and *C. ovatus*. One of the best cultivars is 'Marie Simon', with flesh-colored flowers.

C. sanguineus (red-stem ceanothus) grows to 10 ft. and has white flowers.

CEDAR. Common name that properly applies to CEDRUS, a genus of evergreen trees with stiff "needles" and erect cones. The name is also applied, with modifying adjectives, to trees and plants of other genera. California incense-cedar is *Calocedrus decurrens*. Canoe-cedar is *Thuja plicata*. Cigar-box-cedar is *Cedrela odorata*, also known as Spanish- or West-Indian-cedar. Ground-cedar is *Lycopodium complanatum*. Incense-cedar is *Libocedrus*. Japanese-cedar is *Cryptomeria japonica*. Red-cedar refers to several species and varieties of JUNIPERUS. Stinking-cedar is *Torreya taxifolia*. White-cedar refers to *Chamaecyparis thyoides*, *Tabebuia pallida*, and *Thuja occidentalis*.

CEDAR-APPLE RUST. This is one of the worst of several diseases that attack the leaves and fruits of apple trees. The life history of *Gymnosporangium juniperi-virginianae* is typical of most RUSTS. The disease alternates life cycles on *Juniperus* spp. (wild juniper or red-cedar) and apple trees.

Chocolate brown, corky "cedar-apples" (actually galls) are the response of the red-cedar to the irritation caused by this fungus in the leaf tissues. Beginning in spring and during warm rains for several months, gelatinous orange-yellow horns, made up of hundreds of spores, grow out from depressed areas on the surface of the "apples." As the weather clears, the spores are liberated and carried by the wind to the leaves and twigs of apple trees or flowering crabapples, causing light yellow spots on the upper surface of the leaves. Later, swelling on the underleaf surfaces discharge spores, which are blown back to red-cedars, on whose twigs or leaves the fungus lives over winter, forming a small, rounded enlargement the next spring, which increases in size during the summer, and the second spring matures as a gall or cedar-apple. Thus, the fungus spends four or five months on the apple host, and eighteen or more months on the red-cedar.

Three species of red-cedar are susceptible to this rust, namely *J. virginiana* (eastern red-cedar), *J. scopulorum* (western red-cedar), and *J.*

horizontalis (creeping red-cedar). Some varieties of *Malus* (apple) are susceptible, and others are more or less resistant, depending on the locality. Foreign species of crabapples (with the exception of *Malus sylvestris*) have been found immune and should be used in place of the native varieties in gardens. In apple-growing regions, rust is controlled by eradicating all red-cedars within a mile of any orchard.

On the apple, rust can be controlled with applications of fungicide. Consult the agricultural extension service for local guidelines.

CEDAR-OF-LEBANON. Common name for *Cedrus libani*, a wide-spreading evergreen tree with dark green needles. See CEDRUS.

CEDRELA (se DREL ah). A genus of mostly subtropical or tropical, deciduous or evergreen trees of the Meliaceae (Mahogany Family), with colored, fragrant wood of commercial value. The foliage resembles that of *Ailanthus*, and some of the species are grown for ornament or avenue trees in warm places. *Cedrela* is propagated by seed, cuttings of mature wood, and root cuttings over heat.

PRINCIPAL SPECIES

C. odorata (West-Indian-cedar, Spanish-cedar, cigarbox-cedar), native to the West Indies and South America, is grown for its fragrant wood, extensively used for making cigar boxes. It grows to 100 ft. and bears loose clusters of yellowish flowers.

C. sinensis, from China, grows to 50 ft., has long panicles of white flowers, and is hardy in southern New York and southern New England.

C. toona, from the Himalayas, often attains 70 ft. and has fragrant, white flowers; it has been planted as an ornamental in Florida.

CEDRUS (SEED rus). A genus of Asiatic and North African coniferous trees belonging to the Pinaceae (Pine Family), commonly known as cedar. They are grown for their hardiness, growth habit, needle color, and general ornamental value, though they are not entirely hardy.

The three species are large, wide-spreading evergreens with many stiff needles in a whorl or cluster. They bear quite large, oval cones, which are erect on the branches and fall apart at maturity. There are some unusual cultivars available.

PRINCIPAL SPECIES

C. atlantica (atlas cedar) has feathery, bluish green foliage with 3-in. cones. Pyramidal when young and flat topped with horizontal branches when older, it grows to a height of 50 ft. Cv. 'Argentea' has silver-blue needles. 'Fastigiata' has narrow, upright habit. 'Glauca' has grayish blue color. 'Glauca Pendula' has weeping branches with blue needles. Hardy in Zones 6–7.

C. brevifolia (cypress cedar) is similar to *C. libani* but is less hardy and has shorter needles and cones.

C. deodara (deodar cedar), from the Himalayas, has very graceful, drooping branches with 2 in. long needles and cones up to 5 in. long. Hardy in Zones 7–9. Cv. 'Aurea' has yellow needles. 'Kashmir' and 'Shalimar' are much hardier selections with bluish green color. Cv. 'Pendula' has weeping branches.

C. libani (cedar-of-Lebanon), with dark green, needles 1 in. long and cones 4 in. long, grows to about 50 ft. and is a very striking specimen tree; native to Asia Minor and hardy in Zones 6–8. Cv. 'Glauca' has bluish or silvery white foliage. 'Pendula' has drooping branches. 'Stenocoma' is an extremely hardy form.

CEIBA (say EE bah) **pentandra.** A very large (to 120 ft.) tropical tree belonging to the Bombacaceae (Bombax Family), commonly known as kapok or silk-cotton tree. It has immense spreading branches, a very large trunk sometimes 30 ft. in diameter, thin buttresses or surface roots that may extend 30 ft., and compound, deciduous leaves. White or rose-colored flowers (the petals hairy outside) are followed by capsular fruit, woolly inside and containing many woolly seeds. The cottony material inside the seed capsules is kapok, widely used for stuffing pillows, life preservers, etc. Interesting as well as valuable, this tree is planted as a specimen tree in Zones 10–11.

CELANDINE. Common name for *Chelidonium majus*, a weedy herb with yellow flowers, sometimes grown in wild gardens; see CHELIDONIUM.

Lesser-celandine is *Ranunculus ficaria*, see RANUNCULUS. Tree-celandine is *Macleaya cordata*; see MACLEAYA.

CELASTRACEAE (sel as TRAY see ee). The Stafftree Family, a widely distributed group of trees and shrubs, often climbing. The botanical name, signifying "evergreen," refers to the bright fruits that persist through the winter. They are really pods, splitting at the summit to reveal red seeds. The genus *Paxistima* is sometimes cultivated, principally in borders; species of *Celastrus*, *Euonymus*, and *Maytenus* are grown chiefly as ornamental wall shrubs and trellis covers.

CELASTRUS (se LAS trus). A genus of mostly deciduous shrubs of usually twining habit, belonging to the Celastraceae (Stafftree Family), and commonly known as bittersweet or stafftree. Native in Asia, North America, and Australia, some are very hardy (Zones 4–8) and ornamental, being most effective late in the season when their leaves turn yellow and the yellow fruits open up to reveal crimson-coated seeds. They are useful to cover walls and trellis work, and are especially attractive when allowed to clamber up through an old tree or to ramble at will in rocky places or over rough banks.

They are not particular as to soil or location and grow well in sun or shade. Male and female flowers are borne separately, mostly on the same plant but sometimes on separate plants. This accounts for the nonfruiting of certain specimens. Propagation can be done by seed sown in the fall, by root cuttings, and by cuttings of soft or mature wood.

Celastrus is frequently infested with euonymus scale. Control with a dormant application of an oil spray in early spring.

C. orbiculatus, a Japanese species, is a vigorous climber or rambler to 40 ft. It is distinguished from the native species by more roundish leaves and shorter fruit clusters with yellow capsules.

C. scandens (wax work, false bittersweet) is a native shrub climbing to 20 ft. or more. The fruiting branches, with bright orange capsules and crimson seeds, make attractive and lasting floral decorative material for the home, causing the plant to be rapidly disappearing from the wild.

CELERIAC (se LER ee ak). A variety of CELERY, *Apium graveolens* var. *rapaceum*, grown for its thick, turniplike roots. Seed is sown in spring and the crop grown during summer like celery, but it requires less work because it needs no hilling up or blanching, and its roots are easier to store safely. They can be sliced and eaten raw with salt, used for flavoring soups and stews, boiled like turnips and served with a cream or a hollandaise sauce, or served as a salad.

Celeriac

CELERY. A biennial herb, *Apium graveolens*, of the APIACEAE (Celery Family), whose blanched, crisp leaf stalks are eaten raw or cooked in many different ways. Commercially the crop is grown mainly on reclaimed muck lands with special equipment, but better-quality celery can be produced by home gardeners who give it the necessary attention and whose soil is rich and well supplied with moisture.

EARLY CELERY

For this crop, use a self-blanching variety. Starting in February or early March, fill a seed pan with well-firmed, finely sifted soil. Scatter the seed thinly on the surface, barely cover with sifted soil, press firmly, sprinkle with water, and then keep covered with newspaper and a pane of glass until sprouting starts (in about a month). When seeds have sprouted, remove the newspaper but retain the glass for another week or two. If moisture condenses on it, raise one side slightly for ventilation but not enough to dry the soil. When the seedlings are 1 in. tall, prick them out

and plant 2 ft. apart in flats of similar soil. Place the flats in a coldframe or hotbed until weather and soil conditions permit outdoor planting. At each transplanting, pinch off the outside leaves.

The easiest celery culture demands relatively little work. In early spring, enrich the soil of a bed 4 ft. wide with well-rotted stable or poultry manure forked in 10–12 in. deep and rake the top 6 in. to a very fine texture. Set the plants from the hotbed 6 in. apart in rows 10 in. apart and shade with screens of plaster lath 1 in. apart placed on stakes 18–24 in. above. Plants so treated will blanch themselves. If desired, they can be set farther apart and blanched individually with tiles or paper celery-blanching tubes obtainable from garden suppliers.

LATE CELERY

For an autumn crop, sow seed thinly and shallow in April or early May outdoors in finely prepared, moderately fertile soil. Make the drills 8–10 in. apart. After sowing, firm the soil with the back of the rake and spread burlap snugly over it to check evaporation. Water only when the burlap begins to get dry. When the seed starts to sprout, remove the burlap but provide partial shade for a week or two. When the seedlings are 2 in. high, thin them, setting out the thinned ones so that all plants stand 1–2 in. apart in a similar seedbed.

About mid-July, prepare a space in the garden where a well-fertilized early crop of some sort has been grown and harvested. Before digging, manure it heavily and apply wood ashes (1 lb. to 10 sq. ft.) if available. If manure is scarce or costly, dig a trench 8–10 in. deep, place the manure in the bottom and cover with rich soil until nearly level full, mixing the ashes with the soil, though not directly on the manure. The bed is then ready for the young plants; however, several hours before transplanting, soak the seedbed so the plants will be full of water when moved. Trim them as they are lifted and set them 6 in. apart in rows 10–18 in. apart, depending on the blanching method used. Firm the soil well around them. Keep cultivated until the cool, fall days when blanching time arrives.

Late celery can be blanched with tiles or blanching tubes (as for the early crop), but boards or earth are more often used. Lay 12-in. boards flat on the ground on each side of a row; raise the boards on their edges; work them into the soil a little; and hold them a few inches apart with wire hooks laid across wooden strips nailed across their upper edges. This method is not safe with early celery because the plants might decay.

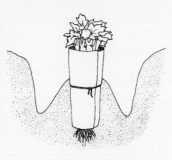

Blanching celery

It is less work than earthing up, which, however, produces the finest quality celery.

To blanch celery by earthing up, first run the wheelhoe with cultivator teeth down each side of the row and close to it. Gather the stalks of celery, wrap them with paper, and then pack enough earth around their bases to hold them erect. With a hand hoe or wheelhoe, throw more earth against the plants. Repeat this process two or three times, raising the soil higher each time. Dig the crop before cold weather sets in; never allow it to freeze.

Storage. There are two basic ways to store celery for the winter: (1) In late fall, as you dig the plants, transplant them close together in deep boxes of soil in a cool, moist, frostproof cellar. Here they will continue to grow and blanch. (2) Dig and replant them closely in a trench 12 in. or deeper and, at the approach of cold weather, cover with an A-shaped board roof with closed ends. Before hard winter sets in, cover this roof with 6–8 in. of manure or other litter. By making the roof in sections, a part of the trench can be emptied at a time without risk of freezing the rest of the crop.

Diseases. Three separate blights attack celery; all can be controlled in the same way. (1) Early blight, caused by *Cercospora apii*, produces dead or ashen-gray velvety areas. (2) Late blight, due to *Septoria apii*, causes brown spots that contain tiny, black fruiting bodies on the leaves and stem. (3) Bacterial blight, caused by *Bacterium apii*, produces reddish brown spots with a yellow halo but without the black fruiting bodies. These symptoms may appear on leaf blade, petiole, or stalk at any stage of the plant's growth. To prevent infection, select seedbed soil that has not grown celery for at least three years and is free from celery refuse.

Insect Pests. Punctures made by the TARNISHED PLANT BUG may cause serious damage. Dust plants with sulfur or spray (so as to hit the bugs) with PYRETHRUM spray. Hand-picking is the only control measure necessary in the case of the celery worm, *Papilio polyxenes*, which is a smooth caterpillar about 2 in. long, green with black cross bands. The adult is the common black swallowtail butterfly; there are two broods a year.

CELERY CABBAGE. A name for the species of *Brassica* commonly called CHINESE CABBAGE.

CELOSIA (sel OH shee ah). A genus of popular annual herbs from the tropics, belonging to the Amaranthaceae (Amaranth Family). The common forms have large, ornamental heads and are good for pot culture or garden beds. Individual flowers are small and not showy, but the crests, besides being colorful and interesting outdoors, can be dried for winter bouquets. Easily grown from seed, they should be started indoors in early spring to produce plants ready to set in the garden in late spring. Plants do best in a fertile soil supplied with plenty of moisture.

C. cristata (cockscomb, woolflower) includes several major varieties, often listed as separate species. Those listed as var. *childsii* grow 12–18 in. high and have large, feathery or plumed, globular heads like balls of wool-chenille, usually red or golden colored. Var. *plumosa* includes forms that grow 2–3 ft. and have dense, plush spikes, usually bright red, in the various shapes of pyramids, grotesquely flattened like the comb of a rooster, or ruffled.

C. floribunda is a branched shrub that grows to 12 ft. and has numerous flowers in tight panicles. It is sometimes grown in southern California.

CELSIA (SEL see ah). A genus of biennial or perennial herbs from Asia and the Mediterranean region with yellow flowers in tall, upright spikes. They resemble the mulleins, to which they are closely related and often crossed to make interesting hybrids. Not quite hardy, they are started indoors and planted in the open in early summer. They can be propagated by cuttings. A few species are commonly known as Cretan-bear's-tail (*C. arcturus*) or Cretan-mullein (*C. cretica*).

CELTIS (SEL tis). A genus of mostly hardy, usually deciduous trees or shrubs belonging to the Ulmaceae (Elm Family), including several species of large trees with cherrylike fruits, valued for shade and ornament, and commonly known as hackberry. They are planted as lawn or specimen subjects. Their rather wide-spreading boughs and light green, elmlike foliage give them an airy, cheerful appearance.

They grow rapidly, especially when young and, not particular as to soil, will thrive in almost any location. Propagation is by seed. Most species are hardy in Zones 3–9.

For the most part, hackberries are free from disease and insect pests. Of the occasional exceptions, the principal disease is a form of WITCHES'-BROOM. The hackberry is also a favorite host for jumping plant lice (psyllas), which can cause deforming galls on foliage and twigs.

PRINCIPAL SPECIES

C. australis, growing to 80 ft., has grayish green leaves, soft and hairy beneath, and orange fruit. It is suitable only for the South.

C. laevigata (sugarberry, Mississippi hackberry) grows to 120 ft. and has long, thin leaves and orange-red fruit that becomes bluish purple. It is native in the southern and south-central states, where it is occasionally planted for shade.

C. occidentalis (sugarberry), a tree growing to 120 ft., has shining green leaves, paler beneath, and orange-red to dark purple fruits. This native

species is planted for shade or lawn specimens in the eastern and midwestern states, but it is usually infected with witches'-broom.

C. reticulata, native to the western states, is a small tree growing to 20 ft. with brownish fruits.

C. sinensis is an Asiatic tree that grows to 60 ft. and has long, wavy-toothed leaves and orange fruit. It is cultivated in mild climates.

CENTAUREA (sen tor EE ah). A genus of annual and perennial herbs with colorful flowers, belonging to the Asteraceae (Aster Family), and known by many common names. The different species are used for many garden purposes, especially in borders, mass plantings, or carpet bedding. Flowering from midsummer to frost, they produce a profusion of blossoms excellent for cutting. Single or double, pompon or plumelike flowers are purple, blue, yellow, rose, or white. In some species, the gray or whitish leaves provide pleasing contrast with other plants.

The annuals are grown from seed started indoors in early spring or in the open ground in mid- to late spring. The foliage types are propagated from cuttings taken in early fall and carried over the winter indoors; or from seed sown in late summer. Perennial kinds can be started from seed in early spring or by root division in spring. The annuals especially often self-sow. All are hardy (perennials surviving in Zones 3–9, depending on the variety) and will thrive under ordinary conditions in any good garden soil if given a sunny location.

Centaurea is subject to diseases such as RUSTS, root rot, and aster yellows. Remove and burn affected specimens. Fungicides are available if chemical control becomes necessary. Be sure to follow all label directions carefully. To avoid problems with aster yellows, do not plant centaureas in the same place where they or asters were grown the previous year. See DISEASE.

PRINCIPAL ANNUAL SPECIES

C. americana (basketflower) grows to 6 ft. and bears solitary, thistlelike flowers generally of rose or flesh color, often 5 in. across. Var. *alba* (star-thistle) bears white, fluffy, double flowers.

C. cyanus (bachelor's-button, bluebottle, cone-flower), growing to 2 ft., is a hardy subject that often reseeds itself. There are single and double varieties with 1½-in. flowers in blue, white, rose, purple, and mauve shades. The plants are woolly white only when young. Some dwarf varieties grow to 10 in. high.

C. moschata (sweet-sultan) is an easily cultivated garden favorite that grows to 2 ft. and has fragrant, white, yellow, or purple, solitary flowers 2 in. across, often beautifully soft and fluffy. Cv. 'Imperial' (giant sweet-sultan) grows to 4 ft. with fragrant flowers of white, rose, lilac, or blue.

PRINCIPAL PERENNIAL SPECIES

C. cineraria (dusty miller) grows to 1 ft. and has white-woolly foliage and large, yellow or purple flowers.

C. gymnocarpa (dusty miller) grows to 2 ft. and has densely woolly foliage and flower panicles of rose or purple mostly hidden by the leaves.

C. macrocephala, growing to 3 ft., has yellow flowers 4 in. across in summer.

C. montana (mountain-bluet, perennial cornflower) grows to 1 ft. and has silvery white young leaves. Several varieties produce flowers of violet-blue, purple, rose, and white.

C. nigra (knapweed, hard-heads), often naturalized, is a coarse, woolly plant that grows to 2 ft. and has solitary, rose-purple flowers about 1 in. across.

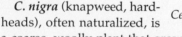

Centaurea montana

CENTAURIUM (sen TOR ee um). A genus of small annual or perennial herbs belonging to the Gentianaceae (Gentian Family) and commonly known as centaury. They grow 4–8 in. tall and in midsummer bear broad, flat clusters of bright red or rose flowers resembling pinks. Especially suited to the rock garden or border, they thrive in light, sandy soil and require protection from full sun and cold weather.

The annuals are propagated by seed sown indoors or out, and the perennials, by seed, division, or cuttings. There are only a few perennial species, and it is best to treat most of these as annual or biennial.

C. chloodes is a fleshy-leaved species, native in England or southwestern Europe.

C. venustum, the species best known in the United States, grows 8 in. tall and bears rose-colored flowers with white throats spotted red.

CENTIFOLIA ROSE. The youngest of the true old European roses; there is some question as to whether these were developed in Holland or the Provence region of France. They have come to us improperly bearing the species name *R. centifolia* and have also been called Provence roses and cabbage roses. They are large, arching bushes, very thorny, with rough-textured foliage and blooms in clusters, usually three. The very full, fragrant flowers have larger outer petals surrounding many smaller petals. Varieties come in shades of white and pink. *R. centifolia* var. *variegata* is a striped variety, delicately penciled pink on a white ground. The centifolia roses, being doubled and filled with petals, are sterile, but the moss roses came from them by way of sporting, a spontaneous mutation in the plant cells.

It should be noted that roses dating from Roman times, called "centifolia," are now thought not to have any relation to the centifolia class, but that any very full petaled variety of the time was so named and did not necessarily possess literally 100 petals. Most of the roses placed in the centifolia class today have many more petals than the hundred petals the name implies.

Well-known selections include 'La Noblesse', 'Petit de Hollande', *R. centifolia* var. *bullata* (lettuce leafed rose), 'Spong', and 'Unique Blanche'.

CENTIPEDE. Literally "hundred-legged," but this insect, belonging to the class Chilopoda of the order Myriopoda, actually has one pair of legs on each of 15–24 segments on a somewhat flattened, cylindrical body. Behind the head is a pair of poison claws with which centipedes attack their prey, usually other insects and small animal life in the soil, where they spend their life. They breathe by means of air tubes and carry two short antennae on the head. Though usually considered beneficial, they constitute a real pest on asparagus in California, where fields are flooded to control them. In the greenhouse, steam sterilization is used. The house centipede is a more delicate form with long, fragile legs. It feeds on flies and other insects that get into the house.

CENTIPEDE GRASS. Common name for *Eremochloa ophiuroides*, an Asian grass useful in hot, dry regions; see EREMOCHLOA.

CENTIPEDE PLANT. Common name for *Homalocladium platycladum*, a tropical shrub with broad, often leafless stems and red to purple fruits; see HOMALOCLADIUM.

CENTRADENIA (sen trah DEE nee ah). A genus of small, shrubby evergreen plants from Central America. Very ornamental for warm greenhouse culture, they have colorful leaves, small pink or white flowers, and capsular fruits. They grow best with plenty of leaf mold and sand in the soil and appreciate liquid manure when established. Propagation is by cuttings.

C. floribunda has slightly angled, reddish stems, leaves red beneath, and clusters of pink flowers.

C. grandifolia has four-winged stems, large leaves bright red beneath, and showy clusters of light rose flowers. Cut sprays are very decorative and last well.

CENTRANTHUS (sen TRAN thus). A genus of annual and perennial plants belonging to the Valerianaceae (Valerian Family), long popular for use in the garden. The small flowers are white or red and borne in dense terminal clusters. The plants grow well in the open border and are easily propagated by seed or division. Perennials are hardy to Zone 4.

PRINCIPAL SPECIES

C. angustifolius is a perennial that grows to 2 ft. and has very fragrant, clear rose flowers.

C. macrosiphon is an annual that grows to 2 ft. and bears very pretty rose flowers.

C. ruber (Jupiter's-beard, red valerian), a very common and handsome feature in old gardens, is a perennial that grows to 3 ft. and has flat-topped clusters of fragrant, crimson or light red flowers blooming all summer. Var. *albus* is a white-flowered form.

Centranthus ruber

CENTROPOGON (sen TRAH poh gahn). A genus of tropical American shrubby plants of somewhat scandent (climbing) habit, belonging to the Lobeliaceae (Lobelia Family). In cultivation they are usually grown in a warm greenhouse, showing to good advantage in hanging baskets. Propagated by cuttings, they thrive best in a sandy, fibrous loam.

C. solanifolius grows to 5 ft. and has 3–6 in., ovate or elliptic leaves and clusters or racemes of scarlet-and-yellow flowers.

CENTURY PLANT. Common name for *Agave americana*, a succulent that was believed to bloom only after it was 100 years old. The name is loosely applied to other plants of similar appearance; see AGAVE.

CEPHALANTHUS (sef ah LAN thus). A small genus of hardy trees and shrubs belonging to the Rubiaceae (Madder Family), comprising about six species, and commonly known as buttonbush. *C. occidentalis*, the one species found in the United States, is widespread naturally in swampy places and therefore is well suited to wet places in gardens; hardy in Zones 5–9. A deciduous shrub to about 6 ft., it is the most common species in cultivation. It has good, glossy foliage and small, tubular, fragrant, white flowers densely packed in long-stalked, globular heads, blooming in late summer.

CEPHALIUM (sef AY lee um). A unique flowering structure occurring in some genera of Cactaceae (Cactus Family) wherein the growth rate of the mature cactus changes dramatically, producing less storage tissue but copious wool and bristles in tight, compacted spirals, thus forming a terminal cap from which flowers and fruits are produced, such as in the genus *Melocactus* (turk's-cap cactus). There are also lateral cephalia in which the structure of the ribs on one side of a columnar cactus changes drastically in the flowering zone, accompanied by copious development of wool and bristles, such as in the genus *Cephalocereus*. There are also "lateral pseudocephalia" where there is development of abundant wool and bristles in the flowering zone, but no structural change in the plant's form, such as in the genus *Pilosocereus* (woolly-torch cactus).

CEPHALOCEREUS (SEF ah loh SEER ee us) **senilis.** The old-man cactus from Hidalgo, Mexico, eventually grows to 30 or even 45 ft. high, clustering from the base. It is one of the most popular cacti as a little potted plant of a few inches tall because of the soft, long, white hairs that completely cover the stem. At one time many members of the Cereanae subtribe, which develop wool in the flowering zone, were placed in *Cephalocereus*. Now those from South America are usually placed in other genera (such as *Austrocephalocereus*, *Coleocephalocereus*, *Buiningia*, or *Espostoa*) and those without a true lateral CEPHALIUM are also placed in other genera (such as *Pilosocereus*), and only *C. senilis*, and *C. hoppenstedtii* from Tehuacan, Mexico, are left in *Cephalocereus*.

CEPHALOTAXUS (sef ah loh TAK sus). A genus of evergreen shrubs and trees native to China and Japan, and commonly known as plum-yew. They are grown for their graceful branches and long, shiny needles. Plants are dioecious, the female producing reddish brown, edible, plum-shaped fruits 1 in. long. Most are hardy in Zones 6–7.

C. fortunii (Chinese plum-yew) grows to 30 ft. and has wide-spreading branches and very attractive, shiny, dark green needles in two flat rows. It grows well in partial shade and develops a beautiful reddish brown bark on the branches and trunk. The fruit is edible when soft.

C. harringtonia (Harrington plum-yew) grows to a height of 30 ft. and has a wide-spreading irregular growth habit. The 1½-in. needles are arranged in two flat rows. Cv. 'Fastigiata' is a slow-growing columnar plant with needles spirally arranged.

CERASTIUM (see RAS tee um). A genus of hardy, herbaceous annuals and perennials belonging to the Caryophyllaceae (Pink Family) and commonly known as mouse-ear chickweed. In full bloom with creeping stems covering the ground, the effect is that of a snowdrift. The 3–6 in. plants are valued for their spreading, mat-forming habit and their attractive, silvery white foliage and showy, star-shaped, white flowers in early summer. These plants are especially suited to the rock garden, and because they

Cerastium tomentosum

prefer sunny locations and dry soil, they are also useful as ground cover or border plants. Propagation is by seed, division, or cuttings taken after flowering. Most species are hardy in Zones 3–9.

PRINCIPAL SPECIES

C. alpinum, native to arctic North America and Europe, grows to 6 in. and has silky hair.

C. arvense (field chickweed, starry grasswort), growing to 10 in., is densely tufted with erect or rising stems and numerous white flowers blooming in the spring. A native in the northeastern states, it can be troublesome in lawns. Its presence indicates a soil that is dry, gravelly or sandy, nitrogen poor, neutral to slightly acid, high in magnesium, and usually calcareous. To control excessive spreading, raise creeping stems with a rake and mow close or dig out small patches.

C. bierbersteinii (taurus cerastium) is a creeper that grows to 6 in. and has woolly gray leaves and white flowers, a good choice for a rock garden. Hardy to Zone 4.

C. grandiflorum is a creeper that grows to 8 in. and has grayish leaves and flowers of transparent white.

C. lerchenfeldianum grows erect to 8 in.

C. tomentosum (snow-in-summer), the most popular and widely grown species, is a hardy, creeping perennial with grayish, downy foliage and abundant white flowers in late spring. Hardy to Zone 4.

Cerastium vulgatum

C. vulgatum (mouse-ear chickweed) sometimes grows to weedy proportions, indicating neutral or basic soils that were recently limed.

CERATONIA (ser ah TOH nee ah) **siliqua.** A handsome evergreen tree native to the eastern Mediterranean region, reaching a height of 50 ft., and commonly known as carob or St.-John's-bread. It is now widely cultivated in warm regions, withstanding a few degrees of frost and succeeding in Zones 9–11. As an orchard crop, grown for its large, flattened, protein-rich, fleshy seedpods, the trees are set 40 ft. apart. The pods, eaten by livestock, are an acceptable human food also used to make a nourishing, fermented drink, as well as coffee and chocolate substitutes. On arid soils, the carob yields a much larger quantity of food than any other crop. Propagation is from seed started under glass and, in the case of preferred varieties, by budding.

CERATOPHYLLUM (ser at oh FIL um) **demersum.** A useful fernlike, freshwater aquarium plant, commonly known as hornwort or coontail. It grows entirely submerged, producing whorls of narrow, bristlelike leaves around the stem. Native to North America, it is hardy in Zones 3–8 and grows in ponds and still waters. In cultivation, it is best suited to the unheated aquarium and should be rooted in the sand of the aquarium bottom.

CERATOPTERIS (ser ah TAHP ter is). A genus of four aquatic plants belonging to the Parkeriaceae (Water-fern Family) and commonly known as water-ferns. They are tender annuals whose roots often extend into the muddy bottoms of ponds or rice paddies. In warm water and bright sun, they quickly build up large masses of lettuce-green foliage. Succulent leaves are borne on inflated stems. In Asia, they are eaten as a vegetable.

C. thalictroides, native in southern Japan, Polynesia, Malaysia, and India, is the most popular species for tropical aquariums. Plantlets form on the fronds, drop off, and float until they can root. When plants are rooted, finely dissected leaves emerge above the surface.

CERATOSTIGMA (ser at oh STIG mah). A small genus of hardy perennial herbs belonging to the Plumbaginaceae (Leadwort Family). Native to the Orient, they have shining leaves and blue, saucer-shaped flowers. Creeping plants growing to 12 in., they are often grown in the border or rock garden, where they continue in bloom late into the fall. They thrive in full sun and good drainage. Propagation is by division or by cuttings rooted under glass during the summer. Most species are hardy to Zone 5.

Ceratostigma plumbaginoides

C. plumbaginoides (leadwort) reaches 10–12 in., producing deep blue flowers from late summer through fall. Hardy to Zone 6.

C. willmottianum is a shrub that grows to 5 ft. and produces bright blue flowers from midsummer through the fall.

CERATOZAMIA (ser at oh ZAY mee ah). A genus of handsome Mexican plants with stiff, palmlike leaves in a whorl at the top of a short trunk. The young leaves are a rich, bronzy, chocolate tint, which later changes to olive green. About six species are grown in subtropical areas. Propagation is by seed, and growth is extremely slow.

CERCIDIPHYLLUM (ser si di FIL um) **japonicum.** A bushy deciduous tree growing to 50 ft., native to Japan, and commonly known as the Katsura tree. It has distinctive rounded heart-shaped leaves and inconspicuous flowers. In autumn, the foliage color varies from yellow to apricot. Thriving in rich, moist soil, it is usually grown for ornament, especially for street and garden planting. It is a popular landscape tree and has no significant disease or insect problems. Propagation is by seed or cuttings of green wood in spring. Cv. 'Pendula', an outstanding as a specimen plant, grows to 25 ft. and has weeping branches. Hardy in Zones 5–8.

CERCIS (SUR sis). A genus of trees and shrubs native in North America, southern Europe, and Asia, belonging to the Fabaceae (Bean Family), and commonly known as redbud or Judas tree. The latter common name derives from tradition, which says that Judas hanged himself on a tree of this group. They are very showy in spring with a profusion of pink or red flowers opening before or as the leaves unfold. Clusters of flowers are produced on the old stems as well as on younger growth. The foliage is handsome, and plants are well suited for the background of shrubberies. They do well in ordinary, well-drained soil but are best transplanted when small, since older plants are difficult to get established. Propagation is by seed or cuttings taken in summer.

PRINCIPAL SPECIES

C. canadensis, found from New Jersey to Florida, is a tall shrub or sometimes a tree that grows to 40 ft. and has a broad, round head. It is the only species really hardy in the North, thriving in Zones 5–9. Very showy in spring, it produces short clusters of pink flowers. Cv. 'Alba' and 'Royal' both have white flowers. 'Pinkbud' has a true, bright pink color. 'Withers Pink Charm' blooms in light pink. 'Forest Pansy' has showy, bright purple spring foliage.

C. chinensis (Chinese redbud) is an Asiatic tree growing to 15 ft., but in cultivation it is usually shrublike. It has glossier leaves and deeper colored flowers than *C. canadensis* but is not as hardy. Hardy in Zones 6–8.

C. siliquastrum (Judas tree) is a shrub or tree of southern Europe, with large, rosy purple flowers. Hardy in Zones 6–8.

CERCOCARPUS (sur koh KAHR pus). A genus of evergreen shrubs or semideciduous small trees of western North America, commonly known as mountain-mahogany. The botanical name comes from Greek words meaning "long, hairy tail," referring to the seed. Succeeding in dry, sunny places, the plants will thrive on dry, rocky, or gravelly slopes in arid temperate regions where conditions are unfavorable to other plants. Sometimes used as shrubs or hedges, they are propagated by seed or cuttings. While most species are hardy in Zones 6–9, *C. ledifolius* and *C. parvifolius* are especially hardy.

CERCOSPORA LEAFSPOT. A plant disease caused by various species of the imperfect fungus *Cercospora* and sometimes called cercospora blight. The spots on leaves are generally reddish brown, of irregular shape, and often have a purplish margin. As the fungus grows, the spots become ashen gray at the center because of the presence of spores. This fungus causes many common leaf spots on trees and shrubs, vegetables, and ornamentals, as well as those on beets, and the early blight of celery. Zinnia leaf spot is very disfiguring.

Since the fungus can live in dead plant material, be sure to clean up the garden carefully in the fall. Dry garden locations are less susceptible than wet areas. If an outbreak occurs, do not plant in the same soil the following season.

CEREANAE (seer ee AY nee). A subtribe of the Cactaceae (Cactus Family) including most of the tall, columnar cacti such as CEREUS.

CEREUS (SEER ee us). A genus of cacti, but many of the plants formerly listed under this heading are now called by other names, such as *Aporocactus*, *Carnegiea gigantea* (the Arizona state flower, which used to be known as *Cereus giganteus*), *Heliocereus* (sun-cereus), *Hylocereus* or *Selenicereus* (moon-cereus). They are all members of the subtribes CEREANAE and *Hylocereanae*.

One species that rightfully retains its name is a common plant in cactus gardens, *Cereus peruvianus*, which does not, in fact, come from Peru.

See CACTUS; CARNEGIEA.

CERIMAN. A common name for *Monstera deliciosa*, a tropical climber with large, perforated leaves and edible fruit; see MONSTERA.

CERINTHE (se RIN thee). A genus of annual and perennial herbs with yellow flowers, native to Europe, and commonly known as honeywort. The plants' popularity with bees is reflected in both the botanic and common names. *Cerinthe* means "wax flower," and was named because of the old belief that bees visited the purple-tipped yellow flowers for wax. The name "honeywort" refers to the abundant nectar secreted by the flowers. The perennials are rarely cultivated, but the annuals are easily grown from seed; *C. majus* is the most common.

CEROPEGIA (see roh PEE jee ah). A genus of about 150 species of herbs or subshrubs belonging to the Asclepiadaceae (Milkweed Family), native to tropical Asia, Africa, and the Malay Peninsula. Some have vinelike stems arising from a caudex or succulent tubers; others have succulent stems, all with intricate and fascinating flowers, some pink to lavender or brown, some hairy, some with ribbonlike lobes, others with structures like little parachutes. The succulent species from South Africa are, floristically, among the most interesting. In temperate regions they are greenhouse plants, usually twining, but some species are erect. They also make excellent houseplants and can be hung outdoors in warm weather. The flowers, more curious than beautiful, are swollen at the base. They require a peaty loam with some sand and fragments of charcoal. Propagation is by cuttings of small side shoots taken in spring and rooted in sand over bottom heat.

C. dichotoma, from the Canary Islands, represents the upright species with tapering, fleshy, clustering stems and tubular, yellow flowers, the long, tapering lobes joined at the tips. Its leaves soon fall and leave behind gray-green stems that stand straight and clustered, resembling a pot of bamboo stakes. It grows to 4 ft. tall and can be a handsome container plant for a mostly sunny and warm place. The fruits are typically paired milkweed pods.

C. woodii (rosary vine, hearts-entangled), from Rhodesia to South Africa, is a popular form with wiry, hanging stems that are set with succulent, paired, mottled, heart-shaped leaves on long, climbing or trailing stems. The peculiarly hooded and ballooned flowers are followed by potato-like tubercles that form at the nodes, resembling beads, and will, in turn, root and form new plants. For best results, remove the tubercles when about ½ in. in diameter and plant them 1 in. deep.

CESPITOSE. Growing in tufts or dense bunches, or forming mats or turf, like *Dianthus deltoides* (maiden pink) or *Phlox subulata*.

CESTRUM (SES trum). A genus of shrubs or small trees native to the tropical Americas, belonging to the Solanaceae (Nightshade Family), and one of the groups commonly known as jessamine. A few species are grown in greenhouses and outdoors in warm regions. As pillar or wall plants outdoors in Zone 10–11, they are attractive in winter with their bright flowers. Propagation is by cuttings.

PRINCIPAL SPECIES

C. diurnum (day jessamine) is a tall evergreen shrub with thick, glossy leaves and white flowers fragrant during the day.

C. elegans is a tall and slender half-climber with loose clusters of red-purple flowers produced over a long season. Cv. 'Smithii' has pale rose-colored flowers.

C. fasciculatum has large flowers in compact and leafy clusters.

C. newelli has relatively larger and more brilliant flowers than *C. fasciculatum*.

C. nocturnum (night jessamine) is a bushy shrub with slender branches and creamy white flowers fragrant at night.

C. parqui (willow-leaved jessamine) has profuse flowers fragrant at night. It is the hardiest of the species but still will not survive frost. Plants are poisonous to cattle and sheep.

CETERACH (SET ur ak). A genus of small, terrestrial, xerophytic ferns grown in greenhouses or warm climates and often classified as *Asplenium*.

PRINCIPAL SPECIES

C. aureum, also listed as *Asplenium aureum*, is a small fern with yellow-green fronds native to the Canary Islands and Madeira. The undersides are covered with dense scales. It is similar to *C. dalhousiae* but is larger and has blade scales.

C. dalhousiae, also listed as *Asplenium alternans*, forms a compact rosette only 2–6 in. high. It is a good rock garden subject in frost-free areas, but requires excellent drainage. It is found in northern India, Mexico, and Arizona.

C. officinarum (rusty-back fern), also listed as *Asplenium ceterach*, is a dwarf fern that grows 2–8 in. and inhabits walls and rock crevices. It has gray-green fronds whose undersides are covered with silvery scales that turn brown later in the season. The sori are hidden beneath the scales. It is more frequently seen in man-made walls than in its natural habitats. It will endure more sun than most wall ferns. It loves mortar and needs some form of lime if potted; however, it is difficult to establish in pots. It is native in Europe, India, and Africa.

CEYLON-GOOSEBERRY. Common name for *Dovyalis hebecarpa*, a small tropical tree that bears edible fruit resembling gooseberries; see DOVYALIS.

CHAENOMELES (kee NAHM el eez). A genus of highly ornamental shrubs belonging to the Rosaceae (Rose Family) and commonly known as flowering-quince. They have glossy leaves, showy flowers in early spring, and hard, green fruits that resemble quince; they are not edible raw but are occasionally used in preserving. Useful in shrub borders, for hedges, or trained against walls, they thrive in any good soil, doing best in a sunny location. Propagation is by seed, root cuttings, and grafting.

PRINCIPAL SPECIES

C. japonica is a low, spreading grower, hardy in Zones 5–8, with spiny branches and bright orange-scarlet flowers. Var. *alpina* is a free-fruiting dwarf form with prostrate branches.

C. speciosa (Japanese-quince) is a vigorous, spiny shrub that grows to 6 ft. or more and has lustrous leaves held late and large, scarlet red flowers in the type species; hardy in Zones 4–8. There are many named varieties with flowers of varying shades from pure white to deep scarlet and some with semidouble flowers.

C. x vilmoriana, a stiff shrub growing to 8 ft., has elliptic leaves and pink-and-white flowers.

CHAENOSTOMA (kee NAHS toh mah). Former name for SUTERA, a genus of African ornamental herbs and shrubs.

CHAFER. A beetle that is a significant pest to roses; see ROSE CHAFER.

CHAIN FERN. Common name for WOODWARDIA, a genus of ferns with sori patterned to suggest a chain.

CHALICE VINE. Common name for SOLANDRA, a genus of woody plants or climbing vines native to the tropical Americas, named for the shape of its flowers.

CHAMAECYPARIS (kam ee SIP ah ris). A genus of evergreen trees of the Cupressaceae (Cypress Family), commonly called false cypress or white-cedar. Young plants often have juvenile, needle-like leaves, while older plants tend to have scalelike leaves.

While they may be 75–100 ft. in the wild, in cultivation all species grow to about 50 ft. Many dwarf and compact cultivars are available and are used in foundation plantings, as specimens, and for hedges. False cypress do best in full sun but may tolerate partial shade. They prefer moist, well-drained soil, a cool climate, and protection from winter wind. Plants should be balled and wrapped in burlap when moved.

False cypresses are relatively free from disease and insect problems. Two gymnosporangium rust diseases may cause deformation or death of white-cedar. One, causing witches'-broom, must be fought by removing the alternate hosts nearby, namely bayberry, sweet-fern, and wax-myrtle. The other rust, causing a swelling of the branches, has *Amelanchier* (shadbush) for its alternate host. JUNIPER blight may cause serious damage following winter injury. The BAGWORM is sometimes found on *Chamaecyparis* but is not usually a serious problem.

PRINCIPAL SPECIES

C. lawsoniana (Lawson false cypress) is a beautiful columnar to pyramidal tree with flat-tened, horizontal branches. Over 200 cultivars being grown include dwarf, color variations, and unusual growth forms, including juvenile foliage. Cv. 'Allumii' and 'Argentea' have silver-blue coloring. 'Aurea' and 'Lutea' have yellow foliage when young. 'Minima Glauca' is a dwarf conical form with blue color. 'Nana' is a dwarf globose form with dark green leaves. Hardy in Zones 6–8.

C. nootkatensis (Nootka false cypress) has drooping, pendulous branches and grows to about 30 ft. under cultivation and nearly 100 ft. in the wild. It is an extremely attractive specimen plant with branches hanging downward in layers. It needs protection from winter wind. Cv. 'Pendula' has very weeping branchlets that are completely vertical to the main branch. 'Glauca' has a bluish green color. Hardy in Zones 5–6.

C. obtusa (Hinoki false cypress) is a tall, slender, pyramidal tree with very dark green, attractive foliage. It is an excellent specimen plant, slow growing with compact habit. There are many popular cultivars being grown. Cv. 'Crippsii' has golden yellow color at the ends of the branches. 'Filicoides' has unusual, flat, fern-like green foliage. 'Gracilis' is a compact, pyramidal form that grows to 12 ft. 'Sanderi' has blue-green foliage on the juvenile form, changing to purple in winter. 'Tetragona Aurea' has bright yellow tips in flat sprays. Hardy in Zones 5–8.

C. pisifera (Sawara false cypress), growing to 75 ft., has a pyramidal shape and a loose, open growth habit. These trees become rather unsightly with age, though beautiful when young. They are not grown much any more, but the many cultivars are widely used in landscaping. Cv. 'Boulevard' is a pyramidal form that grows to 12 ft. and has a silver-blue color in winter. Cv. 'Filifera', growing to 25 ft., has green, threadlike foliage. 'Filifera Aurea' has golden, threadlike branches and grows to 10 ft. 'Plumosa Aurea Nana', growing to 6 ft., has bright yellow, feathery foliage. 'Squarosa Intermedia' is a dwarf, rounded shrub with blue-gray color. Hardy in Zones 4–8.

C. thyoides (white-cedar) is one of the few evergreen trees that will thrive in wet ground and is often planted to screen off unsightly marshes. Hardy in Zones 4–8, it occurs in northern swamps, forming thick stands, and may grow up to 80 ft. high. The wood is light, resists decay, and is used for fence posts, small bridges, arbors, and other garden features. Cv. 'Ericoides' is a dense shrub that turns reddish brown in winter. Cv. 'Andelyensis' is a small, upright shrub.

CHAMAEDAPHNE (kam ee DAF nee) **calyculata.** A hardy evergreen shrub belonging to the Ericaceae (Heath Family) and commonly known as leatherleaf. Hardy to Zone 3, it grows in boggy places in the colder parts of the Northern Hemisphere. It is of spreading habit and grows about

3 ft. high. A sandy-peat soil in a moist place is preferred, and it is most effective when planted in groups. The oblong leaves are rusty beneath, and the nodding, white flowers are borne in leafy terminal racemes in early spring. Propagation is by seed, cutting of mature wood under glass, division, or layers. Var. *angustifolia* has more slender leaves. Cv. 'Nana' grows little more than 12 in. high.

CHAMAEDOREA (kam ee DOR ee ah). A genus of slender, shade-loving palms native primarily from Mexico to Central America, found mostly in the understory of tropical rainforest environments. The stems are mostly ringed or jointed like bamboos, and some species take on a climbing habit. Hardy only in Zones 10–11, a few species are sometimes grown under glass, thriving best under warm, moist, shady conditions.

PRINCIPAL SPECIES
C. elegans (parlor palm) is a graceful, solitary grower to 6 ft., very common in cultivation.

C. glaucifolia grows to 15 ft. and is one of the most decorative with long, glaucous leaves divided into 46 to 80 pinnae in groups of two to four per side.

C. graminifolia is considered the most graceful, having leaves composed of many grasslike pinnae ½ in. wide to 12 in. long, which give it a very graceful appearance.

CHAMAELIRIUM (kam ah LEE ree um) **lutem.** A tuberous-rooted perennial belonging to the Liliaceae (Lily Family), commonly known as blazing-star or devil's-bit. Hardy to Zone 4, it is found from Massachusetts to Illinois and Florida. It grows to 4 ft. and bears bright yellowish white flowers in spikes or sprays from May to July. It needs a moist, peaty soil and a shady location. Propagation is by offsets taken at the end of the blooming season.

CHAMAEMELUM (kam ah MEL um) **nobile.** An aromatic, European herb belonging to the Asteraceae (Aster Family), formerly classified as *Anthemis nobilis*, commonly known as English,

garden, Roman, or Russian chamomile, and used for ground cover or in lawns. A branching, creeping, perennial growing to 1 ft., it has scented foliage. The fragrant, daisylike flowers bloom from late summer to early fall are used in medicine, tea, or cosmetics. Propagation is done by seed or division.

Chamaemelum nobile

CHAMAEROPS (kah MEE rahps). A genus of small palms, commonly known as European fan palms, which usually grow in clumps but may rise on a single trunk to 20 ft. high when suckers are removed.

C. humilis, a single species with many varieties and cultivars available, is the only palm native to Europe. It has large, round leaves cut to the center and is widely grown in the garden or under glass. It is the hardiest palm, with one specimen having lived outdoors as far north as Edinburgh, Scotland. Easily grown in Florida and California (Zones 9–11), it is most effective when grouped as a foreground planting. It benefits from mulching with well-rotted manure during the rainy season and occasional applications of commercial fertilizer.

CHAMOMILE. Common name, also spelled camomile, applied to the two genera ANTHEMIS and MATRICARIA as well as CHAMAEMELUM. They have scented foliage and the typical daisylike flowers of the Asteraceae (Aster Family).

Sweet false chamomile, also known as German- or wild-chamomile is *M. recutita*, the hardy annual that is used for making medicinal tea.

Garden or Russian chamomile, used to make chamomile lawns, is *Chamaemelum nobile*; formerly classified as *Anthemis nobilis*, it was also called Roman or English chamomile.

CHARD. Another name for SWISS CHARD, a variety of the common beet grown for its large leaves and thick leaf stalks.

CHASTE TREE. A common name for *Vitex agnus-castus*, a shrub or small tree with dark green leaves and fragrant flowers; see VITEX.

CHAYOTE. A common name for *Sechium edule*, a climbing tropical vine of the Cucurbitaceae (Cucumber Family), cultivated for its edible tubers and fruit; see SECHIUM.

CHECKERBERRY. A common name for *Gaultheria procumbens*, a creeping shrub better known as wintergreen; see GAULTHERIA.

CHECKERBLOOM. Common name for *Sidalcea malviflora*, a perennial herb related to the mallows, with rosy purple flowers; see SIDALCEA.

CHECKERED-LILY. Common name for *Fritillaria meleagris*, a hardy bulbous herb whose flowers have checkered markings; see FRITILLARIA.

CHEILANTHES (kī LAN theez). A large genus of rock ferns, many from arid situations, with finely dissected foliage composed of beadlike segments in many species, commonly known as lip fern. They are generally small ferns with rather brittle foliage. Frequently they tolerate a long, dry, dormant period. They are excellent plants for pots, rock gardens, or drought-tolerant landscapes and are usually tolerant of full sun. The genus is closely related to *Notholaena*, and species are frequently interchanged.

PRINCIPAL SPECIES

C. argentea (silver cloak fern) is an attractive dwarf with bipinnate fronds 4–8 in. long that are dark green above and have a silvery coating of waxy powder beneath. Native to northern India, China, Japan, and Siberia, it is attractive among rocks when conditions are right and does well in a small pot.

C. clevelandii has green, finely dissected fronds 4–16 in. long.

C. fendleri (Fendler's lip fern) is a tall, bipinnate fern whose lower surface is covered with brown scales rather than hairs. It is common among rocks in northern Mexico and the southwestern states.

C. gracillima (lace fern) is a 10-in., bipinnate fern whose lower frond surface is heavily covered with red-brown hairs. It is native from lower British Columbia to central California and is good for rock gardens.

C. intertexta is a woolier version of *C. gracillima* and grows better at low elevations.

C. lanosa (hairy lip fern) is a bipinnate-pinnatifid to tripinnate fern 8–16 in. high. The lower surfaces of the dark green fronds are covered with dense, gray-brown hairs. It grows on noncalcareous rocky slopes in the midwestern states.

C. lasiophylla (woolly cloak fern) is a small (4–8 in.) pinnate to bipinnate fern that shows the typical "resurrection" behavior of curling its fronds when water is scarce and opening again when moisture is adequate. The fronds are green above and brown-hairy beneath. Although native to Australia, it is quite hardy and good in a sunny rock garden.

C. newberryi (cotton fern) has 8–18 in. fronds that are whitish, woolly, and three times pinnate.

C. siliquosa (Indian's-dream), sometimes placed in the genera *Aspidotis*, *Cryptogramma*, or *Pellaea*, is a dwarf fern with bipinnate to tripinnate fronds 4–8 in. long. The entire margins of the pinnae are reflexed to protect the sori. It is native in northwestern North America to central California and on the Gaspé peninsula of eastern Canada.

CHEIRANTHUS (kī RAN thus). A genus of perennial herbs belonging to the Brassicaceae (Mustard Family) and commonly known as wallflower. Several species rank among the showiest members of the family, with fragrant, yellow or orange flowers in racemes. Native to southern Europe, the showy, velvety blossoms are garden favorites. The many cultivars have charming color variations and double or branching forms. Most are hardy in Zones 5–9.

Seed should be sown early in summer and the seedlings transplanted once or twice and pinched back to induce bushy growth. Young plants are then wintered over in a coldframe and set out in the spring to bloom before hot summer weather. In England the plants are often naturalized in crannies, ruins, and limestone walls and so should be planted in light, loamy soil made sweet with ground limestone. In mild climates they will often live through the winter in the open, coming into full bloom in early spring. Some annual strains bloom the first year from seed.

PRINCIPAL SPECIES

C. allionii is properly listed as *Erysimum hieraciifolium*; see ERYSIMUM.

C. cheiri (wallflower), growing from ½–2 ft., accompanies the daffodils in English gardens, flowering in tones from bright yellow through rich maroon to brown and occasionally purple.

C. × kewensis is a hybrid with flowers 1 in. across, yellow or orange petals, brownish purple on the outside. It is bushy and often used for indoor bloom.

Cheiranthus cheiri

CHELIDONIUM (kel i DOH nee um) **majus.** A weedy biennial or perennial herb belonging to the Papaveraceae (Poppy Family) and commonly known as celandine. Occasionally cultivated in naturalized gardens, it grows to 4 ft. on damp, rich, gravelly soils. Leaves are deeply divided; flowers are yellow, sometimes double, in small umbels; and fruits are slender to 2 in. long. The yellow-orange juice of the plant is slightly caustic and sometimes used in herbal skin medicines. Of European origin, it is widely naturalized in the eastern United States. Var. *laciniatum* has finely cut leaves. Hardy to Zone 5.

CHELONE (ke LOH nee). A genus of hardy, North American perennial herbs closely resembling *Penstemon*, belonging to the Scrophulariaceae

(Figwort Family). Its common name, turtlehead, is derived from the shape of the flowers. Hardy to Zone 4, plants are grown in the wild garden in a damp location that is partially shaded. Propagation is done by seed or division.

C. glabra (white turtlehead, snakehead) grows to 3 ft. and bears whitish or pinkish flowers.

C. lyonii grows to 3 ft. and has rose-purple flowers. Though found wild in the southern Appalachian Mountains,

Chelone glabra

it is perfectly hardy farther north and makes an interesting variation when planted with white-flowered species.

CHEMICAL GARDENING. All gardening is fundamentally chemical gardening. The plant absorbs through the roots certain inorganic chemical substances that are essential for growth and production. This is true whether the plant is growing in a normal soil, in water, in sand, or in gravel. Specifically, however, the term has been applied to a method of growing plants in nutrient solutions with an inert medium for support. See HYDROPONICS; NUTRIENT SOLUTION; WATERING.

CHENILLE PLANT. A common name for *Acalypha hispida*, a tropical shrub with red or white flower spikes; see ACALYPHA.

CHENOPODIACEAE (kee noh poh dee AY see ee). The Goosefoot Family, so called because of the shape of the leaves of some species. It is a widespread group of about 75 genera of weedy herbs and shrubs, often succulent, of which a few are grown for food or ornament. Principal cultivated genera are *Atriplex* (saltbush), *Beta* (beet), *Kochia* (burning bush), and *Spinacia* (spinach). Many others include pestiferous weeds of worldwide importance, such as winged pigweed, Mexican-tea, and Russian-thistle.

CHENOPODIUM (kee noh POH dee um). A genus of plants commonly known as goosefoot or pigweed, and giving its name to the Chenopodiaceae (Goosefoot Family). A few are grown for ornament in the garden and for potherbs, while others are used in medicine or for greens or salad; but they are mainly weeds with mealy foliage, often found in the vegetable garden. Hardy to Zone 3.

PRINCIPAL SPECIES

C. album (lamb's-quarters, pigweed) is a common annual weed from 1–10 ft., found in rich soils. Their uncultivated presence indicates rich soil, intermediate moisture, high organic matter, and a good decay system. When gathered young, the leaves make excellent greens. They are also used in herbal medicines; the seeds, like amaranth, are edible.

C. ambrosioides (American wormseed, Mexican-tea, Spanish-tea) is a strong-smelling herb used for various medicinal purposes.

C. bonus-henricus (good-King-Henry, occasionally called mercury) is a perennial herb that grows to 2½ ft. and has arrow-shaped leaves. It is sometimes cultivated as a potherb or used like asparagus.

C. botrys (feather-geranium or Jerusalem-oak) is a strong-smelling annual with oval or oblong leaves and pretty blossoms in feathery spikes to 2 ft. tall, used for cut flowers.

C. glaucum (oak-leaved goosefoot), introduced from Europe, is a low-branched plant that has pale green leaves with a white undersurface. As a weed, it indicates very rich, moist soil that is neutral to basic and possibly crusted.

C. purpurascens is an annual, often formerly grown in old gardens for its foliage, which is covered with a crystal-like, violet-purple substance.

CHERIMOYA. Common name for *Annona cherimola*, a South American tropical tree grown in warm regions for its tasty fruit; see ANNONA.

CHERRY. Common name for various trees of the genus PRUNUS. The sweet or dessert cherry (*P. avium*) is native to southern Europe and Asia minor; the sour or pie cherry (*P. cerasus*) is probably native to southwest Asia and adjacent Europe; and various other species are native to North America, incuding the Bessey cherry (*P. besseyi*) and the chokecherry (*P. virginiana*). Many flowering cherry varieties have been developed from the Oriental cherry (*P. serrulata*) and the Nanking cherry (*P. tomentosa*).

Plants of other genera to which the name "cherry" is applied include Barbados-cherry, which is *Malpighia glabra*; Cornelian-cherry, *Cornus mas*; ground-cherry, *Physalis* spp.; Indian-cherry, *Rhamnus caroliniana*; Jerusalem-cherry, *Solanum pseudocapsicum*; Madden-cherry, *Maddenia hypoleuca*; Spanish-cherry, *Mimusops elengi*; Surinam-cherry, *Eugenia uniflora*; winter-cherry, *Physalis alkekengi*.

The cultivated sweet cherries are distinctly dessert fruits, to be eaten out of hand or stoned and sugared for the table. Stewing and ordinary canning dissipates their delicate flavor and makes them flat.

Most sour cherries are too tart to eat raw until "dead ripe," when they are also in best condition for canning and for pies; but even when not fully mature, they are excellent for stewing and for pies. For wine making, the riper they are, the better both for flavor and for color.

SWEET CHERRY

P. avium is a tall, pyramidal tree sometimes attaining a height of 100 ft., spreading 75 ft. or more, and living a century or more. The following classes of varieties have originated from it directly or have been produced by hybridization with the sour cherry:

Mazzard. Young seedlings are used as stock for propagation of named varieties of both sweet and sour kinds, and mature trees are common in hedgerows and other uncultivated areas.

Duke. The name is derived from that of one variety, May Duke, which is a corruption of Medoc where the variety originated. Their subacid fruit, intermediate tree size, and other characteristics indicate these varieties to be hybrids between the sweet- and sour-fruited species. Some varieties have light-colored and others dark-colored juice.

Other Varieties. High-quality sweet cherry varieties suited for home use include sweet varieties—Bing, Gold, Napoleon, Stella, Windsor; dukes—Reine Hortense; and morellos—English Morello, Olivet. The wood and buds of sweet cherries are nearly as tender as peaches and do not do well in the hot South or the dry Southwest. They grow well in the Hudson Valley, the Great Lakes region, and the Pacific Coast states, especially California and Oregon.

SOUR CHERRY

P. cerasus includes several hundred varieties, divided into two groups that differ most conspicuously in the characteristics of their fruit. One is the amarelle group, with pale red fruits, colorless juice, moderate acidity, and whitish flesh; the other is the morello group, with dark-colored fruits, red juice, and often strong acidity. Though the fruit of neither can be ranked as dessert quality, that of the former is sometimes moderately pleasant to eat out of hand when fully ripe.

Amarelle trees sometimes exceed 30 ft. in height and 20 ft. in spread and are more erect and larger growing than the morellos, which are often not taller than long-established lilac bushes.

Of the culinary fruits deserving a place in the home garden, the sour cherry should rank high because its ripe fruit can rarely be obtained from stores and markets in good condition unless produced locally and marketed carefully and quickly. Most of such fruit is picked before it has reached full size or developed the characteristic rich flavor of full ripeness. Moreover, unless used within a day of being gathered it loses flavor and before long begins to decay. In the home garden it can be gathered when ripe as wanted and used at once. Because the sweet cherry tree attains great size, it is not suited to small properties, unless budded on dwarfing stock. Even then it is less satisfactory than the dwarf pear or even the dwarf apple, because it may die or become own-rooted and in time grow to standard size. The sour cherries, especially the morellos, being much smaller than the sweet kinds, are suited to small grounds, both as sources of fruit and as ornamental material, for they are beautiful in flower and in fruit. Other good sour varieties are Early Richmond, Montmorency, Meteor, and North Star.

Sour cherries can be grown in a wide range of areas—from New England southward along the coast to Delaware and in the mountains of the Carolinas; from the Great Lakes down the Mississippi Valley, and especially in New York, Ohio, Indiana, Michigan, and Pennsylvania. Because of viral problems, trees tend to be short lived in Zones 3–4.

NATIVE SPECIES

In addition to the sweet and sour cherries in their countless varieties, two North American species are somewhat grown for their fruit. The Bessey cherry (*P. besseyi*) is the parent of the dwarf Rocky Mountain cherry and of its hybrids (with apricots, plums, peaches, and other cherries) originated by Professor N. E. Hansen of South Dakota. These are valuable acquisitions in the prairie states where the sour cherry is not fully reliable and the sweet cherry fails.

The chokecherry (*P. virginiana*) is somewhat cultivated in Quebec, northern Ontario, and other cold parts of the continent for making jellies, jams, sauces, and liqueurs; its improved varieties are grown to some extent for eating raw. Var. *demissa* is native in the western states.

In addition to the Bessey and the chokecherry, other native cherries include the pin cherry (*P. pennsylvanica*) and the sand cherry (*P. pumila*), which are planted mainly for ornament, although they are used to some extent for stocks.

FLOWERING CHERRIES

Within recent years, varieties developed by the Chinese and the Japanese from the Oriental cherry (*P. serrulata*) and from the Nanking cherry (*P. tomentosa*) have attracted wide attention in the United States because of the trees presented by the Japanese government to the United States and planted near the Lincoln Memorial in Washington, D.C. Though other trees of these types have existed much longer in the United States, interest in them has greatly increased their popularity. They are of two general forms: erect but more or less spreading, and weeping; both are among the most beautiful of all flowering trees.

Since many of them are grafted or budded, care must be exercised to prevent the stock from developing undesirable shoots, especially when weeping forms are united with erect stems. Should any shoot or stem develop below the point of union (it is usually erect), it must be immediately removed, for if allowed to develop it will perhaps replace and destroy the valuable part of the tree. Every spring, after growth is well started, the trees should be carefully examined and all sprouts from the stock rubbed off before they become woody—while they are soft.

CULTURE

The sweet cherry is finicky about soil. Since it resents excess moisture, the soil must be deep, gravelly or shaley loams from which surplus water quickly disappears while the moisture supply from below is continuous but not excessive. The sour cherry is far more cosmopolitan and, though it prefers the types of soil just mentioned, will make the best of whatever ground it is placed in, producing good crops even in rather dry and cold regions, provided the supply of moisture is adequate. Moreover, it is not attacked by San José scale and is less subject to other pests that attack the sweet cherry.

SELECTION AND PLANTING

Sweet and sour cherry trees are both budded on two kinds of stock—mazzard and mahaleb (**P. mahaleb**). Though trees budded on the former may cost somewhat more, they should always be given the preference. Commercial cherry growers prefer mazzard stock because the trees develop better than do those on mahaleb stock and are more productive and longer lived; furthermore, the mahaleb, being a dwarfing stock, tends to reduce the size of the trees budded upon it, whether sour or sweet varieties. If it is not possible to purchase trees on mazzard stocks, the next best thing is to plant the mahaleb-budded trees deeply enough so they will develop roots above the point of union and thus become "own-rooted." The point of union can easily be recognized; it shows as a slight crook in the stem 6 or 8 in. above the roots.

Plant one-year sweet cherry trees rather than older, larger specimens if possible, because the branches can then be developed where they are wanted. Since one-year sour cherry trees are generally much smaller, however, it is advisable to plant them about 4 ft. apart in a row and give them clean cultivation for one year before transplanting them to their permanent positions. This reduces the danger of possible damage to such small trees if they are set at the regulation distance apart; it also facilitates training them to good form.

Most sour cherry trees are self-fertile and able to set fruit even when standing alone; but many varieties of sweet cherries fail to bear, not only as isolated trees but also when other varieties growing nearby cannot provide the necessary cross-pollination. Three varieties incapable of pollinating themselves or each other are Lambert, Bing, and Napoleon. When planting any of them, it is necessary to have good pollinators.

When grown in home orchards, morello cherry trees should be given 20 ft. of space; amarelles, 24 ft.; dukes, 30 ft.; and sweet cherries, 35–40 ft. In commercial plantings the distances between trees are usually much less because they are kept severely pruned.

Though the best cherry orchard management involves clean cultivation and cover cropping, sweet cherries will do fairly well planted in a lawn. The sour cherry, being less deep rooting, is less successful in sod but will produce moderately well if bearing trees are fed with a nitrogen fertilizer in early spring. Such feeding is necessary for developing terminal growth.

PRUNING

When two-year cherry trees are planted, the number of branches should immediately be reduced to the three, four, or five best-placed ones, but these should not be cut back because the terminal buds are the most important ones in young trees. Little or no pruning (except the removal of interfering branches) is needed until after the trees begin to bear; some of the interior, heavily shaded branches can then be removed to let light and air into the center of the trees.

When short fruit spurs crowd in sour cherry trees, they can be thinned. When the terminal growths become long, wiry, and naked, they can be cut back to their bases or even farther—into larger branches if these are also rather bare. Both these practices tend to stimulate the development of new shoots; but do not shorten the terminal growths until the trees begin to spread widely, and then prune them only enough to keep the trees shapely and within bounds.

HARVESTING

When cherries are to be used within a few hours it is advisable to pick them without stems because this lessens the chances of breaking the fruit spurs upon which the crop of the following season depends. In picking cherries for sale, the stems (or part of them) must be left attached to the fruit to prevent "bleeding" and to avoid leaving wounds through which decay fungi might enter. Some commercial growers use shears to cut the stems close to the fruit, which is allowed to fall on sheets stretched beneath the trees. A well-grown, full-sized, mature sweet cherry tree will yield one to three bushels of fruit in favorable seasons.

ENEMIES

DISEASES

The most common disease of cherry is brown rot, causing blossom and twig blight and particularly rotting the fruit. The fruit turns brown and soft and is often covered with a grayish mold. For control, see BROWN ROT.

A leaf-spotting fungus may cause almost complete defoliation of trees in years favorable to it. Small, purplish or reddish spots appear on the leaves in early spring and may later fall out, causing a "shot-hole" effect. Leaves turn yellow and fall about the time the fruit ripens, and this early defoliation weakens the trees and makes them susceptible to winter-killing. The fungus overwinters on fallen leaves and the fruiting bodies mature during the tree's blossoming period, shooting out spores during rainy periods. These are carried up to the tree by air currents, and from spots formed on the undersides of the leaves, spores are carried by wind and rain to healthy leaves. The disease occurs on both sweet and sour cherries but is worse on the latter.

A yellow leaf of cherry, resembling leaf spot in some respects, is due to an injured or inefficient root system. Winter injury, wet feet, drought, or unfavorable soil conditions may cause defoliation.

Black knot is frequently found on sour cherry. Abnormal branching, known as WITCHES'-BROOM, is caused by one of the leaf curl fungi. Cut off affected branches several inches below the brooms.

Several viruses affect all of the Rosaceae (Rose Family) and shorten their lives, especially in the North. Since there is no reliable cure, buy virus-free or virus-resistant trees whenever possible.

INSECT PESTS

Wormy cherries are due either to the plum CURCULIO or to fruit flies, of which there are two species: one with an entirely black abdomen and one marked by a series of white crossbands. Both kinds attack cherry, pear, and plum in the northern United States and Canada. Ten months are passed in the soil in a brown pupa case, the flies emerging in early summer and laying eggs in the fruit. The eggs hatch into very small, whitish, legless maggots, which burrow through the flesh. The surface of the fruit appears normal until the maggots are nearly grown, when sunken spots appear. When full grown, the maggot eats its way out, falls to the ground, and enters the resting stage.

The black cherry aphid may cause serious injury to sweet cherries but is seldom serious on sour. Shining black eggs, which winter on smaller branches near buds, hatch as the buds are opening, and the aphids reproduce rapidly. Their presence and feeding cause the leaves of terminal shoots to curl; and the fruit clusters are covered with insects that secrete a honeydew in which a sooty mold fungus grows. See APHIDS.

Wild cherries are favorite hosts for the eastern TENT CATERPILLAR. Unless carefully watched and used as lures on which the moths will lay eggs to be destroyed over winter, such trees should be destroyed.

CHERRY-LAUREL. Common name for ornamental species of PRUNUS, particularly *P. laurocerasus*, a native of eastern Europe and the Orient, grown in the South and California.

CHERVIL (CHUR vil). Common name for two herbs: salad chervil is *Anthriscus cerefolium*, see ANTHRISCUS; and sweet-chervil is *Myrrhis odorata*, see MYRRHIS.

CHESTNUT. Common name for CASTANEA, a genus of hardy, deciduous shrubs, prized for ornament and edible nuts.

CHESTNUT BLIGHT. A fatal disease attacking all native chestnut trees, *Castanea* spp., and responsible for the practical extermination of *C. dentata* (American chestnut) and *C. pumila* (chinquapin) trees throughout most of the eastern states. The cause is a parasitic fungus, *Endothia parasitica*, which gains entrance through wounds or insect injuries in the bark and girdles the stems and trunks of trees of all ages, killing them in a few years. The sticky spores of the fungus are spread by the wind, rain, insects, birds, small animals, and by the transportation of diseased plants, timber, or cordwood from which the bark is not removed.

Believed to have been brought from Japan, the disease was first observed in New York City in 1904, although it was probably established by that time in the surrounding countryside. Spreading rapidly, it killed trees over a steadily increasing territory in spite of vigorous efforts by other states and the United States Department of Agriculture to contain it, and no cure has yet been found.

The measures employed in fighting it have therefore consisted of chemical injections, cutting down diseased trees, burning the bark before using the timber, and investigating the possibility of developing resistant or immune forms of improved chestnut. Japanese species appear to be highly, if not completely, resistant. Work is continuing with the objective of developing by hybridization new forms that will combine the high nut quality of the American species with the resistance of the Japanese species.

See DISEASE; CASTANEA.

CHESTNUT OAK. Common name for *Quercus prinus*, a type of oak tree whose leaves closely resemble those of the chestnut; see QUERCUS.

CHICK PEA. A common name for the legume *Cicer arietinum*, also known as garbanzo; see CICER.

CHICKWEED. Common name for *Stellaria media*, a weed sometimes used for medicinal and culinary purposes; see STELLARIA.

Mouse-ear chickweed and field-chickweed refer to the genus CERASTIUM.

CHICORY. A perennial European herb, *Cichorium intybus*, common as a weed in temperate climates, but whose thick, cultivated roots are roasted and used as a coffee substitute. The leaves of seedlings are used as greens; sometimes those of older plants are blanched like celery, either in autumn or early spring. During the fall and winter, the roots are forced into growth to yield greens known as witloof or Belgian endive, which is used in salads.

For witloof chicory, sow seeds thinly in well-prepared, rich, deep soil in earliest spring, making the rows 15–18 in. apart. Thin when the seedlings are 4 in. high, using the thinnings as greens and leaving plants 6 in. apart in the rows. Keep cleanly cultivated until the leaves meet between the rows. In late autumn dig the roots and, after cutting the tops an inch above the root crown, bury them in a pit or in moist sand or earth in a coldframe or root cellar.

To produce heads, shorten the parsniplike roots from below to 8–9 in. long, bury them upright in damp sand or soil, and cover the tops with 8–9 in. more of damp soil. Keep the temperature at 60°F. In 2–3 weeks blanched heads 5–6 in. long can be cut for use. After harvest, the roots are of no further use.

See also ENDIVE; CICHORIUM.

CHILEAN JESSAMINE. Common name for *Mandevilla laxa*, a woody South American vine with racemes of fragrant, white, funnelform flowers; see MANDEVILLA.

CHILEAN WINE PALM. A common name for *Jubaea chilensis*, a tropical tree with plumlike fruits sometimes used in candy; see JUBAEA.

CHILE-BELLS. Common name for LAPAGERIA, a monotypic genus of twining herbs noted for their showy, drooping flowers.

CHILOPSIS (kī LAHP sis) **linearis.** A deciduous shrub or tree growing to 20 ft., found from Texas to California and Mexico, belonging to the Bignoniaceae (Bignonia Family), and commonly known as desert- or flowering-willow. It bears narrow leaves to 1 ft. long and handsome, crimped, trumpet-shaped flowers. The lilac-colored flowers with two yellow stripes inside are borne in short terminal racemes.

CHIMAPHILA (kī MAF il ah). A genus of North American evergreen herbs or small shrubs belonging to the Ericaceae (Heath Family) and commonly known as pipsissewa or wintergreen. They grow wild in woods from Maine to Alabama and are favorite plants for shady spots in wild gardens. Nodding umbels are made up of white or pink flowers. The leathery, toothed, sometimes marbled leaves grow in irregular whorls on the stem, and the creeping rootstock sends up branches at intervals, thus making the plants useful for ground cover in plantings of conifers or evergreens. They should be given an acid soil rich in leaf mold. Propagation is by softwood cuttings taken when the leaves are half-grown.

PRINCIPAL SPECIES

C. maculata has variegated foliage and very fragrant, white flowers.

C. menziesii is slightly smaller than other species and has a more slender habit and white or pink, nodding flowers.

C. umbellata has shining, dark green leaves and white or rose-pink flowers, borne four to seven in a cluster.

CHIMNEY BELLFLOWER. Common name for *Campanula pyramidalis*, a versatile herb with pale blue or white flowers; see CAMPANULA.

CHIMONANTHUS (kī mah NAN thus). A small genus of deciduous or evergreen shrubs native to China, belonging to the Calycanthaceae (Calycanthus Family), and commonly known as wintersweet or chimney-bellflower.

C. praecox is well worth growing in mild climates (Zones 7–9) for its fragrant, yellow flowers and can be grown as a bush or trained to a wall. It thrives in sandy loam with plenty of leaf mold. Var. *grandiflorus* has larger leaves and flowers but is not as fragrant. Propagation is by seed and cuttings.

CHINABERRY. Common name for *Melia azedarach*, a tropical shade tree whose fruits are sometimes used as beads; see MELIA.

CHINA ROSE. In the late eighteenth and early nineteenth centuries, four important China and tea-scented China roses were brought to Europe. Crossed with the old European roses, they eventually gave rise to repeat-flowering varieties. These China and tea roses were fully developed garden varieties with very smooth stems, few thorns, glossy foliage, and large blooms of exquisitely delicate colors. Their most important attribute was the strongly dominant gene for repeat flowering. They are a good deal more tender than the hardy, old garden rose varieties and can only be grown in conservatories and greenhouses in severe winter climates.

The China rose was known as the 'Monthly Rose' because of its repeat flowering and as the 'Bengal Rose' because of its stopover in India on the way to western European countries. Some of the China rose varieties are 'Old Blush' and 'Hermosa', *R. chinensis* var. *mutabilis*, with yellow blooms turning to pink and then red as they age—a trait they have passed on to such modern roses as 'Masquerade' and 'Circus'. Another is *R. chinensis* var. *viridiflora* (green rose), in which the petals are really made up of deformed sepals.

CHINCH BUG. This small bug, *Blissus leucopterus*, is a sucking insect that attacks lawns and stems of corn. It is very small (¹⁄₁₆ in.) and black with white or brown front wings, brown antennae and legs. Its nymphs are red with white markings or black with white ones. The eggs are white or red. The adults hibernate in clumps of grass.

Chinch bugs are common pests in lawns, especially where there is considerable thatch, and the problem becomes more severe in dry weather. The best way to prevent them is by having a healthy, thatch-free lawn. If an infestation does occur, try applying diatomaceous earth by spreading 15–20 lb. per 1000 sq. ft. of lawn up to four times a year. Mix some soap powder with it for an even more effective solution. Or you can apply a soap-and-water solution every ten to fourteen days.

There are several effective products available from suppliers specializing in natural controls. As with all products, follow the label directions carefully. Consult your local extension service for guidelines for your area.

CHINCHERINCHEE. A common name for various species of ORNITHOGALUM, a genus of bulbous herbs with brilliantly colored flowers, popular for greenhouse culture or cut flowers.

CHINESE CABBAGE. Common name for oriental varieties of *Brassica rapa* (field mustard). In North America, the best-known variety groups are Pekinensis (pe-tsai) and Chinensis (pak-choi); see BRASSICA. Unlike common cabbages, these species quickly run to seed in warm weather without making much of the leafy growth for which they are cultivated.

For early use, sow outdoors in earliest spring; for a fall crop, sow after midsummer. In either case, make the rows 18–24 in. apart and thin the plants when 4–6 in. high; use the thinnings for greens or salad and leave the permanent plants 8–12 in. apart in the row. In 60–70 days, the heads will be ready for use, either raw for salad or slaw, or boiled. Late-maturing heads stored in moist, cool (but frostproof) quarters, will keep about two months.

See also CABBAGE; MUSTARD.

CHINESE EVERGREEN. Common name for *Aglaonema modestum*, a popular houseplant that has dark glossy leaves and thrives in dim corners and soggy soil; see AGLAONEMA.

CHINESE-HAT PLANT. Common name for HOLMSKIOLDIA, a genus of tropical shrubs with curiously shaped flowers.

CHINESE-HOUSES. Common name for COLLINSIA, a genus of annual herbs with bicolored, whorled flowers.

CHINESE-LANTERN PLANT. Common name for *Physalis alkekengi*, a perennial herb grown for its ornamental fruits; see PHYSALIS.

CHINESE MUSTARD. A name loosely applied to various Asiatic species of BRASSICA, the plants somewhat resembling celery cabbage but forming loose, open heads. The leaves are used as potherbs. *B. juncea*, or leaf mustard, is more commonly grown in the United States for this purpose than are the strictly Chinese forms of *B. rapa*. See also CHINESE CABBAGE.

CHINESE PARASOL TREE. Common name for FIRMIANA, a genus of Asiatic trees planted for shade and ornament in the South.

CHINESE SACRED-LILY. Common name for *Narcissus tazetta* var. *orientalis*, a tender herb with creamy white-and-yellow flowers; see NARCISSUS.

CHINESE SCHOLAR TREE. Common name for *Sophora japonica*, an ornamental leguminous tree native to Asia; see SOPHORA.

CHINESE TALLOW TREE. Common name for *Sapium sebiferum*, a tropical tree whose fruits yield a fatty substance used in making candles and soap; see SAPIUM.

CHINQUAPIN. Common name for *Castanea pumila*, a southern species of chestnut; see CASTANEA. Giant-chinquapin is *Castanopsis chrysophylla*, a large evergreen tree; see CASTANOPSIS. Water-chinquapin is *Nelumbo lutea*, better known as the American-lotus; see NELUMBO.

CHIOGENES (kī AHJ en eez). Former botanical name for GAULTHERIA, a genus of low evergreen plants, including creeping snowberry.

CHIONANTHUS (kī oh NAN thus). A genus comprising two species of deciduous trees or large shrubs belonging to the Oleaceae (Olive Family) and commonly known as fringe tree. They are grown for their very fragrant, fringy, white flowers in showy panicles that bloom in early summer. They thrive in sun or partial shade in moist soil, forming a large shrub with multiple trunks or a small tree with a single trunk. Fringe trees are dioecious; male and female trees are necessary to produce the dark blue fruit on the female plant.

C. retusus, native to China, is similar to *C. virginicus* but grows only to 20 ft., has smaller panicles of flowers, and is not as hardy (Zones 6–8).

C. virginicus, native to the Southeast, often grows in very wet areas and has bright yellow fall color. It grows up to 25 ft. high and is an excellent specimen plant for the garden. Hardy in Zones 4–9.

CHIONODOXA (kī ah noh DAHKS ah). A genus of small, bulbous plants of the Liliaceae (Lily Family), native to the mountains of Asia minor and commonly known as glory-of-the-snow. Among the most beautiful of the very early spring-flowering bulbs, their brilliant blues are sometimes varied with white, brightening the garden when few other subjects are seen. Perfectly hardy (to Zone 4), they can be planted in any well-drained, fertile spot and need no protection. The bulbs should be planted in the early fall, 2–3 in. deep and 1–2 in. apart. Natural increase will provide plenty of offsets, or new stock can be grown from seed. Massed plantings around shrubbery or evergreens, and naturalized groups in meadows or on grassy slopes, create a fine effect. The trap-shaped leaves appear at the same time as the flowers. Replanting every third year is advisable, though not always essential. To keep the plants strong and vigorous, the foliage must be left to ripen.

C. luciliae, of which there are many horticultural varieties, some introducing tones of red, is the most widely grown species. Cv. 'Grandiflora' is the largest flowered of all. Cv. 'Tmoli' blooms later than the others.

CHIVES. A hardy perennial herb, *Allium schoenoprasum*, with small, slender, hollow leaves, which are finely chopped and used for flavoring salads, stews, and soups. The abundant dark green, hollow leaves grow 6–12 in. high. Small, round heads of tiny, lavender flowers like pompoms are borne at the top of tough stalks at intervals throughout the summer and early fall. Since both foliage and flowers are attractive in appearance (though onion-scented), the plants are often used for edging flower beds; but unless the flower heads are cut or the seed is gathered promptly, self-sown seedlings may prove troublesome weeds. The small, oval bulbs multiply rapidly, forming clumps.

Cutting a flat of chives

Chives grow best in rich, well-worked soil. Since they are generally grown as perennials in the same place for several years, prepare the bed thoroughly before planting. Rake in compost or dried steer manure at the rate of about 1½ lb. per sq. yd. For a winter supply of fresh chives, plants can be grown in 5-in. pots under fluorescent lights.

Chives are commonly propagated by seed or division. Seed should be sown indoors in early spring in a flat seed box. When the seedlings are a few inches high, they can be cut into squares and planted out, the same depth as they were in the seed box. For pot culture, plant each bunch in a 4-in. pot.

For propagation by division, use two- to four-year-old plants. Dig up the whole plant, shake or wash off the soil, and trim the roots to make division of the clump easy. Divide the clump into several smaller clumps, each containing about eight or ten bulblets. Trim the green tops and trim the roots again, leaving them ½ in. long. Replant the clumps 8 in. apart. For pot culture, use a 5-in. or larger pot. For best results the clumps should be divided every few years.

Chives can be cut when the leaves are as short as 2 in. in early spring; however, it is better to let them grow a little longer. Keep them cut regularly throughout the growing season, or the leaves will toughen. Always cut about ½ in. above the white part of the stems; do not harvest by snipping off the tips.

Chives lose much of their flavor when dehydrated and are useless for salads when they have been frozen. If cut when dry and stored in an airtight container, they will keep well in the refrigerator for three weeks or more.

CHLOROPHYLL. The green-coloring material found in photosynthetic plants. Lack of chlorophyll is sometimes a symptom of CHLOROSIS. See also PHOTOSYNTHESIS.

CHLOROPHYTUM (klor oh FĪ tum). A genus of about 215 tropical herbs belonging to the Liliaceae (Lily Family), closely related to *Antheri-*

cum, and native to the warm regions of Asia, Africa, and South America. In cooler areas, they are grown as greenhouse plants. The flowers are borne in graceful sprays of white, green, or cream, and the foliage of some species is striped lengthwise with yellow. Occasionally grown as border plants in Zones 10–11, they are more commonly used as potted plants or in vases. They are readily propagated by seed, suckers, offsets from the lower stem, and division in the spring.

CHLOROPICRIN. A heavy, colorless, pungent liquid, the active ingredient in tear gas, sometimes used as a fungicide or in soil sterilization; see DISINFECTION.

CHLOROSIS. A reduction in the amount of chlorophyll or green-coloring in a plant, resulting in the paling of its normal green color to yellow, or even white, particularly around the margins of new leaves, while the leaf veins usually remain a darker green. In food plants any type of chlorosis is considered detrimental because lack of chlorophyll means reduced photosynthesis, which is essential to normal plant life and development; however, certain ornamentals with variegated (chlorotic) foliage are purposely propagated. Particularly susceptible plants include azaleas, hydrangeas, rhododendrons, and roses.

The cause is usually attributed to a soil imbalance, especially a lack of essential elements, such as nitrogen, magnesium, or iron in the soil; excessive soil alkalinity, which renders the iron that is present unavailable to the plant; and excess water. Overfertilizing can contribute to chlorosis, as can the addition of too much lime to the lawn. The addition of compost or other organic matter can help to neutralize the basic soil. Too alkaline a soil can also be acidified by adding sulfur or aluminum sulfate; see ACID SOIL.

Infectious chlorosis, transmitted by budding or grafting and occasionally by seed, is usually due to a virus. Chlorosis of lawn grass is usually the result of a lack of iron, which is essential for the production of chlorophyll.

Chlorosis can also be induced artificially by nurseries to promote variegated leaves in some ornamentals. This is done by adding lime to the soil or by depriving the plant of iron, potassium, or nitrogen.

See also PHOTOSYNTHESIS.

CHOCOLATE-LILY. Common name for *Fritillaria biflora*, a small bulbous plant with chocolate-colored flowers; see FRITILLARIA.

CHOISYA (CHOY see ah) **ternata.** A handsome evergreen shrub native to Mexico, belonging to the Rutaceae (Rue Family), and commonly known as Mexican-orange. It will tolerate only a few degrees of frost and thrives best in Zones 10–11. Growing to 6 ft. or more, it has leathery, bright green leaves that show off to advantage the clusters of fragrant, white flowers. These resemble orange blossoms and are produced over a period of several months.

CHOKEBERRY. Common name for three species of ARONIA, a genus of hardy, fruit-bearing shrubs.

CHOKECHERRY. Common name for *Prunus virginiana*, a native tree sometimes cultivated for its fruits. See CHERRY; PRUNUS.

CHOLLA (CHOY ah). Common name for all species of *Cylindropuntia*, a subgroup of the *Opuntia* genus of cactus, which have easily detachable, cylindroid joints or segments rather than the typical flattened, leaflike pads of most members of the genus; see OPUNTIA.

CHORISIA (koh RIS ee ah) **speciosa.** A medium-sized tree from South America, belonging to the Bombacaceae (Bombax Family), and commonly known as floss-silk tree. It is frequently cultivated in warm regions, especially southern California, and is sometimes grown under glass in the North for ornamental effects. It has toothed leaves, a spiny, green trunk, and conspicuous cream or pink flowers 3 in. across and striped with brown at the base. The flowers are followed by pear-shaped capsules filled with seeds covered with cottony or silky floss, which is used to stuff pillows. Propagation is by seed or cuttings. A smooth-trunked form is known. This and selected color forms are often grafted onto seedling stock.

CHORIZEMA (koh ri ZEE mah). A genus of small evergreen shrubs with prickly leaves, mostly native to western Australia, and belonging to the Fabaceae (Bean Family). They rank with the most attractive hardwood plants for spring flowering in the cool greenhouse and can be grown outdoors in Zones 10–11. Indoors they are sometimes trained to wire forms but are generally allowed to grow in a natural, loose manner. Neat little plants in 5-in. pots can be grown from cuttings in a year. They do best at first in a mixture of peat and sand, then later in fibrous loam and peat with a little sand. Potting must be firmly done at all times. Established plants do best plunged outdoors for the summer. Propagation is by seed and by cuttings in the spring.

PRINCIPAL SPECIES

C. cordatum (Australian flame pea) is a shrub that grows to 10 ft. and has loose or open racemes of orange-red flowers with purplish wing petals to 6 in. long.

C. ilicifolium is a medium-sized shrub with weak, slender branches, very showy with its profusion of orange and red-purple blossoms.

C. varium is a shrub that grows to 6 ft. and has flowers similar to *C. cordatum*.

CHRISTMAS-BERRY. A common name for HETEROMELES, a genus of evergreen shrubs or small trees prized for decorative use.

CHRISTMAS CACTUS. Common name for innumerable winter-flowering hybrids of SCHLUMBERGERA.

CHRISTMAS-ROSE. Common name for *Helleborus niger*, a perennial herb that blooms in late winter; see HELLEBORUS.

CHRISTMAS TREES. In different regions, different kinds of evergreen trees are used for Christmas celebration, but almost without exception they are of the coniferous type. The most popular evergreens now being grown and used as Christmas trees are *Pinus sylvestris* (Scotch pine) and its cultivars, *Pseudotsuga menziesii* (Douglas-fir), *Abies concolor* (white or concolor fir), *Abies balsamia* (balsam fir), *Pinus strobus* (white pine), *Pinus nigra* (Austrian pine), *Picea pungens* (Colorado spruce), and *Picea glauca* (white spruce).

The growing of Christmas trees in pastures that are going back to forest or other nonagricultural or marginal land, has become a real business. These Christmas tree farms account for most of the trees now sold at Christmas. Seedling trees can be purchased at cost from the conservation departments of several states or in larger sizes from commercial nurseries. Information as to the planting and care can be obtained from state foresters and state colleges of agriculture.

A decided sentiment has developed in favor of using living Christmas trees. This has spread throughout the country and led nurseries to grow stock especially for this purpose, to be sold in pots, tubs, and containers. Potted trees of various sizes can now be obtained, decorated and enjoyed over the Christmas holidays, and later planted out in the ground in a place previously mulched to prevent its freezing. Since winter is not often an ideal time for planting, however, such specimens often die.

CHRIST THORN. Common name for *Paliurus spina-christi*, a spiny tree of southern Europe and the Orient; see PALIURUS.

CHRYSALIDOCARPUS (kris ah lid oh KAHR pus) **lutescens.** Commonly known as yellow, yellow-bamboo, or areca palm (which is a misnomer since it is not a true *Areca*), this palm has many yellow stems growing in clumps, sometimes 30 ft. high with a spread of 15 ft. The plants are covered with unarmed (spineless), graceful, erect leaves with yellow sheaths. Hardy in Zones 9–11,

the yellow-bamboo palm is grown extensively in south Florida, thriving best in the shade and in a rich, mucky soil. It is extensively grown by florists as a decorative plant, being started easily from seed. Although frequently sold as a houseplant, it does not last long in the hot, dry atmosphere of the average house. *C. madagascariensis*, a larger species, is also grown in south Florida.

CHRYSALIS. The pupa or transformation stage of a butterfly or moth into which the full-grown caterpillar develops. It is oval or cigar shaped, with a horny covering of hardened, gluelike substance exuded from the skin of the larva. The pupae of butterflies are naked chrysalids; those of many moths are enclosed in a soft but tough silken cocoon.

CHRYSANTHEMUM (kris AN the mum). A large genus of annual and perennial herbs, some slightly woody or shrubby at the base, belonging to the Asteraceae (Aster Family), commonly known as mums. Some of the more valued species, especially the pyrethrum and shasta daisy, bear ornamental flowers during the summer. The most famous member, the garden chrysanthemum, is undoubtedly the showiest of all autumn blossoms. Its plants are mostly musk-scented and somewhat coarse of growth, with blooms of amazing diversity in sizes and forms. Its colors vary from white to pale, delicate pastels, tawny bronzes, yellow, purplish, and red. No blue or true purple ever appears, but blends are numerous, and floral production is liberal.

HISTORY

A tiny, yellow daisy was known to Confucius in China after 550 B.C., and seeds from Korea were dispatched to Japan in 386 A.D. In all those countries many new types were developed, and the chrysanthemum became Japan's national flower. *C. morifolium*, in its double form, first appeared in Japan and became the parent of all future double varieties.

In 1764, the chrysanthemum reached England and later France, but its late flowering reduced it to greenhouse culture. A French baker is credited with developing the first seeds leading to earlier varieties. Other French breeders continued, and the pompon, or small, rounded type of blossom was also brought from China. After 1847, some North American gardens had chrysanthemums, chiefly very late pompons called "artemisias."

Because of late blossoms, invariably nipped by hard frosts and mediocre growth habits, the chrysanthemum held only moderate popularity until 1933. In that year, a Connecticut nurseryman introduced his first creation of the set called Korean hybrids. He had bred the wild but vigorous *C. zawadskii* with existing garden varieties to achieve earlier, much hardier, more floriferous kinds. The chrysanthemum quickly came into prominence. While the original Korean hybrids were of single or daisylike flowers, they were intensely bred further into doubles as well. Nearly all the newer varieties have lineage going back to the Korean hybrids. *C. articum* and *C. nipponicum* have also been used by hybridizers, but with less spectacular results.

Shortly after the Korean hybrid's debut, a chance seedling appeared in a Texas nursery. It was low and broad but was covered with hundreds of double pink flowers. Because it resembled a florist's azalea in habit and prolific bloom, it was called "azaleamum." This led to the very widely grown class known as cushions (azaleamum is a trademarked name) and still more fame for the chrysanthemum. Very early to flower, the cushions were also easily grown and well suited for small spaces. Many varieties will bloom by late July after their first year.

USES

In sunny, well-drained borders, individual specimens set at 2-ft. intervals become masses of bloom when little else remains, because they withstand light frosts. Since heights usually vary 1–3½ ft., judicious selection of varieties enhances the whole width of the border. Low growers, like the cushion types, are fine as edging, in urns and tubs, in rock gardens, or in foundation plantings next to evergreens. Chrysanthemums can also be moved while in full bloom if done carefully. If dug up with a ball of soil around them, they can be planted wherever desired. So they can be grown all summer in a reserve area, like a vegetable garden, then moved in the fall.

Most chrysanthemums of taller stature are superb for cutting. The flowers will last two or three weeks in water, but leaves should be removed from the submerged portions of the stem. They are also good when arranged with fall foliage or berried branches. Countless late-blooming varieties are used by commercial greenhouses for bouquets and potted plants. Some compact outdoor types with good color are often lifted with a ball of soil, placed in large pots, and brought inside for added weeks of bloom.

Most late outdoor varieties can be grown in the southern and far western states due to milder climate. In colder climates, varieties not flowering by mid-October are likely to become frozen unless protected on cold nights. Repeated temperatures below 27°F will badly damage most varieties.

CLASSIFICATION

Cultivated chrysanthemums are typically grouped according to two methods. The first classification scheme considers the species from which a variety or cultivar was derived, and the second, devised by the National Chrysanthemum Society, is based on flower form.

SPECIES DERIVATION CATEGORIES

Annual Chrysanthemums. These involve *C. coronarium*, *C. carinatum*, and *C. segetum* and are used for mass plantings for summer and fall bloom.

Feverfews. These forms are all derived from *C. parthenium*. They are hardy perennials grown for their profusion of small, white-rayed flowers with yellow disks.

Pyrethrums. These are cultivars derived from *C. coccineum*. The plants bloom in late spring and summer, and they are frequently used as cut flowers.

Marguerite Chrysanthemums. Also known as Paris daisies, these types come from *C. frutescens*. They are cultivated as annuals in cold climates and can be grown in pots to flower in late winter and early spring.

Perennial Border Daisies. The most recent members of this group are derived from *C. zawadskii*. They are strong, hardy plants.

Common Florist's Chrysanthemums. These are *C. morifolium* hybrids. They occur as bushy garden perennials or as the kinds developed for very large flower heads.

FLOWER FORM CATEGORIES

Single. These have flat disks and five or fewer rows of ray florets.

Semi-double. These have flat disks and more than five rows of ray florets.

Regular anemone. Hemispheric disks are surrounded by five or fewer rows of evenly spaced ray florets.

Pompon. Flowers have a button or globular shape with the disks concealed by incurved ray florets.

Irregular Anemone. These are similar to the regular anemones, but the ray florets are twisted, quilled, or of unequal length.

Regular or Chinese Incurved. Disks are hidden by incurved, overlapping ray florets. The flower heads may be 4–6 in. wide and globular in shape.

Irregular or Japanese Incurved. The overlapping ray florets are wide and twisted. Flower heads are 5–7 in. wide with an open appearance.

Reflexed or Decorative Pompon. These are like the pompon type, but ray florets are reflexed rather than incurved.

Decorative or Aster-flowered Reflex. The flower heads are flattened, and disks are concealed by narrow, reflexed ray florets.

Regular or Chinese Reflexed. These are similar to the regular incurved types, but the ray flowers are reflexed.

Irregular or Japanese Reflexed. These are similar to the Japanese incurved types, but the ray florets are reflexed.

Spoon. These occur in single or double forms. The ray florets have a tubular opening that forms a spoonlike tip.

Quill. The flowers are double, and disks are concealed by a tubular, elongated ray florets with tips spoonlike or closed at the tip.

Threads. These have long, slender ray florets that are straight or slightly curved, and tubular in shape; the closed tips may be slightly coiled or hooked.

Spider. These have tubular ray florets that are curved and twisted with tips obviously hooked or coiled.

CULTURE

Garden chrysanthemums prefer predominately sunny exposures and a well-drained soil of moderate humus content. Planting time is in the spring, after danger of night frosts has ended. In cold climates, mid-May to early July is the favored period. New plants can be placed in small pots, as rooted cuttings without soil or as divisions of older plants. They should be placed 18–24 in. from neighboring material and watered heavily. Wilting plants should be covered with baskets or other protection for a few days, but remove the cover at sundown. As soon as the roots take hold, cover is unnecessary.

When growth reaches 4–6 in., the tips of each shoot are pinched off to encourage bushy development and avoid the need for staking. Also, many more flower stems will appear. The pinching is repeated after each additional 4–6 in. of growth until mid-July. From then on, blossom buds start forming. While chrysanthemums are relatively tolerant of drought, some heavy waterings in dry periods are prudent, especially as the mass of bloom opens.

Plants with larger flowers can be damaged by frosts when fully open, particularly after softening warm spells. Frosts as low as 27°F may only brown the petals while new buds continue unfolding. Temperatures around 22°F may freeze buds. If frost is predicted for any given night, shelters of plastic, burlap, heavy cloth, thick paper, or other material often save the plants. Such shelters should be erected on sticks or poles, as canopies or tents, a few inches above the flowers. If these shelters actually touch the blooms, they act as frost conductors rather than insulators. The covers should drape all the way to the ground. Remove them the next morning.

DISBUDDING

To achieve especially large, perfect flowers, like those grown in commercial greenhouses, quantity must be sacrificed for quality. The plant is trimmed to leave one to four stems in August and staked as the stems elongate. When buds form, all are removed except the top or crown buds on each stem. That bud gradually swells to abnormal size, as all the strength goes into it. Frequent attention is required to remove all new side buds and other strength-taking growths from the leaf axils. When bloom is full, such fine blossoms deserve protection from frosts and heavy rains.

SHADING

This practice is largely for the grower who seeks to force plants into earlier bloom. Since the chrysanthemums normally blossom in the fall when the days are shorter, the light period largely governs the time of flowering. By covering the plants with dark shade cloth or plastic from about 7 P.M. to 7 A.M. each day, the daily light period is considerably shortened. Structures of lath or poles can be erected around large plantings; smaller boxlike frames will do for single clumps. Cloth is draped completely over and around the group or plant to be forced. When buds are nearly ready to show color, shading is halted.

About 60 days of such shading is required to bring a plant into bloom a month ahead of the usual time. Thus, if a variety normally flowering October 20 was desired to bloom September 15, shading should be started July 15.

POTTED PLANTS

Some gardeners enjoy the later-flowering chrysanthemums in pots for indoor display. Commercial growers raise large quantities of them under careful repotting schedules. There is a simple procedure for the average gardener. Plants can be

Chrysanthemum morifolium

set out, pinched, and grown just as for the garden. When cold weather approaches, these plants are carefully dug with a ball of soil and placed in 8–9 in. pots. After a thorough watering, they can be brought inside into a fairly sunny, reasonably cool room. Further watering will be necessary about every third day.

WINTER PROTECTION

Most garden chrysanthemums are inherently hardy against cold, but like other shallow-rooted plants, they can heave out of the ground if not protected against thaws. Also, they do not like constant wetness. A steady winter drainage is important. In late fall, cut the stems down to about 4 in. When the ground is frozen hard, a mulch of 3–4 in. of hay can be loosely applied. Clumps can be stored in coldframes or dug up in late fall with a ball of soil and left to freeze above the ground. When frozen hard, a light cover of hay will keep the plants dry and firm until spring.

When spring arrives, the covering is loosened and gradually removed. All chrysanthemums except cushions, whose summer bloom comes only on older plants, should be properly divided each spring.

PROPAGATION

Seed. If seed is sown by early May, the resulting plants should bloom that autumn, but the extremely hybrid nature of modern types means wide variation. Stem cuttings are easily rooted in sand during late spring and can then be planted directly into the border but must be carefully watered.

Division. This is not only desirable but also affords speedy increase. In spring, when shoots are 1–2 in. high, the clumps are lifted, and strongly-rooted outer stems are torn or cut off. The young divisions are replanted, and the center of the old clump discarded. The resulting plants are healthier and less woody. Undivided plants are likely to become lanky, straggly, and may not flower well if at all.

Cuttings can also be taken of 2–3 in. soft tips in spring. These root readily in any blend of sand, peat, and/or perlite.

ENEMIES

DISEASES

Leaf spot is the most common disease of chrysanthemums, especially on crowded or starved plants. A fungicidal spray or dust prevents spread of brown blotches, and diseased leaves should be removed. Mildew is best prevented by uncrowded plantings in areas with good air circulation and adequate sunlight.

There are several other diseases less common in the home garden than in extensive commercial plantings. Among these is stunt, a virus that once threatened to become serious but now is largely under control due to sanitation and careful roguing of diseased propagating stock. It is evidenced in the garden by runted plants only a few inches tall, yellow foliage, and premature, undersized, off-color blossoms. Since it is probably spread by aster leaf hoppers and by contact with infected plants, affected specimens should be dug up and burned. The disease is most serious in gardens near weedy fields or roadsides, where aster leaf hoppers evidently bring the virus from diseased weeds. Hence, clean cultivation is helpful.

INSECT PESTS

APHIDS and spider MITES, both sucking insects, sometimes appear in hot weather. They are easily controlled with insecticidal soap sprays used according to manufacturers' directions. Various chewing insects, such as beetles, chafers, and tarnished plant bugs, occasionally injure buds and early flowers. Midge is troublesome on rare occasions; small lumps or swellings on the leaves signify their presence as eggs are laid inside. If allowed to go unchecked, the whole plant can be disfigured and crippled. Pick off damaged stems and leaves. PYRETHRUM insecticide is made from certain chrysanthemum blossoms and should never be used to control pests on these plants.

Leaf nematodes can be very serious but happily are not too common. Tiny, invisible insects inside the leaves can suck these leaves dry and brown from the ground up. In wet weather, the nematodes actually swim up the stem. Without good foliage, flowers are largely ruined. Gradually spreading brown areas between the leaf veins are symptomatic of nematode infestation. Carefully inspect newly acquired plants for damage before bringing them into the garden. Infestations can be further avoided by maintaining a rich soil in good tilth, with plenty of compost incorporated for its beneficial microbial populations.

PRINCIPAL SPECIES

C. articum (arctic daisy) is a perennial that grows 12–15 in. and has thick, leathery leaves and white to lilac flowers 2 in. across that bloom profusely in late fall. Native to the Arctic region, it is very hardy and used by breeders as a parent of northland daisies.

C. balsamita (costmary) is a coarse perennial growing to 3 ft. with small heads of yellow disk and white ray flowers.

C. carinatum (tricolor chrysanthemum) is an excellent annual cut flower or garden subject that grows 2–3 ft. high and has single or double flower heads, 2–2½ in. across, of white, red, yellow, or purple rays with a colored ring around a purple disk.

C. balsamita

C. cinerariifolium (dalmatian chrysanthemum, pyrethrum), a perennial, grows 1–2 ft. and has many stems, silvery slashed leaves, and 1-in., white flower heads blooming in early summer. The dried and ground flowers are the most common source of pyrethrum insecticides.

C. coccineum (pyrethrum, painted daisy), also listed as *C. roseum*, is an excellent hardy perennial that grows 1–3 ft. high and has fernlike foliage. It blooms profusely in early summer and often later, with flowers in various shades of pink, red, and white; they may be single, semidouble, or double. It is an ideal cut flower and excellent in borders, especially in groups of

C. cinerariifolium

three to six plants in good sunlight and average soil. The clumps should be divided and reset every few years, best in midsummer. Seeds germinate easily but may not give flowers for several years. Many named varieties are available.

C. coronarium (crown daisy, garland chrysanthemum) is a stout and bushy annual that grows 1½–3 ft. high and is ideal for the garden. Leaves are deeply and compoundly cut. Abundant yellow or whitish flower heads are 1–1½ in. across and sometimes double. Var. *spatiosum* grows to 2 ft. with many leaves and light yellow flowers.

C. frutescens (Marguerite, Paris daisy) grows to 3 ft. and has many white, pale yellow, or pink ray flowers and yellow disks on a branchy plant with a woody base. Although perennial, it is not hardy but is grown by florists as a potted plant, blooming in winter or spring or for cut flowers. It will bloom in any season and is grown outdoors in mild climates.

C. leucanthemum (oxeye or white daisy) is the field perennial commonly encountered as a summer-blooming wildflower in North America. It grows to 2 ft. with white rays and yellow disks.

C. maximum (shasta daisy) is a very popular garden perennial but is often short-lived and grown as a biennial. Flowers are exclusively white, 2–4 in. across, in single, semidouble, frilled, lacinated, or double forms that bloom early through the summer. Excellent in borders and producing superb cut flowers, it grows 2–3 ft. high in heavy clumps and has long, glossy leaves. It needs protection from dampness in winter but should be divided every second year to prevent its drying out. Plants are easily started from seed sown in the spring. There are many named varieties in great demand.

C. maximum

C. morifolium (commercial or florist's chrysanthemum) is an original perennial species that grows 2–5 ft. high and has 2-in. daisies in several colors. It is interesting as a parent of garden kinds, including hundreds of varieties in almost every color except blue. Most fine greenhouse varieties for cutting or potted plant use are developed from the double form, which has been vastly improved.

C. nipponicum (Nippon daisy) is a hardy Japanese perennial that does especially well in coastal areas. It grows 1½–2 ft. high and has solitary, white flower heads 1½–3½ in. across from late summer on; thick, spatulate leaves; and shrubby, woody stems. It has been used in hybridizing with little success; it is best used in gardens near the seashore.

C. parthenium (feverfew) is a hardy, bushy perennial 1–3 ft. high and has abundant, ferny, strong-scented, often yellowish foliage. The profuse clusters of small, single or double, white- or yellow-rayed flower heads are excellent for summer cutting. The entire plant is used in the preparation of medicines and insect repellents. There are several varieties of different height (1–3 ft.), color of foliage, and flower form; the dwarf varieties are good in the border but short lived unless divided annually. It can also be grown from seed. Var. *aureum* (golden-feather) has yellowish leaves and white flowers.

C. rubellum is a hardy, branching perennial that grows 2–3 ft. high and produces abundant clumps of 2–3 in., pink or rose-red daisies blooming in early autumn. It is often an important parent in hybridizing and has led to rubellum hybrids, mostly rather coarse singles.

C. segetum (corn-marigold) is an annual that grows 1½–3 ft. high and has many branches terminating in small, yellow or whitish flower heads. There are several named varieties in cultivation, including 'White Glory', 'Morning Star', 'Evening Star', 'Gold Star', and 'Northern Star'.

C. uliginosum (giant or Hungarian daisy) is a tall (4–7 ft.), late-blooming European perennial, good for planting in the background and tolerant of wet soils. It produces 1–3 in. heads of white flowers and slender, cut foliage.

C. zawadskii (Korean daisy), formerly listed as *C. coreanum* or *C. sibiricum*, is a very hardy, floriferous perennial that grows 18 in. high with

2–2½ in. flower heads of white or rose-tinted rays and yellow disks. It is useful for wild gardens but best known as a parent of the Korean hybrids.

CHRYSOBALANUS (kris oh bah LAY nus). A genus of shrubs or small trees of the Rosaceae (Rose Family), native to the American and African tropics. The chief species is *C. icaco* (cocoplum), sometimes an evergreen tree to 30 ft. but only a bush in its northern range, which is Florida, where it grows on the coast and along streams. It has thick, leathery leaves and small, white flowers that form whitish fruit. A variety is also found with reddish new foliage and purple fruit. The fruits are insipid but sometimes used for preserves.

CHRYSOGONUM (kris AHG oh num) **virginianum.** A low-growing, hairy perennial herb with yellow flower heads, belonging to the Asteraceae (Aster Family), and commonly known as goldenstar or green-and-gold. It is found in the wild growing in dry soils from Pennsylvania to Florida and is sometimes planted in gardens.

CHRYSOPHYLLUM (kris oh FIL um). A genus of tropical evergreen trees of the Sapotaceae (Sapodilla Family), growing to 50 ft. tall in Zones 10–11.

C. cainito (star-apple) is sometimes cultivated in south Florida for ornament and its edible fruit. It has shining leaves, golden brown and silky beneath; purplish white flowers; and almost round, smooth, light purple or green fruit 4 in. across, with a white, usually edible pulp. The star-apple can be grown in a greenhouse, where it requires a moist, hot atmosphere and rich, sandy soil. It is propagated by seed, and by cuttings of ripe wood over heat.

C. oliviforme (satinleaf) is a tropical tree sometimes grown for ornament in south Florida.

CHRYSOPSIS (kris OP sis). A genus of daisylike plants belonging to the Asteraceae (Aster Family) and commonly known as golden aster. They produce yellow flowers on 1–3 ft. stems. Occasional-

ly grown in the border, they are more at home in a dry, sunny part of the wild garden. Propagation is easily done by seed or division. Various species are hardy in Zones 3–9.

C. villosa is a highly variable species with branching, erect or trailing stems, oblong leaves, and dense or loose flower clusters up to 1½ in. across.

CHUFA. Common name for *Cyperus esculentus*; see CYPERUS.

CHYSIS (KĪ sis). A genus of six species of epiphytic or lithophytic orchids endemic to Mexico, Central America, and northern South America. Long, turgid pseudobulbs are covered by grayish, papery sheaths and topped by several plicate, deciduous leaves. Flowers are fleshy and long-lasting, in shades of ivory, yellow, or orange-yellow. These plants do best mounted on cork or coconut husk plaques, or in baskets of a well-draining compost. During growth, the orchids should be watered heavily, and after the leaves drop, kept cool and nearly dry. Hardy to Zone 8 with frost protection, they withstand winter temperatures of 55–60°F. The type species is *C. aurea*.

CIBOTIUM (si BOH tee um). One of several genera of large ferns, collectively known and cultivated as TREE FERNS.

CICADA. This large, wide-headed insect of the family Cicadidae, in the order Homoptera, in summer is often called a locust (which is properly applied to grasshoppers) or a harvest fly (but it is not a fly). Though not serious pests, the females, in laying large groups of eggs, may injure young trees, and the grubs often gnaw tender roots. The length of time between broods varies with the species.

The well-known seventeen-year locust, which does have a seventeen-year lapse between broods, is often called the periodic locust, *Magicicada septendecim*. This one is dark colored, about 1¼ in. long, with transparent wings, red legs, and sucking mouthparts. The females have horny oviposters, which splinter the wood of small branches of fruit trees. The males go through a complex set of body vibrations to produce their loud buzzing "song." After the adult females lay several hundred eggs, the nymphs hatch in several weeks, then drop down and enter the soil to feed for seventeen years. They then come forth, as many as 20,000 to 40,000 from under one tree, work out of their old skins, and by the next day are ready for flight as adults. Local extension services keep track of the predicted dates of emergence, and susceptible plants such as young orchard trees should not be set out at those times. Young trees already in the ground can be protected by cheesecloth or other barriers. Pruning and burning of damaged limbs is advisable after locust damage. In the South, there is a thirteen-year cicada. The one-year, dog-day cicada comes every summer but does little damage.

CICER (SĪ sur) **arietinum.** An annual legume grown as a food crop and popularly known as garbanzo or chick pea. The bushy, hairy herb of the Fabaceae (Bean Family) is native to southern Europe and India, where it is extensively grown as a garden vegetable, the seeds being eaten boiled like peas or roasted like peanuts; more thoroughly roasted, they make an acceptable substitute for coffee. As a field crop they are grown as food for horses.

CICHORIUM (si KOH ree um). A genus of old world herbs of the Asteraceae (Aster Family). Both of the two principal species are grown in the vegetable garden. *C. endivia* (endive) is an annual or biennial with much curled and cut leaves, which are blanched and used as a substitute in hot weather when ordinary lettuce fails to head. The large roots of *C. intybus* (chicory) are used ground as a form of coffee and are also lifted and forced to produce hard, tight heads of white leaves which are used in salads. The flowers of both species are a beautiful shade of blue, and the plants are sometimes used in the border.

See CHICORY; ENDIVE.

CICUTA (si KYOO tah). A genus of moisture-loving perennial herbs belonging to the Apiaceae (Celery Family), native in North America, with small, white, strongly scented flowers in flat clusters. The roots are poisonous, but it is sometimes transplanted to bog gardens or moist spots in the wild garden and is hardy to Zone 5.

C. maculata (water-hemlock) is a perennial herb with small, white flowers in flat- or round-topped clusters, strongly scented foliage, and a

Cicuta maculata

large, poisonous root. It grows to 6 ft., and its finely cut foliage and numerous white flowers make it a bold and striking specimen in the bog or wild garden. It grows naturally in marshes and swampy areas of eastern North America, where it is also known as musquash-root. See POISONOUS PLANTS.

CIGAR FLOWER. Common name for *Cuphea ignea*, a tender Mexican herb whose petal-less flowers resemble cigars; see CUPHEA.

CILIATE. Fringed with small hairs.

CIMICIFUGA (si mi SIF yoo gah). A genus of perennial herbs belonging to the Ranunculaceae (Buttercup Family), commonly known as bugbane. They are tall woodland plants with long wands of very small, white flowers. Useful in the back of a hardy border or in semishaded locations in the wild garden, they are easily propagated by seed or division.

PRINCIPAL SPECIES

C. americana (American or mountain bugbane), native to the southern and central Appa-

C. americana

lachian region, has slender stems 2–6 ft. tall and leaves comprised of three to five oblong leaflets up to 3 in. long. It has long, loose clusters of white flowers.

C. racemosa (black cohosh, black snakeroot) grows to 8 ft. in rich, moist woodland soil. The flowers have an unpleasant odor.

C. simplex is of relatively low growth, not exceeding 3 ft., and is the most effective for planting in the shady border, blooming in autumn.

CINERARIA (si ne RAIR ee ah). Former botanical name, still used occasionally, for woolly perennial species of SENECIO grown in pots for winter flowering.

CINNAMOMUM (sin ah MOH mum). A genus of evergreen trees and shrubs of Asia and Australia, with aromatic leaves and wood. They are mostly of economic rather than horticultural value, although one or two species are grown in Zones 10–11 for ornamental and shade purposes.

PRINCIPAL SPECIES

C. camphora (camphor tree) grows to 40 ft. and has glossy, green leaves that turn yellow to crimson before dropping off. This happens just as the unfolding young leaves are a soft rose-pink shade, quite outclassing in beauty the small, yellow flowers. Commercial camphor is extracted from the wood.

C. cassia (cassiabark tree) is a handsome tree growing to 40 ft., whose bark is used as a substitute for cinnamon.

C. zeylanicum (cinnamon tree) is a small, East Indian tree with long, stiff leaves; the bark yields the popular cinnamon spice.

CINNAMON FERN. Common name for *Osmunda cinnamomea*, a fern with fronds bearing spores that turn a cinnamon color when ripe; see OSMUNDA.

CINNAMON TREE. Common name for *Cinnamomum zeylanicum*, an evergreen tree, whose bark supplies commercial cinnamon; see CINNAMOMUM.

CINNAMON VINE. Common name for *Dioscorea batatas*, a twining vine with edible tubers and cinnamon-scented flowers; see DIOSCOREA.

CINQUEFOIL Common name for POTENTILLA, a large genus of subshrubs or herbs with variously colored flowers.

CIRCAEA (sur SEE ah) **lutetiana.** A weedy herb of the Onagraceae (Evening-primrose Family) with very small, white flowers, commonly known as enchanter's-nightshade. It is a soft, woolly, herbaceous perennial, native to Europe but naturalized in parts of North America, mostly in moist woodlands. It is sometimes used in shady bog plantings and in moist spots in rock gardens. Propagation is by division or rooting offsets in the shade.

CIRRHOPETALUM (seer oh PET ah lum). A genus of 30 species of small to medium-sized, creeping, epiphytic orchids native to India, southeastern Asia, the Pacific Islands, and tropical Africa. The flowers are usually small and often bizarre in appearance. The genus is considered by many taxonomists to be cogeneric with BULBOPHYLLUM, but it is distinguished by umbellate inflorescences. Because of their creeping habit, the plants should be mounted on cork, tree fern, or coconut husk plaques and given a shady, humid environment. They are hardy only in Zones 10–11 and withstand a minimum winter temperature of 60°F. The type species is *C. thouarsii*.

CIRSIUM (SUR see um). A genus of rank-growing, prickly plants of the Asteraceae (Aster Family) with spiny leaves and purple, yellow, and white flowers in heads, commonly known as plumed-thistle. A few species are grown for their bold ornamental effect in the wild garden and are easily propagated from seed.

PRINCIPAL SPECIES

C. altissimum (tall-thistle), a native found in wet meadows, grows from 3–9 ft. and has downy leaves, purple flowers, and a fleshy taproot.

C. arvense (Canada-thistle), introduced from Eurasia and now considered a noxious weed in the United States, reproduces from the smallest piece of creeping root. To control, promptly destroy by digging out the roots, or cut and cover with heavy mulch paper. On lawns, mow frequently just before blossom and do not allow seed to set. It is usually found on rich or heavy soil, and tolerates saline soil.

C. diacantha (fishbone-thistle) is a coarse, prickly biennial herb with purplish heads, native to Asia.

C. lanceolatum, the common pasture or bull-thistle, grows to 5 ft. and has purple heads of fragrant flowers.

C. occidentale is a striking form that grows to 3 ft. and has silvery white foliage topped with large, rose or purple heads.

CISSUS (SIS us). A genus of tendril-climbing shrubs from tropical regions, belonging to the Vitaceae (Grape Family). A few are grown in greenhouses for their decorative foliage or interesting habit; others are grown outdoors doing best in Zones 8–11. Most of them have been known and described under the genus VITIS. Propagation is by cuttings.

PRINCIPAL SPECIES

C. antarctica (kangaroo vine) is a shrubby climber from Australia with thick, glossy leaves. It will not tolerate frost.

C. capensis is now included in the genus RHOICISSUS.

C. discolor (trailing-begonia) is a popular indoor foliage plant from Java. The oblong leaves are mottled with white and pink on the upper surface and reddish purple beneath.

C. incisa (marine-ivy) is a tall, tendril climber of the southern states with fleshy stems and divided leaves.

C. quadrangula is a curious, succulent climber with four-angled and winged stems.

CISTUS (SIS tus). A genus of low, upright shrubs, evergreen or partially so, belonging to the Cistaceae (Rockrose Family), and commonly known as rockrose. The large, handsome flowers resemble roses but are very delicate in texture and fleeting in character. An individual flower lasts only about a day, but a succession keeps up a lasting display for some time. Native to the Mediterranean region, rockroses are sun lovers and do well in a poor, rather dry, light soil where lime is present; hardy to Zone 8. They are tough plants, drought and fire resistant, tolerant of salt, and useful for controlling erosion on banks. The plants suffer from too much pruning and do not transplant well except as young plants from pots. Propagation is by seed, cuttings, and layers.

PRINCIPAL SPECIES

C. crispus grows to only 2 ft. and has crinkled leaves and pinkish flowers.

C. x *hybridus* (white rockrose) has fragrant, white flowers with yellow centers.

C. incanus, formerly listed as *C. villosus*, is a small shrub with hairy leaves and reddish purple flowers.

C. ladanifer is a handsome, medium-sized shrub with clammy leaves, dark green above and white beneath. The flowers are white with a purple blotch.

C. laurifolius, the hardiest, tallest species, grows to 5 ft. The leaves are usually whitish beneath, and the white flowers are marked with yellow blotches.

C. x *purpureus*, a hybrid form with showy purple flowers blotched maroon, grows to 4 ft. and has sticky twigs.

CITRANGE (SIT ranj). A made name for hybrids (produced by Walter T. Swingle of the United States Department of Agriculture) between the common orange and the hardy but inedible trifoliate-orange, *Poncirus* (formerly listed as *Citrus trifoliata*). While dormant, the trees are hardier than oranges (to Zone 8), often surviving temperatures lower than 15°F. There are several species, all of which are worked on trifoliate stock.

Citrangequats are the yellow or orange fruits, 1½–2 in. in diameter, borne by even hardier hybrids of the citrange and the KUMQUAT. They are also used in beverages and for cooking.

CITRON (SIT ron). Generally refers to a large, lemonlike citrus fruit with thick peel that is candied for use in cakes and confectionery. Also the shrub or small tree (*Citrus medica*) that bears it, which is so tender that its cultivation is limited to Zones 10–11. The name "citron" is also applied to the preserving melon (*Citrullus lanatus* var. *citroides*), a variety of watermelon. See CITRUS FRUITS.

CITRULLUS (si TRUL us) **lanatus.** The botanical name of the WATERMELON. Var. *citroides*, the citron or preserving melon, has a small fruit with firm, white flesh, which is used only candied or preserved.

CITRUS. A genus of tropical, evergreen, flowering, usually spiny shrubs and trees native to southeast Asia and the Malay Peninsula, belonging to the Rutaceae (Rue Family). In warmer regions, many species are popular in commercial and home cultivation, some for ornamental purposes, but more for their thick-skinned, pulpy fruits, which are aromatic and juicy.

Edible varieties include: CALAMONDIN; CITRON; GRAPEFRUIT; KUMQUAT; LEMON; LIME; ORANGE; PUMELLO; TANGELO; TANGERINE. For culture, see CITRUS FRUITS.

Popular ornamental varieties include:

C. aurantium (sour orange) is a fine ornamental with fruits sometimes used for marmalades. Once widely used as propagating stock, it has been found susceptible to a virus.

x *Citrofortunella mitis* (calamondin), the hardiest of the citrus hybrids (derived from *Citrus reticulata* x *Fortunella* spp.), is one of the most ornamental, with its dense head of bright green leaves and small, bright orange fruits. The decorative fruits are popular in beverages.

C. x *limonia* (Otaheite orange) is grown as a pot plant in cooler climates. Its origin is unknown, but its compact form; glossy, oblong leaves; fragrant, white flowers pink on the outside; and small, inedible but decorative fruits make this plant popular for indoor culture. Propagation is by seed and by grafting on seedlings.

It requires a very well drained, mellow soil and prefers a place in a sunny window with frequent watering and occasional applications of commercial fertilizer.

CITRUS FRUITS. These form the most important group of tropical and subtropical fruit trees of the world. In the United States some of them may be grown in warm and favored regions from Florida to California and occasionally as ornamental greenhouse or houseplants in the North. Commercially their culture is restricted to southern Florida, the Mississippi Delta, the lower Rio Grande Valley, and southern California. Frost injures all the citrus species in varying degrees. The LIME is the tenderest, being killed by even slight freezing temperatures; the KUMQUAT is one of the hardiest, withstanding temperatures of 15° or even 12°F. Hardiness of tender species can be measurably increased by budding or grafting on seedling stocks of the trifoliate orange, a species hardy even as far north as Washington, D.C. Hybrids of this with the sweet orange are hardy in the warmer parts of the cotton belt where the fruits are used for making beverages and preserves. See CITRANGE.

CULTURE

Citrus fruits will grow in any well-drained garden soil from sandy to clay, but a medium loam is most desirable. In sandy soils, it is difficult to maintain the necessary humus and plant food, while clay soils are harder to work and more difficult to drain.

Propagation is usually done by shield budding on two- or three-year-old seedlings of various stocks, mostly sour orange for good land, rough lemon for sandy soils, and trifoliate orange for heavy ones.

Planting is generally done in winter, the larger species (grapefruit and orange) requiring 25–30 ft. each way, medium species (tangerine and lemon) 20–25 ft., and small ones (kumquat), 15 ft.

To maintain the necessary humus in the soil, a COVER CROP or GREEN MANURE can be used. In the southeastern states, though the trees are sometimes grown in sod, clean cultivation or herbicides are usually used from early spring until the beginning of the rainy season when the cover crop is sown; in the Southwest, the earth is kept bare until fall when the cover crop is sown.

In the East, complete fertilizers are generally applied three times—February, June, and September or October. The element most needed by citrus in most areas is nitrogen, but since soils vary widely, it may be necessary to add other nutrients as well. Check with your local extension service to find what elements may be lacking in local soils.

When the trees are planted, they are generally cut back to 18 or 24 in. to assure low branching. Should sprouts develop from below the bud union they should be rubbed off while succulent, because the wounds will heal more quickly before they have become woody. After the trees are well established, the branches should be thinned in order to leave only four or five for framework limbs. After this they normally form shapely heads with little or no pruning except the removal of dead branches and of excessive shoots, preferably while succulent. Should frost kill parts of the trees, pruning should be delayed until new shoots appear, when the dead parts should be cut out.

All citrus need a good supply of water throughout the year, and especially when the crop of fruit is ripening. Frequent irrigation may be necessary in many regions.

For more information on particular fruits, see CITRANGE; GRAPEFRUIT; KUMQUAT; LEMON; LIME; MANDARIN ORANGE; ORANGE; PUMELLO; TANGELO; TANGERINE.

ENEMIES

Citrus trees probably have more pests than almost any other commercial crop. It is important to plant only certified virus-free trees and be on the constant lookout for possible trouble. The most common insects are mites, scales, and thrips. The larvae of many winged insects can also cause problems, as can aphids.

Melanose and scab are diseases that thrive in warm, moist conditions and attack citrus crops in the Southeast.

The usual spray program includes summer oils in midsummer for mites and scales. Ordinary pesticide and fungicide sprays should control most other insects and disease, but check with other growers or the local extension service to be sure. Eliminate ant colonies in the orchard to reduce the aphid colonies that they cultivate.

CLADANTHUS (klah DAN thus) **arabicus.** An annual herb with strongly odorous foliage, native to southern Spain and Morocco, sometimes grown in the border. It has finely cut, smooth, waxy leaves and bears yellow ray flowers at the tips of the branches.

CLADONIA (kla DOH nee ah) **rangiferina.** A common lichen that grows wild throughout Canada and the northern United States, commonly known as reindeer-moss. It has round, hollow, antherlike stems and branches of silvery gray. It can be cultivated as a ground cover, growing 2–4 in. high and thriving in open ground or partial shade.

CLADRASTIS (klah DRAS tis) **lutea.** A North American native, hardy, decorative tree with fragrant flowers, belonging to the Fabaceae (Bean Family), and commonly known as yellowwood. It is a deciduous, smooth-barked tree with shining leaves and open branches that give an airy effect. The white flowers in racemes 1 ft. long fill the air with fragrance for a great distance. Deep rooting and drought resistant, this tree is particularly attractive because of the showy flowers. Propagation is from seed sown in spring and root cuttings kept cool and moist over winter.

CLAMMY LOCUST. Common name for *Robinia viscosa*, a small tree with pink flowers and sticky hairs on the new growth and pods; see ROBINIA.

CLARKIA (KLAHR kee ah). A genus of hardy annual herbs, native to the western states, belonging to the Onagraceae (Evening Primrose Family), and commonly known as farewell-to-spring or Rocky-Mountain-garland, because in form and color they resemble a garland of almond blossoms. Some annual species native to California, with red, white, lilac, or purple flowers in leafy clusters, are often classified under the separate genus or subgenus *Godetia*.

Excellent for mass planting and growing up to 2 ft. outdoors (taller in the greenhouse), they produce graceful, showy blossoms delicately colored salmon, pink, lavender-purple, red, or white, borne along slender, upright branches. The long, graceful buds, resembling those of the fuchsia, open in summer. The flowers are valuable for cutting, since they will last a long time if gathered while in bud. This makes *Clarkia* an important greenhouse crop as well as a popular garden subject, easily cultivated in sunny locations in any light garden soil. Most grow readily from seed and will often self-sow. Plants seem to thrive better if seed is sown in spring where they are to grow, though seed can be started in the greenhouse in mid-winter and the seedlings transplanted in late spring to stand 9 in. apart, for late spring bloom.

PRINCIPAL SPECIES

C. amoena (satinflower), formerly listed as *Godetia amoena*, is a common wildflower in the western states. It grows to 3 ft. The chalice-shaped flowers vary from rosy purple to white with a darker spot on each petal and frequently double. It is an easily grown annual, blooming freely all summer. Var. *lindleyi*, formerly listed as *Godetia grandiflora*, grows to 12 in. and is the most frequently cultivated kind. It has rose-red flowers with a dark blotch at the center of each petal.

Clarkia amoena

C. breweri (fairy-fans), an attractive annual, forms branched 8-in. mounds and has fragrant, pink flowers with cut petals in early summer.

C. concinna (red-ribbons), formerly listed as *Eucharidium concinnum*, is a dainty annual that grows to 2 ft. and bears charming rose-colored flowers with three-lobed petals. It thrives in ordinary garden soil.

C. gracilis is similar to *C. amoena*, but it has a more crepelike texture on the red petals and there is a soft gradation into white toward the petal base, which is edged with intense red at the very bottom.

C. pulchella is a lower-growing species with slender leaves and flowers ranging from lilac to white.

C. rubicunda (farewell-to-spring), a common western wildflower, has pink flowers marked with a central petal spot in early summer.

C. unguiculata, formerly listed as *C. elegans*, is the commonly grown species, with smooth, reddish stems and growing to 3 ft. under favorable garden conditions and up to 5 ft. when grown under glass. Flowers have spoon-shaped petals that form spidery blossoms in shades of pink, purple, and rose; several double varieties have been developed.

C. williamsonii, growing to 4 ft., has stiff stems that bear large flowers of various colors, with strong crepe undulation to the petals.

CLASPING. Descriptive term for stalkless leaves that wholly or partly surround the twig, such as in the toad-lily or New England aster.

CLAUSENA (klaw SEE nah) **lansium.** A small, Chinese, fruit-bearing tree belonging to the Rutaceae (Rue Family) and commonly known as wampi.

CLAY. The term "clay" refers both to the smallest size minerals in the soil as well as the type of soil that is strongly influenced by the presence of clay minerals. A clay soil will usually have more than 30% clay-size minerals, with sand and silt constituents comprising the remaining minerals. The characteristics of a particular clay soil depends upon the amount and types of clays present.

A clay type soil may show the characteristic clay qualities in greater or lesser degree. These are a smooth greasiness to the touch when moist;

a tendency to become more compact when wet, that is, to "puddle"; and a tendency to then dry into a hard, solid consistency like unbaked brick and, in so doing, to shrink so that broad, deep cracks form in the surface. Through these cracks more moisture from below is lost, depriving any plants that may be growing in the soil, and rendering the soil even less fit for cultivation.

The result of digging or plowing a clay soil when wet is even more disastrous, since it produces large clods or lumps that dry into almost unbreakable solidity. A soil in this condition is almost useless and can be restored only after much hard work and long delay. A clay soil will hold moisture tenaciously, taking a long time to dry out, often because of poor drainage below. Where a clay hardpan underlies loam or sandy soil, this same condition of poor drainage is almost sure to exist.

While many plants will do fairly well in a clay soil with proper handling, the aim should be to make such a soil more friable. This can be done by gradually incorporating sand or quantities of organic materials—manure, compost, peat moss, or whatever is available. In doing this, take care to work the soil only when it is sufficiently dry. Also, frequently vary the depth to which it is plowed or dug so that a smooth, impervious surface will not be created just below the improved arable layer. To break up a stiff clay subsoil, a deep subsoil plowing or trenching can be successful. See also CULTIVATION; DIGGING.

CLAYTONIA (klay TOH nee ah). A genus of spring-flowering perennial herbs belonging to the Portulacaceae (Portulaca Family) and commonly known as spring-beauty. Plants are dwarf, rarely growing over 12 in., and bear white or rose-colored flowers. Growing from deep-seated, hard corms or tubers, they delight in damp, rich soil and partial shade. They are hardy to Zone 4 and well adapted to rock garden use.

PRINCIPAL SPECIES

C. caroliniana, native to eastern North America, grows to 12 in. and has leaves 1–2 in. wide and pink flowers.

C. parvifolia, native to the Pacific Northwest, has one to eight pink or white flowers on spreading or creeping stems. Small bulblets sometimes form in the leaf axils. In some varieties, the basal foliage rosettes can be eaten as vegetable greens.

C. virginica, native to Eastern North America, is not more than 8 in. high with long, narrow leaves and white flowers tinged with pink.

Claytonia virginica

CLEISTOCACTUS (klī stoh KAK tus). A genus of columnar cacti from Argentina and South America (often called torch cactus) characterized by tubular flowers that open only slightly to hardly at all, hence the Latin name *cleisto*, meaning "closed." The most popular species are *C. hyalacanthus*, with basally clustering, erect stems, short, snow-white spines, and crimson flowers; and *C. strausii*, similar but with longer, more yellowish spines. Another interesting species is *C. smaragdiflorus*, less densely spined and with tricolored flowers banded with red, yellow, and green.

CLEMATIS (KLEM ah tis). A genus of herbaceous perennials or woody climbing plants belonging to the Ranunculaceae (Buttercup Family) and widely distributed in temperate regions. They thrive in a well-dug, enriched, light, loamy soil to which lime should be added if lacking.

There are many species of widely differing growth and flower forms, as well as many beautiful hybrids. The bushy species are a good choice for the flower border. The woody, small-flowered kinds are adapted for use on fences, arbors, porches, or rambling in rocky places. The large-flowered hybrids show well on trellises or posts, while some of the less vigorous kinds make good houseplants. Hardiness varies with species from Zone 3–9.

For those that flower off the old wood, pruning consists of removing weak, straggly, and superfluous shoots when dormant. Those that flower from young basal shoots should have all the growth cut back in spring. Propagation is done by seed, layers, division, cuttings under glass, and grafting.

Diseases. Leaf spot and stem rot appear differently on different hybrids. In the garden, the stem near the soil line is usually the only part affected. In greenhouses, water-soaked spots, later becoming tan colored with red margins, occur on the leaves while the girdling lesions at the base of the stem cause the death of the shoots. Supporting the vines and spacing them far enough apart to prevent their matting together will often keep the disease from becoming serious. Remove diseased leaves and infected stubs; take cuttings from disease-free plants; grow young stock in clean beds. See also LEAF SPOT; STEM ROT.

Insect Pests. The clematis borer is a white, brown-headed grub about ⅔ in. long that infests the roots and crowns and sometimes hollows out bases of stems, especially in *C. virginiana* and *C. x jackmanii*. The adult is a clear-winged moth with blackish or violet forewings and transparent, dark-margined hind wings. Moths emerge in summer and lay eggs, the resulting larvae wintering in the roots. Cut out the borers and destroy badly infested plants. See also BORERS.

For red spider, syringe the plants with a forceful stream of water, or dust with sulfur, taking care to coat the undersides of the leaves; see RED SPIDER MITE. Dusting with sulfur will also tend to prevent the ravages of the TARNISHED PLANT BUG. See also INSECT CONTROL.

PRINCIPAL SPECIES

C. alpina is a spring-blooming climber with large, blue, pendulous flowers.

C. connata, also listed as *C. buchananiana*, climbs to 21 ft. with profusions of fragrant, yellow flowers up to 1¼ in. long borne in clusters.

C. flammula (plume clematis) is a slender climber, 12–15 ft. high, with a wealth of fragrant, pure white flowers up to 1¼ in. across in late summer. It grows best in shade and needs occasional pruning.

C. heracleifolia (tube clematis) is stout and erect with a woody base, large leaves of three leaflets, and clusters of lilac flowers in late summer. Var. *davidiana* is more slender with fragrant flowers of deep blue. Hardy to Zone 4.

C. integrifolia, growing to 3 ft., is a summer-blooming species with lavender-blue, bell-shaped flowers. Hardy to Zone 4, it is often used as a border plant. Var. *rosea* is a cerise-pink form.

C. x jackmanii is a beautiful hybrid produced from *C. lanuginosa* and *C. viticella*, and one of the best in its color—rich violet-purple.

C. lanuginosa grows to 6 ft. and bears flat, lavender or white flowers to 6 in. across in early summer.

C. macropetala (big-petal clematis) climbs to 10 ft., producing quantities of large, semidouble, light blue flowers. The plant is bushy and needs support. Hardy in Zones 4–9.

C. microphylla has small leaves and displays 1½-in.,white flowers in spring. A climber reaching 20–30 ft., it clings to trellises and walls.

C. montana (anemone clematis) is a vigorous grower that bears fragrant, white, anemonelike flowers in late spring. Var. *rubens* has reddish young growth and rose or pink flowers.

C. paniculata (sweet autumn clematis) is a vigorous grower and one of the hardiest and easiest to grow. It is conspicuous in late summer with many-flowered panicles of fragrant, white blossoms.

C. recta (ground clematis) grows erect to 4–5 ft. and produces many-flowered panicles of fragrant, white blooms most of summer. Hardy to Zone 4.

Clematis recta

C. tangutica (golden clematis) is a very handsome species that grows to 10 ft. and has golden flowers in early summer and again in fall when the feathery fruits are also attractive.

C. texensis (scarlet clematis) is of moderate growth with handsome, solitary, nodding, urn-shaped flowers in midsummer.

C. virginiana (virgin's-bower) is a native vine, very attractive in hedgerows in midsummer with its long festoons of white flowers in leafy panicles. It does well rambling over slopes and rocky places.

C. vitalba (traveler's-joy) is a tall, vigorous plant with fragrant, greenish white flowers in summer followed by feathery seed heads called old-man's-beard.

C. viticella is a deciduous climber that grows to 12 ft. and has fragrant, blue to rosy purple, bell-shaped summer flowers 2½ in. across.

CLEOME (klee OH mee). A genus of herbs or small shrubs from the tropics, belonging to the Capparaceae (Caper Family). They have white, green, yellow, or purple flowers whose feathery petals and long stamens give them the appearance of orchids. Seed sown outdoors in spring will germinate quickly. When seedlings are 3–4 in. high, thin them out to 2 ft. apart.

Cleome serrulata

C. hasslerana (spiderflower, spider plant), also listed as *C. spinosa*, *C. gigantea*, or *C. pungens*, is an annual species grown in northern gardens. It has a strong, but not unpleasant odor. The plant grows to 4 ft. tall, has rose-purple or white flowers with protruding stamens, and is best used in the border in sandy soil. It is a terrific spreader, self-sowing unless care is taken to remove the seedpods before they ripen.

C. serrulata (Rocky Mountain beeplant) is an annual that grows 2–5 ft. tall and has compound, ovate leaves 1–2½ in. long and dense racemes of showy, pink or white flowers. Native to western North America, it was once commonly planted to attract and feed bees.

CLERODENDRUM (klee roh DEN drum). A genus of deciduous or evergreen trees, shrubs, or herbs with white, violet, or red flowers in terminal clusters, belonging to the Verbenaceae (Verbena Family), and commonly known as glorybower. Native mainly in the tropics, most can be grown only in the greenhouse or outdoors in Zones 10–11. One or two grow and flower fairly well in cooler regions if given a sheltered location and well-drained soil. Propagation is by seed and cuttings.

PRINCIPAL SPECIES

C. bungei, formerly listed as *C. foetidum*, is a Chinese shrub of medium height and not quite hardy. It has rosy red flowers, and the leaves give an unpleasant odor when bruised.

C. philippinum, formerly listed as *C. fragrans*, has fragrant, white flowers and is a useful small shrub for the cool greenhouse. Var. *pleniflorum* has very doubled white blossoms edged with pink and very sweetly fragrant.

C. speciosissimum, formerly listed as *C. fallax*, is a shrub with scarlet flowers from Java, often grown in greenhouses.

C. thomsoniae (bleeding-heart vine) is a popular evergreen twiner for the warm greenhouse. The crimson flowers are set off by white calyxes that persist for a long time, eventually turning purple. It can be trained around a large wire or grapevine-wreath support about 20 in. in diameter. The flowers are produced on new growth, so that the plant can be cut back sharply in late winter or early spring for a summer and autumn of many flowers.

C. trichotomum, from Japan, is a tall shrub or small tree with large, soft leaves. It is conspicuous in mid- to late summer with loose clusters of fragrant flowers set off by red calyxes. The latter persist, making a pleasing contrast with the bright blue fruits. Var. *fargesi*, from China, is somewhat similar but has smaller leaves, and the calyx, green when the flowers open, later turns reddish purple, setting off the turquoise-blue berries. Hardier than others, this species survives to Zone 5, although the tops may be killed back in severe winters.

CLETHRA (KLETH rah). A genus of deciduous or evergreen shrubs or small trees, the only member of the Clethraceae (White-alder Family), closely related to the Ericaceae (Heath Family), and commonly known as summersweet or pepperbush. Native to eastern North America, Asia, and Madeira, they grow best in rather moist, acid soil with peat or leaf mold. Only a few species are hardy, but all have spikes of fragrant, white flowers in summer. Propagation is by seed, cuttings of young shoots, layers, and division.

PRINCIPAL SPECIES

C. acuminata grows to 15 ft. or more and has nodding racemes. Hardy in Zones 6–8, it is found in the mountains from Virginia to Georgia.

C. alnifolia (summersweet, sweet pepperbush) is an upright grower to 10 ft., found in moist places from Maine to Florida, hardy in Zones 4–9. It produces erect racemes of very fragrant, white flowers in summer. It is subject to attacks by red spider if grown in dry places.

C. barbinervis is a large shrub or small tree with a handsome, smooth, mottled bark pattern. Hardy in Zones 6–8, it is the earliest to bloom, producing fragrant, white flowers.

CLIANTHUS (klī AN thus). A genus of tender half-trailing shrubs from Australia and New Zealand, belonging to the Fabaceae (Bean Family), and commonly known as gloryvine. They are usually grown in the greenhouse, trained to trelliswork or light stakes, but can be grown outdoors in a warm climate.

C. formosus (glory pea), formerly listed as *C. dampieri*, has large, showy flowers of remarkable appearance. They are bright red with a velvety, dark purple blotch in the center, borne five or six in a drooping raceme. It is considered excellent for xeriscaping in warm, dry regions. The plant is difficult to grow on its own roots; the usual and most satisfactory method is to graft it on *Colutea arborescens*. This is done by cleft grafting a tiny seedling onto a seedling colutea cut off near the soil; see GRAFTING.

C. puniceus (parrot's-bill) is a shrubby, branched plant that grows to 6 ft. and has eight or more crimson flowers in a raceme. It is easily propagated from cuttings and is a good outdoor shrub in California.

CLIMATE. The general average weather in an area is called its climate. Climates vary from tropical to arctic, with a temperate climate between these two extremes. Climates are warmer near the equator and grow colder at the poles, but there are many factors that influence the climate of a particular area. The higher the elevation above sea level, the colder the climate will be. Nearness to an ocean or large body of water will cause an increase in rainfall and moderation of temperature extremes. Warm or cold ocean currents will affect the climates near a coast, and the nearness of a mountain range and prevailing winds will influence the lows and highs of any climate.

There is a difference between weather and climate. Weather is the temperature, rain- or snowfall, humidity, and other atmospheric conditions at a given moment. Climate is the accumulation of weather effects throughout the year. Since garden plants come from all over the world, their performance in different climates varies greatly. Some plants native to the tropics cannot survive cold weather. Others from a dry climate will rot in climates with a high rainfall. The gardener who understands what to expect from the local climate will be able to choose plants suited to the conditions of that area.

A region or "climate zone" can be defined by the cumulative effects of weather in a given area. The yearly rainfall, low and high temperature range, humidity, and other geographic conditions are approximately the same for the area, and so certain plants thrive and others fail within that zone. See also HALF-HARDY PLANTS; HARDINESS ZONES; HARDY PLANTS.

CLIMBERS. In the popular sense, climbers are any plants used to cover walls, arbors, or trellises, regardless of whether they provide their own means of attachment or have been fastened to their supports. A more limited definition restricts the term to those plants that attach themselves by means of tendrils, stems, or aerial roots, and excludes those that raise themselves above the ground by twisting their stems around a support, being therefore known as twiners.

See also ESPALIER; PRUNING; TRAINING PLANTS; VINES.

CLIMBING FERNS. Common name for certain ferns that climb by twining rachises or other parts, including *Lygodium japonicum* (Japanese climbing fern), see LYGODIUM; and *Stenochlaena palustris* (climbing swamp fern), which makes a handsome houseplant, see STENOCHLAENA.

CLIMBING LILY. A common name for *Gloriosa superba*, a climbing, greenhouse or warm-climate plant with segmented, red flowers; see GLORIOSA.

CLINTONIA (klin TOH nee ah). A genus of hardy herbs with broad leaves, belonging to the Liliaceae (Lily Family), and most appropriate for colonizing in the wild or rock garden. They spread by long rhizomes or underground stems. The white or yellow flowers are followed by attractive berries. Mostly hardy to Zone 3, plants should be grown in rich, moist wood soil in shady spots. Propagation is by seed or division of the roots. The

Clintonia borealis

genus was named for Dewitt Clinton, one of the early governors of New York State, in recognition of his interest in gardening and botany.

PRINCIPAL SPECIES
C. andrewsiana grows to 18 in. and has rose-purple flowers.

C. borealis, common in the northeastern woods, has brilliant blue berries and is the best for naturalizing.

C. uniflora is a western plant with large, starry, white flowers and thrives in peaty soil.

CLITORIA (klī TOHR ee ah). A genus of perennial herbs or shrubby climbers, mostly of the tropics, belonging to the Fabaceae (Bean Family), and commonly known as butterfly pea. Most species are hardy to Zone 9; some are grown under glass; and others can survive cooler climates. Propagation is by seed and cuttings.

PRINCIPAL SPECIES
C. arborescens is a good shrubby twiner for the greenhouse, bearing showy, pinkish flowers.

C. mariana is a low, twining perennial with light blue flowers in summer and is found from New Jersey southward.

C. ternatea is the best species for garden use in the far South, where it is hardy. It makes an attractive twiner for the greenhouse. Flowers are showy blue.

CLIVIA (KLĪ vee ah). A genus of fleshy-rooted evergreen plants belonging to the Amaryllidaceae (Amaryllis Family), commonly known as kafir-lily. Hardy only in Zones 10–11, they are extensively grown as houseplants and greenhouse subjects in cool regions and in shady outdoor locations in warmer areas. They are exceedingly decorative, with large, reddish orange or scarlet, lilylike flowers borne in umbels at right angles to the rather stiff stalks that rise above the drooping, strap-shaped leaves.

Plants are easily raised from seed, and many interesting hybrids have been developed in this way. They can also be propagated by division in the spring, although plants do best if not disturbed for several years. The potting soil should be rich loam and sand with charcoal added to prevent it from becoming acid. During the growing period, water freely and feed with liquid manure. During the resting season, keep the plants in a cool greenhouse and give little if any water.

The most troublesome pest in winter is the mealybug. Remove these small, fleshy, sucking insects, which are enveloped in a mealy, white, spongy, waxlike substance, with a forceful stream of water or with a soft toothbrush and soap, or spray with a contact insecticide.

C. miniata, the commonly grown species, has scarlet flowers, yellow inside, followed by bright red berries.

CLOCHE. A French name for a covering that is placed over a plant or a hill of plants in the garden to protect them from frost and hasten growth. Originally the cloche was a bell-shaped glass device, but today a cloche or row covering may be made of plastic, fiberglass, or spun polyester material.

CLONE (klohn). A clone or clonal variety is a named variety of a plant, the members of which have all originated from the multiplication of a single plant by vegetative (asexual) means, such as grafting, budding, cutting, or division, rather than from seed. In reality, therefore, they all comprise several pieces of one original individual plant.

A clone implies an individual. A race or strain, or a variety reproduced from seed, on the other hand, implies a population or group of individuals. Plants whose distinguishing characteristics fail to come true from seed or that are incapable of producing seedlings are generally propagated as clones.

CLOUDBERRY. Common name for *Rubus chamaemorus*, a species of bramble with white flowers and orange-red fruit; see RUBUS.

CLOVE. One of the segments or bulblets of a garlic or similar bulb. The commercial spice called clove comes from the genus SYZYGIUM.

CLOVER. Common name for TRIFOLIUM, a genus of leguminous herbs with three-lobed leaves, including species known as alsike, crimson, red, and white clover.

Other genera also use forms of this common name. DESMODIUM is tick-clover. LESPEDEZA includes bush- and Japanese-clover. MARSILEA is water-clover. MELILOTUS includes the plants known as bur-, bokhara-, hubam-, and sweet-clover. ORTHOCARPUS includes owls- and prairie-clover. PETALOSTEMON is also called prairie-clover. *Richardia scabra* is Mexican-clover.

CLOWESIA (klow WEE zee ah). A subgenus of five species of epiphytic orchids native to Mexico, Central America, and northern South America. Vegetatively similar to CATASETUM, they have fleshy, bisexual flowers with saccate lips and fringed petals. Basket culture is recommended, with a porous, well-draining compost. They prefer bright, filtered light and require a decided rest after flowering. They are hardy only in Zones 10–11 and withstand a minimum winter temperature of 60°F. The type species is *C. rosea*.

CLUB-MOSS. Common name for LYCOPODIUM, a genus of low, flowerless plants with scalelike leaves, useful for ground covers.

CLUB ROOT. Also called finger-and-toe disease and numerous other descriptive names, this is a fungus spread by a slime mold and resulting frequently in a decline in vigor and often in the death of affected plants. It can be recognized first by a yellowing of the leaves, which may tend to wilt in hot weather. Later it produces a swelling or distortion of the roots of cabbage and other members of the Brassicaceae (Mustard Family). Practically all the cultivated species of crucifers are subject to it, including peppergrass and alyssum.

The club root fungus is spread by contaminated soil and infected manure or plant refuse. To control, try rotating crops yearly. Adding lime to the soil can help. Some cabbage varieties are more disease-resistant; consult your local nursery or seed catalog.

CLUSIA (KLOO see ah). A genus of shrubs and trees from the tropical Americas, belonging to the Guttiferae (Garcinia Family). The commonly grown species, *C. rosea*, has leathery leaves and curious, pink-and-white flowers. It is valuable in tropical landscaping for its drought and salt tolerance, and has proved to be a reliable houseplant.

CLYTOSTOMA (klī toh STOH mah). A genus of evergreen, climbing shrubs from South America, belonging to the Bignoniaceae (Bignonia Family). Closely related to plants of the genus BIGNONIA, they have been grown and described as such. Under tropical or subtropical conditions (Zones 9–11), they are vigorous growers, climbing by leaf tendrils and bearing handsome, funnelform flowers.

Two species are known: *C. callistegioides*, with wavy leaves and flowers with pale purple streaks; and *C. binatum*, with leaves sometimes toothed and mauve-colored, white-throated flowers.

CNEORUM (nee OR um) **tricoccon.** An evergreen shrub of the Mediterranean region and the Canary Isles, commonly known as spurge-olive. It is useful for outdoor planting in Zones 9–11. Its shining, leathery, entire leaves are 2 in. long. Deep yellow flowers growing from the leaf axils are followed by greenish black, three-lobed fruits.

CNICUS (NĪ kus) **benedictus.** A hardy, branching, thistlelike annual, native to the Mediterranean region and the Caucasus, belonging to the Asteraceae (Aster Family), and commonly known as blessed-thistle. The plant tops were used as a tonic and said to be the origin of benedictine liquor. The tops were also used by the American Indians for medicinal purposes. It grows to 2 ft. bearing large heads of yellow flowers with large, leafy bracts, and is used to good effect in the rock garden or wild garden. Seeds are sown in the open ground in early spring where plants are to bloom.

COACH-WHIP. A common name for *Fouquieria splendens*, a cactuslike plant with scarlet flowers; see FOUQUIERIA.

COBAEA (koh BEE ah). A genus of tropical plants, which are the only climbers belonging to the Polemoniaceae (Phlox Family). While perennial under tropical conditions, they are usually cultivated as annuals. They grow readily from seed, best results being obtained by setting the large, flat seeds on edge. In cooler regions, they should be started under glass so as to have well-established plants in pots ready to set out when all danger of frost has passed. Hardy to Zone 9, if planted in a sheltered corner, the flowers continue for some time after the early frosts.

C. scandens (cathedral-bells, cup-and-saucer vine), the principal species, is a rapid and graceful grower to 25 ft. or more, climbing by leaf tendrils. The large, bell-shaped, violet flowers are set off by a large, leafy calyx, which suggests the latter common name. Cv. 'Alba' is a white-flowered form; there is also one with variegated leaves.

COBNUT. Common name for *Corylus avellana* var. *grandis*, a variety of the European hazelnut; see CORYLUS.

COCA. Common name for *Erythroxylum coca*, a tropical shrub cultivated for narcotic drugs; see ERYTHROXYLUM.

COCCOLOBA (koh koh LOH bah). A large genus of tropical and subtropical woody plants, some native along the Florida coast and grown outdoors in Zones 10–11. They grow best in rich, sandy soil and are easily propagated from seed and also by cuttings of ripe wood or by layering.

PRINCIPAL SPECIES

C. diversifolia (pigeon-plum) is a small fruit tree native to the Carribean, tolerant of salt, and valuable in coastal plantings.

C. floridana (pigeon-cherry) bears edible, pear-shaped fruits slightly larger than those of *C. uvifera*.

C. uvifera (sea-grape, shore-grape) is the best-known species. It has large, handsome, glossy leaves veined with white flowers followed by grapelike clusters of edible purple fruit.

COCCULUS (KOHK yoo lus). A genus of herbs, shrubs, or woody plants belonging to the Menispermaceae (Moonseed Family) and commonly known as snailseed. Usually vinelike in habit, they are sometimes used to trail over gateways and arbors. They have attractive foliage and inconspicuous flowers followed by red or black fruit hanging in clusters. Native in the United States and Asia, a few of the evergreen species are grown in pots; others can be grown outdoors as far north as Zone 7 in rich, moist soil. Propagation is by seed or cuttings of half-ripened wood started under glass with bottom heat.

   C. carolinus (Carolina moonseed), a native plant with brilliant red flowers, is hardy in Zones 7–9.

   C. laurifolius, growing to 15 ft., is an evergreen shrub with black fruit, adapted only to Zone 8 and southward. It can be grown in a greenhouse.

COCHLEARIA (kohk lee AIR ee ah) **officinalis.** A small, northern biennial or perennial herb of the Brassicaceae (Mustard Family), with heart- or kidney-shaped leaves and small, white flowers in spring. Commonly called scurvy-grass, it has some medicinal value and is also grown as an annual salad plant in spite of its peculiar flavor of tar. Leaves are ready for harvest in two to three months; successive sowings can be made. Hardy to Zone 3, it prefers cool or partially shaded soil. *C. armoracia*, formerly included in this genus, is now listed as *Armoracia rusticana*; see HORSERADISH.

COCHLIOSTEMA (kohk lee oh STEE mah). A genus of curious and handsome greenhouse herbs native to Brazil and Ecuador, with very short stems and foliage forming a rosette. Two species are cultivated, one with leaves that are deep red on the underside. The flowers of both are violet-blue and borne freely in branched clusters. The soil should be a fibrous loam with peat added and must never be permitted to dry out. The plants also need a humid atmosphere. Propagation is by seed, which should be sown as soon as ripe. Hand-fertilization is necessary.

COCHLOSPERMUM (kohk loh SPUR mum). A genus of tropical evergreen trees or shrubs, hardy only in Zones 10–11. The most common species,

C. vitifolium, has large, yellow, single or double flowers on the end of leafless branches in the spring, before the large, lobed leaves emerge.

COCKSCOMB. A common name for *Celosia cristata*, an annual herb with many flower varieties; see CELOSIA.

COCONUT. The fruit of a tropical palm, *Cocos nucifera*, which grows both inland and along coastlines; the name can be applied to the tree itself. The tree is ornamental in youth, providing an effective screen for windy locations. In old age, its tall stems are picturesque accents in any tropical garden plan.

   The tree is also an important source of many commercial products. The sap is used as a beverage. The husk fiber (coir) is used in making cord, brushes, and other products. The mature nut meat (copra) is edible fresh or dried.

   Although it often grows by the seashore, its roots require fresh water. An annual rainfall of 40 in. or more is necessary for continuous growth. Propagation is by seed (the nut), which takes several months to germinate. Protected by its hard shell and thick husk, the nut can float in the ocean for hundreds of miles and still produce a tree when finally cast ashore.

   Double-coconut is *Lodoicea maldivica*, a species of fan palm remarkable for producing the largest known seeds; see LODOICEA.

COCOS (KOH kohs) **nucifera.** Botanical name for the tropical coconut palm; see COCONUT. The genus once included numerous other species grown for decorative purposes in greenhouses or as houseplants and now classified under other genera, including *Arecastrum*, *Butia*, *Microcoelum*.

COCOZELLE (koh koh zel). Popular name for *Cucurbita pepo* var. *melopepo*, a bush vegetable marrow or summer squash whose elongated, green, striped fruits, picked while the rind can be easily indented with the fingernail, are sliced and fried like eggplant. See SQUASH.

CODIAEUM (koh dī EE um). A genus of tropical shrubs belonging to the Euphorbiaceae (Spurge Family). Commonly known as croton, they are extensively grown in Zones 9–11 and in greenhouses for their highly colored, ornamental foliage, which is extremely variable in form and color.

Massed in a sunny place outdoors, they give a rich, tropical effect and are also useful for vases and window boxes. A mixture of fibrous loam with leaf mold and sand suits them well. In the early stages of growth, they need very warm and moist conditions. While good light is needed to induce bright coloring, some shade may be necessary under clear glass during the brightest weather to prevent leaf burning.

Crotons are subject to leaf spots and rust which luckily are not often serious. Remove badly spotted leaves and dust rusted plants with fungicide. Spider mites can be a serious pest in dry atmospheres.

Propagation is by cuttings of half-ripened shoots under warm and close conditions. Substantial young plants can be secured from old specimens by AIR LAYERING.

SELECTIONS

C. variegatum var. *pictum* includes most of the many varieties in cultivation, which probably originated as seedling or sports forms. They differ greatly in foliage, the leaves ranging from large entire or deeply lobed to long, narrow, and often twisted. The color combinations are often very striking, involving shades of green, yellow, orange, pink, red, and crimson.

Broad-leaved Kinds. Forms with variously colored, unlobed foliage include *andreanum*, yellow with red veinings; 'B. Compte', yellow with red blotches; 'Mrs. Iceton', dark red with rose mottlings; and *reidi*, yellow and red with rosy tints.

Forms with large, lobed leaves are *evansianum*, yellow, veined, and mottled red, and 'Lord Derby', yellow with bright red suffusion.

Long- and Narrow-leaved Kinds. Var. *chelsoni* has drooping and often twisted leaves of yellow tinted bright orange, and shaded crimson. Var. *insigne* has narrow, deep green leaves with red margin and yellow midrib and veins. Var. *interruptum* has twisted, yellow leaves with red markings and an extended midrib. Var. *hanburyanum* is olive green with yellow markings and rosy blotches.

CODLING MOTH. The worst apple pest and cause of wormy apples in the country is the codling moth, *Laspeyresia pomonella*. It also attacks pear, quince, crab apple, English walnut, and wild haws. The larva is a pinky white caterpillar with a brown head, about ¾ in. long, which bores right into the core of the fruit, leaving it full of rotting frass or excrement. It exits through the blossom end of the apple, leaving more brown material at the point of exit. Young larvae also eat the sides of the fruit. The eggs are laid at the blossom end in June, and the larvae, when they leave for the winter, go to crevices in the bark.

The adult moth is dark gray with wavy lines on the forewings, each of which has a large, brown spot. The hindwings are fringed. These moths appear at the time when the blossoms open, reaching a height the week after the petals fall. They lay 50 to 75 small, white eggs on the leaves, twigs, or fruit

Codling moth

during the fourth week after petal drop. The eggs hatch in about a week, and the young larvae are likely to enter the fruit at the blossom end, where they eat and develop for three to five weeks. Then they seek sites for pupation under loose bark or other protected places on the trees or in the debris beneath the trees. In New England, there may be only one generation, but in warmer states, the number rises to two, three, or even four.

Codling moths spend the winter in their last larval instar and pupate in the spring. Corrugated cardboard bands placed around apple tree trunks and then removed and destroyed in spring are excellent for collecting overwintering pests.

Chemical SPRAYING should be carefully timed. Make sure the petals are off the tree or the bees that are doing the pollinating might be harmed. Always follow the label directions carefully. Aside from chemical sprays used in some orchards, gardeners are wise to try such biological controls as **Bacillus thuringiensis** (Bt, commonly available as Dipel, Biotrol, or Thuricide). Other methods worth trying include dormant oil spray, fish oil and insecticidal soap sprays, and water from the hose plus ryania. Paper cups with a bit of molasses in them, suspended in the tree, often trap egg-laying codling moths in the spring. Bands treated with Tanglefoot put around the trunk and suet hung nearby to attract woodpeckers can be effective, as can DIATOMACEOUS EARTH put on the undersides of leaves to deter the moths from laying eggs. Use the horticultural diatomaceous earth, not the kind used for cleaning swimming pools, which has been rubbed smooth of the sharp, prickly, lethal spines.

If the tiny parasitic wasp, *Trichogramma* spp., is used as a control, three applications are advisable: the first during the budding stage, the second during bloom, and the third during petal drop.

CODONOPSIS (koh doh NAWP sis).
A genus of vines and upright plants belonging to the Campanulaceae (Bellflower Family). They can be grown in the border but require winter protection. Propagation is by seed or cuttings. Most are hardy in Zones 5–8.

PRINCIPAL SPECIES

C. clematidea, growing to 3 ft., has charming, pale blue, bell-shaped flowers.

C. ovata, growing to 1 ft., is best suited to the rock garden, where it should be planted at the higher levels in order to show the full beauty of the steel blue flowers spotted yellow and white inside.

C. pilosula, sometimes listed as *C. silvestris*, is a trailing species with twining stems, bloomy foliage, and solitary, greenish or purplish yellow, bell-shaped summertime flowers, 1 in. or more in diameter.

C. vinciflora is a climber with twining stems that bear nodding, blue, bell-like blooms in summer; hardy in Zones 5–9.

COELOGYNE (see LAH jin ee).
A genus of about 125 attractive epiphytic orchids native to southeastern Asia. They have ovoid pseudobulbs, broad, plicate leaves, and many flowers growing from the center of young growths. The medium-sized flowers are racemose and open in shape with narrow petals and sepals and a spreading, three-lobed lip. Colors are white, ivory, or green with contrasting lips.

Species from low altitudes need a warm, humid environment, while those from higher areas should receive cooler and drier conditions. They are hardy to Zone 7 if protected from cold and frost and are best grown in baskets in a loose, well-drained compost placed in lightly filtered shade.

C. pandurata (black orchid) has clear green floral segments and brown-black markings on the fringed lip.

COFFEA (KOF ee ah).
A genus of evergreen shrubs belonging to the Rubiaceae (Madder Family), native to the tropics of Asia and Africa, and commonly known as coffee. More than 25 species have been recognized, some of which are found in greenhouse collections and outdoors in warm climates. Coffee is grown in Zones 10–11 as a shrub for its handsome, shining leaves; fragrant, white flowers; and attractive, red berries. Soil for these plants should be half peat and half loam. Propagation of the ornamental species is by cuttings of ripe wood rooted under glass in moist heat.

C. arabica is grown commercially, the "beans" being the seeds formed within a pulpy fruit; the several varieties have their own distinct flavors.

C. canephora grows larger species and has been hybridized with *C. arabica* to give disease resistance where rust is a problem.

COFFEE.
Common name for COFFEA, a genus of tropical shrubs.

COFFEE-BERRY. Common name for *Rhamnus californica*, a tender evergreen shrub cultivated in California; see RHAMNUS.

COFFEE FERN. Common name for *Pellaea andromedifolia*, a dark, tufted fern native to the western states; see PELLAEA.

COHOSH. Common name for ACTAEA, a genus of herbs native in the North Temperate Zone, with white flowers and red berries. Black-cohosh is *Cimicifuga racemosa*, a perennial herb with malodorous, white flowers; see CIMICIFUGA. Blue-cohosh is *Caulophyllum thalictroides*, an herb with small flowers found in the eastern United States; see CAULOPHYLLUM.

COIX (KOH iks). The most common species in this genus of tall, broad-leaved grasses is *C. lacryma-jobi* (Job's-tears), a popular ornamental garden subject. Although a perennial, it will not tolerate northern winters and so is generally grown as an annual. Seeds should be planted in the open ground not too early in the spring. Plants grow to about 4 ft. and have leaves 2 ft. long and 1½ in. wide. The peculiar, large, hard, grayish to pearly white, round seeds hang in clusters from the sheaths, and it is these seeds, which can be used as beads, that make the grass attractive and give it its common name. The sprays of seeds, if dried before they shatter, are good ornamental material combined with everlastings. In the Orient, the seeds are eaten as a cereal (adlay). See also ORNAMENTAL GRASSES.

COLCHICINE (KOHL ki seen). A fine, yellow, very bitter, and very poisonous powder obtained from corms of the autumn-crocus, *Colchicum autumnale*. It has come into limited horticultural use for experimental purposes because of its ability to modify the development of plants to which it is applied.

Plants are made up of cells of minute size which, multiplying naturally by self-division, cause the plants to grow larger. Each cell contains a nucleus that has within it microscopic bodies called chromosomes, which are responsible for the plant's inherited characteristics and also for the passing on of these characteristics to succeeding generations. As growth takes place, each cell, and each chromosome in it, splits into two and thus, by a complicated process involving the rearrangement of the multiplied bodies, new complete cells are formed. This division, called mitosis, is the stabilizing process insuring the perpetuation of the structure and habits of the parent plants.

When colchicine is applied to a plant part, it sometimes so interferes with this normal process as to cause the formation of new cells, which may have twice, or some other multiple, of the original number of chromosomes, a condition called-polyploidy (see POLYPLOID). This leads to marked changes in the structure, size, and appearance of the plant and, in some cases, even in its reproduction powers, so that a formerly infertile hybrid may become fertile. Increased flower size has been one of the results.

Thus new varieties or strains of plants bearing blossoms of near giant size have been produced by treating the seed or sections of a plant itself with a solution or a lanum paste containing specified amounts of colchicine. After treatment some plants grow with increased vigor even though multiplication of the chromosome count has not been achieved. Colchicine can cause radical changes in plant types and lead to the development of vegetables and flowers having new tastes, odors, or size. Because of the dangerous highly poisonous nature of colchicine, its use in trying to create unusual plants should be approached with great care. This is not an item for use by the home gardener.

COLCHICUM (KOHL chi kum). A genus of cormous plants of the Liliaceae (Lily Family), commonly known as autumn-crocus or meadow-saffron. They are not related to the true crocus, though the flowers of the plants look alike. The species most frequently cultivated, *C. autumnale*, bears clusters of large, pale lavender blossoms in the fall. At its flowering stage, the plant is sometimes known as naked-lady, since the coarse foliage does not appear until the following spring, dying down before midsummer. Do not confuse **Colchicum** with the autumn-flowering forms of the true CROCUS.

The corms are hardy enough to winter over with little or no protection in temperate regions, and left undisturbed, they will flower freely for years. Some can be dug during the dormant season (June and July) and kept for indoor blooming, since they are effective and exceedingly easy to handle. Planted in peat moss in shallow bowls, they blossom with moderate heat and moisture. Indeed, they are so strongly inclined to flower

Colchicum autumnale

that they are sometimes advertised as "bulbs that will flower without soil or water." Of course, while this may happen, the results are inferior.

There are many species, including double forms in purple and white. Other autumn-flowering species include *C. variegatum* and *C. bivonae*, both with checkered markings on the purple petals; *C. sibthorpii*, with large, cup-shaped flowers; *C. speciosum*, with large, violet or pink flowers in clusters; *C. decaisnei*, very late blooming, with flesh-colored flowers; and *C. alpinum*, bearing small, lilac flowers, often in pairs.

Of the less common spring-blooming species, the more important are *C. montanum*, which also blooms again in the fall; and *C. luteum*, the only yellow-flowered member of the genus.

COLDFRAME. A bottomless box placed on the soil or over a pit, in which plants can be started, grown, or stored. It can be covered with a more or less transparent top, frequently an old window sash, to develop and maintain warmth inside it; some solid protective cover can be used to keep out cold and withstand snow, or a slat or other type of screen can provide shade.

Standard dimensions are 6' x 12'; such a frame can be covered with a regulation sash, either glazed or made with one of the several glass substitutes available, which are lighter and not breakable, but less transparent. The length of a coldframe is set by the number of plants it is to hold and the space available. While the coldframe protects the plants and promotes their growth, the only heat it receives or supplies to them is that of the sun. If or when bottom heat is added, the unit is called a hotbed.

Coldframes can be used to start seedlings in advance of the outdoor season, though not so early as in hotbeds; to receive seedlings or other small plants shifted from hotbeds or greenhouses to flats or flowerpots, before they can be set in the open ground—that is, to "harden them off"; to shelter seedlings of hardy plants over winter until they can be planted outdoors in spring; to store hardy and semihardy plants during the winter months; to store hardy bulbs planted in flowerpots or flats during their root-forming periods; and to propagate plants from cuttings, especially during summer.

Coldframe

To be successful, a coldframe must be placed on a well-drained site in full sun or, for forcing purposes, in partial shade if protection during summer is wanted. Shade can be provided by screens of various kinds. It is important that protection from cold winds be supplied, either natural (as by woods or a hill) or artificial (as by a hedge, a fence, or a building). Nearness to the residence, greenhouse, or potting shed and to a supply of water is also important so the plants can be cared for without trouble. While cold-frames are often permanent features of commercial establishments, they can be temporary, movable aids at home. See BOTTOM HEAT; HOTBED.

COLEUS (KOH lee us). A genus of tender annual or perennial herbs belonging to the Lamiaceae (Mint Family). They have brilliantly variegated foliage, which surpasses that of other garden plants for color. Indispensable for grouping on lawns or for ribboning, very well adapted to window box culture, and suitable for potting and bedding, they grow luxuriant foliage of maroon, green, crimson, yellow, and combinations of these colors. The blue or lilac, spiked flowers are less important.

Native to Africa and the East Indies, they are easily cultivated in North American gardens and can be propagated by cuttings rooted in sand at any time. Growing coleus from seed, however, is fascinating, since the seedlings vary greatly in foliage design. Long branches should be pinched back to shape the plants gracefully.

The MEALYBUG, recognized by its soft, white, waxy covering, and WHITEFLY frequently infest the foliage and should be controlled as soon as they appear. Wilt or black-leg, caused by a fungus, may blacken the tissues of single stalks or rot the entire plant. See also DISEASE; GREENHOUSE PESTS.

C. amboinicus (Spanish-thyme), sometimes grown as a houseplant, has aromatic, hairy, fleshy, ovate leaves 1½–2½ in. long and small, pale purple flowers.

C. x hybridus, derived from *C. blumei* and other species, is the common garden or house foliage plant. Really it is a vast collection of subshrubby hybrids with slightly toothed, variously colored leaves and small, blue or lilac flowers.

COLLARDS. A form of kale growing 2–4 ft. high with coarse leaves, borne in tufts, and eaten like greens. Georgia collards, the standard variety, are grown mostly in the South, where seedlings are started like cabbage in late winter for spring use. In the North, for a fall crop, sow in midsummer. The plants are later set 3' x 4' apart and cultivated like cabbage. The name "collards" is also loosely applied to cabbage seedlings grown without transplanting, harvested before heads form, and used as greens. See BRASSICA; CABBAGE.

COLLETIA (koh LE tee ah). A genus of curious, almost leafless shrubs from South America, belonging to the Rhamnaceae (Buckthorn Family). They are remarkable for their odd appearance and stiff, spiny habit. They can be best grown in Zones 7–9 where frost is light. Propagation is by cuttings of side shoots taken with a heel.

C. armata has strong, straight spines and urn-shaped, waxy, white flowers late in the season.

C. paradoxa (anchor plant) has flattened branches with broad spines and small, creamy white flowers in autumn.

COLLINSIA (kah LIN see ah). A genus of attractive, free-blooming annuals in the Scrophulariaceae (Figwort Family), useful in rock gardens, bedding, and wild or meadow gardens, and commonly known as Chinese-houses. They are pretty, generally low, with bicolored flowers arranged in whorls around the stem. The whorl size is smaller at the top, giving a pagoda-like effect in some species, thus the common name. Seeds can be sown outside in the fall if the young plants can be well protected, but spring sowing is usually done in colder areas, as with most annuals. Plants prefer good drainage.

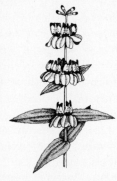

Collinsia heterophylla

PRINCIPAL SPECIES

C. bartsiaefolia is similar to *C. heterophylla* though generally paler in color.

C. heterophylla (Chinese-houses), the principal cultivated species, is a highly variable plant in the wild but is typically about 1 ft. tall and has four to six whorls of flowers with a purple lower lip and a white or lilac upper lip. Other color variants are white, white with lilac, red-purple with purple, etc.

C. tinctoria, a plant of stony slopes, has pale whitish to pinkish flowers on 6–12 in. stems in multiple whorls, with intricate markings and lines within the flower throat and unusual, white-splotched leaves.

C. verna (blue-eyed-Mary) is a hardy herb native from New York to Wisconsin and Kentucky, with blue and purplish flowers.

COLLOMIA (koh LOH mee ah). A genus of pleasing, easily grown annual and perennial herbs belonging to the Polemoniaceae (Phlox Family). Normally only annuals are grown in the garden. Plants start readily from seed, which should be sown where the plants are to stand.

C. cavanillesii, the showiest of the species, has scarlet flowers and grows to 2 ft. high.

C. grandiflora, with salmon-colored flowers, is a coarse annual that grows to 3 ft. and is suitable for use in the wildflower garden.

COLOCASIA (koh loh KAY zee ah). A genus of large-leaved tropical herbs of the Araceae (Arum Family). Hardy in Zones 10–11, some species are grown as garden subjects and display ornamental foliage, the large, heart- or shield-shaped leaves being sometimes 3 ft. long and commonly known as elephant-ear.

C. antiquorum is an ornamental species with very large leaves; in some varieties, these show margins and veinings of purple. This is probably the elephant-ear formerly known and sometimes still listed as *Caladium esculentum*.

C. esculenta (taro) is widely grown in warm climates, especially on islands of the Pacific, and was introduced in the United States by the Department of Agriculture. Their starchy tubers (also known as eddo) are cooked like potatoes. The edible sprouts (commonly called dasheen) are gathered outdoors in spring or forced and blanched in winter for use like asparagus.

COLORADO POTATO BEETLE. These convex, hard-shelled beetles, yellow with black stripes, grow from larvae that are soft and dark red with black spots and black heads. The eggs laid on the undersides of leaves are yellow. The pests are voracious eaters and can defoliate whole rows of plants when they get started. Besides potatoes, they infest eggplants, tomatoes, peppers, and petunias. This beetle used to be a more or less harmless, obscure insect on the plateaus near the Rocky Mountains, but when potatoes were introduced, it rapidly became a major pest. Now it also infests European countries but has been eradicated in England.

larva

adult

Colorado potato beetle

It winters as an adult in the ground, so a spring mulch will help to thwart it. Planting the seed potato pieces right in the mulch will also be helpful. A base of several feet of autumn leaves put on the potato patch to winter over can be used for planting potato pieces covered with a foot or more of hay. The emerging bugs cannot climb up through these mulches to get at the leaves of the plants. Bonemeal, compost, and other enrichments also help.

Companion plantings of horseradish, garlic, marigolds, and bush beans have also proved of some help. The weed *Solanum nigrum* (nightshade) is a good trap plant. Beneficial insects include lady beetles and parasitic tachinid flies. The San Diego strain of *Bacillus thuringiensis* will attack the larvae, as will juvenile-stage predatory nematodes. Adults can be sprayed with rotenone or a rotenone-pyrethrum combination. Floating row covers will be protection from all but the beetles emerging from directly below a particular plant. Extended vigilance is necessary because Colorado potato beetles feed as larvae for 21 days and continue as adults. Most chemical sprays have become basically useless, since the beetles have developed immunity to them.

COLOR IN THE GARDEN. Color is one of the the most striking aspects of garden design. The warm tones of yellow, gold, orange, and red attract attention to those sections of the garden where they are used. Blue and violet, on the other hand, create a quieter, more tranquil mood. Using warm colors makes a planting appear smaller than it actually is, while cool colors make it appear larger. For best results, keep color schemes simple, using more than one or two colors only in a bed of the same plant (zinnias or impatiens, for example).

There are a number of possible harmonies you can select, and these are easily measured on a color wheel. Choose complementary (opposite) colors such as orange and blue or violet with yellow. Split complementary color combines one color with the other to either side of its opposite; examples would be red with blue or red with yellow. Treat pink, a tint of red, the same way as red when designing, and treat violet the same way as purple. Analogus color harmony includes three colors in a row on the wheel, such as yellow, yellow-orange or gold, and orange. Monochromatic design uses different tones of the same color, such as pink and/or red geraniums. Select one harmony and stay with it throughout the bed or border for best effect.

White can blend well with any color or be effective alone. Like pastels, especially light pinks, white is most effective when viewed at night, since it reflects moonlight, streetlights, and garden lights. It is best used when massed alone or as a unifying border. Whites used as buffers between two conflicting colors can often make the design look spotty and disjointed. The same rules that apply to white-flowered plants also apply to white, silver, and gray foliage plants, such as the dusty millers.

COLUMBINE. Common name for AQUILEGIA, a genus of popular spring-flowering perennials, including one species that is the state flower of Colorado. Feathered-columbine is *Thalictrum aquilegifolium*, one of the meadow rues; see THALICTRUM.

COLUMN. A body formed by the union of the pistil with fertile or sterile stamens, which is characteristic of the orchid flower; also, the body formed by stamens alone, such as the tube formed by a union of stamens in the mallows.

COLUMNEA (koh LUM nee ah). A genus of tropical American, vinelike plants belonging to the Gesneriaceae (Gesnera Family). In cultivation they are usually grown in a warm greenhouse, either drooping in hanging baskets or upright, attached to a branch covered with fibrous peat.

The long stems hang vertically and, when in bloom, have a tubular, flaring flower at each node for a spectacular effect. At least 60 species are known from Central and South America, and new ones are frequently found, which means that specialist growers who are also producing hybrids have a great variety to offer.

COMFREY. Common name for SYMPHYTUM, a genus of perennial herbs with coarse, ornamental foliage.

COMMELINA (koh me LĪ nah). A genus of perennial herbs of the Commelinaceae (Spiderwort Family) with jointed stems, grasslike leaves, and short-lived flowers that are generally blue. Commonly called dayflowers, some are weedy, but others can be used as ground covers in the greenhouse or outdoors. Propagate by spring- or fall-sown seed or cuttings rooted over heat.

PRINCIPAL SPECIES

C. angustifolia grows in the southern United States and has blue flowers in purple sheaths.

C. diffusa (formerly listed as *C. nudiflora*), a creeping perennial with small, blue flowers. It is a useful ground cover and can be grown outdoors as far north as Zones 5–6, depending on the conditions. In Florida, it is the most important weed host for celery mosaic disease, hence all mottled or otherwise infected plants should be destroyed.

Two Mexican species, *C. coelestis* and *C. tuberosa*, both suitable for the greenhouse, develop tubers that can be divided.

COMMELINACEAE (koh mel in AY see ee). The Dayflower or Spiderwort Family, so called from the spiderlike appearance of the hairy flower stalks enclosed at the base by flat, sheathing leaves. Principal genera include *Commelina* (dayflower), *Dichorisandra*, *Rhoeo*, *Tradescantia* (spiderwort), and *Zebrina* (wandering-Jew).

COMPANION PLANTING. A term used to describe intercropping for the purpose of putting certain plants near others for mutual benefit, including pest control or the invigorating effect one plant can have on another. Beets and onions both do better growing next to each other, as do corn and pumpkins. There are also some planting combinations that make poor neighbors, such as beans and onions. Benefits include providing some shade, accommodating different root zones, attracting bees and other pollinators, and, through root exudates or aboveground emanations, attracting predators and parasites to control pests.

Companion planting also refers to the practice of growing two or more crops on the same plot of ground with different lengths of time to mature. By the time a short-season crop, like radishes, is ready to harvest, longer-season crops are ready to use the newly vacated space.

Legumes have root nodules containing rhizobial bacteria capable of fixing nitrogen from the air (as plants cannot) and transforming it into nitrates that plants can use. These are planted to provide fertilizer for neighbor plants as well as for themselves. Root vegetables are found to be helped by neighbor legumes.

Many gardeners have rediscovered the ancient habit of planting garlic at random through the garden to take advantage of its allyl sulfide. This substance has been found to kill aphids and onion flies, especially if the garlic is grown in a rich, humus soil that will support the fungi that produce the sulfur compound in the garlic.

Marigolds have also been proven to have powerful, lethal exudates from the roots of the aromatic varieties. They stop the tiny, root-sucking nematodes called eelworms so common in many gardens. Analyzed root exudates have revealed up to 35 compounds, ranging from amino acids, sugars, vitamins, and phosphates to alkaloids and tannins, any of which can have beneficial or repellent capabilities.

Both beneficial and harmful insects are influenced by odors, colors, the shininess of aluminum foil, or the invisible wavelengths coming from all kinds of plants, signaling their attractiveness for such purposes as places to lay eggs. Mutually beneficial influences are believed to exist between asparagus and tomatoes; beans and potatoes; sage, onions, thyme, or mint and plants of the Brassicaceae (Mustard Family). Borage is said to help tomato plants in many ways: attracting bees, deterring tomato worms, strengthening the growth of the plant, and improving the flavor of its fruit. Hot peppers are valuable planted among cabbages and other brassicas, as are catnip and nasturtiums. If planted in the hills with squashes, cucumbers, or pumpkins, nasturtiums will repel squash bugs and cucumber beetles. Horseradish as well as garlic, beans, and marigolds can be useful against the Colorado potato beetle and the corn earworm. Tansy, radishes, and the poisonous castor beans will deter cutworms from beans and brassicas. Turnips and radishes offer protection from harlequin bugs. Fennel, though disliked by many vegetables, will attract the parasitic little wasps that many gardeners buy for pest control.

Roses can be helped by garlic, chives, and plants with poisonous leaves such as rhubarb and elderberry, which have built-in self-protection. As many gardeners have observed, parsley, okra, endive, wormwood, and various Amaryllidaceae (Amaryllis Family) plants, including onions, also have self-protective qualities.

Many books on companion planting and organic gardening give lists of specific recommendations based on varying experiences of gardeners. Often there is the qualification that plants are so subject to conditions of soil, climate, location, and times of planting that the companion plant will not always produce the desired effect. See chart on following page.

VEGETABLE COMPANION GUIDE

	BEAN, BUSH	BEAN, POLE	BEET	CABBAGE	CARROTS	CELERY	CORN	CUCUMBER	EGGPLANT	LETTUCE	MELON	ONION	PEA	PEPPER	RADISH	SPINACH	SQUASH	STRAWBERRY	TOMATO	SPECIAL
Basil	-	-	-	-	-	-	-	-	-	-	-	-	-	X	-	-	-	-	X	-
Beans, bush	-	-	X	X	X	X	X	X	X	X	-	0	X	-	X	-	-	X	-	1
Beans, pole	-	-	0	-	X	-	X	X	X	X	-	0	X	-	X	-	-	-	-	2
Beets	X	-	-	X	-	-	-	-	-	-	-	X	-	-	-	-	-	-	-	-
Cabbage family	X	-	X	-	-	X	-	-	-	-	-	X	-	-	-	-	-	0	X	3
Carrots	X	X	-	-	-	-	-	-	-	X	-	X	X	-	X	-	-	-	X	4
Celery	X	-	-	X	-	-	-	-	-	-	-	X	-	-	-	X	-	-	X	-
Corn	X	X	-	-	-	-	-	X	-	X	-	X	-	-	-	-	X	-	0	-
Cucumber	X	X	-	-	-	-	X	-	-	X	-	X	X	-	X	-	-	-	-	5
Eggplant	X	X	-	-	-	-	-	-	-	-	-	-	-	-	-	X	-	-	-	-
Lettuce	X	X	-	-	X	-	-	X	-	-	-	X	-	-	X	-	-	X	-	-
Marigold	X	X	-	X	-	-	-	X	-	-	-	-	-	-	-	-	-	X	X	-
Melon	-	-	-	-	-	-	-	X	-	-	-	-	-	-	X	-	X	-	-	-
Nasturtium	-	-	-	X	-	-	-	X	-	-	X	-	-	-	X	-	X	-	X	-
Onion	0	0	X	X	X	X	-	X	-	X	-	-	0	X	-	-	X	X	X	6
Parsley	-	-	-	-	-	-	-	-	-	-	-	-	-	-	-	-	-	-	X	-
Peas	X	X	-	-	X	-	X	X	-	-	-	0	-	-	X	-	-	-	-	7
Pepper	-	-	-	-	-	-	-	-	-	-	-	X	-	-	-	-	-	-	-	-
Radish	X	X	-	-	-	-	-	X	-	X	X	-	X	-	-	X	-	X	-	8
Sage	-	-	X	X	X	-	-	0	-	-	-	-	-	-	-	-	-	-	-	-
Spinach	-	-	-	-	-	X	-	-	X	-	-	-	-	-	-	-	-	X	X	9
Squash	-	-	-	-	-	-	X	-	-	-	-	X	-	-	X	-	-	-	-	-
Strawberry	X	-	-	0	-	-	-	-	-	X	-	X	-	-	-	X	-	-	-	-
Tomato	-	-	-	X	X	X	0	-	-	-	-	X	-	-	-	-	-	-	-	10

X good companions   0 bad companions

SPECIAL COMPANIONS

1. savory, tansy
2. savory, tansy
3. all strong herbs
4. sage, no dill
5. no strong herbs
6. savory
7. turnips
8. no hyssop
9. cauliflower
10. mint, no fennel

COMPASS PLANT. Common name for *Silphium laciniatum*, a perennial grassland herb whose leaves point north and south; see SILPHIUM.

COMPOSITE. A composite flower is a compound flower or, more accurately, a head or compact assembly of many small flowers, surmounting or surrounded by leafy bracts forming the involucre. The small flowers can be all of one kind or of different kinds, such as the daisy, which is a typical composite flower. Here the central part is of tiny, tubular disk flowers, while the rim is of ray flowers, whose one strap-shaped petal is greatly enlarged. See also FLOWER.

The Compositae (Composite Family) is now called ASTERACEAE (Aster Family).

COMPOST. The product of a lively pile of organic materials where microorganisms decompose them into a safe, natural fertilizer, crumbly and dark brown like humus and free of disease, insects, and weed seeds. These are killed during the 140–150°F heat generated by the aerobic, oxidizing bacteria that work on the materials. The pile is made in alternating layers of carbon-rich materials, such as dry stalks, hay, and leaves; nitrogen-rich organic materials; and enough air and water to keep the microorganisms active and reproducing. The carbon to nitrogen ratio, when the pile is first made, is usually about 25 to 1; well-oxidized finished compost is about 8 to 1.

When added to the garden as fertilizer and soil conditioner, compost is of greater value than commercial nitrogen-phosphorus-potassium (N–P–K) fertilizer because it recycles and preserves many trace elements and biochemical ingredients needed for good plant growth as well as for the soil microorganisms and earthworms that make nutrients available to root hairs.

MAKING COMPOST

A compost pile, according to its classic model, is made by layering dry, absorbent materials alternately with layers of moist manure or other high-protein or nitrogen-rich materials followed by thin layers of soil or old compost. A handful of superphosphate or potassium-rich Sul–Po–Mag, greensand, granite dust, or a small amount of commercial fertilizer can be added to balance the N–P–K content. Calcium compounds are not recommended because they leach or may block formation of beneficial ion exchanges during the breakdown of complex materials into simpler compounds.

The pile is not usually more than 5 ft. high and 5 ft. wide, but the length can be any size that is convenient. These dimensions provide a width narrow enough for a person to reach over to fork and turn the materials while maintaining enough density to develop and hold the heat. Turning is advisable to allow more air into the heap for use by microorganisms and to allow all materials to be oxidized and thus heated up. If turned, a layered compost heap with or without a bin will be cured into finished compost in a matter of months. Unturned heaps, because part of the process will be anaerobic (without oxygen), will take a year or more. Very fast composting is possible by using plenty of high-nitrogen materials and turning the heap every day or so. Such a heap can make compost in a few weeks. Commercially obtainable tumblers, turned every day, make very good bins for fast composting.

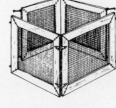
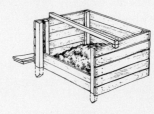

bricks   wire mesh   screen   wood

Compost bins

COMPTONIA (kahmp TOH nee ah) **peregrina.** A fragrant, deciduous, hardy native shrub belonging to the Myricaceae (Bayberry Family), commonly known as sweet-fern. Growing to 5 ft., it has finely cut, fernlike leaves and bears inconspicuous flowers in catkins. It is valuable chiefly as a ground cover or soil binder on dry, sandy slopes. It is particularly good in the wild garden when planted at the base of sumac bushes and is easily grown from seed, division, or layers.

CONE. A compact arrangement of stiff, somewhat leaflike scales beneath which the reproductive bodies are borne. Cones thus form the reproductive processes (or flowers) of the plants called gymnosperms. They are of two kinds, pistillate (female) cones bearing naked ovules and staminate (male) cones bearing sacs that contain pollen. The staminate cones are shed after pollination occurs, while the larger, pistillate cones usually become hard and woody and remain on the tree for some time.

CONEFLOWER. Common name for three genera belonging to the Asteraceae (Aster Family). See ECHINACEA; RATIBIDA; and RUDBECKIA.

CONEHEAD. Common name for STROBILANTHES, a genus of tropical herbs with colorful, cone-shaped flowers.

CONIFER. This is a descriptive term for a tree that bears woody cones containing naked seeds. Pines, hemlocks, firs, larches, etc., are familiar examples. Popularly, the term is used and supposed to refer to any kind of narrow-leaved evergreen, but actually some genera of conifers are deciduous, such as *Larix* (larch) and *Taxodium* (bald-cypress).

Conifers make up the most valuable softwood forests of the world, and they also include some of the most valuable plants used in landscape work, shrubbery borders, and rock gardens. The pines, hemlocks, spruces, firs, junipers, and cedars are used as windbreaks, in groves, as boundary outlines, for backgrounds, as speci-

mens and hedges, and in many other situations. They furnish a quiet note of green that frames or sets off the garden design, acting as an excellent foil for the contrasting texture of deciduous trees and shrubs and the brilliant bloom of smaller growing perennials, annuals, and other plants.

The coniferous genera most commonly used in gardening are, in the northeastern states, ABIES, CHAMAECYPARIS, JUNIPERUS, LARIX, PICEA, PINUS, PSEUDOTSUGA, TAXODIUM, TAXUS, THUJA, and TSUGA. In the South and West, various tender species of the above are used as well as ARAUCARIA, CEDRUS, CRYPTOMERIA, and SEQUOIA. There are many species and numerous varietal and horticultural forms that furnish a multiplicity of material from which the landscape architect and home gardener can choose.

Conifers require little pruning. All that is necessary is to nip out the central bud of lower branches in order to encourage a bushy growth. Many take kindly to severe, repeated shearing and therefore make excellent formal hedges or special garden features.

If the soil is well supplied with humus and the trees are consistently mulched, conifers require little fertilizer except an occasional application of well-rotted manure or bonemeal. Often it is better not to encourage rapid growth, since conifers that grow too rapidly are inclined to be spindly. Certain kinds, especially among the pines, are adapted to and do well in sandy or otherwise rather poor soils.

Conifers should be moved early in the spring, before the new growth starts, or in late summer or early fall after the season's growth has ripened. In transplanting, never allow the roots to dry out, and avoid injuring them, since this reduces the food- and moisture-obtaining mechanism. For this reason, balled and burlaped specimens are more likely to grow than specimens dug up in the field or woodlot, where the roots are less compact and much more likely to be injured. Plant firmly, loosening but not removing the burlap if needed to hold the soil around the roots. Fill the hole with good topsoil and water well when planting. Thereafter, water frequently until the plant is well established, and mulch with rotted leaves or peat moss for the first year or two. Propagation can be done by seed, cuttings, or grafting.

See also EVERGREENS.

CONIOGRAMME (koh nee oh GRAM uh). A genus of several strong-growing ferns native to tropical regions. The fronds are pinnate to bipinnate, and the naked sori follow the veins in a linear pattern. The rhizomes are short and creeping.

C. japonica (bamboo fern), also listed as *Gymnogramme japonica* is a good pot subject with a clumping habit. It is pinnate, 2–4 ft. tall, and has an attractive, light green herringbone pattern running along the center of each pinna. A form with a gold band in the center of each pinna also exists. It is found in China, Japan, South Korea, and Taiwan.

CONIUM (KOH nee um) **maculatum.** A coarse, biennial herb of the Apiaceae (Celery Family), sometimes called winter-fern but more often, poison-hemlock. All parts of the plant are poisonous, sometimes fatal when eaten; but it has a disagreeable taste and smell that make it unlikely to be consumed. This is the hemlock that the Greek philosopher Socrates is reputed to have taken with fatal results. Growing to 4 ft., it has finely cut leaves and small, white flowers in

Conium maculatum

compound umbels. It grows on rich, moist soils. A European herb, it is now naturalized in both North and South America (Zones 4–11) and is valued only as a source of medicine. To control weedy growth, cut rosettes below the surface and pull up. In England, the name "hemlock" refers to this plant, not the evergreen commonly known by that name in the United States and called spruce or hemlock spruce in Europe.

CONOCARPUS (koh noh KAHR pus) **erectus.** A small tree from the tropical American and west African coasts. The gray-green leaves, together with good salt tolerance, make it valuable for landscaping use in Zones 10–11. A silver-leaved variety, var. *sericeus*, is slightly smaller growing and equally useful in locations exposed to salt.

CONTACT POISON. An insecticide used against insects and other creatures, such as mites, that have sucking mouthparts and therefore cannot be controlled with a poison applied to the surface of the plant, but must have it come in direct contact with their bodies. Nicotine, pyrethrum, rotenone, sulfur, and some oils are used as contact insecticides, in either dust or liquid form. See INSECT CONTROL.

CONTAINERS. Various tubs, pots, jugs, and dishes that are suitable for growing plants; see FLOWERPOTS.

CONVALLARIA (kahn val AIR ee ah) **majalis.** A small, graceful, white-flowered herb, hardy and low growing; belonging to the Liliaceae (Lily Family) and commonly known as lily-of-the-valley. Native to Europe and Asia, this perennial is an old favorite both indoors as a potted plant and outdoors, where it often becomes naturalized. It has creeping, underground rootstocks and fleshy crowns, popularly known as "pips," which develop two oblong leaves and a solitary, one-sided spike of fragrant, small, white, bell-shaped blossoms that are excellent for small vase arrangements and are often used for corsages, bridal bouquets, and other decorative purposes.

The fleshy pips are bulblike in their construction and action; the flower embryo is actually present in all ripened, full-size specimens so that only water and moderate heat are needed for the development of flower stems. This makes *C. majalis* one of the most easily handled of all flowering plants and largely accounts for its great popularity.

Because of its beauty, ease of flowering, and availability over the whole year, lily-of-the-valley is also a favorite subject for house culture. Almost any container will do, and where the roots are too long for use in shallow bowls, they can be cut off to the extent of one-half their length without injury. A bowl 6 in. across will accommodate ten to twelve pips, which should stand in an upright position with the fleshy tips extending above the bowl; sand, sphagnum moss, or peat moss should be firmly pressed between and around the roots. Fill the container with lukewarm water and place it near a light window; if water is added as it evaporates to keep the moss or sand moist, the pips will flower in three or four weeks in usual room temperature.

For garden planting, pips should be planted either in late fall or very early spring. For best results, they need a cool, rather densely shaded spot and are perfectly hardy. They can be planted about 6 in. apart, for as soon as they are established, they will begin to propagate and spread over a larger area every year. The planting should be kept free from weeds and not crowded out by other subjects. Flowers can be cut freely, but any removal of the foliage before it has completely died down will interfere with the flower crop the following season.

CONVOLVULACEAE (kahn vul vyoo LAY see ee). The Morning-glory Family, a widely distributed group that is best known horticulturally as twining herbs but includes some erect herbs, shrubs, and rarely trees. The juice is characteristically milky; the flowers are often large and brightly colored, with petals united into a funnelform corolla with a flaring limb. Among the cultivated genera are *Convolvulus*, *Ipomoea* (which includes the common morning-glory and sweetpotato), and *Porana*. Some species are weedy plants, particularly the parasitic *Cuscuta* (dodder) and many species of *Convolvulus*, such as the field bindweed.

CONVOLVULUS (kahn VUL vyoo lus). A genus of annual or perennial herbs commonly known as bindweed. Named from the Latin word *convulvere*, meaning "to entwine," most are trailing or twining plants. They bear funnel-shaped flowers resembling those of the true morning glory (IPOMOEA), to which they are closely related, differing partly in that their flowers remain open all day. This genus lends its name to the Convolvulaceae (Morning-glory Family), and the plants are often listed in catalogs as morning-glory. Dwarf species can be used for bedding, for which they are excellent because they bloom all summer. The tall sorts are good for covering fences or walls, and the tender kinds are cultivated in greenhouses. The blue tones are the most satisfactory shade. A few may naturalize and become troublesome weeds.

C. arvensis (field bindweed) is an introduced, Eurasian, troublesome weed on rich, sandy or gravelly soils in Zones 3–8. It is propagated by seed and creeping roots, which can go down 20 ft. To control, cut as early as possible to prevent spreading.

C. tricolor (dwarf morning-glory), the most commonly cultivated species, is an annual growing 6–12 in. tall, covered with brown hairs, and often branching. The flowers are vibrant blue with a yellow-and-white throat.

COOLHOUSE. A greenhouse or section of one kept especially for growing plants that thrive best in temperatures ranging 35–40°F at night to not over 60°F during the day. Most enclosed porches or small lean-to conservatories answer to this description. Flowers thriving best under these temperature conditions include sweet peas, mignonette, violets, and hardy annuals or perennials grown from seed. Among the many potted plants doing well under similar conditions are old favorites like geraniums and fuchsias.

Some coolhouses are used entirely for carrying plants through their dormant seasons. Agaves, bay trees, some cacti, and other potted plants that cannot survive freezing temperatures outdoors find congenial winter quarters in a coolhouse. Where bench space is available, the coolhouse can even be used for starting extra-early, hardy vegetables, such as lettuce, cabbage, endive, or parsley. See also GREENHOUSE; HOTHOUSE.

COONTAIL. A common name for *Ceratophyllum demersum*, a useful freshwater aquarium plant; see CERATOPHYLLUM.

COONTIE. Common name for ZAMIA, a genus of palmlike tropical plants, especially applied to *Z. floridana* and *Z. integrifolia*.

COPPER BEECH. Common name for two cultivars of *Fagus sylvatica*, both deciduous beech trees with copper-colored foliage; see FAGUS.

COPPER COMPOUNDS. The most familiar form of these materials, used chiefly as fungicides, is BORDEAUX MIXTURE, which has been a standard since 1882 when its fungicidal value was discovered by accident in the vineyards of France.

When solutions of copper sulfate and hydrated lime are mixed, they form fine membranes that cover and protect the foliage. They are practically insoluble in water, but in the presence of a germinating fungal spore or bacterial thallus, they release enough toxic material to kill the disease organism.

COPPERLEAF. Common name for *Acalypha wilkesiana*, a tender shrub with colorful foliage, cultivated in warm regions and greenhouses; see ACALYPHA.

COPROSMA (koh PROHS mah). A genus of tender shrubs or small trees from Australia and New Zealand. The male and female flowers, borne on separate plants, have no decorative value; however, the foliage and colored berries are attractive. The plant can best be grown outdoors only in Zone 11 and warmer regions of Zone 10. Several selections of shrubs or small trees with different leaf colors or growth forms have been produced from the species most often grown, *C. repens* (mirror plant), formerly listed as *C. baueri*. Other cultivars of hybrid origin are used in California, but this useful hedge plant has not been successful in tests in the moist atmosphere of Florida.

COPTIS (KAHP tis). A genus of small, hardy perennial herbs belonging to the Ranunculaceae (Buttercup Family), commonly known as goldthread. The slender root fibers yield a rich yellow dye. White or yellow flowers are borne on long stalks. *C. groenlandica* and *C. trifolia* are hardy to Zone 2 and are sometimes planted in shady, damp places in peaty soil.

CORAL-BELLS. A common name for HEUCHERA, especially *H. sanguinea* and its hybrids, also known as allumroot.

CORALBERRY. A common name for *Symphoricarpos orbiculatus*, a hardy shrub with white flowers and purplish red berries.

CORAL PLANT. Common name for *Jatropha multifida*, a scarlet-flowered shrub or tree, see JATROPHA; also for *Russelia equisetiformis*, a rushlike shrub of the Scrophulariaceae (Figwort Family), see RUSSELIA.

CORAL TREE. Common name for ERYTHRINA, a genus of thorny tropical trees and herbs with showy flowers and pods.

CORALVINE. A common name for *Antigonon leptopus*, a tendril climber with handsome racemes of rose-pink flowers; see ANTIGONON.

CORDATE. Heart-shaped, particularly referring to a leaf. Compare OVATE.

CORDIA (KOHR dee ah). A large genus of tropical trees and shrubs, some vinelike, belonging to the Boraginaceae (Borage Family). A few may be found in greenhouse collections, or growing outdoors in Zones 9–11, many species blooming several times a year. They thrive in any light, rich soil and are propagated by seed and cuttings.

PRINCIPAL SPECIES

C. boissieri is a sprawling shrub or small tree with white flowers in terminal clusters. It is more cold hardy (to Zone 9) than other species, which are strictly for frost-free areas.

C. lutea is a sprawling shrub with an almost constant display of yellow flowers in terminal clusters.

C. sebestena (geigertree) is a large evergreen shrub or small tree of the Florida Keys. It has bell-shaped, orange-scarlet flowers in large terminal clusters.

CORDON. A fruit tree (usually dwarf) or shrub trained to one or more straight, unbranching stems that are supported upright, horizontally, or obliquely on a trellis or against a wall in a more or less geometrical design. The cordon is a simple form of ESPALIER. Its advantages for fruit trees are the saving of space and the production of superior fruit, which because it is borne close to the stems and receives adequate room and sunlight, develops to perfection. While all of the stone fruits can be so trained, the fruits most commonly handled in this way are apples and especially pears. See TRAINING PLANTS.

CORDYLINE (kor di LĪ nee). A genus of sparingly branched, upright shrubs of the Agavaceae (Agave Family). They are closely related to *Dracaena* and are used in much the same way in interiors and tropical landscapes. The long leaves are crowded at the top of the stems and gradually droop from an upright to a graceful hanging position.

Propagation is by tip cuttings of sections of stem rooted in a free-draining mix. Growth is best in a similar potting medium.

PRINCIPAL SPECIES

C. australis is an elegant, sparingly branched plant with slender leaves that arch out from the central new growth.

C. indivisa, formerly listed as *Dracaena indivisa*, is similar to *C. australis* but is somewhat stockier. It is relatively hardy but is mostly grown as a greenhouse ornamental or to plant vases and window boxes in colder regions. In one form, it is a familiar plant in subtropical bedding arrangements.

C. terminalis, formerly listed as *Dracaena terminalis*, has wide, sword-shaped leaves. Many cultivars have been developed, ranging in size from 'Baby Doll', with leaves less than 6 in. long, to some that grow to 20 ft. overall, with leaves 4 ft. long. The color range is equally great, from plain green, red-edged, variously red-sectored, vibrant maroon, to the almost black 'Black Prince', and tricolor red, yellow, and green of 'Kiwi'. The leaves are long lasting when cut and are useful for flower arrangements; it also makes a good greenhouse ornamental.

COREOPSIS (koh ree AHP sis). A genus of annual and perennial herbs belonging to the Asteraceae (Aster Family) and commonly known as tickseed. Ranging in height 1½–4 ft. and bearing flowers of yellow, orange, red, or brownish purple, they are grown as much for cutting as for their long season of garden decoration, blooming from early summer to frost. Both annuals and perennials succeed in any good soil and a sunny location. Several species native to the western states and formerly listed as *Leptosyne* have been moved to this genus.

The annual species, sometimes known as *Calliopsis*, provide some of the gayest, hardiest, and most easily grown of garden materials. Their yellow, maroon, crimson, and pink flowers on wiry stems make excellent bouquet material. They are not easily transplanted but are grown from seed started outdoors in spring. Plants should be thinned to stand 10 in. apart.

The perennial forms can be started from seed, from cuttings of growing wood taken in summer, or by divisions of the roots made in mid- to late spring. In the border they make a brilliant showing, the toothed petals forming a ring around a darker colored disk. Tall varieties are effective grouped with dwarf compact types as edgings.

PRINCIPAL SPECIES

C. basalis (goldenwave calliopsis), formerly listed as *C. drummondi*, grows to 12 in. and has 2-in. heads of golden yellow or brownish purple flowers especially good for cutting or bedding.

C. bigelovii, *C. californica*, and *C. stillmanii* are low annuals from the western states, with ferny rosettes of finely dissected foliage and showy displays of yellow daisies 2 in. across that bloom over a long season. Thriving in full sun and excellent drainage or sterile soils, they make attractive wildflower displays or meadows. Seed is best started indoors.

C. gigantea (giant coreopsis) is similar to *C. maritima*, but large, woody trunks growing to 4 ft. high give the plant a palmlike appearance in the spring and a bizarre appearance when dormant in summer.

C. grandiflora is a perennial species that grows to 2 ft. and has leafy stems and solitary heads to 2½ in. across with yellow ray flowers.

C. hamiltonii is similar to *C. bigelovii* but has smaller leaves and 1-in. flowers, blooms over a longer season, and is easily grown from seed.

Coreopsis grandiflora

C. lanceolata is a perennial with large, orange-yellow flower heads 2 in. across on long, graceful stems. Var. *flore-pleno* has double flowers. Hardy to Zone 6.

C. maritima (sea-dahlia) is a tender, short-lived perennial from the western states that has large clumps of finely dissected, succulent, ferny foliage from a woody base in the spring, followed by bouquets of large (4-in.), yellow daisies, then goes completely dormant for the summer.

Coreopsis lanceolata

It requires full sun and good drainage.

C. tinctoria (calliopsis) bears flowers of yellow rays with crimson-brown at the base and brownish purple disks. They grow taller than *C. basalis* and thrive in sunny borders.

CORIANDER. Common name for the flavoring herb *Coriandrum sativum*; see CORIANDRUM.

CORIANDRUM (koh ree AN drum) **sativum.** An annual herb of the Apiaceae (Celery Family), commonly known as coriander or cilantro. It is grown for its aromatic seeds which are used as one of the ingredients in curry powder and to flavor some liqueurs. The seeds are used in Latin American cooking, and the leaves, known as Chinese parsley, are used in Chinese cooking.

The seed is sown in early spring in rows about 12 in. apart. Seedlings should be thinned to 4 in.

Coriandrum sativum

apart; transplanting should never be attempted. Plants will grow about 2 ft. high. Leaves can be gathered at any point in their growth. In midsummer, ripened seed heads are gathered and dried on sheets, then beaten with flails or rubbed between the hands to separate the seeds.

CORIARIA (kor ee AIR ee ah). A small genus of herbs or shrubs grown chiefly for their ornamental berries. They grow well in good garden soil in a sunny location but are not hardy where frosts are severe.

C. japonica, the best-known species, is a shrub of medium height with pale green, frondlike stems and leaves. The bright red berries in summer later turn black.

C. terminalis is usually herbaceous and has black fruit. Var. *xanthocarpa* has translucent yellow berries that remain decorative for a long time.

CORK TREE. Common name for PHELLODENDRON, a genus of ornamental trees with attractive, aromatic foliage.

CORM. A shortened, fleshy, erect underground stem with inconspicuous, scalelike leaves. It closely resembles, and is often mistakenly called, a bulb (like the "bulbs" of gladiolus and crocus), but actually it is distinguished by being more definitely a modified stem. The stem character of bulbs is obscured by their very fleshy leaves.

From the prominent terminal bud and smaller ones in the axils of its scalelike leaves, corms develop new plants and often small subsidiary corms known as cormels. *Caladium*, *Colchicum*, and *Gladiolus* all grow from corms.

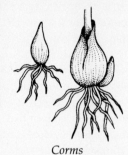

Corms

CORN. An annual American cereal grass, **Zea mays**, also known as maize. Its field varieties are grown for fodder and grain; the sweet kinds, for their ears of immature seeds; certain "popping" varieties, for making popcorn; and a few kinds as ornamentals, for their attractive foliage; see ZEA.

Sweet corn, **Z. mays** var. **rugosa**, is horticulturally the most important, being grown throughout the United States, Mexico, and Canadian border provinces. There are many varieties with differing characteristics, including color, size, or arrangement of seeds, as well as plant size and habit.

CULTURE

Sweet corn thrives best in warm, well-drained soils, especially those enriched by plowing under heavy clover sod or lavish dressings of manure. The soil can hardly be too rich, and the crop will not thrive in poor, thin soils without liberal feeding. In such places, a generous dressing of complete, quickly available, commercial fertilizer composed of nitrate of soda, muriate of potash, and superphosphate give fairly successful results.

Soil preparation is the same as for early spring garden crops but should be done immediately before seeding if possible. Since all varieties are tender, it is risky to have seedlings appear before the last spring frost. In the home garden, however, the satisfaction of occasionally pulling an extra early crop through is well worth the cost of seed and labor. Similarly, it is worth risking the loss of a late crop by sowing even after midsummer, if planting an early maturing variety that will reach an edible stage before the first frost. Sometimes a crop can be saved from an early frost by cutting and standing the stalks in shocks; many of the ears will continue to ripen to edible condition.

In the case of small plots, time can be gained by soaking the seed overnight, by sprouting it for a week before sowing, or by starting plants indoors, in hotbeds, in dirt bands or pots of clay or paper and transplanting to the garden after the weather has become settled.

Planting in hills for cultivation in both directions with a rotary tiller or garden tractor is suitable in large areas of rough, stony, or gravelly land, but in small plots and well-tilled soils, sow-

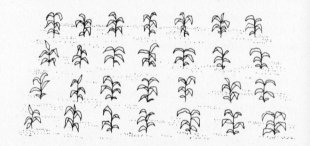

Block planting corn

ing in drills and leaving the plants of dwarf varieties 6–8 in. apart in the rows and spacing taller varieties 8–12 in. will yield the most and best corn with the least work, especially if a wheelhoe is used at weekly or ten-day intervals. The distance between the rows will depend on the size of the varieties and the tools used—from 18–24 in. for dwarf kinds to 30–36 in. for tall kinds. Corn must be planted in blocks of at least four rows to ensure pollination.

Popcorn. **Z. mays** var. **praecox**, is sown at the same time as the earliest sweet corn and given the same cultivation. It is allowed to mature fully and then is cut and shocked like field corn so it will dry out thoroughly. The ears are then removed, shucked, and stored in dry quarters such as a warm attic.

HARVESTING

Corn is ready for the table when shortly past the "milk stage," which is easily recognized after a little practice. The silks should be dry and black, and the husk leaves will have a characteristic appearance of maturity. In general, if the ear feels plump and firm when grasped, it is ready. For home use, it is better to harvest too young than too old.

In gathering, grasp the stem just below the ear with one hand and the ear with the other and twist in opposite directions. The ear will break off at a joint just below it. The shorter the time between gathering and serving, the better, because the sugars in the kernels rapidly change to other, less flavorful compounds. After gathering the last ear on a stalk, bend the stalk down and break or cut it off close to the ground. If left standing, it would use water and plant food to no purpose; cut while still green, it can be fed to livestock or used as the basis of a compost heap.

ENEMIES

The many diseases and insect pests are usually controlled on commercial crops by cultural methods, crop rotation, and the destruction of all refuse or waste materials that might harbor pests and disease. In the home garden, special efforts may be possible and well worthwhile.

DISEASE

Bacterial wilt known as Stewart's disease attacks all varieties of sweet corn but is most destructive on the early yellow types. Favored by high temperatures, it results in plants that are dwarfed, wilted, and dried up, looking as though they have been frosted. Small drops of yellow slime may ooze from the cut ends of stalks. The causal bacterium is carried in the seed and in old plant refuse and may be transmitted by the twelve-spotted cucumber beetle or by flea beetles. To avoid the disease, use seed from healthy plants. Where attacks are severe, plant late varieties. Seed of fairly resistant strains developed by crossing can be tried.

Corn smut caused by a fungus is usually seen wherever corn is grown as black swellings on ears and tassels. The first symptom is a pale, shining, swollen area. The white covering membrane becomes darker and finally bursts, releasing a powdery mass of black spores. Gather and burn smutted ears and stalks before this happens.

INSECT PESTS

The corn earworm, which is 2 in. long when full grown, begins to injure plants when the ears are in silk, continuing to be active until harvest time. Its presence is evidenced outside by moist castings on the silk. Inside the husk, the grains may be eaten down to the cob. Molds may follow the feeding of the larvae. The earworm may attack other plants, such as cotton, tomato, and tobacco. It can be controlled with mineral oil squirted into the silks while green, four or five days after the silks appear.

Bent or broken tassels indicate the presence of the well-known European corn borer, a

Preventing earworms

flesh-colored worm with fine, black dots, about 1 in. long when full grown. It attacks many herbaceous plants, especially corn, sorghum, smartweed, pigweed, and dahlias. Full-grown larvae hibernate in the cornstalks and stems of weeds, pupating in late spring. The yellowish brown moths, with irregular, wavy, dark bands, emerge from June to August and lay eggs on the undersides of the leaves. When the eggs hatch, in a week or less, the larvae soon bore into the leaves, leaf stems, stalks, and corn ears. In most infested regions, there is only one generation each year, but in New England there are two. The most effective control measure is to destroy all cornstalks and weeds in the fall, cutting the corn as close to the ground as possible, not leaving more than 2 in.

The southern corn rootworm is the larvae of the twelve-spotted cucumber beetle, which injures corn and other food plants, such as peanuts, beans, and cucurbits, in warm regions. The grubs feed on the roots and buds, boring through the crown at the base of the plant. Insecticides are futile against this rootworm stage but can be used to destroy the beetles as they feed on aboveground portions of the plants. Crop rotation helps to control this pest.

For other corn insect pests and their controls, see ARMY WORM; CHINCH BUG; CUTWORM; GRASSHOPPER;INSECT CONTROL; JAPANESE BEETLE; WIREWORM; GRUBS.

CORNEL. Common name for a few species of dogwood, including *Cornus canadensis* and *C. mas*; see CORNUS.

CORNELIAN-CHERRY. Common name for *Cornus mas*, the earliest-flowering species of dogwood; see CORNUS.

CORNFLOWER. Common name for *Centaurea cyanus*, an annual herb frequently cultivated for its attractive flowers; see CENTAUREA.

CORN-SALAD. Common name for *Valerianella locusta* var. *olitoria*, grown for use as a potherb or salad; see VALERIANELLA.

CORNUS (KOR nus). A genus of shrubs, trees, and a few herbs, including the principal members of the Cornaceae (Dogwood Family), and commonly known as dogwood. Among the most useful of hardy ornamentals, they are important for their flowers, twig colors, fruits, growth habit, and bark patterns. Native in temperate regions of the Northern Hemisphere, one or two are herbs, and some grow to be fair-sized trees, but most are free-growing shrubs. *C. florida* (flowering dogwood) is one of the most beautiful features of the early spring landscape in the Atlantic coastal

Cornus florida

otatoes and a favorite for garden planting wherever it will grow.

Dogwoods are adapted for many garden purposes and grow well in ordinary soil. For shady locations, few shrubs are better. The forms with colored stems are very effective in winter and grow, showing to good advantage, when grouped near water, especially if old wood is cut out every year.

Propagation is from fall-planted seed, which will germinate in the spring. Dogwoods will also grow from softwood cuttings. Shrub types can be reproduced by layering.

ENEMIES

While many species are relatively free of disease and insect problems, some (like *C. florida*) are not. Crown CANKER is the most serious disease. Symptoms are smaller, lighter green leaves, dieback of branches, cankers on trunks, and death of the tree. It is caused by the fungus *Phytophthora cactorum*, and there is no reliable cure.

Leaf spot, another fungal disease causing brown spots on the leaves, can be controlled by gathering and burning all leaves in the fall. See LEAF SPOT.

A serious disease has attacked *C. florida* in the eastern states. It is an airborne fungus that kills leaves, flowers, and branches in the spring, and trees ultimately die. It is worse in shady areas and during wet, humid weather. There is no control at present. Thousands of flowering dogwoods have died from this disease. Planting trees in sunny locations, watering during drought, mulching under trees, fertilizing, and good air circulation are beneficial preventive measures.

Borers have always been a problem on dogwoods. Keeping trees well fertilized, watered, and mulched is important in keeping borers away. Scale is sometimes a problem but can be controlled with an oil spray. See SCALE INSECTS; BORERS.

PRINCIPAL SPECIES

C. alba (Tatarian dogwood) is an upright shrub from western Asia, growing to 10 ft. and conspicuous with its blood red branches. Its flat heads of creamy white flowers are followed by clusters of white or bluish-tinted fruits. Var. *sibirica* is a less vigorous grower with coral-red branches. Good variegated leaf forms are cv. 'Argenteo-marginata', with leaves edged white; 'Gouchaultii', with leaves variegated yellowish and pink; and 'Spaethi', with leaves broadly edged yellow. Hardy to Zone 3.

C. alternifolia (pagoda dogwood), found from New Brunswick to Georgia, is a handsome, large shrub or small tree whose whorled branches in horizontal tiers give it a distinctive appearance. It has dark blue fruits.

C. amomum (silky dogwood), found from Massachusetts to Tennessee, is a vigorous shrub with purple branches. It has yellowish flowers and blue or partly white fruits. Leaves have hairy or silky undersides.

C. canadensis (bunchberry, dwarf cornel) is a native herb that grows only a few inches high. It requires a cool, rich soil in a partly shaded place and is often slow in getting established in gardens. It has a whorl of about six leaves, from the center of which

Cornus canadensis

come the tiny, greenish flowers surrounded by four to six white bracts. Later it bears round, scarlet berries in tight clusters.

C. capitata, a tender species from the Himalayas, is a partly evergreen, large shrub or small tree with pale yellow bracts and strawberrylike fruits.

C. controversa is the Asiatic form of *C. alternifolia*, growing much larger and flowering several days earlier.

C. florida (flowering dogwood), found from Massachusetts to Florida, is one of the most beautiful of small trees. It is handsome in early spring with its four white, blunt-ended bracts surrounding the dense heads of small, greenish flowers, and again in fall with scarlet fruits and gorgeous leaf coloring. The flower buds are conspicuous

all winter. There are many beautiful cultivars now available.

C. kousa (kousa dogwood) is a large shrub or small tree from Asia, blooming in early summer with showy, white, pointed bracts. This is a spectacular tree in bloom, with flowers in flat sprays above the horizontal branches of green leaves. With age, it develops a fine exfoliating, mottled bark pattern. Edible fruits on 1-in. stems are the size and color of a large raspberry. Fall color is a showy reddish purple or scarlet. It should be planted below eye level to really appreciate its beauty. It is usually disease and insect free. Cv. 'Milkyway' produces many more flowers and fruit.

C. mas (cornel, cornelian-cherry) is a large Asian and European shrub or small tree, conspicuous as the earliest spring-flowering species with small, yellow clusters opening and fading before the appearance of the lustrous leaves, which remain green until late in the fall. It bears large, red, edible fruits in late summer. The bark is of close texture and is dark colored, remaining on the trunk for several years. It is valuable in shady locations and tolerates dry soil better than most dogwoods. Cv. 'Aureo-elegantissima' has leaves variegated creamy white and pink. Hardy to Zone 5.

C. nuttalli, native in western North America, is the giant of the dogwoods, growing to 75 ft. or more, and is considered the most beautiful of the genus, bearing four to six white or pinkish bracts and bright red or orange fruit. It is not hardy in cold regions.

C. officinalis, the Asiatic form of *C. mas*, is hardy in Zone 5. It differs most noticeably in the bark, which is reddish and peels into papery shreds about the second year.

C. racemosa is a gray-branched shrub of dense habit with white flowers in early summer. In fall, its appearance is striking, with white fruits (which are attractive to many birds) on red stems, the latter remaining colorful long after the fruits have gone. Hardy to Zone 4.

C. sanguinea (blood-twig dogwood) is a European species with dark red branches, greenish white flowers, and black fruits. Cv. 'Viridissima' has green branches and fruits.

C. sericea (red-osier dogwood), found from Newfoundland to Virginia, spreads by underground stems. It has dark red branches and white or bluish fruits. Cv. 'Flaviramea' is outstanding in winter with its yellow branches. Hardy to Zone 3.

COROKIA (koh ROH kee ah). A genus of evergreen shrubs native to New Zealand and belonging to the Cornaceae (Dogwood Family). They are easily grown in good garden soil but are hardy only where frosts are light (to Zone 9). The small, yellow, fragrant flowers opening in spring are followed by orange or red berries.

C. cotoneaster, the most attractive species, has wiry, interlaced branches; small leaves, whitish beneath; and bright yellow, star-shaped flowers.

COROLLA. The inner set of floral leaves or petals, which are of delicate texture, usually brightly colored, and often scented. See FLOWER.

CORONA. In a flower, an outgrowth of the receptacle forming a crown around the stamens, on or just inside the corolla, like the conspicuous cup of the daffodil or the fringed crown of the passion flower; or an outgrowth of stamens united to form a tube, like the hood crowning the stamen tube of the milkweeds. See FLOWER.

CORONILLA (kor oh NIL ah). A genus of shrubs and herbs from the Mediterranean region and western Asia, belonging to the Fabaceae (Bean Family). The shrubby species, deciduous or evergreen, are very attractive in form, with pinnate leaves and tufts of yellow flowers. They grow well in sandy loam in a warm, sunny place but are not entirely hardy where frosts are severe. Others are naturalized and hardy in Zones 3–9.

PRINCIPAL SPECIES

C. emerus (scorpion-senna) is a medium-sized shrub, deciduous or evergreen according to climate. It has abundant yellow, pealike, red-tipped flowers from late spring to midsummer.

C. valentina var. *glauca* is an attractive evergreen of medium height, with glaucous leaves and fragrant, clear yellow flowers produced over a long season.

C. varia (crown-vetch) is a straggly European herb with pinkish white, pealike flowers borne in dense heads and blooming all summer. Naturalized in some states, it is most effective as a ground cover, growing to 2 ft. high. It is very hardy and attractive, now widely used on sunny slopes along highways and banks for erosion control.

Coronilla varia

CORREA (KOR ee ah). A genus of tender Australian shrubs belonging to the Rutaceae (Rue Family). They are good decorative plants for the greenhouse, making shapely, free-flowering specimens. Plants grow best in a mixture of fibrous peat and sharp sand, and the shoots need pinching to induce a good, bushy growth. Propagation is by cuttings or by grafting.

C. alba is a relatively compact grower with small, white flowers. It is good stock on which to graft the showier kinds.

C. reflexa, formerly listed as *C. speciosa*, is the best-known species. It is a slender grower and profuse bloomer with nodding tubular flowers of scarlet with yellowish green tips. There are several good forms.

CORTADERIA (kor tuh DEE ree uh). A genus of tall-growing, perennial grasses called pampas grass, native to South America, and one of the showiest of the ornamental varieties. The long, silky plumes, borne in late summer, remain beautiful for many weeks. They can be cut and dried for winter house decoration as soon as they are fully developed. Cortaderias are very similar to members of the genus GYNERIUM.

Pampas grass thrives in a rich, light, sandy soil in a sheltered position among shrubs or on the

lawn. It is not hardy in the North but can be grown there as an annual, from seed sown under glass in spring. Seedlings are first transplanted to a coldframe for hardening and then, when 1–2 ft. high, to their perma-
nent location. In warm re-gions, clumps can be divided. See also ORNA-
MENTAL GRASSES.

C. rudiuscula grows to 6 ft. and has leaves to 4 ft. long and purple or yellow panicles.

C. selloana grows to 20 ft. and has very long

Cortaderia selloana

leaves about ¾ in. wide and white or pink panicles. Cv. 'Rosea' has pink plumes.

CORTICIUM.
A minute, partially saprophytic fungus, the cause of the rhizoctonia disease of potatoes, and one of the fungi causing damping-
off in seedlings and also stem and root rot. Plants in the garden most likely to be attacked belong to the Pink, Mustard, Bean, Nightshade, and Aster families. To discourage attacks of this fungus in seedbeds, water from below, provide excellent ventilation without drafts, and spread a thin layer of dry sand over the surface of the soil between the seedlings. See also DISEASE; FUNGUS; and discussions of specific plants.

CORYDALIS
(koh RID al is). A genus of herbs belonging to the Fumariaceae (Fumitory Family) with interesting, irregular, yellow, blue, purple, or rose flowers resembling those of a bleeding-
heart. They are easily cultivated in any ordinary garden soil but prefer partial shade. Propagation is by seed or division, and in some species, by tubers. Most are hardy in Zones 4–9.

PRINCIPAL SPECIES
C. cava var. *albiflora*, growing 6–8 in., is a spring-flowering species with pure white flowers. Its foliage dies back in summer.

C. lutea, growing to 9 in., blooms in spring and autumn. Well suited to the border, wall, or rock garden, it produces great profusions of stems that bear clusters of tubular, yellow flowers.

C. nobilis (Siberian corydalis) grows to 30 in. and has white blossoms with purple margins. It tends to die back after flowering.

C. sempervirens is an annual that occasionally grows 2 ft. high and has brilliant pink-and-yel-
low flowers.

C. thalictrifolia, a perennial that grows 1

Corydalis nobilis

ft., has yellow flowers in spreading racemes and delicately cut foliage like that of a meadow rue.

CORYLOPSIS
(koh ri LAHP sis). A genus of decid-
uous shrubs belonging to the Hamamelidaceae (Witch-hazel Family) and commonly known as winter-hazel. Native to China and Japan, they are cultivated for ornament. It has delicately scented, yellow flowers borne in nodding clusters and opening in early spring, before the leaves appear. They thrive in a light, rich soil. Where winters are severe, they do best in a pro-
tected location; hardy in Zones 6–8. Propagation is by seed or layers.

PRINCIPAL SPECIES
C. glabrescens is the hardiest of the genus, doing well to Zone 5. It grows to 15 ft. with fragrant, pale yellow flowers appearing in spring.

C. gotoana, with pale yellow flowers, is the largest grower and hardier than most.

C. pauciflora is a spreading shrub that grows to 6 ft. It has pale yellow flowers, larger than other species. Hardy to Zone 6.

C. spicata has heart-shaped leaves about 4 in. long and early-blooming, bright yellow flowers. It is one of the most beautiful deciduous shrubs.

CORYLUS
(KOR il us). A genus of hardy deciduous shrubs or small trees belonging to the Betu-
laceae (Birch Family) and commonly known as hazel, hazelnut, or filbert. They are native to the northern temperate regions of North America,

Europe, and Asia and have long been cultivated for their edible nuts. Some species are grown for their ornamental foliage, which may be colorful all year or turns yellow or red in the fall. The golden yellow male flowers in pendulous catkins are also attractive in early spring. They thrive in any good, well-drained soil and are propagated by seed, suckers, layers, budding, and grafting.

PRINCIPAL SPECIES

C. americana (American hazelnut), a large shrub or small tree growing to 25 ft., is the common native species.

C. avellana (European hazelnut, cobnut) is a bushy shrub growing to 15 ft., occurring in many varieties and long cultivated for its nuts. Distinctive forms are cv. 'Aurea', with yellow leaves, and 'Contorta', with twisted and curled branches.

C. colurna (Turkish hazel) is a southern European tree that forms a handsome, pyramidal head and sometimes grows to 80 ft. tall.

C. cornuta (beaked hazelnut) is a native shrub that grows to 10 ft. and is conspicuous in fruit, with the bristly involucre constricted above the nut to form a long beak.

C. maxima (filbert) grows to 30 ft. and has many varieties grown for the large nuts. Cv. 'Purpurea' is an ornamental form with dark purple leaves. Removing a portion of the old growth each spring induces young growth, which produces larger and better-colored leaves.

C. sieboldiana (Japanese hazelnut) is a large bush that grows to 15 ft. and has young leaves often marked reddish in the middle. The nuts are enclosed in a bristly, constricted involucre.

CORYMB. A broad, more or less flat cluster of short-stalked flowers, the outer ones blooming first. The blossoming progresses toward the center of the cluster. Contrast CYME.

CORYPHA (KOR if ah). A genus of about eight species of monocarpic palms native to tropical Asia and Australia. Two are occasionally cultivated in Zones 10–11, where they require a fertile, moist soil with ground limestone added. They are seldom grown as greenhouse plants.

C. elata (Gebang or Buri palm) grows to 60 ft. or more and matures to flowering stage in 30 to 80 years.

C. umbraculifera (talipot palm) is a tree native to Ceylon and the Malabar coast. Growing to 80 ft., it has a stout, ringed trunk and spines found only on the stalks. The palmate leaves are 12–16 ft. across, very lightweight, and easily folded up like a fan. After reaching maturity, at 20 to 80 years, the tree produces clusters of creamy blossoms, the largest inflorescences found in the plant kingdom.

COSMOS (KAHZ mohs). A genus of tall annual herbs native in Mexico and Central America, belonging to the Asteraceae (Aster Family). They have feathery foliage and single or double blossoms with broad, silky rays, usually white to rosy lilac or yellow to scarlet. Ranging 1–10 ft. high, they are grown for late summer bloom in the tall border, where the late-flowering species withstand first frosts.

They thrive in average soil but prefer a light, rather poor texture and flourish in either sun or partial shade. Cosmos should be started from seed outdoors in mid- to late spring and covered to a depth of ¼ in. When the plants are 3 in. tall, thin out to not less than 2 ft. apart. As they reach a height of 2 ft., pinch the tops so they will branch out. Frequent cultivation around the base of plants is beneficial as long as it is not deep

Cosmos support

enough to injure the roots. To support a group of tall cosmos, place three or four stakes around the plants and circle them with a cord.

Stem blight attacks mature plants (both indoors and out), but not young ones. Infection appears first as small, brown spots, which gradually enlarge until the stem is girdled, after which the parts above suddenly wilt and die. Remove diseased branches as they appear, and in autumn, pull up and burn all plants and plant parts. Wilting of plants may also follow injury caused by the STALK BORER.

PRINCIPAL SPECIES

C. bipinnatus, the most cultivated species, is extremely tall, sometimes growing to 10 ft., bearing white, pink, lilac, or crimson flower heads 3 in. across with yellow disks. There are early and late, single or double forms.

C. diversifolius is a low, tuberous-rooted perennial, reaching 16 in., usually grown as an annual. The velvety, red rays, with red disks, are sometimes tinged dark purple.

Cosmos bipinnatus

C. sulphureus, growing to 6 ft., has 3-in. heads of pale yellow rays and darker yellow disks.

COSTMARY. Common name for *Chrysanthemum balsamita*, a coarse perennial with yellow disk and white ray flowers; see CHRYSANTHEMUM.

COSTUS (KAWS tus). A genus of strong-growing, soft plants belonging to the Zingiberaceae (Ginger Family). The common name, spiral ginger, describes the arrangement of the leaves around the stem, which is accentuated by spiraling of the stem itself. In most species, the flowers are large and showy but open only one or two at a time from a pinecone-like set of bracts at the top of the leafy stems. Some have leaves that are deep red and bluish green below. All are interesting plants for the tropical garden or northern greenhouse if there is enough room to spare. They are heavy feeders, but not particular as to soil.

COTINUS (koh TĪ nus). A genus of small trees or shrubs belonging to the Anacardiaceae (Cashew Family) and commonly known as smoketree. They thrive in well-drained, not too rich soil and are propagated by seed or cuttings.

C. coggygria (European smoketree), native from southern Europe into China, produces a smoky effect. It is a bushy shrub that grows to 15 ft. and is outstanding in summer with large panicles of feathery, filmy fruiting panicles. The foliage takes on good coloring in the fall. Hardy in Zones 5–8.

C. obovatus (American smoketree, chittamwood) is native to the southern states but is fairly hardy in sheltered locations in Zones 5–8. It is a large shrub or small tree that grows to 30 ft. or more and has rounded, 6-in. leaves. Its fruiting panicles make very little show, but it is one of the most brilliant woody plants in fall when the leaves turn orange and scarlet.

COTONEASTER (koh toh nee AS tur). A genus of deciduous or evergreen shrubs found in the temperate regions of Europe, northern Africa, and Asia (mostly in China), belonging to the Rosaceae (Rose Family). Most of them are hardy to Zone 5 and rank among the most useful of shrubs for ornamental planting. They are outstanding for their attractive habit of growth and colorful fruits. A few white-flowered species are conspicuous in bloom, and in some the foliage takes on brilliant coloring in the fall. All kinds thrive in an open, sunny location and well-drained soil. In general, plants from pots are the most easily established. Propagation is effected by seed, cuttings, and layers. Many cotoneasters make excellent ESPALIER plants.

The sudden death and blackening of shoots from the tips may be due to the bacterial disease FIRE BLIGHT. To control, carefully remove all infected branches, dipping pruning shears in a disinfectant after each cut, and cut back to several inches below the visibly affected portion. The small, circular, dark gray SAN JOSÉ SCALE is frequently present. See also INSECT CONTROL; SCALE INSECTS; SPRAYING.

PRINCIPAL SPECIES

There are many species, of which the most important for garden use can be divided into four groups according to their size, growth patterns, and other characteristics.

DWARF SHRUBS

These include dwarf or prostrate growers of spreading habit with small, dark green, sometimes evergreen leaves and red fruits. They are good for planting on slopes and in rock gardens.

C. adpressus grows to 18 in., the stems often rooting. It has pink flowers and the leaves turn dark red in the fall. Hardy in Zones 5–7.

C. dammeri is a creeping evergreen with white flowers and long, trailing branches that root as they grow. Hardy in Zones 6–8.

C. horizontalis (rock cotoneaster) has a distinct, two-ranked habit of branching. It makes a good wall plant and is effective when sprawling over a boulder in the rock garden. It has pinkish flowers. Var. *perpusillus* is a handsome, even more dwarfed form, but is very susceptible to fire blight. Hardy in Zones 5–7.

C. microphyllus (rockspray) is a dwarf evergreen shrub with dense, spreading habit, small, white flowers, and abundant red berries. It is a good rock garden plant; hardy in Zones 6–8.

LARGE SHRUBS

These have white flowers and red fruits.

C. frigidus grows to 20 ft. and is one of the most beautiful in flower and fruit. It does well on the West Coast but is not hardy in the North.

C. hupehensis is a medium-sized shrub of graceful habit with conspicuous clusters of flowers in spring and large, bright red berries that drop in early fall. The leaves remain green late and finally turn yellow. Hardy in Zones 6–8.

C. multiflorus is similar to *C. hupehensis* in appearance but is not very free fruiting; in this respect, var. *calocarpus* is better than the type. Hardy in Zones 4–7.

C. pannosus, an outstanding species, grows to 6 ft. and has graceful, arching branches and leaves white beneath. Hardy in Zones 7–8.

C. racemiflorus is a spreading shrub that grows to 8 ft. Var. *soongoricus* is one of the showiest, with pink fruits. Hardy in Zones 4–7.

C. salicifolius is often regarded as the best of the tall evergreen species, with dark green, leathery leaves and flower clusters about 2 in. across. A fine espalier plant, this species has a lovely arching habit and is very showy in flower and fruit. Hardy in Zones 6–8.

RED-FRUITED TYPES

These species have reddish flowers and red fruits.

C. bullatus is a broad, round-topped bush, the tallest of the red-fruited kinds. Var. *floribunda* has arching branches and abundant fruit.

C. dielsianus is similar to *C. divaricatus* but is of a looser habit, with arching branches to 10 ft. Hardy in Zones 6–8.

C. divaricatus makes a dense, wide-spreading bush to 6 ft. and has shining, dark green leaves. Hardy in Zones 5–7.

C. franchetii is a densely branched, upright evergreen of graceful habit and with orange fruit. Hardy in Zones 6–8.

C. zabelii is a medium-sized shrub with slender, arching branches and dull green leaves that turn yellow in the fall. Var. *miniatus* has orange-red fruits and is one of the outstanding berried shrubs. Hardy in Zones 5–7.

BLACK-FRUITED TYPES

These species have reddish flowers and black fruits, and are the least showy in fruit. Some are desirable for their good, vigorous growth and often brilliant leaf coloring in the fall.

C. foveolatus is a vigorous grower, outstanding in fall when its leaves turn orange and scarlet. Hardy in Zones 5–7.

C. lucidus is a strong, upright grower and good hedge plant, holding its lustrous green leaves until late in the season. Hardy in Zones 4–7.

COTTON. Common name for GOSSYPIUM, a genus of tropical shrubs or woody herbs that produce the commercial fiber. Lavender-cotton is *Santolina chamaecyparissus*; see SANTOLINA.

COTTON FERN. Common name for *Notholaena newberryi*, a western native fern whose feathery fronds have a powdery surface.

COTTON ROOT ROT. A fungal disease that attacks cotton and other plants in arid parts of the Southwest. See DISEASE; FUNGUS.

COTTONWOOD.   A common name for POPU-LUS, a genus of hardy deciduous trees; especially for *P. deltoides* and related native species.

COTULA (KOH tyoo lah). A genus of annual or perennial herbs native in the Southern Hemisphere and belonging to the Asteraceae (Aster Family).   One or two species are sometimes grown in rock gardens for their low mats of interesting foliage. They need a light, sandy soil and are propagated by seed and division. Hardy to Zone 8.

C. *dioica* has stems about 1 ft. long and small, dark green, somewhat divided leaves and small heads of pale yellow flowers. It has been popular in carpet bedding.

C. *squalida* has soft, hairy stems and much-divided, fernlike leaves.

COTYLEDON (kah teh LEE dun). A genus of small, succulent southern African shrubs in the Crassulaceae (Orpine Family). *Cotyledon* once included the genus *Echeveria* from Mexico and has recently been reduced even further by separation of the genus *Tylecodon* (the name is an anagram) on the basis of deciduous leaves with alternate arrangement, whereas the leaves of *Cotyledon* are evergreen, their arrangement decussate—that is, opposite in pairs. Among the most interesting and attractive species are C. *undulata*, with pairs of powdery white leaves with wavy margins, and C. *tomentosa*, with fuzzy, green leaves and orange flowers. Old standbys such as C. *paniculata* and C. *reticulata* are now generally accepted in *Tylecodon*.

COTYLEDON LEAF. The first leaf of a germinating plant, commonly called a "seed leaf" because it exists in embryo form inside the seed before the plant has begun to grow. The number of cotyledons present in a seed is used to divide flowering plants into two classes: Monocotyledoneae, with one cotyledon, and Dicotyledoneae, with two cotyledons. They contain stored food and nourish the young seedling until it has developed true leaves.

COUCH GRASS. Common name for some species of the genus AGROPYRON, including some weeds and valuable forage crops.

COUPLET FERN. Common name for *Dennstaedtia bipinnata*, a large, leathery fern from tropical rain forests; see DENNSTAEDTIA.

COURGETTE. Common name in Great Britain for *Cucurbita pepo*, the green squash, which is better known in the United States as ZUCCHINI; see also CUCURBITA.

COVER CROP. Any crop sown toward the close of the growing season, either where a temporary crop has been harvested or between permanent plants, to cover the ground until early spring. It benefits the garden in several ways. It prevents the loss of surface soil and plant food, especially on slopes, through erosion. It prevents the leaching of soluble plant foods, which are taken up in the plants and returned when the crop is turned under.

Crops that hold their leaves through the fall and winter add humus to the soil if turned under in spring. It checks growth of weeds and encourages ripening of woody plants from midsummer on by using up available plant food. It can increase the supply of available nitrogen in the soil, especially when a legume or other nitrogen fixer is grown. It can reduce the supply of available nitrogen and check woody growth if a nitrogen-consuming crop is grown. Winter cover crops prevent or reduce the effects of alternate freezing and thawing that may damage crop roots.

In vegetable gardens, a cover crop can be sown broadcast among the rows or growing crops any time after midsummer. Though much of it may be destroyed in harvesting the late crops, what survives will be worth more than its cost. A cover crop should always be turned under in spring while still green and succulent; otherwise the work is harder to do and the crop breaks down and decays slowly.

See also GREEN MANURE.

COWBERRY. Common name for *Vaccinium vitis-idaea*, a creeping evergreen shrub with dark red berries; see VACCINIUM.

COW HERB. Common name for *Vaccaria pyramidata*, a pink-flowered annual herb, also called cow-soapwort; see VACCARIA.

COWLILY. Common name for NUPHAR, a genus of aquatic herbs similar to waterlilies.

COW-PARSNIP. Common name for HERAC-LEUM, a genus of herbs with large flower clusters.

COWPEA. A tender annual legume from Asia, *Vigna unguiculata*, with several varieties ranging from bushlike to trailing, not climbing, vines. As a farm crop it is grown chiefly in the South for forage and GREEN MANURE. In the North it is often grown in the summer for green manure, being sown in spring after danger of frost has passed, and plowed or dug under when the ground is needed, but in any case before pods form. Since it grows rapidly, it can thus be used to follow crops of early-maturing vegetables, such as radishes, spinach, or lettuce, as a soil-improving measure. Sow 1 oz. to 25–30 sq. ft. broadcast on small areas, or drill in at the rate of about five pecks per acre on larger spaces. See also VIGNA.

COWSLIP. A common name of Anglo-Saxon origin, associated with several plants of different families. The most common and accepted use is for *Primula veris*, a yellow primrose from Europe; see PRIMULA. *Caltha palustris* (marsh-marigold), whose flowers have showy sepals but no petals, is also called cowslip. American-cowslip is DODECATHEON, a genus of perennials with spurred flowers. Cape-cowslip refers to LACHENALIA, a genus of lilylike herbs. Virginia cowslip is *Mertensia virginica*, a popular garden herb with drooping, blue flowers; see MERTENSIA.

CRAB APPLE. Common name for various species of shrubs and trees of the genus MALUS, also known as crab apples, and planted for their showy flowers or fruits, or both. All do well in the northern United States and adjacent Canada, but not in the South, except in the mountains. They constitute one of the most useful spring flowering groups or ornamentals. Their culture, training, and pruning are much the same as those of the apple.

Both wild and cultivated varieties are susceptible to FIRE BLIGHT. The wild crab, *Malus coronaria*, was probably the first host of the apple and cedar rust, but Bechtel's crab (*M. ioensis* cv. 'Plena') is always severely rust-ed when grown in close proximity to red cedar.

Crab apples

Since crab apples are subject to most of the insect pests attacking apple trees, wild crabs near an apple orchard should be cut down to remove sources of infestation.

Most crab apple trees bear fruit, although a few are sterile. The fruit of any of the species can be used in jelly, each species and variety having a more or less distinctive flavor, although some produce fruit so small it is hardly worth the trouble. Many of the cultivars have attractive red, pink, or purple blooms, and some, such as the dolgo crab, *M. dolgo*, have fairly large fruits. Choose a kind that is resistant to scab, so as to minimize spraying, and for small lots, one that is grafted on dwarfing roots.

SELECTIONS

Carmine crab, *M.* x *atrosanguinea*, grows to 15 ft. and has unfading, deep rose blossoms.

Chinese apple or ringo crab, *M. prunifolia* var. *rinkii* grows to 15 ft. and has white blooms.

Chinese flowering crab, *M. spectabilis*, grows to 25 ft. and has extra large, pink or rose-colored flowers.

Garland or sweet crab, *M. coronaria*, grows to 30 ft. with large, rose flowers changing to white.

Hall crab, *M. halliana*, grows to 18 ft. and has large, deep rose flowers.

Japanese flowering crab, *M. floribunda*, grows to 25 ft. and has profuse, large, red flowers, paling to almost white.

Prairie crab, *M. ioensis*, to 30 ft., has white or bluish flowers and is the latest to bloom.

Rivers crab is a variety of *M. spectabilis*, with double pink flowers.

Sargent crab, *M. sargentii*, grows only 6 ft. and bears large, white flowers.

Siberian crab, *M. baccata*, to 40 ft., has small, white flowers.

Siebold or Toringo crab, *M. sieboldi*, grows to 15 ft. and has blush pink flowers.

Southern crab, *M. angustifolia*, is a semievergreen that grows to 25 ft. and has large, pink or rose flowers.

CRABGRASS. Common name for many herbs that are occasionally used for ornament and in pastures but are generally obnoxious weeds, particularly in lawns. The name is applied especially to DIGITARIA, a genus of herbs belonging to the Poaceae (Grass Family).

The leaves and flower-bearing stems bend for the lawn mower, making it very difficult to cut off the seed-bearing tops. Moreover, pieces of crabgrass scattered by the mower are likely to take root where they fall. The pest can be controlled by raking the sod vigorously with a steel rake so as to loosen the plants and make them stand upright, when they can be more easily mown or, better, cut by hand. Areas so treated should be reseeded with good grass seed in the fall, since crabgrass and other weeds can be crowded out by a dense, vigorous sod. If raking and mowing is not effective, the grass should be cut out with a hoe or pulled up by hand before the plants go to seed. If seeding is prevented, the above methods should clean a lawn of the weed in two or three seasons; see WEEDS.

CRAMBE (KRAM bee). A genus of cruciferous herbs sometimes grown for ornament. *C. maritima* (sea-kale) is raised for its young shoots, which are blanched and used like asparagus. The perennial kinds are hardy to Zone 6.

CRANBERRY. Several trailing evergreen species of *Vaccinium*. The name is believed to be a corruption of "crane berry" in allusion to the curved, necklike form of the flower-bud stem.

Cape Cod in Massachusetts and parts of New Jersey and Michigan are the leading cranberry-producing regions. This plant is not grown in gardens for its fruit and rarely, if ever, as an ornamental. With the discovery that the tops of the plants cut off in the fall make excellent mulch for perennial beds and borders, the cranberry has attained importance in the eyes of gardeners, prompting the business of gathering, bailing, and selling this mulching material. Cranberries, like other plants of the Ericaceae (Heath Family), require acid conditions for growth.

False blossom, a viral disease causing malformation of the flower, stunting of the plant, and a witches'-broom effect is transmitted by the blunt-nosed leaf hopper, a small, active insect. Control the latter and thereby prevent the spread of the disease by flooding the bog with water. Flooding until late May also helps control the black-and-yellow headed cranberry worm and the cranberry fruit worm.

PRINCIPAL SPECIES

V. macrocarpon (large, American, or trailing swamp cranberry), with long stems (often 4 ft.), relatively larger leaves, and much larger fruits, is the species cultivated commercially for its berries used in making the jelly or sauce inseparably associated with turkey. It is grown in specially constructed, sand-covered bogs, provided with ditches and dams to permit flooding or draining.

V. oxycoccus (small or European cranberry) has small leaves, dark green above and powdery white below, and little, red berries.

V. vitis (mountain cranberry, cowberry, foxberry) is a low creeper often used as a ground cover among shrubbery, attractive with its shiny, little leaves and small, dark red berries, which often persist until spring.

CRANBERRY BUSH. Common name for *Viburnum trilobum* and *V. opulus*, both shrubs with edible fruits like cranberries; see VIBURNUM.

CRAPE JESSAMINE. Common name for *Tabernaemontana divaricata*, an attractive flowering shrub grown outdoors in warm regions or potted in the greenhouse; see TABERNAEMONTANA.

CRAPE-MYRTLE. Common name for *Lagerstroemia indica*, an attractive tender shrub with panicles of colorful flowers with fringed petals; see LAGERSTROEMIA.

CRASSULA (KRAS yoo lah). A genus of succulent herbs and shrubs, mostly from South Africa, belonging to the Crassulaceae (Orpine Family). They have opposite, fleshy leaves and clusters of small, white, rose, or yellow flowers. They are sun lovers and thrive best in sandy loam with a small proportion of leaf mold. During the growing season they can be watered as freely as ordinary plants, but in the resting period they should be kept drier. Propagated by cuttings of stems and leaves, and occasionally by seed. See CACTUS.

PRINCIPAL SPECIES

C. barbata is a charming miniature; its small, green leaves margined with thick, white hairs.

C. falcata has thick, gray, sickle-shaped leaves and spectacular, bright crimson flowers.

C. x *morgan's beauty* (incorrectly called *C.* x *morgan's pink*) is the popular miniature, hybrid with compact bouquets of bright pink flowers.

C. ovata is currently considered the valid name for the common and popular jade plant, which in the past has correctly been referred to as *C. argentea*, *C. portulacacea*, and *C. obliqua*, all now considered synonyms, and incorrectly as *C. arborescens*, an entirely different species.

C. teres is interesting with tight, lumpy columns of leaves that make it look like a rattlesnake tail.

CRASSULACEAE (kras yoo LAY see ee). The Orpine Family, a group of characteristically fleshy plants that are widely distributed, chiefly in dry places. Important cultivated genera include *Adromischus, Cotyledon, Crassula, Dudleya, Echeveria, Kalanchoe, Pachyphytum, Sedum*, and *Sempervivum*.

CRATAEGUS (krah TEE gus). A genus of hardwood trees and shrubs belonging to the Rosaceae (Rose Family) and commonly known as haw, hawthorn, or thornapple. The botanical name is derived from the Greek word meaning, appropriately, "strength," for the trunks frequently have a muscular appearance, the wood is hard, and the branches are exceedingly tough.

This extensive group includes many native species valuable for ornamental planting, nearly all hardy, and all attractive in habit of growth, in blossom, and in fruit. They are long-lived and slow growing. They have attractive, white, pink, or occasionally red flowers, usually clustered and followed by decorative, small, applelike fruits; in some species these remain on the branches until midwinter, and in others they are juicy enough to be made into jelly. The branches are spiny, and the deciduous foliage often turns brilliant red or orange in the fall. Of generally small size, often branching horizontally, and frequently showing symmetrical, flat-topped forms, the various hawthorns are valuable in the shrubbery border, where their distinct planes carry up from the lower shrubs to the trees in the background. Their abundant flowers render them excellent lawn specimens, and some species make fine hedges. The efficient thorns make the plants useful as boundary barriers, but because the thorns are sharp, avoid planting where there are small children.

CULTURE

Hawthorns grow readily in almost any soil, even in limey clay, and thrive in open woodlands or exposed, sunny locations. If properly handled, they readily develop a fibrous root system and, when properly root trimmed, are easily transplanted. Almost all species endure trimming and, if cut back when reset, become established quickly. In pruning, however, care should be taken to preserve the rugged character of the tree, for when leafless, the wide-spreading, thorny branches are most picturesque in effect.

All American hawthorns come true from seed, which should be rubbed free from the pulp or separated by soaking the fruit in water until the flesh has decayed. Sow the seed in flats and keep them in a cool cellar or shade-house for two years, watering them occasionally, since germination does not take place until the second spring, or sometimes the third. Transplant the seedlings within a year to encourage the formation of a fibrous root system. Rare cultivars are grafted on seedling stock of *C. laevigata*.

Diseases. The most prevalent leaf disease of hawthorns is a fungal leaf spot. The small, reddish brown spots may cover the leaves which turn yellow and drop off, sometimes until the plant is completely defoliated. Where the disease persists, the shrubs should be sprayed with BORDEAUX MIXTURE several times, beginning as the young leaves form.

Several of the apple and juniper rust fungi attack this host; see JUNIPER, RUSTS. FIRE BLIGHT causes twig blight and canker; to control, prune out diseased parts.

Insect Pests. A lace bug, if abundant, may turn the leaves yellow or stippled white by sucking out the plant juices; it can be killed by spraying thoroughly with a contact insecticide.

A strong stream of water will help to control woolly apple APHIDS. Red spider injury can be prevented by dormant spraying with a miscible oil or controlled during the summer with a sulfur spray. Remove and burn twigs infested with the thorn limb borer. See also INSECT CONTROL.

PRINCIPAL SPECIES

C. crus-galli (cockspur thorn) has wide-spreading, rigid, often drooping branches covered with long thorns. The showy flowers are followed by small, round, dry-fleshed, red fruits, often remaining on the tree all winter. The glossy leaves take on brilliant autumn coloring. The cockspur thorn sometimes reaches 40 ft. but can be kept bushy by pruning. If the plants are close-set as a hedge, the long, sharp thorns produce an almost impenetrable barrier. Cv. 'Inermis' is thornless.

C. laevigata (English hawthorn, May tree), formerly listed as *C. oxyacantha*, is the plant of English literature and for which the ship *Mayflower* was named. It grows to 15 ft., forming a bush or small tree. Its white flowers are followed by bright red fruit. Cv. 'Paulii' (Paul's scarlet) has bright scarlet, double flowers and is the form most frequently seen in the United States. It is an exceedingly showy plant and valuable for the small garden since it never becomes very large. Unfortunately, it is very susceptible to defoliation by the hawthorn leaf spot.

C. mollis, native to the Midwest, is a handsome species with short, stiff thorns, glossy leaves, and small, scarlet, pear-shaped fruits that drop soon after ripening in August. It is the state flower of Missouri.

C. phaenopyrum (Washington thorn), growing to 30 ft., is native to the southern states. It has slender thorns and flowers in dense clusters, succeeded by lustrous, coral-like fruits that remain on the branches into midwinter. It makes an excellent hedge.

C. punctata (dotted haw), a small, wide-limbed tree, grows to 30 ft., may be almost spineless, and has large, red, pear-shaped, dotted fruit.

CREAMCUPS. Common name for *Platystemon californicus*, a native annual herb of California; see PLATYSTEMON.

CREEPERS. As generally regarded, creepers are not especially different from climbers and vines. To some, any plant that is or can be used for covering a wall is a creeper. More specifically, the term refers to trailing plants that root along the stem. These range from little plants that creep along the ground, such as *Veronica filiformis*, up to a plant like *Hedera helix* (English ivy) that is both a good ground cover and a high-climbing vine. Many plants use the term "creeper" in their common names: canary creeper is *Tropaeolum peregrinum*; creeping-Charlie or creeping-Jenny is *Lysimachia nummularia*; creeping-snowberry is *Gaultheria hispidula*; Virginia creeper is *Parthenocissus quinquefolia*.

CREEPING-CHARLIE. Common name for two creeping herbs: *Lysimachia nummularia*, belonging to the Primulaceae (Primrose Family), is often found carpeting damp ground with shiny leaves and yellow flowers, see LYSIMACHIA; *Pilea nummularifolia*, belonging to the Urticaceae (Nettle Family), is a tender species with creeping stems, see PILEA.

CRENATE. Term for the toothed margin of a leaf in which the teeth are rounded and point toward the apex of the leaf. Sometimes it refers to any leaf margins with rounded teeth and can be combined with another term to complete the description; thus the leaf of black cottonwood is finely crenate-serrate, that is, with small, round teeth pointing toward the tip. See also LEAF.

CRESCENTIA (kre SEN tee ah) **cujete.** A tropical American tree of the Bignoniaceae (Bignonia Family), commonly known as calabash tree. Attaining 40 ft., with broad head and spreading branches, it is grown for the smooth, globular fruits, which may measure 1 ft. or more across, and the hard, woody shells, which are made into water vessels, "calabash pipes," and other objects. The shell can be made to assume various forms if constricted during growth.

CRESS. Common name for various annual and perennial herbs of the Brassicaceae (Mustard Family) used as salads and garnishes and characterized by their piquant flavors.

Though easily cultivated, usually giving leaves ready for cutting in less than two months (and later crops thereafter), the plants quickly run to seed in hot weather and so should be started early in the spring or in midsummer for fall harvesting. In common with other crucifers, cress show prominent white blisters on the leaves—the so-called white rust, *Abulgo candida*. To prevent it, destroy infected refuse; keep down cruciferous weeds; practice crop rotation.

Blistercress is a name for some popular garden flowers, species of ERYSIMUM.

Garden cress, *Lepidium sativum*, is popular as a garnish or salad in Europe; see LEPIDIUM.

Indian cress, better known as garden nasturtium, is *Tropaeolum majus*; see TROPAEOLUM.

Pennycress is THLASPI, a genus of flowering herbs, including cultivated and weedy forms.

Rockcress names many species of flowering ARABIS. Purple- or false rockcress is AUBRIETA, a genus of low-growing perennials.

Stonecress refers to numerous dwarf, flowering herbs of the genus AETHIONEMA.

Upland or winter cress refers to species of BARBAREA), hardy European biennials naturalized in parts of North America.

Watercress, *Nasturtium officinale*, is the best known in North America; see NASTURTIUM.

CRESTED FERN. A common name for *Dryopteris cristata*, which has pinnae resembling the slats of a shutter; see DRYOPTERIS.

CRIMSON FLAG. A common name for *Schizostylis coccinea*, a tender herb related to iris, with crimson flowers; see SCHIZOSTYLIS.

CRINUM (KRĪ num). A genus of bulbous plants, usually evergreen and fragrant, one of which is native to our southern states. The leaves are thick and strap-shaped. There are many species, hybrids, and varieties, ranging from trumpet- to star-shaped flowers but always characterized by a very long flower tube. The colors range from pale pink to wine red and white.

All through the extreme South, these plants are seen flourishing in a great many gardens. Hardy to Zone 7, they seem to withstand neglect and severe treatment and still bloom and propagate profusely. They are tender subjects that will not winter over in northern regions without special protection. For this reason, together with the fact that they resent disturbance and reestablish themselves slowly when started from dry bulbs, their use in northern gardens is very limited.

PRINCIPAL SPECIES

C. americanum (swamp-lily), native to the Gulf states, has showy, white flowers that bloom in winter and spring.

C. asiaticum (St.-John's-lily or poison bulb), with fragrant, white flowers, is important in commercial trade and suitable for pot culture.

C. pedunculatum, the true species, has greenish tinged, white flowers with bright red anthers.

CRITHMUM (KRITH mum) **maritimum.** A perennial herb of the Lamiaceae (Mint Family), commonly known as samphire. The fleshy herb grows 1 ft. high or less and has cut leaves and inconspicuous flowers in umbels. A European seashore plant, it is occasionally grown in the border or in the herb garden as a salad. It thrives best in sandy or gravelly soil, in an open, sunny location, and is propagated by division or by seed sown as soon as ripe.

CROCOSMIA (kroh KAWS mee ah). A genus of cormous plants native to South Africa, belonging to the Iridaceae (Iris Family), and commonly known as coppertip or montbretia. The appearance and culture are similar to those for the closely related genus *Tritonia*, also called montbretia. Crocosmias grow to 2 ft. or more and have irislike leaves. They have a long bloom period in late summer, producing flowers in shades of scarlet, orange, and red.

Crocosmia sp.

Propagation is usually done by dividing the corms in early spring, but plants can also be produced from seed sown as soon as it is ripe. They thrive in a sunny location with light afternoon sun and good garden soil. Although usually hardy only in warm climates, they have been known to survive in cooler climates with winter protection.

A hybrid species, *C.* x *crocosmiiflora*, and the larger-flowered *C. masoniorum* are most commonly planted, but exciting new forms are being developed in Britain.

CROCUS (KROH kus). A genus of hardy cormous or bulbous herbs of the Iridaceae (Iris Family), comprising many species from which the modern varieties have been developed. Seasonally, crocuses are divided into two main groups—those that flower in the fall, and the much more important and better-known spring-flowering crocuses. The former type must not be confused with COLCHICUM, a member of the Liliaceae (Lily Family) but called autumn-crocus because of the similar appearance of the flowers.

FALL CROCUSES

Corms of the autumn-flowering crocuses are obtainable in July and August and should be planted during those months or their flower buds may start to develop and spoil while the bulbs are out of the ground. They flower in advance of the foliage and, being mostly of the rosy lavender shades, make bright spots of color in the early fall garden. The slender leaves appear in spring and, if allowed to develop and die down naturally, store up food for a crop of flowers for the ensuing fall. If uncrowded, the bulbs can be undisturbed for years, but when they become too thick they should be respaced.

SPRING CROCUSES

Because of their brilliant coloring in the very early spring before most other flowers appear, the spring crocuses are deservedly extremely popular. The best effects are obtained when they are massed, but informal plantings of individual colors can also be made in front of shrubbery or evergreens, on the edge of perennial borders, or scattered through grass that can be left without mowing for several weeks. If the foliage is left uncut to die down naturally, the corms will propagate from year to year and will continue to bloom profusely until they become crowded, when, as suggested for fall species, they should be

Crocus vernus

dug up and replanted while dormant in midsummer. Since the corms are inexpensive, some gardeners plant them directly in the lawn, mow them down along with the grass after the flowers fade, and plant a new crop of bulbs year after year.

Corms of spring-flowering crocuses should be planted not later than November, spaced about 3 in. apart, and set about 3 in. deep. Where the winters are severe, some protection is advisable until the plants are well established.

SELECTIONS

Crocus colorings range from pure yellow through the various lavender and blue shades to pure white. There is a constant improvement in varieties, so current bulb catalogs should be consulted in order to locate the finest kinds.

Among the 40 or more species, the best known for spring flowering are the yellow *C. angustifolius* (cloth-of-gold crocus); the lilac or white *C. imperati*; the lilac or white, often purple striped, *C. vernus*; and the yellow *C. flavus* (Dutch crocus). A great many hybrids of these and others are on the market. The best autumn-flowering species are *C. sativus* (saffron crocus), usually bright lilac in color, whose stigmas furnish the medicine, dye, and seasoning known as saffron; and *C. speciosus*, with feather-veined lilac flowers.

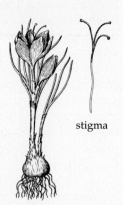

stigma

Crocus sativus

ENEMIES

While crocuses grown as undisturbed perennials in lawns, borders, and gardens do not usually call for insect or disease control measures, darker flecks on the flowers indicates the presence of a viral disease resembling the BREAKING of tulips. A decay of the bulbs is caused by fusarium fungus, and a storage rot, by BOTRYTIS. The fungus causing dry rot of gladiolus corms also affects crocus. See also BULBS.

CROP ROTATION The practice of alternating various crops on a given area as a matter of convenience in operating, or to enhance soil fertility, control pests and diseases, or increase crop yields. The same crop grown year after year or season after season on the same plot of ground will deplete the soil of the nutrients needed by that particular plant. In the home garden setting, rotation is practiced when the corner for growing tomatoes one year becomes the place for growing cabbage the next.

As one means of controlling plant diseases caused by bacteria or fungi living in the soil, this practice "starves out" the disease-producing organism by keeping susceptible plants off the area for a sufficient number of years. On lands inhabited by the club root organism, cabbage and other cruciferous plants should be grown only once in four to six years. A long rotation should also be practiced for the control of black rot on cabbage and cauliflower. A three-year rotation of corn helps to avoid corn smut.

Although long-term crop rotation is often impractical in the small home garden, changing the planting site each year or even shifting individual crops from place to place prevents accumulation in the soil of the pathogens of aster wilt, gladiolus corm disease, tulip blight, and nematodes. If all types of rotation are impossible, the only way to overcome a serious soil infestation is to remove the soil to a depth of 6–8 in. and either sterilize it or replace it with fresh, uninfected soil.

CROSS. Another name for a HYBRID. To "cross" is to hybridize. See PLANT BREEDING.

CROSSANDRA (kraws AN drah). A genus of African herbs or subshrubs valued in partial shade in tropical gardens and as greenhouse subjects. The terminal spikes of yellow or orange flowers emerge a few at a time from between closely pressed bracts and are produced even in shade, making this a useful houseplant. New colors and sizes are being introduced as growers become interested in producing this as a crop.

CROSSVINE. Common name for *Bignonia capreolata*, a flowering vine; see BIGNONIA.

CROTALARIA (kroh tah LAIR ee ah). A large genus of shrubs and herbs belonging to the Fabaceae (Bean Family), mostly grown for ornament or forage crops. They have sweet pea–like flowers and swollen pods that give rise to the common name "rattlebox." The shrub varieties can be propagated by cuttings, but plants are usually raised from seed, which is first soaked in warm water.

PRINCIPAL SPECIES

C. capensis grows to 5 ft. and has golden yellow flowers to 1 in. long. It is native to South Africa and grown in south Florida.

C. retusa (golden-yellow sweet pea) is an annual that grows to 3 ft. and has racemes of about twelve yellow flowers streaked with purple.

C. mucronata is a perennial that grows to 8 ft. and bears yellow flowers striped with brown. In warm climates it is sometimes grown as a GREEN MANURE.

CROTON. Common name for CODIAEUM, a genus of tropical shrubs of the Euphorbiaceae (Spurge Family). *Croton* is also the botanical name of a large genus, mostly of trees and shrubs belonging to the same family, but is of no special garden value. *C. tiglium* is a small tropical tree that yields the powerful purgative, croton oil.

CROWBERRY. Common name for *Empetrum nigrum*, a heathlike evergreen shrub with edible, black berries; see EMPETRUM.

CROWN. This term has three different meanings in connection with plants: (1) The part of a plant, particularly of a tree, above the first branching of the stem—its foliage- and flower-bearing region. In this sense, in a bulb, corm, tuber, or budded rhizome, it is the summit from which the green leaves or the main stem arises. (2) An organ or group of organs formed in a circle, like the cup of a daffodil or the whorl of leaves above the flowers of *Fritillaria imperialis* (crown-imperial). (3) In any herbaceous perennial, such as *Delphinium*, the portion of the plant at or just below the surface of the ground where the stem emerges from the root.

CROWN FERN. Common name for *Blechnum discolor*, a fern that forms a symmetrical rosette over a stout rhizome; see BLECHNUM.

CROWN GALL. A bacterial disease manifested on various woody or herbaceous plants in the form of tumorlike enlargements at the crown or on aerial portions, or else by an excessive production of roots and shoots. Other names for the gall formations are crown knot, root knot, and cane galls; excessive root development usually goes under the name of hairy root. The latter is common on fruit trees, especially apple, but the galls are found on many ornamental plants—roses, blackberries, raspberries, grapes, and daisies are particularly susceptible. The galls are irregularly globular, with a more or less convoluted surface, and may vary in size up to six to ten times the diameter of the stem from which they originate.

To control crown gall, clean nursery stock must always be planted. Diseased and healthy stock should never be mixed, nor should plants be heeled in soil that may have produced plants with crown gall, since the bacteria live in the soil. If there is any doubt as to the health of the stock purchased for the garden, place it in a copper sulfate solution (1 oz. to 4 gal. water) for one hour before planting. Prevent wounding plants when cultivating them. Galls on aerial portions can be removed, but disinfect the pruning knife before and after cutting.

CROWN-IMPERIAL. Common name for *Fritillaria imperialis*, a showy bulbous herb with nodding, bell-shaped flowers; see FRITILLARIA.

CROWN-OF-THORNS. Common name for *Euphorbia milii*, a shrubby plant with spiny, curving stems; see EUPHORBIA.

CROWN ROT. This disease, also called root rot or sclerotium rot, is very prevalent on ornamentals in the northeastern states and occurs to some extent also in the Midwest. It has been reported on *Aconite, Ajuga, Aquilegia, Campanula, Cos-*

mos, Delphinium, Dianthus, Dracocephalum, Erigeron, Eupatorium, Hosta, Iris, Penstemon, Phlox, Physostegia, Trillium, Valeriana, Viola; and nearly a hundred other plants are known to be susceptible. The name of the fungus that causes it, *Sclerotium delphinii*, is indicative of the heavy losses in delphinium beds. Another species, *S. rolfsii*, is responsible for a similar disease of many southern plants.

The first symptoms usually appear with the beginning of warm, humid weather. A sudden yellowing of shoots is followed by rapid wilting and drying. Sometimes the rapid decay of the crown causes the plants to topple over without preliminary wilting. When plants are crowded or cover the ground closely (as does *Ajuga reptans*), large plantings seem literally to disappear in the course of two or three days, only a few black, dried strands being left where there was luxuriant green growth a few days before. As the plants wilt, the crowns and surrounding soil are overrun with white fungus threads (hyphae), in which the resting bodies (sclerotia) are formed. The latter are about the size and shape of mustard seed and are first white, then reddish brown. There may be so many that the ground looks red.

The sclerotia are able to remain alive in the soil for months or even years. If there has been continued trouble from crown rot, the best control is to destroy all of the plants and either replace the soil or disinfect it with a fungicide drench; see DISINFECTION. Since this is not often feasible, the next best method is to remove and burn all the diseased plants.

CROWN-VETCH. Common name for *Coronilla varia*, a pinkish-flowered herb; see CORONILLA.

CRUCIFER. A descriptive term for any plant belonging to the BRASSICACEAE (Mustard Family), including some important vegetables, garden flowers, and troublesome weeds.

CRYOPHYTUM (krī oh FĪ tum). Former botanical name for succulent plants now classified in the genus MESEMBRYANTHEMUM.

CRYOSOPHILA (krī oh SAW fil ah). A genus of palms native to Mexico and South America, formerly listed as *Acanthorrhiza*, and commonly known as rootspine palms. The fan-shaped leaves cut into many segments are bluish green above and pale beneath. The slender trunk is covered, especially toward the base, with a network of aerial roots that have hardened into darkened spines.

Hardy to Zone 9, these trees are frequently planted outdoors in Florida and can be used in gardens farther north. They thrive in rich humus soil in a partially shaded spot. In cooler climates, they can be grown in the greenhouse or as a potted plant in the window; in either case, they should be shaded from direct sunlight. Water well but never so much that the roots stand in water. Plants should be shifted only when necessary, and repotting should be done when roots are in active growth during spring or summer.

C. nana is a small tree whose grayish trunk has short spines. The leaves are 2 ft. long, 1 in. wide, green above, and silvery on the underside.

C. warscewiczii grows 20 ft. or taller and has long root spines at the base of the trunk, which becomes smooth toward the top. The leaves are green above and silvery underneath and show a conspicuous vein pattern when dry.

CRYPTANTHUS (krip TAN thus). A genus of small, tropical foliage plants belonging to the Bromeliaceae (Pineapple Family). Epiphytic in the wild, they are often grown in warm greenhouses; they are effective in pans and thrive in a mixture of fern fiber and sphagnum moss with broken brick and charcoal. Ample moisture is needed in the growing season, but little in winter. Stiff, spreading leaves with spiny edges form a rosette that almost hides the dense heads of small, white flowers. Propagation is by division.

PRINCIPAL SPECIES

C. acaulis has wavy, dark green, recurved leaves, white and scurfy beneath.

C. bivittatus has dull green leaves marked with two buff or reddish lengthwise stripes and brown beneath.

C. zonatus has crinkly leaves marked with transverse bands of white, green, or brown.

CRYPTOCORYNE (krip toh koh RĪ nee). A genus of tropical, submerged aquatic plants with reddish flowers that resemble small callas, belonging to the Araceae (Arum Family), including excellent subjects for indoor aquariums. Two types are fairly common, one with broad, somewhat heart-shaped leaves and one with straplike leaves. These are especially valuable in aquariums that receive too little light for good development of the more common oxygenating plants.

CRYPTOGRAMMA (krip toh GRAM ah). A genus including about four species of dimorphic ferns found in the North Temperate Zone. They have short, creeping or ascending rhizomes and recurved margins that protect the sori. They are rare and should not be collected from the wild.

PRINCIPAL SPECIES

C. acrostichoides (parsley fern, American rockbrake), sometimes listed as a variety of *C. crispa*, is a small, North American fern that grows 3–6 in. tall among barren rocks. It has bipinnate to tripinnate, evergreen fronds, the fertile ones taller than sterile ones, and stout, ascending rhizomes.

C. crispa (parsley fern) is a small fern with many clustered fronds that inspire its common name. It has 2–8 in., tripinnate to quadripinnate fronds that grow from a creeping rhizome. Native to Europe, Afghanistan, and Asia Minor, it is difficult to cultivate, being an inhabitant of mountain screes where water runs continuously at the roots, while the fronds are in full sun. It cannot tolerate lime of any sort.

C. stelleri (slender cliff-brake) is a dainty, fragile fern that grows 3–6 in. tall with pinnate-pinnatifid fronds arising from a creeping rhizome. Extremely difficult to cultivate, it is deciduous and grows on cool, moist limestone ledges in northern North America, Asia, and Europe.

CRYPTOMERIA (krip toh MEE ree ah) **japonica.** A large evergreen tree of striking form and unique foliage character, native to Japan, belonging to the Taxodiaceae (Taxodium Family), and commonly known as Japanese-cedar. It is the only member of the genus, but there are numerous cultivars. It attains a height of 125 ft. in its native land. In the United States it grows as far north as Massachusetts in sheltered locations near the coast but suffers in severe winters, the foliage being occasionally killed in irregular patches. From Philadelphia southward it develops into a beautiful pyramidal tree.

The angular, pointed foliage is arranged spirally around the stem. Growing in tufted masses, it creates a distinctive and attractive effect. As cold weather approaches, it takes on a purple hue like that of native junipers. This tree, suitably located, adds interest and beauty to any garden. Both its color and the modeling of the foliage masses are immediately noticeable and set it off from other evergreens. Cryptomerias can be grown from seed or cuttings taken late in the fall. Hardy in Zones 6–7.

There are some excellent cultivars available. 'Compacta' is compact and conical with bluish green needles. 'Elegans' is a bushy plant that grows to 12 ft. with soft, feathery juvenile foliage. 'Elegans Nana' is a dwarf, compact form that grows to 3 ft. 'Cristata' has fasciated coxcomb growth and is a very unusual large shrub. 'Lobbii' is a compact pyramidal form that grows to 50 ft. with shiny needles that stay green all winter. 'Vilmonniana', a small, compact dwarf growing to about 2 ft., makes a wonderful rock garden specimen. 'Tansu' is a new compact dwarf plant growing to 18 in. and excellent for rock gardens.

CRYPTOSTEGIA (krip toh STEE jee ah). A genus of tropical vining shrubs of the Asclepiadaceae (Milkweed Family), usually grown for ornament in the warm greenhouse and commonly known as rubbervine. Propagated by cuttings, they are easy to grow in a mixture of loam and peat.

C. grandiflora has thick, glossy leaves and twisted flower buds. The funnel-shaped, reddish purple flowers turn pale with age. This plant has been widely cultivated in India for rubber obtained from the juice.

C. madagascariensis is a good climber with showy flowers of white or pink.

CTENITIS (ten EE tis). A large genus of 150 pantropical ferns with finely dissected fronds.

C. sloanei (Florida or American tree fern) is not a true tree fern, but it does form a short trunk covered with woolly, reddish brown scales. The much-divided fronds can grow 6–7 ft. It is quite uncommon and grows in southern Florida and the tropical Americas. It can be grown in a humus-rich soil but should not dry out.

CUBAN LILY. Inappropriate but common name for *Scilla peruviana*, a flowering bulbous plant native to southern Europe; see SCILLA.

CUBÉ. A tropical, leguminous plant, *Lonchocarpus* spp., that is pounded up and thrown into streams by some inhabitants of countries where it grows. It kills or paralyzes fish so they can be easily caught. Though harmless to people, the poisonous agent in the plant, known as ROTENONE, is an effective botanical insecticide. Extracted from the cubé roots, it is used in the making of contact, and to some extent stomach, poisons for plant protection. See INSECT CONTROL.

CUCUMBER. An annual, trailing or tendril-climbing Asiatic herb, *Cucumis sativus*, grown for its immature, green fruits, which are used as pickles, in salads, and sometimes cooked. Gherkins are small-fruited varieties or small immature fruits of standard ones that are harvested early for pickling.

There are two general classes of cultivated varieties. The English forcing kinds bear slender, nearly spineless fruits, often more than 3 ft. long, with few seeds. The common or garden cucumbers include several types and many sizes. The English kinds are grown only under artificial conditions in greenhouses, while the common kinds can be grown in hotbeds, coldframes, outdoor gardens, and commercial farms.

Cucumbers grow male and female flowers on the same plant. Pollination is usually needed from the male to the female for fruit formation, although plant breeders have developed all-female varieties that are self-fertile. In choosing the all-female kinds, it is vital to understand whether the variety needs a pollinator planted. In seed catalogs, normal cucumbers are described as monoecious (plants with both male and female flowers) and gynoecious (plants with mostly female flowers). Some cucumbers classified as all-female do in fact set

Cucumber buds

a small portion of male flowers—just sufficient to ensure pollination. When a cucumber sets 100% female flowers and is self-fertile, it is known as pathenocarpic. These are available in both indoor and outdoor varieties

Other Cucumbers. Bur- or star-cucumber, *Sicyos angulatus*, is an annual vine sometimes grown for screening but is often a weed; see SICYOS. Mock- or wild-cucumber, ECHINOCYSTIS, is a genus of North American climbers, often planted to cover arbors because of their small, profuse flowers and large foliage. Squirting-cucumber, *Ecballium elaterium*, is a trailing perennial herb cultivated for its curious fruits.

CULTURE

Being tender, cucumbers can be grown outdoors only in frostless weather. Since they do not transplant well, they are generally grown from seed sown where the plants are to remain. Plants can, however, be started indoors in flowerpots, berry boxes, or the soil of inverted sods. They require warm soil—preferably a sandy loam—full sun, abundant and readily available food, and protection from disease and insects—especially cucumber beetles, which feed on the plants and spread the destructive wilt disease.

Outdoor Planting. Enrich the ground and prepare it for seeding after the weather has turned consistently warm. Make hills 4' x 4' apart for small, early kinds, and 4' x 6' for large, late ones. If the soil is naturally poor or lacking in humus, work a pitchfork-full of well-decayed manure into each hill. Scatter a dozen seeds in a 1-ft. circle in each hill and bury them ½ in. deep. It is advisable to cover each hill with a melon plant protector until after the vines begin to run, to keep out cucumber beetles. When the plants are nicely under way, thin out the inferior ones, leaving not more than five to each hill. Keep the soil cultivated as long as it can be done without injuring the spreading vines.

Greenhouse Culture. To force garden cucumbers indoors, start the plants in flowerpots of good soil two weeks before their spaces in the greenhouse will be ready. Transplant into beds of rich soil 18–24 in. apart in rows 30–36 in. apart. Train the vines on rough cords suspended from the roof or a framework. With proper care, good plants should begin to bear in six or eight weeks and yield up to 100 fruits each.

English frame cucumber plants for winter cropping are started in the fall, 80 to 100 days before the fruits are wanted. If grown for spring and early summer use, sow seed in February or March. When bees are not available indoors, the pistillate flowers must be hand-pollinated.

Harvesting. For small pickles (gherkins), gather the cucumbers when only 2–3 in. long—about six weeks from sowing. For "dill" size pickles, harvest when 4–6 in. long. For slicing, pick fruits when they are plump and cylindrical but before they bulge in the middle or show a yellowish tinge at the blossom ends. Daily picking during hot weather will prolong the fruiting season.

Enemies. Cucumbers are subject to bacterial wilt, mosaic, anthracnose, and angular leaf spot. The most troublesome pests are pickle worm, squash bug, cucumber beetles, and aphids. For pest and disease controls, see enemies under CUCURBITA.

CUCUMBER-ROOT. Common name for *Medeola virginica*, a native herb with edible roots and whorled leaves, also known as Indian cucumber-root; see MEDEOLA.

CUCUMBER TREE. Common name for *Magnolia acuminata* and *M. macrophylla*, both hardy, pyramidal trees grown for their showy flowers; see MAGNOLIA.

CUCUMIS (KYOO kyoo mis). A genus of tender, mostly Asiatic and African, vinelike herbs. Four species are grown in North America for their variously formed succulent fruits, which are edible, interesting, or both. The most important species are *C. melo* (melon) and *C. sativus* (cucumber).

PRINCIPAL SPECIES

C. anguria (West India or bur gherkin) grows wild in Florida and Texas; its odd, small, prickly fruits are sometimes used as pickles.

C. dipsaceus (hedgehog or teasel gourd), from Arabia, is grown as curiosity or ornament for its hard, bristly fruits.

C. melo (MELON, muskmelon), with trailing stems and rounded leaves, is widely cultivated in many forms for its fleshy fruit. Many varieties are popularly and indiscriminately classed as cantaloupes, but that name correctly applies only to one group. Cultivation has produced cultivated forms divided into several classes based on original varieties.

The Cantaloupensis group (cantaloupe) produces fruit with hardy, scaly or warty rinds and is not commonly grown.

The Chito group (mango or orange melon, lemon cucumber) has small, firm fruits used as pickles or preserves.

The Conomon group (oriental pickling melon) produces fruits used like the Chitos but is little grown in North America.

The Dudaim group (dudaim melon) is sometimes cultivated for its marbled, fragrant fruits.

The Flexuosus group (snake or serpent melon) produces curious, long, coiled, or twisted fruits.

The Inodorus group (winter or cassaba melon) includes strong-growing kinds whose large, mildly scented fruits keep well into winter.

The Reticulatus group (muskmelon, netted melon) produces important commercial crops of medium or large fruits with orange flesh and netted rinds.

C. sativus (CUCUMBER) is the common garden vegetable. Var. *anglicus* is the strong-growing, English forcing type with almost spineless fruits.

CUCURBITA (kyoo KUR bee tah). The principal genus of the Cucurbitaceae (Cucumber Family), including tendril-bearing, annual or perennial, vinelike herbs that, except in cultivated bush varieties, root at the joints. A member of the genus is called a cucurbit. See also GOURD; PUMPKIN; SQUASH; ZUCCHINI.

DISEASES

Bacterial wilt is one of the most serious troubles of cucumber, squash, muskmelon, and pumpkin, especially east of Kansas and north of Tennessee. The bacteria clog and destroy the sap tubes of stem and leaf, frequently causing a crop loss of 20%. Starting with a single leaf, the wilting gradually spreads through the entire plant. The bacillus that causes it can overwinter in the digestive tract of the twelve-spotted cucumber beetle, hence control of the disease is directed largely at control of the beetle. Pull up and burn diseased plants.

Anthracnose is usually more severe on watermelons than on other cucurbits but sometimes occurs in epidemic proportions on cucumbers and muskmelons. All parts of the plant above ground may be affected, showing yellow and water-soaked spots on the leaves, later enlarging and turning brown; a blackened or scorched condition of the vines; water-soaked sunken spots covered with masses of buff-colored spores on the fruits. Control by crop rotation and planting seeds treated with a fungicide.

Downy mildew, a fungus common in areas of cool, wet nights and humid days, produces irregular yellow spots on leaves, which later curl and die. Try planting mildew-resistant varieties. If necessary spray with BORDEAUX MIXTURE or another general-purpose fungicide every ten days.

Mosaic, a viral disease also known as "white pickle" is, along with bacterial wilt, the most important cucurbit disease. The leaves are dwarfed and distorted, the plants stunted, and the fruit knotted and blotched with yellow and green. Cucumbers and squash are seriously affected, and muskmelon vines are stunted, but watermelon is only slightly susceptible. There are several weed hosts—milkweed, pokeberry, ground cherry, and wild cucumber—from which the disease is carried by insects. Such hosts should be destroyed in and around the garden.

INSECT PESTS

Of many insects that attack cucurbits, the most serious is probably the striped cucumber beetle. Overwintering yellow, black-striped adults devour leaves and stems of tender, young plants and may infect them with cucumber wilt. To prevent this, plants can be covered with cheesecloth, or heavily mulched. Late planting may help, as will choosing resistant varieties. Spraying with insecticide may be necessary in serious cases; begin spraying cucumbers soon after seeds germinate, using a pyrethrum-rotenone combination at weekly intervals.

The twelve-spotted cucumber beetle, which feeds on a large number of food plants, is more serious in the South. Control measures are as for the striped beetle.

The pickleworm, another southern pest, is a slender, green worm with a row of black spots. To control it, plant early and destroy waste materials and old vines by burning.

The squash vine borer, *Melittio satyriniformis*, a white, grublike caterpillar with a dark head, prefers squash and pumpkin but may attack all cucurbits. It tunnels in the main stem near the ground and can be killed by slitting the stem with a knife. Hand-pick bugs, and try an onion or garlic spray. Companion plantings of nasturtiums, calendulas, or marigolds can help.

The melon aphid or louse is most troublesome on cucumber and melon. It feeds on the underside of leaves, causing them to curl. Ladybugs or predatory lacewings are an excellent control. Pests can also be rinsed off with water. If necessary, use a contact insecticide.

The squash bug, also called stink bug because of its offensive odor, lives over the winter in trash and attacks plants as soon as they are up by puncturing the leaf tissues and petioles.

Although a sucking insect, the rusty brown adult is resistant to contact sprays. Companion planting with radishes, marigolds, or nasturtiums may help. Crop rotation is essential; remove vines from the garden at the end of the season.

See also INSECT CONTROL.

PRINCIPAL SPECIES

C. ficifolia (Malabar gourd), a native of eastern Asia, is grown for ornament.

C. foetidissima (also listed as *C. perennis*), the Mexican calabazilla, which grows wild as far north as Nebraska, bears inedible fruits.

C. maxima is the parent species of the cultivars 'Mammoth', 'Chile', 'Hubbard', 'Boston Marrow', and the curious turban (or "squash-within-a-squash") types.

C. moschata includes squashes that resemble pumpkins, such as the winter crookneck and cushaw.

C. pepo includes summer, autumn, and bush pumpkins; vegetable marrow; acorn, pattypan, scallop (or simlin), zucchini (or courgette), and summer crookneck squash; and yellow-flowered gourds.

CUCURBITACEAE (kyoo kur bit AY see ee). The Cucumber or Gourd Family, which includes the cucurbits and many other useful plants. Besides the genus *Cucurbita,* many members are grown for edible fruit, among them *Benincasa*, *Citrullus* (watermelon), *Cucumis* (melon and cucumber), *Lagenaria*, *Luffa*, and *Sechium*. Chiefly ornamental forms are *Abobra*, *Bryonia*, *Coccinia*, *Cyclanthera*, *Ecballium*, *Echinocystis*, *Melothria*, *Momordica*, *Sicana*, and *Trichosanthes*.

CULTIVAR. A term for a "cultivated variety," one that was produced in cultivation. The origin of the cultivar may or may not be known. A "variety" is a group of like plants that originated in the wild though they may also be cultivated.

CULTIVATION. This word has two meanings in gardening. One application is the care and maintenance of a particular type plant, as in the cultivation of roses. In this sense, cultivation includes the watering, weeding, and feeding of plants. The other use of this term describes the act of hoeing or working the soil after seeds have been sown or plants have been established. The soil is cultivated to keep down weeds and break down the soil crust, allowing for better aeration. Cultivation around plants needs to be done with care so that the root system is not damaged. Shallow cultivation with a hoe or forked tool is the most common method, but cultivation of the soil is also done with electric or gas-powered tillers, with hand tools, or by raking.

Never cultivate wet soil, since this may damage the soil structure by pushing out air pockets and compacting it too tightly. This is especially true of heavy clay soil. During warm weather, cultivation can dry the soil by encouraging evaporation, so frequent cultivation during droughts should be avoided. By using a mulch instead of cultivation to control weeds during the summer, water will be conserved and the soil temperature kept low. See also DIGGING; DOUBLE DIGGING; TRENCHING.

CULTIVATOR. Any implement used to loosen the soil and destroy the weeds around crops is considered a cultivator. The device can be as simple as a hand cultivator, which has a rake or rakes to drag the soil. Mechanical cultivators consist of various types of replaceable, adjustable tines, or teeth, attached to a frame, which can be manipulated to fit the width to be covered and the depth the teeth are to penetrate. Large cultivators are drawn by tractors and can work two or three rows simultaneously.

The work done varies according to the styles of teeth used. Some have only one type of teeth, usually spikes or shovels; others have interchangeable teeth, including rakes, spikes, shovels, disks, and cutaways (disks with deep notches cut in their margins).

Rakes and spikes do the best work on light soils in which they scratch the surface and destroy weeds. Rakes kill sprouting weeds, and spikes kill larger plants. Disks, usually set at a slight angle to the direction of pull, slice the surface and throw the soil either toward or away from the rows of plants. They are useful also (especially when weighted) for cutting and mixing sod with surface soil. Shovels can be used in the same way, either for hilling the plants or raising the soil between the rows. Cutaway teeth break down clods of heavy soil and reduce the surface to an even level and texture.

Rotary tillers, often used for cultivation, consist essentially of a gasoline motor and various types of narrow teeth that, rotating at high speed, break up and stir the soil, incorporating manure and other material without the preliminary operation of plowing. Also, the push of the revolving teeth helps to propel the machine.

See also TOOLS; ROTARY TILLER.

CUMIN. Common name for the spicy herb *Cuminum cyminum*; see CUMINUM.

CUMINUM (KYOO min um) **cyminum.** A small, European annual herb belonging to the Apiaceae (Celery Family), with finely cut leaves and clusters of small, white or rose flowers. The seeds are used as an ingredient in curry powder and for flavoring pickles, soups, and chili. Both plants and seed are commonly called cumin. Plants are easily raised from seed.

CUNILA (kyoo NĪ lah) **origanoides.** A hardy, native perennial herb of the Lamiaceae (Mint Family), commonly known as stone mint. It is grown in the border for its profusion of bloom or in the herb garden for its leaves, which are sometimes used for tea. Growing to 1 ft., it has small, purple-pink, two-lipped flowers in flat-topped clusters and small, oval leaves. It needs a light, dry, sandy soil and can be propagated by seed or division.

CUP-AND-SAUCER VINE. A common name for *Cobaea scandens*, an annual vine with attractive flowers; see COBAEA.

CUP FERN. Common name for DENNSTAEDTIA, a genus of ferns with cup-shaped indusia.

CUPFLOWER. Common name for NIEREMBERGIA, a genus of tropical flowering perennials, usually grown as annuals. A few species are also called whitecup.

CUPHEA (KOO fee ah). A large genus of tropical and subtropical American herbs belonging to the Lythraceae (Loosestrife Family). Only a few kinds have been generally grown, and these mostly in greenhouses or outdoors in Zones 9–11. The herbaceous varieties are easy to raise from seed as tender annuals, and the shrubby varieties are propagated from cuttings.

C. hyssopifolia (false heather, Mexican-heather) is a small, woody plant with tiny leaves and deep or pale pink flowers. It is common in warm regions as a ground cover or in borders.

C. ignea (cigarplant, cigar flower), also sold as *C. platycentra*, is a small, twiggy species. Its tubular flowers are 1 in. long and have bright red calyxes tipped with gray, black, and white, suggesting the common names.

CUPID'S-DART. A common name for CATANANCHE, a perennial herb with long, narrow leaves and heads of ray and disk flowers.

CUP PLANT. A common name for *Silphium perfoliatum*, a grassland perennial with flowers cupped by the upper leaves; see SILPHIUM.

CUPRESSUS (kyoo PRES us). A genus of large trees suited only to mild and warm regions, including the principal members of the Cupressaceae (Cypress Family), and commonly known as cypress. Some have very dark foliage and are very distinctive in form, attaining 80 ft. Most of them are hardy only in the Gulf states and in California (Zones 6–9). They thrive in deep, sandy loam soil and are ornamental in youth and picturesque in maturity, living to a great age. Some are dense and bushy, some are flat topped with horizontal branching, and others are sharply pyramidal and compact.

The canker disease of Monterey cypress in some regions of the West Coast kills the top branches and patches of bark. Trees may be killed or so deformed as to lose their ornamental value. There is no cure for this canker, so all affected branches should be removed promptly.

The cypress bark scale turns the limbs of Monterey cypress yellow, then red or brown, and may seriously damage thickly planted hedgerows. It may also attack the Arizona and Guadaloupe cypress and incense-cedar. Spray in late summer and again in midautumn with a miscible oil emulsion. See also INSECT CONTROL.

PRINCIPAL SPECIES

C. arizonica (Arizona cypress), being native to the southern half of Arizona, is particularly adapted to dry soils and drought conditions. Narrowly pyramidal to a height of 40 ft., it can be effectively used to frame entrances and doorways. Hardy to Zone 6.

C. macnabiana (MacNab cypress) grows to 20 ft. and has fragrant foliage. It is the hardiest species; although native to southern Oregon and California, it is hardy from Massachusetts to Missouri and southward. Bushy and slow of growth, it is especially valuable in garden design.

C. macrocarpa (Monterey cypress) is found along the coast of California but will grow throughout the southern states as far north as Virginia. Attaining a height of 40 ft., it is pyramidal in youth, becoming flat topped in old age with ascending branches and a bare high trunk. It would fit in well with dwarf evergreens of similar character and lends itself to dry rock gardens near the sea.

C. sempervirens (Italian cypress) grows to 80 ft. In its native southern Europe and western Asia, it is famous as a garden subject, having been used for centuries. Its foliage is dark green, and its form is like that of the Lombardy poplar. The narrow, columnar cv. 'Stricta' has been extensively used in California. Hardy to Zone 7.

CURCULIGO (kur KYOO li goh). A genus of tropical plants belonging to the Hypoxidaceae (Stargrass Family). They are dwarfs of palmlike appearance with arching, corrugated leaves. Useful ornamental subjects for the warm greenhouse, they are hardy to Zone 9 and will tolerate heavy shade. They thrive in a mixture of fibrous loam, old cow manure, and sand. Propagation is by division.

C. capitulata, the principal species, has dark green leaves to 3 ft. long and a dense spike of yellow flowers; the spike is recurving and usually appears just above the ground.

CURCULIO. A name for various kinds of snout beetles or weevils, some of which are troublesome fruit pests. The plum curculio (*Conotrachelus nenuphar*), a native species, attacks plum, peach, apple, pear, and other stone and pome fruits. It is generally distributed east of the Rocky Mountains from Canada southward. The adult, about ¼ in. long, is brown, mottled with gray, and has four humps on its back. It feeds on the blossom to some extent, but the chief injury is the shallow feeding cavities and crescent-shaped scars on the fruit, caused when the female lays an egg in a cavity and then, just in front, makes a crescent-shaped slit that leaves the egg in a kind of pocket.

Curculio adult

The young larvae, grayish white with a small, brown head, eat into the fruit, causing it nearly always to fall to the ground before ripening. After two to four weeks, the larvae leave the fruit, burrow into the soil, and pupate in earthen cells, the adult beetles emerging in about a month. It overwinters in the adult stage, becoming active when night temperatures reach 68–70°F. Besides being probably the chief cause of wormy cherries on trees in small orchards or in cities, the plum curculio is harmful in that it spreads spores of the BROWN ROT fungus.

Because of a peculiar habit of feigning death when disturbed by drawing their legs and snout close to the body and falling to the ground, curculios can be controlled by what is known as the "jarring method." A sheet is placed under the tree, whose trunk is hit with a wooden or cloth-covered mallet; the insects fall onto the sheet and can be destroyed. Jarring trees each morning for six weeks after blossoming is advisable.

Since rotenone sprays need many repetitions and are even then not wholly effective, chemical sprays are sometimes used to control this pest. Consult your local extension service for spraying recommendations and follow directions explicitly. Clean cultivation around the trees is an important measure, and all fruit dropped early from peaches, plums, or apples should be raked up and destroyed.

The apple curculio, a less important pest resembling the plum curculio, makes a large number of skin punctures close together and causes apples to become misshapen and knotty. General orchard sanitation methods should be practiced, and wild hawthorns and crabs (which are the curculio's native food plants) should be removed from within a half mile of the orchard.

See SNOUT BEETLE; WEEVIL; BEETLES.

CURCUMA (kur KYOO mah). A genus of vigorous tropical herbs belonging to the Zingiberaceae (Ginger Family). They can be grown outdoors in Zones 10–11, but they thrive in rich soil in a warm greenhouse. They have a thick, tuberous rootstock, stems that grow to 10 ft., and large leaves that dry off soon after flowering. The flowers are borne in showy spikes, each flower surrounded by a leafy bract, and the whole spike crowned with a colored tuft. During the plant's resting stage, the soil should not be kept bone dry, or the tubers will shrivel. Propagation is by division or tubers planted in spring.

PRINCIPAL SPECIES

C. domestica, sometimes listed as *C. longa*, is an Asiatic perennial with long-stalked leaves and spikes of yellow flowers with tufts of white bracts. The dried rhizomes yield the turmeric of India, used as a condiment and dye.

C. petiolata (queen-lily) has dense spikes of pale yellow flowers and rosy purple bracts.

C. zedoaria, formerly listed as *C. pallida*, has leaves with silky undersides and yellow flowers, the lower bracts being green and the upper ones white tinged with carmine.

CURRANT. Common name for two popular, unrelated fruits and the plants that produce them. The first is the dried fruit of small grapes (a variety of *Vitis vinifera*) exported from the Mediterranean region of Europe; the name is a corruption of Corinth from where the product was originally shipped. The second kind of currant is the small, red, white, or black, globular berry borne in clusters by various species of RIBES.

Indian-currant is *Symphoricarpos orbiculatus*, a species of snowberry; see SYMPHORICARPOS.

SELECTION

Vitis is rarely grown in the United States, but *Ribies* spp. are found in both home and commercial plantings throughout the northern two-thirds of the country. The red and white varieties, both developed from the European species *R. sativum*, are the most important in home gardening, and the reds are a market fruit.

The black currant, *R. nigrum*, is grown by those who enjoy its peculiar flavor in jam and jelly. Since it is the alternate host of destructive white pine blister rust disease, it should not be planted near white pine trees.

The following species of *Ribes* are grown mainly for ornament: *R. americanum* or *R. floridum* (American black currant), with creamy flowers and black fruit; *R. aureum* (golden currant), with yellow flowers and purplish fruit; *R. odoratum* (buffalo currant), with fragrant, yellow flowers and black fruit; and *R. triste* (swamp red currant), with purple flowers and red fruits . None of these has been much improved by man as far as the edibility, yield, or fruit is concerned.

CULTURE

Currant bushes are of outstanding hardiness; even the blossoms that appear in early spring withstand the frosts that destroy the flowers of other fruits. They are grown successfully almost to the Arctic Circle but are at their best where the soil is moist and the air is cool and humid. They will not, however, tolerate either heat or dryness, so except in the mountains, or under shade and irrigation, they fail in hotter, drier regions.

The soils best suited to currants are moist but well-drained silt and clay loams, especially those well supplied with humus. On lighter (sandy) soils they are usually less successful. All too often they are neglected in home gardens, resulting in bushes choked with worthless stems, overgrown with sod and weeds. These bushes become food for currant worms, which strip off the foliage; plant lice, which suck the juices of the leaves; and borers, which destroy the older stems. Such plants frequently give small yields of inferior fruit; however, no bush fruit is easier to keep free of such enemies and to maintain in high productivity of choice fruit.

Planting. Currant bushes should be planted approximately 6 ft. apart. Because of their shallow roots, a deep mulch is advisable, one that can be left in place and added to each year. If additional fertilizer is needed, the mulch can be pulled aside in early spring to apply manure, compost, or other organic or chemical fertilizer; then the mulch is replaced. Commercial growers either keep the bed cultivated, use herbicides, or between the plants raise a cover crop that is turned under each year.

Pruning. The most effective management allows only the best two of each year's usually numerous young shoots to remain; the inferior ones are cut down to the base shortly after midsummer so as to concentrate all the plant food in selected stems, which become sturdy and highly productive. These stems begin to bear the second season, increase their yield the third, and reach their maximum the fourth; thereafter the quantity, size, and quality of the berries rapidly declines. Hence the importance of cutting out the oldest stems after they have borne their third crop—that is, at the end of their fourth summer. All cut stems should be burned at once to destroy any borers that may be present in them. This method restricts the number of stems left after the summer pruning to a maximum of eight.

ENEMIES

Diseases. Blister rust, a disease that alternates between plants in the Saxifragaceae (Saxifrage Family) and white pines, causes currants to be a forbidden fruit in some areas. Black currants are often the most deadly hosts of the disease, but

experts recommend a distance of at least 900 ft. between any currant bush and white pine. Anthracnose shows up as purplish or brown spots on the leaves and can be controlled by fungicides.

Insect Pests. Aphids and scale can be controlled by insecticides applied early. Currant borers sometimes infect the canes, and currant stem girdlers may infect the tips of the branches. Currant worms attack the leaves in early summer, but all three are easily controlled with a mild insecticide. Choose one that will wash off early, since the fruit ripens early.

CURRANT TOMATO. Common name for *Lycopersicon pimpinellifolium*, a spreading, rather weak-growing species of tomato that is native to Peru. It produces clusters of 10–25 fruits, only slightly larger than currants, and is used mainly for hors d'oeuvres and garnishing. The plants are sometimes grown as curiosities or ornamentals. They also make an excellent summer cover for unsightly piles of brush.

CUSCUTA (kus KYOO tah). A genus of one of the few plants that are true parasites, commonly known as dodder, lovevine, strangleweed, goldthread, devil's-hair, and hell-bind). The genus is closely related to morning-glories, but they are leafless, twining, parasitic seed plants without chlorophyll, which attach their yellow, orange, or pink, threadlike stems to various cultivated and wild plants, taking their food from these hosts by means of sucking organs (haustoria).

Especially menacing to clover, alfalfa, and flax, dodders are sometimes found on ornamentals, having been seen strangling chrysanthemum, dahlia, helenium, petunia, Virginia- creeper, trumpet vine, English ivy, and other vines. The dodder flowers, small and white, pink, or yellowish, appear in clusters from early June to the end of the growing season. The seeds, ripening from July until frost, are produced in great abundance, and only clover or alfalfa seed free from dodder seed should be purchased. Seed firms use special apparatus to remove it, but if there is doubt as to the purity of the seed intended for planting, send it to your state seed laboratory for testing. Portions of ornamentals attacked by dodder should be freed of it or removed before it sets seed. Dodder is sometimes used to produce medicines and red dye.

CUSHAW. A common name for *Cucurbita moschata*, a species of squash of variable form but mostly oblong with a large, smooth crookneck. It is used in fall and winter, hence another common name is winter crookneck squash. See SQUASH; PUMPKIN.

CUT FLOWERS. Cut flowers, such as those used in flower arangements, depend on proper conditioning and maintenance if they are to keep their fresh appearance for a reasonable period. Flowers cut specifically for drying are known as EVERLASTINGS. A section of the garden, preferably in a secluded but sunny spot, can be devoted to flowers to be used for cutting. Thus, the main border need not be denuded when the flowers are desired indoors.

The general rules for conditioning most flowers are the same, but there are specific things to do for various blooms. It is best to cut plant material in the evening, because sugar has been stored in the plant tissue all day. The next best time to cut is early morning, and the poorest time is the middle of the day.

Flowers should be cut with a sharp knife or garden clippers. Cut the stem on a slant and remove all unnecessary foliage. Immediately place the stem up to its neck in a bucket of water. Place the flowers in a cool room out of the sunlight for at least six hours or overnight, preferably in a dark cellar where the temperature is relatively low, until they are to be arranged in vases or packed for shipment. A darkened room will slow the development of the blooms, while placement close to an indirect light source will open the blossoms.

Certain flower stems need special treatment. Brittle stems, such as those of chrysanthemums, should be broken to expose greater surface for water intake. Woody stems, such as lilac, should be peeled back and split an inch or so. Milky stems, such as poppies, must have their ends sealed with a flame or by dipping them momentarily in boiling water.

In placing flowers in a container, be sure that it is spacious enough to permit circulation of air and proper absorption of water. Jamming them into a narrow vase chokes the flowers and shortens their life. Cut flowers survive longest if kept out of direct drafts and away from bright sunlight. They keep best in a cool and humid environment.

Plant water should be changed daily to prevent accumulation of bacteria. When changing the water, remove half an inch or so from the ends of the stem with a clean, slanting cut. This reopens the water-absorbing vessels. Leaves that would be submerged should be removed from the stems, especially in the case of asters, calendulas, chrysanthemums, and dahlias, which become foul quickly.

CUTTINGS. Vegetative tissue of a plant severed from the parent for the purpose of reproduction. They can be inserted in water, sand, soil, peat moss, or some other medium, where they form roots and/or shoots and become new plants. By this method of PROPAGATION as well as by DIVISION, LAYERING, or BUDDING, plants that are identical with the parent are reproduced. In this way, a new form that has been created by hybridization, or discovered as a variation or SPORT from the normal type, is propagated and a stock of plants is built up. Seeds from such new forms, if produced (sometimes such plants are sterile), will not be the same as the parent, but cuttings will reproduce in kind the plant from which they were severed.

Cuttings provide a simple, convenient, and inexpensive method for increasing the stock of a particular plant. Most plants are easily multiplied by this method; some are propagated more favorably by division, layering, grafting, or budding; and though herbaceous plants are commonly propagated by seed, many can also be grown from cuttings or layers when desired.

Cuttings can be classified either according to the plant parts—such as roots, tubers, rhizomes, stems, or leaves—or according to the stage of development of the parts—such as dormant, ripe, or hardwood cuttings, or active (green, immature or softwood) cuttings.

HARDWOOD CUTTINGS

Hardwood cuttings are generally used in propagating grapes, such soft-wooded trees as willows and poplars, and bushes such as gooseberries and currants. In late autumn after the leaves have fallen, the stems are cut to the desired length, generally 5–12 in. (A), tied in bundles, and buried—butt ends up—below the frost line in the soil. Or, they can be taken in winter and buried in vermiculite, sand, peat moss, or sphagnum moss, and kept moist and cool in a cellar (B). Cuttings made in fall and winter form good calluses (protective coverings of new cells on the cut surfaces) and therefore root more freely than spring cuttings.

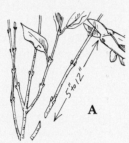

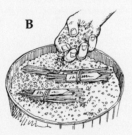

When spring comes, the callused hardwood cuttings are unearthed, dipped in a rooting compound (C), and planted, usually 4–8 in. apart, erect or slanting, preferably in light, well-drained soil with adequate moisture provided for the butt (D). Both root and stem development will be facilitated if the lower buds

on the cuttings, especially on short-segmented stock, are removed. Plants grown outdoors from such ripe or hardwood cuttings can be transplanted to nursery rows or (in the case of grapes, especially) to permanent quarters after the first season.

SOFTWOOD CUTTINGS

Green or softwood cuttings are generally rooted in greenhouses or coldframes or, on a small scale, in boxes or pots in a warm room in the house. The "wood" should be taken from vigorous plants at a stage when it breaks with a snap when bent. If it merely crushes between the fingers, it is too young to use; if it bends without breaking, it is too old. After a little practice, the favorable stage can be easily recognized.

Convenient lengths for softwood cuttings are 3–6 in. The base should be cut just below a node, or joint. The top should be cut slanting with a bud (or node from which a bud will sprout) just below the tip. There should be two or three nodes on each cutting. Lower leaves are cut off to reduce transpiration and decomposition in the rooting medium; they would die anyhow when covered over. If the remaining leaves are large, as on a begonia, from a third to a half of each is cut away to reduce evaporation from such a large leaf surface. Some of the leaf surface should be left to carry on the life processes while the cutting is forming roots.

Vermiculite (medium or coarse grade) or this plus perlite make an ideal rooting medium. Both these items are sterile (free of plant pathogenic organisms) as purchased. Sand or fine gravel that has been washed free of all clay and organic matter is also used for rooting cuttings. To wash sand, a bucket is filled half with sand; a strong stream of water from the hose is turned into the sand. When the water runs off clear, the sand is satisfactory for root cuttings, although it is not sterile. Mixtures of peat moss and washed sand or perlite are also good. Beach sand is never used, since it is too salty.

To prepare a propagating bed, a container about 3 in. deep with numerous drainage holes is filled with rooting medium, leveled, and watered thoroughly. If the medium contains sand or fine gravel, it is compressed with a block of some sort and slits or holes are opened to receive the cuttings. It is necessary to firm the medium again around the cuttings. If the mix does not contain sand or gravel, the cuttings are simply poked 2 in. deep into the mix. After planting or "sticking" the cuttings, they are watered.

From the time the cuttings are removed from the parent plant, they are always kept moist and cool (except for plants like CACTUS, which need to have their cuttings left out for a few days to dry out and callus before being stuck).

The rooting bed should be in a location with good, indirect light and good ventilation. The cuttings are kept constantly moist. If the weather is hot, covering the cuttings with a piece of newspaper that can be kept moist with a fine spray from time to time may be helpful for the first few days. BOTTOM HEAT will shorten the rooting time and, with cuttings that are more difficult to root, makes the difference between rooting and not rooting. For material that is still more difficult to root, INTERMITTENT MIST is a further aid.

When roots are ½–¾ in. long, the cuttings can be transferred to 3-in. flowerpots, one to a pot, and again given plenty of water to encourage their growth. When the roots fill these pots, the young plants should be shifted to the next size larger, and so on until they reach the largest size pot required or until they are set outdoors. See POTTING; POTTED PLANTS.

LEAF CUTTINGS

Mature leaves of some plants with or without a petiole or stem can be rooted. If the petiole is left on, as for African-violets, it serves as a stem. For leaves without petioles, such as Rex begonias, the leaf blade is placed flat on the rooting medium, pegged down with toothpicks, and the main veins cut with a razor or sharp knife at 1–2 in. intervals. The container is then covered with a piece of glass or clear plastic to maintain a saturated atmosphere. Plantlets with roots will form at the vein cuts, and then the covering is gradually removed to acclimatize the plantlets to drier air. In a few weeks after acclimatization, the plantlets are cut apart and individually potted.

Gloxinia leaves, when inserted in sand, form tubers at the base of the stem. When dried and rested for a while, they can be planted like ordinary tubers. Hyacinth leaves placed in wet sand often develop bulblets at their base.

ROOT CUTTINGS

Root cuttings can be used to propagate plants that naturally produce suckers from their roots—such as red raspberries and blackberries. In a sense, these are simply small divisions. In the spring, dig up the parent plant, cut off bits of the root, the thickness of a lead pencil and 2–4 in. long (A). The parent plant can either be replanted or discarded. If it is to be replanted, cut back the top drastically to have no more top than roots. The part of the root that is closest to the main root of the plant is considered 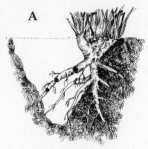  the top of the root cutting. Some propagators cut the top straight across and the bottom at a slant to aid in keeping track.

Plant cuttings in a rich loam and provide sun and moisture. When planting the roots of woody shrubs or trees, bury them so that just the top is exposed, and then cover them with ¼ in. of sharp sand or vermiculite (B).

Rhizomes, which are not really roots but underground stems, are treated similarly. The potato is the best example of cuttings made from a tuber. See also DIVISION.

CUTWORM. A name given to the larvae or caterpillars of many species of moths of the Noctuidae, including *Amathes migrum*, *Agrotis orthogonia*, and *Peridroma saucia*, which cause various types of injury on many kinds of plants, except those with woody stems. Crops seriously affected (especially in young stages) are beans, cabbage, clover, corn, cotton, tomatoes, and tobacco, but ornamental seedlings newly set out are often attacked as well. Some species are indigenous, and others are migrant, moving north each year.

Cutworm

The worms usually winter as small larvae in the soil under plant debris. In the spring, the smooth, dull gray, green, or brown, ravenously hungry caterpillars destroy tender, young plants as they are set out. Generally they cut them off at or near the surface of the ground, but some species of cutworms climb up and eat the leaves. If disturbed, they curl up and play dead until unobserved, then swiftly burrow out of sight. In early summer, the worms pupate and the somberly colored moths emerge soon afterward. Usually there is only one generation per year.

Cutworm prevention

Collars of newspaper or flexible cardboard wrapped around the stalks of transplants and other young plants, or a stick inserted beside the stem will frustrate the cutworm, which attacks by encircling the stem. A spray of **Bacillus thuringiensis** (Bt, commonly available as Biotrol, Dipel, or Thuricide) or introduction of predatory nematodes or parasitic trichogramma wasps will also act as controls for this widespread pest.

CYANOTIS (sī ah NOH tis). A genus of perennial herbs with weak or creeping stems, native in warm regions, and belonging to the Commelinaceae (Spiderwort Family). They resemble TRADESCANTIA and are grown under similar conditions in the greenhouse.

C. kewensis (teddy-bear vine) grows in prostrate form and has reddish, hairy stems and rosy purple flowers.

C. somaliensis (pussy-ears) has narrow, triangular leaves and dense heads of blue flowers.

CYATHEA (sī ATH ee ah). One of several genera of large ferns collectively known and cultivated as TREE FERNS.

CYCAD. Common name for a family of palmlike plants, including the attractive sago-palm; see CYCADACEAE.

CYCADACEAE (sī ka DAY see ee). The Cycad Family, an ancient group of palmlike plants, cone bearers rather than flowering, and even more primitive than the pines and other conifers. Principal cultivated genera include **Cycas** (sago-palm), **Dioon**, and **Encephalartos**.

CYCAS (SĪ kas). A genus including some of the largest members of the Cycadaceae (Cycad Family), with trunks that may reach 20 ft. tall and 30 in. in diameter. Commonly called sago-palm, the plant resembles a palm or tree fern with its terminal whorl of many featherlike leaves but is not related to either of these groups.

The plants are a striking part of tropical landscapes and are also used as houseplants. They do not grow well with wet feet but are not otherwise fussy about soil, as long as there is no deficiency of micronutrients, particularly manganese. Propagation is by seed, or by careful removal and rooting of small plants that form as swellings on the side of the trunk.

C. circinalas (queen-sago) has leaves up to 8 ft. long with broad, flat leaflets. Hardy in Zones 10–11.

C. revoluta (king-sago) usually has leaves less than 4 ft. long, and the leaflets have margins bent downward with a sharp tip. Hardy in sheltered spots at the southern edge of Zone 9.

CYCLAMEN (SĪK lah men). A genus of European and Asiatic plants that bear attractive flowers with sharply reflexed petals and heart-shaped leaves mottled with white among the veins.

Started from seed, which comes true to color, cyclamens take fifteen to eighteen months to reach maturity. They produce cormlike tubers, but these are seldom used in commercial propagation because they do not form plants as free flowering as specimens raised from seed.

Seed sown in early winter will germinate after the tuber has formed below ground in about two months. When two leaves appear, set several plants in a 4–5 in. pot. A fresh, fibrous, well-drained loam containing one-fifth well-rotted horse manure is best for their potting mixture. Move each plant to a 3-in. pot when root growth demands the space. Plants can be set out-

Cyclamen persicum

doors in the summer and shifted again there. They require abundant light but some shading on hot summer days.

Great care must be taken in raising cyclamens in the greenhouse, since they have numerous enemies. See that healthy plants are not too wet and that they have proper ventilation.

Diseases. A soft, slimy bacterial rot that affects the crowns of cyclamens results in stunting, wilting, and loss of leaves. Destroy infected plants.

Various fungi, including gray mold or botrytis blight, may appear on the leaves of plants kept too wet. Destroy infected parts, clean up rubbish around pots, ventilate to keep plant surfaces free from moisture, and use care in watering.

Another fungus causes conspicuous stunting and reddish brown diseased areas on the corms but rarely kills plants. The best control measure is to plant seeds from healthy plants in new or sterilized soil.

Insect Pests. The cyclamen mite is a serious problem on both greenhouse and outdoor plants. This minute animal feeds in the crevices of the tips of plants or buds, resulting in stunted and distorted plant growth. Severely infested plants do not flower. The broad mite, a related species, often causes a downward puckering of the leaves and a silvery, blistered appearance on the under-

side. Dusting frequently with fine sulfur is somewhat effective. Potted plants can also be immersed for fifteen minutes in water at 111°F. Strict greenhouse sanitation is important, and fumigation can be done if necessary. Knotty growths or galls on the roots may be due to NEMATODES. See also GREENHOUSE PESTS.

PRINCIPAL SPECIES

C. hederifolium (baby cyclamen), formerly listed as *C. neapolitanum*, has colorful foliage and late-blooming, white or pink flowers with magenta markings.

C. persicum, coming in all shades of red and white, is the large-flowered florists' cyclamen from which many hybrids have been developed by constant breeding and selection.

C. purpurascens, formerly listed as *C. europaeum*, is a small European native with rose-purple flowers, whose tubers are gathered from the wild and planted in gardens. When obtainable in North America, this species blooms in August in rock gardens in the northern states and Canada.

CYCLAMEN MITE. A common garden pest; see MITES.

CYCLANTHERA (sī klan THEE rah). A genus of annual or perennial vines, native mostly in tropical America, belonging to the Cucurbitaceae (Cucumber Family). One or two species are grown as ornamental vines for screening purposes and are treated as tender annuals. They climb by tendrils.

C. brachystachya grows to 10 ft. and has three-angled or lobed leaves and short, spiny, usually curved fruits that burst open when ripe.

C. pedata, growing to 10 ft. or more and has leaves of five to seven narrow leaflets and oblong fruit about 2 in. long, often with soft prickles.

CYDONIA (sī DOH nee ah). A genus of shrubs or small trees from the Middle East, bearing edible fruits, belonging to the Rosaceae (Rose Family), and commonly known as QUINCE. Hardy to Zone 4. *C. oblonga* has long been cultivated for its fruit, which is used in the making of choice preserves, while others are ornamental. *C. sinensis* (Chinese quince) is a large shrub or small tree that grows to 20 ft. and bears light pink flowers in spring and yellow, woody, fragrant fruits, often 7 in. long, in autumn.

CYMBALARIA (sim bah LAIR ee ah). A small genus of creeping perennial herbs belonging to the Scrophulariaceae (Figwort Family). The plants are tender in cold climates but seed themselves and thrive in moist and partly shaded locations. Some are grown as ground covers outdoors, in the greenhouse in vases or hanging baskets, or on walls. Propagation is by seed or by division of the long stems.

C. muralis (Kenilworth-ivy), the best-known species, is a small, trailing, shade-loving perennial herb that bears lilac-blue flowers with yellow throats. It is native to Europe but naturalized in the northeastern United States. It is sometimes grown as an evergreen ground cover or to drape walls, but it is even more common as a decorative trailer in greenhouses.

CYMBIDIUM (sim BID ee um). A genus of about 70 species of epiphytic or terrestrial orchids from the Asian subtropics. They are well known and popular among orchidists because of their near hardiness (to Zone 8 with ample moisture and Zone 5 if protected from frost) and easy culture.

The pseudobulbs are short, and the leaves are leathery or thin, long, lanceolate, and often decorative. The flowers are showy and fleshy in shades of white, rose, green, deep mahogany, and purple. The dorsal sepal hoods the lip, which is tubular in shape, enclosing the prominent column. The lip is often marked with gold striations and contrasts in color with the sepals and petals.

These plants can be grown outdoors in temperate regions. All require a well-drained, humusy compost of sphagnum moss, peat, sand, and dried cow manure with abundant water at the roots and high light and humidity. Some plants need a decided rest after growth is complete. The type species is *C. aloifolium*.

CYMBOPOGON (sim boh POH gahn). A genus of tall, mostly perennial grasses, natives of the tropics (hardy in Zones 10–11), and useful for border planting. They grow to a height of 6 ft. and have fragrant leaves to 3 ft. long and ¾ in. wide, covered with a whitish bloom. The flower clusters may be 2½ ft. long. *C. nardus* (citronella grass) has tapering, lancelike spikelets, while those of *C. citratus* (lemon grass) are linear and not tapering. *C. choenanthus* (camel-hay) is a dwarf species, growing to 2 ft., with the joints of its flower clusters covered with hair. Citronella oil, used as a deterrent against mosquitoes, is derived from *C. nardus* and other species. See ORNAMENTAL GRASSES.

CYME. A more or less flat-topped, often branched cluster of flowers in which those in the center bloom first. The blossoming moves outward toward the perimeter of the cluster. Contrast CORYMB.

CYNARA (SIN ah rah). A genus of about a dozen old world, thistlelike perennial herbs with large, purple, blue, or white flowers. *C. scolymus* (French or globe ARTICHOKE) and *C. cardunculus* (CARDOON) are cultivated as vegetables.

CYNODON (SĪN oh dahn) **dactylon.** Commonly known as Bermuda grass, a creeping perennial grass that is propagated from springs, sod, or plugs but spreads by means of runners or stolons. The narrow leaves, to 2 in. long, are rough on top. Bermuda grass might be called the "Kentucky bluegrass of the South," for it is one of the most important pasture and lawn grasses for that region.

Cynodon dactylon

Preferring a fertile, rather heavy soil that is not too wet, but able to grow on light sand and tolerate a more alkaline condition than most crops, it thrives throughout the hot weather but cannot survive hard freezing. Bermuda grass will turn a strawlike color with the onset of cool temperatures in the fall, and it remains that way throughout the winter until spring.

Established from Virginia southward and westward to Arizona and California, Bermuda grass is widely used for athletic fields and golf courses as well as lawns, but owing to its persistent character in frost-free regions, it sometimes becomes a bad weed in cultivated fields. See LAWN.

CYNOGLOSSUM (sin oh GLAHS um). A genus of rather weedy herbs belonging to the Boraginaceae (Borage Family) and commonly known as hound's-tongue. Plants grow about 2 ft. tall, with stiff, hairy leaves, the shape of which inspired the common name. Although they are of little interest in the garden, they are occasionally grown for their blue flowers. Propagation is by seed.

PRINCIPAL SPECIES

C. amabile (Chinese-forget-me-not), one of the more common species, is a biennial used for bedding, borders, or rock gardens. Its small, fragrant flowers are blue, pink, or white.

C. nervosum is larger and showier than most other species.

C. virginianum is a frequently naturalized perennial, with clusters of oblong flowers ½ in. across.

C. wallichi, an annual, has racemes of very small, blue flowers.

Cynoglossum amabile

CYPERACEAE (sī pur AY see ee). The Sedge Family, a group of perennial grasslike herbs distinguished from the grasses by their solid, three-angled stems, the leaves borne in closed sheaths, and the very different flowers borne on spikes. Distributed around the world, sedges are commonly found in low, marshy places and are principally cultivated as ornamentals in water gardens; only a few genera are commonly grown, including *Carex*, *Cyperus*, and *Scirpus*.

CYPERUS (sī PEE rus). A genus of moisture-loving herbs, including some perennials commonly grown in Zones 9–11. The genus lends its name to the Cyperaceae (Sedge Family).

PRINCIPAL SPECIES

C. alternifolius (umbrella plant) grows 3–4 ft. high and resembles a miniature clump of palm trees. A splendid plant for the shallow water at the edge of the pond or for the large aquarium, it requires rich soil and, as long as its roots are wet, thrives equally well indoors or outside. Indeed, it survives as a houseplant under conditions where other plants cannot. The leaf crown will produce new plants if cut off and pressed flat into damp sand or moss. Cv. 'Gracilis' is smaller and better suited for use in aquariums than the type.

C. esculentus (nutsedge, chufa) is a reedlike herb that is grown in the southern states chiefly as food for poultry and pigs. Its many roots are hard, little tubers, often called nuts, and can be eaten roasted or cooked.

Cyperus esculentus

C. papyrus (papyrus, paper plant), the plant from which the ancient Egyptians made paper, grows 10–15 ft. tall in summer and displays a moplike crown of fine, grassy leaves at the top of each stem. It should be planted in a box of rich soil and submerged in shallow water. Since it is tender, this will facilitate moving it indoors when frost approaches. Propagation is by seed or by division of the root clump in the spring or early summer while the plant is in peak growth.

CYPHOMANDRA (sī foh MAN drah) **betacea.** A South American shrub commonly known as treetomato. It has fragrant, pinkish flowers and is sometimes grown in northern greenhouses or outdoors in Zones 9–11 for its egg-shaped, mildly acid fruits.

CYPHOSTEMMA (sɪ FAWS tem ah). A genus of southern and tropical African succulents in the Vitaceae (Grape Family), formerly included in the genus *Cissus*. Some members have spectacularly caudiciform, highly succulent trunks, such as *C. juttae* or *C. bainesi*. *C. cramerana*, from Namibia, grows to 12 ft. tall. The flowers are small and inconspicuous, but the fruits are quite large, colorful, and attractive. Propagation is predominantly from seed in the more succulent species.

CYPRESS. Common name for CUPRESSUS, a genus of trees suited to mild and warm regions.

The bald-cypress of swampy areas is *Taxodium distichum*, of which pond-cypress is a variety; and Montezuma-cypress is *T. mucronatum*. Cypress vine is *Ipomoea quamoclit*, a showy annual vine; see IPOMOEA. False cypress is the genus CHAMAECYPARIS. Standing-cypress is the scarlet-flowered herb *Ipomopsis rubra*; see IPOMOPSIS. Summer-cypress is the annual *Kochia scorparia*; see KOCHIA.

CYPRIPEDIUM (sip ruh PEE dee um). A genus of orchids native to temperate zones of Asia, Europe, and North America, commonly known as lady's-slipper or moccasin flower. Often growing 3 ft. high, the plants have fans of plicate, deciduous leaves. They are terrestrial with fibrous roots. Showy flowers of pink, yellow, or green have an erect dorsal sepal, a synsepalum (united lateral sepals), and long, twisted petals. The lip is an inflated pouch.

Cypripedium sp.

They are hardy in Zones 1–8 if protected from freezing, withstanding a minimum winter temperature of 55°F, and are marginally hardy in Zones 9–11. Some native species are seen in wild gardens; however, they are protected and should never be collected from their natural surroundings. They do well in shade when kept moist, planted in sand mixed with peat, leaf mold, and sphagnum moss.

C. reginae, formerly listed as *C. spectabile*, is the state flower of Minnesota and has white petals striped with rose or purple in early summer. The type species is *C. calceolus*.

CYRILLA (sir IL ah). A genus of deciduous or semievergreen shrubs or trees commonly known as leatherwood. *C. racemiflora* has tough, fibrous bark and tough, flexible shoots that can be bent and twisted without breaking. Hardy in Zones 6–9.

CYRTOMIUM (sir TOH mee um). A genus of medium-sized ferns with tough, glossy, pinnate fronds. The rhizomes are nearly erect.

PRINCIPAL SPECIES

C. caryotideum (dwarf holly fern), native to Asia and Hawaii, is a small, compact fern growing 6–12 in. and thriving in pots. It can be grown in the garden in warm-temperate or subtropical areas in acid, humus-rich soil and semishade.

C. falcatum (holly or Japanese holly fern) is a popular houseplant in many countries and is grown in the garden where suitable. The glossy, dark green, pinnate fronds have pinnae whose toothed edges give it the appearance of Oregon holly. Native to China, Japan, and Korea, it is hardy to Zone 7, or 6 if grown in a protected spot. Cultivars include 'Butterfieldii', 'Mayi' (Cristata), and the commonest, 'Rochfordianum'.

C. fortunei is very similar to *C. falcatum* and is native to the same regions, but it has more erect, paler green, dull fronds and narrower, more numerous pinnae.

CYSTOPTERIS (sis TAHP tur is). A genus of small ferns with delicate, bipinnate to quadripinnate fronds that are deciduous in cold areas. Both the generic name and the common name, bladder fern, refer to the bulbils that form on the rachis and pinnae rachis of some species. A few species, native and hardy in most of North America, do well in the garden in proper soil.

PRINCIPAL SPECIES

C. bulbifera (berry or bulblet bladder fern) is an easily grown fern that, with suitable growing conditions, can clothe an area with its 12-in. fronds in a short time. It spreads by dropping the bulblets that form on the reverse of the fronds and soon take root. Unwanted plants are easily pulled. It is bipinnate and grows in crevices of limestone rocks. It also does well in walls. It is native to Canada and the northern states, where it frequently hybridizes with *C. fragilis* and *C. protrusa* to produce the fertile hybrids *C. laurentiana* and *C. tennesseensis*.

C. fragilis (fragile fern) is a dainty fern whose rhizomes spread soil to form sizable colonies. It has 5–15 in., bipinnate-pinnatifid fronds. Its common name comes from the brittleness of its fronds. It is very hardy and is commonly found in North America and moist regions of the world, especially in rocky woodlands and near streams.

C. montana (mountain fragile fern) is a rare species with a far-creeping rhizome and tripinnate-pinnatifid, deltoid fronds. It is found in North America, mostly in Canada, and the boreal areas of Europe and Asia.

CYTISUS (SIT is us). A genus of attractive shrubs native in Europe, Asia, and Africa, belonging to the Fabaceae (Bean Family), and commonly known as broom. This genus is closely related to GENISTA and includes some species formerly classified there. The species are deciduous or evergreen and in some cases almost leafless. One or two are popular greenhouse plants, and several can be grown outdoors in Zone 5 if given suitable conditions. Still others are good for rock garden planting. They require full exposure to sun and wind with perfect drainage at the roots and pre-

fer poor soil to rich. The taller kinds are likely to become straggly unless pruned back after flowering. Small plants are easier to establish than larger ones. Propagation is by cuttings, layers, and grafting.

PRINCIPAL SPECIES

C. canariensis (genista) is an evergreen shrub sold by florists for winter and spring flowering under glass, especially at Easter. It grows well in a sandy loam. After flowering, the plant should be trimmed back to a compact shape and plunged outdoors during the summer.

C. x *kewensis* is very similar to *C. albus*.

C. multiflorus (white Spanish-broom) is a slender grower to 3 ft. and has a profusion of white flowers.

C. nigricans is a slender grower to 4 ft. and has spikes of clear yellow flowers in midsummer.

C. x *praecox*, one of the showiest, is a vigorous growing hybrid to 10 ft. and has a mass of sulfur yellow flowers. Hardy to Zone 7.

C. albus, with creamy white flowers, is a ground cover adaptable to rock gardens or slopes.

C. purpureus, with purple flowers and prostrate habit, is suitable for planting in rock gardens or on slopes where hardy.

C. racemosus (genista) is very similar to *C. canariensis* in use and appearance.

C. scoparius (Scotch broom) is a semihardy European shrub growing to 10 ft. that has become naturalized in some parts of North America. It is valuable for planting on dry, gravelly banks and makes a good showing with its bright green stems and abundant yellow, pealike flowers. Cv. 'Andreanus' is more tender, with striking flowers of yellow and crimson. Hardy to Zone 6.

C. supinus is a hardy, low shrub of dense habit with terminal heads of yellow flowers that bloom in summer.

D**DABOECIA** (dah BEES ee ah) **cantabrica.** A low evergreen shrub native in Ireland and southwest Europe, belonging to the Ericaceae (Heath Family), and commonly called Irish heath. Compatible with other heaths and heathers, it is suitable for planting in the rock garden, thriving in peaty soil, but it requires winter protection, being hardy only to Zone 7. It grows to a foot or more and has small, shining green leaves, whitish beneath, and relatively large, loose, bell-like nodding sprays of purple flowers. There are a number of cultivars on the market. 'Alba' is a white-flowered form, and 'Bicolor' has flowers striped white and purple. Propagation is by cuttings of half-ripened shoots under glass.

DACTYLIS (DAK ti lis). A genus of perennial grasses, hardy to Zone 5. The most important species is *D. glomerata* (orchard grass), planted in meadows and pastures, sometimes included in lawn seed mixtures for shady areas. Except that it is quick-growing and will withstand shade, it is not a desirable lawn grass, since it is coarse and makes a bunchy turf. Var. *variegata*, with silver-striped leaves, is a dwarf ornamental sometimes planted in borders.

DAFFODIL. Common name often applied indiscriminately to any kind of NARCISSUS, but which correctly refers to several of the hardy species, especially the larger, single-flowered trumpet sorts. It is not the same as jonquil, which refers to only one narcissus species.

Peruvian-daffodil is *Hymenocallis narcissiflora*, a South American species of spider-lily; see HYMENOCALLIS.

DAHLIA (DAHL yuh). A genus of tender perennial herbs that grow from tuberous roots and are usually treated as half-hardy annuals. Flowers vary widely in color, including nearly all colors except blue.

Native to the mountains of Mexico, the plants, called Acoctii by the natives, were first discovered in the 16th century by a Spanish physician sent by King Philip II to study the natural history of the region. About 1789, plants and seeds were sent to Europe, and Andreas Dahl, a Swedish botanist and student of the great Linnaeus, became so involved in its study and development that the genus was ultimately named for him. The original species was called *D. variabilis* (now listed as *D. pinnata*), and thousands of hybrids have been developed as a result of its variability. Many other forms, including the cactus dahlias, have been developed from species discovered later.

CLASSIFICATION

For exhibition purposes, the American Dahlia Society divides the genus into general categories, largely dependent on flower shape.

1. Incurved Cactus. Fully double flowers with margins of the majority of the floral rays revolute (rolled or quilled) for at least half their length, the floral rays tending to curve toward the center of the flower.

2. Straight and Recurved Cactus. Fully double flowers with the margins of most of the floral rays revolute for half their length or more, the floral rays being recurved or straight.

3. Peony. Open-centered flowers with not more than three rows of ray florets regardless of form or number of florets, with the addition of smaller curled or twisted floral rays around the disk.

4. Semicactus. Fully double flowers with the margins of most of the floral rays revolute for less than half their length.

5. Formal Decorative. Fully double flowers, rays generally broad, either pointed or rounded at tips, with outer floral rays tending to recurve and central floral rays tending to be

Formal decorative

cupped, all floral rays in somewhat regular arrangement.

6. Informal Decorative. Fully double flowers, floral rays generally long, twisted or pointed, and usually irregular in arrangement.

7. Ball. Fully double flowers, ball-shaped or slightly flattened, floral rays in spiral arrangement, blunt or rounded at tips, and quilled or with markedly involute margins; 2 in. or more in diameter.

Anemone

8. Anemone. Open-centered flowers with only one row of ray florets regardless of form or number of florets, with the tubular disk florets elongated, forming a pincushion effect.

9. Single. Open-centered flowers with only one row of ray flowers regardless of form or number of florets.

Single

10. Pompon. Fully double flowers, ball-shaped or slightly flattened, floral rays in spiral arrangement, blunt or rounded and quilled, or with markedly involute margins; less than 2 in. across.

11. Collarette. Open-centered flowers with only one row of ray florets, with the addition of one or more rows of petaloids, usually of a

Colarette

different color, forming a collar around the disc.

12. Miscellaneous. This group accommodates any dahlia not fitting into the other groups. Other categories are sometimes listed, including Miniature Decorative, Duplex, Mignon, Orchid-flowering, and Dwarf.

SOIL AND SITE

There is a common but erroneous impression that dahlias are not particular about soil or location. Since they are native to hot, high, dry climates, all dahlias need well-drained soil. In wet, heavy, poorly drained soils where water settles, plants cannot thrive and will usually die. Under favorable conditions, however, a single tuber planted at the beginning of the growing season will produce five to fifteen tubers, depending on the variety, forming a clump by the end of the season. This shows the gross feeding capacity of the plant, whose rootlets shoot out from the tubers in all directions. Dahlias grow best in well-drained, loamy soil mixed well with humus or decayed leaf mold.

PLANTING

Midspring after all danger of frost is passed is the best planting time; the exact dates depend on the locality and season. Being of tropical or subtropical origin, a dahlia plant can be easily and sometimes seriously checked and stunted if hit by a late freeze or a spell of cold, wet weather in early spring.

Sufficient space should be allowed in planting. Leave 3 ft. between plants in the row and at least the same distance between rows for the taller decorative kinds. For the miniatures, less space is needed. For best results, however, dahlias of any type should never be crowded.

After the soil has been prepared and stout stakes driven at the correct distances before planting (so that the roots will not be injured), the soil should be drawn away from a stake and a tuber laid flat on the soil with the new growth or sprout end nearest the stake. The depression must be deep enough so that when the soil is replaced gradually as growth preceeds, at least 6 in. of soil will cover the tuber.

As plants grow, the stems should be securely (but not tightly) fastened to the stakes, preferably with some wide fabric. Strips of strong cloth about 1 in. wide will prevent damage to the hollow, pithy stalks during storms or high winds. Cord is not suitable, since it will often cut through the hollow stake. See TYING.

DISBUDDING

When plants reach a height of 12 in., the tips can be pinched out, leaving two sets of two leaves each remaining on the plant. At the junction of each of these four remaining leaves with the main stem, a new flowering branch will take the place of the single main stem whose tip was removed. This will retard the flowering season from ten days to two weeks, which is desirable since the finest flowers are always produced on the younger, more tender growth. All flower buds should be removed until early August, after which they can be allowed to mature.

Flower buds will appear as growth proceeds. A center bud and two side buds form at the end of each flower stalk. At the junction of each leaf and stalk below the tip, three more buds will appear. The leaves are on opposite sides of the stalk, and flower buds always appear in threes. For large exhibition flowers, allow the tip or center bud to remain, pinching out the two side buds. The two series of buds next below the terminal or tip bud should then be removed, taking care that the leaves are not injured, since foliage counts for points as well as flowers in the exhibitions. This disbudding should give the terminal bud a stem 18–24 in. long. It can be further lengthened by removing the third series of bulbs.

Disbudding is only done to the decorative forms (both formal and informal), to straight and incurved cactus forms, and to the peony-flowered types. It should not be practiced with the colarettes, miniatures, and others where a wealth of bloom is preferred over the size of the individual blossoms.

FEEDING AND CULTIVATING

Assuming the soil contains plenty of humus-making material and is well drained, dahlias will require regular applications of a complete fertilizer at intervals of about one month beginning when the plants are 12 in. high. Such a fertilizer should be high in phosphoric acid and potash content and relatively low in nitrogen, since the plants are naturally leafy. Under no circumstances should ordinary stable manure be used alone, as it would produce a rank growth of foliage and only a few poor flowers.

Cultivation must follow every application of fertilizer and every rain so that a dust mulch (not more than 1–2 in. deep) is maintained at all times. This makes the plant food available for the roots and keeps weeds in check. Green cover crops of rye, vetch, or similar plants grown over the winter and turned under in the early spring to decay will keep dahlia soil in ideal condition.

Where it is desired to hasten growth for backward plants or to meet exhibition dates, liquid manure can be applied. Sulfate of ammonia, nitrate of soda, or urea can be used at the rate of not more than 1 tsp. per gallon of water and applied at intervals of two or three weeks. These are not complete foods, however, and will not take the place of more balanced formulas; they supply nitrogen only and are used only for forcing purposes.

BLOOMS FOR EXHIBITION

To be in best form, exhibition blooms should be cut in the early morning or late evening, never during the heat of the day. Sharp garden shears should be used, and the cut made on a long angle to allow plenty of water to enter the stem cells. If the stem is cut squarely across, or torn or pinched together by a dull knife, the crushed arteries will not absorb water freely. As soon as it is cut, the bloom should be deeply immersed in plain cold water and placed in a cool, dark, shaded location for six hours. In this time, it will absorb all the water needed and will be ready for showing or decorative use. If the stem is shortened daily by about an inch with a clean, long-angled cut and fresh water is supplied, the flowers should stay in perfect condition for five days.

FALL CARE

After plants have been cut down by a killing frost, remove the tops, leaving stubs 6 in. tall. Allow the clumps to remain in the soil for ten days or two weeks to thoroughly ripen, after which they can be removed. Use great care in digging, so that the narrow neck that connects the tuber and clump is not injured or the tender neck broken; otherwise a blind tuber results. When the clumps have dried out so the soil shakes freely from them, they can be stored for the winter in dry quarters where they will not freeze or dry out as a result of exposure to the air. A cellar with the same conditions that keep stored potatoes in good condition will suit dahlias. The clumps can be packed in boxes or barrels, either covered with any light, perfectly dry material such as bran or sawdust, or wrapped well in dry newspaper and stored where they cannot absorb dampness. Cold rooms partitioned off in the cellar where the temperature remains in the forties will prove ideal.

PROPAGATION

Dahlias can be propagated by division of the clumps, by cuttings taken from growing plants, and by seed. Division is the most common home garden method. Tubers from divided clumps or cuttings made in either spring or fall will all reproduce true, while seedlings may vary.

Division. Plants do not grow from an eye, like the potato; growth starts only at the junction of the narrow neck of the tuber and the tough wood of the old stem or stalk. In dividing a clump, therefore, each individual tuber must be cut with some portion of the old stalk attached to the neck of the tuber and with the skin of the neck unbroken; otherwise no growth will result.

Tuber division

Growth of the sprouts in early spring is a guide to the division of the clumps, which is the common garden practice.

Cuttings. Commercial growers expose clumps to heat, light, and moisture during February or early March, when growth quickly starts. When a new sprout has formed at least two sets of leaves, it can be cut off cleanly with a sharp blade just below the first set of leaves nearest to the tuber. Without tearing, cut off the lowest set of leaves and insert the cutting up to the second set of leaves in sand in a hotbed or propagating box. The cuttings root readily in moist sand and will soon need to be transplanted into light soil and

kept shaded for a few days to prevent wilting. It is advisable to spray them with a gentle mist two or three times a day until they are well started. Thereafter, gradual exposure to sun and air will soon harden them off ready for their permanent bed.

Cuttings can also be taken from green, growing plants during August or early September. Taken from nonflower-bearing branches, they should be treated as above, started in the smallest sized pots and shifted to larger ones as necessary and encouraged to grow until the tops are cut down by frost. The tubers should remain in the pot and be stored for the winter. Taken out at planting time, although they may be curiously twisted from growing in a pot, they can be treated like any other tuber.

Seed. Dahlias can be propagated from seed sown indoors in early spring and planted out at the usual time. They will bear flowers and form tubers during the same growing season, but they will not reproduce true to the parent. Unless systematically handcrossed by experienced breeders, seedling plants rarely have exceptional value; if not superior (or at least equal) to existing varieties, such plants should be destroyed. Experienced growers, knowing that a change of soil, different climatic conditions, and excessive food are all important factors in producing variability of this remarkable plant, use this method to produce new varieties.

DISEASE

Dahlia stunt, which makes plants short and bushy with excessive side branches, can be caused by feeding insects or by mosaic disease. Mosaic is characterized by yellowish or pale green bands along the leaf veins or by general mottling, roughening, curling, or crinkling of the leaves. Affected plants do not recover and should be destroyed to prevent spreading. The disease is carried in cuttings and root divisions as well as aphids, but not in seed or soil. Resistant varieties should be grown.

Three wilt diseases can affect dahlias. One is a soft, wet bacterial soft rot, showing a yellow ooze when the stem is cut. The other two are caused by fungi that leave browned stems and decay stored root tubers. Remove wilted plants and the soil immediately surrounding them as soon as possible, and select healthy plants for propagation. To prevent tubers from rotting in storage, the clumps can be dusted with sulfur.

Mildew, a white coating over the leaves, may appear late in the season but is not particularly serious. It is readily controlled by dusting with sulfur.

INSECT PESTS

Dahlias are sometimes attacked by the common stalk or stem borer—grayish brown, white-striped larvae that cause wilting and sometimes the death of plants. Their presence is often evidenced by small holes and exudations of sawdust near the base of the stem. If discovered in time, they can be killed and the plant saved by carefully slitting the stem lengthwise with a sharp knife, by probing with a flexible wire, or by injecting carbon-bisulfide or other sulfer compounds. Since the insects attack many weeds, where the inconspicuous adult moths lay eggs in the fall, keeping all weeds cut down in the vicinity of the garden will largely control these pests.

The European corn borer attacks dahlias. Its control is difficult because it attacks so many hosts, including both useful plants and weeds. In most infested regions, there is only one generation each year, but in New England there are two. The most effective control measure is to cut plants and weeds in the fall as close to the ground as possible. Spraying with rotenone will kill young borers before they enter the stalks.

Chewing insects, such as the grasshopper, can cause problems, but they can be prevented or controlled by spraying with a stomach poison.

Plants stunted by the feeding activities of other insects, including leaf hoppers, thrips, or plant bugs, will recover if the pests are destroyed with pyrethrum or other suitable sprays. The active tarnished plant bug causes blackening or unequal development of the flower beds; cleaning up garden rubbish where the insect may winter is one control method.

See also INSECT CONTROL.

PRINCIPAL SPECIES

D. coccinea forms a slender plant that grows to 4 ft. high and has single, typically eight-petaled flowers that are scarlet above and lighter below. It is not often cultivated.

D. excelsa (flat tree dahlia), *D. imperialis* (bell, tree, or candelabra dahlia), and *D. maxoni* are all tall, more or less woody forms that grow to 20 ft. and have single, usually eight-petaled flowers in shades of pink, red, and lavender. They are sometimes grown in warm regions.

D. juarezi is the parent of the cactus dahlias.

D. mercki (bedding dahlia) is a slender plant to 3 ft. tall with finely cut foliage and erect, single, lilac flowers.

D. pinnata (or *P. variabilis*) is the parent species of the familiar garden dahlias.

D. popenovi grows to 4 ft. with single scarlet flowers with eight-quilled petals. It is believed to be an even older form than *D. juarezi*, possibly the ultimate ancestor of the cactus dahlia.

DAHOON. Common name for *Ilex cassine*, an evergreen holly native from Virginia southward; see ILEX.

DAISY. Common name for numerous members of the Asteraceae (Aster or Daisy Family), especially *Bellis* and *Chrysanthemum*.

African daisy, known in California as freeway daisy, is *Arctotis*, with white, yellow, and violet flowers; also *Lonas*, from the Mediterranean, with yellow flowers; and sometimes *Gerbera*, better known as Transvaal daisy.

African golden daisy refers to species of *Dimorphotheca*, better known as cape-marigold.

Arctic daisy is *Chrysanthemum arcticum*, a hardy low-growing perennial with white or lilac flowers.

Barberton daisy is the pastel-colored *Gerbera jamesonii*.

Blue daisy is *Felicia*, a tender African subshrub with solitary heads of yellow disk and blue ray flowers.

Cape daisy is the annual *Venidium fastuosum*, also known as monarch-of-the-veldt.

Crown daisy is *Chrysanthemum coronarium*.

Daisy bush or daisy tree refers to the tropical *Olearia*.

Easter daisy is *Townsendia exscapa*.

English daisy is *Bellis perennis*, the daisy of literature, a hardy dwarf perennial with rounded double flower heads of white and pink.

Globe daisy is *Globularia trichosantha*.

Korean daisy is *Chrysanthemum coreanum*, a hardy plant with single white flowers.

Michaelmas daisy refers to many leafy fall-blooming forms of ASTER.

Nippon daisy is *Chrysanthemum nipponicum*.

Orange daisy is *Erigeron aurantiacus*.

Oxeye daisy is the common wildflower *Chrysanthemum leucanthemum*.

Painted daisy is *Chrysanthemum coccineum*.

Paris daisy is *Chrysanthemum frutescens*.

Seaside daisy is *Erigeron glaucus*.

Shasta daisy is *Chrysanthemum maximum*.

South African daisy is *Gazania*.

Swan river daisy is *Brachycome iberidifolia*.

Transvaal daisy is *Gerbera jamesonii*.

White daisy is *Chrysanthemum leucanthemum* or *Layia glandulosa*.

Yellow daisy is *Rudbeckia hirta*, better known as black-eyed-Susan.

DAISY TREE. Common name for OLEARIA, a genus of tender evergreen shrubs and trees of the Asteraceae (Aster Family).

DALECHAMPIA (day le CHAM pee ah) **roezliana.** A small, upright or climbing tropical shrub belonging to the Euphorbiaceae (Spurge Family). Hardy in Zones 10–11, it is grown in greenhouses for its large and attractive rosy pink bracts. Inside the two large outer bracts are smaller ones placed among the small male and female flowers, which are curiously shaped and yellowish in color. It requires perfect drainage and a mixture of sandy loam, peat, and leaf mold. Propagation is by cuttings.

DALLIS GRASS. Common name for *Paspalum dilatatum*, a South American grass introduced in the Southeast as an ornamental or pasture grass; see PASPALUM.

DAMASK ROSE. Very ancient, and probably acquiring its name by distribution to western lands from the area dominated by the city of Damascus around the time of the Crusades, though these roses are thought to be native to regions farther east. Damask roses were also widely distributed during Roman times, but unlike the Gallica roses, which naturalized easily, these required good cultivation. Grown in monastery gardens during the dark ages, they returned to prominence in the sixteenth century.

Damask roses are thorny, arching shrubs with small clusters of pink or white blooms, which are intensely fragrant. *R. damascena trigintipetala* is grown in the Kazanlik Valley of Bulgaria for attar used in the perfume industry.

The repeat-flowering form of the damask rose, *R. damascena semperflorens* (autumn damask), led to the development of the damask perpetual or Portland roses and took part in the development of the Bourbon roses through a natural cross with the pink China rose.

Well-known varieties include 'Mme. Hardy', 'Celsiana', 'Leda', Painted Damask, 'Ispahan', and 'Marie Louise'.

DAMMAR-PINE. Common name for AGATHIS, a genus of tall evergreen trees of the Araucariaceae (Araucaria Family).

DAMPING-OFF. A name given by gardeners to the wilting and death of seedlings just before or just after they emerge from the soil. When, instead of the uniform, well-filled rows of seedlings expected in a flat or seedbed, one finds rows thin and broken by many bare spots, or when many of a good stand of seedlings suddenly collapse or fall over on the ground and die, it is usually the disease called damping-off that is responsible.

The cause is not one specific organism, as with most plant diseases, but may be any one of several fungi that live in the soil near the surface and, under favorable conditions, enter the plants just as they come out of the ground. The slender, tender stems shrivel up and the plants topple over. Overly thick planting and high humidity are factors favoring the development of these fungi, which can cause losses up to 90–100% of an entire planting.

Damping-off

There is no way to cure or save a seedling affected by damping-off. Such plants should be discarded along with the surrounding soil. If the disease appears in the corner of a hotbed, it can sometimes be prevented from spreading by prompt action to correct the conditions that favor it. Ventilate and dry off the bed; remove the dead plants with some of the soil if they are restricted to a limited area. A practice among commercial growers is to heat some fine sand in the oven and sprinkle it lightly on the soil among the uninfected seedlings with a view to killing or preventing the spread of the fungus.

Damping-off can be largely prevented by treating, before sowing, either the soil or the seed with heat or with chemicals. In greenhouses where steam is available, it is the best means for soil sterilization. At home, treat small lots of soil by baking it in an oven for the time required to bake a potato placed in the center of the flat or pan of soil.

Red copper oxide (purchased as cuprous oxide or under various trade names) markedly improves the stand of many vegetable and flower seedlings. Use at the rate of only a small pinch of the material to an ordinary packet of seeds, shaking the seeds and dust together in a bottle. Red copper oxide as a spray (4 tsp. to 3 gal. water) is also useful in preventing damping-off of young seedlings. Spray the surface of the soil immediately after first watering, and spray the plants as they appear above ground.

See also DISINFECTION; DISEASE.

DANDELION. Common name for the widespread, yellow-flowering herb TARAXACUM.

Dwarf- and mountain-dandelion are common names for the genus KRIGIA whose species resemble the common dandelion.

DAPHNE (DAF nee). A genus of small deciduous or evergreen shrubs belonging to the Thymelaeaceae (Mezereum Family) and native in Europe, northern Africa, and Asia. They are chiefly valued for their fragrant spring flowers, sometimes resembling those of candytuft. They thrive best in well-drained, sandy loam well supplied with leaf mold. Hardiness varies, but most thrive to Zone 6.

PRINCIPAL SPECIES

D. x *burkwoodii* (Burkwood daphne) is a hybrid that grows to 4 ft. and has fragrant pinkish white flowers and red fruit. This is a vigorous growing plant and is easier to grow than other species; hardy to Zone 4. Two outstanding cultivars are 'Somerset', with bushy growth to 4 ft., and 'Carol Mackie', a very hardy and beautiful plant, leaves edged with cream color.

D. cneorum (garland flower, rose daphne) is a choice low evergreen with dense clusters of very fragrant pink flowers in spring, and often a second crop in the fall. Light soil or peat moss spread over the base of a plant induces stem rooting and the development of a larger clump; hardy in Zones 5–7.

D. genkwa is a slender deciduous shrub from China with pale lilac flowers appearing before the leaves; hardy to Zone 5.

D. laureola (spurge-laurel) is an evergreen shrub that grows to 4 ft. and has large, shining green leaves and yellowish green flowers in early spring. It grows best in partial shade and moist soil and is only hardy to Zone 7.

D. mezereum (mezereum, February daphne) is a European deciduous shrub that has become naturalized in some parts of the United States. Its very fragrant lilac-purple flowers appear before the leaves, often in early spring. In the summer it is attractive with scarlet fruit. Hardy to Zone 6.

D. odora (winter daphne) is an evergreen that grows to 4 ft. with dense heads of very fragrant white or purplish flowers. It is hardy to Zone 7 but is a good plant for the cool greenhouse.

DAPHNIPHYLLUM (daf ni FIL um). A genus of handsome, small evergreen trees or shrubs native to China and Japan, and belonging to the Euphorbiaceae (Spurge Family). They grow slowly and can be cultivated only where frosts are light; generally hardy to Zone 8. A partly protected location with rich, moist soil in which lime is present suits them best.

D. humile is a dwarf form with oval leaves and dark blue fruit.

D. macropodum, growing to 30 ft., is the best-known species. Its twigs are red when young, and the large, handsome leaves, glaucous beneath, somewhat resemble those of a rhododendron. The flowers are not conspicuous, but the fruits are bloomy black.

DARLINGTONIA (dahr ling TOH nee ah). A genus of insectivorous plants of the Sarraceniaceae (Sarracenia Family), occurring in limited areas of springs and bogs in northern California and southwestern Oregon but offered throughout the country as a houseplant. Their leaves, from 3–30 in. long, grow from a rootstock in an annual rosette and are modified into a pitcher shape, the fused half of the leaves forming a lid decorated with an attractive crimson and green tonguelike appendage. The leaves are hollow, fascinatingly colored, and covered with honey glands so that insects are lured within them and drowned in the liquid secreted at the hollow base. Darlingtonias are not hardy in the north (hardy to Zone 7) but in several instances have

Darlingtonia californica

wintered over. They are generally grown in greenhouses, under the same conditions as *Sarracenia* and other allied species, in a soil of perlite and peat. They must be kept constantly moist and benefit from being in a saucer of standing water. They appreciate being crowded and the roots kept cool. Propagation is done by seed or division.

D. californica (California pitcher-plant or cobra-lily) has tubular leaves and an arched hood marked with translucent areas that admit light into the interior. The yellowish to brownish red flowers appear on a 2-in. stem and are 1¼ in. across, blooming from May to July.

DASHEEN. A common name for the natural or forced sprouts of *Colocasia esculenta*; see COLOCASIA.

DASYLIRION (da si LEER ee un). A genus of desert plants of the United States and Mexico, belonging to the Liliaceae (Lily Family), and commonly called sotol. They are short-trunked, stiff plants with long and narrow leaves crowded near the top to form a more or less dome-shaped head. They are very striking in bloom with dense-panicled racemes of small whitish flowers towering high above the crown of leaves. They are sometimes grown in pots or tubs for formal decoration and are propagated by seed.

D. glaucophyllum has glaucous leaves to 4 ft. long, the margins armed with small teeth. The flower stems grow 12–18 ft. high.

D. wheeleri (spoonflower) has leaves to 3 ft. long, armed with brown-tipped teeth and with long, usually drooping racemes on stems 9–15 ft. The leaves of this species are long, stiff, and very slender except at the base, which is broad, ivory-colored, highly polished, and spoon-shaped where they overlap one another. They have become popular, collected and sold in large numbers for use in flower arrangements.

DATE. The fruit of a palm tree, *Phoenix dactylifera*, which has been cultivated in arid regions for about 5000 years. Although date palms have been grown in Florida and California and some other parts of the United States for more than a century, the trees yield poorly because the temperatures are not continuously high enough to ripen the fruit.

Commercial growing in North America, which started about 1890 in Arizona, was stimulated by importation of superior varieties by Walter T. Swingle of the U. S. Department of Agriculture. It is now well established in irrigated fields in California, Arizona, and parts of Texas. Since the male and female flowers are borne on different trees, and inferior seedless dates develop from unpollinated flowers, natural pollination is supplemented by tying branches of male flower clusters among the female flower clusters during peak fertilization periods.

Propagation of choice varieties is by suckers, which develop from the base to 10 ft. up the trunk. Trees three to six years old are moved in spring to favored locations in warm soil, and their tops are reduced. Such trees should start bearing fruit at five or six years old and should be producing 100–200 lb. fruit annually at ten to fifteen years. The fruit clusters are generally cut before they are fully ripe and are matured somewhat like bananas in a warm room. See PHOENIX.

DATE-PLUM. Common name for *Diospyros lotus*, a small deciduous Asiatic tree, a species of PERSIMMON.

DATURA (dah TYOO rah). A genus of annual or perennial herbs, shrubs, or trees found in warm regions, belonging to the Solanaceae (Nightshade Family), and commonly known as thorn-apple. They are mostly coarse, strong-smelling plants, but a few are grown for the sake of their large trumpet-shaped flowers. They are easily cultivated, some being treated as tender annuals. The woody species are propagated by cuttings. Most parts of the plants are poisonous if eaten. Many plants formerly included in this genus are now classified under BRUGMANSIA.

D. metel (also listed as *D. cornucopia*) is an annual that grows to 5 ft. and bears large, often double flowers, whitish inside and violet outside, with a purple calyx.

D. stramonium (thorn-apple, jimsonweed, Jamestown weed) is a tropical annual growing to 5 ft., widely naturalized in the United States on rich, alluvial, or gravelly soils. It has erect white or violet flowers. Its leaves, seeds, and very prickly fruit are poisonous when eaten, and for some individuals contact causes a skin irritation. Its growth indicates low potassium if stunted and low phosphorus if stems are purple. To control, hoe plants as soon as they are recognized and burn plants with mature seeds. Hardy to Zone 3.

DAUCUS (DAW kus) **carota.** An herb of the Apiaceae (Celery Family), with finely cut foliage and filmy white flowers in umbels, commonly known as Queen-Anne's-lace. It is a common weed, in North America. Sometimes used in herbal medicines, the root is edible, but the cores are tough. The seeds can be used to make a flavorful tea, but swallowing the seeds should be avoided since they will tickle the throat. The dry seed heads are often used in dried flower arrangements.

Daucus carota

Var. *sativa* is the common CARROT.

Queen-Anne's-lace tolerates low nitrogen and a range of pH levels. Its size indicates deep soil with some degree of fertility, but it will tolerate dryer conditions where soil could stand improvement. Cultivation of the plant induces germination. Hardy to Zone 3, it is a companion to peas, leaf lettuce, chive, and red radishes. To discourage its spread as a weed, mow as the flowers appear.

DAVALLIA (dah VAL ee ah). A genus of epiphytic evergreen ferns found in trees and on mossy boulders. Broadly triangular fronds rise from a thickened, hairy, creeping rhizome, suggesting the common names of rabbit's-foot or hare's-foot fern. The sori are close to the margin and generally united. They make excellent houseplants and are especially good for hanging baskets.

Pot them carefully so as not to bury the rhizomes, in a coarse epiphytic mixture. Give plenty of diffused light, and water sparingly during rest periods. Old fronds frequently die and drop off. Many species mistakenly sold under other names are *D. trichomanoides*.

PRINCIPAL SPECIES

D. canariensis (Canary Island hare's-foot fern) is a graceful fern with broad tripinnate, lacy fronds and thick rhizomes. It is excellent for pot or basket culture and is slow growing but long-lived. It is native to the Canary Islands, Spain, and Portugal.

D. fejeensis (rabbit's-foot fern), native to the Fiji Islands, is a highly desirable quadripinnate fern with ½-in. brown rhizomes. It makes excellent, long-lived basket plants that can grow to a very large size. Cv. 'Plumosa' is a common form with graceful, highly dissected, drooping fronds.

D. griffithiana (also listed as *Humata tyermannii*), from India and southern China, is tripinnate to quadripinnate, and the rhizomes are covered with white or yellowish scales. It is very similar to *D. mariesii*, which differs by having brownish rhizome scales.

D. solida, found in the Malay archipelago, Australia, and the Pacific Islands, is an attractive basket fern with shining, dark green fronds 2–4 ft. long. The fronds are tripinnate to quadripinnate and have a purplish hue when young. The ½-in., brown, scaly rhizomes grow straight out from the basket, rather than hang. Cultivars include 'Ornata' and 'Ruffled Ornata'.

D. trichomanoides (squirrel's-foot fern) is the most common form in trade, although it is often misnamed or confused with *Humata tyermanii*. It has a tidy growth habit, producing 12-in. tripinnate to quadripinnate fronds and wandering brown rhizomes. Native to Malaysia, New Guinea, and Indonesia, in suitable climates it can be grown as a ground cover.

DAVIDIA (dah VID ee ah) **involucrata.** A pyramidal deciduous tree commonly known as dove tree. It is exceedingly beautiful when in bloom, with dense heads of small, inconspicuous flowers surrounded by very large cream-colored drooping bracts converging in such a way as to resemble a white dove, thus the common name. The green, plumlike fruit is 1½ in. across. The tree grows to a height of 50 or 60 ft. and has graceful oval leaves 6 in. long, silky beneath. Propagation is by seed or cuttings of half-ripened wood. Hardy in Zones 6–8.

This interesting tree, so spectacular in bloom, was discovered in China in 1869 by the Abbé David, for whom it was named. In 1901, plant explorer E. H. Wilson, on an expedition sponsored by a large English nursery firm, rediscovered it and introduced it into cultivation in England in 1902, and into the United States via the Arnold Arboretum two years later.

DAYLILY. Common name for HEMEROCALLIS, a genus of perennial herbs with successive showy flowers, each lasting one day.

DEBREGEASIA (dee bre jee AY see ah). A genus of trees and shrubs of Asia and Africa, belonging to the Urticaceae (Nettle Family). One species, *D. longifolia*, is sometimes grown as an ornamental. It is a large, deciduous shrub or small tree, easy to grow, but not hardy where frosts are severe. It is conspicuous because of its foliage, the large, handsome leaves being dark lustrous green above and white beneath. The flowers are tiny and inconspicuous, but the orange-red, mulberrylike fruits are decorative.

DECIDUOUS. This term describes trees, shrubs, or vines that shed their leaves in winter, as opposed to EVERGREENS, which hold their leaves throughout the year. Shedding leaves is common in broad-leaved plants, serving to reduce loss moisture through evaporation. The word is also used by botanists to describe any portion of a plant that falls off in natural course, such as flower parts, bud scales, or fruits.

DECODON (DEK oh duhn) **verticillatus.** A perennial herb belonging to the Lythraceae (Loosestrife Family), commonly known as swamp loosestrife or water-willow. It has woody stems and long leaves and sometimes grows quite tall. The showy clusters of magenta flowers are a common sight along marshy pond edges and swamps of the eastern states during the summer. It is a desirable plant for colonizing around ponds and in very wet areas.

DECUMARIA (dek yoo MAIR ee ah). A genus of climbing shrubs belonging to the Saxifragaceae (Saxifrage Family). *D. barbara*, native to North America, grows well in a rich, moist soil and partial shade. It is a handsome shrub growing to 30 ft., climbing by aerial rootlets, and clinging firmly to walls and tree trunks. It has glossy leaves and produces a mass of small, fragrant white flowers in early summer.

DEER. These graceful, fleet-footed creatures can cause problems in gardens near woods, creeks, and rural areas. Deer love to browse tender trees, shrubs, and vegetables. In localities where deer abound and are protected by law, they often do considerable damage to orchards and even to home gardens. Barriers, dogs, and various scent repellents can be helpful in keeping deer out of the garden.

Individual trees and shrubs can be covered with wire or plastic net cages to keep the deer away from them during the time when they are most vulnerable.

The most effective permanent protection is fencing or a hedge so high that the animals cannot jump over it and so strong or dense they cannot break though. Deer can easily jump over an 8 ft. fence to get into a garden, but in small gardens or orchards, they seldom bother. Here, wires strung at 2 ft. and 3 ft. may be adequate. Deer shy away from anything they do not understand, such as the nearly invisible wires. Note, however, that such wires can be dangerous to humans.

Dogs fenced in or near the garden can frighten deer; however, they must be trained or restrained to prevent them from doing their own form of damage. Deer have a delicate sense of smell, and manure or scent from a member of the cat family, or blood meal, may discourage them. Indians used to spread their personal scent (urine) around their gardens to protect them.

A repellent spray can be made by mixing 2 eggs, 1 cup water, 1 cup milk, and 3 drops soap. Spray new tender growth every week or two to protect the plants but let you smell your flowers. These repellents are best used in autumn when deer damage is at its highest.

DEERBERRY. Common name for *Vaccinium stamineum*, a deciduous shrub with white or purple-tinged flowers and large inedible berries; see VACCINIUM.

DEER FERN. Common name for *Blechnum spicant*, a pinnate fern that forms a rosette; see BLECHNUM.

DEERFOOT. Common name for the perennial herb *Achlys triphylla*, native to wooded areas of the Pacific coast.

DEER-GRASS. A common name for RHEXIA, a genus of low perennial herbs, usually with purple flowers.

DEHISCENCE. The method or process by which the seedpod or the anther of a flower opens to discharge its contents, which are seeds in the first case and pollen grains in the second.

DELONIX (de LOHN iks). A genus of tropical trees belonging to the Fabaceae (Bean Family), formerly included in the genus *Poinciana*. *D. regia* (royal-poinciana, flamboyant) is one of the most brilliant of tropical flowering trees, commonly planted in warm regions, especially Florida. It is a wide-spreading tree that grows to 40 ft. and has 2-ft. leaves with 10 or 20 leaflets, and bright scarlet flowers 3–4 in. across in clusters followed by flat, woody pods to 2 ft. long. A yellow-flowered form is also seen occasionally.

DELOSPERMA (del ah SPUR mah). A genus of more than 100 plants native to South Africa, some of which produce mats of succulent foliage and daisylike flowers, which thrive in hot, sunny rock gardens. Only two species are in wide circulation in the United States, but a number of other attractive species are being tested and introduced. Propagation is by seed, division, or cuttings. Some delospermas are not reliably hardy, but the following two are hardy from Canada to the southern states.

D. cooperi has prostrate stems with curved, 1½–2 in. leaves, almost round and narrowing to a point. It produces its bright cerise flowers from early summer until frost.

D. nubigena has small, roundish foliage and produces its yellow flowers in midspring.

DELPHINIUM (del FIN ee um). An important genus of annual and perennial herbs commonly known as larkspur. Although the most widely known form is the popular garden delphinium — with dense or branched spires of attractive blossoms in shades of blue, or in the hybrids lavender, purple, or rosy mauve, rising from 3–8 ft. high — there are smaller, more delicate, less important species having yellow, white, or red blossoms. The flowers of all species are somewhat irregular, the sepals forming the spur and petal-like outer parts while small petals, clustered around the sta-

Delphinum cultivar

mens, form the "bee," so prominent in some forms. The leaves, usually cut, are clustered at the base or are on the flowering stalks.

CULTURE

Even casually grown, delphiniums are extremely hardy (most surviving in Zones 3–7) and make satisfactory garden plants, but if given a little special consideration, they reward the grower many times over. Fine plants depend upon sun, circulation of air, and a rich, light, alkaline soil. To ensure air circulation, mature plants should stand at least 2 ft. apart. To maintain a highly alkaline soil condition, it is advisable to sprinkle a "light snow" of agricultural lime over the soil once or twice during the growing season. A well-balanced commercial fertilizer (containing about 5% nitrogen, 10% phosphates, and 5% potash) should be given to plants in the early spring, following directions supplied by the manufacturer.

The popular garden varieties, if cut to the ground after blooming, will often produce a second set of blossoms later in the summer. A second feeding should be given after a ten-day rest period following the cutting down. It is almost a necessity to stake the taller varieties early in the season to prevent damage by high winds and storms. Although certain diseases are almost always associated with delphiniums, if the plants have all the sun, air, and lime they need and are well watered during prolonged dry spells—in short, if they are kept strong and vigorous— infection is rare. Except in the most extreme climates, winter protection is not needed.

Planting. Although nothing can take the place of delphiniums in the herbaceous border, they are usually at their best when grown in rows by themselves. In either case, madonna lilies, Canterbury-bells, daylilies, or some other plant that enjoys or tolerates the same conditions can be planted in front of them for decorative effect, allowing the 2-ft. clearance for circulation of air.

By sowing seeds in an outdoor frame, sheltered from the sun, in midsummer when the first crop of seed has ripened, one can have, the following year, small plants that will blossom in between the first and second flowering of the older stock.

A coldframe, or wooden flat with the bottom knocked out and set into the soil, is ideal for summer-sown seed, as it simplifies the matter of giving protection against storms or intense heat with stretched burlap. After the seed is sown, the bed should not be allowed to dry out. The plants will be large enough to move by early fall but still should be given the protection of a coldframe or mulch of leaves. Transplanting should be done at least a month before frost to give the seedlings time to establish themselves. Since few delphinums can be trusted to come true from seed, all the young plants should be taken care of to permit a selection of the best colors and types later on. By late spring, set plants in their permanent places in the garden.

Seeds can be sown in frames in the early fall when rains and the lack of intense summer heat make an ideal condition for their growth. In spring the young plants can be set in rows in the propagating bed or in the vegetable garden until of sufficient size to place in the border.

Old established plants in the garden will begin to bloom in early summer and will often bloom again in early fall. For midsummer flowers, seeds can be sown in the greenhouse or hotbed in winter, the seedlings pricked out into pots, and the young plants set out in the garden in spring. When an old clump of delphiniums becomes so thick that air cannot circulate through the stalks, it should be lifted and divided into three clumps of approximately the same size. See DIVISION.

The annual species are easily raised from seed. This is sown, in cool regions, either indoors or in the open in ordinary soil during late spring; and in warmer regions, in the fall.

DISEASES

A bacterial disease called BLACK SPOT causes irregular black spots on the upper leaf surfaces and sometimes on the stems; it is unsightly but not often serious. The similarity between its name and the term "blacks" used to describe mite injury has confused many lecturers and writers, so that the wrong remedy is often recommended for mites. To control the bacterial black spot, remove all old plant parts in autumn and drench the crowns with a solution of copper sulfate in early spring. Remove infected leaves as soon as noticed. If much injury has been noted in previous years, spray two or three times during the spring with BORDEAUX MIXTURE.

A most serious fungus disease of delphiniums is CROWN ROT. Plants suddenly wilt or topple over, and at the crown one can usually see the small, red resting bodies and the white mycelium or threadlike vegetative part of the fungus. Carefully remove each diseased plant with the surrounding soil and drench the vacant space and adjacent plants with a copper sulfate solution. It is important to take care of infected plants immediately since the fungus is able to infect a great many other perennials.

Other root rots are due to various bacteria, fungi, or other organisms and cultural defects such as too high a soil temperature, insufficient moisture, too compact a soil, and the use of manure too close to plant crowns. Rots following cutting back of flower stalks can be somewhat prevented by disinfecting tools between cuts.

Mildew, prevalent on the West Coast and late in the season in eastern gardens, is controlled with sulfur or copper fungicides.

Stunt, or CHLOROSIS, a virus disease, causes dwarfing of the plant and flower heads and mottling of the foliage. Remove and destroy diseased plants.

The annuals are particularly subject to diaporthe blight, characterized by a premature withering of basal leaves at the approach of flowering and patches of dead tissue on stems at the point of leaf attachment. Remove infected plants to save neighboring healthy ones. Plant seed obtained from disease-free sources, and change the planting site the year after an attack.

See also DISEASE.

INSECT PESTS

The cyclamen mite causes very severe injury, curling and distorting the leaves and blackening the flower buds, which is said to have "the blacks." The mites are too small to be seen with the naked eye, and since the general appearance is that of a disease rather than insect injury, the wrong control measures are frequently applied. Remove infested parts and spray frequently both early and late in the season with rotenone. Dusting with sulfur between sprays can also help.

Leaves that are cupped downward probably

have aphids clustering underneath. Red aphids are exceedingly common on annual larkspurs and require treatment. See APHIDS.

Slugs can be at least partly controlled by sprinkling lime or spreading sifted ashes around the plants. See SLUGS.

See also INSECT CONTROL.

PRINCIPAL SPECIES

While there is no particular structural distinction, it has become customary among gardeners to restrict the use of delphinium as a common name to highly bred perennial species, hybrids, and varieties in which the flower spikes have developed, while the annual and native species with smaller, looser, less imposing form are more commonly called larkspur. This distinction, however, is not absolute or consistent.

HYBRIDS

Among the best-known hybrid strains are the Wrexham Hybrids, called hollyhock-flowered, and those sent out by Blackmore and Langdon. These two strains were developed in England. Other interesting hybrids have been produced by both French and North American growers.

D. x *belladonna* (garland larkspur), also listed as *D. cheilanthum* or *D. formosum*, is a tall, branched sort, supposedly from Siberia. It is a product of *D. elatum* x *D. grandiflorum*, with rich blue sepals over long yellow petals. It is most like *D. elatum* but is lacking a pronounced central raceme.

D. x *cultorum* refers to any number of hybrids whose origin is uncertain.

PERENNIALS

Many perennial species have been highly developed to produce flower spikes of remarkable size, beauty, and variability as well as other hybrids. Most of them are native to California.

D. californicum (coast larkspur) grows to about 6 ft. and bears hairy white, sometimes purplish flowers in long spikes.

D. cardinale (scarlet larkspur) is a native species with spikes of bright red, loosely arranged flowers.

D. elatum (bee or candle larkspur, delphinium) is a tall, erect perennial with spirelike clusters of rather small, blue to purple flowers, which will bloom again in fall if stalks are cut back after spring flowering. Many of the tall garden varieties and hybrids have been derived from it to produce gigantic spikes of large, often double flowers.

D. grandiflorum (bouquet larkspur) is a perennial that often blossoms the first year with large blue or white flowers on plants about 3 ft. tall.

D. nudicaule (red larkspur) bears bright red flowers loosely arranged in spikelike form and relatively blunt leaves.

D. trolliifolium (cow-poison, poison larkspur), a weak-stemmed herb with blue-and-white flowers, occasionally planted but usually found in the wild along the West Coast where it causes great trouble among herds of horses and cattle, although apparently it is not toxic to sheep. The seeds have insecticidal properties and should not be eaten.

D. variegatum (royal larkspur) grows 1½ ft. tall and has purple flowers.

ANNUALS

Blue predominates in the annual larkspurs, but the colors range from white through pink and blue to deep purple. The wandlike spikes of loose racemes bear many flowers above the feathery, soft green foliage. These annuals are easily raised from seed. This is sown in cool climates either indoors during early spring or in the open, in ordinary soil, during late spring; and in warm regions, during the fall.

DENDROBIUM (den DROH bee um). A huge genus of about 1500 species of showy, evergreen or deciduous, epiphytic and lithophytic orchids native to southeastern Asia, Japan, the Philippines, Australia, New Zealand, and New Guinea. Generally they have erect, several-noded pseudobulbs and thin to leathery leaves growing in ranks along the stem. Colorful flowers are pendent or produced singly. They are small to large in size and are all colors but black. Each flower has a mentum or spur attached to the column and lateral sepals. Shapes vary depending on the species. In some types, petals and sepals are twisted and narrow; in others, broad and flat. In some, the lip is hairy or fringed. Most are long-lasting, but a few are ephemeral.

The evergreen types should be grown in warm and moist conditions; they are hardy to Zone 9 with frost protection. Deciduous ones are variously hardy to Zone 7 and need high humidity and warmth during growth but require a cooler, drier atmosphere during the fall and winter. Generally, *Dendrobium* plants do best when slightly underpotted. All require strong light. The type species is *D. moniliforme*.

DENDROCALAMUS (den droh KAL ah mus). A genus of treelike grasses included among the BAMBOO tribe, commonly known as giant bamboo, and hardy in Zones 10–11. *D. membranaceus*, with bright green mature culm (or trunk), will grow up to 70 ft. in protected spots in California. *D. strictus* (male bamboo) is 20–50 ft. high when mature.

DENDROCHILUM (den droh KĪ lum). A genus of approximately 100 species of unusual epiphytic orchids noted for chains of small, delicate, white-to-ivory flowers pendent from graceful racemes. They are native to a wide area of tropical and subtropical Asia, the Philippines, and New Guinea. The pseudobulbs are tufted, narrow, and ovoid, with one narrow, leathery leaf.

The plants need an open, well-drained compost, moderate shade, warmth, and abundant water while growing. They are best grown in shallow pots with many drainage holes. The roots should not be disturbed. Hardy to Zone 9 with frost protection, they withstand winter temperatures of 55–60°F. The type species is *D. aurantiacum*.

DENDROMECON (den droh MEE kahn) **rigida.** An evergreen shrub belonging to the Papaveraceae (Poppy Family) and commonly known as bush or tree poppy. Growing to 10 ft., it has narrow, leathery, glaucous leaves with prominent veins, and the golden yellow flowers are very similar to single poppies. Native to California, it

is hardy only to Zone 6 but can stand some frost if given protection such as is afforded by a wall. Propagation is by seed, which is very slow to germinate.

DENNSTAEDTIA (den STED ee ah). A genus of about 70 ferns native to the tropics and subtropics, including only one found in eastern North America. The indusia are cup-shaped, giving the genus its common name of cup fern. All are terrestrial, with creeping rhizomes rapidly forming large colonies; their use is precluded in small gardens because of this habit. Where ample space is available, they are very ornamental and long-lived. They can be grown in containers but must be frequently divided.

PRINCIPAL SPECIES

D. bipinnata (couplet fern) is a large, pinnate to bipinnate leathery fern. Common in the rain forests of tropical America and naturalized in Florida, it is an attractive plant for the large, shady tropical garden but needs plenty of room.

D. cicutaria is a large fern native to rain forests of South America and the West Indies. It can be grown in the shady garden or in a large container in the greenhouse.

D. davallioides (lacy ground fern) is a four- to five-pinnate fern from Australia, found in shaded forests and along stream banks. Dark green, lacy fronds are spaced along the creeping rhizomes, which spread freely in the garden.

D. punctilobula (hay-scented fern) is a deciduous fern that grows 1–2 ft. and has thin-textured, bipinnate to bipinnate-pinnatifid, yellowish-green fronds. Common in the northeastern states and Canada, it occurs in open, well-drained meadows and forest clearings and is usually too aggressive for any but the largest garden.

DENTARIA (den TAY ree ah). A genus of small herbs belonging to the Brassicaceae (Mustard Family), commonly known as toothwort. They have white, toothlike roots and clustered white, rose, or lavender flowers and are used in the rock garden or for colonizing in the wild garden. The two species most commonly grown are *D.*

diphylla (pepperroot), with clustered white flowers; and *D. laciniata*, with white or lavender blossoms.

DENTATE. Toothed, particularly a sharply toothed leaf with teeth somewhat large and at right angles to the blade.

DEODAR. Common name for *Cedrus deodara*, a cedar tree with graceful drooping branches; see CEDRUS.

DERRIS (DAIR is). A genus of tropical plants of the Fabaceae (Bean Family). One or two species contain a resinous substance used by natives of the tropics to temporarily poison streams, thus paralyzing the fish and making them easier to catch. More recently, the roots of *D. elliptica* have been made into powders or extracts and offered under various proprietary names as contact insecticides. See ROTENONE; INSECTICIDE.

DESERT-CANDLE. A common name for EREMURUS, a genus of bulbous plants with rosettes of basal leaves and colored flowers on tall stalks.

DESMAZERIA (dez mah ZAIR ee uh) **sicula.** An annual grass, commonly known as spike grass. Native to the Mediterranean region, it is sometimes grown for its feathery sprays, which are used in either green or everlasting bouquets. It is a small plant, about 1 ft. tall, with narrow leaves to 6 in. long and flowering heads 2–3 in. long made up of small individual spikelets. Seeds should be sown where the plants are to grow.

DESMODIUM (des MOH dee um). A genus of herbs and shrubs belonging to the Fabaceae (Bean Family), commonly known as tick-trefoil or tick-clover. Nearly all the species grow in dry woods and fields, and are sometimes planted in the border or wild garden, although their chief use is as forage plants.

PRINCIPAL SPECIES

D. canadense, native from eastern Canada to Oklahoma, is a somewhat weedy perennial growing to 8 ft. in the wild, with oblong leaves to 4 in. long and clusters of irregular pink or purplish flowers followed by jointed pods that are distributed like those of beggarweed.

Desmodium canadense

D. motorium (telegraph or moving plant), formerly listed as *D. gyrans*, is a tender Asiatic species with purple flowers. It is sometimes grown as a greenhouse oddity for the leaflets, which have the power of moving in several directions. Though a perennial, it is generally treated as an annual and is grown from seed.

D. tortuosum (beggarweed), formerly listed as *D. purpureum*, is a forage plant grown on moist land in the southern states. Its common name is derived from the twisted seedpods, which cling like burrs and may be carried long distances by animals or people.

DEUTZIA (DEWT see ah). A genus of deciduous shrubs native in Asia and belonging to the Saxifragaceae (Saxifrage Family). They are attractive in early summer with their wealth of flowers, mostly white but some tinged pinkish. They do best in well-drained soil with plenty of humus. In cold climates, some need a protected position and even then are not entirely hardy in severe winters. Numerous hybrids and varieties have been developed. Propagation is by seed, by cuttings of green or hard wood, and by layering.

PRINCIPAL SPECIES

D. gracilis is one of the best dwarf shrubs, of graceful habit and bearing large clusters of pure white flowers. Hardy to Zone 5.

D. x *lemoinei*, a hybrid between *D. gracilis* and *D. parviflora*, makes a broad, rounded bush with large clusters of white flowers. Hardy to Zone 4.

D. x *magnifica* is a showy form with double white flowers in dense, long panicles. Hardy to Zone 6.

D. scabra is a tall shrub with brown branches, rough leaves, and erect clusters of white flowers often tinged pink. The form known as 'Pride of Rochester' has large, double white flowers tinged rose. Hardy to Zone 5.

DEVIL'S-BIT. A common name for *Chamaelirium lutem*, a perennial herb with yellowish flowers and tuberous roots; see CHAMAELIRIUM.

DEVIL'S-PAINTBRUSH. A common name for *Hieracium aurantiacum*, an herbaceous weed with red, orange, or yellow flowers, a serious pest in meadows and hayfields; see HIERACIUM.

DEVIL'S-TONGUE. Common name for *Amorphophallus rivieri*, a tropical herb whose attractive flowers have an offensive odor; see AMORPHOPHALLUS.

DEVIL'S-WALKING-STICK. A common name for *Aralia spinosa*, a spiny flowering shrub; see ARALIA.

DEVILWOOD. Common name for *Osmanthus americanus*, an evergreen shrub with whitish bark and fragrant flowers, native to the southern United States; see OSMANTHUS.

DEWBERRY. A common name for forms of trailing blackberries, *Rubus flagellaris* (American), *R. ursinus* (Pacific), and their fruit; see BLACKBERRY.

DIAMOND FLOWER. Common name for *Ionopsidium acaule*, an annual herb with tiny violet or white flowers; see IONOPSIDIUM.

DIANELLA (dī ah NEL ah). A genus of fibrous-rooted perennials belonging to the Liliaceae (Lily Family), with grasslike leaves and whitish or blue flowers in loose clusters followed by blue fruits. In mild climates (Zones 10–11) the plants can be grown outdoors, but elsewhere a greenhouse or other frostproof location is necessary.

DIANTHUS (dī ANTH us). A large genus of mostly hardy perennial and annual herbs variously known as carnation, picotee, sweet-William, and pink. Virtually every species is a spicy, fragrant, beautifully flowered plant. The blossoms are often pink or lavender but also may be white, yellow, rose, or purple. Many have spots, bands, or other patterns on the flowers.

Dianthus barbatus

With the exception of a few alpine species that thrive best in cool climates, dianthus can be raised almost anywhere with confidence, many especially suited to the rock garden. Various species are hardy to Zone 2. Enjoying sunshine and delighting in a moist soil of ordinary garden composition, the plants generally bloom in the spring.

Which of the many species and hybrids the gardener chooses depends largely on the type, scale, climate, and location of the garden. Though there are more than 120 species of *Dianthus*, those listed below are of the greatest importance to the average gardener.

CULTURE

It is best to increase the perennial varieties by layering or by cutting (taken with a heel). Cuttings will sometimes root better if taken from the new growth of plants grown in pots. Seed can be used; planted in spring or summer, it yields flowers the second season. Annuals are propagated by seed sown in the spring.

The grass pinks are grown easily from seed, which germinates in less than a week. They prefer a rich, well-drained soil containing lime, though they will thrive almost anywhere in a sunny location. Frequent cutting as soon as flowers begin to fade will prolong the period of bloom.

Carnations. As a greenhouse crop, carnations are grown from cuttings about 3 in. long taken from the base or stems of stock plants in late fall and early winter. Inserted in sand kept moist over mild bottom heat, they are sufficiently rooted for potting up in a month and are shifted to larger pots from time to time as necessary. They are hardened-off in spring so they can be set out in the field in late spring. After a summer outdoors, they are benched in midsummer so as to come into bloom as the weather gets cold. Some growers get excellent results by growing their plants under glass year-round, thus avoiding planting out in spring and moving indoors in fall.

Carnation

ENEMIES

Diseases. In all kinds of dianthus, sudden wilting or rotting at the base of the plants may be due to root or crown rot. Anthracnose causes the death of the branches of hardy pinks, the leaves first turning yellow and then brown. For control measures, see CROWN ROT; ANTHRACNOSE.

Wilt diseases and STEM ROT are probably the most serious carnation troubles. Brown lesions appear on the stem at the surface of the soil, followed by wilting and yellowing of the leaves. Remove diseased plants or parts as soon as noticed, and use only healthy plants for propagation. Soil sterilization is sometimes helpful. Care should be taken to prevent wounding plants by rough handling or too close cultivation.

Blight or LEAF SPOT, also known as branch rot, shows as ashy white, circular spots on the leaves, the centers of the spots being covered with dark fungus growth. It may cause girdling and death of the branches. Spray plants with a fungicide such as BORDEAUX MIXTURE containing a good spreader before they are placed in the benches and every few weeks thereafter.

Yellowish or reddish brown pustules on the backs of leaves are symptoms of rust. Hand pick infected leaves before the pustules break. Spray regularly with fungicide or lime sulfur, or dust with sulfur. These measures will also prevent other minor leaf spots. In greenhouses, try to keep proper humidity and dry foliage.

Insect Pests. Red spiders can be kept down by dusting with sulfur or spraying with a weak solution of lime sulfur. See RED SPIDER MITE.

PRINCIPAL SPECIES

D. x *allwoodii* (Allwood hybrids) is a hardy hybrid race named for the original hybridizers, the Allwood Brothers of England, who produced it by crossing *D. plumarius* with *D. caryophyllus*. It comes in a wide range of colors with petals entire or variously fringed. The tufted foliage is generally firm, broad, and somewhat glaucous. These pinks bloom freely in summer with the clove scent of *D. plumarius* and the heavy texture of carnations. There are many named varieties, but mixed seed produces flowers of fine quality on plants that can be propagated from cuttings. Var. *alpinus* has shiny leaves, large rose and pink flowers a little later in summer, and is an excellent rock garden plant. It prefers lime soils.

D. alpinus, from the Alps, has large, odorless, dark-colored, crimson-spotted flowers with relatively short tufts of shining green, pointed foliage and is excellent in the rock garden.

D. arenarius is a good rock garden specimen whose fragrant white flowers have deeply cut petals.

D. barbatus (sweet-William) is a faintly scented species that grows 1½–2 ft. tall and has smooth, flat, broad green foliage and profuse flowers of purple, red, rose, or white in large bracted heads. Some forms are double. This is a popular species with many excellent named varieties that bloom in spring and early summer. Though perennial, the plants are best treated as biennials. There is also an annual group about 15 in. tall, which blooms in late summer and early fall the first year from seed.

D. brevicaulis, suited to the rock garden, grows only 1 in. high and has tiny, ¼ - ½ in.

leaves and ½-in. purple flowers.

D. caesius, also listed as *D. gratianopolitanus* (Cheddar pink), a hardy European native, is a desirable rock garden species, forming compact mats of foliage and producing fragrant rose-colored flowers with toothed petals on 3–12 in. stems.

D. carthusianorum (clusterhead pink), grows 18–36 in. and blooms throughout the summer with single heads of pink to magenta flowers.

D. caryophyllus (carnation, clove pink) is the predominant, fragrant species, generally associated with florists or greenhouse use. Native to southern Europe and in cultivation for more than 20 centuries, the carnation has become generally known in North America as a plant 2–3½ ft. tall, with a brittle, slightly branching stem, narrow opposite leaves, and large, terminal double flowers, usually ruffled or toothed, generally in shades of red, white, and pink and occasionally yellow or purple. Variegations occur, but usually on body colors of yellow or white. "Selfs" are the flowers of one solid color; the flowers are known as "flakes" when striped with one color, "bizarres" if striped with two or three, and "picotees" if the petals are merely edged or bordered with another color. The Grenadins include strongly perfumed flowers of one color. The Flamands are large flowers, always double, and higher in the center. There are two main groups among the highly developed large-flowered forms. The outdoor or border carnations, including the Marguerite types, are delightful though seldom grown in the United States since they require cooler summers than we can offer. Among the florist's or greenhouse carnations is the perpetual flowering type, known as the American carnation; the red form of this type is the state flower of Ohio.

D. chinensis (annual pink) will flower from seed the first season and are called annuals, but they are really short-lived perennials. The foliage is glabrous, green, and tufted. Plants grow 12–18 in. tall with somewhat branching stems. The flowers are solitary or loosely assembled, only slightly fragrant if at all, and 1 in. across in tones of red, lilac, or white. There are many fine varieties, of which *heddewigii*, with rich, velvety flowers, is one of the best.

D. deltoides (maiden pink), with small, deep red, crimson-eyed, fragrant flowers on numerous branchlets, does well in the rock garden.

D. glacialis var. *neglectus* (glacier pink) is a good rock garden specimen with small, odorless, red-purple flowers, the toothed petals tawny beneath.

D. knappii is not a handsome plant but is treasured by some gardeners for its clusters of yellow flowers, each with a purple spot.

D. monspessulanus grows 8 in. tall and 12 in. across and bears fragrant, pink to carmine, 1–1½ in. flowers in spring and summer.

D. myrtinervius, one of the choicest rock garden species, has minute foliage and numerous deep pink flowers.

D. neglectus, also listed as *D. pavonius*, bears red, 1-in. flowers in summer and does well in the rock garden.

D. pavonius has trim grassy tufts and large purplish-red flowers. There also are a number of named cultivars; three desirable ones for the rock garden are 'Tiny Rubies', 'La Bourbrille', and 'Spotty'.

D. plumarius (grass pink) is an old-fashioned species universally cultivated in borders and at path edges and is distinguished by a clovelike fragrance. The mat-forming plants have smooth, whitish foliage and grow to 18 in. high. Simple or branched stems bear two or three highly fragrant flowers with fringed petals of rose, purple, or white (or particolored), blooming from early to midsummer. There are many named varieties, one of the most popular being *semperflorens*. Some are double. The grass pinks have been hybridized to produce a wide range of large-flowering varieties with colors running from white to rich crimson, with beautiful zonings or stripes. Combinations with carnations have produced hardy strains.

D. superbus (lilac pink) grows 1–2 ft. and bears fragrant, lilac to rose-purple, deeply fringed flowers in summer.

DIAPENSIA (dī ah PEN see ah). A genus of small, tufted, evergreen plants found in North America, northern Europe, and Asia. *D. lapponica*, found on mountaintops of New York and New England, is sometimes grown in rock gardens. It is hardy to Zone 2, requiring a cool situation in gritty soil with peat or leaf mold. Under favorable conditions it forms a low, dense tuft, usually only 1–2 in. high, with white, bell-shaped flowers.

DIAPENSIACEAE (dī ah pen see AY see ee). The Diapensia Family, so named by Linnaeus because the parts of the flower are in fives. The members of the family are low-growing, evergreen woody shrubs or perennial herbs restricted to the North Temperate Zone. *Diapensia*, *Galax*, *Pyxidanthera*, and *Shortia* are genera sometimes cultivated as ground covers and in rockeries.

DIASCIA (dī ASH ee ah) **barberae.** A small, half-hardy South African annual belonging to the Scrophulariaceae (Figwort Family), and commonly known as twinspur. The flowers have round teeth or spurs on the lower petals, which inspired the common name. The plant is a slender low-grower whose sprays of rose or violet flowers are borne on leafy 1-ft. stems. The mottled yellow throat suggests the plant's kinship to *Nemesia*. Twinspur is a good border or potted plant, easily raised from seed in light, well-drained soil and full sun. It should be started indoors and transplanted to stand 6 in. apart. Pink and orange hybrids are also available.

DIATOMACEOUS EARTH. A fine, silica-rich powder made from ancient sea-bottom deposits of diatom shells, useful to deter insect pests by piercing the exoskeletons or internal organs of such insects as gypsy moths, codling moths, lygus bugs, boll weevils, thrips, mites, slugs, snails, cornworms, flies, and nematodes. It is effective against mildew and brown rot too. To avoid hurting the beneficial insects, applications must be timed carefully. Since it dessicates the insect, it is less effective in hot, very humid weather. Use the horticultural type of diatomaceous earth (commonly available as Permaguard); the type made for use in swimming pools is useless because it lacks sharp edges.

DIBBLE. A pointed tool, also called a dibber, often merely a short, stout stick, but often with a bent handle or grip and a metal-shot point, used to make holes in soft ground for planting bulbs or setting small plants. The term is also used as a verb, meaning the practice of using the tool. To do this correctly, thrust the dibble into the soil, remove it, lower the plant roots into the hole, then press earth firmly against them all the way to the bottom. Unless this is done carefully, air pockets may be left below the surface in which the roots will hang and dry, injuring and possibly killing the plant.

DICENTRA (dī SEN trah). A genus of charming, hardy, long-lived perennial herbs commonly known as bleeding-heart. They have attractive, fernlike foliage, and their dainty, heart-shaped blossoms with spurred petals are usually rose-red or white but in some species are yellow or straw colored. *Dicentra* was formerly known as *Dielytra*, and plants are still sometimes listed in catalogs under that name.

Dicentras grow best in deep, mellow soil in a sunny, sheltered spot and increase in beauty year after year if undisturbed but well cared for. Propagation is easily done by division of the crown or the roots. If roots are cut in 3-in. pieces and set in rich loam, new plants will soon start.

PRINCIPAL SPECIES

D. canadensis (squirrel-corn) is a North American woodland perennial, useful in shaded rock gardens. It has greenish white flowers nodding in loose sprays. The root consists of many small tubers, giving rise to the common name. Hardy in Zones 4–8.

D. chrysantha (golden-eardrops), native to California, is an interesting species for the border. It has numerous golden heart-shaped flowers in erect panicles and pale, bluish green cut leaves. Hardy to Zone 8.

D. cucullaria (Dutchman's-breeches) has

small, white, yellow-tipped flowers with widely spreading spurs. Growing 10 in. high, it is a native species hardy in Zones 3–9 and is easily naturalized in rich soil in open rocky woods.

D. eximia (bleeding-heart) is the native wild species and has nodding, dull rose-pink blossoms with rounded spurs. It grows readily in cool, moist soil in the wild garden or a sheltered corner of the rock garden. If watered, it will bloom all summer. Hardy in Zones 4–8.

Dicentra cucullaria

D. formosa (western bleeding-heart) is very similar to **D. eximia**, but it varies in color from white to deep rose. Hardy in Zones 4–8. Var. *oregana* (sometimes listed as **D. glauca**) bears flowers in nodding clusters.

D. ochroleuca has yellow or cream-colored blossoms.

D. spectabilis is the old-fashioned garden favorite, forming a leafy clump to 2 ft. tall; it is covered in spring with drooping clusters of bright pink, drooping blossoms held gracefully above the finely cut foliage. Hardy in Zones 4–8.

D. uniflora is a tiny plant suitable for the rock garden. Its white or pink flowers, rising singly above the ferny leaves, have recurved petals and rounded, sacklike spurs.

Dicentra spectabilis

DICHELOSTEMMA (dī kel oh STEM ah). A genus of cormous plants in the Amaryllidaceae (Amaryllis Family) with a wide variety of floral forms. Useful bulbs to naturalize in wild or rock gardens in warmer regions and usually hardy to Zone 8, they can also be grown in pots elsewhere if given winter protection. Easy to start from seed, though often taking three to five years, they generally offset cormlets freely.

PRINCIPAL SPECIES

D. ida-maia (firecracker flower) is perhaps the most exciting species with 2-ft. stems arising from grassy foliage, producing a terminal pendulous cluster of crimson-red tubular flowers tipped with green. This plant does best with semishade and a dormant summer period.

D. multiflorum (ookow) grows 2–3 ft. tall and has pale blue flowers clustered into a 4-in. sphere, making it an excellent cut flower.

D. pulchellum (blue-dicks), formerly listed as **Brodiaea capitata**, is an easily grown herb with funnel-shaped, blue-lilac flowers clustered into 3-in. heads atop 2-in. stems.

D. volubile (snake-lily, twining brodiaea) is another attractive oddity with glistening, hourglass-shaped pink flowers clustered into a 3-in. head atop a stem that can grow to 10 ft. and twines on itself or branches to raise its flowers into

Dichelostemma pulchellum

the sunlight. Best in some shade, it can also be grown in pots.

DICHORISANDRA (dī koh ree SAN drah). A genus of perennial herbs from tropical America, belonging to the Commelinaceae (Spiderwort Family) and sometimes sold as blue-ginger. One or two are occasionally grown in the warm greenhouse and outdoors in warm regions. They thrive in a mixture of loam, leaf mold, and sand, requiring a liberal supply of water when growth is active. Propagation is by seed, cuttings, and division.

D. musaica grows to 18 in. high, with spotted stems and large, oval, dark green leaves marked with numerous short, transverse white lines, the underside being deep reddish purple. It has bright blue-and-white flowers in a short spike.

D. thyrsiflora grows to 4 ft., with large, glossy green leaves and rich, dark blue flowers with yellow stamens in a dense compound inflorescence.

DICKSONIA (dik SOH nee ah). One of several genera of large ferns, collectively known and cultivated as TREE FERNS and closely related to *Cibotium*. Hardy to Zone 10, it is suitable only for cool greenhouse or hothouse culture.

DICOTYLEDON. A member of one of the two great classes of angiosperms, or flowering plants, the other being the monocotyledons. Dicotyledons are distinguished by (1) two plump, wing-like embryo- or seed-leaves (cotyledons); (2) leaf-veins forming an open network and ending freely at the leaf margin; (3) flowers typically, though not necessarily, with parts grouped in series of four or five; and (4) the food or water vessels in the stem arranged concentrically, forming the "rings" of woody stems. Contrast MONO-COTYLEDON.

DICTAMNUS (dik TAM nus) **albus.** A hardy, bushy perennial with numerous common names including burning bush, fraxinella, dittany, and gasplant. It is notably long lived but resents transplanting once it is established. Growing in a sunny location, a single plant has been known to outlive three generations of one family. The rather strong, lemon-scented plants, which are about 3 ft. high and as broad, make a fine display all summer and are especially striking when the loose spires of flowers surmount the foliage. While the original species, *D. albus*, sends up 9–12 in.

Dictamnus albus

spikes of white blooms, cv. 'Purpureus' has pink flowers with red veins. On sultry summer evenings, the volatile oil emitted as a vapor by the plants will flash when touched off with a lighted match; this unique property gives rise to two of the common names.

Seed sown an inch deep in the open ground as soon as ripe in autumn will sprout well the following spring. Seedlings should be transplanted to stand 4–6 in. apart when a few inches tall and again spaced 12 in. apart the following spring. Give clean cultivation both years and set the plants in their permanent positions (preferably a dry, sunny spot) the third spring. From that time forward, they should bloom every year. Hardy in Zones 3–8.

DICTYOSPERMA (dik tee oh SPURM ah). A genus of feather-leaved, tropical palms commonly known as princess palms. They have trunks to 40 or 50 ft., crowned with long, drooping, unarmed (spineless) leaves with red or yellow nerves and stems.

D. album, found in the Mascarene Islands of the Indian Ocean, is a stately tree with graceful, feathered leaves, glossy above. Young plants of its var. *rubrum* have beautiful, glossy, deep green leaves with red veins and margins.

It thrives in sandy soil or in limestone foundations and needs shade when the plants are young. In the North, princess palms are grown in warm greenhouses, with temperatures of at least 75°F during the day and never below 60°F at night. They should be planted in peat and loam, or loam and sand mixed with well-rotted cow manure, and receive frequent waterings. The plants are most attractive when young and used as table decorations.

DIDIERIACEAE (did ee air ee AY see ee). A most extraordinary family of succulent trees and shrubs from Madagascar, similar in superficial appearance to the Fouquieriaceae (Ocotillo Family) of the Southwest deserts, which similarly put out small, fugacious, or short-lived leaves during periods when rain is available, and which quickly dry and fall during periods of drought. The family includes the genera *Didierea*, *Alluaudia*, and *Alluaudiopsis*. All species are choice and quite outlandish in appearance.

DIDYMOCHLAENA (di di moh KLEE nah) **truncatula.** A widely grown fern, favored among fern enthusiasts because of its glossy, symmetrical foliage, commonly known as tree maidenhair fern. It has 2–4 ft., bipinnate to tripinnate fronds that are a striking pink or red when young. Native to South America, Africa, India, and Malaysia, this tropical fern is an excellent container plant.

DIEBACK. A symptom of plant disease consisting of the progressive death of a terminal shoot from the tip backwards. This may be caused by an organism, insufficient moisture, or severe temperatures. Many plants of indeterminate annual growth normally die back to some extent over the winter, but an abnormal amount of dying back in roses or other woody shrubs may be due to insufficient maturing of tender growth before cold weather starts. Feeding of such plants too late in the season, especially with nitrogenous substances, can cause this. See DISEASE.

DIEFFENBACHIA (deef en BAK ee ah). A genus of shrubby, upright tropical American evergreen plants with fleshy stems, belonging to the Araceae (Arum Family), and commonly known as dumb cane. They are usually grown in warm greenhouses for their large, soft, handsome leaves, which are variously spotted and feathered with white, cream, or yellow markings.

There are many cultivars on the market, some of them tissue-propagated in order to attain uniformity and to rapidly bring sufficient quantities to salable size. Dieffenbachias make durable and showy indoor foliage plants, growing 18 in. to 8 ft. tall and more. Some have leaves almost entirely creamy white with green edging; others are variously marked with white to creamy yellow and silvery spots or veins.

The plants thrive in a mixture of fibrous loam and peat with sand and are appreciative of a little very old manure. Propagation is by cuttings of the leafy top or by cutting up the old stems into short pieces. The common name is derived from the acrid sap causing temporary loss of speech if applied to the mouth; be careful in handling the plant, since the juice is very acrid and toxic.

A bacterial leaf disease produces reddish spots with yellow margins, often followed by wilting. Do not crowd plants, and avoid overwatering.

PRINCIPAL SPECIES

D. x *bausei* is a showy hybrid with broad, yellowish green leaves, blotched dark green and spotted white, on white stems.

D. imperialis has handsome shining green leaves marked yellow and white, up to 2 ft. long and 12 in. wide.

D. maculata (spotted dumb cane), formerly listed as *D. picta*, is very showy with shiny green leaves blotched with white and yellow. It produces several handsome forms with varying leaf markings.

D. seguine (mother-in-law plant), growing to 10 ft., has dark green leaves spotted with transparent white blotches.

DIERAMA (dī ur AY mah). A genus of bulbous plants of South Africa, belonging to the Iridaceae (Iris Family). They can be grown outdoors in mild climates and are sometimes grown in greenhouses. They thrive under the same treatment as IXIA.

D. pendulum has narrow leaves and lilac flowers on stems growing to 4 ft., drooping at the ends.

D. pulcherrimum has narrow, sword-shaped leaves drawn to a slender point and reddish purple, drooping flowers borne on spikes growing to 6 ft. long.

DIERVILLA (dī ur VIL ah). A genus of low, spreading deciduous shrubs of North America, belonging to the Caprifoliaceae (Honeysuckle Family), and commonly known as bush honeysuckle. Hardy in Zones 5–8, diervillas are little shrubs forming a mat of underground stems and are useful for massing, edging the front of shrubberies, or holding banks in shape. They are not particular as to soil, do well in partial shade, and are propagated by suckers.

D. lonicera, native from Newfoundland to North Carolina, grows to 3 ft. and has oval, long-pointed leaves to 4 in. long and small yellow flowers, usually in threes, appearing early in summer.

D. sessilifolia is native from North Carolina southward but is hardy to Zone 4. It grows to 5 ft. and has four-angled stems, leaves to 6 in. long, and pale yellow flowers in three- to seven-flowered clusters in early summer.

DIGGING. Digging the soil by hand was the preliminary step in preparing a plot of ground before the development of power tilling machines. The digging process was done with a narrow shovel or spading fork in early spring after the soil had dried to the point that it was workable. After digging or tilling, manure and compost can be added to the soil. The deeper the soil is worked, the better the air and water circulation there is around the roots of the plants. Digging to a depth of 12–15 in. is ideal, though most digging is done to the depth of the spade or shovel blade used. The purpose of digging is to loosen and turn each section of soil so that the debris and weed seeds on the surface of the soil are turned under and the dark topsoil just below the surface is brought to the top. See also DOUBLE DIGGING; CULTIVATION; TRENCHING.

DIGITALIS (di ji TAL is). A genus of biennial and perennial herbs with tall handsome flowers, belonging to the Scrophulariaceae (Figwort Family), and commonly known as foxglove. Native to Europe and western Asia, they are popular garden plants and hardy to Zone 4. Their long flower spikes, on stems 3 ft. tall or more, are crowded with large, thimblelike blossoms all drooping toward one side and beautifully spotted on the outer or inner surface. Foxgloves are useful for naturalizing among shrubs or placing in a background of a hardy border.

Easy to grow in the garden, as long as they have some shade, foxgloves will thrive in any ordinary soil. They are generally propagated by seed or by division following the cultural rules for perennials. Seed for biennial species can be sown in the spring or summer, producing flowering plants the second season.

PRINCIPAL SPECIES

D. ferruginea (rusty foxglove) is a perennial or biennial growing to 6 ft. The flowers are rusty red, downy outside, and the lower lip is bearded.

D. grandiflora (yellow foxglove), formerly listed as *D. ambigua*, is a perennial or biennial that grows to 3 ft. and has hairy foliage. The yellowish flowers are 2 in. long and are marked with brown.

D. laevigata is a perennial that grows to 3 ft. and has yellow flowers, spotted purple.

D. lanata (Grecian foxglove) is a perennial or biennial growing to 3 ft. high. Flowers are 1 in. long and nearly white, with fine veins.

D. lutea (straw foxglove) is a perennial that grows to 2 ft. and has flowers of yellow or white, ¾ in. long.

D. nervosa is a perennial with small, yellowish flowers in long, dense racemes.

D. purpurea (foxglove) grows to 4 ft. and has flowers 3 in. long, purplish in color, and somewhat spotted. A widely naturalized species, it has been used in medicines for centuries. Var. *alba* produces white flowers. Cv. 'Gloxiniiflora' has wide-mouthed flowers and longer spikes than others of the species.

Digitalis purpurea

D. x *sibirica* is a hairy perennial with yellowish flowers.

DIGITARIA (di ji TAIR ee ah). A genus of annual or perennial, often weedy herbs belonging to the Poaceae (Grass Family), and commonly known as CRABGRASS or finger grass. The inflorences are slender, fingerlike spikes, rounded on one side, flat on the other, and more prominent than the inconspicuous flowers they carry.

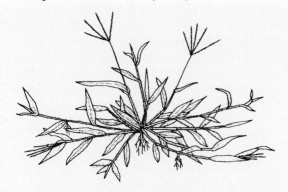

Digitaria sanguinalis

D. sanguinalis (hairy crabgrass) is an annual with branching stems that grow to 3 ft. and often spread by roots at the base. The ⅜ in. wide leaves have a smooth or rough, hairlike texture and grow from hairy or pimply sheaths. The flowers are borne in 6-in. spikes grouped with a few or several clustered together at the base, usually with a few whorls just below them. In Europe and the western United States, it is used for forage and hay, but in the eastern and southern states, this is a noxious weed, especially on lawns.

DILL. Common name for the flavoring herb *Anethum graveolens*; see ANETHUM.

DILLENIA (di LEN ee ah). A genus of Australian or Asian trees, one of which, *D. indica* (hardy in Zones 10–11), is grown in the warmest parts of the United States for its large, showy, white or yellow flowers, often exceeding 6 in. across, and for its tart, fleshy fruits. While normally evergreen, it is likely to drop its leaves in dry seasons.

DIMORPHOTHECA (dī mor foh THEE kah). A genus of annuals and perennials, sometimes listed as *Osteospermum*, belonging to the Asteraceae (Aster Family), and commmonly known as cape-

marigold or star-of-the-veldt. South Africa contributed this choice and colorful group of flowers to our gardens. They are herbs or subshrubs bearing solitary terminal heads of ray and disk flowers in orange, yellow, purple, blue, or white and are ideally suited to low beds, borders, or rock gardens as a source of color late in the season. Growing from 1–2 ft. tall in warm, sunny locations, they do best when given a long season, flowering from early summer until frost. The plants, spreading in habit, are covered with an abundance of large, daisylike blossoms that generally expand in the sunlight but close toward evening.

In California and other mild regions, they are splendid winter plants if seed is sown in the late fall. In other areas, seed is generally sown indoors in early spring or outdoors a little later. The perennial species are propagated by cuttings.

PRINCIPAL SPECIES

D. aurantiaca is a perennial, often shrubby, which blooms during its first season. Flower rays are orange-yellow. There are many hybrids in white, sulfur yellow, golden yellow, salmon, rose, apricot, and ecru.

D. cuneata is a small, branching, sticky shrub with yellow flowers.

D. plurialis, formerly listed as *D. annua*, is a rough, hairy annual whose flower rays are white or yellowish above and purplish on the underside. Var. *ligulosa* is a double form whose white rays have yellow or purple undersides. Var. *ringens* has a deep blue ring around the center.

D. sinuata, formerly listed as *D. calendulacea*, is a hairy annual with orange-yellow flowers.

DIOECIOUS. A term applied to plants in which the two kinds of sex organs are borne on different individuals. The flowers bearing only the male reproductive elements are called staminate; those bearing the female egg cells are pistillate flowers. In contrast, monoecious plants are those bearing both kinds of flowers on the same individual. These terms apply only to plants in which the stamens and pistils occur in separate (unisexual) flowers. In so-called perfect (bisexual) flowers, the male and female organs are found together in a single blossom. See FLOWER.

DIONAEA (dī oh NEE ah) **muscipula.** A perennial insectivorous herb native to swampy regions of the Carolinas, belonging to the Droseraceae (Sundew Family), and commonly known as Venus flytrap. The plants have white flowers to 1 in. across borne on stems 12 in. tall, and rosettes of leaves consisting of two hinged blades set with sensitive hairs. When these are touched by an insect, the halves of the leaf close to form a trap. The entrapped insect dies, and its juices are absorbed by the plant.

These plants are sometimes grown in botanical collections in greenhouses, where they should be potted in silver sand and black silt with a surface of chopped sphagnum moss. The pots should be set in an inch of water and kept in a moist atmosphere in full sunshine.

See also INSECTIVOROUS PLANTS.

DIOON (dī OON). A genus of slow-growing cycads, native to Mexico, with stiff, feather-shaped leaves at the top of a trunk that may reach 6 ft. in height after many years. Hardy to the southern edge of Zone 9.

DIOSCOREA (dī ohs kor EE ah). A genus of herbaceous twining vines from warm regions, closely related to the Liliaceae (Lily Family), and commonly known as yam or sweet-potato (which more correctly refers to a species of *Ipomoea*). Several species are cultivated in the tropics for their large, edible tubers, which are handled and used like potatoes. A few are grown in greenhouses for their handsome foliage. Easy to grow, they are propagated by seed, tubers, and cuttings. See also YAM.

PRINCIPAL SPECIES
D. alata (winged, white, or water yam) is distinguished by four-winged or angled stems. It produces tubers up to 3 ft. long and weighing up to 100 lb., but these are of coarse texture and inferior flavor. The smaller varieties are preferred for culinary use.

D. batatas (cinnamon vine, Chinese yam) is a tall climbing vine from China, with slender twining stems. It is useful as a porch vine where a heavy screen is not desired. It is tuberous-rooted and fairly hardy in cold regions, where it is herbaceous. In the tropics, it is often cultivated for the edible tubers that grow up to 3 ft. long, deep in the ground. Attractive shiny leaves are conspicuously ribbed and veined. Small clusters of cinnamon-scented white flowers are borne in the leaf axils, where little tubercles are formed and can be used to start new plants.

D. bulbifera (air-potato) is a tall slender climber, remarkable for its large, angular tubers, which develop in the leaf axils and may become a foot long and weigh several pounds. The root-tubers, when produced at all, are small. It is native to Asia and the Philippines.

D. discolor. A decorative greenhouse species with leaves mottled in several shades of green, white along the midrib, and rich purple beneath.

D. trifida (yampee, cush-cush) is a tender vine with small tuberous roots.

DIOSMA (dī OZ mah) **ericoides.** A heathlike shrub native to South Africa, belonging to the Rutaceae (Rue Family); it is the only member of its genus and is commonly known as buchu. It is sometimes grown under glass and also outdoors in very warm regions, Zones 9–11. The foliage is pleasantly aromatic, and the small white flowers, freely produced, are useful as fillers in table decorations. When grown in a pot, it requires a mixture of fibrous loam with peat or leaf mold and plenty of sharp sand. Plants should be cut back hard after flowering to induce a good bushy habit. Propagation is by cuttings of young wood.

Because a related plant, *Adenandra fragrans*, was once known as *Diosma fragrans*, its common name, breath-of-heaven, is frequently applied to this plant as well.

DIOSPYROS (dī AWS pi ros). A genus of widely scattered trees and shrubs belonging to the Ebenaceae (Ebony Family), and commonly known as persimmon. Most are ornamental and interesting, but they are also grown for their edible fruits and harvested for commercial lumber. Deep taproots make them difficult to transplant. The trees are usually dioecious, with male or female flowers, so both should be planted to ensure fruit production.

D. kaki (Japanese persimmon), an attractive ornamental tree growing to 25 ft., is cultivated for its large, sweet, bright orange to red fruit. It is commonly grown and eaten in Asia and occasionally in the United States. It can be grown in warm regions, but it is not hardy in the North. There are many cultivars available. Hardy in Zones 7–9.

D. virginiana (common persimmon), a tree growing to 50 ft., is native from Connecticut to Florida and west to Texas. The sweet, small, orange fruits are produced late in the fall and should be eaten raw only when very soft. They also make a delicious pudding. Several cultivars are available. Hardy in Zones 4–9.

DIPELTA (dī PEL tah). A genus of deciduous shrubs of China, belonging to the Caprifoliaceae (Honeysuckle Family). They are hardy to Zone 6 and grow well in any good soil in a location that does not get too hot and dry. Propagation is by cuttings of half-ripened and mature wood.

D. floribunda, the hardiest species, is a large, handsome shrub that grows to 15 ft. In early summer it produces a profusion of clusters of funnel-shaped, pale rose flowers with orange markings. Large, conspicuous, and persistent bracts are borne at the base of the clusters.

DIPLADENIA (dip lah DEE nee ah). Former name for a genus of flowering vines now known as MANDEVILLA.

DIPLAZIUM (dip LAY zee um). A genus of 400 tropical species of ferns from China, Japan, and Korea, only a few of which are found in the North American trade. Several make very attractive container plants, varying from quite dwarf to 2–3 ft. high. Enthusiasts who grow ferns from spores should look for spores of *D. subsinuatum* (also

listed as *D. lanceum*) and *D. tomitaroanum*, a choice, very dwarf Japanese species; both have simple fronds. *D. esculentum* (vegetable fern) is an interesting and edible escapee into Florida from southeastern Asia.

DIPSACACEAE (dip suh KAY see ee). The Teasel Family, a group of herbs bearing dense heads or spikes of small flowers subtended by stiff-hooked bracts. The common name is derived from the use of the dry, ripe spikes of species of *Dipsacus* (the "teasels" of the textile industry) for fluffing or teasing the nap of cloth. A few genera include ornamental subjects, such as *Cephalaria*, *Morina*, and *Scabiosa*.

DIPSACUS (DIP sah kus). A genus of tall, hairy or prickly, thistlelike herbs commonly known as teasel. A few species are grown as ornamentals in the wild garden or shrubbery border. Started from seed, they are easily established and, indeed, are likely to escape and become weeds. The genus lends its name to the Dipsacaceae (Teasel Family), to which it belongs.

PRINCIPAL SPECIES

D. pilosus, growing to 4 ft., is a bristly plant with yellowish white flowers in round heads.

D. sativus (Fuller's teasel), formerly listed as *D. fullonum*, grows to 6 ft. and has lavender flowers in dense heads. The bracts on the seed heads are sharp and spinelike. These dry, bristly heads are used in the textile industry for raising a nap on fabrics, no machinery having been invented to replace them.

D. sylvestris (common teasel) is only slightly different from *D. fullonum*. Both species are valuable bee plants.

DIRCA (DUR kah). A small genus of North American shrubs with attractive foliage, valued for their early flowers, and commonly known as leatherwood.

D. palustris has tough, fibrous bark and tough, flexible shoots that can be bent and twisted without breaking. It grows best in moist soils and is hardy in Zones 5–9.

DISA (DĪ sah). A genus of approximately 130 species of terrestrial orchids native to tropical and South Africa. The plants have subterranean tubers with stoloniferous roots. The flowers are resupinate, colorful, and exotic in shape; petals are fused to the column, and the lip is barely discernible. The dorsal sepal is erect, spurred, and helmet-shaped; lateral sepals are broad and spreading.

The plants are classified as warm or cool growing. The warm types are hardy only to Zone 9 and withstand a minimum winter temperature of 60°F. The cool types are hardy to Zone 5 with frost protection and will withstand temperatures down to 50°F. Difficult to establish, *Disa* plants need a dense compost of live sphagnum moss and peat. The cool-growing types need a cool, moist, shady environment with constant moisture at the roots during growth. Warm-growing plants need a dry rest after the stems die back. The type species is *D. uniflora*.

DISBUDDING. The practice of destroying buds on young shoots for some desired end, usually the enhancement of the quality and size of flowers. For instance, bush roses normally develop several flower buds on each stem. If all are allowed to bloom, the flowers will be small and imperfect; but if all except the terminal bud are destroyed as soon as they can be reached with the fingernail, the single flower remaining will be larger and more perfect in form with a longer stem. Early disbudding also tends to foster quick new growth lower down on the plant and helps maintain a succession of bloom the whole season through. Chrysanthemums, dahlias, and various other plants produce specimen and exhibition blooms when their flower and branch buds are so treated.

Newly planted grapevines are often allowed to develop a shoot from each of two or three buds, only to have all but one cut off the following spring. It is a better practice to disbud all but the strongest of such shoots, leaving only one leaf on each as soon as the base of the selected shoot has become partially woody. It thus gets most of the available plant food and usually becomes strong enough to bear fruit the next season—a year earlier than the usual practice. For the same reason, during the second and third years, shoots that start at a point lower than is desirable for arms, and those between the upper and lower arms, are destroyed when an inch or less in length. The sooner they are removed the better.

Experiments have shown that fruit trees can be much stronger structurally if disbudded instead of being permitted to branch at will. The practice starts with the unbranched one-year tree—the whip—with its terminal bud intact and plump. Groups of three buds located at the heights desired and a foot or more apart are chosen for development and all others except the terminal or topmost one are destroyed. These selected buds can all be expected to develop branches. In the spring of the second year the most favorably placed and the best-developed branch in each group is chosen to form a part of the permanent framework of the tree, the others being cut back close to the trunk. The same practice when repeated on the main branches tends to make a symmetrical, well-balanced, structurally strong tree.

DISEASE. Disease in plants is most simply defined as "any deviation from a normal condition." Generally this means an injurious condition or process caused by the continued irritation of some chief factor, which may be either an environmental condition or a living organism. Diseases caused by environmental conditions such as drought, excessive moisture, lack of proper nutrients or overfeeding, improper soil acidity, too low or too high temperatures, gas or electrical injury, or injury resulting from industrial processes are called physiological diseases.

Viral diseases are difficult to classify and are recognized chiefly by a mosaic or mottled effect on the foliage or by a yellowing and stunting of the plant. Mycoplasma and rickettsia, which are bacterialike organisms, also cause diseases of plants, with symptoms similar to viral disease symptoms.

Plant injury caused by the chewing and sucking of insects is not considered true plant disease; but the disturbance caused by nematodes (eelworms) resulting in typical symptoms such as browning of the tissues and gall formation, is generally so considered. Plant parasites that cause disease in the generally accepted sense are bacteria, slime molds, fungi, and a few higher plants such as dodder and mistletoe.

Symptoms are evidences of plant disease produced in or by the plant itself. Signs are evidences of the pathogen, or disease-producing organism, such as fruiting bodies or mycelium. It is necessary for the gardener to recognize a plant disease or the group to which it belongs in order to select and apply proper control measures. An understanding of a few of the fundamental symptoms and signs will help in consulting the literature concerning specific diseases and in asking for special help. In contacting experiment stations and other sources of information about the garden troubles, provide a typical specimen of the affected plant whenever possible. In any case, give a complete, careful description of the symptoms and signs noted. Too often such a query takes the form of "My elm is sick; what shall I do about it?"

COMMON SYMPTOMS OF PLANT DISEASE

Symptoms can be either local, such as a spot or canker, or general, as in the case of wilt or damping-off. They are classed as necrotic, which means resulting in death of the tissues involved; hypoplastic, resulting in underdevelopment; or hyperplastic, resulting in overdevelopment of tissues or functions.

Some common necrotic symptoms are:

Blight. Sudden killing of shoots, foliage, or blossoms by a pathogenic organism.

Canker. Sunken lesions in stems, branches, trunks, or roots of trees or shrubs.

Damping-off. The rapid rotting at the base, or wilting of seedlings. They may be damped-off in such a young stage that they do not even emerge from the soil.

Dieback. The dying backward from the tip of twigs and branches of trees and shrubs. May be a symptom of winter injury, of fungus attacks, or of wet soil.

Mummification. Wrinkling and drying of fruits into a hard mass called a "mummy," consisting of an intermingling of host plant and fungus tissue. See BROWN ROT.

Rot. Dead tissue in a more or less advanced stage of decomposition. Rots can be soft, hard, dry, or wet and caused by either bacteria (as the soft rot of iris) or by fungi (as the crown rot of ornamentals).

Scorch. Sudden death and browning of large areas of leaves or fruits—due to drought, heat, or spray injury.

Shot-hole. A spotting of leaves followed by dropping out of diseased areas; certain kinds of leaves, such as cherry, have a special tendency in this direction. May be due to fungi or to spray injury.

Spot. A more or less circular, dead area developed in leaves or fruit; usually brown in the center but often surrounded by reddish or yellow zones.

Wilt. The clogging or poisoning of the vascular (circulatory) system of a plant, resulting in drooping or dieback and usually the death of the entire plant.

Among the common hypoplastic symptoms (those showing underdevelopment in size or differentiation of organs) are some particularly characteristic of viral diseases, such as:

Chlorosis. Subnormal development of the green color in a plant.

Mosaic. A mottling or incomplete chlorosis.

Rosetting. The crowding of the foliage into a rosette due to the shortening of the internodes of the stems.

Stunting. A reduction in size.

Yellows. A general chlorotic condition.

Examples of hyperplastic symptoms (those showing overdevelopment in size or differentiation of organs) are:

Callus. Tissue overgrowth in response to wounding.

Curl. Abnormal bending, curling, or crinkling of leaves due to overdevelopment of one side.

Fasciculation or witches'-broom. Clustering of organs due to adventitious development of shoots.

Scab. Definite, usually circular, somewhat raised lesions on fruits, tubers, stems, and leaves.

Tumefaction. Tumorlike swellings or galls produced on woody portions of plants due to the action of bacteria or fungi.

SIGNS OF DISEASE-CAUSING AGENTS

There are various signs of disease-producing organisms, such as:

Exudation. A mixture of plant sap and the disease-causing organism, as illustrated by the bacterial ooze seen on fire blight cankers and the gummy substance formed in brown rot.

Fruiting Bodies. These fungus growths may be soft brown cups arising from mummies on the ground, such as BROWN ROT; small black dots in the center of stem or leaf lesions; or large sporophores coming out of tree trunks, such as BRACKET FUNGI. See also FUNGUS.

Mycelium. A white weft at the base of the plant (as in sclerotinia rot) or dark radiating strands in a leaf spot disease such as black spot of rose. The mycelium is the growing part of a fungus.

Odors. These are characteristic of certain diseases, especially the soft rot of iris.

Sclerotia. Hard, more or less spherical, resting bodies of a fungus, black in the case of botrytis blight of peonies, reddish brown in crown rot.

Spores. These may appear as grayish mold on buds (as in botrytis blight), gray pustules on fruit (in brown rot), reddish pustules on stems and leaves (in rusts), or black sooty masses (in smuts).

Despite popular belief to the contrary, the prevalence of plant disease is nothing new; some of the present-day troubles go back to the earliest human records. But the spread of plant diseases has kept pace with the advance methods of transportation and the severity of its attacks with the more intensive culture of special crops. Disease-producing organisms are transported in or on seed, tubers, nursery stock, and soil and plant debris by boat, train, automobile, and airplane, as well as by the older natural forces of air and water currents, birds, and insects.

Local dissemination of plant disease is accomplished by wind and wind-splashed rain, by insects—the honey bee is responsible for spreading fire blight organism, and aphids and leaf hoppers carry the virus of certain mosaics—and by dogs, cats, field mice, and other animals, especially humans. Gardeners themselves (through their hands, clothing, and tools) are often unwittingly responsible for spreading disease around their own and their neighbors' gardens. Hence, always take sanitary precautions when working with diseased plants. If you cut off a blighted peony bud covered with spores, do not carry it openly around the garden on the way to the trash pile; put it in a bag immediately. If you pull up a slimy, diseased iris plant, do not touch a healthy one until you have washed your hands thoroughly with soap and water or dipped them in disinfectant. Above all, do not divide your iris and give some to your neighbors without disinfecting the rhizomes and fans; see IRIS. Likewise, disinfect pruning tools after cutting off a diseased plant part before touching them to a healthy subject. See DISINFECTION.

BACTERIAL DISEASES

Many serious plant diseases are caused by bacteria. While the symptoms may be similar to those of fungus diseases, the latter's characteristic signs, such as fruiting bodies and spores, are absent. The following kinds of symptoms are typical of those shown by bacterial diseases :

Blights, such as fire blight of apples and ornamentals, bean blight, bacterial blight of lilacs; rots, such as soft rot of iris, black rot of crucifers; wilts, as cucumber wilt; leaf spots, as black spot of delphinium; and overgrowths, such as gladiolus scab, crown gall.

Bacteria that cause plant disease can be spread by almost anything, including the carelessness of the gardener, especially during wet weather; by wind-splashed rain; and by insects, sometimes within them as in the case of cucumber wilt, and sometimes on the outside of their body as the iris borer spreads bacterial soft rot. Fortunately, bacteria that cause plant disease are not of the group that forms resistant resting bodies called spores, so the spread of bacterial diseases through the air is not as common as that of fungus diseases, whose spores can be carried long distances by wind and air currents.

Since these diseases in plants are difficult, if not impossible, to cure, precautions should be taken to avoid them, by preventing infection and by developing immunity or increased resistance to the organisms in improved varieties of plants.

PHYSIOLOGICAL DISEASES

These are not parasitic, but rather environmental troubles, due not to living organisms, but to conditions under which the plants are growing, such as:

Malnutrition. Deficiences of nutrients in the soil weakens many plants. Lack of sufficient nitrogen causes yellowing and stunting. Lack of iron prevents chlorophyll development and consequently causes poorly colored foliage. Calcium is necessary for normal leaf development, phosphorus for the formation of proteins, and potassium for carbohydrate development (for example, there is a disease called "potash hunger" of potatoes). A deficiency of magnesium also causes chlorosis or poor foliage color, as in the "sand drown" of tobacco. For such diseases, the remedy is of course to supply fertilizers rich in the deficient element, but this must frequently be done by the trial-and-error method.

Overfertilization. Symptoms of overnourishment and excesses of soluble salts in the soil can be foliage color that is too dark and suppression of reproductive organs, or their transformation into other organs. An excess of nitrogen can cause rank, succulent plant growth and lower the quality of fruits and vegetables as well as resistance to disease. Plants fed too late in the season may be "soft" and unable to withstand winter.

Improper Soil Acidity. Too acid a soil can result in definite symptoms of disease in almost all plants except those requiring a special acid condition; on the other hand, such plants as rhododendron and laurel, which prefer acid conditions, do exceedingly poorly in neutral or alkaline soil.

Unfavorable Water Conditions. Much winter injury is due to lack of available water, either through freezing of the soil or actual drought. Trees will show the effects of one or two seasons of drought for several years. Conversely, too much water in the soil can so reduce the supply of oxygen that the plants die. Acid rain will also have a detrimental effect on many plants.

Unfavorable Temperatures. Too-high temperatures cause tipburn and scald. Too-low temperatures cause dieback, bud injury, and frost cankers.

Pollutants. Manufacturing or industrial pollutants are responsible for many diseases. Vapor, dust, or fumes from melting tar compounds are distinctly injurious. Trees may suffer not only from lightning but also from electrical discharges from transmission lines. Leakage of natural gas into the soil is a fairly common source of trouble in greenhouses and gardens along streets. Even a slight leakage of gas causes a slow but very thorough poisoning, from which there is not much chance of recovery. In detecting such leakage, scientists use certain plants very sensitive to small amounts of gas, such as the tomato or sweet pea.

Smoke injury is another hazard near large industrial centers. The chief injury is done by sulfur dioxide; when large amounts are present in the air, there is rapid disappearance of chlorophyll in the leaves, followed by death. When small amounts are present, symptoms are retarded growth, failure to blossom and set fruit, early shedding of leaves, and eventual death.

Poor Protective Measures. Diseases due to practices employed in trying to control other diseases include injury during seed disinfection, fumigation, or spraying.

VIRAL DISEASES

This group of plant diseases is caused by microscopic organisms that can be transmitted from diseased to healthy individuals. No visible organisms or causal agents are known, since the viruses can pass through fine filters. Viral diseases take the form of infectious chlorosis or foliage or flower variegation; leaf roll (of potatoes); curly top (of sugar beets); rosetting; stunting; and the various so-called mosaics, whose chief symptom is a mottling of the leaves often accompanied by dwarfing or malformation of the flowers.

Some viral diseases, such as tobacco mosaic, can be transmitted merely by touching. Others are transmitted only by budding or grafting. A few are transmitted through seed, as bean mosaic, some both by grafting and insects, and many chiefly by insects. Most mosaics are carried by insects: cucumber mosaic by the melon aphis and the striped cucumber beetle, curly top by a leaf hopper, and so on through a long list.

There are no protective measures known by which viral diseases can be controlled, so the chief precaution against them is the immediate removal of all diseased individuals, a practice known as "roguing."

DISINFECTION. This means the direct destruction of a disease-producing organism in any way associated with the host plant or present in its immediate environment. The term includes disinfection of the plant in a dormant or active condition; disinfection of plant parts such as seeds, bulbs, and tubers; and soil disinfection.

TREATING PLANT PARTS

Disinfection of seeds and other plant parts is accomplished with hot water or various chemicals. Hot-water seed treatment is practiced to protect against loose smut, black rot, and to destroy nematodes, flies, and mites in bulbs, especially narcissus and other flowering kinds. The procedure varies depending on the plant material and the pathogen or pest involved.

Many fungicides are available for treating seed and other plant parts to prevent the spread of disease. Of the chemicals used for soil sterilization, all are highly poisonous to humans and are not always recommended for use by the gardening public. Sodium chloride was first found to be a seed disinfectant when a cargo of wheat, lost off the coast of England in the seventeenth century, was later salvaged in good condition—freed from the smut fungus by the immersion in salt water.

Copper sulfate, next developed as a cereal seed disinfectant, has since been largely replaced. Contact your local garden center or extension service to find the best choice for your particular plant problem. In lieu of chemical sterilants, and more in line with today's thinking about the environment, is the use of beneficial microflora. They come in powder form, are simple to use, and are nonpoisonous to humans and the environment. At the Santa Barbara Botanic Garden nursery, for example, two different ones are used: one to add to the water for seed sowing and another to add to the medium for containers. There are no doubt other companies producing similar products. See appendix for suppliers.

When pruning diseased plants, a pathogen is readily spread from diseased to healthy plants on the blades of the tools being used. Between cuts and certainly between plants, the cutting edge of the tool should be dipped in denatured alcohol or another disinfectant solution.

SOIL DISINFECTION

This can be accomplished through the use of heat, electricity, or chemicals. Partial sterilization, or pasteurization by heat, can be accomplished by placing soil in a metal container and baking it in an oven, by heating it with electricity, or by treating it with hot water or steam. It requires that moist soil or pot mix be heated to 140°F and kept at that temperature for 30 minutes. When cooled it is ready to use. Most all pathogens will be killed, whereas many of the beneficial microorganisms will not be. Sterilization (180°F for 30 minutes) of the soil is less desirable, as it kills all the beneficial microorganisms as well.

For sterilization, steam is probably the most satisfactory means, although it is usually applicable only to large greenhouses unless a portable boiler is available for treating outdoor seedbeds. Steam can be applied either through loose tile or perforated pipe buried in the soil or by means of a large inverted pan. Limited amounts of soil can be sterilized in a large pressure cooker like those used for canning operations.

Boiling water can be used for soil sterilization

where only a small area is to be treated, but it has the disadvantage of puddling the soil. Enough must be applied to thoroughly saturate the soil—about 7 gal. per cubic ft. This method controls nematodes and soil fungi near the soil surface but is not very successful for deep sterilization. Small (4-in.) flower pots full of soil or pot mix immersed for 5 minutes in boiling water will probably give satisfactory results.

Some chemicals such as Vapam, methyl bromide, and chloropicrin can be used to sterilize soil. Contact your local extension service regarding their use and possible hazards.

Sulfur can occasionally be used as a soil fungicide, especially for the suppression of common scab of potatoes. Apply 1 lb. to 100 sq. ft. and thoroughly cultivate it in advance of planting. The amount of sulfur may have to be varied somewhat to correspond with the initial acidity of the soil.

DISK FLOWER. One of the individual florets that make up the center of the flower head of such composite plants as the daisy. They are so small and so compactly arranged that the whole head, whether or not it has a border of strap-shaped, petal-like ray flowers, has the appearance of, and is often mistaken for, a single flower. See also RAY FLOWER.

DISPORUM (dī SPOH rum). A genus of perennial herbs belonging to the Liliaceae (Lily Family) and commonly known as fairy-bells. They have slender rootstocks, leafy stems, and drooping white or yellowish flowers, solitary or borne in clusters, and are followed by attractive red or yellow berries. Native in wooded areas, they are very lovely in the wild garden, especially when in fruit, and are similar to Solomon's-seal in growth, but usually are grown in drier situations. Propagation is by seed or division. Most are hardy in Zones 7–9.

PRINCIPAL SPECIES

D. hookeri grows to 2 ft. and has green flowers followed by scarlet berries. Var. *D. oreganum* has creamy white flowers.

D. lanuginosum has greenish flowers and red fruit.

D. maculatum, growing to 2 ft., has yellowish flowers dotted with black.

D. smithii, growing to 3 ft., has whitish flowers to 1 in. and bright yellow berries.

DITCHMOSS. Common name for *Elodea canadensis*, a perennial aquatic herb with floating, whitish flowers; see ELODEA.

DITTANY. A common name for *Dictamnus albus*, a shrubby flowering perennial that emits a flammable oil; see DICTAMNUS.

DIVISION. A form of vegetative propagation in which one or more new plants are separated from the parent plant. A "division" is a plant removed from another plant. To divide a plant successfully, you must examine its growth habits. Certain woody shrubs and herbaceous perennials, including mock orange and shasta daisies, expand the size of their clumps by growing numerous new plants all around them. These are easy to divide because the outer plants have roots (A).

Plants with fleshy roots also increase in a manner that makes division possible. Lilies, daffodils, and similar plants can be periodically lifted from the soil and their roots split apart and replanted (B).

Many plants will spread by sending out suckers from their roots; they can be divided by digging up the sucker plants. For example, blackberries and red raspberries are easy to propagate in this

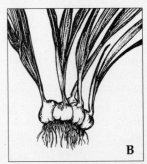

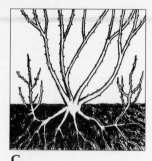

C

D

way. Poplars, willows, black locust, wild cherry, and many other plants often send up new trees from their roots. Sucker plants sometimes sprout a long distance from the parent plant (C).

Others, including tropical plants such as pineapple and banana, produce sucker-type offshoots or offsets close to their trunk, which can be removed to start new plants. Offsets are sometimes tricky to start successfully because it is difficult to get a good root on each one when you cut it from the parent.

Many vines, ground covers, and similar plants, both herbaceous and woody, creep in all directions, root, and create new plants in a process called natural layering. Wild grapes, kudzu, water-hyacinth, and myrtle, for example, often spread over a large area in this manner. They can become either a useful covering for an unsightly eroded spot, or real pests. It is easy to dig up and divide the newly formed plants.

Divisions and/ or separations are made by simply pulling a plant apart at the crown or basal plate as

Dividing a clump

with narcissus bulbs, or cutting with a sharp knife as with peony roots, clippers for chrysanthemums, and a saw or axe for a large *Philadelphus* or bamboo clump. The division may or may not have roots; if it does not, it will root when treated like other CUTTINGS. If a plant is pulled apart, before replanting, the raw edges of the break are smoothed with a knife or clippers, and the wound is touched with a fungicide such as dusting or soil sulfur or a rooting compound with a fungicide. This lessens the possibility of infection. Plants with modified roots, such as dahlia, are divided in such a manner that a piece of the old stem with an eye (shoot bud) remains attached to each division. The eyes are located on the stalk near the attachment with the tubers and are easy to locate as the plant begins to awaken in spring before replanting.

Suckers that develop from plants such as red raspberry and snowberry are dug individually (D). Stolons (slender branches) that naturally take root, as in red-osier dogwood, are similarly cut apart. Crowns or rooted buds that form, usually at the tips of rhizomes, toward the close of the growing season and push forward in the soil are often severed and planted; the best example of this type is lily-of-the-valley.

Still more specialized instances of division or separation are the bulblets formed in the leaf axils of tiger lilies and other kinds, the plantlets formed in the margins of bryophyllum leaves, and the fronds of various ferns.

Taken as a whole, division and separation are two of the easiest methods of propagation that gardeners can utilize in increasing plants suited to these types of multiplication. See LAYERING; PROPAGATION.

DIZYGOTHECA (dī zig oh THEE kah) **elegantissima.** A shrub or small tree native to Polynesia, belonging to the Araliaceae (Aralia Family), and commonly known as false aralia. The fingerlike leaflets are slender on young plants, and the leaves get coarser with age. It is a reliable houseplant provided that it is not overwatered.

DOCK. Common name for RUMEX, a genus of biennial and perennial herbs.

DODDER. Common name for CUSCUTA, a genus of leafless, parasitic vines.

DODECATHEON (doh dek ah THEE ahn). A genus of small North American perennial herbs belonging to the Primulaceae (Primrose Family), commonly known as shooting-star or American-cowslip. They have basal leaves and rounded clusters of nodding flowers resembling cyclamens. The blossoms are white, purple, or rose-colored, with reflexed petals, the jointed stems making a beaklike projection, which inspired the common name of shooting-star.

Plants grow naturally in half-shady woodland or rather damp mountain meadows. When cultivated, they should be planted in moist, humus-rich soil in the partly shaded rock or wild garden, taking care there is good drainage. Hardiness varies depending on the species. Propagation is by seed or division.

PRINCIPAL SPECIES

D. clevelandii (western shooting-star), growing to 18 in., has rather small leaves and purple flowers with a yellow base and beak; the color occasionally varies to white.

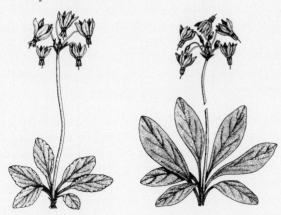

D. clevelandii   *D. meadia*

D. dentatum grows to 12 in. or more, with leaves to 10 in. and yellowish white flowers borne two to four in a cluster with very short beaks.

D. hendersonii is similar to *D. clevelandii* but has deep purple beaks.

D. jeffreyi is a relatively tall grower with erect leaves to 1 ft. and many-flowered umbels of deep rose-red flowers with purple beaks.

D. meadia (eastern shooting-star), one of the largest, grows to 2 ft. and has rose-colored flowers, white at the base, and leaves up to 6 in. long. It runs into many forms, including cv. 'Album' and 'Splendidum'.

D. poeticum, with leaves to 4½ in., has prettily colored flowers of rose-pink with concentric circles of yellow and crimson.

D. pulchellum has smooth, light green leaves and rose-red flowers on stout stems; it is especially suited to the rock garden.

DODONAEA (doh doh NEE ah) **cuneata.** A tropical shrub commonly known as hopbush. It is generally viscid (sticky) and has small flowers and winged fruits.

DOGBANE. Common name for APOCYNACEAE, a large family of mostly tropical herbs, shrubs, or trees grown for ornament, edible fruit, or medicinal products. Common dogbane is the genus *Apocynum*.

DOGTOOTH-VIOLET. A common yet misleading name for various white, yellow, and pink forms of ERYTHRONIUM species, which are hardy perennial herbs of the Liliaceae (Lily Family), not a violet.

DOGWOOD. Common name for CORNUS, an important genus of deciduous shrubs, trees, and a few herbs, widely cultivated in temperate regions.

DOLICHOS (DOH li kohs). A genus of tropical twining plants belonging to the Fabaceae (Bean Family). In the tropics, several species are grown for food, forage, or cover crops. In the United States, a few are grown in gardens for ornamental purposes. They are rapid growers, to 10 ft. or so, with wisteria-like flowers of red or white followed by attractive seed pods. They do best if planted where they are to stand.

D. lablab (hyacinth bean, bonavist, lablab) is a tender perennial usually grown as an annual. It has large, three-part leaves and stiff spikes of reddish purple flowers. It is not particular as to soil and can be sown outdoors when weather becomes warm, or started in pots under glass. Var. *giganteus* is of larger growth with white flowers.

D. lignosus (Australian pea) is a perennial, evergreen in warm regions, with smaller leaves than *D. lablab* and rosy purple or white flowers. It is a useful trellis vine.

DOMBEYA (dahm BAY ah). A genus of shrubs or small trees of Africa, sometimes grown in greenhouses, and one or two outdoors in Zones 10–11. They are rapid growers, with mostly large, heart-shaped or palmate leaves and umbels of showy flowers. Propagation is by seed or cuttings.

Some breeding work has been done to produce smaller hybrids suitable for the garden, but as colorful as these are, they have proved difficult to propagate and are not often seen. *D. burgessiae*, *D. x cayeuxii*, and *D. wallichii* are all large-growing shrubs with pink balls of flowers.

DOODIA (doo OH dee ah). A genus of small container ferns native to Australia and New Zealand. Hardy only in Zones 10–11, they are seldom seen but well worth growing because of their easy culture and the striking color of the new fronds. Useful in the greenhouse for edging and underplanting, they will tolerate overhead watering and prefer shade but must have perfect drainage.

There are several species available in trade, all rather similar, forming compact bushy plants 8–24 in. tall with once-pinnate fronds colored red, violet, or bronze when young, and often in fancy crested, plumed, and pendulous forms.

PRINCIPAL SPECIES

D. aspera (hacksaw fern) is a tough, pretty, pinnatifid fern with spear-shaped fronds, growing 18–24 in. tall. Fronds are soft red when young, and stipes are suffused with pink. It colonizes easily and can be used as a ground cover in a suitable climate.

D. caudata (small rasp fern) is a small, pinnate fern growing 6–12 in. It forms clumps rather than colonies and is excellent for pot culture.

D. media is a relatively large species with 2 ft. long, pinnate-pinnatifid fronds.

DORITIS (doh RĪ tus). A genus of monopodial orchids, with one species valued for its ability to hybridize with other members of Sarcanthinae orchids (*Phalaenopsis*, *Vanda*), producing intergeneric hybrids. The genus is native to Sri Lanka, India, and tropical southeastern Asia and was first described by nineteenth-century English botanist John Lindley.

The plants are small and epiphytic, with oval, leathery, distichous leaves on a short stem. Many showy medium-sized flowers, in shades from white to bright fuchsia, rise on stiff, erect spikes from between the leaves. Oval dorsal and lateral sepals are equal in size and color. The petals are usually reflexed. The three-lobed lip has two lateral lobes and a larger, undulating midlobe; two antennae lie behind the lateral lobes at the base of the lip.

Hardy in Zones 10–11 with protection from cold (minimum winter temperature 60–65°F), plants do best in baskets containing a porous, well-drained medium. The plants need high humidity, moderate shade, and warmth and should never dry out. They tend to form clumps, growing into excellent specimens.

DORMANCY. A condition of inactivity of seeds, roots, buds, or shoots of plants characterized by a suspension of growth and a reduced metabolic rate. Plants living in environments with seasonally extreme temperatures (hot or cold) or moisture availability often avoid the rigors of the season of stress by ceasing activity and becoming dormant.

Many plants of arctic and temperate regions produce growth inhibitors, such as abscisic acid, in response to the short days and long nights of late summer and autumn. These substances cause active growth to cease, resting buds to form, leaves to shed, and plants to enter dormancy even before winter arrives. Even if autumn weather is warm enough for continued growth, these plants will remain dormant, since many species require the cold temperatures of winter to break down the growth inhibitors. Increases in the amounts of gibberellin produced by a plant in the spring can also enhance the deactivation of growth inhibitors and hasten the resumption of growth and flowering.

Many species produce seeds that are dormant and require specific environmental conditions or internal requirements to be met in order to germinate. Seeds can be either inhibited or stimulated to germinate by the presence of light. High or low temperatures or the absence of sufficient moisture can also cause seeds of a given species to remain in a dormant condition. The matching of environmental conditions for germination with the ideal conditions for growth of seedlings has obvious survival values.

DORONICUM (doh ROH nik um). A genus of perennial, daisylike, yellow-flowered herbs, native to Europe and temperate Asia, belonging to the Asteraceae (Aster Family), and commonly known as leopard's-bane. They are among the earliest of the family to bloom in spring gardens and are popular for border planting. The leaves are oval or slightly heart shaped, numerous, with petioles at the base thinning out, and are often stemless along the flower stalks.

Doronicum plantagineum

Doronicums thrive under average conditions but prefer a rich loam and full sun. Stock can be increased readily by yearly divisions (after the plants are through flowering) or can be grown from seed. Most species are hardy in Zones 4–8.

PRINCIPAL SPECIES

D. clusii, growing to 2 ft., has solitary flowers and basal leaves.

D. cordatum, formerly listed as *D. caucasicum*, grows 2 ft. high and has one flower to a stem; the heart-shaped leaves are coarsely toothed.

D. grandiflorum grows to 1 ft., producing large yellow flowers in the spring. It is compact in growth habit but suitable for cutting.

D. pardalianches, growing to 4 ft., has hairy stems bearing up to five flower heads.

D. plantagineum, the best known and most commonly grown species, grows 5 ft. high and bears large, solitary flowers 2–4 in. across; the roots are tuberous.

DORSTENIA (dor STEEN ee ah) **crispa.** One of a few succulent members from tropical East Africa of this genus in the Moraceae (Mulberry Family). The "crisped" or wavy margined leaves are borne in terminal tufts; the inflorescence, or flowering head, looks a bit like a fig turned inside out. It has acute, radiating, fingerlike bracts that give it a strange sunburst-like appearance. The actual flowers are extremely tiny, as are the seeds, which are forcefully expelled when ripe, with subsequent seedlings coming up at random. The largest succulent member is *D. gigas*, from Socotra, with a very thick succulent caudex that grows to 3–4 ft. tall, with the caudex or stem nearly a foot and a half thick.

DORYANTHES (doh ree AN theez). A genus of large succulent plants belonging to the Agavaceae (Agave Family), commonly known as spear-lily. Native in dry regions of Australia, they are sometimes grown in California or in greenhouse collections. They usually attain a good size before flowering, and when fully grown they may have as many as 100 leaves 6 ft. long. Propagation is by suckers.

D. excelsa has sword-shaped leaves to 4 ft. long and a flower stem to 18 ft. bearing scarlet flowers 4 in. across in a round head.

D. palmeri has arching leaves to 6 ft. long and a many-flowered panicle of funnel-shaped red flowers, whitish on the inside, on a tall stem.

DORYOPTERIS (dor ee AHP tur is). A small genus of tropical ferns that grow in a chemical-poor, alkaline soil with perfect drainage. Where hardy, they will grow in rock gardens if conditions are not too wet, but they are better off as houseplants.

D. concolor is a small (4–12 in.), dark green, clump-forming fern with palmate fronds. It is widely distributed throughout Central and South America, Africa, Asia, and Australia. Some botanists list this fern in the genus *Cheilanthes*, which grows in the same conditions.

D. pedata (hand fern), native to Mexico and Central and South America, is an attractive little fern, growing 4–16 in., with dark green fronds resembling the outline of a hand or a maple leaf. Each frond is carried on a wiry black stipe. Var. *palmata* is an even more attractive form, with proliferous buds from which new plants are easily grown.

DOUBLE DIGGING. This technique for preparing garden beds involves, in essence, rotating the soil. Begin by removing a spade's depth and width of soil along one row and turning over a spade's depth of soil beneath the top layer.

Double digging

Then dig up the next spade's depth and width of soil and placing it into the first trench. Continue down the length of the bed in this manner and fill in the final row with the soil removed from the first row.

See also DIGGING; CULTIVATION; TRENCHING.

DOUBLE FLOWER. A flower in which the petals are multiplied beyond the usual number found in the species. Doubling is usually an inherent character, not susceptible to modification by culture or environment. The extra petals often appear to replace stamens or pistils that have become suppressed or transformed into the petal-like shape or condition.

DOUGLAS-FIR. Common name for *Pseudotsuga menziesii*, a common evergreen tree with bluish needles and drooping cones; see PSEUDOTSUGA.

DOUGLASIA (dug LAS ee ah). A genus of small alpine herbs belonging to the Primulaceae (Primrose Family), differing from *Primula* and *Androsace* in their branching growth. They bear yellow or rose flowers, solitary or in somewhat rounded flat clusters. Douglasias will do best on a north-facing slope of the rock garden and are difficult to cultivate in southern regions. They should be given sharp drainage but never allowed to dry out entirely. They are increased by seed, division, or cuttings.

D. vitaliana, native to Europe, is the most easily grown. Its stems lie on the ground and are tipped with small rosettes of leaves and nearly stemless long-tubed yellow flowers.

DOVE TREE. Common name for *Davidia involucrata*, a deciduous tree from China whose flowers resemble white doves; see DAVIDIA.

DOVYALIS (doh vee AY lis) **hebecarpa.** A small, tropical tree native to Ceylon and India, commonly known as ceylon-gooseberry. It grows outdoors in Zones 10–11 and bears edible fruits whose velvety covering and purple color resemble ripe gooseberries.

DOWNY MILDEW. Common name of fungi that produce loose white tufts or downy masses on the surface of the host. Sometimes known as false mildew, it grows inside the host plant, sending sporangiophores out through the stomata of the plant to create the downy patches on the leaves.

Although many chemical fungicides are available, gardeners are increasingly realizing that they can control adequately with practicing clean gardening techniques, getting rid of diseased plants, and choosing more disease-resistant varieties.

See also MILDEW; FUNGUS; DISEASE.

DRABA (DRAY bah). A genus of small, tufted, hardy annual or perennial herbs belonging to the Brassicaceae (Mustard Family). They are useful in the rock garden, having a neat habit and thriving in porous soil and a sunny position. The four-petaled flowers are typically yellow or white and appear early in the year. Propagation is by seed, division, or cuttings. Hardiness varies depending on the species, with some perennials thriving in Zones 3–6.

PRINCIPAL SPECIES

D. aizoides (Whitlow-grass), well suited for use in rock gardens in Zone 5, is a low-growing annual that forms a cushionlike mound with narrow, acute leaves ½ in. long and small yellow or white flowers in early spring.

D. bruniifolia produces minute tufts with orange-yellow flowers on short stems, excellent for troughs or small gardens. Var. *olympica* is a choice form. It grows well in pieces of tuff.

D. dedeana, with white flowers, is an excellent garden form.

Draba sp.

D. fladnizensis sends up greenish white flowers from a cushionlike tuft.

D. lasiocarpa, formerly listed as *D. aizoon*, grows about 4 ft. high, with narrow, rigid, hairy leaves and pale yellow flowers.

D. rigida, producing tiny plants and flowers, is not summer-hardy in hot climates but is worth growing as an annual because of its bright yellow winter flowers.

D. sibirica has creeping stems to 12 in., making a soft green mat with bright yellow flowers.

DRACAENA (drah SEE nah). A genus of ornamental plants with brilliant, often variegated foliage, belonging to the Agavaceae (Agave Family) and widely distributed in the tropics. Many properly belong to the closely related genus *Cordyline* but are sold and grown as *Dracaena*. One or two can be grown outdoors in Zones 10–11, but they are mostly popular as ornamental greenhouse foliage plants.

Dracaenas are easily grown but need a light, rich soil and, to promote quick growth, plenty of heat and moisture. They do not need large pots, but to maintain the bright leaf colors of the variegated forms, good light is needed in winter. When established they can stand ordinary greenhouse conditions, and some of them (notably *D. fragrans* and *D. surculosa*) tolerate indoor conditions fairly well. They are subject to red spider, scale, and mealybugs. For control and preventive measures, see HOUSEPLANTS.

Plants are propagated easily. The leafy tops of "leggy" plants can be taken as cuttings or made into new specimens by AIR LAYERING. Young plants are obtained by cutting up the old stems into pieces about 1 in. long, but better ones in shorter time come from the underground "toes" or fleshy extensions of the stem.

PRINCIPAL SPECIES

D. deremensis, from tropical Africa, includes many cultivated forms. Cv. 'Bausei' has leaves with a central white stripe. 'Janet Craig' has extremely durable, plain green leaves. 'Warneckii' has thin white lines through silvery green leaves. There are also compact forms of both 'Janet Craig' and 'Warneckii', which make rosettes of leaves growing slowly 6–10 in. tall. These make excellent tabletop plants.

D. draco (dragon tree), sometimes grown in California, is a long-lived tree growing to 30 ft. or more with sword-shaped leaves of bluish green. It can be grown outdoors in the tropics. A famous specimen at Tenerife in the Canary Islands grew 70 ft. high with a trunk diameter of 15 ft.; it was one of the oldest trees ever known.

D. fragrans is a popular decorative plant with handsome, shining, green recurved leaves. Cv.

'Lindenii' has marginal bands of creamy white or yellow. Cv. 'Massangeana' has a broad yellow stripe down the center.

D. goldieana is a magnificent foliage plant. The handsome leaves are marked with alternate crossbars of dark green and silvery gray.

D. indivisa is now listed as *Cordyline indivisa*; see CORDYLINE.

D. marginata, from Madagascar, has narrow, sword-shaped leaves with a thin purple banding on the edges. Cv. 'Tricolor' has colorful leaves striped with green, white, yellow, and pink; good light brings out the contrasting colors.

D. sanderana, a slender grower, has leaves marked with broad white margins. It soon becomes leggy and should be frequently propagated.

D. surculosa, formerly listed as *D. godseffiana*, is one of the best houseplants, forming a slender bushy plant with leaves freely spotted white.

D. terminalis is now listed as *Cordyline terminalis*; see CORDYLINE.

DRACOCEPHALUM (dray koh SEF ah lum). A

genus of hardy annual and perennial flowering herbs, belonging to the Lamiaceae (Mint Family), and commonly known as dragonhead. Their two-lipped flowers of blue, purple, and sometimes white are borne in whorls in the axils of the leaves or in spikes. These plants are not of great horticultural value but sometimes make pretty groups in a rather moist, shady part of the border. They are easily raised from seed or cuttings, but their flowers, produced in early summer, are very fleeting, not lasting at all in hot, exposed locations. Most species are hardy to Zone 2.

PRINCIPAL SPECIES

D. bullatum is an excellent subject for a shady corner of the rock garden, with almost round, hairy leaves and bright blue flowers.

D. calophyllum var. *smithianum*, also listed as *D. forrestii*, is a relatively low grower with finely cut leaves, white-hairy beneath, and whorled, blue-purple flowers.

D. moldavica is a charming annual species with blue or white flowers in long leafy racemes.

D. nutans, 1 ft. tall, has rather large, bright blue flowers in drooping spikes.

D. ruyschiana is a perennial that grows erect to 2 ft. with bluish flower spikes and hairy leaves.

DRACUNCULUS (dra KUN kyoo lus). A genus of

tuberous herbs of the Araceae (Arum Family), native to the Mediterranean region. *D. vulgaris* is sometimes grown as a curiosity in greenhouses or outdoors in mild climates. It has interesting leaves divided into ten or more segments from a bow-shaped base, and a large purple spathe with a vile odor.

DRAGONHEAD. Common name for DRACO-

CEPHALUM, a genus of hardy annual and perennial herbs with fleeting blossoms. False dragonhead is PHYSOSTEGIA.

DRAGONROOT. Common name for *Arisae-*

ma dracontium, a tall perennial herb with greenish bracts containing berries; see ARISAEMA.

DRAGON TREE. Common name for *Dracaena*

draco, a large-leaved tree native to the Canary Islands and sometimes grown in California; see DRACAENA.

DRAINAGE. The removal of excess water.

Most plants and trees, except aquatics, will die if water stands on their roots for any length of time. Their root development is also hampered by too much moisture in the subsoil even where the surface conditions are satisfactory. To remove excess water, gardeners use various forms of drainage, the simplest of which is to plant on sloping ground. Swamps or flat ground in danger of flooding can be ditched, the ditches leading to an outlet. If no outlet is available, in some situations a large "dry" well can be dug through the subsoil and hardpan to some more porous layer beneath. This is usually filled with stones, topped with cinders and gravel.

For lawns and gardens where ditches are objectionable, underdrainage can be used. Narrow ditches are partly filled with stone, cinders, or coarse gravel and a layer of straw or other material to prevent the replaced topsoil from washing down into the drainage and clogging it.

Porous drain tiles can be laid end to end in a ditch with enough gravel (or strips of building paper) to prevent the soil from washing in and silting them up. The ditch is then filled with soil. Where there is any considerable flow of water, as under land that has springs and wet spots, or in soils so heavy that they do not warm up in the early season, tile drainage is better than stone, and the ditches should be spaced only a few feet apart and placed deep enough so as not to be disturbed in cultivating the soil. In regions where plenty of flat stone is available, a skilled person can build good permanent drains to carry any flow of water by laying two rows of stones in the bottom of the ditch and capping these with larger flat stones, preferably two or three layers.

For rock and alpine gardens, drainage material is often laid under the entire area, sometimes in conjunction with an underground irrigation system. Sloping ground can be dug out to a depth of 24 in. or more and the excavation filled half-way with cinders and stone chips. Perforated water pipes are then laid so that a continual flow of water seeping out of the small holes will drain away rapidly, thus simulating the water from melting snow that trickles through the ground all summer on high mountains. Pipes and drainage are covered with alpine soil. See also ALPINE PLANTS.

Potted Plants. Drainage for potted plants is provided by the hole in the bottom of the pot. A piece of broken pot (potshard) is laid over it, concave side down, to prevent the soil from slipping out. For alpine plants, several potshards are thrown in, sometimes enough to half-fill the pot. This is called drainage, but its purpose is equally to furnish a reservoir of moisture as well as to drain, since the fragments of pot soak up quantities of water and remain damp for a long time, affording good root hold for alpine plants. This same practice is followed in seed pans and flats, especially for alpines and heaths. Cinders and stones are often used in the drainage instead of potshards, but best of all, because of the large amount of water absorbed, is broken soft brick.

DROPWORT. Common name for *Filipendula vulgaris*, a perennial herb with fernlike foliage and white flowers; see FILIPENDULA.

DROSERA (DRAH ser ah). A genus of small insectivorous herbs, commonly known as sundew. They bear white, red, or pink flowers in clusters on slender stems above rosettes of leaves that are covered with glistening sticky hairs.

Insects become entangled in these hairs, and leaves gradually bend inward toward the center, effectively trapping the victim. Their sticky excretion then turns to an acid substance, which acts on the insect and permits it to be digested, much as gastric juices act on human food. See also INSECTIVOROUS PLANTS.

Sometimes grown in the greenhouse, sundews should be planted in pots with mucky soil covered with sphagnum moss, and the pots set in saucers of water to assure a constant supply of moisture at the roots. They must have full sunshine and are easily propagated by seed, cuttings of the rootstock, or division.

D. filiformis has threadlike leaves covered with glistening purple hairs and white to purple flowers on stems 2 ft. tall.

D. rotundifolia, a common species found throughout Europe, Asia, and North America, has round, glistening, hairy leaves to 1½ in. and white to red flowers on stems up to 10 in. long.

DROUGHT GARDENING. With careful planning and attention to growing conditions, healthy plants can be grown when the water needs of a garden are not met, even for an extended period of time, by the available rainfall. Furthermore, efficient and conservative watering practices enable the gardener to make best use of limited water while significantly improving yields.

The availability of water should be a consideration when planning the size and location of the garden. In times of drought, a small, intensively grown garden will yield the most, yet require the least water. Although the garden should receive at least six hours of direct sunlight a day, a location that receives some afternoon shade allows for better moisture retention by the soil. Nearby buildings will provide shade and protection from wind that robs plants of moisture by speeding up evaporation losses. Trees or shrubs also provide shade and wind protection but will compete with garden plants for scarce water supplies, and so are best kept at a distance. A northern or eastern slope is preferable to a south- or west-facing slope, but a level area is best because water and nutrient loss from runoff is dramatically reduced. If water is severely restricted, consider growing plants in containers.

When deciding what types of vegetables to grow, it may be wise to evaluate them by the amount of water they require over a season for healthy growth. Vegetables such as beets, carrots, lettuce and other greens, onions, turnips, and various types of cabbage are considered to be water efficient because they produce the greatest amount of food with the least amount of water. In sharp contrast are the inefficient water consumers, such as corn, which requires 54 gal. water per plant to produce just two ears of corn. Some plants, such as lettuce, cauliflower, onions, and corn are quite sensitive to prolonged periods without water, while other plants, such as sweet-potatoes, watermelons, and pumpkins are less sensitive to drought. Agricultural extension services can give advice regarding the drought-resistant varieties best suited to local areas.

Special attention should be given to soil quality and composition. Soil that is rich in nutrients, and organic matter, that is well aerated and moisture retentive, will be more productive in a dry season. The ideal soil is a sandy loam with added organic matter, such as compost, to improve the soil's ability to retain water, while making it more friable and fertile. Plants in a healthy soil will grow vigorously, developing strong root systems to seek out water.

Plan on grouping together plants with similar moisture requirements to make watering easier.

Wide-row planting offers many advantages to the dry-weather gardener. More plants can be grown in less space. Dense bands of plants form a living mulch that reduces water loss by evaporation and keeps plant roots cool. Watering is simpler with the use of soaker hoses placed directly on the seed beds, or with irrigation furrows dug between the rows.

Ideally, the garden should receive about an inch of water each week. If supplemental watering is required, apply it slowly, uniformly, and to a depth of 5–6 in. Apply water when the air is still, preferably in the morning. One of the easiest and most efficient methods of applying water to plants is with a commercial or homemade drip irrigation system. Irrigation trenches and basins are also effective ways to water plants. Due to the excessive waste of water by evaporation, the use of sprinklers is not recommended. Application of a mulch can reduce evaporation of water from the soil by as much as 70%. A layer of mulch also helps to moderate soil temperature, prevents crust formation on clay soils, prevents the growth of weeds, and can add to the organic content of the soil. Mulch should be spread when the soil is warm and wet.

See also XERISCAPE; IRRIGATION.

DROUGHT-TOLERANT PLANTS. Certain herbs and shrubs are especially suited to growing in dry conditions; see XERISCAPE.

DRUPE. The term for a fruit developed from one carpel or ovary cell in which the outer part is soft and fleshy, and the inner part is a single hard seed or stone, the shell enclosing a kernel. Typical drupes are cherry, almond, and peach. Blackberries and raspberries are composed of many small drupes or druplets joined together.

DRYAS (DRĪ ahs). A genus of dwarf evergreen plants belonging to the Rosaceae (Rose Family), commonly known as mountain avens. Native to far northern or mountain regions of North America, Europe, and Asia, they are well suited to the rock garden. They form a low ground cover with a somewhat shrubby base and white or yellowish solitary flowers followed by decorative, feathery seed heads. They are difficult in the South, and need a sunny site with sharp drainage. Propagation is by seed or cuttings.

PRINCIPAL SPECIES

D. drummondii has nodding yellow flowers that often do not open well.

D. octopetala, the best-known species, has dark green, wrinkled leaves, whitish beneath, and white, eight-petaled flowers that stand erect.

Dryas octopetala

D. x *suendermannii*, a hybrid of *D. drummondii* and *D. octopetala*, has nodding flowers, yellow in bud but white when open.

DRYING-OFF. The practice of reducing the moisture in pots or other plant containers in order to ripen bulbs or give plants a rest between periods of forcing. It is usually done gradually; often the containers are laid on their sides or tilted under greenhouse benches or in the shade outdoors.

DRYNARIA (drī NAR ee ah). A genus of epiphytic tropical ferns that are very ornamental and can be grown on garden trees in suitable climates. In colder climates, they are good for pot culture. They have short, broad, sterile, humus-collecting "nest" fronds that brown early, and long pinnate or pinnatifid fertile fronds.

D. quercifolia (oak-leaf fern) is a widespread and common plant growing 1–4 ft. and typical of the genus. It has broad, furry rhizomes and dark green fronds, of which the sterile is shaped like an oak leaf. It is a fine, spreading garden subject for the tropics and handsome in the house or greenhouse. It requires a coarse epiphytic pot-ting mix. *D. fortunei* is similar but considerably smaller. Both are found in southeastern Asia.

DRYOPTERIS (drī AHP tur is). A large genus of ferns distributed in nearly all wooded parts of the world, including many species of temperate regions, of robust habit and excellent for garden culture. The sterile fronds of most species are evergreen and grow 1–4 ft. tall, with short underground rhizomes and terminal crown. The indusia occur in various places on the fronds, but all are shield- or kidney-shaped. Plants prefer well-drained woodland leaf mold with some sand, in considerable shade, with plenty of water during the growing season. They hybridize readily, producing many sterile hybrids and great taxonomic confusion. There are some fertile hybrids.

PRINCIPAL SPECIES

D. aemula (hay-scented buckler fern) is an attractive fern growing 1–2 ft. with purple-brown stipes and pale green, triangular fronds that smell pleasantly of hay when stroked. It is easy to cultivate in rich, rocky woodland soil with plenty of water during dry spells. It is found in the temperate regions of Europe.

D. affinis (scaly male fern), also listed as *D. borreri* or *D. pseudomas*, is a large fern, growing 2–5 ft. It is often confused with *D. filix-mas*, but it is semievergreen, and new growth is a golden green with coppery stipes. Native throughout Europe and the temperate and subtropical areas of southwestern Asia, it thrives in cool climates in a moist, well-drained soil. Several very decorative varieties are cultivated, including 'Congesta Cristata', 'The King', 'Polydactyla', and 'Ramosissima'.

D. x *boottii* (Boott's shield fern) is a sterile hybrid of *D. cristata* and *D. intermedia*, found in northeastern North America.

D. x *campyloptera* is a fertile hybrid between *D. expansa* and *D. intermedia*. It is a large (2–3 ft.) fern frequently seen in the moist deciduous woods of the Appalachian Mountains and New England.

D. carthusiana (narrow buckler fern) is a common, graceful species whose light green fronds can be weeds in nurseries, greenhouses, and gardens. Native throughout North America and Europe, it is very hardy and deciduous in cold areas.

D. x *clintoniana* (Clinton's shield fern) is a fertile hybrid between *D. goldiana* and *D. cristata*. It is a large (2–4 ft.) evergreen hardy fern growing in moist woods and swamps of eastern North America.

D. cristata (crested shield fern) is not crested in the usual sense, but its pinnae are joined to the rachis in a horizontal plane, like the slats of a shutter. It grows 2–4 ft. high and is found in wet areas of temperate regions throughout the world. It is easily cultivated in a moist, shaded location.

D. cycadina (shaggy shield fern) is an outstanding small fern growing 8–16 in., with masses of black scales covering the entire stipe. It can be grown in shade or partial sun in moist, well-drained soil. It ranges from temperate and subtropical India to China and Japan.

D. dilatata (broad buckler fern) is a large, robust fern growing 1–5 ft. high, with very broad fronds. It is easy to grow in partial shade and rich, leafy soil. It is found in Greenland and in temperate and subtropical areas of Asia, South Africa, North America, Europe, and Japan.

D. erythrosora (autumn or roseate wood fern) is a beautiful small fern growing 12–18 in. Its outstanding rosy new fronds may be bright red in colder areas. At maturity the fronds become a glossy dark green with a leathery texture. In summer, bright red sori are produced. This fern will thrive in both shade and partial sun as long as drainage is good and there is plenty of moisture. It is from the temperate and subtropical areas of China, Japan, and Korea. In 1976, the very interesting var. *prolifica* was introduced. It is substantially different from the species, the pinnae being quite narrow, producing a lacy effect. As a houseplant, and in humid garden conditions, it forms bulbils on the upper surface of the fronds, from which new plants are produced. It is hardy to Zone 7.

D. filix-mas (male fern) is a large fern growing 2–5 ft. The species is pinnate to bipinnate and can be deciduous or evergreen. Evergreen forms should have old fronds removed in late winter to allow the innumerable new croziers to emerge in the spring. It is easy to cultivate in a semishaded location in humus-rich, acid to neutral soil. It is quite variable in the wild, having many varieties, some extremely ornamental; some of the more attractive cultivars include 'Barnesii', 'Crispa', 'Cristata Martindale', 'Linearis Cristata', and 'Linearis Polydactyla'. Although rare in North America, found primarily in eastern Canada, it is distributed throughout the mountains of India, Greenland, and Europe, being one of the most common ferns in Britain. In medieval times it was believed to be the male counterpart of *Athyrium filix-femina* (lady fern), but ferns have no sexes in this sense, and these two belong to different genera.

D. fragrans (fragrant wood fern) is a small fern that grows 2–12 in. and has overlapping pinnae. The undersides of the fronds are covered with scales and glandular hairs. The hairs, when brushed, produce a floral odor that give this fern its common name. It is found in the subarctic regions of Asia, Europe, and North America.

D. goldiana (giant or Goldie's wood fern) is a strong-growing, large, deciduous fern that grows 3–4 ft. and is found in cool, moist woodlands. It is very hardy and native throughout the northeast and north-central United States.

D. intermedia (evergreen wood fern) is very similar to *D. carthusiana* but has blue-green fronds. It is very hardy, easily grown, and abundant in eastern North America.

D. lepidopoda is an attractive fern whose croziers are covered with black scales. The new fronds are copper-colored; growing 1–2 ft., they turn dark green at maturity. It is found in mountainous areas of China and northern India.

D. ludoviciana (southern shield fern) has 2–4 ft. fronds forming an erect clump of leathery dark green. It grows in wet woods on limestone outcroppings and at the edges of swamps in the southeastern states. The fertile pinnae, occurring only at the tips of the fronds, are much narrower than the sterile ones. The pinnae are not turned horizontally as they are on *D. cristata*, which is thought to be a hybrid offspring of this species.

D. marginalis (marginal shield fern) produces leathery, dark green fronds 1–2 ft. long that form clumps on rocky woodland slopes throughout northeastern North America. The location of the sori near the margins of the fronds gives the plant its common name.

D. submontana is a small bipinnate fern that grows 6–8 in. and has broad, blue-green, leathery fronds. Native to mountainous limestone areas in the temperate regions of Europe and North Africa, it is easily cultivated.

D. tokyoensis is a small fern that grows 1–2 ft., forming a rosette of dark green fronds. Native to Japan and Korea, it can be cultivated in rich, acid soil in a shady location.

D. uniformis is a 1–2 ft. fern with broad short fronds. A good garden candidate, requiring acid loamy soil, it is native to China, Korea, and Japan.

D. varia (Japanese holly fern) is a medium-sized, ornamental fern that grows 1–2 ft. and has leathery, triangular, dark green fronds. The stipe is covered with dark scales. It needs shade and an acid humusy soil.

D. wallichiana, attaining 2–4 ft., is truly beautiful when well grown. Spring brings a profuse number of uncoiling croziers, which are light green and have numerous reddish black scales. The mature fronds are bright green with prominent veins on the pinnules. Though slow to mature, it is worth the wait. A shady situation suits it best. It is native to high mountains, growing under shrubs and trees in subtropical and temperate regions of Africa, China, India, Japan, and South and Central America.

DUCKWEED. Common name for *Lemna minor*, a tiny aquatic plant that forms attractive colonies on the water surface; see LEMNA.

DUDLEYA (DUD lee ah). A genus of crassulaceous (succulent) plants with over 40 species (similar to *Echeveria*) from western United States and northwestern Mexico, particularly near the Pacific Ocean. Many are covered with a powdery white bloom. *Stylophyllum* and *Hasseanthus* are generally considered to be subgenera of *Dudleya*. The *Dudleyas* are characterized by the broad and persistent attachments of the leaf bases. Plants have either cylindrical or flat, oval or oblong leaves in rosettes. Excellent for the arid rock garden or drought-tolerant garden in warm regions; hardy to Zone 9.

PRINCIPAL SPECIES

D. brittonii, from northern Baja California, is one of the largest and most attractive species, with rosettes up to about a foot and a half in diameter and white as if covered with chalk.

D. cymosa has grayish green or purplish green, flat rosettes and bright yellow to scarlet flowers on 10-in. stalks.

D. edulis has clusters of 6 in. long, fingerlike, pale green leaves and showy white clusters of fragrant, starlike flowers appearing in June.

D. farinosa (coast dudleya) has flat-leaved rosettes in bright green or chalky grey about 6 in. across and creamy yellow, partially closed flowers on 18-in. stalks.

D. pulverulenta (chalk dudleya) has huge, whitish gray rosettes, up to 18 in. across, with 2 ft. tall stalks of scarlet flowers.

D. virens and *D. viscida* have greener leaves and fragrant pink flowers opening flat.

DUMB CANE. Common name for DIEFFENBACHIA, a genus of ornamental greenhouse shrubs with toxic sap.

DUNE GRASS. Common name for *Elymus arenarius*, a grass useful in sandy soils; see ELYMUS.

DURANTA (dur ANT ah). A genus of tropical American woody shrubs or small trees belonging to the Verbenaceae (Verbena Family). One or two species are commonly grown in Zones 10–11 and occasionally in greenhouses. Most species have lilac or purple flowers, but white-flowered forms are also known. They are propagated by seed or cuttings.

D. repens (golden-dewdrop, pigeonberry, skyflower) sometimes has spiny branches. Flowers are lilac colored in loose panicled racemes and followed by yellow berries.

D. stenostachya has spineless branches; lilac-colored flowers are borne in slender racemes, and the fruit is yellow.

DUSTING. Dusting is the application of insecticides or pesticides in dry form with a stream of air as the propellant (as opposed to SPRAYING) to prevent or control harmful organisms on plants. The ancients scattered lime and other materials on plants to protect them against disease, and the use of dry sulfur in the control of powdery mildew on grapes was common in the United States as early as 1848.

Most of the control products commonly recommended for gardeners, alone and in combination, can be bought in either spray or dust form. This leaves the gardener the choice of spraying, dusting, or both. The advantages and disadvantages of each method may help in making a choice.

ADVANTAGES OF SPRAYING

1. Garden supply stores generally stock a greater variety of spray materials than dusts.

2. Sprays leave a less conspicuous residue on the foliage.

3. Plant diseases are more easily controlled by spraying because sprays adhere longer, making fewer applications necessary.

4. Weather conditions do not limit spraying as much as dusting, which is less effective in windy weather or on dry foliage.

5. Sprays can be directed higher and more accurately and do not drift as much as dusts, hence they can be used on trees more effectively.

6. Dust clouds tend to drift and settle in places other than those to which they are being applied, so there is a greater possibility of irritation and harm to people, animals, or plants from poisonous dusts than from poisonous sprays. Because of this, weed killers should not be applied as dusts or fine mists, and respirators should be worn when using all dangerous materials.

7. For effective coverage of a given area, spraying is more economical than dusting.

ADVANTAGES OF DUSTING

1. Dusts are much lighter than sprays (1 lb. dust equals about 5 gal. spray in coverage). This makes application much easier.

2. With dusts there is no messy measuring or mixing. You simply put them in the duster and proceed.

3. Dusts can be left in the duster ready to use again with little likelihood of damage to the duster, whereas sprays, being corrosive, must be carefully cleaned out of the equipment after each use.

4. Dusting equipment is usually simpler to operate.

5. One can do a thorough job of dusting much more quickly than spraying.

6. Dusts penetrate dense foliage and reach the undersides of foliage more readily than sprays.

7. Dusts are less likely to injure foliage than sprays.

8. There is less danger of poisonous residues remaining on fruit or vegetables from dusts because dust washes off more readily.

9. Though dusts cost more, there is a saving of time and labor in application.

DUSTING RECOMMENDATIONS

Applications of poisonous dusts can be dangerous for the worker. Never inhale dusts. A mask or respirator, goggles, and protective clothing are advisable. The instructions on pesticide containers should always be read before applying poisonous material, even if just to refresh the user's memory. The instructions should always be followed. This means preparation and cleanup may take as long or longer than the application of the pesticide to the plants. Protective measures may seem unnecessary or even extreme, but an accidental lungful of poisonous pesticide cannot be undone.

Bordeaux mixture or a copper-lime dust on a plant covered with dew will be helpful against many fungi. Protection from aphids is possible by using a poisonous nicotine dust, where permitted by law. Some dusts can be dispensed from their containers. Others need various kinds of equipment.

WHEN TO DUST

Plants are best dusted when they are damp or wet and the weather is calm. That usually means waiting until evening or early morning for best results. Always dust lightly but thoroughly, coating the entire plant (and especially the undersides of leaves) with a thin layer of dust. Repeat weekly or as often as necessary to keep the growth covered. A heavy application of dust is not only unsightly but can also be injurious. As honey bees and other beneficial insects, animals, or birds may be affected by chemical dusts, treatment should always be timed to avoid their active times. Contact your local extension service for advice on the best timing for your area.

APPLICATION EQUIPMENT

Equipment for applying dusts ranges from the primitive and wasteful can with small holes punched in the cover, through hand and power dusters, to airplane and helicopter devices for dusting forests and large acreages of crops. Small plastic squeeze-bottle dusters are the easiest devices to use when only a few plants are concerned. They tend to pour when held pointing downward and should not be held at rest in that position.

For larger areas, various hand dusters of the plunger, dustgun, or bellows type are available. The most effective have easier action than others, produce a better and more uniform dust cloud,

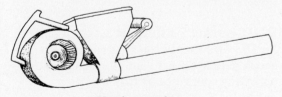

Hand rotary duster

do not pour dust when held downward, and are equipped with an extension tube with a fishtail dust nozzle for directing dust to the lower parts of plants and the undersides of low-growing leaves.

One of the best types of the small hand dusters is the rotary duster. Some have an extension rod allowing the spray to be directed upwards.

These are lightweight and easily held in one hand. The air blast produces a continuous, even dust cloud that will reach plants up to 10 ft. tall with a minimum of effort. A considerable number of plants and shrubs can be dusted in a short time with this type of duster. A battery-driven model is also available.

The larger knapsack dusters, suitable for gardens up to several acres are of two types—the rotary fan type operated by a crank and the bellows type operated by a lever. They are supported by shoulder straps and fit comfortably at first, but operation for any extended length of time is wearing on the operator. The rotary fan type is most suitable for row crops, while the bellows type is best suited for individual plants, small trees, and shrubs. Also available are motorized knapsack dusters in which the fan is driven by a lightweight engine. They are both easy and convenient to use in gardens where expensive motorized dusters drawn by tractors are impractical.

DUSTY MILLER. A common name for many plants with white woolly foliage, including *Senecio cineraria*, *Artemesia stellerana*, *Centauria cineraria*, *Centauria gymnocarpa*, *Lychnis coronaria*, and *Chrysanthemum ptarmiciflorum*.

DUTCH BULBS. The popular hardy bulbs that are planted in the fall for spring bloom have become known as Dutch bulbs. This is not because these flowers had their origin in Holland, but because the Dutch adopted them and have grown them for centuries to a greater extent and greater degree of perfection than any other country.

Principally the group includes *Tulipa*, hardy *Narcissus*, *Hyacinthus*, *Crocus*, and, to a lesser extent, the bulbous *Iris*, *Scilla*, *Chionodoxa*, *Eranthis*, *Muscari*, and *Galanthus*.

The bulb fields of Holland comprise an area approximately 50 miles long and two miles wide, along the North Sea coast. Situated mainly below sea level, and protected by manmade dikes, they are crisscrossed with canals, which provide a constant source of moisture (water table) at a controlled depth. These conditions permit the highest types of mass horticultural development in the world.

North American gardeners now import more than 500 million bulbs from Holland each year, of which about a third are tulips. Most of these bulbs are planted in gardens to bloom for a period extending from a few seasons to many years, depending on the particular type of bulb and the care it is given.

Dutch bulbs are among the easiest flowers to grow, and demand little in preparation or special materials. While soil preparation and enrichment are always of value in cultivating any plant life, they are, strictly speaking, not necessary in the case of bulbs. All the latter require is average soil and simple cultivation methods.

Bulbs have been constructed by nature so that they carry their own food for the period of germination and preliminary growth. Actually they are whole but dormant plants—roots, stems, leaves, and blossoms—which are telescoped into a budlike structure. The actual bulb consists mostly of plant food. Depending on the particular flower, for normal growth, bulbs are planted 3–6 in. apart.

DUTCH ELM DISEASE. This very serious disease of elms was first observed in 1919 in Holland, whence its name; but its origin is not known. Four infected trees were found in Ohio in 1930, the number later increasing to eleven. It is now believed that the fungus *Ceratocystis ulmi* entered this country in elm logs imported from Europe for making furniture veneer (now excluded by a federal quarantine) and shipped to factories in a number of eastern and central cities.

The fungus is known to be parasitic only on the elm and the related zelkova. The disease can occur in either acute or chronic form. In the former, wilting begins in the younger leaves and advances rapidly down the branches; an entire tree may be near death in as short a period as four weeks. In the chronic form, wilting occurs in one or several branches of the tree following conspic-

uous yellowing of the foliage. This yellow "flag" is one of the chief symptoms looked for in scouting for infected trees. Such a tree may live for three or more years before its inevitable death.

If twigs from a diseased tree are cut across, a brown discoloration is seen in the sapwood. The same discoloration may be present in the case of VERTICILLIUM WILT.

Several elm insects carry the fungus. The most important in North America is a small bark beetle, *Scolytus multistriatus*. Adult beetles emerging from diseased wood during the summer months feed in the crotches of young twigs or in leaf axils, chewing through the bark to the cambium, wounding the tree and inoculating it with the disease fungus. Later they go again to dead or dying parts of weak trees and lay their eggs in vertical galleries; the larvae eat their way sideways from the main gallery and pupate, and later the beetles chew their way out, leaving exit holes.

Dutch elm disease has been held in check with a program combining sanitation, spraying, and chemotherapy. In sanitation, pruning and removal of all unhealthy wood or trees is attempted. In spraying, trees are protected against the elm bark beetle by applications of insecticides that are formulated to be effective in this particular use. In chemotherapy, benomyl or other fungicides are injected into the vascular system of the tree; this is costly and is usually reserved for particularly valued trees.

DUTCHMAN'S-BREECHES. Common name for *Dicentra cucullaria*, a perennial herb whose small, yellow-tipped white flowers have widely spreading spurs; see DICENTRA.

DUTCHMAN'S-PIPE. Common name for *Aristolochia durior*, a hardy woody vine with large leaves and small pipe-shaped flowers; see ARISTOLOCHIA.

DWARF FRUIT TREES. Dwarf fruit trees grow less vigorously than standard trees, are smaller at maturity, begin to produce blossoms and fruits at an earlier age following planting, yet they bear fruits as large and tasty as those on standard-sized trees. The tree is composed of two grafted parts, the root or rootstock and the scion or top variety. It is the rootstock that determines the growth characteristics of the top: whether a tree will be dwarfed and how much, and also whether it can be successfully trellis trained if this is desired. Therefore, in buying dwarf trees, it is important to know if the rootstock is very dwarfing or semidwarfing; it is especially important to choose the correct rootstock when selecting apple, pear, and sweet cherry trees because of the great differences in vigor, size, blossom, and fruiting time between the dwarf and standard varieties. Several commercial nurseries grow dwarf trees, and they are normally available through retail distributors or mail order. Local nurseries or extension services can give advice regarding varieties best suited and available in your area.

PLANTING

To be assured of adequate pollination of blossom, plant two or more varieties of each kind of fruit. The usual planting distance is 12′ x 12′, or if trees are planted in a single row, they can be spaced as close as 8 ft. apart. If the area is open enough for sunshine, there is room for six or eight dwarf trees in the spread of a single well-grown standard apple or sweet cherry tree. In cold climates, peach, nectarine, and apricot trees should be placed in locations most sheltered from direct winter winds. Plant trees only where ample sunlight will be available to them; fruit trees will not do well in the shade. Espalier or trellis-training on walls of buildings, on fences, and arbors, is a special variation of growing dwarf trees and requires concentrated and drastic pruning and tying of branches; when grown in this manner, dwarf fruit trees provide ornamental appeal in the landscape.

Trees should be planted as early as possible, as soon as the frost is out of the ground and the soil is workable and not overly soggy. If trees are planted too late, the tops will leaf out before the roots become established; this can prevent normal growth and delay fruiting for a year or two.

Roots should not be allowed to dry out prior to planting. Bare-rooted trees require a hole 12–15 in. deep and 18 in. across, large enough to accommodate the roots spread out in a natural position. Trees in burlap or containers need only to be placed at the right depth with as little disturbance as possible of the soil around the roots. Remove the containers carefully. Good topsoil should be packed around the roots leaving no air pockets. The graft union, the bulged and somewhat roughened area a few inches above the topmost roots, must be a few inches above the soil level. If the union is below the soil level, the scion may take root and negate the dwarfing effect of the rootstock.

After planting, leveling, and packing, soak the soil around the roots. Additional watering at two-week intervals will help the root system become established. Fertilizer is not needed at planting, nor during the first growing season, unless the soil is extremely poor. However, beginning the second year, apply ¼ lb. of a 10–10–10 fertilizer per tree; increase to ½–¾ lb. per tree after five years of growth. Well-rotted manure and compost material are excellent natural fertilizers, which also supply organic matter to the soil. Lawn grass clippings scattered under trees can also be helpful.

PRUNING

Pruning cannot be standardized; each tree is a special case requiring individual attention and good judgment. Although dwarf trees are not pruned as heavily as standard or full-sized trees, they are pruned at planting to ensure proper development, and later on to remove weakened wood, water sprouts, and suckers and to foster vigor and fruitfulness. Unnecessary cutting should be avoided.

All cuts should be made with sharp tools, clean and close to the trunk or the particular lateral branch involved. At planting, a one-year-old apple tree is usually cut back to 3 ft. high after planting, and most lateral branches are removed. A two-year-old tree 5–6 ft. high is headed back to 3½–4 ft. from the ground, and all but two or three well-placed lateral branches are cut back.

Early in the second spring, prior to the start of growth, select three or four branches with wide-angled crotches, placed from 20 in. above the ground and 8–10 in. apart on the trunk. These branches should point in opposite directions to

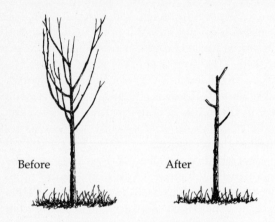

Pruning a one-year-old dwarf apple tree

provide good tree conformity. Remove other branches. All subsequent pruning should consist of thinning out weak wood, water sprouts in the centers of the trees, suckers from the crown or roots, and cutting back scaffold limbs to lateral branches. Prune out broken branches and those interfering with the more desirable branches. Peaches usually are pruned more severely then apples. Sweet cherries need only light thinning and corrective pruning. Plum and apricot trees need very little pruning while young and moderate thinning out and heading back as they grow older. Thinning of fruit is also important in the quality and regular quantity of harvests. See also PRUNING and articles regarding individual plants.

DWARF PLANTS. Dwarf plants are of interest and value for garden planting, especially in restricted areas. Dwarf forms of species can occur naturally or can be developed through plant breeding. Certain plants are also dwarfed by mechanical manipulation, such as grafting on stocks of a dwarfing nature, by stem and root pruning, or by otherwise interfering with the normal process of growth.

In the case of annuals, or plants grown as such (whether flowers or vegetables), it is a real triumph for the plant breeder to get a dwarf strain that will reproduce true from seed. In recent years gardens have been enriched as the result of much painstaking work along these lines.

In the case of dwarf forms of perennials, either herbaceous or woody, that may not reproduce true from seed (or in some cases not set seed at all), propagation is done by cuttings or other vegetative method. Dwarfing by manipulation (called bonsai) has been carried out to the greatest perfection by Chinese and Japanese gardeners in their handling of false cypress, junipers, pines, and other evergreen and deciduous shrubs and trees. By a carefully studied system of pruning and training, watering and feeding, they have been able to keep specimens of these naturally large-growing plants dwarfed and in small containers to a ripe old age. See also BONSAI; DWARF FRUIT TREES.

DYCKIA (DĪK ee ah). A genus of tropical perennial herbs belonging to the Bromeliaceae (Pineapple Family). They have stiff, rather succulent leaves edged with sharp spines. Native principally to Brazil but also found in other southern South American countries, they live in open, semidry areas mostly in rocky territory. Flowers, generally yellow or orange, are borne on tall spikes produced from a compact rosette. They are excellent subjects for tropical rock gardens or as houseplants, with treatment similar to cacti and other succulents, except that dyckias prefer a more acid soil than cacti. Propagation is by offshoots or seed.

D. brevifolia is excellent for succulent collections, forming a compact rosette that divides and subdivides, eventually becoming large masses. Green leaves are heavily spined, and yellow flowers are borne on tall spikes.

D. fosterana is striking and showy, forming a compact ball-rosette of many silvery, deeply serrated leaves 3–5 in. long and bearing orange flowers on 12-in. spikes. It is excellent as a houseplant or in a tropical rock garden.

E

EARDROPS. A common name sometimes applied to FUCHSIA, also called lady's-eardrops, because of the shape of the flowers. Golden-eardrops is a common name for *Dicentra chrysantha*, a tall perennial related to bleeding-heart; see DICENTRA.

EARTHING-UP. Hilling or heaping soil around the roots of plants. The purpose may be to increase root hold, as with corn; to cover the tubers of potatoes to prevent sun scorch and to provide drainage between the rows in heavy soil; to blanch the stalks of celery; or to protect half-hardy plants in winter.

EARTHWORM. The valuable *Annelida*, also called land worms and fishing worms, help in the garden and the compost heap. They are segmented worms that live in moist soil containing decaying organic matter, which they eat along with the soil itself. They crawl out at night to feed or to escape flooded burrows when there is heavy rain. When they burrow through the soil, they suck up both minerals and organic matter, including larvae, eggs, and seeds as well as plant debris. The food is ground up in the pharynx, neutralized by calcium carbonate secreted by glands, and then pulverized in the gizzard by the small stones and mineral particles ingested from the soil. When the food reaches the intestines, it is digested, and the indigestible parts are excreted as "castings," a very valuable addition to the soil or compost. It has been estimated that in an acre of land, the worms may bring 35,000 pounds of soil to the surface. From opening and enriching the soil, the worms provide conditioning of great value. Earthworms, therefore, should not be killed or poisoned, even though they may cause certain disfigurations on lawns and golf courses. Gardeners wishing to buy worms to help in making compost should order "red worms."

EARWIG. Chewing insects of the order Dermaptera (meaning "skin wing") resembling beetles in their hard wing covers but distinguished from them by pincerlike appendages at the tail end. The hind wings are folded both lengthwise and crosswise. Earwigs are troublesome plant pests in the South and on the Pacific Coast, feeding on the petals of flowers and on fruits and vegetables. In other regions they are rarely of pest proportions. The females lay eggs in the soil and then watch over them until hatched and during the first few nymph instars. One generation is produced per year in temperate climates. Earwigs can be trapped in lengths of bamboo or used rolls of paper towels or a flowerpot or other container stuffed with paper poised on a stick; they crawl into such traps at dawn and then can be emptied into a water-kerosene mixture or into a frog or fish pond to be eaten. The name refers to an old belief that earwigs would crawl into the human ear for protection.

Earwig

EASTER LILY. Common name for *Lilium longiflorum*, a white-flowering bulb, and similar species forced for Easter bloom; see LILIUM.

EBONY. A name applied to the wood of a number of trees, and hence to the trees themselves, especially Asiatic species of DIOSPYROS.

Green-ebony is *Jacaranda mimosifolia*, native to South America and sometimes grown in northern greenhouses; see JACARANDA.

Mountain-ebony is *Bauhinia variegata*, native to India and China, now widely planted in Florida; see BAUHINIA.

ECCREMOCARPUS (ek rem oh KAHR pus) **scaber.** A climbing vine native to Chile, belonging to the Bignoniaceae (Bignonia Family) and commonly known as gloryflower. Hardy only to Zone 10, it can be grown as an annual in the North. It flowers well if sown early and grown in light, rich soil in a warm location. It climbs by means of tendrils at the ends of bipinnate leaves. The tubular, orange-red flowers are about an inch long and are borne in loose racemes.

ECHEVERIA (ek ee VEER ee ah). A genus of succulents of the Crassulaceae (Orpine Family), having leaves in rosettes and small flowers, usually in spikes. Among the most popular and attractive of succulents, its leaves are colored in various soft pastel shades, some with white, pruinose pow-

Echeveria pulvinata

der, some with short, fuzzy felt, and some with eyelashlike hairs along the margins.

   E. elegans is an old favorite, with glaucous, bluish leaves and pink and yellow flowers. Also popular is *E. pulvinata*, with fuzzy green leaves blushed red. Choice novelties are *E. laui*, with white, rounded, pruinose leaves, and *E. shaviana*, with thin, delicate, pinkish to bluish leaves with wavy margins. The large, cabbage-headed *E. gibbiflora* and some of its many hybrids can be quite spectacular.

   Most are of easy culture, given a bright location for best color, a well-drained, porous planter mix, and generous but well-spaced waterings. Propagation is by offset, seed, and even leaves, which often produce plantlets at their base when placed on damp and shaded soil.

ECHINACEA (ek ee NAY see ah). A genus of perennials native to North America, belonging to the Asteraceae (Aster Family); closely related to

Rudbeckia, including several known as coneflower. They are bushy plants with showy, daisylike flower heads often 6 in. across, with raised bronzy centers. A fine source of cut flowers, they are also useful for bold landscape effects, giving two months or more of bloom. They like rich, sandy loam and thrive in dry or exposed spots. Spring-sown seed will give bloom the following year. Clumps can be divided, but this should not be done too often. The genus takes its botanical name from a Greek word for hedgehog, suggested by its bristly seed heads.

Echinacea purpurea

PRINCIPAL SPECIES

   E. angustifolia grows to 2 ft., with lance-shaped leaves and heads of light purple with dark disk flowers often 1 in. high.

   E. pallida, growing to 3 ft., has rose-purple or white flowers with long, drooping rays.

   E. purpurea (purple coneflower) grows to 5 ft., bearing broad, oval leaves and purplish rose to white flowers with drooping rays. Cv. 'Bright Star' has reddish purple flowers; 'Magnus' has large, nondrooping, rose-colored flowers; 'White Lustre' has white flowers with a bronze cone; and 'White Swan' has white flowers with a dark cone.

ECHINOCACTUS (ek in oh KAK tus). A genus that at one time included most ribbed, globular cacti; redefined by Britton and Rose in *The Cactaceae* to include only a few species from North America. These are the barrel cactus types with woolly fruits and flowers. *E. grusonii* (golden-

Echinocactus

barrel) is deservedly one of the most popular cacti. *E. parryi* and *E. platyacanthus* are from Mexico. *E. polycephalus* and *E. horizonthalonius* both occur in the southwestern states. Some more conservative botanists also include *Astrophytum* and *Homalocephala* (Texas horse-crippler cactus) in this genus.

ECHINOCEREUS (ek in oh SEER ee us). A most popular genus of rather small, mostly clustering cacti with large, showy flowers and impressive and attractive spination. Some species have edible fruits. Often called hedgehog cactus, it is from Mexico and the southwestern United States. Of the species occurring natively in the Southwest are *E. engelmannii* (strawberry cactus), with large, reddish purple flowers and long, variously colored spines; and *E. triglochidiatus* (claret-cup cactus), with outstanding orange-red flowers. Other choice species are *E. albatus*, with snowy white spines and magenta flowers; and *E. knippelianus*, almost spineless, with long, hairlike spines and whitish to pink flowers.

ECHINOCYSTIS (ee kī noh SIS tis). A genus of annual and perennial vines native to North and South America, belonging to the Cucurbitaceae (Cucumber Family); commonly known as mock or wild cucumber and wild balsam-apple.

E. lobata is a fast-growing annual, widely distributed in the eastern states, and is useful as a temporary screen or to drape fences and arbors. It has deeply lobed leaves, clusters of small white or greenish flowers, and egg-shaped, prickly fruit. Plants are easily grown from seed.

ECHINOPS (EK in ahps). A genus of thistle-like perennial and biennial herbs belonging to the Asteraceae (Aster Family) and commonly known as globe-thistle. They have flowers in round heads; scales surrounding the flowers are often metallic blue in color. Because of their bold, prickly, white woolly foliage as well as their flowers, they are most decorative as background plants in the border or when planted among shrubbery. Propagation is easily done from seed,

division, or root cuttings. Most are hardy to Zone 3.

PRINCIPAL SPECIES

E. exaltatus (Russian globe-thistle) is the largest of the species, often growing to the size of a lilac bush (10 ft. or more).

E. humilis, native to Siberia, grows to 4 ft., with silvery, cobwebby foliage and large blue flower heads.

E. ritro (small globe-thistle) grows to 2 ft., with finely cut, white downy leaves and steel-blue flowers that bloom all summer.

E. sphaerocephalus (great globe-thistle) grows to 8 ft., with white or bluish flower heads to 2 in., somewhat cobwebby stems, and rough, hairy leaves.

Echinops sp.

ECHINOPSIS (ek in AHP sis). A genus of mostly globular, clustering, spiny cacti; included among the barrel cactus group, native to South America. This genus is characterized by large, white flowers that look a bit like Easter lilies and have given the genus the nickname Easter-lily cactus. Plants of this genus are very desirable in cultivation and are well suited for use in dish gardens. Exceedingly attractive hybrids have been produced with other cactus genera that have more colorful flowers. See also PARAMOUNT HYBRIDS. For culture see CACTUS.

E. eyriesii is a desirable species whose white flowers have a delicate fragrance.

E. multiplex (barrel or Easter-lily cactus) is the most common species. Its blossom is a beautiful pink, rising from a little round cushion into a long, slender tube. The plant multiplies rapidly and can be propagated by division.

Some authorities include *Trichocereus*, a genus of columnar South American cacti, some of which (*T. terscheckii*) reach dimensions to rival our saguaro (see CARNEGIEA) but have similar, large, mostly nocturnal white flowers, with hair on the outside of the flower tube (like *Echinopsis*). One of the most common species of *Trichocereus* is *T. spachianus*, a species with short spines and ribbed, basally branching stems to about 3 ft. tall, a species popular for under stock for grafting.

ECHIOIDES (ek ee OY deez) **longiflorum.** A perennial version of *Arnebia decumbens*, formerly listed as *A. echioides* and commonly known as prophet flower. This species does not grow as large (to 1 ft.), and the purple spots on the yellow flowers fade away entirely, leaving the blossoms yellow. Propagation is by seed, division, or cuttings, and the plant is hardy to Zone 4. For comparison, see ARNEBIA.

ECHIUM (EK ee um). A genus of rough-haired or bristly, annual or biennial, sometimes perennial herbs belonging to the Boraginaceae (Borage Family) and commonly known as viper's bugloss. They have purple, rose, or white flowers in coiled racemes or showy spikes. Some of the species from the Canary Islands are often planted in California. All thrive and flower well in poor soil in open, sunny locations. They produce only a profusion of leaves if planted in too rich a soil. Propagation of the annuals and biennials is by seed and of the perennials by seed, layering, or cuttings.

PRINCIPAL SPECIES

E. candicans is a shrub growing to 6 ft., with white-haired foliage and white or blue-and-white flowers in profuse spikes.

E. fastuosum is a shrub growing to 6 ft., with purple or dark blue flowers in dense spikes.

E. giganteum is a shrub growing to 10 ft., with white-haired leaves and white flowers.

E. lycopsis (formerly listed as *E. plantagineum*) has been extensively hybridized, with larger red as well as blue and purple flowers developed.

E. vulgare (blueweed) is a bristly annual or biennial Eurasian weed widely naturalized in the United States. It grows to 2½ ft., with profuse foliage and rose-pink buds followed by blue flowers in panicles. In the eastern states it has escaped and become a troublesome weed in open fields, thriving on dry, gravelly soils, especially on limestone in Zones 4–8.

E. wildpretii, formerly listed as *E. bourgaeanum*, is a branching shrub growing to 10 ft., with white-haired foliage and rose-colored flowers in large, flat-topped clusters.

EDELWEISS. Common name for *Leontopodium alpinum*, a perennial tufted herb with starlike floral leaves; see LEONTOPODIUM.

EDGING. Plants can be arranged attractively to define the edge of a flower bed or border, or of a lawn, path, driveway, or other specific area within any landscape. In a well-kept garden, such a boundary or division line between lawn and path, lawn and border, path and border, etc., is neat and definite without being stiff, harsh, or obtrusive.

Plants used along the margins of beds, borders, or elsewhere to outline definite areas should be of small, compact growth. If annuals, they should have a long season of bloom and be easily kept within bounds. If perennials or of shrubby form, they should be sufficiently dwarf and tolerant of clippings or pruning if necessary.

Edging plants are used in both formal and informal plantings. For the formal bed, a grass strip or close-clipped hedge of low-growing evergreens, such as *Buxus* (box) or a dwarf form of *Berberis* (barberry), is appropriate. For the shrubbery border, *Pachysandra terminalis* (Japanese-spurge), *Taxus cuspidata* (Japanese yew), or *Myrtus* (myrtle) are often used. The more informal herbaceous border is often edged with a combination of low-growing perennials such as *Arabis* (rockcress), *Dianthus* (pink), *Iberis* (candytuft), *Phlox* (especially dwarf phlox), or *Viola* (violet). For the annual border, *Alyssum*, *Lobelia*, *Ageratum*, *Iberis*, *Torenia*, and many other low-growing annuals make a charming edge.

EDRAIANTHUS (ed ray AN thus). A genus of low-growing perennial herbs native to the

Mediterranean region and belonging to the Campanulaceae (Bellflower Family). They are very much like and sometimes classified with WAHLENBERGIA. Plants bear nodding, bell-shaped flowers of blue, violet, or purple, and are useful in the rock garden, where they should be given a light soil rich in new humus and watered freely. Propagation is by seed or division. Most are hardy to Zone 5.

PRINCIPAL SPECIES

E. dalmaticus has broad, toothless leaves and funnel-shaped flowers.

E. graminifolius is grassy and tufted with 3-in., bladelike leaves. Flower clusters bloom in early summer.

E. pumilio is a very low grower, no more than 1 in. high, bearing stalkless violet flowers in late spring.

EELGRASS. Common name for species of VALLISNERIA, a genus of aquatic plants useful in aquariums.

EELWORM. A common name for harmful types of NEMATODES—microscopic, eel-like organisms that normally infest soils and plant or animal tissues. While many kinds are apparently beneficial or harmless, some are destructive plant pests (true plant parasites), causing diseases of various kinds, such as root knots, leaf galls, and bulb injury, in many ornamental and agricultural plants.

These pests are successfully controlled by planting marigolds, especially French or Mexican varieties, whose root exudate will deter them, especially during the next year after planting. There are also beneficial predatory nematodes that are parasitic on soil-inhabiting pests and are available commercially for introduction as a form of biological control.

EGGPLANT. A tropical perennial herb or subshrub, *Solanum melongena* var. *esculentum*, grown as an annual for its large, fleshy, pear-shaped purple or white fruits, which are used as a vegetable.

The snake- or serpent-eggplant, *S. melongena* var. *serpentinum*, has long slender fruits with curved tips. The scarlet- or tomato-eggplant, *S. integrifolium*, is a spiny annual grown for ornament.

Eggplants are tender, slow-growing, and easily checked and stunted by temperatures below 50°F. In northern gardens, they should be started indoors four to six weeks before they can be safely planted outdoors. To lessen the shock of transplanting, when the seedlings have developed their third true leaves, shift to 2½ or 3-in. flowerpots. Shift again to a larger size when necessary, and set in the garden 2–3 ft. apart after the weather has become warm. The soil should be warm, well drained, and light but rich. Thereafter they need clean cultivation, watering in very dry weather, and protection against potato beetles. In warm climates, seed may be sown in an outdoor seedbed, and when the seedlings are 6 in. high, they may be moved directly to the garden.

Eggplant

Well-grown plants in good soil will produce two to five large fruits each, so the number needed may be calculated this way. Fruits may be used when sufficiently large and richly colored in the case of the purple kinds, as long as the seeds are soft. When autumn frost threatens, cut them with several inches of stem, place in ventilated baskets, and store in a cool, moist cellar where they should keep until late December.

Eggplant may be subject to the same bacterial wilt as that affecting tomatoes. Plant disease-resistant varieties whenever possible.

The eggplant flea beetle punctures the leaves and stunts plants in the seedbed. A pyrethrum-rotenone combination spray is often recommended. This also hinders the eggplant lace bug. The Colorado potato beetle is frequently injurious; see INSECT CONTROL.

EHRETIA (e RET ee ah). A genus of deciduous and evergreen trees and shrubs of tropical and subtropical regions, belonging to the Boraginaceae (Borage Family). They are not particular as to soil but, with one or two exceptions, can be grown only in warm climates.

PRINCIPAL SPECIES

E. acuminata, hardy to Zone 5, is a small tree with large, oblong, saw-edged leaves and big panicles of small, white, scented flowers in summer.

E. dicksonii is smaller and more tender than *E. acuminata* and has large, roundish, hairy leaves and fragrant clusters of white flowers.

E. microphylla (Philippine-tea) is a large, tender shrub with small leaves in clusters and flowers borne singly or two to four together.

EICHHORNIA (īk HAWR nee ah) **crassipes.** A showy, tender, perennial, aquatic herb commonly known as water-hyacinth. It grows luxuriantly and is cultivated in ponds and aquariums for its attractive foliage. Though hardy only to Zone 10, in fresh waters of Florida it has attained the status of a major pest, growing so rampantly as to obstruct traffic in some rivers.

In the tank or pond, its submerged hanging roots are a valuable refuge for newly spawned fish. The leaf stems are enlarged to form bladders or floats that sustain the heavy masses of leaves and blooms at the water's surface. In shallow water, the plants root in the soil and flower more freely than when floating unattached. The beautiful flowers, pale blue with markings of darker blue and yellow, are borne in groups of six or eight on a loose spike rising about 1 ft. above the leaves.

ELAEAGNACEAE (el ee ag NAY see ee). The Oleaster Family, a group of trees and shrubs mostly distributed in tropical regions of the Northern Hemisphere, usually covered with silvery or yellow-brown scales. The flowers are without petals, and the fruit is a berrylike structure imbedded in the fleshy calyx. The genera—*Elaeagnus* (oleaster), *Hippophae* (sea-buckthorn), and *Shepherdia* (buffalo berry)—are grown for ornament and somewhat for their fruit.

ELAEAGNUS (el ee AG nus). A genus of ornamental North American, European, and Asiatic shrubs and small trees of the Elaeagnaceae (Oleaster Family). Generally slow growing, they are easy to cultivate, making a good hedge or windbreak shrub. They have fragrant, inconspicuous flowers followed by sometimes edible fruit of various colors, and some species have spiny branches. Some species are hardy in cool regions and deciduous, while others are southern evergreens. A sunny location in well-drained soil is most favorable. Propagation is by seed, grafting, and cuttings of mature or half-ripened wood.

PRINCIPAL SPECIES

E. angustifolia (Russian-olive, oleaster) is a hardy deciduous shrub or tree growing to 30 ft., with small, gray-green leaves, silvery beneath, forming rather dense masses. It is a pleasant tree for the garden border, changing from silver to green in gentle breezes. In late spring the tubular flowers, silver outside and yellow inside, are rather inconspicuous but emit a spicy fragrance of great carrying power. If pruned severely, it will make a dense plant suitable for screens and windbreaks. Hardy in Zones 3–7.

E. commutata (silverberry), formerly listed as *E. argentea*, attains 12 ft. and is found from eastern Canada to Utah. Its axillary, fragrant flowers are followed by short-stemmed silvery fruit. Hardy in Zones 3–5.

E. macrophylla, a southern evergreen growing to 12 ft., is highly ornamental, with large, broad, shining leaves, silvery beneath. These, combined with red fruit that follows the autumn flowers, make a brilliant picture. Hardy in Zones 7–8.

E. multiflora (gumi, cherry elaeagnus) is a useful northern shrub, growing to 6 ft. with fragrant flowers but most noted for its long-stemmed scarlet-spotted edible fruit. Hardy to Zone 5.

E. pungens (thorny elaeagnus) is a tall evergreen shrub with very fragrant, late fall flowers followed by red fruit that has silvery and brown scales. There are several cultivars with variegated leaves. Hardy in Zones 6–9.

E. umbellata (autumn-olive) is a large shrub growing to 15 ft. high by 15 ft. wide, with fragrant white flowers blooming in spring, followed by tart red fruits. Birds spread the seeds everywhere, and it has become a persistent weed in many places. Hardy in Zones 4–8.

ELAEOCARPUS (el ee oh KAHR pus). A genus of southern European, tropical trees and shrubs, grown extensively in the southern states and California. They have showy flowers in racemes and are propagated by cuttings or seed. *E. reticulatus*, treated as a shrub in the greenhouse, has creamy white flowers and blue fruit. *E. dentatus*, a tree growing to 60 ft., has leathery leaves, white flowers in drooping racemes, and purplish gray fruits.

ELAPHOGLOSSUM (el af oh GLAHS um). A very large genus of ferns with simple, dimorphic fronds. Mostly native to the American tropics, they are usually grown in greenhouses and require abundant moisture and good drainage.

E. callifolium is a small to medium-sized glossy green fern that inhabits tree trunks and boulders in the rain forests of Australia, Malaysia, and Indonesia. It can be grown in pots on an epiphytic mix.

E. crinitum (elephant-ear fern) is a striking fern with black scales on the stipes and fronds. The fronds are simple and broadly ovate. Native to South America and the West Indies, it is difficult to cultivate, needing constant high humidity or mist.

ELDER. Common name for SAMBUCUS, a widely distributed genus of mostly large deciduous shrubs, with white flowers followed by red or black berries.

ELECAMPANE. Common name for *Inula helenium*, a perennial herb with large clusters of yellow flowers; see INULA.

ELEPHANT-EAR. Common name for COLOCASIA, a genus of tropical herbs cultivated for their ornamental foliage and some varieties for their edible tubers. Elephant's-ear refers to CALADIUM, a genus of large-leaved herbs often grown in greenhouses for their variegated foliage.

ELEPHANT FERN. Common name for ANGIOPTERIS, a genus of tropical ferns with heavy rhizomes and a striking pattern on the stems and fronds. Elephant-ear fern is *Elaphoglossum crinitum*, a tropical fern with simple, ovate fronds; see ELAPHOGLOSSUM.

ELEPHANT GARLIC. A common name for *Allium scorodoprasum*, a close relative of the onion, also known as sand leek and giant or Spanish garlic. Its appearance, with long, pointed bulbs or "cloves" used for flavoring, is very much like the common garlic, *A. sativum*, but the whole plant is somewhat larger, and the flowers are light purple instead of white. The 3-ft. flower stalk (scape) is leafy from the base to the middle and topped by a small white bulb that bears purple bulbils. Bulbs also form underground at the base of the stem.

Elephant garlic is a hardy perennial but is usually grown as an annual. Like onions, it should be grown in soil that is well prepared by adding compost or manure the preceding fall, then tilling and firming the soil in early spring. It requires plenty of sun and good drainage. Staking may be necessary to support the aerial bulbils when they become heavy.

Propagation. The underground bulbs should be divided and replanted. Aerial bulbils can also be planted. This should be done as early in spring as possible. Fall planting is only recommended when winters are very mild. Plant them 6 in. apart and 2 in. below the soil surface.

Harvesting. Like onions, the bulbs can be lifted

when the tops are quite dry, then left in the sun long enough so that any dirt on the surface is dry. They can be braided by the tops or packed in crates or netted bags.

ELETTARIA (el e TAY ree ah). A small genus of perennial, aromatic herbs of the Zingiberaceae (Ginger Family), native to the East Indies. Plants are occasionally found in greenhouse collections, for they bear varicolored flowers in great profusion.

E. cardamomum (Cardamom) produces aromatic seeds that are well known as a spice and used in medicine. The plants, which are hardy only to Zone 10, should be grown in moist, shady places. They are propagated by root division and by seed, which is contained in ¾ in. long capsules. Plants grow to 10 ft., with large leaves, hairy beneath, and white flowers with a lip of yellow and blue stripes.

ELEUSINE (el yoo SĪ nee). A genus of grasses including many weed and forage and some ornamental plants, native to Europe but extensively naturalized in the United States. The species are all annual, flat-leaved, tufted in character with spikelets borne in five-branched, umbrella-shaped form.

E. coracana (African-millet) grows to 4 ft. and bears broad spikes 1½ in. long.

E. indica (wiregrass) is flower-bearing, prolific, and generally considered a weed. Growing from 1–2 ft., it has spreading spikes to 4 in. long.

ELM. Common name for ULMUS, a genus of tall deciduous trees native to the North Temperate Zone. The Elm Family is ULMACEAE.

ELODEA (el oh DEE ah). A genus of useful aquatic herbs, whose botanical name comes from the Greek word meaning "marshy" and commonly known as waterweed, ditchmoss, or waterthyme. This genus includes some of the most valuable plants for oxygenating aquariums where fish are kept. The tender, perennial, branching stems grow 3 in. to 4 ft. long, depending on the depth of the water. Flowers are inconspicuous, but the small whorled or opposite leaves form an attractive green lacework through the water. Variously hardy to Zone 3, plants propagate freely from cuttings and can be grown rooted or floating. For the aquarium, cultivated stock is preferable to that collected in the wild.

E. canadensis (ditchmoss), sometimes listed as *Anacharis canadensis*, has whitish flowers that float on the surface and is commonly found in slow-moving streams and ponds throughout the summer.

ELSHOLTZIA (el SHOHLT zee ah). A genus including several species of herbs or subshrubs belonging to the Lamiaceae (Mint Family). The most valuable for gardens is *E. stauntonii* (mint shrub), a Chinese hardy deciduous semiwoody shrub growing 4–5 ft. high. It grows best in a sunny position and fairly rich soil. The dense, one-sided spikes of purplish pink flowers open in September and October. The shoots should be pruned back about half their length in the spring. The genus name is likely to be confused with *Eschscholzia* (California poppy), unless carefully noted.

ELYMUS (EL i mus). A genus of tall-growing annual or perennial grasses native to temperate regions of both hemispheres and commonly known as wild-rye or Lyme grass. Some species are planted on banks or at the back of borders in the garden. A species often planted as a binder in sandy soils is *E. arenarius* (sea lyme grass or dune grass), growing to 5 ft., with leaves 1 ft. long, and beardless spikes 10 in. long. Several other species range 3–10 ft. tall and bear spikes from a few to 15 in. long. See BINDING PLANTS.

EMBRYO. A plant (or animal) in the earliest and most rudimentary stage of its development; in the flowering or seed-bearing plants it is the plantlet contained in the seed.

EMILIA (ee MIL ee ah). A genus of low-growing annual and perennial plants belonging to the

Asteraceae (Aster Family) and commonly known as tasselflower or Flora's-paintbrush. The slender stems are tipped by small, rayless, many-colored flower heads surrounded by soft white bristles (pappi); they resemble tiny paintbrushes. Native in southern Europe, they will grow in any sunny corner and self-sow, blooming from midsummer to frost.

E. javanica (formerly listed as *E. sagittata*), the common garden species, is an annual growing to 18 in., with scarlet flowers in loose clusters. Var. *lutea* has yellow flowers.

E. sonchifolia is similar to *E. javanica*, but flowers are rose or purple, rarely white.

EMMENANTHE (em en AN thee). A genus of annual herbs of the Hydrophyllaceae (Waterleaf Family), native to western North America, and bearing long-lasting yellow or whitish pink bell-shaped flowers in drooping racemes. Best sown outdoors in light, well-draining soil, or started indoors and set out after the danger of frost is past.

E. penduliflora (whispering-, golden-, or yellow-bells), a dwarf California species, grows in densely branched mounds about 10 in. tall, covered with drooping racemes of yellow flowers that eventually dry papery and whisper in a breeze.

EMPETRUM (em PET rum) **nigrum.** A hardy, evergreen, heavily branched, prostrate, heathlike shrub, commonly known as crowberry. Hardy in Zones 3–6, it is widely distributed in the Northern Hemisphere. It has inconspicuous flowers, the male and female forms being borne on separate plants, and the pistillate (female) flowers being followed by edible black berries. It is a good plant for the rock garden and thrives in a lime-free soil of sandy loam with plenty of peat or leaf mold. Propagation is by cuttings.

EMPRESS TREE. Common name for *Paulownia tomentosa*, a sturdy, mid-sized tree with large leaves and conspicuous violet flowers; see PAULOWNIA.

ENCEPHALARTOS (en sef ah LAHR tohs). A genus of beautiful, palmlike plants from South Africa, belonging to the Cycadaceae (Cycad Family). They have stout, usually branchless trunks and a rosette of stiff, spiny-tipped foliage. Aside from their ornamental value, they are interesting botanically, being ancient forms and occupying an intermediate place between flowering and spore-bearing plants. Hardy only to Zone 10, they are successfully grown outdoors in south Florida but only under glass in the North. Of slow growth, they need heat, moisture, partial shade, and a rich, sandy soil containing fiber. Propagation is by suckers, which sprout around the base. Of the 20 or more species, some have trunks entirely under ground, and others rise to 30 ft.; few are in cultivation. *E. villosus* has an orange-yellow fruit considerably larger than a pineapple.

ENCYCLIA (en SIK lee uh). About 150 species of epiphytic orchids native to Mexico, the West Indies, and northern South America. The genus is sometimes considered synonymous with *Epidendrum*, but taxonomists have designated members of the family in which the lip is free from or only partially fused to the column and which have pseudobulbs as belonging to the genus *Encyclia*. They produce several to many flowers, ranging in color from white to green or violet. They hybridize easily with other members of the tribe Epidendreae to form important man-made genera (including *Epicattleya*). The flowers of this genus are generally smaller and less showy than those of *Cattleya*.

During active growth, they should be given ample water and bright light and kept warm. Basket culture is recommended, and a porous, well-drained compost is needed. Hardy to Zone 7 with frost protection, depending on the species, they generally withstand minimum winter temperatures of 55–60°F. The type species is *E. viridiflora*.

ENDEMIC. A term describing a native species that grows in a specific, localized area.

ENDIVE. A hardy biennial or annual herb, *Cichorium endivia* is grown for use in salad or as a potherb; often called curly endive or escarole in markets and kitchens. For summer use, sow the

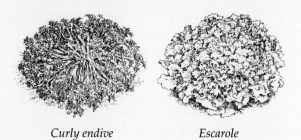

Curly endive   *Escarole*

seed thinly in early spring in a hotbed; a cold-frame; or, as soon as the garden can be dug, in a seedbed for later transplanting, or even directly in the garden rows. Make the latter 18–20 in. apart, and thin or set the plants 12–15 in. apart. Keep cleanly cultivated.

For autumn and winter harvesting, make successional sowings three weeks apart from June until August in the North, and 4–6 weeks longer in the South. Though the plant is hardy, the leaves may be injured by severe frost, so protect them on cold nights. Transplanting to a cold-frame as fall approaches is a favorite method.

To blanch the inner leaves for salad, tie the outer ones together above the crowns, or cover individual plants with drain tiles or blanching tubes. Be sure the plants are dry when this is done, or the centers may rot. Should rain occur while the blanching is occurring (it requires 2–4 weeks), uncover the heads, let them dry, and re-cover them. Blanching is not required when the crops are grown for greens.

The long blanched heads of the witloof chicory, *C. intybus*, are also known in many places as Belgian endive; see CICHORIUM.

ENDYMION (en DIM ee ahn). A genus of the Lili-aceae (Lily Family) and commonly called wood-hyacinth, this bulb is hardy to Zone 6 and lends itself well to naturalizing in woodland gardens and under shrubs. The name "hyacinth" refers to its form in that the flowers are bell shaped,

though looser in form than those of a true hyacinth, and with narrower leaves.

There are three to four species; perhaps the best known is *E. hispanicus*, which originally had blue flowers, but now there are various culti-vars. 'Alba' is white; 'Rosea' is pink flowered.

E. nonscriptus (English-bluebell) is a looser form with deep blue flowers; in the British Isles it covers acres of ground with blue in the spring.

ENKIANTHUS (en kee ANTH us). A genus of hardy deciduous Asiatic shrubs belonging to the Ericaceae (Heath Family). They thrive in a rather moist, sandy, acid soil supplied with peat or leaf mold. In habit, they are stiffly upright with whorled branches and are distinctive in appear-ance year-round. The long slender clusters of nodding yellow-orange flowers that open in spring are very attractive, although not always showy. In the fall, the leaves assume gorgeous shades of yellow, red, and orange. Propagation is by seed, cuttings, or layers.

PRINCIPAL SPECIES

E. campanulatus (red-vein enkianthus) is a tall shrub with pendulus, bell-shaped, yellowish flowers, veined with red and of unusual appear-ance. It is one of the most brilliantly colored shrubs in the fall. Hardy to Zone 5.

E. cernuus grows to 15 ft. and has white flow-ers. Var. *rubens*, with red flowers, is more hand-some. Hardy to Zone 6.

E. perulatus, which grows to 6 ft., has urn-shaped, white flowers opening in advance of the leaves, which are mostly yellow in the fall. Hardy to Zone 6.

ENTELEA (en te LEE ah) **arborescens.** A shrub or small tree from New Zealand, belonging to the Tiliaceae (Linden Family). It is hardy to Zone 10 and has been planted in southern California as an ornamental. It has large heart-shaped, toothed or slightly three-lobed leaves. The white flowers are 1 in. across and borne in flat clusters.

ENTEROLOBIUM (en ter oh LOH bee um). A genus of tropical trees, hardy to Zone 10, with feather-form leaves and large pods used for cattle feed. It is one of several trees known as eartree.

ENTIRE. A term referring to any leaf or leaflike part whose margin is continuous and not to any extent toothed or indented. While it usually means that a leaf is unlobed, it is sometimes used for a lobed leaf to indicate that the margins of the lobes are not toothed.

EOMECON (ee oh MEK uhn) **chionantha.** A half-hardy, early-blooming perennial herb belonging to the Papaveraceae (Poppy Family) and commonly known as snow poppy. The white, poppy-like flower clusters are borne on reddish, branching stalks 9–12 in. high. Leaves are pale green, heart shaped, and grayish beneath. Native to China, it is hardy as far north as Zone 7. Propagation is by division of the rootstock.

EPACRIS (EP ah kris). A genus of heathlike evergreen shrubs from New Zealand and Australia, sometimes grown as potted plants in a cool greenhouse. They thrive under the same treatment as ERICA, but are easier to propagate and grow from cuttings.

E. *longiflora* (Australian- or fuchsia-heath), also listed as E. *autumnale*, has rosy carmine and white flowers mainly in spring but also at other seasons.

EPAULETTE TREE. Common name for PTEROSTYRAX, a genus of hardy deciduous trees and shrubs with white flowers.

EPHEDRA (e FED rah). A genus of small, bushy, broomlike shrubs found in arid places in various parts of the world, commonly known as Mormon-tea or joint-fir. They are of peculiar appearance, with jointed and apparently leafless green or gray stems, somewhat resembling horsetails. Most are not hardy in the North but are useful as ground cover in warmer regions for erosion control on sterile soils or in wild gardens and drought-tolerant landscapes. E. *californica* is a densely branched, grayish stemmed shrub growing to 3 ft. tall with significant spread. E. *viridia* is a bright green, twiggy shrub growing to 4 ft.

EPIDENDRUM (ep uh DEN drum). A genus of over 1000 species of epiphytic, terrestrial, or lithophytic orchids; first defined by eighteenth century Swedish botanist Carolus Linnaeus. They are distributed throughout the Americas from North Carolina to Argentina. Many are "reed stem" orchids without pseudobulbs, having instead long reedlike canes, a major difference from the genus *Encyclia*. Also, the lip and column are fused.

The flowers vary widely in size, shape, and color, ranging from white and yellow to rose, scarlet, or purple. These orchids thrive in baskets of porous, well-drained compost and need bright light. Reed-stem types can be grown in the ground in full sun. Terrestrial types should be grown in humusy porous or sandy soil. All require abundant water. While many are hardy to Zone 7, they should be protected from cold, withstanding minimum winter temperatures of 55–60°F. The type species is E. *nocturnum*.

EPIGAEA (e pi JEE ah) **repens.** An attractive spring-blooming creeping evergreen belonging to the Ericaceae (Heath Family), commonly known as mayflower or trailing-arbutus. It is the state flower of Massachusetts and one of the choicest wildflowers found in the eastern states, but it is not common in cultivation, despite many attempts to establish it in gardens. Hardy to Zone 3, it requires an acid, peaty soil in a shady place and seems to like association with *Tsuga* (hemlock). Wild plants are protected by law in several states and will seldom thrive in gardens, so it is necessary to start with nursery-grown plants. Prepare a good location in a moist spot and work in plenty of peat moss and sharp sand.

Propagation can be achieved by division and layers, but the best plants are obtained from seed. They should be sown as soon as ripe, using a mixture of peat moss and sand in a well-drained flat. Cover with a shaded pane of glass and look for the seedlings in about four weeks. When large enough to handle, plant them singly in small pots; plunge these in moss and keep cool and shaded at all times. When this method is followed, plants usually begin to flower in their third year.

EPIGYNOUS. A term applied to a flower in which petals, sepals, and stamens are inserted above the ovary and are attached to it. In such a case, as illustrated by the iris or apple, the ovary appears below the flower, not within it, and is said to be inferior. See OVARY.

EPILOBIUM (ep il OH bee um). A large genus of herbs or subshrubs native in temperate regions of the world, belonging to the Onagraceae (Evening-primrose Family) and commonly known as willow herb. They have willowlike leaves, small white or sometimes yellow flowers, and long fruit pods or capsules. Mostly hardy in Zones 4–9, they are among the easiest plants to grow. Although one or two may be grown in borders, for the most part they are better placed in the wild garden and by the waterside. Propagation is by seed, division, and runners.

PRINCIPAL SPECIES

E. angustifolium (fireweed, blooming-Sally), found all across the northern states, is a tall, robust perennial that spreads rapidly by means of underground runners. It bears long ter-
minal spikes of rosy
purple flowers. Var.
album has been im-
proved in cultivation
and is a useful white-
flowering border plant.

E. dodonaei is a rela-
tively small plant with
rosemarylike leaves and
reddish flowers crowd-
ed at the ends of the
branches.

E. hirsutum (codlins-
and-cream) is a soft,
hairy, clammy plant

Epilobium angustifolium

with leafy clusters of pale purple or white flowers. It grows to about 4 ft. and spreads rapidly and widely by underground runners.

E. nummularifolium, from New Zealand, is a small creeping plant with tiny white flowers, valuable as a ground cover in the rock garden.

EPIMEDIUM (ep i MEE dee um). A genus of hardy perennial herbs belonging to the Berberidaceae (Barberry Family) and commonly known as barrenwort. They have small leaves that are bronzy when young and almost evergreen in sheltered spots. Small, waxen, red, pink, yellow, or white flowers are borne in delicate, airy racemes.

Epimedium grandiflorum

Because of their attractive foliage, barrenworts are eminently suited to the rock garden but may also be planted in a shady portion of a border garden or along a wooded path. They are easily increased by division of the roots; most are hardy in Zones 3–7.

PRINCIPAL SPECIES

E. alpinum, growing to 1 ft., is a European species seen mainly in var. *rubrum*, which has red-edged leaves and red flowers.

E. grandiflorum (long-spur epimedium), formerly listed as *E. macranthum*, native to Japan, grows to 9 in. with red and violet, white-spurred flowers in early summer. Varieties produce various colors, including var. *niveum* in white; var. *roseum* in rose-red; and var. *violaceum* with purple spurs.

E. pinnatum (Persian epimedium) has yellow, red-spurred flowers with different shades and sizes represented in several good varieties.

E. warleyense grows to 10 in. and has coppery orange sepals and yellow spurs.

EPIPHYLLUM (ep i FIL um).

A genus of epiphytic cacti from tropical America, formerly known as *Phyllocactus*. The generic name means "from the leaf," but the plant is actually leafless, the "leaves" being flattened, green, leaflike stems. The flowers are large, showy, white, and bloom at night.

Many spectacular hybrids, called orchid cacti, have been produced. These are diurnal (day flowering) and vary in shades of red, purple, pink, orange, yellow, and combinations thereof. Developed from jungle cacti, orchid cacti thrive in light shade, moderate warmth, fresh air, and need frequent mistings or sprayings. Their culture is quite different from most other cacti.

EPIPHYTE.

A term for specialized plants that fasten themselves on the trunk or branches of other plants, usually trees. Commonly called "air plants," epiphytes are variously modified to cling, to obtain and store water, and to catch drifting humus, since they usually have no contact with actual soil but only with humus that clusters around their base. Some of them put out air roots or scalelike organs to absorb air and moisture; various kinds are grown as curiosities in the greenhouse. They are not parasites, which attach themselves to live plants in order to use their sap, or saprophytes, which live on the tissues of dead plants. Epiphytes use other plants merely as supports to reach a location that assures sufficient air and light.

EPIPREMNUM (e pi PREM num).

A genus of climbing, tropical perennials native to Malaysia, belonging to the Araceae (Arum Family) and commonly known as pothos, ivy arum, or devil's-ivy. Usually greenhouse or houseplants, they climb by means of stem rootlets and produce heart-shaped leaves and spadiceous flowers (tiny blooms on a spike). The commonly grown species is *E. aureum*, a climbing or trailing vine with yellow-blotched green leaves. Varieties have yellow or white-and-green variegated leaves and stems.

EPISCIA (e PISH uh).

A genus of tropical plants belonging to the Gesneriaceae (Gesneria Family). They make luxuriant foliage plants, beautiful with or without flowers. There are hairy or smooth-leaved kinds and others with contrasting veins or zones. The five-lobed, long-tubed flowers are all fringed, some more noticeably than others. Blossoms may be white, yellow, pink, red, blue, or lavender, and spotted, marked, or lined.

Episcias are best displayed when allowed to trail and grow unimpeded, as from a shelf or hanging basket. They grow strawberrylike stolons one after the other, and these soon produce a magnificent cascade of foliage. The effect is highlighted by the blossoms, which arise in the leaf axils, in some varieties only seasonally, in others almost constantly. If space does not permit the fullest spreading for episcias, they may be cut back into a rounded bushy form. Root the plantlets along the cut-off stolons by pinning them to the soil.

Plants thrive in semisunny to semishady conditions and warm temperatures with humidity 30% or more. They are very sensitive to sudden drops in temperature, and a modest chill of 50–55°F can make the leaves appear frost damaged. If this happens, keep them on the dry side for a time and do not fertilize; the plant should recover when warmth returns. The soil should be equal parts loam, sand, peat moss, and leaf mold, kept evenly moist with biweekly feedings except in late fall and early winter. Propagation is by rooting the stolons.

E. reptans (flame-violet), formerly listed as *E. coccinea* or *E. fulgida*, was the first species to attract commercial attention. Its bronzy pebble-surfaced leaves with distinctive green or silver veining have become a familiar sight wherever tropical plants are grown.

Today there are dozens of other species and cultivars available, including 'Cleopatra', which has mostly pink and white leaves with only a touch of silvery green.

EQUISETUM (ek wi SEE tum). A genus of flowerless perennials commonly known as horsetails. They are vascular wetland plants allied to ferns and club-mosses and are useful for holding banks and covering waste areas. They have hollow, jointed stems with leaves reduced to mere scales at the joints. Spores (not seeds) are borne in cone-like spikes.

E. hyemale (scouring-rush) is a species native to Eurasia and Pacific North America, with slender evergreen stems growing to 4 ft. It is suitable for naturalizing.

ERAGROSTIS (er ah GROS tis). A genus of medium-sized grasses, some annuals, some perennials, valued for their delicate ornamental sprays, which consist of small spikelets carried in open panicles. There is considerable confusion between the individual species, which grow between 1½–3 ft. tall, with leaves 4–12 in. long, and panicles 4–15 in. long. *E. tef*, an annual growing to 3 ft, is known as teff. *E. elegans*, *E. interrupta* and *E. japonica*, all known as love grass, are annuals growing to 3 ft., useful for bouquets. See ORNAMENTAL GRASSES.

ERANTHEMUM (ee RAN thee mum). A genus of tropical herbs and shrubs, belonging to the Acanthaceae (Acanthus Family). Its botanical status and relations have been confused and several plants known and grown as *Eranthemums* are now reclassified to other genera. At present the most common species recognized by botanists as belonging here is *E. pulchellum* (formerly known as *E. nervosum*). This is a good plant to be grown in the greenhouse for blue winter blooms in the warm greenhouse and also a popular shrub for outdoor planting in Zones 10–11. It is easy to grow from cuttings of young wood, but needs light, rich soil with plenty of moisture and ample sunlight.

ERANTHIS (air ANTH us). A genus of small, tuberous rooted, hardy perennials belonging to the Ranunculaceae (Buttercup Family) and commonly known as winter-aconite. Its bright yellow blooms resembling buttercups and whorls of shiny leaves appear in the earliest spring with the snowdrops. It thrives in half-shade and leafy soil and is especially well suited to rock gardens. Tubers are usually planted in autumn; to avoid disturbing them, their location should be marked before the foliage dies down after flowering. Most are hardy in Zones 5–9.

E. hyemalis grows to 8 in. and has long-stemmed, finely cut foliage and flowers to 1½ in. across.

E. sibirica grows about 4 in. high and has relatively small flowers and few petals.

EREMOCHLOA (air im OH kloh ah) **ophiuroides.** Commonly known as centipede grass, it was introduced from Asia; recommended for lawns

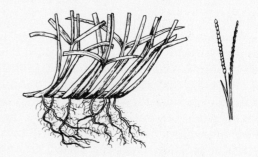

Eremochloa ophiuroides

and pastures in the South, where it has been tested by a Florida experiment station. It spreads by means of runners, is able to withstand drought, and is propagated by cuttings (called stolons), which are planted in spring and summer in well-prepared soil.

EREMURUS (air im YOOR us). A genus of tall, desert-dwelling bulbs belonging to the Liliaceae (Lily Family) and commonly known as desert-candle, foxtail lily, or giant-asphodel. There are some 38 species of Asian origin, as well as many hybrids, including the hardiest and some of the most spectacular species of the tall desert lilies. Long, slender leaves spring from the fleshy, rope-like roots in dense basal rosettes. Above them rises the stout, sometimes 8 ft. long flower stalk clothed for half its length with close-set, starry blooms, which last for several weeks. The eremurus has become popular both as a stately border subject and as a florist's flower.

Since seedlings develop slowly, the purchase of sizable plants is advisable. They are not the easiest bulbs to grow, but once established they do well to Zone 5 if given some winter protection. Because they are on tall, leafless stems, they show up best if planted in front of a dark background like an evergreen hedge. They also need well-drained, rich, fibrous soil containing sharp sand and a sunny location to grow well. Most are hardy in Zones 4–9.

Eremurus elwesii

The plants die back after flowering, but foliage growth reappears in early spring and must be protected against late frosts. A mound of wood ashes drawn over the crown or a watertight box filled with dry leaves will give winter protection. Established plants should never be disturbed, for the roots are very brittle.

PRINCIPAL SPECIES

E. elwesii is one of the common species grown in home gardens. Reaching a height of 6–9 ft., its ovate, lanceolate, somewhat fleshy leaves grow to 3 ft., and its many flowers are pink with a dark midvein.

E. himalaicus is a popular subject with white flowers.

E. lactiflorus reaches a similar height but has bright yellow flowers.

E. robustus (giant desert-candle) grows up to 10 ft. high with 2 ft. long leaves and, in early summer, 2–3 ft. spikes of flowers ranging from white to orange, yellow, and bright pink.

E. stenophyllus, formerly listed as *E. bungei*, has orange-yellow flowers.

ERIANTHUS (air ee AN thus). A genus of stout, tall-growing plants belonging to the Poaceae (Grass Family), collectively known as the plume grasses. They are good plants for borders or the background of lawns from New York southward (hardy to Zone 5). They are perennials but are mostly grown as annuals, attaining a height of 10–12 ft. in a season, with long flat leaves. *E. ravennae* (ravenna grass), the tallest, has leaves 3 ft. long and about ½ in. wide; the plumelike panicles may be as long as 3 ft. See ORNAMENTAL GRASSES.

ERICA (AIR ik ah). A large genus of evergreen shrubs native in Europe and south Africa, belonging to the Ericaceae (Heath Family) and commonly known as heath. They are closely related to the genus CALLUNA (commonly known as heather) but may be distinguished by their needlelike or very narrow leaves, usually in whorls and spread apart. In mild regions they are attractive for outdoor grouping. They require lime-free soil and thrive where there is plenty of leaf mold or peat. Mostly hardy to Zone 6, some do well in colder climates if given sheltered positions. Several species make excellent houseplants; they hold their flowers well and are often grown by florists for Christmas and Easter. Potted plants do best when firmly potted in fibrous peat and coarse sand. To keep them shapely, trim back after flowering. The soft-wooded varieties are easier to grow than the hard-wooded ones, but all of them require considerable attention.

Erica sp.

PRINCIPAL SPECIES

HARDY TYPES

These survive fairly well in colder regions, especially when placed in sunny positions in the rock garden or well-drained slopes. Evergreen boughs placed over them in winter will keep the foliage in good condition. Most are hardy in Zones 6–8.

E. carnea (spring heath) grows about 1 ft. high, with leaves in fours and reddish flowers from winter to late spring. A few popular cultivars are 'Springwood Pink' with deep pink flowers, 'King George' with crimson blooms, and 'Springwood White' with white flowers.

E. terminalis (Corsican heath), formerly listed as *E. stricta*, has stiff branches with leaves in fours and is usually more upright. The flowers are rosy purple in late summer. The hybrid x *darleyensis* (darley heath) has fine, needlelike foliage and purplish pink flowers and is one of the earliest ericas to grow. Hardy to Zone 6.

E. tetralix (cross-leaved heath) is a twisted and branched little shrub with leaves in threes and rosy purple flowers appearing in late spring. It is hardier than most, surviving in Zones 4–7.

E. vagans (Cornish heath) grows to 1 ft. or more, with leaves in fours or fives and pinkish flowers in summer.

TENDER SPECIES

These thrive only in mild regions or under cool greenhouse conditions.

E. arborea (tree heath) grows to 20 ft. in favored climates. It has leaves in threes and bears an abundance of white fragrant flowers in spring. Several forms are grown.

E. hyemalis has leaves in four and rosy pink flowers, tipped white. It is one of the easiest and most popular for indoor culture.

E. lusitanica (Spanish heath) grows to 12 ft. with leaves from three to five in a whorl and pink flowers in early spring.

E. mediterranea grows to 10 ft. and has leaves in fours or fives and red flowers in spring. Several forms are grown in mild regions.

E. melanthera is a good species to grow in pots for winter bloom. It has leaves in threes and

bears a profusion of pinkish flowers with conspicuous black anthers.

E. ventricosa has leaves in fours and pink flowers with swollen tubes. There are several good color forms of this beautiful species.

ERICACEAE (e ri KAY see ee). The Heath Family, an important group of shrubs and small trees, is widely distributed but strongly prefers regions with acid soil conditions. Plants belonging to this family are described as ericaceous. A large, much-varied family, some species, like the blueberry, are grown for food; many others are highly ornamental subjects grown for foliage and showy flowers. Some family members are fine broad-leaved evergreens. Also included are some of our finest flowering shrubs. There are about 70 genera and nearly 2000 species in the family, more than 800 belonging to the genus *Rhododendron*, including the azaleas. Other common representatives are *Andromeda*, *Arctostaphylos* (bearberry), *Calluna* (heather), *Enkianthus*, *Epigaea* (trailing-arbutus), *Erica* (heath), *Gaultheria* (wintergreen), *Gaylussacia* (huckleberry), *Kalmia* (mountain-laurel), *Ledum*, *Leucothoâ*, *Pieris*, and *Vaccinium* (blueberry and cranberry).

Ericaceous plants come from all parts of the world, many being mountain plants. They almost invariably prefer acid soils, and most will tolerate nothing else. Although some prefer open locations, nearly all will do well in semi-shade; many, particularly the evergreen types, need protection from sweeping winds. As a general rule, the cultural directions given for RHODODENDRON apply to other ericaceous plants, all of which prefer peaty soils.

ERIGENIA (er ee JEE nĭ ah) **bulbosa**. A low-growing, tuberous-rooted, almost stemless herb belonging to the Apiaceae (Celery Family) and commonly known as harbinger-of-spring. It is native in open deciduous woods from the Mississippi River eastward, and its small clusters of white blossoms are among the earliest of spring flowers.

ERIGERON (e RIJ ur awn). A genus of annual and perennial herbs belonging to the Asteraceae (Aster Family) and commonly known as fleabane or wild-buckwheat. These plants have flower heads of white, rose, or violet ray flowers and yellow disk flowers. Some of the species are cultivated in the border, others are naturalized in the wild garden, while a few are grown in the rock garden. Easily cultivated, they should be planted in warm, sandy soil in full sun. Fleabanes are propagated easily by seed or division. Various species are hardy in Zones 6–9.

Aster yellows, a virus disease, causes yellowing and stunting; control by removing and burning infected plants.

Erigeron speciosus

PRINCIPAL SPECIES

E. alpinus, growing to 3 in., has delicate pink daisylike flowers.

E. aurantiacus (double orange daisy), growing to 9 in., has brilliant orange blossoms blooming throughout the summer. It is very showy in the rock garden at a time when bloom is needed.

E. caucasicus, growing to 10 in., has rosy lavender flowers blooming in profusion throughout the summer.

E. compositus, growing to 2 in., has feathery gray foliage and pale lavender flowers.

E. karvinskianus is a trailing alpine perennial growing to 18 in., with white or pink daisylike flowers blooming all summer and autumn. It blooms the first year from seed and should have winter protection in cold climates.

E. pulchellis (poor-Robin's-plantain), native to eastern North America, is a biennial or short-lived perennial growing to 2 ft.; it has rounded leaves and 2–3 in. heads of blue, pink, or white ray flowers.

E. speciosus is a perennial growing to 2 ft. and has violet-rayed flowers to 1½ in. across in flat-topped clusters blooming over a long period. Cv. 'Pink Jewel' is a free-flowering plant with single pink flowers in early summer. Cv. 'Grandiflorus' has large blue-purple flowers in summer.

Many horticultural varieties of erigeron are available, including 'Darkest of All', with deep violet-blue flowers; 'Forester's Darling', with semidouble pink flowers; 'Prosperity', with semidouble blue flowers; 'Rose Triumph' with large double pink flowers; and 'Strahlenmeer', with soft blue flowers.

ERINUS (e RĪ nus). A hardy European mountain perennial belonging to the Scrophulariaceae (Figwort Family). It forms low, dense tufts and is commonly grown in partly shaded places in the dry rock wall or in crevices in the rock garden. Early in April it bears small, rosy purple flowers rising 3–4 in. above the matted foliage. It is easily grown from seed or divisions and self-sows readily. Several color forms are available.

Erinus sp.

ERIOBOTRYA (air ee oh BOHT ree ah) **japonica.** A small subtropical evergreen Asian tree or shrub belonging to the Rosaceae (Rose Family), sometimes called Japan-plum, but more commonly known as loquat. It is grown as a home garden fruit from Florida westward to California, where it is also planted for its plum-like yellow or orange fruit, which is delicious whether eaten raw or in pies or preserves. These develop in spring from fragrant white flowers borne in panicles. Plants are occasionally grown under glass in pots as ornamentals. Though the tree will grow in any good soil, it does best in clay loams and needs an area 25–30 ft. in diameter. Bacterial dieback can be a problem. Hardy to Zone 8.

ERIOGONUM (air ee AW guh num). A genus of annual herbs and subshrubs belonging to the Polygonaceae (Buckwheat Family), represented by many species in western America, sometimes known as wild-buckwheat. Extremely variable, from dense alpine mats to huge coastal shrubs, it is a genus with great horticultural potential for dryer areas. Many species are of special appeal to rock gardeners but are also extremely valuable for drought-tolerant landscapes in warmer regions. Suited to poor, well-drained soils in full sun, they generally flower in late summer.

PRINCIPAL SPECIES
LOW, MAT-FORMING SPECIES

E. kennedyi is a densely packed mat of tiny gray leaves forming a silver mound 3–4 in. tall and 18 in. wide, with whitish flowers in ball-like heads to 6 in. Like all the mat-forming types, this is ideal for rock gardens, walls, and path edges.

E. lobbii produces clustered rosettes of 1–2 in. long, elliptic, silvery brown leaves lying flat on the ground and creamy to rose-pink clusters of flowers on stems up to 6 in. long, arching flat over the foliage.

E. ovalifolium, forms a silvery gray mat of spoon-shaped leaves about 4 in. high, with yellow or pink flowers in tight or loose heads.

E. umbellatum (sulfur flower) forms a mat or low shrub, 4–24 in. tall, of oval, green 2-in. leaves, which set off large heads of sulfur-yellow flowers.

Eriogonum umbellatum

E. ursinum (talus buckwheat) forms loose mats of shiny green or woolly leaves in loose rosettes, with stout stalks bearing 3-in. clusters of creamy flowers.

MID-SIZED OR LOW SHRUB SPECIES

E. compositum has 6-in. arrow-shaped leaves forming a large mound 1 ft. tall with huge 8-in. clusters of cream or yellow flowers on 2½-ft. stalks.

E. grande rubescens (Santa Cruz Island buckwheat) grows in 8-in. mounds of greenish foliage topped in August with 18-in. stalks of rich rose-pink clusters.

E. latifolium (coast buckwheat) forms mounds of grayish foliage to 1 ft. with cream to pink clusters 2 in. across that age darker bronze.

E. saxatile has branched clumps growing to 8 in. with stems covered with felty, white, undulate leaves 1 in. long and wiry spikes of whitish pink flowers to 18 in.

LARGE TYPES

E. arborescens (island buckwheat) is a woody shrub growing to 4 ft. with a treelike branching pattern and creamy 5-in. clusters of flowers appearing in August.

E. fasciculatum (California buckwheat) is a bushy subshrub growing to 4 ft. tall with a great spread; it has green or gray foliage and 4-in. creamy flower clusters in June. This species is useful for sterile soils.

E. giganteum (St.-Catherine's-lace) is a tender shrub growing to 4 ft. tall and 5 ft. wide, with white-woolly 4-in. leaves and huge, diffuse flower clusters to 18 in. wide in September; excellent for arrangements.

ERIOPHORUM (air ee oh FOHR um). A genus of herbs belonging to the Cyperaceae (Sedge Family), commonly known as cotton-grass. They are native to bogs of the North Temperate and Arctic Zones and are sometimes planted along pond edges or in the bog garden for their ornamental cottony seed heads.

ERIOPHYLLUM (air ee oh FIL um). A genus of annual or perennial herbs or subshrubs native to western North America, members of the Asteraceae (Aster Family) and useful in the wild or meadow garden or drought-tolerant landscapes.

PRINCIPAL SPECIES

E. confertiflorum (golden-yarrow) is a subshrub with stiffly erect branches 8–24 in. tall; it has small dissected gray leaves and yarrowlike clusters of golden flowers that bloom in June. Hardy to Zone 9.

E. lanatum (Oregonsunshine) is a short-lived perennial growing to 6–18 in.; it has deeply lobed leaves covered with woolly hairs and produces showy 1½-in. yellow daisies over a long season.

*Eriophyllum
confertiflorum*

E. staechadifolium is a loose, tender subshrub growing to 3 ft. tall and 6 ft. wide with grayish lobed leaves and clusters of yellow flowers in July.

ERITRICHIUM (air i TRIK ee um). A small genus of handsome low-growing alpine plants commonly known as alpine-forget-me-not. The vivid blue flowers make every rock gardener want to grow these, but few succeed. If seedlings grow, they seldom flower and are short-lived. The ultimate alpine challenge, they are best admired and photographed at 12,000 ft. in the Alps or Rocky Mountains.

ERODIUM (air OH dee um). A genus of annual and perennial herbs belonging to the Geraniaceae (Geranium Family) and commonly known as heron's-bill or stork's-bill. A few species are used in the garden, but the greater number are planted as forage crops. Those species cultivated on the edge of the border or in the rock garden should be planted in a sunny location in gritty loam to which a little lime has been added. Valuable because of their long blooming period, they are propagated by seed or division. Most are hardy in Zones 6–9.

PRINCIPAL SPECIES

E. chamaedryoides, growing to 3 in., has white, rose-veined flowers blooming nearly all year. It is a dainty alpine, suitable for a shady corner in the rock garden.

E. chielanthifolium, growing to 4 in., has silvery, fernlike leaves and white flowers veined with rose to ¾ in. across. It is a charming alpine species native to Spain and Morocco and is perfectly hardy in the North.

E. corsicum, growing to 6 in., forms rosettes of downy foliage covered with pink, rose-veined flowers all summer.

E. glutinosum (heron's-bill) grows to 18 in. and produces long seed pods that resemble a bird's pointed beak.

E. macradenum, growing to 1 ft., has pale lavender blossoms, the two upper petals marked with large purple spots.

E. manescavii, a European native, is the tallest species, growing 1 ft. or more, and has magenta flowers to 1½ in. across. It is a vigorous plant but is rather difficult to combine with others because of the strong color of the blossoms.

Erodium glutinosum

E. trichomanifolium grows to 5 in. and has violet flowers veined with pink; it is a good rock garden subject.

EROSION. This refers to two distinct actions, one that is constructive and is a phase of soil formation, the other destructive, contributing to the injury of soil.

The first type is weathering, disintegration, and washing or blowing away of rocks and soil. Rocks are split and chipped by frost and by plant roots, dissolved by chemical action of rainwater and soil seepage, worn away by stream action or by sand blowing in the wind. The resulting finely powdered rock, mixed with humus or decayed vegetable and animal matter, is soil.

The second type is soil erosion. The washing or blowing away of the topsoil (and sometimes even the subsoil) is a great natural force. Soil erosion is most rapid on cultivated, sloping land where heavy rains wash out channels and carry off many tons per acre of topsoil; in drought times the wind whirls such soil away as dust.

Preventive measures include planting hills, slopes, and banks with trees, shrubs, forage crops, permanent ground cover, or strong grass; covering less steep inclines with permanent sod; and plowing sloping land only when in good condition and when it is to be quickly replanted. While still small, erosion channels should be blocked with stones, brush, anchored straw, and fast-growing trees; otherwise the channels deepen to torrent beds. Where possible, hillsides that must be cultivated should be terraced to break the flow of water; or level trenches can be plowed or strips of sod left at right angles to the slope. The best control for wind erosion is planting vegetation with strong roots.

ERUCA (e ROO kah). A genus of the Brassicaceae (Mustard Family). The species *E. vesicaria* var. *sativa* (rocket-salad, roquette) is grown for use as greens. This half-hardy annual herb is grown like spinach for spring and fall salads, but in hot weather it quickly goes to seed. Seed is sown outdoors when the weather is settled and in early fall. In six to eight weeks, the leaves can be used. To reduce their natural strong flavor, they can be grown rapidly and cut often. Sometimes listed in catalogs as arugula. See GREENS.

ERYNGIUM (air IN jee um). A genus of mostly perennial plants with spiny leaves and flowers in dense heads or spikes, belonging to the Apiaceae (Celery Family) and commonly known as eryngo. The steel-blue or gray foliage of the larger species is most attractive in the border, while the smaller kinds are well suited to the rock garden. The taller types provide excellent cut flowers that can be dried for winter bouquets. Eryngos should be planted in light, rich soil in an open, sunny location. They are easily propagated by seed sown as soon as ripe or by division. Most are hardy in Zones 4–6.

PRINCIPAL SPECIES

E. agavifolium, growing to 5 ft., is usually grown for its attractive foliage, which forms

rosettes up to 2 ft. across. Flowers are suitable for dried bouquets.

E. amethystinum, growing to 1½ ft., has small blue flowers surrounded by narrow bracts and is hardy to Zone 2 or 3.

E. maritimum (sea-holly), growing to 1 ft., has broad, spiny, grayish blue leaves and pale blue heads of flowers surrounded by tiny bracts.

E. x *oliveranum*, growing to 3 ft., has broad cut leaves and blue flowers 1½ in. long, surrounded by very narrow stiff bracts.

E. yuccifolium (rattlesnake-master) has yucca-like leaves up to 2 ft. long and round, white, green-tinged, summer blossoms good for drying.

Eryngium yuccifolium

ERYSIMUM (ah RIS im um). A genus of hard annual, biennial, or perennial herbs belonging to the Brassicaceae (Mustard Family) and commonly known as blistercress or wallflower, which also refers to the genus *Cheiranthus*. They have white, yellow, orange, blue, or lilac flowers. Some of the smaller species are excellent plants for the rock garden or the edge of the sunny border and are easily cultivated. The perennials are hardy in Zones 3–6, depending on the species.

Erysimum capitatum

RECOMMENDED ROCK GARDEN SPECIES

E. alpinum has clear yellow flowers. It frequently blooms when only 6 in. high and continues to flower until frost. It reseeds nicely but is never a pest.

E. capitatum (Douglas's or coast wallflower),

native to western North America, is a biennial growing erect to 18 in. with simple or branching stems bearing narrow, slightly hairy leaves about 3 in. long and yellowish or white flowers.

E. hieraciifolium (Siberian wallflower), sometimes listed as *Cheiranthus allionii*, is a short-lived perennial with small, vivid orange blossoms continuing in bloom over a long season. It blooms freely about tulip time and is so bright and cheerful and self-sows so readily that it is a good addition to any garden.

E. pulchellum (hedge mustard) grows to 1 ft. or more, producing profuse yellow-orange flowers in the spring.

E. purpureum is a low-growing Asian species with purple flowers.

ERYTHRINA (air i THRĪN ah). A genus of leguminous trees, shrubs, and some herbs with showy flowers and pods, belonging to the Fabaceae (Bean Family).

The tree species are commonly known as coral tree or coral bean. They are grown in the open in Zones 10–11. In the tropics, some species are used for shade trees in coffee and cacao plantations, known there as "immortelles." Coral trees are easily propagated from seed or from cuttings of mature wood. Stem borers kill the branch tips and thus can be a serious problem.

Among the 20 or more species grown in California, *E. crista-galli* is one of the most attractive. It forms a small, bushy tree whose branch tips carry clusters of long, slender, orange-scarlet blooms.

ERYTHRONIUM (er i THROH nee um). A genus of bulbous, early spring-blooming herbs of the Liliaceae (Lily Family), with graceful nodding flowers and often richly mottled leaves. Common names are dogtooth-violet, fawn or trout lily, and adder's-tongue; others are applied locally. The plants are particularly attractive in the rock garden or naturalized in masses in the wild garden; they should be planted in light soil full of humus in partially shaded places. Unless they are given a natural woodland condition, a winter mulch of

decayed leaves and ashes is beneficial.

The plants are propagated by seed, and some species spread naturally by means of underground rootstocks. The best time for obtaining new stock or for replanting is when the leaves die away after flowering. The bulbs should be planted not less than 3 in. deep, and finer effects are obtained by massing or planting them in groups rather than as individual plants.

ENEMIES

Speckling of leaves, followed by shriveling and falling over on the soil, is caused by a fungus that develops resting bodies, sclerotia, which produce spores in the spring. Remove and destroy infected plants, taking the adjacent soil with them. See FUNGUS; SCLEROTIUM.

PRINCIPAL SPECIES

E. americanum (trout lily), growing to 12 in., is the species commonly known in the East. The leaves are richly mottled, and the yellow flowers

Erythronium americanum

have recurved petals. It often grows in great colonies on the edge of the woodland and increases rapidly by offsets.

E. californicum (fawn lily), growing to 1 ft., with cream-colored flowers and richly marked leaves, is a western species that can naturalize very easily. Var. *bicolor* (white or yellow) is very fragrant.

E. citrinum, growing to 8 in., has white flowers marked at the base with deep citron yellow.

E. dens-canis (dogtooth-violet), growing to 6 in., with mottled leaves and white, yellow, pink, or purple flowers, is the Eurasian form commonly grown abroad.

E. grandiflorum (avalanche lily), growing to 2 ft., has green leaves and bright yellow flowers. Cv. 'Robustum' is a large form.

E. hendersonii (fawn lily), growing to 1 ft., with mottled leaves, has strongly recurved, purple flowers.

Erythronium grandiflorum

E. montanum, growing to 1½ ft., with slightly recurved white flowers, grows in profusion on the high slopes of mountains in Oregon and Washington, but because it starts so late, it is difficult to cultivate in the East.

E. multiscapoideum, a dainty species growing to 6 in., with creamy white, yellow-centered flowers, is generally sold as *E. hartwegii*.

E. oregonum, formerly listed as *E. giganteum*, grows to 1½ ft., with beautifully mottled brown and green leaves and large creamy flowers touched with maroon at the base; it is one of the most beautiful of the species.

E. revolutum, growing to 1 ft., has white flowers tinted lavender or purple.

ERYTHROXYLUM (e ri THROK si lum) **coca.** A shrub growing to 12 ft., native to western South America and the West Indies. It is cultivated in tropical climates for the narcotic drug cocaine, which is obtained from the leaves. The leaves, dried and mixed with a little lime, are chewed by Peruvian Indians to prevent hunger and fatigue while on journeys and while working.

ESCALLONIA (es kah LOH nee ah). A genus of handsome shrubs from South America, mostly evergreen, belonging to the Saxifragaceae (Sax-

ifrage Family). They can stand some frost but are not hardy where winters are severe; they thrive near the seaside. When well suited to the climate, and in a rather light and well-drained soil, they make dense, moundlike bushes from 6–15 ft. or more in height. Some species have been successfully used as hedges and also trained as vines. In most cases, the young growth glistens with resinous glands. The flowers, usually tubular in shape, are borne in clusters of white, pink, or red. Most of the species are summer bloomers, but one or two flower in autumn. They are easily propagated by cuttings.

PRINCIPAL SPECIES

E. bifida grows to a large bush with very sticky branchlets and white flowers. The long and narrow glossy green leaves are finely toothed.

E. x *langleyensis* is one of the best of the hybrid forms, usually growing as a low shrub. It has graceful arching branches, small leaves, and short racemes of rosy carmine flowers.

E. rubra var. *macrantha* is dense and spreading, with thick, oval, shining leaves and clusters of rosy crimson flowers. It is a good hedge plant where hardy.

E. virgata is a branched, deciduous species with white flowers in leafy racemes; it is the hardiest of the group.

ESCAROLE. A name used (mainly by greengrocers and cooks) for the salad or pot herb *Cichorium endiva*, also known as ENDIVE.

ESCHSCHOLZIA (esh SHOLT zee ah). A genus of annual or perennial herbs of the Papaveraceae (Poppy Family), commonly grown as annuals. The most widely known and popular species is *E. californica* (California poppy), which grows wild in and is the official flower of the state for which it is named. The plants sometimes grow to 2 ft. but are usually lower and spreading, with bluish green, finely cut foliage and attractive satiny-petaled flowers to 2 in. across, varying from pale cream to deep orange. The flowers, which are slender rather than cup-shaped like other poppies, vary considerably in form as well as color, double forms occasionally occurring.

California poppies are attractive border or edging plants, blooming profusely all summer and even after the first frosts. They thrive in ordinary garden soil and are easy to grow. Seed can be sown very early in spring (or later if desired) where the plants are to stand. They should be thinned out later, since they will not stand transplanting. If well protected with a light, loose covering of leaves, plants will often winter over and bloom extra early the following spring; plants also may develop from self-sown seed.

Eschscholzia californica

Other species sometimes seen in rock gardens or wildflower meadows are *E. caespitosa*, growing to 18 in. but usually smaller, with 1½-in. yellow or pale orange flowers in great profusion; and *E. lobbii*, a diminutive plant growing to 8 in., with tiny 1-in. flowers of soft yellow or gold, excellent for pot display.

ESPALIER (es PAL yer). This term is used both for a trellis or lattice on which a fruit tree is trained and for a tree so handled. This practice is more common abroad than in the United States, where the long, hot growing season is not so well adapted to keeping the plants under strict control. It has the advantages of saving space, of giving the trees maximum care and, when necessary, shelter, and of helping produce high-quality fruit. It is therefore sometimes followed in small gardens or in sections of large estates that are in the charge of expert gardeners skilled in the art.

In employing the espalier system, dwarf trees (mainly pear or apple, but any of the stone fruits if desired) are used, and the branches, restricted to a definite, symmetrical number, are trained in a single plane parallel to the support, either horizontally, vertically, or diagonally. The branching is started low, and by constant heading back (pinching of unwanted shoots) and tying of the stems to the trellis, the desired form and design of branches is developed; the fruits are allowed to form on selected spurs at uniform intervals.

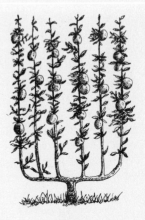

Espalier

This training and spacing results in giving all the fruit maximum light and air; trees on espalier trellises are therefore less likely to suffer from abrupt temperature changes than those grown close against walls. See TRAINING PLANTS.

ETIOLATED. Blanched or whitened from lack of sunlight. The term is generally applied to spindly plants that have been grown in darkness and in whose tissues the green color bodies (chloroplasts) have been changed to white (leucoplasts).

EUCALYPTUS (yoo kah LIP tus). A genus of rapidly growing, broad-leaved, evergreen trees of subtropical and temperate climates, many of them commonly known as gum trees. Members of the Myrtaceae (Myrtle Family), they grow to great size and are of ornamental value, having attractive gray-green or bluish, lance-shaped or ovate leaves on pendulous twigs. Some are profuse bloomers, bearing umbels of white or pink flowers, which are a valuable source of honey. There are dwarf types of some species, while juvenile forms of others are grown as foliage plants. Some endure extremes of heat and cold, and the whole group is notably free from insects because of the strong aromatic oil in the wood. Propagation is by seed sown under screens.

PRINCIPAL SPECIES

E. camaldulensis (red gum), growing to 200 ft., is resistant to drought and withstands great heat, yet it endures some frost. It will thrive in an alkaline soil and survive flooding for a prolonged period.

E. globulus (blue gum) is the species most often planted in the United States. It is a rapid grower, particularly suited to dry soil, and makes a fine windbreak. A majestic tree, it grows to 300 ft. and bears flowers 1½ in. across. Var. *compacta* is well suited to garden use, being dwarf with a round, compact form.

Eucalyptus globulus

E. sideroxylon (red ironbark) is a tall tree with dark, persistent bark. Var. *rosea* has rose-colored flowers. Var. *pallens* has red blossoms. Both varieties are profuse bloomers.

Other species include: *E. botryoides* (bastard mahogany), *E. resinifera* (red-mahogany), and *E. robusta* (swamp-mahogany).

EUCHARIS (YOO kah ris). A genus of bulbous herbs with long-stemmed, broad basal leaves and dazzling clusters of fragrant flowers, belonging to the Amarylidaceae (Amaryllis Family), and native to the Colombian Andes. The flowers are purest white with pale green in the daffodil-like cup and are lightly lemon scented. Greenhouse subjects except in subtropical climates, they are unrivaled for beauty and freedom of bloom; however, even without flowers, a well-grown eucharis makes a fine foliage plant, in some ways better suited to interior decoration than the ubiquitous *Spathiphyllum* (peace-lily).

The bulbs should be planted in coarse fibrous soil with charcoal and sand. Flowering is stimulated by free watering and full sunshine. Plants are relatively pest free, but mealybugs can be a problem on the leaf reverses along the main stem. Remove them with cotton swabs dipped in dena-

tured alcohol or spray with an insecticidal soap solution. Repeat weekly until clear. See also MEALYBUG.

E. grandiflora (Amazon-lily, star-of-Bethlehem) is a popular greenhouse subject. There are some smaller species in cultivation, which collectors enjoy.

EUCOMIS (YOO koh mis) **punctata.** A bulbous, South African herb of the Liliaceae (Lily Family), commonly known as pineapple flower. Its raceme of green and brown flowers is borne 1 ft. above a rosette of many large, purple-spotted, lance-shaped leaves and is topped by a cluster of leafy bracts, something like the pineapple. The plant is hardy to Zone 10, where bulbs can be left in the ground all year; in the North, they are grown only in greenhouses.

EUGENIA (yoo JEE nee ah). A genus of evergreen trees and shrubs of the Myrtaceae (Myrtle Family), mostly tropical and subtropical. Many species formerly included in this genus are now classified in the genus SYZYGIUM, but this genus retains the fruiting species, such as *E. uniflora* (Surinam-cherry, pitanga), a tropical shrub or small tree with fragrant white flowers and eight-ribbed, crimson, edible fruits; and *E. brasiliensis* (Brazil-cherry, grumichama); as well as ornamentals that are valued for their fine leaf texture.

EULALIA (yoo LAY lee uh). Common name for *Miscanthus sinensis*; see MISCANTHUS.

EULOPHIA (yoo LOH fee uh). About 300 species of small to large (3 ft. high) terrestrial orchids native to the tropics worldwide but prevalent in Africa. Pseudobulbs rise from underground tubers or corms. Several to many showy flowers in shades of rose, white, purple, and green are borne on erect spikes. The leaves are leathery or soft and plicate. The petals are broader than the sepals, with a three-lobed lip the same color as the petals. Two lateral lobes partially enclose the column; the lip may be spurred.

Plants prefer a mixture of peat, sphagnum

moss, sand, and dried cow manure, and they do best in filtered shade. When in growth, they should be watered abundantly. Variously hardy to Zone 7, some species will withstand a mild frost and can be grown outdoors with protection. The type species is *E. guineensis*.

EUONYMUS (yoo AHN i mus). A genus of deciduous or evergreen shrubs, small trees, creeping ground covers, or climbing vines, widely distributed in temperate regions, belonging to the Celastraceae (Stafftree Family), and commonly known as spindle tree. They are mostly upright (a few prostrate species do well in sun or partial shade) and are not particular as to soil. The flowers are inconspicuous, but most have colorful fruits. Most of the deciduous kinds, and a few of the evergreen, are hardy in cool climates. The latter make good hedges or ground covers, thriving under city and seaside conditions. Propagation is by seed, layers, and cuttings.

ENEMIES

Euonymus stems are often afflicted with aerial CROWN GALL tumors; the only remedy is cutting out infected portions. Various leaf spots of minor importance may disfigure foliage. Mildew, prevalent in the South and West, can be controlled with fungicides or sometimes merely by a stream of water directed against the shrub under high pressure. See also LEAF SPOT; MILDEW.

The chief pest is the euonymus scale, which is common on most species and also on bittersweet. The female resembles the oyster-shell scale; the male is white and slender; the young appear in early spring, and successive generations feed on both wood and foliage until late fall. Spray thoroughly in early spring with a miscible oil and in the summer, as the young scales hatch, with a white-oil emulsion and sulfur insecticide mixture. Do not use an oil spray if the temperature is nearing 90°F. Consult a local extension service for recommendations. See also SCALE INSECTS.

PRINCIPAL SPECIES

E. alata (winged euonymus), native to Asia and hardy in Zones 4–8, is a wide-spreading deciduous shrub to 8 ft. or more, distinguished by its corky-ridged branches. The leaves turn a brilliant red in the fall, and when these have fallen, the small but numerous brightly colored fruits are conspicuous. Cv. 'Compacta' is a dense, rounded form suitable for a hedge.

E. americanus (strawberry bush) is a native North American deciduous shrub growing to 8 ft., hardy to Zone 6, of undistinguished habit and inconspicuous flowers, but spectacular in fall with pink, warty fruits and scarlet-covered seeds.

E. atropurpurea (burning bush, wahoo) is a large native deciduous shrub or tree growing to 25 ft., with small purple flowers. The leaves turn yellow in fall, and the fruit is scarlet. Hardy in Zones 5–9.

E. europaea is a European deciduous shrub or tree to 25 ft., hardy in Zones 4–7. It is very showy in the fall with smooth, pinkish red fruits. There are forms with fruit of varying color, from white to crimson.

E. fortunei (formerly listed as *E. radicans*), native to Asia and hardy in Zones 5–9, is a trailing evergreen that can climb to 40 ft. or more on a rough surface by means of stem rootlets. It is extremely variable and useful in all its forms. Var. *vegeta* has larger leaves of dull green and handsome fruit. It makes a good low-spreading bush, tight hedge, or high climber on a wall and is very hardy. Cv. 'Carrierei' is somewhat similar but has lustrous leaves and is not such a good climber. Var. *acuta* is a glossy, pointed-leaved form, useful as a ground cover or to cover a low wall. Cv. 'Colorata' is similar but the leaves turn reddish-purple in the fall. 'Minima' (sometimes called *E. kewensis*) has tiny dark green leaves marked white along the veins, a good choice for the rock garden. 'Emerald and Gold' is low growing, to 2 ft., with yellow-margined leaves. 'Gracilis' has leaves variegated with white, pink, or yellow. 'Dart's Blanket', about 16 in. high and spreading as a ground cover, is somewhat salt tolerant and has dark green, waxy leaves that turn purple underneath in the fall.

E. japonica, from Asia, is a tender evergreen growing to 15 ft., with dark green, glossy leaves. It is a good screen or hedge plant for seaside gardens and tolerates shade well. There are numerous cultivars with white and yellow variegated leaves. Hardy to Zone 7.

E. radicans (winter creeper) is a slow-growing vine, excellent for covering walls.

EUPATORIUM (yoo pah TOH ree um). A large genus of flowering herbs, belonging to the Asteraceae (Aster Family), comprising a number of good specimens for the ornamental border, wild garden, or greenhouse. Many are hardy to Zone 3. The hardy types are very easily cultivated, thriving in ordinary, good, light garden soil. While they can be grown from seed, propagation is usually done from root division in spring.

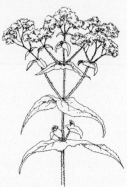

Eupatorium purpureum

Two root and crown diseases, CROWN ROT and rhizoctonia rot may be responsible for the sudden wiping out of stands of this plant. At the first indication of wilting, remove all diseased plants.

A BOTRYTIS blight may kill tops back to a lesion a few inches from the ground, but prompt removal of infected portions often allows side shoots that grow from below the lesion to continue blooming.

PRINCIPAL SPECIES

E. coelestinum (mist flower, hardy- or perennial-ageratum), a native plant to 3 ft. Blooming from late summer until late in the fall, its blue to violet flowers in delicate, fluffy heads closely resemble the true AGERATUM, but the plant is taller. It grows well in sun or shade and makes a pleasing color combination planted in a sunny border with bright-hued Mexican zinnias.

E. corrolata (flowering-spurge) is a very hardy species growing 18–36 in. with tiny flowers framed by white bracts. The smooth leaves are 1½–2 in., turning red in the fall.

E. ianthinum, with violet flower clusters, is a

tender Mexican species easily grown in the northern greenhouse and readily propagated from cuttings.

E. perfoliatum (boneset, thoroughwort) grows 2–3 ft. with grayish white flowers in flat-topped clusters. It was once used in medicines and is often seen in old gardens.

E. purpureum (Joe Pye weed) is a tall, rank-growing species with rose or rose-purple flowers in large open clusters, useful for naturalizing in the wild garden in low, marshy ground. The common name derives from a belief that the plant was used for medicinal purposes in the early days of Massachusetts by an Indian doctor called Joe Pye. Other similar species known as Joe Pye weed are the smaller *E. maculatum*, growing to 6 ft., and *E. verticillatum*, growing to 8 ft. with purple flowers in rounded clusters.

E. rugosum (white snakeroot), formerly listed as *E. urticaefolium*, grows to 4 ft. with massed heads of white flowers. It was once used to produce medicines. If chewed, it is poisonous and is a problem where cattle graze.

EUPHORBIA (yoo FOR bee ah). A very large and diverse genus, widely distributed in tropical and temperate climates, commonly known as spurge and comprising the principal genus of the Euphorbiaceae (Spurge Family). Some are desert plants and assume a cactuslike form; some are leafy tropical shrubs; and others are hardy herbaceous perennials and annuals. They have abundant milky juice, which in many species has poisonous properties.

There are many hardy species suitable for the rock garden and border; many of them are quite weedy. Other larger succulent species are grown in cool-climate greenhouses or outdoors in warm areas. One species, *E. pulcherrima*, with its brilliant scarlet bracts, is the popular winter-flowering poinsettia.

CULTURE

The fleshy kinds are hardy only to Zones 10–11 and are grown under similar conditions to those required by cacti, adding interest to any collection of succulents. They thrive in a porous and not very rich soil. Propagation is by cuttings, which grow best if dried somewhat before being placed in a mixture of sand and charcoal.

Shrubby plants, like *E. pulcherrima*, are often potted or greenhouse subjects. They can be cut back after a rest period and grown on, but usually young plants are produced annually from cuttings. These are rooted at intervals starting in spring in order to have plants of different sizes. Hardy only in warmer parts of the sunbelt, they can be grown outdoors during the summer in cool climates but require uniform conditions of warmth and moisture after being transferred to the greenhouse.

The herbaceous perennials, mostly hardy to Zone 7 or colder, are propagated by seed or division. A few annual kinds are easily grown from seed and are useful for the flower garden.

Poinsettias. Grown as potted plants, poinsettias do best in a mixture of half loam and fourths of dried cow manure and leaf mold. They are grown from cuttings about 3 in. long, set three in a small pot, and kept in a close atmosphere in a warm frame until rooted. Afterward they are shifted into larger pots, thus avoiding the checks caused by abrupt shifting; disturb the roots as little as possible.

Euphorbia pulcherrima

One large plant or a few small ones can be flowered in a 5–7 in. pot. When flowering is over, the plants should be dried off and allowed to rest in a warm place for three to four months. Then they can be cut back, brought into light and heat, and forced into growth in spring to supply new cuttings. A gift plant rested and cut back, if grown on slowly or plunged outdoors over summer, will sometimes bloom again. Plants must receive full light and sunshine at all times and should be protected from sudden changes of temperature.

MEALYBUG infestations are a common problem on poinsettias. The poinsettia root aphid can be controlled by dusting the earth ball and the inside of the pot with insecticidal dust or by submerging the earth ball in a mild insecticide solution. Poinsettias and other euphorbias suffer a phytotoxic effect from insecticidal soap sprays.

See also HOUSEPLANTS; INSECT CONTROL.

FLESHY SPECIES

E. canariensis grows to 20 ft. and has thick four- to six-angled stems and black spines.

E. grandicornis is one of the most striking in appearance, with broadly winged, angled stems and large spines.

Euphorbia lactea

E. lactea (spotted spurge) is a fast grower of candelabrum form with three- or four-angled branches marked with a white band down the middle. It is often used for hedges in warm regions.

E. meloformis (melon spurge) is a curious plant with deeply angled, melon-shaped main stems, which are deeply ribbed and practically leafless, but may have small offsets attached. It is hardy in Zones 10–11.

E. milii var. *splendens* (crown-of-thorns) has flexible stems to 4 ft. long, well armed with stout spines. It can be trained to a form and is attractive with its bright red bracts produced most of the year.

E. tirucalli (milkbush) is easily cultivated, forming a small succulent tree with a dense head of slender round branches whose sap is poisonous.

SHRUBBY SPECIES

E. fulgens (scarlet-plume) is a small shrub with slender drooping branches bedecked with small orange-scarlet bracts, very decorative and lasting as cut sprays. It is best grown from annual cuttings and kept under warm conditions.

E. pulcherrima (poinsettia, Christmas flower) is a tropical shrub growing to 10 ft. or more in its native environment. Although suitable for garden culture in frost-free regions (Zones 10–11), it is more commonly grown under glass for Christmas decoration. Its large flat rosettes of rich red bracts surround central clusters of small yellow flowers. In var. *plenissima*, some of the flowers have been transformed into red bracts, giving the appearance of doubling. Var. *alba* and *rosea* are forms with white and pink bracts. Yellow-bracted poinsettias have been introduced, adding to the array of reds, pinks, white, and marbleized bicolors. Cultivars have also been developed for growing in cooler greenhouses, thus being more energy efficient.

HERBACEOUS SPECIES

E. corollata (flowering spurge) is native to eastern North America, growing to 3 ft. and making an attractive show in the flower border with its white bracts. It is also useful for cutting.

E. cyathophora (fire-on-the-mountain) is an annual with toothed leaves. It is very similar to and sometimes cultivated as *E. heterophylla*, but its upper leaves and bracts are red or red based.

E. cyparissias (cypress spurge) is a small, fine-leaved perennial, which has long been cultivated and is now naturalized in the eastern states. It is a good ground cover on dry banks, its narrow dark green leaves giving it a mosslike appearance.

E. epithymoides forms a rounded clump 12 in. or higher and is very attractive in spring flower gardens with its yellow floral leaves.

E. heterophylla (Mexican fireplant) is a bushy, easily cultivated annual growing to 3 ft.; it has leaves of varying shapes, the upper leaves and bracts marked with green or purple, never red. This name is often misapplied to forms of *E. cyathophora.*

E. lathyris (caper spurge, moleplant) is a stout, unbranched annual or biennial growing to 3 ft., with oblong or lance-shaped leaves, native to Europe and naturalized in North America. One of its common names is derived from its reported use for repelling moles and gophers when planted in the garden.

E. marginata (snow-on-the-mountain) is an old annual flower-garden favorite, growing to 2 ft.; it has white bracts and margins on the upper leaves.

E. myrsinites is a fleshy prostrate plant with gray-green leaves and attractive yellow flower heads in early spring. It shows to good advantage in stony places.

Euphorbia marginata

E. wulfenii is a somewhat woody perennial herb growing to 3 ft., with two-horned yellow glands and tight spirals of oblong leaves.

EUPHORBIACEAE (yoo for bee AY see ee). The Spurge Family, an important group of herbs, shrubs, and trees of varied habit, includes many ornamental forms and many plants of economic importance, which yield edible nuts and fruits, rubber, and valuable medicinal products. Some are cactuslike, and most are characterized by a milky, acrid juice. The flowers vary widely in form: in poinsettia, the showy parts are actually colored bracts. Among the cultivated genera are *Acalypha*, *Aleurites*, *Breynia*, *Codiaeum*, *Euphorbia*, *Hevea*, *Manihot*, *Pedilanthus*, *Phyllanthus*, *Ricinus*, and *Sapium*.

EUROPEAN CORN BORER. An inch long, grayish pink caterpillar, *Ostrinia nubilolis*, followed by a yellow-brown, nocturnal moth that lays white eggs on lower surfaces of leaves. Two or three generations are produced each year. Emerging larvae feed on leaves before moving to corn stalks. It also infests grasses and flower stalks. To feed, the borer enters a stalk, which can be split below the bore hole to remove it. It will winter over in the bore hole, so fall cleanup is

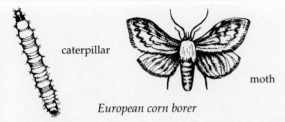

caterpillar

moth

European corn borer

very important. The eggs are often eaten by lady beetles, lacewings, and braconid and trichogramma wasps. To reduce the risk of attack, plant corn early and use early varieties. Resistant kinds include 'Butter and Sugar', 'Apache', and 'Wonderful'. Soil should be 40°F for two days before planting. Another control is spraying with **Bacillus thuringiensis** (Bt, commonly available as Biotrol, Dipel, or Thuricide). See also BORERS.

EURYA (yoo RĪ ah). A genus of Japanese evergreen shrubs allied to the CAMELLIA and thriving under similar conditions and best grown in Zone 10. *E. japonica*, the species usually cultivated, is a tall shrub or small tree. The handsome, glossy leaves are either roundish or long, with toothed edges. The var. *variegata* is a handsome, decorative plant for the cool greenhouse, thriving in sandy loam, with peat or leaf mold. The flowers are small and inconspicuous but have an unpleasant odor.

EURYALE (yoo RĪ ah lee) **ferox.** An aquatic herb belonging to the Nymphaeacaea (Waterlily Family), with large, deep green, round, platterlike leaves (1–4 ft. across) with turned-up rim and a network of air pockets on the spiny purplish underside. The small flowers (2 in. across) are deep purple. The plant is native to India, where it is cultivated for the edible seeds. As a self-sowing annual, it is hardy to Zone 5.

EUSTOMA (YOO stoh mah) **grandiflorum.** A very showy annual or short-lived tender perennial member of the Gentianaceae (Gentian Family),

native from Nebraska to Mexico, and commonly known as prairie gentian. Grayish green clasping waxy leaves on stems 1½–3 ft. hold large, open bell-shaped, satiny flowers of deep purple, white, or pink. It is little cultivated but worthy of a place in the border. Select color forms are widely available. Easily grown from seed or cutting, it can be extended by starting seeds in summer and carrying them over winter in a frame, the plants blooming early the following summer. It should be planted in dry, loamy soil in an open, sunny location.

EUSTREPHUS (YOO stree fus). A genus of Australian twining plants belonging to the Liliaceae (Lily Family). They are easily grown in pots or a greenhouse border and outdoors in warm climates (Zones 10–11). The light blue flowers are clustered in the leaf axils and are followed by orange-colored berries. Plants provide good material for decorative work.

EUTERPE (yoo TUR pee). A genus of slender feather palms, some of which are commonly known in Brazil as Assai palms. They have erect trunks, often in clumps and showing the ringed scars of fallen leaves. The leaves are spineless and feathery. Native to warm parts of South America and the West Indies, these palms are not reliably hardy even in Florida, but they are often grown indoors, where they require moist air and rich soil, supplemented with overhead sprinkling.

E. oleracea (wild cabbage palm) has edible terminal bulbs, which are processed as hearts of palm; harvesting them kills the plant. It also has edible fruit.

E. edulis, grown occasionally in Florida, has clumps of slender trunks to 100 ft., wide-spreading leaves, and large clusters of purple-black fruit.

EVENING-PRIMROSE. Common name for OENOTHERA, a large and widely distributed genus of day- or evening-blooming, annual, biennial, and perennial herbs. The Evening-Primrose Family is ONAGRACEAE.

EVERGREENS. A term applied to plants that hold their foliage from season to season, often for a long period of time—some pines retain their needles for fifteen years. Eventually the leaves are shed and replaced by new ones, but so gradually that the loss is not noticed. Climatic conditions have a great deal to do with whether a plant is evergreen or not; it may retain its foliage in a mild climate, but shed its leaves in the winter when planted in the North, even though it is perfectly hardy. *Ligustrum vulgare* (common privet) is entirely evergreen in the South but only partially so north of Philadelphia.

KINDS OF EVERGREENS

For horticultural purposes, evergreens may be conveniently divided into two classes: (1) the narrow-leaved evergreens (including most conifers), which have needlelike, scalelike, or flat leaves; and (2) the broad-leaved evergreeens. The word CONIFER means strictly trees or shrubs bearing woody cones containing naked seeds; it is often considered synonymous with evergreen, but botanically it includes a few trees, such as the larches, which are distinctly deciduous.

Evergreens have innumerable uses in landscape work and in the garden, especially the slow-growing kinds that are also long-lived, giving stability to the landscape design or garden picture. There is great variation in their color, from the somber green of some of the spruces to the frosty silver of many of the firs and the bronze and purple hues of the junipers, while cultivars provide gold and white effects, especially valuable as accent points and for contrast. The larger species are best used for windbreaks or for specimens in large lawns or other expanses, where they increase in stateliness and beauty through the years and form an appropriate background for flowers and deciduous autumn foliage.

CULTURE

Narrow-leaved Evergreens. The best time to transplant evergreens is in the spring when the buds are swelling or in autumn after the new growth has ripened. Nursery-grown specimens are much more easily transplanted than those collected from the wild, for in the nursery the root system has been kept compact and bushy by repeated transplantings. Also, the plants are delivered with a ball of earth wrapped in burlap, which prevents the roots from drying out.

Dig a hole considerably larger than the burlapped rootball, and without removing the covering, set the plant in the hole at just about its previous level. Then unfasten, open out, and leave the burlap; it will rot in time. Fill the hole with good topsoil at the same time so as to settle the soil. Be sure

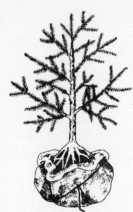

Transplant with burlap covering on rootball

the earth is well settled, leaving no air pockets. Then spread an inch or two of mulch on the surface to prevent evaporation of moisture from the roots. There should be a slight depression rather than a mound around the base of the plant. This will hold the water in instead of shedding it. Water daily if necessary until the plant is well established. The drying out of newly planted evergreens is a common cause of loss.

If evergreens are deeply mulched, the ground will not freeze so far down and the plants will be able to secure moisture from the soil even in winter, which is helpful since they have no true dormant season.

Well-rotted manure is probably the best fertilizer for evergreens. Sometimes a balanced plant food or one rich in nitrogen is given to stimulate growth. This should be dug into the soil and the area well watered. It can also be applied in solution or in holes driven at 2-ft. intervals down to the feeding roots.

Broad-leaved Evergreens. These are handled essentially in the same manner as narrow-leaved kinds, but tender species can be dug and heeled-in over winter where they will not be injured by hard freezing and set out again in the open in the spring. Specimens planted in spring or fall are the most likely to make rapid growth. As with narrow-leaved kinds, properly balled nursery-grown plants are more successfully moved than collected stock from the wild.

Many of the broad-leaved evergreens belong to the Ericaceae (Heath Family), *Rhododendron* and *Kalmia* being outstanding examples. These plants thrive best in an acid soil and, for the most part, require partial shade. Therefore, a suitable location should be selected and the ground prepared with great care. They should be planted in soil free from lime, rich in humus, and provided with good drainage. If available, a location under the light shade of high conifers is ideal. After planting, water them thoroughly. Mulch with leaves, pine needles, wood chips, or similar material. If the soil is well supplied with humus, and if a plentiful leaf mulch is maintained, any special feeding is best done with fertilizers of an acid-forming nature. After the plants have become established, the soil surrounding the plants should be disturbed as little as possible, for the roots are very near the surface, and there is a definite mycorrhizal association between the feeding roots of ericaceous plants and certain fungi.

ENEMIES

Physiological Troubles. Some of the most conspicuous diseases of evergreens are due not to fungi, bacteria, or other living organisms, but to physiological conditions. Trees that retain their foliage throughout the year need a constant supply of moisture. Winter drying, resulting in a reddening or browning of the needles, is caused by the rapid loss of water from the leaves when the water in the soil is frozen and cannot be taken up by the roots. Root freezing or other injury has the same result. Strong winds or intense sunlight may increase evaporation to such an extent that parts of the plant wilt and die.

Simple precautions will help protect valuable evergreens from such troubles: apply a mulch to prevent root freezing and excessive evaporation of water from the soil, and water generously late in the fall. Providing additional shade by means of a windbreak gives evergreen plants an extra advantage against early spring sun and wind.

Fungal Diseases. Needle cast (defoliation of conifers) is caused by several fungi. The needles show yellowish or brown bands and later turn entirely yellow or brown and drop off. Sometimes they exhibit the round or oblong, black fruiting bodies of the fungus. Young trees, which are more subject to these diseases than old ones, should be sprayed with BORDEAUX MIXTURE before rainy periods when the spores are most likely to be spread and start new infections.

Heartwood and root decay, though most serious in forests, can damage specimen trees. The most destructive of the heartwood type is the pecky wood decay that gives the heartwood around the decayed area a purplish tinge, fills the affected reddish wood with holes or pockets, and produces a triangular, shelflike fruiting body at old branch wounds; see BRACKET FUNGI. Another wood decay common in the western states appears as large, rusty brown, hoof-shaped fruiting bodies emerging from branch stubs. Heartwood diseases can be prevented to a great extent by careful pruning and proper care of all wounds, especially broken branch stubs. All broken limbs should be sawed off evenly against the tree and the wound, if over 2 in. across, covered with a dressing. Cavities should be properly cleaned out and treated. See TREE SURGERY.

Basal decay is usually more important among ornamental conifers than are the wood rots. One kind occurring in pine, fir, larch, spruce, hemlock, and arborvitae may spread from the roots upward into the trunk for several feet. The usual result is the uprooting of the tree in a heavy wind. The soft, red-brown, umbrella-shaped fruiting bodies grow from exposed or lightly buried roots. The mushroom root rot is common on many kinds of coniferous trees; see ARMILLARIA ROOT ROT. The control of root diseases is somewhat difficult. Remove diseased parts of roots and the fungus fruiting bodies. Dig an "isolation ditch" around diseased trees to prevent the spread of infection.

Insect Pests. All types of evergreens are subject to attacks by spider mites, which give the plants a brownish or grayish, pale appearance. Examined closely, the needles are seen to be mottled brown or gray and covered with fine webs. Small reddish eggs and the tiny mites can be seen with a magnifying glass. Occurring abundantly with the approach of warm weather, mites can cause serious injury. Spray early in the season, before new growth starts, with a miscible oil or an oil emulsion diluted according to manufacturer's directions for evergreens. After growth starts, syringe forcibly with the hose, dust with sulfur on warm days, or spray with lime-sulfur (summer strength) or with a rotenone compound. See MITES; RED SPIDER MITE; SPRAYING.

Scale insects attack pines, spruces, hemlocks, and junipers. Spray before growth starts with a dormant oil. Lime-sulfur (1 to 9) should be substituted in spraying those types of juniper in which the leaves form a cup.

See also INSECT CONTROL.

EVERLASTINGS. Many flowers are extensively used for permanent winter bouquets because they retain their form and color when dried. Some or all of them may be known by the French word "immortelle." Many of them are also attractive subjects for the garden or greenhouse. Most everlastings of the hardy garden belong to the Asteraceae (Aster Family), with papery ray florets coming in delicate colors.

Cutting. The best time for harvesting depends largely on the type, but a few general rules can be applied. Asters and related flowers should be cut just as the buds are fully developed and are beginning to open. Otherwise the blossoms may turn brown or spread too wide and shatter or fall apart when dry. *Gomphrena* should be picked only when the flowers are well matured. *Gypsophila* (baby's-breath) and *Limonium* (sea-lavender) can be picked whenever the flowers are of suitable form and can be used at once in dry bouquets.

Drying. After cutting, strip off the leaves. Flowers should be hung in small bunches tied together with heads downward in warm dry quarters with good ventilation, out of strong sun-

light. Do not attempt to arrange them in vases until the last bit of moisture has left the stems. If stored in an upright position, the heads will bend over and dry in distorted shapes, but drying upside down will retain a more natural form.

For curving sprays, a few fresh stems can be hung singly over a rounded surface, such as that made by tacking heavy paper to the edge of a shelf, rounding it out well, and tacking the lower edge to the underside of a shelf. In arranging dried flowers in bouquets, a bunch of dried sphagnum moss, shredded paper, or a few inches of clean dry sand will help keep them in place.

Drying flowers

Grasses. Many annual grasses are well suited for drying and arranging with everlasting flowers. Although they usually do not retain their color when dried, most are easily dyed, taking color much more satisfactorily than many everlasting blossoms, with the exception of *Briza*, whose glossy surface must be treated before it will take dye. All dried grasses are useful even without coloring. Any of them can be preserved if cut at the proper time, just before the flowers open. Then tie the grasses in small bunches and hang them in the shade where there is good ventilation. If not needed immediately, when the bunches are thoroughly dry, pack them away, but not in a dusty place. Cutting the grasses at various stages of growth will provide additional variety. See also ORNAMENTAL GRASSES.

EVODIA (ee VOH dee ah). A genus including numerous deciduous and evergreen trees and shrubs native to Asia and Australia, and belonging to the Rutaceae (Rue Family). Three or four species from China are the hardiest, but they are not extensively planted. They are small trees, distinguished by their handsome compound, aromatic leaves. The small whitish flowers are borne in panicles in summer and are followed by showy black seeds. They grow well in ordinary garden soil, and the seeds germinate readily. Various species are hardy in Zones 5–9.

E. danielii (Korean evodia), a small, wide-spreading tree growing to 30 ft., has dark green leaves with seven to eleven leaflets. Bees love the small white flowers, which bloom from mid to late summer.

E. hupehensis grows to 50 ft. with five to nine leaflets and is not quite as hardy as *E. danielii*.

EXACUM (EK sa kum). A genus of summer-blooming, European annual, biennial, or perennial herbs belonging to the Gentianaceae (Gentian Family). The flat-petaled, white, lilac, or purplish blue flowers are borne in branching clusters atop leafy stems. Usually they are grown from seed as potted plants, though hardy in warm climates. Seed can be sown in light, well-drained soil in March or, for larger specimens, the previous August. Shade from hot sunlight.

E. affine (Persian- or German-violet), with bluish flowers, and *E. macranthum*, whose purplish-blue flowers are ringed with yellow in the throat, are both biennials about 2 ft. high. *E. zeylanicum* is an annual whose smaller blue flowers have blunter petals.

EXHIBITIONS. Growers of flowers and vegetables may wish to exhibit them or enter them into judged competition. Most exhibition of plants takes place at fairs and garden clubs or at the meetings of special growers' clubs. Usually there are standards and specific rules about preparation and presentation of the plant material, which can be obtained from the organization sponsoring the exhibition. There are also exhibitions of floral arrangements.

EXOCHORDA (eks oh KOR dah). A genus of hardy deciduous shrubs from Asia, belonging to the Rosaceae (Rose Family), resembling some of the spiraeas, and commonly known as pearlbush.

They grow best in a rather light, rich soil in a sunny place and are among the most attractive of spring-flowering shrubs. Their white flowers in terminal racemes are followed by capsular fruits with winged seeds. They should be pruned back after flowering to keep them in good shape. The species listed are hardy in Zones 5–8. Propagation is by seed or softwood cuttings.

PRINCIPAL SPECIES

E. giraldii is very similar to *E. racemosa* but is more vigorous. Var. *wilsonii* is stronger still and more floriferous—the best of the group.

E. korolkowii, one of the earliest shrubs to leaf out in spring, has darker and denser foliage than the others but is not so floriferous.

E. x macrantha, a hybrid between *E. racemosa* and *E. korolkowi*, resembles the first-named parent but is more upright and vigorous.

E. racemosa (common pearlbush), of rather slender, spreading habit, grows to 10 ft. and bears racemes of pearly buds and pure white flowers.

EXOTIC. A term used as a noun or adjective, meaning not native, applied to a plant introduced from a foreign area. *Mesembryanthemum crystallinum* (iceplant) is native to South Africa but is exotic elsewhere; goldenrod is native to the United States but is an exotic plant in Europe. In contrast with exotic as a noun, we have indigen, of which the corresponding adjective form is "indigenous."

EXTENSION SERVICES. In addition to local garden centers, Cooperative Extension Services are excellent sources of information on agricultural enterprises in specific areas. Many provide soil-testing services (usually for a fee). They also give advice regarding suitable plants for a given area and insect or disease control for home gardens as well as commercial crops. Extension personnel are located in county or area offices and substations in each state as well as agricultural colleges of state universitites. For more specific information, contact the Cooperative Extension Service nearest you. See listings in appendix.

EYE. A term variously applied in horticulture as (1) to the dark center of such flowers as *Thunbergia* (black-eyed Susan); (2) to the sunken buds on certain tubers like the common potato; (3) to the branch buds on stems of shrubs, trees, and woody vines and the shoots of herbs asexually propagated. In cases (2) and (3), the term is most frequently used in connection with propagation, such as in single-eye or two-eye cuttings.

F

FABACEAE (fah BAY see ee). The Bean Family, formerly known as Leguminosae (Pea Family), a large group comprising herbs (many of them climbing), widely distributed in diverse situations in most parts of the world.

Of great significance horticulturally is the fact that all leguminous plants have microorganisms (rhizobia) inhabiting their roots and have the peculiar property of being agents in the transformation of atmospheric nitrogen into nitrogenous compounds available for the use of the plants. This is accomplished by certain soil bacteria that invade the roots of legumes, form colonies, and irritate the root tissues, which develop characteristic nodules. Here the bacteria obtain carbohydrates from the plant and carry on the nitrogen-fixation process, storing up the resulting nitrogenous food material. This, if not used by

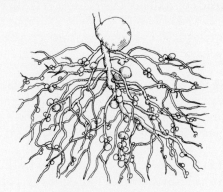

Nitrogen-fixing nodules

the plant itself, is added to the soil when the plant dies and its roots decay, thereby becoming available for other plants. Thus, besides being able to secure the nitrogen they need (even when there is an insufficient supply in the soil), legumes actually add to that supply and, as far as the nitrogen is concerned, leave the soil more fertile than before they grew. For this reason, legumes such as clovers, vetches, and soybeans are commonly included (to be plowed under) in crop rotations to increase the nitrogen content of the soil as well as to add humus as they decay.

Among the many useful genera in this important family are: *Acacia, Adenanthera, Albizia, Amorpha, Baptisia, Calliandra, Cassia, Ceratonia, Cercis, Chorizema, Cladrastis, Clitoria, Coronilla, Cytisus, Desmodium* (trefoil), *Dolochos, Erythrina, Genista, Gliricidia, Indigofera, Laburnum, Lathyrus* (sweet pea), *Lens* (lentil), *Lotus, Lupinus, Medicago* (alfalfa), *Mimosa, Phaseolus* (bean), *Pisum* (pea), *Robinia* (locust), *Sophora, Tamarindus, Trifolium* (clover), *Vicia* (vetch), *Vigna*, and *Wisteria*.

FABIANA (fay bee AYN ah). A genus of small, heathlike shrubs of the Solonaceae (Nightshade Family), commonly known as false heath. They are native to South America and are hardy only to Zone 9. *F. imbricata*, the best-known species, is sometimes grown in a cool greenhouse and also outdoors in mild climates. It is a branching shrub growing to 8 ft. and has small, overlapping, scalelike leaves and small white flowers freely produced. Propagation is by cuttings.

FAGACEAE (fah GAY see ee). The Beech Family, which includes *Fagus* (beech), *Quercus* (oak), and *Castanea* (chestnut), all woody trees or shrubs distributed mostly in the temperate and subtropical regions of the Northern Hemisphere. Male flowers are borne in catkins; female flowers are clustered or solitary; the fruit is a nut enclosed in a cup or burr.

FAGUS (FAY gus). A genus of hardy deciduous trees belonging to the Fagaceae (Beech Family), and commonly known as beech. Related to oaks and chestnuts, they are hard wooded, long-lived, and beautiful in their light gray bark and various forms. The common name is said to be derived from a Saxon word meaning "book," as records were written on the bark and on tablets made of its wood. There are several species, all natives of the North Temperate Zones of North America, Europe, and Asia, but only two, with their numerous varieties, are often grown in gardens.

All are round-headed, spreading trees growing to 80 ft. or more that have smooth, light-colored bark. They are among the most decorative of garden subjects in form, color, cleanliness, and grace. The species are very similar, but the varieties include forms with brilliantly colored and finely cut leaves, weeping or pendulous branches, and other interesting characteristics. Spring fills them with heads of staminate flowers, which are followed by three-cornered burry nuts containing edible kernels.

The beech thrives best where soil is protected by a mulch of its own leaves. It is customarily stated that they are partial to limestone soil, but fine specimens and large stands are found on acid soils, preferring rather dry hillsides. Propagation is by seeds stratified over winter and sown in spring. Seedlings should be frequently transplanted to prevent the development of long taproots, since the trees suffer if these are injured.

The trees are particularly free from dead branches, insect pests, and fungi; however, a serious bark disease associated with the presence of the beech scale and the fungus *Nectria*, prevalent in Canada, has spread through the northeastern states. Use a dormant application of an oil spray to check the scale and also to control woolly aphids that cover the undersurface of the leaves of the European beech with disfiguring white masses. A sulfur insecticide can also be used when the young leaves first appear. See also INSECT CONTROL.

A mottle-leaf or scorch disease, resulting in premature leaf fall, is prevalent on American beech, but the exact cause is not known.

PRINCIPAL SPECIES

F. grandifolia (American beech) grows to 75 ft. in cultivation and over 100 ft. in the wild. It has handsome, smooth, clean, gray bark on the trunk and limbs. It is a large, majestic tree, strikingly beautiful, particularly in winter, but makes an effective background for early-flowering shrubs and perennial borders. Its surface roots make it difficult to grow much of anything under the tree, but moss does well and is very satisfactory as a ground cover. Fall color is a beautiful russet to bronze. This tree makes a dense shade with age and is long-lived. Hardy in Zones 4–9.

F. sylvatica (European beech) has darker bark and smaller, darker green, relatively shining, toothless leaves that turn reddish brown in the fall and remain on the tree most of the winter. Growing to a height of 60 ft., with a spread of about 45 ft., it is a large, noble specimen tree with age and is best planted in parks and wide-open areas. The fall color is excellent, ranging from bronze to copper shades, with branches reaching the ground. All upright forms can be clipped, forming excellent hedges. Hardy in Zones 5–7, the European beech is less sensitive to unfavorable conditions, and there are numerous varieties of great merit.

FALLUGIA (fah LOO jee ah). A genus of one species, *F. paradoxa*, native in the western United States, and a member of the Rosaceae (Rose Family). It is a low, spreading, deciduous shrub bearing 1½-in. white flowers followed by attractive heads of feathery-tailed fruits. Hardy as far north as Massachusetts (to Zone 7), it requires a well-drained, stony soil in full sun. Propagation is by seed or layers.

FALSE ACACIA. Common name for *Robinia pseudoacacia*, a tall tree with thorny branches, fragrant white flowers, and reddish brown pods that hang on the tree all winter; see ROBINIA.

FAMEFLOWER. Common name for TALINUM, a genus of fleshy herbs including many popular rock garden species.

FAMILY. A group of plants comprising few or many genera, the members of which are sufficiently alike in general characteristics to show somewhat close relationship and to justify their being classed together. In some families (known as natural families), such as the grasses, the asters, and the crucifers, the similarities and relationship are obvious. In other families, such evidences are obscure, even to botanists, and the affinities so doubtful that the grouping of the genera is more or less tentative.

Generally the characteristics identifying a family are indicated in one prominent genus that gives the family its name. Thus, Rosaceae is the Rose Family. Names of plant families can be easily recognized because they all end in "ceae," as in Rosaceae, Campanulaceae, Rubiaceae, etc.

For other classification information, see GENUS; SPECIES; VARIETY.

FAN PALM. Common name for a number of palms with broad, fan-shaped leaves, sometimes cut all the way to the center into many segments and known as "palmate" leaves. "Costapalmate" leaves are also ribbed. Well-known examples belong to the genera *Corypha, Livistona, Sabal* (palmetto), and *Washingtonia*.

FANWORT. A common name for CABOMBA, a genus of aquatic plants with finely cut submerged leaves.

FAREWELL-TO-SPRING. A common name for CLARKIA, a genus of annual herbs—often wildflowers in the western states, referring especially to the early summer-flowering forms.

FASCIATION. A botanical term for a common malformation in plant stems resulting in an enlargement and flattening, as if several stems were fused together.

FASTIGIATE. Erect, narrowing toward the top. A term applied to trees of slender or pyramidal form, in which the branches spring from a single trunk, gradually lengthening from top to bottom, as in the lombardy poplar and contrasted with the vase-form of the American elm.

FATSHEDERA (fats HED ur ah). An interesting houseplant whose name comes from the fact that it is a hybrid between a species of *Fatsia* and one in the genus *Hedera*. Both genera belong to the Araliaceae (Aralia Family) but are not as closely related as most plants that are able to hybridize successfully. The hand-shaped leaves are intermediate in size between the two parents. A moist but well-drained soil and a moderate tempera-

ture is best for this plant. When used in the garden, a frost-free but cool location is the most successful, although the plants have been successfully grown in Zone 7 in sheltered sites.

FATSIA (FAT see ah) **japonica.** An evergreen shrub or small tree belonging to the Araliaceae (Aralia Family). It has large, glossy, deeply lobed leaves and long panicles of white flowers. Sometimes grown under glass in the North, it makes a stately plant of subtropical appearance outdoors in Zones 9–11. Propagation is by seed and cuttings.

FAWN LILY. Common name for *Erythronium californicum*, a cream-colored spring-flowering bulb native to California; the name is also sometimes applied to other species of ERYTHRONIUM.

FEIJOA (fi JOH ah). A genus of South American trees and shrubs belonging to the Myrtaceae (Myrtle Family), and sometimes called Pineapple-guava.

F. sellowiana, a beautiful evergreen shrub from Brazil, is the only species commonly grown in the United States. It was introduced into California chiefly for its aromatic and edible fruits, but apart from this, it is a worthwhile ornamental. It can stand a few degrees of frost and is hardy to Zone 9. Growing to about 15 ft., it thrives best in a loamy soil with plenty of humus. The oval, glossy green leaves are silvery beneath. Cup-shaped flowers of white and crimson have conspicuous clusters of dark red stamens. The egg-shaped fruit is green with a red flush. Propagation is by seed, cuttings, and layers.

FELICIA (fee LIS ee ah). A genus of herbs or subshrubs native to Africa and hardy only in Zones 10–11, belonging to the Asteraceae (Aster Family), and commonly known as blue daisy. They bear solitary flower heads with yellow disks and sky blue rays.

The shrubby species, which can be propagated by cuttings, are sometimes grown under glass for winter bloom and outdoors in warm regions.

The annuals, easily grown from seed, are useful fillers in the rock garden.

F. amelloides (blue-marguerite), a low shrubby plant, is an old-time greenhouse favorite valued for its sky blue flowers on long, wiry stems.

F. bergerana (kingfisher daisy) is a low, spreading annual with bright blue flowers of a rather unusual shade.

FELT FERN. A common name for *Pyrrosia lingua*, an epiphytic fern with simple, rather fleshy and hairy fronds; see PYRROSIA.

FENNEL. A perennial herb, *Foeniculum vulgare*, grown for its culinary uses; see FOENICULUM. Fennel flower is NIGELLA, a genus of bright-flowered annuals.

FERN ALLIES. A group of genera including *Equisetum*, *Isoetes*, *Lycopodium*, *Psilotum*, and *Selaginella*, which have several characteristics in common with ferns. These are the lack of seeds or flowers, vascularity (in which they differ from more primitive plants), and reproduction by means of spores. They have no distinct fronds, but the small leaves, each with a single vein, are arranged on simple or sometimes branched stems. The spores are also borne differently.

The fern allies are at about the same evolutionary level as the ferns, but obvious differences point out that if they did come from a common ancestor, divergence occurred at a very early stage of evolution. Botanists generally believe that ferns are more closely related to higher plants, including the conifers, cycads, and flowering plants. Because their life cycles are so similar to ferns and they are cultivated in the same way, this group continues to be called fern allies.

FERNS. Thoreau once said, "Nature made ferns for pure leaves." He was right; it is primarily for the great beauty of their leaves, the endless variety of forms, and the range of subtle shades of green that we treasure these plants. They are always pleasing, not depending on any special season for their appeal as flowering plants do.

They are surprisingly easy to grow, and there is a place for them in every house and garden.

The history of ferns goes much farther back into the shadows of time than does the history of the human race. The first primitive ferns, which appeared at the beginning of the Carboniferous Period, are now extinct. Our knowledge of those ferns is based on fragmentary fossils of pieces of roots, stems, fronds, sporangia, and spores. They are, however, in such an excellent state of preservation that even internal structures can be studied in detail. In fact, fossils of equisetum-like plants are little different from the modern forms of *Equisetum*, a genus of fern allies. Prehistoric ferns and their allies were the great trees in the Paleolithic forests.

WHAT IS A FERN?

Ferns have roots, stems, and leaves, just like other vascular plants. The striking difference is that ferns do not produce flowers and therefore lack seeds. They reproduce by means of spores, as did their primitive ancestors, in a life cycle that is unique and fascinating.

The roots of a fern are black and wiry, quite shallow, and attached to a modified stem or rootstock called a rhizome. The rhizome may be subterranean, or it may run along the surface of the ground or cling to rocks and trees. Some ascend to form the tree ferns of the tropical rain forests. The rhizome is usually covered with hairs or scales—small, very thin, membranous outgrowths—which may be black, white, or colored, adding interest when the rhizome is visible.

From the rhizome arises the stalk, or stipe, which supports the leaves, or fronds. The stipe may also be covered with hairs or scales, in shades of brown, silver, or black. The stalk can arise from the rhizome singly or in clusters, depending on the species, and contains the vascular system that carries food and water between the rhizome and the frond.

The frond is what we visualize when we think of a fern. Fronds may be simple, as in *Asplenidum nidus* (bird's-nest fern) or compound, the divided form customary to most ferns. Compound fronds have divisions known as pinnae, and when further division of the pinnae exists, these divisions are called pinnules. Even further division may be present, and thus the frond may be 1-, 2-, or 3-pinnate (referred to as pinnate, bipinnate, and tripinnate). The ultimate division is known as a segment. The part of the stalk to which the pinnae are joined is called the rachis. If the frond is cut at least half the distance to the rachis, it is said to be pinnatifid rather than pinnate. If the pinnae are cut to the rachis but the pinnules are cut only partially, the frond is pinnate-pinnatifid. Many combinations of cutting exist.

Fronds

The frond segments not only perform the usual leaf functions of photosynthesis, but also bear the reproductive spores. These spores are contained in sporangia, tiny capsules made of a single layer of cells, which in turn are grouped in clusters called sori. The sori are usually found on the undersides of the frond, and the beginning fern grower may mistake them for scale insects. The sori are usually protected by a cellular membrane called an indusium. These indusia have differing shapes, according to the genera of the fern, and are important aids to identification and classification. If there are no indusia, the sori are said to be naked. Sometimes the sori are protected by the rolled-over or reflexed edge of the pinna.

Fronds that bear spores are called fertile, and those without spores are sterile. Ferns may have both fertile and sterile portions on the same frond, as does *Osmunda claytoniana* (interrupted fern), or they may have some entirely fertile fronds that are the same size and shape as the sterile ones, like *Dryopteris marginalis* (marginal shield fern). Some ferns are dimorphic, that is, they have two different-looking types of fronds, one fertile and the other sterile. In some species,

these two types are very similar at first glance, but with closer observation we spot the somewhat different size or shape of those fronds bearing spores, as in *Dryopteris cristata* (crested fern). In other dimorphic species, the sterile frond is very obviously different, as in *Onoclea sensibilis* (sensitive fern) and *Matteuccia struthiopteris* (ostrich fern).

When conditions are right, the spores are released, and millions are borne away on the wind. If and when they come to rest in a moist and shady niche, a fascinating life cycle begins. In as little as two weeks, depending on conditions, a tiny heart-shaped, membranous body called the prothallium develops. It is usually about ¼ in. across. On the underside are found the male and female sex organs called the antheridium, where the sperm are formed, and the archegonium, where the eggs are formed. When the temperature is right and moisture is present, the sperm swim from the antheridium to the archegonium and fertilization takes place. The fertilized egg grows a tiny root down into the soil; a first leaf curves upward through the notch of the heart-shaped prothallium; and from it a stem begins growing laterally. The prothallium nurtures the new plantlet until it has developed roots and fronds sufficient to take up nourishment and start photosynthesis on its own. It is now recognizable as the fern we know and is called a sporophyte. It will continue to bear this name no matter how large it becomes. When the new sporophyte is mature, at the proper season sporangia are formed, spores are released, and the cycle begins over again. The descriptive scientific term for this cycle is alternation of generations.

GROWING FERNS INDOORS
HUMIDITY

Growing ferns indoors was much easier before the advent of central heating, which raises room temperatures and reduces humidity levels to a point not compatible with healthy ferns. Disadvantages can be overcome with a little ingenuity, however. There are many beautiful tropical ferns that will thrive at 65–75°F. Humidity can be raised in a number of ways; the simplest is to group plants on a tray filled with a layer of pebbles that are kept nearly covered by water. This raises the humidity considerably in the immediate area. The use of a misting bottle also helps, as does a room humidifier. Consider using the evaporative type rather than the atomizing type, which lays an annoying mineral dust on every surface in the room, including plant leaves.

LIGHT

Light is the next important factor to be considered. A site at a north window is ideal, an east window is good, but direct south or west window light should be avoided, although a thin curtain placed between ferns and the windowpane will modify the light sufficiently. If no suitable windows are available, the use of a fluorescent light fixture is an excellent alternative. Two ordinary cool-white lamps in an inexpensive fixture will give ideal light for growing ferns. If you wish to mix flowering plants with the ferns, use one cool-white lamp and one warm-white lamp in the fixture, putting the ferns at the ends and the other plants in the center where the light is more intense. Some fern lovers grow and propagate hundreds of plants in a "plant room" filled with shelves lit by fluorescent fixtures. Even an extra closet can be used in this way, and a basement with an even temperature is a good spot for quantity growing.

SOIL

The soil for indoor ferns is easily mixed in quantity by the grower and is more consistent in quality and content than commercial mixtures. A simple basic mix is 2 gal. screened sphagnum peat moss, 1 gal. perlite, 1 gal. vermiculite, 1 tbsp. superphosphate, 2 tbsp. ground limestone, and 6 tbsp. 5–10–5. Mix these well and store in a covered container. Do not add water until just before using, then add only enough to moisten. If you wish to eliminate the superphosphate and 5–10–5, feed with a quarter-strength liquid fertilizer each time you water. This soil has the advantage of no weed seeds, insect eggs, or disease organisms. Starting with healthy plants and giving them good care will minimize troubles.

Ferns need repotting more often than the average houseplant. Some can fill the pot with roots in three or four months. For this reason, slight overpotting is permissible.

WATER

Healthy ferns grow vigorously and need daily water monitoring in the beginning. Check to see if they need water by feeling the weight of the pot, noticing the color of the soil surface, and thrusting a finger into the soil about ½ in. below the surface. If the soil feels dry, add water until it flows freely from the drainage hole. Do not water until it feels dry again. A little water every day is a good way to overwater and build up too many minerals in the soil. If clay pots are used, it will be necessary to water more often than with plastic or glazed pots. Be alert for pests when watering. This is also a good time to groom plants by removing dead fronds, leaves, and blossoms. Good care will reward you with handsome, disease-free plants.

ENEMIES

If you start with healthy plants, use a sterile planting medium, and follow good cultural procedures, you should have minimal problems with pests and diseases. However, occasional lapses do produce a stressed plant, and problems can develop. The most common fern pests are four sucking insects.

Scale. The shiny brown discs are often confused with sori by beginning gardeners. See SCALE INSECTS.

Aphids. Also called green fly, the immature forms may be green, yellow, or black; they cluster on tender new growth. See APHIDS.

Mealybugs. These look like little tufts of cotton, usually appear in the axils of pinnae and rachis or other snug, hidden areas such as the junction of stipe and rhizome. See MEALYBUG.

Spider Mites. These minuscule relatives of the spider can take over the leaf surfaces of under- or overwatered plants, particularly if the humidity is very low. They produce yellowed leaves and a covering of fine webs. A hand lens is needed to detect them. See MITES.

It is hoped that pests will be detected before

they are widespread. Checking for pests when watering helps prevent problems. The appearance of ants is cause for alarm, since they spread some sucking insects by cultivating them for their excreted honey dew. Sticky spatters of this honey dew on lower leaves and shelves are also indicators of trouble.

Ferns are extremely sensitive to toxic insecticides. They should not be used except in extreme situations, for the fern's sake as well as for the sake of the environment and the grower. A few mealybugs can be eliminated by a cotton swab or a paintbrush dipped in isopropyl alcohol and touched to the offender. Pests, even aphids, can be hand-picked, followed by spraying with an insecticidal soap. Wait 20–30 minutes, then follow with a rinse at the sink. This should take care of the immediate problem. Isolation, vigilance, and repetition is the watchword for the next few weeks as possible eggs hatch. A heavy infestation can be handled in two ways: either destroy the plant or, if it is truly precious, use a stronger insecticide, following the instructions on the label and handling it with great care. Do not use any oil-base insecticides. For best results, use a powdered insecticide suspended in water. The fern may lose some or all fronds but may recover. Ferns with tough, leathery fronds can often be rescued from scale infestations this way, but the more delicate ferns, such as the maidenhairs, are often lost when heavily infected.

In high-humidity areas, there may be some trouble with mold on the fronds. This can be prevented by good ventilation, while at the same time controlling drafts. In winter, if you have a room humidifier, a small electric fan in the corner of the room will keep the air moving slightly; just make sure it does not blow directly on the ferns. Water only at soil level; do not wet the fronds. Also, not spacing plants too closely cuts down the spread of pests.

SELECTIONS

Very few ferns from the temperate and colder regions can be used as houseplants. They tend to flourish during a short period of clement weather and then go dormant for the extended months of winter. Most tropical ferns, however, adapt well to the home and do not have such a pronounced dormant period; their growth merely slows down and they need less water and no fertilizer during this period.

Ferns that make good houseplants are *Asplenium nidus* (bird's-nest fern); various forms of *Nephrolepis exaltata* 'Bostoniensis' (Boston fern); *Pteris cretica* (Cretan brake); the various footed ferns such as *Davallia trichomanoides* (rabbit's-foot fern), *Humata tyermannii* (bear's-foot fern), and *Polypodium aureum* (golden polypody); *Cyrtomium falcatum* (Japanese holly fern); *Rumohra adiantiformis* (leather fern); and many more. Refer to individual fern entries for their uses and culture.

FERNS IN THE GARDEN

Most ferns have adapted to shade over many eons, but there are also a few that have adapted to living in the blast of full sun, such as the xerophytic ferns of the North American deserts. Whatever your garden conditions, you are sure to find ferns that you can grow.

There are two interdependent factors upon which good fern culture depends: a constant supply of moisture and soil that drains well yet holds the necessary moisture. The best soil is a mixture of humus (compost, peat, or other organic matter that retains water) and soil particles of a size that permits excess water to drain rapidly yet retains some water in the pore spaces. Clay particles are too fine and tend to hold too much water too long. Coarse sand lets too much water drain away too rapidly. Interestingly enough, the solution to both these problems is about the same: add humus, which opens up the clay soil to facilitate drainage and also helps to hold moisture in sandy soil.

The planting bed, made up of carefully prepared soil, should be at least 12 in. deep; 18 in. would be better. Check the drainage capacity of the underlying soil by pouring some water into a preliminary hole of the same depth and making sure it drains fairly rapidly. If it doesn't, consider making a raised bed, which takes much less work than breaking up hardpan.

Two other factors that must be considered are light and nutrition. While most ferns prefer shade, no plant will grow in truly dense shade. High shade is ideal; this admits bright light and even some direct sun, usually in the early morning or late afternoon hours. Dappled shade is just as good, where the overhead canopy is sparse enough that alternate patches of light and shade travel across the undergrowth as the sun moves across the sky. This can be achieved by judicious pruning. The degree of shade determines moisture need, so ferns planted in sunny spots will require watering.

Fern nutrition is not a real problem. If you are generous with compost and leaf mold, both in the soil and as a mulch, you are also supplying a good portion of the nutritional needs. A light meal of fertilizer at the beginning of growth in the early spring is not essential, but it will help your ferns to grow and spread more vigorously.

SELECTIONS

The following ferns are excellent for the starting fern gardener in temperate zones. *Adiantum pedatum* (maidenhair fern), *Athyrium filix-femina* (lady fern), *Athyrium niponicum* (Japanese painted fern), *Cystopteris bulbifera* (bulblet bladder fern), *Cystopteris fragilis* (fragile fern), *Dryopteris marginalis* (marginal shield fern), *Osmunda cinnamomea* (cinnamon fern), *Osmunda claytonia* (interrupted fern), *Osmunda regalis* (royal fern), *Polystichum acrostichoides* (Christmas fern), and *Thelypteris hexagonoptera* (broad beech or southern beech fern). Specific uses and culture are discussed under each genus entry.

PROPAGATION

There are two basic methods of propagating ferns: asexual (vegetative) and sexual. Asexual propagation produces a clone or exact duplicate of the parent plant. Sexual reproduction by means of spores produces a plant with the same species characteristics, but varietal or hybrid characteristics cannot be counted on to reappear in the offspring.

VEGETATIVE METHODS

The most frequently used and easiest method of vegetative propagation is simple division, separating a clump or mat of ferns into two or more pieces, then replanting and nursing these rhizomatous divisions until they are established. With house ferns, this is best done after the dormant period when the fern is about to commence active growth, or during the active growth period. The actively growing rhizome will soon send new roots into the surrounding soil. It is prudent to carefully monitor watering of newly divided and repotted plants.

Epiphytic ferns with aerial rhizomes, such as those of the footed ferns, can be multiplied by severing a section of rhizome, preferably containing at least one frond, and pegging it onto the surface of slightly moist vermiculite in a closed propagating box. Under fluorescent lights, or in a brightly lit area with no direct sun, rooting will occur in a month or so. The rooted rhizome can then be planted on the surface of a pot of epiphytic medium, covering the roots but not the rhizome. Cover with a plastic bag for a week or two, and it will soon develop into a new plant. Several of such rooted divisions can be used to plant hanging baskets. Water sparingly until the basket contains plenty of roots.

In the garden, ferns can be divided at almost any time. The ideal time, however, is just as the croziers are unfolding in the spring. Rapid root growth under ideal conditions will quickly establish the new division. The end of summer, before the onset of dormancy, is the next best time. The warm days and cool nights of early fall will aid in the establishment of new roots before freezing. Carefully water when needed, and when freezing occurs mulch well with straw or pine needles to protect against alternate freezing and thawing. If you must divide a fern during the summer, chances of success are quite good if you are vigilant about shading, protecting from drying winds, and watering.

Another means of vegetative propagation is by means of runners or stolons. The tip of the stolon is pegged down, or shallowly buried in a pot of damp, porous medium. When rooting is accomplished and a new plantlet started, the runner can be severed from the parent plant. This is a common way of multiplying Boston fern and its cultivars.

One of the most interesting methods of asexual propagation is by means of the bulbils or plantlets that form on the fronds of certain ferns. Such ferns are described as viviparous. Examples are *Asplenium bulbiferum* (mother fern), *Cystopteris bulbifera* (bulblet bladder fern), and *Polystichum setiferum* (soft shield fern). The bulblet bladder fern multiplies itself by dropping bulbils from the backs of its fronds, and the surrounding area is soon covered with young ferns. It makes an excellent ground cover for this reason. Bulbils can also be collected and sown elsewhere in a suitable area. The tiny plantlets on the fronds of the mother fern can be gently removed and placed on the surface of moist vermiculite in a closed, transparent container. Place the container in bright light, such as under a fluorescent lamp, and the plantlets will soon form roots. They can then be potted in a proper fern mix where they will soon grow into vigorous plants. Whole fronds containing plantlets of such ferns as *Polystichum setiferum* can be removed, pegged down on moist propagating medium, and treated in the same manner. By the time roots have formed, the plantlets can be easily but carefully removed from the original frond, potted in a suitable mix, and planted in the garden when large enough.

PROPAGATION FROM SPORES

There are almost as many methods of propagating ferns sexually as there are propagators. It is not the difficult task that one might expect. With fresh spores, success is almost guaranteed. Members can obtain spores from fern society exchanges (see resources in appendix), or they can be collected from the wild or from other gardens. Collection must be done at the proper time; consult your local extension service or fern society for recommended collection dates.

Examine the sporangia closely, with a magnifying glass if necessary. Young sporangia are whitish green. As they mature, a gradual change occurs from light to medium brown. At full maturity, they become dark brown, almost black, round, and plump. There are a few species whose mature spore color does not follow this rule but is gold or green. If the sporangia have a lighter, fuzzy look, it is too late; the sporangia have opened, and the spores are gone. Cut a frond whose sporangia are medium brown. Place it, sporangia side down, on a sheet of smooth typing paper that is folded down the center. Place another sheet over it, and carefully place the sheets between the pages of a book, being careful to keep the sporangia side down. Close the book and wait a few days. Then open the book, remove the upper sheet, carefully lift the frond, and as you refold the bottom sheet, the dark spores will collect in the crease. Remove from the spores any bits of frond that have broken off. With careful handling, there should not be much debris. Carefully tap the spores from the crease into a small vial or clean medicine capsule; label it carefully and store in a cool, dry place.

Some spores, such as those of the Osmundaceae, which are green at maturity, must be sown within a day or two, or they die. Others can be saved and sown over a much longer period, but the sooner spores are sown, the faster they germinate, and the better the chance of sufficient growth occurring before plants are overwhelmed by such contaminants as molds and algae.

When sowing spores, the most important factor is the cleanliness of the containers, the medium they contain, and the tools used. It is impossible to actually sterilize your equipment, but most contaminants can be removed by simple kitchen methods. A variety of containers can be used—any shallow vessel with a transparent lid, such as a clay pot covered by a piece of glass, a plastic glass covered by transparent wrap, or small plastic pots put in a transparent box after sowing. The plastic containers should be soaked in a solution of a 1:10 proportion of laundry bleach to water for 30 minutes and allowed to drain upside down on a clean paper or linen towel. If using glass-covered clay pots, heat both cover and pot in the oven at 280°F for 30 minutes.

The medium should be pasteurized ahead of time, by moistening and heating it at 280°F for 30 minutes. An oven-roasting bag pierced by an oven thermometer is useful for this purpose. Longer heating is not necessary or desirable. It is important not to use any garden soil at this stage. African-violet mix or any high-peat potting soil is fine; some brands are prepasteurized.

After the slightly moist soil is placed in the containers, the spores can be gently tapped from the storage container, or directly from the folded paper if you have just collected them. Do not sow thickly, or the tiny sporophytes will not be able to penetrate the thick layer of prothallia that results. Using a bleach-sterilized spray bottle and boiled water, mist well and cover the container with a clear top. Place pot(s) in a tray of cooled boiled water until both pots and medium are wetted. Allow to drain well.

At this stage, all containers should be placed in a warm, brightly lit place. A shelf beneath fluorescent lamps is ideal. Fresh spores may germinate in as little as two weeks, but the prothallia will not be visible to the naked eye for another month or so. If the prothallia are present, and no sporophytes emerge, carefully flood with boiled water, just as carefully pour it off, and re-cover. This will provide the moisture needed by the sperm to enable them to swim to the eggs.

When the sporophytes have two or more fronds, small pieces of the prothallial mat can be separated and spaced out on the surface of the pasteurized planting medium, either in a large pot or in a plastic box pierced with drainage holes. Either container should have a transparent cover. When the little ferns have grown to about 2 in., they can be moved into individual pots. They should still be kept in a humid atmosphere for a while and gradually weaned away from it as they grow. Hardy ferns can be planted out when spring arrives, but they should be mulched the first winter.

There are other methods to try, but all rely on the same principles of cleanliness, humidity, light, and warmth.

As you give more and more room to ferns,

don't feel guilty; just keep in mind the words of George Schenk, that evocative garden writer who says, "These are the plants that put wings on the garden. Nothing else . . . affords us quite the visual buoyancy of ferns. They lighten the garden, and so they lighten the gardener."

FEROCACTUS (fair oh KAK tus). A genus of very spiny, often large cacti including most barrel cacti, which in most cases are so large that they are suitable only for extensive and complete collections. Some of the smaller species can, however, be included in any collection where they prove desirable for pot or garden culture. All species of *Ferocactus* are native to Mexico and the United States. Desert types are fairly hardy. For cultural directions, see CACTUS.

PRINCIPAL SPECIES

F. acanthodes (California fire-barrel) is attractive with reddish to yellowish spines, but it is slow growing.

F. lindsayii, with purplish stems, is one of the newer species.

F. macrodiscus is one of the smaller species, with flattened, solitary stem and candy-cane striped flowers.

FERTILIZATION. In flowers this refers to the union of male reproductive bodies (pollen) with female reproductive bodies (eggs) to produce offspring (seeds). Do not confuse with POLLINATION or with fertilizing in the sense of improving soil by increasing its fertility or supply of available plant food.

FERTILIZER. Any material that supplies nutrients to growing plants is a fertilizer. Strictly speaking, the term includes farm MANURE, which must first be decomposed before the nutrients become available to the plant. Most gardeners, however, make a distinction between manures and fertilizers. In classifying fertilizers, such terms as artificial, natural, mineral, chemical, prepared, and manufactured all have their limitations, and even the terms "organic" and "inorganic" must be qualified. Commercial fertilizer is generally thought of as manufactured or processed material sold in bags or bulk loads, as contrasted to fresh or rotted unprocessed manure sold in bulk. For example, manure that is dried, shredded, and bagged is considered a commercial fertilizer.

ORGANIC FERTILIZER

Organic fertilizers are substances produced by animals and plants, or derived from them. They include animal excrement, carcasses, blood, bone, and other packinghouse by-products, refuse from fisheries and fish oil factories, and oil meals left after extraction of vegetable oil (such as castor powder and cottonseed meal), and brewery or tobacco wastes. Among the sewage sludges, activated sludge is a fertilizer, but digested sludge is not, since it is used primarily to improve the physical condition of the soil. Materials such as straw, leaves, garden refuse, and garbage, when composted are sometimes known as artificial manures.

Using organic materials instead of synthetic commercial fertilizers is one of the two main aims of organic gardeners and farmers—the other being the use of various biological methods of pest control (see BIOLOGICAL CONTROL). Compost, manures, tilled-in cover crops, nonpoisonous soil additions such as cottonseed meal, blood meal, fish emulsion, seaweed, and inorganic materials such as the naturally occurring green sand and granite dust, rock phosphates, and self-improving and dolomitic lime are preferred to the quickly effective nitrogen-phosphorus-potassium (N–P–K) commercial fertilizers. The fast actions of high concentrations of commercial fertilizers are thought to upset the natural balancing of comparatively slow processes in the soil. Users of the quick methods have often overlooked many of these slow processes whose complicated actions have sustained plant growth over the millennia.

Other soil improvements provide valuable fertilizer. One is the practice of cover cropping during dormant periods, frequently called GREEN MANURE, in which often a legume crop (such as soybean, clover, vetch, peas, or beans) provides nitrogen. Winter rye, millet, and rape are also valued as cover crops. Rape has special benefits because of its quick growth and mass of green material. When these crops are plowed in, their substance adds organic matter good for tilth and nutrition. Mulches of organic material that will decay into the soil are another source of nutrients. Recommended are peat moss, ground bark, wood chips, and coco or buckwheat hulls. Straw, hay, and grass clippings spread on the garden are other sources. Such mulches also help to retain moisture in the soil, moderate the temperature, and give protection from winds and heavy downpours.

The humus and humic acids from organic fertilizers aid the essential microorganisms in the soil as commercial fertilizers do not. Air and water in the soil and soil texture are also enhanced.

INORGANIC FERTILIZER

Inorganic fertilizers include products derived from natural mineral deposits, such as Chilean nitrate of soda; manufactured or synthetic products, such as ammonium sulfate; and by-products of steel mills and factories.

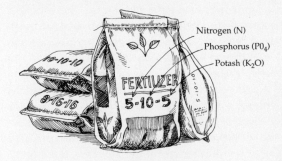

Nitrogen (N)
Phosphorus (PO_4)
Potash (K_2O)

Fertilizer bag

Materials used primarily to improve the soil's physical condition or to change its reaction are considered soil amendments, but to the extent that they supply a needed nutrient, they are also fertilizers. Most fertilizers furnish one or more of the three elements most commonly deficient in soils, namely, nitrogen (denoted by the chemical symbol N), phosphorus (P), and potassium (K). These are not present in elemental form but are chemically combined with oxygen and/or other elements, both in the fertilizer bag and in the soil. It is the custom in the United States to give the analysis of fertilizers in terms of nitrogen (N), phosphate (PO_4), and potash (K_2O); these major nutrients are always listed in that order. Thus, the figure 5–10–5 means: 5% nitrogen, 10% phosphate, and 5% potash. A fertilizer analysis shown as 0–15–30 means no nitrogen, 15% phosphate, and 30% potash. Fertilizers that contain all three nutrients are known as complete fertilizers. Those with only one or two nutrients are called incomplete or special fertilizers.

No fertilizer nutrients come in pure form. They all contain other substances, some of which may play only a minor role in plant nutrition, have no value, or may be harmful in certain situations. For example, muriate of potash is an excellent source of potassium, but the chloride it contains is injurious to certain crops.

COMMERCIAL FERTILIZERS

Factory-mixed fertilizers are indispensable to modern agriculture and are very useful to the home gardener as well. Home mixing is possible, and in some instances results in lower cost, but the labor involved seldom justifies the practice. Factory-mixed fertilizers usually contain a number of products so selected as to provide the various nutrients in the proportions required for any particular analysis. Choice of ingredients is governed in part by their blending properties and, of course, cost is an important factor. Frequently the same nutrients in a single mix come from several different materials. For example, nitrogen can be supplied by nitrogen solution alone (concentrated form of soluble nitrogen), or it can come from urea and sulfate of ammonia, or from urea, ammonia, nitrate, and castor powder.

Fillers are usually included in mixed fertilizers, not as adulterants, but as conditioners and dilutants—substances that are quite essential to the mixing of commercial fertilizer. The fillers in modern fertilizer mixes usually contain lime and organic material such as dried, digested sludge, rather than sand, as was once the case.

The purchase of fertilizers should be governed by the chemical analysis of the product as shown on the label rather than by the brand name. State laws require the registration of fertilizers, and a package label giving the guaranteed analysis (that is, the percentage of nitrogen, available phosphates, and water-soluble potash present).

There is usually little difference between fertilizer brands having the same analysis. For ordinary use a 5–10–10 formula in one brand is likely to be as good as the same analysis of any other brand. However, in the more specialized fields, differences in fertilizer ingredients need to be taken into account. For example, the grower who wants a fertilizer containing slow-acting organic nitrogen needs to know whether the nitrogen comes from urea or a more slowly available material, such as castor powder or blood meal. Unfortunately this information is not usually provided.

Liquid Fertilizers. In general, commercially available liquid fertilizers need to be diluted before use. To save time and effort in mixing, a proportioner can be used. One end is attached to

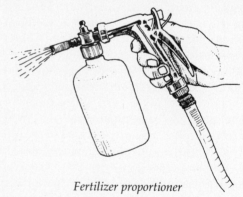

Fertilizer proportioner

a regular water hose and the other is connected to a container of concentrated liquid fertilizer solution. During operation, the solution is diluted to the correct proportion.

FERTILIZER USE

Slowly available organic nitrogen is recommended for lawns or slow-growing ornamental shrubs and trees. The alternative is to apply a mineral fertilizer in smaller repeat doses. This will supply the needs of the plant during the growing season without having too high a concentration when the plants are small.

Soil tests and the crop grown should be the basis for determining the fertilizer analysis required. In the small garden a general-purpose mix, such as 5–10–5 or 5–10–10 will usually be satisfactory. The large garden or lawn may have need for more than one grade of fertilizer. Because soils, crop requirements, climate, and weather differ widely, it is impossible to give specific recommendations on fertilizer formulas, and it is unwise to generalize. Consult your local extention service for advice.

FESCUE (FES kyoo). Common name for FESTUCA, a widely naturalized genus of perennial grasses.

FESTUCA (fes TOO ka). A genus of temperate-zone, perennial grasses, commonly known as fescue, some of which have become naturalized in North America. They will grow on a wide variety of soils and will tolerate moderate to heavy shade, depending on the type and variety.

New turf-type varieties of *F. arundinacea* (tall fescue) render them suitable for use on lawns and athletic fields. Sometimes used alone, they can

each) can hasten the process of establishment. Tall fescues are for the most part tolerant of drought conditions as well as wear and have some tolerance to salts. They are ideal for the low-maintenance lawn. Non-turf varieties have been used for forage in the transition zone.

Fine fescues include species with relatively fine leaf blades. Similar to a pine needle, they can be rolled between the thumb and index finger. Other species, like *F. elatior* (meadow fescue), are often used for other purposes since they tend to form a bunchy turf and are therefore unsuitable for lawns, though they are sometimes used in grass mixtures for shady places and for meadows and pastures. Most are shade tolerant but will not stand up under heavy wear.

PRINCIPAL SPECIES

F. ovina (sheep fescue) is coarse and unsuitable for lawns, but some varieties are useful for other purposes. Var. *duriuscula* (hard fescue) will tolerate some drought conditions. Var. *glauca* (blue fescue), growing to 12 in. tall, has striking blue-green foliage and a low tufted growth habit. It is quite hardy and attractive as an edging plant.

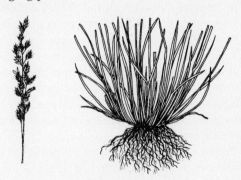

Festuca rubra

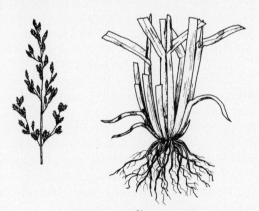

Festuca arundinacea

also be used in combination with other grasses. Being a bunch type of grass, tall fescues can take the better part of a growing season to form a complete growing surface. Mixing them with perennial ryegrasses and Kentucky bluegrasses (20%

F. rubra (chewing or creeping fescue) is a low-growing bunch type of grass used in low maintenance lawn mixes. It has some knitting action through rhizomes.

FETTERBUSH. Common name for *Lyonia lucida*, a flowering evergreen shrub of the Ericaceae (Heath Family); see LYONIA.

FEVERFEW. Common name for *Chrysanthemum parthenium*, a highly variable perennial with white flowers.

FICUS (FĪ kus). A genus of trees, shrubs, and woody vines, widely distributed in tropical and warm temperate regions, belonging to the Moraceae (Mulberry Family). Some are grown as ornamental plants in greenhouses and outdoors in Zones 10–11 where *F. carica*, known as the common FIG, is grown for its sweet, edible fruits.

Of the more than 800 species known, only about 30 are grown in any quantity. Several species of *Ficus* together make up the major tree components of indoor landscaping, and plants are also sold with several trunks braided together and in other bizarre, knotted forms. Propagation is by cuttings, air layering, and commercially by tissue culture.

HOUSEPLANT CULTURE

The requirements of indoor specimens is simple. If given sunlight, rich potting soil, and an ample supply of water during the growing season, most will thrive despite the dry air of most homes. During the summer they benefit from being placed outdoors (in the pot) in a sheltered corner where they will not be damaged by wind.

Because they grow rapidly, especially if occasionally fed with liquid manure, they should be repotted once a year. Rubber plants are generally grown to one stem or sometimes two, but excellent specimens can be obtained by pinching them back to make them branch and training them into compact, sturdy forms.

Propagation. When a plant becomes too large or the long stems ungainly, it is desirable to alter its habit. This can be done in two rather simple ways. One is to cut it back to within a foot of the soil, encouraging new shoots to appear at the base. Many growers, however, object to losing the top of the plant and prefer AIR LAYERING, which enables them to make two plants out of one. There are two easy ways to do this. One is to tie a ball of sphagnum moss around the base of a young shoot at a point where the stem has been notched or scarred to stimulate the formation of

roots. Keep the moss moist, and when new roots are found spreading through, cut the shoot from the parent branch and pot it as a new plant.

The other, more common method is to make an upward incision about halfway through the stem at a point near the lowest leaves and keep the cut open by inserting a pebble or small piece of wood. Then split a 3–4 in. flowerpot in two vertically, place it around the cut portion, fill it with moss or loose absorbent soil, and bind the pot tightly in place with wire. Keep the material moist at all times, and within several weeks, young roots will develop from the wound. Then sever the rooted specimens from the old stem; pot it up carefully in a new whole pot; and you will have two plants, since the parents will develop side branches.

Using a propagating box, the gardener can increase plant stock by cutting off the upper part of a stem and using short pieces with one leaf each. Put these cuttings in sand in the propagating box and maintain bottom heat and a humid atmosphere.

Insect Pests. Mealybugs and scale insects commonly infest *Ficus* houseplants. The circular scale is dark reddish and stands out prominently from the leaf. Morgan's scale is somewhat similar but flatter. Often soft scale also infests these plants. All these pests can be controlled fairly easily; see HOUSEPLANTS; MEALYBUG; SCALE INSECTS.

PRINCIPAL SPECIES

In their wild form, a group of species (and especially *F. benghalensis*) commonly known as banyans, are noted for the age, size (some to 100 ft. high), and shape they attain; they spread to form secondary trunks when aerial roots take hold in the soil. This striking characteristic form is one of the wonders of the plant world.

F. aspera (clown fig) has rough, strongly variegated leaves.

F. benjamina (weeping fig) is the most common interior plant and is a tree for huge open spaces in frost-free areas. Aerial roots form secondary trunks growing in the "banyan" habit.

F. carica is valued in mild regions for the edible fruit; see FIG.

F. elastica (rubber plant) is a common interior plant—this one with large, glossy leaves in a variety of shades of green, red, and also variegated. Its sturdy, enduring growth, long life, simple cultural requirements, and large handsome leaves—anywhere from 3–12 in. long and about a third as wide—have offset its stiff, sometimes ungainly form and made the rubber plant a favorite for years. Oblong or elliptical in shape with small abrupt points, the leaves are glossy and dark green above and dull or lighter green on the underside.

F. lyrata (fiddleleaf fig) gets its common name from the shape of its leaves. It is also grown as a houseplant and is more compact in form than *F. elastica*, with large, oblong, cabbagelike leaves with an irregular outline, a deep green color, and conspicuous veins.

F. montana is a ground cover with oak-shaped leaves.

F. pumila is a creeping type that covers walls and tree trunks in the South and makes good hanging basket plants.

F. retusa var. *nitida* (Indian-laurel fig) also takes interior conditions well. It is attacked by thrip that must be controlled to keep the young leaves from damage. Variegated forms of this and *F. benjamina* are available.

F. sagittata is an interesting form similar to *F. pumila*.

F. sycomorus (Pharaoh's fig, sycamore), a small tree of Egypt and Syria, also listed as *Sycomorus antiquorum*, has historical interest as the sycamore of the Bible; it has been grown to some extent in south Florida.

FIESTA FLOWER. Common name for the western flowering annual *Pholistoma auritum*; see PHOLISTOMA.

FIG. Common name for *Ficus carica*, a small tree or large spreading bush of warm, temperate climates grown for its pear-shaped "fruit." This is actually a swollen, hollow receptacle with a small opening in the end opposite the stem, completely lined with tiny flowers that develop into the true fruits—the "seeds" of the fig.

In Zones 9–11, it is a favorite garden and local market subject, and from the warmer parts of these regions, the fresh fruit is shipped to cooler areas. In California, the Smyrna fig is grown commercially for drying.

In colder zones, plants are sometimes grown outdoors during summer and dug in late fall with large balls of earth that are kept moist in a cool place until spring; the plants are set out-

Ficus carica (fig)

doors again when the weather becomes mild. They can also be grown in tubs moved in and out as the weather demands, and they are often grown in greenhouses, being treated like hothouse grapes with their branches trained horizontally to save space and increase the yield. So handled, a plant can be expected to ripen two or even three crops in a year.

Though figs can be grown from "seeds" taken from fresh "fruits," the product of the resulting plants is so variable that plants are more commonly propagated from dormant wood cuttings taken from mature trees in winter or early spring. For best results, these should be 4–5 in. long, cut through their nodes, and set with their tips even with the soil surface. In good soil they will be ready to transplant to the nursery row (there set 2 ft. apart) the following spring; the next year they can be planted in their permanent positions, 18–25 ft. apart.

Though the fig does best in heavy soils well supplied with moisture, it can be grown successfully in a sandy soil if firmly packed and kept moist by occasional watering. Under these conditions, NEMATODES give less trouble than in light, loose, dry soils. Shading the soil, mulching deeply, and irrigating during dry spells also promote growth and fruit production.

Ordinary figs produce fruit anywhere in Zones 9–10, but the high-quality Smyrna fig fails except where a small wasp (see FIG WASP) is present in numbers. It enters the immature figs, pollinates the flowers, and causes the development of the fleshy fruit to edible size. Since the discovery of the part this insect plays in fig production, and the development of methods of raising it and establishing it in orchards, the growing of Smyrna figs for drying has become a large, successful commercial activity in southern California.

FIG WASP. The palatability of the Smyrna fig depends on the pollination of the flowers (which line the inside wall of the so-called fruit) by a small wasp, *Blastophaga psenes*, imported from Asia for this purpose. If the flowers are not fertilized, seeds do not form, and the characteristic flavor is lacking. The female fig wasp comes from the male tree (called the caprifig) covered with pollen to lay her eggs in the fleshy receptacles borne by the female trees, where the pollen is dropped or rubbed off against the flowers. The male wasps are wingless and never leave the tree where they develop from larvae in small galls. The females gnaw their way out of the galls, and become covered with pollen as they emerge and seek the small opening at the end of the fig.

At one time, figs containing mature wasps were strung among the branches of the Smyrna fig trees, but this spread BROWN ROT. More recently, the wasps have been reared in sterile incubators to be released in fig orchards.

FIGWORT. Common name for SCROPHULARIA, a genus of herbs and shrubs grown for medical and ornamental purposes. The Figwort Family is SCROPHULARIACEAE.

FILAMENT. A threadlike body; particularly the anther-bearing stalk of a stamen. See FLOWER.

FILBERT. Common name for CORYLUS, a genus of deciduous trees planted for ornament and for their edible nuts.

FILIPENDULA (fi li PEN dyoo lah). A genus of hardy perennial herbs, belonging to the Rosaceae (Rose Family), and sometimes known as meadowsweet. Filipendulas resemble certain spireas, having very finely cut leaves and small white, pink, or purple flowers borne in clusters. They are showy, easily grown plants for the border, and some species are of such robust growth that they can be naturalized by the edges of streams or ponds. All are increased by seed or division; various species are hardy in Zones 3–9.

PRINCIPAL SPECIES

F. camtschatica is a tall species with lobed leaves and white flowers.

F. palmata, growing to 4 ft., has large, pale pink flowers in late summer.

F. purpurea grows to 4 ft. and has pink or purple flowers. One of the handsomest species, it is often forced in pots indoors and should be given winter protection in colder regions. Var. *alba* has white blossoms. Var. *elegans* has white flowers with prominent red stamens.

F. rubra (queen-of-the-prairie), native from Pennsylvania to Kentucky, grows about 8 ft. high and has large clusters of exquisite, peach-blossom pink flowers.

F. ulmaria (queen-of-the-meadow) is native to Asia and is a garden escapee in the eastern states. Sometimes cultivated in hardy borders, it grows to 6 ft. and has cut leaves, white woolly beneath, and white flowers in dense panicles.

Filipendula ulmaria

Var. *aurea* is the same as the species type but has yellow-green leaves.

F. vulgaris (dropwort), native to Europe and Asia, grows 2–3 ft. tall and has tuberous rootstocks, beautiful fernlike foliage, and sprays of delicate white flowers in summer. Unlike other species, it withstands drought conditions.

FILMY FERNS. A group of delicate, often diminutive plants having a single layer of cell tissues that produces a transparent texture through which the veining and bristlelike receptacles for the sporangia can be seen. The group includes two genera, *Hymenophyllum* and *Trichomanes*, which differ only slightly. Dripping cliffs and dank ravines are their habitat, and a moist atmosphere is essential for their growth. They can only be cultivated indoors in specially built structures that can maintain the precise conditions they demand. Occasionally the smallest ones can be maintained in a terrarium. A few temperate zone species are far more abundant in southern England and Ireland than in North America. *H. tunbrigense* (Tunbridge fern) and *T. boschianum* are found in the southeastern states.

FINOCCHIO (fi NOH kee oh). Native (Italian) and common name for sweet or Florence fennel, *Foeniculum vulgare* var. *azoricum*, grown for its edible thickened leaf stalks; see FOENICULUM.

FIR. Common name for ABIES, a widely varied genus of handsome pyramidal hardy evergreen trees belonging to the Pinaceae (Pine Family).

The common name is also applied to other genera. China-fir is *Cunninghamia*. Douglas- or red-fir is *Pseudotsuga*. Joint-fir is *Ephedra*. Summer-fir is *Artemisia gmelinii* cv. 'Viridis'.

FIRE ANT. Common name for a vicious biting ant, *Solenopsis invicta*, introduced to the southern states from South America; see ANTS.

FIRE BLIGHT. A serious bacterial disease affecting apples, pears, quinces, and many ornamental shrubs, among them shadbush, Japanese quince, cotoneaster, hawthorn, species of prunus, firethorn, rose, and spirea. Affected portions are black or brown with the appearance of having been scorched. In spring the blossoms may be blighted and the twigs die back rapidly, with dark, drooping leaves. During the summer, infection may spread to the larger limbs and main trunk where "hold-over" cankers may form in which the bacteria can survive the winter. The disease is spread chiefly by insects, especially bees, and by wind-blown rain.

The blossom blight phase can be avoided by choosing disease-resistant varieties. Also avoid overfertilizing. Eradication is the chief means of control. To do this, break off or prune out all blighted blossom clusters and remove all diseased limbs and twigs, cutting several inches below the visibly blighted part. After each cut, disinfect the pruning tool with 70% denatured alcohol or a solution of 9 parts water to 1 part bleach. Wash and dry tools after use. Consult your local extension service for safe guidelines for your area.

FIRECRACKER-FLOWER. Common name for the scarlet-flowered *Dichelostemma ida-maia*, native to California; see DICHELOSTEMMA.

FIRETHORN. Common name for PYRACANTHA, a genus of shrubs, mostly thorny, with showy berries.

FIREWEED. A common name for *Epilobium angustifolium*, a robust perennial with long spikes of rosy purple flowers; see EPILOBIUM.

FIRMIANA (fur mee AY nah). A genus of Asiatic trees belonging to the Sterculiaceae (Sterculia Family), and variously known as Chinese parasol, phoenix, or varnish tree. They resemble plane trees (the genus *Platanus*) and are grown for shade as street or lawn specimens in the South. Trees are propagated by seed, easily transplanted, and hardy to Zone 9.

C. simplex, native to China and Japan, is a deciduous tree that grows to 50 ft. and has lobed leaves 1 ft. across. Cv. 'Variegata' has white markings on the leaves.

FISHHOOK CACTUS. Common name for some species of FEROCACTUS, because of their hooked or barbed spines.

FISHTAIL PALM. Common name for decorative trees with leaves spreading at the tips like fish tails, especially the genus CARYOTA. Thorny-fishtail palm refers to AIPHANES.

FITTONIA (fi TOH nee ah). A genus of tropical perennial herbs belonging to the Acanthaceae (Acanthus Family), grown for their hairy, beautifully veined foliage. They make excellent houseplants and are especially useful in terrariums and fluorescent-light gardens. The small two-lipped flowers are quite inconspicuous, being borne in slender spikes beneath bracts. Fittonias are useful low or creeping foliage plants, often grown beneath greenhouse benches or in shade where few other plants thrive. Plants should be potted in a soil of equal parts of loam, leaf mold, and sand. They should be kept shaded and grown in a temperature never lower than 55°F.

F. gigantea grows to 18 in. and has short-pointed leaves veined with rosy red.

F. verschaffeltii has dark green leaves beautifully veined with red. Var. *argyroneura* has white-veined leaves. Var. *pearcei* has leaves with carmine veins and hairless undersides.

FIVE-SPOT. Common name for *Nemophila maculata*, a California annual whose white flowers bear purple spots on each of the five lobes.

FLACOURTIA (flah KOOR tee ah). A genus of tropical shrubs and trees, sometimes spiny, and of no particular value. One shrubby species, *F. indica*, is an Asiatic species that has been introduced to California and Florida for its edible fruit and is given the common names ramontchi, governor's-plum, and batoko-plum. It is not particular as to soil but will not tolerate frost. The small, yellowish flowers are followed by cherrylike, dark maroon, pulpy fruits which are used for jams and preserves.

FLAMBOYANT. A common name for *Delonix regia*, a flowering tropical tree; see DELONIX.

FLAMINGO FLOWER. Common name for *Anthurium andraeanum*, a popular greenhouse plant bearing large heart-shaped leaves and brilliant orange-red to white, calla-like bracts surrounding the flowers.

FLANNELBUSH. Common name for *Fremontodendron californicum*, a tender, drought-resistant shrub with showy yellow flowers; see FREMONTODENDRON.

FLAT. A shallow box (1) in which seed is sown (usually indoors), (2) to which seedlings are transferred (pricked out) as soon as they are large enough to handle, and (3) from which such seedlings are transplanted to a hotbed, frame, or outdoors when of suitable size. Flats are especially handy for the small gardener, as they make possible more and better work in a given time than any other means of handling seedlings. Back-breaking labor over a frame is eliminated, for flats can be brought indoors where sowing and transplanting can be done on tables or benches of convenient height, regardless of the weather. Moisture control is easier than in outdoor beds, with a resulting bonus of better plants. If evenly spaced, the number of plants in flats of uniform size can be estimated at a glance. When it comes time to transplant, each plant can be lifted from the flat with ample soil around its roots.

Flats made from soap boxes and other miscellaneous containers can be satisfactory in themselves, but they are not ideal because the irregular sizes tend to waste space, and being made of light, cheap lumber, they are not durable. The size of the standard flat varies somewhat with the geographical area (18" x 18" x 2¾" outside dimensions is common), and while they were all previously made of wood (cypress or redwood), plastic is now the favored material. Flats always contain numerous drain holes.

When preparing the seedbed, a single page of an old telephone book or newspaper is placed on the bottom of the flat so that the planting medium does not fall through. On this, loose, friable soil (⅓ loam, ⅓ leaf mold or other humus, and ⅓ sharp sand well mixed and sifted) is spread to within ½ in. of the top. After this has been firmed slightly with a brick or block of wood (especially in the corners), a thin (⅛-in.) layer of even finer soil, resifted, is spread loosely on the surface in which the seed is sown. Prior to sowing, however, the soil should be well moistened either with a fine spray or by placing the flat half its depth in water until the soil is saturated; then let it dry until in good shape for sowing.

Preparing the seedbed

Since the seedlings do not remain long in the flat, the soil mixture needs little or no fertilizer supplement; it is simply a medium for seed germination and as such needs only to maintain the required moisture and temperature conditions.

FLAX. Common name for LINUM, a genus of herbs grown both for commercial and garden purposes. The common name is also applied to other plants. East Indian or yellow flax is a species of *Reinwardtia*. Mountain- and New-Zealand-flax are species of PHORMIUM. Toadflax refers to a few species of LINARIA.

FLEABANE. A common name for ERIGERON, a genus of annual and perennial herbs with variously colored ray and disk flowers.

FLEA BEETLE. The Alticinae, a subfamily of the Chrysomilidae (Leaf Beetle Family) is named for the insects' habit of jumping like fleas when disturbed. The various species go by names of the plants they attack, such as eggplant, grape, potato, spinach, strawberry, and sweet potato flea beetles. Some kinds have been released to fight weeds, such as those in Wisconsin used to fight Canada thistle. Others, like the potato flea beetle (*Epiyrix cucumeris*), spread diseases

Flea beetle

such as early potato blight, sometimes causing the death of the plants. The striped flea beetle, *Phyllotreta striolata*, attacks most members of the Brassicaceae (Mustard Family).

Adults are ⅕ in. or smaller and are rarely seen because they quickly hop away. They emerge from the soil in spring, attack plants immediately, and lay eggs on or at the base of the plants. The root-eating larvae are tiny, whitish, elongated forms up to ⅕ in., which later pupate in the soil. There can be several generations each year.

Infestations can be controlled by several methods. FLOATING ROW COVERS provide fairly good protection, and rotenone dusts are effective on adults. Flea beetles are also repelled by sprinklings of DIATOMACEOUS EARTH. The larvae are attacked by juvenile parasitic nematodes. Sticky white cardboard hung near the top of vulnerable plants also helps. Plants shaken over a towel or tissue will drop quite a few flea beetles. Other preventives include late planting, cleaning up debris where the pests hide over the winter, tilling infested soil, and keeping plants healthy and well watered.

FLEECEFLOWER. Common name for a few species of POLYGONUM, especially the flowering vines *P. aubertii* and *P. baldschuanicum*.

FLEUR-DE-LIS. Common name for *Iris germanica* var. *florentina*, a German variety of iris that has been adopted as the royal emblem of France; the name is also used loosely for other species of IRIS.

FLIES. Though the familiar housefly (*Musca domestica* of the order Diptera) can be a dangerous transporter of disease organisms, many other flies are beneficial.

BENEFICIAL SPECIES

The tachinid and cluster flies include 1300 species of beneficial parasitic insects that lay eggs that develop into consuming larvae inside the hosts of over 100 kinds of caterpillars. Tachinid flies look like hairy houseflies, some with large bristles on the abdomen. Be careful to protect these flies. See also WASPS.

Tachinid fly

The syrphid or hover flies are equally valuable parasites. These flies are often seen hovering and darting above flowers; many of them are bright colored and more like bees or wasps than like houseflies. Sometimes they are even classified as WASPS. They eat many aphids as well as decaying vegetable matter. The lar-

Hover fly

vae are naked and legless, rather slender, with a pointed front and no visible head. The adult hover fly is yellow and black and is a good pollinator, since it feeds on pollen and nectar. The white larvae look like tiny, transparent slugs and eat enormous quantities of aphids and have been known to eat up to 900 aphids before maturing.

Soldier flies (Stratiomylidae) are medium-sized, wasplike insects either dark or bright colored. These, too, can be seen near flowers, but they are fairly sluggish. The larvae or maggots, as fly larvae are called, are leathery, elliptical, and flattened. Some are aquatic; others are found under bark or in decaying matter. Some are found in the nests of sawflies and other Hymenoptera.

European crane flies, which look like big mosquitos, are of little benefit. Their maggots are gray-brown and leathery, often called leatherjackets. Some are predacious; others are not. Birds usually keep them under control. Aphid flies are also predacious.

See also INSECTS, BENEFICIAL.

PEST SPECIES

Among damaging flies, there is the carrot rust fly, whose maggots infest carrots. The best control is to plant carrots late (early summer and after). Tea leaves planted with the seeds sometimes help, as will pulverized wormwood put around the base of carrot plants. Repellent companion plants include onions, leeks, and garlic.

The cherry fruit fly, which looks like a housefly, lays its eggs in cherries, and the maggots consume the fruit. The insects drop to the ground when fully grown, so it is important to clean up beneath the trees and to use sprays such as rotenone or yellow sticky bands and traps—four hung in small orchards, or one per acre in large orchards. A jar of half ammonia and half water placed below the trap is helpful.

Hessian flies, *Phytophaga destructor*, are small black insects with long legs. They emerge from their pupae in early fall to lay red eggs on the upper surface of leaves of early wheat, rye, and barley. In a few days, the maggots appear and start rasping the stems to get at the sap. They have been a pest ever since Revolutionary War days when they came to this country, evidently in the straw bedding of the Hessian soldiers. Infested wheat is stunted in the fall, and plants may die during the winter. Others come up in the spring with weak straws that often break in the wind. Some of the larvae that live in the stems or leaf sheaths survive the winter, pupate, and then the adult females lay up to 300 eggs before dying. Late planting is one control, and dates should be determined with the help of the local extension service. Volunteer wheat and infected stubble should be destroyed. Crop rotation helps, as does proper fertilization. Resistant varieties include 'Ottawa', 'Ponca', 'Pawnee', 'Dual', 'Russell', and many others.

Walnut husk flies spend the winter in cases beneath walnut trees. The adults emerge in late

August to eat foliage for several weeks and then mate and lay eggs in the husks of the walnuts. The larvae then attack both husks and kernels, turning them brown and inedible. Infected and dropped nuts can be put in water to drown the maggots.

See also FRUIT FLY; INSECT CONTROL; WHITEFLY.

FLOATING-HEART. A common name for NYMPHOIDES, a genus of aquatic plants with heart-shaped leaves and delicate flowers.

FLOATING ROW COVERS. Extremely lightweight, breathable plastic covers for vegetables and flowers. Floating row covers protect plants from wind, cold, and insects while admitting air, water, and sunlight. The cover edges should be secured, and thus sealed, with stones,

Floating row cover

soil, or stakes. Remove covers from plants that are pollinated by bees when plants begin to flower.

FLORET. One of the individual, usually small, flowers that make up a dense flower cluster; in particular one of those comprising the head of a composite or the spike of a grass. See FLOWER.

FLORIBUNDA. This rose class was developed by Poulsen in Denmark early in the twentieth century by crossing a polyantha with a hybrid tea. First called hybrid polyantha, the floribunda name was given to the class by Dr. J. H. Nicholas. Early floribundas are repeat flowering, cluster blooming, hardy bedding roses. As the class developed, they became very close to the HYBRID

TEA ROSE in form. Today the blooms are like smaller hybrid teas in single stems and small clusters. It may be said they are merging into the hybrid tea class. The grandiflora class represents a merging of the floribunda with the hybrid tea, but it is not an accepted class in some countries, where the varieties pertaining to it remain floribundas. Many varieties are marketed in other countries as hybrid teas or as "flora-tea" roses.

Some early floribundas were 'Ellen Poulsen', introduced in 1911, 'Else Poulsen' and 'Kirsten Poulsen' in 1924, and 'Betty Prior' in 1935. 'Rosenelfe', introduced in 1939, was the first hybrid tea–type floribunda.

Well-known varieties are 'Europeana', 'Iceberg', 'Gene Boerner', and 'Angel Face'.

FLORICULTURE. The growing of flowers for sale, usually in a greenhouse environment for use as cut flowers, potted plants for ornamentation, or any other plant material for decorative use. Growers in the floriculture industry must produce a high-quality product free from any blemish or weather injury, making the controlled environment of a greenhouse necessary. Timing is crucial to many floriculture crops, since the bulk of fresh and potted flower sales occurs at particular seasons. Manipulating light and temperature allows the commercial floriculture grower to time peak bloom for specific dates. Most commercial floriculturists sell their product wholesale to florists or other retailers.

FLOSS-SILK TREE. Common name for *Chorisia speciosa*, a warm climate tree whose seeds are covered with cottony or silky floss; see CHORISIA.

FLOSSFLOWER. Common name for AGERATUM, a genus of attractive annuals with fluffy blue or white flowers.

FLOWER. From the gardener's standpoint, the flower is one of the most important features of plant material because of its aesthetic qualities—color, texture, fragrance, form, etc. To the plant, however, it has a different and even greater significance, because it constitutes the reproductive apparatus by which the higher plants propagate themselves; through fertilization (the union of reproductive bodies) and the production of seed containing new plants in embryo.

REPRODUCTIVE FUNCTION

In simple flowers, such as trillium, a flower stalk (peduncle) terminates in a fleshy pad (receptacle), to which other flower parts are attached. The outermost parts of the flowers are

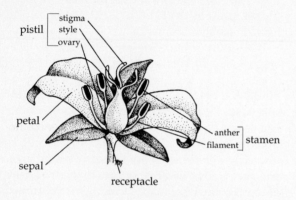

Trillium, a simple flower

the sepals, which are usually small, green, leaflike structures that cover and protect the flower while it is in the bud. Collectively all the sepals are called the calyx, which is Latin for "cup." In some species the sepals are fused together forming a tubular calyx, and in other species they resemble petals. Immediately inside the sepals are the petals, which may take on a variety of forms, some species having petals fused together into a tube, and others having petals that are free and unattached. On some flowers, all the petals are symmetrical, but on others, they take irregular forms. Collectively the petals form the corolla, or "small crown" in Latin.

In the center of the flower are the sexual parts, the male stamens and the female pistil. There may be one or several pistils depending on the species, but most flowering plants have more than one stamen. The stamen consists of a slender stalk (filament), to which pollen-bearing sacs

(anthers) are attached. The pistil has three major components, whose shapes may vary widely among species. The upper surface of the pistil, which receives pollen grains, is the stigma. The stigma is attached to the ovary at the base of the pistil by a usually slender tissue known as the style. Inside the ovary is a chamber containing the ovules, the female sex cells, which mature into seeds after fertilization.

When the flower is at the right stage for fertilization, the stigma is covered with a sticky substance that holds any pollen grain that comes in touch with it. Such a grain from a nearby flower is usually brought there by an insect. Once in place on the sticky stigma, it commences its true life function. It begins to develop a tubelike projection, which pushes itself through the surface of the stigma, extends in length, pushing downward, growing through the entire length of the style, until it reaches the ovary at the base. There it seems to seek out an ovule, touches it, and through a microscopic change in the cells of both the ovule and the tube at the point of contact, fertilizes the ovule, which then develops into a seed.

Many such pollen grains may settle on the stigma of a single flower, send their elongating tubes into the ovary, and thus bring about the development of a whole capsule-full of seeds. Every plump pea in a pod has been fertilized in this manner; the small flat ones are the ovules that no pollen has reached. Every ripe kernel of corn has been touched by a pollen tube that has grown all the way down the silk—each strand of which is the style of a flower of corn.

FLOWER TYPES

Not every flower, of course, has its parts arranged like the trillium above. In the *Campanula* (bellflower), the ovary is a swollen portion of the receptacle just below the calyx instead of inside the corolla. An ovary thus placed characterizes an inferior (epigynous) flower. If the ovary lies within the flower, as in the trillium, the flower is superior (hypogynous).

In the *Oenothera* (evening-primrose), the ovary is still farther down, for the calyx forms a long tube with four green sepals at the top and a four-celled ovary at the base. All parts of the evening-primrose are in multiples of four. There are four separate petals in the corolla; eight stamens are attached to them at the base, and the stigma expanding in the very center is divided into four sections.

Other flowers, such as those of plants in the Rosaceae (Rose Family), have an ovary position called perigynous, that is intermediate between superior and inferior. In these flowers, the stamens form a ring that encircles the ovary and the sepals, and petals are attached to the receptacle at the level of the middle of the ovary.

Flowers of the buttercup have a less definite number of parts. While there are usually five sepals, the number of petals in different species ranges from 5 to 20. The stamens are numerous and of indefinite number, and the ovary is split into many single-celled units called carpels, which arise in a thimblelike mass from the receptacle.

In the Liliaceae (Lily Family), the flower parts run characteristically in threes. Think of the spring Easter lily; look closely at one of the scillas when it comes up in the garden in spring; or in midsummer, one of the tiger lilies in the border. In any of these, you will find no definite calyx but only a spreading, funnel-shaped corolla with six pointed lobes. Botanists call three of these lobes the calyx and the other three the corolla, but the word perianth (which in any flower refers to the calyx and corolla, or the "floral envelope," together) is a more convenient term.

In some cases, the showy parts of the flowers are sepals rather than petals. In other cases, still different structures known as bracts are quite showy, standing between the true leaves of the plant and the perianth of the flower. Sometimes they resemble leaves, as in the leafy branch halfway up the stem of an anemone. Sometimes they resemble sepals, lying close beneath the flower, as in hepaticas. In other cases they resemble petals, as in dogwood and poinsettia.

A large aggregation of bracts, such as that which upholds the flower head of a chrysanthemum or thistle, is called an involucre.

COMPOSITE FLOWERS

In the Asteraceae (Aster Family, also known as Composite or Daisy Family), which includes asters, chrysanthemums, thistles, and many other familiar plants, each flower is really a head consisting of innumerable flowers, or florets, as

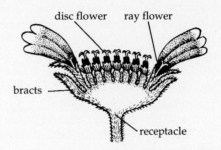

Tidy-tips, a composite flower

can be seen in tidy-tips. The small flowers or florets share a common, broad receptacle, which is usually enclosed from below by many leafy bracts. The ray flowers usually form a ring around the outside of the head. Each ray flower has a relatively long, straplike petal, which upon close inspection can be seen to be several small petals fused together. In the center of the flower head are the even smaller disk flowers, with minute, tubular corollas. The stamens and pistils in these flowers are surrounded by the petals, but they are usually so small that magnification is required to see them clearly. Many species in the Asteraceae (Aster Family) have sterile ray flowers that lack stamens and pistils entirely.

The dandelion head consists of ray flowers exclusively. The ageratum head, on the other hand, consists of only disk flowers; thistles, ironweed, and gayfeather are also in this class. In *Centaurea* (cornflower), the marginal flowers take on the aspect of rays but retain the tubular character of the disk flowers. The head is one of several ways in which flowers may be arranged. For others, see INFLORESCENCE.

REGULAR AND IRREGULAR

A glance at the flower of an apple tree, a petunia, or a tulip, reveals each part duplicated around the circle, that is, all the petals are alike in form, and other parts correspond to them. This radial symmetry gives them the name of "regular" flowers. In an irregular flower, there is only bilateral symmetry. An orchid, for instance, has one petal often developed into a lip, as in the cattleyas, or into a pouch, as in the lady's-slippers.

The snapdragon, lobelia, and lupine are other types of irregular flowers; in them, two petals are united into an upper lip and three petals into a lower lip of distinctive form. In the sweet pea (in fact, in virtually all members of the Fabaceae, or Bean Family), while the sepals are fairly regular, two of the petals are united to form an upright keel, which encloses the stamens and pistil; two more form wings, one at either side of the keel; and a fifth is broadened out to form the standard or banner, which stands at a right angle to the keel. Flowers of the violet are made irregular chiefly by the spur, which is an elongated nectar sac developed from one of the sepals.

POLLEN AND SEED DISPERSAL

Floral modifications are adapted to suit and promote the method of pollination or mode of seed distribution upon which the plant largely depends.

POLLINATION

The showy portions of the flower have evolved to attract insects to carry pollen on their rough bodies from the anthers of one flower to the stigma of another. The glands of the fragrant nectar found in some flowers doubtless serve the same purpose. When a moth or bee comes to sip the nectar, or a hummingbird to eat small insects, it catches loose grains of pollen on its body, then flies to another flower to feed, and unwittingly leaves the pollen on the sticky stigma there. See also POLLINATION.

Some flowers have neither petals nor sepals but seem to rely for attractiveness on a large, leafy bract called a spathe. In these, such as *Arisaema triphyllum* (jack-in-the-pulpit) plants, the actual flowers are structures of the simplest sort—a cluster of stamens comprises a male flower, a single-celled ovule, a female flower, and many of these are crowded on the columnar spadix, which the spathe more or less completely surrounds.

Some flowers are so particular as to the type of insect performing the pollination that they are especially constructed to respond only to certain ones. The snapdragon, for instance, has a mouth that can be opened only by a bee; a crawling ant cannot gain entrance there. Some tropical plants have a throat so long that only a certain moth with a long proboscis can reach the pollen. In the iris, the stigma has been developed into three widely separate parts, resembling three extra petals, and bearing the sticky surface for receiving pollen more or less underneath a protective shelf. The adaptations of the orchid to pollination by special insects have been the subject of volumes of scientific writing.

The majority of flowers produce more vigorous seed when they have been cross-pollinated —that is, they receive pollen from another plant of the same kind—or at least close pollinated by another flower from the same plant. Yet some are formed so that only the pollen from their own stamens can reach their pistils. Such flowers are called self-pollinated.

Each kind of flower has its own peculiarities in this respect, and many devices are employed to fulfill these requirements. In certain flowers, to induce cross-pollination, the stigma does not become sticky until after the pollen is shed. In others, the stigma may ripen first, receive pollen from outside sources, and then, its function completed, dry up at the time the stamens within the same flower begin to shake out their pollen.

SEED DISTRIBUTION

When the time comes for seed dispersal, some plants provide their seeds with feathery wings, like the dandelion and milkweed. Others, especially trees such as maple, ailanthus, and elm, send their seeds on the wind with winged fruits. Other plants have their seeds carried by means of burrs. Seeds of aquatic plants usually have special apparatus for floating, while seeds of some plants, including violets, garden-balsam, and witch-hazel, are shot out with such force when their capsule bursts that they fall clear of the parent plant where they can start growing, under favorable circumstances, or be carried elsewhere.

FLOWER CLASSIFICATION

The form of the flowers is the basis of classification. By this method, orders, families, genera, species, and varieties of the plants are identified and named (see PLANT NAMES AND CLASSIFICATION). It is chiefly the genera and species that are of concern to the gardener, though the identification of certain varieties means recognition of often superior plants for garden use, while a knowledge of the main families of flowering plants is helpful in recognizing and choosing new garden subjects and estimating what may be expected of them.

FLOWERPOTS. A container in which plants are grown, either temporarily or permanently. They used to be made almost exclusively of clay, but now the plastic pot is a commonly used competitor. For various special purposes, pots are also made of concrete, peat moss, paper, glazed crockery, glass, or wood. Large plastic or wooden pots or tubs are used for large foliage plants such as palms, particularly in hotel lobbies and large reception rooms.

Plastic and porous clay pots come in many sizes, from 1–12 in. or more in diameter, and are of various depths depending on their intended use. Most have a drainage hole in the bottom.

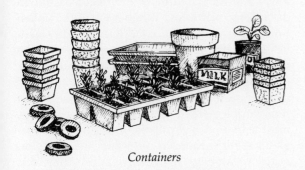

Containers

The standard and most common shape is about twice as wide at the top as at the base.

Seed pans, bulb pans, and azalea pans are actually shallow pots varying from 2–6 in. deep and 6–8 in. across. They are used for starting small seeds, rooting cuttings, forcing bulbs, and growing shallow-rooted plants.

Clay Pots. When using brand new clay pots, of any kind, they should be soaked a few minutes in water before planting; otherwise, they will draw water from the soil and rob the plants. Previously used or dirty pots of any kind, besides being unsightly, may contain disease organisms and should always be washed, and scrubbed if necessary, prior to re-use. A good disinfectant is household bleach and water in a solution that is slick to the touch. One advantage to nonporous pots is that they are so much easier to clean. A white crust on the upper edge of a clay pot is accumulated salts from the water; the worst of this can be removed by soaking for a few minutes in water.

Peat Pots. Pots made of compressed peat moss are sometimes used for starting plants that do not like to have their root system disturbed during transplanting. These pots retain moisture, and

Peat pot

the roots easily penetrate their walls, which become soft and disintegrate into the soil when they are set in the ground.

Paper Pots. Pots made of thin but strong waterproof, flexible cardboard or roofing paper are used for growing, and especially for shipping young plants, such as vegetables and annual or perennial ornamentals. Made with interlocking but easily opened bottoms, they can be left on the plants when they are set out to keep the root ball intact. The rim, if allowed to stand slightly above the soil level, helps to ward off cutworms. Some kinds of paper pots will eventually break down and let the roots spread into the soil.

Nonporous Pots. Nonporous pots of plastic or glazed crockery are now common, especially for houseplants. Extensive experiments have revealed interesting facts about the distribution of roots in the soil in porous and nonporous containers, the different rates of evaporation from them, and other factors affecting plant growth. In a greenhouse where the air is moist and conditions are kept uniform, the old-style clay pot is entirely satisfactory; however, where the air is almost always dry and the temperature liable to fluctuate, the nonporous type requires less attention and less frequent watering while insuring better results and stronger, more vigorous plants.

FLUORESCENT LIGHT. Tubular, low-watt electric lamps useful for promoting growth of indoor plants; see ARTIFICIAL LIGHT.

FOAMFLOWER. Common name for *Tiarella cordifolia*, an eastern wildflower with delicate blossoms and interesting color variations; see TIARELLA.

FOENICULUM (fee NIK yoo lum) **vulgare.** A hardy, perennial European herb, commonly known as fennel, grown as an annual or biennial for its aromatic seeds and fragrant leaves, both of which are used for flavoring. Since the seed is slow to sprout, sow it in early spring. The plants require full sunlight but only the simplest culture in any good garden soil. In places, it has become a pestiferous weed, giving an unpleasant flavor to the milk and butter of cows that eat it, as do garlic and wild onion.

Foeniculum vulgare

In var. *azoricum* (Florence fennel or finnocchio, sometimes incorrectly called anise) the greatly enlarged leaf bases form a bulblike structure 3–4 in. in diameter and are called the "apple." When blanched by earthing up, it can be cooked as a vegetable or eaten raw; the stalks, resembling anise-flavored celery, can also be eaten raw. As the plants grow rapidly, make successional sowings two weeks apart. This variety is often incorrectly listed as *F. dulce*, which lacks the thickened base.

FOLIAGE PLANTS. A wide range of plants are grown for the decorative value of their leaves rather than for their flowers. In some cases the foliage is highly and variously colored, as in the genus *Codiaeum*, the various forms of which are known as crotons. With many others, while the foliage may be green, their general habit of growth, as well as the pleasing character of the individual leaves, renders them of outstanding decorative value.

Foliage plants associate well with flowering plants and serve to show off their floral beauty to better advantage. In general, they are of a much more permanent character than flowering plants and on the whole require less cultural skill to secure effective results.

A great many are available for the adornment of greenhouses, conservatories, and other indoor settings—ranging all the way from such large and permanent occupants as palms down to the lowly but colorful forms of Rex begonias and the deciduous caladiums. While some of the woody foliage plants require good light conditions to develop their best color, a great many will thrive under shadier conditions than are suitable for most flowering plants. An annual repotting is usually sufficient to keep them in good condition, supplemented by feeding when growth is most active. A sharp lookout should be kept at all times for such insect pests as scale, red spider mites, mealybugs, and thrips; appropriate control measures should be taken as soon as their presence is detected.

PALMS

In general, palms are of easy culture, obtainable in various forms, and most useful and lasting in decorative groups or as single specimens.

In large glass structures they can be planted in beds, but most kinds can be maintained in good condition for some time in comparatively small pots or tubs. They appreciate feeding and should never be allowed to get really dry. The following are good examples, and details concerning them will be found under their respective genera: *Archontophoenix cunninghamiana*, *Caryota urens*, *Chamaedorea glaucifolia*, *Chrysalidocarpus lutescens*, *Howea belmoreana*, *Licuala grandis*, *Livistona chinensis*, *Phoenix roebelenii*, *Rhapis excelsa*, and *Thrinax radiata*.

See also PALMS.

FERNS

This great group of flowerless plants contains a great many forms notable for their grace of habit and beauty of leaf form. Ferns are highly valued to combine with both flowering plants and cut flowers. In view of their diversity of form and varied shades of color, a greenhouse devoted entirely to ferns can be a place of utmost attractiveness all year round. The following are good examples in their respective groups: *Alsophila australis*, *A. tricolor*, *Blechnum gibbum*, *Cibotium schiedei*, and *Dicksonia antarctica*. All of these develop trunks of varying length in maturity and are known as TREE FERNS. Large and well-grown specimens are very imposing and stay in better condition if the trunks are kept moist. See also FERNS.

HERBS WITH SHOWY LEAVES

Species of *Alocasia* make very handsome potted plants. *A. cuprea*, *A. korthalsii*, *A. sanderana*, and various hybrids are distinguished for the size, shape, and beautiful markings of their leaves. *Anthurium crystallinum*, *A. magnificum*, *A. veitchii*, and *A. warocqueanum* are magnificent foliage plants when well grown. Fancy-leaved species of *Caladium*, forms of *C. bicolor* and *C. picturatum*, are showy for indoor decoration and can also be used outdoors in subtropical bedding. *Calathea* spp. will tolerate a lot of shade and occur in good variety. *C. ornata*, *C. roseopicta*, *C. veitchiana*, and *C. zebrina* are among the best.

Cissus discolor shows its highly colored leaves

to advantage either trained on a form or grown as a vine. The many colorful forms of *Coleus blumei* can be quickly grown into large handsome specimens for decoration; they are also popular for summer bedding. *Gynura aurantiaca* (velvetplant) produces leaves of good color when grown in a well-lighted location in the greenhouse. *Monstera deliciosa*, *Philodendron melanochrysum*, *P. verrucosum*, and *Xanthosoma lindenii* are interesting and attractive members of the Araceae (Arum Family), well worth a place in choice collections.

Caladium sp.

SHRUBBY FOLIAGE PLANTS

Some of these are hard wooded, and while they can be kept in fairly good condition for some years, it is wise to keep the young plants coming along from cuttings.

Abutilon savitzii is a rather dwarf member of the group but attractive, with silvery-edged leaves; it is useful as a summer bedding plant or for greenhouse adornment. *A. pictum* cv. 'Thompsonii' is a strong grower with large lobed leaves blotched creamy white and yellow. The variegated form of *A. megapotamicum* is very useful and attractive for furnishing baskets and vases. *Acalypha wilkesiana* and its varieties make good bushy plants with handsome bronzy-green leaves, blotched or mottled with coppery, orange, red, and crimson shades. *Begonia* x *argenteo-guttata*, *B. metallica*, and *B. sanguinea* are shrubby species well worth growing for their foliage alone.

The common *Ficus elastica* (rubber plant) and its variegated form have long been known for their ability to stand tough treatment; and the same is true of *F. lyrata*. The showiest of the group is *F. aspera*, but it is not of such robust growth, and its thin leaves, blotched with creamy white, are rather tender. *F. benjamina*, an extremely popular indoor tree, lives on indefinitely once adapted to reduced circumstances indoors; branches may need pruning back in spring by as much as one-fourth to one-third their length.

Hibiscus rosa-sinensis cv. 'Cooperi' has leaves marked with crimson-and-white variegations that are especially showy in young plants. *Pandanus* spp. (screw-pine) are very useful decorative plants in the juvenile state and make imposing specimens when planted out with plenty of room to develop. *P. baptistii* is the easiest to handle, having no prickles; but *P. veitchii* and *P. sanderi* are very popular in spite of their spiny character. *Sanchezia speciosa* and *Strobilanthes dyeranus* make handsome plants, with the best leaf coloring found in young specimens.

ANNUALS

Annuals and other plants that can be grown as annuals include a number of good foliage plants especially valuable in summer bedding arrangements. They can be raised annually from seed sown indoors early in the year. Gray-leaved plants are always most effective, and prominent among them are the so-called dusty millers, including *Senecio cineraria* and its varieties, *S. vira-vira*, *Centaurea cineraria*, and *C. gymnocarpa*. *Chrysanthemum parthenium* (feverfew) occurs in various forms of neat compact plants with yellow foliage. For dark crimson foliage effects, the highly developed, colored-leaf forms of *Beta vulgaris*, the common garden beet, are most effective. *Amaranthus tricolor* cv. 'Splendens' is a striking and colorful plant with leaves of rich red marked with yellow and bronzygreen. *Artemisia gmelinii* cv. 'Viridis' (summerfir) and *Kochia scoparia* (summer-cypress) make very neat, compact specimens with feathery foliage.

Albizia distachya, with straight stems and finely cut leaves, gives a very graceful effect. Young plants of *Eucalyptus globulus* (blue gum) are very striking. *Melianthus major* is attractive with light green leaves of good size cut into nine to eleven leaflets. The various forms of *Ricinus communis* (castor bean) are outstanding for bold and stately effects.

HARDY FOLIAGE PLANTS

A number of herbaceous perennials and subshrubs with good foliage value can be selected for use in flower gardens and shrub borders. *Artemisia abrotanum* (old-man), *A. stellerana* (old-woman), and *A. ludoviciana* var. *albula* (silver-king) give bushy, gray and silvery effects. *Lavandula angustifolia* (lavender) and *Santolina chamaecyparissus* (lavender-cotton) are also effective silvery subshrubs, good in connection with rockwork. *Cerastium tomentosum* and *Stachys byzantina* are good for low silvery mats and patches—the latter being best when flower stems are cut off early.

The old-fashioned *Dianthus plumarius* (pink) would be well worth growing for its glaucous foliage, even if it never flowered. In some places the blue-green *Ruta graveolens* (rue) can be used to produce an unusual effect. *Macleaya cordata* (plume-poppy) is too big and spreading for the average flower border, but a clump in a corner, or with shrubs, can be one of the most effective things in the garden, both in bloom and at other times.

FOLLICLE. A type of simple, many-seeded fruit or seedpod that opens along only one suture. It may occur alone, as in milkweed, or as one section of a compound ovary, as in delphiniums or peonies.

FONTANESIA (fahn tah NEE zee ah). A genus of deciduous shrubs of western Asia, resembling LIGUSTRUM in their leaves and clusters of small white flowers. Belonging to the Oleaceae (Olive Family), these shrubs are easily grown in ordinary garden soil, and are readily propagated by seed or cuttings. There are only two species: *F. phyllyreoides*, growing to 10 ft., is only halfhardy and has small, grayish green leaves. *F. fortunei* is a taller shrub with glossy leaves held late in the fall and is hardy to Zone 5.

FORCING. The growing of plants outside their natural seasons. Forcing is most often used to speed up the maturation of a plant. Heating cables, coldframes, plastic covers, and greenhouses are commonly used to force plants.

FORGET-ME-NOT. Common name for MYOSOTIS, a popular genus of hardy, low-growing herbs with bright flowers. Cape- and summer-forget-me-not refer to species of ANCHUSA, a genus of herbs whose blue flowers have red-and-white markings. Chinese-forget-me-not is *Cynoglossum amabile*. Creeping-forget-me-not is *Omphalodes verna*, a perennial herb with blue flowers and prolific runners; see OMPHALODES.

FORSYTHIA (for SITH ee ah). A genus of hardy deciduous shrubs, native in Asia, and belonging to the Oleaceae (Olive Family). With their wealth of brilliant yellow flowers appearing before the leaves, they are among the showiest of spring-flowering shrubs. Hardy in Zones 5–9, they are not particular as to soil and do well in partial shade as well as in the open. They also have lovely foliage, the slender, clean-looking leaves being carried late into the fall and sometimes becoming handsomely olive or purplish in color. Propagation is by cutting of green or mature wood and by layers.

Nodular outgrowths, or galls, ¼–1 in. in diameter are caused by a fungus and may occur along forsythia stems, which should then be removed and burned.

PRINCIPAL SPECIES

F. x *intermedia* (border forsythia) is a hybrid of *F. suspensa* and *F. viridissima*. Growing to 10 ft., it has clustered yellow flowers on arching branches. There are several useful cultivars, including 'Spectabilis', a strong grower with the largest and showiest flowers of the group, and 'Spring Glory', with an abundance of pale yellow flowers.

F. ovata is a Korean species, the hardiest species (to Zone 5) and also the earliest to bloom. It has amber-yellow flowers borne singly.

F. suspensa grows to 8 ft. or more, with slender branches, often bending to the ground and rooting at the tips. In bloom, it forms a golden yellow mound. Var. *sieboldii* (weeping forsythia) has more slender branches and can be used effectively to cover a wall or arbor. Hardy to Zone 5.

F. viridissima is conspicuous with its bright green stems and leaves, which turn dark purple in the fall. It is rather stiff, more tender than most, and later to bloom. Cv. 'Bronxensis' is an important dwarf, compact form that grows only 12 in. high, spreading to 3 ft., and has smaller leaves. Hardy to Zone 5.

FORTUNELLA. A genus of small tropical evergreen trees related to citrus; see KUMQUAT.

FOTHERGILLA (faw thur GIL ah). A genus of deciduous shrubs of North America, belonging to the Hamamelidaceae (Witch-hazel Family). They are branched, of medium height, and thrive best in moist, sandy loam with plenty of peat or leaf mold. The flowers, though without petals, present very conspicuous clusters of long white stamens tipped with yellow anthers; they are quite fragrant and smell like honey. In the fall, the leaves assume very colorful tones. Propagation is easiest by root cuttings or suckers.

F. gardenii, of dwarf slender habit, has small flower clusters opening before the leaves, which turn crimson in autumn. Hardy in Zones 5–8.

F. major, the best known, is a roundish, compact shrub that grows 10 ft. or more with orange-yellow leaves in the fall. Hardy in Zones 5–8.

FOUNDATION PLANTING. Plants can be added along the foundations of buildings to hide cellar walls or to tie the architecture in with the site. Tightly clipped evergreens have often been chosen for this duty, but other options are available, such as flowering shrubs, planters, even food plants.

Perennials are popular because they add interesting foliage textures and a changing variety of colorful blooms to an otherwise green landscape. The best perennials to use near a house are those that will develop into good-sized plants but not spread out too much. Because they are always on display, they should have attractive foliage and look nice even when not in bloom.

When planting evergreen or flowering shrubs, begin by placing the tallest (at maturity) at the corners and on each side of doorways, and use progressively lower plants in between. Large clumps of the more massive perennials can also be planted this way.

Planting close to any structure raises problems not generally encountered in more open spaces. The obvious question of light and shade requirements should be considered. In selecting spots for plants, be careful to avoid water runoff from the roof, which is likely to pummel anything planted in its path. For most plants, the soil should be carefully prepared first by digging to loosen the soil as much as possible, especially for large plants or shrubs, since root space will naturally be limited by the foundation barrier.

Especially around new structures, be careful to remove any rocks or scraps of building material that may be buried near the foundation. Soil chemistry may be affected, depending on the construction material used, permitting excessive acid or lime to leach into the soil. While this may not be apparent for some time, it sometimes explains lack of vigor in foundation plantings, and is easily corrected once the problem is identified; see ACID SOIL.

FOUNTAIN GRASS. Common name for *Pennisetum alopecuroides*, a tall, perennial ornamental grass from China; see PENNISETUM.

FOUQUIERIA (foo kee AIR ee ah). A genus of cactuslike plants of the semitropical desert of the southwestern United States and northern Mexico, belonging to the Fouquieraceae (Ocotillo Family), and commonly known as candlewood. In the dry season, leaves of the spiny shrubs or small trees fall, leaving the slender, erect stems that resemble dead sticks. In the rainy season, they flame with brilliant flowers borne in slender panicles or racemes to 10 in. long.

The chief species, *F. splendens* (ocotillo, vine cactus, coach-whip), has furrowed, spiny, whip-like branches, tiny leaves, and terminal tassels of scarlet, hummingbird-pollinated flowers about 1

in. long. In the deserts of the southwestern United States and Mexico, ocotillo is often used as a fence because of its formidable spines, and the stems often take root and form a living fence.

The other genus of the family is the monotypic *Idria*, whose only member, the cirio or boojum tree, forms a dominant and otherworldly element in the vegetation of north-central Baja California, looking like enormous, upside-down carrots. By the most recent classification, it has been included in *Fouquieria*.

Similar to the boojum are the barrel trees of central Mexico, *F. fasciculata* and *F. purpusii*, both with enlarged succulent blue-green stems and small white flowers.

FOUQUIERIACEAE (foo kee air ee AY see ee). A family of North American xerophytic to succulent trees and shrubs, commonly known as the Ocotillo Family, and including the genus FOUQUIERIA. All members of this small family have small "fugacious" leaves that appear virtually overnight when the rains start, only to dry up and fall as soon as it dries out again, thus conserving precious moisture against loss through transpiration.

FOUR-LINED PLANT BUG. The sucking insect *Poecilocapsus lineatus*, a true bug, is generally considered an enemy of currants, but it also attacks many weeds, ornamentals, garden vegetables, and even fruit trees east of the Rocky Mountains. The young nymphs are bright red and the adults are greenish yellow with four distinct black stripes down the wing covers. The eggs winter over in slits in the canes of currants and other plants, and hatch in late spring. The feeding of the young bugs causes small whitish dots on the upper surfaces of the leaves, which may turn brown and drop off while new growth may wilt. When this pest infests chrysanthemums, it leaves black spots on the leaves. It is also about the only pest to attack the Lamiaceae (Mint Family). Kerosene emulsion or pyrethrum spray can be used to kill the nymphs, but frequent and thorough spraying will be necessary.

Insecticidal dusts may prove effective, and diatomaceous earth should also be tried.

FOXGLOVE. Common name for DIGITALIS, a genus of herbs cultivated for their flowers and for medicinal purposes.

FRAGARIA (fra GAY ree uh). A genus of herbs including the cultivated STRAWBERRY.

FRAGILE FERN. Common name for *Cystopteris fragilis*, a hardy but dainty fern with brittle fronds; see CYSTOPTERIS.

FRAME. An abbreviated name for a COLDFRAME, a topless, bottomless box used to grow plants. Compare HOTBED.

FRANCOA (fran KOH ah). A genus of perennial herbs with mostly basal leaves, native to Chile, and belonging to the Saxifragaceae (Saxifrage Family). They are useful border plants in mild regions and are sometimes grown in the cool greenhouse. Propagation is by seed or division; most species are hardy to Zone 8.

F. ramosa (maiden's-wreath) is relatively tall and has a woody base and arching spikes of white flowers on a branching stem.

F. sonchifolia has leaves with rounded lobes and leaf stalks strongly winged at the base. It bears a long-stemmed raceme of pink flowers.

FRANGIPANI. Common name for PLUMERIA, a genus of tropical shrubs, and for the perfumes derived from them.

FRANKLINIA (frank LIN ee ah). A monotypic genus belonging to the Theaceae (Tea Family) and formerly listed as *Gordonia alatamaha*. The one species, *F. alatamaha*, is commonly known as the Franklin tree, named in honor of Benjamin Franklin. Once native to Georgia, it was discovered by John Bartram in 1770 and has never been seen in the wild since. Fortunately, Mr. Bartram brought a few seedlings back to Philadelphia where he propagated and disseminated this rare

and lovely small tree. All *Franklinia* seen today are direct descendants of these original seedlings. Though difficult to get established, it can be grown as far north as Boston in sheltered locations. It prefers moist, acid soil and is propagated by seed, layers, or greenwood cuttings under glass.

Franklinia is a large shrub or small tree that grows to 30 ft. and has 6-in.-long leaves that turn bright orange or red in the fall. The beautiful, fragrant, white, 3-in. flowers with bright yellow stamens resemble single white roses and bloom from midsummer to early fall. This is a very unusual, aristocratic specimen plant for any garden and is worth the effort wherever it can be grown. Hardy in Zones 6–9.

FRANKLIN TREE. Common name for FRANK-LINIA, a genus comprised of one rare, small tree once native to Georgia and now surviving only through cultivation.

FRAXINELLA. A common name for *Dictamnus albus*, a shrubby flowering perennial that emits a flammable oil; see DICTAMNUS.

FRAXINUS (FRAK si nus). A genus of large deciduous trees of the Oleaceae (Olive Family), commonly known as ash. Mostly hardy, they are important landscape subjects and sources of timber. Two native species, white and green ash are most commonly cultivated.

Ash can be propagated best by moist stratification at 65°F for 60 days followed by 1200 days at 33–40°F. Cultivars and clones are budded onto seedling understocks. They make rapid growth and, since they are dioecious and seedlings can be quite a problem, only male cultivars and clones should be planted.

Oyster-shell scale attacks ash but can be controlled with a dormant oil spray. Carpenter worms and other borers can be controlled with insecticides. See also INSECT CONTROL; SPRAYING.

PRINCIPAL SPECIES

F. americana (white ash), native throughout the United States, is high branching with an oval shape, growing to over 100 ft. in the wild and about 75 ft. in cultivation. Due to numerous disease and insect problems, it is not commonly grown. Cv. 'Autumn Purple' and 'Autumn Applause' are male clones with handsome purple color in the fall. Hardy in Zones 3–9.

Fraxinus americana

F. excelsior (European ash) grows 70 to 120 ft. or higher and has a rounded and spreading outline. Attractive dark green leaves keep their color until late in the fall. This species has been cultivated for centuries in Europe and Asia, where many cultivars are grown. 'Aurea' is more compact and slow growing, with showy yellow stems and branches in winter and outstanding deep-yellow fall color. 'Pendula' is a small, rounded tree with weeping branches. 'Hessei' is a newer male clone that has shiny, dark green leaves, an oval to rounded form, and hardy, vigorous growth to 60 ft. Hardy in Zones 4–7.

F. nigra (black ash) is a wetland or swamp species native to eastern North America. It grows to 75 ft. and has flowers appearing before the leaves. Its wood is highly prized for making splint baskets.

F. ornus (flowering ash), native to Europe, grows to about 50 ft. high and spreads about as wide, with fragrant, showy white panicles of flowers in late spring. It makes a fine specimen plant and, although not often seen or grown in the United States, has been cultivated in European gardens for over 300 years. Hardy in Zones 5–6.

F. pennsylvanica (green ash), a North American native with upright, spreading habit, grows to 60 ft. and is also subject to disease and insect problems. Cv. 'Marshall's Seedless' is a male clone with glossy, dark green foliage and yellow fall color. Hardy in Zones 3–9.

FRECKLEFACE. Common name for HYPOESTES, a genus of tropical herbs that have green leaves spotted with pink, red, or white.

FREESIA (FREE zee ah). A genus of South African bulbous plants that are important as a commercial florists' cut flower but are of limited value to the home gardener in most parts of the country because of the special conditions and handling needed for them to flower.

The bulbs are produced commercially in southern California, where freesias are a popular and beautiful garden flower; they are planted outdoors in early fall and bloom profusely in midwinter. As a conservatory or home greenhouse subject, the bulbs can be planted in pots, boxes, or benches in the early fall to flower in about three months. Hardy only in Zones 10–11, their success is largely governed by correct regulation of the temperature, which should be maintained at about 50°F. Plenty of ventilation and a well-drained soil should also be provided. After they flower and the foliage becomes yellow, the corms are dug, dried out, and kept for replanting the following autumn. Handled in this manner, they can be grown year after year with no deterioration.

The fusarium corm disease or rot, prevalent in many kinds of bulbs and affecting different freesias to varying degrees, has been so destructive in certain greenhouses that growing freesias has been practically abandoned. The dry-rot fungus of gladiolus also attacks freesias. Breaking, a virus disease prevalent on tulips, shows in freesias as a concentration of color in certain areas on the blossoms.

SELECTIONS

The many kinds of freesias available range from pure white through yellow, orange, opal, lavender, and pink with some interesting combinations. Most are forms or hybrids of two principal species. *F. armstrongii* has white flowers shaded with orange and purple. *F. refracta* has several varieties, including *alba* and *xanthospila*, both white; *leichtlinii*, pale yellow; and *odorata*, bright yellow. The hybrids, collectively listed as

F. x *hybrida*, are constantly showing improvement in form and habit as well as interesting variations in color, doubleness, and fragrance.

FREMONTODENDRON (free MAHN toh den drun) **californicum.** A handsome, evergreen, southern California shrub or small tree belonging to the Sterculiaceae (Sterculia Family), formerly listed as *Fremontia*, and commonly known as flannelbush. Though hardy only to Zone 8, it will tolerate a few degrees of frost if given a sunny position against a wall. It is completely drought resistant and needs excellent drainage. It has small, lobed leaves, resembling those of a palm, and produces a mass of large, cup-shaped yellow flowers in early summer. Propagation is by seed and softwood cuttings.

FRINGE TREE. Common name for CHIONANTHUS, a genus of trees or shrubs with showy flower panicles.

FRITILLARIA (fri ti LAIR ee ah). A large genus of bulbous plants with drooping bell-shaped flowers, belonging to the Liliaceae (Lily Family), and commonly known as fritillary.

The species vary widely in flower. Colors range from yellow to orange, scarlet, or crimson, while many are checkered in greenish, brown, or purple. Some blossoms are tightly grouped on stem tops, while others have fewer, more scattered flowers on smaller plants.

Fritillaries are generally hardy in Zones 4–9. Bulbs should be planted in early fall for flowering the next spring. The gray bulb rot of tulips may attack fritillaries, as may the lily mosaic disease. Plants that are stunted with mottled flowers should be discarded.

seed head

bulb

Fritillaria biflora

PRINCIPAL SPECIES

F. agrestis (stinkbell) is a California native whose yellowish green flowers have a disagreeable odor; hardy in Zones 9–11.

F. biflora (mission-bells, black or chocolate lily) is a small plant with flowers of a deep chocolate tint, blooming in early spring.

F. camschatcensis (Kamchatka or black lily) blooms in early spring and has dark maroon flowers.

F. imperialis (crown-imperial) is a showy species with a large cluster of nodding yellow, orange, or crimson bell-shaped flowers tightly grouped around the top of a stem 3–4 ft. high. The bulb and whole plant have a curious odor, which deters moles and gophers. Bulbs require wide spacing and deep planting in exceedingly rich earth; hardy to Zone 4.

F. lanceolata, a western species, has attractive green and purple or brown flowers.

F. meleagris (snake's-head, checkered lily, guinea-hen-tulip), with its many varieties, is the most commonly grown. Hardy to Zone 4, it is a spring-flowering form native to the western states and temperate regions of Europe. Relatively few scattered blossoms, with curious spots and veins of purple and maroon, are borne on fairly small plants.

F. pallidiflora is a western species whose greenish yellow flowers mature to pure yellow.

F. pudica is a western species with golden yellow blossoms.

F. recurva is a western species with orange and scarlet flowers.

FROGS. These primarily aquatic AMPHIBIANS are helpful as insect predators.

FROND. The entire leafy portion of any fern, including the apparent stem (stipe), the midrib, or extension of the apparent stem (rachis), and the green blade. The true stems of the ferns are either below or on the surface, sometimes abbreviated into a mere surface base for the fronds. A frond differs from a leaf in that it may bear reproductive cells on its surface and develops from a coil. See FERNS. Frond is also a term applied to the leaves of palms and cycads.

FROST. The steady frosts of midwinter do less damage than late spring and early autumn frosts, which find plants unprepared. Injury in autumn is expected and seldom causes much concern. The chief damage occurs in spring, when sap is flowing, buds are bursting their covers, and flowers are opening. Fruit crops may be completely destroyed by killing frost after the flowers have opened; this damage runs into millions of dollars per year.

At times, early fall frost occurring just after good growing weather will split the bark or wood of shrubs and trees, causing serious injury, especially to evergreens. For this reason, woody plants should never be fertilized later than early summer. Nor should any fertilizer or manure be applied between midsummer and Thanksgiving. Cultivation of the soil also should be discontinued during this period, watering restricted after September, and the soaking in preparation for winter delayed until all likelihood of stimulating growth has passed.

Warm spells in winter, by bringing up the sap in such trees as maples and followed by intense cold, cause frost cracks to open in the trunks, through which much sap is later lost. As a treatment or partial remedy for frost cracks in any bark or wood, filling with tallow and wrapping has been recommended. Better still is prevention, which means placing species likely to make fall growth or early sap flow where they will not feel the warmth of the sun, and where the ground will remain frozen late, as on a north slope or at the north side of a building or woodland. This is a common method of preventing the killing of peach buds in early spring. A heavy mulch also helps delay spring growth but should not be put in place until early winter.

In order to foresee and combat frost, its nature must be understood. A storm is normally followed by clear weather and (in the Northern Hemisphere) northerly winds—masses of cooler air moving in with the higher air pressure. The

sky clears. Toward evening the wind drops to a complete calm, and, if the temperature at sunset is 40°F or lower, frost can be expected. The clearer the sky, the greater is the probability of frost; it increases with high barometric pressure and absence of wind. Under these conditions heat is lost rapidly from the surface of the ground, plants, and other objects by radiation. Plants are still further cooled by evaporation of their moisture, and the drier the air, the faster the evaporation and consequent cooling will take place. Frost is likely to occur at any time during the night and may last all night.

Tables and charts giving the normal expected dates for the first frosts in the fall and the last in spring have been published by the National Weather Bureau, local extension services, and other agencies. They are useful in determining the earliest advisable planting time for numerous vegetables.

In the extreme south of Florida, Texas, and California, frosts occur only in winter and are rare, but their very rarity results in extensive damage, and lemon, grapefruit, and orange groves can suffer severely. The fruits themselves are sometimes frozen and lost. The trees, which are evergreen, may be partly or wholly killed. Farther north, the greatest damage is done later to the flowers of apple, peach, and related fruits, resulting in loss of a season's crop but seldom injuring the trees if varieties have been well chosen. Fruit trees blooming during the season of probable frost are so constantly in danger that the owners, aided by government forecasts, are on the alert all through the spring months.

Small fruits, especially cranberries, which are grown in low bogs, may also be injured, as may young or newly set out vegetable or ornamental plants. Magnolia flowers in the north are cut by frost more often than not, and blossoms of the flowering dogwood are occasionally nipped. Frost injury can be lessened by choice of site for garden or orchard. Fruit trees or other vulnerable plants should be placed on rising ground rather than at the bottom of a valley. A hilltop or northern slope will also protect by holding back the bursting of buds in spring until there is less likelihood of cold. In planting in natural frost pockets, frost-resistant varieties should be used.

PROTECTIVE MEASURES

Often the effects of late spring and early autumn frosts upon tender plants growing outdoors can be prevented by simple, inexpensive, easily applied precautions or by prompt treatment in the early morning after a cold snap. In a small way, individual plants can be covered to reduce the radiation of heat from the plants and from the earth. Since any covering of the ground will check radiation, small plants can be protected to a certain extent by covering them with newspapers, sheets, large inverted flower pots, crocks, peach baskets, tents of paper, boxes, or any like device. Straw scattered to a depth of several inches is often effective. For taller plants, burlap shades can be arranged. Choice small flowers or even whole rows of flowers can be shielded by a CLOCHE. This is a series of rods, plastic pipes, or branches thrust into the ground in an arch over a bed or row of plants and covered with plastic film. The ends of the film are gathered and weighted. This forms a miniature temporary greenhouse.

It should be remembered that stopping radiation from the root of the plant does not prevent air cooled by radiation a few inches away from flowing in around the plant and freezing it. Flower pots, boxes, and straw are therefore more effective than covers open at the sides, but even slight protection may be enough to maintain a nonfreezing temperature in the warmer season. Potted plants can be brought under shelter at any threat of frost, and when danger is evident, it may even pay to take up newly transplanted ornamentals of a tender nature, carry them under shelter until the cold wave has passed, then set them in the open again.

When a slight frost does occur, especially in the absence of such precautions as those mentioned, it is often possible to save plants, provided these efforts are made before the sun strikes them. In the garden, treatment consists of drenching the foliage with cold water in order to "draw the frost." Even such tender plants as dahlias, cannas, tomatoes, and melons can thus be saved, provided the temperature has not been more than a degree or two below freezing.

Potted and movable plants that have been frozen should be taken immediately, before the sun strikes them and they have a chance to thaw, to a shaded coldframe or lighted cellar, where the air, though above freezing, is cold; there they can be allowed to thaw as slowly as possible. Once badly frozen, annuals can seldom be brought back to health and should be thrown away.

FRUIT. Botanically and strictly speaking, fruit is the ripening ovary of a FLOWER, including its contents and any closely adhering parts. Examples are cucumber, pepper, tomato, apple, plum, raspberry. Sometimes the term is applied to the ripe or ripening reproductive part of any plant together with the part containing it—like wheat, barley, almond, blueberry, and peach.

The word "fruit" may refer to a specialized reproductive body of any kind (like the spore of a fungus), including any modified plant part in which it is developed. By extension of this thought, it may refer to various consolidated forms of inflorescence, including the cone of a pine.

FRUIT FLY. Strict quarantine and confiscation of fruit at U. S. borders is the result of the devastating pest *Ceratitis capitata* (Mediterranean fruit fly). The female pierces the skin of fruits, especially oranges, and lays her eggs within the fruit so the maggots sponge up the liquid of the fruit and ruin it. They feed in the fruit for ten to fourteen days. It is the most destructive member of the family, attacking 100 different kinds of plants. The female lays up to 800 eggs in a fruit. They hatch in nine to twenty days, and there can be twelve or fifteen generations each year.

The fly is somewhat smaller than a housefly and yellowish in color. No real control is available, but experiments are under way with *Opius oophilus*, which may prove to be a parasite on fruit fly eggs. See also INSECT CONTROL; FLIES.

FRUITING BODY. A structure in which spores of a FUNGUS are borne. A mushroom is an example of the larger, more complex types.

FRUIT IN THE GARDEN. A wide range of fruit for baking, for use in jams and jellies, or for eating fresh is surprisingly easy for home gardeners to grow. Even in limited space, dwarf trees, container-grown plants, and hanging strawberry baskets provide ample fruit with relatively little care. Many fruit trees and bushes are attractive additions to the home landscape throughout the season, including the bright pink peach blossoms in spring or the fall-ripened orange fruits of a leafless persimmon.

It is important to prepare the soil, assemble the required tools and materials, and even dig the holes in advance, so that stock can be planted as soon as it arrives. Most fruit trees and bushes require annual pruning and a sensible program of pest and disease control; however, they do not need as much day-to-day care as do most vegetables and flowers.

Many fruits are not adversely affected by moderate fluctuations in weather, but certain climatic details must be considered carefully when growing fruit. In addition to a season of warm weather, most temperate climate fruits need a dormant season of chilly weather. To determine which fruits are best suited to your area, contact your local extension service.

See also DISEASE; DWARF FRUIT TREES; HARVESTING; INSECT CONTROL; PROPAGATION; PRUNING; SPRAYING, and individual fruit entries.

FUCHSIA (FYOO shah). A genus of plants native to Mexico, South America, and New Zealand, longtime indoor and garden favorites, and sometimes called lady's-eardrops because of the form of the flowers. They are shrubs or trees in their native environment, but in the United States they are generally cultivated indoors as potted plants. They are also often bedded out in summer in northern gardens, while in milder climates they are grown outdoors all year. They make a lovely hanging basket plant.

As a common name, fuchsia is also applied to plants of other genera. California-fuchsia is *Zauschneria californica*; see ZAUSCHNERIA.

Fuchsia species differ widely in their appearance and growth habit, some being only 18 in. tall and others reaching 20 ft. or more. In the commonly cultivated species, the maximum height is about 12 ft. All species are shrubby and grow rapidly. The leaves are simple and usually small. Plants are generally of erect form, and they produce long branches whose extremities bear beautiful pendulous flowers in great profusion. The blossoms produced outdoors in July and August and indoors nearly all winter range in color from rose, red, and purple to white. The calyx,

Hanging fuchsia

consisting of four parts, generally is reflexed and colored to contrast beautifully with the corolla, which also has four parts.

CULTURE

Fuchsias are often trained and pruned to form standards or large pyramids with one central stem. In developing the pyramidal shape, all shoots except the leader must be pinched in, carefully and systematically. Growth of fuchias is so rapid that, with proper outdoor conditions (Zones 9–11), they can be used to cover walls and fences.

Medium-rich garden soil that contains some leaf mold is best; the plants also like a rather humid atmosphere and partial shade. Plants that are grown from seed should be started in the greenhouse in midwinter and can then be set out in late spring.

Propagation is most often done by cuttings of soft greenwood handled as follows: After the plants have finished blooming indoors, they should be rested by putting them in a cool, dry place and withholding water, except for the small amount needed to keep the wood from drying. Start watering and feeding them again in early winter and in a few months there should be enough new shoots for cuttings. Do not use hardwood. Take cuttings with two joints and root them in the propagating bed. As soon as they are rooted, they should be planted in 2-in. pots of rich soil composed of loam and leaf mold with a slight quantity of sand. Shift to larger pots as growth makes it necessary, and in repotting cut back the branches slightly. Pinch off the ends of new growth frequently to produce stocky plants. Cuttings so handled should make good plants in 6-in. pots by the following fall. Full exposure to the light, a moist atmosphere, and water as needed are essential, especially when the plants are young. Cuttings of outdoor-grown plants can be taken in the fall.

Control red spider mites by syringing the plants occasionally with water. The greenhouse whitefly and mealybugs may also cause problems; for control measures, see GREENHOUSE PESTS.

PRINCIPAL SPECIES

Florists grow few of the natural species, most of their attention being centered on the increasing number of hybrids. Most catalogs list only hybrid varieties.

F. arborescens is a tall species that grows up to 25 ft. and has leaves that are 8 in. long but flowers only ½ in. long in pink or purplish.

F. fulgens grows to 4 ft. and has 7-in. leaves and 3-in. red flowers.

F. x hybrida, one of the best cultivated forms and commonly grown in conservatories and window gardens, is probably derived from *F. magellanica* and *F. fulgens*. Its leaves are 4 in. long. The flowers, sometimes 3 in. long and sometimes double, have crimson calyxes and purple petals, occasionally rose or white.

F. magellanica (hardy fuchsia) is usually a low shrub, but it sometimes grows up to 20 ft. when trained on walls. Its leaves are 2 in. long, and the flowers are small (only ½ in. long) with red calyxes and blue petals. This species, which has numerous varieties, is commonly grown outdoors in warm climates.

F. procumbens (trailing-queen) is a vine from New Zealand with orange-and-purple flowers.

F. splendens has scarlet flowers with small greenish petals and long protruding stamens.

F. triphylla grows to 18 in. and has small leaves and cinnabar-red flowers 1½ in. long.

FUMARIA (fyoo MAIR ee ah) **officinalis.** An herb belonging to the principal genus in the Fumariaceae (Fumatory Family). It grows 2–3 ft. tall and has finely cut leaves and racemes of small flesh-colored or purplish flowers tipped with crimson. It was once considered to have medicinal value but has little horticultural value.

FUMARIACEAE (fyoo may ree AY see ee). The Fumitory Family. The name, which means "smoky," is perhaps derived from the odor of some species of *Fumaria*. The members are delicate herbs native to the North Temperate Zone and closely related to those of the Papaveraceae (Poppy Family) but differing in having a watery instead of a milky juice. Leaves are deeply cleft, and the flowers are very irregular. *Adlumia*, *Corydalis*, and *Dicentra* (which includes dutchman's-breeches and bleeding-heart) are the chief cultivated genera.

FUMIGATION. The control of undesirable plant-infesting (or other) undesirable organisms by toxic fumes given off by substances called fumigants. Fumigation is particularly valuable in greenhouses and other enclosed spaces.

Which chemical fumigant to use and its dosage rate are determined partly by the kinds of plants and insects to be treated and partly by the tightness of the building. For specific fumigants and their use, consult your local extension service or nursery. The directions for use of any poisonous fumigant should be read and carefully followed.

FUNGAL DISEASES. Maladies caused by various kinds of FUNGUS. The majority of plant diseases fall in this category. They can be recognized by their symptoms, such as leaf spot, wilt, rot, or blight (some of which may resemble symptoms of bacterial diseases); and especially by their signs, which include the fungus fruiting bodies or spores. For positive identification, it is often necessary to examine these spores under the microscope or to grow the fungus from material taken from the diseased plant, in the laboratory, on artificial culture media. See DISEASE.

FUNGICIDE. A material used to protect plants against or to inactivate or kill fungi, primarily those that cause plant diseases. Fungicides are of two kinds: eradicants, materials used to kill or inactivate the fungi or bacteria existing in the soil, on seed, on the plant, or in the plant (chemotherapy); and protectants, materials used to protect susceptible plant parts externally or internally in advance of the invasion of fungi or bacteria.

There is a wide variety of fungicides on the market today. Always read the directions on the label carefully and follow the recommendations.

FUNGUS. A low order of organisms, more complicated in structure and therefore higher up the scale than bacteria and slime molds, but lower than plants. Fungi vary widely in size, form, and appearance, but all are characterized by a lack of chlorophyll, the green substance that gives true plants their characteristic color. Because chlorophyll is essential to the manufacture of food, fungi cannot make their own food but must obtain it from plants or animals, which are called hosts. Fungi that live on dead tissues, whether animal or vegetable, are called saprophytes; those that derive their food from living organisms are called parasites, a term also applied to animals that do the same thing. Many are both parasitic and saprophytic at different stages in their life cycle. A few, such as the rusts, smuts, and mildews, are known as obligate parasites because direct contact with living tissue is necessary for them to grow.

One group of fungi, the mushrooms, includes valuable edible, or interesting ornamental forms; others are familiar to most of us as the molds and mildews that appear on spoiled foodstuffs or in damp places. In horticulture, fungi are of greatest significance as the cause of the majority of plant diseases.

FUNKIA (FUNG kee ah). Former name (still found in catalogs) for HOSTA, a genus of fleshy-rooted plants with attractive foliage and long flower stems, commonly known as plantain lilies.

FUNNELFORM. Term describing tube-shaped flowers that widen toward the end of petals that are often fused, including morning-glories and many types of lilies.

FURCRAEA (fur KREE ah). A genus of succulent desert plants from the tropical Americas, belonging to the Amaryllidaceae (Amaryllis Family). They look like species of AGAVE and are grown under similar conditions. Their flowering size and age is very uncertain, and once they send up their tall stems, which bear many greenish white flowers in loose panicles, they usually die. They are easily propagated from the numerous bulblets that are borne in the flower clusters.

PRINCIPAL SPECIES

F. bedinghausii has a trunk that grows to 3 ft., leaves 33 ft. long, 30 to 50 in a rosette, and a flower stem 12–15 ft. high.

F. hexapetala has a rosette of 25 to 30 bright green leaves with edges armed with brown hooked prickles. The flower stem grows to 15 ft.

F. foetida has a short trunk, a rosette of 40 to 50 leaves that often grow to 8 ft. long, and a wide-spreading flower panicle on stems to 30 ft. high.

FUSARIUM. A soil fungus with various species that are widespread and cause wilts in a great variety of plants. The symptoms are root or stem rots. The white vegetative portion (mycelium) and the spore masses usually have a pink or purple cast. Some of the serious fusarium diseases are aster wilt, cabbage yellows, and wilts of flax, potato, tomato, and cotton. Control measures include soil disinfection and planting improved, resistant varieties.

GAILLARDIA (gay LAHR dee ah). A genus of annual, biennial, and perennial herbs native in North America, belonging to the Asteraceae (Aster Family), and commonly known as blanketflower. Often grown as cut flowers, they do best in full sunlight in a light, open, well-drained soil. The hardy annual types, reaching a height of 2 ft., bear large, showy, solitary heads with yellowish or reddish rays and purple disks from June to frost. All types produce their flowers on long stems, which makes them ideal for indoor decorative purposes. The annuals are more beautiful than the other types, and the double

Gaillardia aristata

varieties are considered handsomer than the singles. Grown alone, in the border or in beds, the flowers, with their contrasting colors, make an effective display.

The annuals and biennials are grown from seed sown indoors or in the garden. The perennials can be propagated by seed, division of the roots, cuttings taken in August or September, or root cuttings taken in early spring. Plants occasionally self-sow.

PRINCIPAL SPECIES

G. amblyodon is a rather hairy annual with excellent red or brownish red flowers.

G. aristata is a perennial and one of the last plants in the garden to die back in autumn. It grows to 3 ft. and bears 4-in. heads of yellow ray flowers.

G. pulchella is the most popular annual species. Its heads are 2 in. across, and the ray flowers are yellow shaded with rose-purple at the base. Var. *picta* produces larger heads in varied shades. Cv. 'Lorenziana' shows enlarged and tubular rays.

GALANTHUS (gah LAN thus). A genus of small, hardy, bulbous plants of the Amaryllidaceae (Amaryllis Family) commonly known as snowdrop. They bear drooping, bell-shaped white flowers on stalks about 1 ft. tall, above a few basal leaves. Their chief value is their extreme earliness, for they bloom before any other bulbous subject, often before the snow disappears. This and the little blossoms both suggest the common name snowdrop.

The common snowdrop is *G. nivalis*, but *G. elwesii* is much larger, and there is also a double form. All three have drooping white flowers with greenish stripes on the petals. They are perfectly hardy (to Zone 4) and can be planted outdoors without protection.

The bulbs should be planted 3–4 in. deep in early fall in their permanent location, since they resent disturbance. They naturalize readily in semishaded locations in meadows or on grassy slopes and, left alone, will bloom profusely from year to year without further attention.

Galanthus nivalis

Snowdrops are susceptible to the gray mold of BOTRYTIS blight, so do not plant any bulbs harboring the minute, hard, black resting bodies (sclerotia). If sclerotia are solely on the outer scales, they can be removed and the naked bulb saved for planting.

GALAX (GAY laks) **urceolata**. A stemless perennial herb, formerly listed as *Galax aphylla*, belonging to the Diapensiaceae (Diapensia Family). It has stiff, shining, heart-shaped or rounded leaves up to 5 in. across and small white flowers in spikes 9–15 in. high. Native from Virginia to Georgia, it is fairly hardy (to Zone 4), thriving in sandy loam with peat or leaf mold and suitable for a ground cover in a partly shaded place. Propagation is by division.

The leaves are used by florists for wreaths and other decorative work. They keep well in cool storage and take on a bronzy tint in the fall that makes them additionally attractive.

GALEGA (gah LEE gah). A small genus of hardy (Zones 3–9), bushy perennial herbs with white, purple, or blue pealike flowers in thick clusters, which are good for cutting. Two commonly grown species are *G. orientalis*, from the Caucasus, and *G. officinalis* (goat's-rue), from Europe and Asia, with its four botanical varieties, *alba*, white; *compacta*; *hartlandii*, lilac; and *carnea*, rose.

GALIUM (GAL ee um). A genus of slender temperate-climate herbs belonging to the Rubiaceae (Madder Family) and commonly known as bedstraw. Some have square stems and all have stalkless leaves in whorls and abundant clusters of very small white or yellow flowers. They are grown mainly in rock gardens for the light, airy effect similar to that of baby's-breath. Most species are hardy in Zones 4–9.

PRINCIPAL SPECIES

G. boreale (northern bedstraw) is native over much of North America and popular for rock garden use.

G. mollugo (wild madder, great or white bedstraw, false baby's-breath) is a 3-ft. perennial weed introduced from Europe to the eastern states.

G. odoratum (woodruff, sweet woodruff or woodroof) sometimes listed as *Asperula odorata* is a fragrant perennial that grows to 12 in., erect or spreading.

Galium odoratum

The 1½-in. leaves are borne in whorls with rough edges. Small white flowers are borne in loose clusters.

G. verum (yellow bedstraw) is a good rock garden and bank plant, it but sometimes becomes a pest weed in the eastern states.

GALLICA ROSE. Very ancient and called by many confusing names such as "Crimson Damask," these roses are quite distinct from the damasks. Gallicas are short, rounded bushes that will sucker widely on their own roots and form dense thickets. Colors are all shades of pink, red, and purple; many striped and spotted flowers can be found in this class.

A whole industry was built upon *R. gallica officinalis*, which was grown for several centuries around the town of Provins, about 35 miles southeast of Paris, where the town was said to be lined with apothecary shops, all selling conserves, syrups, and powders made from the rose. Gallica roses have the characteristic of dried petals retaining and intensifying the fragrance, which made them ideal for potpourri and other uses. Rose products were thought to be a cure-all in ancient times, partly, no doubt, because of the fragrance. More scientific factors may have been the fact that the method of preparing rose waters resulted in a sterile product; and the high vitamin C content of roses.

R. gallica officinalis, along with its striped sport, 'Rosa Mundi', is still regarded as one of the best garden subjects among the gallicas, all excellent subjects for large or small gardens. Others include 'Tuscany', 'Tuscany Superb', 'Cardinal de Richelieu', 'Charles de Mills', and 'Belle de Crecy'.

GALLS. Deformations or overgrowths of plant tissues caused by the irritation produced by bacteria, fungi, or insects.

GALPHIMIA (gal FIM ee ah). A genus of American shrubs and small trees belonging to the Malpighiaceae (Malpighia Family), often sold under the older name *Thryallis*. The plant flowers throughout the warm seasons in Zones 10–11 and is always bright with clear yellow flowers. Propagation is by seed or by cuttings in midsummer.

GALTONIA (gawl TOH nee ah).

A small genus of South African bulbs of the Liliaceae (Lily Family), commonly known as giant summer-hyacinth. In midsummer they produce tall spikes bearing fragrant, white or greenish, drooping, bell-shaped flowers. The basal leaves are stout and strap shaped. Bulbs are tender in the temperate zone and must either be heavily mulched (after being planted in a protected location) or dug up in early fall, stored in a frost-free place over winter, and planted out when the soil warms in the spring. They propagate naturally by offsets but can also be raised freely from seed. The principal species is *G. candicans*, whose white flowers are borne on stems 3 ft. high.

GAMOPETALOUS.

A term applied to a flower with petals wholly or partly fused to form a corolla tube, as in the morning-glory or salvia. Gamopetalous corollas are differentiated into two regions, the tube and the more or less flaring portions, called the limb.

GARBANZO.

A common name for the legume *Cicer arietinum* also known as chick pea; see CICER.

GARDENIA (gahr DEE nee ah).

A genus of shrubs or small trees native in subtropical regions of the Eastern Hemisphere, and belonging to the Rubiaceae (Madder Family). They will grow outdoors in Zones 9–11, but they are also grown extensively under glass for cut flowers, popular as corsage material and mostly produced in winter.

CULTURE

Under glass, gardenias need warm, moist conditions during their growth season, and young plants (preferably not over two years old) give best results, although it is possible to keep older plants going. They are grown in pots or benches and thrive best in good fibrous loam with one-third old cow manure and a little sand. Gardenias grow best in definitely acid soil with a pH of 5.0 to 5.5.

Propagation is by cuttings rooted under close conditions in winter. Great care should be taken not to infect cuttings with phomopsis canker, which appears as brown dead areas containing black fungus fruiting bodies on stems and branches. Use a very sharp knife and dip the cuttings in a fungicidal dust or, even better, plant them in a sterilized rooting medium.

Gardenia jasminoides

Owing to the fact that gardenias seem fussy and sometimes refuse to do well even for expert greenhouse growers, professional gardeners are loath to recommend them for house culture because of the dry heat and varying conditions found in most homes. Yet many homeowners manage to keep the plants in good condition for years and to get successive crops of the popular sweet-smelling flowers. The secret is largely one of keeping the atmosphere sufficiently moist, giving plants enough (but not too much) water in the soil, and misting often. Plants should be protected from drafts and temperature changes of any kind. They need a bright, sunny location during the winter and slight shade part of the time in summer, but not out in the garden where winds can buffet them.

Enemies. Leaf spots are checked by sanitary measures, such as removal of spotted leaves. Use of sterilized soils prevents root knot; see NEMATODES. Bud drop, a nonparasitic disease, is induced by too high a temperature and humidity, and sometimes by overfeeding. Too alkaline a soil may produce chlorotic leaves.

Whiteflies, mealybugs, and soft scale can be controlled by spraying with insecticidal soap until clear. Remove mealybugs and soft scale by rubbing with a cotton swab dipped in denatured alcohol. For other recommendations, see GREEN-HOUSE PESTS.

PRINCIPAL SPECIES

G. jasminoides (cape jessamine) is a bushy shrub that grows to 6 ft. and has thick, glossy evergreen leaves and waxy-white, heavily scented flowers with nine petals. The double-flowered varieties are the most popular, and some growers have developed specially selected forms with larger flowers. It is also extensively grown in greenhouses for cut flowers sold by florists, and as a potted plant.

G. thunbergia has long leaves. The large, eight-parted, fragrant white flowers have long tubes and spathelike calyxes.

GARLIC.

A hardy perennial bulb, *Allium sativum*, native to the Mediterranean region of Africa and Europe, and closely related to onions. Unlike that of the onion, the garlic bulb separates beneath a papery, super-ficial skin, into divisions or "cloves." It is usually grown as an annual for the pungent and distinctive flavor of its bulbs, which are used as a seasoning. The leaves are long, narrow, and flat, and flowers are borne on top of a tough stalk that grows about 2 ft. tall. The flowers are white umbels enclosed in a sheath, sometimes also containing bulbils.

Garlic plant

ELEPHANT GARLIC, *Allium scorodoprasum*, also known as giant garlic, is a close relative, very similar to *A. sativum*, but is larger in all respects and somewhat milder in flavor.

CULTURE

The plant, which rarely produces seed, is of the easiest culture and does best in only moderately fertile soil. In rich deep soil the tops become overdeveloped.

Propagation is usually done by dividing the compound bulbs into individual cloves. As early in the spring as the soil is workable, the cloves should be planted in rows 18–24 in. apart with the cloves 6 in. apart and 2 in. deep. The soil should be tilled and firmed before planting. Fall planting is only advisable in warm climates. Once rooted, the cloves should not be transplanted. They can be grown in window boxes or pots (one clove to each 5-in. pot), but container growing is seldom satisfactory.

Garlic bulb

Garlic needs plenty of sunshine; if grown in cold damp areas, it is usually of inferior quality. It grows well in a moist, sandy loam with a pH of 5.5 to 8.0. Soil prepared for onions is suitable. To allow the maximum development of the bulbs, pick off any flower heads that appear, and keep the soil in a loose and friable condition. Cultivate regularly to keep weeds down.

Watering is important; it is best to keep a balance between excessively wet or dry conditions. If the developing bulbs suffer drought, their growth will be checked, and bulbs will ripen prematurely. Then when irrigated, the newly developing cloves will sprout. If watered excessively, bulb quality and keeping quality will be impaired. As with onions, all water should be withheld when the tops start to dry and the bulbs ripen.

Harvesting and Storing. Garlic should be harvested, dried, and stored in much the same way as onions. In autumn, when the leaves have died, dig up the plants, braid their tops, and hang them in an airy place to dry. The cloves can be peeled, chopped, and frozen, but it is difficult to contain the flavor and smell. It is generally not practical to dry and powder garlic at home, since the flavor is inferior to fresh garlic. Although the foliage may have culinary uses, the cloves will suffer if these are cut; instead, grow GARLIC CHIVES for their fresh leaves.

GARLIC CHIVES.

A perennial herb, *Allium tuberosum*, also known as Chinese or Oriental chives. Closely related to onions, it is used like chives in cooking but has a flavor more like garlic. The dark green leaves grow about 16 in. tall. They are not hollow like ordinary chives, *Allium schoenoprasum*, and are triangular rather than round in cross section.

CULTURE

Although they withstand some frost, garlic chives are not as hardy as ordinary chives. In climates with long, severe winters they may be killed unless given some protection.

Garlic chives thrive in the vegetable garden in well-worked soil enriched with compost or dried manure. In cooler climates, a well-drained, sheltered, sunny position is necessary. In hot, dry climates, some shade may be required. Water the plants regularly, and keep them free of weeds. Unless seed is wanted, remove flower stems and flower heads as they appear to promote foliage growth.

For a small crop of leaves ready to use during the first year, seed

Garlic chives

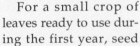

should be started indoors in early spring. When the tiny grasslike seedlings are large enough to handle, they will transplant easily. Lift them gently from the soil, trim the roots to ½ in. long, bunch ten or twelve together, and plant them.

Mature plants can also be divided in spring. In climates with mild winters this can also be done in the fall. Dig up the whole plant, wash the soil off the roots, and trim them to about 12 in. long. The little bulblets can then be separated easily. Bunch six or eight together and replant them about 10 in. apart.

Indoor Culture. To grow garlic chives indoors, use a 4-in. square pot or a 5-in. round one. When the plants grow and fill the container, divide the plants and repot into two or more pots. They can also be grown in a sunny window box but need to be dug and divided every year.

Harvesting. With a sharp utility knife, cut the greens about ½ in. above ground level. Do this whether you need many or few leaves. It will stimulate growth.

GARRYA

(GAR ee ah). A genus of ornamental evergreen shrubs of western North America, commonly known as silk-tassel bush. They are distinctive because of the long, drooping catkins of greenish white flowers, borne on shoots of the previous year, the male and female forms on separate plants. The male catkins are larger and of more striking appearance. Plants are propagated by cuttings or layers and are not easy to transplant except from pots. They are hardy only to Zone 8.

G. elliptica, the best-known species, grows to over 10 ft. in favorable localities and is a good-looking shrub with dark green, oval leaves, gray underneath.

GAS PLANT.

A common name for *Dictamnus albus*, a shrubby flowering perennial that emits a flammable oil; see DICTAMNUS.

GASTERIA

(gas TEE ree ah). A genus of small, mostly stemless succulent plants originally included in the genus *Aloe*, belonging to the Liliaceae (Lily Family), and native in South Africa and Namibia. Hardy in Zones 10–11, a few species are grown in succulent collections indoors and also make good window plants. Their leaves are thick and fleshy, more or less tongue shaped, rough, and either two-ranked or in rosettes. The flowers are green, white, red or pinkish, somewhat inflated or pot-bellied (hence the genus name), and are borne in loose clusters on arching stems. They need good drainage and do well in pans in a mixture of sandy loam with broken brick and a little leaf mold.

PRINCIPAL SPECIES

G. armstrongii is one of the most interesting, with thick, textured, dark green, oppositely arranged leaves that look like fat green tongues.

G. maculata has a rather twisted arrangement of shining green leaves that grow to 6 in. long and have large white spots.

G. pulchra has glossy, dark green leaves up to 12 in. long in spiral ranks with white spots.

G. sulcata has short, dull green, strap-shaped leaves with greenish dots.

G. verrucosa has rough, dull gray leaves that grow to 6 in. long with many small white warts.

GAULTHERIA (gawl THEE ree ah). A genus of evergreen shrubs, erect or prostrate, widely distributed in North and South America, Asia, and Australia, belonging to the Ericaceae (Heath Family). Variously hardy in Zones 2–7, they thrive in cool, acid soil, and merit use as a ground cover in the rock garden. They are also good for evergreen shrub border planting, growing best in sandy, peaty soil and a rather moist and partly shaded location. Propagation is by seed, cuttings, layers, and division.

PRINCIPAL SPECIES

C. hispidula (creeping-snowberry) has small, bell-shaped flowers in late spring followed by dainty white berries clustered among the small glossy oval leaves. It can be propagated by seed, division, or cuttings and is hardy in Zones 2–7.

G. procumbens (wintergreen, teaberry, checkerberry) is a low plant with creeping stems, native from Canada to Georgia. The oval, leathery leaves make a fine tea or can be eaten fresh. It has

Gaultheria procumbens

nodding white flowers borne singly and edible, scarlet, berrylike fruits. Hardy in Zones 4–7.

G. shallon (salal), native in the western states, grows to 2 ft. or more and makes a good undershrub. It has rather large, heart-shaped leaves; panicles of pinkish white bell-shaped flowers; and dark purple edible fruits. The foliage is popular for use in floral arrangements. Hardy in Zones 6–7.

GAURA (GAW rah). A small genus of perennial North American herbs belonging to the Onagraceae (Evening-primrose Family), with spikes of white flowers, occasionally planted in wild gardens or hardy borders.

G. coccinea is a midwestern plant that grows to 2 ft. and has white, pink, or scarlet flowers.

G. lindheimeri, native from Louisiana to Texas, grows to 4 ft. tall and has loose clusters of white flowers.

GAYFEATHER. Common name for LIATRIS, a genus of showy perennials with heads of purple or white flowers borne on wandlike stems.

GAYLUSSACIA (gay loo SAY shee ah). A genus of North American berry-bearing shrubs valuable for both foliage effect and fruit, belonging to the Ericaceae (Heath Family), and commonly called huckleberry. They grow best in a shady area in acid, sandy soil. Fruits are blue or black and usually edible, similar to blueberries but with ten hard little seeds that crack loudly when chewed, thus suggesting another popular name, "crackerberry." Huckleberry leaves are sprinkled on the underside with resinous dots not found on blueberry leaves. Though the huckleberry can be eaten and grown like blueberries, their culture is not commonly attempted nor recommended.

PRINCIPAL SPECIES

G. baccata (black huckleberry) is a deciduous shrub that grows to 3 ft. with glossy black sweet edible fruit in late summer. Hardy in Zones 3–8.

G. brachycera (box huckleberry) is a very rare, evergreen ground cover species that grows to 12 in. high. Very attractive pink, bell-like flowers are produced in spring followed by blue edible fruits in late summer. This plant is stoloniferous, spreading underground about 6 in. per year. All seeds produced are sterile, so colonies in the wild are from one plant. Isolated colonies are rare and found only in Pennsylvania, Delaware, West Virginia, and Tennessee. The largest colony, near New Bloomfield, Pennsylvania, is estimated to be about 13,000 years old and now reputed to be the oldest living plant in the world. This one plant has covered a distance of 1¼ miles and is now preserved by the state of Pennsylvania. Clones of box huckleberry are now propagated and used for landscape purposes. Hardy in Zones 6–7.

G. dumosa (dwarf huckleberry) is a deciduous shrub that grows to 1½ ft. high and has black fruit that appears in late summer and is edible but has little taste. Hardy in Zones 3–9.

G. frondosa (dangleberry) is a deciduous shrub that grows to 6 ft. and has bell-shaped, purplish flowers followed by glaucous, swee,t edible, dark blue fruit in late summer. Hardy in Zones 5–9.

GAZANIA (gah ZAY nee ah). A genus of low herbs, annual or perennial, native to South Africa, belonging to the Asteraceae (Aster Family), and commonly known as South African daisy. Old-time favorites for flowering in the cool greenhouse and for summer bedding outdoors, they have rather narrow leaves of varying form, mostly covered beneath with dense, white woolly hairs. The flowers range from white through orange and yellow to scarlet and are beautifully spotted at the base of the petals. Like many South African flowers, they close at night. Sandy loam with humus and a sunny location suit them well. Propagation is by seed, division, and cuttings. Often included in wildflower seed mixtures, the types most commonly grown are selections of *G. ringens* or the trailing species *G. uniflora*.

GAZEBO. A design for a garden shelter that is built into a wall, developed from the watch tower in a medieval palace wall or battlement.

GELSEMIUM (jel SEE mee um) **sempervirens.** A twining, evergreen shrubby plant commonly known as Carolina yellow jessamine, the state flower of South Carolina. Native from Virginia to Central America and hardy in Zones 7–9, it is grown in mild climates as a ground cover, useful for draping porches or covering banks. Its fragrant, funnel-shaped yellow flowers are followed by beaked seed capsules. Propagation is by cuttings.

GENIPA (JEN ip ah) **americana.** A tropical American tree, best grown in Zones 10–11. It has large yellowish or white flowers and large (3-in.) brown berries that can be eaten fresh, preserved, or used in beverages; commonly known as genip or genipap.

GENISTA (je NIS tah). A genus of deciduous or half-evergreen shrubs found in Europe, Asia, and Africa, belonging to the Fabaceae (Bean Family), and commonly known as broom. They are closely allied to CYTISUS, several species having been referred to that genus; the common genista grown by florists especially for Easter is *C. canariensis* or *C. racemosus*.

Genistas are ornamental shrubs with showy yellow or white flowers, thriving in dry, sandy soil in mild climates and showing well on sunny banks. Some are used to produce yellow dyes. Most are hardy to Zone 6, but a few species survive in colder climates in sheltered locations. Propagation is by seed and cuttings.

PRINCIPAL SPECIES

G. germanica is an upright, spiny little shrub with rather small flowers. Hardy to Zone 5.

G. hispanica (Spanish broom) is a densely branched prickly shrub that grows to 2 ft. and has clusters of golden yellow flowers in late spring. Hardy to Zone 7.

G. lydia (Lydia woodwaxen) is a low-growing ground cover with yellow flowers and many pendulous branches. Hardy to Zone 7.

G. pilosa is a small prostrate grower to 12 in. with rooting branches and short clusters of yellow flowers in late spring. Hardy to Zone 5.

G. sagittalis is another dwarf species, featuring two-winged branches. Hardy to Zone 5.

G. tinctoria (dyer's greenweed) is an upright, slender shrub that grows to 3 ft. and has striped branches and yellow, many-flowered terminal clusters. Var. *plena* is a form with double flowers. Hardy in Zones 5–7.

GENTIAN. Common name for GENTIANA, a genus of mostly perennial herbs. The Gentian Family is GENTIANACEAE. Prairie gentian is *Eustoma grandiflorum*, a related annual herb with bell-shaped purple flowers; see EUSTOMA.

GENTIANA (jen shee AY nah). A large genus including at least 350 species of herbs comprising the primary members of the Gentianaceae (Gentian Family), mostly perennial, famous for their rich blue flowers, and commonly known as gentian. There are some species with purple, white, yellow, and even pink flowers. Some of the flowers are pleated, striped, spotted, or fringed; almost all are beautiful. Some are suitable for the perennial garden. The alpine species do best in a well-drained rock garden where they are watered and fed often. All are generally regarded as heavy feeders.

Gentiana andrewsii

The best method of propagation is by seed. Sowing the fine, fresh seedpods in a coldframe where they receive nature's cycles of chilling and warming usually results in excellent germination.

PRINCIPAL SPECIES

TALL SPECIES

Among the taller-growing varieties suitable for the garden are several easily raised perennials.

G. andrewsii (closed or bottle gentian) is an eastern woodland species that blooms in late summer. It carries dark blue or greenish white, partially or entirely closed flowers in terminal clusters on erect stems 15–20 in. tall. They are drought and heat tolerant.

G. asclepiadea (willow gentian) displays large blue trumpets at the end of 15–30 in. stems and in the top of leaf nodes. The more moisture it has, the more magnificent the plant becomes. It is suitable for woodland or shady perennial bed planting.

G. lutea, growing to 6 ft., has yellow flowers in the leaf axils on the top half of a leafy stem.

G. macrophylla grows erect stems 12–24 in. tall that carry clusters of pale blue flowers.

G. pneumonanthe has slender, deep blue, erect flowers on slim stems with fine leaves. It should be kept moist.

ROCK GARDEN SPECIES

G. acaulis bears large trumpets of rich blue spring flowers on ground-hugging foliage. Native to the Alps, it is one of the finest rock garden species. A number of forms are available.

G. decumbens includes a large group of Asian gentians that produce a rosette of foliage and sprawling stems tipped with trumpet flowers in summer. The group is extremely variable. Seed offered as *G. decumbens* may produce choice, compact plants with large, richly colored flowers, or the plants may be mostly foliage with a few insignificant blooms.

G. farreri is a fall-blooming gem. A mature plant will be surrounded with procumbent stems bearing large, open, blue trumpets. This is closely related to the choice *G. ornata* and *G. sino-ornata*.

G. scabra is one of the desirable fall-blooming, heat-tolerant, Asian gentians. Several varieties are also available. Var. *saxatilis* grows close to the ground.

G. verna is a dainty, spring-blooming, blue gentian from the Alps. The individuals are smaller and the petals open out.

GENTIANACEAE (jen shee ah NAY see ee). The Gentian Family, an almost wholly herbaceous group, principally native to temperate climates. The flowers are regular and bisexual with fused petals and exhibit some of the best blues known in horticulture. Only a few genera are cultivated, principally *Exacum* and *Nymphoides*; many species of *Gentiana* are valued but are difficult to grow.

GENUS. A group of plants constituting a subdivision of a family, and containing groups of species more or less closely related and having certain obvious structural characteristics in common. Like a species, a genus is a somewhat arbitrary concept designed to simplify identification and indicate a relationship; hence, its definition is subject to differences of opinion. Members of a genus resemble each other more than they do members of other genera; all oaks, for example, are more alike than they are like any of the willows.

The first part of a plant's botanical or scientific name is that of the genus to which it belongs; the second part, a qualifying adjective indicating "what kind," is the species name. Thus, *Betula* is the name of the genus to which all birches belong, and *Betula papyrifera* indicates the paper birch, a particular species. See also PLANT NAMES AND CLASSIFICATION; FAMILY; SPECIES; VARIETY.

GEONOMA (jee oh NOH mah). A genus of small, shade-loving palms from Central and South America. Most attractivie in a young state, a few are grown under glass. They require abundant water and are hardy only in tropical conditions.

PRINCIPAL SPECIES

G. elegans grows to 6 ft. and has a slender reed-like stem and leaves to 12 in. long, usually divided into five or seven segments, or rarely three.

G. gracilis is very graceful with dark green, arching leaves made up of many narrow leaflets.

G. schottiana grows to 10 ft. and has leaves to 3 ft. long divided into many narrow leaflets tapering to a tail-like point.

GERANIACEAE (jur ay nee AY see ee). The Geranium Family, so called from the Greek word for "crane," suggested by the beaked fruit. Widely distributed herbs, a few are woody. Most of the cultivated kinds are grown solely for ornament, but some species of *Pelargonium* furnish the perfumery oil called rose geranium. The nearly regular flowers have five petals, five sepals, a lobed ovary, and one, two, or three times the number of petals. The house and bedding plants commonly known as geraniums are species of *Pelargonium*; the genera *Geranium* and *Erodium* are hardy plants of simple culture.

GERANIUM (jur AY nee um). A large genus of mostly perennial herbs widely distributed in temperate regions and commonly known as crane's-bill, referring to the long beaklike projection on the seed. They have mostly lobed or divided leaves and showy flowers of various colors, sometimes to 1½ in. across but mostly under ½ in.

Geranium sp.

Geraniums are useful plants for the rock garden and flower border. Mostly hardy to Zone 6, they grow well in any good soil, and some are well adapted for naturalizing. Propagation is easily done by seed, cuttings, or division. They are subject to the same pests as *Pelargonium*.

Other Geraniums. As a common name, geranium is applied to several unrelated plants. The common geraniums grown in florist, home, and garden culture belong to the genus PELARGONIUM, which includes the Lady Washington and zonal hybrids. Beefsteak-geranium is *Begonia* x *rex-cultorum*. California-geranium is *Senecio petasites*. Feather-geranium is *Chenopodium botrys*. Mint-geranium is *Chrysanthemum balsamita*. Strawberry-geranium is *Saxifraga stolonifera*.

PRINCIPAL SPECIES

G. argenteum is a perennial or biennial that grows only a few inches high and has silvery, divided leaves and large pink flowers.

G. dalmaticum is a good rock garden subject with pink flowers. There is also a white form.

G. himalayense, formerly listed as *G. grandiflorum*, grows 12 in. or more and has leaves that are deeply five-lobed and pale lilac flowers.

G. ibericum grows to 18 in. and has leaves that are deeply seven-lobed and showy panicles of violet-purple flowers in midsummer. Cv. 'Album' is a good white form.

G. maculatum is the common North American species, thriving in moist places and showy in summer with pale rosy purple flowers.

G. pratense grows to 3 ft. and has seven-lobed leaves and large bluish purple flowers.

G. psilostemon is a vigorous and free-flowering species from Armenia, with dark red flowers spotted black.

G. robertianum (herb Robert, red-robin) is a small, attractive, annual or biennial, North American native with small, bright crimson or purplish rose flowers and deeply cut leaves. It colonizes readily from seed.

G. sanguineum, a useful rock garden subject, makes a rounded plant about 18 in. high with five- to seven-lobed leaves and large reddish purple flowers. Several color forms are on the market, including white and clear pink kinds. Var. *prostratum*, often grown as *G. lancastrense*, is a small, compact form with rosy pink flowers.

GERBERA (GER be rah) **jamesonii.** An herb belonging to the Asteraceae (Aster Family), and commonly known as Transvaal, African, Barberton, or veldt daisy. This tender South African perennial has attained tremendous popularity as a florists' cut flower, following the introduction of an improved, large-flowered, scarlet type, and the development of variously colored hybrids. They are hardy only in Zones 10–11, and in cool climates they are usually grown as greenhouse or window plants.

The plants bloom over a long winter season, producing long-petaled, daisylike flowers 2–4 in. across on exceedingly long stems. The flowers are excellent for cutting, stand well above a rosette of gray-green leaves, and are solid-colored in many pastel shades, from pale amber through salmon and rose to a rich ruby red.

GERMINATION. Popularly speaking, this term refers to the beginning of plant growth from a seed. Botanists give it more specific meanings: the resumption of growth by the dormant embryo in a seed under the favorable combined influence of moisture, heat, and oxygen; and the start of growth from a seed or spore. See SEEDS; SCARIFICATION.

GESNERIA (jes NEE ree ah). A genus of about 60 species of perennial herbs and shrubs belonging to the GESNERIACEAE (Gesneria Family), and native to the West Indies and northern South America. They make outstanding small house plants, thriving in the same conditions as *Saintpaulia* (African-violet). Most are also ideal for terrariums and growing under fluorescent lights.

PRINCIPAL SPECIES

G. citrina is a rare and distinctive form with bright yellow, tubular flowers and leathery green leaves on short upright or spreading stems.

G. cuneifolia has narrow, dark green, glossy leaves in a low rosette. The tubular red firecracker flowers bloom all year. Cv. 'Quebradillas' has orange-yellow tubular flowers in everblooming profusion.

G. pedicellaris, formerly listed as *G. christii*, has showy clusters of everblooming red tubular flowers. The narrow wavy leaves form compact rosettes with a bubbly texture.

Hybrids. 'Lemon Drop' bears showers of bright yellow flowers all year amid narrow, dark green, leathery foliage. 'Sun Drop' is very dwarf and compact with clusters of yellow tubular flowers and narrow, glossy, leathery leaves.

GESNERIACEAE (jes ne ree AY see ee). The Gesneria Family, a group of mostly herbaceous plants, widely distributed in the tropics. The stems are commonly fleshy and prostrate but in the woody kinds are erect and climbing. A number are frequently cultivated for their very large, showy tubular flowers. Among these are *Achimenes*, *Aeschynanthus*, *Alloplectus*, *Episcia*, *Kohleria*, *Saintpaulia*, *Sinningia*, *Smithiantha*, and *Streptocarpus*.

GEUM (JEE um). A genus of erect, generally dwarf, flowering perennials belonging to the Rosaceae (Rose Family) and commonly known as avens. They are easy to grow, excellent for cutting, and adapted to the rock garden, borders, or beds. Bearing yellow, red, or white flowers freely from late spring through fall, the plants thrive best in light, rich, well-drained soil in open, sunny situations. Propagation is by seed sown in the open ground in the spring, or by division of the roots in the fall. There are 20 or more species, including many satisfactory varieties cultivated in the United States. Most are hardy in Zones 5–9.

PRINCIPAL SPECIES

G. x *borisii* is a hybrid of *G. reptans* and *G. bulgaricum*. It has a compact growth habit, to 1 ft. high, and bears orange-red flowers in late spring through early summer.

G. bulgaricum grows to 2 ft. and has large, heart-shaped terminal leaflets. Flowers are bright yellow or orange.

G. coccineum has heart-shaped foliage and bright red flowers 1 in. across. Var. *flore pleno* is a double variety, best used in the border.

G. montanum, growing 6–9 in., has golden yellow flowers 1½ in. across. A form with orange-red flowers is sometimes listed as a separate species, *G.* x *heldreichii*.

G. peckii, growing to 2 ft., has few, if any, lateral leaflets. Its yellow flowers are 1 in. across.

G. quellyon (Chilean avens), formerly listed as *G. chilense*, is a hairy plant 1–2 ft. high. The leaves have a large terminal leaflet and many smaller lateral leaflets. The dazzling scarlet flowers, at their best in summer, are 1½ in.

Geum quellyon

across. Var. *plenum* is double. Probably the most popular catalog variety is 'Mrs. Bradshaw', which blooms all summer, bearing fully double brilliant orange-scarlet flowers. Cv. 'Lady Stratheden' is a semidouble yellow form. Cv. 'Orange Queen' bears double orange-scarlet blossoms. Cv. 'Lionel Cox', of compact growth to 8 in. high, produces spring bloom of creamy yellow flowers touched with pink.

G. reptans, with 1½-in. yellow flowers, grows to 6 in. and develops long runners.

G. rivale (Indian-chocolate, water avens), growing to 2 ft., is naturally a bog plant and has small, coppery pink flowers with a purple calyx. Hardy to Zone 3, it should receive consistent moisture.

GIBBERELLINS. A group of growth-regulating chemicals found in plants. They are primarily used to increase the length of plant stems and to hasten the germination of those kinds of seeds that are difficult to germinate.

GILIA (GIL ee ah). A genus of annual, biennial, or perennial herbs, mostly native to western North America, belonging to the Polemoniaceae (Phlox Family). They are easily cultivated in the flower garden, and seed can be sown where plants are to bloom.

PRINCIPAL SPECIES

G. achilleifolia is a bushy annual that grows to 2 ft. or more and has finely divided leaves and dense clusters of blue or purple flowers.

G. aggregata and *G. rubra* are now listed in the genus IPOMOPSIS.

G. capitata is an annual growing to about 2 ft. with dense, roundish heads of light blue flowers.

G. laciniata is a dwarf annual with finely divided leaves and few-flowered clusters of rose, blue, or lilac blossoms.

G. tricolor (bird's-eye gilia) is an annual that grows to 3 ft. and has loose clusters of lilac or violet flowers marked yellow, very freely produced.

GILLIFLOWER. Common name derived from the French *giroflée*, sometimes spelled gillyflower or gilloflower. The name is said to have been first given in Italy to plants of the Caryophyllaceae (Pink Family), especially species of

Dianthus (carnation); the gilliflower of Chaucer and Shakespeare was **D. caryophyllus**. More recently the name has been applied to **Matthiola incana** (stock) and to **Cheiranthus cheiri** (wallflower). In England in the seventeenth century, the name "Queen's-gilliflower" was applied to **Hesperis matronalis**.

GINGER. Common name for many genera and species both in and out of the ZINGIBERACEAE (Ginger Family). The ginger spice of the market consists of dried rhizomes of a tropical plant, **Zingiber officinale**, see ZINGIBER.

Wild-ginger is the common name for the genus ASARUM, including plants common in eastern woodlands. Red ginger is **Alpinia purpurata**, and shell ginger is **A. zerumbet**; see ALPINIA.

GINKGO (GINK goh). An Asiatic genus of hardy deciduous trees belonging to the Ginkgoaceae (Ginkgo Family). The genus is commonly represented by one species, **G. biloba**, often called maidenhair tree because its attractive deeply cut leaves resemble enlarged forms of the popular maidenhair fern (**Adiantum**). It grows to 120 ft. and has characteristic diagonally upright form and flowers in loose catkins, followed (in the case of pistillate trees) by yellowish, foul-smelling fruit. It is native to northern China and Japan and is the sole survivor of a family widespread in early geologic times.

The ginkgo is often used as a street or park tree, or for planting as a specimen where a picturesque effect is desired. Because of the rather leathery texture of the leaves, it is free from insect pests and disease. It is also resistant to drought, air pollution, and heat, and will grow in most any soil. Fall color is a brilliant yellow. The small leaves often blow away, which saves raking.

There are many different forms available. Cv. 'Fastigiata' is especially upright in growth. 'Laciniata' has cut leaves. 'Macrophylla' has larger leaves than the type. 'Sentry' is a new clone with very narrow, upright growth; it is often planted along streets and in narrow spaces in the landscape. Hardy in Zones 5–9.

GINSENG (JIN seng). Common name for the genus PANAX of herbs much valued by the Chinese, who use it in tea and medicine. The Ginsing (or Aralia) Family is ARALIACEAE.

GLABROUS. A term meaning "not hairy," as illustrated by the stem of the bush poppy or the leaves of the orpine (**Crassula argentea**). It is often incorrectly used to mean smooth, which properly refers to plant parts that are not only free from hairs, but also not rough or gritty to the touch. Do not confuse with GLAUCOUS.

GLADIOLUS (glad ee OH lus). A genus of tender cormous plants of the Iridaceae (Iris Family). Its leaves are swordlike and grow fan-shaped, inspiring the common name sword-lily. Flowers are borne on tall, upright spikes that have as many as 25 flowers on a spike under ideal culture. Flowers open from the bottom upward, five to ten being open at one time.

Gladiolus fall into three general classifications: the tender, small, spring-flowering ones that have their origin in tropical Africa; the winter-hardy species from the Mediterranean region of Europe; and the summer-flowering ones from southeast Asia. The Asian species are by far the most popular.

The summer-flowering gladiolus can be found in hundreds of varieties, and still new ones appear each year from the hybridists' gardens. They cover an unusually wide range of size, color, and petal formation. In size, they range from the miniatures, some of which have florets little more than an inch in diameter, to the giant ones that may produce florets up to 10 in. across. Varieties can be found in almost every color and shade from pure white through the deep black-reds, including some of the few known green flowers. Many popular ones are bicolor, and those with blendings of several colors are known as smokies. There is no true blue-colored gladiolus, but the violet shades approach the blue.

Most varieties have round, rather broad petals, which may be plain, ruffled, crinkled, or needle-pointed. In addition, others are laciniate, some are orchidlike, and still others are doubled. Fragrance in gladiolus has been elusive, but breeders have been able to produce that in some cases.

HISTORY OF GLADIOLUS

The hybridization and improvement of the gladiolus began at least as far back as 1807 when William Herbert produced seedlings from some of the African species being brought to England. Interest developed rapidly in both England and on the European continent. The modern summer-flowering gladiolus had its real beginning with the introduction of the hybrid *G.* x *gandavensis*, which had been developed by Bedinghaus, gardener for the Duc d'Aremburg.

In North America, the John Lewis Childs firm on Long Island was one of the first to popularize and improve the gladiolus. Luther Burbank included this flower among his many hybridizing projects. Because of the improved elements of grace, coloring, and ease of growth and propagation, Burbank revolutionized gladiolus breeding. In 1932, Professor E. F. Palmer of Canada introduced the variety 'Picardy', the first variety with very large flowers to result from crossing the *G.* x *gandavensis* and *G. primulinus* strains.

GLADIOLUS CULTURE

Few flowers are as adaptable to various climates and soil conditions as the gladiolus. Its cultural requirements are rather simple. It will grow well in almost any type of rich soil if it has the two absolutely necessary features of full sun and good drainage. However, it does not compete well with roots from woody plants and will not remain healthy in waterlogged soil.

Gladiolus corms are tender and in most areas will not winter over in the ground, although this has been done successfully in mild climates or where winter protection has been given. The general practice, however, is to lift the corms each fall and to plant them again the next year. They should be dried off promptly after the flowers have faded, whether grown indoors or in pots, as they are likely to rot if stored away moist. The corms can be planted in the spring as soon as the soil is warm. Plantings can be continued up to within 90 days of heavy freezes.

The corms are planted in trenches for the cutting garden or in clumps in the flower border, 4–5 in. deep, depending on the size of the corm, in soil that has been well worked. A slightly acid soil is best. Moderate fertilization is desirable; the fertilizer should have a low nitrogen and a high phosphate content, a formula of 3–8–6 being good. The soil around the plants should be kept loose and friable (easily crumbled) at all times for best results.

Plenty of water given either naturally or by irrigation is helpful in growing top-quality blooms. The feeding roots of the gladiolus grow out from the plant toward the middle of the rows. Therefore, fertilizer is best fed in ribbons about 8 in. from the row, and when the plant has made fair growth, cultivation should be shallow.

When the plants are grown for cut flowers, the removal of any part of the foliage (with the spike) interferes with the normal development of the new corm. If two or three of the broadest leaves at the base of the plant are allowed to remain, a fair crop can result, but maximum corm development can only come if the whole plant is left intact. After the flowers wither, the spike should be removed since the development of a seedpod draws heavily upon the whole plant structure and in time decreases the size of the new corm.

About six weeks after the blooming period is over, the corms will be ready for digging. With spading fork or other convenient tool, loosen the soil around the plant and lift it free. The old tops should then be cut off close to the top of the new corm. Set these corms out to dry in a warm, airy place, not in full sun, and permit them to dry for about three weeks. At this time the old corm can be broken from the new and discarded. The new corms should then be stored in suitable containers in a basement or other fairly cool location. It is important that corms be stored so that air can move around them during the storage period. Corms should not be planted again until after they have gone through this.

BLOOMS AND CORM SIZE

Corms that measure 1½ in. diameter are known as the "first size" in the case of most varieties; and this size is recommended for general garden use. Under good cultural conditions, however, corms of much smaller size will flower equally well, for the flower bud is a progressive one and will develop from even a small cormel when the right conditions prevail. The age of the corm, which can be determined by the size of the root plate or flattened basal area from which roots arise (the smaller the root plate, the younger the bulb), is almost as important in determining the quality of the corm as is the size. After they attain their normal growth, gladiolus corms do not continue to improve with age, but on the contrary, become less valuable. The corm planted in spring is not the same one that is harvested that fall. The old corm (A) withers during the growing period as a new one forms on top of it (B).

PROPAGATION

Propagation of gladiolus is done by planting the small, hard-shelled cormels (C) that are found attached to the parent corm at digging time and growing them into corms. Some varieties pro-

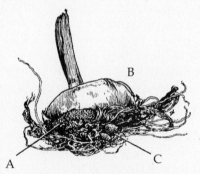

Gladiolus corm development

duce these cormels in greater profusion than others, and some produce cormels that will germinate much more readily than others. In general, large and soft-shelled cormels germinate readily. Hard-shelled types can be encouraged to germinate by soaking them in water for several hours before planting, or by cracking the shell.

Cormels are planted in trenches about 2 in. deep. The soil must be packed firmly about them and kept fairly moist until germination has been induced. During the storage period these cormels should be kept in as cool temperatures as possible, but above freezing. Quarters that are too warm will throw them into deep dormancy. Cormels are treated as other corms at digging time. They will reach full size in an average of two years.

Because of their interest in gladiolus and the ease with which the mechanics of hybridization are carried out, many amateur gardeners carry out their own breeding programs. Each flower bears both the anthers, or pollen-bearing organs, and the stigma, or female part. Cross-pollination is accomplished by dusting the pollen from the anthers of the pollen parent onto the end portion of the stigma of the seed-bearing parent. Pollen must be dry to be useful. Parent selections are made according to the aims and judgment of the breeder. Once the flowers have been hand-pollinated, they should be covered immediately to keep insects away.

After fertilization has taken place the seed will develop in the ovaries. It is permitted to ripen on the flower stem. After it is ripe, the seed is gathered, kept over winter, and in the spring, planted about ½ in. deep in a specially prepared seedbed. A majority of the seed will grow into small corms the first season. Over winter these are handled just like regular corms and are planted the next spring in the garden. Selection is made as the flowers bloom, and propagation of the selected flowers is repeated by growing cormels as directed above.

Hybridization calls for good judgment in the defining of aims, in the selection of parents for the desired qualities you want to combine, and in knowing when real improvement has been achieved.

ENEMIES

Insect Pests. The most important insect enemy of gladiolus is THRIPS, small blackish insects about ¹⁄₁₆ in. long that can be seen with the naked eye. They cause damage by sucking the juices from the growing plant, especially from the flower spike as it is developing, thus producing a brownish or blasted effect. To control, the corms can be soaked in a gallon of water to which a tablespoon of disinfectant has been added. Or, a specially prepared dust can be purchased and put on the corms during the storage period to kill any thrips they may harbor. Corms are planted with this insecticidal dust on them. Always follow directions of the label carefully.

After the plants have reached a height of 8–10 in., they can be sprayed or dusted at ten-day intervals until bud spikes begin to appear. The life cycle of the thrips is about ten to twelve days, so it is more effective to follow a short, concentrated spray schedule than it is to spray sporadically throughout the season.

Diseases. The diseases of gladiolus can be divided into three general classes: fungal diseases, bacterial diseases, and viral diseases.

Yellows caused by a fusarium fungus, has been called the most common and important disease of this plant. It causes slowing of growth and a yellowing of the leaf between the veins, and often a rotting of stored corms. Later the yellow turns to brown as the disease spreads, and eventually the plant dies. Since it cannot be detected until damage has been done, can remain virulent in the soil for some years, and cannot be cured by any known method, the greatest hope of the gladiolus grower is to prevent its getting into the planting by being exceedingly careful to buy only healthy stock.

Other fungus diseases are rots of one kind or another. The amateur gardener will have trouble distinguishing which is which, but general rules for treatment will hold for all.

Dry rot, *Sclerotinum gladioli*, produces hard lesions on the corms. Small brown spots may appear on the leaves above ground level. The best way to handle any cases where fungus trouble is suspected is to ROGUE out infected plants. Also, remove some of the soil where the plant was growing. Good drainage of the soil is very important. Quick drying of the corms at digging time is another preventive measure. Storage should be in a dry location. The use of a fungicide on the corms or in the soil at planting time will also aid in preventing disease.

Two forms of blight caused by fungus may be encountered. These are red spot, *Stemphylium*, and leaf blight, *Botrytis gladioli*. Each causes small spots of rotting on the foliage and flowers. In red spot these lesions have a tiny red center. In botrytis, the spotting is dark brown with a lighter brown center. Both stemphylium and botrytis have the same effect, making the flowers useless and spreading rapidly only under foggy or humid conditions. Neither disease is prevalent under most conditions. At least partial control can be achieved by a fungicidal spray. In climates where humidity is a special problem, only varieties known to resist these diseases should be planted.

There are two forms of virus that attack *Gladiolus*. One is known as mild mosaic and can be identified by white flecking on the leaves. In most cases the flower is not harmed. The other form of virus is white break, which causes a white, woody breaking of the color on the flowers and a narrowing and stunting of the leaves. There is no known cure for these virus diseases. Diseased plants should be rogued to prevent spread of the virus to other plants.

Fortunately, most gladiolus varieties are not affected by viruses. Gardeners will have little trouble with gladiolus diseases if they begin with healthy stock, rogue any affected plants, spray or dust during the growing season, and make certain that corms are planted in well-drained locations.

PRINCIPAL SPECIES

G. callianthus, formerly classified as the genus *Acidanthera*, is a summer-blooming herb native to tropical and southern Africa. Where the growing season is too short for outdoor bloom, it is sometimes grown in gardens and then brought indoors. It can also be grown indoors in pots. The cream-colored, long-tubed flowers with dark centers are up to 2 in. across, drooping on short, slender stalks from a 12–18 in. stem. Hardy in Zones 10–11.

G. x *colvillei* is a robust hybrid that grows 18–24 in. tall and has narrow leaves and nearly erect scarlet and bright yellow flowers. Cultivars have white, pink, or pure red blossoms.

G. x *gandavensis* is a vigorous hybrid that grows 2–4 ft. tall and has broad sword-shaped leaves and many-flowered spikes of red and reddish yellow blossoms.

G. x *hortulanus* (garden gladiolus) is a broad term for several varieties and cultivars that have lost or outgrown their original classification. Most are sturdy, vigorous growers with flower spikes of highly variable form and color.

G. illyricus is a European native that grows 1½–3 ft. high and has long leaves and reddish, purple, or bluish flowers.

G. tristis grows 24 in. tall and has slender stems bearing prominently ribbed, cylindrical leaves that grow up to 18 in. long. The fragrant yellowish white flowers are marked with purple and open at night. Cultivars are available with red, purple, or white flowers.

GLAUCIUM (GLOW see um). A genus of easily cultivated garden flowers native to Europe, belonging to the Papaveraceae (Poppy Family), and commonly known as horned or sea poppy. There are annual, biennial, and perennial species, but all are usually grown as annuals. They are started from seed in sunny locations where their large orange, yellow, or red flowers and dissected bluish leaves adorn the garden throughout the season.

PRINCIPAL SPECIES

G. corniculatum is an annual that grows to 18 in. Its red flowers have a black spot at the base of each petal.

G. flavum is an annual that grows to 3 ft. high and has bluish foliage and long stems bearing yellow or orange flowers followed by long, slender seed pods.

G. oxylobum, formerly listed as *G. leiocarpum*, is a perennial that grows less than 2 ft. tall and has yellow flowers.

GLAUCOUS. Covered or whitened with a waxy bloom that rubs off, as on the skin of an apple; a term used to describe the surface texture and appearance of leaves, stems, fruits, and other plant parts. Do not confuse with GLABROUS.

GLECHOMA (gle KOH mah) **hederacea.** A hardy, creeping, mat-forming perennial, formerly listed as *Nepeta hederacea*, commonly known as field-balm, gill-over-the-ground, or ground-ivy. It has blue flowers and is often used for ground cover in shady spots.

GLEDITSIA (gle DIT see ah). A genus of broad-headed, deciduous, mostly thorny trees belonging to the Fabaceae (Bean Family) and commonly known as honey-locusts. They are frequently used for shade trees and other ornamental purposes. Propagation is by seed sown in spring after being soaked in warm water or acid.

G. aquatica (water- or swamp-locust) is a low, branching tree that grows to 60 ft. and has a spiny trunk, lacy foliage, inconspicuous pealike flowers, and large pods. It grows in wet and swampy areas of the South. Hardy in Zones 8–9.

G. triacanthos (honey- or sweet-locust) grows to 60 ft. and has a trunk and branches armed with stout, rigid, three-forked spines 3–4 in. long. The leaves are feather form and finely divided. Inconspicuous greenish flowers are followed by flat, glossy brown or black pods. This species has been somewhat overused in landscape, street, park, or specimen plantings and is not grown anymore; it has been replaced by thornless cultivars. It is quite susceptible to webworm defoliation, cankers, and attacks of the honey-locust borer. Cv. 'Moraine' is thornless, nonfruiting, and quite resistant to webworm attacks. 'Sunburst' is thornless and has bright yellow leaves in spring changing to green in early summer. 'Shademaster', thornless and nonfruiting, has ascending branches and dark green leaves. Hardy in Zones 4–9.

GLOBEFLOWER. Common name for TROLLIUS, a genus of perennial herbs with flowers resembling double buttercups.

GLOBE LILY. Common name, along with globe-tulip, for certain species of CALOCHORTUS, a western genus whose graceful stems carry nodding flowers of fine white, yellow, or rose color.

GLOBULARIA (gloh byoo LAIR ee ah). A genus of shrubby little plants found mostly in the mountains of southern Europe and Asia. They have small blue (rarely white) flowers in rounded heads. Sometimes grown in rock gardens, they require a moist and partly shaded location. Propagation is by division or seed. Most are hardy in Zones 5–9.

PRINCIPAL SPECIES

G. cordifolia is a tiny prostrate grower that has leaves notched only at the tips and tiny heads of blue flowers on short stems.

G. nudicaulis is similar to *G. trichosantha* but is a bit larger and has naked flower stems.

G. trichosantha (globe-daisy) is a neat little plant a few inches high. It has toothed leaves about 1 in. long and pale blue, fluffy flowers in small (½-in.), rounded heads on leafy stems.

GLORIOSA (gloh ree OH sah). A genus of tropical, climbing herbs with lilylike, yellow or red flowers and tall, weak stems, belonging to the Liliaceae (Lily Family), and commonly known as glory lily. They grow from long tubers and are attractive, summer-flowering climbers under glass. Native in tropical Africa and Asia, they grow well outdoors only in Zones 10–11.

Plants can be bedded outdoors as far north as New York for summer flowering; however, the growth under such conditions is short and less floriferous. The dormant tubers are started in pots early in the year. They do best in a rather rough, turfy loam with leaf mold, and they appreciate liberal feeding when growth is well under way. The flowers are very colorful and of curious form, with wavy, reflexed segments and long, spreading stamens. Propagation is by tuber division or by offsets.

G. rothschildiana has crimson flowers with oblong, strongly reflexed segments, margined yellow and broadening to a yellow base. There are varieties with pale yellow and reddish purple flowers.

G. superba (spider or climbing lily) grows to 5 ft. or taller and bears yellow, orange, or red flowers with narrow, crisped segments.

GLORYBOWER. Common name for CLERODENDRUM, a genus of highly variable, mostly tropical plants with colorful flowers in terminal clusters.

GLORYBUSH. Common name for TIBOUCHINA, a genus of tropical American shrubs with purplish flowers.

GLORY LILY. Common name for GLORIOSA, a popular, tropical genus of the Liliaceae (Lily Family).

GLORY-OF-THE-SNOW. Common name for CHIONODOXA, a genus of blue, pink, or white spring-flowering bulbs.

GLORY PEA. Common name for *Clianthus formosus*, a tender trailing shrub with large, showy, drooping, scarlet flower clusters; see CLIANTHUS.

GLOXINIA (glahk SIN ee ah). A genus of Brazilian herbs with richly colored flowers belonging to the Gesneriaceae (Gesneria Family). The showy bell-shaped flowers are violet, purple, white, or reddish and often marbled or spotted with darker shades. They rise 6 in. above the large, downy, conspicuously veined leaves. Gloxinias grow from scaly rhizomes and require similar treatment to florists' "gloxinia."

As a common name, gloxinia refers to *Sinningia speciosa*, which is commonly known in the florist trade; see SINNINGIA.

GLYCYRHIZA (glī ki RĪZ ah) **glabra.** A perennial herb of southern Europe and southwestern Asia that grows to 3 ft. and has pale blue, pealike flowers in spikes and short, flat pods. Of no special garden value, it is, however, grown commercially for its roots, which yield the licorice used in medicine and flavorings. Grown in rich, moist soils from seed or division, it is hardy to Zone 9.

GNAPHALIUM (nah FAY lee um). A genus of woolly herbs, hardy and widely distributed throughout the world. They have small heads of mostly yellow flowers, resembling tiny everlastings. Only a few have been cultivated, and the best known are now referred to other genera. *Helichrysum petiolatum* was listed as *G. lanatum*; *Leontopodium alpinum* (edelweiss) was *G. leontopodium*; and *Antennaria margaritacea* was *G. margaritacea*.

GOAT'S-RUE. Common name for *Galega officinalis*, a hardy perennial herb with pealike flowers; see GALEGA.

GODETIA (goh DEE shee ah). A group of annual flowering herbs comprising a subgenus of CLARKIA but sometimes listed separately.

GOLDEN ASTER. Common name for CHRYSOPSIS, a genus of perennial herbs with yellow, daisy-like flowers.

GOLDEN-CLUB. Common name for *Orontium aquaticum*, a hardy, aquatic perennial with conspicuous yellow flower spikes rising above the water; see ORONTIUM.

GOLDEN-DEWDROP. A common name for *Duranta repens*, a subtropical American shrub or small tree with lilac flowers and yellow berries; see DURANTA.

GOLDEN-EARDROPS. Common name for *Dicentra chrysantha*, a perennial herb with panicles of golden flowers and fernlike leaves; see DICENTRA.

GOLDEN-GLOW. Common name for *Rudbeckia laciniata* var. *hortensia*, a tall, smooth plant related to the black-eyed-Susan; see RUDBECKIA.

GOLDEN-LARCH. Common name for PSEUDOLARIX, one of the few deciduous genera of the Pinaceae (Pine Family).v

GOLDEN-MARGUERITE. Common name for *Anthemis tinctoria*, a short-lived perennial herb with yellow ray flowers; see ANTHEMIS.

GOLDEN-RAIN TREE. Common name for *Koelreuteria paniculata*, a wide-spreading tree that bears large clusters of yellow flowers; see KOELREUTERIA.

GOLDENROD. Common name for SOLIDAGO, a genus of perennial herbs with showy flowers.

GOLDENSEAL. A common name for *Hydrastis canadensis*, a low perennial herb with attractive berries and thick yellow rootstocks; see HYDRASTIS.

GOLDEN-SHOWER. Common name for *Cassia fistula*, a greenhouse tree with large leaves and loose clusters of pale yellow, pealike flowers; see CASSIA.

GOLDEN-STARS. Common name for the genus BLOOMERIA, especially the popularly cultivated *B. crocea*, with golden yellow flowers in an airy sphere, about 4 in. across on 18-in. stems.

GOLDEN-YARROW. Common name for *Eriophyllum confertiflorum*, a 2-ft. perennial with heads of yellow flowers; see ERIOPHYLLUM.

GOLD FERN. Common name for PITYROGRAMMA, also called goldback or golden-backed fern, a genus of ferns characterized by a gold or silvery farina on the fronds.

GOLDFIELDS. Common name for LASTHENIA, a genus of Californian herbs with yellow flower heads.

GOLDILOCKS. Common name for *Aster linosyris*, a perennial herb with small heads of yellow flowers in clusters; see ASTER.

GOLDTHREAD. Common name for COPTIS, a genus of perennial herbs with slender root fibers.

GOMPHRENA (gahm FREE nah). A genus of herbs with white, red, or violet flower heads, which somewhat resemble those of a clover, useful for bedding and cut flowers or everlastings. Propagation is by seed, which should be started indoors since it does not germinate well in the open ground. Remove the cottony coating before sowing.

G. globosa (globe amaranth), the best-known species, is an annual, erect and branching, that grows to 18 in. tall and has variously colored blossoms. Flowers for drying should not be picked until well matured, toward the end of summer. While drying, protect them from rats, which are fond of the seeds.

Gomphrena globosa

GONIOPHLEBIUM (gaw nee oh FLEB ee um). A generic name sometimes used for the fern *Polypodium subauriculatum*; see POLYPODIUM.

GOODYERA (GOOD yer ah). A genus of small, hardy, terrestrial orchids, formerly listed as *Epipactis*, and commonly known as rattlesnake-plantain. The beautifully veined and variegated leaves resemble the pattern of the markings on a rattlesnake; for that reason they were once considered an antidote for snake bites. The small white flowers, united above into a helmet over the unfringed lip, grow in spikes, sometimes 12 in. high. Generally found in open woods in acid soil, rattlesnake-plantains can be grown in the wild garden if planted in conditions similar to their natural habitat with a plentiful supply of leaf mold.

G. pubescens, with leaves to 2 in. and veined with white, is the most common species in eastern woodlands.

GOOSEBERRY. Various species of thorny bushes closely related to the currants and generally included with them in the genus RIBES; some botanists, however, separate them into the genus *Grossularia*.

As a common name, gooseberry is applied to several plants that are not related to the real gooseberry, including the following: Cape-gooseberry refers to *Physalis peruviana* and *P. pruinosa*. Ceylon-gooseberry is *Dovyalis hebecarpa*. Otaheite- and star-gooseberry refer to *Phyllanthus acidus*. Southern-gooseberry is *Vaccinium melanocarpum*.

Some of the species (namely two), have produced improved varieties whose fruit is used in North America while immature for making jam, jelly, and pie, and in Europe when ripe as a dessert. North American varieties (developed from *Ribes hirtellum*) are mostly inferior in size and quality to European kinds (developed from *R. grossularia*) some of which are as large as hen's eggs. In North America, these so-called English gooseberries fail to produce well partly because of our hotter, drier summers and partly because of their greater susceptibility to mildew, but mainly because of neglect. Given proper care they are fairly successful.

The bushes are exceedingly hardy and can be grown in very cold climates; in warm ones they must be sheltered from the heat. Rich, heavy, but well-drained soils suit them best. They should stand 6 ft. apart to favor cross-cultivation and facilitate fruit picking. Each year several to many shoots grow from the base of the bush. If allowed to remain, they reduce the quantity and lower the quality of the berries; therefore, all but the two sturdiest should be removed not later than when the fruit is harvested. At this time also the stems that have borne three times should be cut out because thereafter they decline in productivity.

For general cultural directions and recommendations for control measures to use against anthracnose, leaf spot, powdery mildew and the imported currant worm, see CURRANT. The gooseberry fruit worm causes infected berries to color prematurely, then either dry up or decay. Such fruit should be gathered promptly and destroyed.

GOOSEBERRY TREE. Common name for *Phyllanthus acidus*, a tropical tree grown for its tart fruit, which is used for pickles and preserves; see PHYLLANTHUS.

GOOSEFOOT. Common name for various species of CHENOPODIUM, a genus of glandular shrubby herbs with medicinal and culinary uses. The Goosefoot Family is CHENOPODIACEAE.

GOPHERS. There are several species of small, burrowing, pouched rodents or pocket gophers, widely distributed in the United States, especially west of the Mississippi. Although, like the earthworm, this animal performs a service by stirring and mixing the soil and making it arable, collectively gophers are called the "western gardener's public enemy No. 1," because of the damage they do to agricultural crops of all kinds. In contrast to the mole, they live strictly on vegetable material and are destructive to a wide range of plant life. Roots, bulbs, and tubers, including potatoes and other garden vegetables, suffer from their depredations.

Shallow burrows and the loose, crescent-shaped mounds of earth surrounding the tunnel openings injure and disfigure fields, pastures, and lawns. Their burrows are deeper and the

Pocket gopher

only surface indication of their presence is the scattered mounds of pushed-up earth where they enter and leave. In irrigated regions, gopher burrows in ditch banks can cause washouts, floods, and water scarcity, representing thousands of dollars lost to the community. Gardeners and farmers go to considerable trouble to keep

gophers out of their gardens or to combat them by various means.

Owl nest boxes may attract owls, which naturally prey on gophers. Spurge (*Euphorbia lathrus*) repels gophers but must be planted in the perimeter to exclude them. The gopher snake, another valuable help in controlling this pest, should not be killed or harmed but, on the contrary, encouraged to live in western gardens.

In the Northwest, the term "gopher" is applied to a striped ground squirrel, and in the Gulf States it refers to a burrowing turtle, neither of which are of particular importance to gardeners.

GORDONIA. A genus of evergreen or deciduous trees or shrubs belonging to the Theaceae (Tea Family). They have glossy, decorative foliage and flowers resembling camelias. They should be planted in moist, acid soil and can be propagated by seed, layers, or greenwood cuttings under glass.

G. alatamaha (Franklin tree) is now listed as *Franklinia alatamaha*; see FRANKLINIA.

G. lasianthus (loblolly-bay), native to the southeastern states, is an evergreen tree that grows to 60 ft. and has glossy, dark green leaves and showy white, fragrant, long-stemmed flowers 2½ in. across, which bloom for nearly two months in summer. Hardy in Zones 8–9.

GORSE. A common name for ULEX, a genus of spiny, semihardy shrubs with fragrant flowers.

GOSSYPIUM (gah SIP ee um). A genus of tropical, woody herbs of the Malvaceae (Mallow Family), and furnishing one of the world's most important crops. Several species are grown as an annual field crop to furnish commercial cotton, and sometimes in northern greenhouses for interest, flower shows, or educational purposes.

The plants have lobed leaves and purplish or yellow flowers, which are followed by fruits called "bolls," within which the seeds are attached to a fibrous lint.

Though seldom used as ornamentals, cotton plants are attractive, with their large, mallowlike flowers. Two species are occasionally grown in mild climates for their decorative effect: **G. davidsonii** has yellow flowers that are purple at the base; **G. sturtianum** is an Australian native that has purple flowers with dark center.

GOURD.

A common name loosely applied to any member of the Cucurbitaceae (Cucumber Family), including pumpkin, squash, cucumber, and melon. It is now restricted (in North America) to the ornamental, inedible-fruited species of cucurbits, of which there are many popular forms.

Most gourds are tender annuals, either trailing or climbing by means of tendrils. They thrive in the full sun, in well-drained, rich soil. Usually the seed is sown where the plants are to remain, but sometimes, to save time, it is started on inverted sods or in small flower pots, the plants being set outdoors after the danger of frost has passed.

The common gourds are yellow-flowered varieties of **Cucurbita pepo**, whose many varieties includes the common PUMPKIN; see also SQUASH. Hedgehog or teasel gourd is **C. dipsaceus**; see CUCURBITA.

Calabash, serpent, snake, and white-flowered gourd are forms of the annual vine **Lagenaria siceraria**, which also includes the dishcloth maté (or utensil gourd of Paraguay); see LAGENARIA. The true calabash is not a gourd but is the fruit of a tropical tree, **Crescentia cujete**, of the Bignoniaceae (Bignonia Family).

Gooseberry gourd is **Cucumis anguria**; see CUCUMIS.

Serpent gourd also refers to **Trichosanthes anguina**; see TRICHOSANTHES.

GOUT PLANT.

Common name for **Jatropha podagrica**, a tropical shrub with bright red flowers; see JATROPHA.

GOUTWEED.

Common name for **Aegopodium podagraria**, a weedy perennial herb with white flowers, sometimes planted in poor soil; see AEGOPODIUM.

GRAFTING.

Any process whereby a part (scion) taken from one plant is made to unite with and grow upon another part of a plant (stock). The scion can be a single bud (see BUDDING), a small twig bearing a few to several buds, a piece of stem (as of a cactus), a terminal shoot (as of an evergreen), or a fragment of root of a desirable variety. As the two parts of a graft grow together, they are said to form a union.

Grafting is a method of PROPAGATION in which the primary purpose is either to increase the chances of the scion's making successful growth by giving it a new foundation in the form of a more vigorous root system than it had before, or to change over the form, character, fruit-bearing quality, etc., of the stock plant or tree by substituting some other variety for its original top.

The operation can also create a tree or plant bearing two or more distinct varieties of flower or fruit, or two kinds (staminate and pistillate) of flowers, in which case the chances of successful pollination of the latter are increased. Grafting provides a way to work up a stock of plants that cannot successfully or quickly be increased by other asexual means, such as division, layering, or rooting of cuttings.

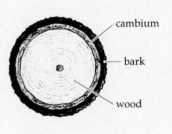

Cross-section of stem

To be successful, grafting must ensure and maintain intimate contact between the cambium tissues of scion and stock, that is, the layer of growing cells that is just under the bark and outside the wood. Most grafting is done with dormant scions, which means in winter or early spring, unless the scions can be kept dormant in cold storage until the stock plants are in best condition to receive them. This is illustrated in budding, which is usually done in midsummer. Scions so kept for future use should be carefully labeled and kept moist and cool so they will neither shrivel nor start into growth.

After the scion and stock have been cut and adjusted (by any of the methods described below), they are tied in place (if necessary), after which the whole area of wounded surface is covered with tree seal, melted paraffin, or GRAFTING WAX or wound with grafting tape to prevent the drying of the parts and to exclude moisture and disease organisms.

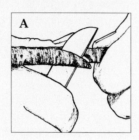

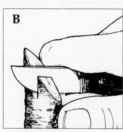

Many kinds of grafting are practiced by expert plant growers for special purposes or with specific plants, but the techniques that are best suited to the average gardener's needs are whip, cleft, side, and bridge grafting.

WHIP OR TONGUE GRAFTING

In this method, both scion and stock (of about the same diameter) are cut on a long slant, about 1 in. long (A); a slit is made in the middle of each cut surface (B), and the two are fitted together so that the tongue of one fits into the slot of the

Whip grafting

other. They are then bound firmly (C) and if they are to be exposed to the air, they can also be covered with grafting wax.

CLEFT GRAFTING

This is the simplest method, and the one generally used in working over old trees—either to make a worthless seedling or other specimen produce good fruit, or to make it possible to grow more than one variety on a tree.

Stock branches ½–2 in. in diameter are cut squarely across where the bark is smooth (A). These stumps are then split to a depth of about 1½ in. (B) and the slit is pried apart until it will

admit a scion. This is previously cut to a slender wedge shape at the bottom (C), they are usually 4–6 in. long and bear three or four buds. The scion is inserted in the split stock and adjusted so that its lowest bud is just above the stock and on the outside (D). Also, the scion is slanted slightly outward so that its cambium layer is certain to be in contact with that of the stock at at least one point.

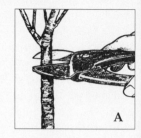

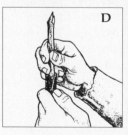

Cleft grafting

As a rule the pressure of the wood is enough to keep them in place, but the graft can be tied with cord or tape if necessary. The entire top of the stock to below the base of the split is then covered with grafting wax.

SIDE GRAFTING

In this method a cut is made downward into the stock just beneath the bark, and the scion (its base cut in a wedge shape) is thrust beneath the bark, tied there, and waxed. The stock above the graft can be cut off, or not. This method is especially useful for developing branches at bare spaces along trunks and main limbs.

BRIDGE OR REPAIR GRAFTING

This method is used to establish new sap connections across large wounds such as those made in winter when mice gnaw the bark of trees. Water sprouts, being long and lusty, make the best scions for this work. The edges of the wound are trimmed back to healthy wood at the top and bottom where slots are cut at four or five points around the trunk. The scions are cut long enough to fit into corresponding slots above and below so as to have a slight bow outward, and each scion is cut, slanting at each end so that the smooth part will fit against the trunk to which it is tacked firmly. All cut and injured surfaces are then covered with grafting wax or wound with waxed cloth. Trees so treated can be saved, even though completely girdled since, in time, the scions will not only form unions at the top and bottom, but will also grow together to form a new exterior trunk.

GRAFTING WAX. A more or less pliable protective material used to cover cut surfaces on woody plants, especially those made in grafting. It is usually made of resin, beeswax, and beef tallow and is commercially available.

GRAMINEAE (gram in AY ee). Former botanical name for the POACEAE (Grass Family).

GRAMMATOPHYLLUM (grah MAT oh fil um). A genus of twelve species of large epiphytic orchids native to southeastern Asia, Indonesia, New Guinea, the Philippines, and Polynesia. Its large, round, showy flowers are shades of green-yellow with orange-brown spots. The plants need abundant water during growth and should be grown in bright light in a porous, well-draining compost. Hardy to Zone 9, they withstand a minimum winter temperature of 60°F. *G. speciosum*, the type species, attains a height of 25 ft. or more in its native habitat.

GRANADILLA. Common name for the edible fruit of several species of PASSIFLORA.

GRANDIFLORA. This rose class was created by a cross between the hybrid tea and floribunda roses. 'Queen Elizabeth', the archetype, maintains a standard that few other roses have reached. It is a large, hybrid tea type (see HYBRID

TEA ROSE), blooming in small clusters on a very large bush. Since the blooms, though large, are somewhat smaller than most hybrid tea blooms, and the plant is generally larger than the average hybrid tea plant, it might be more appropriately called "grandibush" instead of grandiflora. It should be noted that many countries have not accepted this class name. Other roses that have been placed in the grandiflora class include 'Aquarius', 'Pink Parfait', and 'Sonia'.

GRAPE. A pulpy, edible berry borne in clusters of vines of the genus VITIS. Its cultivated varieties belong to three important groups. The European species, *V. vinifera*, with more than 1500 varieties, has been cultivated in mild parts of the Eastern Hemisphere from prehistoric times, but in North America it consistently failed until means were discovered (by grafting it upon stocks of North American species) to prevent its destruction by grape root louse or phylloxera. Except when grafted on such resistant stocks, it still fails wherever this pest is established. It is the leading species on the Pacific Coast, especially in California where much of the nation's grape crop is produced.

As a common name, grape refers to several other plants. The Grape Family is VITACEAE. Cape or evergreen grape is *Rhoicissus capensis*; see RHOICISSUS. Oregon-grape is *Mahonia nervosa*; see MAHONIA. Sea-grape is COCCOLOBA.

NATIVE GRAPES

The most important North American species, the fox grape, *V. labrusca*, is native from Massachusetts to the Allegheny Mountains and southward to Georgia. Its first important variety, Catawba, was disseminated in 1823, and its second, Concord, in 1854. Since then, more than a thousand varieties have been introduced. These two are still leading commercial varieties.

From the Potomac River southward, the native muscadine grape, *V. rotundifolia*, has been cultivated in gardens since colonial days. It is not grown commercially (except occasionally for local markets) because it "shatters" or drops off its clusters when ripe.

Grapes are ideal for the home garden. Their vines can be trained on porches, pergolas, arbors, and summer houses, where they are as attractive and useful as any other ornamental vine, not to mention their regular production of red, white, or blue fruit. By selecting varieties that ripen successionally, one can make the fruiting season cover a full two months; and with simple home storage facilities, the fresh grape season can be extended to six months or even longer. Once planted, the vines can be allowed to take care of themselves, but they will not produce as well as when trained by the easily understood and applied principles discussed below. Thus cared for, they may remain productive for 50 years or longer.

CULTURE
SOIL AND PLANTING

Though sandy or gravelly loams are preferred for commercial grape growing, any fairly deep, well-drained, moderately fertile soil will produce abundant crops. Soils excessively rich in nitrogenous matter are undesirable because they tend to produce a rank growth of stems and foliage, but little fruit. Fertilizers are best applied in the spring. On a poor soil, an application of 1 lb. of 5–10–10 fertilizer per vine scattered over as much ground as it is likely to cover when the growth starts will help develop shoots. See FERTILIZER.

Commercial grape growers generally prefer planting first-class one-year vines because they are vigorous. Two-year vines are also popular but generally cost more. It probably makes little difference which is chosen provided that the planting is done correctly and followed by good care afterward. Never should vines older than two years be planted because their root systems are usually seriously reduced in digging.

BUILDING THE TRUNK

After planting, cut off all puny shoots and reduce the strongest one to only two or three joints, each carrying a plump bud. In vineyard practice, all three buds are allowed to develop shoots, but two of these are cut off before the following spring. Then the strongest is cut back to two or three buds and the process repeated. The idea here is to get a strong trunk or main stem with which to start the third spring.

A better practice is to shorten the weaker shoots to only one joint and one leaf as soon as the lower joints of the strongest have become woody—usually after six or eight weeks of

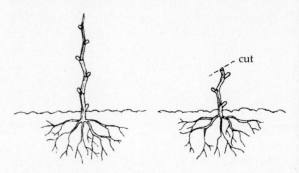

Cut newly planted grapes back to develop strong trunks.

growth. This concentrates the plant food in the remaining shoot, which becomes strong enough to serve as the main trunk of the vine and, the following year, perhaps to produce some fruit-bearing shoots. This method starts fruit production a year sooner than the usual vineyard treatment. The only reason for allowing the extra shoots to develop at all is to provide against loss of the main shoot by the possible accident of having it broken off.

The main shoot should be tied vertically, but loosely, to a stout bean pole or other support 6–8 ft. long. If it grows more than 3 ft. during the first season, it will be strong enough to bear some fruit the following year, but it should be cut back by at least 50% before the spring of that year. Vines considerably less than 30 in. long should be cut back to only three joints and made to start over again and develop stronger stems under the treatment already described.

No trellis, arbor, or other permanent support need be given until the spring of the second year. Then, if the vine is in open ground, it can be merely a stout stake; or, if the plant is by a porch, veranda, or arbor, a heavy wire (No. 9 or 8), preferably of copper, will serve. This should be securely fastened at the ground and at the top so the main stem can go straight up and become a trunk from which the branches will be developed during the second year.

PRUNING

As in all other pruning for the production of flowers or fruit, it is essential to understand how and where the plant bears its blossoms—on which the fruits depend. Each year the grapevine develops, from buds formed the previous year, long green shoots that bear leaves and tendrils. Examination of the shoots shows that a tendril occurs opposite a leaf at nearly every node (joint) and that the tendrils show many variations — including single and branched strands, some of which bear a few grapes while others have lost the tendril habit and become clusters of fruit.

All of these green parts—leaves, tendrils, and clusters—are borne on shoots that start to grow in spring. Most of them develop from buds formed the previous year in the angles of the leaf stems. After the leaves fall in the autumn, these buds can be easily seen at each joint on the shoot (now called a "cane"), where they and the joints serve as guides at pruning time. If their number is reduced, the shoots that develop from the remainder are strengthened and made more prolific, yielding higher quality fruit than unpruned, untrained vines can ever bear. Furthermore, the vines can be kept within desired bounds and trained in any desired direction.

The only time that grapevines should be pruned is in winter, or in cold climates, very early spring when they are dormant. At that time, with the above principles of growth in mind, the pruning is based on several considerations. (1) Puny shoots bear no fruits and should be cut off. (2) "Bull" canes—overgrown, burly, very long ones—also are generally sterile; therefore, cut them out at their starting points. (3) Reduce, in both number and length, those canes that are about the thickness of a lead pencil; they are the ones whose green shoots, produced the following summer, will bear fruit.

Commercial grape growers generally limit the number of canes to two, four, or sometimes six, each pair trained horizontally at approximate right angles to the main trunk, and each allowed to bear only six to ten buds, depending on the strength of the vine.

RECLAIMING OLD VINES

Old vines that have been neglected for years need severe pruning, so severe, in fact, that it may be wise not to do it all at once, but instead to spread it over two or more years, depending on the size of the vine.

First, find the main trunk and begin cutting away the growth that is more than 8 ft. from the trunk. You will probably collect a large pile of prunings in a short time, and the old vine will look absolutely butchered. Dig, or pull out any canes that have taken root, and either replant them elsewhere or destroy them. The goal is to establish a compact plant with all of the grape-bearing area close to the main trunk where it will be most productive.

This type of heavy pruning will stimulate a lot of new growth during the summer, and it must be either cut back or thinned out, so that only a limited number of strong lateral canes will result. Train the new canes

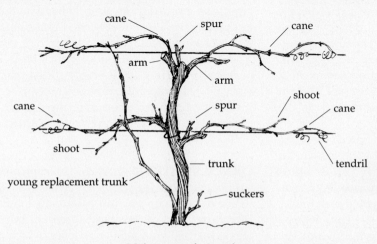

Major parts of grapevine

along wires or over an arbor. After the vine is under control, prune it heavily each year so it will maintain its compact shape, and gradually allow one of the young, vigorous sprouts to replace the old main stump.

Treat grape canes as biennials; let them grow one year, produce the next, then remove them. While the two-year-old canes are bearing, guide some new ones along the same wire so they can become the bearing canes the following year.

Training (as distinguished from pruning) consists in placing the canes and shoots so as to take best advantage of sunlight and air. It allows for wide divergence of preference. On arbors and other high supports, the best plan is to train the main trunk direct to the top and to cut back the canes on it each year to mere "spurs" of only one to three buds—two being preferred.

The chief advantages of this method are: first, that the fruit will be borne on the shoots developed from these spur buds from near the ground to the top of the vine; and, second, that there will be less work needed for pruning, spraying, and gathering the fruit, and it will be easier than when the vines are allowed to clamber without restraint to the top of the arbor, resulting in unsightly growth with stems crowded overhead, leaving trunks bare closer to the ground.

ENEMIES

DISEASES

Black rot is the most destructive fungus disease of grapes, directly attacking and destroying the berries and spotting the leaves. The fungus overwinters in shriveled, mummied, rotted fruit, putting out a crop of spores to infect new growth in the spring. The best control is to pick all fruit and not leave any to rot on the vine or on the ground nearby.

Downy mildew of grapes has spread from the United States to Europe, causing great losses. On the leaves it first shows as pale yellow spots accompanied by downy white tufts beneath. Later, flowers and fruits are blighted and rotted. Powdery mildew may occur in late summer as a fine white coating on the upper sides of the leaves but appears too late to do serious damage.

INSECT PESTS

The grape berry moth is the cause of most of the wormy grapes in the United States. The grape berries are webbed together and drop from the stems when about the size of garden peas, or small holes are eaten in nearly ripened berries. The ½ in. long, greenish gray worms with brown heads pass the winter and pupate in grayish silken cocoons, the small grayish purple moths emerging in spring.

The adult grape root worm, also very destructive, is a small, gray-brown leaf beetle that eats chainlike holes in the leaves; the larvae devour small root fibers and the bark of larger roots. Other pests include the grape flea beetle, rose chafer, Japanese beetle, grapevine beetle, sphinx caterpillar, and, sometimes, the spotted grapevine beetle.

In the case of all pests consult your local extention service for safe guidelines for the use of insecticides. Always follow the instructions on packages carefully.

GRAPE FERN. Common name for BOTRYCHIUM, a genus of succulent ferns with grapelike clusters of sporangia.

GRAPEFRUIT. An evergreen, semitropical citrus fruit tree (*Citrus* x *paradisi*), grown mainly in Florida, southern Texas, and California for its large, fine-grained fruits, usually borne in bunches that suggest huge, few-berried grape clusters. It was originally cultivated as a hybrid or mutant from the pumello, *C. maxima*, which bears larger, coarser-grained fruit singly, rather than in clusters. The grapefruit, though generally a commercial orchard tree, is occasionally a home garden subject, hardy to Zone 9. For culture, see CITRUS FRUITS.

GRAPTOPHYLLUM (grap toh FIL um) **pictum.** A tropical shrub with purple or crimson flowers, native to New Guinea, and commonly known as caricature plant. It has large, green or purplish leaves marked with yellow blotches, which often suggest the profile of a human face; large, wide-open flowers are purple or crimson. Hardy in Zones 10–11, it is sparingly cultivated as a greenhouse curiosity or in shady tropical gardens. Propagation is by cuttings.

GRASS. Common name for many plants belonging to the POACEAE (Grass Family), with bladelike leaves, including many lawn, forage, grain, and weed plants.

GRASSHOPPER. A number of insect species belonging to the Acrididae of the order Orthoptera. They are large, usually green or brown winged creatures that are more familiar to us as remarkable jumpers, being equipped with long, powerful hind legs. Grasshoppers may have been the destructive "locusts" of ancient times. They should not be confused with the so-called locusts that sing in trees during the summer, which are harmless species of CICADA.

Various species of grasshoppers occur all over the world and attack a great variety of wild and cultivated crops, doing tremendous damage when in great numbers. The eggs winter over in inch-long packets about an inch below the soil surface in uncultivated ground such as field margins and waste land. The young hoppers that emerge late in spring look like the adults except in size and lack of wings. They soon begin to feed, completing their growth by midsummer but continuing to feed until frost.

GRASS-PINK ORCHID. Common name for CALOPOGON, a genus of moisture-loving orchids with grassy leaves.

GRATIOLA (gra TĪ oh lah) **aurea.** A low-growing annual herb with small, golden-yellow flowers, commonly known as goldenpert or golden-hedge-hyssop. It grows in wet ground from Maine to Florida and is useful for covering damp banks of ditches and ponds.

GRAY MOLD. Common name sometimes applied to BOTRYTIS blights because of the fluffy gray masses of spores.

GREENBRIER. Common name for SMILAX, a genus of woody vines including some used as decorative foliage by florists and some that are annoying weeds.

GREENHOUSE. A glass- or plastic-roofed building used for the propagation or maintenance of plants. Though often built as a separate structure with independent heating equipment, it can be combined with a garage (if small) or with a residence, especially in the form of a conservatory or sun room. There are many styles and types available from a variety of sources.

A convenient location where the greenhouse will receive maximum sunlight and minimum shadow is most important. The plans should consider not only the initial house but also present and prospective grade, the shape of the area, heating arrangements, and possible enlargements.

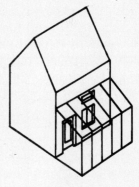

Greenhouse

The great demand for amateur or home greenhouses has stimulated leading greenhouse-construction firms to develop standard sizes and unit features that fit together something like sectional bookcases. The purchaser benefits not only in reduced costs for standard sizes and equipment, but also because it is possible start with a few units and expand as interest, skill, and experience develop.

Ventilation. Different types of vents serve to reduce the air temperature and humidity inside the greenhouse. Ventilators, comprising about 10% of the roof area, should be placed preferably on both sides of the ridge, each side to be operated independently on the lee side of the wind to avoid downdrafts of air during cold weather. There are several styles of regulators, made to lift several ventilators at once from a narrow crack to full capacity, thus providing for complete and immediate control of air flow. Ventilators can be placed at the sides, but such a location is not as essential or as desirable as the ridge. In warm dry climates, however, side vents are essential for more rapid air circulation during periods of high temperature.

With advancing electronic technology, heating, cooling, and humidity control can be completely automated (as can plant watering) or completely or partially manual. Complete automation, of course, is the most expensive initially and needs a fail-safe arrangement and an available repair service, but the freedom from concern, particularly on a cold spring day with alternating full sun and overcast must be experienced to be appreciated.

Heat. How you heat your greenhouse is determined largely by what is practical locally. For the small greenhouse a forced air heater, conveniently controlled by a thermostat, is much less expensive initially depending on the availability of electricity, gas, and oil. As a general rule, gas or oil heat is the most economical in the North, with electricity best in the South where relatively little heat is necessary except during the coldest spells of winter. All gas or oil units need to be properly vented, otherwise plants may be damaged and dangerous fumes may build up. Many small greenhouses, if attached to a dwelling, can be warmed by extending the existing home heating system.

Since no single item of greenhouse construction is so important, the capacity of the heating system should always be calculated by a specialist in greenhouse heating.

Pest Prevention. Attacks by diseases and insects usually start as a result of error in management. Knowledge of the conditions under which such pests increase and spread, plus keeping plants vigorous through good cultural practices will reduce the danger of attack. Keep the premises clean by destroying all debris and affected plant parts. It is far easier and more important to maintain healthful conditions than to reestablish them after infection has occurred.

Keep a watch out for any insect or disease problems and deal with them immediately.

Plants that are grown in biologically active (not sterile) soil that is kept uniformly and adequately moist are less likely to fall prey to pest and disease. Most insect problems can be controlled by weekly spraying with insecticidal soap; however, this is not recommended for members of the Euphorbiaceae (Spurge Family) or nasturtiums, since it has a phytotoxic effect on them. See also GREENHOUSE PESTS.

PLANT HANDLING

Under the handling of plants, the following general principles are most important.

Conditions. Practically every plant grown in the greenhouse has a normal period of activity and season of bloom. It is wise to keep conditions favorable to the plant rather than forcing the plant to adapt itself to grow under unnatural conditions.

Its natural habitat suggests the type of treatment that is best for each plant species. Imitation of soil, light, temperature, and moisture conditions under which the plant grows naturally usually leads to success in culture. The fact that a plant is found naturally in a swamp, a tropical region, or on a mountainside does not necessarily mean it will fail under different conditions. The original habitat merely hints at the probable successful method of treatment.

Dormancy. Most plant species do not grow continuously but go through an inactive or rest period. For example, hardy bulbs, such as tulips, rest between late spring and early autumn; cacti rest during dry seasons. Plants should be given similar rest periods when grown under the artificial conditions of greenhouse culture.

Growth Stages. Each plant species must reach a definite stage of growth. Vegetative development and reproduction rarely occur coincidentally. Woody plants, such as azaleas, must have well-ripened wood before flowers can be expected; otherwise any blooms that may develop will be inferior and short-lived. The frequency at which plants are shifted from pot to pot, particularly in the case of herbaceous plants, acts as a partial control of the time of flowering and fruit production. If kept in small pots too long, they will blossom prematurely or die. If shifting frequently to successively larger pots, the period of vegetative growth is lengthened. Maintenance in one pot for a period of time tends to check growth and encourage flowering. Fertilizers applied during the early stages encourage vegetative growth; withheld until growth is well advanced, they induce flowering and increase the size of flowers and fruit.

Each plant has its own typical means of propagation, usually by seed, but often by some vegetative (asexual) method, such as layering, division, grafting, or cuttings. The vegetative methods frequently produce better plants than seed-grown ones, and they are always true to variety (except for bud sports; see SPORT).

GREENHOUSE PESTS. Many insects and diseases cause problems in the greenhouse, but conditions in a greenhouse are usually particularly favorable for pests. Since the ordinary control methods are difficult because of the close conditions and sensitivity of many indoor plants to sprays, the best control is prevention, which means exclusion. When infestation does occur, more aggressive controls may be necessary.

INSECTS

The insect pests that attack greenhouse plants are in many cases the same as those that attack the same or related crops in the garden.

Sucking Insects. Many sucking insects cause problems in the greenhouse. The scales include the small hard, brown, and armored kinds and the larger, soft tortoise scales common on oleander, fern, and palm. The soft mealybugs form white clusters on coleus, orchid, poinsettia, ivy, and other plants. The small dark-bodied greenhouse orthezia is covered with waxy filaments.

Aphids of various colors weaken plants and distort young growth. Whiteflies are tiny, snow-white, four-winged creatures that rise up from the plants in swarms when disturbed and cover plants with a sticky material, in which a sooty black fungus grows. Greenhouse thrips whiten and fleck leaves with yellow and distort flower buds. Red spider mites cover the undersurface of leaves with fine webs and turn the upper surface yellow. The cyclamen mite blackens the buds and distorts the leaves.

Chewing Insects. Several chewing insects are troublesome under glass. The greenhouse leaf tier is a pale green caterpillar that encloses one or more leaves in a web. Leaf rollers act first as miners and then as chewers. The Florida fern caterpillar is dark green. There are many species of cutworms. The corn earworm likes to eat chrysanthemum buds. The strawberry rootworm feeds on rose leaves as an adult beetle and injures the roots as a grub. The chrysanthemum midge makes cone-shaped galls on the leaves, and the rose midge distorts the flower buds. Wireworms, white grubs, sowbugs, millipedes, and the garden centipede may work in the soil feeding on the roots, while nematodes cause galls on the roots or leaves, which disfigure and often kill the plants.

Prevention. To prevent insect problems, greenhouses (meaning the soil and benches as well as the rest) should be cleaned by heat, steam, or other sterilization or heavy fumigation in the intervals between crops, and all plants should be carefully inspected before they are admitted. Soil used in filling the benches should be carefully inspected to see that it does not contain wireworms, white grubs, eelworms, cutworms, or other insects. Infested soil should be sterilized by steam when possible; see DISINFECTION and individual pest entries.

Eradication. Many insects and related pests in greenhouses are most easily controlled by FUMIGATION. Those that work in the soil are controlled by soil sterilization with steam or chemicals and sometimes by the use of poison baits.

If fumigation is not possible, spraying with contact insecticides may become necessary for the control of scales, mealybugs, and other sucking insects. Insecticidal soap sprays are most effective and entirely safe on most plants, but they must be used consistently and mixed exactly according to manufacturer's directions. Do not spray plants in direct sun, and read the label for more specific guidance. Nasturtiums and members of the Euphorbiaceae (Spurge Family), including poinsettias, suffer a phytotoxic effect from insecticidal soap sprays. See also INSECT CONTROL.

DISEASES

The spread of plant disease is encouraged in greenhouses, where plants are already in close proximity, by the practice of overhead watering. Plants soaked with the hose, especially on cloudy days when they cannot dry off rapidly, are very susceptible to botrytis blight or to becoming covered with mildew. Rose black spot and mildew are more prevalent in early fall before the temperature is well regulated. Painting the heating pipes with sulfur is one of the remedies for mildew. Removal of all diseased plant parts, spacing the plants well apart, and keeping humidity low will do much toward preventing the spread of plant disease in the greenhouse. Specific control measures are discussed under articles on the various diseases and the plants they affect. See also DISEASE.

GREEN MANURE. Certain crops can be grown and turned under to fertilize and improve the soil. The idea of using crops to improve the soil is not a new one; the Chinese have been using green manures for nearly 3000 years, and the ancient Greeks and Romans practiced green manuring extensively.

It was only in the late nineteenth century that scientific explanations for the benefits of green manures began to be understood. It is now known that this method speeds up the natural system of creating rich soil, which is typically built up over the centuries as natural vegetation dies and decomposes. By raising crops, then chopping them up, and tilling them under, the same process is accelerated, and the benefits to the soil are apparent much more quickly.

Green manures that are planted in order to prevent the leaching of nutrients out of the soil are called catch crops. Green manures that remain in the garden over the winter, protecting the soil from erosion and temperature extremes, are referred to as cover crops. All green manure techniques overlap in their contributions to the improved quality of the soil.

BENEFITS

By turning under green manure crops, the gardener provides ideal conditions in which soil organisms, especially microorganisms, will flourish. A healthy population of soil organisms benefits the soil in several ways: They decompose organic matter in the soil, releasing nutrients that plants can use, thereby reducing the amount of chemical fertilizer usually needed. They create HUMUS, organic matter that helps the soil hold water and retain nutrients. The mild acids produced by soil microbes help dissolve nutrients otherwise tied up in the insoluble minerals of the soil. They help suppress plant diseases and parasites carried by the soil. Some microorganisms, especially those associated with roots of legumes—such as alfalfa, beans, peas, and vetch—convert or "fix" nitrogen in the air and add it to the soil's fertility. When turned under, alfalfa is the best of the nitrogen-fixing crops, adding as much as 200 lb. nitrogen per acre.

Green manures can also improve soil structure, crowd out weeds, bring up minerals from the subsoil, and encourage the growth of earthworms, which aerate and enrich the soil with their castings. Green manures can also provide food, forage, or aesthetic value.

METHODS

Green manure can be planted wherever a bare spot exists in the garden. When a crop is harvested, it can be replaced with a green manure, possibly an edible one such as beans or peas. In the fall, after the last cultivation, cowpeas, buckwheat, and ryegrass will fill in vacant spots quickly. In cool climates, annual ryegrass makes a good winter cover crop for areas that will be planted with a new crop early in the spring. Hairy vetch, kale, and winter rye will resume growth in the spring, so these can be planted where late crops such as corn, squash, and melons will be planted. In the South, good cover crop choices include crimson, bur, or yellow sweet clover and vetch, field peas, lupine, rye, oats, barley, or wheat.

For a two-year rotation, divide the garden into two plots. Plant garden crops in one, and grow manures for the entire season in the other. Switch uses of the plots the next year. In a three-year rotation, a different third of the garden is planted with green manures each year.

In order to gain maximum benefits from green manures, they should be turned under by hand or with a rotary tiller before they go to seed. To add the maximum nutrients to the soil, the green manure crop should be turned under while it is still fairly young, green, and succulent. A vegetable crop can be planted in the same spot in as little as two weeks. For greater increase of the organic content of the soil (humus), allow the green manure to become more woody and mature; then the soil should be ready for planting six to eight weeks after the manure has been turned under.

GREENS. Plants whose succulent leaves and stems, steamed or boiled, are served as a vegetable. While growing, they are usually called by their popular, individual names or referred to collectively as potherbs. In general, as they are most in demand in early spring, the hardy annuals are often sown in the fall and wintered under mulches or in coldframes. They are also started during late winter in greenhouses, hotbeds, or coldframes, or sown at the earliest possible moment outdoors in spring.

Since greens must be succulent and tender, the annuals must be grown rapidly in loose, very rich soil, well drained but well supplied with moisture. The perennials can be hastened by placing coldframes or plant forcers over them as soon as the ground has thawed. The latter include pokeweed, sorrel, dock, dandelion, and chicory.

Among the many weeds and wild plants used as greens are the following: buckhorn plantain, chicory, dandelion, various cresses, dock, goosefoot (or lamb's-quarters), mustard, pigweed, pokeweed, purslane, sorrel, and marsh-marigold.

Hardy annuals suitable for spring sowing include: chervil, Chinese amaranth, Chinese artichoke, Chinese mustard, Chinese cabbage, corn-salad, kale, nasturtium, orach, and spinach. The seed can be obtained at seed stores or through mail-order catalogs.

Species that can be sown in the fall and wintered over for spring use are spinach, dandelion, fetticus, kale, and collards. For summer and autumn use, the most popular are Swiss chard and New Zealand spinach. In addition, the following are often used as greens: beet tops, turnip sprouts, and thinned out seedlings of cabbage and related plants.

GREVILLEA (gre VIL ee ah). A genus of Australian trees and shrubs belonging to the Proteaceae (Protea Family) of the Southern Hemisphere. One or two species are grown for ornament in the United States, either under glass or outdoors in Zones 10–11.

G. robusta (silk-oak) is the best-known species. In its native land, it is a fast-growing tree to 150 ft. As a greenhouse subject, it is easily grown from seed, forming one of the most decorative of fern-leaved plants and doing well in 4- or 5-in. pots. In warmer regions, it is used as a shade tree, and there the curiously shaped, orange-yellow flowers add to the beauty of the foliage.

G. thelemanniana is a spreading shrub that grows to 5 ft. and has finely cut leaves and curious red flowers tipped with green.

GREWIA (GROO ee ah). A genus of trees or shrubs belonging to the Tiliaceae (Linden Family) and found in warm regions of Asia, Africa, and Australia. *G. biloba*, from China and Korea, is the hardiest species and can be grown as far north as southern New England. It is a shrub that grows to 8 ft. and has large leaves, toothed and sometimes three-lobed, and small clusters of pale yellow flowers in summer. *G. occidentale* is a South African shrub or small tree with finely toothed leaves and purple flowers, hardy only in the warmest parts of the United States.

GRINDELIA (grin DEE lee ah). A genus of coarse western North American perennial herbs belonging to the Asteraceae (Aster Family), and commonly known as gumplants. They bear large yellow, generally sticky, flowers and are sometimes planted in poor soils for ornament. *G. stricta* var. *venulosa* (dune gum plant) makes an effective ground cover mat, growing 6 in. tall and spreading 8 ft.; it has 3-in. yellow daisies in June and July. Other species can be effective in the wild or meadow garden for late-season color. Hardy to Zone 9.

GRISELINIA (gri sel IN ee ah). A genus of evergreen trees or shrubs of New Zealand, belonging to the Cornaceae (Dogwood Family). They can be grown outdoors only in Zones 10–11. Male and female flowers are borne on separate plants; if plants of the two sexes are planted in close proximity, the female, or pistillate, ones bear bunches of green, grapelike berries. They grow well in ordinary soil and can be propagated by cuttings.

G. littoralis forms a large shrub or small tree. It has oval, pale green, leathery leaves; will stand clipping; and where hardy, is an excellent subject for seaside gardens.

G. lucida is a smaller grower but has much larger leaves, up to 6 in. long.

GROMWELL. Common name for LITHOSPERMUM, a genus of annual and perennial herbs. False gromwell is *Onosmodium*, a seldom-cultivated genus of the Boraginaceae (Borage Family).

GROUND BEETLES. There are up to 2500 species of ground beetles (Carabidae) in the United States, most of them beneficial in the garden. Their large, shiny black forms can be seen running through the grass or under stones or debris. Others are blue, green, or brown with many longitudinal fine stripes or ridges and sometimes spots. The long predatory larvae feed at night and destroy many caterpillars.

The peculiar bombardier beetles, *Brachinus*, ward off predators by hitting them in the face with smokelike gas shot from abdominal glands. These beetles are reddish brown with black wing covers and are often found under rotten logs.

The 1-in. beetle, *Calosoma scrutator*, is many-colored, with violet or green wings. The searcher and fiery hunter ground beetles climb trees to hunt for prey. The European ground beetle is the one introduced to New England to attack gypsy moths and brown-tailed moths. See also INSECTS, BENEFICIAL.

The smaller, diurnal tiger beetles, of the family Cicindelidae, are equally predatory, both as larvae and adults. The hump-backed larvae live in cylindrical tunnels in the soil, awaiting prey at the upper openings of their tunnels. They have powerful mandibles.

GROUND-CEDAR. A common name for *Lycopodium complanatum*, a species of clubmoss; see LYCOPODIUM.

GROUND-CHERRY. A common name for PHYSALIS, a genus of perennial herbs grown for their ornamental fruits.

GROUND COVERS. A term applied to a plant or group of plants of special value for covering the ground, especially beneath trees or on banks where grass does not thrive. Selection of ground cover material must consider all aspects of the area to be planted, including slope, available light, moisture, desired height, maintenance, traffic, and accessibility among others.

A wide variety of plants from different families are used as ground covers in different situations. In hot, dry regions, certain succulent plants are useful, while low shrubs can be useful in harsher climates. Grasses, annuals, and sods are good for areas where a quick cover is needed, while slower-growing perennials may be desirable for permanent planting.

As for any planting, the soil should be prepared and fertilized to suit the plants selected; it is usually cultivated deeper than for bedding plants. Weeding and mulching are especially important until the plants are established. Spacing is also an important consideration. Larger plants, such as junipers and other low shrubs, will require at least a few feet between plants and will grow to fill the intervening space, while grasses and other small herbs can be seeded quite close together.

The accompanying chart gives a few recommendations for covering selected locations. Other good ground covers are BINDING PLANTS, FERNS, and ORNAMENTAL GRASSES.

GROUND-IVY. A common name for *Glechoma hederacea*, a mat-forming perennial with blue flowers; see GLECHOMA.

GROUNDNUT. Common name for *Apios americana*, a perennial vine belonging to the Fabaceae (Bean Family), cultivated for its edible tubers and as bee plants; see APIOS.

GROUND-PINE. Common name for *Lycopodium obscurum*, a genus of ground-covering club-mosses; see LYCOPODIUM.

GROUNDSEL. Common name for SENECIO, a large and variable genus of herbs and woody

GROUND COVERS

PLANT NAME	HARDINESS (Zones)	HEIGHT	BANKS & SLOPES	BEDS & BORDERS	UNDER TREES	FLOWERS
Ajuga spp.	3–4	3–10 in.	yes	–	yes	yes
Artemisia stellerana	3–4	to 2 ft.	yes	–	–	–
Calluna vulgaris	5	to 18 in.	–	yes	–	yes
Convallaria majalis	4	6–12 in.	–	yes	yes	yes
Cotoneaster spp.	5	1–3 ft.	yes	yes	–	–
Euonymus fortunei	4	2–24 in.	yes	yes	yes	–
Hedera spp.	6–8	to 50 ft. long	yes	yes	yes	–
Hosta spp.	4	10–24 in.	–	yes	yes	–
Juniperus spp.	3–6	1½–10 ft.	yes	yes	–	–
Liriope spicata	5	to 10 in.	yes	–	yes	–
Lonicera japonica	5	to 20 ft.	yes	–	–	yes
Pachysandra terminalis	5	to 9 in.	yes	yes	yes	–
Parthenocissus quinquefolia	4	to 50 ft.	yes	–	–	–
Primula spp.	5	6–12 in.	–	yes	yes	yes
Rhododendron spp.	6–7	1–3 ft.	–	yes	yes	yes
Rosa spp.	6–7	to 20 ft.	yes	yes	–	yes
Sedum spp.	3–8	2–24 in.	some spp.	yes	–	yes
Thymus serpyllum	4	4 in.	–	yes	–	yes
Veronica spp.	4–5	4–15 in.	–	yes	yes	yes
Vinca minor	5	to 10 in.	yes	yes	–	yes

plants, many of which are weeds.

Groundsel-bush is *Baccharis halimifolia*; see BACCHARIS. Giant-groundsel is *Ligularia wilsoniana*; see LIGULARIA.

GRUBS. A grub is the larva of an insect. Usually this term is used to specify the larval stage of a beetle, as caterpillar specifies that of a moth or butterfly, and maggot that of a fly. Grubs of the Japanese and June beetles can be particular nuisances.

JAPANESE BEETLE grubs, which usually live under the grass of lawns, are plump and white.

The larvae of the June beetle, *Phyllophaga* spp., are called white grubs. They have smooth, curved bodies—white except for the swollen, dark-colored posterior portion, six thoracic legs, large brown heads, and distinct jaws. Their size ranges ½–1 in. long, distinguishing them from the smaller but otherwise quite similar larvae of other beetles. They feed on the roots of grass, corn, wheat, potatoes, strawberries, and other plants, and are likely to be numerous in sod land or long-established strawberry beds. The larvae of oriental beetles and rose chafers can be controlled with methods similar to Japanese and June beetle grubs.

White grub

The most reliable control for common grub infestations is milky spore disease, which can be inserted into the ground every foot or so to a depth of several inches. This organism, BACILLUS POPILLIAE (commercially available as Doom), is best put in the ground in fall or spring, allowing 10 oz. of the powder to 2500 sq. ft. The grub feeds on the powder and dies, then its body releases millions more spores. By the second year, the spores are quite effective and remain so for 15 to 20 years. Cooler soil temperatures reduce the effectiveness of Doom in northern regions, taking longer for it to control grub infestations.

BACILLUS THURINGIENSIS (Bt, commonly available as Biotrol, Dipel, or Thuricide) is another effec-

tive control. If introducing bacteria is not desirable, fall plowing or tilling will help to destroy grubs and expose them to wild birds, chickens, or hogs, which will eat them.

To control the adults, use commercial traps with a floral lure or phermone (sex attractant). Rotenone is also effective but should be sprayed only after dark when bees will not be affected. See also INSECT CONTROL.

GRUGRU PALM. Common name for *Acrocomia aculeata*, a West Indian tree whose nuts yield an oil sometimes used in soap and other cosmetics; see ACROCOMIA.

GUADALUPE PALM. Common name for *Brahea edulis*, a stout palm tree with fan-shaped leaves and sweet black fruits; see BRAHEA.

GUAIACUM (GWĪ ah kum). A genus of trees and shrubs of the tropical Americas. The common name of lignum-vitae, meaning "wood of life," may refer to its medicinal properties; however, the plant's commercial value is in its lumber, which is very hard and dense and is known by the same common name as the tree.

The rather ornamental plants have leathery, finely cut leaves and small, blue or purple flowers. Hardy in Zones 10–11, they grow slowly but are sometimes seen in California and Florida gardens. *G. officinale* has evergreen leaves and grows to 30 ft. in dry soil.

GUANO. An organic fertilizer, now used less often than it once was. It consists of the accumulated excrement of wild birds with some admixture of dead birds themselves, decayed feathers, fragments of fish and seaweed, etc. It is obtained from dry coastal areas, chiefly in South America, where vast numbers of seabirds have gathered for many years. Owing to the heavy depletion of the deposits and the increasing availability of manufactured (synthetic) fertilizers, it has become relatively unimportant.

Peruvian guano, collected from a group of islands off the coast of Peru, contains about

10½% nitrogen and 10% phosphoric acid. Guanos containing larger percentages of phosphorus come from the West Indies and from islands in various parts of the Pacific Ocean. In general, however, guano is considered primarily a nitrogenous fertilizer.

GUAVA. Common name for *Psidium*, a genus of tropical American trees belonging to the Myrtaceae (Myrtle Family). The common guava, *P. guajava*, some of its varieties, and a few other species are grown in Zones 10–11 for their edible fruits, generally used in jellies and beverages. They are not particular as to soil except that it be well drained. Propagation is by seed or, in the case of the better varieties, by budding.

P. guajava grows to 30 ft. and bears roundish yellow fruit up to 4 in. long, with white, yellow, or pink, aromatic flesh.

P. littorale (strawberry guava), formerly listed as *P. cattleianum*, is a smaller and hardier tree with purplish red fruits; these are about half the size of the other, and their flesh is white.

GUERNSEY-LILY. Common name for *Nerine sarniensis*, a tender bulbous plant with crimson lilylike flowers; see NERINE.

GUINEA-HEN-TULIP. Common name for *Fritillaria meleagris*, a hardy bulbous herb whose flowers have checkered markings; see FRITILLARIA.

GUM. A common name applied alone, in combination, and rather loosely to trees (and one herb) of different species, genera, and even families. Various species of EUCALYPTUS are known as gum trees.

Gum, cotton gum, or tupelo gum refers to *Nyssa aquatica*, a large tree native to the swamps of the southern states. Sour, black, and pepperidge gum refer to *N. sylvatica*, a larger tree native from Maine to Texas. See NYSSA.

Sweet gum is *Liquidambar styraciflua*, a huge deciduous tree with brilliant fall color; see LIQUIDAMBAR.

Gum arabic tree is *Acacia nilotica*, a leguminous tree grown for its sap; see ACACIA.

Gum plant is GRINDELIA, a genus of western North American herbs related to asters.

GUMBO. A popular name in the South for *Abelmoschus esculentus*, more commonly known as OKRA.

GUMMOSIS. The formation and exudation of clear or amber-colored gums that harden into solid masses on the surface of affected parts. Caused by a fungus, it is a common symptom on lemon and lime tree bark near ground level, especially when wet soil is in contact with the bark. Prevent by planting trees so that the lateral roots spread out at ground level, by choosing disease-resistant varieties, and avoiding watering at the base of the tree. If gummosis occurs, cut away the infected bark and an area of good bark surrounding the injury. The wood need not be removed. Expose the lateral roots by removing all soil around the trunk.

GUNNERA (GUN er ah). A genus of perennial herbs native to South America and the Antipodes. It is successful only as far north as the cooler parts of Zone 9 if given heavy protection. The leaves are hurt by frost, but the plant will not take very hot weather either; it thrives in Great Britain. The principal species is *G. manicata*, which has a stout, creeping rootstock and huge, lobed leaves that grow to 6 ft. or more across on prickly stems to 6 ft. or more high. The greenish flowers are borne in a dense, tapering spike to 3 ft. long. It is a plant of majestic appearance and requires rich, moist soil in a sheltered but sunny location. Propagation is by seed and division.

GUZMANIA (guz MAY nee ah). A genus of tropical American herbs belonging to the Bromiliaceae (Pineapple Family). A few are grown for ornament in the warm greenhouse, and they also make good houseplants. They have stiff erect leaves in basal rosettes, with the flowers usually surrounded by long showy bracts. Plants thrive in a mixture of fern fiber and sphagnum moss with broken charcoal, and they require an abundance of water during the summer.

G. lingulata has leaves that grow to 18 in. long and dense drooping heads of yellow and purple flowers with red bracts.

G. monostachia, formerly listed as *G. tricolor*, has rich green sword-shaped leaves to 18 in. long. The flower spike is longer than the leaves and is clothed with bracts of yellowish green streaked with black, and the upper ones tinged red. The flowers are white.

GYMNOCALYCIUM (jim noh kal IS ee um). A genus of succulents from South America, commonly called chin cactus because of large protuberances or bumps under each spine cluster. The generic name means "naked calyx" and refers to the fact that the large, beautiful, colorful, waterlily-like flowers have no wool or hair on the flower tubes. These cacti are interesting and of easy culture, flowering readily. *G. denudatum* is a wonderful plant with tightly appressed spines (like flattened spiders) and large white flowers. An orange-red stemmed sport (or mutant) without chlorophyll, developed in Japan and grafted onto tender, dark green *Hylocereus* understock, became intensely popular in flower shops and even supermarkets throughout the world, sold under the names ruby-ball, red-cap, or hibotan.

GYMNOCARPIUM (jim noh KAHR pee um). A genus of small to medium-sized boreal ferns with fronds widely spaced on creeping rhizomes.

G. dryopteris (oak fern) is a small, dainty fern with 8–12 in. high, deltoid, bipinnate fronds of yellow-green. It inhabits wet woods in northern North America, Asia, and Europe.

G. robertianum (limestone oak fern) is a rare fern that grows 9–18 in. tall and has triangular bipinnatifid fronds. It is native to northern regions of Europe and North America, growing on limestone rocks in shaded woodlands.

GYMNOCLADUS (jim NAHK lad us). A small genus of large, deciduous, dioecious or polygamous trees of the Fabaceae (Bean Family).

G. dioica (Kentucky coffee tree), native to the eastern and central states, is a sturdy tree growing to 100 ft. It is often used for its bold, decorative effect in large plantings. It has coarse twigs and few branchlets with large, compound leaves. The greenish white flowers in large clusters borne at the ends of the branches are followed by thick, curved pods that remain on the tree all winter and contain dark seeds 1 in. wide. As the Latin species name suggests, it is dioecious, with both male and female trees needed to produce fruits. It thrives in rich soil and is propagated by seed or cuttings. Hardy in Zones 4–8.

GYMNOGRAMME (jim noh GRAM ee). A generic name used by many botanists for some species of CONIOGRAMME.

GYMNOSPERM. A term (from the Greek words meaning "naked seed") applied to the large group of plants that produce seeds on the open surfaces of scales that make up a cone. The group is further distinguished from the flowering plants, or angiosperms (which bear seeds enclosed in a case), by frequently having evergreen, needle-, scale-, or fern-like leaves. The gymnosperms are a very ancient group represented today by cycads, yews, ginkgos, and the conifers like pine and spruce. See PLANT NAMES AND CLASSIFICATION.

GYNERIUM (gī NEER ee um). A genus of perennials in the Poaceae (Grass Family). The most common, *G. sagittatum* (uva grass), grows up to 40 ft. and bears silky, plumelike terminal panicles 3 ft. long with drooping branches. It is much like *Cortaderia* except for botanical details of the flowers. The leaves have finely toothed edges. The plant is used as an ornamental in warm regions. See ORNAMENTAL GRASSES.

GYNURA (gī NYOO rah) **aurantiaca.** A tropical member of the Asteraceae (Aster Family), commonly known as velvet plant. It is native to Java, where it sometimes escapes cultivation and makes a branching, shrubby plant to 3 ft. high.

Hardy only in Zones 10–11, it is usually grown under glass as a potted plant, in the same manner as COLEUS, and rarely exceeds 18 in. The orange flower heads consist of rather inconspicuous but foul-smelling disk flowers only; the charm of the plant is in the purple velvet effect on the densely hairy, soft green leaves. The velvet plant should be given rich potting soil, abundant moisture, and full sunlight to bring out the color of the foliage. It is propagated by cuttings or seed.

GYPSOPHILA (jip SOH fil ah). A genus of hardy annual and perennial herbs belonging to the Caryophyllaceae (Pink Family) and commonly known as baby's-breath. These airy plants are extremely graceful, though they are devoid of conspicuous foliage. Bearing many tiny blossoms on delicate-looking, but sturdy, well-branched stalks, the plants produce a misty effect in the border or rock garden. They thrive in almost any location and generally bloom through the summer. The plants are propagated by seed sown in the open, by division, and occasionally by cuttings. Gypsophila is fine for cut flower mixtures. Hardiness varies with the species from Zones 3–8.

Gypsophila paniculata

PRINCIPAL SPECIES

G. acutifolia is a tall perennial, greatly branched, with white flowers larger than *G. paniculata*.

G. cerastioides (mouse-ear gypsophila) is a downy, creeping perennial that grows to 4 in. and bears white flowers with pink veins.

G. elegans, a hardy annual growing to 2 ft., has many cultivars, including 'Covent Garden', to 18 in., with large white flowers good for cutting; 'Giant White', to 18 in., with blooms 15–20% larger than 'Covent Garden'; and 'Red Cloud', to 18 in., with carmine to mid-pink blooms.

G. muralis is an annual species that grows to 1 ft. and has solitary and axillary rose flowers.

G. paniculata is one of the most interesting perennials, bearing white flowers on plants 3 ft. high. It is excellent massed as a border plant. Among the named doubles are 'Bristol Fairy', 'Ehrlei', 'Pink Fairy', and 'Perfecta'. If cut before the flowers are fully open, the graceful sprays can be dried for use in winter bouquets.

G. repens (creeping gypsophila) is an excellent perennial species that grows to 6 in. tall and bears pale pink blossoms in summer; it is well adapted to rock garden use.

GYPSUM. This material, also known as landplaster, is chemically known as sulfate of calcium. Containing about 14% calcium, it was formerly considered a satisfactory source of lime for soils. However, while it can help acid soils somewhat and generally improve soil structure, it is not a liming material and will not neutralize acids. It is most commonly used in agriculture to help reclaim soils that have excess sodium, which can harm plants by adverse effects both on plant nutrient availability and on soil structure. When used, it should be applied in finely ground form. Gypsum forms up to 50% of the less common commercial acid phosphate (ordinary superphosphate), but it is not contained in concentrated superphosphate.

Gypsum is sometimes used as a carrier for insecticide dusts. It has also been recommended for dusting over iris rhizomes after soft rot and borers have been cut out.

GYPSY MOTH. This devastating pest, *Lymantria dispar*, belonging to the Lymantriidae, escaped from an experimental laboratory in Medford, Massachusetts, where it was brought from Europe in the latter part of the nineteenth century as a possible silkworm. Though held in check by strict quarantine at the Massachusetts border, it has now spread to 25 states and strips millions of acres a year where not controlled. It attacks forest trees and shrubs, defoliating 500 different kinds.

The adult male moths are brown and the females white. The caterpillars are dark colored and very hairy with blue tubercles on the front half of the body and red ones on the rear half. They hatch out in April, feed voraciously and grow rapidly to mid-June. They feed at night and crawl down to spend the day in debris beneath the tree. They can be caught by bands of burlap

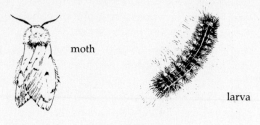

moth

larva

Gypsy moth

strips that are treated with Tanglefoot or other sticky material and placed around the trunk to thwart their return for the night. The trap works best if a collar or skirt of folded material is placed at chest height. Examine the bands daily and kill all trapped caterpillars. By July, if still feeding, the caterpillars can reach 2 in. or more. Females lay mounds of 300 to 500 pale tan eggs; since the females cannot fly, all eggs are laid on the soil surface. Gather them to shake or drop into kerosene and water; wear gloves, since they cause a rash. Defoliation puts a strain on trees when they produce new leaves, so they need fertilizer during the summer. Evergreens do not send forth new leaves after defoliation, so protection for those trees must come from prevention.

If sprayed twice in the spring with **Bacillus thuringiensis** (Bt, commonly available as Biotrol, Dipel, or Thuricide), the infestation can be reduced to 15%. Around this time, the caterpillars are ¾ in. long; later they are too large for effective control by Bt. After exhausting their food supply the caterpillars weaken and can be infected with nuclear polyhedrosis virus (NPV); their bodies become limp as a result. At this time the U.S. Forest Service gathers the bodies to make a control spray from them. It only takes about ten bodies to make gallons of Gypchek, as it is called. It has been 90–100% successful in control projects.

About 45 kinds of birds eat the caterpillars, and so do squirrels, chipmunks, and white-footed mice. Two flies imported from Europe parasitize the caterpillar: **Compsilura concinnata**, a tachinid fly, and **Sturnia scutellata**, whose only host is the gypsy moth. The first fly inserts a living larva into the caterpillar with her ovipositor. It hibernates as a small larva there, consuming the pest. The second lays eggs on foliage eaten by the caterpillar; its insides are destroyed when the eggs develop into larvae. They later hibernate in puparia in the soil as pupae. Other parasites and various wasps have also been tried as controls. See also INSECT CONTROL.

H

HABENARIA (hab en AIR ee uh). A genus of about 500 species of terrestrial orchids found on all continents, commonly known as rein orchid or fringed-orchis. They are mostly found in North American bogs, growing in filtered shade in acid, humusy soil. Plants and flowers are small or large and variously colored, with yellow, orange, and red predominating. The flowers are spurred at the base, some with fringed lips. Hardy to Zone 7, many species can withstand a slight frost and can be grown outdoors with frost protection in mild climates. The plants should never dry out completely while in growth. After flowering, the stems die back, and the fleshy tubers stay underground. Plants should be kept dry until new shoots appear; then watering is resumed. The type species is *E. macroceratitis*.

HABERLEA (hah bur LEE ah). A genus of small alpine plants belonging to the Gesneriaceae (Gesnaria Family), with nodding blue or lilac flowers on stems 4–6 in. high. These Balkan relatives of African-violets can best be grown by placing their rosettes in a north-facing wall niche or on the north side of a rock garden. Propagation is by seed or by leaf cuttings. Two species are known: *H. ferdinandi-coburgii* and *H. rhodopensis*.

HABIT. In gardening, the manner of growth, whether tall, dwarf, upright, spreading, trailing, open, dense, or otherwise.

HABITAT. The kind of environment where a plant grows naturally or is indigenous. For example, plants can be found growing in woodland, field, seashore, marsh, lakeshore, and other habitats.

HACKBERRY. Common name for CELTIS, a genus of deciduous trees and shrubs belonging to the Ulmaceae (Elm Family).

HAEMANTHUS (hee MAN thus). A genus of showy, bulbous South African plants belonging to the Amaryllidaceae (Amaryllis Family), and commonly known as blood-lily. The white or red lilylike flowers are borne in dense ball-like heads on long stalks, often preceding the broad, luxuriant leaves. They are grown indoors in cool regions for spring and summer bloom or outdoors in the ground in warmer sections of the Sunbelt.

For pot culture, plant the bulbs in the fall in equal parts of peat and loam made friable with sand, covering the lower half of the bulb only. Water frequently and syringe the foliage daily until the blooms begin to fade. Then gradually dry off the plants, leaving the bulbs undisturbed in the pots, and store until the following autumn. Propagation is by offsets.

There are a number of species and various named forms. *H. katharinae* is one of the most beautiful with large apple-green leaves to 14 in. long and 6 in. wide. Its brilliant red flowers are borne in clusters sometimes 9 in. across.

HAKEA (HAY kee ah). A genus of Australian evergreen shrubs belonging to the Proteaceae (Protea Family), a few species of which are grown for ornamental use. They are good drought resisters and, although usually hardy only in Zones 10–11, they can stand a few degrees of frost. Propagation is by seed and cuttings.

PRINCIPAL SPECIES

H. elliptica is a compact shrub with white flowers. The young growth opens with a rich bronzy tone and is very showy.

H. laurina (sea-urchin) is a tall shrub or small tree with narrow leaves about 6 in. long and round clusters of crimson flowers with yellow styles. It is the showiest of all in bloom.

H. suaveolens is a large shrub of rounded form with needlelike leaves and tiny, white, sweetly scented flowers.

HALESIA (HAYL zee ah). A genus of deciduous trees or large shrubs commonly known as silverbell or snowdrop tree. Although native to North America, the genus is named after the eighteenth century plant physiologist Stephen Hales, who was educated at Corpus Christi College in Cambridge, England. Valued for their handsome drooping, bell-shaped, white flowers in early spring, they thrive in any well-drained soil and, in the North, appreciate a well-sheltered position. They are propagated by seed (best sown in the fall), layers, or root cuttings.

PRINCIPAL SPECIES

H. carolina is the best-known species. In a favorable climate, it forms a tree that grows to 40 ft. and has spreading branches, but in the North, it is usually a tall shrub. Hardy in Zones 5–8.

H. diptera is similar to *H. carolina* but it is smaller and less hardy (to Zone 6).

H. monticola grows to nearly 60 ft. in the South and is hardy as far north as Zone 6. It has relatively large leaves and flowers.

HALF-HARDY PLANTS. In a given climate, these are plants injured by severe weather or requiring special care part of the year. Plants that need a heated greenhouse in winter are called "tender." These terms are not used strictly, either of them often being applied to any condition short of complete hardiness. Annuals are half-hardy where they must be started indoors and not set outdoors until warm weather. Half-hardy perennials will live through some winters only to be killed by an unusually severe season. Or they may require special protection in the form of mulch, shade, or windscreen, or need to be wintered under glass in a coldframe. Among woody plants and trees, those that die to the ground but are root-hardy and spring up again can be called half-hardy.

For comparison, see HARDY PLANTS.

HAMAMELIDACEAE (ham ah mel i DAY see ee). The Witch-hazel Family, a group of trees and shrubs common to warm temperate regions, and including a few ornamental genera, such as *Hamamelis*, *Corylopsis*, and *Liquidambar*.

HAMAMELIS (ham ah MEL is). A genus of hardy deciduous shrubs or small trees native to North America and Asia, commonly known as witch-

hazel. They are of special interest because of their season of bloom, which is from late fall to early spring. The fragrant flowers with narrow, wavy petals are borne in clusters. They are vigorous and bushy, with good foliage that turns yellow and orange in the fall. Hard-shelled fruits that shoot out seeds are visible on trees in autumn.

Witch-hazels do well in sandy loam, and the native kinds can stand more shade and moisture than those from Asia. Propagation is by seed (which usually does not germinate until the second year), by layers, and also by grafting. Most species are hardy in Zones 4–8.

PRINCIPAL SPECIES

H. x *intermedia* is an outstanding hybrid between *H. japonica* and *H. mollis*. A shrub or small tree, it grows to 15 or 20 ft. and blooms in winter, often depending on the weather. Flowers vary in color from yellow-orange to red. Hardy to Zone 5.

H. japonica (Chinese witch-hazel) is a shrub or tree that grows to 30 ft. The flowers have bright yellow petals and purplish calyxes.

H. mollis, a Chinese shrub or tree growing to 15 ft., is the showiest of all the witch-hazels. The leaves are grayish white beneath, and the sweetly fragrant flowers have golden yellow petals and a purplish red calyx. The flowers bloom in late winter, lasting a long time in the cold weather. It is a wonderful specimen plant for the garden. Hardy to Zone 6.

H. vernalis, native in the southern states, grows to 10 ft. and opens its yellow petals from a dark red calyx in winter. Hardy to Zone 5.

H. virginiana (common witch-hazel), native from Canada to Florida, is a large shrub or tree that grows to 20 ft. It is conspicuous because the fragrant, light yellow flowers appear while the leaves are falling, or as late as December, and are quite showy if leaves have already fallen. It grows in sun or shade and is hardy to Zone 4.

HAMELIA (hah MEE lee ah). A genus of evergreen shrubs of tropical and subtropical America, belonging to the Rubiaceae (Madder Family). A few are grown in Zones 9–11 for their showy flowers and dark-colored berries. If the tops are cut down by frost, the plants sprout readily again from below. Propagation is from seed and by cuttings of half-ripened wood.

H. patens (scarletbush) is a large shrub with long leaves, usually in threes, and branching clusters of bright orange-red flowers produced over a long season. These are followed by attractive dark berries, also very lasting.

HAMMOCK FERN. Common name for *Blechnum occidentale*, a stoloniferous fern useful for ground cover in subtropical to tropical regions, elsewhere as a houseplant; see BLECHNUM.

HANGING BASKETS. Hanging basket planters tastefully filled with handsome foliage and flowering plants contribute to the adornment of a window or the decoration of any room. Baskets are available in different forms and various materials, such as wire, willow or wickerwork, terra cotta, plastic, and wood. When watering is needed, baskets can be plunged into the water and allowed to drain off before being put back in place. If wood, plastic, metal, or terra cotta containers are used, drainage holes must be provided. Rustic earthenware or back-covered baskets are suitable if they have an inner plant basin properly providing for drainage.

CULTURE

The soil depends on the plants to be grown, but most mixes should be half loam, one-fourth sand, and one-fourth well-decayed leaf mold or humus. This should be pressed firmly around the roots to avoid settling or washing out.

Indoor baskets containing flowering plants will need a sunny exposure as close to the window as possible, while foliage plant collections do not generally require or want direct sunlight. Baskets containing foliage plants exclusively can hang at the north or shady side of a room.

Watering must be done with great care. In ordinary room temperatures, baskets can be watered every second or third day if the plants are actively growing. Overwatering, keeping the soil saturated, should be avoided, but it should never be allowed to become bone dry either.

Free circulation of fresh air is as necessary as sufficient water; however, direct cold drafts are distinctly harmful.

As soon as the plants in a newly arranged basket are well established and growing, the soil should be enriched once a month, either by dipping it in or watering with a weak solution of liquid manure or fertilizer.

HARBINGER-OF-SPRING. Common name for *Erigenia bulbosa*, a low tuberous herb with white flower clusters in early spring; see ERIGENIA.

HARDENBERGIA (hahr den BUR jee ah). A genus of twining herbaceous or shrubby vines of Australia, belonging to the Fabaceae (Bean Family). They are sometimes trained over rafters and pillars in the greenhouse or grown outdoors in very warm regions. They like a peaty and well-drained soil, and under glass they do better in a prepared border or solid bed than in pots. Propagation is by seed or cuttings of young growth.

H. comptoniana has three to five leaflets and small blue or violet flowers borne in a long raceme. *H. violacea*, formerly listed as *H. monophylla*, usually has single leaflets and rosy purple flowers.

HARDENING-OFF. The process of gradually allowing young indoor-started plants, seedlings, or tender grafted subjects to be accustomed to the cold and wind of the outdoors. Plants protected from the elements are not tolerant of an immediate move to the outside. Aside from colder temperatures, hardening-off can prepare plants for lower humidity, wind, and sun. The home gardener can use a covered deck or porch to harden-off newly purchased bedding material or vegetable starts. In hotbeds or coldframes, plants are given increased ventilation and are eventually left open to the sky entirely unprotected, except when the weather is unfavorable. Plants can be hardened-off for a few days to a couple of weeks, depending on the weather and condition of the plant. Decreasing the food and water that reaches a plant will also help toughen up the soft succulent growth that makes new plants so susceptible to weather damage.

Hardening-off also refers to adjusting a plant to very reduced light as found in most homes. Houseplants are usually propagated under relatively high light conditions. Unless the light is gradually reduced over a two- to three-week period, the foliage, particularly the older leaves, may turn yellow or pale green and drop off.

HARDHACK. Common name for *Spiraea tomentosa*, a low shrub native to the eastern states with steeple-like, rosy purple flowers; see SPIRAEA.

HARDINESS ZONES. All gardens are influenced greatly by the local CLIMATE, or average weather conditions. Aside from the obvious differences of freezing cold winters in northern regions and blistering hot summers farther south, individual areas have more subtle differences, affected by rain or snowfall, humidity, altitude, prevailing winds, and other aspects of weather.

For many years, horticulturists have used hardiness zones to match plants with the areas where they can be grown successfully. The imaginary lines that designate these zones for gardeners are general guidelines and are not rigid guarantees that the climate within that zone will stay uniform. These zones are approximate, since relatively tiny differences in altitude, even differences in density of buildings or trees can influence the local climate. Areas are assigned hardiness zones so that when plants are described they can be labeled as hardy to certain zones. This reassurance is especially important for gardeners ordering plants by mail or nursery owners bringing in stock from a distant location.

Hardiness zones define the average annual minimum temperature in a region and rate the hardiness of a plant (or temperature range it will tolerate). There are more specific zones used by other garden authorities, and a number indicating a hardiness zone is often included in plant descriptions. The accompanying map gives a guideline of average temperatures throughout North America. In 1990, for the first time in 25 years, the map was revised by the research service of the United States Department of Agriculture (USDA) to include new and more precise information. Including Canada, Mexico, Alaska, and Hawaii for the first time, this map is divided into eleven zones based on the range of average minimum temperatures, with Zone 11 being almost frost free and Zone 1 covering the coldest regions of Canada. Small areas of microclimates are also added to indicate cool pockets at high elevations and hot spots in large metropolitan areas and sheltered valleys.

See also HARDY PLANTS; HALF-HARDY PLANTS; WEATHER.

HARDPAN. A layer of impervious soil, sometimes found (and sometimes created) just below the surface or topsoil. It is usually composed largely of clay or other fine-textured soil that has become compacted or puddled until its particles are practically cemented.

To remedy the condition, tilling with a special plow can be enough to break up the formation. When the hardpan has once been broken up, sand or sifted ashes can be worked into it, to prevent further compacting. As rapidly as possible, generous quantities of organic material (humus) should be incorporated, to improve the physical condition, to promote aeration of the soil, and to add to other factors that constitute fertility.

HARDY PLANTS. These are plants that live and thrive in a given climate. The word "hardy" is most often used to mean "capable of enduring cold," but since there is no word to signify the ability to live through heat, wet, or drought, all these conditions are sometimes included under one word. Thus, a plant that is hardy in Labrador but usually dies in the heat of Florida or the drought of Arizona can be called "not hardy" in those warmer climates.

In practice, however, writers speaking of hardy plants commonly mean those that survive

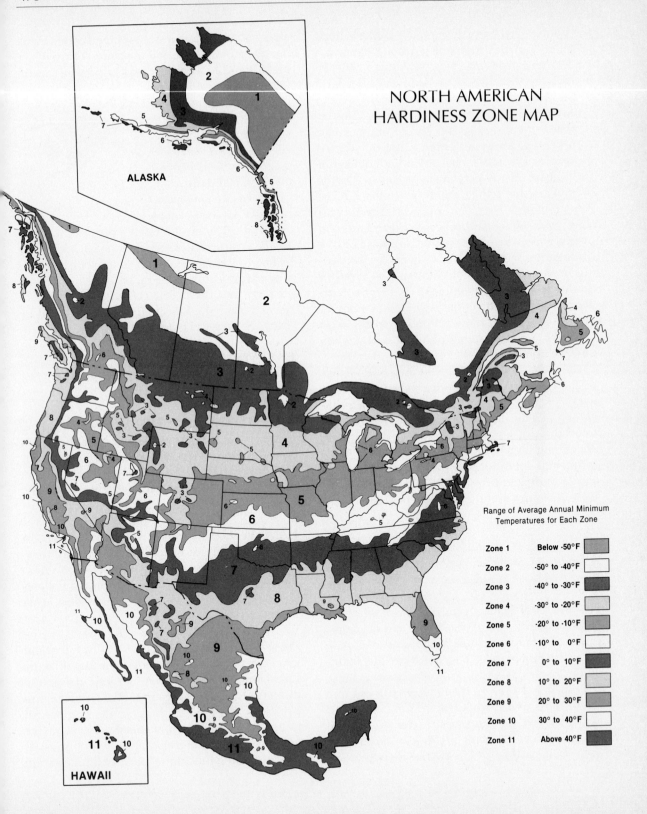

NORTH AMERICAN
HARDINESS ZONE MAP

ALASKA

HAWAII

Range of Average Annual Minimum
Temperatures for Each Zone

Zone 1	Below -50°F
Zone 2	-50° to -40°F
Zone 3	-40° to -30°F
Zone 4	-30° to -20°F
Zone 5	-20° to -10°F
Zone 6	-10° to 0°F
Zone 7	0° to 10°F
Zone 8	10° to 20°F
Zone 9	20° to 30°F
Zone 10	30° to 40°F
Zone 11	Above 40°F

the winter in the northern states and perhaps southern Canada. Plants that are not hardy are called tender or HALF-HARDY PLANTS. Hardy annuals are those whose seed can be sown early in the open ground, the seedlings being able to withstand spring frosts, like peas or poppies, as opposed to half-hardy and tender annuals like tomatoes or zinnias, which must be started indoors, or if outdoors, not sown until danger of frost is past. Hardy perennials such as columbine or rhubarb die to the ground in winter, but the roots remain alive to put up new growth year after year. Trees and other woody plants are hardy when the entire growth remains alive through the winter. Woody plants are so variously affected by climate that special types of hardiness are often mentioned. A plant is bud-hardy when the flower buds formed in summer or autumn to bloom the following spring pass through the winter uninjured; root-hardy when only the upper part of the plant dies in winter.

The accompanying hardiness map of the United States gives a general idea of the climate in various regions. A map of such a large area cannot indicate the inevitable variations that are sure to occur within narrow territorial limitations, depending largely on elevation and other environmental conditions. However, the relationships of different regions is brought out, and these zones are useful guidelines in garden planning.

HAREBELL. Common name for *Campanula rotundifolia*, a slender perennial herb with blue flowers in loose racemes; see CAMPANULA.

HARLEQUIN BUG. A sucking insect, *Murgantia histrionica*, that feeds on the sap of plants, causing them to wilt, turn brown, and die. Also called fire bug or calico bug, it is especially injurious to brassicas and plants of the Solanaceae (Nightshade Family). It is gaudy with red and black spots and is about ⅜ in. long, flat, and shield-shaped. An unpleasant odor causes it to be included in the stink bug group. Producing three generations per year, the insects in all

stages of development are found on plants by the dozen from early spring to winter. Tiny white, black-banded eggs are laid in packets on the underside of leaves. The eggs hatch in four to seven days and develop to nymphs, which suck so much that Brassicaceae (Mustard Family) plants wilt and die.

Harlequin bug

There is no satisfactory spray or dust except sabadilla. The most effective control measures are the destruction of adults in the fall and spring by hand-picking and the use of trap crops such as mustard, kale, turnip, or radish, which are planted early and then sprayed with kerosene and burned after the insects have congregated on them. See INSECT CONTROL.

HASTATE. Halberd-shaped; said of a triangular leaf whose pointed basal lobes spread sideways. Compare with SAGITTATE.

HAUSTORIA. Specialized rootlike sucking organs by means of which certain higher-plant parasites, such as dodder and mistletoe, and certain fungi, such as rusts and mildews, obtain their food from the tissues of the host plants on which they live.

HAWKWEED. Common name for HIERACIUM, a genus of weedy or ornamental herbs with brilliant red, orange, and yellow flowers. Golden-yellow-hawkweed is *Tolpis barbata*, a yellow-flowered annual sometimes grown as an ornamental; see TOLPIS.

HAWORTHIA (hah WORTH ee ah). A succulent genus of small, mostly stemless members of the Liliaceae (Lily Family) from southern Africa. The numerous, usually greenish white flowers are produced on 6–12 in. long stalks and are all rather similar and not particularly showy, but the leaves show considerable variety and unusual and interesting functions. Many of the leaves are "windowed," that is, with translucent, window-like areas that allow sunlight to enter for production of chlorophyll deep within the leaf.

Perhaps the most remarkable species are those with truncated leaves that look as if they had been cut off with a knife, the truncated ends windowed, such as *H. truncata* or *H. maughanii*. *H. bolusii* and *H. arachnoidea* (also listed as *H. setata)* have long hairs or soft bristles along the margins that give them a delicate appearance. Others, such as *H. pumila* (also listed as *H. margaritifera)*, have white, pearl-like tubercles all over the rich green leaves.

HAWTHORN   Common name for CRATAEGUS, a genus of hardy, deciduous, flowering, usually thorny shrubs or small trees.

The name is sometimes applied to other plants. India-hawthorn is *Raphiolepis indica*, and Yedda-hawthorn is *R. umbellata*. Water-hawthorn is *Aponogeton distachyus*.

HAY-SCENTED FERN.   Common name for *Dennstaedtia punctilobula*, a deciduous fern with thin-textured fronds, common in the northeastern states; see DENNSTAEDTIA.

HAZEL.   Common name for CORYLUS, a genus of deciduous trees also known as hazelnut, planted for ornament and for their edible nuts.

The name "hazel" is also applied to other plants. Chilean-hazel is *Gevuina avellana*. Winter-hazel is the genus *Corylopsis*. Witch-hazel is the genus *Hamamelis*; the Witch-hazel Family is HAMAMELIDACEAE. Victorian-hazel is *Pomaderris apetala*.

HEAD.   A term sometimes applied to any dense flower cluster or INFLORESCENCE but generally used to refer particularly to the type found in members of the Asteraceae (Aster Family) (see COMPOSITE), and in clovers and a few other plants.

HEAL-ALL.   Common name for *Prunella vulgaris*, a low, purple-flowered weed sometimes used in herbal medicines; see PRUNELLA.

HEART ROT.   Rot of the heartwood of a tree caused by various wood-destroying fungi, mainly of the basidiomycete or mushroom group. Their presence in apparently sound trees is frequently known by the appearance of bracket fungi, which are the fruiting bodies of the fungus growing within. Infection usually takes place through wounds such as broken branch stubs. Heart rot weakens a tree and renders its timber of little value.

See also FUNGUS; TREE SURGERY.

HEARTSEED.   Common name for CARDIOSPERMUM, a genus of tender climbing herbs with single white spots on the seeds.

HEATH.   Common name for ERICA, a genus of shrubs or small trees with needlelike leaves; often confused with heather, which more correctly refers to the genus CALLUNA. The Heath Family is ERICACEAE.

The name also refers to other genera. False heath is FABIANA, a genus of small greenhouse shrubs with little white flowers. Irish heath is *Daboecia cantabrica*. Mountain heath is the genus PHYLLODOCE.

HEATHER.   Common name for CALLUNA, a genus of hardy flowering shrubs, closely related to and frequently confused with *Erica* (heath).

HEATING CABLE.   An electric cable of low voltage that is placed under pots or flats, usually in a greenhouse or HOTBED. The gentle BOTTOM HEAT provided by a heating cable encourages quick germination of seeds and speeds up formation of roots on cuttings.

HEAT INJURY.   Too high a temperature—either natural outdoors or artificial in houses or greenhouses—can result in retarded growth and failure to produce mature flowers and fruit; sun burn or sun scald of leaves, flowers, or fruit; formation of heat cankers on stems; defoliation; premature ripening of fruits; or death of an entire plant.

HEAVENLY-BAMBOO. Common name for *Nandina domestica*, an Asiatic shrub with attractive foliage, flowers, and berries, belonging to the Berberidaceae (Barberry Family), and not related to the true bamboos; see NANDINA.

HEAVING. The lifting action exerted by a soil during the winter under the influence of ground frost or alternate freezing and thawing; see FROST.

HEBE (HEE bee). A genus of shrubby or small treelike plants with leathery leaves and pink, purple, or white flowers borne in small clusters. Belonging to the Scrophulariaceae (Figwort Family), they are mostly native to New Zealand. Plants resemble *Veronica*, with which they were once grouped, except that hebes are woody and usually evergreen.

The best-known species are *H. speciosa*, an evergreen shrub that grows to 5 ft. and has reddish purple flowers in 4-in. racemes; and *H. traversii*, a small shrub with 3-in. racemes of white flowers.

HEDEOMA (hed ee OH mah) **pulegioides.** A small purple-flowered annual herb belonging to the Lamiaceae (Mint Family), commonly known as American-pennyroyal. It is naturalized along wood roads from Quebec to Kansas and occasionally transferred to the wild garden because the odor of the leaves (resembling that of European pennyroyal, which is *Mentha pulegium*) is said to be offensive to mosquitos.

HEDERA (HED ur ah). A genus of evergreen ivy, generally considered vines, but actually high-climbing shrubs belonging to the Araliaceae (Aralia Family), and commonly known as ivy. The botanical name *Hedera* is the ancient Latin name for ivy.

Ivy has many uses, from covering walls, rocks, tree trunks, and trellises, to carpeting bald spots in shady places and edging beds and borders. It makes a good houseplant, especially to train around a window or to plant in hanging baskets.

Ivy is easily propagated by cuttings and layers,

and for slow-growing choice varieties, sometimes by grafting. Pieces of stem placed in water root readily and remain decorative for some time if it is not desired to plant them. Seeds, which should be sown when ripe, are usually slow to germinate. Although winter injury to plants can be severe, most species are hardy in sheltered places to Zone 5, surviving winter in better condition in shaded locations.

PRINCIPAL SPECIES

H. canariensis (Algerian ivy) is native to the Canary Islands and northern Africa. It has deep green, shiny leaves 5–7 in. across with four to seven lobes. It is similar to *H. helix*, but it has reddish twigs and petioles, and its leaves are more broadly spaced along the stems. Var. *variegata* has yellowish white leaf margins.

H. colchica (Persian ivy) is an evergreen species bearing 4–10 in. oval, unlobed leaves, which are thick and dark green. Var. *dentata* has slightly toothed leaves.

H. helix (English ivy) is the principal species. Famous in literature as well as horticulture for its long life, it clings by aerial rootlets and is able to cover brick and stone walls with a dense, thick

Hedera helix

mantle of glossy green. Old plants of the original species produce flowering shoots of different appearance from the normal creeping or climbing growth, the familiar three- to five-lobed leaves being replaced by usually rounded entire leaves. Small clusters of inconspicuous greenish flower clusters appearing in the fall are followed by black berries.

HEDGE. A continuous and close planting of trees, shrubs, or occasionally (for temporary results) tall quick-growing annuals, along a boundary to protect and enclose the garden, or along a division line within the garden to set one portion apart from another. The term does not necessarily imply a rigidly pruned and restrained growth; however, splendid walls of living green developed by proper pruning are among the finst elements of a garden.

The pruned and shaped hedge belongs wherever a stone or similar wall might be properly used and is almost as effective as a protection.

The unsheared hedge belongs to a more casual environment and requires more room; however, it is not strictly naturalistic, even if permitted to grow in a natural manner. Being composed of just one kind of plant, instead of two or more (as compose a natural thicket), a hedge cannot give the impression of natural wild growth. It is sophisticated without being as dignified or refined as a clipped hedge. Bear this in mind when choosing hedge plants for any position; the untrimmed hedge can easily degenerate from casual to untidy in appearance.

Planting. Hedge plants are spaced according to the type of plant and the demands of the gardener. Common deciduous shrubs are usually planted 9 in. apart. Finer deciduous material and most evergreens are better set at least 18 in. apart, while some of the larger-growing evergreens will do even better at 24 in. This ensures the roots adequate room for feeding right from the start and makes it unnecessary to remove alternate plants in the future as growth advances.

Form. To ensure dense growth from the ground up, deciduous plants are usually cut back to within a few inches of the ground when planted. Material especially grown for hedges in a nursery may not need such handling, but generally cutting back of about 30% of the tip growth is always needed. The properly shaped hedge is narrower at the top than at the bottom, and the top should be rounded rather than flat. The sloping sides admit abundant light to the lower branches and prevent them from pining away and giving the hedge an open and leggy look. Also, a somewhat narrower and rounded top sheds snow instead of accumulating a heavy load that causes bending and breaking.

Maintenance. To establish correct form, planting is supplemented by clipping along the sides of the plants but not between them.

Annual clipping of deciduous hedges should be done just as the first strong growth of the season is slowing down—in late spring, depending on the locality—and again in late summer after the secondary growth is made if a shaggy appearance makes it necessary.

Evergreens grow more slowly and usually do not need clipping until well past midsummer; they should never be severely pruned. Simply shape them and, once they have filled out, maintain that shape.

HEDYCHIUM (he DIK ee um). A genus of tropical herbs of the Zingiberaceae (Ginger Family), mostly natives of India, and commonly known as ginger-, butterfly-, or garland-lily. Mostly hardy only in Zones 10–11, in frostless regions they are favorites in the open garden, and in colder climates they are greenhouse plants.

They are robust growers, attaining 3–8 ft., and have highly ornamental foliage similar to that of *Canna* and sprays of showy fragrant flowers of various colors—white and cream through orange and pink to scarlet. In the open, most of them flower in the summer; under glass, they can be coaxed to bloom almost continuously. They require a rich soil, preferably a peaty loam with a little sand and a generous proportion of well rotted manure. Plenty of water must be given, with an occasional complete immersion of the pot during the growing period. An application of liquid manure should be given at intervals, and while growing the plant needs abundant light and a moist atmosphere. After blooming, the rootstocks are lifted, dried off gradually, rested in a cool place, and repotted in new soil in spring or early summer. Propagation is by division just before repotting.

H. coronarium (garland-lily, butterfly ginger) with white flowers, and the similar *H. flavum*, which is yellow, are both strongly fragrant. *H. coccineum* and *H. gardneranum* are more erect, with showier heads of reddish orange flowers.

HEDYOTIS (hed ee OH tis). A genus of small, tufted, North American herbs, formerly listed as *Houstonia*, belonging to the Rubiaceae (Madder Family). They have pretty little white, blue, or purple flowers. Some species are grown in the rock garden, and most thrive in moist, semishaded situations. They are delicate plants but easily grown in the wild garden and variously hardy to Zone 4. Propagation is by division of the clumps.

PRINCIPAL SPECIES

H. caerulea (bluets), a low perennial with solitary white, blue, or violet flowers with a yellow eye, is the common form seen in the eastern states. Unlike other members of the genus, it must be planted in the open, where its profusion of white blooms gives damp meadows the look of a light snow cover.

H. floridana is a southern species that has purple flowers.

Hedyotis caerulea

H. michauxii (creeping bluets), formerly listed as *Houstonia serpyllifolia*, grows to 10 in. with prostrate stems that bear relatively large, deep violet-blue flowers.

H. nigricans, formerly listed as *Houstonia angustifolia*, is a taller plant than other species, with white to purple flowers in flat-topped clusters; it is the species commonly seen in the southern states.

H. purpurea, from the central states, has several stems to 18 in. long that bear purple or lilac funnelform flowers in long terminal clusters. There are several varieties native in different parts of North America.

HEDYSCEPE (hee di SEE pee) **canterburyana.** A feather-leaved palm formerly listed under *Kentia* and commonly known as umbrella palm. It is found wild only in the Lord Howe Islands in the South Pacific, where its tall trunk is crowned by broad, feathery, overarching fronds and reaches a height of 30 ft. It has been grown successfully outdoors in south Florida and southern California. Thriving in rich, moist loam, it should be sheltered from direct rays of the sun, especially in the juvenile stage. When grown under glass, the umbrella palm requires a heavy potting soil enriched with well-rotted manure, frequent watering, a night temperature never below 60°F, and partial shading throughout the year.

HEEL. The small piece of two-year or older stem left at the base of a cutting (see CUTTINGS) taken for propagation purposes. Usually it is either the first joint of the old wood below the extension of young wood; or, when the young stem grows at an angle, it is merely a thin slice of such wood.

HEELING-IN. Storing dormant plants in trenches by covering them with soil until conditions are favorable for planting. It is most often practiced with dormant nursery stock before the ground has been prepared. For winter storage dig the trenches from east to west on well-drained bare ground. Make the north side vertical; the south, a long slope. Across this slope lay a slanting row, or single layer of plants, their roots toward the opposite (vertical) end, and only their tops extending beyond the soil level. Cover them—roots and stems, almost to the tops—with soil, sifting and packing it in around them. Lay on another single row and cover it, and so on until the trench is full of overlapping, slanting alternate rows of plants and soil. The trench can be made as long as necessary by extending it at

Heeling-in

the vertical end. When heeling-in newly received small trees or shrubs, remove all packing material to prevent mice from nesting in it. Dormant deciduous shrubs so stored will pass the winter safely but should be dug and planted in early spring before they make much growth.

HELENIUM (he LEE nee um).

A genus of mostly perennial herbs native to North America belonging to the Asteraceae (Aster Family) and commonly known as sneezeweed. They are coarse and erect in habit, bearing yellow or bronze flower heads, either solitary or in flat-topped clusters, in late summer or fall. A number of the perennial species are cultivated in rich, loamy soil in the border, preferably in the rear, for height and early autumn bloom. Some of the more weedy species can be massed in the wild garden.

Helenium autumnale

They are easily increased by seed, division, and cuttings. If attacked by white aphids on the roots, they should be lifted, the roots thoroughly washed, and the plants reset in another section of the border. Most are hardy in Zones 5–9, with a few thriving in Zone 3.

PRINCIPAL SPECIES

H. autumnale grows to 6 ft. and has long, rather narrow leaves and 2-in. flower heads whose rays shade from lemon-yellow to deep red on the varieties.

H. bigelovii, growing to 4 ft. high, is a decorative plant with richly colored flowers, the disks brownish and the rays clear yellow.

H. flexuosum, growing to 3 ft., has clustered heads of flowers with brownish or purplish disks and drooping yellow or brownish yellow rays.

H. hoopesii grows to 3 ft. and has yellow flower heads to 3 in. across lasting well in the border and also when cut.

HELIANTHELLA (hee lee an THEL ah). A genus of western North American perennial herbs of the Asteraceae (Aster Family), with long-stemmed yellow or brownish heads of flowers from summer to autumn. Hardy to Zone 8.

HELIANTHEMUM (hee lee AN the mum). A genus including more than 120 species of perennial herbs or low subshrubs, native to North America and the Mediterranean, and commonly known as sun-rose or frostweed. They are suitable for ground cover, rock gardens, or border planting, thriving in dry limestone soil and full sun. Yellow, rose, white, or purple flowers appear from midsummer to fall on plants 6–24 in. high. The plants must be protected in cold regions. Propagation is by seed sown in spring, by greenwood cuttings, or by division. Most are hardy in Zones 6–9.

H. nummularium (rock-rose) is the most common and hardy species. It grows to 12 in. and bears yellow flowers 1 in. across. There are numerous varieties with colorful flowers, including *albo-plenum*, double white; *aureum*, deep yellow; *cupreum*, copper variegated with yellow; *macranthum*, white with yellow blotches; *mutabile*, pale rose changing to lilac or nearly white; and *roseum*, pale rose (also in a double form).

HELIANTHUS (hee li AN thus). A genus of coarse annual or perennial herbs of the Asteraceae (Aster Family), popularly known as sunflower. The flower heads, with yellow rays and yellow, purple, brown, or almost black centers, range from a few inches to more than a foot in diameter. The small ones are borne in clusters, the large ones as a rule singly or at intervals along tall, stout stems. Sunflowers are widely cultivated in Russia, India, and Egypt, an oil being extracted from the seeds, and the resulting oil-cake being fed to livestock. The ripening seeds are also eaten as nuts.

Sunflowers are easily grown from seed, but perennial kinds are also propagated by division, or from offsets. They make excellent border and background material.

Applications of sulfur dust will control not only the sunflower rust, which produces yellow-brown spore pustules on the backs of the leaves, but also the powdery mildew that appears late in the season.

The larvae of the sunflower maggot may occur in such numbers inside the stalks as to cause them to fall over. The adult fly can be controlled by spraying with a general-purpose insecticide such as rotenone-pyrethrum.

PRINCIPAL SPECIES

H. annuus (sunflower), reaching heights of 12–15 ft. and developing huge heads 12 in. across, is the common garden subject. A North American native plant, widespread over the western prairies, it is at times a pernicious weed in Kansas and adjacent states. Nevertheless, it is the Kansas state flower. Several horticultural forms have been developed, with attractive wine-red and chestnut shades and combinations of lemon-yellow and orange. These forms are smaller and more appropriate for the border; the taller type should be planted

Helianthus annuus

only as background material or at the edge of the vegetable garden where pole beans can be allowed to climb the stalks and where the heads will furnish valuable poultry food or winter provender for the birds.

H. decapetalus (thinleaf sunflower) is one of the hardy sunflowers with numerous small heads of yellow flowers that, in the horticultural varieties, vary through coppery and purplish tones. They bloom over a long period and, though rather coarse for the herbaceous border, make striking groups in shrubbery.

H. tuberosus (JERUSALEM-ARTICHOKE, girasole) is a tall-growing perennial with edible, potatolike roots.

HELICHRYSUM (he li KRĪ sum) **bracteatum.** A hardy annual belonging to the Asteraceae (Aster Family), commonly known as strawflower and called immortelle in France. Growing 1–3 ft. tall, it is considered one of the finest of all everlastings for the home garden.

Flowers should be cut when partially open and dried slowly in a cool place, heads downward to keep the long stems straight; see EVERLASTINGS. The stiff, overlapping scales, which form the showy part of the flower head, come in a wide range of soft and brilliant shades. Propagation is by seed, either sown outdoors or started indoors for earlier bloom; also by cuttings. A rich, loamy soil is preferred.

HELICODICEROS (he li koh DIS ur us) **muscivorus.** A tuberous-rooted plant belonging to the Araceae (Arum Family), and commonly known as twist arum. It grows to 18 in. with leaves parted into fingerlike divisions and hairy spadix or spikelike flower clusters shaded by purple-hairy spathes twisted at the throat into a horizontal position. Though a floral curiosity, this plant is seldom grown because of the vile odor, which attracts carrion flies and other insects. Started in autumn indoors, it will flower in the spring. It can be propagated by division.

HELICONIA (he li KOH nee ah). A genus of large tropical herbs with leaves and plant form similar to those of a small banana. The flowers are variously colored, with their display accentuated by colored bracts at the base of each one. These may be spaced apart or pressed together, and the whole may stand erect or hang.

The plants are gross feeders, growing and flowering best with ample water and light. Many species and cultivars have been introduced for warm regions or greenhouse use.

H. psittacorum are small to medium height (2–4 ft.) and free flowering throughout the year. Others, such as *H. bihai* (wild-plantain), *H. humilis* (lobster-claw), and *H. wagnerana* are more seasonal. All stop growth when the temperature drops to 60°F.

HELIOCEREUS (hee lee oh SEER ee us). A genus of cacti (sun-cereus) popular for greenhouse or lath-house cultivation. Easy to culture and growing quickly, their blossoms can scarcely be surpassed in size and brilliance. Specimens have been known to produce over 100 buds and blossoms at one time. The flowers, about 9 in. across, are brilliant crimson and violet-mauve.

There are many hybrids produced by cross fertilization, and especially fine buds are often grafted onto other stock. Of tropical origin, they need warmth, not too dry conditions, and a particularly loose but rich planting mix, as for most epiphytic cacti. For cultural information, see CACTUS.

HELIOPHILA (hee lee AWF il ah). A small genus of South African herbs belonging to the Brassicaceae (Mustard Family), having racemes of blue flowers and narrow, hairy leaves. They are treated as half-hardy annuals, the seed started indoors and the seedlings set out after danger of frost is over; seed can also be sown in late spring where the plants are to stand.

H. linearifolia is a desirable greenhouse cut-flower subject for its abundance of delicate sky blue flowers, although the petals close at night.

H. pilosa, growing 6–24 in., has light blue flowers varying to lilac and yellow. It can be forced in the greenhouse or used as a bedding plant in the border where it will bloom in summer.

HELIOPSIS (hee lee AHP sis). A genus of hardy perennial herbs belonging to the Asteraceae (Aster Family), commonly known as oxeye. With yellow, sunflowerlike heads 2½ in. across on plants up to 5 ft. tall, they are best relegated to informal borders or wild gardens. Seeds sown outdoors in ordinary dry soil, even in an exposed situation, will produce flowers for cutting the second year. Most are hardy in Zones 4–9.

Heliopsis helianthoides

H. helianthoides and *H. scabra*, the latter with rough-haired stems, have both given rise to numerous varieties in several tones of yellow and orange, some with double flowers.

HELIOTROPE. Common name for HELIOTROPIUM, a genus of half-hardy and greenhouse plants with fragrant, violet flower clusters. Garden-heliotrope is *Valeriana officinalis*; see VALERIANA.

HELIOTROPIUM (hee lee oh TROHP ee um). A genus of half-hardy plants with small, deep violet flowers, commonly known as heliotrope. Because of their pleasantly scented, attractive flower clusters, the plants have long been in summer border gardens and in use by florists. They are common greenhouse plants, but they can be grown outdoors year-round in Zones 10–11 and the milder regions of Zone 9. They are otherwise grown outdoors as summer annuals and will succumb to the first frost of autumn.

Somewhat woody at the base, heliotropes can be developed into standard or tree forms by early and continued pruning of all side branches, but they are best known as border plants, giving their fragrant bloom amid rough-veined leaves from early summer until heavy frost. Easily cultivated, heliotropes are also used as potted plants. They can be kept in the same pot for several years. They should be given liquid manure in the growing season.

Propagation is best accomplished from softwood cuttings placed in flats containing equal parts of leaf mold and sand. They require heavy shading for the first week and ample moisture from the very beginning. Plants should be potted in ten or twelve days, or as soon as they have rooted, or they may be attacked by a destructive fungus. A light soil is best in the pots.

PRINCIPAL SPECIES

H. arborescens, formerly listed as *H. peruvianum*, is the source of most garden forms of heliotrope. It bears fragrant, deep violet to white flowers from late spring to early autumn and grows 4–6 ft. high. Whether grown as a standard, a potted plant, or a bedding plant, it cannot tolerate frost.

H. curassavicum (seaside heliotrope) is a short-lived annual forming a creeping mass 6–24 in. high. Small white or blue flowers are borne in spikes and bloom in summer and early autumn. Smooth, somewhat succulent leaves are linnear or obovate, to 1½ in. long.

HELIPTERUM (hee LIP tur um). A genus of annuals grown for winter bouquets as everlastings, belonging to the Asteraceae (Aster Family), and sometimes distributed by seed suppliers as *Acroclinium*. One of the daintiest of annuals, it is easily cultivated. Seeds are generally sown outdoors where plants are to grow, though they can be started indoors to produce earlier flowers. Plants stand 1–2 ft. tall and should be placed 6–12 in. apart.

PRINCIPAL SPECIES

H. humboldtianum (also listed as *H. sanfordi*), the most popular species, bears small flowers in ball-shaped clusters 1½ in. across. The color is deep, rich, golden yellow, but outer bracts have a greenish tinge. For dried flowers, they should be cut when the buds are opening, stripped of leaves, tied in bunches, and hung in a shady place. As they dry, the flowers will open. They will retain their color for years.

H. manglesii (Swan River everlasting), sometimes listed under *Rhodanthe*, is slender, growing to 1½ ft., with loose heads about 1½ in. across of white to bright pink blossoms. Cv. 'Maculatum' has red spots on the white bracts.

H. roseum is an excellent, commonly grown species. It grows to 2 ft. high, with heads of rose or white flowers not clustered, and is often used in dried flower arrangements.

HELLEBORE. Common name for HELLEBORUS, a genus of hardy, perennial, fibrous-rooted herbs, and for an insecticide made from the roots of plants of the genus VERATRUM, commonly known as false hellebore or white-hellebore.

Usually distributed as a dry powder, hellebore insecticide is comparatively nonpoisonous to humans but is a slow stomach poison for insects. It is an old, well-known material but is expensive and not effective unless fresh. Its use is recommended only in certain cases, as in the control of the currant worm, when a more dangerous poison is not advisable. See INSECT CONTROL.

HELLEBORUS (he li BOHR us). A genus of fibrous-rooted European perennial herbs belonging to the Ranunculaceae (Buttercup Family) and commonly known as hellebore. Most species are hardy in Zones 3–8 and bloom in earliest spring or even midwinter. Several kinds have become naturalized in North America. All parts of the plant are poisonous if eaten.

Hellebores should be planted in partial shade in rich, moist soil and should not be disturbed once established. A fern bed gives them excellent protection winter and summer. They are also excellent subjects in a shrubbery border or rock garden. If the flowers are wanted primarily for cutting, plants should be grown in beds of good garden loam

Helleborus niger

mixed with sand and top-dressed with well-rotted manure. If the plants are to be forced under glass, strong specimens should be potted up in late summer or fall and gradually brought into a warmer temperature. The flowers, which can thus be secured at any period of the winter, last well when cut. Propagation is by division of the roots or by seed. Seedlings bear flowers in the third year.

PRINCIPAL SPECIES

H. foetidus, growing to 2 ft., flowers in late winter and spring. Both flowers and stems are a bright lemon-green. The foliage is compact, glaucous, and evergreen. Hardy to Zone 6.

H. lividus var. *corsicus*, native to the Mediterranean, grows to 18 in. and produces clusters of

2-in., green, saucerlike flowers. The evergreen foliage is glaucous and toothed.

H. niger (black hellebore, Christmas-rose) grows to 12 in. and has colorful divided foliage. Large attractive white, greenish, or slightly purplish flowers up to 5 in. across are borne on relatively long stems and resemble wild roses or anemones, with prominent yellowish stamens. Blossoms appear in late winter or very early spring, before most other spring flowers.

H. orientalis (Lenten-rose), of which there are many attractive varieties, blooms early, bearing purplish flowers in clusters.

H. purpurascens, growing 9–12 in., has large, palmate, deeply lobed leaves and 2–2½ in. violet blooms appearing in early spring.

H. x sternii, growing to 2 ft., has toothed gray leaves and pinkish lime to creamy 1½-in. flowers borne in clusters and opening from late winter to early spring.

H. viridis opens its broad, yellowish green, buttercuplike flowers earlier than almost any other spring-flowering subject in the garden.

HELONIAS (hel OH nee as) **bullata.** A bulbous perennial herb belonging to the Liliaceae (Lily Family), commonly known as swamp-pink. It has thin, dark green, clustered leaves 6–15 in. long and bears 30 pink or purplish flowers clustered atop stalks up to 2 ft. high. Hardy to Zone 5 and found in bogs and wet places in the eastern states, it is a handsome plant for the wild garden and is very easily propagated by division.

HELXINE (helk SI nee) **soleiroli.** Former botanic name for *Soleirolia soleirolii*, a creeping perennial herb commonly known as baby's-tears; see SOLEIROLIA.

HEMEROCALLIS (hem ur oh KAL is). A genus of flowering herbs commonly known as daylilies, including some of the most frequently planted perennials in North American gardens, and described by some as the perfect flower. A few species originated in central Europe, but most are native to Japan and eastern Asia, where they have been depicted in paintings and textiles since ancient times. These plants are valued in many countries not only for their beauty, but also for their medicinal uses and edible buds, flowers, and roots.

Daylilies grow from fibrous roots, which are more fleshy than those of most other herbaceous perennials. The foliage is grasslike, and the flowers are borne on tall leafless stems (scapes). Because their flowers are similar, daylilies are frequently confused with the true lilies, of the genus *Lilium*, including Easter lilies, madonnas, or regals, which all grow from bulbs.

The genus name *Hemerocallis* is from the Greek word meaning "beauty for a day." Although a few open in the evening and persist through the next day, the flowers of most daylily plants open in the morning, then fade and die by early evening. However, a mature daylily produces sufficient buds to ensure continuous blooming for many weeks, a blooming period longer than that of most perennials.

CULTURE

Although some have been developed specifically for cultivation in warm or cold zones, thousands of the modern daylily types, like their forbearers, grow well in a wide range of climates. They enjoy a sunny location, but the red and pink varieties produce better color when they are protected from direct afternoon sun.

Daylilies should be planted 18–36 in. apart depending on whether they are miniature or full sized. They prefer fertile, well-drained, soil with a pH of 6 to 7. They are useful for border plantings, as individual clumps, as foundation plants, in rock gardens, as ground covers, and they can also be grown in planters, pots, or other containers. Most plants will live indefinitely with little care and will continue to bloom if the clumps are divided every six to ten years, preferably in early spring or late summer, after the flowers have faded.

Daylilies need plenty of water, especially during the blooming season. Applying a mulch of organic matter 2–3 in. thick is of great benefit to keep the soil from drying out rapidly. Add more mulch and fertilizer each year. Be careful never to overfertilize the plants, however, because overnourished plants will produce more foliage and fewer blooms.

SELECTIONS

The genus *Hemerocallis* is comprised of approximately two dozen oriental species, most of them characterized by their vigor, hardiness, dependability, and ease of propagation. In addition to raising daylilies, many growers find hybridizing them a fascinating, and sometimes profitable, hobby.

Over 32,000 named and registered cultivars have been developed from the original rust-colored, lemon-yellow, and early orange varieties. Daylilies now range in height from a few inches to over 6 ft. tall. Flowers may be as small as violets or as large as 9 in. across. The petals may be ruffled or smooth, and all one color or a combination of several colors. Many have contrasting blotches, halos, and edgings against a single, pale background shade. The spectrum of colors include nearly every shade except black, white, and blue.

The American Hemerocallis Society classifies daylilies by the hardiness of the foliage, which results in the following divisions.

Dormants. Considered to be the hardiest daylilies, their foliage turns brown and dies back in the late fall, both in the North and South.

Evergreens. These are the least hardy types. Their foliage remains green all winter but becomes dormant in cooler climates. Some evergreen cultivars can be grown in the North with winter protection.

Semi-evergreens. The foliage of these plants always becomes dormant in the North but stays green for part of the winter in warmer climates before turning brown. They vary considerably in hardiness, and some are able to survive in most of the United States and lower Canada.

Cultivars and Hybrids. Although the number of daylily cultivars is large, and many different assortments are offered by nurseries, a few are regarded as classics in their category. The large-flowering, fragrant, yellow 'Hyperion', devel-

oped in 1924, is probably the hybrid most commonly grown. 'Ed Murray' is a popular red; 'Dance Ballerina Dance', a famous, large ruffled pink; 'Joan Senior', a classic near-white; 'Kindly Light', the standard among those with spider-type blooms; 'New England Night', an outstanding very dark red. 'Stella de Ora', a low-growing, small-flowering cultivar that produces golden yellow blooms for many weeks, is considered one of the best of the long-season bloomers. Many of these classics are used as breeding stock for developing new hybrids.

PRINCIPAL SPECIES

H. altissima has very clear night-blooming flowers and grows very tall.

H. aurantiaca (orange daylily) is an orange-flowered evergreen.

H. dumortieri (early daylily) is a vigorous species with early-blooming orange flowers.

H. fulva (tawny daylily) is the tawny roadside species that has gone wild in much of North America. Cv. 'Europa', the best-known form, is an excellent ground cover and is used in shady wild gardens.

H. liliasphodelus (lemon daylily), also listed as *H. flava*, is quite fragrant, and it was a favorite among the old-time cultivated daylilies.

H. middendorffii (Middendorff daylily) is a dwarf with pale orange flowers.

H. multiflora (mayflower daylily) has a great many orange flowers on each stalk.

HEMIONITIS (hem ee oh NEE tis). A genus of small terrestrial ferns with broad, palmately or pinnately lobed fronds and shorter-stalked sterile fronds. The sporangia are borne along the veins. Most kinds produce small plantlets in the notches of the fronds, from which new plants are easily propagated. All but one are native to the American tropics.

H. arifolia is a pretty little fern that grows 4–6 in. and has simple, heart-shaped, glossy, dark green fronds. It needs a warm place in strong light, a well-drained alkaline soil mix, and strict avoidance of overpotting. It is native to the tropics of southeastern Asia.

H. palmata (strawberry fern) has palmate fronds shaped like those of a strawberry. Native to Central and South America and the West Indies, it is 4–12 in. tall and makes a charming pot plant, requiring the same conditions as *H. arifolia*. Like *H. arifolia*, it can be propagated by means of plantlets that form on the fronds.

HEMLOCK. Common name for TSUGA, a genus of coniferous evergreens with horizontal branches; small, soft, flat needles; and attractive little cones.

The name is also applied to other genera. Ground-hemlock is *Taxus canadensis*, a low, spreading species of yew; see TAXUS. Poison hemlock refers to the genus CONIUM, renowned for causing the demise of the Greek philosopher Socrates. Water-hemlock is *Cicuta maculata*, a flowering perennial herb with strong-scented foliage and poisonous roots; see CICUTA.

HEMP. Common name for *Cannabis sativa*, an annual herb once grown as a source of rope fiber; see CANNABIS. The name "hemp" is also applied to other fibrous plants. Bowstring-hemp is SANSEVIERIA. Manila-hemp is *Musa textilis*; see MUSA. Sisal-hemp is *Agave sisalana*; see AGAVE.

HENNA. Common name for *Lawsonia inermis*, a tropical shrub grown for ornament and dye; see LAWSONIA.

HEPATICA (he PAT ik ah). A genus of small hardy herbs distributed throughout the Northern Hemisphere, belonging to the Ranunculaceae (Buttercup Family), and sometimes known as liverleaf. They have three-lobed evergreen leaves; new ones appear after the flowers, which may be white, lavender, purple, blue, or pinkish. Natives of open, rich woodlands, they bloom in the very early spring and are desirable plants for the shady rock garden. They produce more flowers if fertilized. Propagation is by seed or division.

PRINCIPAL SPECIES

H. acutiloba is a North American native that has leaves with three-pointed lobes.

H. americana is an American species that has rounded lobes.

H. nobilis, from Eurasia, is like *H. americana*, but it has larger flowers.

H. transsilvanica, native to Romania, has toothed lobes.

Hepatica acutiloba

HERACLEUM (her ah KLEE um). A genus of perennial or biennial herbs of the Northern Hemisphere, belonging to the Apiaceae (Celery Family), and commonly known as cow-parsnip. They are coarse growers with large-lobed or compound leaves and minute white, purplish, or pink-tinted flowers in enormous umbels. Propagation is by seed or division. Hardy to Zone 3.

H. sphondylium var. *montanum*, formerly listed as *H. lanatum*, is a native species that grows to 6 ft. and has large leaves, white beneath, and umbels of white flowers 1 ft. across.

H. mantegazzianum, a species from the Caucasus region, grows to 9 ft. or more and has deeply cut leaves 3 ft. long and large white flowers in umbels 4 ft. across.

HERBARIUM. A collection of dried, pressed plants mounted on sheets of paper and used in the study of botany. Besides thousands of private herbaria, there are large collections in botanical gardens, natural history museums, and universities, many open to the public.

HERB ROBERT. A common name for *Geranium robertianum*, an attractive annual or biennial with red or purplish flowers and deeply cut leaves; see GERANIUM.

HERBS. The broad botanical definition uses the word to mean a nonwoody, vascular plant. However, the term is now generally used to mean plants and shrubs that are mostly aromatic and whose leaves, flowers, stems, bulbs, or roots can be used for flavoring, teas, medicine, candies, and perfume, or just for their fragrance.

The pronunciation of the word "herb" is so often the subject of controversy, that it seems desirable to note that it has long been the custom in England to sound the initial "h," whereas in the United States it has been the custom to ignore it and pronunce the word "urb."

Culinary herbs are plants whose leaves, flowers, stems, seeds, bulbs, or roots can be used for flavoring cooked foods, salads, and drinks. It does not refer to potherbs, which include any plant cultivated for "greens."

A garden (or section of the garden) can be devoted to the cultivation of herbs. All of the plants listed in the accompanying chart have a place in any herb garden, for many are fragrant and ornamental, as well as being useful in the kitchen. Potherbs are better grown in the vegetable garden. Most culinary herbs thrive best and develop the finest flavor when grown in a moderately fertile, fibrous garden loam, though various species require different levels of warmth, light, and moisture.

PROPAGATION

The seeds of many herbs are small and some are slow to germinate. Sowing under controlled conditions in greenhouse, coldframe, or under fluorescent lights gives best results for such varieties. The resultant seedlings can then be pricked out into small pots and grown on for a few weeks before hardening them off and transplanting them into a well-prepared bed in the garden.

LAYERING

This is one of the easiest methods of propagating herbs, often happening naturally as herbs put down roots where their stems touch the soil.

Simple Layering. Select a stem of the parent herb near the soil and bend it down to fasten it to the ground. Before burying it, make an incision just below a node, cutting at a slant halfway through the stem. Peg the branch down with 8-in. pieces of bent coat-hanger wire, cover with soil, and water. Placing a brick over the buried wound helps to keep it in place and to conserve moisture. After about six to eight weeks, check

for new root growth from the wound. Plants layered early in the year can be transplanted by fall.

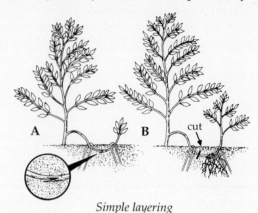

Simple layering

Mound Layering. Suitable for bushy herbs, mound layering (or stool layering) can produce several new plants from one original. Mound the soil up around the center of the plant, burying the center branches and keeping them constantly covered with soil. If done in the fall, the plants

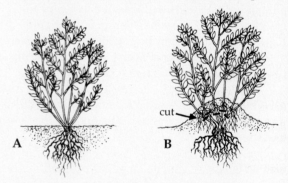

Mound layering

will have formed new roots within the mound by late spring. After strong new growth, cut off the stems and plant each separately.

HARVESTING

Gather leaf herbs before the first blossoms begin to open and in the early morning before the sun gets hot but after it has had time to dry the dew on the leaves. At this time the leaves contain the largest percentage of essential oils. Either hang them in small bunches or spread them thinly on sheets or trays in an airy, warm

HERB CULTURE

PLANT (common name)	LIFE SPAN HARDINESS	HEIGHT (inches)	SOIL SATURATION	LIGHT	DISTANCE APART (inches)
Agrimonia eupatoria (agrimony)	P H	24–36	well drained, ordinary	some shade	10
Allium ascalonicum (shallots)	P H	15	rich, well drained	full sun	8
Allium sativum (garlic)	P H	12	well drained, rich	full sun	6
Allium schoenoprasum (chives)	P H	8–12	rich	full sun	8
Allium tuberosum (garlic chives)	P H	30	rich	full sun	10
Aloysia triphylla (lemon verbena)	P T	to 96	light, well drained	full sun	24–36
Anchusa spp. (alkanet)	P H	24	well drained, light, sandy	some sun	18
Anethum graveolens (dill)	A H	36	light, sandy	sheltered, full sun	10
Angelica spp. (angelica)	B H	84	moist, rich	part shade	36
Anthriscus cerefolium (chervil)	A H	6	well drained, ordinary	some shade	8
Artemisia abrotanum (southernwood)	P H	36	ordinary	full sun	48
Artemisia absinthum (absinthe)	P H	48	poor, light	full sun or part shade	36
Artemisia dracunculus (tarragon)	P H	24	well drained, light	full sun	12
Borago officinalis (borage)	A H	36	well drained, ordinary	sun or part shade	18
Calendula officinalis (pot-marigold)	A H	24	well drained, light, sandy	full sun	12
Carum carvi (caraway)	B H	24	ordinary	full sun	8
Chamaemelum nobile (English or Roman chamomile)	P H	12	well drained, light	full sun	6
Chrysanthemum cineraiifolium (pyrethrum)	P H	18–24	well drained, limed	full sun	18
Coriandrum sativum (coriander)	A H	24–36	ordinary	full sun	4

Symbols:

A – annual	B – biennial	H – hardy	P – perennial	T – tender

PLANT (common name)	LIFE SPAN HARDINESS	HEIGHT (Inches)	SOIL SATURATION	LIGHT	DISTANCE APART (inches)
Crocus sativus (saffron crocus)	P H	3	rich, well drained	full sun or part shade	6
Foeniculum vulgare (fennel)	P H	60	well limed	full sun	18
Galium odoratum (sweet woodruff)	P H	8–10	moist, leafy	full shade	12
Galium spp. (bedstraw)	P H	36	dry, sandy	full sun	24
Hyssopus officinalis (hyssop)	P H	18	well drained, light	full sun or part shade	12
Inula helenium (elecampane)	P H	96	moist, light	full sun	30
Laurus nobilis (bay)	P T	40 ft.	well drained, ordinary	full sun	varies
Lavandula spp. (lavender)	P H	12–30	well drained, light	full sun	24–36
Levisticum officinale (lovage)	P H	72–84	moist, rich	some shade	36
Marubium vulgare (horehound)	P H	24	well drained, light, sandy	full sun or part shade	10
Matricaria recutita (wild-chamomile)	A H	24	well drained, sandy	full sun	8
Melissa officinalis (lemon-balm)	P H	48	well drained, sandy	full sun or part shade	18
Mentha pulgium (European pennyroyal)	P H	prostrate	moist, heavy	part shade	6
Mentha spp. (mint)	P H	36	rich, moist	full sun or some shade	18
Monarda spp. (wild-bergamot)	P H	36	ordinary, moist	full sun or part shade	18
Myrris odorata (sweet cicely)	P H	24	rich, moist	part shade	24
Nepeta cataria (catnip)	P H	36	sandy, dry	full sun	18
Ocimum basilicum (sweet basil)	A T	18	rich	full sun	12
Ocimum basilicum cv. 'Minimum' (bush basil)	A T	8	well drained, rich	full sun	12
Origanum majorana (sweet marjoram)	P T	9–12	rich, light	full sun sheltered	12

Symbols:

A – annual   B – biennial   H – hardy   P – perennial   T – tender

PLANT (common name)	LIFE SPAN HARDINESS	HEIGHT (inches)	SOIL SATURATION	LIGHT	DISTANCE APART (inches)
Origanum spp. (oregano)	P H	18	light, dry	full sun	18
Pelargonium graveolens (rose geranium)	P T	36	well drained, light	full sun	36
Petroselinum crispum (parsley)	B H	8–12	rich	full sun or part shade	8
Pimpinella anisum (anise)	A T	24	ordinary	full sun	4
Poterium sanguisorba (salad burnet)	P H	18	dry, ordinary	full sun	12
Rosmarinus officinalis (rosemary)	P H/T	48–60	well drained, light	full sun	36
Rumex spp. (sorrel)	P H	30	rich, moist	full sun	18
Ruta graveolens (rue)	P H	24	well drained, poor	full sun or part shade	24
Salvia spp. (sage)	P H	18	sandy, limed	full sun	24
Santolina spp. (santolina)	P H	24	light, well drained	full sun	36
Satureja hortensis (summer savory)	A H	18	light, rich	full sun	8
Satureja montana (winter savory)	P H	8	poor, well drained	full sun	12
Symphytum spp. (comfrey)	P H	24–36	well manured, heavy	full sun	36
Tanacetum vulgare (tansy)	P H	36	ordinary, well drained	full sun	48
Thymus citriodorus (lemon thyme)	P H	12	sandy, well drained	full sun	18
Thymus herba-barona (caraway thyme)	P H	semiprostrate	sandy, well drained	full sun	8–12
Thymus serpyllum (wild thyme)	P H	low, creeping	sandy, well drained	full sun	4
Thymus vulgaris (garden thyme)	P H	10	sandy, well drained	full sun	12
Verbascum spp. (mullein)	B H	96	poor, dry	full sun or shade	18–24

Adapted from *Growing and Using Herbs Successfully,* by Betty E. M. Jacobs (Storey Communications, Inc., 1981), with permission from the publisher.

Symbols:

A – annual	B – biennial	H – hardy	P – perennial	T – tender

place, indoors or out, in the shade. Some people place the bundles in paper bags with air holes punched in them to reduce exposure to light and dust. Herbs can also be dried in a dehydrator. When the leafy parts become crisp, rub them gently off the stems and store in airtight jars in the dark, to prevent loss of flavor and color. They can be rubbed to a powder when needed for use.

Later in the season, if a few seeds fall when the plant is tapped gently, that is the right moment to collect the seed heads. They should be cut off, dropped into a paper bag, and carried to the drying area where they can be spread out. Ideally a current of warm, not hot, dry air should pass continuously over them. Do not crowd them. When the smaller stems are brittle, the seeds can be rubbed off and spread out for further drying, turning then daily for a week. They will need further watching once they are put in airtight jars to be sure there is no condensation. If there is, further drying will be necessary.

HERCULES'-CLUB. Common name for *Aralia spinosa*, a very spiny small tree; see ARALIA. It also refers to *Zanthoxylum clava-herculis*, a spiny shrub belonging to the Rutaceae (Rue Family); see ZANTHOXYLUM.

HERMANNIA (hur MAN ee ah) **verticillata.** A South African straggly subshrub with bell-like flowers, formerly listed as *Mahernia* and commonly known as honey-bell. It is usually grown in greenhouses as a hanging plant or trained to a form. The leaves are small and finely cut. In spring it bears a profusion of nodding, very fragrant yellow flowers. It is easily grown from cuttings.

HERNIARIA (hur nee AIR ee ah). A genus of small, trailing herbs belonging to the Caryophyllaceae (Pink Family), commonly known as burstwort or herniary. There are annual and perennial evergreen kinds with greenish flowers, native to sandy places in Europe, western Asia, Africa, and the Canary Islands. Species are variously hardy to Zone 3.

H. glabra forms dense mats of mosslike foliage that turns bronzy red in winter. It is used to some extent in carpet beds, in rock gardens, and between stepping stones. Plants thrive in ordinary garden soil and are propagated by division or seed.

HESPERALOE (hes pur AL oh). A genus of herbs very similar to *Yucca*. *H. parviflora*, found in Texas, has long narrow leaves to 4 ft. and nodding rose flowers. Hardy only in Zones 10–11, it is grown outdoors in the southern states and under glass in colder climates.

HESPERIS (HES pur is). A genus of hardy biennial and perennial herbs of erect, branching habit, commonly known as rocket. They bear showy, pyramidal spikes of white, rose, or mauve-purple flowers, good for summer cutting. Plants are 1–3 ft. tall; their colorful display is enhanced by the sweet fragrance of the blooms.

Hesperis does best when given a sunny location in the border. Propagation is by seed sown in spring or indoors somewhat earlier; the resulting plants will flower the following season. Most species are hardy in Zones 3–9. Mottling of the foliage and curling of the leaves is the sign of mosaic, a virus disease. To control, remove and destroy infested plants.

H. matronalis (sweet or dame's rocket, dame's-violet) is a coarse, branching perennial with purple to white, single and double flowers that have a delightful fragrance, which is accentuated in the evening. Plants often

Hesperis matronalis

self-sow, but better results come from handling them as biennials, sowing some seed every year for plants to blossom the next year.

HESSIAN FLY. Common name for *Phytophaga destructor*, a small black insect especially damaging to wheat, barley, and rye crops; see FLIES.

HETERANTHERA (het ur AN thur ah). A genus of bog herbs with small white, blue, or yellow flowers and creeping or floating stems. There are several species. *H. dubia* has small yellow flowers. *H. reniformis* has blue flowers. Both grow readily in damp spots in bog gardens in Zones 7–11.

HETEROCENTRON (het ur oh SEN trahn) **elegans.** A creeping Mexican vine formerly listed under the genus *Schizocentron*. It is a charming plant worthy of being more widely cultivated in warm regions (Zones 10–11), indoors, in porch baskets, or window boxes. The stems root at the joints, forming thick carpets on the ground, and bear deep blue flowers 1 in. wide. It can be grown in shade or sun in any light warm soil and is easily propagated by seed or cuttings.

HETEROMELES (het er oh MEE leez). A genus of large evergreen shrubs or small trees belonging to the Rosaceae (Rose Family) and commonly known as toyon or Christmas-berry. Native to California and hardy in Zones 8–9, *H. arbutifolia* is largely used for ornamental planting, prized for its profusion of bright red berries appearing in winter, which are in great demand for decorations at Christmastime, hence the common name. It has shining, dark green, sharp-toothed leaves and panicles of white flowers.

HEUCHERA (HYOO kur ah). A genus of perennial herbs, usually of dwarf, compact growth habit, native to western North America, belonging to the Saxifragaceae (Saxifrage Family), and commonly known as alumroot or coral-bells. Blooming from all summer, they are valuable for the low border or rockery.

In a good loamy soil and sunny location, the plants produce mats of deep green, sometimes tinged white or red, from which rise slender stalks bearing airy clusters of tiny bell-shaped flowers, which are good for cutting. Plants are propagated from seed sown in spring and by division in spring or fall. Various kinds are hardy to Zone 3.

PRINCIPAL SPECIES

H. americana (palace-purple) grows to 24 in. and blooms in sprays of greenish white flowers with foliage that stays purple year round.

H. x *convallaria* has flowers resembling lily-of-the-valley.

H. micrantha grows to 24 in. and bears loose panicles of white flowers tinged yellow to blue.

H. sanguinea (coral-bells) is the most commonly cultivated species in the United States. Hardy to Zone 4, it grows 12–24 in. and bears bell-shaped flowers about ½ in. long with prominent coral-colored calyxes. There are many cultivars, among them 'Alba', with white flowers; 'Gracillima', a slender form; 'Hybrida', a robust type with large flowers of various colors developed from crimson; and 'Maxima', featuring dark crimson flowers.

Heuchera sanguinea

HEVEA (HEV ee ah) **brasiliensis.** A tropical tree of the Euphorbiaceae (Spurge Family), commonly known as the Para rubber tree. It is now the main commercial source of natural rubber, which is produced from its milky sap.

HIBISCUS (hī BIS kus). A variable genus of widely distributed herbs, shrubs, and small trees belonging to the Malvaceae (Mallow Family) and commonly known as rose mallow. The genus is generally divided into four groups: annuals, herbaceous perennials, hardy shrubs, and tropical shrubs and trees.

Improved forms of the native species have been developed with large showy flowers. Popularly known as mallow marvels and giant-flowering marsh mallows, they are usually listed as hybrids of the perennial *H. moscheutos*.

Several armored scale insects and the white fly attack hibiscus in the greenhouse and can be controlled by fumigation; see SCALE INSECTS; FUMIGATION. Outdoors *H. syriacus* is often seriously infested with aphids, which are checked by rinsing with a strong stream of water or spraying with insecticidal soap or other contact insecticide. See APHIDS; INSECT CONTROL.

PRINCIPAL SPECIES

Annuals. The annual species of hibiscus are easily raised from seed.

H. sabdariffa (roselle, Jamaican-sorrel) grows in warm regions and is cultivated for its yellow flowers with fleshy calyxes, from which sauces, jellies, and a cooling drink are made. The plant is easily grown like the tomato, plants being set 18–24 in. apart in rows 3–4 ft. apart. The bolls are gathered before they become woody and are used either fresh or dried.

H. trionum (flower-of-an-hour) grows to 2 ft. and has deeply divided leaves and sulfur-yellow flowers with dark centers. It is useful in the flower border.

Herbaceous Perennials. This group contains some good garden species valuable for late summer flowering. Propagated by seed or division, they will grow almost anywhere but appear to best advantage in moist soil in the flower border or shrubbery.

H. coccineus is native to southern swamps and has slender lobed leaves and large rose-red or crimson flowers. It is not hardy in cold climates but has been used as a parent in the production of garden forms.

H. lasiocarpus, formerly listed as *H. icanus*, is found in southern swamps and resembles *H. moscheutos* but has smaller leaves and flowers of pale yellow, pink, or white with a crimson eye.

H. militaris is found in wet places from Pennsylvania southward. It has hastate leaves and large white or pink flowers with a purple eye. It has been used in hybridizing.

H. moscheutos (swamp rose mallow, marsh mallow) is a perennial herb that grows to 4 ft. and has leaves entire or three-lobed and blush or rose flowers 8 in. across clustered in the leaf axils. Native to Europe, this species has become naturalized in moist places in the eastern states and has been used in the production of many garden forms. Hardy in Zones 5–9. Var. *moscheutos*, formerly listed as *H. oculiroseus*, found in southeastern coastal swamps, is less hardy than the species. It has white flowers with crimson centers.

Hibiscus moscheutos

Shrubs. The shrub species are increased by seed, cutting, and grafting.

H. rosa-sinensis (Chinese hibiscus), the state flower of Hawaii, is a tropical shrub or tree that grows to 30 ft. in warm climates. It is a favorite potted plant in greenhouses and is valued for its large, showy flowers of various colors, sometimes double. Old plants can be cut back annually and grown on for several years. Among the various forms, var. *cooperi* is conspicuous, with narrow leaves variegated white and small scarlet flowers.

H. schizopetalus is a tall tropical shrub from Africa with slender drooping branches and curious drooping flowers of red or orange-red. The petals are recurved and deeply cut, with stamens hanging far beyond.

H. syriacus (rose-of-Sharon, shrub-althaea) is a tall, hardy upright shrub of rounded form, valued for its late-summer flowering season and colorful blossoms. There are numerous garden forms with colors ranging from white to pink, red, and bluish purple. Some have double flowers, and some have variegated leaves. They thrive best in well-drained soil.

HICKORY. Common name for several species of CARYA, a genus of deciduous trees planted for ornament and some for their edible nuts.

HIERACIUM (hī ur AY shee um). A genus of perennial herbs belonging to the Asteraceae (Aster Family) and commonly known as hawkweed. Many species have become very troublesome weeds in the eastern states, but a few are attractive in the border with their brilliantly colored flowers. They are easily grown from seed and propagated by division of the rooting stem. Hardiness varies (Zones 3–5), depending on the species.

PRINCIPAL SPECIES

H. aurantiacum (orange hawkweed, devil's-paintbrush), a perennial herb bearing red, orange, or yellow flowers in heads on slender, erect stalks above flat rosettes of leaves, is a serious pest in meadows and hayfields, especially on dry, sterile, or gravelly, mostly acid soil. Its bitter juice makes it unpalatable to cattle.

H. venosum (rattlesnake weed, poor-Robin's-plantain), though ornamental with bright yellow flowers, is usually a troublesome weed.

H. villosum (shaggy hawkweed), the most desirable form for the border, grows to 2 ft. with golden yellow flowers and silvery white foliage.

HILLS-OF-SNOW.
Common name for *Hydrangea arborescens*, a North American shrub with showy clusters of white flowers.

HIPPEASTRUM
(hip ee AST rum). A genus of bulbous herbaceous plants with large, lilylike flowers, native only in South America, belonging to the Amaryllidaceae (Amaryllis Family), and commonly known as amaryllis. Various species and many hybrids are grown as houseplants and summer garden subjects. The strong, stout, erect stems bear several enormous flowers of white, pink, or red (or those colors combined) above a clump of broad, swordshaped leaves.

Bulbs of hybrids are commercially produced in enormous quantities in the southern states. For outdoor planting in those localities, and for greenhouse and home flowering in the North, there is nothing among the bulbous plants that is as readily handled or that produces more effectively showy flowers. The blossoms range in color from various shades of pink to deepest red. In the South, the foliage is evergreen except when cut down by frost.

The bulbs must be lifted and stored in dry sand over winter. When new bulbs are received, they should be potted at once and maintained in an even temperature of about 65°F. The flowers often appear before the foliage. After blooming, the potted plant can be plunged outdoors when the weather becomes warm. Taken inside in the fall, it will be ready to flower again in the early spring.

Hippeastrum sp.

PRINCIPAL SPECIES

H. aulicum (lily-of-the-palace) grows to 2 ft. tall and bears large, paired, green-throated red flowers. Hardy in Zones 10–11.

H. x *johnsonii* has large red flowers with white veins.

H. puniceum, formerly listed as *Amaryllis equestre*, is a beautiful soft pink form that grows abundantly in Florida and other southern states. It adapts well to home and greenhouse conditions in the North.

HIPPOPHAE
(hip POH fee). A genus of deciduous ornamental shrubs or trees with spiny branches, belonging to the Elaeagnaceae (Oleaster Family), commonly known as sea-buckthorn. *H. rhamnoides* is the species most commonly grown. This is a very hardy (to Zone 4) shrub or small tree, native to Europe and Asia. It is not particular as to soil, is drought resistant, and often suckers freely. The narrow silvery gray leaves make it very conspicuous. The small yellow flowers are of separate sexes, produced on different plants, so it is necessary to have male and female plants nearby to assure a crop of the showy orange-colored berries.

HIRSUTE. Rather coarsely hairy; used particularly in reference to leaves and twigs.

HISPID. Clothed with erect, stiff hairs, as in species of borage.

HISTIOPTERIS (his tee AHP tur is). A genus of tropical ferns that is very adaptable but apt to become weedy. *H. incisa* has fronds that will scramble through other vegetation, often growing over 15 ft. long. The bipinnate to quadripinnate fronds are very attractive but are frequently damaged by grubs. It can be grown in containers or in the ground. It is found in tropical regions throughout the world.

HOARHOUND. Spelling variation of horehound; see MARRUBIUM.

HOARY. Covered with a close grayish white down, like the fruit of the pasqueflower or the young branches of the silk-oak.

HOBBLEBUSH. Common name for *Viburnum alnifolium*, a North American shrub with conspicuous clusters of white flowers followed by purple-black berries; see VIBURNUM.

HOE. A tillage tool that in its simplest form consists of a thin, flat blade set nearly at right angles to its long handle. There are many varied forms for special purposes.

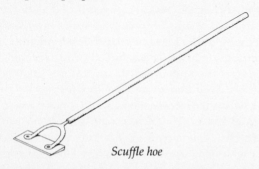

Scuffle hoe

Used for weeding, the common hoe should be handled as a chopping or slicing tool, not a drawing implement. Thus used, it will leave a level soil surface completely loosened with all weeds cut off and exposed to the killing rays of the sun. The various types of scuffle hoes do the same work but are slid along just under the surface, not lifted or chopped.

See also CULTIVATION; TOOLS.

HOFFMANNIA (hawf MAN ee ah). A genus of tropical American herbs or shrubs usually grown in warm greenhouses for their colored foliage. They are easily grown from cuttings, and old plants make good specimens if cut back in spring.

PRINCIPAL SPECIES

H. discolor is a dwarf, hairy plant and has purple stems, leaves olive green above and rich red beneath, and small red flowers.

H. ghiesbreghtii grows to 4 ft. and has four-angled stems; leaves a foot or more long, dark velvety green above and red purple beneath; and small yellow flowers, spotted red.

H. regalis has plaited leaves about 9 in. long, shining dark green above and deep red beneath.

HOG-PEANUT. A common name for AMPHICARPAEA, a genus of trailing perennials sometimes used for ornament but often becoming pestiferous weeds.

HOHERIA (hoh HEE ree ah). A genus of shrubs or small trees, white flowered and evergreen or nearly so, native to New Zealand, and belonging to the Malvaceae (Mallow Family). They can be grown outdoors only in Zones 9–11. *H. populnea*, the largest of the group, grows to 30 ft., has oval leaves to 5 in. long, and bears a profusion of flowers about 1 in. across followed by clusters of winged seeds. *H. sexstylosa* grows to 15 ft. or more, with long, narrow leaves and flowers less than an inch across. *H. angustifolia* has smaller leaves and flowers.

HOLLY. Common name for ILEX, a genus of trees and shrubs grown for their shiny foliage and colored fruits. The Holly Family is AQUIFOLIACEAE.

The name is also applied to other genera. African-holly is *Solanum giganteum*. Mountain holly is *Nemopanthus*, another genus of the Holly Family. Sea-holly is *Eryngium maritimum*.

HOLLY FERN. Common name for several species of POLYSTICHUM, including the Anderson's, Braun's, California, Dudley's, giant, mountain, and western holly ferns. *Cyrtomium falcatum* is called dwarf or Japanese holly fern; see CYRTOMIUM.

HOLLYHOCK. Common name for ALCEA, a genus of annual, biennial, or perennial herbs, cultivated for their flowers.

HOLMSKIOLDIA (hohlm SKEE ohl dee ah). A genus of shrubs belonging to the Verbenaceae (Verbena Family) and commonly known as Chinese-hat plant. The petals of the flowers form an inch-long tube hanging below a saucer-shaped calyx, giving the plant its common name. These shrubs are valuable in landscapes in Zones 10–11 for their bright displays several times a year, when the flowers occur in profusion on long, arching branches. Propagation is by cuttings, and the plants will tolerate a wide range of soil types.

H. sanguinea, the most common species, has brick-red flowers. A lemon-yellow variety is also known.

H. speciosa has a purple tube and lavender "hat."

HOLODISCUS (hoh loh DIS kus). A genus of ornamental shrubs belonging to the Rosaceae (Rose Family) and native to the western United States. In gardens they prefer a well-drained soil in a sunny location. Some species are hardy to Zone 4. Propagation is by seed and layers.

H. discolor (ocean-spray, cream bush), the principal species, is a large spreading shrub that grows to 15 ft. and has slender, arching branches, making a good accent plant on a lawn. It has rather small, somewhat lobed leaves and is conspicuous in summer with its large drooping or erect panicles of small creamy white flowers. Instead of falling, these later turn an attractive tan color, continuing in that condition for some time.

H. microphyllus (mountain-spray) is an ornamental shrub with creamy flowers on drooping stems.

HOMALOCLADIUM (hoh mah loh KLAD ee um) **platycladum.** A tropical shrub of the Polygonaceae (Buckwheat Family) with broad, ribbonlike, shiny stems, often leafless in the flowering stages, and commonly known as ribbonbush. The small, inconspicuous, greenish flowers are followed by a decorative, red, berrylike fruit, which later turns dark purple. It is also called centipede plant because of its numerous long, straggling branches. Native to the Solomon Isles, it is grown in greenhouses or outdoors in Zones 10–11, principally for its curious appearance. As a potted plant it attains a height of 4 ft., but as a garden subject it may reach 12 ft. Easily cultivated, it is propagated by cuttings and occasionally survives light frosts.

HONESTY. A common name for LUNARIA, a genus of flowering herbs often used for dried bouquets.

HONEY-BELL. Common name for *Hermannia verticillata*, a South African shrub of weak, straggly habit, usually grown as a hanging greenhouse plant; see HERMANNIA.

HONEYBUSH. Common name for MELIANTHUS, a genus of tropical evergreen shrubs.

HONEYSUCKLE. Common name for LONICERA, a genus of ornamental shrubs and vines valued for their showy, fragrant flowers and decorative fruit.

The common name is also used to describe other genera and species. The Honeysuckle Family is CAPRIFOLIACEAE. Bush honeysuckle is *Diervilla*. White swamp-honeysuckle is *Rhododendron viscosum*. Himalayan honeysuckle is

Leycesteria formosa. Cape-honeysuckle is *Tecomaria capensis*. Jamaica-honeysuckle is *Passiflora laurifolia*. French-honeysuckle is *Hedysarum coronarium*.

HONEYWORT. Common name for CERINTHE, a genus of mostly annual herbs with sweet, colorful flowers.

HOODIA (HOO dee ah). A genus of small, succulent tropical herbs belonging to the Asclepediaceae (Milkweed Family). They have large showy yellow or purple flowers and cactuslike foliage. In cool climates they are grown in greenhouse botanical collections.

HOP. Common name for fruit of the genus HUMULUS.

HOP-HORNBEAM. Common name for OSTRYA, a genus of hardy, deciduous, hard-wooded trees belonging to the Betulaceae (Birch Family).

HORDEUM (HOR dee um). A genus of annual and perennial members of the Poaceae (Grass Family), native to temperate zones of the Eastern and Western Hemispheres, where they are hardy to Zone 3. *H. jubatum* (squirrel-tail grass) is a biennial or perennial ornamental, growing to 2½ ft. The 4-in. nodding heads have barbed beards often 3 in. long. Propagation is by seed, usually sown where the plants are to grow. Any ordinary soil is satisfactory, provided there is plenty of sun. The flower spikes are gathered just after their emergence from the sheath and are dried for use in winter bouquets. *H. vulgare* is the wild species from which barley, the cereal crop, has been developed. See ORNAMENTAL GRASSES.

HOREHOUND. Common name for *Marrubium vulgare*, which is frequently used for flavoring candies and lozenges; also spelled hoarhound. See MARRUBIUM.

HORMONE. A substance produced in one part of a plant that affects the function or regulates the action of another part. There are root-forming, flower-forming, and other process-regulating substances present in plants as hormones. Because of their characteristic actions, they are sometimes popularly referred to as chemical messengers, and, because various chemical compounds found elsewhere or synthesized have been discovered to have somewhat similar growth-inducing or growth-regulating effects, they too are called hormones. Used in low concentrations, these synthetic materials are now being used in the manufacture of proprietary liquids and powders used on many plants to stimulate or hasten growth responses.

See also AUXIN; CHEMICAL GARDENING; ROOTING COMPOUNDS.

HORNBEAM. Common name for CARPINUS, a genus of hardy deciduous trees with smooth bark and very hard wood.

Hop-hornbeam refers to OSTRYA, a similar genus of trees with dark brown bark and hoplike fruit clusters.

HORNET. Common name given to several species of large social wasps (Vespidae), especially the European hornet, *Vespa crabro*, and the bald-faced or white-faced North American hornet, *Vespa maculata*.

The European species, which may be more than an inch long, is dark brown with bands of orange-yellow. It builds nests in hollow trees and, in gathering wood for construction, tears pieces of bark from the stems of lilac, boxwood, arborvitae, and other trees or shrubs. The work often suggests that of a novice using a dull saw, the bark being torn away to the cambium and the stems sometimes being girdled. The hornets also appear to feed on the sap flowing from the wounds. They

Hornet

are generally active in the evening and can be caught in lighted traps, or a rotenone spray can be used but only after dusk when bees have stopped working.

Other hornets, such as the North American species, are useful predators on certain flies and caterpillars. See also WASPS.

HORNWORM. These large green caterpillars, of the Sphingidae, with a horn on their heads are either tomato hornworms (*Protoparce quinquemaculata* or *Manduca quinquemaculata*) or tobacco hornworms (*M. sexta*). They also infest eggplants, peppers, and potatoes, as well as other plants of the Solanaceae (Nightshade Family). Sometimes both kinds of larvae can be found feeding on the same plant. The 3–4 in. long hornworms can be distinguished by their white stripes; the tomato hornworm's stripes are V-shaped; the tobacco hornworm's stripes are diagonal. The end horn on both is black and almost straight.

Hornworm

The 2 in. long, dark brown, spindle-shaped pupae hibernate in the soil, with the moths emerging in the spring. The moths, which are 4 in. long and gray with yellow or white markings, lay greenish yellow eggs on the undersides of leaves. The eggs hatch in a week, and the larvae feed and grow for three or four weeks. They are easy to see and pick off at this stage. When fully grown, they enter the soil about 3 in. deep and pupate. One generation per year is produced in the North, with two or three in the South. Control by *Bacillus thuringiensis* is very effective, especially in early stages of the larval growth. Trichogramma wasps and rotenone can also be tried. Timed plantings also help. Consult your local extension service for the correct dates. Never kill hornworms that have growing white larvae sticking out of their bodies. These are the result of the parasitic brachonid wasp, which lays her eggs on the hornworms and thus produces many more beneficial parasites.

HORNWORT. A common name for *Ceratophyllum demersum*, a useful aquarium plant; see CERATOPHYLLUM.

HORSEBRIER. Common name for *Smilax rotundifolia*, a vicious climbing weed found from the Carolinas to Texas; see SMILAX.

HORSE-CHESTNUT. Common name for AESCULUS, a genus of hardy deciduous trees planted for their shade and showy flowers.

HORSERADISH. A large-leaved, hardy European perennial herb, *Armoracia rusticana*, which has become a weed in moist ground in cool parts of North America. It is cultivated for its white-fleshed, pungent roots which are grated and used as a flavoring.

The plant does well in practically all deep, moist but well-drained soils of moderate fertility. Since it produces no seed, small roots trimmed from the large ones after harvest are used to start new plantings in spring. They are cut about six inches long, square across the upper end, and slanting on the lower end so they will be planted "right end up," 10–15 in. apart in shallow furrows 30–36 in. apart, with the upper ends 4 in. below the surface.

The horseradish flea beetle feeds on this plant and watercress. The tiny insects are black with yellowish wing covers, and the larvae may burrow in the petioles, killing some of the leaves. Wood ashes sprinkled lightly on the plants repel the beetles. Garlic sprays are also effective.

HORSERADISH TREE. Common name for *Moringa pterygosperma*, a deciduous tree, planted in the tropics for ornament and for its edible parts; see MORINGA.

HORSETAIL. Common name for EQUISETUM, a genus of flowerless perennials allied to ferns and club-mosses.

HORTICULTURE. The cultivation of plants. The word comes from the Latin *hortus*, meaning "garden," but the term is usually taken to include ornamental and vegetable gardening, landscape planting, fruit growing, and related activities, both around the home and commercially as in orcharding or truck gardening. There is an increasing tendency, however, to popularly restrict the term to noncommercial activities.

HOSE. The familiar garden hose, made of flexible tubing of rubber or vinyl often reinforced with fabric, is one of the essential tools of a garden or greenhouse. As such it should be of good quality and handled with proper care.

Common hose sizes are ½ and ⅝ in. inside diameter. Thin, all-vinyl hoses are inexpensive and lightweight but often subject to twisting, kinking, and splitting. Heavier, reinforced hoses are worth the extra expense for most uses. Garden hose lengths begin at 25 or 50 ft., and the size increases in 25-ft. increments.

Porous garden hoses, plugged at one end and known as soaker hoses, are used along garden rows to provide even water distribution. All hoses are equipped with standard connections for attachment to taps and various nozzles or other equipment. There are many handy accessory connections to simplify the attachment of hose to faucet or to meet other watering needs. See SPRINKLING; WATERING.

HOST. An organism that harbors a parasite. Since a disease-producing organism is not always strictly parasitic (i.e., obtaining its food directly from the host plant), the term "suscept" has been introduced to indicate any living organism in which disease has been introduced by another organism. However, the older word "host" is still used loosely to cover all cases of one organism victimized by another.

HOSTA (HAH stah). A genus of perennial herbs with thick, fleshy, durable roots, belonging to the Liliaceae (Lily Family), formerly listed as *Funkia*, and commonly known as plantain lily. They have large, conspicuously ribbed leaves and blue or white, funnelform flowers in loose clusters.

Native to China and Japan, they are widely planted for their foliage effect. The clumps of large glossy leaves make excellent accents at corners of beds or in foundation planting, while a row along a driveway gives a definite finish to the edge of the lawn. They should be planted in rich soil, and many species grow well in the shade. Propagation is by division. Various species are hardy to Zone 3.

Hosta sp.

The reddish spore bodies of CROWN ROT fungus can form so thickly around the base of plantain lilies that they actually color the ground. Control by removing any diseased plant and the surrounding soil.

PRINCIPAL SPECIES

H. crispula grows about 3 ft. high and has pointed oval, white-margined leaves to 8 in. long. The funnelform lavender flowers are 2 in. long and are borne in loose, many-flowered racemes.

H. fortunei (fortune's plantain lily) has thick gray-green leaves with yellow veins. It blooms in summer, sending up 3-ft. stalks with light mauve blooms. Cv. 'Albomarginata' is more widely grown than the species, with thinner, paler foliage.

H. lancifolia (narrow-leaved plantain lily), formerly listed as *H. japonica*, grows to 2 ft. and has dark green leaves 5 in. long and dark violet flowers that fade with age.

H. plantaginea (fragrant plantain lily) has graceful sprays of fragrant flowers rising, late in summer, 2½ ft. above the large, heart-shaped, deeply ridged leaves, which are 10 in. long and 6 in. wide.

H. undulata has wavy-margined leaves splotched with creamy white.

H. ventricosa (blue plantain lily), formerly listed as *H. caerulea*, has deep green leaves 9 in. long and 5 in. wide, and blue flowers in long, loose racemes up to 3 ft. high.

HOTBED. A bottomless box with a more or less transparent removable top, used to grow plants out of local season. It differs from a COLDFRAME chiefly in that it is artificially heated so it can be used earlier (and later) and operated during more inclement weather. When its source of artificial heat ceases or is removed, a hotbed becomes a coldframe in effect and service.

In the past, hotbeds were heated exclusively by fermenting organic materials (especially fresh horse manure), by warm air flues, hot water or steam pipes, or by warm air from a heated house basement. These sources are still used where local conditions make them economical or otherwise desirable. Electricity has proved so convenient, adaptable, and satisfactory that both commercial and amateur gardeners are adopting it widely, adding BOTTOM HEAT with low voltage cables, plates, or grids.

The time to start a hotbed depends on the local conditions, kinds of plants being grown, growing time available, outdoor temperature to be overcome, and available heat. Hardy plants can be started long before tender ones and can also be set out in the open ground sooner. Generally speaking, hotbeds can be put into service six to eight weeks before the soil can be dug or plowed in the garden.

After sowing, water and ventilate carefully. Without enough water the young plants will be burned by the heat and dryness; without adequate fresh air (not cold drafts) they will grow weak.

Successful management of a hotbed depends mainly upon providing ample space between seedling plants, watering early in the day (never toward night), regulation of the temperature by ventilation (except where it is electrical and thermostatically controlled), and ventilating carefully, as much as is safe and increasingly as the season advances.

In severe cold weather, hotbeds and coldframes need the protection of mats held in place by wooden shutters, wires, or other devices. The old-fashioned, homemade straw mats have been largely replaced by manufactured kinds, such as fabric mats of quilted burlap, canvas, plastic (see SARAN CLOTH), or other waterproof material, obtainable at garden supply stores. Hotbeds, but more often coldframes, are also sometimes covered with lath or slat latticework frames so as to provide partial shade as the spring advances and the sun's rays become stronger.

See also COLDFRAME; VENTILATION.

HOT CAPS. Individual tent-shaped coverings of wax paper or plastic that, acting as miniature greenhouses, are used to protect tender young plants from excessive wind or cold.

Hot cap

HOTHOUSE. A glasshouse (greenhouse) that is kept artificially heated for the purpose of growing tender exotic or subtropical plants, or for the production of fruits, flowers, or vegetables outside of their normal season.

See also GREENHOUSE.

HOTTENTOT-FIG. A common name for *Carpobrotus edulis*, a fleshy-leaved perennial that has showy flowers and edible fruits; see CARPOBROTUS.

HOTTONIA (hah TOH nee ah). A genus of perennial aquatic herbs belonging to the Primulaceae (Primrose Family), commonly known as water-violet, including two species sometimes used in aquariums and hardy in Zones 3–8. *H. palustris*, the European species, is preferable to *H. inflata*, which is native to North America. The erect, submerged stems and creeping rootstocks of both species are practically leafless and not ornamental, but handsome spikes of pale violet flowers make up for this deficiency.

HOT WATER TREATMENT. A general term for different methods of disinfecting to destroy plant diseases or insect pests. They are used in the sterilization of soil, in treating seed, in treating flower bulbs for nematodes and bulb flies, and in the control of cyclamen mites.

For the treatment of seed, those with impermeable seed coats (quite common among the Fabaceae or Bean Family), the seed is placed in an appropriately sized container (not aluminum) and four to five times its volume of nearly boiling water (190°F or more) is poured over the seed. The seed is left in water to cool overnight (12–24 hours) and is then sown as usual. For prompt germination of seeds with impermeable seed coats they must be treated as above, scarified, or given some other treatment to open the seed coat to moisture and gaseous exchange so germination can occur. If not so treated, germination will be slow and sporadic over months or years.

HOUND'S-TONGUE. Common name for CYNOGLOSSUM, a genus of herbs sometimes grown for their small flowers.

HOUSEPLANTS. Plants grown in rooms of ordinary homes, rather than subjects requiring a greenhouse and expert care. One or a few single plants can be artfully placed, or a whole window space can be occupied. The plants can be hardy or tender, but they should be well adapted to withstand average house conditions—dry atmospheres, high or uneven temperatures, and inadequate light. The best places for houseplants are near windows in rooms that get the most sunshine. A saucer should be provided for each pot, and small pebbles, coarse sand, or sphagnum moss in the saucer are helpful in permitting excess water to seep from the pot instead of lying about the roots of the plant. Since the water evaporates from the saucer, it helps create the moist atmosphere that most plants need.

TYPES AND CULTURE

Bulbs. The bulbous plants are in a class by themselves. Generally they can be grown in sandy soils, in comparatively small pots, and allowed to make root growth in a dark cool location before being brought into the light and heat and encouraged to flower. Tulips, daffodils, and hyacinths grow best in soil, while paperwhite narcissus and Chinese sacred-lily can be grown in bowls of water containing only pebbles to support them. See BULBS.

Shrubby Plants. The shrubby class includes most of the climbing plants as well as those of an evergreen nature, most of which do not bloom until late winter or early spring, and the majority of which can be cultivated best in small pots. The aim with all such plants is to encourage summer growth so they will be well ripened before entering their resting period. These plants require lower temperatures and much less water and light until growth starts naturally, when they should be given more heat, light, and water.

Herbaceous Plants. The young and tender or softwood group, grown from cuttings or seed, require all possible light and considerably more water at all times, since they are actively growing. Rapidly growing flowering plants especially need abundant water, heat, and exposure to direct sunlight. Tropical plants, such as palms, ferns, dracaenas, pandanus, and foliage plants in general, normally are resting during the winter, prefer subdued light, and should receive water sparingly.

Soil and Potting. Soil for potted houseplants should be made up generally of one-half loamy garden soil, one-fourth well-rotted leaf mold or fine humus, and one-fourth sand. To each wheelbarrow load of such soil should be added one 4-in. potful of complete, high grade fertilizer, then the mass should be thoroughly mixed together and screened to get rid of stones and debris.

Comparatively small pots are needed at first. Do not overpot by placing small plants in large pots; when necessary (as indicated by a dense growth of roots) they can be shifted into larger

HOUSEPLANT CULTURE

LATIN NAME	COMMON NAME	LIGHT	MOISTURE
Aglaonema spp.	Chinese evergreen	low	moist
Araucaria heterophylla	Norfolk-Island-pine	high	moist
Asparagus spp.	asparagus-fern	medium	moist
Begonia spp.	begonia	medium	moist
Chlorophytum spp.	chlorophytum	medium	moist
Cissus discolor	trailing-begonia	medium	moist
Codiaeum variegatum var. *pictum*	croton	high	moist
Coleus hybridus	coleus	medium	wet
Cycas spp.	sago-palm	medium	moist
Dieffenbachia spp.	dumb cane	medium	moist
Dizygotheca elegantissima	false aralia	medium	moist
Dracaena spp.	dracaena	medium	moist
Ficus elastica	fig, rubber plant	high	dry
Gynura aurantiaca	velvet plant	medium	moist
Hedera helix	English ivy	low	moist
Howea spp.	kentia palm	low	moist
Maranta spp.	prayer plant	medium	moist
Monstera deliciosa	Mexican-breadfruit	low	moist
Nephrolepis exaltata cv. `Bostoniensis'	Boston fern	medium	wet
Peperomia spp.	peperomia	high	dry
Philodendron spp.	philodendron	low	moist
Spathiphyllum spp.	peace-lily	low	moist
Tolmiea menziesii	piggyback plant	medium	moist
Zebrina pendula	wandering-Jew	low	moist

High Light. Place plants within a few feet of a window that faces south or east. During summer you may have to move plants back a few feet, particularly close to Venetian blinds, or close shear curtains during the sunniest part of the day to prevent foliage burn. If plants are getting too much sun, the leaves closest to the window will fade, become flaccid, and may be scorched.

Medium Light. Plants will grow well in a window that faces north or west. A southern or eastern exposure where light intensity is reduced by buildings, curtains, or trees is also good for plants in this category.

Low Light. Plants can be placed several feet from the window for long periods of time. However, if they show light-deficiency symptoms, such as stretching toward the light source, faded leaf markings, or smaller than normal leaves, move them closer to a window.

Dry. Water thoroughly when the top half of the soil in the container feels totally dry to the touch.

Moist. Water thoroughly when the top inch of soil in the container feels totally dry to the touch.

Wet. Keep the soil evenly and constantly moist, but never soggy.

Adapted from *Keep Your Gift Plants Thriving*, by Karen and Jim Solit (Storey Communications, Inc., 1986), with permission from the publisher.

pots. On the other hand, do not attempt to underpot by crowding large roots into pots too small for them. In potting, do not fill a pot with soil; leave a ½-in. space between the soil and the rim for watering. Pot firmly by pressing down the soil with the thumbs while rotating the pot, until pulling a leaf from the plant will not dislodge it. Old pots should be thoroughly cleaned by scrubbing before reuse, and new clay pots should be soaked and allowed to absorb all the water they can hold, but they should not be wet during the actual operation of potting. Small stones or pieces of broken pot (potshards) must be placed over the hole in the bottom to permit drainage while preventing the soil from escaping. In pots 4 in. and larger, an inch of coarse material, such as gravel, potshards, cinders, or sifted ashes, should be placed in the bottom to assist drainage.

Holiday Plants. Christmas and Easter plants, poinsettia, cyclamen, primula, Jerusalem-cherry, even gardenia, and many lesser subjects can all be kept in bloom and sturdy for weeks if faded flowers, seedpods, and imperfect leaves are promptly removed and the plants are not given too sunny a position.

If it is desired, these holiday gift plants (while not really houseplants since they come from the hot, moist atmosphere of the greenhouse to very different conditions in the home) can be grown for flowering another season. After flowering is over, watering should be gradually withheld and the plant allowed to rest for a few weeks. They should never become bone dry at the roots, but should receive just sufficient water to keep them alive. Then, at the approach of warm weather, cut them back to a compact, symmetrical shape and plunge the pots to the rim in the garden in a semishaded location. As they grow, keep them pinched back to shape and in the fall, before frost, take them up and indoors. If conditions are not too difficult for them (dry air is the greatest problem), they will probably bloom again, though perhaps not as early and never as satisfactorily as the first time. Consequently it is usually desirably to raise or purchase young plants for flowering in the home.

All indoor plants require additional food during their active growing and flowering seasons. At three- or four-week intervals they can receive liquid food made of a good high-grade complete commercial fertilizer, which can be purchased in various forms and should be applied according to manufacturer's directions.

The accompanying chart gives culture advice for common foliage houseplants. See also HANGING BASKETS, POTTED PLANTS; WINDOW BOXES.

HOUSTONIA (hoo STOH nee ah). Former botanical name for HEDYOTIS, a genus of small perennial herbs with pale bluish or purple flowers.

HOVEA (HOH vee ah) **longifolia**. A small ornamental shrub from Australia, belonging to the Fabaceae (Bean Family). Plants are rarely cultivated, and then in a cool greenhouse or, sometimes, outdoors in warm regions (Zones 10–11). The flowers, mostly deep blue or purple, are small but freely produced in clusters. When grown in pots, the plants need frequent pinching when young to induce bushy growth. Their flowering season is early spring, and they resent being grown in unnecessarily large pots and being overwatered.

HOWEA (HOW ee ah). A genus of feather-leaved palms, formerly known as *Kentia*. They have gracefully arching, feathery, spineless leaves over 7 ft. long in mature specimens, and trunks ringed with scars of fallen leaves. The two species, *H. belmoreana* and *H. forsterana* are grown outdoors in frostproof regions of California but do not grow well in the climate of Florida. In the juvenile state, however, they are two of the most popular palms for indoor pot culture, tolerating dry conditions, dim light, and even considerable abuse remarkably well. In the greenhouse they start readily from seed sown in light soil and given bottom heat of 80°F. Pot the seedlings in rich soil, preferably of rotted sod without manure, and keep the air moist. After four months, give a night temperature of 60°F, monitoring carefully for SCALE INSECTS.

HOYA (HOY ah). A genus of mostly climbing, tropical evergreen shrubs belonging to the Asclepiadaceae (Milkweed Family). About 200 species are known and many are grown in greenhouses or window gardens. They have thick fleshy leaves and umbels of fragrant wavy-textured flowers. They are not difficult to grow in a mixture of fibrous loam and peat, with some charcoal. Good drainage is important, since they will not tolerate stagnating water at the roots. Keep them in the resting stage during winter but do not cut off the old flower stalks, since they produce flowers for several years.

PRINCIPAL SPECIES

H. bella is a small bushy grower that bears white flowers with crimson centers.

H. carnosa (wax plant), from Asia, is the best-known species. It is a twiner with rooting stems and grows to 8 ft. or more. The clustered flowers are whitish with a pink center.

H. imperialis is a very tall climber with reddish brown flowers to 3 in. across in drooping umbels.

HUCKLEBERRY. Common name for GAYLUSSACIA, a genus of fruit-bearing shrubs. The name is erroneously applied to *Vaccinium*, which is more commonly and appropriately known as blueberry. True huckleberries are easily distinguished by large, bony seeds in the fruit and resinous dots on the underside of the leaves. Although huckleberries can be eaten and grown like blueberries, their culture is not commonly attempted nor recommended. See GAYLUSSACIA; BLUEBERRY.

Garden-huckleberry is a popular name for *Solanum nigrum*. He-huckleberry is *Lyonia ligustrina*. Reflecting the confusion between true huckleberries and blueberries, hairy-huckleberry refers to *Vaccinium hirsutum*, and squaw-huckleberry is *V. stamineum*, which is correctly called deerberry.

HUDSONIA (hud SOH nee ah). A genus of hardy heathlike shrubs comprised of three species. They bear numerous bright yellow flowers but are short-lived and seldom cultivated. They are hardy to Zone 5 and propagated by seed.

PRINCIPAL SPECIES

H. ericoides, extending far to the west, grows in dry, sandy areas.

H. montana grows in the mountains of North Carolina.

H. tomentosa (beach heather) grows on sandy shores and dunes near the Atlantic coast from New Brunswick to North Carolina.

HUMATA (hyoo MAT ah). A genus of small, rhizomatous, epiphytic ferns similar in appearance and growth habit to *Davallia* and frequently mistaken for them. *D. griffithiana* is often listed in this genus. They are native from Madagascar to the Pacific Islands.

H. tyermannii (bear's-foot or silver-rabbit's-foot fern) is a readily available and popular basket fern from China. Its creeping rhizomes are covered with white scales that give them a silvery appearance. Tripinnate to quadripinnate-pinnatifid, dark green fronds grow 8–12 in. long.

HUMEA (HYOO mee ah). A genus of herbs or shrubby plants native to Australia and belonging to the Asteraceae (Aster Family). Only one species, *H. elegans*, is grown to any extent. The plants are of interest for summer flowering in the greenhouse or outdoors in Zones 10–11. The leaves are sweet scented, and the brownish red flowers are borne in terminal, loose-branched, drooping panicles.

HUMULUS (HYOO myoo lus). A genus of tall, vigorous vines with rough stems and leaves. Besides being important in brewing, they are of some ornamental value. Native in North America, Europe, and Asia, they are grown for ornament, and one species for its fruit, the hops used in brewing.

H. japonicus, a vigorous and fast-growing annual vine, has leaves more deeply cut than *H. lupulus*. It will make 10–20 ft. of growth in a season from seed sown in May.

H. lupulus (common or European hop) is an herbaceous perennial with fast-growing, twining stems, sometimes attaining 30 ft. in a season. It has become widely naturalized in North America and is a good screen plant for the summer, interesting with its clusters of papery, pale yellow hops, which have a distinct heavy odor.

HUMUS. This is the organic or nonmineral material that makes up a large part of any fertile productive soil that is in good condition. It consists of the more or less decomposed remains of vegetable and animal matter—that is, plants themselves, dead animals from microscopic organisms right on up, and all kinds of manures.

Humus can accumulate in a soil naturally, as leaf mold in an undisturbed forest, dead grasses in a meadow or pasture, or peat formed by dead water plants accumulating at the bottom of ponds and bogs. It can be formed during decomposition of organic materials, or added to and incorporated in the soil in the form of manure, granulated peat moss, compost, green manure crops turned under to rot, or many other substances. While this variety of sources and the fact that it is constantly undergoing change makes it impossible to give any definite description of humus, its general character is that of a black or brown, loose, porous, absorbent substance such as can be scraped up from the forest floor where no fires or human interference have prevented natural decay.

HUNNEMANNIA (hun em MAN ee ah) **fumariifolia.** A Mexican perennial herb, the only member of the genus, belonging to the Papaveraceae (Poppy Family), and commonly known as golden-cup, Mexican tulip poppy, or bush-eschsolzia since it resembles a tall, bushy California poppy. In the United States, it is grown as a half-hardy annual, because plants from spring-sown seed will flower in late summer of the first season, continuing until cool weather. The yellow tulip-shaped flowers, 3 in. across, are borne on upright plants to 2 ft. tall. Catalogs often list cv. 'Sunlite', which grows to 24 in. and produces double, 2–3 in. blooms. They need full sun but thrive in ordinary garden soil, withstand drought well, and often survive conditions that are fatal to many

other plants. *Hunnemannia* is good for the border and for cut flowers, which will last more than a week indoors if gathered before they are fully open. Plants frequently self-seed.

HUTCHINSIA (hu CHIN see ah). A genus of small hardy herbs belonging to the Brassicaceae (Mustard Family), resembling DRABA. They have entire or cut leaves and small, white flower clusters.

H. alpina is a minute, tufted perennial suitable for the alpine or rock garden, where its flowers appear during the spring and summer. It should be grown in a moist, semishaded position and can be increased by seed or by cuttings.

HYACINTH. Correctly applied, this is the common name for HYACINTHUS, a small genus of flowering bulbous plants, including the popular Dutch hyacinths.

The name is also applied to a number of other plants. Grape-hyacinth is the genus MUSCARI. Giant summer-hyacinth, or summer-flowering-hyacinth is GALTONIA. Hyacinth bean is the flowering perennial vine *Dolichos lablab*; see DOLICHOS. Water-hyacinth is *Eichhornia crassipes*; see EICHHORNIA. Wild-hyacinth refers to several plants, including *Camassia scilloides*; see CAMASSIA. Star-hyacinth and starry-hyacinth are *Scilla amoena* and *S. autumnalis*; see SCILLA. Wood-hyacinth refers to species of ENDYMION.

HYACINTHUS (hī uh SIN thus). A small genus of true bulbous plants, commonly known as hyacinth. The chief species is *H. orientalis*, a native of Asia Minor, from which most of the present-day hyacinths for outdoor and indoor use have descended. With the massive trusses of perfectly shaped flowers, in white, occasionally yellow, and many tones of red, purple, and blue, hyacinths provide a distinctive type of sturdy, formal beauty in the early spring garden. As houseplants, they are easy to force in late winter and early spring, when their bright colors are truly welcome, notwithstanding the sweet, at times almost overpowering fragrance.

Hyacinth bulbs (except the Roman type) are

produced almost exclusively in Holland, where favorable soil and climatic conditions, plus generations of experience, combine to give splendid results. For commercial use, hyacinth bulbs do not naturally propagate fast enough, so growers employ an artificial method of propagation that involves a hollowing out of the bulbs to stimulate the formation of bulblets. This work requires expert knowledge and special treatment, so it is not an easy activity for the amateur.

Hyacinthus orientalis

Hyacinth bulbs are offered in catalogs in various sizes. The size of a forced flower truss is almost entirely determined by the measurement of the bulb; a medium-sized bulb is considered best for general garden use.

DUTCH HYACINTHS

Garden Culture. Fresh bulbs of medium size of the so-called Dutch hyacinths, the kind universally grown in gardens, are essential for good effects. They are available from September through the fall months and should be planted as early as possible to permit root development before the ground gets cold. Prepare the soil by spading and enriching; then plant the bulbs 4 in. deep and 6 in. apart for the larger sizes, and correspondingly closer for the smaller ones.

In the spring, trusses can be picked for use as cut flowers without damage to the bulb, but the foliage must be allowed to remain and die down naturally. Nothing is to be gained by digging and replanting the bulbs unless they are being crowded out by other garden subjects. Each year there will likely be a diminishing of the size of the bloom, however; and since there is nothing that can be done to materially alter the condition, the continued production of large, full flower trusses year after year will ordinarily require constant

renewing of bulbs. For names of the best and most popular varieties in each color, consult the current catalogs of bulb dealers who keep up with the production of new and improved kinds.

Indoor Culture. Hyacinth bulbs planted singly in 5-in. pots in September can be forced into bloom by Christmas. Single bulbs can also be flowered with fair satisfaction in the familiar hyacinth glasses or vases. In using pots, place broken crockery for drainage in the bottom of each pot. Fill loosely with a rich mixture of leaf mold, loam, and sand; then press each bulb firmly into the pot until the crown is at soil level. Next, bury the pots 8–10 in. deep in the ground or in a coldframe. In two months or less, when the roots are developed and a pale sprout shows well above the bulb, bring the pots indoors, but keep them in a cool, dark corner until the sprouts turn green. Thereafter, good window light (but not extreme heat) and frequent watering will bring the flowers into bloom.

Liquid manure applied from the time the buds appear will improve the flowers. If a flower shoot begins to show buds while very short, it can be drawn up to give a larger truss by placing an inverted flower pot or a cone of paper over it for a week or so. Pots brought in from outdoor storage at intervals will provide successive crops of flowers until spring.

ROMAN HYACINTHS

Another small class of tender hyacinths is known as the Roman, or French Roman, type. Produced commercially in southern France and Italy, these bulbs are used outdoors in the United States only in the extreme south. They are distinguished from the Dutch type of northern gardens in that they produce several graceful, loose-flowering spikes from one bulb instead of the usual compact, single spike. The best of them are white.

For indoor growing, the bulbs can be planted from late summer through the early fall months in bowls of peat moss and kept in a cool, dark place until they are well rooted and the tops show a growth of an inch or two. Transferred then to a light window, they will ordinarily bloom about Christmas. If desired, several bulbs can be planted in a pot, following the same steps recommended for Dutch hyacinths.

ENEMIES

Hyacinth yellows was one of the first diseases of plants known to be caused by bacteria. Water-soaked stripes in the foliage followed by yellowing and withering of leaves and flower stalks, and a yellow, soggy rot of the bulbs are the chief symptoms. Each infected bulb, together with the surrounding soil, should be carefully removed. Another bacterial disease causes the bulbs to become a sticky, white, slimy mass soon after they are dug. Burn all such bulbs.

A sclerotina rot causes yellow blotches on the leaves and small, raised, dark spore bodies (sclerotia) on the outer bulb scales. Sterilize the soil to kill the sclerotia, and ventilate the bulbs well during storage. See also BULBS; SCLEROTINA ROT.

HYBRID. Offspring of two parents that differ genetically, that is, are dissimilar in one or more characteristics. Thus a hybrid is the result of cross-fertilization; a cross. See PLANT BREEDING.

HYBRIDIZATION. The mating or crossing of two dissimilar plants with the intention of creating a new and different progeny. See PLANT BREEDING.

HYBRID MUSK ROSE. Some of the early hybrid musk roses were raised by Peter Lambert in Germany during the early twentieth century. About twenty years later, the Rev. J. H. Pemberton in England developed a great many more varieties. They are a very mixed group, and the influence of the musk rose is remote; the major characteristics of the class are strongly multiflora, but the hybrid musk name is generally accepted.

Hybrid musk roses are strong growing and repeat blooming in small clusters. Many are few-petaled, but some are quite double. Most are delicate shades of various colors that fade to near white, but there are some bright colors. A few bloom in large clusters of many small flowers. In general they resemble larger FLORIBUNDA roses.

Most, but not all, are strongly fragrant, and some have the musk fragrance reminiscent of sweet peas. Some hybrid musk roses are 'Penelope', 'Vanity', 'Robin Hood', and 'Belinda'.

HYBRID PERPETUAL ROSE. This class, developed from crosses between Bourbon roses and the China and tea roses, were the main garden roses from about 1840 to 1880. In the latter part of the nineteenth century they were crossed again with tea roses, forming the modern hybrid tea class.

Hybrid perpetual roses are not really perpetual blooming, but rather give some repeat bloom, mostly in the fall. In France they were called hybrid "remontant," which gives a better picture of their blooming habit. They can be divided into three groups: the earliest hybrid perpetuals, like 'Baronne Prevost', introduced in 1842, had very much the "old rose" form; the middle group, like 'Victor Verdier', raised in 1859, had very full, globular form; and the later group, such as 'American Beauty', named 'Mme. Ferdinand Jamain' in France, 1875, was very close to the modern hybrid tea in form. Hybrid perpetuals resemble long, leggy hybrid teas. Many of them have much larger, more double blooms in shades of white, pink, and red, some of the whites having a pale yellow cast, and some of the reds age to purple shades.

Some of the famous hybrid perpetuals are 'La Reine' (1842), 'General Jacqueminot', also known as General Jack or the Jack Rose (1853), 'Fisher Holmes' (1865), and 'Frau Karl Druschki' (1901).

HYBRID RUGOSA ROSE. The rugosa hybrids vary widely, whereas the species rugosa rose and its color sports are dense, neatly rounded shrubs with deep mint-green, deeply engraved (rugose) foliage. They have repeat-blooming, fragrant, informal flowers and decorative hips like small cherry tomatoes. Some of the hybrids are close to the species, but others are different in almost every way. The species rugosas fit into the old garden rose category, and all the rugosa hybrids are modern shrub roses; see ROSE.

Some hybrid rugosas repeat bloom and others do not; some have rugose foliage and some do not; some produce decorative hips while others do not. The species rugosas and most hybrids are all very thorny.

Much work has been done with hybrid rugosas in the attempt to bring the good garden qualities and hardiness of the species into the modern rose gene pool, and much progress has been made in the modern shrub rose category. So far, however, it has not proved possible to bring the good qualities so sought after into the more formal hybrid tea and floribunda classes.

Some well-known hybrid rugosas are 'Hansa', 'Thérèse Bugnet', 'Blanc Double de Coubert', and 'Henry Hudson'.

HYBRID TEA ROSE.

Often considered the ultimate development in form and beauty, the hybrid tea rose is high centered, with its petals unfurling evenly, maintaining a symmetrical outline. Flowers bloom in shades of white, pink, combined pink and yellow shades, red, combined yellow and red shades, mauve, and unusual russet shades of pink and yellow. So far no true shades of blue or brown (pansy color) have been developed.

The hybrid tea rose was developed in the late nineteenth to early twentieth century from crosses between tea roses and the hybrid perpetuals that were the main garden roses of the mid- and late 1800s. In the early years of the twentieth century, Joseph Pernet-Ducher of France bred 'Soleil d'Or' from 'Persian Yellow', the double form of *R. foetida*, and 'Antoine Ducher', a hybrid perpetual. This was the basis for the Pernetiana roses, which merged into the hybrid teas, giving them the potential for bright, pure yellow as well as brilliant orange-red.

In 1867, 'La France' was sent out by Guillot Fils, of France, and it later was declared to be the first hybrid tea of superlative distinction.

The most famous hybrid tea is 'Peace', introduced in 1945. It was bred by Francis Meilland of France and is also known in France as 'Mme. A. Meilland', as 'Gloria Dei' in Germany, and as

'Gioia' in Italy. Other famous hybrid teas include 'Lady Mary Fitzwilliam' (1882), 'Mme. Caroline Testout' (1890), 'Ophelia' (1912), 'Mrs. Sam McGredy' (1929), and 'Crimson Glory' (1935).

Popular hybrid teas are 'Bewitched', 'Chrysler Imperial', 'Color Magic', 'Dainty Bess' (a single, five-petaled rose), 'Fragrant Cloud', 'Garden Party', 'King's Ransom', 'Miss All-American Beauty' (known as 'Maria Callas' in Europe), 'Pascali', 'Tiffany', and 'Tropicana'.

HYDRANGEA

(hī DRAN jee ah). A genus of deciduous shrubs native in Asia and North and South America, belonging to the Saxifragaceae (Saxifrage Family). They are valued for their large clusters of showy white, pink, or blue flowers, which are long lasting, often with enlarged, sterile, marginal flowers; in some cases all the flowers are sterile.

CULTURE AND SELECTION

Hydrangeas thrive best in a rich, moist soil and flower freely in an open location, but they will grow under varying conditions. Rather severe pruning should be practiced and the weak growth thinned to encourage strong shoots for good flower heads.

Several species are hardy to Zone 4, but some are not. In the tender group is **H. macrophylla**, a fine plant for seaside gardens in mild climates. It is sometimes preserved outdoors in colder regions by tying up the branches in late fall and banking up the soil around it. It is also a good plant for forcing under glass and is largely grown for the Easter trade. Numerous cultivars have been developed.

Hydrangea macrophylla

Blue hydrangeas are very popular, and sometimes a seeming miracle occurs when plants propagated from the blue variety produce pink flowers. This is due to a change in soil acidity; blue flowers are produced in an acid soil. Hence, growers of potted plants often add iron or aluminum sulfate to the soil. Outdoors, a sandy soil and addition of peat moss, leaf mold, or any other acid-creating material will aid in keeping blue varieties blue.

Most kinds of hydrangea are readily propagated by cuttings of half-matured shoots under glass, also by hardwood cuttings, layers, suckers, or divisions. Good plants can be grown in one year from cuttings. The young plants can be plunged outdoors in pots for the summer or planted out in a sunny place to be lifted and potted in the fall.

PRINCIPAL NORTH AMERICAN SPECIES

H. arborescens is an upright shade-loving shrub that grows to 10 ft. and has rounded clusters of white flowers, only a few of which are sterile. Cv. 'Grandiflora' (hills-of-snow) is more generally planted for its large, profuse clusters of white, all sterile flowers, which bloom early and turn greenish in late summer. Best results are obtained by cutting the shoots to the ground each spring. Hardy in Zones 4–9.

H. quercifolia (oakleaf hydrangea), a southern species but hardy to Zone 5, is a distinguished shrub that grows to 6 ft. and has large lobed leaves that turn wine color in the fall. The long panicles of flowers, many of them sterile, open in early summer and turn reddish purple in the fall.

PRINCIPAL ASIATIC SPECIES

H. anomala is a high climber to 50 ft., clinging firmly to walls and tree trunks by aerial rootlets. Without support, it is a straggling, prostrate bush. It is very slow to get established but has good clean foliage and is conspicuous in early summer with large white flower clusters bearing only a few sterile blossoms. Hardy in Zones 5–7.

H. aspera var. *sargentiana* is a striking shrub with hairy stems, purplish young growth, and large leaves. The large, flat clusters of bluish violet, fertile flowers surrounded by sterile white flowers, are very showy. It can be grown outdoors only in mild regions and prefers partial shade.

H. heteromalla, formerly listed as *H. xanthoneura*, is somewhat similar to *H. macrophylla* but has larger leaves and a more vigorous growth habit. It has loose, convex clusters of white flowers with large, sterile flowers. Var. *wilsonii* is a good form with narrower and glossy leaves.

H. macrophylla (bigleaf hydrangea) grows to 12 ft. in favored climates and has broad, handsome, thick, shining leaves. It occurs in forms with blue, pink, or white flowers borne in flat or rounded clusters. Many cultivars are grown, some with very large clusters of all sterile flowers of varying shades. Hardy in Zones 7–9.

H. paniculata, one of the hardiest, can assume the size and form of a small tree. It has long panicles of white flowers with few sterile blossoms and is a handsome, late flowering shrub. Cv. 'Grandiflora' (peegee hydrangea) has very large panicles of almost all sterile flowers. It has been planted everywhere, especially in New England where it thrives; hardy in Zones 4–8.

HYDRASTIS (hī DRAS tis) **canadensis.** A low perennial herb belonging to the Ranunculaceae (Buttercup Family) and commonly known as orange-root or goldenseal. It grows nearly 12 in. tall and has thick yellow rootstocks, broad basal leaves, and inconspicuous greenish white flowers without petals, followed by beautiful crimson, raspberrylike fruits. When commercial plantings of goldenseal are made for its medicinal roots, the beds are covered with laths to give the required shade. Occasionally cultivated in gardens for the beauty of its leaves and fruits, it should be planted in rich, moist soil in a partially shaded position and liberally mulched with humus. Plants are hardy in Zones 2–8 and are propagated by seed or division.

HYDRIASTELE (hī dree ah STEE lee) **wendlandiana.** A feather palm from Australia, frequently planted in south Florida, where it becomes a small tree with graceful, arching, spineless leaves and large bunches of fruit at the top of the trunk. In the greenhouse it requires abundant water and a temperature of about 65°F. It responds well to fertilizers, especially when kept pot-bound. It also makes an excellent, easily handled houseplant. This botanical name is sometimes incorrectly applied to *Ptychosperma elegans*, a similar tropical tree.

HYDROPHYLLUM (hī droh FIL um). A genus of

six or more hardy North American plants, mostly perennial, useful in the wild garden or in rich, shaded locations, and commonly known as waterleaf.

   H. canadense is one of the perennial species good for planting around shrubbery, where they colonize, take care of themselves, and form a very attractive foliage mass. It grows to about 2½ ft., and its lobed, palm-shaped leaves are 12 in. across. Clusters of small, greenish white or violet flowers appear in early summer.

HYDROPONICS. A term coined for the grow-

ing of plants in artificial nutrient solutions without the need for soil. The key aspects of growing plants under hydroponic, or soilless, culture include the characteristics of the nutrient solution used to water and feed the plant; the medium or method used to support the plant; and the method of applying the solution to the plants. A variety of media are used to grow plants hydroponically: sand, gravel, perlite, vermiculite, combinations of these materials, or no media at all—the plant roots in water.

   See also NUTRIENT SOLUTION; SOILLESS CULTURE.

HYLOCEREUS (hī loh SEER ee us) undatus. The

best-known species of a prized genus of cultivated cacti, commonly known as night-blooming cereus or Honolulu-queen. It is grown all over the world but is most renowned in Hawaii, where hedges of it bear thousands of blossoms at once, scenting the surrounding air. It sends forth many aerial roots and grows readily from cuttings. In colder climates it should be treated like other species of tropical origin and grown in a lathhouse or greenhouse as conditions warrant. For soil requirements and culture, see CACTUS.

HYMENOCALLIS (hī men oh KAL is). A genus of

summer-blooming bulbs of the Amaryllidaceae (Amaryllis Family), commonly called spider-lily. Their leaves are narrow or strap-shaped, and their strange white flowers appear in flattened clusters at the top of long, rather stout, naked stems. Some species are grown in the greenhouse for winter bloom; others are grown in the garden for summer bloom and the bulbs lifted after flowering and stored over winter. They are propagated by offsets.

PRINCIPAL SPECIES

   H. caribaea, with long, narrow, shining leaves and fragrant white flowers with very narrow petals, blooms in winter under glass.

   H. caroliniana (formerly listed as *H. occidentalis*) and *H. rotata* are spring-flowering species, charming when naturalized in wild gardens of their native southern states.

   H. narcissiflora (basketflower, Peruvian-daffodil), formerly listed as *H. calathina*, is a summer-blooming plant from South America. It has white flowers with a funnel-shaped fringed crown, striped with green, and long, threadlike stamens. Some catalogs and gardeners still call it by its former generic name, *Ismene*.

HYMENOPHYLLUM (hī men oh FIL um). One of

the genera collectively known and cultivated as FILMY FERNS because of the transparent quality of their fronds.

HYMENOXYS (hī men

AHK sis) **grandiflora.** A hardy perennial wildflower resembling sunflowers, belonging to the Asteraceae (Aster Family), and commonly known as old-man-of-the-mountain or alpine-sunflower. It forms mats of feathery leaves 3–4 in. long and covered with cottony white hairs. Stems up to 12 in. tall bear 3–4 in. heads with about 30 bright

H. grandiflora

yellow ray flowers surrounding a domed cluster of small, densely packed disk flowers. The flower heads are surrounded by many woolly bracts.

Native above timberline in the Rocky Mountains, old-man-of-the-mountain requires conditions that replicate the alpine tundra and high meadows. Ideal in rock gardens in Zone 4 and colder, it thrives in full sunlight and moist well-drained soil rich in gravel and limestone. Propagation is by seed collected in late summer when fruits are ripe. These should be planted ¼ in. deep in their permanent location or in flats of coarse soil left outdoors for the winter. Transplant seedlings as soon as they are sturdy and several inches high to avoid hindering the taproot.

HYPERICUM (hī PUR ik um). A large genus of perennial herbs and shrubs, commonly known as St.-John's-wort. Some are weedy, but most species are decorative, usually having bright yellow flowers with profuse stamens and often evergreen foliage. They are grown in rock gardens or borders, and the species that sucker readily are used for ground covers in the landscape.

Hypericum calycinum

They grow easily in loamy or sandy soil, and their blooming period is prolonged if they are given a semishaded position. The more tender species should be placed in the rock garden where they can have winter protection. St.-John's-worts grow readily from seed, but the creeping species are also propagated by division and suckers. Most are hardy in Zones 4–9.

PRINCIPAL SPECIES

H. ascyron is a perennial that grows 2–6 ft. tall and has golden flowers 2 in. across and oblong leaves 5 in. long. Hardy to Zone 3.

H. calycinum (Aaron's-beard, rose-of-Sharon) is a low shrub with evergreen foliage and beautiful, large, golden flowers. Spreading by suckers, it is suitable for ground cover and hardy if given winter protection.

H. frondosum, formerly listed as *H. aureum*, is a deciduous shrub that grows to 3 ft. and has bluish green foliage and flowers nearly 2 in. across. Hardy to Zone 5.

H. kalmianum is a low, hardy shrub with evergreen leaves and yellow flowers 1 in. across in flat-topped clusters.

H. x *moseranum* (goldflower), a hybrid between *H. calycinum* and *H. patulum*, is an attractive shrub that grows to 2 ft. with drooping branches and loose clusters of yellow flowers to 2½ in. It is most attractive massed in the border or grown as a potted plant. Hardy to Zone 7.

H. patulum is a shrub that grows to 3 ft. and has large solitary or clustered flowers in midsummer. Hardy to Zone 7. Cv. 'Henryi' is a more vigorous form with larger flowers and needs winter protection.

H. prolificum is a fairly large shrub with small flowers in flat-topped clusters and narrow, evergreen leaves.

HYPOESTES (hī poh EST eez). A genus of herbs commonly known as freckleface because of the small green leaves heavily splashed with pink spots. They have long been enjoyed as an indoor novelty plant or as garden subjects in Zones 10–11. New varieties with very bright pink, red, or white coloring have been developed in Europe, and the plants are now grown on a larger scale. Culture is simple in any good potting soil, and propagation by cuttings is fast and sure.

HYSSOPUS (his OHP us) **officinalis.** A hardy European perennial herb or subshrub commonly known as hyssop, grown as a culinary and medicinal herb and as an ornamental. It is readily propagated by cuttings and division, or by seed sown in early spring, either in drills 18 in. apart and the plants thinned to 12 in. or in seed beds, the seedlings to be transplanted in early summer. Hardy to Zone 4, light and limey soils suit it best.

I

IBERIS (ī BEE ris). A genus of small to medium-sized herbs, belonging to the Brassicaceae (Mustard Family), and commonly known as candytuft. The botanical name is derived from "Iberia," the former name for Spain, where they are native. Some are half-hardy annuals and others, evergreen perennials; both types are low growing, thrive in any ordinary garden soil, and require little special care. Originally flowering in white, the

Iberis sempervirens

genus has lent itself well to hybridization and now comes in many pastel tints.

Seeds of the annual kinds should be sown outdoors, because the plants are difficult to move. If started early in the spring, the plants will bloom within two months, since germination and growth are rapid. Keep the soil loose around the plants, and to produce large flowers, thin out the buds. Used in the rock garden or as an edging plant, the annual varieties (some of which are fragrant) will bloom throughout the season if not allowed to go to seed. Successive sowings are advised for best results.

The perennial candytuft is a compact plant, somewhat woody at the base. White flowers bloom only in the spring and become lilac with age. Seeds can be sown in the fall for next season's early bloom. Propagation can also be done by dividing the roots. Among the perennials, hardiness varies, some thriving to Zone 3.

PRINCIPAL SPECIES

I. amara (rocket candytuft) is a small, hairy annual with large, white, fragrant flowers.

I. gibraltarica (Gibraltar candytuft) is an ever-

green perennial with light purple or lilac flowers in flat clusters.

I. pinnata is a closely branching annual growing to 16 in. Flowers are white with a lilac tinge and are often slightly fragrant.

I. sayana is a compact, dainty form suitable for a trough or small rock garden.

I. sempervirens (edging candytuft), the most commonly grown species, is an evergreen with flowers in racemelike heads. It is frequently used at the edge of perennial beds, forming neat mounds of foliage covered with white blossoms. Several cultivars are available. Var. *correifolia* has close clusters of white flowers.

I. umbellata (globe candytuft), the common garden annual, grows to 16 in. and branches freely. Numerous cultivars have flowers of pink, violet, purple, red, or carmine.

ICEPLANT. Certain succulent, ground-covering members of the Aizoaceae (Carpetweed Family). Commonly applied to *Carpobrotus edulis*, a fleshy leaved perennial with showy flowers and edible fruits; see CARPOBROTUS.

The name is even more appropriately applied to *Mesembryanthemum crystallinum* (sometimes listed as *Cryophytum crystallinum*), an annual, mat-forming mesemb with icy looking papillae; see MESEMBRYANTHEMUM.

ILEX (ī leks). A genus of evergreen and deciduous glossy-leaved trees and shrubs noted for their brilliant red berries and commonly known as holly. The hollies are of great ornamental value in the garden as small specimen trees, hedges, and in the shrubbery border.

All hollies grow best in rich, rather moist soil; though they are slow growing, the evergreen species make remarkably fine hedges. Propagation is from seed, which should be stratified, since they do not germinate until the second year. Most species are propagated by cuttings of ripened wood, and some cultivars are grafted.

Hollies should be moved in spring before growth starts, or in the fall. Many of the species are dioecious, that is, they have the pistillate or berry-forming flowers on one plant and the staminate flowers on another. Since much of the charm of the plants is in the berries, care should be taken to plant (especially in the case of deciduous species) mostly pistillate specimens, with a few staminate ones to ensure pollination of the others.

Ilex sp.

The chief insect pest of holly is a leaf miner, which produces winding, yellowish brown mines in the green leaves. The young maggots, hatching from eggs laid on the underside of the leaves, work in the new foliage throughout the season and winter there. Control by picking and burning infested leaves and spraying with an insecticidal soap solution during late spring and early summer.

PRINCIPAL SPECIES

I. aquifolium (English holly) is exceptionally beautiful, since it bears large, dense clusters of berries, but it is not as hardy as the native kinds. It is native to Europe, North Africa, and western Asia. An occasional specimen will survive even southern New York winters in sheltered locations, but the species does best in the moister, more equable climate of western Washington and Oregon, where it is grown commercially for Christmas greens. The best cultivar is 'Albomarginata', with bright red berries and silvery white leaf margins. There are many other cultivars occasionally grown in gardens. Hardy in Zones 6–9.

I. cassine (dahoon) is an evergreen species with small yellow fruits, native in swampy areas from Virginia southward.

I. cornuta (Chinese holly), native to China, is a large, rounded shrub that grows to 10 ft. and has very shiny, showy foliage. The most popular cultivar is 'Burfordii', with glossy, convex leaves and abundant orange-red fruit. This unusual cul-

tivar produces its fruit parthenocarpically (without fertilization), so male and female plants are not needed for pollination. Hardy in Zones 7–9 (6 in sheltered locations).

I. crenata (Japanese holly) is an exceedingly fine evergreen for general use in the garden, making a good background or formal specimen shrub. It is native to Japan and is hardy in Zones 5–8. Many outstanding cultivars are grown. Cv. 'Convexa' is very hardy, compact, and somewhat spreading; it grows to 8 ft. and has shiny, convex leaves. 'Helleri' is a dwarf with horizontal branches that grow to about 3 ft.; it does well in warm regions but is tender in the North. 'Green Dragon' and 'Dwarf Pagoda' are both very dwarf plants with tiny, shiny leaves, excellent for bonsai and rock garden culture. 'Hetzii' is a more compact selection of 'Convexa', but it is not quite as hardy.

I. decidua (possum-haw), a southern native, is a deciduous shrub or tree with orange or red berries, found in swampy environments.

I. glabra (inkberry, winterberry) is a hardy evergreen species native from Massachusetts to Mississippi. Although the black fruit lacks the showy effect of the red-berried species, the excellent smooth, dark foliage is effective in shady northern corners; it thrives in wet areas and acid soil. Cv. 'Compacta' is a dense-growing dwarf plant. Hardy in Zones 5–9.

I. laevigata (smooth winterberry) should be used more extensively for the winter beauty of its clustered scarlet berries on bare stems. In the wild garden, it should be massed in swampy areas but will also grow in the border. Hardy in Zones 4–9.

I. x meserveae (Meserve holly) is an exciting group of new hybrids developed by Kathleen Meserve. They are hardy, compact, vigorous-growing plants that have blue-green foliage and abundant fruit. Outstanding clones are 'Blue Angel', 'Blue Maid', 'Blue Prince', 'Blue Princess', 'Blue Stallion', and 'Golden Girl' (with yellow berries). Hardy in Zones 5–9.

I. opaca is one of the most handsome of our native shrubs, found from Massachusetts to

Florida and Texas. This species, among others, has been extensively used for Christmas greens. Due to excessive collection, wild specimens are now protected by law in several states. With its spiny evergreen foliage and brilliant red berries, a well-grown specimen makes a decorative contrast when planted in front of coniferous evergreens. Over 1000 cultivars have been found or developed. Hardy in Zones 5–9.

I. paraguariensis (Paraguay-tea, yerba-de-maté) is a tropical evergreen tree cultivated in its native South America, where the leaves are an important source of tea. Hardy in Zones 10–11.

I. pendunculosa (longstalk holly) is native to China and Japan. It has entire leaves and red berries on 1 in. long stems. Hardy in Zones 5–8.

I. verticillata (black-alder, winterberry) is a deciduous species similar to *I. laevigata*. It supplies the berried twigs that florists use to brighten up holiday wreaths. It is especially good for border plantings if given sufficient moisture and acid soil. Hardy in Zones 4–9. There are a number of outstanding cultivars. Cv. 'Sparkleberry' has abundant, bright red fruits. 'Winter Red' is a heavy-fruiting bushy plant that grows to 8 ft. and has bright red berries. 'Apollo' is a male selection to be planted with 'Sparkleberry' for good fruit set. 'Christmas Cheer' is free-fruiting with red fruit and upright shape.

I. vomitoria (yaupon, cassena) is an evergreen shrub or small tree that grows to 25 ft. and has scarlet berries. Native from Virginia to Florida and Texas, it was once used in medicine by the Indians. Hardy to Zone 7.

IMMORTELLE. A common name, from the French word meaning "everlasting," for many flowering annuals that are dried for winter bouquets, especially applied to species of XERANTHEMUM and HELICHRYSUM.

IMMUNIZATION. The art of rendering a crop 100% resistant to attacks by specific organisms or pests generally established in an area. Natural immunity can be developed by selection and propagation of individuals that show marked resistance, or by crossing plants that are desirable but susceptible to a given trouble with less desirable but more resistant forms. Numerous attempts at artificial inoculations have been made on plants, but so far no success has been attained.

IMPATIENS (im PAY shens). An interesting genus of annual greenhouse, border, and wildflower garden plants, belonging to the Balsaminaceae (Balsam Family). They differ so in form and habit that their relationship is only revealed by the spur formed by one of the three sepals and by the ripe pods, which, if touched, quickly curl and expel the seeds. This latter characteristic is responsible for its common names, touch-me-not and snapweed. Most thrive under moist, shady conditions, but newer strains, known as New Guinea impatiens, tolerate full sun.

Impatiens capensis

PRINCIPAL SPECIES

I. balsamina (garden balsam), native to tropical and subtropical regions, is often grown in the border, with double, roselike blooms in white, lavender, lemon yellow, and many shades of red crowded close to leafy spikes 12–18 in. tall. Improved hybrids with fuller flowers of peach-blossom pink have also been introduced. Though a tender subject, plants set out in early summer from seed sown indoors in spring will continue blooming through the autumn after most other annuals are gone. They require ample moisture, some shade, and plenty of room. Several transplantings, leaving them finally 2 ft. apart, are often desirable. Pinch off the first buds, and remove sideshoots if heavy central spikes of bloom are desired. Grown alone, balsam is suitable for low hedges because of its upright habit. It is a fast grower and will respond to extra attention such as the addition of fertilizer to the soil, the best enrichment being liquid manure. Full exposure to sun and an adequate supply of water are also essential for best results. Many gardeners have produced shorter plants with more double flowers than normal by transplanting them two or three times during the summer. When grown in the greenhouse, balsam can be increased by cutting.

I. capensis and *I. pallida* (touch-me-not, jewelweed) are self-sowing native species, good for the wild garden or in wet spots along the shore of a pond or stream. During most of the summer they will bear a profusion of small golden blossoms dangling above the foliage of these bushy, but watery stemmed plants.

I. glandulifera, formerly listed as *I. roylei*, is a purple-flowered garden annual that is grown from seed and requires little care. Although rather coarse in habit, it serves well to fill in vacant spots in the garden from late summer to early fall.

I. wallerana, formerly listed as *I. sultani* or *I. holstii*, is the most popular species. This tender annual adds a splash of color to any shady spot in the garden. Flowers on the 8–14 in. plants may be red, orange, white, salmon, violet, pink, or bi-color. The foliage is green or bronze, depending on the cultivar. The plants are valued for their ability to withstand shady conditions and for their clean, neat habit. They provide excellent results when grown in hanging baskets, pots, or other containers. Since these plants are very sensitive to cold temperature, the seeds should be started early indoors and set outside only after all danger of frost has passed.

IMPERFECT FLOWER.

A flower in which either stamens or pistil are lacking, in contrast to a hermaphrodite or PERFECT FLOWER. It is thus unisexual, as distinguished from bisexual. When flowers of each sex are borne separately but on the same plant, the individual (or species, if it is a distinguishing characteristic) is said to be monoecious. When the flowers of each sex are borne only on separate plants, these plants (and the species) are dioecious.

See also FLOWER; STERILITY; SELF.

INARCHING.

A type of plant propagation, also known as approach grafting, in which one plant (scion) is joined to another plant (stock) while each continues to grow on its own roots. When the union is accomplished, the scion is severed from its original plant, becoming thereafter a part of the stock plant.

See also GRAFTING.

INCARVILLEA

(in kahr VIL ee ah). A genus of Asiatic herbs including several showy and fairly hardy perennials that were brought from China and established with great success in North American gardens. Growing from 18–24 in. high, the plants produce terminal clusters of red or yellow blooms that are borne above a basal group of vivid green leaves resembling those of *Ailanthus*. The tubular flowers have a broadly expanded, five-lobed rim.

Often incorrectly called hardy gloxinias, incarvilleas thrive in rich but light, well-drained soil in a sunny border. Propagation is by root division or by seed sown in spring and summer for bloom the following year. Hardy in Zones 6–9, winter protection is recommended in colder climates. The young growths forming above the rootstock in summer can be cut off and rooted as cuttings under glass.

I. delavayi is the best-known species, growing 2 ft. tall and bearing rose-purple flowers with yellow tubes. *I. mairei* var. *grandiflora* is similar to *I. delavayi* but has fewer rose-red flowers on a less vigorous plant.

INDEHISCENT.

A term applied to a fruit that does not have regular sutures or valves to disperse the seeds it contains. For comparison, see DEHISCENCE.

INDIAN-BEAN.

Common name for *Catalpa bignonioides*, a flowering deciduous tree of the southeastern states; see CATALPA.

INDIAN-CUP.

A common name for *Silphium perfoliatum*, a grassland perennial with flowers cupped by the upper leaves; see SILPHIUM.

INDIAN-PAINT. A common name for *Lithospermum canescens*, an orange-flowered perennial similar to forget-me-nots; see LITHOSPERMUM.

INDIAN-PAINTBRUSH. Common name for species of CASTILLEJA, known for the brilliant orange or red bracts surrounding their flowers.

INDIAN-PIPE. A common name for *Monotropa uniflora*, a unique flowering plant without chlorophyll; see MONOTROPA.

INDIAN-TURNIP. Common name for *Arisaema triphyllum*, a familiar woodland herb that has three-parted leaves and mottled flowers; see ARISAEMA.

INDICATOR PLANT. A species that by its presence indicates the type of environment present. For example, *Stanleya pinnata* (prince's-plume) indicates soils rich in selenium, an element tolerated by this species but few others. Likewise, sphagnum moss indicates wet, acidic conditions, while *Typha* (cattail) indicates wet environments, and *Hepatica acutiloba* (sharp-lobed hepatica) is generally indicative of neutral to alkaline soil conditions.

INDIGO. Common name for INDIGOFERA, a genus of deciduous shrubs and perennial herbs with attractive flowers.

The name is also applied incorrectly to other plants. Bastard indigo is *Amorpha fruticosa*. Wild-indigo is *Baptisia*, a genus of leguminous herbs with colorful flowers. False indigo may be either AMORPHA, a genus of deciduous shrubs with blue or white flowers, or BAPTISIA.

INDIGOFERA (in di GAWF er ah). A genus of deciduous shrubs and perennial herbs mostly from warm regions of the world, belonging to the Fabaceae (Bean Family), and commonly known as indigo. The shrubby species are attractive summer-flowering shrubs of light and graceful habit. The number of leaflets in each leaf varies with the species. They do well in light loam and a sunny location. A few are fairly hardy and, if killed back, usually renew themselves from the base. Propagation is by seed and cuttings.

PRINCIPAL SPECIES

I. amblyantha, from China, grows to 6 ft. and has seven to eleven leaflets and dense clusters of large, bright rose flowers. Hardy to Zone 6.

I. gerardiana is a slender Himalayan shrub with leaves of 13 to 21 leaflets and long racemes of purplish rose flowers. Hardy to Zone 6.

I. kirilowii, from Korea, grows erect to 3 ft., with seven to eleven leaflets and dense clusters of large, bright rose flowers. Hardy to Zone 5.

I. potaninii is a graceful Chinese species that grows up to 5 ft. high with nine to eleven leaflets and lilac-pink flowers in drooping clusters. Hardy to Zone 6.

INDOOR GARDENING. Since ancient times, gardeners have endeavored to create optimum growing conditions for their plants indoors as well as outdoors. The art of bonsai has been practiced for centuries in the Orient. Container-grown fruit trees are depicted on the walls of Egyptian tombs. The ancient Romans tended herbs and roses in primitive greenhouses. With sufficient knowledge and care, modern indoor gardens can simulate almost any plant's natural environment and grow exotic foliage plants, tubbed fruit trees, splendid tropical flowers, climbing vines, desert cacti, fancy vegetables, culinary herbs, even a salad garden. It is possible to get a head start on spring by forcing bulbs and starting seedlings indoors, to prolong indefinitely the life of a treasured gift plant, or to overwinter prized outdoor plants by moving them indoors when frost first threatens.

In varying degrees, all plants require light, food, warmth, and moisture. When considering which plants to grow indoors, it is best to match the growing conditions that are available with the needs of the plant. A greenhouse provides a growing environment far superior to an indoor room, but less-than-ideal conditions can be remedied in a number of ways. Dim interior light can be supplemented with artificial lights. Low-levels of humidity can be improved by grouping plants, by setting the pots in shallow trays filled with water and stones, and by conscientiously misting the foliage. Suitable ambient temperatures can be supplied by moving the plants from one location in the home to another, if necessary. Knowledge of a plant's natural, seasonal growth cycle should dictate the schedule by which fertilizer is applied and the amount of water required. During periods of dormancy, the rate of photosynthesis and the plant's need for food and water are lower than during periods of active growth or flowering. Overwatering and overfeeding are the two most common and avoidable houseplant killers.

Plants can be grown in almost any container imaginable. Dishpans, cachepots, hanging baskets, urns, tubs, pickle jars, lunch boxes, and pots of plastic, terra-cotta, peat, porcelain, stoneware, or glass. Regardless of the container, the size and shape of the plant can be guided by pinching, pruning, and repotting when necessary. The gardener can propagate indoor stock by seed or vegetatively by using root or crown divisions, stolons, and suckers, by air layering, or by rooted cuttings.

Serious infestations of damaging pests are best prevented by maintaining the health of houseplants, washing the foliage regularly, using a sterile potting mix, providing adequate air circulation, and by keeping a watchful eye out for any symptoms of disease, evidence of damage, or presence of pests. Once discovered, pests can be physically removed by washing the infected plant with soap and water, or in extreme cases by treating with insecticide. Whether it is growing on a sunny windowsill or in a spacious conservatory, it is often best to destroy or at least quarantine a diseased plant before the infection has an opportunity to spread to neighboring plants.

See also FLOWERPOTS; GREENHOUSE; HOUSEPLANTS; WINDOW BOXES.

INFERIOR. Beneath, below, or under. An inferior ovary is one that appears to be beneath the flower rather than within it, because of the inser-

tion of the calyx, corolla, and stamens on the summit of the ovary. See EPIGYNOUS.

INFLORESCENCE. A term meaning, strictly, the arrangement of flowers on a plant; it is also applied to the individual flower cluster and, sometimes, to its manner of unfolding or opening. The many forms of flower clusters or arrangements fall into several quite distinct groups, which provide one of the means of distinguishing flowers. The term "head" is sometimes applied to any flower cluster but this is inaccurate, since a head is a special type.

A single flower borne at the end of a stem (as in the poppy) is called "solitary." Sometimes blossoms occur in pairs as in *Linnaea borealis* (twinflower). Beyond this, the arrangement can take on any of the typical forms described below. The stalk of a single flower or flower cluster is called a peduncle (in bulbous plants it is usually termed a scape); in a cluster, the stalk of a single flower is a pedicel. If a cluster or flower has neither peduncle nor pedicel, it is said to be sessile, meaning that it is set directly against the main stem. See FLOWER.

SPIKE

This is a slender, usually erect but sometimes drooping, arrangement of flowers (either sessile or on very short stalks) along the sides of a common stem. In the spikes of Timothy (herd's grass) or of cattail, the flowers are sessile; in that of the common lavender, they have short peduncles. In the spikes of the common grape-hyacinth and the hollyhock, flowers may be sessile or short stalked.

Raceme. This differs from a spike only in that the flower stalks are longer, giving a looser effect, as in the lily-of-the-valley or fireweed.

Panicle. This is an extension of the raceme in which the flower stalks are branched, giving a loosely pyramidal form as in oats and many other grasses, also astilbe and *Aralia spinosa* (Hercules'-club). When a shortening of the peduncles makes the panicle more compact, as in the lilac, the term "thyrse" is often used.

Catkin or Ament. This is another sort of spike,

compact, sometimes short and rounded, usually supplied with a bract or scale beneath each minute flower. Birch and willow bear catkins; and the cone, as in the pine, is actually an inflorescence of this type.

Spadix. Another spikelike form, this is a fleshy column bearing densely packed sessile flowers. The whole structure usually arises from a partly enveloping sheath called a spathe. Jack-in-the-pulpit and anthurium are good examples, their large green or colored spathes being often mistaken for the corolla of a large single flower.

OTHER FORMS

Departing from the spike form, there are the following types of inflorescence.

Whorl. Flowers are said to occur in whorls when more than two surround the stem at exactly the same level.

Umbel. Here a number of flower stalks arise from a common center in such a way that the flowers are carried at about the same height, forming a flattened or slightly rounded cluster. All members of the Apiaceae (Celery Family), of which the wild carrot or Queen-Anne's-lace and the blue laceflower are examples, have this sort of inflorescence. The umbel is "simple" if the peduncles are undivided, or "compound" if they are branched.

Cyme. Here the flower stalks rise from a common point to approximately the same level, but the intermediate divisions are irregular, filling up the intervening space, as in the common elder or snowball (*Viburnum*). In this type the flowers at the center of the inflorescence open first.

Corymb. In this type the flower stalks, instead of growing from a common point, originate at different points along the stem. Since the lowest are the longest, the others becoming progressively shorter, the flowers are borne at about the same height, forming a flattened or slightly rounded surface, as in the verbena. They differ from those of a cyme in that they open first around the margin and then progressively inward. The flower of the pear is an example, whereas that of the apple forms an umbel. A modification of the corymb that is sometimes rec-

ognized, in which the flowers are more compactly placed, is the fascicle, as in sweet-William.

Head. This is a dense spherical, ovoid, or cylindrical flower cluster borne at the end of a stem, as in clovers, the globe amaranth, and *Echinops* (globe-thistle). The name is also applied to the flower cluster of the Asteraceae (Aster Family), as illustrated by the aster or daisy, in which a compact round mass of disk flowers may be surrounded by a fringe of flattened, strap-shaped ray flowers (see COMPOSITE). A composite flower head may consist of all disk or ray flowers, or the two sorts may be mingled in varying proportions or modified into intermediate shapes.

INKBERRY. Common name for *Ilex glabra*, a hardy evergreen species of holly with black berries; see ILEX.

INOCULATION. In its relation to gardening and plant growing, this term, like many others, refers sometimes to harmful and sometimes to beneficial acts and results. A simple definition is the depositing of infectious material (called the inoculum) on or in an "infection court," which is any place in or on a host plant where infection can be set up; this may be a wound, a water pore, breathing pore (stoma), nectary, leaf surface, seed surface, or root hair. An inoculum may consist of any portion of the organism causing the infection (called a pathogen), such as spores, mycelium, bacterial thallus, insect eggs, etc.

In many—perhaps most—cases, inoculation is the first step in the development of an injurious plant DISEASE, but there are certain infectious organisms that establish a useful or helpful relationship (symbiosis) with the host plant.

INORGANIC. Not living, such as rock or sand, as contrasted with "organic," or living matter (or compounds produced or derived from living organisms), which comprises the plant and animal life of the world.

The mineral basis of the soil in which plants grow is inorganic; but any fertile garden soil is a mixture of such materials with more or less organic constituents, such as bacteria, fungi, and insects; and the decomposing remains of plants or animals, which, having once been alive, are of organic origin.

Plant foods added to the soil in the form of commercial fertilizers are generally inorganic, but the same chemical elements of nutrition that they provide—such as nitrogen, phosphorus, potassium, calcium, etc.—can also be supplied to the soil in the form of organic fertilizers, such as manures and composts, since the plant substances composing these composts have previously obtained the chemical elements from the soil.

INSECT CONTROL. Several kinds of formulas and concoctions are available for controlling insect pests. Many gardeners and farmers have learned to their sorrow that harsh chemical insecticides of the sort developed during and since World War II have, instead of controlling pests, actually caused pest increases in the long run. Many alternative methods, including botanical and biological controls, are effective against insect pests without harmful side effects.

There are two general categories of insect poisons. Those called stomach poisons are for chewing insects. Contact poisons penetrate through the breathing pores or somehow smother insects that have piercing and sucking mouthparts. Insecticides are chemical, organic, bacterial, or abrasive in nature and can be made from a wide variety of materials.

BIOLOGICAL AND ORGANIC INSECT CONTROLS

Though there is considerable danger to humans, wildlife, the soil, water sources, and nontarget species of insects from chemical sprays, there is far less environmental pollution from biological controls. In a period of transition to more or less complete biological control of pests, an approach known as INTEGRATED PEST MANAGEMENT (IPM) is receiving increasing emphasis. It can involve using some harsh chemicals on very specific target dates to stop dangerous buildup at times when a particular species is most prolific.

Otherwise, most of the controls are biological, including introducing beneficial predators or applying various physiological controls. See INSECTS, BENEFICIAL; BIOLOGICAL CONTROL.

With the increasing trend toward organic gardening, many alternatives to dangerous chemicals have come into common use. Physiological controls including abrasive substances, bands (see BANDING TREES), barriers, BRAN MASH, and various REPELLENTS have become common in battling garden pests. Sprays or dusts known as botanical insecticides, made from many plant parts, are often very effective. Other sprays made from ground-up bodies of the same species have succeeded in keeping away some insects.

ABRASIVE SUBSTANCES

DIATOMACEOUS EARTH, which clogs and rasps the insect, is a good contact poison. Made of needle-sharp fragments of sea shells and fossils and now commercially available, it is less problematic than many substances. Cutworms, grubs, and caterpillars can be pierced and wounded, or at least repelled by this scratchy material. Wood ashes, saved over the winter and used as a repellent during the spring and summer works in the same way to irritate or wound pests. These two materials can be more effective as dusts than as sprays if carefully applied to surfaces the insects frequent.

BOTANICAL FORMULAS

These include contact and stomach poisons made from various plant parts. The strongest and most hazardous are those made from the so-called botanicals: pyrethrum, rotenone, ryania, and sabadilla. One or more of these substances can be combined with copper or sulfur fungicides. Available commercially are mixtures of rotenone, pyrethrum, and ryania; one is called Tri-excel, but it is also available under other names. Though most botanical preparations are relatively safe, commercial formulas are often mixed with more dangerous chemicals, so check on the synergists added to see whether they are safe, and always follow label directions carefully. Other effective mixtures can be made from common herbs and plants such as garlic, onions, and hot peppers. An insecticidal principle is also found in nicotine. See SPRAYING; DUSTING.

Herbal Formulas. As many gardeners have noticed, insects normally avoid certain plants, especially strong herbs such as parsley, tansy, bee balm (except bees), feverfew, horseradish, rhubarb, elderberry, castor beans, wormwood, and others. Such plants can provide materials for useful repellent sprays. Grind or pulverize the leaves or leaves and flowers, add a little soap and water, steep, and strain to make the spray. Bury the mash around the plant to be protected.

Garlic. A spray proven in several university tests and by many home gardeners is made from garlic. Its toxic principle, allyl sulfide, has been extracted and made into a spray capable of killing 99% of the mosquito larvae at the test site. In the home garden, garlic spray can show almost equally good results if the spray is made correctly. One recipe involves soaking 3 oz. minced cloves of garlic in mineral oil or fish emulsion for 48 hours, then adding about a pint of soapy warm water (use soap, not detergent). Store this mixture in china or glass, and dilute 1 part garlic mixture to 20 parts water for the spray. Another version is to dissolve half a cake of a pure, mild soap in 1 gal. hot water and add 2 mashed garlic cloves plus 4 tbsp. hot pepper. Because garlic is a powerful antibiotic, it can be used against plant diseases also. Onions, chives, and ornamental *Allium* species can be added as boosters or used to make milder sprays by themselves.

Hot Red Peppers. These make a useful spray, especially if the whole pods are used. Some soap will help, but as with all soap sprays, it is wise to wash off the soap after the insect control has worked.

Hellebore. A good old-fashioned insect poison has been made from the roots of *Veratrum* spp. (false hellebore, white-hellebore). It is a stomach poison for chewing insects, many bothersome beetles, and caterpillars. It is available commercially, or false hellebore seeds can be purchased from some nurseries for home preparations. Once used to poison arrow tips, it is poisonous to humans and animals if ingested. One formula is

1 oz. hellebore dust to 2 gal. water, with a little lime or flour added. See HELLEBORE.

Nicotine. A highly toxic extract, derived from tobacco, that was once common in commercial sprays, fumigants, and homemade mixtures for use against aphids and other soft-bodied insects. Its effectiveness varies depending on the concentration, and there may be harmful side-effects on humans, plants, and animals. See NICOTINE.

Pyrethrum. This is made from the dried flowers of *Chrysanthemum cineraiifolium*. Pyrethrum's insecticidal principles are pyrethrins I and II, and cinerins I and II, both unstable because they decompose in sunlight and are easily hydrologized. More useful on adults than larvae, it stuns many kinds of insects; often the stunned insects must be destroyed later, though sometimes they die naturally. Pyrethrum is not usually lethal to bees or lady beetles in normal doses, but excessive application may prove fatal to many beneficial insects. The poison is short lived and does not build up as some of the hard chemicals have done. Seeds of this chrysanthemum are available, so you can grow your own. To make the spray, use ground-up flower heads in water with a little soap added. Though rarely dangerous for mammals, it can cause dermatitis in some people. See also PYRETHRUM.

Rotenone. This is usually made from *Derris elliptica*, *Cubé barbasco*, and other tropical plants. It also occurs in a perennial weed, *Tephrasis virginiana* (devil's-shoestring), of which the ground roots will provide 5% rotenone. This toxin will act as both stomach and contact poison on all insects. It will not harm humans and other warm-blooded animals but will kill beneficial fish as well as insects. It is best to use it after dusk to avoid harming bees and other pollinators and away from water sources where fish might be affected. Rotenone is available in 1% and 5% concentrations, the first adequate for control of many pests. Cubé is common in commercial preparations. See also ROTENONE.

Ryania. This botanical is made from the powdered roots of a South American shrub, *Ryania speciosa*. It is effective in controlling codling moths, corn borers, cranberry fruit worms, aphids, and Japanese beetles and can be used with some degree of safety close to harvest. Ryania makes pests sick enough to lose their appetites; some are not killed by it but are put into a state of flaccid paralysis. It soon breaks down to harmless components, having little effect on mammals and generally doing less harm than many other insecticides. You can buy 100% powder and mix it ½ oz. to 1 gal. water. It is good for attacking persistent pests; however, stronger sprays may be needed. Apply five sprayings per season for severe pests.

Sabadilla. This potent insecticide is made of powdered seeds from a South American and Mexican plant of the Liliaceae (Lily Family), and it tends to become stronger as it ages. It has been used for several centuries against grasshoppers, webworms, army worms, codling moths, and aphids. It is also recommended for control of lygus bugs, squash bugs, chinch bugs, harlequin bugs, blister beetles, and many pest larvae. It is seldom harmful to mammals, but many people have allergic reactions to sabadilla dust, which can be very irritating to the nose, throat, and eyes.

Other Formulas. Milder, but often effective, are sprays made from chips of quassia (a Latin American tree) boiled in water, with or without toxic larkspur seeds. This spray attacks aphids, sawflies, caterpillars, and some other insect larvae, but it spares bees and lady beetles.

BACTERIAL CONTROLS

The highly successful *Bacillus thuringiensis* (Bt), a bacteria that sickens insects, is a good stomach poison for controlling caterpillars. It is available from many nurseries as Biotrol, Dipel, or Thuricide. When sprayed on plants attacked by any kind of caterpillar or wormlike larva, the pest eats the disease organism and is so affected that it cannot recover. Cabbage butterfly worms are easily controlled by this spray, and it is also useful against codling moths, gypsy moths, cutworms, and some grubs. Also very useful against Japanese beetles and other in-ground grubs is *Bacillus popilliae* (milky spore disease),

sold commercially as Doom. See also BIOLOGICAL CONTROL.

HORMONE FORMULAS

Insect growth regulators (IGR), including pheromones and the recently developed hormones that delay or distort the growth patterns or sex capabilities of insects, have met with some success. Final results of the long-term effects of such compounds on the species and neighboring organisms, however, are not fully known. Some gardeners, therefore, are very cautious about using this approach to pest control. At first it was believed to be species specific, but later it was found that extremely small amounts affected many more insects than the one pest targeted for control. Juvenile hormones delay and keep postponing the insect's ability to grow to the next phase or instar or to ever reach adulthood. The molting hormones cause molts out of phase and distort the natural sexual pattern of development. It cannot yet be assumed that these substances will never have any unforeseen side effects on other fauna or the environment. As the head of the insectary Rincon-Vitove said, "Nature resists single answers," and tinkering with hormones is certainly no simple matter.

See also PHEROMONE.

INORGANIC INSECT CONTROLS.

CHEMICALS

Though highly efficient in killing insects and often used in small- and large-scale gardening, chemical insecticides are seldom ideal or even effective in the long term. Many insects build up resistance to chemicals. The insects that are natural enemies of the relatively small percentage of insect pests are usually eliminated as well; thus the predators will cease to keep the pests under control.

Related effects include the buildup to pest proportions of insects that were previously found to be merely minor nuisances, such as the tobacco budworm in the South or the cabbage looper and beet army worm where they were not serious pests before. The population of the omnivorous leaf roller exploded as a side effect of organophosphorus and chlorinated hydrocarbon sprays used for other targets. Such explosions have probably been due to the destruction of natural enemies. Added to these ironies are the dire effects of accumulations of such chemicals in widespread poisoning of food crops as well as poisoning birds, fish, and animals that consume poisoned plants, water, or insects. Because of the very long-lasting effects of a spray like DDT, its traces can be found in foods, animals, birds, and humans for many years.

Common insecticides in previous years included many arsenical compounds as stomach poisons, the most common being lead arsenate, which is no longer legal. Substitutes of fluorine compounds have also been used, although some do burn leaves. One, cryolite (sodium aluminum fluoride), though insoluble in water, has been used as a dust or spray. It must not be mixed with lime or other alkaline compounds. Its tolerance figure was 7 ppm.

OILS

Among contact sprays, oil is a very old insecticide. Kerosene is used more than other types of oils, and it frequently occurs in emulsions. Summer oils of higher fractions are used with water to control scale insects, whiteflies, and mealybugs on trees and ornamentals with ¼–2% oil used. Dormant oil sprays used in the spring on tree pests are made from still heavier oils. Prepared emulsions are diluted to 2–5% concentrations.

Oils were once used for coating water surfaces to check developing mosquito larvae, but this practice is no longer permitted. The water source is often polluted, hampering fish and other creatures dependent on it. For dormant and simple oil sprays, see SPRAYING.

OTHER COMPOUNDS

Insecticidal soap is a modern, effective spray of many uses. Boric acid has proved useful against cockroaches. Even plain water, or water with a small amount of detergent or soap flakes added, applied as a forceful spray can clean away insects quite efficiently—especially aphids and whiteflies.

If used discriminately, sulfur can be used to kill insects; however, it will kill both pests and beneficial insects. Never combine sulfur with oil sprays. Use of the very toxic lime-sulfur mixture was once common, but it is rare today.

INSECTARY. Some universities, government agencies, or private establishments breed and raise insects for use in biological control programs. Nurserymen, seedsmen, and home gardeners can order these beneficial insects (including lady beetles, praying mantises, tiny parasitic wasps, lacewings, predatory mites, and nematodes) for distribution or use. See appendix or consult your local extension service for suppliers of beneficial insects.

INSECTICIDAL SOAP. A type of contact insecticide; see SPRAYING.

INSECTICIDE. A chemical or organic agent used for INSECT CONTROL.

INSECTIVOROUS PLANTS. A term applied generally to various kinds of plants that supplement the food they obtain from the soil and air by trapping insects in specially modified leaves, dissolving out their soluble juices by means of special secretions, and absorbing the nutrients. This nutrient solution is especially rich in nitrogen, which these plants are particularly in need of, since they generally grow in bogs and other wet places and have scanty roots.

Pitcher Plants. One familiar group includes plants of the Sarraceniaceae (Sarracenia or Pitcher Plant Family), including the genera *Sarracenia* and *Darlingtonia*. All of these, as suggested by the common name, have leaves modified into a sort of pitcher or hooded-trumpet form, often brightly colored and sometimes adorned with conspicuous appendages. The hollowed leaves may also be provided with honey glands that help to attract insect prey. Downward-pointing hairs line the leaves and urge the trapped insects toward the accumulated liquid in the bottom of the receptacle but prevent them from climbing up. Once bogged in the secretion, the victim dies and is digested by the plant.

Owing to this method of feeding, **Darlingtonia** (California pitcher plant) has been advertised as carnivorous, meat-eating, and the like, sometimes with the unwanted recommendatation that it be fed a daily ration of meat.

Sundews and Flytraps. *Drosera* (sundew) represents a type of insect-consuming plant that has small, rounded leaves covered with glistening, sticky hairs that, when an insect touches them and is caught by the sticky secretion, gradually fold over upon it until it is firmly held. The sweet secretion turns to a sort of gastric juice that acts on the prey and prepares it for assimilation by the leaf, which later spreads out its hairs again and is ready for more game.

Another member of the Droseraceae (Sundew Family) is *Dionaea* (Venus flytrap), whose two-lobed leaves are covered with glandular hairs and fringed with stiff bristles. When an insect lights on one of these leaves, the two halves come together like the jaws of a trap, the marginal bristles interlocking. The trapped insect dies and is dissolved and absorbed; then the plant opens and sets its leaf trap again.

From other families, interesting genera that also have the ability to trap and digest insects are *Nepenthes*, *Utricularia*, and *Pinguicula*.

Culture. Species of pitcher plants and sundews can be grown in bog gardens or greenhouses, and even in the home with special care. Small insectivorous plants grown as houseplants do well in live sphagnum moss and distilled rather than tap water.

INSECTS. Eighty percent of all animals on this planet are insects of the order Arthropoda. There are a million species described in scientific literature, and entomologists estimate only 10% are known. Of the insects now known, most are either neutral or beneficial in effect to humans. Those that are injurious are so primarily because they compete with man for food and fiber crops or adversely affect human health and comfort. See also INSECTS, BENEFICIAL; INSECT CONTROL.

Most insects have a hardened outer covering or exoskeleton, jointed legs in pairs, and a body con-sisting of distinct segments. The Hexapoda have six legs and usually two pairs of wings in their adult stage. Only one group are true "bugs," though the term is commonly used for all insects, and even for bacteria and viruses when those organisms cause brief illnesses in humans. Crustacea, such as crabs, shrimp, and lobsters, are members of the order Arthropoda, as are sowbugs.

Each insect has three body regions: the head, with compound eyes and two antennae of feelers; the thorax, with usually three pairs of legs; and a segmented abdomen. It breathes through pores called spiracles along the sides of its abdomen and thorax.

Insects grow by passing through several stages of development. This metamorphosis can be "complete" or "incomplete." If incomplete, the stages are egg, nymph, and adult. If complete, the stages are egg; larva, grub, or maggot; pupa; then adult. Nymphs are similar to adults, only smaller; there may be several molts when the wingless nymphs shed old skins for new. In the last molt, the nymph more closely resembles the adult and forms wings. Grasshoppers, aphids, leaf hoppers, and many others undergo incomplete metamorphosis.

The first stage of complete metamorphosis is the egg, laid on leaves, usually the undersides, in crevices on bark or other places, in debris under plants, in the soil, or as parasites in the bodies of other insects. The egg hatches into a larva, entirely different from the adult in form. It is usually wormlike, a caterpillar or bare oval creature, usually legless but sometimes with prolegs that grasp prey. The larvae of flies are called maggots; those of beetles are grubs. Caterpillars are the larvae of moths and butterflies. They all have mouthparts and eat vigorously. Larvae molt several times, shedding hardened skin and wriggling out for new expansion. Each molt is called an instar, and there may be up to six molts before the larvae pupate, which is the resting stage during which the pupa stays quiet and changes into an adult. Some spin cocoons for protection; some go into the soil; some hide under bark; or some, like flies, stay in the last larval skin. Special devices are made for the safe escape of the adult when it is developed. Some adults live a short life, almost entirely devoted to egg-laying—sometimes mating, sometimes not.

A few insects, like stink bugs, undergo no metamorphosis; they just hatch and then enlarge by roughly five nymph stages until adults. Throughout, they have identical mouthparts. In gradual metamorphosis there are molts, but when there is no molting, the insects, such as silverfish, just grow in size. Some kinds may molt after sexual maturity as do the crustaceans.

Mature insects have pairs of antennae, very sensitive to touch and to radiation from plants and other insects, including mates. Many have two sets of eyes: simple ones called ocelli, probably very sensitive to light; and two large compound eyes on either side of the ocelli, with a few to thousands of hexagonal lenses.

There are significant differences in the mouthparts of insects, important to note in choosing the means to control them. Some are chewing insects with strong mandibles used in grinding, cutting, tearing, fighting, and, in bees, for molding wax. They move laterally. The maxilla on each has several parts: the palp or palpus, which feels and probably smells and tastes, and some chewing sections, one with teeth. There is a sort of tongue and glands that salivate and sometimes make silk.

Other insects suck and rasp, or pierce and suck. The rasping ones include the thrips, and these have mouthparts with styletlike sections. Those that pierce and suck are very common, including stink bugs, mosquitoes, and those that siphon or lap up liquids. The stink bugs have long jointed beaks that lie between the legs when not in use. In the beak's groove is the needlelike structure that does the piercing and sucking, usually with four hairlike stylets, two as mandibles, two as maxillae. Mosquito mouthparts, with six stylets, are efficient for stinging and sucking blood. Houseflies have sponging mouthparts; their fleshy proboscis comes down from the head. Its spongy surface has capillary canals that collect the liquid food. These insects have palpi, as do the siphoners such as moths and butterflies. There is a long, hollow proboscis that coils up when not in use. Bees have chewing-lapping mouthparts. The tongue structure is long and hairy; its labial palpi form a lapping tube to gather nectar. In some insects, both larval and adult forms are capable of puncturing plant cells and injuring them; in some, one stage is injurious, the other is not; in many cases neither do damage to plants. Moths and butterflies, as adults, cannot hurt plants, but as larvae, like that of the gypsy moth, they can do great damage.

KINDS OF INSECTS

True Bugs. These include squash bugs, assassin bugs, chinch bugs, lace bugs, and stink bugs, among others. They are the Hemiptera, whose front wings, thickened and narrowed at the base, meet to form a triangle, thinner at the tip. Their sucking mouthparts can cause considerable injury to the host plants. These true bugs (like the grasshoppers and crickets, the Orthoptera) undergo gradual metamorphosis. The Orthoptera have narrow, leathery front wings and broad, thin hind wings. The group includes praying mantises, the beneficial predators, and the walking-stick insect. Some, like grasshoppers, have large, strong hind legs.

Beetles. The Coleoptera, the beetles, are the largest order of all. Their hardened front wings meet in a line down the middle of the back. They have chewing mouthparts, both as larvae and as adults, and undergo complete metamorphosis. See BEETLES.

Moths and Butterflies. Lepidoptera include moths and butterflies, with scaly coverings on their wings and often on their bodies. They undergo complete metamorphosis and in the pupal stage often spin cocoons. Many butterflies are harmless, but many moths have chewing larvae that are very destructive. See BUTTERFLIES; CATERPILLARS.

Flies. Diptera, the fly order, have sucking mouthparts, one pair of wings, and as adults are rarely damaging to plants. The larvae, called maggots, live in both decaying and living plant tissues. This group includes many beneficial insects, such as the syrphid and tachinid flies, as well as the robber flies. See FLIES.

Bees, Ants, and Others. Hymenoptera includes families of very beneficial parasitic insects, such as the ichneumons, chalcids, and braconids as well as some families of sawflies and several wheat pests. Bees and ants also belong to this order. They usually have chewing mouthparts, with the larvae of the parasites chewing away and destroying the bodies of their hosts. Some adults are carnivorous. See BEES; ANTS.

Thrips. The thrips (both singular and plural) belong to the order Thysanoptera. It has smaller, slender wings, rasping, sucking mouthparts, and undergoes a gradual metamorphosis. It is especially injurious to gladiolus and in recent years to sugar maples in the form of pear thrips. See THRIPS.

Termites. Isoptera is the order of yellowish, soft-bodied termites. Commonly called white ants, they are not ants at all. One of the few animals that can digest cellulose due to symbiotic protozoa in their system, these pests have biting mouthparts and eat wood in buildings and trees. Their metamorphosis is gradual. See TERMITES.

Earwigs. The order Dermaptera are commonly called earwigs. These are like beetles but have pincerlike rear appendages. See EARWIG.

Aphid Lions. Neuroptera is the order of the so-called aphid lions or lacewings. They undergo complete metamorphosis, and both larvae and adults have chewing mouthparts. They are highly beneficial to the gardener, since they eat other insects. See LACEWING.

INSECTS, BENEFICIAL.

For millions of years, many insects have preyed on or parasitized other insects. Practically all of the potential pest species have been controlled by beneficial insects, thus maintaining the balance of nature. Without such control, insects could easily have overrun the world and conquered mankind by destroying the main sources of food, clothing, and building materials. In recent decades, however, import of exotic species, widespread monoculture, and unforeseen side effects of wide-spectrum chemical sprays have changed the patterns of nature.

The spraying of hard pesticides that began in the middle of the twentieth century has killed off many of the beneficial insects. Unfortunately their population often takes longer to recover than that of the target pests. In fact, the phenomenon of resurgence or upset, as it is called, occurs when the target insect rebuilds in numbers so rapidly that the predators and parasites cannot catch up. Furthermore, the pests often develop resistant strains that do not succumb to hard chemicals even after repeated attempts, which may cause more spray deaths of the beneficial insects, themselves able to control the pests. Another detrimental effect of spraying has been the increased population of some pest species, as happened when the tobacco budworm and beet army worm became pests after sprays to control boll weevils were in common use.

PARASITIC AND PREDATORY INSECTS

Parasitic insects lay one or more eggs in the host; these eggs develop into larvae and eat out the body of the host from within. The host can be an egg, a larva, or occasionally an adult. The ovipostor varies from species to species, sometimes short and strong, sometimes long and delicate but very piercing, even capable of going through wood to reach an egg. Some parasites lay eggs on leaves, which then will be eaten by the host insect.

Among the most active and persistent parasitic insects are the very small wasps of the order Hymenoptera and some flies of the order Diptera. Lacewings of the order Neuroptera, praying mantises of the order Orthoptera, and several famous beetles of the order Coleoptera are predatory insects, which are usually larger than the prey. They chew or suck the juices of the insects they control, each species having mouthparts suitable for the method of attack. The delicate green LACEWING, whose larvae are called aphid lions, is a very effective predator with a wider range of victims than the lady beetle, controlling aphids, army worms, and Colorado potato beetles.

PREDATORY BEETLES

The Vedalia lady beetle (or ladybug), imported from Australia in the late nineteenth century, was the first spectacularly successful biological control applied by plant scientists to the cottony-cushion scale infesting the citrus groves of California at the time. The 500 shipped in were ready to go to work both as adults and larvae. They proliferated very well and spread quickly in other orchards. Now several strains of lady beetles are available from any commercial insectary. To be useful in the garden, the beetles must be beyond the stage of ovarian diapause and ready to eat the aphids, mealybugs, and scales they feed on, and also ready to lay eggs. In ordering, ask for "preconditioned" lady beetles; reports of failure with these predators are usually due to their not being preconditioned. See also LADY BEETLE.

Ground beetles are also beneficial, as are the green syrphid maggots that prey on aphids, leaf hoppers, and others as they inch along ready to capture prey with their hooked, fanglike mouthparts. Adults, called flower flies, can be seen in the garden hovering almost motionless over flowers. Mites can be controlled by larger predatory mites, also on the market as members of the Phytoseiidae. These are rather slow to work, but they reproduce rapidly and can keep ahead of an infestation of red spider mites, for example. Root nematodes can be controlled by the predatory nematodes, *Neoaplectana carpocapsae* (Nc). They can be purchased by the millions.

WASPS

Thousands of species of tiny parasitic wasps are of great value. Some resemble large WASPS, others are so like hairy FLIES that they have actually been classified as flies. Among the very smallest are the chalcid wasps, under two millimeters. They are squat, stocky, and black or metallic, though sometimes yellow. Their elbowed antennae vibrate intensely when hunting for a host to pierce, usually one of the whiteflies, scales, mealybugs, or aphids.

Not quite as small as the chalcids, but still too tiny to bite through human skin, are the braconid wasps—more wasplike in build, with a longer, stronger ovipositor extending from the rear of the abdomen and straight antennae. Their wings are delicate and filamentous. When laying an egg, the stinging ovipositor is swung under the body to thrust into its victim. These predators include the commercially available *Trichogramma evanescens*, which lays on many caterpillars, such as the tomato hornworm, where the eggs develop to consuming larvae and then pupate in cocoons that can be easily seen protruding from the destroyed hornworm. Never kill a worm in that condition, because in time it will give forth many more beneficial parasites.

Rather like the braconids are the ichneumonids, brown, yellow, or black, and with longer stinger ovipositors. They seek out borers, the larvae of many moths, butterflies, beetles, and various solitary bees and other wasps. The ovipositor is so sharp it easily penetrates wood to get at a victim inside a stem.

Others are tachinids, also sometimes called flies because of their spiny or hairy appearance. They are larger and often visible in gardens where they visit and pollinate the musky flowers that honey bees avoid, such as marigolds. They often lay eggs on the outside of victims or on leaves to be eaten by the insect. Some of them lay larvae. The wasp *Encarsia formosa* can help to eliminate an infestation of whiteflies in the greenhouse.

Sometimes the beneficial adult wasp herself sucks the body juices or blood from the victim to get protein for further egg making. In various chalcid and ichneumon species the feeding tube is molded by the parasite. Sometimes, as with other chalcids, for example, the insect is a hyperparasite—that is, she lays eggs in eggs already there to develop into parasites. Sometimes she merely pierces that egg and ruins all chances of destruction by the pest because the pierced egg won't develop.

The egg laying capacity of some of these wasps is extraordinary. The lifetime count for one tachinid studied was 6000. It is common for chalcids to lay 100 to 200 eggs on the outside of a host. Others lay up to 1500 during a season.

MANTIDS

Praying mantises are also useful predators. Their egg cases can be bought and hung on limbs to develop. Unlike many other beneficial insects that eat or attack only a few pest species, these relatively large insects are omnivorous, eating beneficial insects along with the pests, so they should be placed where a pest buildup is expected. See PRAYING MANTIS.

OTHER PREDATORS

Other beneficial insects that eat or attack pest insects include ant lions, fireflies, damsel bugs, pirate bugs, and assassin bugs. Still others overcome pest weeds such as prickly-pear cactus in Australia and the leaf beetle of the *Chrysolina* sp., which managed to wipe out klamath weed in the West.

MANAGEMENT OF BENEFICIAL INSECTS

Insectaries are studying and bringing out more beneficial predators and parasites every year. The devouring capacities of these beneficial insects indicate how helpful to the gardener they can be. The larva of a lady beetle can eat 400 aphids in a day, and the adult in its lifetime can eat 5000 aphids. A fourth-instar lacewing larva can devour 1000 to 1500 citrus red mites per day.

Predatory insects work fast and can accomplish control of quite large infestations quickly. They tend to move on in search of another source of prey, unless they merely tide over with nectar, sap, or honeydew until a new buildup occurs. Parasites effect control more slowly and regularly feed on nectar, sap, pollen, and honeydew as they hunt for victims, so prey in low densities are adequate for parasites. Predators, followed by working parasites, can be a good way to introduce biological control to your garden or greenhouse.

Good management for beneficial insects in the garden would also include providing flowers in bloom all summer, water, nesting and hiding sites (especially to the north of the garden), and a barrier of plants to the south, since pests often approach from that direction. A shallow ditch and grass down the center of the garden provides a place for the helpful insects to move safely or to rest. Watch for pest concentrations and move the

beneficial insects to those places where they like to feed. If you do not buy them, find beneficial insects yourself in the open and bring them in to proliferate. Use a good insect guide for identification, and learn how various species need to be handled. See also BIOLOGICAL CONTROL; INTEGRATED PEST MANAGEMENT (IPM); INSECT CONTROL.

INSERTED. Attached, such as an organ to its support. The sepals, petals, and stamens of potentilla are said to be inserted on the receptacle below the ovary, making the insertion or manner of attachment that is called "hypogynous." If they were inserted above the ovary, the flower would be termed "epigynous." See OVARY.

INTEGRATED PEST MANAGEMENT (IPM). This is an approach to pest management that uses several aspects of biological control to discourage a pest, in contrast to the conventional single approach to pest control, which generally calls for spraying a given insect with a specific chemical. IPM programs have been developed for insects, vertebrates, and pest plants, as well as household pests; and they have beneficial results both in agricultural settings and in the garden. Only when there is an unmanageable buildup of a pest population are chemical sprays used, and then they are carefully timed to target the peak of pest populations. The guiding principle in IPM is to give nature a free hand to maintain a natural balance. Creative nonintervention sets up conditions that favor insects, birds, and mammals that keep pests in check.

One of the primary efforts in IPM is to attract and conserve beneficial insects (see INSECTS, BENEFICIAL). Untreated fields have been analyzed to find the best pest control practices and natural enemy complexes. Natural enemy complexes are predators, parasites, and pathogens that attack pests as antagonists; this can be one of the most important facets of biological control. Sometimes those organisms are helping by merely occupying niches, using resources, and taking the place of more harmful pests that might come into the garden or orchard. Weeds support this community of organisms and also help with insect control. Practitioners of IPM also plant crops on schedule to avoid growth and maturity during peak insect activity. Special attention is given to developing a rich, humusy soil, to using mulches instead of herbicides, and to assuring that residues of crops plowed under are kept free from contamination by hard chemicals. Cleanup and sanitation are carefully included. On some large farms, huge vacuum cleaners are used to collect and destroy pests.

A growing concern about protecting crops from dangerous chemicals and protecting the environment from pollution, runoff of nitrates, and poisonous sprays has led many farmers and gardeners to adopt IPM practices. Crop yields, though sometimes lower the first year, soon become plentiful. Moreover, the IPM program proves to be significantly less costly than programs involving expensive fertilizers and sprays. During the 1980s IPM began to be widely taught in extension services and agricultural colleges.

To take advantage of IPM for insect control in your garden, develop a good habitat for beneficial insects, which includes a "house" for them to live in, suitable food, and some protection. Insects regulate each other by competition and food supply, and they will seldom be a problem when set against each other. See also BIOLOGICAL CONTROL; INSECT CONTROL.

INTENSIVE CROPPING.
Various planting practices designed to obtain maximum crop returns from specific areas, like planting short-season vegetables where they will be harvested before slower-growing kinds planted with them need the space.

INTERCROPPING.
A type of intensive cropping in which quick-maturing crops are planted between the rows of slower-growing plants to get maximum use from a plot of land.

INTERMITTENT MIST.
Rooting cuttings by periodically misting them (automatically) with water usually gives a high percentage of rooting in the shortest possible time. Since the foliage is kept moist, the cuttings can be made longer, 4–6 in. In many cases, with intermittent mist, cuttings can be rooted in full sun. One additional step is necessary in establishing the rooted cuttings: once rooted, either before or after potting, they must be hardened-off (acclimatized) to the normal drier environment. This can be done by increasing the interval between mistings or reducing the light for a few weeks.

Intermittent mist is used with or without BOTTOM HEAT and can be used for germination of seed as well as root cuttings. It is a relatively inexpensive low pressure system requiring water-line pressure of 20–60 p.s.i. The ultimate is a high pressure (400–500 p.s.i.) fog system. In a glasshouse or shadehouse this system can be used for house cooling, frost protection, and insecticide-fungicide application in addition to propagation. While the fog system is expensive compared to a simple mist system, it is much more versatile.

INTERRUPTED FERN.
Common name for *Osmunda claytoniana*, a fern with abbreviated pinnae covered with brown spores; see OSMUNDA.

INULA
(IN yoo lah). A genus of perennial, mostly hairy herbs usually with yellow flowers, belonging to the Asteraceae (Aster Family). Most species are hardy (Zones 3–9) and thrive in average garden soil if given a sunny location. Propagation is easily done from seed or division. Perhaps a half dozen of the 50 or more European species are cultivated as showy border subjects.

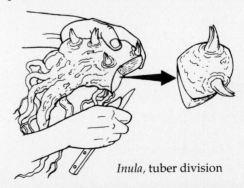

Inula, tuber division

PRINCIPAL SPECIES

I. ensifolia cv. 'Gold Star' grows in 2-ft. clumps with 2½-in., rose-pink flowers and fernlike foliage. Hardy to Zone 4.

I. helenium (elecampane) grows to 6 ft. and has velvety leaves. It is extremely susceptible to MILDEW and, unless protected, is likely to show a thick coating of white over the leaves by midsummer.

I. oculus-christi grows to 2 ft. with silky leaves.

I. orientalis (Caucasian inula), formerly listed as *I. glandulosa*, is a relatively tall, hairy species.

Inula helenium

INVOLUCRE. A whorl or rosette of scalelike bracts around the base of a flower cluster as in members of the Asteraceae (Aster Family) and Apiaceae (Celery Family).

INVOLUTE. Rolled inward from each side; said of a leaf or other flat body whose margins curl inward upon the body. Compare REVOLUTE.

IONOPSIDIUM (ī oh nahp SID ee um) **acaule.** A small annual herb native to Portugal and North Africa, belonging to the Brassicaceae (Mustard Family), and commonly known as diamond flower. Grown in gardens and greenhouses, it produces a profusion of small violet or white blossoms. It requires moist soil, partial shade, and protection from drying winds. Seed can be sown in early spring for summer blossoming, and in midsummer for fall bloom. Plants started in the fall can be kept over winter in pots for spring use.

IPHEION (IF ee ahn). A genus of the Amaryllidaceae (Amaryllis Family), including a few species of South American origin, and commonly called spring starflower. It is an invaluable bulb for naturalizing in a shrub border that gets little annual disturbance. The popularly cultivated form is *I. uniflorum*, which has nearly flat, slightly glaucous leaves to ⅜ in. wide. The flowers are borne on 6–8 in. stems and are pale blue with bright orange stamens.

IPOMOEA (ī poh MEE ah). A genus of mostly herbaceous plants belonging to the Convolvulaceae (Morning-glory Family) and commonly known as morning-glory. Some are important decorative species, while others are pernicious weeds. There has been considerable confusion between this genus and *Convolvulus* (bindweed), while the former genera *Calonyction* (moonflower) and *Quamoclit* (star-glory) have been reclassified under *Ipomoea*. Thus, species of the four groups are sometimes found under different names in catalogs and lists.

Many species of *Ipomoea* can be used to cover fences, trellises, walls, or banks, their large, dark green, usually heart-shaped leaves making an excellent screen, with trumpet-shaped flowers of many beautiful colors borne in bright profusion on summer mornings. Others can be grown in pots. One is an important commercial crop.

Morning-glories are easily grown in any fairly good soil, either indoors or out. Hardy in Zones 10–11, most are only cultivated as annuals. They grow rapidly in almost any moderately rich garden soil. Seed should be sown where the plants are wanted as soon as danger from frost is past. The tubers of the half-hardy perennial kinds should be dug in fall in cold climates and kept indoors away from frost over winter. When seeds are sown, germination can be hastened by soaking overnight in warm water or by filing or cutting a small notch in the horny outer coat. The perennial forms can also be propagated by division, though the customary method is layering, or by cuttings rooted indoors or in a hotbed.

PRINCIPAL SPECIES

I. acuminata (blue dawnflower), formerly listed as *I. leari*, is a twining perennial bearing large heart-shaped leaves and numerous white-throated blue or purple flowers that turn pink with age.

It is good for the warm greenhouse or, in warm regions, for covering embankments.

I. alba (moonflower), formerly listed as *C. aculeatum*, is sometimes grown under glass in cool regions and outdoors where it is warmer. A tropical twining vine, it grows to 20 ft. high in good soil, bearing large heart-shaped leaves. Fragrant flowers to 6 in. across are white and trumpet-shaped with a broad, flat rim; they open in the evening and usually close before noon. Several forms are offered under various names. Plants are easily grown as tender annuals.

I. batatas (SWEET-POTATO), native to the tropical Americas, is a small-flowered species, now cultivated worldwide as a commercial crop.

I. coccinea (star ipomoea), formerly listed as *Q. coccinea*, is an annual that grows to 20 ft. and has heart-shaped leaves and scarlet, yellow-throated flowers. Varieties have lobed or divided leaves and larger flowers including yellow or orange forms. It thrives in light soil and full sun.

I. horsfalliae, one of the best of the tropical species, is suitable mainly for greenhouse cultivation, producing white, pink, or magenta flowers.

I. leptophylla (bush morning-glory, moonflower) is a shrubby western native, which grows in exceedingly dry places and produces purple-throated, rose-pink flowers.

I. x *multifida* (cardinal climber), formerly listed as *Q.* x *sloteri*, is a hybrid with palmately lobed leaves and crimson, white-throated flowers. It grows best in light soil and full sun.

I. nil, one of the most popular morning-glories in cultivation, is the source of the large-flowered Japanese or imperial forms (sometimes called *I. imperialis*), which bear blue, purple, pink, or rose flowers and leaves varying from heart-shaped to lobed. The vines grow rapidly, often blooming in six weeks from seed.

I. pandurata (wild sweet-potato vine, man-of-the-earth) is a beautiful hardy vine with a tuberous perennial root, trailing or twining stems, and purple-throated white flowers. Native from Connecticut to Florida and Texas, it frequently escapes cultivation to become one of the worst weed pests known.

I. purpurea (common or tall morning-glory), the most commonly grown species, appears in many color varieties, including double forms. It will grow well on string or wooden trellises, wire poultry netting, old tree trunks, or stone walls. Seeds can be saved from the vines for the next year's sowing.

I. quamoclit (cypress vine, star-glory), formerly listed as *Q. pennata*, is a slender annual twiner with leaves divided into fine, threadlike segments. Flowers are showy scarlet; a white form is available. Widely naturalized in the American tropics, it grows rapidly in light soil and full sun.

I. tricolor (morning-glory) grows to 10 ft. and has purplish blue flowers 4–5 in. across. It is a tender perennial grown as an annual, with many cultivars available.

IPOMOPSIS (ī poh MAHP sis). A genus of annual, biennial, or perennial herbs, mostly native to western North America, belonging to the Polemoniaceae (Phlox Family), and formerly included under the genus *Gilia*. The leaves are variously hairy and may be entire or finely dissected and almost needle-like. Salver-shaped or tubular flowers in various colors are borne in clusters. The plants are easily cultivated in the garden, thriving in relatively dry conditions. Propagation is by seed, which can be sown where plants are to bloom.

Ipomopsis aggregata

I. aggregata (scarlet gilia), native to California, is a biennial that grows to 2 ft. and has 2 in. long, linear leaves. The showy flowers of scarlet, yellow, pink, or nearly white are borne in long, dense clusters.

I. rubra (standing-cypress), growing in pyramidal form to 6 ft., is a hardy biennial or perennial herb native to dry parts of the southeastern United States. It has finely dissected leaves resembling cypress needles. The tubular scarlet flowers are borne in narrow panicles with orange or yellow markings. Each flower lasts only a few days, but the succession lasts long as blooming progresses downward from the top of the stem.

Ipomopsis rubra

IRESINE (ī re SĪ nee). A genus of bushy, erect or climbing herbs and small shrubs belonging to the Amaranthaceae (Amaranth Family) and commonly known as bloodleaf. They are native to tropical or semitropical regions and are grown like coleus as houseplants or in summer beds for their foliage, although the flowers are inconspicuous. Propagation is by cuttings.

I. herbstii grows to 6 ft. and has notched leaves of purplish red or green, veined with yellow. Cv. 'Aureo-reticulata' has greenish red leaves veined with yellow.

I. lindenii has narrow, sharp-pointed red leaves.

IRIDACEAE (ī ri DAY see ee). The Iris Family, a group of widely distributed, mostly low-growing perennial herbs with fleshy rootstocks, corms, or bulbs. The leaves are long and narrow; the flowers are subtended by bracts, with six petals and sepals inserted on the rim of the ovary; stamens are three instead of six as in other families of the same order, such as Liliaceae (Lily Family). The family yields some medicinal products, such as orris root and the drug saffron, and many of the choicest ornamentals. Chief cultivated genera are *Acidanthera*, *Babiana*, *Belamcanda*, *Crocosmia*, *Crocus*, *Freesia*, *Gladiolus*, *Iris*, *Ixia*, *Lapeirousia*, *Moraea*, *Neomarica*, *Sparaxis*, *Tigridia*, *Tritonia*, and *Watsonia*.

IRIS (Ī ris). The principal genus of the Iridaceae (Iris Family), one of the largest and most important groups of garden plants. In ancient mythology, Iris, symbolizing the rainbow, is often referred to as the "goddess of the rainbow," but she had no such important position on Olympus. She was the personal attendant and messenger of Hera, spouse of the great Zeus. Her name has been perpetuated in a great genus of plants because of their unusual color quality—a shimmering changeability under varying lights and positions, which has given us the adjective "iridescent." This quality was contained in her garb, says an old author who wrote, "Iris, of saffron wings, displaying against the sun a robe of a thousand varying colors."

Iris sp.

The iris, as we now know it, is a comparatively modern type that is of paramount importance in gardens, blooming in late May and early June, after the tulips and before the peonies and roses. Its development into garden material came about during the late nineteenth to early twentieth centuries. This development was confined principally to one subdivision of a large group of irises, known as the bearded or pogon types because of a strip of hairy growth, a "beard," on the three divisions of the flower, known as the falls, which usually droop or are barely horizontal.

This beard, according to botanists, is a guide or signal to insects seeking nectar. It leads them to the store hidden deep in the heart of the flower. In going after the nectar, they must come in contact with the flower's seed-producing organs.

Thus, they pick up some of the pollen from the stamen placed above the beard of one flower and carry it on their bodies to fertilize other flowers. The iris is so constructed that flowers are not self-fertilizing; seed is produced only through the unintentional agency of insects or by plant breeders who deliberately perform the same function.

The iris' method of pollination has resulted in the wonderful development of the modern iris, because, of all garden subjects, it is perhaps the most easily controlled and handled for hybridizing purposes. Even a rank amateur can breed new iris varieties.

HISTORY

The iris has long been used in heraldry and for ornamental designs because of its distinct form. This consists of three upright divisions, known as the standards; three lower divisions, known as the falls; and in between are three-strap-shaped divisions, known as the style branches. It is classically represented in the fleur-de-lis, which is the national symbol of France.

Few irises were grown in our ancestors' gardens. They occupied a position of rather minor importance and were known as "flags" or flower-de-luces. There was a gray-white, the old time orris, which yielded fragrant powder of orris root used in cosmetics and tooth powders. One of the oldest of common garden plants, this was botanically known as *I. florentina* (Florentine iris).

Another old cultivated type was a purple iris, often known as a German iris for no good geographical reason. For a time this gave its name to the entire group of tall bearded irises. Native European forms occasionally found included a pale yellow, a yellow with brown falls, and a tall, handsome lavender (*I. pallida*).

Intercrossing the European forms produced thousands of varieties now in commerce and cultivation. The ancient varieties have taken a relatively minor place in the modern iris, aside from furnishing two outstanding characteristics that add to the plants' garden value—namely, hardiness and variety of coloring.

The real beginning of the modern iris came with the introduction from the eastern Mediterranean countries of new species with huge flowers and tall stems, attaining heights of 4 ft. or more, a stature previously unknown in bearded irises. The first of these was *I. amas*, discovered in the provence of Amasia in Asia Minor. While lacking in great height, it first brought huge flowers and can be found in the background of many modern irises. Next came *I. trojana*, huge and tall, found near the site of ancient Troy; *I. cypriana*, from the island of Cyprus; *I. mesopotamica*; and *I. ricardi*. The finest of the modern irises contain a mixture of several of these strains. Iris breeders, having incorporated the good qualities of the Asiatic forms, started working for hardiness, vigor of growth, and freedom of bloom.

This rather sketchy outline of the origin of the modern garden iris has direct bearing on the garden use and value of this plant. While the oriental forms gave great height and size, they also brought to the previously ironclad bearded iris an element of tenderness and some cultural difficulties that iris fanciers soon recognized.

IRIS CLASSIFICATION

Botanists divide the genus *Iris* into two large divisions: those growing from rhizomes and those growing from bulbs. A third, relatively minor division consists of only one anomalous species, *I. nelapensis*, which is neither bulbous nor strictly rhizomatous.

The bulbous and rhizomatous irises are further subdivided by botanists and horticulturists. The subgroups given below are variously determined by flower form, species derivation, and habit. The popular bearded cultivars are particularly numerous and are classified by horticulturists according to plant height. For descriptions and lists of new cultivars, consult the publications of organizations such as the American Iris Society.

RHIZOMATOUS IRISES

Bearded (Pogon) Irises. These have a beard or pattern of hairs on the falls. They are sometimes collectively referred to as German irises. The old-fashioned flags belong to this group.

Miniature dwarfs are under 10 in.

Standard dwarfs (Lilliputs) are 10–15 in.

Intermediates are 15–28 in.

Miniature Talls (table iris).

Border Iris.

Standard Talls are over 28 in.

Regalias have hairs in a line on the falls and standards.

Pseudoregalias have hairs in a line on the falls.

Onococychis have hairs scattered on the falls. These are thought to be the biblical lilies-of-the-field.

Crested (Evansia) Irises. This is a small group with cockscomb-like crests on the falls.

Beardless (Apogon) Irises. These have smooth falls without any beard or crest. The group includes numerous widely distributed species. Horticultural forms include the Siberian, spurious, Louisiana, and Japanese irises.

BULBOUS IRISES

Irises growing from bulbs are included in two subgenera, *Xiphium* and *Scorpiris*.

Xiphium Irises. This group includes the English, Dutch, and Spanish forms, all with large erect standards.

Scorpiris. This includes the Juno irises with very small, spreading or down-curved standards.

CULTURE

The culture of most irises is simple. There are only two requirements—sun and good drainage. Plants grow well in almost any soil, but they are most satisfactory and less susceptible to disease, such as root rot, in soils of only moderate fertility. While they need to be fed occasionally and the finest bloom quality is developed in richer soils, the soft growth produced by too much food is susceptible to root, the worst of iris diseases. A hot wet season and resulting lush growth also seem to encourage disease.

The iris should not be crowded by other plants that overshadow it or mat closely around the roots and foliage. It needs air and sunshine, but half a day of full sun will suffice.

Although some form bulbs, most irises grow from rhizomes, fleshy underground stalks that bear the true stringy roots. These rhizomes branch and eventually overcrowd each other, so it is necessary to dig and replant the clump at certain intervals—usually from three to five years under ordinary culture. Otherwise parts of the clump become choked and will not produce a good flower crop. Some growers avoid the need for too frequent digging and replanting, which can destroy a clump effect, by carefully cutting out crowding rhizomes when working fertilizer into the soil.

When an iris makes vigorous growth and a large clump but produces no bloom, the best treatment seems to be to dig, divide, and replant it. If it still does not bloom, discard it.

Planting. In planting an iris, the root should be reduced to a single section of the rhizome with a single fan of leaves. Half the length of the leaves should be cut off to balance the disturbance of the roots. The rhizome should be planted horizontally with a light covering of soil, not more than 1 in. and even less in light soils. An old and frequently quoted direction said, "Plant it like a duck on the water, half in and half out of the soil;" but this may lead to heavy losses from heaving during the first winter after planting. If planted a little too deep, the rhizomes adjust to the plants' needs by working their way toward the surface. Bearded irises should be planted after their blooming season, but the sooner thereafter the better.

In planting different iris varieties, especially the tall bearded kinds, pay attention to the heights of different kinds, which are usually given in catalogs; otherwise a tall plant may eclipse a lower-growing beauty.

Soil and Feeding. Heavy clay soils must be broken up for the successful growth of the bearded iris. Washed sand and peat moss or other humus material are excellent for this purpose. Very light sandy soils need occasional addition of humus in the form of old manure, compost, or peat moss; in such soils, however, the peat moss is sometimes too slow to disintegrate.

A number of old theories regarding iris requirements have been disproved. Bearded irises do not need lime unless the soil is very acid. They do need calcium, which is best applied in the form of GYPSUM. The use of fresh manure is inadvisable since it can burn plants, but they can stand it as a mulch if there is no actual contact with the plants.

ENEMIES

Disease. Most iris diseases are fostered by the humidity maintained by too luxuriant foliage growth. Cutting the leaves back to 8–10 in. fans after flowering helps greatly in disease control.

Rhizome (or soft) rot, a bacterial disease due to *Bacillus carotovorus* and common on many vegetables and ornamental plants, causes a rotting of fleshy rhizomes and is responsible for the loss of many valuable iris plants. All rhizomatous kinds are susceptible. The first visible symptom is a browning and withering of the foliage tips, followed by a watersoaked appearance at the base and the collapse of leaves and shoots. A cream-colored bacterial ooze may appear on the rotting leaves, and the fleshy portions of the rhizomes disintegrate into a soft, wet, slimy, yellowish, foul-smelling mass within the intact epidermis. If the rot is allowed to spread, the characteristic unpleasant smell may spread throughout the garden. Infection takes place through wounds, many of which are made by the iris borer (see below).

Combat the rot by lifting all infected plants and burning those most seriously affected. From the others, cut out all soft portions, then dip in a disinfectant solution. If the disease has been severe, sterilize the soil. When possible, removal of the old soil and replacing it with fresh earth is even better. Leave the treated rhizomes in the sun for a day or so, and space them well when replanting, being careful to leave the top of the rhizome exposed. Keep the soil light and well drained by incorporating sand or sifted coal ashes. This procedure is also helpful in controlling other diseases and insect pests.

Leaf spot is more common and destructive to Siberian irises than is generally realized. The elliptical reddish-bordered spots with a grayish center dotted with black fruiting bodies of the fungus occur largely on the upper half of the leaf, but in severe cases all the foliage dies prematurely with consequent weakening of the rhizomes and often death of the plant in a year or two.

Since the fungus lives in old leaves on the ground, the best control is careful removal and burning of all dead and diseased leaves in the fall.

In CROWN ROT, which can be serious in crowded iris beds, the leaf bases and flower stalks are rotted and covered with numerous reddish brown sclerotia. Remove such leaves and stalks, and drench the soil with a good disinfectant. If necessary, remove and treat plants as for rhizome rot.

A bacterial leaf blight can be serious in midsummer during wet seasons; sanitary measures are the primary control. Mosaic. a streaking of the foliage with light and dark green areas, occurs chiefly in the bulbous irises.

Insect Pests. The most dreaded insect pest of iris is the borer, *Macronoctua onusta*, which is extremely injurious itself and is almost inevitably followed by soft rot. Eggs laid in the fall near or on the basal leaves hatch sometime in April. The larvae eat their way down inside the leaves, increasing in size until, when they reach the rhizome, they are 1–1½ in. long, soft, fat, and pinkish tinged, with a brown head. They pupate in the soil near the base of the plants in late summer, and the moths, violet-brown with black markings, emerge in the fall to lay their eggs. In its early stages the borer's presence can be recognized by a wet stain along the edges of the leaves, followed by a ragged appearance. In small plantings, many of the larvae can be killed by squeezing all leaves that show the wet stain firmly between the thumb and forefinger, starting at the ground and pulling upward. Some growers recommend covering the iris beds with dry leaves in the fall and burning them over quickly to kill the eggs, but this often injures the plants. It is better to cut away the old dead leaves and destroy them, thus getting rid of the eggs that would produce borers the following season. In spring, dust weekly with insecticide. The best way to get rid of borers is to dig up and examine all the plants just after flowering, cut out any borers found, then treat the rhizomes with disinfectant as for soft rot. If this procedure is followed every three or four years, when the irises should be divided anyway, the borers should be kept fairly well under control.

Aphids can be controlled by spraying with a pyrethrum-soap or nicotine-soap solution.

RHIZOMATOUS IRISES

BEARDED TYPES

The bearded iris class breaks into natural divisions based on season and style of growth, both important qualities in the garden. These are the dwarfs, the earliest of all; the intermediates, a rapidly developing class; and the tall bearded class, which is the most important. They give a season of bloom extending from spring to early summer, one class merging into another. The intermediates are actually results of crossing the early dwarfs and the late, tall bearded irises.

The dwarf irises furnish material for beautiful garden combinations with the daffodils and other early spring bulbs. The earliest of the type and one of the first irises grown in North American gardens is *I. atroviolaceae*, which produces tiny red-purple blooms. It was cultivated by the pioneers and is delightful with yellow crocus, the forsythias, and the earliest spring bulbs. There is also a great variety of dwarf irises in a fairly wide and increasing color range, all making fine material for garden pictures, with the daffodils, early tulips, primroses, and other early perennials and bulbs.

The dwarfs merge into the intermediate class, which receives due attention from hybridists. New and attractive varieties are intermediate both in blooming season and size between the dwarfs and the tall bearded class. Gardeners use this fine type in combination with various tulips to produce wonderful spring garden pictures. The intermediates have a season of about two weeks and overlap the tall bearded season by a few days, thus giving a continuous iris pageant.

The tall bearded irises provide material for some of the finest garden pictures of the entire season. The flowers, with their marvelous and gorgeous as well as delicate and elusive colorings, are especially effective when planted with the late May and early June perennials, such as daylilies, columbines, hardy pinks, iceland pop-

pies, coral-bells, and the perennial flax.

Oncocyclus Irises. There are a number of iris species of great beauty but exceedingly difficult to grow, notably the huge, curiously marked and colored oncocyclus iris, of which *I. susiana* (mourning iris) is the best known. They are subjects for the expert or for the gardener willing to give them special culture and conditions.

Regelia Irises. The regelia group also includes beautiful members but is difficult to handle. Between these two groups there are hybrids, which are somewhat easier to grow. There are also a few hybrids between the easily grown tall and dwarf bearded and the oncocyclus types; they exhibit great and unusual beauty and many more are likely to become popular, bringing new types to this remarkable race of garden plants. A good one among them is 'William Mohr', a hybrid between the ancient bearded iris variety *parisiana*, and the rarely beautiful species *I. gatesi*.

CRESTED TYPES

This group is distinguished by the presence of a notched ridge instead of a beard. These little irises popular in rock gardens offer a field of beauty quite distinct from their more stately relatives. In general, the bulbous ones should be grown where they will have a baking period during the summer. The rhizomatous ones will grow almost anywhere. Flowers are available in all colors, except true red; some have beautiful patterns.

BEARDLESS TYPES

There are several dry or bearded irises. Unlike the bearded types, they require constant moist conditions and prefer heavy soils. A few are swamp natives and semiaquatic plants, such as *I. versicolor* (wild blue flag).

Siberian Irises. The best-known and most useful beardless types are a large class known as Siberian irises. They bloom along with the tall bearded class in white or many tones of blue, and some modern varieties include reddish tones. They have narrow grasslike foliage, tall slender stems, and graceful blooms of medium size produced in great profusion, making them among the most ornamental of all irises. There are many named varieties and most are impervious to all but the most exceptional heat and drought.

These irises are among the finest for cutting purposes, being stronger than the more fragile and rather ephemeral, tall bearded kinds. Much improvement has been made in this class, particularly in rich, dark, almost velvety textures formerly lacking, also in increasing the height, which sometimes reaches 50 in.

Siberians should be planted in the early spring before growth is well started or in the early fall, allowing time for them to become established. They like a rich, heavy soil with good moisture-retaining qualities and will stand some fertilizing. They are most effective in masses or single clumps and are ideal for planting beside pools where conditions suit them perfectly. Plants gradually form thick clumps but are best left alone, since they do not require frequent division like the bearded types. Propagation is easily done from seed.

Species closely allied to the Siberian irises have been introduced from China, bringing new red and yellow tones to this class. These include *I. chrysographes*, *I. forresti*, and others.

Spurious Iris. A highly decorative type, *I. spuria*, produces distinctive and attractive flowers toward the end of the season for tall bearded and Siberian irises. Just why it was dubbed the "spurious" iris has never been explained. It is represented by stately plants with fine all-season foliage of good height. Under some conditions, such as prevail in parts of California, it grows so vigorously that it is useful only in larger gardens. This is not true in most regions, however, and these irises are easily cultivated.

The best known and most striking of this group is the gold-banded iris, *I. ochroleuca* and its varieties, which have huge tall-stemmed creamy blooms with yellow patches on the falls. It is beautiful planted with delphiniums and pink climbing roses.

Others of this group, smaller in stature but with similar graceful foliage and blue or purple flowers, are more or less well known. 'Mt. Wil-son', typical of the class, blooms in pale blue and is frequently planted in striking combinations with umbellatum lilies. 'Lord Wolseley' blooms in deeper blue.

Louisiana Iris. The happy discovery, in the Louisiana delta country and other southern regions, of what appear to be new beardless iris species opened a prospect of an entirely new race for garden use including previously unknown colors. They range from white to deep purple with all the intermediate tones of yellows, reds, and blues. The flowers also vary in size and shape. Although native to the South, they have been successfully grown all over the United States.

The forerunners of these types, which seem to fall close to them structurally, were *I. fulva*, a coppery red flower native to the more southerly states but hardy in the North; *I. hexagona*, with blue-purple flowers; and *I. foliosa*, with lush foliage that hides the light blue blooms.

Japanese Iris. Perhaps the most magnificent of all is *I. kaempferi*, the Japanese type with its ruffled blooms lasting through July, sometimes 12 in. across in all manner of blues, red-purples, and white with a great variety of mottlings, specklings, and stipplings as well as self (solid) colors. They require abundant moisture—almost swamp conditions during their spring growing season—and then a dryer resting season when they withstand much drought safely. They need an acid soil in order to endure and flourish. In the average garden they will survive for two or three years, then dwindle and disappear. They are so beautiful, however, that they are well worth replacing, and those whose garden conditions suit them are truly fortunate.

Since Japanese irises are readily grown from seed, some gardeners maintain a supply by this method, but the seedlings are seldom as fine as the named varieties carefully selected from thousands of seedlings. There is much confusion regarding the names of these irises owing to carelessness of exporters who have sent the same iris under different names at different times or different irises under the same name.

BULBOUS IRISES

An important class of greenhouse irises grows from bulbs. The best known and most generally cultivated are the Spanish, Dutch, and English types. The Dutch type has become the most important, being an improvement on the older Spanish type, which it resembles.

Spanish and Dutch Irises. Before the tall bearded irises became popular, Spanish irises were often grown in gardens, until a federal quarantine prohibited the importation of many kinds of foreign plants. Spanish irises were obtainable very cheaply and, although short-lived, they were easily replaced.

Now that the Dutch irises (initially suspected of being tender) have been tested by gardeners and found to grow as readily as the Spanish, they have increased in popularity in North American gardens. Both Spanish and Dutch kinds require light well-drained soil for best growth outdoors. They also require late fall planting because they make a fall growth of foliage. The colors vary, including white, yellow, blue, and bronze.

English and Other Bulbous Irises. The English iris (which really comes from Spain) is another handsome bulbous subject. It requires a moist, heavy soil in order to flourish. It has heavier foliage than the Spanish and in bloom resembles a miniature Japanese iris. Most bulbous irises bloom toward the middle or end of June, just as the tall bearded types are waning.

PRINCIPAL SPECIES

I. cristata (crested iris) is a rhizomatous species native in the southeastern states. It is a vigorous dwarf that grows 4–6 in. high and bears faintly fragrant, lavender-blue flowers with yellow crests. It does best in partial shade and is good for large gardens. There are several varieties blooming in blue, white, or purple.

I. danfordiae (Danford iris) is a bulbous reticulata type that grows to 12 in. and has yellow-orange flowers spotted with olive green.

I. ensata (Japanese or sword-leaved iris) grows 2–3 ft. high and bears two to four white, blue, purple, or red-violet flowers often marked with contrasting veins.

I. foetidissima (gladwin iris) is a beardless rhizomatous species growing to 18 in. The flowers are inconspicuous, but the plant is cultivated for its large pods containing round red seeds used in dried arrangements. The evergreen leaves emit an offensive odor when bruised.

I. fulua (copper iris) is a beardless rhizomatous species that grows 2–3 ft. and has brightly colored flowers from coppery orange to salmon. It thrives in wet places.

I. germanica (German iris) is a bearded rhizomatous species that grows 2–3 ft. and bears white to lilac or purple flowers with yellow beards. It yields the orris root used in medicines, perfumes, and tooth powders.

I. gracilipes makes dainty fans of fine foliage and carries airy, quarter-sized lavender flowers. There is also a white form.

I. hoogiana (redbeard iris) is a regalia rhizomatous species that grows to 30 in. and has flowers of white or pale to dark grayish blue.

I. kaempferi (Japanese iris) is a beardless rhizomatous species that grows to 2 ft. high and has red-purple flowers marked with yellow.

I. lacustris (lake iris) is a relatively small plant, easily grown if given partial shade, moisture, and an occasional dressing of leaf mold.

I. laerigata (rabbit-ear iris) is a beardless rhizomatous species that grows to 2 ft. and has flowers of blue or purple and sometimes white.

I. minutaurea is a challenge to flower. It requires scree conditions and blooms when the foliage is 5–6 in. high. A successful plant is covered with small yellow flowers dotted with brownish purple.

I. nepalensis grows to 2 ft. and has dark violet and white flowers with violet veins and yellow markings.

I. pallida (orris) grows to 3 ft. and has scapes bearing two to three scented, lavender-blue flowers with brown-purple veins and yellow-tipped white beards. It is one of the irises grown for the production of orris, obtained from the powdered dry rhizome and used in perfumery.

I. persica (Persian iris), belonging to the bulbous Juno group, grows to 6 in. and has violet-scented, greenish blue flowers marbled with bright yellow.

I. pseudacorus (yellow flag) is a beardless rhizomatous species that grows to 5 ft. high and has yellow flowers often veined with violet or brown. It grows well in wet places.

I. pumila (dwarf bearded iris) is an adaptable plant that is found growing naturally from the seaside to the mountains. It grows 4–8 in. and has low, sturdy foliage with relatively huge 3–4 in., very early blooming flowers in a wide range of colors, especially yellow or lilac.

I. reticulata (netted iris), a small bulb belonging to the reticulata group, grows to 2 ft. It is easily cultivated, especially in the rock garden, and is available in several color forms but usually has deep violet to purple flowers marked with orange and white. One of the earliest spring bulbs, it thrives in a sheltered corner where it will come up with the snowdrops and often bloom while snow is still around it.

I. siberica (Siberian iris) is the parent of many beardless rhizomatous hybrids and varieties. It grows 2–4 ft., and its scapes bear two to four white to lilac or purple flowers.

I. susiana (mourning iris), a traditional garden favorite, is an onocyclus rhizomatous type growing 12–18 in. with bright violet to purple flowers.

I. tectorum (roof iris) is an easy grower, larger in all its parts than most kinds suited to the rock garden.

I. versicolor (blue flag) is a beardless rhizomatous species that grows 2–3 ft. and has blue flowers marked with yellow. It is the common wild iris that thrives in wet places. Skin irritation may result from handling the rootstock.

Iris versicolor

I. xiphioides (English iris) belongs to the xiphium bulbous group and grows 1–2 ft. with white to lavender or dark blue flowers marked with yellow.

I. xiphium (Spanish iris) is a bulbous species that grows 1–2 ft. and has large flowers of white, yellow, blue, purple, or slate-blue marked with a yellow or orange patch. Its many forms include the Dutch iris, which is one of the best for forcing potted blooms.

IRISH HEATH. Common name for *Daboecia cantabrica*, a small, half-hardy, evergreen shrub of the Ericaceae (Heath Family); see DABOECIA.

IRON. Besides being one of the principal commercial minerals, iron is also one of the elements essential to plant growth. It is present in sufficient quantities in practically all soils. Iron causes some of the characteristic soil colors—red, yellow, etc.—and is a constituent of chlorophyll, the green matter of plants, without which the manufacture of food in the leaves (and consequently normal growth) is impossible. When for any reason plants fail to assimilate iron, their foliage becomes white or nearly so, in mottled designs or over large areas; they are then said to be chlorotic, or suffering from CHLOROSIS. Sometimes young shoots develop more rapidly than iron can reach them, causing the newly formed leaves to be pale or white instead of green for a time.

Iron compounds are used in gardening to some extent as fungicides and weed killers. The most common of these is iron sulfate, which is sometimes used to spray plants infected with fungi, though it is not as efficient as copper sulfate.

IRONWOOD. Common name for CARPINUS, OSTRYA, and various other trees characterized by exceptionally hard wood.

IRREGULAR. A type of flower in which not all parts are alike. Examples are the two-lipped snapdragon, the highly modified orchid, the lobelia and mint with two petals distinctly unlike the other three, the nasturtium with its long spur formed by one sepal, the gladiolus with petals of different shapes, and many other types. All these are different from any regular flower, such as that of the apple or potato, whose perianth is the same seen from every side.

IRRIGATION. A general term for the process of watering crops by any method, but especially that of distributing water in quantity over land surfaces. In arid regions of the western United States, elaborate and costly construction and equipment, including dams, reservoirs, machinery, flumes, ditches, furrows, etc., are often employed in irrigating orchards and field crops such as sugar beets, alfalfa, and the like. In normally humid areas where irrigation is used more to meet drought emergencies, to improve crop quality, or to hasten growth, sprinkler systems are more common, both on commercial fields and in smaller home gardens. Here water is conducted in pipes under pressure and distributed through nozzles to fall in rainlike drops. Effective irrigation is a valuable insurance of success in plant growing and lawn care.

Overhead Irrigation. Overhead irrigation or sprinkling presents five outstanding advantages over flood or ditch irrigation.

1. It saves time in applying water.

2. Its ideal application in the form of artificial rain does not pack down the soil or injure plants, flowers, or fruits.

3. It is capable of soaking the soil in summer as soon as a crop has been harvested, in advance of plowing or digging for a succeeding crop, to provide ideal conditions for seed germination and rapid plant growth.

4. It can help to protect tender plants such as beans and dahlias against frost in the late spring and early autumn by creating a moist atmosphere in the evening, and to help save them if slightly frostbitten by thawing them out in the early morning before the sun strikes them.

5. It is effective in putting applications of plant food into solution and in washing off any commercial fertilizer that, lodged on the foliage, might burn it.

There are a number of types of sprinklers available that can be connected to hoses or installed as more permanent systems. The two main types used are oscillating sprinklers (which can rotate 180° from being almost parallel and close to the ground to perpendicular and then parallel to the ground on the opposite side) and pulsating sprinklers (which can rotate a complete 360° circle parallel to the ground if desired).

Hose Irrigation. One type of sprinkler irrigation is a hose that is perforated at regular intervals, giving in effect a flexible pipe system for use on the ground along curving borders. Another type of hose is made of a durable but porous material through which water seeps slowly enough so as not to wash the soil, but rapidly enough to moisten a considerable area as the water spreads sideways by capillary attraction. This can be used either on cultivated soil or on the lawn.

Drip (Trickle) Irrigation. Semiflexible tubing with perforations or emitters at regular intervals allows water to slowly drip out of the openings. Tubing can be placed on the soil surface, under a mulch layer, or buried beneath the surface. It is a most efficient form of irrigation, using the least water while keeping plants well supplied, and can be adapted to most garden situations.

Drip irrigation

Other Methods. Another type of irrigation, especially adaptable to specimen plants, consists of sinking flower pots, tin cans with perforated bottoms, or short lengths of drain tile vertically near such plants and filling them with water as frequently as necessary. This carries the moisture down to the root and is economical when a limited supply makes it impossible to thoroughly soak all the soil between rows or plants.

Vegetables and berry plants grown in rows can be irrigated by the western method of running water into shallow furrows beside or between the rows until the ground is soaked and then filling the furrows with loose soil to prevent the wet surface from drying hard and causing rapid evaporation.

See also SPRINKLING; WATERING.

ISOETES (I soh ET eez). A genus of FERN ALLIES with quill-like cylindrical leaves rising from an underground corm and giving them the common name quillwort. They are mostly aquatic and are sometimes used in aquariums. They are mainly from temperate regions and are rarely tropical.

ITEA (IT ee ah). A genus of deciduous or evergreen trees or shrubs with simple alternate leaves, mostly from tropical or temperate Asia, belonging to the Saxifragaceae (Saxifrage Family). The one North American species, *I. virginica* (sweetspire), a deciduous shrub growing to 8 ft., is the only one at all hardy in the North (to Zone 5). The tops may die back after a severe winter, but it soon makes up from below. It is a useful summer-flowering shrub and is very adaptable as to soil and location but is best grown on moist ground. The white, slightly fragrant flowers are borne in upright racemes, and in the fall the leaves turn a brilliant red. Propagation is by seed, cuttings, and root division.

ITHURIEL'S-SPEAR. Common name for *Triteleia laxa*, a cormous member of the Amaryllidaceae (Amaryllis Family), native to California and producing large, spherical heads of pale blue-lilac flowers; see TRITELEIA.

IVY. Common name for HEDERA, a genus of twining shrubs, including Algerian, English, and Persian ivies. The name "ivy" is also applied to other plants. American-ivy, Boston-ivy, and Japanese-ivy are species of PARTHENOCISSUS. Cape-ivy and German-ivy are species of SENECIO. Devil's-ivy or ivy arum belongs to the genus EPIPREMNUM. Ground-ivy belongs to the genus GLECHOMA. Ivy gourd is *Coccinea graudis*. Kenilworth-ivy is *Cymbalaria muralis*. Marine-ivy is *Cissus incisa*. POISON-IVY is a species of RHUS.

IXIA (IK see ah). A genus of about 30 South African herbs related to the iris. Growing from corms, they produce slender, grasslike leaves and long, slender spikes up to 18 in. of small, funnel- or bell-shaped flowers in showy colors, borne several on a stem. They flower in the spring but are tender, so their use in North American gardens is restricted to warm regions. Like many South African bulbs, *Ixia* seems to prefer the West Coast conditions and grows splendidly there. In the East, it has proved difficult to handle. Normally hardy to Zone 7, it is ideal for patio pot cultivation almost everywhere.

They should be planted in late fall, about 3 in. deep, with sand in the bottom of each hole. A winter covering is essential in the northern part of their range, but a coldframe can also be used. Spring-planted corms will bloom in summer, while those planted in a cool greenhouse in early fall will provide winter flowers.

There are many horticultural forms ranging from white to pink, red, lilac, and yellow. Several species are cultivated. *I. maculata* grows to 2 ft. and bears dense spikes of flowers, originally yellow with a dark purplish blotch at their base but now with many hybrids in various colors. *I. columellaris* blooms in mauve and blue; *I. speciosa*, crimson; and *I. leucantha* var. *lutea*, deep yellow. *I. viridiflora* has interesting flowers of pale green with black throats.

IXIOLIRION (ik see oh LEE ree ahn). A genus of Asiatic summer-blooming herbs belonging to the Amaryllidaceae (Amaryllis Family) and commonly known as Siberian-lily. They have bulbous rootstocks and violet or blue lilylike flowers in flattened clusters. Since the species are tender (hardy to Zone 7), the plants must be dug in the fall and the bulbs stored in frostproof quarters until spring.

IXORA (ik SOH rah). A genus of tropical evergreen shrubs often grown in warm greenhouses and outdoors in Zones 10–11, belonging to the Rubiaceae (Madder Family). They are among the most handsome of tropical woody plants, bushy, with attractive foliage and clusters of showy flowers. They are not difficult to grow and do well in a mixture of fibrous loam and peat with sharp sand. For sizable plants, use the compost in as rough a state as possible and pot firmly. Specimen plants in large pots can be kept going for several years without repotting if fed liberally with liquid manure. Give the plants a short rest after flowering and then prune to shape. Light shade is desirable during the hottest weather. Propagation is by cuttings.

I. coccinea and *I. chinensis* or their hybrids are the most commonly grown. *I. acuminata* is a tall-growing, white-flowered species. *I. duffii* 'Superking', formerly listed as *I. thyrsiflora*, is a spectacular large-flowered, scarlet species.

J

JABOTICABA. Common name for *Myrciaria cauliflora*, a tropical fruit-bearing shrub; see MYRCIARIA.

JACARANDA (jak ah RAN dah). A genus of tropical American trees or shrubs belonging to the Bignoniaceae (Bignonia Family). Some species are grown as street trees or lawn specimens in Zones 9–11. Plants are occasionally seen in cooler regions as small greenhouse specimens or used in subtropical arrangements. Propagation is by seed or cuttings of half-ripened wood.

J. cuspidifolia has large leaves and clusters of long, pointed, violet-blue flowers.

J. mimosifolia (green-ebony) has elegant, finely cut, fernlike leaves and loose clusters of large blue flowers.

JACKFRUIT. Common name for *Artocarpus heterophyllus*, a tropical Asiatic tree related to breadfruit; see ARTOCARPUS.

JACK-IN-THE-PULPIT. A common name for *Arisaema triphyllum*, a familiar woodland herb with three-part leaves and mottled flowers; see ARISAEMA.

JACOBEAN-LILY. Common name for *Sprekelia formosissima*, a flowering tropical plant of the Amaryllidaceae (Amaryllis Family); see SPREKELIA.

JACOB'S-LADDER. A common name for *Polemonium caeruleum*, a perennial herb that has feathery foliage and drooping flowers; see POLEMONIUM.

JACQUEMONTIA (jak MAWN shee ah). A genus of subtropical and tropical climbing plants, belonging to the Convolvulaceae (Morning-glory Family). They can be grown outdoors in Zones 10–11. The principal species is *J. pentantha*, a twining perennial that has a shrubby base and bears loose clusters of violet-blue flowers. Propagation is by seed or cuttings.

JAMESIA (JAYM zee ah). A genus of deciduous shrubs native to the Rocky Mountains, belonging to the Saxifragaceae (Saxifrage Family). *J. americana* is hardy and thrives in any well-drained garden soil in a sunny place. It grows to 4 ft. and bears short clusters of white flowers in early summer. Propagation is by seed or cuttings of ripened wood.

JAPANESE BEETLE. The rapidly spreading beetle, *Popillia japonica*, was first found in the United States about 1915. The spread would have been rather slow by flying only, but Japanese beetles have traveled on shipments of plant products and by truck and automobile, rapidly increasing in population in each area it reaches. The wave of great abundance drops in several years, so control becomes more possible.

Japanese beetle

The shiny, bronzy beetle is around ⅓ in. long and has five white tufts along the sides of the abdomen, six legs, and tough wings. The larval form of the beetle, the grub, can do considerable damage before it emerges from the soil, where the eggs were laid. For controls, see GRUBS.

The trap plants placed at the edge of a garden to deter Japanese beetles from the vegetables and flowers you wish to protect should include light-colored flowers (especially white roses if you don't mind sacrificing a few), evening primroses, Virginia creeper, and knotweed.

These beetles are easy to see and pick off by hand, and various repellent substances, such as wheat flour or a dusting of hydrated lime, can be applied to plants. There are also commercially available traps that can be very successful.

JAPANESE GARDEN. The Japanese ideal of garden making is to reproduce for intimate enjoyment the loftiest aspect of nature—those natural scenes that are not otherwise available for daily contemplation. Scenes of wild and rugged splendor—mountains, forests, cascades, chasms, promontories, abysses—are common features in Japanese garden designs. In general, the design is based on a theme with a central idea, with all elements selected to contribute to this one thought.

Japanese designs utilize natural forms of wood in its natural state, stone, and bamboo for building materials, exploiting natural features such as gnarled branches or unusual rock formations. Water is always desirable, in the form of a pool, rivulet, or even a dry brook, all of which should be as close as possible to natural form.

The planting material is selected to resemble the effect of natural growth long undisturbed. This means no mixed beds or borders. One type of flower is the feature of its season, and evergreen material in shrub or tree form should be strongly dominant, but never in assorted kinds.

JAPANESE LAWN GRASS. Common name for *Zoysia japonica*, a creeping perennial also known as Korean lawn grass; see ZOYSIA.

JAPANESE PAGODA TREE. Common name for *Sophora japonica*, an ornamental leguminous tree native to Asia; see SOPHORA.

JAPANESE-QUINCE. Common name for *Chaenomeles speciosa*, a vigorous ornamental shrub with lustrous leaves and scarlet flowers; see CHAENOMELES.

JASMINE (JAZ min). Common name for JAS-MINUM, a genus of tropical and subtropical shrubs grown for their showy, fragrant flowers. Other plants have been called jasmines because of their fragrance; however, they can be distinguished in that true members of the genus *Jasminum* are spelled "jasmine" and those of other genera, "jes-samine." Both are pronounced the same way. See also JESSAMINE.

JASMINUM (jaz MIN um). A genus of tropical and subtropical, deciduous or evergreen shrubs, sometimes climbing, and commonly known as jasmine. Belonging to the Oleaceae (Olive Family), they are widely distributed in warm climates and can be grown outdoors in the warmer parts of the United States. Some are grown in greenhouses for their showy, fragrant flowers produced in winter. They grow well in good loamy soil and are propagated by cuttings and layers.

PRINCIPAL SPECIES

J. nudiflorum has yellow winter flowers and grows in sheltered spots.

J. officinale (poet's jasmine) is a long, vining shrub that may reach 30 ft. The delicate, compound leaves and slender, white, fragrant summer flowers make this a fine wall or arbor covering as far north as Washington, D.C.

J. sambac is a shrub, almost always blooming in warm regions with fragrant white flowers that are fully doubled in the variety 'Grand Duke'.

J. volubile (*J. simplicifolium* in the Florida trade) and *J. multiflorum* (downy jasmine) are common landscape plants in south Florida.

JATROPHA (jah TROH fah). A genus of tropical trees and shrubs belonging to the Euphorbiaceae (Spurge Family), commonly known as coral plant or lucky leaf. They have a long flowering season in Zones 10–11.

PRINCIPAL SPECIES

J. integerrima, also listed as *J. hastata*, is a shrub or small tree that is constantly bright with red flowers.

J. multifida (coral plant) is a scarlet-flowered shrub or tree.

J. podagrica (gout plant) is interesting for its swollen base, palmate leaves, and bright red flowers.

JEFFERSONIA (jef ur SOH nee ah) **diphylla.** A hardy woodland perennial herb native to Virginia and adjacent states, belonging to the Berberidaceae (Barberry Family) and commonly known as twinleaf. Its generic name was given in honor of Thomas Jefferson. It is an attractive plant that grows to 12 in. and has two-parted leaves and dainty white flowers 1 in. across. Hardy to Zone 3, it can be easily grown in the wild or rock garden, where it should be given a moist, humus-rich soil.

JERUSALEM-ARTICHOKE. Common name for *Helianthus tuberosus*, a perennial species of sunflower with edible tubers resembling potatoes. The common name is a misnomer on two counts: it is not an artichoke, and it is native to North America, not the Middle East. Jerusalem is a corruption of girasole, the Italian name for sunflower, given to the plant when it was carried back to Europe by early explorers in North America.

Jerusalem-artichoke

The plant grows to 6 ft. and has coarse, hairy foliage surmounted by bright yellow flowers 2–3 in. across, but it is grown more as a vegetable than for ornament. Its potatolike tubers, which are a delicious fall, winter, and early spring vegetable when scalloped or steamed and served with a bechamel or hollandaise sauce, compare with cauliflower in their delicate but distinct flavor. When cooked, it differs from potato and sweetpotato in never being mealy. It also makes a delicious pickle.

Since it often becomes a pestiferous weed, it should always be planted where it can do no harm—in a corner, or around the compost heap. Here it will bloom profusely in late summer and produce tubers abundantly without crowding other garden crops. It produces no seeds. When the tops die, cut them down and use them (with dead leaves and other garden refuse) to cover the patch and prevent deep freezing of the ground, so tubers can be dug as needed all winter. Digging and storing a supply in the fall is not advisable, since the tubers shrivel in storage. One planting will last indefinitely without care, though feeding will improve the size and yield of tubers. When harvesting, leave enough tubers in the ground to stock the bed for another year.

JERUSALEM-CHERRY. Common name for *Solanum pseudocapsicum*, a small shrubby relative of the eggplant and potato, cultivated primarily as a potted plant for its decorative fruits.

JERUSALEM THORN. Common name for *Parkinsonia aculeata*, a tropical, spiny, flowering tree; see PARKINSONIA. It also refers to *Paliurus spina-christi*, a spiny tree with greenish yellow flowers and brown fruits; see PALIURUS.

JESSAMINE (JAZ min). A common name for a number of fragrant plants. African, confederate, Malayan, or star jessamine is *Trachelospermum jasminoides*; see TRACHELOSPERMUM). Cape jessamine is *Gardenia jasminoides*; see GARDENIA. Carolina yellow jessamine is the genus GELSEMIUM. Chilean jessamine is *Mandevilla laxa*; see MANDEVILLA. Crape jessamine is *Tabernaemontana divaricata*; see TABERNAEMONTANA. Orange jessamine is *Murraya paniculata*; see MURRAYA.

This common name also refers to plants of the genus JASMINUM, but these are more appropriately termed "jasmine." Both names have the same pronunciation.

JETBEAD. Common name for *Rhodotypos scandens*, a deciduous shrub of the Rosaceae (Rose Family), native to Japan; see RHODOTYPOS.

JEWELWEED. A common name for *Impatiens capensis* and *I. pallida*, two annual herbs with golden flowers; see IMPATIENS.

JIMSONWEED. Colloquial corruption of Jamestown weed, which is a common name for *Datura stramonium*, a coarse, toxic weed; see DATURA.

JOE PYE WEED. Common name for *Eupatorium purpureum*, a rank-growing herb that has rose or purplish flowers in large, open clusters; see EUPATORIUM.

JONQUIL. A common name often erroneously applied as a synonym for daffodil to any sort of hardy NARCISSUS; it is correctly applied only to the species *N. jonquilla*.

JOSEPH'S-COAT. Common name for *Amaranthus tricolor*, an annual herb with colorful foliage; see AMARANTHUS.

JOSHUA TREE. Common name for *Yucca brevifolia*, a grotesquely shaped tree of the southwestern deserts; see YUCCA.

JOSS FLOWER. A common name for *Narcissus tazetta* var. *orientalis*, a tender bulb that bears clusters of small flowers; see NARCISSUS.

JUBAEA (joo BEE ah) **chilensis.** A large, unarmed feather palm, commonly called Chilean wine palm, syrup palm, or in Chile, coquito. It grows to 30 ft. and has a stout, columnar trunk 3 ft. or more in diameter surmounted by a crown of feather-form leaves 4½ ft. long. It produces plumlike, 1½ in. long, one-seeded fruits with fibrous flesh, which look like miniature coconuts and are called monkey's coconuts. A syrup or honey is made from the sap; in Chile they are used in candy. Due to commercial harvesting of the sap, few wild stands remain. As a garden subject, it is a handsome palm and grows well in California but does not thrive in Florida. It is frequently grown under glass in climates where the night temperature is 50°F. Large specimens in tubs are seen in subtropical gardens.

JUDAS TREE. Common name for CERCIS, a genus of flowering shrubs or trees, especially for *C. siliquastrum*, a European native with purplish flowers.

JUGLANS (JUG lans). A genus of deciduous trees including the principal members of the Juglandaceae (Walnut Family), and commonly known as walnut. It includes the black walnut, butternut, and some strains of the English or Persian walnut that are hardy in the North, and other

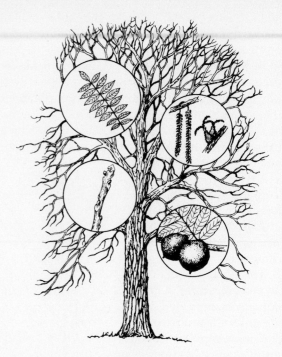

Juglans nigra

West Coast species requiring a warm climate. The walnuts are ornamental because of their attractive form and cheerful, airy appearance. The vibrating pinnate foliage permits breezes to pass through, yet it casts ample shade. The delicious nuts and comparative freedom from leaf-eating insects add greatly to their value. Generally clean branched, with strong trunks, they make large domes and swing their graceful foliage close to the ground. One species is grown commercially in California for its nuts; several others yield superior timber for furniture, gun stocks, etc.

Rich, moist soils develop the finest specimens. Walnuts were formerly grown entirely from seed, but improved kinds are now commonly grafted or budded on seedlings of the black or California species.

Brown LEAF SPOT causes a generally unhealthy condition of black walnut and butternut trees. The irregular brown spots appear on the leaves in early summer, and the fungus winters in the dead leaves.

The walnut caterpillar is a serious pest. The black, 1½ in. long caterpillars with white, spiny hairs feed in groups on the leaves and rear up both ends when disturbed. Pick up and burn nuts that drop prematurely after being injured by the butternut and walnut curculios. Spray before leaf growth starts in the spring with a miscible oil to control oyster-shell and walnut scales. The walnut aphid, which may produce extensive honeydew, can be controlled by washing pests off or with insecticide. See also APHIDS; CATERPILLAR; INSECT CONTROL; SCALE INSECTS; SPRAYING.

PRINCIPAL SPECIES

J. ailantifolia (Japanese walnut), formerly listed as *J. sieboldiana*, is very hardy and is often planted in the northern states. It grows rapidly and has dense, luxuriant foliage. It is a desirable ornamental for garden and grounds.

J. californica (California walnut) varies from a 50-ft. tree in rich soil to a shrub at 3000 ft. elevation. It has been extensively used as a street tree and as stock for budding the English walnut.

J. cinerea (butternut, white walnut) is a worthy ornamental, but it has a more spreading form and is not so long-lived as *J. nigra*; however, it endures moister soil. The nuts of this species have always been esteemed. They are customarily picked while young and green. The hard wood is used for furniture and interior trim. The sap, bark, and all green parts of the tree have the characteristic staining properties of the tribe, the juice quickly oxidizing to a dark brown color on exposure to the air.

J. nigra (black walnut) is best known and planted as a shade or avenue tree because of its majestic form and general beauty. Given rich soil, room, and sunlight, it will attain 150 ft. Spreading, round-headed, and long-lived, it provides abundant shade and background for home or garden. The roots of black walnut, or soil conditions caused by them, have a toxic effect on rhododendrons and other ornamentals, so the two kinds of plants should not be planted in close proximity.

J. regia (English or Persian walnut) is fairly compact, as befits an orchard tree, but deserves a place in the lawn or garden background. It is a handsome, semihardy tree valued for its decorative value as well as its nuts. The bark is silvery gray and smooth as compared with the rough, dark barks of other species. Originally native to the Middle East, it is hardy from California through the South and along the Atlantic Coast to Massachusetts. If grafted on roots of *J. nigra*, it becomes hardy in the northern states, ripening its nuts before frost. Varieties of this species provide most of the commercial walnut products.

JUJUBE. Common name for ZIZIPHUS, a genus of tropical and subtropical shrubs and trees.

JUNCUS (JUNG kus). A genus of stiff, grasslike, perennial herbs commonly known as rush. They grow in wet areas and have unbranched, round stems; narrow, flat, grassy leaves; and small clusters of greenish or brownish flowers. Some of the smaller rushes (sometimes obtainable from dealers) are grown in pots or planted in bog gardens. They are hardy to Zone 4.

J. balticus is tufted in growth and has greenish flowers edged white.

J. effusus (common rush) with a soft stem to 4 ft. high, widely distributed in the North Temperate Zone, is used for making woven mats. Its varieties *spiralis* and *vittatus*, the latter with yellow stripes, are decorative forms.

JUNE BEETLE. Members of the genus *Phyllophanga*, and also called June bugs, May beetles, or May bugs. As grubs in their larval stage, these common leaf chafers are very destructive soil pests. Of the 250 species in the United States, some live a two-year cycle, especially in warmer regions, and some a three-year cycle. Each female lays 150 to 200 eggs in the soil, usually in permanent pasture, lawns, or grassy wastes, rarely in clean clover or alfalfa fields or under row crops. The white grubs feed on roots of grasses and grain crops, as well as roots of strawberries, potatoes, onions, and other plants; for control, see GRUBS.

A few species live in one-year cycles, and a few

in four year cycles. In a two year cycle, both larvae and adults stay in the ground during the winter, with the larvae feeding on the roots and the most damage occurring in the second year. In the fall of the second year, the larvae pupate with the adult emerging from that stage but staying in the pupal cell in the ground until the following spring. Then the adult, a large, brownish beetle, emerges to attack at night such trees as poplar, oak, linden, willow, ash, maple, and walnut. In the three-year cycle, the grubs feed below the ground during a second summer and winter before emerging. Crops should not be planted in infested, newly plowed sod ground.

JUNIPER. Common name, meaning "forever young," for JUNIPERUS, a genus of evergreen trees and shrubs belonging to the Cupressaceae (Cypress Family).

JUNIPERUS (joo NIP ur us). A genus of about 70 species of small or medium-sized evergreen trees and shrubs belonging to the Cupressaceae (Cypress Family) and commonly known as juniper (an ancient name meaning "forever young"); some species are known as red-cedar. They have small, mostly gray-green leaves and blue or reddish berrylike fruits. Some species are among the best ornamentals, often used in landscaping. The majority are hardy even in the coldest parts of the United States, preferring rather dry sandy or gravelly soil, with full exposure to wind and sun, but tolerating average soil conditions, resenting only shade and wet ground.

TYPES AND USES

In form, junipers vary from dense, columnar trees to trailing ground cover. The taller, columnar forms are used in both formal and informal planting, giving the same effect as the Italian cypress, which is not as hardy. The dense, spirelike growth, however, is essentially a character of young trees; after 20 or 30 years, the top growth tends to slow or stop, the branches spreading to a domelike crown in *J. virginiana* (red-cedar), *J. chinensis* (Chinese juniper), and their varieties. Among the best slender forms are the columnar

Chinese, and the red-cedar varieties of *J. chinensis*, including cv. 'Canaerti', 'Glauca', and 'Keteleeri'. Of the smaller upright forms, several dense, decorative ones have become popular, but most of them are short-lived under average conditions. The Irish and Swedish junipers are narrow and quick growing. The Greek and variegated Chinese kinds are slow growing and exceedingly compact.

Longer lasting is the irregularly spreading, massive Pfitzer juniper, indispensable for evergreen border and foundation planting, especially since it will endure some shade for a time. Other spreading types of lower habit are the savin, Japanese red-cedar, and var. *depressa* of *J. communis* (common juniper).

A number of creeping junipers, especially cultivars of *J. horizontalis* (creeping juniper), can be used for ground cover in full sun, to hold steep banks, in the rock garden, or as an exposed evergreen border edging.

Shades of color in juniper foliage should be studied in arboretums or nurseries since they are striking, though hard to describe, and often change with the seasons. The junipers show all variations of blue-green and gray-green with pinkish and purplish tints and blooms, and deep purple winter color in some kinds. The fruits, though usually small, are ornamental, blue with a white bloom, and are plentiful on the red-cedars. On the rare Formosa juniper, they are orange-brown, while the Syrian juniper bears brown edible fruits an inch in diameter. Fruit of common junipers is used in making gin and oil of juniper. Many junipers, such as red-cedar, are dioecious, only the female plant producing fruit.

Juniper leaves are of two kinds: needle shape on young seedlings and leading shoots, and scalelike on the twigs of older trees. The young are often bristle tipped, while the older, scale-shaped ones cling close to the twig, forming what is called whipcord foliage, because it resembles a braided cord.

CULTURE

Junipers can be propagated from seed, cuttings, or grafting. Seeds should be collected and cleaned, then stratified for about four months. Most junipers are grown from cuttings taken in summer, fall, or winter, and most root easily. Cuttings produce a larger plant more quickly than by seed. Cultivars are also grafted on understock of *J. virginiana* and *J. chinensis*.

The chief requirements of junipers are sunlight, drainage, and cultivation. When shaded even slightly, most varieties are subject to scale and red spider, which weaken and disfigure them. Dormant sprays of miscible oil (about 1 to 40) or insecticidal soap solutions during the growing season control both these pests, but no control is really satisfactory in shade. Junipers placed in full sun and well cultivated will seldom suffer any infestation, and the columnar, Chinese, Canaert, and some other junipers are nearly immune. They need little pruning but can be trimmed when out of shape or pruned in formal plantings. Most species are hardy in Zones 2–9.

Juniper cultivars of the past have originated in foreign countries, but recent North American selections seem more resistant to disease. The red heartwood of the larger trees is very durable in the ground, making red-cedar posts one of the most desirable kinds for rustic fences and arbors. "Cedar" chests are made of red-cedar, whose aromatic oil repels moths.

ENEMIES

Many junipers are subject to RUSTS and blights that can spread to other plants. A serious twig blight prevalent in nurseries is also common on eastern ornamental red-cedars during wet springs. The tips of the twigs die, turning light tan, and in young trees the fungus may spread to the trunk. During rains, spores are carried from diseased leaves and infect nearby trees. Prune out brown diseased twigs and spray two or three times every two weeks with BORDEAUX MIXTURE, beginning when the new growth starts.

Several species of rust fungus cause diseases of the common red-cedar and other junipers. The life history of the ever-present apple and cedar rust, *Gymnosporangium juniperi-virginianae*, is typical. Its stages of development alternate on the two hosts. See CEDAR-APPLE RUST.

Cedar hawthorn rust is caused by a fungus that attacks hawthorn, mountain-ash, cultivated apple, and pear as alternate hosts. This rust makes small, round, perennial galls which produce a crop of spore horns each year.

Cedar quince rust, caused by another fungus, attacks pear, apple, chokeberry, shad, and hawthorn. It causes spindle-shaped swellings of the branches of red-cedar and common mountain juniper on which orange-red spore pustules develop. Removal of one of the hosts is the only way to control the disease.

Among the insect pests, the juniper webworm is becoming serious on *J. communis*. It forms webbed masses within which the reddish brown, white-striped larvae feed. Pyrethrum sprays applied with enough force to enter the webs are effective. See also CATERPILLAR; WEBWORM; INSECT CONTROL.

PRINCIPAL SPECIES

J. californica (California juniper) grows to 40 ft. and has large, reddish brown fruit. It is a good plant for desert areas.

J. chinensis (Chinese juniper), growing to 60 ft., is similar to red-cedar but has brighter green foliage. There are many cultivars: 'Aurea' (golden Chinese juniper) has yellow-tipped foliage; 'Aureo-globosa' is a dense, dwarf kind with yellow new growth; 'Japonica' (Japanese juniper) is a spreading, dark green selection; 'Pfizeriana' (Pfizer juniper) is a massive, spreading, dense, blue-green form; 'Pyramidalis' forms a narrow, compact column; 'Sargentii' is a pale green selection that makes a good ground cover; 'Variegata' forms a broad pyramid with dense, upright branches streaked white; 'Kaizuka' (Hollywood juniper) is dark green with upright, twisted growth habit; 'Robusta Green' is upright, growing to 12 ft., and has brilliant green foliage; 'Maney' is bushy and 6 ' x 6 ' and is good for cold climates; 'Old Gold' has gold foliage and grows in a compact, spreading habit.

J. communis (common juniper) is a shrub or small tree, usually spreading, with needle leaves. Cv. 'Aurea' (golden juniper) has yellow young leaves. 'Compressa' is a slow-growing dwarf form, and 'Depressa' (prostrate juniper) is spreading, with ascending branches.

J. conferta (shore juniper) is a ground cover that grows 1 ft. high and spreads 8 ft. over the ground. It has black fruits.

J. horizontalis (creeping juniper, creeping red-cedar) is a ground cover with many varieties and cultivars. Cv. 'Douglasii' (Waukegan juniper) has bluish foliage that turns purple in winter. 'Bar Harbor' is a creeping form with blue-green foliage, purple in winter. 'Wiltonii' is a low form that grows 6 in. high and has spreading, blue-green foliage. 'Blue Chip' is silvery blue.

J. sabina (savin) is a spreading, rather low, dark green species. Var. *arcadia* grows to 1 ft. high, has green foliage, and is resistant to juniper blight. Cv. 'Broadmoor' grows 2–3 ft. high and 4 ft. wide and has bright green, feathery foliage. 'Fastigiata' (column savin) is a narrow, upright, dark green form. 'Tamariscifolia' (tamarix savin) is dense, low, spreading, and gray-green.

J. scopulorum (western, Colorado, or Rocky Mountain red-cedar) is a western form similar to *J. virginiana* with a narrow, pyramidal shape, growing to 30 ft. Cv. 'Blue Heaven' has striking blue color all year. 'Gray Gleam', 'Platinum', and 'Moffetii' all have silver-gray color and narrow, upright growth. Hardy in Zones 4–8.

Juniperus scopulorum

J. silicicola (southern red-cedar) grows to 50 ft. and has drooping branchlets.

J. squamata is a pale blue-green ground cover. Cv. 'Meyeri' (fishtail juniper) is dense, irregularly upright, and pale blue-gray. 'Prostrata' grows flat along the ground.

J. virginiana (red-cedar) is a tree that grows to 75 ft. and is common throughout the eastern United States. It has upright branches or a wide-spreading shape. It has many varieties and cultivars that can be used for hedges, windbreaks, topiary work, and specimens in the landscape. It should not be planted near apple trees since it is a host for the CEDAR-APPLE RUST fungus. Cv. 'Canaerti' (Canaert red-cedar) is dark green and columnar; 'Globosa' (globe red-cedar) is a compact dwarf; 'Keteleeri' is dense and upright; 'Kosteri' is a dwarf type; 'Pendula' (weeping red-cedar) has pendulous branches.

JUSTICIA (jus TISH ee ah). A genus of the Acanthaceae (Acanthus Family), now including many garden species formerly classed in other genera. They are easily grown favorites in southern gardens, and many make good greenhouse plants, since they are free blooming and not at all fussy. Under glass, the best results are obtained with young plants, the shoots of which should be pinched early to induce a bushy growth. They thrive in good loamy soil with periodic extra feeding.

J. brandegeana (shrimp plant), formerly listed as ***Beloperone guttata***, is native to the American tropics and has closely pressed pink bracts between the white flowers, which inspired the common name. It is similar to ***Acanthus*** but has much more slender two-lipped flowers in long curving spikes made showy by brick-red overlapping bracts, which inspire the common name. Although less frequently cultivated than its interesting form deserves, it is sometimes seen in the open ground in the southern states or as a houseplant in cooler regions. Growing to 18 in. tall, the plant requires rich, well-drained soil and delights in full sunshine and considerable warmth. It is propagated by cuttings since seed is difficult to get started. There are several varieties available, some that are more compact, others with several chartreuse or nearly yellow bracts.

J. carnea (ribbonbush, plumeflower) is a medium-sized shrub with heads of long, slender flowers produced several times a year. Forms with pink, white, or yellow flowers are produced in this species or the very similar *J. aurea*.

K

KAEMPFERIA (kam FEE ree ah). A genus of stemless herbs belonging to the Zingiberaceae (Ginger Family). The leaves of several species are attractively marbled or variegated, hence their common name, peacock plant. Foliage dies to the ground in winter. Flowers in some appear before the new leaves in spring, but in all there is a succession of bloom over a long period. They are good for indoor pot culture in cool regions or as a garden plant in Zones 10–11 grown in a rich, moist soil.

KAINIT. A low-grade potash fertilizer obtained as a by-product from mines. In commercial mixtures, it contains 12–16% potash in the sulfate form, but this is adulterated with common salt (sodium chloride), which may make up as much as a third of the material, and other compounds. Unless it can be secured cheaply, kainit is not an economical or for that matter desirable way to supply potash to the soil. If used, it should be applied well in advance of planting—a full season or more if possible—so that the undesirable constituents that can injure young plant roots have time to leach out.

KALANCHOE (kal an KOH ee). A genus of crassulaceous succulents mostly from southern and tropical Africa and Madagascar but also with species occurring in India and some southwestern Pacific islands. They are notable for their colors and textures as well as their ease of propagation; in some species rooted plantlets will form along the margins of the leaves while still growing on the parent plant, and in others, pieces of leaf will readily root and grow new plants.

Kalanchoe blossfeldiana

Cultural requirements are the same as for other succulents—a porous, gritty soil, ample moisture during the growing period, abundant sunshine, and freedom from drafts. If the potting soil is first sterilized, nematodes are not likely to infest the roots, and if excessive moisture is avoided, plants are less likely to be attacked by a phytopthora wilt and stem rot favored by dampness.

Some species have lovely pastel shades of pink, blue, or lavender; others have felted or hairy leaves and stems in various shades of gray and brown, such as *K. tomentosa* (panda plant) or *K. beharensis* (elephant's-ear). Various cultivars of red-flowered *K. blossfeldiana* have become staples in the flower markets for their abundant, long-lasting, and multicolored flowers. *K. pinnata* (leafplant) is a succulent tropical perennial, easily cultivated as a houseplant, with greenish or yellow flowers that wave in the breeze and new plantlets forming in the notched leaves.

KALE. A common name for several nonheading varieties of the hardy biennial cabbage, *Brassica oleracea*, grown for its foliage, which is used as greens. In home gardens it is generally grown during the fall and early winter, seed being sown in late spring, either where the plants are to mature or in seedbeds; in the latter case, transplanting can be done 4–6 weeks later. Its culture differs in no way from that of CABBAGE. See also BRASSICA.

KALMIA (KAL mee ah). A genus of mostly evergreen shrubs, native in North America, belonging to the Ericaceae (Heath Family), with several species referred to as laurels. Their leaves contain a poisonous element that can prove fatal to sheep, goats, and calves that browse on the plants. Some are among the best of broad-leaved evergreens for northern gardens and are very valuable for ornamental plantings, especially when massed.

Hardy in Zones 3–9, they thrive best in partial shade in sandy or peaty, very acid, not too dry soils, but they will also grow out in the open and in sunny loam if free of lime. In sunny places, a continuous mulch is invaluable. Propagation is by seed, cuttings of half-ripened wood under glass, layers, and grafting and tissue culture.

PRINCIPAL SPECIES

K. angustifolia (sheep-laurel, lambkill) grows to about 3 ft. and has narrow, light green leaves, pale beneath. It has rose-pink or crimson flowers, borne in lateral clusters. The common names were given because the leaves were thought to be especially poisonous to sheep; actually there is more evidence of the dangerous nature of **L. latifolia**. Hardy in Zones 3–8.

K. latifolia (mountain-laurel, calico bush) is one of the most beautiful of shrubs in the United States and is perhaps the best broad-leaved flowering evergreen for northern gardens, hardy to Zone 5. It is the state flower of Connecticut and Pennsylvania. The showy flowers are borne in terminal clusters, varying in color from white to deep rose, with purple markings inside. The leaves are thought to be poisonous.

KALOPANAX (kal oh PAN aks) **pictus.** A large shade tree from eastern Asia, belonging to the Araliaceae (Aralia Family), and commonly known as castor aralia. It grows to about 60 ft. high and has large, palmate leaves and a tropical appearance. Young branches have numerous prickles. Masses of small white flowers bloom in late summer.   It has no significant disease or insect problems. Hardy in Zones 5–7.

KAPOK. A common name for *Ceiba pentandra*, a large, spreading tropical tree; see CEIBA.

KATSURA TREE. Common name for *Cercidiphyllum japonicum*, a deciduous tree or shrub with distinctive foliage, planted for ornament; see CERCIDIPHYLLUM.

KEEL. Term for a flower part that forms a ridge shaped like a boat's keel; more particularly, the structure formed by the two lower petals of a sweet pea or other papilionaceous flower that are united along the lower edge.

KENILWORTH-IVY. Common name for *Cymbalaria muralis*, a tender, trailing evergreen variously grown for ground cover or greenhouse decoration; see CYMBALARIA.

KENTUCKY BLUEGRASS. Common name for *Poa pratensis*, a perennial grass often used in lawns; see POA.

KENTUCKY COFFEE TREE. Common name for *Gymnocladus dioica*, a large, coarse-branched tree with flower clusters followed by persistent seedpods; see GYMNOCLADUS.

KERRIA (KER ee ah) **japonica.** A Chinese deciduous shrub belonging to the Rosaceae (Rose Family) and commonly known as Japanese kerria; it is the only member of its genus. Growing to 8 ft., it has an attractive, arching growth habit and abundant, single, golden yellow flowers in late spring, and sometimes there is a scattering throughout the season. The light green, twiggy stems are very decorative in winter. Cv. 'Pleniflora' usually grows taller and can be trained on porches or against a wall; the double flowers are much showier and at least twice as long as the species. There are also varieties with white or yellow variegated leaves.

Kerria is not particular as to soil but prefers a well-drained and sheltered position, doing well in partial shade. Generally hardy in Zones 5–9, it may be killed back at the top if overexposed to below-zero temperatures.

A disfiguring leaf and twig blight causes reddish brown leaf spots; if it is severe, the leaves may turn yellow and die prematurely. On stems, several spots may run together to form long cankers, the bark splitting and the twigs being gradually killed. To control, cut out diseased shoots and rake up and destroy dead leaves.

KIGELIA (kĭ JEE lee ah) **pinnata.** A tropical African tree of the Bignoniaceae (Bignonia Family), having leaves in threes and claret-colored, bell-shaped flowers in drooping panicles. The common name "sausage tree" is derived from the rough, gourdlike fruits to 18 in. that hang on cordlike stems several feet long.

KING PALM. Common name for ARCHON-TOPHOENIX, a genus of feather palms.

KINNIKINICK. Common name for *Arctostaphylos uva-ursi*, an attractive prostrate shrub with mealy red berries, also known as bearberry; see ARCTOSTAPHYLOS.

KIWI. A common name for *Actinidia chinensis*, a handsome twining vine that produces the popular kiwi fruit; see ACTINIDIA. The name also refers to a cultivar of *Cordyline terminalis*, an ornamental tropical shrub; see CORDYLINE.

KLEINIA (KLĪ nee yah). A genus of interesting succulent members of the Asteraceae (Aster Family), today mostly lumped together with SENECIO, from which they differ principally in their lack of rayflorets. Species of particular interest are *K. haworthii*, from South Africa, with spindle shaped leaves and stems that are densely whitefelted, and *K. pendula*, the "Inch Worm" from tropical East Africa to Arabia, with red flowers and purple-lined stems that arch back to earth, root again, arch out again, etc.

KNIPHOFIA (nī FOHF ee ah). A genus of the Liliaceae (Lily Family), including some of the most startling of autumn-blooming plants, with dense, cigar-shaped spikes of red and yellow tubular flowers rising like skyrockets above other garden subjects so that it draws attention from everything around it. Appropriately called torch lily, red-hot-poker, or poker-plant, *Kniphofia* is also sold under its former botanical name *Tritoma*.

Seed sown under glass in very early spring will sometimes produce flowering

Kniphofia uvaria

plants the following autumn. Hardy to Zone 7, when set outdoors after all danger of frost has past, the young plants should be given a loose, well-drained, rather poor soil in a sheltered but sunny location. In cool regions, the rhizomes should be dug up in the fall and stored in dry earth at a cool, but not freezing, temperature. Seed can also be sown outdoors in early summer, the plants being set in a permanent location the following spring. Old rhizomes can be divided to produce strong new plants, and when offsets arise, they too can be used for propagation.

KNOTWEED. Common name for species of POLYGONUM, a genus of weedy herbs with tiny flowers. The Knotweed Family is POLYGONACEAE.

KOCHIA (KOH kee ah). A genus of fast-growing, shrublike, ornamental annuals belonging to the Chenopodiaceae (Goosefoot Family) and commonly known as summer-cypress, Belvedere, burningbush, or Mexican firebush. The small but dense foliage is a clear bright green in spring and a somewhat deeper shade all summer, then turns bronze-red after frost. Plants grow 1½–4 ft. high and are compactly pyramidal or rounded. They are easily grown in moderately rich soil from seed sown in the open ground in late spring or started indoors earlier. Their formal shape and uniform size adapt them for use as a temporary hedge or tall border for walks or drives, but they are apt to become weedy and aggravate people prone to hay fever.

K. hyssopifolia is a relatively small plant with long, narrow leaves.

K. scoparia (Belvedere, summer-cypress), the best-known species, and its var. *trichophylla* are most often used in borders.

KOELREUTERIA (kel roo TEER ee ah). A genus of oriental trees belonging to the Sapindaceae (Soapberry Family).   The trees have compound leaves and are beautiful when in flower.

K. paniculata (golden raintree) is a wide-spreading tree that grows to 30 ft. It bears large clusters of showy yellow flowers in midsummer, followed by three-part, bladdery capsules. Native to Asia, it is hardy in sheltered locations as far north as Zone 5. It is rather short-lived but adaptable in its soil requirements and resistant to drought, so it is often planted in the south central states. Propagation is by seed, planted in autumn or stratified over winter, and by root cuttings. Catalogs occasionally list this tree under the common name "varnish tree," which properly applies to *Rhus verniciflua*.

KOHLERIA (koh LEE ree ah). A genus of tropical American herbs belonging to the Gesneriaceae (Gesneria Family), including some species that formerly comprised the genus *Isoloma*. The blossoms are tubular or bell shaped, opening a few at a time at the top of short stems and giving a long-lasting display. Several species and hybrids are grown in northern greenhouses for their orange-purple or scarlet flowers, and breeding work has added a range of colors to the existing species.

KOHLRABI. A hardy form of *Brassica oleracea*, sometimes called stem turnip. Although a biennial, it is grown as an annual spring and fall vegetable for its pale green or purple, swollen turniplike stem. It is ready for the table while tender and small, about 2–3 in. thick; when larger it becomes woody and strong flavored. Seed is usually sown in rows directly in the garden, though sometimes, for earlier harvesting, it is started in hotbeds, coldframes, or outdoor seedbeds. In any case, the plants should stand a little further apart than beets in rows 12–18 in. apart. The crop is managed like turnips.

KOLKWITZIA (kohl KWIT zee ah) **amabilis.** A deciduous, upright shrub from China, the only member of its genus, belonging to the Caprifoliaceae (Honeysuckle Family), and commonly known as beautybush. Hardy in Zones 5–8, it is a very desirable plant, growing to 10 ft., with a particularly graceful form and good foliage throughout the season. It does not flower until fully established but then becomes one of the loveliest

flowering shrubs in late spring. The bell-shaped flowers are soft pink with a yellow throat, and distinction is added by the bristly white hairs with which the flower stalks and sepals are clothed. Propagation is by cuttings of growing wood in late summer.

KOREAN LAWN GRASS. Common name for *Zoysia japonica*, a creeping perennial better known as Japanese lawn grass; see ZOYSIA.

KRIGIA (KRIJ ah). A genus of small annual or perennial herbs belonging to the Asteraceae (Aster Family) and commonly known as mountain- or dwarf-dandelion. These bright, attractive plants are native in North America and are good rock garden plants; they do not become weedy like the common dandelion (*Taraxacum officinale*). They have leafy stems and heads of yellow or orange ray flower heads about 1 in. across. They grow readily in any pocket of light sandy loam and are propagated by seed.

K. montana, a perennial growing to 1 ft., has very narrow leaves and bright golden flowers.

K. virginica, an annual growing to 1 ft., has oval leaves to 8 in. and red to orange flowers.

KUDZU (KOOD zoo). Common name for *Pueraria thunbergiana* and *P. lobata*, twining vines with large tuberous roots, sometimes grown for ornament, fodder, or erosion control, but often becoming weeds; see PUERARIA.

KUMQUAT. Common name for *Fortunella*, a small genus of Chinese evergreen shrubs differing only in small details from *Citrus* and grown in Florida as one of the less important CITRUS FRUITS. The trees, which attain 10 or 12 ft. and are somewhat hardier than the sweet orange (to Zone 9), make ornamental plants for the North and are grown outdoors in the South for the elongated fruits about the size of small plums and the color of oranges. These are aromatic, edible raw, and good for preserving, besides being decorative on the table. Hybridized with various forms of *Citrus* to vary size and quality of fruit.

LABELING. Plants, bulbs, packets of seed, and trees should always be labeled when bought, sold, traded, or moved to a new site. It is easy to lose track of the name of a variety and is often impossible to identify it again with certainty. Labels for such temporary purposes are usually made of wood, plastic, or paper. When bought in quantity, wood labels are cheap; they can be notched and wired for attaching to trees, stakes, or cords, and larger sizes can be sharpened for thrusting into the ground or into a pot or bundle. Labels made of narrow strips of plastic or heavy waxed paper—printed or plain, and slit so they can be wrapped and quickly fastened around any stem or trunk—are even more convenient.

Temporary labels are also useful to mark single plants or flowers from which to propagate or collect seed. Newly sown rows, seedbeds, and seed pots are often marked with wood labels, except in the case of seeds that germinate very slowly and may need more lasting markers. Names should be written with pencil or permanent ink.

There are many kinds of permanent metal tree labels. Those of zinc can be written on with black carbon pencil. Paper-thin copper labels can have names written with a metal stylus or large nail when the label is placed over a backing of soft cardboard; these will last indefinitely and be inconspicuous when the weathered copper turns a dark color. Properly surfaced plastic holds lead pencil writing well, but even when tinted green it may be conspicuous.

LABIATAE. Former name for the LAMIACEAE (Mint Family).

LABRADOR-TEA. Common name for *Ledum groenlandicum*, a dwarf evergreen shrub with small white flowers in spring; see LEDUM.

LABURNUM (la BUR num). A genus of small deciduous trees or large shrubs from southern Europe and Asia, belonging to the Fabaceae (Bean Family), and commonly known as golden-chain. Where hardy (Zones 5–7), they rank among the most beautiful of flowering trees, with their three-part leaves and long, drooping clusters of yellow flowers followed by flat leguminous fruits. They need well-drained soil and can withstand city conditions very well. Propagation is by seed, layers, and, in the case of choice varieties, by budding and grafting.

PRINCIPAL SPECIES

L. alpinum (Scotch laburnum) is native in southern Europe, and not Scotland as the common name might imply. It is the hardiest species, surviving to Zone 5. It grows to 20 ft. and has long flower clusters that open about two weeks later than other species.

L. anagyroides (common laburnum) grows to 30 ft., but it is hardy only to Zone 6. The showy yellow flowers are borne in pendulous clusters to about 8 in. long.

L. x *watereri*, a hybrid between *L. alpinum* and *L. anagyroides*, grows to 15 ft. and is hardy in Zones 6–7.

LACE BUG. Approximately 100 species of lace bugs (Tingidae) are found in the United States, with the sycamore lace bug, *Corythucha ciliata*, as a common example. They infest other trees and shrubs, such as rhododendron and azaleas, as well as cotton, feeding on the underside of leaves and drawing out sap. Adults are identified by the reticulated and lacelike appearance of their wings. Their feeding accounts for the stippled, discolored or yellowed look of the leaves and the unthrifty foliage on sycamores and hawthorns. Oak lace bugs, *C. arcuata*, are also common. Nine weeks are required for the life cycle, and they produce two or more generations each year. Lace bugs are true bugs.

LACE FERN. Common name for *Cheilanthes gracillima*, a bipinnate fern with red-brown hairs on the lower frond surface; see CHEILANTHES.

LACELEAF. Common name for *Aponogeton fenestralis*, an aquatic herb with veiny leaves, also known as latticeleaf; see APONOGETON.

LACEWING. These members of the order Neuroptera are some of the most efficient predators among the beneficial insects used for biological control; and thus, they deserve special care. The green lacewing, *Chrysopa carnea*, is readily available commercially for introduction into the garden. The brown lacewings (Hemerobiidae) and powdery lacewings (Contopterigidae) may also be available. Lacewings are known to be voracious eaters of aphids, mealybugs, scales, and whiteflies, as well as mites. They are extremely important in integrated pest management (IPM) in apple orchards. Be careful not to kill or injure these delicate benefactors.

The adults of green lacewings, with beautiful, lacy, delicate, green wings and golden eyes, are much larger than the adults of brown and powdery lacewings. They are often seen at night when attracted by lights, so protect them from banging into lamps or fixtures and hurting themselves. The adults eat pollen and nectar, and it is wise give them a food source and encourage them to

Adult lacewing

Lacewing eggs

reproduce. They set the eggs on long, delicate, 10-mm stalks, laying about 30 per day. These stalks protect the eggs from predators, especially any lacewing larvae nearby. Eggs hatch in about five days, and the resulting larvae go through four instars within two or three weeks. They then pupate in white cocoons for ten days.

The larvae, commonly called aphid lions, have grabbing mandibles for attack. They are alligator-shaped grubs that hold up their victims to suck out the juices and to prevent their clinging to the base from which the larvae caught them. They are useful for controlling aphids, army worms, and Colorado potato beetles. One larva

can eat over 400 victims a day—mealybugs and whiteflies, or the eggs of mites, thrips, or other lacewings. It is wise, therefore, to spread out the lacewings when you buy them.

Feed the egg-laying adults; if well fed, a female can lay up to 2000 eggs. The best food sources are flowers with pollen and nectar or honeydew. If such foods are not practicable, provide brewer's yeast, which is useful to have on hand for several of the commercially available insects used for biological control. Spread the yeast with some sugar and water on sheets of paper attached to plants or impaled on a stake. This practice of feeding lacewings is especially important when using them in greenhouses to control pests. Also provide water, either by misting or by using a wad of cotton hanging from a bottle of water attached to a branch or laid on the soil.

Individual lacewings have been known to consume 1600 mites in one day and up to 12,000 during the several instars of their larval growth. In all, lacewings will work as controls for two or three weeks, if well provided. See also INSECTS, BENEFICIAL.

LACHENALIA (la ke NAY lee ah). A genus of small South African bulbous plants of the Liliaceae (Lily Family), closely related to the squills, and commonly known in the United States as cape-cowslip and in England as leopard lily. Native to the Cape of Good Hope, the plants have broad, basal leaves and 9-in. spikes of red, yellow, or white bell-shaped blossoms, either erect or cylindrical and drooping.

They are easily flowered in a cool greenhouse in winter and will give six weeks of bloom. Many are suited to window gardens or hanging baskets. Plant in August, ½ in. deep, using six bulbs to a 6-in. pot, in a rich loam soil with leaf mold, peat, and sand, adding 1 part bonemeal to 50 parts soil. Store in a well-protected coldframe until late November, when pots can be brought inside. Water weekly with liquid manure when growth starts.

After bloom is over and the leaves and stems wither, water must be gradually withheld. When thoroughly dry, the bulbs should be stored in their pots until the following August. The bulblets should then be removed and placed in separate pots. Ripened seed germinates readily, blooming the first season.

L. tricolor, with yellow, red-tipped flowers, is the best-known species. It has varieties with interesting color variations.

LACTUCA (lak TYOO kah). A genus of mostly tall annual and perennial herbs of the Northern Hemisphere, belonging to the Asteraceae (Aster Family). The species are generally weedy and are not considered garden subjects, but *L. sativa* (LETTUCE) is an important salad plant.

LACY GROUND FERN. Common name for *Dennstaedtia davallioides*, an Australian fern with lacy fronds spaced along the spreading rhizomes; see DENNSTAEDTIA.

LADY BEETLE. Also called ladybugs or ladybird beetles, *Hippodamia convergens*, and *Rodolia cardinalis* are small, round beetles with red, brown, or tan bodies and black spots. These common, beneficial insects are frequently seen outdoors and are seen inside when they come in for the winter. Save the clusters of yellow eggs on the underside of leaves and also the larvae, which are tapered blue and black, with orange spots and long legs or spiny backs. Both larvae and adults are very active consumers of aphids, scales, mites, and mealybugs (10 to 50 daily). The orange industry in California was saved when a lady beetle species from Australia was imported to use as biological control for cottony cushion scale.

Lady beetle

Lady beetles can be purchased from insectaries. When ordering, specify that you want "preconditioned" lady beetles. That is, they should be beyond the aggregation phase of ovarian diapause and in a state to feed and lay eggs; if not in the correct phase, introduced lady beetles usually fly off and do not stay to develop and eat the local pests. Release them gently at the base of infested plants, either in the early morning or in the evening, preferably spacing them out over several days. Watch for and protect the eggs and larvae. See also INSECTS, BENEFICIAL.

LADYBELL. Common name for ADENOPHORA, a genus of perennial herbs grown for their bell-shaped flowers.

LADYBUG. Another name for the LADY BEETLE, often a beneficial garden insect.

LADY FERN. Common name for ATHYRIUM, a genus of ferns cultivated for their lacy fronds.

LADY-OF-THE-NIGHT. Common name for *Brunfelsia americana*, a greenhouse shrub with showy white fragrant flowers; see BRUNFELSIA.

LADY'S-MANTLE. Common name for ALCHEMILLA, a genus of low-growing herbs.

LADY'S-SLIPPER. Common name usually referring to PAPHIOPEDILUM and sometimes CYPRIPEDIUM, hardy orchids with delicate flowers.

LAELIA (LAY lee uh). An important genus of approximately 75 epiphytic or lithophytic (rupicolous) orchid species distributed from Mexico and the West Indies through northern South America. Breeding readily with other genera in the Epidendreae tribe, intergeneric forms are among the most beautiful orchids in cultivation. Leathery leaves top ovoid, cylindrical, or hollow pseudobulbs. One to many small or large showy flowers rise from pseudobulbs in a wide range of colors including white, yellow, orange, red, blue, and purple. The flowers resemble those of the *Cattleya* genus, but generally the sepals, petals, and lip are narrower, and the lip is not as showy.

They are tropical or subtropical, so should be given warmth (minimum winter temperature of 60°F), with the exception of the Mexican species (including *L. anceps*), which can withstand several degrees of frost. *L. anceps* is being used to produce winter-hardy intergeneric cattleya-type orchids. They are best grown in baskets of porous, well-draining compost or mounted on slabs of cork or tree fern bark. The type species is *L. grandiflora*.

LAGENARIA (la je NAY ree ah) **siceraria.** A tender annual vine belonging to the Cucurbitaceae (Cucumber Family), commonly known as calabash or white-flowered gourd. The genus name comes from the Latin *lagen*, meaning "bottle," referring to the curious hard-shelled fruits, which are decorative and sometimes useful as utensils, coming in a great variety of shapes and sizes. The plant makes an excellent temporary screen, growing rampantly to 40 ft., bearing roundish and slightly musk-scented white flowers.

Start seeds 1 in. deep and 4 in. apart in rich, light soil in full sun. Water freely in dry weather and give liquid manure occasionally. Gather the gourds when yellow and hang indoors to dry.

LAGERSTROEMIA (lah gur STREE mee ah). A genus of shrubs or small trees belonging to the Lythraceae (Loosestrife Family). Blooming freely in warm weather, they are widely cultivated from the Sunbelt northward to Zone 7 and are root-hardy even farther north. Flowers occur on new wood, so young plants, even seedlings, bloom in the first season of growth and are often known as the lilac of the South. Miniatures and dwarfs have been developed, some having a cascade habit suited to hanging baskets and window boxes.

L. indica (crape-myrtle) is a deciduous shrub that grows to 20 ft. and has panicles of attractive flowers with fringed petals. There are numerous cultivars, including 'Alba', with white flowers; 'Purpurea', purple; 'Rosea', pink; and 'Rubra', reddish purple. Breeding work at the National Arboretum introduced a number of newer varieties that are resistant to mildew. This resistance, as well as the handsome chestnut color of the trunks, has come from *L. fauriei*, which was introduced from Japan. Most forms have been given names related to native American tribes and are recognizable in catalogs by this means. They have all been extensively tested and are highly recommended for freedom of flowering and general vigor. A range of dwarf varieties, which grow only about 3 ft. tall, has also been developed and is useful where lower shrubs are needed.

The crape-myrtle is a Chinese plant, but it is grown widely throughout the southern states where it blooms profusely for several months, as specimen shrubs, as hedges, and for background planting; in many places it has become naturalized. In cooler climates, it can be grown in a pot or tub in a cool greenhouse, and if cut back severely, will bloom several times a year. It is root-hardy to Zone 6 if given winter protection. Although it dies to the ground, it will send out a vigorous growth in the spring and bloom profusely. It is easily raised from seed, the young plants blooming the first summer. Propagation is also done with cuttings of ripe wood.

Disease. Powdery mildew is common on crape-myrtle in the Gulf states. Minute, deformed shoots covered with a white coating appear in early spring, followed by circular white patches on the young leaves. The white coating then spreads over all of the shoots. In midsummer the disease is not conspicuous, but it reappears in the fall. A single application of commercial lime-sulfur, diluted 1 to 80 and used as soon as the buds burst in the spring, will help to control it.

Insect Pests. Aphids, if abundant, can cause defoliation; also, the honeydew that they secrete supports the sooty-mold fungus, which gives the leaves a black smutty appearance. Spray with a sulfer compound or other contact insecticide to control both problems.

LAGURUS (lah GOO rus) **ovatus.** An annual grass commonly known as hare's-tail grass or rabbit-tail grass. Native to the Mediterranean region, it is now naturalized in California and is grown as a garden ornamental, sometimes indoors in pots, and also for use in dry winter bouquets. It prefers a warm location and well-drained soil; it reaches a height of 1 ft. and has leaves 4 in. long and less than ½ in. wide. The spikelets have dense, woolly heads, 2 in. long and rather broad. See ORNAMENTAL GRASSES; EVERLASTINGS.

LAMARCKIA (lah MAHR kee uh) **aurea.** A tufted annual grass (goldentop), grown for ornamental purposes, naturalized in California, though native in southern Europe. Growing to 1 ft., it has soft, glabrous leaves 6 in. long and ¼ in. wide and bears awned spikelets, purplish or golden-yellow in color, clustered in one-sided glossy panicles 4 in. long. See ORNAMENTAL GRASSES.

LAMBKILL. Common name for *Kalmia angustifolia* a hardy evergreen shrub with light green leaves and clusters of rose-pink or crimson flowers; the leaves were thought to be especially poisonous to sheep; see KALMIA.

LAMB'S-EARS. Common name for *Stachys byzantina*, a woolly perennial with purple flowers; see STACHYS.

LAMB'S-QUARTERS. Common name for *Chenopodium album*, an annual weed sometimes used for greens; see CHENOPODIUM.

LAMIACEAE (lam ee AY see ee). The Mint Family, formerly called Labiatae, a widely distributed group of plants, many of which are grown for their flavor or odor, for ornament, or for medicine. Most of the North American kinds are garden subjects and sweet herbs. Mints have characteristically four-sided stems and are rich in a fragrant, volatile oil. Their flowers are grouped in flat heads or crowded into spikes, the petals of individual flowers fusing to form the characteristic irregular two lips. Among the genera cultivated are *Dracocephalum, Hyssopus, Lavandula, Leonotis, Marrubium, Mentha* (mint), *Monarda, Nepeta, Origanum, Physostegia, Rosmarinus* (rosemary), *Salvia* (sage), *Scutellaria, Teucrium,* and *Thymus* (thyme).

LAMIUM (LAY mee um). A genus of European annual and perennial herbs belonging to the Lamiaceae (Mint Family) and commonly known as dead-nettle. A few of the species are grown in borders and rock gardens; most are hardy in Zones 3–9. Dead-nettles are easily cultivated and are propagated by seed or division. Some varieties have naturalized themselves and become weeds.

Lamium maculatum

L. maculatum (spotted dead-nettle) with white-striped leaves is the most commonly grown species, though not the most striking in appearance, growing 12 in. or taller. The opposite, toothed leaves, though resembling those of a nettle, are not prickly to the touch. The whorled flowers, usually purple-red or white, are hooded.

LAMPRANTHUS (lam PRAN thus). A genus of succulent, branching plants of the Aizoaceae (Carpetweed Family), resembling the genus MESEMBRYANTHEMUM, in which they were once included. Averaging 2 ft. high, they have narrow, fleshy leaves and large, showy, brilliantly colored flowers; they are effective in sunny rockeries and dry borders but are hardy only in Zones 10–11. Seed is sown in spring in light, well-drained soil, and the seedlings are thinned later to 6 in. Many varieties, in golden yellow, red, violet, or purple, are offered by nurseries.

LANCEOLATE. Shaped like a spearhead; a term applied particularly to leaves that are several times longer than broad, narrowed toward each end, and broadest one-third of the distance from the base, like those of the pussy willow.

LANDSCAPING FABRIC. A woven or feltlike material used like mulch to block out weeds, conserve moisture, or warm the soil. This fabric is usually topped with an attractive mulch, such as bark chips or gravel. Landscaping fabric is usually sold in rolls of various lengths so it can be spread out between trees and shrubs. It is of a porous nature so that water and oxygen can penetrate the barrier but weeds cannot.

LANTANA (lan TAN ah). A genus of shrubby plants, resembling VERBENA (to which they are related), native chiefly to Central America and north to the Gulf states; desirable both as greenhouse and garden plants, hardy in Zones 10–11.

L. camara, the principal species, originally tall and scraggly, has been developed into a number of low, compact, full-flowered varieties whose flowers in flattish clusters vary or change from brilliant yellow through orange to red. Widely grown as a greenhouse subject, being easily started from seeds or cuttings, it is excellent as a summer bedding plant, blooming continuously until nipped by the frost in autumn. Plants desired for indoor bloom in late spring can then be pruned back severely, potted in fresh soil, and kept in a cool greenhouse over winter. If new stock is wanted, prune the outdoor plants and pot them up in September and take cuttings from the new growth indoors. Give the young plants a fairly high temperature during their early growth.

L. montevidensis (weeping or trailing lantana), a low sprawling plant with rosy lilac flowers, makes an effective ground cover in the South and, when set out once continual warm weather is assured, also in northern regions.

LAPAGERIA (lap ah JEE ree ah) **rosea.** A tall, twining, evergreen, summer-blooming herb belonging to the Liliaceae (Lily Family) and commonly known as Chile-bells or Chilean-bellflower. The leaves and tendrils indicate its relation to *Smilax*. Its large, showy, lilylike flowers drooping in rosy or crimson spotted bells are typical of the Lily Family. However, there is no bulb. The flowers ripen into fleshy, beaked fruits, and propagation is done by seed, cuttings, or shoots layered in sandy peat. The shoots, sometimes 20 ft. long, climb on walls or trellises.

Hardy in Zones 10–11, this is a choice subject for cool greenhouses or gardens in mild climates, but its culture is exacting. Well-drained soil is essential, as are shade and careful watering. The genus was named in honor of Napoleon's wife, Josephine de la Pagerie. There are a number of lovely varieties, including the rare and beautiful *albiflora*, which looks just like the species but has creamy white flowers with a light pink blush.

LAPEIROUSIA (la pe ROO see ah). A genus of African bulbous plants that have red or blue flowers similar to *Freesia*. Generally hardy to Zone 8, they can be grown in the open in cooler climates if planted in light soil and given winter protection. They are also frequently grown in greenhouses for winter flowers. Since the bulbs propagate rapidly, they should be divided often. The two species grown are *L. laxa*, with bright scarlet flowers in a one-sided spike, 1 ft. high; and *L. juncea*, with rosy flowers growing on 2-ft. stalks.

LARCH. Common name for LARIX, a genus of deciduous, coniferous ornamental and timber trees belonging to the Pinaceae (Pine Family).

Golden-larch is *Pseudolarix kaempferi*, another deciduous conifer with feathery, pale green leaves that turn yellow in autumn; see PSEUDOLARIX.

LARIX (LAIR iks). A genus of deciduous coniferous trees belonging to the Pinaceae (Pine Family) and commonly known as larch. They are unusual in that they shed their needles in the fall. They are planted as ornamentals for their stately form and soft texture, and for the pleasing, delicate effect of the new growth early in the spring. Larches are also valuable as a source of timber. Among the hardiest of all trees, they do well in almost any soil or location, preferring moderate moisture. Growth is very rapid, especially in young seedlings.

Larches usually take a "Christmas tree" shape with long, straight branches and short needles tufted like a pine. Species are grown from seed sown in fall or spring in shaded beds and treated like spruce or pine. The seedlings, which should be given plenty of room to develop, are easily transplanted after the leaves have fallen.

DISEASES

The larch canker disease, first serious in Europe, has spread to the United States, especially to New England. The cankers (open wounds surrounded by rough and enlarged callus rolls) occur on the trunk, often near the base, and resinous material oozes from the tree. Specimens growing under adverse conditions are most likely to be attacked, the fungus gaining entrance through branch stubs and other wounds; healthy, vigorously growing trees cannot be directly infected. Prevent by proper care and feeding, careful pruning, and wound protection; see TREE SURGERY.

Several rust fungi attack larch needles. One has willow as the alternate host. Another is associated with poplar, while a third requires birch for the completion of its life cycle; see RUSTS.

Needle cast is common on larch. The mistletoe that causes witches'-broom on spruces also attacks this genus.

INSECT PESTS

The larch casebearer is one of the primary insect enemies. It hibernates as a larva in a silk-lined case attached to the branches and main trunks. As new needles are formed, the larvae drill and mine into them, eating as far as they can without leaving their cases. Filmy gray moths are seen in early to mid-summer, and in autumn a new brood of larvae is hatched. See also CASEBEARER.

The other primary enemy is the woolly larch aphid, which makes the foliage look as though it has been dusted with flour or small particles of woolly matter. Young hatch from eggs at the base of the leaves in spring. Spraying with an insecticidal soap solution at that time helps control them. See also APHIDS.

The green, black-headed larva of the larch sawfly defoliates extensive areas of larch forests and occasionally injures ornamental trees. See also SAWFLY.

PRINCIPAL SPECIES

L. decidua (European larch), growing to 100 ft., is a strong-growing ornamental and is valued for its lumber. Var. *pendula* (weeping larch) has very drooping branches. Hardy in Zones 3–6.

L. × *eurolepis* (Dunkeld larch) is an attractive hybrid of the European and Japanese species. It is resistant to canker and aphids. Hardy in Zones 2–5.

L. kaempferi (Japanese larch), growing to 90 ft., is an ornamental species with striped bark and bright-yellow leaf color in autumn. Hardy in Zones 5–7.

L. laricina (American larch, tamarack) is a stiff swamp tree that grows to 60 ft.; it also does well on drier ground. Hardy in Zones 2–4.

LARKSPUR. A common name for DELPHINIUM, especially for the annual and native Eurasian perennial species, which are less showy than many highly developed perennials and hybrids.

LARVA. An insect in the first stage of its growth or metamorphosis after leaving the egg. It is the growing stage of an insect with complete metamorphosis; a nymph is the corresponding stage of an insect with gradual metamorphosis. See INSECTS.

A larva is usually wormlike and strikingly different from the adult form, from which it is separated by a pupal, or resting, stage. The larvae of moths and butterflies are usually called caterpillars; those of beetles, grubs; and those of flies, maggots. Larvae grow in size by undergoing a series of molts; each successive stage is called an instar.

LASTHENIA (las THEE nee ah). Commonly known as goldfields, these small annual herbs are native to the Pacific Coast. Usually reaching 6 in., they

Lasthenia californica

give a brilliant display of small yellow daisies in the spring and are easily grown from seed. Although there are many species, most of which look alike, the most commonly grown are *L. californica*, growing about 1 ft. tall with 1-in. flowers; *L. minor*, about 6 in. tall with spreading branches and 1-in. flowers; and *L. macrantha*, about 8 in. tall on leafy stems with 2-in. flowers.

LASTREOPSIS (las tree AHP sis). A genus of medium-sized terrestrial ferns used as bedding plants in warm climates and also as potted plants. The fronds are triangular and bipinnate to quadripinnate. Most like plenty of water, but some are tolerant of moderate dryness when established.

LATANIA (lah TAY nee ah). A small genus of fan palms from the Mascarene Islands in the Indian Ocean. The trees may grow to 50 ft., and many are remarkable for the brilliantly colored veins and midribs of the leaves; thus they are popular garden subjects in south Florida (Zones 10–11).

They can be grown successfully in heavy, fertile, well-drained soil with some lime added. They should be well watered and shaded when young. In cooler climates, where they are extensively grown in warm greenhouses, they require a light well-drained soil, shading throughout the year, and abundant water. Where conditions are satisfactory, they are also attractive houseplants.

PRINCIPAL SPECIES

L. borbonica and *L. commersonii* are old names sometimes listed in catalogs for seeds of *L. lontaroides*.

L. loddigesii is a relatively rapid grower whose leaves have bluish blades, sometimes tinged reddish in young plants.

L. lontaroides, one of the most striking species, has crimson leaf stalks and ribs.

L. verschaffeltii, a very slow growing kind, has 5-ft. leaves with orange stalks.

LATH HOUSE. A more or less permanent structure of timber framework with the top, sides, ends, or all three covered with lath spaced to give broken shade. It is a valuable aid in both home gardening and commercial plant growing in regions where intense sunlight is a major problem. In such places, a lath house often corresponds in usefulness to the greenhouse of colder localities, though it can also serve to supplement a small greenhouse in an especially well equipped garden layout. It also provides a pleasant place in which to do potting, grafting, flower arrangement, and other tasks that do not require special conditions but cannot be comfortably performed out in the sunlight. The design and construction of lath houses are not standardized but

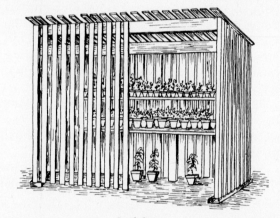

Lath house

are usually worked out to suit the convenience of the user, the requirments of the location, or the demands of a crop such as palms, camellias, begonias, asparagus ferns, etc., all of which are commonly grown under lath houses.

LATH SHADE. A simple and inexpensive method of protecting soil and plants from direct sunlight. Usually it is made by nailing plaster lath to supporting light boards or furring strips of convenient lengths—often 6 ft. to correspond with that of the regulation hotbed. The laths can be laid crosswise only, or in two directions at right angles. If spaced the width of a lath apart, the former arrangement casts stripes, and the latter checks of shade, which sweep across the area covered as the sun moves. Such shades are sometimes fastened to permanent frames equipped with short legs, or with supports tall enough to stand beneath. The former are used mostly for protecting little plants, seedlings, or cuttings; the latter, for sheltering potted plants or broad-leaved evergreens from the summer sun outdoors.

LATHYRUS (LATH ir us). A genus of leguminous herbs including more than 200 species occurring throughout the world, variably known as sweet, perennial, or everlasting pea. The vines or erect plants, including both annuals and perennials, with tendrils and showy flowers ranging from white to shades of red, yellow, and purple, are mostly cultivated for ornament; a few species bear edible seeds, while others are poisonous.

The perennials are propagated by seed or cuttings in ordinary soil and will tolerate partial shade; most are hardy in Zones 3–9. The annuals require a deep, moist soil and full sunlight. Ample support should be provided and the flowers should be kept picked to lengthen the blooming season.

PRINCIPAL SPECIES

L. japonicus (beach pea), is a widely distributed perennial species with attractive rosy-purple flowers, found on sea and lake shores around the world, and is often used to bind sandy soils in seashore gardens. Although the blossoms, which are borne in small, short-stemmed clusters, are similar to but less showy and fragrant than those of *L. odoratus*, the foliage is attractive. Since the plant is hardy and easy to grow, it is well worth a place in the garden.

L. latifolius (sweet, perennial, or everlasting pea), a broad-leaved, tall-growing perennial, is not fragrant but is excellent for general garden use because it can be trained on pillars, trel-

Lathyrus latifolius

lises, or wires to fill in any gaps. Varieties include *albus*, with white flowers; *rosea*, a clear pink; and *splendens* (pride-of-California), shrubby and blooming in dark red and purple.

L. odoratus (sweet pea) is a familiar annual climber that grows to 6 ft. or more but requires a support on which to climb as well as plenty of room, air, and generous feeding. Valued for its color and fragrance, it is available in many flower forms (including plain, wavy, or ruffled petals), heights, and colors (including solids, stripes, and mottled patterns). There are two distinct forms. The summer-flowering sweet pea must be sown as early as the ground can be worked. The other, a winter-flowering type chiefly used for greenhouse production of cut flowers, can be grown outdoors in warm regions. Var. *nanellus* (Cupid, dwarf, or bedding sweet pea) is a nonclimbing type that forms a low, compact plant suitable for use in beds and borders, where they bloom throughout the summer.

LAURACEAE (lor AY see ee). The Laurel Family, a widely scattered group of aromatic trees and shrubs principally native to warm climates. Leaves are usually leathery and evergreen. Flowers are petal-less, with six sepals inserted below the ovary. A few, such as avocado, nutmeg, cinnamon, and camphor, are grown for ornamental and commercial uses. Genera of horticultural interest are *Cinnamomum*, *Laurus*, *Lindera*, *Persea*, *Sassafras*, and *Umbellularia*.

LAUREL. Common name for LAURUS, a genus of evergreen trees. The Laurel Family is LAURACEAE.

The name is also used in connection with plants of other genera. California laurel is *Umbellularia californica*; see UMBELLULARIA. Cherry-laurel is *Prunus caroliniana* or *P. laurocerasus* (which is also called English-laurel), and Portugal-laurel is *P. lusitanica*; see PRUNUS. Indian-laurel is *Ficus benjamina*; see FICUS. Mountain-laurel is *Kalmia latifolia*, and Sheep-laurel is *K. angustifolia*; see KALMIA. Spurge-laurel is *Daphne laureola*; see DAPHNE.

LAURUS (LAHR us). A small genus of evergreens belonging to the Lauraceae (Laurel Family). *L. nobilis* (laurel, sweet bay), the only regularly cultivated species, is native in southern Europe and is the laurel of classical times. Its leaves are used both fresh and dried for flavoring. It grows as a shrub or tree to 30 ft. or more, and it has rather large, lanceolate, leathery, and aromatic leaves; greenish yellow flowers; and black berries. Hardy to Zone 7, it can stand several degrees of frost and thrives best in good loamy soil with leaf mold. In mild regions it is a good hedge plant, and it can stand hard pruning. It is the best evergreen for use on steps and terraces as a

Laurus nobilis

tub plant, and it can be trimmed into various shapes, the usual form being that of a round-headed, small standard tree.

LAURUSTINUS. Common name for *Viburnum tinus*, a useful evergreen shrub with glossy green leaves and pinkish white flowers; see VIBURNUM.

LAVANDULA (la VAN dyoo lah). A genus of fragrant herbs or shrubs commonly known as lavender. They are evergreen or almost evergreen, depending on the climate, with small white, blue-violet, or dark purple flowers on spikes. *L. angustifolia*, the most common species, is a Mediterranean subshrub grown for ornament in the garden and for its sweet scent when dried. The dried flowers are used to fill sachets and to perfume clothing and linens. Commercially, the flowers and the green parts are used for making "oil of spike," aromatic vinegar, and lavender water. *L. officinalis*, *L. spica*, and *L. vera* were names formerly used for this species.

True lavender, only hardy to Zone 5, is little grown in cold climates, where it must be protected over winter by mulching with straw. It is more popular, therefore, in the milder Pacific Coast and in the South. Since seed produces variable plants, propagation is commonly by cuttings taken as soon as the new growth has attained a

length of 2–4 in., either in early summer or after harvesting in early fall. These are set in a shady place, 4 in. apart, and are kept cultivated for a year. Then they are transplanted not less than 2 ft. apart in permanent quarters in dry, light, limey, friable soil and full sunlight. In such locations they thrive best, develop the maximum fragrance, and are least likely to be injured in the winter. They will grow in wet soil, but do so poorly; in rich soil they become lush and sappy; however, in either wet or rich soils, they lack fragrance and succumb to frost easily.

Lavandula angustifolia

LAVATERA (lav ah TEE rah). A genus of usually tall, branching, fast-growing annual herbs and several shrubby perennials belonging to the Malvaceae (Mallow Family) and commonly known as tree mallow. The annuals, including some splendid hybrids, are colorful with mallowlike flowers and are easily grown in any average garden. The perennials are especially suited to the climate of the West Coast. Raised from seed without special attention, even the perennials will bloom within a year, but they should never be transplanted.

PRINCIPAL SPECIES

L. arborea (tree mallow) is a shrubby biennial that grows 6–10 ft. tall and has dark-veined magenta flowers.

L. assurgentiflora, the most common shrubby species, is a dense, round-headed plant growing to 6 ft. or more with large, bright red flowers. It tolerates dry sandy soil, wind, and salty air.

L. trimestris, the most common annual species, grows 2–6 ft. high and bears large, rose-red, mallowlike blossoms in the axils of its maple-shaped leaves.

LAVENDER. Common name for LAVANDULA, a genus of fragrant herbs. Sea-lavender is LIMONIUM. Lavender-cotton is *Santolina chamaecyparissus*; see SANTOLINA.

LAWN. With the increasing interest in gardening and the increased attention to landscaping the home grounds, the lawn is being recognized as the starting point of garden design. As the setting, frame, or approach to the dwelling, a good lawn appreciably increases the market value of any residential property.

PREPARATION AND CONSTRUCTION

In planning and making a lawn, keep in mind that it is a long-term proposition, and that a good foundation (including drainage, soil texture, and food supply) is essential in providing a successful environment for the grass plants. This calls for artificial drainage if necessary, thorough preparation of the soil, an ample supply of organic matter, grading that is artistically effective as well as practical from the point of view of upkeep, and the use of good seed mixture and plenty of it.

Grade the soil so that water will drain evenly. Check for high or low spots by stretching a string between two pegs at ground level. Low spots should be filled to prevent puddling. Where the

Checking soil level

soil is already good and drainage conditions are satisfactory, preparation need not be deeper than 6–8 in. If the soil is heavy and inclined to stay wet, drain tile should be laid.

IMPROVING THE SOIL

If there is doubt as to the lime or food needs of the soil, samples should be sent (before any work is started) to the nearest soil testing laboratory or agricultural extension service for analysis and recommendations. Heavy soils can be lightened by incorporating sand or some form of humus, such as peat moss; one bale to 300 sq. ft. worked into the upper 4 in. of soil is a good application. On the other hand, a light, sandy soil is also improved and given more "body" by a similar

addition of peat moss or other organic material.

If there is time, a GREEN MANURE crop can be grown and plowed under to add to the supply of organic matter in the soil. Natural (animal or barnyard) manures are less desirable in making a lawn because they are likely to contain many weed seeds, which may continue to germinate over several years. Thoroughly rotted manure in which weed seeds have been killed by fermentation is safer, but its plant food value may be doubtful. A "balanced" or "complete" commercial lawn fertilizer of what is called a 5–10–5 formula (that is, containing 5% nitrogen, 10% phosphates, and 5% potash) or its equivalent, worked or rototilled into the upper 6–8 in. of soil at the rate of 25–40 lb. per 1000 sq. ft., will supply available nourishment for the new grass as well as a supply of food later on. After the soil is thus prepared it is advisable to water it well to allow it to settle and firm, then let it stand for two days before sowing.

If lime is needed to correct an acid condition, it should be applied on the surface and raked in at the rate of 35 lb. hydrated lime or 50 lb. ground limestone per 1000 sq. ft. If this can be done some months before the lawn is made, so much the better.

SEED MIXTURE

The seed mixture must be suited to the location and climate as well as to the soil and the sun or shade conditions. Reputable lawn seed companies carry mixtures for special purposes, and it is generally more satisfactory for amateurs to use one of these than to mix their own. Good clean seed is never cheap, but the use of the highest quality mixture for a given purpose is a good investment.

Kentucky bluegrass (*Poa pratensis*) is a standard kind for a neutral loam in a sunny situation. The fescues are particularly useful for dry, slightly shady locations where the soil is neutral or mildly acid. For moisture, shade, and a heavy soil, rough-stalked meadow grass (*Poa trivialis*) can be good. See POA; FESTUCA.

With the advent of turf-type perennial ryegrasses (*Lolium perenne*), it is advantageous to use a mixture containing at least 20% of this grass seed. The perennial ryegrass will germinate within 5–7 days (depending on the temperature and rainfall) and will give a quick cover to the lawn as well as some protection to the Kentucky bluegrass seed, which takes much longer to germinate (two or more weeks). It might be worth noting that the quality of many of the turf-type perennial ryegrasses are so good that they alone will make an acceptable lawn. See LOLIUM.

Turf-type fescues (*Festuca arundinacea*), will also make an acceptable lawn, one that will withstand considerable traffic, as well as drought conditions, after it is established. Incorporation of 20% perennial ryegrass and 20% Kentucky bluegrass with the tall fescue seed will speed up the establishment rate. This mixture is often used on athletic fields.

SEED SOWING

The best time to sow lawn grass seed is in the late summer to early fall; this practice cuts down on the competition offered by weeds and takes advantage of the fall rains. Unless given a fine start, a spring-sown lawn may burn out in summer. However, if necessary, spring seeding is entirely possible. Whatever the season, loosen the soil with a steel rake to the depth of 1 in. just before sowing. Then divide the seed into equal parts, half to be sown as you walk back and forth in one direction (north and south) and the rest as you go back and forth at right angles over the same area. A calm day permits more even distribution and a cloudy one assures more moisture in the soil.

As soon as the seed is sown, the surface can be raked with a fine-tooth rake or covered with not more than ½ in. of top-dressing (half sand and half loam). The ground should be rolled (not too heavily) to firm the earth around the seeds and promote quick germination. On a small area, the firming can be done with a plank or the back of a spade. If the sowing is done in late spring, a covering of burlap or even newspapers can be laid over the area to prevent drying and baking; but this must be removed as soon as the young grass appears.

Watering should be done at first gently and with a fine sprinkler to prevent washing. It should be done often enough to keep the soil and seeds from drying out. When there is not adequate rainfall, water the seedbed for 15–20 minutes, three times per day. After the grass is well started, the waterings should be more thorough and less frequent. Deep watering encourages the development of deep roots upon which the future success of the lawn largely depends. Shallow watering or sprinkling tends to bring the roots near the surface, where they are quickly affected by the heat.

In mowing a new lawn, set the blades to cut not less than 1½–3 in. above the ground. As the turf becomes thick, it can be mowed closer,

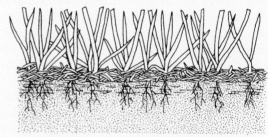

Matted thatch from infrequent mowing

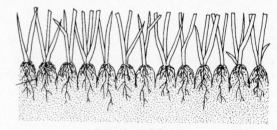

Grass free of thatch

although the longer it can be left the better for the grass. If mowing is done frequently so that the clippings are less than 1 in. long, they will not leave matted thatch to smother the grass or turn brown and unsightly, and they can be left on the ground, thereby slightly reducing fertilizer needs.

CARE OF THE LAWN

An established lawn should be raked in the early spring to remove any debris that has accumulated over the winter, such as fallen twigs, leaves, etc. Patches of dead grass or weeds should be raked out also. If the lawn is to be spot-seeded, an application of fertilizer is in order. Check by having a soil test to see whether lime is needed; if it is, apply the recommended amount. Distribute the appropriate seed or seed mixture over the areas in need of renovation, making sure that the seed is evenly dispersed over the bare areas. Rake the seed in slightly and cover the patches with ¼ in. of topsoil. Keep areas moist. A pre-emergent weed preventer can be applied, but make sure that it is a safe one and that it will not inactivate the lawn seed. See WEEDS. If the lawn comes through the winter in good shape, then an application of fertilizer in late spring will be necessary. Once again a pre-emergent herbicide may be necessary. Consult your local extension service for pesticide recommendations.

Summer maintenance consists mainly of thorough watering during dry spells, mowing as often as necessary, and preventing annual weeds from seeding. It is better to water thoroughly once or twice a week than to sprinkle daily. If weeds are not allowed to seed, in the course of two or three seasons they will be crowded out by vigorously growing grass. It is not advisable to fertilize during the hot summer months unless plenty of moisture is provided to make the food available.

Early fall, however, is a particularly good time for lawn feeding. The current season's weed crop should have been eliminated by this time, so all the nourishment supplied will be available for the grass. Fallen leaves should not be allowed to remain on the lawn, for instead of protecting the grass as might be supposed, they are inclined to suffocate it.

Under ordinary circumstances no winter mulch is needed. Walking on lawns when the ground thaws during mild spells in winter should be avoided, since it is likely to cut up the turf and leave holes and a rough surface.

When a lawn needs patching or renovating, do not merely sprinkle some seed on the bare spots. Rake the spots vigorously, or, better, loosen the soil with a spading fork, work in a little fertilizer and fresh compost, rake to a smooth level surface, sow the seed thickly, and treat like a new lawn.

SPECIAL PROBLEMS

THE SHADED LAWN

Lawns in shaded areas need special attention. Correct drainage by incorporating peat moss in the upper 6–8 in. of soil or by grading so that water will not stand there. For seeding, use a special, good quality seed mixture of shade-enduring grasses. The best shade-tolerant grasses in suitable localities (like the northeastern United States) are chewing, hard fescue, and rough bluegrass (**Poa trivialis**), the latter requiring soil that is constantly moist. Shade-tolerant varieties of Kentucky bluegrass are also available. Perennial ryegrasses have some shade tolerance. If the shade is cast by trees, deeper preparation of the soil and more frequent and more liberal feeding will be needed to supply food for the grass as well as for the tree roots. A good plan is to work a fertilizer rich in organic matter into the soil 10–12 in. deep, from a point 1 ft. or so from the tree trunk as far out as the branches spread. Thereafter, the top 6 in. of the soil can be prepared as already directed for new lawn making.

Both in applying fertilizer and in mowing, remember that a lawn in the shade has a more delicate turf than one in the sun. Weed control, however, is usually simpler since most of the worst weeds also like a sunny exposure. Where the shade is so dense that grass cannot be made to grow, a ground cover, or a mulch might be advisable.

THE SLOPING LAWN

Slopes demand special attention. The home owner, in planning the grounds, should avoid making grassy slopes that are going to be difficult to mow or to keep from drying out. If grade conditions cannot be corrected, it may be best to give up the idea of grass and deliberately create a wildflower meadow or other natural garden. Various ground covers could be used, or even woody plants. If grass is chosen, however, the crest and the bottom of a slope should be gently curved so as to avoid corners where the mower either will not cut or will gouge the soil. Special lawn grass mixtures for slopes are recommended because of their deep-rooting quality, but this is an important characteristic in any grass mixture, and deep preparation of the soil will encourage it. Hydroseeding is another option for seeding slopes. It sprays on the seed in a suspension of water; seed also can be sprayed on with fertilizer and a fiber mulch. The latter method is used to prevent the seed from eroding and from drying out.

A temporary trench around the top of a slope will help to prevent the soil from washing while the grass is starting; or a nurse crop of oats or rye can be sown thinly with the grass seed to hold the earth until the grass roots are established. Such a nurse crop should not be allowed to grow more than 4 in. high or it will cut off air and light from the young grass; usually it is most conveniently mowed with a scythe—as, indeed, all fine lawns once were.

Sometimes it is advisable to lay strips of sod at the top and bottom of the slope and sow seeds in between. The sown area can be covered with 2–3

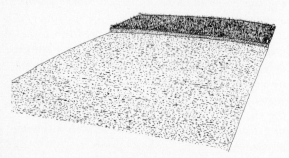

Sod at the top of a slope

in. of straw, which can remain until the grass is nearly tall enough to mow, or burlap can be stretched across the seeded area and pegged securely to the sod strips. If the slope is very

steep, it may be necessary to sod throughout. Here, or wherever sodding is done, sods should be cut 1 ft. wide and as long as can be handled, and 1 in. deep as uniformly as possible. They should be laid smoothly, at right angles to the slope, on a freshly raked seed bed, butted snugly together, and, when all are in place, patted down with a sod-tamper, or rolled. Wooden pegs can be driven through the sod to keep it from sliding down the slope. Water the sods thoroughly. See also SOD.

LAWNS IN THE SOUTH

Several factors make lawns in the South a unique problem. What the southern home owner wants, and what is so difficult to find, is grass that will make a green lawn for the entire year, withstanding the hot summer (which is an even harder test than northern winters). Preparation is a bigger job in the South, for even a fairly good soil won't do: first-class conditions are needed for a good lawn. A garden plot that has been fertilized and nurtured for years would make a fine lawn.

For hot dry places, Bermuda grass can be sprigged, plugged, or sodded. It makes a good lawn from June to October but is discolored by the first heavy frost. If an annual such as Italian ryegrass is sown over the Bermuda lawn in the early fall, it will keep the lawn green until the Bermuda grass starts again in the spring, thus giving a good-looking lawn throughout the year. Perennial ryegrasses are also used for the same purpose.

In the lower South, where the soil is sandy, St. Augustine, centipede, and Bermuda grasses are used. The first named is particularly well-adapted to coastal areas. Grown from sprigs or sod, it makes a presentable lawn if mowed frequently. Species of **Zoysia**, especially **Z. matrella** (manila grass), are sometimes used for lawns in southern states as well.

DISEASES, INSECTS, AND INJURY

Trouble spots on the lawn can be caused by unhealthy grass, unfavorable weather conditions, burning from unequal distribution of fertilizers, attacks of insects, fungus diseases, cultural problems, or any one of a number of soil conditions that inhibit growth.

Brown Patch. Of the fungus diseases, the best known is probably "large brown patch," caused by a common soil-inhabiting fungus. The browned area, which is usually more or less circular, may vary from an inch to several feet in diameter; it is usually bordered with a dark green ring of recently affected grass. Sometimes wefts of the fungus mycelium can be seen on the grass. The disease is most apt to develop in hot, humid weather and is fostered by overwatering, excessive soil acidity, and poor drainage.

The disease called "small brown patch" or "dollar spot" is caused by another species of fungus that causes a brown patch but differs in that the spots are a lighter brown and never more than 2 in. across. For diagnosis and control measures for your area, contact your local extension agent.

Snowmold. Caused chiefly by *Fusarium nivali*, snowmold is prevalent when the snow is melting, but it is serious only in northern regions. Whitish gray, dead, slimy areas appear in the grass, often accompanied by a fluffy white growth of the fungus mycelium. The disease is favored by late fall feeding and winter mulching and can be checked or prevented by any treatment of the soil that tends toward rapid drying of the turf during spring thaws. If prevalent and repeatedly troublesome, the disease can be prevented. See SNOWMOLD.

Damping-Off. New seedling grass may be damaged by several fungi. To prevent problems, avoid overwatering or overfertilizing newly seeded areas. See DAMPING-OFF.

Grubs. Lawns may be damaged by the larvae of Japanese, June, and other beetles. The adult beetles lay their eggs in the soil during the summer months. The eggs hatch and the larval form of the beetle, the grub, is born. The grubs at first feed on grass roots just below the surface, but on becoming full grown in the fall, they burrow deeper and there pass the winter. Early fall injury may resemble drought injury, the turf being soft and spongy. If large numbers of grubs are present, so much of the root system may be cut off that the turf can be lifted up from the soil like a loose, thick carpet. Such injury is most severe in exposed, unshaded sections of the lawn. See GRUBS for control measures.

Chinch Bug. This bug, formerly notorious as a corn and grass pest in the Midwest, has caused serious damage to lawns in some parts of the East, the injured areas being killed outright. When large patches of brown appear on the lawn, this bug may be the cause. The presence of the small black-and-white bugs can be tested by pushing a bottomless coffee can a few inches into the soil, filling it with water, and watching to see if the bugs float up. See CHINCH BUG for controls.

Sod Webworms. These pests are most apt to cause injury in hot dry seasons. If you have lots of moths flying around the lawn, they are probably adult webworms. They lay their eggs on the grass. The young caterpillars hatch and feed on grass leaves, form protective silken webs, and later build silk-lined tunnels along the surface of the soil, into which cut-off blades of grass are dragged. They feed at night and can be detected with a flashlight. Badly infested turf becomes ragged brown in appearance, and much damage can be done in a short time. See WEBWORM for controls.

Earthworms. Worms are usually considered beneficial factors in soil building and conditioning; their injury to grass (if any) is debatable. Damage to lawns chiefly consists of heaving and unsightly piles of castings.

Moles. Although they eat injurious grubs and insects, they may also do considerable damage to lawns by burrowing about and throwing up mounds above their tunnels. Besides being unsightly, the mounds pull the earth away from the grass roots, causing the turf to wilt and even die. Moles are hard to control, especially in loose soils where they are less likely to limit their travels to a few routes or burrows. The best way to control moles is to get rid of the larvae and other grubs that they feed on. Eliminate their food source and they will disapear. See GRUBS, MOLES for control measures.

LAWN MOWER. See MOWING.

LAWSONIA (law SOHN ee ah) **inermis.** A tropical shrub widely grown for decoration in warm climates; the source of henna dye. It bears clusters of small, fragrant flowers, white or rose colored. In the West Indies, where it has become naturalized, it is known as mignonette tree.

LAYERING. A method of vegetative propagation in which roots are encouraged to form on stems that are still part of the parent plant. After the roots have formed, the section of the stem bearing them is severed from the original plant and is handled as a separate individual. As with the other asexual propagation methods (in which no union of the sexes or production of seeds is involved), layering reproduces a plant exactly, without variation such as may occur in plants raised from seed. Layering is a development of a wholly natural phenomenon, since many kinds of plants—especially vines, trailers, and slender, drooping, woody bushes—will root of their own accord when a section of stem comes in contact with a moist substrate. Layering is best done in the spring or at the beginning of a growth cycle. Five principal methods of layering have been developed from nature's cruder forms.

PRINCIPAL METHODS

Simple Layering. This is done by bending and covering branches (except the tips, which must be kept uncovered to maintain circulation) with soil and holding them in position with pegs, stones, or earth clods until rooted. In a modified form of this method the stems are laid in shallow trenches prior to anchoring or pegging. The branches are often twisted, scraped, cut, or otherwise slightly wounded on the underside at the points where rooting is desired to encourage the quick formation of roots. See HERBS for illustration.

Modified Continuous Layering. This is popular for the propagation of certain grape varieties and other vines whose cuttings root poorly. In spring, canes of the previous year's growth are pegged down in shallow, open trenches. When shoots several inches long have developed along

these canes, the latter are wounded on the underside of the points where the shoots are, and soil is piled on these points and around the base of the shoots. After roots have formed, the canes are cut between the rooted shoots, which are transplanted and carried on as separate plants.

Compound or Serpentine Layering. This consists of bending flexible stems in a series of curves along the ground so that the down sections, or "troughs," are in contact with soil and

Compound layering

the up sections, or "crests," are in the air (A). Cut plants apart when roots have formed (B).

Mound, Hillock, or Stool Layering. This is done by cutting bushes, such as quince, gooseberry, and blueberry, back to within a few inches of the

Potting the new plants

ground in spring and heaping earth over the stumps. These send up shoots, which develop roots in the mound of earth. The following spring the rooted shoots are broken apart and planted in nursery rows or (if large enough) in their permanent positions. Rhododendrons are sometimes propagated by mound layering. See HERBS for illustration.

Chinese, Air, or Pot Layering. This is a greenhouse or home practice employed chiefly on stiff, erect-growing plants, such as dracaena, croton, oleander, and rubber plants that have become leggy and unsightly. See AIR LAYERING; PROPAGATION; RUBBER PLANT.

LAYIA (LAY yah). A genus of daisylike annual plants native to western North America. A few species are common and easily grown in the open, sunny border. For early blooms, the seeds can be started in a hot-bed, but they will grow well if planted where the plants are to stand.

L. glandulosa (white-daisy) is an attractive, early-blooming plant that grows to 18 in. and has rather sticky, narrow leaves and flowers in heads, the rays white or tinged with rose.

L. platyglossa (tidy-tips) is a pretty California wildflower that grows to 12 in. and is now often used in the border; the flowers have yellow rays tipped with white.

Layia platyglossa

LEADER. The upright tip of any tree that grows with a central trunk. In spruce, fir, pine, etc., the leader is usually an unbranched shoot with buds at the top from which spring the following year's extension of the leader and a new whorl of branches. When a tree of this type develops two or more leaders, all but one should be cut away. If the tip of the leader is injured, the tree stops growing in height until a new leader can develop, often two or three years later; and the trunk will be crooked at that point. A new and straight leader can be established in one growing season by immediately bending up the nearest branch (the strongest of a whorl) and tying it to a stake as close to a vertical position as possible. Thus aided, it will eventually dominate the others and become the leader.

LEADPLANT. A common name for *Amorpha canescens*, a small shrub with hairy leaves and purplish flowers; see AMORPHA.

LEADWORT. Common name for PLUMBAGO, a genus of tender shrubby plants grown in greenhouses or warm climates for their colorful flowers. The Leadwort Family is PLUMBAGINACEAE.

LEAF. An expansion of or extension from the stem of the plant; the leaf's function is to convert carbon dioxide and water into carbohydrates. The typical form consists of a broad blade connected to the branch by a petiole, or stalk.

The vessels that transplant food and materials from the root through the stem continue into the leaf and at its base (as well as on the stem where a leaf falls) are evident as tiny dots. In the leaf they appear as veins. Thus, there is a continuous system throughout the plant for bringing raw materials to the leaves and distributing manufactured food from them throughout the entire plant.

The inner tissue of the leaf is thin walled, and with the aid of the vital substance chlorophyll (which also gives plant parts their green color), it is equipped to manufacture food. In the presence of sunlight, the chlorophyll acts on the carbon dioxide of the air and on the soil solution brought up from the roots and builds up the basic food substances—sugar and starch, giving off oxygen in the process.

Protecting the leaf is an epidermis covered with a waxy cuticle and stomata, or pores, which regulate the giving off of excess water (see TRANSPIRATION). The epidermis, the structure and shape of the individual leaf, and even the whole plant organism—as in the arrangement of the many leaves on a plant—are all modified according to the habit of the plant, in order to protect the leaf against unfavorable external conditions and to obtain the maximum amount of sunlight it needs to do its work.

See also LEAVES.

LEAF CURL. A disease affecting peach, raspberry, and some woody bushes such as rhododendron. Symptoms include thickened, curled leaves with yellowish or reddish tints. To control, remove diseased leaves and discard them away from the plant. To help prevent further outbreaks, spray with a lime-sulfur fungicide in the dormant season before buds begin to swell. See also PEACH.

LEAF HOPPER. *Empoasca fabae* (potato leaf hopper) and others are sucking insects belonging to the same order (Homoptera) that includes the aphids. They occur throughout the world and attack all wild and cultivated plants. When they are abundant, plants show a lack of vigor and retarded growth, and the leaves usually have a whitened, stippled, or mottled appearance. Certain species, particularly the potato leaf hopper, cause the tips of the leaves to wither and die as if they had been scorched, the condition being called "hopperburn." Besides the direct injury they do, leaf hoppers are harmful because they carry the virus of certain plant diseases, such as aster yellows. The adults are small, active, slender-winged insects of various colors, usually found on the underside of leaves and hopping or flying for

Leaf hopper

short distances when disturbed. The best control measure is a contact insecticide with soap added. Since the insects move quickly, not all will be hit with one application of spray.

Northern leaf hoppers go south for the winter, returning in the spring to attack apple buds or young maple foliage and beans and other garden plants later on. They lay one egg per day for two to 20 days. There is one generation per year.

Controls include DIATOMACEOUS EARTH sprinkled on vulnerable plants, FLOATING ROW COVERS, insecticidal soap, and ROTENONE—used after dark when bees have returned to their hives. See also INSECT CONTROL.

LEAF MINER. Any number of kinds of insects, including *Liriomyza* spp. and *Fenusa pusilla* (birch leaf miner), which are small enough to live and feed between the upper and lower epidermis of a leaf. The tunnels they make show as winding white trails or broad, whitish spots on the green leaf surface.

On garden plants and trees like columbines, boxwood, or birches, which are particularly affected, the most practical plan is to remove and destroy the unsightly mined leaves. Cultivate surrounding soil in the fall to expose pupae to predators. Leaf miners are difficult to control by spraying unless this is accurately timed to get the adult insect as it emerges from the leaf or to prevent it from laying eggs in the half-opened leaves. Sprays of NICOTINE compounds are sometimes recommended. See also INSECT CONTROL; SPRAYING.

Leaf miner damage

LEAF MOLD. A friable mixture of decayed leaves and varying quantities of earth that accumulates naturally on forest floors. A similar material can be produced for the garden in compost heaps. See also COMPOST; LEAVES.

LEAFPLANT. Common name for *Kalanchoe pinnata*, a succulent tropical perennial easily cultivated as a houseplant and propagated from new plants that form in notches in the leaves; see KALANCHOE.

LEAF ROLL. The rolling of leaves can be caused by many things: waterlogged soil, excessive quantities of fertilizer, insects, bacteria, or fungi. The rolling is usually first observed on lower leaves, spreading upward on the plant. Generally the damage is only temporary and the plant recovers, often bearing a normal crop of fruit or flowers. The disease on potatoes specifically designated as leaf roll is a viral disease; see POTATO.

LEAF ROLLER. *Urbanus proteus* on beans and *Calpodes ethlius* on cannas are small, green or bronze caterpillars that roll up a single leaf, or fasten several together, and feed within the resulting tent. Fruit-tree leaf rollers, oblique-banded leaf roller, red-banded leaf roller, and strawberry leaf roller are among the more common species. The caterpillars can be controlled by hand-picking and by *Bacillus thuringiensis* (Bt, commonly available as Biotrol, Dipel, or Thuricide). Spray early to kill these pests before the leaves become curled. See INSECT CONTROL.

LEAF SPOT. A discolored area on a leaf with a more or less definite outline; a symptom of disease. When the areas involved are large and indefinite, the symptom is termed blotch or, sometimes, blight. Leaf spots frequently have centers of brown or light-colored or dead tissue with a dark or reddish margin of more recently affected tissue. Small black dots in a leaf spot are the fruiting bodies of a fungus containing spores. If they are absent it may mean that the spot is of bacterial origin or merely that the fruiting stage has not been reached.

Spotted leaves should be raked up in the fall and destroyed, not added to the compost pile. During the growing season, occasional spotted leaves on a plant should be removed and destroyed. Control a specific leaf spot disease with appropriate fungicides recommended for that disease and its host plant by your local extension service. See also FUNGICIDE; FUNGUS.

LEAF TIER. The greenhouse leaf tier is a moth whose active, slender green larvae cover several leaves with a single web or draw the parts of a single leaf together and eat the undersurfaces of the leaves. They attack many plants in the greenhouse and also in the garden. The adult moths, brownish with wings crossed by dark wavy lines, emerge from cocoons that are formed within the rolled-up leaves. Outbreaks of

Leaf tier

aspen, beech, and holly leaf tiers are sometimes severe. Control by sanitary measures and fumigating the greenhouse and the garden with *Bacillus thuringiensis* (Bt, commonly available as Biotrol, Dipel, or Thuricide).

See also INSECT CONTROL.

LEATHER FERN. Common name for *Rumohra adiantiformis*, a tropical fern that has tough, durable fronds; see RUMOHRA.

LEATHERLEAF. Common name for *Chamaedaphne calyculata*, an evergreen shrub found in cold-region bogs; see CHAMAEDAPHNE.

LEATHERWOOD. Common name for *Cyrilla racemiflora* (see CYRILLA) and the genus DIRCA due to the tough, fibrous nature of their bark and shoots.

LEAVES. Fallen leaves have excellent plant food value in their content of nitrogen, potash, and phosphoric acid and are even more valuable because of the vegetable matter that they add to the soil as they decay and become HUMUS. Humus increases the water-holding capacity of the soil, and its acid reaction helps break down the mineral elements of the soil. The accumulation of leaves (as leaf mold) in forests is part of the explanation of the sustained soil fertility, even though no fertilizer is ever supplied. Therefore, gather and save all disease-free leaves and use them either for mulching or for making COMPOST.

Useful as a winter mulch around shrubbery, leaves can be placed around rose bushes and piled on rows to reduce or prevent freezing of the ground. Leaves used as winter mulch must not be allowed to pack down over the crowns of perennial plants like strawberries, delphinium, foxglove, and the like, partly because they may smother the plants and also because a soggy mat is not only poor insulation but, on the contrary, freezes and adds to the damage it is supposed to protect against. Leaf mulches should not be applied until after the ground has frozen.

When oak, especially red oak, leaves are available, they make an excellent mulch for rhododendrons, mountain-laurel, and other plants that require acid soil. Here, however, they should remain undisturbed from year to year, with more added on top as those underneath decay.

LEDUM (LEE dum). A genus of hardy evergreen shrubs of North America, belonging to the Ericaceae (Heath Family). They are dwarf plants, not exceeding 3 ft. in height and often shorter. They have attractive, narrow evergreen leaves with rolled edges, fragrant when bruised, and clusters of white flowers in spring and early summer. Hardy in Zones 3–5, they prefer a boggy, sandy, peaty soil and seem to do equally well in sun or partial shade. Propagation is by seed, layering, and division. Seedlings are very slow growing.

L. groenlandicum (Labrador-tea) has narrow dark green leaves, densely covered with rusty hairs beneath, and flowers with five to seven stamens. The leaves are said to have been used as a substitute for tea during the Revolutionary War.

L. palustre (wild-rosemary) is similar to *L. groenlandicum* but has smaller leaves and ten stamens in the flowers.

LEEA (LEE ah). A genus of tropical, shrubby plants belonging to the Leeaceae (Leea Family), similar to grapevines but without tendrils.

L. amabilis, the best known in cultivation, is a handsome plant for the warm greenhouse and is often used to climb pillars. It does well in a rich loamy soil. The leaves are divided into five or seven leaflets that are bronzy green and of velvety texture, with a broad white stripe. Var. *splendens* has red stems and leaves with bright red markings. Propagation is by cuttings.

L. coccinea, a shrub with deeply cut leaves, is useful as an interior plant and outdoors in warm climates. A purple-leaved form is known.

LEEK. A hardy, biennial herb, *Allium ampeloprasum* var. *porrum*, closely related to onions but of milder flavor, grown for its flat, solid leaves and enclosed stems, which are frequently blanched and served like asparagus or used to season soups and meat dishes.

Leeks thrive in a temperate or cool-temperate climate. A light, rich, friable, moist but well-drained soil is ideal, but any good garden loam with a pH as high as 8.0 will give satisfactory results. The ground should be prepared as for onions, with compost or manure added to well-worked soil the preceding fall, then the surface raked and firmed by rolling or treading on it in early spring.

Leek

Leeks are a slow-growing crop, so seed should not be sown directly into the permanent bed. To grow leeks best, sow the seed thinly in a seedbed in early spring. For an early winter and/or late spring crop, sow in a seedbed eight weeks before the last spring frost is expected. Seedlings should be ready for transplanting to their permanent positions in about ten weeks. When the seedlings are 3 in. high, prick them out, setting the thinnings 1–2 in. apart in other nursery or seedbeds. When the plants are plump as straws, cut their tops back about one-half and transplant to the garden 12–15 in. apart in shallow trenches.

When the plants are about ten weeks old, lift then from the seedbed, trim the roots to about an inch long and the leaves to about 8 in. Now they are ready to plant. Make narrow holes 8 in. apart and 6 in. deep with a dibber. Set a plant in each hole and fill with water; this will wash the soil down to cover the roots. Soil should not be packed tightly around the stems. As the plants grow, they will fill the hole. Setting the plant this deep will produce blanched stems without the trouble of growing plants in trenches.

The first leeks should be ready for harvesting a

few weeks before the first frost. In mild climates, plants can be left in the ground and dug as needed. For winter use, dig the plants and set them in moist soil either in a coldframe that can be protected during cold weather or in a cellar where the air is moist and the temperature low. In climates where the ground freezes hard and deep, dig plants as late as is practical and store them in a cool, frost-free place in sand. They can also be sliced and frozen. Leeks do not dry well.

LEGOUSIA (le GOO see ah). A genus of small annual herbs, formerly listed as *Specularia*, and closely resembling *Campanula* (bellflower). They have violet, blue, or white wheel-shaped or broadly bell-shaped flowers and are used in the rock garden or border, growing from seed sown where they are to stand.

L. pentagonia, formerly listed as *S. pentagonia*, is a hairy-leaved plant with five-angled buds and small, solitary blue flowers.

L. speculum-veneris (Venus's-looking-glass), formerly listed as *S. speculum*, is often used as an edging plant and bears violet-blue or white, toothed flowers to 1½ in. long, one to three together in the leaf axils.

LEGUME. Any plant of the FABACEAE, or Bean Family; also the fruit of a member of this family, a flat, dry pod that opens on two sides, including peas and beans.

LEGUMINOSAE. Former name for FABACEAE, the Bean Family.

LEIOPHYLLUM (lī oh FIL um). A genus of dwarf, compact shrubs of North America, belonging to the Ericaceae (Heath Family), and commonly known as sand-myrtle. Hardy to Zone 5, they thrive best in a sandy, peaty soil and can stand partial shade as well as an open situation. They are useful in the rock garden and for bordering evergreen plantings. Propagation is by seed or layers.

L. buxifolium is a twiggy, compact shrub growing to about 2 ft., very attractive in late spring when studded with small white or pinkish flowers. There are several cultivars available.

LEMMAPHYLLUM (lem ah FIL um). A genus of small, creeping, epiphytic ferns whose thick, succulent fronds look nothing like most ferns. Five species are found in eastern Asia.

L. microphyllum is a tiny, charming fern with glossy green, fleshy fronds only ½–1½ in. long. The sterile fronds are fat and oval; the fertile ones are long and slender with the sori in rows on each side of the midvein. The plants do well in tree-fern baskets and on slabs, the wiry, slender rhizomes creeping over the entire surface. They need a coarse, well-drained mix.

LEMNA (LEM nah) **minor.** A tiny, floating aquatic plant commonly known as duckweed, used in many aquariums and pools. Individual plants are almost insignificant, very small and simple in structure. Plants are hardy in Zones 4–9, and under favorable conditions with plenty of light and warmth, a colony of them soon forms attractive floating patterns of rich green on the water surface. It is necessary, especially in the aquarium, to thin its masses periodically so fish and submerged plant material do not suffer from the lack of light and reduction of oxygenating surface. Some species of fish will occasionally eat duckweed.

LEMON. A small, spiny, evergreen, semitropical tree, *Citrus limon*, which bears acidic citrus fruit. Though grown on a commercial scale in the United States, mainly in California, it is an important garden fruit in the warmer parts of the whole citrus belt. The trees are more subject to frost injury than those of the orange, but less than those of the lime. Hardy in Zones 10–11, both trees and fruits prefer a dry, cool summer climate. The trees are often grown indoors in large flower pots or tubs for ornament. For culture, see CITRUS FRUITS.

Water-lemon, *Passiflora laurifolia*, is a tropical South American vine with white flowers and edible yellow fruit; see PASSIFLORA.

LEMON-BALM. Common name for *Melissa officinalis*, an aromatic herb; see MELISSA.

LEMON VERBENA. Common name for *Aloysia triphylla*, a white-flowered shrub with lemon-scented foliage; see ALOYSIA. VERBENA is the botanic name for another genus and common name for Verbenaceae, the family to which both genera belong.

LENTIL. An annual, semiclimbing, leguminous herb *Lens culinaris* (formerly listed as *L. esculenta*), grown for its small, flattened, nutritious seeds, which are used like dried beans. For a garden crop, seed is sown like peas in early spring in drills 18–30 in. apart in sandy loam and given ordinary cultivation. The seed keeps best if left in the pods when harvested.

LEONOTIS (lee aw NOH tis). A genus of shrubby plants from South Africa, commonly known as lion's-ear. The plants bear two-lipped, yellow or orange-scarlet flowers in dense whorls around the tall, leafy, square stems—which mark the Lamiaceae (Mint Family). They are suited to bold effects in the border in warm climates (Zones 10–11), or to pot cultivation in greenhouses for midwinter bloom. Seed of annuals should be sown early in the hotbed, ¼ in. deep, and set out later in well-drained, sunny soil. Perennials are propagated by division and cuttings, and the shrubby kinds by cuttings rooted under glass in early spring. During the summer, the plants growing outdoors should be pinched frequently to produce a compact, uniform shape. Only a few of the many species are often cultivated. *L. leonuris* grows to 6 ft. and has orange-red flowers in September; its dwarf form, var. *globosa nana* does not exceed 2½ ft. in height.

LEONTOPODIUM (lee ahn toh POH dee um). A genus of hardy, tufted, perennial herbs belonging to the Asteraceae (Aster Family). Several species are suitable for the rock garden, although none is particularly showy.

L. alpinum (edelweiss) is the most frequently grown. It has white-woolly foliage and inconspicuous flowers in heads surrounded by starlike clusters of floral leaves resembling pearly everlastings. Native to the high mountains of central Asia and Europe and especially associated with the Swiss Alps, it is a favorite alpine subject for rock gardens. It requires scree conditions and full sunlight, and it is easy to grow from seed.

Leontopodium alpinum

LEONURUS (lee on YEW rus). A genus of weedy herbs, originally native to Europe and Asia, naturalized in the United States, belonging to the Lamiaceae (Mint Family), and commonly known as motherwort. Of coarse habit, they grow 2–3 ft. high and have small leaves and prickly, two-lipped, purple, pink, or white flowers closely set around a single spike. Though occasionally seen in gardens, their tendency to self-sow makes them dangerous guests. When desired, they are easily raised from spring-sown seed in any ordinary soil. Hardy in Zones 4–7.

L. cardiaca (common motherwort) blossoms through the summer. The plant top, harvested at flowering time, has been used in herbal remedies of Europe and Russia, though contact with the plant may cause skin irritation.

LEOPARD MOTH. *Zeuzera pyrina*, an enemy of elm, maple, and other shade trees, native to Europe, first found in the United States in 1882, and now well established along the Atlantic Coast. The pinkish white, partly grown larvae, with dark brown spots, winter in burrows in the heartwood of infected trees. In the spring they start feeding and burrowing, then pupate in their tunnels, the moths emerging from June to early autumn. The latter, 2–3 in. across are very striking when the wings are expanded; they are white, blotched and spotted with blue and black. Eggs are laid in dark crevices and hatch in ten days, the young borers soon working their way to the heartwood of the branch. Two or three years are required for a life cycle.

During the fall and winter months, control by cutting and burning all infested branches, recognizable in early fall by the wilted leaves and the numerous holes through which sawdust is thrown out. The larvae can be killed by painting accessible twigs with a pine-tar, creosote, insecticide mixture. See INSECT CONTROL.

LEOPARD PLANT. Common name for *Ligularia tussilaginea* var. *aureo-maculata*, a tall perennial with spotted foliage; see LIGULARIA.

LEOPARD'S-BANE. Common name for DORONICUM, a genus of daisylike perennial herbs. The name is also applied to *Senecio doronicum*; see SENECIO.

LEPIDIUM (lee PID i um). A genus of Asiatic annual, perennial, or biennial herbs of the Brassicaceae (Mustard Family), commonly called peppergrass. They have small white or greenish flowers and finely cut leaves.

The species are of little horticultural interest, except *L. sativum*, the common garden cress, which is grown for its pepper flavor as a salad or garnish. It is widely popular in Europe and deserves to be better known in North America. This is the cress of the tea-time English sandwiches of mustard and cress.

Cress grows quickly and is well suited to cooler temperatures; the richer the soil, the better. Sow seed thickly in narrow drills 10–12 in. apart in earliest spring and at weekly intervals until late spring. If sown later than this, the plants become strong flavored and quickly go to seed. Seedlings appear in three or four days, grow rapidly, and can be cut with shears in three or four weeks. If the cutting is not too close, two or three more cuttings can be made. Plants can also be grown indoors and are ready to eat in eight to ten days, generally giving much better results than outdoor sowing. Hardy to Zone 3.

See CRESS for other cultivation information.

LEPTODACTYLON (lep toh DAK ti lawn). A genus of attractive shrubs of western North America belonging to the Polemoniaceae (Phlox Family). They have prickly, needlelike foliage and showy, 1½-in., fragrant flowers in pink or white. Hardy to Zone 9, they are useful in a wild garden, rock garden, or drought-tolerant landscape. Generally grown from seed or cuttings, they need a sterile, well-drained, rather dry soil.

L. californicum (prickly phlox) is a shrub about 3 ft. tall and is covered with satiny pink flowers in spring.

L. pungens (granite phlox) is a low shrub, usually under 1 ft., with a profusion of whitish or pinkish flowers in spring.

LEPTOSPERMUM (lep toh SPUR mum). A genus of evergreen shrubs or small trees of Australia and New Zealand, belonging to the Myrtaceae (Myrtle Family). They are grown outdoors in Zones 10–11 and are sometimes seen in greenhouse collections. Those in cultivation are upright shrubs with slender branches and small, stiff leaves. In spring they are most attractive with a profusion of white or pinkish flowers. Propagation is by cuttings.

L. laevigatum (Australian teatree) is a white-flowered shrub that has been used especially in California for the reclamation of loose, shifting sands.

L. scoparium is a good spring-flowering, woody plant, producing a mass of white flowers when well grown. Its var. *bullatum* is an improved form with larger leaves and flowers, and var. *chapmanii* is a form with bright rose flowers.

LESPEDEZA (les pe DEE zah). A genus of herbs or subshrubs belonging to the Fabaceae (Bean Family) and commonly known as bush-clover. Some species are grown as forage or green manures, while one or two of the hardy Asiatic species are valuable in the garden for their late flowers. The roots are hardy in the North, and plants thrive in light soils and sunny locations. Propagation is by seed or division.

PRINCIPAL SPECIES

L. formosa is a graceful and handsome plant with a profusion of rosy purple flowers in long, drooping racemes in early autumn.

L. japonica is similar to *L. formosa* but has white flowers.

L. striata (Japanese- or Korean-clover) is grown for hay or green manure in warm regions.

LETTUCE. A hardy annual herb, *Lactuca sativa*, and the most important salad plant grown in North America for its edible leaves. Varieties are generally grouped according to their shape and characteristics: heading or cabbage lettuces; leafing or curled lettuces, with crinkly leaves, not in heads; and cos or ROMAINE LETTUCE, whose leaves form long, erect, columnar heads, the interiors more or less blanched.

CULTURE

Lettuce is a salad plant and therefore must be grown rapidly in what is called quick soil. This means well-drained, friable ground in which there is a constant supply of moisture and ample readily available plant food. Since the plant is hardy, it can be started in a coldframe one month, or in a hotbed two months, before outdoor sowing is possible. A first planting of a 3–6 ft. row of thinly sown seed should give enough early plants for an ordinary family. Similar successional sowings should be made in outdoor seedbeds at intervals of ten to fifteen days until midspring or later. The main reason for successional sowings is that as warm weather approaches the plants become bitter and quickly go to seed.

In the garden the lettuce rows should be not less than 12 in. apart for small-growing kinds or 15 in. apart for large ones. The plants should be thinned first while less than 2 in. tall to stand 2 in. apart; a second time when they begin to crowd, each alternate plant being removed; and a third time in the same fashion when the remainder become crowded. The thinnings in the first two cases can be transplanted if not needed for the table.

In home gardens the loose-leaf varieties will usually be found most satisfactory because they are the easiest to grow to perfection, unless conditions are exceptionally favorable. Romaine or cos lettuce, though a so-called summer type, requires partial shade in hot, sunny, dry summers. Shade can be provided by lath or cheesecloth screens.

When garden space is restricted, lettuce plants can be set alternately with cabbage or similar plants or the rows can alternate with those of parsnips, salsify, and other slow-growing crops. In this case the lettuce is used first. On the other hand, quicker maturing crops like radish, spinach, and onion sets can be grown between the lettuce plants.

Harvesting. To have lettuce reach the table in best condition the plants should be pulled or cut early in the morning while still wet with dew or at latest before the sun has wilted the leaves. The plants should then be washed and set in a cool place where the air does not circulate much. This will maintain the morning crispness. If the lettuce is shaken almost dry, placed in a tightly closed container, and kept in the refrigerator, it will retain its crispness for a week.

ENEMIES

Lettuce diseases, including two kinds of rot, a tipburn, and certain virus troubles, are sometimes very destructive. Because the leaves are to be eaten, spraying and dusting are potentially dangerous. The chief control measures are removal of lettuce refuse, crop rotations, and the eradication of weeds in the vicinity. Bottom rot starts in the bottom leaves lying on the ground and destroys first the blades and then the midribs. Drop or sclerotinia rot attacks chiefly greenhouse lettuce, as does the gray mold rot. See BOTRYTIS.

Tipburn results from high temperatures in combination with other unfavorable weather conditions and in midsummer may destroy many plants.

To control aphids (which carry a mosaic or virus disease of lettuce), cover the crop with floating row covers. To check slugs, which are fond of lettuce, surround the plants with lime, fine coal ashes, or soot.

LEUCHTENBERGIA (look ten BURG ee ah) **principis.** Commonly known as agave cactus, this true cactus has a superficial resemblance to an *Agave* by virtue of the elongated blue tubercles, each of which bears long papery spines. It is a greenhouse plant that bears striking yellow flowers and requires the same treatment as the ECHINO-CACTUS. To propagate, offsets should be well dried at the base and potted in soil of broken brick and peaty loam, or by seeds, which must be sown as soon as ripe in shallow pans over heat.

LEUCOCRINUM (lew koh KRĪ num) **montanum.** A native, spring-blooming herb of the western United States, commonly called mountain, sand, or star lily. It has a rootstock or rhizome, narrow grasslike leaves, and fragrant, tubular white flowers, starlike in form, growing in clusters. Although attractive, it is nearly impossible to cultivate, and collection only destroys native stands, since no one grows it from seed.

LEUCODENDRON (loo koh DEN drawn). A genus of South African trees or shrubs belonging to the Proteaceae (Protea Family). They are grown outdoors in Zones 10–11, particularly in California. The best-known species, *L. argenteum* (silvertree), is one of the most noted trees of the Cape of Good Hope region, where it grows to 30 ft. It is a showy and interesting plant by reason of its large narrow leaves, densely covered with silky, silvery white hairs and closely set upon the stems. It is propagated by seed. Dried leaves are shipped from South Africa and are used for decorative purposes.

LEUCOJUM (loo KOH jum). A genus of bulbous plants with drooping white flowers, belonging to the Liliaceae (Lily Family) and commonly known as snowflake. In the North, they are hardy in the border with winter protection, and in some areas of the South they have become naturalized. They are easily grown, bulbs being planted 3 in. deep in well-drained soil in the perennial or shrubbery border or rock garden; they should remain undisturbed for as long as possible.

PRINCIPAL SPECIES

L. aestivum (summer snowflake) has long, strap-shaped leaves and bears two to eight white, green-tipped blossoms clustered on a stalk 1–1½ ft. high in late May.

L. autumnale has very slender 9-in. flower stalks bearing from one to three blossoms. This species is not as satisfactory for cultivation as others, since it requires a sheltered location and winter protection.

L. vernum (spring snowflake) has white blossoms, usually borne singly and appearing about a month after the early snowdrops.

LEUCOTHOE (loo KOH thoh ee). A genus of deciduous and evergreen shrubs native in Asia and North and South America, belonging to the Ericaceae (Heath Family). Leucothoes grow best in a moist, sandy peat soil and shade or partial shade. Propagation is by seed, cuttings, division, and rooted tips of older branches where they touch the ground.

PRINCIPAL SPECIES

L. axillaris differs only slightly from *L. fontanesiana*, chiefly in having a smaller and shorter-stemmed leaf, with flower buds greenish instead of reddish. Hardy to Zone 6.

L. fontanesiana, formerly listed as *L. catesbaei*, is found from Virginia southward but is hardy to Zone 5. It is one of the handsomest broad-leaved, shade-loving evergreens. It grows to 6 ft. and has arching branches and large, lustrous, purplish green leaves, which in the open take on a bronze autumn tone. The nodding white flowers, with a very unpleasant odor, are borne in clusters along the stem in early spring. This is a good plant to use in protected places, especially near the waterside, or to mass in front of rhododendrons or kalmias.

L. racemosa (sweetbells) is an upright grower to 10 ft. and is found in moist places from Massachusetts to Louisiana. The leaves are deciduous and turn scarlet in autumn. The small but attractive white or pale pink bell-like flowers have a sweet fragrance and bloom from late May to June. Hardy in Zones 6–9.

L. recurva, found from Virginia southward, closely resembles *L. racemosa* but is of more spreading habit. It will tolerate drier conditions than most, and its leaves also turn scarlet before falling. The fragrant, white, bell-like flowers bloom in early spring before the leaves. Hardy in Zones 6–8.

LEVISTICUM (lev IS tik um) **officinale.** A hardy flavoring herb of the Apiaceae (Celery Family), commonly known as lovage. It grows to 6 ft. or more and has glossy, dark green, compound leaves and greenish yellow flowers in umbels. It is grown for aromatic seeds used in tea, candy, and liqueurs; leaves for tea; and flowers and foliage for oil to flavor tobacco or perfume. Propagation is by seed (sown in fall) or by division. Once established it needs little care but plenty of root room, thriving in a deep, rich soil.

Levisticum officinale

LEWISIA (loo IS ee ah). A genus of low-growing deciduous or evergreen perennial herbs of the Portulacaceae (Portulaca Family). They have smooth, fleshy leaves, often in rosettes, and charming waxy or satiny cactuslike flowers in white, pink, rose, and blends of yellow and peach. All native to the western states, they are outstanding treasures for the rock garden. They are perfectly hardy but are more of a challenge to grow in the South due to humidity.

Because the fleshy root and leaves are subject to rot, many gardeners succeed by planting them vertically, in walls or on steep slopes in the rock garden. A collar of gravel beneath the rosette also helps keep the foliage dry. Propagation is easy from seed. In the spring, small side rosettes can be treated as cuttings and rooted in sand.

PRINCIPAL SPECIES

DECIDUOUS KINDS

The deciduous group requires a loose, gritty soil, full of humus and well watered but also well drained.

L. brachycalyx has oblong, light green leaves and white flowers veined with rose.

L. nevadensis has short-stemmed white flowers tinted lavender.

L. oppositifolia has a few narrow leaves and solitary flowers tinted rose, on stems 6–12 in. high.

L. rediviva (bitterroot) has a dense rosette of narrow leaves, above which rise beautiful silky, short-stemmed blossoms 1½ in. across, varying in color from white to deep rose.

Lewisia rediviva

This is the state flower of Montana, where it covers acres of land with bloom in the spring.

EVERGREEN KINDS

The evergreen species of *Lewisia* should be planted in sandy silt mixed with leaf mold. The crown should be set 1 in. above the surface of the soil and filled around with stone chips and pea-sized gravel. This rough, loose material will assure perfect drainage of water from the axils of the leaves.

L. columbiana, growing 6–9 in. high, has densely overlapping green leaves and branched clusters of lovely white to light pink flowers striped with dark pink.

L. cotyledon is the most varied evergreen species. Many beautiful hybrids are on the market, having flowers of many shades of pink, orange, white, and even yellow.

L. tweedyi has exquisite salmon-pink blossoms nearly 2 in. across, one to three on a stem, rising just above the thick, fleshy leaves. Since the root of this species is very large, it should be given plenty of room. This lovely plant has been known to have over 200 blossoms open during a season. A choice white form is also available.

LEYCESTERIA (lī ses TEER ee ah) **formosa.** An attractive Himalayan deciduous shrub belonging to the Caprifoliaceae (Honeysuckle Family) and commonly known as Himalayan honeysuckle. It grows to 6 ft. and is hardy to Zone 7. The white flowers, tinged purple, are arranged in whorls, in drooping, leafy racemes. The leafy bracts are purple, and the flowers, which open in summer, are followed by reddish purple berries. Propagation is by seed and cuttings of green or mature wood.

LIATRIS (lī AY tris). A genus of showy North American perennial plants belonging to the Asteraceae (Aster Family) and commonly known as gayfeather or blazing-star. The small heads of purple or white flowers are generally borne close against long, wandlike stems. Attractive throughout midsummer and well into autumn in the wild, they are also effective when massed in the flower border. Plants are easily raised from seed or by division of the clumps and do not resent transplanting. Most are hardy to Zone 3.

Liatris pycnostachya

PRINCIPAL SPECIES

L. graminifolia grows to 3 ft. and has purple flowers and long, grasslike leaves. The flower stalks are sometimes branching.

L. ligulistylis grows to 12 in. and has rose-purple flower heads in flattened clusters.

L. punctata grows to 12 in. or more and has heads of rose-purple flowers in dense spikes.

L. pycnostachya grows to 5 ft. and is excellent when planted in masses. Unlike many other tall plants, these dense purple spikes to 18 in. long open their flowers from the top downward.

L. scariosa, growing to 6 ft., is pubescent and bears bluish purple flowers, often purple tipped, in interrupted racemes.

L. spicata grows to 6 ft. and has long spikes of purplish rose flowers. Var. *montana* has shorter spikes on dwarfer, stouter plants.

LIBERTIA (li BUR tee ah). A genus of tender perennial plants of the Iridaceae (Iris Family), native to Chile and New Zealand, and named for Marie A. Libert, a Belgian botanist. Plants grow to 3 ft. and have evergreen, swordlike foliage and large white flowers appearing in early summer. These are lovely border plants for the warmest climates and should be planted in spring or fall in rich sandy soil and lightly covered in winter. The creeping, fibrous rooted rhizomes can be divided in spring, or seed can be sown in the coldframe from late summer through autumn. Most species have white flowers, *L. grandiflora* being especially free flowering; but *L. caerulescens* has blue flowers.

LICHEN. An organism comprised of fungal and algal cells living together symbiotically. They are rootless, stemless, flowerless, and leafless; usually gray-green or rusty-gray but sometimes brighter in color; and cling closely in flat or ruffled mats to rocks, tree bark, and the bare ground, where more complex forms of plant life could not obtain a foothold. Their fruiting bodies (containing spores) occur as knobs, disks, or cups, usually brightly colored. Lichens are found in every zone. Of very slow growth, they attain great age that may run into several centuries.

The lichen is the result of the close association of two very different growths for their mutual advantage (called symbiotic association). One, an alga, with the power of manufacturing plant food but easily dried by the sun, is fed upon by a white, threadlike fungus, unable to produce its own food but capable of absorbing and retaining moisture. In return for its food obtained from the alga, which it enwraps completely, the fungus furnishes the necessary shade, moisture, and protection for its companion. Between them, by chemical and mechanical action, they not only live and grow, but actually build up a thin layer of soil on which mosses can subsist; there they die, thus producing additional soil where higher orders of plants can grow.

Lichens supply certain dyes and drugs, and several species are edible; one supplies the so-called Iceland-moss. Another is believed identical with the manna of the Israelites. The so-called reindeer-moss is a branching lichen. While not garden subjects to be cultivated, they are interesting when introduced as features of a rock or wild garden, or in miniature garden arrangements such as terrariums.

LICORICE. Common name for *Glycyrrhiza glabra*, a perennial herb used for flavoring; see GLYCYRRHIZA.

LICORICE FERN. Common name for *Polypodium glycyrrhiza*, a small fern whose rhizomes taste of licorice; see POLYPODIUM.

LICUALA (lik yoo AY lah). A genus of small fan palms native to tropical Asia, Australia, and the Pacific islands. They grow single or clumped trunks and long-stemmed, rounded, fan-shaped leaves. In the juvenile stage, these handsome palms make decorative specimens handled as tub plants in the warm greenhouse. They must have plenty of water and shade from intense sunlight. *L. grandis*, the best-known species, has a single stem growing to 6 ft. and is leafy for at least half its height when young. Propagation is by seed started in pans with bottom heat.

LIGHT. Light is vital to all green plants; in fact, they cannot live without it. Plants feed themselves largely by turning the chemical elements contained in water and air into sugar, which supplies nearly all their needs and which they store for future use in the form of starch. Light is the fuel or energy source by which water and air are thus combined in the cells of a leaf. Without light, no sugar or starch can be made; when the stored supply is used up, the plant dies.

Some plants require direct sunlight; others can use indirect or diffused light, such as that on the north side of a rock or in the shade of thick woods, and may die if exposed to the direct rays of the sun. There are also some plants that prefer special combinations of light and shade, a few hours of full sunlight and shade the balance of the day, scattered spots of sunlight falling through the trees, or the light of the sky on a steep northern slope, where direct sunlight never falls. Most plants adapt themselves to different degrees and kinds of light by changing their leaf structure to suit conditions. Soft, thin leaves grown in shade often burn brown when moved into sunlight and later drop off, when smaller, thicker leaves have grown to take their place. It is therefore best not to move plants from shade to sun, or, if it must be done, to move them at a season when the sun is low.

In the Northern Hemisphere, the sun gives most light in June, when it is highest, and least in December, when lowest. The difference is made greater by the frequency of cloudy weather in winter. House and greenhouse plants often suffer from lack of light in winter, especially because not all the light passes through ordinary window glass. All possible light should be given to these winter plants, though some need shielding from the unnatural heat of sunlight passing through glass.

Houseplants should be placed in the brightest part of the room, and hotbeds and coldframes built so that the sash slopes southward, to admit more direct light rays. Greenhouses should be laid out scientifically with the glass sloped to invite maximum light and to prevent the burning effects that result when light passes through a lens. Successful house- and greenhouse plants are usually those that can adapt themselves easily to different amounts of light, or which prefer shade. Artificial light is helpful to supplement daylight in greenhouses, and experiments tend to show that with the right size and type of bulbs used, electric light will help greatly in promoting the health and growth of plants that would soon die without it. See ARTIFICIAL LIGHT.

In spring, outdoor plants begin their growth more in response to light than to heat, with the result that early blossoms like those of magnolia, peach, and dogwood, and the leaves of such evergreens as rhododendron are sometimes injured by getting under way in advance of late spring frost. Plants of these types should therefore be given less light by being placed on a northern slope or on the north side of a building or woodland.

LIGNUM-VITAE. Common name for trees of the tropical genus GUAIACUM and for lumber produced from them.

LIGULARIA (lig yoo LAIR ee ah). A genus of perennial herbs native to western Europe and the Far East, belonging to the Asteraceae (Aster Family), including some formerly grouped with *Senecio*. They have broad basal leaves showily marked and bear numerous yellow flower heads on 5-ft. stems. This is a striking plant for the garden border and is easily grown from seed sown in spring ⅛ in. deep in ordinary garden soil and the plants thinned later. Hardy in Zones 4–8.

PRINCIPAL SPECIES

L. dentata, growing to 5 ft., has large purple, bronze, or green leaves with maroon undersides and stems. It prefers shade and moist soil.

L. japonica is a bold plant for landscaping. Hardy to Zone 7.

L. przewalskii, growing 30–36 in., sends up showy spikes of yellow blooms.

L. tussilaginea (leopard plant), formerly listed as *L. kaempferi* var. *aureo-maculata*, is a tall perennial with yellow, sometimes white or rose, spotted leaves. The variety name means "gold-spotted."

L. vetchiana, growing 4–5 ft., produces tall, slender, golden spikes above distinctive 16-in., toothed leaves.

L. wilsoniana (giant-groundsel) grows to 5 ft. with yellow flowers in heads.

LIGULE. A strap-shaped body where leaf blade meets sheath in the grasses; and the narrow and moderately long corolla of the ray flowers of composites. The term is derived from a Latin word meaning "little tongue."

LIGUSTRUM (li GUS trum). A genus of deciduous or evergreen shrubs native in Europe, Asia, and Australia, belonging to the Oleaceae (Olive Family), and commonly known as privet. They are valuable for ornamental use, especially as hedge or screening material, but sometimes for specimen plantings. They have clean foliage, spikes of flowers in summer, and usually black or bluish black berries borne in great profusion and mostly remaining all winter.

Not particular as to soil, privets are well adapted to withstand shade, city, and seaside conditions. Propagation can be done by seed but is easiest from cuttings. The evergreen species are not hardy, and even some of the deciduous ones are killed back in severe winters. If pruned back, they grow up vigorously and more bushy than before. Some species are well adapted for close clipping and trimming in fancy shapes. *L. ovalifolium* is largely used for this purpose but is killed to the ground by below-zero temperatures. *L. amurense*, while not quite as good looking, is much hardier. For a tall hedge or screen, *L. vulgare* is effective, keeping its leaves green and holding them until quite late.

PRINCIPAL SPECIES

L. amurense (Amur privet) is a Chinese shrub of upright growth to 15 ft. It holds its light green leaves late and produces slightly bloomy berries. It is one of the hardiest and is a good hedge plant for Zones 4–7.

L. x *ibolium* is a hybrid between *L. ovalifolium* and *L. obtusifolium*, somewhat hardier (Zones 5–7) than its parents.

L. japonicum is a handsome, bushy evergreen that grows to 10 ft. and has flower panicles to 6 in. long. It is useful in warm climates for topiary, hedges, and containers. Hardy to Zone 7.

L. lucidum (glossy privet) is a large shrub or small tree, sometimes used for street planting in warm regions and useful for topiary, hedges, or specimen plantings. It is cultivated in China for the white wax exuded from the bark as the result of insect activity. It is very showy in bloom, with panicles about 10 in. long. Hardy to Zone 8.

L. obtusifolium is a hardy Japanese shrub with

wide-spreading and curving branches, bearing small, nodding panicles of flowers and heavily laden all winter with bloomy black berries. Var. *regelianum* is a low, dense form with almost horizontal branches, making a very handsome shrub for foreground planting. Hardy in Zones 5–8.

L. ovalifolium (California privet), a native of Japan, is upright and grows to 15 ft. It has handsome shining foliage and creamy white flowers, the odor of which may be unpleasant. Cv. 'Aureo-marginatum' (golden privet) is less vigorous and needs good soil in a sunny place to show to best advantage. Hardy in Zones 6–8.

L. sinense (Chinese privet) grows to 12 ft. or more and makes a very showy flowering shrub in summer. Hardy in Zones 7–9.

L. tschonskii, formerly listed as *L. acuminatum*, is a Japanese species of somewhat spreading habit, to 6 ft. The leaves drop early in the fall, but it has shining black berries.

L. x *vicaryi* (golden vicary privet) is a deciduous species with white flowers in the spring and lovely foliage. Hardy to Zone 5.

L. vulgare (European privet) is a shrub that grows to 15 ft. and has flower clusters to 3 in., popular as a hedge. Hardy to Zone 4.

LILAC.
Common name for SYRINGA, a genus of large deciduous shrubs belonging to the Oleaceae (Olive Family), popular for their showy, fragrant flowers.

LILIACEAE
(lil ee AY see ee). The Lily Family, a large, important group of plants widely distributed but most abundant in warm regions. Though most are perennial herbs, dying down after flowering to a crown of fleshy underground stems, some are woody or treelike. A few are grown for food, like species of *Asparagus* and *Allium* (onion), but the family is most noted in contributing some of the finest of ornamentals. Flowers are large, regular, and showy; sometimes small ones are clustered. Flower parts are typical in size; both petals and sepals are alike, colored, and inserted below the ovary instead of above, as in other families of the general lily alliance.

Genera most commonly cultivated are *Allium*, *Aloe*, *Anthericum*, *Asparagus*, *Asphodeline*, *Asphodelus*, *Aspidistra*, *Bowiea*, *Bulbocodium*, *Calochortus*, *Camassia*, *Chionodoxa*, *Chlorophytum*, *Colchicum*, *Convallaria* (lily-of-the-valley), *Eremurus*, *Fritillaria*, *Galtonia*, *Gloriosa*, *Hemerocallis* (daylily), *Hosta* (plantain), *Hyacinthus* (hyacinth), *Kniphofia*, *Lachenalia*, *Lilium* (lily), *Liriope*, *Muscari*, *Ophiopogon*, *Ornithogalum*, *Paradisea*, *Rohdea*, *Ruscus*, *Scilla*, *Smilax*, *Tricyrtis*, and *Tulipa* (tulip).

LILIUM
(LIL ee um). A genus of true bulbs including the principal members of the Liliaceae (Lily Family), commonly known as lily. As with most other bulbous subjects, the native sources of origin are largely confined to water-bound locations; therefore, the islands and coastal regions of the Orient and the Mediterranean Sea, together with both coasts of the United States, are important contributors of different species of this important and beautiful flower.

Lily bulb

Lily bulbs, in all instances, are composed of fleshy, overlapping scales and are of a size usually proportionate to the stem and flowers produced. The erect stems bear both spear-shaped leaves and funnel- or bell-shaped flowers with six petals; the outer three are sometimes smaller than and overlap the inner three.

In the United States, horticultural trade custom has divided lilies into two main groups. The first takes in all of the garden kinds—both white and colored—and designates them as "hardy lilies;" the second comprises the tender, white, so-called Easter lilies, some of which can, however, be flowered outdoors as summer bedding subjects.

PROPAGATION

There are several ways by which lilies can be successfully propagated. With commercial growers, the approved practice—which amateurs eager to raise large quantities of lilies can follow—is to select the finest-appearing lily stalks at the time of flowering and to use the bulbs that produce them as propagating stock. This ensures constant improvement, which may not be attained when other means are employed. The plants marked at flowering time are carefully dug and the bulbs are separated. When the normal planting time approaches, these bulbs are broken apart scale by scale (A), and the scales are planted out in rows (B). Tiny bulbils form at the base of the scales where they were separated from the main bulb, and each one produces a top growth (C). When this dies down in the normal manner, the bulbils are lifted to be replanted the next season. Repeated replantings ultimately produce flowering-size bulbs, the time needed for this development differing with the variety of lily. In many types, the second year's planting will give a crop of a size suitable for garden planting.

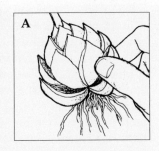

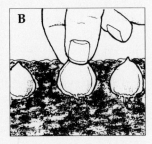

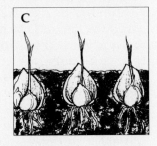

Another method widely employed is the planting of seed. Here again the selection of seedpods from the finest stalks is important. It should be noted, however, that variations will likely occur in all lilies grown from seed. At the same time, most lilies are heavy seed producers so the planting of seed is the quickest way to develop a stock.

The seed, harvested during the summer, can be sown in greenhouses or coldframes in late fall, or outdoors in early spring. Bulbils, varying in size according to the variety and the treatment given them, will, with subsequent replantings, develop into flowering-size bulbs. *L. regale* (regal lily) grows especially well from seed, and this is the method chiefly employed in commercial production of vast quantities of this variety.

There are also three methods of what can be called natural propagation. The most intensive is by means of the small bulbs that form along the stalk under the ground from just above the bulb to the surface of the soil. Their number can be increased by deep planting or by hilling up the bulbs as the stalks grow so as to lengthen the portion below ground level. The bulbs so formed are usually quite large, and in the case of many varieties, will reach flowering size after being grown on for one additional season.

Second, there are the aerial bulblets that form in the axils of the upper leaves of some species. In the tiger lily, such bulbils are quite prolific, and there are several other species that produce them about as freely. These bulbils should be carefully watched at about flowering time so they can be gathered when ripe, but before they fall to the ground. Planted whenever the bulbs of the parent stock are planted, the bulbils will increase in size annually, and in two or three seasons they will produce flowering-size bulbs.

Finally, there is the natural division of the bulb itself, which is quite important to the gardener whose plantings are likely to remain undisturbed for several years. Under such conditions, varieties that have become well established will be found to have increased considerably. The whole clump of bulbs should then be lifted after the foliage has died down naturally and the new bulbs that have formed around the original one can be pulled apart readily. Since all lily bulbs dry out quickly when exposed, immediate replanting should be done.

CULTURE

Growers agree that the most essential factor in the successful cultivation of lilies is good drainage. An ideal soil is a porous loam with a gravelly subsoil; but if a given soil is too heavy or too light and sandy, it should be dug out to a depth of 3 ft., a layer of stones or gravel placed at the bottom, and this covered with a good, friable, fertile, fibrous loam.

The depth of planting varies with the species; normally it should be about three times the height of the bulb. That is, if the bulb is 3 in. high, its base should be 9 in. deep when planted. According to rooting habits, there are two main classes of lilies. Those of one class produce roots from the base of the bulb only; the other kind develop feeding roots along the stem between the bulb and the surface of the ground.

Base-rooting (BR) lilies require shallow planting and depend on available plant humus food in the surface soil for their nourishment. It is advisable to mix well-rotted manure with the soil to a depth of 6 in., where the base of the bulb will be, to encourage the downward growth of the basal roots. Base-rooting lilies often lie dormant the first year after planting or send up only a weak, nonflowering shoot, because the heavy roots have been destroyed in storage and transit. Lilies that are carefully transplanted do not suffer this damage and resulting check.

Stem-rooting (SR) lilies require deep planting so as to have maximum root-producing stem area. They usually bloom well the first year, and it is desirable to incorporate bonemeal into the first 18 in. of soil, to add to the nourishment they can derive from the humus and plant food already present.

Whether lilies are grown in a bed by themselves or in the border in combination with perennials, they require a year-round mulch to keep the soil mellow and to conserve moisture. Fresh manure should never be used, but partially decayed leaves are excellent if the soil is rich; well-rotted horse or cow manure is essential if the soil lacks humus. Many lilies do well in the shrubbery border, where their roots are kept cool and their stems are supported by the surrounding plants, their blossoms reaching up into the sunlight.

In certain species the bulbs are composed of very loose scales under which water may collect and cause rotting. To prevent this, plant them on their sides on a layer of sharp sand. Indeed, a handful of sand placed in the bottom of the hole when planting any kind of lily is an advisable rot preventive.

The following list of species includes special cultural requirements of important stem-rooting and bulb-rooting lilies.

ENEMIES

Mosaic, the most serious lily disease, is prevalent in all parts of the world, and all species of *Lilium* (and the related genus *Fritillaria*) are more or less susceptible. *L. auratum*, *L. longiflorum*, and *L. speciosum* are more susceptible than *L. canadense*, *L. hansonii*, or *L. regale*. It is caused by a virus that is carried from diseased to healthy lilies by the melon aphid. It is not transmitted through the seed nor by contaminated soil.

Affected plants exhibit marked stunting, often with distortion and twisting of stems and leaves, deformed flowers, and mottling of the foliage into light and dark areas. The virus invades all parts of the plant except the seed, and affected plants never recover, but die. To control, plant only bulbs known to be healthy, if possible, or if practical, raise lilies from seed. In plantings, remove all mosaic-infected plants as soon as detected. In greenhouses, frequent fumigation to control aphids checks the spread of mosaic. Forcing at a slightly higher temperature increases the percentage of perfect bloom. See also MOSAIC.

Another virus disease affecting the tops of lily plants is known as "yellow flat." The leaves become pale and curl downward. The control is the same as for mosaic.

BOTRYTIS blight, a serious fungous disease, appears first as conspicuous orange-brown spots on the foliage; these are followed by a blighted or burned appearance and rotted buds. Diseased areas may be covered with a gray mold. Small, black spore-bearing bodies (sclerotia) formed on dead leaves and stems give rise to early spring infection, and the disease spreads very rapidly in moist weather. To prevent it, gather and burn all dead stalks and leaves in the autumn, and apply a fungicide in the spring as soon as new growth appears, repeating two or three times. In green-houses, keep the humidity low. Infected bulbs should be lifted and destroyed.

If bulb rots are seen when bulbs are dug, cut away rotted portions and soak bulbs in a fungicide for an hour or so.

The bulb mite causes considerable injury to lily bulbs, but no satisfactory method of control has been developed, since methods used against mites in other bulbs may be injurious to lilies. Plant only sound, healthy bulbs; destroy infected plants; and store at low temperatures when bulbs are out of the ground. A brown-and-yellow aphid is often present in great numbers on the underside of lily leaves from midsummer through fall. Spray the underside of foliage with contact insecticide.

PRINCIPAL SPECIES

The following list comprises the most important *Lilium* species suitable for garden culture in the United States. Since the principal ones are of foreign origin, they are given first, then the native kinds, and finally some foreign ones of value but which require expert handling. At the end of each species description, BR indicates base-rooting, and SR indicates stem-rooting (see culture above). The figures indicate planting depth measured from the base of the bulb to the surface of the soil.

COMMON FOREIGN SPECIES

L. auratum (goldbanded or goldband lily of Japan), growing to 6 ft., is one of the largest and handsomest of lilies. The large, fragrant, flaring trumpet flowers are ivory white with broad yellow bands down the center of each petal and purple blotches on the inner surface. Plant in soil rich in humus but free from lime. Of the several varieties, *platyphyllum* is large and especially vigorous. Cv. 'Rubrum' has crimson instead of yellow bands, and 'Pictum' has a crimson tip on each band. SR, 9–12 in.

L. brownii is a beautiful Japanese species. Flowers are trumpet shaped with creamy white inside petals surrounded by rose-purple outside petals. It grows readily in the open border in light, sandy soil. The bulb should be planted on its side on a bed of sand so water will not collect under the scales and induce rot. SR, 8 in.

L. bulbiferum (orange lily) is native to the mountains of southern Europe and grows to 6 ft. tall. Flowers are chalice shaped, orange or saffron colored, and spotted with crimson. A robust species for the border, it grows well in any good garden soil and eventually forms dense clumps. SR, 5 in.

L. candidum (Madonna or Annunciation lily) is a well-known and important garden species from southern Europe and Asia. Flowers are pure white and horizontally borne, with short, flared trumpets. The bulbs, obtained principally from France, are available in midsummer and should be planted then. They produce a rosette growth in the fall, which begins to lengthen in early spring, the flowers appearing in late June on stems 3–4 ft. tall. BR, 4–5 in.

L. chalcedonicum (scarlet Turk's-cap lily) is a 4-ft. species native to Greece. Flowers are bright scarlet with rolled-back petals and a disagreeable odor. It is easily grown in a sunny location and will endure a limey soil. Cv. 'Maculatum' is darker red spotted with purple. BR, 5 in.

L. concolor (star lily), growing to 4 ft., comes from China and Japan. Flowers are usually erect, unspotted, and ranging in color from yellow to bright scarlet. Var. *pulchellum* frequently shows spotted flowers. It should be planted in the rock garden in full sun. BR, 4 in.

L. davidii is a tall (6-ft.) Chinese lily with cinnabar-red, black-spotted flowers. A hardy species, it is easily grown in the open border. SR, 6 in.

L. hansonii is a fine Japanese species that grows to 5 ft. Drooping flowers with reflexed petals are bright yellowish orange with purplish brown spots. It grows readily in the border but should be planted in partial shade to prevent flower bleaching. SR, 6 in.

L. henryi is a tall (to 9 ft.), robust species from China. The lemon to orange-yellow flowers are reflexed and look like those of *L. speciosum*. Sometimes 20 blossoms are borne on one stem, making some support desirable; this lily is therefore an excellent species to plant among rhodo-dendrons. SR, 10 in.

L. japonicum, a Japanese species, grows to 2 ft. tall. Broad, funnel-shaped flowers are pale pink to rose in color. A beautiful lily, it thrives in the peaty soil under rhododendrons and kalmias but is not reliably hardy in the New England states. SR, 8 in.

L. x *maculatum*, a hybrid derived from *L. elegans* and *L. thunbergianum*, is a dwarf Japanese species in which the orange-red flowers with purple-black spots are held erect. There are many horticultural forms showing great variations in color and height. They grow well in sunny borders or rock gardens. SR, 6 in.

L. martagon (Martagon or Turk's-cap lily) has drooping flowers with recurved petals produced in tiers or whorls along stems that grow 6 ft. tall. They are purplish red to violet-rose, spotted with deep red at the base. This species and its white and purple varieties will grow in sun or shade. SR, 5 in.

L. medeoloides (wheel lily) is an oriental species that grows to 2½ ft. Drooping flowers with recurved petals are scarlet with apricot shadings and black spots. SR, 6 in.

L. monadelphum is a sturdy Caucasian species with 5–6 ft. stems and golden yellow flowers often spotted with purple. It should be planted in partial shade but will not flower until the second year. Var. *szovitsianum* (also listed under *Colchicum*) is straw colored with black spots. BR, 5 in.

L. pensylvanicum (candlestick lily), a Siberian species, has orange-red, black-spotted flowers borne erect on stems 2–3 ft. tall. SR, 5 in.

L. pomponium (lesser Turk's-cap lily) is an Italian species with 2–3 ft. stems and drooping, bright red flowers spotted with purple. It responds readily to cultivation in sunny gardens. BR, 5 in.

L. pumilum (coral lily) has nodding, brilliant scarlet flowers on slender stems from 1½–3 ft. high. It is a popular rock garden or border species. SR, 5 in.

L. pyrenaicum (yellow Turk's-cap lily) is native to the Pyrenees and grows easily in the open border to 3–4 ft. Flowers are greenish yellow with purple spots. Cv. 'Aureum' is deeper yellow. BR, 5 in.

L. regale (regal lily) is a useful and magnificent Chinese species introduced early in the twentieth century. Growing from 3–4 ft. tall, it bears flowers in large terminal clusters. They are long and trumpet-shaped, with white, lilac, and brown shadings on the outside and shading to yellow on the inside base. Unlike many lilies, this species adapts itself well to garden conditions and propagates readily from seed. SR, 12 in.

L. rubellum, a Japanese species, has umbels of one to nine fragrant, rosy pink flowers to 3 in. long borne horizontally on 2–3 ft. stems. It grows best in sandy or gravelly soil and is excellent in a border of deciduous shrubs or a rock garden. SR, 6 in.

L. speciosum is an important, showy species from Japan, including several varieties grown commercially for cut flowers as well as in gardens. The white flowers flushed with rose are reflexed, slightly drooping, and borne in groups on stems to 4 ft. This lily is easy to grow in the open, sunny border, or among small deciduous shrubs. Chief cultivated selections are cv. 'Album', pure white; 'Kraetzeri', white tinged with green; 'Magnificum', white with crimson shadings; 'Roseum', carmine pink; and 'Rubrum', deep rose. SR, 8–12 in.

L. x *testaceum* (Nankeen lily) is generally considered a hybrid between *L. candidum* and *L. chalcedonicum*, having foliage, habit, and time of flowering similar to those of the former. The flowers are flat, slightly reflexed, and apricot colored. Plant in the open border among tall-growing perennials. BR, 5 in.

L. tigrinum (tiger lily) is native to China and Japan, though now common in North American gardens and elsewhere, having naturalized in many places. It grows 3–4 ft. high and has large heads of reflexed, orange-red flowers with purplish black dots and is easily established under average garden conditions over a wide range. Var. *splendens* is taller and more highly colored, while var. *flore-pleno* is semidoubled with several rows of petals. SR, 9 in.

NORTH AMERICAN NATIVE SPECIES

L. bolanderi (thimble lily) is a California species with bell-shaped, deep crimson, purple-spotted flowers; it should be grown amid shrubbery. SR, 6 in.

L. canadense (meadow lily) is found along the Atlantic Coast from Canada to Georgia. The flowers on 3–5 ft. stems are small, drooping, and funnel-shaped, varying in color from orange-yellow to red. There are several varieties including *rubrum*, *parvum*, and *flavum*. In the wild it grows in damp meadows, but when cultivated it does well in sun or partial shade in a moist, well-drained location. SR, 10 in.

L. catesbaei (southern red lily) is native to the southern states from North Carolina to Florida. Bright orange-red, erect flowers have many purple spots. BR, 4 in.

L. columbianum is native to western North America. Flowers are drooping, bright reddish orange, and spotted purple with reflexed petals. Not reliably hardy in the East, it should be grown in semishade in acid soil. BR, 6 in.

L. grayi, a native of Virginia and North Carolina, is closely related to *L. canadense*. The drooping, funnel-shaped flowers are rich crimson blotched with purple at the base. It thrives in loose, peaty soil among rhododendrons or kalmias. BR, 5 in.

L. humboldtii is a tall (6-ft.) species from California. Flowers are drooping, reflexed, and rich orange-red with maroon spots. The var. *magnificum* is larger. Plant in open woodland or among tall shrubbery in peaty soil. BR, 5 in.

L. kelloggii is a California species characterized by large trusses of delicate, reflexed flowers of pinkish purple banded with yellow and maroon dots. It grows best in half-sunlight in a mixture of sand and peat. BR, 5 in.

L. maritimum (coast lily) is a California species found growing close to the shore. The stems, 3–5 ft. tall, bear reddish orange flowers spotted purple. It should be grown in a moist, well-drained spot free from lime. BR, 4 in.

L. michiganense, similar to *L. canadense*, is native to Michigan, Minnesota, and Missouri. Red colors predominate in its flowers. It grows to 5 ft. in rocky woods and has a branching rhizome. SR, 10 in.

L. pardalinum (leopard lily) is a very fine species from California and Oregon, where it grows to 8 ft. The flowers droop on the stalk and are bright orange-red with dark crimson spots on reflexed petals. There are several forms varying in color and height. It should be grown in a moist, well-drained, peaty soil in full sun. It grows from a rhizome and requires shallow planting.

Lilium pardalinum

L. parryi is a California species that grows 3–4 ft. tall. Flowers are sweet scented and pale lemon-yellow. Plant in shrubbery in loamy soil with a gravelly subsoil. BR, 5 in.

L. philadelphicum (orange-cup lily) is an eastern North American species. Flowers are cup-shaped, scarlet shading to yellow at the base, and purple spotted. Plant in acid, dry soil in sun or shade. SR, 5 in.

L. rubescens (chaparral lily) is native to California and Oregon. It bears fragrant white flowers with purple shadings erect in large heads on 6-ft. stems. It should be grown in acid soil amid shrubbery. BR, 5 in.

Lilium philadelphicum

L. superbum (American Turk's-cap lily) is native to the Atlantic Coast from New Brunswick to Georgia. The tall stems bear orange-red flowers spotted with purple. This beautiful lily should be grown on the edge of the woodland in moist, peaty soil near a stream or in shrubbery in the open. SR, 9 in.

L. umbellatum (western orange-cup lily) is native to the midwestern states. Bearing erect red or orange flowers on stems up to 2 ft, it resembles *L. philadelphicum*.

L. washingtonianum is a grand lily from California and Oregon with drooping funnel-shaped, sweet-scented flowers of pure white, tinged purple or lilac borne on 4–6 ft. stems. Plant in moist, well-drained soil in partial shade. SR, 10 in.

FOREIGN LILIES FOR THE SPECIALIST

L. bakeranum, from Burma and China, grows 3 ft. high. It bears broad, funnel-shaped flowers to 2½ in. across, colored creamy white with many brown spots at the base. It should be handled in pots, plunged in summer and taken into a cool cellar for winter. SR, 8 in.

L. callosum is an oriental species with small, drooping, orange-colored flowers borne abundantly on 2–3 ft. stems. Plant in full sun. SR, 8 in.

L. carniolicum is a southern European species with fragrant, recurved, orange-yellow and red flowers dotted purple-black, 2 in. or less in diameter. SR, 6 in.

L. duchartrei, native to western China, grows from small bulbs and has slender stems to 4 ft. tall. The flowers are white with inside spots of reddish brown. Plant in a well-drained, shaded part of the rock garden. SR, 4 in.

L. lankongense is a western Chinese species whose slender stems, 1–2 ft. tall, support reflexed flowers that are white with a purplish cast and spotted crimson. This species grows best in full sunlight. SR, 5 in.

L. leichtlinii is a fine Japanese species with reflexed flowers of citron-yellow, heavily spotted with purple, and borne on stems to 6 ft. tall. Grow in light, loamy soil in the open. SR, 6 in. There are several forms, including var. *maximowiczii*, which has salmon-red flowers.

L. leucanthum (Chinese white lily) is a beautiful species closely resembling *L. brownii* with long, drooping, milky white, funnel-shaped fragrant flowers with a greenish cast on the outside and tinged with yellow in the throat. Since it is not hardy, it should be raised in the greenhouse. SR, 9 in.

L. myriophyllum is a Chinese species that grows to 4 ft. Flowers are greenish white with a yellow cast and often red outside. It should be grown in the open. Var. *superbum* (commonly called *L. sulphureum*) is a rare, vigorous form of exceptional beauty. The flowers are sulfur yellow with streaks of claret red on the outside of the petals. The name *myriophyllum* is often applied to *L. regale*. SR, 10 in.

L. neilgherrense is a tender species from India that grows to 4 ft. Sweet-scented, pale sulfur yellow flowers are up to 10 in. long. SR, 9 in.

L. philippinense is a low-growing (to 1½ ft.) species from the Philippines. It is rather easily produced from seed and is attracting considerable attention as a result. The flowers are large, trumpet shaped, and pure white tinged with green. Var. *formosanum* is white with reddish purple shadings on the outside. It is not hardy but is easily grown in the greenhouse. SR, 8 in.

L. sargentiae comes from western China. Flowers, borne horizontally on 6-ft. stems, are milky white, occasionally with a greenish throat and purple shadings on the outside. It is hardy but much more subject to disease and should be grown among low shrubbery in the sun. SR, 9 in.

EASTER LILIES

The various forms of the well-known white Easter lily are all developments of one Japanese species, *L. longiflorum*. For the most part, they show only slight differences that would not be noticed by the amateur but are important to the commercial grower who selects varieties and strains on the basis of such factors as size and texture of the flower, date of flowering, temperature requirements for forcing, length of stem, etc.

Bermuda was the first region to grow bulbs of this species commercially, and for many years it had a virtual monopoly on the world's markets. The kind grown there, although sometimes referred to as a species (*L. harrisii*), is actually *L. longiflorum* var. *eximium*. It is a fine, large lily of excellent texture and form, but for a time its culture was threatened with extinction by a serious disease that appeared on the island early in the twentieth century. By the time measures for controlling and preventing it were perfected, the Japanese had begun to develop other varieties and had fostered a world demand that they continue to supply. Some of the Japanese forms fit particularly well into the needs of the flower business because they can safely be kept in cold storage for long periods and taken out to be forced at any time, thereby providing for a succession of flowers throughout the year instead of only at Easter time as in the past.

Lilium longiflorum

For greenhouse culture, bulbs of any of the kinds mentioned above are planted in pots—one bulb to a 6-in. pot is the usual practice—and either placed under a bench in a coolhouse or plunged outdoors (away from frost) until the root system has developed and top growth begins to appear above the soil in the pots. They can be brought in to full light and, gradually, to a forcing temperature, from 60–70°F, at which flowers will open in 110 to 120 days.

Though usually considered essential greenhouse plants, Easter lilies can be planted out in spring in the North and will bloom well in the garden in summer. In the South and California, they are used extensively in border plantings.

LILY. Common name correctly applied to members of the genus LILIUM and of LILIACEAE (Lily Family). The term is often used in the common names of many other genera that resemble true lilies, especially members of the AMARYLLIDACEAE (Amaryllis Family). The ever popular daylilies are species of HEMEROCALLIS. Fairy-lily refers to ZEPHYRANTHES, a genus of colorful flowering bulbs. Foxtail lily is EREMURUS, a genus of tall desert plants.

LILY-OF-THE-NILE. A common name for *Agapanthus umbellatus*, a tender, bulbous herb grown in greenhouses for its bright flowers; see AGAPANTHUS.

LILY-OF-THE-VALLEY. Common name for *Convallaria majalis*, a perennial herb with small white bell-like flowers; see CONVALLARIA.

LILYTURF. Common name for LIRIOPE and OPHIOPOGON, two genera belonging to the Liliaceae (Lily Family) and used for ground cover.

LIME. A compound of calcium, often used to alter chemical solutions or soil conditions. Limestone is the carbonate; quicklime, the oxide; and slaked or hydrated lime, the hydroxide. All three forms are used to improve soils and to reduce acidity or sourness, while quicklime and hydrated lime also have many uses in the preparation of sprays, dusts, and whitewash.

For most garden purposes, ground limestone is preferred, since it comes finely powdered, is easy to handle, and is not caustic. Lime should be applied to acid soils well before planting crops that need only slightly acid or alkaline conditions. Mixing the ground lime into the soil as thoroughly as possible (perhaps with a rotary tiller) will accelerate its effect on the soil. It usually contains some magnesium in addition to the calcium, and the analysis printed on the bag should be noted, since lime with more than 25% magnesium is not desirable unless the soil is very low in magnesium.

Most vegetables and some flowering plants benefit if lime is spread in winter and mixed thoroughly with the soil as soon as it can be worked. Average soil will take 100–200 lb. a year on a plot 50 ft. square; less should be applied on light, sandy soil and more on clay. It should not be used for acid-loving plants. It is valuable in combination with leaf mold and compost, hastening their decay, releasing plant food, and neutralizing acidity. Lawns of bluegrass and a few other lime-loving grasses can be sprinkled with hydrated lime, but other lawns are better without it. It is often scattered around the roots of iris, delphinium, and other lime-loving plants.

By liming, the soil is changed in chemical nature. Not only is it made less acid, but also phosphorus is altered to forms that make better plant food, while some injurious elements are made harmless. Lime also helps the complicated process by which soil bacteria, especially those that live in the roots of legumes, put valuable nitrogen in plant food form.

Lime is an ingredient in sprays such as lime-sulfur, BORDEAUX MIXTURE, and others, as well as dusting materials. Plain hydrated lime is a convenient insecticide for currant and cabbage worms. Mixed with tobacco dust finely ground, it will control aphids and other insects if simply thrown over the plants by hand two or three times at intervals of a few hours. Since it is harmless, the dust can be used freely except on acid-soil plants; what falls to the ground acts as a good fertilizer. Lime alone or mixed with tobacco, if dusted on young peas, beans, and other plants, will repel rabbits. Whitewash made with lime and water, and a little glue sometimes added as a binder, is sometimes painted on the trunks of orchard trees to destroy insect pests. It can also be used on boards in coldframes, greenhouses, and other structures for the same purpose; it acts somewhat as a wood preservative.

See also ALKALINE SOIL; CALCIUM; SOIL; LIMESTONE.

LIME-LOVING PLANTS

Gardens grown on land with a limestone subsoil, or that are naturally alkaline by containing lime in the soil, will need to grow lime-tolerant plants. These plants are the opposite of acid-loving plants, such as rhododendrons and azaleas, which could never survive in a soil with lime.

Trees for Lime Soil. These include ornamental crabs, flowering cherries and plums, pears, hawthorn, and mountain-ash, which are all flowering trees. Evergreen trees and shrubs that do well with lime are yews, juniper, and black pine.

Shrubs for Lime Soil. Roses do very well as long as the soil is well worked and holes are deeply dug before planting. The wild roses or species of roses do especially well. *Kerria japonica* (Japanese-rose), mock orange, flowering currant, honeysuckle, and all kinds of *Cotoneaster* thrive on lime soil. *Buxus* (common boxwood) is a natural under lime conditions. *Forsythia* and *Clematis* prefer a more alkaline or lime soil over an acid one.

Flowers for lime soil. Aside from the roses already mentioned, many perennial flowers, such as delphinium, aster, salvia, poppy, primula, phlox, and carnation bloom well. Bulbs do quite well in a lime soil, especially crocus and daffodils.

LIME TREE. A small, tropical, thorny evergreen tree, *Citrus aurantiifolia*. It has 3-in. oval leaves and white flowers followed by greenish yellow fruits. Fruits are of two types, a strongly acidic kind commonly grown in the United States and the Caribbean, and a sweet type grown in India and Latin America. In the United States, because of its tenderness to frost (hardy only in Zones 10–11), growth is restricted almost entirely to gardens in the southern tip of Florida and southern California. Seedling trees are named for their place of origin, such as Key lime and Mexican lime. For culture, see CITRUS FRUITS.

LIMESTONE. Natural rock consisting mainly of calcium carbonate mixed with some magnesium carbonate. It is the principal rock of large sections of the United States, giving rise to alkaline soil and hard water (where the acid rainwater leaching through dissolves the stone). Because alkaline or neutral soil improves most garden crops, finely ground limestone is often spread on the vegetable garden. Lime is entirely safe, will not burn plants, and so can be used generously if needed.

Limestone is often used for rock gardens, partly because large stones of it are comparatively lightweight and easily handled, and partly because many alpine plants prefer it. For these lime-loving alpines, a mulch of limestone chips proves effective.

See also ALKALINE SOIL; CALCIUM; LIME.

LIMNANTHEMUM (lim NAN the mum). A botanical name sometimes used for NYMPHOIDES, a genus of aquatic herbs commonly known as floating-heart.

LIMNANTHES (lim NAN theez) **douglasii.** An annual herb commonly known as meadow-foam. This attractive little plant grows in masses in low, damp places in the western states and is lovely in wild gardens, creating a sheet of brilliant color in the early spring. Excellent for bedding, as a border annual, or naturalized in meadows and lawns, it is easily raised from seed. It has deeply cut, yellowish green leaves and fragrant, 1½ in. wide white, pink, or yellow flowers. The blossoms may be pure white; some are shaded toward the base into pink or yellow, depending on the variety.

LIMNOCHARIS (lim NOH kah ris). A genus of tropical American aquatic herbs whose large leaves with milky juice are lifted above the water. The flowers, which open in July, are composed of three petals and three sepals.

L. flava, the principal species, rises 12–18 in. above the water surface with blunt, velvet-green leaves and green and yellow flowers. Hardy only in Zones 10–11, it is readily cultivated in the greenhouse in warm tanks or outdoors in shallow ponds through the summer. Propagation is by root division or runners.

LIMONIUM (lim OH nee um). A genus of flowering herbs belonging to the Plumbaginaceae (Leadwort Family) and commonly known as statice, sea-pink, or sea-lavender. The perennials are hardy to Zone 3 and are often grown for decoration in greenhouses, rock gardens, borders, and for dried bouquets. The branching plants bear narrow leaves that form rosettes. Small spiked or clustered flowers have a papery texture and come

Limonium latifolium

in shades of white, yellow, rose, lavender, or blue. Whether left on the plants or cut for fresh or dried bouquets, they are exceedingly long-lasting.

L. latifolium is a perennial with delicate lavender flowers, somewhat resembling *Gypsophila* and similarly used both fresh and dried. It favors a dry location in the garden or greenhouse.

L. sinuatum is a biennial or perennial whose white flowers have persistent calyxes occurring in blue, pink, lavender, or yellow. A low rosette of dandelionlike leaves forms the base for the stiff, angular, branching flower stalks.

LINANTHUS (lī NAN thus). A genus of annual herbs of the Polemoniaceae (Phlox Family), commonly known as flax flower or California phlox. The opposite leaves are usually divided to the base and appear to be whorled. The funnelform flowers, often fragrant, are arranged in more or less dense terminal heads in soft tones of pink, violet, yellow, blush, and white. Plants are grown from seed, chiefly in the West, where some of the species are native. It should be sown thickly in

Linanthus grandiflorus

light soil. The best species are **L. grandiflorus**, growing to 18 in. with long flowers in white, lilac, or pink; and **L. dianthiflorus**, with tufted, 6-in., entire, threadlike leaves and smaller flowers.

LINARIA (lī NAY ree uh). A genus of rather low-growing annual, biennial, and perennial herbs of the Scrophulariaceae (Figwort Family), some trailing and others erect. The flowers, which come in a wide variety of pastel shades, resemble miniature snapdragons and are lovely in wildflower gardens and meadows, especially on sandy or gravelly soil.

The annuals are of easy culture from seed, which is generally sown indoors. The perennials are equally simple to grow, the usual method of propagation being division, though seeds should produce flowering plants the second year.

PRINCIPAL SPECIES

L. alpina is a low, spreading, rock garden plant with fine, frosty leaves and bright violet flowers with an orange palate.

L. anticaria is a low-branched plant for shady rock pockets, with blue-and-white, lilac-spurred flowers.

L. bipartita (cloven-lip toadflax) is an erect annual, also in violet and orange, with varieties in all purple and all white.

L. cymbalaria (Kenilworth ivy) is now classified as *Cymbalaria muralis*, but is often found in catalogs under the former name. Some other species with single axillary flowers and palmately veined leaves are now placed in the same genus; see CYMBALARIA.

L. marocanna is a fast-growing, hardy annual 15 in. tall. For garden culture, it is offered in a mixture of shades of crimson, orange, and blue; its cv. 'Fairy Bouquet' is shorter and has a more compact habit of growth.

L. vulgaris (toadflax, butter-and-eggs), with yellow-and-orange flowers on erect plants, is a common roadside weed throughout most of the world. It has medicinal herb and dye applications.

Linaria vulgaris

LINDEN. Common name for TILIA, a genus of handsome deciduous trees of the North Temperate Zone. The Linden Family is TILIACEAE.

LINDERA (lin DER ah). A genus of deciduous or evergreen aromatic shrubs or trees, native in temperate and tropical regions of Asia and North America, belonging to the Lauraceae (Laurel Family), and formerly listed as *Benzoin*. Only a few of the nearly 60 known species are hardy in cold regions, most growing in Zones 5–9.

L. benzoin (spicebush, wild-allspice), formerly listed as *B. aestivalis*, is a hardy, native deciduous shrub for shade, growing to 10 ft. in moist places from New England southward. Fragrant yellow flowers are without petals but numerous enough to be conspicuous in early spring, before the leaves. The plant is attractive again in the fall with its clear yellow leaves and scarlet fruits.

LINEAR. Narrow and more or less long, with margins parallel, like the leaves (or needles) of pines.

LINNAEA (lin NEE ah) **borealis.** A dainty, trailing evergreen belonging to the Caprifoliaceae (Honeysuckle Family) and commonly known as twinflower. It has small glossy leaves and fragrant pink or white, bell-shaped flowers nodding in pairs from slender, erect stems. Var. *americana* has more tubular flowers to ½ in.

Twinflowers can be naturalized in the wild or rock garden if given a cool, moist situation and acid soil rich in peaty humus. Hardy to Zone 2, they can be propagated by division or cuttings of green or half-ripened wood. The botanical name comes from the botanist Linnaeus, who is said to have favored the flower.

LINUM (LĪ num). A genus of narrow-leaved herbs and shrubs with both garden and commercial uses, including the principal members of the Linaceae (Flax Family), and commonly known as flax. There are several annuals and perennials popular in the garden for their delicate, five-petaled flowers in shades of blue, white, yellow, or red and borne on extremely slender stems. The genus lends its name to the Linaceae (Flax Family), to which it belongs.

Placed in full sun in the garden, the plants will bloom abundantly but will not stand frost. Seeds of the annual species can be sown where the plants are to stand, or they can be started indoors with the perennials and set in the garden later. Though some are hardy in Zones 4–5, most perennials should be protected from cold, and some will bloom the first year from seed.

PRINCIPAL SPECIES

L. flavum (golden flax), with bright yellow flowers, is a half-hardy perennial that is excellent for border planting.

L. grandiflorum (flowering flax), with its varieties, is the species most commonly grown and one of the few popular annuals.

L. monogynum, from New Zealand, has large, showy white flowers but is seldom grown.

Linum flavum

L. narbonense is one of the best for rock gardens. It has large, sky blue flowers with white markings in the center and white stamens.

L. perenne, with blue or sometimes white flowers, is the most reliably hardy perennial. Var. *lewisii* (blue or prairie flax), native to western North America, is even more robust with larger leaves and flowers.

Linum perenne

L. suffruticosum var. *salsoloides*, a native of the Alps, has white flowers with a purple eye but is not often grown.

L. usitatissimum (flax) is grown commercially to produce both linen and linseed oil.

LION'S-EAR.
Common name for LEONOTIS, a genus of herbs and shrubs of the Lamiaceae (Mint Family).

LIP.
One of the parts formed by the calyx or corolla of a flower when organized into (usually two) unequal divisions, like the plants of the Lamiaceae (Mint Family); also the labellum of an ORCHID.

LIPARIS
(lī PAIR us). A genus of 250 species of terrestrial, lithophytic, or epiphytic orchids native to tropical and subtropical regions, and commonly known as twayblade. They have broad leaves nearly 6 in. long. Small blossoms in shades of green, yellow, orange, and purple are borne in many-flowered racemes rising 10 in. above the foliage.

Epiphytic or lithophytic species need a porous, well-draining compost, and terrestrial types, a humusy compost. They can be used in wild gardens; all species require shade and a moist environment. Hardy to Zone 7 with frost protection, they withstand minimum winter temperatures of 55–60°F. The type species is *L. loeselii*.

LIP FERN.
Common name for CHEILANTHES, a genus of ferns with finely dissected foliage usually composed of beadlike segments.

LIPPIA
(LIP ee ah). An old genus of tender herbs and shrubs belonging to the Verbenaceae (Verbena Family). The principal members are now classified under other genera: *L. citriodora* (lemon verbena) is now *Aloysia triphylla*; see ALOYSIA. *L. canescens* is *Phyla nodiflora* var. *canescens*; see PHYLA. *L. repens* is *Phyla nodiflora* var. *rosea*; see PHYLA.

LIQUIDAMBAR
(lik wid AM bur). A genus of huge deciduous trees belonging to the Hamamelidaceae (Witch-hazel Family).

PRINCIPAL SPECIES

L. formosana (Formosan gum), from China, has yellow to red fall color and grows to 60 ft. Hardy in Zones 6–7.

L. orientalis (oriental sweet gum) is a smaller species from Asia Minor, growing to 25 ft. tall.

L. styraciflua (American sweet gum), native from Connecticut to Florida and Mexico, has shining, maplelike leaves colored brilliant yellow to red and purple in the fall. In winter, it has an interesting furrowed bark and persistent spiny fruit balls. Sweet gum grows very well in wet, poorly drained areas as well as drier areas and is hardy in Zones 6–9.

LIRIODENDRON (lee ree oh DEN drun) **tulipifera.**
A deciduous tree belonging to the Magnoliaceae
(Magnolia Family) and commonly known as tulip
tree or tulip-poplar. It has bluish green, lobed
leaves abruptly cut off at the tips; fall color is
bright yellow. In late spring, it bears solitary bell-
shaped, greenish yellow flowers marked with
orange at the base and followed by long, conelike
fruits.

One of the finest trees of the Eastern Seaboard
and Midwest, the tulip tree grows to 200 ft. in the
wild and 100 ft. in cultivation in congenial surroundings. It is
handsome, with
a beautiful clean,
straight trunk,
which is some-
times as much as
10 ft. in diame-
ter.It thrives best
in rich, moist
soil and is prop-

Liriodendron tulipifera

agated by seed. This tree is admirably adapted
for park or street planting but is difficult to transplant; young trees should be moved in early
spring. Hardy in Zones 5–9.

LIRIOPE (lee REE oh pee). A genus of stemless,
smooth, evergreen perennial herbs belonging to
the Liliaceae (Lily Family) and commonly known
as lilyturf. They have broad, grasslike foliage
and small, purplish to whitish flowers in spikes
blooming in late summer and fall. They are easily grown in containers indoors or on the summer

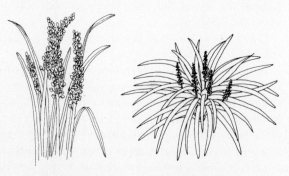

Liriope muscari   Liriope spicata

patio. Hardiness varies with the species. Within
their range, they are useful as a ground cover
over large areas, since they are indifferent to
shade or sun, and are readily propagated by root
division.

L. muscari grows 15–20 in. tall and has deep
lilac flowers that suggest grape-hyacinths; it is
hardy to Zone 6. Var. *variegata* (yellow-striped
lilyturf) has yellow-striped leaves and is hardy to
Zone 7.

L. spicata (creeping liriope) is a small, narrow-
leaved form with pale lavender flowers. Hardy
to Zone 4, it is a good choice for window boxes or
hanging baskets.

LITCHI (LĪ chee) **chinensis.** A Chinese evergreen
tree belonging to the Sapindaceae (Soapberry
Family), commonly known as lychee. Its fruits
are popular in warm regions, where they are
eaten fresh. In cool regions, the fruit is better
known in dried form, the sweetish, raisinlike
pulp and its single large seed being enclosed in a
thin, rough, brown, papery shell; the whole thing
about 1 in. in diameter. It is hardy to Zone 9 and
is often planted as a garden tree in south Florida
and California. It should be given ample room,
about 40 ft. Deep, loamy soils with ample moisture suit it best. Once established, it will tolerate
slight frosts.

LITHOCARPUS (lith oh KAHR pus). A small
genus of deciduous trees belonging to the
Fagaceae (Beech Family). They rank halfway
between the oaks and chestnuts and are confined
chiefly to the Orient. However, one species, *L.
densiflorus* (tanbark-oak), is native to the dry
hillsides and ravines of Oregon and California. It
is valued commercially as a source of tannin, and
it makes a distinctive ornamental specimen. The
tanbark-oak makes a splendid garden tree in the
far West and South, reaching a height of 80 ft. or
more. Its evergreen leaves are yellow and
downy in spring, and a profusion of yellow flowers in erect catkins appears in midsummer.
Propagation is by seed, cuttings, or layers.
Hardy in Zones 8–9.

LITHODORA (lith oh DOH rah). A genus of perennial herbs formerly listed as *Lithospermum*. *L. diffusa* and its named selections 'Grace Ward' and 'Heavenly Blue' are all outstanding additions to a rock garden. Sprawling, evergreen branches with fine foliage carry flowers of brilliant blue. The plants flower over many weeks, beginning in early spring, and reproduce readily from cuttings. Hardy to Zone 6.

LITHOPS (LITH ops). A most remarkable genus of tiny mimicry plants from South Africa and belonging to the Aizoaceae (Carpetweed Family). Each plant consists of just two fused, highly succulent, varicolored, windowed leaves (that is, leaves with translucent areas allowing sunlight to enter the leaf) and yellow to white flowers that push up through the cleft between the leaves. Each year the old leaves shrivel and dry as a new pair develops. They are among the marvels of the succulent world; old plants have been found that are up to 250 years old. They resemble in color and shape the pebbles among which they grow, and they sometimes cluster with age. They demand a fairly strict dormant period, particularly during the part of the cycle when the new pair of leaves is forming, and lots of sun and fresh air.

LITHOSPERMUM (lith oh SPUR mum). A genus of hairy perennials or annuals, related to forget-me-nots, belonging to the Boraginaceae (Borage Family), and commonly known as gromwell. They have heavy foliage and blue, white, or yellow flowers in heavy clusters or spikes. They are easily grown from seed and cuttings in any average soil. One species has long been cultivated as a medicinal herb and is included in many lists for the herb garden. Other species are occasionally used in the wildflower garden, border, or rock garden. Plants and seeds of North American species are offered by dealers as wildflowers. Hardy to Zones 3–4.

PRINCIPAL SPECIES

L. canescens (puccoon, Indian-paint), native to eastern North America, is a perennial that grows to 12 in. and has orange flowers. The root was

once used by Native Americans to make red dye.

L. incisum is a perennial that grows to 12 in. or more and has yellow flowers.

L. multiflorum is a perennial that grows to 2 ft. and has light yellow blossoms.

L. officinale, a perennial growing to 4 ft., is usually only cultivated for medicinal purposes.

LIVERWORT. Common name for members of the group of flowerless plants known as hepatics or, botanically, *Hepaticae*. These, together with a second large class, the mosses, make up the Bryophyta, the second main division of the plant kingdom. Liverworts are flat green, red, or yellow-brown, ribbonlike or stemmed, and scaly-leafed growths that creep closely along the bark of living trees in damp woods, on shady banks, or on rocks. Do not confuse it with the genus *Hepatica*, which is a group of true flowering plants of the Ranunculaceae (Buttercup Family).

LIVISTONA (liv is TOH nah). A genus of fan palms native from Asia through the Pacific islands. There are a number of beautiful and decorative kinds with large, fan-shaped leaves on spiny stalks and panicles of small whitish flowers growing from the leaf axils.

Several species are grown in California and Florida, including *L. australis* and *L. chinensis*. These palms require a heavy, moist soil; sandy soils can be made suitable by adding clay and well-rotted manure. In cooler climates, these two vigorous species are easily grown in the greenhouse in a rich light soil with a night temperature of 60°F.

L. australis (Australian fan palm) grows to 60 ft. and has a dense crown of dark green, almost round leaves.

L. chinensis (Chinese fan or fountain palm), from central China, is a stout, low-growing tree to 30 ft. topped by a heavy crown of leaves 6–8 ft. across. This is the source of the familiar palm-leaf fans exported from China. In North America, it is a popular subject grown in large pots or tubs for porch, terrace, or garden decoration in summer.

LIZARDS. These AMPHIBIANS are often helpful in the garden.

LOAM. A medium-texture soil that it is a mixture of sand, silt, and clay particles and organic material in such proportion that their influences blend together with none dominating. Loam is easily worked, usually fertile, and acceptable to nearly all plants. Gradations in texture are often referred to as "sandy loam" or "clay loam."

See also SOIL.

LOBELIA (loh BEE lee ah). A genus of herbs with mostly blue or red irregular flowers in close or long spirelike clusters. As garden plants, the species fall naturally into two groups, annuals and perennials.

Plants are grown easily from seed, which should be started indoors in midwinter to have blooming-size specimens ready to set out in May. In a cool climate, the border of annual lobelia will continue in bloom until autumn. Even where the summer is hot, the plants, if cut back and given plenty of water, will usually keep on blooming. Annuals can also be propagated by seed collected in late winter from plants wintered in the greenhouse. Perennials are propagated by seed, division, or offsets and are usually hardy to Zone 2.

PRINCIPAL SPECIES

L. cardinalis (cardinal flower, Indian-pink), a perennial growing to 4 ft., has narrow leaves and a spire of intense crimson flowers. This is one of the most beautiful of North American native plants, growing naturally in damp, half-shaded situations and sometimes in the shallow water of slowly moving streams. It is raised from seed or propagated by offsets. Plants will often grow in a well-watered border, although a woodland setting is more appropriate.

Lobelia cardinalis

L. erinus, one of the most popular small border subjects, is a low-growing plant from South Africa with blue or violet flowers and green or deep bronzy red foliage, grown as a hardy annual. Var. *alba* has white flowers. Var. *gracilis*, with long, slender branches, is more suitable for the cutting garden than border plantings. Var. *compacta* grows short and close.

L. inflata (Indian-tobacco), native to the southern states, is a hairy annual that grows to 3 ft. and has light blue flowers

L. siphilitica, native from Maine to Louisiana, is a sturdy perennial that grows to 3 ft. It bears racemes of flowers in a charming shade of clear blue and grows readily in moist soil in half-shaded situations.

LOBULARIA (lahb yoo LAIR ee ah) **maritima.** A popular perennial treated as an annual, belonging to the Brassicaceae (Mustard Family), formerly listed as *Alyssum maritimum*, and commonly known as sweet-alyssum. *Lobularia* is distinguished from the true alyssum by differences in flower structure and color. True alyssums have yellow flowers, while those of sweet-alyssum vary from deep purple to pure white. These sweet-scented plants grow in uniform height only 3–6 in. tall but spread up to 12 in. and are especially useful in borders, edgings, rock gardens, hanging baskets, planters, or annual ground cover plantings.

Native to the Mediterranean region, lobularias branch and flower freely from late spring until frost, producing an abundance of little blossoms. They can be grown by beginners with assurance of success, being equally at home in beds, pots, or window boxes and thriving in a sunny location. After danger of frost, seed can be sown outdoors where the plants are to grow. However, seed does not always germinate well in open ground and is best started indoors and the plants set out in spring. Some varieties, especially the double white, can be propagated only by cuttings. These can be taken at any time during the summer and will root easily in a coldframe or even in the open border in a somewhat shaded location.

LOCUST. Common name for ROBINIA, a genus of native trees and shrubs belonging to the Fabaceae (Bean Family). Black locust is *R. pseudoacacia*. Honey-locust refers to GLEDITSIA, a genus of usually thorny trees frequently planted for ornament; water- or swamp-locust is *G. aquatica*.

LODOICEA (loh doh IS ee ah). A genus of spineless fan palms, commonly known as double-coconut because of the very large, double-lobed seed. *L. maldivica* grows naturally only on the Seychelles Islands in the Indian Ocean, where it grows to 100 ft. high with a straight, slender trunk 12 in. in diameter, crowned by the heavy, fanlike leaves 5–10 ft. long. It is remarkable for producing the largest known seeds in the vegetable kingdom. These huge lobed nuts, sometimes 18 in. long, require ten years from the time of flowering to ripen.

LOGANBERRY. Common name for *Rubus ursinus* var. *loganobaccus*, a variety of Pacific dewberry; see BLACKBERRY.

LOISELEURIA (loh is e LOO ree ah). A genus of low, evergreen, procumbent (prostrate) shrubs with opposite leaves and small white or pink flowers, belonging to the Ericaceae (Heath Family), and commonly known as alpine-azalea. One species, *L. procumbens*, of the subarctic regions, forms a low mat of evergreen foliage covered with small white or pink flowers. It requires excellent drainage, peaty soil, and a north-facing site in alpine and rock gardens. Only northern gardeners are apt to succeed with this challenging plant.

LOLIUM (LAH lee um). A genus of grasses grown in pastures, meadows, and sometimes lawns, commonly known as ryegrass. Turf-type perennial ryegrasses are widely used on lawns, alone or in combination with other grasses. They usually germinate in five to seven days (depending on temperature and irrigation or rainfall). They supply moderate shade for other slower growering kinds. *L. multiflorum* (annual ryegrass) and

L. perenne (perennial ryegrass) are used on lawns where other, nonturf types are not suitable.

Lolium perenne

LOMATIA (loh MAY shee ah). A genus of trees or shrubs of Australia and Chile, belonging to the Proteaceae (Protea Family). They are sometimes grown in the cool greenhouse or outdoors in Zones 10–11. In pots they thrive in a mixture of equal parts of loam, peat, and sand; good drainage is essential. They are of interest chiefly for their elegant foliage. *L. ilicifolia* has prickly, hollylike leaves. *L. silaifolia* is an Australian shrub with attractive, divided foliage which is dyed and used by floral decorators under the name crinklebush. *L. ferruginea*, from Chile, is a graceful plant with finely divided leaves and yellow and scarlet flowers with rusty hairs.

LOMATIUM (loh MAY shee um). A genus of perennial herbs belonging to the Apiaceae (Celery Family), found in dry soil in the western United States. They are nearly or quite stemless, varying according to species from 2–30 in. tall, and have dissected leaves and flat heads of small yellow, white, or purple flowers, many with showy seed heads.

Few of the 60 species have been developed in cultivation, but some are adaptable to rockwork, the front of large borders, or gravelly soil in the wild garden. The plants thrive in full sun or partial shade and well-drained soil. Plants do well on sunny banks, but ample moisture is important during the growing season. Mostly hardy to Zone 8, the plants' active growth occurs from winter through spring, and they can become weedy if not carefully tended. Propagation is most easily done by seed, and plants usually flower the second spring.

L. dasycarpum, found wild along the California coast, has lacy foliage. Its 2-in.-long stems support clusters of five-petaled, greenish yellow flowers covered with fuzzy hairs, making them look white. The shoots of this low-growing species appear in winter from a long, thick, branching taproot. Each plant has up to ten flattened stems that grow for

Lomatium dasycarpum

several inches along the ground, then rise and turn purplish as flowers appear in early spring.

LONG-DAY PLANT. A term applied to plants in which flower bud formation is initiated by exposure to relatively long day lengths (fourteen hours or more) and suppressed by exposure to shorter day lengths. In actuality, these plants respond to short dark periods rather than long days.

LONICERA (lahn IS er ah). A genus of deciduous or evergreen shrubs widely distributed throughout the Northern Hemisphere, belonging to the Caprifoliaceae (Honeysuckle Family), and commonly known as honeysuckle. The genus includes bushes, climbers, and trailers, as well as some of the most popular and useful ornamental shrubs. Easily cultivated, they are not particular as to soil and in general prefer open, sunny locations, although some do well in partial shade. The bush forms are valuable for use in mixed shrub plantings or for screening purposes; some attain large size if grown as single specimens with ample room for development. The climbers are good on fences or trellises. *L. japonica* (Japanese honeysuckle) and some others make

good ground covers, though at times becoming a nuisance by spreading and choking out other plants. Honeysuckles are propagated by seed, cuttings of mature wood, and layers.

BUSH SPECIES

L. x *bella* (belle honeysuckle) is a shrub that grows to 8 ft. and has pink or white flowers, red fruit, and good foliage. Cv. 'Candida' has pure white flowers, and 'Rosea' has deep pink flowers. Hardy in Zones 5–7.

L. fragrantissima (winter honeysuckle) is a stout, half-evergreen shrub that grows to 8 ft. and has handsome leathery leaves. It is especially valued for its sweet-scented creamy white flowers in late winter and early spring, and for its leaves that remain green well into winter. Hardy in Zones 5–8.

L. maackii (Amur honeysuckle) is a stout, upright grower, to 15 ft., and has large dark green leaves. About the last species to bloom, it is very conspicuous with large white to yellow flowers. The dark red fruit is ripe in early fall. Var. *podocarpa* is shorter and more spreading, with leaves and fruit retained later. It is tolerant of dry conditions and hardy in Zones 3–6.

L. morrowii is a wide-spreading shrub that grows to 8 ft. and has white to yellow flowers and blood red fruit. The leaves hang on and continue green until quite late. Hardy in Zones 4–6.

L. nitida (boxleaf honeysuckle) is an upright evergreen that grows to 6 ft. and has small leaves, creamy white flowers, and bluish purple fruit. It makes a good hedge in mild regions. Hardy in Zones 7–9.

L. pileata is evergreen or half-evergreen, of almost prostrate growth, with white flowers and dark purple fruit. It is excellent for a shady place in the rock garden. Hardy in Zones 5–8.

L. tatarica (Tatarian honeysuckle), one of the most common members of the genus, bears a profusion of pink or white flowers, followed by dark red fruit. Unfortunately this species has become a weedy pest in many areas, seeding itself everywhere. Hardy in Zones 4–7, it is very viable, some of the best forms being cv. 'Grandiflora', with large white flowers; 'Rosea', with flowers rosy pink outside and paler within; and 'Lutea', with yellow fruit.

CLIMBING SPECIES

L. caprifolium, twining to 20 ft., has leaves bluish beneath, yellowish white or purplish flowers, and orange-red fruit. Native to Europe and Asia, it is naturalized in parts of the eastern United States. Hardy in Zones 6–8.

L. x *heckrottii* is a hybrid, supposedly between *L. americana* and *L. sempervirens*. It has purple-and-yellow flowers lasting all summer. Hardy in Zones 5–9.

L. japonica is evergreen or nearly so, with twining stems 15–30 ft. and very fragrant white flowers tinged purple. It is a good porch vine and excellent ground cover, especially for steep slopes. Cv. 'Halliana' is very similar but has pure white to yellow flowers; 'Aureo-reticulata' has small leaves netted yellow. Great caution should be taken before planting this on any property. It is extremely aggressive and has become a weedy, shrubby vine in the eastern United States, destroying native wildflowers, ground covers, ferns, shrubs, and small trees. Birds spread the seeds everywhere, and it is difficult to eradicate once established. Hardy in Zones 5–9.

L. periclymenum (woodbine), common in English hedgerows, is a very attractive climber with whorls of fragrant yellowish white flowers. Hardy in Zones 6–8.

L. sempervirens (trumpet honeysuckle) is a tall climber with dark green leaves, bluish beneath; orange-yellow to scarlet, yellow-tubed flowers; and red fruits. Hardy in Zones 5–9.

LOOSESTRIFE. Common name for two genera of perennials, LYSIMACHIA, with yellow flowers, and LYTHRUM, which blooms in shades of pink or purple. The Loosestrife Family is LYTHRACEAE. Swamp loosestrife is *Decodon verticillatus*, a moisture-loving perennial with magenta flowers; see DECODON.

LOQUAT. Common name for *Eriobotrya japonica*, a subtropical tree or shrub producing plumlike edible fruit; see ERIOBOTRYA.

LORANTHACEAE (loh ran THAY see ee). The Mistletoe Family, a widely distributed group of chiefly shrubby plants with jointed stems, parasitic upon trees. The leaves may be broad but are sometimes scalelike. The flowers are small, and the fruit is a berry that germinates on the host plant, into which the parasite sends its feeding roots. They are grown commercially for Christmas decoration.

LOROPETALUM (loh roh PET ah lum). A genus of attractive but tender evergreens from China, belonging to the Hamamelidaceae (Witch-hazel Family). Only one species, *L. chinense*, is cultivated. A medium-sized shrub, thriving best in peaty and gritty soil, it can be grown outdoors only in very warm regions. In early spring it produces a mass of white flowers with strap-shaped petals.

LOTUS (LOH tus). A genus of shrubs and herbs belonging to the Fabaceae (Bean Family) and commonly known as trefoil. Native to Europe and Asia, and introduced to the United States, they thrive in sunny, dry locations and are valuable for ground cover in the rock garden and on banks. They have irregularly pinnate leaves and yellow, purple, or white pealike flowers. Propagation is by seed or, for plants with woody stems, by cuttings.

As a common name, lotus refers to several AQUATIC PLANTS, especially those of the genera NELUMBO and NYMPHAEA, including tropical species native to Africa, India, and Egypt.

PRINCIPAL SPECIES

L. berthelotii is a tender, branched, dwarf shrub with curious scarlet flowers, suitable for greenhouse use or warm-climate gardens.

L. corniculatus (bird's-foot trefoil, ladies'-fingers, babies'-slippers) is a low, hardy perennial introduced from Europe and sometimes grown for forage. It has a sprawling habit with many small yellow flowers from usually red buds.

L. jacobaeus (St. James trefoil) is tall and shrubby with flowers varying from dark purple to yellow.

L. tetragonolobus (winged pea) is a trailing annual with sparse, purplish red flowers, pods are edible when young.

LOVAGE. Common name for *Levisticum officinale*, a hardy flavoring herb of the Apiaceae (Celery Family); see LEVISTICUM.

LOVE-IN-A-MIST. A common name for *Nigella damascena*, an annual herb with colorful flowers; see NIGELLA.

LOVE-LIES-BLEEDING. Common name for *Amaranthus caudatus*, a coarse annual herb with crimson flowers; see AMARANTHUS.

LUCULIA (loo KYOO lee ah). A genus of tender shrubs from the Himalayas, with large, leathery leaves and showy corymbs of salver-shaped flowers in white, rose, or red. They are easily cultivated under glass in moderate temperature and bloom through midwinter. They can be set outside in summer. Syringe often with clear water to avoid attacks of red spider. Young plants can be raised from cuttings taken after the flowering period and should be gradually hardened-off by reduced temperatures.

LUDISIA (loo DISH ee uh). This is one of a group of jewel orchid genera, so called because of their lustrous, richly colored foliage. Only one species, *L. discolor*, comprises this genus of terrestrial plants native to China and southeastern Asia. The genus is synonymous with *Haemaria*.

The foliage is purplish with attractive red or gold venation. Many small ivory flowers top erect spikes rising from the center of the leaves. Succulent rhizomes creep across the top of the planting medium, which should not be allowed to dry out. Plants root at nodes along the rhizomes. Pseudobulbs are not evident. These shade-loving orchids do best in shallow pots, planted on top of a compost made of peat, sphagnum moss, and sand. Hardy only to Zone 10 with cold protection, they withstand minimum winter temperatures of 55–60°F.

LUDWIGIA (lud WIG ee ah). A genus of bog or aquatic plants related to the evening primrose. The rather small yellow flowers are borne close to the stems. They can be grown either from seed or cuttings, but most species are little known and seldom cultivated. A few species, formerly listed as *Jussiaea* and commonly known as primrose-willows, can be propagated by seed planted in pans submerged in shallow water or by cuttings and division. Hardiness varies with the species, to Zone 4.

PRINCIPAL SPECIES

L. alternifolia is a perennial that grows to 3 ft. and is sometimes used in the wild garden.

L. longifolia, formerly listed as *Jussiaea longifolia*, is a tender annual growing to 6 ft., with narrow, long-pointed leaves and yellow flowers.

L. mulertii is an aquarium plant from the tropics, attractive with its brightly colored foliage.

L. peploides, formerly listed as *Jussiaea repens*, is a tender annual with oval leaves, small yellow flowers, and creeping stems that root at the nodes.

LUFFA (LOO fah). A genus of tropical climbing herbs with large yellow flowers and cylindrical oblong fruits of the familiar cucurbitous type. When ripe, these have dry, papery shells that contain a network of strong fibers. This network can be detached from the softer tissues and used as a tough fabric for washing purposes; hence the popular names: washrag-, towel-, dishcloth-, fleshbrush-, and vegetable-sponge-gourd. The young *Luffa* fruits are eaten in some tropical countries. Hardy only in Zones 10–11, culture is the same as for other warm-climate gourds.

LUNARIA (loo NAIR ee ah). A genus of flowering herbs belonging to the Brassicaceae (Mustard Family) and commonly known as honesty, moneyplant, or satinflower. Only two species are frequently cultivated. Both

Lunaria annua

are branching and grow erect 2–3 ft. high. They bear single flowers that range from purple to white. Their interesting flat, papery seedpods are commonly used in dried bouquets. The plants are easily grown from seed and thrive in partial shade.

L. annua, also listed as *L. biennis*, has pods rounded at both ends, 2 in. long and nearly as wide. Although it can be grown as an annual if started early enough, it is best treated as a biennial, the satiny pods produced the second season.

L. rediviva is a perennial with leaves closely and sharply toothed. Its pods taper at both ends and last much longer than the wider ones of *L. annua*.

LUNATHYRIUM (loo nah THĪ ree um). Name used by some botanists for *Athyrium thelypteroides*, a species of lady fern; see ATHYRIUM.

LUNGWORT. Common name for PULMONARIA, a genus of creeping perennials with blue or purple flowers.

LUPINE. Common name for LUPINUS, a genus of annual and perennial herbs grown for ornament, cover crops, or forage. False lupine is THERMOPSIS, a genus of yellow-flowered perennials.

LUPINUS (loo PĪ nus). A genus of annual and perennial herbs, or sometimes shrubs, belonging to the Fabaceae (Bean Family), and commonly known as lupine. They are grown chiefly for ornamental purposes, though some species are useful for cover crops or forage. In the United States, the ornamental forms are popular bed and border subjects, growing best in well-drained, alkaline soil.

Lupines are distinguished by their deeply cut foliage, which has many lancelike rays radiating from the end of the leaf stalk. The blue, yellow, white, or rose flowers, shaped like those of peas, are borne in great profusion on long-stemmed spikes and bloom in May and June. If the plants are cut back after the first bloom is over, they will often produce a second showing of flowers.

Many fine garden hybrids are constantly being made available in addition to a number of species that are well worth growing because of their easy culture and attractive flowers. The perennials are more popular than the annuals, though both are excellent for display purposes. The perennials should be planted in masses for the best effects. The annuals are good as cut flowers and in mixed beds, where they often continue to bloom until late summer.

Plants generally grow to 3 ft. high, thriving in either sun or partial shade. They are mostly hardy in Zones 7–9 but do not thrive in hot areas. Propagation is by seed sown in the open where the plants are to grow, since they are tap-rooted and resent transplanting. The perennials can also be propagated by division.

ANNUAL SPECIES

L. densiflorus is a California native that grows to 18 in. and has white, yellow, and red flowers blooming in late spring.

L. hirsutus is an easily grown, blue-flowered species useful for ornament, fodder, or green manure planting.

L. luteus is a European species that grows to 2 ft. and has fragrant yellow flowers. It thrives in the poorest soil and is important as a green manure crop and as a garden ornament.

Lupinus nanus

L. nanus (sky lupine) grows 12–16 in. high and produces white or soft blue flowers in early summer. It is a good wildflower garden plant since it blooms best in poor soil.

L. succulentus (purple annual lupine), a succulent wildflower native to southern California, grows to 2 ft. and has clusters of deep purple or blue blooms.

Lupinus succulentus

L. texensis (Texas bluebonnet), formerly listed as *L. subcarnosus*, is a blue-flowered species native to Texas, where it is the state flower.

PERENNIAL SPECIES

L. argenteus is a silvery-leaved species native to the West Coast. It grows to 3 ft. and has rose, violet, or white flowers.

L. perennis is a hardy plant about 2 ft. tall that has downy foliage and abundant flowers, usually blue but varying to pink and white.

L. polyphyllus, native from Washington through California, grows to 5 ft. tall and usually has blue flowers. Many strains are available in a variety of soft-hued colors. Cv. 'Gallery Series' is a dwarf form that grows to 20 in.

Lupinus perennis

LYCASTE (lī KAS tee). About 35 species of epiphytic or terrestrial orchids native to Mexico, Central America, northern South America, and the West Indies. The plants have short, thick, furrowed pseudobulbs and large deciduous, plicate leaves.

Inflorescences rise from the bases of pseudobulbs, bearing single or several fleshy flowers. They are large, showy, and fragrant, in colors from white and blush-pink through green and rich yellow or orange. The flowers may be 4½ in. across. Three sepals are similar in size and color, the dorsal sepal being perpendicular to the lateral sepals. The petals are generally smaller than the sepals and are parallel to the column, which they almost enclose. The three-lobed lip is hinged to the column foot and is nearly the same size as the petals.

These plants do well in a porous, well-drained compost in pots. After the leaves drop, the plants should rest, dry, in a cool spot. As new shoots appear, the plants should be placed in filtered light and high humidity, and given little water until the roots start to grow. They should be watered freely when in full growth. Hardy to Zone 7 with protection from freezing, they withstand minimum winter temperatures of 50–55°F. The type species is *L. plana*.

LYCHNIS (LIK nis). A large genus of herbs with brilliantly colored flowers, including annuals, biennials, and perennials, belonging to the Caryophyllaceae (Pink Family), closely related to the genus *Silene*, and known by various common names. The dominant color in the genus is red, and the five petals, which expand broadly at the top of the long calyx tube, are characteristically notched in the center or sometimes deeply divided into two segments.

All are easily raised from seed and usually propagate themselves readily once established. If seeds are sown early indoors, most species will give their first bloom in the garden in early to mid-summer. If cut back immediately after blooming, the plants may flower again in the fall. They will do well in ordinary soil, even in rather dry locations; they especially love sun. Perennials can be propagated by division. Hardy in Zones 3–9.

PRINCIPAL SPECIES

L. alba (evening campion) is now listed as *Silene alba*; see SILENE.

L. alpina, a good species for rock garden use, grows to only 1 ft. and bears bright rose-pink flowers with narrow, two-lobed petals blooming in late spring.

L. x arkwrightii cv. 'Vesuvius' is a large hybrid cross between *L. chalcedonica* and *L. x haageana*, producing heads of large orange-red, star-shaped blooms in summer and maroon foliage with a bronze tint.

L. chalcedonica (scarlet-lightning, Maltese-cross, Jerusalem-cross) is a perennial with gleaming scarlet flowers an inch across, each petal indented half its length, forming large rounded clusters atop 2–3 ft. stalks. Flowers vary from rose to white, and there are double forms.

L. coeli-rosa (rose-of-heaven) is a free-flowering annual that grows 9–18 in. tall and bears a single broad rose-red flower opening at the top of each stalk. White- and purple-flowered forms are among the many developed varieties, some accented with eyes.

L. coronaria (rose campion, mullein pink, dusty miller) is a branching biennial or perennial, usually treated as an annual, with white-woolly leaves and large crimson flowers terminating each branchlet. It is sometimes listed in catalogs as *Agrostemma coronaria*.

Lychnis coronaria

L. coronata is an early summer bloomer bearing smooth, green leaves and loosely clustered, cinnabar or salmon-colored flowers 2 in. across with toothed petals. The plant is somewhat tender and usually biennial in cultivation.

L. flos-cuculi (cuckooflower, ragged-robin) is a hardy, rapidly spreading perennial with red to white flowers clustered atop erect stems, each petal deeply cut into four segments.

L. flos-jovis (flower-of-Jove) is a hardy perennial with erect flower stalks rising from rosettes of coarse-haired leaves; it bears clusters of small bright pink or rose-red blossoms.

L. x haageana is an early summer–flowering hybrid perennial with brilliant scarlet flowers 2 in. across, borne two or three together on plants 12–15 in. high.

L. pyrenaica is a small, prostrate plant suited to rock crevices; it has pink and white flowers.

L. viscaria (German catchfly) is a tufted perennial with clustered small red flowers. Varieties are white, pink, or striped and sometimes double.

L. x walkeri is a long-blooming hybrid perennial with carmine-flowered and silvery-haired leaves.

LYCIUM (LIS ee um). A genus of deciduous or evergreen shrubs distributed throughout the temperate and warmer regions of both hemispheres, belonging to the Solonaceae (Nightshade Family), and commonly known as matrimony-vine or box-thorn. They are sometimes spiney

and of more or less loose and clambering growth, well adapted for ornamental planting against walls and fences, and doing well on rocky slopes. Small flowers are followed by brightly colored berries. Not particular as to soil, they can tolerate dry places. Thought should be given to their location due to the suckering habit of most species, which may be a nuisance in some situations. Most species are tender, but a few are hardy to Zones 5–6. Propagation is by seed, cuttings, layers, and suckers.

L. chinense has slender, arching, and often prostrate branches to 12 ft., usually spineless and holding the leaves until late in the fall. It bears a profusion of small purple flowers in early summer, followed by a showy display of orange-red berries about an inch long.

L. halimifolium is upright with arching branches to 10 ft., usually spiny, and holding green leaves quite late. The flowers and scarlet, oval fruits are somewhat smaller than those of *L. chinense*.

LYCOPERSICON (li koh PUR si kahn). A genus of annual and perennial herbs native to South America and other warm regions, belonging to the Solanaceae (Nightshade Family), including all forms of the familiar TOMATO.

L. lycopersicum, one of the most popularly cultivated vegetables in commercial and home gardens, is a tender perennial growing to 10 ft. but is widely cultivated as an annual. Many hybrids and cultivars are available in addition to the natural varieties. Var. *cerasiforme* (cherry tomato) has clustered fruit about ¾ in. in diameter. Var. *pyriforme* bears pear-shaped fruit a little larger than the cherry type.

L. pimpinellifolium (currant tomato) is a perennial usually grown as an annual for its red fruits about ½ in. in diameter.

LYCOPODIUM (li koh POH dee um). A genus of primitive, evergreen, flowerless plants with scalelike leaves, commonly known as club-moss or ground-pine, and the only horticulturally interesting member of the Lycopodiaceae (Club-moss Family). They are useful as ground cover in shady woods, but since it is difficult to transplant and establish a colony of mature plants, they should be increased by cuttings. Being allied to the ferns (see FERN ALLIES), they do not produce seeds, but propagate by minute spores borne on spikes or in the leaf axils. Many native species were ruthlessly collected for use as Christmas greens, but they are now protected by law in many states. A few species can be propagated from cuttings, making collection of entire plants unnecessary.

PRINCIPAL SPECIES

L. clavatum (running-pine) has creeping stems to 9 ft. long. The mycorrhizal roots make it difficult to move successfully.

L. complanatum (ground-cedar) has upright, sometimes fan-shaped, scale-covered branches.

L. lucidulum (shining club-moss) lacks the mycorrhizal fungus and is adaptable to garden use. It can be rooted from cuttings by pressing a short section (5–6 in. long) horizontally into damp sand, leaving the top above the sand. Protected from drying out, it should produce a well-rooted plant.

L. obscurum (ground or princess-pine) has stems that growg underground and send up tree-like branches to 10 in. high. It can be cultivated like *L. lucidulum*.

LYCOPUS (LĪ koh pus). A genus of moisture-loving aromatic herbs belonging to the Lamiaceae (Mint Family), commonly known as water-horehound and sometimes called bugleweed. Many species, varying from 1–3 ft. high, are well distributed in moist ground throughout the United States, preferring a deep, rich soil. The leaves are toothed or pinnatifid. Tiny bell-shaped flowers are white or pale blue, clustered in axillary whorls in midsummer.

Three species are common: *L. virginicus* and *L. uniflorus*, the latter being more slender and smoother; and the widespread *L. americanus*, distinguished by its deeply pinnatifid leaves. *L. europaeus* is also commonly grown in ornamental gardens.

LYCORIS (lī KOH ris). A genus of bulbous plants belonging to the Amaryllidaceae (Amaryllis Family), with lilylike red, orange, white, or pinkish lavender flowers that appear after the narrow leaves have entirely disappeared. Several species are imported to the United States from China and Japan, where they are native. Most species are grown under glass or are hardy outdoors to Zone 7 with winter protection. Bulbs are planted in the open border in soil rich in humus in order to maintain

Lycoris squamigera

the vigorous growth essential to the production of handsome clusters of flowers. The lush foliage appears in the early summer but soon ripens and dies; in August the lovely flowers suddenly appear on naked stalks. Because of this pattern of blooming without foliage, the plants should be surrounded by some type of ground cover, such as snow-in-summer (**Cerastium tomentosum**) or lavender petunias.

PRINCIPAL SPECIES

L. africana (golden spider-lily) is a half-hardy species with narrow, grayish green leaves and bright red, orange, or yellow flowers appearing atop stout stems. It is usually grown under glass but is generally hardy in the border with winter protection.

L. radiata (red spider-lily), often treated as a pot plant, has small, bright red blossoms in clusters. The leaves appear in winter, and the flowers bloom later in the year. It is usually very hardy. Cv. 'Alba' has white flowers.

L. squamigera, sometimes listed in catalogs as *Amaryllis hallii*, probably the most popularly cultivated species, has fragrant clusters of lavender-rose blossoms 3 in. long, rising on naked stalks 2–3 ft. high. Its various common names (mystery-, magic-, or resurrection-lily, naked-lady) refer to the sudden late-summer appearance of the flower stalks with no foliage. Cv.

'Purpurea' has darker flowers. The species and cultivar are both hardy to Zone 5.

LYGODIUM (lī GOH dee um). A genus of mostly tropical ferns that climb by means of twining rachises. The fronds extend themselves as they climb, sometimes as high as 30 ft. The pinnae are forked in half, and each pinnule appears to be a complete pinna. On fertile pinnae, which occur at the ends of the fronds, the sporangia are borne on fingerlike projections. The plants can form tangled thickets in swampy areas.

L. japonicum (Japanese climbing fern) makes a handsome show if planted in a container with strings, wires, or poles for it to climb. It dies back periodically, but after a rest period and removal of the dead fronds, it will soon thrive again. The bipinnate fronds can be several feet long, and the sterile pinnae have elongated triangles. The fertile pinnae are similarly divided but not as elongated. Native to eastern Asia, it is hardy to Zone 7 and has escaped cultivation in the southeastern coastal states, where it has become a pest.

L. palmatum (Hartford fern) has fronds 3–4 ft. long. The sterile pinna halves are palmate, split into six narrow pinnules. Fertile pinnae are much smaller and divided into several segments. It inhabits sandy bogs and swamps, but only in a few spotty locations. Although it is native to the eastern and southern states, it is very rare, protected by law in most areas, and should never be collected.

LYONIA (lī OH nee ah). A genus of deciduous or evergreen shrubs native in North America, the West Indies, and Asia, belonging to the Ericaceae (Heath Family). They are bushy shrubs, not often planted but suitable for massing. They thrive in moist, sandy, peaty soil and shade or partial shade. Propagation is by seed, cuttings, and layers. Only one or two species are hardy beyond Zone 6.

PRINCIPAL SPECIES

L. ligustrina (maleberry, he-huckleberry), found from Maine to Florida, is a deciduous shrub growing to 12 ft. In early summer it bears small white flowers in leafless racemes. In the fall the leathery oval leaves take on colored tints.

L. lucida (fetterbush), found from Virginia southward, is an evergreen that grows to 6 ft. and has lustrous leaves and white or pink flowers in leafy racemes.

L. mariana (staggerbush), found from Rhode Island to Florida, is deciduous and grows to 6 ft. Its nodding white or pinkish flowers are borne in leafless racemes.

LYSICHITON (lī si KIT un). A genus of moisture-loving herbs belonging to the Araceae (Arum Family), including two species similar in form to *Symplocarpus foetidus* (skunk-cabbage) but not as malodorous. It is sometimes planted near ponds or in bog gardens.

L. americanum (yellow-skunk-cabbage), native to the western states, has 5 ft. long leaves. The spadix and spathe are bright clear yellow.

L. camtschatensis (white-skunk-cabbage), native to eastern Asia, has shorter leaves than the American species and a white spadix and spathe.

LYSIMACHIA (lī sim AY kee ah). A genus of European perennial herbs with yellow flowers, belonging to the Primulaceae (Primrose Family), and commonly known as loosestrife. Only a few of the many species are suitable for the garden, the rest of them being weedy and invasive. The following are fine choices for the border or for naturalizing in a partially shaded spot. Mostly hardy in Zones 4–9, they all require moist soil, particularly if they receive little or no shade. Propagation is by seed or division.

PRINCIPAL SPECIES

L. barystachys grows to 2½ ft. and has white flowers in loose racemes, drooping when first opening.

L. ciliata (fringe loosestrife) has open spikes of yellow flowers above purple foliage. Full sun enhances their color.

L. clethroides (shepherd's-crook), commonly available, grows to 3 ft. and has white flowers in terminal spikes that bloom in summer, taking the form of a shepherd's crook.

L. *dubia* grows to 2 ft. and has attractive rose-colored flowers clustered on spikes.

L. *nummularia* (money-wort, creeping-Charlie, creeping-Jenny) is a low, trailing plant with bright yellow flowers and round, shiny leaves, often found bordering ponds or ditches. It is useful as a ground cover in shady places but can be a pest in lawns.

L. *punctata* (yellow loosestrife) produces spikes of bright yellow blooms in early summer.

Lysimachia punctata

LYTHRACEAE (lĭth RAY see ee). The Loosestrife Family, a group of mostly tropical herbs, shrubs, and trees. Several genera are grown for ornament, including *Cuphea, Lagerstroemia, Lawsonia,* and *Lythrum.*

LYTHRUM (LITH rum). A genus of slender annual or perennial, moisture-loving herbs commonly known as loosestrife. Several North American species are hardy to Zone 4 and are easily cultivated and useful for border planting and naturalizing. Pink, purple, or magenta flowers may be borne singly or in clusters. The genus lends its name to the Lythraceae (Loosestrife

Lythrum salicaria

Family). Plants are easily cultivated in moist soil. Propagation is by seed or division.

PRINCIPAL SPECIES

L. *alatum,* native throughout North America, is an erect perennial that grows to 4 ft. and has oblong leaves and solitary purple flowers.

L. *flexuosum,* from the Mediterranean region, grows erect or prostrate with oblong or linear leaves and solitary, funnelform purple flowers.

L. *hyssopifolia* is an annual that grows to 2 ft. and has scattered flowers of pinkish purple.

L. *salicaria* (spiked or purple loosestrife) is sometimes known as willow-herb for its willow-like leaves. Originally introduced from Europe, it has wandlike spikes of deep magenta flowers, which color broad stretches of eastern marshlands in late summer. It self-sows and has escaped cultivation to become an invasive weed in some areas. 'Roseum superbum' is a popular cultivar that grows 4–5 ft. tall and has larger, paler rose flowers. It thrives in well-drained but well-watered soil.

L. *virgatum* is similar to L. *salicaria* but has narrower leaves and paired or clustered flowers-borne in open, leafy sprays. Some of its cultivars, including 'Dropmore Purple' and 'Morden Pink', are splendid border plants.

LYTOCARYUM (lī toh KAR ee um) **weddellianum.** A Brazilian feather palm, formerly listed under various genera, including *Cocos* and *Syagrus.* In its native habitat, it grows to 7 ft. with slender, frondlike foliage dropping nearly to the ground. The slow symmetrical growth of this species makes it the most popular of dwarf palms for pot culture. In the juvenile state, the glossy deep green leaves spread in an almost perfect circle. It is occasionally grown outdoors in Florida, where it requires abundant moisture. Although it may survive a few degrees of frost, it should be protected during cold weather with a covering of evergreen branches. For culture, see PALMS.

M

MAACKIA (MAK ee ah). A genus of oriental deciduous trees and some shrubs with attractive foliage and whitish, pealike flowers in erect panicles. The species imported and grown from seed are hardy to Zone 5. They thrive in any soil but bloom best when in a sunny location.

MACADAMIA (mak ah DAY mee ah) **ternifolia.** An evergreen tree from Australia, belonging to the Proteaceae (Protea Family), and commonly known as Queensland nut. Cultivated in the warmest parts of the United States for its large, edible nuts, it also has merit as an ornamental tree. It can stand mild frost and dry conditions but grows best in deep, moist, loamy soil where it may attain 50 ft. It has whorls of shining leaves up to 1 ft. long and bears white flowers in clusters about as long as the leaves, and nuts that are smooth and shining.

MACFADYENA (mak FAD yen ah) **unguis-cati.** An evergreen vine commonly known as cat's-claw because of the clawlike tendrils by which it clings. It has been listed as *Doxantha unguis-cati* and *Bignonia tweediana*. Usually grown in the greenhouse, it can tolerate a few degrees of frost outside, though it is generally hardy only in Zones 10–11. It is too robust a grower for pot culture, but the roots need to be somewhat restricted, either in a long box or narrow border, in order to induce free flowering. The bright yellow trumpet-shaped flowers are up to 4 in. across.

MACLEAYA (mah KLAY ah) **cordata.** A tall-growing perennial herb, formerly listed as *Bocconia cordata* or *B. japonica*, belonging to the Papaveraceae (Poppy Family), and commonly known as plume poppy or tree-celandine. Very different from the ordinary poppy, its feathery sprays of small, petal-less flowers are held high above the large, grayish green, lobed leaves. It makes an effective background for perennials or tall accent near the house or in the shrubby border. The small flowers are followed by slender, drooping plumes of seed vessels, as attractive as the flowers. Propagation is easily done by removing and resetting the numerous suckers that form at the base of the plant. If set in rich soil, they will rapidly develop to blooming size but may become invasive if not tended carefully. Hardy in Zones 4–9.

Macleaya cordata

MACLURA (mah KLOOR ah) **pomifera.** A medium-sized spiny deciduous tree belonging to the Moraceae (Mulberry Family) and commonly known as Osage-orange. It has fairly long, bright green leaves, and the flowers are not showy. The female tree is conspicuous when bearing the large, greenish yellow, orangelike fruits, which are inedible. Although native from Arkansas to Texas, it will survive farther north. It grows well even on rather poor land and makes a fine hedge. It survives repeated browsing by livestock. At one time it was largely grown for its leaves, used as a substitute for mulberry for feeding silkworms. The Osage Indians, who valued its wood for making bows, called it bow-wood. Because of its durability in the ground, it is good for fence posts and railroad ties. Propagation is by greenwood and root cuttings under glass. Hardy in Zones 5–9.

MADDER. Common name for many shrubby or herbaceous plants belonging to the RUBIACEAE (Madder Family).

MADEIRA VINE. Common name for *Anredera cordifolia*, a flowering vine frequently grown for ornament; see ANREDERA.

MADIA (MAY dee ah). A genus of sticky, strongly aromatic annual and perennial herbs belonging to the Asteraceae (Aster Family) and commonly known as tarweed. Some species close their yellow, daisylike flowers in bright sunlight but will be open in the morning and evening, on overcast days, or in partial shade. *M. elegans* (showy tarweed), a robust annual good for dry or wild gardens, grows 2–6 ft. Its many 4-in. yellow daisies are often marked with bronze at the petal base, all summer and fall. *M. nutans* (nodding madia), a small spring annual, grows to 4 in. and has many 1-in. yellow flowers; ideal for rock gardens.

MADRONE. A common name for *Arbutus menziesii*, a large tree native to California with white flowers followed by small red fruits; see ARBUTUS.

MAGNOLIA (mag NOH lee ah). Common and botanical name for a genus of more than 85 species of deciduous and evergreen trees and shrubs distributed throughout North and Central America and Asia. It is the principal genus of the MAGNOLIACEAE (Magnolia Family).

The evergreens are not as hardy as the deciduous kinds. Many of them are spectacular in the blooming season, bearing probably the largest flowers of any cultivated tree; these range from white, through yellow and pink to purple. The tree is not especially graceful in form, but the astonishing spring transformation from naked branches to a mass of gorgeous fragrant flowers never fails to win admiration.

From the Orient come slow-growing dwarf species and hybrids that blossom before the leaves appear and provide some of the most striking and useful garden types. In view of their early blossoming habit, they are best placed against an evergreen background.

Most magnolias thrive in a rich, porous soil that is moderately moist; they prefer sandy or peaty loam. Specimens are difficult to transplant and must be carefully balled and wrapped and not trampled when reset, to avoid breaking and bruising the roots. The native kinds should be moved just as growth begins. The Asiatic species and hybrids should be moved when in bloom, since the roots are tender and will not heal except when the plant is growing. Pruning must be done during the growing season, since dormant

trees do not easily heal their wounds.

Magnolias are propagated from seed and greenwood cuttings, and by layering or grafting on potted stock in the greenhouse. For grafting, *M. tripetala* is preferred because of its superior fibrous roots, although *M. acuminata* is also used.

The magnolia scale is large (½ in. across), soft, and resembles the tulip tree scale. Since the young winter over in a partly grown state, the best control is a dormant application of a safe, miscible oil. See SCALE INSECTS.

PRINCIPAL SPECIES

M. acuminata (cucumber tree), growing to 100 ft., is hardy from New York west and southward (Zones 4–8). The large greenish flowers of this imposing, pyramidal tree are distinguished with difficulty from the leaves. The flowers are followed by conspicuous seeds.

M. campbellii is an Asiatic species that grows to 80 ft. Its 10-in. flowers are white and pink inside and purple outside. Hardy from Virginia southward (Zones 7–9).

M. fraseri grows to 50 ft. and bears leaves 1½ ft. long and flowers 10 in. across. Hardy from Virginia southward (Zones 6–9).

M. grandiflora (bull-bay), an evergreen growing 50–100 ft., is the grandest tree of the tribe. It grows along the coast from North Carolina to Texas but may survive in sheltered locations up to Boston. It has long, lustrous leaves and is very showy in bloom from April to August, with 8-in. flowers like giant roses. This is a magnificent specimen plant in any garden at any time of the year. In the western states, it tends to be a problem, with leaves and flower parts falling from spring to fall. There are some fine cultivars now being grown. 'Edith Bogue' is the hardiest selection, surviving to –24°F. 'Majestic Beauty' has flowers to 12 in. across and larger, longer leaves. 'St. Mary' is very floriferous and grows to 20 ft. in a dense, shrubby shape. 'Little Gem' is a newer dwarf cultivar that grows to 10 ft. and has smaller leaves and flowers. 'Samuel Sommer' has flowers to 14 in. across with twelve petals. Hardy in Zones 6–9.

M. heptapeta (Yulan), formerly listed as *M. denudata*, is a deciduous tree native to China that grows to 50 ft. and bears fragrant 6-in. flowers before the leaves appear.

M. hypolenica, formerly listed as *M. obovata*, is an Asiatic tree that grows to 100 ft. and is hardy from New York southward. Its large leaves are almost silvery white beneath, and its fragrant 7-in. flowers are followed by cylindrical scarlet fruits 8 in. long. Hardy in Zones 7–9.

M. kobus is a hardy Asiatic species whose white flowers often completely cover the tree in early April before the foliage appears. It grows to 30 ft. in a dense, symmetrical habit. Hardy in Zones 4–7.

M. macrophylla (large-leaved cucumber tree) is similar to *M. acuminata* but grows to only 50 ft. and has larger leaves and white flowers.

M. sieboldii is a small Asiatic tree that grows to 20 ft. It has one of the most beautiful blossoms of any magnolia; the fragrant, white, cup-shaped flowers with many crimson stamens bloom for a long period starting in May. Hardy in Zones 6–7.

M. x soulangiana is a hardy Asiatic hybrid that grows to 30 ft. high. It is a prolific bloomer and one of the most often planted kinds. In the North, the flowers bloom profusely in early April and are often killed by frost and freezing temperatures. Its 6-in. fragrant flowers are white inside and brilliant purple outside. There are many cultivars with blossoms of white, rose, red, and other shades. Hardy in Zones 5–9.

M. stellata (starry magnolia) is a hardy, bushy Asiatic native that grows slowly to 15 ft. It is a showy plant with sweet, narrow-petaled white flowers about 3 in. across. It blooms with the early daffodils in April, before the foliage appears. In the North, the blossoms are frequently damaged by late frost. Hardy in Zones 4–8.

M. tripetala (umbrella tree) grows to 30 ft. and has leaves nearly 2 ft. long. The 10-in. white flowers, blooming in spring, are of unpleasant odor; these are followed by rose-red fruits. Hardy in Zones 5–8.

M. virginiana (sweet- or swamp-bay) varies from shrub size to a tree of 30 ft. and is hardy from Massachusetts along the coast southward to Florida and Texas, where it is evergreen. Its fragrant flowers are 3 in. across and bloom from late spring through early fall. This is an unusual magnolia, since it often grows in very wet areas. The leaves are silvery white beneath. There is a new cultivar for northern areas that stays evergreen to –17°F. Hardy in Zones 6–9.

MAGNOLIACEAE (mag noh lee AY see ee). The Magnolia Family, a group of trees, shrubs, or sometimes vines, mostly native to North America and Asia. Many forms of *Magnolia* are valued as ornamentals because of the beauty of their flowers and foliage as well as their ready response to cultivation. The genus *Liriodendron* (tulip tree) yields timber and fine ornamental trees.

MAHOGANY. Common name for *Swietenia mahagoni*, a tropical evergreen whose wood is highly valued; see SWIETENIA. The Mahogany Family is MELIACEAE.

The common name is also applied to other plants. Bastard mahogany is *Eucalyptus botryoides*; red-mahogany is *E. resinifera*; swamp-mahogany is *E. robusta*; see EUCALYPTUS. Mountain-mahogany refers to the genus CERCOCARPUS.

MAHONIA (mah HOH nee ah). A genus of handsome evergreen shrubs found in North and Central America, Europe, and Asia, belonging to the Berberidaceae (Barberry Family). They are outstanding for their glossy evergreen foliage, showy yellow flowers, and bluish white fruit.

Most species are tender, but a few are hardy as far north as Zone 4, where they do best in a location sheltered from wind and hot sun. They grow well under trees, especially where the soil is inclined to be moist, and are fine for massing. Some kinds spread freely by suckers. Propagation can be done by seed, cuttings, and division of the parent plant.

PRINCIPAL SPECIES

M. aquifolium (Oregon grapeholly, holly-leaved barberry) grows to 3 ft. or more. It has handsome, spiny, lustrous dark green leaves of five to nine leaflets, which take on a bronzy tone in fall. The clusters of abundant yellow flowers are showy in spring, and later the bluish black, bloomy fruits are attractive. Hardy in Zones 4–8.

M. bealei (leatherleaf mahonia) grows to 12 ft. with handsome leaves of nine to fifteen leaflets with a few spiny teeth, and large clusters of fragrant pale yellow flowers. Hardy in Zones 6–8.

M. nervosa (Oregon-grape), a western native, is a dwarf and free-suckering species with large lustrous leaves of eleven to nineteen leaflets. It is the state flower of Oregon. Hardy to Zone 6.

M. repens (creeping mahonia) is a low grower of stoloniferous habit, only 12 in. high, and has bluish green leaves of three to seven leaflets. Hardy to Zone 6.

Mahonia repens

MAIANTHEMUM (may AN the mum) **canadense.** A spring-blooming, low-growing perennial herb, native from eastern Canada to the southern Appalachian range, belonging to the *Liliaceae* (Lily Family), and commonly known as wild lily-of-the-valley or Canada-mayflower. Young shoots have a single leaf, but at flowering stage, the stem produces two or three leaves. The plants bear 2-in. plumes of small (½-in.), white, bell-shaped flowers, each with two petals and two sepals; they resemble blossoms of the true lily-of-the-valley. After pollination by bumblebees, the sweetly fragrant flowers are fol-

Maianthemum canadense

lowed by berries containing several tiny, round, white seeds. The berries turn from speckled green to bright red as the foliage yellows in late summer. The berries are quickly consumed by mice, chipmunks, and birds.

Wild lily-of-the-valley is an exceptionally adaptable wildflower, useful for planting in cool soils where it forms mats of foliage. Although it will grow in ordinary soil, it prefers mildly acidic soil rich in humus. It will thrive and produce large leaves in shady locations; however, in sunny spots, the shoots tend to be more densely packed and flower more abundantly with smaller leaves.

Plants are most commonly propagated by dividing the rhizomes in the fall, cutting 2-in. pieces with at least one greenish bud each. Set the divisions about 6 in. apart and ¾ in. deep, moisten the soil, and mulch for the winter. The new plants will usually flower the following spring. Although propagation from seed is time consuming, it is not difficult. In late summer, collect the fruits and separate the seeds from the pulp. Immediately plant the seeds ⅓ in. deep in the desired location or in flats left outdoors for the winter. Once established, plants will spread rapidly on their own.

MAIDENHAIR FERN. Common name for ADIANTUM, a popular genus of ferns distinguished by their wedge-shaped, stalked pinnules (leaflets). Tree-maidenhair fern is *Didymochlaena truncatula*, a popular fern with glossy, symmetrical foliage; see DIDYMOCHLAENA.

MAIDENHAIR TREE. Common name for *Ginkgo biloba*, an attractive, hardy, deciduous tree with fernlike leaves; see GINKGO.

MAIZE. A native Indian name often used in England for *Zea mays*, which is better known as CORN in the United States.

MALAY-APPLE. Common name for *Syzygium malaccense*, a tropical tree with reddish flowers and berries; see SYZYGIUM.

MALCOLMIA (mal KOHL mee ah). A genus of low, grayish annuals and perennials, commonly known as Malcolm or Mahon stock, of which three species are grown in North American gardens for their small, scentless flowers of white, lilac, or pinkish purple. Seed is sown in the fall or started indoors for early blooming; outdoors for later flowers.

M. maritima (Virginia stock), the best-known species, is an annual that grows to 12 in. and bears graceful sprays of small flowers. It is easily cultivated and best when sown biweekly for successional bloom, preferably in the front of a sunny border planting. Seeds sown in the fall will give flowers early in spring.

MALE FERN. Common name for *Dryopteris filix-mas*, a large deciduous or evergreen fern; see DRYOPTERIS.

MALLOW. Common name for MALVA, a genus of mostly perennial herbs, including both weeds and garden subjects. The Mallow Family is MALVACEAE.

The common name is also applied to other genera. False mallow is *Malvastrum*. Globe mallow is *Sphaeralcea*. Jew's-mallow is *Corchorus olitorius*. Musk mallow refers to *Malva moschata* or *Abelmoschus moschatus*. Poppy mallow is the genus CALLIRHOE. Prairie mallow is *Sphaeralcea coccinea*. Rose mallow and marsh mallow are the genus HIBISCUS. Tree mallow is LAVATERA.

MALOPE (MAL oh pee). A genus of mallowlike annuals common in European gardens. The large purple, rose, or white flowers will continue to open from early summer until frost if the seeds are sown early in a good garden soil. Malopes are excellent cut flowers, since the blooms last a long time if placed in water after cutting.

MALPIGHIA (mal PIG ee ah). A genus of flowering evergreen trees or shrubs. Native to the tropical Americas, they are grown outdoors in Zones 10–11 and in greenhouses in cooler regions. Propagation is by seed and cuttings.

PRINCIPAL SPECIES

M. coccigera is a bushy shrub that grows to 3 ft. and has small, roundish, spiny leaves and pale pink flowers; sometimes used for dwarf hedges in warm climates.

M. glabra (Barbados-cherry), the principal species, grows to about 15 ft. with shining, oval leaves and rose-red flowers with a fringed edge. The fruit is red, about the size of a cherry, rich in vitamin C and is highly esteemed in the tropics.

M. urens (cowage, cow-itch) is a small shrub with oblong leaves, pink or pale purple flowers, and edible fruit. It has long been cultivated in Europe despite the stinging hairs on the undersides of the leaves.

MALUS (MA lus). Botanical name for all the apples, sometimes treated as a subgenus of PYRUS. These include important species of mostly deciduous trees, rarely shrubs, native in cool-temperate regions of the Northern Hemisphere, and belonging to the Rosaceae (Rose Family). Many are valuable as orchard fruits or ornamentals; see APPLE and CRAB APPLE.

PRINCIPAL SPECIES

M. x *atrosanguinea* makes a small, bushy tree that is very showy with rosy-carmine flowers.

M. baccata (Siberian crab) is a handsome tree that grows to 40 ft. and has snowy white flowers and small red or yellow fruit.

M. communis, *M. pumila*, *M. domestica* (common apple), considered to be the ancestors of modern apples, probably originated in Europe or western Asia and have been grown for many centuries. They have white flowers with a trace of pink and may grow to more than 40 ft. in height.

M. coronaria (wild sweet crab) grows to 30 ft. and is very handsome in spring with pink-and-white fragrant flowers and is subject to cedar rust. The fruits are like small green apples, hard and sour, but good in jelly.

M. floribunda (showy crab) is a large shrub or small tree, very floriferous with carmine-tipped buds but pale flowers; especially showy in autumn with pea-sized yellow fruit.

M. halliana is usually of bushy habit, with glossy leaves and deep rose colored flowers. Cv. *parkmanii* has double pink flowers.

M. hupehensis is of stiff, upright growth, with fragrant white or tinted flowers, resembling a cherry tree when in bloom.

M. ioensis (prairie crab) is a tree that grows to 30 ft. and has large blush or pink flowers; it is subject to cedar rust. Cv. 'Plena' (Bechtel's crab) has very showy, double pink flowers.

M. × micromalus makes a shapely little tree, one of the showiest with its pink flowers and red fruit.

M. prunifolia (plum-leaved apple) is very showy in bloom with large white flowers, and in autumn with yellow or red fruit.

M. sargentii, a compact bush growing to 6 ft., is very ornamental with red-tipped buds and white flowers, and later with small, dark red fruit.

M. spectabilis (Chinese flowering apple) grows to 25 ft. and has showy pink flowers, fading to white.

M. toringoides has lobed leaves, creamy white flowers, and yellow or red fruit.

M. × zumi is a shapely tree of pyramidal habit that grows to 20 ft.. It has pink buds and white flowers followed by small red fruit.

MALVA (MAL vah). A genus of perennial and a few annual herbs, some useful in the flower garden, and others persistent garden weeds, all commonly known as mallow. They have five-parted, rose or white, silky or papery-petaled flowers. Easily cultivated in any ordinary garden soil with plenty of light and warmth in Zones 4–9, they are inclined to self-sow and escape from cultivation. The genus lends its name to the Malvaceae (Mallow Family).

PRINCIPAL SPECIES

M. alcea is a perennial with deep rose or white flowers similar to those of *M. moschata* and is often found naturalized by the roadside. Hardy to Zone 4.

M. moschata (musk mallow) is a European perennial with rose or white flowers and finely cut leaves. Native to Europe and northern Africa,

it is sometimes cultivated and is often seen as a garden escapee in England and North America.

M. rotundifolia (common or round-leaved mallow) is a common biennial or perennial barnyard weed with very small white flowers followed by flat, wrinkled, green fruits, often called cheeses.

M. verticillata grows to 8 ft. and has rounded leaves and white or purplish flowers about ½ in. long. Var. *crispa* has curly leaves sometimes used as a garnish in place of parsley.

Malva alcea

MALVACEAE (mal VAY see ee). The Mallow Family, a widely distributed group of herbs and shrubs of economic and horticultural importance. The family yields many ornamental subjects and a few grown for food, medicine, and fibers. The outstanding representative is *Gossypium*, the source of commercial cotton. Among other genera in cultivation are *Abutilon*, *Althaea*, *Callirhoe*, *Hibiscus*, *Lavatera*, *Malope*, *Malva* (mallow), *Malvaviscus*, *Sidalcea*, and *Sphlaeralcea*.

MALVAVISCUS (mal vah VIS kus). A genus of shrubby plants, mostly from the tropical Americas, belonging to the Malvaceae (Mallow Family), and commonly known as turk's-cap or sleeping-hibiscus. A few species are well known in outdoor gardens in Zones 10–11 or under glass in cooler climates. Propagation is by cuttings.

M. arboreus (wax mallow), the principal species, is well known in greenhouses and is a good houseplant. In pots, it grows 2–3 ft. high and has a long blooming season. The flowers are usually bright scarlet, resembling those of *Abutilon* but not fully opening. There are several varieties with variable flowers.

MAMMEA (ma MEE ah). A genus of West Indian trees of which one large species, *M. americana*, is grown in Zones 10–11 for its globular, russet, rather rough, leathery-skinned, apricot-flavored fruit. It has generally failed in California, but it has succeeded in Florida as far north as Palm Beach. In rich soil the tree becomes one of the most striking of West Indian subjects, often attaining a height of 60 ft. with a trunk 3–4 ft. in diameter, displaying glossy, thick foliage and abundant fragrant, white flowers.

MAMMILLARIA (mam il LAIR ee ah). One of the largest, most varied, and popular groups of cacti, the so-called nipple cactus or pincushion cactus, mostly from Mexico, sometimes classified as Neomammillaria. The flowers are small and colorful, mostly red, pink, magenta, white, and yellow, appearing in a ring around the apex in the previous year's growth, rather than from the apex as in the related *Coryphantha* cactus. The tubercle is divided in two, the spine-bearing portion at the tip of the tubercle, the flower-bearing portion at the base, often protected by wool. The fruits are colorful and naked, devoid of spines, hairs, or scales. Some species bear hooked central spines; in others the spines are all straight. Most species are choice.

Among the most remarkable in the genus are the dwarf species, in the wild hardly bigger than the tip of your little finger but with flowers up to 2 in. long, including: *M. carmenae*, with soft yellow spines and golden yellow flowers; *M. laui* and its varieties, with white to yellow, soft to stiff spines and bright pink flowers; *M. saboae* and its varieties; and *M. theresae*.

PRINCIPAL SPECIES

M. bocasana (powder-puff cactus) has soft, long, silky white hair for radial spines; hooked central spines; and long, white axillary hairs.

M. elongata (golden-stars) comes in several cultivated forms, usually with naked or slightly wooly spines and red flowers about ½ in. long.

M. guelzowiana with spectacular, large, purple-red flowers and many spines.

M. hahniana (old-woman cactus) bears long, white hairs in irregular clusters, with spines that shed easily. The ¾-in. flowers are purplish red.

M. plumosa (feather cactus) has soft, white, feathery spines and scented, pale yellow flowers.

MANDARIN ORANGE. Common name for *Citrus reticulata*, whose varieties include tangerine and Satsuma. The trees are only slightly hardier (to Zone 9) than the sweet orange, *C. sinensis*. The name is sometimes given to the fruit of the MANGOSTEEN, *Garcinia mangostana*.

MANDEVILLA (man de VIL ah). A genus of twining evergreen shrubs from South America, belonging to the Apocynaceae (Dogbane Family), hardy only in Zones 10–11. They are handsome and showy flowering plants for the intermediate greenhouse, where they can be grown either in a border and trained to the roof, or in pots trained on stakes or a wire form. They thrive in a mixture of fibrous peat and loam, with coarse sand and broken charcoal added. Keep them moderately warm and dry during the resting stage in winter. In early spring, when new growth is starting, prune back the side branches and repot, or renovate the soil. Give a little extra heat until growth is well under way. Propagation is by root cuttings with bottom heat.

M. boliviensis and *M. splendens* are the species usually grown. There are also named forms of garden origin, with clusters of large, showy, funnelform flowers in white, yellow, and shades of pink with yellow markings.

M. laxa (Chilean jessamine), formerly listed as *M. suaveolens*, is a woody vine with racemes of fragrant, white, funnelform flowers. Sometimes grown in the greenhouse or outdoors in warm regions, it does not take kindly to pot culture.

MANDRAGORA (man drah GOR ah) **officinarum.** An old European medicinal herb commonly known as mandrake or love-apple. The leaves are large, nearly hiding the solitary, purple or yellowish, bell-shaped flowers. Hardy in Zones 4–9, plants grow readily to about 1 ft. high in rich, warm, loamy soil and are propagated by seed or division. Formerly grown in herb collections, they are sometimes seen in wildflower gardens. From the thick, tuberous roots, often branching into humanlike forms, an aphrodisiac was concocted in ancient times, and many superstitions still linger about the plant, which has poisonous qualities.

MANDRAKE. Common name for *Mandragora officinarum*, an old European medicinal herb; see MANDRAGORA. The name is also sometimes applied to *Podophyllum peltatum*, which is better known as mayapple; see PODOPHYLLUM.

MANETTIA (mah NET ee ah). A genus of tropical American twining plants belonging to the Rubiaceae (Madder Family). A few species are grown in greenhouses and are useful to drape trellises and rafters or to train on forms. They can also be used outdoors for summer flowering in a sunny place. They have a long blooming season, and some attention should be given to training and trimming to prevent the growth from becoming a tangle. Propagation is by cuttings.

M. cordifolia var. *glabra* has large flowers that are more than 1 in. long and crimson throughout.

M. inflata, formerly listed as *B. bicolor*, is perhaps the best-known species, bearing bright, tubular flowers of red, tipped with yellow, and somewhat swollen at the base.

MANGIFERA (man JIF er ah) **indica.** Botanical name for the tropical evergreen tree that produces the common MANGO.

MANGO. Common name for *Mangifera indica*, a tropical Asiatic evergreen tree grown in Zones 10–11 for its large, peachlike fruits. These are ranked among the world's choicest fruits in color, aroma, flavor, and food value. In nature, the tree often exceeds 75 ft. in height and 100 ft. in spread; in gardens, by proper pruning, it can be kept less than half as large. It needs well-drained but moisture-retentive soil. It can be grown from seed, but the best varieties are propagated by grafting and budding.

MANGOSTEEN. Common name for *Garcinia mangostana*, a pink-flowered Malayan tree whose pulpy, reddish purple fruits are among the world's choicest. This tree can be grown in the United States only in Zone 11 and the very warmest part of Zone 10. It needs well-drained but moist soil and complete absence of cold.

MANIHOT (MAN i hot). A genus of tropical American plants of which a shrub, *M. esculenta* (cassava, manioc), is the most important. It is cultivated for its long, thick, tuberous, starchy roots, which are a starch staple and also furnish commercially produced tapioca. Hardy only in Zones 10–11, it thrives in rich, light soil.

MANILKARA (man il KAR ah) **zapota.** A tropical evergreen tree of the Sapotaceae (Sapodilla Family), commonly known as sapote or sapodilla. It has broadly oval leaves to 16 in. long and white flowers to ½ in. across. The tree bears abundant edible, brownish fruit with red or yellowish, translucent, melting, sweet flesh and one hard seed. It is native to Central and South America, popularly cultivated in Mexico and the West Indies, naturalized in the southern tip of Florida, and is often grown in southern gardens, but it cannot endure any frost. Propagation is by seed, which is planted in fertile, heavy clay or sandy loam soil after the heavy husk is removed; trees should stand about 30 ft. apart.

MANURE. Animal and vegetable matter used to enrich soil. The value of a manure depends on its ability to supply those plant foods that quickly disappear from the soil under heavy cultivation and heavy cropping. Compounds of nitrogen, potash, and phosphorus are the first to become exhausted. Of these, nitrogen is the hardest to replace. The soil content of organic matter or humus, though less accurately measurable and less fully explained by chemistry, is even more important to maintain. All these needs are supplied by ordinary manure. Even carefully composted manures may carry weed seeds; chemical fertilizers are desirable and often substituted because they do not. Just as humans cannot stay healthy on a diet wholly of food in tablet form, plants outside the laboratory will not thrive indefinitely on chemical fertilizers alone. These can be used as stimulants and sources of special food in conjunction with manure. Some kinds can be added to the manure itself rather than to the soil. Superphosphate, phosphate rock, and gypsum scattered lightly over fresh manure either in the stall or on the compost heap not only add their own fertilizing value to the value of the manure, but they prevent the escape of important nitrogen compounds.

Stable manure is in demand not only for spreading on the soil, but also for use in hotbeds and mushroom houses. In hotbeds its fermentation can be used to furnish heat to force growth and keep out frost.

Cow and hog manures are usually kept on the farm and are seldom sold in quantity except from feedlots. They are valuable because they do not generate much heat and are particularly desirable for making liquid manure, or "manure tea."

Manure that has been dried and shredded, like the commercial sheep or cow manure sold in bags, is usually highly concentrated, but much of the heating capacity has been removed by drying; also, the shredding makes it safe to sprinkle thinly on lawns, or even on the perennial border, if care is taken to keep the particles well scattered, for even small piles may generate heat. Otherwise it should be handled like fresh manure. Rabbit manure also is sometimes available in quantity and should be treated the same as poultry manure. Stockyard products such as dried blood, tankage, etc., being organic materials, might be classed as manures but are more conveniently considered as fertilizers.

Green Manure. A growing crop, especially of high-nitrogen leguminous plants, can be turned under to rot in the soil. In small-scale gardening it is not as feasible as on the farm to give up ground for a whole season to a green manure crop or to use crop rotations that call for plowing under grass or clover sod. In the vegetable garden, however, some manure can be grown in the late fall and early spring by sowing winter rye or rye and vetch. See GREEN MANURE.

Compost. Cornstalks, weeds, sods, grass clippings, green garbage, leaves, and straw—in short everything of vegetable (but not woody) nature can be made to supply nearly as much plant food as manure. None of these materials should be burned in the well-regulated garden, unless badly infected with serious plant pests or diseases. Compost piles can be enriched by adding fertilizers. See COMPOST.

USING MANURE

Composted manure can be used more effectively than fresh because top-dressings can be placed where most needed in addition to the bulk applications turned under. In the vegetable garden, leaf crops should be given more manure than root crops, especially carrots, which are best not manured at all. In the flower border, manure should be used sparingly on perennials subject to root rot, such as iris or delphinium. Annuals thrive best when heavily manured. Plants of the squash and melon group like a large shovelful in the bottom of the hill, but this method should not be used except for rank-growing annuals. It is a mistake to place manure in the bottom of the hole when transplanting any woody subject. The quick growth that follows may mean disaster to the plant, which instead of increasing the top, should be spending its energies on root growth to prepare for drought and frost. Manure should be used on transplanted shrubs and trees only as a top-dressing and only in late fall or winter, the purpose being to keep out frost rather than to fertilize. Of course, incorporation of thoroughly rotted manure with soil in advance of planting is always in order.

Fresh stable manure should not usually be placed on the soil, except in fall on plowed land or land to be turned in the spring. It is better if first composted, watered, and occasionally turned with a fork. Soil mixed through the manure as it is turned will slow the fermentation and lessen the danger of overheating. When the interior of the pile is no longer warm to the touch, the manure is ready for use on the garden.

Poultry manure, which also heats if allowed to ferment, should be mixed with its own bulk of soil and composted before applying, since it may injure plants that it touches if spread on the ground while fresh.

Amounts of manure or compost to be used in the garden are not easily stated, and if stated are not easily followed because different lots will differ in strength. If it is properly rotted or composted, however, much manure can be used without danger, and any excess plant food is carried for the most part from year to year, which is not true in the case of soluble fertilizers. On the other hand, every bit that is added is helpful, so no gardener should spurn a supply of manure, however small. A load or two of manure delivered late each winter is good fare for the average small garden, when supplemented with compost and fertilizers.

It is estimated that well-rotted manure weighs about 810 lb. per cubic yard. On this basis, one ton of such manure represents very close to 2½ cubic yards.

LIQUID MANURE.

Since plants can use (that is, take in through their roots) only food that is in solution, solid manures and fertilizers take effect slowly, depending on rainfall or artificial watering to dissolve them. When quick results are desired, such as flowers to be forced for sale or for exhibition, manure and fertilizers are often dissolved in water, and the resulting liquid manure, or "manure tea," is applied to the soil. This must be done carefully, using a weak solution, applying it only to soil that is already moist, and preferably adding more water immediately afterward.

For ordinary garden needs, liquid manure is made by hanging a sack of rotted cow, sheep, or chicken manure in a large container of water for a couple of days, then dipping out the dark liquid (or drawing it off through a spigot) and diluting it to the color of weak tea, when it is safe to apply with a sprinkling can. Do not use it more than once a week. Any animal manure used in gardening will make liquid manure, but it must be rotted or dried, not fresh. It is a mistake to use liquid manure or any other forcing treatment except at or just before flowering time, or on sickly plants, because forced growth is not hardy, and plants require weeks or months to recover from the strain of forcing.

See also COMPOST; FERTILIZER; SOIL.

MANZANITA. Common name for ARCTO-STAPHYLOS, a genus of evergreen trailing shrubs to small trees.

MAPLE. Common name for ACER, a genus of handsome, deciduous, hardy, and usually long-lived trees. Flowering-maple is ABUTILON, a genus of herbs and small shrubs.

MARANTA (mah RAN tah). A genus of tropical American herbs grown in warm countries and in greenhouses for their ornamental foliage and commonly known as prayer plants. The types that have become popular houseplants, for their beautiful leaves that fold upward at night, include *M. leuconeura* and its varieties.

M. arundinacea (arrowroot) has starchy roots that yield commercial arrowroot and tapioca. Growing to 6 ft., it has leaves 12 in. long and 4 in. wide and bears white flowers, but it is generally grown only for its edible product. An acre of arrowroot will commonly yield about 14,000 lb. of rootstocks, from which about 2100 lb. of the dry starches will be obtained.

Many plants cultivated under this genus name are properly listed under *Calathea*.

MARANTACEAE (mar an TAY see ee). The Maranta or Arrowroot Family, a group of perennial herbs with rootstocks formed in clumps. Principal genera are *Calathea* and *Maranta*.

MARGUERITE. Common name for various daisylike plants of different genera, principally *Chrysanthemum frutescens*, with variously colored flowers popular in the florist trade. Blue-Marguerite is *Felicia ammeloides*; golden-Marguerite is *Anthemis tinctoria*; and hardy-Marguerite is *A. tinctoria* var. *kelwayi*.

MARIGOLD. Common name for TAGETES, a popular genus of brightly colored annual flowers, including those known as African or Aztec, French, and sweet-scented marigolds. Several other plants are also known by this common name. Bur-marigold refers to BIDENS, a genus of weeds propagated by seeds (burs) that hook onto passing objects. Cape-marigold is the genus DIMORPHOTHECA. Corn-marigold is *Chrysanthemum segetum*. Desert-marigold is *Baileya multiradiata*. Fig-marigold refers to the genus MESEMBRYANTHEMUM and sometimes to AIZOACEAE (Carpetweed Family). Marsh-marigold is *Caltha palustris*; see CALTHA. Pot-marigold is *Calendula officinalis*; see CALENDULA.

MARIPOSA LILY. Common name, along with Mariposa-tulip, for many species of CALOCHORTUS, attractive bulbous herbs with variously colored cup- or trumpet-shaped flowers, native to western North America.

MARJORAM. Common name for flavorings derived from various species of ORIGANUM. Sweet marjoram is *O. majorana*.

MARKER CROPPING. The practice of sowing quick-sprouting seed (especially of forcing radish varieties) in the same rows and at the same time with seed of plants that germinate slowly or whose seedlings are hard to see. The "marker" seed leaves appear in a few days.

MARROW. Also called vegetable marrow, various types of *Cucurbita pepo* (bush squash) are popular in Europe but less known in North America despite their easy culture and culinary use. As a summer squash, they are high-quality vegetables, easily prepared for the table with a minimum of waste. The fruits are not scalloped, watered, or irregular like many other varieties, but are oblong, uniform, thicker fleshed, and much heavier when ready for use. While often served boiled like summer squash, they are especially good when cut in slices and fried like eggplant. For culture, see SQUASH.

MARRUBIUM (mah ROO bee um). A genus of herbs in the Lamiaceae (Mint Family). *M. vulgare* (horehound, hoarhound) is an aromatic perennial with woolly white foliage and whitish flowers. Its chief use is for flavoring candies and lozenges to be used for throat afflictions. The plant is hardy to Zone 3 and thrives in any dry soil. Often spreading as a weed, seeds may be distributed by the hooked teeth on the calyx catching onto fur or clothing.

Marrubium vulgare

MARSH-MARIGOLD. Common name for *Caltha palustris*, a moisture-loving herb whose flowers have showy white, pink, or yellow sepals; see CALTHA.

MARSILEA (mahr SIL ee ah). A widely distributed genus of about 65 aquatic ferns, commonly known as pepperwort, water fern, or water-clover. Plants are distinguished by floating leaves that resemble four-leaf clovers. They float in deep water, but the stipes stand erect in shallow areas. The slender, creeping rhizomes root in bottom mud. Hardy to Zone 7, they reproduce by means of spores contained in sporocarps, specialized organs near the base of the stipes. They can be grown in containers of water, aquariums, even in tubs of wet soil.

PRINCIPAL SPECIES

M. drummondii, from Australia, has leaflets covered with whitish hairs and is commonly cultivated in greenhouses. It thrives in pots of rich soil kept in water-filled saucers.

M. macropoda (water-clover) has upper stipes and pinnae covered with long golden hairs. It is native to Texas.

M. quadrifolia is a European native that grows wild in the eastern states, especially in New England. It makes an attractive water cover, but if not controlled it is likely to become a nuisance.

MASDEVALLIA (maz duh VAL ee uh). A genus of 300 small to medium-sized epiphytic or terrestrial orchids native to Mexico, Central America, and northern South America. These plants have no pseudobulbs but grow in dense clusters with a single oval leaf on each stem.

The flowers are among the most unusual of all orchids. Pendulous or erect inflorescences bear one to several, often brightly colored flowers. The basally united sepals are the showiest parts of the flowers; the free part spreads to form long tails. The petals are inconspicuous, and the lip is small. Colors are combinations of red, purple, and white.

The plants do well in pots with a well-drained, porous compost. Day and night temperatures should not vary more than 20°, with minimum temperatures of 50–55°F. These plants thrive in moist, shady, cool conditions and should never dry out. The type species is *M. uniflora*.

MASK FLOWER. Common name for ALONSOA, a genus of orange- or red-flowered tropical herbs often grown as annuals.

MASSACHUSETTS FERN. Common name for *Thelypteris simulata*, a moisture-loving fern with lance-shaped fronds, found mostly in New England; see THELYPTERIS.

MATRICARIA (mat ri KAY ree ah). A genus of rather weedy, mostly annual herbs belonging to the Asteraceae (Aster Family) and commonly known as matricary or German-chamomile. They have finely cut foliage, often disagreeably scented, and small flower heads with yellow disk florets and sometimes white rays. A few of the species are grown in the border,

Matricaria recutita

others in old-fashioned herb gardens for medicinal purposes. They grow readily to 2 ft. or less in any good garden soil. The perennials are propagated by seed and division; the annuals and biennials can be grown from seed sown where the plants are to stand.

M. aurea is a small annual with dull yellow flowers.

M. recutita (wild-chamomile, sweet false chamomile), formerly listed as *M. chamomilla*, is a hardy, branching annual with sweet-scented foliage and daisylike flowers to 1 in. across. It is often used for making medicinal tea.

MATRIMONY-VINE. Common name for LYCIUM, a genus of clambering shrubs with inconspicuous flowers and brightly colored berries.

MATTEUCCIA (mah TOO see ah). A genus of ferns that includes two species of similar appearance and cultural needs, commonly known as ostrich ferns.

M. orientalis is distinct in that it only grows 1–3 ft. and its blades do not taper at the base.

M. struthiopteris, also listed as *M. pensylvanica*, is a tall and vigorous fern found growing in shaded, sandy swamps in the northeastern states. It often reaches 5 ft. in the wild but is seldom taller than 3–4 ft. in the garden. It is a beautiful subject for moist situations; it will also do well, but not grow as large, in drier environments. The sterile fronds are broad, tapering below, and palmlike. The fertile fronds, which appear in July, resemble ostrich plumes, though shorter, stiff, and with pinnae rolled back to protect the sporangia. It prefers moist soil, through which the stolons travel and send up new plants at intervals.

MATTHIOLA (ma THĪ oh lah). A genus of annuals and perennials, named for the Italian botanist Matthioli, belonging to the Brassicaceae (Mustard Family), and commonly known as stock. Two species with many cultivars are grown for ornament in the garden or greenhouse, both bearing colorful flowers in terminal clusters.

Culture varies with the species or variety. Plants are subject to white maggots, which destroy the roots if watering is not done carefully. In the early stages, watering should be done with a fine spray used in the morning if weather is cold or at night when warm. Early spraying with water helps to check the flea beetle, which sometimes eats the leaves of young plants. Later, only the soil should be watered and care taken to keep moisture off the foliage. Stocks may also suffer from bacterial blight, mosaic, or stem rot. In all cases diseased plants should be removed immediately.

M. incana (queen or Brampton stock) is a perennial or biennial grown for late summer and autumn blossom in the garden or greenhouse. A sturdy, erect plant 1–2½ ft. tall, it bears flowers usually double and in a wide range of colors, with purples and pinks predominating. It should be grown from seed sown in late spring in the open for bloom about fifteen months later. When the seedlings are 2 in. high, they should go into separate pots to be set in a frame for protection from rainy or cold weather. The following spring they can be transplanted to the spot where they are to bloom. For greenhouse culture, they can be started in flats in late summer, taken inside in the fall, and the earliest brought into bloom in early spring. Plants do best in moist, cool conditions. The many subspecies have variable flower color and form. Var. *annua* (ten-weeks or intermediate stock), the most popular type and usually grown as an annual, is quick to come into bloom (about ten weeks from seed-sowing), producing fragrant flowers ranging from white through lilac to crimson and borne on handsome spikes, the double flowers forming rosettes.

M. longipetala var. *bicornis* (evening or Grecian stock) is a hardy, straggling, branchy annual, that grows to 15 in. high and is cultivated for its small, sweet-scented, lilac blossoms, which are inconspicuous by day, but open toward evening or after a shower. The blooming period is from midsummer to early fall. Plants are grown from seed sown indoors or outdoors. The mature seedpods bear two conspicuous horns.

MAXILLARIA (mak sil AIR ee uh). A genus of about 300 species of epiphytic or lithophytic orchids from the American tropics and subtropics. Plants have tufted (caespitose) habit or have pseudobulbs with an elongated rhizome.

The flowers are often small and inconspicuous, while some are larger, showy, in shades of white, yellow, brown, and dull crimson. Most produce several to many flowers, varying in size from minuscule to 6 in. across. The three sepals are alike in size and color; the dorsal sepal is perpendicular to the other two. Petals are much smaller than the sepals and are the same color. The three-lobed lip is attached to the column, and the side lobes nearly enclose the column.

Hardy to Zone 9 with frost protection, the plants require warm, moist conditions (minimum winter temperatures of 60–65°F) and bright light (to 3000 footcandles). They are best planted in baskets of porous, well-drained medium or mounted on slabs of cork or tree fern bark.

M. ramosa is the type species. *M. tenuifolia* has the fragrance of coconut custard.

MAYAPPLE. Common name for *Podophyllum peltatum*, a shade-loving herb with conspicuous leaves and insipid fruits; see PODOPHYLLUM.

MAYFLOWER. Common name for *Epigaea repens*, an attractive, spring-blooming, creeping evergreen; see EPIGAEA.

MAYTENUS (may TEN us). A genus of evergreen shrubs and trees with leathery leaves, formerly listed as *Gymnosporia*, belonging to the Celastraceae (Stafftree Family). The two species most frequently seen are *M. cassinoides*, an erect shrub with small white flowers from the Canary Islands; and *M. serratus*, a spiny shrub from Abyssinia. They are propagated by seed or cuttings.

MAZUS (MAY zus). A genus of hardy, low, creeping herbs belonging to the Scrophulariaceae (Figwort Family) and native from Asia to Australia. Most species bear blue or white flowers in terminal, nonsymmetrical racemes. They have toothed or cut leaves that form rosettes and are grown as ground covers due to their mat-forming habit and simple culture. Propagation is by seed or division.

PRINCIPAL SPECIES

M. japonicus bears ¾–in. blue flowers, with brown-spotted lower lips, on stems up to 1 ft. tall.

M. pumilio is like *M. reptans* but has larger leaves and smaller flowers.

M. reptans, most frequently used, has small, coarsely toothed, bright green leaves and bluish purple or white, mimulus-like flowers. It is quite hardy and, like *M. pumilio*, spreads so rapidly in the rock garden that it is best confined to rock crevices and steps.

MEADOW-BEAUTY. A common name for RHEXIA, a genus of low-growing perennial herbs, usually with purple flowers.

MEADOW-FOAM. Common name for *Limnanthes douglasii*, an annual herb with bright flowers, native in damp western meadows; see LIMNANTHES.

MEADOW-RUE. Common name for THALICTRUM, a genus of perennials related to buttercups, useful for border and wild-garden planting.

MEADOWSWEET. Common name for species of SPIRAEA, especially *S. alba*, a deciduous shrub with white flowers. The name is sometimes applied to FILIPENDULA, a genus of hardy perennial herbs.

MEALYBUG. These white, cottony-looking insects of the Pseudococcidae attack many ornamental and greenhouse plants and all citrus species. Of worldwide distribution, they belong to the same family as SCALE INSECTS. They are of two types: the citrus or short-tailed mealybugs, which produce living young; and the long-tailed mealybugs, which have long, waxy processes resembling tails and reproduce by eggs. These are carried by the females in cottony, waxy sacs

found chiefly at the axils of branching stems or leaves of infested plants. In greenhouses, the eggs hatch in about ten days, producing flattened, oval, smooth-bodied, light yellow, six-legged bugs that crawl over the plants, sucking the sap and soon beginning to secrete the white waxy covering.

Mealybug

The young females, called nymphs, go through three instars in two to three weeks, then spend four days as young adults and four more as pregravid adult females. Finally, they have fourteen more days as egg-laying adults. The eggs are deposited 300 to 600 in cottony, waxy sacs on the undersides of leaves, in the forks of branching twigs or other protected places, and hatch in ten to fourteen days. The young start extruding the white waxy covering that makes mealybugs look fluffy. The males develop wings, but the females do not. The males, however, never feed; their only function is to fertilize females.

Mealybugs are especially troublesome on soft-stemmed plants. They can be numerous on succulents, coleus, fuchsia, cactus, croton, ferns, heliotrope, geranium, gardenia, and begonia. They also attack orchids, poinsettias, dracaena, and chrysanthemums. Since they extrude honeydew, they attract ants as well as the sooty mold that grows on honeydew. Citrus plants have been particular victims of mealybugs, but use of parasites such as the ladybug, *Cryptolaemus montrouzieri*, and the effective *Tetracnemus pretiosus* have saved millions of dollars for California orchardists.

Biological control can also be provided by LACEWING insects, which will work at cooler temperatures than some other control parasites or predators. Effective sprays include insecticidal soap, summer white oil in emulsion, and sulfur solutions with or without soap flakes. PYRETHRUM and ROTENONE can also be tried. Test leaves of delicate plants before using to see whether the mixtures are likely to burn the leaves. See INSECT CONTROL; SPRAYING.

MECONOPSIS (mek ahn AHP sis). A genus of annual, biennial, and perennial herbs belonging to the Papaveraceae (Poppy Family) and commonly known as Asiatic poppy. They have yellow juice and yellow, reddish, or blue four-petaled flowers borne singly or in clusters. An attractive group of plants for the border or rock garden, they thrive outdoors only in the Pacific Northwest or where the summers are cool and humid and winters are mild. They should be planted in a rich, warm, sandy loam in a sheltered, half-shaded location. The perennials are

Meconopsis cambrica

propagated by seed or division of the roots; and the annual and biennial species, by seed started early under glass. The annuals are planted after danger of frost is over. Biennials and perennial seedlings are carried over the summer in pots and planted out in the fall.

PRINCIPAL SPECIES

M. betonicifolia, a perennial growing to 6 ft., has bluish violet flowers to 2 in. across in flat-topped clusters. Var. *baileyi* is considered one of the finest blue flowers in cultivation but is difficult to grow in the eastern states. It should be sheltered from the intense heat and drying winds of summer and given applications of liquid manure at the flowering season.

M. cambrica (Welsh poppy) is a perennial that grows to 1½ ft. and has large, solitary, pale yellow flowers and finely cut leaves with a silvery bloom beneath. Cv. 'Frances Perry', with scarlet flowers, is a relatively recent introduction. Hardy to Zone 6.

M. grandis grows to 2 ft. and bears 4–5 in. blue and violet flowers on erect 2-ft. stems.

M. heterophylla (wind or flaming poppy) is now listed as *Stylomecon heterophylla*; see STYLOMECON.

M. horridula grows 3–4 ft. and has 2-in. blue, red, or white flowers on clustered, hairy stems.

M. integrifolia (Chinese yellow poppy) is a biennial that grows 1½–3 ft. It has long, narrow leaves and clusters of yellow flowers, each 6 in. across. Unlike those of other species, these flowers have five to ten petals.

M. napaulensis (satin poppy), formerly listed as *M. wallichii*, is a perennial that grows to 6 ft. and forms a mound of finely cut silvery foliage bearing pale blue flowers to 2 in. across.

M. regia, growing 3–4 ft., sends up large spikes of yellow, poppylike flowers. The unique prostrate leaves are silver or gold, arranged in dense rosettes.

M. superba grows to 3 ft. and produces 2–3 ft. stems of creamy white flowers in its second year of growth. The leaves are clothed in grayish hairs.

M. villosa, growing to 2 ft., is a spring-blooming species with nodding yellow flowers above tawny gold foliage.

MEDEOLA (med ee OH lah) **virginiana.** A perennial herb with an edible tuberous root, belonging to the Liliaceae (Lily Family), commonly known as cucumber-root. It grows naturally in moist soils from Nova Scotia to Minnesota southward and has slender stems growing to 3 ft. Leaves are borne in two whorls, the lower with five to nine leaves up to 5 in. long and the upper one with three to five smaller leaves. The flat clusters of small, greenish yellow flowers appear in the upper leaf whorl in early summer and are followed by dark purple berries.

MEDICAGO (me di KAY goh). A genus of leguminous herbs and some shrubs, commmonly called medic, bearing small, pealike flowers in heads or racemes followed by twisted leguminous fruits. Some species are grown for ornament, but the most important, *M. sativa* (alfalfa, lucerne), is a valuable forage and hay crop, especially on irrigated land. In orchards it is sometimes grown as a cover crop. The young sprouts are a popular salad garnish; see SPROUTS.

MEDINILLA (me di NIL ah). A genus of shrubby tropical plants with attractive flowers and foliage, including some striking subjects for the warm greenhouse. They are not suited to strong sunlight but will not flower well in heavy shade either. Good fibrous loam with sharp sand suits them well, and firm potting is necessary to produce good flowering wood. Propagation is by cuttings, best rooted singly in peat and sand.

PRINCIPAL SPECIES

M. magnifica has handsome, leathery, evergreen leaves and pendulous panicles of deep pink or reddish flowers with showy rose-pink bracts.

M. teysmannii bears upright panicles of rose-pink flowers without bracts.

M. venosa has 1-in. pink flowers and 3–6 in. oblong leaves on reddish brown stems.

MELALEUCA (mel ah LOO kah). A genus of shrubs or trees of Australia, belonging to the Myrtaceae (Myrtle Family), and commonly known as bottle-brush. They have attractive, somewhat leathery leaves and dense spikes or heads of conspicuous flowers. Several species are grown in Zones 10–11; however, one has become a major pest. They are well able to withstand drought.

PRINCIPAL SPECIES

M. armillaris is a graceful shrub or small tree with slender, drooping branches; soft, slender, linear leaves; and round spikes of white flowers.

M. ericifolia has feathery, heathlike foliage and spikes of yellowish white flowers.

M. hypercifolia has bright green leaves and dense spikes of brilliant red flowers.

M. quinquenervia (cajeput or punk tree) sometimes grows to 80 ft. and is well able to withstand salt water and wind. Its thick, spongy bark peels in thin layers and is used for many purposes. The flowers are creamy white. This species has become a major pest tree in south Florida, where it has invaded thousands of acres of the Everglades; because it crowds out native vegetation, its planting is now prohibited there.

M. thymifolia is a dwarf species with thymelike leaves and red flowers.

MELIA (me LEE ah). A genus of deciduous or evergreen trees and shrubs native in tropical Asia and Australia, belonging to the Meliaceae (Mahogany Family), and commonly known as bead tree. The species *M. azedarach* has many common names, including chinaberry and pride-of-India. Popular for shade and ornament, it has become widely distributed throughout Zones 9–11 and will tolerate a few degrees of frost. Often a deciduous tree, it grows to 50 ft. and has graceful pinnate foliage. The fragrant, lilac flowers are borne in loose panicles. The oval, yellow fruits hang for a long time, and in some countries the seeds are threaded as beads. Var. *umbraculiformis* (Texas umbrella tree) grows with an umbrella-like effect. Var. *floribunda* is a very floriferous form, flowering when small.

MELIACEAE (mel ee AY see ee). The Meliaceae (Mahogany Family), a group of tropical hardwood trees and shrubs. Principal cultivated genera include SWIETENIA, commonly known as mahogany; CEDRELA and MELIA, popular for shade and ornament.

MELIANTHUS (mel ee ANTH us). A genus of strongly scented, evergreen shrubs native to South Africa, belonging to the Sapindaceae (Soapberry Family), and commonly known as honeybush. They can be grown outdoors only in Zones 10–11.

M. major, which grows to 10 ft. in California, has gray compound leaves 1 ft. or more long, with a winged stem and stipules united at the base to form a leafy collar. The sweetly scented, reddish brown flowers are borne in racemes 1 ft. long.

M. minor has smaller leaves with stipules not united and upright racemes of dull red flowers.

MELICOCCAS (me li KOH kus) **bijuga.** A tropical American tree commonly known as mamoncillo, Spanish-lime, or genip; it is grown for its juicy, edible fruits, which are smaller than those of *Genipa americana*, an unrelated tropical tree also called genip.

MELILOTUS (mel i LOH tus). Commonly known as sweet-clover or melilot, this genus of hardy, annual and perennial, leguminous herbs of the Fabaceae (Bean Family) are native to Asia and the Mediterannean region, where they have long been prized as forage crops. Naturalized in the United States, they are generally regarded as weeds or, at best, valuable bee plants, though improved strains are being increasingly grown as a hay, green forage, and pasture crop.

MELISSA (mel LIS ah) **officinalis.** An aromatic perennial herb belonging to the Lamiaceae (Mint Family) and commonly known as common-, lemon-, bee-, or sweet-balm. It is grown in the home herb garden for seasoning and is also used in cosmetics, liqueurs, and medicine. It grows to 2 ft. and has small, two-lipped flowers in late summer. The leaves have a decided lemon odor and flavor. Of European origin, it is widely naturalized in North America. Hardy in Zones 4–9, it is easily propagated by seed or division. There is also an attractive, golden, variegated-leaf form.

Melissa officinalis

MELON. Common name for the fruits and plants of several Asiatic or African annual herbs of the species *Cucumis melo*. One or more kinds can be grown in most of the United States and warmer regions of Canada as outdoor crops; or, in colder areas, they do well in hotbeds and protected coldframes. The honeydew and casaba varieties are grown commercially in warm regions but require too long a season to be successful in the North. While the name "cantaloupe" is popularly used as a synonym for muskmelon, it correctly refers to a variety rarely if at all grown in North America.

WATERMELON is also a cucurbit but belongs to a different genus, *Citrullus lanatus* or *C. vulgaris*.

One of its varieties (*citroides*) is called citron or preserving melon. The latter name is also applied to a plant of yet another cucurbitus genus, *Benincasa hispida*.

CULTURE

Melons thrive best in highly fertile, light, sandy loams, warm weather, and sunny locations. Tender annuals, melons require a growth season of at least 100 frost-free days. They "sulk" or become diseased in cold and damp weather and are easily killed by frost. With adequate protection in spring and fall, they can be successful in home gardens but must be grown rapidly.

Since melons are difficult to transplant, seed is generally sown right in the garden. For early fruiting and to overcome the handicap of a short season, plants can be started indoors. Be sure to harden the plants off well before setting them out. When the weather has settled, either sow a dozen seeds or set two to four plants in each hill. Space the hills 5' x 5' or 4' x 6' apart. If seed is sown, destroy all but the best two to four plants in each hill when they are well started.

If the soil is not naturally rich, thoroughly mix a large forkful of well-decayed manure or a pound of high-grade complete fertilizer in each hill before sowing or transplanting. Cultivate the soil weekly, shallow near the plants, deeper farther away.

Melon plants can be either monoecious (with unisexual flowers) or dioecious (with both male and female flowers). Since only the females bear fruit, using pollen from the males, it is always advisable to grow a number of plants close enough together so that they can be pollinated.

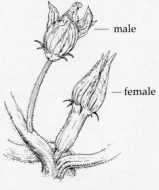

Melon flowers

When the plants begin to "run," lay the vines lengthwise along the rows to permit continued tillage and facilitate harvesting.

Harvesting. Market melons are usually disappointing because they are gathered too immature and are transported under refrigeration, thus failing to develop their natural flavor. When allowed to ripen fully on the vine, however, the flavor can also be impaired. An experienced eye recognizes melons that are just ready for picking. The way to learn these signs is to examine the stem ends of the fruit. Until cracks appear around the stem union, the fruit is too immature to gather. When cracks show all around the stem, they are ready to be harvested. There are also differences in color, netting, and a sort of glisten that one comes to recognize. After gathering, keep the fruit in a warm place one or two days before using it.

Enemies. Unless protected against insects, especially while young, melons may be killed by a wilt disease that these creatures carry from plant to plant. In fact, melons are subject to all the same diseases and insect pests as cucumbers and the other cucurbits. In addition, the melon worm is frequently injurious, especially in warmer regions. The adult is a white moth with brown bands along the wing margins; the caterpillar is mottled greenish yellow, about 1 in. long. Control by planting some squashes ahead of melons to serve as a trap crop; using insecticidal sprays or dusts; and destroying vines and waste fruits as soon as the crop is harvested.

MENISPERMIACEAE (men is per MAY see ee). The Moonseed Family, a largely tropical group of herbaceous or woody climbing vines. Principal genera include *Menispermum* and *Cocculus*.

MENISPERMUM (me ni SPERM um). A genus of hardy, woody, climbing vines commonly known as moonseed. There are two species, one native in North America and the other in Asia, but both are hardy in Zones 4–8 and are suitable for draping fences, arbors, and trellises. Propagation is by seed and cuttings of ripened wood.

M. canadense is found in rich lowlands from Quebec to Georgia. It grows to 10 ft. or more and has large, heart-shaped, lobed leaves; small,

greenish yellow flowers; and bunches of black berries like tiny grapes. These contain a flattened, crescent-shaped stone, from which the common name is derived. *M. dauricum*, from Asia, is very similar, but it is smaller and has more shield-shaped leaves and smaller fruiting clusters.

MENTHA (MEN thah). A genus of herbs of the Lamiaceae (Mint Family), having aromatic leaves and inconspicuous flowers and readily identified by their aroma and square stems. They are generally cultivated for their essential oils or, in the herb garden, for their leaves. They grow easily in any good garden soil in a moist location with some sun.

Mentha pulegium

Mints are easily raised by runners, but be sure to cut off at least a 2-in. piece of root with at least one node on each piece. Propagation can also be done by division or cuttings. A few good varieties can be raised from seed; *M. pulegium* (pennyroyal) and *M. requienii* are particularly desirable. In many parts of the eastern states, members of the Mint Family have escaped from old gardens and become naturalized.

The classification of varieties of *Mentha* is difficult because they easily cross and hybridize. Even with the same variety, the flavor can vary depending on the soil and climate in which they are grown.

PRINCIPAL SPECIES

M. × *piperita* (peppermint) is a hybrid between *M. aquatica* and *M. spicata*. It grows to 3 ft. and has long spikes of lilac-pink flowers in autumn. Plants are extensively cultivated for the strong essential oil and make a popular tea. Var. *citrata* (bergamot mint), also listed as *M. citrata*, has a lemon scent when crushed. Hardy to Zone 3.

M. pulegium (European pennyroyal) can be propagated by seed or vegetatively by cutting off and replanting tiny pieces of the rooted stem. Easily grown in the herb garden if given winter protection of straw or leaves, it has small, oval leaves and bluish lavender flowers. The most common variety has a prostrate habit, though there is a rare upright variety.

M. requienii is a creeping species with minute, roundish leaves with a very strong peppermint scent and flowers that are bluish lavender in summer. It makes a good ground cover in shade or semishade and can be propagated from seed.

M. spicata (spearmint) grows to 2 ft. and has strongly aromatic leaves and purple or white flowers in whorls on a spike. Hardy to Zone 3.

M. suaveolens (apple mint), often listed as *M. rotundifolia*, grows to 2 ft. and has woolly gray-green leaves and pale pink flowers. It has a minty flavor for making mint sauce.

MENTZELIA (ment ZEE lee ah).

A genus of herbs or shrubs of western North America, usually with rough-textured foliage and barbed hairs, commonly known as blazing-star. They often have showy flowers of white, yellow, or orange.

M. laevicaulis, 3–5 ft. in height, has flowers of satiny yellow, 4–6 in. across, opening late in the day through early morning in summer; a biennial of hot, rocky slopes.

M. lindleyi is an annual that grows 1–2 ft. and has large, single, five-petaled, golden-yellow flowers with an orange base and a very satiny sheen surrounding a showy brush or cluster of stamens. A central flower stalk arises from a rosette of lobed gray leaves. Seed should be sown in a sunny, well-drained, poor soil.

Mentzelia lindleyi

MERRYBELLS.

Common name for UVULARIA, a genus of hardy perennials with drooping yellow flowers.

MERTENSIA (mur TEN see ah).

A genus of perennial herbs belonging to the Boraginaceae (Borage Family) and having delightful, blue, white, or purple bell-shaped blossoms in graceful nodding clusters. Hardy in Zones 3–9, they are suited to the informal border or for naturalizing in the wild garden. They are charming in combination with white flowers of *Trillium grandiflorum* and thrive in a half-shady location and soil abundantly supplied with humus. Since the foliage disappears entirely after the plants bloom, it is advisable to plant them among ferns, which will conceal the bare soil. Mertensias are propagated by seed and, with difficulty, by division.

PRINCIPAL SPECIES

M. ciliata (mountain-bluebell), a Rocky Mountain native, grows to 3 ft. and has a profusion of smooth, grayish green leaves and blue bell-shaped flowers produced from bright pink buds.

M. nutans, with lovely azure blooms in slender, graceful panicles, is found in the western states and is charming planted among evergreen ferns in a wild garden.

M. sibirica is an Asiatic form with long racemes of purplish or light blue flowers, sometimes varying to white.

Mertensia ciliata

M. virginica (Virginia-bluebells, Virginia-cowslip) is the most widely planted species. It grows to 2 ft. high and has smooth leaves and nodding flower clusters. The pink buds contrast delightfully with the drooping, blue flowers. Var. *rubra* has pink blossoms, and a pure white form is occasionally found.

Mertensia virginica

MESCAL BEAN. Common name for *Sophora secundiflora*, an evergreen shrub or tree with violet-blue flowers, native to the Southwest; see SOPHORA.

MESEMBRYANTHEMUM (mez em bree ANTH em um). Meaning "midday flowers," one of several succulent genera in the Aizoaceae (Carpetweed Family). Many of them have striking, glistening, icelike points on the foliage. The group, original-

Mesembryanthemum sp.

ly very large, has gradually been broken up by botanists, and so many species have been placed in other genera that few now go under the name *Mesembryanthemum* in botanical lists.

Mostly natives of hot, dry, barren portions of South Africa, the plants are tender in the North and do particularly well on the West Coast because of the dry climate. When grown in pots they should be given a light, dry, gritty soil and excellent drainage, care being taken to water them from below.

PRINCIPAL SPECIES

M. crystallinum (iceplant), sometimes listed as *Cryophytum crystallinum*, a South African species naturalized in southern California, is an annual, mat-forming mesemb that develops dense, succulent, icy looking papillae that make the plant look as if it were kept in a deep-freeze. It is the most commonly grown species and produces white to deep pink flowers.

M. deltoides has small, rose flowers of a satiny texture and toothed, triangular leaves misted with a gray bloom.

M. multiflorum is a white-flowered, rather woody plant with straight branches covered with three-angled, grayish green leaves.

M. speciosum is of shrubby growth to 2 ft. and has showy, scarlet blossoms and short, flattened leaves, glistening when young.

M. spectabile bears purple flowers on trailing woody stems covered with pointed, three-angled, grayish green leaves.

METROSIDEROS (me troh si DEE ros). A genus of trees and shrubs, sometimes climbing, and mostly native to New Zealand. They belong to the Myrtaceae (Myrtle Family) and are closely allied to CALLISTEMON (bottlebrush) from Australia, requiring the same culture.

PRINCIPAL SPECIES

M. excelsus (New Zealand Christmas tree) is a tree that grows to 70 ft. and has dark red flowers.

M. perforatus is a climber with leathery, shining leaves and white flowers. It grows to about 5 ft. in pots, but in its native forest it climbs to the tops of the tallest trees.

M. tremuloides is a small tree of Hawaii with narrow, shining leaves and bright red flowers.

MEXICAN BEAN BEETLE. *Epilachna varivestis*, an orangy tan beetle with eight black spots on each wing cover, is very destructive on bean plants from the time the first true leaves appear. The beetles feed for a week or so, then lay yellow eggs, which develop into spiny, yellow larvae in another week. The larvae also eat the bean plants and then

Mexican bean beetle

pupate after three to five weeks. There can be two or more generations per summer.

Fall plowing helps to control these beetles, and interplanting with garlic, marigolds, potatoes, radishes, and turnips may also help. Sprays from garlic, hot pepper, and onion will deter feeding. Lime and soap, pyrethrum, and rotenone have also been useful. Be sure not to use rotenone until after the bees have returned to the hive at dusk. The little parasitic wasp *Pediobius foveo-latus* is also recommended, as is hand-picking the eggs and adult beetles. Larvae can be treated with *Bacillus thuringiensis* (Bt). See also INSECT CONTROL; BEETLES.

MEXICAN-ORANGE. Common name for *Choisya ternata*, a tropical evergreen shrub with flowers resembling orange blossoms; see CHOISYA.

MEXICAN-STAR. Common name for *Milla biflora*, a bulbous herb of the Liliaceae (Lily Family), often incorrectly listed as *Bessera elegans*; see MILLA.

MEXICAN-SUNFLOWER. Common name for TITHONIA, a genus of herbs or shrubs whose brilliant flowers resemble sunflowers, grown in warm regions and in greenhouses.

MICE. Of the many species found in the United States, only a few have any significant economic impact on crop destruction. Mice live and hide either on or just below the surface of the ground in unsightly runways made by themselves or by moles and gophers. They can cause damage to grass roots, bulbs, and the tender bark and young roots of trees and shrubs.

The injury to trees and shrubs consists not only of gnawing of the bark, which may girdle and kill the plant, but also in leaving open wounds through which bacteria and spores of fungi can gain entrance and cause disease. These small animals sometimes carry fungus spores on their feet and thus both injure and inoculate a tree at the same time. Unfortunately, such pernicious activity is ordinarily carried on beneath the surface of either snow or earth, and before it is discovered, the damage has usually gone too far to be remedied. Gardens should be inspected regularly for damage.

CONTROLS

Valuable trees, especially newly planted fruit trees, can be protected by wrappings or guards of wire, wood veneer, or plastic. Natural agents that hold the meadow mouse in check are hawks, owls, snakes, skunks, and—near ponds—the bullfrog. Catnip attracts cats, which control mice. Owls, encouraged by nest boxes, find mice to be tasty treats. Weasels and snakes are other predators.

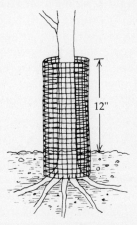

Mouse tree guard

Susceptible bulbs can be planted in wire cages made with a mesh fine enough so the pest cannot get through (up to ½ in.). Sometimes a whole bed is lined with such barriers. Mice do not like daffodils, hyacinths, scilla, or grape-hyacinths, so these can be planted if you lose other bulbs. When straw and similar materials are used for protecting roses and other shrubs it should not be put on until the ground has frozen so that mice will not nest in it. Mice and chipmunks can be discouraged by placing small snap-back traps in the runways, but these should be placed in covered runways to prevent catching birds.

Nut-tree leaves, sassafras, camphor, spurge, onion, mint, or dog fennel will deter mice. Traps and jiggling contraptions that vibrate the soil can also be used against them. Pieces of lava rocks soaked in garlic are effective as repellents, and garlic sprays put into runways will repel most rodents. Castor beans (*Ricinus communis*) and emulsions of castor oil and water are also effective; of course the beans should be buried where children and domestic animals cannot get them.

MICHAELMAS DAISY. Common name for many leafy fall-blooming forms of ASTER.

MICHELIA (mī KEE lee ah). A genus of Asiatic trees or shrubs belonging to the Magnoliaceae (Magnolia Family). The best known in cultivation is *M. figo* (banana shrub), which has also been listed as *M. fuscata* or *Magnolia fuscata*. Hardy to Zone 8, it is a popular evergreen shrub in the southern states where it grows to about 15 ft. The young growth is covered with soft, brown hairs, but later the leaves are smooth. The brownish purple flowers, an inch or more across, produced from late spring to early summer, emit a strong banana fragrance. Propagation is sometimes from seed but mostly by cuttings of ripened wood, under glass.

MICONIA (mī KOH nee ah) **calvescens.** A woody, tropical American plant, formerly listed as *M. magnifica*, and one of the most striking foliage plants. The broad, wavy-margined leaves 2 ft. or longer are lustrous green above and reddish bronze beneath with prominent, light-colored veins. Sometimes grown in the warm greenhouse, the plant needs good fibrous loam with old manure or leaf mold, plenty of water, and protection from direct sunlight. Propagation is by cuttings.

MICROGRAMMA (mīk roh GRAM ah). A generic name used for many species of POLYPODIUM.

MICROMERIA (mīk roh MEE ree uh). A genus of perennial herbs of the Lamiaceae (Mint Family), commonly known as savory. They have small leaves and tiny, two-lipped flowers. Hardy to Zone 7, they can be grown in the rock garden and are propagated by seed or cuttings. *M. piperella*, from southern Europe, is semishrubby in growth and bears small, rosy purple flowers in clusters. *M. chamissonis* (yerba buena) is now listed in the genus SATUREJA.

MICROPROPAGATION. Another name for TISSUE CULTURE.

MIDGE. The midge is a small fly, sometimes called a gnat. The larvae feed inside leaves and flowers, causing them to distort. They pupate in warty growths, called galls, on leaves, stems, and flower buds. Any such growths should be picked off and burned or destroyed. One kind of midge larvae, the APHID MIDGE or Aphidoletes, is beneficial to gardeners, but since these pupate in cocoons on the ground, they will not be harmed by destroying the galls formed by other midges.

Midge gall

MIDRIB. The large central vein of a leaf, usually existing as a ridgelike extension of the petiole; or a similar main ridge on any leaflike part.

MIGNONETTE. Common name for RESEDA, a genus of annual herbs valued as bee plants. Mignonette vine is *Anredera cordifolia*, a tropical vine; see ANREDERA. Mignonette tree is *Lawsonia inermis*, a tropical tree that yields henna dye; see LAWSONIA.

MILDEW. The common name for certain types of fungi and for the diseases they cause. There are two groups: the powdery mildews (ascomycetes) and the downy mildews (phycomycetes); see FUNGUS. The chief characteristic of the latter is the tufts or downy masses of mycelium or white vegetative tissue, usually on the undersurface of leaves. DOWNY MILDEW is probably the most important group.

The powdery mildews live for the most part on the surface of host plants, making a cobwebby growth of MYCELIUM, which assumes a white powdery appearance with the formation of chains of minute spores (conidia). From the surface mycelium, special rootlike sucking organs (haustoria) penetrate the cells of the host plant and there obtain food. Small, round, black bodies (perithecia) are scattered through the white mycelial growth.

Mildew is more prevalent in cloudy, humid weather and on plants grown in shade. The young shoots and buds may be curled and distorted and the entire plant may be somewhat dwarfed. Roses, phlox, and lilacs are especially subject to attack, but powdery mildews can be readily held in check by dusting plants with fine sulfur or another appropriate FUNGICIDE recommended for your area and host plant.

MILFOIL. Common name for ACHILLEA, a genus of hardy herbs. Water-milfoil is *Miriophyllum*.

MILKY SPORE DISEASE. See BACILLUS POPILLIAE.

MILK-THISTLE. Common name for *Silybum marianum*, an annual or biennial thistlelike herb with large, purplish flower heads; see SILYBUM.

MILKWEED. Common name for ASCLEPIAS, a genus of perennial herbs with milky juice. The Milkweed Family is ASCLEPIADACEAE.

MILLA (MIL ah). A bulbous herb of the Liliaceae (Lily Family) often incorrectly referred to as *Bessera elegans*, native to the Southwest, and commonly known as Mexican-star. Attractive in border plantings, it sends up a stalk 18 in. tall bearing one to five star-shaped, waxy blossoms nearly 3 in. across. Flowers are fragrant and will last for many days. Plants are hardy to Zone 9. In cooler regions, the small bulbs should be planted in the spring; then in late summer, after the foliage has matured, they should be taken up and stored in a frost-proof place until the following year. *Milla* can also be grown indoors, placing the BULBS in containers.

MILLET. Common name for certain grasses used for hay or forage. See PANICUM; PENNISETUM.

MILTONIA (mil TOH nee uh). A genus of 20 species of epiphytic orchids native to Costa Rica, Panama, southeastern Brazil, and Paraguay. Short, compressed pseudobulbs bear two narrow, thin leaves.

The inflorescences rise from the base of the pseudobulb with one to several medium-sized flowers on scapes. The flowers are showy and long-lasting, in shades from straw-color, yellow-green to chestnut-brown and rose-purple. Shapes vary widely; some are open and star shaped, and others have wide-spreading lips with narrow petals and sepals.

There are two divisions in the genus: a flat, pansy type (Colombian) and one resembling *Odontoglossum* (Brazilian type), with a more open shape. The pansy types have been separated into a newer genus, MILTONIOPSIS. Flowers of this group have lips with a distinctive waterfall-like pattern surmounted by a crest at the apex. Many hybrids have been made by breeding both types with allied genera such as *Oncidium*, *Brassia*, *Aspasia*, and *Odontoglossum*. Flowers of these man-made hybrids are spectacular and often bizarre.

Colombian types need constant cool temperatures in the range of 50–70°F. The Brazilian ones tolerate warmer temperatures (withstanding minimum winter temperatures of 60°F) and can be grown with *Cattleya*, being given a little less light. Those with clustered pseudobulbs do best potted in a porous, well-drained medium; those with creeping rhizomes do best in baskets in a similar medium. All require abundant water and bright filtered light while growing, less water when pseudobulbs attain their growth.

Type species are *Miltonia spectabilis* and *Miltoniopsis vexillaria*.

MILTONIOPSIS (mil toh nee AHP sis). A genus of five species of epiphytic or lithophytic plants formerly included in the genus MILTONIA, native to Costa Rica, Panama, and the northern Andes in South America. Clustered, flattened pseudobulbs are topped by several leaf-bearing sheaths. Flowers are large, flat, and often marked with exotic patterns or blotches and streaks. Base colors are white, pink, or red-purple. The broad lip is distinguished by a rigid callus and a waterfall-like pattern in a color contrasting with the base. Plants prefer small pots with a porous, well-drained compost in a shady, moist location. They require copious watering during growth and withstand a minimum winter temperature of 55°F. The type species is *M. vexillaria*.

MIMOSA (mi MOH sah). A genus of shrubby or herbaceous plants native mostly in the tropical Americas, belonging to the Fabaceae (Bean Family). Most of them are spiny and have attractive, feathery leaves, which in some species are very sensitive. Some of the shrubby kinds are planted for ornament in warm regions. Mimosas thrive under the same treatment as ACACIA; in fact, "mimosa" is the name used by florists for blooms of some *Acacia* species, particularly *A. dealbata*.

M. pudica (sensitive or humble plant), a perennial in the tropics, is often grown as an annual in the flower garden or under glass and is easily started from seed. It has a spiny stem, long-stemmed leaves cut into many leaflets, and round lavender-colored flower heads. The chief interest lies in the extremely sensitive leaves, which recoil at the slightest touch, the leaflets folding together and the leaf stalk drooping. After a time, they assume their original form. Frequently grown as a curiosity, it is treated as an annual in cool climates, seed being sown in ordinary garden soil in full sunshine. Grown in the house or cool greenhouse as a potted plant, it is easily propagated by cuttings rooted in sandy soil.

MIMULUS (MIM yoo lus). A genus of tender annual or perennial herbs or shrubs, sometimes listed under the genus *Diplacus*, belonging to the Scrophulariaceae (Figwort Family), and commonly known as monkey flower. The flowers, which have been compared to a grotesque face, are large, spotted, oddly shaped, and two-lipped in shades of brilliant yellow, flesh, crimson, maroon, or white.

Mostly hardy in Zones 5–9 and native to the Pacific Coast, they are excellent for containers, hanging baskets, and for house or greenhouse culture. Several species can be grown successfully in a wildflower garden or border garden. They should have some shade, protection from wind,

and plenty of water, though the semishrubby species do well in the sun.

Plants can be grown from cuttings and divisions. More often they are propagated from seed sown from winter to spring in loam, leaf mold, and sand and kept in a temperature of 60°F until they germinate. They will bloom the first year.

PRINCIPAL SPECIES

M. aurantiacus (bush mimulus) is a shrubby plant that grows to 4 ft. and has apricot or yellow flowers.

M. cardinalis grows 1–3 ft. and has scarlet flowers and prefers rich, moist soil.

M. cupreus (Mexican-star) is an annual that grows to 6–9 in. and has yellow flowers that bloom in summer, turning shades of copper as they mature. Cv. 'Red Emperor' has flowers of an especially showy red.

M. guttatus grows to 2 ft. and has yellow flowers. It is easily transplanted or started from seed. Hardy to Zone 9.

M. x *hybridus* (monkey flower), also listed as *M. tigrinus*, is a hybrid that grows 1 ft. tall and produces flowers in many colors made more striking by stripes and spots.

M. lewisii grows to 2½ ft. and has dark red blooms and sticky, gray-green leaves. It needs less moisture than most species.

M. longiflorus grows 2–3 ft. and has 3-in. cream to salmon-pink blooms and shiny foliage with silvery new shoots. It cannot withstand severe winters.

M. luteus, a prostrate perennial, bears yellow flowers spotted with red or purple and is the source of most garden varieties.

M. moschatus (musk plant) is a low, spreading perennial with pale yellow, brown-spotted flowers, usually grown for the musklike fragrance of its leaves.

M. nanus grows only 2–6 in. high and has many ¾-in. purple flowers with patches of white. It is not especially hardy but can be grown successfully in greenhouse pots.

M. ringens (Allegheny monkey flower) is a perennial wildflower common in the eastern states. It grows to 4 ft. and bears toothed, oval leaves and narrow, two-lipped flowers varying in color from blue to violet, pink, or white.

MIMUSOPS (mi MYOO sops). A genus of tropical evergreen trees of the Sapotaceae (Sapodilla Family), with leathery leaves and milky juice; planted in warm countries for ornament, as well as for edible fruits, oil, rubber, and other products. *M. balata* grows to 100 ft. and yields rubber of fair quality. *M. elengi* (Spanish-cherry) is a much smaller tree and is valued for its edible yellow berries.

MINIATURE ROSE. In 1918 a Major Roulet discovered miniature roses growing in pots on window ledges in a village in Switzerland; and the villagers said they had been growing them for over a hundred years. This rose was considered to be a form of *R. chinensis* cv. 'Minima' and was given the name of *R. rouletii*, now 'Rouletii'.

A miniature rose named 'Pompon de Paris', thought by many authorities to be the same rose with variations in characteristics occasioned only by differences in culture, was widely sold as a pot plant in France from 1839.

In the 1930s and 1940s, Jan deVink in Holland and Pedro Dot in Spain introduced miniature rose varieties that were sold in the United States. In the 1950s, Ralph Moore began his prolific output. By the 1970s, the miniature rose explosion was under way.

Miniature rose plants are exact replicas of their larger relatives. While they started out as 8–12 in. mature plants, many have now been introduced that are much larger, to the point where a new class of "in-between" roses has come into being, midway between the miniatures and the floribundas. This class has not yet received an official name, being variously called miniatures, patio roses, sweetheart roses, and mini-floras. Interestingly, the smallest of the miniature roses are now often called "micro-minis."

Some of the famous early miniatures include 'Baby Gold Star', 'Cinderella', 'Perla de Alcanada', 'Perla de Montserrat', and 'Tom Thumb' or 'Peon'.

Other popular miniature roses include 'Baby Darling', 'Rise-n-shine', 'Starina', and 'Toy Clown'.

Some climbing miniature roses have been developed for use in hanging baskets or as ground cover or carpeting as well as for small trellis work. Examples of these are 'Jeanne Lajoie', 'Nozomi', and Sweet Chariot'.

MINT. Common name for many aromatic herbs of the genus MENTHA, including peppermint, spearmint, and apple mint. Horse-mint is *Monarda punctata*; see MONARDA. The Mint Family is LAMIACEAE.

MIRABILIS (mi RAB il is). A genus of perennial herbs from the American tropics, grown in gardens as tender annuals. Some have tuberous roots, which can be taken up and stored over winter. About a dozen species are grown in the warmer parts of the United States. Propagation is by seed sown in the open ground.

M. jalapa (four-o'clock, marvel-of-Peru), the most popular species, does not open its flowers until late afternoon except on dull, cloudy days. It is a well-branched plant about 3 ft. tall and has bright foliage and fragrant, long-tubed blossoms in shades of white, red, or yellow with attractive markings. It blooms from midsummer to frost and is useful as a summer hedge, plants then being set 1 ft. apart. In the border, plants develop best when planted 2 ft. apart.

M. longiflora has larger flowers of violet, white, or red.

MISCANTHUS (mis KAN thus) **sinensis.** One of the best ornamental grasses for northern regions, commonly known as eulalia grass. It makes attractive clumps for the border or around the lawn, and once established, it will remain for years. Any good soil is suitable. It grows from 4–10 ft. tall and has leaves to 3 ft. long and 1 in. wide with a striking whitish midrib. The silky, plumelike panicles grow to 2 ft. The leaves of cv. 'Gracillimus' (maiden grass) are narrow and channeled; those of 'Variegatus'(striped eulalia grass) have white or yellow stripes; and those of 'Zebrinus' (zebra grass), yellowish bands. Eulalia sometimes escapes from gardens and grows wild. See also ORNAMENTAL GRASSES.

MIST FLOWER Common name for *Eupatorium coelestinum*, a perennial herb resembling an ageratum; see EUPATORIUM.

MISTLETOE. Common name for the many members of the LORANTHACEAE, a large family of green parasitic plants that infest the branches of various kinds of trees. In the United States they are represented mainly by the genus *Phoradendron*, of which the species *P. flavescens* is found throughout the south Atlantic states, forming dense bunches 1–3 ft. across. The stems are smooth and green; the small, rounded leaves are yellowish green, thick, and persistent; and the inconspicuous flowers are followed by waxy, white berries. The plant is sold during the Christmas holidays because it resembles the traditional mistletoe (*Viscum album*) of Europe, which for centuries has been a romantic yuletide symbol with vague religious or sentimental significance. It is also the state flower of Oklahoma. The oak mistletoe of California is *P. villosum*.

MISTLETOE AS A DISEASE

This is one of the few higher plants that are capable of causing plant disease. In the southern and Pacific states it is a common pest of many shade trees, producing on their branches globular masses from a few inches to several feet in diameter. These parasitic masses obtain food from their host by means of rootlike parts called haustoria. If mistletoe is present in abundance it is a distinct menace to the host tree and in extreme cases may kill it. It can usually be kept under control by breaking off the brittle growths, but sometimes the masses must be removed by pruning so as to get rid of the haustoria embedded in the wood.

Dwarf mistletoes (*Arceuthobium* spp.) parasitize conifers and are particularly important pathogens in forest stands of the mountain and Pacific states, where about 20 species of ash, walnut, black locust, and boxelder were affected.

MITCHELLA (mit CHEL ah) **repens.** A very attractive, evergreen trailer native to eastern North America and eastern Asia, commonly known as partridgeberry, squawberry, or twinberry. Because it roots at the stems, it can be used to good advantage to carpet shady places in the rock garden or as a ground cover under evergreen trees. Small-berried specimens in glass bowls are featured by florists at Christmas time. It has dark green, rounded leaves often marked with white lines. The fragrant twin flowers are white with a pinkish tinge and followed by scarlet berries ⅓ in. in diameter. Var. *leucocarpa* has white fruits. Plants are hardy to Zone 3 and easily propagated by rooted portions of the stems.

MITELLA (mi TEL ah). A genus of delicate but hardy woodland herbs belonging to the Saxifragaceae (Saxifrage Family), commonly known as bishop's-cap or mitrewort. They have heart-shaped basal leaves and small, white or greenish flowers.

M. diphylla, the most pleasing species for the wild garden, has white flowers in a slender raceme sometimes 8 in. long. It is propagated by seed or division. Hardy to Zone 4, it should be grown in rich leaf mold or in woodland soil in the shade.

MITES. These pests are very small members of the class Arachnida, which includes spiders, daddy-long-legs, ticks, and scorpions, all with four pairs of legs, not three as with insects. The unsegmented body is connected to the head, and they lack antennae and true jaws. They do have compound eyes. Some are so small they are practically microscopic. Mites feed by sucking juices. The larger predatory mite is a useful control for the small mites and is available commercially. Unfortunately, DDT and other hard chemicals have brought about enormous population imbalances of mites, because those insecticides killed off the beneficial predators and parasites on these pests. Also, mites have often built up resistances to miticides; new strains toxic to humans have also developed.

The very common red spider mites are detectable by their reddish discoloration of the leaves and the very fine webs that appear on the undersides, making them look mealy or powdery. They come to indoor plants and to many outdoor shrubs and trees. Control is possible with rotenone, pyrethrum, and sulfur sprays and dusts. Rotenone should only be used after dusk when it will not affect bees. See RED SPIDER MITE.

The very common and pestiferous cyclamen mite causes blackened buds and leaves on cyclamens, African-violets, and snapdragons indoors and on delphiniums and many other plants outdoors. To prevent pests from spreading, keep plants well spaced and beware of handling healthy plants after infested ones, since the tiny, colorless mites are nearly invisible on hands and clothing. Affected plants are best destroyed, but sometimes they can be saved by immersing the whole plant in water of 110°F for 10–15 minutes.

Cyclamen mite

Trombidiidae is a family of valuable harvest mite scavengers common in leaf litter. Predatory mites, *Phytoseiidae* spp., are available in three categories effective against red spider mites, two-spotted mites (also very common), and many others. When ordering them, specify the humidity and temperature of each area you need to treat, with temperatures varying from 80–100°F, and humidity from fairly high where cooler to lower where hotter. Introduce them at the beginning of an infestation, or at least order them as soon as possible when the infestation becomes apparent. Before they arrive, use insecticidal soap for a knock-down spray. Weekly applications may be needed for very heavy infestations of mites. The rate of introduction is two predators on every second infested plant. See also INSECT CONTROL.

MITREWORT. Common name for MITELLA, a genus of woodland herbs with heart-shaped leaves. False mitrewort is TIARELLA, a genus of woodland herbs with racemes of delicate flowers.

MOCCASIN FLOWER. A common name for CYPRIPEDIUM, a genus of orchids better known as lady's-slipper.

MOCK ORANGE. Common name for PHILADELPHUS, a genus of deciduous shrubs of the Saxifragaceae (Saxifrage Family), cultivated for their showy fragrant flowers. The California mock orange is *Carpenteria californica*; see CARPENTERIA.

MOLD. A term applied to loose, black, friable soil rich in humus and practically synonymous with LEAF MOLD.

The term is frequently used loosely to cover certain fungi that do not belong in any one botanical group but that show some superficial resemblances. All of them are more or less cottony, cobwebby, velvety, or powdery organisms occurring on decaying organic matter and frequently producing fermentation and decay. BOTRYTIS blight of peonies is often called gray mold. The black sooty fungus often growing on aphid honeydew is called SOOTY MOLD. For control, see various types of mold and their host plants.

MOLES. Moles are unspectacular garden residents and rather unjustly blamed for damage they don't do. These small mammals with minute eyes often covered with skin, small concealed ears, and soft, iridescent fur, live almost entirely underground, feeding on smaller animal life, such as slugs, grubs, Japanese beetles, and earthworms. The related, smaller shrews have long, pointed snouts and velvety fur. They may do considerable damage to lawns as they tunnel underground, but both creatures are beneficial in gardens since they feed on insects.

The presence of moles is usually known only by the raised ridges of turf or earth pushed up from beneath as they burrow. One species, the star-nosed mole, which has a long tail and curious fingerlike appendages on its nose, does not make ridges, but throws dirt up in a mound. It is true that grass roots die out above the burrows (because the moisture supply is disrupted), causing yellow streaks to appear, but it is a mistake to take it for granted that the mole is feeding on the roots. They take nothing in the way of plant food, and their activities are entirely concerned with the hunt for worms, insects, and even mice, which are destructive to plant roots and bulbs as well as tree trunks. They are powerful destroyers of beetle larvae without threatening birds, toads, and other natural insect pest controls.

Star-nosed mole

To best control moles, eliminate the grubs they feed upon. Try using milky spore disease, which can be effective when used according to directions. See also BIOLOGICAL CONTROL.

MOLINIA (moh LIN ee uh). a genus of tufted perennial grasses hardy to Zone 5. One species, *M. caerulea*, is sometimes grown for ornament; see ORNAMENTAL GRASSES.

MOLTKIA (MOHLT kee ah). A genus of woody perennial herbs, 6–18 in. tall, with flowers in varying shades of blue. Several species, including *M. petraea* and *M. suffruticosa* are suitable for rock garden use. Hardy to Zone 6.

MOLUCCELLA (mahl yoo SEL ah). A genus of annual herbs belonging to the Lamiaceae (Mint Family) and commonly called molucca-balm. They are easily raised from seed sown in spring. For earlier blooms, they can be started indoors and set out after danger of frost has passed.

M. laevis (bells-of-Ireland, shellflower), a popular garden subject, has whorls of fragrant, white

flowers surrounded by bell-shaped, green bracts. As plants mature, the flowers drop off and the bracts dry to a golden straw color. When picking flowers for drying, remove the foliage, leaving only the bracts. Staking the plants during the summer will produce long, straight stems.

Removing foliage

MOMORDICA (moh MOHR di kah). A genus of annual or perennial tendril-climbing plants of the tropics, belonging to the Cucurbitaceae (Cucumber Family). Two species are sometimes grown in gardens as ornamental vines, treated as tender annuals; that is, started outdoors after frost danger is past, or preferably earlier indoors. They require a light, rich soil. Plants have deeply lobed leaves, yellow flowers, and fruits that are very decorative when they burst open after ripening.

M. balsamina (balsam-apple), common as a weed in the southern states, is a moderate grower that bears oval, orange fruits to 3 in. long.

M. charantia (balsam-pear), the more commonly cultivated species, is larger and has orange-red, oblong fruits about 8 in. long.

MONARCH-OF-THE-VELDT. A common name for *Venidium fastuosum*, a flowering herb better known as cape daisy; see VENIDIUM.

MONARDA (moh NAHR dah). A genus of annual or perennial, rather coarse, aromatic herbs belonging to the Lamiaceae (Mint Family). They have the square stems and opposite leaves characteristic of the family and bear showy, usually red or lavender flowers in clusters.

Easily grown, monardas can be naturalized for the wildflower garden, and they are occasionally used in the border. Propagation is easily done by division in the spring. If allowed to go to seed in a corner of the garden, some species will attract birds. Hardy in Zones 4–9.

PRINCIPAL SPECIES

M. didyma (Oswego-tea, bee-balm) grows to 3 ft. and has scarlet flowers surrounded by red-tinted bracts at the summit of leafy stalks. A brilliant, mint-scented perennial with a long season of bloom, it is appropriate grown in a natural setting. Var. *alba* blooms in white, and var. *salmonea* has yellowish pink blossoms.

M. fistulosa (wild-bergamot) is a strongly scented perennial that has lavender or lilac blossoms with purple or whitish bracts in clusters atop 3-ft. stalks. Native from New England to Colorado, it is easily transplanted. It grows well on a dry, sunny slope in the wildflower garden, and is effective in the border, especially planted in combination with perennial phlox.

Monarda fistulosa

M. punctata (horse-mint) bears 1-in. flowers of purple and yellow in axillary or terminal clusters. Hardy in Zones 6–9.

MONARDELLA (muh NAHR del ah). A genus of annual and subshrubby perennials of the Lamiaceae (Mint Family), native to western North America, and commonly known as coyote mint or deer mint. The foliage is aromatic, and flowers are arranged on spherical heads held above the foliage. Mostly hardy to Zone 8, these plants are useful for the rock garden or small-scale drought-tolerant landscapes, preferring poor, dry sites. Propagation is by seed, cuttings, or division.

PRINCIPAL SPECIES

M. lanceolata is an annual of poor soils, growing to 1 ft. with showy heads of rose-lilac flowers.

M. macrantha is a low, trailing, bright green leaved herb with 1½-in., bright scarlet flowers; it grows best in some shade.

M. odoratissima (mountain mint) is similar to *M. villosa* but has bright green leaves and larger, showier flower heads about 2 in. across with rose-purple blossoms and oval bracts.

M. villosa, the most common species, is an 18-in. shrub with 1-in. gray-green leaves and ½-in. flowers in showy heads of purple, lilac, or white.

MONEYPLANT A common name for LUNARIA, a genus of flowering herbs often used for dried bouquets.

MONEYWORT. Common name for *Lysimachia nummularia*, a trailing herb with yellow flowers and round leaves; see LYSIMACHIA.

MONKEY FLOWER. Common name for MIMULUS, a genus of tender herbs or shrubby plants with oddly shaped flowers.

MONKEY-PUZZLE. Common name for *Araucaria araucana*, an evergreen tree with stiff, sharply pointed leaves, which make it difficult to climb, "even for a monkey." See ARAUCARIA.

MONKSHOOD. Common name for ACONITUM, a genus of perennial, highly poisonous herbs grown for their showy flowers.

MONOCARP. A plant that flowers and fruits once, then dies soon after. All annuals and biennials are monocarps, as are some perennials, such as the century plant.

MONOCOTYLEDON. The class of flowering plants, including the grasses, sedges, rushes, lilies, iris, orchids, aroids, palms, and their relatives, which have only one seed leaf, or COTYLEDON, as contrasted with the rest of the flowering plants, the dicotyledons, which have two seed leaves. The monocotyledonous plants, or "monocots" as they are sometimes called, are further characterized by parallel veining in the leaves, by having the food- or water-vessel vertical tubes scattered unevenly through the stem (not arranged in rings around the center), and by having the parts of the flower characteristically (though not necessarily) arranged in threes. Contrast with DICOTYLEDON.

MONOECIOUS. A term applied to plants that bear flowers of different "sexes," that is staminate and pistillate, on the same individual. See FLOWER; contrast with DIOECIOUS.

MONOTROPA (mahn oh TROH pah) **uniflora.** A leafless saprophytic herb belonging to the Pyrolaceae (Pyrola Family), commonly known as Indian-pipe, and ghost or wax plant. Each naked stem bears a nodding, waxy flower. It is remarkable among higher (flowering) plants because it contains no chlorophyll. It is native to damp, shady woods in the Northern Hemisphere.

MONSTERA (MAHN stur ah). A genus of strong, handsome woody climbers from the tropical Americas, belonging to the Araceae (Arum Family). The best-known species is *M. deliciosa* (Mexican-breadfruit, Ceriman), which can be grown in a pot but is most imposing when planted out in a warm greenhouse and allowed to grow at will against a wall or other support. It is conspicuous because of its large leathery, irregularly cut and perforated leaves and cordlike aerial roots. The clublike flower spike (spadix) rises from a creamy white enveloping leaf or bract (spathe) about 12 in. long. The spadix eventually develops into a conelike edible fruit with the flavor of pineapple and banana. It is propagated by stem cuttings rooted in a mixture of sand and leaf mold with heat.

MONTANOA (mon tah NOH ah). A genus of shrubs or small trees from Mexico and Colombia, belonging to the Asteraceae (Aster Family). Hardy in Zones 10–11, they are sometimes grown under glass for winter bloom or outdoors in summer for a subtropical effect. *M. bipinnatifida*, the principal species, grows to 8 ft. and has large, handsome, hairy leaves deeply cut and 3-in. flower heads with white ray petals. It is easily grown from seeds sown under glass in spring.

MONTBRETIA. Common and former botanic name for TRITONIA and CROCOSMIA, two genera of flowering corms closely related to *Gladiolus*.

MOONFLOWER. Common name for some species of IPOMOEA, a genus of tropical vines with showy flowers.

MORACEAE (moh RAY see ee). The Mulberry Family, a widely distributed group of herbs, shrubs, trees, or sometimes vines. It includes many horticultural subjects and yields commercial products including fiber, rubber, food for silkworms, hops, and edible fruits such as breadfruit, figs, and mulberries. The osage-orange (*Maclura*) is widely used for hedges, and others are of general interest. Principal cultivated genera are *Artocarpus*, *Broussonetia* (paper mulberry), *Ficus* (fig), *Maclura*, and *Morus* (mulberry). The small flowers are borne in heads or spikes; the male and female organs are on separate flowers, the pistils sometimes being borne on the inner surface of a hollow receptacle, as in the fig.

MORAEA (moh REE ah). A genus of plants resembling and closely related to the Iris. Mostly from Africa, they are not hardy in cool climates but are grown extensively in California and Florida. They have corms or rootstocks; narrow, grasslike leaves; and clustered white, red, yellow, or lilac flowers, which last only a day. In cold climates, the corms or rootstocks must be planted in the spring, lifted before frost in the fall, and stored like those of the *Gladiolus*.

M. neopavonia, 1–2 ft. tall, has brilliant red flowers with a blue- or green-black mark at the base of each petal.

MORINDA (moh RIN dah). A genus of trees, shrubs, and climbers of the Rubiaceae (Madder Family), widely spread throughout the tropics. Hardy in Zones 10–11, some species have edible fruit, and others yield dyes. *M. citrifolia* (Indian-mulberry), the best-known species, is a small tree with large leaves and small heads of white flowers, followed by yellowish, fleshy fruit. A red dye is obtained from the flowers and a yellow one from the roots. *M. royoc*, native to Florida and the West Indies, is a low, branching shrub with spreading and somewhat climbing stems.

MORINGA (moh RING gah) **pterygosperma.** A deciduous tree of the East Indies, formerly listed as *M. oleifera*, and commonly known as horseradish tree. Hardy in Zones 10–11, it is planted in the tropics for various purposes, including the ornamental effect of its fragrant, white flowers, its edible root, and its seeds, from which oil is extracted for use as a base in perfumes and cosmetics, among other purposes.

MORNING-GLORY. Common name for IPO-MOEA, a large genus of tropical vines, most with heart-shaped leaves and colorful, short-lived flowers. The Morning-glory Family is CONVOLVU-LACEAE.

MORUS (MOH rus). A genus of hardy long-lived deciduous trees commonly known as mulberry. They are grown in the United States for the edible, though rather insipid, berrylike fruits and in the Orient for the leaves, on which silkworms are fed. Most species are hardy in Zones 5–8.

Mulberries have practically no ornamental use. They seed everywhere and become a nuisance. There is no significant fall color; the fruit is messy; and a number of diseases and insects cause problems. The fruit is relished by birds and are quickly excreted on clean laundry and anything else nearby. The trees are interesting because of the variability of their leaves, several forms often being found on the same tree. The flowers are not showy, and male and female are borne in separate catkins.

PRINCIPAL SPECIES

M. alba (white mulberry) is a Chinese tree that grows to 50 ft. and is of rounded form with shining, light green leaves variously lobed. It bears an abundance of sweet, white, pinkish, or purple fruit. Seedlings showing a good deal of variation are often found along the roadside.

M. nigra (black mulberry) is an Asiatic tree that grows to 30 ft. and has a short trunk and broad round head. It has large, rough, dull green leaves tapering to a point and usually not lobed. It bears large, dark-colored fruits and is not entirely hardy in the North.

M. rubra (red or American mulberry) is a native North American tree that grows to 60 ft. or more. Its large, variable leaves turn bright yellow in the fall. The dark purple fruit is edible, but the tree is more often grown for ornament.

MOSAIC. A viral disease having as its chief symptom mottling of the foliage caused by light yellow areas arranged on the leaves in a kind of mosaic pattern. This is accompanied by general dwarfing of the plant and sometimes by the curling and crinkling of the leaves. See also DISEASE.

MOSS. Minute green plants with leafy stems and minute rootlike parts, densely packed together to form velvety cushions or growing in clusters resembling tiny ferns or trees. They form the second of two classes that make up the second great division, Bryophyta, of the plant kingdom, the other class being the Hepatics, or liverworts.

Most mosses are ½–1 in. high. However, a very common moss, *Polytrichum commune* (haircap moss) will grow 12 in. high. Mosses reproduce by spores that are very light and can blow through the air for hundreds (perhaps thousands) of miles.

Mosses grow on rocks and damp banks, on dead or living trees, and on the surface of shallow waters and are found in all humid climates over a wide range of altitudes and degrees of heat or cold. It is believed that mosses, lichens, and hepatics, the triple link between aquatic and land plants, may have been the first vegetation to appear on the earth and that they may have reigned supreme for a time.

Mosses build up plant tissue and capture dust and debris from the wind, thus providing, with the decay of older plants, sufficient soil for the sprouting of fern spores and later of the seeds of herbs, shrubs, and trees in time. They thus play an important part in establishing plant growth in previously barren places. Indeed, the storage of dust by rock mosses and of mud by aquatic mosses has actually directed the earth's covering of vegetation. There are many genera and hundreds of species. The main division is between those that live on land, including rocks and trees, and those that live in the water.

The most important mosses from a gardener's standpoint are the peat or bog types. These are usually of large, loose growth, changing color with variations in the weather, as they spread over the foothold for larger plants. The mossy surface shows only the tops of the very plants whose underparts died long before and are being gradually transformed into peat. Bogs so formed, if eventually drained, make rich crop lands. Ancient peat deposits are dug up and used for fuel in certain parts of the world, or are ground and added to garden soil to increase its moisture-retaining quality and improve its texture as peat moss. See PEAT.

On account of its spongy, absorptive quality, moss of the genus *Sphagnum* is largely used in packing plants for shipping. Sphagnum moss is also an excellent medium for germinating many seeds. It is one of the few plants known to contain a bacteria that produces an antibiotic that prevents damping-off of seedlings.

Mosses help to prevent erosion. They can absorb moisture rapidly, since they have no waxy covering on their leaves as do other plants, and can survive drought conditions better than grass. Since most mosses prefer shade and acid soil, they have been used as ground covers for shady areas. Gardening with moss is being seen more and more; even replacing shady grass lawns with moss and other ground covers. Mosses never have to be mowed, watered, or fertilized once established. They are ideal substitutes for shady areas where the soil is acid and grass is difficult to grow.

Another important use of mosses is as indicators of air pollution problems in cities and suburbs. Most mosses cannot tolerate air pollution and quickly die or disappear from a location where they may have flourished for years.

MOSS-PINK. Common name for *Phlox subulata*, a low perennial herb with many flower color variations; see PHLOX.

MOSS ROSE. Moss roses were very popular during the Victorian age. They are sports (naturally occuring mutations) of the CENTIFOLIA ROSE. Mossy glands appear on the sepals and calyx tube of the flower bud, and even on the stems in some varieties. The green moss of the centifolias is slightly sticky to the touch and smells of pine.

Repeat-flowering moss roses developed as sports of the damask perpetual or Portland roses. The moss of the damask perpetual moss roses is brownish and rather sparse, though it still has the pine fragrance. Repeat blooming can be rather sparse, too. Nevertheless, these are all charming roses.

'Common Moss' is the best known of the centifolia moss roses, while 'Salet' is the most commonly grown of the damask perpetual moss roses. 'Crested Moss' (also known as Napoleon's Hat) is considered not to be a true moss rose, but rather a parallel centifolia sport, having a fringe just on the edges of the sepals, giving the three-cornered-hat effect.

MOTHER-OF-THOUSANDS. A common name for *Cymbalaria muralis*, a tender ground cover or trailing plant, better known as Kenilworth-ivy; see CYMBALARIA. The name is also applied to *Saxifraga stolonifera*; see SAXIFRAGA.

MOTHERWORT. Common name for species of weedy flowering herbs of the genus LEONURUS.

MOTH ORCHID. Common name for PHALAENOPSIS, an orchid genus with mothlike flowers.

MOUNTAIN-ASH. Common name for SORBUS, a genus of ornamental trees and shrubs grown for their flowers, foliage, and showy fruit.

MOUNTAIN-LAUREL. Common name for *Kalmia latifolia*, a hardy evergreen flowering shrub that is invaluable for ornamental plantings but has foliage that may be poisonous to sheep, goats, and calves. It is the state flower of Connecticut and Pennsylvania; see KALMIA.

MOUSE-EAR CHICKWEED. Common name for some species of CERASTIUM, a genus of low, tufted, herbaceous plants; some used in borders, others mere weeds.

MOWING. A mower is any mechanical device for expeditiously cutting lawn grass to uniform, even height. The reel-type mower consists of a series of five or more curved, steel strip blades that revolve rapidly as the machine moves forward. The revolving blades draw and cut the grass leaves against a sharp, horizontal, stationary blade, which is held at the bottom but is adjustable to vary the length of grass left above the ground. A roller behind the blades helps to support the machine and firm the turf after it has passed. Ratchets in the wheels permit the blades to revolve in only one direction, slipping when the mower is drawn backward. This type of mower is made in various sizes and grades, some operating by pushing, others by a motor.

The rotary mower, generally more common and expensive than the reel mower, is powered by a gasoline or electric motor. It has only one blade shaped something like a propeller with two

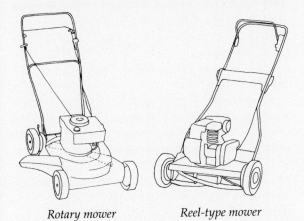

Rotary mower   *Reel-type mower*

cutting edges. The blade revolves horizontally, parallel to the ground, with a cutting action similar to a knife or scythe. The rotary's cut is not the scissorlike operation of the reel mower and therefore it is cleaner cutting. The chassis of the rotary mower has four wheels instead of the reel's two.

One notable advantage of the rotary mower is that it will cut tall and coarse grasses through which a reel mower cannot be driven. Working on a lawn that is not entirely level, the rotary is less likely to scalp the top of any high spots. A disadvantage is that the rotary will not cut closer than an inch high, but few lawns (those of only bent grass) require such close cropping. The rotary blade can be removed and sharpened easily with a file, while reel blades require skilled attention and careful adjustment.

In cutting wet grass, some rotary mowers tend to discharge matted clumps of clippings. If clippings are to be left on the lawn so they can sink into the soil and turn to humus, they will be dispersed if the machine is driven in a direction that will throw the clippings on the still uncut portion of the lawn.

With either type of mower, it is important to see that the lawn is free from sticks, stones, dog bones, or other obstructions before beginning to cut the grass. Such objects may knock chips out of reel blades. With a rotary mower, they can be very dangerous if the whirling blade throws them out at a high velocity. Do not allow children or pets anywhere near a rotary mower in operation. Another danger with the rotary lies in stepping too close and jeopardizing one's toes.

Many kinds of both reel and rotary mowers are available. Self-propelled and riding mowers are more practical for large areas than the push variety. Attachments are available to collect cut grass and leaves or to distribute clippings evenly over the lawn. Good mowing can be done only with a good machine of adequate size and in good condition, with blades kept sharp and mechanisms well oiled.

MOWING

The mowing of a new lawn should begin when the young grass is 2–3 in. tall. For the first few times it should not be cut too close to the soil or the soil will be so exposed to the sun that it may be baked and the grass roots killed. Later, as the turf thickens, the cutting can be closer depending on the condition and quality of the soil, the moisture supply, the weather, the vigor of the grass, and the amount or purpose of use the lawn receives.

The frequency of mowings should be such that clippings will not become too heavy to leave on the surface. There they will gradually rot and add to the humus in the soil without flattening the living grass or causing mold or mildew. If the trimmings are long and coarse, it is better to rake them up and add them to the COMPOST pile.

Do not mow a lawn when the ground is so wet and soft that the operator's feet or pressure of the mower will injure, compact, or puddle the surface. Refrain from mowing during hot, dry weather when the grass makes little growth. Also, stop mowing in the fall as soon as vigorous growth stops so the lawn can go into winter with a good protection of sod.

The use of the lawn mower should be supplemented around tree trunks and along beds, borders, paths, and other boundaries by the use of a string trimmer or suitable edging shears. This is better than damaging the bark of trees and shrubs by mowing too close to them or breaking down the sod edges of flower beds by running the mower into them while attempting to trim edges closely. See also LAWN.

MUEHLENBECKIA (myoo len BEK ee ah). A genus of shrubby tropical plants belonging to the Polygonaceae (Buckwheat Family), formerly listed as *Calacinum*, and commonly known as wireplants. They have wiry stems, alternate leaves, and small unisexual flowers in short clusters, followed by berrylike fruits. Sometimes seen in greenhouses, they can be grown in hanging baskets and outdoors in warm climates. Propagation is by seed or cuttings. Due to reclassifications, some species may be listed under *Homocladium*.

PRINCIPAL SPECIES

M. australis is a stout twining vine that grows to 25 ft. with 1–3 in. oblong leaves, small greenish flowers in dense panicles, and black fruits.

M. axillaris is a prostrate, twining plant or sprawling bush that makes a low, matted clump.

M. complexa (wirevine, maidenhair vine, mattress vine), with rounded leaves, is similar to *M.*

australis but hardier, smaller in all features, and well suited to basket culture. It is a thickly interlaced, twining plant from New Zealand, best grown in hanging baskets under glass. Popular in California, it has proved drought resistant, and is used to cover embankments as a high climber. The greenish white flowers are inconspicuous, but the female flowers develop into fleshy cups holding the seed. Var. *trilobata* has deeply lobed, fiddle-shaped leaves.

MUHLENBERGIA (myoo len BUR jee ah). A genus of perennial grasses native to eastern North America. Although not generally cultivated, they are often found in rich, gravelly soils and are commonly eaten by livestock. Early in the growing season, the stems are short and erect, resembling *Cynodon dactylon* (Bermuda grass), but as the season progresses, they become more slender and branching, bearing spike or panicle seed heads. The plants reproduce by seed or by creeping rootstocks.

M. frondosa (satin grass) is a perennial weed found in fields, along roadsides, and various waste places in eastern North America. It has decumbent stems growing from scaly, knotted rootstocks and flat, rough-textured leaves. Numerous dense panicles, usually tapered to a point, are borne on the end of the branches, producing pointed grains usually surrounded by a chafflike bract.

M. schreberi (nimblewill, wire grass), a common weed in pastures, along roadsides, or in old orchards in the eastern states, grows 1–3 ft. tall and has very branched stems that frequently root at the lower nodes, without clusters of scaly rootstocks. It produces chestnut-brown grains usually without bracts.

MULBERRY. Common name for MORUS, a genus of deciduous trees with variable foliage and fruit. The Mulberry Family is MORACEAE.

The name is also applied to other plants. French-mulberry is *Callicarpa americana*. Indian-mulberry is *Morinda citrifolia*. Paper mulberry is *Broussonetia papyrifera*.

MULCH. Mulch is an application of material such as straw or leaves, spread on the surface of the ground around plants. Mulch helps control weeds, maintain a more uniform soil temperature, and conserve moisture in the soil.

In vegetable and flower gardens, a mulch should be of such loose, organic material. They check evaporation, and when dug or cultivated in, they decay, ultimately increasing the soil's HUMUS content. Coarse materials such as whole corn and other stalks, bark chips, straw, and marsh or salt hay are used for mulching fruit trees, grapevines, berry bushes, and ornamental shrubbery. Clean straw spread between strawberry rows performs the additional function of keeping the ripening berries off the ground, clean, and less liable to mildew or mold.

Nature can be encouraged to provide a winter mulch by spreading brush over the areas to be protected. The winds will blow leaves among the twigs, which will hold them in place and also prevent them from becoming matted down and sodden. Otherwise, winter mulches must be applied with caution and not until the ground has frozen. Sometimes, as in the strawberry bed, this is important mainly because it prevents running a loaded cart or wheelbarrow down the rows until the frozen crust is thick enough to support it. In the case of hardy bulbs, the delay in mulching keeps mice from building nests in the material, burrowing in the soft ground beneath it, and eating the bulbs.

Mulches around fruit trees, bushes, and vines can be removed in early spring or (if not too coarse) turned under according to the preference of the gardener and the soil's need of humus. Around some plants, mulch can be left from year to year, and always should be in the case of rhododendrons and related plants. Coarse mulches on strawberry beds must be removed from the plants, either to the spaces between the rows or altogether, as soon as nearby grass begins to show green. This rule also applies to hardy bulbs and perennials. Fine materials such as buckwheat hulls or finer residue from well-rotted manure can be allowed to remain, to be gradually incorporated with the soil by cultivation. It is advisable to remove mulches gradually, a little at a time over two weeks or more, to harden the new spring growth without exposing it to damage by late frosts.

Wherever obtainable at reasonable cost, salt marsh hay is highly recommended, mainly because it does not contain grass and weed seeds, but also because it is clean, does not mat down and become soggy, and can be gathered up in the spring and used year after year—as it regularly is on bulb fields around the world. Cranberry tops, trimmed from the bogs each fall, are baled and marketed from Massachusetts growing regions. The tough, tangled stems are wiry and springy, letting light and air penetrate to the plants covered and making it a very desirable and lasting mulch for perennials.

With the growing realization of the importance and value of mulches (and with the reduced supply of manure), new materials are constantly being sought, discovered, or devised, sometimes with considerable success. Inorganic materials used as mulch include stone chips, plastic, woven fabric, and gravel.

A number of types of synthetic materials are available for use as mulches or to cover plants and soil as well. LANDSCAPING FABRIC can be used as a weed-blocking mulch, often covered with bark chips or gravel to make them less obtrusive. The use of black plastic sheeting to cover the soil surface between plants warms the soil, which can be very beneficial to heat-loving vegetables like tomatoes and eggplants. It eliminates most weed growth and helps reduce evaporation from the soil. Transplants can be set into the soil through holes in the plastic. Clear plastic, when pulled tightly over the soil surface, will serve as well as black plastic, but it may permit weed growth if it is not secure and tight around the edges. A woven polyester fabric sheeting, "reemay," is used as a row or plant cover but also functions as a mulch by warming the soil somewhat and letting in rainfall while lessening evaporation. A number of other types of mulches are also available. See accompanying mulch chart.

MULCH MATERIALS

MATERIAL	APPEARANCE	INSULATION VALUE	RELATIVE COST	THICKNESS	WEED CONTROL
Aluminum foil	poor	fair, reflects sun's heat	very high	one layer	good
Asphalt	poor	fair	high	½–1 in.	fair
Asphalt paper	poor	good, absorbs heat from sun	high	1 layer	excellent
Bark, chopped	good	good	moderate	2½–3 in.	good
Buckwheat hulls	good	good	high	1–1½ in.	good, may sprout
Burlap	poor	fair	moderate	1 layer or more	poor
Cocoa bean hulls	good–excellent	good, absorbs heat from sun	high in most areas	1 in.	good
Coffee grounds	good	fair	low, but not plentiful	never more than 1 in.	good
Compost	fair	good	high, supply usually limited	1–3 in.	good
Cork, ground	fair–good	excellent	high	1–2 in.	good
Corncobs, ground	good	good	low in Midwest	2–3 in.	excellent
Cottonseed hulls	good	good	low in the South	1–2 in.	good
Cranberry vines	good	fair	low in some areas	3–4 in., 2 in. if chopped	fair–good
Evergreen boughs	poor	good for wind protection	low	1–several layers	fair
Fiberglass	poor	excellent	high	3½–6 in.	excellent
Grass clippings	poor if not dried, may have unpleasant odor	good	low	1 in. maximum	fair
Green ground (cover crops)	fair	good once sod is thick	low	allow to grow to full height	good
Growing ground cover	excellent	fair	moderate	1 layer	fair
Hay	poor, unless chopped	good	low, if spoiled	6–8 in., 2–3 in. if chopped	good

MULCH MATERIALS

PENETRATION	WATER RETENTION	SOIL MOISTURE SPEED	DECOMPOSITION COMMENTS
poor, unless perforated	excellent	no decomposition	Aphids shy away from foil-mulched plants. Should be removed and recycled.
fair	fair–good	decomposes in in about 1 year	Complicated to apply in home gardens.
poor, unless perforated	good	extremely slow if at all	Difficult to manage, tears. Must be carefully weighted and removed each fall.
good	good	slow unless composted before use	Must be replaced only every two years. Can be stringy, difficult to manage.
excellent	fair	slow	Easy to handle. May be blown around in high wind or splashed by rain.
excellent	fair	slow	Excellent for preventing erosion on slopes. New grass grows right through it.
good unless allowed to mat	good	slow, adds nitrogen to soil	Sawdust can be added to improve texture and increase water retention. May develop mold. Has chocolaty smell.
fair, may cake	good	fairly rapid	Use carefully. May prevent ventilation. Best used in container gardens.
good if well rotted	good	rapid, adds nutrients	Partially decomposed compost is an excellent feeding mulch.
good	good	very slow, has little effect on soil nitrogen	Odorless. Stays in place nicely once it has been soaked.
fair, soak before applying	excellent	nitrogen fertilizer should be added to mulch	Avoid close contact with stems of plants because of heat generation.
good	good	fairly rapid	Will blow in the wind. Has fertilizer value similar to cottonseed meal.
good	good	fairly rapid	Excellent winter cover mulch. Pea vines have similar characteristics.
good	fair	slow	Good for erosion control. Should be removed from perennials in spring.
fair, will get soggy and mat	good	no decomposition	Unpleasant to handle. Totally fireproof. Mats are better than building insulation.
good if not matted	fair	rapid; green grass adds nitrogen	Can be mixed with peat moss. After drying can be spread thinly around young plants.
good	good	decomposing legumes and cover crops are rich in nitrogen	Should be harvested or tilled directly into the soil.
good	good	will live from one year to the next	Includes myrtle, pachysandra, etc. Use where you are not going to walk.
good	good	rapid, adds nitrogen	Second- or third-growth hay that has not gone to seed is ideal.

MATERIAL	APPEARANCE	INSULATION VALUE	RELATIVE COST	THICKNESS	WEED CONTROL
Hops, spent	fair	fair, heats up when wet	low where available	1–3 in.	good
Leaf mold	fair	good	low	1½ in.	fair–good
Leaves	fair	good	low	4–6 in.	good
Manure	poor–fair	good	moderate–high	as thick as supply allows	fair
Muck	poor	fair	moderate	1–2 in.	fair
Oak leaf mulch	good	good	low	2–4 in.	good
Oyster shells, ground	good	fair	high	1–2 in.	fair
Paper	poor, can be covered with soil	fair	low, but specialized mulch paper is expensive	1–several layers	good
Paper pulp	poor	fair	moderate	½ in.	fair
Peanut hulls	good	good	low where plentiful	12 in.	good
Peat moss	good	good	moderate–high	1 in.	good
Pine needles	good–excellent	good	low	1–1½ in.	good
Polyethylene	poor, but can be covered	fair, some colors absorb heat	moderate–high	1–6 mil.	excellent
Poultry litter	poor	fair	low–moderate	½ in.	fair
Pyrophyllite	fair	fair	high	1–3 in.	fair
Redwood bark chips	excellent	good	high	2–3 in.	fair
Salt hay	good	good	moderate, less if you gather it	3–6 in.	good, contains no seed
Sawdust	fair–good	good	low	1–1½ in.	good
Seaweed, kelp	poor	good as a winter mulch	low in coastal areas	4–6 in.	excellent

PENETRATION	WATER RETENTION	SOIL MOISTURE SPEED	DECOMPOSITION COMMENTS
good	good	slow, rich in nitrogen and other nutrients	Avoid close contact with trunks and stems because of heating.
fair, if not too thick	good	rapid	An excellent feeding mulch. Use like compost.
fair, likely to mat	good	fairly slow, adds nitrogen	Contributes many valuable nutrients. Can be chopped and mixed with other things.
fair–good	good	rapid, adds nitrogen, packaged mixes may have harmful salts	Should be at least partially rotted. Supplies many nutrients.
good, but will splash and wash away	fair	rapid	Very fertile. Can be mixed with other materials to improve texture.
good	good	slow	Recommended for acid soil plants. Has only slight influence on soil pH.
good	good	slow	Works like lime. Will raise soil pH.
poor, unless perforated	good	slow, unless designed to be biodegradable	Can be shredded and used effectively.
fair	good	rapid, nitrogen-rich as side-dressing	Requires special equipment. Useful in deep planting operations. Good way to recycle.
good	good	rapid, adds nitrogen	Can be mixed with other material for superior appearance. May splash in rain.
poor, absorbs much water	poor, draws moisture from soil	very slow	Adds little or no nutrients to soil. Valuable only as a soil conditioner.
excellent	good	slow, very little earthworm activity	Often used with acid-soil plants, but can be used elsewhere.
poor, unless perforated	excellent	no decomposition	Contributes nothing to the soil. Must be handled twice a year. Various colors available.
good	fair	very rapid, adds nitrogen	Should not be used unless mixed with dry material. Excellent fertilizer.
good	fair	extremely slow	Should be considered a permanent mulch.
fair, repels water in some cases	fair	very slow, add to nitrogen to application	Earthworms avoid redwood. It acts as an insect repellent in some cases.
good, does not mat	good	slow	Can be used year after year. Is pest free. Good for winter protection.
fair	fair	slow unless weathered; robs soil nitrogen	Has high carbon content. Does not sour soil. Very little earthworm activity.
fair	good	slow, adds nitrogen	Provides sodium, boron, and other and potash trace elements. Excellent for sheet composting.

MATERIAL	APPEARANCE	INSULATION VALUE	RELATIVE COST	THICKNESS	WEED CONTROL
Stinging nettle mulch	fair	fair	low	1–3 in.	fair
Stone, crushed	excellent	good, depending on color	high	2–4 in.	fair, except shale
Straw	fair, unless chopped	good	low–moderate	6–8 in., 1–2 in. if chopped	good, avoid oat straw for weed control
Sugar cane (bagasse)	poor–fair	good	moderate	2–3 in.	good
Tobacco stems	good	good	high	1–2 in.	good
Vermiculite	excellent	excellent	high	½ in.	good
Walnut shells	excellent	good	low where plentiful	1–2 in.	good
Wood chips	good	good	moderate	2–4 in.	good
Wood shavings	fair	fair	low	2–3 in.	fair

MULLEIN. Common name for VERBASCUM, a genus of biennial herbs. Cretan-mullein is *Celsia cretica*; see CELSIA. Mullein pink is *Lychnis coronaria*; see LYCHNIS. Rosette-mullein is RAMONDA.

MURIATE OF POTASH. This chemical compound, also called potassium chloride, is a convenient commercial fertilizer for soil known to lack potash. While commercial grades differ in quality, the average potassium content is about 35–50%, which is equivalent to 44–60% potash in oxide form. It is about as soluble as common salt, which it resembles, but it promptly combines with clay and humus in the soil and is not leached away by drainage water as nitrogen is. In other words, it remains until it is taken up by plants. When used alone, it should be applied not more than 3 lb. to 100 sq. ft., and it is better to make several applications at intervals than one large one. See also POTASH; FERTILIZER.

MURRAYA (mu RAY ah) **paniculata.** A shrub or small tree of the Rutaceae (Rue Family), used as a hedge in warm regions, and commonly known as orange jessamine. It can be grown as a pot plant in the greenhouse or outdoors in warm regions. In pots it needs good soil and liberal feeding. It has glossy, pinnate leaves and very fragrant white flowers produced in successive crops during the late spring and summer, followed by clusters of red fruits. Propagation is by seed.

MUSA (MYOO zah). A genus of treelike herbs commonly known as bananas. There are ornamental species with brightly colored bracts around the flowers that eventually emerge from the rolled leaves making up the "trunk" of the plant. The popular edible fruits come from selections of *M. acuminata* and *M.* x *paradisiaca*; see BANANA. The forms that are usually cooked before they are good to eat are known as plan-

PENETRATION	WATER RETENTION	SOIL MOISTURE SPEED	DECOMPOSITION COMMENTS
good	fair	fairly rapid	Has helpful insect-repelling qualities.
good	fair	extremely slow	Should be considered permanent mulch. Contributes some trace elements through leaching.
good	good	fairly slow, nitrogen fertilizer is helpful	Should be seed-free if possible. Straw is highly flammable.
good	good	rapid due to sugar content	Needs to be replenished often. Has fairly low pH. Mix with lime.
good	good	slow	Nicotine is an effective repellent of some insects.
good	good	extremely slow	Totally sterile. Recommended for hothouse use. Will blow and splash outdoors.
good	good	very slow	Will furnish good trace elements. Resists fire.
good	good	fairly slow, little effect on soil nitrogen	May contain carpenter ants, but does not retain tree diseases.
good	fair	very rapid, will use up soil nitrogen	Hardwood shavings are better than pine or spruce. Chips or sawdust make better mulch.

tain. Some ornamantal species have leaves splashed with red or have colored bracts on the infloresence.

M. ensete (Abyssinian banana) bears inedible fruit but is one of the most ornamental species. It is often grown from seed, which, being very hard, should have holes filed in them or be soaked for 48 hours in warm water before being planted in a propagating bench with bottom heat. The young plants should be potted up in good soil and kept at a night temperature of 65°F. While small, they can be used outdoors during the frost-free months for tropical effects; in time, however, they become too large to move in and out conveniently for any but the largest conservatories. Mature plants are big and not too beautiful, except for their imposing size.

M. textilis (Manila-hemp, Abaca), with leaves up to 6½ ft. long, has been cultivated to produce rope fiber from the sheaths of the leaf stems.

MUSACEAE (myoo ZAY see ee). The Banana Family, a group of stout tropical herbs often becoming woody and of great stature. Genera usually cultivated are *Ensete* and *Musa* (banana).

MUSCARI (mus KAIR ee). A genus of small bulbous plants of the Liliaceae (Lily Family), commonly known as grape-hyacinth. Their charming, tiny, blue or white bell-shaped flowers in spikelike racemes appear very early in the spring. Grape-hyacinths should be planted in drifts in the border or the rock garden, or among shrubs, preferably in light loam, though they grow readily under almost

Muscari botryoides

any good garden conditions. Hardy to Zone 4, they are propagated by seed or offsets and multiply naturally very rapidly.

M. botryoides, with its dark blue, beadlike flowers, is well known in old gardens and has become naturalized in orchards and other grassy places in many regions. Its cv. 'Album' has white flowers, while those of 'Caeruleum' are bright blue. Cv. 'Heavenly Blue' is much larger and is charming planted in combination with some pink, white, or yellow tulip species.

M. comosum cv. 'Montrosum' (feathered-hyacinth) is interesting because of its peculiar flowers, which are sterile and cut into fringelike shreds.

MUSHROOM. Properly speaking, this refers to any large, fleshy fungus growth whether edible, inedible, or poisonous. The name is often limited to those kinds that have conspicuous, umbrellalike "caps," also correctly called toadstools, though this term is popularly applied to poisonous or supposedly poisonous kinds as distinguished from edible mushrooms. Among the edible fungi that can loosely be called mushrooms, but that do not form caps and therefore are not "toadstools," are chanterelles, puff-balls, morels, clavarias, truffles, and pore-, horse-, and liver-fungi. All these varying forms are actually the spore-carrying fruit bodies of fungi whose growing parts are masses of threadlike tissue in the soil. The spores are small and dustlike when ripe—as can be seen by breaking open an old brown puff-ball.

Though some species can be cultivated by dusting their spores or transplanting clumps (with more or less attached earth) to supposedly favorable spots in the garden, only the common mushroom, *Agaricus campestris*, has so far become a real crop plant. With the introduction of special varieties and strains, it has become an important commercial product.

GROWING MUSHROOMS

Cultivating mushrooms is distinctly different from most vegetable gardening techniques and requires some special conditions and equipment.

The growing medium consists of well-composted manure contained in plastic dishpans or wooden trays about 2' x 3' and 12 in. deep. The compost is seeded with spawn, which can be purchased from a laboratory. In about three weeks' time, a cottony growth of mycelia will cover the surface of the compost. At this time, a moist, slightly alkaline overlay of peat and compost, called a casing, is added to a depth of 1–1½ in. Frequent light waterings and a newspaper mulch help maintain a high moisture content while the mushrooms grow up through the casing. Fully mature mushrooms are ready to harvest six or seven days after the casing is applied, and blooms of mushrooms should occur every ten to fourteen days for two to three months. Mushrooms will grow in a temperature range of 58–72°F but prefer cooler temperatures, which slow their rate of production and extend the growing season. Kits that supply growing medium, tray, and spawn are frequently available from seed companies and made available to the home grower through catalogs.

POISONOUS MUSHROOMS

Although many species of mushrooms are great delicacies, many others are toxic and even fatal if ingested. The two poisonous species most often eaten, mistaken for the safe and edible meadow mushroom or because of their attractive appearance, are *Amanita phalloides* (destroying-angel, death-cap) and *Amanita muscaria* (fly amanita, fly mushroom). If it appears that either of these has been eaten, contact a doctor immediately, since ingestion of either can be fatal.

The destroying-angel has a white, brownish, greenish, or yellowish cap, white gills, and a ringed stem rising from a cup at the base. Thus, it differs from the common meadow mushroom, which always has pink or brown gills beneath the cap and no cup at the base.

The fly amanita has a brilliant orange or yellow cap spotted with white warts, white gills, and a ringed stem rising from a swollen base covered with concentric rings of the fluffy cup. It is frequently found under birch trees and in open pine woods.

MUSK MALLOW. Common name for *Malva moschata* and *Abelmoschus moschatus*, both flowering perennial herbs of the Malvaceae (Mallow Family. See MALVA; ABELMOSCHUS

MUSKMELON. Common name for the netted or nutmeg types of the casabas or winter melons, all originating from the species *Cucumis melo*. Compare CANTALOUPE. See also CUCUMIS; MELON.

MUSTARD. Common name for various species and varieties of the genus BRASSICA. They are half-hardy annual herbs whose leaves are used for salads and potherbs; their seeds—whole or ground, alone or mixed with other spices—are used to flavor foods and as a condiment; and from these seeds is obtained colza, or oil of mustard, a counterirritant. Other species are pestiferous weeds, especially in grain fields.

As a common name, mustard also refers to other plants. The Mustard Family is BRASSICACEAE. Hedge- or treacle-mustard is a catalog name for ERYSIMUM, or blistercress.

For salad and potherb use, sow seed of any of the mustards thinly outdoors in rows 12 in. apart in earliest spring and at weekly intervals until a month before hot weather, and again in the fall until six weeks before winter. For a winter supply, sow from November until March in coldframes or cool greenhouses. Gather by shearing the plants while young and tender—for salad when they are 4 in. high and for greens when 6 in. high. If not sheared too closely, a planting will give two or three cuttings. Hot weather makes the leaves too strong for most tastes, especially for salad. See also GREENS; POTHERB.

MUTISIA (myoo TIS ee ah). A genus of interesting tendril climbers from South America, belonging to the Asteraceae (Aster Family). They can be grown in greenhouses or outdoors in very warm regions, doing best in a sandy loam with leaf mold added. Propagation is by cuttings.

M. clematis, the best-known species, grows to 20 ft. or more and has pinnate leaves and 2-in. heads of red flowers.

M. decurrens grows to 12 ft. and has orange-scarlet flowers.

M. ilicifolia grows to 15 ft. and has hollylike leaves and heads of white or rose flowers.

MYCELIUM. The fundamental structure or vegetative part of a fungus, consisting of delicate, branched tubular or filamentous threads called hyphae; see FUNGUS.

MYOSOTIS (mī oh SOH tis). A genus of low-growing, hardy, annual, biennial, or perennial herbs belonging to the Boraginaceae (Borage Family) and commonly known as forget-me-not. They are grown for their blue, white, or pink flowers and thrive in cool, partly shady locations with moist soil. Forget-me-not is the state flower of Alaska.

Myosotis sylvatica

While the dwarf varieties are among the most delightful of all edging plants, bearing their small bright flowers early in the season, other varieties are excellent for waterside planting or for naturalizing in the wild garden. In combination with pansies or English daisies, they are good in the rock garden or as a ground cover in the rose garden. The tall varieties, growing to 18 in., will spread and trail over a large area. Most of the perennials are hardy to Zone 3, but winter protection of all species is desirable.

If seed is sown early, blossoms may be produced the same year, though generally flowers are borne only the second year, appearing from early spring until late summer. The foliage, which is rather small and smooth and of a clear light green, accentuates the delicate beauty of the flowers. The annual species will self-sow.

If cut and placed in water, branches bearing flower buds will continue blooming for a long time and often will develop roots so they can be potted and grown on. Root clumps of the perennial kinds can be divided to produce new plants.

PRINCIPAL SPECIES

M. arvensis is similar to *M. sylvatica*, with blue or white flowers.

M. azorica is a perennial bearing blue flowers with a whitish center.

M. laxa, a perennial, has blue flowers with yellow centers.

M. scorpioides is a perennial with white, pink, or yellow centers. Var. *semperflorens* is a dwarf form.

M. sylvatica is annual or biennial that grows 8–24 in. and has flowers with yellow centers and petals varying from blue to white or pink. There are many forms, sometimes listed as *M. alpestris*, *M. dissitiflora*, *M. lithospermifolia*, or cv. 'Robusta Grandiflora'.

MYRCIARIA (mur see AHR ee ah) **cauliflora.** A large, slow-growing shrub native to Brazil, belonging to the Myrtaceae (Myrtle Family), and commonly known as jaboticaba. This is one of the best plants for a small garden or sunny patio (Zones 10–11) if grown in rich, moist soil. White flowers and delicious thick-skinned black fruits the size of a large grape are formed two or three times a year directly on the trunks, which at other times are attractive with scaling red-brown bark.

MYRICA (MEER ik ah). A genus of evergreen and deciduous shrubs or small trees widely distributed in the temperate and warmer regions of both hemispheres, belonging to the Myricaceae (Bayberry Family), and commonly known as waxmyrtle, bayberry, or sweetgale. They are grown for their attractive aromatic foliage and decorative grayish or purple fruits. Wax is obtained from the fruit of some species, and the fruit of others is edible.

They need a lime-free soil and most appreciate peat or leaf mold, but *M. pensylvanica* and *M. californica*, of the East and West Coast respectively, grow well in sandy, sterile soil. Only one or two species are hardy in cold climates. Propa-

gation is by seed, layers, and suckers.

PRINCIPAL SPECIES

M. californica (California bayberry), found from California to Washington, is a large evergreen shrub or slender tree with reddish purple fruit. It will grow in poor, sandy soil but is hardy only to Zone 7.

M. cerifera (wax-myrtle) is a large evergreen shrub or small tree, native from New Jersey to Texas. It does best in moist, peaty soil and has small, grayish white, waxy fruits, which yield a wax used in making candles. Hardy to Zone 7.

M. faya (candleberry myrtle), from the west coast of Europe and Africa, grows to 25 ft. and has smooth, waxless leaves to 4½ in. long. Hardy in Zones 10–11.

M. gale (sweetgale) is a deciduous shrub growing to 5 ft., with yellowish fruit surrounded by two bracts in dense catkins. It suckers freely and prefers a moist, peaty soil. Hardy in Zones 2–5.

M. pensylvanica (bayberry) grows to 8 ft. and is found from Nova Scotia to Florida. It has dull green, almost evergreen leaves that emit a resinous fragrance when crushed. In winter it is conspicuous with clusters of grayish fruits whose waxy covering has been used for making fragrant candles. It thrives in poor soil and is hardy in Zones 3–6.

M. rubra, a small tree from the South Pacific, occasionally grows to 60 ft. and has 5-in. leaves. The small purplish fruits are edible and sometimes used in beverages.

MYRIOPHYLLUM (mee ree oh FIL um). A genus of widely distributed, mostly aquatic herbs commonly known as water-milfoil. Several species are cultivated in aquariums and pools, while others are pernicious weeds. In aquariums, they help to provide oxygen for fish. Below the water surface, their long, graceful stems are densely covered with finely dissected leaves, which make this group the most feathery of all the aquatics. Hardiness varies (Zones 5–11) depending on the species. A few species are found in freshwater lakes, and one imported kind has become a serious pest.

PRINCIPAL SPECIES

M. aquaticum (parrot's-feather, water-feather), formerly listed as **M. proserpinacoides**, is a favorite, not for its submerged foliage, but for the delicate green masses of foliage produced above the water. Potted in rich soil and submerged at the edge of the pool or in the aquarium, with adequate warmth and light, plants quickly produce myriads of trailing stems encircled with whorls of feathery leaves. It is hardy to Zone 8 and especially useful for relieving the austere lines of a formal pool or a fountain basin. Indoors, planted in a water-tight hanging basket, it is as charming as any fern.

M. heterophyllum is a temperate species found in eastern North America, with thick stems bearing feathery underwater foliage in whorls of four to six leaflets and emergent lance-shaped leaves to 2 in. long.

M. hippuroides (western-milfoil), found in wet areas of the Pacific states, has finely cut submerged leaves and linear to lance-shaped leaves at the water surface.

M. spicatum (Eurasian-milfoil) is an introduced species that has become a serious pest, crowding out native vegetation in North American lakes. It is distinguished by whorls of four feathery leaves divided into 12 to 21 pairs of leaflets. The stems grow to 8 ft. long, and flowers are produced in interrupted spikes.

M. verticillatum (myriad leaf) is native to northern North America, Europe, and Asia. It has flowers arranged in spikes. The foliage includes submerged leaves in whorls of four to five leaflets and relatively small, finely cut leaves showing above the surface of the water.

MYRRH. Common name for the fragrant herb *Myrrhis odorata*; see MYRRHIS.

MYRRHIS (MUR is) **odorata.** A perennial herb native to Europe, belonging to the Apiaceae (Celery Family), and commonly known as myrrh, sweet cicely, or sweet-chervil. It has finely cut leaves and bears small, white flowers in umbels followed by shiny, ribbed fruits 1 in. long. It was once highly esteemed as a potherb or for salad, having a flavor like licorice. It is now occasionally grown in garden borders for the fragrant white flowers. Hardy to Zone 4, it is easily propagated by seed sown as soon as it ripens, or by root cuttings.

Myrrhis odorata

MYRTACEAE (mur TAY see ee). The Myrtle Family, an important and distinctive group of aromatic tropical trees and shrubs with thick evergreen leaves, including many ornamental subjects. The genera most commonly cultivated are *Callistemon*, *Calothamnus*, *Eucalyptus*, *Eugenia*, *Feijoa*, *Leptospermum*, *Melaleuca*, *Metrosideros*, *Myrtus* (myrtle), *Pimenta*, *Psidium*, *Rhodomyrtus*, and *Tristania*.

MYRTLE. Common name for MYRTUS, a genus of attractive, mostly subtropical, evergreen shrubs. The Myrtle Family is MYRTACEAE.

The name is also applied to several plants that belong to other botanical families. Crape-myrtle is *Lagerstroemia indica*; see LAGERSTROEMIA. Running-myrtle or periwinkle-myrtle is *Vinca minor*; see VINCA. Sand-myrtle is the genus LEIOPHYLLUM. Wax-myrtle is *Myrica cerifera*; see MYRICA.

MYRTUS (MUR tus). A genus of attractive, evergreen shrubs or small trees found mostly in subtropical regions and commonly known as myrtle. They are very ornamental for outdoor planting in Zones 9–11 and are often grown as potted

Myrtus communis

plants in cooler regions, thriving in well-drained, loamy soil with leaf mold added. Propagation is by cuttings of half-ripened shoots under glass, and by layers.

The principal species is **M. communis**. This is the myrtle of the ancients, who used it in different forms on festive occasions. Native to the Mediterranean area, it is a handsome, bushy evergreen that grows to 10 ft. and has glossy, dark green, scented leaves and fragrant, white flowers followed by blue-black berries. It makes a good hedge or screen plant in Zones 9–11, and a good pot or tub plant for summer porch or terrace decoration in cooler regions. There are variegated-leaf forms and several named varieties, which differ chiefly in the size and shape of the leaves. **M. ugni** is now classified as **Ugni molinae**.

NAEGELIA (nay JEE lee ah). Former botanical name for SMITHIANTHA, a genus of herbs suited to greenhouse culture.

NAILWORT. Common name for PARONYCHIA, a genus of annual and perennial herbs with tiny flowers.

NAKED-LADY. A common name given to species of COLCHICUM and LYCORIS, since the leaves and flowers do not appear at the same time. Naked-lady-lily refers to *Amaryllis belladonna*; see AMARYLLIS.

NANDINA (nan DĪ nah) **domestica.** A beautiful evergreen shrub native to China and Japan, belonging to the Berberidaceae (Barberry Family), and commonly known as heavenly-bamboo (although not related to the true bamboos). It is popular in warmer regions for its graceful foliage, winter coloring, and berries. The finely cut leaves are tinted pink when young, then in winter change from green to red. The loose terminal clusters, to 1 ft. long, of small, white flowers are followed by bright red berries. Though generally considered tender, it can stand some frost and is hardy in Zones 6–9. The roots are hardy to Zone 5, where plants have survived below-zero temperatures and sent up new tops in the spring. It grows well in a light, moist, loamy soil, with plenty of leaf mold. Propagation is by seed or cuttings. Cultivars worth growing are 'Alba', with white fruit; 'Harbor Dwarf', very compact (growing to 2 ft.) with purplish leaves in winter; and 'Atropurpurea Nana', a compact plant (growing to 2 ft.) with red leaves in winter.

NANNYBERRY. Common name for *Viburnum lentago*, a tall bush with white flowers and edible berries, native to eastern North America; see VIBURNUM.

NAPTHALENEACETIC ACID. One of several synthetic growth regulators. There are many uses for this AUXIN. See HORMONE.

NARCISSUS (nahr SIS us). A genus of chiefly spring-flowering bulbous plants belonging to the Amaryllidaceae (Amaryllis Family). The hardy forms are commonly called daffodils and sometimes jonquils, though the latter is the correct name of only a single species. They are universal favorites in gardens of the North Temperate Zone and are also popular subjects for indoor and greenhouse culture as well; tender kinds with smaller flowers in clusters are easily forced to bloom indoors in bowls of pebbles or peat moss. Narcissi are characterized by flowers of white, yellow, or orange with six flaring perianth segments that surround a central tube of varying lengths, known as the trumpet, cup, corona, or crown. The leaves, which are generally smooth and linear, appear with the flowers.

In the United States, confusion exists because the accepted terms "narcissus," "daffodil," and "jonquil" are not clearly understood or differentiated. Narcissus, though actually the name of the entire genus, in this country commonly applies to the sweet-scented, usually tender, cluster types. Daffodil is the common name by which the trumpet varieties are usually known, but many people use it loosely for all of the hardy garden narcissus in which the yellow color predominates. Jonquil is a true classification (*N. jonquilla*) of the hardy narcissus distinguished by nearly round, rush-like leaves and small, deep yellow, sweet-scented flowers appearing in clusters on the stem. In some regions, however, all hardy trumpet *Narcissus* species are called jonquils.

NARCISSUS CLASSIFICATION.

The greatest development of the narcissus has taken place in England and Ireland, where professional gardeners and serious-minded amateurs have taken the original species and early hybrids, and with ever progressive cross-fertilization, developed many charming new forms in endless variety, showing improvement in size, form, color, and flowering date. Similar work has been done by some expert bulb growers in Holland and the United States.

In the early stages of narcissus development, botanists tried to classify the new types in accordance with the wild species that they most nearly resembled. In some cases, species were named for the introducer who developed them (such as **barri** or **leedsi**). However, by the early twentieth century, classifications were confused at best. On January 1, 1950, the Royal Horticultural Society of London adopted a revised classification scheme for *Narcissus*. This system categorizes primarily by flower form: trumpet-shaped, large-cupped, small-cupped, flat-cupped, double, and those with several flowers to a stem. Some of the resulting eleven divisions are further subdivided by flower color combinations: perianth colored and corona colored, perianth white and corona colored, etc. The characteristics of narcissus attributable to species derivation provide the basis by which some of these plants are classified: i.e. all hybrids in which the characteristics of *N. triadrus* are clearly evident are grouped together in the division that bears the name of the original species from which the hybrids were derived.

All members of this genus are naturally prolific hybridizers; they have been cross-bred and selected extensively by horticulturists, resulting in an increasingly bewildering array of named cultivars, which number in the many hundreds. Some of the more common and long-standing varieties are given below. For a more comprehensive list of narcissus varieties, consult *The Classified List of Daffodil Names* and the *Tulip Yearbook*, both published by the Royal Horticultural Society of London.

NARCISSUS DIVISIONS

Trumpet Narcissus. The corona is as long as the perianth or longer. The strong, large flowers occur one per stem; 16–20 in. tall. This is the best-known group of narcissus, commonly referred to as daffodils. Cultivars include 'King Alfred', a favorite since Victorian times; 'Mt. Hood', an all-white form, and many bicolor varieties. Subdivisions are by flower color combinations:

A. Perianth colored; corona colored, not paler than the perianth.

B. Perianth white; corona colored.

C. Perianth white; corona white, not paler than the perianth.

D. Any color combination not included above.

Large-cupped Narcissus. In this division, the corona is more than a third the length of, but not as long as the perianth. Flowers are borne one to a stem; 14–20 in. tall. Cultivars include the showy 'Amor', the pure white 'Duke of Windsor', and pink and white 'Salome'. Subdivisions A through D are the same as for trumpet narcissus types.

Small-cupped Narcissus. The corona on this flower is very small, measuring less than a third the length of the perianth. The large petals emphasize the colored cups beautifully. One fine-shaped flower is borne on each stem; average height is about 20 in. Varieties include the early-blooming 'Barrett Browning' and the sweet-scented, late-blooming 'Queen of Narcissi'. Subdivisions A through D are the same as for trumpet narcissus types.

Double Narcissus. Rather than the characteristic trumpet-shaped corona, the centers of these flowers are filled with an abundance of little petals that give a ruffled appearance; 14–18 in. tall. Cultivars include the fragrant, golden 'Tahiti', and 'Cheerfulness', an old favorite first introduced in the 1920s.

Triandrus Narcissus. Members of this group resemble *N. triandrus*. Each has slender foliage and one to six small nodding flowers per stem; 9–14 in. tall. Most are deliciously fragrant. Varieties include 'Silver Chimes', with six or more flowers per head and 'Thalia', often referred to as the orchid-flowering daffodil. Subdivisions by flower color are as follows:

A. Cup or corona not less than two-thirds of the length of one perianth segment.

B. Corona less than two-thirds the length of perianth segments.

Cyclamineus narcissus. All hybrids that resemble the species *N. cyclamineus*, which is native to marshes of the Pyrenees. Each stem bears one or more drooping flowers, the petals of which are reflexed and give the appearance of a cyclamen flower; 8–10 in. tall. These are the earliest bloomers. Cultivars include 'February Gold', the long-time mainstay of the early spring garden, and 'February Silver', its silver-white counter-part. Subdivisions A and B are the same as for triandrus narcissus types.

Jonquilla Narcissus. All are hybrids of the species *N. jonquilla*. The common name "jon-quil" is correctly applied only to members of this division. Each stem bears two to six sweet-scent-ed flowers; 14–16 in. tall. Cultivars include 'Tre-vithian', an old favorite. Subdivisions A and B are the same as for triandrus narcissus types.

Tazetta Narcissus. Sometimes referred to as the polyanthus narcissus, all are hybrids of *N. tazetta* and are the oldest form of narcissus in cultivation. This is the flower that inspired the classical Greek legend about Narcissus, the boy who fell in love with his own reflection. Each stem bears four to eight small, very fragrant flow-ers; 16–18 in. tall. Cultivars include 'Cragford', 'Paperwhite', and 'Galilea', all well-suited to indoor forcing.

Poeticus Narcissus. Members of this division show the characteristics of the species *N. poeticus*. Commonly known as poet's daffodils, these have been in cultivation since the Middle Ages, and they continue to grow in profusion around old European castles. Among the fra-grant varieties in this division are the old-fash-ioned favorites, 'Actaea' and 'Peasant's Eye'; 15–18 in. tall.

Species and Wild Forms or Wild Hybrids. See list of principal species at the end of this entry.

Other. All narcissus that cannot be included in any of the above divisions.

GROWING NARCISSUS OUTDOORS

Narcissus are not desirable for formal plant-ings; they show off to best advantage when they give the impression of not having been planned or planted. Their color and gracefulness permit many charming effects at a season when little else is blooming in the garden. For small gardens, small plantings of separate varieties is very effec-tive. With the exception of the tazetta kinds, all narcissus are hardy, which means that they can be grown outdoors in the temperate zone, though some winter covering is recommended in exposed places.

Uses and Sites. Narcissus are largely employed to produce naturalized effects. For this purpose, the older, short cup varieties and the smaller trumpet kinds are preferable to the newer, more refined hybrids, which are less like-ly to continue flowering over a period of years. Mass plantings in grassy slopes, meadows, and woodland borders or along the banks of streams give an annual array of flowers; they need little attention until the bulbs become so crowded that both number and size of flowers diminish. The bulbs can then be taken up, sepa-rated, and replanted.

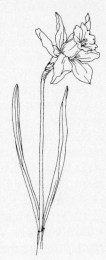

Narcissus sp.

Planting. For new plant-ings, the bulbs, which are available from September on through the fall months, should be planted as soon as possible. For further instructions on growing conditions and planting, see BULBS.

Lifting and Storing. It is important to keep the foliage in a green condition as long as possible, for it is between the flowering period and the dying of the foliage that the flower buds for the following season are made. If the bulbs are to be lifted, it should be done as soon as the foliage has entirely withered. The curing and storing of nar-cissus bulbs involves some risk, and there is nothing to be gained by keeping them out of the ground; digging, and replanting should be car-ried on simultaneously. As the bulbs are lifted, those that fall apart readily should be separated, but no attempt should be made to pull apart those that adhere at the base. Care must be taken to prevent the sun from shining directly on the bulbs while harvesting is in progress, as this will result in scalded spots that may start to decay. Care should also be taken to prevent bruising.

Where dormant storing is unavoidable, it can best be done in shallow wooden trays with an air space at the bottom. They should be placed where there is an abundance of air but away from moisture. A shed with low eaves but no sides is ideal. In the early stages of drying, the bulbs should be stirred frequently.

GROWING NARCISSUS INDOORS

The varieties of the tender tazetta or cluster narcissus are the most readily flowered indoors. The most popular type is the pure white cv. 'Paperwhite' (*N. grandiflora*). 'Soleil d'Or', the pure yellow cultivar, ranks next in popularity, while the combination cream and yellow kind (var. *orientalis*), commonly known as Chinese sacred-lily, is also used extensively. The double form of this latter type, which is called 'Double Roman Constantinople', is very fragrant, but its lightweight stems are hardly strong enough to support the heavy flowers.

Indoor narcissus

Bulbs of these varieties are available from early fall through midwinter and can be planted at any time during this period. Early plantings will produce flowers in late November, but the time required for flowering shortens as the season develops, so that plantings made at Christmas will flower in about three weeks. Successive plantings will, therefore, provide flowers over a long period. See BULBS for instructions on blooming narcissus in water.

The hardy types are more difficult to handle indoors, but they can be successfully flowered indoors with a preliminary outdoor planting. The bulbs should be planted in receptacles with drainage holes (clay flower pots are best) in good garden soil or peat moss. The pots should be plunged outdoors (that is, buried so their rims are below the surface) and covered with a foot or more of leaves, straw, or sifted ashes to prevent the frost from penetrating and the soil from drying out. If this is done before the ground freezes, the bulbs should have developed a good root system by the first of the year (this can be determined by examining one pot). They are then ready to be brought into the house, where the atmosphere should be humid and the temperature not above 60°F for the first ten days. Thereafter it can gradually be raised to 70°F. Strong light should not be allowed until the shoots turn green. Abundant water is required.

ENEMIES

Most species are susceptible to mosaic or gray disease, a virus that causes streaking of flowers and foliage, and small and fewer bulbs. Basal rot, caused by a species of fusarium fungus inhabiting the soil, begins at the root plate or base of the scales and spreads into the central portion of the bulb, the rotted tissue being purplish brown, dry, and spongy. The large trumpet narcissus is principally affected; the jonquil, poeticus, and tazetta types are highly resistant. This is principally a problem for commercial growers, and there is little that gardeners can do about it. The acidity of the soil may also be an important factor.

Two other fungi, forms of BOTRYTIS, cause diseases. One is fairly common; the other has become important in fields of the Pacific Northwest where it has completely destroyed the foliage but has not caused bulb rot. Leaf scorch appears as yellowish, reddish, or brown areas at the tips of the leaves, followed by reddish brown raised spots. It kills the leaves several weeks early.

PRINCIPAL SPECIES

N. bulbocodium (hoop-petticoat daffodil, petticoat daffodil) is native to Portugal, Spain, and southern France and grows about 15 in. tall. It bears nearly odorless, solitary flowers in shades of yellow with widely flaring trumpets and very narrow spiky perianth segments. Several forms are available, including var. *conspicuus*.

N. jonquilla (jonquil), originally from southern Europe and Algeria, grows 18 in. tall and bears two to six fragrant flowers to a stem. The coronas are 1 in. long with a wavy edge and are less than half as long as the perianth. Leaves are 18 in. long, narrow, and rushlike. Many forms are available, including cv.'Simplex'.

N. poeticus (poet's narcissus) is native to southern Europe, especially Greece. Its leaves are narrow and up to 18 in. long. The flowers are usually solitary, white, and very fragrant—used to make perfume. The corona is very short, wavy, rimmed with red, and much shorter than the perinath.

N. tazetta has large bulbs and relatively broad, flat leaves to 18 in. long. It bears four to eight fragrant, white flowers with perianth tubes up to 1 in. long. Var. *orientalis* (Chinese sacred-lily) has three or four creamy white and yellow flowers clustered at the end of slender 12-in. stalks; it is popular throughout the Orient, cultivated outdoors along the Pacific Coast, and widely grown indoors in bowls of water with the bulbs supported by pebbles.

N. triandrus (angel's-tears), originally from Spain and Portugal, has leaves about 12 in. long, narrow, and rushlike. The flowers occur one to six per stem in shades of pale yellow to pure white. The corona is at least half as long as the perianth. Available forms include cv. 'Albus'.

NASTURTIUM (nas TUR shum).

As a common name, nasturtium refers to TROPAEOLUM, a genus of familiar garden herbs cultivated for ornament and sometimes for their edible parts.

Botanically, *Nasturtium* refers to a genus of succulent herbs, which usually grow in running water and are commonly known as watercress. *N. officinale* is the primary species commercially cultivated in specially constructed, concrete water beds for its pungent flavor in salads.

NATIVE.

A term applied to a species, genus, or even family of plants indicating its origin in a particular region. Do not confuse with "naturalized," which means introduced and growing wild in a new place. For example, a species of *Lythrum* (purple loosestrife), long ago introduced into North American gardens from Europe where it was native, has now become completely naturalized in eastern North America, growing freely in the wild.

NATIVE PLANTS.

Every section of the United States has trees, shrubs, and flowers particularly beautiful as a part of the natural landscape. In recent years, appreciation has grown for their suitability in landscape work, especially in informal plantings.

Not long ago it was exceedingly difficult to obtain native plants from nurseries, but now many dealers specialize in them, and as the demand grows, we will see more and more of the rarer and lovelier plants preserved through their proper use and appreciation.

On the Atlantic seaboard, for example, the flowering dogwood (*Cornus florida*) reaches its highest degree of loveliness. While people once had to seek wild specimens and transplant them to their gardens (all too often unsuccessfully), plants can now be obtained from nurseries, not only in the common white form, but also in the rarer pink and double varieties. All through the eastern states these and other dogwood species and many of the viburnums, all attractive in flower and fruit, can be used most effectively. Full advantage also can be taken of the beauty of mountain-laurel and rhododendron, including pink, white, and flame-colored azaleas. Other shrubs—such as hollies, wild cherries, plums, chokeberries, shadbush, hawthorns, spicebush, sweet pepperbush, gordonia, and fringe tree—combined with plantings of native trees, are also characteristic of this region.

Every region has characteristic plants that can, and should, be used more often in home plantings, and to that end, they should be made available by commercial horticulturists.

CONSERVATION OF NATIVE PLANTS

One safeguard of native wild plants is the Federal Endangered Species Act of 1973, administered by the United States Fish and Wildlife Service. This act gives protection to those native species that are recognized as endangered in the United States. However, this law applies only to federal lands and to interstate traffic of rare plants. The protection of endangered wildflowers on other public and private lands is left up to the states, as is the protection of species that might become locally rare or endangered through collection by native-plant suppliers and wildflower fanciers. State laws protecting wildflowers are far from uniform, and even where there is protective legislation, the enforcement of these laws is sometimes weak.

In addition to state laws concerning the protection of native plants, the wildflower gardener is faced with moral and ethical considerations that do not confront the gardener of cultivars. Essential to the enjoyment and appreciation of wild native plants is the respect for living things in their native habitats. The wildflower gardener's code of conduct should protect naturally occurring populations of native plants, not only to let others enjoy them, but also to preserve the ecological roles these plants play. Individual actions do make a difference, both positively and negatively. Wildflower gardeners have the chance to counteract the tragedy of habitat destruction and reduction in native populations occurring around the world.

CONSERVATION GUIDELINES*

1. Let your acts reflect your respect for wild native plants as integral parts of biological communities and natural landscapes. Remember that if you pick or disturb wildflowers, your action affects the natural world, and that the cumulative effects of the actions of many people can be particularly harmful.

2. Do not dig or take cuttings from native plants in the wild except as part of rescue or salvage operations sponsored by responsible organizations.

3. Encourage the use of regional native plants in home and public landscapes, but before obtaining wildflower plants or seeds for your home landscape, learn enough about their cultural requirements to be sure you can provide a suitable habitat.

4. If you collect seeds from the wild, collect a few seeds or fruits from each of many plants and only from common species that are locally abundant. Purchase wildflower seeds only from companies that collect responsibly.

5. Purchase live wildflower plants only from suppliers or organizations that propagate their own plants or purchase their material from those who propagate them. Ask sellers about the origin of plants you are considering buying. If there is any doubt about the plant's origin, do not purchase it.

6. Be cautious and knowledgeable in the use of exotic wildflowers. While many of these non-native wildflower species can be attractively used in gardens and landscapes, some species are overly aggressive, becoming weeds that may displace native species. Become aware of your state's noxious weed laws by contacting your state Department of Agriculture or local extension service.

7. When photographing or closely inspecting wildflowers, be careful not to trample plants nearby.

8. If you pick wildflowers, dried seed stalks, or greens for home decoration, use only common species that are abundant at the site. Leave enough flowers or seeds to allow the plant population to reseed itself. Avoid picking herbaceous perennials such as wild orchids, jack-in-the-pulpits, or gentians that, like daffodils, need to retain their vegetative parts to store energy for next year's development. Avoid cutting slow-growing plants such as running-cedar, club-mosses, or partridgeberry for Christmas wreaths or other decorations.

9. Become familiar with your state's wildflower protection laws. If your state does not have laws protecting wildflowers, or if the existing laws are weak, support the passage and enforcement of strong and effective legislation for the preservation of native plants. Report unlawful collection of plants to proper authorities and, when necessary, remind others that collecting plants or disturbing a natural area is illegal in parks and other public places.

10. If you learn that an area with wildflowers is scheduled for development, notify a native plant society in your region. Discuss with the

developer the possibilities of compatible development alternatives or of conducting a wildflower rescue or salvage operation.

11. It is important to protect information about the locations of rare species. If you discover a new site of a plant species that you know is rare, report it to responsible conservation officials, such as your state's Natural Heritage Program, a native plant society, Nature Conservancy chapter, or the United States Fish and Wildlife Service, as soon as possible and before discussing it with others.

*Adapted for broader applicability from the Virginia Wildflower Preservation Society's "Wildflower Conservation Guidelines."

See also WILDFLOWERS.

NECTARINE. A type of peach, *Prunus persica* var. *nucipersica*, with smooth, not furry, skin. Both trees are the same, and either fruit may emerge from the other, by sport or from seed. Hardy to Zone 7 and most frequently grown on the Pacific Coast, its culture is the same as for PEACH except that the fruit needs more protection against CURCULIO.

NECTARY. A glandular surface or organ in a flower that secretes nectar to attract insects, which by visiting different flowers, bring about pollination.

NECTRIA CANKER. A diseased area caused by infection by a fungus of the cortex and cambium region of trees. It is generally localized in relatively small areas on the trunk, spreading slowly from year to year. Each year the cambium at the margin of the canker forms a new callus, which is subsequently killed by the fungus (a species of the genus *Nectria*) so that the area consists of concentric rings of callus. At certain times of the year small fruiting bodies (perithecia) of the fungus are found on the recently killed bark near the margin of the canker.

Nectria cankers are common on nearly every species of hardwood and on many of the larger shrubs. Plants are seldom killed outright, but the open wound created furnishes entrance for insects and wood-destroying fungi. Cankers should be identified and removed in their initial stages. See TREE SURGERY.

NEILLIA (NEE lee ah) **sinensis.** A species of Asian deciduous shrubs belonging to the Rosaceae (Rose Family) and closely related to *Spiraea*. They are graceful spreading shrubs with bright green leaves, more or less lobed, and small, pink or whitish flowers in terminal clusters blooming in late spring. Propagation is by seed or cuttings of greenwood under glass. Hardy to Zone to 7.

NELUMBO (ne LUM boh). A genus of aquatic plants belonging to the Nymphaeaceae (Waterlily Family), commonly known as lotus. Sacred to the ancient Hindi, the plants spread westward and were valued by the old Egyptians as well. The leaves, blooms, and curious seedpods are perhaps the most striking single feature in Egyptian architecture and decoration.

From June through August, the flowers bloom on high stems that tower over the wide, blue-green, silver-sheened leaves, which float or extend above the water and may be 6 in. to 3 ft. across. Like those of many waterlilies, the flowers open on three successive days before they fade. In a good location with plenty of sun and rich soil, the plants thrive and good-sized roots will produce flowers the first season. Hardy to Zone 4, once set, nelumbos bloom freely and, unless the roots are actually frozen, suffer little from the cold.

Planting should be done in the spring when warm weather has definitely arrived. Treatment should be much the same as for other waterlilies (see NYMPHAEA), and they can be grown in half-barrels or tubs if a pond or other larger body of water is not available.

N. lutea (American-lotus, water-chinquapin) produces seeds that were used as food by the American Indians. It is perfectly hardy and easily cultivated, rewarding the grower with magnificent yellow blossoms up to 10 in. across.

N. nucifera (sacred-, East-Indian-, or Egyptian-lotus), formerly listed as *N. speciosum*, has been the parent of many varieties whose large showy, fragrant blooms stand up to 5 ft. out of the water, and range in color from pure white to dark rose-red. They are mostly hardy only in Zones 10–11.

NEMASTYLIS (nem ah STĪ lis). A genus of tender bulbous plants belonging to the Iridaceae (Iris Family), with grassy leaves and blue or purple flowers. Resembling blue-eyed-grass, they are seldom grown in gardens.

N. acuta (prairie iris) has leaves to 12 in. long and bright blue flowers lasting for only a day. It is native from Tennessee to Texas but hardy to Zone 6.

NEMATANTHUS (ne mah TAN thus). A genus of small woody plants, often trailing, suitable for basket culture. The flowers are red or orange, usually tubular, but often with a constriction near the throat or a bell shape, giving an interesting form. Belonging to the Gesneriaceae (Gesneria Family), their cultural requirements are similar to other epiphytic members of the family.

NEMATODES. These threadlike, microscopic worms (also called eelworms and round worms) infest many cultivated and wild plants, usually within the plants, entering at the root or as ectoparasites, attacking through plant cell walls. Some are pathogenic on humans, animals, and all plants. Others are parasitic and beneficial in controlling other nematodes and even, sometimes, grubs of Japanese beetles and other soil-dwelling pests.

Soil samples are very likely to contain nematodes, both free-living and plant-attacking genera. They can whip themselves several feet in the soil, but most nematode movement comes from movement of the soil. Because there are so many different kinds of nematodes, soil samples (including root samples and some water) should be examined by experts to determine what sort of controls should be applied. One reliable control comes from planting marigolds, preferably French or Mexican, which exude a killing essence from their roots. This effect is actually stronger the second year after planting and persists to the third year.

PEST SPECIES

Plants attacked by nematodes develop root galls or root knots and suffer dwarfing, poor flowering, or pale and distorted leaves and stems. Where they wound the plant when feeding, diseases often develop. This pest is especially prevalent in the South, where females lay up to 500 eggs a day. The life cycle is only 30 days. In some species, the male is scarce or unknown.

One important nematode is the stem and root nematode of hyacinths, phlox, and narcissus. It causes leaf distortion with tiny "spicules" and discolored rings on the bulbs. Dormant bulbs should be soaked in water kept at 110–115°F for 2½ hours. Distorted phlox stems and flowers are signs of nematode infestation. Remove and burn any infested plants as soon as the pest is discovered.

The common root knot nematodes cause swollen galls on roots and dwarfed, pale plants. These galls provide winter quarters for the tiny worms. They return to the upper foot of soil in the spring unless already controlled by marigold exudate. For flats with infested soil, the best treatment is to dip the whole flat in water kept at the boiling point for several minutes. This works better than merely pouring on boiling water. In greenhouses, steam treatment is used as well as flame pasteurizers.

Rotation of crops and planting of resistant species are other means of control. The natural fungus of most value in damaging nematodes is especially encouraged by rich organic matter in the soil, so it is wise to keep adding compost and other plant material to the soil. This fungus sends out a ring that squeezes the nematode. Other fungi are toxic. Fallow ground, especially in May and June, helps to starve nematodes. In a system sometimes practiced in the South, the fallow year is succeeded by a year of keeping chickens on the plot, then a year growing corn. After that cycle, vegetable crops are again introduced. Choice of fairly resistant vegetables is still advisable; these include broccoli, brussels sprouts, garlic, leek, onions, Jerusalem-artichoke, turnip, rhubarb, and spinach. Cyst nematodes do not thrive in acid or alkaline soils, so in an acid soil the safest crop would be potatoes; in alkaline, cabbages and beets.

The sting nematode in the South can be controlled by turning under cover crops of CROTA-LARIA spp. and by rotating hot peppers with watermelon, for example. This nematode helps to eradicate plants such as crabgrass, ragweed, and cocklebur.

The leaf nematode is a serious pest on chrysanthemums as well as other greenhouse plants. Sterilized soil and sand are the best preventives. Since nematodes need moisture, avoid watering leaves.

BENEFICIAL NEMATODES

Very powerful controllers of pest nematodes are the parasitic nematodes, available commercially as juvenile or Nc (*Neoaplectana carpocapsae*) nematodes. These parasites attack insects as well as nematodes, which have their larval stage in the soil. They stand on their tails and sway in search of a host, frequently a nematode. After entering the host, this parasite releases killing bacteria, which feed on the host's body and kill it in about two days. Then the parasite feeds on the body of the host and reproduces. The cycle takes about a week. The new generations continue to control nematodes and such other soil dwellers as borers, root weevils, cutworms, and others for the rest of the season. Most if not all beneficial nematodes require a humid environment for success.

One other parasitic nematode has been used to control the boll weevil, which infests cotton. It penetrates the young weevil, eats up its stored fat, and causes the pest to emerge from hibernation in search of more food. It emerges too early and starves to death because there is no cotton yet ready for it to attack.

NEMESIA (ne MEE see ah). A genus of small, half-hardy South African herbs belonging to the Scrophulariaceae (Figwort Family). The bright yellow, orange, or red blossoms resemble miniature snapdragons. There are many intermediate shades and colors in cultivated strains, and a close planting of these brilliant little flowers creates an effect resembling a mosaic of jewels.

Nemesias should be started in early spring in the hotbed or greenhouse and planted in the open in late spring. They should be set close so that the frail stems can support one another. Where the summers are not too hot, they will bloom continuously for several months. The plants are also charming in window boxes.

N. strumosa, the most widely cultivated species, grows to 2 ft. and bears racemes of white, yellow, or purple flowers with spotted throats. Var. *suttonii* has larger flowers in more varied colors. Var. *nana compacta*, one of the prettiest forms, is excellent for an edging.

Other species occasionally found in gardens include *N. floribunda*, *N. lilacina*, and *N. versicolor*.

NEMOPANTHUS (nee moh PAN thus) **mucronatus.** An ornamental deciduous shrub of the Aquifoliaceae (Holly Family), commonly known as mountain holly. It is native from Newfoundland to Wisconsin and Virginia, mostly in moist ground. It is a well-branched shrub growing to 10 ft.; the young branches are purplish but later turn gray. It has medium-sized, bright green leaves that turn yellow in the fall. The whitish flowers are inconspicuous, but the red berries stand out. It grows well in shade and in acid environments such as mountaintops and bogs. Propagation is by seed. Hardy in Zones 3–7.

NEMOPHILA (nuh MAH fil ah). A genus of delicate annual herbs, mostly native to California, with cut leaves, sometimes rough haired, and blue or white flowers borne singly or occcasionally in racemes. Plants are low

Nemophila menziesii

growing and spreading. If seeds are sown early in spring in a semishaded spot in the border, or on the edge of the wild garden, the small, bright flowers will appear continuously all summer. The species most widely grown, *N. menziesii* (baby-blue-eyes) has delightful, clear blue, wide open or broadly bell-shaped flowers on short stems above the prettily cut leaves. *N. maculata* (five-spot) has five-lobed white blossoms, the tip of each petal marked with dark purple.

NEOMARICA (nee oh mah RIK ah) **northiana.** A tropical perennial herb formerly listed as *Marica northiana* and commonly known as apostle plant. It has long, narrow leaves and white, yellow, or blue flowers on long, flat, leaflike stalks. The flowers resemble those of iris, to which the plant is related, but are short-lived. It makes an excellent houseplant, blooming in winter and spring. Hardy only in Zones 10–11, plants will survive the winter outdoors in Florida when properly mulched. Propagation is by division of the clumps.

NEOREGELIA (nee oh red JEL ee ah) **marmorata.** A colorful epiphytic herb from South America, formerly listed as *Aregelia marmorata*, belonging to the Bromeliaceae (Pineapple Family), and commonly known as marble plant. It has rosettes of light green leaves to 16 in. long and 2½ in. wide with a dark-mottled base and sheath. The blue or lavender tubular flowers are about 1½ in. long. It is most often grown as a houseplant and is cultivated like other bromeliads. Many forms with mottled or red-tipped leaves are hybrids but are often listed under this name.

NEPENTHES (ne PEN theez). A genus of insectivorous plants with small, clustered flowers, native to the tropical Orient. Many fancy named cultivars are now grown in North America. They are known as pitcher plants because the expanded midrib of the leaf forms a pitcherlike receptacle, with a hooded tip often brightly colored and furnished with winged fronts, lids, and spring collars. These characteristics apparently attract

insects into the receptacle, from which they cannot escape. Finally they fall to the bottom and are dissolved by a fluid secreted by the plant.

Nepenthes are grown in greenhouses in pots or hanging baskets of sand, peat, and sphagnum moss in a temperature never below 65°F. They are propagated by seed or cuttings of ripened wood. Growers sometimes use live sphagnum moss as the growing medium and keep it moistened with distilled water.

N. hookerana has pale green pitchers marked with purple, to 6 in. long and 3 in. wide, sometimes doubly fringed.

N. mirabilis, formerly listed as *N. phyllamphora*, has pale or reddish green pitchers to 6 in. long and 1½ in. across with narrow frontal wings.

NEPETA (ne PET ah). A genus of annual or perennial herbs of the Lamiaceae (Mint Family), some naturalized in the United States. Mostly odorous, with toothed or cut leaves and whorls of blue or white flowers borne in spikes or clusters. The genus is of importance chiefly as a source of medicinal products, but there are several species useful in the garden, particularly as ground covers in shady places. All are of easy culture and propagated by seed or division.

PRINCIPAL SPECIES

N. cataria (catnip, catmint) is a perennial that grows to 3 ft. high and has pale, downy foliage. It has whitish or pale purple flowers ¼ in. long borne in dense spikes up to 5 in. long and blooming from mid- to late summer. The plant, common in old gardens and now widely naturalized, has a characteristic pungent odor that is highly attractive to cats. Hardy to Zone 3.

N. hederacea (ground-ivy) is now listed as *Glechoma hederacea*; see GLECHOMA.

Nepeta cataria

N. mussinii is a branching perennial that grows 1–2 ft. and is covered with whitish down. The flowers, blue with dark spots, grow to ½ in. long in long racemes. It is frequently confused with *N.* x *faassenii* (Persian ground-ivy), a perennial hybrid valued for its gray-green foliage but often growing in unkempt form.

NEPHROLEPIS (nef roh LEP is). A genus of subtropical and tropical terrestrial ferns including some excellent houseplants; many species and their cultivars are widely propagated commercially throughout the world. They are poor spore producers and are usually propagated by division or by rooting stolons. Tissue culture is a popular method of commercial propagation. The species thrive under less than ideal conditions and produce dense crowns of long fronds. Under ideal conditions, the fronds of species may grow to 10 ft. long. Several species have become naturalized in Florida.

PRINCIPAL SPECIES

N. acuminata has 4–7 ft., pinnate fronds that bear both fertile and sterile pinnae. The fertile pinnae are deeply lobed, producing an attractive effect in combination with the wider sterile pinnae at the base of the fronds. It can be grown in tropical gardens or as a large container plant.

N. biserrata (sword fern) has 4-ft., drooping fronds with drooping pinnae. It is an invasive fern found in tropical regions worldwide.

N. cordifolia (tuberous sword fern) has bright green, pinnate fronds 10–30 in. long that bear closely spaced, strongly auricled pinnae. The roots often have small, scaly tubers. Native in Africa and Asia, it is sometimes epiphytic on palmettos but is usually a colonizing terrestrial that becomes weedy in tropical regions and can be grown as a potted plant. Cv. 'Duffii' is a sterile form with abbreviated round pinnae and crested tips.

N. exaltata (sword fern) is a tropical American fern with stiff, upright, pinnate fronds that grow 8–9 ft. under ideal conditions. It is not much different from other species, but mutation has produced many interesting varieties. The first was cv. 'Bostoniensis' (Boston fern) which appeared in an 1870 shipment of ferns to Boston. From this arose a multitude of mutants that have been widely cultivated. Caution must be used in watering the finely dissected foliage of some of these cultivars, since they are prone to rot. Technically, each cultivar should include the name 'Bostoniensis', but this is rarely done. The many cultivars include 'Bostoniensis Aurea', 'Bostoniensis Compacta', 'Childsii', 'Elegantissima', 'Falcata', 'Fluffy Ruffles', 'Gracillima', 'Hillsii', 'Lycopodioides', 'Mini Ruffle', 'Rochfordii', 'Shadow Lace', 'Silver Balls', 'Susi Wong', 'Verona', and 'Whitmanii'. There has been much confusion in naming because it has been difficult to accurately describe the differences between cultivars, and many old cultivars have been given new names through error or dishonesty. Most of these cultivars are produced commercially by tissue culture. One of the most recently introduced, cv. 'Dallasii' (Dallas fern), is said to be even more tolerant of adverse conditions than the original Boston fern.

NEPHTHYTIS (nef THĪ tis). A small genus of herbs belonging to the Araceae (Arum Family), native to western Africa. They have thick rhizomes, slender stems, and long-petioled, arrow-shaped leaves. One species, *N. afzelii* is cultivated in warm climates and offered as a foliage plant for home or greenhouse decoration. They do well in relatively poor growing conditions and are usually grown climbing on bark supports.

NERINE (ne RĪ nee). A genus of brilliantly flowered South African plants belonging to the Amaryllidaceae (Amaryllis Family). Hardy only to Zone 9, they are favorites for greenhouse cultivation because of their mass of crimson or scarlet blooms late in the fall; white and rose blossoms are occasionally seen. The flowers, which have recurved, 1-in.-long petals and long, bright red stamens, are borne in large umbels at the top of a leafless stem (scape) 12 in. or taller.

The leaves appear after the flowers are gone.

At this time, the plants need the greatest care with plenty of sunshine, frequent sprinklings of the leaves, persistent watering of the roots, and occasional applications of liquid manure. When the leaves finally turn yellow, the pots should be laid on their sides in the sun for the bulbs to ripen. In late summer, top-dress the pots with rotted manure, soak them well, and return them to the greenhouse bench. Do not repot the plants for about five years. The offsets can be used to produce new plants.

N. sarniensis (Guernsey-lily) and *N. curvifolia* var. *fothergilli* are the most often seen.

NERIUM (NEE ree um). A well-known genus of evergreen shrubs with showy flowers, native to southern Europe and Japan, and belonging to the Apocynaceae (Dogbane Family). Commonly known as olean-der, they are usu-ally grown in pots or tubs for green-house, window garden, or porch decoration and outdoors in Zones 8–11. Despite the fact that the stems and leaves are poisonous if eaten by people or ani-

Nerium oleander

mals and are beloved by scale insects and mealy bugs, they have long been popular shrubs. Plants thrive in loamy soil, and it is not difficult to have good specimens if attention is paid to resting and cutting them back after flowering and subse-quently shaping and feeding them when growth is active. Well-ripened shoots are essential for free flowering, so they should be fully exposed to air and light. Propagation is by cuttings of mature wood, which are often rooted in water.

Oleanders may be infested with mealy bugs, soft scale, and white or oleander scale. To control all these, fumigate greenhouses or spray plants with insecticide. In Florida, a fungus often causes WITCHES'-BROOM on this host. The plants are stunted and flower production ceases. Prune out all brooms together with 12 in. of the branches on which they are growing; then spray with a fungi-cide. Burn all prunings.

N. oleander (oleander, rose-bay), native to southern Europe, is the most widely grown species. It may attain 20 ft. and is attractive at all times with its dark green, leathery leaves up to 8 in. long. The large, showy, spring and summer flowers are borne in terminal clusters, rosy red in the type species. There are numerous varieties ranging in color from white to bright red, and with double as well as single flowers.

NERTERA (NUR te rah) **granadensis.** A slender, creeping perennial native to the Southern Hemi-sphere, formerly listed as *N. depressa*, and com-monly known as bead plant. The flowers are inconspicuous, but the orange-colored berries make it a handsome little plant when in fruit. It is sometimes grown in northern greenhouses, where it merits attention as a window plant. In regions where the climate is not severe, it makes a good ground cover for shady places, showing to advantage in the rock garden. It requires a sandy soil with leaf mold. Propagation is by seed or division.

NETTLE. Common name for URTICA, a genus of herbs usually bearing stinging hairs. The Nettle Family is URTICACEAE. Dead-nettle is LAMIUM, a genus of border or rock garden plants of the Lamiaceae (Mint Family).

NEUTRAL SOIL. Soil neither acid nor alkaline. On a scale of one to fourteen, neutral soil has a pH value of seven. Few soils are exactly neutral, but in practice, soils can be described as neutral when they vary between pH 6.8 and 7.2. Acid soil can be made neutral by adding lime; alkaline soils, by adding aluminum sulfate, sulfur, or tan-nic acid. See also ACID SOIL; ALKALINE SOIL; PH.

NEW ZEALAND SPINACH. A tender, pros-trate, annual herb of the Southern Hemisphere, *Tetragonia tetragonioides*, grown for its succulent leaves and branch tips, which are used as summer greens. While New Zealand spinach is very similar to ordinary spinach when cooked, it has a much wider usefulness for home gardens for several reasons. It thrives in the hot weather that spinach cannot stand, is easier to grow, and can be cut repeatedly all summer. Having more open growth, it does not collect much sand and requires less washing; in other respects, it is cultivated the same as ordinary SPINACH.

NICANDRA (nī KAN drah). A genus of Peruvian annual herbs, similar to *Physalis* but with showier flowers, somewhat grown for ornament in warm climates or greenhouses. *N. physalodes* (apple-of-Peru, shoo-fly plant, fly-poison plant) is an old-fashioned garden favorite with blue flowers, easily grown from seed. It is reputedly able to kill houseflies if crushed leaves and shoots are mixed with milk and left where flies can eat it.

NICOTIANA (ni koh tee AY nah). A genus of annual or perennial, occasionally shrubby herbs belonging to the Solanaceae (Nightshade Family) and commonly known as tobacco. Various species have been cultivated for commercial tobacco production or for garden ornament. Several species, commonly called flowering tobacco, have sticky, hairy foliage and long-tubed white, yellow, pink, rose, red, greenish, or purple flowers, which usually open at night and almost invariably are delightfully fragrant.

All the types commonly cultivated are native to the South American tropics and are very sensitive to frost. They prefer light, rich soil in a warm, sheltered location. Although they frequently self-sow, it is advisable to start plants from seed sown early in the spring in the greenhouse or hotbed. Plants should be hardened-off gradually and not set out until the weather has turned warm.

The many diseases and insect pests of commercial tobacco crops are seldom troublesome on garden plants. Ornamental species, however, are frequently infested late in the season with the greenhouse whitefly. Spraying with a contact insecticide may be effective; see INSECT CONTROL.

PRINCIPAL SPECIES

N. alata (flowering tobacco) may grow up to 5 ft. high, but most cultivars are 1–3 ft. The flowers droop as if wilted during the day, then open in the evening. Var. *grandiflora* (jasmine tobacco) is grown for its fragrant blossoms.

N. bigelovii (Indian tobacco) yielded tobacco for native Indians in the southwestern states.

N. glauca (tree tobacco) is a quick-growing plant naturalized in the dry hill regions of Texas and southern California. It grows to 20 ft. or more, becoming woody and treelike.

N. x *sanderae* is a hybrid that grows to 3 ft. and has carmine-rose flowers. Some of the cultivars are striking plants for the annual border.

N. sylvestris, a tall, graceful plant, is topped with showerlike clusters of starry, white flowers with long, slender tubes, which open in the daytime but are not fragrant.

N. tabacum is cultivated to produce commercial tobacco crops.

NICOTINE. Extract of tobacco, sometimes used in commecial and homemade insecticides. It is most often used as a spray or greenhouse fumigant to control aphids, but its effectiveness varies depending on the concentration. Nicotine solutions, especially nicotine-sulfate, were once common but have largely been replaced by other formulas. Due to its highly toxic nature, nicotine may have harmful side-effects on humans, plants, and animals and should be used with care, if at all, especially on fruits and vegetables.

NIDULARIUM (nid yoo LAIR ee um). A genus of Brazilian epiphytic herbs belonging to the Bromeliaceae (Pineapple Family). They have prickly edged leaves in rosettes, and among the foliage are red, white, or purple stemless flowers surrounded by brightly colored bracts.

Hardy only in Zones 10–11, they are usually grown in warm greenhouses in pots, baskets, or slatted cribs filled with fibrous material. They should be watered sparingly in the winter when dormant, but given plenty of moisture in summer when growth is active. The two best-known species are *N. innocentii*, with 12-in. leaves and white flowers surrounded by brilliant scarlet bracts; and *N. fulgens*, with thick clusters of white-and-lavender flowers and bright red bracts set close in the axils of the white-spotted leaves.

NIEREMBERGIA (nee rem BUR jee ah). A genus of low-growing, half-hardy perennials or subshrubs native to South America, belonging to the Solanaceae (Nightshade Family), and commonly known as cupflower. Excellent in the rock garden because of their dwarf stature—seldom more than 6 in.—they are also used in the open border. Because of their numerous pale violet or white flowers of slightly irregular cup shape and sometimes with purple centers, they are occasionally grown as potted plants and are excellent for baskets or vases.

Hardy to Zone 7, most species are perennial in the tropics but are treated as annuals in cooler climates. They will flower the first season from seed sown indoors early. The plants require a warm, protected situation, especially during the early stages of their development. If grown indoors or in warm regions as perennials, they can be propagated by cuttings.

N. gracilis and *N. repens* (whitecup) have white, blue, or rose-tinted flowers and creeping stems that take root and by which the plants can be propagated.

N. scoparia grows to 3 ft. and is shrubby and branching. Its flowers are white with lilac or blue tints and yellow throats.

NIGELLA (nī JEL ah). A genus of attractive, hardy annual herbs belonging to the Ranunculaceae (Buttercup Family) and commonly known as fennel flower. Plants have blue, yellow, pink, red, or white flowers and very finely cut foliage, which probably suggested the common name. Seed can be sown in spring as early as the ground can be worked, or even in the fall, since the small plants from fall-sown seed often survive the winter and bloom quite early in the summer.

N. damascena (love-in-a-mist, devil-in-a-bush) grows to 18 in. and bears blue, white, red, or pur-

ple flowers surrounded and partially concealed by the finely cut, green leaves of the involucre. The flowers, which last well when cut, are most attractive in mixed bouquets.

N. sativa (fennel flower), from the Mediterranean region, has solitary blue flowers without a surrounding lacy involucre. The seeds, known as black cumin and used for seasoning in Europe, are not the same as the common spice derived from *Cuminum cyminum*.

Nigella damascena

NIGHT-BLOOMING CEREUS. A common name that applies to various genera and species of cacti, including CEREUS, SELENICEREUS, HYLOCEREUS, EPIPHYLLUM, and many other genera of the Cereanae and Hylocereanae subtribes that have white, night-blooming flowers.

NIGHTSHADE. Common name for several species of SOLANUM, especially *S. nigrum*.

The Nightshade Family is SOLANACEAE. Deadly nightshade is *Atropa belladonna*, which is cultivated only for medicinal purposes; see ATROPA. Enchanter's-nightshade is *Circaea lutetiana*; see CIRCAEA.

NITRATE. The main chemical form of nitrogen that plants take from the soil for their use. Although most of the nitrogen in soils occurs as organic molecules in humus, it is converted first to ammonium and then rapidly to nitrate (see NITRIFICATION) before it is used by most plants. While nitrates are readily available to plants, they are not held at all by most soils and readily leach below the root zone after large amounts of rainfall or irrigation and can, therefore, pollute ground water if excessive quantities are used.

Some nitrogen fertilizers have nitrate in them —calcium nitrate, Chilean nitrate, potassium nitrate, and ammonium nitrate—with all but the last not very commonly found in stores. Other nitrogen fertilizers, such as ammonium sulfate and urea, will be readily converted to nitrates once added to the soil.

NITRIFICATION. The changing of crude compounds of nitrogen into, first, ammonia, then nitrites, and finally nitrates, in which form the nitrogen becomes available for the use of plants as food. This progressive change is brought about in the soil or in other substances containing nitrogen in complex forms (like stable manures or humus), by the action of so-called nitrifying bacteria. If conditions are unfavorable for the activity of these organisms (one such condition being a lack of oxygen), then another sort of bacteria, the denitrifying kind, gets to work and breaks down valuable nitrates, releasing much of the nitrogen in gaseous form, which is thus lost to the plants.

Recommended methods of handling manure, compost, and soil are designed to foster nitrification, prevent denitrification, and thereby improve the fertility of the soil.

NITROGEN. An essential element for all living things where it is found in combination with carbon and other elements to form many molecules such as proteins. It is needed in relatively high amounts by plants as well as animals. In soils it is found mainly as organic molecules in humus, with some present in ammonium, and as nitrate (the main form of nitrogen used by most plants). It is also found in the air as a colorless, tasteless, odorless gas comprising about 78% of the atmosphere. While this gas is of little direct use to most plants, it can be used by certain bacteria, such as those living in roots of legumes, which provide a source of available or fixed nitrogen for the plant.

While all plants need nitrogen in relatively large quantities (compared to their needs for other nutrients), the ones needing the most nitrogen are those that develop a large amount of leafy growth, such as cabbage, tomatoes, and corn. Nitrogen is found in many organic materials, such as manures, composts, grass clippings, and the like. One of the reasons to keep adding a variety of organic materials to soils is to keep plants well supplied with available nitrogen.

There are many types of commercial nitrogen fertilizers available, such as ammonium sulfate, ammonium nitrate, and urea. Fertilizers containing nitrogen are frequently sold as mixtures with phosphate and potash. When commercial nitrogen fertilizers are used, it is best to make more than one application to plants, with some added before planting or transplanting, and some added later as a side-dressing near the developing plant.

Be careful not to stimulate trees and shrubs by adding nitrogenous fertilizers between early summer and late fall, because they may not prepare for winter temperatures and could be injured by frost or other weakening conditions.

Since it is a frequent limiting factor to the growth of plants, nitrogen should be conserved and added to the soil on a regular basis.

NODE. That part of a stem at which leaves and buds have their origin. The spaces between nodes are called "internodes." It is from the node that new plants arise in propagation by suckers, stolons, rhizomes, and runners. Also, it is the presence of nodes that distinguishes underground stems from roots, which also branch out but not from buds.

NOISETTE ROSE. This class originated in 1811 with a natural cross between the pink China rose and the musk rose in the garden of a rice grower named Champneys, who showed the resulting plant (now called 'Champney's Pink Cluster') to his friend, a nurseryman named Noisette, who sent seeds to his brother in France.

The Noisettes were quickly crossed with tea roses, and many everblooming climbers resulted. Unfortunately, they are very tender and so are only grown in mild climates. Some famous Noisettes are 'Blush Noisette', 'Lamarque', and 'Maréchal Niel'.

NOLANA (noh LAN ah). A genus of trailing, perennial herbs, grown as annuals, with flowers resembling morning-glories, but of greater substance. Native to Peru and Chile, these basket plants (which are also useful in the border or among rocks) prefer a sunny exposure and will thrive in dry soils and hot climates. Seed is best sown where the plants are to grow, though it is possible to start them indoors and transplant later. *Nolana* combines well with *Portulaca*, which requires about the same conditions.

N. acuminata, formerly listed as *N. lanceolata*, is entirely covered with short, whitish hairs. The deep blue blossoms, 2 in. across, have yellowish white, spotted throats.

N. paradoxa has stems growing to 1 ft. or longer and leaves spotted and streaked with purple above. The showy tubular, blue flowers, 2 in. across, have white throats, yellow inside. Var. *violacea* has violet blossoms.

NOPALEA (noh PAY lee ah). An interesting genus of cacti whose peculiar red flowers set them apart from the similar OPUNTIA. The flower does not open but is erect at the edge of the flat joint, with exserted stamens and with the pistil exserted beyond the stamens.

One species that should be included in any large garden collection is *N. cochenillifera* (cochineal plant), a rapid grower formerly of commercial importance as the host plant for the cochineal insect from which a brilliant red dye was made prior to the development of cheaper aniline products.

NORFOLK-ISLAND-PINE. Common name for *Araucaria heterophylla*, a handsome evergreen; see ARAUCARIA.

NOTHOLAENA (noh thoh LEE nah). A genus of small, warm-climate, drought-tolerant ferns. They are closely related to *Cheilanthes*, and some botanists advocate combining the genera. They are all native in North America but can be grown outdoors only in the southwestern states or indoors with expert care.

PRINCIPAL SPECIES

N. aurea (golden cloak fern), also listed as *Cheilanthes bonariensis*, is an 8–24 in. fern with narrow, pinnate-pinnatifid fronds whose lower surface is covered with white to light brown hairs. It is found in southern California and Arizona southward to Chile and Argentina.

N. fendleri (Fendler's cloak fern), also listed as *Cheilanthes cancellata*, common in the southwestern states, has a zigzag rachis that gives it another common name, latticework cloak fern. It has triangular fronds 5–14 in. long, arising from a scaly-hairy brown rhizome. It is five- to six-pinnate with very small pinnae.

N. newberryi (cotton or Newberry's cloak fern) has broad, pointed, feathery fronds 8–10 in. long with powdery leaf surfaces that appear silvery. The black stipes grow from scaly rhizomes. Native to Baja and southern California, it enjoys more shade than other species.

N. sinuata (wavy cloak fern), also listed as *Cheilanthes sinuata*, is an 8–24 in. fern that grows throughout the southwestern states to South America but is very difficult to cultivate. It has narrow, pinnate-pinnatifid fronds with three to six lobes per pinna.

NOTHOSCORDUM (noh thoh SKOR dum). A small genus of bulbous, onionlike plants of the Liliaceae (Lily Family), known as false garlic. They have yellow or white flowers in flattish clusters and grasslike leaves. Native to the southern United States and Mexico, they are not hardy in cold climates. If grown in the garden, the bulbs should be dug in the fall. They can also be grown as pot plants. *N. bivalve* grows to 16 in. with yellowish flowers. *N. inodorum* has leaves to 1 ft. and fragrant, blush-white flowers lined with deep pink, borne on stems to 2 ft. tall.

NOTOCACTUS (noh toh KAK tus). A genus of South American cacti ("noto-" meaning "southern"), easy for the beginning collector since most species are not only attractive in spination and appearance, but are easily cultivated and will flower readily even as rather young plants.

Recommended species are *N. scopa*, with dense, soft, bristly silver and reddish spines, and large, satiny yellow flowers; *N. haselbergii* (sometimes segregated as *Brasilicactus*), with short, fine, silvery, bristly spines and dazzling red to orange-red flowers; and *N. leninghausii* (sometimes segregated as *Eriocactus*), a many-ribbed, shortly columnar, basally clustering species with soft, hairlike golden spines and large, satiny yellow flowers.

NUPHAR (NOO fahr). A genus of aquatic plants of shallow ponds with large, green, floating leaves similar to waterlilies, formerly classified as *Nymphozanthus*, and commonly known as cowlily, yellow-pondlily, or spatterdock. Golden yellow, globelike flowers are 5 in. across. A few species are grown in aquariums, while others are attractive pond subjects.

Hardy to Zone 2, the plants are mostly native to the western United States, growing in stagnant waters and still pools, where mud bottoms supply nourishment and a foothold for its heavy creeping rootstocks. In cultivation, plants respond to the same treatment as NYMPHAEA. Propagation is by seed or division.

N. advena (sometimes listed as *Nymphaea advena*) has flat, green, heart-shaped leaves that float or stand slightly above the water to frame groups of cup-shaped, yellow, lilylike flowers. The species is hardy to Zone 2, but in northern regions the pure yellow species is replaced by a variety tinged with a purplish tone.

NUT. As commonly understood, any fruit whose seed is enclosed in a leathery, woody, or bony rind or shell, more or less separable from the seed itself. The term is also applied to the "meat" or "kernel." Botanically speaking, it is an INDEHISCENT, single-celled, single-seeded hard fruit.

NUTRIENT SOLUTION. A solution of chemical salts that will supply to a plant all of the mineral elements needed for growth in proper portions and at the proper concentrations, cus-tomarily used in HYDROPONICS. The term is also sometimes used to refer to any watering solution that contains some plant nutrients.

NYCTAGINACEAE (nik tah gin AY see ee). The Four-o'clock Family, a group of herbs, shrubs, and trees widely distributed in warm regions but chiefly confined to the Americas. A few genera are grown for ornament, chiefly *Abronia*, *Bougainvillea*, and *Mirabilis*.

NYMPH. The name given, during its growing stage, to an insect that undergoes gradual or incomplete metamorphosis in its life cycle. The nymph corresponds to the larva (grub) of an insect that undergoes complete metamorphosis. Though a larva, such as a caterpillar, differs greatly in appearance from the adult moth or butterfly, a nymph is similar in shape and body construction to its adult. Nymphs grow by molting or shedding their skin, and each successive stage between two molts (called an instar) is more like the adult than the preceding one. With the final molt, the nymphal stage passes over into the adult stage without the intervention of an inactive or pupal stage such as occurs in insects with complete metamorphosis.

NYMPHAEA (nim FEE ah). A genus of large-flowered, fragrant plants entirely aquatic in habit and well known in both wild and cultivated forms as waterlily. About 40 species from all parts of the tropic and temperate zones with their many hybrids offer a wide range of color and size of bloom and foliage to satisfy any setting. Plants are perennial, growing from submerged rootstocks, and have broad, floating foliage and showy flowers. The genus is roughly divided into two groups: the tender ones (tropical and subtropical in origin) and the hardy ones.

HARDY NYMPHAEAS

The hardy waterlilies can be planted directly in the bottom of large, natural ponds if the more desirable container planting is not possible. Unless actually frozen, plants will survive over the winter as far north as Zone 1. These hardy forms present a wide variety of shapes, colors, and sizes of bloom, including the best of the yellow kinds and others ranging from pure white to

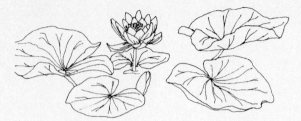

Nymphaea odorata, a hardy waterlily

deep vermilion, bronze, or copper. In most hardy species, the flowers float on the water surface, while some kinds raise the blossoms slightly above the water.

TROPICAL NYMPHAEAS

The tropical waterlilies are usually grown as annuals in cool climates, started from seed each year and set out in the pool or pond as soon as the weather permits. The tropicals are more spectacular in the size of bloom and leaf. Their flowers are displayed on fine, erect stems well above the water and can be used as cut flowers. Plants grow quickly during the summer and bloom until hit by frost. They offer fragrant exotic charm not found in the hardy sorts and cover an infinitely varied palette of blue, violet, purple, pink, deep rose, and dark red. They lack the yellow and copper tints of the hardy lilies, so most color schemes of any extent call for planting both types.

The tropicals are divided into two classes of day- and night-blooming. By judicious planting, the grower may have lilies in flower 24 hours a day in even a very small pool.

CULTURE

To grow waterlilies successfully, plenty of good, rich soil is imperative. They are gross feeders, and particularly the large night-bloomers, which make heavy leaf growth, must have plenty of food to keep them at their best through the entire summer.

Over a period of months, topsoil of a some-

what heavy texture should be first piled in layers and then thoroughly mixed with cow manure in a half-and-half mixture; horse manure (used in the same proportion) is not quite as good. If neither is available, sheep manure at the rate of 1 part to 8 or 10 parts of topsoil is excellent. In addition to the manure, ground bonemeal, dried blood, or other concentrated fertilizer can be added.

Waterlily roots, when unconfined, tend to spread, and the more delicate species are often choked by the rank growth of stronger varieties. To check this spreading and to make general culture easier, the common practice is to grow individual plants in a box, tub, or other suitable container and submerge the whole. The choice of container should vary according to the need of the occupant, but at least a cubic foot of good rich soil must be allowed for each plant; larger species demand more root room and more soil. With small boxes, the soil must be renewed each year, at which time the root can be divided.

PROPAGATION

To raise waterlilies from seed, sow in small pots of well-sieved, sandy loam and submerge in water in a warm, sunny location. When sufficient growth has been made, pot up the seedlings in fertile soil. If seed is to be sown directly in a pond, roll each one in a ball of clay and drop in the desired location.

Hardy waterlilies are usually grown from dormant rootstocks, which should be planted just below the soil surface at an angle slightly off horizontal. They can be set out as early as mid-April. If planted directly in the pool rather than in a container, either put them in a small basket of soil or press them down into the bottom and weigh with a small stone. Direct planting can be done in 1–2 ft. of water.

Tropical waterlilies are usually purchased as growing plants. When the temperature is stabilized at 70°F, they should be set out with the leaf crown just above the top of the soil. Growers commonly put a shallow layer of clean sand or fine gravel on top of the soil to hold it down and keep the pool clean. The depth of water above the crown should be 8–16 in. Shallow water allows the sun to warm the young plants. One of the great advantages of container planting is that by putting blocks under the box, plants can be set in any depth of water.

PLANTING

Waterlilies should not be too crowded; plant 3–6 ft. apart—more for larger varieties—in a position receiving maximum sunlight. Plenty of light and heat are essential to bring them to perfection. If plants need extra food during the growing season, they can be given additional nourishment by shoveling a bag full of dried blood or one of the specially formulated commercial fertilizers down among the roots.

WINTER PROTECTION

Hardy waterlilies can be wintered in the pond or pool unless it freezes solid. A small pool should be covered with boards and blanketing of straw or leaves placed on top. If the pool has to be drained, fill it with straw or other mulch, being careful to amply protect root boxes (if left in place) against the invasion of rats and mice. Containers are best cared for by removing them to the cellar and covering them with burlap, which should be moistened often to keep the soil damp enough to ward off dry rot.

USEFUL NYMPHAEA VARIETIES

Growers list many fine varieties of both hardy and tropical waterlilies. Each season, new hybrids are introduced, but the following list includes some well-proven and easily obtained suggestions.

HARDY NYMPHAEAS

Apricot to Copper-red. *N.* 'Aurora' and *N.* 'Comanche'.

Pink and Red. *N.* x *marliacea* 'Rosea', *N.* 'W. B. Shaw', *N.* 'Attraction', and *N.* 'Rose Arey'.

White. *N.* x *marliacea* 'Albida', *N. alba* 'Gladstoniana', *N. odorata* var. *gigantea*, and *N. tetragona*.

Yellow. *N.* x *marliacea* 'Chromatella' and *N. sulfurea* 'Sulfurea Grandiflora'.

TROPICAL NYMPHAEAS, NIGHT-BLOOMING

Pink and Red. *N.* 'Devoniensis', *N.* 'Emily Grant Hutchings', and *N.* 'Red Flare'.

White. *N. lotus* var. *dentata* and *N.* 'La Reine de Los Angeles'.

TROPICAL NYMPHAEAS, DAY-BLOOMING

Blue. *N. caerulea* (Egyptian-lotus), *N. gigantea hudsoniana*, *N.* 'Blue Beauty', and *N. capensis* var. *zanzibariensis* and cv. 'Azurea'.

Pink. *N. capensis zanzibariensis* 'Rosea', *N.* 'General Pershing', and *N.* 'Mrs. C. W. Ward'.

Purple. *N. capensis zanzibariensis*, *N.* 'Panama Pacific', and *N.* 'August Koch'.

White. *N. flavovirens* and *N.* 'Mrs. George H. Pring'.

NYMPHAEACEAE (nim fee AY see ee). The Waterlily Family, a group of aquatic herbs much used in garden pools, of which *Nymphaea* (waterlily) is the typical genus.

NYMPHOIDES (nim foh Ī deez). A genus of aquatic plants sometimes listed as *Limnanthemum*, belonging to the Gentianaceae (Gentian Family), including three flowering perennial species commonly used in garden pools, tub gardens, and aquariums. Plants have delicate flowers and are commonly called floating-heart because of the leaf shape. Because their growth habit is similar but daintier, they compliment plantings of larger waterlilies with a minor variation. Hardiness varies with the species to Zone 4.

N. indica (water-snowflake) has the typical, light green, heart-shaped leaves and yellow-centered white flowers minutely fringed like snowflakes. It blooms profusely throughout the summer but is not hardy enough to leave in the outdoor pool where winters are cold.

N. peltata is fairly hardy, with typical waterlily-like leaves and a profusion of rich yellow flowers.

NYSSA (NIS ah). A small genus of North American deciduous trees commonly known as tupelo or, in the South, as gum tree. The small, greenish white flowers are followed by purple or blue fruits, and simple leaves turn a brilliant red in early autumn. They grow naturally in moist situations in the southern half of the United States.

Since they have long roots and few rootlets, transplanting is difficult, especially larger trees. They are easily propagated from seed, either stratified or sown as soon as ripe.

N. aquatica (tupelo, cotton gum) is similar to *N. sylvatica*, native mostly to swamps of the southern states, and hardy in Zones 6–9.

N. sylvatica (black, pepperidge, or sour gum) is a hardy, slow-growing, cylindrical tree that grows to 50 ft. high. Its foliage is excellent during the summer and turns flaming, shiny red in the fall. The bold, crooked, twiggy branches make a picturesque outline against the sky in winter. Hardy in Zones 4–9.

O

OAK. Common name for QUER-CUS, a genus of mostly deciduous and some evergreen trees and a few shrubs belonging to the Fagaceae (Beech Family).

The name is sometimes applied to other plants. Jerusalem-oak is *Chenopodium botrys*. Poison-oak is *Rhus toxicodendron* or *R. diversiloba*. She-oak is the genus *Casuarina*. Silk-oak is *Grevillea robusta*. Tanbark-oak is *Lithocarpus densiflorus*.

OBEDIENT PLANT. Common name for PHYSOS-TEGIA, a genus of perennials whose flowers can be set at any angle.

OBLANCEOLATE. Shaped like a spearhead but with the broadest portion two-thirds of the distance toward the apex, like the leaves of *Ilex cassine* or *Myrica cerifera*. Compare LANCEOLATE.

OBOVATE. Egg-shaped in outline, like the leaves of the shellbark hickory, the broader portion of the leaf being toward the apex. Compare OVATE.

OCIMUM (OH sim um). A genus of half-hardy annual or perennial herbs or small shrubs of the Lamiaceae (Mint Family), commonly known as basil. It is esteemed for flavoring and its pleasingly scented foliage; once used for medicinal purposes.

An annual of the tropics, it is tender and should not be attempted outdoors until the weather is warm. It grows easily from seed, which should be started indoors. Plants should be transplanted or thinned to stand about 9 in. apart. A well-enriched soil in a sunny location is preferred. The small flowers are white or purple. The leaves may be either green or purple and can be cut fresh as needed.

Ocimum basilicum

Plants cut back to produce leaves for drying will develop successive crops of foliage until early fall. At that time, strong plants can be lifted and potted up to supply a winter crop indoors.

O. basilicum (sweet or common basil) is an annual that grows to 2 ft. 'Minimum' (bush basil) is a cultivar; see also HERBS.

OCONEE-BELLS. Common name for *Shortia galacifolia*, an evergreen herb with roundish, leathery leaves and white flowers; see SHORTIA.

OCOTILLO. Common name for *Fouquieria splendens*; see FOUQUIERIA. The Ocotillo Family is FOUQUIERIACEAE.

ODONTOGLOSSUM (oh DAHN toh glah sum). About 300 species comprise this genus of epiphytic or lithophytic orchids from the montane areas of tropical and subtropical central and northern South America. They are mostly large plants with compressed pseudobulbs topped by leathery leaves. Their erect inflorescences bear one to several showy flowers in racemes or panicles. Sepals, petals, and lips are usually spreading and crisped, and are often marked with exotic patterns of spots, bars, and stripes. Colors range from white, yellow, and green to rich brown, violet, and crimson.

This genus is an important member of the Oncidiinae, and flowers produced from such intergeneric breeding are exceptionally long-lasting and beautiful with exotic patterns. Hardy to Zone 7 if protected from freezing, the plants generally need cool conditions, withstanding minimum winter temperatures of 50–60°F. They require high humidity at all times and should be shaded in hot weather. A porous, well-drained compost is needed, and fresh air is critical. The type species is *O. epidendroides*.

ODONTONEMA (oh dahn toh NEE mah). A genus of shrubby tropical American plants belonging to the Acanthaceae (Acanthus Family). *O. schomburgkianum*, sometimes listed as *Thyrscanthus rutilans*, is the principal species.

OEDEMA. A physiological disease, also called dropsy, possibly caused by too much water in the soil, that results in swellings on leaves and other organs, giving a blistered appearance. Overfertilizing with nitrates is believed to induce the condition.

OENOTHERA (ee noh THEE rah). A large genus of annual, biennial, and perennial herbs of wide distribution, consisting of two distinct main groups. One includes the evening-primroses, which open late in the day and close toward morning, and the other, the sundrops, which remain open during the sunlight hours, forming attractive clumps. There are species in both groups that are stemless, or more or less prostrate, and useful in the rock garden. The culture in both types is easy as long as they are given dry soil and full sunlight. Propagation is by seed or, in the perennial species, by division of the clumps. Most are hardy in Zones 4–9.

Evening-primroses. Peculiarly, the evening-primroses open suddenly with a quick, nervous motion that can be seen and heard, exposing yellow, red, pink, rose, or white corollas, which attract night-flying moths. They are among the best of the evening garden flowers and are excellent for mixed beds and borders, growing in branching form from 1–3 ft. tall and producing large blossoms continuously. With their soft, poppylike blooms decorating the tops of the upright spikes, they give the effect of candelabras.

Sundrops. The sundrops, valuable especially in the perennial border, bear flowers generally yellow on plants 2 ft. tall.

PRINCIPAL SPECIES

O. acaulis (dandelion-leaved sundrop) is a biennial or perennial; at first without stems, it later develops spreading branches. Growing 6–12 in. tall and blooming in summer, the plants bear long-tubed, yellow, blue, or white flowers 4 in. across.

O. argillicola, 2–4 ft. high, can be grown as a biennial or perennial. Bushy plants bear 2–4 in. yellow flowers.

O. biennis (common evening-primrose) is a coarse, erect, simple or branched biennial growing to 3 ft. tall. The yellow flowers are 2 in. across. This weedy species is widely naturalized and is common in fields and waste areas. The southern var. *grandiflora* has larger flowers.

Oenothera caespitosa

O. caespitosa, a stemless perennial growing to 4 in., bears 2–3 in., white flowers that turn a rose color as they mature. Swordlike, gray-green leaves form a cushion of foliage.

O. cheiranthifolia, growing 9–12 in., produces yellow flowers above silver foliage throughout the summer. It prefers full sun and poor soil.

O. erythrosepala, a strong candidate for the border, grows 3–4 ft. and sends up spires of 2½–3½ in. yellow, bell-like flowers from summer into autumn.

O. fruticosa, a perennial growing to 3 ft., is semiwoody at the base and has reddish stems. The showy yellow flowers, to 2 in. across, open during the day. Cv. 'Major' bears flowers in profusion and is bushy in habit. Var. *youngii* is strong, stocky, and a prolific bloomer.

Oenothera hookeri   *Oenothera missouriensis*

O. hookeri (giant evening-primrose), growing 2–6 ft., produces impressive spires of 3-in., yellow flowers maturing to green.

O. missouriensis (Missouri evening-primrose) is an easily cultivated, trailing perennial to 1 ft.

with extremely showy evening flowers at least 3 in. across and long tubed. Hardy to Zone 5.

O. pallida grows 12–18 in. high with fragrant, white flowers aging to pink.

O. speciosa, growing to 18 in. and spreading quickly by rhizomes, has light pink, 2-in. flowers that bloom during the day. Hardy to Zone 5.

O. tetragona, growing 2–3 ft., is a perennial but is usually treated as an annual. It creates many-flowered clusters of 1½-in., yellow flowers. In cv. 'Fireworks', the flower buds are bright red before opening. Hardy to Zone 5.

OFFSET. A plant that develops from the base of a "mother" plant, such as the small "chickens" of the common houseleek, *Sempervivum tectorum*, known as hen-and-chickens.

OIL SPRAYS. A method of insect control; see SPRAYING.

OKRA. A tall, tropical African annual herb *Abelmoschus esculentus*, formerly listed as *Hibiscus esculentus*, and also called gumbo. Its long, ribbed pods are used while green and tender for thickening soups, catsups, and stews or as a vegetable. They can be canned, dried, or used fresh. The fully formed but unripe seeds of larger pods can be shelled and cooked like peas.

Okra

Since the plants, similar to hibiscus, have large, striking leaves and handsome yellow, red-centered blossoms, they can be used as ornamentals in the flower garden or the front of the shrubbery border.

Okra thrives in any good garden soil in full sunlight with clean cultivation. The seeds tend to rot in wet soil, so good drainage is essential. Since the plants are sensitive to frost, the weather must be settled before they are started. They are hard to transplant unless started in flowerpots, which should be done a month before it is safe to

set them outdoors. If the growing season is long enough, sow seed outdoors 1 in. deep. Rows for tall varieties should be 2–3 ft. apart; for dwarfs 18 in. The tall plants should stand 30 in. apart; the shorter ones, 15 in.

The powdery mildew common on phlox occasionally infects okra, and a fusarium wilt causes yellowing and death. With a view to avoiding disease, grow seedlings in uninfected seedbeds and plant them in clean soil. The spinach aphid and the corn earworm may also feed on okra.

OLEA (OH lee ah). A genus of evergreen trees and shrubs lending its name to the Oleaceae (Olive Family), to which it belongs, and are commonly known as olive. Various species are native to the warm regions of Europe and Asia and are commonly grown in orchards or as street trees in California. Hardy to Zone 9.

O. africana is a small tree from Africa and China with smaller fruits than the common species.

O. europaea (common olive) is a tree that grows to 25 ft. and has gray-green, oval leaves. The small, edible fruits are shiny black when ripe and usually pickled or made into olive oil.

OLEACEAE (oh lee AY see ee). The Olive Family, a group of temperate-climate trees and shrubs, a few of which are grown for ornament and one, the olive, for its fruit. The flowers, which have a four-cleft calyx and four-cleft tubular corolla, are grouped into three tribes, their dominant genera being *Fraxinus* (ash), *Syringa* (lilac), and *Olea* (olive). Among other genera widely cultivated are *Chionanthus*, *Forsythia*, *Jasminum*, *Ligustrum* (privet), *Osmanthus*, and *Phillyrea*.

OLEANDER. Common name for NERIUM, a well-known genus of tropical evergreen shrubs. Yellow-oleander is *Thevetia peruviana*; see THEVETIA.

OLEARIA (oh lee AIR ee ah). A genus of evergreen shrubs and trees from New Zealand and Australia, belonging to the Asteraceae (Aster Family), and commonly known as tree aster or daisy tree. They will tolerate a few degrees of frost but grow outdoors only in warmer regions. They do well near the seashore if not too exposed. Propagation is by seeds and cuttings.

Of the principal species, *O.* x *haastii* is the hardiest. It makes a compact bush that grows to 8 ft. and has grayish green, small, leathery leaves, silvery beneath, and clusters of white, daisylike flowers. *O. stellulata* grows to about 5 ft. and bears large leafy heads of white flowers. Seedling forms with flowers of rosy pink to blue have been developed.

OLEASTER. A common name for *Elaeagnus angustifolia*, a deciduous shrub or tree with dense masses of gray-green leaves and fragrant flowers in late spring; see ELAEAGNUS. The Oleaster Family is ELAEAGNACEAE.

OLIVE. Common name for OLEA, a genus of evergreen trees or shrubs native to warm regions of Europe and Asia. The Olive Family is OLEACEAE. Fragrant olive is *Osmanthus fragrans*, a flowering Asiatic tree popular as a greenhouse plant; see OSMANTHUS.

OMPHALODES (ohm fah LOH deez). A genus of low-growing annuals and perennials with white or blue flowers resembling forget-me-nots, belonging to the Boraginaceae (Borage Family), and commonly known as navelwort or navelseed. Of easy culture and thriving in sun or shade if given sufficient moisture, they are often grown in the border or rock garden. Propagation of annuals is from spring-sown seed, and perennials, by division. Most are hardy to Zone 6.

PRINCIPAL SPECIES

O. linifolia, growing to 18 in., is an annual with clusters of gray-green leaves and white, slightly fragrant flowers on branching stems.

O. luciliae, with rose flowers turning bluish, is a popular garden perennial, which should be grown in well-drained limestone soil.

O. verna (creeping-forget-me-not) is a frequently grown perennial with blue flowers in early spring, resembling true forget-me-nots. It produces runners freely, spreading quickly over bare spots in the rock garden or naturalizing readily on the edge of a pond.

ONAGRACEAE (oh nah GRAY see ee). The Evening-primrose Family, a group of mostly herbs principally limited to the temperate portions of the Western Hemisphere. The flowers have four clawlike petals around a tubular calyx. Among the genera providing popular ornamental garden subjects, mostly of easy cultivation, are *Clarkia*, *Epilobium*, *Fuchsia*, *Gaura*, *Lopezia*, *Ludwigia*, *Oenothera* (evening-primrose), and *Zauschneria*. *Ludwigia* and *Trapa* are aquatic forms.

ONCIDIUM (ahn SID ee um). A genus of over 750 very small to very large epiphytic, lithophytic, or terrestrial orchids native to the tropics and subtropics of North, Central, and northern South America and the West Indies. Commonly called the dancing-lady orchids, these plants and their flowers vary widely in shape, size, and color.

The leaves may be long, narrow, and thin; equitant (fan-shaped); terete (round and pencil-shaped); "mule-eared" and leathery. Pseudobulbs may be ovoid, round, or flattened. Flowers are few to many, some borne on long scapes, others rising on short inflorescences. They may be tiny to large (4 in. across). Colors are predominantly yellow but may be crimson, pink, white, chocolate-brown, or green. The lip is the distinctive part of the flower, being broad and crisped on the edges with a prominent crest under the column.

Bred with other members of the Oncidiinae, intergeneric hybrids of this group produce long-lasting flowers of great beauty. Most do well in baskets containing a porous, well-draining medium, while some are best mounted on slabs of cork or tree fern. They prefer filtered light and protection from freezing, with minimum winter temperatures of 55–60°F. Most need high humidity and ample water during growth. The type species is *O. variegatum*.

ONION. A hardy biennial herb, *Allium cepa*, grown usually for its firm, ripe, white bulbs but also for its immature stems (known as bunch onions or scallions), which are eaten raw as a relish or salad, and for its tender young leaves that are used for seasoning. See ALLIUM for related species.

CULTURE

The numerous varieties are propagated in four ways: from seed; from sets, or little bulbs grown from seed the previous season but checked in their development by thick sowing, usually in poor soil; from "multipliers" or "potato onions," each consisting of two to several "hearts" that develop new stems when planted and contain one to several new hearts when mature; and from "top onions" or bulblets that develop in place of flowers, at the tops of the flower stems.

Top onion

Seed-raised onions are the most important commercially, because it is their ripe bulbs that can be shipped or stored for use during the winter. Top, tree, and Egyptian onions are useful in home gardens because the tops can be broken apart and the bulblets planted like sets to produce early young onions. The plants raised from bulblets, if allowed to mature, produce new tops crowded with more bulblets and perhaps a few flowers. Plants grown from sets should be used while young, since they usually produce inferior bulbs.

Soil and Planting. The soil for onions should be loose and well drained but well supplied with humus and highly retentive of moisture. When possible, especially if it is heavy, the soil should be plowed or dug in the fall and left rough over the winter so that the frost can mellow it. As early in spring as it can be worked, it should be raked fine and the seeds sown promptly. Seed sprouts slowly, and the shallow-rooted seedlings need moisture to help them through their baby stages. Late-sown onion seed is almost sure to fail. Though thick sowing is usually recommended, thin sowing is more economical of seed and will involve less work in thinning. Only choice seed should be sown.

If desired, seedlings can be started in a coldframe or hotbed four to six weeks earlier than outdoors and transplanted 4–6 in. apart in the garden. They should then be larger than a piece of spaghetti. Seedlings started in nursery beds or even in the open garden rows can also be transplanted at about the time the first thinning is done. In the home garden, several thinnings are desirable, each one (after the first) giving young onions that can be used green or boiled. Clean culture is essential throughout the season but especially during the early stages.

Sets and bulblets of top onions are planted in early spring, 1–2 in. apart. In 4–6 weeks they can be used as green onions.

Harvesting. When the tops of most of the bulbs in the row or bed begin to ripen and yellow, a light roller can be run over it to break down the rest of the crop and hasten the ripening of the bulbs. Since thick necks, or scullions, do not keep well, they should be pulled and used as soon as possible. When all the tops have died, or just before cold weather arrives, pull or dig the crop in the early morning, leave the crops on the ground for a day or two to dry, then place them loosely in crates and store under cover where free air circulation will dry them further. When thoroughly dry, they should be cleaned and, for winter, stored in dry, frostproof quarters.

DISEASES

The most important of the diseases affecting onions are smut, downy mildew, fusarium basal rot, and neck rot. The fungus that causes smut lives from year to year in the soil. It injures chiefly seedlings, which show black smutty lesions on the leaves and die early. It can be controlled by burning the affected plants and practicing crop rotation. Onions grown from sets are not subject to smut.

The DOWNY MILDEW fungus lives on the seed and in old refuse, and affected plants turn yellow and die. A three- or four-year crop rotation is advisable. Cultivate the soil only when it is dry.

Fusarium basal rot causes the roots to turn pink, shrivel, and die. To offset the loss of those roots, feed the plants well.

Neck rot occurs in storage after the onions are dug. To prevent it, store them in slatted crates and maintain low temperature and humidity.

INSECT PESTS

The chief insect pests are onion thrips and maggots. Thrips blanch and deform the leaves, the injury being worse in hot, dry weather. Spraying with insecticide kills many thrips but does not entirely control them. Some success has followed scattering moth balls along the row, but excessive use of these will hamper beneficial elements in the soil. Spraying onion plants with water from a hose, limiting the force so it will not knock down the plants, can deter thrips.

The onion maggot is the larva of a small fly. Hatching from eggs laid on the base of plants or in cracks in the soil, the young maggots feed on the stem. Young plants usually die, but in older plants the maggots work into the bulb. Burn all onion tops, trash, and grass surrounding an onion field. Practice a three- or four-year rotation of the onion crop. Organic gardeners have interplanted with radishes. The maggots prefer the radish root to the onion and so congregate on the radishes, which are then pulled and destroyed.

ONOCLEA (ah noh KLEE ah) **sensibilis.** A coarse, terrestrial fern found in moist soils, commonly known as sensitive or bead fern. The only member of its genus, it is dimorphic with characteristically unique fertile fronds. The pinnules curl tightly around the sori so that each stalk resembles a stick covered with green beads. The sterile fronds are 10–20 in. tall, pinnate to bipinnate, the pinnae having wavy margins. Although winter hardy, it is sensitive to cold and browns easily. It should not be introduced into the garden, except in a controlled situation, because it spreads quickly and is difficult to eradicate. It will take full sun if given plenty of moisture. It is found throughout eastern and central North America from Newfoundland and Saskatchewan through Florida and Texas.

ONOPORDUM (ahn oh POR dum). A genus of annual, biennial, and triennial herbs belonging to the Asteraceae (Aster Family) and commonly known as thistle. They have woolly, prickly leaves and attractive, rounded heads of white or purple flowers. Native to Europe, a few are grown in the border, where they thrive in any well-drained soil. Plants are easily propagated from seed sown where the plants are to stand.

O. acanthium (Scotch thistle) is the best-known species among those cultivated for ornament in wild gardens and borders, but it may become weedy if neglected. A biennial growing sometimes to 9 ft., it has prickly leaves covered with white down and heads of lavender flowers 2 in. across. This is the thistle of song and story inseparably associated with Scotland. The story goes that Robert Bruce's armies were made aware of enemies approaching Stirling Castle when one barefoot invader cried out after stepping on a sharp thistle spine.

ONOSMA (ohn AHS mah). A genus of annual, biennial, and perennial herbs, sometimes shrubby, belonging to the Boraginaceae (Borage Family). Native from the Mediterranean to the Himalayas, only a few are cultivated. Yellow, purple, or white, bell-like flowers are borne in one-sided clusters from midsummer to autumn. The tubular or urn-shaped corollas with attached stamens make the blossoms extremely attractive, especially when grown in the rock garden among plants with light foliage. The taller species are good for borders. Propagation is by seed or by cuttings taken in summer. Plants thrive in full sun or partial shade.

PRINCIPAL SPECIES

O. alboroseum is a perennial from Asia Minor with rounded, oblong leaves and velvety, white flowers 1 in. long, which turn pink and then bluish with age.

O. stellulatum, the most commonly cultivated species, grows 8 in. tall with golden, inch-long, tubular flowers.

O. tauricum (golden-drop), from southern Europe, is similar to *O. stellulatum* but has lower, longer bracts.

OPHIOGLOSSACEAE (oh fee oh glahs AY see ee).

The Adder's-tongue Family, a group of ferns, of which two genera (*Botrychium* and *Ophioglossum*) are cultivated.

OPHIOGLOSSUM (oh fee oh GLAHS um). A

genus of terrestrial and epiphytic ferns distributed throughout most of the world, commonly known as adder's-tongue ferns. From a brief, fleshy rhizome arises an erect, entire, ovate or kidney-shaped sterile frond. A taller fertile frond is made up of a naked stipe, which terminates in a narrow cylindrical spike formed of two rows of round sporangia without indusia.

These plants frequently appear during rainy periods. They are primitive ferns in the same family as *Botrychium*, but *Ophioglossum* fronds emerge erect rather than bent over, and the fronds are entire rather than divided. They should not be collected, not only because they are rare, but also because they are nearly impossible to transplant or cultivate.

O. pendulum (ribbon fern) is an epiphytic tropical species. It resents disturbance, but if it is moved with its host intact, it will continue to grow in a greenhouse. Its fronds are shining, green ribbons that hang vertically and are very ornamental. Native to Madagascar, southeastern Asia, and Australia, it is frequently seen in public conservatories.

O. petiolatum is an exception to the norm of the genus because it occurs in abundance and is easy to cultivate. It is frequently found in moist meadows from Arkansas to Florida.

OPHIOPOGON (ahf ee oh POH gun). A small

genus of low, evergreen perennials from the Orient, belonging to the Liliaceae (Lily Family), formerly listed as *Mondo*, and commonly known as lilyturf, or snake's-beard. Generally cultivated as greenhouse foliage plants for their lilylike leaves, these sod-forming plants are also useful as ground covers or edging plants. They are easily grown in sun or shade and propagated by root division.

M. jaburan, the best-known species, has 2–3 ft. leaves and white flowers followed by bluish fruits.

M. japonicus has relatively small leaves and bears flowers below the mat of foliage.

OPUNTIA (oh PUN tee ah). Probably the best-

known genus in the Cactaceae (Cactus Family), it is the most widely distributed in its native habitat, which extends from Canada to the tip of South America. There are many interesting and beautiful species suitable for culture in both house and garden. There are two major subgenera whose names are so descriptive that they effectively differentiate them. The *Cylindropuntia* have cylindrical stems, while the *Platyopuntia* have flat stems or pads.

The *Cylindropuntia* group includes the famed cholla of the southwest, which, though of little economic value, is sometimes used as a supplementary forced forage in arid regions. Members of this group have easily detachable, cylindroid joints rather than the typical flattened, leaflike pads of most members of the genus. Many species have barbed spines, including *O. bigelovii* (teddy-bear cholla) and *O. fulgida* (jumping cholla) from the southwest United States and northwest Mexico. The spines of the latter are barbed and often enclosed in papery sheaths; the spines enter the flesh much more easily than they come out, so they seem to jump when you accidentally brush against them. Because of this, some forms of considerable beauty are not recommended for cultivation. Many, however, are highly desirable. Some species form virtual trees with trunk and branches.

Most authorities include *Nopalea* and *Consolea* under *Opuntia*.

O. microdasys (old-man cactus) and *O. rufida* are spineless and quite attractive, with tufts of red, white, or yellow glochids at each areole, but they are far from harmless. The glochids are tiny and hard to see, but barbed and quite irritating. In fact, they are the source of what used to be sold as itching powder. Virtually all *Opuntias* bear glochids, a characteristic of the genus, which, together with the barbed spines, make many collectors shun them all. They do, however, have among the most beautiful of cactus flowers, mostly large and satiny, with wrinkled, spineless blue pads and magenta flowers. Another choice Californian, *O. erinacea* var. *ursina* (grizzly-bear cactus) has long, white, hairlike spines and yellow flowers.

The *Platyopuntia* (prickly-pear cactus) group is of greater economic value. Used to some extent as a forage, these plants are also cultivated for their edible fruits. Hardy forms are common along the

Opuntia platyopuntia

Atlantic Coast as far north as New York. *O. ficus-indica* (Indian-fig) is cultivated in tropical countries for its fruit.

For propagation and care, see CACTUS.

ORACH. Common name for the annual herb *Atriplex hortensis*, grown mainly as a potherb; see ATRIPLEX.

ORANGE. Common name for both plant and fruit of several species of the genus *Citrus*. The orange blossom is the Florida state flower. for culture, see CITRUS FRUITS.

Important sweet oranges are: common or sweet orange, *C. sinensis*, with many horticultural varieties including the navels. Popular hybrid oranges include the Kings, which have excellent flavor and readily separable skins, the temples (*C.* x *nobilis*), and the tangelos (*C.* x *tangelo*). Satsuma, the hardiest of the commercial citrus, and tangerines are types of Mandarin oranges (*C.*

reticulata). For ornamental species, see CITRUS.

The name "orange" is also used in connection with many noncitrus plants. Trifoliate-orange belongs to the genus PONCIRUS. Mexican-orange, *Choisya ternata*, is an evergreen shrub grown outdoors in warm climates and in greenhouses for its fragrant, showy, white flowers. Mock-orange, *Philadelphus*, is a genus of hardy shrubs grown for their white or creamy flowers, fragrant in many species. Another mock-orange or wild-orange, *Prunus caroliniana*, is the cherry-laurel, an evergreen tree native from North Carolina to Texas; see PRUNUS. Osage-orange, *Maclura pomifera*, is a tree often used for hedges on rather poor soils as far north as southern Michigan. Otaheite orange is *Citrus* x *limonia*.

ORANGEROOT. Common name for HYDRASTIS, a low perennial herb with thick yellow roots, basal leaves, and raspberrylike fruits.

ORCHARD. A planting of deciduous fruit or nut trees. Citrus fruits (which are evergreens) are generally said to be grown in groves, which, however, are identical to orchards in layout and management. An orchard can be either a home or commercial proposition, depending on its size and purpose. See also FRUIT IN THE GARDEN.

ORCHID. Common name for plants of the Orchidaceae, one of the most highly prized of all plant families.

DESCRIPTION AND CHARACTER

The Orchidaceae comprise the largest family of flowering plants, including up to 1000 genera, 25,000 species, and 100,000 hybrids. Orchids are found throughout the world, except in major deserts and the Arctic circles, but most are native to temperate, tropical, or subtropical regions. They are monocotyledons, or single-leaf plants, and may be terrestrial, epiphytic, lithophytic, or saprophytic. Most are epiphytic (living on other plants but not extracting nourishment from them) or terrestrial (growing in soil or on the ground). Saprophytic orchids derive nourishment from decayed plants and usually lack chlorophyll. Lithophytic plants grow on a substrate on rocks. Some orchid plants are less than an inch high; others may grow over 15 ft. high. Orchid flowers vary widely in color, form, and size. Some blossoms may be so tiny they are best examined under a magnifying glass, while others are flamboyant, plate-sized flowers.

The Orchid Family is comprised of 40 subtribes, twelve tribes, and three subfamilies. Once thought to be so rare and difficult to cultivate that only the rich could afford them, a wide variety of orchids are now grown through modern cultivation methods by thousands of hobbyists. Even species formerly seen only in rare plant collections or botanical gardens are grown by many hobbyists.

Orchids belong to one of the plant families that can be hybridized across genera. Many natural hybrids are found in the wild. Today, bigeneric and trigeneric orchids are common, and intergeneric orchids containing six or more genera are not uncommon. By cross-breeding orchids from different climates, using plants of robust habit with others of varying color and pattern, exquisite intergeneric orchid hybrids of great vigor and even hardiness are available—many bloom several times a year.

The orchid hobbyist has many options for housing plants. A free-standing backyard greenhouse can accommodate a collection of several thousand orchids. Construction costs are not prohibitive, but given orchids' sensitivity to temperature, heating and cooling costs in a cool or temperate climate should be considered before undertaking such a project. A lean-to greenhouse attached to the side of the home is inexpensive to maintain, but such a shelter may cost almost as much as a free-stand-

Potted orchid

ing unit. The orchid lover can raise plants under lights in a basement, spare room, sun porch, solarium, or even on a rooftop. Thousands of hobbyists grow windowsill orchids in kitchens, bathrooms, or hobby rooms.

Orchid plant costs are now within the reach of everyone. Seedlings near blooming size may cost only a few dollars and mature plant divisions can be purchased for little more. In the United States, many plant nurseries, mostly located in Hawaii or along the coasts, specialize in orchids, although there are major growers in every large metropolitan area. Other growers are located in Japan, Thailand, Taiwan, Belgium, Germany, and the United Kingdom. All orchids are protected by endangered-species treaties, which the United States honors. As such, they are protected from being collected from the wild in every country where these treaties are in effect. The hobbyist should always purchase healthy plants from a reputable dealer.

ORCHID TYPES

SYMPODIAL ORCHIDS

These include those with pseudobulbs (erect lateral branches rising from a rooted horizontal stem) and rhizomes (rooted horizontal stems) for storing food and water. Important genera in this category include *Broughtonia*, *Cattleya*, *Dendrobium*, *Epidendrum*, *Laelia*, and *Oncidium*.

Flower spikes are terminal or axial, and flowers emerge from the tops or bases of the pseudobulbs, with new growth rising from the base of the pseudobulbs.

MONOPODIAL ORCHIDS

Plants in this group grow upright on a single stem. Flowers are borne on axillary inflorescences, with aerial roots growing along the stem, usually between the leaves. Such plants have no subterranean roots or rhizomes in which to store water or nutrients and must be watered and fed more often than sympodial orchids. Principal genera in this category include *Vanda* and *Phalaenopsis*.

Terrestrial orchids grow in humusy compost and leaf mold on the forest floor, in swamps and bogs, or in open savannas. Some terrestrial orchids are sympodial, with short rhizomes from which the next year's growth ensues. Few of them have pseudobulbs; their roots may be thick and fleshy, fibrous, or tuberous.

FLOWERS

Orchid flowers are unique. They are zygomorphic, meaning the flower can be divided into two equal halves in only one plane. They are also irregular, having dissimilar petals. Orchid flowers have three sepals and three petals. One petal is usually larger and more distinctive than the other two, contrasting in color with the rest of the flower parts. This is the lip or labellum, and is a landing platform for the pollinator. It may be lobed, saccate, fringed, or spurred—it may even mimic an insect to attract its pollinator.

Although all orchids are fragrant, their aromas are vastly different. Some are fragrant at night to attract a night-flying pollinator. Such orchids are usually white or light-colored. Some orchids have little aroma, but others emit a powerful musky fragrance. Still others have a foul, putrid odor.

Reproductive organs of the orchid are unique. Pistils and stamens are united into a gynandrium, or column, which bears the pollen. The pollen is formed into agglutinated masses of hard, waxy grains called pollinia. The inferior ovary (located below the column) has floral parts attached to its apex and contains thousands of minuscule seeds.

CULTURE

A green thumb is not necessarily standard operating equipment for cultivating orchids. Application of common sense and tender, loving care are required, and the "t.l.c." does not always take priority. Some orchids do better with minimal attention and even neglect.

They have basic needs of fresh, buoyant air; protection from excessive cold or heat; adequate, good quality water; a porous, well-draining compost for support; enough light to produce chlorophyll; and food on a regular basis.

Temperature. Besides the distinctions between epiphytic and terrestrial species, orchids are classed by climate: tropical and subtropical (thriving only in warm climates) or hardy (requiring intermediate or cool conditions).

Warm-growing orchids and their hybrids are the most commonly cultivated. They require special protection from heat as well as cold, with fresh, buoyant air and high humidity (75%). Minimum winter night temperatures should not go below 60–65°F in their growing environment. Although most can tolerate near-frost conditions for a short time, cold inhibits growth and flowering. Daytime temperatures should be 70–85°F. They can also tolerate temperatures higher than 90°F for a short time, but if the leaves feel warm to the touch, the plant should be cooled immediately by misting.

Light. Light is critical. Most orchids do best if given morning and late afternoon sun. Plants subjected to noonday and hot afternoon sun may suffer leaf damage from sunburn, affecting the health of the plant. A basic rule is that if an orchid has thick, leathery leaves, it can tolerate strong sunlight (to 4000 footcandles). If its leaves are thin and dark, it needs less light (3000 footcandles or less). Generally, monopodial vandaceous orchids with thick strap or terete leaves and strong aerial roots should be grown in high light (4000–5000 footcandles). Phalaenopsis-type orchids should be given about 3000 footcandles.

Water. Water is one of the most important and least understood aspects of orchid culture. Water quality is critical. Softened water contains salt and will kill most orchid plants. Heavily chlorinated water can damage plants; however, the treated water of most municipalities does not contain enough chlorine to cause harm. If the only water available is chlorinated city water, it can be stored in buckets overnight to allow the chlorine to dissipate. The best water for orchids is collected rain, distilled water, or water purified by reverse osmosis.

Monopodial orchids should be watered over the entire plant, including the aerial roots. They need to be watered more often than sympodial orchids. Roots of the sympodial and terrestrial orchids may rot if the potting medium becomes waterlogged. It is imperative to water them thoroughly and let the plants dry completely (the medium stays moist while the water drains off). Increasing humidity keeps orchids from drying out in too much heat or wind. It is a good idea to wet down the floor of the orchid house in hot, dry weather, increasing humidity and cooling the area.

Seedlings should be misted often, usually every other day. If the collection is small, the plants should be watered individually, not submerged in a tub of water where other plants have been standing, because this practice spreads disease and infection. With few exceptions, orchids should be watered in the morning, allowing leaves to dry before nightfall to avoid fungus infections.

Air. Orchids cannot tolerate stagnant air. In nature they live on trees, along stream banks, and on rocky outcroppings—always with fresh, moist air present. They are susceptible to air pollution caused by automotive exhausts and poorly ventilated or malfunctioning heaters in greenhouses or other growing areas. In the greenhouse or lean-to, air should be admitted at the peak of the roof and at the base of the structure, permitting cool air to enter from the base and circulate through the plants, while warm air is exhausted through upper vents. In the home, open windows or floor fans near the plants will provide moving air. Humidity can be supplied by placing plants on pebble-filled trays filled with water. The plants should sit on the pebbles, not in the water. In the greenhouse or lean-to, benches can be made of hardware cloth or rot-resistant wood lath. A newer innovation is a sturdy plastic bench in a lattice pattern. Ample space should be allowed between pots so the plants do not touch. This also prevents the spread of disease.

Food. Food is another misunderstood aspect of orchid culture. Orchids need nutrients regularly, but they should not be overfed. Each orchid species has different fertilizing requirements. It is best to water the plants thoroughly before fertilizing, so the food is absorbed quickly without burning the plant with fertilizer salts. As a rule, orchids should be fed every ten days with a diluted (half strength), balanced (20–20–20), water-soluble fertilizer applied to the entire plant and its medium. Plants in growth do well with an application of high nitrogen (30–10–10) fertilizer once a month, followed by a high phosphate (10–30–10) fertilizer on the following application.

Healthy orchid leaves are normally medium green in color, tough and leathery, and stand upright. If plants have dark green, floppy, weak leaves, it indicates they may have been fed too much nitrogen-rich fertilizer, resulting in a weakened, nonflowering plant. Pots should be leached of fertilizer salts every month by flushing them with clear water; otherwise plants may suffer damage caused by the buildup of fertilizer salts on the pot. A sign of fertilizer salts damage is blackened root tips. Resting plants need less fertilizer than do those in growth.

Potting Material. Orchid potting media varies. The medium should be porous, long-lasting, easy to work with, and of sufficient mass to support the plants. Orchids do not grow in soil. Even terrestrial ones grow in a humusy compost made up of leaf mold and bark collected at the base of trees or on the banks of streams. The compost for epiphytes can be coconut husk fiber, charcoal chunks, lava rock, tree fern fiber, fir bark, cork chunks, or any number of porous, inorganic materials. A newer introduction is New Zealand sphagnum moss, a long-fibered sphagnum moss grown on the South Island of New Zealand. This easily handled, clean, long-lasting fiber presents an attractive appearance.

Terrestrial orchids need a fairly dense medium or combination of media, such as peat, pearlite, sphagnum moss, sand, and leaf mold.

Plaques for mounting orchids can be coconut husks, cork, cedar or cypress slabs with a wad of sphagnum moss or coconut husk fiber backing roots to maintain moisture at the roots until the plants are established.

PROPAGATING

Orchids are propagated by seed, clonal division, and through tissue culture. The easiest, cheapest, and most reliable method is division, which assures growers of receiving exact duplicates of the plants they have divided.

POTTING AND DIVISION

Before potting orchids, all tools and pots should be cleaned and sterilized. All cutting tools should be flamed or submerged in a sterilizing solution (50% household bleach; or trisodium phosphate) after any cut is made on a plant. New pots can be sterilized by soaking in a solution of 25% household bleach. Used pots should be thoroughly cleaned, all debris removed, and soaked for 30 minutes in the bleach solution. These precautions are important to prevent the spread of disease.

Dividing and Potting Sympodial Orchids. All dead roots and leaves should be trimmed from the plant being divided. If the plant grows in all directions (i.e., if new leads appear on front and back bulbs), the plant can be divided into three or four bulb divisions by cutting through the rhizome between two pseudobulbs. If the plant grows in one direction, the division should be made so there are live eyes (beginning growth at the base of a pseudobulb) on one or more of the bulbs at the back of the plant (back bulbs).

The pot should be large enough to accommodate several years' growth and have ample drainage holes in the bottom. Plastic pots do not absorb water or fertilizer salts and are less expensive and easier to handle than clay pots. Plants in plastic pots do not need to be watered as often as those in clay; they also last longer. They tip over easily, however. Clay pots do not upset as easily but are heavier and break easily. Fertilizer salts tend to adhere to clay pots. Orchid baskets are made of teak, cedar, redwood, or wire. They are attractive and permit perfect drainage. Plastic net pots provide good drainage and are inexpensive.

Before planting, the pot should be filled with potting medium. It is not necessary to add stones or pottery shards in the bottom of the pot; in fact, they provide a hiding place for bugs, snails, and slugs that may injure the plant. The plant is set on top of the compost, and the medium is filled in around the roots, packed tightly enough to hold the plant steady without wobbling. The tops of the rhizomes should be exposed and the pseudo-bulbs should be erect. The plant can be held erect by clamps attached to the rim of the pot across the rhizomes. The base of the plant should be level with the top of the pot.

Vandaceous orchids require little compost, and most do best in baskets with aerial roots hanging free. Many growers simply support vandaceous plants in baskets with no added compost, watering them three or four times a week. Phalaenopsis-type orchids need a porous compost of sphagnum moss, coconut husk fiber, fir bark, medium agricultural charcoal, or tree fern. Their aerial roots should hang free, and the plant itself should be tipped to prevent water from standing in the crown, because the plants are susceptible to crown rot.

Monopodial orchids can be divided by being topped or cut on the stem between the aerial roots. At least four aerial roots should remain above the point where the stem is severed. If sufficient live roots remain, a new plant may also start from the bottom half of the plant.

When to Divide. The time to divide orchids is after flowering, when the new growth is no more than 1–2 in. high. Orchids can be repotted at any time if care is taken not to disturb healthy roots.

STARTING SEED

Propagating from seed is time-consuming, delicate work. In nature, a friendly fungus is present that facilitates the germination of the tiny seeds that fall from the ripened pod onto the substrate. This cannot be duplicated in greenhouses or the backyard garden. Seeds are collected from green pods, placed on an agar surface in sterile flasks, and germinated in a warm, well-lighted and ventilated room. After the seeds germinate, the plantlets are replated onto other flasks a year or two after sowing. When the plantlets are several inches high, they are unflasked and 15 to 20 plantlets are put into a community pot. A flask may provide plants for many community pots. In several years, the plantlets are big enough to be transferred to individual pots, where they stay until they are nearly flowering size. As they mature, they are moved to larger pots. The potting medium for seedling plants is usually denser than it is for mature plants, and seedlings require frequent watering. The process from unflasking to maturity may take as long as ten years in some species. Generally, orchids reach blooming size seven years from flasking. Mature plants may resemble either or both plants that made the seed.

TISSUE CULTURE

In this method of propagation, active cells (usually at root tips and apex of a floral shoot) are surgically removed from the live orchid plant. The microscopic pieces of tissue are placed in a special nutrient solution, sealed in a flask, and revolved on a rotary table. In time, the pieces produce plantlets genetically identical to the plant from which the tissue was extracted. This procedure produces virus-free orchid plants and relatively inexpensive clones of rare or exceptional specimens. Leaf tip culture follows the same process.

OFFSETS

These sometimes grow off the mature plant. Species of *Dendrobium* and *Phalaenopsis* are especially likely to produce offsets. When the small plant develops roots and more than one set of leaves, it can be carefully cut away from the mother plant and potted.

ENEMIES

INSECT PESTS

A number of insects attack orchids, the most prevalent being scale, mealybugs, thrips, spider mites, aphids, cockroaches, slugs, and snails. To combat these pests, it is best to isolate the infected plant and treat the specific creature. It is important to take great care when handling any insecticide or fungicide. Avoid breathing any dust or fumes and wear protective gloves, surgical mask, long-sleeved shirt, and long pants.

Scale is the most common insect that attacks orchids. It is evidenced as a hard, white or red dot or a white powder seen on pseudobulbs or stems, especially tender parts. Scales suck juice from the plant, causing it to become weak and stunted. For a minor infestation, a cotton swab or toothbrush soaked in rubbing alcohol scrubbed lightly over the infected area is effective. This treatment should also be repeated every seven

days for a period of three weeks. See SCALE INSECTS for further controls.

Snails and slugs are chewing insects that attack plants at night. Cleanliness is the first step in controlling these creatures. They hide in decayed foliage, under damp wood, or in potsherds. Wrapping a bit of cotton around the flower stem keeps snails and slugs away from the flowers. For control measures, see SNAILS; SLUGS .

Roaches are an insidious pest on orchids. They chew new roots and flowers and often invade pots and baskets, hiding under drainage shards. Household sprays are helpful, but oil-based sprays should not be used on orchids. Follow directions on product labels carefully.

Mites are sucking insects that particularly attack soft-leaved orchids. They flourish in a dry atmosphere and multiply in hot weather. Vulnerable plants should be watered frequently in hot weather. See MITES for control information.

Other pests are thrips, ants, grasshoppers, squirrels, rats, and mice, all if which do great damage to orchid plants and flowers.

DISEASES

Diseases of orchids are difficult to detect and control. It is wise to discard any plant that is infected with rot or fungus. Cleanliness is the best method for keeping orchid diseases in check. Sterilized tools are important, since disease can be spread through open cuts.

Fungus diseases include black rot, crown rot, and root rot. They are easily spread from plant to plant. Most fungus diseases appear as black or purplish spots. New leaders may turn black and slimy and have a foul odor. Botrytis causes leaf tips and flowers to become spotted. Like most fungi, it is accelerated by a damp, cold environment. Diseased plants should be kept dry and placed where they will receive fresh air, and the affected parts cut away well below the evidence of the infection. Good sanitation and uncrowded benches help prevent problems with fungi.

Bacterial diseases sometimes attack orchids; brown spot, in particular, is a problem with *Phalaenopsis*. It appears as a sunken brownish spot on the leaf, gradually spreading to the crown.

Bacterial bulb rot often attacks *Cymbidium*. Any diseased plant should be isolated and kept dry. Diseased portions should be cut away with sterile tools, leaving only healthy tissue.

Viruses are incurable diseases in orchids. They are systemic through the entire plant. These diseases are infectious, and it is imperative to use sterile tools and pots whenever plants are being divided or potted to prevent their spread. Plant viruses are detectable only through laboratory analysis. Affected plants may develop color break (unsightly brownish or black streaks) in the flowers, malformed lips, and necrotic or longitudinal raised reddish streaks on new leaves. A plant suspected of having a virus should be isolated and tested; local extension services can advise the grower where plant analysis is done. If it is determined that the plant has a virus, the plant should be burned. Common orchid viruses include cattleya flower break and color break (commonly called tobacco mosaic virus or TMV), ringspot, cymbidium mosaic, and cymbidium necrotic ringspot virus.

Chemicals used to treat orchid diseases and kill insects are toxic. The grower should always take great care when applying chemicals, using the exact dosage recommended on the label. To prevent diseases and avoid insects that prey on weakened plants, the grower should always start with healthy, vigorous plants. Sanitation around the plants and in the growing area will help maintain disease-free, healthy plants. For further control information, see entries under the names of individual diseases.

HOUSING ORCHIDS

The free-standing orchid greenhouse should be built so the longest sides face north and south. Lean-to structures should be attached to the east or northeast side of the house. In the home, a sunny bay window, bathroom, or kitchen window make excellent growing areas. Many hobbyists raise orchids under lights in basements and even on rooftops. In the home, orchids should be protected from the sun's rays, which are intensified by window glass. Filmy curtains can be used to screen orchids, with care taken to ensure the plants receive adequate ventilation. In the greenhouse or lean-to, roller slat shades or shade cloth, a plastic screening available in various percentages of screening (55–75% are usually best), can be used to shade the orchids from the afternoon sun. Greenhouse ventilators should be built into the peak and base of the structure.

Greenhouse size depends on the quantity and size of plants to be housed. A bi-level or tri-level greenhouse works well where land space is limited. In such houses, terrestrial orchids do well on the lowest level, with seedlings and orchids requiring less light placed on the second level, and plants requiring high light hanging from rods above the second level. Benches can be flat or stepped in tiers, and made of nonrusting, rot-resistant materials that allow ventilation and drainage. Flat benches should be wide enough for the grower to reach across easily, and of a comfortable height. Aisles should be wide enough for an adult to pass easily between the benches. Greenhouse height depends on whether plants will hang over benches and should be high enough for an adult to stand erect.

ORCHIDS FOR DIFFERENT ENVIRONMENTS

The following orchids can be grown outdoors in temperate climates: *Arethusa* grows in acid, swampy areas. *Bletilla* prefers humusy, rich soil. *Calopogon* grows in swampy savannas. *Cymbidiums* and *Cypripediums* tolerate various habitats. *Epidendrum* requires full sun and loose, open soil. *Habenaria* tolerates various habitats. *Oeceoclades* thrives in shade and humusy soil. *Orchis* tolerates various habitats. *Spiranthes* requires sandy, well-drained soil.

ORCHIDS FOR SMALL SPACES

Ascocenda, Ascocentrum, Broughtonia and its hybrids, small *Cattleyas*, and *Laelias* need bright light and high humidity. *Phalaenopsis, Doritis*, and their hybrids require light shade and high humidity.

POPULAR INTERGENERIC HYBRIDS

This is a partial listing of the most popular intergeneric hybrids and the parent genera. New forms are introduced every day.

Aeridovanda = Aerides x *Vanda*

Ascocenda = Ascocentrum x *Vanda*

Brassidium = Brassia x *Oncidium*

Brassocattleya = Brassavola x *Cattleya*

Cattleytonia = Cattleya x *Broughtonia*

Colmanara = Miltonia x *Odontoglossum* x *Oncidium*

Doritaenopsis = Doritis x *Phalaenopsis*

Epicattleya = Epidendrum x *Cattleya*

Laeliocattleya = Laelia x *Cattleya*

Miltassia = Miltonia x *Brassia*

Miltonidium = Miltonia x *Oncidium*

Odontioda = Odontoglossum x *Cochlioda*

Potinara = Brassavola x *Cattleya* x *Laelia* x *Sophronitis*

Sophrocattleya = Cattleya x *Sophronitis*

Sophrolaelia = Laelia x *Sophronitis*

Sophrolaeliocattleya = Cattleya x *Laelia* x *Sophronitis*

ORCHID CACTUS. Common name for hybrids of the cactus genus EPIPHYLLUM.

ORCHID TREE. Common name for species of BAUHINIA, a genus of tropical oriental trees that are popular in south Florida for their purple or white flowers.

ORCHIS (OR kis). The orchid from which the Orchidaceae (Orchid Family) derives its name, a Greek word, meaning "testicle," referring to the ovoid, underground tubers of this terrestrial genus. The plants are widely distributed through Europe and Asia to China and in North America. The leaves form a basal rosette, with an erect inflorescence bearing many small, brightly colored flowers in shades of white, pink, purple, and occasionally yellow or green. Sepals and petals are united into a hood enclosing the lip and column. Plants are hardy to Zone 3 if protected from freezing in extremely cold areas. They are best planted in a humusy, well-drained medium and should be given abundant water while growing. The ground roots of several species are used as a tapioca-like food called salep. The type species is *O. militaris*.

As a common name, fringed-orchis refers to HABENARIA, another orchid genus with red to yellow flowers found in North American bogs.

OREGANO. Common name for the flavoring herb derived mainly from species of ORIGANUM. Commercially produced oregano is often a mixture of *Origanum* or similar herbs of other genera.

OREGON-GRAPE. Common name for *Mahonia nervosa*, a small evergreen shrub with yellow flowers and blue berries. It is the state flower of Oregon; see MAHONIA.

ORGANIC. Living, as contrasted with nonliving or inorganic, and referring to both plants and animals, their patterns of growth, action, reproduction, and often to the beneficial processes of decay. Decaying matter, as in manures and composts, is known to be of great value when added to the soil for the improvement of the soil tilth, structure, moisture retention, and as a basis for the life of essential microorganisms that carry on the biochemical reactions in the soil solution necessary for plant nutrition.

The term "organic" is also used to describe methods of gardening and farming and the food grown by these methods. The term indicates the absence of synthetic chemicals from fertilizers, herbicides, and pesticides used in crop cultivation. The aim of organic gardening and food production is to follow and enhance nature's own methods of growing and balancing populations of flora and fauna.

ORGANIC MATTER

The term "organic matter" refers to the naturally occurring plant and animal resources in the soil, compost, or humus and to the organisms that live in the soil. Dead plant and animal parts are subject to the continuing processes of decay by microorganisms and earthworms. The biochemistry of the processes means the breakdown of complex carbon compounds, combinations with minerals in the soil, and a balancing of soil components. Humus has negatively charged ions that attract such positive ions as those of sodium, potassium, iron, copper, and boron. When synthetic chemicals are added or have been added in the past, humus acts as a buffer to help rebalance the soil, especially if the chemicals have caused a buildup of sodium nitrates.

Organic matter enriches the soil solution, helps drainage, temperature, soil structure, movement and nourishment of roots, and the entry of air and water into the soil. It incorporates whatever is tilled into the soil, whether weeds, leaves, carcasses, manure, or compost, any of which can help to maintain the life cycles by replacing nutrients and soil resources removed by cropping. It also aids in the control of soil diseases through its antibiotic qualities. Physically it protects the soil from damage by high winds, heavy downpours, and droughts.

ORIGANUM (oh RIG ah num). A genus of perennial herbs of the Lamiaceae (Mint Family), including those commonly known as oregano and marjoram used as flavorings for dressings and sauces. When the common name of oregano is found on packaged dried herbs, the contents may have come from any one of a number of *Origanum* species or similar herbs.

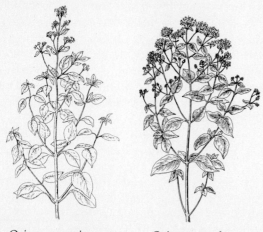

Origanum majorana   *Origanum vulgare*

Since the seed is very small, sow it in a seed pan; prick out the seedlings into flats; water them carefully and shield from strong sunlight until they are growing well, then transplant to the garden 12 in. apart in rows 18 in. apart. Gather for drying just before flowering begins.

O. majorana (sweet marjoram), formerly listed as *Majorana hortensis*, is a tender perennial usually cultivated as an annual and valued for its aromatic foliage used in cooking.

O. onites (pot marjoram), *O. heracleoticum* (winter sweet marjoram), and *O. vulgare* (oregano, wild marjoram) are perennials, hardy to Zone 3.

ORNAMENTAL GRASSES. The ornamental grasses are frequently related to their more utilitarian counterparts, which are used as food plants, forage crops, and lawn grasses. When used as decorative subjects in the flower garden or landscape design, ornamental grasses lend an air of elegance and tropical lushness. Many produce attractive sprays that compare favorably with any flower in the garden for their beauty in both green and everlasting bouquets.

The use of ornamental grasses may be limited by the amount of space they require. Although some are useful as border or clump plantings, others are not easily confined to a small patch in the garden. Some also require a good deal of headroom, since they can attain a height of 20 ft. when mature. A few are rather particular about soil and climate, although most of the perennial types require only minimal attention once they are established.

Propagation of ornamental grasses is usually by seed or division. The hardy annuals are grown from seed, which is sown in beds that will not restrict the growth of the seedlings. Poor growth will result if seedlings or transplants are grown in cramped quarters. Perennials are propagated in early spring by seed, offsets, stolons, or division. Grasses with variegated foliage usually will not come true from seed and should only be propagated by dividing the clumps.

SELECTIONS

Agrostis nebulosa (cloud bent grass) is a dwarf annual with leaves 8 in. long and 6-in. panicles of fine branches; see AGROSTIS.

Arrhenatherum (oat grass) is a genus of early-summer, low-growing grasses whose green and white leaves are attractive as a border or single clump; see ARRHENATHERUM.

Arundo (giant reed), a genus of perennials including the tallest and most spectacular of the ornamental grasses, grows 8–20 ft. and has bright green, broad leaves (variegated in some species). Reddish plums over 12 in. long appear at the end of stalks in late summer. The woody stems are sometimes used to make reeds for musical instruments. It prefers deep, rich soil, lots of sun, and a warm climate. See ARUNDO.

Briza (quaking grass) is a genus of annuals that grow about 24 in. tall and have spikelets that tremble in the slightest breeze. They are lovely in dried bouquets and grow readily from seed sown in early spring. See BRIZA.

Coix lacryma-jobi (Job's-tears) is a perennial that grows up to 4 ft. and is cultivated as an annual in cool climates. The grayish to pearly white seeds are large and can be used as beads or in dried arrangements. In the orient, the seeds are eaten as a cereal (adlay). See COIX.

Cortaderia selloana (pampas grass), one of the showiest of the perennial grasses, grows 8–20 ft. tall and has an abundance of showy white plumes in late summer. Cv. 'Rosea' has pink plumes. They grow in ordinary soil with full sun. Although not hardy in cold climates, they can be grown as annuals. The plumes can be cut and dried for winter arrangement. See CORTADERIA.

Erianthus ravennae (plume grass) resembles pampas grass but is shorter. It is a perennial that grows 8–12 ft. tall and is cultivated as an annual in the North. It thrives in full sun and ordinary soil. See ERIANTHUS.

Festuca ovina var. *glauca* (blue fescue) is a perennial that grows 12 in. tall and has striking blue-green foliage in a low, tufted habit. It is quite hardy and useful as an edging plant. Many related species are also useful. See FESTUCA.

Juncus effusus (common rush) is not a true grass but is especially useful for grassy ornamental plantings in wet areas. It is a perennial herb that grows to 4 ft. and has unbranched, round stems; flat, grassy leaves; and small clusters of greenish or brownish flowers. It is sometimes used for making woven mats. See JUNCUS.

Miscanthus sinensis (eulalia grass) is an excellent ornamental perennial that grows slowly to 10 ft. There are several good cultivars with attractive color variations. See MISCANTHUS.

Pennisetum setaceum (fountain grass) is a tender perennial that grows 3–4 ft. and has narrow leaves and 12-in. plumes that vary in color from copper to rose. It is native to Ethiopia and can be grown as an annual in cooler climates. See PENNISETUM.

Phalaris arundinacea var. *picta* (ribbon grass), one of the hardiest and most easily cultivated perennial grasses, grows 2–4 ft. high and has green-and-white striped leaves.

Stipa pennata (European feather grass) is a perennial that grows to 3 ft. high, cultivated for its feather plumes that may be 12 in. long. It is not hardy in cold regions. See STIPA.

Other useful grasslike ornamentals include CYPERUS (umbrella plant) and various kinds of BAMBOO.

ORNITHOGALUM (or ni THAHG ah lum). A genus of bulbous herbs of the Liliaceae (Lily Family), from Europe and Africa, with white, reddish, or yellow lilylike flowers in clusters at the top of a leafless stalk. The hardy species are often left in the ground from year to year, but tender sorts, grown in pots or window gardens, are brought indoors as soon as cold weather arrives. Propagation is by offsets.

PRINCIPAL SPECIES

O. arabicum, a Mediterranean species suitable for greenhouse culture, grows to 2 ft. and has leaves 2 ft. long and 1 in. wide. The fragrant flowers borne in racemes are white with shining black pistils. It is sometimes called chincherinchee in the florists' cut-flower trade.

O. caudatum (sea-onion) grows to 3 ft. and has leaves 2 ft. long and 1½ in. wide. The flowers, 1 in. across in long racemes, are white with green centers. It makes a good greenhouse subject.

O. miniatum (chincherinchee, star-of-Bethlehem), formerly listed as *O. thyrsoides* var. *aureum*, has deep golden yellow flowers.

O. narbonense, attractive in the greenhouse, grows to 2 ft. and has leaves 1½ ft. long and ½ in. wide and racemes of white flowers with green midveins.

O. nutans, native to the northern states, grows to 2 ft. tall and has leaves 18 in. long and ½ in. wide, bearing nodding clusters of 2-in. flowers that are white on the inside and green with white margins outside.

O. pyramidale is hardy, growing to 2 ft. The leaves and flowers are similar to *O. narbonense* but only half as large; the flower clusters are long and narrow.

O. thyrsoides (chincherinchee) grows to 1½ ft. and has leaves 1 ft. long and 2 in. wide and dense clusters of white flowers about ¾ in. across. Best suited to greenhouse culture, it is a popular florist flower with a reputation for lasting long.

O. umbellatum (star-of-Bethlehem), native to the northern states, grows 6–12 in. tall. Its leaves are linear with a midvein, 1 ft. long, and slightly wider than those of *O. nutans*. The flowers are starlike, 1 in. across, white inside, green margined with white outside, and borne in flattened clusters of 5 to 20 blossoms.

ORONTIUM (oh RAWN shee um) **aquaticum.** A handsome, aquatic, perennial herb native to North America, belonging to the Araceae (Arum Family), and commonly known as golden-club. Emerging above the water surface, it produces a conspicuous 2-in. spike or spadix covered with tiny yellow flowers at the tip and shading to white and then red at the base as the blooms age. The elliptical leaves are rich, dark green, and grow to 12 in. above the water. Perfectly hardy to Zone 3, it is well suited to the pond or any marshy spot.

ORPINE. Common name for *Telephium,* a seldom-grown genus of herbs belonging to the Caryophyllaceae (Pink Family). The Orpine Family is CRASSULACEAE and includes mainly succulent herbs and shrubs.

ORTHOCARPUS (or thoh KAHR pus). A genus of annual and perennial herbs of western North and South America, commonly known as owl's-clover. *O. purpurascens*, a California species, is sometimes grown in gardens for its spikes of purple or crimson, tubular flowers.

Orthocarpus purpurascens

OSAGE-ORANGE. Common name for *Maclura pomifera*, a spiny deciduous tree with bright green leaves and greenish yellow, inedible fruits; see MACLURA.

OSIER. Common name for those species of SALIX (willow) whose light stems or branches are used for wickerwork, especially *S. viminalis* and *S. purpurea.*

Red-osier dogwood refers to *Cornus sericea* and *C. stolonifera*, North American shrubs belonging to the Cornaceae (Dogwood Family); see CORNUS.

OSMANTHUS (ahz MAN thus). A genus of evergreen shrubs or small trees belonging to the Oleaceae (Olive Family). They have attractive foliage and clusters of small, very fragrant flowers. They are too tender to grow outside in cold climates, although *O. heterophyllus* may survive to Zone 5 in a sheltered location. They grow well in ordinary soil and can tolerate partial shade. Propagation is by cuttings of half-ripened wood under glass.

PRINCIPAL SPECIES

O. americanus (devilwood) grows to 40 ft. It has whitish bark, 3–5 in. shining leaves, and short clusters of fragrant, yellowish white flowers in early spring. Native in the southern United States, it is hardy in Zones 6–9.

O. delavayi is a Chinese shrub that grows to 6 ft. and has small, dark green, leathery leaves and fragrant, white flowers in early spring.

O. x *fortunei*, a hybrid between *O. heterophyllus* and *O. fragrans*, grows to 6 ft. It has large, oval, spiny leaves and white flowers in the fall. Hardy to Zone 7.

O. fragrans is an Asiatic tree that grows to 30 ft. It is well known in cultivation as a greenhouse shrub and is valued for its yellowish white, very sweet scented flowers in winter and spring. Hardy to Zone 8.

O. heterophyllus, formerly listed as *O. ilicifolius*, is a Japanese shrub that grows to 20 ft. and has spiny, glossy green, oval leaves and small, fragrant, white flowers that bloom from early to late fall. Cv. 'Myrtifolius' has small, narrow leaves. 'Rotundifolius' is a dwarf form with roundish leaves. 'Argenteo-marginatus' and 'Aureus' have white and yellow variegated leaves. Hardy in Zones 6–8.

OSMOSIS. The movement of water across a semipermeable membrane from a region of low salt or sugar concentration to a region of higher concentration. When two different liquids are separated by a thin membrane, the flow is from lighter to denser. Thus, the soil solution carrying plant food in weak solutions is absorbed through the walls of the root hairs because it is not as concentrated as the liquid sap inside the root cells. On this same principle, soluble plant food, such as a concentrated commercial fertilizer, should be applied in small quantities at a time, not too close to the plant roots, and in connection with prompt, generous applications of water. Otherwise the soil solution around the fine roots may be made more concentrated than the liquid in the roots, which will rupture the cell walls as it is drawn out by osmotic pressure.

OSMUNDA (ahs MUN dah). A genus of ferns represented by three species that are common and hardy in the United States from Maine to North Carolina and west to Minnesota. They are excellent ferns for the garden, needing only plenty of water and responding lustily to ideal conditions of drainage and typical fern soil. They differ from other ferns in having the fertile fronds so contracted that they lose all suggestion of a frond and resemble instead a spray of minute flowers going to seed, thus the common name "flowering ferns." All have green spores that should be sown when fresh or they will not germinate. They grow 3–5 ft. high and are excellent background plants. The new, uncurled croziers, especially of *O. cinnamomea* and *O. claytoniana*, can be cooked and eaten like asparagus. Plants should be protected from heavy winds, and old fronds should not be removed until spring. The rhizome fibers are harvested for use as a growing medium for epiphytes called osmundine.

PRINCIPAL SPECIES

O. cinnamomea (cinnamon fern) grows 2–4 ft. tall and has broad, pinnate, blue-green sterile fronds and fertile ones bearing spikes of spores that turn a cinnamon color when ripe in early June. The sterile fronds can be distinguished from those of *O. claytoniana* by the tufts of brown hair under the bases of the pinnae.

O. claytoniana (interrupted fern) grows 1–3 ft. tall and has pinnate fronds. Halfway to the summit, the fertile fronds bear three or four pairs of abbreviated pinnae contracted and covered with brown spores. These hang down when ripe and give the plant an appearance unique among all ferns.

O. regalis (royal fern) is one of the stateliest and most celebrated of all northern ferns. Its fronds are 1–5 ft. tall, bipinnate, with pinnae widely spaced. The reddish pink fronds in early spring are particularly lovely. The sporangia are borne in flowerlike panicles at the tips of the fronds. It likes abundant moisture but must have good drainage.

OSTRYA (AWS tree ah). A genus of small, hardy, deciduous, hard-wooded trees native to the Northern Hemisphere, belonging to the Betulaceae (Birch Family), and commonly known as hop-hornbeam or ironwood.

O. virginiana (hop-hornbeam, ironwood) is the only species regularly cultivated. It makes a fine small tree that grows to 30 ft. and has drooping branches, dark brown flaky bark, and hoplike fruit clusters. It has no serious disease or insect problems and does well in sun or partial shade but is somewhat difficult to transplant. Hardy in Zones 4–9.

OSWEGO-TEA. Common name for *Monarda didyma*, a perennial herb with red, pink, or white flowers; see MONARDA.

OTHONNA (oh THOH nah) **capensis.** A South African herb or shrub belonging to the Asteraceae (Aster Family), formerly listed as *O. crassifolia*, and commonly known as little-pickles. The only regularly cultivated member of the genus, it makes a good hanging-basket plant for the conservatory or window garden. It has slender, drooping stems; fleshy, cylindrical leaves that resemble small cucumbers; and small heads of yellow flowers produced over a long season. It is easily grown and propagated by stem cuttings.

OVARY. The more or less bulbous part of the pistil within which are contained one or more ovules. Flowers with stamens, petals, and sepals originating around the base of or below the ovary are said to have a superior ovary; when these parts are inserted around the summit of the ovary and seem to rise from it, the ovary appears not within but beneath the flower, which is said to have an inferior ovary. See FLOWER.

OVATE. Term applied to the leaves and leaflike parts, meaning "egg shaped" in outline, the point of attachment being at the broad end. See LEAF. Compare CORDATE; OBOVATE.

OVULE. A body contained within the ovary of the flower, which when fertilized by the sperm cell contained in the pollen grain becomes a seed.

OXALIS (ahk SAL is). A genus of small, rather delicate, bulbous or tuberous herbs, including the principal members of the Oxalidaceae (Wood-sorrel Family), and commonly known as wood-sorrel. Some are useful in rock gardens, others for bedding, for hanging baskets, as potted plants, or for greenhouse decoration. The native species are characterized by their cloverlike leaves which, like the flowers, close at night. Most are hardy to Zone 8, but some thrive in colder climates. The flowers, usually in pastel shades, have five petals that expand above a cone-shaped tube.

Whether raised from bulbs, tubers, rootstock, or seed, plants grown outdoors are best if started in spring. Both indoor and outdoor subjects require an acid soil composed of a porous mixture of leaf mold, sand, and loam. Liquid manure applied from time to time when the plants are nearly mature will encourage the production of good flowers.

As a common name, blue-oxalis refers to *Parochetus communis*, a trailing tropical plant with cloverlike leaves and rich blue flowers; see PAROCHETUS.

HARDY SPECIES
O. acetosella (shamrock) is an early-blooming European native naturalized in the eastern United States.

O. bowiei is a South African native, useful in the rock garden, with rose-red flowers that continue to open all summer.

O. corniculata var. *atropurpurea*, often sold as *O. tropaeoloides*, is a purple-leaved bedding plant with yellow flowers.

Oxalis montana

O. montana (wood-sorrel) is the familiar species with inverted heart–shaped leaflets borne in threes and often folded down the middle. Native to woodlands in the northern United States and Canada, it is useful for naturalizing. The sour-tasting leaves and flowers are sometimes used to make tea or as a salad or cold drink garnish. In early summer, it has solitary white or pink flowers with pink veins. Hardy to Zone 4.

O. oregana (redwood-sorrel), native to the Pacific Northwest, has creeping rhizomes and is good for ground cover in the shade. Growing to 10 in. tall and nearly stemless, it has pink, white, or rose-colored flowers. Leaflets are 1½ in. wide and borne in threes.

O. rosea, the true species, has loosely clustered pink flowers.

O. rub (often sold as *O. ro* has rose, lilac, or white flowers clustered on long stalks.

Oxalis oregana

HALF-HARDY SPECIES

O. adenophylla is a low, compact plant with many narrow leaflets arranged like rays and large flowers of white or pink with darker veins.

O. crassipes has 8–18 in. flower stalks bearing small, pink blooms through most of the year in warmer regions.

O. deppei has white flowers and dark green leaves with purple bands. It is good for greenhouse culture.

O. enneaphylla is similar to *O. adenophylla*.

O. hirta has deep violet, rose, or purple flowers and leaves of three narrow leaflets.

O. lasiandra (often sold as *O. rosea* in several color forms) has large leaves with five to ten leaflets and flowers crowded in umbels.

O. latifolia bears small, pink to lavender flowers on 6-in. leaf stalks.

O. ortgiesii, a good greenhouse plant, is somewhat succulent, having yellow flowers and leaflets with pointed instead of rounded lobes.

O. pes-caprae (Bermuda-buttercup), also listed as *O. cernua*, is a tender herb from South Africa and is naturalized in Florida and the West Indies. It bears yellow flowers on stalks that rise above the often purplish leaves.

O. purpurea, also listed as *O. variabilis*, is a low-growing, spreading plant but is usually not invasive. It grows 4–5 in. tall and has red flowers

and cloverlike leaves. White, lavender, and pink varieties are available as cv. 'Grand Duchess'.

O. valdiviensis is a perennial that is generally raised as an annual. It has yellow flowers with brown stripes inside borne in clusters on 6-in. stalks.

O. versicolor grows 8 in. tall and has small (½-in.) leaflets and bears striped flowers of white, yellow, and purple.

OXERA (ahk SEE rah) **pulchella.** A shrubby climbing plant belonging to the Verbenaceae (Verbena Family). Apparently the only cultivated member of the genus, it is usually grown in a warm greenhouse or outdoors in Zones 10–11. It is an interesting winter-flowering climber, bearing clusters of fragrant, white, trumpet-shaped flowers, 2 in. or longer. It does well in a mixture of fibrous peat and loam with sand and is propagated by cuttings.

OXEYE. Common name for HELIOPSIS, a genus of perennial herbs with yellow flowers. Oxeye daisy is *Chrysanthemum leucanthemum*; see CHRYSANTHEMUM.

OXLIP. Common name for *Primula elatior*, a garden perennial with abundant yellow flowers in spring; see PRIMULA.

OXYDENDRUM (ahk si DEN drum) **arboreum.** A slow-growing, pyramidal tree growing to 30 ft., belonging to the Ericaceae (Heath Family), and commonly known as sourwood or sorrel tree. It is native to the United States and makes a superb small specimen tree that is beautiful all year, with drooping branches; small, white flowers in summer; and dark green leaves turning red and purple in the fall. Hardy in Zones 5–9, it grows best in acid, well-drained soil and full sun. Propagation is by seed or cuttings.

OXYTROPIS (ahks ee TROH pis). A large genus of perennial herbs or small, shrubby plants, found mostly in the mountainous regions of Europe, Asia, and North America, belonging to the

Fabaceae (Bean Family), and commonly known as locoweed or crazyweed. A number of these legumes form attractive, ground-hugging mats that are excellent subjects for the rock garden. Propagation is easily done by seed or division. They are hardy in cool regions but can be difficult to grow in heat or humidity. A few species are very vigorous and apt to become weedy.

PRINCIPAL SPECIES

O. campestris is a European species with cream-and-purple, winged flowers borne on scapes 12 in. high.

O. lambertii, a western locoweed with ground hugging habit, has attractive, hairy stems and variable flower colors of white, purple, and carmine.

O. splendens grows to 18 in. high and has blue or purple flowers borne in racemes above 10-in. elliptic leaves.

OYSTER PLANT. Common name for *Tragopogon porrifolius*, commonly known and cultivated as SALSIFY. Spanish-oyster plant is *Scolymus hispanicus*; see SCOLYMUS.

P

PACHYPODIUM (pak i POH dee um). A genus of very choice succulents in the Apocynaceae (Dogbane Family) with remarkable swollen caudices or fat, succulent stems. *P. lamerei* and *P. geayi* have been grown extensively from seed in recent years and are popularly sold under the name Madagascar-palm, though they are palmlike only in superficial appearance, with their terminal tuft of long, linear to lanceolate leaves. The trunks are straight and quite spiny, branching dichotomously only after flowering. They will take fairly tropical conditions and will not tolerate much frost.

PACHYSANDRA (pak is AN drah). A genus of low, dense perennial herbs or subshrubs, evergreen or partly so, belonging to the Buxaceae (Box Family), and variously known as spurge. Some make useful ground covers and are propagated by cuttings.

P. *procumbens* (Allegheny-spurge) has less attractive foliage than *P. terminalis* and is usually deciduous. The greenish white flowers with purple markings rise from the base of the stem in early spring. Hardy in Zones 5–8.

P. *terminalis* (Japanese-spurge) is one of the most useful evergreen ground cover plants available, especially for planting under trees. Hardy in Zones 5–9, it can also be used to advantage to cover banks and anywhere grass will not grow or is not desirable, particularly in shady places. The terminal spikes of white flowers open early in spring and are attractive to bees. The fruit (not often seen) is a soft, white berry. Var. *variegata* has leaves marked white. Cv. 'Silver Edge' (silver-edge-spurge) is less hardy (Zones 6–9).

PACHYSTACHYS (pak ee STAY kiss). A genus of small shrubs from tropical America, belonging to the Acanthaceae (Acanthus Family). They bloom at the tips of the new shoots with slender tubular flowers growing out from a group of closely pressed bracts. *P. lutea* (yellow shrimp plant) makes a good potted plant, thriving in any good potting soil. Propagation is by cuttings.

PAEONIA (pee OH nee ah). A genus of hardy, perennial, herbaceous or shrubby plants belonging to the Ranunculaceae (Buttercup Family), commonly known as peony, and long favored as decorative garden subjects. Plants have thickened rootstocks and large, handsome flowers in shades of white, pink, or red blooming in early spring.

CLASSIFICATION

The peonies most widely grown are divided by horticulturists into two classes. The herbaceous forms include numerous varieties developed from *P. albiflora* and *P. officinalis*. The tree peonies are forms of *P. suffruticosa*, a Chinese shrub that grows to 6 ft. and was once widely grown but is now replaced by newer herbaceous forms.

Single

Flowers of the herbaceous peonies are classified by many variations in shape and color.

Single. Few petals and profuse stamens.

Japanese

Japanese. Wider, conspicuous stamens.

Bomb. Some stamens changed to narrow petals.

Bomb

Semidouble. A number of stamens changed into broad, petal-like parts.

Crown. Both stamens and carpels are petal-like.

Rose. Completely double flowers, both stamens and carpels having become petals.

Semidouble

CULTURE

Peonies are among the most popular and satisfactory of garden perennials. Their blooms are showy without being coarse and range in color from white

Rose

through pink and red to the darkest purple, with a few yellows among the newer types. Their foliage is decorative from early spring to fall, and they are absolutely hardy in Zones 5–9. They are effectively used in the border in combination with other perennials, especially grouped as accents. Although peonies are generally thought of as large perennials for the formal garden or larger specimen plantings, a few dainty species add miniature peony charm to the rock garden. They thrive best in a not-too-heavy soil that has been well dug and enriched. In spring, they should be planted so that the buds or "eyes" are not covered more than 3 in. deep. Since the plants are heavy feeders, it is good to give them an annual top dressing of bonemeal or well-decomposed manure mixed with rich soil from the compost heap. Sometimes peonies do not produce the characteristic blooms the first year after planting. Once established, if properly fed,

Peony planting

they will increase in size and produce beautiful blooms for ten or twelve years without division.

Herbaceous peonies are easily forced in the greenhouse for winter bloom. The clumps are dug early in the fall and kept in a coldframe until needed. When brought into the greenhouse and kept in a temperature of about 60°F, the flowers will appear in six to eight weeks.

Propagation. The preferred method is dividing clumps in the fall. New plants can be started from seed, but the seedlings will not bloom until the third year. Some improved varieties, especially the tree peonies, can be increased by grafting the eyes onto tubers of growing plants.

ENEMIES

Botrytis Blight. The most common disease of peonies, this is likely to be very destructive during wet seasons. It has also been called bud blight, bud blast, or gray mold. In reality, there are two blights, one early and one late, caused by different species of the same fungus, **Botrytis paeoniae** and **B. cinerea**. Early in the spring, young shoots suddenly wilt and fall over, turning black and showing masses of gray-brown spores. If nothing is done, these spores are later carried to developing buds, which turn black and cease growth. Botrytis blight is usually the unsuspected cause of failure of peonies to bloom. Older buds may be blasted. The stems may take on a brown appearance in places. There may be irregular dark areas on the leaves, spreading rapidly during rain. Decay and crown rot may extend all through the season.

The chief means of control are thorough sanitary measures. In late fall, cut all stalks just below the surface of the ground, removing as much of the stalk as possible without injuring the bud. This destroys many resting bodies (sclerotia) that would be sources of spring infection. Promptly remove any infected shoots in the spring and all diseased buds, flowers, and leaves during the season. In doing this, carry a paper bag to collect all diseased material, then burn it. Diseased parts carried around uncovered will scatter spores.

Other Rots. Occasionally other rots, including phythophthora blight and sclerotinia stem rot, may kill the shoots. These can be controlled by the same measures as botrytis blight.

Nematode root knot, caused by a microscopic eelworm is especially serious in sandy soils in the eastern states. Affected roots are irregularly knotted or gnarled, and the weak, spindling, stunted plants gradually die. Dig unhealthy looking plants in the fall, remove all infected roots, divide the healthy portions, and replant them. Dormant roots can be treated in hot water at 120°F for 30 minutes. In planting new roots and treated ones, avoid soil where the disease has occurred. See NEMATODES.

Insect Pests. There are not many insects that disturb peonies. The ROSE CHAFER is especially fond of this plant and should be removed by hand-picking and the insects destroyed. If stalks are left standing, they are likely to be infested with oyster-shell scale. Ants are often seen on the buds, but they are merely feeding on a sticky secretion and cause no injury.

PRINCIPAL SPECIES

P. delavayi is a shrubby form that grows to 3 ft. and has crimson blossoms 2 in. across.

P. lactiflora, formerly listed as *P. albiflora*, has flowers with eight or more pink or white petals. Many of the garden forms have been derived from this species, including pink and white double varieties.

P. lutea is a shrubby plant with yellow flowers, sometimes used by hybridists to expand the color range of garden peonies.

P. mlokosewitschii (Caucasian peony) has

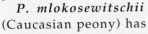

Paeonia lactiflora

large, yellow flowers with golden anthers and gray- to blue-green foliage that turns brown in winter.

P. officinalis (common peony) grows to 3 ft. and has single flowers varying from white to dark crimson. This is the old garden favorite, usually seen with double white, rose, or red blossoms. Var. *festiva* has white flowers with crimson centers.

P. suffruticosa (tree peony), sometimes listed as *P. moutan*, is a shrubby species from China that grows to 6 ft. It is widely grown throughout the Orient, and more sparingly in North America. It is a much-branched shrub with white, rose, purplish, or red flowers to 12 in. across. There are several varieties, including var. *humei*, with whitish, semidouble, dark-centered flowers; and *papaveracea*, whose poppylike blossoms have dark-blotched, satiny petals. It is usually propagated by grafting improved kinds on nonblooming tubers of herbaceous species.

P. tenuifolia, an excellent choice for the rock garden, grows to 1½ ft. with finely cut, fernlike foliage and small, erect, dark crimson flowers.

PAINTBRUSH. A common name for three plants, *Hieracium aurantiacum* (devil's-paintbrush or hawkweed), a field weed with orange flowers, see HIERACIUM; *Emilia javanica* (Flora's-paintbrush or tasselflower), a garden annual with small, red flowers, see EMILIA; and *Castilleja californica* (Indian-paintbrush), a perennial with bright red flowers and bracts, see CASTILLEJA.

PAK-CHOI. Common name for certain varieties of *Brassica rapa*, known as Chinese cabbage; see BRASSICA; CHINESE CABBAGE; MUSTARD.

PALIURUS (pal ee YOO rus). A genus of spiny deciduous trees native to the Orient and southern Europe, belonging to the Rhamnaceae (Buckthorn Family).

P. spina-christi (Christ or Jerusalem thorn) is sometimes grown in the United States but is not hardy north of Washington, D.C. This is a spreading shrub or small tree that grows to 20 ft. The dark green foliage is attractive, but, following greenish yellow flowers, the real interest is the brownish fruits shaped like a low-crowned, wide-brimmed hat. It needs a sunny location and well-drained soil. Propagation is by seed, layers, and root cuttings.

PALMETTO. Common name loosely applied to several plants but properly referring to SABAL, a genus of tropical American fan palms, including the cabbage and dwarf palmettos.

Blue-palmetto is *Rhapidophyllum hystrix*. Scrub- or saw-palmetto is the trailing plant *Serenoa repens*; see SERENOA.

PALMS. Decorative and useful, woody tropical plants, mostly trees, some bushy, and a few climbers, forming the botanical family Palmaceae. This is one of the most outstandingly beautiful groups of the plant world. The stately trunks and the feathery foliage of many of the

2000 or more species give the characteristic note to the tropical landscape. Those most frequently seen have a cylindrical trunk, from a few to 100 or more feet in height, in some species smooth, in others armed or spiny, and in many covered with the sheaths of old leaves. Most palms bear their leaves in a crown at the tip.

TYPES AND CONDITIONS

For horticultural convenience, palms are divided into two broad groups according to the type of foliage. The fan palms have broad leaves palmately divided; in some species they may be 10 ft. across. The other group is made up of feather palms, with leaves divided in feather form—cut into segments from the midrib; these have occasionally grown nearly 50 ft. in length. Sometimes the foliage, and occasionally the fruit, is armed with sharp spines or prickles.

Many palms are grown outdoors in Florida, the Gulf states, and California; a few are native in the southern states. Among these, the sabals and other palmettos will endure several degrees of frost. The royal types add immeasurable dignity when planted along avenues or driveways and to frame vistas. The coconut palms are particularly lovely as they bend over ocean beaches. The stiff fans of the palmettos form good evergreen background for the garden picture, and plants used singly make excellent accents. The feathery plumage and beautiful flowers and fruit of other species add a unique interest to the tropical and semitropical garden.

PALMS IN THE GARDEN

The outdoor culture of palms varies widely with the location and the species, but in general, most of them will not endure frost and should be planted in a somewhat protected position sheltered from too-intense sun as well as from cold winds. Many of the more tender types suffer more from exposure to sun than from cold. The soil, which is inclined to be sandy in most warm regions otherwise suited to palms—such as Florida or California, should be enriched with well-rotted manure. This should also be used to mulch the roots during the rainy season. Although palms will survive poor soil conditions, frequent applications of a well-balanced fertilizer will promote growth and enhance the beauty of the plants.

Many palms drop their leaves. These should not be raked away, since they provide a natural humus as they gradually rot around the base. Although palms are associated with sandy places, water is required for their best success, especially in the dry season. Lacking it, growth will be slow. Hardiness depends upon the age; young specimens often perish in a cold snap while older trees come through unscathed, even with several degrees of frost.

Disease. Black scorch of the date palms, prevalent in the southwestern states, is reduced by destroying infected trunks, leaves, and litter. In California, a penicillium disease, which may kill ornamental palms, appears as discolored linear streaks in leaves of *Phoenix canariensis*; as deformed and retarded growth in *Washingtonia filifera*, for which the resistant *W. robusta* should be substituted; and as trunk cankers on other palms, which should be surgically treated as soon as discovered.

PALMS AS HOUSEPLANTS

Outside tropical regions, palms are best known as houseplants. A number of species are easily cultivated by anyone under ordinary home conditions. They require relatively little sun and often grow surprisingly well indoors, where the atmosphere is usually too hot and dry for most plants.

For success with palms in the house, a few basic conditions should be satisfied. The most important is never to allow a palm to be chilled

Cocos sp.   *Phoenix roebelenii*

by a sudden cold draft from an open door or window. This will cause the leaves to turn brown and eventually drop. Since palms are not expensive in small sizes, it is better to buy a new one than to try restoring a chilled plant to health and beauty.

Another requisite is to water thoroughly whenever necessary but never to allow stagnant water to stand in the pot or the saucer beneath it. It is best to water palms from below, by setting the pot in a basin of water and allowing it to stand there until the surface soil is damp. This treatment once a week is far better than sprinkling the soil daily.

To keep the leaves clean, sponge them frequently with clear water. Regular syringing with a fine spray and considerable pressure will normally check insects such as scale, thrips, and red spider mites.

Repotting should be done only when absolutely necessary, and preferably in spring or early summer. In shifting, do not move to too large a pot; a single size larger than the former container is about right, since potted palms do best when their roots are confined. A good potting soil contains equal parts of turfy loam, sand, and leaf mold mixed with dried manure. Add a 4-in. pot of coarse bonemeal to each bushel of this mixture.

PALMS IN THE GREENHOUSE

For years palms have been stately greenhouse subjects in botanical garden collections as well as private conservatories. They are also widely grown commercially in many regions, both in small sizes for sale as houseplants and in larger sizes for use as decorative material in hotel lobbies and comparable large spaces.

In the greenhouse, the majority of palms succeed best with a temperature range of 60°F at night and 70–80°F during the day. In the heat of summer, they should be shaded and a humid atmosphere should be maintained by frequent watering and constant spraying of the foliage. Adequate ventilation should be assured day and night in order to check fungus diseases, which thrive in a hot, moist atmosphere. See also GREENHOUSE.

Enemies. To control a leaf spot or anthracnose that may kill the tips of the leaves and cause spotting, carefully cut off all dead lower leaves and burn them. See LEAF SPOT; ANTHRACNOSE.

Mealybugs and many kinds of scales infest palms in greenhouses and other indoor conditions, but most infestations can be treated fairly simply. Mealybugs are checked by spraying with an insecticidal soap solution. The scales can be wiped off the leaves of a small stock of plants with a soft cloth dipped in a soapy solution. Larger infestations may require fumigation. See also MEALYBUG; SCALE INSECTS; INSECT CONTROL; GREENHOUSE PESTS.

PAMPAS GRASS. Common name for CORTADERIA, a genus of showy South American grasses.

PANAX (PAY naks). A genus of Asiatic and North American perennial herbs commonly called ginseng, valued by the Chinese as medicine and popular in tea. The plants require cool, moist, deep, well-drained soil and shade supplied either by tall forest trees or slat sheds. If fresh seed is sown as soon as it is gathered, it may germinate the following spring; if dried, it may require a year longer. Seedlings can be sold or transplanted in the fall or spring when one or two years old. Roots four or five years old can be dug for export.

Panax quinquefolius

The only species of interest are *P. pseudoginseng* (Asiatic ginsing), *P. trifolius* (dwarf or groundnut ginseng), and *P. quinquefolius* (American ginseng). The last mentioned is gathered wild (and occasionally grown) for export. At one time exploited, today it has little status as a garden crop.

PANCRATIUM (pan KRAY shum). A genus of interesting white- or green-flowered bulbous plants of the Amaryllidaceae (Amaryllis Family). The white cup bearing the stamens in some species resembles the trumpet or crown of a daffodil. The cultivated species, some of which are mistakenly identified as *Hymenocallis*, require a rather high temperature, good ventilation without drafts, frequent syringing, abundant water, and a rich, loamy soil containing about ⅕ well-rotted cow manure. While flowering, they can be given a cooler, airier location; after flowering, water should be greatly reduced until their resting period. After a few weeks on a bench in a coolhouse and occasional watering, they are ready to grow again. Unless crowded, it is better to top-dress them than to disturb their roots. If offsets develop, they can be used for propagation, rooting them in a mixture of sand, leaf mold, and peat. Seed can also be used. Young plants should be kept moist and given plenty of sun.

The hardiest species, useful for summer bloom in milder climates, is *P. illyricum*, bearing 6 or more flowers at the top of a scape 1 ft. tall. The evergreen, fragrant, white-flowered *P. maritimum* has a cup 1 in. long within a perianth that extends 1½ in. above the tube.

PANDANUS (pan DAY nus). A large genus of tropical trees or shrubs commonly known as screw-pine, because of the spiral formation of the prickly margined, swordlike leaves along the main stem. They are handsome and easily cultivated as potted plants for the house, succeeding best in sandy loam with charcoal and leaf mold intermixed. They require good drainage with plenty of water in summer but are best kept moderately dry in winter when no water should be allowed to lodge in the leaf axils. The plants are inclined to raise themselves out of pots due to the downward growth of the roots.

PRINCIPAL SPECIES

P. baptistii has short stems and green leaves about 1 in. wide, some striped white.

P. pygmaeus (pigmy pandanus) is a low, spreading shrub less than 2 ft. high in the center, which sends out branches from the base in all directions, with the leaves at the ends of the branches gray-green beneath.

P. sanderi is short stemmed, with leaves 2 in. or wider and yellow stripes lengthwise along the margins.

P. veitchi has spiny leaves up to 2 ft. long and 3 in. wide, dark green in the center and bordered with white. It is a handsome houseplant, largely employed in a young state for table use. For this purpose, propagation is by offsets or suckers rising from the base, which should be cut with a sharp knife as soon as they are large enough to be detached. The cuttings are then inserted singly in small pots, the crown of each cutting being kept well up, and the pots plunged in a closed frame with little water given until the roots are formed. Propagation can also be done by seed. During the winter, the foliage will benefit from occasional gentle spongings with warm, slightly soapy water, dried off with a damp sponge.

PANDOREA (pan DOHR ee ah). A genus of vigorous growing, evergreen vines or climbing shrubs from Australia and South Africa, belonging to the Bignoniaceae (Bignonia Family). They grow outdoors in warm regions but can tolerate a few degrees of frost. A sunny location and rich soil suits them best. Propagation is by seed and cuttings of green wood.

P. jasminoides (bower plant) is a climbing shrub with clusters of a few white blossoms with pink throats.

P. pandorana (wonga-wonga vine) is the least showy species, with panicles of many whitish yellow flowers spotted purple; however, it is worth growing for the fine foliage alone.

PANICLE. A loose, spirelike arrangement of flowers (INFLORESCENCE) on a stalk; a branched raceme. The blossom of *Astilbe* (Japanese-spirea) is an example.

PANICUM (PAN i kum). A rather large genus of annuals and perennials of the Poaceae (Grass Family). They are of little garden interest, but some are important grain and forage plants, while others are troublesome weeds. They are hardy to Zone 5.

PRINCIPAL SPECIES

P. capillare (witch grass) is usually a weed but is sometimes grown for its large, loose spikes for fresh or dry bouquets. An annual, it grows to 2 ft. and has leaves 1 ft. long and ½ in. wide. The branches of the panicles, which may be 14 in. long, are extremely slim and spreading. See WEEDS.

P. miliaceum (millet), grown for hay and forage, is the best-known species of agricultural interest.

P. virgatum (switch grass), a perennial growing to 6 ft. but otherwise much the same as *P. capillare*, can be raised from seed for ornament.

PANSY. Common name for certain hybrid and garden species of violet; see VIOLA.

PAPAVER (pah PAY vur). A genus of annual and perennial herbs commonly known as poppy. This group can be recognized by its large, showy flowers with paperlike petals of clear color on long stems and by its milky juice. The garden species and their varieties have a great range of color and are widely planted for their decorative value and easy culture, thriving in beds, borders, and rock gardens. The Papaveraceae (Poppy Family) is named for this genus.

There are few true perennials, including *P. orientale* and *P. bracteatum*; all others are annuals or perennials that bloom the first year from seed. Seed for the annual species is sown in the fall or very early in spring in a light, warm soil and an open, sunny location where the plants are to stand, and the seedlings thinned out, since they are exceedingly difficult to transplant. The perennials can be propagated

Papaver orientale

by seed, division, or root cuttings made in late summer. These should be planted in full sun, and in gritty, well-drained soil, since standing water causes the roots to rot. Hardiness varies with the species, but many of the perennials may be challenging in hot climates.

Bacterial blight causes black lesions on stems, leaves, floral organs, and seedpods of oriental and corn poppies. The leaf tissues between the black spots turn yellow, then brown, and the leaf falls. If the stems are girdled, the plants die. The only known control is to destroy the plants in infected beds and disinfect the soil.

The black bean and spinach aphids both infest poppies, but both pests can be controlled by thoroughly rinsing the undersides of leaves with a stiff stream of water or treating them with a contact insecticide; see APHIDS.

PRINCIPAL SPECIES

P. alpinum (alpine poppy), also listed as *P. burseri*, is a low-growing perennial native to the Alps. A delicate plant with finely cut, grayish foliage and fragile, white or yellow, delightfully scented blossoms, it should be planted in a sunny, well-drained location in soil composed largely of rock chips and sand. Hardy in Zones 5–9, it is attractive and suited to the rock garden but is relatively short lived; thus, it should be routinely propagated from seed. Varieties are available in a wide range of colors including red, orange, pink, yellow, and white.

P. atlanticum has hairy basal leaves and flower stems up to 1½ ft. The single blooms are orange or red. Hardy in Zones 7–9.

P. bracteatum is a perennial, one of the parents of the oriental hybrids but differing from *P. orientale* in its solid-colored petals and leafy bracts below the flowers.

P. californicum (western poppy) is an annual with brick-red flowers marked with green at the base of the petals. It should not be confused with the true California poppy, which belongs to the genus *Eschscholzia*.

P. glaucum (tulip poppy) is an annual with grayish green foliage and cup-shaped, scarlet flowers 4 in. across, borne on 2-ft. stems.

P. nudicaule (Iceland poppy) is a perennial that grows to 1 ft. and blooms the first year from seed; it is hardy in Zones 2–9 but rarely lasts more than three years in the garden. It has charming white, orange, or reddish fragrant flowers with a number of brilliant varietal forms.

P. orientale (Oriental poppy) is a perennial that grows to 3 ft. or more and has large, coarsely cut leaves covered with bristly hairs. The natural flowers are brilliant scarlet blotched with black at the base of each petal. Many varieties have been developed, extending the color range from pale pink through salmon to maroon. Though their blooming season is short, they are hardy in Zones 2–9 and give a most brilliant effect in the border, and later their fading foliage can be concealed if perennial baby's-breath is planted among them.

P. rhoeas (corn, Flanders, or Shirley poppy) is the annual red field poppy of Europe and Asia, usually having cinnabar-red flowers. It is a weed on waste areas on a wide range of soils that are neutral to weakly acid but is rarely a problem in the United States. Some varieties are cultivated as ornamentals, and many strains are available in shades varying from pure white through pink and rose to bright scarlet, without the dark base, both single and double blooms.

P. rupifragum is a perennial with finely cut leaves and pale red blossoms borne on 1½-ft. stalks. It should be planted in poor, sandy soil in the rock garden, since it becomes weedy when grown in rich ground. Hardy in Zones 7–9.

PAPAVERACEAE (pah pay vur AY see ee). The Poppy Family, a group of largely familiar herbs, many of them choice flower garden subjects. Genera commonly cultivated are *Argemone*, *Chelidonium* (celandine), *Dendromecon* (tree poppy), *Eschscholzia* (California poppy), *Glaucium*, *Hunnemannia* (tulip poppy), *Macleaya*, *Meconopsis*, *Papaver* (poppy), *Platystemon*, and *Romneya*.

PAPAYA. Common name for *Carica papaya*, a tropical, treelike herb and its edible fruits, sometimes known as Pawpaw or Papaw. The plant grows erect, unbranched, and palmlike, often to 20 ft., and has a crown of seven-lobed leaves, each 2 ft. wide, from the axils of which hang 20 to 50 melonlike, yellow-skinned, pink- or yellow-fleshed fruits, which ripen successively for several weeks and may weigh 10–15 lb. each. While immature, these are cooked like squash; when ripe, they are eaten like muskmelons, with which their flavor is sometimes compared. The unripe fruits yield the medicine papain.

Though the plants are easily propagated from seed, the best varieties are grafted. They require sunny positions, well-drained, rich loam, and frequent cultivation.

PAPER BIRCH. A common name for *Betula papyrifera*, a hardy deciduous tree with attractive white bark; see BETULA.

PAPHIOPEDILUM (paf ee oh PED il um). About 60 species of terrestrial or lithophytic orchids native to southeastern Asia, China, New Guinea, the Solomon Islands, and the Philippines, commonly known in cultivation as lady's-slipper. Plants do not have pseudobulbs, but thick, spreading roots are formed at the base of the plant. Leaves are leathery, sometimes mottled, distichous, and long.

One to several waxy flowers are borne on erect inflorescences. The fused lateral sepals form a synsepalum, and the erect dorsal sepal sometimes hoods the labellum (pouch). The dorsal sepal is often distinctively marked with stripes, spots, and warts. Petals are horizontal, usually twisted and elongated, and often marked with hairy warts. In some species, the petals droop and continue to lengthen as the flower matures. The lip is an inflated pouch. Flowers vary in color and size, some being diminutive, while others are stately. Colors are palest blush-rose, chrome-yellow, green, mahogany, and wine-black.

There are two kinds of *Paphiopedilum* growing in warm and cool conditions. All species require shady, humid conditions and should be planted in a well-drained compost of peat, sphagnum moss, and charcoal. Adding a small amount of agricultural lime to the topsoil several times a year is beneficial. Hardy to Zone 6 if protected from frost, they withstand minimum winter temperatures of 55–60°F. The type species is *P. insigne*.

PAPYRUS. Common name for the tall sedge, *Cyperus papyrus*, also known as paper plant; see CYPERUS.

PARAFFIN. The use of melted paraffin to cover grafts instead of the familiar GRAFTING WAX or tree seal. Not only the graft but the entire scion is covered with the melted (but not hot) paraffin, and in many cases the entire top of dormant plants, such as rose bushes and some fruit trees, are dipped in paraffin to check evaporation and keep them in better condition between digging and storage. This treatment has become widespread in nursery culture, especially in connection with the so-called packaged roses, in which the roots are embedded and sealed in a mass of peat moss, the whole plant being enclosed in a carton for sale by various retailers.

Paraffining has also been practiced on budded plants, but with somewhat less success, owing to the greater susceptibility of the tender buds to injury. Nevertheless, the use of paraffin, which can be obtained anywhere and kept in the right condition for application with a soft brush in a simple heating pot, is an easy method of covering any sort of propagation wound and of preventing evaporation and drying of the tops of dormant, deciduous plants; it can well be investigated by home gardeners.

PARAMOUNT HYBRIDS. Globular, clustering cactus hybrids with spectacular colored flowers. Harry Johnson of Paramount Cactus Gardens, formerly in Paramount, California, hybridized ECHINOPSIS, which has large, white, nocturnal flowers, with *Lobivia*, another South American genus but with diurnal (day-blooming) flowers. The resultant hybrids are spectacular, with large, colorful flowers that stay open during the day

and last for several days. 'Orange Glory', with rich, yellow-orange flowers, and 'Stars & Stripes', with predominantly light pink and dark rose striped flowers, are among the prettiest.

PARASITE. A plant or animal nourished by another to which it attaches itself or within which it establishes itself. Generally the presence of the parasite produces a diseased condition, but this is not always true. The term "pathogen" is used to cover all disease-producing organisms, whether they are parasitic or not.

PARATHELYPTERIS (pa rah thuh LĪP tur is). A subgenus of ferns included in the larger group THELYPTERIS.

PARKINSONIA (pahr kin SOH nee ah). A genus of tropical or subtropical trees or shrubs belonging to the Fabaceae (Bean Family). The principal species is *P. aculeata* (Jerusalem thorn, ratama), a small, thorny, evergreen tree with feathery, pendulous branches and loose clusters of fragrant, yellow flowers. It is often used as a hedge plant in Zones 10–11 and can tolerate very dry conditions. It has been tried in greenhouses but does not thrive in pots. Propagation is by seed.

PARNASSIA (pahr NAS ee ah). A genus of small perennial herbs found in the North Temperate Zone, belonging to the Saxifragaceae (Saxifrage Family), commonly known as grass-of-Parnassus. They are interesting for planting in partly shaded, moist places, blooming in late summer. The white flowers, marked with greenish or yellowish veins, are borne singly. Propagation is by seed or division.

PRINCIPAL SPECIES

P. asarifolia, found in the mountains of Virginia and North Carolina, grows to 20 in. and has kidney-shaped leaves and flowers 1 in. across.

P. fimbriata is native in the northwestern states and is distinguished by its fringed-petaled flowers.

P. glauca, formerly listed as *P. caroliniana*, is common in moist northern meadows and swamps; it grows to 12 in. or more and has ovate leaves about 2 in. long and flowers 1 in. across or larger.

P. palustris, found in Europe and Asia as well as North America, has relatively small leaves and flowers.

PAROCHETUS (pa roh KEE tus) **communis.** A tropical, perennial trailer with cloverlike foliage, belonging to the Fabaceae (Bean Family), and commonly known as shamrock pea or blue-oxalis. It has cobalt-blue pealike flowers with pink wings. Useful for pot or hanging-basket culture, it blooms nearly all year. The soil should be a mixture of sand and humus, and pots should be placed in a partially shaded position. Plants can also be grown in a cool, sheltered location in the rock garden, but they are seldom hardy in cool climates.

PARONYCHIA (par oh NIK ee ah). A genus of small annual or perennial, mostly hardy, tufted herbs belonging to the Caryophyllaceae (Pink Family) and commonly known as whitlowwort or nailwort. They are well suited for rock work, walls, and carpet bedding. The perennial Mediterranean species are especially favored for the silvery bracts surrounding the insignificant flowers. Found in the wild growing over mountain rocks, they provide interest in hot and sunny, but not humid, rock gardens.

P. argentea is a low, prostrate perennial with egg-shaped leaves and small, whitish, crowded flowers. They are free-growing plants forming neat patches 1 ft. or more in diameter.

P. argyrocoma (silver whitlowwart, silverling) is an upright, perennial native from Maine to Georgia. It grows to 8 in., forming broad mats covered with silvery downy hairs, straight leaves, and flat clusters of small flowers.

PARROTIA (pah ROH shee ah) **persica.** A small deciduous tree native to the Middle East and belonging to the Hamamelidaceae (Witch-hazel Family). It is hardy to Zone 5, but in cultivation it usually takes the form of a large shrub. It does well in acid soil that is loamy and well drained in a protected location. The flowers are more curious than beautiful; they are without petals but have conspicuous purple stamens and appear before the leaves, which take on brilliant coloring in the fall, turning from yellow to orange and then scarlet. Propagation is by seed and layers.

PARROT'S-FEATHER. Common name for *Myriophyllum aquaticum*, an aquatic plant with finely cut leaves; see MYRIOPHYLLUM.

PARSLEY. Common name for the biennial herb *Petroselinum crispum* often used for flavoring or garnishing; see PETROSELINUM. The Parsley (or Celery) Family is APIACEAE.

PARSLEY FERN. Common name for species of CRYPTOGRAMMA, a rare genus of ferns with curved margins. Southern parsley fern is the succulent *Botrychium australe*; see BOTRYCHIUM.

PARSNIP. A biennial herb, *Pastinaca sativa*, grown for its long, thick, white, sweet roots, which are used as a vegetable from late autumn to early spring. Cow-parsnip is HERACLEUM.

To produce straight, unbranched roots, the plants should be grown in deep, rich, moist soil. Because they require a long season to develop and the seed is slow to sprout, sow it in early spring in rows 18 in. apart, scattering seeds of a quick-growing forcing radish at 3-in. intervals to mark the rows. Use the radishes when they are of edible size, and weed and thin the parsnip seedlings to stand 6 in. apart. Cultivate cleanly all season until the foliage touches between the rows. Beginning in late fall, dig as needed. Some can be stored in a root cellar or a pit for winter use when the ground is frozen, but leave enough in the ground for spring use, since they are not injured by freezing. In spring, dig as needed until new tops start to grow, then dig all that remain and store them in a cold place to prevent sprouting. As long as they do not start to grow, spring-dug parsnips are better than fall-dug ones.

PARTHENOCISSUS (pahr thin oh SIS us). A genus of deciduous, high-climbing vines native to North America and Asia, belonging to the Vitaceae (Grape Family). They cling closely to walls and other supports, mostly by means of tendrils with adhesive tips. They thrive in any good soil that is not too dry and, when established, cover a large space. Propagation is by seed, cuttings, and layers. Enemies are the same as for AMPELOPSIS, with which members of this genus were once associated.

PRINCIPAL SPECIES

P. henryana is a tender Chinese vine of moderate growth, hardy in Zones 7–9. Its five-parted leaves are marked white along the veins and purple beneath. Leaf coloring is developed best under glass or outdoors in a partly shaded location.

P. quinquefolia (Virginia creeper, American-ivy) is a handsome, tall climber, native from New England southward, hardy in Zones 5–8. It clings to walls or tree trunks and is also an excellent cover on steep banks. Its large leaves, which turn scarlet and crimson in autumn, are five-parted, clearly distinguishing it from poison-ivy, with which it is sometimes confused.

P. tricuspidata (Boston-ivy, Japanese-ivy) is a high-climbing and close-clinging Asiatic vine, hardy in Zones 5–8. Its glossy, three-lobed or three-parted leaves of varying size make a very dense, flat covering, especially on brick walls, and give a brilliant patch of orange and scarlet in fall.

PARTRIDGEBERRY. A common name for *Mitchella repens*, an evergreen trailer with fragrant flowers and scarlet berries; see MITCHELLA.

PASPALUM (pas PAL um). A large, widely distributed genus of mostly perennial and some annual grasses. They are distinguished by one or many flattened racemes with hard, papery bracts surrounding the flowers. Various species are grown for ornament, lawns, and pasture forage.

P. dilatatum (dallis grass) was introduced from South America as an ornamental and is now naturalized in the southeastern states as far north as New Jersey. It is a perennial and grows 5–6 ft. tall. The leaf blades are 10 in. long and ½ in. wide. There are three to five racemes about 3 in. long with a fringe of long, silky, white hairs.

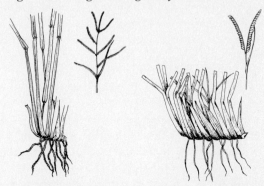

Paspalum dilatatum   *Paspalum notatum*

P. notatum (bahia grass) is a perennial with stems that grow to 2 ft. Native to South and Central America, it has been introduced in the southeastern states as a pasture or ornamental grass. There are several varieties available, some in commercial lawn seed mixtures, with flat or folded leaf blades and usually paired, curved racemes of glossy spikelets.

PASSIFLORA (pas i FLOR ah). A large genus of mostly tendril-climbing vines, the principal member of the Passifloraceae (Passion Flower Family). Some species are grown in greenhouses, as climbing houseplants, or outdoors in warm regions for their interesting and ornamental flowers; others are grown for their edible fruits. The flowers have an unusual structure, thought by early discoverers to be emblematic of the crucifixion of Christ. They can be grown in pots or planted out in a border if intended to cover a large area. They do well in a fibrous loam with leaf mold and appreciate liquid manure when growth is active. Propagation is by seed or cuttings.

PRINCIPAL SPECIES

P. alata has winged stems and large, fragrant flowers of crimson, purple, and white. Edible yellow fruits are about 5 in. long.

P. x *alatocaerulea* is a hybrid that has fragrant flowers of white and pink, with the crown purple, blue, and white.

P. caerulea is a slender but vigorous grower with flowers 3–4 in. across in a mixture of white, blue, and purple, followed by egg-shaped, yellow fruits. One of the best of several named forms is 'Constance Elliott', which has fragrant, white flowers.

P. edulis (passion fruit) has white-and-purple flowers smaller than most of the species, and purple fruit about the size of a hen's egg. It is grown as a commercial crop in Australia.

P. flavicarpa, with yellow fruit, is grown as a commercial crop and thrives at lower altitudes than the purple-fruited kinds.

P. incarnata (maypop) is native from Virginia to Texas and has white, pink, and purple flowers followed by edible yellow fruit.

P. laurifolia (water-lemon, Jamaica-honeysuckle), from South America, has entire leaves and large, white flowers spotted with red and purple, followed by edible yellow fruit.

P. manicata is a rapid and vigorous climber, suitable for outdoor planting in warmer regions. It makes a fine show with its profusion of bright scarlet flowers set off with a blue crown.

P. quadrangularis (granadilla) is one of the chief species grown for fruit. It is a tall, strong grower with large, fragrant, white, red, and purple flowers and yellowish green fruits to 9 in.

P. racemosa, with deeply lobed leaves, is one of the best of the red-flowered species and has been largely used in hybridizing.

PASTEURIZATION. Partial sterilization with heat, often used to prepare soil before planting; see SOIL PASTEURIZATION.

PATHOGEN. Any disease-producing organism, often but not always parasitic; see PARASITE.

PAULOWNIA (paw LOH nee ah). A genus of trees from China, belonging to the Scrophulariaceae (Figwort Family). They have large leaves resembling those of *Catalpa* and large, erect clusters of beautiful, violet, gloxinia-like flowers. The genus and common name for *P. tomentosa* were given in honor of Anna Paulowna, princess of the Netherlands.

P. tomentosa (princess or empress tree) is a sturdy, medium-sized tree that grows to 40 ft. and has conspicuous, fragrant, violet flowers in clusters 1 ft. long followed by pods that remain on the tree all winter. It is planted as a specimen or avenue tree in mild climates and is hardy in Zones 6–9. It will withstand salt air and is therefore a good choice for shore properties. Farther north it is root-hardy, dying to the ground each winter and in the spring sending up vigorous shoots covered with huge leaves, which permits its use as a screening foliage plant as far north as Montreal. If possible, it should be sheltered from strong winds. It grows best in a light, warm loam and can be propagated easily by seed.

PAWPAW. A common name for two North American plants, usually *Asimina triloba*, a tree bearing aromatic fruits that are almost black when ripe; see ASIMINA. Pawpaw less commonly refers to the melonlike fruits of the tropical herb *Carica papaya*, which is better known as PAPAYA.

PAXISTIMA (pak SIS ti mah). A genus of low-growing evergreen shrubs native to North America and closely related to *Euonymus*. Hardy to Zone 5, they seem to thrive best in well-drained, neutral to alkaline soil. They are a good choice for rock gardens or ground covers. Propagation is by layers, cuttings, or rooted divisions.

P. canbyi, native to the mountains of Virginia, forms a dense mat up to 1 ft. high with trailing and rooting branches. It grows well in the open or partial shade.

P. myrsinites, native from British Columbia to California, grows to 2 ft., is somewhat stiffer, and prefers partial shade.

PEA. The genus *Pisum*, including annual, herbaceous, tendril-climbing vines belonging to the FABACEAE (Bean or Pea Family) and grown mainly for their edible seeds and pods.

Horticulturally, varieties fall into four groups. (1) The original species is *P. sativum*, which climbs about 6 ft. and bears pods 4 in. or longer. (2) The edible-podded varieties, listed as var. *macrocarpon*, are also tall and bear soft, 6-in. pods. (3) The dwarf varieties, listed as var. *humile*, grow 15–36 in. tall and bear small pods. (4) The field peas, listed as var. *arvense*, are grown as a source of dried peas, for forage, or for green manure. The first three kinds have white flowers; the last, pinkish blossoms with lavender wings and greenish keels.

Garden varieties of peas are further divided into smooth-seeded and wrinkle-seeded kinds. Since the smooth-seeded kinds are somewhat hardier and not so likely to rot in cold, damp soil, they can be sown about a week earlier; however, they are of poorer quality and should only be planted in limited quantity to provide earlier peas. Taking less space and yielding a harvest in less time from sowing, the dwarf and half-dwarf,

Pea pods

wrinkle-seeded varieties that don't need staking are more popular than the tall kinds, but they are less prolific and have a much shorter season.

Snap peas are plump, edible-podded peas that grow fat peas that are far sweeter than the old types of edible-podded peas, or "sugar peas." The original sugar snap is a tall vine that grows to 6 ft. When picked, it is necessary to break off the stem section and with it a stringy suture along the top of the pea.

OTHER PEAS

Australian pea is *Dolichos lignosus*; see DOLICHOS. Beach, bedding, black, cupid, dwarf, everlasting or perennial, grass, and sweet pea are all forms of LATHYRUS. Butterfly pea is the genus CLITORIA. COWPEA refers to the genus VIGNA, which includes black-eyed pea, *V. unguiculata*

var. *unguiculata*; and catjang pea, *V. unguiculata* var. *cylindrica*. Chick pea, also known as garbanzo, is *Cicer arietinum*; see CICER. Glory pea is *Clianthus formosus*; see CLIANTHUS. Rosary pea is *Abrus precatorius*; see ABRUS. Shamrock pea is *Parochetus communis*; see PAROCHETUS. Winged pea is *Lotus tetragonolobus*; see LOTUS.

CULTURE

PLANTING

Some gardeners prefer to make successional sowings of early, wrinkle-seeded varieties. A better plan is to sow early, all at one time, several varieties that require different periods for maturing, because the pea is a cool-season crop, and early sowings get a better start and yield more abundantly than those made after the ground has become drier and warmer. Tall kinds take longer to mature than dwarfs, so the two types, even if planted at the same time, bear fruit at different periods.

Though peas are essentially a spring crop, some of the quick-growing varieties, especially the round-seeded ones, can be sown after midsummer for autumn use. However, unless there are frequent showers or overhead irrigation is employed, the autumn crop is likely to be disappointingly small.

It is most important to sow peas thinly, especially the tall varieties. Plants of the dwarf kinds should never be closer than 3 in., or those of the tall sorts, less than 4 in. apart in the rows. If the amount of seed usually recommended (1 lb. or pint to 100 ft. of single row) is sown to ensure a good stand, the seedlings should be thinned to suitable distances. Thin planting will result in increased yields and also make the seed go farther. The earliest sowing (of round-seeded varieties only) should be made 3–4 in. deep; the later ones, not more than 2 in.

Should the ground be somewhat dry at sowing time, the seed can be soaked overnight, then spread out in the morning until the surface water has evaporated. After sowing, firm the soil by treading on the rows. Soaking is especially advisable in growing an autumn crop, for soaked seed should sprout several days earlier than dry seed, and the plants grow more lustily. However, if the soil is wet and the weather cold, soaked seed might decay rather than germinate.

SUPPORTS

Tall varieties need to be supported by brush or a trellis. The dwarf kinds are usually allowed to sprawl on the ground, though it is much better to support them so they can be more easily cultivated and harvested.

Birch branches or small saplings make the best pea-vine brush supports because they are very twiggy, and when the season ends, they can be removed with the vines and burned. Branches from a severely pruned privet hedge are also good. Poultry netting (2 in. mesh or larger, the height depending on the variety) is popular, being easily set up and tied to stout stakes. At the end of the season it is easily taken down, rolled up, and cleaned of dead vines by being held and turned over a hot fire. If stored under cover, it will last for years. More recently a plastic mesh has been introduced specifically for supporting pea and other vegetable vines, but it is not as dis-

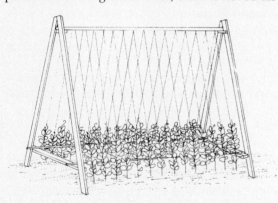

An A-frame trellis

posable as brush or as easily cleaned and durable as wire mesh. An A-frame trellis can be made easily from 2" x 2" supports, with cord or twine strung between the top and both bottom supports. The peas will climb the support from two parallel rows.

To avoid damaging the plants and to stimulate their growth, the support should be placed firmly as soon as the peas are sown. Netting should be

placed while the seedlings are not much more than 1 in. high. The bottom of the wire or other support should be 2–3 in. above the soil. It is common to sow tall varieties in double rows 6–8 in. apart with the trellis between them and with pairs of rows 2½–3 ft. apart. This space can be planted with short-season crops such as spinach, lettuce, onion (sets), and radishes sown at the same time as the peas but harvested before the pea vines get tall enough to shade them.

Dwarf varieties are often sown in groups of four rows only 6–8 in. apart with 2–3 ft. left between the rows to permit picking two rows from each side. Unless the vines are supported, however, this method gradually results in a jungle of vines and difficult picking. If no support is to be given, single-row sowing will be more satisfactory, but in this case, the vines must be turned first to one side and then to the other to allow cultivation.

ENEMIES

Diseases. Several bacteria and fungi attack peas, causing discoloration on the leaves and fruit as well as stunted, unhealthy plants. Powdery mildew is most serious during warm, humid weather, covering the plant with a dense, white coating. Most diseases can be avoided by growing disease-resistant, early, and quick-maturing varieties. To prevent recurrent problems, rotate pea crops every few years and dig vines and turn refuse under immediately after harvesting.

See also CROP ROTATION.

Insect Pests. The pea aphid and a weevil are the only insects likely to be serious. The aphid stunts the plants and causes severe crop losses. The adult weevil, a brownish beetle ⅕ in. long, spotted with gray, dark brown, and white, lays eggs on the surface of newly formed pods. When they hatch, the larvae drill through the pods and into the peas.

PEACH. Common name for *Prunus persica*, a small tree native to China, cultivated since ancient times for its fruit and, in some forms especially, for its ornamental bloom (see PRUNUS).

The NECTARINE, *P. persica* var. *nucipersica*, is a natural mutation of the peach; that is, either fruit may emerge from the other by sport or seed.

The peach is the most adaptable of all tree fruits for home gardens. It can grow nearly everywhere in the United States, southern Ontario, and coastal British Columbia, where the winters are not colder than -15°F. Unless the wood is well matured and remains dormant until spring, however, it may be injured by even mild winters, and spring frosts may destroy the blossom buds or the newly set fruits. The peach blossom is the state flower of Delaware, where the fruit is an important commercial crop.

Peach orchards rarely last longer than twelve years, but with exceptional care they may be continued profitably for more than twice as long, and individual trees may reach 30 or even 40 years.

In selecting peach varieties for the home garden, choose those recommended as suitable for the region and of highest dessert quality. Among the best varieties are Elberta, Redhaven, Cresthaven, Belle of Georgia, Saturn, Madison, and Reliance, which is hardy in the North. Contact your local extension service or nursery for recommendations.

CULTURE
Peaches are propagated by summer-budding desired varieties on stocks grown from seed sown early the previous spring. In the South, where the work is done in early summer, new trees (called June buds) develop the same year and are ready to plant in the autumn. In the North, where the budding is done after midsummer, the buds remain dormant until spring. They then grow the entire season and are called one-year trees. No older trees should be planted because the loss of roots of such trees would make recovery slow if at all. Peach trees should be spaced to allow a spread of 25 ft.

After planting, the tree should be pruned. Select three or four of the strongest branches to save, and clip off the others. The remaining branches and the main stem above the topmost branches should be shortened so as to concentrate plant food in the remaining buds.

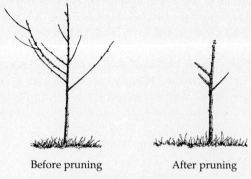

Before pruning   After pruning
Newly planted peach tree

Though the peach does best in sandy soils, it readily adapts itself to all but heavy and rich ones. In these, growth is likely to be excessive and will suffer in winter. Yet the possession of unfavorable soil should not deter anyone from planting peaches for home use, since heavy soils can be lightened and rich ones thinned by growing nitrogen-consuming crops beneath the trees.

In home gardens the soil around peach trees can be mulched, or it can be cultivated and kept weed free. In any case, a circle at least 2 ft. in diameter should be kept cultivated around each trunk to discourage borers.

A simple test will determine when fruit is ready to harvest. Use the fleshy part of a thumb to press the skin of the fruit. A peach is ripe when it gives a little to a thumb press.

PRUNING
Before the buds swell in the second spring, all shoots not needed to form the framework must be cut off. The only later pruning needed (until after the trees begin to bear fruit) is merely to encourage good form and to keep the interior open to admit light and air.

Since the fruit is borne mostly on long, one-year shoots developed mainly from the terminal and adjacent buds, peach trees tend to extend rapidly and to break down from the weight of the crop. To prevent such accidents, reduce these shoots 50–74% each spring while the tree is still dormant. After the trees are six years old, some two- and three-year-old branches should be cut to reduce the spread and leverage.

No tree is less likely to be overpruned than the peach. Heavy pruning of dormant trees tends to produce new shoots with blossom buds which will bear fruit the following season. These buds can easily be recognized because they are rounded, whereas branch buds are pointed. Other fruit buds are borne on short, wiry shoots along the main branches. After the fruit has ripened, these spurs generally die.

ENEMIES

DISEASES

Peach Leaf Curl. This fungal disease is most serious in the northern states, where repeated attacks will kill a tree. The tissue of the leaves is puckered along the midvein, resulting in a curling and distortion and a glistening yellow or reddish color. Most of the leaves fall soon and are replaced by a new crop, but this lowers the vitality of the

Peach leaf curl

tree, interferes with or prevents the setting of fruit, and makes the trees more susceptible to winter killing. The fungal spores live over the winter on the buds and can be controlled by spraying with a fungicide at any time during the dormant period when the temperature is well above freezing. Fall spraying is regarded as preferable.

Brown Rot. The soft, brown decay caused by a fungus is responsible for the familiar grayish brown spore masses and later the wizened, mummied fruits. Cankers are often formed and gum is frequently exuded. For control, see BROWN ROT.

Peach Scab. Also known as freckles and black spot, this causes small, round, olive-black spots on the fruit six weeks after the petals have fallen, followed by cracking and premature dropping of diseased fruits.

Phony Disease of Peach. Occurring in the commercial peach growing regions of Georgia and Alabama, this trouble is caused by a rickettsia-like organism. Affected trees produce short terminal growth, profuse lateral branching, deep green foliage, and undersized fruits. The latter suggested "pony peach" as a name for the disease, but when it was mistakenly passed along as "phony" peach, the name stuck. Trees do not apparently die of this disease, but they never recover and are best destroyed.

Other Diseases. Powdery mildew, sometimes present on young twigs and leaves can be controlled by spraying with sulfur or a chemical fungicide. Several viral diseases such as little peach and yellows also bother the trees, but they cannot be controlled, so the trees should be destroyed. Some of these viruses spread from wild cherry trees, which should be eradicated if growing within 500 ft. of cultivated trees.

INSECT PESTS

The best-known insect pest of peaches is the peach borer. Its larvae work in the trunk at or near ground level, producing gummy masses of reddish borings. The adult is a brilliant yellow-and-black, hornetlike moth. Peach trees should be examined for signs of injury in June and September and any borers killed by inserting a flexible wire into the tunnels, enlarging the opening slightly with a sharp knife if necessary. Banding the lower portion of the trunk during the summer while the moths are in flight helps prevent infestation. See also BORERS.

Some control of infestation is possible by spraying the trees several times in July and August with an insecticide. Since each region varies in climate, obtain a spray recommendation for peach pest control from your local extension service.

PEANUT. A tender, annual, herbaceous vine, *Arachis hypogaea*, belonging to the Fabaceae (Bean Family), grown in warm regions for forage and hay, as a soil improver, and for its pods—the familiar peanuts that are also called goobers, pindars, and ground-nuts.

The plants will not stand frost and require a long season to mature. Commercially they are important only from Virginia south and westward, but they are sometimes grown as a garden novelty as far north as Massachusetts and Michigan. In such places, however, they ripen few or no pods unless the season is favorable.

Once all danger of frost is past, seeds of the thick-shelled varieties should be removed from the pods and scat- tered about 10 in. apart in rows 30 in. apart. The thin- shelled varieties are usually sown without shelling. Sandy loam soils suit them best, and clean cultivation is needed until the plants are well established.

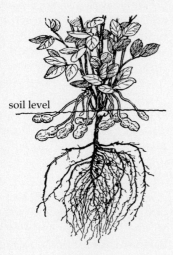

soil level

Peanut plant

The showy, yel- low flowers are staminate. The productive pistil- late flowers are inconspicuous. After being fertilized, they bury themselves in the ground, where the seedpods, or peanuts, develop. When frost has killed the tops, the plants are pulled or dug and allowed to dry for a while before the pods are removed. If the pods are fully grown, they should be kept dry and carefully roasted for use.

When peanut plants are grown as forage, live- stock are driven onto the field, where cattle will browse the foliage and hogs will root for the nuts. For hay, the crop must be cut before frost; after drying, it is stacked on slat platforms.

Hog-peanut is a common name for species of AMPHICARPAEA.

PEAR. Common name for trees, and their fruit, of the genus PYRUS of which two species are grown in North America: the European pear, *P. communis*, which includes all the dessert and the best culinary varieties; and *P. pyrifolia* (Chinese sand pear), noted for the grittiness of its fruit.

As a common name, "pear" refers to several unrelated plants. Alligator-pear is *Persea ameri- cana*, better known as AVOCADO. Balsam-pear is *Momordica charantia*. Prickly-pear is a genus of cactus; see OPUNTIA. Vegetable-pear is *Sechium edule*, or CHAYOTE.

CULTURE

Pears are more limited in their range than apples because of less resistance to both cold and heat. They have a wider northern, but more lim- ited southern range than peaches. Commercially they succeed best from New England to Michi- gan and on the Pacific Coast; in home gardens, they are best in both these regions and in moun- tainous areas and near rivers and lakes large enough to keep the air humid. In the dry air and cold winters of the prairie states, failure is likely.

Although the pear succeeds best in heavy, moderately fertile soils retentive of moisture, it can be planted in any well-drained soil. As with the APPLE, one-year trees are best for planting because the frame branches can be trained to give a strong top. Since some varieties are highly sus- ceptible to fire blight, the trunk and the lower parts of the frame limbs should be kept free from small twigs and fruit spurs, which can easily become infected.

Standard pear trees should be allowed spaces of 30 ft. in diameter; dwarfs, 15 or perhaps 12 ft. Dwarfs, propagated on quince stocks, are espe- cially desirable in home gardens.

Tillage and fertilizing are the same as for the apple, except that nitrogenous fertilizers must be used more cautiously to prevent lush growth, which is more likely to be attacked by blight than firmer tissues. For this reason, mulching and sod culture are more desirable than clean cultivation.

Pruning and training are similar to that of apple, except that a larger number of secondary branches can be allowed to remain as reserves in case of blight attack.

Harvesting. Pears should never be allowed to ripen on the trees. They should be gathered when, upon being bent upward, they separate at the union between the stems and the fruit spurs that bear them. The ripening process is complet- ed in storage, where they will ripen more evenly. As with other fruits, cold retards ripening and heat hastens it.

ENEMIES

DISEASES

Fire blight is the most prevalent and serious of pear diseases. The use of nitrogenous fertilizers increases susceptibility to it. During periods of rapid growth, it causes twigs and branches to die quickly, leaves to turn black, and twigs to hang. Remove all blighted parts several inches below the diseased portions, disinfecting the pruning tools with a chlorine bleach solution between cuts. To prevent fire blight, plant trees that are blight resistant and, if possible, avoid overfertilizing. Call your local extension service if the disease gets beyond the stage where you can control it by pruning.

There are two rust diseases of pear leaves and fruit. The eastern form is similar to apple rust and also has red cedar as its alternate host; the western form completes its cycle on incense cedar. Several leaf spot diseases may occasionally cause defoliation; if they are prevalent, spray with fungicide or lime sulfur.

INSECT PESTS

Most of the insects that bother pears can be controlled by the same spray schedule as for apples. Since apples and pears bloom at different times, however, it is difficult to combine the first sprayings. The pear also has a different collection of insect pests, so it is a good idea to learn what to look for and be ready to make additional sprayings if necessary to protect the tree and its crop. See also APPLE.

Injury by the pear psylla dwarfs the leaves, produces brown areas, and often causes defoliation. This small, sucking insect has at least four broods in a season. The tiny, reddish brown, fly-like adults pass the winter under the bark and in trash, and lay their eggs around the buds in early spring. The young (nymphs) during their first three stages are covered with honeydew, which supports an infestation of SOOTY MOLD, and this can sometimes cover large portions of the tree. Other insect pests are the pear leaf blister mite, which produces brownish blisters on the foliage; the pear thrip, which causes the developing buds to turn brown and shrivel; and the pear midge, which infests small pears with maggots, causing them to drop.

The sinuate pear borer is injurious in eastern gardens, causing sinuous, or winding, tunnels in the inner bark and sapwood. Pears may also be attacked by aphids, brown-tail moths, coddling moths, gypsy moths, fall webworms, false tarnished plant bugs, New York weevil, quince curculio, and scurfy scale.

VARIETIES

Selection of varieties is more restricted than with apples because some do better as standards, others as dwarfs, and still others must be "double worked," that is, grafted on pear stock already made dwarf by previously being grafted on quince.

In localities where the pear can be grown, dessert varieties deserve outstanding popularity among home garden fruits for several reasons. Early varieties cannot be successfully marketed in best, or usually even in good, condition; no other temperate-climate fruit compares with them in aroma, lusciousness, or range of flavors; they can always be grown to greater perfection in small plantings than in commercial orchards; assorted varieties ripen successively over a season from midsummer to midwinter or later. Standard pear trees grow far too large for most suburban backyards, so dwarfs are recommended. Although they do not produce as much fruit, they are easier to prune, harvest, spray, and are attractive in all seasons.

Among pears recommended for home gardeners are Anjou, Bartlett, Bosc, Comice, Honeysweet, Kieffer, Tyson, and Seckel. Northern gardeners may want to try the hardier varieties: Golden Sweet, Luscious, Mendel, Parker, and Patten.

The fact that some varieties of pears are self-sterile need not alarm the home pear grower, provided that several varieties are planted fairly close together so bees can carry pollen from one flower to another.

PEARLBUSH. Common name for EXOCHORDA, a genus of hardy shrubs with white flowers.

PEARLY EVERLASTING. Common name for ANAPHALIS, a genus of woolly perennials often dried for winter bouquets.

PEAT. Organic material obtained from extensive deposits of partly decomposed plants, usually found in wet areas. For garden use, it is processed into various products, including peat moss and compressed peat pots (see FLOWERPOTS).

Peat Moss. After being dried and ground, processed peat moss has a light, porous texture that makes it a good soil conditioner. Its value is based mainly on its ability to absorb and hold moisture, although it is also used to lighten heavy soils and can be used as a mulch or rooting medium. When it is used as a MULCH, however, its absorbent texture may draw moisture out of the soil. Because of its acidity, peat is most useful in growing ericaceous and other acid-loving plants.

Although it naturally has a low nutrient content, it can be combined with decaying compost or manure. The best and most common peat moss is sphagnum peat, a crumbly brown material commercially available in bags or bales. Since a bag of peat moss is dry and greatly compressed, it is often lumpy and slow to take up moisture at first. The bag can be opened and the contents broken up a bit and left outdoors, so that it can absorb rain and become soft, loose, and absorbent before needed for use. Otherwise, a small quantity (for filling pots, flats, and other uses) should be soaked in water and then squeezed partly dry, making it easier to handle and mix with the soil.

See also HUMUS.

PECAN. Common name for *Carya illinoinensis*, a valuable, nut-bearing tree in the HICKORY group of the Juglandaceae (Walnut Family). Its natural range is from Indiana to Mexico; in Texas there are great natural groves and extensive orchards. Large commercial orchards are also found in Georgia, Alabama, Louisiana, Oklahoma, and Mississippi. The pecan is not quite hardy in the North but has been planted successfully from the 43rd parallel in the North to the Gulf and also in the western states.

It is a deep-rooting, long-lived, large (to 150 ft.), vigorous tree that grows best in fertile soil, rich in humus, on land that has been under cultivation for a number of years. In an orchard, trees should be in rich soil, spaced widely—at least 30–40 ft. apart, but 50–70 ft. is best because the tree must have adequate light for good production. Intercropping with cotton, corn, and peaches is a common practice until the trees come into bearing. A tree eight to ten years old will bear 5–25 lb. of nuts.

Pecans do not come true from seed and are difficult to start from cuttings; therefore, much work has been done with budding and grafting in order to perpetuate desirable varieties.

The pecan is invested with many of the same insect enemies as hickory. Spraying with an insecticide during the spring and summer will control the pecan-bud moth and the pecan-leaf casebearer. Trees should be sprayed with insecticide for casebearers immediately after the nuts have set, and with a fungicide for pecan scab.

Bitter pecan is *Carya aquatica*, a smaller tree found in swampy areas of the South; see CARYA.

PEDICULARIS (ped ik yoo LAIR is). A genus of annual and perennial herbs belonging to the Scrophulariaceae (Figwort Family), commonly known as wood-betony or lousewort. They have spiked clusters of whitish or reddish two-lipped flowers and are suitable for the wild garden. Care should be taken to give them plenty of their native wood soil, since some species are dependent on mycorrhizal association. Propagation is by seed or division.

PRINCIPAL SPECIES

P. canadensis (wood-betony), the common woodland species, grows to 18 in. and has soft-hairy, fernlike leaves that are more attractive than the rather dull reddish or yellowish flowers.

P. groenlandica

P. groenlandica (elephant-heads, little-pink-elephants) is a hardy alpine perennial. Toward the base, the 6–24 in. stems have fernlike leaves 2–10 in. long and, at the top, spikes of small, pink flowers that resemble tiny elephant heads.

P. lanceolata grows to 3 ft. and bears purple or sometimes white flowers.

PEDILANTHUS (pee dil ANTH us). A genus of small, succulent plants of tropical America belonging to the Euphorbiaceae (Spurge Family). **P. tithymaloides** (redbird-cactus, jewbush), the principal species, is an attractive plant for the warm greenhouse or outdoors in warm regions. It grows 4–6 ft. high and has fleshy stems and dark green leaves, the midrib being keeled below. The showy part of the flower cluster is the red or purple involucre. Vars. *variegatus* and *cucullatus* both have white-edged leaves, and in the latter, the edge is turned up, somewhat cup-shaped. The plants are propagated by cuttings, which should first be dried at the base.

PEDIOCACTUS (pee dee oh KAK tus). A genus of hardy but hard to grow cacti native to the United States and commonly known as the Great Plains cactus. This group includes some most remarkable mimicry plants, such as the group sometimes called *Navajoa*, with stiff spines; **P. peeblesianus** (sometimes classified as the monotypic *Pilocanthus*), with long, hairlike spines; and even occasionally includes *Toumeya*, with spines that remarkably resemble dried grass. These are among the most difficult cacti to maintain in cultivation.

PELARGONIUM (pel ahr GOH nee um). A genus of flowering herbs, including the common geranium, related to but quite distinct from the genus *Geranium*. Another common name, stork's-bill, is a Latin translation of the genus name, suggesting the shape of the fruit. Besides the geranium so often used for bedding and potting, *Pelargonium* includes the old-fashioned window plant known as the Martha Washington geranium, **P. domesticum**, and other important houseplants.

SELECTIONS

The introduced cascade geraniums, from crosses between bedding geranium and the ivyleaf sorts, are more heat tolerant than the standard ivyleaf cultivars and are splendid for hanging baskets and window boxes. A host of different scented geraniums have been brought into cultivation, along with numerous hybrids, some of which have showier flowers and a longer blooming season than the typical species.

There also have been developed a large number of miniature and dwarf geraniums that mature under 12 in. The Deacon hybrids, developed by an English rector, are intermediate in size between dwarf and standard bedding geraniums, and they flower unusually well in window gardens and greenhouses.

A group, known as fancyleaf geraniums, comes in all sizes and a number of odd and rare kinds, such as cv. 'Bird's Egg', which has flower petals speckled in a contrasting color, and carnation-flowered types that have petals notched as if cut with pinking shears.

One succulent geranium, **P. echinatum**, is an odd and relatively rare form, easily and often mistaken for a cactus because of its thorny stems. In the winter and spring it grows rapidly. When provided with sunlight for several hours daily, the stems will be laden with white flowers, the upper petals of which are marked by a perfectly heart-shaped crimson spot, hence the common name "sweetheart geranium." During summer and fall, the plant goes dormant, loses all its leaves, and needs to be kept dry.

CULTURE

Hardy only in Zones 10–11, pelargoniums are usually cultivated as houseplants or summer bedding subjects. They thrive in light, sunny to semisunny conditions with temperatures on the cool side (50–70°F) in winter, except Martha Washingtons, which require 60°F or colder in order to set buds. They thrive in the humidity of the average house, preferably 30% or more, with plenty of fresh air circulation. Soil should be 3 parts loam to 1 part each of sand and peat moss; add a teaspoonful of steamed bonemeal to each

5-in. pot. Pack this medium firmly around the roots. Water thoroughly, then not again until the surface is dry.

The plants flower best when slightly pot-bound; overpotting is particularly unwise for the miniatures. Fertilize biweekly during active growth and flower but not at all during resting periods; the Martha Washington and ivyleaf varieties rest in winter.

Propagate by rooting cuttings in spring for winter bloom, in autumn for the following spring and summer. Bedding geraniums, once propagated entirely from cuttings, are now often grown from hybrid seeds in order to assure virus-free stock.

ENEMIES

DISEASES

Several diseases affect pelargoniums, but most of them can be checked by clean and careful cultivation.

Under humid conditions, botrytis blight attacks both blossoms and leaves, quickly covering them with a soft, gray mold. Bacterial leaf spot shows first as a water-soaked dot, which turns brown and irregular or circular in outline; the leaf tissue between the spots eventually turns yellow and dies. Cercospora leaf spot causes small, light brown or red spots with a darker border. Control all three by placing plants well apart and giving plenty of light and air, picking off diseased flowers and leaves, watering carefully so as not to splash the tops, and keeping the level of humidity low.

Leaf crinkle, a virus disease serious in greenhouses, causes irregular yellow spots on ruffled, dwarfed leaves, which later drop off. Since the disease is usually transported by infected cuttings, propagating stock should be carefully inspected.

Blackleg, a disease of cuttings and young plants, causes a blackening and rotting of stems and petioles. Avoid it by using fresh or sterilized sand in the cutting bench.

Dropsy or edema, a physiological disease, causes water-soaked spots, later brown and corky on the leaves, which turn yellow around them and later drop off, checking the plant's growth. The disease is usually worse in late winter after dark weather and may be caused by warm, moist soil stimulating root action while cool, moist air prevents transpiration. To control, keep the air dry and the temperature even, and do not overwater. Diseased plants may recover if set outdoors when warm weather comes.

INSECT PESTS

Whiteflies almost invariably infest Martha Washingtons and may spread to other species. Eradicate by weekly spraying with insecticidal soap until clear. Tiny, green geranium worms can be troublesome, especially outdoors in summer. Hand-picking is an effective means of control, or use a commercial insecticide labeled specifically for this application.

PRINCIPAL SPECIES

P. domesticum and its varieties are the common Martha or Lady Washington geraniums that are popular as window plants.

P. graveolens (rose geranium) is a woody perennial that grows to 3 ft. Probably of hybrid origin, it is half-hardy and generally cultivated in the greenhouse. The deeply lobed leaves are fragrant and soft haired. Rose-colored flowers with red spots or veins are borne in umbels. It yields an oil that is used in the perfume industry and is sometimes used for flavoring or jelly.

P. odoratissimum (apple or nutmeg geranium) is a sprawling plant that has branches to 18 in. long and fragrant, obtuse leaves 1 in. across. White flowers, sometimes veined with red, are borne in umbels of five to ten blossoms. It is a source of geranium oil sometimes used in perfumes.

Pelargonium graveolens

P. peltatum, one of the ivyleaf geraniums, is a trailing species popular for hanging baskets or houseplants.

P. zonale is a parent of many hybrids and varieties of bedding plants with leaf markings suggesting the common name "zonal geranium."

PELLAEA (pe LEE ah). A genus of small ferns commonly known as cliff-brakes. They grow in tufts, chiefly on limestone cliffs. Most species are dark or bluish green, with dark, polished stipes and marginal indusia. Several species are native to the United States, but they require ideal conditions for garden culture, preferring exposed locations, light soil, and constant moisture at the roots but none from above. A mulch of gravel will help them to retain moisture. For houseplant species, provide a mix of 2 parts peat or leaf mold, 1 part loam, and 1 part very coarse sand or fine gravel.

PRINCIPAL SPECIES

P. andromedifolia (coffee fern) is a western species that grows 4–24 in. tall and has creeping rhizomes and tripinnate fronds with oval pinnules. Frequently seen in California and on the Baja peninsula, plants grow naturally on noncalcareous rocks.

P. atropurpurea (purple cliff-brake) has a short, creeping rhizome and 6–20 in. long fronds of leathery texture, pinnate above and bipinnate below. The pinnules are smooth and blue-green, the stipes purplish to black. It is found in much of North America and south to Guatemala.

P. hastata is a good houseplant or greenhouse subject with delicately textured, pinnate fronds 18 in. long. Many of the pinnules have three broad lobes. Native to Africa, it needs acid, loamy soil in a bright, airy environment.

P. mucronata (bird's-foot fern) grows 3–16 in. and has bipinnate to tripinnate fronds and pinnules often folded in half. It is found in California and the Baja peninsula.

P. ovata grows 8–24 in. tall from a creeping, wiry rhizome on calcareous soil and rocks. The zigzag fronds are tripinnate with oval pinnules. It is common in Texas and tropical America.

P. rotundifolia (button fern) is a very popular houseplant, growing 2–8 in. It has dark green, polished fronds with firm, round, buttonlike, little pinnules. It likes an acid, humus-rich, well-drained soil with constant moisture.

P. viridis (green cliff-brake) is a South African species that grows in clumps of light green fronds. It does well in the house or greenhouse, needing perfect drainage, warmth, and plenty of light. It appreciates a little lime.

PELLIONIA (pel ee OH nee ah). A genus of tender perennial herbs belonging to the Urticaceae (Nettle Family). Creeping at the base, with ornamental foliage and variable leaves, they are valuable in window boxes and hanging baskets, thriving in rich sandy loam and a moist atmosphere. Propagation is by division of the roots and cuttings rooted in sandy soil.

P. daveauana has succulent, creeping, prostrate stems to 2 ft. long with alternate leaves, narrow or elliptic-oblong, 1–2½ in., of a bronzy olive green, slightly tinged or marked with a broad, irregular band of bright green.

P. pulchra has leaves tinged dull purplish underneath.

PELTANDRA (pel TAN drah) **virginica.** A perennial herb native in eastern North American bogs, commonly known as arrow arum. It has glossy, dark green leaves shaped like arrowheads on long leaf stalks and bears white flowers. Hardy to Zone 5, it is sometimes grown in margins of water gardens. Propagation is by seed or division of the tuberous root.

PELTATE. Shield- or target-shaped, as applied to circular leaves whose stalks are attached at a point within the circumference of the lower leaf surface. Peltately veined refers to veins radiating in all directions from the point of attachment of the petiole, as in a peltate leaf, like that of *Tropaeolum* (garden nasturtium).

PENNISETUM (pen i SEE tum). A genus of grasses including some species grown for grain and forage as well as several graceful and highly ornamental and perennial kinds. They are native to the tropics and subtropics but are widely grown both as garden plants and for cutting and drying as winter decoration.

Seed should be started indoors or in hotbeds in spring and the seedlings grown on in small pots with plenty of room to develop. When planting them in the garden, allow 12–18 in. between clumps. See ORNAMENTAL GRASSES.

PRINCIPAL SPECIES

P. alopecuroides (fountain grass) is a perennial from China that grows to 4 ft. and has narrow 2-ft. leaves and 6-in. silvery and purplish spikes.

P. americanum (pearl, Indian, or African millet) is grown for its grain.

P. latifolium, from South America, grows 5 ft. tall or more and has leaves 1 ft. long and 1 in. wide, and nodding, green, bristly spikes borne several on a stem and therein different from the others, which have solitary heads. It prefers a sandy loam in well-drained soil and a sheltered site. In the North, plants can be lifted in the fall and wintered under glass.

Pennisetum setaceum

P. setaceum (fountain grass) grows to 4 ft. tall, with very narrow leaves to 2 ft. long. The spikes, 1 ft. or longer, are strikingly colored—purple, coppery red, and rose. Of Ethiopian origin, it can be grown as an annual in cooler climates.

P. villosum, sometimes listed as *P. longistylum*, is from Abyssinia, with short leaves and 4-in. purplish spikes at the end of a plumelike stem. Somewhat hardier than other species, it will grow in any ordinary soil and is a good plant for the sunny border. It is perennial but is best grown as an annual.

PENNYROYAL. Common name given to a number of herbs in the Lamiaceae (Mint Family). European pennyroyal is the "sweet herb" *Mentha pulegium*; see MENTHA. American-pennyroyal, commonly found flowering purple along wood roads, is *Hedeoma pulegioides*; see HEDEOMA. Bastard pennyroyal, a species of bluecurls, is *Trichostema dichotomum*; see TRICHOSTEMA.

PENSTEMON (pen STEM awn). A genus of perennial herbs and low shrubs in the Scrophulariaceae (Figwort Family) and commonly known as beardtongue. Almost all are native to North America, and many are well known for their showy flower spikes. Of the several hundred species, only a few dozen are grown in gardens, mostly as rock garden specialties, or naturalized in wild or meadow gardens, or in drought-tolerant landscapes. Some are useful in the garden border, especially types referred to as *P. gloxinioides*, which include many showy, mid-sized plants with dozens of color selections. Flowers range from clear red to reddish purple, pink, lavender, purple, white, yellow, and blue. These must be treated as a tender bedding perennial in the North or raised as tender annuals from seed. Penstemons generally need excellent drainage with not too much water; they are subject to sudden wilt caused by the crown rot organism. Propagation is by seed, cuttings, and division.

PRINCIPAL SPECIES

P. acaulis is a dwarf, forming mats of fine foliage with blue flowers.

P. acuminatus, growing to 2 ft. and of stiff habit, has glaucous leaves and blue flowers.

P. anguineus, growing 1–3 ft. tall, has green, leafy basal rosettes and airy spikes of purple flowers; good for open woodland.

P. angustifolius has slender leaves and stems to 2 ft., crowded with blue flowers.

P. azureus forms an 18-in. subshrub with grayish leaves and rich, sky-blue flowers.

P. barbatus, growing 2–6 ft. tall, has slender stems with pink or red flowers and is useful in the back of the border.

P. caespitosus is a dwarf species that forms mats with pale blue to purple flowers.

P. centranthifolius (scarlet bugler), a useful background plant, grows 3–5 ft. tall and has gray, basal leaves and narrow, scarlet flowers; it is native in California and Arizona.

P. cobaea grows to 2½ ft. and has large, purple flowers.

P. cyananthus, growing to 3 ft., has bright blue flowers.

P. davidsonii forms a dense, spreading mound under 12 in. tall with large, lilac flowers.

P. digitalis, growing to 5 ft., has white, inflated flowers and is a good background subject.

Penstemon cyananthus

P. eatonii, native from California to Utah, grows erect to 3½ ft. and has thick basal leaves and bearded, scarlet flowers.

P. glaber is a handsome plant that grows to 2 ft. with large, blue flowers.

P. grandiflorus is a good wildflower garden species or tall border plant that grows up to 6 ft. tall. It has stout, glaucous leaves and stems with numerous large, lavender-blue flowers.

Penstemon eatonii

P. hartwegii grows to 4 ft. and has large, drooping, red flowers. It does well in a border garden or moist meadow.

P. heterophyllus grows 1–3 ft. tall and has bright green leaves and blue to rose flowers.

P. hirsutus, native to the eastern United States, grows to 3 ft. tall. It has fine-haired leaves to 4½ in. long, often toothed. The tubular, 1-in. flowers are scarlet or purplish and nearly closed at the throat. Several cultivars have been introduced.

P. menziesii grows to 12 in. high from a woody base with violet-blue flowers all summer.

P. newberryi (pride-of-the-mountain) forms a loose mound under 12 in. tall with reddish leaves and a profusion of bright rose-red flowers.

P. pinifolius, growing less than 12 in. tall, has tiny, needlelike leaves and tubular, scarlet flowers blooming all summer.

P. rupicola forms a gray-leaved mound under 6 in. tall and has deep rose to lilac flowers.

P. spectabilis, growing to 5 ft., has pale green, clasping leaves and large, open flowers in rose-lavender or azure. It is useful in a moist meadow or border garden.

Penstemon spectabilis

P. strictus (Rocky Mountain penstemon), growing to 2½ ft., bears royal blue to purple flowers ¾–1¾ in. long on the upper half of the stem and narrow leaves on the lower half.

P. unilateralis, growing to 2 ft., has showy blue flowers and is best when planted in masses.

Penstemon strictus

PENTAS (PEN tas). A genus of African herbs and subshrubs, sometimes grown in the warm greenhouse for winter bloom or as bedding plants in warm regions. Water and spray freely when growth is active, and pinch the shoots to induce a compact habit. Propagate by cuttings in spring. The principal species, **P. lanceolata**, has clusters of flesh pink flowers. Var. **kermesina** has showier flowers of carmine-rose. White and various shades of red are available. These are good nectar sources for butterflies.

PEONY. Common name for PAEONIA, a genus of hardy perennial herbs and shrubs cultivated for their handsome flowers.

PEPEROMIA (pep ur OH mee ah). A genus of annual or perennial, herbaceous, creeping, succulent plants belonging to the Piperaceae (Pepper

Famly). A host of new peperomias have been introduced. They appeal to the collector and make superb houseplants, adapting readily to varied lighting conditions. Small-growing, with ornamental leaves, they are well suited for use as foliage plants in greenhouses or in hanging baskets. Equal parts of loam, leaf mold, and sand makes a satisfactory soil. The plants should be kept at a warm temperature, watered carefully, and shaded during the summer.

P. argyreia, formerly listed as *P. sandersii*, has leaves to about 5 in. long with dark reddish stems. Varietal forms have colored stripes between the leaf veins.

P. maculosa has fleshy, egg-shaped, bright shining green leaves to 7 in. long and erect stems spotted with brown or purple.

PEPPER.

PEPPER. The fruit of *Capsicum* spp., plants belonging to the Solanaceae (Nightshade Family), sometimes called pimiento. Most are grown as annuals, although in their warm native countries they are actually shrubs. They bear small, white or slightly tinted flowers and attractive fruit in the form of edible, many-seeded berries that vary in color and size from very hot to mild or sweetly pungent.

Ornamental pepper

There are only two important species. Most of the common peppers, sweet, hot, and ornamental, are forms of *C. annuum* or *C. frutescens*. Before fruit formation, the two species appear to be identical, but in *C. frutescens*, flowers are frequently borne in clusters of two or more to a node. Many varieties of *C. annuum* are cultivated for their different fruits; see CAPSICUM.

CULTURE

The plants are tender and must be started indoors. Seed should be sown in flats six to eight weeks before the plants can be set outdoors. The seed requires two to three weeks to germinate. Seedlings are pricked into small flowerpots or 2 in. apart in flats, and they should be kept growing steadily without check until all danger of frost has passed. When transplanted to the garden, they should stand 12–18 in. apart in rows 2–3 ft. apart and be given clean and frequent cultivation. They do best in well-drained but moist, light, warm soil that is well supplied with humus but not overly rich.

For potted plants, they are grown and repotted as necessary to fruit in 5-in. pots with rich soil and adequate drainage.

When gathering the fruits, do not pull them off, since this is likely to injure the plants. Instead, cut them with a knife or pruning shears, but only a short piece of stem, to avoid poking holes in other fruits. When the first fall frost threatens, gather all the fruits both large and small and store in a cool cellar where the air is not dry, where they may keep until December or later.

ENEMIES

Of the several diseases of peppers, anthracnose or fruit rot, is the most widespread, causing depressed, soft lesions in the fruit, covered with dark fungal mycelium and pink spore masses. Since sunburned fruits are the most seriously affected, spray plants with a fungicide such as BORDEAUX MIXTURE to hold the foliage.

Pepper fruits are susceptible to sun scald and blossom-end rot, physiological diseases that also affect tomatoes. Healthy plants with good leaf cover prevent sun scald. Regular watering during dry spells and high calcium content in the soil prevents blossom-end rot.

For the spinach, melon, and potato aphids that sometimes infest peppers, use a strong spray of water from the hose to wash the pests away; or try a soap spray. Some control of the pepper maggot, which infests the fruits and causes decay, can be obtained by dusting the plants and fruit with DIATOMACEOUS EARTH in midsummer to discourage adults from laying eggs; otherwise, infested fruits should be removed and destroyed immediately.

PEPPERGRASS. Common name for LEPIDIUM, a genus of cruciferous plants, grown for salad or garnish.

PEPPERMINT. Common name for *Mentha* x *piperita*, a perennial herb whose essential oil is distilled and used for flavoring and as a medicine; see MENTHA.

PEPPERROOT. Common name for *Dentaria diphylla*, a perennial herb with toothlike roots and clustered white flowers; see DENTARIA.

PEPPER TREE. Common name for SCHINUS, a genus of subtropical trees.

PEPPERVINE. Common name for *Ampelopsis arborea*, a climbing shrub with finely cut leaves and purple fruit; see AMPELOPSIS.

PEPPERWORT. Common name for MARSILEA, a genus of fernlike aquatic plants whose leaves resemble four-leaf clovers.

PERENNIALS. Plants that live more than two years are known as perennials, as distingushed from annuals, which live only one season, and biennials, which mature and die after two. Although trees and shrubs are perennial in habit, the term is generally applied to herbaceous plants whose roots continue to live, sending up new branches and flower stems in spring. Some perennials live indefinitely, while others tend to die out after three or four years unless the roots are taken up, divided, and replanted every few years. These relatively short-lived kinds are know as imperfect perennials. Many plants that are hardy perennials in warm climates can be cultivated as annuals in colder regions. While some perennials will flower the first season from seed if sown early, they are often not at their best until the second year or even later.

As new plants come into bloom and old ones pass, the garden presents changes almost from week to week, constantly giving the gardener something to look forward to. Only a few peren-nials bloom all season, and most of them, in congenial surroundings, increase in beauty as they mature. With judicious selection and arrangement of plants, one can be assured of continuous change from early spring until fall. The accompanying chart gives guidelines for selecting and planting common garden perennials.

PLANTING

Soil. Because a perennial bed is permanent, it should have a deep, adequate foundation with suitable drainage. The gardener should spare no efforts to prepare the bed thoroughly, digging the soil to a depth of at least 12 in. Any available source of humus will reinforce the soil with a balanced, available plant food. Economy of effort lies in thorough preparation at the start, so that the soil will not require renewal or elaborate attention for several years.

Seed Sowing. The most inexpensive method of growing most perennials is from seed, but for a first-year start it may be desirable to buy a few established plants. While not all perennials will come true from seed, especially hybrids, most can be started this way. In warm regions, seed can be sown in the fall, enabling the plants to get a start and make vigorous growth early in spring and mature before the heat of summer. In colder climates, seed should be sown early enough to make good growth before winter; some are sown in the spring at the same time as many annuals, others in the summer, a few in early fall, and still others started indoors.

Other Propagation Methods. If suitable stock is available, many perennials are best propagated by vegetative methods, including division of the roots, rooting shoots or stolons, and cuttings of roots or stems. The best time to take cuttings is in the spring when the parent plants are at their peak growing rate. Root cuttings are best made in mid- or late summer, so that they will grow into good plants by the following spring. See also PROPAGATION.

SUMMER CARE

If a perennial bed is made well in the beginning, thoroughly worked, and well supplied with humus and plant food, it will require only

PERENNIAL PLANTING GUIDE

GENUS	MATURE HEIGHT (inches)	SPACING (inches)	MONTHS OF BLOOM	COLOR	SOIL	pH	SUN EXPOSURE
Achillea	18–36	12–18	7–9	r,w,y	g	N	s/ps
Ajuga	5–10	10–15	5–6	b,w	g	N	s/ps
Anthemis	24–36	12–18	7–9	y	g	N	s
Artemisia	5–48	12–24	7–9	foliage	d	N/A	s
Astilbe	24–48	12–18	6–8	p,r,w	g/m	N	s/ps
Centaurea	18–36	10–18	6–8	b,p	g/d	N	s
Chrysanthemum	6–36	12–24	7–11	p,r,w,y	g	N	s
Coreopsis	12–36	12–15	6–8	y	g	N	s
Dianthus	4–8	12–15	6–8	p,r,w	g	N	s
Dicentra	12–30	12–20	5–8	p,w	g/m	N	ps
Dictamnus	24–36	12–20	6	p,w	g/d	N	s
Echinacea	30–36	12–24	7–9	p	g/m	N	s
Echinops	24–48	12–24	7–8	b	g/m	N	s/ps
Euphorbia	24–36	12–15	4–6	y	d	N	s
Gaillardia	15–30	12–20	6–9	r,y	g/d	N	s
Geum	15–24	12–18	6–8	r,y	g	N	s
Gypsophila	6–48	12–36	6–8	p,w	g/d	N	s
Helenium	24–48	12–18	8–9	r,y	g	N	s
Heliopsis	36–48	15–24	7–9	y	g/d	N	s
Hemerocallis	24–40	18–24	7–9	p,r,y	g/m	N	s/ps
Heuchera	12–18	10–15	6–9	p,r,w	g	N	s/ps
Hosta	18–38	12–24	7–9	p,w	g/m	N/A	sh/ps
Iberis	6–15	10–15	4–9	w	g	N	s/ps
Iris pseudacorus	30–36	18–24	6–7	y	m	N	s
Iris sibirica	24–36	12–18	6	b,p,w	m	N	s
Iris versicolor	30–36	18–24	6–7	b	m	N	s
Lilium (Oriental hybrids)	24–84	30–36	8	r,p,b	g	N	s/ps
Lupinus	30–48	12–18	6–7	b,r,w,y	g	N	s
Lychnis	12–38	12–18	6–8	y,r	g	N	s

(see guide to symbols on p. 724)

GENUS	MATURE HEIGHT (inches)	SPACING (inches)	MONTHS OF BLOOM	COLOR	SOIL	pH	SUN EXPOSURE
Nymphaea	12–18 across	24–30	6–9	b,p,r,w,y	wp	N	s
Paeonia	20–24	18–20	5–6	r	g	N	s
Papaver	36–40	16–18	6	p,y	g	N	s
Phlox paniculata	24–40	12–18	6–8	b,p,r,w	g	N	s
Platycodon	15–24	12–18	6–9	b,p,w	g	N	s/ps
Primula	5–24	10–15	4–6	b,p,r,w,y	g/m	A	ps
Rudbeckia	24–36	18–24	7–9	y	g	A	s
Salvia	36–60	12–18	6–8	b	g	A	s
Sedum	6–24	8–15	7–9	p,r,w,y	g	A	s
Stachys	8–18	9–15	6–7	foliage	g/d	A	s/ps
Thalyctrum	36–60	12–18	5–8	p,w,y	g/m	A	s/ps
Thymus	3–8	9–12	6–8	p,r,w	g/d	A	s

COLORS: b = blue, purple shades; p = pink, lilac shades; r = red shades; w = white; y = yellow, orange shades.

SOIL: g = general, loamy garden soil; d = dry soil; m = moist soil; w = wet soil; wp = water plant.

pH: N = normal (6 to 6.5); A = more acid (below 6.0); L = prefers some lime.

SUN EXPOSURE: s = full or mostly full sun; ps = part sun or light shade; sh = medium to dense shade.

Adapted from *Successful Perennial Gardening* by Lewis and Nancy Hill (Storey Communications, Inc., 1988), with permission from the publisher.

occasional cultivation with a hoe or other tool to keep down weeds and lessen evaporation during the growing season. Low ground covers planted among the perennials will help prevent weeds and will shade the soil from hot sun. Beds can also be mulched with peat moss, buckwheat hulls, or lawn clippings to keep the soil cool, prevent baking, check evaporation, and prevent weed growth. The most important cultivation is done when the bed is uncovered each spring and the winter mulch can be dug under to keep up the humus supply.

Watering. Casual spraying is not only inadequate, but is actually worse than not watering at all, because it merely wets the top layer of the soil, resulting in shallow root development. To be effective, watering must be thorough; continue until water begins to stand in puddles on the surface. Then do not water again until it is definitely needed. Early in the morning is the best time to water, since damp foliage overnight in warm weather contributes to the spread of fungus diseases.

WINTER PROTECTION

When perennials are purchased from a local nursery, they are likely to be hardy in that zone. However, perennial gardens usually come through the winter better when given some sort of protection or mulch. Mulch should not be applied until the ground has frozen. Another purpose of mulching is to protect the evergreen foliage of plants like hollyhock, foxglove, candytuft, and sweet-William from damage caused by exposure to ice and snow. The simplest mulch is a loose layer of leaves from hardwood trees. Oak leaves are better than those of maple, which are softer and mat down tightly when soaked with rain or snow. Keep the mulch light enough not to smother the plants; a few inches will be sufficient. In the spring, the protection should be removed as soon as a reasonable amount of growth has appeared. Do not wait until the shoots are big enough to be damaged by removing the material and forking over the soil.

Proper cultivation, adequate feeding, and garden cleanliness will help keep perennials clear of diseases. In general, when a plant is found to be diseased, the tops should be cut back and destroyed. If a second attack is apparent when new growth comes from the roots, it is often wise to remove and destroy the plant and the soil around it. Fungus and mildew can be prevented by appropriate sprays and careful attention to when and how watering is done. In all cases, the aim should be to prevent the occurrence of disease if possible; next, its prompt care when detected; and finally, removal of a seriously diseased specimen before it spreads infection to other plants. See also DISEASE; INSECT CONTROL.

PERESKIA (per ESK ee ah). A genus of Mexican, West Indian, and South American cacti in which the broad, flat leaves are persistent to the extent that they can be called evergreen. They are succulent in appearance but possess the one unmistakable characteristic that marks them as cacti, namely, the areole or center of growth. In cold climates they are greenhouse plants easily propagated from cuttings. They are often used as a stock for grafting. The flowers, which differ from those of other cacti in that they have stems (others are sessile), appear either singly or in drooping clusters. They are single and range from white to rose.

P. aculeata (lemonvine cactus) is slender plant that starts out erect and then becomes a vine that grows to 30 ft. It has lemonlike leaves and an edible fruit. It is grown more as a stock for grafting other cacti (especially *Schlumbergera*) than it is grown for its own sake.

PERFECT FLOWER. A flower that has both stamens and pistils and is therefore capable of both producing pollen and developing seeds, though it may not be able to fertilize itself. Because it possesses both male and female organs, it can be called a hermaphrodite, or a bisexual flower. See also FLOWER.

PERGOLA. A garden structure, similar to an arbor, originating in Italy and designed to support grapevines.

PERIANTH. The floral envelope as a whole; that is, normally the calyx and corolla together or the calyx alone when there is no corolla.

PERILLA (pee RIL ah). A small genus of the Lamiaceae (Mint Family), consisting of half-hardy annual herbs native to India and China. They are cultivated for the highly colored foliage, which is sometimes used for summer bedding and subtropical effects in the garden. Plants thrive in any light, loamy soil. Propagation is by seed started over gentle heat in early spring, then gradually hardened-off and placed in the border in late spring.

P. frutescens, the common garden form, has dark bronzy purplish foliage with crisped and fringed margins. It is cultivated in the Orient for its oily seeds and is somewhat naturalized and weedy in the eastern United States.

PERIPLOCA (pe RIP loh kah). A genus of deciduous or evergreen climbing shrubs belonging to the Asclepiadaceae (Milkweed Family) and commonly known as silkvine. Though of tropical origin, they are hardy in the United States if given winter protection in colder regions. They need well-drained soil in a sunny location and are well adapted to climb arbors and trellises. Propagation is by seed, cuttings, or layering.

P. graeca is a vigorous deciduous vine that grows to 40 ft. and has dark green, shining leaves held late and loose clusters of greenish or brownish purple flowers.

P. sepium, a shorter and more slender species

with smaller leaves and flowers, is the hardiest; its leaves turn yellow in the fall.

PERISTROPHE (pe RIS troh fee). A genus of tropical herbs or shrubs belonging to the Acanthaceae (Acanthus Family). *P. speciosa*, the one most commonly grown, is a bushy shrub often grown in pots for winter flowering in the greenhouse. The flowers are violet-purple, and it thrives under the same treatment as JUSTICIA.

PERITHECIUM. A closed fungal fruiting body, spherical or flask-shaped, containing sacs (*asci*) in which the sexual spores are contained. See FUNGUS; compare APOTHECIUM.

PERIWINKLE. Common name for VINCA, a genus of trailing, flowering herbs. Madagascar-periwinkle is *Catharanthus roseus*; see CATHARANTHUS.

PERNETTYA (pur NET ee ah). A genus of low evergreen shrubs belonging to the Ericaceae (Heath Family) and commonly known as prickly heath. Native to South America, they are hardy only to Zone 7. They do best in peaty, rather moist soil in a sunny location and are well placed in the rock garden or with evergreen shrubs. They have small, spiny pointed, glossy green leaves and small, white or pinkish nodding flowers in early summer. The pealike fruits are very colorful, varying from white to red or dark purple. Propagation is by seeds, cuttings, layers, and suckers. *P. mucronata*, the principal species, is a bushy grower 2–3 ft. tall, occurring in various forms with different colored berries.

PERPETUAL FLOWERING. A term applied to varieties of flowering plants that, instead of bearing flowers during a brief period of their active growth season, continue to bloom as long as growth goes on.

PERSEA (PUR see ah). A genus of broad-leaved, evergreen trees, some of which are planted extensively for ornament in warm countries. The most important species, however, is *P. americana*, which bears the AVOCADO.

P. borbonia (red- or bull-bay) is a large tree native to the South and is sometimes planted for ornament. Hardy to Zone 7.

PERSIMMON. Common name for DIOSPYROS, a genus of trees cultivated for ornament as well as for their edible fruit and valuable wood.

PEST CONTROL. See INSECT CONTROL; INTEGRATED PEST MANAGEMENT (IPM).

PESTICIDE. See INSECT CONTROL; INTEGRATED PEST MANAGEMENT (IPM).

PETAL. One of the inner series of floral leaves that together make up the COROLLA. See FLOWER.

PETALOSTEMON (pet ah loh STEE mun). A genus of mostly perennial North American herbs commonly known as prairie-clover. They bear flowers in small spikes. Several species are grown in wildflower or rock gardens.

B. purpureum is a perennial native to central and western North America. It grows to 3 ft. and has narrow, ¾-in. leaflets in groups of three to five and 2-in. spikes of violet or red flowers.

B. villosum (silky prairie-clover), found

Petalostemon purpureum

in central North America, grows to 2 ft., upright or along the ground. Its oblong leaflets to ½ in. long are densely covered with soft hairs, and the rose-purple or occasionally white flowers are borne in 4-in. spikes.

PETREA (pet TREE ah). A genus of tropical American, scandent or vining, shrubby plants belonging to the Verbenaceae (Verbena Family). The principal species, *P. volubilis* (purple-wreath, sandpaper vine), is a twining shrub grown outdoors in Zones 10–11 and sometimes farther north under glass, where it is usually trained to a support or form. It has oblong, wavy leaves and very showy purple flowers in a slender cluster. It thrives in a compost of equal parts of fibrous loam and peat, with the addition of some old cow manure and sharp sand.

PETROSELINUM (pet roh sel IN um). A biennial herb of the Apiaceae (Celery Family), commonly known as parsley. Seeds need to be fresh and should be soaked in warm water before sowing. In the garden it is slow to germinate, so it is better to sow varieties being grown for the leaves indoors under controlled conditions. A sowing in early spring and another in midsummer should keep a supply of green leaves all year round, especially if some protection can be given or plants are potted indoors in winter.

Moss curled parsley   Italian parsley

P. *crispum* (moss curled parsley), sometimes listed as *P. hortense* or *Carum petroselinum*, is the familiar curly leaved herb. Var. *neapolitanum* (Italian parsley) is the plain leaved form. Var. *tuberosum* (turnip-rooted parsley) is grown for its edible roots. This variety should be sown in the garden in early spring. Both varieties can be used for flavoring, but the curly leaved type is considered best for garnishing.

PE-TSAI. Common name for certain varieties of *Brassica rapa*, which are sometimes called Chinese cabbage. It has become popular for its cylin-drical heads of crisp green leaves with a tender, white central core. It can be eaten raw or cooked and, like other brassicas, does better in the cool weather of spring and autumn than in summer. See also BRASSICA; CHINESE CABBAGE; MUSTARD.

PETUNIA (pe TOO nee ah). A genus of highly ornamental, hardy or half-hardy annuals or perennials belonging to the Solanaceae (Nightshade Family). Best results are obtained when the perennials are grown as annuals. Petunias are one of the most popular commercially produced bedding plants, grown in beds, borders, window boxes, pots, tubs, and hanging baskets. Plants range in height from about 6 in. to over 18 in. Later in the growing season, lanky plants can be cut back, resulting in new, shorter growth. Flower colors of some of the original species were white and purple; however, new hybrid species of the garden annual type range from white to red to pink, purple, blue, yellow, and bicolor.

P. x *hybrida*, the most commonly grown kind, is a cross between *P. violaceae* and *P. axillaris*. This plant performs best if given a sunny location in the garden in well-drained soil. Plants can be started from seed indoors several weeks before they are to be set outside. Petunias can tolerate cool growing temperatures and actually benefit from temperatures of 50–55°F, which promote compact growth and branching. Although the coolness may delay flowering, the blossoms are larger.

There are several types of petunias available from seed catalogs. These include grandiflora singles, taller plants that produce a relative few, very large flowers. In contrast, multiflora singles are shorter, producing a greater number of smaller flowers on plants that are better able to withstand adverse weather conditions. Both grandifloras and multifloras are available with double flowers. These types are not as popular as the single types because of their less than adequate performance in the garden. The floribunda, a cross between grandiflora and multiflora types, has become increasingly popular. It combines the large flower size of the grandiflora with the abundant bloom and weather-hardiness of the multiflora. The 'California Giant', one of the original types of petunias cultivated in the nineteenth century, has very large flowers (over 6 in. across) and is occasionally still produced as a specimen plant in the greenhouse.

PEYOTE (pay YOH tee). A common name for any member of the genus *Lophophora* but most specifically *L. williamsii*, a most unique but notorious little cactus, with soft, blue-gray, spineless stems and tufts of cottony wool in the areoles. The plant contains various hallucinogenic alkaloids; for this reason the United States government has made it an illegal plant to possess, except for members of the Native American Church, who consume peyote as part of their religious rites.

pH. One of the most important soil factors in cultivating most plants is the acidity or alkalinity of the soil. This is measured on the pH scale, ranging from 0 (most acidic) to 14 (most alkaline) with a value of 7 indicating neutral conditions. The pH units are based on multiples of ten, so a pH of 4.0 is ten times more acidic than a pH of 5.0, and 100 times more acidic than a soil with a pH of 6.0.

The pH of the soil is important because it directly and indirectly influences the availability of nutrients essential for plant growth. Nutrients such as phosphorus, calcium, potassium, and magnesium are most available to plants when the soil pH is between 6.0 and 7.5. Under highly acid (low pH) conditions, these nutrients become insoluble and relatively unavailable for uptake by plants. However, iron, trace minerals, and some toxic elements such as aluminum become more available at low pH. High soil pH can also decrease the availability of nutrients. If the soil is more alkaline than pH 8, phosphorus, iron, and many trace elements become insoluble and unavailable for plant uptake.

The availability of nitrogen is also influenced by pH. Much of the nitrogen that plants eventually use is bound within organic matter, and the conversion of this bound nitrogen to forms available to plants is accomplished by several species of bacteria that live in the soil. When the pH of the soil drops below 5.5, the activity of these bacteria is inhibited, and little nitrogen is made available to the plants. At about the same pH levels there is a general decline in most forms of bacterial activity and an increase in the activity of soil fungi. This shift in soil biology may further influence which plants can survive and which cannot.

The usual pH range of soils is from about 4 to about 8. Typically in the humid eastern United States, the precipitation is sufficient to remove large amounts of potassium, calcium, magnesium, and other alkaline nutrients. As a result, the soils in humid regions tend to be acidic, with pH values below 7. In the arid western states, the situation is quite different. There, substantially less precipitation falls, and as a result, the alkaline constituents can maintain soil pH significantly higher than 7.

Local soil pH varies because of differences in bedrock geology, acid rain, or the vegetation present. In general, regardless of the geographic region, locations with limestone or marble bedrock have soils with increased alkalinity, and locations with granite bedrock have acidic soils. Certain species of plants can also increase the acidity of the soil through the addition of organic matter with a low pH. The dead foliage of pines, spruce, fir, oaks, and many of the heath plants can acidify the soil as it decomposes. In cool, wet areas, the growth of sphagnum and other mosses can also create acidic conditions.

See also ACID SOIL; ALKALINE SOIL.

PHACELIA (fa SEE lee ah). A genus of annual or perennial herbs belonging to the Hydrophyllaceae (Waterleaf Family). The blue, white, or lilac flowers are borne in clusters or curled cymes. Many species are of straggly growth habit or poor color, but some are popular garden subjects. Most grow in full sun on well-drained soil, which should be kept moist early in spring while the plants are becoming established. The annual forms are propagated by seed, which should be scarified and soaked in water overnight, then kept in the dark until germination occurs.

PRINCIPAL SPECIES

P. bolanderi is a perennial with lobed, 5-in., fuzzy leaves and lilac, saucer-shaped flowers 1½ in. across. It makes a good ground cover in filtered light. Hardy to Zone 9.

P. campanularia (California-bluebells) is an annual that grows 12–18 in. tall and is native to desert regions of the southwestern United States. The intense blue, blue-purple, or rarely white, bell-shaped flowers bloom in early summer. The leaves are basically elliptic or ovate with coarsly tooth-ed edges. The plants are especially attractive in mass plantings.

Phacelia campanularia

P. divaricata is a low, spreading annual 1 ft. across with lilac, saucer-like flowers, good for rock gardens.

P. tanacetifolia (purple-heliotrope, bee-food) is a tender annual that grows erect, 1–3 ft. high.

Phacelia tanacetifolia

The stems and feathery divided leaves are covered with short, stiff hairs. The ½-in. lavender-blue flowers, borne in numerous fiddlehead clusters, attract numerous honey bees.

PHAIUS (FAY us). A genus of 30 species of medium-sized to large terrestrial orchids commonly known as nun orchids, distributed throughout tropical Asia, Africa, Indonesia, New Guinea, and the Pacific Islands. The leaves are large, pli-

cate, thin-textured, and often deciduous. The pseudobulbs are short and round. Long-lasting showy flowers are large with broad, flat sepals and petals and a tubular lip. Their colors are white, yellow, rose, and purple-brown.

Plants prefer a well-drained compost of peat, leaf mold, sphagnum moss, and sand. Hardy to Zone 7, they do not withstand winter temperatures of less than 60°F. Copious water should be given during growth, plus shade and humidity. When growth is complete, plants should be dried out and kept slightly cooler. The type species is *P. grandifolius*.

PHALAENOPSIS (fal en AHP sis). A popular genus of about 40 species of epiphytic or lithophytic orchids indigenous to southeastern Asia, Indonesia, the Philippines, and Australia, commonly called moth orchid because of its white, mothlike flowers. The plants are monopodial, with large, oval, dark or mottled green leaves, often maroon underneath, and many fleshy aerial roots. There are two types: *Phalaenopsis* plants, with succulent, oval leaves, and *Paraphalaenopsis*, with narrow, pencil-shaped, terete leaves.

The flowers are several to many, borne on arching inflorescences. Although mostly white, some are yellow, red, pink, and mauve, many with concentric barring or striping on petals and sepals. *Phalaenopsis* flowers have broad and round sepals and petals, and the three-lobed lip is small, usually striped in yellow or red. In some species the lip has cirri, or antennae, at the base of the midlobe. *Paraphalaenopsis* flowers have narrow, erect, slightly twisted dorsal sepals, with spreading lateral sepals. Petals are reflexed and slightly twisted. The three-lobed lip has erect lateral lobes and a forward-projecting midlobe. Colors are white, yellow, or dull orange.

Both types do well in baskets of porous, well-drained compost with roots hanging free. Plants need moderate to light shading, high humidity, and should never be allowed to dry out. These plants are tender (hardy in Zones 10–11) and must be protected from frost, withstanding minimum winter temperatures of 60–65°F. The type species is *P. amabilis*.

PHALARIS (FAHL ahr is). A genus of annual and perennial ornamental grasses native to Europe (and one species to North America) and hardy to Zone 3. They were commonly cultivated for ornament in gardens of the past. Propagation of the perennial types is by division and the annual types, by seed.

Phalaris canariensis

P. arundinacea var. *picta* (ribbon grass) is an attractive perennial with slender, green to yellow and white striped leaves. It is one of the hardiest, most easily cultivated forms and grows 2–4 ft. tall.

P. canariensis (canary grass) is a European annual naturalized in North America, whose glossy yellow seeds are fed to caged birds.

See also ORNAMENTAL GRASSES.

PHASEOLUS (fah SEE oh lus). A genus of annual or perennial herbs belonging to the Fabaceae (Bean Family), native in warm regions, and including a few familiar edible subjects. Mostly of twining habit, they are grown chiefly for their edible pods and seeds. For culture, see BEAN.

PRINCIPAL SPECIES

P. caracalla is now listed as *Vigna caracalla*; see VIGNA.

P. coccineus (scarlet runner bean) has somewhat tuberous perennial roots but is grown mostly as an annual. A tall, slender twiner with bright scarlet flowers and long, edible pods, it is often grown for ornament on porches and arbors.

P. limensis (lima bean) is a tender high climber with white or creamy flowers but is valued for its edible and highly nutritious seed. Var. *limenanus* is bush or dwarf lima.

P. vulgaris (kidney bean, haricot) is a tall, twining annual with white, yellowish, or violet flow-

ers. Var. *humilis*, a nonclimbing form, is the common field and garden bean. There are a great many named varieties, most of which are used in the green pod stage, though a few are grown for the dry seeds.

PHEASANT'S-EYE. Common name for the genus ADONIS; also applied to *Narcissus poeticus*, see NARCISSUS.

PHEGOPTERIS (feg AHP tur is). Botanical name sometimes used for a group of ferns included in the genus THELYPTERIS.

PHELLODENDRON (fel oh DEN drun). A genus of ornamental trees native to eastern Asia, belonging to the Rutaceae (Rue Family), and commonly known as cork tree. They have particularly attractive, aromatic foliage and bear abundant black fruit, which remains for a long time after the leaves have fallen. They are adapted to a wide variety of soils, growing vigorously when young. *P. amurense*, the species most commonly planted, grows from 30–50 ft. high and has a broad, rounded head; it is easily started from seed. Hardy in Zones 4–7.

PHEROMONE. Pheromones are scents given off by insects and animals in order to communicate with other members of the same species. Often these scents are used to attract mates, but they can also warn of danger or announce a food source. Many pheromones have been isolated and used in commercially available traps. Pheromone traps have become an important method of INSECT CONTROL.

PHILADELPHUS (fil ah DEL fus). A genus of North American and Eurasian deciduous shrubs belonging to the Saxifragaceae (Saxifrage Family), commonly known as mock orange. Mostly of medium size, they are valued for their great display of white or creamy, fragrant flowers in early summer. Most species are hardy to Zone 5, unless noted otherwise. They are not particular as to soil, provided it is not soggy or poor. They tolerate shade better than most flowering shrubs. Propagation is by seed, layers, or cuttings of greenwood or hardwood.

PRINCIPAL SPECIES

P. coronarius (common, sweet, or European mock orange) is perhaps the oldest cultivated species. It grows to 10 ft. and bears racemes of creamy white flowers, the most fragrant of the species.

P. delavayi, an Asian native, is a strong grower to 15 ft. and has large, very fragrant flowers, the petals somewhat fringed. Hardy to Zone 6.

P. x *lemoinei*, the first of the hybrids, is a small, graceful shrub with slender stems, fine leaves, and a wealth of small, very fragrant flowers. Some of the best forms of this hybrid are 'Avalanche', 'Mont blanc', 'Candelabra', 'Erectus', all with single flowers; and 'Boule d'Argent', with double flowers.

P. lewisii, native to North America, is a vigorous grower with arching branches and large, slightly fragrant flowers in dense racemes. Hardy to Zone 7.

P. pubescens, native to North America, grows to 10 ft. and has dark green leaves and racemes of slightly fragrant flowers.

P. purpurascens is one of the best. Native to Asia, it grows to 12 ft. and has spreading and arching branches, small leaves, and rather small, cupped flowers, very fragrant and offset with a bright purple calyx. Hardy to Zone 6.

P. x *splendens*, a chance hybrid, supposedly between *P. grandiflorus* and *P. lewisii*, is one of the handsomest of the larger kinds, with clusters of pure white flowers to 3 in. across.

P. x *virginalis* has large, semidouble flowers that bloom in the spring. Good forms are 'Bouquet Blanc', 'Argentine', 'Glacier', and 'Virginal'.

PHILODENDRON (fil oh DEN druhn). A genus of usually climbing, shrubby, tropical American plants belonging to the Araceae (Arum Family). Popular as houseplants, they are sometimes grown under glass and thrive in a warm and moist atmosphere; hardy only in Zones 10–11. They can be grown in pots, the climbing forms doing well planted outside and trained to a wall or pillar. A compost of fibrous loam and peat, with sand, suits them well. Propagation is by cuttings of the tops or stem lengths.

PRINCIPAL SPECIES

P. bipennifolium (horsehead or fiddle-leaf philodendron) has leathery, dark green, sagittate leaves.

P. bipinnatifidum is a short-stemmed species with large, divided leaves and a spathe or calla-like flower bract about 8 in. long, reddish brown on the outside and white within.

P. cordatum (heart-leaf philodendron) is the ubiquitous species known to the uninitiated simply as ivy. The ovate leaves grow to 18 in. long and 10 in. wide or even larger. In its juvenile stage this species makes a highly satisfactory houseplant for hanging baskets or can be trained into various shapes.

P. giganteum is a climber with leaves to 3 ft. long and 2 ft. wide. The spathe is almost 12 in. long, purplish outside and red inside.

P. mamei is a dwarf with large, handsome leaves marked silvery white.

P. scandens (heart-leaf philodendron) is a common species most commonly grown in var. *micans* (velvet-leaf) and *oxycardium* (parlor-ivy, common philodendron).

P. selloum is mixed in the trade with *P. bipinnatifidum*. It is one of the most popular large, self-heading (nonclimbing) philodendrons. In the house its large girth can often be best displayed by setting the pot on a pedestal 3–4 ft. tall so that the leaves will spread up and out, giving the effect of an indoor tree.

P. squamiferum has distinctly five-lobed leaves and figures in the parentage of numerous modern hybrids.

P. verrucosum is a beautiful climber with medium-sized leaves of satiny green with metallic shadings above, lined with bands of maroon beneath. The leaf stems are red and bristly.

PHLEBODIUM (fle BOH dee um). A genus of ferns in which a number of botanists place *Polypodium aureum*; see POLYPODIUM.

PHLEUM (FLEE um) **pratense.** A perennial grass and one of the most important hay plants. Commonly known as Timothy—in England as herd's grass—it has leaves to 1 ft. long and cylindrical, short, bearded spikes, sometimes 6 in. or more long at the end of stiff stems that may attain 5 ft. in rich soils. Seed is sometimes included in low-priced lawn grass mixtures because it is cheap and starts quickly, giving a good green growth soon after seeding. It is undesirable as a lawn grass, however, and mixtures

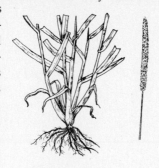

Phleum pratense

containing it should be avoided. Also, Timothy hay should not be used as a winter mulch, since it will scatter seed in the beds and require interminable weeding thereafter.

PHLOMIS (FLOH mis). A genus of perennial herbs or shrubby plants belonging to the Lamiaceae (Mint Family). They are rather coarse growers, suitable for the wildflower garden or as a natural shrub. Propagation is by seed, cuttings, and division.

P. fruticosa (Jerusalem-sage) is a shrubby plant to 4 ft. and has crinkled, sagelike leaves, white beneath. It has many-flowered whorls of yellow flowers opening in summer in the eastern states and sometimes flowering all winter in southern California.

P. tuberosa is a vigorous perennial herb with tuberous roots and dense whorls of purple flowers. It is native in southern Europe but has become naturalized in the eastern United States.

PHLOX (flahks). A genus of hardy, erect or diffuse, tall or tufted perennials and a few annuals, mostly native to North America and some to northern Asia. Many species and hybrids grow in mats of springtime color, with showy flowers of red, pink, violet, blue, buff, or white.

As a common name, phlox also refers to other plants. The Phlox Family is POLEMONIACEAE. Night-phlox is *Zaluzianskya capensis*, a South African annual grown indoors for ornament and fragrance.

CULTURE

The perennial species and varieties are among the best and most popular of garden plants. Some of the species are dwarf, creeping plants suitable for rock gardens or for the front of the mixed border. The taller forms are well adapted for bedding purposes or for the rear of mixed border plantings.

Most species are hardy in Zones 3–9 and all are very easily cultivated, the tall-growing perennials thriving in any good bed or border, but succeeding best in rather heavy soils of good depth. During dry weather, a top mulch of humus or peat is helpful, as well as occasional thorough watering.

Propagation. The dwarf species do not seed very readily and are propagated mainly from cuttings or root division. Cuttings inserted in a coldframe during summer and then shaded will form good plants for the following spring. Taller-growing varieties can be propagated from seed (which should be saved from extra fine varieties only) or by cuttings of the young stems, shoots, or roots. The roots can be cut into short lengths and treated like seed. Old clumps can also be lifted, separated, and replanted in early spring. It is advisable to destroy self-sown seedlings, since they have a strong tendency to revert back to the original lavender color.

ENEMIES

Diseases. Preventive measures for most diseases of phlox are the destruction of all plant tops and fallen leaves in the fall and proper division and spacing of plants.

Powdery MILDEW covers both top and bottom of the leaves in midsummer with a white fungal growth whose black fruiting bodies (perithecia) can be seen later. It is most prevalent on plants that are crowded and in damp or shady places.

LEAF SPOT appears as brown spots, first on the lower leaves, which may die, and progressively on the other leaves up the stem. It can be very serious on certain varieties, but the cause is not known.

Insect Pests. Phlox is subject to a nematode or eelworm that causes root galls. The more destructive stem nematode (which also attacks narcissi) causes stunted plants; swollen, cracked stems; narrow, crinkled leaves; and inhibited flowering. Remove and destroy affected plants with surrounding soil. See NEMATODES.

The most serious pest on phlox is the RED SPIDER MITE, which infests the undersides of leaves, turning them light yellow and giving the plant a general unthrifty appearance. Looking closely on the undersurface, one can see the tiny red mites enclosed in a webby mass. Plants in full sun in hot, dry weather are more subject to mite damage. Dusting with sulfur, as for mildew, will often keep the mites in check. Spraying with the hose is also useful.

The phlox bug, which punctures tender shoots and sucks the sap, can be controlled with an insecticidal soap spray, but this is not usually necessary. Common stalk BORERS occasionally tunnel in phlox stems.

PRINCIPAL SPECIES

P. amoena, a southern native, produces a small cartwheel of clear pink flowers. The furry stems of the new growth are also attractive.

P. bifida (sand phlox) is a dwarf, tufted, hairy perennial with awl-shaped lower leaves about ¼ in. long. Flowers are violet to white with a violet tube. Var. *alba* is an outstanding choice that looks like a drift of snowflakes completely covering the foliage.

P. carolina (Carolina phlox) blooms in late spring with white to magenta, ¾-in. blooms. The foliage is glossy and resists the problems of red spider mites and mildew. Cv. 'Miss Lingard', with white flowers, is an excellent form, and 'Rosalinde' is similar with pink flowers. Early-flowering forms are cultivated as *P. suffruticosa*.

P. diffusa (spreading phlox), native to the northwestern United States, is a prostrate, branching perennial that grows in 6-in. clumps. It has linear leaves ½ in. long and lilac, pink, or white flowers ½ in. across, usually borne singly on leafy bracts.

P. divaricata (blue phlox, wild-sweet-William) is the common woodland native. It grows 9–18 in. high and has oblong leaves 2 in. long. Pale violet, blue, lavender, or mauve flowers are borne in clusters in spring and early summer. There are several color forms, including var. *alba*, *lilacinia*, *laphami*, and cv. 'Fuller's White'.

P. drummondii (annual or Drummond phlox) grows 12–15 in. high and has oval to tapering leaves and erect stems a little branched at the top. Large heads bear individual large flowers of many color forms, varying from white to scarlet and lilac to purple with a darker eye. Native to Texas, it is strong and sturdy in growth habit and shows well if grown in masses.

P. glaberrima has smooth, glossy, lanceolate leaves and pinkish purple

Phlox drummondii

flowers that bloom in summer. Var. *triflora* is similar to *P. carolina* but has narrower leaves.

P. paniculata (summer perennial phlox) grows to 4 ft. high and has oblong to oval leaves 4–5 in. long. In the original species, flowers are purple, but they now vary into many colors and shades; they are borne in large terminal clusters in summer and early autumn. The many forms have been blended and intermixed to a great degree, comprising what is now called garden phlox.

P. stolonifera (creeping phlox) is a common, hairy, creeping perennial with tapering oval leaves about 3 in. long and purple or violet flowers in flat clusters blooming in spring and early summer.

P. subulata (ground- or moss-pink) is a low perennial, forming mats about 6 in. high. Oval evergreen leaves are about ½ in. long. It grows best in acid soil. Early spring flowers vary from pinkish to white or purple; there are various color forms available. A number of choice selections made by H. Lincoln Foster and carrying the name "Millstream" (such as 'Millstream Daphne' and 'Millstream Jupiter') provide a wide range of colors. Two choice miniature forms are 'Laura', pale pink, and 'Snee-wichen', white.

Phlox subulata

P. suffruticosa, an early-flowering form of *P. carolina*, grows about 3 ft. high and has leaves to 5 in. and flowers from purple to rose and white.

PHOENIX (FEE niks). A genus of palms commonly known as date palms. Some species have no evident stem, while others have tall trunks nearly covered with the bases of old leaf stalks. Almost all of them sucker profusely from the base. They have plumey leaves and bear a profusion of edible fruit. One species produces important commercial crops, while others are grown for fruit or ornament outside in Zones 9–11 and as potted plants in cooler climates.

PRINCIPAL SPECIES

P. canariensis (Canary Island date palm) is a tall, strong tree with wide-spreading leaves on yellow stalks. It is extensively planted in Zones 9–11 as an avenue tree or garden specimen. It requires regular watering and frequent applications of fertilizers rich in ammonia, phosphate, and potash. As a potted plant, it is excellent for porch, sun room, or patio decoration, enduring hot sun and severe summer storms.

P. dactylifera is widely grown commercially for its fruit in the warmer states as well as in Europe and Asia, where it is one of the oldest and most valuable of cultivated trees; see DATE.

P. roebelenii (pygmy date palm) is a graceful dwarf grown in Florida in shady locations with rich, moist, loamy soil. In the North it is a popular greenhouse subject or houseplant, easily handled and very desirable because of its slow growth.

P. rupicola, a Himalayan species, is a small, symmetrical tree with glossy, bright green foliage. It requires rich, moist soil and protection from cold when young.

P. sylvestris (wild date palm), planted in Florida and California gardens, resembles *P. dactylifera*, but has more beautiful arching crowns of bluish green leaves and great bunches of inedible orange fruit. The trunks are studded with old leaf stalks, which furnish an excellent growing medium for ferns and native orchids.

P. zeylanica (blue date palm) grows in clumps with foliage rivaling that of the Colorado blue spruce in color.

PHOLISTOMA (foh li STOH mah). A small genus of annual herbs native to the Southwest and Mexico. *P. auritum* (fiesta flower) shows a profusion of lilac-blue flowers in open woodlands in early spring.

PHORMIUM (FOR mee um). A genus of tall perennial herbs belonging to the Agavaceae (Agave Family) and native to New Zealand, where they are valued for their very strong fiber. They are grown outdoors in Zones 9–11 as ornamentals. In cooler climates, they are grown inside or in tubs to be set outside in summer and wintered in a cool greenhouse. Propagation is by seed or division.

P. colensoi (mountain-flax) grows to 7 ft., has less rigid leaves, and bears yellow flowers.

P. tenax (New-Zealand-flax) grows to 15 ft. and has long, narrow leaves and numerous dull red flowers in clusters on a long stem. It has showy color forms, one variegated and one showing reddish purple foliage.

PHOSPHATES. A general term for compounds of phosphorus, one of the three elements essential to all plant growth that are most frequently lacking in soils. The source of phosphates commonly used as plant food in the organic group is animal bone, which is obtainable in the form of bonemeal of different degrees of fineness, either raw or steamed, the latter containing less nitrogen as a result of the treatment. In plants, phosphorus hastens maturity, stimulates root growth, and contributes to seed formation.

Among inorganic commercial fertilizers, the chief phosphate carrier is a natural phosphate rock, ground and sold either raw or after treatment with acid to make it more soluble. Ordinary superphosphate (produced with sulfuric acid) contains about 8% of the element phosphorus, or 20% phosphate, and is sold as 0–20–0. Concentrated (or triple) superphosphate, made with phosphoric acid, contains about 20% of the element phosphorus, or about 46% phosphate, and is sold as 0–46–0 (composition may vary).

PHOTINIA (foh TIN ee ah). A genus of evergreen and deciduous shrubs or small trees native to Asia, belonging to the Rosaceae (Rose Family). The deciduous species are mostly hardy to Zone 5, growing well in a sunny location. The evergreen species are less hardy, tolerating only a few degrees of frost. Both kinds do well in a light, sandy loam and are propagated by seed cuttings of half-ripened wood under glass and by layers.

PRINCIPAL SPECIES

P. x *fraseri*, a hybrid between *P. glabra* and *P. serrulata*, is an evergreen shrub that grows to 15 ft. and has showy, new, red leaves in the spring. The flowers have a bad odor. Hardy to Zone 8.

P. serrulata (Chinese photinia), an evergreen shrub or tree, grows to 25 ft. with long, leathery, glossy, dark green leaves tinted crimson when young. The flower clusters, about 6 in. across, are followed by round, red berries. Hardy to Zone 8.

P. villosa is a large deciduous shrub with somewhat spreading branches, good clean foliage, and clusters of hawthornlike flowers in early spring. The leaves are colorful in autumn, and the bright red berries persist into winter. Hardy to Zone 5.

PHOTOPERIODISM. A term for the effect of relative length of daylight exposure (photoperiod) upon the growth and flowering (reproduction) of plants. It has been learned that flowering plants fall into four groups. In a SHORT-DAY PLANT, flower bud formation is initiated in a relatively short day length (about ten to twelve hours) and suppressed by increasing the length of the day. In a LONG-DAY PLANT, flower bud formation is initiated by exposure to a relatively long day length (fourteen hours or more) and suppressed by decreasing the length of the day. Indeterminates are plants that bloom with more or less readiness under all light periods. In intermediates, flowering is initiated by a zone or band of day lengths of median duration but inhibited by day lengths either above or below the band.

The length of the light period is more important than the light intensity. In actuality, plants respond more to the length of the dark period, and short photoperiodic effects can be reversed by a brief flash of light during the night. Other features of plant growth, such as stature, bulk, production of seeds or oil, are influenced by the photoperiod, although other factors, such as temperature, moisture, humidity, and food supply have a bearing upon the behavior of all these plants.

PHOTOSYNTHESIS. From the Greek words meaning "light" and "putting together," this term refers to the process by which the green leaves of plants, in the presence and with the aid of sunlight, manufacture sugars and starches from the carbon dioxide absorbed from the air and water and raw food materials taken in from the soil by the roots, releasing oxygen in the process.

Fundamentally, food is a form of stored energy. Thus, this manufacture of sugar and starch in the leaf is the conversion of radiant energy of the sun into these compounds. This is effected by microscopic bodies called "chloroplasts," which contain the green pigment (chlorophyll) that gives plants their characteristic color and without which the vital process of photosynthesis cannot take place.

PHYLA (FĪ lah). A genus of tender herbs and shrubs of the Verbenaceae (Verbena Family); most species formerly classified as *Lippia*. Plants have rose, purple, or white flowers clustered in spikes. The species commonly cultivated is *P. nodiflora* var. *canescens* (creeping-lippia, carpet-grass, matchweed). It has a creeping, spreading stem and small heads of lilac flowers and is often grown as a ground cover in California and other warm regions. Since it spreads rapidly in dry, poor soil, it is a very acceptable substitute for grass. The small flower heads are easily removed by the lawn mower, and because the plant spreads by creeping branches and not by seed or underground stems, there is no danger of its becoming a dangerous weed. Var. *rosea* has rose-colored flowers.

PHYLLANTHUS (fil AN thus). A genus of tropical herbs, shrubs, or trees, formerly listed as *Xylophylla* and belonging to the Euphorbiaceae (Spurge Family). Hardy in Zones 10–11, a few species are grown in the tropics for their edible fruits, and others are useful ornamental plants for the greenhouse. Propagation is mostly by cuttings, sometimes by seed and layers.

PRINCIPAL SPECIES

P. acidus (Otaheite-gooseberry, gooseberry tree, star-gooseberry) is a tree with small panicles of reddish flowers. Cultivated in the tropics (especially in the West Indies) and naturalized in south Florida, its tart fruits are used for pickling and preserves.

P. emblica (emblic) grows to 30 ft. The branches are clothed with many small leaves, giving it the appearance of a fir or hemlock. It bears edible fruits.

PHYLLITIS (fi LĪ tis) **scolopendrium.** A fern with entire fronds up to 18 in. long, commonly known as hart's-tongue fern, and sometimes listed as *Asplenium scolopendrium*. It is native to Europe and Asia and is found very locally in limestone areas of North America, especially the Niagara region. It does well in European rock gardens but is difficult to establish in the United States. It must have a moist, shady, limey situation protected from wintry winds. Hundreds of varieties have appeared naturally in Great Britain over the

years; not all are cultivated, but some are grown successfully as houseplants. Some of the many cultivars are 'Crispum', 'Crispifolium', 'Cristatum', 'Laceratum', 'Marginatum', 'Muricatum', 'Ramo-cristatum', 'Sagittatum', and 'Undulatum'.

PHYLLODOCE (fil LOHD oh see). A genus of dwarf evergreen shrubs from the arctic regions of Europe, Asia, and North America, belonging to the Ericaceae (Heath Family), and commonly known as mountain-heath. They are suitable for the rock garden and require a moist, peaty soil in a partly shaded location. Most are difficult to grow in hot, humid climates. Propagation is by cuttings or layers.

PRINCIPAL SPECIES

P. breweri is usually under 1 ft. high and has dark green leaves and pink flowers.

P. caerulea grows about 6 in. high and has pink or purple, urn-shaped flowers.

P. empetriformis makes a low-growing mat of small, dark green, shining leaves and heads of rosy purple, bell-shaped flowers. There are several cultivars with white or pink flowers.

PHYLLOSTACHYS (fil oh STAY kis). One of several genera of plants of the Poaceae (Grass Family), commonly known as BAMBOO. It comprises tall, grassy Chinese and Japanese shrubs with stems flattened on one side.

P. aurea (golden bamboo), growing to 15 ft., has yellow canes and graceful leaves 5 in. long, smooth above with a bloom beneath. This is one of the "running" bamboos that spreads by means of long, underground stems.

P. nigra (blackjoint bamboo), hardy and slow growing but reaching 25 ft., has plumelike foliage and canes that turn black the second year.

PHYSALIS (FIS ah lis). A genus of tender, annual or perennial herbs belonging to the Solanaceae (Nightshade Family) and commonly known as ground-cherry or husk-tomato. Some are grown in the garden for the large, bright-colored, inflated and papery calyxes and others for their small, edible, papery-husked fruits. Most are natives of warm climates and are tender, so plants should be started early indoors, gradually hardened-off, and set out in a warm, sheltered spot after danger of frost is over. Various species are hardy in Zones 3–9.

PRINCIPAL SPECIES

P. alkekengi (winter-cherry, Chinese-lantern, strawberry-tomato) grows to 2 ft. and bears small, white flowers followed by large, balloon-like calyxes that become 2 in. long when the plant is in fruit and turn to orange-red "flaming lanterns" when ripe. Arranged along stiff stems, they are effective for indoor winter decoration. Pods develop the second year on dense bushes. Propagation from seed is easy, and the plants often self-sow; also, rhizomes can be divided or cuttings rooted. It is a perennial and forms long, tuberous roots that are not killed by frost, spread-

Physalis alkekengi

ing all over flower beds and becoming a great nuisance; the plants should be grown only where their aggressive growth can be controlled.

P. ixocarpa (tomatillo) is an annual from Mexico, now grown farther north. The clear yellow flowers are followed by a round, sticky, purple berry surrounded by a purple-veined calyx. The edible fruit is harvested green for use in Mexican cuisine.

P. peruviana (cape-gooseberry) is a tropical plant that grows to 3 ft. and has yellowish flowers followed by a yellow berry enclosed in a swollen, long-pointed calyx. Native to South America, the common name reflects its widespread cultivation in South Africa.

P. pruinosa (strawberry-tomato, dwarf cape-gooseberry) is a stout-branched, gray-haired,

native annual with buff-yellow flowers followed by edible, tomato-flavored fruit about the size of a cherry and covered by a large, hairy calyx.

PHYSOSTEGIA (fī soh STEE jee ah). A small genus of hardy perennial herbs belonging to the Lamiaceae (Mint Family), commonly known as false dragonhead, and sometimes called obedient plant, presumably because the flowers remain at any angle to which they are turned. Hardy in Zones 3–9, they succeed in any good soil but thrive best in cool, moist locations and partial shade. Propagation is by seed or by root division.

Physostegia virginiana

P. virginiana grows 2–3 ft. high and has narrow, tapering leaves 5 in. long and irregularly notched. The flowers are flesh-colored to purplish, about 1 in. long in spikes at the branch tips. The stems are erect and herbaceous, dying down in winter. There are also white and pink varieties.

PHYTEUMA (fī TOO mah). A sizable genus of hardy perennial herbs, curious members of the Campanulaceae (Bellflower Family). The unusual flowers often look like clusters of small urns. The smaller species are suitable for the rock garden, where they thrive in rock crevices or scree conditions. They are easily propagated from seed.

PRINCIPAL SPECIES

P. charmelii is a petite species with dark blue flowers.

P. comosum is an intriguing flower form that H. Lincoln Foster describes in his book *Rock Gardening* as ". . . a weird cross between a stemless artichoke and a porcupine—odd, bewitching, and improbable."

P. hemisphaericum is a compact plant with blue or whitish flowers.

P. scheuchzeri grows 12–18 in. high and has violet-blue flowers.

P. sieberi grows to 6 in. high and has dark blue flowers.

PHYTOLACCA (fī toh LAK ah). A genus of herbs, shrubs, trees, and occasionally climbers native to North America and commonly known as pokeberry or pokeweed. They have undivided leaves and small flowers in terminal clusters followed by fleshy berries. Some parts of the plants are poisonous, but others are edible.

P. americana (poke, skoke), native from Maine to Florida and to Mexico, grows 12 ft., dying to the ground each fall. It is a strong-smelling plant but bears attractive, small, purplish white flowers in long racemes followed by reddish purple berries with a staining juice. The stems and leaves are smooth, often with a bloom or purplish tinge, and the plant makes a clean, attractive foliage growth for the wild garden. The seeds and roots are deadly poisonous, but young growth is sometimes used as a substitute for asparagus. Great care should be taken when gathering in order to avoid including any of the poisonous root.

PICEA (pī SEE ah). A genus of coniferous trees belonging to the Pinaceae (Pine Family) and commonly known as spruce. The stiff leaves are diamond shaped in cross section, and twigs are roughened where needles have been shed. The cones are pendent and persistent. There are many species native in North America. In their various forms, spruces are exceedingly useful and ornamental. The large types are especially valuable for park or landscape planting, and the slower-growing species for the home grounds.

Most spruces are hardy and grow best in full sun but will tolerate some shade. They will grow in almost any kind of soil if there is good drainage and sufficient moisture. Because of their shallow rooting habit, they are easily transplanted. The dense, close foliage and strong branches make spruces excellent for windbreaks or shelter belts. Several species, including *P.*

abies and *P. glauca*, endure severe pruning and are often used as hedge plants. They can be raised from seed and cuttings. Rarer varieties are grafted on seedling stock of *P. abies*.

Diseases. Spruces grown as ornamentals are fairly free from diseases. Several rust fungi may attack leaves, twigs, or cones. Three of them, causing blisters on spruce needles, have alternate hosts in members of the Ericaceae (Heath Family), including *Ledum groenlandicum* (Labrador-tea), *Andromeda* spp. (bog-rosemary), and *Chamaedaphne calyculata* (leatherleaf). Other rusts develop alternately on wild varieties of *Rubus idaeus* (red raspberry) and *R. pubescens* (dwarf raspberry). A different type of rust, requiring only one host, causes the falling of one-year-old needles of Engelmann spruce in the Northwest. WITCHES'-BROOM is caused by a rust fungus. See also RUSTS; DISEASE.

Insect Pests. One of the most serious insect pests is the gall aphid, which attacks especially Norway spruce but may infest red and black spruces, causing cone-shaped galls at the base of young shoots, preventing twig growth. These are caused by the feeding of the young nymphs, which remain in the gall pockets until late summer. Then they emerge and lay eggs from which the overwintering females are hatched. Control by removing infested twigs during the winter and by spraying with a sulfur or soap solution before growth starts in the spring. A miscible oil spray can be carefully applied at that time. See also APHIDS; INSECT CONTROL; SPRAYING.

Several insects damage the foliage. The spruce mite webs over the needles in a manner similar to the common red spider mite; see MITES. The light green larvae of the spruce leaf miner mine in and web together the needles; see LEAF MINER. Caterpillars of the spruce budworm feed on new needles and those of the preceding season, webbing them together and severing them at the base. See also CATERPILLAR; BUDWORM.

Sawflies are an increasing concern. The European spruce sawfly has become well distributed in Canada since its introduction. The yellow-headed spruce sawfly occurs both in Canada and across the northern United States. A pest of forest trees, it also occurs on ornamental spruces, which can be treated by oil SPRAYING. See also SAWFLY.

Weak trees of red, white, and black spruce infested by bark beetles should be removed and destroyed; see BARK BEETLE. Leaders may be attacked by the white pine WEEVIL. The BAGWORM can also cause serious problems.

PRINCIPAL SPECIES

P. abies (Norway spruce) is a tall, pyramidal tree that grows to 60 ft. and has horizontal branches; drooping branchlets; shiny, dark green needles; and long, drooping, brown cones to 7 in. Although a native of Europe, it is one of the most common of cultivated evergreens in the eastern states; despite its attraction in youth, it becomes unkempt with age. It has many varietal forms, some with variegated foliage, including the green and white cv. 'Argentea'. Dwarf varieties suitable for the

Picea abies

rock garden include 'Pumila' and 'Pygmaea', not exceeding 2 ft. Cv. 'Nidiformis' (bird's-nest spruce) is a popular, spreading dwarf growing to 3 ft. high and 6 ft. wide. Cv. 'Pendula' includes a group of clones with weeping branches. Hardy in Zones 3–7.

P. engelmannii (Engelmann spruce), a native of the western states, grows to 50 ft. and has bluish green foliage and slender branches borne in close whorls. It forms a slender, pyramidal tree much more graceful than the widely planted *P. pungens*. Cv. 'Glauca' has steel-blue needles. Hardy in Zones 3–7.

P. glauca (white spruce), growing to 50 ft., has ascendant branches and drooping branchlets; leaves somewhat bluish green with a strong aromatic odor when crushed; and small, glossy, light brown cones to 1½ in. long. The foliage is dense

and close in young trees, making them highly ornamental. Cv. 'Conica' (dwarf Alberta spruce) is a very compact, slow-growing, pyramidal plant that grows to 10 ft.; it needs full sun, good air circulation, and a cool location to prevent red spider mite infestation. Hardy in Zones 3–6.

Picea glauca

P. mariana (black spruce), which yields spruce gum, usually does not grow more than 60 ft. tall. It has dull or bluish green squared needles to ¾ in. long and cones about 1½ in. long. It is native from Alaska to Virginia and hardy to Zone 2.

P. omorika (Serbian spruce), native to Yugoslavia, is a very graceful specimen plant that grows to 50 ft. and has a slender trunk and weeping branches. Cv. 'Nana' is a rounded shrub that grows to 8 ft. Hardy in Zones 4–7.

P. orientalis (Oriental spruce) is an attractive, dense, narrow, pyramidal tree that grows to 50 ft. and has horizontal branches and very small, shiny, dark green needles. It is a choice specimen tree, native to the Caucasus and Asia Minor. Hardy in Zones 4–7.

P. pungens (Colorado spruce), a western native growing to 50 ft., has horizontal branches that form a regular pyramidal growth. The rigid, spiny leaves are bluish green, silvery white, or occasionally dull green. The cones are 4 in. long. The foliage color is so striking that the species should be used with discretion; it has been badly abused in indiscriminate foundation groupings. There are many important

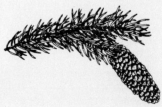

Picea pungens

cultivars: 'Glauca' (Colorado blue spruce) has bluish green needles; 'Glauca Prostrata', with very silver-blue foliage, grows flat as a ground cover; 'Hoopsii' is an outstanding specimen plant with a pyramidal shape and very silvery color; 'Montgomery' is a dwarf, oval shrub with silver-blue needles; 'Thompsonii' forms a pyramidal tree with light silver-blue, very thick needles. Hardy in Zones 3–7.

PICKERELWEED. Common name for *Pontederia cordata*, a hardy aquatic herb with blue-violet flowers; see PONTEDERIA.

PICOTEE. A type of *Dianthus* (carnation) characterized by a marginal band of color on each petal contrasting with the solid body color of yellow or white. The term is also applied to *Begonia* and other similarly bicolored flowers.

PIERIS (pī EER is). A genus of evergreen shrubs or small trees from North America and Asia, belonging to the Ericaceae (Heath Family). They thrive best in a sheltered, shady position and a rather moist, sandy soil with peat or leaf mold. If planted in hot, dry, sunny areas, they are very susceptible to diseases and pests. Attractive year-round, they are excellent as specimen plants in rock gardens, mass plantings, or mixed with other plants.

PRINCIPAL SPECIES

P. x *brower's beauty* is a hybrid between *P. japonica* and *P. floribunda*, a dense, compact plant with shiny, dark green leaves. Hardy in Zones 5–8.

P. floribunda, sometimes listed as *Andromeda floribunda*, is a wide-spreading, dense shrub growing to 6 ft. Native from Virginia southward, it is desirable for its hardiness (Zones 5–8) and fragrant flowers in spring. It has dull green leaves and nodding white flowers in upright panicles. The flower buds are conspicuous all winter.

P. japonica is a larger and faster-growing upright evergreen shrub to 12 ft., very handsome in form with lustrous leaves delicately tinted when young. Hardy in Zones 5–8, it is outstanding for the garden and a beautiful sight during spring when it blooms with drooping panicles of white, slightly fragrant flowers. In cooler climates the blooms are sometimes winter killed.

PIGEON-PEA. Common name for the tropical shrub *Cajanus cajan*; see CAJANUS.

PIGEON-PLUM. Common name for *Coccoloba diversifolia*, a small tree native to the Caribbean; see COCCOLOBA.

PIGWEED. A common name for species of AMARANTHUS, especially *A. retroflexus* and *A. hybridus*; also for the genus CHENOPODIUM (goosefoot), especially *C. album*.

PILEA (PĪ lee ah). A genus of tropical, annual or perennial herbs of the Urticaceae (Nettle Family). Some are creeping and many are weedy, but a few species are worth growing in greenhouses or warm gardens (Zones 10–11). They thrive best in a moist compost of loam and leaf mold to which a little sand has been added. Propagation is by seed, cuttings, or division of the roots.

PRINCIPAL SPECIES

P. cadieri (aluminum plant) has silver-striped leaves on erect, 12–15 in. stems.

P. microphylla (artillery plant) is an annual or biennial with branched, fleshy stems from prostrate to 12 in. high and leaves not over ¼ in. long. Its common name reflects the plant's habit of forcibly discharging its pollen from the staminate flowers when mature.

P. nummulariifolia (creeping-Charlie) is a perennial with creeping stems that root at the joints. The oval leaves are as much as ¾ in. across.

P. serpyllifolia is a superior plant of similar appearance to *P. microphylla* although it grows slightly larger.

PILULARIA (pil yoo LAIR ee ah). A genus of aquatic ferns similar in basic structure to other water ferns; however, the fronds are simple, rushlike spikes with no pinnae. *P. americana* (American pillwort) is found in wet pond edges or transient pools in scattered sites throughout the southern and western states. *P. globulifera* (European pill-wort) is native throughout Europe from Scandinavia to Portugal.

PIMELEA (pi MEL ee ah). A genus of Australian evergreen shrubs commonly called riceflower. A few species are sometimes grown in greenhouses and outdoors in Zones 9–11. They are raised from semi-ripe wood cuttings, taken in spring and kept in a moderate temperature in partial shade until well rooted, then potted. Thereafter they are kept in moist but well-drained soil and shifted to larger pots when necessary. They should begin to bloom the second spring.

PIMENTA (pi MEN tah) **officinalis.** An evergreen tree growing to 40 ft., native to the West Indies and Central America, and commonly known as pimento or allspice. The tree has leathery foliage, white flowers, and dark brown, berrylike fruits, which are dried and used for flavoring.

PIMIENTO. A name derived from the Spanish "pimienta" meaning "pepper," applied to the genus CAPSICUM and to certain of its cultivated sorts.

PIMPERNEL. A common name for ANAGALLIS, a genus of small herbs with small, starlike flowers of red, blue, or white.

PIMPINELLA (pim pi NEL uh). A large genus of the Apiaceae (Celery Family). A few species are occasionally planted in borders. The most common is *P. anisum* (anise), the seeds of which are used in medicine and in cooking as a seasoning. It is an erect annual plant that grows to 2 ft. and has deeply notched leaves and small, white or yellow, clustered flowers, which are used to flavor some

Pimpinella anisum

liquors. The seeds are sometimes used in flavorings, medicines, or perfumes. Plants thrive in full sun and are easily grown from seed in the herb garden. Seed should be planted in spring in rows of loamy, well-worked soil where the plants are to stand.

PINACEAE (pin AY see ee). The Pine Family, a large group of gymnosperms, or evergreen cone-bearing plants (see CONIFER). It comprises resinous trees and shrubs of wide distribution, including many ornamentals and timber producers. The leaves are typically needle- or scale-like, mostly evergreen, and borne in condensed clusters. Male and female organs are in different flowers of the same plant and are borne on the upper surfaces of modified leaves that make up the characteristic cones. Many members are of horticultural importance, among them *Abies* (fir), *Araucaria*, *Cedrus* (cedar), *Larix* (larch), *Picea* (spruce), *Pinus* (pine), *Pseudotsuga*, and *Tsuga* (hemlock).

PINCHING. The removal or shortening of young shoots, to maintain a symmetrical plant form, to encourage the development of buds, or to enhance flower or fruit development. It is usually done without regard to the bud position. See DISBUDDING.

Pinching

PINCUSHION CACTUS. A common name for members of the genus MAMMILLARIA.

PINCUSHION FLOWER. A common name for SCABIOSA, a genus of annual and perennial herbs with flowers whose nobbed stamens protrude beyond the florets.

PINE. Common name for PINUS, a genus of evergreen trees including many species with needles in clusters. The Pine Family is PINACEAE.

The common name "pine" is applied to several trees and plants belonging to other genera. Cypress-pine is *Callitris*. Dammar-pine and kauri-pine refer to *Agathis*. Ground-pine and princess-pine refer to *Lycopodium*. Norfolk-Island-pine is *Araucaria heterophylla*. Screw-pine refers to the genus *Pandanus* and the family Pandanaceae. Umbrella-pine is *Sciadopitys verticillata*.

PINEAPPLE. A South American bromeliad, *Ananas comosus*, whose familiar aromatic fruit resembles a large, fleshy pinecone, thus giving the plant its common name, which also refers to several other plants. The Pineapple Family is BROMELIACEAE. Pineapple flower is a common name for *Eucomis punctata*, a bulbous herb with green and brown flowers; see EUCOMIS. Pineapple-guava refers to FEIJOA, a genus of tropical trees and shrubs, sometimes ornamental, and bearing edible fruits.

The pineapple plant consists of a rosette of stiff, thick, sharp-pointed, prickly edged leaves and resembles a century plant. From the center rises a stem sometimes 4 ft. high; near its summit, this swells to a fruit that consists of a spike or head of flowers, all parts of which are consolidated into one succulent mass, surmounted by a crown or tuft of leaves.

Any well-drained but moisture-retaining soil will grow edible pineapples. Plants are propagated commercially from suckers (called ratoons) that develop at the base of the old plants as they die after the fruit has developed. They are treated as cuttings until they root in the fields and go into a regular fertilization program to grow the plant up to fruiting size. In the home, the top leaves can be twisted out of the fruit itself, cleaned of a few of the smaller leaves, and set into a shallow jar of water to root before going into a pot to grow on.

PINGUICULA (pin GWIK yoo lah). A genus of small, stemless herbs, widely distributed in moist areas, belonging to the Lentibulariaceae (Bladderwort Family), commonly known as butterwort.

They have a sticky substance on the leaves that attracts and traps insects. The pretty, little, solitary flowers are variously colored yellow, purple, or white. They can be grown only on rocks in the bog garden or in a moist part of the rock garden. Propagation is by seed or offsets. *P. vulgaris* grows to 6 in. and has violet or purple flowers ½ in. long.

PINK. Common name for DIANTHUS, a genus of flowering herbs, including species known as cheddar, clove, garden, grass, maiden, pheasant's-eye, or Scotch pink. The Pink Family is CARYOPHYLLACEAE.

The name is also applied to several species of related genera, such as *Lychnis coronaria* (mullein pink), *Silene virginica* (fire pink), *S. acaulis* (cushion pink), and *S. caroliniana* (wild pink); see LYCHNIS, SILENE.

Other plants using this common name include *Helonias bullata* (swamp- or stud-pink), *Phlox subulata* (moss- or ground-pink), and the genera ARMERIA and LIMONIUM, both known as sea-pink.

PINNA. One of the leaflets of a fern frond or similarly formed "pinnately compound" leaf, which means one with an arrangement of leaflets on either side of a common petiole.

PINNATE. Descriptive term for compound leaves shaped like a feather with leaflets on both sides of a central stem.

PINUS (PĪ nus). An important genus of coniferous trees including about 80 species and commonly known as pine. Most species are confined to the North Temperate Zone, but some are found on mountains in the tropics. The genus is most easily recognized by the needlelike leaves, which are generally longer than in other conifers and are always grouped in bundles or clusters (called fascicles) of from two to five (or sometimes a single needle), the number being an important factor in distinguishing the species.

Widespread in their distribution, the pines are extremely adaptable to varied climatic conditions and, with their many forms and types, supply indispensable material for ornamental use as well as the production of timber, turpentine, and other commercial products.

For landscape work, in either parks or home grounds, there are pine species for every situation: fast- and slow-growing kinds, some with silvery foliage, and others showing a green of almost somber darkness. While most of them grow to 100 ft. or more, some are medium-size or dwarf in habit.

For use in the eastern states, in groves, or as specimen trees, *P. strobus* (white pine) is eminently suitable, not only because it is the characteristic forest tree of the region, but because it is graceful in youth, sturdy and compact in middle life, and most picturesque in age with its great trunk and often wide-spreading branches.

Pinus strobus

For background planting, the red pine, with its glossy green needles, makes a less somber effect than the rapid-growing Austrian pine that is often used for that purpose. The short, bluish green needles of the Scotch pine make a pleasing contrast when planted with darker pines or spruces. *P. rigida*, *P. virginiana*, and *P. banksiana* are useful soil binders on dry, sandy slopes.

CULTURE

Pines, as a rule, will grow well in rather poor but well-drained sandy loams, since they prefer a light diet rather than an overabundance of plant food. It is much better to plant nursery-grown trees, which have been frequently root-pruned or transplanted and caused to develop a fibrous root system. For forest planting, one-year-old seedlings are generally used.

In planting pines, remember that they love light and will become scraggly and unsightly or die out when shaded. Many pines are susceptible to salt damage and air pollution.

They are most easily propagated by seed sown in spring in prepared beds, in frames, or in the open. Later the young seedlings should be shaded from intense sunlight.

DISEASES

White Pine Blister Rust. The blister rust of white pine damages all pines that have needles in clusters of five. The rust fungus destroys the bark, girdling twigs and branches. The rust cannot spread from one pine to another but must first infect a plant of one of the alternate hosts, usually currants and gooseberries. See also WHITE PINE BLISTER RUST; RUSTS.

Other Fungus Diseases. Stem blister rusts attack two- and three-needled pines. The alternate hosts of one are *Comptonia peregrina* (common sweet fern) and *Myrica* spp. (sweetgale), which should be removed from the area 200 ft. wide around western yellow, scrub, and pitch pines. Young pines in gardens or nurseries may be stunted or killed by this rust; after ten years of growth, they are more resistant. Young trees are also susceptible to the rust that infects two- or three-needled species (except pitch pine) and has species of *Comandra* as alternate hosts.

Another fungus is destructive to shore, lodgepole, and western pine west of the Rocky Mountains. The fungus affects weeds of the genus *Castilleja* but does not require them as alternate hosts in order to spread.

A stem blister rust is generally distributed throughout the United States, causing witches'-broom, bark swellings on pines, and leaf pustules on oaks. Remove infected young pines. See WITCHES'-BROOM.

Blister rust fungi sometimes cause the defoliation of pines. The most common of them completes its life cycle on asters and goldenrod.

INSECT PESTS

Pine Shoot Moth. The European pine shoot moth is especially serious on red and Scotch pines but may infest other species. The brown caterpillars feed on the buds, tunnel in the new shoots, kill the terminal buds, and make the lateral shoots become leaders. A distinctive crooked condition known as bayonet growth results.

Small, reddish brown moths emerge in early summer and lay eggs on the new buds. The presence of larvae is indicated in autumn by small masses of pitch over the entrance holes. To control, remove and burn infested shoots. Consult your local extension service for advice about use of insecticide sprays when the moths are emerging, and again when the young borers are hatching. See also CATERPILLAR.

White Pine Weevil. The white pine weevil, a small brown gray-mottled SNOUT BEETLE, kills leaders of white and other pines during midsummer. To control, cut and burn infested tips early. Spray with a lime-sulfur solution (1 to 9) in spring before growth starts. Banding the base of leaders with cotton may help. Feeding trees to keep them in a vigorous condition is advisable since the weevil, like certain other insects, attacks weaker trees first. See also WEEVIL.

Pine Tip Moth. The small, white, block-headed larvae of the pine tip moth burrow into the tips of shoots or buds, causing side shoots to develop. Often a gummy resin collects at the injured place. Spray growing tips with a sulfur insecticide at weekly intervals during early summer. Cut off and destroy infested twigs in fall and winter.

Sawfly. Pine needles are fed upon by various species of SAWFLY larvae, which may do considerable damage before their work is noticed. Handpick the caterpillars or apply rotenone; consult your local extension service for advice.

False Pine Webworm. Webbed masses of brownish or greenish excrement on terminal twigs of various pines are caused by the green or brown larvae of the false pine WEBWORM. Control in the same manner as for sawfly larvae.

Pine Bark Aphid. Fluffy white masses on bark and shoots of white pine bark indicate the pine bark aphid, which, by sucking the tree juices, causes poor growth, yellow needles, defoliation, and sometimes death. Rinse thoroughly with a strong stream of water. See also APHIDS.

Spittle Bug. Another sucking insect is the SPITTLE BUG, whose grayish nymphs are found in the center of frothy masses of white spittle. Spray insecticides do not always penetrate the spittle, but some control can be gained by dusting with ROTENONE. See also INSECT CONTROL; DUSTING.

Pine Leaf Scale. The white, elongated pine leaf scale on needles of pines and related conifers can be controlled by spraying carefully in early spring with a miscible oil or oil emulsion, or with nicotine-sulfate when the young are hatching in late spring. See also SCALE INSECTS; SPRAYING.

PRINCIPAL SPECIES

P. banksiana (jack pine) may grow to 75 ft. but is usually smaller and shrubby. The paired needles are bright or dark green, stiff, twisted, and up to 1½ in. long. It thrives on poor soils and is hardy to Zone 2.

P. bungeana (lacebark pine), native to China, is a striking specimen tree that grows to 50 ft. Its handsome mottled bark is similar to the plane tree or sycamore. Dark green needles are in bundles of three. Hardy in Zones 5–8.

P. canariensis (Canary Island pine) grows to 100 ft. and has drooping branches that bear glossy, light green needles up to 12 in. long grouped in threes on yellowish branches. The drooping cones may be 8 in. long.

P. cembra (Swiss stone pine) grows about 75 ft. and has dense, brown branches, dark green needles clustered in fives, and oval cones to 3½ in. long. It is native to Europe and Asia, hardy to Zone 3, and grows very slowly.

P. contorta var. *latifolia* (lodgepole pine), formerly listed as *P. murrayana*, is a tree that grows 75–150 ft. tall and has stiff, twisted needles at least 2 in. long in pairs. It is native to western North America and is hardy to Zone 4.

P. coultri (big-cone pine) grows to 75 ft. and bears dark bluish green needles 12 in. long and grouped in threes. Aptly named, it bears cylindrical cones, which may be 14 in. long. Native to California, it can be grown in sheltered locations as far north as Zone 7.

P. densiflora (Japanese red pine) is a rapid-growing tree, at length forming a rather wide-spreading, strongly branched head. The slender, sharp-pointed, blue-green needles are 5 in. long and clustered in pairs. Cones are 2 in. long. It is quite hardy in the North but sometimes suffers from winter injury. Hardy in Zones 4–7.

P. edulis (piñon pine) is a shrub or small tree that grows to 25 ft. tall and has stout needles, which may be grouped in clusters of two to five, usually three. Its cones produce the edible piñon nuts. It is native throughout the southwestern states to northern Mexico and is hardy to Zone 5.

P. elliottii (slash pine) grows to 100 ft. and has deep green, paired or triplet needles up to 5 in. long and cones to 6 in. long. Hardy to Zone 8, it is cultivated commercially in the southeastern states for lumber, turpentine, rosin, and pulp.

P. flexilis (limber pine) is a hardy species found from Alberta to Texas and California. The needles, 3 in. long, are in bundles of five, and the oval cones are 6 in. long. It is a beautiful specimen tree that grows to about 50 ft. and has a fine blue-green color. Hardy in Zones 5–7.

P. jeffreyi (Jeffrey pine) has bloomy needles 5–10 in. long in fascicles of three and conic or oval cones 5–12 in. long. Native from southern Oregon to the west coast of Mexico, it is hardy to Zone 6.

P. koraiensis (Korean pine) forms a dense, pyramidal growth and has dark green needles 4 in. long in bundles of five and long cones. This compact, slow-growing pine is excellent for specimen planting.

P. lambertiana (sugar pine) is a tall species, growing 200 ft. or more. Its sharp, 4-in. needles have white lines on the back and are grouped in clusters of five. The cylindrical cones may be 12–20 in. long. Native from Oregon to Baja California, it is hardy to Zone 6 but needs winter protection from high winds.

P. monophylla (single-leaf piñon pine) is similar to *P. edulis* but has mostly single, cylindrical needles and is native from Idaho to northern Mexico; hardy to Zone 6.

P. monticola (western white pine) grows to 200 ft. and has bluish 4-in. needles in groups of five and cylindrical cones 5–8 in. long. A valuable source of timber, it is native from British Columbia to California and is hardy to Zone 6.

P. mugo (Swiss mountain pine), usually shrubby in growth, has bright green, paired leaves to 2 in. long and cones to 2½ in. long. Cv. 'Compacta' is a dense, rounded form. Var. *mugo* (mugho pine) is a prostrate shrub. Hardy in Zones 3–7.

P. nigra (Austrian or black pine) has pyramidal growth at first and later becomes flat-topped with stout branches. The needles are stiff, dark green, to 6½ in. long in clusters of two. The 3 in. long cones are somewhat oval. Austrian pine is sometimes killed in the eastern and

Pinus nigra

midwestern states by diplodia tip blight, an airborne fungus that kills twigs, branches, and eventually the entire tree. This pine can be grown for Christmas tree production, since young trees are apparently immune to the blight. Hardy in Zones 5–7.

P. palustris (longleaf pine) grows to 100 ft. and has cylindrical cones. The common name comes from its dark green needles clustered in threes, which may be up to 18 in. long on young trees and 9 in. on mature specimens. Commercially, the trees yield timber, pulp, and turpentine. It is native to the southeastern states and hardy to Zone 7.

P. parviflora (Japanese white pine), growing to 40 ft., is a hardy tree of dense growth with bluish green needles to 1½ in. long in bundles of five, forming tufts at the tips of the branches. It is widely used for bonsai. Hardy in Zones 5–7.

P. ponderosa (ponderosa pine) grows up to 200 ft. and sometimes taller and has dark green, triplet needles 5–11 in. long and oval or oblong cones 3–8 in. long. It is a valuable timber tree native throughout western North America and hardy to Zone 6.

P. radiata (Monterey pine) grows 75 ft. or more and bears bright green needles 4–6 in. long in groups of three and conic or oval cones 7 in. long. Often planted for timber in warm climates, it is native to California and Mexico and is hardy to Zone 7.

P. resinosa (red pine) is upright and domelike in youth, later wide-spreading with rather drooping branches. The dark green, glossy needles are grouped in pairs, and its light brown cones are 2½ in. long. It is very hardy and is useful for planting with the white pine. Hardy in Zones 3–8.

Pinus resinosa

P. sabiana (digger pine) is a Mexican native that grows 40–80 ft. tall and has bluish green needles 9–12 in. long in groups of three and oval cones about 5 in. long.

P. strobus (white pine) is symmetrical and pyramidal first, later wide-spreading with soft, bluish green needles to 5 in. long in clusters of five. The brown, cylindrical, pendent cones are up to 4 in. long and often gracefully curved. A sprig of leaves and cones constitutes the state flower of Maine. Several cultivars have been developed: 'Fastigiata' is of narrow, upright growth; 'Glauca' has grayish green needles; 'Nana' is a bush form; 'Prostrata' has trailing branches; 'Compacta' is a dense, rounded shrub to 3 ft. high and 6 ft. wide. Hardy in Zones 4–8.

P. sylvestris (Scotch or Scots pine) has spreading, drooping branches; stiff, bluish green, often twisted needles to 3 in. long in clusters of two; and cones 2½ in. long. This extremely hardy and useful European tree is extensively planted in the eastern states. Cv. 'Argentea' has silvery needles; 'Fastigiata' grows in upright, narrow form; and 'Watereri' has bluish gray leaves and columnar growth. This species is best used for Christmas trees, since it is short-lived and rather unattractive with age. Hardy in Zones 3–8.

Pinus sylvestris

P. taeda (loblolly pine), native from New Jersey to Texas, grows to 100 ft. tall and has 6–9 in., bright green needles in threes and cones 3–5 in. long. It is hardy to Zone 7 and is used commercially for timber and pulpwood.

Pinus taeda

P. thunbergiana (Japanese black pine) is a large tree that grows to 130 ft. high and forms a broad, pyramidal head of drooping branches. The bright green, sharp-pointed needles are 4½ in. long and bundled in pairs. The cones are 3 in. long and somewhat oval. Native to Japan, it is perfectly hardy in the North. Cv. 'Oculus-Draconis' has needles banded with two yellow stripes. This is one of the best pines for salt tolerance and is widely used for seashore plantings. It has a very irregular growth habit, with every specimen forming a different shape. Hardy in Zones 6–7.

P. virginiana (scrub or Jersey pine) grows 30–50 ft. tall and bears paired needles about 3 in. long and twisted cones to 2½ in. long. Native to the eastern United States, it thrives on poor soil and is hardy to Zone 5.

P. wallichiana (Himalayan pine) is a graceful tree with soft, grayish green, drooping needles to 8 in. long in bundles of five. The cylindrical cones are up to 10 in. long. It can be hardy as far north as Zone 6 if planted in a sheltered location.

Pinus virginiana

PIPSISSEWA. Common name for CHIMAPHILA, a genus of evergreen herbs or shrubs found in eastern woodlands.

COLOR KEY

ANNUALS

PERENNIALS & BULBS

HERBS, VEGETABLES, & FRUIT

ROSES

FOLIAGE PLANTS

SHRUBS & TREES

HOUSEPLANTS

NATIVE PLANTS & WILDFLOWERS

DORIS DEWITT

ANNUALS

A border of annuals.

Browallia speciosa.

Ipomoea tricolor (morning-glory).

Iberis umbellata (globe candytuft).

Salpiglossis sinuata (painted-tongue).

Centaurea cyanus (bachelor's-button).

Cosmos bipinnatus (garden cosmos).

Lobelia erinus.

Impatiens wallerana.

Lobularia maritima (sweet-alyssum).

Pelargonium sp. (geranium), top; *Centauria* sp. (dusty miller), middle; *Petunia* sp., bottom.

ANN REILLY

ANN REILLY

Salvia splendens (scarlet sage).

Coleus x *hybridus* in variety.

Nicotiana alata (flowering tobacco).

ANN REILLY

Celosia cristata (cockscomb) cv. 'New Look'.

Celosia cristata (cockscomb) cv. 'Jewel Box Red'.

ANN REILLY

ANN REILLY

ANN REILLY

Tagetes erecta (Aztec marigold) cv. 'Perfection Gold'.

Tagetes patula (French marigold) cv. 'Red Marietta'.

ANN REILLY

Tagetes patula (French marigold) cv. 'Golden Gate'.

ANN REILLY

ANN REILLY

Antirrhinum majus (snapdragon) cv. 'Rocket'.

Zinnia sp., top; *Dianthus* sp., bottom.

Ageratum houstonianum (garden ageratum).

Calendula officinalis (pot-marigold).

Catharanthus roseus (Madagascar-periwinkle).

Begonia semperflorens (wax begonia).

GAY BUMGARNER

PERENNIALS & BULBS

Perennial daisies.

Galanthus nivalis (snowdrops).

Tulipa sp.

Narcissus cv. 'Small Talk'.

Allium giganteum (giant onion).

Muscari botryoides (grape-hyacinth).

Hyacinthus cv. 'Carnegie'.

Crocus spp.

Lilium longiflorum (Easter lily).

ANN REILLY

ANN REILLY

Dahlia cv. 'Randi Dawn'.

Convallaria majalis (lily-of-the-valley).

Anemone sp. (windflower).

DAVID M. STONE

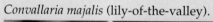

MARY NEMETH

Gladiolus cv. 'King's College'.

Ranunculus asiaticus (Persian buttercup).

Iris siberica (Siberian iris).

Chrysanthemum sp., cushion type.

Chrysanthemum sp., cushion type.

Alcea rosea (garden hollyhock), with traditional five petals.

Alcea rosea (garden hollyhock), with double, fringed petals.

ANN REILLY

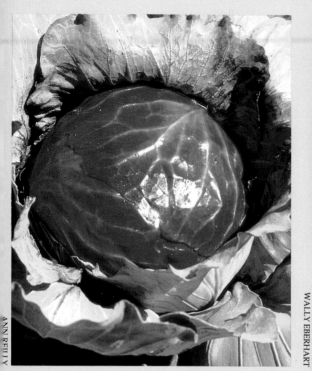

Brassica oleracea var. *capitata* (red cabbage).

Beta vulgaris (beet).

Brassica oleracea var. *capitata* (savoy cabbage).

Allium cepa (garden onion).

Curcubita pepo (squash).

Solanum melongena var. *esculentum* (eggplant).

Rhaphanus sativus (radish).

Cynara scolymus (French artichoke).

Capsicum annuum var. *grossum* (bell pepper).

Lycopersicon lycopersicum (tomato) cv.'La Roma'.

Lactuca sativa (lettuce) cv. 'Iceberg', 'Romaine', 'Red'.

Brassica oleracea var. *gemmifera* (brussels sprouts), top; var. *acephala* (kale), bottom.

GAY BUMGARNER

DAVID M STONE

MARILYN WOOD

Pyrus communis (pear), cv. 'Bosc'.

Malus (apple) cv. 'Red Delicious'.

Cucumis melo (muskmelon).

Citrullus lanatus (watermelon).

Rubus alleghieniensis (sow-teat blackberry).

Ribes uva-crispa (European gooseberry).

Fragaria (strawberry), cv. 'Ozark Beauty'.

Ribes sativum (currant).

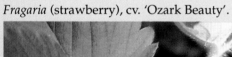

Citrus limon (lemon).

Citrus x *paradisi* (grapefruit).

Prunus serrulata (Japanese flowering cherry).

Poncirus trifoliata (hardy-orange).

Vaccinium angustifolium (lowbush blueberry).

ROBERT E. LYONS

Petroselinum crispum (parsley).

DAVID M. STONE

Mentha spicata (spearmint).

Foeniculum vulgare var. *azoricum* (florence fennel, finocchio).

ANN REILLY

JOHN A. LYNCH

Anethum graveolens (dill).

ROBERT E. LYONS

Salvia officinalis (sage).

Thymus praecox (mother-of-thyme).

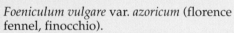

ANN REILLY

Cuminum cyminum (cumin).

Origanum vulgare (oregano).

Pimpinella anisum (anise).

Origanum majorana (sweet marjoram).

Carum carvi (caraway).

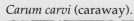

Ocimum basilicum (basil).

HERBS,
FRUIT,
&
VEGETABLES

JOHN A. LYNCH

DAVID M. STONE

Left: Harvesting vegetables. Above: *Nepeta cataria* (catnip), left; *Prunus persica* (peach), right.

ANN REILLY

Paeonia (peony) cv. 'Vivid Rose'.

BETSY FUCHS

Digitalis purpurea (foxglove).

Myosotis scorpioides (forget-me-not).

Astilbe x *arendsii* (false spirea).

PRISCILLA CONNELL

JOHN A. LYNCH

Dicentra spectabilis (bleeding-heart).

Lathyrus latifolius (sweet pea).

Dianthus barbatus (sweet-William).

Echinacea purpurea (purple coneflower).

HAL HORWITZ

Aster novae-angliae (New England aster).

Aster laevis (smooth aster).

MARY NEMETH

HAL HORWITZ

LOIS MOULTON

Delphinium sp.

Primula sp. (primrose).

Aquilegia sp. (columbine).

Iris, bearded type, cv. 'Cameo Cascade'.

Phlox paniculata (summer perennial phlox).

Phlox subulata (ground-pink).

Coreopsis grandiflora.

Hemerocallis (daylily) cv. 'Minute Man'.

Hemerocallis sp. (daylily).

Heilanthus annuus (sunflower).

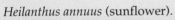

ROSES

Floribunda cv. 'Simplicity'.

Old Garden Rose, Damask cv. 'Mme. Hardy'.

Old Garden Rose, Gallica cv. 'Rosa Mundi'.

Rosa rugosa.

Rosa rugosa var. *alba*.

Hybrid Tea cv. 'Garden Party'.

Hybrid Tea cv. 'Color Magic'.

Hybrid Tea cv. 'Bewitched'.

Grandiflora cv. 'Gold Medal'.

ANN REILLY

Miniature cv. 'Stars 'n' Stripes'.

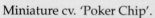

Miniature cv. 'Poker Chip'.

ANN REILLY

ANN REILLY

Miniature cv. 'Simplex'.

Large-flowered Climber cv. 'America'.

ANN REILLY

Floribunda cv. 'Gene Boerner'.

Grandiflora cv. 'Sonia'.

Floribunda cv. 'Sunsprite'.

Old Garden Rose, Moss cv. 'Henri Martin'.

ROBERT E. LYONS

FOLIAGE PLANTS

Mixed Grasses

Erica vagans (Cornish heath).

Helleborus orientalis (Lenten-rose).

Hosta crispula (plantain lily).

ANN REILLY

Stachys byzantina (lamb's-ears).

Artemesia schmidtiana (silvermound).

ANN REILLY

ANN REILLY

Calluna vulgaris (heather).

Artemesia stellerana (beach wormwood).

JOHN J. SMITH

Gypsophila paniculata (baby's-breath).

ANN REILLY

Osmunda cinnamomea (cinnamon fern).

Botrychium virginianum (rattlesnake fern).

Matteuccia struthiopteris (ostrich fern).

Dennstaedtia punctilobula (hay-scented fern).

MARY NEMETH

Onoclea sensibilis (sensitive fern).

ROD PLANCK

Pteridium aquilinum (bracken fern).

Pteris sp. (brake fern).

ROD PLANCK

Adiantum pedatum (northern maidenhair fern).

DAVID M. STONE

ROBERT E. LYONS

Eritrichium sp. (alpine-forget-me-not).

Polytrichum communis (haircap moss).

Cladonia rangiferina (reindeer-moss).

Lycopodium obscurum (ground-pine).

Pachysandra terminalis (Japanese-spurge).

Euphorbia marginata (snow-on-the-mountain).

WALLY EBERHART

Alpine meadow.

PAUL MARTIN BROWN

Pennisetum alopecuroides (fountain grass).

Sisyrinchium angustifolium (blue-eyed grass).

Sasa veitchii (kuma bamboo).

ANN REILLY

Phalaris arundinacea var. *picta* (ribbon grass).

Festuca ovina var. *glauca* (blue fescue).

ANN REILLY

BOB RASHID

Cortaderia selloana (pampas grass).

SHRUBS
&
TREES

Left: Azalea garden. Above:
Rhododendron cv. 'Blue Peter'.

Prunus subhirtella cv. 'Pendula' (weeping Higan cherry).

AL BUSSEWITZ

ANN REILLY

Magnolia sp. (magnolia).

MARLYN WOOD

GREGORY CRISCI

ANN REILLY

JOHN A. LYNCH

Malus sp. (crab apple).

Cornus florida cv. 'Rubra' (pink flowering dogwood).

MARILYN WOOD

PHILIP E. KEENAN

VALORIE HODGSON

Acer saccharum (sugar maple).

Ginkgo biloba (maidenhair tree).

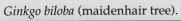

GAY BUMGARNER

AL BUSSEWITZ

Quercus palustris (pin oak).

Sorbus sp. (mountain-ash).

PHILIP E. KEENAN

Rhododendron hybrid.

Lonicera tatarica (Tatarian honeysuckle) with *Lonicera japonica* (Japanese honeysuckle), inset.

Forsythia sp.

HAROLD BARNETT

Syringa vulgaris (common lilac).

Hibiscus syriacus (rose-of-Sharon).

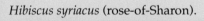

JOHN J. SMITH

ANN REILLY

Rhododendron hybrid.

Kalmia latifolia (mountain-laurel).

DOROTHY S. LONG

Hydrangea macrophylla (bigleaf hydrangea).

VIRGINIA TWINAM SMITH

HOUSEPLANTS

Left: Orchid display at Shaw's Gardens, St. Louis, Missouri. Above: *Echeveria* sp., left; *Senecio* sp. (cineraria), right.

ANN REILLY

Begonia x *tuberhybrida* (tuberous begonia).

ROBERT E. LYONS

Begonia rex (painted leaf begonia).

Abutilon hybridum (flowering-maple).

ROBERT E. LYONS

ANN REILLY

Aechmea fasciata (living-vase).

Cyclamen persicum (cyclamen).

JOHN A. LYNCH

Caladium sp. (elephant's-ear).

DAVID M. STONE

Opuntia sp. (prickly-pear cactus).

Mammillaria sp. (pincushion cactus).

Schlumbergera bridgesii (Christmas cactus).

Opuntia bigelovii (teddy-bear cholla).

Pereskia grandifolia (leaf cactus).

Ferocactus acanthodes (California fire-barrel).

Phalaenopsis orchid, cv. 'Zauberrot'.

Laelia orchid.

Cymbidium orchid, cv. 'Red Beauty'.

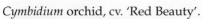

Paphiopedilum orchid (lady's-slipper).

Miltonia orchid, cv. 'Rodeo'.

Dendrobium orchid.

Masdevallia orchid.

Cattleya orchid.

Vanda orchid.

Cypripedium orchid.

NATIVE PLANTS
&
WILDFLOWERS

Left: *Eschscholzia californica* (California poppy).
Below: *Sanguinaria canadensis* (bloodroot), lower left;
Tradescantia virginiana (spiderwort), lower right;
Viola papilionacea (common blue violet), upper left;
Cornus canadensis (bunchberry), upper right.

ALL PHOTOGRAPHS IN THIS SECTION BY HENRY W. ART

Rudbeckia hirta (black-eyed-Susan), top; *Rosa carolina* (pasture rose), bottom.

Callirhoe involucrata (poppy mallow).

Iris versicolor (wild blue flag).

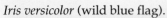

Physostegia virginiana (false dragonhead).

Clarkia amoena (farewell-to-spring).

Phacelia campanularia (California-bluebells).

Monarda fistulosa (wild-bergamot).

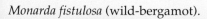

Eriogonum umbellatum (sulfur flower) with *Phlox diffusa* (spreading phlox).

Hedyotis caerulea (bluets).

Layia platyglossa (tidy-tips).

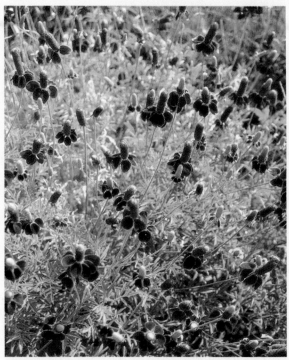

Ratibida columnifera (Mexican-hat).

Lilium pardalinum (leopard lily).

Gaillardia pulchella (blanket flower).

Salvia coccinea (scarlet sage).

PIQUERIA (pik EE ree ah). **trinervia.** A tropical herb belonging to the Asteraceae (Aster Family), grown by florists for winter bloom, and distributed under the name "stevia" (which correctly refers to another genus). Growing to 3 ft., it has narrow, oval, toothed leaves about 3 in. long and is extensively cultivated for its graceful sprays of small, white clusters of flowers which are combined with bolder blossoms in bouquets. It is also sometimes grown as a bedding plant.

Easily raised from seed, cuttings, or division, it will thrive in sun or shade. Pinching back makes for compact, free-flowering plants. During the winter, the plants should be cut back. In early spring, the new growth can be rooted as cuttings and later potted. Plants can be set outdoors after danger of frost is over and grown there until fall, when they are again potted and grown indoors for winter bloom.

PISTIA (PIS tee ah) **stratiotes.** A small, tender, floating perennial herb belonging to the Araceae (Arum Family) and commonly known as water-lettuce. Often used in aquariums and warm ponds, its floating rosette of pale green, fluted leaves are velvety to the touch, and the pendent mass of feathery roots is mostly ornamantal. It prefers a partly shaded location and temperatures of 70–80°F. Young plants develop from side runners.

PISTIL. The central organ of a flower, consisting of one or more parts (carpels), each of which consists of a style (stem), stigma (apex), and basal ovule-bearing ovary. In compound pistils (composed of more than one carpel), the carpels are merged to form what appears to be a single organ, though the styles and stigmas may be either fused or independent. Because they contain the cells that when fertilized become seeds, pistillate flowers are often referred to as "female" flowers. See FLOWER.

PISUM (PEE sum). A genus of leguminous plants of which the most important, *P. sativum*, is the common garden PEA.

PITCAIRNIA (pit KAIR nee ah). A genus of greenhouse perennial herbs, rarely shrubs, native to the tropical Americas, and belonging to the Bromeliaceae (Pineapple Family). They have narrow leaves in rosettes with red, yellow, or nearly white flowers borne in spikes or clusters. They thrive in a well-drained mixture of rich loam and leaf mold. Propagation is by offsets.

P. corallina has both small and long, tapering leaves to 3 ft., about 4 in. wide and spiny edged. The flowers are coral-red and borne in clusters on red stalks 12 in. long.

PITTOSPORUM (pi TOS poh rum). A genus of evergreen trees and shrubs native to the Southern Hemisphere. The genus lends its name to the Pittosporaceae (Pittosporum Family). Several species are grown outdoors in Zones 9–11, and one or two under glass, usually by experts. They have attractive foliage and clusters of small, mostly fragrant flowers. Useful for hedges, specimen planting, and some as avenue trees, they are propagated by seed, cuttings, or by grafting on *P. undulatum*.

PRINCIPAL SPECIES

P. crassifolium (karo) is a tall shrub or small tree from New Zealand. It has thick, leathery, shiny leaves and terminal clusters of red or dark purple flowers. It makes a good windbreak.

P. eugenioides (tarata) is a tall shrub or slender tree often used in California for clipped hedges and ornamental groupings.

P. phillyraeoides (willow pittosporum) is a tree of the Australian desert, resembling a weeping willow.

P. rhombifolium (Queensland pittosporum) can be grown as a pot plant or an avenue tree. It has yellow-orange fruits that remain decorative for a long time.

P. tenuifolium (tawhiwhi) is a symmetrical, compact tree to 30 ft.; one of the best for screening purposes, it tolerates close clipping. Var. *purpureum* has green growth that turns purple later in the season.

P. tobira (tobira, Japanese pittosporum), a good hedge plant in warm regions, is the one commonly grown under glass. It has thick, leathery leaves and clusters of fragrant, yellowish white flowers. Var. *variegata* is a form with white-marked leaves. Cv. 'Wheeleri' is a dwarf form that is useful for ground cover in southern gardens.

Pittosporum tobira

P. undulatum (Victorian-box) is a shrub or tree to 40 ft., often planted in southern California and highly prized for its very fragrant flowers.

PITYROGRAMMA (pit ee roh GRAM ah).

A small genus of xerophytic terrestrial ferns from subtropical and tropical America and Africa, also naturalized in Asia. They are characterized by a coating of white or yellow farina on the undersides of the fronds with sori appearing as black flecks on this background.

PRINCIPAL SPECIES

P. argentea (goldback fern) is a bipinnate fern that grows 6–10 in. and has fronds curling upward at the edges. It is a decorative pot plant that needs plenty of light and a fast-draining soil.

P. calomelanos (silverback fern) has bipinnate to tripinnate fronds up to 3 ft. tall. The farina on the lower surfaces varies from white to pale yellow. Common in the Central and South American tropics and the West Indies, it probably has escaped from gardens to naturalize in Florida. It is found mainly in disturbed sites, scree slopes, and open woods.

P. chrysophylla (gold fern) is an attractive bipinnate plant that is similar to *P. calomelanos* but smaller, growing only 4–16 in. Native to the West Indies, it does well in a container or in the tropical garden.

P. triangularis (California gold fern) is a small fern that grows 4–8 in. high and has triangular, bipinnate fronds backed with gold farina. The stipe is twice as long as the rachis. It grows among rocks in the western states and Mexico. Fronds often curl when moisture is low.

PLANE TREE. Common name for PLATANUS, a genus of deciduous trees grown for shade and for their unusual bark.

PLANTAGO (plan TAY goh). A genus of the Plantaginaceae (Plantain Family), including herbs and shrubby plants, marked mostly by basal leaves and inconspicuous flowers in heads or spikes. They include several troublesome weeds, but a few are grown for ornament. All are easily propagated by seed.

As weeds on lawns, plantains should be dug out but can only be eradicated by cultivating dense and vigorous turf so they cannot find a foothold; see WEEDS.

PRINCIPAL SPECIES

P. cynops is a shrubby plant that grows to 1½ ft. and has whitish flowers in heads ½ in. long.

P. lanceolata (narrow-leaved or buckhorn plantain) is an unattractive, widespread weed on lawns. It indicates compacted, dense, wet-worked, or trampled soils with a range of nitrogen, water, and pH but usually moist and acid. While the plant tolerates a low level of potassium, the potassium content of the leaves is proportional to the content in the soil. To control, hoe out individual plants. If this plant is all that your lawn will grow, till it up, fertilize, add compost, and reseed. The wilted leaves and seeds are sometimes used in herbal remedies and cooking.

Plantago lanceolata   *Plantago major*

P. major (broad-leaved plantain) is a common lawn weed that grows on soils with a wide range of nitrogen and pH, an intermediate amount of water, and little humus.

P. maritima grows as an annual, biennial, or perennial, with flowers in spikes to 5 in. long. Found by the seashores of Europe, Asia, and North America, it indicates sodium in the soil and grows in areas with a wide range of fertility.

P. patagonica is an annual that grows to 1 ft. and has very small flowers in dense spikes.

P. psyllium (fleawort) is a branching annual with narrow, hairy leaves and dense ½-in. flower spikes.

PLANTAIN. Common name for PLANTAGO, a genus of troublesome weeds. It also refers to other members of the Plantaginaceae (Plantain Family), including a species of MUSA, which includes the common banana, and several unrelated plants. Plantain lily is HOSTA. Poor-Robin's-plantain is a species of ERIGERON and sometimes of HIERACIUM. Water-plantain is ALISMA. Wild-plantain is one of the HELICONIA.

PLANT BREEDING. The creation of new horticultural varieties or the improvement of existing varieties by selection, hybridizing, and other means. The best-known plant breeder of modern times—probably because he was the most publicized—was Luther Burbank, but breeding has been practiced for hundreds of years in Europe and thousands in Japan and China. Today hundreds of horticulturists—scientific, professional, commercial, and amateur—are carrying it on in all parts of the world, with all kinds of plants and with varying degrees of success. Nearly all popular flowers, vegetables, and fruits have been bred away from their natural condition, in some cases so far that scientists cannot decide what that natural condition was. The difference between a delicious or a winesap apple and the hard, sour, worthless fruit of a wild apple seedling is due to plant breeding, as is the change from the weed queen-Anne's-lace to the garden carrot.

SELECTION

A batch of seedlings of any wild plant, when carefully compared, will show considerable differences in size, habit, flower color, fruit, etc. The first step in practical plant breeding is to select from a great number of seedlings of the plant to be improved, one or more that are better than all the rest. By this method alone, the pecan nut has been improved from something not much better than the hickory to the thin-shelled, full-meated pecan of commerce.

Selection plays a part in the breeding of all plants, but principally in connection with two other methods, both of which cause wider variations from the normal plant than are ordinarily found in nature.

One of these methods is cultivation. Seedlings of cultivated plants tend to vary more than those grown from seeds of similar plants found in the wild; and the higher the degree of cultivation, and the longer it is continued, the greater the variations will be. They may take the form of bud sports—sudden, unaccountable changes in the character of a single branch, such as a red-flowering branch of a white rose. Bud sports can occur anywhere, and not only plant breeders and nurseries but gardeners too should watch for them , because when desirable, they can usually be propagated as new varieties. Dwarf plants, variegated foliage, and other changes of the nature of bud sports may come in batches of cuttings, induced apparently by propagation. In all these cases the variation is provoked by some form of cultivation.

HYBRIDS

A second means of inducing variation is hybridizing. Plants produce seed naturally by POLLINATION. Pollen (the minute, dustlike cells in the anthers) from one flower falls or is carried by wind or insect to the pistil of that flower or another flower on the same or another plant. Fertilization then takes place, and seed begins to form at the base of the pistil. Some plants, like wheat, do not have to be crossed and are self-pollinated; but the great majority of ordinary plants produce poorer seed or none at all when self-pollinated.

If the pollen comes from a different variety or species, the offspring is called a HYBRID. Thus, a wild blackberry and a red raspberry were crossed to produce the purple loganberry, which is therefore said to be a hybrid between the two. Hybrids, according to the laws of Mendel, are usually alike in the first generation. Thus, when the blackberry and raspberry were hybridized, if hundreds of the resulting hybrid seedlings had been raised, all of them would probably have resembled the loganberry in appearance. However, if a loganberry (already a hybrid) is crossed either with a similar hybrid or with a blackberry or a raspberry, the resulting seedlings will show much variation, some with purple fruit, some with red, and with various combinations of growth habit.

ARTIFICIAL POLLINATION

Plant breeders use various methods of artificial pollination to produce hybrids, depending on the kind of plant. Sometimes pollen is collected by touching one flower's anthers with a fine brush until the pollen clings to it, then touching the brush to the stigma of the flower to be pollinated. Sometimes pollen is collected in quantity by shaking or scraping the flowers over a sheet of paper. A simpler way is to take the stamen from one flower and touch its tip to the stigma of the other flower. With plants that bloom at different seasons, it is better to save the pollen of the earlier flower rather than force the later one, but both methods are used. Some pollen will remain potent a month or more if the plucked stamens are put in an envelope and allowed to dry. Plant breeders usually cut away the stamens so that the flower's own pollen cannot reach the pistil, and cut away the petals to remove a possible insect pollinator's landing platform, or tie a paper bag over the flower or flower cluster to keep insects from pollinating it with pollen from other flowers. A label is then attached, carrying a record of the cross or a number referring to a filed record.

GENETIC DEVELOPMENTS

Developments in the science of plant breeding include the treatment of parent plants or their reproductive cells in various ways to change the nature, arrangement, and number of the chromosomes and other bodies by which inheritance of characters are transmitted. Experiment includes

exposure to x-rays, high-frequency electrical currents, and treatment with a drug colchicine (obtained from the autumn-crocus), which so shocks a plant as to increase the number of its chromosomes per cell. See POLYPLOIDY. These methods are interesting and can lead to developments from which gardeners may benefit.

PLANT FOODS AND FEEDING. Under cultivation, crops are usually harvested instead of returning to the soil naturally. Cultivation of soil also increases the breakdown of organic matter (humus). Hence, after a number of years, soil exhaustion sets in, and the supply of one or more of these elements becomes deficient. The minerals and humus carrying them must then be added to replace the elements taken out. This is the purpose of soil improvement, the adding of manure, compost, commercial fertilizers, lime, and other materials. By feeding each crop the minerals it needs and removes in growing, the soil is prevented from again becoming exhausted, and its fertility is maintained. Obvious signs of soil exhaustion are stunted and yellow growth; lack of flowers, fruit, or seeds; and poor root development.

Experienced gardeners keep on hand a supply of various plant foods, not only manure and compost, which are general soil builders containing both vegetable matter and many plant food elements in limited amounts, but also special foods especially rich in certain elements that meet the special needs of particular crops or unusual conditions. Manures and composts are turned under by plowing or spading and mixed with the soil as it is cultivated; or are added on the surface, to be cultivated in if fine enough, or left as a mulch. The art of plant feeding, however, may require an understanding of the nature of the many mineral or commercial fertilizers and knowing how to apply them. Each vegetable, flower, and tree has likes and dislikes, but certain general principles of fertilizing can be stated. For more information on soil additives, see COMPOST; FERTILIZER; GREEN MANURE; HUMUS; LIME; MANURE; PEAT; SOIL; SOIL AMENDMENT.

In the vegetable garden, a soil with manure, compost, and lime added and plowed in (or better, deeply spaded) may need no further nutrients; however, if needed, fertilizers can be scattered on the surface. For broadcasting in this way, the following amounts can be used per 100 sq. ft.: 1 lb. muriate or sulfate of potash, ammonium sulfate, or nitrate of soda; 2–4 lb. complete fertilizers or cottonseed meal; and 5–10 lb. superphosphate, horn shavings, ground limestone, or wood ashes. Any such material applied during the summers should be used in relatively smaller quantities; indeed, it is always better to apply several small doses at intervals than a heavy application at one time.

SELECTING PLANT FOODS.

Various plants use nutrients at different rates, and the choice of food can alter the type and form of growth. Excessive nitrogen should not be used on crops in which seed or fruit production is desired, such as tomatoes, as opposed to stem or leaf crops like celery or cabbage. Potatoes should not be given surface manure or lime but should receive a good application of balanced fertilizer. Root crops are helped by liberal quantities of muriate of potash, and beets, by lime and manure; but no lime or manure should be applied for carrots. Onions relish some lime and either a balanced fertilizer or superphosphate and sulfate of potash.

For all leaf crops, especially lettuce, nitrogen is particularly necessary, and general fertilizers and manure are also needed. Squash and melons also respond to nitrogen and benefit by large amounts of manure and balanced fertilizers. Nitrogen is good on young tomato plants too but should be given only at planting time, a balanced fertilizer being added soon after.

Flower Gardens. Annual flowers require heavy feeding with manure (preferably worked into the soil well in advance—or for the previous crop) and fertilizers, especially those that are quickly soluble. If grown for exhibition, they should receive applications in liquid form when the buds form. They can be given the maximum quantity of any plant foods except nitrogen, which should be used moderately (if at all) on young plants.

Perennials vary greatly in their requirements but should not be fed as much as annuals, since they must grow at a moderate rate to prepare for the winter. The more concentrated fertilizers, particularly nitrates, should be avoided. Commercial fertilizers are generally beneficial early in spring and should be worked into the ground rather than left on the surface. Chief reliance should be placed on manure, compost, and bonemeal rather than chemical stimulants. Since there are hundreds of kinds of perennial plants, there are naturally exceptions, including plants that respond to some special fertilizer and will not tolerate others.

Lawns. Lawns from which new growth is constantly being removed are continually in need of feeding, and many special foods are recommended. The ground for new lawns should be thoroughly prepared, well-rotted manure being worked in to a depth of at least 10 in. and fertilizer raked into the surface 3–4 in. After a year or two, if no food were provided, the sod would become thin and poor with the exhaustion of the original food supply. Therefore, even new lawns should be dressed with finely shredded manure, rich compost, or peat moss in the late fall. A balanced fertilizer should be broadcast in early spring, about 40 lb. per 1000 sq. ft.; water this in immediately and thoroughly. To heighten the vigor and color of the grass, ammonium sulfate, ammonium nitrate, or a high-nitrogen complete fertilizer can be added occasionally, using about 2 lb. per 1000 sq. ft. Since almost any good plant food will help a lawn, it is advisable to use first one, then another, rather than a single kind.

Trees and Shrubs. Mature shrubs and trees do not need fertilizing if their roots can be kept covered at all times with a natural mulch of leaves. The root system of a tree or spreading shrub usually reaches about as far as the spread of the branches, and the feeding roots will be found mainly on or near this outer zone. It is where the drip from the branches falls, therefore, that a mulch is most useful.

Moisture-loving trees, such as elm and Lombardy poplar, and lusty-feeding shrubs like privet, send their roots out many yards farther than their branches, but these rank growers do not usually need mulching or special feeding. Sod is not a good cover for tree roots, especially those of evergreens. Large white pines will sometimes die in a few years on a lawn, but plant around them a wide bed of rhododendrons with a permanent heavy mulch of leaves, and they will flourish indefinitely.

If a mulch is not practicable and the tree cannot get its normal supply of nitrogen nutrients as the mulch decays, it must be fed. Fertilizers can be scattered on the surface if it is loose soil, or placed in small holes made about 2 ft. apart over the feeding root area. In the latter method, the holes should not be more than 12–18 in. deep, since the active feeding roots lie mostly near the surface, just below the layer of leaf mold that would be their natural food source in a forest. Rotted or composted manure, compost, and other animal or vegetable matter makes the best tree food. Rapid-growing kinds like maple and elm may do well on commercial fertilizers. Trees should never be forced with nitrogen, which gives a quick, succulent, nonresistant growth. Commercial tree foods high in nitrogen should not be used on most trees.

Houseplants. Potted plants can be fed by mixing the food with their potting soil and repotting when the nutrients are exhausted. Or a complete commercial fertilizer can be sprinkled on the surface, giving a teaspoonful to a 5-in. pot once every few months. Prepared foods in powder or tablet form for dissolving in watering solutions are usually satisfactory and very convenient.

PLANTING.
Plants are added to the garden either by starting new plants from seed or more often by transplanting a seedling shrub or tree from some other location into the home garden soil.

STARTING SEEDS INDOORS
Seeding can take place in flats or small pots indoors, which are then moved into the garden once seedlings have developed. Seeds can also be planted directly in the soil, usually in the spring. Use these tips for planting seeds indoors and for setting out later:

1. Use a container with a drainage hole.

2. Use a clean, quick-draining planting medium. Peat moss, vermiculite, and packaged soil mixes are good examples.

3. Sow the seeds at the proper depth—just barely cover tiny seeds.

4. Keep the medium moist, but not wet, at all times. A spray bottle makes a good watering device.

5. Use a plastic or glass covering to seal in humidity while the seedlings are very young.

6. Give the seeds gentle bottom heat to hasten germination. Setting flats on top of the refrigerator or dryer is a good alternative to specialized heating cables.

7. Thin the seedlings before the second set of leaves is formed. When seedlings are crowded together, they do not transplant well.

8. Give maximum sunlight to indoor seedlings after they have sprouted.

9. Turn the container often to keep the young seedlings from growing toward the light and developing irregular forms.

Once the seedlings have sprouted a second set of leaves (its first set of true leaves), they can be transplanted to larger pots or, weather permitting, moved outdoors during the day until they become adjusted to the new environment. Most plants need a week or more to become accustomed to the outdoors. See HARDENING-OFF.

PLANTING SEEDS OUTSIDE
Before planting seeds directly into the ground, the soil must be cultivated, fertilized, and watered if necessary. Follow these steps for direct seeding:

1. Hoe or cultivate the top 6–8 in. of soil, removing any stones, weeds, and debris.

2. Add compost, manure, or chemical fertilizer to the soil and work it in well. It is especially important to work chemical granular fertilizers into the top 6 in. of soil to avoid fertilizer burn.

3. Water the soil lightly if it is dry to the touch.

4. If it is necessary to sow the seeds in a straight line, use the straight edge of a board or tie a string between two stakes to mark the line.

5. Large seeds can be poked into the ground so that they are covered with soil about half as deep as their diameter. Medium-sized seeds can be planted in a shallow ditch made by pressing the edge of a hoe into the soft ground. Barely cover the top of the soil and then cover with a dusting of fine soil or sand. Firm the soil down on top of all seeds after planting to ensure that they make good contact with the soil.

6. Once the seeds are planted it is important to keep the soil moist at all times.

The length of time required for seeds to germinate or sprout depends on the type of seed and the temperature of the soil. If seeds are planted very early in the spring when the soil is cold and wet, they may rot. Check the suggested planting date on the seed packet; some seed producers will recommend starting seeds indoors in flats rather than direct sowing in the ground.

See also TRANSPLANTING; SEEDS.

PLANT NAMES AND CLASSIFICATION.
Classification is the systematic arrangement of plant groups that expresses these relationships in terms of evolution, or descent from common ancestors.

Plants differ most obviously in structure, and this is the principal basis of classification. Minor structural differences, such as the size, shape, color, and number of leaves, are regarded as unstable characters since they do not breed true (see PLANT BREEDING). The number, structure, and arrangement of flower parts, however, are more constant and therefore are important factors in identifying and classifying plants.

Proper classification calls for an orderly nomenclature, or system of naming. Because names in Latin (the accepted scientific language) are internationally used, they are preferable to common names that may mean different things to different people in different places. When their construction and significance are understood, such "scientific" names are no more diffi-

cult to use than the "common" ones, and of course they are more definite and accurate. The real gardener makes use of both kinds. The unit of classification is the plant individual, which is said to belong to a "species," that is, a group of plants so nearly alike in their more stable characters that they differ no more than offsprings of the same parent.

The familiar quaking aspen (*Populus tremuloides*) is such an individual. All aspens taken together form a distinct and easily recognizable group called a "genus." A species, then, is a collection of closely related individuals, and a number of such species (it may be many or few) make up the genus. The two categories, genus and species, in that order, give the individual plant its botanical or "official" name. *Populus* is the name of the aspen genus, that is, all the poplars and aspens; *tremuloides*, the specific name, tells what kind of aspen, thus classifying it. Thus, *Populus tremuloides* is the name of an aspen (*Populus*) that is like all the other aspens in general characteristics but is further identified as a quaking aspen.

VARIETIES AND THEIR NAMES
Within a species, plants may differ among themselves to some degree, by minor and less stable variations. These give rise to "varieties," or subdivisions of a species; each member of a variety has the determining characteristics of its species but differs slightly from the species. *Betula papyrifera* var. *cordifolia*, for example, is a variety of *B. papyrifera* (paper birch), differing from it by being somewhat smaller, more restricted in locale, and with broader, heart-shaped leaves. Often a variety bears the name of its discoverer or producer, like *Acer platanoides schwedleri*, or the Schwedler maple. Races, strains, and clones are other terms used to describe subdivisions along horticultural or cultural lines.

According to botanical usage, the generic part of a plant name is capitalized. In the style followed in this book, the species and variety parts of the name are not; however, botanists and horticulturists are not agreed to this latter point, so variation will be found in different publications. In strict botanical usage, abbreviation of the name of the person who first listed the plant is also part of the name (as **Acer saccharum Marsh.**—meaning the sugar maple as named by Humphrey Marshall). Since this information is rarely needed by practical gardeners, it is usually omitted.

FAMILIES, ORDERS, AND CLASSES

In classification by genetic and evolutionary relationships, similar species (**Betula papyrifera**, **Betula lenta**, and so on) are grouped into a genus, in this case **Betula** (birch). The birch genus, however, is closely related to four other genera, namely the **Alnus** (alder), **Carpinus** (hornbeam), **Ostrya** (ironwood), and **Corylus** (hazelnut). Such an aggregation of related genera is called a family—in this case, the Betulaceae or Birch Family, named after its principal genus. The fact that all plant family names end in -aceae makes it easy to recognize them.

A further, somewhat more distant relationship is that between different families. The Rosaceae (Rose Family), for instance, is grouped with the Fabaceae (Bean Family), the Hamamelidaceae (Witch-hazel Family), and four other families to which it bears certain structural resemblances, to form the Rosales (Rose Order). Similarly, the Betulaceae (Birch Family) is akin only to the Fagaceae (Beech Family), which includes the oaks, so these two families are grouped together into the order Fagales. Here also there is a distinguishing form of the name, all plant orders ending in "-ales."

Each order of flowering plants in turn falls into one of two subclasses, which are distinguished by profound structural differences. Grasses, palms, lilies, and orchids are members of the subclass Monocotyledoneae (MONOCOTYLEDON), but the bulk of garden plants falls into the subclass Dicotyledoneae (DICOTYLEDON).

These two subclasses, each composed of orders, families, genera, and species, together comprise the class Angiospermae, or plants that bear seeds inside a receptacle called an ovary (see FLOWER). These are the plants one thinks of when speaking of flowers, but conifers, which belong to the other great class, the Gymnospermae, or naked-seeded plants, also bear flowers in the botanical sense of the word. The cones of the pine and the berries of the yew and juniper are the mature female flowers that bear the seeds, the male flowers being less conspicuous.

The plant kingdom is subdivided into two major groups: the Tracheophyta, or vascular plants, having xylem and phloem for the conduction of water, nutrients, and organic compounds; and the Bryophyta, or nonvascular plants, such as mosses and liverworts, which lack such a conductive system. The Tracheophyta in turn are placed into two major divisions based on whether they produce seeds (as with the gymnosperms and angiosperms) or spores (as with ferns, club-mosses, and horsetails).

See also FAMILY; GENUS; VARIETY and other terms used in this article; also STANDARD.

PLATANUS (PLAT ah nus). A genus of large, ornamental, deciduous trees native to southern Europe, Asia, and North America, comprising the Platanaceae (Plane Tree Family), and commonly known as plane tree, sycamore, or buttonwood. They are characterized by bark that peels off in large patches and by dense, lobed, maplelike leaves. Frequently used for street planting and other ornamental purposes, the trees grow to a massive shapeliness.

Though they thrive best in rich, moist soil, some species are quite tolerant of city conditions, and they will tolerate severe pruning. They are excellent shade trees, and their mottled white and gray trunks, from which the bark falls in shreds or plates, gives them a most distinctive character. Propagation is by cuttings of green or ripened wood, layers, and seed.

PRINCIPAL SPECIES

P. x acerifolia (London plane) is a hybrid between **P. orientalis** and **P. occidentalis**. It is commonly planted as a street tree, since it is hardy as far north as Massachusetts and to a considerable extent is free from disease.

P. occidentalis (buttonwood, sycamore) is a hardy species native to the eastern states and grows to 150 ft. It is spectacular when dormant, with its white upper branches shading to green and brown toward the base. Planting is not recommended, however, since it is highly susceptible to disease.

Platanus occidentalis

P. orientalis (oriental plane) grows to 100 ft. and has a short trunk and broad head. This is the old-world plane, native to southeastern Europe and western Asia and is not frequently seen in the United States. Trees marketed under this name are usually hybrids.

P. racemosa, native to southern California, has an interesting appearance, with coarse foliage and gnarled habit; however, it is susceptible to disease.

PLATYCERIUM (pla ti SEE ree um). A genus of epiphytic ferns with broad and uniquely forking fronds, commonly known as staghorn ferns. They are tropical and require warm greenhouse care. Some of the smaller species can be grown as large houseplants. In the wild they grow on rocks and trees in a vertical orientation; in cultivation they look and grow best when mounted on large slabs of tree fern fiber or rot-resistant wood modified to hold an epiphytic medium. The sterile shield fronds soon cover the slab. Plants need bright light out of the hot sun and plenty of water. When the days are shorter and growth has slowed or stopped, much less watering is needed. The sporangia form on large patches of the fertile fronds. They can be propagated by the removal and growing on of small offsets called pups. A few species are hardy enough to be grown outdoors in Zones 10–11. There are a number of species and cultivars in trade, but a few are commonly available.

PRINCIPAL SPECIES

P. bifurcatum (common staghorn fern) is the most commonly available form. It grows rapidly and is thus rewarding to the grower. The foot-

wide, sterile shield fronds are round to kidney-shaped, and the forking fertile fronds can reach 3 ft. in length. The sporangia form on the upper surface of the farthest forms. Plants from the temperate regions of Australia are quite hardy and will survive actual frost, but specimens of the same species from more tropic regions are not so tough. It is also found in New Guinea and Indonesia.

P. grande produces upright sterile fronds divided into blunt lobes at the apex. The forking fertile fronds can be 6 ft. long, and the semicircular spore patches arise at the first forks. Native to the Philippines, it must be kept at a temperature above 60°F.

P. vassei resembles *P. bifurcatum*, but the fertile fronds are more erect, and the shield fronds are tougher and more leathery. It is not so hardy and should be kept above 40°F.

PLATYCLAYDUS (pla ti KLAY dus) **orientalis.** An attractive tree with dense foliage, formerly included in the genera *Thuja* or *Biota* and commonly known as oriental arborvitae. The leaves are arranged in flat, vertical sprays on two-ranked branchlets. It is not as hardy as *Thuja*, doing best in Zones 6–7, and only grows to about 30 ft. There are many cultivars with great diversity of form and foliage color.

PLATYCODON (pla ti KOH don) **grandiflorum.** An herbaceous perennial belonging to the Campanulaceae (Bellflower Family) and commonly known as balloonflower. Showy white or blue blossoms develop from buds that resemble little balloons. The flowers, borne at the end of slender, leafy stems, are bell or star shaped, large, and rich blue in the species and white in the var. *album*. Hardy in Zones 3–9, this useful, 1–2 ft. tall

P. grandiflorum

plant is especially adapted for use in rockeries or garden borders. There are also dwarf forms, such as 'Baby Blue', and some with semidouble flowers, such as 'Hakone Double Blue'. Many gardeners consider this the most beautiful hardy plant in cultivation. It thrives best in deep, well-drained, sandy loam soil. Propagation is easily done by seed sown in early spring.

PLATYSTEMON (pla tee STE mon) **californicus.** This low, annual herb native to California is the only member of its genus belonging to the Papaveraceae (Poppy Family) and is commonly known as creamcups. Its leaves are narrow or oblong, and it bears white to pale yellow flowers 1 in. across, singly on long stems; it is sometimes grown in gardens and wildflower meadows.

PLEUROTHALLIS (ploo roh THAL is). The largest genus of new-world orchids, there are approximately 1000 species native to the tropical Americas. They are small to medium-sized epiphytic plants with erect, one-leafed stems rising from creeping rhizomes. They do not have pseudobulbs. Leaves are oval and succulent. Flowers are generally small, one to several, on a stem rising from the leaf axil. The flowers vary widely in size and shape; in some the dorsal sepal has a long tail and nearly encloses the lip. The petals are long and narrow, reflexing backward. The lip is usually cordate and sometimes fringed. Lateral sepals are often fused. Many flowers are streaked with contrasting colors, which may be yellow, crimson, white, purple, or green. They do well in baskets of porous, well-drained compost or mounted on slabs of cork or tree fern. Hardiness and temperature ranges vary, since their habitats may be tropical rain forests or cooler cloud forests, but all should be protected from cold. Most plants prefer moderate shading and high humidity and should not be allowed to dry out. The type species is *P. ruscifolius*.

PLUM. Common name for various small trees of the genus PRUNUS, cultivated for their smooth-skinned, bloom-covered fruit. Plums are divided into three general groups—European, Japanese, and American. Their diverse origin explains the widely different cultural requirements and adaptations of the different groups.

The common name "plum" often applies to other genera. Coco-plum refers to *Chrysobalanus icaco*. Date-plum is *Diospyros lotus*. Governor's-plum is *Flacourtia indica*. Hog-plum is *Spondias mombin*. Jambolan-plum is *Syzygium cumini*. Japanese-plum is *Eriobotrya japonica*. Kaffir-plum is *Harpephyllum caffrum*. Marmalade-plum is *Manilkara zapota*. Natal-plum is *Carissa grandiflora*. Pigeon-plum is *Coccoloba diversifolia*. Spanish-plum is *Spondias purpurea*.

SELECTION

The common plum, *P. domestica*, probably originated in southeast Europe. It includes most of the dessert varieties and all of the prune plums cultivated in commercial fruit-producing areas from New England to Michigan and on the Pacific Coast. As home garden fruits, many varieties can be grown farther north and others in the mountains southward to Georgia. They are less reliable in the southern and prairie states.

Since the so-called Japanese (though probably Chinese) species, *P. salicina*, was first introduced into North America in 1870, many its varieties have proved far wider adaptability to be grown farther north and south, and with greater prospect of success in the prairie states. Among them are some of excellent dessert quality.

The North American plums have originated from several species whose natural range extends from the Canadian Northwest to the Gulf states and from the Mississippi River to the Rocky Mountains. Outside of this area they should not be planted because they are of lower quality than are the dessert varieties of both European and Japanese species and because the more humid atmosphere encourages brown rot.

Besides these three groups, several other species are grown in gardens for fruit or ornament but not commercially. Among them are the apricot plum or Simon plum, *P. simonii*, popular mainly in California; the beach plum, *P. marati-*

ma, native along the Atlantic Coast to Virginia and planted in sandy soils for its flowers and rather astringent fruits used for making jam and jelly; and the Pacific Coast native plum, *P. sub-cordata*, grown for ornament and fruit.

At least two different varieties within the same family are usually necessary for good pollination in order to produce fruit. Variety selection is tricky; consult your local extension service and nurseries for recommendations as to what varieties are available and best suited to your area.

ENEMIES

Diseases. The BROWN ROT fungus is particularly destructive to plum fruits, rotting them, covering them with soft, gray spore masses, and turning them into mummies. Where possible, remove infected fruit from the tree and destroy it, and rake up all fallen fruit.

The common black knot disease, which may be destructive to both wild and cultivated plums and cherries, is hard to control. The fungus causes hard swellings covered with charcoal-black fruiting bodies on twigs, small branches, and even larger limbs. Prune off all affected twigs and branches during the winter and remove and destroy whole trees if badly infected. Black knot is nearly impossible to control with sprays.

Two common leaf diseases (leaf blight and bacterial black spot) cause brown spots, which fall out, giving a shot-hole effect. For other controls, see PEACH.

Insect Pests. The European fruit leucanium, a convex, reddish brown, soft scale, and the San José scale are best controlled with a dormant oil spray. There are several aphids that infest plums—the green apple, spinach, mealy plum, and rusty plum aphids—as well as the fruit bark beetle, the peach borer, and the plum curculio (which cuts crescent-shaped marks in the fruits).

PLUMBAGINACEAE (plum baj in AY see ee). The Leadwort Family, a group of widely distributed herbs and shrubs preferring salty soil conditions. Many species are useful outdoors in rock and border gardens or for bedding. A few are grown indoors, and some have medicinal properties. *Armeria*, *Ceratostigma*, *Limonium*, and *Plumbago* are the genera most cultivated.

PLUMBAGO (plum BAY goh). A genus of subtropical herbs and small shrubs commonly known as leadwort. Hardy only in warm climates, they are cultivated indoors in cold climates for the handsome spikes of purplish, blue, sometimes white or red, phloxlike blossoms borne on the branching tips.

Propagation is by seed, by cuttings of nearly mature wood, or by division. They thrive in a turfy soil with some sand. Old plants should be cut back in the spring to within 1 in. of the base. Young plants need pinching back several times to assure bushy growth.

P. auriculata, formerly listed as *P. capensis*, is a popular climbing species with flowers of azure blue. Cv. 'Alba' has white flowers.

P. indica is similar to *P. auriculata* but has purplish red blossoms.

PLUMERIA (ploo MEE ree ah). A genus of tropical American trees belonging to the Apocynaceae (Dogbane Family). Both the plants and perfumes derived from them are commonly known as frangipani. Popular in warm climates, the shrubs and trees have milky juice and large, waxy, fragrant, funnelform flowers. Propagation is by cuttings.

P. obtusa is a shrub or small tree that grows to 20 ft. with 7-in. oblong leaves and white flowers.

P. rubra is a tree that grows to 25 ft. and has stubby branches. Many different flower colors have been developed, some by hybridization with other species.

PLUMOSE. Featherlike, like the plumy hairs or bristles making up the modified calyx of certain asters such as thistles and blazing-star (*Liatris*).

PLUNGE. To sink a flowerpot containing a growing plant rim-deep in the soil or cinders of a greenhouse bench, coldframe, or outside ground, usually done between flowering periods.

POA (POH ah). A genus of small, mostly perennial grasses often used in lawns, commonly known as bluegrass. Hardiness varies according to the species (to Zones 2–3). Bluegrass does best in a neutral to slightly sweet (alkaline) soil in a moist, moderately cool climate, forming a thick, even turf that is self-perpetuating under favorable conditions. Irrigation may be required in hot, dry summers. Bluegrass lawns are grown from seed, sown alone, or mixed with perennial ryegrasses. Most northern sodded lawns consist of all or mostly **P. pratensis**. See LAWN.

PRINCIPAL SPECIES

P. compressa (Canada bluegrass) is coarser textured and less valuable for most lawns than its southern relative. Canada bluegrass, however, is more adaptable to varying soil and climatic conditions and, though not so highly thought of, is often used in lawn seed mixtures for low-maintenance lawns. It is a perennial but is very stemmy in its growth habit, with creeping rhizomes of a bluish green tinge; not a desirable lawn grass.

P. pratensis (bluegrass or Kentucky bluegrass), the principal species, is the standard lawn grass in temperate and northern regions. Though native to Europe and Asia, it has become naturalized in North America and is a valuable feature of some of the rich meadows and pastures of some regions of the United States, especially in

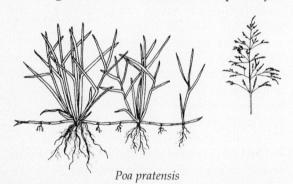

Poa pratensis

Kentucky, the state whose name it bears. It is a hardy, tufted perennial, which uncut may grow to 3 ft. in favorable locations, with leaves ½ in. wide and 6 in. long. The inflorescence or seed head is a panicle growing to 8 in.

P. trivialis (rough bluegrass) is a perennial with stems to 3½ ft. tall. The leaves are ⅛ in. wide, emerging from rough-textured sheaths. Infloresences are about 2 in. long with tiny spikelets, conspicuous nerves, and a weblike cov-

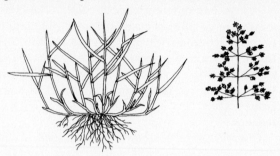

Poa trivialis

ering at the base. Native from southern Europe to western Asia and northern Africa, it is grown throughout much of North America and is often available in mixtures for meadows and pastures.

POACEAE (poh AY see ee). The Grass Family, formerly known as Gramineae, a large group of monocotyledonous plants, comprising more than 500 genera, a third of which grow in the United States.

Grasses are characterized by their long, narrow, two-ranked leaves, which clasp the stem and bear a small appendage called a ligule (or sometimes a tuft of hairs) on the stem side where the sheath flattens into the blade. The flowers, which are usually minute, are borne in spikelets, each flower consisting of two or more bracts. The lowest one or two, always empty, are called glumes; the next, containing the floret, are the lemmas; and within is a two-nerved bract called the palea. The flower has no definite perianth (calyx and corolla). There are usually three stamens, but there may be anywhere from one to six. The two styles surmount a single, one-celled ovary containing one ovule, which becomes a seed, in many cases a common grain.

One group among the ORNAMENTAL GRASSES, mostly hardy annuals grown from seed, is raised for its attractive sprays, used in both green and everlasting bouquets. Examples are the genera

Agrostis, Briza, Coix, Eragrostis, Hordeum, Lagurus, Pennisetum, and *Stipa.*

For outdoor ornamental effects, another group of tall perennials, especially the larger varieties, may figure in landscape design, creating tropical effects in the garden. They like a fairly rich soil in a protected position and are propagated in early spring by division, stolons, or offsets, and sometimes by seed. Examples are *Arrhenatherum, Arundo, Cortaderia, Elymus, Erianthus, Festuca, Gynerium, Miscanthus, Pennisetum* (*P. japonica*), *Phalaris, Setaria,* and *Uniola,* as well as the bamboos.

Lawn grasses are perennials, in many cases improved or selected strains of wild species. They are chosen for their ability to make a turf of green throughout the year, and numerous mixtures are available for various locations and purposes, such as in shade and for banks, seaside, or southern conditions. Grass seed mixtures usually contain a quick-starting but short-lived kind to serve as a nurse crop with slower-growing but more permanent kinds. Lawns are also established by planting stolons of certain kinds of grass, or squares or strips of sod. See also LAWN.

PODOCARPUS (poh doh KAHR pus). A genus of evergreen trees and shrubs, native to subtropical regions of Australia, South America, Asia, and Africa, belonging to the Podocarpaceae (Podocarpus Family). Some species are grown outdoors in the warmest regions of the United States, and occasionally under glass elsewhere, for their attractive foliage. They do well in a mixture of sandy loam and peat. Propagation is by seed or cuttings.

PRINCIPAL SPECIES

P. alpinus, from Australia, is the hardiest species and will tolerate considerable frost. It is usually a dense, rounded bush.

P. gracilior (weeping podocarpus), from Africa, grows to 70 ft. and has thin, pointed leaves to 3 in. long. It is often grown as a decorative plant in pots or tubs.

P. macrophyllus (southern-, Japanese-yew), from Japan, grows to 60 ft. and has narrow, dark green, glossy leaves in a dense spiral formation. Var. *maki,* usually shrubby, has smaller leaves.

P. totara (Totara-, mahogany-pine), from New Zealand, grows to 100 ft. but in cultivation is often a bush less than one-tenth of that height. It has small, rigid, leathery leaves of a bronzy tone.

PODOPHYLLUM (poh doh FIL um) **peltatum.** A perennial herb found in shady spots, commonly known as mayapple and sometimes called mandrake. It is conspicuous for its large, lobed, shield-shaped leaves, which die down in midsummer. In May it produces waxy, white, cuplike flowers with a disagreeable scent that hang from the fork of the stems. These are followed by lemonshaped fruits called

Podophyllum peltatum

the apples, which have an insipid, sweetish taste. The mayapple grows prolifically in many parts of the eastern states and makes an excellent ground cover on open, sandy banks or under trees in partial shade. Hardy to Zone 5, it thrives in rich, moist soil and is easily propagated by seed or division.

POGONIA (poh GOH nee ah) **ophioglossoides.** A small terrestrial orchid native to temperate zones of Asia and to North America, commonly known by many common names, including rose pogonia and snake-mouth. It has a single dainty, pale rose or white, fragrant flower 1 in. long with oval sepals and petals and a pale pink lip, veined with rose and crested with yellow-brown hairs. It should be grown in bog gardens in strongly acid soil or in sphagnum moss.

POINCIANA. Former botanical name for the genus CAESALPINIA of prickly tropical shrubs. As a common name, royal-poinciana refers to *Delonix regia;* see DELONIX.

POINSETTIA. Common name for *Euphorbia pulcherrima*, a tropical herb commonly sold at Christmas time; see EUPHORBIA.

POISON-BULB. A common name for *Crinum asiaticum*, a bulbous plant with fragrant, white flowers; see CRINUM.

POISON-HEMLOCK. Common name for *Conium maculatum*, a poisonous herb of the Apiaceae (Celery Family); see CONIUM.

POISON-IVY. Common name, frequently used interchangeably with poison-oak, for three species of RHUS, deciduous or evergreen shrubs or vines belonging to the Anacardiaceae (Cashew Family), notorious for their toxic effects upon contact with the skin. All three are attractive but widespread pests throughout the United States, growing in meadows, along roads, scrambling over fences, and frequently creeping into the garden, where it is a real menace. Hardy to Zone 3.

SPECIES

Rhus diversiloba (Pacific poison-oak) is a shrub that grows to 8 ft., or sometimes climbs. Its leaves have three toothed or lobed leaflets up to 3 in. long, smooth on both sides. The flowers are greenish in axillary panicles, followed by whitish fruit. It is native from British Columbia to Baja California.

Rhus radicans (poison-ivy) is sometimes a shrub, rarely a tree, and most often a vine climbing high by means of aerial roots on tree trunks. Common in shaded woodlands, along roadsides, or scrambling over rocks and fences throughout North America, this is a beautiful vine, the foliage taking on red and orange hues in the fall. It is distinguished by leaves of three somewhat oval, pointed leaflets, glossy above and slightly hairy beneath. The small, greenish flowers, in loose clusters, are followed by small, grayish, round fruits, which remain on the plant during the winter. It is sometimes mistaken for the harmless *Parthenocissus quinquefolia* (Virginia creeper), which can easily be distinguished by its five-part leaves, compared to the three-lobed leaflets of poison-ivy.

Rhus toxicodendron (poison-oak) is a shrub that grows to 6 ft. and has leaves of three-lobed or rounded leaflets, hairy on both sides; panicles of greenish flowers; and whitish fruits usually covered with soft hair. It is generally found in the eastern United States during the summer and is frequently confused with *R. radicans*.

SYMPTOMS AND REMEDIES

All three species have the same toxic qualities. Many people are susceptible to the poisonous oil called toxicodendrol, contained in the leaves, bark, roots, and fruit. In those not immune, it causes rashes, extreme itching and burning of the skin, swelling, and often a feeling of extreme lassitude. Severe cases can incapacitate the victim, and fatal consequences are not unknown.

Different authorities recommend different remedies, but severe cases should be treated by a physician. The rash can be avoided if the toxic oil can be removed from the skin soon after contact. As soon as possible after exposure, thoroughly wash hands and all exposed skin with a strongly alkaline soap, such as a yellow laundry soap. Make a profuse lather, apply with a soft brush or cloth, and rinse well, repeating the process three or four times, taking care not to break the skin. Then dab the skin with cotton soaked with equal parts of grain alcohol and water. Repeat this several times, using fresh cotton each time. Never use poisonous wood alcohol.

ERADICATION

Poison-ivy can be killed by spraying or otherwise treating the plants with a solution of 3 lb. common salt to 1 gal. water over an area 3 yards square. Large plants can be killed by cutting the vines at or below ground level and saturating the bases with brine, giving a second application after two weeks. Sheep and goats will eat the plants and can be fenced in to clear areas of poison-ivy. Never burn the plants; the fumes are as toxic as touching the plant and worse if inhaled. Chemical herbicides can be useful; consult your local extension service for recommendations.

POISONOUS PLANTS. Plants with poisonous qualities can be divided into two groups: those causing irritation to the skin when touched and those that are toxic when eaten. There are several popular garden subjects that are poisonous if eaten. Many other plants can be considered toxic or irritating to especially sensitive individuals.

No plant should ever be ingested until it has been positively identified as edible. Different parts of plants that produce edible crops may prove toxic, such as the leaves of rhubarb or wild cherry. Even edible plants at the wrong stage of development can be toxic; many plant parts are edible when mature and poisonous when green, or edible when green and toxic when mature. Some plants may be toxic when raw but edible if cooked. In any case, it is always best to be sure of a plant's edible or poisonous nature.

The most common plants that cause skin rashes and irritation belong to the genus **Rhus**, including POISON-IVY, poison-oak, and poison sumac. There are several others, including some garden subjects, which have similar toxic properties. Severe reactions should always be treated by a physician. Many types of MUSHROOM are rightly feared for their toxic qualities.

There are also many popular garden subjects with toxic qualities. The accompanying chart includes many common garden plants and describes which parts are toxic on contact or poisonous if eaten. This list is not necessarily complete; do not assume a plant is edible if it is not listed here. Contact experienced growers or your local extension service for further information.

POISONOUS PLANTS

LATIN NAME (common name)	POISONOUS PARTS	TOXIC ON CONTACT	TOXIC IF EATEN	COMMENTS
Aconitum spp. (monkshood)	leaves, roots		x	Known to be fatal, even in small quantities
Actaea spp. (baneberry)	all		x	Parts are toxic, berries and roots known to be fatal
Aesculus spp. (horsechestnut, buckeye)	nuts		x	Known to be fatal
Agrostemma githago (corncockle)	all		x	
Amianthium muscaetoxicum (fly-poison)	all	x	x	Highly toxic if touched or eaten
Anagallis arvensis (scarlet pimpernel)	all		x	
Anthemis cotula (mayweed, dog-fennel)	leaves	x		Skin irritant, common weed in grain fields
Argemone mexicana (prickly poppy)	all		x	
Arisaema triphylla (jack-in-the-pulpit)	root	x	x	Root is an irritant and astringent
Arnica spp. (arnica).	all		x	
Asclepias tuberosa (butterfly weed)	stems, leaves, roots		x	
Baptisia tinctoria (wild indigo)	leaves, shoots		x	Known to be toxic

LATIN NAME (common name)	POISONOUS PARTS	TOXIC ON CONTACT	TOXIC IF EATEN	COMMENTS
Buxus sempervirens (boxwood)	all		x	
Calla palustris (wild calla)	all		x	Toxic if eaten raw
Caltha palustris (marsh-marigold)	all		x	Toxic if eaten raw
Campsis radicans (trumpet creeper)	all	x		Irritating in varying degrees to many people
Caulophyllum thalictroides (blue cohosh)	all		x	
Cestrum spp. (jessamine)	all		x	
Chamaelirium luteum (devil's-bit)	all		x	
Chelidonium majus (celandine)	all		x	
Chenopodium ambrosioides (Mexican-tea)	leaves		x	Dried leaves have been used in teas but are toxic if eaten raw
Chenopodium botrys (Jerusalem-oak)	leaves		x	
Ciccuta maculata (water-hemlock)	all, especially roots		x	Known to be fatal
Clematis spp. (clematis)	all		x	
Conium maculatum (poison-hemlock)	seeds, leaves, roots		x	Known to be fatal, even in small amounts
Convallaria majalis (lily-of-the-valley)	berries		x	
Cornus spp. (dogwood)	fruit		x	Slightly poisonous
Crotalaria sagittalis (rattlebox)	raw seeds		x	
Cypripedium spp. (lady's-slipper, moccasin flower)	all	x		Irritating in varying degrees to many people
Cytisus scoparius (Scotch broom)	raw seedpods		x	
Daphne mexreum (daphne)	all		x	
Datura stramomium (jimsonweed)	all		x	Known to be fatal
Delphinium spp. (larkspur)	seeds, foliage, roots		x	Known to be fatal if eaten in sufficient quantity
Dicentra spp. (dicentra)	all		x	
Digitalis purpurea (foxglove)	leaves		x	
Equisetum spp. (horsetail)	all		x	

LATIN NAME (common name)	POISONOUS PARTS	TOXIC ON CONTACT	TOXIC IF EATEN	COMMENTS
Eupatorium rugosum (white snakeroot)	all		x	Known to be fatal
Euphorbia spp. (spurge)	all	x	x	All parts toxic if eaten; juice of some species may irritate skin
Gelsemium sempervirens (yellow jessamine)	all		x	Known to be fatal
Gymnocladus dioica (Kentucky coffee tree)	raw seeds, fruit pulp		x	
Hedera helix (English ivy)	berries		x	
Helleborus niger (Christmas-rose)	all, especially leaves		x	
Heracleum lanatum (cow-parsnip)	whole plant	x	x	Tall plant found in wet areas; causes rash, effects similar to poison-ivy
Hydrangea spp. (hydrangea)	all		x	
Hydrastis canadensis (golden-seal)	all		x	
Ilex spp. (holly)	leaves, berries	x		
Iris spp. (blue flag)	all, especially roots		x	
Kalmia spp. (mountain-laurel, lambkill)	leaves, shoots		x	Known to be fatal; especially dangerous to children
Lantana camara (lantana)	all		x	Known to be fatal
Lathyrus spp. (sweet pea)	seeds		x	
Ligustrum vulgare (privet)	all		x	
Lobelia spp. (lobelia)	all		x	
Lupinus spp. (lupine)	seeds		x	
Melia azedarach (chinaberry)	all		x	
Menispermum canadensis (Canada moonseed)	fruit		x	Resembles wild grape, but fruit is known to be fatal if eaten in sufficient quantity
Mirabilis spp. (four-o'clock)	all		x	
Momordica charantia (balsam-apple)	all		x	
Morus spp. (mulberries)	unripe fruit, raw shoots		x	

LATIN NAME (common name)	POISONOUS PARTS	TOXIC ON CONTACT	TOXIC IF EATEN	COMMENTS
Narcissus spp. (daffodil)	juice	x		Juice may irritate skin when plants are handled
Nerium oleander (oleander)	leaves		x	
Ornithogalum umellatum (star-of-Bethlehem)	bulbs, leaves		x	
Orontium aquaticum (golden-club)	rootstocks, seeds		x	
Parthenocissus quinquefolia (Virginia creeper)	berries		x	May be fatal if eaten in sufficient quantity
Peltandra spp. (arrow arum)	all		x	Toxic if eaten raw
Phoradendron flavescens (mistletoe)	all		x	Known to be fatal
Physalis spp. (ground-cherry)	leaves, unripe fruit		x	
Phytolacca americana (pokeweed)	root, seeds, leaves, mature stems		x	Known to be fatal.
Podophyllum peltatum (may-apple)	roots, leaves, seeds, green fruit		x	
Primula spp. (primrose)	whole plant	x	x	Several species cause rashes; effects similar to poison-ivy
Prunus spp. (wild black cherry)	withered leaves, raw seeds		x	Quite poisonous and known to be fatal
Ranunculus spp. (buttercups)	all		x	
Rhamnus spp. (buckthorn)	leaves, fruit		x	
Rheum rhaponticum (rhubarb)	leaves		x	Leaves are toxic, but stems are edible
Rhododendron spp. (azalea, rhododendron)	all		x	Known to be fatal
Ricinus communis (castor-bean)	fruit		x	Known to be fatal
Robinia pseudoacacia (black-locust)	roots, bark, leaves, seeds		x	Sometimes known to be fatal
Sambucus spp. (elderberry)	all		x	Ripe berries are edible, but stems, leaves, and unripe berries can be toxic
Sanguinaria canadensis (bloodroot)	all		x	
Saponaria officinalis (bouncing-bet)	all		x	
Solanum spp. (nightshade)	varies with species			Some species are highly toxic even though related to edible plants, including the common potato and eggplant

LATIN NAME (common name)	POISONOUS PARTS	TOXIC ON CONTACT	TOXIC IF EATEN	COMMENTS
Solanum carolinense (horse-nettle)	all		x	
Solanum dulcamara (bittersweet)	berries		x	Sometimes fatal
Solanum nigrum (deadly nightshade)	berries		x	Fruit is very poisonous, especially when green
Symplocarpus foetidus (skunk-cabbage)	raw leaves		x	
Tanacetum vulgare (common tansy)	all		x	Known to be fatal if eaten in sufficient quantity
Urtica dioica (stinging nettle)	leaves	x		Skin irritant; effects seldom last long
Veratrum spp. (false hellebore)	all		x	All parts poisonous; root known to be fatal
Wisteria spp. (wisteria)	seeds		x	Highly toxic, even in small quantities
Zephyranthes atamasco (atamasco-lily)	leaves and bulbs		x	
Zygadenus venenosus (death-camas)	all		x	All parts poisonous; root fatal

POISON SUMAC. Common name for *Rhus vernix*, a tree or shrub found in damp, marshy ground; it is toxic when touched. See RHUS; POISON-IVY.

POKEBERRY. Common name for PHYTOLACCA, a genus of woody or herbaceous plants with small flowers in terminal clusters followed by fleshy berries; also known as pokeweed.

POKERPLANT. Common name for KNIPHOFIA, a genus of red and yellow flowering plants of the Liliaceae (Lily Family).

POLEMONIACEAE (poh le moh nee AY see ee). The Phlox Family, a group of occasionally woody, widely distributed herbs principally native to North America. It supplies many flower-garden ornamentals and subjects for greenhouse culture, principally from the genera *Cantua*, *Cobaea*, *Collomia*, *Gilia*, *Phlox*, and *Polemonium*.

POLEMONIUM (poh le MOH nee um). A small genus of tall or dwarf, hardy perennials or, rarely, annuals belonging to the Polemoniaceae (Phlox Family) and commonly known as Jacob's-ladder. The blue, violet, or white flowers are showy, and the finely cut foliage resembles fern fronds. Plants are easily cultivated in any ordinary, good garden soil, but they flourish best in a deep, rich, and well-drained loamy soil. The low-growing forms fit well in the rock garden, while taller ones are better suited for backgrounds in the flower garden. They can be grown from seed or propagated by division of the roots. Most are hardy in Zones 3–7.

Polemonium boreale

PRINCIPAL SPECIES

P. boreale, also listed as *P. richardsonii*, is a dwarf species that grows 6–9 in. high and has 15–21 leaflets and many leafy, downy stems and a faint odor of musk. Var. *pulchellum* has smaller flowers of violet or white.

P. caeruleum (Jacob's-ladder, charity, Greek-valerian) is a perennial that grows 2–3 ft. high and has feather-shaped leaves and narrow, egg-shaped, sometimes variegated leaflets. Drooping flower clusters are bright blue with yellow stamens. Cv. 'Album' bears white flowers, and 'Blue Pearl' has lilac-blue ones.

P. reptans (creeping-Jacob's-ladder) grows to 12 in. and has narrow leaves of 7–11 sharp-pointed, egg-shaped leaflets. Stems are leafy and smooth, and the roots are creeping. Light blue, sometimes white, drooping flowers are borne in loose clusters. It is a good choice for the front of the border or in rock gardens.

P. viscosum (skunk-weed, sticky polemonium), also listed as *P. confertum*, is an attractive plant native to the southern Rocky Mountains; it grows to about 4 ft. and has ill-scented, sticky, downy leaves of 30 to 40

Polemonium viscosum

leaflets about ⅕ in. long. Blue or violet flowers are about ¾ in. long with tubes longer than the corollas.

POLIANTHES (pah lee AN theez). A genus of tuberous herbs from Mexico, belonging to the Agavaceae (Agave Family), and bearing racemes or spikes of intensely fragrant flowers.

There are about twelve species, the most important in horticulture being *P. tuberosa* (tuberose), which is grown as a houseplant and widely as a commercial cut flower. It forms a fleshy, bulblike rootstock or tuber. The top part of this stock is covered with the broadened bases of the old leaves. From its short, rosettelike growth of spear-shaped, grasslike foliage arises a solitary flower stalk, which in summer and autumn bears many waxy, white, funnel-shaped, usually double flowers. Tuberoses are one of the few so-called bulbous stocks that are commercially produced almost exclusively in the United States.

POLLARD. To cut a tree back to its crown or trunk, or to cut out the main central branch, in order to induce the luxuriant growth of new shoots. Only certain species respond satisfactorily. In North America, willow trees are perhaps the most familiar subjects, the resulting shoots—called osiers, withes, or wickers—being used in making furniture, baskets, and other wickerwork. The olive is handled similarly, old trees being thus renewed.

POLLEN. This dusty substance, seen in many opening flowers and inconspicuous in others, consists of the male sex cells of flowering plants. Developed in the anthers that surmount the stamens of a flower, pollen grains exhibit great diversity in size, character, and design so that many species can be identified by their distinctive pollen grains when these are studied under a microscope. They are variously adapted to conveyance by the wind, insects, birds, or mammals, depending on the species.

POLLINATION. The transfer of pollen from the anther of one flower to the stigma of another. Accomplished in nature by wind, insects, birds, or mammals, it can be brought about by plant breeders or home gardeners through artificial means, in which case the process is called hand pollination or artificial pollination. Although pollination is one of the steps in the process of reproduction by seed, FERTILIZATION is also necessary. The two terms are often confused but should be sharply distinguished, for fertilization does not always follow pollination. For the explanation of cross-pollination, self-pollination, and other terms, see FLOWER, PLANT BREEDING.

Plants exhibit many wonderful adaptations and mechanisms developed for the purpose of aiding pollination. Many species are entirely dependent upon bees and other insects for the transfer of their pollen and, hence, for the perpetuation of their kind. This is especially true of those forms with imperfect flowers or that are self-sterile. Some plants, especially in tropical regions, have flowers pollinated by bats, while hummingbirds pollinate many species that have red, pendent flowers. Others depend upon the wind for pollination; wind-borne pollen will sometimes float for hundreds of miles on the wind currents of the upper atmosphere. Pollen from species normally insect-pollinated is generally not adapted to flying in the wind and often possesses special features that aid insects. Flower colors, odors, and nectar of blossoms are considered adaptations for the purpose of attracting pollinators and aiding cross-pollination.

See also FERTILIZATION; FLOWER.

POLYGALA (poh LIG ah lah). A genus of ornamental annual and perennial herbs and shrubs widely distributed through temperate and warmer regions, including the principal members of the Polygalaceae (Milkwort Family), and commonly known as milkwort. They comprise the principal cultivated members of the Polygalaceae (Milkwort Family), with irregular flowers somewhat similar to orchids. Some of the shrubby, tender species are grown indoors or outdoors in very warm regions. The hardy native species do well in light soil and partial shade. Propagation is by seed and cuttings.

PRINCIPAL SPECIES

P. chamaebuxus is a creeping evergreen shrub with yellow flowers, native to Europe and hardy to Zone 6. Var. *grandiflora* has yellow flowers with purple wings.

P. x *dalmaisiana* is a free-blooming, bushy plant with rosy purple flowers, hardy only to Zone 9 and sometimes grown indoors.

P. paucifolia (fringed polygala, flowering-wintergreen) is a pretty, trailing perennial with light rosy purple flowers, native and hardy to Zone 4.

POLYGONACEAE (pah li goh NAY see ee). The Buckwheat or Knotweed Family, a group of erect or climbing herbs, shrubs, and trees widely distributed in both warm and cold climates. Species of several genera are cultivated for ornament and a few for food; among these are *Antigonon*, *Coccoloba*, *Muehlenbeckia*, *Polygonum*, *Rheum* (rhubarb), and *Rumex*.

POLYGONATUM (poh lee GAHN ah tum). A genus of perennial herbs with greenish pendulous flowers, belonging to the Liliaceae (Lily Family), and commonly known as Solomon's-seal. They have creeping roots on which each year's growth scars show prominently. From the roots rise leafy, arching, graceful stems with small, white or greenish, bell-shaped flowers hanging from the leaf axils; these are followed by handsome, blue or black fruits. Plants should be grouped in humus-rich soil in a shady part of the wild garden or among ferns at the north side of the house. They are easily propagated by seed or division.

Polygonatum biflorum

PRINCIPAL SPECIES

P. biflorum grows up to 4 ft. and has relatively few flowers in each cluster; it is the species most commonly seen in the wild.

P. commutatum, growing to 8 ft., makes outstanding groups.

P. latifolium and *P. multiflorum* are European natives.

POLYGONUM (poh LIG oh num). A large genus of annual or perennial herbs and undershrubs found throughout the world but rare in the tropics. They belong to the Poligonaceae (Buckwheat Family) and are known by various common names, including knotweed, smartweed, and fleeceflower. Several species are worth growing for their climbing habit and fragrant flowers. Leaves of most species are typically large; the flowers are minute but often massed in showy spikes or clusters.

The desirable species are easily cultured in any ordinary, good garden soil. Annuals can be grown from seed sown in the open in spring, while perennials are generally propagated by division.

PRINCIPAL SPECIES

P. affine (Himalayan fleeceflower), growing 12–18 in., is a fast-growing and hardy (to Zone 3) perennial that will tolerate a wide range of conditions. It has red flowers on 2–3 in. spikes from August through October. Since it can be invasive, it is best relegated to marginal areas.

P. amplexicaule (mountain-fleece) is a perennial that grows to 3 ft. and has heart- to egg-shaped leaves up to 6 in. long and stems to 2–3 ft. The flowers are bright rose-red or white, single or in clusters 2–6 in. long, borne in the autumn.

P. aubertii (China fleecevine, silver lacevine, fleeceflower), a well-known perennial, is a fast-growing climber to 25 ft. and has twining, woody stems and a wealth of foamy, greenish white, fragrant flowers borne in long clusters in late summer. It has been found hardy as far north as Zone 5 and appears to be entirely free from plant diseases.

P. aviculare (knotweed, knotgrass) is a troublesome weedy herb with close-set spikes of minute flowers, but it is sometimes used in wildflower gardens and natural plantings.

Polygonum aviculare

P. baldschuanicum (fleeceflower) is a perennial similar to **P. aubertii** but has pink flowers and is better suited to the western and southern states.

P. bistorta (snakeweed) var. **superbum** is a perennial that grows 3 ft. high in sun to partial shade and is hardy to Zone 3. It produces pink flowers borne on spikes from late spring through midsummer.

P. capitatum (pinkhead knotweed), growing to 6 in., is an evergreen perennial that is native to the Himalayas and hardy to Zone 6. It has pink flowers and a low, trailing habit that makes it suitable for ground cover in warmer regions. It will grow in sun or shade and can be invasive.

Polygonum bistorta

P. multiflorum is a Japanese climbing perennial with tuberous roots; it is evergreen in mild climates and has greenish white flowers in slender clusters.

P. orientale (prince's-feather) is an annual that produces fine plants if raised in slight heat and given rich soil.

P. persicaria (lady's-thumb) is an annual with 2-in. spikes of pink or purplish flowers.

P. polygaloides is a dwarf western annual with white or pink flowers.

P. sachaliense (sacaline) is a coarse, rampant, perennial vine that must be used, if at all, with discretion.

POLYPLOID. A term given to the condition that exists when a plant (or animal) has a greater number of sets of chromosomes than are normally found in an individual of that species or variety. Starting with any family or genus, the species having the lowest number of chromosome sets would be considered a diploid, that is, having one set of chromosomes from each parent. If that same species has a variety with chromosome sets in any multiple of that lowest number (twice, three times, four times as many, etc.), that variety would be considered a polyploid. Since the number of chromosomes is an influential factor in their ability to combine and pair off during the process of reproduction, a polyploid may have, or be able to transmit, qualities that a hybrid offspring of diploid parents cannot possess or pass on. Thus, a hybrid normally unable to reproduce at all, if a polyploid, might be able to do so.

All this would be of little practical interest to gardeners were it not that plant breeders have found ways to create polyploids, such as by treating plants with the drug COLCHICINE. The marigold variety 'Tetra', much larger than the type from which it was developed, was introduced as a polyploid that resulted from such treatment.

POLYPODIACEAE (pah li poh dee AY see ee). The Fern Family, which embraces three-fourths of the fern world. The members are mostly low plants of varying habits, without distinct trunks and growing mostly from prostrate rhizomes. The fronds or leaflike parts are usually feather-formed, always bearing tiny spore cases on the underside (when fertile). By this latter characteristic, they are distinguished from the so-called flowering ferns, grape ferns, and other fern allies. The Polypodiaceae is sometimes known as the True Fern Family. It includes most of the cultivated FERNS.

POLYPODIUM (pah li POH dee um). A large genus of ferns with creeping, forking rhizomes. They are usually epiphytic and mostly tropical. The fronds are united to the rhizomes at a pronounced joint. The blades may be simple or pinnate, infrequently more divided. The sori are large and circular, without indusia, in one or more rows halfway between midvein and margin. The species vary greatly in size.

PRINCIPAL SPECIES

P. aureum (golden polypody, rabbit's-foot fern), also listed as *Phlebodium aureum*, is a vigorous and bold species for warm conditions. The broad, 3–4 ft. long, pinnatifid fronds have a curious shape, the terminal segment being very long, and the rachis, winged. The abundant, raised, golden-yellow sori give the plant one of its common names. It needs plenty of water and occasional dilute fertilizer when actively growing. It can be grown in the garden in warm areas and makes an excellent, if somewhat large, potted plant. There are several cultivars, including 'Mandaianum', 'Cristatum', 'Leatherman', and 'Ekstrand', with strikingly ruffled, blue-green fronds. It is common in peninsular Florida and is also found in most of tropical America.

P. australe (southern polypody) can be grown in the temperate garden under the usual fern conditions with the addition of grit to ensure excellent drainage. It is also excellent for basket or pot culture. It is often confused with *P. vulgare* but has narrower, rougher-textured fronds. Native to Europe and the nearby Atlantic islands, it is successful in the warmer temperate regions. There are several cultivars, including 'Cambricum', 'Barrowii', 'Oakley', and 'Semilacerum'.

P. fauriei is very similar to *P. formosanum* but has a more slender, scaly rhizome.

P. formosanum (caterpillar fern) is a most unusual and attractive basket fern with glaucous, wormlike rhizomes and pinnatifid fronds that can hang 1–2 ft. It needs a coarse epiphytic mix, moisture, and a well-ventilated spot. Native to Japan, Taiwan, and southern China, it is hardy in warm temperate and subtropical regions. There is one cultivar, 'Cristatum', which is not really crested but gives that effect due to the emergence of several fronds from a single point on the rhizome.

P. glycyrrhiza (licorice fern) is a small (4–16 in.), pinnatifid fern whose rhizomes taste of licorice. Native from Alaska to California, it is difficult but suitable for culture in temperate to subtropic regions; it needs a sheltered spot in the garden.

P. x *interjectum*, a European species, is a stable hybrid between *P. australe* and *P. vulgare*. It is similar to both its parents and grows in similar conditions but will tolerate more moisture.

P. loriceum is often confused with *P. formosanum* but differs in having dark green, curling rhizomes and larger, more erect fronds. It is from Central and South America, Mexico, and the West Indies.

P. lycopodioides, also listed as **Microgramma lycopodioides**, is a small fern that grows 2–8 in. and has entire, slender fronds and spreading rhizomes covered with light scales. It is epiphytic and excellent for hanging baskets. Native to Central and South America, Mexico, and the West Indies, it needs warm, moist conditions.

P. phyllitidis (strap fern) is a good plant for the greenhouse, with long, leathery, shining fronds and running stems. Grow in shallow pots, using plenty of peat or half-decayed leaf mold, and water generously but provide good drainage.

P. piloselloides, also listed as **Microgramma piloselloides**, is a tiny plant, growing only 2–3 in., with entire, 1–3 in. sterile fronds and longer, narrower fertile fronds, sometimes with toothed margins. The fronds have an obvious short stalk and are closely spaced on wiry, creeping rhizomes. It needs high humidity and can be grown in a pot or basket filled with epiphytic medium.

P. polypodioides (resurrection fern) is a small fern that grows 2–4 in. It copes with drought by curling its fronds to reduce water loss and expands again when moisture becomes available. It is similar to *P. virginianum* but is smaller and not hardy. It is epiphytic, often growing on tree trunks in North, Central, and South America.

P. sanctae-rosae is an interesting 1–2 ft. pinnatifid fern with buff-colored scales covering the surfaces of erect fronds. Native to Mexico and Central America, it is epiphytic and requires a coarse mixture and a bright, warm, airy, humid location.

P. scouleri (leather polypody) is a small fern similar to *P. virginianum* but has broader fronds and fewer, broader pinnae. It is found near the shore on rocks and trees along the West Coast of the United States.

P. subauriculatum, also listed as *Goniophlebium subauriculatum*, is an epiphytic fern that makes an outstanding basket plant where there is sufficient space for weeping fronds that can be 4–8 ft. long. Cv. 'Knightiae' is the form usually grown. It needs a warm, humid but airy environment. Native to northern India, China, New Zealand, and Australia, it can be grown outdoors in tropical regions.

P. thyssanolepis (scaly polypody) is a 2–20 in. high fern with deeply lobed, leathery fronds whose undersides are covered with pale scales. Its rhizomes are thin and much branched. Common from Arizona and Texas to South America, it is a good basket plant in an epiphytic mix.

P. vacciniifolium, also listed as *Microgramma vacciniifolia*, is a small fern that grows 2–4 in. with creeping rhizomes bearing widely spaced, almost stemless entire fronds less than 2 in. long. The rhizomes are covered with white scales. It is very similar to *P. piloselloides* but has smaller, rounder sterile fronds and is slower growing. Native to South America, it is a good basket plant requiring warmth and high humidity.

P. virginianum (common polypody, rockcap fern) is common in much of North America except the far South and West, growing on boulders, cliffs, and decaying logs. Its dark green, pinnatifid fronds are 5–10 in. long with pinnae joined along their blades. It is evergreen and fine for filling in spaces in the shaded rock garden. It transplants readily, but should be cut carefully from the tangled mats in which it grows.

P. vulgare (common polypody) is very similar to *P. virginianum*, but its fronds are longer and wider, and its rhizome tastes sweet. It is found in Africa, China, Japan, and Europe, but like its North American twin, it inhabits rocks and walls, and its garden culture is the same. It is excellent in the well-drained rock garden and is common in European gardens as a ground cover under shrubs. There are many attractive cultivars, including 'Bifidum', 'Cornubiense', 'Trichomanoides', and 'Cristatum'.

POLYPODY. Common name for many species of the fern genus POLYPODIUM that grow on rocks and logs.

POLYSCIAS (poh LIS ee ahs). A genus of tropical shrubs or trees that make attractive foliage plants for the greenhouse. They grow well in a mixture of fibrous loam, leaf mold, and a little old manure, with sand and charcoal to make it porous. Propagation is by cuttings of the leafy tops, or by heel cuttings from an old plant. Almost any size piece will root, provided that the medium is not kept too wet.

PRINCIPAL SPECIES

P. crispata (chicken-gizzard) takes its common name from the leaf shape and may grow in green and variegated forms.

P. filicifolia (fernleaf) has very dissected leaves.

P. fruticosa (Ming aralia) and var. *crispa* (parsley aralia) have very finely divided leaves.

P. guilfoylei (roseleaf) shows much variety in the degree to which the leaves are cut, green, and variegated, including the very dark green 'Black Aralia'.

P. pinnata (Balfour, dinnerplate) has large, round leaflets.

POLYSTICHUM (poh
LIS ti kum). A genus of small to medium-sized terrestrial ferns that are crown-forming with an ascending rhizome. The fronds are narrow or broad, usually pinnate or bipinnate, and frequently toothed. The sori are covered by an umbrella-shaped indusium.

Polystichum sp.

PRINCIPAL SPECIES

P. acrostichoides (Christmas fern) is one of the most familiar and handsome, North American ferns, with narrow, 1–2 ft., pinnate, evergreen fronds. The sori are distributed thickly on the upper third of the blade. The pinnae are auricled and show some variation, usually near summer's end. It is abundant in moist woods in eastern North America.

P. aculeatum (hard shield fern) is a strong-growing plant that attains 3 ft. in a good environment, thriving in moist woodland conditions with a little lime in the soil. The fronds are pin-

nate to bipinnate and of a firm texture, thus the common name. There is a theory that it may be a hybrid between *P. lonchitis* and *P. setiferum*. Var. *pulcherimum* is considered one of the most beautiful British ferns, found in northern England, Scotland, and rarely Ireland.

P. andersonii (Anderson's holly fern) is an attractive fern that grows 1–4 ft. and has pinnate-pinnatifid to bipinnate fronds. There is a proliferous bud near the tip of each hollylike frond. It is frequently found in northwestern North America, growing on cool, moist, rocky slopes and in wet woodlands. It is easily cultivated in similar garden situations.

P. braunii (Braun's holly fern) is a very hardy, beautiful bipinnate fern that grows 1–4 ft. and thrives in rich, acid soil and a shady location. It is common in northern regions of North America and is found in Europe, Japan, and China.

P. x *californicum* (California holly fern) has tall, 2½-ft., pinnate-pinnatifid fronds about 8 in. wide. It is a usually fertile hybrid between *P. munitum* and *P. dudleyi* and is found growing from California to Washington.

P. cystostegia (mountain shield fern), native to New Zealand, is a little, bipinnate fern, growing 4–10 in. high. Generally found in high alpine scrubland, it is very hardy and ideal for rock garden use.

P. dudleyi (Dudley's holly fern, Dudley's shield fern) is a bipinnate fern that grows to 3 ft. and is found in moist California woods.

P. lonchitis (mountain holly fern) is a pinnate fern with narrow, bristly fronds ranging from 6–24 in. high. It is found in moist, shaded rock crevices on high mountains and is common in northern and western North America, Asia, and Europe.

P. munitum (giant holly fern, western sword fern) is a tall, pinnate fern that grows 2–6 ft. and resembles *P. acrostichoides*. It does well in the garden and is quite cold tolerant. It is abundant in northwestern North America.

P. polyblepharum is a tall, pretty fern that grows 2–4 ft. and has a rosette of shiny, dark green fronds. New fronds are intriguingly scaly.

It likes rich, organic, acid soil and is native to China, Japan, and Korea.

P. x *scopulinum* (western holly fern, Eaton's shield fern) is a fertile hybrid between *P. lemmonii* and *P. munitum* and has pinnate fronds about 12 in. tall and 2½ in. wide. It makes a nice rock garden plant and is native from Washington to Idaho, Utah, and California.

P. setiferum (soft shield fern) is a moderately robust, bipinnate fern that grows 2–5 ft. and is popular in temperate gardens around the world. It grows in a rosette of arching, dissected fronds that are semievergreen. Many plantlets are produced along the rachis, from which new plants start, frequently forming whole colonies when conditions are right. It likes woodland conditions in the garden but can take a bit more sun than most woodland ferns. It is often confused with *P. aculeatum* but is larger and more vigorous.

P. tsus-simense is a small, bipinnate fern that grows 12–18 in. and has narrow, triangular fronds with a firm, leathery texture. Native to China, Korea, and Japan, it can be used in the rock garden in the warmer temperate zones. Indoors it is suitable for basket or pot culture.

POLYTRICHUM (pah li TRIK um) **communis.** An evergreen moss, commonly known as haircap moss. It makes an attractive ground cover with a starlike whorled form. Its resistance to drought and direct sunlight make it relatively unique among the mosses, which normally prefer moist shaded locations.

POMADERRIS (poh mah DER is). A genus of trees and shrubs from Australia and New Zealand, belonging to the Rhamnaceae (Buckthorn Family). One or two species are grown for ornament in Zones 10–11. Propagation is by cuttings of half-ripened shoots.

P. apetala (Victorian-hazel) grows to about 20 ft. and has leaves that are white beneath and long clusters of greenish white flowers without petals.

P. elliptica grows to 8 ft. and has leaves with white undersides and clusters of bright yellow flowers.

POME. A fleshy fruit composed of several parts (carpels) naturally grown together, containing a parchmentlike inner layer (endocarp), which contains the seeds. Typical examples are the apple, pear, and quince. Compare BERRY; DRUPE; FRUIT.

POMEGRANATE. Common name for the fruits of a large, subtropical bush, *Punica granatum*. It is grown for its brilliant orange-red flowers, and commercially, for its large, juicy, pulpy fruits about the size of oranges, with many seeds enclosed in a leathery rind. There is a dwarf form, var. *nana*, suitable for greenhouse culture and small gardens. Other varieties have white, red, variegated, and double, striped flowers.

In the Gulf states and other warm areas, the pomegranate is a popular garden subject and is grown commercially in deep, heavy loams. In orchards, bushes are set about 15 ft. apart; for hedges, they are set 6–8 ft. apart. They are propagated by seed and layering but chiefly by hardwood cuttings taken in spring.

PONCIRUS (pawn SI rus) **trifoliata.** A small, spiny, deciduous tree native to China, belonging to the Rutaceae (Rue Family), and commonly known as hardy- or trifoliate-orange. It is used as propagating stock to make citrus more hardy, but the fruit is bitter and inedible. In warm regions, it is also used for ornamental planting, and long, sharp spines make hedges of it impenetrable. The fragrant, white flowers are followed by small, very aromatic, very acid, lemonlike fruits. Hardy in Zones 6–9.

PONDWEED. Common name for POTAMOGETON, a genus of aquatic herbs found more often in the wild than in cultivation. Cape-pondweed (*Aponogeton distachys*) is another aquatic plant frequently cultivated for its attractive, fragrant flowers; see APONOGETON.

PONTEDERIA (pahn te DEE ree ah) **cordata.** An aquatic herb found in shallow waters of eastern North America, commonly known as pickerelweed. It has large, arrow-shaped leaves borne on long stalks rising about 1 ft. above the water surface. The spikes of blue-violet flowers are profuse and most attractive. Hardy to Zone 3, it is useful for planting in shallow waters (about 10–12 in. deep) along pond or lake margins. Propagation is usually by division. Most aquatic plant dealers keep it in stock.

POPLAR. Common name for POPULUS, a genus of hardy deciduous trees widely distributed throughout the temperate zone.

POPPY. Common name for PAPAVER, a genus of annuals and perennials with showy flowers. The Poppy Family is PAPAVERACEAE.

The common name is also applied to other genera. Asiatic, Chinese yellow, satin, and welsh poppy are species of MECONOPSIS. Bush poppy or tree poppy is DENDROMECON. California poppy is *Eschscholzia californica*. Canyon or Matilija poppy is *Romneya*. Celandine poppy is *Stylophorum diphyllum*. Flaming or wind poppy is *Stylomecon heterophylla*; see STYLOMECON. Horned or sea poppy is the genus GLAUCIUM. Mexican or prickly poppy is the genus ARGEMONE. Plume poppy is *Macleaya*. Poppy mallow is the genus CALLIRHOE. Snow poppy is *Ecomecon chionantha*. Tulip poppy is *Hunnemannia fumariifolia*. Water-poppy is *Hydrocleys nymphoides*.

POPULUS (PAHP yoo lus). A genus of hardy, deciduous, soft-wooded trees widely distributed throughout the temperate zone, belonging to the Salicaceae (Willow Family), and variously known as poplar, aspen, and cottonwood. Aspen refers mostly to smaller-growing species, particularly those having flat leaf stems, which cause leaves to shake and flutter in the slightest breeze. Poplars grow readily in any soil, and the cottonwood species are found growing naturally in low land near rivers. They are easily propagated by seed or hardwood cuttings and often reach heights of 90 ft.

They have alternate leaves and bear flowers in catkins followed by seeds often surrounded by cottony hairs. Because of their rapid growth, they are extensively planted in dry prairie regions for windbreaks and along avenues, but also for ornamental purposes. They are also grown commercially as a source of pulpwood. Poplars are not generally long-lived, and since their long roots are likely to find their way into drains and clog them up, or upheave pavements, they should be placed with care. Their graceful trunks and their light, airy leaves rustling in the slightest breeze combine to make them cheerful, companionable trees, but those species with conspicuously white-lined leaves should be placed among darker-leaved deciduous trees or in front of evergreens to get the full beauty of their form and coloring.

Because of its symmetrical columnar effect, the Lombardy poplar is frequently planted for accents and boundaries, but in the eastern states it is short-lived and within a few years becomes unsightly. In the western states, it attains great size and beauty and can be used in landscape work with confidence if planted among other types to avoid monotony.

ENEMIES

Poplars are subject to several types of diseases. At least four leaf rusts, with alternate hosts on hemlock, larch, and fir, may interfere with the growth of young trees. The European poplar canker frequently kills Lombardy poplars in the nursery and trees recently set out. For this reason, this species is no longer recommended for planting. Cytospor, a canker that is destructive during periods of drought, can be prevented by keeping trees in a vigorous, healthy condition by proper feeding and watering.

Insects that feed on poplar foliage include the willow leaf beetle, satin moth, spiny elm caterpillar, and cottonwood leaf beetle. See BEETLES; CATERPILLAR; INSECT CONTROL.

The oyster-shell scale is a common pest, and the poplar and willow curculio, the native poplar borer, and the cottonwood borer can be very injurious. For the latter two, prune and burn badly infested limbs. See also BORERS; CURCULIO; SCALE INSECTS.

PRINCIPAL SPECIES

P. alba (white poplar, abele) is a wide-spreading tree that grows to 90 ft. or taller and has coarsely lobed, triangular leaves, dark green above with whitish or grayish down beneath. Native to Europe and Asia and naturalized in North America, it is very hardy, even along the north Atlantic Coast, surviving in Zones 4–8. Cv. 'Nivea', with leaves densely white beneath, is found in many regions as an escapee in the United States where,

Populus alba

suckering freely, it has become quite a nuisance. Other cultivars are 'Pyramidalis', of close, columnar form; 'Globosa', small with a rounded head; and 'Pendula', with drooping branches.

P. balsamifera (balsam poplar, hackmatack balm-of-Gilead), sometimes listed as *P. candicans*, has glossy, heart-shaped leaves. Native across northern North America, it is a moderately long-lived tree of stately appearance, growing 75–100 ft. tall. On the home grounds, the staminate form should be planted because the seeds borne by the pistillate tree are surrounded by dense cottony hairs, which become unsightly if they accumulate on the ground. The white wood is of coarse and poor quality, but the trees are rapid growers in almost any soil, especially in wet areas, and are widely used for windbreaks where better subjects will not thrive. The wood is commercially harvested for pulp, plywood, and paper products. Hardy in Zones 2–9.

P. deltoides (cottonwood), native to eastern North America, grows to 90 ft. and has a wide crown and 7-in., ovate leaves.

P. fremontii (Fremont cottonwood), native to the southwestern states and hardy to Zone 7, grows to 90 ft. and has small, triangular leaves. Var. *wislizenii* (Rio Grande cottonwood) has yellowish green leaves, is larger in all dimensions, and is native and hardy throughout the Southwest to Zone 5.

P. grandidentata (large-toothed aspen) is an Atlantic Coast native, very similar to *P. tremuloides* but relatively smaller with rough-edged leaves.

P. nigra (black poplar) has triangular leaves, light green beneath. It is best known through its cv. 'Italica' (Lombardy poplar), of distinct columnar growth; once popular, it is now rarely planted due to its susceptibility to a serious canker disease. Hardy in Zones 4–9.

P. sieboldii (Japanese aspen) has oval to wedge-shaped leaves and is hardy to Zone 6.

P. tremula (European aspen), growing to 60 ft., has flattened leaf stalks, tilting the leaves and causing them to flutter in the slightest breeze. It is native in Europe but is also found in Asia and North Africa. Cv. 'Erecta' is a narrow, upright form from Sweden, which may replace the Lombardy poplar in cultivation. Cv. 'Pendula' has drooping branches. Hardy in Zones 2–7.

P. tremuloides (quaking or American aspen), a North American native, is a small tree with leaves hung on such slender stalks that they flutter restlessly. The clear yellow of the autumn foliage, especially in the western forms, in contrast with the silvery white of its trunk and limbs, makes a most pleasing effect in woodland planting. Hardy in Zones 1–9.

P. trichocarpa (western balsam poplar) grows to 18 ft. and has broad, oval leaves 5–10 in. long, rounded at the base and whitish or rusty on the underside. Native to western North America, it is hardy to Zone 5.

PORTULACA (por tyoo LAH kah). A widely distributed genus of hardy, sometimes edible, mostly perennial, fleshy, more or less succulent, low-growing or ascending herbs, sometimes becoming troublesome weeds, and commonly known as purslane. The genus lends its name to the PORTULACACEAE (Portulaca or Purslane Family).

The flowers, which open only in sunlight, are available in many strains with a wide variety of colors, including red, orange, white, purple, yellow, or pink in both single and double forms.

Customarily treated as half-hardy annuals, purslanes can be used for massing in beds, as edging plants, in rock gardens or on walls, and on bare sunny banks. Hardy in Zones 5–9, they succeed in any good garden soil, preferring a mixture of loam, leaf mold, and coarse sand in a sunny location. Seed should be sown where plants are to grow, but since it is very fine, a more even distribution can be obtained by mixing it with dry soil or sand before sowing.

P. grandiflora (rose-moss, sunplant), a popular plant for warm, sunny locations in the garden, is a low grower, to 12 in., with scattered leaves about an inch long. Flowers are red, white, or yellow, sometimes striped, up to 1 in. across.

P. oleracea var. *sativa* (purslane, pusley) is a persistent, yellow-flowered, annual weed of eastern vegetable gardens, sometimes used as a potherb. Small portions of the fleshy pink stems spread from the crown and will take root under adverse conditions, and whole plants pulled up and thrown aside will often stay alive long enough to permit the taproot to bend over and re-

Portulaca oleracea

enter the ground. As a weed, it can be destroyed by spraying with iron-sulfate. Complete removal, however, is not always desirable. The tips, gathered young, before flower buds develop, are like New Zealand spinach, and can be enjoyed as a salad green, and the stems as a pickle. In the garden, purslane spreads over the soil surface, making a living mulch; in cornfields, it uses less water and nutrients than those it preserves in the soil; thus, removing it will hamper crop yields. Hardy to Zone 3, it should be managed so it does not crowd too much. Var. *giganthes* is an ornamental form with double flowers.

PORTULACACEAE (por tyoo lah KAY see ee). The Portulaca or Purslane Family, a group of widely distributed fleshy herbs, chiefly native to the tropics of the Western Hemisphere. Cultivated genera include *Calandrinia*, *Claytonia*, *Montia*, *Portulaca*, and *Talinum*.

POTAMOGETON (poh tah moh GAY tahn). A genus of aquatic herbs native in tropical and temperate regions, commonly known as pondweed. Variously hardy to Zone 3, most are attractive in appearance, with elliptic, grasslike, or straplike leaves, some beautifully veined. They are seldom cultivated satisfactorily, however, and are more likely to be a nuisance in the lily pond.

POTASH. A general term for compounds of potassium, one of the most essential elements for plant growth that are frequently lacking in soil. The name "potash" was given when material was obtained by steeping wood ashes in an iron pot. In addition to the natural oxide and carbonate so obtained, the name "potash" has been extended to include the other forms now used as fertilizers.

It helps strengthen stem and leaf growth, and generally improves flower, fruit, seed, and root crops. It is especially valuable on potatoes, beets, and onions. Under ordinary cultivation, the soil becomes exhausted, calling for the use of manure, compost, and special potash fertilizers. The oldest and one of the best sources is wood ash, for any vegetable matter yields potash when burned. Ashes from the fireplace or woodstove, though small in bulk, contain as much as 7% potash and should be scattered on the soil of the vegetable and flower garden whenever available in winter or stored in a dry place for use in spring. Small quantities can be applied to the lawn also, if sprinkled thinly, but none should be used on any acid-soil or evergreen plants, since the ash contains some lime.

Of the chemical potash fertilizers, the most common and least expensive is muriate of potash (potassium chloride), which contains about 40% of the element potassium, or 60% potash, and is sold as 0–0–60. Other forms sometimes available in stores include potassium sulfate and the mixed potassium and magnesium sulfates (sometimes sold as "sul-po-mag"). Potassium is also found as a constituent of complete fertilizers, which also contain nitrogen and phosphate.

POTATO. A tropical and subtropical perennial herb, *Solanum tuberosum*, now extensively grown in temperate countries for use as a vegetable, a source of starch, and other commercial purposes. It is closely related to eggplant, tomato, and pepper, and like them, it is tender to frost.

As a common name, potato also refers to other plants. Air-potato or yam is *Dioscorea bulbifera*; see DIOSCOREA. SWEET-POTATO is *Ipomoea batatas*.

Potatoes thrive best in sandy loam soils rich in humus, well drained but retentive of moisture, and well supplied with potash. However, a satisfactory crop can be grown in any good garden soil. Manure, if used, is best applied to the previous crop or plowed under the previous autumn so it will become well decayed before the potatoes are planted. The soil should not be limed within a year prior to planting because lime, as well as wood ashes (which are 30% lime) and fresh manures, tend to make the tubers scabby. Plowing under clover-sod or other leguminous green manure crop is a good preparation for potatoes. The land should be deeply tilled or dug and made fine by harrowing or raking or both. Also, commercial fertilizer rich in potash can be worked in either over the whole area or in the furrows (or hills). Keep the fertilizer from coming in direct contact with the "seed" (cut tubers) or it may burn them. Always mix the fertilizer with the soil below where the tubers are to be planted; the roots will go down to it.

PLANTING

In the home garden, potatoes are generally planted in hills, 3–4 in. deep and 18–24 in. apart, but planting in drills involves less labor and generally gives more satisfactory results. In this case the seed pieces are dropped in furrows 3–5 in. deep at intervals of 6–8 in.; or, preferably, two pieces together at intervals of 15–18 in., thus forming hills. The space between rows should be not less than 18 in.

The former practice of earthing up the hills or rows not only wastes time and labor but also, except in wet land, produces poorer results than level culture. At the last cultivation, however,

Earthing up

slight earthing up may be advisable to prevent exposing any tubers to the light, which makes them green, tough, and undesirable.

SEED

For seed purposes choose tubers that are well formed, of moderate to large size, and with shallow eyes (this type is better for peeling). Small tubers and the tip ends of large ones (the end where the eyes are crowded together) should be discarded because they produce many shoots that compete with one another and thus reduce the yield. The remainder of each tuber should be cut in

Cutting tubers

large pieces, each bearing at least one eye, preferably two, and not more than three.

The most important step in securing early potatoes is choosing a quick-maturing variety. The time between planting and harvest can be shortened still further by spreading the seed potatoes one layer deep where they will be in strong sunlight and a temperature of 60°F or more for two or three weeks before planting. Instead of developing long, brittle, white shoots, as potatoes usually do toward spring when stored in dark, damp cellars, these light-exposed tubers develop short, tough, dark colored rosettes which, if not broken off when planted, will rapidly develop into plants. In warm, rich, sandy loams the time between planting and harvesting can thus be reduced to seven or even six weeks in the case of the earliest varieties.

MAINTENANCE AND HARVEST

Potatoes should be kept green and vigorous throughout the season, being cultivated (not too deep nor too close) regularly. When the vines die or are killed by frost, and before the ground freezes, dig carefully with a spading fork when the soil is not wet. Let the tubers dry for a few hours, then gather them, taking care not to bruise them, and store in a dark, moist, cool (just above freezing) cellar or pit. Early potatoes can be dug as soon as they are large enough to use, a few hills at a time as needed.

ENEMIES

DISEASES

The potato seems to be subject to more diseases than other vegetable, but the severity of any one trouble depends largely on the section of the country and on weather conditions. Late blight (due to *Phytophthora infestans*), which caused the great Irish famine of 1844, is probably the most generally destructive. Wet seasons favor the disease, which first shows as water-soaked areas on the leaves, with a white mold on the underside. Tubers are rotted as a result of spores being washed down into the soil. Consult your local extension service for recommended control measures for your region and soil.

Rhizoctonia rot, another fungus, appears as brown, corky sclerotia (spore bodies) on the potato skins, often thought to be merely dirt. The cooking quality is not affected, but if such potatoes are used for seed, the seedlings may be girdled and die. Avoid planting when the soil has become too warm, and use only disease-free seed potatoes.

Common SCAB affects chiefly the appearance of the tubers. Plant resistant varieties, and keep the soil acid.

For black leg, which is a bacterial soft rot of the base of the stem, use disease-free seed potatoes.

Fusarium wilt causes rapid collapse of the plant. In cutting seed, discard tubers showing discoloration. The symptoms of the several virus diseases of potatoes are indicated by the names—mosaic, leaf roll, spindle tuber, and yellow-dwarf. Control consists in use of seed from clean fields and the control of insect carriers, namely, aphids and leaf hoppers.

INSECT PESTS

About six insects are likely to be serious pests. The best known is the COLORADO POTATO BEETLE; both the larvae (soft, dark red with black head and spots) and the adults (convex-, hard-shelled beetles with black stripes) feed on the foliage, and there are two generations a year. Pick off the beetles and egg cases from the leaves. Unless you have a big patch with an unusual attack, you probably will not need to resort to sprays.

The very small, shiny, jet-black potato flea beetle eats small, round holes in the leaves until they appear sievelike; see FLEA BEETLE for controls. For the potato aphid, a large pink or green plant louse, spray with homemade onion spray, introduce ladybugs, and remove wild rose bushes from the vicinity; see APHIDS.

POTENTILLA (poh ten TIL ah). A genus of about 500 mostly hardy subshrubs or herbs, rarely annuals, native to the Northern Hemisphere, belonging to the Rosaceae (Rose Family), and commonly known as cinquefoil or five-finger. The flowers are usually yellow and sometimes white, but in the hybrid forms there are shades of orange, red, crimson, and pink in both single and double forms. They are

Potentilla sp.

suitable for beds and borders, and some species are good subjects for rock gardens and bare banks. They thrive in sunny locations in any ordinary garden soil but prefer sandy soils. They can be readily propagated by seed or by division of the roots. The hybrid forms are more cultivated than the species, both for appearance in the garden and for cutting, the flowers being borne from midsummer to autumn. Most species are hardy in Zones 5–9.

PRINCIPAL SPECIES

P. anserilla (silverweed) is a low creeper with yellow flowers.

P. atrosanguinea (Himalayan cinquefoil) bears blood red flowers on 18-in. plants.

P. crantzii, formerly listed as *P. alpestris*, is a perennial that grows from to 12 in. and has basal leaves of five wedge-shaped leaflets deeply cut in the upper half. Bright yellow flowers about 1 in. across are borne in summer. Cv. 'Pygmaea' forms a mat suited to the rock garden.

P. fruticosa forms a shrub 2–4 ft. high and has feather-shaped leaves of narrow, tapering, downy leaflets up to an inch long. Sparse yellow flowers 1½ in. across are borne in summer. It is hardier than most species, to Zone 3. Often used as a hedge, there are a great many varieties, including cv. 'Abbottswood', growing to 2 ft. with white flowers; cv. 'Gold Star', to 3 ft. with large, yellow flowers; and cv. 'Sunset', to 3 ft. with red-orange flowers.

P. nepalensis cv. 'Miss Willmott' is an especially recommended variety bearing rose-colored flowers.

P. nitida is a good rock garden mat with rose-colored flowers.

P. recta is a large plant with sulfur flowers; hardy to Zone 3. Cv. 'Warrenii' is tall with clear yellow flowers.

P. tabernaemontani has spring blooms of bright yellow with dark green, toothed leaflets. Growing to 3 in., the plants are mat forming, spreading up to 2 ft., and may be evergreen in warmer areas.

P. x *tonguei* grows 8–12 in. and has 1-in., light yellow flowers with red centers.

P. tridentata is evergreen and hardy to Zone 2. It grows to 6 in. and serves well as a ground cover, preferring dry, acid soil conditions. Flowers are small, white, strawberrylike from May through summer. Cv. 'Minima' is similar but lower growing.

P. villosa, a native of China, grows about 1 ft. high and has leaves parted into three leaflets, coarsely toothed, silky above and hairy beneath. Flowers are creamy white.

POTERIUM (poh TAIR ee um). A genus of herbs and subshrubs belonging to the Rosaceae (Rose Family) and native to Europe, Asia, and northern Africa. They are closely related to SANGUISORBA but are distinguished by having male and female flowers on the same plant.

Poterium sanguisorba

P. sanguisorba (salad burnet) is a perennial that grows 6–18 in. and has nearly hairless basal leaves and ½-in., green or purplish flowers. It is widely naturalized in North America and hardy to Zone 3.

POTHERB. Any plant whose succulent young parts are boiled and eaten as GREENS, such as spinach, mustard, fetticus, and cabbage.

POTHOS. A common name for EPIPREMNUM, a genus of tropical plants used for ground cover, hanging baskets, or houseplants.

POTTED PLANTS. A term applied to plants grown in flowerpots and similar containers for their decorative effect. Such plants may be either flowering subjects, such as begonias, calceolarias, cyclamens, kalanchoe, or primulas; bulbous materials, such as Easter lilies, hyacinths, tulips, and the like; or foliage plants, such as aspidistras, crotons, dracaenas, ferns, or palms. Potted plants can be grown from seed, from cuttings, or as grafted specimens. See also HOUSEPLANTS; FLOWERPOTS; INDOOR GARDENING.

POTTING.

The transferring or potting up of plants from seedling flats, cutting benches, and other propagating quarters to flowerpots; also the repotting, or shifting of larger plants from one pot to another. Though the operation is simple, failure to perform it properly is a common cause of failure with potted plants.

For a proper start, seeds should be sown thinly in seed pans or flats so the seedlings will have room to grow without becoming spindly, until they have formed their second pair of true leaves. At this stage they can either be pricked out into other flats to develop for two to four more weeks or potted directly in 2½–3 in. pots. See PRICKING-OUT; TRANSPLANTING.

Cuttings should also be given plenty of space to develop roots. The best stage at which to pot them is when their roots are not more than ½–¾ in. long. If done much sooner, they are likely to develop slowly; if done later, they are more difficult to handle and are liable to suffer a check through the breakage of roots.

There are many suitable media for potting; one is composed of equal parts of garden loam, sand (not beach sand), and peat moss. There are also bagged sterilized mixes available at most nurseries. These are usually artificial mixes (no soil) made up of perlite, peat moss, and perhaps vermiculite plus fertilizer. When ready to use, any medium should be uniformly mixed and moist. A good test for moisture is to squeeze a handful hard; if any water comes out, the soil is too wet; if it falls apart quickly when the hand is opened, it is too dry; if it retains its shape as squeezed and merely cracks slightly, it is damp enough.

Correct potting of cuttings and seedlings consists of placing each plant in the center of its container at the same depth at which it stood in the seedbed or the cutting bench, firming the soil around the roots, and refraining from filling the pot with soil. In a 3-in. pot, ½ in. (proportionally more in larger pots) must be left between the soil surface and pot rim to hold water. If the soil is even with the rim, the water runs off instead of soaking in, and the plants die or suffer from thirst.

Monitoring and care until the plants have become established is important. The pots must be set level, otherwise they will not hold enough water. Partial shade is nearly always necessary for newly potted plants. The density of the shade depends on the season and the strength of the sunlight. Less shade is needed in winter than in summer.

Never let the plants suffer for lack of moisture. When watering, always fill the water reservoir (the area between the top of the medium and the top of the pot lip). After watering, some surplus water should drain out of the drain hole. This drainage of excess water is imperative when using water high in total soluble salts. Watering is best done early in the morning so the wetted foliage will be dry by sundown.

KNOCKING OUT

Just as soon as the developing plant has used all the food in the small pot and filled the soil space with its roots, it must be shifted to a larger container, or it will be stunted. Experienced growers can recognize the shifting stage at a glance; the novice can determine it by "knocking out" the plant thus: place one hand, palm down, on top of the pot with the plant stem between the first and second fingers; turn the pot and plant upside down and firmly tap the

Knocking out

pot with the heel of the free hand. The ball of soil will slide into the other hand. If only a few roots are visible, the plant is not ready for a shift and should be replaced in the pot, the bottom of which should then be tapped to firm the ball of soil back into the pot. Never press the loosened ball back into the pot (as is done in potting a plant the first time) since it might break the roots. If, however, the roots have formed a fairly dense network around the outside of the earth ball, and especially if they are becoming dark colored, the plant is ready to be shifted at once. Shift the plant only to the next larger size container. An over-size container and a little too much water can easily kill a newly repotted plant.

Be sure the soil is merely moist when a plant is knocked out. If very dry, the ball may fall apart; if wet, the soil may puddle and later bake.

SHIFTING

Always have the ball of soil moist when it is repotted. If it is dry, no amount of watering later will wet it. Always use clean pots.

Before placing a plant in the next larger size pot, break and shake the surface soil off as far down as the roots because it has been depleted of its original supply of plant food by the plant and by leaching. The plant is then placed on some good soil in the new pot, more soil is added around the sides and on top of the root ball, the soil is gently firmed with the thumbs, and the bottom of the pot is then given a sharp rap on the bench to further firm the soil. As before, avoid setting the plant either too deep or too shallow.

While the plants are in 2½–4 in. flowerpots, they need little or no special drainage, but from the time they are in 5-in. pots, they require it. Drainage is provided by placing a curved piece of broken pot, convex side up, over the drainage hole and a few other pieces on top of it. This not only allows excess water to pass out, but also admits the necessary air to the soil. A half-inch or so of drainage material is enough.

See also PLANTING.

POTTING SHED. That part of a greenhouse or other garden shed (or sometimes a separate structure) in which indoor gardening operations are done, such as potting plants and bulbs, making cuttings and grafts, and where the necessary sup-

plies and appliances for such work are kept. In large greenhouse establishments, the potting shed is centrally located with respect to the different houses. In the small garden, the potting shed can often be conveniently combined with the tool shed. In addition to convenient tool storage, where they will be out of the way but ready to use, the potting shed should provide bins for storing soil-mixture ingredients as well as places for safe storage of seeds, bulbs, spray materials, commercial fertilizers, flowerpots and saucers, flats, and the numerous other supplies that are needed.

PRAIRIE-CLOVER. Common name for PETALO-STEMON, a genus of perennial herbs with spikes of pealike flowers.

PRAIRIE-DOCK. Common name for *Silphium terebinthinaceum*, a grassland perennial with smooth foliage and daisylike flowers; see SIL-PHIUM.

PRAIRIE GENTIAN. Common name for *Eustoma grandiflorum*, an annual herb with bell-shaped, purple flowers; see EUSTOMA.

PRAYING MANTIS. The praying mantis, *Mantis religiosa*, belonging to the Mantidae in the order Orthoptera, is a large, predacious insect of great value as an eater of other insects, though it also cannibalizes its own species at times. Its name is derived from its long, efficiently grasping front legs on a long thorax. The legs fold back in a praying sort of position so they get great leverage for attack. Eggs, which can be bought commercially for use as a beneficial insect in the garden, are laid in masses held together by a kind of glue and can often be seen stuck to branches in the southern states, where they are most common. The insects overwinter in these

Praying mantis

hardened egg cases, coming forth in the summer as nymphs, which are especially voracious, even eating beneficial insects and pollinators.

The praying mantis is highly useful as a biological control in the garden and greenhouse. Neither mantids nor their egg cases should be destroyed. Many species can be found in the United States, including the Carolina, the Chinese, and the European. See INSECTS, BENEFICIAL.

PRETTY-FACE. Common name for *Triteleia ixioides*, a cormous herb bearing yellow flowers with a purple stripe.

PRICKING-OUT. A process of transferring tiny seedling plants from seed pans to flats or small pots, or from crowded rows in one flat to another flat, where they are spaced about an inch apart each way. The purpose is to give the seedlings room for normal development until large enough to transplant and also to prevent their becoming spindly and weak as they inevitably will if left crowded. It is usually done using a stick

Pricking-out

cut in a V-shape at one end, the plantlet being lifted out and replanted where wanted. See also TRANSPLANTING; POTTING.

PRICKLY-PEAR. Common name for members of the subgenus *Platyopuntia*; see OPUNTIA.

PRIDE-OF-CALIFORNIA. Common name for *Lathyrus latifolus* var. *splendens*, a shrubby, leguminous herb with bright-colored flowers; see LATHYRUS.

PRIMROSE. Common name for PRIMULA, a large genus of flowering herbs popular in greenhouse and garden culture. The Primrose Family is PRIMULACEAE. Other plants known as primroses include OENOTHERA (evening-primrose) of the Onagraceae (Evening-primrose Family); as well as greenhouse plants of the genus STREPTOCARPUS (cape-primrose).

PRIMULA (PRIM yoo lah). A large genus including about 400 species of usually low-growing perennial herbs belonging to the Primulaceae (Primrose Family) and commonly known as primroses. These popular greenhouse and garden plants are noted for their cheery vivid flowers that are available in nearly any color or combination desired (except blue), with white, pink, and yellow predominating. The flower parts always occur in fives, the tubular corolla being topped by five spreading lobes. The foliage grows in rosettes that may range in size from 2 in. to 2 ft.

Primula x polyantha

across. Some kind of primrose is suitable for every type of garden site from bog to woodland or rock garden; they are especially effective in shady borders and in mass plantings.

There are several hundred species of varying habits, all but about five are native to the North Temperate Zone, with most being well adapted to the cool and moist conditions of Britain and the Pacific Northwest. Primroses do not tolerate hot, dry summers but will thrive where proper conditions can be provided. They require a site that allows for good drainage, ample moisture, and protection from wind and midday sun. Although deep shade will inhibit flowering, most species prefer partial shade, especially during the hottest part of the day. The soil should be somewhat heavy, slightly acidic, and rich in organic material such as peat moss, compost, or leaf mold. Most primroses also benefit from a summertime mulch and a winter covering of evergreen boughs.

Propagation. Primroses should be divided as necessary, about every two to four years. This is the simplest method of propagation for named cultivars or hybrids. Plants should be divided in the spring, after flowering, or in late summer when they begin to go dormant. When large numbers of plants are needed, the reliable species are easily propagated by seed, which is sown indoors in late winter, or in spring in a cold-frame. Early fall is the best time to transplant the seedlings to their permanent site, where they should be left undisturbed. The alpine species are best sown in summer, when the seed is ripe; seedlings can be set out the following spring.

Primula sp.

Diseases. Seedlings and young plants are sometimes killed by DAMPING-OFF but can be prevented by careful attention to soil conditions, watering, and ventilation.

Gray mold or BOTRYTIS blight is most prevalent indoors, but it may occur in the garden during humid weather and rapidly rot the plants. In the greenhouse, destroy badly diseased plants, isolate infected plants from others, and reduce the water supply. If possible, water from below to avoid wetting the leaves.

Primroses may also be affected by ROT, RUSTS, yellows, LEAF SPOT, or ANTHRACNOSE.

Insect Pests. Primroses are subject to attacks from the primrose flea beetle, a metallic blue insect that is rather plentiful, usually first appearing in late spring. A second generation from eggs laid in summer winters over in adult form in protected locations. See also FLEA BEETLE.

Plants in the garden are sometimes eaten by SLUGS, and the WHITEFLY may be troublesome in greenhouses.

The tiny RED SPIDER MITE is a persistent primrose pest, especially troublesome indoors where it may be sufficient to spray several times with clear water or, for bad infestations, with an insecticide. Outdoor cleaning and burning of all rubbish and weeds will keep down all kinds of pests.

See also INSECT CONTROL; GREENHOUSE PESTS.

PRINCIPAL SPECIES

P. auricula (auricular primrose), growing to 8 in., has been extensively hybridized to produce a variety of flower colors, some fragrant, and some with centers that contrast with the outer petals. Blossoms are 1 in. wide. It requires winter protection, and some greenhouse forms are available.

P. denticularia (Himalayan primrose) grows to 10 in. and has solitary, ½-in. flowers of violet, lilac, or white appearing in spring before the foliage.

P. japonica (Japanese primrose), a fine, vigorous species, grows to 2 ft. and has dense umbels of rose, purple, or white flowers an inch wide or larger appearing in whorls one above the other in early summer. Useful in pots or in the garden, it requires constant moisture, rich soil, and shade.

P. juliae (Julia primrose) is a dwarf that grows only 3 in. and has tiny, rose, red, or crimson-violet flowers on 2-in. stalks. The wrinkled foliage forms small tufted mounds that make a good mass planting.

P. x *polyantha* (polyanthus) is a popular hybrid growing to 12 in. It has rounded leaves tapered toward winged stems. Flowers of various colors are solitary or borne in umbels.

P. sieboldii (Japanese star primrose) grows 8–12 in. and bears flowers 2 in. wide crowded in umbels. Blossoms are pink, purple, blue, or white, often with a contrasting center. This species is more sun and drought tolerant than most, but the foliage dies back in summer.

P. veris (cowslip primrose) grows 6–8 in. and bears nodding bundles of ½-in., yellow flowers with orange centers, sometimes double and fragrant. The foliage dies back in summer.

P. vulgaris (English primrose) grows to 6 in. and requires rich soil and mulch in summer. It has variable 1½-in. flowers, usually yellow, but blue forms are available; they may be double and numerous or solitary.

PRIMULACEAE (prim yoo LAY see ee). The Primrose Family, comprising widely distributed herbs abundant principally in the Northern Hemisphere. Among the best-known genera are *Anagalis*, *Androsace*, *Cyclamen*, *Dodecatheon*, *Lysimachia*, *Primula*, and *Soldanella*.

PRINCE'S-FEATHER. Common name for two plants, mostly applied to *Amaranthus hybridus* var. *erythrostachys*, a showy annual; see AMARANTHUS. It is also applied to *Polygonum orientale*, an annual herb related to buckwheat; see POLYGONUM.

PRINSEPIA (prin SEE pee ah). A genus of deciduous shrubs from Asia, belonging to the Rosaceae, (Rose Family). *P. sinensis*, native to Manchuria, and the best-known species, is a spiny, slender-branched shrub that grows to 6 ft. or more, thriving in a sunny location on well-drained soil. It is hardy in Zones 4–7 and is about the earliest shrub to come into leaf, which makes it conspicuous when most others are still bare. The small, bright yellow flowers appear in clusters from the axils of the opening leaves. The fruit is cherrylike and edible but is not freely produced. Propagation is by seed and cuttings.

PRIVET. Common name for LIGUSTRUM, a genus of deciduous and evergreen shrubs valuable for hedges and landscaping.

PROBOSCIDEA (proh boh SID ee ah). A genus of sticky-haired, annual and perennial herbs, commonly known as proboscis flower or unicorn plant. They have large, long-stemmed leaves and large, purple flowers. The okralike fruits, which can be pickled when young, become woody when ripe and have long, curved, sharp-pointed beaks.

P. fragrans (martynia), the most common species, is native from Delaware to Illinois, southward and westward to New Mexico. It is grown both for ornament and to produce vegetables. In the latter role, its soft, immature fruits are pickled, either alone or mixed with other vegetables.

In cool climates, seed must be started indoors, then the plants set in the open ground and spaced like cucumber hills after danger of frost has passed. In warm regions, seed can be started outdoors, and all but three or four seedlings should be thinned from each hill.

PROPAGATION. The increase in number, or multiplication, of plants to perpetuate the species or variety. Also the process and methods employed to promote natural increase in some plants and to bring increase about under conditions when it would not otherwise take place. It is based on natural principles that constitute the science of propagation and upon methods of handling that constitute the art.

Methods, of which there are many, can be grouped in two classes: those dependent upon seeds and spores; and those that employ vegetative tissue. Because reproduction by seed is dependent upon the previous activity of the reproductive organs (stamens and pistils), it is called sexual. Reproduction by vegetative tissue (which includes cuttings) is termed asexual because no union of parent plants is involved. Spores are asexual, usually one-celled, reproductive bodies of flowerless plants. Practically speaking, however, reproduction by spores (as in mushrooms and ferns) is considered a sexual process.

Nearly all farm and garden crops and many flowers are grown from seeds. Notable exceptions are Irish potatoes and sugar cane which, though they produce some seed, are propagated asexually; so are Jerusalem-artichokes, tarragon, sweet-potato, horseradish, and most of the tree and bush fruits whose seedlings, though true to species characteristics, rarely reproduce true to variety, the fruit of the seedlings being inferior to that of the parent variety. Hence the necessity of producing all such plants by asexual methods.

The propagation of plants by asexual methods depends primarily upon the activity of the cambium. This is a layer of very thin tissue composed wholly of young, easily broken cells filled with protoplasm from which new plant tissues are formed. This vital layer separates the bast and sieve tissues (phloem) from the wood (xylem) and in most common trees forms a continuous sheath between bark and wood extending from root tips to topmost buds. Upon it depends all growth of woody plants—the lengthening of roots and branches and the increase in girth of all parts. The healing of wounds that penetrate deeper than the bark also depends upon cambium activity, since it develops protective callus tissue over them.

In propagation by CUTTINGS, a callus must form over the severed base prior to the development of roots; in LAYERING, cambium action hastens root development if the buried parts of the stems were previously wounded. In successful GRAFTING, the cambium of stock and scion unite and the callus formed from the edges of these wounds covers the exposed internal tissues and protects them from drying and decay.

In both sexual and asexual propagation methods, home gardeners and commercial nurseries have relied largely upon traditional rules, which have proved only partially successful. Seeds of many plants have taken months or even years to germinate, and cuttings have failed altogether or have given poor results when handled by ordinary methods. Thanks to experiments and investigations, many propagation problems have been solved in recent years and further improvements are clearly on the way. The alert propagator should keep abreast of new discoveries and become familiar with at least some of the methods worked out by scientists and proved in the trial grounds of various institutions.

See BULBS; SEEDS; DIVISION; GRAFTING.

PROPHET FLOWER. Common name for *Echioides longiflorum*, a perennial herb with yellow flowers, very similar to *Arnebia decumbens*; see ECHIOIDES; ARNEBIA.

PROSTANTHERA (prohs tan THEER ah). A genus of shrubby plants native to Australia, belonging to the Lamiaceae (Mint Family), and commonly known as mintbush. They are studded with resinous glands and are usually strong scented. Cultivated for their simple, abundant flowers, they are sometimes grown under glass and outdoors only in Zones 10–11. Propagation is by seed or softwood cuttings.

PRINCIPAL SPECIES

P. lasianthos (Victorian-dogwood) has toothed, oblong leaves pale beneath and white flowers tinged red.

P. nivea is a handsome shrub that grows to 6 ft. and has slender leaves and snow white flowers, sometimes tinged with blue, in leafy racemes.

P. rotundifolia has small, roundish leaves and purple flowers in short, close clusters.

PROTEA (PROH tee ah). A genus of trees, shrubs, or stemless perennials, outstanding plants native to the Cape of Good Hope and comprising the principal members of the Proteaceae (Protea Family). At one time they were among the most popular greenhouse plants, but today they are seldom seen outside botanical gardens. They are unusual-looking plants with leathery leaves and large, round flower heads accented by scaly and usually colored bracts. Sandy peat, with good drainage, careful watering, and a sunny, airy location are the chief cultural requirements. A number of species are now grown commercially as cut flowers.

P. cynaroides, one of the outstanding species in its native habitat, has white flowers and pink-tipped bracts. When the flower heads first open, they are full of a honeylike substance which is collected and made into sugar.

P. speciosa, with silky white flowers and bracts, was once one of the most popular species.

PRUNE. Originally this term referred to any plum; in modern North American usage, it means a dried plum or any meaty, not juicy, variety of plum that can be easily dried without spoiling. Though various prune varieties are grown in the eastern states, they are not dried there commercially because the air is too humid. The American prune industry is mostly confined to the Pacific Coast states.

PRUNELLA (proo NEL ah). A genus of small perennial herbs belonging to the Lamiaceae (Mint Family), sometimes called brunella. They bear purple or violet flowers in close-set heads or spikes. The plants are rather weedy but can be used in the shady part of the border or rock garden. They grow well in any garden soil, are easily naturalized in the wild garden, and are propagated by seed or division.

P. grandiflora (self-heal), the species most often found in catalogs, is a European plant that grows to 1 ft. and has purple flowers. Various cultivars include 'Alba', 'Rosea', and 'Rubra'. Hardy in Zones 5–9.

Prunella grandiflora

P. vulgaris (self-heal, heal-all) is a low, hardy, and rather weedy perennial herb, native to Europe and often naturalized in North America, thriving on a wide range of slightly acid soils. It may grow up to 2 ft., stems often lying on the ground. It has blunt spikes of purple or blue flowers, but there are occasional white forms. It tolerates being walked on and mowed. As its common names suggest, it has been used in herbal medicines. Hardy in Zones 3–9.

PRUNING. The removal of dead or living plant parts to benefit those that remain, to increase flower or fruit production, or to improve the form of the pruned tree, bush, or vine.

Every decaying branch and stub is a menace to the life of a tree because, through it, decay may work into and destroy the heartwood and make the trunk hollow and weak. Hence the importance not only of removing all dead, dying, and diseased branches, but also of detecting in advance those that are likely to be starved by being shaded or to become broken or diseased or to otherwise threaten the well-being of the tree. When the smaller of such branches are removed and the cuts made carefully (as directed below),

the healing will be quicker and the opportunity for disease to gain entrance lessened.

PRINCIPLES OF PRUNING

The underlying principles of pruning can be grouped under three headings: true pruning, or the removal of plant parts to increase either the number or improve the quality of the flowers (and therefore the fruit) or to improve the character of the plant; simple training, or the location of individual branches in structurally favorable positions and the removal of those less favorably placed; and training the plant in some more or less unnatural form.

Gardening literature is full of pruning rules, but since many apply to specific aims, conditions, or plant species, apparent contradictions are common. It is therefore important to understand the following fundamental principles, rather than to adopt mere rules.

1. Constant good management of plants is of primary importance; pruning is secondary. It will not offset abuse or neglect of necessary tillage, plant feeding, or control of plant pests.

2. Climate and locality influence both the need for and the effects of pruning; methods that are right under one set of conditions must be avoided or modified under others. For instance, from Delaware southward, along the Atlantic seaboard, where the air is humid, winter pruning may do no harm; but in the prairie states, where it is dry and cold, so much water may be lost through winter-made wounds that trees may be killed; again, in hot, dry regions, sun scald of the trunks and branches may follow heavy pruning of trees previously neglected.

3. Pruning does not change the natural habit of a plant; pruned plants resume their normal habit when left to themselves. A sprawling tree like that of the Rhode Island Greening apple cannot be made to grow erect like one of Northern Spy, or vice versa. Pruning should seek merely to correct faults and maintain the natural form of the variety.

4. Plants of the same variety or species vary in habit according to their age and must be pruned more or less differently at different ages. Plants

when young tend to make rapid, erect growth; as they approach bearing age they reduce this rate, preliminary to flower and fruit production.

5. Drastic pruning of branches stimulates or favors stem or wood production because the supply of food taken up by the full root system is forced into a smaller percentage of top with the result that latent buds develop into branches. Gardeners prune weak shrubs and trees to promote increased top growth.

6. Drastic pruning of the roots reduces wood production and so can be used to induce fruitfulness. Its effects resemble the withholding of food, for it reduces the quantity of sap supplied. A plant thus or otherwise checked in its normal growth promptly sets about reproducing itself—that is, forming flower buds.

7. Water sprouts and suckers develop because of some disturbance of a plant's physiological balance, especially after excessive pruning or the destruction of large amounts of top by insects or diseases. They indicate vigor of root and a more or less inactive top.

8. The uppermost buds on branches usually grow most vigorously, particularly in young plants. When a shoot is shortened, a side or "axillary" bud (one formed in the angle of a leaf stalk) becomes an "uppermost" bud and, instead of remaining dormant, develops a shoot to take the place of the lost leader. This will be larger than any shoot produced from a bud lower down on the stem.

9. Shoots developed from terminal (end) buds usually grow straight ahead; those from branch buds on the sides of shoots, always at an angle. Advantage can be taken of this to spread or contract a tree or bush or to fill gaps between branches by so pruning it that the topmost bud remaining points in the desired direction.

10. Pruning trees in summer favors flower and fruit production; pruning in winter stimulates leaf and branch production. Trees and shrubs pruned while dormant strive to replace the parts removed with new ones; the result is the forced development not only of flower buds, but also of leaf and shoot buds that would otherwise have remained dormant. Thus, severe dormant pruning is followed by much top growth but often reduces yield. This does not apply in the case of the GRAPE.

11. Excessive growth can be converted into flowering or fruiting "spurs" by shortening them.

12. Removal of small branches and twigs can be used as a means of thinning the fruit and thus promoting annual bearing. To practice it the pruner must know how the variety bears its blossom buds. It is a less costly method of thinning than the removal of the developing fruit in midsummer, but it requires careful determination of the proportion of flower buds that will set fruit. See BLUEBERRY; BUD.

13. The healing of wounds is affected by the kind and vigor of the plant, the length and location of the stubs, the smoothness or roughness of the cut surfaces, the health of the wood, and the season when made.

If pruning wounds are small and made shortly before or during spring, growth may be so speedy as to close them before midsummer. But if they are large with ragged surfaces, decay organisms are likely to enter, especially if the pruning is done between July and February, after active growth has stopped. In such cases not only does the wound surface dry, but the dryness penetrates beneath the bark, which raises, widens the wound, and delays healing. The sooner the edges of ragged wounds are trimmed and protected from drying, the more likely healing is to occur.

Swabbing the wound surface with tree seal or other commercial material available at the nursery or with antiseptic and covering it with the following lotion will prevent drying. Melt 1 lb. first-grade resin and 1 oz. beef tallow over a gentle heat, then add 8 oz. alcohol. Keep tightly corked in a wide-mouthed bottle and apply with a small brush. Should the lotion become thick, add a little alcohol.

The healing of tree wounds differs from that of animal wounds in that callus or scar tissue has no connection with the tissues beneath. Its only functions are to stop the loss of water and prevent the entrance of decay. Its formation is so slow that, unless the wound is protected, decay starts before the callus seals the surface.

14. Though wood dressings do not themselves hasten healing, they may serve to prevent the entrance of disease and/or insects, are harmless to growing tissues, are antiseptic, and serve to protect the wound surface until the callus forms. Properly made wounds smaller than ½ in. across, especially those made just before spring growth starts, heal so quickly they need not be dressed. Larger wounds can be dressed advantageously provided the young tissues are not injured.

TYPES OF PRUNING

REMOVING LARGE LIMBS

To remove a large branch, make three separate cuts as follows: (1) about a foot from the main trunk, saw from below through the limb until the saw binds—possibly a third of the branch diameter; (2) a few inches beyond this cut, saw downward through the limb until it falls—the undercut will prevent the branch tearing off a strip of bark down the tree, as almost always happens if the first cut is made

Removing a large limb

from above; (3) remove the stub that is left by again sawing from above and so close to the main trunk that a smooth, flush wound results. While this will be larger than if the branch were cut farther out, it will heal more quickly with little chance of the decay infection that almost always attacks a stub.

PRUNING NURSERY STOCK

This should be done as soon as the plants are delivered and unpacked if it has not already been done at the nursery. Before planting, shorten slightly every root of the thickness of a lead pencil, and cut back any injured roots to sound wood. Make the cuts with a sharp knife and preferably on a slant, with the surface of the

wound facing down. Touching all these fresh root cuts with dusting or soil sulfur or a root-inducing hormone powder with fungicide added may be helpful.

After planting, reduce the tops of all except one-year trees at least 50%, and preferably 75%, to balance the reduction of the feeding root area suffered even under the most careful handling. Before reducing the top, however, decide which branches to retain so as to develop a structurally strong specimen. Whenever possible, let the main branches start a foot or more apart on the trunk and point in different directions. Three or four are enough to start with—others can be developed later. Shorten these "frame" limbs 30–50%, and cut off all others.

It is not advisable to cut the main stem because if that is done branches tend to develop in a bunch just below the cut and make the tree structurally weak at that point. If a young tree exhibits such a bunch of branches, cut off all but the best one. To avoid receiving such stock, insist that the nursery provide trees that have not had their leaders cut. Better still, buy only one-year whips, which are usually branchless, permitting the development of branches exactly where wanted by the simple expedient of pinching off any others during the first spring and summer.

CORRECTING A Y-CROTCH

If an otherwise desirable tree has two main branches forming a sort of Y with its tendency to split when the tree gets older, the condition can be corrected in three ways: (1) remove one branch (the smaller) close to the trunk, i.e., close to the other that is to be left as the leader. Since this is likely to cause a rather large wound and serious drying that may injure the tree, a better plan is (2) to shorten the smaller branch considerably and the larger one only a little. This makes the former a subordinate side branch on the latter. (3) Often the best plan of all in the case of a newly planted tree is to cut back the poorer branch to a 6-in. stub, which is left for two years and then trimmed off close to the main trunk the second spring. The smaller wound at the end of the stub does not dry out the trunk or interfere

PRUNING GUIDE

FRUITS

LATIN NAME (common name)	WHEN TO PRUNE	METHOD
Cydonia oblonga (quince)	early spring	Cut back young trees to form low, open head. Little pruning of older trees is required except to remove dead and weak growth.
Malus sp. (apple)	winter or early spring	Train tree for low head. Prune moderately. Keep tree open with main branches well spaced around tree. Avoid sharp V-shaped crotches
Prunus persica (peach)	early spring	Prune vigorously—remove half the previous year's growth. Keep tree headed low and well thinned out.
Prunus spp. (plum)	early spring	Remove dead and diseased branches. Keep tree shaped up by cutting back rank growth. Prune moderately.
Prunus spp. (cherry)	winter or early spring	Prune moderately—cut back slightly the most vigorous shoots.
Ribes spp. (currant)	early spring	Remove old unfruitful growth. Encourage new shoots.
Ribes spp. (gooseberry)	early spring	Same as currant; cut back new shoots at least 12 in. high and side shoots to two buds.
Rubus spp. (blackberry)	after bearing and in summer	Remove at ground level canes that bore last crop. In summer cut back new shoots 3½ ft. high.
Rubus spp. (raspberry)	after bearing and in summer	Remove at ground level in fall the canes that bore last crop. In summer, head back new canes 20–22 in. high.
Vitis spp. (grape)	late winter or early spring before sap starts	Requires heavy pruning of old wood to encourage new bearing wood. Remove all old branches back to main vine. Cut back the previous year's new growth to four buds.

SHRUBS AND VINES

LATIN NAME (common name)	WHEN TO PRUNE	METHOD
Berberis spp. (barberry)	early spring	Little pruning is required except to remove a few old branches, occasionally to encourage new growth. Head back as necessary to keep plant in shape.
Buddleia spp. (butterfly bush)	early spring	Cut out all dead wood. Remove some old branches and head-in as necessary to keep plant properly shaped.
Campsis radicans (trumpet vine)	early spring	Prune side branches severely to the main stem.
Clematis spp. (clematis)	spring	Cut out weak growth but save as much old wood as possible.
Cornus florida (flowering dogwood)	after flowering	Remove dead wood only.

LATIN NAME (common name)	WHEN TO PRUNE	METHOD
Cornus spp. (dogwood)	spring shoots.	Varieties grown for colored twigs should have the old growth removed to encourage bright colored new
Deutzia spp. (deutzia)	after flowering	Remove a few older branches and all dead wood. Do not let growth get too dense.
Diervilla spp. (bush honeysuckle)	after fruiting	Cut out some old branches. Keep bush open.
Forsythia spp. (forsythia)	after flowering	Remove a few older branches at the ground each year and head back new growth as necessary.
Hibiscus syriacus (rose-of-Sharon)	when buds start	Cut out all winter-killed growth back to live wood.
Hydrangea spp. (hydrangea)	early spring	Remove dead and weak growth. Cut old flowering stems back to two buds. Certain varieties should be cut back to the ground.
Kalmia latifolia (mountain-laurel)	after flowering	Prune very little—remove a few old branches at the ground from weak, leggy plants to induce growth from the roots.
Malus spp. (crab apple)	early spring	Prune moderately—cut out dead and broken branches and suckers.
Parthenocissus quinquefolia (Virginia creeper)	spring	Clip young plants freely. Older plants require little pruning except to remove dead growth and some thinning.
Philadelphus spp. (mock orange)	after flowering	Cut out dead wood and a few old branches to thin out plant.
Rhododendron spp. (rhododendron, azalea)	after flowering	Treat same as *Kalmia latifolia* (mountain-laurel).
Rosa hybrids (tea and perpetual hybrids)	spring after frosts	Cut away all dead and weak growth and shorten all remaining branches or canes to four buds for weak growers and five buds for vigorous sorts.
Rosa spp. (climbing roses)	after flowering	Cut out about half of old growth at the ground and retain the vigorous new shoots from the root for next year's flowers. Head back as necessary.
Sambucus spp. (elderberry)	after fruiting	Prune severely—remove half of season's growth.
Symphoricarpos spp. (snowberry)	early spring	Thin out some old branches and cut back last season's growth to three buds of the part remaining.
Syringa spp. (lilac)	after flowering	Remove diseased and scaly growth. Cut off old flower heads, and cut out surplus sucker growth.
Viburnum spp.	early spring	Prune lightly—remove all dead or weak growth and a few of the old branches.
Weigela spp. (weigela)	after flowering	Prune lightly—remove all dead or weak growth, and head in as necessary. Cut out a few old branches at the ground to induce new growth.

with the sap movement, and since the stub does not increase in size, the wound left when it is finally cut off is proportionally smaller and more likely to heal over rapidly.

SPUR PRUNING

This consists of the reduction of shoots to only a few joints and buds. It is practiced mostly on dwarf fruit trees and usually in late spring or summer, though sometimes in winter. It consists of pinching off the young shoots. See GRAPE.

HEADING-IN

This process shortens young growths and is done to correct bad habits or to promote fruit bearing. In the former case, the main governing factors are extent or rate of growth, distance between trees, character of trees (dwarf or standard), and preference as to form. Annual growths of 3 ft. in young or unfruitful trees can be shortened 30–50% to make the head thicken up. In rampant, mature trees such treatment may aggravate the trouble, which may have been caused by excess of plant food or previous excessive or faulty pruning. In such cases, checking growth is essential. Heading-in is often practiced with dwarf trees to maintain proportion of top to root and to keep the trees small and fruitful.

Pinching-off. In this form of heading-in, the immature shoots are shortened while still small. Its chief purposes are to foster flower and fruit bud development, keep the trees small, maintain desired forms of plants, thin the fruit, and ensure balance between the tops and roots of dwarf trees. Properly, it consists of pinching the soft shoots with the thumbnail.

Disbudding. Pinching-off of buds that would become branches or flowers where not desired is mostly employed to produce specimen or exhibition flowers such as roses, chrysanthemums, and dahlias. It can also be employed to develop structurally strong trees.

See also TRAINING PLANTS.

CLIPPING

Also called shearing, this is the removal of small growths so as to develop and maintain plants in more or less unnatural forms, as in hedges. Strictly speaking, it is not pruning.

PRUNING ORNAMENTALS

Ornamental trees, shrubs, and woody vines, when pruned at all, are more often wrongly pruned than are fruit trees. All too often they are sheared or clipped in fantastic or formal shapes while dormant and thus shorn of their greatest beauty—their flowers. Usually, all they need is annual attention.

When a branch grows beyond the balance, beauty of form or convenience, cut it off at its starting point so as not to leave an ugly prong. Any hole left in the plant by such a step will soon fill up with new growth.

Cut out dead, diseased, and dying stems whenever they are seen because they menace the health of other parts, prevent the entrance of sunlight and air, and waste the water pumped into the diseased and dying stems by the roots. Similarly, when bushes become crowded with stems, thin out the old, failing, puny, and worthless ones.

To obtain the finest display of bloom, it is necessary to know how and where the individual species produce their blossom buds, which might otherwise be pruned off. On this basis they fall into two classes:

1. All shrubs and trees that bloom during early spring develop their flower buds during the previous year. If they are pruned while dormant, and especially if clipped to some set shape, many buds and blossoms are destroyed. The correct time to prune them is within a week or two after the flowers have fallen—while the plants are in leaf. They then have the balance of the growing season in which to develop more and better blossom buds for the following year.

2. Shrubs and trees that blossom from late spring forward develop their blossom buds earlier during the same season. They can therefore be pruned to advantage while dormant or just as growth is starting.

EVERGREENS

Never prune evergreens, either coniferous or broad-leaved, in winter, because the additional evaporation from the cut surfaces might kill them. Prune them just as growth is starting in the spring. Rampant shoots appearing during the growing season can be pinched back or headed when noticed. Usually evergreens require little pruning beyond the removal of dead, diseased, or injured branches.

Winter killing of branches often upsets the pruning program because it necessitates extensive cutting. When it occurs, wait until the living parts can be distinguished from the dead ones, then prune accordingly. Trees whose branches apparently matured the previous autumn are benefited by heavy pruning, while those that did not ripen their wood well may be injured by such treatment. In cases of severe winter killing, delay of needed pruning until the trees are growing well permits the easy identification of dead wood.

PRUNUS (PROO nus). The stone fruits, an important genus of the Rosaceae (Rose Family). These mostly deciduous shrubs and small trees, found chiefly in the North Temperate Zone include valuable orchard fruits as well as purely decorative kinds. Many are hardy in the North and very showy when flowering in spring, although after a severe winter most of the flower buds may be killed. They thrive best in a well-drained loam soil; to avoid injury by late frosts, it is desirable to plant them in northern exposures where they will be less likely to start into growth early. Propagation is by seed, grafting, and budding. See also ALMOND; APRICOT; CHERRY; NECTARINE; PEACH; PLUM.

PRINCIPAL SPECIES
PLUM GROUP

P. americana is a native plum, usually a small, twiggy, and thorny tree, with small, yellow or red fruit.

P. cerasifera (cherry plum, myrobalan) is a small, slender tree often used as stock for grafting and is a useful hedge plant, commonly employed as such in England. It has varieties of weeping form with variously colored leaves, including var. *pissardii*, a handsome purple-leaved form, often grown as an ornamental or to provide colorful shoots for cutting.

P. domestica, from Europe and Asia, is the parent of many garden plums.

P. hortulana (wild-goose plum), native in Kentucky and adjoining areas, is a small tree with red and yellow fruit.

P. insititia (damson plum, bullace) has smaller leaves and fruit than *P. domestica*; it includes the popular Green Gage variety.

P. maritima (beach plum) is a native, sometimes thorny, bush found chiefly in coastal areas and well adapted for planting in sandy soil. The profuse small, white flowers are followed by mostly red or deep purple bloomy fruit, rather bitter for eating raw but excellent for jelly or jam.

P. salicina (Japanese plum) is a spreading tree with yellow or light red fruit, often pointed; very hardy and cultivated in several varieties.

P. spinosa (sloe, blackthorn) is a thorny ornamental shrub often used in hedgerows and poor soils in its native Europe for its early spring blooms, which appear before the purplish leaves. White and pink varieties are available. Its small, blue or black astringent fruits are used for flavoring liqueur. Hardy to Zone 5, it grows to 12 ft.

CHERRY GROUP

P. avium (sweet cherry) is a tall, pyramidal tree with birchlike bark and clusters of white flowers. It is cultivated in many named forms, the common seedling forms, with small fruits known as mazzard cherries; often used as stocks.

P. besseyi (western sand cherry) is a dwarf, spreading species valued on the Great Plains for its sweet fruit. It has been used for crossing with other species and also as a stock to give hardiness and induce dwarfing.

P. cerasus (sour cherry), a small, round-headed tree, is cultivated in many forms for the acid fruit used for pies, preserves, etc. Varieties include the morellos and amarelles.

P. mahaleb (mahaleb cherry) grows to 30 ft. and has small, white, fragrant flowers that open after the leaves are well out; it is often used as grafting stock for other cherries.

P. serrulata (Japanese flowering cherry) is a Japanese species that has yielded many beautiful flowering cherry varieties and cultivars.

P. subhirtella (Higan cherry) is the spring-blooming cherry of Japan, a large shrub or small tree that bears a profusion of blush or pink flowers. Cv. 'Pendula' is a well-known weeping form.

P. tomentosa (Nanking cherry, Hansen's bush cherry) is a spreading shrub to 10 ft., with white or tinted flowers early, and reddish, edible fruit.

BIRD CHERRY GROUP

P. padus (European bird cherry) is a tree that grows to 40 ft. and has fragrant white flowers in loose, drooping clusters followed by black fruit. The wood is valued for building.

P. pensylvanica (wild red cherry) is a bushy shrub or tree that grows to 40 ft. and has red-barked, slender branches, small, white flowers in umbels, followed by light red fruit in summer.

P. serotina (black cherry) is a fine native timber tree, growing to 100 ft., the outer bark dark brown, the inner bitter and aromatic. The flowers are in long, loose racemes that open when the leaves are well out and are followed by purplish black fruit.

Prunus serotina

P. virginiana (chokecherry) is a wild shrub or tree growing to 30 ft. It has rough, speckled bark, white flowers in short, dense racemes with the leaves, and red fruit. It is cultivated in Quebec, northern Ontario, and other cold parts of the continent for fruits used in jellies, jams, sauces, and liqueurs. Improved varieties are sometimes grown for eating raw. Var. *demissa* is native in the western United States.

CHERRY-LAUREL GROUP

P. caroliniana (cherry-laurel) is an evergreen tree that grows to 40 ft. and is found from North Carolina southward. It has small, creamy white flowers and is also known as wild-orange and mock-orange.

P. laurocerasus (cherry-, English-laurel) is an evergreen shrub or small tree with large, glossy leaves and fragrant, white flowers in short clusters. It is often used for hedge and screening purposes in mild climates. Cv. 'Schipkaensis', a smaller form, is hardy in sheltered places in Massachusetts.

P. lusitanica (Portugal-laurel) is a handsome evergreen shrub with thick, glossy, leathery leaves and white flowers in clusters longer than the leaves. It is often grown as a tub plant in cold climates and outdoors as an ornamental in warmer regions. Hardy in Zones 7–9.

ALMOND, APRICOT, AND PEACH GROUP

P. armeniaca (apricot) is a round-headed tree with pinkish or white flowers, cultivated for its choice fruit in many named varieties.

P. davidiana is a slender, peachlike tree with blush flowers very early. It is hardy in the North, but the flower buds are often winter-killed.

P. dulcis var. *dulcis* (sweet almond) is a peachlike tree, the source of the important nut. It is one of the showiest in early spring with delicate, pink flowers but is not hardy in cold climates.

P. mume (Japanese apricot) grows to 30 ft. and has a rounded crown; it is hardy in the North when worked on plum stock. Very decorative forms with double white and double pink flowers are known as Japanese flowering plums.

P. persica (peach) is a small tree that bears pink flowers, very showy when in bloom, and is valued for its choice, slightly downy fruit in many named varieties. There are also double pink- or white-flowered forms and some with purple leaves. Var. *nucipersica* (nectarine) has smaller, smooth-skinned, very choice fruit.

P. tenella (Russian almond) is a hardy, dwarf, compact bush with early pink flowers.

P. triloba (flowering almond) is a hardy bush with clear pink flowers. Cv. 'Multiplex' has double, rosy pink flowers.

PSEUDERANTHEMUM (soo de RAN the mum). A genus of shrubby tropical plants belonging to the Acanthaceae (Acanthus Family). They make good free-flowering subjects for the warm greenhouse. After flowering, old plants can be rested, cut back, and grown on into good specimens. Propagation is by cuttings.

PRINCIPAL SPECIES

P. atropurpureum is a showy plant with purple leaves about 6 in. long and clusters of purple-centered flowers.

P. reticulatum has green, wavy leaves to 10 in. long, marked with a yellow network. The flowers are white with reddish purple spots.

P. tuberculatum is a neat, white-flowering shrub with small leaves, and branches covered with small, wartlike growths.

PSEUDOBULB. The water- and food-storage organ formed by the swelling internodes of stems of orchid plants. Shapes and sizes vary greatly depending on the genus and species.

PSEUDOLARIX (soo doh LAR iks) **kaempferi.** A coniferous deciduous tree belonging to the Pinaceae (Pine Family) and commonly known as golden-larch. The feathery, needlelike leaves in dense bundles are pale green in summer and turn golden yellow in autumn. The tree is graceful with whorled branches, slender and drooping. Although native to China, it is hardy in Zones 5–7 and is quite free from insect pests and diseases. It should be planted in moist, well-drained soil in a sheltered, sunny position and is particularly beautiful when placed in front of dark green evergreens. Propagation is by seed.

PSEUDOTSUGA (soo doh TSOO gah). A genus of coniferous evergreen trees belonging to the Pinaceae (Pine Family) and variously known as fir or spruce (though those common names are more correctly applied to other genera). They have needlelike leaves and drooping cones with trident-shaped bracts. They are of symmetrical, pyramidal growth, resembling the true firs (*Abies*) but easily distinguished from them by the drooping cones and more flexible leaves. In their natural habitat, they are valuable forest and timber trees, but they thrive in cultivation. Propagation is by seed. Most species are hardy in Zones 4–6.

A needle-cast disease of Douglas-fir causes yellow tips on the older needles during the winter and brown mottling in the spring. Remove and destroy infected needles and spray with BORDEAUX MIXTURE in the spring.

PRINCIPAL SPECIES

P. japonica has glossy leaves notched at the tip and 2-in. cones.

P. macrocarpa (bigcone-spruce) has drooping branches and cones to 7 in.

P. menziesii (Douglas-fir), formerly listed as *P. douglasii*, is one of the fastest growing and most satisfactory of evergreens for parks or home grounds, reaching a height of over 200 ft. in its native Rocky Mountains. It has beautiful bluish green needles and drooping brown cones to 4½ in. long on horizontal branches with drooping branchlets.

Pseudotsuga menziesii

In age, it sometimes has a trunk 12 ft. in diameter with 2 ft. thick, cinnamon-brown bark and no branches up to 100 ft. from the ground. As a young tree, it makes a regular pyramidal growth with branches that sweep to the ground. It is a valuable timber tree in the western states and one of the most beautiful evergreens for landscape work. It thrives in a light, rather acid, sandy loam, and groups tend to do better than single specimens because of their mutual protection from high winds. The trees transplant easily. A few cultivars are grafted on seedling stock of the species.

P. sinensis has notched leaves and 2½-in. cones.

PSIDIUM (SID ee um). A genus of tropical shrubs and trees that produce the edible GUAVA.

PSILOTUM (sil OH tum). A genus of FERN ALLIES with no roots or leaves but only underground stems and erect branches. *P. nudum* is occasionally found growing on trees and logs in wet woods in the southern states and Mexico.

PSYCHOTRIA (sī KOH tree ah). A genus of shrubs belonging to the Rubiaceae (Madder Family), they are useful shade plants in warm climates. Three species are native to Florida, where *P. nervosa* is known as wild-coffee. As greenhouse plants, they are valued for their glossy leaves and heads of white flowers followed by red or black berries. Hardy in Zones 10–11.

PTELEA (TEE lee ah) **trifoliata.** A North American shrub or small tree growing to 25 ft., belonging to the Rutaceae (Rue Family), and commonly known as hop tree. The dark green, trifoliate leaves have good value in a mixed planting and are highly aromatic. Small, very fragrant yellowish flowers are borne in dense clusters and followed by interesting and decorative hoplike seeds. It is not particular as to soil but is partial to shade. Propagation of the species is by seed; of varieties, by layering or grafting. Cv. 'Aurea' has rich yellow leaves that fade to green in August. Hardy in Zones 4–9.

PTERIDIUM (te RID ee um). A fern genus with one extremely widespread species. There are several regional varieties, including four found in North America; however, it is not easy for the amateur to spot the fine distinctions between them. Many botanists recognize most of the varieties as distinct species because they often grow together and maintain their differences.

P. aquilinum (bracken) is a strong, aggressive, yet attractive fern that covers woodland floors, hillsides, and pastures. The fronds are lovely light green as they unfurl in spring, and in autumn they are shades of russet, cream, and brown. The plant has tough, spreading, much-branched rhizomes that go deep in the soil. Fronds are triangular, bipinnate to tripinnate, sometimes quadripinnate, and can be as tall as 15 ft. The croziers and rhizomes have been used as food but are suspected of containing carcinogenic toxins. The dried fronds were often used in the past to stuff mattresses and pillows. It is dangerous to introduce this fern into the garden, unless it can be confined by barriers going deep into the ground. Var. *cristatum* is an attractive form that might be used in this way.

PTERIS (TER is). A genus of about 250 species of tropical and subtropical ferns, variously known as brake ferns. Many are cultivated as garden plants where hardy, and a few are available as container plants in temperate areas. There are many more beautiful species that could be grown. Most have vigorous root systems and need repotting at least twice a year.

Pteris cretica

A fast-draining fern mix is suitable for most, but a few need added lime. They require plenty of water (less in winter); drying of the roots is usually fatal. They are easily grown from spores, and the young plants grow very rapidly. Several species have escaped and naturalized in Florida.

PRINCIPAL SPECIES

P. argyrea (silver brake), also listed as *P. quadriaurita* cv. 'Argyrea', is a 2–4 ft. tall, pinnate to bipinnate fern with stunning silver-variegated fronds. Native to India, it is one of the most popular cultivated brakes and makes an excellent container plant.

P. cretica (Cretan brake) is a 16–24 in., pinnate to bipinnate plant that is widespread and is spreading further by naturalizing. Native to Africa, southern Europe, and Asia, it is a good houseplant if lime is added to the potting mix. Cultivars include 'Albo-lineata', 'Albo-lineata Cristata', 'Distinction', and 'Wilsonii'.

P. ensiformis (sword brake) is a small (6–12 in.), bipinnate fern common to tropical forests and mangrove fringes, and it often colonizes walls and gardens. Native to Asia and Australia, it is an excellent houseplant with an attractive cultivar, 'Victoriae', which has white stripes on each side of the midrib and comes true from spores.

P. tremula (Australian or tender brake) is an

attractive, lacy, tripinnate fern that grows quickly, its bright green fronds reaching 4 ft. in height. It is easily grown as a container plant.

P. vittata (ladder brake) is a large, bipinnate fern with fronds up to 4 ft. long. It needs plenty of light and water but excellent drainage. It is found in South Africa, Asia, Japan, and Australia.

PTEROCARYA (ter oh KAY ree ah). A genus of deciduous Asiatic trees belonging to the Juglandaceae (Walnut Family), commonly known as wingnut. They are rapid-growing trees with divided leaves and winged nutlets. Most are hardy in Zones 6–8.

P. fraxinifolia (Caucasian wingnut), native to Iran, grows to 50 ft. and is occasionally grown for its wide-spreading branches as a shade tree. It has no significant disease or insect problems.

PTEROSTYRAX (ter oh STĪ raks). A genus comprising two species of deciduous Asiatic trees or shrubs with white flowers, commonly called epaulette tree. Both species prefer a moist, sandy loam and are propagated by seed or softwood cuttings. Hardy in Zones 5–8.

P. corymbosus is shrubby with relatively small leaves and flower clusters.

P. hispidus is a very fast growing tree to 30 ft. and has a broad head and slender branches. The oblong leaves, to 7 in. long, resemble those of the elm. The abundant creamy white, pendulous panicles of fragrant flowers in spring make it highly desirable.

PTYCHOSPERMA (tī koh SPUR mah) **elegans.** An interesting feather palm from Australia and neighboring islands, it is a slender tree that grows to 25 ft. and has graceful, arching, featherform leaves to 3 ft. long. Cultivated in south Florida, it thrives in rich, moist soil. It has been listed under various names, especially *Hydriastele wendlandiana*, which correctly refers to a different tree.

PUBESCENT. Covered (but not matted) with hairs, particularly short, soft, downlike, and not very dense hairs, like those on the underside of the leaves of hardy catalpa, the twigs of the flowering dogwood, or the throat of the flower of *Crocus vernus*. "Puberulent" means "somewhat pubescent."

PUCCOON. A common name for *Lithospermum canescens*, an orange-flowered perennial similar to forget-me-nots; see LITHOSPERMUM.

PUERARIA (pew er AY ree uh) **thunbergiana.** A twining Asiatic perennial vine belonging to the Fabaceae (Bean Family), commonly known as kudzu. It has large, tuberous roots; large, three-part, somewhat lobed leaves; spikes of fragrant, purple flowers; and large, flat, hairy seedpods. Hardy to Zone 5, in the North it usually dies to the ground in winter, and in favorable conditions it grows from 40–60 ft. long each summer. Halo spot, a bacterial disease, causes conspicuous spotting of the leaves. To avoid the disease, plant roots from disease-free fields and do not use cuttings.

Pueraria thunbergiana

P. lobata is similar to *P. thunbergiana* but has more deeply lobed leaflets and is chiefly grown as an ornamental. It is used to cover hillsides to prevent erosion and has been unsuccessfully planted as cattle fodder and as a source of starch from the fleshy roots. Plant to control its growth, because in fertile soil, kudzu will cover fences, houses, trees, barns, etc., and in a short time. It has been referred to as a vegetable form of cancer.

PULMONARIA (pul moh NAY ree ah). A genus of European perennial herbs, closely related to the forget-me-not, belonging to the Boraginaceae (Borage Family), and commonly known as lungwort. They have creeping rootstocks; large basal leaves, often mottled; and blue or purple flowers in flat-topped clusters. Attractive, decorative plants for the border, they thrive best in a semi-shaded position in rich, moist soil. They can be grown from seed or propagated by division of the clumps. Most are hardy in Zones 3–8.

PRINCIPAL SPECIES

P. angustifolia grows to 1 ft. and has dark blue flowers. Vars. *aurea* and *azurea* are other color forms.

P. montana grows to 1½ ft. with bright green leaves and violet flowers.

P. officinalis has spotted leaves and odd, reddish flowers fading to violet.

P. saccharata (Bethlehem-sage) grows to 1½ ft. and has white-spotted leaves and whitish or reddish violet flowers. Cv. 'Mrs. Moon' is an attractive plant during most of the year, popular for its easy cultivation, moderate spreading habit, and pink flowers maturing to blue. Cv. 'Sissinghurst White', is a newer cultivar much like 'Mrs. Moon', but it has pure white flowers.

Pulmonaria saccharata

PULSATILLA (pul sah TIL ah). A genus of hardy perennial herbs, commonly known as pasque-flower. They are related to and often grouped under the genus ANEMONE, but a number of taxonomists prefer to maintain their separate identity. Pulsatillas are a large group, many of which are ideal subjects for the rock garden. The airy seed heads are as decorative as flowers.

PRINCIPAL SPECIES

P. cernua, native to Japan, is a compact species with nodding, wine-red flowers.

P. patens with bluish violet blooms, is now widely listed as *Anemone patens*; see ANEMONE.

P. vulgaris is a choice and easy plant for the rock garden with a number of forms available. Cv. 'Rubra', with deep red flowers, is perhaps the most choice.

PUMELLO. Common name for *Citrus maxima*, a tropical evergreen tree from which the better-known *C.* x *paradisi* (GRAPEFRUIT) was derived. The pumello, also known as shaddock, is a smaller tree distinguished from the grapefruit by its fruits, which are coarser grained, borne singly, yellow to orange, globose to pear shaped, and very large (sometimes to 20 lb.!). The giant fruit is popular in southeast Asia and China and is sometimes grown in the United States as an ornamental curiosity. Very tender, it is hardy only in Zones 10–11. For culture, see CITRUS FRUITS.

PUMPKIN. A name loosely applied, sometimes interchangeably with "squash," to the plants and edible fruits of several species of CUCURBITA. The field pumpkin popular at Halloween is *C. pepo* var. *pepo*.

Pumpkins thrive best in the full sun and in rich, well-drained, light soils. Generally the seed is sown where the plants are to mature. Where the season is short, growth can be hastened by sowing them on inverted sods, or in berry boxes or flowerpots, from which the plants are transplanted to the open ground after the danger of frost has passed. Frequently, field varieties are planted (as partner crops) in vacant hills in cornfields. Bush varieties are set 4–5 ft. apart, and vining kinds, 10–12 ft. Generally only one plant is grown on each hill. In soil less than moderately rich, a forkful of well-decayed manure should be mixed with the soil at each stand.

The fruits must be gathered before frost touches them, handled as carefully as eggs to prevent bruising and consequent decay, laid in a sunny place or in a coldframe or deep straw, covered in cold and wet weather until the shells become hard (in about two weeks), and then stored where the air is dry and the temperature does not fall below 50°F. Thus handled they should keep until after midwinter.

Pumpkin vines may be attacked by downy mildew, bacterial wilt, and anthracnose but are not often seriously injured. The squash bug and squash vine borer are the worst insect pests.

See also CUCURBITA; SQUASH.

PUNCTATE. Dotted with pits, such as the resinous depressions on wax-myrtle leaves. They may be colored or translucent, on the surface or internal.

PUNICA (PYOO ni kah) **granatum.** A large, subtropical bush grown for its brilliant orange-red flowers and fruits, commonly known as POMEGRANATE.

PUNK TREE. Common name for *Melaleuca quinquenervia*, an Australian tree with bark that shreds in conspicuous strips. Planting this tree is prohibited in south Florida, where it is an aggressive weed; see MELALEUCA.

PUPA. The stage during which an insect undergoing complete metamorphosis changes from the larva or grub to the adult stage. During this stage (sometimes erroneously called a "resting stage") locomotion and feeding cease, respiration is reduced, and all available energy is devoted to the development of wings, legs, mouthparts, and other appendages of the adult and to the maturing of the reproductive organs. A pupa may be naked and exposed (in which state it is called a chrysalis), or enclosed in a case, which may be anything from a folded leaf to a silken cocoon.

PURSLANE Common name for *Portulaca oleracea*, a persistent succulent weed sometimes used as a potherb; see PORTULACA; WEEDS. The Purslane or Portulaca Family is PORTULACACEAE.

Winter purslane is the edible herb *Montia perfoliata*.

PUSCHKINIA (push KIN ee ah). A genus of small bulbous plants belonging to the Liliaceae (Lily Family). They resemble the early-flowering squills (see SCILLA) but are not so brilliantly blue, the small, nodding blossoms in loose clusters being striped pale blue and white. Only one species, *P. scilloides* is commonly grown. It grows to 6 in. and is charming in the rock garden or border. Plants will spread slowly if left undisturbed. Var. *libanotica* has smaller flowers.

PUSSY WILLOW. Common name for *Salix discolor*, a deciduous shrub with large, silvery catkins; see SALIX.

PUSSY-TOES. Common name for ANTENNARIA, a genus of perennial herbs with basal clusters of woolly leaves.

PUTTYROOT. Common name for *Aplectrum hyemale*, a North American orchid with yellowish brown flowers; see APLECTRUM.

PUYA (POO yah). A genus of large, dry-region, South American herbaceous plants that have dense rosettes of spiny-edged leaves and spikes of yellow, purple, or blue flowers. Related to BROMELIA, they require the same sort of treatment whether in outdoor gardens or, as sometimes grown, in greenhouses.

PYCNANTHEMUM (pik NAN thee mum). A genus of North American perennial herbs belonging to the Lamiaceae (Mint Family) and commonly known as mountain mint. They produce heads or flat-topped clusters of small, purple or white flowers in late summer or fall. Of easiest culture, they are hardy to Zone 5 and are often grown in the wild garden.

P. flexuosum has slender stems and whitish lavender flowers.

P. virginianum, which grows 1–3 ft. high, has fragrant, mintlike leaves and flowers in dense heads.

PYRACANTHA (pī rah KAN thah). A small genus of Asiatic evergreens, mostly thorny shrubs, belonging to the Rosaceae (Rose Family) and commonly called firethorn. Their masses of white flowers are followed by many brilliant orange-red "berries"—really diminutive apples or pomes. Propagation is by seed, cuttings, layers, and grafting.

Where hardy, these are beautiful shrubs for such various purposes as climbing a wall, forming a hedge, or as dense bushes in the shrub border. They are particularly effective on a slope. A sunny location in well-drained soil suits them best. They do not transplant readily.

Sudden browning or blackening and dieback of twigs could be due to FIRE BLIGHT, a bacterial disease common on apples and several ornamental shrubs. To control, prune out diseased shoots well below the infected area with pruning shears dipped after each cut in a disinfectant, such as a mercuric bichloride solution. Scab is a common problem affecting the fruit, causing it to turn brown and fall off prematurely. Spray with lime-sulfur (1 gal. to 30 gal. water) early in spring, before growth begins and before flowering.

PRINCIPAL SPECIES

P. coccinea (scarlet firethorn) grows to 6 ft. as a bush or to 20 ft. against a wall. It is hardy in Zones 6–9, with some cultivars thriving in Zone 5. It has oval leaves 1 in. or longer and striking, bright orange-red berries. Cv. 'Lalandei' is hardier and more vigorous with showy orange-red fruit. 'Aurea' has yellow fruit.

P. crenulata grows to 20 ft. and has lustrous, bright green leaves and orange-red berries; hardy to Zone 7. Var. *flava* has yellow fruit.

P. koidzumii (Formosa firethorn), used widely in the South, has masses of red berries and grows about 12 ft. high and 12 ft. wide. Cv. 'San Jose' is a wide-spreading shrub; 'Victory' has an upright, arching habit and dark red fruit; 'Waterei' grows to 8 ft. high and 8 ft. wide and is almost thornless, with dark red fruit. Hardy to Zone 8.

P. x *mohave*, with abundant orange-red fruits is quite resistant to scab and fire blight.

P. x *teton*, a hybrid with yellow-orange fruits, is resistant to scab and fire blight.

PYRETHRUM (pī REETH rum). A former genus of plants in the Asteraceae (Aster Family), now considered part of the genus CHRYSANTHEMUM. As a common name it is applied by florists to *Chrysanthemum coccineum* (or *C. roseum*), a perennial with finely cut foliage, bearing in spring or summer flower heads of white to lilac or crimson on long, erect stems.

The common name also applies to *C. cinerariifolium*, one of the species from which the botanical insecticide is produced. This insecticide should not be used on chrysanthemums. In gardens the name is also applied to *C. parthenium*, better known as feverfew.

PYRETHRUM INSECTICIDE

This is the botanical insecticide extracted from dried, daisylike flowers of three species of chrysanthemum by hot carbon dioxide under high pressure (in a process like that used to decaffeinate coffee). The most common source is *C. cinerariifolium*, which, though once produced in quantity in California, is more recently grown and produced in Kenya because of the economic advantages.

In the plant, four esters make up the toxic pyrethrin principle. They are subject to decomposition by sunlight, so as well as being quick acting, pyrethrum has little residual effect. For natural pyrethrum, no tolerance has been established; for synthetic, it is 2–4 parts per million. Commercial preparations for sprays usually have a concentration of about .10%. A spreader of soap makes the action of pyrethrum more effective. When used to control fleas on animals, the preparation is made as a dust. The only pure, strong pyrethrum available is at a veterinarian's or a pet shop. Some commercial mixtures should be examined to see whether they contain hard toxic chemicals. Others are composed of supplements like sesame oil or asarinin.

One effective pesticide, Tri-excel, is supplemented with two other botanicals: ROTENONE and ryania. Rotenone products should not be used until dusk or very early in the morning when bees and other beneficial pollinators are not out working.

To make your own pyrethrum insecticide, gather flower heads of *C. cinerariifolium* when two or three rows of petals have opened in the central disk, and when the flowers are free of dew or raindrops. Dry them in the sun or in an oven at very low heat, leaving out the stems. Put 10 grams in a light-proof bottle with 4 oz. of denatured alcohol. Shake well and let stand for 24 hours; then filter. The result will be a .1% solution, but on exposure it becomes stronger as the alcohol evaporates. Since pyrethrum can be released when the flower head is crushed, it is possible to use this insecticide in dust form from the crushed flower parts instead of making a spray. This is useful to control cabbage worms, mosquitoes, and sometimes hornets. Such dust, cut with inert ingredients, is often available at garden centers and farm suppliers.

PYROLA (pī ROH lah). A genus of dwarf, evergreen, perennial herbs commonly known as shinleaf or wintergreen. They bear waxy, white, purple, or greenish flowers atop slender stalks. Since they need very acid soil, it is impossible to grow them in the average garden, but if carefully handled, they can be grown in a wildflower garden in a soil kept continuously acid with a mulch of oak leaves. They are also likely to do well under pine trees. Hardy to Zone 3.

PRINCIPAL SPECIES

P. elliptica has evergreen leaves and white flowers. It has a creeping underground root system, and frequently, colonies of the plants can be found.

P. rotundifolia, the European form, has white flowers.

P. virens, formerly listed as *P. chlorantha*, with greenish white flowers, is found in North America, Europe, and Asia.

Pyrola sp.

PYROLACEAE (pīr oh LAY see ee). The Pyrola, Shinleaf, or Wintergreen Family; some scientists combine this group with plants of the Ericaceae (Heath Family). Its members, mostly evergreen, are low herbs found in northern regions. The flowers are small and regular, and in *Pyrola* (shinleaf) are borne on an upright, leafless stalk.

PYROSTEGIA (pir oh STEE jee ah). A genus of evergreen climbing shrubs belonging to the Bignoniaceae (Bignonia Family). *P. venusta*, for-

merly listed as *P. ignea*, is the principal species; it is a popular vine outdoors in warm regions (Zones 10–11) and is sometimes grown under glass. The leaves have two or three leaflets, and the tendrils, by which it climbs, are three-parted. It has showy, drooping clusters of reddish orange flowers with reflexed lobes. Propagation is by cuttings.

PYRROSIA (pee ROH see ah). A genus of small to medium-sized epiphytic ferns with a thick layer of hairs on the back of the fronds. The naked sori cover the dorsal frond surface.

P. hastata is an excellent basket fern with 6–10 in., three-lobed fronds growing from a short, creeping rhizome. It is native to China, Korea, and Japan and needs a freely draining mixture.

P. lingua (felt or tongue fern) is a suitable plant for greenhouse or pot culture. It has simple, oblong or linear fronds 6–10 in. long, rarely lobed, rather fleshy and hairy, growing from creeping, scaly rhizomes. They like peaty soil with coarse sand, doing best in shallow pots or baskets and used for ground cover in California. There are many striking cultivars, including 'Contorta', 'Cristata', 'Nana', 'Tsunomata', and 'Variegata'.

PYRUS (PĪ rus). An important genus of mostly deciduous trees, rarely shrubs, native in cool-temperate regions of the Northern Hemisphere belonging to the Rosaceae (Rose Family), and commonly known as PEAR. The group includes valuable orchard fruits and many good ornamentals, showy in spring when in bloom, and attractive in fall with their colorful fruit. Most of them are hardy in the North and easily cultivated in well-drained soil. Propagation is by seed and, in the case of named varieties, by budding and grafting.

PRINCIPAL SPECIES

P. arbutifolia is correctly listed as *Aronia arbutifolia*; see ARONIA.

P. calleryana is a handsome, free-flowering, Chinese species with glossy leaves very colorful in autumn. Cv. 'Bradford' is a tall, vigorous ornamental and is attractive as a street tree.

P. communis (common pear) is a large, upright, long-lived tree, showy in spring with clusters of white flowers and cultivated for its fruit in many named varieties.

P. melanocarpa is correctly listed as *Aronia melanocarpa*, see ARONIA.

P. salicifolia is a small tree with slender, more or less drooping branches, silvery, willowlike leaves, and creamy white flowers.

QUAILBUSH. Common name for *Atriplex lentiformis*, a shrub native to saline soils of California, useful for erosion control; see ATRIPLEX.

QUAMASH. Common name for CAMASSIA, a genus of bulbous plants with racemes of blue or white flowers.

QUARANTINE. A regulation or statute promulgated and administered under the law by the local, state, or federal government for the purpose of preventing the spread of injurious insects or plant diseases. It may either completely prohibit the entry or movement of plant or other material (in which case it is an embargo), or merely regulate by requiring preliminary inspection and certification either of the material or the premises or locality where it was grown.

There are several hundred quarantines —federal and state—now in effect, although many of them are relatively local or limited in application. A number of them deal with staple crops rather than those of interest to the home gardener. Additional information can be secured from the Department of Agriculture in Washington, D.C., and from state extension services.

QUEEN-ANNE'S-LACE. Common name for *Daucus carota*, a flowering plant that includes the common carrot; see DAUCUS.

QUEEN-OF-THE-MEADOW. Common name for *Filipendula ulmaria*, a tall perennial herb sometimes cultivated for its dense panicles of white flowers; see FILIPENDULA.

QUEEN-OF-THE-PRAIRIE. Common name for *Filipendula rubra*, a tall perennial herb with peach-pink flowers; see FILIPENDULA.

QUEENSLAND NUT. Common name for *Macadamia ternifolia*, an Australian tree cultivated for ornament and for its edible nuts; see MACADAMIA.

QUERCIFILIX (kwer si FEE liks) **zeilanica.** A tiny, scarcely known dimorphic fern whose sterile fronds vaguely resemble oak leaves. The fertile fronds are contracted into a few linear segments. There are no indusia. The only species known in cultivation, it is native to tropical and subtropical regions and can be grown in a small pot of fast-draining fern mix.

QUERCUS (KWUR kus). A genus of magnificent, mostly deciduous trees and a few shrubs belonging to the Fagaceae (Beech Family) and commonly known as oak. They have inconspicuous flowers borne in catkins or spikes and oblong or roundish fruits called acorns, set in cuplike involucres. Beautiful in all their various forms, oaks are usually wide spreading with great trunks, often tall and majestic. They are valuable forest trees as well as useful for ornamental purposes in landscape design. Some of the low-growing species are excellent for dry, rocky hillsides. The foliage, often beautifully cut, is always interesting and in many species assumes brilliant autumn coloring. The evergreen species, with their hollylike leaves, grow mostly in the southern states, California, and Oregon; but almost all the deciduous species are hardy. Many oaks grow in swampy ground, but others, especially red oaks, prefer drier soil.

All can be propagated by seed sown as soon as gathered, but the varieties are grafted in the greenhouse on potted stock, preferably on *Q. robur*. Sometimes in the South, evergreen species are propagated by layers or cuttings.

Diseases. Practically all species of oak are subject to leaf blister, caused by a fungus that is common throughout the United States but is more injurious in the South. Blisters appear on the leaves before they are full grown, often causing them to curl. Control measures used for peach LEAF CURL should be successful, including a spray of BORDEAUX MIXTURE after the leaves fall and before the buds swell.

Four species of powdery mildew attack oak leaves. Where necessary, control can be obtained by spraying with wettable sulfur. Anthracnose or scorch, caused by a fungus and common on the plane tree, may cause complete or partial defoliation of white oaks. Spray three times with BORDEAUX MIXTURE at two-week intervals, beginning when the leaves are half grown; also destroy fallen leaves. Several species of blister rust fungi (see RUSTS) have their alternate stage on oak leaves. One of them injures two- and three-needled pines, and if the pines are more valuable in a certain location, the oaks should be removed to eliminate the menace to the pines.

Insect Pests. The list of insects attacking oaks is a long one, but few are of great importance. Scales are controlled by a dormant spray with a miscible oil. For protection against many leaf-eating insects, the foliage should be thoroughly sprayed with insecticide in the spring. In certain localities and years, the cankerworm will practically denude the trees. Caterpillars of the gypsy, brown-tail, and forest moths as well as the American silkworm, forest tent caterpillar, and orange-striped oak worm may all feed on the leaves. Cecropia and luna moth caterpillars also feed on the leaves but are generally harmless. The California oak moth is a destructive pest of live oaks on the Pacific Coast. A late-summer as well as spring spray may be needed to control the two broods. Leaf rollers that may attack oaks are controlled by spraying the trees with insecticide before the leaves begin to curl. Control of several conspicuous leaf miners can be difficult. For other controls, see INSECT CONTROL; CATERPILLAR; LEAF ROLLER; LEAF MINER; SCALE INSECTS.

PRINCIPAL SPECIES

Q. agrifolia (California live oak), growing to 100 ft., is a handsome tree with spiny-toothed, glossy evergreen leaves, native to California. Hardy to Zone 9.

Q. alba (white oak), growing to 75 ft., is one of the most characteristic and noble trees of the northern states. It should be planted where it will have room to show its majestic proportions and the full beauty of its autumn coloring, often a striking wine-red or purple. Growing best in a rather moist soil, it is quite adaptable, but it is slow growing and hard to transplant. White oaks

are long-lived trees, with some individuals found to be over 500 years old. Hardy in Zones 3–9.

Q. coccinea (scarlet oak), growing to 80 ft., is excellent for dry locations. The bright green foliage becomes brilliant scarlet in autumn. Hardy in Zones 4–9.

Q. ilicifolia (bear or scrub oak) is a branching deciduous shrub growing 10 ft. or taller bearing 4½-in. leaves with paired, toothed lobes and whitish undersides. It is native to the eastern United States and is hardy to Zone 5.

Q. imbricaria (shingle oak), growing to 60 ft., has slender, drooping branches in youth but becomes round-topped with age. The foliage is glossy dark green above, downy beneath, and becomes russet-red in the fall. Hardy in Zones 4–8.

Quercus ilicifolia

Q. kelloggii (California black oak), a West Coast native, grows 80 ft. or more and has 6-in. oblong leaves divided into narrow, sharply toothed lobes and may have fuzzy undersides.

Q. lobata (valley oak) grows to 100 ft., bearing 3-in., lobed leaves with grayish fuzz underneath.

Q. macrocarpa (burr oak) grows 80 ft. or more and has leaves to 10 in. long with large terminal lobes and grayish hairs on the undersides. Native to eastern North America, it is an important source of lumber.

Q. nigra (water oak) grows to 60 ft. and has small, 3-in., obovate leaves. It transplants easily and is used as a street or shade tree in Zones 6–9.

Q. palustris (pin oak), growing to 60 ft. or more, forms a symmetrical, pyramidal head with long, pendulous branches. The foliage assumes a bright red in autumn. Because of its erect, symmetrical, and rather rapid growth and ease of transplanting, it is often used for landscaping. Cv. 'Sovereign' has lower branches that remain horizontal to the trunk. Hardy in Zones 4–8.

Q. phellos (willow oak), growing to 60 ft., has narrow leaves like a willow and a pyramidal shape when young. It grows best in wet areas and is used as a street or shade tree in Zones 5–9.

Q. prinus (chestnut oak), formerly listed as *Q. montana*, grows to 70 ft. or more, thriving in dry ground and valuable for ornamental planting in the eastern states. It develops deeply ridged bark with age. The foliage resembles that of the chestnut and turns dull orange in autumn.

Q. robur (English oak), growing to 50 ft., is a stout, wide-spreading tree greatly valued for its historical associations. It has many horticultural varieties, including cv. 'Fastigiata', of upright growth, and cv. 'Pendula', with drooping branches. Hardy in Zones 4–8.

Q. rubra (red oak), growing to 80 ft., is a handsome round-topped tree with spreading branches and foliage that turns a dark shade of red in the fall. Hardy in Zones 4–8.

Quercus rubra

Q. velutina (black oak) is a rapid-growing tree attaining 75 ft. or more. It has slender branches and an open head of glossy foliage that develops little fall color. Hardy in Zones 3–9.

Q. virginiana (live oak), growing to 60 ft. and very wide spreading, has elliptic evergreen leaves that are glossy above and downy beneath. This long-lived species is native, well appreciated, and often cultivated in the southern states. Hardy only in Zones 7–9.

QUILLAJA (kwil AY ja) **saponaria.** An evergreen tree of the Rosaceae (Rose Family), commonly known as soapbark tree. It has small, shining, leathery leaves and white flowers ¾ in. across in terminal clusters. Its bark has saponaceous and medicinal qualities. Not hardy in the North, it is sometimes grown as a greenhouse tree or outdoors in Zones 9–11. Propagation is by cuttings rooted under glass.

QUILLWORT. Common name for ISOETES, a genus of FERN ALLIES with cylindrical leaves.

QUINCE. Common name for various shrubs grown for fruit or ornament, belonging to the Rosaceae (Rose Family). Some species have long been cultivated for fruit used in the making of choice preserves. The common quince, *Cydonia oblonga* (formerly included with apples and pears as *Pyrus cydonia*), is a wide-spreading shrub or small, crooked tree of slow growth. It thrives best in deep, heavy, moist, not overly rich soil, where, however, the fruit produced is dull, greenish yellow instead of the rich, golden yellow characteristic of lighter soil. The ornamental Japanese- or flowering-quince, often listed as *Cydonia,* is now part of the genus CHAENOMELES.

CULTURE

For home fruit production, one or two specimens should yield an ample supply, since a mature bush should bear two to four pecks of fruit annually. Because of the beauty of the flowers as well as the ripe fruit, quinces deserve a place as ornamental plants, provided a circular space of 15 ft. or more in diameter is allowed for each plant.

Since they are shallow-rooted plants, they do better under mulch than if the soil is cultivated. Thus treated, they are also less liable to fire blight because the growths are less sappy and therefore more resistant to attack. The aim should always be moderate, not luxuriant, growth, and this can be gained partly by the sparing use of nitrogenous fertilizers and manures.

Quince blooms rather late in spring and bears its flowers on green shoots of the current season. It is prone to set more fruit than it can develop to full size, however, so all defective and crowded ones should be removed while small. This is easily done a week or two after the flowers fade while the stems are still soft enough to permit pinching them off. Pruning consists merely of removing dead, dying, and superfluous branches while the plants are dormant.

One-year or two-year bushes are better to plant than older ones. They can then be trained in either tree or bush form. The advantage of the tree form is that borers are more easily controlled, while in the bush form, fire blight can more easily be kept in check and new stems can be induced and encouraged when necessary. See control of these and other quince enemies under APPLE.

Disease. Fire blight is a common disease of both common and flowering quinces. Infected wood must be removed with great care. The quince rust has juniper as its alternate host. It produces deep orange spores in white cluster cups on the backs of the leaves and on the fruit. A leaf and fruit blight common on pear may seriously injure quince trees, and the black rot of apple may occur. For control measures, see FIRE BLIGHT; RUSTS; PEAR; APPLE.

Insect Pests. Until the advent of the oriental fruit moth, the quince curculio was the most destructive pest of this tree. These small, gray snout beetles appear in midsummer, and the flesh-colored grubs tunnel through the fruit. Two thorough applications of insecticide, when the beetles appear and begin to lay eggs, give some control. Several APHIDS, the CODLING MOTH, and the SAN JOSÉ SCALE commonly infest quince.

QUISQUALIS (kwis KWAW lis) **indica.** A tropical shrub of vigorous climbing habit, sometimes grown in warm greenhouses, and commonly known as rangoon-creeper. It thrives best when planted out in a summer bed of fibrous loam, peat, and sand. In summer it bears loose clusters of fragrant flowers with long, green calyx tubes and petals that open white and age to red over the course of one or two days. After flowering it needs a resting period and later severe pruning to induce vigorous new growth. Propagation is by softwood cuttings. Hardy in Zones 10–11.

R

RABBITS. Sometimes rabbits can cause problems by nibbling on vegetables, young fruit trees, and flowers. To protect fruit trees, wrap the lower 2 ft. of trunk with chicken wire, or perforated plastic, extending 2 in. into the ground. Dried blood sprinkled around is also an effective repellent, but it attracts dogs and must be replaced after a rain. Epsom salts (2 tsp. per 1 qt. water) or powdered rock phosphate sprinkled on young leaves makes them unpalatable until washed off. Rabbits dislike onions, so interplant these with cabbage, lettuce, peas, and beans. Other plant materials that are repellent are aloe, tobacco, cayenne, black pepper, and an ornamental *Senecio cinerara* (dusty miller). A row or two of soybeans planted along the edge of the garden will keep rabbits eating them instead of more valuable vegetables. For temporary protection, a movable cage of poultry fence or chicken wire can be placed over young plants as needed. Live traps, which allow the release of pets that wander into them, can also be used to catch the animals, which can then be transported to other areas.

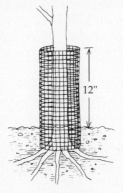

Tree guard

RABBIT'S-FOOT FERN. Common name for some species of DAVALLIA (also called hare's-foot fern), suggested by their hairy, creeping rhizomes; and for *Polypodium aureum*, a tropical fern with long, curiously shaped fronds; see POLYPODIUM. Silver-rabbit's-foot fern, *Humata tyermannii*, is a popular basket fern with silvery scales; see HUMATA.

RACE. A term in plant breeding that means a strongly marked group of individuals capable of coming true from seed. Cultivated races are somewhat similar to botanical varieties, but they are usually highly developed forms, originating in cultivation and generally requiring more or less selection to keep them from degenerating. See PLANT BREEDING; STRAIN; VARIETY; CLONE.

RACEME. An elongated, slender flower cluster in which each flower is borne on a stalk (pedicle) of its own rather than close against the main stalk (peduncle) as in a spike. A raceme may be erect or drooping, and loose or compact, depending on the length of the pedicels.

RACHIS. The continuation of the twig into the flower cluster to form the main axis, which bears the flowers and individual flower stalks making up the inflorescence; also the main axis of a fern leaf.

RADERMACHERA (ra dur mak AIR ah) **sinica.** A tropical tree, formerly listed as *Stereospermum*, and commonly known as baby-doll. Already small in nature, it is treated with growth retardants for use as a houseplant. The large compound leaves are a shiny dark green and contrast well with other simple shapes in the interior.

RADISH. An annual herb, *Raphanus sativus*, grown for its crisp-fleshed roots of various sizes, shapes, and colors. In the case of the rat-tailed or aerial radish, it is the long, soft, thick pods that are pickled or used in a salad.

Root radishes are of three classes: small, globular or oblong spring varieties, white, pink, or red in color, which reach edible size in three to five weeks; somewhat larger, oblong or slender, pink or white summer varieties; and white or black winter varieties that require cool conditions, grow to large (sometimes enormous) size, and are used fresh or stored like turnips. Small radishes are eaten raw; the larger kinds are occasionally boiled and served like turnips.

Aerial radish

To be crisp, mild, and of the best quality, radishes should grow rapidly and be used as soon as large enough. This means frequent small sowings that fit well into the garden scheme as interplant-ings between larger, slower-growing crops and also to mark rows of seeds that start slowly. Forcing radishes can be grown 1–2 in. apart in rows only 6–8 in. apart; the larger kinds need up to 12 in. or more between rows and correspondingly more space between the plants. Before planting, sift out and discard small, light seeds. Make suc-cessional sowings every

Early small radish

week or so, first in the hotbed from late winter until early spring; then outdoors until late spring, using the summer kinds for the later plantings.

After midsummer, sow the large winter kinds that would become hard, stringy, and strong fla-vored if started in hot weather. Dug before frost and stored in a cool place, these will keep for sev-eral weeks. For use, peel and cut the tender, crisp roots lengthwise in thin slices.

A white rust occurring on many crucifers is most serious on radish, causing prominent

Late radish

white blisters on the leaves and thickened, dis-torted stems. Spraying is not recommended, but crop rotation, cultivating to keep down crucifer-ous weeds, and burning all infected crop refuse are advisable preventive measures against this and other radish troubles, which are chiefly those discussed under BRASSICA.

The most common insect pests are aphids, the cabbage root maggot, and flea beetles. These can be kept out of small plantings by protecting with floating row covers.

RAFFIA. Dried vegetable fiber made from the peeled cuticle of leaves of a certain palm tree (*Raphia farinifera*) and used for tying plants to stakes, for bunching vegetables, in budding, and for various other gardening purposes. It is light, inexpensive, clean, easy to use, and surprisingly strong. Raffia eventually rots under the influ-ence of moisture and weather, so it should not be used for permanent tying, but it is unusually good in the flower garden. It is somewhat easier to handle if slightly moistened.

RAGGED-ROBIN. A common name for *Lych-nis flos-cuculi*, a perennial herb with red to white flowers clustered atop erect stems; see LYCHNIS.

RAGWORT. Common name for SENECIO, a genus of herbs, shrubs, and trees, including climbers and succulents.

RAISED BEDS. These are garden beds, especial-ly seedbeds, elevated 6–10 in. above walkways that run between them. Because rainwater runs off the raised beds into the walkways, this tech-nique improves the drainage and aeration of the cultivated soil. It enables a gardener to plant on time in the spring, despite heavy rains that threaten to waterlog other gardens; thus, low-lying wet areas can be converted into productive garden spaces.

Due to an increased surface area exposed to sunlight, the soil in a raised bed can be up to 10°F warmer than that of a conventional garden. This encourages the growth of warm-weather crops such as melons and tomatoes, and allows the northern gardener to keep crops such as kale and spinach growing long after the first frost.

Because traffic is restricted to walkways between the raised beds, the soil does not become compacted, remaining deep and loose. Once plants are established, crops can be irrigat-ed easily by running water down the walkways.

Raised beds are suitable for many different cli-mates and soil types. Although fall is the most popular time of year to construct them, raised beds can also be made in the spring or late summer with equal success. The beds are formed by raking up well-cultivated garden soil from walkways 18–20 in. wide to form beds that are 15–16 in. wide and elevated 4–10 in. above the walkways. Compost or fertilizer can be added to the beds, which are then leveled off with the back (tines up) of a garden rake; they are now ready for planting.

RAISIN. Originally a term for grape clusters; now popularly it refers to dried grapes, mostly *Vitis vinifera* and various currant and muscat types that have been sun dried and processed. In the United States, most raisins are produced in California. See also GRAPE.

RAKING. The garden rake is primarily a tillage tool that, in its simplest form, consists of short metal or wooden teeth or tines attached to a bar set at right angles to a long handle. Its principal uses are to draw together loose materials, including leaves or grass clippings; to break up soil clods; and to level and make soil surfaces fine. The simple form is varied in many ways to adapt the tool to special purposes. Variations involve differences in size, number, shape, length, closeness, or arrangement of the tines and the material of which the tool is made.

The leaf rake is especially adapted for gathering leaves and grass clippings. The long, flexible tines sweep up grass clippings and leaves without injuring the grass. In gathering leaves and twigs, the rake should be used with long, sliding strokes, the tines being lifted only enough to clear the debris.

In fitting soil and preparing a seedbed, use the garden rake, alternating push and pull strokes,

Top: leaf rake
Bottom: garden rake

letting the teeth touch only the top of the clods at first, then sinking them gradually until they work freely in the pulverized soil. Sometimes it helps to turn the large rake over and use the flat top to break large clods and fill hollows or uneven spots. To break up a crust and create a dust mulch, rake only 1 in. deep or less, letting part of the weight of the tool rest in the hand nearest the head and propelling it with the other. This same delicate action is most effective in destroying a new crop of weeds, especially if the rake is moved back and forth with a slight sideways movement to cover every inch of surface. Where seeds are planted a full inch or deeper, this raking can be done in two directions at right angles over the whole planted area, thereby uprooting a host of weeds that would call for much more work later.

See also CULTIVATION; LAWN.

RAMONDA (rah MAWN dah). A genus of herbs belonging to the Gesneriaceae (Gesneria Family). They have rosettes of hairy leaves and broad, bell-shaped, blue, pink, or white flowers. The ramondas are exquisite rock garden plants and, though difficult to grow, are worth the care that they require. They need perfect drainage. Many growers succeed by planting them on the north-facing side of a rock wall or in vertical crevices in the rock garden. Propagation is easy from seed. Mature plants can be divided, and leaf cuttings will also root.

PRINCIPAL SPECIES

R. myconi, from the Pyrenees, is the most commonly grown species. Its leaves are quite hairy, and the lavender-blue bells are charming. It is also found with white or pink flowers.

R. nathaliae, from the Balkans, is very similar to *R. myconi* but is not as hairy. It is also found in several color forms.

R. serbica, from the Balkans, has smaller flowers than other species.

RANGOON-CREEPER. Common name for *Quisqualis indica*, a climbing tropical shrub with fragrant, white to red flowers; see QUISQUALIS.

RANUNCULACEAE (rah nun kyoo LAY see ee). The Buttercup or Crowfoot Family, a hardy group of mainly herbaceous, but sometimes woody, plants. Many of the genera are favorite flower-garden plants, and some, such as *Aconitum*, yield powerful drugs. Other cultivated species include *Adonis*, *Anemone*, *Aquilegia* (columbine), *Cimicifuga*, *Clematis*, *Delphinium*, *Eranthis*, *Helleborus* (hellebore), *Nigella*, *Ranunculus*, and *Trollius*.

RANUNCULUS (rah NUN kyoo lus). A widely distributed genus of annual, biennial, or perennial herbs, commonly known as buttercup or crowfoot. Some are found wild, and others are grown in the flower garden, border, or rockery. Most of the species are perennial, and only a few have been modified into variously colored forms and doubles. The common plants bear yellow, white, or red blossoms with mostly five sepals and petals and many stamens.

Ranunculus sp.

Most of the buttercups are propagated from seed or by division of the plants in the spring. Most of the crowfoots are yellow, but there are several white species, especially in the batrachium group, which includes bog or aquatic plants. Many crowfoots are adaptable to rock garden use, all preferring well-drained soil and a sunny location; hardiness varies according to species.

PRINCIPAL SPECIES

R. aconitifolius (aconite buttercup) grows 3 ft. high and just as wide and has stalks of numerous white, buttercup-like blossoms. The attractive leaves are much like those of *Aconitum* (monkshood). Hardy in Zones 4–8.

R. asiaticus (Persian or turban buttercup) is often used by florists. Its newer cultivars produce white, pink, red, orange, and yellow flowers, including dwarf and giant double forms. Other features of this species are its simple or only slightly branched habit of growth to 1½ ft. high and the long-stalked, bright yellow flowers with hairy sepals. Var. *superbissimus* is taller and produces larger flowers. Perennial and hardy to Zone 7, it is grown in the greenhouse or outdoors in the summer.

R. ficaria (lesser-celandine) grows to 6 in. and bears 1-in., yellow flowers in spring. Glossy leaves are 2 in. long and disappear during early summer.

R. gramineus (grassy buttercup) grows to 12–18 in. with chalice-shaped yellow blossoms and blue-gray, reedlike foliage. Hardy to Zone 8.

R. pyrenaeus grows 6–9 in. and produces white, cup-shaped flowers; it is a strong candidate for the rock garden.

R. repens (creeping buttercup), one of the best rock garden species, grows 6–12 in. and bears yellow flowers through the summer. Its runners root at the joints, and the flower sepals are slightly hairy. Var. *pleniflorus* has double flowers. It is perennial and hardy in Zones 3–8.

RAPE. Common name for *Brassica napus*, grown for its oily seeds in India and Europe.

RAPHANUS (RAF ah nus) **sativus.** The cruciferous herb from which the cultivated RADISH has been developed.

RAPHIA (RAY fee ah). A genus of feather palms, mostly native to tropical Africa and commonly known as raphia palms. They have relatively short trunks (to 30 ft. tall) and magnificent spreading leaves, sometimes 65 ft. long and 8 ft. wide.

R. farinifera from Madagascar, growing to 30 ft., is one of several species grown in south Florida. Among its leaves, it bears 6-ft. clusters of fruit sometimes weighing 300 lb. The young, folded leaves are used to produce the fiber called RAFFIA, a favorite material for tying up plants or bunches of vegetables and used commercially for making baskets, fabrics, and other products.

RASPBERRY. Erect perennial plants of the genus RUBUS (brambles) and therefore closely related to blackberries. They have woody, usually prickly, biennial stems and are cultivated for their delicious fruits in red, yellow, purple, and black varieties. See also BLACKBERRY.

Although some red and yellow raspberries grown in North America belong to the European species, *R. idaeus*, the majority belong to its North American variety, *strigosus*. All these propagate themselves naturally by suckers, which develop from the roots, especially when the latter are injured or broken. The many varieties of black raspberries belong to the native American species, *R. occidentalis* (blackcap raspberry, thimbleberry), and propagate by the tips of

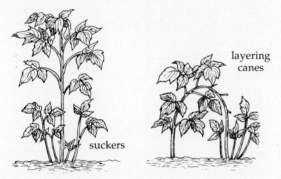

Raspberry propagation

their young canes bending over to the ground and taking root. Purple types, which are hybrids of these two species, may propagate by one or the other of their parents' methods.

Black varieties are less hardy than the reds. Raspberries will not stand drought or heat, so they cannot be grown successfully in the South, except in high altitudes or with special care as to moisture and partial shade.

SELECTION

Lists of raspberry varieties seem almost endless in nursery catalogs; it may be beneficial to consult other local growers, nurseries, or your local extension service to learn which are best suited to your area. One-year-old, No. 1 grade, disease-free plants are best for establishing new plantings.

Red and black varieties are desirable for eating fresh, while yellow and purple are popular as dessert fruits. All four are excellent for canning, jam, and juice. Black varieties are less hardy than reds. Purple raspberries are a cross between blacks and reds. Varieties of all colors are available to produce from early to late in the season.

Among the reds are everbearing raspberries that are highly desirable for the home garden. Given a little extra attention, they will produce two crops in a season. They require plenty of plant food and, especially, sufficient moisture in the soil to make food available during hot, dry weather. Unless the ground is moist, the buds that produce the fall crop will fail to develop or the fruit fail to ripen. A constantly maintained mulch is perhaps the easiest and cheapest means of assuring fall fruiting, although, if it is available, overhead irrigation is even better. The fruit is borne in the fall on the current year's new canes, so if only the fall crop is wanted, all the canes should be cut to the ground each fall after bearing. If both summer and fall crops are wanted, only the two-year canes should be cut after the summer crop is harvested.

CULTURE

Raspberries thrive in any well-drained soil if liberally supplied with humus and moisture. Black kinds do better than red ones in light soils. When plants are set out, the stems should be cut back close to the ground. This tends to develop sturdy new shoots and a strong root system, whereas if the original stems are left, the plants may die even though they at first seem to thrive and may even bear some fruit the first season.

Though raspberry plants produced from suckers can be planted with safety in the fall, those grown from tips (like black raspberries) should be planted only in spring. The reason is that the former can be set deeply enough to withstand any heaving of soil over winter, whereas the latter, which must be set with their buds no deeper than the soil surface, are likely to be heaved out of the ground and killed by alternate thawing and freezing. Spring setting is, therefore, best for all bramble fruits.

Varieties that propagate only by stem tips tend to form clumps or hills and are not easily kept in place if the tips are not allowed to root at will and thus give rise to a veritable jungle. This is easily prevented by pinching the succulent young tips when they reach 30–36 in. high.

Popular distances to set suckering varieties are 3 ft. between plants and 5 or 6 ft. between rows. The spaces between plants in the rows can be allowed to fill up with new ones developed from suckers. Black raspberries are generally spaced 4 or 5 ft. apart with 6 or 7 ft. between the rows. The first year, strong plants can be allowed to develop two shoots; weak ones should be permitted only one.

Harvesting. Like blackberries, raspberries should be so ripe that they fall off the vine when barely touched. If you must tug the fruit to harvest, the berry is not ripe.

As soon as the last fruit has been gathered, the old canes and the puny new ones should be cut out; the former will die during winter anyway, and the latter will produce no fruit. Three to five sturdy stems should be left on each plant to fruit each year. While they are dormant, cut them back to 4 ft. or 4½ ft. to encourage side branching. In gardens it is often more desirable to grow all raspberries (and blackberries) under a permanent, year-round mulch than attempt constant cultivation. This conserves moisture, supplies humus, saves the labor of cultivation, and prevents unwanted suckers growing from cut roots.

ENEMIES

Diseases. Raspberries are bothered by several diseases. The most serious is mosaic, a virus disease for which there is no cure. Infected plants should be destroyed. Plant certified, disease-free, virus-resistant varieties only, and keep the plants at least 100 ft. away from black raspberries and wild brambles. The disease is spread by aphids, which can fly only short distances. Anthracnose, showing up as gray spots on the leaves, can usually be controlled by pruning out the infected parts. Cane blight and spur blight, which often kill the entire canes, can also be controlled by a fungicide. By spraying the canes early, before the leaves open, and again after the leaves are fully grown, most diseases can be controlled; but when infection is bad, it may be advisable to spray again just after harvest.

Insect Pests. The cane borer, red-necked cane borer, and cane maggot, all attack the canes. Pruning off the affected parts and destroying them, and spraying early in the season usually controls them. The raspberry fruit worm eats both leaves and fruit, as does the Japanese beetle. Red spider mites may be problems during some years. Insecticides applied in early summer, before the fruit forms, usually keep them under control, although it may also be necessary to repeat the sprays after the berries are picked.

RASP FERN. Common name for *Doodia caudata*, a small fern growing in clumps and excellent for pot culture; see DOODIA.

RATIBIDA (ra ti BID ah). A genus of annual and perennial herbs belonging to the Asteraceae (Aster Family), formerly classified as *Lepachys*, and commonly known as coneflower or Mexican-hat. The slender, branching, hairy stems bear drooping, yellow flower heads, which resemble the daisylike black-eyed-Susan, having brownish disks and yellow ray flowers, but the foliage is more delicately cut, and the disk of the flower is more than 1 in. high. Hardy in Zones 3–9, *Ratibida* is closely related to *Rudbeckia*, and its culture is very similar. Two species of these beautiful wildflowers native to the western prairies are now in common cultivation, and both are easily raised from seed.

R. columnifera (Mexican-hat, prairie coneflower) grows to 3 ft. and has distinctive heads of black cones surrounded by yellow and red ray flowers.

Ratibida columnifera

The species and var. *pulcherrima* are biennial or perennial and can be started from seed sown early in the spring in the border where plants are to grow.

R. *pinnata* (gray-headed coneflower) has yellow ray flowers surrounding a tall, gray cone. The leaves are hairy, alternate, and compound. This perennial will bloom continuously throughout the summer if seeds are started early indoors and the seedlings are set in the open in a sunny location. It thrives in dry soils and will reach a height of 4 ft.

RATTLESNAKE FERN. Common name for *Botrychium virginianum*, a deciduous fern with triangular fronds; see BOTRYCHIUM.

RATTLESNAKE-MASTER. Common name for *Eryngium yuccifolium*, a perennial herb with spiny leaves and greenish white flowers; see ERYNGIUM.

RATTLESNAKE-PLANTAIN. Common name for GOODYERA, a genus of small terrestrial orchids with variegated leaves.

RAVENALA (ray ve NAY lah) **madagascariensis.** A tropical plant of remarkable appearance, having a palmlike trunk and large, bananalike leaves arranged to form a large, fan-shaped head. Small specimens are sometimes seen under glass, and it can be grown outdoors in the warmest regions of the United States. In the tropics it grows to 30 ft. high. It received its popular name, traveler's tree, from the fact that water held in the flower bracts and leaf stalks is likely to be a lucky find for any thirsty traveler who comes upon the tree.

RAY FLOWER. One of the large, usually brightly colored, petal-like, strap-shaped florets that form the radiating border of the flower head of many plants of the Asteraceae (Aster Family), such as the daisy, marguerite, sunflower; or, massed together, a head, as in the dandelion. When associated with DISK FLOWER clusters, as in the daisy, ray flowers lose their reproductive function; only the disk flowers are pollinated and bear seed. The ray flower thus becomes primarily an organ of insect attraction, the petals of its corolla fusing into a flattened, showy ray.

REBUTIA (reb YOO tee ah). A delightful group of miniature cacti from central South America. Large, colorful flowers with long tubes mostly arising from around the base of the plants, forming rings or crowns of blossoms, hence the name "crown cactus." Easy to grow and easy to flower, most species are desirable. R. *albiflora* has delicate, white flowers. R. *costata* blooms in a rich, buttery yellow. R. *grandiflora* has large, red flowers. R. *heliosa* has a dense covering of silver-gray spines, pressed flat against the stems, and bright orange flowers.

RECEPTACLE. The apex of the flower stalk upon which the floral parts are borne. It is also called "torus" and is often remarkably modified. The "fruit" of the strawberry in which the seeds, called achenes, are embedded. In the East Indian lotus, the receptacle is greatly enlarged, but it is to enclose the seeds, not to form a berry.

REDBUD. Common name for CERCIS, a genus of deciduous shrubs or trees with showy flowers.

RED-CEDAR. Common name for several species of JUNIPERUS that are not true cedars but rather a separate group of evergreen trees and shrubs belonging to the Cupressaceae (Cypress Family).

RED-RIBBONS. Common name for *Clarkia concinna*, a dainty annual with rose-colored flowers; see CLARKIA.

RED SPIDER MITE. A common name for *Tetranychus* spp. It is not really a spider, or an insect, but a tiny, eight-legged mite. This pest is common in greenhouses, on houseplants, vegetables, and ornamental plants in the garden and on many trees and shrubs, both deciduous and evergreen.

The leaves show the results of its sucking of the juices, becoming blotched with pale yellow and reddish brown spots and gradually dying and dropping. The underside of the leaves appears to have been dusted with fine, white powder, but if magnified, this is seen to consist of empty wrinkled skins and minute eggs suspended on strands of fine silk webbing along which move the small, green, yellow, black, or red mites.

Red spiders can often be held in check, especially in the house and greenhouse, by syringing plants with a forceful stream of water. Unless this is done early in the day, the watering may make conditions more favorable for disease infections by leaving the atmosphere moist at night. The large, predatory mite is the recommended biological control. Lacewings, lady beetles, or insecticidal soap can also prove effective.

REDTOP. Common name for the coarse grass *Agrostis alba*; see AGROSTIS.

REDWOOD. Common name for *Sequoia sempervirens*, a giant evergreen tree native to the Pacific Coast; see SEQUOIA.

REGNELLIDIUM (reg nel ID ee um). A genus of tropical aquatic ferns from Brazil and Argentina. They grow in mud among other vegetation, with long stipes carrying paired leaflets that arise from a creeping rhizome. They can be cultivated in containers of warm water and are very sensitive to cold.

REGULAR. A flower form in which all the members of one set of floral organs are the same: all sepals alike, all petals alike, all stamens alike, the carpels alike. Looking at the center of the flower, the parts are repeated or radiate about it (having radial symmetry), as in the lilies and most members of the Ranunculaceae (Buttercup Family).

REHMANNIA (ray MAN ee ah). A genus of perennial herbs of the Scrophulariaceae (Figwort Family), comprising plants with sticky, hairy foliage and showy, two-lipped, tubular, pale or brownish flowers with brilliant colored throats. Hardy in Zones 10–11, they are grown as greenhouse plants in cooler areas. Propagation is by seed or cuttings. *R. elata*, growing to 6 ft., has rose-purple flowers to 3 in. across, the throat dotted with yellow and red. *R. glutinosa* has large, solitary, yellowish flowers with purple veins and throats.

REINHARDTIA (rīn HAHR tee ah). A genus of small, spineless, dwarf palms formerly listed as *Malortiea*. Native to Central America, they are fairly popular outdoors in Zones 10–11 and elsewhere under glass. The best-known species are *R. gracilis*, which grows to 8 ft. and has ribbed, toothed leaves; and *R. simplex*, with additional pinnae at the base and cleft tips on the leaves.

REPELLENTS. Various substances or other plants that deter harmful pests. Protection is provided not by killing, but by making the plant repugnant to the pest because of the odor, texture, surface color, or other characteristic.

For example, wood ashes on squash plants drive back squash bugs. DIATOMACEOUS EARTH around the base of plants fends off many insects. Slugs are repelled by lime, sand, or other substances that scratch or dry their flesh. Wheat flour will clog and dry out the skins of other insects, too. Soot will repel, as will creosote, and coal tar oils. Soaps are excellent repellents and very easy to apply in sprays with water. Bands of newspaper or cloth with or without Tanglefoot or other sticky substances repel attackers that climb up trunks and stalks to get at the leaves of plants. Dusts made from botanicals can be either lethal or repellent.

Genetic alterations of plants have been used to make plants more hairy, for instance, and thus repellent. Other alterations have changed the smell of plants to mask the normally attracting odor. Hollow stems have been altered to solid stems, thus foiling the sawfly. Some plants can be bred to become tolerant of attackers like aphids.

The practice of COMPANION PLANTING is based on the observation that many plants, especially strongly scented herbs and onions or other members of the Amaryllidaceae (Amaryllis Family), naturally fend off insect pests. Well-known combinations include tomatoes and asparagus, basil and tomatoes, chives and carrots, onions and lettuce, marigolds with plants subject to nematodes, nasturtiums with cucumbers, and garlic or sage with many plants.

See also INSECT CONTROL; INSECTS, BENEFICIAL.

RESEDA (re SEE dah). A genus of tender herbs with thick stems and coarse foliage, commonly known as mignonette. They are grown in gardens and greenhouses for their dense, fragrant flower spikes.

Reseda odorata

R. odorata is an annual species grown outdoors and in greenhouses for the fragrance of its stout, oval spikes of greenish, yellow, or sometimes reddish flowers, which individually are inconspicuous. It is often planted by beekeepers because it helps to yield a large amount of excellent honey. The sweet-scented plants are excellent for pots or boxes, valuable in the bed or border, and suitable for culture as cut flowers, particularly in the improved forms.

REST PERIOD. A time when plants temporarily slow or cease growth processes; see DORMANCY.

RESURRECTION FERN. Common name for *Polypodium polypodioides*, a small fern that curls and expands its fronds depending on the moisture available; see POLYPODIUM.

RESURRECTION PLANT. Common name for two plants that have the common habit of curling up when dry and opening out again when supplied with moisture, including *Anastatica hierochuntica*, an annual from the Middle East, see ANASTATICA; *Selaginella lepidophyulla*, a mosslike herb native from Texas to South America, see SELAGINELLA.

REVOLUTE. Rolled backward or downward, as a coiled tendril, or a leaf or petal whose margin rolls backward from the apex (as in the cactus or quilled form of dahlia). Compare INVOLUTE.

RHAMNACEAE (ram NAY see ee). The Buckthorn Family, a widely distributed group of small trees and shrubs. Important genera are *Ceanothus*, *Colletia*, *Hovenia*, *Pomaderris*, *Rhamnus*, and *Zizyphus*.

RHAMNUS (RAM nus). A genus of deciduous or evergreen shrubs or small trees, commonly known as buckthorn. Found chiefly in the temperate regions of the Northern Hemisphere, several are quite hardy and worth a place in shrub borders for their handsome foliage and attractive fruits. They are not particular as to soil and will tolerate some shade. Propagation is by seed, best sown in fall, and by cuttings or layers.

PRINCIPAL SPECIES

R. californica (coffee-berry) is a tender, evergreen, berry-producing shrub cultivated in California.

R. caroliniana (Indian-cherry) is a deciduous shrub or tree that grows to 20 ft. and has attractive, finely toothed leaves and greenish flowers followed by flattened clusters of berries that turn from red to black. Hardy in Zones 6–9.

R. cathartica (common buckthorn) is native to Europe and Asia but has become naturalized in parts of the United States. It is a vigorous grower, to 20 ft., and bears glossy black berries. Hardy in Zones 3–7, it does well in dry soil and is a good hedge plant.

R. crocea (red-berry) is a tender, dwarf, evergreen shrub with stiff, spiny branches, handsome foliage, and red berries. Native to California, it is hardy to Zone 8.

R. purshiana is a small, handsome tree from the western states. Hardy to Zone 7.

RHAPHIOLEPIS (raf ee OHL ep is). A genus of evergreen shrubs native to China and Japan, belonging to the Rosaceae (Rose Family). They can only be grown outdoors where the climate is mild, Zones 9–11, but their range can be extended a little if they are trained to a wall. A well-drained soil with plenty of humus is preferable. Propagation is by seeds, cuttings, or layers.

PRINCIPAL SPECIES

R. x *delacourii* is a hybrid between *R. umbellata* and *R. indica*, with pink flowers and intermediate habit.

R. indica (Indian-hawthorn) grows to 5 ft. with shiny, leathery foliage, clusters of fragrant, white flowers tinged with pink, and small, black fruits.

R. umbellata (yedda-hawthorn) grows to 12 ft. or more and is the hardiest species. It has thick, lustrous, dark green leaves and dense clusters of fragrant, white flowers.

RHAPIS (RAY pis). A genus of reedlike oriental palms commonly known as lady palm. Two species, *R. humilis* and *R. excelsa*, are popular subjects for moderately heated greenhouses or as lawn specimens in warm climates (Zones 9–11). See also PALMS.

RHEUM (REE um). A genus of strong-growing Asiatic perennials, of which the most important is *R. rhabarbarum*, the vegetable RHUBARB. Other species, notably *R. officinale*, are used for bold foliage effects.

RHEXIA (REK see ah). A genus of low-growing, mostly purple-flowered perennial herbs commonly known as meadow-beauty or deer-grass. They are native in the eastern states, hardy to Zone 5, and suitable for summer bloom in moist wild gardens and sometimes in borders. Propagation is by seed or tubers.

R. mariana is a relatively tall plant with cylindrical, hairy stems and small, pale purple flowers.

R. virginica, an attractive little wildflower, has

Rhexia virginica

a square, winged stem and clusters of rosy purple blossoms 1 in. or more across. It grows natu rally in neutral soil and thrives in the garden if given sufficient moisture.

RHIPSALIS (RIP sal is). A genus of cacti very different from other genera of the Cactaceae (Cactus Family). The flowers are white, delicate, small, and individually somewhat insignificant; in quantity they make quite a show, as do the little, round, white to translucent fruits. It is the virtually spineless and graceful stems that are the main appeal. The plants are epiphytes in nature, growing in the tropics on the branches of trees or clambering over rocks, often with only aerial roots.

Perhaps the most graceful and lovely is *R. heteroclada* with green branches that divide and redivide in increasingly smaller segments, creating magnificent, cascading plants. Another of the many interesting and attractive species is *R. paradoxa* with curious alternately angled, long, hanging stems. *R. cassutha* (mistletoe cactus) is odd and interesting, not beautiful. Its common name comes from a fancied resemblance of its stems and white berries to those of true mistletoe.

Rhipsalis is the only genus of cactus with a few members (possibly only variants of one species) that occur natively outside of the Americas, undoubtedly spread to Africa from South America by birds at some prehistoric time.

RHIZOME. An underground or rootlike stem, from the joints (nodes) of which spring true roots and stems of new plants that can be cut from the parent and treated as separate individuals. While some rhizomes are as slender as the overground stem, most are thickened by

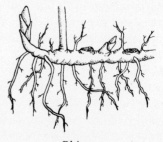

Rhizome

the storage of food material that sustains the plant over winter or during dormant periods.

While the function of rhizomes as a means of propagation is especially apparent in the rapid underground spread of many grasses, notably quack grass and witch grass, it is also a valuable method of reproducing many garden plants.

RHODODENDRON (roh doh DEN dron). An immense genus including over 800 species of mostly evergreen and deciduous shrubs, and a few trees and epiphytic plants. They are native to the temperate regions of the Northern Hemisphere and have been found on all continents except Africa and South America. In addition to the hundreds of species, there are huge numbers of hybrids available, with more being introduced each year. Some have been cultivated for over a century, and over 4000 species, varieties, and hybrids have been cataloged in North America alone. There are many excellent dwarf rhododendrons for the rock garden. The plants selected depend on the scale of the garden.

Rhododendrons prefer moderate temperatures and moist climates, and are ideally suited for cultivation in the coastal northwestern states. While all rhododendrons require some sunlight in order to flower, some prefer the deep shade provided by a nearby tree or other sunscreen; others are more sun-tolerant. They grow best in a highly organic, well-drained soil protected by a layer of mulch to conserve moisture and to reduce frost penetration in colder areas. The evergreen species usually need to be shaded from harsh winds and direct sun, especially in winter. They can be propagated by seed, by layers, or by rooting semi-hardwood cuttings in sand.

SELECTIONS

Although gardeners and nurseries usually consider them as separate groups, the genus *Rhododendron* includes plants commonly referred to as azaleas. There are no constant botanical differences between them, so the following distinctions are not completely reliable. Generally speaking, the azaleas are mostly deciduous with funnel-shaped flowers, while the rhododendrons are usually evergreen and have larger, bell-shaped flowers borne in terminal clusters, but there are exceptions to this rule.

The genus is divided by horticulturists into 43 series, which are further subdivided. Botanists divide *Rhododendron* into eight subgenera and their subdivisions, based on the various characteristics of the leaves and flowers. For more information about the genus and descriptions of the many cultivars, consult the publications of

Potted azalea

the American Rhododendron Society and the American Horticultural Society.

PRINCIPAL SPECIES

R. catawbiense (catawba rhododendron, mountain rosebay, purple laurel) is an evergreen shrub or small tree that grows 10–20 ft. tall. It has shiny green leaves that are paler beneath, and lilac to purple flowers. One of the most reliable and cold-tolerant species, it is one of the parents of the Catawba hybrid group.

R. caucasicum (Caucasian rhododendron) is an evergreen shrub to 3 ft. tall, infrequently cultivated as an ornamental specimen. Its leaves are 2–4 in. long and rusty brown on the undersides. The flowers are pink to yellowish white and up to 2 in. across. It is one of the parents of the Caucasicum hybrid group.

R. fortunei (fortune's rhododendron) is an evergreen shrub that grows to 12 ft. The leaves are 4–8 in. long, and the fragrant flowers are lilac to pink in color. It is one of the parents of the Fortunei hybrid group.

R. griffithianum (Griffith rhododendron) is an evergreen shrub that grows to 12 ft. or more, with leaves 4–12 in. long. The flowers are slightly fragrant, white to pink in color, sometimes frilled, and considered by some to be among the most beautiful of rhododendron flowers. Many excellent hybrids of the Griffithianum group have been bred from this species.

R. indicum (indica azalea) is an evergreen azalea shrub that grows to 6 ft. and has leaves about

1½ in. long. The flowers are 2½ in. across and vary in color from rose to scarlet. Native to Japan, this species should not be confused with the Indian hybrid azaleas. Some varieties are used for indoor forcing.

R. japonicum (Japanese azalea) is a very hardy deciduous shrub that grows to 6 ft. and has leaves up to 4 in. long. The flowers range in color from yellow to salmon or brick red and have a distinctly unpleasant odor. It is one of the parents of the Molle hybrid azaleas.

R. kaempferi (torch azalea) is a deciduous to semi-evergreen shrub that grows to 8 ft. and has leaves up to 2½ in. long and fuzzy on both sides. The funnel-shaped flowers are pink, orange-red, rosy scarlet, or bright red. The foliage turns reddish in autumn. This species has been used to produce several groups of hybrid azaleas, including the Kaempferi hybrids.

R. luteum (pontic azalea) is a deciduous shrub that grows to 12 ft. and has leaves up to 5½ in. long and hairy along the margin and midrib. The flowers are funnel shaped, yellow, and very fragrant. It is one of the parents of the Ghent hybrid azaleas.

R. mucronulatum (Korean rhododendron) is a deciduous shrub that grows to 8 ft. and has leaves up to 3 in. long and somewhat scaly. The flowers are broadly funnel shaped and rose-purple in color. This is a very early-flowering species with flowers appearing before the foliage unfurls.

R. nakaharae is an attractive deciduous species, small and ground hugging, with orange-red flowers.

R. schlippenbachii (royal azalea), considered to be one of the finest of the deciduous azaleas, is a shrub that grows to 15 ft. and has 2–4 in. leaves arranged in clusters at the ends of the twigs and turning yellow, orange, or scarlet in autumn. The flowers are pink with brown spots borne three to six in a cluster.

R. viscosum (swamp-honeysuckle, swamp azalea) is a summer-bloom shrub native to North America, bearing fragrant, white flowers.

R. yakusimanum (yako rhododendron), from Japan, is a compact evergreen shrub growing to about 3 ft. The oblong leaves are up to 3 in. long and have dense, white hair on the undersides. The bell-shaped flowers are white to pink in color. It is especially suited to the rock garden. It and its hybrids are handsome in foliage and flower. They are both cold- and heat-tolerant shrubs, successful throughout much of North America.

R. yedoense (yodogawa azalea) is a deciduous or semievergreen shrub growing to 5 ft. The leaves are narrow, up to 3 in. long, hairy beneath, and turn purplish in autumn. The double flowers are rosy purple in color.

RHODOTYPOS (roh doh TĪ pus) **scandens.** A deciduous, upright, spreading shrub growing to 6 ft., native to Asia, belonging to the Rosaceae (Rose Family). Commonly known as jetbead, it is the only member of the genus. Hardy in Zones 5–8, it is a valuable ornamental shrub for general planting. Its clean, bright green foliage is particularly noticeable in the fall when many other shrubs are bare. The large, white, four-petaled flowers are borne singly, mostly in late spring but sometimes sparingly during the summer. It has shiny black fruits that persist until spring, then lie dormant for a year, and finally give rise to seedlings, which appear in abundance around the old plant.

RHOEO (REE oh) **spathacea.** A Mexican and West Indian plant of the Commelinaceae (Spiderwort Family), formerly listed as *R. discolor*, and commonly known as Moses-in-the-cradle. Somewhat similar to *Tradescantia*, it has succulent, dark green leaves, purple beneath, up to 1 ft. long, and crowded on 8-in. stems. The somewhat flattened clusters of white flowers are partly hidden by two boat-shaped bracts. Cv. 'Variegata' has leaves attractively striped yellow. Both forms make decorative foliage plants for the greenhouse and can be grown in the open in Zones 10–11, where they are occasionally found naturalized. A dwarf, densely tufted form is popular as a ground cover in south Florida, and a green variety is occasionally seen.

RHOICISSUS (roh i SIS us) **capensis.** A tropical evergreen vine from South Africa, belonging to the Vitaceae (Grape Family), formerly included in the genus *Cissus*, and commonly known as cape or evergreen grape. A vigorous grower climbing by tendrils, it is sometimes grown in greenhouses and often planted in southern California for its decorative foliage or interesting habit. The fruit is used in jelly, and the roots are said to make good cattle fodder.

RHUBARB. A stout, hardy perennial herb, *Rheum rhabarbarum*, also known as pie plant. Its thick leaf stalks are used principally in spring and early summer, stewed or made into pies and preserves. The leaves are not edible raw or cooked.

Spinach-rhubarb, also known as sorrel or dock, is *Rumex abyssinicus*, a hardy perennial whose leaf stalks are used like rhubarb and leaves like spinach.

Rhubarb requires rich soil, well supplied with moisture. Propagation is easily done in spring by dividing established clumps; each piece should have at least one eye. Set plants 4–5 ft. apart each way with their crowns 4 in. below the surface; tramp them in place, give clean cultivation, and feed generously. No stalks should be pulled until the second year, and then only sparingly. Thereafter they can be pulled until the stalks become dry and hollow. Thus treated, clumps should pro-

Rhubarb flower stalks

duce well for at least 20 years, though it may be advisable to dig, divide, and replant some of them in new, well-prepared soil every eight or ten years. Calculate one or two clumps for each member of the family for an ample supply.

In gathering, do not break off the stalks, but grasp firmly close to the base and remove it whole with a quick jerk. When flower stalks appear, remove them promptly to conserve the strength of the plants.

Plants in the garden can be forced for winter and extra early spring use by covering them with drain tiles, peach baskets, barrels, or deep baskets around which fresh horse manure is packed to create warmth; or deep coldframes can be placed over them. Again, clumps can be dug in late fall, after freezing weather, and planted in soil in a cellar or beneath greenhouse benches for a forced winter crop.

Leaf spot produces conspicuous reddish brown, circular spots. The only control measure called for is the removal of old leaves in the fall.

The bean and spinach aphids, the European corn borer, the common stalk borer, and the yellow woolly bear may infest rhubarb. The rhubarb curculio, when feeding and laying eggs, makes holes in the stalks, which exude drops of sap. The only remedy is to gather the adult black snout beetles. See INSECT CONTROL.

RHUS (ROOS). A genus of deciduous or evergreen shrubs, small trees, or vines, widely distributed in temperate and subtropical regions, belonging to the Anacardiaceae (Cashew Family), and commonly known as sumac. Some of them are virulently poisonous, and others are used for commercial purposes, but the majority are decorative and suitable for ornamental planting. Most of the sumacs have compound leaves that assume brilliant scarlet colorings in the fall, though a few western species have simple evergreen leaves. The flowers, usually small, occur in large panicles. In many species, these are followed by dense fruit heads, often a fine deep red, soft and velvety, and retaining their beauty well into winter. Many of the native types grow well in dry, poor soil and are useful for massing on barren hillsides. The deciduous species are generally more hardy (to Zone 3); the evergreen species require a warmer climate.

PRINCIPAL SPECIES

R. aromatica (fragrant sumac) is a low, spreading shrub, one of the best cover plants for dry, rocky slopes. It has highly aromatic, three-part leaves, short spikes of yellow flowers in spring, and hairy, red fruit. Hardy in Zones 4–9.

R. copallina (shining sumac) grows to 30 ft. and is conspicuous with dark green, glossy leaves with a winged leaf axis. Hardy in Zones 5–9.

R. diversiloba (Pacific poison-oak), native to the western states, is a shrub that grows to 8 ft., or sometimes climbs. It has the same poisonous qualities as **R. radicans**. Its leaves have three-toothed or lobed leaflets, smooth on both sides. See also POISON-IVY.

R. glabra (smooth sumac) grows to 15 ft. and has smooth, bloomy stems. It is very handsome in the fall with bright red foliage and scarlet fruit heads. Hardy in Zones 3–9.

R. javanica grows to 25 ft. and is distinguished by having wings on the leaf axis and often on the leaf stems. It is the showiest in bloom, with large panicles of creamy white flowers in late summer.

R. ovata (sugarbush), a native of the southwestern United States, is an evergreen shrub with light yellow flowers and dark red, hairy fruits.

R. radicans (poison-ivy) is a high-climbing vine on tree trunks, sometimes a shrub, or rarely a tree, common in shaded woodlands and along road-sides throughout North America. It is a beautiful vine but is extremely irritating to most people, causing extensive rashes after contact with the skin. It is iden-

Rhus radicans

tified by leaves of three somewhat oval, pointed leaflets, glossy above and slightly hairy beneath, with red twigs. The small, greenish flowers, borne in loose clusters, are followed by small, grayish fruits. See also POISON-IVY.

R. succedanea (wax-tree) is a poisonous, tender, Japanese species that grows to 30 ft. and has nine to fifteen lustrous leaflets. From the whitish fruit, a waxlike substance is obtained and used in candlemaking.

R. toxicodendron (poison-oak) is a shrub that grows to 6 ft. and has leaves of three lobed or rounded leaflets, hairy on both sides. It is generally found in the eastern states and is frequently confused with **R. radicans**, with which it shares the same toxic qualities. See also POISON-IVY.

Rhus toxicodendron

R. typhina (staghorn, Virginian, or velvet sumac) grows to 30 ft. and has branches densely covered with velvety hairs. It bears handsome foliage that is especially colorful in the fall. Cv. 'Dissecta' is a handsome selection with finely cut leaves. Its red fruit in the fall makes a delicious pink lemonade when steeped in hot water. Hardy in Zones 4–8.

R. verniciflua (varnish, lacquer tree), native to China and Japan, is an ornamental but poisonous tree that grows to 60 ft. and has large leaves of eleven to fifteen leaflets and long, drooping clusters of whitish flowers followed by smooth, pale yellow fruit ¼ in. across. It yields the famous varnish or lacquer of Japan, used on highly polished woodenware.

R. vernix (poison sumac) is a tree or shrub that grows to 20 ft. and has leaves of seven to thirteen leaflets, smooth above and soft-hairy beneath; greenish white flowers in loose panicles; and grayish white, flattened fruits ⅕ in. across. Although the foliage turns a brilliant orange and scarlet in autumn, it should not be planted since, like **R. radicans**, it can be extremely toxic. It grows naturally in swamps and marshy ground throughout eastern North America; hardy in Zones 5–9.

Rhus vernix

RHYNCHELYTRUM (rīn CHEL it rum) **repens.** A member of the Poaceae (Grass Family), commonly known as natal or ruby grass, often grown in the South (hardy to Zone 9) either for forage or in garden border plantings. It is a perennial but is usually grown as an annual from seed. It has leaves to 8 in. long and shining, open racemose flower clusters either pink or reddish brown. See ORNAMENTAL GRASSES.

RHYNCHOSTYLIS (rin koh STĪ lis). A genus of four species of vandaceous orchids from India, Malaysia, Indonesia, and the Philippines, commonly known as fox-tail orchids. They are epiphytic plants with short, leafy stems, no pseudobulbs, and thick aerial roots. The leaves are thick, leathery, and distichous. Many fragrant, showy flowers are densely clustered in drooping racemes. Sepals and petals are spreading, with the saclike lip adnate to the base of the column foot. The lip has a backward-pointing spur. The base color of the flower is white with red, magenta, or blue spotting. Plants do well in baskets containing charcoal or a porous, well-drained compost. They require bright light (3600 footcandles), copious water, and warm conditions (minimum winter temperature 60–65°F). They hybridize with other vandaceous orchids to produce colorful long-lasting intergeneric hybrids. The type species is *R. retusa.*

RIBBONBUSH. Common name for *Homalocladium platycladum*, a tropical shrub with broad, often leafless stems and red to purple fruits; see HOMALOCLADIUM.

RIBES (RĪ beez). A large genus of mostly deciduous shrubs native in temperate regions and belonging to the Saxifragaceae (Saxifrage Family). Some species are grown for their edible fruits (see CURRANT; GOOSEBERRY), others for the decorative value of their flowers and foliage. Most are hardy in Zones 3–9 and grow well in any good loamy soil. They can be propagated by seed, cuttings of green and mature wood, or layers.

Currants and gooseberries are alternate hosts of the destructive WHITE PINE BLISTER RUST disease and therefore should not be grown in the vicinity of valuable white pine stands. Some species are controlled by interstate quarantine regulations.

PRINCIPAL SPECIES

R. americanum (American black currant) has drooping racemes of whitish flowers. The leaves turn yellow and crimson in the fall. Hardy in Zones 3–7.

R. nigrum (European black currant) is the parent of cultivated black currants.

R. odoratum (buffalo currant) is a bushy shrub that grows to 6 ft. and is very ornamental in early spring with yellow, clove-scented flowers that appear with the leaves. It is sometimes confused with *R. aureum*, which is very similar but smaller in every way and has less-fragrant flowers. Hardy in Zones 5–7.

R. sanguineum grows to 12 ft. and is very showy with a profusion of rosy red flowers. Cvs. 'Atrorubens' and 'Splendens' are less vigorous forms with darker flowers. Hardy in Zones 6–8.

R. sativum (currant), a western European species, has given rise to the cultivated red and white currants. Cv. 'Macrocarpum' (cherry currant) has larger red fruits.

R. speciosum, native to California, is one of the showiest species, with long, pendulous, fuschia-like, bright red flowers. A tender evergreen, it is hardy only to Zone 8.

R. uva-crispa (European Gooseberry), formerly listed as *R. grossularia*, grows to 3 ft. and has spiny stems and large, hairy, green-, yellow-, or red-veined fruits.

RICCIA (RIK see ah). A genus of small plants belonging to the group called liverworts or hepatics, often found on stagnant pools associated with duckweed. The small, flattened part (thalus) is only ⅛ in. wide but may be 1–2 in. long and branched.

R. fluitans is grown in indoor pools and aquariums. The plant bodies float on the surface without roots, sometimes forming mats, but they develop root hairs if they come in contact with soil.

RICINUS (RIS in us). A genus of herbaceous plants native to tropical Africa and belonging to the Euphorbiaceae (Spurge Family). Growing quite large when wild in the tropics, some are cultivated as annuals for their attractive foliage, as rodent repellents, and for medicinal products.

For garden plants, seeds can be started under glass and transplanted outdoors in spring. The soil can be clay or sandy loam but should have good drainage.

R. communis (castor-bean, castor-oil plant), growing 5–8 ft., is an attractive, annual foliage plant with deeply lobed, palmlike leaves 3 ft. long. It is commonly grown as a background or screen and for its attractive seedpods. Caution should be used in the placement of these plants because the seeds are toxic. Several widely differing varieties are available.

RINGING. Removing a narrow strip of bark from around the stem of a growing plant without, however, cutting into the wood. It is done to induce the formation of flowers, fruits, or both, at points above the cut, a result achieved through the fact that the elaborated plant food descending from the leaves cannot pass the gap so created and is consequently utilized in the parts above. Grape canes are often ringed to produce large berries and exhibition clusters of fruit. The quality of such fruit is usually inferior to that normally produced.

RIVINA (rī VĪ nah). A genus of delicate herbs belonging to the Phytolaccaceae (Pokeweed Family), native to the southern states and the tropical Americas. *R. humilis* (rouge plant), the cultivated species, is a slender plant that grows to 3 ft. and bears white or rosy flowers followed by ornamental, berrylike fruits. Grown in the greenhouse or as a summer annual outdoors, it is propagated by seed or by cuttings started over bottom heat in the spring.

ROBINIA (roh BIN ee ah). A genus of highly ornamental North American trees and shrubs belonging to the Fabaceae (Bean Family), commonly known as locust. They are hardy subjects characterized by graceful feather-form leaves and showy blossoms in long, drooping clusters, which are followed by flattened, glossy brown or nearly black pods. They are widely planted for decorative purposes, easily transplanted, and grow well under ordinary conditions—even in dry, thin soil. Propagation is by seed, cuttings, suckers, root cuttings, and division.

About the only disease of locust is wood decay that follows a borer injury; however, several insects are very destructive. Black locusts have been ruined in certain regions by BORERS, whose presence is first shown by sawdust protruding from holes that later become ugly scars. Cut and burn badly infested trees and try SPRAYING the bark (not the foliage) of valuable specimens. The CARPENTER WORM is fond of locust. Also, a general browning of black locust leaves from the vicinity of New York City southward can be due to the feeding of the LEAF MINER, a small, reddish, black-marked beetle.

PRINCIPAL SPECIES

R. hispida (rose-acacia), growing to 10 ft., is a large, attractive shrub with rose-purple flowers, native from Virginia southward. Its suckers can become a problem. Hardy in Zones 6–8.

R. pseudoacacia (black, yellow, or common locust; false or black-acacia) is a tall tree of the eastern and central states. It may attain 40–80 ft. and has thorny branches with grayish brown, heavy, deeply grooved bark. The very fragrant, white flowers in long, pendent racemes cover the tree in late spring. Flattened, reddish brown pods 4 in. long hang on the tree all winter, rattling in the wind when they become dry. It is an excellent tree for reforestation, especially in poor soils where noth-

Robinia pseudoacacia

ing else will grow. Since it often produces suckers from the roots and is frequently attacked by borers and leaf miners, it is not a good tree for the home landscape. Hardy in Zones 4–8.

R. viscosa (clammy locust) is a small tree that grows to about 30 ft. and has pink flowers. Its young growth and pods are covered with sticky hairs. Hardy in Zones 4–6.

ROCAMBOLE. Common name for a little-cultivated variety of garlic but often erroneously applied to *Allium scorodoprasum*, which is better known as giant garlic or ELEPHANT GARLIC.

ROCKCAP FERN. Common name for *Polypodium virginianum*, an evergreen fern usually found growing on boulders, cliffs, and decaying logs; see POLYPODIUM.

ROCKCRESS. Common name for ARABIS, a widely cultivated genus of herbs with white, pink, or purple flowers.

ROCKET. Common name for HESPERIS, a genus of hardy herbs with showy, pyramidal flower spikes. Sweet rocket or dame's rocket is *Hesperis matronalis*.

The common name is also applied to other plants. Rocket-salad is the strong-flavored salad plant *Eruca vesicoria* var. *sativa*; see ERUCA. Rocket or yellow rocket also refers to *Barbarea vulgaris*; see BARBAREA.

ROCK GARDEN. A rock garden is one intended primarily for the culture of alpine plants. Its construction should be an attempt to reproduce as nearly as possible the conditions under which these plants thrive in the wild state and to present to the eye a natural and pleasing appearance.

LOCATION

A successful rock garden can be made almost anywhere except in dense shade or marshy ground. It can be of any size from a few square yards up to several acres. A rather sunny slope is probably the best location since sun is essential to the success of many rock plants, and the slope

makes possible an effect of height without troublesome or costly construction. A natural outcropping of rock is a bonus.

If there is any choice, the garden should have an eastern exposure; that is, it should be open to or slope toward the east. South, west, and north are the next choices in order of desirability. The reason for this is that, while most of the plants enjoy sun, they do best when not subjected to its direct rays during the hottest part of the day. A western exposure can be made very satisfactory, however, by the judicious planting of a tree such as white birch, which will cast thin and scattered shade during the early afternoon. Apple trees, kept very much thinned out, are also effective as well as decorative. In the South, a successful rock garden can be developed in filtered light beneath a tall, deciduous tree.

Aside from the matter of exposure, some judgment should be exercised in choosing a site for the rock garden. Such a garden can be built in the middle of a flat lawn, but great skill is required to give it a natural appearance in such a location. It is far better at the edge of the lawn, with a background of small trees and shrubs.

MATERIALS AND CONSTRUCTION
THE ROCK

Practically any kind of rock will do for the construction, weathered limestone being probably the best, and round field boulders the least desirable. Many gardeners and all suitable plants favor tuff, a porous volcanic rock that holds moisture like a sponge and is full of little channels for the roots of plants. Tuff, however, must be imported into most neighborhoods at considerable expense and always has an artificial appearance unless carefully used by an expert. The safest rule is to use whatever rock prevails in the neighborhood and attempt to have it all of the same character; although this is not essential.

The beginner's most common faults in constructing a rock garden are a tendency to place stones on end or to place them formally at regular intervals, which is equally unnatural. A little time spent in examining a natural outcropping before beginning the construction will be well spent. By always recalling the fact that whatever looks natural is right, you will avoid a great many pitfalls.

When a site has been chosen and its limits marked off, the area should be dug out to a depth of at least 1 ft., or preferably more, especially in low ground. One condition that plants almost invariably demand is good drainage. The excavation should, therefore, be a little more than half full with broken stone, broken bricks or tile, or coarse gravel. This material can be piled a little higher in spots where the final construction will be high. Next, add a layer of sand, gravel, or finer cinders and thoroughly wash this with the hose. The matter of drainage cannot be stressed too strongly. It is a comparatively easy matter to water a rock garden when it is too dry but, if it is improperly drained and a spell of wet weather occurs, nothing can be done and the choicest plants will rot away overnight.

SOIL

To provide the sharp drainage required in a rock garden, a mixture of equal parts of sand, pea gravel, and bark or other humusy material plus some superphosphate to promote flowering works well. Different areas within one garden can be amended to suit specific plants. For example, add peat for ericaceous plants; add more gravel for succulents; or add lime for the few plants that truly require a limey soil.

There are several principles that must be followed to get the best results in the above ground construction. In the first place, a large proportion of rock plants send their new roots to a surprising depth, even down into the drainage material. There should, therefore, be good depth of soil (at least 1 ft.) wherever there is to be planting. Rocks set into a slope should slant into the hill and downward; this makes them less likely to come loose and will also help to slow down any runoff and direct the moisture inward toward the roots of the plants. Steep slopes should be avoided because they wash out in heavy rain, burying the plants below as well as uncovering the roots of those above. A terraced construction, with gentle slopes on the terraces and miniature cliffs or

ledges separating them, is probably the most satisfactory. Steeper slopes can be used if occasional flat rocks are sunk into the slope in a vertical position with just their top edges showing so they will check the wash. Planting of dense, creeping plants such as thyme is also helpful, but nothing will completely prevent the erosion of a steep slope.

TERRACE CONSTRUCTION

The making of a terraced rock garden, particularly on a small scale, is quite simple. When the drainage has been built up almost to the ground level, a layer of soil is thrown over this and thoroughly washed in. This washing in is important throughout the construction, as it prevents any possibility of air pockets into which roots might stray and reduces to a minimum later settling, which would otherwise quite alter the contours of the finished garden. Next, lay an irregular rim of rock around the edge of the area, some stones being almost flush with the ground and others rising well above it. Fill this enclosure with the soil mixture and thoroughly soak it with the hose as before.

On the low plateau thus formed, construct another terrace in the same way, sinking all rocks firmly so that they do not move when used as stepping-stones. Remember that irregularity in the width and height of the terraces is essential and that the grain of the rock should tend to run in one general direction. This terracing process can be continued until the desired height is reached. Occasional gaps in the terrace walls, one above the other, will give the impression of miniature valleys or gullies.

When the construction has been completed, top-dress the soil with stone chips. Gravel will serve the same purpose—which is to slow down the evaporation of moisture, keep the foliage of the plants off the ground, and prevent spattering of mud onto low-growing blooms during heavy rains.

Paths in the rock garden are best made of flat stepping-stones sunk flush with the ground level, since they look more natural than gravel and require less care than grass.

MORAINES AND SCREES

The more experienced rock gardener will probably want to include a moraine. In nature this is the mass of rocks, stones, and gravel plus a small amount of silt that is deposited at the foot of a melting glacier. The proportion of soil in this debris is almost negligible, yet there are some plants that thrive under just such conditions. A moraine is usually a sunny slope watered from underneath by the melting snow and ice of the glacier. This watering from underneath as well as the manner of its deposit is what distinguishes the moraine from the scree, which is the mass of broken rock at the base of a cliff, formed by the accumulation of fragments torn loose by frosts and rock slides. In other words, the scree is a "dry moraine" as far as the rock garden is concerned.

Many gardeners prefer to have a sloping concrete basin a foot or so below the surface as a foundation for the moraine, but this is not really

Rock garden

necessary unless the ground below is very sandy and likely to drain off the supply of moisture too rapidly. Otherwise, the foundation of the drainage is the same as for the rest of the rock garden. Instead of building up with the regular soil mixture, however, use one part of that to four or more parts of gravel, sand, and broken stone. The moraine feature should be a gentle slope in

the valley of the rock garden with cliffs on each side and higher construction at the top.

The underground watering is supplied in various ways. If the concrete foundation is used, a trickle of water in at the top is sufficient. Otherwise, one of the best methods is to run a perforated pipe up the middle of the valley a few inches below the surface. This pipe should be fitted with a valve so that only a very little water will flow, otherwise the moraine will turn into a swamp. The water can be turned off entirely in wet weather and, of course, in winter. See also ALPINE PLANTS.

WATER

Water is always an addition to the rock garden; a little trickle of a stream running into a small pool and overflowing into a bit of boggy ground offers great possibilities both in construction and planting. Eight or 10 in. is deep enough for a pool of this type and, while ordinary waterlilies will find this rather shallow, such plants as **Nymphoides indica** (water-snowflake) and **Hydrocleys nymphoides** (water-poppy) will be ideally suited. Certain primulas, irises, etc., will enjoy the bog. See also AQUATIC PLANTS; BOG GARDEN; and individual genus entries.

CARE AND PLANT MATERIALS

MAINTENANCE

The care of a rock garden is easier than that of an ordinary herbaceous garden. Of course it should be kept free of weeds since it does not take long for a strong-growing weed to smother some of the more delicate rock plants.

Periodic watering is essential since the soil is likely to dry out due to its porous nature; and it is quickly affected by the wind as well as the sun. Rock plants are not as quick to show the effects of drought as are ordinary plants. They turn brown slowly and seldom wilt but indicate their displeasure in lack of growth and scantiness of bloom.

In the spring, it will often be found that some plants have been forced out of the ground by the heaving action of frost. These should be pressed back into place or actually taken up and replanted if necessary. At this time it is just as well to top-dress the whole garden, that is, add a thin layer of good soil mixture. In the case of plants that form dense mats, this layer of gritty soil can be spread right over them and washed in with a little sprinkling or worked in with the fingers. This ensures thorough covering of the roots and supplies fresh nourishment for the spring growth.

PLANTING

In planting the rock garden, there is a great wealth of material upon which to draw. It has been said that there are 40,000 different plants suitable for this type of culture; whatever the number, there are a great many readily available beautiful and interesting plants that are easily grown under these special conditions. There are whole genera all of whose numerous members are typical and desirable rock plants, except the few that are not hardy; notable among these are ***Androsace, Dianthus, Draba, Saxifraga, Sedum,*** and ***Sempervivum.***

The ideal rock plant should be a freely flowering, hardy perennial of neat habit and dwarf stature, easily grown but not a rampant spreader. Below is given a list of plants that, generally speaking, fulfill these conditions. Some excep-

tions have been included either on account of their beauty of foliage and neatness of habit alone, even though the bloom is insignificant, or because, while somewhat difficult of culture, they possess exceptional beauty that more than offsets this disadvantage. Such plants as arabis, aubrieta, and alyssum should be cut back after flowering to keep them neat and in good condition.

The accompanying chart gives information to help the gardener get started. Plants are listed by primary blooming seasons, but many flower on into the next season, particularly from late spring into summer and from summer into autumn. Many spring-flowering species bloom again in the fall. Following the name of each plant is the height or growth habit, the flower color, best light exposure, and other comments such as the preferred propagation method if other than seed (such as bulb, corm, etc.) and best type of soil.

The best times to plant are in the spring as soon as frosts are over and the ground becomes workable, and in the early autumn. Bulbs and corms should be planted in autumn except those of ***Colchicum*** and fall crocuses, which must be planted in August during their dormant season.

ROCK GARDEN PLANTS

EARLY SPRING FLOWERING

PLANT NAME	HEIGHT	FLOWER COLOR	LIGHT REQUIREMENTS	COMMENTS
Adonis amurensis	1 ft.	yellow	sun or light shade	
Anemone pulsatilla (pasque-flower)	9 in.	blue to purple	sun	dry conditions
Arabis procurrens	1 ft.	white	sun	
Aubrieta spp.	3 in.	blue to purple	sun	mat forming
Chionodoxa luciliae	6 in.	blue	sun	grows from bulbs
Crocus angustifolius	4 in.	yellow	sun	dry conditions, grows from corms
Crocus imperati	6 in.	lavender	sun	dry conditions, grows from corms
Crocus sieberi	3 in.	lavender	sun	dry conditions, grows from corms

PLANT NAME	HEIGHT	FLOWER COLOR	LIGHT REQUIREMENTS	COMMENTS
Crocus tomasinianus	4 in.	lavender	sun	dry conditions, grows from corms
Dicentra formosa	10 in.	pink	sun or light shade	
Eranthis hyemalis (winter aconite)	3 in.	yellow	shade	
Erythronium hendersonii (trout-lily)	1 ft.	purple	light shade	grows from bulb
Fritillaria meleagris cv. 'Alba'	1 ft.	white	light shade	grows from bulb
Galanthus elwesii (snowdrop)	6 in.	white	sun	grows from bulb
Galanthus nivalis (snowdrop)	4 in.	white	sun	grows from bulb
Gentiana acaulis	4 in.	blue	sun	
Helleborus niger (Christmas-rose)	1 ft.	white	part shade	prefers rich soil
Iris reticulata	10 in.	purple	sun	
Narcissus asturiensis	4 in.	yellow	sun	grows from bulb
Narcissus minor	4 in.	yellow	sun	grows from bulb
Phlox subulata	4 in.	various	sun	mat forming
Primula denticulata	8 in.	various	sun	
Pulmonaria angustifolia (lungwort)	8 in.	blue	sun or light shade	
Trillium grandiflorum	16 in.	white	shade	prefers acid soil
Tulipa dasystemon	4 in.	yellow, white	sun	prefers dry soil, grows from bulbs
Tulipa kaufmanniana	8 in.	yellow, red	sun	grows from bulbs

LATE SPRING FLOWERING

PLANT NAME	HEIGHT	FLOWER COLOR	LIGHT REQUIREMENTS	COMMENTS
Ajuga pyramidalis cv. 'Metallica Crispa' (bugleweed)	4 in.	blue	sun or light shade	
Allium moly	1 ft.	yellow	sun or light shade	
Armeria maritima (thrift)	10 in.	pink	sun	dry conditions
Aurinia saxatilis	10 in.	yellow	sun	dry conditions
Bellis rotundifolia (English daisy)	5 in.	white	sun	

PLANT NAME	HEIGHT	FLOWER COLOR	LIGHT REQUIREMENTS	COMMENTS
Campanula elatines var. *garganica*	6 in.	blue	sun	
Campanula portenschlagiana	5 in.	blue	sun	good for crevices
Cerastium alpinum	4 in.	white	sun	trailing habit
Chrysanthemum alpinum	8 in.	white	sun	
Chrysogonum virginianum	6 in.	yellow	sun or light shade	
Corydalis lutea	8 in.	yellow	sun or shade	
Cymbalaria aequitriloba	½ in.	lavender	light shade	mat forming
Dianthus arenarius	8 in.	white	sun	dry conditions
Dianthus pavonius	5 in.	pink	sun	dry conditions
Erythronium revolutum	1 ft.	white, lavender	light shade	grows from bulbs
Geranium cinereum	6 in.	pale pink	sun	
Globularia nudicaulis	8 in.	blue	sun	
Gypsophila repens	6 in.	pink, white	sun	
Helianthemum nummularium	8 in.	various	sun	prefers alkaline soil
Hypoxis hirsuta (star-grass)	10 in.	yellow	sun or light shade	
Iberis sempervirens (candytuft)	1 ft.	white	sun	
Iris cristata	4 in.	blue	sun or light shade	dry conditions
Linum perenne var. *alpinum* (flax)	6 in.	blue	sun	
Lychnis alpina	3 in.	pink	sun	
Muscari botryoides cv. 'Album'	8 in.	white	sun	grows from bulbs
Myosotis alpestris (forget-me-not)	6 in.	blue	sun	
Oenothera caespitosa	6 in.	white	sun	
Oenothera missouriensis	10 in.	yellow	sun	
Papaver alpinum	6 in.	various	sun	dry conditions
Phlox divaricata	1 ft.	lavender	sun or light shade	dry conditions
Potentilla alba	4 in.	white	sun	
Potentilla verna nana	2 in.	yellow	sun	mat forming
Primula japonica	18 in.	various	sun or light shade	moist conditions
Primula juliae	4 in.	red	sun	
Saxifraga macnabiana	16 in.	white	sun	dry conditions
Saxifraga paniculata	6 in.	white	sun	dry conditions
Sedum dasyphyllum	3 in.	white	sun	mat forming

PLANT NAME	HEIGHT	FLOWER COLOR	LIGHT REQUIREMENTS	COMMENTS
Sedum pulchellum	4 in.	rose-purple	sun or light shade	trailing habit
Sedum ternatum	4 in.	white	sun	
Silene caroliniana var. *pensylvanica* (wild-pink)	6 in.	pink	sun or light shade	
Stachys corsica	½ in.	white	sun	dry conditions, mat forming
Thymus serpyllum	2 in.	purple	sun	mat forming, grows on rocks
Tiarella cordifolia	6 in.	white	shade	
Tulipa linifolia	6 in.	red	sun	dry conditions, grows from bulbs
Veronica prostrata	3 in.	blue	sun	trailing habit
Viola gracilis	8 in.	lavender	sun	
Viola pedata	4 in.	violet	sun or light shade	prefers acid soil

SUMMER FLOWERING

PLANT NAME	HEIGHT	FLOWER COLOR	LIGHT REQUIREMENTS	COMMENTS
Allium carinatum	18 in.	pink	sun	dry conditions, grows from bulbs
Allium cyaneum	6 in.	blue	sun	grows from bulbs
Allium stellatum	18 in.	pink	sun	grows from bulbs
Astilbe chinensis cv. 'Pumila'	1 ft.	pink	sun or light shade	moist conditions
Astilbe simplicifolia	8 in.	pale pink	sun or shade	dry or moist conditions
Campanula carpatica	1 ft.	blue	sun	
Campanula cochleariifolia	5 in.	blue	sun	grows well in crevices
Campanula rotundifolia	14 in.	blue	sun	dry conditions
Campanula tommasiniana	6 in.	purple-blue	sun	
Ceratostigma plumbaginoides	1 ft.	blue	sun or light shade	
Cyclamen purpurescens	4 in.	crimson	sun	
Digitalis grandiflora (yellow foxglove)	2 ft.	yellow	sun or light shade	
Erodium chamaedryoides	2 in.	pink	sun	
Eryophyllum caespitosum	1 ft.	yellow	sun	
Gentiana lagodechiana	4 in.	blue	sun or light shade	
Gentiana septemfida	5 in.	blue	sun or light shade	

PLANT NAME	HEIGHT	FLOWER COLOR	LIGHT REQUIREMENTS	COMMENTS
Gentiana sino-ornata	4 in.	blue	sun or light shade	
Geranium sanguineum var. *prostratum*	6 in.	pink	sun	
Hypericum reptans		yellow	sun	trailing habit
Inula ensifolia	9 in.	yellow	sun	
Lavandula angustifolia cv. 'Munstead'	18 in.	lavender	sun	
Mentha requienii	½ in.	white	sun or light shade	mat forming
Nierembergia repens	3 in.	white	light shade	trailing habit
Parnassia palustris	6 in.	white	sun	moist conditions
Potentilla fruticosa (shrubby cinquefoil)		yellow	sun or light shade	prefers poor soil
Saponaria ocymoides	6 in.	pink	sun	
Saxifraga cortusifolia	8 in.	white	light shade	
Scutellaria alpina	6 in.	violet	sun	trailing habit
Sedum ewersii	5 in.	purple	sun	trailing habit
Sedum sieboldii	4 in.	pink	sun	prostrate habit
Sedum spurium	4 in.	bright pink	sun	trailing habit
Sempervivum (houseleek)	characteristics vary with species			
Silene schafta	6 in.	pink	sun	
Teucrium chamaedrys	8 in.	pink	sun	
Thymus citriodirus	6 in.	pink	sun	mat forming

AUTUMN FLOWERING

PLANT NAME	HEIGHT	FLOWER COLOR	LIGHT REQUIREMENTS	COMMENTS
Aster linariifolius	4 in.	blue	sun	trailing habit
Chrysanthemum arcticum	14 in.	white	sun	
Colchicum autumnale cv. 'Album'	6 in.	white	light shade	grows from corms
Colchicum autumnale cv. 'Roseum'	6 in.	pink	light shade	grows from corms
Colchicum speciosum var. *bornmuelleri*	8 in.	rose or lilac	light shade	grows from corms
Crocus longiflorus	5 in.	lilac	sun	dry conditions, grows from corms
Crocus speciosus	6 in.	lilac	sun	dry conditions, grows from corms

ROCKROSE. Common name for CISTUS, a genus of drought-resistant, evergreen shrubs bearing showy flowers.

ROCKSPRAY. Common name for *Cotoneaster microphyllus*, a spreading evergreen shrub with white flowers and abundant red berries; see COTONEASTER.

RODGERSIA (rah JUR see ah). A genus of hardy, ornamental, shrubby herbs, native to China and Japan, belonging to the Saxifragaceae (Saxifrage Family). Their five-lobed leaves spread like a wide-open hand, and they bear showy terminal clusters of small, white or yellowish white flowers resembling those of the astilbe. Rodgersias will grow in sun or shade if sheltered from high winds and prefer moist, peaty soil. Propagation is by seed or division.

PRINCIPAL SPECIES

R. aesculifolia grows to 6 ft. and has palmate leaves and flat clusters of white flowers.

R. pinnata grows to 3 ft. and has large panicles of white flowers tinted pink in summer. Hardy to Zone 3.

R. podophylla (bronze-leaf), native to South America, has light green foliage in spring, changing to a metallic bronze in summer. The plant reaches a height of 3–5 ft., and the leaves average 20 in. across. Hardy in Zones 5–8.

R. tabularis has round, green, semilobed leaves that form a low, 3-ft. mound. The small flowers are white, borne in numerous panicles 6–9 in. long in early summer.

ROGUE. A name given by plant breeders to a variation, usually inferior, from a given or standard type. Roguing, in plant breeding, is the removal of such undesired or deviating individuals as they occur in a seedling population, in order to purify or "fix" the variety, race, or strain. See PLANT BREEDING.

Roguing of individual plants affected by infectious diseases is also done to control and prevent the spread of the diseases. It is especially important in fighting virus diseases. See DISEASE.

ROHDEA (ROH dee ah) **japonica.** An Asiatic herb of the Liliaceae (Lily Family), commonly known as lily of China. It is grown indoors in the North and outdoors in warm climates as a reliable foliage plant. It has broad, leathery, basal leaves to 2 ft. long, but only 3 in. wide. Small, rounded, bell-shaped flowers in short spikes are almost hidden in the foliage and are followed by large, round, red berries. *Rohdea* is hardy as far north as Washington, D.C. and makes an excellent houseplant, doing well even in a cool window. There are a number of varieties with variegated leaves. They are highly regarded in China and Japan, where the many varieties are intensively grown by wealthy enthusiasts.

ROLLER. A cylinder of wood, concrete, or metal mounted to rotate on an axle and equipped with a handle or towing bar and used to compact loose soil. Though deep preparation of the soil is desirable, excessive air spaces interfere with the upward passage of moisture from the subsoil reservoir. The surface of a seedbed should remain loose; hence the roller should be followed by a weeder, harrow, or rake to create a dust mulch that will check loss of moisture by evaporation.

The efficiency and ease of operation of rollers depend more on their height and width than weight. Of two rollers of equal weight, the higher, narrower one will press soil harder. It will also be easier to operate because less of its surface is in contact with the ground, and the longer distance between axle and rim affords greater leverage in moving it. Rollers should be pulled, not pushed, over soft ground to cover foot or wheel marks. Types consisting of two or more cylinders mounted on one axle are easier to operate than one-piece types, especially around curves and when turning, because the sections turn independently without dragging or scraping.

To firm a winter-heaved and water-loosened lawn prior to the first spring mowing, a roller should be used as soon as the frost is out of the ground.

ROMAINE LETTUCE. A group of lettuce varieties belonging to a single species, *Lactuca sativa*, also known as cos lettuce. They grow 12–24 in. high and form cylindrical or conical heads that tend to blanch at the center. They are valued in England, and a few have become popular in North American gardens, although the hot summers do not favor them. These few, however, are gaining in popularity as both greenhouse and outdoor crops. Seed can be sown outdoors at any time

Romaine lettuce stalk

from early spring until late summer and well-formed heads gathered in ten weeks or less. See LETTUCE.

ROMNEYA (RAHM nee ah) **coulteri.** A showy perennial herb belonging to the Papaveraceae (Poppy Family), commonly known as California tree poppy or Matilija poppy. Native to southern California and Mexico, it grows to a height of 8 ft. and has many branches and attractive foliage, the finely cut, rich gray leaves having a slight bloom. Pointed buds develop into huge, fragrant, crinkly petaled white flowers up to 6

Romneya coulteri

in. across with bright golden clusters of stamens in the center. Var. *trichocalyx* is similar to the type but has more rounded, hairy buds. Plants spread by runners when established and are excellent for the back of the border, banks, or drought-tolerant landscapes. Hardy to Zone 7, they should be given a warm, sheltered position in light, rich, well-drained soil and full sun.

Propagation is by root cuttings in autumn or by seed. Seed is slow to germinate and needs scarification; plants may take several years to attain blooming size. Plants should be cut back to the ground before being transplanted, but even then failure is likely to result when they are moved.

RONDELETIA (ron de LEE shee ah). A genus of tropical evergreen shrubs or trees, some of which are still grown in the greenhouse and outdoors in Zones 9–11 but not as much as in former years. They bear large clusters of showy, fragrant flowers. They thrive in a mixture of loam, peat, and sand and are propagated by cuttings. Young shoots need pinching to induce a bushy growth. Principal species include: *R. odorata*, with showy clusters of yellow-throated, red flowers and *R. cordata*, with pink flowers.

ROOT. The descending axis of a plant. It penetrates the soil, absorbs moisture and nutrients, and acts as a support and anchor for the stem. Its structure is particularly adapted to fulfill these twin functions of nutrition and support. The pith region is a storage place for reserve foods; this concentration of foods gives many roots (such as the carrot) a high food value. Around the pith is a cylinder of vessels that either carry manufactured food down to build up the growing root tips or pump raw material up the stem.

Fibrous roots

Surrounding this cylinder is a thick layer of tissue that strengthens the root, and over all is a protecting epidermis. Long, threadlike root hairs branch out into the soil, increasing the absorptive surface of the root; and at the tip of each root is the delicate, yet surprisingly strong growing point. It is the growing point and the root hairs that are most frequently damaged in careless or ignorant gardening practices, especially in transplanting.

ROOTBALL.
The rounded mass of roots and soil that cling to a plant, tree, or shrub when it is removed from a pot or dug from a bed. Successful transplanting is promoted by keeping this ball intact so that the fine feeding-roots are disturbed as little as possible.

Shrubs and trees prepared for sale or shipment with the rootball encased in a protective covering of burlap, usually secured with twine, are said to be "balled and burlapped," designated in nursery catalogs as "B & B." When planted, a balled and burlapped shrub can be placed in the prepared hole with the burlap intact. Once the twine is removed, the burlap will decay in the soil as the root system grows.

To form a good rootball around a plant that must be moved, the soil must be moist but not wet. Sandy soil does not lend itself well to the formation of a rootball.

ROOTING COMPOUNDS.
These materials are receiving much attention at the hands of scientists, commercial breeders, and home gardeners. There are two kinds: natural (made by plants themselves) and synthetic. Other names applied to them are growth substances, growth regulators, growth-promoting substances, plant hormones, or auxins. In addition to inducing or speeding up the formation of roots, they can influence plant growth, generally in a number of other ways, including promoting or retarding it.

ROOT NODULES.
Small swellings or enlargements on the roots of leguminous plants caused by nitrogen-fixing bacteria (rhizobia), which have the power of taking nitrogen from the atmosphere and "fixing" it in a form available for the use of plants. See FABACEAE.

ROOT PRUNING.
The reduction of root length as a horticultural operation includes three types: it may occur as an unavoidable trimming of the roots of nursery stock when being dug; it may mean the trimming back of injured roots to sound wood to favor healing and the establishment of new feeding roots; and it may involve the cutting of roots without digging in order to check vegetative growth or to restrict the space in which the plants are allowed to develop. This last method is used in the block system of growing vegetable seedlings at regularly spaced intervals in flats, the soil being cut between them in both directions in weekly intervals. Specimen nursery trees are often similarly treated by special tools in order to stimulate the formation of a compact ball well supplied with fine roots. Root pruning is also a preliminary step in moving a large tree; in that case it consists of digging a trench a foot or so wide and twice as deep around the tree as far from the trunk as the radius of the desired ball. This is done a full season ahead of the actual transplanting, by which time the severed roots will have developed enough young feeding roots to make the moving operation less of a shock to the tree.

ROOTSPINE PALM.
Common name for CRYOSOPHILA (formerly listed as *Acanthorrhiza*), a genus of fan palms including medium-sized trees with spiny trunks.

ROSA
(ROH za). An important plant genus of more than 250 species native to the North Temperate Zone. For species hybrids and cultivars (cultivated varieties), see ROSE.

Rosa species are woody plants varying from low shrubs to tall climbers with basal, lateral, and sublateral branches called canes. They are described as thorny, although roses do not have true thorns; they have prickles, bristles, hairs, glands, and pubescence. Leaves are alternate and compound with uneven numbers of leaflets. Flowers are usually a single row of petals, most commonly five, in colors of pink or white with some species yellow and a few red.

Botanists of all ages have differed widely on questions related to the genus *Rosa*. They have agreed it is difficult to define *Rosa* species. *R.*

centifolia, *R. chinensis*, and *R. damascena* have come to us as fully developed garden plants with double flowers improperly bearing species names. *R. roxburghii* (chestnut rose) was first discovered in its double form and given the species name; later the single form, the true species, was discovered and given the name *R. roxburghii* var. *normalis*. *R. alba* is generally believed to be a species hybrid, and some experts think it was originally a cross between *R. canina* and *R. gallica*. These are only a few examples of points of confusion.

Many species roses make good garden plants and will thrive in ordinary garden soil, though it is wise to give them conditions as near to their native habitat as possible, fertilizing very little if at all. The most widely grown species of rose, *R. hubonis* (Father Hugo's rose or golden rose of China) does best in unimproved soil. Other excellent garden subjects include *R. eglanteria* (sweetbrier rose or Shakespeare's eglantine), *R. pendulina* (alpine rose), *R. rugosa* and its color sports var. *alba* and var. *rubra*, *R. foetida* (Austrian brier) and its color sport var. *bicolor* (Austrian copper rose).

R. carolina (pasture rose), native throughout eastern North America, is a slender, very prickly branching plant

Rosa carolina

that grows to 3 ft. or more. It has narrow, ovate, 1½-in. leaflets in groups of five to nine and produces solitary pink flowers 1½–2 in. across with red hips.

R. canina, *R. multiflora* cv. 'Manettii' (formerly listed as *R. chinensis* var. *manettii*), and 'Fortuniana' (formerly listed as *R.* x *fortuniana*) have been widely used as understocks for budded plants of cultivated varieties in order to give vigor, though other vigorous roses may also be used for the purpose. See ROSE.

R. multiflora, a Japanese rose, when imported to this country rapidly became invasive and has been designated a noxious weed in several states.

Rose hips, the seedpods that form after the flower petals fall, are high in vitamin C and have been used as food supplements in some countries, notably in England during World War II, when schoolchildren gathered *R. canina* hips.

Among species roses used in garden situations can be found *R. acicularis* (arctic rose or polar rose), the Lady Banks Roses, *R. banksiae* var. *banksiae* in white and var. *lutea* in yellow—both vigorous but tender, climbing *Rosa* varieties; *R. farreri* var. *persetosa* (threepenny bit rose); *R. glauca* (red-leaved rose), formerly listed as *R. rubrifolia*; *R. pomifera* (apple rose); *R. primula* (incense rose); *R. spinosissima* (Scotch or burnet rose); *R. virginiana* (shining rose); and *R. wichuraiana* (memorial rose).

ROSACEAE (roh ZAY see ee). The Rose Family, an important group of trees, shrubs, and herbs of various habits, widely distributed throughout the North Temperate Zone and contributing many major ornamental forms and fruit-yielding subjects, besides a few of medicinal value. The flowers include many colors, with white and pink shades predominating. The petals are borne on the margin of a usually hollow receptacle that in some species becomes fleshy and enlarged to form the apple and strawberry fruits. Most of the cultivated forms are hardy; some of the most important genera in gardening include *Alchemilla*, *Amelanchier*, *Aronia*, *Aruncus*, *Chaenomeles*, *Cotoneaster*, *Crataegus* (hawthorn), *Cydonia*, *Duchesnea*, *Eriobotrya*, *Exochorda*, *Filipendula*, *Frageria* (strawberry), *Geum*, *Gillenia*, *Heteromeles*, *Holodiscus*, *Kerria*, *Mespilus*, *Osteomeles*, *Photinia*, *Physocarpus*, *Potentilla*, *Prunus* (the stone fruits), *Pyracantha*, *Pyrus* (the pome fruits, including apple and pear), *Raphiolepis*, *Rhodotypos*, *Rosa*, *Rubus* (brambles, including raspberries and blackberries), *Sanguisorba*, *Sibiraea*, *Sorbaria*, *Sorbus* (mountain-ash), *Spiraea*, *Stephanandra*, and *Stranvaesia*.

ROSARY-PEA. A common name for *Abrus pre-catorius*, a vine of the Fabaceae (Bean Family) whose brilliant red-and-black, poisonous seeds are sometimes used as beads; see ABRUS.

ROSE. References to roses can be found throughout history and in the folklore and literature of every land. In ancient times roses were grown for medicinal purposes. In the middle ages they were grown for medicine, conserves, and perfumes. In more modern times, roses are grown for the perfume industry, as cut flowers for the florist industry, and as garden flowers. In every age, roses have been grown for their beauty and decorative value.

Roses traveled widely from very early times. That roses were taken to every part of the Roman Empire is only an example of a phenomenon that happened on a smaller scale in innumerable other instances. Roses were brought back to western European countries from the Crusades, and later, in the age of the plant hunters, roses were brought from China and the east to England, France, and other European countries. Roses were also taken to countries in the Southern Hemisphere. While roses are native only to the Northern Hemisphere, it should be remembered that all the roses we speak of here were already fully developed garden varieties, though species roses were also distributed in the same way, being used in such instances as garden subjects and also as understocks for budded plants that lived on and naturalized after the top graft had died out.

Because ancient garden roses, now referred to as "old garden roses," were hardy, thrifty plants, able to survive periods of neglect and in some cases to naturalize, they are still with us, and we can grow in our gardens the same roses grown by the Romans, the Crusaders, and the Empress Josephine, who collected every then-known rose variety in her garden at Malmaison.

CATEGORIES

Roses are generally divided into two categories: old garden roses and modern roses. Roses that are grown for the perfume and related industries fit into the former group; roses grown under glass for the florist trade fit into the latter group. (In a few cases, varieties are grown both for the greenhouse and the garden; the cultivar 'Sonia' is a good example of this.)

The important old European garden roses were the gallicas, damasks, albas, centifolias, and mosses. To this list we must add the Chinas and the tea-scented China roses that arrived in Europe at the end of the eighteenth century and the beginning of the nineteenth century. At the next stage of development in rose history come the Portlands or perpetual damask and perpetual damask moss roses, and the Bourbons. This takes us well into the nineteenth century, where we see the development of the hybrid perpetuals, the forerunners of today's modern hybrid teas.

Of the modern roses there are hybrid teas, grandifloras, floribundas, miniature roses, which trace their beginnings back to the early nineteenth century but were only fully developed in the twentieth century.

Climbing roses and roses classified simply as shrub roses fit into both old garden rose and modern rose categories. Roses are not true climbers, but some varieties produce long canes that can be trained as climbers.

Many climbers can be divided into two groups: large-flowered climbers, which generally bloom in small clusters; and ramblers, which have large flowering heads made up of very small individual flowers. Most of the climbing roses that fit into both these categories bloom only once a year and do not repeat bloom later in the season. In the late nineteenth and early twentieth centuries, a number of repeat-blooming polyantha roses were developed from the once-blooming ramblers. These are small, ever-blooming shrubs, which, crossed with the hybrid tea roses, gave us the floribunda roses developed during the early to mid-twentieth century.

Other climbers developed as sports of hybrid tea and floribunda roses, and these are mostly all repeat blooming. Sporting in plants is not fully understood but can be described as a spontaneous mutation in the plant cells, giving rise to climbing varieties of bush roses, different colors of bloom, etc.

Roses must be propagated vegetatively, since they will not come true from seed. New varieties of roses are bred by crossing the two varieties chosen to be the parents and by rigorous selection of the resulting seedlings.

In ancient times rose growers watched for new and improved forms and increased them by propagation of cuttings and suckers (possibly only on own-root plants). In more recent times, nurseries planted great quantities of bee-crossed seeds, choosing the best of the resulting seedlings for vegetative propagation. Since the latter part of the nineteenth century when hybridization came to be understood, crosses have been made by rose breeders, and new and improved forms have been developed much more quickly than in past centuries.

The grandiflora class can be understood as a cross between the hybrid tea and floribunda classes; however, it is not an acknowledged classification in many countries, where roses we place in the grandiflora class remain in the floribunda. As the floribunda class has progressed, the varieties within it have become closer to the hybrid tea class and are sometimes called floribunda hybrid tea–type.

At the other end of the scale, many miniature roses have been bred so large that they now form a group variously called mini-flora, patio roses, sweetheart roses, and "in-between" roses.

Around the beginning of the present century, a class of roses were bred by Joseph Pernet-Ducher of France, combining the hybrid perpetuals and hybrid teas of the time with Persian Yellow, the double form of the Austrian Brier (*R. foetida*), and they were called hybrid Pernetianas for a time. Eventually they merged into the hybrid tea class and the Pernetiana class was eliminated.

The development of modern roses is not static, but ever changing. We can be sure new roses will continue to evolve, especially now that we can see into the future and imagine what the results of genetic engineering may prove to bring—possibly even a true blue rose.

CLASSIFICATION

The major rose classes have been given above. There are other classes that fit in one way or another and in some instances fit into both the old garden rose and modern rose categories. Sometimes rose classes are listed by nurserymen as "use" classes, such as the newly developed shrub rose varieties advertised as "ground cover" roses, more accurately described as "carpeting" roses. Another very new group is the English rose group that represents a cross between old garden rose types and the repeat-blooming capabilities of modern roses. Of the Scotch roses, a few of them fit into the old garden rose category while most fit into the modern shrub rose variety.

The Noisette roses, representing a cross between the musk and the China or tea-scented China roses, are mostly climbers of ever-blooming habit and, being very tender, are mostly grown in mild climates. The hybrid musk roses are only remotely connected to the musk roses and show more strongly their multiflora heritage, but the name hybrid musk has been accepted for the class. They fit in as modern shrub roses. While *R. rugosa* and its color sports var. *alba* and var. *rubra* are naturally occurring species roses and have been placed in the old garden rose category, the hybrid rugosas are all placed with the modern shrub roses. It should be noted that species roses can be placed in the old garden rose category or in the modern rose category depending on the date of their discovery, 1867 being the dividing line determined by the American Rose Society.

Much folklore, legend, and misinformation has been printed about roses and continues to be printed in books, articles, and publications of rose societies. Just as botanists disagree about *Rosa* species on the scientific level, so rose experts and rose authorities disagree on many aspects of rose history. *R. gallica* var. *officinalis* (apothecary rose) was confused with damask roses over several centuries and is referred to as the "Red Damask" in many old books. Its sport, *Rosa mundi,* was confused with a damask rose and may be pictured in books under the caption York and Lancaster. The true 'York and Lancaster' is a damask rose, but a pink-and-white particolored rose with some pink petals and some white petals in the same flower, not a deep pink-and-white striped rose.

Many roses have been placed, for a time, in whatever class the nurserymen thought would sell best, and classification of roses is generally difficult to approach logically. As time goes by, however, roses are grouped with those to which they show close affinity, and with few exceptions, the classes sort themselves out pretty well.

On another level, separating legend from historical fact is an interesting if confusing exercise, complicated by the legends being presented in literature as if they were fact.

PLANTING

In most cases, roses should be planted in an open, sunny position with good drainage. While in the past double digging was mandated, it is now thought that roses do not require such deep soil preparation. It is still a good idea, however, to provide as much improvement as is practical. The addition of one-third by volume of peat moss and/or compost is minimal. Roses thrive best in slightly acidic soil, so agricultural lime or sulfur can be added to bring the pH to a nearly neutral or slightly acidic state. If very much soil preparation is required, it is best to accomplish it a full season before planting. Gypsum can be used to improve soil without changing the pH. The addition of compost will improve both sandy and clay types of soil.

Roses are planted mainly in two ways: as dormant, bare-root plants and as potted roses obtained from local nurseries in leaf and often in flower. Carefully set potted roses in place, making sure that the budhead (often referred to as the bud union) is at ground level. The bottom of the container should be taken off before setting in place in the planting hole, and then the sides can be removed. The use of boxed roses advertised to be planted in their boxes should be avoided; if such roses are selected, they should be removed from the box and treated as bare-root plants.

Dormant bare-root rose plants should never be allowed to dry out. They should be left in their plastic bag until ready to plant and then placed in buckets of water where they can safely remain for several hours. They should be examined and any damaged canes or roots pruned off. In planting, the roots should be spread out as much as possible over a cone of improved garden soil, making sure the budhead is at ground level. Rosarians in cold winter climates sometimes plant the budhead an inch or two below ground level, while growers in mild climates tend to make sure the budhead is well exposed. The planting hole should be filled in and the rose well watered. Then it should be hilled up with garden soil (to prevent dessication of the canes) until the new growth starts, when the extra soil should be carefully and gradually washed away with a stream of water from the garden hose to avoid breaking off tender new growth.

Tree or standard roses, where the top variety is budded onto a tall standard, a sturdy rose cane especially selected for the purpose (which is, in turn, bud grafted onto a vigorous understock), should be planted as outlined above, but with the addition of a strong stake with secure ties carefully placed so as to afford protection from strong winds, especially after the top growth becomes fully developed. These roses can make outstanding accents in the garden landscape. Half-standards are available in some countries.

CULTIVATION

Fertilizer should not be given to newly planted roses; after they have bloomed, they can be fertilized slightly. Established roses should be given fertilizer early in the spring, and twice more during the growing season. Some rosarians prefer to fertilize more often with lighter applications. Fertilizer should be withheld in the fall to encourage roses to become dormant and so withstand the rigors of winter. Any balanced fertilizer can be used just as effectively as a special rose formulation.

Roses require lots of water, and if the drainage is good, as it should be, it is almost impossible to overwater. In very warm climates, where there is little if any winter season and summers are very hot and dry, roses will go into a dormant state in midsummer. They should be given what water can be spared, but they will recover well in the cooler days of fall. This will depend in large part on the varieties chosen.

In severe winter climates, roses require some protection. Here again, it is important to choose varieties that will withstand winter conditions best. Many forms of winter protection are used by rosarians in cold climates, from mounding with garden soil, compost, or leaves, perhaps with some material forming a retaining collar, to styrofoam cones or panels covering the entire rose bed. Climbers can be laid down and covered with garden soil or leaves held in place with burlap or some other suitable material. Rose bushes can be dug out on one side so they can be tipped over and covered with soil, compost, etc. Each gardener must find a favorite method based on the severity of the climate, including the microclimate of the particular property.

PROPAGATION

Because of the variety of roses available, most people do not find it necessary to propagate their own plants. Propagation is not difficult, however, and can be very rewarding.

During peak bloom, a cutting should be taken from a stem that had a good flower. As soon as the bloom shatters, the wood is mature enough to make a cutting. Another way to test for mature wood is to push a thorn (prickle) off the stem by pressing with the thumb on the side; it should pop off easily.

Remove the top part of the stem, down to the first five-leaflet leaf, and cut just below the lowest five-leaflet leaf; your cutting should be about 6 in. long and have at least three leaf axils. The top leaf should be retained and the others trimmed off. Dip the bottom end in rooting hormone compound and insert in potting mix made up of sterile soil with sharp sand added. Avoid using vermiculite in the potting mix, as it does not drain well, and a good air mix is important to the growth of roots. Cuttings can be placed in trays or pots, under mist or in plastic bags to keep humidity high during rooting. Roots will form in about six weeks, when the rooted cuttings can be gradually hardened-off and the tent or enclosure removed.

Many rose growers root new cuttings in place in the garden by covering them with large jars, such as restaurant-sized mayonnaise jars, which are left in place until the following spring, or until the new growth gets too large. They are then removed gradually, for a short time at first and then for longer periods each day until they can be left off entirely. The surest way to root rose cuttings is under a misting tent, but some growers have good luck with other methods.

There really is no such thing as softwood and hardwood in roses, since roses have canes with a central pith. Many people do think of the young growth as softwood and the older, woody-appearing growth as hardwood, but the terms are misapplied.

HARDINESS

On the question of hardiness, it should be noted that many roses do not succumb to low temperatures if the change is gradual. Damage results when fluctuating temperatures occur. Most winter damage is due to dessication in drying winds and winter sun when the ground is frozen and the plant is unable to take up moisture. Much depends on the vagaries of the season and upon the microclimate. A sheltered location will often ensure the survival of a rose that may be borderline hardy. Therefore it is difficult to place rose varieties in climate zones. One can say in general that some species and most old garden roses are very hardy, and that as rose development gets closer to the modern rose, some hardiness is lost. Some roses in the modern rose category, however, are relatively hardy. The China and tea roses are, for the most part, quite tender, and the modern hybrid tea is hardier than the tea rose but not as hardy as the hybrid perpetual from which it was developed. Floribundas are a little more hardy than hybrid teas, but as they merge into the class, there is a wider range of hardiness among them, and within the hybrid tea class as well.

ENEMIES

Roses are subject to a variety of pests and diseases, particularly if grown as a single crop. Those who wish to do a minimum of spraying interplant their roses with other garden shrubs and flowers. The choice of disease-resistant varieties is important. Major problems will be BLACK SPOT, MILDEW, and RUSTS among the fungal diseases (see FUNGUS), depending somewhat on the area in which one gardens. Preventive sprays can be used against the fungal diseases. Aphids are the most common pests and can be dealt with by washing them off with a strong stream of water, or with two applications of a pesticide a week or ten days apart to break the breeding cycle. The most serious pests in some areas and in some seasons are THRIPS, Japanese BEETLES, MIDGE, and spider MITES.

New developments in fungicides and pesticides come about rapidly in the effort to find more effective, less dangerous spray materials. Read labels completely, follow directions to the letter, and buy only the amount you can use in one season. The shelf life of spray materials has been found to be much shorter than previously believed. In addition, since insects can build up a resistance to pesticides, the gardener may decide to switch to another type in succeeding years or may wish to try an improved, newly developed product. See also DISEASE; INSECT CONTROL.

MULCHES

Various mulches are used to retain moisture and keep down weeds. The material used should be something readily obtainable in your area. Some gardeners swear by a dust mulch, which means frequent light surface cultivation and hand weeding. Popular mulches include ground bark chips, buckwheat hulls, cocoa hulls, bagasse (sugar cane), grass clippings, spoilt hay, seaweed, shredded leaves, and compost. Peat moss is a good soil additive but should not be used as a mulch unless mixed with other material, such as compost. Nonorganic mulches, such as black plastic mulch, are not recommended for roses, since water and fertilizer need to be applied at the drip line, not at the base of the plant.

PRUNING

Roses should be pruned in early spring when the new growth buds, which occur in the leaf axils, can be seen pushing forth. The best flowers will appear on second-year canes, and some older canes should be removed, as well as all thin, twiggy growth (smaller than pencil thickness). Any diseased canes, those showing canker, for example, should be removed, and any crossing canes that may damage each other in heavy winds should be reduced to one free cane.

It is possible to shape the bush by pruning to a bud that is headed in a desirable direction. Generally it is recommended to prune to an outward facing bud.

Although the early spring pruning is the major pruning of the year, taking place when the bush is defoliated and the structure can be seen, cutting flowers during the growing season should also be thought of as pruning and should be done according to the same principles; that is, for the good of the bush. Exceptions will be made when long stems are wanted for special occasions. In general, cut just above an outward-facing, five-leaflet leaf; the new flowering stem will come from that leaf axil.

SELECTING PLANTS

The question of which rose varieties to choose for winter hardiness, for disease resistance, and for good performance in special situations is one that can only be answered by experience. This does not have to be accomplished purely by trial and error. Reading about roses, studying rose catalogs, and talking with other rose enthusiasts in your area will all be helpful. The American Rose Society publishes a yearly buyer's guide called *Handbook for Selecting Roses*. Their ratings are national, which means an average has been taken. A few roses that are highly rated for exhibition may not perform well in your garden, while many roses with a low national rating will thrive in special areas, such as coastal or desert gardens, severe winter or hot climates, etc. Regional districts of the American Rose Society and some local chapters publish a rating guide but usually concentrate only on newly introduced varieties. Nevertheless, it is helpful in many ways to join a plant society.

In regard to all the older classes of roses, it is helpful to join the Heritage Roses Group and receive their publications. The reference section of the local library, or better yet, the nearest botanical garden library, may contain information on roses and on national or local rose organizations.

ROSE CHAFER. This beetle, *Macrodactylus subspinosus*, is a significant pest on roses. Its long, slender, half-inch body is light tan, with wings less hard and horny than other beetles. The spiny legs are long and prominent. Besides roses, it infests peonies and grapes, and it also attacks hydrangeas, hollyhocks, iris, foxglove;

Rose chafer

fruit trees such as apple, cherry, peach, and pear; and raspberries and strawberries. The beetles come in swarms in late May to early June, going first to roses and peonies, then to young grapes and various kinds of foliage. The feeding period lasts three to four weeks. Eggs, laid in sandy soil, hatch within two weeks into small, white grubs, which feed on grass roots. They then burrow into the ground for the winter.

Milky spore disease, *Bacillus popilliae*, which is inserted into lawns for control of Japanese beetles, will also control rose chafer grubs. Handpick individual beetles or shake plants over a sheet to collect infestations of adult beetles. Cheesecloth, mosquito netting, or floating row covers will make good barriers against them.

ROSE MALLOW. A common name for HIBISCUS, a genus of showy-flowered perennial herbs.

ROSEMARY. Common name for *Rosmarinus officinalis*, whose leaves are used in seasoning and medicine; see ROSMARINUS. Bog-rosemary is ANDROMEDA. Wild-rosemary is *Ledum palustre*; see LEDUM.

ROSE-OF-JERICHO. A common name for *Anastatica hierochuntica*, a small annual herb, and for *Selaginella lepidophylla*, a mosslike herb, both noted for shriveling when dry and opening when given moisture; see ANASTATICA; SELAGINELLA.

ROSE-OF-SHARON. A common name for *Hibiscus syriacus*, a hardy, upright, summer-flowering shrub; and for *Hypericum calycinium*, a low, shrubby species of St.-John's-wort. See HIBISCUS; HYPERICUM.

ROSETTE. A clustering growth habit, which may be a natural arrangement of the foliage, as in sempervivum, dandelions, and other plants, or else a symptom of disease, such as peach rosette and the rosette of wheat. See DISEASE.

ROSINWEED. Common name for SILPHIUM, a genus of grassland perennials with daisylike flowers.

ROSMARINUS (rohz mah RĪ nus) **officinalis.** A hardy evergreen subshrub belonging to the Lamiaceae (Mint Family). Native to southern Europe and Asia, the plants have been cultivated for centuries, chiefly for aromatic leaves, which are used in seasoning and yield an oil used in medicine. Small, light blue flowers are borne in early spring, in loose clusters that grow from the leaf axils; the blossoms help to produce prize flavored honey. The foliage is white and woolly beneath and

Rosmarinus officinalis

dark and shiny above. Plants grow to a height of 2–6 ft. and last for years if given winter protection. Hardy to Zone 6, they prefer dry, well-drained soil and full sun. In Pacific Coast states where the soil is dry and rocky, they are planted as hedges.

ROSSIOGLOSSUM (rah see oh GLAH sum). A genus of six species of epiphytic orchids endemic to the cordilleras in Central America, initially described by twentieth century German botanist Friedrich R. R. Schlechter. They are closely related to *Odontoglossum* but are distinguished from that genus by a free lip that forms a right angle with the column.

They produce large, colorful flowers that are mostly yellow with red-brown marks. The plants should be grown in moderate shade and ample water. Hardy to Zone 5 if protected from freezing, they withstand minimum winter temperatures to 55°F. The type species is *R. grande*.

ROT. A disintegration of tissues; decay; putrefaction. As a symptom of plant disease, rot may be hard, soft, wet, or dry. See DISEASE.

ROTARY TILLER. A rotary cultivating machine with metal tines that dig the soil, usually powered with a gasoline motor, although some are electric. The rotary tiller is a versatile machine used to turn over sod or soil, prepare beds for seeding, cultivate between rows, till under crop residue, or mix in mulches, compost, or fertilizer.

In use, the operator walks behind or to one side, steering the device with a pair of handles that angle up and back from the body of the machine. Small tillers without wheels are driven by the rotating metal tines that pull the machine

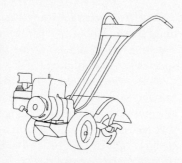

Rotary tiller

forward as they till the soil. In larger models, the tines revolve in front or in back of a pair of wheels. Most large models have forward and

reverse features for greater control. Many tillers feature optional attachments such as furrowers, edgers, aerators, and de-thatchers. Rototiller is a common name in trade.

ROTATION OF CROPS. See CROP ROTATION.

ROTENONE. An insecticide and miticide extracted from the ground-up roots of plants such as *Derris elliptica*, *Lenchocarpus* spp. (cubé), and *Tephrosia virginiana* (devil's-shoestring), and other plants containing the effective principle. The tropical plants are sometimes used in hot climates to paralyze fish in streams to make them easy to catch. When using this now popular insecticide, be careful to keep it away from fish ponds and water sources.

Rotenone is useful as both a contact and stomach poison and is not toxic to humans. However, it is toxic to bees, wasps, and other good pollinators and so should only be applied to garden plants after bees have gone to their hive for the night. Both sprays and dusts are used, sometimes combined with PYRETHRUM and ryania, or an all-purpose fungicide. In recent years, cubé has been the primary source for commercial rotenone mixtures. One-percent strength is usually sufficient for protecting vegetables. Five percent is used for severe cases and for attacking ticks and fleas on dogs. Rotenone is recommended for use with flea beetles, leaf rollers, thrips, corn earworms, cucumber beetles, and the Mexican bean beetle, as well as many others. See also INSECT CONTROL.

ROUGE PLANT. Common name for *Rivina humilis*, a tender annual with white or rosy flowers and berrylike fruit; see RIVINA.

ROYAL FERN. Common name for *Osmunda regalis*, a stately northern fern with widely spaced pinnae; see OSMUNDA.

ROYAL PALM. Common name for ROYSTONEA, a genus of feather palm trees commonly planted for their majestic habit and vigorous growth.

ROYSTONEA (roy STOH nee ah). A genus of majestic feather palms native from northeastern South America through the Caribbean to Florida and commonly known as royal palms. The tall trunks (50–100 ft.) are often swollen in the middle. The graceful, wide-spreading heads are made up of arching leaves 10–15 ft. long with 3-ft. leaflets (pinnae). Because of their extremely rapid growth, resistance to fire, disease, and winds, and their adaptability to a variety of soils, the trees are valued for street and specimen planting in the southern states (Zones 10–11). They grow rapidly from seed and often take root in the wild on plate rock, the roots getting their nourishment from the fallen leaves and flowers.

PRINCIPAL SPECIES

R. borinquena (Puerto Rican royal palm) has a trunk 50 ft. or taller that is swollen toward the top, bearing a crown of featherlike fronds 10 ft. long.

R. oleracea (Carribean or South American royal palm) grows 100 ft. or taller with the trunk enlarged at the base and cylindrical toward the top. Its huge leaves, up to 20 ft. long, form a spreading, erect crown.

R. regia (Cuban royal palm) is the most common cultivated species, growing 75 ft. or more. Its trunk is larger at the base and swollen or of equal thickness through the middle and then tapered at the top. Some of the 15-ft.-long leaves are erect and some drooping, forming a rounded crown. Male and female flowers are borne together in clusters of purple followed by dark red or purple fruits less than an inch in diameter.

RUBBER PLANT. Common name for *Ficus elastica*, a common houseplant with glossy, oblong leaves; see FICUS.

RUBBER TREE. Common name for several tropical plant species. *Castilla elastica* produces milky juice that was once a common source of rubber; see CASTILLA. *Hevea brasiliensis* (Para rubber tree) has become the main commercial source of natural rubber; see HEVEA. *Ficus elastica*, an ornamental belonging to the Moraceae (Mulberry Family), is sometimes called India rubber plant or tree.

RUBBERVINE. Common name for CRYPTOSTEGIA, a genus of tropical vining shrubs usually grown for ornament and sometimes for economic purposes.

RUBIACEAE (roo bee AY see ee). The Madder Family, a large, distinct group of plants, mostly tropical. It furnishes many ornamental forms, chiefly greenhouse subjects, and yields many economic products such as coffee, quinine, dyes, and medicine. Common genera include *Asperula*, *Bouvardia*, *Cinchona*, *Coffea*, *Coprosma*, *Galium*, *Gardenia*, *Genipa*, *Hamelia*, *Hoffmannia*, *Ixora*, *Luculia*, *Manettia*, *Pentas*, *Rondeletia*, *Rubia*, and *Serissa*.

RUBUS (ROO bus). A large genus of shrubby plants native mostly in the temperate and colder regions of the Northern Hemisphere, belonging to the Rosaceae (Rose Family), and commonly known as brambles. Most have prickly, and usually biennial, stems. Some are grown for their edible fruit; others for their ornamental stems, foliage, and flowers. They thrive in open locations and good loamy soil and are propagated by seed, layers, suckers, and root cuttings.

For cultivation and edible species, see BLACKBERRY; RASPBERRY.

NORTH AMERICAN SPECIES

R. allegheniensis (sow-teat blackberry) is a highbush blackberry with leaves of three or five leaflets, from which some of the cultivated species have originated.

R. chamaemorus (cloudberry) is a hardy, herbaceous species with white flowers and orange-red fruit; a good rock garden plant.

R. deliciosus (Rocky Mountain flowering raspberry), native to Colorado, is a good, hardy, thornless ornamental shrub with currantlike leaves and showy, roselike, white flowers. Hardy in Zones 4–6.

R. flagellaris (American dewberry) is a trailing blackberry with stems usually several feet long;

one of the parents of the cultivated dewberries.

R. hispidus (swamp dewberry) is a slender trailer with glossy, half-evergreen leaves and no prickles; a good ground cover for moist places.

R. occidentalis (blackcap raspberry) is an erect, moderate grower with glaucous, prickly canes that arch to the ground where the tips root, producing new plants. It is the source of good cultivated varieties.

R. odoratus (flowering raspberry), native to the eastern states, is an erect, thornless shrub growing to 6 ft. or more with large-lobed, maplelike leaves and showy, rosy purple flowers blooming most of the summer. It thrives in partial shade and moist soil and is hardy in Zones 4–6.

R. spectabilis (salmonberry) is an almost spineless, hardy, perennial-stemmed species with purple or rose-colored flowers and salmon-colored, edible fruit.

R. ursinus (Pacific dewberry) is a trailing blackberry whose varieties include the well-known boysenberry, loganberry, and youngberry.

ASIATIC SPECIES

R. illecebrosus (strawberry raspberry, balloonberry) is a dwarf, Japanese, nearly woody, herbaceous bramble planted for its ornamental foliage. The stem is winter-killed to the ground in the North, but new shoots the following season produce large, fragrant, white flowers and scarlet fruit, which is good for stewing or canning.

R. phoenicolasius (wineberry) is similar to and grown like the trailing blackberries, preferably on a trellis, usually more for ornament than for its small, soft, red, rather insipid, though sometimes acid fruit. In cold localities and when grown on wet soils, it often winter kills but then generally sends up new shoots from the crown.

EUROPEAN SPECIES

R. idaeus (European raspberry) is the source of some of the cultivated forms. Var. *strigosus* is the American red raspberry, which is also cultivated in improved forms.

R. laciniatus (cutleaf blackberry) grows to 20 ft. in a mild climate. With finely cut leaves and large, black fruit, it makes an attractive plant for dressing an arch.

R. ulmifolius var. *bellidiflorus* is an ornamental form with double pink flowers. Var. *inermis* (evergreen thornless blackberry) is often grown in mild regions.

RUBY GRASS. Common name for *Rhynchelytrum repens*, a flowering grass cultivated in warm climates; see RHYNCHELYTRUM.

RUDBECKIA (rood BEK ee ah). A genus of annual, biennial, or perennial herbs with conical disks in daisylike flowers, belonging to the Asteraceae (Aster Family), and commonly known as coneflower. Native to North America, these coarse, summer-blooming herbs have showy terminal heads of yellow ray flowers and cone-shaped, brown, yellowish, or purplish black disk clusters. Including the well-known black-eyed-Susan of the fields, rudbeckias are sturdy plants that in pioneer days were mainly familiar wildflowers. Today's descendants are popular garden subjects.

Thriving in any soil and doing equally well in full sun or partial shade, they make a welcome addition to the yellow border, continuing their bloom well into autumn. Propagation is by seed sown indoors or outdoors, by cuttings, or by division of the roots.

PRINCIPAL SPECIES

R. fulgida cv. 'Goldsturm' is a perennial that grows to 24 in. tall in Zones 3–9. Its bushy form carries large quantities of bright yellow flowers good for cutting.

R. hirta (black-eyed-Susan) is a hardy perennial that can be grown as an annual. Perhaps the most familiar species, it has vivid yellow, dark-centered flower heads borne in abundance on rough-haired plants 2–3 ft. tall. It is the state flower of Maryland. Cv. 'Gloriosa Daisy' is a popular garden variety.

Rudbeckia hirta

R. laciniata var. *hortensia* (golden-glow) is a tall, smooth plant, hardy in Zones 3–9.

R. subtomentosa grows 4–5 ft. tall with flowers of yellow rays surrounding dark brown cones and foliage on hairy stems. Hardy to Zone 5.

R. triloba (brown-eyed-Susan) is one of the most attractive species, with many branches bearing quantities of small but showy flowers.

RUE. Common name for RUTA, a genus of aromatic and medicinal perennial herbs. The Rue Family is RUTACEAE. Goat's-rue is *Galega officinalis*; see GALEGA. Meadow-rue is the genus THALICTRUM. Wall-rue is the fern *Asplenium ruta-muraria*; see ASPLENIUM.

RUELLIA (roo EL ee ah). A genus of widely distributed, generally hairy herbs or shrubs belonging to the Acanthaceae (Acanthus Family). They bear flat or funnelform flowers in shades of blue, violet, white, rose, red, and occasionally yellow or orange. The tropical species are known collectively in England as Christmas-pride.

Frequently grown outdoors in warm climates (Zones 10–11), they are easily grown in the greenhouse. Seed should be sown in the spring in sandy soil and the seedlings potted in soil composed of sand, peat, leaf mold, and loam. They should be watered freely in summer and when in bud in the fall, being given liquid manure as a stimulant. Plants can also be propagated by cuttings taken in spring or summer and by division.

PRINCIPAL SPECIES

R. ciliosa, native from New Jersey to Texas and hardy in the North, grows to 2½ ft. and has stemless, blue or lavender flowers to 2 in. across borne singly or in clusters.

R. graecizans, formerly listed as *R. amoena*, grows to 2 ft. and has tapered oval leaves on winged stems and clusters of bright red flowers.

R. macrantha, from Brazil, grows to 6 ft. and has rosy purple, bell-shaped flowers to 3 in. borne singly in the leaf axils. It is an excellent, easily cultivated plant for the greenhouse.

R. tuberosa is a hairy plant that grows to 2 ft. and has thick roots and showy pink flowers.

RUFFLE PALM. Common name for AIPHANES, a genus of very spiny trees resembling fishtail palms.

RUGOSE. Wrinkled, or marked by fine, depressed lines, like leaves of *Prunus tomentosa*.

RUMEX (ROO meks). A genus of about 100 widely distributed hardy herbs in the Polygonaceae (Buckwheat Family), mostly biennial and perennial, and many of them troublesome WEEDS. Some inhabit dry areas; others prefer marshy lands. They are popularly known as dock and sorrel. The name "sorrel" is sometimes applied to the whole genus but particularly to the low-growing species with spearhead-shaped, fleshy, sour but edible leaves, which are sometimes used for salad or to flavor soups.

Two or three of the sorrels are cultivated in California and some of the southern states, but they are hardy to Zone 3. They are long-lived perennials, sustaining frequent and severe cutting. The young leaves in spring are an excellent green; later the leaves are sometimes used for medicinal purposes.

Less popular are the species commonly known as dock (although the common name sometimes refers to the entire genus). This large group of biennial and perennial herbs has stout taproots and large, smooth leaves, usually with wavy margins, placed alternately on tall stems. Greenish flowers without petals are arranged in whorled clusters and are followed by fruits of leathery red or brown. Hardy to Zone 3, most of them are troublesome weeds, common in pastures and along roadsides, but a few have useful landscape qualities. Some dock roots yield a dye, and astringent medicines are made from others.

PRINCIPAL SPECIES

R. acetosa (sour dock) is an indicator of moderate nitrogen on moist, acid, alluvial soil. It tolerates low phosphorus on acid soils and tends to spread in lawns after ammonium sulphate is added.

R. acetosella (sheep sorrel) is an indicator of a nitrogen-poor, acid soil that has a poor balance of calcium, magnesium, sodium, and potassium. It is tasty in soup, steamed as a green, or as a sour zest in salad.

R. crispus (curled dock) is an indicator of a moderate level of nitrogen and a low level of calcium. Often found on sour, wet patches of compact soil with insufficient drainage, it tolerates low potassium and can be controlled by improved drainage and added lime.

R. hydrolapathum (giant water dock), a European native growing 4–6 ft. high, is sometimes used with good results in landscaping along water courses.

R. hymenosepalus (canaigre, tanner's dock), native to western North America, is a perennial growing to 3 ft. Its roots contain tannin that is used in preparing leather, and the leaves and stems are edible.

R. patientia (spinach dock, herb patience), a perennial, grows to 6 ft.

R. scutatus (French sorrel) is a hardy perennial growing to 18 in. and is characterized by its heart-shaped, fleshy leaves. It is the only species that is not too acid for salads.

R. venosus (wild-begonia, sour greens) is a perennial native to the northwestern United States and adjacent Canada. Growing to 18 in., it has oblong leaves and red flowers and is sometimes cultivated for its showy, winged fruits.

Rumex scutatus

RUMOHRA (roo MOH rah). A genus of tropical ferns endemic to the Southern Hemisphere, including only one species known in cultivation.

R. adiantiformis (leather fern) has tough, durable fronds often used in floral arrangements. It makes an excellent houseplant, requiring only moderate watering and enduring lower humidity than most ferns. When grown in tropical gardens, its fronds grow 2–5 ft. It is found in Africa, Australia, Polynesia, and South America.

RUNNER. A long, slender, trailing stem that may take root and produce new plants wherever its leaf and bud parts come in contact with the soil. Runners are especially valuable in propagating some plants quickly and inexpensively, like the strawberry, which forms runners in July after the blooming period. Many ornamental

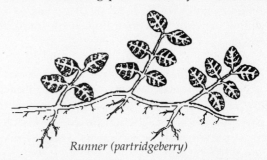

Runner (partridgeberry)

plants also spread and increase naturally by runners or can be induced to do so. Of course, where increase in size or number is not wanted, the frequent removal of runners is a necessary aspect of cultivating plants that form them.

RUSCHIA (RUS kee ah). A genus of flowering, succulent shrubs from South Africa, belonging to the Aizoaceae (Carpetweed Family), including many species formerly listed in the genus *Mesembryanthemum*. Growing prostrate or erect and sometimes tufted, they have stiff, angular, bluish green leaves with darker spots. The pink, red, white, or purple flowers are solitary or borne in clusters and have lobed calyxes. The taller, shrubby species are suitable for planting outdoors in a warm, sunny location or potted indoors in a sunny, well-ventilated place. The lower, tufted kinds also make good houseplants. Propagation is easily done by seed or cuttings.

RUSCUS (RUS kus). A Mediterranean genus of low evergreen shrubs belonging to the Liliaceae (Lily Family). They are valuable for undergrowth in dark places, spreading by suckers.

R. aculeatus (butcher's-broom), which grows to about 3 ft., is the best-known species. It has green stems and glossy, leaflike, flattened stem branches from the middle of which the small, white flowers are borne in clusters, the male and female usually on separate plants. The fruit is a large, red berry. Cultivated since before 1750, the dried and dyed foliage sprays are often used by florists and sold for decorative purposes during the Christmas season. Hardy to Zone 8.

R. hypoglossum and *R. hypophyllum* are smaller plants with elliptic or ovate leaves and yellow or white flowers followed by small, red fruits.

RUSH. Common name for JUNCUS, a genus of grasslike perennials grown in wet areas. Flowering-rush is *Butomus umbellatus*, an aquatic perennial with rose-colored flowers resembling irises; see BUTOMUS. Scouring-rush is EQUISETUM, a genus of fern allies.

RUSSELIA (rus SEL ee ah). A genus of shrubby plants of the American tropics, belonging to the Scrophulariaceae (Figwort Family), and commonly known as firecracker plant. They are often grown in greenhouses and outdoors in Zones 10–11. They have a long season of bloom, and by reason of their pendulous habit, are well adapted for hanging baskets. They thrive in rich, light soil and are easily propagated by cuttings.

R. equisetiformis (coral plant), the principal species, is an Australian shrub. It is a branching plant that grows to 4 ft. and has drooping, rush-like stems bearing a profusion of small, tubular, scarlet flowers. It is popular in southern gardens and northern greenhouses.

R. sarmentosa, from Central America, is a shrub that grows to 6 ft. and has angled stems, toothed ovate leaves about 3 in. long, and clusters of red flowers.

RUSSIAN-OLIVE A common name for *Elaeagnus angustifolia*, a deciduous shrub or tree with dense masses of gray-green leaves and fragrant spring flowers; see ELAEAGNUS.

RUSTS. A name used to designate either a group of fungi or the diseases produced by them. The name is taken from the easily recognized iron-rust color of the spore pustules. Many of the rusts occurring in garden and greenhouse, such as those on hollyhock or snapdragon, can be controlled by application of suitable fungicides recommended for specific areas and plants. Rusts that require two different hosts on which to complete their life cycle are more frequently controlled by the removal of the host that is least important in the area being protected. Control of some rusts is also being achieved by breeding resistant varieties, as in the case of wheat, asparagus, and snapdragon. Plants attacked by rusts do not usually die but may be dwarfed and yellowed. Certain rusts cause accelerated growth in the form of galls or WITCHES'-BROOM.

RUST FUNGI

The common name "rust," of the fungal order Uredinales is suggested by the conspicuous reddish orange spore pustules observed in certain stages of the life cycle of typical forms. Rust fungi are obligate parasites, that is, they cannot grow unless in contact with living plant tissue. The mycelium, which is made of threadlike hyphae, grows between the cells of the host plant and feeds by means of specialized sucking organs (haustoria) that penetrate the cell walls. Five different types of spores (reproductive bodies) may be formed during the life of a single rust, but not all are found in every species.

Rusts are of two general types: first, those that pass all the stages of their life cycle on a single host and are called autoecious; and, second, those that spend part of their life on one kind of plant and the rest on another kind of plant called an alternate host. Hollyhock and asparagus rusts are well-known garden examples of autoecious rusts, requiring no alternate hosts. The important black stem rust of wheat, barley, rye, and many grasses (caused by the fungus *Puccinia graminis*) is an excellent example of a rust of the second type (heteroecious) and can be used to demonstrate a typical life cycle with its different stages. While the details are of interest mainly to scientists, it is helpful for gardeners to know the complicated history of some of their plant troubles.

First or Red Spore Stage. Urediniospores or summer spores are formed in spore pustules called uredinia. Reddish brown streaks or pustules on the cereal hosts are the first signs of this rust. Successive crops of spores formed are carried by the wind to healthy plants.

Second or Black Spore Stage. Teliospores or winter spores are formed in telia. Dark-colored spore cases (sori) appear on the wheat in late summer or early fall; but the spores do not germinate until spring, when they produce small, colorless sporidia.

Third or Sporidium Stage. Sporidia or basidiospores develop. These spores cannot reinfect wheat but germinate only if the wind carries them to leaves, twigs, or fruit of certain species of barberry.

Fourth, Pycnial, or Spermagonial Stage. Pycniospores are formed in pycnia. Yellowish areas appear on the upper surface of barberry leaves. Spores that formed in the minute, flask-shaped bodies of these areas are necessary for the development of the next stage.

Fifth or Cluster Cup Stage. Aeciospores are formed in aecia. Clusters of tiny, yellow-orange cups form on the undersurface of barberry leaves and are filled with chains of yellow spores. These chains cannot reinfect barberry but must return to wheat, where they start a new life cycle.

The WHITE PINE BLISTER RUST is another heteroecious rust of great economic importance, currants and gooseberries being the alternate hosts. The rust affecting cedar and apple is particularly injurious to the apple fruit; on the cedar it produces the gall-shaped deformations commonly known as cedar-apples (see CEDAR-APPLE RUST). Deformations caused by other rusts may take the form of excessively bushy growths of shoots at the end of tree limbs; these are known as WITCHES'-BROOM. For control or prevention of such rusts, removal of the alternate host from the vicinity of the desired species is the principal method.

RUSTY-BACK FERN. Common name for *Ceterach officinarum*, a dwarf fern with gray-green fronds; see CETERACH.

RUTA (ROO ta). A genus of perennial, aromatic, and medicinal or culinary herbs with finely cut leaves, commonly known as rue. Native to the Mediterranean region, all are hardy to Zone 4. They can be propagated by seed or division.

PRINCIPAL SPECIES

R. chalepensis grows to 2½ ft. with elliptic leaflets about ½ in. long. The flowers are borne in flat-topped clusters and have fringed petals.

R. graveolens (common rue, herb-of-grace) is a shrubby evergreen plant that grows to 3 ft. and has yellowish flowers and much- divided, pungent-smell-ing, bitter-flavored leaves, which may cause skin irritations. It is often found in the eastern states escaped from old gardens.

Ruta graveolens

R. montana grows to 18 in. The narrow, linear leaflets are hairless and covered with a bloom. The flowers have lobed petals.

RUTABAGA. A hardy biennial variety of *Brassica napus*, also known as Swedish-turnip or Swede, and cultivated as an annual vegetable. It differs from the turnip structurally in having bloom-covered leaves, a more elongated and leafy top, and much more fibrous roots. In cultivation it requires four to six weeks longer to mature and more distance between plants and rows. Because it needs cool weather and moist soil to develop, it is sown in early summer for winter use.

See also BRASSICA; TURNIP.

RUTACEAE (roo TAY see ee). The Rue family, a group of frequently evergreen, mostly woody, aromatic plants distributed in tropical and subtropical regions. Most of the genera yield a characteristic pungent or aromatic oil, and some include medicinal, ornamental, and odorous species. The family is best known for the important citrus fruits. Some species with inedible fruits are valued for hybridizing. Genera commonly cultivated are *Boronia*, *Casimiroa*, *Choisya*, *Citropsis*, *Citrus*, *Correa*, *Dictamnus*, *Diosma*, *Evodia*, *Fortunella*, *Murraya*, *Phellodendron*, *Poncirus*, *Ptelea*, *Ruta*, *Severinia*, *Skimmia*, and *Triphasia*.

RYANIA. One of the botanical insecticides; see INSECT CONTROL.

RYE. Common name for SECALE, a genus of grasses grown for grain, straw, or green manure. Ryegrass is LOLIUM, a genus of pasture grasses. Wild-rye is ELYMUS, a genus of useful binders.

S

SABADILLA. A botanical insecticide ; see INSECT CONTROL.

SABAL (SAY bahl). A genus of about 20 species of palms, commonly known as palmetto, distinguished by their spineless leaves and growing to various heights up to 90 ft.; some have no stem above the ground level. They are found in marshy districts from North Carolina to Florida and southward throughout Mexico to Venezuela. Found in some localities in groups of only a few trees in the rich, black soil of Florida river valleys, it may grow by thousands, covering large areas.

All the species of sabal that make trunks are of great beauty in the North. Several are grown as tub plants in the greenhouse and moved outdoors in summer. South American species require hothouse conditions. Propagation of all kinds is by suckers.

S. minor (dwarf palmetto), growing only 3–4 ft., has very short, erect stems and stiff, bluish or green, nearly flat leaves in ribbed segments.

S. palmetto (cabbage palmetto, palm, or tree) derives its common name from the terminal bud, which can be eaten, boiled like a cabbage or processed as hearts of palm; however, collecting this bud kills the plant. In the wild it has an erect stem 20–60 or rarely 80 ft. tall with a trunk diameter of 12–15 in. The long-stemmed, fan-shaped leaves measure 5–8 ft. across the blade. This species is the most favored for cultivation. If well cared for, it will thrive on poor, sandy soil. It is widely grown along avenues and roads in the southern states and used generally in landscaping effects.

SABATIA (sa BAT ee ah). A genus of hardy annual or biennial herbs of the Gentianaceae (Gentian Family), commonly known as rose gentian. They have white, rose-pink, or rose-purple wheel-shaped flowers in flat-topped clusters. Native to eastern North America and seldom cultivated, they are handsome plants well worth a place in the border or rock garden, where they should be planted in a moist, peaty soil.

SADLERIA (sad LEE ree ah). One of several genera collectively known and cultivated as TREE FERNS.

SAFFLOWER. Common name for CARTHAMUS, a genus of spiny-leaved annuals grown for ornament, dye, and medicinal products.

SAFFRON. Common name for *Crocus sativus*, a lilac-flowered, fall-blooming cormous herb; see CROCUS.

SAGE. Common name for SALVIA, a large genus of herbs and shrubs. The common name is also applied to other genera. Bethlehem-sage is *Pulmonaria saccharata*. Jerusalem-sage is *Phlomis fruticosa*. Sagebrush, the state flower of Nevada, is *Artemisia tridentata*.

SAGITTARIA (sa jit AIR ee ah). A genus of perennial aquatic herbs belonging to the Alismataceae (Water-plantain Family) and commonly known as arrowhead. They are most attractive planted on the edge of a pond, displaying their white, buttercuplike flowers and arrow-shaped leaves. Some species are excellent for providing oxygen in aquariums. They are variously hardy to Zone 5 and are propagated by division, seed, or tubers.

PRINCIPAL SPECIES

S. engelmanniana is excellent for naturalizing in colonies in shallow water, the arrow-shaped leaves and clustered white flowers creating an attractive effect.

S. montevidensis (giant arrowhead) is often grown in aquariums and lily ponds. It has large, white flowers and sometimes reaches a height of 6 ft. It is tender in cold climates but has become naturalized in the warmer states.

S. sagittifolia (old-world arrowhead) grows to 4 ft. and bears white flowers with purple spots. The underground tubers are eaten in eastern Asia.

SAGITTATE. Shaped like an arrowhead, like the leaves of the genus *Sagittaria*; that is, long-triangular with the sharp basal lobes projecting downward. Compare HASTATE; CORDATE.

SAGO-PALM. Common name for CYCAS, a genus of palmlike tropical trees.

SAGUARO. Common name for *Carnegiea gigantea*; see CARNEGIEA.

ST. AUGUSTINE GRASS. Common name for the creeping perennial *Stenotaphrum secundatum*; see STENOTAPHRUM.

ST.-JAMES'-LILY. Common name for *Sprekelia formosissima*, a flowering tropical plant of the Amaryllidaceae (Amaryllis Family); see SPREKELIA.

ST.-JOHN'S-BREAD. Common name for the fleshy seedpods of *Ceratonia siliqua*, a Mediterranean evergreen tree, better known as carob; see CERATONIA.

ST.-JOHN'S-WORT. Common name for HYPERICUM, a genus of perennial herbs and shrubs with showy yellow flowers.

SAINTPAULIA (saynt PAW lee ah). A popular houseplant with fuzzy-hairy leaves, belonging to the Gesneriaceae (Gesneria Family), and commonly known as African- or Usambara-violet. *S. ionantha* is the best known, but many other species are grown and figure in the genes of thousands of modern cultivars.

First brought into cultivation in Germany late in the nineteenth century, these plants did not get a foothold in North America until the introduction of numerous cultivars in 1936. Since then, the African-violet has become the world's most popular houseplant. One well-known grower alone distributes more than 50 million specimens annually in the United States, Germany, England, Japan, Spain, Holland, Australia, and South America.

Saintpaulia

CULTURE

Although very commonly grown, African-violets frequently do not bloom or grow properly for one of several reasons. Careful culture, however, can ensure healthy, attractive plants. When you bring a flower-covered plant home, it may stop blooming after a few weeks. It needs time to adjust. Be gentle, and situate it in the best spot available. New buds should appear in a few weeks.

Light. A plant may produce several symptoms due to insufficient light. Growth "bolts" upright, like lettuce in hot weather. Leaf stems grow unusually long as the plant reaches toward light. No blooms are produced. This condition can be corrected by increasing natural light. All species need bright light and some direct sun, except in hottest weather or in the Sunbelt. In a fluorescent-light garden, position plants so that leaves are 6–10 in. beneath two 20–40 watt bulbs that are lighted 14–16 hours out of every 24. Replace tubes after one year of use. A combination of generic warm and cool white bulbs produces a balance of rays that will nurture root, leaf, and flower production.

Temperature. Below 60°F African-violets are discouraged from blooming. Temperatures above 80°F also thwart budding and encourage diseases (various rots) and mealybugs.

Watering. Always use water of room temperature or slightly warmer, especially in winter. Cold water harms the roots, and if dropped on the leaves causes unsightly white or yellow disfigurations, especially if sunlight strikes the droplets.

Feel the surface soil with your fingers. "Nicely moist" at all times is ideal for African-violets. Dryness to the point of slightly wilted leaves means no blooms. Soggy wet soil is also harmful. If excess water is trapped in the pot, root and crown rot will set in; however, it may be possible to salvage leaf cuttings.

Atmosphere. African-violets need fresh air that circulates freely. Space plants with this in mind, and protect them from hot or cold drafts. If air is extremely dry, the foliage may grow, but not the blooms. Group plants on pebbles in trays kept filled with water but never so deep that the pots actually stand in water.

Potting and Propagation. Repot plants at least once a year, ideally in late winter or spring, or when a burst of bloom is desired about three months later.

Young African-violets tend to grow and bloom more readily than old ones. Old plants can be replaced by starting leaf cuttings, which root readily. Select a mid-sized leaf, neither the oldest nor the youngest and cut it so the leaf has 1 in. of stem (petiole) attached. Insert the stem part almost 1 in. deep in a clean rooting medium and keep constantly warm and moist in bright light. New plants will appear from the base of the stem where rooting first occurs and can be removed and potted separately when large enough to handle.

The flowers can also be cross-pollinated. Seedpods take several months to ripen, and seedlings may come into bloom in six to twelve months.

Soil and Feeding. Use only ingredients that are naturally sterile or have been pasteurized. One good mix is equal parts packaged all-purpose potting soil, sphagnum peat moss, and clean sharp sand or perlite. There are also some excellent packaged mixes blended especially for African-violets.

Correct soil pH is important; African-violets do well in a slightly acid to neutral or slightly alkaline soil, pH 6.5 to 7.5. Acidity brings out leaf redness and intensifies flower blues. Too acid a soil can prevent bloom. Correct by watering with ½ tsp. agricultural lime added to 1 qt. water. If all conditions apparently needed do not produce bloom, the soil may be too alkaline (sweet); correct by watering three times at monthly intervals with a solution of ½ tsp. cider vinegar to 1 qt. water.

Old depleted soil may keep plants alive but not blooming. At this time, they should be repotted or fertilizer should be added. Many commercial fertilizer products are available specifically for African-violets, but follow manufacturer's directions carefully. Too much fertilizer can cause bunching and distortion of new growth. If this happens, flush out toxic salts by watering heavily several times within a few hours, draining between applications.

Maintenance. Keep all withered or discolored leaves promptly picked. If a plant is dusty, shower it with tepid water and allow it to drain and dry before placing in direct sun.

If plant stems have grown several inches, snaking over the edge of the pot, a "neck" job is required. Replant it, removing the bottom soil and roots, and lower the stem as necessary. Add fresh soil at the top so the lowermost leaves emerge at the new soil surface.

Except for the natural trailers, most modern African-violets bloom best if kept to a single main crown of leaves. Remove all developing suckers (offsets) as soon as they can be discerned from the flower buds. A nail file or knife can be used to extricate the suckers with a minimum of damage to the parent.

Insect Pests. Cottony mealybugs are readily visible except when they hide in crevices; rub them off with a cotton swab dipped in denatured alcohol. Tiny cyclamen mites cause new leaves and flower stems to be distorted. Control them by using a miticide, such as insecticidal soap, thoroughly dipping the affected plants on a weekly basis as necessary.

SALAL. Common name for *Gaultheria shallon*, a native western shrub with heart-shaped leaves, pinkish white flowers, and purple fruits; see GAULTHERIA.

SALIX (SAY liks). A large genus of soft-wooded trees and shrubs, commonly known as willow and some species as osier. Some forms are erect, others are weeping or even prostrate. All have deciduous leaves and bear staminate and pistillate flowers on separate trees in the form of catkins that, due to the covering of silky hairs developed in some species, are conspicuous in spring before the leaves appear. Willows differ widely in size, from the white willow with lofty, furrowed trunk and spreading branches to a tiny, prostrate shrub found in the Arctic regions.

CULTURE

Willows are planted as ornamental trees and valued for their quick growth, pleasing form, and graceful foliage. The silvery catkins or "pussy willows" of some species, and the bright golden or orange twigs of others, make a bright and cheering spot of color in the winter landscape. Willows are also cultivated for basket-making material.

Because of its extensive root system, the willow is exceedingly valuable for soil binding and to prevent erosion along river courses. It is often planted near lakes and ponds to hold the shoreline. Preferring moist locations but able to grow in unfavorable locations, willows naturalize readily. While not especially long-lived, they grow so rapidly that they are often used as nurse trees for others slower in growth that need partial shade while young.

Growing readily from cuttings (sometimes broken branches lodging along the shore of a stream strike root and start new plants without human help), willows can also be raised from seed, which should be planted as soon as ripe. The weeping types are sometimes grafted on upright stocks to create a standard form.

ENEMIES

Diseases. A leaf and twig blight in the New England states is the most important willow disease. The fungus *Fusicladium saliciperdum* has killed or injured hundreds of large trees. It overwinters in cankers on the twigs and blights the young leaves as they emerge from the bud. Four or five applications of a fungicide such as BORDEAUX MIXTURE will give protection; the first should be made before the buds open, a second two weeks later, a third as the leaf tips emerge, a fourth when the leaves are half to two-thirds grown, and the last when they are full size. See also BLIGHT.

Leaf rusts are common on willows, and occasionally a "tar spot" occurs similar to that on maples. Rusts, and one or two leaf-spotting fungi, may cause defoliation, but raking and burning fallen leaves will ordinarily keep them under control. See also RUSTS.

Insect Pests. The imported willow beetle is a common pest. Both the shiny, dark metallic blue beetles ⅛ in. long and the bluish-black alligator-like larvae feed on the leaves, the former chewing holes and the latter skeletonizing them. There are two broods each year. See also BEETLES.

Many other insects feed on willows, among them various types of APHIDS, the fall WEBWORM, GYPSY MOTH, poplar leaf beetle, poplar tent maker, satin moth, and spiny elm CATERPILLAR. The oyster-shell scale commonly infests willow, and the poplar and willow CURCULIO bores into the trunks and twigs of pussy willows. See also BEETLES; INSECT CONTROL; SCALE INSECTS.

PRINCIPAL SPECIES

S. alba (white willow), growing to 75 ft., has lance-shaped leaves to 4 in. long. The catkins appear with the leaves. Native throughout the Eastern Hemisphere, it has become widely naturalized in North America. There are a number of varieties: *chermesina* has brilliant red twigs; *sericea* has leaves with silky undersides; *tristis* has yellow, weeping branches; *vitellina* has leaves with bloomy undersides and very yellow branches. Hardy in Zones 2–8.

S. babylonica (weeping willow), growing to 30 ft., has exceedingly long, graceful, drooping branches, narrow leaves to 6 in. long, and catkins appearing with the leaves. Cv. 'Crispa' is a curious form with twisted and curled leaves. Hardy in Zones 5–8.

S. caprea (goat willow, sallow), growing to 25 ft., has rather broad leaves to 4 in. and large, handsome catkins before the leaves. Cv. 'Pendula' (Kilmarnock willow) has crooked branches. Hardy in Zones 5–8.

S. discolor (pussy willow) is well known for its large, silvery catkins, which appear in late winter or early spring before the leaves. It grows to 20 ft., sometimes in tree form, but more often forms a shrub to about 10 ft. In either form it is attractive and worthy of being extensively planted, not only because of the catkins, but also because of its symmetrical growth. It does well in dry ground as well as moist locations and is easily propagated by cuttings. Plants can be pruned hard to encourage more catkins. Hardy in Zones 2–8.

S. purpurea (purple osier), a shrub growing to 9 ft. with whitish-undersided leaves, has escaped in many places. Its branches are frequently used in basket weaving. Var. *lambertiana* has thick purple branches. Cv. 'Pendula' has drooping branches; 'Gracilis' has narrow leaves and delicate branches. Hardy in Zones 4–8.

S. repens (creeping willow) forms a low shrub that is useful for binding soil on moist banks.

S. viminalis (common osier), growing to 30 ft., has lance-shaped, silvery leaves to 10 in. and catkins that appear before the leaves. It is a Eurasian plant that has become established in North America. Its lithe stems or branches make this the species most commonly used for basket weaving material.

SALMONBERRY. Common name for *Rubus spectabilis*, an almost spineless bramble with colorful flowers and edible fruit; see RUBUS.

SALPIGLOSSIS (sal pi GLAW sis) **sinuata.** A branching, half-hardy annual herb from Chile, belonging to the Solanaceae (Nightshade Family), and commonly known as painted-tongue, velvet flower, or paisley flower. It grows about 2 ft. high and bears funnelform flowers 2½ in. long and wide, of velvety texture and in many subtle colors, including rich tones of purple, blue, and red. The strikingly veined interior of the blossoms gives them an exotic beauty. All the cultivated types are forms of this species or its var. *superbissima*, which is more upright or columnar than branching.

Plants thrive best in sandy soil and partial shade. A soil that is not excessively rich gives the best and most colorful flowers. The branches do not spread much, so individual plants need comparatively little elbow room and are easily tucked between perennials where they get the desired amount of shade. Pinching out the center while the plant is small encourages branching. The stems are wiry and slender, and a few forms have greater lasting qualities when cut.

The seeds are extremely fine and, unless carefully handled, are likely to be buried too deep or washed away. Whether started in a seed box in the house during early spirng or planted in a carefully marked row outdoors when the soil has started to warm, they should be sprinkled on the surface and pressed into the soil, then covered with newspaper or muslin that is kept moist. After the seeds have germinated, the plants mature without difficulty but should not be allowed to suffer a check or be stunted. For winter flowering indoors, sow seeds in midsummer and pot up the young plants carefully in the fall.

SALSIFY. A hardy biennial, *Tragopogon porrifolius*, also called oysterplant, grown for its long, fleshy, edible, white roots. In form they resemble parsnips, but they are smaller and flavored like oysters.

The common name is also applied to other plants. Black-salsify is *Scorzonera hispanica*. Spanish-salsify is *Scolymus hispanicus*.

Salsify succeeds best in light, rich, mellow, deep soil. Sow seeds thinly an inch deep in rows 15 in. apart. When the seedlings are 3 in. high, they should be thinned to 4 in. apart and thereafter be given clean cultivation.

Since the plants require a long season to develop usable roots, seed must be sown as soon as the ground can be worked in spring. They are hardy, so some of the roots can be left in the ground like parsnips until the following spring. They must be dug before growth starts. This practice is even better than digging and storing them in the fall, because they tend to shrivel more than parsnips and become tough if stored indoors. Winter supplies should be dug late and stored preferably in outdoor pits.

SALSOLA (SAL soh lah) Commonly known as Russian-thistle, this genus of rampant, bushy, annual herbs dry into rounded masses of stems and become "tumbleweeds" to be blown along by the wind, scattering seeds as they go. Its leaves are small, stiff, grayish, and spiny tipped; flowers are small, solitary, and unattractive. Hardy in Zones 3–9, this plant is most common in the prairie states, along railways and waste land. In gardens it is not likely to become troublesome if it is destroyed before it goes to seed. Its presence inhibits many other plants, including grain, and is a warning to check soil conditions. It grows in dry, sandy or saline, nitrogen-rich soil with low calcium, magnesium, and manganese and usually neutral pH.

SALTBUSH. Common name for the genus ATRIPLEX of shrubs found in salty areas. A few species are cultivated as potherbs under the common name ORACH.

SALT HAY. Hay grown on salt marshes is exceedingly valuable for mulching, first because it is inclined to be firm and stiff, not likely to mat down and freeze solid, and second, because it is free from seed, both of its own kind and that of weeds. Large quantities are used on commercial bulb farms, the hay being carefully raked off the rows in spring, stacked, and used year after year. It is equally useful for mulching perennial borders, strawberry beds, and similar plantings in the home garden, but it is not so suitable as a cover crop or source of humus to be plowed under or added to the compost heap.

See also MULCH.

SALVER-SHAPED. A corolla in which the limb or border is flat and flares abruptly from the long, slender tube, as in phlox and nicotiana.

SALVIA (SAL vee ah). A large and widely distributed genus of herbs, subshrubs, and shrubs belonging to the Lamiaceae (Mint Family) and commonly known as sage. It includes several valuable garden perennials whose flowers grow in spikes, racemes, or panicles on tall stems in blue, red, pale yellow, or white and variations. Others have more or less ornamental value and various culinary or medicinal applications. They range from 2–4 ft. high.

Some species are only half-hardy in temperate climates and must be treated as annuals. Some of the best, however, are extremely hardy, and this, combined with their simple cultural requirements, makes them popular plants. Any average garden location suits them, although they are at their best when planted in an enriched loamy soil where they get sun most of the day. Some of the species are grown as culinary or medicinal herbs. The hardy species should be propagated by division when the clumps become large. The best time to do this is in spring, as soon as the plants appear above the ground.

PRINCIPAL SPECIES

S. apiana (bee or white sage, greasewood) is a subshrub, 3–8 ft. high, with white to pale lavender flowers and white-haired leaves to 3½ in. long. Native to southern California, they are occasionally grown in the border, but their chief use is as bee plants.

S. argentea (silver salvia) is an extremely hardy species and highly decorative throughout the season. Its large, to 8 in., woolly leaves form rosettes in early spring and are responsible for the common name. Graceful sprays of white, yellowish, pale rose, or blue flowers are borne in midsummer on stems about 3½ ft. high, which should be staked so they will not be broken off by wind or storms.

S. azurea is similar to *S. pitcheri* but is slightly shorter and has lighter blue flowers. Var. *grandiflora* is really *S. pitcheri*.

S. coccinea (native scarlet sage) is a tender perennial that can be grown as an annual. It prefers full sun on well-drained soils. Stems up to 2 ft. tall bear heart-shaped leaves and scarlet flowers.

S. farinacea (mealy or mealycup sage) grows nearly 4 ft. tall, forming a large, soft clump of silver foliage and lavender flowers.

Salvia coccinea

S. nemorosa (violet sage), variously listed as *S. virgata* var. *nemorosa*, *S.* x *superba*, or *S.* x *sylvestris*, is a hardy perennial that grows 3 ft. or more and has large, loose clusters of flowers ranging from light blue to purple. It should be staked to avoid wind or storm damage.

S. officinalis (common or garden sage) is a hardy European subshrub of lesser ornamental value but is cultivated for its aromatic leaves, which are extensively dried for seasoning meats and cheese. Seeds should be sown thinly indoors or outdoors in seed beds. Transplant when plants are large enough to move, setting them at least 18 in. apart and giving clean cultivation. Established plants persist for years. Cv. 'Holts Mammoth' is the best variety, but since it bears no seed, it is propagated by layers and cuttings. Because the plants often exceed 3 ft. in diameter, they should be planted that far apart.

Salvia officinalis

S. patens (blue sage), a popular, adaptable species, grows about 2 ft. high and has flowers of ultramarine blue. Some growers dig up its roots in the fall and store them away from frost until it is time to replant in the spring, thus making the plants last for several years.

S. pitcheri is the finest of the truly hardy species that remain in the garden for years. It provides the deepest and purest of salvia blues, coming into bloom in late summer and continuing to bear its 1-in. flowers until frost, along thin, nimble stems about 4 ft. high. If not staked from early summer on, the plant takes on a semiprostrate and less tidy appearance. Once allowed to grow on the ground, the plants cannot be straightened up. As the new growth appears late in the spring, the stakes should remain in place from year to year to prevent plants from being spaded up, and as a reminder to tie the stems to them. Native to the midwestern states, it is sometimes listed as var. *grandiflora* of the lower-growing, southern native *S. azurea*.

S. sclarea (clary) is a hardy biennial with scented leaves and bluish flowers. It is sometimes used to flavor food and as a source of oil for perfumes.

S. splendens (scarlet sage), the best-known and most-used species, is a small, tender shrub grown for its brilliant flowers. It tends to be overused and misused. Its vivid color does not combine easily with other flower shades, and it is therefore advisable to use the plant by itself against a background of greens. The same caution applies to many of its vivid varieties and cultivars, such as 'Bonfire', 'Harbinger', and 'Scarlet Dragon', though not to the white var. *alba*. All are usually treated as annuals in cool regions, started in seed boxes indoors during early spring and set out in the garden when the soil is warm.

SALVINIA (sal VIN ee ah). A small and interesting genus of flowerless aquatic herbs that form large, floating annual colonies in quiet waters. Their simple, round or oval fronds that spring from thin rhizomes float on the water surface or creep on wet mud. Although not true ferns, they are an interesting novelty for the fern fancier to grow in a tub of water, which they fill. There are ten species found in tropical regions.

S. natans, the species commonly grown in ponds and aquariums, soon spreads over a large area, although each plant consists of only two very small, oval leaves.

SAMARA. A hard, dry, winged fruit, as of the ash or elm. Two samaras may be joined together, forming a double samara, as in the maple.

SAMBUCUS (sam BYOO kus). A genus of large, rather coarse, deciduous shrubs or small trees with compound leaves, belonging to the Caprifoliaceae (Honeysuckle Family) and commonly known as elder. They are widely distributed in temperate and subtropical regions. Both the large, flat heads of showy white flowers and the dense clusters of small, red or black berries are attractive, and the latter are a favorite bird food. Elders are very effective when planted in groups, and while not particular as to soil and location, do especially well in partial shade and rich, moist soil. Most species are hardy to Zone 4. The berries of *S. nigra* and *S. canadensis* are prized for making elderberry wine and jelly or combining with apples in pies. Propagation is by cuttings, and some kinds by suckers.

PRINCIPAL SPECIES

S. caerulea (blue elder), from the western states, sometimes grows to 50 ft. The branches are bloomy when young, and the blue-black, edible berries are covered with a heavy bloom. Hardy to Zone 6.

S. canadensis (American or sweet elder) grows to 12 ft. and suckers freely. It is the most handsome in bloom, with flower clusters to 10 in. across; later it hangs heavy with purplish black, edible berries. Cv. 'Aurea' has leaves of golden yellow and red berries. 'Adams' has much larger fruit in larger clusters. 'Rubra' has red fruits. Hardy in Zones 4–9.

S. nigra (European elder) grows to 30 ft. and bears yellowish white flowers in clusters to 8 in. across, followed by shining black, edible berries. Cv. 'Albo-variegata' and 'Aureo-variegata' are sometimes grown for the sake of their white-and-yellow variegated leaves. The color is more intense when they are planted in a sunny position. Hardy to Zone 6.

S. pubens (American red elder), growing to 15 ft., bears rather loose, pyramidal, not very showy flower clusters to 4 in. across. When the scarlet berries ripen in early summer, however, it is one of the outstanding shrubs of the countryside. Hardy in Zones 4–8.

S. racemosa (European red elder) grows to 12 ft. and has dense, oval flower clusters about 3 in. long and showy scarlet berries in early to midsummer Cv. 'Plumosa' is a cut-leaved form with leaflets divided to about the middle. Hardy in Zones 4–7.

SANCHEZIA (san CHEE zee ah). A genus of South American herbs or shrubs. The species, *S. speciosa* (formerly listed as *S. nobilis*), is grown for ornamental purposes in warm greenhouses or outdoors in the South. It is a shrubby plant to 5 ft. and has attractive leaves up to 1 ft. long and yellow flowers borne in dense terminal panicles from the axils of bright red bracts. Cv. 'Ellen' is more compact and has brighter contrast between its yellow veins and green leaves. Propagation is by cuttings.

SAND. From the gardener's standpoint, sand consists of the mineral part of the soil—minute rock fragments ranging from very fine (still coarser than clay or silt) to coarse (finer than the smallest grade of gravel). Chemically, it is almost pure quartz or silica and consequently plays little or no part in providing plants with food. Also, since its structure is very porous, it cannot hold moisture but dries out and warms up quickly. These qualities make sand, alone, impracticable as a garden soil, but they render it a valuable additive for stiff, heavy clays to make them looser and more friable, or to loosen over-fibrous peaty soils to give them more body and substance. For many crops, what is known as sandy loam cannot be surpassed, provided it is kept supplied with humus and the essential plant food elements.

Such a soil is easy to cultivate, well drained, quick to dry off after rains to permit cultivation, ready for planting early in the spring, free from stones, and not inclined to puddle and bake when dried out by the sun. If it becomes extreme in any of these respects, it can easily be improved by generous additions of manures, by turning under green manure crops, or by otherwise incorporating additional HUMUS.

Sands vary in character according to their origin. Those formed by the action of water consist of individual grains rounded like tiny boulders—as found on ocean or lake beaches and in riverbeds. Those not subject to water action have sharp grains, as found in builders' sand and gravel pits. Beach sand, if not impregnated with sea salt, can be used to lighten and aerate heavy soils. Sharper sand is an excellent medium for rooting many kinds of cuttings; for some plants it should be mixed with peat moss for this purpose.

It is also used for stratifying hard seeds over their ripening period.

Sand has also gained importance as a medium for growing experimental and commercial crops of various greenhouse plants, such as carnations, sweet peas, and others. See HYDROPONICS.

SANDPAPER VINE. Common name for *Petrea volubilis*, a tropical woody vine with blue flowers and showy fruits; see PETREA.

SAND-VERBENA. Common name for ABRONIA, a genus of low or trailing annual and perennial herbs with showy, fragrant flowers.

SANGUINARIA (san gwi NAIR ee ah) **canadensis.** A perennial herb native in eastern and Central North America, belonging to the Papaveraceae (Poppy Family), and commonly known as bloodroot. The red juice of its roots was once used as body paint by the Indians. It grows in rich, moist woodlands and is easily grown in the wild garden, where it can be propagated by seed or division. It has attractive white flowers in April and May on stems 8 in. high; large, lobed leaves; and a prominent rootstock.

Sanguinaria canadensis

SANGUISORBA (san gwee SOR bah). A genus of the Rosaceae (Rose Family) commonly called burnet. The hardy perennial herbs, usually with cut leaves and small, white, red, or purplish flowers in heads or dense spikes, sometimes reach a height of 6 ft. Most species are grown as ornamental plants in the border. They are propagated from seed and by division. *S. officinalis* (great burnet or burnet bloodwort) grows to 5 ft. and has dark purple flowers in short spikes. A European plant hardy to Zone 3, it has often escaped in North America. Closely related to *Poterium*.

SAN JOSÉ SCALE. This pest, *Comperiella bifasciata*, sucks up the sap from leaves, fruit, and wood of apple, peach, pear, and other fruit trees, lowering the vitality of the branches, and even killing them. The mature female is the size of a pinhead, living under the protective covering it forms over its yellow body. Where it feeds, it leaves a red stain, especially on tender new wood and fruit. The adults are sedentary, but the young are crawlers, sometimes blown from tree to tree. Oil emulsion is a control to be used early and again late in the spring. These pests often attract ants for the honeydew they exude. Controls include lady beetles and chalcid wasps, especially *Aphytis luteolus* and *A. mytilaspidis*. See INSECT CONTROL; SCALE INSECTS.

SANSEVIERIA (san se VEE ree uh). A genus of perennial herbs belonging to the Liliaceae (Lily Family) and commonly known as snake plant or bowstring-hemp. They have very thick, stiff leaves often mottled with white, and clustered flowers on slender stalks.

Hardy in Zones 10–11, they are grown as garden subjects in warm climates. In cool climates they are grown as house or porch plants, requiring little sun and doing best in a rather heavy soil. When grown indoors, the leaves should be washed frequently with warm soapy water and then sponged off with clear water. A few species are frequently seen, and many unusual forms have become favorite collectibles. Cultivars come in miniature forms and with highly colorful variegated leaves.

S. trifasciata cv. 'Laurenti', from Africa, has creamy yellow, lengthwise stripes on the leaves.

S. zeylanica, from Ceylon, grows to 2½ ft. and has hollowed leaves banded with white.

SANTOLINA (san toh LĪ nah). A genus of low evergreen shrubs, native to Europe and Asia, belonging to the Asteraceae (Aster Family), and hardy in Zones 6–8.

S. chamaecyparissus (lavender-cotton), a stiff, broadly branching, fine-leaved subshrub, grows to 2 ft. and has silvery gray, woolly foliage remaining throughout the winter. The small, globular, yellow flower heads are of less importance than the foliage. Native to the Mediterranean region, this old-fashioned plant is said to be one of the first raised in North American gardens. It is easily cultivated in a sunny location and propagated by cuttings taken either before frost or in the spring from plants that have been wintered in a coldframe.

S. virens, growing to 15 in., is a spreading plant with green, needlelike leaves. The yellow flowers,

Santolina chamaecyparissus

borne in summer, are small and buttonlike. Propagation is by seed or cuttings.

SANVITALIA (san vi TAY lee ah). A genus of small, annual, North American herbs, belonging to the Asteraceae (Aster Family). The small (¾-in.), yellow, daisylike flowers with purple centers first appear on the trailing stems in early summer and continue to bloom until frost.

S. procumbens is the most commonly grown species and is easily started from seed. Best growth is obtained in full sun and light, well-drained soil. Plants are well suited for bedding, borders, rock gardens, and hanging baskets.

SAPINDUS (sah PIN dus). A genus of tropical trees and shrubs including the principal members of the Sapindaceae (Soapberry Family), commonly known as soapberry. They bear leathery fruits that contain a soapy substance, saponin, which is used for cleaning purposes by tropical natives. A few species are grown for ornament in warm climates, doing well even in dry, rocky soil. Most species are only hardy to Zone 9. Propagation is by seed or cuttings in the spring.

PRINCIPAL SPECIES

S. drummondii, growing to 50 ft., is deciduous with yellowish white flowers and round, yellow fruit that becomes black. It is more hardy than other species (to Zone 6).

S. mukorossi, growing to 60 ft., is a brittle evergreen tree whose orange-brown fruit has a very soapy quality.

S. saponaria, growing to 30 ft., is evergreen with pinnate leaves; small, white flowers in racemes to 10 in. long; and a small, round, shining, orange-brown fruit.

SAPIUM (SAY pee um) **sebiferum.** A tropical tree belonging to the Euphorbiaceae (Spurge Family) and commonly known as Chinese tallow tree or vegetable-tallow. It grows to 40 ft. and has a milky, poisonous juice; sharply pointed leaves that turn bright crimson with age; and flowers in spikes. It has been planted for shade or ornament in Zones 8–11, where it has widely naturalized. In China and various equatorial countries it is cultivated for its fruits whose fatty covering is used in making candles, soap, and a dressing for cloth. Propagation is by seed or cuttings. This tree is adaptable to many different soils and is free of disease and insect problems.

SAPODILLA. A common name for *Manilkara zapota*, a tropical evergreen tree grown for its edible fruit; see MANILKARA.

SAPONARIA (sap oh NAY ree ah). A genus of hardy European annual and perennial herbs belonging to the Caryophyllaceae (Pink Family) and commonly known as soapworts. They have white, pink, or red flowers in clusters and are very easily cultivated, with some species suited to the rock garden. Propagation is by seed or division. Most species are hardy in Zones 3–8.

PRINCIPAL SPECIES

S. caespitosa (Pyrenees soapwort), growing to 6 in., is a tufted plant with rose flowers. It does well tucked into the crevices of a dry, stone retaining wall. Hardy to Zone 6.

S. lutea, a small tufted plant whose clusters of

yellow flowers have violet stamens, is a charming subject for the rock garden.

S. ocymoides (rock soapwort), a perennial growing to 9 in., is a trailing, soft-haired plant with pink flowers in flat-topped clusters, often used on walls and in the rock garden. Var. *splendens* has larger, intense pink flowers.

S. officinalis (bouncing-bet) is a perennial, often 3 ft. tall, native to Asia and widely naturalized along roads and railroad tracks in the eastern United States. It has crowded terminal clusters of white or pinkish flowers to 1 in. across, blooming throughout the summer.

Saponaria ocymoides

SAPOTE. Common name applied to various genera of tropical trees bearing edible fruits, including *Manilkara zapota*, a tropical evergreen tree also known as sapodilla; see MANILKARA.

Black-sapote is *Diospyros ebenaster* of the Ebenaceae (Ebony Family); see DIOSPYROS.

White-sapote is *Casimiroa edulis*, a Mexican tree growing to 50 ft; see CASIMIROA.

SAPROPHYTE. A plant that obtains nourishment from dead, decaying organic matter, differing from a parasite, which is nourished by a living host. Many fungi are both parasitic and saprophytic. Many saprophytic plants lack chlorophyll and therefore lack the ability to photosynthesize.

SARAN CLOTH. A relatively long-lasting green or black plastic cloth that gives various degrees of shading depending on the tightness of the weave—30% shade, 65% shade, etc. It is used in place of lath for shade houses, to cover small greenhouses and even benches within a greenhouse.

SARCOCOCCA (sahr koh KOHK ah). A genus of attractive evergreen shrubs from Asia belonging to the Buxaceae (Box Family), commonly known as sweet box. The glossy green leaves are their chief attraction, the clusters of small, whitish, fragrant flowers that open in early spring being inconspicuous. They need a mild climate to grow best, but one or two species can survive northern winters in a sheltered location. Not particular as to soil, they are stoloniferous and are an excellent ground cover for shady areas. Propagation is by division or cuttings.

S. hookerana grows to 6 ft. in a mild climate. It has narrow leaves to 3 in. long and blue-black fruits. Var. *humilis* is smaller, growing to 2 ft. Hardy to Zone 6.

S. ruscifolia can grow to 6 ft., has roundish leaves and red fruits, and is hardy to Zone 7.

SARRACENIA (sar ah SEE nee ah). A genus of small, insectivorous plants, commonly known as pitcher plants. The genus lends its name to the Sarraceniaceae (Sarracenia Family). Their basal leaves (often attractively mottled or splashed with various colors) are hollow, forming receptacles, sometimes with a wing along one side and a lid at the top. Insects trapped within them are drowned in the liquid held in the hollow base and gradually absorbed, thereby supplying the plant with nitrogenous food; see INSECTIVOROUS PLANTS. The single, nodding flowers range from yellow to purple.

Hardiness varies from Zones 3–11, depending on the species. Some hardy kinds can be grown in the bog garden. Other tender kinds can be grown in the greenhouse in pots filled with sandy soil covered with sphagnum moss and kept standing in saucers of water in full sunlight. They are grown from seed and hybridize easily.

PRINCIPAL SPECIES

S. alata, formerly listed as *S. sledgei*, has erect-lidded, green pitchers to 2½ ft. with red and yellow veins and yellowish, fragrant flowers.

S. flava (trumpet pitcher plant) has erect, trumpet-shaped, crimson-throated pitchers to 3 ft., veined yellow-green to green or entirely crimson. Yellow flowers to 4 in. across are pungent smelling. Hardy to Zone 7.

S. leucophylla, formerly listed as *S. drummondii*, is an attractive southern species with green, purple-veined, trumpet-shaped pitchers to 4 ft. and equipped with an erect, wavy-margined lid; flowers are purple.

S. minor has purple-veined, white- and yellow-blotched pitchers to 2 ft. and yellow flowers.

S. psittacina has prostrate leaves to 6 in. splotched and veined purple; a white, strongly bent lid; and purple to greenish purple flowers to 2 in. across.

S. purpurea (common pitcher plant) is a widespread native species found in cold mountain bogs from the East Coast to the Rocky Mountains. Its leaves are often 10 in. long, and it has purple or greenish flowers 2 in. across. Hardy to Zone 3.

S. rubra has erect pitchers to 20 in. with purple veins and a bent-over lid. Flowers are crimson and scented like violets.

SASA (SAH sah). A genus of dwarf or medium-sized shrubs of the Poaceae (Grass Family), one of those commonly known as BAMBOO. Distinguished from other bamboos by their small size, *Sasas* have cylindrical stems and graceful leaves, often toothed or hairy. Some are hardy enough to be planted as far north as Washington, D.C. *S. bicolor* produces stems to 2 ft. long and has small leaves. *S. veitchii* (kuma bamboo) has stems to 2 ft. or slightly taller and spreads fast by underground runners. The lance-shaped, dark green leaves have white edges.

SASSAFRAS (SAS ah fras). Common and botanical name for a genus including three species of aromatic deciduous trees belonging to the Lauraceae (Laurel Family). They are handsome pyramidal trees with light green, peculiarly lobed foliage, which assumes brilliant hues in autumn. The yellow flowers, borne in racemes, are followed by beautiful blue fruits on fleshy, red stems.

Trees should be planted in light soil in an open, sunny location. Propagation is by seed sown

immediately upon ripening, root cuttings, or suckers. It is very difficult to transplant older trees because of their long taproots. This tree is ordinarily not injured by insects, but the JAPANESE BEETLE is especially fond of it.

S. albidum, the North American species, attains 50 ft. or more and is hardy in the North. The leaves vary in shape from entire to three lobed, and the fruit is very ornamental. It is often planted for its decorative form and brilliant autumn-foliage colors of deep orange, scarlet, and purple. Hardy in Zones 5–8.

SATINFLOWER. A common name for LUNARIA, a genus of flowering herbs often used for dried bouquets. The name also refers to a few species of CLARKIA.

SATUREJA (sat yoo REE jah). A genus of hardy, aromatic herbs and small evergreen shrubs of the Lamiaceae (Mint Family). Several varieties are grown in the border for the fragrant, tiny, white flowers in the leaf axils. Some are low growing and of special value in both rock and wild gardens. They do well in any soil; the annuals can be propagated by seed, the perennials by seed or division in the spring.

Since the seed is minute, it should be sown indoors in seed pans, and the seedlings pricked off into flats and later transplanted outdoors when large enough.

Satureja hortensis

The plants should stand 15 in. apart. They will thrive in any good garden soil in full sunlight. Most species are hardy to Zone 5.

PRINCIPAL SPECIES

S. calamintha (calamint) is more commonly listed as *Calamintha nepeta*; see CALAMINTHA.

S. douglasii (yerba buena) is sometimes listed as *Micromeria chamissonis*, the "good herb" of early Spanish settlers in California, who made tea of the aromatic leaves.

S. hortensis (summer savory), growing 12–18 in., is an important and useful culinary herb whose aromatic leaves are used, either green or dried, for flavoring salads, sauces, stuffings, soups, stews, and all kinds of bean dishes for its digestive properties.

S. montana (winter savory) is a perennial herb or subshrub, growing 6–12 in., also cultivated for its flavor and used like summer savory.

Satureja montana

SAUROMATUM (saw roh MAY tum) **guttatum.** A tropical herb belonging to the Araceae (Arum Family) with large flowers resembling jack-in-the-pulpit, sometimes cultivated under the name red-calla. It has long, pointed spathes marked with dark purple spots and one long leaf cut into segments. It is sometimes grown as an oddity in the greenhouse, but the large tubers of this curious, dull-colored arum will survive in the open border in Zone 7 if given winter protection.

SAVORY. Common name for culinary herbs of the genus SATUREJA. Summer savory is *S. hortensis*; winter savory is *S. montana*.

SAW FERN. Common name for *Blechnum serrulatum,* a common tropical swamp fern with creeping rhizomes; see BLECHNUM.

SAWFLY. Insects belonging to the suborder Symphyta, part of the same order as the bees and wasps (Hymenoptera), and so named because of the sawlike egg-laying apparatus of the female, who uses it to cut pockets in the plant tissue in which the eggs are placed. Actual injury (usually a skeletonizing of the leaves) is done only by the larvae, which are called false caterpillars or slugs, since they are usually covered with a slimy coat-

ing. Many kinds of shade trees and shrubs may be attacked by the sawfly larvae, which will be noted coiled over the edges of the leaves.

Important members of this group are the cherry and pear slug, the three rose slugs, and the imported currant sawfly. Sawflies on conifers are becoming increasingly destructive. Mugho and Austrian pines may have lost nearly all their needles and be near death before the well-camouflaged larvae are discovered. Other sawflies attack white pine and spruce. Since these are

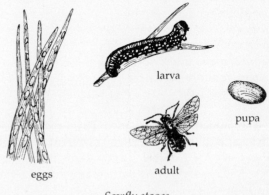

larva

pupa

eggs   adult

Sawfly stages

chewing insects, sprays such as rotenone and ***Bacillus thuringiensis*** (Bt, commonly available as Biotrol, Dipel, or Thuricide) can be tried for control. See INSECT CONTROL.

SAXIFRAGA (saks IF rah gah). A large genus of mostly hardy perennials, with a few annuals and biennials, commonly known as saxifrage or rockfoil. They are found on mountaintops and in rocky places in much of the world. The flowers can be white, yellow, orange, red, pink, purple, or rose. Some are attractively spotted. The leaves are variable, often found in a rosette at the base of the plant. Nearly all are beautiful and highly interesting subjects that are very desirable in the rock garden, in troughs, or in planted walls, being valued as highly for the decorative appearance of the foliage as for the flowers.

Saxifrages are easily raised from seed but may be lost if transplanted at too early a stage. Experts recommend keeping the small seedlings in the same pot for more than a year before moving. Established plants can be increased by rooting rosettes or by division. Once established, the plants need little winter protection. Those encrusted with lime need to be grown in a gritty medium with a high pH. Most of the alpine species do not survive in the heat and humidity of the South. On the other hand, the tender *S. stolonifera* (strawberry-geranium) is an excellent ground cover in the South but marginally hardy farther north.

Saxifraga sp.

SELECTIONS

The numerous species of saxifrages have been divided into fifteen or sixteen different sections. Those in each group share common characteristics. Rock gardeners are particularly interested in the following sections:

Dactyloides Group. These are the mossy saxifrages. In cool climates, they run about with abandon, act as beautiful ground covers, and flower in the springtime. They are intolerant of heat and humidity.

Euaizoonia Group. These include the encrusted saxifrages. They have rosettes of silvery leaves edged with a white crust and springtime sprays of beautiful flowers. Because they interbreed readily, both in the garden and in the wild, accurate identification is sometimes difficult. No rock gardener would go wrong by seeking out *S. paniculata* or any of its choice cultivars. The rosettes of *S. cochlearis* are beautifully encrusted, and each small leaf is shaped like a spoon.

Kabschia Group. These are some of the most beautiful cushion species and hybrids, like *S.* x *burserana*. Most of the members of this section are desirable rock garden plants.

Robertsonia Group. These species have aboveground rhizomes, usually toothed leaves, and spotted flowers, like *S. umbrosa*.

PRINCIPAL SPECIES

S. x *burserana* of the kabschia group, is hardy to Zone 6 and grows in 4-in.-high tufts of small, pointed, grayish silver leaves and white flowers. Varieties and cultivars include forms with different colors and flower shapes.

S. callosa has dense rosettes of 5-in. leaves, reddish at the base, surrounding flower stems that bear branching panicles of white flowers, often with reddish spots. It is native to southern Europe and is hardy to Zone 6.

S. cochlearis, belonging to the euaizoonia group, has silvery gray rosettes of 1-in., rounded leaves and 10-in. stems that bear white flowers not quite an inch across in spring. Native to the Alps, it is hardy to Zone 6.

S. cortusifolia, growing to 18 in. high, has fleshy, roundish, lobed, long-stemmed, shiny green leaves 3–4 in. wide that form rosettes. It bears irregular, white flowers in loose panicles on tall stems. Native to eastern Asia, it is hardy only to Zone 7 and thrives in woodland conditions with shade and a soil of acid leaf mold.

S. cotyledon grows 24 in. or taller and has tongue-shaped, toothed leaves to 3 in. long and fragrant, white flowers that are veined with pink. Cultivars may have white flowers spotted with red and variable leaf color. It is generally hardy to Zone 6.

S. cymbalaria is a half-hardy, low, spreading annual with tiny, star-shaped, yellow flowers. It is native in the region from southeastern Europe to northern Africa and naturalizes readily by self-sowing.

S. x *macnabiana*, growing to 12 in. high, is a hybrid with red-spotted white flowers and foliage that forms green rosettes and turns rich colors in autumn. Plants marketed under this name are more likely forms of either of its parents, *S. callosa* and *S. cotyledon*.

S. paniculata, native and hardy to Zone 2 and belonging to the euaizoonia group, is a popular plant with 1½-in. leaves that form basal rosettes and pale yellow, purple-marked flowers ½ in. across that bloom in midsummer. There are many varieties and cultivars with a wide range of growth habits and flower colors.

S. stolonifera (strawberry-geranium) is an easily cultivated perennial useful for ground cover and excellent as a potted plant. Its leaves may be up to 4 in. across, with veins on the top and reddish on the underside. White, asymmetrical flowers about an inch across are borne in erect spikes. Plants are very hardy (to Zone 2), should be kept moist, and are propagated by rooting small plantlets that form on the runners.

S. umbrosa (London-pride), one of the robertsonia group, is a perennial with pink or white spring flowers on 6-in. stems. The foliage grows in funnel-shaped rosettes 6–12 in. high. Native to Europe and hardy to Zone 7, it is especially popular in England. Varieties offer different flower shape, color, and size. Plants offered under this name may be forms of *S.* x *urbium*.

S. x *urbium* (London-pride saxifrage), a European perennial useful for ground cover, is similar to *S. umbrosa* but has longer leaf stems, more pointed leaves, and bigger flowers.

S. virginiensis (early or Virginia saxifrage), native to eastern North America and hardy to Zone 3, grows to 12 in. high and has rosettes of toothed, oval leaves to 3 in. long and small, white flowers. It is noted for growing in rocky hillsides and firmly rooting itself among stone crevices.

SAXIFRAGACEAE (sak si frah GAY see ee). The Saxifrage Family. Principal cultivated genera include: *Astilbe*, *Bergenia*, *Carpenteria*, *Deutzia*, *Escallonia*, *Heuchera*, *Itea*, *Hydrangea*, *Philadelphus* (mock-orange), *Ribes* (currants and gooseberries), *Saxifraga*, and *Schizophragma*.

SAXIFRAGE. Common name for SAXIFRAGA. The Saxifrage Family is SAXIFRAGACEAE.

SCAB. Definite, more or less circular, usually slightly raised and roughened, ulcerlike lesions on fruits, tubers, leaves, or stems of plants, resulting from the overgrowth of epidermal and cortical tissues. The name is also used for the disease as well as the symptom, such as apple scab and potato scab.

Common scab, affecting potatoes especially, is caused by an actinomycete that spreads rapidly in dry alkaline soils. Control by using GREEN MANURE, and avoid adding lime, wood ashes, or fresh manure, all of which will add to the alkaliity. Also, try rotating potatoes with other crops, waiting at least three years to grow potatoes in the same place again.

SCABIOSA (skab ee OH sah). A genus of annual or perennial herbs with showy flower heads, belonging to the Dipsacaceae (Teasel Family). One common name, "mourning-bride," refers to the very dark colors of some species, while the name "pincushion flower" was inspired by the nobbed stamens that protrude beyond the florets. Scabiosas are easily grown in an open, sunny location from seed started indoors or planted in the open ground in late spring. Perennial forms are mostly hardy in Zones 3–9. Seedlings of the annual *S. atropurpurea* should be set 6–8 in. apart. If pinched back while small, they will make bushy, 2-ft. plants. Flowers will be produced all summer if seed heads are not allowed to form. As cut flowers, scabiosas last well, and their odd color range makes them effective in bouquets.

PRINCIPAL SPECIES

S. atropurpurea has cut leaves and dark rose or white flowers. The various cultivars show interesting differences in height and form.

S. caucasica (pincushion flower) is a perennial that grows to 2 ft. and has pale blue flowers in rather flat heads, which are surrounded by a grayish involucre. Varieties, handsomer than the type, include: *goldingensis*, with large, deep lavender blossoms; *magnifica*, bluish lavender; and *alba*, white. Among the cultivars are: 'Fama', which grows to 20 in. and has long-

Scabiosa caucasica

stemmed, lavender blooms suitable for cutting; and 'Mount Cook', which grows to 24 in. and has long-stemmed, white blooms late spring to fall.

S. columbaria has lilac-blue flower heads on long stalks.

S. japonica is a very attractive perennial that grows to 2 ft. and has finely cut foliage and large heads of dark purple-blue flowers.

S. stellata cv. 'Drumstick' (paper-moon) produces blooms of blue that soon turn to bronze. The globe-shaped seed heads can be used in arrangements of everlastings.

SCABROUS. Rough or gritty to the touch because of short, stiff hairs or points, such as the surface of certain leaves, like those of *Echium*.

SCAEVOLA (skay VOH lah). A genus of coastal plants with deceptively soft-looking, large leaves. *S. plumieri*, native to Florida, and *S. taccada* (formerly listed as *S. frutescens*), from Hawaii, are widely used in Zone 11 and the warmer parts of Zone 10, especially where a fast-growing informal hedge with high salt tolerance is needed.

SCALE. A much-reduced leaf, generally without chlorophyll and usually modified to perform a protective function, such as covering buds. Often, however, a scale may be vestigial, that is, a survivor of an ancestral character and without a function on the plant.

A pine cone is composed of scales that bear and protect the bodies that later produce seed; the scales of buds are old-growth leaves investing the embryo shoot and leaves with a protective covering capable of many modifications to shield them against severe weather, birds, and insects. See BUD; LEAF.

SCALE INSECTS. The cottony-cushion scale, *Icerya purchasi*, a scourge in California in the 1880s and distributed in many parts of the United States, has become the most famous of all scale pests because it was the occasion for importing the vedalia lady beetle, which established the validity of biological control by completely con-

quering this destructive scale. This and other lady beetles have become the standard control for all scales, as well as mealybugs. See INSECTS, BENEFICIAL; LADY BEETLE.

Scale insects fall into two groups: (1) the armored scales (Diaspididae), which have distinct, hard, separable shells or scales over their delicate bodies; and (2) the tortoise or soft scales, with shells not separable from the bodies. Though a few are born alive, most armored scales reproduce by eggs protected under the mother's shell. Before settling down as adults to a permanent position, the young crawl around until they find a good place to insert their threadlike mouthparts into the bark or leaf to start sucking. The molted skin of the young becomes part of the scale of the adult along with wax exuded from the insects' bodies.

Scale insects

Various forms of these members of the order Homoptera include the orchard pest called oyster-shell scale, which is small, gray, ⅛ in. wide, and of oyster-shell shape. It also infests peonies and roses. The female overwinters with 50 to 60 white eggs, from which the young emerge in spring to crawl some distance before emitting wax to form a brownish shell.

Scales emit honeydew, and the black scale's sweet emission attracts a covering of sooty mold to make it black. The SAN JOSÉ SCALE is a black-brown pest covered with a grayish bloom. It spots the fruit on orchard trees and, when in great numbers, sucks the vigor from the tree and sometimes kills it.

The scurfy scale is a gray-white scale appearing on dogwood, willows, and elms (where they still exist). The whitish evergreen scales such as pine leaf scale and juniper scale are both common. Some plants, such as Scotch-broom and some maples confer an immunity on attacking scales so that lady beetle treatment is ineffective. In this case, using dormant oil sprays to control this pest is advisable. Contact insecticides such as ROTENONE can be swabbed or sprayed on scales that get on houseplants. A strong contact spray or soap suds, followed by a clear water syringe, can be effective on large palms and rubber plants. Hand-picking, swabbing with alcohol, or scrubbing with an old toothbrush are other possible methods of control. Soap and lime sprays can be useful. Parasitic WASPS such as *Metaphycus helvolus* and the widely effective LADY BEETLE called *Chilococorus nigritis* are available from insectaries.

SCALLION. A popular name, corrupted from the botanical name, *Allium ascalonicum*, an aromatic herb that is closely related to the onion; see SHALLOT.

SCAPE. A stalk arising directly from the crown of the root and bearing one or more flowers but no foliage leaves, as in *Pyrola* (shinleaf) and *Sanguinaria* (bloodroot).

SCARBOROUGH-LILY. Common name for *Vallota speciosa*, a South African bulb with strap-shaped leaves and clustered lilylike flowers; see VALLOTA.

SCARIFICATION. A technique for hastening germination of dormant hard-shelled seeds by notching or scratching the surface; see SEEDS.

SCARLET BUGLER. Common name for *Penstemon centranthifolius*, a California and Arizona perennial with scarlet flowers; see PENSTEMON.

SCARLET RUNNER BEAN. A twining perennial bean, *Phaseolus coccineus*, grown as an annual in cold countries for its brilliant flowers and large edible seeds; see BEAN.

SCARLET SAGE. Common name for *Salvia splendens*, a tender shrub frequently planted for its colorful flowers; see SALVIA.

SCHEFFLERA (shef LER ah). A genus of trees with large, handlike leaves, belonging to the Araliaceae (Aralia Family). Two species are grown in tropical landscapes or as houseplants in colder climates.

S. actinophylla (Queensland umbrella tree), sometimes listed as *Brassaia actinophylla*, is common in gardens in Zones 10–11 and is one of the mainstays of interior landscaping. In the garden it will reach 40 ft. and flower with an octopuslike inflorescence of bright red stalks and tiny flowers followed by black fruits.

S. arboricola (dwarf schefflera) is more modest in size in all its parts than *S. actinophylla* and is widely used for hedges in Zones 10–11 as well as for interiors. This species propagates well from cuttings as well as from seed.

SCHINUS (SKĪ nus). A genus of semitropical, southwestern and South American trees, two of which are common outdoors in California and Florida, also sometimes grown in northern greenhouses, mainly for their ornamental fruits. One species, however, has become naturalized and is an aggressive weed. Both of the common species are dioecious (bearing male and female flowers on different plants) and are propagated by seed and cuttings.

S. molle (California pepper tree), growing to 50 ft., has graceful, pendulous branches and long panicles of yellowish flowers followed by long-lasting, rose-colored berries. It has been extensively planted as a lawn, park, and street tree but is subject to attack by black scale (see SCALE INSECTS), which is a menace to citrus orchards.

S. terebinthifolius (Brazilian pepper tree), growing to 20 ft., became popular as an ornamental, replacing *S. molle* because it is less prone to black scale. It is of more rigid form, with leaves very dark above and lighter below. Its bright red fruit, borne in drooping clusters, lasts well and makes attractive indoor decorative material. In central and south Florida, however, it has been so widely planted, its seed spread by birds, and the plant so vigorous, that its rapid spread is threatening the native vegetation in many places. Planting of this aggressive weed is now prohibited in many places.

SCHISANDRA (skī SAN drah). A small genus of deciduous twining shrubs of Asia and North America, belonging to Schisandraceae (Schisandra Family), but closely related to *Magnolia* and commonly known as magnolia-vine. Propagation is by seed, greenwood and root cuttings, layers, and suckers.

S. chinensis, the principal species, is hardy in Zones 5–7 and is useful for vining trees and fences. Thriving in a rather moist, sandy loam and partial shade, it grows to 20 ft. with bright, medium-sized leaves; clusters of small, fragrant, pink flowers; and small, bright red berries. The flowers being dioecious, plants of both sexes must be planted together to ensure fruit.

S. coccinea, the only species native to North America, can only be grown in Zones 7–9. It has purplish crimson flowers and scarlet berries.

SCHIZAEA (skī ZEE ah). A genus of ferns in which the fertile fronds are threadlike, topped by a tiny cluster of contracted pinnae, and the sterile fronds are grasslike. They are rare, very difficult to cultivate, and should never be collected from the wild.

S. germanii is a very rare species occasionally seen in Florida and tropical America. Both sterile and fertile fronds are upright, and the fertile ones are topped with a few upright, contracted, narrow (½-in.) segments bearing the sporangia.

S. pusilla (curly-grass fern) is a difficult-to-find fern with 1–2 in. grasslike sterile fronds often curled like a stretched-out spring. The fertile fronds are 2–4 in. tall and topped by six or seven tiny yellow-brown pinnae. It is not showy and is of interest only to the fern enthusiast. It is native to the acid pine bogs in the northeastern states.

SCHIZANTHUS (skī ZAN thus). A genus of large, showy annual or biennial plants, native to South America, belonging to the Solanaceae (Nightshade Family), commonly known as butterfly flower or poor-man's-orchid. They have finely cut foliage and daintily graceful, red, gold, yellow, white, violet, lilac, bluish, or pink flowers good for cutting. Plants are grown easily outdoors in the summer or as large specimens in pots in the greenhouse for winter and early spring bloom. For summer bloom in the garden, seed can be started under glass in early spring or planted outdoors later when the soil is warm. When transplanting, pinch out the tops of the young plants to make them bushy. Spray with water when the weather is hot, for they do better in a cool summer climate than where the heat is intense. For greenhouse culture, sow seeds in pots in early fall in light, rich soil, shifting the seedlings as they grow, eventually to 12-in. pots, again pinching out the tops and staking; these plants will bloom from late winter through spring.

PRINCIPAL SPECIES

S. pinnatus grows to 4 ft., varying greatly in color and markings. The lower lip of the flower is usually lilac or violet.

S. retusus is a dwarf form with orange on the notched upper lip of the flowers, which come in many beautiful color variations. Cv. 'Grahamii' grows to 5 ft. with rose or violet flowers.

S. x wisetonensis, a hybrid between *S. pinnatus* and *S. retusus* cv. 'Grahamii', shows many interesting variations in tone and color.

SCHIZOPETALON (skiz oh PET ah lahn) **walkeri.** A little South American annual belonging to the Brassicaceae (Mustard Family). It grows to about 1 ft. and is frequently cultivated in the border or in frames for its fragrant, purple or white flowers with fringed petals and borne in erect racemes. Seeds can be sown in the open in spring, and the plants will bloom throughout the summer. Plants from later sowings can be carried in coldframes over winter for early spring bloom.

SCHIZOPHRAGMA (skiz oh FRAG mah). A genus of tall, climbing, deciduous shrubs of east Asia, belonging to the Saxifragaceae (Saxifrage Family), commonly known as climbing-hydrangea. They climb by means of aerial rootlets and are slow in getting established; however, they are well worth waiting for if used to cover a wall or tree trunk. Propagation is by seeds, greenwood cuttings under glass, and layers.

S. hydrangeoides (Japanese hydrangea-vine), the best-known species, grows to 30 ft. and bears its loose, white flower clusters in midsummer. Often confused with *Hydrangea petiolaris*, it is, however, easily distinguished when in flower because the sterile marginal flowers consist of only one sepal an inch or more long, instead of four as in the HYDRANGEA. It also flowers later in the summer and the leaves are thicker and more coarsely toothed.

S. integrifolium is not nearly so tall but bears clusters of larger, sterile flowers. It is not hardy in the North.

SCHIZOSTYLIS (skiz OHS ti lis) **coccinea.** A fleshy-rooted South African herb belonging to the Iridaceae (Iris Family) and commonly known as crimson flag or Kafir-lily. It has narrow leaves and showy, tubular, crimson flowers, which are usually grown for cutting. If planted out in late spring in rich soil, it will bloom profusely in the summer. Plants taken up and potted in early fall will bloom again during the winter in the greenhouse.

SCHLUMBERGERA (shlum ber JEE rah) **truncata.** A popular species of Brazilian epiphytic cactus, sometimes called crab cactus because the flattened, green, leaflike joints look somewhat like the flat back legs of a crab. *S. truncata* is one of the parents, along with *S. russelliana* of the many hybrids known collectively as Christmas cactus (and sometimes as Easter cactus), referring to the approximate time of their flowering; the most popular is *S. bridgesii*. Its drooping branches are tipped with zygomorphic (that is: asymmetrical) flowers. There are crimson, salmon, magenta, pink, and white hybrid variants, all of which are delicately lovely. The stems are green, jointed, flattened, leaflike, virtually spineless pads. The parents of various Christmas cacti are epiphytic cacti from the tropical Americas, which need

light shade or filtered light, warmth, and an especially loose, rich, well-draining planting mix. They should be kept from drying out completely.

A common practice is to graft this species onto a more robust stock—often an upright stem of *Pereskia*—which results in a large bush plant, very showy when in bloom. It is also used in hanging pots or baskets. If cuttings are inserted a few inches apart, they soon produce a thick, graceful mass of foliage. See also CACTUS.

Schlumbergera bridgesii

SCHOMBURGKIA (shahm BUR kee ah). A genus of twelve species of hollow-bulbed epiphytic orchids native to tropical North America, the West Indies, Central America, and northern South America. Many fragrant, colorful flowers, varying in shape and hue, are borne on long, arching scapes. Petals and sepals are often twisting, with a broad, spreading lip. The plants are used in breeding with other members of the Epidendreae. They do best in baskets containing a porous, well-draining medium in full sun. They require much water during growth. Hardy in Zones 10–11 with frost protection, they withstand minimum winter temperatures to 60°F. The type species is *S. crispa*.

SCIADOPITYS (sī ah DAH pit us) **verticillata.** A tree native to Japan, belonging to the Taxodiaceae (Taxodium Family), and commonly known as umbrella-pine. It is a slow-growing, pyramidal evergreen with handsome foliage, the glossy needles, 5–6 in. long, growing in whorls of 15 to 35. Its common name comes from the shape it assumes in age, when the branches become more loose and drooping while the head grows broader. A choice selection for landscape planting, it will grow to 30 ft. and thrives best in a rather sheltered position in partial shade in a well-watered loam or clay soil. Propagation is usually from seed. Hardy in Zones 4–8.

SCILLA (SKIL ah).

A genus of small bulbous plants belonging to the Liliaceae (Lily Family), commonly known as squill, wild-hyacinth, or bluebell. The flowers of some species provide perhaps the most beautiful blue in the garden. The hardy types (to Zone 4) are of the simplest culture, increasing rapidly by offsets and self-sown seeds. Blooming early in the spring, they are lovely in the border or rock garden, or naturalized in the grass, where they should be fed occasionally with top-dressings of well-rotted manure.

Scilla sp.

PRINCIPAL SPECIES

S. amoena (star-hyacinth), grows to 6 in. and has relatively long, strap-shaped leaves and white, or blue flowers.

S. autumnalis (autumn squill, starry-hyacinth), growing to only 6 in., has wheel-shaped, rose-colored blossoms appearing in autumn.

S. peruviana (Cuban lily) is a greenhouse species from southern Europe, despite its name. It has long, broad leaves and many-flowered clusters of reddish, white, purple, or blue blossoms. It is often planted in the border in mild climates.

S. siberica (Siberian squill) has one to three small, drooping, intensely blue flowers on a rather short stalk rising above the narrow leaves, which are 4–6 in. long. Blooming very early, it should be given a sheltered location.

SCION.

The piece of an improved variety of plant (bud or cutting) that is inserted into the stock in the process of GRAFTING.

SCIRPUS (SKUR pus).

A genus of large, coarse perennials belonging to the Cyperaceae (Sedge Family) and commonly known as bulrush. Sometimes planted in shallow pond borders or as a background in bog gardens (and one in the greenhouse), they have grasslike leaves bearing flowers in small spikes. Propagation is by division, seed, or suckers. Hardiness varies with the species, to Zone 3.

PRINCIPAL SPECIES

S. acutus grows to 9 ft. and has solitary or clustered spikelets.

S. atrovirens has leafy stems growing to 4 ft. and spikelets in heads.

S. cernuus grows to 12 in. and has many drooping stems and solitary spikelets. It is grown in the greenhouse in damp pots and is prized because of its graceful habit.

S. holoschoenus is stiff and rushlike with a few narrow leaves and spikelets in dense heads.

S. lacustris grows to 9 ft. and is apparently leafless, forming a mass of spikes terminating in dense headlike clusters.

S. tabernaemontani grows to 2 ft. and bears flat-topped clusters of spikelets.

SCLEROTINIA ROT.

A stem rot and wilt of various garden vegetables and ornamental plants caused by a fungus. It is common on lettuce (where it is known as lettuce drop), carrots, beans, celery, cucurbits, crucifers, and tomatoes. Occasionally it affects aquilegia, calendula, peony, delphinium, sunflower, and other perennials and annuals. The symptoms are chiefly a soft rot at the base of the plant involving also the lower leaves, followed by a wilting of the entire plant. In moist weather the crown of the plant may be covered by a thick weft of white mycelium and black resting bodies (sclerotia) in the rotting tissues. The fungus can be distinguished from that causing CROWN ROT by the black color of the sclerotia, the size (up to ½ in.), and the more luxuriant and prominent mycelium. The control measures for the two diseases are the same, including removal of the diseased individuals and application of a suitable fungicide.

SCLEROTIUM. A dense, compact mass of fungus threads (hyphae) combined with food materials in the form of oil and other compounds. The name comes from a Greek word meaning "hard," since sclerotia are generally more or less round, elongated, cylindrical, globular, or ellipsoidal masses with a hard outer covering. They vary in size from a pinhead to some unusual forms as big as a cantaloupe and may be reddish brown, brown, or black in color. They are resting bodies that serve to carry the fungus over periods unfavorable for its growth. Loose in the soil or in bits of plant debris, they live through the winter and are ready to initiate infection in the spring. Common plant diseases that depend chiefly on sclerotia for overwintering are CROWN ROT, SCLEROTINIA ROT, rhizoctonia rot, and BOTRYTIS blight. See also FUNGUS.

SCOLYMUS (SKOHL im us) **hispanicus.** A hardy biennial herb commonly known as golden-thistle or Spanish-oysterplant. It has toothed leaves and is grown for its long, edible taproots. These are larger and milder-flavored than those of salsify but are used in the same way as a fall, winter, and spring vegetable.

SCORCH. The sudden death and browning of large, indefinite areas in leaves and fruits; a symptom of disease caused by drought, excessive heat, toxic action of fungicides or insecticides, or sometimes by bacteria or fungi. See DISEASE.

SCORZONERA (skor zoh NAIR ah) **hispanica.** A hardy perennial herb raised as an annual vegetable for its long, slender roots, known also as black- or Spanish-salsify. The young leaves are also sometimes used as a salad. Grown like a parsnip or ordinary SALSIFY, it can be used in the fall or left in the ground until spring, and then, before growth starts, dug and stored in a cold place.

SCOURING-RUSH. Common name for *Equisetum hyemale*, a fernlike perennial herb; see EQUISETUM.

SCREW-PINE. Common name for PANDANUS, a genus of tropical trees or shrubs with spiral leaf formation.

SCROPHULARIA (skrawf yoo LAIR ee ah). A widely distributed genus of strong-smelling perennial herbs and subshrubs commonly known as figwort. The botanical name comes from their supposed medical value in treating cases of scrofula. The plants are not very showy but are sometimes used in borders or natural gardens. Most are hardy to Zone 4.

S. lanceolata (lanceleaf figwort) is a native species growing to 8 ft. with rather narrow leaves and clusters of small, green and purple flowers.

S. marilandica (Maryland figwort) grows to 10 ft. and has grooved stems; large, dark green leaves; and dull purple or greenish flowers.

SCROPHULARIACEAE (skrahf yoo lair ee AY see ee). The Figwort Family, mostly temperate herbs and, rarely, shrubs or trees; including many with medicinal value, chiefly *Digitalis* (foxglove). Many other genera are cultivated, among them *Calceolaria*, *Collinsia*, *Penstemon*, *Verbascum*, and *Veronica*.

SCRUB-PALMETTO. Common name for *Serenoa repens*, a trailing, branching palm with fanlike leaves; see SERENOA.

SCUTELLARIA (skyoo tel AIR ee ah). A genus of usually perennial herbs or shrubby plants belonging to the Lamiaceae (Mint Family) and commonly known as skullcap. They have two-lipped, scarlet, yellow, blue, or violet flowers and are sometimes planted in the border or rock garden, where they grow to 12 in. or less. The herbaceous species are propagated by division and the shrubs from cuttings. Most are hardy to Zone 5.

PRINCIPAL SPECIES

S. alpina spreads rapidly and bears purple or white flowers 1 in. long in thick clusters. Hardy in Zones 3–9.

S. angustifolia grows to 6 in. with rather large, solitary, violet-blue flowers in the leaf axils.

S. indica has bluish flowers in dense clusters to 4 in. long. Var. *japonica* is lower with darker blue flowers.

S. orientalis is low growing with gray-green foliage and yellow flowers over a long season.

S. resinosa has soft-haired, gray foliage and charming, blue or purplish flowers.

S. ventenati, with scarlet flowers in long racemes, is grown in the greenhouse.

SCYPHULARIA (skī fyoo LAIR ee ah). A genus of ferns related to and closely resembling the genus *Davallia*. *S. pentaphylla*, also listed as *D. pentaphylla*, is a popular basket fern with 1–2 ft., drooping, leathery fronds. Its fronds are more coarsely divided than those of *Davallia*, and the brown rhizome scales are not ciliate, a distinction seldom noticed by the average fern grower. Native to Java and Polynesia, it is long-lived and easily cultivated.

SEA-GRAPE. Common name for *Coccoloba uvifera*, a tropical tree with grapelike clusters of edible fruit; see COCCOLOBA.

SEA-HOLLY. Common name for *Eryngium maritimum*, a perennial herb with pale blue flowers and spiny foliage; see ERYNGIUM.

SEA-OATS. A common name for UNIOLA, a genus of grasses with showy panicles.

SEA-ONION. Common name for *Urginea maritima*, which yields medicinal squill, see URGINEA; and for the green-and-white flowering *Ornithogalum caudatum*, see ORNITHOGALUM.

SEAWEED. Various kinds of seaweed are gathered, allowed to decay in heaps, and then used as manure, since they provide humus, some nitrogen, and a fair amount of potash. Plenty of water should be applied to the pile where it is rotting, to wash out salt from the seawater; rain and freezing weather will hasten this seasoning. When well rotted, seaweed can be spread 3–4 in. deep and plowed or spaded into the soil. It varies considerably in its composition but on the average may contain .5% nitrogen, .2% phosphorus, and 1% potash. Liquid fertilizers made from seaweed are commercially available.

SECALE (suh KAY lee). **cereale.** A hardy annual grass commonly known as rye, grown on farms for its grain and straw but in orchards and gardens as a GREEN MANURE and COVER CROP for the purpose of adding to both the humus and plant-food content of the soil.

In the vegetable garden, seed can be scattered among maturing crops during August and September and lightly raked or cultivated in, care being taken not to injure the growing crops. The resulting green crop can be dug or plowed under in the late fall, or it can be left as a cover-crop and dug in early in the spring.

On land from which a fall crop is harvested any time before freezing weather, rye can be broadcast, for even if it does not germinate immediately, it will be ready to sprout at the first warm spell and make some growth before time to plow in the spring. Fall-sown rye will usually make a good start and survive any ordinary winter. In spring it must be plowed or dug under while soft, succulent, and less than 1 ft. high. If left too long, there may be difficulty in covering it; also, woody stems take longer to rot and are a much poorer source of humus.

SECHIUM (SEE kee um) **edule.** A vine of the Cucurbitaceae (Cucumber Family), often planted in the tropical Americas for its edible tubers and fruit and commonly known as chayote. It is a hardy perennial in Zones 9–11, suitable for growing in both Florida and California, or even farther north in regions with a long growing season if treated as an annual.

The fruit is pear shaped, green or white, 3–4 in. long, contains one large seed, and is often boiled and prepared in various ways. The tubers are harvested after two years' growth. The leaves supply forage, and young parts are used as greens or potherbs. Start plants where they are to stand, 8–12 ft. apart, planting the whole fruit.

SEDGE. Common name for CAREX, a large genus of grasslike perennials. The Sedge Family is CYPERACEAE.

SEDUM (SEE dum). A large genus of hardy, succulent or fleshy, erect or prostrate members of the Crassulaceae (Orpine Family), including some formerly listed as *Gormania*, and commonly known as stonecrop and live-forever. The botanical name is derived from the Latin word meaning "to sit" after their characteristic habit of "sitting" or affixing themselves on rocks and walls. Some are herbaceous perennials, dying to the ground in winter, while many are evergreen. Native

Sedum sp.

to the temperate and frigid zones, they are easily grown in cold climates and increasingly popular with the cultivation of rock gardens. The flowers are usually white or yellow, sometimes pink or blue. Leaves are highly variable—opposite, alternate, and sometimes in whorls.

Sedums are exceptionally adaptable and useful in almost any location. Some are favored for their spreading capacity, others for rock work and edging, some for carpet bedding, some are grown in mixed borders because of their greater height, and still others are frequently used as potted plants. In naturalistic plantings, they can be allowed to spread extensively, but some may be invasive.

CULTURE

Like most plants, sedums have preferences, growing particularly well in a light, loamy soil in open, sunny locations. No rock garden can be considered quite complete without its quota of sedums, along with saxifrages and sempervivums. Children will often develop an interest that will extend to many other plants if they are encouraged to set young plants in chinks in the walls or use them as carpet bedding in the paths.

All sedums are easily grown from seed, which can be sown in late summer. The seedlings can be wintered over with a slight covering and will be ready for transplanting to their permanent places in spring. Seed can also be spring sown. Stock can be multiplied by division of the tufts in early spring. Propagation can also be done from cuttings rooted in sandy soil and kept shaded until well started.

Humus or well-rotted leaf mold enriched with a good, complete fertilizer, can be worked lightly into the soil around the plants to good advantage. If weeds are kept out, the plants tend to remain noticeably free from disease. Being quite hardy, sedums need little winter protection other than a few leaves put on late in the season to prevent heaving of the soil.

PRINCIPAL SPECIES

S. acre (gold-moss) is a low, creeping evergreen greatly favored for its spreading capacity. It bears leaves less than ¼ in. long and yellow flowers in summer. Var. *aureum* has bright yellow leaves in spring and provides a mossy, golden carpet for use on walls, rocky ledges, and stone garden paths.

S. aizoon produces numerous small, yellow to orange flowers in late summer and is useful for edging.

S. album is a dark green, creeping evergreen that forms compact mats. Handsome flat heads of white flowers bloom in midsummer. Several varieties produce foliage of different shades.

S. anglicum, a self-sowing biennial that gives an evergreen effect, grows about 2 in. high and has compact gray foliage and white summer flowers.

S. brevifolium is a creeping evergreen with small leaves densely crowded along the stems and small, whitish flowers in midsummer.

S. cauticola is a clump-forming species that produces a loose circle of stems, about 15 in. across, with roundish, gray-blue foliage. Small heads of rosy flowers at the stem ends bloom from late summer to early fall.

S. dasyphyllum forms tiny, gray-blue beads of foliage with pinkish flowers in midsummer. A choice, mat-forming sedum, it is considered one of the best of the group.

S. divergens, native to the western states, produces tiny, green, jellybean-like leaves on 4-in. stems. It forms an attractive ground cover that turns reddish in sun.

S. ewersii, growing to 1 ft., is a stocky plant with short, thick leaves and pink to purple leaves. A somewhat tender evergreen, it is good for houseplant culture.

S. hispanicum is an annual or biennial with gray-green leaves and pink flowers in midsummer. Var. *minus* is a dwarf form (to 2 in.) often used in carpet bedding.

S. kamtschaticum is an evergreen that grows 6–9 in. and has strong clumps of dark, glossy green foliage on prostrate stems, bearing orange-yellow flowers in mid- to late summer.

S. lydium is a shapely, dwarf evergreen often used for rock work, edging, and carpet bedding. Its leaves are tipped with red, and tiny, white or pink flowers bloom in late summer.

S. morganiaum (donkey- or burro-tail) produces long stems that trail over the sides of hanging plants up to 4 ft. Leaves are thick, almost round, fleshy, light green, and closely spaced. The pink to red flowers are rarely seen. Hardy only to Zone 9, it makes a good houseplant, thriving in partial shade and sheltered from wind.

S. oregonense, formerly listed as *Gormania oregana*, is native to the western states and has grayish rosettes of leaves about 2 in. across and ringed pink along the margin. Whitish flowers are borne on 6-in. stems.

S. populifolium is an evergreen subshrub with fragrant, white to pinkish flowers in late summer.

S. pulchellum is a handsome, but little known, North American native evergreen that grows to 1 ft. and has slender, trailing or ascending branches and rosy purple flowers.

S. rhodanthum is an erect perennial, native to the Rocky Mountains. It grows to 1 ft. and has stout rootstocks, very leafy stems, and rose-colored flowers in late summer.

S. x rubrotinctum (Christmas-cheer, pork-and-beans) produces yellow flowers and small, nearly globular leaves turning bronze-red in the sun and borne on weak stems. Growing no more than 6–7 in. tall, it makes a vigorous ground cover in Zones 9–11 and is good for houseplant culture.

S. rupestre is a creeping evergreen that reddens with age and in dry weather. Flowers are golden yellow in summer.

S. sarmentosum, from the Orient, is a fast-spreading, prostrate evergreen of yellowish tinge with bright yellow flowers.

S. sexangulare is a dwarf, creeping evergreen with densely crowded, rich green leaves and yellow flowers in summer.

S. sieboldii, much like *S. cauticola*, produces pink flowers from late summer to mid-autumn. Fleshy, nearly round, slightly notched leaves about 1 in. long are grouped on single stems 8–9 in. long that hang over the sides of a pot or trail on the ground. In autumn, the plants turn bronze-red and then die back to the ground in winter. Hardy to Zone 3, they require partial shade and occasional water. An attractive form with variegated leaves is available.

S. spathulifolium, native to the western states, forms low, flat-leaved rosettes 2 in. across in various shades of green, whitish gray, or purple. It bears curved sprays of bright yellow flowers on 6-in. stems and grows well in shaded sites.

S. spectabile, because of its greater height, is grown largely in the mixed border and is fre-

Sedum spectabile

quently used as a potted plant. It is a robust, upright perennial to 1 ft. that has light green foliage and numerous small, pink flowers in early fall. Cv. 'Autumn Joy', a popular perennial, is probably a cross between *S. spectabile* and *S. telephium*. Its flowers turn from pink to salmon to red in late summer through autumn. The leaves are light green on upright stems.

S. spurium (two-row stonecrop) is a spreading, mat-forming, evergreen perennial, 2–6 in. high, with dense, broad heads of pink and white flowers in mid- to late summer. Cold weather turns the foliage red, but the stems stay red all year. Hardy to Zone 3, it is an excellent choice for year-round ground cover.

S. telephium has deep bronze to dark green foliage and clusters of red flowers 2–3 in. across blooming in late summer. Cv. 'Emerald Carpet' forms a dense, green mat 4 in. high and has yellow flowers.

SEED DISINFECTION. Treatment of seed before planting with either a dust or a liquid disinfectant to prevent infection by bacterial or fungal disease. See DISINFECTION.

SEEDS. Seeds are fertilized, ripened ovules or eggs of flowering plants. Each contains a rudimentary plant (the embryo), which while dormant is protected by various coats and is supplied, either in or around its seed leaves (cotyledons), with stored food sufficient to start its active life and carry the seedling until its cotyledons reach light, turn green, and with the aid of light begin to manufacture their own food (see PHOTOSYNTHESIS). Since seed development results from the fertilization of the ovules by pollen produced in the stamens of the same or some other flower, reproduction of plants by seed is termed "sexual" as distinguished from the "asexual" processes of division, cuttings, etc.

Seeds vary widely in size, from those of the begonia, which are dustlike, to those of the double-coconut (*Lodoicea maldivica*), which are often 12–18 in. long and weigh up to 40 lb. each. They also exhibit a marvelous diversity in form. In many cases the form is a special adaptation to assist in the distribution of the seed, such as the "wings" of the maple and tulip-tree and the "parachutes" of dandelion and milkweed, for wind transportation, and various burrs and hooks, which attach their seeds to animals. In other instances they have impervious coats that enable them to survive digestion in animals' stomachs; still others are buoyant and waterproof for long periods and thus suited for transportation by water.

DORMANCY AND GERMINATION

Relatively few seeds will sprout as soon as they mature. Even under ideal germinating conditions most of them remain dormant for what is called a rest period, which varies in length in different plant groups. Such periods are thought to be necessary for certain chemical changes related to the ripening of the seed.

Mangrove seeds sprout while still attached to the branches, and some cereal grains germinate during wet weather while still in the heads. Some vegetable and flower seeds of the mustard, grass, lily, bean, and aster families start into growth within a few days; others (carrots and parsnips) require about a month, while the rest period of many shrubs, trees, and perennials often exceeds a year. See DORMANCY.

Investigations have disclosed means of shortening these dormant periods in some cases, thus reducing the cost of starting the plants and the risk of losses from drying, decay, and the depredations of mice and other pests. Agents used to hasten germination include different combinations of chemicals, moisture, heat, freezing, and other treatments. One important and long-practiced method for seeds with internal dormancy is cold STRATIFICATION.

Another type of seed dormancy is caused by seed coats of some species that are impermeable to moisture absorption and/or gaseous exchange, both of which are necessary for germination. Impermeable seed coats can be opened (the dormancy nullified) by scarification or hot water. Scarification is the perforation of the seed coat with some implement—knife, file, or sandpaper. For the hot

Scarification

water treatment, 190–212°F water in a quantity three or four times the volume of the seed is poured over the seed and left to cool overnight (12–24 hours) before sowing.

When dormancy occurs, it is nature's way of ensuring that seed in the wild will germinate only in spring or at the optimum time for that particular plant in its particular environment. Dormancy is not present in most garden seeds.

It should be kept in mind that seeds, though dormant, are living organisms and must be properly treated if they are to give satisfactory results. Naturally, all they need in order to grow is favorable conditions. Their vitality (or lack of it) is established by their maturity, the weather conditions during harvest time, and their treatment during harvesting and storing.

Well-ripened seeds harvested under favorable (dry) conditions and properly stored should retain their vitality for the maximum time characteristic of the species. Seeds of some plants germinate poorly if more than a few weeks old; those of others will sprout well after being stored for ten years or more. Stories about seeds sprouting after having been in tombs or the pyramids for centuries are usually publicity schemes or newspaper yarns.

Seeds harvested during humid weather are usually less viable (capable of growth) than those gathered under dry conditions. Seeds once injured never regain their vigor. Heating while in storage always reduces vitality.

HOW SEEDS GERMINATE

The popular idea is that seed germination or sprouting is the first step in plant growth; actually it is merely the resumption of activity by the dormant young plant in the seed. The factors essential to germination are viable seed, moisture, air, and favorable temperature. The degrees of the last three factors needed vary considerably with different kinds of plants. Briefly, the process of germination is as follows: the seed absorbs water, which enables enzymes in the seed to convert stored starches into sugars. These contribute to the growth of plant cells and tissues; this increases the size of the embryo, which, becom-

ing active, bursts through the water-softened seed coat—and a seedling plant is started on its way.

Both the time and the depth to sow seed outdoors are influenced by soil moisture and temperature, as well as seed size. Seeds sown deeply in moist, cool soil in early spring often decay because, even though the air is mild, evaporation of soil water keeps the soil too cold for them. Seeds sown too shallow in summer, especially if the soil is not packed firmly around them, find so little moisture to absorb that they remain practically dry and fail to sprout. Hence, early spring sowing should be shallower than late spring and summer sowing of the same kind of seed.

Other than this, the only general guidelines to follow are: (1) seeds of hardy plants can be sown earlier in spring, in wetter ground, and somewhat deeper than those of tender plants; (2) strongly viable and fresh seed can be sown more deeply than weak and old stock; (3) in spring, when the soil is damp, it should be firmed but lightly over the seeds (if at all), whereas in summer when the ground is relatively dry, it must be packed hard to permit the rise of moisture from the subsoil; and (4) seeds of large size can be sown deeper than small ones, especially when the ground is dry. A general rule for planting is to sow seeds at a depth that measures two to three times the diameter of the seed.

Small seed, like portulaca or petunia, are sown in containers and should not be covered at all but watered lightly after sowing and the container covered with a piece of glass or clear plastic and a piece of newspaper. The newspaper will help to maintain a saturated atmosphere around the seed and prevent overheating. Sowing too deep will cause the buried seedlings to run out of stored food before the leaves reach the light and can start manufacturing additional food. When the seeds begin to sprout, the paper should be removed. When the temperature rises too high or the air gets too moist, forming mist on the glass, tilt or remove the glass for ventilation and to prevent DAMPING-OFF or the drawing of the seedlings into tall, weak, spindly plants. When germination is complete, the glass should gradually be removed over a week or so. The seedlings should receive good filtered light but no full, direct sunlight. The seedbed must be kept moist at all times once the seed is sown.

The popular practice of soaking pea, bean, corn, and other garden seeds is not always desirable; if continued too long, the seed can become waterlogged and decay when planted in moist or cold soil.

Though seeds that sprout strongly usually make the best plants, there are exceptions. Double-flowering ruffled petunia seed produces both lusty and puny seedlings; the former develop into sturdy plants that bear single flowers and later produce seed; the less vigorous seedlings produce the desired double flowers but no seed.

Since the value of seed depends primarily on its ability to germinate, testing the seed before planting it is very worthwhile. Under the laws of most states, this must be done and the approximate germination percentage certified by the dealer before the bulk seed is sold. State agricultural authorities also take samples of seed on the open market and test them both for viability and for purity—that is, trueness to variety and also freedom from chaff, dirt, and weed seed—as a check against the dealers' representations. These activities are a safeguard and help for gardeners, but often the latter find it interesting or desirable to make their own tests—of surplus seed that has been stored for a year or more, or of the home-grown seed.

SAVING SEEDS

The growing and saving of seeds from garden crops for sowing purposes is a highly developed activity and demands intimate knowledge of the plants concerned. The grower of vegetables or flowers—and especially the home gardener—may well leave the work to seed growers, hybridists, and other specialists who devote their lives to originating new varieties or to the maintenance of the purity of established strains. With heirloom or very old varieties, of which there are many, it may be imperative for home gardeners to save their own seed, since it may not be available from seed companies.

Seed production is carried on along two lines. One involves plant breeding and the selection and multiplication of new, improved varieties so produced. The other is the maintenance of stocks of seed true to type, strain, or variety by rigorous roguing—the removal from the growing seed crop of all inferior or slightly different plants.

In both directions there are unlimited opportunities for the skilled professional or commercial grower, for there is always a demand for both new and improved varieties and for good seed, true to variety. Quality product in both classes of seed commands premium prices; but to develop one and maintain the other, a working knowledge of the laws of plant breeding and selection, and familiarity with seed harvesting, drying, cleaning, and storage are essential. Of the two activities, the former is likely to appeal most to the beginner, mainly because of the appeal to his inexperienced eye of the possibility of becoming a second Luthur Burbank.

The amateur gardener who may want to save the seed of some especially fine plants should realize, first, that the progeny of a hybrid plant is almost certain to differ more or less widely from its parent. Probably less than 1% will come true. If only seed from these true ones is saved and planted, and if this process is repeated year after year, the percentage of true to type plants may increase until, in time, the stock of seed may be practically 100% true. For best results, start slowly and work gradually and carefully according to the following rules:

1. Make sure that the seed is fully ripe before gathering the heads, pods, or other fruit.

2. Spread the heads, pods, or other parts thinly on cloth or clean boards or trays, preferably in the shade or indoors where the air is dry and in motion.

3. Make sure that these enclosing parts are thoroughly dry before separating the chaff and waste from the seed itself.

4. After removing the trash, place the clean seed in containers that permit free access of air—cotton sacks are good.

5. Store where the air will be dry and the temperature preferably below 50°F, that is, in a refrigerator. If the refrigerator defrosts automatically, the seed must be kept in a moisture proof container. Seed should be stored out of reach of mice and other pests.

If there is any likelihood of insect infestation (weevils are especially common as seed pests), treat seed in an airtight container with a few napthalene crystals or flakes for 24 hours.

There are a number of exceptions to the above storage conditions, including all seeds that are fleshy to some degree, such as acorns (oak seed), and the seed of many tropical species. These must be sown immediately (or kept moist and cool until sown), for as the seed dries, its viability decreases until the seed is dry and dead.

The length of time common garden flower and vegetable seed will remain viable (that is, able to sprout strongly and produce sturdy seedlings) varies widely with the species and variety, and the care taken in harvesting and storing the seed. Some seeds, such as those of chervil and martynia, rarely retain their germinating power longer than one year; whereas seed of celery, cabbage, cucumber, and various other vegetables and flowers may sprout well after ten years or even more. Seeds of highly developed strains may have a shorter longevity than less highly bred strains. Seed not fully mature when gathered or that was stored before fully dry, or kept at too high a temperature and/or too high a relative humidity may sprout very poorly or not at all whenever planted. In any case, it is advisable to make tests before doing any actual planting.

SIMPLE SEED TESTING

Commercial seed testers and those of state departments have special apparatus for making delicate tests of many lots of seed, but for home testing of seed purity, one really needs only stout, white paper or cardboard on which to spread samples, tweezers to pick out small seeds, a 6-in. plant label whittled to a thin edge and pointed for separating seeds from impurities, and a magnifying glass to examine seeds for impurities and identification.

To make a simple but adequate germination test, place a disk of white blotting paper in a shallow dish, wet it, and on it scatter 25 to 100 seeds; cover with another matching disk of moistened blotting paper, and then with an inverted dish or piece of glass. Keep the device at room temperature and apply water gently to the paper often enough to keep it moist. After the third day, gently remove the upper blotter, count any seeds that have sprouted, and do so from day to day for a couple of weeks. The percentage of seeds that actually sprout will give an idea of the viability of the seed; the relative numbers that sprout before and after the middle of the test period supply a guide as to whether the seed should be sown thickly or thinly.

SEED-SOWING POINTERS

Seedage, as the sowing of seeds is called, involves all the fundamentals thus far considered and includes the following practical points:

Seeds can be classified as large and small; and, according to the kind of plants they produce, as hardy or tender to frost, annual, biennial, or perennial.

As far as size is concerned, the main consideration is depth of planting, which often determines where they should be started. Most large seeds can be sown in the open ground. Medium-sized ones can be sown either outdoors or under glass. Minute seeds, like those of thyme and petunia, should always be started in seed pans or flats.

Seeds of hardy plants like radish and poppy can be sown as early in spring as the ground can be worked—and should be, in order to get the benefit of the cool moisture at the time. Seeds of tender plants must not be sown outdoors until the ground is warm and only just moist.

Seeds of tropical and subtropical plants, such as eggplant, tomato, and *Cobaea*, are best sown under glass several weeks before it would be safe to sow them outdoors.

Seeds of half-hardy and tender annuals can be treated the same way for early results or sown outdoors, either in nursery beds for transplanting or in the open ground, when the flowers are wanted in their normal summer season.

Biennials, such as Canterbury-bells and dandelion for greens, can be sown at any time between early spring and midsummer; given necessary protection over winter, they will mature the following spring or summer. Biennials are often started outdoors in midsummer for the following season's bloom, but more, larger, and finer flowers should result from spring-sown seed.

Seeds of hardy perennials are often sown in greenhouses, hotbeds, and coldframes during winter. Home gardeners without such facilities can use seed pans or flats in a sunny window or can prepare special sheltered, outdoor seedling beds in which to sow as early as possible in spring. The seedlings started indoors are pricked out into flats and a month or so later transplanted to nursery rows where they are grown for one season so as to be a good size for planting in their permanent quarters that fall or the following spring. It is usually advisable to sow seeds more thinly than the nursery or package recommends. This avoids crowding the seedlings, making them spindly and weak. For the same reason, it is essential to prick out or transplant the seedlings before they begin to crowd. This work is best done on cloudy days, in the evening, or just before a rain. When done under glass, the seedlings should be given some shade for a day or two.

In the garden, soil in which seeds are sown should be freshly sifted or dug and finely raked so as to be porous while still retaining enough moisture to favor germination. Always firm the soil over the seeds to bring them in contact with the moisture film that envelopes the soil particles. Soils for merely starting seedlings should be only moderately fertile—poor is better than rich—because this will stimulate root rather than top development and facilitate transplanting later.

Outdoors, the cultivation should be given three or four days after sowing in order to kill weeds whose seeds, being already in the soil and moist, are sure to germinate before the crop seeds can start. This first cultivation is the most important of all because by killing the first crop of weeds,

one tends to reduce the number of later weeds.

Gardeners can take advantage of the difference in speed of germination by sowing a few seeds of a quick-starting kind in or along the rows of slow-growing kinds to show where the rows are. The best crop for this purpose is a forcing variety of radish because its seeds (dropped 3 in. apart) will sprout within three or four days. The roots will reach edible size in less than a month, and the foliage will shade the rows just enough to help the growth of the more permanent or full-season crop. When the radishes are harvested, the regular crop can be given its first thinning and weeding.

SELAGINELLA (sel ah ji NEL ah). A genus of flowerless herbs with scalelike leaves, commonly known as spike-moss. They are grown for the beauty of their mossy foliage and are considered one of the FERN ALLIES. Some species are hardy, but those species most interesting horticulturally are grown in greenhouses to cover the soil in benches, pots, or baskets; as specimen plants for table decoration; or in terrariums.

The hardy kinds are easily cultivated in damp shady woods. In the greenhouse, new growth will start readily from old plants chopped up and scattered over soil, which is then covered with glass or plastic and kept at 70°F.

PRINCIPAL SPECIES

S. apoda forms mats to 16 in. across and has pale green leaves. It is frequently seen in lawns and damp woods or meadows of the eastern United States.

S. braunii, with straw-colored foliage and an erect stem over 12 in. high, is often used in porch boxes.

S. kraussiana, from Africa and naturalized in the southeastern states, is a bright green, mossy perennial with creeping stems, often used to carpet soil in tropical regions.

S. lepidophylla (resurrection plant, rose-of-Jericho), native from Texas to South America, is a curious mosslike herb with rather stiff branches to 4 in. long covered with small, scalelike leaves and forming flattened, tufted rosettes. When dry the plant curls up into a tight grayish ball, the form in which it is distributed. When put in water it expands and becomes green, and it can thus be alternately dried and "resurrected" a number of times. It can also be grown on soil as a decorative houseplant.

S. martensii, often grown for cut foliage, has long, graceful stems and very fine, pale green leaves.

S. pallescens, formerly listed as *S. emmeliana*, is from the American tropics. Growing to 12 in., it has bright green leaves and makes an attractive fernlike specimen for pot culture.

SELECTION.

The process of choosing an individual or a group of individuals for the preservation of desirable characters or for further breeding operations, eliminating all others. In a systematic attempt to develop an improved variety or strain, a plant breeder might first cross (or hybridize) two plants showing certain desirable characters, and then by practicing selection, separate out from the progeny of that cross the individuals closest to the desired ideal. These might be used for further crossing; or, if of sufficient merit, they could be propagated by cuttings, division, or other asexual methods, so as to build up a stock of plants of the new kind for introduction. See PLANT BREEDING.

SELENIA

(se LEE nee ah). A genus of small North American herbs belonging to the Brassicaceae (Mustard Family), with finely cut foliage and yellow flowers. They are interesting annuals, which can be readily grown from seed in any sunny spot in the wild or rock garden. *S. aurea*, with golden-yellow flowers, bears flat seedpods similar to those of *Lunaria*.

SELENICEREUS

(se le ni SEER ee us). The name (meaning "moon-cereus") of a genus of slender cacti, climbing in habit. It includes some of the best-known and most beautiful of the night-blooming cereus.

S. macdonaldiae is a wonderful sight when in bloom, with flowers 15 in. in diameter. It grows rapidly, its slender, cylindrical stems reaching to lengths of 15 or 20 ft. in a single season. Semi-aerial in character, it roots easily and under cultivation is happy in soil. Of tropical origin, it should receive greenhouse treatment in colder climates. Several other species of this genus are also favorites in cultivation. See CACTUS.

SELF.

In plant breeding, self-pollination, or selfing, means the use of a plant's own pollen upon its own stigmas to produce self-fertilized progeny. This results in seed production without crossing or hybridizing. See PLANT BREEDING.

SEMPERVIVUM

(sem per VĪ vum). A genus of succulent plants in the Crassulaceae (Orpine Family). The genus, commonly called house-leeks, is named from the Latin words meaning "live forever," alluding to the well-known tenacity of many species, especially *S. tectorum*, the common or roof houseleek.

The genus comprises 50 or more species of succulent herbs or subshrubs of variable habits, often stemless and developing young plants from offsets in the leaf axils.  Those grown in the United States are mostly hardy, and many seem to be hybrids of a few basic species. The alternate leaves are thick and fleshy, frequently forming compact rosettes, and often are red spotted toward the tips. In the "spider-web" forms, the entire plant appears to be covered with silvery cobwebs. Mature rosettes produce spectacular

Sempervivum tectorum

flowering stems, after which those rosettes die. Blossoms, borne in dense heads, are variously colored—white, pink, greenish, yellow, or purplish. All the hardy forms are well suited for rock crevices, wall plantings, and borders; the more tender or greenhouse kinds are valuable as succulents indoors and as summer carpet-bedding plants outdoors. The smaller plants are popular for dish gardens, terraria, and other miniature arrangements.

CULTURAL DIRECTIONS

Sempervivum succeeds well in any good garden soil and will thrive even in sandy wastes. Consequently, they are unsurpassed for rock gardens or covering dry banks or old walls. They were once popular in formal gardens as edging plants.

Plants are easily raised from seed sown in spring or late summer and carried over winter with slight protection. Young plants, which spring up at the base of old ones, can be easily separated and grown on as new individuals.

No plants are more easily cultivated than *S. tectorum*. They require no care other than preventing weeds from crowding them out. They respond well to a shallow cultivation of the soil around them. They are shallow rooted and thrive on a light mulch of humus or peat moss during hot weather but do not require further feeding.

Occasionally, plants are found covered with orange-red rust pustules. Remove and destroy individuals if badly rusted, and dust others with fine sulphur. CROWN ROT may also occur. Otherwise, *Sempervivum* grows free from pests and plant diseases and, like many other shallow-rooted rock plants, needs no winter protection other than a thin covering of leaves or other light litter applied in early winter to prevent heaving or lifting of roots out of the soil. Where children have gardens of their own, some of these interesting and easily grown plants should be included.

PRINCIPAL SPECIES

S. arachnoideum (cobweb houseleek, hen-and-chickens) grows only 3–4 in. high. Gray-green, hairy leaves in tight rosettes are joined by a lacy, silvery web; it has red flowers in June. Varieties range from tiny to medium size, and many are fine for rock gardens and for edging borders.

S. arenarium is a sand-loving species that grows to 9 in. and forms tiny, globular clumps of bright green leaves and pale yellow flowers.

S. atlanticum has pale red, 1-in. flowers in summer on 1-ft. stems; the slender, smooth, pale green leaves are tipped with reddish brown when mature.

S. braunii, to 9 in., has leaf rosettes about 2 in. across and dull yellow flowers in July.

S. calcareum, from France, attains 1 ft. and has smooth leaves with red-brown tips and pale red flowers in summer.

S. ciliosum, from Bulgaria, produces tight rosettes of hairy foliage.

S. fimbriatum is an 8–10 in. hybrid with reddish leaves tipped with hairs. It has bright red flowers in July.

S. flagelliforme is low growing (4 in.) and has tiny rosettes of woolly leaves with 1-in., red flowers close against them.

S. globiferum grows to 1 ft. and has rather few 1-in., yellow flowers flushed purple inside in summer.

S. montanum has tightly packed leaf rosettes and bright purple flowers in June, on 6-in. stems.

S. x *schotti* has pale red flowers on 1-ft. stems in summer. The leaves have reddish brown tips.

S. soboliferum is a popular form with pale yellow flowers in dense heads 4 in. across in summer. New rosettes are attached to the parent plant by slender threads.

S. tectorum is the best-known species with many names, including roof houseleek and hen-and-chickens. It has leaf rosettes to 4 in. across, hairy stems to 1 ft. high, and pink to red flowers about 1 in. across.

S. triste is a rarer form of *S. tectorum*, with the upper part of the leaves suffused with red-brown and bright red flowers on 1-ft. stems.

SENECIO (sen EE see oh). A very large and variable genus of herbs, shrubs, and trees widely distributed throughout the world, belonging to the Asteraceae (Aster Family), and commonly known as groundsel or ragwort. They include some climbers, some succulents, some hardy herbaceous perennials, some noxious weeds, and the potted plant that florists call cineraria. Some species formerly included under *Senecio* are now listed under *Ligularia*. The woody species are native in South Africa, Central and South America, and Australia. In general, senecios are easy to grow in good, loamy soil. They are propagated by seed, cuttings, and division.

PRINCIPAL SPECIES

S. articulatus (candle plant) is a branching plant that grows to 2 ft. and has flat, lobed leaves and heads of white flowers lacking ray petals. Hardy only in Zones 10–11, it is often grown in succulent collections.

S. aureus (golden ragwort) is a hardy, herbaceous perennial that grows to 2 ft. and has golden flower heads in late spring.

S. cineraria (dusty miller, silver groundsel) is a tender, branching perennial with white, woolly stems and leaves, often cultivated for its silvery gray and finely cut foliage, and popular for window boxes or bedding arrangements of all kinds. Seed is started indoors in winter for transplanting outdoors when danger of frost has passed. Plants can also be propagated in late summer or fall from tip cuttings, if space is available to winter these where they can be kept somewhat dry and in temperatures above freezing. Hardy to Zone 6.

S. compactus is a dwarf, dense shrub from New Zealand, with small leaves and yellow flowers in leafy clusters.

S. cruentus (cineraria), a short-stemmed, woolly perennial, is grown by florists as a winter-flowering potted plant. It can be grown outdoors in Zones 9–11. The large, velvety, generally toothed leaves are often completely obscured by the daisylike flowers in shades and combinations of purple, red, blue, pink, and white. Native to the Canary Islands, the

Senecio cruentus

species is the parent of many hybrids that grace greenhouses and homes with even larger and more brilliant blossoms. While plants can be carried over, fresh stock is usually grown every year from seed sown in spring or early summer, depending on the season in which flowers are wanted. The soil should be a fine, sandy loam containing about one-third leaf mold. When seedlings are large enough to handle, they should be potted up and kept moist and cool. Liquid manure is beneficial after the buds appear. Double-flowered varieties are also propagated by cuttings of strong shoots that arise after the flowering tops are removed.

S. doria, growing to 4 ft., has showy yellow flowers. Hardy in Zones 6–9.

S. doronicum (leopard's-bane) is a hardy, herbaceous perennial with heads of orange-yellow flowers 2 in. or more across; popular for border plantings.

S. elegans (purple ragwort) is an old-time garden annual with yellow disk flowers and purple ray petals. There are forms with white, rose, and crimson flowers and some double forms.

S. grandifolius, native to Mexico, is a large shrub that grows to 15 ft. and has leaves to 18 in. long and heads of yellow flowers.

S. greyi is a New Zealand native shrub with leathery leaves about 3 in. long, white beneath, and yellow flowers.

S. jacobaea (ragwort groundsel, tansy ragwort) is a biennial or perennial with divided leaves and heads of yellow flowers. Hardy to Zone 4 and widely naturalized, it is a troublesome weed in the north Atlantic and Pacific coasts and the subject of a biological control program of the United States Department of Agriculture. Three insects were introduced to bring the weed into balance with other meadow and pasture plants. White-spotted cattle that eat this plant are photosensitized and become susceptible to sunburn.

S. kleinerii, growing to 12 in. or more, is an attractive, easily tended houseplant that seldom needs repotting. It is hardy only in Zones 10–11 and needs abundant light.

S. macroglossus (wax vine, cape-ivy) is an herbaceous, climbing perennial with handsome ivylike leaves and yellow flowers. It does well in the cool greenhouse.

S. maritima (silver-dust), growing to 8 in., is a perennial usually treated as a half-hardy annual. It creates a mound of silver-white, fernlike leaves, which are attractive for bedding or edging.

S. milkanioides (German-ivy) is a slender twiner with dark green, angled leaves and heads of small, yellow flowers. A popular window garden plant, it is hardy to Zone 9.

S. petasitis (velvet groundsel, California-geranium) is a robust, tender perennial that grows to 8 ft. and has large, soft-lobed leaves and many-headed panicles of yellow flowers. Hardy to Zone 9, it is a good winter-blooming plant for the greenhouse.

S. pulcher (showy groundsel) grows erect to 4 ft. and is fairly hardy (to Zone 6) in well-drained soil. It has a white, cobwebby appearance. Showy heads to 3 in. are made up of yellow disk flowers with reddish purple ray petals.

S. rowleyanus (string-of-beads) is a common potted plant in the western states, where it is hardy to 25°F and requires shade in hot regions. It is a succulent with long, single stems that hang from a pot or trail on the ground. The leaves are ½ in. long, round, and fat. The small, white flowers are aromatic.

S. scandens, a woody climber to several feet, has grayish green leaves and heads of yellow flowers. It is often confused with *S. mikanioides*.

S. speciosus, a perennial growing to 1 ft., is a good plant for the greenhouse with showy basal leaves and heads of bright purple flowers.

S. tanguticus is a stout, herbaceous perennial that grows to 7 ft. and has broadly ovate leaves divided into toothed segments and numerous heads of yellow flowers borne in pyramidal terminal panicles.

S. vira-vira, formerly listed as *S. leucostachys*, is similar to *S. cineraria* but is less stiff and has more finely cut leaves. It is used in bedding arrangements and for window boxes.

S. vulgaris (common groundsel) is an annual introduced from Europe and widely naturalized to become a bad weed in some regions.

SENNA. Common name for CASSIA, a genus of herbs, shrubs, and trees common in tropical areas and belonging to the Fabaceae (Bean Family).

SENSITIVE FERN. Common name for *Onoclea sensibilis*, a fern with pinnules curled to look like a stick covered with green beads; see ONOCLEA.

SENSITIVE PLANT. A common name for *Mimosa pudica*, a curious tropical plant whose leaves recoil when touched; see MIMOSA.

SEPAL. One of the outer set of floral leaves, which collectively make up the calyx. See FLOWER.

SEQUOIA (se KWOY ah) **sempervirens.** A giant coniferous tree, the only member of its genus, belonging to the Taxodiaceae (Taxodium Family), and commonly known as redwood. This tree, native only to the Pacific Coast ranges of the United States, is the largest tree in North America and one of the largest in the world. It grows to a majestic height of 365 ft., with trunk circumferences to 80 ft. The small, scalelike leaves are similar to hemlock needles. The wood is reddish in color and very valuable for building homes, furniture, etc., since it resists decay and does not burn. Some of the giant specimens in California are estimated to be over 3000 years old. It can be propagated from seed but is rarely grown in gardens. Fortunately, a number of groves of these trees have been preserved in California. Hardy to Zone 7.

The giant-sequoia is *Sequoiadendron giganteum*, a closely related tree, which does not grow as large and differs in some technical details; see SEQUOIADENDRON.

SEQUOIADENDRON (se kwoy ah DEND ron) **giganteum.** A giant coniferous tree growing to 250–300 ft., native to the West Coast, and commonly known as giant-sequoia, big tree, or giant-redwood. The only member of its genus, it belongs to the Taxodiaceae (Taxodium Family). It has needlelike foliage and is closely related to the pines but is distinguished in that the cone scales lack separate bracts and have more seeds. It differs from the *Sequoia* in that it does not grow as large and has ovate to lanceolate leaves, smooth buds, and larger scales on the cones.

SERENOA (se re NOH ah) **repens.** A member of the Palmaceae (Palm Family), commonly known as saw- or scrub-palmetto. It has trailing, branching stems bearing fanlike leaves 2½ ft. across and cut into 20 or more parts. The fragrant flowers are followed by almost round, black fruits. In the wild, this plant covers vast areas of sandy soil from South Carolina throughout Florida and Louisiana. The cut tops or "crowns" are sent north for Christmas decorations, remaining fresh and green for a long period. Plants are occasionally grown in the North in cool conservatories, and small specimens make good, slow-growing potted plants.

SERVICEBERRY. A common name for fruit-bearing species of AMELANCHIER, a genus of North American shrubs or small trees.

SESAME. Common name for *Sesamum indicum*, a tender annual herb whose seeds are used as a seasoning; see SESAMUM.

SESAMUM (SES ah mum) **indicum.** A tender annual herb commonly known as sesame. It is cultivated for its tiny seeds, which have a nutlike flavor and are used in various baked goods. The popular Arabian Nights command "open sesame" probably derives from the ripened pods that burst suddenly to eject the seeds. The plant was familiar in ancient Egyptian and Persian cultures, where the seeds were

Sesamum indicum

ground into flour, and it is still used in Near East cooking. The plants also make good ornamental subjects growing 2–3 ft. tall with long, pointed, dark green, slightly hairy leaves and spikes of bell-shaped flowers blooming in summer.

Sesame is a warm-climate herb and needs a long, hot growing season of at least four months to flower and set seeds. It grows best from Zone 7 southward. Seed is best started outdoors in sufficiently warm climates, because it resents transplanting. It should be sown ¼ in. deep after all danger of frost has passed and night temperatures are above 60°F. In cooler regions, it can be started indoors in individual pots. Germination takes about a week, and plants should be set outdoors about 6 in. apart when the weather is warm enough. Plants require no special care. They thrive in full sun and average soil. Add fertilizer at planting time, and water when the ground starts to dry out.

To harvest the seeds, cut the mature pods before they burst open. Cut the stems off at ground level and place them upside down in a paper bag, which will catch the seeds as the pods open.

SESSILE. Without a stalk and seated directly upon the support; a term applied to any stalkless organ that is commonly stalked, such as a flower or leaf.

SETARIA (see TAY ree uh). A genus of tropical, annual and perennial grasses, commonly known as bristle grass. Many of the numerous varieties have colored spikes and are grown as ornamentals. *S. palmifolia* (palm grass) is a perennial, often grown in the far South as ornamentals and in greenhouses in the North. It grows to 6 ft. and has folded leaves 2 ft. long and 3 in. wide. The spikelets are borne in branching terminal racemes on stems 2 ft. long. One form has striped leaves. *S. italica* is foxtail millet.

SHADBUSH. A common name for AMELANCHIER, a genus of attractive North American shrubs or small trees.

SHADE CLOTH. A woven material used to protect and shade plants. Shade cloth can be used in a greenhouse on top of the glass or suspended just over the heads of sun-sensitive plants. It can be used in the field to shade row crops or draped over a frame to grow shade-loving plants. Its use is often seasonal, the shade cloth brought out at the start of the summer to shade sun rooms or greenhouses and then removed once the burning rays of the sun subside in the fall.

SHAGBARK HICKORY. Common name for *Carya ovata*, a handsome, ornamental hickory tree with gray bark that breaks up into shaggy shreds, and delicious nuts; see CARYA.

SHALLOT. A small, mild-flavored species of onion, *Allium ascalonicum*, also known as scallion, which is a corruption of the botanical species name. The plant grows to 18 in. tall, producing hollow leaves like other onion species. Occasionally, violet flower heads are produced, which are typical of the allium shape. The bulbs vary in shape and color depending on the strain. The leaves are eaten raw or used for flavoring. The flavor of true shallots is distinctive and much more subtle than other

Shallot bulbs

alliums. When buying bulbs, gardeners should be sure they are getting genuine shallots and not a variety of multiplying onions. It may be advisable to deal with a specialist grower.

CULTURE

Although they are hardy perennials, shallots are generally grown as annuals. They will thrive in a relatively wide variety of soils, except heavy clays or wet locations. Ideal conditions are like those suited to common onions: rich, moist loam with compost or manure added the preceding fall and then tilled and firmed in early spring.

The plants need plenty of sun, especially toward the end of their growth. Water need not be given as frequently as for onions, but the soil should not be allowed to dry out completely in the early stages of growth. Do not leave plants covered with a mulch in wet weather, since this could cause the bulbs to rot.

Plants should not be transplanted once they have rooted. When cultivating to check weeds, take care not to damage the newly forming bulbs just below the surface.

The better strains of shallots do not set seed and are generally grown from sets. To propagate, break up the bulb clusters, remove the loose skins, and plant the bulbs singly about 8 in. apart. Press them into well-firmed soil, so that they are just below the surface.

If the soil conditions permit, shallot bulbs can be planted in late winter or very early spring, since the plants will grow at low temperatures and freezing weather does not damage them; their normal annual cycle of growth stops soon after midsummer. Especially in regions with hot summers, bulbs are best planted in the fall to mature by spring before hot weather sets in. Even where winter weather is severe, fall sowing may give better results. Experimenting over a few years will determine what works best in specific areas.

Harvesting. When the leafy tops are turning brown, bulbs can be lifted and left to dry on the surface if the weather is dry and sunny. In inclement weather, bulbs should be spread on a wire rack under cover so that air can circulate around them. At this stage it is important to keep them from getting wet. The bulbs can be peeled, chopped, bagged, and frozen, but this is not really necessary. If stored in bags or airy crates in a dry place with a temperature of about 60°F, they will keep almost indefinitely.

SHAMROCK. Common name for certain plants with three leaflets, especially *Oxalis acetosella* and *Trifolium repens*. The shamrock was supposedly used by St. Patrick as a symbol for the Holy Trinity and is now widely associated with

Irish heritage. Several other plants are reputed to be the true shamrock, including some cresses.

SHAMROCK PEA. Common name for *Parochetus communis*, a tropical trailer that has cloverlike foliage and pink-and-blue flowers; see PAROCHETUS.

SHASTA DAISY. Common name for *Chrysanthemum* x *superbum*, a hardy, summer-flowering hybrid; see CHRYSANTHEMUM.

SHEARS. There are two basic types of garden shears, scissorlike cutting tools consisting of a beveled blade pivoted and operating against a flattened "anvil" or two beveled blades facing and pivoting against each other. They are used for various cutting tasks, such as gathering flowers or fruits, pruning, thinning, hedge trimming, and edging beds or borders. Countless styles and sizes of one-hand and two-hand shears (the latter often called lopping shears or loppers) are available from garden suppliers. Some are excellent, and others are undesirable for various reasons, including poor design or material and faulty or cheap construction.

When choosing pruning shears, the following features should be considered:

1. The blades should be made of first-class steel, because a keen edge is essential to good work and prevents unnecessary damage to the plant being cut.

2. The tool should work freely. After a cut has been made, smaller types should open promptly through the action of a spring. The style of spring is mainly a personal preference; it should be sufficiently strong but not too difficult to operate and shaped and attached so that it is not likely to catch in twigs, snap out of place, or pinch the user's hand.

3. When closed, the blades should unite to form one narrow point that can be easily inserted between branches without injuring the bark.

4. The handles should be alike and without projections so that the tool can easily be reversed in the hand, allowing the blade to be placed against the plant part from which a piece is to be cut without bruising it.

5. The blade should not enter a slot, but should engage its opposing jaw like scissor blades (or close down on it like a knife on an anvil). Slots are likely to become clogged and interfere with speedy operation.

6. For general tree work, shears should be fairly heavy. A 10-in. size is suitable for an average man; for women and children, smaller sizes are easier and less tiring to work with. Smaller shears are also better for trimming twigs and small branches or cutting flowers. A special type of shears for picking flowers or fruit grasps and holds the cut stem to prevent dropping the blossom or fruit.

Two-handed shears also come in many sizes and styles. Those with slender, short metal shanks inserted in long, wooden handles are not good, because in spite of ferrules, they are weakest where they should be strongest. In the best kind, only the hand grips are wood, and the blades are extensions of lever handles.

Unless shears (especially lopping blades) are kept sharp, they are prone to injure the tree or shrub being cut. They should not be used to cut branches that are obviously larger than they were made for. A pruning saw will handle these more easily and with less danger of injuring the tree. See PRUNING; TOOLS.

Single-hand clippers

Grass shears are mostly single-hand clippers that work like spring-loaded scissors. They may be made of one piece of spring steel shaped to keep the blades apart except

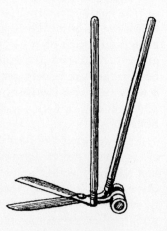

Upright grass shears

when squeezed together, or they may be shaped and pivoted so that the blades work horizontally as the handles are worked vertically in a some-

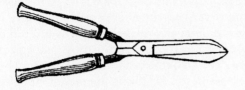

Hedge shears or loppers

what easier position. One such device includes a long handle and lever arrangement that permits the operator to stand while trimming grass edges.

Hedge shears are mostly two-hand tools with blades about as long as the handles, so that, operated like scissors, they make a long cut and permit rapid work. Gas or electrically operated shears have series of teeth that work back and forth like those of a mowing machine. They are only suitable for light work or small growth.

SHEATH. Any tubular part surrounding or encasing another part; such as the leaves of the bromeliads that sheath one another, or the leaf base surrounding the stem in grasses.

SHEEPBERRY. Common name for *Viburnum lentago*, a tall bush with white flowers and edible berries, native in eastern North America; see VIBURNUM.

SHEEP-LAUREL. Common name for *Kalmia angustifolia*, a hardy evergreen shrub with light green leaves and clusters of rose-pink or crimson flowers; the leaves were thought to be especially poisonous to sheep; see KALMIA.

SHEPHERDIA (she PUR dee ah). A genus of shrubs or small trees of North America, belonging to the Elaeagnaceae (Oleaster Family) and commonly known as buffalo-berry. They are hardy to Zone 3, able to withstand extreme cold and dry conditions, and do well near the seaside. Male and female flowers are borne on separate plants. Propagation is by seed, best sown in the fall.

S. argentea is a tall, thorny shrub with silvery leaves and oval, red, edible fruits, valued for jellies or conserves. It is attractive for contrast in mixed shrub plantings and is useful for hedges.

SHIELD FERN. Common name for several species of ferns, especially belonging to the genera DRYOPTERIS, which includes the Boott's, Clinton's, crested, marginal, shaggy, and southern shield ferns; and to POLYSTICHUM, which includes the hard, mountain, and soft shield ferns. Variegated shield fern is *Arachniodes simplicior*; see ARACHNIODES.

SHINLEAF. Common name for PYROLA, a genus of low, evergreen, perennial herbs.

SHOESTRING FERN. Common name for *Vittaria lineata*, a fern with narrow, entire, hanging, dark green fronds; see VITTARIA.

SHOOTING-STAR. A common name for DODE-CATHEON, a genus of perennial herbs with spurred flowers.

SHORT-DAY PLANT. A term applied to plants in which flower bud formation is normally initiated by relatively short day lengths (ten to twelve hours) and suppressed by exposure to longer day lengths. The actual stimulation of these processes is longer dark periods rather than short light ones.

Typical plants of this category are chrysanthemum, poinsettia, cosmos (late varieties), certain varieties of dahlias, African-marigold, ageratum, tithonia, most of the golden rod, most native asters, and aquilegia. Such plants can be forced into earlier bloom by shading them with opaque black cloth. This is a common commercial practice with growers of chrysanthemums, especially in greenhouses. The shading is started just prior to the time of normal bud setting, the cloth covering being applied at an appropriate hour in the late afternoon and left on until nightfall. The practice is continued for several weeks, the length and time of shading depending on the latitude and the variety being grown. Conversely, the use of artificial light to supplement daylight will delay bud setting in this type of flower. By following these practices, a certain variety of chrysanthemum can be brought into bloom early by shading, at a normal period by giving it natural light, and at a later period by the use of supplementary artificial light.

See also LONG-DAY PLANT; PHOTOPERIODISM.

SHORTIA (SHAWR tee ah). A genus of low, evergreen, stemless herbs belonging to the Diapensiaceae (Diapensia Family), with nodding, white, bell-shaped flowers. They are delightful little plants for the rock garden or as an underplanting for rhododendron and kalmia. They require a shaded position in acid, humus-rich soil and should be mulched regularly with oak leaves. They seldom set seed and should be propagated by division or runners.

S. galacifolia (oconee-bells) has roundish, wavy-margined, rather leathery leaves similar to those of *Galax* and charming white flowers nearly 1 in. across. First discovered in 1788 in the mountains of Carolina, it has never been found wild anywhere else.

S. uniflora (nippon-bells), native to Japan, is very similar to the Carolina species but has more heart-shaped leaves.

SHRIMP PLANT. Common name for *Justicia brandegeana*, a tropical plant with closely pressed, pink bracts around white flowers; see JUSTICIA.

SHRUB-ALTHAEA. A common name for *Hibiscus syriacus*, a hardy, upright, summer-flowering shrub; see HIBISCUS.

SHRUBS. Shrubs are woody plants of bushy habit in varying sizes, developing several stems instead of a single trunk as does a tree. The use of shrubs in gardening is, of course, taken for granted; everyone knows about shrubs in a general way, but far too often they have not received the consideration to which they are rightly entitled. Considering the permanent character and importance in the garden and landscape picture, less imagination has been displayed in the selection and arrangement of shrubs than of any other group of garden plants. As a result, too many plantings are dull and uninteresting for the greater part of the year.

One reason for this is the monotonous repetition of a few well-known kinds. Every shrub has a value for some particular use and place, but when planted without regard to position, or with little or no consideration given to harmonious arrangement, a pleasing result can scarcely be expected. One need only point to the indiscriminate overplanting of the sterile form of *Hydrangea paniculata*.

SELECTING AND USING SHRUBS

Shrubs can be used to emphasize or define spaces in the garden, and wonderful effects can be achieved with seasonal color. Every location has its own special requirements as to what and where to plant.

SELECTION

Before selecting a shrub, there are several important things to be considered, such as the location and exposure, whether open to air and sunlight or subject to various degrees of shade; and the character of the soil, whether naturally heavy and retentive of moisture or light and dry, and whether it is acid, neutral, or alkaline. The amount of space determines whether a dwarf, medium, or large-growing shrub is required.

The various purposes for which shrubs can be used range from carpeting the ground to clothing a high wall. They can be used to screen out unsightly objects, to unite the foundation walls of a building to the ground, to display the individual charm and beauty of a single specimen, to group together for a mass effect, to squeeze close together in hedge form, or to grow as a ground cover. Whatever the purpose, there is a wealth of plant material from which to choose. In a large area, it is possible to use greater variety and to plant for mass effect. For a small yard, make the selection from a few choice and favorite kinds.

SEASONAL EFFECTS

There is much to be considered in shrub plant-ing besides the great burst of growth and flower in the early part of the season. Some thought should be given to year-round effects, which means a study of form, winter twig color, foliage and fruiting timing and color, as well as floral display. Shrubs can bring cheer with flowers before the official arrival of spring or prolong the garden interest with a bright display of fruits or colored stems later in autumn and winter. Some species gain added value by holding their leaves green after others are bare, for example, the hybrids *Symphoricarpos* x *chenaultii* (snow-berry) and *Spiraea* x *vanhouttei*. There are numerous berry shrubs that have continued interest after the leaves have fallen.

SHRUBS FOR VARIOUS PURPOSES

The groups suggested below are not to be regarded as complete for every place and pur-pose, but rather as examples. In favored climates a much wider selection, of course, is possible.

Broad-leaved Evergreens. Unfortunately only a comparatively few can be grown in cool climates, which makes these few all the more important. They are worth special care and mostly prefer a sheltered and partly shaded place. Examples are the native rhododendrons and certain hybrids of *Leucothoe fontanesiana* (mountain-laurel), and the native Japanese species of *Pieris*. The many forms of *Calluna* (heather) are fine for sandy, sunny locations, as are several species of *Erica* (heath), though they are not quite as hardy. Another prostrate and easily grown plant in this group is *Arctostaphylos uva-ursi* (bearberry).

Several of the evergreen species of *Euonymus* are hardy and useful for various purposes, from carpeting bare spots under trees to covering walls, making informal hedges, or focusing on accent plants. The related *Paxistima canbyi* makes a very desirable evergreen mat. In a shel-tered place, the evergreen *Berberis* (barberry) and the allied *Mahonias* may do very well. The same can be said of *Buxus* (box or boxwood) and cer-tain of the hollies (*Ilex* or *Nemopanthus*). The only *Viburnum* that can stand much frost is *V.*

rhytidophyllum, a very handsome shrub where hardy. *Daphne cneorum* is a choice plant for rock gardens and edging foundation plantings.

Shrubs with Lasting Foliage. Deciduous shrubs that retain their green leaves late in the fall are often desirable, and the following are good in this as well as other respects: *Acanthopanax sieboldianus, Buddleia alternifolia, B. davidii, Cotoneaster hupehensis, C. simonsii, Forsythia* x *intermedia, F. viridissima, Kerria japonica, Ligustrum amurense, L. ovalifolium, Lonicera fragrantissima, L. morrowii, L. maackii* var. *podocarpa, Lycium chinense, Rhamnus frangula, Stephanandra incisa, Symphoricarpos* x *che-naultii, Viburnum alnifolium, V. lantana,* and *V. plicatum* var. *tomentosum*.

Shrubs for Shady Places. The following do well in shady locations under ordinary soil con-ditions.

Large specimens include: *Cornus alternifolia, C. mas, C. stericea,* deciduous species of *Euony-mus, Hamamelis virginiana, Lindera benzoin, Viburnum alnifolium, V. cassinoides,* and *V. den-tatum*.

Medium and smaller growers include: *Clethra alnifolia, Deutzia gracilis, Diervilla lonicera,* all kinds of *Forsythia, Hydrangea arborescens, Ker-ria japonica, Symphoricarpos albus,* and *Xan-thorhiza simplicissima*.

Early-flowering Shrubs. In regions where win-ter is severe, no flowers are more welcome than those appearing early in the year. A few shrubs belong with the advanced group that herald the season's display. *Daphne mezereum* sometimes opens its fragrant flowers in midwinter. Some of the genus *Hamamelis* (witch-hazel) may show even before that, such as *H. japonica, H. mollis,* and *H. vernalis*. The showy flowers of the relat-ed *Corylopsis* open in advance of the leaves, *C. spicata* being considered one of the best. One of several good qualities of *Lonicera fragrantissima* is that its sweetly scented flowers make their presence known before winter has quite gone. Two taller shrubs with early, yellow blooms are *Lindera benzoin* and *Cornus mas*. *Forsythia ovata* is the earliest of this showy group. *Vibur-*

num carlesii is a delightful shrub that should be in every garden for its spicy-scented and handsome, early flowers.

Summer and Late-flowering Shrubs. After the great burst of spring and early summer bloom has passed, there still remain a few flowering kinds to carry along the display well into autumn. For midsummer, there are several forms of *Spiraea japonica* and *S.* × *bumalda*, particularly the cv. 'Anthony Waterer'. *Cytisus nigricans* and *C. supinus* are good shrubs for a sunny place, as are the garden forms of *Potentilla fruticosa*, which continue in flower more or less all summer. Of larger growth and very showy are *Hypericum frondosum* and *H. prolificum*. *Itea virginica* and, later, *Clethra alnifolia* are conspicuous with their fragrant, white flowers in erect racemes. *Hydrangea quercifolia* is outstanding with its huge panicles, and *H. arboresceus* var. *radiata*, with its flat, white heads and silvery leaves, gives a cool appearance in a shady spot. Later in the season, *H. paniculata* cv. 'Grandiflora' is conspicuous with its long, loose, white panicles. *Stewartia*, with showy white flowers, are beautiful in midsummer. *Abelia* × *grandiflora* begins to show well at this time and continues until frost. The forms of *Hibiscus syriacus* give a striking display of color in late summer. *Clerodendrum trichotomum* is valued for its large, fragrant flowers, which are quickly followed by colorful fruit. *Buddleia davidii* blooms from midsummer until frost.

Shrubs with Colorful Fruit. There is a wealth of good material in this group, and it is rightfully receiving more attention from planters as the several kinds do much to prolong the interest beyond the actual growing season. Such genera as *Berberis, Cotoneaster, Cornus, Euonymus, Ilex, Lonicera, Ligustrum*, and *Viburnum* contain many species that will give a varied and colorful display, in some cases lasting throughout the winter. Some of the rose shrubs such as *Rosa rubrifolia, R. rugosa*, and *R. villosa* are also valuable in this respect. Species of *Callicarpa* have lilac- and violet-colored fruits, and the brightest blue is found in *Symplocos paniculata*. *Hippophae rhamnoides* is outstanding with its orange-colored fruit. Some species of *Eleagnus* have orange or silvery fruits. *Symphoricarpus albus* has the most conspicuous white fruit.

Shrubs with Colored Stems and Twigs. This group is outstanding for providing color masses in winter, and the intensity of the color increases as spring approaches. They are often placed in association with waterside plantings but will do well in drier places. The brightest coloring is developed in the open. Various *Cornus* (dogwood) and *Salix* (willow) species have brilliant red or yellow stems. *Kerria japonica* and *Forsythia viridissima* show well with stems of bright green.

CULTURE

SOIL AND PLANTING

While most plants, with the exception of those belonging to the Ericaceae (Heath Family), are not especially particular as to the pH of the soil, they do appreciate thorough preparation in the form of deep digging, especially where there is a hard subsoil. It pays to break up the soil at least 2 ft. deep. The shrubs are likely to be in their location for a long time and feeding can be taken care of later on when established, but the addition of organic matter in the form of really old, rotted manure or leaf mold, placed below the roots at planting time is advisable.

Planting of most shrubs can be safely done in the fall when growth is mature, except perhaps in low, wet places. A generous mulch will protect the plants from the bad effects of freezing and thawing so common in northern winters. Spring planting can be started as soon as the soil is dry enough to work freely.

SPACING

In planting shrub borders, a common fault is to space them too close for proper development of good growth. It should be recognized that the individual plant does not develop as fully when grouped as it does when planted as a single specimen. Close planting for immediate effect is all very well if thinning out and rearrangement are done as soon as crowding takes place. Too often, however, this is entirely neglected, and the resulting tangle is not only a mass but a mess. The proper spacing will depend, of course, on the ultimate size of the particular shrubs. It will vary from 2–3 ft. with the smaller growers and up to 6 ft. or more for the more vigorous kinds. Some of the more robust herbaceous perennials make good temporary fillers between shrubs.

ARRANGEMENT HINTS

Something to consider in the grouping of various kinds is harmony of composition with respect to habit of growth and quality of foliage. A gradual transition from coarse to fine foliage is generally better than too great a contrast. In arranging the planting, a more pleasing effect is obtained by grouping three or more of a kind together. Certain large, upright growers such as *Caragana arborescens*, *Chimonanthus praecox*, *Cornus alternifolia*, *Halesia carolina*, *Hibiscus syriacus*, and *Viburnum sieboldii*, can be used to good effect singly as accent plants.

Using dwarf and spreading shrubs in the front of a border can hide the bare legs of taller specimens and unite the planting with the ground. Such examples as *Abelia* x *grandiflora*, *Deutzia gracilis*, *Itea virginica*, *Kerria japonica*, *Stephanandra incisa*, *Spiraea* x *bumalda*, *Spiraea thunbergii*, and *Symphoricarpos* x *chenaultii* work well for this purpose.

For FOUNDATION PLANTING, the chief object is to unite the building and the ground in order to create a harmonious appearance with the architectural style. This requires careful consideration in selecting plants for year-round effect. Foliage and forms are more important than the fleeting floral display. It is not generally necessary to completely hide the foundation walls. Pleasing and interesting arrangements can be worked out with selections of broad-leaved evergreens, dwarf forms of the coniferous type, and the choicest dwarf and medium-growing deciduous shrubs.

PRUNING

The general appearance and well being of shrubs depend a good deal on the manner in which pruning is practiced. Everyone knows that pruning is necessary, but many do not understand the principles that should govern the use of pruning shears. Too often the natural form is marred by a general trimming instead of careful thinning out of old wood to promote vigorous young growth. Except where desirable for special effects, overly sheared specimens give a spotty and unnatural appearance.

Study the habits of the individual shrub before beginning any pruning operation. In general, shrubs that flower before midsummer should receive most of their pruning immediately after flowering. This will consist chiefly in the removal of a certain amount of old growth from the center and perhaps a little shortening back to suit the position. Those that flower later need pruning before growth starts, since their flowers are borne on the current season's growth.

In dealing with neglected or overgrown specimens, it is sometimes necessary to be very drastic and to cut everything back to within a foot or so of the ground just before growth starts. Sad-looking specimens can be wonderfully renewed in this way, especially if the soil is stirred up and fertilized at the same time. In pruning shrubs for the effect of colored stems in winter, they can be entirely cut back to the ground in spring. If the gap this leaves for a time is objectionable, cut back only the oldest stems each year.

SICANA (si KAY nah) **odorifera.** A vine belonging to the Cucurbitaceae (Cucumber Family), commonly known as Cassabanana. Native to South America, this fast-growing and lengthy vine can be grown as an annual in the United States. Its chief appeal is for its aromatic, decorative, edible fruits; these are orange-crimson, smooth, slender, and nearly cylindrical, up to 2 ft. long.

SICYOS (SIK yohs) **angulatus.** An annual climbing vine, native to North America, belonging to the Cucurbitaceae (Cucumber Family), and commonly known as star or bur cucumber. It is a fast grower, to 20 ft. or more, and is sometimes used for screening purposes but is more often fought as a weed. It has sharply angled or lobed leaves; small, whitish flowers; and short spiny fruits.

SIDALCEA (si DAL see ah). A genus of perennial and annual herbs belonging to the Malvaceae (Mallow Family) and commonly known as prairie mallow. They grow 2–3 ft. tall and bear spikes or clusters of white, pink, or purple flowers like miniature hollyhocks. Grown from seed, cuttings, or divisions, sidalceas should be planted in rich, sandy soil. The cultivated species are generally perennial, many of them blooming over a long season. Hardy in Zones 5–9.

PRINCIPAL SPECIES

S. candida is a pure white–flowered species that is native to the Rocky Mountains.

S. × *hybrida* includes a number of hybrids, some having pink or satiny rose flowers.

S. malviflora (checker-bloom) is a California native perennial, with rosy purple blossoms in many-flowered racemes; hardy to Zone 8. Var. *atropurpurea* has purple flowers. Var. *listeri* has mallowlike blossoms of silky pink.

S. oregana has deep pink flowers to ¾ in. long.

Sidalcea malviflora

SIDE-DRESSING. The addition of manure, compost, or other soil amendments is usually best before or after the growing season, but some plants need additional food. In relatively poor soil or new gardens especially, fertilizer material can be placed on the surface of the ground, between rows in the garden as opposed to that plowed or spaded under. Any plant food added after growth begins must be applied as a side- or top-dressing, unless dissolved in water. Direct use of manure, compost, nitrogenous fertilizer, or other soil amendments close to developing plants during the growing season is generally inadvisable since it may burn them. However, fertilizer can be applied in the garden by sprinkling it in a shallow along a row furrow around the plants 5–6 in. away from the stems, where the nutrients leach into the soil before coming in contact with the plant roots.

Different vegetable crops require varying amounts of food during the stages of their development. During the first stage, plants develop their roots and basic structure. At the second stage, when they start to blossom, they need extra food to set fruit and seed-pods. It is not usually a good idea to fertilize before the second stage, since it may encourage

Side-dressing of fertilizer

lush foliage and extraneous roots to develop, which ultimately delays the harvest.

SILENE (sī LEE nee). A genus of annual, biennial, or perennial herbs belonging to the Caryophyllaceae (Pink Family) and commonly known as catchfly or campion. Various species are clustered, erect, or vinelike in form. Many have showy flowers of red, pink, or white and are highly decorative in the border or rock garden. A few are good greenhouse subjects. They have a long season of bloom, through the summer and well into the fall, and are easily grown in a light, warm soil. The annuals are propagated by seed and the perennials, by seed, division, or cuttings. If the annual seed is sown in the fall, much earlier bloom will be secured. Hardiness varies with species, generally from Zones 3–8.

PRINCIPAL SPECIES

S. acaulis (cushion pink, moss campion) is found in high mountain areas, forming a beautiful mat hardly more than 2 in. high with short-stemmed, rich pink to reddish purple flowers ½ in. across, blooming over a long summer season. Hardy in Zones 4–8, it is very good in the rock garden but is a challenge for all but the expert grower. It starts readily from seed but is difficult to maintain and flower; it needs sun and sharp drainage. Var. *alba* is a white-flowered form.

S. alba (evening campion), formerly listed as *Lychnis alba,* bears white flowers that open in the evening. The plant is somewhat sticky and includes double-flowered perennial or biennial forms in cultivation.

S. armeria (sweet-William catchfly) is a smooth, annual plant that grows to 2 ft. and has clusters of rose or white flowers in mid- to late summer. Seed should be sown in the fall or very early spring where the plants are to stand.

S. californica (Indian pink) has bright red flowers atop several 6–18 in., branched stems. It grows well in light shade and needs moisture during the start of the flowering season.

Silene californica

S. caroliniana (wild-pink), sometimes listed as *S. pennsylvanica,* grows to 10 in. and has white or rose flowers in flat clusters in spring. It is a good subject for the border or wildflower garden. Hardy in Zones 5–8.

S. compacta is a biennial that grows to 2 ft. The foliage has a bloom, and pink flowers are borne in heads 3 in. across surrounded by the upper leaves. It is best propagated by seed.

S. flavescens grows to 8 in. and has yellowish, hairy foliage and bright yellow flowers.

S. hookeri, growing to 5 in., produces beautifully fringed, rose or salmon-pink flowers 2 in. across. Hardy in Zones 4–8 but difficult to grow in the East, it can be remarkably fine in the rock garden where conditions are suitable.

S. laciniata (Mexican campion, Indian pink) grows to 5 ft. and has glowing red flowers. Var. *purpusi* is a dwarf form with cardinal red flowers and is much better for the border than the species.

S. maritima is an attractive perennial that grows to 1 ft. The foliage has a bloom, and the white flowers have balloonlike calyxes. Cv. 'Robin White Breast' has double, white flowers. Hardy in Zones 5–8.

S. pendula is an annual that grows to 10 in. and has soft, hairy foliage and flesh-colored flowers in graceful, drooping racemes in summer. Var. *alba* is pure white. Var. *ruberrima bonnettii* is purplish.

S. quadrifidia (alpine catchfly), formerly listed as *S. alpestris,* grows 4–12 in. high and has sticky foliage and glistening white flowers in summer. It is best suited to the rock garden or edge of the border. Hardy in Zones 3–8.

S. regia (royal catchfly) grows to 4 ft. and has deep, glowing scarlet flowers in panicles in midsummer. It is exceptionally fine when naturalized in the wild garden.

S. schafta (moss campion) grows to only 6 in. and has soft-haired leaves in rosettes and rose or purple flowers. Hardy in Zones 5–8, it is fine for the rock garden.

S. stellata (starry campion) is a woodland perennial with white, nodding flowers to 3 ft. tall, blooming all summer. It is more appropriate in a wildflower garden than in the border. Hardy in Zones 5–8.

S. virginica (fire pink) grows to 2 ft. and has brilliant scarlet or crimson flowers with notched petals borne in nodding clusters from late spring until early fall. Perennial and hardy in Zones 3–8, it provides an excellent note of color in the border and works well in the wildflower garden.

SILK-COTTON TREE. Common name for *Ceiba pentandra,* a large tropical tree whose woolly seed produces the commercial kapok of pillow stuffing; see CEIBA.

Silk-cotton tree or red silk-cotton is also applied to *Bombax ceiba,* another source of commercial fiber.

SILK-TASSEL BUSH. Common name for GARRYA, a genus of tender, ornamental evergreen shrubs.

SILK TREE. Common name for *Albizia julibrissin,* a flowering, ornamental Asiatic tree frequently cultivated in the southern states; see ALBIZIA.

SILPHIUM (SIL fee um). A genus of tall, coarse perennials of prairie grasslands, belonging to the Asteraceae (Aster Family), and commonly known as rosinweed. They have heads of yellow disk and ray flowers resembling sunflowers and are suitable for the back of the sunny, open border. They are hardy to Zone 3 and easily propagated by seed or division.

PRINCIPAL SPECIES

S. integrifolium has entire leaves and flower heads to 2 in. across borne in late summer.

S. laciniatum (compass plant) grows to 12 ft. and has rough leaves that point north and south, hence the common name. Large flower heads to 5 in. across bloom continuously from July to September.

Silphium laciniatum

S. perfoliatum (cup plant, Indian-cup) grows to 8 ft. and has upper leaves that surround the stem, giving rise to the common names. The heads are 3 in. across.

S. terebinthinaceum (prairie-dock) grows to 10 ft. and has almost smooth foliage and many 3-in. flower heads that make it one of the most decorative species.

SILT. A term applied to a soil type intermediate in texture between sand and clay. While if rubbed between fingers it feels soft and smooth like clay, rather than gritty like sand, it does not tend to puddle and bake to the same extent as clay, nor does it dry out as quickly as sand. Ordinarily, however, it is deficient in humus or organic matter and can be greatly improved for crop production purposes by having manure, peat moss, leaf mold, or other vegetable matter incorporated with it. Since it usually contains a fair amount of mineral matter, it is a good basis for a useful garden soil. In fact, a good silt loam is an excellent type for most garden plants except those that are expected to make quick early-spring growth.

SILVERBACK FERN. Common name for *Pityrogramma calomelanos*, a tropical fern with whitish or yellowish farina on the lower surfaces; see PITYROGRAMMA.

SILVERBELL. Common name for HALESIA, a genus of deciduous trees and shrubs covered with drooping, bell-shaped, white flowers in spring.

SILVERBERRY. Common name for *Elaeagnus commutata*, a deciduous shrub with fragrant flowers followed by silvery fruit, found from eastern Canada to Utah; see ELAEAGNUS.

SILVER LACE VINE. Common name for *Polygonum aubertii*, a twining woody vine with profuse, fragrant flowers; see POLYGONUM.

SILVERROD. Common name for *Solidago bicolor*, a white-flowered species of goldenrod; see SOLIDAGO.

SILVERVINE. Common name for *Actinidia polygama*, a twining shrub with variegated leaves, fragrant flowers, and yellow fruit; see ACTINIDIA.

SILYBUM (SIL i bum). A genus of thistlelike herbs of the Asteraceae (Aster Family), having spiny, white-spotted leaves and large heads of purplish flowers. They grow well in a sunny spot in any good garden soil and will bloom the first year from seed.

S. marianum (blessed-, holy-, milk-, or St.-Mary's-thistle) is an annual or biennial that grows to 4 ft. and has spiny, glossy leaves and rose-purple heads of flowers 2½ in. across, surrounded by spiny bracts. A European native, it has become naturalized in California.

SIMMONDSIA (sim MAWN zee ah) **chinensis.** A subtropical evergreen shrub related to *Buxus* (boxwood) and commonly known as goatnut or jojoba. It is somewhat grown for ornament and for its edible fruits or oily seeds.

SINNINGIA (si NIN jee ah). A genus of Brazilian plants belonging to the Gesneriaceae (Gesneria Family) and best known through *S. speciosa*, known in the florist trade as gloxinia, which correctly refers to another genus. The plants are usually started in a warm greenhouse; seeds are planted in shallow flats in soil composed of equal parts of finely sifted leaf mold, sand, and peat. Later the seedlings are potted in equal parts of leaf mold, loam, and peat. Young plants are shifted several times and shaded from direct sunlight.

Sinningia speciosa

Care should be taken not to wet the leaves when watering. Plants bloom in late summer, and after the flowers and leaves have matured, water is withheld to encourage tubers to ripen. When mature, they are stored in sand for the winter at a temperature of 45°F. These tubers will start into growth the following spring. Rare varieties are grown from leaf or stem cuttings.

Also of interest to indoor gardeners are the many species and cultivars of miniature sinningias. *S. pusilla* grows hardly an inch tall, with tiny brown-veined, olive green leaves and pale lavender flowers on delicate pedicels to 1 in. high. It is nearly everblooming and makes a treasure for any small terrarium or bottle garden. Many other species, varieties, and cultivars are available from specialists and through plant exchanges sponsored by the American Gloxinia and Gesneriad Society.

SISYRINCHIUM (si si RINK ee um). A genus of small, North American perennials belonging to the Iridaceae (Iris Family) and commonly known as blue-eyed-grass. They have fibrous roots, grasslike foliage, and small, blue or yellow flowers. Growing wild in rich meadows or swamps, they make most attractive colonies in an open, rather moist spot in the wild garden. They are easily propagated by seed or division. Hardiness varies with species.

PRINCIPAL SPECIES

S. angustifolium grows to 2 ft. and has pale green leaves and deep violet-blue flowers ¾ in. across. Hardy in Zones 3–9.

S. bellum (blue-eyed-grass) is often grown in California; there are many named forms available, with flowers ranging from violet to white.

S. bermudiana grows 1–2 ft. and has grassy leaves and violet-blue flowers. Hardy to Zone 9.

S. californicum grows to 1 ft. high and has bright yellow flowers.

S. striatum grows 18–24 in. high with gray-green leaves, similar to those of iris. It produces an

Sisyrinchium bellum

abundance of star-shaped, creamy flowers in early summer. Hardy to Zone 7.

SKIMMIA (SKIM ee ah). A genus of evergreen shrubs from Asia, belonging to the Rutaceae (Rue Family). They are slow-growing, handsome, dwarf shrubs, best grown in Zones 7–9 or in Zone 6 with winter protection. They prefer a rather moist loam and partial shade. In cold climates, they can be grown in pots for their attractive foliage and decorative berries. They grow well in acid, sandy loam with peat or leaf mold and are able to withstand moderate industrial pollution. Propagation is by seed or cuttings.

S. japonica, the most commonly grown species, is a dense shrub to 5 ft. and has pale, yellowish green leaves. In this species, male and female flowers are borne on separate plants, the staminate flowers being very fragrant. They should be planted in a group in order to ensure a crop of the round, scarlet berries, which remain in good condition from September to June.

S. reevesiana is of more dwarf habit with dark green leaves, perfect flowers, and oval, dark red berries freely produced.

SKOKE. A common name for *Phytolacca americana*, a strong-smelling plant with attractive flowers and fruit; see PHYTOLACCA.

SKULLCAP. Common name for SCUTELLARIA, a genus of short perennial herbs with colorful, two-lipped flowers.

SKUNK-CABBAGE. Common name for *Symplocarpus foetidus*, a malodorous herb planted for ornament in bog gardens; see SYMPLOCARPUS. Yellow- and white-skunk-cabbage are species of LYSICHITON, which are similar but not so smelly as the true skunk-cabbage.

SKUNKWEED. Common name for *Polemonium confertum*, a low-growing perennial herb with blue flowers; see POLEMONIUM.

SLAT HOUSE. A structure made of timber framework covered with lath spaced to give broken shade inside; see LATH HOUSE.

SLIP. Another name for CUTTINGS.

SLOE. A common name for *Prunus spinosa*, also known as blackthorn, a shrub or tree grown as an ornamental or for its fruits, which are used for flavoring liqueur; see PRUNUS.

SLUGS. These pests are related to snails, clams, and oysters of the phylum Mollusca (mollusks). Snails and slugs are called "gastropods," meaning "stomach on the foot." The shells of snails are reduced to small disks on the backs of slugs. Both leave a slimy trail where they have moved themselves along by means of a secreted slime. Two slugs are common: the gray field slug and the giant or spotted slug.

Slugs work at night destroying young and tender seedlings and newly set transplants. In the day they hide in the earth under clods or under boards or sticks, stones, and debris. Slugs can be gathered and then destroyed by sprinkling salt on them, which dehydrates them and turns their bodies orange.

The well-known trap for slugs is a jar lid or shallow container set at soil surface and filled with beer or a solution of brewer's yeast. The yeast in the beer attracts them, and the alcohol dissolves their slime so they are prevented from leaving the container and drown. Commonly used deterrents for slugs include sprinkling sand, wood ashes, crushed egg shells, and diatomaceous earth in 3–6 in. circles around the plants to be protected. A wormwood drench of the ground or mulches of oak leaves or tobacco stems will also deter slugs. BRAN MASH will attract slugs and then dry and harden on their skins, preventing them from moving. A commercial aromatic pellet called Slug-off will mask the odor of the attracting plant and thus deter the attacking slugs.

Slug

SMARTWEED. Common name for several weedy herbs and vines of the genus POLYGONUM, sometimes used in wild gardens and borders.

SMILACINA (smī lah SEE nah). A genus of perennial woodland herbs belonging to the Liliaceae (Lily Family) and commonly known as false Solomon's-seal or false spikenard. They have creeping rootstocks, leafy stems, and small, whitish flowers in terminal racemes followed by shiny, red or greenish berries. They are easily colonized in the wild garden and are propagated by seed or division.

Smilacina racemosa

S. racemosa, growing to 3 ft., is found all over North America and has plumelike clusters of creamy white flowers and red berries. Var. *amplexicaulis* is a western form.

S. stellata (starflower), growing to 20 in., has few-flowered clusters of starry blossoms and will grow in the shade of evergreens.

SMILAX (SMĪ laks). A genus of widely distributed, mostly woody, tendril-climbing vines belonging to the Liliaceae (Lily Family) and commonly called greenbrier. Some species form bothersome thorny thickets. They are little cultivated, but the foliage of some native species is cut and used for decorative purposes, especially by florists. The common smilax of the florists, however, is *Asparagus asparagoides*; see ASPARAGUS. Most North American native species are found in Zones 6–9.

PRINCIPAL SPECIES

S. glauca (catbrier or sawbrier) is partially evergreen with oval leaves and sometimes covered with a bloom and black berries. It grows in thickets of eastern North America, spreads rapidly by underground runners, and may cause great annoyance in shrubbery plantings in dry ground or around the edge of a garden because of its strong, smooth, almost wiry stems armed with needle-sharp spines. It is a hard pest to eradicate; determined grubbing out of the roots is probably the best method of extermination.

S. herbacea (carrion flower) is a native perennial herb with black fruits, distinguished by the foul odor of its flowers.

S. lanceolata (Florida smilax, Jackson-brier), native in the southern states, is a high-climbing evergreen with large, fleshy tubers. Its leafy stems are often used in floral arrangements.

S. rotundifolia (horsebrier) is a woody, climbing vine with thorny stems; rounded, glossy leaves; and blue or black fruit. Native from eastern Canada to Texas, it spreads rapidly by underground stems and is often a pernicious weed.

S. walteri, found in swamps in sandy regions, bears coral-red berries and is useful in winter decorations.

SMITHIANTHA (smith ee ANTH ah). A genus of tropical American herbs belonging to the Gesneriaceae (Gesneria Family), formerly listed as *Naegelia*, and commonly known as temple-bells. There are some extraordinarily beautiful species that grow about 20 in. tall and have soft, heart-shaped leaves and brilliant, tubular flowers 1½ in. long in clusters. In cool climates, plants are raised in a warm greenhouse from rootstocks started in boxes and lightly covered with soil. They are potted up in 5–6 in. pots filled with rich, porous soil with plenty of drainage material at the bottom. After blooming, the rhizomes should be stored under greenhouse benches and given water occasionally. Propagation is by runners or offsets.

S. cinnabarina has leaves covered with red or purple hairs and drooping, cinnabar-red flowers spotted with white.

S. zebrina has soft-hairy leaves veined with purple-red and spotted red-and-yellow flowers.

SMOKETREE. Common name for COTINUS, a small genus of trees or shrubs with feathery foliage, belonging to the Anacardiaceae (Cashew Family).

SMUT FUNGI. A group of disease-causing organisms so named because of the sooty-black, ripe spore masses that usually break up into a fine, dustlike powder. Smuts attack many cultivated hosts as well as wild plants. The corn and onion smuts are probably most familiar to the gardener, but those affecting wheat, oats, barley, rye, rice, and sorghum are of great economic importance. The parts most frequently destroyed are either the kernels (seeds) or the entire flower cluster. The fungi can live and grow only on their hosts, but the spiny, heavy-walled, dark spores serve as resting bodies and are able to live in refuse for a long time and then infect the plants with which they come in contact.

In corn smut, infection results in large, boil-like overgrowths on ears and sometimes on tassels. In the loose smuts of cereal grains, the young kernels are reduced to a smutty mass consisting of disintegrated flower parts, mycelium, and spores. There is also a "stinking smut" of wheat, so called because of its foul odor. Onion smut causes dark pustules on the seedlings.

Corn smut is controlled by the removal and burning of the smut boils before the masses break. Cereal smuts are prevented or controlled by the use of clean seed, by crop rotation, and by seed disinfection.

SNAIL FLOWER. Common name for *Vigna caracalla*, a perennial, twining vine related to the kidney bean; see VIGNA.

SNAILS. There are many kinds of snails, belonging to the phylum Mollusca, mostly harmless in the garden. In California, however, where French snails were introduced as a food crop (escargot), they have become a common pest. Since snails work at night, a good way to track them down is to find where they hide during the day—usually in low, shady branches or under woodpiles, boards, and garden debris. The trail of slime that snails and slugs leave when they move along the ground will help the gardener to locate their patterns of movement. Scratchy and irritating substances put in their paths (such as lime, dry sand, wood ashes, or diatomaceous earth) will help deter these pests, which are often found in the shade of the north side of buildings.

When gathering snails to get rid of them, have a pail of salty water or water and kerosene ready to drop them in. Both are lethal. Also be vigilant in early summer to find and destroy eggs. They can often be found in dark places between leaves, such as the leaves of a head of lettuce, though snails do not eat lettuce. They do not eat tomato leaves either but do attack and eat large holes in the fruit. Scratchy deterrents at the edge of gardens and floating row covers can often help in the control of these pests. Their natural predators include salamanders, snakes, and turtles.

SNAKE GOURD. Common name for *Trichosanthes anguina*, an annual vine with curious, serpent-shaped fruits; see TRICHOSANTHES.

SNAKEHEAD. A common name for *Chelone glabra*, a moisture-loving perennial with whitish or pinkish flowers.

SNAKE-LILY. Common name for *Dichelostemma volubile*, a pink-flowering member of the Amaryllidaceae (Amaryllis Family); see DICHELOSTEMMA.

SNAKEROOT. Common name for *Cimicifuga racemosa*, a moisture-loving wildflower with malodorous blossoms; see CIMICIFUGA.

SNAKES. With snakes as with other animals, the gardener must make a choice. It is the prevailing prejudice against reptiles that makes the consideration of snakes in gardens particularly difficult. Notwithstanding the aversion of many people to all kinds of snakes, and the well-warranted fear of the poisonous kinds, snakes as ordinarily found in gardens merit entirely different consideration.

Among the many species found in the United States, only four are poisonous. Most snakes are harmless to humans and desire merely to be left alone. Many of them are powerful aids in the control of insects, field mice, and many other creatures that are definitely injurious to plant life. If one's dislike of snakes is so intense as to make them objectionable, one may choose to get rid of them. Before doing this and depriving the home and garden of some beneficial predators, however, the development of a little familiarity might breed not contempt, but tolerance and perhaps even respect and liking. Various field guides and other references can provide useful information.

POISONOUS SNAKES

Of the four that are truly dangerous, the rattlesnake is easily recognized by its characteristic warning sound. In color it varies according to region; generally it is yellowish or brown with cross bands and markings of darker brown or black. The sides are lighter in color and the body darkens toward the tail. The head is of the diamond shape common to many species of poisonous snakes.

The copperhead, dangerous because of its habit of striking without warning and often apparently without due provocation, is found from the northeastern states to Wisconsin and southward, usually in rather damp places. It sometimes strays into gardens, yards, or even into outbuildings. Of a distinct reddish coloring, it has hazel-brown saddle markings

Copperhead snake

and copper-yellow shading along the sides and head. Many studies have shown it to be extremely useful in the destruction of insect and animal pests, but its ready use of a dangerous weapon necessarily calls for its removal from human proximity.

The other two poisonous North American snakes occur only in the far South and are not likely to get in the gardener's way. The water moccasin or cottonmouth, related to the rattler and the copperhead, does not often stray from the deep swamps. The tiny coral snake might be encountered by a Florida gardener, but its bright colors and the warnings of local experts should make its recognition easy.

BENEFICIAL SNAKES

The harmless garter snake, found throughout the United States in various forms, is the one most commonly found in gardens. It is usually harmless and scarcely able to break the skin with a bite, although when cornered it manages to put up a good fight. Its food is composed largely of insects and small animals such as mice, frogs, toads, etc.

The two snakes whose presence causes the least consternation are the green snake and the grass snake. Both are strictly insect and insect larvae eaters and are harmless to humans or other animals. Unfortunately they are the prey of many of the smaller carnivorous animals and flesh-eating birds.

Probably the most maligned of all the snakes beneficial to the gardener and farmer is the milk snake. Despite the old superstition that it hangs around barns and houses in order to steal milk, it has no interest in milk whatsoever. It preys on rats, mice, gophers, and other rodents that infest the buildings and vicinity. Although its reddish coloring and black markings frequently lead this snake into being mistaken for the copperhead, the milk snake really belongs to the same

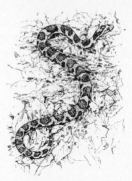

Milk snake

family as the king snake, a redoubtable killer of rattlers and copperheads. In all probability, milk snakes also account for more than a few dead young rattlers. They are not poisonous but can give nasty bites.

Among the other snakes found in close proximity to humans and their activities, the black, pilot black, hog-nosed, pine, and corn snakes all have good and bad points, depending entirely on the perspective. A snake with no redeeming value in the garden is the common water snake. In any of its many varieties it is not poisonous, but it can give a vicious bite—and does so on the slightest provocation. Squat and ugly in appearance, it preys almost entirely on the life of ponds and streams. Frogs and the young of any water fowl are common victims.

SNAKE'S-HEAD. Common name for *Fritillaria meleagris*, a hardy, bulbous herb whose flowers have checkered markings; see FRITILLARIA.

SNAPDRAGON. Common name for ANTIRRHINUM, a genus of annual or perennial herbs with racemes of colorful flowers.

SNEEZEWEED. Common name for HELENIUM, a genus of annual or perennial herbs with yellow or bronze flowers.

SNEEZEWORT. Common name for *Achillea ptarmica*, a perennial herb with small, white flowers; see ACHILLEA.

SNOUT BEETLE. In this group of beetles (Curculionidae), the head is prolonged forward and downward, forming a cylindrical snout that may range in length from a short beak to one much longer than the entire rest of the body. The snout enables the beetle to eat soft, underlying plant tissues. With the mouthparts at the end of the long snout, the insect makes a hole deep into the tissues of plants and fruit to lay its eggs there. Later the larvae, footless grubs inside the fruit, eat the flesh away.

Many species of snout beetles are very destructive, especially on beans, roses, and fruit crops. The plum curculio also attacks apples and many stone fruits; the well-known cherry "worm" is the grub of this snout beetle. The cotton boll weevil is probably the most destructive southern member of this group. The imbricated snout beetle, dull silvery white with brown markings, gnaws holes in many kinds of garden vegetables and fruits and also in the bark of trees and shrubs. Minor infestations can be controlled by hand-picking.

See also CURCULIO; WEEVIL; BEETLES.

SNOWBALL. Common name for several kinds of VIBURNUM, a genus of deciduous shrubs and trees, particularly the forms with showy, white flowers.

SNOWBERRY. Common name for SYMPHORICARPOS, a genus of hardy, deciduous, berry-producing shrubs; especially *S. albus*.

SNOWDROP. Common name for the genus GALANTHUS, early spring-blooming, hardy, bulbous herbs with drooping, white flowers.

SNOWFLAKE. Common name for the genus LEUCOJUM, small, hardy, bulbous herbs with white flowers. Water-snowflake is *Nymphoides indica*; see NYMPHOIDES.

SNOW-IN-SUMMER. Common name for *Cerastium tomentosum*, a creeping perennial herb that produces abundant white flowers; see CERASTIUM.

SNOWMOLD. A lawn or turf disease most severe in the northern United States. White patches, due to the cottony growth of the fungus *Fusarium nivale*, appear on the grass just as the snow is melting in early spring. Often there is a fluffy white growth of the mycelium. The disease can be controlled by avoiding late-fall fertilizing in wet areas. Any treatment of the soil that tends toward rapid drying of the turf in spring will also help prevent snowmold.

SNOW-ON-THE-MOUNTAIN. Common name for *Euphorbia marginata*, a flower garden favorite, with white bracts and the upper leaves margined white; see EUPHORBIA. The name also refers to *Aegopodium podagraria* var. *variegatum*, a somewhat weedy perennial occasionally used in edge plantings; see AEGOPODIUM.

SOAPBERRY. Common name for SAPINDUS, a genus of tropical trees whose fruit contains a soaplike substance.

SOAP SPRAYS. A type of contact insecticide; see SPRAYING.

SOAPWORT. Common name for SAPONARIA, a genus of hardy herbs with white, pink, or red flowers.

SOD. The surface layer of a lawn or other stretch of closely mown grass; also a small section cut out of such an area to be used elsewhere. Thus used, the word corresponds to "turf," as used in English gardening. Sodding (the operation of placing sods to cover an area of bare ground), while more expensive than raising grass from seed, is a convenient and valuable method of securing a good turf almost immediately; also in places where seed cannot be sown, or where the soil is likely to wash, as on terrace slopes, along narrow borders, etc. Even in developing a larger stretch of lawn than could economically be sodded, sods can often be used to advantage to outline the area or perhaps cut it up into squares. The soil within the strips is then brought to the exact level of the grass ready for seeding.

SOD CUTTING

Sods can be cut from out-of-the-way corners of a large lawn for use in more important places, or from good, dense sod. Sod growers sow sod as a crop, replacing a plot with rich topsoil and reseeding it as soon as it has been stripped of its turf. Commercial sod growers use mechanical sod harvesters and pile the strips on pallets for shipping. Sods are usually cut 1 ft. wide and of uniform thickness (usually 2 or 3 in.), depending on the depth of the root growth. The size can also vary with each sod grower. The strips should be cut with a regular half-moon edger kept very sharp and worked along the edge or edges of a heavy plank. Each strip is cut free by sliding the edger, a sharp spade, or a special sod-cutting tool

Skimming sod

under it at a uniform depth. The strips are then cut in 1–3 ft. lengths, depending on the denseness and strength of the turf. To handle well, sod should be neither dry nor wet; the important thing is to have a good, loamy soil that will not shake loose from the roots at the slightest movement. Good sod cannot be cut from sandy soil.

It is best, of course, to reset sod without delay. Allowing it to sit without placing it will cause it to decline.

LAYING SOD

Before laying sod, prepare the soil as in making a lawn, rake it smooth, and when loose and uncompacted, leave it just about as high as the desired finished level. Lay the sods carefully, first along the margin of the area, then side by side toward the center. Fit the edges close together, adding or removing a little sod beneath as may be necessary to produce a level surface. When an area a few sods wide is laid, it is best to go over the entire sodded area with a lawn roller. Then soak it thoroughly. Irrigate daily to keep the sod-soil interface constantly moist. Thereafter treat the area like a regular lawn or grass border. See also LAWN for how to sod on a slope.

SOIL. This is the surface layer of the earth that supports plant life. It is the composite result of disintegration and decomposition of diverse kinds of rocks; the effects of climatic and other physical conditions; the activities during the lives and of animals and plants that exist on or in the ground; and the decay after their deaths. As these conditions vary, so do the composition, character, color, and depth of the soil.

SOIL CHARACTERISTICS

Soils that form and remain where the "bed rocks" are located have characteristics typical of the rocks from which they are developed. Soils that form mainly from the decomposition of vegetable matter in swamps must be thoroughly drained before they can be used for cultivated plants. They are generally too acid for most vegetables and flowering plants, and so must be dressed liberally with lime and made neutral or somewhat alkaline before being used.

Soils that are or were carried by water, wind, glacier, or other agency naturally differ considerably from the types just described.

MINERAL COMPOSITION

Of the four main contributing factors, the composition of the fundamental inherited minerals is generally the most influential in determining the type of a soil. When limestone rock disintegrates, it forms clay soil with an alkaline reaction. Such soils are often so fine grained that the particles run together and thus make drainage, plowing, digging, and cultivation difficult. Upon being improved and lightened, however, they become retentive of moisture and plant nutrients, and as a rule constitute a class of highly desirable soils for tree, bush, and vine fruits. Also, when properly managed they are among the most productive for grains and vegetables.

On the other hand, when granites or sandstone disintegrate, they form sandy soils that, unless carefully treated, allow too rapid a passage of water and with it the loss of dissolved plant nutrients. Soils formed from sandstone rocks contain little or no alkali and, in fact, are usually more or less acid. Hence, they are especially adapted to such plants as rhododendrons, azaleas, blueberries, and other acid-soil types. See ACID SOIL.

TEXTURE

Soils vary not only according to their basic mineral (rock) composition, but also according to the size of the particles (fine or coarse) and the proportion of decaying animal and vegetable matter or HUMUS. Humus varies widely in amount in different soils and different times. A peat or muck soil may be nearly all humus, a sand may contain practically none, and a loam may have just the right amount for average garden requirements. Humus is, however, restricted to the upper level of cultivated soil, or in nature to the zone in which plant roots live and die. The underlying soil is usually devoid of it. Since humus is constantly breaking down into simpler substances, cultivation tends to hasten this change, as does the heat of southern regions. From the soil specialist's standpoint, there are three main sizes of mineral particles: sand, 2 to $\frac{1}{20}$ mm; silt, $\frac{1}{20}$ to $\frac{1}{200}$ mm; and clay, less than $\frac{1}{200}$ mm. Based on that classification, soils are defined in this way: sands contain less than $\frac{1}{5}$ silt and clay; sandy loams have $\frac{1}{5}$ to $\frac{1}{2}$ silt and clay but not more than 20% clay; silt loams are more than 50% silt and clay with less than $\frac{1}{5}$ clay and more than $\frac{1}{2}$ silt; clay loams are more than $\frac{1}{2}$ clay and silt with less than $\frac{1}{2}$ silt and 20–30% clay; clays are more than 50% silt and clay combined and more than 30% clay. Two other types of soil in which organic matter dominate physical properties are peat, with 65% or more of organic matter; and muck, with 25–65% well-decomposed organic matter mixed with much clay, silt, or sand.

STRUCTURE

The particles of minerals and humus are usually naturally formed into larger aggregates that may be of a variety of sizes and shapes. The extent of development of aggregates and the degree of a soil's compactness greatly influence the quality of soil. The structure of a soil as it relates to the growth of plants is called tilth. A soil has good structure or tilth if it is easily worked and prepared for a seedbed or transplants, stores plentiful amounts of water yet drains excess water easily, and allows for good root development.

DEPTH

Soil depth varies greatly. A soil may be a mere film formed upon rocks partly by the decay of lichens, algae, and other lowly plants, and partly by the destruction of the rocks by these plants and by frost action. Or soil may be several feet deep as in river valleys; near the Mississippi, for instance, nature has laid down rich deposits.

From the gardener's viewpoint, soils are divided into two parts. Topsoil, the upper surface or soil proper, is a generally dark layer, richer in plant nutrients and especially in humus than the underlying layer or subsoil. Although most cultivated plants distribute their roots mainly if not altogether in the surface layer, many crops and trees may penetrate the subsoil to an astonishing depth.

FERTILITY

The capacity of soils to produce plants differs widely and can be judged with a fair degree of accuracy by mere observation. Even without the knowledge that certain species of plants are associated with specific soil types or conditions, it is possible for a person without a knowledge of botany to roughly determine the general character of a given soil area.

Where the natural vegetation is luxuriant, the soil quality is almost sure to be good. Where growth is sparse and scrawny, the opposite is usually true, although the cause may be abuse of a formerly good soil by humans. Such superficial methods of judging soils can be very helpful when several places are being considered in the search for a prospective home, or when one is trying to find the best site on a piece of property for a vegetable garden or special landscape feature.

No matter how poor a soil is, it can almost always be improved, although in some cases the cost would be so high or the time required so long that it would be more economical to replace barren earth with imported topsoil.

If a soil is wet, "cold," and late, drainage will dry, aerate, and warm it. If it is heavy and sticky, it will be helped by the addition of sand and especially humus in the form of manure, green manures, compost, or cover crops plus late-autumn plowing or digging and early-spring top-dressing with lime or wood ashes. These operations will tend to lighten it and make it more retentive of moisture, warmer, and easier to work. If it is excessively sandy, additions of humus reinforced with lime will give it more body. If it is lacking in plant nutrients, these can be added in many forms. See FERTILIZER; MANURE; PLANT FOODS AND FEEDING.

SOIL MANAGEMENT

In the great majority of cases, the gardener must make the best of the soil conditions at hand. The first step is ensuring adequate DRAINAGE, so plants receive adequate moisture but do not stand in water. Next comes the removal of superficial, undesirable materials upon or in the surface layer—such things as stumps, roots, stones, boulders, and other objects, including leftover building materials and rubbish.

TILLAGE

Cultivation, the next step, is the treatment of the earth itself. As a general rule, only a few inches (approximately 4–7 in.) are plowed or dug. In gardens, soils are sometimes deepened and greatly improved by DOUBLE DIGGING or TRENCHING. These practices, together with the subsequent harrowing and raking are done not only to bury sod and trash, and to mix manures and fertilizers with the topsoil, but also to loosen the soil mass so that plant roots can penetrate it and various helpful microorganisms (bacteria) find it a suitable medium in which to perform their functions. These practices also increase the porosity or capacity of the ground to absorb and retain water and increase the aeration, or ability of the soil to admit air, which is as necessary to root development and activity as are water and plant nutrients.

One cause of poor soil is lumpiness, which may result from working the soil when it is too wet. More often, however, it is due to plowing or digging when too dry. To prevent the condition, therefore, study the soil type and choose a time for plowing or digging when the soil is just moist enough to turn and crumble nicely, and before it tends to turn up in the form of dry clods. It is important that the newly plowed furrows or freshly dug soil be harrowed or raked into uniform friability with the least possible delay, to conserve as much moisture as possible in the soil. In a small garden, bed, or border, raking should be done as soon as a few square yards have been dug with the spading fork, which should be used to break each clod as it is turned.

Just when to dig or plow can be determined by considering several factors. If the soil surface glistens with moisture, it is too wet. Dig up random chunks of soil in the area to be worked and examine the surface for excess moisture. Squeeze a handful, if it holds its shape fairly well when the hand is opened, with only a few cracks showing, it is in good condition. If it leaves mud on the hand, it is too wet, and if it falls apart readily and is more or less dusty, it is too dry.

TROUBLESHOOTING

Poor soils may result from excessive cultivation without restoring vital conditions, natural poor texture and shortage of nutrients, or working the soil when too wet or too dry.

Maintaining Humus. Soils are often made poor by depleting their supply of HUMUS through mismanagement or the failure to add organic material such as manure. With the cost and difficulty of obtaining manure outside rural areas, gardeners have been too prone to rely on chemical fertilizers for needed plant food and to neglect to provide any other kind of humus. Actually it is comparatively easy to do this in several inexpensive ways. First, all fallen leaves, cut and pulled weeds, lawn clippings, trimmings, stems of plants, vegetable waste from the kitchen, and similar organic materials should be used. Either bury them directly in part of the garden alloted to the purpose for a season, or let it rot in a compost pile. Leaves and lawn clippings can also be used as a mulch and then worked into the soil. Second, grow a catch crop, cover crop, or GREEN MANURE and dig or plow under while still green and soft to supply the necessary succulent vegetable matter. Such materials, upon decaying, become humus.

Remember that losses of humus are due partly to chemical burning. Gaseous products of oxidation are constantly being given off from decomposing humus, and unless they are reabsorbed by the soil, they are usually lost into the air. Also, the activities of microscopic forms of life in the soil help to break down the complicated organic materials into simpler compounds that are taken up by plants, leached away, or released into the air until nothing is left in the soil except the mineral constituents.

The loss of humus generally occurs most rapidly in sandy soils because of their more open structure, better drainage, and therefore higher temperature.

Puddling. When soil (especially clay and loess) is mismanaged by being tilled while too wet, the soil mass becomes dense and plant roots find it difficult to penetrate. The finer particles become wedged between the coarser ones, and moisture and air are driven out. The soil soon becomes hard and difficult to plow or dig. When it is turned up, it forms clods that, on drying, bake to almost bricklike hardness.

Hardpan. Another undesirable condition in a soil is the existence of hardpan, a layer of impermeable soil just below the topsoil. It may be a natural condition, or it may have been induced by plowing the soil when too wet, or repeatedly at the same depth until a sort of floor is formed. A hardpan prevents the downward passage of water after a rain and also the normal upward passage of water from lower levels to the surface layer.

This makes the surface soil cold in spring, as a result of the chilling effect of evaporation of the excess water retained above the hardpan, and later, dry in summer, because after the excess surface moisture has evaporated, too little comes up from below to replace it.

A hardpan should therefore be broken up. On a small scale, this can be done by using a pickax in the bottoms of the furrows, or by double digging. On a larger scale, it can be done by following the ordinary plow with a deep-tilling chisel subsoil plow that penetrates several inches below the bottom of the furrow and lifts, breaks, and loosens but does not invert the hard layer. Moderate explosives are sometimes used to accomplish the same object.

Lacking Nutrients. Soils commonly become unproductive due to a lack of nutritive substances. When it is understood that the soil is a complicated chemical arena in which myriad microscopic creatures play important roles, it is easy to understand that mismanagement and neglect will quickly impair, if not destroy, the very purpose for which gardeners use the soil.

Available plant nutrients are reduced in a soil by continuous cropping and by losses of soluble materials in the drainage water. These and similar losses can be replaced through the addition of compost, manures, and fertilizers or growing green manures and cover crops. Soils become less productive as they become too acid for certain plants or too alkaline for others. The accumulation of alkali salt at or near the surface may create soil solutions too strong for plants to thrive. Such conditions can usually be corrected in humid climates by drenching the soil surface to dilute and wash the undesirable materials to levels below reach of the plant roots.

Materials actually poisonous to plants are sometimes developed in soil as the result of life processes of certain plants or animals. Some of these may be poisonous to other plants. Their presence is not characteristic of any particular kind of soil condition, because the interminable natural changes in soil effect constant variation in the amounts of the poisonous substances.

Toxic conditions may be caused by several elements, including (1) poor drainage and ineffective ventilation or aeration of the soil, which may be remedied by several methods; (2) deficiency of lime; (3) continuous cropping with the same or related plants, which drain specific nutrients, correctable by crop rotation; (4) undesirable or unbalanced minerals in the soil, such as aluminum, manganese, and silica compounds, which may be a result of insufficient lime; (5) the presence of unfavorable or absence of favorable microscopic organisms, especially bacteria; (6) the presence of harmful pollutants in the soil.

SOIL AMENDMENT.

This is any material added to a soil to act as an indirect fertilizer, favorably influencing plant growth through its effect on the soil structure or quality rather than by actually adding plant food, as a fertilizer does. It might also be called a soil conditioner.

Beneficial effects of soil amendments include (1) the conversion of unavailable plant food; (2) the improvement of the physical condition of the soil; (3) the neutralizing of an acid condition of the soil; (4) the making of neutral or alkaline soils more acid and thus more favorable for certain plants, such as rhododendrons and blueberries.

Lime in various forms, muck, peat moss, salt, sulfate of iron, soot, coal ashes, and aluminum sulfate are all soil amendments. See also SOIL.

SOILLESS CULTURE.

This term is loosely applied to growing plants in nutrient solutions, no matter what the method. It can correctly be applied to growing in water cultures. When sand or cinders are used for support, it is difficult to draw the line where soilless culture leaves off and soil culture begins. Soil, as generally defined, is made up of sand, silt, clay, and humus. Actually the only difference between soilless culture and culture in the soil is the technique of handling the nutrient solution. See also CHEMICAL GARDENING; HYDROPONICS; NUTRIENT SOLUTION.

SOIL PASTEURIZATION.

Pasteurization implies partial sterilization of soil with heat. Soil for flats, seed pots, and greenhouses sometimes needs to be pasteurized to get rid of damping-off organisms and other infections of the soil. Pasteurization differs from complete sterilization in that a lower temperature is required. One method is to put the soil three or four inches deep in a big pan, moisten it well, and insert a meat thermometer. Bake it at a low heat in the oven until it reaches 140–145°F, the temperature just hot enough to kill pathogens. It can be used as soon as it is cool.

If beneficial organisms are destroyed, the quality of the soil is injured, so do not let the temperature go higher than 145°F. Complete sterilization usually occurs at 180–185°F. Compost or other organic fertilizers added to the mixture can restore beneficial microorganisms. Boiling water poured over a flat will also effect sterilization. Cover the flat with aluminum foil and stick a thermometer through it. The moist mix is kept at the required temperature for 30 minutes and then is cooled before use. See also DISINFECTION.

SOIL TESTING.

A number of factors may influence soil fertility without being readily apparent. If plants fail to grow in soil that should have been ideal, chemical tests can determine the presence or absence of significant elements. Although detailed analysis of the soil is not usually practicable for the ordinary gardener, samples can be sent to the nearest testing facility.

Conditions as to acidity or alkalinity are constantly changing, and they can be easily tested by anyone. Not only can acidity be increased or decreased by the fertilizers used and the plants grown, but it can also be much greater in one part of the garden than in another. When to use lime or where to put an acid-soil plant are common gardening questions.

Tests should be made before planting definitely acid- or alkaline-loving plants; also whenever such plants show signs of lowered vitality. If the pH reading of the soil samples taken from near their roots has shifted toward neutral since the last test, corrective additions of lime, aluminum sulfate, or oak leaves can be added to the soil immediately, according to whether less or more acidity is needed.

With the simplest, inexpensive soil-testing sets sold in seed stores, a sample of dry soil is saturated with liquid and allowed to stand for a minute, then the liquid is run off and examined. A pH reading (measure of acidity) is based on matching the liquid with a color chart furnished with the set. A reading of seven is neutral; higher than seven, alkaline; and lower than that, acid.

Some soil-testing kits also allow the gardener to determine the need for plant nutrients; where results are critical, however, it is usually better to send samples to a laboratory for analysis.

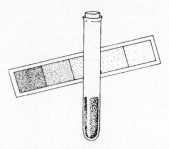

Simple soil-testing kit

In preparing soil samples, care should be taken to get a typical representative sample by collecting small quantities from at least half a dozen places in the area in question, mixing them thoroughly in a very clean container, and testing or sending about a pound of the mixture. A good way to collect the soil is to make borings with a soil auger or large carpenter's auger (not one that is needed for delicate woodwork) to the full depth of the cultivated layer of the plot. A small trowel or spade can be used, the point being to mix all such samples before sending them.

In submitting such a soil sample to a laboratory, it is helpful to describe the piece of land, tell how it has been handled, what has been grown, and any nearby environmental factors that may have some effect on the neighborhood (especially industrial or other agricultural activity). With this information, the report can include recommendations as to any treatment needed, such as liming or fertilizing, to make the soil suitable for the desired crop or planting.

See also ACID SOIL; ALKALINE SOIL.

SOLANACEAE (soh lah NAY see ee). The Nightshade Family, a large group of more or less poisonous plants abundant in the warmer regions of the earth. Principal cultivated genera are *Atropa*, *Browallia*, *Brunfelsia*, *Capsicum* (pepper), *Cestrum*, *Cyphomandra*, *Datura*, *Fabiana*, *Hyoscyamus*, *Iochroma*, *Lycium*, *Lycopersicon* (tomato), *Mandragora*, *Nicotiana* (tobacco), *Nierembergia*, *Petunia*, *Physalis*, *Salpichroa*, *Salpiglossis*, *Schizanthus*, *Solandra*, *Solanum* (including the eggplant and potato), and *Streptosolen*.

SOLANDRA (soh LAN drah). A small genus of tall, woody plants or climbing vines native to the tropical Americas, belonging to the Solanaceae (Nightshade Family), and commonly known as chalice vine, named for the shape of its flowers. Usually grown indoors, though sometimes grown outdoors in warm regions, they like plenty of sunlight at all times and a soil that is not too rich, since rampant growth produces few flowers. The growing and flowering season is from fall to spring. While the plants are resting in summer, keep them on the dry side. They object to much root disturbance, but top dressings of new soil will suffice for two years or more. Propagation is by cuttings of half-ripened shoots taken with a heel.

S. grandiflora (trumpet flower), from the West Indies, is the tallest grower, reaching 30 ft. or more. It has thick, leathery leaves and fragrant flowers nearly a foot long, white or yellowish with pale yellow corollas.

S. guttata, from Mexico, growing to 12 ft. or more, has leaves to 6 in. long and fragrant flowers about 9 in. long, yellow with purple spots or feathering on the corollas. *S. maxima* is similar, but the corollas are deep gold with purple lines.

SOLANUM (soh LAY num). A genus of herbs, shrubs, vines, and trees of the Solanaceae (Nightshade Family). Many are of horticultural value. Others are used medicinally or as vegetables, including the POTATO, EGGPLANT, and JERUSALEM-CHERRY. The species have compound or simple leaves and white, blue, yellow, or purple, bell- or wheel-shaped flowers followed by berries, which are often decorative. Most solanums can be raised from seed, others from cuttings or by division.

To produce well-fruited specimens, seed should be sown in February and the young seedlings potted up and later plunged outdoors (pots and all) after danger of frost has passed. Occasional shifts into larger pots during the spring and summer bring flowering-size plants into 5–6 in. pots by September, when they should be brought indoors.

Solanum pseudocapsicum

Indoors they are highly susceptible to damage from gas fumes and drafts, against which they should be carefully protected. After their winter fruiting season is over, the branches can be cut back to within 2–3 in. of the main stem. When the weather grows warm, the plants, still in their pots, are plunged outdoors in a sheltered spot for the summer. The shoots that have been pruned off can be rooted as cuttings to provide new plants.

PRINCIPAL SPECIES

S. capsicastrum (false Jerusalem-cherry, ornamental-pepper) is a small Brazilian plant, resembling the fruit-bearing species, especially *S. pseudocapsicum*, equally attractive for indoor culture. It has scarlet or deep orange, oval or pointed fruits lasting only a short time.

S. dulcamara (bittersweet) is a shrubby, European vine that grows to 8 ft. and bears violet flowers followed by poisonous red berries. Naturalized throughout North America, it makes an attractive climber in the wild garden.

S. giganteum (African-holly), occasionally cultivated in southern California, is a shrubby, Asiatic plant growing to 25 ft. It has prickly leaves and lavender or blue flowers followed by round, red berries.

S. integrifolium (scarlet- or tomato-eggplant), a spiny annual, grows to 3 ft. tall and has clusters of white flowers and scarlet or yellow fruit.

S. jasminoides (potato vine, jessamine nightshade) is a shrubby climber to 10 ft. and has starry, bluish white flowers. It is native to Brazil and is grown under glass in the North and outdoors in the South and California.

S. melongena bears lavender flowers and purple fruit. Var. *esculentum* is the common EGGPLANT in which the fruit is usually purple but may be white, striped, or yellowish. Var. *depressum* is the dwarf eggplant. Var. *serpentinum* (snake or serpent eggplant) has fruits that are 12 in. long, 1 in. thick, and curled at the end.

S. muricatum (melon-pear, pepino) is a spiny, South American, shrubby herb with blue flowers and edible, 6-in., purple fruits with yellow flesh.

S. nigrum (black nightshade, garden-huckleberry) is an annual, weak-stemmed plant that sometimes lies on the ground and sometimes grows erect to 2 ft. It has small, white flowers followed by black berries. The leaves and immature berries are poisonous to humans and livestock, but the ripe berries are edible. Improved forms are offered and sometimes cultivated as wonderberry and sunberry. Often found in the shade, it is inhibited by wormwood and white mustard but is stimulated by clover. Plants can be topped to encourage spreading and used as a living mulch. It grows wild in warm climates, where its presence indicates an overcropped, loamy or gravelly soil, rich in nitrogen with neutral to basic pH and an intermediate moisture level.

S. pseudocapsicum (Jerusalem-cherry) is a small, shrubby plant cultivated for its small, globular, scarlet or yellow, edible fruits. It is an attractive houseplant or outdoor ornamental in warm regions. Since the fruits ripen among the shiny, dark leaves in December, it is also called Christmas berry or Christmas-cherry. Though a dwarf form is generally grown, plants will sometimes attain 4 ft.

S. tuberosum, the "Irish" POTATO, originally native to the Andes, is cultivated as a food plant of worldwide importance.

S. wendlandii is a showy climber grown in greenhouses and outdoors in warm regions. It has lilac-blue flowers 2½ in. across and in California reaches 50 ft. if planted in full sun.

SOLDANELLA (sohl dah NEL ah). A genus of perennial herbs belonging to the Primulaceae (Primrose Family), having nodding, blue, violet, lavender, mauve, or white flowers. Native to the mountains of Europe, these beautiful, little flowers should be grown in moist, shady locations in the rock garden. They are propagated by seed or division and hardy to Zone 4.

PRINCIPAL SPECIES

S. alpina has kidney-shaped leaves. It produces its pale lavender-blue flowers in early spring on stems 3–6 in. high.

S. minima, a charmer, grows to 4 in. and has tiny, rounded leaves and pale bluish purple, tubular flowers with darker markings.

S. montana is the largest (to 15 in.) and showiest of the group. It has clear blue or violet, wide-open flowers in late spring and rounded, leathery leaves 2–3 in. across.

S. pusilla is very similar to *S. minima* but is larger in all dimensions. It grows to 6 in. and has leaves about ½ in. across and blue to purplish, solitary flowers in late spring.

SOLDIER BEETLE. These beneficial beetles resemble fireflies. The larvae are helpful predators. Do not confuse with SPINED SOLDIER BUG, which is not a beetle. See also BEETLES; INSECTS, BENEFICIAL.

SOLEIROLIA (soh le ROHL ee ah) **soleirolii.** A small, creeping, perennial, mosslike herb with rooting stems, native to Corsica and Sardinia, belonging to the Urticaceae (Nettle Family), formerly classified as *Helxine soleirolii*, and known most commonly as baby's-tears, but also called creeping nettle, Paddy's-wig, or Irishman's-wig. Hardy in Zones 10–11, it is used in conservatories, window gardens, and outdoor rock gardens in warm climates, creating a dense mat of bright green. Propagation is done by stem cuttings.

SOLIDAGO (soh li DAY goh). A genus of erect perennial herbs belonging to the Asteraceae (Aster Family) and commonly known as goldenrod. Many minute heads of golden yellow, rarely white flowers make plumelike, showy masses that brighten the countryside in many parts of North America throughout late summer and fall. In a popular survey conducted by a magazine, goldenrod was approved as the national flower of the United States, but it has not been officially recognized. Alabama, Kentucky, and Nebraska have made it their official state flower.

Solidago sp.

Goldenrods are extensively planted in English gardens in combination with the fall asters and Michaelmas daisies. A collection of goldenrods and asters in a natural garden is easily made, since both plants are moved very readily and propagate rapidly. Hardy in Zones 3–9, goldenrods become weedy in rich soil, however, and should therefore be handled with care in cultivation. They bloom the second year from spring-sown seed. Old clumps should be divided in the spring. Since goldenrod, like aster, is host for an orange rust of pine needles during part of its life, plants should be removed from valuable stands of pine trees; see RUSTS.

PRINCIPAL SPECIES

S. altissima, one of the handsomest species, grows 3–6 ft. high and has large, pyramidal panicles of small, golden flowers.

S. bicolor (silverrod) is relatively small and has white flowers crowded on slender spikes.

S. caesia (wreath goldenrod) grows about 2 ft. tall in semishade, producing smooth foliage, sometimes with a bloom, and flowers in leaf axils or in terminal clusters.

S. canadensis, one of the most common species, usually grows 3–4 ft. tall and has large, pyramidal panicles of very small flowers.

S. nemoralis grows to 2 ft. and has grayish, soft-haired leaves and long-lasting flowers in one-sided panicles.

S. odora (sweet goldenrod) grows 1½–4 ft. high and has anise-scented leaves and flower panicles lasting many weeks.

S. speciosa is tall and has nearly smooth leaves and bright yellow flowers in compound panicles.

SOLLYA (SOHL ee ah). A genus of evergreen climbing shrubs native to Australia. They are hardy outdoors in Zones 9–11 and are sometimes grown under glass. *S. heterophylla* (bluebell-creeper), the principal species, grows to 6 ft. high and has slender, twining stems and variable leaves from narrow to oval. The blooming stage is very attractive with brilliant blue flowers borne in loose clusters. In the South it is a popular plant for scrambling over banks, boulders, and low fences. Propagation is by seed and cuttings.

SOLOMON'S-SEAL. Common name for POLYG-ONATUM, a genus of perennial herbs with greenish, pendulous flowers. False Solomon's-seal is SMILACINA, a genus of woodland perennials.

SOOTY MOLD. The leaves of many trees often become coated with a sooty black covering in midsummer. The damage is chiefly to their appearance, unless the coating is so heavy as to shut out sunlight and interfere with the normal leaf processes. The condition is caused by fungi related to powdery mildews but in which the mycelium is dark-colored instead of white. These fungi are not parasitic to the extent of sending feeding rootlets into the leaf tissue but obtain nourishment either from the sugary solutions exuded from the leaves or from insect secretions known as honeydew. Sooty molds, which frequently follow infestations of aphids and the citrus whitefly, can be controlled by destroying the insects with suitable CONTACT POISON.

SOPHORA (soh FOR ah). A genus of deciduous trees belonging to the Fabaceae (Bean Family). Showy when in bloom, they have ornamental value for lawn or garden planting. They have decorative, pinnate foliage and conspicuous, long panicles of fragrant, yellow, white, or violet flowers. Some are evergreen and grow only in the South. They thrive in soils varying from rather dry to moist, well-drained, sandy loam. Propagation is by seed or grafting.

PRINCIPAL SPECIES

S. japonica (Japanese pagoda tree, Chinese scholar tree), growing to 75 ft. or more, is native to China and Korea. The dense, round-headed tree bears yellowish flowers in panicles 15 in. long. It is particularly desirable in the garden because of its late summer flowering, when most woody plants are past bloom. Against a background of evergreens, the long chains of flowers are even more effective. Cv. 'Fastigiata' has an upright growth habit; 'Regent' grows quickly and has an oval crown, glossy leaves, and flowers when only about six years old; 'Pendula' is a weeping form. Hardy in Zones 5–8.

S. secundiflora (mescal bean) is an evergreen shrub or tree growing to 40 ft. It has fragrant, 1-in.-long, violet-blue, pealike flowers in early spring. Native to the southwestern states, it is hardy only to Zone 8.

S. tetraptera and *S. microphylla* are tender evergreens that grow to 40 ft. and have small, yellow leaves and abundant, good-sized, golden yellow blossoms. Hardy to Zone 8.

SOPHRONITIS (sawf roh NĪ tis). An important genus of several colorful, dwarf species of epiphytic orchids native to western Brazil and Paraguay, many from mountainous regions. Each pseudobulb bears one leathery leaf and one to several large, brightly colored flowers on a short inflorescence. Sepals and petals are broad and flat, and the lip is small. Colors are scarlet, orange-red, and violet.

The importance of this genus in producing commercial intergeneric hybrids in the Epidendreae tribe is incalculable. Nearly all of the red or orange *Cattleya* hybrids have *Sophronitis* in the background. All of the genera *Sophrocattleya*, *Sophrolaeliocattleya*, and *Potinara*, and many others, have a heritage from *Sophronitis*.

The plants do well mounted on cork, tree fern, or other slabs. Since they are small plants that retain little moisture, they should be watered frequently and never allowed to become dry; however, they require perfect drainage. Hardy to Zone 9 if protected from frost, their minimum winter temperatures should be 50–55°F. They do well in bright, filtered light. The type species is *S. cernua*.

SORBARIA (sor BAIR ee ah). A genus of hardy, deciduous, Asiatic shrubs belonging to the Rosaceae (Rose Family), formerly classed with the true *Spiraea*, and commonly known as false spiraea. They have handsome pinnate leaves and attractive, large plumes of creamy white flowers in summer. Hardy in Zones 3–7, they are not particular as to soil and can stand some shade but thrive and show to best advantage near water. False spiraeas are good for banks but can be a problem in other areas since they sucker profusely and spread quickly. Propagation is by suckers and root or stem cuttings.

S. arborea (tree-spirea) is the tallest and most handsome, growing to 15 ft. or more, but it is hardy only to Zone 5. It has large, drooping panicles of small, pure white flowers in summer.

S. sorbifolia grows to about 10 ft. and spreads freely by suckers. It is one of the earliest shrubs to unfold its leaves in spring and has plumes of creamy white flowers by early summer.

SORBUS (SOR bus). A genus of deciduous trees or shrubs belonging to the Rosaceae (Rose Family) and commonly known as mountain-ash. Native in temperate regions of the Northern Hemisphere, they are cultivated for their ornamental foliage, attractive flowers, and clustered fruits. They are propagated by seed, budding, and grafting.

PRINCIPAL SPECIES
S. alnifolia (Korean mountain-ash), one of the best ornamentals, grows to 50 ft. in oval form. It has simple, dark green leaves, orange-red fruits, and orange fall color. Hardy in Zones 4–7.

S. americana (American mountain-ash, dogberry) grows to 30 ft. and has leaves of eleven to seventeen narrow, saw-toothed leaflets that are greyish on the undersides. It is very showy in the fall with bright red fruits. Its native range is from Newfoundland southward at high elevations to North Carolina. Hardy in Zones 3–7.

S. aria (white beam tree) is a handsome European species that grows to 50 ft. and has orange-red fruits. Its sharply toothed, entire leaves have white undersides. It will tolerate dry and exposed locations. Hardy to Zone 6.

S. aucuparia (European mountain-ash) is a round-headed European tree growing to 50 ft. or more. Its nine to eleven leaflets are shorter and more rounded than those of *S. americana*, but it is equally showy in fruit. There are several forms of this species. Cv. 'Fastigiata' is of narrow, pyramidal habit. Var. *pendula* has long, drooping branches. Cv. 'Xanthocarpa' has orange-yellow fruit. Hardy in Zones 4–6.

S. torminalis (wild service tree) is a widespreading European tree that grows to 80 ft. and bears orange-red fruits. It has attractive, light green leaves with angular lobes, turning bright red in the fall. Hardy in Zones 6–7.

SORGHUM (SOR gum). A genus of tall, European grasses with broad, coarse-textured leaves and some with large, tassel-like seed heads. There are both annual and perennial species, some hardy to Zone 7. It has numerous varieties, some that are useful forage crops and others grown for the grain or other products, including kafir-corn, feterita, durra, and broom-corn. Other important species are *S. halepense* (Johnson, means, or aleppo grass), cultivated as a pasture grass in the South but often escaping as a pernicious weed, and *S. sudanense* (Sudan grass).

SORREL. A common name for RUMEX, a genus of perennial herbs; the name is particularly applied to the low-growing species with edible leaves. Indian- or Jamaican-sorrel is *Hibiscus sabdariffa*; see HIBISCUS. Wood-sorrel is a species of OXALIS.

SORREL TREE. Common name for *Oxydendrum arboreum*, a small deciduous tree that is excellent for specimen planting, with its drooping branches, white flowers, and brilliant fall coloring; see OXYDENDRUM.

SOTOL. Common name for DASYLIRION, a genus of large, treelike desert plants with small, whitish flowers.

SOUR GUM. Common name for *Nyssa sylvatica*, a hardy deciduous tree valued for its fall color and picturesque outline; see NYSSA.

SOURWOOD. Common name for *Oxydendrum arboreum*, a small deciduous tree with drooping branches, white flowers, and brilliant fall coloring; see OXYDENDRUM.

SOUTHERNWOOD. Common name for *Artemisia abrotanum*, a shrubby perennial with yellowish flowers; see ARTEMISIA.

SOWBUG. Common in old or neglected greenhouses, in hotbeds, and wherever there are dampness and rotting wood, this creature is not a true insect but a crustacean, related to the crayfish. Sowbugs have five pairs of walking legs, two pairs of antennae, and unlike insects, they have no trachea and breathe by blood gills. Sometimes called pillbugs, they are flat bodied, oval, light gray or slate colored, up to ½ in. long, and roll up into a small ball resembling a pill when disturbed; in that state they can be quite easily brushed off into a dustpan. They are usually found in damp, warm places at the surface of the ground, under boards or trash, and in other protected places. They injure greenhouse plants by feeding on the roots but are often found in gardens as well. Keep strawberry beds dry, especially by using sand as a mulch. About one year is required for the life cycle, but all stages can be found in a greenhouse at the same time.

Sowbug

SOYBEAN. Common name for *Glycine max*, also called soya or soja bean. It is an erect, annual, leguminous herb from China and Japan that sometimes grows to 6 ft. and has inconspicuous, white or purple flowers and pendent, brownish, hairy pods. An important human food crop and source of various commercial products in the Orient, it is more common in the United States as a forage crop and a valuable warm-weather green manure or COVER CROP throughout the country. See also BEAN.

SPADING. The spade and the spading fork are tools used to dig the soil in preparation for sowing and planting. The chief uses are to bury weeds and manures—both applied dressings and green manure crops; to aerate the soil and increase its porosity and water-absorbing and holding capacity; to bring plant food from lower levels nearer to the surface and thus favor plant development; and to provide a deep, loose, friable seedbed or growing medium.

The common spade has a rather thick, usually flat, steel or wrought-iron blade. The straight (sometimes curved) cutting edge, guided by the wooden handle, is pressed into the ground with a foot placed on its upper end. In general form, the shovel resembles the spade but is usually round in outline, of more concave form, has low, raised sides, and is made of thinner metal; thus, it is adapted more for scooping and throwing sand, gravel, or loose earth than for cutting dense soil.

Both spades and shovels are made in many forms. The four most used in home gardening have long or short handles, either straight or with a D-shaped hand hold. The styles with long, straight handles are less effective than the others, since their shorter curved blades do not penetrate the soil as deeply as do the straight spade blades. Also, their smooth, round handles are harder to manipulate, especially in turning soil over. The short or D-handled spade and digging fork penetrate the soil deeply when their blades or tines are thrust vertically downward and are designed to pry up and turn over lumps or clods of earth. For all soils except dry, sandy ones, the D-handled spading fork is the best digging tool. Where the soil is sandy and loose, the solid blade of the spade is better.

The common (but wrong) way to dig with either fork or spade is to thrust the tool into the ground at an angle. This not only removes or loosens a shallower layer of soil but also demands more stooping than does the correct way. It is much harder and less effective work; it does not bury weeds, grass, manure, and other surface material and yet demands fully as much time and effort as the right way. The resulting shallow stratum of soil does not provide as good a rooting medium and dries out quickly.

The proper technique is to thrust the tines or blade vertically full depth into the soil. With the foot, force the cross piece at the top of the blade down flush with the soil, then pry up the clod, invert it completely in the air, and dump it upside down in the furrow. Finally, slice or crumble it with glancing blows of the tool. Thus, all trash will be buried deeply where it will most readily decay, and the clods will be broken up ready for the rake to make the surface still finer in readiness for seeding and planting. A well-spaded plot is level, clean, and uniform.

In heavy soils, the work can be lightened by making clods only half as wide as in medium and light ones, where the spade is usually thrust 6–10 in. or more from the edge of the undug soil. Always dig to full spade depth, except that shallow soils should not be dug or plowed to full depth the first time. This would bring up too much inert, unaerated subsoil. Deepen a new soil gradually, digging about 1 in. deeper each year and mixing this thin layer of new subsoil with manure or humus and richer surface earth as it is turned up.

Never dig more ground in one day than can be sown or planted that same day, because seeds and plants will start best in freshly turned soil. If a rain should occur before seeding or planting, the surface might become so heavily caked that re-digging might be necessary. This rule is especially important when the ground is very dry, as in midsummer. Seed sown in freshly dug ground

and well firmed can be expected to give a full stand of plants. If the soil dries out, newly planted seed is at a distinct disadvantage.

Another good practice when digging is to use a steel rake as soon as four or five furrows have been dug across the area. The gardener can thus stand on firm, undug ground while raking, and avoid tramping on soft, newly turned soil. Even more important, it will allow the maximum amount of moisture retention in the soil. In any case, always rake immediately after digging; never postpone this work from morning until afternoon.

See PLANTING; RAKING; SEEDS; TRENCHING.

SPADIX. A form of spike composed of a fleshy axis in which the flowers are often deeply imbedded, as in the aroids; the whole is subtended or shielded by a large, arching, and frequently colored bract called the spathe. See INFLORESCENCE.

SPANISH-BROOM. Common name, along with weaver's-broom, for *Spartium junceum*, an ornamental shrub from Europe, belonging to the Fabaceae (Bean Family); see SPARTIUM.

Spanish broom also refers to a true broom belonging to the genus GENISTA and listed as *G. hispanica*. White Spanish broom, *Cytisus multiflorus*, belongs to the other genus commonly identified as broom; see CYTISUS.

SPANISH-LIME. Common name for *Melicoccas bijuga*, a tropical tree grown for its edible fruits; see MELICOCCAS.

SPANISH-MOSS. Common name for *Tillandsia usneoides*, an epiphytic herb that grows on trees in warm climates; see TILLANDSIA.

SPARAXIS (spah RAK sis). A genus of South African, bulblike herbs of the Iridaceae (Iris Family), commonly known as wandflower. The narrow, grasslike leaves and clusters of flowers grow from corms.

Plants are set outdoors in the spring for summer bloom, since they are not hardy in cool climates. After the plants have blossomed, allow the foliage to ripen until the end of July, then lift the corms and store them in a dry place until the following spring. When forced under glass, five or six corms are planted in a 6-in. pot, and the pots are placed in a cool, frost-free pit for several weeks to allow roots to form. They are then brought into a cool greenhouse and kept at a temperature of 55°F until after flowering, when the foliage is allowed to ripen before the bulbs are removed from the pots and stored.

S. *tricolor*, growing to 18 in., is the most common species. It has purplish flowers with yellow throats and dark spots on each segment.

SPARMANNIA (spahr MAN ee ah). A genus of handsome shrubs from South Africa, belonging to the Tiliaceae (Linden Family), and commonly known as African-hemp. Plants have dense foliage and heavy heads of white bloom in early summer, rivaling the viburnums. Under greenhouse culture, they average 6 ft. in height, but outdoors in Zones 10–11 they may attain 20 ft. They require full sunlight and a rich loam soil with peat and sand. Cuttings are propagated under unshaded glass in April.

Of the two species, *S. africana* is the more desirable. Its var. *flore-pleno* (double flowered) is less free flowering. *S. ricinicarpa*, formerly listed as *S. palmata*, is of lower growth with deeply lobed leaves.

SPARTIUM (SPAHR shee um) **junceum.** An upright shrub to 10 ft., belonging to the Fabaceae (Bean Family), and commonly known as Spanish- or weaver's-broom. It has slender, rushlike branches and racemes of large, golden yellow, sweetly scented, pealike flowers. Hardy as far north as Philadelphia, it is much planted in the western states on dry, rocky banks, where it blooms almost all year-round. Propagation is by seed or greenwood cuttings.

SPATHE. A large, hoodlike bract subtending and arching over a spike or other inflorescence, usually in such cases called a SPADIX. The spathe

is frequently colored and somewhat petal-like, as in the calla.

SPATHIPHYLLUM (spath ee FIL um). A genus of herbs belonging to the Araceae (Arum Family) and sometimes known as peace-lily. They have become important plants for interior use, with breeding and selection producing plants that flower at all heights from 1–6 ft. Their flower form is typical of the family, with a fleshy spike of tiny flowers surrounded by a showy modified leaf (spathe). The spathe in this case is creamy white, contrasting well with the long, slender, dark green leaves.

SPATHODEA (spa THOH dee ah). A genus of strikingly handsome tropical trees of the Bignoniaceae (Bignonia Family), with evergreen, pinnate leaves and clustered, bell-shaped, scarlet, yellow, or orange flowers with a leathery calyx. Most species are hardy only in Zones 10–11. *S. campanulata* is occasionally planted in the southern states and is commonly used as a street tree in the tropics. It requires a rich, moist soil and is propagated by seed or cuttings.

SPATTERDOCK. A common name for NUPHAR, a genus of aquatic plants with large, green, floating leaves similar to waterlilies.

SPAWN. Common name for the whitish, fibrous, vegetative part (mycelium) of certain fungi, from which the conspicuous, aboveground, spore-bearing parts, called mushrooms, toadstools, shelf fungi, etc., are developed. Seed catalogs refer to this material prepared in the form of dry bricks of peatlike appearance or in other forms. It is planted in the cultivation of edible mushrooms.

SPEARMINT. Common name for *Mentha spicata*, a perennial used for flavoring; see MENTHA.

SPECIES. A group of plants comprising a subdivision of a genus and including individuals with the capacity to freely interbreed. In a plant name, the first word indicates the genus, and the second is the species. Thus, the familiar white oak is **Quercus alba**, "Quercus" signifying the whole oak genus, and "alba" (Latin for "white"), the group or species, of which any member resembles in essential characteristics all other white oaks more than it does any other kind of oak.

Because of the natural variation of plants, it is almost impossible to separate them into absolute categories; thus, small (though sometimes striking) differences between plants of one species—as in shape, color, or number of leaves—give rise to smaller groups called "varieties." Stable characters that determine grouping into species include such constant features as number, structure, and arrangement of flower parts; these are retained and passed on through generations when members of the same species mate. The mating of members of different species constitutes what is called crossing or hybridizing, the result being a cross or hybrid. Species, therefore, although an arbitrary term used to indicate close relationship, really represents a primary genetic relationship and is regarded as the unit of classification.

See PLANT NAMES AND CLASSIFICATION; FAMILY; GENUS; VARIETY.

SPEEDWELL. Common name for VERONICA, a genus of annual or perennial herbs with blue, purple, or white flowers.

SPHAERALCEA (sfee RAL see ah). A genus of herbs and shrubs cultivated in warm regions (Zones 8–11) and greenhouses for their orange, red, or violet, mallowlike flowers and commonly known as globe-mallow.

S. ambigua (desert-mallow), native to deserts of the south-western United States, is a shrubby perennial that endures freezing

Sphaeralcea ambigua

winter temperatures and hot desert conditions. It grows 1½–3 ft. high and has stems and leaves covered with gray hairs. The maplelike leaves are 1–2½ in. across and has rounded lobes and scalloped edges. Numerous red-orange flowers are borne near the tips of the branches.

SPHAEROPTERIS (sfair AHP tur is). One of several genera collectively known and cultivated as TREE FERNS.

SPHAGNUM. A name given to about 300 species of mosslike plants found in all northern temperate countries, also called bog moss and sometimes, loosely, peat moss. Although occasionally used while alive and green, it is more familiar to gardeners in a processed form, which is largely used in making compost for growing water-loving plants (like pitcher plants), for propagating cuttings, for mulching, and especially for wrapping the roots of roses and other perennials before shipping them. Its value is based on its high absorbency and water-holding capacity, due to its peculiar cell construction and spongelike texture. Even as it decays and loses some of its body, it continues to be useful for mulching and lightening soil, thereby becoming more like real peat moss, which is largely made up of decomposed sphagnum deposits laid down centuries ago. Wild sphagnum bogs are fragile and are protected in some areas. See also PEAT.

SPHINX MOTH. Very large, heavy-bodied moths with long, narrow wings, belonging to the Sphingidae, and also called hawk or hummingbird moths. The larvae, called hornworms, are large, smooth caterpillars, usually green, about 3 in. long when full grown, and with a prominent backward or projecting horn near the tip of the abdomen. Injurious members of this group are the tomato and tobacco hornworms (*Manduca* spp.) and the catalpa sphinx.

SPICEBUSH. Common name for *Lindera benzoin*, a native shrub with small, yellowish, fragrant flowers and scarlet fruits; see LINDERA.

SPIDERFLOWER. Common name, along with spider plant, for *Cleome hasslerana*, a tropical herb with white or purplish flowers, cultivated as an annual; see CLEOME.

SPIDER-LILY. Common name usually applied to the bulbous genus HYMENOCALLIS. In the South, it sometimes refers to species of LYCORIS; golden spider-lily is *L. africana*.

SPIDER MITE. See RED SPIDER MITE; MITES.

SPIDERWORT. Common name for TRADESCANT-IA, a genus of grasslike, purple-flowered perennials. The Spiderwort Family is COMMELINACEAE.

SPIKE. An elongated, spirelike INFLORESCENCE in which the individual flowers are without stalks (sessile) and borne close against the main flower stalk. A head of timothy grass or wheat is an example, as is the willow catkin.

SPIKE HEATH. Common name for *Bruckenthalia spiculifolia*, a flowering evergreen shrub with needlelike leaves; see BRUCKENTHALIA.

SPIKENARD. Common name for *Aralia racemosa*, a North American woodland shrub with aromatic roots; see ARALIA. False spikenard is SMILACINA, a genus of woodland wildflowers similar to Solomon's-seal.

SPINACH. A short-season herb grown and used as greens or salad. Its horticultural forms are grouped as prickly-seeded (*Spinacia oleracea*) and round-seeded (var. *inermis*).

Seed can be sown as soon as the ground can be worked; successional sowings can follow until midspring. Plants from later sowings quickly run to seed, so for summer greens, NEW ZEALAND SPINACH should be substituted. In cool climates, sowings of the true spinach can be made again in August and September for autumn use.

The soil should be well drained and abundantly supplied with humus and quickly available plant food. Because it keeps the leaves freer from sand and lessens the necessity for washing, a peat or muck soil is especially desirable; large commercial crops are grown in muck-bed areas in the northern states. After putting the soil in fine condition, make rows 12 in. apart and sow the seed thinly (one every inch) to reduce the labor of thinning, which is done when the plants get their first true leaves and should leave plants 3–6 in. apart. Cutting can usually start in six to eight weeks, the plants being harvested successively as they become big enough to use until the crop is cleaned up.

Spinach can be carried over winter beneath light straw mulches or in uncovered coldframes. By covering the frames with a sash before the crop is wanted, the plants can be started into growth, making supplies available all winter. For early spring use, seed can be sown during February in hotbeds or coldframes.

Spinach

Enemies. There are several leaf diseases of spinach, but no spraying is advised because of the nature of the crop. Seed treatment with benomyl has been very successful in controlling damping-off.

The most common pest is the spinach aphid, and the best control is probably a rotenone-pyrethrum spray if flushing with water and other controls are unsuccessful; see APHIDS.

SPINACH-BEET. A name sometimes used for SWISS CHARD.

SPINDLETREE. Common name for EUONYMUS, a genus of ornamental shrubs, small trees, and climbers of many forms.

SPINE. A sharp-pointed and rigid growth of indeterminate size, usually arising as a direct outgrowth of the stem or branch, as on the honey locust, or less often on leaf margins, as on the holly. Spines are less woody than thorns.

SPINED SOLDIER BUG. *Podisus* spp., belonging to the stink bug family (Pentatomidae), is a beneficial predator on the Colorado potato beetle. It is broad and flat like other stink bugs, with sharp spines and the pronotum extended. It also preys on the Mexican bean beetles, its larvae feeding on the pests. Before this predator arrives from the insectary to act as a biological control, it is advisable to use a rotenone spray of 5%, but only after dusk when bees and pollinators have gone to their hives for the night. The rotenone should be well diluted in water. Cease the spraying three days before releasing the spined soldier bug larvae. They will remain in the nymphal state for three weeks, after which the adults work for nearly two months more. They can thus benefit the garden for 85 days if the habitat and food supply are suitable. Their action is to harpoon their prey, inject toxin, and bring about paralysis of the victim in about a minute. They also attack moth larvae and sometimes hunt down cabbage loopers and earwigs. These predators have only been on the market since 1988. See INSECTS, BENEFICIAL; STINK BUG.

SPIRAEA (spī REE ah). A large genus of deciduous shrubs native to the temperate regions of the Northern Hemisphere, belonging to the Rosaceae (Rose Family), and commonly known as spirea. The common name "spirea" or "Japanese-spirea" is also applied to ASTILBE, which florists force into bloom for late winter and early spring sale. Blue-spirea is *Caryopteris incana*, see CARYOPTERIS. False spirea is the genus SORBARIA. Rock-spirea is *Holodiscus dumosus*; see HOLODISCUS.

CULTURE

Many of the species, as well as numerous hybrids and cultivars, are hardy in Zones 4–9. They are mostly small or medium-sized, profusely blooming shrubs with white the dominant color. The early-flowering group is all white, but the late-flowering group comprises some with pink or reddish flowers. Early-flowering species should be pruned right after flowering, the pruning consisting of thinning out old wood rather than cutting back. Later bloomers are best cut back fairly hard in spring.

Spireas prefer a sunny location and will grow in any good soil but thrive best in a rich, moist loam. They are propagated by seed and easily from cuttings of green and mature wood.

EARLY-FLOWERING SPECIES

S. x *arguta*, a hybrid between *S. thunbergii* and *S.* x *multiflora*, is very similar to the former but is showier in flower. Hardy in Zones 5–7.

S. cantoniensis is bushy to 4 ft., with dense, showy umbels of flowers in early summer and blue-green leaves held late in the season. Hardy in Zones 7–9. Cv. 'Lanceata', with narrow leaves and double flowers, is even more tender.

S. nipponica, blooming in early summer, is a vigorous shrub that grows to 8 ft. in a rather stiff form. It has dark green leaves, bluish beneath, held late in the fall, and showy umbels of white flowers. Hardy in Zones 4–8.

S. prunifolia (bridalwreath) is hardy in Zones 5–8. Cv. 'Plena' grows to 6 ft. and has upright, slender branches; dark green, shining leaves that turn brilliant orange-scarlet in the fall; and double flowers that last a long time.

S. thunbergii, the earliest species to bloom, is a twiggy shrub to 5 ft. and has slender, arching branches; feathery, bright green leaves that turn orange to scarlet in the fall; and small, pure white flowers. Hardy in Zones 5–8.

S. x *vanhouttei*, a hybrid between *S. cantoniensis* and *S. trilobata*, resembles the latter but is larger and showier. Hardy in Zones 4–8, it is one of the most floriferous and popular of shrubs.

S. veitchii, the latest of the spring-flowering group, grows to 12 ft. and has spreading, arching branches, dark green leaves, and flat clusters of creamy white flowers in early summer. It is a good background plant, hardy in Zones 6–8.

LATE-FLOWERING SPECIES

S. albiflora is a dwarf, compact Japanese shrub with a profusion of white flowers; hardy in Zones 5–7.

S. x *billiardii*, a hybrid between *S. douglasii* and *S. salicifolia*, grows to 6 ft. and bears pink flowers in late summer. Hardy in Zones 4–6.

S. bullata is a dwarf Asiatic shrub with dark green, crinkled leaves and pink flowers, suitable for the rock garden. Hardy in Zones 5–7.

S. x *bumalda* is a hybrid between *S. japonica* and *S. albiflora*, hardy in Zones 4–8, with flowers white to deep pink. Two of the best-known forms are 'Anthony Waterer', a dwarf and compact form with crimson flowers; and 'Froebelii', of taller growth but also with crimson flowers.

S. decumbens is a European species of prostrate growth with white flowers.

S. japonica is a bushy, upright shrub that grows to 6 ft. and has flat clusters of deep crimson flowers. Hardy in Zones 4–8, it is a variable species with several cultivars.

NATIVE NORTH AMERICAN SPECIES

S. alba (meadowsweet) grows to 6 ft. and has white flowers in long, leafy clusters; hardy in Zones 4–7.

S. densiflora, a western native, is a dwarf, bushy shrub with attractive clusters of rose-colored flowers; hardy in Zones 6–7.

S. douglasii, another western species, grows to 8 ft. and is very handsome with rosy pink flowers in long, dense panicles. Hardy in Zones 5–7, it spreads by suckers.

S. tomentosa (hardhack, steeplebush) is a low shrub common in moist places in the eastern states and is showy in late summer with panicles of rosy purple flowers. Hardy in Zones 4–7.

SPIRANTHES (spī RAN theez). A genus of about 300 mostly terrestrial orchids native to the temperate and subtropical zones of the world, commonly known as lady's-tresses. Their roots are fibrous or tuberous, and the leaves at the stem base are usually insignificant. The flowers, which are highly variable in shape, color, and size, are often borne in spiral racemes. The blossoms are usually small, in shades of white to green and rarely in scarlet, orange, or yellow. Plants can be colonized in the wild garden, doing best in an acid, sandy, perfectly drained soil in filtered shade and humid conditions during growth. They need a dry rest after the flowers die back. Most are hardy to Zone 4.

SPITTLE BUG. The family Cercopidae includes small, sucking insects that live on grass and plant stems and surround themselves with a frothy, whitish foam. This foam is often called "frog spittle." It is secreted by the nymphs, which beat the secretion until foamy. The emerging adult is small and dark, like a more robust leaf hopper with small antennae between the eyes. Spittle bugs fly little, just hopping away if disturbed. They lay eggs in the stems or in angles of the axils. They overwinter in the egg stage. These

Spittle bug

insects are relatively harmless unless there is a large rise in numbers, when they can be injurious, especially to legume crops. Sprays do not penetrate the foam, but rotenone dust has been somewhat successful as a control. The little green nymph can be pinched out of the spittle by hand. See INSECT CONTROL.

SPLEENWORT. Common name for ASPLENIUM, a genus of ferns with tufted growth and wiry stipes. Lobed spleenwort is *Asplenosorus* x *pinnatifidus*, a hybrid between *Asplenium* and *Camptosorus*; see ASPLENOSORUS. Silvery-spleenwort is *Athyrium thelypteroides*, a large and graceful deciduous fern; see ATHYRIUM.

SPOONFLOWER. Common name for the leaves of *Dasylirion wheeleri*, often used in flower arrangements; see DASYLIRION.

SPORE. A body of microscopic size that serves to disseminate and reproduce fungi, ferns, and club-mosses, corresponding to a seed in the higher plants. Spores are of two types: those formed as a result of the union of two elements that represent male and female, and termed "sexual" or "perfect" spores; and those formed directly from hyphae (fungus threads) without the intervention of a breeding act, and called "asexual" or "imperfect" spores. See FERNS; FUNGUS; SEEDS.

SPORT. Name given to an abrupt deviation from type; in scientific language, a mutation. The term usually refers to a bud sport (somatic mutation) such as the sudden, unexplainable occurrence of a branch bearing pink roses on a bush normally having only red flowers. This usually implies a genetic or hereditary change within the affected plant cells, so that the new character becomes fixed; that is, self-perpetuating and heritable. Many popular kinds of roses, carnations, apples, and other valuable plants called clonal varieties by scientists have risen as bud sports. See CLONE, PLANT BREEDING; for contrast, HYBRID.

SPOTTING-OFF. A synonym for PRICKING-OUT, transplanting seedlings from the seedbed to another container.

SPRAYING. There are two basic methods of applying insecticides and fungicides to plants—spraying and dusting; see DUSTING for discussion of advantages and disadvantages of each. Spraying is the application of agents such as suspensions, emulsions, or solutions of insecticides or fungicides under pressure through nozzles that distribute the liquid in very fine droplets over the surface to be treated.

Most spray materials are available in two forms. Wettable powders go into suspension when mixed with water. Emulsifiable concentrates, solutions of agents in an organic solvent that, in turn, is made to disperse in water as an emulsion. A few come in the form of water miscible solutions. Wettable powders must be kept in suspension while spraying by shaking or an agitator in the sprayer. They are generally safer on foliage than emulsifiable concentrates but leave more conspicuous residue. Emulsifiable concentrates generally do not require agitation once they are dispersed in the water and may be slightly more effective on insects. Most fungi-

cides are purchased in wettable form. Many pests can be controlled with less dangerous home mixtures and alternative control methods that are gaining in popularity.

The choice of the spray material depends on accurate identification and knowledge of the habits of the targeted plant enemy as well as knowledge of how the agent works. The modern organic insecticides, with a few exceptions, are specific for certain pests or groups of pests and are not necessarily limited by the insect's method of feeding on plants.

In controlling plant diseases, it is frequently not enough to know that the trouble is a fungal leaf spot or a blight, since the fungicide needed may depend on actual species of the organisms causing it. Certain well-known diseases can be readily identified by the gardener, but the determination of others and the organisms causing them must be left to the scientist. When in doubt, consult your local agricultural extension service.

SELECTING PESTICIDES

There are many types of insecticidal sprays available to control garden pests. Gardeners attempting to have a biologically balanced garden should avoid wide-spectrum, hard chemical sprays. If cultural practices, including the introduction of beneficial insects, bacilli, and natural repellents, do not give enough control, mild or strong organic sprays are often the next step.

The number of products and formulas appearing under trade names is constantly increasing. Many of these products are similar and control the same pests according to the information on the labels. This is most confusing to home gardeners and growers who are trying to find the most effective solution for certain pests or groups of pests. Insects and diseases vary greatly in their susceptibility to different treatments. It is important to read all the information on labels carefully and to know what to look for on a label when making a selection.

In controlling plant diseases, the timing of applications is particularly important, because once a fungus has entered the plant, most fungicides are useless in stopping the infection. Most fungicides are preventives and must be used before a disease has started to form a protective barrier between the plant and the disease-producing organisms.

Both home gardeners and commercial growers can obtain lists of spray materials available and spray schedules for various crops or plants in the area from a local agricultural extension service. These recommend formulas and timing of applications based on the stage of plant development or the time of year.

DORMANT SPRAYS

Applying materials on plants for pest control when they are dormant or inactive, normally after leaf drop in the fall and before the start of new growth in the spring, are called dormant sprays. In practice they are usually applied in the early spring from a month before right up to the time when new growth begins. Dormant spraying is a protective insurance against some insects and diseases that spend the winter in dormant stages on trees and shrubs.

Dormant sprays must act as contact poisons to kill the overwintering eggs and insects hidden in cracks or bark crevices, on the undersides of twigs, and around leaf scars and buds. Many but not all dormant pest stages on plants are susceptible to dormant spray materials. For the few that are impervious, such as cankerworm and tent caterpillar eggs, sprays must await their active stages.

OIL SPRAYS

These are used chiefly for spraying plants in a dormant condition, usually early in the spring before the buds come out. Non-toxic oils are safe and effective for coating insect eggs to prevent them from hatching. These sprays are often supplemented by sticky bands around the trunks of trees to prevent the attacking insects from crawling up to the leaves. Miscible oils are stable emulsions. Other oil emulsions, with larger droplets, break down quite quickly. Miscible oils, available under various trade names, are usually made from mineral or vegetable oils and are diluted with water at the rate of 1 part to 15 or 25 parts. Follow directions on the container.

Dormant oil sprays are usually applied to the point of runoff, so that eggs will be coated, causing the embryo to suffocate. Always follow label directions carefully. Some trees, especially some spruces, should not be treated with oil sprays.

Lubricating oil emulsions, also available commercially and diluted 1 part to 25 or 35 parts of water, were often used, before the days of modern biological control, for killing scale insects and other pests on orchard and other deciduous trees. Check to see whether the oil is separating out of the emulsion; if it is, the spray is no longer safe to use.

Use oil sprays only on bright, clear days when the temperature is above 45°F and not likely to get colder. The spray should dry quickly. Do not use where there are cups or crevices for the spray to collect in. Evergreens can be sprayed before new growth starts, but use on upright junipers (as well as hard maples) can be injurious.

Lightweight summer oils have been used on such garden and greenhouse pests as whiteflies, mealybugs, and red spiders. Rogon is recommended for the transition from hard chemicals to biological control. Lady beetles and other modern controls are more frequently used. Sprays made from PYRETHRUM are sometimes combined with a little kerosene.

SOAP SPRAYS

Soaps are valued as contact insecticides, having been one of the earliest poisons for soft-bodied insects. At the present time, soap is not often used alone as a spray, except perhaps against a few aphids on houseplants; but it is used to a considerable extent as a flux in making oil emulsions and as a spreader for pyrethrum sprays. Fish oil soap is made by combining fish oil with water and caustic potash or soda. Sodium soaps are hard or laundry soaps.

The amount of soap that can be safely used varies from ½–3 oz. per gallon of diluted spray, depending on the insect to be controlled and the kind of plant to be sprayed. Insecticidal soaps are now available in concentrates and sprays for controlling a number of insect pests of garden and house plants.

SPRAYING EQUIPMENT

Modern gardeners have a number of types of sprayers to choose from, including hose applicators of the proportioner type, aerosol applicators, hand atomizers, slide sprayers, compressed air sprayers, knapsack sprayers, bucket pumps, hydraulic power sprayers, and mist blowers. More than one type may be necessary to take care of all situations around the home or garden.

Hose Applicators. The proportioner types are very popular with home gardeners, for they make spraying rela-
tively easily. They consist of a glass or plastic jar with a siphoning device in the cover attachable either at the faucet end or at the nozzle end of the hose. When the water is

Hose-end sprayer

turned on, the concentrated spray material is taken up and diluted with the water in a predetermined proper dilution for spraying. They come equipped with a nozzle that is adjustable for both fan-shaped spray for close-up spraying or a long stream suitable for the upper parts of trees that are not too tall. Some hose sprayers produce a more uniform spray than others, and those equipped with a shut-off valve are preferable.

Hand Atomizers. The hand atomizer sprayer is a handy type of spray applicator for houseplants or a limited number of small, outdoor plants. It usually comes in pint or quart size and produces a fine mist with suspensions, emulsions, or solutions by operating a hand plunger.

Slide or Trombone Sprayers. There are two types. One is attached to the cover of a quart container; the other is equipped with a 4–6 ft. hose that can be placed in any convenient bucket containing the spray solution. The nozzle is adjustable for close-up or long-distance spraying. The pumping action is tiring, and it is difficult to get good coverage on the undersides of low-growing plants with such sprayers.

Compressed Air Sprayers. The compressed air type of sprayer is still popular for general garden use. It consists of an air pump mounted in an airtight chamber, which is never filled more than three-fourths full with spray material. Pressure is secured by pumping air into the tank like blowing up a tire. The high pressure gives a good spray at

Tank sprayer

first, but as the pressure goes down, the spray gets poorer, and frequent stops for adding air to the tank are necessary.

Knapsack Sprayers. Carried slung on the back and operated by pumping a handle with one hand and manipulating the spray nozzle with the other, knapsack sprayers are too heavy and tiring for the average home gardener. Their advantages over compressed air sprayers include an agitator to keep the spray mixed and a large air chamber to produce a steady spray pressure.

Bucket Pumps. These are simple or double acting, that is, they produce either an intermittent or a constant spray. They are clamped into bucket or other suitable spray containers. Two people are usually required for efficient operation, one pumping and the other spraying. There should be a long enough hose to enable the person spraying to move around a tree or bush without having to move the bucket too often.

SPREADERS AND STICKERS

Many substances are combined with pesticides to enhance sticking, spreading, or wetting qualities; to aid in dilution or uniform dispersion; or to increase toxicity to pests. These substances include adhesive or sticking agents, wetting and spreading agents, emulsifying agents, diluents or carriers, and synergists.

A good sticker has the function of prolonging the retention of sprays or dusts on plants.

Spreaders and wetters aid liquid sprays in wetting waxy surfaces and spreading evenly over them by reducing the surface tension of the water. All three characteristics are desirable in most spray applications; substances having all three are generally used.

Diluents or carriers are used to decrease the amount of active ingredient in a spray or dust so that it can be evenly dispersed in small quantities over a given surface. Water is the usual diluent for sprays, but a number of finely ground inert materials can be used in dusts. These include clays such as pyrophyllite, kaolin, or bentonite; talcs; and botanical flours such as walnut shell, redwood bark, soybean, and peanut shell flour. Alkaline diluents including water from limestone areas should not be used with pesticides that are not compatible with alkalis.

SPRAY INJURY

The application of chemical compounds in the form of sprays or dusts to leaves and other plant parts may produce various types of injury when label directions are not followed, weather conditions are not right, or applications are made carelessly. Crops differ in their sensitivity to spray chemicals and may exhibit varying responses such as spots, shot holes, burning , stunting, yellowing, defoliation, cankers, die-back, blight, and even death. Frequently the symptoms of such injury resemble those of true diseases.

Lime-sulfur may cause yellowing and leaf drop on apples, russeting of fruit, especially in hot weather, and is too injurious on peaches in the summer to be used at all.

Copper sprays, including BORDEAUX MIXTURE, may cause russeting of fruit and defoliation on stone fruits and are not recommended on them except low-soluble copper on cherry trees after picking. Their weekly use in the vegetable garden may produce stunting of young plants and paling of leaf margins or brittleness and spotting of older plants.

SPREKELIA (spre KEE lee ah) **formosissima.** A bulbous herb native to Mexico and South America, belonging to the Amaryllidaceae (Amaryllis Fam-

ily), and sometimes listed as *Amaryllis formosissima*. Seen in Peru by early Spanish explorers, the color reminded them of the knights of St. James and thus suggested the common names Jacobean- or St.-James'-lily. Growing to about 1 ft., it bears brilliant scarlet flowers to 4 in. long. The bulbs are covered with a black skin.

The plants are half-hardy and do well in the open border in mild regions, where the bulbs should be planted in May. After they bloom in June, the bulbs are allowed to ripen until fall, then lifted, dried, and stored away from frost over winter. Plants can also be grown in pots indoors, treated like AMARYLLIS; or, it is suggested, in glasses like HYACINTHUS. They are easily propagated by offsets.

SPRING-BEAUTY. Common name for CLAYTONIA, a genus of common wildflowers with white or rose-colored flowers.

SPRING-STARFLOWER. Common name for *Ipheion uniflorum*, an onion-scented, bulblike plant with bluish white flowers; see IPHEION.

SPRINKLING. Devices that break up streams of water into rainlike drops are a good means for watering gardens and lawns. Sprinklers are available in many patterns and types. Adjustable hand nozzles often have an opening that can be changed to emit anything from a long solid stream to a short, broad cone of fine spray.

Hose sprinkling attachment

Mechanical devices attached to a hose are placed on the lawn and automatically operated by water pressure to revolve or otherwise throw fine streams of water over a wide area. The type used for a given purpose should be selected according to the nature and amount of work to be done. See IRRIGATION.

There are two common problems with sprinkling as generally done in gardens: it is often started too early in the season before the moisture is needed; and during really dry weather, too little water is applied. In both cases, more harm than good generally results.

Sprinkling should never be started until after the season is well advanced, because the water stored deep in the soil during the winter keeps working upward toward the surface from the time the ground thaws until early summer. The time to begin will depend largely on the winter's precipitation and the amount and frequency of spring rain. Sprinkling started too early keeps the surface soil so moist that plants are stimulated to develop their roots close to the surface instead of going down to the deeper, more permanent supply of soil moisture where they are more likely to find water throughout the season even if the surface dries and is baked by the sun.

The second wrong practice often results because, in dry weather, the surface soil becomes muddy and deceives the inexperienced gardener into believing that enough water has been applied. Actually the water has not even reached the roots, which may be in an almost powdery, dry earth below a thin layer of mud from which the water quickly evaporates. Deep roots get no benefit, while the shallow ones, as in a lawn, are attracted to the surface stratum and then, when it dries, are worse off than if no sprinkling had been done.

Sprinkling should always be continued on in any one spot until the soil has become thoroughly drenched. Then do not sprinkle that place again until the plants appear definitely in need of more water. The best time of day to sprinkle is toward or during the evening, so that evaporation losses and waste will be reduced to a minimum. Sprin-

kling can be done in the greenhouse at any hour of the day, but precautions must be taken to avoid burning the foliage as a result of the concentration of focusing of the sun's rays. No such precaution is needed in the case of plants outdoors.

It is a valid criticism of sprinkling, even when it is done correctly, to suggest that as a rule the practice of WATERING or IRRIGATION—both of which imply the more abundant use of water—are better than sprinkling as a phase of garden management.

SPROUTS. A simple, inexpensive method of indoor garden can be employed to produce fresh vegetables in the form of freshly sprouted seeds that are easily started in a jar on the windowsill. Sprouting transforms seeds into nutritious vegetables richer in vitamins and minerals than the original seed.

Good edible sprouts can be grown from alfalfa seeds, mung beans, sunflower seeds, wheat, rye, barley, millet, oats, soybeans, garbanzos, peas, lentils, pintos, kidney beans, and navy beans. These can be used fresh in sandwiches and salads, with cooked vegetables, in baked goods, and many other ways.

Use only seeds intended for direct human consumption. Seeds intended for planting are often chemically treated with toxic fungicides. Heat-dried seeds are not always viable. Most seeds will increase in volume six to eight times when they sprout. Start with 3–4 tbsp. dry seeds or a cup of grain or beans in a quart jar, preferably with a wide mouth. Fill the jar with warm water to soak seeds, and place in a warm, dark area overnight. Cover the top of the jar with cloth or mesh and secure with a rubber band and drain out the excess water; if the sprouts are left sitting in water, they will mold. Rinse the sprouts twice daily until they sprout, and make sure they have adequate ventilation. The exact time for sprouts to mature will vary. They can be put in direct sunlight for the final day to develop the chlorophyll in them. Ripe sprouts should be refrigerated and will keep for several days.

The following list includes suitable seeds for sprouting, the amount per quart of water, and approximate time required for sprouting.

Alfalfa seeds	3 tsp.	3–4 days
Barley	1 cup	3 days
Garbanzos	1 cup	3 days
Lentils	¾ cup	3 days
Mung beans	¾ cup	2–3 days
Oats	1 cup	2–3 days
Peas	¾ cup	3–4 days
Pintos	¾ cup	3–4 days
Soybeans	1 cup	3 days
Sunflower seeds	1 cup	2 days
Wheat	1 cup	3 days

SPRUCE. Common name for PICEA, a genus of evergreen trees belonging to the Pinaceae (Pine Family); they have whorled branches, needlelike leaves, and drooping cones.

The name sometimes refers to PSEUDOTSUGA, another genus of the Pinaceae, especially to *P. macrocarpa* (bigcone-spruce).

SPUR. A modification of one or more petals or sepals so that they are fused to form a tubelike structure, as in larkspur or columbine. The tube is usually filled with a sweet fluid (nectar) so the spur is, or was at one time, a pollination device; for insects to reach the nectar they must first brush over the stamens and pistils, thereby distributing pollen among different plants. See also POLLINATION.

SPURGE. Common name for EUPHORBIA, a diverse genus of herbs, shrubs, and treelike plants, variously known as garden subjects, houseplants, or weeds. It includes those called caper, cypress, flowering, and melon spurge. The Spurge Family is EUPHORBIACEAE. The name is also applied to a few unrelated plants. Allegheny-, Japanese-, mountain-, and silver-edge-spurge belong to the genus PACHYSANDRA.

SPURGE-LAUREL. Common name for *Daphne laureola*, an evergreen shrub with yellowish green flowers in early spring.

SPURGE-OLIVE. Common name for *Cneorum tricoccon*, a tropical shrub with yellow flowers followed by greenish black fruits; see CNEORUM.

SQUASH. The corrupted, abbreviated Indian name for the fruit and the plant of several annual cucurbits or members of the Cucurbitaceae (Cucumber Family).

All squashes are tender to frost, so they must be sown or planted after the weather is warm, but early enough so that early or fall frost will not destroy them before their fruits mature. Since they are difficult to transplant, seed is best sown where the plants are to remain, though sometimes it is started on inverted sods or in berry boxes or flowerpots so as to artificially lengthen short seasons. Squashes revel in well-drained, rich, light soils and full sunlight. Bush varieties are usually spaced 4–5 ft. apart and running kinds, 10–12 ft. apart. Clean cultivation is necessary until the plants occupy the ground.

Harvesting. Summer squash should be gathered as soon as large enough to use—while their rinds are still soft enough to indent easily with the fingernail. If allowed to mature, the fully ripe fruits will be less desirable for the table, and also the plants will tend to stop bearing. Winter kinds, on the other hand, should be allowed to remain until frost threatens, then gathered and handled as carefully as ripe peaches to avoid bruises, for these soon result in rot. To harden the rinds, lay them singly on straw in a sunny exposure for two weeks; but protect them in cold and wet weather. If then stored in dry air and at a temperature above 50°F, they will often keep until spring; in humid air and at lower temperatures they may decay in a few weeks.

Enemies. Squashes are not especially subject to disease but may be attacked by downy mildew, bacterial wilt, and anthracnose. The most important insect pests are the squash bug and the squash vine borer, whose presence is disclosed by piles of sawdust. To control, pick off bugs and interplant with nasturtiums, calendulas, or marigolds, which discourage such pests. Try an onion-water or garlic spray if pests are persistent.

SQUASH BUG. This pest, *Anasa tristis*, attacks all cucurbits—melons, pumpkins, gourds, and all squashes. Its adult, reddish brown body is flattened, as with other true bugs, and it develops from a dark red egg to four nymph instars, the first green, the others gray, until it reaches the darker-colored adult stage. The green nymphs, with pink antennae and legs, have

Squash bug

stink glands on their abdomens; the adults, on the thorax. When crushed, these bugs give off a disagreeable odor.

Apparently this bug injects a toxin into the leaves of the plant, for they rapidly wilt and turn gray. The bugs are likely to swarm all over the vines and soon kill the plants if not controlled. Since the adults overwinter under dead leaves and garden trash, one necessary control is to clean up the garden and burn debris after harvest.

Use a good fertilizer to strengthen the vines before the bugs attack, which usually occurs when the vines begin to run. An effective biological control is one of the tachinid FLIES. Wood ashes make a good dust, but be careful not to scorch the leaves of the plant. Sabadilla is a potent dust or spray control, especially during the five-week maturing period of the nymphs. Avoid hitting beneficial bugs, however, such as the assassin bug.

Companion plantings of nasturtiums have a deterrent effect. Plant their seeds in the hill when you plant the squash. As much as possible, hand-pick the bugs or knock them into kerosene and water. Find and destroy the eggs, which are three-sided and laid singly or in clusters of 15 to 50 below leaves or on stems. These hatch in five to ten days after laying. Early, prolific yellow squash and black magic zucchini are vulnerable to squash bugs, but royal acorn squash is resistant to this pest.

SQUASH VINE BORER. An insect pest especially damaging to squash plants; see BORERS.

SQUILL. Common name for SCILLA, a genus of small, spring-blooming bulbs with racemes of white, blue, or purple flowers. Medicinal-squill is the genus URGINEA.

SQUIRREL'S-FOOT FERN. Common name for *Davallia trichomanoides*, a tidy fern with finely cut fronds and brown rhizomes; see DAVALLIA.

STACHYS (STAY kis). A genus of coarse, weedy herbs or shrubs belonging to the Lamiaceae (Mint Family) and commonly known as betony or woundwort. They have white, yellow, purplish, or scarlet flowers in whorls or spikes. Mostly hardy in Zones 4–9, they thrive in rich, sandy loam in full sun and can be propagated by seed, cuttings, or rooted runners. A few species are of interest in the garden.

PRINCIPAL SPECIES

S. affinis (Chinese- or Japanese-artichoke), formerly listed as *S. sieboldii*, is sometimes grown for its edible tubers; see ARTICHOKE.

S. corsica is a soft-haired annual with small leaves that makes a close carpet covered with large, pale pink blossoms.

S. germanica is a white-woolly perennial that grows to 4 ft. tall and has small, white or rose-purple flowers.

S. grandiflora is an especially hardy perennial (to Zone 2). It grows to 3 ft. and has soft-haired leaves and violet flowers 1 in. long. Its varieties produce different flower colors, including *superba*, intense purple; *alba*, white; and *robusta*, rose-pink.

S. lanata (lamb's-ears), also listed as *S. byzantina* or *S. olympica*, is a hardy, strong-

Stachys lanata

growing perennial with purple flowers and thick foliage covered with a dense, white wool. It is valued chiefly as a foliage bedding plant.

STAGHORN FERN. Common name for PLATYC-ERIUM, a genus of epiphytic ferns with broad, forking fronds.

STAKING. The practice of supporting tall plants and vines with stakes can be done for one or more of the following reasons: to save space; to prevent tall stems or flowers (such as dahlia) from being broken by wind; to facilitate gathering a crop (such as climbing beans); or to keep clean, improve the quality, and reduce the tendency to disease of the fruit (such as tomato).

Staking includes keeping individual plants off the ground with a single stake or with several (connected stakes are called supports); and also "brushing" sweet peas and tall-growing varieties of garden peas by placing twiggy branches or small saplings beside the rows for the vines to

Staking

climb on. The use of lattice or chicken wire might not be called "staking" but would serve the same purpose.

Brush, stakes, and bean poles should always be put in position as soon as seed has been sown. If this step is delayed, there is a risk of injuring the roots that increases as the roots grow. When setting out dahlia tubers or any kind of plants, the stakes should be put in place before or when planting is done to avoid injuring the bulbs or rootballs, as often happens when pointed stakes are driven into the ground after planting.

Stakes should be chosen in relation to the height and size of the plant's expected growth as well the exposure and prevalence of wind. Wire tomato cages are good substitutes for traditional staking in the vegetable garden and around tall perennials. The cages are placed so that the wire legs surround the young plant, which is held upright by the sides of the cage. Another type of wire stake can be made from a stiff wire coat hanger bent into a half circle at the end to support the plant stems.

STALK. The stem or support of an organ, like the petiole of a leaf, the peduncle of a flower or flower cluster, the pedicel of one flower in a cluster, the filament of a stamen, or the stipe of a pinnately compound leaf.

STALK BORER. This common pest, *Papaipema nebris*, is found invading stalks of many plants throughout the country east of the Rocky Mountains. They bore and tunnel in stems of giant ragweed, dahlia, and iris, as well as whole acres of corn when not under control. They also infest cotton and many other plants and grasses, including hollyhock, rhubarb, lily, potato, and tomato.

The caterpillar larvae feed in the stalks, growing to 1½ in. before pupating and hatching into brown moths in late summer. They have only one

Stalk borer

generation each year, but the females have been known to lay up to 2000 eggs. These eggs overwinter attached to the stems of wild hosts, so cleanup around the edges of the garden and of nearby fields is an important control measure. Slitting the stalks and killing the caterpillar with a knife or wire is another possibility. Like other caterpillars, it can be controlled with a spray or dust of ***Bacillus thuringiensis***. Spraying the area where the borer feeds could also act as a control. See also BORERS; INSECT CONTROL.

STAMEN. That part or organ of a flower that bears pollen grains. It is composed of a thread-like stem (filament) bearing a two-celled sac (anther) containing reproductive bodies or pollen grains in which are germ cells. When a pollen grain reaches the pistil of a flower, it grows, penetrates the pistil, and releases the sperm cells that fertilize egg cells in the ovary. Consequently, the stamens are often considered the male organs of the flower. They are arranged around the pistil and just within the corolla or circle of petals. See FLOWER.

STAMINATE. A flower containing only the stamens, or male reproductive organs, as distinguished from one that is pistillate, that is, possessing the female organs. A PERFECT FLOWER has both kinds of organs. The term is also applied to an individual plant or tree with only staminate flowers. When the two kinds of flowers are borne separately, the plant is dioecious.

STANDARD. Botanical term for the more or less erect upper petal of the sweet pea or similar papilionaceous flower. The term is also applied to each of the three inner segments of iris flowers, which are erect and narrow to a claw, in contrast to the three relaxed and hanging outer segments known as falls. Iris standards are variously described, according to their position, as domed, cupped, flat, or arching.

Horticulturally, the term has several applications, chiefly, perhaps, in connection with fruit trees. A standard fruit tree, as popularly understood in the United States, is a tree allowed to attain the natural size and development of its species. (Contrast with DWARF PLANTS.)

Among British gardeners, the term is sometimes similarly used but also has a more specific designation, namely, a dwarf tree trained to stand without the support of a wall, trellis, or stake. Contrast with ESPALIER and CORDON; see also TRAINING PLANTS.

Still another application refers to rose bushes trained in tree form, whether grown on their own roots or grafted or budded. In each case, the "trunk" or stem is grown to the desired height before flowering branches are allowed to develop and form a head. Other shrubs, both flowering and fruit bearing, are similarly trained. Among the more common are quince, currant, and gooseberry. In North America, however, the standard, or tree form, is not desirable because of the attacks of borers.

STANHOPEA (stan HOH pee uh). A genus of 25 species of unusual epiphytic, lithophytic, or terrestrial orchids distributed throughout the American tropics, commonly known as el toro. Rigid and furrowed pseudobulbs are topped by large plicate leaves. Several large, showy flowers are borne at the end of pendent inflorescences that emerge from the base of the pseudobulb and grow downward.

The complex lips of the fleshy, fragrant flowers are made up of three parts. A hypochile (basal third), usually boat shaped, is attached to the column. The second part, or mesochile, has two hornlike projections (hence the common name, which is Spanish for "the bull") that are usually parallel to the upper part of the lip and sometimes curled around it. The third part, or epichile (upper third), is cordate or oblong. The lip itself has little color, but the column, extending nearly to the end of the lip, is winged and strongly marked with chestnut or mahogany. Reflexed dorsal and lateral sepals are larger than the petals, which are reflexed and undulant. Sepals and petals are yellow to cream and marked with chestnut-brown or mahogany. The flowers, which may be 7 in. across, last only a few days.

Plants do best in moderate shade and high humidity when planted in baskets in a very porous, loose compost to permit the inflorescences to penetrate the medium and hang below the pot. They should never dry out and need warm temperatures, withstanding winter temperatures to 60°F. The type species is *S. insignis*.

STAPELIA (stah PEEL ee ah). One of several extraordinary genera of succulent plants from southern and tropical Africa, Arabia, and India, belonging to the Asclepiadaceae (Milkweed Family), and commonly known as starfish flower. These plants, including *Stapelia*, *Orbea*, *Caralluma*, *Huernia*, and *Hoodia*, are characterized by fly-pollinated, five-pointed corolla flowers richly textured and colored, often in flesh tones, often hairy and usually smelling like rotten meat. The flowers are among the most fantastic in the entire plant kingdom. They are grown in green-houses in the North and in a light, open, sandy soil with excellent drainage. During winter they rest and should have little water; in summer, as they come into flower, they need more. They are propagated by cuttings.

Orbea variegata, still popularly listed as *Stapelia*, has short, succulent stems and yellow-ish-to-cream flowers mottled with purple-brown blotches; it is commonly and easily grown.

S. gigantea has enormous, hairy, yellowish flowers with transverse red lines and wrinkles. It is also fairly common, easy to grow, and quite remarkable for the size of its flowers, which can be over a foot in diameter.

STAPHYLEA (sta fi LEE ah). A genus of deciduous shrubs or small trees found in temperate regions of the Northern Hemisphere, belonging to the Staphyleaceae (Bladdernut Family), and commonly known as bladdernut. They have attractive, compound foliage; greenish white flowers in mostly nodding clusters; and inflated, bladder-like fruits. Useful for mixed shrub plantings, they are not particular as to soil and location but do best in a rather moist, partly shady spot. Propagation is by seed, layers, and cuttings.

PRINCIPAL SPECIES

S. colchica, from the Caucasus region, grows to 12 ft. and has three or five leaflets, erect or nodding clusters of fragrant flowers, and fruits 4 in. long. It is sometimes grown in pots for forcing. Hardy to Zone 5.

S. holocarpa, from China and considered to be the most handsome species, has white or pinkish flowers opening before the leaves. It grows up to 25 ft. or more, has three leaflets, and pear-shaped fruit about 3 in. long.

S. pinnata (European bladdernut) grows to 15 ft. and has 4-in. oblong leaves and flowers in nodding, 5-in. panicles.

S. trifolia (American bladdernut) is an upright shrub growing to 15 ft., found from Quebec to Georgia. It has leaves composed of three leaflets, flowers in nodding clusters about 2 in. long, and fruit up to 3 in. long.

STAR-HYACINTH. Common name for *Scilla amoena*, a bulbous, white- or blue-flowered, spring-blooming herb; see SCILLA.

STAR-OF-BETHLEHEM Common name for *Ornithogalum umbellatum*, a hardy spring-blooming bulb with clusters of starlike, white flowers; see ORNITHOGALUM. The name is also applied to *Eucharis grandiflora*, a greenhouse bulb with fragrant, white flowers; see EUCHARIS.

STAR-TULIP. Common name for certain species of CALOCHORTUS with bell-shaped flowers, native in the West from Mexico to Oregon.

STATE FLOWERS. The flowers chosen as symbolic of the various states are in some cases native wildflowers or trees; in others, garden flowers; and in still others, introduced plants that have become associated with the region. They have been selected for diverse reasons—through sentiment, because of their prevalence, or to give the state prominence commercially. Also, they have been selected in various ways. In many states, the flower has been named by the legislature; in others, it has been officially proclaimed by the governor; and in many sections it was elected by the people or by schoolchildren.

Some states seek to preserve wildflowers in danger of extinction by bringing them to public notice, as Arizona did with the saguaro and New Mexico, with the yucca; while others merely wish to commemorate the beauty of certain plants at blooming season, as illustrated by the magnolias of Louisiana and the rhododendrons of West Virginia. See chart on following page.

STATICE. Common name for LIMONIUM, a genus of flowering herbs often used in everlasting bouquets. Botanically, *Statice* was once a genus that included plants now classified as *Armeria* or *Limonium*.

STAUNTONIA (stawn TOH nee ah) **hexaphylla.** A tender woody vine from eastern Asia. It has evergreen leaves and clusters of small, white,

STATE FLOWERS

Alabama	goldenrod	*Solidago canadensis*
Alaska	forget-me-not	*Myosotis* spp.
Arizona	giant saguaro	*Carnegia giganteus*
Arkansas	apple blossom	*Malus* spp.
California	California poppy	*Eschscholtzia californica*
Colorado	Colorado columbine	*Aquilegia caerulea*
Connecticut	mountain-laurel	*Kalmia latifolia*
Delaware	peach blossom	*Prunus persica*
Dist. of Columbia	American beauty rose	*Rosa* (hybrid)
Florida	orange blossom	*Citrus sinensis*
Georgia	Cherokee rose	*Rosa laevigata*
Hawaii	hibiscus	*Hibiscus rosa-sinensis*
Idaho	Lewis mock-orange	*Philadelphus lewisii*
Illinois	native wood violet	*Viola* spp.
Indiana	zinnia	*Zinnia elegans*
Iowa	wild rose	*Rosa suffulta*
Kansas	sunflower	*Helianthus annuus*
Kentucky	goldenrod	*Solidago patula*
Louisiana	southern magnolia	*Magnolia grandiflora*
Maine	pine cone and tassel	*Pinus strobus*
Maryland	black-eyed-Susan	*Rudbeckia hirta*
Massachusetts	trailing-arbutus	*Epigaea repens*
Michigan	apple blossom	*Malus* spp.
Minnesota	showy lady's-slipper	*Cypripedium reginae*
Mississippi	southern magnolia	*Magnolia grandiflora*
Missouri	downy hawthorn	*Crataegus mollis*
Montana	bitterroot	*Lewisia rediviva*
Nebraska	November goldenrod	*Solidago serotina*
Nevada	sagebrush	*Artemisia tridentata*
New Hampshire	purple lilac	*Syringa vulgaris*
New Jersey	violet	*Viola* spp.
New Mexico	yucca	*Yucca* spp.
New York	rose	*Rosa carolina*
North Carolina	oxeye daisy	*Chrysanthemum leucanthemum*
North Dakota	wild prairie rose	*Rosa arkansana*
Ohio	scarlet carnation	*Dianthus caryophyllus*
Oklahoma	mistletoe	*Phoradendron serotinum*
Oregon	Oregon hollygrape	*Mahonia nervosa*
Pennsylvania	mountain-laurel	*Kalmia latifolia*
Rhode Island	violet	*Viola* spp.
South Carolina	Carolina jessamine	*Gelsemium sempervirens*
Tennessee	iris	*Iris* spp.
Utah	sego-lily	*Calochortus nuttallii*
Vermont	red clover	*Trifolium pratense*
Virginia	flowering dogwood	*Cornus florida*
Washington	coast rhododendron	*Rhododendron macrophyllum*
West Virginia	great rhododendron	*Rhododendron maximum*
Wisconsin	native violet	*Viola* spp.
Wyoming	Indian-paintbrush	*Castilleja coccinea*

very fragrant flowers followed by round, green berries splashed with scarlet. Hardy to Zone 8, this handsome plant is used in the South to cover old stumps or small trees, and if planted in moist, rich ground, it will eventually grow to 40 ft.

STEEPLEBUSH. Common name for *Spiraea tomentosa*, a low shrub native to the eastern states with steeplelike, rosy purple flowers; see SPIRAEA.

STELIS (STEL is). A genus of more than 200 species of small, tufted epiphytic or lithophytic orchids native to the American tropics and the West Indies. Numerous small flowers are yellow to green, often spotted with purple. The plants should be potted in a porous, well-draining compost and kept in a shady, moist location. They are allied to the genus *Pleurothallis* but differ in the construction of petals and sepals. Hardy to Zone 5 if protected from freezing, they should be maintained in temperatures not below 55–60°F in winter and not above 75°F in summer. The type species is *S. ophioglossoides*.

STELLARIA (stel AIR ee ah). A genus of perennial herbs belonging to the Caryophyllaceae (Pink Family). A few are cultivated for various purposes, but some species may be weeds.

S. *holostea* (Easter-bells) is a temperate-region, root-creeping plant with erect, downy stems to 2 ft. tall, bearing terminal clusters of numerous small, white flowers in late spring. Native to Europe and tending to spread freely, it has escaped from gardens to become a weed in some areas. It should be reserved for planting on dry banks where grass will not grow.

S. *media* (chickweed) is a weed that grows to 2 ft. and has opposite leaves and small white flowers. Originally a European native, it has become naturalized over much of North America (Zones 2–10) and has been used for medicinal purposes and as food for fowl and caged birds. Good-tasting in salads or steamed as a green, chickweed is high in vitamin C. Presence of chickweed indicates a soil rich in nitrogen, neutral pH, and high surface organic matter. If stunted, it indicates a low phosphorus level. It is very troublesome in rich soil of the border or vegetable garden and in frames, spreading fastest during the cool months of the growing season. It usually dies back when garden plants get large and does not interfere with them, and so, it makes an excellent winter COVER CROP. To control in lawns, rake with a stiff rake and then mow close. In gardens, shallow cultivate when seedlings are small.

Stellaria media

STEM. The ascending axis of a plant from which leaves, flowers, and fruits develop. Since the stem is the continuation of the root, the internal structure of that part is carried up to the stem. The principal modification is the addition of tissue, which adds rigidity to the stem and enables it to fulfill its chief function of support.

Stems take special forms according to different functions they sometimes perform, such as food storage, propagation, and specialized kinds of support. Examples of these are tubers, rhizomes, stolons, crowns, bulbs, and tendrils.

STEM ROT. Any plant disease (or the symptom or phase of a disease) that causes the destruction of stem tissue, either by dry or soft decay. See DISEASE.

STENANTHIUM (sten AN thee um). A genus of tall herbs of the Liliaceae (Lily Family) with grasslike leaves and clusters to 2 ft. long of small, whitish or greenish flowers. Some of the tropical species are grown in the greenhouse, others are decorative in the wild garden or border. Grown from seed, they should be planted in light, rich soil in partial shade. *S. robustum* (featherfleece) grows to 5 ft. tall and has long, narrow leaves and greenish flowers. *S. gramineum* has still narrower, grassy leaves and pure white flowers.

STENOCHLAENA (sten oh KLEEN ah). A genus of about five species of tropical, climbing, epiphytic ferns. They can be grown in humid greenhouses but soon grow out of bounds as houseplants.

S. palustris (climbing swamp fern), native to India, southern China, and Australia, has leathery, pinnate fronds up to 4 ft. long. It makes a handsome basket plant requiring plenty of moisture and bright light.

STENOTAPHRUM (ste no TAF rum) **secundatum.** A warm-season perennial grass widely used on southern lawns, especially in coastal areas, and commonly known as St. Augustine grass. It will grow on a wide variety of soils but prefers well-

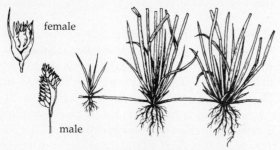

female

male

Stenotaphrum secundatum

drained, sandy conditions. This dioecious member of the Poaceae (Grass Family) is coarse-textured and produces stolons that are both fairly thick and long. It is somewhat tolerant of shade and salt. An aggressive grass, propagated by seeds, sod, or plugs.

STEPHANANDRA (stef ah NAN drah). A genus of deciduous shrubs from Asia, belonging to the Rosaceae (Rose Family). They are graceful and are appropriate for the front of shrub borders or planting on rocky slopes. Propagation is by cuttings and division.

S. incisa grows 4–7 ft. and has wide-spreading, slender branches densely arranged and triangular, deeply lobed leaves that take on reddish purple tints in the fall. Its small clusters of tiny, white flowers are freely produced. In severe winters the stems may be killed back, but young growth springs freely from the base.

STEPHANOTIS (stef ah NOH tis). A genus of twining tropical shrubs belonging to the Asclepiadaceae (Milkweed Family). They are valued for the clusters of fragrant, pure white, tubular flowers flaring to a star shape, which are traditional in wedding decorations.

S. floribunda (Madagascar jessamine) is the best-known species, valued for its clusters of fragrant, waxy, white flowers. It has thick, shining, green leaves, with flowers freely produced and very lasting. It requires a warm temperature and thrives best in turfy loam. The shoots can be trained over a frame or carried along the rafters or wires. It is a favorite plant of the mealybug, and a grower may well feel proud of a really clean plant. Propagation is by cuttings of half-ripened shoots.

STERCULIACEAE (stur kyoo lee AY see ee). The Sterculia Family, a group of tropical, softwood shrubs and trees, rarely herbs, and sometimes vines. The bark of some species yields commercial fibers, and several are grown for ornament. One kind furnishes the cola-nut. The flowers are usually clustered in panicled or axillary whorls, often without petals, and with five or more stamens forming a tube. Among the cultivated genera are *Brachychiton*, *Cola*, and *Firmiana*.

STERILITY. Unfruitfulness, or failure of plants to bloom, set seed, or produce functional offspring, may be of many kinds and degrees. Anything that causes a break in the chain of events necessary for flowering, pollination, fertilization, or fruition may be a factor. The condition may be due to heredity and/or the environment.

When plants cannot be crossed successfully because some inherent physiological or chemical factor prevents fertilization, they are said to be incompatible, and the condition is called cross-incompatability. If, as commonly occurs, a plant will not set seed to its own pollen, it is said to be self-incompatible or self-sterile.

Among the environmental factors affecting fruitfulness are the weather, the season, nutritional conditions, diseases, and insects. Some crosses may be successful under greenhouse conditions but not outdoors.

Sterilities and their causes are of great practical importance to plant breeders, fruit growers, seed producers, and all who wish to raise superior seedlings. See PLANT BREEDING.

STERILIZATION. The act or process of rendering a medium sterile or free from living bacteria or other organisms. Complete sterilization of soil to control the disease-causing agents (pathogens) in it is seldom desirable since the result would be the death of all organisms, beneficial as well as harmful. The usual aim is, therefore, only a partial sterilization, pasteurization, or DISINFECTION.

STERNBERGIA (stern BUR gee ah). A genus of European bulbous plants of the Amaryllidaceae (Amaryllis Family) with narrow leaves and crocuslike flowers, generally appearing in autumn. Plant them 6 in. deep in a rather heavy soil in full sun where the bulbs can ripen thoroughly in summer.

S. lutea, growing very profusely throughout Palestine, is thought by some to have been the biblical "lilies of the field." It has golden yellow, funnel-shaped flowers and resents transplanting, increasing in numbers if left undisturbed.

A lesser-known species, charming in the rock garden, is *S. fischerana*, which comes from the Caucasus and blooms in spring.

STEVIA (STEE vee ah). A genus of sturdy perennial herbs belonging to the Asteraceae (Aster Family), only occasionally seen in gardens. *S. ivaefolia* and *S. purpurea* are the species usually grown. The name "stevia" is commonly used by florists for *Piqueria trinervia*; see PIQUERIA.

STEWARTIA (stoo AHR shee ah). A genus of deciduous shrubs or trees from North America and Asia, belonging to the Theaceae (Tea Family). While not commonly planted, they are among the most outstanding of flowering shrubs, with their large flowers like single roses blooming in summer, excellent fall color, and beautiful bark. They thrive in a sandy loam with peat or leaf mold added and prefer partial shade. Propagation is by seed, cuttings of almost mature wood, and layers.

PRINCIPAL SPECIES

S. koreana (Korean stewartia) is a shrub or tree that grows to 20 ft. and has 3-in., white flowers in summer; purplish red foliage in autumn; and beautiful mottled, flaking bark with orange, gray, and reddish brown colors together on the same tree. Hardy to Zone 6.

S. malacodendron (silky stewartia), native from Virginia southward, is a handsome shrub that grows to 12 ft. and has flowers up to 4 in. across with purple stamens. Hardy in Zones 7–9.

S. ovata (mountain stewartia), formerly listed as *S. pentagyna*, is native from North Carolina southward and grows to 15 ft. It has white, wavy-petaled flowers with white stamens and yellow anthers. Var. *grandiflora* is a rare form with larger flowers and conspicuous purple stamens. Hardy to Zone 5 or 6.

S. pseudocamellia (Japanese stewartia) is a Japanese shrub or tree that grows to 30–40 ft. and has showy flowers with orange-colored anthers and a wonderful smooth, mottled bark. In the fall, the leaves turn brilliant red, orange, and yellow. Hardy in Zones 5–8.

S. sinensis is a Chinese shrub or tree that grows to 30 ft. and has fragrant, white flowers, 2 in. across. Hardy to Zone 6.

STIGMA. In flowering plants, the apex or terminal extension of the pistil, usually at the summit of a stalk (style). It may or may not be enlarged but is usually roughened, sticky, or otherwise prepared to receive and retain pollen grains. See FLOWER.

STINGING NETTLE. Common name for *Urtica dioica*, a widespread herb known for the irritating sting of its leaves and stems; see URTICA.

STINKBELLS. Common name for *Fritillaria agrestis*, a bulbous herb whose flowers have a disagreeable odor; see FRITILLARIA.

STINK BUG. Various species of the Pentatomidae are distributed throughout the United States. Their common name refers to the offensive odor given off by these shield-shaped bugs. The stink bug of the West, *Chlorochroa sayi*, attacks peas, beans, and potatoes as well as wheat, other grains, and sunflowers, both as nymphs and as adults. The southern, green stink bug is larger, ⅝ in. long, and infests especially beans, which it distorts, and also cabbage, corn, dogwood, elderberry, okra, and sometimes orange and apple. Control by hand-picking, careful cleanup, and the botanical insecticide sabadilla.

The one-spotted stink bug is also called the spined stink bug. This ¾-in. pest feeds on tomatoes, eggplant, and other plants, causing blemishing called catfacing. The related HARLEQUIN BUG, a flat, black bug with red markings, is a serious pest on cabbage and other members of the Brassicaceae (Mustard Family).

The two-spotted stink bug, *Perillus bioculatus*, however, is a welcome bug in the garden because it is a useful and beneficial predator. It attacks army worms, cutworms, and the larvae of beetles and various caterpillars.

See INSECT CONTROL.

STIPA (STĪ pah). A genus of tall grasses grown mainly for ornament, often called spear, feather, or needle grass. They grow to 3 ft. tall and have leaves rolled inward at the edges and small, bearded spikelets borne in clusters. They are among the most beautiful of the small ornamental grasses for the garden or border. They can be grown from divisions of the clumps or from seed. Most are hardy to Zone 5.

PRINCIPAL SPECIES

S. elegantissisima (Australian feather grass) has sparse foliage, but the bearded, purple spikelets in panicles are half the height of the plant.

S. pennata (European feather grass) has conspicuous feathery plumes up to 12 in. long. It is not hardy in cooler climates.

S. tenacissima (esparto grass) is a tough, branching species grown for ornament and fiber.

STIPULE. One of the two small, leaflike appendages sometimes appearing at the base of a leaf stalk. Their function seems to be to protect the buds, as in the tulip tree, but sometimes they exist as prickles, glands, or tendrils. Occasionally they take the form of leaves, as in the pansy.

STOCK. A common name for plants in two genera of flowering herbs. MALCOLMIA includes those known as Malcolm, Mahon, or Virginia stock. MATTHIOLA includes evening, Grecian, queen, Brampton, ten-weeks, intermediate, and Dresden stock.

STOKESIA (stoh KEE zee ah) **laevis.** A perennial herb belonging to the Asteraceae (Aster Family), found from South Carolina to Louisiana, and commonly known as Stoke's aster. It bears blue or purplish blue flowers in heads to 4 in. across and has grayish green foliage. Cv. 'Alba' has white flowers, 'Caerulea', blue, and 'Rosea', pink. Stokes' aster is a charming, erect, branched plant growing about 15 in., most attractive in groups in the middle of the border. It blooms freely over

Stokesia laevis

a long period and is easily grown from seed or propagated by division. It requires an open, sunny position in light, rich soil and should not become too dry.

STOLON. A form of stem or, more accurately, a branch or shoot given off at the summit of a root. It may grow either just above or just below the soil surface, take root at the tip or at several joints, and form one or more new plants. This kind of stolon, commonly called a runner, is a means of propagating many plants, including strawberries.

Stolon

STOMACH POISON. An insecticide used to destroy chewing insects, either mixed with edible materials to form a bait, or applied as a spray or dust covering plants so thoroughly that the insect, in eating the plant tissue, will get a fatal dose. In the past, stomach poisons often contained arsenic, but materials such as HELLEBORE, ROTENONE, and other materials have replaced it. The pathogen *Bacillus thuringiensis* (Bt) and botanicals such as sabadilla are commonly used. See INSECT CONTROL.

STONECRESS. Common name for AETHIONEMA, a genus of dwarf, flowering herbs.

STONECROP. Common name for SEDUM, a genus of succulent perennials popular for rock garden culture.

STONE FRUIT. A common name for a fruit like cherry or peach, botanically known as a DRUPE.

STONE MINT. Common name for *Cunila origanoides*, a flowering perennial of the Lamiaceae (Mint Family); see CUNILA.

STOOL. A clump of suckers together with the plant base from which they spring. A grass or grain plant is said to be stooling when it throws up stalks other than the primary stalk. In some cases, as in the gooseberry, suckers so formed are used as a means of propagation—LAYERING. Surplus suckers above those wanted for reproduction should be removed.

STORK'S-BILL. Common name for ERODIUM, a genus of annual and perennial herbs, sometimes ornamental but usually planted for forage. The name is sometimes applied to PELARGONIUM.

STRAIN. A group of individuals within a variety or race, which constantly differ in one or more characters from the varietal or racial type. An illustration would be an improved sort of pea, bean, or other vegetable developed from a well-known variety by a grower who would produce a supply of seed or plants to be sold as his or her strain of the given variety. It should be kept in mind, however, that a catalog variety or strain bearing the name of a grower or firm cannot always be clearly differentiated from the variety of which it is supposed to be an improvement. Compare VARIETY; RACE; SPORT.

STRANVAESIA (stran VEE see ah). A genus of evergreen shrubs or small trees native to Asia, and belonging to the Rosaceae (Rose Family). They have handsome foliage and clusters of small, white flowers resembling those of the hawthorn. The fruits are small, red-orange berries. Plants thrive in a well-drained, loamy soil with humus and grow best in Zones 8–9.

S. davidiana, the principal species, grows up to 20 ft. and has oblong leaves to 4 in. long and scarlet berries. Var. *undulata* has wavy leaves and orange-red berries and is hardier.

STRAP FERN. Common name for *Polypodium phyllitidis*, an attractive greenhouse fern with long, leathery fronds and running stems; see POLYPODIUM.

STRATIFICATION. A process that uses moist, cold or sometimes moist, warm conditions to trigger germination of certain kinds of seed. In the wild, this seed, after ripening in summer, would not normally germinate until the following spring. Thus, they would undergo one winter (moist, cold period) before germination. With other types of seed, two moist, cold periods (with an intervening moist), warm period are necessary for complete germination.

Stratification

Cold stratification requires temperatures of 35°–40°F for various lengths of time depending on the species, usually one to three months. Warm stratification requires temperatures of 68°–86°F usually for less than three months. For warm or cold stratification, the seed must always be kept moist.

In practice, in a cold winter climate the seed can be sown outdoors and germination will occur in spring as temperatures increase. In warm winter climates, to conserve space or simply to hasten germination, the seed can be placed along with moist (not drippy wet) peat moss or vermiculite (three to six times the volume of the seed is enough) in a sealed container or plastic bag, and placed in a refrigerator but not in the freezer unless 32°F temperature is required. If stratification is to be for three months, the seed should be examined every other week from two months on, to make sure germination has not started. If it has started, small, white primary roots will be showing, and the seed should be sown immediately. Some kinds of seed require warmer temperatures for germination and will not start to germinate until placed in a warmer situation. See also SEEDS.

STRATIOTES (strat ee OH teez) **aloides.** A perennial aquatic herb commonly known as water-soldier or water-aloe. Native to Europe, it is ornamental in the aquarium. It has clusters of narrow, pointed, tooth-edged leaves, stiff and spiny enough to give it the common name crab's-claw in some localities. Hardy to Zone 3, it is especially interesting for its curious habit of remaining rooted in the pond bottom and entirely submerged during the winter months. When the water becomes warmer in spring, aided by the buoyant growth of new leaves, it floats to the surface to display its three-petaled, white blossoms. In the fall, its blooming over, it sinks again to the bottom.

STRAWBERRY. A low-growing, stemless perennial that propagates rapidly by long runners and bears highly prized red berries in late spring. The cultivated strawberry resulted from European hybridizing of the Virginian strawberry, *Fragaria*

virginiana, from eastern North America, and the Chilean strawberry, *F. chiloensis*, from the Pacific Coast of South America. It is the most widely grown of all our fruits, and there are varieties suited to every state and Canadian province.

When buying plants it is important to purchase only certified, hardy, disease-resistant plants. Most are being produced by tissue culture, which ensures they are disease free.

CULTURE

Soils that will grow good vegetables, if well drained and in good physical condition, are suitable for strawberries. Organic matter should be added if needed either as manure or compost or by turning under a sod crop.

The strawberry bed should be a sunny site without shade of trees or buildings or the competition of tree roots. Trouble from frost, leaf spot, and fruit rot can be avoided if good soil drainage and air circulation are present. Avoid planting after tomatoes until two years have elapsed, and eliminate perennial weeds before planting.

PLANTING

Strawberries are usually set as early in the spring as soil condition and weather permit. Potted plants can be set any time during the spring, summer, and fall. In the South, fall planting of bare-rooted plants is also possible.

Strawberries are usually grown in the matted row. The plants, which are set in a row, produce many runner plants, which take root around the mother plant and bear fruit the following year.

Strawberry runner

With vigorous varieties that produce many runners and favorable growing conditions, the row becomes overcrowded and the crop and berries are much smaller than where the number of runners are limited. For best results with the matted row, the runner plants should be spaced around the mother plant as they develop until they are spaced about 6 in. apart in a row 18 in. wide. Thereafter all runner plants are removed.

A better method is the hill system. The plants are set a foot apart in the row and all runner plants are removed as they appear. Two, three, or four rows can be set this way with 12 in. between the rows. An alley 3 ft. wide is left, and additional beds can be set. This method results in maximum production of fruit per unit of area and the berries are larger than those crowded in matted rows.

too deep
correct
to shallow

Correct depth for planting strawberries

Strawberry plants are set with the crown even with the surface of the ground. Dormant plants set early will not need watering, but freshly dug plants may need to be watered, especially if they are set late and the weather is dry. Fertilizers, unless used very carefully, should not be used at planting time, but a weak solution of liquid fertilizer applied twice a week after planting can get the plants off to a good start.

CARE

Summer care consists mostly of weed control, which can be done by cultivation, hoeing, or mulching. Preemergent herbicides can also be used to prevent the sprouting of seeds that might have been in the soil or were blown into the area.

The blossoms, which appear a few weeks after planting, should be removed to prevent fruiting during the first year, which reduces plant vigor. Any fruit obtained from first-year fruiting is at the expense of the crop a year later.

Fertilizers may not be needed on garden soils that have been well fertilized while growing vegetable crops for several years. On less fertile soils, 1–2 lb. of balanced fertilizer such as 5–10–10 to each 100 ft. of row can be applied as a side dressing at the first hoeing. In late summer another application is desired to stimulate fruit bud formation, which occurs during the fall months. Fertilizers should not be applied to the bed in the spring of the fruiting year.

In the bearing year, irrigation may be needed if the weather is dry. Rainfall and water from irrigation should total about 1 in. per week. If applied directly to the plants by trickle irrigation, less rotting of berries is likely. Plantings in good vigor can be renewed for a crop the second year by cleaning up the weeds after harvest, fertilizing and caring for the bed as during the first year.

In the fall, the bed should be mulched with straw, marsh hay, or similar material after a few hard frosts, but before the ground starts to freeze. The mulch is spread over the plants to a depth of 3 in. In the spring, part of the mulch is raked into the alley between the rows. The leaves and blossoms push through the remaining mulch, which keeps the berries clean during splashing rain.

Everbearing strawberries fruit more or less continuously during the summer and fall. They are best grown in hills with all runners removed. Mulching, high fertility, and ample moisture are essential for good crops. Blossoms are removed until early to mid-summer, after which they are permitted to develop.

Harvesting. An even red color is not always the perfect indication of ripe fruit. Some varieties have light-colored or even greenish tips when ripe. A taste test is the best indicator of ripeness.

SELECTION

Many good varieties are available, each region having its own list. North of the latitude of Washington, D.C., Sparkle is one of the best varieties, being of excellent dessert quality and suitable for freezing. Catskill, Midland, Fairfax, and Empire are also good sorts. South of Washington, D.C., Blakemore is widely cultivated, but Dixieland, Pocahontas, Earlidawn, Redglow, and Surecrop are considered favorably. Albritton is grown in North Carolina, and Klonmore in

Louisiana, while in Florida, Missionary and Florida 90 are favorites.

The Midwest grows many of the northern varieties as well as Robinson, Armore, and Vermilion. Marshall has long been a West Coast favorite because of its high quality and suitability for preserving and freezing.

Other varieties worth trying in various regions are Cardinal, Dunlap, Redchief, Sunrise, and Surecrop. Everbearing varieties are Ogallala, Ozark Beauty, Tristar, and Superfection. The alpine strawberry, *Fragaria vesca*, is occasionally grown in gardens. The berries are small, long pointed, soft, and with a mild characteristic flavor. The plants bear fruit from summer to fall.

STRAWBERRY FERN. Common name for *Hemionitis palmata*, a small tropical fern with palmate fronds; see HEMIONITIS.

STRAWBERRY-TOMATO. Common name for species of PHYSALIS, especially *P. alkekengi*, a perennial herb grown for its ornamental fruits.

STRAWFLOWER. Common name for *Helichrysum bracteatum*, a tall annual with colorful flowers that are often used for dried bouquets; see HELICHRYSUM.

STRELITZIA (strel IT see ah). A genus of South African herbs belonging to the Cannaceae (Canna Family) and commonly known as bird-of-paradise flowers. They are popular in florist shops and flower shows but are not often grown outside of California. The showy blossoms are oddly shaped, resembling a bird taking flight, and borne in rigid, boatlike bracts with several petals united to form the tongue. Several species can be grown under glass in tubs or outdoors in warm climates (Zones 10–11). Propagation is by division or suckers and occasionally by seed started in moist heat.

PRINCIPAL SPECIES

S. alba, formerly listed as *S. augusta*, is a treelike form growing to 18 ft. Its white flowers have purplish bracts, sometimes 15 in. long.

S. nicolai (giant bird-of-paradise), a popular landscape plant in tropical and subtropical areas, grows 12–15 ft. high and has great heads of blue or whitish flowers over a long season. It can be grown indoors but is not likely to flower there.

S. reginae, growing to 3 ft., is a trunkless plant with long leaves. The yellow flowers have dark blue tongues and purple boatlike bracts.

STREPTOCARPUS (strep toh KAHR pus). An important genus of stemless herbs native to South Africa and Madagascar, belonging to the Gesneriaceae (Gesneria Family), and commonly known as cape-primrose. Most species have broad basal leaves, showy blue or purple blooms, and capsular seedpods (the genus name coming from the Greek words meaning "twisted fruit").

The genus has been greatly expanded so that there are miniatures only 6 in. tall and larger, showier hybrids that have a visual impact similar to *Sinningia* (florists' gloxinia) or *Saintpaulia* (African-violet). A subclass, known as *Streptocarpella*, includes plants of more succulent habit, which make superb and nearly everblooming hanging-basket subjects, usually with flowers in blue or lavender-purple standing out from the small, hairy leaves on long, thin pedicels.

Cape-primroses are easily cultivated in a cool greenhouse planted in rich, loose soil with sand. Seed sown in mid- to late winter should produce blooming plants by the following winter, which should be discarded after flowering. Plants can also be propagated by leaf cuttings and division.

PRINCIPAL SPECIES

S. dunnii has single leaves to 3 ft. long and rose or reddish flowers borne on 12-in. stems.

S. x kewensis, a hybrid between *S. dunnii* and *S. rexii*, has leaves 2–3 ft. long and numerous mauve-purple flowers with striped throats on 12-in. stems.

S. rexii bears several leaves to 8 in. long. The mauve flowers are borne on 12-in. stems.

S. saxorum has blue or purplish flowers borne on thin pedicels that boost them out from the mass of soft-haired leaves. The effect is showy, and the various cultivars make outstanding hanging basket plants outdoors in warm weather or indoors at other times, in bright open shade or with some direct sunlight.

S. *wendlandii*, the most striking of this handsome group, produces a single leaf to 2 ft. long, like S. *dunnii*. Its violet-blue flowers are borne on stems 2½ ft. high.

STREPTOPUS (STREP toh pus). A genus of small, woodland herbs belonging to the Liliaceae (Lily Family), commonly known as twisted-stalk. Native to North America, Europe, and Asia, they resemble Solomon's-seal but are branching in habit. Small, pink or white, bell-shaped flowers grow from the leaf axils. They are excellent material for the wild garden, requiring partial shade and rich, moist soil. The flowers are followed by bright red berries that hang like tiny Japanese lanterns, making a bright color note amid the green. Propagation is by seed or division of the creeping rootstock.

S. *amplexifolius* grows 2–3 ft. tall with pairs of greenish white flowers followed by scarlet berries hanging from the leaf axils, each flower stem appearing knotted.

S. *roseus* has solitary, rosy purple flowers.

STREPTOSOLEN (strep toh SOH len) **jamesonii.** This evergreen shrub, native to South America and belonging to the Solanaceae (Nightshade Family), is a popular plant for outdoor grouping in very warm areas (Zones 10–11) and is an old favorite in northern greenhouses. It is sometimes grown in standard form for summer bedding arrangements but does well in pots, thriving in a sandy loam with leaf mold or old manure. It is very showy in bloom with clusters of orange-red flowers at the ends of slender shoots. Old plants can be cut back and grown on year after year. Propagation is by cuttings.

STROBILANTHES (stroh bi LAN theez). A genus of tropical Asiatic herbs and shrubs commonly known as conehead. The botanical name comes from the Greek words *strobilos* meaning "cone" and *anthos*, "flower." Hardy in Zones 10–11, they are sometimes used as bedding plants in frost-free areas and can be grown in greenhouses in cooler regions. Growth requires abundant heat and moisture; they are propagated by cuttings started in sandy soil under heat.

S. *dyeranus*, growing to 3 ft., is a shrubby greenhouse plant with purplish, iridescent leaves and spikes of violet flowers.

S. *isophyllus* has pink or blue-and-white flowers growing in clusters from the axils of the long, narrow leaves.

STROMANTHE (stroh MAN thee). A genus of tropical herbs of the Marantaceae (Maranta Family), grown principally for their foliage.

S. *porteana*, the species most often cultivated, has broad, green leaves to 1 ft., barred with white above and purple beneath. The blood red flowers are borne in racemes to 6 ft. It should be grown in a warm greenhouse where the night temperature does not drop below 65°F, shielded from direct sunlight, and in soil composed of rich loam, leaf mold, and sand. Propagation is by division of the rootstocks or by cuttings.

STUNT. A common name for diseases whose chief symptom is a dwarfing of the plant, with shortened internodes (spaces between the stem joints). The condition is usually produced by a virus (see DISEASE), but sometimes eelworms are the primary cause. There are, for example, two stunts of DAHLIA, one a virus and the other a nematode or EELWORM disease.

STYLE. The column or pillar in the flower that extends above the ovary and is capped by the STIGMA. The style varies considerably in length or may be absent in some flowers, as in the poppy.

STYLOMECON (stī LOH mek ahn) **heterophylla.** A tender annual herb belonging to the Papaveraceae (Poppy Family), formerly listed as *Meconopsis heterophylla*, and commonly known as wind or flaming poppy. A handsome decorative plant, it grows to 2 ft. and has solitary flowers borne on stems that sway in the breeze. The bright red-orange, purple-centered flowers are 1–2 in. wide with four silky petals surrounding purple filaments amd bright yellow anthers. The leaves are 1–6 in. long and deeply cut with rounded lobes. The seedpods are oddly shaped capsules ½ in. long that resemble a ribbed toy top.

Stylomecon heterophylla

Wind poppies thrive in variable light conditions, but they do best if planted in moderately moist soil with good drainage and partial shade. They are propagated by seed, which should be scratched lightly into the soil and then kept moist but not wet until the flowering period has passed. Seed should be started in the fall in the plant's native range (western California) and in the spring elsewhere. In its natural range, wind poppy will self-seed, forming attractive clumps in the garden.

STYLOPHORUM (stī LAH for uhm) **diphyllum.** A perennial herb belonging to the Papaveraceae (Poppy Family) and commonly known as celandine poppy. It bears deep yellow flowers to 2 in. across in clusters, blooming in early spring. Growing to 1½ ft., it is quite charming in the wild garden and is easily transplanted, thriving in rich soil and partial shade. Hardy to Zone 4.

STYRAX (STĪ raks). A genus of deciduous or evergreen trees or shrubs widely distributed in tropical and warm temperate regions of America, Asia, and Europe and commonly called storax. They are attractive in bloom, with racemes or drooping clusters of showy white flowers followed by inconspicuous, fleshy or dry fruits. Useful in the shrubbery border and charming when planted as single specimens on the lawn, they do best in light, sandy, loamy, well-drained soil in a sheltered location. Hardiness varies

according to species, Zones 6–9. Propagation is by seed, layering, grafting on *Halesia carolina*, and, rarely, by cuttings.

PRINCIPAL SPECIES

S. americanus grows to 10 ft. and has oval leaves and few-flowered racemes of fragrant ½-in. blossoms. It is found wild from southern Virginia to Florida and is hardy to Zone 5.

S. grandifolius grows to 12 ft. and has fragrant, many flowered racemes; it is hardy to Zone 6.

S. japonicus is a shrub that grows to 30 ft. and has light, open, graceful branches and fragrant, drooping, bell-shaped flowers. It is hardy to Zone 5.

S. obassia grows to 30 ft. and has almost round leaves that are velvety beneath and has many-flowered racemes of pure white blossoms in late spring. Hardy to Zone 5.

S. wilsonii is a compact, branching shrub that grows to 10 ft. and has three to five flowers in a cluster. It is remarkable for its tendency to bloom when very small.

SUBSHRUB. A term used to designate a partly shrubby plant, one having persistent but not hard-wooded stems. Examples are southernwood, Japanese-spurge, and lavender-cotton.

SUBSOIL. A term applied to the layer of soil immediately under the ordinary cultivated and frequently enriched topsoil. Lying anywhere from a few inches to a foot or more below the surface, it is penetrated by plant roots of large and exceptionally vigorous subjects. Because it has long been undisturbed and is poorly aerated and devoid of humus or organic matter, the subsoil cannot support the beneficial microorganisms essential to the manufacture of plant food in the soil and therefore is unsuited to growing crop plants. This unfertile condition can be gradually corrected by several methods, including subsoil planting or TRENCHING; incorporating manure or other humus; and growing sturdy, especially deep-rooting plants for a few seasons.

Stiff, lifeless subsoil is naturally associated with heavy clay soil formations. A sandy or gravelly subsoil may be just as lacking in humus and just as unsuitable for most crops, but it is easier to break up and improve and does not interfere with drainage of excess water as does a clay subsoil or HARDPAN. On the other hand, it may sometimes be so porous that the topsoil does not remain sufficiently moist for the needs of the plants grown in it; added humus improves this condition.

See also SOIL.

SUCCESSION CROPPING.

The practice of replacing an early crop after harvest with one that will occupy part or all of the balance of the growing season.

SUCCULENTS.

Fleshy plants whose leaves are able to store water, including many CACTUS species. Native to the arid regions of the world, these plants have adapted to their conditions by assuming a wide variety of shapes. Some are as round as an orange, as *Euphorbia obesa* and *E. meloformis*. Others of the *Cissus* group are shaped like old tree stumps. The well-known Joshuatree (*Yucca brevifolia*) holds up arms to heaven.

The thin, broad leaves of plants from regions that have abundant rainfall would lose too much water through evaporation in the dry air of desert areas. Leaves of the succulents are likely to be very thick and fleshy, small, or even entirely absent, replaced by thorns or spines. Stems, too, are frequently thick and sometimes many-angled.

INTERESTING TYPES

Among the succulents are plants with stems like a series of organ pipes. One of these resembles a geranium when it sends out its leaves. There are succulent plants so like the stones among which they grow that it is a difficult task to find them. These are the stone plants or living-rocks of South Africa. In these same deserts can be found the curious window plants, such as the *Lithops*, *Fenestrarias*, and others. These, because of climatic conditions, long ago retired into the ground, their only connection with the outer world (except when they bloom) being through the flat, translucent tops of their leaves which lie on the surface and let in light.

Haworthias and *Crassulas* sometimes have fleshy leaves laid so closely upon one another that they form a solid column or sphere. Some of the succulents protect themselves by turning the edges of their leaves toward the sun.

In the last few years, interest in these plants has grown, and they are now planted extensively indoors and out. It is understandable that they have become popular, since many of them have large and beautiful flowers. Deserts blossom at certain times with shades of pink, crimson, scarlet, orange, yellow, or white from these succulents. Some of the tiny plants are almost completely hidden by their large flowers.

KINDS OF SUCCULENTS

We find a surprising number of plant families represented among the succulents. The great family of Cactaceae (Cactus Family) includes many of the better-known genera. They are found, with few exceptions, in the Western Hemisphere, especially in the southwest United States, Mexico, and South America. Here are the true cacti, the *Echinocactus* and *Cereus*, often of large growth; the *Echinocereus*, with low growth; the *Ferocactus*, globular to cylindric in shape; the *Mammillaria*, with many globular or cylindrical species, covered with tubercles; the *Opuntias* (prickly-pears), which thrive in many desert places; the *Epiphyllums* (or *Phyllocactus*), mostly epiphytes or air plants, with branches often flat and leaflike; and many others.

In the Liliaceae (Lily Family) we find *Aloe*, *Astroloba*, *Gasteria*, and *Haworthia*, as well *Sansevieria*, often used in dark areas of houses and apartments. These plants, which are related to true lilies, occur in many forms, from tree *Aloes*, such as *A. cooperi* and *A. bainesi*, to low-growing ones. Among the *Astroloba*, *Gasteria*, and *Haworthia* are many small types suitable for rock gardens in the milder parts of the country and for sunrooms in the North. They can be streaked, striped, turned and twisted, flattened, or angled in an enormous variety of interesting shapes.

In the Agavaceae (Agave Family) we find the *Agave* genus, to which group the century plant belongs, as well as many of the more familiar ones, and the genera *Beaucarnea*, *Calibanus*, *Hesperaloe*, *Nolina*, and *Yucca*.

The Asclepiadaceae (Milkweed Family) has a fascinating collection of forms, found generally in South Africa. There are carion-flowers (*Stapelia*), with stiff-angled stems bearing large and strangely beautiful star-shaped flowers along or at the top of the stems, attractive in spite of the sometimes unpleasant odor. Others are *Hoodia*, with flat, widely opened flowers in exquisite shades of creamy pink or buff; *Huernia*; and *Trichocaulon*. Also in this family we have fascinating succulents in the genera *Ceropegia* and *Brachystelma*.

The Crassulaceae (Orpine Family) includes *Adromischus*, *Cotyledon*, *Crassula*, *Dudleya*, *Echeveria*, *Kalanchoe*, *Pachyphytum*, *Rochea*, *Sedum*, and *Sempervivum*. Some of these genera have many species with handsome flowers that are often fragrant. Others are well-known rock garden plants, stonecrop and hen-and-chickens among them. Valuable plants for indoor or outdoor gardens, they sometimes smother everything else with their rapid growth.

Then there is the big Euphorbiaceae (Spurge Family), with hundreds of wonderful succulents, including the well-known *E. splendens* (crown-of-thorns), and *E. caput-medusae* (Medusa's-head), with its snaky looking stems. *E. obesa* and *E. meloformis* are the fat and melon-shaped euphorbias. Madagascar is the home of some of the most interesting and attractive *Euphorbias*, including delightful dwarf species such as *E. francoisii*, *E. capsaintmariensis*, *E. platyclada*, *E. neohumbertii*, *E. vigueri*, and many more of the most interesting and desirable succulents.

Succulent members of the Asteraceae (Aster Family) come from *Kleinia*, *Senecio*, and *Othonna*, while the Portulacaceae (Portulaca Family) contributes *Anacampseros*; some of these are covered with a white, cobweb-like wool, and others have silvery white, papery scales and look more like bird droppings than plants.

There is also the immense group formerly called *Mesembryanthemum* but now divided into many different genera. The stone plants and the window plants belong here and the greatest variety of almost unbelievably strange forms. The true *Mesembryanthemum* of South Africa make thick carpets of growth, their small, succulent leaves very green and attractive, and their masses of daisylike flowers covering the plants with white, yellow, orange, pink, scarlet, or magenta. The flowers have a glittering effect, due to their surface texture, which acts like thousands of tiny mirrors reflecting the light. These are easily grown indoors and in California and Florida but are not hardy in the North.

All too often people think only of the more common cacti when they think of succulents, but the variety of succulents is nearly endless. For instance, the remarkable Didieriaceae from Madagascar are all somewhat succulent, as are the Fouquieriaceae (Ocotillo Family) from North America, with remarkable succulent members such as the *Idria* or boojum tree. There are some remarkable succulents in the Dioscoreaceae (Yam Family), such as members of the genus *Testudinaria* or *Dioscorea*, and succulent aroids, such as *Zamioculcas zamiifolia*, a succulent that can be grown from leaves, an ideal houseplant that does well with little light and can go without water for months.

CULTURE

Some of the North American succulents are hardy in the latitude of New York, and many are already being grown there. Warmer regions furnish conditions suitable for nearly all of them, but the smaller South African ones will be improved by a little shelter from summer rains. Both kinds (North American and South African) do well as sunroom plants. They grow easily and like the fairly cool sunroom temperature better than the hot air of greenhouses. They must, however, be protected from frost. They need to have fresh air; this is very important. Water can be given when the plants are growing but must be withheld almost entirely when they are resting. They should be watered from below.

Succulents do well in ordinary soil but require good drainage. They grow easily from cuttings, but these should be laid on a shelf or put in completely dry sand for a week or more, or the cut end should be dipped in powdered charcoal; otherwise they will be likely to rot. Contact insecticide preparations will protect from APHIDS. Fumigation with naphthalene vapor at a temperature of 88–95°F is effective for eradicating red spider. For mealybugs and woolly aphids, use alcohol on cotton. See also INSECT CONTROL.

SUCKER. A short or subordinate stem springing from a bud at the summit of the root. The term is also applied to shoots that arise from buds that arise anywhere on an apple. True suckers are sometimes used to propagate the plant, since their leaf nodes take root when bent into the soil. See LAYERING; PROPAGATION.

SUFFRUTICOSE. Half-herbaceous and half-woody; the condition found in so-called sub-shrubs, which have herbaceous stems and branches that die down yearly to a woody base.

SUGARBERRY. Common name for *Celtis laevigata*, a large southern tree with colorful fruits; and sometimes applied to *C. occidentalis*, native to the eastern and midwestern states; see CELTIS.

SUGARBUSH. Common name for *Rhus ovata*, an evergreen shrub native to the southwestern states; see RHUS. Sugarbush is also a popular term in the United States for a grove of sugar maple trees.

SULCOREBUTIA (sul kor ee BYOO tee ah). Similar in appearance and culture to *Rebutia* and equally highly recommended for beauty of forms and flowers, this group of small, clustering cacti, also from central South America, includes many recently discovered species. *S. arenacea* has dark brown stems; short, white, pectinate spines; and yellow flowers. *S. candiae* has chocolate brown stems and golden yellow spines and flowers. *S. rauschii* has velvety, bluish purple, round stems;

tiny, black spines; and large, magenta flowers. The variety in the group is seemingly endless.

SULFUR. Sulfur is one of the chemical elements essential to the growth of plants. It ranks close to phosphorus in both the amount used by crops and the supply in the soil; but it is rarely if ever necessary to add sulfur to increase fertility, especially under garden conditions. See also FERTILIZER; PLANT FOODS AND FEEDING.

LIME-SULFUR

Lime-sulfur was first used in Australia as a sheep dip and introduced into California about 1880 as an insecticide to control San José scale. The fact that peach trees thus sprayed for scale were free from leaf curl disease revealed its fungicidal value. However, its possibilities as a summer fungicide were not discovered until nearly 30 years later when it was substituted for BORDEAUX MIXTURE in the control of apple scab. It has become a standard fungicide for use on fruits, including apple, pear, and quince. Lime-sulfur can be purchased as a liquid or powder.

OTHER COMPOUNDS

Potassium Sulfide. This is an old compound used as a stainless spray on ripening fruit and by some florists to combat mildew. Use at the rate of 1 oz. to 3 gal. water, spraying immediately after mixing.

Wettable Sulfurs. These are dry preparations that mix readily with water and are obtainable ready for dilution. They are prepared by mixing the sulfur with various fluxes, such as glue, diatomaceous earth, flour, or dextrin, and are more noticeable on the plants than sulfur dusts.

Colloidal Sulfur. This is a manufactured, extremely finely divided form in which the particles are much smaller than could be produced by grinding. When mixed with water, they form a very fine suspension.

Sulfur Dusts. Specially prepared powders are fine enough to pass through a 300-mesh sieve. Ordinary flours of sulfur should never be used for dusting, since the particles are too coarse for adequate coverage and may cause burning. Usually some substance such as talc, called a "fluffer," is added to the sulfur dust to prevent it from packing and to make it flow evenly. The dust controls fungus diseases and can be mixed with a powdered insecticide to control insect pests as well.

Sulfur dusts are particularly useful against powdery mildews, rust, and rose diseases, especially black spot. Black spider and the broad mite (see MITES) are also controlled with sulfur dusts applied when the temperature is 70°F or warmer. The dust can be obtained with a green coloring agent to make it less conspicuous on the foliage; however, if properly applied, the cheaper, yellow sulfur is not objectionably noticeable, and it is better for ornamental plantings than liquid sulfur sprays. At one time, nicotine was commonly added to control aphids but has largely been replaced by other contact insecticides.

See also INSECT CONTROL.

SUMAC. Common name for RHUS, a genus of trees, shrubs, and vines widely distributed throughout North America and including mostly ornamental and some poisonous species.

SUMMERSWEET. A common name for CLETHRA, a genus of flowering shrubs or small trees, especially *C. alnifolia*.

SUNDEW. Common name for DROSERA, a genus of insectivorous plants with sticky-haired foliage.

SUNDROPS. A common name for species of OENOTHERA, including annuals and perennials grown for their large, yellow flowers.

SUNFLOWER. Common name for HELIANTHUS, a genus of tall, coarse herbs with daisylike flower heads. Alpine-sunflower is *Hymenoxys grandiflora*, a perennial wildflower found above timberline; see HYMENOXYS.

SUPERPHOSPHATE. The most common forms of commercial fertilizer phosphorus used in farming and gardening are two types of superphosphate. Both materials are made by treating

ground rock phosphate (found in large deposits in the southern Atlantic states and northern Africa) with acid in order to render the phosphorus more soluble and thus available to plants.

Ordinary superphosphate, no longer commonly used in commercial agriculture but available in seed and garden supply stores, is made by treating the ground rock with sulfuric acid. It contains about 8% of the element phosphorus, or 20% phosphate, and is labeled as 0–20–0. Ordinary superphosphate contains gypsum (calcium sulfate) as a manufacturing by-product.

Concentrated (or triple) superphosphate is made by treating the ground rock with phosphoric acid and contains about 20% of the element phosphorus, or about 46% phosphate, and is labeled as 0–46–0 (composition may vary).

See also FERTILIZER; PHOSPHATES; PLANT FOODS AND FEEDING.

SURINAM-CHERRY. Common name for *Eugenia uniflora*, a tropical shrub or small tree with white flowers and red fruits; see EUGENIA.

SUTERA (SOO tur ah). A genus of African herbs or shrubby plants belonging to the Scrophulariaceae (Figwort Family), formerly listed as *Chaenostoma*. Hardy to Zone 9, they are usually grown in greenhouses and occasionally planted outdoors in mild climates. The flowers are showy, white, yellow, or reddish, somewhat starry in shape, and borne in racemes. Propagation is by seed or cuttings.

S. hispida, frequently planted in California, is a perennial that grows 2 ft. high and is sometimes shrubby. The flowers are pinkish or white.

SUTURE. A line along which a fruit (especially a pod or capsule) splits open to emit its seeds. Milkweed, pea, radish, and garden balsam are examples.

SWAINSONA (swayn SOH nah). A genus of herbs or shrubby plants native to Australia, belonging to the Fabaceae (Bean Family), and commonly known as senna pea. They are grown outdoors in warm regions, and a few are old greenhouse favorites. Under glass they thrive in a mixture of sandy loam with leaf mold. If given a sunny location and a root area that is restricted in a pot, tub, or narrow border, they produce pealike flowers freely over a long period, followed by swollen pods. Old plants can be cut back and grown on again, but young plants generally give best results. When the plants are established they appreciate liquid manure. Propagation is by seed or cuttings.

S. galegifolia (swanflower, winter sweet pea) has long, supple branches and is usually trained as a climber. It has graceful leaves composed of 11 to 21 leaflets, and long-stemmed clusters of deep red flowers. Var. albiflora, with pure white flowers, is more generally grown for decorative purposes. Other forms sometimes grown are var. rosea, with pink flowers, and var. violacea, with rosy violet flowers.

S. greyana grows to 3 ft. and has whitish young growth; it bears large, pink flowers in long, upright racemes. Its leaflets are larger than those of S. galegifolia, to 1 ½ in. long.

SWAMP-HONEYSUCKLE. Common name, along with swamp azalea, for *Rhododendron viscosum*, a summer-blooming shrub with fragrant, white flowers; see RHODODENDRON.

SWAMP-LILY. Common name for *Crinum americanum*, a bulbous herb with white flowers native in the southern states.

SWAMP-LOCUST. Common name for *Gleditsia aquatica*, a large, spiny tree with lacy foliage found in southern swamps; see GLEDITSIA.

SWEET-BAY. Common name for *Magnolia virginiana*, a hardy shrub or tree with fragrant flowers blooming from May through September; see MAGNOLIA.

SWEETBELLS. Common name for *Leucothoe racemosa*, an upright shrub with colorful leaves and attractive, fragrant flowers; see LEUCOTHOE.

SWEET CICELY. A common name for the fragrant herb *Myrrhis odorata*; see MYRRHIS.

SWEET CORN. A name given to the smaller-growing varieties of *Zea mays*, commonly grown for their edible ears and distinguished from field corn, which is grown for forage or grain; see CORN.

SWEET-FERN. Common name for *Comptonia peregrina*, a hardy shrub with fernlike leaves; see COMPTONIA.

SWEET-FLAG. Common name for *Acorus calamus*, a moisture-loving herb with grassy leaves and greenish flowers; see ACORUS.

SWEETGALE. Common name for MYRICA, a genus of deciduous shrubs; especially for *M. gale*, which bears catkins and small fruits.

SWEET GUM. Common name for *Liquidambar styraciflua*, a huge deciduous tree with brilliant fall color; see LIQUIDAMBAR.

SWEETLEAF. Common name for SYMPLOCOS, a genus of tender shrubs or small trees with abundant flowers followed by small fruits.

SWEET-POTATO. A tropical, perennial, trailing herb, *Ipomoea batatas*, grown for its swollen, tuberlike roots, which are a popular winter vegetable. Sweet-potatoes are grown commercially from New Jersey southward and westward but will sometimes mature in gardens from Connecticut to southern Michigan. They are not suited to the small garden because the vines of individual plants often extend 10 ft. or more.

Other Sweet-potatoes. The common name "sweet-potato" is often, though incorrectly, used for DIOSCOREA, which is more accurately identified as yam. Wild sweet-potato vine or man-of-the-earth is another perennial of *Ipomoea* (*I. pandurata*) native from Connecticut to Texas. It sometimes becomes a bad weed if neglected. The roots are not eaten, but the vine is ornamental in a rough way and, if kept under control, makes a good cover for stumps, back fences, etc. Also it is very hardy, the roots surviving in below-zero temperatures if they are well mulched. On this account it is sometimes offered as wild or perennial morning-glory.

CULTURE

The crop thrives best in a sandy loam, but any warm, well-drained soil will give good yields. It is grown from rooted draws or sprouts, which are broken or slipped from tubers planted in hotbeds about a month before the last expected frost. Manure is spread in furrows made 6 in. deep and 4 ft. apart, then covered with soil raised about 6 in. by plowing from

Planting sweet-potatoes

each side of each furrow toward it so as to form a ridge. The plants (then about 6 in. long) are set 5 in. deep and 15 in. apart in these ridges and given clean cultivation. To prevent the vines from taking root after they start to run, they are lifted and moved every couple of weeks.

When frost has killed the tender tips of the vines, the crop is dug and allowed to dry on the ground for a few days. Bruised and frosted roots are discarded, and the perfect ones are placed in barrels in layers alternating with layers of dry sand and stored in dry, warm quarters.

Disease. Sweet-potatoes are subject to some diseases in the field and to storage rots, which are of more interest to the housekeeper than to the gardener. Soft rot is widely known as the cause not only of the soft decay of the potato tuber, but also of the black bread mold. The disease spreads from one infected tuber to all in contact with it; hence, in handling the tubers, take care not to bruise or break the skin.

Numerous garden diseases of this crop include fusarium stem rot, black rot, foot rot, scurf, Texas root rot, and leaf blight and spot. Resistant seed selections, use of clean plant beds, and crop rotation are the general control measures recommended. The leaf diseases are not serious enough to call for protective measures.

Insect Pests. Aphids, blister beetles, leaf hoppers, and tortoise beetles are pests, but the sweet potato weevil is of chief importance. This snout beetle feeds on leaves, vines, and roots of this host and of morning-glory. Thoroughly clean fields at harvest time so as to leave nothing for the insect to winter in.

SWEETSHRUB. Common name for CALYCAN-THUS, a genus of deciduous North American shrubs with aromatic fragrance.

SWEETSPIRE. Common name for *Itea virginica*, a native American, deciduous shrub with racemes of small, white flowers; see ITEA.

SWEET-SULTAN. Common name for *Centaurea moschata*, an annual herb with fragrant flowers; see CENTAUREA.

SWEET-WILLIAM. Common name for *Dianthus barbatus*, a hardy perennial herb bearing colorful flower heads; see DIANTHUS. Wild-sweet-William is *Phlox divaricata*; see PHLOX.

SWIETENIA (swī TEEN ee ah) **mahagoni.** A tropical evergreen tree commonly known as mahogany. Its dark red wood is valued for furniture and interior finish. Trees are often planted in warm regions for ornament and shade in gardens, parks, and along streets.

SWISS CHARD This plant, often called leaf or spinach beet, is a variety of the common beet, *Beta vulgaris*, grown for its large leaves used as greens and for its broad, thick, pale or white leaf stalks used like asparagus.

Rhubarb chard is a newer strain, whose stalks and larger leaf veins are dark, rich, ruby red, resembling

Swiss chard

those of rhubarb. While equally as good for eating as the type, it is also a brilliantly ornamental plant while growing and attractive for use in flower arrangements.

Culture for Swiss chard is the same as for beets except that the plants should be at least 12 in. apart in rows at least 18 in. apart. As the outer leaves attain usable size they can be cut or broken off close to the crown. Others will develop from the center, so one planting will yield from midsummer until frost. See also BEET; BETA.

SWORD FERN. Common name for species of NEPHROLEPIS, also including tuberous sword fern; and for *Polystichum munitum* (western sword fern), see POLYSTICHUM.

SWORD-LILY. A little-used common name for GLADIOLUS, a popular genus of cormous herbs bearing spikes of flowers.

SYAGRUS (sī AY grus). A genus of feather palms from Brazil, usually small and sometimes stemless. They have graceful, feathery leaves, not armed or spiny except occasionally on the leaf stems. Some species yield palm kernel oil, and a few are planted for ornament. For culture information, see PALMS.

S. weddelliana is now listed as *Lytocaryum weddellianum*; see LYTOCARYUM.

SYCAMORE. Common name for a number of deciduous trees, the most interesting in North America being *Platanus occidentalis*, cultivated for ornament in warmer regions; see PLATANUS.

In Europe, the maple species *Acer pseudoplatanus* is called sycamore; see ACER.

The sycamore of the Bible, a small fig tree native to Egypt and Syria and now cultivated in south Florida, is botanically listed as *Ficus sycamorus*; see FICUS.

SYMPHORICARPOS (sim for i KAHR pohs). A genus of deciduous shrubs of North America, belonging to the Caprifoliaceae (Honeysuckle Family), and commonly known as snowberry.

They are of upright, slender, spreading habit, a good choice for the front of a shrub border or for underplanting. The flowers are rather inconspicuous, the chief decorative value being in the clustered fruits. They are tolerant of most soil conditions and do equally well in sun or partial shade. Not all species are entirely hardy. Propagation is by seed, cuttings, and suckers.

PRINCIPAL SPECIES

S. albus (snowberry) is a slender shrub that grows to 3 ft. and has oval leaves, sometimes lobed on young shoots; small, pinkish, tubular flowers; and large, round, snow white berries. Var. *laevigatus*, which grows to 6 ft., has larger leaves and fruit clusters. Hardy in Zones 3–7.

S. x *chenaultii*, a hybrid between *S. orbiculatus* and *S. mycrophyllus*, has slender, spreading branches and graceful foliage, which hangs on and remains green quite late. It is one of the best "facers" for a shrub planting. The berries are deep pink with whitish streaks and are usually not abundant. Hardy to Zone 5.

S. orbiculatus (coralberry, Indian-currant) is a twiggy grower to 6 ft. and has dull green, oval leaves and white, bell-shaped flowers. The leaves stay green late, and the plant is conspicuous well into winter with its dense clusters of dark purplish red berries. Hardy in Zones 3–7.

SYMPHYTUM (SIM fit um). A genus of coarse, herbaceous, perennial, European herbs belonging to the Boraginaceae (Borage Family) and commonly known as comfrey. Certain species were once thought to have medicinal value, but its internal use is no longer advised and may in fact be harmful. A few are now used in the border for the sake of their large, hairy foliage, which is much more beautiful than the small, blue, purplish, or yellow flowers. They are easily

Symphytum sp.

cultivated and are tolerant of shade. Remove the flower stalks of those grown for their foliage and propagate by seed, division, or root cuttings, Species are variously hardy in Zones 3–9.

PRINCIPAL SPECIES

S. asperum (prickly comfrey) grows to 5 ft. and is sometimes used as a forage plant.

S. grandiflorum grows to 2 ft. and has thick mats of hairy, oblong leaves and creamy yellow, ¾-in. flowers that bloom in spring.

S. officinale (common comfrey) grows 2–3 ft. and has escaped from cultivation in parts of North America. Var. *variegatum* has highly ornamental leaves variegated with white.

SYMPLOCARPUS (sim ploh KAHR pus) **foetidus.** A coarse perennial herb belonging to the Araceae (Arum Family), commonly known as skunk-cabbage. It has heavy roots, broad leaves 3 ft. long, and a bloom consisting of a spadix or spike rising from a brownish calla-like spathe, interesting in form but with a heavy fetid odor. Skunk-cabbage, native in low, swampy areas throughout the eastern states and hardy to Zone 3, is often planted in wild or bog gardens for the ornamental effect of the large leaf clumps and the color inflorescence.

SYMPLOCOS (SIMP loh kohs). A large genus of deciduous or evergreen trees or shrubs mostly distributed in tropical and subtropical regions, commonly known as sweetleaf. The genus lends its name to the Symplocaceae (Sweetleaf Family).

S. paniculata (Asiatic sweetleaf), a large shrub or small tree with slender, spreading branches is the only species hardy in the North. In spring it produces an abundance of small, white flowers in short panicles, and in fall it is conspicuous with bright blue fruits. It is best transplanted when small and thrives in good, ordinary soil and a sunny location. Propagation is by seeds (which are slow to germinate), cuttings under glass, and layers.

S. tinctoria (sweetleaf) is an evergreen species with dense clusters of yellowish, fragrant flowers and orange-brown fruit.

SYNTHYRIS (SIN thī ris). A genus of small perennial herbs of the Scrophulariaceae (Figwort Family), bearing white or purple flowers in very early spring. Charming in the rock or wild garden, they should be planted in an acid soil, rich in humus, and in partial shade; hardy to Zone 8. Propagation is by seed or division of clumps.

S. reniformis, from western North America, grows to 9 in. and has scalloped, roundish leaves and clusters of small, blue or purple flowers.

SYRINGA (si RIN gah). A genus of large, mostly hardy, deciduous shrubs belonging to the Oleaceae (Olive Family) and commonly known as lilac. They are easily cultivated and popular for their free-flowering, fragrant qualities and very ornamental bloom. The flowers are borne in large panicles, ranging in color from pure white to deep crimson, through many shades of pale

Syringa sp.

purple, with some near pink and blue. They may be single or double and are usually very fragrant.

The common lilac, *S. vulgaris*, is one of the best-loved shrubs and is often found in the countryside, marking the site of a former dwelling. More than 400 cultivars of this old favorite have been developed as the result of skilled work by plant breeders. Besides these, all of which flower in spring, there are several good Asiatic species that extend the season of bloom, ending with the so-called tree lilacs, which flower early in the summer.

CULTURE

Lilacs are tolerant of almost any soil and location but thrive best in a rich, well-drained soil and open site. They appreciate lime and respond well to applications of bonemeal and dressings of rotted manure from time to time. Should they get overgrown and scrawny, they can be completely renovated by cutting back after blooming.

Lilacs can be forced to bloom readily and are largely grown for this purpose in Europe.

Propagation is by cuttings of half-ripened and mature wood, by suckers, and by layers. Varieties are often budded or grafted on stock of common lilac or *Legustrum* (privet) for quicker growth, but generally own-rooted material is preferable. Grafting on privet stock is frequently the cause of graft blight, which becomes progressively acute from year to year. It causes yellowing, thickening, and brittleness of foliage, leaf roll, premature defoliation, and general malformation of bushes.

ENEMIES

Diseases. Two diseases of lilac have similar symptoms and are controlled in the same manner. They are bacterial blight, which causes mostly black spots on the succulent young leaves and stems, and Phytophthora blight, in which the spots are dark brown. Either may kill suckers back to the parent stem. To avoid these troubles do not let the bushes become crowded, cut out dead branches, and prune to let in sun and air.

The most common and conspicuous lilac disease is MILDEW, but, coming in late summer, it is not very destructive. It is unsightly, however, and if unchecked, is apt to weaken the bushes.

Insect Pests. Both the oyster-shell and euonymus scales attack lilacs. Control with a dormant oil application before growth starts in the spring, followed by an insecticidal soap spray in the summer if necessary. Presence of the lilac borer in stems is indicated by the wilting of individual shoots and fresh borings hanging from the stem. See also BORERS; SCALE INSECTS.

The giant hornet sometimes injures plants by tearing the bark from the stems for use in nests, and by feeding on the sap. The lilac LEAF MINER is an introduced pest that first tunnels in the leaves and then webs them together and skeletonizes them.

EARLY-FLOWERING SPECIES

S. x *chinensis* (Chinese lilac) is supposedly a natural hybrid between *S. vulgaris* and *S. persica*. It is a fast grower and free bloomer, similar to its exotic parent in habit but with more massive clusters of reddish purple flowers. Hardy to Zone 7.

S. laciniata (cutleaf lilac) grows to 6 ft. and has deeply cut leaves and pale purple flowers all along the branches. Hardy in Zones 5–8, it is especially successful in the warmer climates.

S. meyeri is a small, compact bush growing to about 4 ft. and is very attractive early in the season with small, reddish purple flowers; it produces a second crop in the fall. It is not susceptible to the mildew common in most species. Cv. 'Palibin' is a compact, dwarf form. Hardy in Zones 4–7.

S. oblata is a stout, compact grower with broad, leathery leaves that turn wine color in the fall, an unusual occurrence with lilacs. It is one of the earliest to bloom, with compact, roundish clusters of pale purple flowers. Var. *dilatata* is a good form of more graceful habit, with loose clusters of purplish pink flowers. Hardy in Zones 4–7.

S. x *persica* (Persian lilac) grows to 10 ft. and has slender branches of graceful habit. It is very showy in bloom with large, loose clusters of pale purple flowers. Hardy to Zone 7.

S. vulgaris (common lilac), the state flower of New Hampshire, is a large, upright shrub that grows to 20 ft. and usually has pale purple flowers. Cv. 'Alba' is the common white form. The single and double cultivars in varying forms are commonly called French lilacs. In general they have larger individual flowers and heavier clusters, but not all are as fragrant as the type. Hardy in Zones 4–7.

LATE-FLOWERING SPECIES

S. josikaea (Hungarian lilac) is tall and narrow with dark green, lustrous leaves and small, violet-colored flowers in rather short clusters.

S. microphylla (littleleaf lilac) is a graceful plant that grows to 6 ft. and has small leaves and loose clusters of pale purple flowers. Hardy in Zones 5–8.

S. x *prestoniae* (Preston lilac), with pink flowers in early summer, is a hardy, bushy plant that grows to 8 ft. and is resistant to mildew. It has showy panicles of slightly fragrant flowers and good foliage. Choice cultivars are 'Isabella', with extra large, pink panicles, and 'Donald Wyman', with deep pink flowers. Hardy in Zones 3–7.

S. reticulata (Japanese tree lilac), formerly listed as *S. japonica*, grows to 30 ft. or more and has a short trunk and reddish brown bark, similar to a cherry. It is conspicuous in early summer with large, showy panicles of creamy white, unpleasantly scented flowers. Hardy in Zones 4–7.

S. villosa makes a dense, rounded shrub to 12 ft. and has warty stems, large leaves, and rosy purple to whitish flowers. Hardy in Zones 3–7.

SYSTEMICS. The name given to chemicals that are absorbed by the plant's tissues to invade the entire system of the plant and make it all poisonous to attacking pests, especially sucking insects such as aphids. It is often applied to the soil around infected plants to be taken up by the roots and circulated to other plants. This is a potentially dangerous control method and should not be used on food plants. See INSECT CONTROL.

SYZYGIUM (si ZĪG ee um). A genus of small, tropical, Asiatic trees producing fruits that are eaten fresh or used in cooking, jellies, or confections, and also yielding a popular spice. Many species were once included in the genus *Eugenia*.

S. aromaticum (clove tree) is a tropical tree that grows to 30 ft. and is cultivated to produce the commercial spice known as cloves, which are the dried flower buds.

S. malaccense (Malay-apple, pomerack) is a Malayan tree with a large, thick head, reddish purple flowers, and fragrant, apple-flavored, red berries.

Other cultivated species include *S. cumini* (jambolan-plum), *S. jambos* (jambos, rose-apple), and *S. paniculatum* (Australian-brush-cherry).

T

TABEBUIA (ta bee BOO yah). A genus of deciduous or evergreen trees belonging to the Bignoniaceae (Bignonia Family) and bearing large, white, pink, or yellow flowers nearly 3 in. long. They are cultivated for lumber in the tropics and are valuable ornamentals in south Florida and California.

PRINCIPAL SPECIES

T. caraiba (silver trumpet tree), formerly listed as *T. argentea*, is a small tree with silvery leaves and a gnarled trunk. It produces a mass of yellow blooms in Zone 11 and the warmer parts of Zone 10, usually when the tree has briefly lost its leaves.

T. chrysotricha (golden trumpet tree) has leaves with rusty hairs. Its flowering habit is similar to *T. caraiba*, but the trees will tolerate a little frost without damage.

T. heterophylla (pink trumpet tree), formerly listed as *T. pallida*, has white to deep pink flowers in one main flowering in the spring and additional small bloomings through the year. Hardy only to Zone 11 and warmer areas of Zone 10.

T. impetiginosa, often distributed as *T. palmeri*, has a flowering habit similar to *T. caraiba*, but the flowers are brilliant pink flushed with yellow in the throat. It is as hardy as *T. chrysotricha* but prefers dry winters.

TABERNAEMONTANA (tah bur nee mon TAN ah). A genus of evergreen trees or shrubs of the tropics, belonging to the Apocynaceae (Dogbane Family). They are attractive plants for shrub borders in warm regions and are sometimes grown in pots under glass. Propagation is by cuttings.

T. divaricata (crape jessamine, pinewheel flower), occasionally listed as *Ervatamia coronaria*, is a shrub that grows 6–8 ft. and is sometimes cultivated as a potted plant in the greenhouse. It has glossy, green leaves and frequent crops of single or double, waxy, white flowers about 2 in. across clustered in the forks of the branches. Some selections are more fragrant than others. The double-flowered var. *florepleno* is the form most commonly grown.

T. grandiflora grows up to 6 ft. and has leaves about 5 in. long and clusters of yellow flowers over 1 in. across.

TACCA (TAK ah). A genus of tropical, tuberous-rooted, perennial herbs with large leaves at the base of stems that are surmounted by brown or greenish flowers in dense, round-topped clusters. Below the clusters are showy, leaflike bracts from which arise long, threadlike flower stems that bear no flowers in most species. In cool regions, the plants can be grown in greenhouses and should be given rich soil with excellent drainage. As they bloom in summer, water should be withheld and the plants rested over winter. They are propagated by division.

T. chantreiri (batflower) has dark red-brown flowers and bracts, hence its common name.

T. leontopetaloides, formerly listed as *T. pinnatifida*, has finely cut leaves sometimes 4 ft. across and is grown in the tropics as a source of arrowroot, which is obtained from the ground tubers. It has greenish and purplish flowers.

TAGETES (tah JEE teez). A genus of strong-scented annual herbs often grown in the garden for their brilliant midsummer bloom and commonly known as marigold. Marigolds have been developed and hybridized to produce many forms, from the giant Africans or Aztecs to the tiny French types. Varieties are available for many purposes, including beds, borders, massing, or cutting. They bloom from midsummer until frost, with solitary or clustered heads of yellow, orange, brownish, or reddish ray and disk flowers borne on branching plants 1–3 ft. tall.

Realizing the popularity and wide applicability of the well-known forms, plant breeders and in particular one prominent American seedsman, have developed a great array of improved and enlarged types of special interest. There are handsome hybrids in which the brilliant red tones of the French splash flowers of real African size and form. A unique race, developed from plants found in the Far East, lacks the tiny oil sacs found in the leaves of most marigolds as well as the characteristic sharp fragrance. Another nearly odorless kind has the oil sacs, but they apparently do not function. There is also an extra large flowered strain created by treating parent plants with COLCHICINE and thus producing a so-called tetraploid condition; the resulting novelty was therefore named 'Tetra.' Along with these flower developments have also come increased size and vigor of plants, greater bushiness, and other qualities favored in the garden.

CULTURE

Native to Mexico and South America, marigolds are thoroughly hardy throughout the United States and will succeed almost anywhere with little attention. They thrive in any ordinary garden soil in sunny locations. In fact, the French varieties do better in rather poor soil, since rich earth encourages rank growth of the finely cut foliage, which may subordinate the gay blossoms. Plants are propagated by seed sown indoors in early spring or outdoors when danger of frost has past. They are free from or withstand disease better than most other annuals.

French marigolds have the added benefit of controlling injurious nematodes when grown near vulnerable plants such as tomatoes. Its root exudate is very effective in eliminating the nematodes, not only during the season they are planted, but also for one or two years afterward.

If a bacterial wilt similar to that of tomatoes and related plants attacks marigolds, destroy the diseased plants. A fungus wilt and stem rot appear as a blackening and shriveling of stems near the soil line followed by wilting and death. Remove infected plants and sterilize the soil before replanting; see DISINFECTION. In moist weather, gray mold may attack flowers, which should be removed and burned. Slugs and Japanese beetles are fond of marigolds; see SLUGS and JAPANESE BEETLE for control measures.

PRINCIPAL SPECIES

T. erecta (Aztec or African marigold), once supposed to be native to Africa, is really a Mexican species that grows 1½–3 ft. tall. The compact tubular or quilled petals of its flower heads make a large globe of golden yellow or orange. New cultivars of varying size, with double flowers, and without the typical odor, are constantly being introduced.

T. lucida (sweet-scented marigold) is botanically a perennial but is cultivated as an annual. The small orange-yellow heads grow in dense terminal clusters. Leaves are toothed, not deeply cut. Plants grow about 18 in. tall.

T. patula (French marigold) is more profuse than the Aztec type. Plants bear smaller (1½ in. across), solitary flowers, often two-toned in yellow and red, with flat and overlapping petals. Branching from the base, the plants grow about 18 in. tall and produce blossoms admirably suited for cutting. This species includes color variations and dwarf selections, which are compact little bushes with feathery, dark foliage, covered with brilliant buttons of flowers and excellent for bedding, edging, and cutting.

T. tenuifolia, sometimes listed as *T. signata*, is a tall plant with few-rayed yellow flowers. The species is better known in its dwarf form, var. *pumila*, which makes a compact, fernlike, little bush of delicate fragrance, covered all summer with tiny, single, orange blossoms.

TALINUM (tah LĪ num). A genus of small, fleshy perennial herbs belonging to the Portulacaceae (Portulaca Family) and commonly known as fameflower. Erect clusters of pink, red, or yellow flowers last only a short time. Several species are delightful, hardy additions to the rock garden or border; others are grown in pots or tubs as houseplants. They are propagated easily from seed or division.

T. paniculatum, growing to 2 ft., has red to yellowish flowers in clusters to 10 in. long. A form with white-edged leaves is often grown indoors.

T. triangulare, growing to 1½–2 ft. tall, has red or yellowish flowers in long racemes. Native to the tropical Americas, it is an excellent border plant and also is used as a potherb.

TALIPOT PALM. Common name for *Corypha umbraculifera*, a palm tree that grows to 80 ft. with enormous, fan-shaped leaves; see CORYPHA.

TAMARACK. Common name for *Larix laricina*, a hardy, deciduous, coniferous species of larch tree; see LARIX.

TAMARINDUS (tam ah RIN dus) **indica.** A medium-sized tree belonging to the Fabaceae (Bean Family) and very common through the tropics where the pulp around the seeds in its long pod is used as a fresh fruit, in drinks, or as a flavoring for chutneys and curry. It has a beautifully detailed yellow flower that is too small to be appreciated except at close quarters. It will tolerate some salt and the poor rocky soils of south Florida but responds better to richer, moister conditions.

TAMARISK. Common name for TAMARIX, a genus of deciduous shrubs and trees native to Europe and Asia, and cultivated for ornament.

TAMARIX (TAM ah riks). A genus of deciduous shrubs and trees native to Europe, Africa, and Asia and commonly known as tamarisk or salt cedar. They are of graceful habit and unusual appearance with their long, slender branches and heathlike leaves. The small, pinkish flowers, freely borne in loose racemes or panicles, give the plants a very feathery appearance. In gardens, it is generally best to keep them in a bushy form by annually cutting back the long growth. They grow well in dry, sandy soil, especially near the sea, and can be used as windbreaks. Propagation is by seed or cuttings of growing wood. A few species are hardy as far north as Zone 4.

PRINCIPAL SPECIES

T. aphylla, formerly listed as *T. articulata*, grows to 30 ft. and is often used as a windbreak in dry regions of California. It is distinguished by jointed branches and tiny, sheathing leaves.

T. parviflora, one of the hardiest species, grows to 15 ft. and has reddish bark and pink flowers in spring.

T. ramosissima, formerly listed as *T. odessana*, is hardy and grows upright to 6 ft. It has purple branches and large panicles of pink flowers blooming in mid- to late summer.

TANACETUM (tan ah SEE tum). A genus of annual and perennial herbs of the Asteraceae (Aster Family), commonly known as tansy. They have aromatic, pinnately cut foliage and clusters of small, tight heads of very small, yellow disk flowers. A few are grown in the garden for medicinal purposes and occasionally for flavoring like sage. Although small amounts of the young leaves and flowers make a good seasoning, they contain an oil that is toxic if taken in large quantities. Hardy to Zone 3, they can be easily propagated by seed or division and require no special care or soil conditions. They spread quickly and so need plenty of room.

Tanacetum vulgare

T. vulgare (common tansy), a perennial growing to 3 ft., is a native European plant but has escaped and become naturalized all over the United States in waste places and along the roadside. Its var. *crispum* has larger, much more finely cut foliage.

TANBARK-OAK. Common name for *Lithocarpus densiflorus*, a tall tree native to California and Oregon, valued for ornamental planting and as a source of tannin; see LITHOCARPUS.

TANGELO. Common name for *Citrus paradisi* x *reticulata*, a hybrid citrus fruit whose parents were the grapefruit and the tangerine. The fruit is smaller than a grapefruit, which it resembles in appearance; but it resembles a tangerine in the looseness of its skin. Its flavor may be similar to both. Hardy in Zones 10–11. See CITRUS FRUITS.

TANGERINE. Common name for varieties of *Citrus reticulata*. The top and bottom of the 2–3 in. orange fruit are depressed, and segments and skin separate easily from each other. Hardy to Zone 9. For culture, see CITRUS FRUITS.

TANKAGE. A comparatively quick-acting organic fertilizer. Its composition varies greatly, the nitrogen ranging from 4–10% and the phosphoric acid from 7–12%.

TANSY. Common name for the genus TANACE-TUM, including herbs grown for ornamental, medicinal, and culinary use.

TAPE-GRASS. Common name for VALLISNERIA, a genus of aquatic plants useful in aquariums.

TARAXACUM (tah RAK sah kum) **officinale.** A stemless herb of the Asteraceae (Aster Family) and commonly known as the dandelion. It has leaves in deeply cut, spear-shaped rosettes and flat, solitary, bright yellow heads of exclusively disk flowers on naked hollow stems. Of European origin, it is now naturalized in almost every temperate climate, Zones 2–9, and is often an annoying weed, especially in lawns.

It is collected from the wild and is sometimes cultivated for culinary and medicinal purposes. Many European growers have developed special strains, some with very

Taraxacum officinale

large and very curly leaves. The leaves make excellent greens for salads or potherbs in the spring. A sweet wine is made from the blossoms. The root is roasted for a coffeelike drink. Many herbal remedies are based on this common plant.

When grown as a salad or potherb crop, dandelions should be planted 1 ft. apart each way in light, fertile loam. A light crop of leaves can be gathered the first fall after seeding, but plants are usually allowed to stand until the following spring when the leaves are harvested like spinach; or they can first be blanched by gathering and tying the leaves together, placing pots over the plants, or covering them with large cans

or sand. The blanching lessens the bitter flavor, which increases as the plants age. Dandelions can also be handled like chicory, that is, the roots dug in the fall and forced in a cellar or hothouse to produce blanched heads resembling barbe de capucin.

This bright-flowered herb says much about the soil. It prefers clay or deep, heavy soil, and its presence indicates a soil that is rich in nitrogen, phosphorus, potassium, and magnesium but is low in calcium and humus. It shows levels of moderately high raw organic matter, intermediate moisture, and neutral to basic pH. A low phosphorus level stunts its growth. Dandelions tend to sprout the year after lime is added to an acid plot.

Dandelion is a good "mother plant," improving the vigor of nearby plants, and its roots attract earthworms and open up hard soils. It withstands alkaline salts, increases soil permeability, and is actually healing your yard by growing in it. When herbicides are sprayed on a lawn, soil fungi are killed, destroying the soil structure, so herbicides can actually encourage dandelions. Compost and soil acidifiers are better to discourage dandelions and stimulate grass.

As a weed, the dandelion has spread over vast areas by means of its small, plumed seeds that are carried by the lightest breeze. Once established, the plants are hard to dislodge because of their long, fleshy taproot which, when just the tops are cut, promptly sends out new leaves and flowers; the latter cut in full bloom will sometimes mature seeds while lying on the ground.

If you really do not want dandelions on your lawn, they can be discouraged by cutting off the tops before seeds form, increasing drainage and acidity, or feeding with ammonium sulphate or high nitrogen organic fertilizer (like chicken manure) and something to acidify the soil. The acidity discourages dandelions, and the grass crowds it out.

The only practical way to completely eradicate dandelions from a lawn is to pull out each plant, root and all, by hand if the grass is very young and the turf tender, or, in firmer sod, with two spades or a weeding spud. Afterwards, fill the holes they leave with a bit of soil and a pinch of grass seed. This should be done before the plants have bloomed, and roots should be promptly burned or otherwise effectively disposed of.

TARNISHED PLANT BUG. The small, brown *Lygus lineolaris*, a true bug, is a widespread pest on cultivated and wild plants and grasses. The ½–¾ in. adults get their tarnished look from the golden speckles on their wings. The eggs are laid in the stems, midribs, or leaves and in buds of herbaceous plants, including many fruit trees, where the adults attack buds in spring and cut off blossoming and fruiting. After feeding, they migrate to other plants to lay eggs in flowers or leaves. The very small, emerging nymphs are greenish with black dots. They develop through five instars. In one season

Tarnished plant bug

there can be four or five generations, and in the South these pests go on breeding all winter. They are often found on wild mustard, goldenrod, aster, and vegetable, fruit, or alfalfa crops. These pests overwinter as adults and feed on buds and new growth in early spring.

The lygus bug (*L. elisus* or *L. hesperus*), familiar in the Southwest and West, is a similar pest, somewhat smaller and lighter in color with a similar life cycle and similarly controlled.

The most effective control is careful cleanup and elimination of the weeds the bugs use for overwintering. Sabadilla and pyrethrum are somewhat effective, and sticky traps of white cardboards covered with Tanglefoot or other trapping material hung near top leaves in early spring are also successful in catching many bugs before they lay eggs. Put the traps out when the temperature has reached 60–65°F.

TARO. A common name for *Colocasia esculenta*, a tropical herb cultivated for food and ornament; see COLOCASIA.

TARRAGON. Common name for *Artemisia dracunculus*, a perennial herb whose leaves are used for seasoning. See ARTEMISIA; HERBS.

TARWEED. Common name usually applied to the genus MADIA, a group of sticky annuals and perennials with yellow, daisylike flowers that close in strong sunlight. The name is sometimes applied to a few other glandular summer composites in the West.

TASSELFLOWER. A common name for *Amaranthus caudatus*, a coarse annual herb with crimson flowers, see AMARANTHUS; and for EMILIA, a genus of annuals with colorful rayless flowers.

TAXACEAE (tak SAY see ee). The Yew Family, a group of resinous evergreen trees and shrubs distributed in warm regions throughout the world. The leaves are needle- or scale-like. Male and female organs are in separate flowers on the same plant, the staminate flowers being conelike. The fruit is a hard-coated seed surrounded by a fleshy disk, the whole resembling a berry. Some species are grown for landscape planting, mostly of the genera *Cephalotaxus*, *Podocarpus*, *Taxus* (yew), and *Torreya*.

TAXODIUM (tak SOH dee um). A genus of evergreen and deciduous trees and shrubs comprising the principal members of the Taxodiaceae (Taxodium Family), a subfamily of the Pinaceae (Pine Family). They thrive in wet or swampy locations and are planted for their picturesque effect and feathery, ornamental foliage.

T. distichum (bald-cypress), the best-known species, is a deciduous tree growing to 50 ft. with a trunk sometimes 6 ft. in diameter. It has light brown, flaky bark; small, light green, needlelike leaves; and a head, at first narrow, then broad and rounded. As the trees grow older, the trunks grow large and give rise to cypress "knees," which bring air to the roots when the swamps are flooded. The bald-cypress grows naturally in swamps from Delaware to Florida but is hardy as far north as New England and is excellent in parks or in extensive landscaping, especially where there is wet, swampy soil. They are comparatively free from insect pests, but the larvae of a small moth may brown the foliage by feeding on it. Var. *nutans* (pond-cypress), also listed as *T. ascendens*, is similar but more columnar, with appressed leaves. Hardy in Zones 5–9.

T. mucronatum (Montezuma-cypress) is a cone-bearing Mexican evergreen planted for ornament in California and the South. Hardy to Zone 8.

TAXUS (TAKS us). A genus of evergreen trees and shrubs with broad, flat leaves (needles), native throughout the Northern Hemisphere, and commonly known as yew. They grow slowly and have many uses in the landscape and gardening, ranging in height from a dwarf bush a foot or so high to a 60-ft. tree. The low-growing forms are among the most useful of evergreens for small gardens. Their leaves are broader than those of fir or spruce and extend on either side of the stems, producing a flattened, soft effect. The rich, dark green foliage remains uniform in coloring throughout the year, and the pistillate plants are colorful in fall with scarlet, berrylike fruits. While the flaky fruits are edible, the seeds they surround are poisonous, so small children should be kept away from *Taxus*.

Yews withstand hard clipping well; being of dense habit, they make good hedge plants and are excellent for any form of topiary work. A rather moist loam suits them best, but they grow in ordinary soil with plenty of humus and do well in sun or shade. Propagation is by seed, cuttings of half-ripened or fully matured shoots under glass, and sometimes by grafting in the case of varieties.

The most important pest of yews is the black vine weevil whose larvae feed on the roots. The tops of the plants turn yellow, then brown, and severely injured plants may die. The adult black beetles hide by day and feed on foliage at night, when they can be jarred off onto a cloth and dropped into a pail of kerosene and water. See also WEEVIL; BEETLES.

PRINCIPAL SPECIES

T. baccata (English yew) grows to 40 ft. with a short, wide trunk and a broad head. It lives to an old age but is only hardy to Zones 6–7. There are numerous named cultivars, some of which are hardier than the type. Cv. 'Adpressa', with irregular growth, has long, spreading branches; good forms of this are 'Erecta', of bushy, columnar habit, and 'Aurea', one of the best of the so-called golden yews. 'Dovastoni' is wide spreading with pendulous branches, making a handsome lawn specimen. 'Elegantissima' is a compact and ornamental form with young leaves striped pale yellow. 'Fastigiata' (Irish yew) is a handsome columnar form with heavy growth and very dark green leaves. 'Repandens' makes a low-spreading mound and is one of the hardiest.

T. canadensis (Canadian yew, ground-hemlock) is a very hardy, low-spreading native usually found in dense shade. In cultivation it will grow in the open and become less straggly, but the foliage is likely to become discolored by the winter sun. Hardy in Zones 3–6.

T. cuspidata (Japanese yew) is a large shrub or tree that grows to 30 ft. It is somewhat similar to *T. baccata* but has darker green leaves yellowish beneath. There are both upright and spreading forms. Cv. 'Nana' is a good shrubby form of slow growth with short needles. It is very dense and compact when young, later spreading widely. 'Capitata' is a pyramidal form growing to 30 ft., or less with pruning for formal shape. Hardy in Zones 4–7.

T. x *media* is a hybrid between *T. baccata* and *T. cuspidata*. Two of its outstanding forms are cv. 'Hatfieldii', of dense, bushy form; and 'Hicksii', of columnar habit. Its seedlings show interesting differences in leaf form and growth habit. Hardy in Zones 4–7.

TEA. The tea sold commercially is derived from the leaves of *Camellia sinensis*; see CAMELLIA. The word "tea" is also applied to several other plants, whose leaves or other parts are sometimes steeped for beverages. Appalachian-tea or teaberry is *Viburnum cassinoides*. Australian-tea tree is *Leptospermum laevigatum*. Crystal-tea is *Ledum palustre* and Labrador-tea, *Ledum groenlandicum*. Mexican- or Spanish-tea is *Chenopodium ambrosioides*. New-Jersey-tea is *Ceanothus americanus*. Oswego-tea is *Monarda didyma*. Paraguay-tea is *Ilex paraguariensis*. Philippine-tea is *Ehretia microphylla*.

TEABERRY. A common name for *Gaultheria procumbens*, a creeping shrub with leathery leaves, and for *Viburnum cassinoides*, a rounded shrub with finely toothed leaves. See GAULTHERIA; VIBURNUM.

TEA ROSE. There has been much speculation as to how the tea roses were named. Some authorities think they were named for the fragrance of fresh tea leaves (not the cured and processed product), while others think the name came from the fact that early roses were shipped over long sea voyages in tea chests. Still others have described the fragrance as fruity, specifically like stone fruits.

The tea roses are closely related to the China roses, having smooth stems with glossy foliage and lightly fragrant blooms of superb shape and delicate colors. They typically have the long central petals surrounded by evenly unfurling outer petals that have been the inheritance of our modern hybrid tea. They are extremely tender. Many superlative climbing forms exist.

Some famous tea roses include 'Gloire de Dijon', 'Mme. Bravy', and 'Maman Cochet'.

It should be pointed out that many people today refer to the hybrid tea as a "tea rose," thus confusing the classes.

TEASEL. Common name for DIPSACUS, a genus of coarse, prickly biennial herbs. The Teasel Family is DIPSACACEAE. Teasel gourd is *Cucumus dipsaceus*, an annual related to the cucumber; see CUCUMIS.

TECOMA (te KOH mah). A genus of upright shrubs native from Florida to South America, belonging to the Bignoniaceae (Bignonia Family).

They are grown outdoors in Zones 10–11 and sometimes in pots under glass for their showy flowers. Several species formerly listed here have been reclassified to other genera.

PRINCIPAL SPECIES

T. alata, formerly listed as *T. smithii*, is a supposed hybrid of Australian origin. It has eleven to seventeen leaflets and large, showy panicles of yellow flowers tinged orange.

T. garrocha (trumpetbush) is a graceful plant to about 5 ft. and has leaves of seven to eleven leaflets and fragrant clusters of yellow or pink, scarlet-tubed flowers in panicles or racemes.

T. stans (yellow-elder, yellowbells), sometimes listed as *Stenolobium stans*, has yellow, bell-shaped flowers borne in loose clusters. A free-flowering tropical shrub, which may form a small tree with the appropriate early pruning, it is native along the Gulf Coast to Florida, where it is popular for ornamental planting.

TECOMARIA (tek oh MAYR ee ah). A genus of half-climbing tropical shrubs belonging to the Bignoniaceae (Bignonia Family). The most commonly grown is *T. capensis* (cape-honeysuckle). Native to South Africa, it is a good porch or trellis plant for warm regions (Zones 10–11). It has handsome pinnate leaves and clusters of showy, orange-red or yellow flowers, produced almost continuously. Spring pruning ensures a good growth of flowering wood. Propagation is by seed and cuttings.

TECTARIA (tek TAIR ee ah). A genus of rather coarse terrestrial ferns. They can be cultivated in warm greenhouses or outdoors in tropical regions. Most are rather large for houseplants. Several form viviparous bulbils on the fronds.

T. gemmifera is an easily grown fern with bipinnate to quadripinnate fronds 2–5 ft. long. Many bulbils are produced on the upper surfaces of the leaves. These can be used to start new potted plants to replace the parent when it becomes too large. The fronds are thinly textured and suffer in low humidity. It is native in Africa and the Seychelles.

TEFF. Common name for *Eragrostis tef*, an ornamental annual grass; see ERAGROSTIS.

TELEGRAPH PLANT. Common name for *Desmodium motorium*, a tender leguminous plant with the peculiar property of being able to move its leaves; see DESMODIUM.

TELLIMA (TEL i mah) **grandiflora.** A woodland perennial plant of western North America, belonging to the Saxifragaceae (Saxifrage Family), commonly known as false alumroot. It has almost round, toothed leaves. The greenish flowers, which become red, have finely fringed petals like snowflakes and are borne on long racemes to 3 ft. It is easy to naturalize in woodland gardens or in moist, open areas and is hardy to Zone 6. The plant is self-sowing once established.

TEMPLETONIA (tem pul TOH nee ah) **retusa.** An Australian shrub belonging to the Fabaceae (Bean Family). It is a tall plant with leathery leaves and pealike, red flowers, commonly known as coral-bush. In Zones 10–11 it succeeds in fairly light soil and blooms in winter.

TENDRIL. A very slender, flexible appendage that serves to support a plant by clinging to or winding around some other object, as in the cucurbits and sweet peas. Tendrils are sometimes provided with disklike attachments that permit them to cling to flat surfaces, as in the Virginia creeper. Being coiled like a spring, they are able to hold a plant and still allow some movement without pulling loose, and to draw closer by contracting.

TENT CATERPILLAR. Also called the apple tree, American, or Eastern tent caterpillar, this is the larvae of the moth, *Malacosoma americanum* belonging to the Lasiocampidae. Common throughout the United States in the spring, it often completely defoliates orchards and sometimes ornamental trees and shrubs, and fills wild cherry, apple, and other trees along roadsides with large, unsightly nests.

The winter is passed in the egg stage, with gray or dark brown, shiny egg masses about ½ in. long encircling small twigs as though a bit of gum had been wrapped around them and then varnished. The eggs hatch just as the apple leaves unfold, and the tiny worms at once attack them, at the same time forming a colony in the nearest branch fork and building a weblike nest

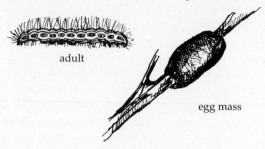

adult

egg mass

Tent caterpillar

for protection at night and in wet weather. As the caterpillars crawl out to feed, they leave a silken trail behind, which may connect several nests over the tree. In about a month the caterpillars, full grown and 2 in. long, black with bluish markings and a white stripe down the back, leave the nests and crawl along the ground, fences, or buildings. They pupate in dirty whitish cocoons, fastened on tree trunks, under bark or shingles, or on any sort of litter.

The small, heavy-bodied moths appearing in early summer have short, reddish brown wings with white bands. There is one brood each year; "tents" seen in midsummer or later are caused not by this pest but by the fall WEBWORM.

A regular spray program will control the tent caterpillar in orchards. In gardens and home grounds, the nests can be removed by burning—if the work is done carefully so as not to injure the tree. A better plan is to wipe them out in the crotches with rags moistened with kerosene, gasoline, or some full-strength contact spray. The sooner this is done, the easier and more pleasant and effective it is. The best means of control is by pruning off and burning the twigs carrying the egg masses. Do this any time while the leaves are off the trees, when the masses can be easily seen against the sky. Birds and other insects (including parasites) are natural enemies of the tent caterpillar and a natural balance is gradually established so that after the pest has been abundant for four or five years, it usually disappears for the same length of time.

The tiny, beneficial trichogramma WASPS can be applied to fruit trees at the budding, blooming, and petal-drop stages. Sprays made with *Bacillus thuringiensis* (Bt, commonly available as Biotrol, Dipel, or Thuricide) on leaves under attack can also be effective.

The related forest tent caterpillar is a pest of woodlands but may defoliate shade trees such as poplar, maple, and oak. The blue-headed caterpillar has a line of silvery, diamond-shaped spots down the middle of the back. Again the winter stage is the egg, ½ in. long, laid in light brown masses on the twigs of host plants.

See also INSECT CONTROL; SPRAYING.

TERMINAL. The end or apex of a stem, foliage branch, or shoot bearing a flower cluster. The term is commonly used as an adjective, as "the terminal bud," meaning the one at the end of a shoot. Because this bud is responsible for the continuation of the growth of the stem in its original direction, the shape of the plant can be modified by removing or destroying it. See also BUD; DISBUDDING.

TERMINALIA (tur mi NAY lee ah). A genus of tropical trees, mostly from south Asia, where they are valued for ornamental and economic purposes. *T. catappa* (tropical-almond, myrobalan) has been introduced into southern Florida for street planting. It is a deciduous, stately tree that grows up to 80 ft. and has horizontal branches in whorls. The leaves grow to a foot long, are clustered at the ends of branches, and turn a rich red before falling. The fruit is a nut of good flavor and in the tropics yields a valuable oil.

T. muelleri (black-olive), growing to only about 30 ft., is useful for smaller spaces. The deep purple fruits resemble olives, inspiring the common name.

TERMITES. These wood-infesting insects, of the order Isoptera, are called white ants, but they differ from true ants by not having a slender waist. They occur in all parts of the world but are much more numerous in the tropics. They may attack woody plants in the garden but are more seriously destructive to buildings, fence posts, and any type of structure made of wood or with wooden framework. The fact that they work within the wood, giving no sign of their presence until much damage may have been done, makes them all the more dangerous.

To prevent infestation, great care should be taken to avoid having woodwork come in direct contact with the earth. The foundations and framework of infested buildings should be replaced with metal or stone, or wood treated with creosote or other preservative. Exterminating companies make a special business of finding the colonies, killing the termites, and treating all woodwork against infestation.

TERRARIUM. A container, usually glass, in which small plants are grown and arranged to suggest a natural landscape. The success of a terrarium, like any other garden, depends on its design and the suitability and practicability of the plant material used. Woodland plants will do fine with partial sunlight; however, if flowering plants are used, it needs plenty of sun.

MAKING A TERRARIUM

The native woodland terrarium is perhaps the easiest and most interesting to make. The first step is the preparation of the container. Almost any type of glass-sided container will work; the most common and easiest to plant and maintain is a leaky discarded aquarium or other rectangular glass case. Panes of window glass can be fastened together with strong tape and placed in a base made of a baking or roasting pan.

Place an inch or so of gravel in the bottom. On this, sprinkle a layer of ground or broken up charcoal to keep the terrarium sweet. Then add leaf mold or humus to receive the actual planting. It is best to group plants with similar growing requirements. Interesting bits of bark, lichens, sticks, pebbles, and other bits might also be worked into a terrarium scheme.

Planting. As in a larger garden, differences of level add charm and character to the terrarium and serve to better display the plants. Set small rocks in place to help attain this effect, and pile the leaf mold up behind them in the desired contours. Pockets should be made to hold the larger plants. Be careful to tamp leaf mold well around the roots of larger plants. Smaller ones should be planted with their crowns just above the soil. With the large plants and ferns in place, the terrarium is ready for the surface covering of moss, which should be packed tightly around the protruding rocks and on top of the raw humus. Next lay in the bits of lichen-covered bark and other decorative material; then water with a fine spray.

Naturally it must be provided with a glass cover. Experience will determine whether the cover should be kept tight, partly open, or entirely off. When the glass becomes clouded with condensed moisture, give more ventilation. As long as the air is clear, the terrarium can be kept covered or nearly so.

Bottle Garden. This is simply a terrarium using a large bottle as the container. Its planting differs from a regular terrarium only in that work must be done with long forceps and tamping sticks, and the original plant material must be small enough to fit through the neck of the bottle without injury. Once set in place, plants tend to grow rapidly and fill the entire space. A little more ingenuity and patience may be required, but the effect is worthwhile.

Desert Terrarium. A desert or arid terrarium is started in much the same way as the woodland type. Obviously it will contain desert rather than woodland plants. The drainage layer of gravel and charcoal is hardly necessary, and the soil layer is sandy rather than loamy and rich in humus. The desert terrarium needs more sun and air than a woodland type.

TESTUDINARIA (tes too din AIR ee ah). A genus of the Dioscoreaceae (Yam Family) with many interesting caudiciform, succulent members. *T. ele-*

phantipes, from South Africa, and *T. macrostachya*, from southeastern Mexico, both have leafy, vinelike stems arising from a large, fleshy, succulent, mostly aboveground caudex which becomes barky and neatly fissured with age, resembling a great tortoise shell—a most curious type of succulent. It was from the Mexican species, often referred to as *Dioscorea macrostachya*, that the ingredients of the birth control pill were first isolated. Propagation is from seed, but since the flowers are unisexual, both male and female plants are necessary to obtain seed.

TETRAGONIA (tet rah GOH nee ah) **tetragonioides**. An annual herb commonly known as NEW ZEALAND SPINACH, grown as a hot-weather substitute but requiring similar culture to ordinary SPINACH.

TEUCRIUM (TOO kree um). A genus of herbs or shrubby plants, widely dispersed throughout the temperate and warmer climates, belonging to the Lamiaceae (Mint Family), and commonly known as germander. Many have showy flowers. Hardiness varies with species in Zones 5–9. A few are hardy in the North and well adapted for rock garden or flower border planting. Others are suitable for greenhouse culture. They are not particular as to soil, but a light sandy soil seems to suit them best. Propagation is by seed, cuttings, or root divisions.

PRINCIPAL SPECIES

T. canadense (American germander) is a creeping form, with pale rose flowers blooming in summer. There seems to be great variation in height among plants of this species, some growing 6–8 in. high and others, up to 3 ft.

T. chamaedrys is a procumbent, shrubby plant with stems about 1 ft. high and loose spikes of reddish purple or rose-colored flowers.

T. fruticans (tree germander) grows up to 6 ft., forming a very attractive shrub with silvery foliage and blue flowers. In mild climates, it has a long flowering season and is recommended for dry places.

T. marum (cat-thyme), from the Mediterranean region, is a small, much-branched, tender shrub with short spikes of purplish pink flowers. Cats are said to be very much stimulated by it.

T. montanum is a low, prostrate shrub with creamy or pale yellow flowers, making a fine effect in mass.

THALIA (THAY lee ah). A genus of large, perennial herbs of the Marantaceae (Maranta Family). They do best planted in wet ground or in shallow water, but most species are suited only to the greenhouse or to very mild climates, although some are hardy to Zone 6.

T. dealbata has leaves from 6–9 in. long, lightly powdered like those of *Canna*, and borne on stalks from 1–4 ft. tall. The small, purple flowers are carried high on a very long stem. Where the climate is mild enough, this is a splendid plant for waterside use.

T. geniculata is similar to *T. dealbata* but is much larger. It grows from 5–10 ft. tall, and its leaves are up to 2 ft. long.

THALICTRUM (thah LIK trum). A genus of perennial herbs belonging to the Ranunculaceae (Buttercup Family), commonly known as meadow-rue. Some are very decorative in the border and others are charming when naturalized in the wild garden. They have attractive cut foliage and numerous clustered flowers without petals but with numerous large, drooping stamens and sometimes showy sepals. They create a remarkably fine effect if planted in combination with subjects of heavier growth habit, such as iris or peonies. Almost all the species are easily grown in a light, rich, loamy soil, but a few of the tall-growing, native species thrive in moist, swampy land. Propagation is by

T. aquilegifolium

seed or division. Most species are hardy in Zones 4–8.

PRINCIPAL SPECIES

T. aquilegifolium (feathered-columbine), a European native, grows to 3 ft. and has rosy purple, clustered flowers blooming in early summer.

T. delavayi, with purple or lavender flowers on tall stems, provides light, feathery bloom in the back of the border.

T. dioicum is a native plant growing to 2 ft., easily grown in dry woodland soil.

T. dipterocarpum is a tall, late-blooming species with pyramidal clusters of rosy mauve or purple flowers brightened by drooping, golden stamens.

T. flavum grows to 4 ft. and has creamy yellow flowers with numerous bright yellow stamens.

T. glaucum (dusty meadow-rue), also listed as *T. speciosissimum*, has grayish blue foliage and 4-ft. stems bearing yellow flowers that bloom in early summer.

T. minus is a low grower with greenish yellow flowers, excellent in the rock garden.

T. polygamum, growing to 8 ft., bears large clusters of feathery, white flowers. It grows naturally in damp, open meadows and is easily colonized on the edge of the bog garden.

T. rochebrunianum (lavender mist) bears sprays of long-standing, lavender blooms with yellow stamens in the latter half of summer. It grows 4–6 ft. and usually requires staking.

THEA (TEE ah) **sinensis.** Former botanical name for *Camellia sinensis*, an evergreen shrub or tree that is grown for commercial tea; see CAMELLIA.

THELYPTERIS (the LIP tur is). A genus of ferns not recommended for purposes other than naturalizing, since they can be invasive. They have creeping or ascending, scaly rhizomes, and the large fronds are pinnate to tripinnate, mostly pinnate-pinnatifid. Four species are common in the eastern states, and a multitude are found throughout the tropical, subtropical, and temperate regions of the world. Most members of this genus were once listed under *Dryopteris*; some botanists divide this group into splinter genera, including *Christella*, *Mycrothelypteris*, *Oreopteris*, and *Phegopteris*.

PRINCIPAL SPECIES

T. hexagonoptera (broad beech or southern beech fern), also listed as *Phegopteris hexagonoptera*, is pinnate to bipinnate and grows 1½–2 ft. tall. It is similar to *T. phegopteris*, but the basal pair of pinnae spread out rather than curve down. Also, the pinnae are connected by wings on the rachis. Common in North America, it spreads quickly in shaded woodlands.

T. noveboracensis (New York fern), also listed as *Parathelypteris noveboracensis*, is an attractive but invasive fern with erect, pinnate-pinnatifid fronds 1–2 ft. tall, which arise at intervals from a long, creeping rhizome. It is useful as a ground cover in open woods and under shrubs, where it can be contained. It is abundant in damp woodland areas in eastern North America.

T. palustris (marsh fern) is a pinnate-bipinnate fern whose creeping rhizomes form colonies of plants 4 ft. high in wet, lime-free locations. The fertile pinnae appear much contracted because of their inrolled edges. It is found in temperate to subtropical areas of North America and Europe.

T. phegopteris (long beech or northern beech fern), also listed as *Phegopteris connectilis*, is a pinnate to bipinnate fern that grows 8–20 in. high and has thin, pale green fronds. It differs from *T. hexagonoptera* in that the two basal pinnae turn strongly downward and the pinnae are not connected by a winged rachis. It is common in moist woods in the United States, Canada, and Asia.

T. simulata (Massachusetts fern), also listed as *Parathelypteris simulata*, grows 1½–3 ft. tall and has lance-shaped, pinnate-pinnatifid fronds and is found in coniferous and cranberry swamps. It can be cultivated in deep, moist, peat-rich soil with plenty of shade. There are rare, spotty colonies in northeastern North America, with a greater concentration in New England.

THEOBROMA (thee oh BROHM ah) **cacao.** A tropical tree, commonly known as cacao, whose seeds are the commercial source of cocoa and chocolate.

Hardy only in Zones 10–11, it is native and extensively cultivated in Central and South America. A wide-branched evergreen to 25 ft., it bears large flowers that produce seed pods to 1 ft. long and 4 in. thick with a hard, leathery shell containing up to 40 "beans," some an inch wide. These are prepared for manufacture by washing and fermentation. Propagation is generally from seed. Trees, when 1–2 ft. tall, are planted 10–15 ft. apart; they bear fruit in about 4 years.

THERMOPSIS (thur MAHP sis). A genus of perennial herbs with racemes of yellow flowers, resembling and related to lupines, belonging to the Fabaceae (Bean Family), and commonly known as false lupine. Useful in the garden and hardy to Zone 3, they are easily grown in light, rich soil in an open, sunny location. Propagation is by seed or division.

PRINCIPAL SPECIES

T. caroliniana is the best-known species. It grows to 4 ft. and bears its yellow, pealike blossoms in midsummer. Although it is a rather coarse plant, it is good for bold effects in perennial borders.

T. montana is very similar to *T. caroliniana*, but it only grows to 2 ft. and its flowers form shorter, less dense racemes.

T. rhombifolia grows 1 ft. high and also has yellow flowers.

T. caroliniana

THEVETIA (the VEE shee ah) **peruviana.** A tropical American tree, commonly known as yellow-oleander and in Florida as trumpet flower. It grows to 30 ft. and has narrow, evergreen leaves to 6 in. long and fragrant, 2–in., yellow flowers.

THIMBLEBERRY. A popular name loosely applied to blackberries and raspberries generally, but properly applied to the blackcap raspberry, *Rubus occidentalis*; see RASPBERRY.

THISTLE. Common name given to several genera of plants, many of them troublesome weeds but applied particularly to the genus ONOPORDUM, a group of woolly, prickly leaved herbs with attractive rounded heads of white or purple flowers often associated with Scotland.

The common name is also used in connection with other plants. Blessed-thistle refers to both *Cnicus benedictus* and *Silybum marianum*, the latter also known as holy-, milk-, or St. Mary's-thistle; see CNICUS, SILYBUM. Fishbone-thistle is *C. diacantha* of the genus CIRSIUM, which is known as plume-thistle. Globe-thistle is the genus ECHINOPS. Golden-thistle is *Scolymus hispanicus*; see SCOLYMUS. Plumless-thistle is the genus CARDUUS. Russian-thistle is a SALSOLA.

THLASPI (THLAS pee). A genus of annual and perennial herbs with loose clusters of white, pink, or purple flowers, belonging to the Brassicaceae (Mustard Family), and commonly known as pennycress. Native to temperate and cold climates and mountainous altitudes throughout the world, some are widely distributed weeds, while others are cultivated for their racemes of small flowers. Still others are raised for their large, flat, ornamental pods, which are occasionally used in winter bouquets.

Although some of the perennials can be propagated by division and cuttings, they and the annuals are usually grown from seed. The seedlings should be transplanted to partly shaded locations in naturally moist soil, usually in rock gardens. The species best known in North America are all perennials.

PRINCIPAL SPECIES

T. alpestre grows 12–18 in. high and has white flowers with a reddish tinge.

T. rotundifolium grows to 8 in. and has lilac flowers.

T. stylosum grows in low tufts with 1-in. racemes of rose-tinted flowers.

THORN. Alone this is generally used as a common name for the genus CRATAEGUS, including those known as thornapple (which also refers to the genus DATURA), English hawthorn, and cockspur, Washington, or white thorn. It is also applied in various forms to many different genera. Black-thorn is *Prunus spinosa*. Box-thorn is LYCIUM. Broom-thorn is *Ulex europaeus*. Camel- and kangaroo-thorn are species of ACACIA. Christ-thorn is *Paliurus spina-christi*. Fire-thorn and evergreen-thorn are species of PYRACANTHA. Hedge-thorn is *Carissa bispinosa*. Jerusalem-thorn is *Parkinsonia aculeata*. Lily-thorn is *Catesbaea spinosa*. Mysore-thorn is *Caesalpinia sepiaria*.

THRIFT. A common name for ARMERIA, a hardy genus of flowering perennials.

THRINAX (THRĪ naks). A genus of slender, spineless fan palms, commonly known as silver palms because of the light-colored undersurface on the leaves. Several species are native and extensively cultivated in Florida or nearby islands.

T. morrisii is one of the most beautiful species, with a trunk up to 30 ft. tall, sometimes elevated 3 ft. above the ground by the massed roots, and surmounted by a wide head of fan-shaped leaves. This lovely palm thrives in sun or shade, preferring rich, moist loam. In sandy soil, it responds well to additions of organic fertilizer.

THRIPS. Tiny insects with rasping and sucking mouthparts belonging to the order Thysanoptera, meaning "fringed" or "bristled wings." They are slender, about ⅛ in. long, and agile. Destructive species include the gladiolus, greenhouse, onion, and pear thrips. The thrips injury is sometimes called white blast from the white flecks on plants at the time of attack. Affected branch tips then wither, curl up, and die.

Thrips

The greenhouse thrips deposit eggs in slits in leaves. They hatch after about a week into very active nymphs that rasp the leaves and then suck up the juices. There are four molts before the brown adults, with four narrow wings, are formed.

Insecticidal soap, diatomaceous earth, pyrethrum, and rotenone sprays have proved useful on various species. Predatory nematodes can also be introduced into the soil near vulnerable plants. The pests eat the nematodes, which then destroy them from within. See also INSECT CONTROL.

THUJA (THOO yah). A genus of coniferous evergreen trees belonging to the Pinaceae (Pine Family), well known in many forms as the arborvitae. They grow best in cool locations, either in wet soil, sandy loam, or sand with water near the surface, but suffer from heat and cold in dry locations. The foliage is dense, scalelike (sometimes juvenile or needlelike), waxy to the touch, and fragrant.

Thuja plicata

Landscape plans today make extensive use of arborvitae as screens for privacy, protection for more tender plants, windbreaks, hedges, and as specimen plants. Many new dwarf cultivars are being used as accent plants in rock gardens. Care must be taken when pruning arborvitae. Do not prune beyond the green growth, as this will create a dead spot on the plant that usually will not grow back. They can tolerate partial shade but will have a less dense growth habit. Avoid plantings in hot, dry areas because of the susceptibility to red spider. Propagation is by seed or by cuttings taken in midwinter through early spring.

PRINCIPAL SPECIES

T. occidentalis (American arborvitae, white-cedar) often grows to 60 ft., retaining its dense, pyramidal form. Very useful in landscaping, with infinite variety in shape, color, foliage, and size, it is found in all the northern states and higher elevations to North Carolina and Tennessee and is suitable for backgrounds, hedges, and accents. The dwarf forms are admirable material for carrying out designs or for foundation planting. There are many desirable cultivars. Hardy in Zones 3–8.

T. orientalis is now listed as *Platyclaydus orientalis*; see PLATYCLAYDUS.

T. plicata (western red-cedar, giant arborvitae, canoe-cedar) is native from Alaska to northern California and Montana, where it may grow to a height of 200 ft., but under cultivation, only to about 50 ft. A beautiful tree, it has great drooping, fernlike branches, will endure close shearing, and is occasionally grown as a specimen tree or screen for privacy. Its durable wood makes it a valuable timber tree in the western states. Hardy in Zones 2–7.

THUJOPSIS (thoo YAHP sis) **dolobrata.** A Japanese evergreen tree belonging to the Pinaceae (Pine Family). It grows to 25 ft. and has graceful, frondlike branchlets. There are several cultivars: 'Nana' is dwarf with lighter-colored leaves; 'Variegata' has white-tipped branchlets; 'Hondae' is taller with smaller leaves. Hardy in Zones 6–7.

THUNBERGIA (thun BUR ji ah). A genus of about 75 species of tender, climbing plants from tropical regions, belonging to the Acanthaceae (Acanthus Family), and sometimes called clockvine. Several are grown for greenhouse decoration. When planted outside, they grow and flower freely, producing blossoms of white, buff, blue, scarlet, or purple. In very warm regions, some are grown as ornamental vines on trellises and arbors. *T. alata* and its varieties are the hardiest forms, although a slight frost cuts their top growth to the ground. In cooler climates, they can be grown as annuals and displayed in hanging baskets or window boxes. Thunbergias bloom in late summer and autumn. Propagation is by seed, cuttings, or layers.

PRINCIPAL SPECIES

T. alata (black-eyed-Susan vine) is a twining perennial to 8 ft., often grown as an annual for greenhouse bloom or outdoors, where it flowers in late summer. The flowers are mostly buff with a dark purple throat. Two good varieties are *alba*, white, and *aurantiaca*, orange, both with dark centers.

T. erecta is a medium-sized, straggly shrub. The dark purple flowers are borne singly but in great profusion. A white-flowered form is also grown.

T. grandiflora is the commonest of the blue-flowered species. It is a tall climber with large, heart-shaped leaves and bell-shaped flowers borne singly or in short, drooping racemes.

T. laurifolia is a strong, woody climber, one of the best for winter flowering in the greenhouse. The large, pale blue flowers are borne in clusters.

THYME. Common name for THYMUS, a genus of aromatic herbs. Spanish-thyme is *Coleus amboinicus*; see COLEUS.

THYMELAEACEAE (thi mee lee AY see ee). The Mezereum Family, a group of warm-climate trees and shrubs with tough, acrid bark. Useful genera include *Daphne*, *Dirca*, and *Pimelea*.

THYMUS (TĪ mus). A genus of aromatic herbs or shrubby plants of the Lamiaceae (Mint Family), commonly known as thyme, long cultivated and valued as both ornamental and culinary herbs. They have small, lavender or pink flowers. In the rock garden, their fine foliage makes excellent carpeters for the edges. When planted in the seams of a rock path, they soften the appearance and provide delicious fragrance when crushed or stepped on.

A large number of thymes, including some of the variegated ones, though suitable for rock garden usage, should not be planted among rare alpine plants, since they may be invasive.

Thymus vulgaris

Many other species, including *T. herba-barona* (caraway thyme) are suitable for the rock garden, and others, for planting in the border as fragrant ornamentals. They all grow well in a light, well-limed soil, in full sun. Some species can be propagated from seed and many by cuttings and/or division. Various species are hardy to Zones 4–5.

T. vulgaris (garden or common thyme) and the hybrid *T.* x *citriodorus* (lemon thyme) are shrubby plants, important for their flavor, and belong in the herb garden.

Thymus x *citriodorus*

T. serpyllum (wild thyme) is often confused with *T. praecox* (mother-of-thyme), of which there are several attractive cultivars, including 'Albus', with white flowers; 'Roseus', with pink flowers; and 'Cocinneus', with crimson flowers. All of these make an excellent ground cover in full sun and a fairly dry location.

TIARELLA (tī ah REL ah). A genus of small, perennial woodland herbs belonging to the Saxifragaceae (Saxifrage Family), commonly known as false mitrewort. They have small, delicate flowers in racemes, and their simple or compound leaves assume beautiful bronzy red tones in the autumn. Hardy to Zone 4, false mitreworts are delightful when colonized in the wild or rock garden, and they are easily propagated by seed or division.

T. cordifolia (foam-flower), found in the eastern states, grows to 12 in. and bears small, white flowers. There are interesting color variations in cv. 'Purpurea',

Tiarella cordifolia

with reddish purple flowers, and 'Marmorata', with marbled foliage.

T. unifoliata, a western form, grows to 2 ft., bearing panicles of feathery flowers.

TIBOUCHINA (ti boo SHEEN ah). A genus of tropical American shrubs and herbs with large, purple flowers, commonly called glorybush. Grown under glass or outdoors in Zones 10–11, they are handsome plants for conservatory decoration, grown either in bush form or to adorn a wall or pillar. For bush forms, pinch the strong shoots at intervals and train in shape. They grow easily from cuttings and thrive in a rich, loamy soil.

T. granulosa is a large species, reaching 40 ft. in its native Brazil, with brilliant, purplish violet flowers.

T. urvilleana, formerly listed as *T. semidecandra*, grows to 10 ft. or more and has soft, hairy leaves and showy, violet-colored flowers up to 5 in. across.

TICKSEED. One of the common names for BIDENS, a genus of weeds propagated by seeds (burrs) that hook onto passing animals.

TIDY-TIPS. Common name for *Layia platyglossa*, a daisylike annual of western North America whose yellow ray flowers are often tipped with white. See LAYIA.

TIGER LILY. Common name for the orange-flowered species *Lilium tigrinum*; see LILIUM.

TIGRIDIA (tī GRID ee ah). A small genus of tender biennial herbs, native from Mexico to Peru, belonging to the Iridaceae (Iris Family), and commonly known as tigerflower. Growing from bulbs, they produce short, saberlike foliage. Forked, leafy stalks bear a quick succession of irislike flowers, whose striking beauty is seldom equaled. While the individual blossoms last only a day, there are enough on each stalk to provide a display over a considerable period.

T. pavonia, the most important species, grows to 2½ ft. in great profusion in the Mexican hills.

Its flowers are normally red, spotted yellow and purple, but there are varieties providing interesting yellow, white, and lilac effects. Var. *grandiflora* has very large flowers. Hardy to Zone 6.

TILIA (TIL ee ah). A genus of handsome hardy deciduous trees commonly known as linden, basswood, and in England as lime. Distributed throughout the North Temperate Zone, they are valuable timber and ornamental trees. Though easily grown in most soils, they need plenty of moisture in order to thrive.

Tilia americana

They are generally pyramidal in form, some species becoming more irregular with age. They have been extensively planted because of their dense, attractive foliage and the abundant fragrant, yellowish flowers that add to their beauty. Also, they produce a uniform landscape along avenues or entrance driveways. Lindens are important bee forage trees from which a very fine honey is produced.

Lindens are propagated by seed, which requires two years to germinate, and by layers or cuttings. Named cultivars of special value are sometimes grafted in spring or budded in summer on common stocks.

PRINCIPAL SPECIES

T. americana (American basswood, American linden) grows to great size and has been used as a street tree, but use is limited because of its size and the popularity of other species. Hardy in Zones 3–7.

T. cordata (littleleaf linden), native to Europe, is an excellent shade tree that grows to 60 ft. and has an oval to pyramidal shape and small, shiny green foliage. Cv. 'Greenspire' is widely used as a street tree with a single, straight leader. Hardy in Zones 4–7.

T. x *europaea* (European linden), with smaller leaves and generally more pyramidal shape, has also been a favorite street tree; however, the suckers can prove troublesome. Hardy in Zones 4–7.

T. platyphyllos, a large-leaved species, grows to 75 ft. and has several varieties with colored branchlets, deeply cut leaves, pyramidal habit, and other variable characteristics. Hardy in Zones 4–7.

T. tomentosa (white or silver linden) grows to 70 ft. and has more upright branches. It endures heat and dryness more than other species. Hardy in Zones 5–7.

TILIACEAE (til ee AY see ee). The Linden or Basswood Family, a group of trees and shrubs widely distributed in warm and tropical regions, with some ranging into the temperate zone. The sap is mucilaginous, and the bark is tough, that of the genus *Tilia* (linden) yielding commercial fiber, and a species of *Corchorus* yielding jute. *Sparmannia* is a greenhouse subject, and forms of *Tilia* are well-known shade or ornamental trees.

TILLAGE. In general, this means all practices relating to the management of land in crop production—manuring, plowing, harrowing, disking, rolling, and cultivation (loosening the surface of the soil to increase air circulation, conserve moisture, and destroy weeds).

TILLANDSIA (ti LAND zee ah) **usneoides.** A slender, drooping, American epiphytic herb ("air plant") of the Bromeliaceae (Pineapple Family), commonly known as spanish-moss. It has long, slender, gray, mosslike stems covered with tiny leaves and very small, inconspicuous flowers. The "moss" is used commercially for packing and in the manufacture of various materials. Many *Tillandsia* species are grown, including some with large, blue flowers set off by pink bracts.

TIMOTHY. Common name for the perennial hay grass *Phleum pratense*; see PHLEUM.

TISSUE CULTURE. A term for a relatively new laboratory technique, also called micropropagation, used for mass producing plants. Very small

sections (about 1-mm cubes) of vegetative plant tissue, often bud or root tips, are induced to grow under asceptic conditions in a completely controlled environment. First, large amounts of callus tissue are produced. This tissue is then divided into small sections or chunks and placed in a different medium, which induces formation of shoots; then an alteration in medium induces the individual shoots to form roots. All this is done in test tubes or other small glass containers. Once the plantlets are formed, it is necessary to take them out of their closed asceptic environment, pot them individually or in flats, and adapt them to greenhouse conditions. The acclimatization step is often rather difficult. This propagation method is usually cost effective only when about 1000 or preferably several thousand multiples of one plant are needed.

Tissue culture or micropropagation has opened up a whole new field. Not only is it the quickest method of vegetative mass reproduction, but it is now ushering in perhaps the ultimate plant breeding technique—genetic engineering—in which the DNA (the determiner of all physical traits) is added to and subtracted from individual cell nuclei with resultant changes in the plant traits. A plant is then produced from the single genetically altered cell. Since genetic engineering is not limited to plant life (insect DNA has been added to plants), it opens up moral and ethical questions that have not been thoroughly addressed, much less answered.

TITHONIA (ti THOHN ee ah). A genus of robust herbs or shrubby plants native in Mexico and further south, belonging to the Asteraceae (Aster Family), and commonly known as Mexican-sunflower. The principal species, *T. rotundifolia*, also known as *T. speciosa*, is a very robust grower, sometimes attaining a height of 12 ft. in six months from seed. The flowers are brilliant orange-red, about 3 in. across, with the top of the flower stem inflated. They commonly flower late in summer, but an early-flowering strain is also available.

TOADFLAX. Common name for a few species of LINARIA, including hardy wild herbs.

TOAD LILY. Common name for TRICYRTIS, a genus of perennial lilies, usually with spots on the flowers.

TOADS. These AMPHIBIANS look like frogs but often live away from water sources.

TOBACCO. Common name for NICOTIANA, a genus of annual or perennial herbs including ornamental plants and commercial crops. Tree tobacco is *N. glauca*. Indian-tobacco refers to *N. bigelovii* and to *Lobelia inflata*, a hairy annual with blue flowers; see LOBELIA.

TOBIRA. A common name for *Pittosporum tobira*, an evergreen shrub with leathery leaves and fragrant flowers; see PITTOSPORUM.

TOLMIEA (tol MEE ah) **menziesi.** A hardy herb native to the Pacific Northwest, belonging to the Saxifragaceae (Saxifrage Family), and commonly known as piggyback plant or youth-on-age. It has rounded, toothed leaves and small, green and brown flowers in slender racemes. Hardy to Zone 7, it is useful in the rock garden or as a houseplant. It has the charming habit of producing embryonic plants at the sinus of mature leaves, inspiring the common names. These small plants can be pinned down to moist soil, rooted, and then severed from the parent and potted separately.

TOLPIS (TOHL pis). A genus of herbs with heads of yellow flowers, belonging to the Asteraceae (Aster Family). *T. barbata* (golden-yellow-hawk-weed), an annual growing to 2½ ft., is native to southern Europe. It is occasionally used in the border and is easily grown from seed sown where the plants are to stand.

TOMATO. A tropical herb, *Lycopersicon lycopersicum*, related to the eggplant, pepper, and potato. Tomato varieties offer a wider range of choices and uses than those of most other vegetables. In size, the fruits vary from the so-called currant varieties weighing less than an ounce, to mammoth, meaty sorts weighing over a pound each. The plum, pear, and cherry varieties (named for their shapes) and others somewhat larger are so desirable for salads and for preserving that every home garden should have a few plants. In flavor, some are highly acidic, while others are almost sweet. Many are exceedingly juicy and so are well adapted for making beverages; others are meaty and almost seedless and thus are desirable for slicing or canning whole.

The strawberry- or husk-tomato is *Physalis pruinosa*. Tree-tomato is *Cyphomandra betacea*, a South American shrub.

CULTURE

GARDEN TOMATOES

In its native South American habitat, the tomato is a perennial; in temperate climates, however, it is grown as an annual. Since it requires a relatively long season, seed is usually started indoors or in sheltered beds four to eight weeks before the earliest date when plants can be safely set outdoors. The seedbed should be light and friable but not rich, since forced growth is likely to be spindly and weak.

Seed and Planting. If seed is sown thinly in flats or beds (not more than three to the inch), much stronger plants will result than from thicker seeding. When the seedlings have their second pair of true leaves, they should promptly be pricked into other flats 4" x 4" apart or into 3-in. flowerpots. Delay leads to crowding, stunting, and unsatisfactory plants. It is also better to grow them steadily but slowy at a rather low temperature (50°F) than at a higher heat, because they then suffer less of a check when set outdoors in less favorable surroundings.

Set the plants in the open after all danger of frost has passed. They should then be stocky, sturdy, and dark green. Tall, spindly, yellowish plants are not worth planting—and certainly not worth buying.

Feeding and Cultivation. Any well-drained garden soil will grow good tomatoes, especially if well supplied with humus. Manures and nitrogenous fertilizers must be used with caution, because they tend to develop oversized plants and few, small, inferior fruits. Ground bonemeal and superphosphate tend to promote sturdy plants; sulfate and muriate of potash and wood ashes foster abundant, high quality fruit, so they can be used freely.

Where cultivation can be done in two directions, plants can stand as close as 3' x 3', though up to 4 ft. apart is better. In home gardens, plants can be trained on trellises, stakes, cages, or other

Tomato cage support

supports for appearance, to save space, and because the fruit supported up in the light and air is better able to resist diseases than if the plants sprawl on the ground. They also tend to keep the fruit clean, prevent premature decay, and facilitate gathering. Wire supports or cages can be purchased or made at home. If trained to stakes and cultivated in only one direction, plants can be set 24 in. apart or even less.

ENEMIES

DISEASES

Many diseases of tomatoes may be serious in certain localities, but several are generally distributed. A number of them can be avoided or controlled to a large extent by using clean seed (see SEED DISINFECTION), planting healthy stock, burning all crop refuse, and thoroughly cleaning the area in autumn. Certain diseases are best prevented by growing resistant varieties. This is especially true of fusarium wilt, which shows first as wilting, yellowing, and dying of the leaves from the lower part of the plant upward, followed by death of the entire plant.

The familiar blossom-end rot, appearing as water-soaked areas that later turn black on the blossom ends of the fruit, is due to irregular watering and lack of calcium in the soil. Plant in good, moisture-retentive soil, cultivate well, and give plenty of water.

Plants showing the virus disease mosaic (which can be recognized by yellowing and mottling of the leaves and stunting of the plant), should be burned.

INSECT PESTS

The CUTWORM is one of the most serious pests of young plants. The potato and spinach aphids, which commonly infest tomato, can be controlled by fitting the lower stem section with a paper collar. A rotenone-pyrethrum spray can be used against the greenhouse WHITEFLY, which may bother outdoor tomatoes as well. Soil nematodes should be controlled by planting nematode-resistant varieties.

Large green worms or caterpillars with a projection or horn on the back (the tomato hornworm and the related tobacco hornworm) that feed on the leaves should be picked off but not killed if a parasitic wasp is evident; see HORNWORM. The adult moth is mottled gray and brown with a wingspread of 4–5 in.

If stems are infested by a striped caterpillar, the common stalk borer, the only course is to destroy the plants and set out new ones.

TOMATO HORNWORM. *Manduca quinquemaculata*, a common caterpillar pest on tomato plants; see HORNWORM.

TOMENTOSE. Covered with a rather dense matting of short, soft, woolly hairs, like the leaves of mullein. Compare WOOLLY.

TONGUE FERN. A common name for *Pyrrosia lingua*, an epiphytic fern with simple, rather fleshy and hairy fronds; see PYRROSIA.

TOOLS. Garden tools are any implements or devices by which garden work is lightened, improved, or done more quickly than is possible by hand alone. This general category includes hand tools, such as spades and rakes, and power tools, such as lawn mowers and rotary tillers.

Until amateur gardeners begin to appreciate the time- and labor-saving characteristics of good tools designed for specific purposes, most of them either buy blindly or restrict themselves to fewer and poorer tools than the nature of their work would warrant. Generally it is not essential or even advisable to spend a large sum of money at the start for a complete assortment. After the few fundamental tools such as digging fork, hoe, and rake have been bought, others can be added as needed or desired.

COST AND QUALITY

For most gardeners, time is usually at a premium. Money spent for tools that enable a larger amount of work to be done in a given period is really an investment in time. From another standpoint, one of the greatest satisfactions in amateur gardening is to use the best adapted tool for each type of work; such tools lessen labor, speed work, and give the pleasure of doing work in the best way.

A good tool may cost more than a poor one, but this difference is more than offset by the better work it does and the increased time it will last. Because a good tool is made of better materials than a poor one, it will keep its edge better, give better service, and wear out rather than give out. Its initial cost will almost certainly be less than that of the two or three cheap ones that it will most likely outlive.

In choosing any equipment, especially lawn mowers or hand-power machines like garden rollers, avoid getting a size too large for the person who is to operate it.

CARE OF TOOLS

Because of their relatively high initial cost and because keeping them in good condition adds to the satisfaction of their use, tools should always be properly maintained and stored.

Storage. Exposure to weather soon rusts them, as does storing them in a wet cellar or basement. Dampness soon destroys the edge of cutting tools, spades, rakes, and hoes and rusts other parts. The tool shed or other quarters should always be dry to prevent rusting, and lighted to make tools easy to find or put away.

An excellent way to store tools with long, straight handles, such as rakes and hoes, is upright in racks with holes bored for the handles in the lower horizontal member. D-handled spades and forks are best hung on hooks screwed into the wall.

Small tools such as saws, trowels, shears, and hand weeders are best stored in well-ventilated cupboards hung on hooks screwed into doors and inside surfaces. This doubles the storage space without requiring much increased depth.

Cleaning. Because tools cost money and because care increases their useful life, it is important to clean every tool promptly after it has been used. Moist soil is easily cleaned from metal parts by scraping with a flat-ended stick, but after it has dried, it is difficult to remove if it contains much clay. The longer soil is allowed to adhere to a tool, the more rust is likely to develop as a result.

Seasonal Maintenance. At the close of each season, all tools should be examined and all machines overhauled. Worn and broken parts should be replaced and every implement repaired, sharpened, oiled, repainted, or otherwise renovated to put it in proper condition. Oiling all bearing parts (especially of lawn mowers during the season and particularly at the season's end) is one of the most important but most commonly neglected of all tool-care essentials. Lack of lubrication is one of the chief reasons that machines wear out.

Rust. Rust must be fought constantly, not only because it makes work more difficult, but because it shortens the life of tools. When tools are overhauled at the close of the season, they should be thoroughly cleaned with kerosene to remove grease, caked oil, and dirt. Similarly, all nuts and bolts should be soaked in kerosene and then given a few drops of heavy oil or vaseline so they will work easily. Finally, all metal parts should be swabbed with oil (automobile waste oil will do) before they are put into storage for the winter.

One convenient way to oil such tools as spades and rakes is to put clean sand in a long narrow box, saturate it with oil, and work tools back and forth in it a few times before hanging them up. Otherwise use an oily rag.

Sharpening. Sharp tools perform better work more quickly and with less effort than dull ones. With knives, shears, saws, and other tools used in pruning, budding, grafting, and cutting garden flowers, the keener the edge, the cleaner the cut, and the quicker the healing. Well-sharpened spades, hoes, sickles, scythes, or similar tools will reduce work, perhaps more than any shortcut.

Frequent regular attention to sharpening throughout the season is far easier and better than one general spring or fall sharpening. Usually all that is needed for the larger, heavier implements is a large, flat file, though a grinding wheel will save time and effort, especially in keeping hoes and spades in good condition. Sharpening stones, graded by abrasiveness and hardness, are available for tools such as sickles, scythes, knives, and shears.

If bent corners or nicks occur on spades, hoes, and other tools, they should be filed down and the blade given an edge, preferably on a short angle, because this will be less prone to damage again when striking unseen obstructions like stones. Nicks in knives and shears do not necessarily require grinding to be removed. Small nicks can be disregarded because later sharpening will eliminate them. However, large ones may ruin the tool or make heavy grinding necessary. Nothing can take the place of experience in deciding such a question.

There is a great variety of sharpening devices available. For the proper technique for each tool, consult manufacturer's directions, a local dealer, or someone experienced in sharpening.

TOOTHWORT. Common name for DENTARIA, a genus of perennial herbs with toothlike roots and clustered flowers.

TOP-DRESSING. Manure, compost, fertilizer, or other plant food material placed on the surface of the ground, as opposed to that plowed or spaded under. See also MULCH.

TOPIARY. The training or pruning of plant material into various objects or geometric shapes. It has been practiced in gardens since the Middle Ages and is seen at its best in some formal English gardens.

In its simple forms, it may consist of clipping and forming the end plants of a hedge into balls, piers, or pyramids; or of accenting a clipped hedge at intervals or rectangular spacing with a round or square finial. This breaks the monotony of a long, regular hedge, serves to accent entrances or frame vistas, and is highly desirable when done with discretion.

More advanced specimens of topiary pieces include geometrical cubes, balls, pyramids, or combinations of such forms, or in figures such as birds, animals, and the like. These are interesting accents but must be used only in tidy formal gardens where the gardener has time to keep the training and pruning severely in hand.

The best evergreen materials for topiary work are *Buxus suffruticosa* (box); *Taxus cuspidata* (yew), *T. brevifolia*, and hybrids; and *Tsuga caroliniana* (hemlock). The best deciduous material is found in varieties of *Ligustrum* (privet). *Fagus* (beech), *Carpinus* (hornbeam), and *Crategus* (hawthorn) can also be used for large, simple forms. *Hedera helix* (English ivy) trained over wire supports is also very attractive.

TOPSOIL. The upper soil layer—usually from 6 in. to about 10 in. in depth—of soil, which is normally the most fertile and in which the majority of feeding plant roots are found. Its ability to grow plants is due largely to its humus, the fact that it is aerated, and its content of bacteria and other microscopic organisms that give life to a soil, and which are lacking in the SUBSOIL.

TOP-WORKING. Completely changing over the top of a seedling or tree that bears poor fruit, by grafting it to one or more desired varieties, usually by the cleft method; see GRAFTING. This operation, usually done to old or at least well-developed trees, is naturally a severe one, so it is sometimes done gradually. That is, perhaps a third of the large branches are grafted one year, another third the second year, and the remainder the third year, by which time the initial grafts will have probably begun to make growth.

TORENIA (toh REE nee ah). A genus of annual and perennial herbs belonging to the Scrophulariaceae (Figwort Family) and commonly known as wishbone flower. They bear two-lipped flowers resembling small gloxinias. Native to tropical Asia and Africa, they are treated as garden annuals in cool regions or are occasionally grown in the greenhouse. In Florida, where they grow readily from self-sown seed, they are grown along water courses or in dry, sandy soils. They succeed best, however, in a partially shaded position and require regular watering. Propagation is by seed or cuttings, and plants should not be set outdoors until the ground is warm.

Torenia fournieri

PRINCIPAL SPECIES

T. asiatica has dark bluish purple flowers 1½ in. long.

T. baillonii has predominantly yellow flowers marked with red-purple.

T. fournieri has violet and blue flowers marked with yellow.

TORREYA (tor EE ah). A genus of handsome evergreen trees belonging to the Taxaceae (Yew Family). Native to North America and Asia, most are hardy to Zone 7. They have needlelike leaves and drupelike seeds with covering. Propagation is by seed or cuttings of side shoots.

T. californica (California-nutmeg) forms a rounded tree to 60 ft. at maturity. The leaves have a strong odor when crushed.

T. taxifolia (stinking-cedar), growing to 40 ft., is a somewhat spreading tree, native to Florida. Its yewlike foliage, when bruised, emits a fetid odor. It bears dark purple, drupelike fruits.

TORTOISE BEETLE. *Metriona bicolor* (golden tortoise beetle) and *Chelymorpha cassidea* (argus tortoise beetle), also called sweet-potato beetles or gold bugs because they are golden and striped, mottled, or spotted with black. The larvae have conspicuous, horny spines, including two long ones at the posterior end, on which they pack all of their dirt and excrement.

The feeding of these turtle-shaped beetles is usually confined to plants of the Convolvulaceae (Morning-glory Family), but they sometimes feed on milkweed, raspberry, or corn. They eat round holes in leaves or devour them completely.

A ROTENONE spray can be used for control, but avoid using this until after dusk when bees and other pollinators have returned to their hives for the night. See BEETLES; INSECT CONTROL.

TOUCH-ME-NOT. A common name for species of IMPATIENS that bear pods that curl to eject the seeds when touched.

TOYON. A common name for HETEROMELES, a genus of evergreen shrubs or small trees.

TRACHELIUM (tra KEE lee um). A genus of perennial herbs or small shrubs belonging to the Campanulaceae (Bellflower Family), native to southern Europe, and commonly known as throatwort. They have simple leaves and tubular blue flowers. Only *T. caeruleum* is commonly seen. Sometimes growing to 3 ft., it has clusters of small flowers varying from dark blue to white. A perennial plant, it is grown outdoors in the South and as a greenhouse plant or garden annual in the North. Propagation is by seed or cuttings. Hardy to Zone 8.

TRACHELOSPERMUM (tray kel oh SPURM um) **jasminoides.** A southern Asiatic vine belonging to the Apocynaceae (Dogbane Family) and commonly known as African, Malayan, or star jessamine. The woody, evergreen vines have opposite leaves and very fragrant, white, flat-topped clusters of salverform flowers, each 1 in. across. Var. *variegatum*, with green-and-white leaves, sometimes tinged reddish, is said to be hardier. In cool climates it is grown in greenhouses, where it can be a satisfactory climber, although it takes several years to develop a large specimen. It can also be grown in tubs, trimmed to bush form, and wintered indoors in a cool place. In the southern states, where it is a favorite vine, it is grown in the open and known also as confederate jessamine.

TRACHYMENE (tray ki MEE nee). A genus of Australian or Asian herbs with delicate blue or white flowers in flattish clusters resembling those of Queen-Anne's-lace and also belonging to the Apiaceae (Celery Family).

They are represented in North America by *T. coerulea* (blue laceflower), a handsome annual from Australia that has gone through phases of popularity for garden and greenhouse culture and listed in many catalogs under the former generic name *Didiscus*. The dainty plant, growing to 2½ ft. tall, blooms from July to November. Its flat or rounded clusters of clear blue flowers with slender tubes suggest miniature lace parasols. The blossoms make graceful cut flowers and are extensively grown by florists.

The plant is also an easily cultivated garden subject. It is best placed in a moist, cool, sunny location. Seed should be sown outdoors where plants are to stand as soon as all danger of frost has passed. Later they should be thinned to have 1 sq. ft. of room per plant. Since seed germination is slow, it is sometimes advisable to start plants indoors in pots so they can be set outdoors with the least possible disturbance of the roots. For winter flowering in the greenhouse or conservatory, plants can be grown from seed in the bench or carefully potted up from the garden before frost occurs.

TRADESCANTIA (trad es KAN tee uh). A genus of herbs belonging to the Commelinaceae (Spiderwort Family) and commonly known as spiderwort. They are of various habits, some erect, others trailing; some are grown in the open, others under glass or in hanging baskets. The indoor species are usually grown for their foliage, but several of the hardy species make attractive border plants with white, rose-purple, or blue flowers. All are easily grown from seed, divisions, or cuttings.

PRINCIPAL SPECIES

T. x *andersoniana* cv. 'Purple Dome' has purple flowers in summer. The foliage flops over after flowering and should be cut back. Hardy in Zones 4–9.

T. fluminensis (wandering-Jew) is a trailing South American plant that roots at the stem joints. It has smooth, fleshy stems and leaves, and its white flowers are hairy inside. The leaves are very green, especially when the plants grow where there is little light. Hardy only to Zone 8, it is often used to edge greenhouse benches, in window boxes, or as houseplants. It requires a constant supply of moisture in order to grow luxuriantly. Stem cuttings root easily in water and can then be potted. Var. *variegata* has yellow-and-white striped leaves, but this coloration is seen only when the plant grows in full light, the foliage returning to the ordinary green form when shaded.

T. ohieusis, formerly listed as *T. reflexa*, is native to damp areas in the central and southern states. It has very narrow, grasslike leaves and blue or white flowers on 3-ft. stems.

T. subaspera, formerly listed as *T. pilosa*, grows to 3 ft. and has lilac-blue flowers. It is native from southern Pennsylvania to Missouri and is hardy in Zones 4–9.

T. virginiana (common spiderwort) is a native plant, hardy in Zones 4–9. It grows to 3 ft. and has long, reedlike leaves and dark violet-purple flowers 1–2 in. across

Tradescantia virginiana

that bloom nearly all summer. Var. *alba*, with white flowers, and var. *coccinea*, with red flowers, are interesting forms.

TRAGOPOGON (trag oh POH guhn). A genus of biennial or perennial herbs with yellow or purple heads of ray flowers and commonly known as goat's-beard. They are native to Europe and widely naturalized throughout North America.

T. porrifolius (salsify, oysterplant) is a biennial grown for its edible root; see SALSIFY.

T. pratensis (meadow salsify) is a biennial that grows to 3 ft. and has yellow flowers 2¼ in. across, occasionally cultivated for ornament.

TRAILING-ARBUTUS. Common name for *Epigaea repens*, an attractive, spring-blooming, creeping evergreen; see EPIGAEA.

TRAILING-QUEEN. Common name for *Fuchsia procumbens*, a trailing vine with orange-and-purple flowers; see FUCHSIA.

TRAINING PLANTS. The methods and practices of developing plants according to specific aims, either for constructional strength, as in the disposition of framework branches of trees and shrubs; for the developing of symmetrical forms as in the shaping of pot plants; for the arrangement of the stems of vines according to systems that promote flower or fruit production; for the restriction of the development of certain plants to dwarf stature; and for various other objects.

TRAINING TREES

Properly understood and conducted, training is an educational rather than a corrective process. It endeavors to prevent, or at least reduce, the necessity for pruning. With no group of plants is this objective so important but at the same time so frequently neglected as in the growing of shade trees. Though, as a rule, growers cut off the lower branches of such trees, either to facilitate cultivation of the soil around them or to develop branchless trunks up to desired heights, probably not one tree in a hundred is ever afforded further training as to the position, arrangement, direction, length, or balance in size of its branches.

The all too common result of such neglect is that when such dead or crowded branches are removed, the cutting is incorrectly done, leaving stubs through which decay enters the main trunks and thus dooms the abused trees to untimely breakdown. In other cases, where two main branches are allowed to develop to practically uniform size in the form of a Y, the result is that when loaded heavily with ice or snow, and especially when subjected to the extra strain of high wind, one or both of these branches may crash to the ground, thus leaving a lopsided tree or merely a stump.

These same remarks apply with less force to fruit trees, at least as grown by well-informed commercial and amateur fruit growers. Modern fruit growers demand either two-year trees that have never been topped (that is, had their leaders or main stems cut) or one-year-old, unbranched whips on which they can develop branches exactly where wanted and suppress all others before they have become woody or even before they have developed from the buds.

The most recently developed and most satisfactory method of training fruit trees is to restrict the number of buds to groups of three at various desired heights and specific distances apart on the whips, to destroy all others and, beginning in the spring of the following season, to select the best-placed branch in each group, cutting off all the others with a sharp knife close to the stem.

This plan permits the grower (1) to have the framework (sometimes erroneously called scaffold) branches located so far apart—a foot or more—that no two will pull directly against each other and thus tend to break down; and (2) to have the branches point in different directions so that when viewed from above they suggest the spokes of a wheel, thus laying the foundation for systematic development, which can be further promoted by selecting the secondary branches by the same method.

Though these same principles are equally applicable to shade trees, most planters of such ornamentals prefer to plant specimens with at least some branches already developed. In that case, choose specimens that have no Y-crotches, in which the main branches are far apart, that have the leader or tip intact, that have no ugly crooks in trunks or branches and, always, those that are of small size, because they are easier to train, most certain to grow, and least costly to buy. After planting such trees, cut out, cleanly and close to the trunk, all inferior and badly placed branches and reduce the number of secondary branches. This will produce better results than shortening the branches, which is almost certain to create undesirable crooks and bunches of branches.

On side hills and in narrow quarters, fruit trees are sometimes trained in conventionalized fan form by restricting the branches to a single plane at approximate right angles to the slope of the hill. A second advantage of this system is the increased distribution of the light and air, which results in fruit of higher color and quality.

A disadvantage of the system is that it demands attention several times each season, since branches that start to develop apart from the desired form must be suppressed. If possible, this should be done while the shoots are green and succulent—during May or early June. While succulent they can be bent over and pulled off with scarcely any effort, whereas if allowed to mature they must be cut. When they are pulled off, no new branches are likely to develop at the same points, but when cut, water sprouts are likely to appear around the wounds and call for additional later pruning.

To produce and maintain fruit trees in dwarf form requires, first, grafting or budding the desired varieties on dwarfing stocks; second, the annual removal of all roots that develop above the graft (if a root operation); and third, frequent attention during the growing season to pinching out superfluous shoots and preventing undue extension of those that are desired; unless restricted, supposedly dwarf trees will probably become half or even full standard size. See also CORDON; DWARF FRUIT TREES; ESPALIER.

TRAINING VINES

Vines can be satisfactorily trained only when their individual nature is understood and when methods are adopted to meet the specific charac-

teristics of each. They naturally fall into three general groups: (1) those that cling to walls, trees, and other supports by means of rootlike organs on their stems (English ivy; trumpet creeper); (2) those that hold fast to supports by means of tendrils (grape, holly; Virginia creeper, partly) or by modified leaves (clematis, coiling leaf stems; garden pea, tendrils at the ends of the leaves); and (3) those that coil around their supports (wisteria, false bittersweet, or *Celastrus*).

Training of clinging vine species consists mainly in leading the growing tips in desired directions on masonry walls. Do not let such vines attach themselves to wooden walls or they may wedge themselves beneath or between the clapboards or shingles and pry them off.

Tendril-climbing vines require supports around which their tendrils can twist or to which the holdfasts on these tendrils can become attached. They rarely give such trouble as clinging or twining vines do.

Coiling or twining vines must also be given supports around which they can twist. They must not be allowed to grow around shrubs, saplings, or tree limbs because they do not give and in time will strangle and often kill such support growths. They can, however, be grown over dead trees or stumps. Rampant vines like wisteria if trained on verandas or other attached parts of a house may actually pull their supports apart. In general, the training of vines (except grapes) consists mainly in directing the growth where wanted and in reducing the branches to desired numbers.

In grape training the main object is to secure abundant fruit. Though this is generally considered as pruning, it is equally a matter of training because the underlying principles are modified to meet the ideas of the grower. Thus there are dozens of systems followed, most of which produce fruit in abundance. See GRAPE.

TRAINING SHRUBS

So-called climbing roses and other shrubs such as weeping forsythia (*F. suspensa*), which are not strictly climbers, can be trained to reach heights of 10–15 ft. by restricting the stems to a few or only one to be tied loosely at various points to stakes or arbors or on the front of (not led through) trellises. By pinching off the lower shoots, these stems will become trunklike below and very branching above. To cover the lower parts of the trellises, other plants (of the same or of different kinds) can be employed and similarly treated, but with shorter trunks. Even such sturdy shrubs as Japanese flowering quince can be trained on walls in this fashion.

Bush roses can be trained in almost any form desired. One popular form is the so-called standard or treelike form. This is accomplished by tying the single stem to a stake and preventing the development of branches below the point chosen for the head. Such branches should be removed just as the buds are starting to develop into shoots. Standard form plants are often created by grafting the desired sort at the top of an erect-growing plant of the desired height.

One of the simplest but most pleasing styles of training is that of making stiff-stemmed, erect-growing annuals (zinnia and cosmos) and perennials grown as annuals (dahlia and delphinium) grow treelike. All that is necessary is to pinch off the growing tip (an inch or less) of the young stem just above a leaf stalk when the plant is only 4–6 in. high. Branches will soon develop from the buds in the angles of the remaining leaves and will extend outward and upward in somewhat shrublike form. After these branches have grown 3–4 in. long, they can also have their tips similarly pinched to increase the number of branches. This will tend to thicken the tops and increase the number of blossoms, though the size of each flower will probably be smaller than on plants not so trained. The overall effect will be more striking because of the abundance of flowers.

One precaution is necessary when this type of training is done: the plants must be set farther apart, because they will need the extra space in which to spread.

TRANSPIRATION. The process by which water is given off by the leaves of a plant. It is accomplished and regulated by the stomata, or minute openings or pores on the surface of the leaf. These openings are formed or bounded by kidney-shaped guard cells that, with an abundance of water in the leaf, become turgid and distend the pore, permitting moisture to be given off. When the leaf's supply of water is low, they become flaccid and collapse, thus diminishing the opening and checking transpiration.

It is estimated that a large sunflower plant can give off a quart of water daily this way, and an average oak tree during its five active months, about 28,000 gallons. From this, one can readily imagine the effect of transpiration on the temperature and humidity of the environment.

The greatest transpiration activity takes place during full sunshine. For that reason, flowers should not be cut at such times, since there is likely to be insufficient water in the stems to prevent wilting.

TRANSPLANTING. The process of removing plants from one place and resetting them in another. When small seedlings are lifted from the rows in a flat or from seed pans, separated, and replaced at uniform distances in other pans or flats, the term PRICKING-OUT is generally used. The first transplanting is done to give them space in which to develop, until they are either potted or planted in more permanent quarters a few weeks later. Crowded seedlings quickly become slender or spindly, weak, and useless.

For early spring planting outdoors, seedlings can be started in greenhouse benches or hotbeds, pricked out into flats or coldframes, and later moved to the garden, or sometimes, as with melons, onions, etc., they are transplanted only once—to the open ground. For later harvesting, seed can be sown thinly in outdoor nursery beds when the weather is favorable and the seedlings later transplanted to their permanent quarters.

Transplanting almost invariably injures some of the delicate feeding rootlets and thereby checks the growth of the plant to some extent. It offers various advantages, however—including that of stimulating the development of a good, compact root system—so the most improved methods should be used.

First, plants to be pricked-out or transplanted should be prepared for the operation. With seedlings and small plants, this means watering them well several hours before they are to be moved; this makes them plump and tends to prevent the soil from falling from their roots. Second, the soil where they are to be placed should be freshly dug, finely raked, and moist (but not wet) so as to help them become established and soon resume normal growth activity. Third, should considerable loss of roots be unavoidable, part of the top (leaves) should be removed to balance such root loss. Fourth, transplanted plants, especially succulent seedlings, should be shaded from full sun for a few days.

Within limits, the younger the plant, the more likely it is to survive the operation and suffer little check. Short, stocky, herbaceous plants transplant better than weak, spindly, "leggy" ones. Those started under glass but gradually inured to outdoor conditions such as lower temperatures and strong sunlight (see HARDENING-OFF) will resist unfavorable weather better than those not so prepared. Further, those that have been pricked-out and transplanted once or twice while small, or root pruned (see ROOT PRUNING), will withstand the shock of final transplanting because the preliminary processes restricted the roots to a smaller area than they would otherwise occupy. Consequently they suffer less root injury when moved.

Always transplant in cloudy, cool, and damp weather if possible; or at least wait until the cool of the evening. If the next day proves hot or windy, cover the plants to prevent excessive evaporation.

Firming the soil around the roots of transplanted plants is important because it stimulates the rise of water by capillary action from the deeper sources of supply to within reach of the roots. Since a compacted soil surface evaporates more water than a loose one, however, the surface soil should be stirred and loosened immediately after the plant is definitely planted. On top of the layer of loose soil so created, it is advisable to spread

an additional MULCH of peat moss, compost, buckwheat hulls, or other loose material to effect the same result.

Sprinkling newly set plants is never advisable because it wets only the immediate surface. Whenever necessary, watering should be deep and thorough. For best results, form a shallow basin of loose soil around each plant and fill it once or more before mulching the plant. Wait until the water has sunk in and the soil formed a light crust; then loosen it an inch or so deep before it really bakes.

Plants with taproots transplant with difficulty, unless the main vertical root is cut while small and thus is made to send out horizontal side roots. Plants carrying considerable foliage for the size of the roots—like lettuce or cabbage—may also prove difficult unless the amount of leaf surface is reduced by about a third.

Potted plants and those grown in transplanting boxes transplant easily because each has its roots compactly surrounded by a ball of earth. This should be well moistened before the plant is set out. Shrubs, woody vines, and trees from a nursery, if container grown, can be planted at any time; however, the best time is early spring or fall. If field grown and purchased with bare roots or balled in burlap, they are usually planted while dormant. Any broken or injured roots

Seedlings in a transplanting flat

should be cut back to sound wood. The holes should be dug wide and deep enough to accommodate all the roots without having to bend or overlap them. The topsoil and subsoil from the hole should be placed in separate piles, and in filling the hole, use the topsoil first, working it well around the roots with the fingers or a blunt stick. Settle it well by watering or tramping firmly, then add the subsoil and firm that well also.

Transplanting seedlings

Leave a depression around the plant so that rain or water applied in dry spells will soak into the roots and not away from them. After planting, the branches should be pruned to balance any loss of roots and to start the formation of the top of the plant. See PRUNING.

Large trees can be moved in winter with balls of frozen soil if prepared for the operation in advance. This is, however, more a task for an expert tree mover than for the gardener. Similarly, it is better to transplant nursery-grown trees with compact root systems than wild plants with spreading roots that are sure to be injured. See also EVERGREENS.

TRAPA (TRAY pah). A genus of Asiatic aquatic herbs producing nutlike fruits, belonging to the Onagraceae (Evening-primrose Family), and commonly known as water-chestnut. They have both floating and submerged leaves and small flowers. Various species are hardy to Zone 6 but are mostly grown in aquariums.

T. bicornis (ling-nut) has fruit 3 in. across with two strongly curved spines shaped like a bull's horns.

T. natans (water-chestnut) has dainty, mottled, pinnate, floating foliage in a rosette, and small, inconspicuous white flowers. The nutlike fruit with four spiny angles is formed under the leaves and drops off when ripe. It is edible, usually cooked. Native in Eurasia and Africa, it is a naturalized weed in several North American rivers.

TRAUTVETTERIA (trawt ve TEE ree ah). A genus of tall, hardy perennial herbs belonging to the Ranunculaceae (Buttercup Family), occasionally planted in the wild garden.

T. carolinensis has small, white flowers to ½ in. across in clusters and large, lobed leaves. It will grow readily if planted in rich soil and is easily propagated by division of the roots in early spring or late fall.

TRAVELER'S-JOY. Common name for *Clematis vitalba*, a tall, flowering vine; see CLEMATIS.

TRAVELER'S TREE. Common name for *Ravenala madagascariensis*, a tropical plant with a palmlike trunk and fan-shaped head of bananalike leaves; see RAVENALA.

TREE. A tree is a woody plant with a single stem or trunk, usually without branches to a height of 10 ft. but crowned at the top with spreading branches, and growing at least 20–25 ft. There are numerous exceptions, such as the many firs, spruces, and red-cedars, which have close-set branches from the ground up. Another type of exception is found in trees of shrubby or declining form, often with multiple stems or trunks. The term "tree form" or STANDARD is applied to plants that have a single stem with a compact and globular or weeping top.

Trees can be divided into two broad classes: evergreen and deciduous. Evergreen trees hold their foliage—which may be needle-shaped or broad-leaved—throughout the year. Although the foliage is completely replaced every few years, the young leaves are constantly growing to replace the old ones, so the tree is never bare. Deciduous trees shed their foliage in the fall. They are usually broad-leaved, but a few needle-leaved trees belong in this class.

TREE FERNS. Common name for a large group of modern ferns that are similar to the great tree ferns of the Coal Age but not related to them. They are not even closely related to each other, occurring in several different families. Species of various genera are included in this generalized group, the most commonly cultivated forms belonging to *Alsophila*, *Cycathea*, and *Sphaeropteris* (Cyatheaceae); BLECHNUM (usually grown as houseplants) and *Sadleria* (Blechnaceae); *Cibotium* and *Dicksonia* (Dicksoniaceae). *Ctenitis sloanei* (American or Florida tree fern) is not a true tree fern but does develop short, scaly trunks; see CTENITIS.

Some of these ferns reach a height of 30 ft. or more; some *Cythaea* in New Zealand actually attain as much as 80 ft. In cultivation they will seldom grow to more than 10–15 ft. They differ from the low-growing ferns in possessing elongated, trunklike stems that bear fronds at their summits, while in the low types, fronds are produced from horizontal creeping stems or abbreviated surface crowns. Smaller, epiphytic ferns often volunteer in the fibers of the trunks.

Smaller species can be grown in tubs. A few even thrive in pots when they are very young, but they soon outgrow small containers. Some require a tropical greenhouse, others only a cool greenhouse, but none will endure a temperate climate where they will be exposed to any frost. Generally they are not difficult to grow if replanted regularly as they increase in size, in a porous soil composed of coarse peat, coconut fiber, and some sand. They should be kept shaded and well watered, including the fibrous stems, except when resting.

TREE GUARD.
Any device employed to protect an individual tree from possible or probable injury. The protection can be merely two or more stakes placed around the trunk, which is tied to the stakes, thereby receiving support as well as protection. The guard should be firmly fixed in the ground and the tree should be tied or braced by pieces of

Tree support

rope or wire run through lengths of old hose, so they will not cut into the bark; all too often, a well-intended guard does more harm than good because this point is neglected. Other guards are effective against gnawing rodents and other animals; see MICE.

TREE-OF-HEAVEN.
Common name for *Ailanthus altissima*, a quick-growing deciduous tree; see AILANTHUS.

TREE SURGERY.
To prevent the spread of fungi and infection that may enter a tree through cuts or wounds, all broken branch stubs should be removed and all pruning cuts should be made smooth and flush with the surface of the supporting trunk. In removing large limbs, three cuts should be made to prevent the tearing of the bark when the limb falls (see PRUNING). The surface of the cut should be left smooth and the cut (or any other wound in a tree trunk) should be somewhat pointed at the top and bottom to encourage callus formation. All dressed surfaces should be watched for tendencies to blister, crack, or check and should be repaired annually.

Cavity work involves cutting out decayed wood. With heartwood decay it is usually impossible to tell when all the infected wood has been removed; and often, if all of the decayed matter were removed, the tree would be so weakened as to be a menace. Decay of the sapwood can usually be taken care of efficiently. Excavate discolored and water-soaked wood until the sound portion is reached; smooth the surface of the cavity and shape it so that water cannot remain in any hollow; make the final cut along the edge of the bark and sapwood with a sharp knife; cover the cambium with a coat of shellac; then paint the remainder of the cavity with a wound dressing. Deep cavities should be cleaned and shellacked, then a ½–¾ in. hole should be drilled from outside upward to the base (lowest point) of the cavity so any water that enters the cavity will drain out. A cavity and its drain hole should be checked periodically to see they are clear of leaves and other refuse.

It is not necessary to fill the cavity. The only reasons for doing so are to give improved appearance and to provide a foundation surface for callus growth. Contrary to popular belief, filling a cavity does not increase the strength of the tree. It should be remembered that large scars will always be conspicuous, that the tree may never entirely heal, and that unless the tree is particularly valuable, sentimentally or otherwise, the cost of extensive cavity work might better be spent in replacing the tree with a sound specimen. Ordinarily the homeowner will find it more satisfactory to employ an experienced tree surgeon before attempting a major operation.

TREE-TOMATO. Common name for *Cyphomandra betacea*, a tropical shrub that has fragrant, pinkish flowers and acid fruits; see CYPHOMANDRA.

TRELLIS. Any open structure of wood erected for the support of climbing plants, sometimes used alone as a screen. The simplest form is composed of light strips nailed vertically and horizontally to a framework of heavier wood with the spaces between the parallel laths about equal to the strips themselves.

TRENCHING. A method of digging or spading soil to a greater depth than ordinary digging reaches. This deep digging of the soil loosens up the subsoil for superior root penetration. See also CULTIVATION; DIGGING; DOUBLE DIGGING.

TRICHOMANES (trī KAH man eez). One of the genera collectively known and cultivated as FILMY FERNS.

TRICHOSANTHES (trī koh SAN theez) **anaguina.** An annual vine of the Cucurbitaceae (Cucumber Family), commonly known as serpent or snake gourd. Raised in India for its edible fruits, it has large, almost round, lobed leaves; racemes of flowers with finely cut petals; and very slender, gourdlike fruits from 1–6 ft. long, usually curved and coiled like a serpent. It can be raised in cool areas if treated as a tender annual. Start the seeds indoors and set the plants out in very rich soil after all danger of frost is over.

TRICHOSTEMA (trik oh STEE mah). A genus of herbs of the Lamiaceae (Mint Family), hardy to Zone 9, and commonly known as woolly blue-curls, locally as ramero. *T. lanatum* is a shrubby perennial suitable for the wild garden or as a background plant for rock gardens. The plant reaches 4 ft. in height and has narrow leaves, downy beneath, and attractive blue flowers ½ in. long and covered with blue or purple wool.

TRICYRTIS (trī SUR tis). A genus of half-hardy, perennial, Asiatic herbs belonging to the Liliaceae (Lily Family) and commonly known as toad lily. They have rootstocks, leafy stems, and purple-spotted, bell-shaped flowers. Usually grown in pots in cold climates, they can be used outdoors in Zones 4–8 if given adequate winter protection. Propagation is by division.

PRINCIPAL SPECIES

T. flava grows to 20 in. and has yellow flowers, spotted dark purple inside.

T. hirta has hairy leaves and white blossoms spotted with purple and black.

T. latifolia has yellow, purple-spotted flowers on 18–24 in. stems.

T. macropoda, from China and Japan, has violet flowers spotted purple, borne in clusters on 2–3 ft. stems.

TRIFOLIATE ORANGE. Common name for *Poncirus trifoliata*, a semihardy citrus species used as an ornamental plant and as propagating stock to make citrus more hardy. It is hardy to Zone 6, but the fruit is bitter and inedible. See PONCIRUS.

TRIFOLIUM (trī FOH lee um). A genus of annual, biennial, or perennial herbs belonging to the Fabaceae (Bean Family) and commonly known as clover. They have divided leaves consisting of three leaflets and very small, white, red, purple, or yellow flowers, pealike in form but borne in dense, soft, rounded heads. Some are low growers, while others may be up to 3 ft. high. A few species are cultivated for ornament; others are important forage, COVER CROP, green manure, or LAWN planting.

They are grown from seed sown (broadcast) in very early spring, sometimes before the frost is out of the ground. They are not particular as to soil so long as it is not sour or wet.

Diseases are not usually important on garden clovers, but the characteristics of the more common of them are worth noting. LEAF SPOT shows as small, brownish purple spots, each with a central disklike fruiting pustule on the upper surface. The leaves turn yellow and often drop off. Early cutting is recommended. The leaves of red clover are frequently whitened by powdery MILDEW and may serve to infect cowpeas, larkspur, lima and spring beans, lupines, peas, and turnips. Several RUSTS cause pustules on the leaves, but they are not dangerous.

Early mowing provides the most satisfactory control of most insect pests on clover, such as the greenish white cloverhead caterpillar, which feeds in the flower heads of red clover; the clover leaf hopper, which sucks the sap from the leaves, causing white spots; the clover leaf weevil, a dark brown-striped, brown beetle, which eats notches in the leaves; pea APHIDS; and clover MITES. The greenish clover bud weevil, which cuts slits in the stem just above the lateral buds is the most destructive pest of clover in the midwestern states, and there is no satisfactory control.

PRINCIPAL SPECIES

T. agrarium, *T. alexandrinum* (Egyptian clover), and *T. filiforme* are yellow to yellow-white forms.

T. alpestre grows about 10 in. tall and bears purple flowers.

T. hybridum (Alsike clover), which originated in the Alsike parish of Sweden, is a tall, slender-stemmed perennial with white blossoms. It is valuable on cool, moist lands and is excellent for hay, pasture, and if sown thickly, as a cover crop.

T. incarnatum (crimson clover) grows 2–3 ft. and has tall, deep crimson flower spikes. Some-

times grown for forage and cover crops, it is one of the most ornamental species, especially massed in the wild garden or among rock plants. It should be sown by midsummer so it can be well established before cold weather. As a cover crop, it is ideal for sowing among garden vegetables that will be gathered during autumn, scattering 1 oz. seed to 150–200 sq. ft. Enough plants should survive even the digging of such crops as potatoes and parsnips to make a worthwhile stand. Even though winter may kill it, it leaves vegetable matter that enriches the soil. If the cover crop survives the winter, it should be dug or plowed under while only 1 ft. high before the stems become woody.

T. pratense (red clover), the state flower of Vermont, is a relatively low grower used for forage or cover crops and is sometimes pleasing when planted in clumps in the border.

T. repens (white clover, shamrock) is reputed by some to be the signature plant of Ireland. This low, creeping perennial with small, round, white heads is often included in lawn seed mixtures with the idea that the plants will start quickly, sheltering slower-growing grasses while they are getting established, and later die out as the more permanent grasses spread.

Trifolium repens

The usual allowance is 5% of the total amount of seed sown. If sown alone, twice as much must be used. It can also be propagated by runners. Cv. 'Kentish Wild White', produced on old pastures in Kent, England, is better than the species because it lasts longer and, in lawns, blooms later and more sparsely.

T. rubens has purplish red flowers, usually in paired heads. It can be used in the flower garden, either in borders or in the rock garden.

TRILISA (tril EES uh) **odoratissima.** A perennial herb belonging to the Asteraceae (Aster Family) and commonly known as Carolina-vanilla. It forms a shrubby plant to 3 ft. and has heads of purplish flowers without rays and foliage that smells of vanilla when bruised. Native from North Carolina to Florida, it is best grown in light soil and is hardy to Zone 8. Propagation is by seed sown in autumn or by division.

TRILLIUM (TRIL ee um). A genus of hardy perennial herbs of the Liliaceae (Lily Family), having short, thick rootstocks, leaves in threes, and three-parted flowers that may be white, pinkish, violet, or greenish. They are beautiful woodland plants, growing naturally in semishade in moist soil, rich in humus. Hardy to Zone 4, they are easily transferred to the wild garden, and some species grow well in the border, even in city gardens. The best time to transplant trilliums from the woods is midsummer after the foliage has ripened, but they can be moved successfully even when in full bloom and can also be grown from seed sown as soon as it is ripe.

PRINCIPAL SPECIES

T. catesbaei, growing to 1½ ft., has rose or pink flowers to 2½ in. on drooping, 2-in. stems.

T. cernuum (nodding trillium), growing to 1½ ft., has a small, white, drooping flower.

T. chloropetalum, native to the northwestern United States, grows on stout stems to 2½ ft. tall with stemless, ovate leaves to 6 in. long, often mottled. The large (3½ in. long) maroon to greenish yellow or white flowers are followed by winged fruit.

T. erectum (purple or red trillium, wake-robin) grows to 1 ft. and has purplish red flowers with a

disagreeable odor. It is most effective in groups in the wild garden.

T. grandiflorum (white trillium) grows to 1½ ft. tall and has white flowers that change to rose-pink. It is one of the most handsome species, responding well to cultivation and increasing rapidly in the wild garden or shady border. The flowers have no noticeable scent.

T. nivale, growing to 6 in., has erect or drooping, 1-in., white flowers.

T. ovatum, growing to 1½ ft., has fragrant,

T. grandiflorum

white flowers changing to rose-pink. Similar to *T. grandiflorum*, it is easily grown but is more suitable for the wild garden than the border.

T. petiolatum, growing to 6 in., has purple, stemless flowers to 2 in. that scarcely show above the forest floor.

T. pusillum, growing to 8 in., has erect, pink flowers about 1 in. across.

T. recurvatum, growing to 1½ ft., has erect, brown-purple blossoms.

T. rivale, growing to 8 in., has erect, purple-marked white flowers.

T. sessile (wake-robin), growing to 1 ft., has a purplish or greenish, erect flower that is set without a stem in the midst of three mottled leaves. Var. *californicum* has purple, rose, or white flowers to 4 in. across and spotted leaves; cv. 'Rubrum' has red-purple leaves.

T. undulatum (painted trillium), growing to 2 ft., has a white flower veined with purple at the base of the petals that is followed by a brilliant red berry, most attractive in the summer.

TRISTANIA (tris TAY nee ah). A genus of trees and shrubs from Australia, belonging to the Myrtaceae (Myrtle Family), sometimes grown in greenhouse collections and hardy to Zone 9. *T. conferta* (Brisbane-box), the principal species, is a handsome evergreen tree to 150 ft., very valuable

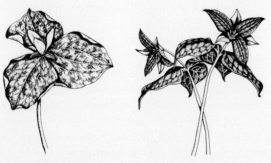

T. chloropetalum   *T. erectum*

in hot, dry regions, where it can withstand difficult conditions. The leaves, which grow to 6 in. long, are crowded at the ends of branches. Small, white flowers are borne in clusters.

TRITELEIA A showy genus of cormous plants in the Amaryllidaceae (Amaryllis Family), native to the western states and useful for naturalizing in the wild or rock garden. Most are hardy to Zone 7 and can be grown protected in pots in colder regions. Easy to grow from seed in a well-drained soil, they take three to five years to flower and require a dormant summer period.

PRINCIPAL SPECIES

T. hendersonii is a real beauty with 6-in. heads of bright white flowers with a deep purple central stripe.

T. hyacinthina (white brodiaea) has pure white flowers with 4-in. heads.

T. ixioides (pretty-face, yellow brodiaea) varies in height from 4–24 in. and has 6-in., spherical heads of pale or bright yellow flowers with an external, purple central-petal stripe.

T. laxa (triplet-lily, Ithuriel's-spear), formerly listed as *Brodiaea laxa*, is the most widely grown species, producing 2 in. long, crepelike, blue-lilac flowers arranged in 8-in. spheres. Var. 'Queen Fabiola' has darker purple flowers with 5-in. heads.

TRITONIA (trī TOHN ee ah). A genus of half-hardy, South African cormous plants of the Iridaceae (Iris Family), formerly classified and commonly known as *Montbretia*. They produce slender spikes of brightly colored flowers in summer and grasslike leaves to 18 in. long. Because of the perishable nature of the blossoms, *Tritonia* are not good cut-flower subjects. Grown in clumps or mass plantings in the garden, however, each corm produces several flower spikes and provides a wealth of beauty over a long period. Various species and hybrids produce different shapes and sizes of flowers ranging from bright yellow to red and sometimes spotted.

They are closely related to *Gladiolus* but are cultivated differently; once planted, they form permanent clumps in a perennial or mixed flower border. Not reliably hardy in cold climates, they should be lifted and stored over winter in a frost-free place and covered with sand, fine sawdust, or slightly moist earth. The corms propagate naturally by producing offsets—quite abundantly in some species, but slowly in the case of many of the new hybrids. They can, with benefit, remain undisturbed for several years.

T. crocata, the most commonly grown garden form, is hardy to Zone 7. It produces many bright orange flowers 2 in. across on a 2-ft. stem. They like well-drained, fairly rich soil and bloom late spring to early summer.

TROLLIUS (TROH lee us). A genus of perennial herbs belonging to the Ranunculaceae (Buttercup Family) and commonly known as globeflower. They have lobed or cut leaves. The white, orange, or yellow flowers resemble large, double buttercups. Growing naturally in swampy situations, they adapt themselves well to garden conditions if planted where the soil is not too dry. They can also be placed on the edge of a bog garden or near a pool. Propagation is by seed or division. Most are hardy in Zones 3–8.

Trollius sp.

PRINCIPAL SPECIES

T. acaulis grows to 3–12 in. and has yellow, 2-in. flowers; it is a good choice for rock gardens and the front of borders.

T. europaeus grows to 15 in. and has large, rounded, lemon yellow flowers blooming from May to July; it is attractive in the border.

T. laxus (spreading globeflower) is native to swampy meadows in the northeastern states and is sometimes grown in rock gardens.

T. ledebourii, also listed as *T. chinensis*, is a relatively large species from Siberia with open, clear yellow flowers.

T. pumilis grows 6–12 in. and has yellow, 1½-in. flowers and finely cut, mounded foliage.

TROPAEOLUM (troh PEE oh lum). A genus of tender, dwarf or climbing herbs with showy flowers, native to South America, and commonly known as nasturtium. They have succulent stems; shield-shaped, lobed, or finely cut leaves; and usually orange, red, or yellow spurred flowers in single and double forms, often with fringed lower petals. Many species are perennial in mild climates, but all are treated as annuals in cooler regions.

Tropaeolum sp.

Seed is sown in the open in the spring, or earlier in a hotbed or in pots or boxes in the house. The plants will bloom most prolifically if given a rather poor soil in a northern exposure.

Nasturtiums may suffer from a bacterial wilt common on tomatoes, eggplant, potatoes, and peppers, so they should not be grown near or in soil where those plants have previously been infected. Destroy diseased plants and sterilize the soil. See DISEASE; DISINFECTION.

An almost inevitable pest of this plant seems to be the black bean aphid, which infests the stems and undersides of leaves, curling and distorting them. The leaf miner may make serpentine tunnels in the leaves; control by destroying infested leaves. See APHIDS and LEAF MINER for control measures.

PRINCIPAL SPECIES

T. majus (garden nasturtium), the most commonly grown species, is a somewhat succulent annual vine with large blossoms, which in the species are orange or yellow, but cultivars show a wide range of colors from pale straw to dark reddish purple. The round, ribbed, green seedpods have a peppery flavor and are sometimes pickled while young. Flowers, leaves, and young seedpods are often called Indian-cress. Var. *nanum* (Tom Thumb nasturtium) is a dwarf form that has proved excellent for edging a border. Many other cultivars and hybrids produced with *T. minus* have been developed to produce attractive colors, double forms, fragrances, and habits. Most are grown from seed like the species, but since some produce no seed, they must be propagated by cuttings.

T. minus is a dwarf form with flowers 1½ in. across.

T. peregrinum (canary-bird flower) is a popular quick-growing annual vine with small, lobed leaves, ideal for covering trellises, often reaching a height of 15 ft. The dainty, curiously cut yellow blossoms with curved, green spurs resemble canary birds in flight.

T. speciosum is a slender perennial vine with small, attractive, scarlet flowers and finely divided foliage. It is hardy in warm regions of the southern and western states. For summer bloom in cooler climates, the small, tuberous roots can be planted out after danger of frost is over.

TROUT LILY. A common name for species of ERYTHRONIUM, a genus of nodding, spring-blooming flowers of the Liliaceae (Lily Family).

TROWEL. A small, shovel-like tool consisting of a blade and a handle of metal or metal and wood, for use in one hand. The blade resembles a curved spade or scoop. Many styles and sizes are distributed by garden suppliers, each adapted for some more or less specific purpose in planting or transplanting bulbs, plants, cuttings, and so on.

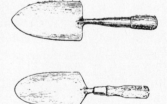

Trowels

The best style is made of one piece of steel with a cone-shaped socket and a wooden handle driven in and firmly held by a riveted pin extending through both. It usually costs more than the type made with a ferrule, the "one-piece," pressed-metal style, or any of the double-ended combinations of trowel and weeder. A strong, well-shaped, well-balanced trowel has many uses, lasts for years, and is worth extra money and good care.

TRUMPETBUSH. Common name for *Tecoma garrocha*, a tender shrub with colorful, fragrant flowers; see TECOMA.

TRUMPET CREEPER. Common name for CAMP-SIS, a genus of shrubby deciduous vines with showy flowers, also known as trumpet vine.

TRUMPET FLOWER. Common name for *Bignonia capreolata*, a showy evergreen vine native as far north as Virginia. The name is also applied to species of the tropical genera SOLAN-DRA and THEVETIA.

TSUGA (TSOO gah). An important genus of North American and Asiatic coniferous evergreen trees belonging to the Pinaceae (Pine Family) and commonly known as hemlock. The horizontal branches bear small, soft, flat needles and attractive little cones. Hemlocks are less formal in outline than the firs (*Abies*) and spruces (*Picea*), for though their limbs spread horizontally, they branch repeatedly into many small branchlets, which generally droop most gracefully. With their fine, feathery foliage, they are most beauti-

Tsuga sp.

ful in youth, but they attain great dignity in age and are among the finest evergreen trees for park, lawn, or specimen planting and windbreaks. Various species are hardy in Zones 4–7.

Hemlocks will stand severe pruning, growing dense and velvety, and are often used for hedges. Since they have fibrous roots, they can be moved easily, especially if root-pruned in preparation. They grow best in a rather acid, well-drained but moist soil. Propagation is by seed or cuttings;

and the varieties, by grafting on *T. canadensis*.

In general, hemlocks are less attacked by fungus diseases than pine, spruce, or fir. Two species of blister rust fungi affect the leaves of Canada hemlock. One has its alternate stage on *Rhododendron* and *Vaccinium*. The other completes its life cycle on *Hydrangea*. A third rust produces dirty white pustules on cones, twigs, and needles and uses poplar as its alternate host. One rust, requiring no alternate host, may kill the needles or cause reddish, swollen pustules on them and on twigs, which should be pruned off and burned. See RUSTS.

The hemlock span-worm feeds on the new growth and sometimes completely strips trees. The flat-headed, spotted hemlock borer works under the bark of living, injured, and dying hemlock and spruce trees. The adult beetle is bronze with three small, whitish spots on each wing cover. Cut down infested trees in late winter and burn the bark. See BORERS; INSECT CONTROL.

Hemlock scale has become a serious problem on hemlocks in the eastern United States, killing thousands of young and large trees. The hemlock woolly aphid has also become a serious problem. See APHIDS; SCALE INSECTS.

PRINCIPAL SPECIES

T. canadensis is the species most grown in the eastern states. It is very hardy and often naturally forms groves on the northern side of ravines from Nova Scotia to Alabama. There are many garden forms. Cv. 'Albo-spica' has white-tipped young branchlets. 'Compacta' is a dwarf form with short branchlets and short leaves. 'Microphylla' has very small needles. 'Nana' is a very small form suitable for the rock garden. 'Pendula', also listed as *T. sargentii*, forms a flat-topped bush with pendent branchlets. 'Coles Prostrate' is a dwarf, spreading plant to 1 ft. high.

T. caroliniana, a southern native, is a smaller tree with dark green needles. Of compact growth, it is graceful but not always hardy. 'Compacta' has a dense, round-topped growth.

T. heterophylla (western hemlock) grows 125–200 ft. tall and has drooping branchlets and 1-in. cones.

TUBER. A short, swollen, underground stem gorged with reserve food. Being really a kind of stem, a true tuber bears buds (eyes), which are small and covered with tiny scales. Because of these buds and its large content of stored food, a tuber is able to give rise to a new plant and support it until its

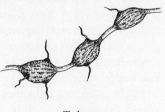

Tubers

own feeding roots develop. A perfect example of a true tuber is the common Irish potato. Horticulturists speak of root tubers, stem tubers, and crown tubers, but only the stem type truly merits the name.

TUBEROSE. Common name for *Polianthes tuberosa*, a Mexican herb that produces tuberous roots and fragrant flowers; see POLIANTHES.

TUBEROUS BEGONIA. Common name for several species of BEGONIA, especially *B.* x *tuberhybrida*.

TUFF. A porous rock formed by cooled lava and volcanic ash. It generally has a texture of gravel or sand and is especially useful in the rock garden because it holds moisture like a sponge and is full of little channels for roots to take hold.

TULIP. Common name for TULIPA, a popular genus of flowering bulbs. Members of the genus CALOCHORTUS are also called tulips and include globe-, star-, and butterfly-tulips. Mexican tulip poppy is *Hunnemannia fumariifolia*, a perennial herb grown in warm climates; see HUNNEMANNIA.

TULIPA (TOO lip ah). A genus including probably the most popular of the bulbous spring flowers of the North Temperate Zone, commonly known as tulip. It is a group of true bulbs of the Liliaceae (Lily Family), developing several long, broad, pointed leaves and a single scape that bears usually one erect, cup-shaped or bell-shaped flower

with six petals (actually petals and sepals). The flowers, of satiny texture, occur in a wide range of colors, pure, broken, and combined; they appear with the leaves in spring from bulbs planted in the fall.

TULIP HISTORY

Introduced into Europe from Turkey in 1554, tulips have figured prominently in floral history ever since and have gained increasing favor everywhere. The famous "tulipomania" of Holland in the seventeenth century, during which fortunes were invested in the bulbs and their culture and vast sums were lost through wild speculation, is schoolbook history. While fabulous prices then paid for a single bulb of a new variety have never been equaled, there has continued to be a strong desire on the part of growers to create or possess new kinds of outstanding merit.

Tulipa sp.

Tulips grow readily from seed, and this is the means chiefly employed for producing new varieties. Many new kinds also appear naturally as mutations (sports)—that is, a bulb, for some unaccountable reason, suddenly bears a flower that is different in either form or color from what its variety would normally produce. If the bulb retains this difference when grown on for another season, it may become the nucleus of another new kind, a stock of which is built up by the natural tendency of the plant to develop small new bulbs at the base of a large one. These (except in the case of sports) reproduce their parent.

Holland is the home of commercial tulip production (see DUTCH BULBS), but tulips thrive in other water-bound regions of the North Temperate Zone.

TULIPS IN THE GARDEN

Bulbs can be planted as soon as they are available from dealers in early September, or they can be set out any time thereafter until the ground actually freezes. The size of the bulb has a definite bearing on the size of the flower that will be produced. With most varieties, bulbs measuring 1½ in. in diameter will make the best showing the first year.

Prepare the soil thoroughly by spading it deeply and enriching with bonemeal or well-rotted manure. If possible, do not use a location that was planted with tulips the year before.

Tulips should be set out in accordance with a prearranged plan to bring out the effect desired. The planting of mixed colors rarely produces a satisfactory result. For those who wish a wide assortment of colors, spot planting of individual varieties is best. Where formal bedding is desired, the single early or double early sorts (see below) will be preferable since their stems are shorter and therefore do not need a background to show them off to best advantage. The longer-stemmed and later-flowering groups make their best appearance when planted in front of shrubbery or evergreens or when massed in a perennial border.

In design planting, a good plan is to dig out the whole space that the bulbs are to occupy to the depth of 4–6 in., place the bulbs in the desired position about 6 in. apart, and replace the soil.

Although tulips are hardy in the North Temperate Zone, a slight winter covering is always an advantage and sometimes a necessity in exposed places. It must not be applied until the ground has frozen. It can be of leaves, hay, or straw and should be removed in spring as soon as the new growth peeps through.

Tulip bulbs produce their leaves and flowers on the same stem. If the blooms are cut so low as to remove part of the foliage, the future flowering quality of the bulbs will be lessened. Except for special cutting, therefore, the faded flowers should be removed close to the top of the stem and before they begin to form seedpods, since seed draws heavily upon the stored vitality of the bulb. The foliage should then be encouraged to remain green as long as possible, for during the growing period after flowering, the new bulbs are being formed for the next year. When plant-

ing new tulip bulbs every year, the old bulbs can be removed as soon as they finish flowering; their remaining in the ground will reduce the chances of producing good quality flowers in the same location next year.

As soon as the foliage is completely withered, the bulbs can be lifted. Several smaller bulbs (bulblets) will be found in place of the large one planted. These should be stored in an airy, dry location; in a few weeks they can be cleaned, sorted as to sizes, and replanted. Any bulb that measures 1 in. or more in diameter will likely provide a flower the next season. The smaller sizes can be planted in rows in a separate part of the garden to grow into flowering-size bulbs in one to three years, depending on the soil and other conditions that may affect their growth.

TULIPS INDOORS

Although forced by florists both for cut flowers and as pot plants for midwinter and early spring trade, tulips are usually not as satisfactory for ordinary home forcing as are hyacinths and narcissi. This is principally because tulips require a longer period of preparation, which is best given by burying them outdoors in the pots or flats in which the bulbs are planted, 1½–2 ft. deep and covering them with soil. Here they can and should be subjected to hard freezing temperatures until it is time to bring them indoors, when they will be well rooted. See also BULBS.

ENEMIES

The most common tulip trouble is a spotting and rotting disease known as "fire." Small, circular spots on petals and leaves increase in size, the margins appearing water soaked and the centers gray. In moist weather, the leaves and blossoms quickly decay and become covered with the brownish gray mold typical of BOTRYTIS blights. The fungus spores are carried to healthy plants by tools, animals running through the garden, splashing rain, and air currents. Tulips wounded in digging are easily infected.

ROGUE out all infected plants as soon as noticed; cut off each blossom as soon as it has finished blooming, and cut the leaves down to the soil level as soon as they turn yellow. Before planting bulbs, examine them carefully and remove all bulb scales containing the small, black sclerotia of the fungus. It is better not to plant tulips on the same land two years in succession. Spraying two or three times in early spring with a weak BORDEAUX MIXTURE will help to control the disease.

Gray rot of bulbs is only occasionally destructive in the United States. Soil disinfection is advisable as a preventive measure.

A virus disease is responsible for the sudden color change in tulips known as BREAKING. The odd flowers that result were long considered and named as a distinct type—and some growers still regard them as such.

The only insect generally destructive to tulips is the bulb mite. For control, see BULBS.

CLASSIFICATION

For centuries, tulips have been the subjects of extensive horticultural hybridization and selection. Up to 150 species have been derived from the original tulip species, and several thousand hybrids and cultivars have resulted from the crossbreeding of the species or "botanical" tulips.

According to the revised classified list and international register of tulip names, garden tulips are categorized by a combination of the following features: relative blooming time, flower form, and species derivation. This complicated method of classification results in the following scheme:

Single Early Tulips. Earliest blooming of the ordinary garden forms; 9–16 in. Some varieties are scented. Choice cultivars include 'Beliona', 'Princess Irene', and 'Van der Neer'.

Double Early Tulips. These tulips have large, double blooms reminiscent of peonies and bloom in early spring. They all originated as sports of a popular old variety called 'Murillo'. The stems are rather short and sturdy; most plants do not grow more than 12 in. high. 'Peach Blossom' is a popular cultivar.

Triumph Tulips. These flower in midseason. Varieties are the result of crossbreedings of single early tulips and late-blooming types, especially the Darwin tulips. The flowers are large and borne on strong stems, growing 16–26 in. tall, usually under 20 in. 'Apricot Beauty', and 'Garden Party' are popular cultivars.

Darwin Tulips. These tall, late-blooming tulips are probably the most popular class. Flowers are cup shaped and range in color from white to purple-black, growing 16–26 in. The Darwin and cottage tulips are sometimes considered together in a single class called single late tulips. Common forms are cv. 'Duke of Wellington', 'Golden Age', and 'Queen of the Night'.

Darwin Hybrid Tulips. The result of hybridizations of Darwin tulips and *T. fosteriana*, they are the giants of the tulip garden and bloom in late spring. Colors range from deep yellow to scarlet, and the average plant height is 24–28 in. Cv. 'Gudoshnik', 'White Jewel', and 'Olympic Flame' are the common forms.

Lily-Flowered Tulips. These bear elegant, long-waisted blooms with pointed petals that curve outward at the tips. They are late bloomers with many color varieties and average 28–30 in. tall. Cv. 'Queen of Sheba', 'Maytime', and 'Red Shine' are common.

Cottage Tulips. These late-blooming tulips with large, egg-shaped flowers standing on long stems include some of the multiflowering or bouquet types and average 24–30 in. tall. Some have green feathering on the petals. They are often considered together with Darwin tulips in one class heading called single late tulips. Common cultivars are 'Golden Harvest' and 'Rosy Wings'.

Parrot Tulips. These varieties arose as mutations (sports) of other tulips. The large flowers have twisted, cut or feathered petals, and the stems are long and fairly weak; average height is 20–26 in. Many color variations are found, some with streaking and green flecks. Popular cultivars are 'Blue Parrot', 'Flaming Parrot', and 'Fantasy'.

Double Late Tulips. The peony-flowered tulips have heavy blossoms with full, ruffled center petals and bloom in late spring. The flowers are carried on tall, strong stems, usually 18–24 in. tall. Popular cultivars include 'May Wonder', 'Mt. Tacoma', and 'Angelique'.

Kaufmanniana Tulips. Hybrids of *T. kaufmanniana* (water-lily tulip). The very early blooming flowers are often bicolored, and the foliage is often beautifully mottled or striped. Colors range from creamy white to salmon to scarlet. Plants are only 6–9 in. tall. Common cultivars are 'Kaufmanniana' and 'Shakespeare'.

Fosteriana Tulips. Hybrids of *T. fosteriana*. Tulips of this division produce the largest flowers and the longest stems (14–18 in.) of the early-blooming types and range in color from luminous white to brilliant scarlet. The foliage is often striped or mottled. Principal cultivars are 'Orange Emperor', 'Red Emperor', and 'White Emperor'.

Greigii Tulips. Hybrids of the wild, oriental *T. greigii*, these are prized not only for their orange-red blossoms, but also for their distinctive moss-green foliage, which is attractively striped, mottled, and wavy margined. The petals are finely pointed and edged in creamy white or yellow. They flower in midseason and grow 8–20 in. tall. Cultivars include 'Cape Cod', 'Oriental Splendor', and 'Plasir'.

Other. Natural species, their varieties and hybrids.

PRINCIPAL SPECIES

The wild forms of tulips and some of their hybrids are referred to as species or botanical tulips. These original wild forms, ancestors of all the common garden tulips, are native to the Old World, from the Mediterranean region to Japan. Species or botanical tulips are easily cultivated and are best suited for use in the rock garden or in low borders.

T. acuminata (Turkish tulip) grows 1–1½ ft. high and has narrow leaves. Blooming in midsummer, it has 4-in., yellow or pink flowers with narrow, papery petals and hairs inside near the base. Hardy to Zone 4.

T. clusiana (lady or candy-stripe tulip) has narrow foliage folded lengthwise. The flowers are small and fragrant; the three pinkish red outer petals are margined with white, and the three inner petals are a creamy white. The center is purplish in color. It blooms midseason and

grows to 15 in. It is native to Iran and Pakistan but has been naturalized in southern Europe.

T. fosteriana has ovate leaves, and the large, vivid scarlet flowers open up flat to reveal a yellow-margined black center. This species is suitable for massing. It is a native of Turkestan.

T. gesnerana has rounded, blade-shaped leaves and cup-shaped flowers that open broadly. The petals are a dull crimson or scarlet, and the center is yellow-margined olive to black. This species is indigenous to eastern Europe and Asia Minor. It is the botanical tulip from which most of the tall, late-blooming common garden tulips were derived.

T. kaufmanniana (water-lily tulip), native to Turkestan, grows 5–10 in. tall with oblong foliage and large, starlike flowers that vary in color from creamy white to yellow, scarlet, or pink. The petals are brilliantly striped with carmine, and the center is yellow. This species is perennial and will come up annually for years.

T. praecox is a tender species from Italy. It has stout stems about 2 ft. high and oblong leaves 1 ft. long. The flowers can be up to 3½ in. long and are dark red with a yellow-and-green mark at the base and orange or green on the outside.

T. sylvestris, from the Middle East, grows to 1 ft. high and has two or three leaves up to 10 in. long. It has fragrant, bright yellow flowers tinged with red and borne solitary or in pairs, nodding in buds but becoming erect as they open. It spreads to form large clumps but does not bloom readily. Some cultivars grow larger and flower more freely.

T. wilsoniana is a Turkish species growing only 8 in. high but is tougher than most. It has narrow 4–5 in. leaves in groups of five. The flowers are brilliant red with black marks at the base and yellow anthers.

Many other tulip species, hybrids, and varieties, especially the smaller ones, are used for rock garden planting.

TULIP TREE. Common name for *Liriodendron tulipifera*, a flowering deciduous tree excellent for park or street planting; see LIRIODENDRON.

TUNBRIDGE FERN. Common name for *Hymenophyllum tunbrigense*, one of several plants collectively known and cultivated as FILMY FERNS.

TUPELO. Common name for NYSSA, a genus of handsome deciduous trees whose leaves turn brilliant red in the fall.

TURBINICARPUS (tur bin i KAHR pus). A small genus of fascinating Mexican cacti, mostly an inch or two in diameter. Easily cultivated and easily grown from seed. Many have unusual spination, varying from acicular to hairlike to papery to fuzzy white spines. Favorites are any of the varieties of *T. schmiedickeanus*, such as the diminutive var. *gracilis*; *T. laui*, with large, white to pink flowers; or the remarkable *T. valdezianus*, with tiny spine clusters like lacey, white doilies.

TURF. The mat of grass plants, their interwoven roots the entangled soil that forms the body of any stretch of LAWN. The term is often used interchangeably with SOD, although the latter refers particularly to the grass mat when removed in strips or squares to be used elsewhere in sodding.

TURKEY-BEARD. Common name for XEROPHYLLUM, a genus of tall, hardy lilies.

TURK'S-CAP CACTUS. The name given to a most remarkable group of globular cactus, namely *Melocactus*, distinguished by a unique terminal flowering structure called a CEPHALIUM, forming a cap of wool and bristles atop the cactus in which the red flowers and bright red fruits appear.

TURMERIC. A spice and dye made from the roots of *Curcuma domestica*; see CURCUMA.

TURNIP. A semihardy biennial selection of *Brassica rapa* var. *rapifera*, grown as an annual for its enlarged roots, which are served as a vegetable or used for flavoring soups and stews. It differs from the Swedish-turnip or rutabaga by its closer grouping of leaf stems, its hairy (not bloom-covered) leaves, the flatter or more globular form of the swollen root, an almost naked taproot, and light-colored flesh that is purple on the upper surface in some varieties.

As a common name, Indian-turnip refers to *Arisaema triphyllum*, better known as jack-in-the-pulpit; see ARISAEMA.

To grow tender roots for summer use, sow seed thinly in early spring in well-prepared, moderately fertile, well-drained soil. Make the drills 12–15 in. apart. When the seedlings are 4–6 in. high, thin them to stand 6–8 in. apart. Cultivate every seven to ten days until the foliage touches between rows.

Gather the roots for use when 2–3 in. thick. If allowed to grow larger, they become woody and strong flavored, or the plants may go to seed, especially in hot weather.

For autumn and winter use, sow after midsummer but manage like the spring crop. When cold weather approaches, dig the roots, cut off the tops, and store the roots in a cool, dry place. Keep the air moist and the temperature as near 32°F as possible without freezing. These conditions prevent shriveling and decay. For other culture and pest information, see BRASSICA.

TURNIP-ROOTED CELERY. Thick-rooted celery varieties used for flavoring; see CELERIAC.

TURNIP-ROOTED CHERVIL. A biennial vegetable grown for its small, dark gray, carrotlike roots; see CHERVIL.

TURTLEHEAD. Common name for CHELONE, a genus of handy, summer-flowering, moisture-loving perennial herbs.

TUSSOCK MOTH. Usually considered a shade tree pest, the white-marked tussock moth, *Hemerocampa leucostigma*, is sometimes destructive in orchards. Foliage of all kinds of trees, except conifers, is skeletonized by the yellowish black, hairy, striped caterpillar, which has a long, narrow tuft of black hairs projecting from each side of the head and one from the tail, and two bright red spots and four white tufts of hair on the back. The male moths are dark brown with strong wings; the females, like those of the cankerworm, are wingless.

The eggs, laid in the fall in conspicuous, stiff, white masses attached to trunks, branches, or dead leaves, hatch in late spring, the larvae becoming full grown in July and spinning cocoons on the trunk. Larvae of a second generation feed on the trees in late August and early September.

Many parasites and hyperparasites live on this caterpillar, thus keeping it somewhat under control. Other control can be achieved by daubing overwintering egg masses with creosote. Especially valuable trees can be protected with sprays of *Bacillus thuringiensis* (Bt,

Tussock moth caterpillar

commonly available as Biotrol, Dipel, or Thuricide). See also CATERPILLAR; INSECT CONTROL.

TWAYBLADE. Common name for LIPARIS, a genus of orchids with broad leaves and many-flowered racemes, and *Listera*, a genus of dwarf terrestrial orchids.

TWINBERRY. A common name for *Mitchella repens*, an evergreen trailer with fragrant flowers and scarlet berries; see MITCHELLA.

TWINFLOWER. Common name for *Linnaea borealis*, a trailing evergreen with bell-shaped flowers; see LINNAEA.

TWINLEAF. Common name for *Jeffersonia diphylla*, a woodland perennial with two-parted leaves and dainty, white flowers; see JEFFERSONIA.

TWINSPUR. Common name for *Diascia barberae*, an annual herb with sprays of rose or violet flowers; see DIASCIA.

TWISTED-STALK. Common name for STREPTOPUS, a genus of woodland lilies with pink or white, bell-shaped flowers.

TYING. In gardening, this term means the fastening of plants to stakes, trellises, and other supports. When not done properly or done with the wrong materials, tying may do more harm than good. Avoid using hard strings and thin wires, because they tend to cut or girdle the soft tissue of many plants. Paper- or cloth-covered wires make good plant ties, as do pipe cleaners and strips of cloth.

Loop tying method

There are two very simple and effective methods to tie plants to supports. The first way is to place the tie or other strip between the plant stem and the stake, bringing the ends around the stake and tying them firmly so the knot is away from the plant. Then bring the ends around the plant stem and tie it in a loose loop. In

Figure-eight tying method

the figure-eight method, make a loose loop around the plant stem, cross it, and tie the ends securely around the stake. Either way, the loop should not be tight enough to strangle the plant.

Climbing plants are often fastened to arbors, walls, and arches by tying them to a trellis framework. Masonry walls can support climbing plants if nails are fastened to the walls first and the plants then secured to the nails.

TYPE. The specimen upon which a species is based. To belong to the same species, other plants must approximate this "type specimen" in certain general characteristics. This is the ideal representation of a species.

TYPHA (Tī fah). A genus of tall, perennial, swamp-dwelling herbs commonly known as cattails. They have creeping rootstocks; narrow, flat leaves; and odd, brown flowers in dense, blunt spikes on unbranched stems up to 10 ft. tall. They are often planted in the bog garden, or in colonies along streams or ponds for their stately and decorative effect. The leaves are used for chair seats or in basketry. Plants grow readily and propagate naturally, but

Typha sp.

they can be propagated more rapidly by division or by seed planted in pots that are kept in warm water.

PRINCIPAL SPECIES

T. angustifolia (narrow-leaved cattail, small bullrush), narrow to North America, Europe, and Asia, grows to 6 ft. and has flower spikes light brown in color with a bare segment separating the male and female parts and leaves not over ½ in. wide.

T. latifolia (common cattail, nailrod, bullrush) grows to 10 ft. and has dark brown spikes, usually with no space between the male and female zones, and leaves to 1 in. wide.

T. minima is a small European species that grows only 2½ ft. high. It has very narrow leaves, only ⅛ in. wide, and flower spikes like those of *T. angustifolia* but darker brown and only ⅜ in. in diameter.

U **UEBELMANNIA** (oo bul MAN ee ah). One of the newer and most sensational discoveries in the Cactaceae (Cactus Family) is this new genus with a handful of members from Brazil, discovered and described by Horst and Buining in the 1960s. *U. pectinifera* is dark reddish brown with a waxy coating, many acute ribs, and confluent areoles bearing an uninterrupted row of black spines like the teeth of a tight comb. The flowers are small, apical, and greenish yellow.

ULEX (YOO leks). A genus of much-branched shrubs native to Europe, belonging to the Fabaceae (Bean Family), and commonly known as gorse, furze, or whin. They have rigid, dark green, spiny branches and fragrant, showy, yellow, pealike flowers. While not entirely hardy, they may survive in cool climates in favored spots with protection. Propagation is by cuttings or by seed, which should be sown where it is to grow, since this is a difficult subject to transplant.

U. europaeus, the principal species, grows to 4 ft. or more, thriving and flowering well in sandy or gravelly soil in a sunny location. It is a good seaside plant where hardy. The fragrant, yellow flowers are very showy and in mild climates are produced almost continuously. Var. *plenus* has double flowers.

ULMACEAE (ul MAY see ee). The Elm Family, including deciduous trees and shrubs with a watery juice, widely distributed throughout temperate climates. Species of *Celtis* (hackberry) are sometimes planted, and *Ulmus* (elm) has been extensively planted for shade or ornament.

ULMUS (UL mus). A genus of tall deciduous trees native throughout the North Temperate Zone and commonly known as elm. Because of their graceful shape and handsome foliage, consisting of small, simple, alternate, toothed leaves, elms were extensively used for street planting, especially in the eastern United States. Most species are hardy in Zones 3–9.

Diseases. Due to DUTCH ELM DISEASE, *U. americana* (American elm) and others are seldom used or planted. There is still no cure for this disease, which has killed most of the large American elms in the eastern states. New England roads were once lined with these majestic tall trees. This is the most unusual of all the elms because of its "V" or vase-shaped growth habit. Some species of *Zelkova* are similar but are much smaller and not as impressive.

Two other elm wilts are difficult to distinguish from the Dutch elm disease without laboratory culture and study of the fungi (*Verticillium* and *Cephalosporium*) that cause them. Trees affected by these fungi may die or may recover naturally. A virus disease, phloem necrosis, has spread in many areas. No control of this is known except the removal of diseased trees.

Insect Pests. There are many insect pests, and since any agent weakening the tree predisposes it to Dutch elm disease, it is particularly important to protect the trees against insect attack. European and American elm bark beetles, especially, spread Dutch elm disease.

The cankerworm, destructive early in the season, should be controlled by a variety of methods; see CANKERWORM. The elm leaf beetle can be especially destructive in dry seasons. The beetles winter as adults; eat holes in young foliage in early spring; and lay rows of tiny, pearl-shaped orange eggs on the underside of the leaves in early summer. The grubs feed there, skeletonizing the leaves, and then transform to yellow pupae in bark crevices at the base of the tree to produce the yellow or green, black-striped beetles ¼ in. long. See BEETLES; GRUBS.

Other pests that feed on elm foliage include the JAPANESE BEETLE, larvae of the white-marked TUSSOCK MOTH, GYPSY MOTH, spiny elm CATERPILLAR (which develops into the mourning cloak butterfly), fall WEBWORM, and BAGWORM.

Dormant SPRAYING with a miscible oil will control the elm scurfy scale, the chocolate brown European elm scale, and possibly the woolly apple and elm aphids that curl and deform the leaves in early spring. The latter are difficult to fight, but an insecticidal spray before the leaves curl is helpful. See APHIDS; SCALE INSECTS.

PRINCIPAL SPECIES

U. alata (wahoo elm), growing to 40 ft., has a round or open head and branchlets furnished with two wide, corky wings. It is a good avenue tree for the South but is not hardy in the North.

U. americana (American elm), growing to 75 ft., has light gray, fissured bark and upward-sweeping branches with long, pendent branchlets forming the typical "vase" form. It has been all but eradicated by Dutch elm disease.

U. glabra (wych or Scotch elm), growing to 120 ft., forms a rather oblong-shaped head with spreading branches. Since it does not sucker, it is a valuable tree for lawn planting. Especially popular are some of its cultivars: 'Atropurpurea' has purple leaves; 'Camperdowni' (camperdown elm) has a globose head of pendulous branches; 'Crispa' (fernleaf elm) grows slowly and has drooping branches and leaves with ruffled, serrated margins; 'Fastigiata' (Exeter elm) is erect in habit; 'Pendula' (tabletop elm) is a dwarf form with horizontal branches that are stiffly pendent.

U. parvifolia (Chinese elm) is a small, half-evergreen tree useful in mild climates. It makes a very attractive rounded tree that grows to 50 ft. and has tiny, 1-in. leaves and beautifully mottled bark.

U. procera (English elm), formerly listed as *U. campestris*, grows to 60 ft. and has a straight trunk with erect branches forming an oval head, less graceful than the American elm.

U. pumila (dwarf or Siberian elm) is an erect tree introduced and favored for planting in dry, windswept regions. It grows quickly but tends to split apart in storms.

UMBEL. An umbrella-shaped flower cluster (INFLORESCENCE) in which the flower stalks (peduncles) all spring from the same point at the summit of the main stem. The rays so formed, being of nearly equal length, give the cluster its characteristic shape, which may range from nearly flat to domed. Umbels are compound when the flower stalks in turn branch into pedicels on which the individual flowers are borne, as in the carrot. Umbelliferae, the antiquated name for Apiaceae (Celery Family), was derived from the umbels that characterize many of its members. Milkweed and onion flowers also occur in umbels.

UMBELLIFERAE (um bel IF ur ay). Former name for the APIACEAE (Celery Family).

UMBELLULARIA (um bell yoo LAIR ee ah) **californica.** A tall evergreen tree belonging to the Lauraceae (Laurel Family), the only member of its genus, and commonly known as California laurel. Native to California, it sometimes attains a height of 75 ft. and is a very handsome subject with a dense head of lustrous foliage. The leaves are rather narrow, up to 5 in. long, and highly aromatic. The yellowish green flowers are followed by pear-shaped, yellowish or purple fruit.

UMBRELLA FERN. Common name for *Gleichenia,* a genus of forking ferns with clustered, beadlike sporangia.

UMBRELLA PALM. Common name for *Hedyscepe canterburyana*, a tall and broad-headed palm; see HEDYSCEPE.

UMBRELLA-PINE. Common name for *Sciadopitys verticillata*, a Japanese tree related to *Taxodium*; see SCIADOPITYS.

UMBRELLA PLANT. Common name for *Cyperus alternifolius*, a sedge often grown as a houseplant; see CYPERUS.

UMBRELLA TREE. Common name for *Magnolia tripetala*, a hardy tree with long leaves and large, malodorous flowers followed by rose-red fruits; see MAGNOLIA.

Queensland umbrella tree is *Schefflera actinophylla*, a tropical tree often grown as a houseplant; see SCHEFFLERA. Texas umbrella tree refers to *Melia azedarach* cv. 'Umbraculiformis'; see MELIA.

UNDERSHRUB. Any woody plant sufficiently shade tolerant to permit its planting at the base and in the shade of other larger subjects to mask their bare trunks and create an effect comparable to that of natural underbrush. The term is relative rather than specific and may apply to different kinds and sizes of plants depending on the conditions under which they are used.

UNGNADIA (ung NAY dee ah) **speciosa.** A tender, southwestern shrub or small tree growing to 30 ft. and belonging to the Sapindaceae (Soapberry Family). Commonly known as Mexican-, Spanish-, or Texas-buckeye, it is the only member of its genus. It has rosy flowers that open before the glossy leaves in spring and is occasionally planted in the far South. Hardy in Zones 8–9.

UNICORN PLANT. A common name for PROBOSCIDEA, a genus of herbs grown for their curious fruits.

UNIOLA (yoo nī OH lah). A genus of perennial grasses native to southeastern coastal areas and commonly known as sea-oats. Growing to 8 ft., *U. paniculata* bears showy, drooping, and flattened panicles that are faintly tinged with pink and are handsome when dried. Hardy to Zone 6.

URCEOLINA (ur see oh LĪ nah). A genus of bulbous plants of the Amaryllidaceae (Amaryllis Family), with strap-shaped leaves that appear after the scarlet or yellow, urn-shaped flowers borne in umbels on a 1-ft. stem. These are beautiful, lilylike subjects, easily grown in the greenhouse or for summer or autumn bloom in the garden if brought indoors in the fall in their pots or tubs and stored for the winter. The species *U. peruviana*, including those formerly classified as *U. miniata* and *U. pendula*, has rather broad leaves and umbels of two to six bright scarlet or golden, green-tipped flowers.

URGINEA (ur JIN ee ah) **maritima.** A bulbous herb of the Liliaceae (Lily Family) from which is obtained the "squill" of druggists, giving it the common name "medicinal squill." Only half-hardy outdoors, it is sometimes grown in greenhouses for its yellow or rose flowers and is called sea-onion. The plant grows to 3 ft. and has leaves 4 in. wide and 1½ ft. long. It bears a flowered raceme of 50 to 100 small, whitish blossoms atop a 1½-ft., leafless stem. It needs light soil and cool conditions. The flower spikes, which appear before the leaves, last in good condition for many weeks. Propagation is by offsets.

URSINIA (ur SIN ee ah). A genus of South African plants belonging to the Asteraceae (Aster Family) and including about 60 annuals, perennials, and subshrubs. Their vivid orange "daisies" on long, wiry stems stand 2–3 ft. above low tufts of finely cut foliage. The plants bloom profusely from midsummer to late fall, making a colorful addition to the sunny border, and can be potted for continued flowering indoors. The blooms last well when cut. The few available species and hybrids are treated as annuals and easily raised like *Zinnias*, with the same requirements of well-drained soil and hot sunshine.

U. anethoides (jewels-of-the-Veldt) and its hybrids, grow 1–2 ft. tall and have orange flowers with deep purple centers.

U. anthemoides, formerly listed as *U. pulchra*, grows to 18 in. and has orange flowers with brown centers. This species and its hybrids are among the most popular in cultivation.

URTICA (ur TĪ kuh). A genus introduced from Europe, including annual and perennial herbs bearing stinging hairs. Commonly known as nettles, they frequently grow in waste areas. They have some culinary and herbal uses and are rarely troublesome. A good companion plant, nettles are sometimes used to improve the quality of plants, fruits, and herbs grown nearby and may even stimulate the growth of soil microbes. In bio-dynamic gardening, a ferment of nettle is sometimes sprayed as a foliar nutrient and to repel pests.

U. dioica (stinging nettle) is both a hated and loved plant. Contact with hairs on the leaves will sting exposed skin for a short time, but the irritation quickly subsides. The stinging quality of the leaves disappears with drying and cooking. When the young tops are steamed, they make an excellent green, and the dried plants are high-protein fodder. If processed like flax, the mature plants will yield a similar rough but durable fiber. Presence of the plant indicates moist soil rich in nitrogen and humus.

Urtica dioica

URTICACEAE (ur ti KAY see ee). The Nettle Family, a group of herbs, shrubs, and trees often bearing stinging hairs, chiefly native to the tropics. The small, inconspicuous flowers are variously disposed in clusters. A few species (mostly of the genera *Boehmeria*, *Pilea*, and *Soleirolia*) are cultivated for their ornamental foliage, and one is a source of fiber. The family also includes several noxious weeds.

UTRICULARIA (yoo trik yoo LAIR ee ah). A genus of carnivorous aquatic plants and some land-growing air plants, commonly known as bladderwort. They have little horticultural interest, except to the collector. The native species are hardy to Zone 5 and are occasionally gathered for use in the aquarium. The flowers are not showy but have floating, bladderlike leaves equipped with valvelike openings that trap small aquatic creatures. The tropical species are terrestrial or epiphytic, with beautiful orchidlike flowers; they are frequently grown in greenhouses under the same conditions as orchids.

U. longifolia is a tropical species with beautiful violet-and-orange flowers 2 in. across. It should be grown in the greenhouse in baskets containing a compost of sphagnum moss and sand.

U. vulgaris is a hardy, European aquatic plant with floating leaves provided with many bladders. The flowers are yellow on stalks 6–8 in. high. Var. *americana* is the North American form.

UVA GRASS. Common name for *Gynerium sagittatum*, a tall perennial grass with silky panicles; see GYNERIUM.

UVULARIA (yoo vyoo LAIR ee ah). A genus of hardy herbs belonging to the Liliaceae (Lily Family), commonly known as bellwort or merrybells. They are erect perennials that grow from rootstocks and have clasping or stemless leaves and graceful, drooping, yellow flowers 1½ in. long borne at the ends of the stalks. Hardy to Zone 4, they grow naturally in rich, moist woods and can be easily grown in the garden where they are propagated by division.

PRINCIPAL SPECIES
U. grandiflora grows to 18 in. and has pointed leaves and pale yellow flowers.

U. perfoliata, growing to 18 in., has clasping leaves and clear yellow blossoms.

U. sessilifolia is 12 in. tall and has greenish yellow flowers.

V

VACCARIA (vah KAR ee uh) **pyramidata.** An annual herb, formerly listed as *Saponaria vaccaria*, belonging to the Caryophyllaceae (Pink Family), and commonly known as cow herb or cow-soapwort. It has clusters of deep pink flowers and is widely naturalized in North America.

VACCINIUM (vak SIN ee um). A genus of deciduous or evergreen shrubs belonging to the Ericaceae (Heath Family) and widely distributed from the Arctic Circle to the mountains of the tropics. Common names given to different species are BLUEBERRY, cowberry, CRANBERRY, and sometimes huckleberry, which is more correctly applied to the genus GAYLUSSACIA, or GOOSEBERRY, which more often refers to the genera *Ribes* and *Grossularia*.

Some vacciniums are grown especially for the beauty of their colored leaves in fall, others for their edible fruits. They must have a lime-free soil and thrive best in a rather moist, sandy peat. In recent years, free- and large-fruiting cultivars of *V. corymbosum* have been developed, making blueberries a good garden crop where soil conditions are right. Propagation is by cuttings, layers, and division.

PRINCIPAL SPECIES

V. angustifolium (lowbush blueberry) is a dwarf shrub that grows to 2 ft. and is common in eastern North America. Hardy in Zones 3–7, it grows well on dry, sandy hills and furnishes most of the blueberries grown in Maine.

V. corymbosum (highbush blueberry) is a bushy, deciduous shrub that grows to 12 ft. and is found from Maine to Florida. There are numerous cultivars with blue-black berries of fine flavor. It is one of the handsomest shrubs in fall when the leaves turn orange and scarlet. Hardy in Zones 3–8, this species and its cultivars account for most of the blueberries being grown commercially today. See BLUEBERRY.

V. macrocarpon (cranberry) is a creeping evergreen extensively cultivated for its large berries, used for sauce or jelly; see CRANBERRY.

V. stamineum (deerberry) is a branched deciduous shrub that grows to 3 ft. and has pale leaves, white or purple-tinged flowers, and large, inedible berries. Hardy in Zones 6–9.

V. vitis-idaea (cowberry) is a low, creeping evergreen that grows to 8 in. and has small, dark green, shining leaves and dark red, acidic berries. Hardy in Zone 6, it is attractive for edging in the evergreen shrub border. Var. *majus* has larger leaves and fruit, while var. *minus* (hardy in Zones 3–6) is a smaller form that makes a dense mat. Berries are edible when cooked.

VALERIAN. Common name for VALERIANA, a genus of herbs or shrubs with white or rose flower clusters. The common name is also applied to other members of the Valerianaceae (Valerian Family) and a few unrelated plants. African valerian is *Fedia cornucopiae*. Greek-valerian is *Polemonium caeruleum* and sometimes *P. reptans*. Red valerian is *Centranthus ruber*.

VALERIANA (vah lee ree AY nay). A genus of hardy herbs or shrubs with small, white or rose flowers in spikes or flat-topped clusters, commonly known as valerian. They are easily grown for either garden effects or cut flowers and propagated by division.

PRINCIPAL SPECIES

V. arizonica is a small plant with pale pink or white flowers, native to the western states and hardy to Zone 6.

V. officinalis (common valerian, garden-heliotrope), growing to about 4 ft., is an old-fashioned favorite with cut leaves and numerous clusters of small, highly fragrant, pinkish lavender flowers. Var. *alba*, with white flowers, and *rubra*, with red, are pleasing variations. Hardy in Zones 3–8.

V. sitchensis, growing to 2 ft., is not as coarse as *V.*

Valeriana officinalis

officinalis but also has delicate, fragrant, lavender flowers.

V. supina is a little, 6-in., pink-flowered species from Austria, which can be tucked into a hot, sunny spot in the rock garden.

VALERIANELLA (vah lee ree ah NEL uh). A genus of annual herbs with small, rose, blue, or white flowers in flat-topped clusters, grown principally as salad plants, only a few species being used in the border or rock garden. See also GREENS.

V. locusta var. *olitoria* (corn-salad, lamb's-lettuce, fetticus) is an annual grown for use as a potherb or salad. Seed sown broadcast in early fall in rich soil should produce some plants large enough to use before winter. With some protection, the smaller ones should overwinter for very early spring use. In early spring, seed can be sown thickly in drills 12–15 in. apart. Given clean cultivation, this crop should be ready for use within two months. Sown in late spring, it is rarely satisfactory since the plants cannot stand hot weather. *V. eriocarpa* (Italian corn-salad) is similar to *V. locusta* but has longer leaves.

VALLISNERIA (val is NEE ree ah). A genus of perennial aquatic plants commonly known as eelgrass, tape-grass, or wild-celery. Two species, *V. americana* and *V. spiralis*, with submerged leaves, are hardy in Zones 10–11 but popular in aquariums and some water gardens. In addition to their special value as oxygenators, the long, slender, grasslike leaves are extremely decorative. The tiny, three-petaled, pure white pistillate flowers are carried to the surface on spiral stalks. Staminate flowers are produced on the submerged stem and, breaking loose, float to the surface to scatter pollen and accomplish a somewhat haphazard fertilization. Plants also propagate freely by runners.

VALLOTA (val OH tah) **speciosa.** A showy South African flowering bulb belonging to the Amaryllidaceae (Amaryllis Famiy) and commonly known as Scarborough-lily, suitable for greenhouse culture. Plants have strap-shaped leaves and scarlet, lilylike flowers to 2½ in. across in rounded clusters. Cv. 'Alba' has white flowers.

The Scarborough-lily is grown in the North in the greenhouse or as a window plant. It blooms in summer and should be rested in the winter but not entirely dried out, even during its resting period. The bulbs are planted in pots in a mixture of well-rotted manure, sand, fibrous peat, and loam, set as much below the surface as their diameter. Repot only after plants have flowered or when a shift is absolutely necessary, and in doing this, do not disturb or break the roots. It is much better for the bulbs to be crowded than to have too much room. They should always have full sunshine, even during the resting period. Water with liquid manure after the buds have started. They can be grown in the open in warm regions (Zones 10–11), where they will bloom several times a year.

VALVE. One of the parts into which a fruit splits when it opens at maturity, like the two valves of a pea pod.

VANCOUVERIA (van koo VEE ree ah). A genus of small perennial herbs with compound leaves and rather small, white flowers, belonging to the Berberidaceae (Barberry Family), commonly known as inside-out flower. Closely related to *Epimedium*, they are most attractive in the rock garden or used as ground cover in the wild garden. Native to deep forests of the western states, they should be given partial shade and an acid soil. Propagation is by seed or division.

V. hexandra (American barrenwort) grows 1 ft. or taller and has graceful, ruelike foliage and delicate sprays of dainty, white flowers. Hardy to Zone 5.

V. planipetala (inside-out flower), also listed as *V. parviflora*, is native to Oregon and to California, where it grows 7–24 in. high and is a popular ground cover. It has lacy, variably green-colored, evergreen foliage with leaflets 1½–2½ in. long, which may fall in unusually cold weather. White flower clusters bloom in late spring. Hardy to Zone 6.

VANDA (VAN duh). A popular genus of approximately 70 species of monopodial epiphytic or lithophytic orchids native to tropical Asia, Indochina, Australia, New Guinea, and the Philippines, first described by eighteenth-century botanist Sir. W. Jones. Leathery, distichous leaves, interspersed with long aerial roots, grow along the main central stem. Leaves may be strap shaped or terete (pencil-like), and few to many flowers are borne on a horizontal axial inflorescence. The plants often attain considerable size, up to 10 ft. high. The flowers are medium to large, showy, and often fragrant. Sepals are similar in shape and color; the dorsal sepal is usually the broadest. The petals are smaller than the sepals but are similar in shape. A sac or spur at the base of the lip is one of the characteristics of the genus.

Vanda flowers vary widely in color and pattern. They may be spotted or tessellated (checker-patterned) or have a combination of patterns. The colors may be white, blue, green, yellow, rose-purple, or brownish. The texture is often glistening. Many intergeneric hybrids have been made by crossing *Vanda* with *Euanthe* and other related genera. The flowers produced are among the most popular of all orchids, since they are brightly colored and often bloom several times a year.

The plants do well in baskets with little or no compost added. Most are from the tropics and are hardy in Zones 10–11 if protected from frost; winter temperatures should not be less than 60°F. Aerial roots should hang free. If plants are grown without compost, it is important to water them several times a week. *Vanda* requires bright light and high humidity. The type species is *V. roxburghii*.

VANILLA (van IL uh). First studied by botanist Olof Swartz in the eighteenth century, this is the only orchid with commercial value other than cut flowers. The genus *Vanilla* includes about 100 species of terrestrial and epiphytic orchids distributed throughout the tropics of the world. Plants grow as vines, with a thick, fleshy stem that bears a single leaf and roots at nodes in intervals along the stem length. A few species are leafless. The flowers are generally yellow-green with broad-spreading sepals and petals and a long, tubular throat. Clusters of flowers emerge from a short axial inflorescence, opening one at a time, mostly during the morning, and lasting only a few hours.

It is from the fruit of this flower that the commercial vanilla flavoring is manufactured. Flowers are hand-pollinated during the blooming season, and the ripe fruit, a long, shiny, brown pod, is processed to form the vanilla "bean."

Vanilla does best grown in a compost of peat, sphagnum moss, dried cow manure, and leaf mold. It is best to stake the plant, training the vines upward for about 6 ft., then downward toward the pot. Hardy in Zones 10–11 with frost protection, they tolerate minimum winter temperatures to 60°F and require shading from direct sun and high humidity at all times. The type species is *V. mexicana*.

As a common name, Carolina-vanilla refers to TRILISA, a genus of perennial herbs.

VARIETY. A group of individuals within a species but with differences too slight to constitute another species. An ordinary botanical variety is similar to a race or strain of plants that come true from seed to their distinguishing varietal characteristics. A horticultural variety (often indicated in botanical books by the term "Hort.," meaning "hortensis," after it) is practically the same as a variety, except that it has originated under cultivation in a garden, greenhouse, or nursery, often from hybrid ancestry. A geographical variety is a wild group that comes true from seed but is localized in a certain region.

Individuals that are not seed constant and need to be propagated vegetatively are commonly called varieties in trade but are properly clones or clonal varieties. Differences between varieties and species are often hard to determine. Races, strains, and clones are usually subordinate to varieties and are terms seldom applied except to cultivated plants. See RACE; STRAIN; CLONE.

VARNISH TREE. Common name for *Rhus ver-niciflua*, an Asiatic tree from whose fruit is obtained the lacquer used on highly polished woodenware; see RHUS. The name is also applied to a few Asiatic genera, including AILANTHUS, FIRMIANA, and KOELREUTERIA.

VEGETABLE. As popularly understood, this term refers to any plant cultivated for its edible parts. This loose definition includes roots (such as beet, carrot), tubers (potato, Jerusalem-artichoke), stems (celery, cardoon), leaves used raw as salad (lettuce, peppergrass), leaves cooked as potherbs or greens (mustard, spinach), flower buds and heads (French artichoke, cauliflower), fruits (tomato, watermelon), and seeds (peas, sweet corn).

By another popular definition, a vegetable is any plant whose edible part is not very sweet, as distinguished from a fruit, which is used as a dessert.

Botanically considered, all vegetables whose edible parts result from development of pollinated flowers are fruits, including cucumbers, peppers, and beans; see FRUIT. In the soil-handling phase of gardening, vegetable matter, such as humus, is synonymous with plant material, whatever parts of kinds of plants it is derived from.

The accompanying chart gives recommendations on starting and transplanting common vegetables. See individual vegetable entries for further culture information.

VEGETABLE FERN. Common name for *Diplazium esculentum*, an interesting and edible fern from southeastern Asia; see DIPLAZIUM.

VEGETABLE MARROW. A common name for varieties of *Cucurbita pepo*, which are easily cultivated for summer use. See MARROW; SQUASH.

VEGETATIVE REPRODUCTION. Another term for ASEXUAL REPRODUCTION or propagation by cuttings, layering, division, or other methods without the use of seeds. See PROPAGATION.

STARTING VEGETABLES FROM SEED

COMMON NAME (Latin name)	GERMINATION TIME (days)	INDOOR SOWING, (weeks before outdoor planting)	OUTDOOR SOWING (weeks before last frost)
Asparagus (*Asparagus officinalis*)	14–21	12–14	last frost
Bean (*Phaseolus vulgaris*)	7–10		last frost (s)
Beet (*Beta vulgaris*)	10–14		4–6 (s)
Cabbage (*Brassica oleracea*)	10–14	5–7	
Carrot (*Daucus carota*)	14–21		4–6 (s)
Cauliflower (*Brassica oleracea*)	8–10	5–7	
Celery (*Apium graveolens*)	21–25	10–12	
Corn (*Zea mays*)	5–7		last frost

VELTHEIMIA (vel TĪ mee ah). A genus of bulbous herbs from South Africa, belonging to the Liliaceae (Lily Family). The plants have swordlike foliage in basal rosettes and tubular, drooping flowers in dense terminal clusters. Though little known in the United States, they are easily grown, either in a moderately warm greenhouse or outdoors in Zones 9–11. A rich, fibrous soil with charcoal and sand gives best results.

V. capensis has lance-shaped leaves 12 in. long and 1 in. wide with wavy margins. A host of green-tipped, pale pink flowers are borne on 12-in., purple-mottled scapes.

V. viridifolia bears clusters of flowers in yellow tinged with red or purple on 18-in. stalks.

VELVET GROUNDSEL. Common name for *Senecio petasitis*, a perennial herb with heads of yellow flowers; see SENECIO.

VELVET-PLANT. Common name for *Gynura aurantiaca*, a native plant of Java, grown in greenhouses for its attractive foliage; see GYNURA.

VENATION. The kind of pattern formed by the veins of a LEAF. There are two main types. The grasses, lilies, and related plants that make up the monocotyledons are parallel veined, while all the dicotyledons are usually net veined, the multiple branches uniting throughout the leaf, like the cords of a fishnet, and ending freely in the margin.

VENIDIUM (ve NID ee um). A small genus of hardy annuals and perennials from South Africa, belonging to the Asteraceae (Aster Family), and similar to *Arctotis*. Their brilliant orange or yellow flowers, with short, broad petals and large centers, resemble sunflowers. The foliage is densely hairy, the plant compact, averaging 2 ft. in height. Venidiums add an attractive color accent in the border or greenhouse, and the flowers last well when cut. Although several of the available species are hardy in the greenhouse, and some are occasionally grown as perennials in warm regions, they are generally grown from seed started indoors in early spring and treated

STARTING VEGETABLES FROM SEED

TRANSPLANTING, (weeks before last frost)	SPACING (inches)	OPTIMUM SOIL TEMPERATURE RANGE (°F)	DAYS FROM SOWING TO HARVEST**
last frost	10–12	60–85	second season
	3–8	60–85	45–55 (early) 65–75 (late)
	4–6	50–85	50 (early) 80 (late)
4–6	15–18	45–95	62 (early) 110 (late)
	2–4	45–85	60 (early) 85 (late)
4–6	15–18	45–85	120 (early) 180 (late)
last frost	10–12	50–70*	98 (early) 130 (late)
	10–14	60–95	70 (early) 100 (late)

COMMON NAME (Latin name)	GERMINATION TIME (days)	INDOOR SOWING, (weeks before outdoor planting)	OUTDOOR SOWING (weeks before last frost)
Cucumber (*Cucumis sativus*)	7–10	4–6	last frost
Eggplant (*Solanum melongena*)	10–15	8–10	
Lettuce, head Lettuce, leaf (*Lactuca sativa*)	7–10 7–10	4–5 8–10	4–6 (s) 4–6
Lima Bean (*Phaseolus limensis*)	7–10	3–4	last frost
Muskmelon (*Cucumis melo*)	5–7	3–4	last frost
Okra (*Abelmoschus esculentus*)	10–14	4–6	last frost
Onion (*Allium cepa*)	10–14	8–10	6–8
Parsnip (*Pastinaca sativa*)	21–25		6–8
Pea (*Pisum sativum*)	7–10		6–8 (s)
Pepper (*Capsicum annuum*)	10–12	6–8	
Pumpkin, Squash (*Cucurbita* spp.)	7–10	3–4	last frost
Radish (*Raphanus sativus*)	4–6		6–8 (s)
Spinach (*Spinacia oleracea*)	8–10		6–8 (s)
Swiss Chard (*Beta vulgaris*)	7–10		4–6
Tomato (*Lycopersicon lycopersicum*)	5–8	5–7	
Turnip (*Brassica rapa*)	7–10		4–6 (s)
Watermelon (*Citrullus lanatus*)	5–7	3–4	last frost

* In growing celery, daily fluctuation to 60°F or lower at night is essential.

** Time from planting to harvest may depend on variety; transplanted crops may require additional time.

(s) Make successive sowings or plantings every two weeks.

TRANSPLANTING, (weeks before last frost)	SPACING (inches)	OPTIMUM SOIL TEMPERATURE RANGE (°F)	DAYS FROM SOWING TO HARVEST**
last frost	12–15	60–95	60–70
last frost	24–30	75–90	70–85
4–6 (s) 4–6	6–12 10–12	40–80 40–80	60–85 40–50
last frost	4–8	60–85	65–80 (early) 80–95 (late)
last frost	15–18	75–95	80–90
last frost	15–18	70–95	50–60
4–6	6–8	50–95	85 (early) 120 (late)
	3–4	50–70	100 (early) 130 (late)
	2–3	40–75	60–75
last frost	18–24	65–95	60–70 (early) 80–95 (late)
last frost	24–48	70–90	10–120 (pumpkin) 50–80 (early squash) 70–120 (late squash)
	1–2	45–90	22–40 50–60 (winter type)
	4–6	45–75	50 (early) 70 (late)
	6–8	50–85	50–60
last frost	18–24	60–85	65 (early) 100 (late)
	4–6	60–105	40 (early) 75 (late)
last frost	24–30	70–95	75 (early) 95 (late)

as annuals. Because they require space to develop, plants should be spaced 1 ft. apart in full sun and well-drained soil. They will bloom abundantly from summer to late autumn.

V. decurrens has 2-in., yellow flower heads with black centers. It is the best-known species but is rather weedy.

V. fastuosum (cape daisy, monarch-of-the-veldt), the choicest species, has silky grayish foliage and bright orange flowers 4 in. across, with a purplish black zone around a dark center.

VENTILATION.

In horticulture, ventilation is synonymous with airing. In the case of hotbeds heated by fermenting materials, especially manure, this is done partly to replace the air that has become more or less vitiated by the gases of decomposition. In other hotbeds and in coldframes, ventilation removes excessive heat and moisture to develop sturdier plants. See HARDENING-OFF.

Ventilation of coldframes and hotbeds requires careful attention and judgment. In late winter and early spring, alternate sashes must not be slid down and up, as can be done later in warmer weather, since this would result in drafts on the plants immediately under the openings. There are two good ways to avoid harmful drafts while ventilating frames. The upper end of the sash can be raised and held up an inch or more by a block made with steps each an inch higher than the preceding; or the sash can be raised on the sides from which the wind is not blowing. Ventilation given when the sun is shining brightly must be reduced or shut off promptly if the sky becomes overcast, if the wind rises, or if the air becomes colder.

During cold weather, ventilation can start on sunny days at nine o'clock or even earlier, but the sash should be closed in the afternoon when the sun is still shining brightly—not later than four o'clock, often at three—in order to retain as much of the sun's heat as possible. With the advance of the season, ventilation should be increased to make the plants grow sturdy.

See also GREENHOUSE; HOUSEPLANTS.

VENUS FLYTRAP.

Common name for *Dionaea muscipula*, an insectivorous perennial herb native to the Carolinas; see DIONAEA.

VENUS-HAIR FERN.

Common name for *Adiantum capillus-veneris*, a familiar southern fern suitable for rock gardens; see ADIANTUM.

VENUS'S-LOOKING-GLASS.

Common name for *Legousia speculum-veneris*, a violet- or white-flowered annual often used in edge plantings; see LEGOUSIA.

VERATRUM

(vee RAY trum). A genus of hardy perennial herbs belonging to the Liliaceae (Lily Family) and commonly known as white- or false hellebore. They grow to 9 ft. and have large, clasping, ribbed leaves and small, white, greenish, or purple flowers in panicles at the top of the stalk. Variously hardy in Zones 3–9, they are decorative planted along the margin of a stream or pond in the wild garden and can also be used for bold foliage effects in a shaded border. Propagation is by seed or division. The poisonous roots are sometimes processed into a powder or liquid form of insecticide.

PRINCIPAL SPECIES

V. album (European white-hellebore) grows to 4 ft. and has greenish white flowers.

V. californicum, a handsome species from the western states, grows to 6 ft. and has white flowers marked green.

V. nigrum grows 3–4 ft. and has tall, crowded spikes of purple flowers.

V. viride (American white-hellebore) grows 3–4 ft. and has yellowish green flowers. It has been known by many common names, including duck-ratten, earth-gall, devil's-bit, bear-corn, poor-Annie, itchweed, and Indian-poke.

VERBASCUM

(ver BAS kum). A genus of tall, usually biennial herbs of the Scrophulariaceae (Figwort Family), having somewhat woolly or downy foliage and purple, red, or yellow flowers. Commonly known as mullein, they grow readily in any warm, dry soil and are familiar field and roadside weeds in the United States.

Nearly all the species thrive in full sunlight. They are propagated by seed, cuttings, and division and hybridize readily with the genus CELSIA, the result being many new color forms of pink, lilac, rose, or violet.

PRINCIPAL SPECIES

V. blattaria (moth mullein) grows 3–6 ft. tall and has smooth leaves and yellow, lilac-throated flowers. It is a European plant, often found as an escapee from old gardens.

V. chaixii grows to 3 ft. and has white, woolly leaves and yellow flowers with purple stamens; it is an excellent border plant.

V. nigrum, growing to 3 ft., has leaves that are smooth above and downy beneath. The densely clustered, small, yellow flowers have lilac throats and purple stamens.

V. olympicum is a stately species from Greece that grows to 5 ft. and has downy white foliage and bright yellow flowers in tall racemes.

Verbascum sp.

V. phoeniceum (purple mullein) grows to 5 ft. Its leaves are smooth above and soft hairy beneath. The red or purple flowers have prominent purple stamens. Unlike other mulleins, it prefers partial shade, whether in the border or greenhouse. It is a parent of nearly all the pastel-colored hybrids, including *V.* x 'Miss Wilmott', with 5-ft. spikes of pure white flowers; and *V. libani*, with yellow flowers.

V. thapsus (common mullein), a European plant widely naturalized in North America, has a densely woolly rosette of foliage and yellow flowers on stalks up to 6 ft. When

Verbascum thapsus

grouped in the wild garden as a background, it creates a stunning effect. Its growth indicates a dry, gravelly or stony soil rich in nitrogen and low in lime. Mullein was a beloved herb of the Druids, who used it in herbal medicines.

VERBENA (vur BEE nah). A group of perennial herbs sometimes known by the ancient name vervain; it lends its name to the VERBENACEAE (Verbena Family), of which it is the principal genus. Verbenas are grown in gardens for their broad, flat clusters of white, red, or lilac flowers; there are also some shrubby wild forms.

As a common name, lemon verbena is *Aloysia triphylla* (see ALOYSIA) and sometimes refers to *Isotoma petraea* var. *alba*. Sand-verbena is the genus ABRONIA.

CULTURE

Although perennial in warm regions, verbenas are treated as annuals in colder zones, being grown from seed sown in boxes or flats in a sunny window inside, or in hotbeds and greenhouses. The seedlings, after being transplanted at least once, are set outdoors in late spring, about 12 in. apart. Seed can also be sown in the open earlier in the spring to bloom about midsummer. Many varieties of verbena have been developed, and since they do not come true from seed, they must be propagated by cuttings, usually taken in early fall and rooted in moist sand.

Verbena gooddingii

PRINCIPAL SPECIES

V. bonariensis grows to 5 ft. and has tall heads of small, lavender flowers and rather sparse foliage. Hardy to Zone 8.

V. canadensis (clump verbena) is somewhat erect in habit and has spikes of rose, white, or purple blossoms.

V. gooddingii (southwestern verbena) is a low native plant found on sandy soils and in the mountain regions of the desert Southwest.

Lavender flower clusters are borne atop 6–8 in. scapes. The leaves are quite hairy.

V. hastata, perennial and hardy to Zone 3, is a tall plant with spikes of dark blue flowers, native to North America and thriving in damp ground.

Verbena hastata

V. x hybrida (garden verbena), also listed as *V. x hortensis*, is a hybrid race that includes the most widely grown verbenas. They have variously colored flowers and varying growth habits, usually semi-trailing, the shoots rooting readily. The color forms usually seen are one-color, eyed, and striped. They are brilliant and decorative plants, often delightfully fragrant and blooming continuously from early summer until late fall. They are used for massing in beds, for edgings, to fill in spaces in the border left vacant by spring bulbs, and as a ground cover along summer or fall bulbs such as *Gladiolus* and *Lycoris*.

V. laciniata (moss verbena) is a low-growing plant with finely cut leaves and small heads of lavender flowers.

V. officinalis is a European native often found as an escapee in North America. It has pale lavender flowers on 2-ft. spikes.

V. pulchella, also listed as *V. tenera*, has cut leaves and blue or lilac flowers.

V. rigida (tuber verbena), often listed as *V. venosa*, blooms the first year from seed and spreads rapidly, bearing many short spikes of purplish flowers.

V. tenuisecta grows 8–12 in. and has numerous purple flower heads 2½ in. across. Hardy to Zone 6.

VERBENACEAE (vur bee NAY see ee). The Verbena or Vervain Family, a group of herbs, shrubs, and trees distributed throughout temperate and tropical regions. The genus *Tectona* yields teak wood, and many others provide fine garden plants, such as *Callicarpa*, *Caryopteris*, *Clerodendrum*, *Duranta*, *Lantana*, *Petrea*, *Verbena*, and *Vitex*.

VERNATION. The manner in which leaves are arranged in the bud. Determined by cutting the bud at an angle, it is often a valuable guide in identifying plants. The blade may be folded along the veins like a closed fan (plicate), as in maples; or folded lengthwise (convolute), as in roses. The margins may be variously rolled (involute and revolute), as in violets; or the midrib may unroll from base to tip (circinate), as in the ferns.

VERNONIA (vur NOH nee ah). A genus belonging to the Asteraceae (Aster Family), commonly known as ironweed. Stunted by cold, they are perennial herbs in cool climates but reach tree or shrub proportions in the tropics. In late summer, they have showy heads of flowers ranging from white to pink or purple. Some species are grown in hardy borders and wild gardens, being easily handled in good, rich soil and propagated either by seed, divisions, or cutting.

V. altissima grows from New York to Louisiana, sometimes attaining 10 ft.

V. crinita is native from Missouri to Texas, where it usually grows to 12 ft.

VERONICA (vur AHN ik ah). A genus of annual and perennial plants of the Scrophulariaceae (Figwort Family) and occasionally known as speedwell. It was named for the ship that left England with the *Mayflower* but shortly returned because it was not seaworthy. Blue, violet, or white flowers are produced in tightly packed racemes. Highly useful and decorative in the border and rock garden, they are hardy and free flowering, thrive in an open, sunny location or light shade, and are easily propagated by seed or division. Most are hardy in Zones 4–9.

PRINCIPAL SPECIES

V. americana (American brooklime), found in swamps and marshes, is a fleshy, creeping or upright perennial with elliptic leaves and loose racemes of blue or violet flowers.

V. chamaedrys (angel's-eyes, bird's-eyes, germander speedwell) is a compact, mostly evergreen plant spreading to 1 ft. A European native, it can become invasive and has been naturalized in North America.

V. filiformis, with mats of pale green foliage and pinkish lavender flowers in spring, makes a good ground cover.

V. fruticulosa, growing 4–6 in. high, is a spreading shrub with pink or white flowers.

V. gentianoides has long, loose, spikelike clusters of pale lavender flowers veined with blue. Var. *pallida* bears Wedgwood-blue flowers.

V. heidekind grows 9–12 in. and has spikes of pink flowers above mats of gray-green leaves.

V. incana, growing to 2 ft., has white, hoary foliage and porcelain-blue flowers. It is one of the most charming species for the border and is hardier than most (Zones 3–9).

V. maritima, sometimes listed as *V. longifolia*, has long racemes of deep lavender-blue flowers. It is a useful plant for the perennial border and is naturalized in the eastern states. Var. *subsessilis*, with deeper blue flowers, blooms for a long period in moderate shade.

V. multifida, a spreading species, has pale blue or pink flowers and is good in the rock garden.

V. peduncularis, growing to 5 ft., has small, pink-veined, white blossoms and bronzy green foliage forming mounds.

V. repens is a small, creeping perennial with shiny, mossy leaves and blue or pink, almost stemless flowers. It is useful for planting between paving stones or as a ground cover among small spring-blooming bulbs.

V. spicata, to 1½ ft. tall, has blue or pink flowers in spikelike racemes. Var. *alba* has white flowers. Var. *erica* has pink, heatherlike blossoms. Var. *orchidea* has lavender-blue or pinkish flowers and glossy foliage.

V. teucrium, also listed as *V. latifolia*, grows to 1½ ft. and has long racemes of clear blue flowers. It is a valuable ornamental species but is less hardy than most, Zones 5–9. Var. *prostrata*, with rich blue flowers, is a low-growing form excellent in the rock garden.

VERONICASTRUM (vur ah ni KAST rum) **virginicum.** A perennial herb native from New England south and westward, commonly known as culver's-root or culver's-physic. It is a robust plant of stiff habit that grows to 7 ft. and has whorled leaves. In late summer the plant is conspicuous with dense spikes of small, white or pale blue flowers. It is effective in the wildflower garden and thrives best in rich soil and an open location.

Veronicastrum virginicum

VERTICILLIUM WILT. A serious wilt disease of shade trees, especially maple, elm, *Ailanthus*, and a few other woody hosts. Commonly known as maple wilt, it does not generally occur on plants growing naturally in the wild. More maples are being lost each year as a result of this disease, but although attacked trees do not usually recover, there is not the rapid spread to surrounding trees characteristic of the Dutch elm disease. External symptoms are sudden wilting and dying of the foliage on one or more limbs, frequently on one side of the tree or in the top. Sometimes large trees die suddenly, as if their moisture supply had been suddenly cut off. The wood of infected twigs shows characteristic green or brown streaks.

Experiments have determined that a program of generous feeding will arrest the disease in some affected plants. The incidence of the disease can be reduced with adequate watering or rainfall. Verticillium wilt can also affect fruit and vegetables. Crop rotation can help prevent the fungi from becoming established in the soil.

VERVAIN. Common name for some native, seldom-cultivated species of VERBENA, a genus of flowering herbs; sometimes applied to the whole family VERBENACEAE.

VETCH. Common name for the leguminous genus VICIA, especially for species grown for forage and green manure. Other plants called vetch include *Anthyllis vulneraria* (kidney-vetch), *Astragalus* (milk-vetch), and *Coronilla varia* (crown-vetch).

VIBURNUM (vī BUR num). A large genus of deciduous or evergreen shrubs or small trees widely distributed throughout the Northern Hemisphere, belonging to the Caprifoliaceae (Honeysuckle Family). They rank among the most ornamental and useful shrubs for general planting purposes. They are mostly compact and bushy, with attractive foliage that takes on good fall coloring.

Most of them also have showy flowers, followed by decorative fruits. They are good for shrub borders, hedges, roadside plantings, and some make handsome single specimens on lawns. They are not very particular as to soil and location, although generally they prefer a place that is not too dry. Several will tolerate considerable shade. The deciduous species are generally hardy, but only one evergreen species, *V. rhytidophyllym*, can also survive the northern winters. Viburnums do not respond well to pruning. Propagation is by softwood cuttings, hardwood cuttings, layering, and grafting.

PRINCIPAL NORTH AMERICAN SPECIES

V. acerifolium (mapleleaf viburnum, dockmackie) grows to about 5 ft. with slender, upright branches and maplelike leaves. It is a good undershrub and does fairly well in dry places. The yellowish white flowers are borne in small clusters, and the fruit is almost black; neither is very showy. This species is extremely stoloniferous, spreading rapidly, and should be avoided in most gardens and enjoyed in the woods. It is one of the few deciduous trees or shrubs that often has pink to rosy purple foliage in the fall. Hardy in Zones 4–8, it thrives in shade.

V. alnifolium (hobblebush, American wayfaring tree) is a vigorous grower to 10 ft. or more and has large, handsome, dark green, wrinkled leaves turning reddish purple in fall. It has conspicuous, flat clusters of snow white flowers, the outer ones large and sterile, followed by purple black berries. Hardy in Zones 4–7, it is somewhat slow to get established and prefers a moist, shady place.

V. cassinoides (withe-rod, teaberry, Appalachian-tea) is one of the handsomest of native shrubs. In the wild, it is usually found in moist places, sometimes 8 ft. tall. In cultivation in the open it makes a compact, round-headed specimen. It has finely toothed leaves and clusters of creamy white flowers in early summer. In the fall it is outstanding in fruit, with heavy clusters of berries changing in color from yellowish green to pink and blue-black. Hardy in Zones 4–8.

V. dentatum (arrowwood) is an upright, bushy grower to 10 ft. or more and has roundish, coarsely toothed leaves, wide clusters of white flowers in early summer, and blue-black berries. It does well in moist ground and is also good for shady places and under trees in Zones 3–8.

V. lentago (nannyberry, sheepberry) is a tall, hardy bush with white flowers and edible, bluish black berries covered with a bloom. It has long, pointed buds and slender twigs, and is native from northern Canada to Mississippi.

V. prunifolium (blackhaw) is a large shrub or small specimen tree with wide-spreading branches, often the outstanding feature of rocky hillsides in the East and hardy in Zones 4–9. It has handsome foliage and clusters of pure white flowers followed by showy, edible fruit changing from green to yellow, pink, blue, then black.

V. rufidulum (southern blackhaw) grows as a tree to 40 ft. and has wide-spreading branches in warm climates, but in cold regions it is usually a shrub; hardy in Zones 6–9. It has dark green, shining leaves and is distinguished by rusty brown hairs on the leaf and flower stalks. The flowers are pure white in a broad cluster, and the berries are dark blue and bloomy.

V. trilobum (cranberry bush), sometimes listed as *V. americanum*, is the native form of the European *V. opulus*. Hardy in Zones 3–7, it is a large, handsome shrub with three-lobed leaves that turn a brilliant color in fall. It has showy clusters of white flowers, the outer ones large and sterile. The large, heavy clusters of juicy, scarlet berries color easily and remain decorative until spring. The delicious fruit is used like cranberries. Cultivars 'Andrews', 'Hahs', and 'Wentworth' have larger, edible fruits.

PRINCIPAL ASIATIC SPECIES

V. x *burkwoodii*, growing to 8 ft., is an excellent hybrid with fragrant flowers. Hardy in Zones 4–8 and partly evergreen in the South, it has shiny, small, dark green leaves and blooms in the spring with pink buds opening to white flowers with a spicy fragrance. Cv. 'Mohawk' has dark red buds opening to pink and white flowers with a strong, spicy fragrance. Its glossy, green leaves turn orange-red in autumn.

V. carlesii (Koreanspice viburnum) is one of the most desirable shrubs, valued for its very spicy, fragrant, pink-and-white spring flower clusters opening with the leaves. It is of rounded form to 5 ft. and is sometimes grafted, so sucker growths should be checked carefully. Its blue-black berries are not freely produced. Hardy in Zones 5–7.

V. dilatatum is a large and handsome shrub that grows to 10 ft. or more and is free flowering and very conspicuous in fall with an abundance of small, bright scarlet berries often remaining well into winter; hardy in Zones 5–7. Cv. 'Xanthocarpum' has yellow flowers. 'Catskill' is a dwarf plant that grows to 5 ft. and has red fruit. 'Iroquois', growing to 9 ft., has thick, glossy, dark green foliage and large, scarlet fruits.

V. farreri grows to 10 ft. and has short panicles of very fragrant, pink-and-white flowers in advance of the leaves. Hardy in Zones 6–8.

V. x *juddii* (Judd viburnum) grows to 8 ft. and has a rounded growth habit and very fragrant, white flowers. Hardy to Zone 5.

Viburnum x *juddii*

V. plicatum var. *tomentosum* (Japanese snowball) is one of the best of the genus. It is outstanding in form, growing to 10 ft., and has wide-spreading, horizontal branches bearing handsome leaves and showy clusters of white flowers along the upper side. The clusters are conspicuous with an outer ring of large and sterile flowers. It also has attractive fruits that change from scarlet to black. This variety should be planted at or below eye level in the garden or landscape, because the rows of white flowers are on top of green foliage on horizontal branches, not visible from below.

V. rhytidophyllum is a handsome evergreen species that grows to about 10 ft. and has long, dark green, wrinkled leaves yellowish and felt-like beneath. It bears large, flat clusters of yellowish white flowers and fruit that changes from red to black. It needs a protected location for the sake of the foliage and is killed back in below-zero weather. Hardy in Zones 6–8.

V. sargentii is the Asiatic form of *V. opulus* and much like the North American *V. trilobum*. It has larger, sterile flowers than these and is the handsomest of the three in bloom. Hardy in Zones 4–7, it has a good compact form. Cv. 'Flavum' has yellow fruit.

V. setigerum (tea viburnum) is a narrow and upright plant with very handsome leaves but rather plain flower clusters. The fruit are decorative clusters of large, ovoid, scarlet berries. It is hardy in Zones 6–7, but the tops are likely to be killed back in severe winters. The specific name comes from the fact that, in China, Buddhist monks make an infusion known as sweet tea from its leaves.

V. sieboldii is a treelike shrub with bright green, lustrous leaves that give off a disagreeable odor when bruised. The blooms are showy, with large clusters of white flowers followed by berries changing from red to black and soon falling. Hardy in Zones 4–7.

PRINCIPAL EUROPEAN SPECIES

V. lantana (wayfaring tree) is a vigorous shrub that grows to 15 ft. and has light green, wrinkled leaves, white beneath, turning deep red in fall. It has clusters of white flowers and berries that change from red to black. Hardy in Zones 4–7, it will thrive in dry locations and is often used as stock for grafting purposes.

V. opulus (European cranberry bush) grows vigorously to 12 ft. and has three-lobed leaves turning crimson and orange in fall. It has clusters of showy, white flowers and scarlet, juicy fruit. Cv. 'Roseum' (snowball, Guelder-rose) has all sterile flowers in a globose head. It is often attacked by black aphis. 'Xanthocarpum' is a yellow-fruited form.

V. tinus (laurustinus), native to the Mediterranean region, is the most useful of the evergreen species. Bushy to 10 ft. or more, it has glossy, dark green leaves and clusters of pinkish white flowers, which, in mild climates, open during the winter and are followed by black fruits. Hardy to Zone 7.

VICIA (VIS ee ah). A genus of trailing or tendril-climbing, rather weedy herbs belonging to the Fabaceae (Bean Family). They have purple, white, or scarlet flowers and profuse feather-form leaves. Though primarily farm crops, they are useful for improving garden soil, adding nitrogen and humus when dug or plowed under. Some species, commonly known as vetch, are used as forage or green manure crops, others have decorative applications, and one has long been cultivated for food. Vetch will grow in any average soil but prefers one well supplied with lime. In farm regions, escaped vetch has sometimes proved a troublesome weed.

PRINCIPAL SPECIES

V. caroliniana, with loose racemes of white blossoms, is an attractive trailer for sunny slopes in the wild garden.

V. cracca var. *gerardi*, occasionally grown in the border garden, is a hardy annual with purple flowers in short racemes.

V. faba (broad, Windsor, English dwarf, or horse bean) is a vegetable grown as human food for centuries. It is an erect annual plant about 3 ft. high and bears broad pods, sometimes 18 in. long, containing almost round, flat seeds. It is

seldom grown in home vegetable gardens in the United States but is used in the West to fatten cattle. It dislikes extreme heat.

V. gigantea, distributed by dealers of native plants, is a western species sometimes grown in the flower garden for its reddish purple blossoms.

V. sativa (common or spring vetch, historically known as tare) is an annual or biennial grown for forage or cover crop especially in orchards. It will not survive freezing and should be sown in the spring as a soil conditioner over summer.

V. villosa (winter or hairy vetch) is primarily used for green manure, usually sown with rye, equal parts, at the rate of one pint of the mixture per 100 sq. ft. any time during the fall wherever land is vacant.

VICTORIA (vik TOR ee ah) **amazonica.** The first specimen of this South American waterlily to be studied and described was listed as *Victoria regia* and commonly called royal or Victoria waterlily, in honor of England's then reigning queen. The fragrant, night-blooming flowers 6–8 in. across and the large platterlike leaves up to 7 ft. across, give the plant an overpowering beauty and magnificence. The flowers open white and change to pink, then become a deep rose on the second night. Their fragrance is like the odor of pineapples. The enormous, rich green, circular leaves have a curiously turned-up rim 5–6 in. high. The underside is heavily netted with a cross-veining of purplish green air pockets. The stems and veins are spined.

A pool 25–30 ft. across is not too large for a single Victoria. Hardy in Zones 10–11, it requires warmth and full sun at all times. Seeds must never be allowed to dry. As soon as gathered, they should be put in containers of water and kept there until planted. In cooler climates, the plants seldom bloom early enough to ripen seed.

One other species, *V. cruziana*, native to Paraguay, is also cultivated in the United States. It is the most easily cultivated and does well in cooler conditions than *V. amazonica*, thriving in temperatures of 70–75°F.

VIGNA (VIG nah). A genus of annual herbs belonging to the Fabaceae (Bean Family) with leaves in threes and yellowish white or purplish blossoms resembling those of sweet peas. Most species are tender in cold climates and are grown only in warm regions or as short-season, mid-summer subjects for cover crops or forage.

V. caracalla (corkscrew or snail flower), formerly listed as *Phaseolus caracalla*, is a climbing annual vine with flowers in which the keel or lower petal is twisted and resembles a snail shell.

V. unguiculata, formerly listed as *V. sinensis*, is a useful green manure and often grown as a vegetable; see COWPEA. Var. *sesquipedalis* (yard-long or asparagus bean) is raised for its edible pods that are 1–3 ft. long.

VILLOUS. Covered with a nap of fine, soft hairs, not matted, and rather more shaggy than velvety. Many of the *Erigeron* (fleabanes) exhibit this characteristic.

VINCA (VIN kah). A genus of erect or trailing herbs or subshrubs, mostly from warm regions, belonging to the Apocynaceae (Dogbane Family), and commonly known as periwinkle. The cultivated forms are propagated by cuttings and division.

PRINCIPAL SPECIES

V. major is larger in every way than *V. minor* but hardy only to Zone 7. The variegated form, which is usually grown, is used in flowering baskets, vases, and window boxes.

V. minor (running-myrtle, periwinkle-myrtle), the best-known species and one of the most useful of garden plants, is native to Europe but naturalized in some areas. Hardy in Zones 4–9, it thrives under shaded conditions and is one of the best plants to grow beneath trees and in other places where a carpeting effect is desired. It has shining, evergreen leaves

Vinca minor

and attractive violet-blue flowers in spring. There are several varieties, including some white, rosy purple, and double-flowered forms and others with variegated leaves. Var. *bowlesi* is superior to the type in foliage effect and has flowers of a deeper shade of blue, freely produced in spring and again lightly in fall.

V. rosea is now listed as *Catharanthus roseus*; see CATHARANTHUS.

VINE CACTUS. Common name for *Fouquieria splendens*, a cactuslike plant with scarlet flowers; see FOUQUIERIA.

VINES. A large and varied group of plants are included under this general heading, many belonging to the VITACEAE (Grape or Vine Family). In England, the term would be taken to refer only to grapevines, but in the United States, it refers to all kinds of climbing plants as well as certain shrubs with long, flexible shoots that can be trained to serve as vines.

The group comprises a wealth of material available for various situations and purposes. Outdoors, vines are used to cover porches, trellises, arbors, pergolas, and posts; to clamber up old tree trunks or cover the bare ground beneath; to sprawl over rocks; and to cover steep banks. Indoors, they are useful to drape pillars and roof rafters, to cover walls, and in general to add to the floral and foliage effect of a well-kept greenhouse or sunny room. Some are also used to embellish window and porch boxes and hanging baskets in or around the home or other building.

CLIMBING VINES

Vines have developed different methods of supporting their stems. Some produce adventitious roots along one side of the stem, which serve to fix and hold them to such objects as a wall or tree; English-ivy and trumpet vine are good examples of this group. Many cling by means of tendrils, which are often twisted like a spiral spring to combine security with a certain amount of flexibility; gourds, grapes, and peas climb this way. The Boston-ivy attaches itself by means of disks at the ends of the tendrils.

Some vines are supported by their leaves; the stems or petioles, being sensitive to contact with a supporting object, curl around it. Clematis is notable in this group. Many plants have stems that twine around a support, and it has long been a matter of interest that not all twine in the same direction. The hop, for example, turns or winds clockwise, while the morning-glory turns counter clockwise.

PLANTING VINES

An important factor in growing vines, and one often neglected, is the proper preparation of a good location. Most vines are vigorous growers and are expected to remain in the same place for many years. If simply stuck into the ground without regard for soil quality and condition, most kinds are likely to be stunted and become easy prey for insects and diseases. Therefore, break up the soil at least 2 ft. deep over an area at least 3 ft. across for each plant; entirely replace the soil with good loam if necessary, and in any case, enrich it with old manure or leaf mold. If close to a building, watch for buried piles of bricks, mortar, and other rubbish that might interfere with food and moisture for the plants.

As a general rule, planting is best done in spring, and in most cases it is a good idea to cut the plants back severely to induce a good basal growth. Watch the young shoots, and see that they are properly secured from the start. Vines close to a wall are likely to suffer from dryness at the roots, and thorough soaking from time to time will be well worthwhile. Established vines appreciate a mulch of manure and occasional feeding with a good complete fertilizer when growth is active.

VINE SUPPORTS

With the exception of the stem-rooting type, vines used to cover walls will require some kind of support attached to the wall. The old-time shreds and wall nails are still used in some places. Modified forms of this idea are found in wire clips cemented to the wall surface, in wall nails with pliable tips to bend over the stems, and in staples (driven into wooden plugs that in turn are driven into drilled holes) to which the stems

are tied. Stout wires, run through screw-eyes projecting a few inches from the wall, afford a good means of support in many cases.

For porches and against walls that have to be painted from time to time, a good plan is to construct a metal-pipe frame with wire cross-strands or wire netting, and attach it to the wall with hooks. The entire section can then be unhooked and laid on the ground temporarily without damage to the vines. Various forms of wood latticework may best serve the purpose under certain conditions. To form a screen away from buildings, posts with wires threaded through them can be used, and for individual vines out in the open, cedar posts with the branch stubs left on are very satisfactory. In place of a low fence or along a walk or drive, vines can be grown on chains or heavy wires looped in long curves between wood, metal, or masonry posts.

PRUNING

Due consideration should be given to the space to be covered in selecting vines. A vigorous grower planted where there is only space for one of moderate growth means a lot of cutting back, which detracts from the natural beauty of the plant. Of course some pruning is necessary, but as always, the pruning shears should be used with discretion and good judgment. Vines that flower early should be examined right after flowering; lateral growth should be shortened, and some of the old main shoots might be removed to make way for young ones. Vines that flower on shoots of the current season's growth should be pruned in the spring just before new growth starts. It is sometimes advisable to give old plants of English-ivy a hard shearing; if done in the spring, the stems will soon be clothed again with new leaves. Old plants of *Euonymus fortunei* var. *vegeta* will remain more compact and better furnished if some of the laterals are shortened back in spring. Do not allow vines to cover up good architectural features, but by all means let them conceal poor ones.

The accompanying chart compares the features of common vines. For detailed information, refer to the various genera mentioned.

VINE HABITS

LATIN NAME (common name)	HABIT	FEATURES	HARDINESS	USES
Actinidia arguta (tara vine)	twining	large leaves, white flowers, edible fruit	Zones 5–8	train on supports
Akebia quinata (akebia)	twining	deciduous or evergreen foliage, fragrant flowers	Zones 5–8	train on supports
Allamanda spp. (allamanda)	climbing, shrubby	showy flowers, fruit	Zones 10–11	walls, train on supports
Ampelopsis brevipendunculata (porcelain-berry)	twining	colorful berries in autumn	Zones 5–8	train on supports, rocks
Anredera spp. (mignonette)	twining	white flowers in spikes; grows quickly	Zones 10–11	greenhouse, train on supports
Antigonon leptopus (rosa-de-montana)	climbing	bright pink or white flowers	Zones 10–11	greenhouse
Apios americana (groundnut)	climbing, trailing	fragrant, brownish purple flowers	Zones 3–9	slopes, train on supports
Aristolochia durior (Dutchman's-pipe)	twining	large leaves, interesting flowers	Zone 4	train on supports
Asarina barclaiana (asarina)	climbing	heart-shaped leaves, purple flowers	Zone 7	containers, train on supports
Beaumontia grandiflora (herald's-trumpet)	climbing, woody	oval leaves, clustered flowers	Zones 10–11	greenhouse
Bignonia capreolata (crossvine)	trailing, clinging	stiff, evergreen leaves; showy flowers	Zones 6–9	walls, train on supports
Bougainvillea spp. (bougainvillea)	climbing	showy bracts, thorny stems	Zones 10–11	train on supports
Campsis radicans (trumpet creeper)	clinging, trailing	orange-red, tubular flowers	Zone 5	walls, banks, slopes
Cardiospermum halicacabum (heartseed, balloon vine)	twining	interesting, inflated fruit; grows quickly	annual	train on supports
Celastrus spp. (bittersweet)	twining, trailing	rounded leaves, colorful fruit	varies with species	train on supports, slopes
Clematis spp. (clematis)	twining, trailing	attractive flowers, many hybrids	Zones 3–9	train on supports
Clerodendrum thomsoniae (bleeding-heart vine)	twining	evergreen leaves, crimson flowers, white calyxes	Zones 10–11	greenhouse, train on supports
Cobaea scandens (cathedral-bells)	climbing	showy, bell-shaped flowers with leafy calyx; grows quickly	annual	walls, train on supports
Cucurbita pepo var. *ovifera* (yellow-flowered gourd)	trailing	yellow flowers, hard-shelled fruit; grows quickly	annual	slopes

LATIN NAME (common name)	HABIT	FEATURES	HARDINESS	USES
Cymbalaria muralis (Kenilworth-ivy)	trailing	small, shade-tolerant, blue-and-yellow flowers	annual	greenhouse, containers, slopes, banks
Dioscorea batatas (cinnamon vine)	climbing	fragrant, interesting flowers; edible tubers	Zones 10–11	train on supports, light screening effect
Dolichos lablab (hyacinth bean)	twining	large leaves, reddish purple flower spikes; grows quickly	annual	train on supports
Eccremocarpus scaber (gloryflower)	climbing	orange-red, tubular flowers in racemes; grows quickly	annual	train on supports
Echinocystis lobata (mock cucumber)	trailing	clustered green or white flowers, prickly fruit; grows quickly	annual	train on supports
Euonymus fortunei (euonymus)	clinging, trailing	variable, attractive foliage	Zones 5–9	walls, slopes
Forsythia suspensa var. *sieboldii* (weeping forsythia)	shrubby, trailing	abundant yellow flowers before leaves	Zone 5	train on supports, banks
Gelsemium sempervirens (Carolina yellow jessamine)	twining, shrubby	fragrant, yellow flowers	Zones 7–9	ground cover, banks, train on supports
Glechoma hederacea (ground-ivy)	trailing	blue flowers, shade tolerant	Zone 3	banks, containers
Hedera helix (English ivy)	clinging, trailing	dense, glossy foliage	Zone 5	walls, containers
Humulus lupulus (hops)	twining	rough leaves, stems; fragrant, papery, yellow fruits; grows quickly	annual	train on supports, screening effect
Hydrangea anomala (hydrangea)	clinging	attractive foliage, white flowers	Zone 4	walls
Ipomoea spp. (morning-glory, moonflower)	twining, climbing	lush foliage; colorful, trumpet-shaped flowers; grows quick ly	annual	train on supports, banks, slopes
Jasminum spp. (jasmine)	shrubby, sometimes climbing	deciduous or evergreen foliage; showy, fragrant flowers	varies with species	greenhouse, slopes
Lapageria rosea (Chile-bells)	twining, climbing	showy, pink or red, bell-shaped flowers	Zones 10–11	greenhouse, walls, train on supports
Lathyrus latifolius (sweet pea)	twining	showy flowers, broad leaves; grows quickly	Zones 3–9	train on supports
Lonicera spp. (honeysuckle)	twining, trailing, climbing, shrubby	deciduous or evergreen leaves, fragrant flowers	Zones 5–9	train on supports, slopes

LATIN NAME (common name)	HABIT	FEATURES	HARDINESS	USES
Lycium chinense (matrimony vine)	climbing, twining	deciduous or evergreen; often spiny, showy flowers and fruit	Zone 4	rocky slopes, train on supports
Macfadyena unguis-cati (cat's-claw)	climbing	yellow, trumpet-shaped flowers	Zones 10–11	greenhouse benches, train on supports
Mandevilla spp. (mandevilla)	twining, shrubby	showy flowers	Zones 10–11	greenhouse
Parthenocissus quinquefolia (Virginia creeper)	clinging, trailing	compound leaves, colorful in autumn	Zones 5–8	walls, banks, slopes
Parthenocissus tricuspidata (Boston-ivy)	clinging, trailing	lobed leaves, colorful in autumn	Zones 5–8	walls
Passiflora spp. (passionflower)	climbing	showy, fragrant flowers; some have edible fruit	Zones 10–11	containers, greenhouse, train on supports
Pelargonium peltatum (ivyleaf geranium)	trailing	attractive foliage, fragrant flowers	Zones 10–11	containers
Phaseolus coccineus (scarlet runner bean)	twining	showy red flowers, edible pods; grows quickly	annual	train on supports
Plumbago auriculata (leadwort)	climbing	showy, blue or white flower spikes	Zones 10–11	greenhouse
Polygonum baldschuanicum (fleeceflower)	twining	large leaves; small, fragrant, pink flowers	Zone 6	train on supports
Pueraria lobata (kudzu)	climbing	fragrant, purple flowers; lobed leaves	Zone 5	banks, train on supports
Schizophragma spp. (climbing-hydrangea)	clinging	white flower clusters; thick, toothed leaves	Zone 5	walls, tree trunks
Senecio mikanioides (German-ivy)	twining	dark green, angled leaves; small, yellow flowers	Zone 9	containers
Solandra grandiflora (trumpet flower)	climbing	leathery leaves; large, fragrant, white or yellow flowers	Zones 10–11	greenhouse, train on supports
Solanum jasminoides (potato vine)	climbing, shrubby	bluish white flowers	Zones 10–11	greenhouse, train on supports
Solanum wendlandii (nightshade)	climbing	lilac-blue flowers; grows large outdoors	Zones 10–11	train on supports, greenhouse
Stephanotis floribunda (Madagascar jessamine)	twining, shrubby	thick, shiny leaves; fragrant, white flower clusters	Zones 10–11	greenhouse, train on supports
Thunbergia alata (black-eyed-Susan vine)	twining	colorful flowers	annual	containers, train on supports
Thunbergia laurifolia (clockvine)	climbing, woody	clustered, pale blue flowers	Zones 10–11	winter flowering in greenhouse

LATIN NAME (common name)	HABIT	FEATURES	HARDINESS	USES
Trachelospermum jasminoides (african jessamine)	climbing, woody	evergreen leaves; fragrant, white flowers	Zones 10–11	greenhouse, containers
Tropaeolum spp. (garden nasturtium)	climbing, trailing	variable foliage, showy flowers; grows quickly	annual	containers, slopes
Vinca spp. (periwinkle)	trailing	shiny, evergreen leaves; blue flowers	Zones 4–9	containers, slopes
Wisteria spp. (wisteria)	twining	long-lived; showy, fragrant flowers	Zones 5–9	train on supports

VIOLA (VĪ oh lah). A genus of small, usually perennial herbs commonly known as violet or pansy. Some are attractive flower and rock garden subjects, while others are more familiar in florist shops or woodland areas. They bear attractive blue, white, lavender, or yellow flowers in early spring and summer.

Violets are the state flowers of Illinois, New Jersey, Rhode Island, and Wisconsin. All are propagated by seed, division, or offsets.

The pansies include many garden hybrids. These generally have long and branching stems, oval leaves coarsely notched, about 1½ in. long, and stipules ½ in. wide. The flowers are larger than common violets in variously marked combinations of purple, white, or yellow.

CULTURE

Garden Violets. Many species are easily grown as border plants or naturalized on the edge of the woodlands. Set the young plants in rich, loamy soil in a sheltered location in late spring or early fall and mulch well with leaf mold or light, decomposed compost material. With this simple treatment they will bloom for four to six weeks in the spring. They tend to set runners freely, sometimes too much so. To prevent their becoming a matted mass and rapidly "running out," they should be lifted every year, pulled apart, and the young plants reset. In cooler climates, some can be kept in coldframes or cold greenhouses for winter and early-spring cut flowers.

Pansies. In the garden, several hybrid annuals (or perennials treated as annuals) with a wonderful diversity in color and markings are easily grown in beds and borders. They do well in any good, light soil but prefer sandy, loamy, deep planting where the roots can be kept cool, and a location where they will not be overshadowed by trees or directly exposed to the hot, dry sun. Ordinary good garden soil with well-decayed leaf mold, humus, or finely sifted ashes makes an ideal soil.

They are propagated by seed, cuttings, and sometimes by layering. Seed can be sown at any time but is best done in late spring for transplanting in autumn or in late summer for early spring transplants. Sow seed in light soil, cover slightly, and transplant to pots or flats as soon as seedlings are large enough. It is important that good roots be formed and that balls of soil should adhere before the final setting. Cuttings from side-shoots start readily during late summer. If they are bent over, the side-shoots will soon root as layers. In some instances, the old plants can be divided carefully at the roots.

In planting, press roots firmly and deeply in the soil. As soon as the flowering period begins, apply a top mulch of humus or leaf mold. If exhibition flowers are wanted, four to six shoots can be allowed on each plant, the remaining ones being removed or pinched out. If all blossoms are removed until three weeks before the show, the plant will be strengthened and the size of the blossoms increased.

Greenhouse Culture. A number of varieties have been developed especially for greenhouse culture. They are grown in solid beds, the young plants being set in the late spring 8–12 in. apart in rows 10 in. apart. Soil should be composed of 4 parts light loam to 1 part well-rotted manure, well mixed and made definitely alkaline (sweet) with lime. During the summer, the greenhouse should be shaded, cool, and well ventilated. The plants are watered in moderation but never soaked. A mulch of spent manure is excellent to conserve moisture. All runners should be removed, this inducing a compact growth and stimulating flowers to come into bloom in late fall. Very little heat is required during the winter, since violets succeed better when the temperature does not exceed 50°F. Propagation is by division or, preferably, offsets rooted in sand.

ENEMIES

Diseases. Several LEAF SPOT diseases may kill the tissues, forming small or large, circular or irregular, ashy white or brown areas. MILDEW and RUSTS may also be a problem. A widespread leaf spot, known as scab, causes small, red and white spots, which change to light-colored, scalded or blistered areas on leaves and petioles. All such diseases are usually held in check by destroying old leaves in the fall. Gray mold, or BOTRYTIS, is sometimes prevalent in wet weather.

Two root rots affect violets and pansies, one mostly outdoors and the other in greenhouses. Affected plants are yellow, dwarfed, and eventually die, the roots decaying and becoming jet-black. Water the plants early in the day and allow leaves to dry before nightfall. If problems persist, fungicides can be applied, but complete control can be effected only by changing the soil, by soil sterilization, and by the selection of healthy plants for propagation.

Insect Pests. Eelworms may infect violet roots; see NEMATODES. The plants may be infested by pests including the SLUGS, SNAILS, CUTWORM, THRIPS, and yellow woolly bear CATERPILLAR. APHIDS and the RED SPIDER MITE may suck juices

from the plants. In the greenhouse, twisting and distortion of the leaves is due to the gall MIDGE. The LEAF TIER may cause severe injuries; these can be controlled by occasional fumigating for a few hours.

The blue-black grubs of the violet SAWFLY eat the leaves at night. The adult, a small four-winged black fly, lays its eggs in blisterlike incisions in the leaves. See also INSECT CONTROL.

PRINCIPAL SPECIES

V. blanda is a native species with white, sweet-scented flowers. It is charming planted as a ground cover for early spring-flowering bulbs.

V. canina (dog violet) is a garden plant from Europe, with yellow-spurred purple flowers.

V. cornuta (tufted pansy) has very long-spurred flowers. From this species, many garden cultivars have been developed. They are most valuable and decorative for edging the border or for ground cover under roses. Some of the best named forms include 'G. Wermig', forming clumps of rich purple flowers throughout the summer; 'Jersey Gem', a fine, dwarf, free-flowering plant; 'Suttons Apricot', with large, buff flowers tinted orange; 'Golden Yellow'; and a number of others.

V. elegantula, also listed as *V. bosniaca*, has purplish pink blossoms and is a good garden subject.

V. gracilis, from eastern Europe, is a useful rock or wild garden subject with delightful, starry, purple flowers.

V. odorata (sweet, garden, or florist's violet) is a widely cultivated European species. Single forms in blue or white are attractive in border and woodland plantings. A number of cultivars have been developed especially for cultivation under glass, with double forms including 'Marie Louise' and 'Lady Hume Campbell'; and single forms 'Princess of Wales', 'California', and 'Baroness Rothschild'.

V. papilionaceae (common blue violet), whose species name translates to "looks like a butterfly," has delicate, purple-blue or gray-blue petals. The plants are stemless, with flower stalks and heart-shaped leaves rising directly from a branching rhizome just below the soil surface. This violet is unusual because it produces two kinds of flowers. In the spring, leafless stems bear five-petaled flowers with fuzzy beards on the upper petals and purple stripes on the broad bottom petal, which guide pollinating bees to nectar contained in the spur at the base. In late spring and summer, different flowers with closed buds and no petals appear on short, horizontal stems hidden under the leaves; these flowers produce seeds without the aid of insect pollinators.

Viola papilionaceae

V. pedata (bird's-foot violet), with finely cut leaves and purple blossoms, does well in open gardens with acid, sandy soil.

V. x *witrockiana* (pansy, heart's-ease), formerly listed as *V. tricolor* var. *hortensis*, is a familiar garden subject with large, short-spurred flowers in shades and combinations of blue, white, and yellow.

VIOLET. Common name for VIOLA, a genus of small wild and garden herbs with colorful flowers. African-violet and Usambara-violet are names for *Saintpaulia ionantha*. Dame's-violet is *Hesperis matrionalis*. Dogtooth-violet is ERYTHRONIUM. Philippine-violet is *Barleria cristata*.

VIPER'S-BUGLOSS. A common name for ECHIUM, a genus of bristly herbs, including both cultivated and weedy species.

VIRGINIA CREEPER. A common name for *Parthenocissus quinquefolia*, a climbing vine with three-parted leaves; see PARTHENOCISSUS.

VIRGIN'S-BOWER. Common name for species of CLEMATIS, a genus of perennial herbs and flowering vines.

VITACEAE (vit AY see ee). The Grape or Vine Family, a group including erect shrubs and rarely small trees but better known for its woody vines climbing by means of tendrils. In addition to *Vitis* (wild and cultivated grapes), the family includes *Ampelopsis*, *Cissus*, and *Parthenocissus*, which include species cultivated as ornamental vines and wall or trellis covers.

VITAMINS. These much-publicized substances are important regulators for plant growth as well as for the health of people and other animals that consume them. In plant life, vitamins are actually hormones, because they are substances produced in one part of the plant to regulate the function of another part. Many have been studied and their functions isolated.

VITEX (VĪ teks). A genus of deciduous or evergreen shrubs widely distributed in warm and temperate regions, belonging to the Verbenaceae (Verbena Family). One or two species, although not entirely hardy, can be grown to Zone 6. They are valued for their showy flower spikes produced late in the season and are not particular as to soil, providing it is well drained in an open location. Propagation is by layers and greenwood cuttings.

PRINCIPAL SPECIES

V. agnus-castus (chaste tree, hemp tree) is a native of southern Europe, hardy in Zones 6–8. A vigorous shrub, it grows to 10 ft. under favorable conditions, but the shoots are usually killed far back by severe weather. Young shoots from the base produce flowers in the same year. It has very dark green, divided leaves, gray and woolly on the underside, and dense spikes, to 7 in. long, of fragrant, blue, white, or lavender flowers. Cv. 'Alba' is a white form; 'Rosea' has pink flowers.

V. altissima, native to India, is a valuable timber tree that grows to 100 ft. tall and has leaves of three elliptic, 8-in. leaflets that are dark green above and lighter underneath.

V. divaricata grows to 60 ft. high and has oblong leaves of three to five elliptic leaflets that sometimes have hairy midribs. It also has tiny, violet or blue flowers. Native to the Carribean and South America, it yields tannin from the leaves and the wood is used for making shingles.

V. negundo is a Chinese shrub that grows to 10 ft. and has four-sided stems and loose panicles of lavender flowers. Cv. 'Heterophylla' is hardy to Zone 6 and has finely cut leaves and a graceful form.

V. trifolia is a shrub or small tree from Asia and Australia. It grows to 20 ft. and has one to three 3-in., oblong leaflets per leaf and many-flowered, 9-in. panicles of blue or purple flowers. Var. *simplicifolia* is a more sprawling form with single leaflets.

VITIS (VĪ tis). A genus of fast-growing, tendril-climbing, deciduous vines, native to the Northern Hemisphere, mostly in temperate regions, and commonly known as grape, but simply called vine in much of Europe. Some are grown for their ornamental foliage, which in many cases takes on brilliant coloring in fall; others are important vineyard and home garden plants grown for their edible, luscious fruit. Propagation is by seed, cuttings of ripened wood, and layers. For cultivation, see GRAPE.

PRINCIPAL AMERICAN SPECIES

V. acerifolia (bush grape), native to the southwestern United States, is a sprawling, seldom climbing species with leathery, triangular leaves to 5 in. long. Its sweet, black fruits fall soon after ripening.

V. aestivalis (summer grape) is a tall climber found from New York southward, distinguished in foliage by the large, lobed leaves, reddish brown beneath. The berries are bloomy black.

V. berlandieri (Spanish or winter grape) is a southern vine of moderate growth, with large, lustrous leaves and compact clusters of purple berries, ripening late.

V. labrusca (fox grape), native from New England to the southern states, is a strong grower with large, thick, feltlike leaves, dull white to reddish brown beneath. The fruit is purplish black with a strong, musky odor. This is the principal parent of North American cultivated grapes.

V. riparia (riverbank grape) is a vigorous climber found from Nova Scotia southward. It has fragrant flowers, attractive, bright green leaves, and small, purple-black berries.

V. rotundifolia (muscadine, southern fox grape) is found along riverbanks and in rich woodlands of the South, often growing to 100 ft. It has rather small, heart-shaped leaves and dull purple, musky berries.

V. vulpina (frost grape), native from Pennsylvania southward, is a strong, high climber with large, lustrous leaves scarcely lobed, and dull black berries, edible after frost.

PRINCIPAL ASIATIC SPECIES

V. amurensis (Amur grape) is a strong grower with large leaves that turn crimson and purple in fall.

V. coignetiae (crimson-glory vine) is a vigorous, hardy grower with heavy foliage that turns brilliant scarlet in fall.

V. vinifera (wine grape) is the cultivated grape of history, now largely grown in Europe and California in many varieties.

VITTARIA (vi TAIR ee ah). A relatively small genus of subtropical epiphytic ferns. They have clustered rhizomes from which tufts of fronds arise. The fronds are long, hanging, and entire.

V. lineata (shoestring fern) has narrow, entire, hanging, dark green fronds 1–4 ft. long. In the wild, it is an epiphyte on rocks and tree trunks. It makes an interesting container or basket plant and can be grown on a slab of tree fern fiber. It is commonly seen in central Florida, Central America, and the West Indies.

VRIESEA (VREE see ah). A genus of striking greenhouse subjects belonging to the Bromeliaceae (Pineapple Family), native to the tropical Americas and cultivated in south Florida (Zones 10–11). The stiff, spiny leaves, often barred or variegated, grow to 2 ft. long in dense clusters. Flowers borne in flattened spikes are conspicuous for their brightly colored bracts or sheaths. In nature these are mostly epiphytes, but under glass a rich, fibrous soil is required, with liberal watering throughout the summer during active growth. A light sprinkling should be given in winter until flowers form in the earliest spring. Propagation is by suckers, which form around the base of old plants.

PRINCIPAL SPECIES

V. fenestralis, growing to 18 in., has dark-veined leaves tipped with brown and pale yellow flowers with green-spotted bracts.

V. hieroglyphica has leaves banded and irregularly marked with dark green and purple. Its flowers are yellowish.

V. splendens (flaming-sword) has banded leaves and sends up a spectacular inflorescence that retains its bright coloring for several weeks or months. There are numerous cultivars.

W

WAHLENBERGIA (wah len BUR jee ah). A genus of small annual or perennial herbs belonging to the Campanulaceae (Bellflower Family), with nodding, bell-shaped blue flowers, sometimes listed as *Edraianthus*. Especially suited to rock gardens, preferably in the open in well-drained soil, they resemble CAMPANULA and should be given the same culture. The annuals are propagated by seed and the perennials, by seed or division.

PRINCIPAL SPECIES

W. congesta is a creeping perennial with round leaves and small, pale blue blossoms.

W. gracilis is an annual that grows to 1 ft. and has solitary blue flowers ½ in. long.

W. saxicola, an annual, has small leaves and solitary white flowers with blue veins.

WAHOO. Common name for *Euonymus atropurpurea*, a deciduous shrub or tree with scarlet flowers; see EUONYMUS.

WAKE-ROBIN. Common name for TRILLIUM, a genus of perennials with three-part flowers.

WALDSTEINIA (vawld STĪN ee ah) **fragarioides.** A creeping, strawberrylike plant found in the woods from New Brunswick to Georgia and Minnesota, belonging to the Rosaceae (Rose Family), and commonly known as barren- or false strawberry. The plants bear sprays of yellow flowers, but there is no edible fruit. The plants are hardy to Zone 4 and make attractive little trailers for the rock garden, or for rocky ledges, banks, or dry walls, forming a leafy mat. To propagate the plants, divide the roots in March and plant out in the permanent location in full sunlight.

WALKING FERN. Common name for *Camptosorus rhizophyllus*, an unusual prostrate fern; see CAMPTOSORUS.

WALLFLOWER. Common name for CHEIRANTHUS, a genus of showy, flowering perennials. Siberian-wallflower is *Erysimum asperum*.

WALNUT. Common name for JUGLANS, a genus of deciduous trees grown for nuts and timber.

WANDERING-JEW. A common name for two very similar plants of the Commelinaceae (Spiderwort Family). *Tradescantia fluminensis* is a perennial herb with white flowers; see TRADESCANTIA. *Zebrina pendula* is a tender herb with red flowers; see ZEBRINA.

WANDFLOWER. Common name for SPARAXIS, a South African genus of spring-blooming herbs.

WASHINGTONIA (wah shing TOH nee ah). A genus of North American fan palms, extensively grown in Florida, California, and the Gulf states. They have wide fan-shaped leaves and tall trunks covered with dead, drooping foliage resembling a skirt. In the juvenile stage they make excellent specimen plants, and the large trees are often used for avenue planting.

W. filifera (desert fan palm), native near water sources on the border of the Colorado Desert in California, grows to 80 ft. and has a trunk covered under shaggy, hanging old leaves. Hardy to Zone 9, it is planted in Florida but does not thrive near the coast.

W. robusta (thread palm) is tall and slender, sometimes reaching 100 ft. and has a crown of fan-shaped leaves 3–5 ft. across, first erect, then spreading, and eventually drooping. At home in Florida, it is resistant to salt air and flourishes near the seashore, but since it requires a rich, moist soil, it cannot be grown successfully in the high pineland regions.

WASPS. Wasps are part of the order Hymenoptera, comprised of several families of familiar insects, including species beneficial in the garden as well as pests. All adult wasps (and hornets and yellow jackets) have four wings that fold lengthwise like a fan. There are solitary and social wasps, many of them making nests. The female solitary wasp makes her nest alone; the social wasps work together to build nests and to rear young.

The solitary wasps (Eumeninae) make burrows in the ground or in wood or stems, which they provision with caterpillars first paralyzed by a sting. Sometimes they make mud nests to hang from twigs. Each nest has cells in which one egg is laid, suspended by a thread from the cell wall, and sealed inside. The adults are carnivorous, though some also feed on nectar. The bodies of solitary wasps is like the yellow jacket but smaller and more slender.

Encarsia wasp

The social wasps (Vespidae) usually colonize with three castes: females or queens, workers, and males. As with bees, the workers are incompletely developed females. After one season the males and workers die; the females that have been fertilized hibernate, make a new nest, and lay eggs. The hatched larvae feed on the chewed-up insects stocked for them. These include many injurious caterpillars such as the corn earworm.

Among the many small beneficial wasps, some also called FLIES, there are parasites, like *Encarsia formosa*, that lay their eggs in the bodies of other insects with their long, piercing ovipositors. The wasplike Chalcididae are small, dark-colored insects that frequently prey on other insects, by females either directly feeding on insects or laying eggs to produce parasitic larvae in other insects or their eggs. The best known of these tiny wasps is the commercial-

Trichogramma wasp

ly available *Trichogramma evanescens*, usually classed as a chalcid fly, and just one of the 200 or so parasitic beneficial insects in this group. The larvae, which develop within the body of the host, kill it and eat up that body, then emerge to carry on their generations. Other chalcids parasitize the larvae of beetles, flies, moths, and butterflies; some also attack beneficial insect larvae.

Other tiny wasps or flies include the Braconidae, which are important parasites on aphids, moths, and some beetles. When, for instance, a tomato hornworm appears in the garden with white, egglike, little cocoons sticking out all over it, it should not be destroyed, for those are the larvae of brachonid wasps, beneficial insects preparing for adulthood and more generations of insect controls.

Another well-known little wasp is the FIG WASP, which is essential for the fertilization and development of Smyrna figs.

There are also cuckoo or jewel wasps, which lay their eggs in others' nests, thus parasitizing other wasps, bees, and sometimes hornets. These are bright green, blue, red, or purple and only about ½ in. long.

The shiny black pelecinid, a bigger wasp with a long abdomen, feeds on nectar and does not sting. Its larvae are internal parasites of June and Japanese beetle larvae as the grubs get near the surface of the soil before changing to adults.

The large, 1½-in. cicada wasp paralyzes cicadas and maneuvers them, one at a time, to her burrow to lay her egg between the insect's legs to develop there.

Among the Ichneumonidae, another large group, are many important wasps that naturally control harmful caterpillars and sawflies. There are some with ovipositors up to 3 in. long for laying parasitic eggs. These ovipositors are never used for stinging but can be used to pierce wood to get at horntails. Some of the little wasps also lay eggs within other parasitic eggs or larvae, thus becoming hyperparasites.

See also INSECTS, BENEFICIAL.

WATERCRESS. Common name for the herb *Nasturtium officinale*, which grows naturally in wet conditions and is cultivated as a salad or garnish; see NASTURTIUM.

WATER-FEATHER. Common name for *Myriophyllum aquaticum*, an aquatic plant with finely cut leaves; see MYRIOPHYLLUM.

WATER FERNS. A group of ferns quite different from typical ferns. The two obvious differences are that they are truly aquatic and that instead of producing a single type of spore as do the true ferns, both male and female spores are produced and borne in specialized organs called sporocarps. They also do not have fernlike fronds. The two or three families (Marsileaceae, Salviniaceae, and, under debate, Azollaceae) contain five genera: *Azolla*, *Marsilea*, *Pilularia*, *Regnellidium*, and *Salvinia*. Only *Marsilea* and *Pilularia* are found in the cooler temperate regions. An unrelated genus of water fern is CERATOPTERIS, which produces spores more conventionally on the fronds and belongs to the Parkeriaceae.

WATERING. The application of water to plants, both outdoors and indoors, requires more understanding of fundamental principles, more judgment, and more skill than any other gardening practice; yet it is perhaps more often wrongly done than any other gardening task. Too much water is given, or too little, or at the wrong times, wrong temperatures, and so on. The results, though often unsuspected (or at least not associated with their true cause) are frequently serious. Just how to water growing plants involves many subtle factors, but there are a few principal rules.

1. Avoid watering until the soil has become fairly dry, not powdery; then soak it thoroughly. Outdoors this means saturating from several inches to a foot or deeper. Indoors it means enough to wet the soil in the pot or the greenhouse bench from top to bottom. In the latter case, the excess can, of course, drain off, but since this means the loss of soluble plant food by leaching, frequent overwatering is wasteful even though it may not always prove injurious.

2. Avoid keeping the soil continuously wet. It takes experience to know when to water by the appearance of the plants, the flowerpots, the soil surface, and the growing conditions; however, the soil surface should be allowed to dry out between watering.

3. Avoid light—even though frequent—surface sprinkling of outdoor plants and lawns. Such applications are worse than giving none at all, because the moistened stratum of soil is very shallow. The plants are thereby encouraged to develop roots near the surface, and the result is disaster when sprinkling is discontinued for even a few days or when an exceptionally hot spell dries and almost literally bakes the roots.

4. Water actively growing, soft-stemmed large- and succulent-leaved plants abundantly, but dormant and resting, hard-wooded, slow-growing, and small-leaved subjects with restraint. The herbaceous kinds may show signs of flagging and yet recover fully when water is again applied. Woody plants are more likely to suffer seriously, if not die, after they are allowed to dry out. A safe rule to apply to plants in active growth is to water at the first suggestion of flagging.

5. As the amount and character of foliage affect water-using capacity, plants that have been cut back, that have lost their foliage from any cause, or that have become unhealthy must be kept drier than normal until new foliage begins to develop. Similarly, cuttings and newly potted or recently transplanted plants need to be kept fairly dry to encourage the development of root hairs and fibers, which is indicated by the commencement of new leaf and shoot development. One soaking at the time of potting or planting is generally enough, provided the plants are shaded for a few days from strong sunlight.

6. The quantity and character of soil should influence water applications. Loose and warm soils dry out more rapidly than do clays, so they are less likely to become sour if given an excess of water. This principle applies especially in regard to the growing of small plants in flowerpots. Such plants should be kept in small pots until the potting mix becomes filled with roots, then shifted to the next pot size—not a much larger one. Thus the amount of water needed to wet the soil is not likely to be enough to induce souring.

7. During cloudy and muggy weather, watering indoors must not be heavy because it is likely to injure the roots and to produce such humidity of the confined air that the plants will be weakened and made subject to disease and insect attack.

8. Watering greenhouse plants in the morning should be the rule, especially during the winter, so that ventilation can remove the excess before night, when the foliage should always be dry and the air relatively so. Watering of cutting benches and seedlings late in winter afternoons is almost sure to prove disastrous, for DAMPING-OFF is prone to attack plants under this condition. In moderate winter weather, the humidity in a tight greenhouse is likely to be greater than when it is cold, for ventilation is less effective than when the cold outside condenses much of the excess moisture on the glass, thus making the air relatively dry. Therefore, water sparingly during mild winter weather; when it gets cold and clear, you can be more liberal.

9. Usually the only times when watering can be safely done late in the day are during clear weather in summer when there is free ventilation and relatively low humidity. At that season and on bright days, watering with sprinklers during the middle half of the day is likely to produce scalding of the leaves of such plants as Chinese primroses and Rex begonias, unless the plants are adequately shaded.

10. Air temperatures, the location of heating pipes, the strength of the light, and the amount of ventilation must all be considered in greenhouse or conservatory watering practice. Also, the temperature of the water is likely to produce serious effects on plant growth, flowering, and fruiting if it is much more than 10°F below the air temperature.

The best time of day to water lawns, flower beds, borders, and outdoor plantings is generally in the evening, not because the water might burn the foliage during the strong sunshine, but because the loss from evaporation is less. Outdoors, too, watering should be delayed until the plants are actually in need of water, as indicated by slight flagging, and then done generously. Sometimes for larger plants it is most effective to remove the hose nozzle or sprinkler and let the water flow in a gentle stream until a fair-sized area is soaked, then move it to another spot. To avoid washing holes in the lawn or bed, place a piece of board or a square of heavy cloth under the end of the hose.

More sophisticated watering devices for garden include soaker (perforated) hoses, various types of sprinklers, and drip (trickle) irrigation systems; for hydroponic culture, capillary mats and nutrient film systems are used.

See also HYDROPONICS; IRRIGATION; SPRINKLING.

WATERLEAF. Common name for HYDROPHYLLUM, a genus of attractive perennial herbs.

WATER-LETTUCE. Common name for *Pistia stratiotes*, a tender aquatic plant with attractive leaves and feathery roots; see PISTIA.

WATERLILY. Common name for many aquatic plants, especially those in the genus NYMPHAEA. Royal or Victoria waterlily is *Victoria amazonica*; see VICTORIA. The Waterlily Famiy is NYMPHAEACEAE.

WATERMELON. A tropical African, trailing annual vine, *Citrullus latanus* or *C. vulgaris*, belonging to the Cucurbitaceae (Cucumber Family) and cultivated for its large, globular to cylindrical, mottled or striped, green fruits, which are a sweet, refreshing midsummer delicacy.

C. latanus var. *citroides* (citron or preserving melon) produces small, white, hard-fleshed fruits that are used only for preserving. Candied citron, however, is the peel of the fruit from a tree, *Citrus medica*. The Chinese-watermelon (also sometimes called preserving melon) is another cucurbitous plant, *Benincasa hispida*.

Watermelon vines are tender to frost, so seed must not be sown in the open or plants transplanted until the weather has settled. They grow best in full sun and do well in any good garden soil well supplied with humus, and moisture during hot weather. Though they are faster growing than muskmelons, they require longer to mature. Hence, where seasons are short, only early varieties should be grown. Start in hotbeds, coldframes, or greenhouses a month before it is safe to set them outdoors.

Small-growing kinds can be planted 8 ft. apart; larger kinds need 12–20 ft. To avoid weed trouble, it is advisable to prepare the soil in early spring and either keep it cultivated or grow early-maturing vegetable crops in it until melon-planting time. For culture, see MELON.

ANTHRACNOSE is one of the most troublesome watermelon diseases. Stem-end rot and blossom-end rot are common, and ground rot is destructive in the South. The chief control measure for any of these rots is destruction of infected fruit. Watermelon is affected by the same insects as cucumber, and the melon aphid is more serious on watermelon than on cucumber or muskmelon. See also CUCURBITA.

Watermelons are best if left on the vines until really ripe, when the underside becomes hard and yellow, and the tendril nearest the fruit becomes black and shrivels. Also, a ripe melon gives a characteristic dull, thudding sound when tapped with the finger.

WATER-SHIELD. Common name for *Brasenia schreberi*, an aquatic herb with small, purple flowers (see BRASENIA); and for CABOMBA, a genus of aquatic plants with round, floating leaves.

WATER-SOLDIER. Common name for *Stratiotes aloides*, a flowering aquatic plant that sinks in cold conditions; see STRATIOTES.

WATER SPROUT. A succulent shoot or branch produced in a single season from the base, or along the trunk or main limb, of an established tree. It is a natural sequence of severe pruning or other disturbance of the tree's natural equilibrium. Since water sprouts are soft and weak and ordinarily develop where branches are not needed or wanted, they should be cut off close to the trunk as soon as noticed. This does not, of course, apply to the annual growth made by willows and cut back annually for the production of withes or pussy willow sprays.

WATERWEED. A common name for ELODEA, a genus of aquatic herbs with whitish flowers.

WATSONIA (waht SOH nee ah). A genus of sturdy, summer-blooming bulbs from South Africa, belonging to the Iridaceae (Iris Family), and sometimes known as bugle-lilies. They differ from GLADIOLUS only in small botanical characteristics. From 1–6 ft. tall, they have long, sword-shaped leaves and bear scarlet, rose, or white flowers in racemes. Strong plants often branch into several stalks. Most species are hardy to Zone 7. In early May, plant the bulbs 3–6 in. deep with a little sand under each, in an open, sunny border. The soil should be enriched the year before planting with stable manure; do not use fresh manure where it will touch the corms. Bonemeal is an excellent fertilizer for them. Lift the bulbs before freezing weather, remove the tops, and store in a cool, dry, frostproof place. Watsonias bloom from July to September and are a popular source of summer bloom in California gardens. They can also be grown under glass, and since the blooms continue to open after the spike has been cut, they make excellent cut flowers. They can be propagated by seed or the offsets of the corms.

PRINCIPAL SPECIES

W. beatricis has stems 3–4 ft. and basal leaves 3–30 in. long. It has conspicuously pink-tipped bracts and apricot-red flowers. One of its merits is that many blossoms are open at one time.

W. galpinii has 2½-ft. stems with orange-red flowers.

W. marginata has rose-pink, fragrant flowers blooming in early summer.

W. wordsworthiana has 5-ft. stems with purplish lilac flowers up to 1½ in. long.

WAX EMULSIONS. A number of wax preparations that mix readily with water have been devised to spray on woody plants in order to reduce injury caused by drying or freezing foliage during severe weather or during transplanting. Evergreens especially benefit from this treatment. Some rose growers dip all the above-ground parts of a plant in wax while it is still warm; this is thought to keep the plant in better condition over winter while in storage.

WAX GOURD. One of the common names for *Benincasa hispida*, an annual, pumpkinlike vine bearing fruit that is primarily used preserved in cakes and confections.

WAX PLANT. Common name for *Hoya carnosa*, a climbing greenhouse shrub from Asia; see HOYA.

WAYFARING TREE. Common name for *Viburnum lantana*, a European shrub, and *V. alnifolium*, native to North America, both having wrinkled leaves and clusters of white flowers followed by dark berries; see VIBURNUM.

WEATHER. In outdoor gardening, thought must be continually given to changing weather. Moderate heat and sunshine interspersed with frequent rains make the most favorable conditions for plant growth; when other conditions exist, the garden suffers. Intense heat brings need for shade for certain plants; drought calls for sprinkling, and cold, for protection. CLIMATE might be described as the result or composite of accumulated weather conditions.

Weather means sunshine, heat, drought, clouds, fog, rain, WIND, lightning, hail, FROST, snow, sleet, with an occasional flood, tornado, or blizzard. Work in the garden must be planned to suit the weather conditions: planting when rain is expected and weeding when the sun is shining. Sowing of tender annuals must be delayed until danger of frost is past. For these and a hundred such reasons, an understanding of weather is important to gardening.

In all of the United States except the Pacific slope, there is an almost uninterrupted movement of weather conditions from southwest to northeast; thus, storms move at the rate of about 600 miles a day, faster in winter, slower in summer. Storms, which are circular depressions in the atmosphere, may be small or a thousand miles in diameter. They follow one another irregularly, often changing their courses toward the south or north but almost always shifting rapidly eastward. The wind blows from all directions toward these storm centers with a counterclockwise, whirling motion (clockwise in the Southern Hemisphere). Thus, in the United States, as a storm approaches from the west, the wind blows from the southeast or south. If the center passes to the north of the observer, the wind veers to the west and then to the north. If the storm passes to the south, the wind shifts east then north. In the exact center of a storm (and often for some distance around it) there is no wind. The storm area usually brings rain, always clouds, and often higher temperatures. When it has passed, the sky clears, and the air turns colder, unless following storms interfere. The storm center is shown by comparing air pressure (barometer readings) at different points.

The national weather bureau charts weather conditions, showing regions of high and low pressure, storm areas, temperatures, wind directions, and precipitation conditions. The maps based on these reports are given in newspaper and television weather forecasts. These forecasts are not always correct, because sudden and unexpected storm movements often occur; new storms develop, or old ones lose their force.

WEBWORM. A general name for various widely distributed caterpillars that work under the protection of silken webs. The garden webworm, *Achyra antalis*, is a special pest of clover, alfalfa, and some other crops. The parsnip webworm binds together the flower heads of parsnip, celery, and many weeds. Sod webworms are particularly injurious to lawns and corn.

The fall webworm, *Hyphantria cunea*, feeds on many kinds of trees. The presence of this caterpillar is indicated by loosely woven, dirty white webs enclosing the ends of branches but not filling crotches as do the tougher, usually larger (spring) nests of the tent caterpillar, with which they are sometimes confused. The worms are pale yellow, black spotted, and very hairy. They feed on the leaves within the webs, excreting quantities of unsightly black pellets. They attack over 100 North American species of fruit, shade, and woodland trees (but not evergreens).

The winter is passed as a pupa inside a silken cocoon under trash on the ground or under the bark of trees. The nearly snow white moths emerge at intervals during the spring and lay their eggs on the leaves in masses covered with white hairs. The caterpillars feed for a month or six weeks in midsummer, then pupate and produce a second generation in early fall. Control by pruning off and burning all the webs or by treating with *Bacillus thuringiensis* (Bt, commonly available as Biotrol, Dipel, or Thuricide), applied early in the spring. Kerosene sprays have been successful in many cases. Most biological pesticides work best on the larval stage of an insect. Insecticidal soaps, made from naturally occurring fatty acids, can be applied. Always follow directions on the label. See also INSECT CONTROL; CATERPILLAR.

WEDELIA (wed EEL ee ah) **trilobata.** A perennial, evergreen ground cover, native to Florida. It bears an almost year-round show of 1-in., yellow-orange flowers reminiscent of marigolds or zinnias. Hardy only in Zones 10–11 and killed by frost, it recovers quickly. Plants are easily propagated, since they send down roots wherever they touch soil.

WEEDS. Weeding means the removal of undesired plants growing in competition with desired ones. The term "weed" is a relative one, however, because many plants may be useful, beautiful, or interesting where they are wanted, but pernicious elsewhere. White clover, for instance, is a useful and often highly desirable plant in a lawn but is a pest in the strawberry bed.

WEED DISADVANTAGES

Weeds can result in direct loss to the crop grower in a number of ways. They compete with plants growing in the same area for nutrients and moisture and thus reduce the yields of the crop. They provide hosts for diseases that attack related crop plants and offer shelter and food for insects that multiply and attack the desired plants. They increase the amount of labor necessary to bring cultivated crops from planting to harvest. When allowed to grow uncontrolled, they injure the appearance and value of the property and the community. Some weeds put inhibitory chemicals into the air and soil that slow the growth of nearby plants.

WEED ADVANTAGES

Weeds can be vital and beneficial parts of a garden environment in conjunction with all the other resources of nature. Whenever we strive for absolutes like "weed-free," we set ourselves up for frustration and unending work. Gardens can be designed to minimize weeds by increasing plant density, using mulching, catch-cropping, and other strategies. If the garden is properly managed, weeds can provide food and/or shelter for beneficial insects that will control garden pests. Weeds can even attract beneficial insects, providing them with pollen and nectar before and after cultivated plants bloom. Some weeds provide food, herbs, interest, and local flavor to a garden. They can also occupy and cover ground that, if allowed to remain bare, might be eroded by rain or melting snow or lose much soluble plant food by seepage. When plowed or dug under, they and their vegetable matter add to the soil and increase its humus content. Weeds can serve as a volunteer winter COVER CROP in orchards, berry patches, and vineyards. In this capacity, however, weeds are less desirable than a sown cover crop because, if allowed to become established, they may become serious pests.

KINDS OF WEEDS

From the standpoint of their duration, weeds are of three classes. The first class consists of the annuals, which, like goosefoot and purslane, complete their life cycles in one year. In this class belong the "winter annuals," such as shepherd's-purse and chickweed, which start to grow in the autumn but complete their life cycle during the following spring when they bear seed and die. From winter annuals it is an almost imperceptible step to the second class, biennials. These are slow-growing plants such as burdock and wild carrot, which produce only vegetative parts (roots and rosettes of leaves) during one season and bear seed the following year. The third class comprises perennials, plants like Canada-thistle and milkweed, which normally produce seed every year except the first and whose underground parts live for years.

WEED CONTROL

Since annual and biennial plants propagate themselves only by seeds, they can be controlled, first, by preventing their going to seed; second, by cultivating to prevent their getting established; and third, by removing plants that have started growing. Perennials can be similarly controlled while young, but if they are allowed to gain a root hold, they must be fought by destruction of the underground root parts; by chemical treatment; by exposing them to the action of the sun, air, or frost; by choking them out with a smother crop; or by starving them by preventing the development of their green parts by which their food is manufactured.

When weeds are allowed to approach maturity, seed production can be prevented by cutting the tops close to the ground. However, they are much easier to control during the sprouting or young seedling stage, when a slight disturbance of the soil surface is enough to expose their tender rootlets to the sun and air where they will quickly shrivel and die. Herein lies the chief advantage of the steel garden rake, the rake attachments of the wheelhoe, and of other "weeders," implements that penetrate the ground for only a couple of inches.

Mulches can be used to suppress weed growth while preserving or improving the quality of the soil. They generally require little maintenance and improve the growth of desired plants. On large areas, biological controls can economically be used to keep weeds in check.

For removing weeds close to desired plants, hand weeders are essential. There are many styles, some suggesting the bent fingers of an open hand, others like

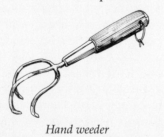

Hand weeder

hooks or claws, still others like knives bent in various forms. All are good for their respective purposes.

HERBICIDES

Most over-the-counter herbicides claim to be biodegradable when used correctly. Some are more like hormones than poisons. However, even with the safest of the weed killers, there is the possibility of a toxic reaction from skin exposure or inhalation. Use all lawn chemicals wisely, consulting your local extension service for information on the newest and safest products. Always follow the directions on the label.

Pre-emergent Herbicides. These are spread on the lawn before certain weeds sprout, creating a film on the soil. They kill grassy annual weeds as they germinate.

Post-emergent Herbicides. These are applied directly to weeds that are already up and growing. These are mostly used to control specific broad-leaved weeds and are "systemic," that is, they are absorbed into the system of the plant. Some post-emergents are "contact herbicides," which kill only the tops of plants and are not effective on thick-rooted weeds like dandelions.

Non-selective Herbicides. These tend to kill any plants, including lawn grass, to which they are applied. There are new, natural, non-selective herbicides on the market made up of fatty acids that are biodegradable and non-toxic to people and pets.

WEEPING TREES. A term for all kinds of trees, large and small, that have pendulous, downward-sweeping branches. It includes two distinct forms, one natural, the other artificially developed. The natural form is exemplified by the weeping willow, weeping beech, and camperdown elm. The artificially produced weeping trees are seen in the weeping mulberry and the many varieties of flowering crab and almond, which have always been favorite subjects for this sort of use. These are made by grafting naturally drooping or prostrate-growing varieties or forms upon straight, woody trunks of an upright form of the same species.

WEEVIL. These pests are related to snout beetles and curculios. The bean weevil (*Acanthoscelides obtectus*), pea weevil (*Sitona pisorum*), and cowpea weevil attack seeds of those plants both in the field and in storage. They are small, shorter than ½ in., dark, and flecked. Their habit is to make small, round holes in the seeds, which are entered by the larvae and consumed from within. The females lay up to 85 or 100 eggs on the seeds or the container, and a new generation is produced in three weeks. In the field, females lay eggs in cracks on the pods. Where conditions are

Bean weevil

favorable, breeding can continue all year. Fumigation of stored seeds with ethylene dichloride or a simple heating have been methods of control. The strawberry root weevil, *Brachyrhinus ovatus*, is also a particular pest.

The boll weevil, *Anthonomus grandis*, which arrived in the United States from Mexico, has had an enormous effect on agriculture in the South. Though in Mexico it fed on various wild plants, in the South its primary host has been cotton, where both adults and larvae consume the flower buds as well as the developed fruit, the bolls. It may also infest okra and hollyhocks. The adult is grayish or yellowish brown with a snout about a third the length of its ¼-in. body. The larvae are fat, wrinkled, legless grubs found only in the buds or bolls.

The adult overwinters in all kinds of places—the bark of trees, gin litter, seed houses, underground, and even in Spanish moss—but average survival is very low. In the spring, first the weevils attack the tender terminal parts of the young cotton plants, then they puncture and feed on the buds to get at the highly nutritious pollen sacs. Eggs are laid in each, one to a bud. The injured buds then drop to the ground or hang withered on the plant. Each female lays about 100 eggs. She can live 50 days, though a few do survive in diapause condition over the winter. Direct application of PYRETHRUM might be effec-

tive, but farmers should consult their local extension service for advice about control.

See also INSECT CONTROL.

WEIGELA (wī GEE lah). A genus of deciduous shrubs belonging to the Caprifoliaceae (Honeysuckle Family) and native to Asia. They spread with more or less pendulous branches, and the clusters of bell-shaped flowers are very showy in spring and early summer. A number of free-flowering and colorful hybrids produced by crossing the different species are now the most popular kinds in gardens.

They thrive in any good garden soil that does not get too dry. While generally considered hardy, most kinds are likely to be killed back somewhat in severe winters unless protected. To keep them healthy, thin out old and straggly wood after flowering. Propagation is by greenwood and hardwood cuttings. Most species are hardy in Zones 5–8.

W. florida, the best-known species, grows to 6 ft. or more and has showy flowers of rose-pink. Var. *venusta*, from Korea, is the hardiest and earliest to bloom. It has smaller leaves and a profusion of dark, rose-purple flowers on arching branches. There are many cultivars with varying form and flowers in shades of white, pink, and red. Hardy to Zone 4.

W. praecox is not unlike *W. florida*, but the flowers are not quite as handsome, though they open earlier. Cultivars flower in shades of white, red, pink, and yellow.

WELSH ONION. Common name for *Allium fistulosum*, also known as Japanese bunching onion, native to Siberia. It has tightly bunched, long white scallions, or hollow leaves, that grow to 12 in. and have a flavor similar to chives but somewhat stronger. The flowers are yellowish white and are borne in umbels. This hardy perennial is evergreen in all but the most severe winters, withstanding temperatures below 0°F. There are varieties suited to climates with hot summers and others good for climates with severe winters. Some seed distributors also list perennial or biennial kinds of Japanese bunching onion. When ordering seed, be careful to state which variety you want.

Soil prepared as for other types of onions—dug and enriched in autumn, then tilled and firmed in early spring—is suitable, though it need not be quite so rich. For winter greens, plants should be in a sheltered, well-drained, sunny spot. Give them some shade where summer temperatures are high. They need little care beyond routine weed control and watering.

Propagation. Seed can be planted in spring or late summer, with germination taking about two weeks. Three- or four-year-old plants can be divided in spring or early summer. The tenderest spring greens and scallions come from summer-sown seed. Mature plants should stand 10 in. apart. Small clumps can be grown in containers. The seedlings can be transplanted at any size; trim their roots to ½ in. long, and cut their tops back.

Harvesting. The green leaves can be cut from early spring to early winter in most climates. Clumps of scallions can be dug during any season when the ground is not frozen too hard. The green leaves dry well, and the scallions can be frozen; however, unless the winter is particularly severe, it is hardly worth the trouble.

WHEELBARROW. A cartlike vehicle for carrying plants, soil, or equipment around the garden. A shallow, boxlike or bowl-like receptacle of wood, plastic, or metal is supported in front by a wheel (sometimes two wheels) and in the rear by a pair of legs or braces. It is pushed or pulled by one person who stands between two shafts at the rear end and carries them at arm's length. Inexpensive wheelbarrows have a solid rubber tire, while better ones feature a pneumatic tire that makes it push more easily, run more smoothly, and do less damage to lawns and other surfaces.

WHISPERING-BELLS. Common name for *Emmenanthe penduliflora*, a dwarf California annual herb with drooping racemes of yellow flowers; see EMMENANTHE.

WHITE CABBAGE BUTTERFLY. This pest, *Pieris rapae*, was introduced from Europe in 1860 and has spread all over the United States, flying even in winter on the Gulf Coast. The butterfly lays her greenish, cylindrical eggs on both sides of the leaves in three to six generations each year. Voracious green caterpillars emerge in about a week, especially bothersome on cabbage (green more than red) and broccoli, but also seen on brussels sprouts, cauliflower, and kale.

The best control is *Bacillus thuringiensis* (Bt, commonly available as Biotrol, Dipel, or Thuricide), but dustings with pyrethrum and rotenone are also used. Use rotenone only after dusk when bees and other pollinators will not be affected. It is easy to crush the eggs to stop development, if you can find them. See INSECT CONTROL.

WHITEFLY. Unless controlled, this tiny member of the Aleyrodidae (*Trialeurodes vaporariorum*) can be a very annoying pest that wilts plants by sucking sap from the undersides of leaves. Commonly known as greenhouse whiteflies, the insects gather in great number on each leaf, usually in greenhouses but also outdoors. If disturbed, they fly up in a fluttering swarm, though they usually pass unnoticed otherwise. They stay on leaves and lay eggs on tiny stalks in circles, which cause them to be called "scales." These hatch into "crawlers," nymphs that suck sap, exude honeydew, and attract sooty mold. After the first stage of

adult whitefly

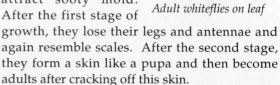

Adult whiteflies on leaf

growth, they lose their legs and antennae and again resemble scales. After the second stage, they form a skin like a pupa and then become adults after cracking off this skin.

They can infest many plants in the greenhouse; and in the garden they particularly attack cucumbers, tomatoes, lettuce, geraniums, ageratums, and members of the Solanaceae (Nightshade Family). When attacked, the plants wilt from loss of sap.

Pyrethrum sprays and insecticidal soap are effective controls. The best biological control is *Encarsia formosa*, one of the tiny parasitic wasps, which will lay her eggs in the developing nymphs. Order early and release two or three times at three-week intervals when the temperature is about 75°F. Sometimes ryania, another botanical, has been used successfully.

See also INSECT CONTROL.

WHITE GRUB. A name for the larvae of the JUNE BEETLE, *Phyllophaga* spp.; see GRUBS.

WHITE PINE BLISTER RUST. The blister rust of white pine, originally introduced from Europe, is now firmly established in North America. All pines having their needles in clusters of five are susceptible. The rust fungus (*Cronartium ribicola* on pines) destroys the bark, girdling twigs and branches. Young trees are killed quickly, older ones more slowly. The rust cannot spread from one pine to another but must first infect a plant of one of the alternate hosts, usually currants and gooseberries, on which the fungus is called by another name (*Cronartium ribicola*). See RUSTS.

Spores from the alternate hosts infect pine needles, whence the fungus mycelium works down into the stems. By the third year, small, brown, dead spots on the yellowed bark are filled with pycniospores. In the spring of the fourth year, the bark cracks, and conspicuous white blisters form and break, discharging the yellow aeciospores. These two stages may occur year after year on a pine until the resulting canker girdles the branch or trunk and kills all parts above. In spring, aeciospores carry the rust back to wild and cultivated currants or gooseberries and start another cycle of disease.

The only feasible control of blister rust lies in the eradication of alternate hosts within a mile of valuable pines in the case of black currants, which are especially susceptible. In some states it is illegal to grow or sell black currant bushes. Other alternate hosts should be kept at least 300 yards from valuable pine plantings.

WHITLOW-GRASS. Common name for *Draba aizoides*, a low-growing perennial useful in rock gardens; see DRABA.

WHORL. A set of three or more leaves or flowers arranged in a complete circle around the stem, such as the leaves of *Medeola virginica* (Indian cucumber root) or the flowers of *Mentha spicata* (spearmint). Compare ALTERNATE.

WIDE ROW PLANTING. A helpful technique for increasing the yield and reducing work in vegetable gardens is to sow seed thickly in a wider row. While the densely planted crop may produce smaller plants, it does give a greater number of plants and thus a larger harvest can be taken from the same space. Vegetables such as lettuce, peas, or beans growing closely together also serve as their own mulch, holding moisture, shading out weeds, and maintaining a steady ground temperature, which encourages a longer spring season for crops that go to seed in hot weather. Other benefits of wide row planting include a savings in time required for weeding and harvesting, easier harvest because plants are close together, and even better-quality produce resulting from more constant growing conditions.

The steps in wide row planting are simple. Start with the standard procedure for preparing any garden soil. Next, mark rows a few feet wide with stakes and string. Rake the area until it is level and smooth; see (A) on next page. Do not make any indentations or furrows. Broadcast seed over the raked area as evenly as possible, sowing a little more thickly than you would in a single row (B). Seeds can be firmed into the soil with the back of a hoe or rake (C). You can even walk on larger seeds to push them into the soil. Cover the seed to the proper depth by raking dirt over them from outside the row (D). Smooth with the back of a garden rake. When the plants are about an inch tall, use a garden rake to thin them. Large-seeded plants should not need thinning.

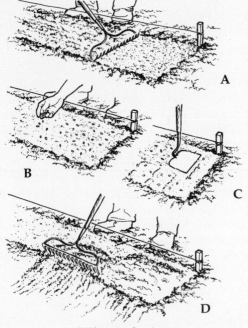

Wide row planting

Of course, not all vegetables should be planted in wide rows. Most warm-season crops, such as corn, tomatoes, eggplant, and peppers, grow quite large and need plenty of sun and heat; these should be allowed plenty of space. However, there is a long list of crops that do well, including many common vegetables and herbs. Among the best choices for this method are beans, beets, cabbage, carrots, chives, dill, garlic, lettuce, mint, onions, parsley, peas, radishes, savory, spinach, turnips, and many others.

WIGANDIA (wi GAN dee ah). A genus of coarse, perennial, Central and South American shrubby plants or herbs, with large, bristly leaves and bell-shaped, blue or violet flowers in one-sided spikes. The hairs on some species may be extremely irritating, which is the basis for the common name "nettlebush." Hardy only in Zones 10–11, they make poor greenhouse plants but are used for bedding plants in subtropical cli-

mates. They are propagated by root cuttings taken in the spring or by seed sown under glass.

W. caracasana, a woody shrub to 10 ft. or more, has toothed, wrinkled leaves 18 by 10 in. and violet, bell-shaped flowers with a white tube. Its var. *macrophylla* is the form usually grown. Other forms sometimes listed separately are probably only varieties of this species.

W. urens grows to 12 ft. and has 1-ft. leaves and violet flowers.

WILDFLOWERS. Any flowering plant that grows without human assistance can be rightfully called a wildflower; however, the distinction should be made between truly indigenous wildflowers and plants that have been imported from other regions by accident or as ornamentals escaped from cultivation.

Some native wildflowers have been grown as garden plants for centuries; many plants that are commonly thought to be domesticated horticultural species, such as annual phlox, cosmos, Virginia bluebells, spiderwort, and California poppy, are actually wildflowers. Some North American wildflowers, such as gayfeather, false dragonhead, and goat's-beard were sent back to Europe by the early settlers and explorers for use as popular garden plants.

Wildflowers are grown for the appreciation of their natural, unaffected beauty and the unstudied look they lend to the landscape. Wildflowers provide a unique opportunity to observe the characteristics of native plants, become familiar with their life cycles, and thereby learn more about the natural environment. An interest in wildflowers may foster an appreciation for the role played by indigenous flora as part of local or national heritage and encourage the protection, preservation, and restoration of native plants.

Wildflowers can be used for many ornamental or accent purposes, and many also make excellent cut flowers. Often wildflowers may be suited to problem areas, such as hot, dry locations or swampy areas. A wildflower garden can be designed to meet a variety of special purposes, including butterfly or hummingbird feeding areas, perfume or fragrance gardens, edible plants, ground covers and hedges, rock gardens, natural selections for specific regions, and container planting.

CULTURE

Native plants are well adapted to the local conditions of their natural habitats. By looking to see what flourishes locally in the wild, gardeners will be able to create a natural-looking garden without a great deal of work or discouragement. Although it is possible to replicate the environment that wild plants like, it is easier and generally more successful to choose plants that are suited to existing conditions.

Plants such as blue flag, cardinal flower, turtlehead, and meadow-beauty thrive in wet soil, while desert-marigold and certain verbenas are ideally suited to parched, sun-baked locations. In any case, cultivation of wildflowers is most successful when you match a species' optimal requirements with naturally occurring conditions in the garden.

Light. While some species are successfully grown only in a rather restricted range of light conditions, others can be cultivated in sunny or shady locations. White baneberry and shinleaf are adapted to deep shade. Purple heliotrope and lance-leaved coreopsis require full sunlight. Bunchberry prefers partial shade but can be grown in full sun, although the plants will be smaller. Spring-flowering wildflowers of deciduous forests, such as spring-beauty, trout lily, and Dutchman's-breeches require full springtime sunlight in order to flower but prefer dense shade thereafter as they go dormant until the following spring.

Perennial wildflowers usually have northern or southern limits that are determined by winter temperatures. Blue-dicks and Our-Lord's-candle are restricted to year-round gardens in warm climates. Wood-betony and pasqueflower can survive even arctic winters. Plants that have evolved in colder zones, such as wild leek and spring-beauty, require winter chilling to continue their life cycles. Plants such as yellow clintonia and bunchberry cannot tolerate hot summer temperatures.

Soil. Wildflowers have diverse soil preferences as well. Some species do well where nutrient levels are high and there is an abundance of

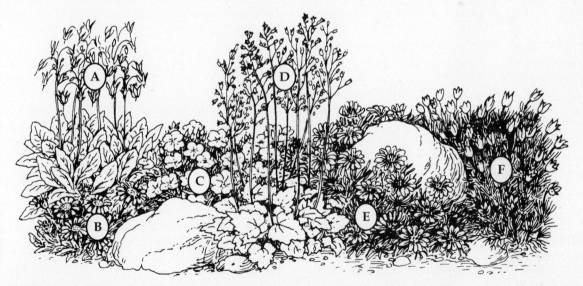

Wildflower Garden: (A) *Dodecatheon meadia* (eastern shooting-star), (B) *Hymenoxis grandiflora* (old-man-of-the-mountain), (C) *Oenothera missouriensis* (Missouri evening-primrose), (D) *Heuchera sanguinea* (coral-bells), (E) *Lewisia rediviva* (bitterroot), (F) *Anemone patens* (pasqueflower)

humus in the soil. Others thrive where there is little organic matter and soil fertility is low. Some species are relatively insensitive to soil acidity, while others grow only in a narrow pH range. In general, soils should be prepared to a depth of several feet; amendments, such as organic matter, should be thoroughly worked into the soil. Sandy soils are best for plants grown in drier conditions. Peat or clay soils are better for plants that prefer plenty of soil moisture.

Care. Once established in a suitable environment, wildflowers require very little maintenance. Damage by pests is practically negligible because of the presence of natural predators that effectively check their numbers. Most wildflowers are pollinated by insects, so the use of insecticides should be avoided. SLUGS seem to relish the taste of certain wildflowers but are easily controlled. Weeding should be done by hand, since many wildflowers are damaged by herbicides.

Propagation. Digging wildflowers from their natural environment, except perhaps where they are imminently threatened by development, is unethical and frequently illegal; see NATIVE PLANTS. Even plants that are not considered to be rare or endangered may become scarce at the edges of their range and should not be removed from the wild. The best way to obtain wildflowers for the garden is to purchase seeds, plants, or planting stock from reputable suppliers who sell nursery-propagated material.

For faster results, live perennial plants can be used. They should be planted when dormant. Although it takes longer to establish in the garden, wildflower seed is available all year, and is less fragile and less expensive than live plants. If seed is collected from the wild, take only a small proportion of the total seed crop only from areas where the plants are abundant. Seed is also available from mail-order suppliers. Although some suppliers carefully formulate seed mixtures that represent native wildflowers of specific regions or habitats, these are more frequently formulated for broad geographic regions and may contain non-native species that are poorly adapted to some areas.

Once a wildflower garden is well established, the plants can be propagated by seed, division of rootstocks, or stem cuttings. To produce the largest numbers of wildflowers, seed should be collected from mature fruits and planted immediately, or in some cases following an after-ripening or some special treatment, such as soaking, chilling, scratching the seed coat, subjecting them to light or darkness, or some combination of these. Perennials can be propagated quickly by the division of their rootstocks, best done when the plant is dormant, usually in the spring or fall. Certain perennials, such as scarlet sage, spiderwort, and some of the penstemons, can be propagated by stem cuttings taken from vigorously growing shoots without flower buds.

More information can be obtained from botanical gardens, arboretums, nature centers, garden centers, native plant societies, horticultural societies, as well as local, state, and national parks and forest services. Many of these organizations conduct field trips, workshops, symposia, and conservation projects and publish a number of magazines, newsletters, and books.

WILD-RICE. The most common name for *Zizania aquatica*, a handsome wetland grass; see ZIZANIA.

WILLOW. Common name for SALIX, a genus of soft-wooded trees and shrubs noted for their graceful foliage and catkins. The name is also applied to other members of the Salicaceae (Willow Family), and a few unrelated plants. Desert-flowering-willow is *Chilopsis linearis*; see CHILOPSIS. Primrose-willow is *Jussiaea*. Water-willow is *Decodon verticillatus*, a species of loosestrife; see DECODON. Willow oak is *Quercus phellos*; see QUERCUS. Willow pittosporum is *Pittosporum phyllyraeoides*; see PITTOSPORUM.

WILTING. The drooping of a plant, caused chiefly by the collapse of cells, may be due to a lack of water but is in many cases a typical disease symptom; see DISEASE. Bacteria may cause wilting by clogging the water-conducting system, and fungi may secrete toxic substances into the plant vessels. Wilting is one of the first symptoms in many root and crown diseases. See also CROWN ROT; SCLEROTINA ROT; FUSARIUM; VERTICILLIUM WILT.

WIND. Changes in WEATHER depend partly on wind, which is therefore useful. Some trees such as pine and juniper require wind to keep them healthy. It helps or stimulates the flow of sap, may rid them of certain insect pests and fungal diseases, helps distribute their pollen and seeds, and tends to prevent or ward off FROST.

Some plants, especially broad-leaved evergreens, will not grow in exposed, windy places. The majority of all plants do better if protected from the strong winds, which may injure through their force, their cold in winter, and more often through their drying effect. Sometimes the contour of the ground will give some protection. Elsewhere, windbreaks should be created.

Damage by wind is of three general kinds; first, the one that makes newly planted trees, especially those such as evergreens with large tops, tilt to one side. Usually this is due to faulty planting, the soil not having been properly packed around the roots and trunks. Preventive measures in such cases are firm packing and staking; see TREE GUARD.

The second class of damage by wind is breakage of branches. Much of this can be prevented by training the trees to avoid weak crotches, especially those in which two branches of practically uniform development form a Y with the trunk. In places subject to disastrous storm winds, planting trees such as silver maple and locust, with their brittle branches, should be avoided. See also PRUNING; TRAINING PLANTS.

Third, wind can cause the tops of certain plants to dry out. Rhododendrons and other broad-leaved evergreens should be placed where little or no wind reaches them, because their tops are dried out much more rapidly in wind than in still air, a situation that is particularly harmful when the ground is frozen and their roots find it difficult to maintain a supply of moisture.

WINDBREAK. Any planting of trees or shrubs on the windward side of a garden, orchard, field, or buildings as protection from the wind. Much garden material that is not injured by extreme cold suffers greatly and may be damaged beyond repair by the buffeting and drying effect of strong winds blowing full on it in summer as well as winter. Gardens near the shore are especially subject to this sort of injury, and often the only possible way of having a garden there is to plant extensive windbreaks between it and the direction of the prevailing wind—usually coming off the water.

Where there is ample ground space, the best form of windbreak is a natural, closely set grove of trees carried far enough in both directions to stay the wind over an area considerably wider than the actual protected space. This width is needed because the protection is based on the principle of shredding up the wind force and scattering it, rather than actually stopping it. The effect of such a planting is much more natural than a series of straight rows of trees.

Evergreen trees are the preferred material for large-scale wind breaks. One large conifer placed in just the right place will afford a surprising degree of protection to a dwelling. A group of three or more, according to the situation, may shelter an area so completely that even high winds will not be felt, although the sound of wind passing through the branches may enhance the garden. In close quarters, a hedge of evergreen or dense deciduous material serves well, especially if the plants are staggered in a double row and given sufficient pruning and care to keep growth compact and thick.

See also HEDGE; PRUNING.

WINDFLOWER. Common name for ANEMONE, a large and versatile genus of perennial herbs with flowering perennial herbs.

WINDOW BOXES. Indoors or out, windows can be filled with narrow containers of plants. Outdoor boxes can be attached below the window or set on a porch railing. Indoors they can be on stands or shelves aranged by the window or set on the windowsill. In either case, special care must be taken to compensate for extremes of sun and temperature that these plants must often endure. Like any container plant, their soil and root space are limited, and they are apt to use up available moisture and nutrients, which must be replenished regularly. They should also be monitored for extreme effects of wind, heat, and cold, which all contribute to loss of moisture.

Although it may be desirable to simply set potted plants in a box, plants can be set directly in boxes as long as they have adequate drainage holes. The best ones are made of rot-resistant wood, such as redwood or cedar made of lumber at least an inch thick to insulate the potting medium and keep it cool and moist. Whether wood or metal, window boxes should measure 8 in. deep (inside measurement) and 8–12 in. wide depending on the distance between window casements. For convenience in handling, a long box can be made in short lengths placed end to end.

INDOOR BOXES

For the most part, these are handled like any other houseplant with a few additional considerations. Location in the room is important. Since flowering plants require lots of sunlight, a window on the south or southeast side of a house, especially a bay window, is best. Foliage plants, however, prefer shaded or subdued light and will do fine with north and west exposures. Supplemental lighting may be necessary; see ARTIFICIAL LIGHT.

Being close to the window exposes them to extremes not encountered by other houseplants or plants set outdoors in the ground. They are more susceptible to loss of moisture, to begin with, and their growing environment is drier than most. Windowsill plants in direct sun should be carefully monitored, since temperatures may soar where there is no breeze or humidity to offset it. This can result in rapid drying of the soil and overheating tender plants. This condition may be further aggravated by being too close to the radiator; even artifical room lighting may generate just enough heat to dry out nearby plants. Humidity and soil moisture can be maintained in several ways. A container of water on the radiator will generate some humidity. Containers can be set in rustproof or plastic pans filled with pebbles and water to keep the plants over but not in water. Sometimes window boxes are planted exclusively with cacti and other succulent plants, which are more tolerant of dry heat.

Cold drafts and dropping nighttime temperatures can be just as deadly as dry heat. Especially in winter, the window should be well secured against draft by caulking or weatherstripping. Plants can be protected from dropping temperatures by moving them away from the window in the evening. This may not be practical for large numbers of plants or those in awkward containers; these can be protected by placing a barrier between the plants and the window: close draperies; cover the plants with newspaper or light fabric; or attach sheets of plastic, cloth, or newspaper to the window frame.

OUTDOOR BOXES

Because of the relatively shallow soil and the increased exposure to cold, plants in outdoor containers are likely to freeze; so it is rarely advisable to grow perennials in window boxes, except in warm regions. They can, however, be planted with annuals for summer effects, and winter effects can be secured with various dwarf evergreens. Such subjects should have good, compact rootballs. They should be planted carefully, usually closer than regular plantings to enhance their effect, and allowed to become established before the boxes are placed in exposed locations. Thereafter, they should receive regular watering, feeding, and care.

WINEBERRY. Common name for *Rubus phoenicolasius*, an ornamental bramble with stems covered with reddish glandular hairs. It bears small, red, edible fruit and is hardy to Zone 6. See RUBUS; for cultivation, see BLACKBERRY.

New-Zealand-wineberry is a common name for *Aristotelia racemosa*, an evergreen shrub of the Southern Hemisphere; see ARISTOTELIA.

WINE PALM. Common name for *Caryota urens*, a graceful tree yielding a sap called toddy or palm wine; see CARYOTA. Chilean wine palm is *Jubaea chilensis*, a tropical tree with plumlike fruits sometimes used in candy; see JUBAEA.

WINGNUT. Common name for PTEROCARYA, a genus of trees of the Juglandaceae (Walnut Family), sometimes grown for ornament.

WINTER. In winter, plants become more susceptible to injury by various elements and need appropriate protection. FROST affects large and small plants from early autumn through spring, causing injuries from foliage damage to uprooting or HEAVING. Snow may weight down and break branches of trees or shrubs. Many trees, both deciduous and evergreen, missing the shade of summer foliage, become more prone to sun scald. Animals, especially rabbits and MICE, cause damage when seeking alternatives to summer food sources.

WINTER STORAGE

When tender, semihardy or even hardy plants that have been growing in the open during summer need a resting period between autumn and spring, or are to be used as stock plants to yield cuttings, they are often stored in "pits" or coldframes until late winter or early spring, when they are taken into the greenhouse. Of the two carrying-over storage places, the pit is better because, as it goes deeper into the ground, the temperature is more easily kept uniform, just above the freezing point. In severe weather, adequate protection in a frame can be assured by covering the sash with mats and shutters to check the radiation of heat and prevent the entrance of cold.

WINTER INJURY

This is damage done by low temperatures occurring after the end of the growing season or before growth starts in the spring, as distinguished from FROST injury. Symptoms of winter injury vary from immediate death of the plant to such localized injury as twig blight, dieback, root killing, bud injury, frost cracks, cankers, winter sun scald, crown or collar rot, and internal necrosis or black heart. It is not only the degree of cold, but also the time in the period of dormancy that influences the amount of injury. Severe weather in early winter causes more injury because plant tissues have not yet become hardened. Also, sudden cold following moderate weather that starts tissues into activity is likely to cause heavy freezing. The presence or absence of a snow cover at the time of freezing also influences the amount of injury. Winter drying of evergreens is caused by the rapid loss of water from the leaves at a time when the water in the soil is frozen and cannot be taken up by the plant roots. See DISEASE.

WINTERBERRY. Common name for various species of ILEX, the genus commonly known as holly.

WINTER CREEPER. Common name for *Euonymus radicans*, a slow-growing vine, good for covering walls.

WINTERGREEN. Common name for *Gaultheria procumbens*, a creeping shrub with edible leaves and berries; see GAULTHERIA. Spotted-wintergreen is CHIMAPHILA, a genus of woodland herbs with pink or white flowers and toothed, leathery leaves. Species of PYROLA are sometimes called wintergreen but are more commonly known as shinleaf.

WIREWORM. These larvae of the click beetle (Elateridae) are familiar to most gardeners as slender, smooth, usually dark brown and hardshelled, but sometimes soft and yellow creatures varying from ½–1½ in. in length. Distributed throughout North America, they attack most

Wireworm

crops belonging to the Poaceae (Grass Family) as well as many other plants, such as corn, clover, beans, potatoes, and turnips, feeding on the roots and tubers. Infested plants have a sickly, stunted appearance and sometimes wilt and die; if pulled up, they reveal little or no root system.

The life cycle covers from two to six years, so control is difficult. It is this pest that makes it inadvisable to plant a garden the first year after plowing up a field or grassland. One effective control is the predatory nematode. Clover as a cover crop and for green manure is also recommended. The worms can be caught in a buried piece of potato or carrot on a string, which is pulled up daily to collect and destroy the pests. In large fields, long crop rotations are advisable. Later summer or fall plowing helps by killing the pupae and also adult beetles before they emerge from the soil. Wireworms are more numerous where the drainage is poor, so drying and aerating plots to be converted also helps to decrease their numbers. Several plowings the fall before planting will also help.

In small gardens or flower beds, the worms can be destroyed by disinfecting the soil. In the vegetable garden, rows of corn planted here and there will often attract the worms and keep them away from other crops. See INSECT CONTROL.

WISTERIA (wis TEER ee ah). A genus of deciduous, twining vines, native to North America and Asia, belonging to the Fabaceae (Bean Family). They rank among the best of the ornamental vines for temperate regions and often attain a large size and old age. While they will grow in almost any soil, they thrive best in a deep, rich loam that does not get too dry. On a wall or building it is best to pay some attention to training the growth. Since their roots are long but not fibrous, the plants are best transplanted when small or from containers.

Wisterias often disappointingly do not flower for many years. Restriction of the root run and shortening back the long shoots in midsummer may aid in the formation of flower buds. The application of superphosphate may also induce blooming. Too much shade can be a problem, and it appears that young plants must reach a certain maturity before beginning to flower, usually about six years after planting. The spring crop of flowers is borne on spurs, and in severe climates the buds are often winter-killed. A small crop of flowers is often produced in late summer on young growth of the current season.

Propagation can be done by seed but is better by cuttings, layers, and grafts. Wisterias are tough vines, mostly hardy in Zones 5–9.

PRINCIPAL SPECIES

W. floribunda (Japanese wisteria) is hardier than the Chinese species. It has thirteen to nineteen leaflets and smaller, more fragrant, violet-blue flowers. Of the several cultivars available, 'Macrobotrys' often bears racemes 3 ft. long, and in Japan, clusters 5 ft. long have been grown. 'Alba' has white flowers, and those of 'Rosea' are pinkish purple.

W. sinensis (Chinese wisteria) is one of the more vigorous climbers of the Northern Hemisphere, growing to 30 ft. It has seven to thirteen leaflets and showy clusters of violet-blue flowers.

W. venusta (silky wisteria), a Chinese species, is one of the hardiest and grows to 30 ft. It has three to nine velvety leaflets, white flowers in short racemes, and velvety pods.

WITCHES'-BROOM. The apt and descriptive name given to a closely grouped cluster of fine slender branches usually arranged more or less parallel to each other and originating from an enlarged axis. Witches'-brooms occur on various kinds of woody plants at the ends of branches and are definite disease symptoms. They may be caused by some of the leaf curl fungi, various species of rusts, and the scaly or dwarf mistletoe. Mostly they are caused by parasitic plant organisms, but the witches'-broom on any hackberry is due to a mite followed by a fungus. See DISEASE.

WITCH-HAZEL. Common name for HAMA-MELIS, a genus of hardy deciduous shrubs or small trees native to North America and Asia. The Witch-hazel Family is HAMAMELIDACEAE.

WITHE-ROD. Common name for *Viburnum cassinoides*, a deciduous shrub with white flowers followed by blue-black fruits; see VIBURNUM.

WOODBINE. Common name in England for *Lonicera periclymenum*; see LONICERA. In North America, the name is often applied to *Parthenocissus quinquefolia*; see PARTHENOCISSUS.

WOOD FERN. Common name for several species of DRYOPTERIS, including the evergreen, fragrant Goldie's, and roseate wood ferns.

WOODLAND STARS. Common name for *Lithophragma*, a genus of small perennial herbs with starry, white or pink flowers.

WOODRUFF. Common name for ASPERULA, a genus of herbaceous perennials grown in semi-shady locations in borders and rock gardens. Sweet woodruff is *Galium odoratum*; see GALIUM.

WOODSIA (WUD zee ah). A genus of small ferns that grow among rocks in temperate to cool-temperate areas of both hemispheres. Most are rare, of no garden value, and should not be collected from the wild. A few are frequently used in rock gardens, however, and easily grown from spores.

PRINCIPAL SPECIES

W. ilvensis (rusty woodsia) is a small fern that grows 3–8 in. and has pinnate-pinnatifid fronds covered on the undersides with hairs and scales that turn brown by midsummer. The stipe is also hairy. An arctic-alpine circumpolar fern found inhabiting cliffs and rocky slopes as far south as Georgia, it has little general garden interest but is among the few species used in rock gardens. It does well in a gravelly soil in any moist crevice.

W. mexicana (Mexican woodsia) is a bipinnate to bipinnate-pinnatifid fern growing 7–11 in. tall. It is frequent on rock ledges of the southwestern states and Mexico.

W. obtusa is a large species that grows to 15 in. and has pinnate-pinnatifid, lanceolate fronds. Common in all of eastern North America, it is a fine rock garden plant if given excellent drainage, moisture, and some shade.

W. oregana (Oregon woodsia) is similar to *W. obtusa* and has roughly the same distribution as *W. scopulina*.

W. scopulina (Rocky Mountain woodsia) is similar to *W. obtusa* but is most frequent in the northwestern states and in a narrow band along the United States–Canadian border.

WOODWARDIA (wood WAHR dee ah). A small genus of medium to large terrestrial ferns found in Asia, Europe, and North America. They are characterized by parallel rows of large, linear sori, suggesting the common name "chain fern." They are acid loving, chiefly found on marshy land, and rank growers, well suited for naturalizing large areas.

PRINCIPAL SPECIES

W. areolata (netted chain fern) resembles a reduced version of *Onoclea sensibilis* (sensitive fern). It is pinnate and grows 1–2 ft. tall. It is dimorphic, the pinnae of the fertile fronds being much narrower than the sterile ones and completely different from the "bead stick" of *Onoclea*. Native in eastern bogs and swamps, in the garden it needs constant and generous moisture.

W. fimbriata (giant chain fern) is a large evergreen fern that grows 3–5 ft. tall and is found in wet forests along the Pacific Coast but is not hardy in the eastern states. It is pinnate-pinnatifid, the lobes sharply pointed. It is almost identical to *W. radicans*, which is distinguished by a proliferous bud on the frond tip.

W. orientalis (Oriental chain fern) grows 4–8 ft. and appears similar to *W. radicans* but differs by having dozens of plantlets on the mature leaves. It is native to temperate eastern Asia but is not hardy in the eastern states.

W. radicans (European chain fern) is a large, luxuriant fern that grows 2–7 ft. and has a very exotic appearance. It is pinnate, with individual pinnae 10–15 in. long. There are large bulbils near the juncture of the rachis and pinnae that drop off and form new plants. It grows in acid swamps and woodland bogs in southern Europe and has escaped and naturalized in Florida.

W. virginica (Virginia chain fern) is a pinnate-pinnatifid fern 2–4 ft. tall that superficially resembles *Osmunda cinnamomea* (cinnamon fern). It is easily distinguished by its creeping habit and lack of a separate fertile frond. It inhabits acid bogs in eastern North America from Quebec to Florida.

WOOLFLOWER. A common name for *Celosia cristata*, an annual herb with many flower varieties; see CELOSIA.

WOOLLY. Bearing long, curly, and matted hairs. Compare TOMENTOSE; VILLOUS.

WORMWOOD. Common name for ARTEMISIA, a genus of aromatic herbs and shrubs.

WORSLEYA (WORS lee ah) **rayneri.** Commonly known as blue amaryllis, this summer-flowering bulb is native to South America. It has broad-bladed leaves and large, lilylike flowers shading from white to lilac or rose. The difficulty of cultivation and the high cost of sizable bulbs keeps these beautiful plants from being more generally used. They should be grown under glass until warm weather in spring and brought in again for winter storage before the first frost.

WULFENIA (wul FEE nee ah). A genus of low-growing, hardy perennial herbs belonging to the Scrophulariaceae (Figwort Family). They bear tubular, blue flowers on 2-ft. stems rising from a clump of basal leaves and are suitable for a shady corner of the rock garden or border. Thriving in rich, moist soil, they should be given excellent drainage since some species have evergreen foliage and decay easily in wet weather or in winter. Plants are hardy to Zone 5 and are propagated by division in spring or autumn and by seed. *W. carinthiaca* grows to 9 in. tall and has small, blue flowers in clustered, slender racemes.

WYETHIA (wī EE thee ah). A genus of large, western North American, herbaceous perennials in the Asteraceae (Aster Family), commonly known as mule's-ears. Large, bold leaves and 4–5 in., yellow daisies appearing in spring make them useful in sun or light shade in a wild or meadow garden. Hardy to Zone 8.

W. amplexicaulis and *W. grandis* are similar species that grow to 2 ft. and have large, glossy, oval leaves and showy, yellow flowers.

Wyethia amplexicaulis

W. helenoides and *W. mollis*, also growing to 2 ft., have soft, woolly, gray leaves and large, yellow flowers.

XANTHISMA (zan THIZ mah). A genus of annual or biennial American herbs of the Asteraceae (Aster Family), commonly known as sleeping daisy. They have narrow leaves and yellow flower heads consisting of ray flowers only and are suitable for planting in dry, open places in the wild garden. They grow readily from seed, which should be sown where the plants are to stand. *X. texana* grows to 4 ft. and has showy yellow heads about 2 in. across that consist of about 20 slender rays.

XANTHORHIZA (zan thoh RĪ zah) **simplicissima.** A stoloniferous deciduous shrub belonging to the Ranunculaceae (Buttercup Family) and commonly known as shrub yellow-root. The only member of its genus, it is native in the eastern states from New York to Florida. It bears drooping racemes of small, star-shaped, brown-purple flowers in early spring, and its sharply cut leaves turn a clear yellow in autumn. The yellow wood of the root and stems give the plant its name. Producing a profusion of suckers, it is a good subject for underplanting in the shrubbery border, or as a ground cover in damp, shady locations or even in sandy soil. It will grow from seed, but since the seedlings are delicate and hard to handle, it is easier to divide old, vigorously growing plants, the pieces soon taking hold and spreading rapidly. Hardy in Zones 4–9.

XANTHOSOMA (zan thoh SOHM ah). A genus of herbs from the tropical Americas, belonging to the Araceae (Arum Family), and commonly known as yautia, tanier, or malanga. Their large, thick leaves on stalks and flowers resemble *Calla.* In the tropics they are grown for their thick, edible, tuberlike, underground stems; in temperate climates, they are ornamental greenhouse plants.

Of the half dozen species, *X. lindenii* (also listed as *Caladium lindenii*) has bright green leaves 1 ft. long with white midribs and veins.

X. sagittifolium, which often exceeds 8 ft. in height, has green leaves 3 ft. long and almost as wide on stems equally long.

XERANTHEMUM (zee RAN them um). A genus of annual herbs belonging to the Asteraceae (Aster Family), grown mainly for their papery flowers, which can be dried and used for everlastings. They are easily grown from seed.

X. annuum (common immortelle), the principal species, grows to 3 ft. and has downy, white foliage and pink, purple, red, or white flowers to 1½ in. across. It has varieties with semidouble and double flowers.

X. annuum

XERISCAPE. The term "xeriscaping" is derived from the Greek word *xeros*, meaning "dry," and is applied to techniques that reduce the water required to maintain gardens. The xeriscaping movement began in the area of Denver, Colorado, in the early 1980s and gathered momentum later in the decade as cities like Los Angeles, California, enacted water-conserving landscaping for new industrial, commercial, and multi-family developments. Adopting these techniques can lead to a 30–80% reduction in water used compared to humid gardening in arid regions.

Xeriscaping stresses the establishment of landscapes adapted to the arid environments around them, rather than trying to transplant and maintain water-consumptive landscapes from humid eastern or tropical areas. Several techniques help to create water-thrifty gardens and landscapes, including reducing the areas devoted to lawns and planting grasses that use less water—like tall fescue; using drought-tolerant plants; adding compost or other materials to soils to increase their water-holding capacity; grouping plants with similar water requirements close together; and, if absolutely needed, installing micro-irrigation systems, such as trickle or drip types that most efficiently meet plants' water needs.

In designing a xeriscape, take advantage of the water draining from roofs, driveways, and impervious surfaces (called hardscapes) for supplemental irrigation. Also, consider planting species with greater water needs in swales and depressions that collect rainwater at the beginning of the dry season. Even water-conserving species may need some watering, but once established they should require only natural rainfall.

Native plants play a natural role in xeriscapes, since they, above all species, are adapted to the local environment. The desert, chaparral, and grassland wildflowers are obvious candidates for water-conserving landscapes. Trees and shrubs such as *Artemesia tridentata* (sagebrush), *Arctostaphylos* (manzanita), *Fremontodendron californicum* (flannelbush), *Spherdia rotundifolia*

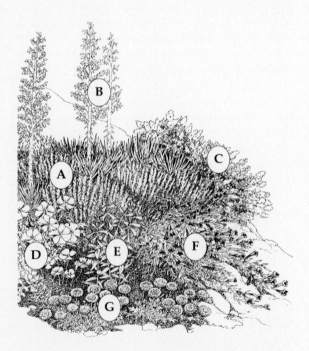

Common xeriscaping plants: (A) *Artemisia tridentata* (sagebrush), (B) *Yucca whippeli* (Our-Lord's-candle), (C) *Ceanothus* sp. (wild-lilac), (D) *Argemone* sp. (prickly poppy), (E) *Penstemon eatonii* (beard-tongue), (F) *Zauchneria californica* (California-fuchsia), (G) *Baileya multiradiata* (desert-marigold)

(buffaloberry), and *Cleome isomeris* (bladder-pod) can also be used quite effectively in xeriscapes. Be sure to prune shrubs periodically so they maintain manageable size; old wood should be removed and new vigorous growth encouraged.

Further information about xeriscaping is available from your local extension service, city or regional water authorities, botanical gardens, or the National Xeriscaping Council, Inc. (see appendix).

XEROPHYLLUM (zee roh FIL um). A genus of hardy perennial herbs native in North America, belonging to the Liliaceae (Lily Family), and commonly known as bear-grass or turkey-beard. They have thick, woody rootstocks and fragrant flowers in racemes. Propagation is by seed or division.

X. asphodeloides, the principal species, is found in pine barrens from New Jersey southward. From the center of a tuft of long, narrow leaves, it sends up a stem to 5 ft. that bears a raceme about 6 in. long of yellowish white flowers in summer. Hardy in Zones 6–9, it is a good plant for the wildflower garden.

Xerophyllum tenax

X. tenax is native to the Pacific Coast and bears large racemes of white flowers with violet stamens. The stiff basal leaves 1–2 ft. long were used by Native Americans to make clothing and baskets. A dense, conical cluster of creamy white, ½-in. flowers fills the upper third of the scape from late spring to midsummer. Hardy in Zones 3–9.

Y

YAM. Common name for various tender ornamental vines, mostly species of DIOSCOREA. Yams are occasionally grown as vegetables in the United States (more often in the tropics), especially *D. alata* (winged, white, or water yam), the best texture and flavor being found in the small varieties whose tubers rarely exceed 1 lb., although some kinds weigh up to 100 lb. The Chinese yam, *D. batatas*, is cultivated more in tropical regions.

In the United States the name "yam" is often wrongly applied to large varieties of the SWEET-POTATO, which belongs to the genus *Ipomoea*.

YANGTAO. A common name for *Actinidia chinensis*, a handsome, twining vine that produces the popular kiwi fruit; see ACTINIDIA.

YARD-LONG BEAN. A common name for *Vigna unguiculata* var. *sesquipedalis*, an herb grown mainly for forage and green manure; it grows flabby pods often 3 ft. long; see VIGNA.

YARROW. Common name for ACHILLEA, a genus of hardy, flowering perennial herbs. Golden-yarrow is *Eriophyllum confertiflorum*; see ERIOPHYLLUM.

YAUPON. Common name for *Ilex vomitoria*, an evergreen shrub or small tree with scarlet berries; see ILEX.

YEDDA-HAWTHORN. Common name for *Rhaphiolepis umbellata*, an attractive, tender shrub with fragrant, white flowers; see RHAPHIOLEPIS.

YELLOW-ELDER. Common name for *Tecoma stans*, a tropical tree or shrub grown in the South for its yellow flowers; see TECOMA.

YELLOWS. A term used to describe diseases caused by several different types of microorganisms in which the major symptom is a yellowing of the plant. Examples of diseases that are termed "yellows" include cabbage yellows, caused by a fusarium fungus; aster yellows, caused by a mycoplasma; and palm lethal yellows, caused by a spiroplasma.

YELLOWTUFT. Common name for *Alyssum murale*, a dwarf perennial herb with yellow flowers; see ALYSSUM.

YELLOWWOOD. Common name for CLADRASTIS, a genus of deciduous trees with long racemes of fragrant flowers.

YERBA BUENA. Common name for *Satureja douglasii*, an herb of the Lamiaceae (Mint Family) whose leaves have been used for tea, and whose tiny, white flowers make them attractive garden specimens; see SATUREJA.

YEW. Common name for TAXUS, a large and variable genus of trees and shrubs with many uses in the landscape and garden. The Yew Family is TAXACEAE.

YOUNGBERRY. Common name for *Rubus ursinus* cv. 'Young', a variety of Pacific dewberry; see BLACKBERRY.

YOUTH-AND-OLD-AGE. Common name for ZINNIA, because the flowers are long-lasting, with some remaining attractive even when others have gone to seed. The name is also applied to *Begonia semperflorens*, presumably for the white-and-green leaves; see BEGONIA.

YOUTH-ON-AGE. A common name for *Tolmiea menziesii*, a rock garden herb or houseplant noted for developing young plants at the base of mature leaves; see TOLMIEA.

YUCCA (YUK uh). A genus of herbaceous and treelike plants of striking character, belonging to the Liliaceae (Lily Family), and native to North America and the West Indies. Some are stemless, and others have woody, scaly trunks, often of majestic height, that rise from clumps of stiff, sword-shaped leaves. The white or violet, cup-shaped flowers, like huge lilies-of-the-valley, are borne mostly in erect clusters or along the stalks. Some emit a heavy fragrance when open at night.

Yuccas are fine for bold, subtropical effects, especially in dry areas. The hardy species can be grown outdoors in cool regions, and many species flourish throughout the southern and western states. A rich but well-drained, fibrous soil and sunny exposure are the best growing conditions. Propagation is by seed (plants often self-sowing), by rhizome or stem cuttings, and by offsets.

PRINCIPAL SPECIES

Y. aloifolia (Spanish-bayonet, Spanish-dagger) grows to 25 ft. Hardy to Zone 8.

Y. brevifolia (Joshuatree) is a grotesquely shaped tree that grows to 30 ft. Native to desert areas of the southwestern states, it is hardy to Zone 7 but is difficult to grow outside its native range.

Y. filamentosa (Adam's-needle) grows to 12 ft. and has leaves edged with fine, white threads. It is commonly grown in northern regions and is hardy to Zone 4.

Y. glauca (soapweed) grows to 8 ft. and has a short, prostrate trunk. Hardy to Zone 2.

Y. gloriosa (Spanish-dagger) grows to 8 ft. and is hardy to Zone 7.

Y. whipplei (Our-Lord's-candle) is the great yucca of southern California and is a glorious sight in bloom.

Yucca filamentosa

YULAN. Common name for *Magnolia heptapeta*, a flowering deciduous tree native to China; see MAGNOLIA.

Z

ZALUZIANSKYA (za loo zee AN skee ah). A genus of South African annual or perennial herbs or shrubby plants belonging to the Scrophulariaceae (Figwort Family). They bear tubular flowers that are very fragrant in the evening. The annual species are frequently cultivated for their ornamental effect as well as for their fragrance. They are grown from seed started in the fall, the plants being wintered over in a coldframe, or from seed started early in the spring in a greenhouse. If planted in light, rich soil, *Zaluzianskya* will start to bloom ten weeks from the time it is set out and will flower through the summer.

Z. capensis (Night-phlox) grows to 18 in. and has soft, hairy, tubular flowers—white inside and purple-black outside.

Z. villosa is a sprawling annual that has narrow leaves and 1-in., white-and-purple flowers.

ZAMIA (ZAY mee ah). A genus of perennial tropical and subtropical plants of the Zamiaceae (Zamia Family), resembling both ferns and palms but actually very distinct from either in their ancestry. The leaves of some species (especially *Z. floridana* and *Z. integrifolia*), commonly known as coontie, are used as decorative foliage by florists, since they are long lasting and do not wither. They have underground, tuberlike trunks and handsome, dark green, feather-shaped leaves forming tufts about 2 ft. high. Grown outdoors in warm regions and under glass in cooler climates, they are especially useful in low plantings and require a mixture of peat, sand, and loam, with ample moisture. They are best propagated by seed. Experienced growers have good success with rooting stem pieces, but it is easy to overwater these before they heal and, by doing so, cause rotting.

Several species are widely grown in subtropical areas, including *Z. pumila* (coontie) and *Z. furfuracea* (cardboard-palm). They are handsome ground covers or specimen plants in the landscape but may elongate too much in indoor pots unless the light is very strong.

ZANTEDESCHIA (zan te DES kee ah). A genus of herbaceous, stout-rooted, South African plants with heart- or spear-shaped, long-stemmed leaves and striking white, yellow, reddish, or spotted lilylike spathes. They are invariably referred to as callas or calla-lilies, although not related to the genus CALLA. Zantedeschias are widely grown in gardens in warm regions and are becoming an important florist crop.

A fungus is responsible for stunting and dry rot of calla roots, accompanied by yellow foliage and reduction in bloom. A bacterial soft rot causes rotting of plants at the surface of the soil, blighting of leaves, and a slimy decay of the rhizome. Discard badly diseased plants and cut out diseased areas in others. To control both dry and soft rots, soak the rhizomes in disinfectant; see BULBS; DISINFECTION. If APHIDS are troublesome on leaves, rinse with water or try a soap solution.

PRINCIPAL SPECIES

Z. aethiopica (calla) is a sturdy, bulbous plant that grows to 2½ ft. and is cultivated by florists. It has smooth, arrow-shaped leaves and a creamy white, flaring spathe with a pointed tip surrounding a yellow spadix. In the North, they are grown in greenhouses and by florists as potted plants and for cut flowers. They are also grown as a perennial outdoors in mild climates for summer bloom in the garden. In cooler climates, the rhizomes should be wintered indoors and planted in very moist ground after danger of frost is over. The plants will bloom profusely during the summer. The plants should be lifted before cold weather in the fall. After being rested for a month or two, they can be potted in soil made rich with well-rotted manure, placed in a fairly sunny spot in a cool greenhouse, watered daily, and given an occasional watering of weak liquid manure. With this treatment they will later bloom in the late winter or early spring, even in a shaded spot. Plants received as gifts in winter can likewise be rested after blooming and then planted in the garden to flower in early fall.

Z. albomaculata (spotted-calla) grows to 2 ft. and has white-spotted leaves. The white spathes are 4–5 in. long, with purple deep in the throat.

Z. elliottiana (yellow calla) requires a leaner soil mixture and more heat than *Z. aethiopica*. Pot the rhizomes in late fall for early spring bloom, or in spring for winter flowers, and keep them dark and slightly dry until the roots begin to form. When they have outgrown their pots, shift them into the next size, using a fibrous soil with plenty of leaf mold and no manure; grow in a moderately warm temperature, feeding with liquid manure from the time flower stalks appear. After the flowering season is finished, ripen off the rhizomes in the pots by gradually withholding water, then store in a dark, cool place.

Z. rehmannii (red- or pink-calla) grows 12–18 in. with narrow, unspotted leaves. The spathes are 4 in. long in pink or light red. Hybrids are available in shades of orange, yellow, and lavender, some against creamy white backgrounds.

ZANTHOXYLUM (zan THOK si lum). A genus of deciduous or evergreen shrubs or trees of tropical and temperate regions, belonging to the Rutaceae (Rue Family). Most are prickly and grown chiefly for their decorative foliage. The small, white or greenish flowers are followed by small pods with shining black seeds. Several species have medicinal value. They are not particular as to soil and can be propagated by seed or by root cuttings.

PRINCIPAL SPECIES

Z. americanum (prickly-ash) is a vigorous native shrub or tree, the hardiest of the group (Zones 4–7).

Z. clava-herculis (Hercules'-club) is native to the South and has a prickly trunk and branches.

Z. schinifolium bears handsome leaves with 13 to 21 leaflets and is the hardiest of the Asian species, doing fairly well as far north as Zone 5 in protected places.

ZAUSCHNERIA (zowsh NER ee ah). A genus of low-growing or trailing, herbaceous perennial herbs or subshrubs in the Onagraceae (Evening-primrose Family). Commonly known as California-fuschia, many are grown for their scarlet,

tubular flowers blooming in late summer and fall; generally hardy to Zone 8. Propagated by seed, cuttings, or division, they are useful in walls, for ground cover, in the wild garden, meadow, rock garden, or in a drought-tolerant landscape.

PRINCIPAL SPECIES

Z. arizonica, growing to 4 ft., is stiff, leafy, and floriferous.

Z. californica grows 1–2 ft., spreading rapidly underground, and has small, gray or green leaves and showy, 3-in., scarlet flowers in late summer; white and pink varieties are available.

Z. cana is a tender subshrub that grows to 3 ft. and has very narrow, gray leaves.

Z. latifolia grows to 18 in. and has oval, green leaves.

Zauschneria californica

Z. septentrionalis, growing 4–6 in., has soft, gray leaves, and is attractive in rock gardens.

ZEA (ZEE ah) **mays.** A plant belonging to the Poaceae (Grass Family), commonly known as CORN or maize. Presumably of Mexican origin, it now consists of many botanical and countless agricultural varieties and strains. Some are cultivated for the succulent stalks and large, coarse leaves used as forage and fodder; others, for the ripened grain to be used as food for humans and animals; still others, for the young tender ears cooked and eaten as a vegetable. There are several varieties of corn with variegated foliage, often grown to divide the vegetable garden from the ornamental grounds. The most common, *Z. mays* var. *japonica*, has leaves striped with yellow, white, or pink and is attractive in flower arrangements and colorful in the garden.

ZEBRA PLANT. Common name for *Calathea zebrina*, a Brazilian perennial grown in greenhouses for its velvety green-striped foliage; see

CALATHEA. The name is also applied to *Aphelandra squarrosa*, whose succulent leaves are marked with white veins; see APHELANDRA.

ZEBRINA (ze BRĪ nah) **pendula.** A tender, trailing plant with red flowers belonging to the Commelinaceae (Spiderwort Family). It is often called wandering-Jew, which more commonly refers to a species of *Tradescantia*, because the plants are very similar when not in bloom. Frequently grown in greenhouses as a hanging foliage plant, its leaves are striped above and red below.

ZELKOVA (zel KOH vah). A genus of deciduous shrubs or trees native to Asia and belonging to the Ulmaceae (Elm Family). They resemble twiggy, small-leaved elms and thrive under the same conditions that favor those trees.

Z. carpinifolia, growing to 50 ft., has a short trunk divided into many stems but is less shapely than *Z. serrata*.

Z. serrata, the principal species, is a good-looking tree, attaining 50 ft. It usually has a short trunk, dividing into many stems with slender, spreading branches forming a round-topped head. This tree tends to grow with a vase shape similar to the American elm and is used as a replacement for it. Cv. 'Village Green' is an outstanding form with rapid growth, reddish fall color, and straight trunk, very resistant to DUTCH ELM DISEASE. Hardy to Zone 6.

ZENOBIA (zen OH bee ah) **pulverulenta.** A small deciduous or partly evergreen shrub native to North America, belonging to the Ericaceae (Heath Family), and commonly known as andromeda. Hardy in Zones 6–9, it thrives best in a sandy, peaty soil and is very conspicuous with its bluish white foliage. The clusters of nodding, white, anise-scented flowers open in late spring. Propagation is by seed and layers.

ZEPHYRANTHES (zef ur ANTH eez). A rather large genus of bulbous plants, most of which are native to the Americas from Pennsylvania southward into the tropics. They produce narrow, grassy leaves and waxy, funnel-shaped flowers that open only in the evening, borne erect on slender, hollow stems. Although they resemble some lilies and are commonly called zephyr-lilies, they are actually members of the Amaryllidaceae (Amaryllis Family). Other common names are rain-lily or fairy-lily, because the flowers appear in the South in great numbers as if by magic as soon as a rainy season starts.

They are grown in the open in the southern and western states. Bulbs should be planted in the early spring, then lifted in the fall and packed in dry soil so they will not shrivel during winter storage.

PRINCIPAL SPECIES

Z. atamasco (atamasco-lily) is the common white, spring-blooming species native in the South and of doubtful hardiness in the North (to Zone 6). It has grassy leaves to 1 ft. long and white, purple-tinged, funnelform flowers to 3 in. in spring.

Z. brazosensis, formerly listed under the genus *Cooperia*, has white flowers tinged red on the outside.

Z. candida is the fall-flowering white species that grows prolifically in warm regions but is not hardy. It is dormant in early summer, but if then planted either in the garden or in the house, it can be quickly and easily flowered.

Z. drummondii is similar to *Z. brazosensis*, but the flowers are slightly smaller and have shorter tubes.

Z. grandiflora has rose-red or pink flowers appearing in early summer and can be used in northern gardens if handled as a tender, summer-flowering bulb. The bulbs should be lifted in the fall, stored frost-free over winter, and planted out in early spring.

Z. rosea is a rose-red, autumn bloomer native to Cuba. Most of the bulbs sold under this name are really *Z. grandiflora*.

ZIGADENUS (zī ga DEEN us). A genus of lilylike perennials, commonly known as camas, some with and some without bulbs, growing about 2 ft. tall and having grasslike leaves and white, greenish, or yellow flowers in clusters. Sometimes grown as pot plants, they are hardy to Zone 4 and occasionally seen in the rock or wild garden. Propagation is by seed or division. Seeds, leaves, and bulbs of some species are poisonous if eaten.

PRINCIPAL SPECIES

Z. elegans (white camas, alkali-grass) has very narrow leaves with a silvery bloom and greenish flowers in clusters to 1 ft. long.

Z. nuttalli (nuttall death camas, poison camas, merryhearts) has rather large flowers ½ in. across in loose clusters.

Z. paniculatus (foothill death camas, sand-corn) is another western species similar to *Z. nuttalli* with yellow flowers and an exceedingly poisonous bulb.

Z. venenosus (death camas), with small, greenish white flowers, is a western species with a very poisonous bulb.

ZINGIBER (ZIN gi ber). A genus of tropical perennial herbs of the Zingiberaceae (Ginger Family), grown in greenhouses in cold climates, for summer bedding in warm regions, and for commercial purposes in the tropics.

Z. officinale yields the ginger spice, which consists of dried rhizomes. It is grown commercially in the East and West Indies, Africa, and China.

Z. zerumbet is grown for its red, pineconelike flower stalks.

ZINGIBERACEAE (zin gi bur AY see ee). The Ginger Family, a group of tropical herbs, some cultivated for their ornamental foliage and habit, and many for dyes, spices, perfumes, and medicinal products. Nearly all are perennials with clumps of short, canelike stems rising from tuberous rootstocks. The most commonly grown are *Alpinia*, *Amomum*, *Curcuma*, *Hedychium*, and *Zingiber* (ginger), all grown in cooler regions only under glass.

ZINNIA (ZIN ee ah). A genus of herbs and small shrubs native to Mexico, belonging to the Asteraceae (Aster Family). The plants are popularly called youth-on-old-age, because the flowers are long-lasting on the plant, some remaining attractive even when others have ripened seed.

The most common garden species is *Z. elegans*, often used for bedding, borders, edging, and cut flowers. Blossom colors include red, yellow, orange, pink, white, green, and several bicolors. Flowers may be as small as 2 in. across in the dwarf varieties or up to 6 in. across in the tall varieties.

Zinnias are most commonly started from seed. They can be sown directly outdoors, or for earlier blooms, they can be started inside several weeks before the last frost. Plants grow best in a light, fertile soil exposed to full sun.

Some foliar diseases may become troublesome when growing zinnias. Space the plants far enough apart in the garden for good air circulation, and avoid splashing water on the plants when watering. If necessary, a fungicide can be applied for additional control; follow the label directions carefully.

Two other species not as well known as *Z. elegans* include *Z. peruviana*, with yellow flower heads and occasionally purple or yellow rays; and *Z. angustifolia*, smaller than *Z. elegans*, with bright orange flower heads.

ZIZANIA (zi ZAY nee uh). An aquatic grass most commonly called wild-rice but also known as Indian-rice, water-rice, and water-oats. Growing along the swampy borders of streams and ponds, it attains a height of 10 ft. in some regions, and when used in the water garden it is a splendid and very handsome grass for a marginal planting. In grocery stores catering to the gourmet tastes, wild-rice brings a good price and is increasingly popular as an accompaniment to poultry, game birds, and other meats.

Hunt clubs and individuals, especially throughout the South, have been sowing great quantities of wild-rice around ponds and in marshes to attract duck and other game birds. The seed is obtainable from almost any seed house. Before planting, it is advisable to put the seed in a coarse cotton bag, attach a rock or other ballast, and soak in water for 24 hours. Sow in water from 6 in. to 5 ft. deep or in any marsh where water stands the year round.

See AQUATIC PLANTS.

ZIZIPHUS (ZĪ zi fus). A genus of deciduous or evergreen shrubs or trees of tropical and subtropical regions of both hemispheres, belonging to the Rhamnaceae (Buckthorn Family) and commonly known as jujube. They are grown mostly in warm climates for ornament and for their edible fruits. Propagation is by seed, root cuttings, and grafting.

Z. mauritiana (Chinese jujube), formerly called *Z. jujuba*, is the chief species and principal source of commercial jujube. This is a deciduous shrub or small tree with slender, prickly branches and light green leaves. Although hardy to Zone 5, it is primarily cultivated in warm climates, especially in China, where a great many varieties are grown for the reddish brown fruits about the size of an olive. The name *Z. mauritiana* has sometimes been restricted to a less hardy, shrubby form, but this appears to be only a variant of the hardier tree, and the name applies to both.

ZONE. Depending on the climate and temperature they require to grow, plants are recommended for various geographic regions or hardiness zones. See CLIMATE; HARDY PLANTS; HARDINESS ZONES.

ZOYSIA (ZOH i see uh). A small genus of creeping perennial grasses of southern Asia, whose fine, compact foliage fits them for use in the southern United States. Hardiness varies according to species (Zones 7–11). The most popular species, *Z. japonica* (Japanese or Korean lawn grass), is commonly used on lawns in the transition zone and is grown as far north as Zone 6. In cooler climates it has a dormancy period lasting from mid- to late fall until mid-spring when it will turn a strawlike brown color. Propagation is by sprigs, sod, or plugs. Other species are *Z. matrella* (Manila grass) and *Z. tenuifolia* (Mascarene grass).

ZUCCHINI. The green squash, *Cucurbita pepo*, is probably one of the easiest and most commonly cultivated garden vegetables, often yielding a bumper crop with minimal effort.

The standard practice is to plant them in hills or mounds. Seeds can be started three to four weeks before the last frost or sown outdoors after it is sufficiently warm (at least 60–70°F). Prepare slightly raised mounds of soil 1–2 ft. in diameter, leaving at least 3 ft. between the mounds for the vines to run. The plants should be spaced at least 6 in. apart. Water deeply at least once a week if there is no rain; avoid wetting the leaves, since this encourages disease. Keep weeds down until the leaves are big enough to shade them out. A mulch of hay between the mounds is helpful to keep out weeds and to keep the fruits clean and dry.

Once the fruit begins to develop, it should be harvested while small and tender (usually less than 6 in. long). Unpicked zucchinis become tough and woody and inhibit the production of more fruits. Oversized fruits can be stuffed, grated for bread, or cooked down for soup stock.

See also CUCURBITA; SQUASH.

ZYGOPETALUM (zī goh PET uh lum). A genus of about 50 species of epiphytic orchids native to Central America and tropical South America. Its flowers are among the most unusual of the orchids. Plants are medium to large, with large, plicate leaves. One to several showy flowers are borne on lateral inflorescences rising from the base of the pseudobulb. The plants need a large pot to accommodate the extremely thick roots. The fragrant flowers have broad, green petals and sepals blotched with rich brown. The crisped and spreading lip is white with vivid purple striations. Plants do well in a porous, well-drained medium. Hardy to Zone 9 with cold protection, plants should not be subjected to temperatures below 60°F. They prefer filtered shade, high humidity, and ample water during growth. Water should not stand on the leaves. The type species is *Z. mackaii*.

Cooperative Extension Services

The following organizations have agricultural research programs and/or information services. Some provide soil-testing services (usually for a fee), and some will give advice regarding plant culture or insect and disease control for home and/or commercial growers.

UNITED STATES

Alabama

Alabama A & M University
Normal, AL 35762

Auburn University
Auburn, AL 36849

Tuskegee Institute
Tuskeegee, AL 36088

Alaska

University of Alaska
Fairbanks, AK 99775

Arizona

University of Arizona
Tucson, AZ 85721

Arkansas

Extension Administration
P.O. Box 391
Little Rock, AR 72203

University of Arkansas
Fayetteville, AR 72701

California

Kearney Agricultural Center
Parlier, CA 93648

University of California
College of Natural Resources
Berkeley, CA 94720

University of California
College of Agriculture and
    Environmental Sciences
Davis, CA 95616

University of California
College of Natural and
    Agricultural Sciences
Riverside, CA 92502

Colorado

Colorado State University
College of Agricultural Sciences
Fort Collins, CO 80523

Fruita Research Center
Box 786
Grand Junction, CO 81502

Connecticut

Connecticut Agricultural
    Experiment Station
P.O. Box 1106
New Haven, CT 06504

University of Connecticut
Storrs, CT 06268

Delaware

Delaware State College
Dover, DE 19901

University of Delaware
College of Agricultural Sciences
Newark, DE 19711

District of Columbia

University of the District
 of Columbia
Washington, DC 20005

Florida

Florida A & M University
Tallahassee, FL 32307

University of Florida
College of Agriculture
Gainesville, FL 32611

Georgia

Fort Valley State College
School of Agriculture
Fort Valley, GA 31030

University of Georgia
College of Agriculture
Athens, GA 30602

Hawaii

University of Hawaii
Honolulu, HI 96822

Idaho

University of Idaho
College of Agriculture
Moscow, ID 83843

Illinois

University of Illinois
College of Agriculture
Urbana, IL 61801

Indiana

Purdue University
School of Agriculture
West Lafayette, IN 47907

Iowa

Iowa State University
College of Agriculture
Ames, IA 50011

Kansas

Kansas State University
College of Agriculture
Manhattan, KS 66506

Kentucky

Kentucky State University
Frankfort, KY 40601

University of Kentucky
College of Agriculture
Lexington, KY 40506

Louisiana

Louisiana State University
Baton Rouge, LA 70893

Southern University and
    A & M College
Baton Rouge, LA 70813

Maine

University of Maine
College of Agriculture
Orono, ME 04469

Maryland

University of Maryland
College of Agriculture
College Park, MD 20742

University of Maryland
Eastern Shore
Department of Agriculture
Princess Anne, MD 21853

Massachusetts

University of Massachusetts
College of Agriculture
Amherst, MA 01003

Michigan

Michigan State University
College of Agriculture
East Lansing, MI 48824

Minnesota

University of Minnesota
College of Agriculture and
    Natural Resources
St. Paul, MN 55108

Mississippi

Alcorn State College
Lorman, MS 39096

Mississippi State University
College of Agriculture
Mississippi State, MS 39762

Missouri

Lincoln University
Jefferson City, MO 65101

University of Missouri
College of Agriculture
Columbia, MO 65211

Montana

Montana State University
College of Agriculture
Bozeman, MT 59717

Nebraska

University of Nebraska
Institute of Agriculture and
    Natural Resources
Lincoln, NE 68583

Nevada

University of Nevada
College of Agriculture
Reno, NV 89557

New Hampshire

University of New Hampshire
College of Agriculture
Durham, NH 03824

New Jersey

Rutgers State University
College of Agriculture
New Brunswick, NJ 08903

New Mexico

New Mexico State University
College of Agriculture
Las Cruces, NM 88003

New York

Cornell University
College of Agriculture
Ithaca, NY 14853

New York State Agricultural
Experiment Station
Geneva, NY 14456

North Carolina

North Carolina A & T
    State University
School of Agriculture
Greensboro, NC 27411

North Carolina State University
College of Agriculture
Raleigh, NC 27695

North Dakota

State University of Agriculture
    and Applied Science
State University Station
Fargo, ND 58105

Ohio

Ohio State University
College of Agriculture
Columbus, OH 43210

Oklahoma

Langston University
Agricultural Research
P.O. Box 730
Langston, OK 73050

Oklahoma State University
College of Agriculture
Stillwater, OK 74078

Oregon

Oregon State University
College of Agriculture
Corvallis, OR 97331

Pennsylvania

Pennsylvania State University
College of Agriculture
University Park, PA 16802

Rhode Island

University of Rhode Island
Kingston, RI 02881

South Carolina

Clemson University
College of Agricultural Sciences
Clemson, SC 29631

South Dakota

South Dakota State University
College of Agriculture
Brookings, SD 57007

Tennessee

Tennessee State University
School of Agriculture
Nashville, TN 37203

University of Tennessee
Institute of Agriculture
Knoxville, TN 37901

Texas

Texas A & M University
College of Agriculture
College Station, TX 77843

Utah

Utah State University
College of Agriculture
Logan, UT 84322

Vermont

University of Vermont
College of Agriculture
Burlington, VT 05405

Virginia

Virginia Polytechnic Institute
    and State University
College of Agriculture
Blacksburg, VA 24061

Washington

Washington State University
College of Agriculture
Pullman, WA 99164

West Virginia

West Virginia University
College of Agriculture
Morgantown, WV 26506

Wisconsin

University of Wisconsin
College of Agriculture
Madison, WI 53706

Wyoming

University of Wyoming
College of Agriculture
Laramie, WY 82071

UNITED STATES TERRITORIES

Guam

University of Guam
College of Agriculture
Mangilao UOG Station
Guam 96923

Puerto Rico

University of Puerto Rico
College of Agricultural Sciences
Mayaguez, PR 00708

Virgin Islands

College of the Virgin Islands
Agricultural Experiment Station
RR 2, Box 10,000
St. Croix, VI 00850

CANADA

Alberta

Alberta Tree Nursery and
    Horticultural Center
RR #6, 17507 Fort Road
Edmonton, AB T5B 4K3

British Columbia

University of British Columbia
Botanical Gardens
6804 Southwest Marine Drive
Vancouver, BC V6T 1W5

Manitoba

Horticulture Section
Manitoba Horticulture
908-401 York Avenue
Winnipeg, MB R3C 0P8

New Brunswick

Department of Agriculture
P.O. Box 6000
Fredericton, NB E3B 5H1

Newfoundland

Department of Forestry and
    Agriculture
Provincial Agriculture Building
Brookfield Road
P.O. Box 8700
St. John's, NF A1B 4J6

Nova Scotia

Nova Scotia Agricultural
    College
P.O. Box 550
Truro, NS B2N 5E3

Kentville Agricultural Center
Kentville, NS B4N 1J5

Ontario

Master Gardener's Program
    (over 20 offices, for the near-
    est location, consult the
    Ontario Ministry of Agricul-
    ture and Food listed in your
    telephone directory)

Prince Edward Island

Prince Edward Island
Department of Agriculture
Research Station
P.O. Box 1600
Charlottetown, PE C1A 7N3

Quebec

Ministère de l'Agriculture, des
    Pêcheries et de l'Alimenta-
    tion (Agriculture, Fisheries
    and Food)
Direction des Communications
200-A Chemin Ste-Foy
Quebec, QC G1R 4X6

Saskatchewan

University of Saskatchewan
Extension and Community
    Relations
Saskatoon, SK S7N 0W0

Botanical Gardens

The following botanical gardens, arboreta, and nature centers have cultivated gardens or natural areas for public display. Some provide additional services and/or have shops where books, seeds, and live plants can be purchased. It is advisable to call ahead when planning a visit, since some facilities are seasonal.

UNITED STATES

American Association of
  Botanical Gardens
P.O. Box 206
Swarthmore, PA 19081

Alabama

Bellingrath Gardens
12401 Bellingrath Gardens Road
Theodore, AL 36582

Birmingham Botanical Gardens
2612 Lane Park Road
Birmingham, AL 35223

Arizona

Arizona-Sonora Desert Museum
2021 North Kinney Road
Tucson, AZ 85743

Boyce Thompson Southwestern
  Arboretum
Route 60
P.O. Box AB
Superior, AZ 85273

Desert Botanical Garden
1201 North Galvin Parkway
Phoenix, AZ 85008

Valley Garden Center
1809 North 15th Avenue
Phoenix, AZ 85008

California

Balboa Park
1549 El Paro
San Diego, CA 92101

Berkeley Botanical Garden
University of California
Centennial Drive
Berkeley, CA 94720

Berkeley Municipal Rose Garden
Euclid Avenue at Bay View Pl.
Berkeley, CA 94704

Luther Burbank Memorial
  Gardens
Santa Rosa and Sonoma Aves.
Santa Clara, CA

Descanso Gardens
1418 Descanso Drive
La Canada, CA 91011

Filoli Center
Canada Road
Woodside, CA 94062

Hearst San Simeon
Department of Parks &
  Recreation
750 Hearst Castle Road
San Simeon, CA 93452-9741

Huntington Botanical Gardens
1151 Oxford Road
San Marino, CA 91108

Living Desert
47-900 South Portola Avenue
Palm Desert, CA 92260

Los Angeles City Garden
Exposition Park
701 State Park Drive
Los Angeles, CA

Los Angeles State and County
  Arboretum
301 North Baldwin Avenue
Arcadia, CA 91007-2697

Lotusland
695 Ashley Road
Montecito, CA

Joseph McInnes Memorial
  Botanical Gardens
Seminary Avenue
Oakland, CA 94613

Mendocino Coast Botanic
  Garden
18220 North Highway 1
P.O. Box 1143
Fort Bragg, CA 95437

Morcom Amphitheater of Roses
700 Jean Street
Oakland, CA 94610

Theodore Payne Foundation
10459 Tuxford Street
Sun Valley, CA 91352

Quail Botanical Gardens
230 Quail Gardens Drive
Encinitas, CA 92024

Rancho Santa Anna Botanical
  Garden
1500 North College Avenue
Claremont, CA 91711

Rose Hills Memorial Park
3900 South Workman Mill Road
Whittier, CA

Santa Barbara Botanic Garden
1212 Mission Canyon Road
Santa Barbara, CA 93105

South Coast Botanic Garden
26300 Crenshaw Boulevard
Palos Verdes, CA 90274

Strybing Arboretum and
  Botanical Gardens
Golden Gate Park
9th Avenue at Lincoln Way
San Francisco, CA 94122

University Arboretum
University of California at Davis
Davis, CA 95616

Colorado

Denver Botanic Gardens
909 York Street
Denver, CO 80206

Longmont Memorial Rose
  Garden
528 North Main
Longmont, CO 80501

Connecticut

Bartlett Arboretum
University of Connecticut
151 Brookdale Road
Stamford, CT 06903

Connecticut Arboretum
Connecticut College
270 Monhegan Avenue
New London, CT 06320-4196

Constitution Plaza
525 Whitney Avenue
New Haven, CT 06511

Elizabeth Park
Municipal Rose Garden
150 Walbridge Road
West Hartford, CT 06119

District of Columbia

Dumbarton Oaks and Gardens
1703 32nd Street, Northwest
Washington, DC 20007

Enid Haupt Garden
Independence Avenue
Washington, DC 20560

Hirschhorn Museum and
  Sculpture Garden
Smithsonian Institution
Independence Avenue SW
Washington, DC 20560

Kenilworth Aquatic Gardens
Douglas Street Northeast
Washington, DC 20019

United States National
  Arboretum
3501 New York Avenue NE
Washington, DC 20002

Florida

Charles Deering Estate
16701 Southwest 72nd Avenue
Miami, FL 33157

Thomas Edison Winter Home
  and Botanical Gardens
2350 McGregor Boulevard
Fort Myers, FL 33901

Fairchild Tropical Garden
10901 Old Cutler Road
Miami, FL 33156

Mounts Botanical Gardens
531 North Military Trail
West Palm Beach, FL 33406

Marie Selby Botanical Gardens
811 South Palm Avenue
Sarasota, FL 34236

Vizcaya Gardens
3251 South Miami Avenue
Miami, FL 33157

Georgia

Atlanta Botanical Garden
1345 Piedmont Avenue
P.O. Box 77246
Atlanta, GA 30357

Atlanta Historical Society
McElreath Hall
3101 Andrews Drive, Northwest
Atlanta, GA 30305

Callaway Gardens
Routes 27 and I-85
Pine Mountain, GA 31822

Savannah
several locations, contact:
Savannah Tourist Information
222 West Oglethorpe Avenue
Savannah, GA 31499

State Botanical Garden of
  Georgia
University of Georgia
2450 South Milledge Avenue
Athens, GA 30605

Hawaii

Foster Botanic Gardens
180 North Vineyard Boulevard
Honolulu, HI

Liliuokalani Garden Park
Banyan Drive and Lihiwai
  Street
Hilo Bay, HI

Pacific Tropical Botanical
  Garden
Lawai Valley
Kauai, HI

University of Hawaii
Maui Agricultural Research
  Center
Kula, HI 96790

Waimea Arboretum
Waimea Falls Park
59-864 Kalanianole Highway
Haleiwa, HI 96712

Idaho

Municipal Rose Garden
Julia Davis Park
1104 Royal Boulevard
Boise, ID 83706

IIllinois

Chicago Botanic Garden
P.O. Box 400
Lake Cook Road
Glencoe, IL 60022

Garfield Park Conservatory
300 North Central Park
Chicago, IL 60620

Abraham Lincoln Memorial
  Garden and Nature Center
2301 East Lake Drive
Springfield, IL 62707

Morton Arboretum
Route 53, East-West Tollway
Lisle, IL 60532

Indiana

Lakeside Rose Garden
1500 Lake Avenue
Fort Wayne, IN 46805

Ball State University Greenhouse
West University Avenue
Muncie, IN 47306

Christy Woods Arboretum
Riverside and Tillotson
Muncie, IN 47306

Jerry E. Clegg Botanic Garden
1854 N. County Road 400, E.
Lafayette, IN 47906

Hayes Regional Arboretum
801 Elks Road
Richmond IN, 47374

Iowa

Arie den Boer Arboretum
408 Fleur Drive
Des Moines, IA 50321

Bicklehaupt Arboretum
340 South 14th Street
Clinton, IA 52732

Des Moines Botanical Center
909 East River Drive
Des Moines, IA 50316

Greenwood Park Rose Garden
48th and Grand Streets
Des Moines, IA

Iowa State University
  Horticultural Gardens
Sixth and Hayber
Ames, IA 50010

Vander Veer Park Municipal
  Rose Garden
2816 East Avenue
Davenport, IA 52803

Kansas

Kansas State University Gardens
17th and Anderson Streets
Manhattan, KS 66502

Kentucky

Bernheim Forest Arboretum
Route 245
Clermont, KY 40110

Tennessee Valley Environmental
Education Center
Land Between the Lakes
Golden Pond, KY 42231

Louisiana

American Rose Center
8877 Jefferson-Paige Road
Shreveport, LA 71119

Hodges Garden
Route 171/P.O. Box 900
Many, LA 71449

Jungle Gardens
Route 329
Avery Island, LA 70513

Live Oak Garden
284 Rip van Winkle Road
New Iberia, LA 70560

New Orleans City Park
Lelong and City Park Avenues
New Orleans, LA

Rosedown Plantation and
  Gardens
Great River Road
P.O. Box 1816
Saint Francisville, LA 70775

Maine

Deering Oaks Park
Deering and Forest Avenues
Portland, ME 04102

Maryland

Brookside Botanical Gardens
1500 Glenallen Avenue
Wheaton, MD 20902

Cylburn Garden Center
4915 Greenspring Avenue
Baltimore, MD 21209

Londontowne Publik House
  and Gardens
839 Londontown Road
Edgewater, MD 21037-2197

William Paca Garden
186 Prince George Street
Annapolis, MD 21401

Massachusetts

Arnold Arboretum
  of Harvard University
The Arborway
Jamaica Plain, MA 02130

Berkshire Garden Center
State Routes 183 and 102
Stockbridge, MA 01262

Boston Public Garden
Arlington and Beacon Streets
Boston, MA

Garden in the Woods
New England Wildflower
  Society, Inc.
Hemenway Road
Framingham, MA 01701

Hopkins Memorial Forest
P.O Box 632
Northwest Hill Road
Williamstown, MA 01267

Walter Hunnewell Pinetum
845 Washington Street
Wellesley, MA 02181

Mount Auburn Cemetery
580 Mount Auburn Street
Cambridge, MA

Norcross Wildlife Sanctuary
Monson-Wales Road
Monson, MA 01057

Sedgewick Gardens at Long Hill
572 Essex Street
Beverly, MA

Smith College Botanic Garden
Lyman Plant House
College Lane
Northampton, MA 01063

Michigan

W.J. Beal-Garfield Botanical
  Gardens
Michigan State University
412 Olds Hall
West Drive
East Lansing, MI 48824

Belle Isle Conservatory and Park
Detroit River, MacArthur Bridge
Detroit, MI

Cranbrook House and Gardens
P.O. Box 801
380 Lone Pine Road
Bloomfield Hills, MI 48013

Dow Gardens
1018 West Main Street
Midland, MI 48640

Fernwood Botanic Garden and
  Nature Center
13998 Range Line Road
Niles, MI 49120

Hidden Lake Gardens
Route 50
Tipton, MI 49287

Matthaei Botanical Gardens
University of Michigan
1800 North Dixboro Road
Ann Arbor, MI 48105

Minnesota

Eloise Butler Wildflower and
  Bird Sanctuary
Theodore Wirth Park
Glenwood Ave. and N. Abbot
Minneapolis, MN 55409

Como Park Conservatory
Midway Pky. and Kaufman Dr.
Saint Paul, MN 55103

Landscape Arboretum
University of Minnesota
3675 Arboretum Drive
P.O. Box 39
Chanahassen, MN 55317

Minnesota Zoological Gardens
12101 Johnny Cake Ridge Road
Apple Valley, MN

Mississippi

American Rose Society Test
  Garden
University of Southern
  Mississippi Campus
Hardy Street
Hattiesburg, MS

Mynelle Gardens
4736 Clinton Boulevard
Jackson, MS 39209

Missouri

Missouri Botanical Garden
4344 Shaw Blouevard
Saint Louis, MO 63110

The Plaza
4625 Wornall Road
Kansas City, MO 64112

Shaw Arboretum
I-44 and Route 100
P.O. Box 38
Gray Summit, MO 63639

Montana

Memorial Rose Park
Brooks Street
Route 93 South
Missoula, MT

Nebraska

Chet Ager Nature Center
2740 A Street
Lincoln, NE 68502

General Crook House
30th and Fort Streets
Omaha, NE 68105

New Hampshire

Fuller Gardens
10 Willow Avenue
North Hampton, NH 03862

New Jersey

Duke Gardens Foundation, Inc.
Route 206
South Somerville, NJ

Frelinghuysen Arboretum
53 East Hanover Avenue
P.O. Box 1295
Morristown, NJ 07960-1295

Princeton University Campus
Princeton, NJ

Tourne Park
Powerville Road
Boonton Township, NJ 07005

New Mexico

Living Desert State Park
Route 285 North
P.O. Box 100
Carlsbad, NM 88220

University of New Mexico
Central Avenue and Yale
  Boulevard
Albuquerque, NM 87131

New York

Bayard Cutting Arboretum
Montauk Highway
Great River
Oakdale, NY 11739

Brooklyn Botanic Garden
1000 Washington Avenue
Brooklyn, NY 11225

Central Park Garden
57th to 110th Streets
and West to Fifth Avenue
New York, NY

Cornell Plantations
100 Judd Falls Road
Ithaca, NY 14850

Highland Park
Mount Hope, Highland Historic
   District
Rochester, NY

Mohonk Mountain House and
   Gardens
Lake Mohonk
New Paltz, NY 12561

New York Botanical Garden
Bronx, NY 10458

Old Westbury Gardens
P.O. Box 430
Old Westbury, NY 11568

Planting Fields Arboretum
Box 58
Oyster Bay, NY

Queens Botanical Garden
42-50 Main Street
Flushing, NY 11355

Root Glen
Hamilton College
107 College Hill Road
Clinton, NY 13323

Sonnenberg Gardens
151 Charlotte Street
Canandaigua, NY 14424

North Carolina

Biltmore Estate Gardens
1 North Pack Square
Asheville, NC 28801

Coker Arboretum
University of North Carolina
Laurel Hill Road
Chapel Hill, NC

Sarah P. Duke Gardens
Duke University
Durham, NC 22706

Elizabethan Gardens
Roanoke Island
Highway 64
Manteo, NC 27954

Reynolda Gardens
100 Reynolda Village
Winston-Salem, NC 27106

Tryon Palace Gardens
610 Pollock Street
New Berne, NC 28563

North Dakota

Gunlogson Arboretum
Icelandic State Park
Highway 5 South
Cavalier, ND 58220

International Peace Garden
Route 281
Dunseith, ND 58329

Ohio

Cedar Bog State Memorial
980 Woodburn Road
Urbana, OH 43078

Crosby Gardens
5403 Elmer Drive
Toledo, OH 43615

Glen Helen
Antioch University
405 Corry Street
Yellow Springs, OH 45387

Holden Arboretum
9500 Sperry Road
Mentor, Oh 44060

Stan Hywet Hall
714 North Portage Path
Akron, OH 44303-1399

Kingwood Center
900 Park Avenue West
Mansfield, OH 44906

Mount Airy Arboretum
5200 Arboretum Road
Cincinnati, OH 45223

Western Reserve
Herb Society Garden
11030 East Boulevard
Cleveland, OH 44106

Oklahoma

Muskogee Azalea Gardens
Honor Heights Park
641 Park Drive
Muskogee, OK 74403

Philbrook Art Center
Formal Gardens
2727 South Rockford Road
Tulsa, OK 74114

Will Rogers Park and Horticultural Center
3500 Northwest 36th Street
Oklahoma City, OK 73112

Tulsa Municipal Rose Garden
   and Memorial Park
Woodward Park
2435 South Peoria Aveue
Tulsa, OK 74114

Oregon

Castle Crest Wildflower
   Gardens
Crater Lake National Park
Crater Lake, OR 97604

Darlington Wayside Arboretum
84505 Highway 101
Florence, OR 97439

Hoyt Arboretum
4000 Southwest Fairview
   Boulevard
Portland, OR 97221

International Rose Test Garden
400 Southwest Kingston Avenue
Washington Park
Portland, OR 97201

Ira's Fountain Park
Southwest Third Avenue and
Market Street
Portland, OR 97201

Leach Botanical Gardens
6704 Southeast 122nd Avenue
Portland, OR 97236

Pennsylvania

John Bartram House and
  Garden
54th St. and Lindbergh Blvd.
Philadelphia, PA 19143

Fairmount Park
East River and Aquarium Drives
Philadelphia, PA

Hershey Gardens
612 Park Avenue
Hershey, PA 17033

Longwood Gardens
U.S. Route 1 and Route 52
P.O. Box 501
Kennett Square, PA 19348

Morris Arboretum
University of Pennsylvania
9414 Meadowbrook Avenue
Chestnut Hill, PA 19118

Pennsbury Manor
400 Pennsbury Road
Morrisville, PA 19067

Phipps Conservatory
Schenley Park
Pittsburgh, PA

Tyler Arboretum
515 Painter Road
Box 216
Lima, PA 19037

Rhode Island

Blithewold Gardens
101 Ferry Road
Bristol, RI 02809

The Breakers
Ochre Point Avenue
Newport, RI

The Elms
Bellevue Avenue
Newport, RI

Green Animals Topiary Garden
Corey's Land
Portsmouth, RI

South Carolina

Brookgreen Gardens
Route 17 South
Murrels Inlet, SC 29576

Columbia Museum of Art,
  Garden
1519 Senate Street
Columbia, SC 29201

Cypress Gardens
3030 Cypress Gardens Road
Moncks Corner, SC 29416

Edisto Rose Garden
Calhoun Drive
Orangeburg, SC

Festival of Houses and Gardens
  Tour
Historic Charleston Foundation
51 Meeting Street
Charleston, SC 29401

Magnolia Gardens
Route 4, Highway 61
Charleston, SC 29414

Middleton Place
Ashley River Road
Charleston, SC 29414

Tennessee

Dixon Gallery and Gardens
4339 Park Avenue
Memphis, TN 38117

The Hermitage
4580 Rachels Lane
Hermitage, TN 37076

Memphis Botanic Garden
Audubon Park
750 Cherry Road
Memphis, TN 38117

Texas

Brown Center Gardens
Lamar University
4205 Park Avenue
Orange, TX

Dallas Garden Center
3601 Martin Luther King
  Boulevard
Dallas, TX 75226

Fort Worth Botanic Gardens
3220 Botanic Garden Drive
Fort Worth, TX 76107

Paseo del Rio
(River Walk)
317 Animal Plaza
San Antonio, TX 78205

San Antonio Botanical Center
555 Sunston Place
San Antonio, TX 78209

Utah

Sugarhouse Park
1602 East 21st Street South
Salt Lake City, UT 84122

Temple Gardens
Temple Square
Church of the Latter-Day Saints
Salt Lake City, UT 84122

Utah Botanical Gardens
1817 North Main Street
Farmington, UT 84025

Vermont

Hildene
Route 7A
Manchester, VT 05254

Vermont Wildflower Farm
Route 7
Charlotte, VT 05445

Virginia

Charles City County and
  James River Plantations
Route 5
Richmond, VA 23220

Colonial Williamsburg
100 Visitor's Center Drive
Williamsburg, VA 23135

Gunston Hall Plantation
10709 Gunston Road
Mayson Neck, VA 22079

Maymont Park
1700 Hampton Street
Richmond, VA 23220

Monticello
Box 316
Charlottesville, VA 22902

Mount Vernon Ladies
   Association
Mount Vernon Memorial
   Parkway
Mount Vernon, VA 22121

Norfolk Botanical Gardens
Airport Road
Norfolk, VA 23518

Stratford Hall Plantation
Robert E. Lee Memorial
   Association
Stratford, VA 22558

Washington

Northwest Native Garden
Point Defiance Park
5402 North Shirley
Tacoma, WA 98407

Rhododendron Species
   Foundation
2525 South 336th Avenue
Federal Way, WA 98063

West Virginia

Cathedral State Park
Route 1
Aurora, WV 26705

Core Arboretum
West Virginia University
P.O. Box 6057
Morgantown, WV 26506-6507

Watoga State Park
Star Route 1
Box 252
Marlington, WV 24954

Wisconson

Alfred L. Boerner Botanical
   Gardens
Whitnall Park
5879 South 92nd Street
Hales Corners, WI 53130

Mitchell Park
Horticultural Conservatory
524 Sout Layton Boulevard
Milwaukee, WI 53217

Olbrich Gardens
3330 Atwood Avenue
Madison, WI

University of Wisconsin
   Arboretum
1207 Seminole Highway
Madison, WI 53711

AUSTRALIA

Botanic Garden of Adelaide
North Terrace
Adelaide, SA 5000 Australia

CANADA

British Columbia

Butchart Gardens
Box 4010, Station A
Victoria, BC V8X 3X4

University of British Columbia
   Botanical Garden
6501 Northwest Marine Drive
Vancouver, BC V6T 1W5

Van Dusen Gardens
5251 Oak Street
Vancouver, BC V6M 4H1

Ontario

Civic Garden Center
Edwards Gardens
777 Lawrence Avenue East
Don Mills, ONT M32 1P2

Humber Arboretum
205 Humber College Boulevard
Toronto, ONT M9W 5l7

Niagra Park Commission
School of Horticulture
Niagra Falls, ONT L2E 6T2

Quebec

Ville de Montreal Jarden
et de l'Institute Botaniques
4101 rue Sherbrook est
Montreal, PQ H1X 2B2

UNITED KINGDOM

England

Cambridge Botanic Garden
Cambridge, Cambridgeshire

Hampton Court Palace
Hampton Court
East Molesey

Oxford Botanic Garden
Oxford, Oxfordshire

Royal Botanic Gardens, Kew
Richmond, Greater London

Sissinghurst Castle
Sissinghurst, Kent

Stourhead Garden
Stouton, Wiltshire

Tresco Abbey Gardens
Tresco, Isles of Scilly
Cornwall

Wakehurst Place
Ardingly
Haywards Heath, Sussex

Scotland

Crathes Castle
Banchory, Kincardine and
   Deeside

Inverewe
Poolewe
Ross, Cromarty and Skye

Royal Botanic Garden
Edinburgh, West Lothian

Wales

Bodnant
Tal-y-cafn, Gwynedd

Horticultural Associations

The following groups are general-interest gardening societies or private institutions that maintain libraries, distribute information, or promote various aspects of horticulture. Their resources vary, and it is best to write for specific information regarding their services.

All-America Selections
1311 Butterfield Road, Suite 310
Downers Grove, IL 60515

**American Community
  Gardening Association**
c/o University of California
Cooperative Extension Service
2615 South Grand Avenue #400
Los Angeles, CA 90007

**American Society of
  Horticultural Science**
701 North Saint Asaph Street
Alexandria, VA 22314

**American Society of Plant
  Taxonomists**
c/o Dr. Samuel Jones
Department of Botany
University of Georgia
Athens, GA 30602

Botanical Society of America
c/o Gregory J. Amderson
Ecology and Evolutionary
  Biology
75 North Eagleville Road
U-43 University of Connecticut
Storrs, CT 06268

**Botanical Society of the British
  Isles**
Department of Botany
British Museum (Natural
  History)
Cromwell Road
London SW7 5BD
England

**Dynamics International
  Gardening Association**
Drawer 1165
Asheboro, NC 27204

Florida Foliage Association
P.O. Box 2507
Apopka, FL 32704

Garden Club of America
598 Madison Avenue
New York, NY 10022

**Horticultural Awareness
  Association**
c/o Christopher VanOosterhout
15830 Cherry Street
Spring Lake, MI 49456

**Indoor Gardening Society of
  America**
c/o Horticultural Society of
  New York
128 West 58th Street
New York, NY 10019

**International Garden
  Horticultural**
Industry Association
26 Pine Street
Dover, DE 19901

**Massachusetts Horticultural
  Society**
Horticultural Hall
300 Massachusetts Avenue
Boston, MA 02115

**Men's Garden Clubs of
  America**
5560 Merle Hay Road
P.O. Box 241
Johnston, IA 50131

**National Asociation of Women
  in Horticulture**
1311 Butterfield Road, Suite 310
Downers Grove, IL 60515

**National Council of State
  Garden Clubs**
4401 Magnolia Avenue
St. Louis, MO 63110

**National Gardening
  Association**
180 Flynn Avenue
South Burlington, VT 05401

**National Junior Horticultural
  Association**
441 East Pine Street
Freemont, MI 49412

National Xeriscape Council
P.O. Box 163172
Austin, TX 78716-3172

**North American Horticultural
  Society**
7931 East Boulevard Drive
Alexandria, VA 22309

Perennial Plant Association
217 Howlett Hall
2001 Fyffe Court
Ohio State University
Columbus, OH 43210

Seed Savers Exchange
RR 3, Box 239
Decorah, IA 52101

Torrey Botanical Club
c/o Dr. H.D. Hammond
New York Botanical Garden
Bronx, NY 10458

**Woman's National Farm and
  Garden Association**
c/o Mrs. C.F. Kirschler
2402 Clearview Drive
Glenshaw, PA 15116

Plant Societies

The following organizations are special-interest groups that focus on various aspects of cultivating specific types of plants. Their resources and member services vary. Write to individual groups for more information.

African Violet Society of America
P.O. Box 3609
Beaumont, TX 77704

American Begonia Society
P.O Box 1129
Encinitas, CA 92024

American Bonsai Society
Box 358
Keene, NH 03431

American Camellia Society
Box 1217
Ft. Valley, GA 31030

American Daffodil Society
2302 Route 3
Byhalia Road
Hernando, MS 38632

American Dahlia Society
c/o James Moore, Jr.
14408 Long Avenue
Midlothian, IL 60445

American Fern Society
Pringle Herbarium
Department of Botany
University of Vermont
Burlington, VT 05405

American Fuchsia Society
San Francisco County Fair
  Building
Ninth Avenue and Lincoln Way
San Francisco, CA 94122

American Gloxinia and Gesneriad Society
5320 Labadie
St. Louis, MO 63120

American Gourd Society
P.O. Box 274
Mt. Gilead, OH 43338

American Hemerocallis Society
c/o Elly Launius
1454 Revel Drive
Jackson, MS 39211

American Herb Association
P.O. Box 353
Rescue, CA 95672

American Hibiscus Society
P.O. Drawer 321540
Cocoa Beach, FL 32932

American Hosta Society
c/o Peter Ruh
9448 Mayfield Road
Chesterland, OH 44026

American Iris Society
7414 East 60th Street
Tulsa, OK 74145

American Orchid Society, Inc.
6000 S. Olive Avenue
West Palm Beach, Florida 33405

American Peony Society
250 Interlachen Rd.
Hopkins, MN 55343

American Plant Life (Amaryllis) Society
P.O. Box 985
National City, CA 92050

American Primrose Society
c/o Larry Bailey
1570 Ninth Avenue North
Edmonds, WA 98020

American Rhododendron Society
14885 Southwest Sunrise Lane
Tigard, OR 97224

American Rock Garden Society
c/o Carole Wilder
221 West 9th Street
Hastings, MN 55033

American Rose Society
P.O. Box 30000
Shreveport, LA 71130

Azalea Society of America
c/o Mrs. William Lorene
8610 Running Fox Court
Fairfax Station, VA 22039

Bonsai Clubs International
2636 West Mission Road #277
Tallahassee, FL 32304

British Pteridological Society
The British Museum
Cromwell Road
London SW7
England

Bromeliad Society
c/o Lina Harbert
2488 East 49th Street
Tulsa, OK 74105

Cactus & Succulent Society of America
c/o Charles Glass
Box 3010
Santa Barbara, CA 93130-3010.

Cymbiium Society of America
c/o Mrs. Richard Johnston
6881 Wheeler Avenue
Westminster, CA 92683

Herb Research Foundation
P.O. Box 2602
Longmont, CO 80501

Herb Society of America
9019 Kirtland Chardon Road
Mentor, OH 44060

Heritage Roses Group
RD 1, Box 299
Clinton Corners, NY 12514

**Indoor Citrus and Rare Fruit
  Society**
176 Coronado Avenue
Los Altos, CA 94022

International Camellia Society
c/o Thomas Perkins III
P.O. Box 750
Brookhaven, MS 39601

**International Carnivorous Plant
  Society**
Fullerton Arboretum
California State University
Fullerton, CA 92634

International Geranium Society
4610 Druid Street
Los Angeles, CA 90032

**International Herb Growers
  and Marketers Association**
P.O. Box 281
Silver Spring, PA 17575

International Lilac Society
Box 315
Rumford, ME 04276

International Oleander Society
P.O. Box 3431
Galveston, TX 55772

International Palm Society
P.O. Box 368
Lawrence, KS 66044

International Turfgrass Society
Agronomy Department
Virginia Polytechnic Institute
  and State University
Blacksburg, VA 42061

International Waterlily Society
P.O. Box 104
Buckeystown, MD 21717

**Los Angeles International Fern
  Society**
c/o Don Woods
9913 Calmada Avenue
Whittier, CA 90605

Marigold Society of America
P.O. Box 112
New Britain, PA 18901

**National Chrysanthemum
  Society**
c/o Galen L. Goss
10107 Homer Pond Drive
Fairfax Station, VA 22039

National Fuchsia Society
c/o Mildred Elliot
15103 McRae Street
Norwalk, CA 90650

**National Wildflower Research
  Center**
2600 FM 973 North
Austin, TX 78725

**North American Fruit
  Explorers**
Route 1
Chapin, IL 62618

**North American Gladiolus
  Council**
c/o James Martin
20337 Township Road 59
Jenera, OH 45841

North American Lily Society
Box 476
Waukee, IA 50263

**Rhododendron Species
  Foundation**
P.O. Box 3798
Federal Way, WA 98063

Saintpaulia International
c/o Mildred Neil
6504 Dresen
Indianapolis, IN 46227

Terrarium Association
Box 276
Newfane, VT 05345

World Aquaculture Society
166 Fraternity
Louisiana State University
Baton Rouge, LA 70803

**World Federation of Rose
  Societies**
J.D. Solis
1686 Hurlingham
Argentina

Landscaping Institutes

The following organizations have specialized programs and/or information resources relating to landscape design.

California State Polytechnic
  University
Institute for Environmental
  Design
3801 West Temple Avenue
Pomona, CA 91768

Iowa State University
Design Research Institute
134 College of Design
Ames, IA 50011

Landscape Architecture
  Foundation
1733 Connecticut Avenue NW
Washington, DC 20009

The Lawn Institute
County Line Road
P.O. Box 108
Pleasang Hill, TN 38578-0108

Louisiana State University
Information Systems Laboratory
Room 216, College of Design
Baton Rouge, LA 70803

University of Arizona
Arizona Agricultural
  Experiment Station
Tucson, AZ

University of Guelph Arboretum
Guelph, ONT N1G 2W1
Canada

University of Kentucky
Kentucky Agricultural
  Experiment Station
Agricultural Sciences Building
  North
Lexington, KY 40546

University of Michigan
Nichols Arboretum
Ann Arbor, MI 48109-1115

University of Pennsylvania
Morris Arboretum
9414 Meadowbrook Avenue
Philadelphia, PA 19118

University of Wisconsin
Wisconsin Agricultural
  Experiment Station
140 Agricultural Hall
Madison, WI 53706

Washington State University
College of Agriculture and
Home Economics Research
  Center
Pulman, WA 99164

Seed, Bulb, and Plant Suppliers

The following suppliers distribute by mail order or retail distribution. Write for catalogs, which may cost a nominal fee.

Kurt Bluemel Inc.
2740 Greene Lane
Baldwin, MD 21013
  Specializes in ornamental grasses, sedges, and rushes; also has perennials, bamboos, ferns, and aquatic plants

Breck's Dutch Bulbs
6523 North Galena Road
Peoria, IL 61632
  Spring and summer bulbs

W. Atlee Burpee Company
Mail Order Catalog Division
Warminster, PA 18974
  Plants, seeds, bulbs, books, tools, and related garden equipment

Comstock, Ferre & Co.
263 Main Street
P.O. Box 125
Wethersfield, CT 06109
  Seeds, specializing in disease-resistant vegetables, annuals, and perennials

Henry Field Seed & Nursery
1723 Oak Street
Shenandoah, IA 51602
  Plants, seeds, tools, and growing supplies for vegetables, fruits, nuts, and flowers

Gurney Seed and Nursery Company
Dept 98-4724 Page Street
Yankton, SD 57079
  Plants and seeds or ornamentals or fruits and vegetables; also tools and canning supplies

Harris Garden Trends Co.
60 Saginaw Drive
Rochester, NY 14623
  Flower and vegetable seeds, tools, and growing supplies

Heritage Gardens
1 Meadow Ridge Road
Shenandoah, IA 51601-0700
  Flowering trees, shrubs, vines, perennials, and bulbs

Inter-State Nurseries
Catalog Division
Louisiana, MO 63353
  Plants and bulbs, specializing in hybrid roses and perennials

Jackson & Perkins Co.
2518 South Pacific Highway
P.O. Box 1028
Medford, OR 97501
  Planting stock, specializing in roses, fruits, vegetables, and bulbs

Johnny's Selected Seeds
Albion, ME 04910
  Vegetables, herbs, flowers, and grains for commercial crops; also growing supplies and books

J.W. Jung Seed Co.
Box 340
335 South High Street
Randolph, WI 53957
  Plants, seeds, bulbs, and supplies for growing fruits, roses, perennials, and various ornamentals

Kelly Nurseries
Catalog Division
Louisiana, MO 63353
  Nursery stock including fruit and ornamental trees, shrubs, vines, and ground covers

Lilypons Water Gardens
P.O. Box 10
6885 Lilypons Road
Lilypons, MD 21717-0010
  Plants, books, and supplies for aquatic gardens

Earl May Seed & Nursery
208 North Elm
Shenandoah, IA 51603
  Plants, seeds, bulbs, tools, and other gardening supplies

Mellinger's, Inc.
2310 West South Range Road
North Lima, OH 44452-9731
  Plants, seeds, bulbs, tools, and other gardening supplies

J.E. Miller Nurseries
1524 West Lake Road
Canandaigua, NY 14424
  Plants and supplies, specializing in fruit, nut, and ornamental trees, shrubs, and vines

Nichols Garden Nursery
1190 North Pacific Highway
Albany, OR 97321
  Plants, seeds, books and supplies, specializing in herbs, vegetables, and flowers for the Northwest

George W. Park Seed Co.
P.O. Box 46
Cokesbury Road
Greenwood, SC 29648
  Plants, seeds, bulbs, tools, and other gardening supplies

Rex Bulb Farms
P.O. Box 774
2586 Washington Street
Port Townsend, WA 98368
  Plants and bulbs, specializing in hybrid lilies

Clyde Robin Seed Co.
3670 Enterprise Avenue
Hayward, CA 94545
  Seeds and books, specializing in wildflowers

R.H. Shumway
628 Cedar Street
P.O. Box 777
Rockford, IL 61105
   *Seeds for vegetables, flowers,
   green manure crops, and fruit
   plants*

Spring Hill Nurseries Co.
6523 Galena Road
Peoria, IL 61632
   *Plants and bulbs, specializing in
   garden flowers, shrubs, ground
   covers, and houseplants*

Stark Brothers Nurseries
Highway 54
Louisiana, MO 63353
   *Plants and supplies, specializing
   in fruit or ornamental trees and
   shrubs, and roses*

Stokes Seeds, Inc.
737 Main Street
P.O. Box 548
Louisiana, MO 63353
   *Vegetable and flower seeds and
   supplies primarily for commercial
   farmers, but also packaged for
   home gardens*

Territorial Seed Company
P.O. Box 27
80030 Territorial Road
Lorane, OR 97451
   *Seeds, bulbs, books, and supplies,
   specializing in vegetables for the
   Pacific Northwest*

Thompson & Morgan
Dept. 13-0 P.O. Box 1308
Jackson, NJ 08527-0308
   Seeds of all types

Tsang & Ma International
P.O. Box 294
425 Harbor No. 6
Belmont, CA 94002
   *Seeds, books, and supplies for
   growing and using oriental vegetables*

K. Van Bourgondien & Sons, Inc.
P.O. Box A
245 Farmingdale Road
Babylon, NY 11702
   *Plants and bulbs, specializing in
   spring or summer bulbs and
   perennials*

Vermont Wildflower Farm
Route 2
Charlotte, VT 05445
   Specializing in wildflower seeds

Andre Viette Farm & Nursery
Route 1, Box 16
State Route 608
Fisherville, VA 22939
   Perennial planting stock

Wayside Gardens
P.O. Box 1
1 Garden Lane
Hodges, SC 29695-0001
   *Plants and supplies, specializing
   in ornamental trees, shrubs,
   perennials, and roses*

White Flower Farm
Route 63
Litchfield, CT 06759-0050
   *Shrubs, perennials, bulbs, books,
   and supplies*

CANADIAN SOURCES:

Alberta Nurseries
P.O. Box 20
Bowden, AB T0M 0K0
   *Plants, seeds, and supplies, spe-
   cializing in vegetables and flowers
   for short-season climates*

Ferncliff Gardens
SS #1
Mission, BC V2V 5V6
   *Specializing in garden perennials,
   including dahlia, gladiolus, iris,
   peonies*

McConnell Nurseries
Port Burwell, ON N0J 1T0
   *Plants, bulbs, and general nurs-
   ery stock, including roses, berries,
   trees, and shrubs*

McFayden Seed Co.
30 Ninth Street, Box 1800
Brandon, MB R7A 6N4
   *Plants, seeds, bulbs, tools, and
   other gardening supplies*

W.H. Perron
515 Labelle Boulevard
Chomeday Laval, QC H7V 2T3
   *Plants, seeds, bulbs, tools, and
   other gardening supplies*

Stokes Seeds
39 James Street, Box 10
St. Catharines, ON L2R 6R6
   *Flower and vegetable seeds for
   commercial and home gardens*

For information on other suppliers, contact:
Mailorder Association of Nurseries, 8683 Doves Fly Way, Laurel, MD 20723
(301) 490-9143

Biological and Organic Gardening Suppliers

The following suppliers produce and/or distribute beneficial insects or other supplies for biological pest control, composting, and soil enhancement. Also consult extension services for names of local suppliers.

Association of Applied Insect
  Ecologists
100 North Winchester Boulevard
Suite 260
Santa Cruz, CA 95050
  Beneficial insects

Bio-Control Co.
P.O. Box 337
57A Zink Road
Berry Creek, CA 95916
  Beneficial insects

Bio-Resources
P.O. Box 902
1210 Birch Street
Santa Paula, CA 93060
  Beneficial insects

Dyna-Prep, Inc.
2215 Broadway
Yankton, SD 57078
  Diatomaceous earth

Fairfax Biological Lab, Inc.
Clinton Corners, NY 12514
  Milky spore powder

The Fertrell Co.
P.O. Box 265
Bainbridge, PA 17502
  Fertilizers and soil amendments

Francis Laboratories
1551 East Lafayette
Detroit, MI 48207
  Natural fertilizers

Green Earth Organics
9422 144th Street East
Puyallup, WA 98373-6686
  Natural lawn care products

Green Pro Services
380 South Franklin Street
Hempstead, NY 11550
  Natural gardening products

Growing Naturally
P.O. Box 54
149 Pine Lane
Pinevillle, PA 18946
  Natural gardening products

Mellinger's
2310 West South Range Road
Lima, OH 44452-9731
  *Fertlilzers, soil conditioners, and
  soil amendments*

Natural Gardening Research
  Center
Highway 48
P.O. Box 149
Sunman, IN 47041
  *Beneficial insects and supplies for
  organic gardening*

Nitron Industries
4605 Johnson Road
P.O. Box 1447
Fayette Ville, AR 72702
  *Organic gardening supplies,
  including natural fertilizers and
  soil enhancers*

Ohio Earth Food, Inc.
13737 DuQuette Avenue, NE
Hartville, OH 44632
  *Natural gardening materials, spe-
  cializing in sea products*

Perma-Guard
1701 East Elwood Street
Phoenix, AZ 85040
  Diatomaceous earth

Reuter Labs, Inc.
8540 Natural Way
Manassas Park, VA 22111
  Natural pest controls

Rincon-Vitove Insectaries
P.O. Box 475
Rialto, CA 92376
  Benficial insects

Ringer Corporation
9959 Valley View Road
Eden Prairie, MN 55344
  *Organic soil amendments, benefi-
  cial insects, garden tools, and
  irrigation equipment*

Safer, Inc.
60 William Street
Wellesley, MA 02181
  *Pest controls, natural soaps, and
  natural herbicides*

Super Natural American
  Distributing Company
13906 Ventura Boulevard
Sherman Oaks, CA 91423
  Natural fertilizers

Unique Insect Control
5504 Sperry Drive
Citrus Heights, CA 95621
  Beneficial insects

Zook & Ranck, Inc.
RD 2, Box 243
Gap, PA 17527
  Fertilizer and soil amendments

Tool and Equipment Suppliers

The following companies manufacture or distribute gardening equipment. Write for catalogs and information regarding local dealers.

Amerind MacKissic, Inc.
P.O. Box 111
Parker Ford, PA 19457
Large power garden tools

Country Home Products
Ferry Road
P.O. Box 89
Charlotte, VT 05445
Mowers, trimmers, clippers, and various garden tools

Garden Way, Inc.
102nd Street & 9th Avenue
Troy, NY 12179-0009
Mowers, rotary tillers, garden carts, and various garden tools

Gardener's Supply Co.
128 Intervale Road
Burlington, VT 05401
Greenhouse kits and garden tools

Kemp Company
160 Koser Road
Lititz, PA 17543
Shredders, chippers, compost-tumblers, and other garden supplies

Kinco Manufacturing
Dept. 7702
170 N. Pascal
St. Paul, MN 55104
Heavy power mowers

Mainline
P.O. Box 526, Dept. GM190
London, OH 43140
Rotary tillers, mowers, and other power tools

Mantis Manufacturing Co.
1458 County Line Road
Huntingdon Valley, PA 19006
Lawn and garden equipment including tillers, chippers, and mowers

The Plow & Hearth
301 Madison Road
P.O. Box 830
Orange, VA 22960
General gardening tools and accessories

Smith & Hawken
25 Corte Madera
Mill Valley, CA 94941
Tools, ornaments, and planting stock